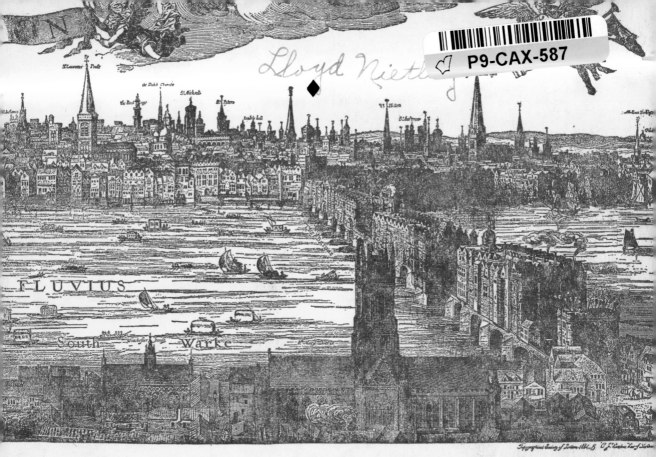

LONDON IN 1890, FROM THE "ILLUSTRATED LONDON NEWS" (*bottom*)

Ruskin

hands = labour.

of the Ruskin's policy

crown = king

Unto this last.

pator. { Marius Epicurean - 863 p.
{ Selections.

from the Divine Service

Bring me my bow of burning gold!
   Bring me my arrows of desire!
Bring me my spear! O clouds, unfold!
   Bring me my chariot of fire!

I will not cease from mental fight,
   Nor shall my sword sleep in my hand,
Till we have built Jerusalem
   In England's green and pleasant land.

BLAKE, "MILTON"

Edited by

B. J. WHITING *Harvard University*

FRED B. MILLETT *Wesleyan University*

ALEXANDER M. WITHERSPOON *Yale University*

ODELL SHEPARD *Trinity College*

ARTHUR PALMER HUDSON *The University of North Carolina*

EDWARD WAGENKNECHT *University of Washington*

LOUIS UNTERMEYER

THE COLLEGE SURVEY

OF

ENGLISH LITERATURE

Volume Two

THE ROMANTIC PERIOD

THE VICTORIAN PERIOD

THE CONTEMPORARY PERIOD

HARCOURT, BRACE AND COMPANY, NEW YORK

PUBLISHERS' PREFACE

The College Survey of English Literature was made in much the same way as English literature itself was—caught up and handed on by the men of one period to the men of another.

As the men of each epoch of English literature were connected with their predecessors only in the transfer of a literary heritage, so the editors of this SURVEY, though more closely associated, are specialists for their periods, each as much at home in the age he edits as he is in his present-day world. Just as every person thinks his own period in time the most crucial and important in history, so each of the seven editors believes the period he edits the most fascinating one of all.

Let us see what this specialization does for the reader of the whole SURVEY. The clatter of reality sounds through the open window of each century, lending intensity and significance to what unfolds on the page. Through our guide, who for all his twentieth-century clothes and manner lives in the age he edits, we hear the ashen thump of a spear shaft being grounded in the court-yard as the minstrel chants in the great hall. We are roused by the cries for bread in the far edges of the street rabble as the virgin queen passes in embroidered silks to her royal barge. We see the dark look of the peasant lover, the terrified white face of the country lass whose innocence has attracted the roving eye of one of King Charles's men. The cautious talk of sedan-chair bearers lends undertone to the patterns of the flute tracing the minuet. Revolution's wave breaks, spuming, against the stout sea wall of an England beginning to feel again; nature burgeons; but we hear, too, the clucking shuttle of bobbins tended by children of seven and nine. There is word that the young queen will marry; commerce rumbles, and there is much loose talk about science mingled with the cries of "Well done! Oh, very well done, sir!" coming faintly up to the manor house from the cricket ground. And so Victoria. . . . Lemonade, and the parish fete, and the growing rumor of war. Then the four years of world struggle, followed by the bickering, disillusioned peace, appeasement, and war again. It's all here, and this is exactly how it happened, and our man saw it and will show you just where and how it occurred.

It was for this sense of reality that the publishers carefully sought for and found that scholar-teacher of each period who could best take you there—intimately, with enthusiasm and accuracy.

The content of this book had an especially interesting development: all seven editors read in manuscript, and offered critical advice upon, the period introduction of each of their colleagues, and similarly commented upon the selections proposed for each period. This advisory work not only brought the broad teaching experience of the whole group of editors into focus with the particular understanding of the specialist in each field, but also made for richness of interpretation and unity of development throughout the SURVEY. Professor Whiting assumed the special responsibility for the Early Period, Professor Millett for the Sixteenth Century, Professor Witherspoon for the Seventeenth, Professor Shepard for the Eighteenth, Professor Hudson for the Romantic Period, Professor Wagenknecht for the Victorian, and Mr. Untermeyer for the Contemporary.

The survey course in English literature is rightly regarded as one of the most important courses in college. In spite of the disproportion between the scope of the literature and the shortness of the time allotted to the course, there is no reason why the student should not form satisfying literary acquaintances through the survey and learn his way to the doors of still other writers whom he will meet often in later courses and in future reading. Accordingly, THE COLLEGE SUR-

VEY gives emphatic space to the major writers—includes, by virtue of its larger page, a greater representation of more of the major writers than is available in comparable anthologies. For instance, the SURVEY has more of the Romances, Chaucer, Shakespeare, Donne, Johnson, Coleridge, Shelley, Keats, Browning, Ruskin, and Arnold than is currently found in similar collections. Such representation permits both intensive study of the major figures and wide choice among their writings. It makes possible the inclusion of complete long selections (*Rasselas*, for example) and satisfying units of works of great length (as Book One of *Gulliver's Travels*, Book Seven of *The Ring and the Book*, much of *The Prelude* and of *In Memoriam*). But inclusion of the major writers alone would show only partially the grandeur and sweep of English literature. The publishers have therefore chosen a page size that is in concurrence with the wish of the editors to present an adequate consideration of all the important literary and social movements of England and to introduce the student to all groups of intrinsically enjoyable literary selections.

The editors felt it would be entirely inconsistent with the importance of Shakespeare as the greatest English writer not to represent him at all in that literary form upon which his reputation primarily rests. Rather than evade this important responsibility on the ground that each individual teacher would want to select the Shakespearean play his sophomores should read, the publishers systematically checked the experience of numerous college teachers against the three plays the editors most strongly recommended. It was, of course, unwise to consider plays which the student had probably read earlier. Similarly, it seemed inadvisable to include a play like *King Lear* which would be too mature for the sophomore to absorb within a limited number of assignments. *The First Part of Henry the Fourth* was thus the play selected, for in it are action, history, humor (what undergraduate can fail to love the bibulous old braggart, Falstaff!)—and some of Shakespeare's tenderest and most moving passages. Sophomores will not have read the play before; it will be within their range; it should be an immediate delight to them. Nothing, of course, prevents the purchase and use by the class of some other play if the instructor wishes it, for the quantity of other representative Shakespearean material is still ample for the course.

The growth and development of the drama has been represented by the inclusion of six significant plays, from *The Second Play of the Shepherds* to Synge's *The Playboy of the Western World*. The plays included coincide with the wish of the editors that no play be included which was not intrinsically interesting, not representative of its time, and not important enough to demand actual study in class.

Freshness of point of view has been constantly sought in the preparation of this anthology. An outstanding example of this is the treatment of *Paradise Lost*. Instead of including the traditional Books One and Two of *Paradise Lost*, the SURVEY includes Book One, complete, lines 1–520 of Book Two (showing the mock-democratic procedure of Hell), lines 376 to the end of Book Nine (showing the temptation in the Garden, which is what this poem is professedly about), and lines 552 to the end of Book Twelve, and, in addition, the *Arguments* of all twelve books. Similarly, in the treatment of Chaucer, not only are "The Prologue," "The Pardoner's Tale," "The Prioress's Tale," and "The Nun's Priest's Tale" included, but also the complete framework of the *Canterbury Tales* is shown by links and synopses.

An earnest attempt has been made to obtain a better balance between prose and poetry than is ordinarily available, in the belief that such a balance will offer more appeal to students. This purpose is discernible in the selections for each period; it is particularly noticeable in the contemporary selections. Some literature of essentially social significance, like that selected from the work of Mill and Morris, will be found, in addition to the belletristic, historical, and personal literature.

For the first time in such a book, the Contemporary Period has received what the publishers feel to be appropriate and varied representation. The six previous periods show the range and temper of English literature; they also whet the sophomore's appetite for a satisfying taste of the literature of his own time. More than two hundred double-column pages of contemporary prose, poetry, and drama are included in THE COLLEGE SURVEY.

Some indication of the value to be had from a collaboration of specialists has already been touched upon. It should be added that the seven period introductions have been so co-ordinated that together they constitute an eighty-thousand-word historical interpretation of the development of English literature; furthermore, each period introduction has been synchronized with the introductions to authors and to individual selections within that particular period. Thus, for example, it is possible to see that Romanticism existed in every period from *Beowulf* and *Sir Gawain and the Green Knight* in the Early Period to Yeats's poetry in our own; one can see the ever changing forms of it appear pronouncedly in the Eighteenth-Century introduction, to burst into elaborate view in that of the Romantic Period. Further, one can see references, let us say in the introduction to Wordsworth, that echo the trends of Romanticism elaborated in the period introduction; and this, again, is echoed in the introduction to a single poem: "Ode on Intimations of Immortality."

The texts used in THE COLLEGE SURVEY are uniformly those of standard editions; for example, the Manly and Rickert edition of *The Canterbury Tales*. In Volume Two the capitalization, punctuation, and spelling of each selection are reproduced exactly as they appeared in an edition approved by the author or accepted as authentic by the readers of his time. Since printing practices were extremely varied before 1800, the capitalization, punctuation, and spelling of the selections in Volume One follow the best modern versions consistent with the flavor of the period in which the selections appeared. The arrangement of authors is based on the dates when they "flourished" rather than on strict chronology. It has been the purpose of the editors, in preparing their introductions and notes, to give effective help to the average sophomore reader without cluttering up his thought with esoteric information.

Much thought has been given toward making the format and illustrations of THE COLLEGE SURVEY attractive and instructive. The four pages of half-tone illustrations preceding each period were designed to show, consecutively, something of the country life of the time, the urban life, the topics the people of the period were most concerned about, and, finally, portraits of the leading literary figures. The wash drawing headpieces, drawn especially for the SURVEY by Mr. Herbert Gute of the School of Fine Arts of Yale University—one of which appears at the beginning of each period—symbolize the nature of the respective periods they introduce. The maps in the end papers were chosen more for their effectiveness as visual aids than for decoration. The reading lists at the end of each section were carefully drawn up not for the scholar, but for the student. A chapter on versification prepared by Mr. Untermeyer will be found in the Appendix, and, following it in Volume One, a list of the English rulers. An essay on the approach to English literature, especially prepared for this anthology by Professor Shepard, has been placed at the beginning of Volume One. It is intended that the student begin with this essay and read with satisfying and growing pleasure the content of THE COLLEGE SURVEY.

English literature is rich, lasting. English cathedrals may crumble into smoking ruin, their cherished windows shattered, their chancels dust; the streets and ghost-haunted lanes of ancient London may become hardly recognizable to recent travelers; the green slopes, the towered lawns, may be scarred with the horror that has marked England's greatest struggle for life. But in English literature all that was England remains, all that was England's endures. No greater hope could be expressed for this book than to have the reader say: Here is England.

CONTENTS

THE ROMANTIC PERIOD

THE VICTORIAN PERIOD

popular

True Greatness in Christianity

THE CONTEMPORARY PERIOD

CONTENTS

The Romantic Period

"Dedham Mill" by John Constable, England's foremost landscape painter. It was nature in a state of dignified simplicity such as this that attracted the poets of the Romantic era. (Metropolitan Museum of Art)

Dove Cottage, home of Wordsworth at Grasmere in the Lake District. (Burton Holmes from Ewing Galloway)

Lower left. A coal mine in England around 1810. The Romantic era witnessed the infancy of the Power Age with its attendant progress and ugliness. (Bettmann Archive)

Lower right. A Scottish farm, 1839. Compare the simplicity of the Scottish country dwelling such as Burns knew with that of the English, which Dove Cottage typifies. (Bettmann Archive)

London, early nineteenth century. Save for pavements, vehicles and fashions, the London street scene of the time of Wordsworth and Keats differed surprisingly little from that of early 1940. (Bettmann Archive)

File cutting in Sheffield. Early in the industrializing of England workers were moved from home workshop to factories. However, this bright, orderly workroom was probably above the average. (Bettmann Archive)

Lower left. An evening party at Brighton Pavilion, from an aquatint by George Cruikshank, the famous artist-caricaturist of the period. Despite the menace of invasion, the dissension within England, and the sympathy with which many of the literary men welcomed "radical" philosophies flourishing abroad, members of society continued to dress and entertain lavishly. (Bettmann Archive)

Below. English textile mill. Machine manufacture considerably altered factory conditions. Production increased by giant strides while actual physical labor was so decreased that women and children were engaged to tend the machines. (Picture Post)

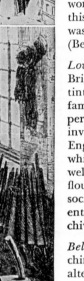

Tintern Abbey. Most of the "romantic" elements of the Romantic Movement are depicted here. The beautiful, the ethereal, Nature, the past, and even the fascination of decay are caught in this scene. (Culver Service)

Chemical lectures. Although this lithograph burlesques the intellectual aspirations of Society in the Romantic era, it clearly indicates the rising interest in science during the early nineteenth century. (American Historical Bureau)

Napoleon at Boulogne. Napoleon, as the champion of the French Revolution, caught the imagination of the young British intellectuals, but, as the ambitious conqueror, stirred the fears of all England. His impact left its traces in much of the literature of the time. Napoleon is shown here constructing a fleet on the French coast for an attack on England. (Brown Brothers)

KEATS
From a painting by W. Hilton, National Portrait Gallery

COLERIDGE
From a painting by Peter Van Dyke

SHELLEY
From a painting by Amelia Curran, National Portrait Gallery

WORDSWORTH
From a drawing by Robert Hancock (Culver Service)

BYRON
From a statue erected by Macgillivray in Aberdeen, 1923

sense), the closer he is to the fountain of goodness. Nature is a manifestation of God, benevolent like Him. When man lives close to Nature and to God, he feels and acts benevolently. Hence men find in their spontaneous emotions, especially their social sympathies, the strongest motives to good conduct. The literary manifestations of these ideas have been called *sensibility*.[7] Such essayists as Addison and Steele in the *Spectator*, such novelists as Richardson in *Pamela*, such poets as Thomson in *The Seasons*, Collins in his odes and songs, and Cowper in *The Task*, treated characters, situations, scenes, and human conduct and motives in accordance with sensibility. After the middle of the century, the writings of Rousseau (for example, *The Confessions*) accentuated the growing tendency toward sentimentality, that is, indulgence in emotion for its own sake. With Collins and Cowper a "confessional strain" was established in English poetry, to be carried on in the poetry of Wordsworth, Byron, and Shelley, and in the essays of Lamb, Hazlitt, and De Quincey.

THE RETURN TO NATURE. Beginning as a reaction against too-exclusive occupation with the urban, this movement was sanctioned by Shaftesbury's teachings. The early nature poets came from the country—Thomson from lowland Scotland, Dyer from Wales. In Thomson's *The Seasons*, 1726–30, and Dyer's *Grongar Hill*, 1727, we find minute and loving notations of natural scenery, the expression of simple pleasure in woods and fields and quiet country life, and the infusion of a strain of moral and religious meditation evoked by natural surroundings. In the poetry of William Cowper (especially *The Task*, 1786) these traits appear fully developed. Thus the eighteenth century left a legacy of ideas about nature that are basic in Romantic poetry: Nature gives calmness and peace to the human mind; it induces a religious feeling; it offers sensible evidence of the beauty and goodness of God; it is the dwelling-place of God; it may be God manifest to us; it quickens social sympathies. Many of these ideas are bound up with Deism and Pantheism, which will be treated later. But fully as important as their ideas is the fact that the eighteenth-century poets, notably Dyer, Collins, Gray, and Cowper, learned to subordinate a landscape to a human mood. That is the essential feature of all great nature poetry.

Meanwhile, more scientific writers were storing up a rich fund of emotional and imaginative experience. Gilbert White wrote *The Natural History and Antiquities of Selborne*, 1789; Erasmus Darwin tried, sometimes ludicrously, in *The Loves of the Plants*, 1789, to poetize vegetable nature; William Gilpin described and illustrated the Highlands of Scotland, the Lake District, and forest scenery; William Bruce reported his explorations of darkest Africa; an American botanist, the Quaker William Bartram, described the wonders of the south Atlantic seaboard and the Gulf region in his *Travels through North and South Carolina*, 1791, which became a favorite in England. All of these books were read by most of the great Romanticists, as Professor J. L. Lowes has excitingly shown for Coleridge in *The Road to Xanadu* (new ed., Houghton Mifflin, 1930).

THE COMMON MAN AND FOLK LIFE. This was parallel to the interest in the return to nature. This too was a protest against typical eighteenth-century absorption in city people, and against the social stratification of England. In Thomson, Gray, and Cowper we find evidence of sympathetic interest in country people's homes and everyday lives, in their welfare, rights, and natural nobility. In fact, Romantic literature was from the first primitivistic, that is, expressive of the belief that rude, simple folk, even savages, exhibit virtues that put civilized people to shame.[8] This tendency was enormously accentuated by the writings of Rousseau, who regarded the arts and sciences as inimical to human happiness and advocated a back-to-nature movement. The savage, the peasant, the mountaineer, the fisherman, the shepherd, were glorified. They lived close to Nature and participated in her primal virtues. Their folklore was a noble source of literary inspiration and material; hence the ballad collections, to be noted later, and hence William Collins's poetic program in *Ode on the Superstitions of the Highlands of Scotland* (written 1749, published 1788), "the whole Romantic School in its germ," to be fully exemplified by Walter Scott. But before the end of the century Burns (*Poems, Chiefly in the Scottish Dialect*, Kilmarnock, 1786), himself a peasant, gave the sturdiest, most genuine, most poetic expression to these ideas about the common man and lowly life. He "showed my youth," says Wordsworth, "How verse may build a princely throne On humble truth."

REDISCOVERY AND REINTERPRETATION OF THE PAST. An antiquarian interest in the Old Norse, Old English, and Celtic languages and literatures soon embraced everything belonging to the Middle Ages and the centuries of British history preceding the "Enlightenment" of the eighteenth. Allan Ramsay, in *The Evergreen* and *A Tea-Table Miscellany*, 1724–27,

[7] See Ernest Bernbaum, *The Drama of Sensibility*, Ginn, 1915, and his *Guide through the Romantic Movement*, Nelson, 1930.

[8] See H. N. Fairchild, *The Noble Savage: A Study in Romantic Naturalism*, Columbia University Press, 1928.

published Scottish ballads, folk songs, and other dialect poetry, and recommended them not only as native to Scotland but as being old, representative of traditional Scottish manners and sentiments. Minor poets like Lady Elizabeth Wardlaw and David Mallet polished folk ballads or wrote imitations that were accepted as genuine antiques. Gray became excited over "Childe Maurice," an old ballad. After the appearance of several collections besides Ramsay's, Bishop Thomas Percy in 1765 issued *Reliques of Ancient English Poetry*, which was a collection of old anonymous ballads together with poems by known early writers, found in a manuscript dating from about 1650. This, one of the three most famous ballad collections in English,[9] became "the Bible of the Romantic Movement," suggesting themes, diction, style, and even critical theory to Coleridge and Wordsworth.

Meanwhile, the Ossianic poems of James Macpherson were making their mark on English literature. Published in 1760–63, these poems, known thenceforth under the comprehensive title *Ossian*, purported to be "genuine remains of ancient Scottish poetry" picked up in fragmentary form among Gaelic-speaking people who had preserved them from the time of their author, Ossian, a bard of the third century. The "old, unhappy, far-off things, and battles long ago," the shadowy landscapes, and the dim, legendary figures of the Ossianic world are presented in a musical prose reminiscent of the Bible. *Ossian* created a furore in Britain and on the Continent. It seemed to justify contemporary idealization of the past and to confirm faith in the virtues of primitive people. It became a storehouse of poetic imagery and phrases for such poets as Coleridge, Wordsworth, Scott, and Byron.[10]

In 1762 (the decade of the *Reliques* and *Ossian*) Bishop Richard Hurd's *Letters on Chivalry and Romance* advocated "the Gothic chivalry" and "the spirit of romance" as superior for poetic purposes to the customs and religion of "Homer's age." In 1764 Horace Walpole published *The Castle of Otranto*, a whimsical, half-cynical horror tale of a medieval Italian nobleman and his family living in an ancient castle. Hurd's *Letters* and Walpole's novel perhaps did most to encourage the "Gothic" vogue, which includes the novels of Mrs. Radcliffe (*The Romance of the Forest*, *The Mysteries of Udolpho*, and others), M. G. Lewis's *The Monk*, William Beckford's *Vathek* (with Oriental setting and diabolism),

and many more. This vogue suggested the poetry of Thomas Chatterton, the Bristol boy who pretended to be the discoveror of manuscript poems by Thomas Rowley, a fifteenth-century monk. It came to flower in such Romantic works as Coleridge's *Christabel*, Byron's *Manfred*, Keats's "The Eve of St. Agnes," and some of the Waverley novels of Scott.[11]

MELANCHOLY. Contemplation of the past often combined with moods of sensibility to produce the poetry of melancholy. Edward Young's *Night Thoughts*, 1742, was the most comprehensive expression of the time spirit on the theme of life, death, and immortality. Robert Blair's *The Grave*, 1743, and Thomas Gray's *Elegy Written in a Country Churchyard*, published in 1751, also treat the theme, the *Elegy* with a power and a beauty that imparted universal qualities to the poem. The lugubriousness of these poems, and the preoccupation of some of them with the physical aspects of death, won for their authors the designation "Graveyard School." Besides establishing a conventional atmosphere of meditation (ruins, ivy, tombs, moping owls, moonlight), the Graveyard Poets suggested one of the greatest themes of Romantic lyric poetry—the debate between Joy and Melancholy, as in Coleridge's "Dejection," Wordsworth's "Ode: Intimations of Immortality," Shelley's "Lines Written among the Euganean Hills," Byron's *Childe Harold*, and Keats's odes.

CRITICAL IDEAS. While imaginative literature was exhibiting the tendencies just described, there was a corresponding development of critical ideas and theories. The new criticism often appears in the prefaces to imaginative works; sometimes it is a part of the substance of these works. Many of the principles and the points of view expressed or implied by the eighteenth-century critics became fundamental in Romantic criticism. Good taste, many of them asserted, is innate, not acquired or dictated by authority. There is need for a change, a fresh start, in poetry, declared Ramsay, Collins, and Young. Originality, Young argued, is superior to imitation and perfect technique. Poetry, maintained Hurd and Young, appeals to feeling and imagination rather than to intellect and reason. An author, argued Thomas Warton, can be rightly judged only in the light of conditions, manners, and ideals of his own age, not those of another; this is the principle of the "historical method," advo-

[9] The other two are Scott's *Minstrelsy of the Scottish Border*, 1802–03, and Francis J. Child's *The English and Scottish Popular Ballads*, 1882–98.   [10] See E. D. Snyder, *The Celtic Revival in English Literature, 1760–1800*, Harvard University Press, 1923.

[11] See Edith Birkhead, *The Tale of Terror: A Study of the Gothic Romance*, Dutton, 1921; Eino Railo, *The Haunted Castle: A Study of the Elements in English Romanticism*, Dutton, 1927; Montague Summers, *The Gothic Quest*, Fortune Press, 1938.

cated in Warton's *Observations on the Faerie Queene of Spenser*, 1754, and *The History of English Poetry*, 1774–81. Shakespeare, Spenser, and Milton take precedence over Homer, Virgil, and Horace, and the medieval Christian tradition, Hurd and Warton held, is superior for literary material to the pagan classical tradition. Shakespeare as a dramatist, Maurice Morgann showed, was not a lawless barbarian, beyond the pale of critical jurisdiction, but a great creative artist expressing his own age and obeying the laws of his own genius.

REVIVAL OF OLDER LITERARY FORMS AND CREATION OF NEW TYPES. Departing from the dominant heroic-couplet form, in 1726 James Thomson brought out the first of *The Seasons* in blank verse reminiscent of Milton. He was followed by Young, Blair, Cowper, Blake, and others, and blank verse became one of the favorite forms for reflective poetry. The Spenserian stanza was revived in William Shenstone's *The Schoolmistress*, Thomson's *The Castle of Indolence*, James Beattie's *The Minstrel*, and Burns's *The Cotter's Saturday Night*, all written between 1737 and 1786. Scott, Byron, Shelley, and Keats were to use this form in famous examples of Romantic narrative and reflective poetry. The revival of the sonnet by Gray, Thomas Warton, Cowper, and W. L. Bowles (*Sonnets*, 1789) was one of the most fruitful developments in lyric poetry, for that form in the hands of Wordsworth and Keats became a fine instrument of Romantic expression. The popular ballad stanza was used in original poems by Ramsay, Percy, Chatterton, Burns, and Cowper; thus was established a precedent for *Lyrical Ballads* and the early poems of Scott. The ode, though it had not been abandoned by the Neoclassical poets of the late seventeenth and early eighteenth centuries, was revivified by Collins and Gray for the treatment of fresh themes. In the *Spectator* papers and in Goldsmith's magazine contributions lay the ancestors of the familiar essays by Lamb, Hazlitt, De Quincey, and Hunt. The variety and the scope of prose fiction were greatly enlarged by *The Castle of Otranto* and its Gothic successors, by attempts at the historical novel like Thomas Leland's *Longsword*, and by the initiation of the thesis or social purpose novel in Godwin's *Caleb Williams*, 1794.

The latter half of the eighteenth century saw an increasing acceleration of the literary tendencies just described. The works of Macpherson, Percy, Chatterton, Walpole, Thomas Warton, Mrs. Radcliffe, Cowper, Bowles, Burns, and Blake—all published after 1750—show that reassertion of feeling and that awakening of imagination which were to characterize the Romantic Period proper. Most of the important Romantic themes, ideas, and attitudes were suggested or stated during these years; meanwhile, the chief forms of Romantic expression were taking shape.

Storm and Stress of Events

The high tide of Romanticism in English literature came during the reigns of George III (1760–1820), George IV (1820–30), and William IV (1830–37). Developments in literature paralleled four great historical movements: (1) the French Revolution; (2) the Napoleonic Wars; (3) the period of reaction, suppression, and continental secondary revolution; and (4) British reform after the defeat of Napoleon. With the two Georges, the political and military leaders, and the events and ideas of the times, the literature is intimately concerned. Human action, emotion, and thought were profoundly stirred by the revolution that, beginning in May, 1789, shook every throne in Europe and transformed the life of every country in the Western world.

The French Revolution began as a protest against the outworn social order based on feudalism, against the privileges of caste, against bureaucracy and despotism. Like the Protestant Reformation, but in the sphere of social relations rather than religion, it was an assertion of the equal value of every human personality. It attempted to reconstruct human society in accordance with theories of the Rights of Man which had been developing, both in France and in England, since the Renaissance. Rousseau was its chief prophet; from him, in Byron's words, came "Those oracles which set the world in flames, Nor ceased to burn till kingdoms were no more." It began in France, not so much because the French common people were oppressed more than any other European people, but because they had leaders who were better educated in political theory. For a while the cause of the French people seemed to be the cause of all mankind.

The early phases stirred hope for the human race. The Estates General met at the Versailles Palace May 4, 1789. The Third Estate (the commons), refusing to sit as one of three houses, to be outvoted by the privileged other two, declared itself *the* National Assembly, invited the other two Estates to join it in one house where it would be numerically superior, and swore not to disband until a constitution had been won. The king, Louis XVI, assented, but gathered his forces, ostensibly to keep order. He was misunderstood. A mob stormed and destroyed the Bastille on July 14. The rest of France followed in this attack on ancient tyrannical authority. The King and the Assembly were compelled to leave the quieter surroundings of Versailles and come to Paris, where the mob could more conveniently exert its pressure.

Between 1789 and 1791 the framing of a constitution, the Declaration of the Rights of Man, and the reorganization of government were undermined by the spread of anarchy in France. Similarly, from 1791 to 1792 the acceptance of the constitution was overshadowed by the growing violence of the extremists (Jacobins) and the steady drift toward war with other countries. The final phase of the Revolution proper, 1792–95, included the proclamation of the Republic of France, the declaration of war "against all kings in behalf of all peoples," the trial and execution (January, 1793) of the King, the Reign of Terror (March, 1793, to the death of Robespierre, 1794), the defeat of the European coalitions against France, and the establishment of the Directory (1795).

At the outset, a majority of the English young and well-educated hailed the French Revolution with joy. The first generation of the Romanticists, Wordsworth, Coleridge, Southey, Hazlitt, Landor, and Scott, were in their late teens when it started. All of them except Scott saw in it the salvation of mankind. "Bliss was it in that dawn to be alive," wrote Wordsworth in his thirties, looking back on his twenties when he knew love and revolution on the soil of France. In the very year of the Terror he wrote a *Letter to the Bishop of Llandaff* justifying the execution of Louis XVI, repudiating caste and privilege, and affirming his faith in the French cause as the cause of humanity. Neither he nor his contemporaries ever forgot the exaltation of those years. And the brave hopes of that early phase were to be revived by the generation of Byron and Shelley, born on the eve or just at the beginning of the revolution, tasting "the apples on the Dead Sea's shore" but rejoicing too that "Mankind have felt their strength, and made it felt."

The course of events gradually disillusioned all but the most inveterate die-hards, such as Hazlitt. War between England and France began in 1793. During the early campaigns young Englishmen like Wordsworth could not join in church prayers for the success of English arms. But the excesses and the blind fury of the revolutionists in their dealings with the institutions of France (religion, the family, and the like), and their early imperialistic invasions of Venice and Switzerland, reputed to be free and democratic, were enough to destroy the revolutionary faith of Coleridge, who wrote his recantation, "France, an Ode," in 1798. England was constantly threatened with invasion, especially in 1796 and 1797, when a French expedition was stirring up rebellion in Ireland. In February, 1797, a small band of blackguards, the scourings of French prisons and penal galleys, under the command of an American, Colonel Tate, actually landed on the coast of Pembrokeshire. A furious mutiny of long-abused sailors in the British fleet for a time almost paralyzed the naval defense. But English victory in the Battle of the Nile lifted the threat of immediate invasion. The war dragged on until 1802, when the Peace of Amiens gave a short breathing-spell for the more deadly struggle to follow.

Since 1795 or thereabout Napoleon Bonaparte had been in control of affairs in France. The second war, to overthrow him, lasted intermittently from 1803 until June, 1815 (Waterloo). During this war England was making a desperate fight for the preservation of its empire and for its own existence. For a time it was alone against Napoleon; again (1803–05) it lived in hourly dread of invasion. The election of Napoleon as Consul for life in 1802, his coronation as Emperor in 1804, the crash of great nations across the waters—all these events re-echo in the poetry of the Romanticists. No better record of the fears, disillusionments, despair, and spiritual anguish of those years can be found than that which Wordsworth wrote in *The Prelude* and in "Poems Dedicated to National Independence and Liberty."

In England, from the beginning of the French Revolution, the situation encouraged dictatorial methods of government. Menaced by invasion from without, the country was torn by dissension within. In London agitators for the independence of the Spanish American colonies embarrassed foreign relations. Many radical associations sprang up to proclaim themselves in sympathy with France and even in favor of the overthrow of the British monarchy. To these Edmund Burke had spoken in *Reflections on the Revolution*, 1790. Agitators like Tom Paine answered him; William Godwin preached philosophical anarchy (*Political Justice*, 1793). The Government, controlled by Pitt and the Tory party, adopted severe measures to repress freedom of speech, of assembly, and of the press. Coleridge's friend Thelwall was among the intellectual radicals tried for high treason, and a shoemaker named Hardy was tried on the same charge, but both were acquitted by sensible English juries. Coleridge and Wordsworth were visited by Thelwall soon after his acquittal. Walking the coast of the Bristol Channel, not far from the spot where the French squadron of 1797 turned back, they were suspected of being French spies. A government spy, whose most noticeable trait was a large nose, was set on their trail. While they were innocently talking about the philosophy of Spinoza, the sleuth shadowed them. To his superior he reported that he could find no harm in them except that they had referred to him as "Spy Nozey." In Birmingham a government-provoked mob wrecked the chemical laboratory of Coleridge's friend Joseph Priestley, who had expressed himself imprudently on issues of the day. The conservatism of the English people tolerated a strong government, in the interest of national defense. By pointing out the dire effects of the revolution in France and the menace of French armies, the Tory party was able to maintain itself against the liberal tendencies of an enlightened minority.

Under Tory leadership the policy of coalitions with absolute monarchies was continued. In 1811, when George III became blind and permanently insane, the Prince of Wales was appointed Regent. No greater enemy of the liberal minority could have come to the fore; none more intolerant and despicable. When Leigh Hunt, a poet and newspaperman, made an offensive personal allusion to him in print, the result was a two-year jail sentence. When, after the defeat of Napoleon, England joined the Quadruple Alliance, the avowed purpose of which was "to preserve monarchical governments and stamp out the spirit of revolution," the cause of liberalism seemed hopeless to such people as Byron and Shelley.

But under peace conditions the agitation for reform, particularly of representation in Parliament, was resumed. The recent example of the American people in winning their independence and then, in the War of 1812, successfully defending it, helped to keep the democratic spirit alive. The frightful economic distress under wartime conditions and afterwar adjustments steadily increased the pressure for reform. From 1815 to 1822, however, the reactionary Tory party, led by firm, narrow-minded men like Castlereagh and Lord Eldon, coped with the spirit of reform by riding it down, as Shelley pictures them in *The Masque of Anarchy*. It was to the two "Bobs"—Castlereagh (Viscount Robert Stewart) and the "turncoat" poet laureate Robert Southey—that Byron dedicated the first and second cantos of *Don Juan*. It was Lord Eldon who refused Shelley the custody of his own children, in part on the evidence of Shelley's moral and political views as expressed in *Queen Mab*. The Government enacted even more severe laws against sedition and

employed a host of spies to ferret out disturbers. Severe outbreaks of mob spirit occurred. One was the "Derbyshire Insurrection"; another, more spectacular, was the "Peterloo Massacre" in 1819, at Manchester, where soldiers broke up a mass meeting of workers, killing several. Shelley heard of the latter in Italy and denounced it in "Song to the Men of England" and "England in 1819."

The death of George III in 1820, though it occasioned two poems that interest us—Southey's *A Vision of Judgment* and Byron's parody, *The Vision of Judgment*—had little effect on the situation. The new king was the old Regent. The Tories, however, realizing that they were losing ground, tried to save themselves by adopting conciliatory and occasional liberal measures. In 1822, the new Minister of Foreign Affairs, George Canning, who had succeeded Castlereagh (a suicide), disregarded the Holy Alliance in acknowledging the independence of the revolting South American countries; in 1823 he supported the Monroe Doctrine with the British Navy; in 1825–27 he shielded the Greeks from Turkish conquest. In 1830, despite the opposition of the Tory party, the Catholic Emancipation bill passed through Parliament. (Lord Byron had spoken in favor of it in 1812.) In 1830, also, the accession of William IV and successful revolutions in France and Belgium against the Bourbons greatly encouraged the liberal cause. Finally, in 1832 the great Reform Bill, a long step toward the guarantee of government by free and equitable representation in Parliament, was passed.

Social and Scientific Drifts

From the outlines of so vast a historical background we need to detach, for better understanding and emphasis, a few details. One of these is the situation, greatly aggravated by war, produced in England by the Industrial Revolution. The early nineteenth century witnessed some of the most painful effects of this transformation of economic and social life by the application of steam power to manufacture and then to transportation. Thousands of home craftsmen were forced by large-scale factory competition to go to the cities for employment or to give up their trades. The dislocation of markets by the long war threw more thousands out of employment, as Wordsworth, for example, shows with moving pathos in the story of Margaret (*Excursion*, Book I). In the mushroom industrial towns of the Midlands there were no housing regulations, few sanitary provisions, no labor laws. With inadequate parliamentary representation, laborers could find no relief through government regulation. The right to strike was not recognized. Only a few generous spirits like Byron had lifted their voices in defense of the Nottingham frame-breakers (saboteurs). Meanwhile, the Corn Laws (a protective tariff on grain) kept the price of foodstuffs out of the reach of the poorest. In the country districts the landlords pocketed the benefits of government protection of agriculture. Tenants, said Shelley, starved or were stabbed in the fields. In the cities, the suffering of the underprivileged sweatshop worker and the streetwalker found utterance in Thomas Hood.

With government oppression and such misery weighing on sensitive souls, it is small wonder that half-baked social schemes were concocted by the intellectuals. The most interesting of these was Pantisocracy, conceived in 1794 by Robert Southey, just out of Oxford; Samuel Taylor Coleridge, recently withdrawn from Cambridge; and Robert Lovell, a young Quaker. Twelve young gentlemen and twelve young ladies were "to sail to America, and, on the banks of the Susquehannah [Pennsylvania], to form a Social Colony, in which there was to be a community of property, and where all that was selfish was to be proscribed." The only result of the Pantisocratic dream, aside from its literary reflections, was wives for Southey and Coleridge—for the latter an incompatible one.

While skepticism and atheism proclaimed themselves through such publicists as Thomas Paine and William Godwin and were "sported" by youngsters like Wordsworth in the 1790's and by Shelley twenty years later, a great religious movement was perhaps saving England from the violence of revolution by arms and bloodshed. Methodism, founded by the Wesleys at Oxford about 1730, and the Evangelical Movement, led by John Newton and William Wilberforce, for reform and regeneration within the Established Church, had been quietly transforming the spiritual life of the English people. The poetry of Coleridge and the later Wordsworth carries on the deep current of religious feeling set in motion by such poets as Cowper.

Early in the nineteenth century the conflict between religion and science that was to rage for over fifty years in England began to take shape. For this was a period of brilliant scientific advancement. In astronomy Sir William Herschel had been calculating the depths of space and the distances of the stars, discovering Uranus with an improved telescope, and preparing the way for the nebular hypothesis (1786). Lagrange had explained why the moon shows only one side of itself, and Laplace, in *Exposition du système du monde*, 1796, had just elaborated the nebular hypothesis. Shelley read such scientific works and embodied them in his poetry. The great astronomer Sir William Rowan Hamilton became a close friend of Wordsworth, furnishing the poet subjects for several poems. James Hutton laid the foundations of modern geology in his *Theory of the Earth*, which was published in the same year as *Lyrical Ballads*, 1798. William Smith, "the father of modern geology," began his work in 1799. The geologists of the period argued over two theories of the origin of the rocks—the Neptunist (action of water) and the Vulcanist (volcanic heat). Wordsworth and Shelley refer to both. In chemistry and physics Sir Humphry Davy, Joseph Priestley, Henry Cavendish, and John Dalton were discovering new elements, gases, and properties of electricity. Wordsworth and Coleridge were friends of Davy and received from him directions for study. One of their reasons for going to Germany in 1798 was to study chemistry. Coleridge and his friends assisted Davy in experiments with nitrous oxide (laughing gas), at parties where guests indulged in sprees of inhalation. At Eton and Oxford Shelley was addicted to scientific dabbling. Coleridge, Wordsworth, and Shelley felt that the future of the world was to be bound up with the progress of science. The Romanticists vacillated between lively admiration for science and fear that it would destroy a spiritual interpretation of the universe. In his moment of optimism about it Wordsworth wrote that "poetry is the breath and finer spirit of all knowledge; it is the impassioned expression which is in the countenance of all Science." The poet, he said, "will be ready to follow the steps of the man of science . . . carrying sensation into the midst of the objects of science itself."

Winds of Doctrine

For an understanding of the literature of the age in its treatment of nature and the problems of religious faith, the hope of immortality, moral conduct, the enjoyment of beauty, and the like, it is necessary to know something about a few philosophical concepts.

Throughout this period, as throughout all ages, there were two opposed systems of philosophy—Materialism (or Naturalism) and Idealism. The contemporary versions of these systems had "ransacked the ages, spoiled the climes."

Materialism conceives of the universe simply as a "brute fact, or collocation of brute facts, under the sway of mechanical law. . . . The apparently rational system of the present cosmos is represented as a happy accident, resulting from one of the infinite casts of nature's dice. The principle of the universe is blind necessity or chance."[12] In other words, Materialism rules out the idea of a conscious, intelligent, purposeful, and benevolent Creator and Ruler of the universe.

The most prominent materialistic philosophy of the period was called *Necessitarianism*. (This is the older term for Determinism.) Its chief professional expounder was William Godwin, in *Political Justice*, 1793, which all the Romanticists read when they were young. Its main basis is included in the definition of Materialism. Its most conspicuous tenet is the law of cause and effect; it denies purposiveness of the universe and freedom of the human will. Every event or action, from the revolution of the earth to the fall of a leaf, from the rise and fall of empires to a baby's smile, happens as a link in a chain of cause and effect, happens inevitably. The universe is an inanimate, soulless machine spinning through its grooves of predestined change. Human beings are automata fulfilling the laws of necessity, under some illusion of free volition, but helpless to do otherwise than as physical and mechanical law compels. The best poetic exposition of necessity appears in Shelley's *Queen Mab*, with a long prose note. Some psychological applications of it are found in Coleridge's *The Rime of the Ancient Mariner* and *Christabel*, in Wordsworth's early poetry, and in Byron's *Manfred*.

The chief materialistic psychology of the period was known as *Associationism*. The fullest treatment of this was David Hartley's *Observations on Man*, 1749. As in Locke's psychology, at birth the human mind is a blank (tabula rasa); there are no innate ideas. All ideas, and the mind itself, are formed ultimately from sensations produced on the nervous system by impressions from without. Simple sensations (color, heat, cold, sound, and so on) produce simple ideas. In accordance with the laws of mental *association* (similarity, contrast, contiguity in time and space, cause and effect, and so on), these simple ideas are combined into complex ideas. With these complex ideas are associated the "intellectual pleasures and pains," which Hartley named and arranged in an ascending scale as Imagination, Ambition, Self-Interest, Sympathy, Theopathy (the feeling for God), and the Moral Sense. An important point of the system is that "All the intellectual pleasures and pains are deducible ultimately from the sensible ones." Thus it is possible to trace the history of our ideas or minds back to the simplest sensations,

to analyze our most complex emotions into their sense elements. Thus, too, the importance of feeding the mind with the right kinds of sensations, of giving it a wholesome social and natural environment. Moreover, Hartley's system contained some suggestions of a development of human personality in three stages—childhood (simple sensation), youth (feeling, esthetic enjoyment), maturity (thought, the moral sense, religion). Coleridge, Wordsworth, and other Romanticists read Hartley, and much of Wordsworth's philosophy of nature was influenced by Associationism.

Diametrically opposed to Materialism is *Idealism* —"any theory which maintains the universe to be throughout the work or embodiment of reason or mind." Plato set up the greatest system of Idealism. According to him, "reality does not belong to the ever-changing world of sense; true being is found in the incorporeal essences or ideas, which communicate to phenomena whatever permanent existence or knowability they possess. These forms exist in a super-sensuous world by themselves. The ideal world of Plato thus is not so much a world of spiritual or self-conscious existences as of abstract reason." [13] *Platonism* is one of the most common elements of thought in the Romantic treatment of the nature of the universe, of means by which the mind knows, of love, and of immortality. Shelley's "Hymn to Intellectual Beauty," for example, is almost pure Platonism.

Neo-Platonism sprang out of Platonism, at Alexandria, Egypt, in the second and third centuries after Christ, among a school of philosophers who investigated the human soul. It embraces the idea that the soul originated in a spirit world (God), descended into earthly forms, through its adaptation to earthly life lost the sense of its divine origin, and returned to God (or Heaven) only by loving spirit as it manifests itself in ever higher and purer forms. By contemplation of ideal values man may free himself from the domination of sense and attain a state of *ecstasy*, in which he becomes one with God. Besides reading the Neo-Platonists (for example, Plotinus and Proclus), the Romanticists absorbed their doctrines at second hand from the poetry of Spenser, Drayton, and other earlier poets and from the Cambridge Neo-Platonic philosophers of the seventeenth century.

Mysticism is an important aspect of Neo-Platonism and other idealistic systems. "Mysticism may be called the belief that man can come into union with the Infinite Being by means of a wholly passive self-surrender to divine influence. The organ in man

[12] J. M. Baldwin, *Dictionary of Philosophy and Psychology*, 3 vols., Macmillan, 1901–05, Vol. 2.

[13] *Ibid.*

by which he thus communes with God is not will or reason; it is not moral nor intellectual, but a hidden faculty of the soul behind them all. In the ecstatic moment of this union, time, space, body, soul, personal existence, all disappear, and man becomes absorbed into the Divine Being."[14] As an element of religious or philosophical thought and experience, Mysticism is of tremendous importance in Romantic poetry. Its greatest poetic exponent was William Blake. Coleridge, Wordsworth, and, to a considerable degree, Shelley exhibit it in such poems as "Tintern Abbey," *The Prelude*, *Prometheus Unbound*, and "Lines Written among the Euganean Hills."

Transcendentalism combines features of most of these forms of Idealism. It emphasizes the intuitive, spiritual, supersensuous aspects of consciousness and experience. It is opposed to *Empiricism* (the doctrine that truth is to be sought and found in the evidence of the five senses). In the theological sense, it holds that the source of religious truth is an organ or process of apprehension transcending (rising above) ordinary sense experience. This organ is variously called religious consciousness, mystical insight, intuition. Through it truth is immediately realized. Romantic Transcendentalism grew out of both Platonism and German Idealism (Kant and Schelling, for example). Coleridge, Wordsworth, Shelley, and De Quincey illustrate it in various ways.

Two terms occurring often in the description or explanation of Romantic thought are Pantheism and Deism. Both have been so loosely used that hard-and-fast explanations are difficult. *Pantheism* views the world and God as indistinguishable and tends to regard deity as an impersonal principle—God is all things; all things are God. *Deism* is the belief that God is not only distinguishable from the world but dwells apart from it and bears to it the relation of a clockmaker to the clock he has made and set going. English Deism, developing in the seventeenth and eighteenth centuries, differed little from orthodox Christianity in its acceptance of the existence of God, of the human duty to worship and obey Him, and of a system of future rewards and punishments; but it broke from orthodoxy in its view of the source of these ideas. It held that they were revealed in God's plan and conduct of the world and that miraculous revelation (the Bible) was and is unnecessary.

Throughout the Romantic Period, the progress of science and the rush and trample of earth-shaking events were making it more and more difficult to believe in the importance and dignity of

[14] James Freeman Clarke, *Events and Epochs in Religious History*, Houghton Mifflin, 1881, p. 276.

human life, in man's moral freedom, in the kindness of Nature, in the existence of God, or, if His existence was assumed, in His love and providence. The spiritual histories of most of the major Romanticists are records of inner conflicts between the claims of Materialism and Idealism. Some of the greatest poems, like *The Prelude* and *Prometheus Unbound*, testify to the reconciliation of those ancient antagonists, the World and the Soul. Great systems meet in such statements as

"the light of sense
Goes out, but with a flash that has revealed
The invisible world."

Flood Tides and Main Currents

English literature of the period 1798–1832, when Romanticism was dominant, has been likened to a flood tide. Drawn by the powerful and mysterious gravitation of cultural destiny, and blown upon by mighty winds from all the shores of the world and of time, this tide flowed in crests and currents, flooding shallows and depths, coves and gulfs.

The first great swell came in with *Lyrical Ballads*. This was followed by currents of verse and fiction from Scott; of criticism and the familiar essay from Lamb, Hazlitt, and De Quincey; of biography and prose fiction, as well as lyric and narrative poetry, from Southey and Landor. Coleridge, Wordsworth, Southey, Lamb, Hazlitt, and De Quincey were intimately associated with one another; in general, they were sympathetic and co-operative. With most of these Scott was acquainted, with several, friendly. Landor, though a friend of two or three, was mostly apart. All of them except De Quincey were born in the decade 1770–80. The wave of this, the first generation of the Romanticists, was at the crest by about 1817. It was followed shortly after by another wave, bearing at its crest Byron, Shelley, and Keats.

The original collaborative program of Wordsworth and Coleridge endeavored to enrich poetic experience by two complementary methods. One, Wordsworth's, was to look intently at common things and familiar life, to rub from them the film which custom had deposited on them, and by directing attention to essential qualities in them to arouse in the beholder a sense of their beauty and mystery. The other, Coleridge's, beginning at the opposite end of human experience, with the faraway, the mysterious, even the supernatural, and putting human nature there, was to make such experience real by truly describing human reactions to it. Both methods, then, had their center of reference in the universal human heart; they began with the understanding and feeling heart; they addressed themselves to the understanding and feeling heart. In another important respect, too, their methods were similar. They adopted for purposes of poetic expression the language of the understanding and feeling heart: Wordsworth, a selection of the language really used by men in a state of excitement; Coleridge, the forthright diction of the old ballads, romances, and other forms of popular literature.

Wordsworth's share of the program involved in the main a reinterpretation of nature, of man's relation to it, and of the relation of both to God; a vindication of the beauty and dignity of common men as he knew them or imagined them to be; and a search for human happiness

"in the very world, which is the world
Of all of us,—the place where, in the end,
We find our happiness, or not at all."

It is not sufficiently recognized that he is also a great poet of the city and of national ideals. His themes, his interests, his ideas, and his technique represent a consummation of such Romantic tendencies as sensibility and self-confession, the return to nature, the glorification of the common man, primitivism, and revival of older poetic forms and styles; and his poetry draws into the focus of an intensely vigorous and independent intellectual experience such concepts as Necessitarianism, Associationism, Neo-Platonism, and Transcendentalism. More than any other poet he completed what the eighteenth century had begun, with the accent of his own personality and with the stress of his age. And more than any other poet he determined the character of nineteenth-century poetry. He is the key to an understanding of many aspects of such varied kinds of poetic experience as Byron's, Shelley's, Keats's, Tennyson's, Arnold's, Meredith's.

As a poet, Coleridge made his greatest contribution in about fifty pages of living poetry, including *The Rime of the Ancient Mariner, Christabel*, "Kubla Khan," "France, An Ode," and "Dejection: An Ode." The first was published in *Lyrical Ballads; Christabel* was designed for the second edition, but was never completed, and was not published until 1816. These two poems and "Kubla Khan" are the greatest triumphs of "the renascence of wonder"; they illustrate perfectly what Coleridge proposed to do in collaboration with Wordsworth. "France" is perhaps the best short political poem of the age; it is the most eloquent condemnation of the French Revolution. "Dejection" is at once a confession of poetic failure, transcendentally explained,

and a triumph of the poetic power which the poet says he has lost. Besides these, Coleridge wrote some delicate and lovely nature poems.

But Coleridge's significance is as great in the field of criticism as in that of original poetry. His criticism of Wordsworth's theory and practice of poetry, his profoundly philosophical exposition of his own theory, his reinterpretation of Shakespeare, and his vindication of ideal values against the growing materialistic philosophy of his own age are more than compensations for his atrophy as poet.

Coleridge's interest in earlier literature and Wordsworth's preoccupation with natural scenery and peasants found original and magnificent parallels in the work of Walter Scott. As an editor and a composer of ballads, as a romancer in the manner suggested by medieval romances and *Christabel*, as a walking and exceedingly articulate encyclopedia of Scottish folklore and history, Scott is the supreme reviver of history. Early in his verse romances and constantly in the great Waverley novels of his middle and later years, he painted a whole gallery of Scottish common people. He knew common people better than Wordsworth did, and his insight into their experience and modes of thought is matched by his power to bring them to life. His native countryside Scott knew as well and as lovingly as Wordsworth knew the mountains and dales of Cumberland. His descriptions of nature are clear and firm, with no touch of mysticism in them. Moreover, Scott was a true singer, in some ranges of song not below Robert Burns.

The chief Romantic essayists were friends of Wordsworth and Coleridge and familiars of their poetic endeavors. Charles Lamb, in letters to Wordsworth, Hazlitt in "My First Acquaintance with Poets," and De Quincey in his memoirs, have left a vivid record of a great literary period in the making. In his own sphere Lamb showed that a vast city is as strange and mysterious and beautiful and lovable as the Lake Country, that a city boyhood is good for a prose *Prelude*, that the old dramatists and prose-writers are as interesting as the romancers, that the essay is as effective for purposes of confession as poetry is, and much more intimate and amusing. Besides criticizing the poetry of Wordsworth, Coleridge, and their contemporaries, Hazlitt enlarged his art on subjects of painting and acting. He is one of the finest critics of the whole range of English literature from Queen Elizabeth down to his own age. And he is a lively and incisive commentator on everyday life, urban and rural (for example, "The Fight" and "On Going a Journey"). De Quincey, younger than the other two, was among the first youthful readers to cheer for *Lyrical Ballads*. He made himself a disciple of Coleridge, contrived to become a friend of the great man, met Wordsworth with trepidation, and settled in the Lake District. His *Confessions of an English Opium-Eater* enlarged the scope and sharpened the psychology of confessional writing. His "On the Knocking at the Gate in *Macbeth*" treats problems of Shakespearean dramaturgy in the spirit of Coleridge. His translations and expositions of such German writers as Jean Paul Richter and Kant spread the knowledge of Transcendentalism in England. His imaginative essays, such as *Suspiria de Profundis* and *The English Mail-Coach*, are prose analogues of Romantic lyrical poems and musical fugues.

Robert Southey and Walter Savage Landor were friends with friends in common among the other Romanticists. The French Revolution excited them into committing undergraduate violence in college, but while Southey gradually turned conservative, Landor remained steadfast to his conception of liberal principles. In different ways they exploited the past—Southey, in homely ballads reminiscent of Coleridge's, later in long narrative poems on Oriental and Welsh themes, then in histories and admirable short biographies; Landor, in his epics *Gebir* and *Chrysaor*, in hundreds of exquisite epigrams and idyls on Greek, Roman, and Italian subjects, and on a larger scale, worthy of comparison with Scott's novels, in the stately portrait galleries of *Imaginary Conversations*. The two men share a similar fate—in being neglected today and in being remembered, if at all, for their short poems and their prose rather than for their ambitious poetic efforts.

The latter phase of the Romantic flood tide brought in Byron, Shelley, and Keats, together with a host of secondary writers, notably Leigh Hunt and Thomas Moore. Crosscurrents sometimes appear to bear them against the tide, but their general movement is in the wake of the crest wave.

With Byron, Shelley, and Keats, a change comes over the spirit of English literature—a change determined largely by the transformation that was taking place in the social and political condition of Europe. Their birth dates—1788, 1792, and 1795, respectively—place them about a generation later than Wordsworth (b. 1770) and Coleridge (b. 1772), the early leaders of revolt against the eighteenth-century order. The older generation, particularly Coleridge and Wordsworth, had, in Legouis' phrase, been "nourished by the faiths and regenerative principles brought into being by the French Revolution; Byron and Shelley did their most characteristic work in the days of the Holy Alliance." Napoleon's bloodstained career and the European reaction against liberty toward absolutism spread over the interval. Byron and Shelley lived in an age of shattered faiths, of cynical political dictatorships, and of profound disillusionment. Between the two generations there were differences in critical theory and in literary practice. The older generation, confounding eighteenth-century Neoclassicism with true Classicism, had rebelled against the literature current in their own age and gone back to the ballad, to medieval romance, and to Spenser, Milton, and the romantic Shakespeare. Byron reacted (in *English Bards and Scotch Reviewers* and *Don Juan*) against the *Lyrical Ballads* theory of poetry and went back to Pope and the humanistic Shakespeare. Keats and Shelley, while showing the influence, both negative and positive, of Wordsworth and Coleridge in ideas and style, "revived the cold ashes of Hellenism"; and (Keats especially) drew inspiration from the Renaissance, largely through the medium of sixteenth- and seventeenth-century English poetry. All three were affected by Italian literature.

Intimate friends from 1816 until Shelley's death in 1822, Byron and Shelley shared certain master passions, but differed, sometimes as widely as the poles, in their philosophical and religious faiths and social theories. They were both fascinated by the past (Greece, Italy, Rome, the East); but whereas to Byron its pageantry and splendor sometimes lighted up the sorry present and consoled his own wounded spirit, to Shelley history, when it interested him at all, was a dark record of man's inhumanity to man, shot through now and then with gleams of heroic self-sacrifice kindling hope for the future. They are both apostles of liberty, but Byron's thought scarcely goes beyond hatred of tyranny, derision of its ministers, and exultation over its destruction. His poetry is a volcanic eruption devastating the social order. Shelley hates tyranny as passionately, but he has a constructive gospel. He envisages a world liberated and transformed by the spirit of intellectual freedom and love. Each treats the characteristic *Weltschmerz* of the 1800's; but whereas Byron is filled with melancholy and despair about everything, including himself, Shelley rises above personal hopelessness into ecstatic contemplation of ultimate salvation for mankind. They both treat the theme of titanism —Byron in *Manfred*, Shelley in *Prometheus Unbound*—but with the difference between nihilism and perfectibility. For a time (1816) the two were influenced by Wordsworth's idealistic interpretation of nature. But after a few splendid speculations (the third canto of *Childe Harold*, and the Augusta poems) on the relationship of his own soul to the cosmos, Byron relapses into his usual dynamic, naturalistic treatment of mountain, woods, and pathless seas as magnificent spectacles and occasional comforters, but not as revealers of higher truths. Shelley, on the other hand, soars above Wordsworth into the Platonic Idealism of "Hymn to Intellectual Beauty" and the dizzy raptures of "Euganean Hills" and *Prometheus Unbound*. Philosophically, Byron is a Necessitarian, theologically, a Predestinarian; Shelley, beginning as a rigorous Necessitarian, ends with a conception of the universe, governed by loving purpose, that goes beyond Plato and approaches Christianity.

An independent, reserved friend of Shelley, and, as he reached his twenties, a distruster of Byron, Keats proudly sailed his own course, sometimes on as perilous seas as those traversed by the Ancient Mariner, more often on those where he could "hear old Triton blow his wreathèd horn." Like Coleridge, he is the poet of "witchery by daylight" ("La Belle Dame sans Merci" and "Lamia") as well as moonlight (*Endymion* and "The Eve of St. Agnes"). Like Shelley, he is fascinated by the ancient beauty of Greece and Italy; like Wordsworth, by the old pagan religion of nature. Like all three, he is an Idealist, drawing his inspiration, however, from the Neo-Platonism of Spenser, Drayton, and seventeenth-century English poets. Whether Beauty embodied herself in physical nature, in ancient sculpture and myth and tale, or in philosophic thought, she was his religion, he was her priest, and poetry was his liturgy. But these themes are not the whole of Keats's poetry. His central and controlling faith, the essence of what he tried to say, is that life, however cruel and ugly in its human aspects of his own day, can be justified by faith in beauty and truth (aspects of the same ultimate reality), and that poetry is one of the great ministers of this faith. Much of Keats's great poetry is about poetry—its origin, its sources, its themes, its ministrations to human life, its relation to truth. Beginning with the Wordsworthian ethics of making poetry a balm to humanity, through its power to inspire sympathy and helpfulness, he resolved this into a nobler and austerer faith in its efficacy for enabling us "to bear all naked truths, And to envisage circumstance, all calm . . . the top of sovereignty."

Thomas Moore and Leigh Hunt are interesting both in themselves and as friends of greater poets. Moore, long an intimate of Byron, and his official biographer, managed to sing movingly about the ancient glories and wrongs of his native Ireland without offending his English friends. In his own way he did for that country a service comparable with that done for Scotland by Scott. Better than most of the Romanticists he understood the technical relations of lyric poetry to music. His songs are still parlor favorites. His Oriental romance *Lalla Rookh*, which used to rest on the marble-topped tables beneath the pampas plumes, lacks the dark, throbbing passion and wildness of Byron's Turkish tales, but is more readable than Southey's long poems about Arabian devil-worshipers and Indian Brahmins. Leigh Hunt, leader of the Cockney School derided by Byron, Moore, and the reviewers, introduced the young Keats to Italian themes, encouraged his early poetic efforts, and gave him two stylistic models—an adaptation of the heroic couplet (as in *Rimini*), which was partly to the good, and a prettified, capersome poetic diction, which was altogether to the bad. But Hunt's steady exposition and defense of Romantic poetry, his felicity in criticizing it by sampling it, and his graceful light essays are more solid claims to remembrance.

The early years of the nineteenth century saw Romantic literature constantly on the defensive. Three great book-review organs—the *Edinburgh Review* (founded 1802), the *Quarterly Review* (1809), and *Blackwood's Magazine* (1817)—lifted the discussion of books from the plane of trade advertising to that of literary criticism. In their attitudes toward writers and their political views they differed. The *Edinburgh*, edited by Francis Jeffrey, Whig in politics, in the main opposed the tendencies of Romantic literature, on grounds of established taste and principles belonging to the earlier, Neoclassical age. This review modified its early opinions of Scott and Byron; but of Wordsworth, never in Jeffrey's lifetime. It ignored Shelley. The Tory *Quarterly*, edited by Scott's son-in-law, J. G. Lockhart, published the famous review of Byron's *Hours of Idleness* that provoked *English Bards and Scotch Reviewers*, and the infamous one of Keats's *Endymion*. It abused Hunt, Hazlitt, Lamb, and Shelley, but treated Wordsworth and the Lake School respectfully and fairly. Its principles were much like those of the *Edinburgh*. *Blackwood's*, edited by "Christopher North" (John Wilson), a young friend of Wordsworth, was kind toward Wordsworth, appreciative of Shelley's poetic genius but hard on his morals and judgment, and harsh to the Cockney School. In these three periodicals were published articles and reviews by Scott, Southey, Hazlitt, and De Quincey. The *London Magazine* (founded in 1820) was a late but brilliant entry into the field. It had the honor of publishing Lamb's *Essays of Elia*, Hazlitt's *Table Talk*, and De Quincey's *Confessions of an English Opium-Eater*. Its brief but distinguished career ended after its editor, John Scott, was killed in a duel. (In those days magazine-editing was a perilous occupation.)

The Attraction of Romanticism Today

The Romantic Period bears many resemblances to our own that make it specially significant for us. Like our own, it was an age of great dreams and hopes that never die; of temporary debacle, catastrophe, and disillusionment; of slowly renewed faith. Its French Revolution, Napoleonic Wars, Congress of Vienna, financial panics, feverish nationalism, secondary revolutions, threats of new wars, and painful economic readjustments correspond roughly to our World War of 1914-18 and its ideals of the world made safe for democracy and small nations, its Russian and German revolutions, its Treaty of Versailles, its aftermath of dictatorships, its depressions, its Munich appeasements, its assaults on small countries, its renewed threat to civilization. Like ours, that period was morally and spiritually bankrupt. It inherited a natural philosophy that pictured the universe as an inanimate machine, and man as a creature helpless in the grasp of a pitiless Necessitarianism, just as we inherited the implications of the evolutionary hypothesis and Behavioristic psychology. It was owner and then receiver in bankruptcy of a social philosophy regarding the nature and the rights of man that promised a new heaven and a new earth, but was strangled in the blood of the counter-revolution and burnt at the stake of a Congress of Vienna. Our parallel of Wilsonian idealism, the Versailles Treaty, and its consequences is only too obvious. Finally, like our own age, it repudiated the esthetics and the literary theory of the previous age.

The biography of the Romantic Period offers great diversity of human temperaments and personalities: the transfigured mystic Blake, the stoical optimist Wordsworth, the flaming sensualist Byron, the full-blooded, masculine Scott, the shining, sky-soaring Shelley, and young Keats bursting Joy's grape against his palate fine. The children of their literary creation are equally diverse.

The literature of the period covers a vast range of human experience, both real and imaginative: Wordsworth's "joy in widest commonalty spread";

Coleridge's phantom-haunted seas of the *Ancient Mariner* and his enchantments of *Christabel;* Landor dining late with guests few but select, or warming both hands before the fire of life; Scott riding the moors of Scotland and ranging the fields of history; Hazlitt walking along the road from Wem to Shrewsbury, the sun of another's genius lighting up his soul as the wintry sun lighted up the puddles along the road; Lamb talking with his dream-children or jesting over Mrs. Battle's whist; Byron wandering "Between two worlds . . . 'Twixt night and morn," or sending lilies to Augusta from the Rhine, or gazing at the moonlit Colosseum.

Besides these general human interests, the literature of the age holds in store for us some more specialized ones. It explored the past and its meaning. Today the age itself and what it recovered are fruitful for an interpretation of our own history. *"Le Romanticisme, c'est la Révolution."* The Declaration of Independence and the Constitution are its American political children. It was extraordinarily bold and vigorous in its philosophical speculations: Naturalism, Determinism, Humanitarianism, perfectibility, Transcendentalism—these are some of the children or familiars of its household. It is therefore a great segment of human thought. It developed a new esthetics and new literary criticism. Understanding of both is indispensable to the enjoyment of beauty and to knowledge of the history of criticism. It explored rigorously the great problems of conduct. In many ways we are inheritors of its ethics and morality—often rebels against both. Even for intelligent protest and rebellion we need to know them. Out of the ruins of a former world and the glorious glimpses of one but recently discovered, the Romanticists erected a new temple for the worship of God, or whatever rules the universe. For many thoughtful people who have not surrendered faith in a presiding personality, purpose, and plan in the universe, or a belief in the kinship and friendliness of Nature, the faith some of the Romanticists held still offers comfort and consolation.

To all of us, therefore, Romantic literature offers values that might be deemed relevant and useful. Since most of it was written by thoughtful and sensitive young men living in a troubled world recognizably like our own, it may help us both as individuals and as citizens of a new world in the making. This vast storehouse of human experience and personalities offers an opportunity for the discipline of fine scholarship, and an abiding source of enjoyment, truth, and hope.

William Wordsworth
1770–1850

"Fair seed-time had my soul," says Wordsworth of his childhood, and adds that he grew up "Fostered alike by beauty and by fear." He was born on April 7, 1770, at Cockermouth, Cumberland, on the edge of the Lake District, in an old brick house near the "bright blue river" Derwent. His father, John Wordsworth, was an attorney, and the law agent and manor steward for Sir James Lowther; his mother, Anne Cookson Wordsworth, the daughter of a dry-goods merchant of the town of Penrith. There were five children, of whom Dorothy (born December 25, 1771) and John (born December 4, 1772) were his favorites. For about a year he attended an infant school at Penrith with Mary Hutchinson, who was to become his wife. Perhaps his first experience of pain and loss came with the death of his mother, when he was eight years old. The death of his father, five years later, completed the breakup of his home life. The children were scattered, William returning to Hawkshead School, which he had entered in 1778. Here, under the motherly care of old Anne Tyson, who boarded him, and under the excellent tutelage of William Taylor, he received a good classical preparation for college. Equally as important, if not more important, was the informal education he received from his natural surroundings in this beautiful region of lakes and mountains and from his rough-and-tumble fellowship with the other middle-class boys of the school (*The Prelude*, Books First and Second). Trapping among the hills (sometimes taking the other boys' catches and feeling uneasy and fearful for the deed), skating on the lake, "borrowing" a boat that was not his own (and taking fright from "the huge and mighty forms" that drove him from the water and troubled his dreams long thereafter), hanging on the giddy edge of cliffs while bird-nesting (and hearing in the wind "strange utterance") —these are some of the Presences of Nature that wrought upon him the impressive discipline of pain and fear, of beauty and joy.

At seventeen, he entered St. John's College, Cambridge University (*The Prelude*, Books Third, Fourth, Sixth). Here his excellent preparation encouraged him to be "an idler among academic bowers." Here he took more interest in his independent reading and in his imaginative life based on communion with natural surroundings than in the curriculum. But here he felt the sacredness of ground which Spenser and Milton and Newton and the other great Cambridge alumni had trod, and he "ran a boisterous course" with the other undergraduates. The two most memorable events of his college years occurred during summer vacations. The first was a half-mystical experience of self-dedication to poetry that came to him one morning after a night spent at a country dance (*The Prelude*, Book Fourth, ll. 309 ff.). The other occurred during his third summer vacation. Instead of staying at Cambridge and preparing for his "senior comprehensive" examinations, due the following January, he set off with a friend, Robert Jones, for the Alps, walking, "hitchhiking," and floating on canalboats across France, then aflame with early ardors of the Revolution (*The Prelude*, Book Sixth).

The years 1791 to 1796 constitute Wordsworth's period of storm and stress. Graduating from Cambridge in January, 1791, he refused to settle down to a vocation. After loafing in London and in Wales, he went to France with the idea of learning French well enough to qualify himself as a traveling companion and tutor to some young gentleman. At Orleans he met two people who profoundly influenced the course of his life, Captain Michel Beaupuy and Annette Vallon. Captain Beaupuy converted him to the cause of the French Revolution, an experience which constituted the second crisis of his life. At Orleans and later at Blois his association with Annette Vallon, a young Frenchwoman, developed into a *liaison* that resulted in her becoming the mother of a child (Carolyn) by him. Torn by the claims of the revolution and of love, he was on the point of casting his lot with the French people, but financial exhaustion that in part prevented marriage or longer residence in France forced him back home. His probable plan to recoup, return, and marry Annette was prevented by the outbreak of war between France and England in 1793. Unless he smuggled himself across the channel in 1793 to visit her, he did not see her again until the short peace of 1802, during which time they met, agreed upon the inadvisability of marriage, and settled the relationship in a manner honorable to him. His agitation over this passion and its frustration, the shock he received when England went to war with France in 1793, his gradual disillusionment in the revolution as it ceased to be a struggle for human liberation and became a bloody and heartless game of power politics, his fruitless search for congenial employment, his homeless wanderings, and the failure of Godwin's rationalism to offer a philosophic stay, all brought him to a spiritual catastrophe in which he "Yielded up moral questions in despair" (*The Prelude*, Book Eleventh).

In the meantime, an event had occurred to make possible the visitation of three good angels. In 1795 a wealthy young gentleman, Raisley Calvert, whom Wordsworth had served as nurse and companion, died leaving him the income from a legacy of about $4500. This enabled him to take a cottage with his beloved sister Dorothy at Racedown, on the southern coast. About the same time he met Samuel Taylor Coleridge. Dorothy and Coleridge brought him back to those sweet counsels between head and heart and to that consolation of nature which he had lost during his period of despair. The growing intimacy of the three young people induced William and Dorothy to move to Alfoxden, in Somerset, to be neighbors to Coleridge, who lived at Nether Stowey, three miles away. From July, 1797, to June, 1798, they were "three persons and one soul," visiting almost daily and writing most of the poems that were to go into *Lyrical Ballads*.

Shortly before this little volume appeared (in September, 1798), the three set out for Germany, to study its language, literature, science, and philosophy. Instead of seriously pursuing any of these, Wordsworth became homesick, wrote the Lucy poems (possibly about some English girl he had known in his boyhood), recorded scenes and incidents of his early life which he was to incorporate later in *The Prelude*, and felt the glow of reviving love for his country. By May, 1799, he and Dorothy had returned and were visiting Mary Hutchinson, whom William was too poor to marry. Late that year he and Dorothy settled in Dove Cottage, Grasmere, within thirty miles of his birthplace. In this neighborhood, the heart of the Lake Country, the poet was to spend the rest of his life.

Compared with the first twenty-nine years, the next fifty-one were "unenriched by strange event." Steady devotion to poetic composition, the results of which appeared in successive editions of *Lyrical Ballads*, *Poems in Two Volumes* (1807), and *The Excursion* (1814) and a collective edition of his poems (1815); his settlement with Annette in 1802 and his marriage with Mary Hutchinson; grief and distress over Coleridge's physical and moral degradation (see

"Dejection: An Ode" and "Resolution and Independence"); indignation at Napoleon's bloody rise to power, and a corresponding growth of patriotic fervor (sonnets of 1802); a steady drift toward political conservatism; a tour of Scotland; the death by drowning of his sailor brother John in February, 1805; the growth of a family; the gradual waning of his power to react vividly to natural beauty, a sense of "the unimaginable touch of time"—these are some of the events and experiences of the middle years recorded in Wordsworth's poetry. He published much verse after 1815, most of it fine in workmanship, some of it recapturing his early freshness and power; but except for *The Prelude* (finished in its first form in 1805, constantly revised thereafter for thirty years, and published posthumously), little of Wordsworth's poetry after 1815 is of interest to any but scholars. Popularity came late to him, but when he died in 1850 he was generally recognized as the greatest and noblest poet of his generation, and Tennyson was proud to receive the laureateship from him, greener because of the head of him that had worn it.

In the phrase "On man, on nature, and on human life, Musing in solitude," Wordsworth names the three great themes of his poetry; he also describes the mood in which his poetry was composed, and suggests the dominant emotional chord that it strikes in the heart of a receptive reader. Whatever vitality of meaning and appeal his poetry may have today derives from the freshness with which he described objects and scenes suggesting these themes, and the power and insight with which he treated their interrelationships.

More than any other poet Wordsworth is concerned with the relation between the inner life of man and the outward life of the world of nature. It was his fundamental conviction that the individual mind is fitted to the external world, and the external world is fitted to the mind. Human happiness was to be found only when "the discerning intellect of Man" was "wedded to this goodly universe In love and holy passion." His own experience and the associational psychology which he learned in his late twenties taught him that the mind of man, with all its ideas, its feelings, its pains and pleasures, was built up from sensations by some mysterious spiritual power in man and in the universe. The ultimate source of all sensations was nature. Nature operated upon his nervous organism in two reciprocal ways, producing emotion and calmness, excitation and peace. Since it was the fount of all his feelings and ideas, he should expose himself to its purest and most beautiful forms. The best attitude toward this source of goodness and truth was not pride in intellect and reason, not hot and selfish striving, but a wise passiveness, an opening of the windows of the soul. The universe itself was spirit. Truth pulsed through it, and the soul must be energized and attuned. Human life was a progressive development of power to respond to the beauty and truth of the universe revealed through nature. In childhood, this response was merely physical stimulation, increased animal activity. In youth, it was feeling and passion, but not reflective thought or deep social sympathy. In manhood, however, it was sensitiveness to "the still sad music of humanity," and "a sense sublime of something far more deeply interfused"; that is, a living knowledge of the spirit of the universe and an ability to unite ecstatically with it in the ultimate of religious experience. Such a votary of nature was Wordsworth at the height of his optimistic faith (as in "Tintern Abbey" and *The Prelude*):

> "well pleased to recognize
> In nature and the language of the sense
> The anchor of my purest thoughts, the nurse,
> The guide, the guardian of my heart, and soul
> Of all my moral being.'

The story of Wordsworth's career as a poet after about 1805 is the story of slow onslaughts on that religion of nature, of brave but not often convincing reassertions of it, of a gradual modification of it in the direction of increasing reliance upon the powers and virtues of man as man, not as a creature of nature, and upon orthodox Christianity. "Resolution and Independence," "Ode to Duty," "Elegiac Stanzas (Peele Castle)," "Ode: Intimations of Immortality," "Composed upon an Evening of Extraordinary Splendour and Beauty"—these most plainly tell the story. Side by side with them and closely connected with them are other poems, such as "My Heart Leaps Up," "To the Cuckoo," and "To a Butterfly," which on smaller scales than "Tintern Abbey" and *The Prelude* show the poet trying to bind his days together, to view human life as an integral, organic, unfolding experience, having its origin and its continuation in eternity.

Through his development of his second great theme, man in this world and in society, Wordsworth made perhaps his most permanent impression upon modern thought and life. If in his poetry of nature he pointed out sources of beauty to which we are no longer so responsive as men once were, and if in his interpretation of its significance he affirms a faith that many good men and women cannot share with him, the same can hardly be said about his treatment of the human figures near the soil whom he painted against his backgrounds of austere mountains and lonely moors and Highland glens. His faith in the dignity and nobility of simple men and women—in his Old Cumberland Beggar, his Simon Lee, his Margaret of the ruined cottage, his Highland women, his Michael, his leech-gatherer—has hardly been subjected to the same discount. Readers as we are of Hardy, Synge, Masefield, Elizabeth Madox Roberts, Ellen Glasgow, Robert Frost, we still accept a literary tradition which he did more to establish than did Cowper, Gray, Crabbe, Burns, and all the eighteenth-century poets together. With the sanction of such poets as Walt Whitman, lonely roads continue to be open schools in which we daily read with delight the passions of mankind.

Today the poetry of William Wordsworth is the inspiration and rallying ground of many cultivated people who believe that the physical universe is a spiritually habitable home for man. Wordsworth is the champion of those who affirm the worth, the dignity, and the nobility of our common humanity. He is on the side of primal human instincts, elemental affections, simple human decency, plain living and high thinking, freedom of the spirit, and a conception of life not as a huddled confusion, a thing of shreds and patches, but as a unified, progressive, infinite experience.

> "Our destiny, our being's heart and home
> Is with infinitude, and only there."
> *The Prelude*, Book VI, ll. 604-05

from THE PRELUDE;

OR, GROWTH OF A POET'S MIND

An Autobiographical Poem

"Several years ago," wrote Wordsworth in "Preface to the Edition of 1814," "when the Author retired to his native mountains, with the hope of being enabled to construct a literary work that might live, it was reasonable that he should take a review of his own mind, and examine how far Nature and Education had qualified him for such employment. As subsidiary to this preparation, he undertook to record, in verse, the origin and progress of his own powers . . . That work [was] addressed to a dear Friend [Coleridge]. . . . The preparatory poem is biographical, and conducts the history of the Author's mind to the point when he was emboldened to hope that his faculties were sufficiently matured for entering upon the arduous labour which he had proposed to himself."

The poem was completed, in the first version, in 1805; read to Coleridge in 1807 (see pages 101–103, below); revised constantly between that date and 1839; and published posthumously in 1850, Mrs. Wordsworth supplying the title and Bishop Wordsworth the subtitle. In 1926 the 1805 version was published by Ernest de Sélincourt, on pages facing the 1850 version, from which our selections are taken.

"*The Prelude*," wrote Professor de Sélincourt, "is the essential living document for the interpretation of Wordsworth's life and poetry." Wordsworth's account of "the origin and progress of his powers" was written in accordance with a transcendentalized modification of Hartley's associationism (see pages 9, 10, and 15). The following selections include several statements of the governing philosophical principle and all the "crises" in Wordsworth's life (pointed out in footnotes). In reading these selections, the student will do well to refer frequently to the preceding biographical-critical sketch of Wordsworth.

BOOK FIRST—CHILDHOOD AND SCHOOL-TIME

When he had left the mountains and received   282
On his smooth breast the shadow of those towers
That yet survive, a shattered monument
Of feudal sway, the bright blue river passed
Along the margin of our terrace walk;
A tempting playmate whom we dearly loved.
Oh, many a time have I, a five years' child,
In a small mill-race severed from his stream,
Made one long bathing of a summer's day;   290
Basked in the sun, and plunged and basked again
Alternate, all a summer's day, or scoured
The sandy fields, leaping through flowery groves
Of yellow ragwort; or when rock and hill,
The woods, and distant Skiddaw's lofty height,

Were bronzed with deepest radiance, stood alone
Beneath the sky, as if I had been born
On Indian plains, and from my mother's hut
Had run abroad in wantonness, to sport,
A naked savage, in the thunder shower.   300

Fair seed-time had my soul, and I grew up
Fostered alike by beauty and by fear:
Much favoured in my birth-place, and no less
In that belovèd Vale to which erelong
We were transplanted;—there were we let loose
For sports of wider range. Ere I had told
Ten birth-days, when among the mountain slopes
Frost, and the breath of frosty wind, had snapped
The last autumnal crocus, 'twas my joy
With store of springes o'er my shoulder hung   310
To range the open heights where woodcocks run
Among the smooth green turf. Through half the night,
Scudding away from snare to snare, I plied
That anxious visitation;—moon and stars
Were shining o'er my head. I was alone,
And seemed to be a trouble to the peace
That dwelt among them. Sometimes it befell
In these night wanderings, that a strong desire
O'erpowered my better reason, and the bird
Which was the captive of another's toil   320
Became my prey; and when the deed was done
I heard among the solitary hills
Low breathings coming after me, and sounds
Of undistinguishable motion, steps
Almost as silent as the turf they trod.

Nor less, when spring had warmed the cultured vale,
Moved we as plunderers where the mother-bird
Had in high places built her lodge; though mean
Our object and inglorious, yet the end
Was not ignoble. Oh! when I have hung   330
Above the raven's nest, by knots of grass
And half-inch fissures in the slippery rock
But ill sustained, and almost (so it seemed)
Suspended by the blast that blew amain,
Shouldering the naked crag, oh, at that time
While on the perilous ridge I hung alone,
With what strange utterance did the loud dry wind
Blow through my ear! the sky seemed not a sky
Of earth—and with what motion moved the clouds!

---

283. those towers, Cockermouth Castle.   **285. river,** the Derwent.

304. Vale, Esthwaite, where Hawkshead School was. **310. springes,** snares or nooses.

Dust as we are, the immortal spirit grows   340
Like harmony in music; there is a dark
Inscrutable workmanship that reconciles
Discordant elements, makes them cling together
In one society. How strange, that all
The terrors, pains, and early miseries,
Regrets, vexations, lassitudes interfused
Within my mind, should e'er have borne a part,
And that a needful part, in making up
The calm existence that is mine when I
Am worthy of myself! Praise to the end!   350
Thanks to the means which Nature deigned to
      employ;
Whether her fearless visitings, or those
That came with soft alarm, like hurtless light
Opening the peaceful clouds; or she would use
Severer interventions, ministry
More palpable, as best might suit her aim.

One summer evening (led by her) I found
A little boat tied to a willow tree
Within a rocky cave, its usual home.
Straight I unloosed her chain, and stepping in   360
Pushed from the shore. It was an act of stealth
And troubled pleasure, nor without the voice
Of mountain-echoes did my boat move on;
Leaving behind her still, on either side,
Small circles glittering idly in the moon,
Until they melted all into one track
Of sparkling light. But now, like one who rows,
Proud of his skill, to reach a chosen point
With an unswerving line, I fixed my view
Upon the summit of a craggy ridge,   370
The horizon's utmost boundary; far above
Was nothing but the stars and the grey sky.
She was an elfin pinnace; lustily
I dipped my oars into the silent lake,
And, as I rose upon the stroke, my boat
Went heaving through the water like a swan;
When, from behind that craggy steep till then
The horizon's bound, a huge peak, black and huge,
As if with voluntary power instinct,
Upreared its head. I struck and struck again,   380
And growing still in stature the grim shape
Towered up between me and the stars, and still,
For so it seemed, with purpose of its own
And measured motion like a living thing,
Strode after me. With trembling oars I turned,
And through the silent water stole my way
Back to the covert of the willow tree;
There in her mooring-place I left my bark,—

340. **Dust as we are.** One of several statements of the
principle in accordance with which the poet's mind and
soul developed.

And through the meadows homeward went, in
      grave
And serious mood; but after I had seen   390
That spectacle, for many days, my brain
Worked with a dim and undetermined sense
Of unknown modes of being; o'er my thoughts
There hung a darkness, call it solitude
Or blank desertion. No familiar shapes
Remained, no pleasant images of trees,
Of sea or sky, no colours of green fields;
But huge and mighty forms, that do not live
Like living men, moved slowly through the mind
By day, and were a trouble to my dreams.   400

Wisdom and Spirit of the universe!
Thou Soul that art the eternity of thought,
That givest to forms and images a breath
And everlasting motion, not in vain
By day or star-light thus from my first dawn
Of childhood didst thou intertwine for me
The passions that build up our human soul;
Not with the mean and vulgar works of man,
But with high objects, with enduring things—
With life and nature—purifying thus   410
The elements of feeling and of thought,
And sanctifying, by such discipline,
Both pain and fear, until we recognise
A grandeur in the beatings of the heart.
Nor was this fellowship vouchsafed to me
With stinted kindness. In November days,
When vapours rolling down the valley made
A lonely scene more lonesome, among woods,
At noon and 'mid the calm of summer nights,
When, by the margin of the trembling lake,   420
Beneath the gloomy hills homeward I went
In solitude, such intercourse was mine;
Mine was it in the fields both day and night,
And by the waters, all the summer long.

And in the frosty season, when the sun
Was set, and visible for many a mile
The cottage windows blazed through twilight
      gloom,
I heeded not their summons: happy time
It was indeed for all of us—for me
It was a time of rapture! Clear and loud   430
The village clock tolled six,—I wheeled about,
Proud and exulting like an untired horse
That cares not for his home. All shod with steel,
We hissed along the polished ice in games
Confederate, imitative of the chase
And woodland pleasures,—the resounding horn,
The pack loud chiming, and the hunted hare.
So through the darkness and the cold we flew,

And not a voice was idle; with the din
Smitten, the precipices rang aloud;   440
The leafless trees and every icy crag
Tinkled like iron; while far distant hills
Into the tumult sent an alien sound
Of melancholy not unnoticed, while the stars
Eastward were sparkling clear, and in the west
The orange sky of evening died away.
Not seldom from the uproar I retired
Into a silent bay, or sportively
Glanced sideway, leaving the tumultuous throng,
To cut across the reflex of a star   450
That fled, and, flying still before me, gleamed
Upon the glassy plain; and oftentimes,
When we had given our bodies to the wind,
And all the shadowy banks on either side
Came sweeping through the darkness, spinning still
The rapid line of motion, then at once
Have I, reclining back upon my heels,
Stopped short; yet still the solitary cliffs
Wheeled by me—even as if the earth had rolled
With visible motion her diurnal round!   460
Behind me did they stretch in solemn train,
Feebler and feebler, and I stood and watched
Till all was tranquil as a dreamless sleep.

　　Ye Presences of Nature in the sky
And on the earth! Ye Visions of the hills!
And Souls of lonely places! can I think
A vulgar hope was yours when ye employed
Such ministry, when ye, through many a year
Haunting me thus among my boyish sports,
On caves and trees, upon the woods and hills,   470
Impressed, upon all forms, the characters
Of danger or desire; and thus did make
The surface of the universal earth,
With triumph and delight, with hope and fear,
Work like a sea? . . . .

BOOK THIRD—RESIDENCE AT CAMBRIDGE

　　The Evangelist St. John my patron was:
Three Gothic courts are his, and in the first
Was my abiding-place, a nook obscure;
Right underneath, the College kitchens made
A humming sound, less tuneable than bees,   50
But hardly less industrious; with shrill notes
Of sharp command and scolding intermixed.
Near me hung Trinity's loquacious clock,

Who never let the quarters, night or day,
Slip by him unproclaimed, and told the hours
Twice over with a male and female voice.
Her pealing organ was my neighbour too;
And from my pillow, looking forth by light
Of moon or favouring stars, I could behold
The antechapel where the statue stood   60
Of Newton with his prism and silent face,
The marble index of a mind for ever
Voyaging through strange seas of Thought,
　alone. . . .

We sauntered, played, or rioted; we talked
Unprofitable talk at morning hours;
Drifted about along the streets and walks,   250
Read lazily in trivial books, went forth
To gallop through the country in blind zeal
Of senseless horsemanship, or on the breast
Of Cam sailed boisterously, and let the stars
Come forth, perhaps without one quiet
　thought. . . .

Beside the pleasant Mill of Trompington
I laughed with Chaucer in the hawthorn shade;
Heard him, while birds were warbling, tell his
　tales
Of amorous passion. And that gentle Bard,
Chosen by the Muses for their Page of State—
Sweet Spenser, moving through his clouded
　heaven   280
With the moon's beauty and the moon's soft pace,
I called him Brother, Englishman, and Friend!
Yea, our blind Poet, who in his later day,
Stood almost single; uttering odious truth—
Darkness before, and danger's voice behind,
Soul awful—if the earth has ever lodged
An awful soul—I seemed to see him here
Familiarly, and in his scholar's dress
Bounding before me, yet a stripling youth—
A boy, no better, with his rosy cheeks   290
Angelical, keen eye, courageous look,
And conscious step of purity and pride.
Among the band of my compeers was one
Whom chance had stationed in the very room
Honoured by Milton's name. O temperate Bard!
Be it confest that, for the first time, seated
Within thy innocent lodge and oratory,
One of a festive circle, I poured out
Libations, to thy memory drank, till pride
And gratitude grew dizzy in a brain   300
Never excited by the fumes of wine

---

439. **with the din,** the beginning of a passage notable for its onomatopoeia (choice of words imitative of natural sounds). 468. **such ministry,** another statement of the principle mentioned in the footnote on l. 340, above. The bird-nesting, boat-stealing, and skating anecdotes are examples of the working of the principle.

61. **Newton with his prism,** one of the beautiful additions to the 1805 version. 254. **Cam,** the river on the banks of which Cambridge stands.

Before that hour, or since. Then, forth I ran
From the assembly; through a length of streets,
Ran, ostrich-like, to reach our chapel door
In not a desperate or opprobrious time,
Albeit long after the importunate bell
Had stopped, with wearisome Cassandra voice
No longer haunting the dark winter night. . . .

             Was ever known
The witless shepherd who persists to drive
A flock that thirsts not to a pool disliked?
A weight must surely hang on days begun
And ended with such mockery. Be wise,
Ye Presidents and Deans, and, till the spirit   410
Of ancient times revive, and youth be trained
At home in pious service, to your bells
Give seasonable rest, for 'tis a sound
Hollow as ever vexed the tranquil air;
And your officious doings bring disgrace
On the plain steeples of our English Church,
Whose worship, 'mid remotest village trees,
Suffers for this. Even Science, too, at hand
In daily sight of this irreverence,
Is smitten thence with an unnatural taint,   420
Loses her just authority, falls beneath
Collateral suspicion, else unknown.
This truth escaped me not, and I confess,
That having 'mid my native hills given loose
To a schoolboy's vision, I had raised a pile
Upon the basis of the coming time,
That fell in ruins round me. Oh, what joy
To see a sanctuary for our country's youth
Informed with such a spirit as might be
Its own protection; a primeval grove,   430
Where, though the shades with cheerfulness were
    filled,
Nor indigent of songs warbled from crowds
In under-coverts, yet the countenance
Of the whole place should bear a stamp of awe;
A habitation sober and demure
For ruminating creatures; a domain
For quiet things to wander in; a haunt
In which the heron should delight to feed
By the shy rivers, and the pelican
Upon the cypress spire in lonely-thought   440
Might sit and sun himself. . . .

  Thus in submissive idleness, my Friend!
The labouring time of autumn, winter, spring,   630
Eight months! rolled pleasingly away; the ninth
Came and returned me to my native hills.

307. **Cassandra,** daughter of King Priam of Troy. She
foretold the fall of Troy. **629. my Friend,** Coleridge, to
whom *The Prelude* was addressed.

BOOK FOURTH—SUMMER VACATION

                'Mid a throng
Of maids and youths, old men, and matrons
    staid,   310
A medley of all tempers, I had passed
The night in dancing, gaiety, and mirth,
With din of instruments and shuffling feet,
And glancing forms, and tapers glittering,
And unaimed prattle flying up and down;
Spirits upon the stretch, and here and there
Slight shocks of young love-liking interspersed,
Whose transient pleasure mounted to the head,
And tingled through the veins. Ere we retired,
The cock had crowed, and now the eastern sky   320
Was kindling, not unseen, from humble copse
And open field, through which the pathway wound,
And homeward led my steps. Magnificent
The morning rose, in memorable pomp,
Glorious as e'er I had beheld—in front,
The sea lay laughing at a distance; near,
The solid mountains shone, bright as the clouds,
Grain-tinctured, drenched in empyrean light;
And in the meadows and the lower grounds
Was all the sweetness of a common dawn—   330
Dews, vapours, and the melody of birds,
And labourers going forth to till the fields.
Ah! need I say, dear Friend! that to the brim
My heart was full; I made no vows, but vows
Were then made for me; bond unknown to me
Was given, that I should be, else sinning greatly,
A dedicated Spirit. On I walked
In thankful blessedness, which yet survives. . . .

BOOK FIFTH—BOOKS

                Yet is it just
That here, in memory of all books which lay
Their sure foundations in the heart of man,
Whether by native prose, or numerous verse,
That in the name of all inspirèd souls—   200
From Homer the great Thunderer, from the voice
That roars along the bed of Jewish song,
And that more varied and elaborate,
Those trumpet-tones of harmony that shake
Our shores in England,—from those loftiest notes
Down to the low and wren-like warblings, made
For cottages and spinners at the wheel,
And sun-burnt travellers resting their tired limbs
Stretched under wayside hedge-rows, ballad
    tunes,   210

328. **Grain-tinctured,** dyed scarlet or purple. **337. dedicated Spirit.** The passage ending here marks Wordsworth's
first personal crisis.

Food for the hungry ears of little ones,
And of old men who have survived their joys—
'Tis just that in behalf of these, the works,
And of the men that framed them, whether known
Or sleeping nameless in their scattered graves,
That I should here assert their rights, attest
Their honours, and should, once for all, pronounce
Their benediction; speak of them as Powers
For ever to be hallowed; only less,
For what we are and what we may become,   220
Than Nature's self, which is the breath of God
Or His pure word by miracle revealed. . . .

A precious treasure had I long possessed,   460
A little yellow, canvas-covered book,
A slender abstract of the Arabian tales;
And, from companions in a new abode,
When first I learnt, that this dear prize of mine
Was but a block hewn from a mighty quarry—
That there were four large volumes, laden all
With kindred matter, 'twas to me, in truth,
A promise scarcely earthly. Instantly,
With one not richer than myself, I made
A covenant that each should lay aside   470
The moneys he possessed, and hoard up more
Till our joint savings had amassed enough
To make this book our own. Through several months,
In spite of temptation, we preserved
Religiously that vow; but firmness failed,
Nor were we ever masters of our wish.

And when thereafter to my father's house
The holidays returned me, there to find
That golden store of books which I had left,
What joy was mine! How often in the course   480
Of those glad respites, though a soft west wind
Ruffled the waters to the angler's wish,
For a whole day together, have I lain
Down by thy side, O Derwent! murmuring stream,
On the hot stones, and in the glaring sun,
And there have read, devouring as I read,
Defrauding the day's glory, desperate!
Till with a sudden bound of smart reproach,
Such as an idler deals with in his shame,
I to the sport betook myself again. . . .   490

BOOK SIXTH—CAMBRIDGE AND THE ALPS

When from the Vallais we had turned, and clomb   562
Along the Simplon's steep and rugged road,

562. **Vallais,** modern Valais, a canton in southwestern Switzerland.

Following a band of muleteers, we reached
A halting-place, where all together took
Their noon-tide meal. Hastily rose our guide,
Leaving us at the board; awhile we lingered,
Then paced the beaten downward way that led
Right to a rough stream's edge, and there broke off;   570
The only track now visible was one
That from the torrent's further brink held forth
Conspicuous invitation to ascend
A lofty mountain. After brief delay
Crossing the unbridged stream, that road we took
And clomb with eagerness, till anxious fears
Intruded, for we failed to overtake
Our comrades gone before. By fortunate chance,
While every moment added doubt to doubt,
A peasant met us, from whose mouth we learned
That to the spot which had perplexed us first   580
We must descend, and there should find the road,
Which in the stony channel of the stream
Lay a few steps, and then along its banks;
And, that our future course, all plain to sight,
Was downwards, with the current of that stream.
Loth to believe what we so grieved to hear,
For still we had hopes that pointed to the clouds,
We questioned him again, and yet again;
But every word that from the peasant's lips
Came in reply, translated by our feelings,   590
Ended in this,—*that we had crossed the Alps.*

Imagination—here the Power so called
Through sad incompetence of human speech,
That awful Power rose from the mind's abyss
Like an unfathered vapour that enwraps,
At once, some lonely traveller. I was lost;
Halted without an effort to break through;
But to my conscious soul I now can say—
"I recognise thy glory": in such strength
Of usurpation, when the light of sense   600
Goes out, but with a flash that has revealed
The invisible world, doth greatness make abode,
There harbours; whether we be young or old,
Our destiny, our being's heart and home,
Is with infinitude, and only there;
With hope it is, hope that can never die,
Effort, and expectation, and desire,
And something evermore about to be.
Under such banners militant, the soul
Seeks for no trophies, struggles for no spoils   610
That may attest her prowess, blest in thoughts
That are their own perfection and reward,
Strong in herself and in beatitude
That hides her, like the mighty flood of Nile
Poured from his fount of Abyssinian clouds
To fertilise the whole Egyptian plain.

The melancholy slackening that ensued
Upon these tidings by the peasant given
Was soon dislodged. Downwards we hurried fast,
And, with the half-shaped road which we had
    missed,   620
Entered a narrow chasm. The brook and road
Were fellow-travellers in this gloomy strait,
And with them did we journey several hours
At a slow pace. The immeasurable height
Of woods decaying, never to be decayed,
The stationary blasts of waterfalls,
And in the narrow rent at every turn
Winds thwarting winds, bewildered and forlorn,
The torrents shooting from the clear blue sky,
The rocks that muttered close upon our ears, 630
Black drizzling crags that spake by the way-side
As if a voice were in them, the sick sight
And giddy prospect of the raving stream,
The unfettered clouds and region of the Heavens,
Tumult and peace, the darkness and the light—
Were all like workings of one mind, the features
Of the same face, blossoms upon one tree;
Characters of the great Apocalypse,
The types and symbols of Eternity,
Of first, and last, and midst, and without
    end. . . .   640

BOOK SEVENTH—RESIDENCE IN LONDON

Rise up, thou monstrous ant-hill on the plain
Of a too busy world! Before me flow, 150
Thou endless stream of men and moving things!
Thy every-day appearance, as it strikes—
With wonder heightened, or sublimed by awe—
On strangers, of all ages; the quick dance
Of colours, lights, and forms; the deafening din;
The comers and the goers face to face,
Face after face; the string of dazzling wares,
Shop after shop, with symbols, blazoned names
And all the tradesman's honours overhead:
Here, fronts of houses, like a title-page, 160
With letters huge inscribed from top to toe,
Stationed above the door, like guardian saints;
There, allegoric shapes, female and male,
Or physiognomies of real men,
Land-warriors, kings, or admirals of the sea,
Boyle, Shakespeare, Newton, or the attractive head
Of some quack-doctor, famous in his day. . . .

Enough;—the mighty concourse I surveyed 220
With no unthinking mind, well pleased to note

---

638. **Apocalypse**, Revelation. See the Book of John.
166. **Boyle,** Robert Boyle (1627–1691), English chemist
and physicist.

Among the crowd all specimens of man,
Through all the colours which the sun bestows,
And every character of form and face:
The Swede, the Russian; from the genial south,
The Frenchman and the Spaniard; from the remote
America, the Hunter-Indian; Moors,
Malays, Lascars, the Tartar, the Chinese,
And Negro Ladies in white muslin gowns. . . .

Oh, blank confusion! True epitome 722
Of what the mighty City is herself,
To thousands upon thousands of her sons,
Living amid the same perpetual whirl
Of trivial objects, melted and reduced
To one identity, by differences
That have no law, no meaning, and no end—
Oppression, under which even highest minds
Must labour, whence the strongest are not free. 730
But though the picture weary out the eye,
By nature an unmanageable sight,
It is not wholly so to him who looks
In steadiness, who hath among least things
An under-sense of greatest; sees the parts
As parts, but with a feeling of the whole.
This, of all acquisitions, first awaits
On sundry and most widely different modes
Of education, nor with least delight
On that through which I passed. Attention
    springs,   740
And comprehensiveness and memory flow,
From early converse with the works of God
Among all regions; chiefly where appear
Most obviously simplicity and power.
Think, how the everlasting streams and woods,
Stretched and still stretching far and wide, exalt
The roving Indian, on his desert sands:
What grandeur not unfelt, what pregnant show
Of beauty, meets the sun-burnt Arab's eye:
And, as the sea propels, from zone to zone, 750
Its currents; magnifies its shoals of life
Beyond all compass; spreads, and sends aloft
Armies of clouds,—even so, its powers and aspects
Shape for mankind, by principles as fixed,
The views and aspirations of the soul
To majesty. Like virtue have the forms
Perennial of the ancient hills; nor less
The changeful language of their countenances
Quickens the slumbering mind, and aids the
    thoughts,
However multitudinous, to move 760
With order and relation. This, if still,
As hitherto, in freedom I may speak,
Not violating any just restraint,

---

228. **Lascars,** East Indians.

As may be hoped, of real modesty,—
This did I feel, in London's vast domain.
The Spirit of Nature was upon me there;
The soul of Beauty and enduring Life
Vouchsafed her inspiration, and diffused,
Through meagre lines and colours, and the press
Of self-destroying, transitory things,   770
Composure, and ennobling Harmony.

BOOK EIGHTH—RETROSPECT—LOVE OF
NATURE LEADING TO LOVE OF MAN

For me, when my affections first were led   121
From kindred, friends, and playmates, to partake
Love for the human creature's absolute self,
That noticeable kindliness of heart
Sprang out of fountains, there abounding most,
Where sovereign Nature dictated the tasks
And occupations which her beauty adorned,
And Shepherds were the men that pleased me
    first. . . .

                                    Yet, hail to you
Moors, mountains, headlands, and ye hollow vales,
Ye long deep channels for the Atlantic's voice,
Powers of my native region! Ye that seize
The heart with firmer grasp! Your snows and
    streams
Ungovernable, and your terrifying winds,   220
That howl so dismally for him who treads
Companionless your awful solitudes!
There, 'tis the shepherd's task the winter long
To wait upon the storms: of their approach
Sagacious, into sheltering coves he drives
His flock, and thither from the homestead bears
A toilsome burden up the craggy ways,
And deals it out, their regular nourishment
Strewn on the frozen snow. And when the spring
Looks out, and all the pastures dance with lambs,
And when the flock, with warmer weather, climbs
Higher and higher, him his office leads   232
To watch their goings, whatsoever track
The wanderers choose. For this he quits his home
At day-spring, and no sooner doth the sun
Begin to strike him with a fire-like heat,
Than he lies down upon some shining rock,
And breakfasts with his dog. When they have
    stolen,
As is their wont, a pittance from strict time,
For rest not needed or exchange of love,   240
Then from his couch he starts; and now his feet
Crush out a livelier fragrance from the flowers

128. **Shepherds . . . pleased me first.** See "Michael,"
especially ll. 21 ff.

Of lowly thyme, by Nature's skill enwrought
In the wild turf: the lingering dews of morn
Smoke round him, as from hill to hill he hies,
His staff protending like a hunter's spear,
Or by its aid leaping from crag to crag,
And o'er the brawling beds of unbridged streams.
Philosophy, methinks, at Fancy's call,
Might deign to follow him through what he does 250
Or sees in his day's march; himself he feels,
In those vast regions where his service lies,
A freeman, wedded to his life of hope
And hazard, and hard labour interchanged
With that majestic indolence so dear
To native man. A rambling schoolboy, thus,
I felt his presence in his own domain,
As of a lord and master, or a power,
Or genius, under Nature, under God,
Presiding; and severest solitude   260
Had more commanding looks when he was there.
When up the lonely brooks on rainy days
Angling I went, or trod the trackless hills
By mists bewildered, suddenly mine eyes
Have glanced upon him distant a few steps,
In size a giant, stalking through thick fog,
His sheep like Greenland bears; or, as he stepped
Beyond the boundary line of some hill-shadow,
His form hath flashed upon me, glorified
By the deep radiance of the setting sun: 270
Or him have I descried in distant sky,
A solitary object and sublime,
Above all height! like an aerial cross
Stationed alone upon a spiry rock
Of the Chartreuse, for worship. Thus was man
Ennobled outwardly before my sight,
And thus my heart was early introduced
To an unconscious love and reverence
Of human nature. . . .

                              Call ye these appearances—
Which I beheld of shepherds in my youth,
This sanctity of Nature given to man—
A shadow, a delusion, ye who pore
On the dead letter, miss the spirit of things;
Whose truth is not a motion or a shape
Instinct with vital functions, but a block
Or waxen image which yourselves have made,   300
And ye adore! But blessèd be the God
Of Nature and of Man that this was so;
That men before my inexperienced eyes
Did first present themselves thus purified,
Removed, and to a distance that was fit:

275. **Chartreuse,** mountains near Grenoble, France, and
the famous monastery situated in them, which Wordsworth
saw in 1790.

And so we all of us in some degree
Are led to knowledge, wheresoever led,
And howsoever; were it otherwise,
And we found evil fast as we find good
In our first years, or think that it is found,   310
How could the innocent heart bear up and live!
But doubly fortunate my lot; not here
Alone, that something of a better life
Perhaps was round me than it is the privilege
Of most to move in, but that first I looked
At Man through objects that were great or fair;
First communed with him by their help.
    And thus
Was founded a sure safeguard and defence
Against the weight of meanness, selfish cares,
Coarse manners, vulgar passions, that beat in   320
On all sides from the ordinary world
In which we traffic. . . . .

BOOK NINTH—RESIDENCE IN FRANCE

France lured me forth; the realm that I had
    crossed
So lately, journeying toward the snow-clad Alps.
But now, relinquishing the scrip and staff,
And all enjoyment which the summer sun
Sheds round the steps of those who meet the day
With motion constant as his own, I went
Prepared to sojourn in a pleasant town,   40
Washed by the current of the stately Loire.

    Through Paris lay my readiest course, and there
Sojourning a few days, I visited
In haste, each spot of old or recent fame,
The latter chiefly; from the field of Mars
Down to the suburbs of St. Antony,
And from the Mont Martre southward to the Dome
Of Geneviève. In both her clamorous Halls,
The National Synod and the Jacobins,
I saw the Revolutionary Power   50
Toss like a ship at anchor, rocked by storms;
The Arcades I traversed, in the Palace huge
Of Orleans; coasted round and round the line
Of Tavern, Brothel, Gaming-house, and Shop,
Great rendezvous of worst and best, the walk
Of all who had a purpose, or had not;
I stared and listened, with a stranger's ears,
To Hawkers and Haranguers, hubbub wild!
And hissing Factionists with ardent eyes,
In knots, or pairs, or single. Not a look   60
Hope takes, or Doubt or Fear is forced to wear,
But seemed there present; and I scanned them all,
Watched every gesture uncontrollable,
Of anger, and vexation, and despite,

All side by side, and struggling face to face,
With gaiety and dissolute idleness.

    Where silent zephyrs sported with the dust
Of the Bastille, I sate in the open sun,
And from the rubbish gathered up a stone,
And pocketed the relic, in the guise   70
Of an enthusiast: yet, in honest truth,
I looked for something that I could not find,
Affecting more emotion than I felt;
For 'tis most certain, that these various sights,
However potent their first shock, with me
Appeared to recompense the traveller's pains
Less than the painted Magdalene of Le Brun,
A beauty exquisitely wrought, with hair
Dishevelled, gleaming eyes, and rueful cheek
Pale and bedropped with overflowing tears.   80

    But hence to my more permanent abode
I hasten; there, by novelties in speech,
Domestic manners, customs, gestures, looks,
And all the attire of ordinary life,
Attention was engrossed; and, thus amused,
I stood, 'mid those concussions, unconcerned,
Tranquil almost, and careless as a flower
Glassed in a greenhouse, or a parlour shrub
That spreads its leaves in unmolested peace,
While every bush and tree, the country through,   90
Is shaking to the roots: indifference this
Which may seem strange: but I was unprepared
With needful knowledge, had abruptly passed
Into a theatre, whose stage was filled
And busy with an action far advanced.
Like others, I had skimmed, and sometimes read
With care, the master-pamphlets of the day;
Nor wanted such half-insight as grew wild
Upon that meagre soil, helped out by talk
And public news; but having never seen   100
A chronicle that might suffice to show
Whence the main organs of the public power
Had sprung, their transmigrations, when and
    how
Accomplished, giving thus unto events
A form and body; all things were to me
Loose and disjointed, and the affections left
Without a vital interest. At that time,
Moreover, the first storm was overblown,
And the strong hand of outward violence
Locked up in quiet. For myself, I fear   110
Now in connection with so great a theme,
To speak (as I must be compelled to do)

77. Le Brun, Charles Le Brun (1619–1690), French historical painter. 81. abode, Orleans (Legouis) or Blois
(Harper).

Of one so unimportant; night by night
Did I frequent the formal haunts of men,
Whom, in the city, privilege of birth
Sequestered from the rest, societies
Polished in arts, and in punctilio versed;
Whence, and from deeper causes, all discourse
Of good and evil of the time was shunned
With scrupulous care; but these restrictions soon 120
Proved tedious, and I gradually withdrew
Into a noisier world, and thus ere long
Became a patriot; and my heart was all
Given to the people, and my love was theirs. . . .

Among that band of Officers was one,
Already hinted at, of other mould—
A patriot, thence rejected by the rest, 290
And with oriental loathing spurned,
As of a different caste. A meeker man
Than this lived never, nor a more benign,
Meek though enthusiastic. Injuries
Made *him* more gracious, and his nature then
Did breathe its sweetness out most sensibly,
As aromatic flowers on Alpine turf,
When foot hath crushed them. He through the
    events
Of that great change wandered in perfect faith,
As through a book, an old romance, or tale 300
Of Fairy, or some dream of actions wrought
Behind the summer clouds. By birth he ranked
With the most noble, but unto the poor
Among mankind he was in service bound,
As by some tie invisible, oaths professed
To a religious order. Man he loved
As man; and, to the mean and the obscure,
And all the homely in their homely works,
Transferred a courtesy which had no air
Of condescension; but did rather seem 310
A passion and a gallantry, like that
Which he, a soldier, in his idler day
Had paid to woman: somewhat vain he was,
Or seemed so, yet it was not vanity,
But fondness, and a kind of radiant joy
Diffused around him, while he was intent
On works of love or freedom, or revolved
Complacently the progress of a cause,
Whereof he was a part: yet this was meek
And placid, and took nothing from the man 320
That was delightful. Oft in solitude
With him did I discourse about the end
Of civil government, and its wisest forms;
Of ancient loyalty, and chartered rights,
Custom and habit, novelty and change. . . .

And when we chanced
One day to meet a hunger-bitten girl, 510
Who crept along fitting her languid gait
Unto a heifer's motion, by a cord
Tied to her arm, and picking thus from the lane
Its sustenance, while the girl with pallid hands
Was busy knitting in a heartless mood
Of solitude, and at the sight my friend
In agitation said, " 'Tis against *that*
That we are fighting," I with him believed
That a benignant spirit was abroad
Which might not be withstood, that poverty 520
Abject as this would in a little time
Be found no more, that we should see the earth
Unthwarted in her wish to recompense
The meek, the lowly, patient child of toil,
All institutes for ever blotted out
That legalised exclusion, empty pomp
Abolished, sensual state and cruel power,
Whether by edict of the one or few;
And finally, as sum and crown of all,
Should see the people having a strong hand 530
In framing their own laws; whence better days
To all mankind. . . .

BOOK TENTH—RESIDENCE IN FRANCE (*continued*)

Cheered with this hope, to Paris I returned,
And ranged, with ardour heretofore unfelt,
The spacious city, and in progress passed 50
The prison where the unhappy Monarch lay,
Associate with his children and his wife
In bondage; and the palace, lately stormed
With roar of cannon by a furious host.
I crossed the square (an empty area then!)
Of the Carrousel, where so late had lain
The dead, upon the dying heaped, and gazed
On this and other spots, as doth a man
Upon a volume whose contents he knows
Are memorable, but from him locked up, 60
Being written in a tongue he cannot read,
So that he questions the mute leaves with pain,
And half upbraids their silence. But that night
I felt most deeply in what world I was,
What ground I trod on, and what air I breathed.
High was my room and lonely, near the roof
Of a large mansion or hotel, a lodge
That would have pleased me in more quiet times;
Nor was it wholly without pleasure then.
With unextinguished taper I kept watch, 70
Reading at intervals; the fear gone by

122. noisier world, Blois (Legouis). **290. A patriot**, Captain Michel Beaupuy.

518. I with him believed, Wordsworth's second crisis— conversion to the revolution, love of man. **51. unhappy Monarch**, Louis XVI

Pressed on me almost like a fear to come.
I thought of those September massacres,
Divided from me by one little month,
Saw them and touched: the rest was conjured up
From tragic fictions or true history,
Remembrances and dim admonishments.
The horse is taught his manage, and no star
Of wildest course but treads back his own steps;
For the spent hurricane the air provides   80
As fierce a successor; the tide retreats
But to return out of its hiding-place
In the great deep; all things have second birth;
The earthquake is not satisfied at once;
And in this way I wrought upon myself,
Until I seemed to hear a voice that cried,
To the whole city, "Sleep no more." The trance
Fled with the voice to which it had given birth;
But vainly comments of a calmer mind
Promised soft peace and sweet forgetfulness.   90
The place, all hushed and silent as it was,
Appeared unfit for the repose of night,
Defenceless as a wood where tigers roam. . . .

                              In this frame of mind,   221
Dragged by a chain of harsh necessity,
So seemed it,—now I thankfully acknowledge,
Forced by the gracious providence of Heaven,—
To England I returned, else (though assured
That I both was and must be of small weight,
No better than a landsman on the deck
Of a ship struggling with a hideous storm)
Doubtless, I should have then made common cause
With some who perished; haply perished too,   230
A poor mistaken and bewildered offering,—
Should to the breast of Nature have gone back,
With all my resolutions, all my hopes,
A Poet only to myself, to men
Useless, and even, beloved Friend! a soul
To thee unknown! . . .

BOOK ELEVENTH—FRANCE (concluded)

Bliss was it in that dawn to be alive,
But to be young was very Heaven! O times,
In which the meagre, stale, forbidding ways   110
Of custom, law, and statute, took at once
The attraction of a country in romance!
When Reason seemed the most to assert her rights,
When most intent on making of herself
A prime enchantress—to assist the work,
Which then was going forward in her name!

235. beloved Friend, Coleridge.   108. Bliss was it, the apex of Wordsworth's hopes for the French Revolution, and with it for mankind.

Not favoured spots alone, but the whole Earth,
The beauty wore of promise—that which sets
(As at some moments might not be unfelt
Among the bowers of Paradise itself)   120
The budding rose above the rose full blown.
What temper at the prospect did not wake
To happiness unthought of? The inert
Were roused, and lively natures rapt away! . . .

Were called upon to exercise their skill,
Not in Utopia,—subterranean fields,—   140
Or some secreted island, Heaven knows where!
But in the very world, which is the world
Of all of us,—the place where, in the end,
We find our happiness, or not at all! . . .

     But now, become oppressors in their turn,
Frenchmen had changed a war of self-defence
For one of conquest, losing sight of all
Which they had struggled for: up mounted now,
Openly in the eye of earth and heaven,   210
The scale of liberty. I read her doom. . . .

I summoned my best skill, and toiled, intent
To anatomize the frame of social life;   280
Yea, the whole body of society
Searched to its heart. . . .

                                        So I fared,
Dragging all precepts, judgments, maxims, creeds,
Like culprits to the bar; calling the mind,
Suspiciously, to establish in plain day
Her titles and her honours; now believing,
Now disbelieving; endlessly perplexed
With impulse, motive, right and wrong, the ground
Of obligation, what the rule and whence   300
The sanction; till, demanding formal proof,
And seeking it in every thing, I lost
All feeling of conviction, and, in fine,
Sick, wearied out with contrarieties,
Yielded up moral questions in despair.

     This was the crisis of that strong disease,
This the soul's last and lowest ebb; I drooped. . . .

                              Then it was—   333
Thanks to the bounteous Giver of all good!—
That the beloved Sister in whose sight

121. The budding rose. The idea is characteristically Romantic.   306. This was the crisis. The preceding passage marks the catastrophe of *The Prelude*—the destruction of Wordsworth's hopes for mankind through the French Revolution.   333. Then it was. Here Wordsworth's account of his recovery begins. Note that he mentions two of his good angels—Dorothy and Nature. The third, Coleridge, was thanked in the 1805 version. Omission of him for 1850 was perhaps due to the estrangement between the two poets.

Those days were passed, now speaking in a voice
Of sudden admonition—like a brook
That did but *cross* a lonely road, and now
Is seen, heard, felt, and caught at every turn,
Companion never lost through many a league— 340
Maintained for me a saving intercourse
With my true self; for, though bedimmed and
   changed
Much, as it seemed, I was no further changed
Than as a clouded and a waning moon:
She whispered still that brightness would return;
She, in the midst of all, preserved me still
A Poet, made me seek beneath that name,
And that alone, my office upon earth;
And, lastly, as hereafter will be shown,
If willing audience fail not, Nature's self, 350
By all varieties of human love
Assisted, led me back through opening day
To those sweet counsels between head and heart
Whence grew that genuine knowledge, fraught with
   peace,
Which, through the later sinkings of this cause,
Hath still upheld me, and upholds me now. . . .

BOOK TWELFTH—IMAGINATION AND TASTE,
HOW IMPAIRED AND RESTORED

There are in our existence spots of time,
That with distinct pre-eminence retain
A renovating virtue, whence—depressed 210
By false opinion and contentious thought,
Or aught of heavier or more deadly weight,
In trivial occupations, and the round
Of ordinary intercourse—our minds
Are nourished and invisibly repaired;
A virtue, by which pleasure is enhanced,
That penetrates, enables us to mount,
When high, more high, and lifts us up when fallen.
This efficacious spirit chiefly lurks
Among those passages of life that give 220
Profoundest knowledge to what point, and how,
The mind is lord and master—outward sense
The obedient servant of her will. Such moments
Are scattered everywhere, taking their date
From our first childhood. . . .

BOOK THIRTEENTH—IMAGINATION AND TASTE,
HOW IMPAIRED AND RESTORED (*concluded*)

From Nature doth emotion come, and moods
Of calmness equally are Nature's gift:

225. **From our first childhood.** See "Ode: Intimations
of Immortality." 1. **From Nature.** Here begins the poet's
statement of one of the cardinal points in his faith. See the
discussion in the biographical-critical sketch.

This is her glory; these two attributes
Are sister horns that constitute her strength.
Hence Genius, born to thrive by interchange
Of peace and excitation, finds in her
His best and purest friend; from her receives
That energy by which he seeks the truth,
From her that happy stillness of the mind
Which fits him to receive it when unsought. 10

Such benefit the humblest intellects
Partake of, each in their degree; 'tis mine
To speak, what I myself have known and felt;
Smooth task! for words find easy way, inspired
By gratitude, and confidence in truth.
Long time in search of knowledge did I range
The field of human life, in heart and mind
Benighted; but, the dawn beginning now
To re-appear, 'twas proved that not in vain
I had been taught to reverence a Power 20
That is the visible quality and shape
And image of right reason; that matures
Her processes by steadfast laws; gives birth
To no impatient or fallacious hopes,
No heat of passion or excessive zeal,
No vain conceits; provokes to no quick turns
Of self-applauding intellect; but trains
To meekness, and exalts by humble faith;
Holds up before the mind intoxicate
With present objects, and the busy dance 30
Of things that pass away, a temperate show
Of objects that endure; and by this course
Disposes her, when over-fondly set
On throwing off incumbrances, to seek
In man, and in the frame of social life,
Whate'er there is desirable and good
Of kindred permanence, unchanged in form
And function, or, through strict vicissitude
Of life and death, revolving. Above all
Were re-established now those watchful thoughts 40
Which, seeing little worthy or sublime
In what the Historian's pen so much delights
To blazon—power and energy detached
From moral purpose—early tutored me
To look with feelings of fraternal love
Upon the unassuming things that hold
A silent station in this beauteous world. . . .

Who doth not love to follow with his eye 142
The windings of a public way? the sight,
Familiar object as it is, hath wrought
On my imagination since the morn
Of childhood, when a disappearing line,

142. **Who doth not love.** This is the second point in
Wordsworth's faith.

One daily present to my eyes, that crossed
The naked summit of a far-off hill
Beyond the limits that my feet had trod,
Was like an invitation into space   150
Boundless, or guide into eternity.
Yes, something of the grandeur which invests
The mariner, who sails the roaring sea
Through storm and darkness, early in my mind
Surrounded, too, the wanderers of the earth;
Grandeur as much, and loveliness far more.
Awed have I been by strolling Bedlamites;
From many other uncouth vagrants (passed
In fear) have walked with quicker step; but why
Take note of this? When I began to inquire,   160
To watch and question those I met, and speak
Without reserve to them, the lonely roads
Were open schools in which I daily read
With most delight the passions of mankind,
Whether by words, looks, sighs, or tears, revealed;
There saw into the depth of human souls,
Souls that appear to have no depth at all
To careless eyes. . . .

   Also, about this time did I receive
Convictions still more strong than heretofore,   280
Not only that the inner frame is good,
And graciously composed, but that, no less,
Nature for all conditions wants not power
To consecrate, if we have eyes to see,
The outside of her creatures, and to breathe
Grandeur upon the very humblest face
Of human life. I felt that the array
Of act and circumstance, and visible form,
Is mainly to the pleasure of the mind
What passion makes them; that meanwhile the
   forms   290
Of Nature have a passion in themselves,
That intermingles with those works of man
To which she summons him; although the works
Be mean, have nothing lofty of their own;
And that the Genius of the Poet hence
May boldly take his way among mankind
Wherever Nature leads; that he hath stood
By Nature's side among the men of old,
And so shall stand for ever. . . .

BOOK FOURTEENTH—CONCLUSION

                          To fear and love,   162
To love as prime and chief, for there fear ends,
Be this ascribed; to early intercourse,

   157. **Bedlamites,** madmen. 280. **Convictions,** one of
Wordsworth's great assertions of the worth and dignity of
human life and of the vitality and beneficence of the universe. The poet is the minister of this faith.

In presence of sublime or beautiful forms,
With the adverse principles of pain and joy—
Evil as one is rashly named by men
Who know not what they speak. By love subsists
All lasting grandeur, by pervading love;
That gone, we are as dust. . . .   170

   This spiritual Love acts not nor can exist
Without Imagination, which, in truth,
Is but another name for absolute power   190
And clearest insight, amplitude of mind,
And Reason in her most exalted mood.
This faculty hath been the feeding source
Of our long labour: we have traced the stream
From the blind cavern whence is faintly heard
Its natal murmur; followed it to light
And open day; accompanied its course
Among the ways of Nature, for a time
Lost sight of it bewildered and engulphed;
Then given it greeting as it rose once more   200
In strength, reflecting from its placid breast
The works of man and face of human life;
And lastly, from its progress have we drawn
Faith in life endless, the sustaining thought
Of human Being, Eternity, and God. . . .

PREFACE

TO THE SECOND EDITION (1800) OF SEVERAL
OF THE FOREGOING POEMS, PUBLISHED,
WITH AN ADDITIONAL VOLUME, UNDER
THE TITLE OF "LYRICAL BALLADS"

   Until the student is ready to take up the "Preface" in
some detail, especially in comparison with Coleridge's
Biographia Literaria, it is well to confine attention to the
passage beginning with the fifth paragraph ("The principal object") and ending with the ninth. This states the
main points of Wordsworth's program—object (including subjects, language, effect sought), differences from
contemporary poetry ("having a purpose," feeling giving
importance to action and situation), and style (negative
and positive features).

THE first Volume of these Poems has already
   been submitted to general perusal. It was published as an experiment, which, I hoped, might be
of some use to ascertain, how far, by fitting to metrical arrangement a selection of the real language of
men in a state of vivid sensation, that sort of pleasure and that quantity of pleasure may be imparted,
which a Poet may rationally endeavour to impart.
   I had formed no very inaccurate estimate of the
probable effect of those Poems: I flattered myself

that they who should be pleased with them would read them with more than common pleasure: and, on the other hand, I was well aware, that by those who should dislike them they would be read with more than common dislike. The result has differed from my expectation in this only, that a greater number have been pleased than I ventured to hope I should please.

Several of my Friends are anxious for the success of these Poems, from a belief that, if the views with which they were composed were indeed realised, a class of Poetry would be produced, well adapted to interest mankind permanently, and not unimportant in the quality and in the multiplicity of its moral relations: and on this account they have advised me to prefix a systematic defence of the theory upon which the Poems were written. But I was unwilling to undertake the task, knowing that on this occasion the Reader would look coldly upon my arguments, since I might be suspected of having been principally influenced by the selfish and foolish hope of *reasoning* him into an approbation of these particular Poems: and I was still more unwilling to undertake the task, because adequately to display the opinions, and fully to enforce the arguments, would require a space wholly disproportionate to a preface. For, to treat the subject with the clearness and coherence of which it is susceptible, it would be necessary to give a full account of the present state of the public taste in this country, and to determine how far this taste is healthy or depraved; which, again, could not be determined without pointing out in what manner language and the human mind act and re-act on each other, and without retracing the revolutions, not of literature alone, but likewise of society itself. I have therefore altogether declined to enter regularly upon this defence; yet I am sensible that there would be something like impropriety in abruptly obtruding upon the Public, without a few words of introduction, Poems so materially different from those upon which general approbation is at present bestowed.

It is supposed that by the act of writing in verse an Author makes a formal engagement that he will gratify certain known habits of association; that he not only thus apprises the Reader that certain classes of ideas and expressions will be found in his book, but that others will be carefully excluded. This exponent or symbol held forth by metrical language must in different eras of literature have excited very different expectations: for example, in the age of Catullus, Terence, and Lucretius, and that of Statius or Claudian; and in our own country, in the age of Shakespeare and Beaumont and Fletcher, and that of Donne and Cowley, or Dryden, or Pope. I will not take upon me to determine the exact import of the promise which, by the act of writing in verse, an Author in the present day makes to his reader, but it will undoubtedly appear to many persons that I have not fulfilled the terms of an engagement thus voluntarily contracted. They who have been accustomed to the gaudiness and inane phraseology of many modern writers, if they persist in reading this book to its conclusion, will, no doubt, frequently have to struggle with feelings of strangeness and awkwardness: they will look round for poetry, and will be induced to inquire by what species of courtesy these attempts can be permitted to assume that title. I hope, therefore, the reader will not censure me for attempting to state what I have proposed to myself to perform; and also (as far as the limits of a preface will permit) to explain some of the chief reasons which have determined me in the choice of my purpose: that at least he may be spared any unpleasant feeling of disappointment, and that I myself may be protected from one of the most dishonourable accusations which can be brought against an Author; namely, that of an indolence which prevents him from endeavouring to ascertain what is his duty, or, when his duty is ascertained, prevents him from performing it.

The principal object, then, proposed in these Poems was to choose incidents and situations from common life, and to relate or describe them throughout, as far as was possible, in a selection of language really used by men, and, at the same time, to throw over them a certain colouring of imagination, whereby ordinary things should be presented to the mind in an unusual aspect; and further, and above all, to make these incidents and situations interesting by tracing in them, truly though not ostentatiously, the primary laws of our nature: chiefly, as far as regards the manner in which we associate ideas in a state of excitement. Humble and rustic life was generally chosen, because, in that condition, the essential passions of the heart find a better soil in which they can attain their maturity, are less under restraint, and speak a plainer and more emphatic language; because in that condition of life our elementary feelings co-exist in a state of greater simplicity, and, consequently, may be more accurately contemplated, and more forcibly communicated; because the manners of rural life germinate from those elementary feelings, and, from the necessary character of rural occupations, are more easily comprehended, and are more durable; and, lastly, because in that condition the passions of men are incorporated with the beautiful and permanent forms of nature. The language, too, of these men has been adopted (purified indeed from what appear to be its real defects, from all lasting and rational causes of dislike or disgust), because such men hourly communicate with the best objects from which the best part of language is originally derived; and because, from their rank in society and the sameness and narrow circle of their intercourse, being less under the influence of social vanity, they convey their feelings and notions in simple and unelaborated expressions. Accordingly, such a language, arising out of repeated experience and regular feelings, is a more permanent, and a far more philosophical language, than that which is frequently substituted for it by Poets, who think that they are conferring honour upon themselves and their art in proportion as they separate themselves from the sympathies of men, and indulge in arbitrary and capricious habits of expression, in order to furnish food for fickle tastes, and fickle appetites, of their own creation.

I cannot, however, be insensible to the present outcry against the triviality and meanness, both of thought and language, which some of my contemporaries have occasionally introduced into their metrical compositions; and I acknowledge that this defect, where it exists, is more dishonourable to the Writer's own character than false refinement or arbitrary innovation, though I should contend at the same time that it is far less pernicious in the sum of its consequences. From such verses the Poems in these volumes will be found distinguished at least by one mark of difference, that each of them has a worthy *purpose*. Not that I always began to write with a distinct purpose formally conceived; but habits of meditation have, I trust, so prompted and regulated my feelings, that my descriptions of such objects as strongly excite those feelings will be found to carry along with them a *purpose*. If this opinion be erroneous, I can have little right to the name of a Poet. For all good poetry is the spontaneous overflow of powerful feelings: and though this be true, Poems to which any value can be attached were never produced on any variety of subjects but by a man who, being possessed of more than usual organic sensibility, had also thought long and deeply. For our continued influxes of feeling are modified and directed by our thoughts, which are indeed the representatives of all our past feelings;

and as, by contemplating the relation of these general representatives to each other, we discover what is really important to men, so, by the repetition and continuance of this act, our feelings will be connected with important subjects, till at length, if we be originally possessed of much sensibility, such habits of mind will be produced that, by obeying blindly and mechanically the impulses of those habits, we shall describe objects, and utter sentiments, of such a nature, and in such connection with each other, that the understanding of the Reader must necessarily be in some degree enlightened, and his affections strengthened and purified.

It has been said that each of these Poems has a purpose. Another circumstance must be mentioned which distinguishes these Poems from the popular Poetry of the day; it is this, that the feeling therein developed gives importance to the action and situation, and not the action and situation to the feeling.

A sense of false modesty shall not prevent me from asserting that the Reader's attention is pointed to this mark of distinction, far less for the sake of these particular Poems than from the general importance of the subject. The subject is indeed important! For the human mind is capable of being excited without the application of gross and violent stimulants; and he must have a very faint perception of its beauty and dignity who does not know this, and who does not further know, that one being is elevated above another in proportion as he possesses this capability. It has therefore appeared to me, that to endeavour to produce or enlarge this capability is one of the best services in which, at any period, a Writer can be engaged; but this service, excellent at all times, is especially so at the present day. For a multitude of causes, unknown to former times, are now acting with a combined force to blunt the discriminating powers of the mind, and, unfitting it for all voluntary exertion, to reduce it to a state of almost savage torpor. The most effective of these causes are the great national events which are daily taking place, and the increasing accumulation of men in cities, where the uniformity of their occupations produces a craving for extraordinary incident, which the rapid communication of intelligence hourly gratifies. To this tendency of life and manners the literature and theatrical exhibitions of the country have conformed themselves. The invaluable works of our elder writers, I had almost said the works of Shakspeare and Milton, are driven into neglect by frantic novels, sickly and stupid German Tragedies, and deluges of idle and extravagant stories in verse.—When I think upon

---

16–22. **Poets . . . creation.** "It is worth while here to observe that the affecting parts of Chaucer are almost always expressed in language pure and universally intelligible even to this day." (Wordsworth)

this degrading thirst after outrageous stimulation, I am almost ashamed to have spoken of the feeble endeavour made in these volumes to counteract it; and, reflecting upon the magnitude of the general evil, I should be oppressed with no dishonourable melancholy, had I not a deep impression of certain inherent and indestructible qualities of the human mind, and likewise of certain powers in the great and permanent objects that act upon it, which are equally inherent and indestructible; and were there not added to this impression a belief, that the time is approaching when the evil will be systematically opposed by men of greater powers, and with far more distinguished success.

Having dwelt thus long on the subjects and aim of these Poems, I shall request the Reader's permission to apprise him of a few circumstances relating to their *style*, in order, among other reasons, that he may not censure me for not having performed what I never attempted. The Reader will find that personifications of abstract ideas rarely occur in these volumes; and are utterly rejected as an ordinary device to elevate the style and raise it above prose. My purpose was to imitate, and, as far as possible, to adopt the very language of men; and assuredly such personifications do not make any natural or regular part of that language. They are, indeed, a figure of speech occasionally prompted by passion, and I have made use of them as such; but have endeavoured utterly to reject them as a mechanical device of style, or as a family language which Writers in metre seem to lay claim to by prescription. I have wished to keep the Reader in the company of flesh and blood, persuaded that by so doing I shall interest him. Others who pursue a different track will interest him likewise; I do not interfere with their claim, but wish to prefer a claim of my own. There will also be found in these volumes little of what is usually called poetic diction; as much pains has been taken to avoid it as is ordinarily taken to produce it; this has been done for the reason already alleged, to bring my language near to the language of men; and further, because the pleasure which I have proposed to myself to impart is of a kind very different from that which is supposed by many persons to be the proper object of poetry. Without being culpably particular, I do not know how to give my Reader a more exact notion of the style in which it was my wish and intention to write, than by informing him that I have at all times endeavoured to look steadily at my subject; consequently there is, I hope, in these Poems little falsehood of description, and my ideas are expressed in language fitted to their respective importance.

Something must have been gained by this practice, as it is friendly to one property of all good poetry, namely, good sense: but it has necessarily cut me off from a large portion of phrases and figures of speech which from father to son have long been regarded as the common inheritance of Poets. I have also thought it expedient to restrict myself still further, having abstained from the use of many expressions, in themselves proper and beautiful, but which have been foolishly repeated by bad Poets, till such feelings of disgust are connected with them as it is scarcely possible by any art of association to overpower.

If in a poem there should be found a series of lines, or even a single line, in which the language, though naturally arranged, and according to the strict laws of metre, does not differ from that of prose, there is a numerous class of critics, who, when they stumble upon these prosaisms, as they call them, imagine that they have made a notable discovery, and exult over the Poet as over a man ignorant of his own profession. Now these men would establish a canon of criticism which the Reader will conclude he must utterly reject, if he wishes to be pleased with these volumes. And it would be a most easy task to prove to him that not only the language of a large portion of every good poem, even of the most elevated character, must necessarily, except with reference to the metre, in no respect differ from that of good prose, but likewise that some of the most interesting parts of the best poems will be found to be strictly the language of prose when prose is well written. The truth of this assertion might be demonstrated by innumerable passages from almost all the poetical writings, even of Milton himself. To illustrate the subject in a general manner, I will here adduce a short composition of Gray, who was at the head of those who, by their reasonings, have attempted to widen the space of separation betwixt Prose and Metrical composition, and was more than any other man curiously elaborate in the structure of his own poetic diction.

In vain to me the smiling mornings shine,
And reddening Phoebus lifts his golden fire;
The birds in vain their amorous descant join,
Or cheerful fields resume their green attire.
These ears, alas! for other notes repine;
A different object do these eyes require;
My lonely anguish melts no heart but mine,
And in my breast the imperfect joys expire;
Yet morning smiles the busy race to cheer,
And new-born pleasure brings to happier men;
The fields to all their wonted tribute bear;

To warm their little loves the birds complain.
I fruitless mourn to him that cannot hear,
And weep the more because I weep in vain.

It will easily be perceived, that the only part of this Sonnet which is of any value is the lines printed in Italics; it is equally obvious that, except in the rhyme and in the use of the single word "fruitless" for fruitlessly, which is so far a defect, the language of these lines does in no respect differ from that of prose.

By the foregoing quotation it has been shown that the language of Prose may yet be well adapted to Poetry; and it was previously asserted that a large portion of the language of every good poem can in no respect differ from that of good Prose. We will go further. It may be safely affirmed that there neither is, nor can be, any *essential* difference between the language of prose and metrical composition. We are fond of tracing the resemblance between Poetry and Painting, and, accordingly, we call them Sisters: but where shall we find bonds of connection sufficiently strict to typify the affinity betwixt metrical and prose composition? They both speak by and to the same organs; the bodies in which both of them are clothed may be said to be of the same substance, their affections are kindred, and almost identical, not necessarily differing even in degree; Poetry sheds no tears "such as Angels weep," but natural and human tears; she can boast of no celestial ichor that distinguishes her vital juices from those of Prose; the same human blood circulates through the veins of them both.

If it be affirmed that rhyme and metrical arrangement of themselves constitute a distinction which overturns what has just been said on the strict affinity of metrical language with that of Prose, and paves the way for other artificial distinctions which the mind voluntarily admits, I answer that the language of such Poetry as is here recommended is, as far as is possible, a selection of the language really spoken by men; that this selection, wherever it is made with true taste and feeling, will of itself form a distinction far greater than would at first be imagined, and will entirely separate the composition from the vulgarity and meanness of

ordinary life; and, if metre be superadded thereto, I believe that a dissimilitude will be produced altogether sufficient for the gratification of a rational mind. What other distinction would we have? Whence is it to come? And where is it to exist? Not, surely, where the Poet speaks through the mouths of his characters: it cannot be necessary here, either for elevation of style, or any of its supposed ornaments: for, if the Poet's subject be judiciously chosen, it will naturally, and upon fit occasion, lead him to passions, the language of which, if selected truly and judiciously, must necessarily be dignified and variegated, and alive with metaphors and figures. I forbear to speak of an incongruity which would shock the intelligent Reader, should the Poet interweave any foreign splendour of his own with that which the passion naturally suggests: it is sufficient to say that such addition is unnecessary. And, surely, it is more probable that those passages, which with propriety abound with metaphors and figures, will have their due effect if, upon other occasions where the passions are of a milder character, the style also be subdued and temperate.

But, as the pleasure which I hope to give by the Poems now presented to the Reader must depend entirely on just notions upon this subject, and as it is in itself of high importance to our taste and moral feelings, I cannot content myself with these detached remarks. And if, in what I am about to say, it shall appear to some that my labour is unnecessary, and that I am like a man fighting a battle without enemies, such persons may be reminded that, whatever be the language outwardly holden by men, a practical faith in the opinions which I am wishing to establish is almost unknown. If my conclusions are admitted, and carried as far as they must be carried if admitted at all, our judgments concerning the works of the greatest Poets both ancient and modern will be far different from what they are at present, both when we praise, and when we censure: and our moral feelings influencing and influenced by these judgments will, I believe, be corrected and purified.

Taking up the subject, then, upon general grounds, let me ask, what is meant by the word Poet? What is a Poet? To whom does he address himself? And what language is to be expected from him?—He is a man speaking to men: a man, it is true, endowed with more lively sensibility, more enthusiasm and tenderness, who has a greater knowledge of human nature, and a more comprehensive soul, than are supposed to be common among mankind; a man pleased with his own passions and volitions, and who rejoices more than

29. "I here use the word 'Poetry' (though against my own judgment) as opposed to the word Prose, and synonymous with metrical composition. But much confusion has been introduced into criticism by this contradistinction of Poetry and Prose, instead of the more philosophical one of Poetry and Matter of Fact, or Science. The only strict antithesis to Prose is Metre; nor is this, in truth, a *strict* antithesis, because lines and passages of metre so naturally occur in writing prose, that it would be scarcely possible to avoid them, even were it desirable." (Wordsworth)

other men in the spirit of life that is in him; delighting to contemplate similar volitions and passions as manifested in the goings-on of the Universe, and habitually impelled to create them where he does not find them. To these qualities he has added a disposition to be affected more than other men by absent things as if they were present; an ability of conjuring up in himself passions, which are indeed far from being the same as those produced by real events, yet (especially in those parts of the general sympathy which are pleasing and delightful) do more nearly resemble the passions produced by real events than anything which, from the motions of their own minds merely, other men are accustomed to feel in themselves:—whence, and from practice, he has acquired a greater readiness and power in expressing what he thinks and feels, and especially those thoughts and feelings which, by his own choice, or from the structure of his own mind, arise in him without immediate external excitement.

But whatever portion of this faculty we may suppose even the greatest Poet to possess, there cannot be a doubt that the language which it will suggest to him must often, in liveliness and truth, fall short of that which is uttered by men in real life, under the actual pressure of those passions, certain shadows of which the Poet thus produces, or feels to be produced, in himself.

However exalted a notion we would wish to cherish of the character of a Poet, it is obvious that, while he describes and imitates passions, his employment is in some degree mechanical compared with the freedom and power of real and substantial action and suffering. So that it will be the wish of the Poet to bring his feelings near to those of the persons whose feelings he describes, nay, for short spaces of time, perhaps, to let himself slip into an entire delusion, and even confound and identify his own feelings with theirs; modifying only the language which is thus suggested to him by a consideration that he describes for a particular purpose, that of giving pleasure. Here, then, he will apply the principle of selection which has been already insisted upon. He will depend upon this for removing what would otherwise be painful or disgusting in the passion; he will feel that there is no necessity to trick out or to elevate nature: and, the more industriously he applies this principle the deeper will be his faith that no words, which *his* fancy or imagination can suggest, will be to be compared with those which are the emanations of reality and truth.

But it may be said by those who do not object to the general spirit of these remarks, that, as it is impossible for the Poet to produce upon all occasions language as exquisitely fitted for the passion as that which the real passion itself suggests, it is proper that he should consider himself as in the situation of a translator, who does not scruple to substitute excellencies of another kind for those which are unattainable by him; and endeavours occasionally to surpass his original, in order to make some amends for the general inferiority to which he feels that he must submit. But this would be to encourage idleness and unmanly despair. Further, it is the language of men who speak of what they do not understand; who talk of Poetry, as of a matter of amusement and idle pleasure; who will converse with us as gravely about a *taste* for Poetry, as they express it, as if it were a thing as indifferent as a taste for rope-dancing, or Frontiniac or Sherry. Aristotle, I have been told, has said, that Poetry is the most philosophic of all writing: it is so: its object is truth, not individual and local, but general and operative; not standing upon external testimony, but carried alive into the heart by passion; truth which is its own testimony, which gives competence and confidence to the tribunal to which it appeals, and receives them from the same tribunal. Poetry is the image of man and nature. The obstacles which stand in the way of the fidelity of the Biographer and Historian, and of their consequent utility, are incalculably greater than those which are to be encountered by the Poet who comprehends the dignity of his art. The Poet writes under one restriction only, namely, the necessity of giving immediate pleasure to a human Being possessed of that information which may be expected from him, not as a lawyer, a physician, a mariner, an astronomer, or a natural philosopher, but as a Man. Except this one restriction, there is no object standing between the Poet and the image of things; between this, and the Biographer and Historian, there are a thousand.

Nor let this necessity of producing immediate pleasure be considered as a degradation of the Poet's art. It is far otherwise. It is an acknowledgment of the beauty of the universe, an acknowledgment the more sincere because not formal, but indirect; it is a task light and easy to him who looks at the world in the spirit of love: further, it is a homage paid to the native and naked dignity of man, to the grand elementary principle of pleasure, by which he knows, and feels, and lives, and moves. We have no sympathy but what is propagated by pleasure: I would not be misunderstood; but wherever we sympathise with pain, it will be found that the sympathy is produced and carried on by subtle combinations with pleasure. We have no knowledge, that is, no general principles drawn from the contemplation of particular facts, but what has been built up by pleasure, and exists in us by pleasure alone. The Man of science, the Chemist and Mathematician, whatever difficulties and disgusts they may have had to struggle with, know and feel this. However painful may be the objects with which the Anatomist's knowledge is connected, he feels that his knowledge is pleasure; and where he has no pleasure he has no knowledge. What then does the Poet? He considers man and the objects that surround him as acting and re-acting upon each other, so as to produce an infinite complexity of pain and pleasure; he considers man in his own nature and in his ordinary life as contemplating this with a certain quantity of immediate knowledge, with certain convictions, intuitions, and deductions, which from habit acquire the quality of intuitions; he considers him as looking upon this complex scene of ideas and sensations, and finding everywhere objects that immediately excite in him sympathies which, from the necessities of his nature, are accompanied by an overbalance of enjoyment.

To this knowledge which all men carry about with them, and to these sympathies in which, without any other discipline than that of our daily life, we are fitted to take delight, the Poet principally directs his attention. He considers man and nature as essentially adapted to each other, and the mind of man as naturally the mirror of the fairest and most interesting properties of nature. And thus the Poet, prompted by this feeling of pleasure, which accompanies him through the whole course of his studies, converses with general nature, with affections akin to those which, through labour and length of time, the Man of science has raised up in himself, by conversing with those particular parts of nature which are the objects of his studies. The knowledge both of the Poet and the Man of science is pleasure; but the knowledge of the one cleaves to us as a necessary part of our existence, our natural and unalienable inheritance; the other is a personal and individual acquisition, slow to come to us, and by no habitual and direct sympathy connecting us with our fellow-beings. The Man of science seeks truth as a remote and unknown benefactor; he cherishes and loves it in his solitude: the Poet, singing a song in which all human beings join with him, rejoices in the presence of truth as our visible friend and hourly companion. Poetry is the breath and finer spirit of all knowledge; it is the impassioned expression which is in the countenance of all Science. Emphatically may it be said of the Poet, as Shakespeare hath said of man, "that he looks before and after." He is the rock of defence for human nature; an upholder and preserver, carrying everywhere with him relationship and love. In spite of difference of soil and climate, of language and manners, of laws and customs: in spite of things silently gone out of mind, and things violently destroyed; the Poet binds together by passion and knowledge the vast empire of human society, as it is spread over the whole earth, and over all time. The objects of the Poet's thoughts are everywhere; though the eyes and senses of man are, it is true, his favourite guides, yet he will follow wheresoever he can find an atmosphere of sensation in which to move his wings. Poetry is the first and last of all knowledge— it is as immortal as the heart of man. If the labours of Men of science should ever create any material revolution, direct or indirect, in our condition, and in the impressions which we habitually receive, the Poet will sleep then no more than at present; he will be ready to follow the steps of the Man of science, not only in those general indirect effects, but he will be at his side, carrying sensation into the midst of the objects of the science itself. The remotest discoveries of the Chemist, the Botanist, or Mineralogist, will be as proper objects of the Poet's art as any upon which it can be employed, if the time should ever come when these things shall be familiar to us, and the relations under which they are contemplated by the followers of these respective sciences shall be manifestly and palpably material to us as enjoying and suffering beings. If the time should ever come when what is now called science, thus familiarised to men, shall be ready to put on, as it were, a form of flesh and blood, the Poet will lend his divine spirit to aid the transfiguration, and will welcome the Being thus produced as a dear and genuine inmate of the household of man.—It is not, then, to be supposed that any one, who holds that sublime notion of Poetry which I have attempted to convey, will break in upon the sanctity and truth of his pictures by transitory and accidental ornaments, and endeavour to excite admiration of himself by arts, the necessity of which must manifestly depend upon the assumed meanness of his subject.

What has been thus far said applies to Poetry in general; but especially to those parts of composition where the Poet speaks through the mouths of his characters; and upon this point it appears to authorise the conclusion that there are few persons of good sense who would not allow that the dramatic parts of composition are defective in proportion as they deviate from the real language of nature, and are coloured by a diction of the Poet's own, either peculiar to him as an individual Poet or belonging simply to Poets in general; to a body of men who, from the circumstance of their compositions being in metre, it is expected will employ a particular language.

It is not, then, in the dramatic parts of composition that we look for this distinction of language; but still it may be proper and necessary where the Poet speaks to us in his own person and character. To this I answer by referring the Reader to the description before given of a Poet. Among the qualities there enumerated as principally conducing to form a Poet, is implied nothing differing in kind from other men, but only in degree. The sum of what was said is, that the Poet is chiefly distinguished from other men by a greater promptness to think and feel without immediate external excitement, and a greater power in expressing such thoughts and feelings as are produced in him in that manner. But these passions and thoughts and feelings are the general passions and thoughts and feelings of men. And with what are they connected? Undoubtedly with our moral sentiments and animal sensations, and with the causes which excite these; with the operations of the elements, and the appearances of the visible universe; with storm and sunshine, with the revolutions of the seasons, with cold and heat, with loss of friends and kindred, with injuries and resentments, gratitude and hope, with fear and sorrow. These, and the like, are the sensations and objects which the Poet describes, as they are the sensations of other men and the objects which interest them. The Poet thinks and feels in the spirit of human passions. How, then, can his language differ in any material degree from that of all other men who feel vividly and see clearly? It might be *proved* that it is impossible. But supposing that this were not the case, the Poet might then be allowed to use a peculiar language when expressing his feelings for his own gratification, or that of men like himself. But Poets do not write for Poets alone, but for men. Unless, therefore, we are advocates for that admiration which subsists upon ignorance, and that pleasure which arises from hearing what we do not understand, the Poet must descend from this supposed height; and, in order to excite rational sympathy, he must express himself as other men express themselves. To this it may be added, that while he is only selecting from the real language of men, or, which amounts to the same thing, composing accurately in the spirit of such selection, he is treading upon safe ground, and we know what we are to expect from him. Our feelings are the same with respect to metre; for, as it may be proper to remind the Reader, the distinction of metre is regular and uniform, and not, like that which is produced by what

is usually called POETIC DICTION, arbitrary, and subject to infinite caprices, upon which no calculation whatever can be made. In the one case, the Reader is utterly at the mercy of the Poet, respecting what imagery or diction he may choose to connect with the passion; whereas, in the other, the metre obeys certain laws, to which the Poet and Reader both willingly submit because they are certain, and because no interference is made by them with the passion but such as the concurring testimony of ages has shown to heighten and improve the pleasure which co-exists with it.

It will now be proper to answer an obvious question, namely, Why, professing these opinions, have I written in verse? To this, in addition to such answer as is included in what has been already said, I reply, in the first place, Because, however I may have restricted myself, there is still left open to me what confessedly constitutes the most valuable object of all writing, whether in prose or verse; the great and universal passions of men, the most general and interesting of their occupations, and the entire world of nature before me—to supply endless combinations of forms and imagery. Now, supposing for a moment that whatever is interesting in these objects may be as vividly described in prose, why should I be condemned for attempting to superadd to such description the charm which, by the consent of all nations, is acknowledged to exist in metrical language? To this, by such as are yet unconvinced, it may be answered that a very small part of the pleasure given by Poetry depends upon the metre, and that it is injudicious to write in metre, unless it be accompanied with the other artificial distinctions of style with which metre is usually accompanied, and that, by such deviation, more will be lost from the shock which will thereby be given to the Reader's associations than will be counterbalanced by any pleasure which he can derive from the general power of numbers. In answer to those who still contend for the necessity of accompanying metre with certain appropriate colours of style in order to the accomplishment of its appropriate end, and who also, in my opinion, greatly under-rate the power of metre in itself, it might, perhaps, as far as relates to these Volumes, have been almost sufficient to observe, that poems are extant, written upon more humble subjects, and in a still more naked and simple style, which have continued to give pleasure from generation to generation. Now, if nakedness and simplicity be a defect, the fact here mentioned affords a strong presumption that poems somewhat less naked and simple are capable of affording pleasure at the present day; and, what I wished *chiefly* to attempt, at present, was to justify myself for having written under the impression of this belief.

But various causes might be pointed out why, when the style is manly, and the subject of some importance, words metrically arranged will long continue to impart such a pleasure to mankind as he who proves the extent of that pleasure will be desirous to impart. The end of Poetry is to produce excitement in co-existence with an overbalance of pleasure; but, by the supposition, excitement is an ₁₀ unusual and irregular state of the mind; ideas and feelings do not, in that state, succeed each other in accustomed order. If the words, however, by which this excitement is produced be in themselves powerful, or the images and feelings have an undue proportion of pain connected with them, there is some danger that the excitement may be carried beyond its proper bounds. Now the co-presence of something regular, something to which the mind has been accustomed in various moods and in a less ₂₀ excited state, cannot but have great efficacy in tempering and restraining the passion by an intertexture of ordinary feeling, and of feeling not strictly and necessarily connected with the passion. This is unquestionably true; and hence, though the opinion will at first appear paradoxical, from the tendency of metre to divest language, in a certain degree, of its reality, and thus to throw a sort of half-consciousness of unsubstantial existence over the whole composition, there can be little doubt but that more ₃₀ pathetic situations and sentiments, that is, those which have a greater proportion of pain connected with them, may be endured in metrical composition, especially in rhyme, than in prose. The metre of the old ballads is very artless, yet they contain many passages which would illustrate this opinion; and, I hope, if the following poems be attentively perused, similar instances will be found in them. This opinion may be further illustrated by appealing to the Reader's own experience of the reluctance ₄₀ with which he comes to the reperusal of the distressful parts of "Clarissa Harlowe," or the "Gamester"; while Shakspeare's writings, in the most pathetic scenes, never act upon us, as pathetic, beyond the bounds of pleasure—an effect which, in a much greater degree than might at first be imagined, is to be ascribed to small, but continual and regular impulses of pleasurable surprise from the metrical arrangement.—On the other hand (what it must be allowed will much more frequently happen), if ₅₀ the Poet's words should be incommensurate with the passion, and inadequate to raise the Reader to a height of desirable excitement, then, (unless the Poet's choice of his metre has been grossly injudi-

cious) in the feelings of pleasure which the Reader has been accustomed to connect with metre in general, and in the feeling, whether cheerful or melancholy, which he has been accustomed to connect with that particular movement of metre, there will be found something which will greatly contribute to impart passion to the words, and to effect the complex end which the Poet proposes to himself.

If I had undertaken a SYSTEMATIC defence of the theory here maintained, it would have been my duty to develop the various causes upon which the pleasure received from metrical language depends. Among the chief of these causes is to be reckoned a principle which must be well known to those who have made any of the Arts the object of accurate reflection; namely, the pleasure which the mind derives from the perception of similitude in dissimilitude. This principle is the great spring of the activity of our minds, and their chief feeder. From this principle the direction of the sexual appetite, and all the passions connected with it, take their origin: it is the life of our ordinary conversation; and upon the accuracy with which similitude in dissimilitude, and dissimilitude in similitude, are perceived, depend our taste and our moral feelings. It would not be a useless employment to apply this principle to the consideration of metre, and to show that metre is hence enabled to afford much pleasure, and to point out in what manner that pleasure is produced. But my limits will not permit me to enter upon this subject, and I must content myself with a general summary.

I have said that poetry is the spontaneous overflow of powerful feelings: it takes its origin from emotion recollected in tranquillity; the emotion is contemplated till, by a species of re-action, the tranquillity gradually disappears, and an emotion, kindred to that which was before the subject of contemplation, is gradually produced, and does itself actually exist in the mind. In this mood successful composition generally begins, and in a mood similar to this it is carried on; but the emotion, of whatever kind, and in whatever degree, from various causes, is qualified by various pleasures, so that in describing any passions whatsoever, which are voluntarily described, the mind will, upon the whole, be in a state of enjoyment. If Nature be thus cautious to preserve in a state of enjoyment a being so employed, the Poet ought to profit by the lesson held forth to him, and ought especially to take care that, whatever passions he communicates to his Reader, those passions, if his Reader's mind be sound and vigorous, should always be accompanied with an overbalance of pleasure. Now the music of harmonious metrical language, the sense of difficulty overcome, and the blind association of pleasure which has been previously received from works of rhyme or metre of the same or similar construction, an indistinct perception perpetually renewed of language closely resembling that of real life, and yet, in the circumstance of metre, differing from it so widely—all these imperceptibly make up a complex feeling of delight, which is of the most important use in tempering the painful feeling always found intermingled with powerful descriptions of the deeper passions. This effect is always produced in pathetic and impassioned poetry; while, in lighter compositions, the ease and gracefulness with which the Poet manages his numbers are themselves confessedly a principal source of the gratification of the Reader. All that it is *necessary* to say, however, upon this subject, may be effected by affirming, what few persons will deny, that, of two descriptions, either of passions, manners, or characters, each of them equally well executed, the one in prose and the other in verse, the verse will be read a hundred times where the prose is read once.

Having thus explained a few of my reasons for writing in verse, and why I have chosen subjects from common life, and endeavoured to bring my language near to the real language of men, if I have been too minute in pleading my own cause, I have at the same time been treating a subject of general interest; and for this reason a few words shall be added with reference solely to these particular poems, and to some defects which will probably be found in them. I am sensible that my associations must have sometimes been particular instead of general, and that, consequently, giving to things a false importance, I may have sometimes written upon unworthy subjects; but I am less apprehensive on this account, than that my language may frequently have suffered from those arbitrary connections of feelings and ideas with particular words and phrases from which no man can altogether protect himself. Hence I have no doubt that, in some instances, feelings, even of the ludicrous, may be given to my Readers by expressions which appeared to me tender and pathetic. Such faulty expressions, were I convinced they were faulty at present, and that they must necessarily continue to be so, I would willingly take all reasonable pains to correct. But it is dangerous to make these alterations on the simple authority of a few individuals, or even of certain classes of men; for where the understanding of an Author is not convinced, or his feelings altered, this cannot be done without great injury to himself: for his own feelings are his stay and support; and, if he set them aside in one instance, he may be induced to repeat this act till his mind shall lose all confidence in itself, and become utterly debilitated. To this it may be added, that the critic ought never to forget that he is himself exposed to the same errors as the Poet, and, perhaps, in a much greater degree: for there can be no presumption in saying of most readers, that it is not probable they will be so well acquainted with the various stages of meaning through which words have passed, or with the fickleness or stability of the relations of particular ideas to each other; and, above all, since they are so much less interested in the subject, they may decide lightly and carelessly.

Long as the Reader has been detained, I hope he will permit me to caution him against a mode of false criticism which has been applied to poetry, in which the language closely resembles that of life and nature. Such verses have been triumphed over in parodies, of which Dr. Johnson's stanza is a fair specimen:—

> "I put my hat upon my head
> And walked into the Strand,
> And there I met another man
> Whose hat was in his hand."

Immediately under these lines let us place one of the most justly-admired stanzas of the "Babes in the Wood."

> "These pretty Babes with hand in hand
> Went wandering up and down;
> But never more they saw the Man
> Approaching from the Town."

In both these stanzas the words, and the order of the words, in no respect differ from the most unimpassioned conversation. There are words in both, for example, "the Strand," and "the Town," connected with none but the most familiar ideas; yet the one stanza we admit as admirable, and the other as a fair example of the superlatively contemptible. Whence arises this difference? Not from the metre, not from the language, not from the order of the words; but the *matter* expressed in Dr. Johnson's stanza is contemptible. The proper method of treating trivial and simple verses, to which Dr. Johnson's stanza would be a fair parallelism, is not to say, this is a bad kind of poetry, or, this is not poetry; but, this wants sense; it is neither interesting in itself, nor can *lead* to anything interesting; the images neither originate in that sane state of feeling which arises out of thought, nor can excite thought or feeling in the Reader. This is the only sensible manner of dealing with such verses. Why trouble yourself about the species till you have previously decided upon the genus? Why take pains to prove that an ape is not a Newton, when it is self-evident that he is not a man?

One request I must make of my reader, which is, that in judging these Poems he would decide by his own feelings genuinely, and not by reflection upon what will probably be the judgment of others. How common is it to hear a person say, I myself do not object to this style of composition, or this or that expression, but to such and such classes of people it will appear mean or ludicrous! This mode of criticism, so destructive of all sound unadulterated judgment, is almost universal: let the Reader then abide, independently, by his own feelings, and, if he finds himself affected, let him not suffer such conjectures to interfere with his pleasure.

If an Author, by any single composition, has impressed us with respect for his talents, it is useful to consider this as affording a presumption that on other occasions where we have been displeased, he, nevertheless, may not have written ill or absurdly; and further, to give him so much credit for this one composition as may induce us to review what has displeased us with more care than we should otherwise have bestowed upon it. This is not only an act of justice, but, in our decisions upon poetry especially, may conduce, in a high degree, to the improvement of our own taste; for an *accurate* taste in poetry, and in all the other arts, as Sir Joshua Reynolds has observed, is an *acquired* talent, which can only be produced by thought and a long-continued intercourse with the best models of composition. This is mentioned, not with so ridiculous a purpose as to prevent the most inexperienced Reader from judging for himself (I have already said that I wish him to judge for himself), but merely to temper the rashness of decision, and to suggest that, if Poetry be a subject on which much time has not been bestowed, the judgment may be erroneous; and that, in many cases, it necessarily will be so.

Nothing would, I know, have so effectually contributed to further the end which I have in view, as to have shown of what kind the pleasure is, and how that pleasure is produced, which is confessedly produced by metrical composition essentially different from that which I have here endeavoured to recommend: for the Reader will say that he has been pleased by such composition; and what more

can be done for him? The power of any art is limited; and he will suspect that, if it be proposed to furnish him with new friends, that can be only upon condition of his abandoning his old friends. Besides, as I have said, the Reader is himself conscious of the pleasure which he has received from such composition, composition to which he has peculiarly attached the endearing name of Poetry; and all men feel an habitual gratitude, and something of an honourable bigotry, for the objects which have long continued to please them: we not only wish to be pleased, but to be pleased in that particular way in which we have been accustomed to be pleased. There is in these feelings enough to resist a host of arguments; and I should be the less able to combat them successfully, as I am willing to allow that, in order entirely to enjoy the Poetry which I am recommending, it would be necessary to give up much of what is ordinarily enjoyed. But would my limits have permitted me to point out how this pleasure is produced, many obstacles might have been removed, and the Reader assisted in perceiving that the powers of language are not so limited as he may suppose; and that it is possible for poetry to give other enjoyments, of a purer, more lasting, and more exquisite nature. This part of the subject has not been altogether neglected, but it has not been so much my present aim to prove, that the interest excited by some other kinds of poetry is less vivid, and less worthy of the nobler powers of the mind, as to offer reasons for presuming that if my purpose were fulfilled, a species of poetry would be produced, which is genuine poetry; in its nature well adapted to interest mankind permanently, and likewise important in the multiplicity and quality of its moral relations.

From what has been said, and from a perusal of the Poems, the Reader will be able clearly to perceive the object which I had in view: he will determine how far it has been attained; and, what is a much more important question, whether it be worth attaining: and upon the decision of these two questions will rest my claim to the approbation of the Public.

THE OLD CUMBERLAND BEGGAR

This and the other following poems about people exemplify the main features of Wordsworth's "Preface" in relation to characters, incidents, and situations from humble or rustic life. With what was said there and with his treatments of these subjects, compare also what he said in *The Prelude* (especially Books Eight; Thirteen, ll. 142–68).

I saw an aged Beggar in my walk;
And he was seated, by the highway side,
On a low structure of rude masonry
Built at the foot of a huge hill, that they
Who lead their horses down the steep rough road
May thence remount at ease. The agèd Man
Had placed his staff across the broad smooth stone
That overlays the pile; and, from a bag
All white with flour, the dole of village dames,
He drew his scraps and fragments, one by one;   10
And scanned them with a fixed and serious look
Of idle computation. In the sun,
Upon the second step of that small pile,
Surrounded by those wild unpeopled hills,
He sat, and ate his food in solitude:
And ever, scattered from his palsied hand,
That, still attempting to prevent the waste,
Was baffled still, the crumbs in little showers
Fell on the ground; and the small mountain birds,
Not venturing yet to peck their destined meal,   20
Approached within the length of half his staff.

Him from my childhood have I known; and then
He was so old, he seems not older now;
He travels on, a solitary Man,
So helpless in appearance, that for him
The sauntering Horseman throws not with a slack
And careless hand his alms upon the ground,
But stops,—that he may safely lodge the coin
Within the old Man's hat; nor quits him so,
But still, when he has given his horse the rein,   30
Watches the aged Beggar with a look
Sidelong, and half-reverted. She who tends
The toll-gate, when in summer at her door
She turns her wheel, if on the road she sees
The aged Beggar coming, quits her work,
And lifts the latch for him that he may pass.
The post-boy, when his rattling wheels o'ertake
The aged Beggar in the woody lane,
Shouts to him from behind; and if, thus warned,
The old man does not change his course, the boy   40
Turns with less noisy wheels to the roadside,
And passes gently by, without a curse
Upon his lips, or anger at his heart

He travels on, a solitary Man;
His age has no companion. On the ground
His eyes are turned, and, as he moves along
They move along the ground; and, evermore,
Instead of common and habitual sight
Of fields with rural works, of hill and dale,
And the blue sky, one little span of earth   50
Is all his prospect. Thus, from day to day,
Bow-bent, his eyes for ever on the ground,

He plies his weary journey; seeing still,
And seldom knowing that he sees, some straw,
Some scattered leaf, or marks which, in one track,
The nails of cart or chariot-wheel have left
Impressed on the white road,—in the same line,
At distance still the same. Poor Traveller!
His staff trails with him; scarcely do his feet
Disturb the summer dust; he is so still   60
In look and motion, that the cottage curs,
Ere he has passed the door, will turn away,
Weary of barking at him. Boys and girls,
The vacant and the busy, maids and youths,
And urchins newly breeched—all pass him by:
Him even the slow-paced waggon leaves behind.

But deem not this Man useless.—Statesmen! ye
Who are so restless in your wisdom, ye
Who have a broom still ready in your hands
To rid the world of nuisances; ye proud,   70
Heart-swoln, while in your pride ye contemplate
Your talents, power, or wisdom, deem him not
A burthen of the earth! 'Tis Nature's law
That none, the meanest of created things,
Of forms created the most vile and brute,
The dullest or most noxious, should exist
Divorced from good—a spirit and pulse of good,
A life and soul, to every mode of being
Inseparably linked. Then be assured
That least of all can aught—that ever owned   80
The heaven-regarding eye and front sublime
Which man is born to—sink, howe'er depressed,
So low as to be scorned without a sin;
Without offence to God cast out of view;
Like the dry remnant of a garden-flower
Whose seeds are shed, or as an implement
Worn out and worthless. While from door to door,
This old Man creeps, the villagers in him
Behold a record which together binds
Past deeds and offices of charity,   90
Else unremembered, and so keeps alive
The kindly mood in hearts which lapse of years,
And that half-wisdom half-experience gives,
Make slow to feel, and by sure steps resign
To selfishness and cold oblivious cares.
Among the farms and solitary huts,
Hamlets and thinly-scattered villages,
Where'er the aged Beggar takes his rounds,
The mild necessity of use compels
To acts of love; and habit does the work   100
Of reason; yet prepares that after-joy
Which reason cherishes. And thus the soul,
By that sweet taste of pleasure unpursued,
Doth find herself insensibly disposed
To virtue and true goodness.

Some there are,
By their good works exalted, lofty minds,
And meditative, authors of delight
And happiness, which to the end of time
Will live, and spread, and kindle: even such minds
In childhood, from this solitary Being,   110
Or from like wanderer, haply have received
(A thing more precious far than all that books
Or the solicitudes of love can do!)
That first mild touch of sympathy and thought,
In which they found their kindred with a world
Where want and sorrow were. The easy man
Who sits at his own door,—and, like the pear
That overhangs his head from the green wall,
Feeds in the sunshine; the robust and young,
The prosperous and unthinking, they who live   120
Sheltered, and flourish in a little grove
Of their own kindred;—all behold in him
A silent monitor, which on their minds
Must needs impress a transitory thought
Of self-congratulation, to the heart
Of each recalling his peculiar boons,
His charters and exemptions; and, perchance,
Though he to no one give the fortitude
And circumspection needful to preserve
His present blessings, and to husband up   130
The respite of the season, he, at least,
And 'tis no vulgar service, makes them felt.

Yet further.——Many, I believe, there are
Who live a life of virtuous decency,
Men who can hear the Decalogue and feel
No self-reproach; who of the moral law
Established in the land where they abide
Are strict observers; and not negligent
In acts of love to those with whom they dwell,
Their kindred, and the children of their blood. 140
Praise be to such, and to their slumbers peace!
—But of the poor man ask, the abject poor;
Go, and demand of him, if there be here
In this cold abstinence from evil deeds,
And these inevitable charities,
Wherewith to satisfy the human soul?
No—man is dear to man; the poorest poor
Long for some moments in a weary life
When they can know and feel that they have been,
Themselves, the fathers and the dealers-out   150
Of some small blessings; have been kind to such
As needed kindness, for this single cause,
That we have all of us one human heart.
—Such pleasure is to one kind Being known,
My neighbour, when with punctual care, each
    week,
Duly as Friday comes, though pressed herself

By her own wants, she from her store of meal
Takes one unsparing handful for the scrip
Of this old Mendicant, and, from her door
Returning with exhilarated heart,   160
Sits by her fire, and builds her hope in heaven.

Then let him pass, a blessing on his head!
And while in that vast solitude to which
The tide of things has borne him, he appears
To breathe and live but for himself alone,
Unblamed, uninjured, let him bear about
The good which the benignant law of Heaven
Has hung around him: and, while life is his,
Still let him prompt the unlettered villagers
To tender offices and pensive thoughts.   170

—Then let him pass, a blessing on his head!
And, long as he can wander, let him breathe
The freshness of the valleys; let his blood
Struggle with frosty air and winter snows;
And let the chartered wind that sweeps the heath
Beat his grey locks against his withered face.
Reverence the hope whose vital anxiousness
Gives the last human interest to his heart.
May never HOUSE, misnamed of INDUSTRY,
Make him a captive!—for that pent-up din,   180
Those life-consuming sounds that clog the air,
Be his the natural silence of old age!
Let him be free of mountain solitudes;
And have around him, whether heard or not,
The pleasant melody of woodland birds.
Few are his pleasures: if his eyes have now
Been doomed so long to settle upon earth
That not without some effort they behold
The countenance of the horizontal sun,
Rising or setting, let the light at least   190
Find a free entrance to their languid orbs,
And let him, *where* and *when* he will, sit down
Beneath the trees, or on a grassy bank
Of highway side, and with the little birds
Share his chance-gathered meal; and, finally,
As in the eye of Nature he has lived,
So in the eye of Nature let him die!

THE REVERIE OF POOR SUSAN

Wordsworth once cited this poem as an illustration of what he meant by his statement, in the "Preface" to *Lyrical Ballads*, "that the feeling therein developed gives importance to the action and situation, and not the action and situation to the feeling." Not the London street scene, not the nostalgic vision evoked by the thrush's song, but Susan's homesickness, is the point of the poem. Wordsworth never describes scenery or tells stories merely for their own sake; human feeling is always the important thing.

At the corner of Wood Street, when daylight appears,
Hangs a Thrush that sings loud, it has sung for three years:
Poor Susan has passed by the spot, and has heard
In the silence of morning the song of the Bird.

'Tis a note of enchantment; what ails her? She sees
A mountain ascending, a vision of trees;
Bright volumes of vapour through Lothbury glide,
And a river flows on through the vale of Cheapside.

Green pastures she views in the midst of the dale,
Down which she so often has tripped with her pail;   10
And a single small cottage, a nest like a dove's,
The one only dwelling on earth that she loves.

She looks, and her heart is in heaven: but they fade,
The mist and the river, the hill and the shade:
The stream will not flow, and the hill will not rise,
And the colours have all passed away from her eyes!

WE ARE SEVEN

The poem illustrates the point that it is foolish and wrong to insist that children have conceptions for which they are not mentally and spiritually ready. (Wordsworth makes this point about this poem and another, "Anecdote for Fathers.")

    —A simple Child,
That lightly draws its breath,
And feels its life in every limb,
What should it know of death?

I met a little cottage Girl:
She was eight years old, she said;
Her hair was thick with many a curl
That clustered round her head.

She had a rustic, woodland air,
And she was wildly clad: 10
Her eyes were fair, and very fair;
—Her beauty made me glad.

"Sisters and brothers, little Maid,
How many may you be?"
"How many? Seven in all," she said
And wondering looked at me.

"And where are they? I pray you tell."
She answered, "Seven are we;
And two of us at Conway dwell,
And two are gone to sea.   20

"Two of us in the church-yard lie,
My sister and my brother;
And, in the church-yard cottage, I
Dwell near them with my mother."

"You say that two at Conway dwell,
And two are gone to sea,
Yet ye are seven!—I pray you tell,
Sweet Maid, how this may be."

Then did the little Maid reply,
"Seven boys and girls are we;   30
Two of us in the church-yard lie,
Beneath the church-yard tree."

"You run about, my little Maid,
Your limbs they are alive;
If two are in the church-yard laid,
Then ye are only five."

"Their graves are green, they may be seen,"
The little Maid replied,
"Twelve steps or more from my mother's door,
And they are side by side.   40

"My stockings there I often knit,
My kerchief there I hem;
And there upon the ground I sit,
And sing a song to them.

"And often after sunset, Sir,
When it is light and fair,
I take my little porringer,
And eat my supper there.

"The first that died was sister Jane;
In bed she moaning lay,   50
Till God released her of her pain;
And then she went away.

"So in the church-yard she was laid;
And, when the grass was dry,
Together round her grave we played,
My brother John and I.

"And when the ground was white with snow,
And I could run and slide,
My brother John was forced to go,
And he lies by her side."   60

19. **Conway,** the county seat of Carnarvonshire, Wales.

"How many are you, then," said I,
"If they two are in heaven?"
Quick was the little Maid's reply,
"O Master! we are seven."

"But they are dead; those two are dead!
Their spirits are in heaven!"
'Twas throwing words away; for still
The little Maid would have her will,
And said, "Nay we are seven!"

SIMON LEE

THE OLD HUNTSMAN;

WITH AN INCIDENT IN WHICH HE
WAS CONCERNED

In the sweet shire of Cardigan,
Not far from pleasant Ivor-hall,
An old Man dwells, a little man,—
'Tis said he once was tall.
Full five-and-thirty years he lived
A running huntsman merry;
And still the centre of his cheek
Is red as a ripe cherry.

No man like him the horn could sound,
And hill and valley rang with glee   10
When Echo bandied, round and round,
The halloo of Simon Lee.
In those proud days, he little cared
For husbandry or tillage;
To blither tasks did Simon rouse
The sleepers of the village.

He all the country could outrun,
Could leave both man and horse behind;
And often, ere the chase was done,
He reeled, and was stone-blind.   20
And still there's something in the world
At which his heart rejoices;
For when the chiming hounds are out,
He dearly loves their voices!

But, oh the heavy change!—bereft
Of health, strength, friends, and kindred, see!
Old Simon to the world is left
In liveried poverty.
His Master's dead,—and no one now
Dwells in the Hall of Ivor;   30
Men, dogs, and horses, all are dead;
He is the sole survivor.

1. **Cardigan**, a county in southern Wales.

And he is lean and he is sick;
His body, dwindled and awry,
Rests upon ankles swoln and thick;
His legs are thin and dry.
One prop he has, and only one,
His wife, an aged woman,
Lives with him, near the waterfall,
Upon the village Common.   40

Beside their moss-grown hut of clay,
Not twenty paces from the door,
A scrap of land they have, but they
Are poorest of the poor.
This scrap of land he from the heath
Enclosed when he was stronger;
But what to them avails the land
Which he can till no longer?

Oft, working by her Husband's side,
Ruth does what Simon cannot do;   50
For she, with scanty cause for pride,
Is stouter of the two.
And, though you with your utmost skill
From labour could not wean them,
'Tis little, very little—all
That they can do between them.

Few months of life has he in store
As he to you will tell,
For still, the more he works, the more
Do his weak ankles swell.   60
My gentle Reader, I perceive
How patiently you've waited,
And now I fear that you expect
Some tale will be related.

O Reader! had you in your mind
Such stores as silent thought can bring,
O gentle Reader! you would find
A tale in every thing.
What more I have to say is short,
And you must kindly take it: 70
It is no tale; but, should you think,
Perhaps a tale you'll make it.

One summer-day I chanced to see
This old Man doing all he could
To unearth the root of an old tree,
A stump of rotten wood.
The mattock tottered in his hand;
So vain was his endeavour,
That at the root of the old tree
He might have worked for ever.   80

"You're overtasked, good Simon Lee,
Give me your tool," to him I said;
And at the word right gladly he
Received my proffered aid.
I struck, and with a single blow
The tangled root I severed,
At which the poor old Man so long
And vainly had endeavoured.

The tears into his eyes were brought.
And thanks and praises seemed to run   90
So fast out of his heart, I thought
They never would have done.
—I've heard of hearts unkind, kind deeds
With coldness still returning;
Alas! the gratitude of men
Hath oftener left me mourning.

LUCY GRAY

OR, SOLITUDE

"Written at Goslar in Germany. It was founded on a
circumstance told me by my Sister, of a little girl who,
not far from Halifax in Yorkshire, was bewildered in a
snow-storm. Her footsteps were traced by her parents to
the middle of the lock of a canal, and no other vestige of
her, backward or forward, could be traced. The body
however was found in the canal. The way in which the
incident was treated and the spiritualising of the character might furnish hints for contrasting the imaginative
influences which I have endeavoured to throw over common life with Crabbe's matter of fact style of treating subjects of the same kind. This is not spoken to his disparage-
ment, far from it, but to direct the attention of thoughtful
readers, into whose hands these notes may fall, to a comparison that may both enlarge the circle of their sensibilities, and tend to produce in them a catholic judgment."
                                              —Wordsworth

Oft I had heard of Lucy Gray:
And, when I crossed the wild,
I chanced to see at break of day
The solitary child.

No mate, no comrade Lucy knew;
She dwelt on a wide moor,
—The sweetest thing that ever grew
Beside a human door!

You yet may spy the fawn at play,
The hare upon the green;   10
But the sweet face of Lucy Gray
Will never more be seen.

"To-night will be a stormy night—
You to the town must go;
And take a lantern, Child, to light
Your mother through the snow."

"That, Father! will I gladly do:
'Tis scarcely afternoon—
The minster-clock has just struck two,
And yonder is the moon!"   20

At this the Father raised his hook,
And snapped a faggot-band;
He plied his work;—and Lucy took
The lantern in her hand.

Not blither is the mountain roe:
With many a wanton stroke
Her feet disperse the powdery snow,
That rises up like smoke.

The storm came on before its time:
She wandered up and down;   30
And many a hill did Lucy climb:
But never reached the town.

The wretched parents all that night
Went shouting far and wide;
But there was neither sound nor sight
To serve them for a guide.

At day-break on the hill they stood
That overlooked the moor;
And thence they saw the bridge of wood,
A furlong from their door.   40

They wept—and, turning homeward, cried,
"In heaven we all shall meet";
—When in the snow the mother spied
The print of Lucy's feet.

Then downwards from the steep hill's edge
They tracked the footmarks small;
And through the broken hawthorn hedge,
And by the long stone-wall;

And then an open field they crossed:
The marks were still the same;   50
They tracked them on, nor ever lost;
And to the bridge they came.

They followed from the snowy bank
Those footmarks, one by one,
Into the middle of the plank;
And further there were none!

—Yet some maintain that to this day
She is a living child;
That you may see sweet Lucy Gray
Upon the lonesome wild.   60

O'er rough and smooth she trips along,
And never looks behind;
And sings a solitary song
That whistles in the wind.

THERE WAS A BOY

Sometimes known as "The Boy of Winander," the poem was written in 1798, published in the 1800 *Lyrical Ballads*, and afterwards incorporated in *The Prelude* (Book Five, ll. 364–97). In *The Prelude* the lines follow a passage in which Wordsworth comments unfavorably upon formal systems of education current in his time. "There Was a Boy," then, would seem to exemplify the best way in which the human soul is evolved. In the moment of tense expectancy, while he is listening for the owls' answer to his hootings, the Boy unconsciously receives a revelation of the beauty of his surroundings. In the Library of Congress murals representing the great poets, a picture of The Boy of Winander represents Wordsworth.

There was a Boy; ye knew him well, ye cliffs
And islands of Winander!—many a time,
At evening, when the earliest stars began
To move along the edges of the hills,
Rising or setting, would he stand alone,
Beneath the trees, or by the glimmering lake;
And there, with fingers interwoven, both hands
Pressed closely palm to palm and to his mouth
Uplifted, he, as through an instrument,
Blew mimic hootings to the owls,   10
That they might answer him.—And they would
     shout
Across the watery vale, and shout again,
Responsive to his call,—with quivering peals,
And long halloos, and screams, and echoes loud
Redoubled and redoubled; concourse wild
Of jocund din! And, when there came a pause
Of silence such as baffled his best skill:
Then sometimes, in that silence, while he hung
Listening, a gentle shock of mild surprise
Has carried far into his heart the voice   20
Of mountain-torrents; or the visible scene
Would enter unawares into his mind
With all its solemn imagery, its rocks,
Its woods, and that uncertain heaven received
Into the bosom of the steady lake.

57. Yet some maintain. Note how this quiet addition throws back over the entire matter-of-fact story a coloring of the supernatural. The effect is somewhat like that achieved by Coleridge in *The Rime of the Ancient Mariner.*

This boy was taken from his mates, and died
In childhood, ere he was full twelve years old.
Pre-eminent in beauty is the vale
Where he was born and bred: the churchyard
     hangs
Upon a slope above the village-school;   30
And through that churchyard when my way has led
On summer-evenings, I believe that there
A long half-hour together I have stood
Mute—looking at the grave in which he lies!

MICHAEL

A PASTORAL POEM

"Written at Town-end, Grasmere, about the same time as 'The Brothers.' The Sheepfold, on which so much of the poem turns, remains, or rather the ruins of it. The character and circumstances of Luke were taken from a family to whom had belonged, many years before, the house we lived in at Town-end, along with some fields and woodlands on the eastern shore of Grasmere. The name of the Evening Star was not in fact given to this house, but to another on the same side of the valley, more to the north."—Wordsworth

Compare *The Prelude*, Book Eight, and the "Preface," which was written for the edition of *Lyrical Ballads* in which "Michael" was first published. Note the significance of the subtitle, "A Pastoral Poem," the poet's account of why and how he became interested in Michael, the emphasis upon Michael's love for his land, the tragic conflict which Michael tries to resolve (love for his land and love for his boy), and the quiet pathos of the conclusion ("And never lifted up a single stone"—said to be Wordsworth's most characteristic line). Note, too, the verse form and the diction.

If from the public way you turn your steps
Up the tumultuous brook of Green-head Ghyll,
You will suppose that with an upright path
Your feet must struggle; in such bold ascent
The pastoral mountains front you, face to face,
But, courage! for around that boisterous brook
The mountains have all opened out themselves,
And made a hidden valley of their own.
No habitation can be seen; but they
Who journey thither find themselves alone   10
With a few sheep, with rocks and stones, and kites
That overhead are sailing in the sky.
It is in truth an utter solitude;
Nor should I have made mention of this Dell
But for one object which you might pass by,
Might see and notice not. Beside the brook
Appears a straggling heap of unhewn stones!

2. Ghyll, northern dialect word for gulley or ravine.
11. kites, hawklike birds.

And to that simple object appertains
A story—unenriched with strange events,
Yet not unfit, I deem, for the fireside,   20
Or for the summer shade. It was the first
Of those domestic tales that spake to me
Of shepherds, dwellers in the valleys, men
Whom I already loved;—not verily
For their own sakes, but for the fields and hills
Where was their occupation and abode.
And hence this Tale, while I was yet a Boy
Careless of books, yet having felt the power
Of Nature, by the gentle agency
Of natural objects, led me on to feel   30
For passions that were not my own, and think
(At random and imperfectly indeed)
On man, the heart of man, and human life.
Therefore, although it be a history
Homely and rude, I will relate the same
For the delight of a few natural hearts;
And, with yet fonder feeling, for the sake
Of youthful Poets, who among these hills
Will be my second self when I am gone.

    Upon the forest-side in Grasmere Vale   40
There dwelt a Shepherd, Michael was his name;
An old man, stout of heart, and strong of limb.
His bodily frame had been from youth to age
Of an unusual strength: his mind was keen,
Intense, and frugal, apt for all affairs,
And in his shepherd's calling he was prompt
And watchful more than ordinary men.
Hence had he learned the meaning of all winds,
Of blasts of every tone; and, oftentimes,
When others heeded not, he heard the South   50
Make subterraneous music, like the noise
Of bagpipers on distant Highland hills.
The Shepherd, at such warning, of his flock
Bethought him, and he to himself would say,
"The winds are now devising work for me!"
And, truly, at all times, the storm, that drives
The traveller to a shelter, summoned him
Up to the mountains: he had been alone
Amid the heart of many thousand mists,
That came to him, and left him, on the heights.   60
So lived he till his eightieth year was past.
And grossly that man errs, who should suppose
That the green valleys, and the streams and rocks,
Were things indifferent to the Shepherd's thoughts.
Fields, where with cheerful spirits he had breathed
The common air; hills, which with vigorous step
He had so often climbed; which had impressed
So many incidents upon his mind
Of hardship, skill or courage, joy or fear;
Which, like a book, preserved the memory   70

Of the dumb animals, whom he had saved,
Had fed or sheltered, linking to such acts
The certainty of honourable gain;
Those fields, those hills—what could they less? had
   laid
Strong hold on his affections, were to him
A pleasurable feeling of blind love,
The pleasure which there is in life itself.

    His days had not been passed in singleness.
His Helpmate was a comely matron, old—
Though younger than himself full twenty years.   80
She was a woman of a stirring life,
Whose heart was in her house: two wheels she had
Of antique form; this large, for spinning wool;
That small, for flax; and if one wheel had rest,
It was because the other was at work.
The Pair had but one inmate in their house,
An only Child, who had been born to them
When Michael, telling o'er his years, began
To deem that he was old,—in shepherd's phrase,
With one foot in the grave. This only Son,   90
With two brave sheep-dogs tried in many a storm,
The one of an inestimable worth,
Made all their household. I may truly say,
That they were as a proverb in the vale
For endless industry. When day was gone,
And from their occupations out of doors
The Son and Father were come home, even then,
Their labour did not cease; unless when all
Turned to the cleanly supper-board, and there,
Each with a mess of pottage and skimmed milk,   100
Sat round the basket piled with oaten cakes,
And their plain home-made cheese. Yet when the
   meal
Was ended, Luke (for so the Son was named)
And his old Father both betook themselves
To such convenient work as might employ
Their hands by the fireside; perhaps to card
Wool for the Housewife's spindle, or repair
Some injury done to sickle, flail, or scythe,
Or other implement of house or field.

    Down from the ceiling, by the chimney's edge,
That in our ancient uncouth country style   111
With huge and black projection overbrowed
Large space beneath, as duly as the light
Of day grew dim, the Housewife hung a lamp;
An aged utensil, which had performed
Service beyond all others of its kind.
Early at evening did it burn—and late,
Surviving comrade of uncounted hours,
Which, going by from year to year, had found,
And left, the couple neither gay perhaps   120
Nor cheerful, yet with objects and with hopes,

Living a life of eager industry.
And now, when Luke had reached his eighteenth
   year,
There by the light of this old lamp they sate,
Father and Son, while far into the night
The Housewife plied her own peculiar work,
Making the cottage through the silent hours
Murmur as with the sound of summer flies.
This light was famous in its neighbourhood,
And was a public symbol of the life   130
That thrifty Pair had lived. For, as it chanced,
Their cottage on a plot of rising ground
Stood single, with large prospect, north and south,
High into Easedale, up to Dunmail-Raise,
And westward to the village near the lake;
And from this constant light, so regular
And so far seen, the House itself, by all
Who dwelt within the limits of the vale,
Both old and young, was named THE EVENING STAR.

Thus living on through such a length of years,   140
The Shepherd, if he loved himself, must needs
Have loved his Helpmate; but to Michael's heart
This son of his old age was yet more dear—
Less from instinctive tenderness, the same
Fond spirit that blindly works in the blood of all—
Than that a child, more than all other gifts
That earth can offer to declining man,
Brings hope with it, and forward-looking thoughts,
And stirrings of inquietude, when they
By tendency of nature needs must fail.   150
Exceeding was the love he bare to him,
His heart and his heart's joy! For oftentimes
Old Michael, while he was a babe in arms,
Had done him female service, not alone
For pastime and delight, as is the use
Of fathers, but with patient mind enforced
To acts of tenderness; and he had rocked
His cradle, as with a woman's gentle hand.

And, in a later time, ere yet the Boy
Had put on boy's attire, did Michael love,   160
Albeit of a stern unbending mind,
To have the Young-one in his sight, when he
Wrought in the field, or on his shepherd's stool
Sat with a fettered sheep before him stretched
Under the large old oak, that near his door
Stood single, and, from matchless depth of shade,
Chosen for the Shearer's covert from the sun,
Thence in our rustic dialect was called
The CLIPPING TREE, a name which yet it bears.

169. Clipping Tree. "Clipping is the word used in the North of England for shearing." (Wordsworth) Still so used in the southern United States.

There, while they two were sitting in the shade,   170
With others round them, earnest all and blithe,
Would Michael exercise his heart with looks
Of fond correction and reproof bestowed
Upon the Child, if he disturbed the sheep
By catching at their legs, or with his shouts
Scared them, while they lay still beneath the shears.

And when by Heaven's good grace the boy grew
   up
A healthy Lad, and carried in his cheek
Two steady roses that were five years old,
Then Michael from a winter coppice cut   180
With his own hand a sapling, which he hooped
With iron, making it throughout in all
Due requisites a perfect shepherd's staff,
And gave it to the Boy; wherewith equipt
He as a watchman oftentimes was placed
At gate or gap, to stem or turn the flock;
And, to his office prematurely called,
There stood the urchin, as you will divine,
Something between a hindrance and a help;
And for this cause not always, I believe,   190
Receiving from his Father hire of praise;
Though nought was left undone which staff, or
   voice,
Or looks, or threatening gestures, could perform.

But soon as Luke, full ten years old, could stand
Against the mountain blasts; and to the heights,
Not fearing toil, nor length of weary ways,
He with his Father daily went, and they
Were as companions, why should I relate
That objects which the Shepherd loved before
Were dearer now? that from the Boy there came   200
Feelings and emanations—things which were
Light to the sun and music to the wind;
And that the old Man's heart seemed born again?

Thus in his Father's sight the Boy grew up:
And now, when he had reached his eighteenth year,
He was his comfort and his daily hope.

While in this sort the simple household lived
From day to day, to Michael's ear there came
Distressful tidings. Long before the time
Of which I speak, the Shepherd had been bound
In surety for his brother's son, a man   211
Of an industrious life, and ample means;
But unforeseen misfortunes suddenly
Had prest upon him; and old Michael now
Was summoned to discharge the forfeiture,
A grievous penalty, but little less
Than half his substance. This unlooked-for claim,

At the first hearing, for a moment took
More hope out of his life than he supposed
That any old man ever could have lost.　220
As soon as he had armed himself with strength
To look his trouble in the face, it seemed
The Shepherd's sole resource to sell at once
A portion of his patrimonial fields.
Such was his first resolve; he thought again,
And his heart failed him. "Isabel," said he,
Two evenings after he had heard the news,
"I have been toiling more than seventy years,
And in the open sunshine of God's love
Have we all lived; yet if these fields of ours　230
Should pass into a stranger's hand, I think
That I could not lie quiet in my grave.
Our lot is a hard lot; the sun himself
Has scarcely been more diligent than I;
And I have lived to be a fool at last
To my own family. An evil man
That was, and made an evil choice, if he
Were false to us; and if he were not false,
There are ten thousand to whom loss like this
Had been no sorrow. I forgive him;—but　240
'Twere better to be dumb than to talk thus.

"When I began, my purpose was to speak
Of remedies and of a cheerful hope.
Our Luke shall leave us, Isabel; the land
Shall not go from us, and it shall be free;
He shall possess it, free as is the wind
That passes over it. We have, thou know'st,
Another kinsman—he will be our friend
In this distress. He is a prosperous man,
Thriving in trade—and Luke to him shall go,　250
And with his kinsman's help and his own thrift
He quickly will repair this loss, and then
He may return to us. If here he stay,
What can be done? Where every one is poor,
What can be gained?"
　　　　　　　　　At this the old Man paused,
And Isabel sat silent, for her mind
Was busy, looking back into past times.
There's Richard Bateman, thought she to herself,
He was a parish-boy—at the church-door
They made a gathering for him, shillings, pence　260
And halfpennies, wherewith the neighbours bought
A basket, which they filled with pedlar's wares;
And, with this basket on his arm, the lad
Went up to London, found a master there,
Who, out of many, chose the trusty boy
To go and overlook his merchandise
Beyond the seas; where he grew wondrous rich,
And left estates and monies to the poor,
And, at his birth-place, built a chapel, floored

With marble which he sent from foreign lands.　270
These thoughts, and many others of like sort,
Passed quickly through the mind of Isabel,
And her face brightened. The old Man was glad,
And thus resumed:—"Well, Isabel! this scheme
These two days, has been meat and drink to me.
Far more than we have lost is left us yet.
—We have enough—I wish indeed that I
Were younger;—but this hope is a good hope.
—Make ready Luke's best garments, of the best
Buy for him more, and let us send him forth　280
To-morrow, or the next day, or to-night:
—If he *could* go, the Boy should go to-night."

Here Michael ceased, and to the fields went forth
With a light heart. The Housewife for five days
Was restless morn and night, and all day long
Wrought on with her best fingers to prepare
Things needful for the journey of her son.
But Isabel was glad when Sunday came
To stop her in her work: for, when she lay
By Michael's side, she through the last two nights
Heard him, how he was troubled in his sleep:　291
And when they rose at morning she could see
That all his hopes were gone. That day at noon
She said to Luke, while they two by themselves
Were sitting at the door, "Thou must not go:
We have no other Child but thee to lose—
None to remember—do not go away,
For if thou leave thy Father he will die."
The Youth made answer with a jocund voice;
And Isabel, when she had told her fears,　300
Recovered heart. That evening her best fare
Did she bring forth, and all together sat
Like happy people round a Christmas fire.

With daylight Isabel resumed her work;
And all the ensuing week the house appeared
As cheerful as a grove in Spring: at length
The expected letter from their kinsman came,
With kind assurances that he would do
His utmost for the welfare of the Boy;
To which, requests were added, that forthwith　310
He might be sent to him. Ten times or more
The letter was read over; Isabel
Went forth to show it to the neighbours round;
Nor was there at that time on English land
A prouder heart than Luke's. When Isabel
Had to her house returned, the old Man said,
"He shall depart to-morrow." To this word
The Housewife answered, talking much of things
Which, if at such short notice he should go,
Would surely be forgotten. But at length　320
She gave consent, and Michael was at ease.

Near the tumultuous brook of Green-head Ghyll,
In that deep valley, Michael had designed
To build a Sheep-fold; and, before he heard
The tidings of his melancholy loss,
For this same purpose he had gathered up
A heap of stones, which by the streamlet's edge
Lay thrown together, ready for the work.
With Luke that evening thitherward he walked: 329
And soon as they had reached the place he stopped,
And thus the old Man spake to him:—"My Son,
To-morrow thou wilt leave me: with full heart
I look upon thee, for thou art the same
That wert a promise to me ere thy birth,
And all thy life has been my daily joy.
I will relate to thee some little part
Of our two histories; 'twill do thee good
When thou art from me, even if I should touch
On things thou canst not know of.—After thou
First cam'st into the world—as oft befalls   340
To new-born infants—thou didst sleep away
Two days, and blessings from thy Father's tongue
Then fell upon thee. Day by day passed on,
And still I loved thee with increasing love.
Never to living ear came sweeter sounds
Than when I heard thee by our own fireside
First uttering, without words, a natural tune;
While thou, a feeding babe, didst in thy joy
Sing at thy Mother's breast. Month followed
    month,
And in the open fields my life was passed   350
And on the mountains; else I think that thou
Hadst been brought up upon thy Father's knees.
But we were playmates, Luke: among these hills,
As well thou knowest, in us the old and young
Have played together, nor with me didst thou
Lack any pleasure which a boy can know."
Luke had a manly heart; but at these words
He sobbed aloud. The old Man grasped his hand,
And said, "Nay, do not take it so—I see
That these are things of which I need not speak. 360
—Even to the utmost I have been to thee
A kind and a good Father: and herein
I but repay a gift which I myself
Received at others' hands; for, though now old
Beyond the common life of man, I still
Remember them who loved me in my youth.
Both of them sleep together: here they lived,
As all their Forefathers had done; and when
At length their time was come, they were not loth
To give their bodies to the family mould.   370
I wished that thou should'st live the life they lived:
But, 'tis a long time to look back, my Son,
And see so little gain from three score years.
These fields were burthened when they came to me;

Till I was forty years of age, not more
Than half of my inheritance was mine.
I toiled and toiled; God blessed me in my work,
And till these three weeks past the land was free.
—It looks as if it never could endure
Another Master. Heaven forgive me, Luke,   380
If I judge ill for thee, but it seems good
That thou should'st go."

                        At this the old Man paused;
Then, pointing to the stones near which they stood,
Thus, after a short silence, he resumed:
"This was a work for us; and now, my Son,
It is a work for me. But, lay one stone—
Here, lay it for me, Luke, with thine own hands.
Nay, Boy, be of good hope;—we both may live
To see a better day. At eighty-four
I still am strong and hale;—do thou thy part;   390
I will do mine.—I will begin again
With many tasks that were resigned to thee:
Up to the heights, and in among the storms,
Will I without thee go again, and do
All works which I was wont to do alone,
Before I knew thy face.—Heaven bless thee, Boy!
Thy heart these two weeks has been beating fast
With many hopes; it should be so—yes—yes—
I knew that thou could'st never have a wish
To leave me, Luke; thou hast been bound to me   400
Only by links of love: when thou art gone,
What will be left to us!—But, I forget
My purposes. Lay now the corner-stone,
As I requested; and hereafter, Luke,
When thou art gone away, should evil men
Be thy companions, think of me, my Son,
And of this moment; hither turn thy thoughts,
And God will strengthen thee: amid all fear
And all temptation, Luke, I pray that thou
May'st bear in mind the life thy Fathers lived,   410
Who, being innocent, did for that cause
Bestir them in good deeds. Now, fare thee well—
When thou return'st, thou in this place wilt see
A work which is not here: a covenant
'Twill be between us; but, whatever fate
Befall thee, I shall love thee to the last,
And bear thy memory with me to the grave."

    The Shepherd ended here; and Luke stooped
        down,
And, as his Father had requested, laid
The first stone of the Sheep-fold. At the sight   420
The old Man's grief broke from him; to his heart
He pressed his Son, he kissèd him and wept;
And to the house together they returned.
—Hushed was that House in peace, or seeming
    peace,

Ere the night fell:—with morrow's dawn the Boy
Began his journey, and when he had reached
The public way, he put on a bold face;
And all the neighbours, as he passed their doors,
Came forth with wishes and with farewell prayers,
That followed him till he was out of sight.   430

A good report did from their Kinsman come,
Of Luke and his well-doing: and the Boy
Wrote loving letters, full of wondrous news,
Which, as the Housewife phrased it, were through-
    out
"The prettiest letters that were ever seen."
Both parents read them with rejoicing hearts.
So, many months passed on: and once again
The Shepherd went about his daily work
With confident and cheerful thoughts; and now
Sometimes when he could find a leisure hour   440
He to that valley took his way, and there
Wrought at the Sheep-fold. Meantime Luke began
To slacken in his duty; and, at length,
He in the dissolute city gave himself
To evil courses: ignominy and shame
Fell on him, so that he was driven at last
To seek a hiding-place beyond the seas.

There is a comfort in the strength of love;
'Twill make a thing endurable, which else
Would overset the brain, or break the heart: 450
I have conversed with more than one who well
Remember the old Man, and what he was
Years after he had heard this heavy news.
His bodily frame had been from youth to age
Of an unusual strength. Among the rocks
He went, and still looked up to sun and cloud,
And listened to the wind; and, as before,
Performed all kinds of labour for his sheep,
And for the land, his small inheritance.
And to that hollow dell from time to time   460
Did he repair, to build the Fold of which
His flock had need. 'Tis not forgotten yet
The pity which was then in every heart
For the old Man—and 'tis believed by all
That many and many a day he thither went,
And never lifted up a single stone.

There, by the Sheep-fold, sometimes was he seen
Sitting alone, or with his faithful Dog,
Then old, beside him, lying at his feet.
The length of full seven years, from time to time, 470
He at the building of this Sheep-fold wrought,
And left the work unfinished when he died.
Three years, or little more, did Isabel
Survive her Husband: at her death the estate

Was sold, and went into a stranger's hand.
The Cottage which was named the EVENING STAR
Is gone—the ploughshare has been through the
    ground
On which it stood; great changes have been
    wrought
In all the neighbourhood:—yet the oak is left
That grew beside their door; and the remains   480
Of the unfinished Sheep-fold may be seen
Beside the boisterous brook of Green-head Ghyll.

LINES WRITTEN IN EARLY
SPRING

The following group of poems, ending with "Tintern
Abbey," illustrates certain cardinal points in Wordsworth's faith: "Lines": 1. Nature and man akin in spirit.
2. Nature alive and consciously sentient. 3. Nature's plan
perfect and holy; and Nature therefore happy; man's out
of harmony, and man consequently miserable. "To My
Sister": 1. Love the law of the world. 2. The receptive
soul of man may be attuned to the Universe. "Expostu-
lation and Reply": 1. The moral sense innate. 2. Nature
a source of truth and wisdom. 3. "Wise passiveness" the
best way to receive truth. "The Tables Turned": 1. Anti-
intellectualism. 2. Opposition to rationalism and scientific
analysis. This group of poems has been the chief basis of
attacks made on Wordsworth's philosophy. It must be remembered that he was in high spirits when he wrote them,
perhaps inclined to be paradoxical; and that in his later
poetry he shows high regard for science, for learning, and
for Reason in her exalted forms; but that even after due
allowance has been made for his mood and the circumstances, they do express his fundamental faith in the natural order and in the intuitive, instinctive elements of the
human mind and spirit.

I heard a thousand blended notes
While in a grove I sate reclined,
In that sweet mood when pleasant thoughts
Bring sad thoughts to the mind.

To her fair works did Nature link
The human soul that through me ran;
And much it grieved my heart to think
What man has made of man.

Through primrose tufts, in that sweet bower,
The periwinkle trailed its wreaths;   10
And 'tis my faith that every flower
Enjoys the air it breathes.

The birds around me hopped and played,
Their thoughts I cannot measure:—
But the least motion which they made,
It seemed a thrill of pleasure.

The budding twigs spread out their fan,
To catch the breezy air;
And I must think, do all I can,
That there was pleasure there.   20

If this belief from heaven be sent,
If such be Nature's holy plan,
Have I not reason to lament
What man has made of man?

TO MY SISTER

It is the first mild day of March:
Each minute sweeter than before;
The redbreast sings from the tall larch
That stands beside our door.

There is a blessing in the air,
Which seems a sense of joy to yield
To the bare trees, and mountains bare,
And grass in the green field.

My sister! ('tis a wish of mine)
Now that our morning meal is done,   10
Make haste, your morning task resign;
Come forth and feel the sun.

Edward will come with you;—and, pray,
Put on with speed your woodland dress;
And bring no book: for this one day
We'll give to idleness.

No joyless forms shall regulate
Our living calendar:
We from to-day, my Friend, will date
The opening of the year.   20

Love, now a universal birth,
From heart to heart is stealing,
From earth to man, from man to earth:
—It is the hour of feeling.

One moment now may give us more
Than years of toiling reason:
Our minds shall drink at every pore
The spirit of the season.

Some silent laws our hearts will make,
Which they shall long obey:
We for the year to come may take   30
Our temper from to-day.

And from the blessed power that rolls
About, below, above,
We'll frame the measure of our souls:
They shall be tuned to love.

Then come, my Sister! come, I pray,
With speed put on your woodland dress;
And bring no book: for this one day
We'll give to idleness.   40

EXPOSTULATION AND REPLY

"Why, William, on that old grey stone,
Thus for the length of half a day,
Why, William, sit you thus alone,
And dream your time away?

"Where are your books?—that light bequeathed
To Beings else forlorn and blind!
Up! up! and drink the spirit breathed
From dead men to their kind.

"You look round on your Mother Earth,
As if she for no purpose bore you;   10
As if you were her first-born birth,
And none had lived before you!"

One morning thus, by Esthwaite lake,
When life was sweet, I knew not why,
To me my good friend Matthew spake,
And thus I made reply:

"The eye—it cannot choose but see;
We cannot bid the ear be still;
Our bodies feel, where'er they be,
Against or with our will.   20

"Nor less I deem that there are Powers
Which of themselves our minds impress;
That we can feed this mind of ours
In a wise passiveness.

"Think you, 'mid all this mighty sum
Of things for ever speaking,
That nothing of itself will come,
But we must still be seeking?

"—Then ask not wherefore, here, alone,
Conversing as I may,   30
I sit upon this old grey stone,
And dream my time away."

THE TABLES TURNED

AN EVENING SCENE ON THE SAME SUBJECT

Up! up! my Friend, and quit your books;
Or surely you'll grow double:
Up! up! my Friend, and clear your looks;
Why all this toil and trouble?

The sun, above the mountain's head,
A freshening lustre mellow
Through all the long green fields has spread,
His first sweet evening yellow.

Books! 'tis a dull and endless strife:
Come, hear the woodland linnet,   10
How sweet his music! on my life,
There's more of wisdom in it.

And hark! how blithe the throstle sings!
He, too, is no mean preacher:
Come forth into the light of things,
Let Nature be your teacher.

She has a world of ready wealth,
Our minds and hearts to bless—
Spontaneous wisdom breathed by health,
Truth breathed by cheerfulness.   20

One impulse from a vernal wood
May teach you more of man,
Of moral evil and of good,
Than all the sages can.

Sweet is the lore which Nature brings;
Our meddling intellect
Mis-shapes the beauteous forms of things:—
We murder to dissect.

Enough of Science and of Art;
Close up those barren leaves;   30
Come forth, and bring with you a heart
That watches and receives.

LINES

COMPOSED A FEW MILES ABOVE TINTERN ABBEY ON
REVISITING THE BANKS ON THE WYE DURING
A TOUR.
JULY 13, 1798

"Tintern Abbey" is a "key" poem. It is *The Prelude* in miniature, completed just before the trip to Germany and in time to get it into *Lyrical Ballads*. Wordsworth composed it in his head, on a trip from Bristol to the Wye country and back, and wrote it down in a hotel at Bristol. "I have not ventured to call this Poem an Ode," he wrote; "but it was written with a hope that in the transitions and the impassioned music of the versification, would be found the principal requisites of that species of composition." The following summary may be helpful to the student in mastering the main ideas and transitions. It should be noted that the three main topics of the theme are restated in the last two lines of the poem—"land-

scape" (its meaning), "to me," and "thy sake" (Dorothy's).

Looking at a landscape near Tintern Abbey which he saw five years before (ll. 1–22) and which now serves as a frame and as material for his reflections, the poet: (1) *recalls* (l. 22) that in the interim his memory of the scene has brought him three "gifts"—(a) sensations sweet that restored him mentally and physically (ll. 22–30), (b) promptings to acts of kindness and love to his fellows (ll. 30–35), and (c) the sublime gift of mystical ecstasy by which he was united with the spirit of the universe and through which he saw into the life of things (ll. 35–49); (2) *reaffirms* frequent consolatory recourse of his spirit to the scene (ll. 49–57); (3) *expresses* the hope that in this present pleasure of seeing the landscape again there is food and thought for future years, though he is changed from what he once was (ll. 58–67); (4) consequently *reviews* his experience of nature—(a) from *boyhood* (parenthetical ll. 73–74), when it gave only sensations and animal pleasures, and (b) from *youth* (ll. 67–85, except 73–74), when it gave only a thoughtless, sensuous rapture, (c) to his present *maturity* (ll. 88–111), when it makes him hear the still, sad music of humanity and brings him into the presence of the divine spirit; and (5), turning to his sister (l. 111), who shares the joy of the present moment with him, *prays* (ll. 119 ff.) that she too will pass from a sensuous enjoyment like that of his own youth to a mature communion, like his, with Nature, which never did betray the heart that loved her, but leads on from joy to joy, to love of man, and to communion with the divine spirit.

Five years have past; five summers, with the length
Of five long winters! and again I hear
These waters, rolling from their mountain-springs
With a soft inland murmur.—Once again
Do I behold these steep and lofty cliffs,
That on a wild secluded scene impress
Thoughts of more deep seclusion; and connect
The landscape with the quiet of the sky.
The day is come when I again repose
Here, under this dark sycamore, and view   10
These plots of cottage-ground, these orchard-tufts,
Which at this season, with their unripe fruits,
Are clad in one green hue, and lose themselves
'Mid groves and copses. Once again I see
These hedge-rows, hardly hedge-rows, little lines
Of sportive wood run wild: these pastoral farms,
Green to the very door; and wreaths of smoke
Sent up, in silence, from among the trees!
With some uncertain notice, as might seem
Of vagrant dwellers in the houseless woods,   20
Or of some Hermit's cave, where by his fire
The Hermit sits alone.

                        These beauteous forms,
Through a long absence, have not been to me
As is a landscape to a blind man's eye:

But oft, in lonely rooms, and 'mid the din
Of towns and cities, I have owed to them,
In hours of weariness, sensations sweet,
Felt in the blood, and felt along the heart;
And passing even into my purer mind,
With tranquil restoration:—feelings too   30
Of unremembered pleasure: such, perhaps,
As have no slight or trivial influence
On that best portion of a good man's life,
His little, nameless, unremembered, acts
Of kindness and of love. Nor less, I trust,
To them I may have owed another gift,
Of aspect more sublime; that blessed mood,
In which the burthen of the mystery,
In which the heavy and the weary weight
Of all this unintelligible world,   40
Is lightened:—that serene and blessed mood,
In which the affections gently lead us on,—
Until, the breath of this corporeal frame
And even the motion of our human blood
Almost suspended, we are laid asleep
In body, and become a living soul:
While with an eye made quiet by the power
Of harmony, and the deep power of joy,
We see into the life of things.

                   If this
Be but a vain belief, yet, oh! how oft—   50
In darkness and amid the many shapes
Of joyless daylight; when the fretful stir
Unprofitable, and the fever of the world,
Have hung upon the beatings of my heart—
How oft, in spirit, have I turned to thee,
O sylvan Wye! thou wanderer through the woods,
How often has my spirit turned to thee!

   And now, with gleams of half-extinguished
      thought.
With many recognitions dim and faint,
And somewhat of a sad perplexity,   60
The picture of the mind revives again:
While here I stand, not only with the sense
Of present pleasure, but with pleasing thoughts
That in this moment there is life and food
For future years. And so I dare to hope,
Though changed, no doubt, from what I was when
    first
I came among these hills; when like a roe
I bounded o'er the mountains, by the sides
Of the deep rivers, and the lonely streams,
Wherever nature led: more like a man   70
Flying from something that he dreads than one
Who sought the thing he loved. For nature then
(The coarser pleasures of my boyish days,
And their glad animal movements all gone by)

To me was all in all.—I cannot paint
What then I was. The sounding cataract
Haunted me like a passion: the tall rock,
The mountain, and the deep and gloomy wood,
Their colours and their forms, were then to me
An appetite; a feeling and a love,   80
That had no need of a remoter charm,
By thought supplied, nor any interest
Unborrowed from the eye.—That time is past,
And all its aching joys are now no more,
And all its dizzy raptures. Not for this
Faint I, nor mourn nor murmur; other gifts
Have followed; for such loss, I would believe,
Abundant recompense. For I have learned
To look on nature, not as in the hour
Of thoughtless youth; but hearing oftentimes   90
The still, sad music of humanity,
Nor harsh nor grating, though of ample power
To chasten and subdue. And I have felt
A presence that disturbs me with the joy
Of elevated thoughts; a sense sublime
Of something far more deeply interfused,
Whose dwelling is the light of setting suns,
And the round ocean and the living air,
And the blue sky, and in the mind of man:
A motion and a spirit, that impels   100
All thinking things, all objects of all thought,
And rolls through all things. Therefore am I still
A lover of the meadows and the woods,
And mountains; and of all that we behold
From this green earth; of all the mighty world
Of eye, and ear,—both what they half create,
And what perceive; well pleased to recognise
In nature and the language of the sense
The anchor of my purest thoughts, the nurse,
The guide, the guardian of my heart, and soul   110
Of all my moral being.

               Nor perchance,
If I were not thus taught, should I the more
Suffer my genial spirits to decay:
For thou art with me here upon the banks
Of this fair river; thou my dearest Friend,
My dear, dear Friend; and in thy voice I catch
The language of my former heart, and read
My former pleasures in the shooting lights
Of thy wild eyes. Oh! yet a little while
May I behold in thee what I was once,   120
My dear, dear Sister! and this prayer I make,
Knowing that Nature never did betray
The heart that loved her; 'tis her privilege,
Through all the years of this our life, to lead
From joy to joy: for she can so inform
The mind that is within us, so impress
With quietness and beauty, and so feed

With lofty thoughts, that neither evil tongues,
Rash judgments, nor the sneers of selfish men,
Nor greetings where no kindness is, nor all   130
The dreary intercourse of daily life,
Shall e'er prevail against us, or disturb
Our cheerful faith, that all which we behold
Is full of blessings. Therefore let the moon
Shine on thee in thy solitary walk;
And let the misty mountain-winds be free
To blow against thee: and, in after years,
When these wild esctasies shall be matured
Into a sober pleasure; when thy mind
Shall be a mansion for all lovely forms,   140
Thy memory be as a dwelling-place
For all sweet sounds and harmonies; oh! then,
If solitude, or fear, or pain, or grief,
Should be thy portion, with what healing thoughts
Of tender joy wilt thou remember me,
And these my exhortations! Nor, perchance—
If I should be where I no more can hear
Thy voice, nor catch from thy wild eyes these
     gleams
Of past existence—wilt thou then forget
That on the banks of this delightful stream   150
We stood together; and that I, so long
A worshipper of Nature, hither came
Unwearied in that service: rather say
With warmer love—oh! with far deeper zeal
Of holier love. Nor wilt thou then forget
That after many wanderings, many years
Of absence, these steep woods and lofty cliffs,
And this green pastoral landscape, were to me
More dear, both for themselves and for thy sake!

THE LUCY POEMS

For mention of the circumstances and possible autobiographical implications of the "Lucy Poems," see page
16. All five poems are elegiac in theme and tone. The
first is a "lover's fancy." The second expresses the poet's
homesickness experienced while he was in Germany. The
third describes at some length the process of growing into
nature; it is a little poetic essay on the education of nature. The fifth describes dying into nature. The fourth
contains two of the most delicate and beautiful nature
similes in English poetry, and illustrates the power of expression inherent in reticence ("And, oh, The difference
to me!").

I

Strange fits of passion have I known:
And I will dare to tell,
But in the Lover's ear alone,
What once to me befell.

When she I loved looked every day
Fresh as a rose in June,
I to her cottage bent my way,
Beneath an evening-moon.

Upon the moon I fixed my eye,
All over the wide lea;   10
With quickening pace my horse drew nigh
Those paths so dear to me.

And now we reached the orchard-plot;
And, as we climbed the hill,
The sinking moon to Lucy's cot
Came near, and nearer still.

In one of those sweet dreams I slept,
Kind Nature's gentlest boon!
And all the while my eyes I kept
On the descending moon.   20

My horse moved on; hoof after hoof
He raised, and never stopped:
When down behind the cottage roof,
At once, the bright moon dropped.

What fond and wayward thoughts will slide
Into a Lover's head!
"O mercy!" to myself I cried,
"If Lucy should be dead!"

2

I travelled among unknown men,
In lands beyond the sea;
Nor, England! did I know till then
What love I bore to thee.

'Tis past, that melancholy dream!
Nor will I quit thy shore
A second time; for still I seem
To love thee more and more.

Among thy mountains did I feel
The joy of my desire;   50
And she I cherished turned her wheel
Beside an English fire.

Thy mornings showed, thy nights concealed
The bowers where Lucy played;
And thine too is the last green field
That Lucy's eyes surveyed.

3

Three years she grew in sun and shower;
Then Nature said, "A lovelier flower
On earth was never sown;
This Child I to myself will take;   60
She shall be mine, and I will make
A Lady of my own.

"Myself will to my darling be
Both law and impulse: and with me
The Girl, in rock and plain,
In earth and heaven, in glade and bower
Shall feel an overseeing power
To kindle or restrain.

"She shall be sportive as the fawn
That wild with glee across the lawn,   70
Or up the mountain springs;
And hers shall be the breathing balm,
And hers the silence and the calm
Of mute insensate things.

"The floating clouds their state shall lend
To her; for her the willow bend;
Nor shall she fail to see
Even in the motions of the Storm
Grace that shall mould the Maiden's form
By silent sympathy.   80

"The stars of midnight shall be dear
To her; and she shall lean her ear
In many a secret place
Where rivulets dance their wayward round,
And beauty born of murmuring sound
Shall pass into her face.

"And vital feelings of delight
Shall rear her form to stately height,
Her virgin bosom swell;
Such thoughts to Lucy I will give   90
While she and I together live
Here in this happy dell."

Thus Nature spake—The work was done—
How soon my Lucy's race was run!
She died, and left to me
This heath, this calm and quiet scene;
The memory of what has been,
And never more will be.

4

She dwelt among the untrodden ways
Beside the springs of Dove,   30
A Maid whom there were none to praise
And very few to love:

A violet by a mossy stone
Half-hidden from the eye!
—Fair as a star, when only one
Is shining in the sky.

She lived unknown, and few could know
When Lucy ceased to be;
But she is in her grave, and, oh,
The difference to me!   40

5

A slumber did my spirit seal;
I had no human fears:
She seemed a thing that could not feel
The touch of earthly years.

No motion has she now, no force;
She neither hears nor sees;
Rolled round in earth's diurnal course,
With rocks, and stones, and trees.

A POET'S EPITAPH

Art thou a Statist in the van
Of public conflicts trained and bred?
—First learn to love one living man;
Then may'st thou think upon the dead.

A Lawyer art thou?—draw not nigh!
Go, carry to some fitter place
The keenness of that practised eye,
The hardness of that sallow face.

Art thou a Man of purple cheer?
A rosy Man, right plump to see?   10
Approach; yet, Doctor, not too near,
This grave no cushion is for thee.

Or art thou one of gallant pride,
A Soldier and no man of chaff?
Welcome!—but lay thy sword aside,
And lean upon a peasant's staff.

Physician art thou? one, all eyes,
Philosopher! a fingering slave,
One that would peep and botanise
Upon his mother's grave?   20

Wrapt closely in thy sensual fleece,
O turn aside,—and take, I pray,
That he below may rest in peace,
Thy ever-dwindling soul, away!

1. **Statist**, statesman or politician.

A Moralist perchance appears;
Led, Heaven knows how! to this poor sod:
And he has neither eyes nor ears;
Himself his world, and his own God;

One to whose smooth-rubbed soul can cling
Nor form, nor feeling, great or small;   30
A reasoning, self-sufficing thing,
An intellectual All-in-all!

Shut close the door; press down the latch;
Sleep in thy intellectual crust;
Nor lose ten tickings of thy watch
Near this unprofitable dust.

But who is He, with modest looks,
And clad in homely russet brown?
He murmurs near the running brooks
A music sweeter than their own.   40

He is retired as noontide dew,
Or fountain in a noon-day grove;
And you must love him, ere to you
He will seem worthy of your love.

The outward shows of sky and earth,
Of hill and valley, he has viewed;
And impulses of deeper birth
Have come to him in solitude.

In common things that round us lie
Some random truths he can impart,—   50
The harvest of a quiet eye
That broods and sleeps on his own heart.

But he is weak; both Man and Boy,
Hath been an idler in the land;
Contented if he might enjoy
The things which others understand.

—Come hither in thy hour of strength;
Come, weak as is a breaking wave!
Here stretch thy body at full length;
Or build thy house upon this grave.   60

MATTHEW

If Nature, for a favourite child,
In thee hath tempered so her clay,

Matthew. The original of Matthew is supposed to have
been William Taylor, Wordsworth's master at Hawkshead.

That every hour thy heart runs wild,
Yet never once doth go astray,

Read o'er these lines; and then review
This tablet, that thus humbly rears
In such diversity of hue
Its history of two hundred years.

—When through this little wreck of fame,
Cipher and syllable! thine eye   10
Has travelled down to Matthew's name,
Pause with no common sympathy.

And, if a sleeping tear should wake,
Then be it neither checked nor stayed:
For Matthew a request I make
Which for himself he had not made.

Poor Matthew, all his frolics o'er,
Is silent as a standing pool;
Far from the chimney's merry roar,
And murmur of the village school.   20

The sighs which Matthew heaved were sighs
Of one tired out with fun and madness;
The tears which came to Matthew's eyes
Were tears of light, the dew of gladness.

Yet sometimes, when the secret cup
Of still and serious thought went round,
It seemed as if he drank it up—
He felt with spirit so profound.

—Thou soul of God's best earthly mould!
Thou happy Soul! and can it be   30
That these two words of glittering gold
Are all that must remain of thee?

THE SPARROW'S NEST

"Written in the Orchard, Town-end, Grasmere. At the
end of the garden of my father's house at Cockermouth
was a high terrace that commanded a fine view of the
river Derwent and Cockermouth Castle. This was our
favourite play-ground. The terrace-wall, a low one, was
covered with closely-clipped privet and roses, which gave
an almost impervious shelter to birds that built their nests
there. The latter of these stanzas alludes to one of those
nests."—Wordsworth

Behold, within the leafy shade,
Those bright blue eggs together laid!
On me the chance-discovered sight
Gleamed like a vision of delight.

I started—seeming to espy
The home and sheltered bed,
The Sparrow's dwelling, which, hard by
My Father's house, in wet or dry
My sister Emmeline and I
      Together visited.   10

She looked at it and seemed to fear it;
Dreading, though wishing, to be near it:
Such heart was in her, being then
A little Prattler among men.
The Blessing of my later years
Was with me when a boy:
She gave me eyes, she gave me ears;
And humble cares, and delicate fears;
A heart, the fountain of sweet tears;
     And love, and thought, and joy.   20

MY HEART LEAPS UP

The briefest treatment of one of Wordsworth's greatest
themes—the endeavor to bind his days together. (See
"Tintern Abbey," "Ode: Intimations," and *The Prelude*,
in the ascending scale of attempts.) The poet rejoices that
his heart leaps up now as it did when he was a boy, because his present response proves the man to be the same
personality as the boy. "Poetry requires a strong persuasion of self-integrity. It is impossible to people who
have forfeited their identity. The imaginative act unifies
the world. Unity is created rather than observed."—
W. L. Sperry, *Wordsworth's Anti-climax*, Harvard University Press, 1935, pp. 165–66.

My heart leaps up when I behold
    A rainbow in the sky:
So was it when my life began;
So is it now I am a man;
So be it when I shall grow old,
    Or let me die!
The Child is father of the Man;
And I could wish my days to be
Bound each to each by natural piety.

RESOLUTION AND
INDEPENDENCE

This poem is important as pointing to a modification
of Wordsworth's faith. The change it suggests can best
be understood by comparing it with the conclusion of the
spiritual-autobiography passage of "Tintern Abbey," be-

9. **Emmeline,** Wordsworth's poetical name for Dorothy.
9. **natural piety,** instinctive love and reverence for the things
of nature. One of the chief points in Wordsworth's teaching was the duty of cherishing the child's instincts and intuitions.

ginning "well pleased to recognise In *nature* and the language of the *sense*." (Italics mine.) To understand the significance of the poem, the student must (1) appreciate
fully what happened to the poet *before* he met the leech-
gatherer—the early-morning high spirits and optimism,
the sudden depression of spirits, the accompanying fears:
"Solitude, pain of heart, distress, and poverty"; and (2)
estimate rightly the *character* of the old man, who is *in*
nature but not *of* nature, who draws his strength not from
the natural order but from religion and the inner resources of the human spirit. Note that in the conclusion
Wordsworth is not merely using the language of prayer;
he is really praying in the orthodox sense ("God . . . be
my help and stay secure").

1

There was a roaring in the wind all night;
The rain came heavily and fell in floods;
But now the sun is rising calm and bright;
The birds are singing in the distant woods;
Over his own sweet voice the Stock-dove broods;
The Jay makes answer as the Magpie chatters;
And all the air is filled with pleasant noise of waters.

2

All things that love the sun are out of doors;
The sky rejoices in the morning's birth;
The grass is bright with rain-drops;—on the moors
The hare is running races in her mirth;   11
And with her feet she from the plashy earth
Raises a mist; that, glittering in the sun,
Runs with her all the way, wherever she doth run.

3

I was a Traveller then upon the moor,
I saw the hare that raced about with joy;
I heard the woods and distant waters roar;
Or heard them not, as happy as a boy:
The pleasant season did my heart employ:
My old remembrances went from me wholly;   20
And all the ways of men, so vain and melancholy.

4

But, as it sometimes chanceth, from the might
Of joy in minds that can no further go,
As high as we have mounted in delight
In our dejection do we sink as low;
To me that morning did it happen so;
And fears and fancies thick upon me came;
Dim sadness—and blind thoughts, I knew not, nor
    could name.

5

I heard the sky-lark warbling in the sky;
And I bethought me of the playful hare: 30

Even such a happy Child of earth am I;
Even as these blissful creatures do I fare;
Far from the world I walk, and from all care;
But there may come another day to me—
Solitude, pain of heart, distress, and poverty.

6

My whole life I have lived in pleasant thought,
As if life's business were a summer mood;
As if all needful things would come unsought
To genial faith, still rich in genial good;
But how can He expect that others should   40
Build for him, sow for him, and at his call
Love him, who for himself will take no heed at all?

7

I thought of Chatterton, the marvellous Boy,
The sleepless Soul that perished in his pride;
Of Him who walked in glory and in joy
Following his plough, along the mountain-side:
By our own spirits are we deified:
We Poets in our youth begin in gladness;
But thereof come in the end despondency and
     madness.

8

Now, whether it were by peculiar grace,   50
A leading from above, a something given,
Yet it befell that, in this lonely place,
When I with these untoward thoughts had striven,
Beside a pool bare to the eye of heaven
I saw a Man before me unawares:
The oldest man he seemed that ever wore grey
     hairs.

9

As a huge stone is sometimes seen to lie
Couched on the bald top of an eminence;
Wonder to all who do the same espy,
By what means it could thither come, and whence;
So that it seems a thing endued with sense: 61
Like a sea-beast crawled forth, that on a shelf
Of rock or sand reposeth, there to sun itself;

10

Such seemed this Man, not all alive nor dead,
Nor all asleep—in his extreme old age:
His body was bent double, feet and head
Coming together in life's pilgrimage;
As if some dire constraint of pain, or rage
Of sickness felt by him in times long past,
A more than human weight upon his frame had
     cast.   70

11

Himself he propped, limbs, body, and pale face,
Upon a long grey staff of shaven wood:
And, still as I drew near with gentle pace,
Upon the margin of that moorish flood
Motionless as a cloud the old Man stood,
That heareth not the loud winds when they call
And moveth all together, if it move at all.

12

At length, himself unsettling, he the pond
Stirred with his staff, and fixedly did look
Upon the muddy water, which he conned,   80
As if he had been reading in a book:
And now a stranger's privilege I took;
And, drawing to his side, to him did say,
"This morning gives us promise of a glorious day."

13

A gentle answer did the old Man make,
In courteous speech which forth he slowly drew:
And him with further words I thus bespake,
"What occupation do you there pursue?
This is a lonesome place for one like you."
Ere he replied, a flash of mild surprise   90
Broke from the sable orbs of his yet-vivid eyes.

14

His words came feebly, from a feeble chest,
But each in solemn order followed each,
With something of a lofty utterance drest—
Choice word and measured phrase, above the reach
Of ordinary men; a stately speech;
Such as grave Livers do in Scotland use,
Religious men, who give to God and man their
     dues.

15

He told, that to these waters he had come
To gather leeches, being old and poor: 100
Employment hazardous and wearisome!
And he had many hardships to endure:
From pond to pond he roamed, from moor to moor;
Housing, with God's good help, by choice or
     chance;
And in this way he gained an honest maintenance.

16

The old Man still stood talking by my side;
But now his voice to me was like a stream
Scarce heard; nor word from word could I divide;
And the whole body of the Man did seem

---

43. Chatterton. See the general introductory essay, page 4.
45. of Him, Burns.

97. grave Livers, a strict religious sect. **100. leeches,** aquatic worms, formerly used for bleeding the sick.

Like one whom I had met with in a dream; 110
Or like a man from some far region sent,
To give me human strength, by apt admonishment.

17

My former thoughts returned: the fear that kills;
And hope that is unwilling to be fed;
Cold, pain, and labour, and all fleshly ills;
And mighty Poets in their misery dead.
—Perplexed, and longing to be comforted,
My question eagerly did I renew,
"How is it that you live, and what is it you do?"

18

He with a smile did then his words repeat; 120
And said that, gathering leeches, far and wide
He travelled; stirring thus about his feet
The waters of the pools where they abide.
"Once I could meet with them on every side;
But they have dwindled long by slow decay;
Yet still I persevere, and find them where I may."

19

While he was talking thus, the lonely place,
The old Man's shape, and speech—all troubled me:
In my mind's eye I seemed to see him pace
About the weary moors continually, 130
Wandering about alone and silently.
While I these thoughts within myself pursued,
He, having made a pause, the same discourse
  renewed.

20

And soon with this he other matter blended,
Cheerfully uttered, with demeanour kind,
But stately in the main; and, when he ended,
I could have laughed myself to scorn to find
In that decrepit Man so firm a mind.
"God," said I, "be my help and stay secure;
I'll think of the Leech-gatherer on the lonely
  moor!" 140

SONNETS

For the autobiographical (experiential and philosophical) significance of the 1802 sonnets, see the biographical-
critical sketch of Wordsworth. A few sonnets which were
written later than 1802 have been added.

COMPOSED UPON WESTMINSTER BRIDGE,
SEPTEMBER 3, 1802

Earth has not anything to show more fair:
Dull would he be of soul who could pass by

A sight so touching in its majesty:
This City now doth, like a garment, wear
The beauty of the morning; silent, bare,
Ships, towers, domes, theatres, and temples
  lie
Open unto the fields, and to the sky;
All bright and glittering in the smokeless air.
Never did sun more beautifully steep
In his first splendour, valley, rock, or hill; 10
Ne'er saw I, never felt, a calm so deep!
The river glideth at his own sweet will:
Dear God! the very houses seem asleep;
And all that mighty heart is lying still!

COMPOSED BY THE SEA-SIDE NEAR CALAIS,
AUGUST 1802

Fair Star of evening, Splendour of the west,
Star of my Country!—on the horizon's brink
Thou hangest, stooping, as might seem, to sink
On England's bosom; yet well pleased to rest,
Meanwhile, and be to her a glorious crest
Conspicuous to the Nations. Thou, I think,
Should'st be my Country's emblem; and should'st
  wink,
Bright Star! with laughter on her banners, drest
In thy fresh beauty. There! that dusky spot
Beneath thee, that is England; there she lies. 10
Blessings be on you both! one hope, one lot,
One life, one glory!—I, with many a fear
For my dear Country, many heartfelt sighs,
Among men who do not love her, linger here.

IT IS A BEAUTEOUS EVENING, CALM AND FREE

"This was composed on the beach near Calais, in the
autumn of 1802."—Wordsworth

It is a beauteous evening, calm and free,
The holy time is quiet as a Nun
Breathless with adoration; the broad sun
Is sinking down in its tranquillity;
The gentleness of heaven broods o'er the Sea:
Listen! the mighty Being is awake,
And doth with his eternal motion make
A sound like thunder—everlastingly.
Dear Child! dear Girl! that walkest with me
  here,
If thou appear untouched by solemn thought, 10
Thy nature is not therefore less divine:
Thou liest in Abraham's bosom all the year;

It Is A Beauteous Evening. **9. Dear Child,** the poet's and
Annette's natural daughter, Carolyn.

And worship'st at the Temple's inner shrine,
God being with thee when we know it not.

ON THE EXTINCTION OF THE VENETIAN REPUBLIC

Once did She hold the gorgeous east in fee;
And was the safeguard of the west: the worth
Of Venice did not fall below her birth,
Venice, the eldest Child of Liberty.
She was a maiden City, bright and free;
No guile seduced, no force could violate;
And, when she took unto herself a Mate,
She must espouse the everlasting Sea.
And what if she had seen those glories fade,
Those titles vanish, and that strength decay;   10
Yet shall some tribute of regret be paid
When her long life hath reached its final day:
Men are we, and must grieve when even the Shade
Of that which once was great, is passed away.

TO TOUSSAINT L'OUVERTURE

Toussaint, the most unhappy man of men!
Whether the whistling Rustic tend his plough
Within thy hearing, or thy head be now
Pillowed in some deep dungeon's earless den;—
O miserable Chieftain! where and when
Wilt thou find patience! Yet die not; do thou
Wear rather in thy bonds a cheerful brow:
Though fallen thyself, never to rise again,
Live, and take comfort. Thou hast left behind
Powers that will work for thee; air, earth, and skies;
There's not a breathing of the common wind   11
That will forget thee; thou hast great allies;
Thy friends are exultations, agonies,
And love, and man's unconquerable mind.

COMPOSED IN THE VALLEY NEAR DOVER
ON THE DAY OF LANDING

Here, on our native soil, we breathe once more.
The cock that crows, the smoke that curls, that sound
Of bells; those boys who in yon meadow-ground
In white-sleeved shirts are playing; and the roar
Of the waves breaking on the chalky shore;—

All, all are English. Oft have I looked round
With joy in Kent's green vales; but never found
Myself so satisfied in heart before.
Europe is yet in bonds; but let that pass,
Thought for another moment. Thou art free,   10
My Country! and 'tis joy enough and pride
For one hour's perfect bliss, to tread the grass
Of England once again, and hear and see,
With such a dear Companion at my side.

NEAR DOVER, SEPTEMBER 1802

Inland, within a hollow vale, I stood;
And saw, while sea was calm and air was clear,
The coast of France—the coast of France how near!
Drawn almost into frightful neighbourhood.
I shrunk; for verily the barrier flood
Was like a lake, or river bright and fair,
A span of waters; yet what power is there!
What mightiness for evil and for good!
Even so doth God protect us if we be
Virtuous and wise. Winds blow, and waters roll,   10
Strength to the brave, and Power, and Deity;
Yet in themselves are nothing! One decree
Spake laws to *them*, and said that by the soul
Only, the Nations shall be great and free.

IN LONDON, SEPTEMBER 1802

O Friend! I know not which way I must look
For comfort, being, as I am, opprest,
To think that now our life is only drest
For show; mean handy-work of craftsman, cook,
Or groom!—We must run glittering like a brook
In the open sunshine, or we are unblest:
The wealthiest man among us is the best:
No grandeur now in nature or in book
Delights us. Rapine, avarice, expense,
This is idolatry; and these we adore: 10
Plain living and high thinking are no more:
The homely beauty of the good old cause
Is gone; our peace, our fearful innocence,
And pure religion breathing household laws.

LONDON, 1802

Milton! thou should'st be living at this hour:
England hath need of thee: she is a fen
Of stagnant waters: altar, sword, and pen,
Fireside, the heroic wealth of hall and bower,

On the Extinction. **8. espouse,** alluding to the annual ceremony in which the Doge of Venice cast a ring into the sea in
token of the wedding of city and sea.   *To Toussaint.* **1. Toussaint,** sobriquet of Pierre Dominique Breda, Negro general
and liberator of Haiti. He was imprisoned by France at the
time this sonnet was written, and died soon after.

Composed in the Valley. **14. dear Companion,** Dorothy, who
accompanied the poet to Calais for the settlement with
Annette.

Have forfeited their ancient English dower
Of inward happiness. We are selfish men;
Oh! raise us up, return to us again;
And give us manners, virtue, freedom, power.
Thy soul was like a Star, and dwelt apart; 5
Thou hadst a voice whose sound was like the sea: 10
Pure as the naked heavens, majestic, free,
So didst thou travel on life's common way,
In cheerful godliness; and yet thy heart
The lowliest duties on herself did lay.

IT IS NOT TO BE THOUGHT OF

It is not to be thought of that the Flood
Of British freedom, which, to the open sea
Of the world's praise, from dark antiquity
Hath flowed, "with pomp of waters, unwithstood,"
Roused though it be full often to a mood
Which spurns the check of salutary bands,
That this most famous Stream in bogs and sands
Should perish; and to evil and to good
Be lost forever. In our halls is hung
Armoury of the invincible Knights of old: 10
We must be free or die, who speak the tongue
That Shakespeare spake; the faith and morals hold
Which Milton held.—In everything we are sprung
Of Earth's first blood, have titles manifold.

WHEN I HAVE BORNE IN MEMORY

When I have borne in memory what has tamed
Great Nations, how ennobling thoughts depart
When men change swords for ledgers, and desert
The student's bower for gold, some fears unnamed
I had, my Country!—am I to be blamed?
Now, when I think of thee, and what thou art,
Verily, in the bottom of my heart,
Of those unfilial fears I am ashamed.
For dearly must we prize thee; we who find
In thee a bulwark for the cause of men: 10
And I by my affection was beguiled:
What wonder if a Poet now and then,
Among the many movements of his mind,
Felt for thee as a lover or a child!

NOVEMBER, 1806

Another year!—another deadly blow!
Another mighty Empire overthrown!

November, 1806. **1. deadly blow,** the battle of Jena, October 14, 1806. **2. Empire,** Prussia.

And We are left, or shall be left, alone;
The last that dare to struggle with the Foe.
'Tis well! from this day forward we shall know
That in ourselves our safety must be sought;
That by our own right hands it must be wrought;
That we must stand unpropped, or be laid low.
O dastard whom such foretaste doth not cheer!
We shall exult, if they who rule the land 10
Be men who hold its many blessings dear,
Wise, upright, valiant; not a servile band,
Who are to judge of danger which they fear,
And honour which they do not understand.

TO H.C.

SIX YEARS OLD

O thou! whose fancies from afar are brought;
Who of thy words dost make a mock apparel,
And fittest to unutterable thought
The breeze-like motion and the self-born carol;
Thou faery voyager! that dost float
In such clear water, that thy boat
May rather seem
To brood on air than on an earthly stream;
Suspended in a stream as clear as sky,
Where earth and heaven do make one imagery; 10
O blessèd vision! happy child!
Thou art so exquisitely wild,
I think of thee with many fears
For what may be thy lot in future years.

I thought of times when Pain might be thy guest,
Lord of thy house and hospitality;
And Grief, uneasy lover! never rest
But when she sate within the touch of thee.
O too industrious folly!
O vain and causeless melancholy! 20
Nature will either end thee quite;
Or, lengthening out thy season of delight,
Preserve for thee, by individual right,
A young lamb's heart among the full-grown flocks.
What hast thou to do with sorrow,
Or the injuries of to-morrow?
Thou art a dew-drop, which the morn brings forth,
Ill fitted to sustain unkindly shocks,
Or to be trailed along the soiling earth;
A gem that glitters while it lives, 30
And no forewarning gives;
But, at the touch of wrong, without a strife
Slips in a moment out of life.

November, 1806. **4. Foe,** Napoleon. *To H. C.,* Hartley Coleridge. **1. fancies from afar.** Compare the hint of preexistence here expressed with the full development of the idea in "Ode: Intimations of Immortality."

THE GREEN LINNET

Beneath these fruit-tree boughs that shed
Their snow-white blossoms on my head,
With brightest sunshine round me spread
   Of spring's unclouded weather,
In this sequestered nook how sweet
To sit upon my orchard-seat!
And birds and flowers once more to greet,
   My last year's friends together.

One have I marked, the happiest guest
In all this covert of the blest: 10
Hail to Thee, far above the rest
   In joy of voice and pinion!
Thou, Linnet! in thy green array,
Presiding Spirit here to-day,
Dost lead the revels of the May;
   And this is thy dominion.

While birds, and butterflies, and flowers,
Make all one band of paramours,
Thou, ranging up and down the bowers,
   Art sole in thy employment: 20
A life, a Presence like the Air,
Scattering thy gladness without care,
Too blest with any one to pair;
   Thyself thy own enjoyment.

Amid yon tuft of hazel trees,
That twinkle to the gusty breeze,
Behold him perched in ecstasies,
   Yet seeming still to hover;
There! where the flutter of his wings
Upon his back and body flings   30
Shadows and sunny glimmerings,
   That cover him all over.

My dazzled sight he oft deceives,
A Brother of the dancing leaves;
Then flits, and from the cottage-eaves
   Pours forth his song in gushes;
As if by that exulting strain
He mocked and treated with disdain
The voiceless Form he chose to feign,
   While fluttering in the bushes.   40

YEW–TREES

There is a Yew-tree, pride of Lorton Vale,
Which to this day stands single, in the midst
Of its own darkness, as it stood of yore;
Not loth to furnish weapons for the bands

Of Umfraville or Percy ere they marched
To Scotland's heaths; or those that crossed the
   sea
And drew their sounding bows at Azincour,
Perhaps at earlier Crecy, or Poictiers.
Of vast circumference and gloom profound
This solitary Tree! a living thing   10
Produced too slowly ever to decay;
Of form and aspect too magnificent
To be destroyed. But worthier still of note
Are those fraternal Four of Borrowdale,
Joined in one solemn and capacious grove;
Huge trunks! and each particular trunk a growth
Of intertwisted fibres serpentine
Up-coiling, and inveterately convolved;
Nor uninformed with Phantasy, and looks
That threaten the profane;—a pillared shade, 20
Upon whose grassless floor of red-brown hue,
By sheddings from the pining umbrage tinged
Perennially—beneath whose sable roof
Of boughs, as if for festal purpose decked
With unrejoicing berries—ghostly Shapes
May meet at noontide; Fear and trembling Hope,
Silence and Foresight; Death the Skeleton
And Time the Shadow;—there to celebrate,
As in a natural temple scattered o'er
With altars undisturbed of mossy stone,   30
United worship; or in mute repose
To lie, and listen to the mountain flood
Murmuring from Glaramara's inmost caves.

THE SOLITARY REAPER

Behold her, single in the field,
Yon solitary Highland Lass!
Reaping and singing by herself;
Stop here, or gently pass!
Alone she cuts and binds the grain,
And sings a melancholy strain;
O listen! for the Vale profound
Is overflowing with the sound.

No Nightingale did ever chaunt
More welcome notes to weary bands   10
Of travellers in some shady haunt,
Among Arabian sands:
A voice so thrilling ne'er was heard
In spring-time from the Cuckoo-bird,
Breaking the silence of the seas
Among the farthest Hebrides.

The Solitary Reaper. **16. Hebrides,** islands off the west coast
of Scotland. Wordsworth wrote this poem during a tour of
Scotland, in 1803, with Dorothy.

Will no one tell me what she sings?—
Perhaps the plaintive numbers flow
For old, unhappy, far-off things,
And battles long ago: 20
Or is it some more humble lay,
Familiar matter of to-day?
Some natural sorrow, loss, or pain,
That has been, and may be again?

Whate'er the theme, the Maiden sang
As if her song could have no ending;
I saw her singing at her work,
And o'er the sickle bending;—
I listened, motionless and still;
And, as I mounted up the hill,   30
The music in my heart I bore,
Long after it was heard no more.

TO THE CUCKOO

O blithe New-comer! I have heard,
I hear thee and rejoice.
O Cuckoo! shall I call thee Bird,
Or but a wandering Voice?

While I am lying on the grass
Thy twofold shout I hear;
From hill to hill it seems to pass,
At once far off, and near.

Though babbling only to the Vale,
Of sunshine and of flowers,   10
Thou bringest unto me a tale
Of visionary hours.

Thrice welcome, darling of the Spring!
Even yet thou art to me
No bird, but an invisible thing,
A voice, a mystery;

The same whom in my schoolboy days
I listened to; that Cry
Which made me look a thousand ways
In bush, and tree, and sky.   20

To seek thee did I often rove
Through woods and on the green;
And thou wert still a hope, a love;
Still longed for, never seen.

And I can listen to thee yet;
Can lie upon the plain
And listen, till I do beget
That golden time again.

O blessèd Bird! the earth we pace
Again appears to be   30
An unsubstantial, faery place;
That is fit home for Thee!

I WANDERED LONELY AS A CLOUD

I wandered lonely as a cloud
That floats on high o'er vales and hills,
When all at once I saw a crowd,
A host, of golden daffodils;
Beside the lake, beneath the trees,
Fluttering and dancing in the breeze.

Continuous as the stars that shine
And twinkle on the milky way,
They stretched in never-ending line
Along the margin of a bay: 10
Ten thousand saw I at a glance,
Tossing their heads in sprightly dance.

The waves beside them danced; but they
Out-did the sparkling waves in glee:
A poet could not but be gay,
In such a jocund company:
I gazed—and gazed—but little thought
What wealth the show to me had brought:

For oft, when on my couch I lie
In vacant or in pensive mood,   20
They flash upon that inward eye
Which is the bliss of solitude;
And then my heart with pleasure fills,
And dances with the daffodils.

SHE WAS A PHANTOM OF DELIGHT

"Written at Town-end, Grasmere. The germ of this poem was four lines composed as a part of the verses on the Highland Girl. Though beginning in this way, it was written from my heart, as is sufficiently obvious."
—Wordsworth

She was a Phantom of delight
When first she gleamed upon my sight;
A lovely Apparition, sent
To be a moment's ornament;

32. **Long after it was heard no more.** Note the importance of memory in many of Wordsworth's lyrics (this; "To the Cuckoo"; "I Wandered Lonely as a Cloud"; and others). 17. **The same.** See "My Heart Leaps Up" and the notes thereon.

She Was a Phantom of Delight. 1. **She,** the poet's wife, Mary Hutchinson.

Her eyes as stars of Twilight fair;
Like Twilight's, too, her dusky hair;
But all things else about her drawn
From May-time and the cheerful Dawn;
A dancing Shape, an Image gay,
To haunt, to startle, and way-lay.   10

I saw her upon nearer view,
A Spirit, yet a Woman too!
Her household motions light and free,
And steps of virgin-liberty;
A countenance in which did meet
Sweet records, promises as sweet;
A Creature not too bright or good
For human nature's daily food;
For transient sorrows, simple wiles,
Praise, blame, love, kisses, tears, and smiles.   20

And now I see with eye serene
The very pulse of the machine;
A Being breathing thoughtful breath,
A Traveller between life and death;
The reason firm, the temperate will,
Endurance, foresight, strength, and skill;
A perfect Woman, nobly planned,
To warn, to comfort, and command;
And yet a Spirit still, and bright
With something of angelic light.   30

ODE TO DUTY

"This ode is on the model of Gray's Ode to Adversity, which is copied from Horace's Ode to Fortune. Many and many a time have I been twitted by my wife and sister for having forgotten this dedication of myself to the stern lawgiver. Transgressor indeed I have been, from hour to hour, from day to day: I would fain hope, however, not more flagrantly or in a worse way than most of my tuneful brethren. But these last words are in a wrong strain. We should be rigorous to ourselves and forbearing, if not indulgent, to others, and, if we make comparisons at all, it ought to be with those who have morally excelled us.

"Jam non consilio bonus, sed more eò perductus, ut non tantum rectè facere possim, sed nisi rectè facere non possim."—Wordsworth

Professor G. M. Harper translated the Latin: "No longer good from taking thought, but led by habit, so that I am not merely able to do right, but cannot help doing right."

The poem marks an important development in the change which began with "Resolution and Independence." Note that here, in order to balance and simplify life, Wordsworth conditionally gives up "the genial sense of youth" (natural impulse, or instinct) for a transcendental, religious guide giving "a repose that ever is the same." With this "genial sense of youth" compare the "something that doth live" of "Intimations."

Stern Daughter of the Voice of God!
O Duty! if that name thou love
Who art a light to guide, a rod
To check the erring, and reprove;
Thou, who art victory and law
When empty terrors overawe;
From vain temptations dost set free;
And calm'st the weary strife of frail humanity!

There are who ask not if thine eye
Be on them; who, in love and truth,   10
Where no misgiving is, rely
Upon the genial sense of youth:
Glad Hearts! without reproach or blot;
Who do thy work, and know it not:
Oh! if through confidence misplaced
They fail, thy saving arms, dread Power! around
      them cast.

Serene will be our days and bright,
And happy will our nature be,
When love is an unerring light,
And joy its own security.   20
And they a blissful course may hold
Even now, who, not unwisely bold,
Live in the spirit of this creed;
Yet seek thy firm support, according to their need.

I, loving freedom, and untried,
No sport of every random gust,
Yet being to myself a guide,
Too blindly have reposed my trust:
And oft, when in my heart was heard
Thy timely mandate, I deferred   30
The task, in smoother walks to stray;
But thee I now would serve more strictly, if I may.

Through no disturbance of my soul,
Or strong compunction in me wrought,
I supplicate for thy control;
But in the quietness of thought:
Me this uncharted freedom tires;
I feel the weight of chance-desires:
My hopes no more must change their name,
I long for a repose that ever is the same.   40

Stern Lawgiver! yet thou dost wear
The Godhead's most benignant grace;

33. Through no disturbance. It was once thought that the death of the poet's brother John had something to do with the change recorded here, but it now seems probable that the poem was written before that event.

Nor know we anything so fair
As is the smile upon thy face:
Flowers laugh before thee on their beds
And fragrance in thy footing treads;
Thou dost preserve the stars from wrong;
And the most ancient heavens, through Thee, are
    fresh and strong.

To humbler functions, awful Power!
I call thee: I myself commend   50
Unto thy guidance from this hour;
Oh, let my weakness have an end!
Give unto me, made lowly wise,
The spirit of self-sacrifice;
The confidence of reason give;
And in the light of truth thy Bondman let me live!

ELEGIAC STANZAS

SUGGESTED BY A PICTURE OF PEELE CASTLE, IN
A STORM, PAINTED BY SIR GEORGE BEAUMONT

A further step along the road marked by "Resolution
and Independence" and "Ode to Duty." This poem is
not merely a comparison of the picture he would have
painted, in the Arcadian optimism of his youth, with the
truer one by Beaumont, but a comparison of his present
outlook with all of his past. The poet sees how cruel nature can be (it had but recently destroyed his brother),
and before this "pageantry of fear" he turns to the
strength of the human heart ("fortitude, patient cheer,"
and so on).

I was thy neighbour once, thou rugged Pile!
Four summer weeks I dwelt in sight of thee:
I saw thee every day; and all the while
Thy Form was sleeping on a glassy sea.

So pure the sky, so quiet was the air!
So like, so very like, was day to day!
Whene'er I looked, thy Image still was there;
It trembled, but it never passed away.

How perfect was the calm! it seemed no sleep;
No mood, which season takes away, or brings: 10
I could have fancied that the mighty Deep
Was even the gentlest of all gentle Things.

Ah! THEN, if mine had been the Painter's hand,
To express what then I saw; and add the gleam,
The light that never was, on sea or land,
The consecration, and the Poet's dream;

1. once, in 1794.

I would have planted thee, thou hoary Pile,
Amid a world how different from this!
Beside a sea that could not cease to smile;
On tranquil land, beneath a sky of bliss.   20

Thou shouldst have seemed a treasure-house divine
Of peaceful years; a chronicle of heaven;—
Of all the sunbeams that did ever shine
The very sweetest had to thee been given.

A Picture had it been of lasting ease,
Elysian quiet, without toil or strife;
No motion but the moving tide, a breeze,
Or merely silent Nature's breathing life.

Such, in the fond illusion of my heart,
Such Picture would I at that time have made: 30
And seen the soul of truth in every part,
A stedfast peace that might not be betrayed.

So once it would have been,—'tis so no more;
I have submitted to a new control:
A power is gone, which nothing can restore;
A deep distress hath humanised my Soul.

Not for a moment could I now behold
A smiling sea, and be what I have been:
The feeling of my loss will ne'er be old;
This, which I know, I speak with mind serene. 40

Then, Beaumont, Friend! who would have been the
    Friend,
If he had lived, of Him whom I deplore,
This work of thine I blame not, but commend;
This sea in anger, and that dismal shore.

O 'tis a passionate Work!—yet wise and well,
Well chosen is the spirit that is here;
That Hulk which labours in the deadly swell,
This rueful sky, this pageantry of fear!

And this huge Castle, standing here sublime,
I love to see the look with which it braves, 50
Cased in the unfeeling armour of old time,
The lightning, the fierce wind, and trampling
    waves.

Farewell, farewell the heart that lives alone,
Housed in a dream, at distance from the Kind!
Such happiness, wherever it be known,
Is to be pitied; for 'tis surely blind.

34. new control. See "Ode to Duty." **36. deep distress,**
the death of John Wordsworth, captain of the *Abergavenny*,
drowned in a storm, February, 1805.

But welcome fortitude, and patient cheer,
And frequent sights of what is to be borne!
Such sights, or worse, as are before me here.—
Not without hope we suffer and we mourn.   60

TO A YOUNG LADY

WHO HAD BEEN REPROACHED FOR TAKING
LONG WALKS IN THE COUNTRY

"Composed at the same time and on the same view
as 'I met Louisa in the shade': indeed they were designed to make one piece."—Wordsworth
The young lady is Dorothy Wordsworth.

Dear Child of Nature, let them rail!
—There is a nest in a green dale,
A harbour and a hold;
Where thou, a Wife and Friend, shalt see
Thy own heart-stirring days, and be
A light to young and old.

There, healthy as a shepherd boy,
And treading among flowers of joy
Which at no season fade,
Thou, while thy babes around thee cling,   10
Shalt show us how divine a thing
A Woman may be made.

Thy thoughts and feelings shall not die,
Nor leave thee, when grey hairs are nigh,
A melancholy slave;
But an old age serene and bright,
And lovely as a Lapland night,
Shall lead thee to thy grave.

YES, IT WAS THE MOUNTAIN
ECHO

Yes, it was the mountain Echo,
Solitary, clear, profound,
Answering to the shouting Cuckoo,
Giving to her sound for sound!

Unsolicited reply
To a babbling wanderer sent;
Like her ordinary cry,
Like—but oh, how different!

Hears not also mortal Life?
Hear not we, unthinking Creatures!   10
Slaves of folly, love, or strife—
Voices of two different natures?

Have not *we* too?—yes, we have
Answers, and we know not whence;
Echoes from beyond the grave,
Recognised intelligence!

Such rebounds our inward ear
Catches sometimes from afar—
Listen, ponder, hold them dear;
For of God,—of God they are.   20

PERSONAL TALK

1

I am not One who much or oft delight
To season my fireside with personal talk,—
Of friends, who live within an easy walk,
Or neighbours, daily, weekly, in my sight:
And, for my chance-acquaintance, ladies bright,
Sons, mothers, maidens withering on the stalk,
These all wear out of me, like Forms, with chalk
Painted on rich men's floors, for one feast-night.
Better than such discourse doth silence long,
Long, barren silence, square with my desire;   10
To sit without emotion, hope, or aim,
In the loved presence of my cottage-fire,
And listen to the flapping of the flame,
Or kettle whispering its faint undersong.

2

"Yet life," you say, "is life; we have seen and see,
And with a living pleasure we describe;
And fits of sprightly malice do but bribe
The languid mind into activity.
Sound sense, and love itself, and mirth and glee
Are fostered by the comment and the gibe."   20
Even be it so: yet still among your tribe,
Our daily world's true Worldlings, rank not me!
Children are blest, and powerful; their world lies
More justly balanced; partly at their feet,
And part far from them: sweetest melodies
Are those that are by distance made more sweet;
Whose mind is but the mind of his own eyes,
He is a Slave; the meanest we can meet!

3

Wings have we,—and as far as we can go
We may find pleasure: wilderness and wood,   30
Blank ocean and mere sky, support that mood
Which with the lofty sanctifies the low.
Dreams, books, are each a world; and books, we
     know,

Yes, It Was. **14–17. Answers . . . Echoes . . . rebounds.**
The idea is transcendental. See the general introductory
essay, page 10.

Are a substantial world, both pure and good:
Round these, with tendrils strong as flesh and blood,
Our pastime and our happiness will grow.
There find I personal themes, a plenteous store,
Matter wherein right voluble I am,
To which I listen with a ready ear;
Two shall be named, pre-eminently dear,—   40
The gentle Lady married to the Moor;
And heavenly Una with her milk-white Lamb.

4

Nor can I not believe but that hereby
Great gains are mine; for thus I live remote
From evil-speaking; rancour, never sought,
Comes to me not; malignant truth, or lie.
Hence have I genial seasons, hence have I
Smooth passions, smooth discourse, and joyous
      thought:
And thus from day to day my little boat
Rocks in its harbour, lodging peaceably.   50
Blessings be with them—and eternal praise,
Who gave us nobler loves, and nobler cares—
The Poets, who on earth have made us heirs
Of truth and pure delight by heavenly lays!
Oh! might my name be numbered among theirs,
Then gladly would I end my mortal days.

SONNETS

NUNS FRET NOT

Nuns fret not at their convent's narrow room;
And hermits are contented with their cells;
And students with their pensive citadels;
Maids at the wheel, the weaver at his loom,
Sit blithe and happy; bees that soar for bloom,
High as the highest Peak of Furness-fells,
Will murmur by the hour in foxglove bells:
In truth the prison, unto which we doom
Ourselves, no prison is: and hence for me,
In sundry moods, 'twas pastime to be bound   10
Within the Sonnet's scanty plot of ground;
Pleased if some Souls (for such there needs must be)
Who have felt the weight of too much liberty,
Should find brief solace there, as I have found.

THE WORLD IS TOO MUCH WITH US

The world is too much with us; late and soon,
Getting and spending, we lay waste our powers:

41. **Lady**, Desdemona, in *Othello*.   42. **Una**, in Spenser's
The Faerie Queene, Book I.

Little we see in Nature that is ours;
We have given our hearts away, a sordid boon!
The Sea that bares her bosom to the moon;
The winds that will be howling at all hours,
And are up-gathered now like sleeping flowers;
For this, for everything, we are out of tune;
It moves us not.—Great God! I'd rather be
A Pagan suckled in a creed outworn;
So might I, standing on this pleasant lea,
Have glimpses that would make me less forlorn;
Have sight of Proteus rising from the sea;
Or hear old Triton blow his wreathèd horn.

ODE

INTIMATIONS OF IMMORTALITY FROM RECOLLEC-
TIONS OF EARLY CHILDHOOD

> The Child is father of the Man;
> And I could wish my days to be
> Bound each to each by natural piety.

As the motto suggests, the "Ode" is one of several
poems in which Wordsworth tries to bind his days together. For discussion of the general theme, see page 17.
Clear recognition of the following main topics may lead
to a comprehension of the poem as a whole. 1. Looking
back at his childhood (stanzas 1–4), the poet misses
something transcendent ("celestial light," "glory," and
so on) which he remembers as resting upon all the scenes
of his childhood, which he is convinced was not the
beauty of nature—for nature in itself is still as beautiful
as ever—but which has passed away. "Whither is fled
the visionary gleam?" 2. The answer (stanzas 5–8) takes
him into a Neo-Platonic (*q.v.*) account of the descent and
forgetfulness of the soul—the soul came from afar, trailing clouds of glory, still conscious of God and its Heavenly
home; Nature and the ways of this earth which it had to
learn made it forget its divine origin and lose the sense
of divine presences. From this point of view, life on this
earth is a progressive despiritualization. 3. If life on this
earth is a progressive disillusionment, how justify it? The
answer (stanzas 9–11) points out, as consolations for what
has been lost ("the celestial light"): first, "That nature
yet remembers" it; second, that this recollection and the
soul's obstinate questionings of sense and outward things
are the surest evidence of the soul's immortality, the
fountain of our purest wisdom; third, that living and
suffering on this earth in primal sympathy with other
creatures give us a tenderness, a wisdom, and a faith to
be acquired in no other way. Therefore, though the poet
has lost the vivid sense of celestial nearness and presence,
he can still view nature and live among men with faith
and imaginative sympathy.

13. **Proteus**, a sea god who could assume any shape he
chose.   14. **Triton**, son of Neptune the sea god. He controlled
the waves by blowing a conch shell.

1

There was a time when meadow, grove, and stream,
The earth, and every common sight,
        To me did seem
        Apparelled in celestial light,
The glory and the freshness of a dream.
It is not now as it hath been of yore;—
        Turn wheresoe'er I may,
        By night or day,
The things which I have seen I now can see no
        more.

2

        The Rainbow comes and goes,   10
        And lovely is the Rose,
        The Moon doth with delight
Look round her when the heavens are bare,
        Waters on a starry night
        Are beautiful and fair;
    The sunshine is a glorious birth;
    But yet I know, where'er I go,
That there hath past away a glory from the earth.

3

Now, while the birds thus sing a joyous song,
    And while the young lambs bound   20
        As to the tabor's sound,
To me alone there came a thought of grief:
A timely utterance gave that thought relief,
        And I again am strong:
The cataracts blow their trumpets from the steep;
No more shall grief of mine the season wrong;
I hear the Echoes through the mountains throng,
The Winds come to me from the fields of sleep,
        And all the earth is gay;
            Land and sea   30
        Give themselves up to jollity,
        And with the heart of May
        Doth every Beast keep holiday;—
            Thou Child of Joy,
Shout round me, let me hear thy shouts, thou happy
        Shepherd-boy!

4

Ye blessèd Creatures, I have heard the call
        Ye to each other make; I see
The heavens laugh with you in your jubilee;
        My heart is at your festival,   40
        My head hath its coronal,
The fulness of your bliss, I feel—I feel it all.
        Oh evil day! if I were sullen
        While Earth herself is adorning,
            This sweet May-morning,

23. **A timely utterance,** "My Heart Leaps Up."

And the Children are culling
        On every side,
    In a thousand valleys far and wide,
    Fresh flowers; while the sun shines warm,
And the Babe leaps up on his Mother's arm:—   50
    I hear, I hear, with joy I hear!
    —But there's a Tree, of many, one,
A single Field which I have looked upon,
Both of them speak of something that is gone:
        The Pansy at my feet
        Doth the same tale repeat:
Whither is fled the visionary gleam?
Where is it now, the glory and the dream?

5

Our birth is but a sleep and a forgetting:
The Soul that rises with us, our life's Star,   60
        Hath had elsewhere its setting,
            And cometh from afar:
        Not in entire forgetfulness,
        And not in utter nakedness,
But trailing clouds of glory do we come
        From God, who is our home:
Heaven lies about us in our infancy!
Shades of the prison-house begin to close
        Upon the growing Boy,
But He beholds the light, and whence it flows,   70
        He sees it in his joy;
The Youth, who daily farther from the east
        Must travel, still is Nature's Priest,
        And by the vision splendid
        Is on his way attended;
At length the Man perceives it die away,
And fade into the light of common day.

6

Earth fills her lap with pleasures of her own;
Yearnings she hath in her own natural kind,
And, even with something of a Mother's mind,   80
        And no unworthy aim,
        The homely Nurse doth all she can
To make her Foster-child, her Inmate Man,
        Forget the glories he hath known,
And that imperial palace whence he came.

7

Behold the Child among his new-born blisses,
A six years' Darling of a pigmy size!
See, where 'mid work of his own hand he lies,
Fretted by sallies of his mother's kisses,
With light upon him from his father's eyes!   90
See, at his feet, some little plan or chart,
Some fragment from his dream of human life,
Shaped by himself with newly-learned art;

A wedding or a festival,
A mourning or a funeral;
    And this hath now his heart,
    And unto this he frames his song:
      Then will he fit his tongue
To dialogues of business, love, or strife;
    But it will not be long   100
    Ere this be thrown aside,
    And with new joy and pride
The little Actor cons another part;
Filling from time to time his "humorous stage"
With all the Persons, down to palsied Age,
That Life brings with her in her equipage;
    As if his whole vocation
    Were endless imitation.

8

Thou, whose exterior semblance doth belie
    Thy Soul's immensity;   110
Thou best Philosopher, who yet dost keep
Thy heritage, thou Eye among the blind,
That, deaf and silent, read'st the eternal deep,
Haunted for ever by the eternal mind,—
    Mighty Prophet! Seer blest!
    On whom those truths do rest,
Which we are toiling all our lives to find,
In darkness lost, the darkness of the grave;
Thou, over whom thy Immortality
Broods like the Day, a Master o'er a Slave,   120
A Presence which is not to be put by;
Thou little Child, yet glorious in the might
Of heaven-born freedom on thy being's height,
Why with such earnest pains dost thou provoke
The years to bring the inevitable yoke,
Thus blindly with thy blessedness at strife?
Full soon thy Soul shall have her earthly freight,
And custom lie upon thee with a weight,
Heavy as frost, and deep almost as life!

9

O joy! that in our embers   130
Is something that doth live,
That nature yet remembers
What was so fugitive!
The thought of our past years in me doth breed
Perpetual benediction: not indeed
For that which is most worthy to be blest;
Delight and liberty, the simple creed
Of Childhood, whether busy or at rest,
With new-fledged hope still fluttering in his
    breast:—
    Not for these I raise   140
    The song of thanks and praise;
    But for those obstinate questionings

Of sense and outward things,
Fallings from us, vanishings;
Blank misgivings of a Creature
Moving about in worlds not realised,
High instincts before which our mortal Nature
Did tremble like a guilty Thing surprised:
    But for those first affections,
    Those shadowy recollections,   150
Which, be they what they may,
Are yet the fountain light of all our day,
Are yet a master light of all our seeing;
    Uphold us, cherish, and have power to make
Our noisy years seem moments in the being
Of the eternal Silence: truths that wake,
    To perish never:
Which neither listlessness, nor mad endeavour,
    Nor Man nor Boy,
Nor all that is at enmity with joy,   160
Can utterly abolish or destroy!
    Hence in a season of calm weather
    Though inland far we be,
Our Souls have sight of that immortal sea
    Which brought us hither,
    Can in a moment travel thither,
And see the Children sport upon the shore,
And hear the mighty waters rolling evermore.

10

Then sing, ye Birds, sing, sing a joyous song!
    And let the young Lambs bound   170
    As to the tabor's sound!
We in thought will join your throng,
    Ye that pipe and ye that play,
    Ye that through your hearts to-day
    Feel the gladness of the May!
What though the radiance which was once so
    bright
Be now for ever taken from my sight,
    Though nothing can bring back the hour
Of splendour in the grass, of glory in the flower;
    We will grieve not, rather find   180
    Strength in what remains behind;
    In the primal sympathy
    Which having been must ever be;
    In the soothing thoughts that spring
    Out of human suffering;
    In the faith that looks through death,
In years that bring the philosophic mind.

11

And O, ye Fountains, Meadows, Hills, and Groves,
Forebode not any severing of our loves!
Yet in my heart of hearts I feel your might;   190
I only have relinquished one delight

To live beneath your more habitual sway.
I love the Brooks which down their channels fret,
Even more than when I tripped lightly as they;
The innocent brightness of a new-born Day
        Is lovely yet;
The Clouds that gather round the setting sun
Do take a sober colouring from an eye
That hath kept watch o'er man's mortality;
Another race hath been, and other palms are
   won.   200
Thanks to the human heart by which we live,
Thanks to its tenderness, its joys, and fears,
To me the meanest flower that blows can give
Thoughts that do often lie too deep for tears.

from THE RIVER DUDDON

AFTER-THOUGHT

I thought of Thee, my partner and my guide,
As being past away.—Vain sympathies!
For, backward, Duddon! as I cast my eyes,
I see what was, and is, and will abide;
Still glides the Stream, and shall for ever glide;
The Form remains, the Function never dies;
While we, the brave, the mighty, and the wise,
We Men, who in our morn of youth defied
The elements, must vanish;—be it so!
Enough, if something from our hands have power
To live, and act, and serve the future hour;   11
And if, as toward the silent tomb we go,
Through love, through hope, and faith's transcend-
   ent dower,
We feel that we are greater than we know.

from ECCLESIASTICAL SONNETS

MUTABILITY

From low to high doth dissolution climb,
And sink from high to low, along a scale
Of awful notes, whose concord shall not fail;
A musical but melancholy chime,
Which they can hear who meddle not with crime,
Nor avarice, nor over-anxious care.
Truth fails not; but her outward forms that bear
The longest date do melt like frosty rime,
That in the morning whitened hill and plain
And is no more; drop like the tower sublime   10
Of yesterday, which royally did wear
His crown of weeds, but could not even sustain
Some casual shout that broke the silent air,
Or the unimaginable touch of Time.

INSIDE OF KING'S COLLEGE CHAPEL, CAMBRIDGE

Tax not the royal Saint with vain expense,
With ill-matched aims the Architect who planned
(Albeit labouring for a scanty band
Of white-robed Scholars only) this immense
And glorious Work of fine intelligence!
Give all thou canst; high Heaven rejects the lore
Of nicely-calculated less or more:—
So deemed the man who fashioned for the sense
These lofty pillars, spread that branching roof
Self-poised, and scooped into ten thousand cells, 10
Where light and shade repose, where music dwells
Lingering—and wandering on as loth to die;
Like thoughts whose very sweetness yieldeth proof
That they were born for immortality.

THE TROSACHS

   "As recorded in my sister's Journal, I had first seen the Trosachs in her and Coleridge's company. The sentiment that runs through this Sonnet was natural to the season in which I again saw this beautiful spot; but this and some other sonnets that follow were coloured by the remembrance of my recent visit to Sir Walter Scott, and the melancholy errand on which he was going."
                    —Wordsworth

There's not a nook within this solemn Pass,
But were an apt confessional for One
Taught by his summer spent, his autumn gone,
That Life is but a tale of morning grass
Withered at eve. From scenes of art which chase
That thought away, turn, and with watchful eyes
Feed it 'mid Nature's old felicities,
Rocks, rivers, and smooth lakes more clear than
   glass
Untouched, unbreathed upon. Thrice happy quest,
If from a golden perch of aspen spray   10
(October's workmanship to rival May)
The pensive warbler of the ruddy breast
That moral sweeten by a heaven-taught lay,
Lulling the year, with all its cares, to rest!

MOST SWEET IT IS WITH UN-
UPLIFTED EYES

Most sweet it is with unuplifted eyes
   To pace the ground, if path be there or none,

Inside of King's College Chapel. **1. royal Saint**, Henry VI, who founded the college in 1441.

While a fair region round the traveller lies
Which he forbears again to look upon;
Pleased rather with some soft ideal scene,
The work of Fancy, or some happy tone
Of meditation, slipping in between
The beauty coming and the beauty gone.
If Thought and Love desert us, from that day
Let us break off all commerce with the Muse: 10
With Thought and Love companions of our way,
Whate'er the senses take or may refuse,
The Mind's internal heaven shall shed her dews
Of inspiration on the humblest lay.

SO FAIR, SO SWEET, WITHAL SO SENSITIVE

So fair, so sweet, withal so sensitive,
Would that the little Flowers were born to live,
Conscious of half the pleasure which they give;

That to this mountain-daisy's self were known
The beauty of its star-shaped shadow, thrown
On the smooth surface of this naked stone!

And what if hence a bold desire should mount
High as the Sun, that he could take account
Of all that issues from his glorious fount!

So might he ken how by his sovereign aid   10
These delicate companionships are made;
And how he rules the pomp of light and shade;

And were the Sister-power that shines by night
So privileged, what a countenance of delight
Would through the clouds break forth on human
  sight!

Fond fancies! wheresoe'er shall turn thine eye
On earth, air, ocean, or the starry sky,
Converse with Nature in pure sympathy;

All vain desires, all lawless wishes quelled,
Be Thou to love and praise alike impelled,   20
Whatever boon is granted or withheld.

IF THOU INDEED DERIVE THY LIGHT FROM HEAVEN

If thou indeed derive thy light from Heaven,
Then, to the measure of that heaven-born light,
Shine, Poet! in thy place, and be content:—
The stars pre-eminent in magnitude,
And they that from the zenith dart their beams,
(Visible though they be to half the earth,
Though half a sphere be conscious of their bright-
  ness)
Are yet of no diviner origin,
No purer essence, than the one that burns,
Like an untended watch-fire, on the ridge   10
Of some dark mountain; or than those which seem
Humbly to hang, like twinkling winter lamps,
Among the branches of the leafless trees;
All are the undying offspring of one Sire:
Then, to the measure of the light vouchsafed,
Shine, Poet! in thy place, and be content.

Samuel Taylor Coleridge
1772–1834

Samuel Taylor Coleridge was born on October 20, 1772, in the vicarage at Ottery St. Mary, Devonshire. His father, the Reverend John Coleridge, besides being vicar of the parish, was master of the grammar school, and by all accounts was learned, absent-minded, and lovable. The last-born in a family of fourteen, young Samuel was indulged by his parents and alternately petted and bullied by his eight older brothers. Hence he was a precocious boy, thrown upon the resources of reading and dreaming. At the age of six he had read such tales as "Jack the Giant-Killer," *Robinson Crusoe*, and the *Arabian Nights*. "One tale," he wrote, years later,

"of a man who was compelled to seek for a pure virgin made so deep an impression on me (I had read it in the evening while my Mother was mending stockings), that I was haunted by spectres, whenever I was in the dark." In the old churchyard of St. Mary's, he loved to read and dream and mope; sometimes he dramatized stories among the gravestones, "cutting down weeds and nettles, as one of the seven champions of Christendom." After a fight in which he used a knife on one of his brothers, he ran away from home with a prayer book in his pocket, fell asleep on the bank of the Otter, and in the night caught a fever that was to afflict him the rest of his life. The old man who was his father once explained "how Jupiter was a thousand times larger than our world and that the other twinkling stars were suns that had worlds rolling round them; and when I came home he shewed me how they rolled round." Thus early, he says, "I regulated my creeds by my conceptions, not by my sight." The death of his father in 1781 broke up this companionship.

In 1782, at the age of nine, he entered Christ's Hospital School in London. His loneliness, his dreamy way of life, and his extraordinary precocity as "the inspired charity boy" are vividly described by his schoolmate Charles Lamb and are recalled in Coleridge's "Frost at Midnight" and *Biographia Literaria*. One day, walking the Strand, in London, and imagining that he was Leander swimming the Hellespont, he unintentionally brushed the pocket of a crusty old gentleman. Challenged as a pickpocket, the boy explained his conduct so eloquently that the old gentleman invited him home and gave him a ticket to a circulating library. As early as 1787 he wrote the first draft of his "Monody on the Death of Chatterton." Before he left Christ's he had walked the London hospitals with his brother Luke and had begun to read and expound the Neo-Platonists. He also formed an acquaintance with Mary Evans that was to ripen into a love affair during his Cambridge years.

In October, 1791, Coleridge entered Jesus College, Cambridge, as a sizar (self-help scholar). Here he read widely and deeply, talked brilliantly about David Hartley, Godwin, the French Revolution, the sonnets of William Lisle Bowles (which he copied and distributed among his friends), Plotinus, and the Cambridge Platonists. He also fell in love with Mary Evans and ran up debts. In despair, he left college and enlisted in His Majesty's Fifteenth Light Dragoons, under the name of Silas Tomkyn Comberbacke. Unable to curry, saddle, or ride a horse, he was transferred to hospital service and became a favorite among the soldiers because he wrote fine love letters for them. His friends begged him out of the army, in time to save him, perhaps, from being killed in France, got him reinstated in college, and arranged about his debts. But he did not remain long at Jesus College.

In June, 1794, on a walking tour he stopped at Oxford and had that momentous meeting with Southey which resulted in the Pantisocracy scheme (to form a Utopian Colony in America) and Coleridge's unhappy marriage with Sarah Fricker. By October, 1795, he was married, settled at Clevedon, in Somersetshire, and writing honeymoon poetry.

He and his wife were living precariously, partly on the income from his lecturing and writing but chiefly on the charity of friends like Joseph Cottle and Thomas Poole. Since Clevedon was too far from a good library, he moved temporarily to Bristol and then, at Poole's invitation, to Nether Stowey. In the notebook of this Bristol library reading he was accumulating the "Chaos" out of which the cosmic order and beauty of "The Rime of the Ancient Mariner" were to be evoked. Editing a short-lived journal, *The Watchman*, lecturing, and preaching in Unitarian chapels occupied his attention until Josiah Wedgwood, the pottery manufacturer, gave him an allowance of £150 per annum. This, says Hazlitt ("My First Acquaintance with Poets"), Coleridge decided to accept while tying his shoe in the parsonage at Wem.

In the meantime the fateful meeting with Wordsworth had occurred. The two young poets exchanged poems and criticisms. At Racedown, where Coleridge visited William and Dorothy, he "leapt over a gate and bounded down the pathless field" into the most fruitful friendship of his and their lives. Dorothy described him thus:

"He is a wonderful man. His conversation teems with soul, mind, and spirit. . . . I thought him very plain . . . for about three minutes: he is pale and thin, has a wide mouth, thick lips, and not very good teeth, longish, loose-growing half-curling rough black hair. But if you hear him speak for five minutes you think no more of them. His eye is large and full, not dark but grey . . . it has more of the 'poet's eye in a fine frenzy rolling' than I ever witnessed."

Of William, Coleridge wrote, "I feel myself *a little man by his side;* and yet do not think myself the less man than I formerly thought myself." By 1797 the "three persons and one soul" were living at Nether Stowey and Alfoxden, three miles apart, in the Quantock hills. From this point of time until after their return from Germany, the stories of the three are practically one story, and that story has been told. The chief events are the writing and the publication of *Lyrical Ballads*, containing "The Rime of the Ancient Mariner" and "Tintern Abbey," the first and the last poem, respectively, included in that epoch-making little volume; the visit to Germany; and Coleridge's suggestion of *The Recluse* and *The Prelude* to Wordsworth. By 1798, however, Coleridge's political thought had outrun Wordsworth's; in "France, An Ode" he abandoned hope for the French Revolution as a means of achieving liberty and fell back on faith in the *spirit* that informs woods, waves, clouds, and the soul of man.

By 1802 Coleridge's life came to be more and more separated from Wordsworth's, though the two remained close friends for five more years and even after a quarrel became partly reconciled for the remainder of Coleridge's life. Coleridge had settled at Keswick, twelve miles from Dove Cottage, in the Lake Country. Here he wrote the second part of "Christabel," begun at Stowey. Here, too, he contracted an unhappy love for Sarah Hutchinson (see his poem "Love"), sister of the Mary who in October, 1802, became the wife of Wordsworth, and felt all the more poignantly the misery of his ill-matched marriage. In desperation he resumed the opium habit which had produced "Kubla Khan," lost "the deep power of Joy," and wrote "Dejection: An Ode," 1802, which, in its earliest form, drains all these springs of grief. Unable to control his personality, he sank into slothfulness, neglected his wife and children, often leaving them to the charity of his brother-in-law Southey, wandered about talking and lecturing, held a government position in Malta, and returned home in time to hear Wordsworth read *The Prelude* to him in 1806. The next year he began a series of public lectures on the English poets, including Shakespeare, that did much to establish his fame as a critic. Placing himself in the hands of a physician friend, James Gillman, and making London his home, he spent the remainder of his life writing and talking as a critic and philosopher. Among his publications in criticism and philosophy are *Biographia Literaria*, 1817; *The Friend*, 1818; *Aids to Reflection*, 1825; and his Shakespearean criticism, brought out posthumously, a large part of it (edited by Thomas M. Raysor) not until the 1930's. He died in 1834.

Coleridge was the most versatile of the Romanticists—the "many-sided Coleridge"; poet, critic, philosopher, moralist, theologian. His was the most fertile and stimulating mind of his generation.

His chief poems were published in *Lyrical Ballads*, 1798 and 1800; *Christabel, Kubla Khan, and the Pains of Sleep*, 1816; *Sibylline Leaves*, 1817; and the collected *Poetical Works*, 1828, 1829, 1834. A score of these poems (some fifty pages) can be read today with pleasure by a cultivated person who has no special scholarly training in the literature of the period. They are among the most transcendently original poems in our language.

One group of them Coleridge himself called "conversation poems." Most of these are in blank verse and treat subjects intimately personal to the poet. "The Eolian Harp," anticipating his honeymoon with "pensive Sara," describes their jasmine-scented cottage and its surroundings at Clevedon, speculates on "the one Life within us and abroad," and identifies this "Life" with God. "This Lime-Tree Bower My Prison" commemorates happy fellowship with Dorothy and William Wordsworth and Charles Lamb during Lamb's visit to Nether Stowey and Alfoxden in 1797. In "Frost at Midnight," the poet, sitting by the cradle of his baby, recalls his own lonely childhood in London, contrasts its bleak surroundings with the "lovely shapes and sounds" the growing child will know, and asserts a faith in the "Great universal Teacher" who shall mold the child's spirit. "The Nightingale," belonging also to the Nether Stowey period, modulates the outpouring of the poet's affection for William, Dorothy, and little Hartley to the music of the bird's song on an April night. "To William Wordsworth," 1806, is a superb poetical review of *The Prelude*. The whole group expresses ideas about nature and human life which anticipate, parallel, or summarize important doctrines of Wordsworth's poetry. For example, both "Frost at Midnight" and "Tintern Abbey" assert the educational influence of nature on the human spirit.

A second group of Coleridge's living poems is composed of pieces marking "The Renascence of Wonder." In these the author goes back to the age of the old ballads and romances for forms, atmosphere, and narrative technique, and sweeps the horizons of the earth and of history for his matter; but he introduces a new ethic and a new psychology in the treatment of his themes, and achieves original and unprecedented effects. Both "The Rime of the Ancient Mariner" and "Christabel" spring out of medieval literary forms; both dramatize or allegorize the conflict between Good and Evil; both make use of hypnotism, "the power of the eye," in their characterization and narrative development; both cast a spell upon the reader, suggesting the interpenetration of the natural and the supernatural worlds. But whereas "The Rime of the Ancient Mariner," in its treatment of offense, expiation, hope, release, and the return of the evil dream, is the complete execution of a deliberate design, "Christabel" snaps at the height of its "witchery by daylight." "Kubla Khan" is "directionless melody" hovering over a dream landscape combining the extremes of beauty and terror. "The Knight's Tomb" is a sigh for the glamour of a long-vanished age.

Coleridge's other poems of unfaded greatness include two odes, "France" and "Dejection," the themes and autobiographical implications of which have already been noted. "Dejection" shows clearly

Coleridge's shift to transcendentalism, most succinctly expressed in the line "And in our life alone does Nature live." With these odes the "Hymn before Sun-Rise, in the Vale of Chamouni" is associated because of its exalted style and the intensity of its religious feeling.

The significance of Coleridge's literary criticism has been partly suggested already. The *Biographia Literaria* account of the origin and purpose of *Lyrical Ballads* and of the defects and excellencies of Wordsworth constitutes one of the three or four master expositions of the Romantic theory of poetry. In this work and in his lectures on Shakespeare, Coleridge became the leader of Romantic criticism. To him criticism was something more than the application of a set of external rules. Previous notions of an opposition between genius and artistic law, he declared, were based on a false notion of the critic's business. Great geniuses are not lawless. They work in accordance with laws that the critic should discover by studying their writings. Since art is vital and organic, it takes different shapes under different conditions of human culture. The critic should take these differences of circumstances into consideration in interpreting and judging works of art. The spirit of poetry persists through the ages, though its form may vary from age to age. It is just as unreasonable to judge Shakespeare's plays by the standards of Greek drama as it would be to judge sculpture by the rules of painting. As a Shakespearean critic Coleridge inaugurated points of view, methods, and interpretations which persist today. His greatest achievement in this field lay in his analysis of Shakespeare's characters—Hamlet, for example—and in his power, as a great poet himself, to enter into and describe Shakespeare's imaginative processes.

ON THE PROSPECT OF ESTAB-
LISHING A PANTISOCRACY
IN AMERICA

Whilst pale Anxiety, corrosive Care,
The tear of Woe, the gloom of sad Despair,
  And deepened Anguish generous bosoms rend;—
Whilst patriot souls their country's fate lament;
Whilst mad with rage demoniac, foul intent,
  Embattled legions Despots vainly send
To arrest the immortal mind's expanding ray
  Of everlasting Truth;—I other climes
Where dawns, with hope serene, a brighter day
  Than e'er saw Albion in her happiest times,   10

With mental eye exulting now explore,
  And soon with kindred minds shall haste to enjoy
(Free from the ills which here our peace destroy)
Content and Bliss on Translantic shore.

TO THE REVEREND
W. L. BOWLES

My heart has thanked thee, BOWLES! for those soft
    strains
  Whose sadness soothes me, like the murmuring
  Of wild-bees in the sunny showers of spring!
For hence not callous to the mourner's pains

Through Youth's gay prime and thornless paths I
    went:
  And when the mightier Throes of mind began,
  And drove me forth, a thought-bewildered man,
Their mild and manliest melancholy lent

A mingled charm, such as the pang consigned
  To slumber, though the big tear it renewed;   10
  Bidding a strange mysterious PLEASURE brood
Over the wavy and tumultuous mind,

As the great SPIRIT erst with plastic sweep
Moved on the darkness of the unformed deep.

THE EOLIAN HARP

COMPOSED AT CLEVEDON, SOMERSETSHIRE

Of this poem Coleridge wrote: "This I think the most perfect poem I ever wrote. Bad may be the best perhaps."

My pensive Sara! thy soft cheek reclined
Thus on mine arm, most soothing sweet it is
To sit beside our cot, our cot o'ergrown
With white-flowered Jasmin, and the broad-leaved
    Myrtle,
(Meet emblems they of Innocence and Love!),
And watch the clouds, that late were rich with light,
Slow saddening round, and mark the star of eve
Serenely brilliant (such should Wisdom be)
Shine opposite! How exquisite the scents
Snatched from yon bean-field! and the world so
    hushed!   10
The stilly murmur of the distant sea
Tells us of silence.

To The Reverend W. L. Bowles, whose *Sonnets*, 1789, impressed the young Coleridge and Wordsworth with the qualities here admirably described. *The Eolian Harp*. **1. Sara**, Sara Fricker, whom Coleridge married in 1795, shortly after this poem was written.

          And that simplest Lute,
Placed length-ways in the clasping casement, hark!
How by the desultory breeze caressed,
Like some coy maid half yielding to her lover,
It pours such sweet upbraiding, as must needs
Tempt to repeat the wrong! And now, its strings
Boldlier swept, the long sequacious notes
Over delicious surges sink and rise,
Such a soft floating witchery of sound   20
As twilight Elfins make, when they at eve
Voyage on gentle gales from Fairy-Land,
Where Melodies round honey-dropping flowers,
Footless and wild, like birds of Paradise,
Nor pause, nor perch, hovering on untamed wing!
O! the one life within us and abroad,
Which meets all motion and becomes its soul,
A light in sound, a sound-like power in light,
Rhythm in all thought, and joyance every where—
Methinks, it should have been impossible   30
Not to love all things in a world so filled;
Where the breeze warbles, and the mute still air
Is Music slumbering on her instrument.

    And thus, my love! as on the midway slope
Of yonder hill I stretch my limbs at noon,
Whilst through my half-closed eye-lids I behold
The sunbeams dance, like diamonds, on the main,
And tranquil muse upon tranquillity;
Full many a thought uncalled and undetained,
And many idle flitting phantasies,   40
Traverse my indolent and passive brain,
As wild and various as the random gales
That swell and flutter on this subject lute!

    And what if all of animated nature
Be but organic harps diversely framed,
That tremble into thought, as o'er them sweeps
Plastic and vast, one intellectual Breeze,
At once the Soul of each, and God of all?

    But thy more serious eye a mild reproof
Darts, O belovèd Woman! nor such thoughts   50
Dim and unhallowed dost thou not reject,
And biddest me walk humbly with my God.
Meek Daughter in the family of Christ!
Well hast thou said and holily dispraised
These shapings of the unregenerate mind;
Bubbles that glitter as they rise and break
On vain Philosophy's aye-babbling spring.
For never guiltless may I speak of him,
The Incomprehensible! save when with awe
I praise him, and with Faith that inly *feels;*   60
Who with his saving mercies healèd me,

18. **sequacious,** following compliantly.

A sinful and most miserable man,
Wildered and dark, and gave me to possess
Peace, and this Cot, and thee, heart-honoured
  Maid!

SONNET

To a Friend Who Asked, How I Felt when the Nurse First Presented My Infant to Me

CHARLES! my slow heart was only sad when first
  I scanned that face of feeble infancy:
For dimly on my thoughtful spirit burst
  All I had been, and all my child might be!
But when I saw it on its mother's arm,
  And hanging at her bosom (she the while
  Bent o'er its features with a tearful smile)
Then I was thrilled and melted, and most warm
Impressed a father's kiss: and all beguiled
  Of dark remembrance and presageful fear,
  I seemed to see an angel-form appear—
'Twas even thine, belovèd woman mild:
  So for the mother's sake the child was dear,
And dearer was the mother for the child.

THIS LIME-TREE BOWER MY PRISON

Addressed to Charles Lamb, of the India House, London

"In the June of 1797 some long-expected friends paid a visit to the author's cottage; and on the morning of their arrival, he met with an accident, which disabled him from walking during the whole time of their stay. One evening, when they had left him for a few hours, he composed the following lines in the garden-bower."
                                        —Coleridge

Well, they are gone, and here must I remain,
This lime-tree bower my prison! I have lost
Beauties and feelings, such as would have been
Most sweet to my remembrance even when age
Had dimmed mine eyes to blindness! They, mean-
  while,
Friends, whom I never more may meet again,
On springy heath, along the hill-top edge,
Wander in gladness, and wind down, perchance,
To that still roaring dell, of which I told;
The roaring dell, o'er wooded, narrow, deep,   10
And only speckled by the mid-day sun;
Where its slim trunk the ash from rock to rock
Flings arching like a bridge;—that branchless ash,

Sonnet. **1. Charles,** Lamb.   **4. child,** Hartley Coleridge.

Unsunned and damp, whose few poor yellow leaves
Ne'er tremble in the gale, yet tremble still,
Fanned by the water-fall! and there my friends
Behold the dark green file of long lank weeds,
That all at once (a most fantastic sight!)
Still nod and drip beneath the dripping edge   19
Of the blue clay-stone.

           Now, my friends emerge
Beneath the wide wide Heaven—and view again
The many-steepled tract magnificent
Of hilly fields and meadows, and the sea,
With some fair bark, perhaps, whose sails light up
The slip of smooth clear blue betwixt two Isles
Of purple shadow! Yes! they wander on
In gladness all; but thou, methinks, most glad,
My gentle-hearted Charles! for thou has pined
And hungered after Nature, many a year,
In the great City pent, winning thy way   30
With sad yet patient soul, through evil and pain
And strange calamity! Ah! slowly sink
Behind the western ridge, thou glorious Sun!
Shine in the slant beams of the sinking orb,
Ye purple heath-flowers! richlier burn, ye clouds!
Live in the yellow light, ye distant groves!
And kindle, thou blue Ocean! So my friend
Struck with deep joy may stand, as I have stood,
Silent with swimming sense; yea, gazing round
On the wide landscape, gaze till all doth seem   40
Less gross than bodily; and of such hues
As veil the Almighty Spirit, when yet he makes
Spirits perceive his presence.

           A delight
Comes sudden on my heart, and I am glad
As I myself were there! Nor in this bower,
This little lime-tree bower, have I not marked
Much that has soothed me. Pale beneath the blaze
Hung the transparent foliage; and I watched
Some broad and sunny leaf, and loved to see
The shadow of the leaf and stem above   50
Dappling its sunshine! And that walnut-tree
Was richly tinged, and a deep radiance lay
Full on the ancient ivy, which usurps
Those fronting elms, and now, with blackest mass
Makes their dark branches gleam a lighter hue
Through the late twilight: and though now the bat
Wheels silent by, and not a swallow twitters,
Yet the still solitary humble-bee
Sings in the bean-flower! Henceforth I shall know
That Nature ne'er deserts the wise and pure;   60
No plot so narrow, be but Nature there,
No waste so vacant, but may well employ
Each faculty of sense, and keep the heart

Awake to Love and Beauty! and sometimes
'Tis well to be bereft of promised good,
That we may lift the soul, and contemplate
With lively joy the joys we cannot share.
My gentle-hearted Charles! when the last rook
Beat its straight path along the dusky air
Homewards, I blest it! deeming, its black wing   70
(Now a dim speck, now vanishing in light)
Had crossed the mighty orb's dilated glory,
While thou stood'st gazing; or when all was still,
Flew creeking o'er thy head, and had a charm
For thee, my gentle-hearted Charles, to whom
No sound is dissonant which tells of Life.

from BIOGRAPHIA LITERARIA

CHAPTER 14

Occasion of the *Lyrical Ballads*, and the objects originally
proposed . . . definitions of a Poem and Poetry with
scholia.

DURING the first year that Mr. Wordsworth and
I were neighbours, our conversations turned
frequently on the two cardinal points of poetry, the
power of exciting the sympathy of the reader by a
faithful adherence to the truth of nature, and the
power of giving the interest of novelty by the modifying colours of imagination. The sudden charm,
which accidents of light and shade, which moonlight or sunset, diffused over a known and familiar
10 landscape, appeared to represent the practicability
of combining both. These are the poetry of nature.
The thought suggested itself (to which of us I do not
recollect) that a series of poems might be composed
of *two sorts*. In the one, the incidents and agents were
to be, in part at least, supernatural; and the excellence aimed at was to consist in the interesting of the
affections by the dramatic truth of such emotions,
as would naturally accompany such situations, supposing them real. And real in this sense they have
20 been to every human being who, from whatever
source of delusion, has at any time believed himself
under supernatural agency. For the second class,
subjects were to be chosen from ordinary life; the
characters and incidents were to be such as will be
found in every village and its vicinity where there is
a meditative and feeling mind to seek after them, or
to notice them when they present themselves.

In this idea originated the plan of the "Lyrical
Ballads"; in which it was agreed that my endeavours
30 should be directed to persons and characters supernatural, or at least romantic; yet so as to transfer
from our inward nature a human interest and a

semblance of truth sufficient to procure for these shadows of imagination that willing suspension of disbelief for the moment, which constitutes poetic faith. Mr. Wordsworth, on the other hand, was to propose to himself as his object, to give the charm of novelty to things of every day, and to excite a feeling analogous to the supernatural, by awakening the mind's attention to the lethargy of custom, and directing it to the loveliness and the wonders of the world before us; an inexhaustible treasure, but for which, in consequence of the film of familiarity and selfish solicitude, we have eyes, yet see not, ears that hear not, and hearts that neither feel nor understand.

With this view I wrote the "Ancient Mariner," and was preparing, among other poems, the "Dark Ladie," and the "Christabel," in which I should have more nearly realized my ideal, than I had done in my first attempt. But Mr. Wordsworth's industry had proved so much more successful, and the number of his poems so much greater, that my compositions, instead of forming a balance, appeared rather an interpolation of heterogeneous matter. Mr. Wordsworth added two or three poems written in his own character, in the impassioned, lofty, and sustained diction which is characteristic of his genius. In this form the "Lyrical Ballads" were published; and were presented by him, as an experiment, whether subjects, which from their nature rejected the usual ornaments and extra-colloquial style of poems in general, might not be so managed in the language of ordinary life as to produce the pleasurable interest, which it is the peculiar business of poetry to impart. . . . [*To be continued*]

THE RIME OF THE ANCIENT MARINER

In Seven Parts

The poem was begun—in collaboration with Wordsworth, who soon dropped out—on November 13, 1797, when the two poets and Dorothy set out on a walking excursion to Linton and the Valley of the Stones; completed, in the first version, March 23, 1798, when Coleridge read it to Dorothy and William; first published in *Lyrical Ballads*, 1798, the first poem in the volume; republished in 1800 with some reduction of the many archaisms; revised between 1800 and 1817; published in its final form, with the addition of the marginal gloss, in *Sibylline Leaves*, 1817. In form it is a ballad, modeled on those of Percy's *Reliques:* one hundred and seven of its one hundred and forty-two stanzas are in regular ballad stanza, 4a3b4c3b, the rest in stanzas ranging from five to nine lines; it follows ballad-narrative technique in the sudden confrontation of characters and unassigned speeches (stanza 1) and in the trick of incremental repetition (see especially ll. 30, 113, 383; and note ll. 59–60, 119–22, 232–35); and it is full of pictures that might have come right out of the old ballads (nodding minstrelsy, bride, and so on). Its theme, stated by Coleridge in the "Argument," has been shown by J. L. Lowes, in *The Road to Xanadu* (Houghton Mifflin, 1930), to have been executed as a "moral and rhythmical harmony": note the conclusion of each of the seven parts, emphasizing the significance of the shooting of the albatross: offense (violating the law of love by the shooting of the albatross—"I shot the Albatross"); penance (appropriately, isolation and loneliness, because the Mariner had broken the law of love—"the Albatross about my neck was hung"); expiation ("Like the whizz of my crossbow"); release (only after the Mariner had been restored to fellowship by blessing the water snakes—"The Albatross fell off my neck," at the climax or dramatic center of the poem); absolution ("The Albatross's blood"); return of the evil dream (inescapable consequence of a wrong action—"Since then . . . I pass like night"). Lowes further shows that the fabric of the narrative includes three intertwisted threads—the *ship's voyage*, the ground plan, factual as an Admiralty report or a captain's log, making a great poem of "Earth, Air, Fire, and Water in their multiform balefulness and beauty"; what Wordsworth called the *spectral persecution* (that is, the revenge by the guardian spirits of the Antarctic); and the *moral idea* of the inescapable consequences of a moral act. This latter, Professor Lowes asserts, includes far more than the so-called moral at the end ("He prayeth best . . ."); it relates the poem fundamentally to human experience, and is thus one of the principal means by which Coleridge attains reality.

ARGUMENT

How a Ship having first sailed to the Equator, was driven by Storms to the cold Country towards the South Pole; how the Ancient Mariner cruelly and in contempt of the laws of hospitality killed a Sea-bird and how he was followed by many and strange Judgements: and in what manner he came back to his own Country.

PART I

An ancient Mariner meeteth three Gallants bidden to a wedding-feast, and detaineth one.

It is an ancient Mariner,
And he stoppeth one of three.
"By thy long grey beard and glittering eye,
Now wherefore stopp'st thou me?

The Bridegroom's doors are opened wide,
And I am next of kin;

The guests are met, the feast is set:
May'st hear the merry din."

He holds him with his skinny hand,
"There was a ship," quoth he.   10
"Hold off! unhand me, grey-beard
    loon!"
Eftsoons his hand dropt he.

The Wedding-Guest is spell-bound by the eye of the old seafaring man, and constrained to hear his tale.

He holds him with his glittering eye—
The Wedding-Guest stood still,
And listens like a three years' child:
The Mariner hath his will.

The Wedding-Guest sat on a stone:
He cannot choose but hear;
And thus spake on that ancient man,
The bright-eyed Mariner.   20

"The ship was cheered, the harbour
    cleared,
Merrily did we drop

The Mariner tells how the ship sailed southward with a good wind and fair weather, till it reached the line.

Below the kirk, below the hill,
Below the lighthouse top.

The Sun came up upon the left,
Out of the sea came he!
And he shone bright, and on the right
Went down into the sea.

Higher and higher every day,
Till over the mast at noon—"   30
The Wedding-Guest here beat his
    breast,
For he heard the loud bassoon.

The Wedding-Guest heareth the bridal music; but the Mariner continueth his tale.

The bride hath paced into the hall,
Red as a rose is she;
Nodding their heads before her goes
The merry minstrelsy.

The Wedding-Guest he beat his breast,
Yet he cannot choose but hear;
And thus spake on that ancient man,
The bright-eyed Mariner.   40

The ship driven by a storm toward the south pole.

"And now the Storm-blast came, and he
Was tyrannous and strong:
He struck with his o'ertaking wings,
And chased us south along.

With sloping masts and dipping prow,
As who pursued with yell and blow
Still treads the shadow of his foe,

23. kirk, church. This form of the word suggests that the
ship sailed from a northern English or a Scottish port.

And forward bends his head,
The ship drove fast, loud roared the
    blast,
And southward aye we fled.   50

And now there came both mist and
    snow,
And it grew wondrous cold:
And ice, mast-high, came floating by,
As green as emerald.

The land of ice, and of fearful sounds where no living thing was to be seen.

And through the drifts the snowy clifts
Did send a dismal sheen:
Nor shapes of men nor beasts we ken—
The ice was all between.

The ice was here, the ice was there,
The ice was all around: 60
It cracked and growled, and roared and
    howled,
Like noises in a swound!

Till a great sea-bird, called the Albatross, came through the snow-fog, and was received with great joy and hospitality.

At length did cross an Albatross,
Thorough the fog it came;
As if it had been a Christian soul,
We hailed it in God's name.

It ate the food it ne'er had eat,
And round and round it flew.
The ice did split with a thunder-fit;
The helmsman steered us through!   70

And lo! the Albatross proveth a bird of good omen, and followeth the ship as it returned northward through fog and floating ice.

And a good south wind sprung up
    behind;
The Albatross did follow,
And every day, for food or play,
Came to the mariner's hollo!

In mist or cloud, on mast or shroud,
It perched for vespers nine;
Whiles all the night, through fog-smoke
    white,
Glimmered the white Moon-shine."

The ancient Mariner inhospitably killeth the pious bird of good omen.

"God save thee, ancient Mariner!
From the fiends, that plague thee
    thus!—   80
Why look'st thou so?"—With my cross-
    bow
I shot the ALBATROSS.

PART II

The Sun now rose upon the right:
Out of the sea came he,
Still hid in mist, and on the left
Went down into the sea.

And the good south wind still blew
    behind,
But no sweet bird did follow,
Nor any day for food or play
Came to the mariners' hollo!   90

His shipmates
cry out against
the ancient
Mariner, for
killing the
bird of good
luck.

And I had done a hellish thing,
And it would work 'em woe:
For all averred, I had killed the bird
That made the breeze to blow.
Ah wretch! said they, the bird to slay,
That made the breeze to blow!

But when the
fog cleared
off, they just-
ify the same,
and thus make
themselves ac-
complices in
the crime.

Nor dim nor red, like God's own head,
The glorious Sun uprist:
Then all averred, I had killed the bird
That brought the fog and mist.   100
'Twas right, said they, such birds to slay,
That bring the fog and mist.

The fair
breeze con-
tinues; the
ship enters the
Pacific Ocean,
and sails
northward,
even till it
reaches the
Line.

The fair breeze blew, the white foam
    flew,
The furrow followed free;
We were the first that ever burst
Into that silent sea.

The ship hath
been suddenly
becalmed.

Down dropt the breeze, the sails dropt
    down,
'Twas sad as sad could be;
And we did speak only to break
The silence of the sea!   110

All in a hot and copper sky,
The bloody Sun, at noon,
Right up above the mast did stand,
No bigger than the Moon.

Day after day, day after day,
We stuck, nor breath nor motion;
As idle as a painted ship
Upon a painted ocean.

And the Al-
batross be-
gins to be
avenged,

Water, water, every where,
And all the boards did shrink;   120
Water, water, every where,
Nor any drop to drink.

The very deep did rot: O Christ!
That ever this should be!
Yea, slimy things did crawl with legs
Upon the slimy sea.

105. We were the first, one of several hints about the
time of the voyage—crossbow, Catholic prayers of the crew
(pre-Reformation touch). Note others.

A Spirit had
followed them;
one of the in-
visible inhabit-
ants of this
planet, nei-
ther departed
souls nor an-
gels; concern-
ing whom the
learned Jew,
Josephus, and
the Platonic
Constantino-
politan, Mi-
chael Psellus,
may be con-
sulted. They
are very nu-
merous, and
there is no
climate or ele-
ment without
one or more.

About, about, in reel and rout
The death-fires danced at night;
The water, like a witch's oils,
Burnt green, and blue and white.   130

And some in dreams assurèd were
Of the Spirit that plagued us so;
Nine fathom deep he had followed us
From the land of mist and snow.

And every tongue, through utter
    drought,
Was withered at the root;
We could not speak, no more than if
We had been choked with soot.

The ship-
mates, in
their sore dis-
tress, would
fain throw the
whole guilt on
the ancient
Mariner: in
sign whereof
they hang the
dead sea-bird
round his
neck.

Ah! well a-day! what evil looks
Had I from old and young!   140
Instead of the cross, the Albatross
About my neck was hung.

PART III

There passed a weary time. Each throat
Was parched, and glazed each eye.
A weary time! a weary time!
How glazed each weary eye,

The ancient
Mariner be-
holdeth a sign
in the element
afar off.

When looking westward, I beheld
A something in the sky.

At first it seemed a little speck,
And then it seemed a mist;   150
It moved and moved, and took at last
A certain shape, I wist.

A speck, a mist, a shape, I wist!
And still it neared and neared:
As if it dodged a water-sprite,
It plunged and tacked and veered.

At its nearer
approach, it
seemeth him
to be a ship;
and at a dear
ransom he
freeth his
speech from
the bonds of
thirst.

With throats unslaked, with black lips
    baked,
We could nor laugh nor wail;
Through utter drought all dumb we
    stood!
I bit my arm, I sucked the blood,   160
And cried, A sail! a sail!

A flash of
joy;

With throats unslaked, with black lips
    baked,
Agape they heard me call:
Gramercy! they for joy did grin,
And all at one their breath drew in,
As they were drinking all.

And horror follows. For can it be a ship that comes onward without wind or tide?

See! see! (I cried) she tacks no more!
Hither to work us weal;
Without a breeze, without a tide,
She steadies with upright keel!　170

The western wave was all a-flame.
The day was well nigh done!
Almost upon the western wave
Rested the broad bright Sun;
When that strange shape drove suddenly
Betwixt us and the Sun.

It seemeth him but the skeleton of a ship.

And straight the Sun was flecked with bars,
(Heaven's Mother send us grace!)
As if through a dungeon-grate he peered
With broad and burning face.　180

Alas! (thought I, and my heart beat loud)
How fast she nears and nears!
Are those her sails that glance in the Sun,
Like restless gossameres?

And its ribs are seen as bars on the face of the setting Sun.

Are those her ribs through which the Sun
Did peer, as through a grate?

The Spectre-Woman and her Death-mate, and no other on board the skeleton ship.

And is that Woman all her crew?
Is that a Death? and are there two?
Is Death that woman's mate?

Like vessel, like crew!

Her lips were red, her looks were free,
Her locks were yellow as gold:　191
Her skin was as white as leprosy,
The Night-mare Life-in-Death was she,
Who thicks man's blood with cold.

Death and Life-in-Death have diced for the ship's crew, and she (the latter) winneth the ancient Mariner.

The naked hulk alongside came,
And the twain were casting dice;
"The game is done! I've won! I've won!"
Quoth she, and whistles thrice.

No twilight within the courts of the Sun.

The Sun's rim dips; the stars rush out:
At one stride comes the dark;　200
With far-heard whisper, o'er the sea,
Off shot the spectre-bark.

At the rising of the Moon,

We listened and looked sideways up!
Fear at my heart, as at a cup,
My life-blood seemed to sip!
The stars were dim, and thick the night,
The steersman's face by his lamp gleamed white;

From the sails the dew did drip—
Till clomb above the eastern bar
The hornèd Moon, with one bright star
Within the nether tip.　211

One after another,

One after one, by the star-dogged Moon,
Too quick for groan or sigh,
Each turned his face with a ghastly pang,
And cursed me with his eye.

His shipmates drop down dead.

Four times fifty living men,
(And I heard nor sigh nor groan)
With heavy thump, a lifeless lump,
They dropped down one by one.

But Life-in-Death begins her work on the ancient Mariner.

The souls did from their bodies fly,—
They fled to bliss or woe!　221
And every soul, it passed me by,
Like the whizz of my cross-bow!

Part IV

The Wedding-Guest feareth that a Spirit is talking to him;

"I fear thee, ancient Mariner!
I fear thy skinny hand!
And thou art long, and lank, and brown,
As is the ribbed sea-sand.

I fear thee and thy glittering eye,
And thy skinny hand, so brown."—

But the ancient Mariner assureth him of his bodily life, and proceedeth to relate his horrible penance.

Fear not, fear not, thou Wedding-Guest!
This body dropt not down.　231

Alone, alone, all, all alone,
Alone on a wide wide sea!
And never a saint took pity on
My soul in agony.

He despiseth the creatures of the calm,

The many men, so beautiful!
And they all dead did lie:
And a thousand thousand slimy things
Lived on; and so did I.

And envieth that *they* should live, and so many lie dead.

I looked upon the rotting sea,　240
And drew my eyes away;
I looked upon the rotting deck,
And there the dead men lay.

I looked to heaven, and tried to pray;
But or ever a prayer had gusht,
A wicked whisper came, and made
My heart as dry as dust.

I closed my lids, and kept them close,
And the balls like pulses beat;
For the sky and the sea, and the sea and
    the sky   250
Lay like a load on my weary eye,
And the dead were at my feet.

But the curse liveth for him in the eye of the dead men.

The cold sweat melted from their limbs,
Nor rot nor reek did they:
The look with which they looked on me
Had never passed away.

In his loneliness and fixedness he yearneth towards the journeying Moon, and the stars that still sojourn, yet still move onward; and every where the blue sky belongs to them, and is their appointed rest, and their native country and their own natural homes, which they enter unannounced, as lords that are certainly expected and yet there is a silent joy at their arrival.

An orphan's curse would drag to hell
A spirit from on high;
But oh! more horrible than that
Is the curse in a dead man's eye!   260
Seven days, seven nights, I saw that
    curse,
And yet I could not die.

The moving Moon went up the sky,
And no where did abide:
Softly she was going up,
And a star or two beside—

Her beams bemocked the sultry main,
Like April hoar-frost spread;
But where the ship's huge shadow lay,
The charmèd water burnt alway   270
A still and awful red.

By the light of the Moon he beholdeth God's creatures of the great calm.

Beyond the shadow of the ship,
I watched the water-snakes:
They moved in tracks of shining white,
And when they reared, the elfish light
Fell off in hoary flakes.

Within the shadow of the ship
I watched their rich attire:
Blue, glossy green, and velvet black,
They coiled and swam; and every track
Was a flash of golden fire.   281

Their beauty and their happiness.

He blesseth them in his heart.

O happy living things! no tongue
Their beauty might declare:
A spring of love gushed from my heart,
And I blessed them unaware:
Sure my kind saint took pity on me,
And I blessed them unaware.

The spell begins to break.

The selfsame moment I could pray;
And from my neck so free
The Albatross fell off, and sank   290
Like lead into the sea.

PART V

Oh sleep! it is a gentle thing,
Beloved from pole to pole!
To Mary Queen the praise be given!
She sent the gentle sleep from Heaven,
That slid into my soul.

By grace of the holy Mother, the ancient Mariner is refreshed with rain.

The silly buckets on the deck,
That had so long remained,
I dreamt that they were filled with dew;
And when I awoke, it rained.   300

My lips were wet, my throat was cold,
My garments all were dank;
Sure I had drunken in my dreams,
And still my body drank.

I moved, and could not feel my limbs:
I was so light—almost
I thought that I had died in sleep,
And was a blessèd ghost.

He heareth sounds and seeth strange sights and commotions in the sky and the element.

And soon I heard a roaring wind:
It did not come anear;   310
But with its sound it shook the sails,
That were so thin and sere.

The upper air burst into life!
And a hundred fire-flags sheen,
To and fro they were hurried about!
And to and fro, and in and out,
The wan stars danced between.

And the coming wind did roar more
    loud,
And the sails did sigh like sedge;
And the rain poured down from one
    black cloud;   320
The Moon was at its edge.

The thick black cloud was cleft, and still
The Moon was at its side:
Like waters shot from some high crag,
The lightning fell with never a jag,
A river steep and wide.

The bodies of the ship's crew are inspired, and the ship moves on;

The loud wind never reached the ship,
Yet now the ship moved on!
Beneath the lightning and the Moon
The dead men gave a groan.   330

They groaned, they stirred, they all up-
    rose,
Nor spake, nor moved their eyes;

It had been strange, even in a dream,
To have seen those dead men rise.

The helmsman steered, the ship moved on;
Yet never a breeze up blew;
The mariners all 'gan work the ropes,
Where they were wont to do;
They raised their limbs like lifeless
    tools—
We were a ghastly crew.   340

The body of my brother's son
Stood by me, knee to knee:
The body and I pulled at one rope
But he said nought to me.

But not by the souls of the men, nor by daemons of earth or middle air, but by a blessed troop of angelic spirits, sent down by the invocation of the guardian saint.

"I fear thee, ancient Mariner!"
Be calm, thou Wedding-Guest!
'Twas not those souls that fled in pain,
Which to their corses came again,
But a troop of spirits blest:

For when it dawned—they dropped
    their arms,   350
And clustered round the mast;
Sweet sounds rose slowly through their
    mouths,
And from their bodies passed.

Around, around, flew each sweet sound,
Then darted to the Sun;
Slowly the sounds came back again,
Now mixed, now one by one.

Sometimes a-dropping from the sky
I heard the sky-lark sing;
Sometimes all little birds that are,   360
How they seemed to fill the sea and air
With their sweet jargoning!

And now 'twas like all instruments,
Now like a lonely flute;
And now it is an angel's song,
That makes the heavens be mute.

It ceased; yet still the sails made on
A pleasant noise till noon,
A noise like of a hidden brook
In the leafy month of June,   370
That to the sleeping woods all night
Singeth a quiet tune.

Till noon we quietly sailed on,
Yet never a breeze did breathe:

Slowly and smoothly went the ship,
Moved onward from beneath.

The lonesome Spirit from the south-pole carries on the ship as far as the Line, in obedience to the angelic troop, but still requireth vengeance.

Under the keel nine fathom deep,
From the land of mist and snow,
The spirit slid: and it was he
That made the ship to go.   380
The sails at noon left off their tune,
And the ship stood still also.

The Sun, right up above the mast,
Had fixed her to the ocean:
But in a minute she 'gan stir,
With a short uneasy motion—
Backwards and forwards half her length
With a short uneasy motion.

Then like a pawing horse let go,
She made a sudden bound: 390
It flung the blood into my head,
And I fell down in a swound.

The Polar Spirit's fellow-daemons, the invisible inhabitants of the element, take part in his wrong; and two of them relate, one to the other, that penance long and heavy for the ancient Mariner hath been accorded to the Polar Spirit, who returneth southward.

How long in that same fit I lay,
I have not to declare;
But ere my living life returned,
I heard and in my soul discerned
Two voices in the air.

"Is it he?" quoth one, "Is this the man?
By him who died on cross,
With his cruel bow he laid full low   400
The harmless Albatross.

"The spirit who bideth by himself
In the land of mist and snow,
He loved the bird that loved the man
Who shot him with his bow."

The other was a softer voice,
As soft as honey-dew:
Quoth he, "The man hath penance done,
And penance more will do."

PART VI

FIRST VOICE

"But tell me, tell me! speak again,   41c
Thy soft response renewing—
What makes that ship drive on so fast?
What is the ocean doing?"

SECOND VOICE

"Still as a slave before his lord,
The ocean hath no blast;

His great bright eye most silently
Up to the Moon is cast—

"If he may know which way to go;
For she guides him smooth or grim.
See, brother, see! how graciously   420
She looketh down on him."

FIRST VOICE

The Mariner
hath been cast
into a trance;
for the angelic
power causeth
the vessel to
drive north-
ward faster
than human
life could en-
dure.

"But why drives on that ship so fast,
Without or wave or wind?"

SECOND VOICE

"The air is cut away before,
And closes from behind.

"Fly, brother, fly! more high, more high!
Or we shall be belated:
For slow and slow that ship will go,
When the Mariner's trance is abated."

The supernat-
ural motion is
retarded; the
Mariner
awakes, and
his penance
begins anew.

I woke, and we were sailing on   430
As in a gentle weather:
'Twas night, calm night, the moon was
    high;
The dead men stood together.

All stood together on the deck,
For a charnel-dungeon fitter:
All fixed on me their stony eyes,
That in the Moon did glitter.

The pang, the curse, with which they
    died,
Had never passed away:
I could not draw my eyes from theirs,
Nor turn them up to pray.   441

The curse is
finally ex-
piated.

And now this spell was snapt: once more
I viewed the ocean green,
And looked far forth, yet little saw
Of what had else been seen—

Like one, that on a lonesome road
Doth walk in fear and dread,
And having once turned round walks on,
And turns no more his head;
Because he knows, a frightful fiend   450
Doth close behind him tread.

But soon there breathed a wind on me,
Nor sound nor motion made:
Its path was not upon the sea,
In ripple or in shade.

It raised my hair, it fanned my cheek
Like a meadow-gale of spring—
It mingled strangely with my fears,
Yet it felt like a welcoming.

Swiftly, swiftly flew the ship,   460
Yet she sailed softly too:
Sweetly, sweetly blew the breeze—
On me alone it blew.

And the an-
cient Mariner
beholdeth his
native coun-
try.

Oh! dream of joy! is this indeed
The light-house top I see?
Is this the hill? is this the kirk?
Is this mine own countree?

We drifted o'er the harbour-bar,
And I with sobs did pray—
O let me be awake, my God!   470
Or let me sleep alway.

The harbour-bay was clear as glass,
So smoothly it was strewn!
And on the bay the moonlight lay,
And the shadow of the Moon.

The rock shone bright, the kirk no less,
That stands above the rock:
The moonlight steeped in silentness
The steady weathercock.

The angelic
spirits leave
the dead bod-
ies,

And the bay was white with silent light,
Till rising from the same,   481
Full many shapes, that shadows were,
In crimson colours came.

And appear in
their own
forms of light.

A little distance from the prow
Those crimson shadows were:
I turned my eyes upon the deck—
Oh, Christ! what saw I there!

Each corse lay flat, lifeless and flat,
And, by the holy rood!
A man all light, a seraph-man,   490
On every corse there stood.

This seraph-band, each waved his hand:
It was a heavenly sight!
They stood as signals to the land,
Each one a lovely light;

This seraph-band, each waved his hand,
No voice did they impart—
No voice; but oh! the silence sank
Like music on my heart.

But soon I heard the dash of oars,   500
I heard the Pilot's cheer;
My head was turned perforce away
And I saw a boat appear.

The Pilot and the Pilot's boy,
I heard them coming fast:
Dear Lord in Heaven! it was a joy
The dead men could not blast.

I saw a third—I heard his voice:
It is the Hermit good!
He singeth loud his godly hymns   510
That he makes in the wood.
He'll shrieve my soul, he'll wash away
The Albatross's blood.

PART VII

The Hermit of
the Wood, This Hermit good lives in that wood
Which slopes down to the sea.
How loudly his sweet voice he rears!
He loves to talk with marineres
That come from a far countree.

He kneels at morn, and noon, and eve—
He hath a cushion plump: 520
It is the moss that wholly hides
The rotted old oak-stump.

The skiff-boat neared: I heard them talk,
"Why, this is strange, I trow!
Where are those lights so many and fair,
That signal made but now?"

Approacheth
the ship with
wonder. "Strange, by my faith!" the Hermit
    said—
"And they answered not our cheer!
The planks looked warped! and see
    those sails,
How thin they are and sere!   530
I never saw aught like to them,
Unless perchance it were

"Brown skeletons of leaves that lag
My forest-brook along;
When the ivy-tod is heavy with snow,
And the owlet whoops to the wolf below,
That eats the she-wolf's young."

"Dear Lord! it hath a fiendish look—
(The Pilot made reply)
I am a-feared"—"Push on, push on!"540
Said the Hermit cheerily.

The boat came closer to the ship,
But I nor spake nor stirred;
The boat came close beneath the ship,
And straight a sound was heard.

The ship sud-
denly sinketh. Under the water it rumbled on,
Still louder and more dread:
It reached the ship, it split the bay;
The ship went down like lead.

The ancient
Mariner is
saved in the
Pilot's boat. Stunned by that loud and dreadful
    sound,   550
Which sky and ocean smote,
Like one that hath been seven days
    drowned
My body lay afloat;
But swift as dreams, myself I found
Within the Pilot's boat.

Upon the whirl, where sank the ship,
The boat spun round and round;
And all was still, save that the hill
Was telling of the sound.

I moved my lips—the Pilot shrieked   560
And fell down in a fit;
The holy Hermit raised his eyes,
And prayed where he did sit.

I took the oars: the Pilot's boy,
Who now doth crazy go,
Laughed loud and long, and all the
    while
His eyes went to and fro.
"Ha! ha!" quoth he, "full plain I see,
The Devil knows how to row."

And now, all in my own countree,   570
I stood on the firm land!
The Hermit stepped forth from the
    boat,
And scarcely he could stand.

The ancient
Mariner earn-
estly entreat-
eth the Hermit
to shrieve him;
and the pen-
ance of life
falls on him. "O shrieve me, shrieve me, holy man!"
The Hermit crossed his brow.
"Say quick," quoth he, "I bid thee say—
What manner of man art thou?"

Forthwith this frame of mine was
    wrenched
With a woful agony,
Which forced me to begin my tale;   580
And then it left me free.

And ever and
anon through-
out his future
life an agony
constraineth
him to travel
from land to
land,

Since then, at an uncertain hour,
That agony returns:
And till my ghastly tale is told,
This heart within me burns.

I pass, like night, from land to land;
I have strange power of speech;
That moment that his face I see,
I know the man that must hear me:
To him my tale I teach.   590

What loud uproar bursts from that door!
The wedding-guests are there:
But in the garden-bower the bride
And bride-maids singing are:
And hark the little vesper bell,
Which biddeth me to prayer!

O Wedding-Guest! this soul hath been
Alone on a wide wide sea:
So lonely 'twas, that God himself
Scarce seeméd there to be.   600

O sweeter than the marriage-feast,
'Tis sweeter far to me,
To walk together to the kirk
With a goodly company!—

To walk together to the kirk,
And all together pray,
While each to his great Father bends,
Old men, and babes, and loving friends
And youths and maidens gay!

And to teach,
by his own ex-
ample, love
and reverence
to all things
that God
made and
loveth.

Farewell, farewell! but this I tell   610
To thee, thou Wedding-Guest!
He prayeth well, who loveth well
Both man and bird and beast.

He prayeth best, who loveth best
All things both great and small;
For the dear God who loveth us,
He made and loveth all.

The Mariner, whose eye is bright,
Whose beard with age is hoar,   619
Is gone: and now the Wedding-Guest
Turned from the bridegroom's door.

He went like one that hath been
    stunned,
And is of sense forlorn:
A sadder and a wiser man,
He rose the morrow morn.

"Christabel" is a fragment composed in bits at various times and places, changes of place having much to do with the scenery of the poem. In form, it is a metrical romance, versified in accordance with the system described in the "Preface" (which is not really new, as Coleridge says; Old English verse and the ballads used it). Its theme is "witchery by daylight." This is developed largely through the suggestion of atmosphere (the Gothic castle with its midnight clock, hooting owl, and crowing cock, its hint of "my lady's shroud," its surroundings of eerie moonlight and fairy wood), and through the character of Geraldine as a witch, or, as has been latterly suggested, a vampire (her strange and wild beauty, her fantastic story, her fainting at the threshold, and her inability to join in praise of the Virgin, her evocation of the mastiff bitch's growl and the flame's flare and the gleam on the shield, her curse on Christabel's mother when Christabel wishes for her, and so on). Geraldine's character is thrown into relief by contrast with the white purity and innocence of Christabel. The bewitchment of Christabel by the power of the eye (reminiscent of the hypnotism of the Ancient Mariner), taking the form of a spell upon her utterance which prevents her from expressing her sense of evil and denouncing her guest, throws into dramatic form the struggle between the powers of Evil and of Good. The conclusion to the poem, never written, would doubtless have shown "That saints will aid if men will call" (l. 330). In Part II, with its scenery of the North Country, Geraldine seems in a fair way to succeed after having literally "vamped" Sir Leoline and momentarily turned the tongue-tied Christabel into a hissing monster; and saints are clearly needed. Bracy the Bard, with his story of the dove and the bright green snake, is the readiest help. He is dispatched, like one of Sir Walter Scott's knights, to the castle of Sir Roland de Vaux of Tryermaine, the alleged father of Geraldine. Here the narrative proper stops short. In the sequel, as Coleridge is reported to have planned it, Bracy's quest is vain. Meanwhile, Geraldine assumes the form of Christabel's absent lover. The return of the true lover puts Geraldine to flight, and the wedding bells ring according to the prophecy in ll. 200–01. (For further details of the proposed completion, see B. R. McElderry's article in *Studies in Philology*, Vol. 33, and A. H. Nethercot's *The Road to Tryermaine*, University of Chicago Press, 1939.) In the absence of Coleridge's own handling of the conclusion in an artistic manner according with the part written, confident interpretation of the poem is perhaps impossible. That it remains a bafflingly beautiful fragment hardly detracts from it.

PREFACE

The first part of the following poem was written in the year one thousand seven hundred and ninety-seven, at Stowey, in the county of Somerset. The second part, after my return from Germany, in the year one thousand eight hundred, at Keswick, Cumberland. . . . It is probable, that if the poem had been finished at either of the former periods, or if even the first and second part had been published in the year 1800, the impression of its originality would have been much greater than I dare at present expect. But for this, I have only my own indolence to blame. The dates are mentioned for the exclusive purpose of precluding charges of plagiarism or servile imitation from myself. For there is amongst us a set of critics, who seem to hold, that every possible thought and image is traditional; who have no notion that there are such things as fountains in the world, small as well as great; and who would therefore charitably derive every rill they behold flowing, from a perforation made in some other man's tank. I am confident, however, that as far as the present poem is concerned, the celebrated poets [1] whose writings I might be suspected of having imitated, either in particular passages, or in the tone and the spirit of the whole, would be among the first to vindicate me from the charge, and who, on any striking coincidence, would permit me to address them in this doggerel version of two monkish Latin hexameters.

> "'Tis mine and it is likewise yours;
> But an if this will not do;
> Let it be mine, good friend! for I
> Am the poorer of the two."

I have only to add that the metre of Christabel is not, properly speaking, irregular, though it may seem so from its being founded on a new principle: namely, that of counting in each line the accents, not the syllables. Though the latter may vary from seven to twelve, yet in each line the accents will be found to be only four. Nevertheless this occasional variation in number of syllables is not introduced wantonly, or for the mere ends of convenience, but in correspondence with some transition, in the nature of the imagery or passion.

PART THE FIRST

'Tis the middle of night by the castle clock,
And the owls have awakened the crowing cock;
Tu—whit!——Tu—whoo!
And hark, again! the crowing cock,
How drowsily it crew.

Sir Leoline, the Baron rich,
Hath a toothless mastiff, which
From her kennel beneath the rock
Maketh answer to the clock,
Four for the quarters, and twelve for the hour;   10
Ever and aye, by shine and shower,
Sixteen short howls, not over loud;
Some say, she sees my lady's shroud.

Is the night chilly and dark?
The night is chilly, but not dark.

[1] **celebrated poets,** Sir Walter Scott and Lord Byron.

The thin gray cloud is spread on high,
It covers but not hides the sky.
The moon is behind, and at the full;
And yet she looks both small and dull.
The night is chill, the cloud is gray: 20
'Tis a month before the month of May,
And the Spring comes slowly up this way.

The lovely lady, Christabel,
Whom her father loves so well,
What makes her in the wood so late,
A furlong from the castle gate?
She had dreams all yesternight
Of her own betrothèd knight;
And she in the midnight wood will pray
For the weal of her lover that's far away.   30

She stole along, she nothing spoke,
The sighs she heaved were soft and low,
And naught was green upon the oak
But moss and rarest mistletoe:
She kneels beneath the huge oak tree,
And in silence prayeth she.

The lady sprang up suddenly,
The lovely lady, Christabel!
It moaned as near, as near can be,
But what it is she cannot tell.—   40
On the other side it seems to be,
Of the huge, broad-breasted, old oak tree.

The night is chill; the forest bare;
Is it the wind that moaneth bleak?
There is not wind enough in the air
To move away the ringlet curl
From the lovely lady's cheek—
There is not wind enough to twirl
The one red leaf, the last of its clan,
That dances as often as dance it can,   50
Hanging so light, and hanging so high,
On the topmost twig that looks up at the sky.

Hush, beating heart of Christabel!
Jesu, Maria, shield her well!
She folded her arms beneath her cloak,
And stole to the other side of the oak.
    What sees she there?

There she sees a damsel bright,
Drest in a silken robe of white,
That shadowy in the moonlight shone: 60
The neck that made that white robe wan,
Her stately neck, and arms were bare;
Her blue-veined feet unsandaled were,

And wildly glittered here and there
The gems entangled in her hair.
I guess, 'twas frightful there to see
A lady so richly clad as she—
Beautiful exceedingly!

Mary mother, save me now!
(Said Christabel,) And who art thou?   70

The lady strange made answer meet,
And her voice was faint and sweet:—
Have pity on my sore distress,
I scarce can speak for weariness:
Stretch forth thy hand, and have no fear!
Said Christabel, How camest thou here?
And the lady, whose voice was faint and sweet,
Did thus pursue her answer meet:—

My sire is of a noble line,
And my name is Geraldine: 80
Five warriors seized me yestermorn,
Me, even me, a maid forlorn:
They choked my cries with force and fright,
And tied me on a palfrey white.
The palfrey was as fleet as wind,
And they rode furiously behind.
They spurred amain, their steeds were white:
And once we crossed the shade of night.
As sure as Heaven shall rescue me,
I have no thought what men they be;   90
Nor do I know how long it is
(For I have lain entranced I wis)
Since one, the tallest of the five,
Took me from the palfrey's back,
A weary woman, scarce alive.
Some muttered words his comrades spoke:
He placed me underneath this oak;
He swore they would return with haste;
Whither they went I cannot tell—
I thought I heard, some minutes past,   100
Sounds as of a castle bell.
Stretch forth thy hand (thus ended she),
And help a wretched maid to flee.

Then Christabel stretched forth her hand,
And comforted fair Geraldine:
O well, bright dame! may you command
The service of Sir Leoline;
And gladly our stout chivalry
Will he send forth and friends withal
To guide and guard you safe and free   110
Home to your noble father's hall.

She rose: and forth with steps they passed
That strove to be, and were not, fast.

Her gracious stars the lady blest,
And thus spake on sweet Christabel:
All our household are at rest,
The hall as silent as the cell;
Sir Leoline is weak in health,
And may not well awakened be,
But we will move as if in stealth,   120
And I beseech your courtesy,
This night, to share your couch with me.

They crossed the moat, and Christabel
Took the key that fitted well;
A little door she opened straight,
All in the middle of the gate;
The gate that was ironed within and without,
Where an army in battle array had marched out.
The lady sank, belike through pain,
And Christabel with might and main   130
Lifted her up, a weary weight,
Over the threshold of the gate:
Then the lady rose again,
And moved, as she were not in pain.

So free from danger, free from fear,
They crossed the court: right glad they were.
And Christabel devoutly cried
To the lady by her side,
Praise we the Virgin all divine
Who hath rescued thee from thy distress!   140
Alas, alas! said Geraldine,
I cannot speak for weariness.
So free from danger, free from fear,
They crossed the court: right glad they were.

Outside her kennel, the mastiff old
Lay fast asleep, in moonshine cold.
The mastiff old did not awake,
Yet she an angry moan did make!
And what can ail the mastiff bitch?
Never till now she uttered yell   150
Beneath the eye of Christabel.
Perhaps it is the owlet's scritch:
For what can ail the mastiff bitch?

They passed the hall, that echoes still,
Pass as lightly as you will!
The brands were flat, the brands were dying,
Amid their own white ashes lying;
But when the lady passed, there came
A tongue of light, a fit of flame;
And Christabel saw the lady's eye,   160
And nothing else saw she thereby,
Save the boss of the shield of Sir Leoline tall,
Which hung in a murky old niche in the wall.

O softly tread, said Christabel,
My father seldom sleepeth well.

Sweet Christabel her feet doth bare,
And jealous of the listening air
They steal their way from stair to stair,
Now in glimmer, and now in gloom,
And now they pass the Baron's room,   170
As still as death, with stifled breath!
And now have reached her chamber door;
And now doth Geraldine press down
The rushes of the chamber floor.

The moon shines dim in the open air,
And not a moonbeam enters here.
But they without its light can see
The chamber carved so curiously,
Carved with figures strange and sweet,
All made out of the carver's brain,   180
For a lady's chamber meet:
The lamp with twofold silver chain
Is fastened to an angel's feet.

The silver lamp burns dead and dim;
But Christabel the lamp will trim.
She trimmed the lamp, and made it bright,
And left it swinging to and fro,
While Geraldine, in wretched plight,
Sank down upon the floor below.

O weary lady, Geraldine,   190
I pray you, drink this cordial wine!
It is a wine of virtuous powers;
My mother made it of wild flowers.

And will your mother pity me,
Who am a maiden most forlorn?
Christabel answered—Woe is me!
She died the hour that I was born.
I have heard the grey-haired friar tell
How on her death-bed she did say,
That she should hear the castle-bell   200
Strike twelve upon my wedding-day.
O mother dear! that thou wert here!
I would, said Geraldine, she were!

But soon with altered voice, said she—
"Off, wandering mother! Peak and pine!
I have power to bid thee flee."
Alas! what ails poor Geraldine?
Why stares she with unsettled eye?
Can she the bodiless dead espy?
And why with hollow voice cries she,   210
"Off, woman, off! this hour is mine—

Though thou her guardian spirit be,
Off, woman, off! 'tis given to me."

Then Christabel knelt by the lady's side,
And raised to heaven her eyes so blue—
Alas! said she, this ghastly ride—
Dear lady! it hath wildered you!
The lady wiped her moist cold brow,
And faintly said, "'tis over now!"

Again the wild-flower wine she drank: 220
Her fair large eyes 'gan glitter bright,
And from the floor whereon she sank,
The lofty lady stood upright:
She was most beautiful to see,
Like a lady of a far countrée.

And thus the lofty lady spake—
"All they who live in the upper sky,
Do love you, holy Christabel!
And you love them, and for their sake
And for the good which me befel,   230
Even I in my degree will try,
Fair maiden, to requite you well.
But now unrobe yourself; for I
Must pray, ere yet in bed I lie."

Quoth Christabel, So let it be!
And as the lady bade, did she.
Her gentle limbs did she undress,
And lay down in her loveliness.

But through her brain of weal and woe
So many thoughts moved to and fro,   240
That vain it were her lids to close;
So half-way from the bed she rose,
And on her elbow did recline
To look at the lady Geraldine.

Beneath the lamp the lady bowed,
And slowly rolled her eyes around;
Then drawing in her breath aloud,
Like one that shuddered, she unbound
The cincture from beneath her breast:
Her silken robe, and inner vest,   250
Dropt to her feet, and full in view,
Behold! her bosom and half her side—
A sight to dream of, not to tell!
O shield her! shield sweet Christabel!

Yet Geraldine nor speaks nor stirs;
Ah! what a stricken look was hers!
Deep from within she seems half-way
To lift some weight with sick assay,

And eyes the maid and seeks delay;
Then suddenly, as one defied,   260
Collects herself in scorn and pride,
And lay down by the Maiden's side!—
And in her arms the maid she took,
    Ah wel-a-day!
And with low voice and doleful look
These words did say:
"In the touch of this bosom there worketh a spell,
Which is lord of thy utterance, Christabel!
Thou knowest to-night, and wilt know to-morrow,
This mark of my shame, this seal of my sorrow; 270
   But vainly thou warrest,
    For this is alone in
   Thy power to declare,
    That in the dim forest,
   Thou heard'st a low moaning,
And found'st a bright lady, surpassingly fair;
And didst bring her home with thee in love and in
  charity,
To shield her and shelter her from the damp air."

THE CONCLUSION TO PART THE FIRST

It was a lovely sight to see
The lady Christabel, when she   280
Was praying at the old oak tree.
   Amid the jagged shadows
   Of mossy leafless boughs,
   Kneeling in the moonlight,
   To make her gentle vows;
Her slender palms together prest,
Heaving sometimes on her breast;
Her face resigned to bliss or bale—
Her face, oh call it fair not pale,
And both blue eyes more bright than clear, 290
Each about to have a tear.

With open eyes (ah woe is me!)
Asleep, and dreaming fearfully,
Fearfully dreaming, yet, I wis,
Dreaming that alone, which is—
O sorrow and shame! Can this be she,
The lady, who knelt at the old oak tree?
And lo! the worker of these harms,
That holds the maiden in her arms,
Seems to slumber still and mild,   300
As a mother with her child.

A star hath set, a star hath risen,
O Geraldine! since arms of thine
Have been the lovely lady's prison.
O Geraldine! one hour was thine—

Thou'st had thy will! By tairn and rill,
The night-birds all that hour were still.
But now they are jubilant anew.
From cliff and tower, tu—whoo! tu—whoo!
Tu—whoo! tu—whoo! from wood and fell! 310

And see! the lady Christabel
Gathers herself from out her trance;
Her limbs relax, her countenance
Grows sad and soft; the smooth thin lids
Close o'er her eyes; and tears she sheds—
Large tears that leave the lashes bright!
And oft the while she seems to smile
As infants at a sudden light!

Yea, she doth smile, and she doth weep,
Like a youthful hermitess,   320
Beauteous in a wilderness,
Who, praying always, prays in sleep.
And, if she move unquietly,
Perchance, 'tis but the blood so free
Comes back and tingles in her feet.
No doubt, she hath a vision sweet.
What if her guardian spirit 'twere,
What if she knew her mother near?
But this she knows, in joys and woes,
That saints will aid if men will call: 330
For the blue sky bends over all!

PART THE SECOND

Each matin bell, the Baron saith,
Knells us back to a world of death.
These words Sir Leoline first said,
When he rose and found his lady dead:
These words Sir Leoline will say
Many a morn to his dying day!

And hence the custom and law began
That still at dawn the sacristan,
Who duly pulls the heavy bell,   340
Five and forty beads must tell
Between each stroke—a warning knell,
Which not a soul can choose but hear
From Bratha Head to Wyndermere.

Saith Bracy the bard, So let it knell!
And let the drowsy sacristan
Still count as slowly as he can!
There is no lack of such, I ween,
As well fill up the space between.
In Langdale Pike and Witch's Lair,   350
And Dungeon-ghyll so foully rent,

306. tairn, a small mountain lake or pond, tarn.

With ropes of rock and bells of air
Three sinful sextons' ghosts are pent,
Who all give back, one after t'other,
The death-note to their living brother;
And oft too, by the knell offended,
Just as their one! two! three! is ended,
The devil mocks the doleful tale
With a merry peal from Borodale.

The air is still! through mist and cloud   360
That merry peal comes ringing loud;
And Geraldine shakes off her dread,
And rises lightly from the bed;
Puts on her silken vestments white,
And tricks her hair in lovely plight,
And nothing doubting of her spell
Awakens the lady Christabel.
"Sleep you, sweet lady Christabel?
I trust that you have rested well."

And Christabel awoke and spied   370
The same who lay down by her side—
O rather say, the same whom she
Raised up beneath the old oak tree!
Nay, fairer yet! and yet more fair!
For she belike hath drunken deep
Of all the blessedness of sleep!
And while she spake, her looks, her air
Such gentle thankfulness declare,
That (so it seemed) her girded vests
Grew tight beneath her heaving breasts.   380
"Sure I have sinned!" said Christabel,
"Now heaven be praised if all be well!"
And in low faltering tones, yet sweet,
Did she the lofty lady greet
With such perplexity of mind
As dreams too lively leave behind.

So quickly she rose, and quickly arrayed
Her maiden limbs, and having prayed
That He, who on the cross did groan,
Might wash away her sins unknown,   390
She forthwith led fair Geraldine
To meet her sire, Sir Leoline.

The lovely maid and the lady tall
Are pacing both into the hall,
And pacing on through page and groom,
Enter the Baron's presence-room.

The Baron rose, and while he prest
His gentle daughter to his breast,
With cheerful wonder in his eyes
The lady Geraldine espies,   400

And gave such welcome to the same,
As might beseem so bright a dame!

But when he heard the lady's tale,
And when she told her father's name,
Why waxed Sir Leoline so pale,
Murmuring o'er the name again,
Lord Roland de Vaux of Tryermaine?

Alas! they had been friends in youth;
But whispering tongues can poison truth;
And constancy lives in realms above;   410
And life is thorny; and youth is vain;
And to be wroth with one we love
Doth work like madness in the brain.
And thus it chanced, as I divine,
With Roland and Sir Leoline.
Each spake words of high disdain
And insult to his heart's best brother:
They parted—ne'er to meet again!
But never either found another
To free the hollow heart from paining—   420
They stood aloof, the scars remaining,
Like cliffs which had been rent asunder;
A dreary sea now flows between.
But neither heat, nor frost, nor thunder,
Shall wholly do away, I ween,
The marks of that which once hath been.

Sir Leoline, a moment's space,
Stood gazing on the damsel's face:
And the youthful Lord of Tryermaine
Came back upon his heart again.   430

O then the Baron forgot his age,
His noble heart swelled high with rage;
He swore by the wounds in Jesu's side
He would proclaim it far and wide,
With trump and solemn heraldry,
That they, who thus had wronged the dame,
Were base as spotted infamy!
"And if they dare deny the same,
My herald shall appoint a week,
And let the recreant traitors seek   440
My tourney court—that there and then
I may dislodge their reptile souls
From the bodies and forms of men!"
He spake: his eye in lightning rolls!
For the lady was ruthlessly seized; and he kenned
In the beautiful lady the child of his friend!

And now the tears were on his face,
And fondly in his arms he took
Fair Geraldine, who met the embrace,
Prolonging it with joyous look.   450

Which when she viewed, a vision fell
Upon the soul of Christabel,
The vision of fear, the touch and pain!
She shrunk and shuddered, and saw again—
(Ah, woe is me! Was it for thee,
Thou gentle maid! such sights to see?)

Again she saw that bosom old,
Again she felt that bosom cold,
And drew in her breath with a hissing sound:
Whereat the Knight turned wildly round,   460
And nothing saw, but his own sweet maid
With eyes upraised, as one that prayed.

The touch, the sight, had passed away,
And in its stead that vision blest,
Which comforted her after-rest
While in the lady's arms she lay,
Had put a rapture in her breast,
And on her lips and o'er her eyes
Spread smiles like light!
                With new surprise,
"What ails then my belovèd child?"   470
The Baron said—His daughter mild
Made answer, "All will yet be well!"
I ween, she had no power to tell
Aught else: so mighty was the spell.
Yet he, who saw this Geraldine,
Had deemed her sure a thing divine,
Such sorrow with such grace she blended,
As if she feared she had offended
Sweet Christabel, that gentle maid!
And with such lowly tones she prayed   480
She might be sent without delay
Home to her father's mansion.
                       "Nay!
Nay, by my soul!" said Leoline.
"Ho! Bracy the bard, the charge be thine!
Go thou, with music sweet and loud,
And take two steeds with trappings proud,
And take the youth whom thou lov'st best
To bear thy harp, and learn thy song,
And clothe you both in solemn vest,
And over the mountains haste along,   490
Lest wandering folk, that are abroad,
Detain you on the valley road.

"And when he has crossed the Irthing flood,
My merry bard! he hastes, he hastes
Up Knorren Moor, through Halegarth Wood,
And reaches soon that castle good
Which stands and threatens Scotland's wastes.

"Bard Bracy! bard Bracy! your horses are fleet,
Ye must ride up the hall, your music so sweet,

More loud than your horses' echoing feet!   500
And loud and loud to Lord Roland call,
Thy daughter is safe in Langdale hall!
Thy beautiful daughter is safe and free—
Sir Leoline greets thee thus through me!
He bids thee come without delay
With all thy numerous array;
And take thy lovely daughter home:
And he will meet thee on the way
With all his numerous array
White with their panting palfreys' foam: 510
And, by mine honour! I will say,
That I repent me of the day
When I spake words of fierce disdain
To Roland de Vaux of Tryermaine!—
—For since that evil hour hath flown,
Many a summer's sun hath shone;
Yet ne'er found I a friend again
Like Roland de Vaux of Tryermaine."

The lady fell, and clasped his knees,
Her face upraised, her eyes o'erflowing;   520
And Bracy replied, with faltering voice,
His gracious hail on all bestowing!—
"Thy words, thou sire of Christabel,
Are sweeter than my harp can tell;
Yet might I gain a boon of thee,
This day my journey should not be,
So strange a dream hath come to me;
That I had vowed with music loud
To clear yon wood from thing unblest,
Warned by a vision in my rest!   530
For in my sleep I saw that dove,
That gentle bird, whom thou dost love,
And call'st by thy own daughter's name—
Sir Leoline! I saw the same
Fluttering, and uttering fearful moan,
Among the green herbs in the forest alone.
Which when I saw and when I heard,
I wondered what might ail the bird;
For nothing near it could I see,
Save the grass and green herbs underneath the old
   tree.   540

"And in my dream, methought, I went
To search out what might there be found;
And what the sweet bird's trouble meant,
That thus lay fluttering on the ground.
I went and peered, and could descry
No cause for her distressful cry;
But yet for her dear lady's sake
I stooped, methought, the dove to take,
When lo! I saw a bright green snake
Coiled around its wings and neck.   550

Green as the herbs on which it couched,
Close by the dove's its head it crouched;
And with the dove it heaves and stirs,
Swelling its neck as she swelled hers!
I woke; it was the midnight hour,
The clock was echoing in the tower;
But though my slumber was gone by,
This dream it would not pass away—
It seems to live upon my eye!
And thence I vowed this self-same day   560
With music strong and saintly song
To wander through the forest bare,
Lest aught unholy loiter there."

Thus Bracy said: the Baron, the while,
Half-listening heard him with a smile;
Then turned to Lady Geraldine,
His eyes made up of wonder and love;
And said in courtly accents fine,
"Sweet maid, Lord Roland's beauteous dove,
With arms more strong than harp or song,   570
Thy sire and I will crush the snake!"
He kissed her forehead as he spake,
And Geraldine in maiden wise
Casting down her large bright eyes,
With blushing cheek and courtesy fine
She turned her from Sir Leoline;
Softly gathering up her train,
That o'er her right arm fell again;
And folded her arms across her chest,
And couched her head upon her breast,   580
And looked askance at Christabel—
Jesu, Maria, shield her well!

A snake's small eye blinks dull and shy;
And the lady's eyes they shrunk in her head,
Each shrunk up to a serpent's eye,
And with somewhat of malice, and more of dread,
At Christabel she looked askance!—
One moment—and the sight was fled!
But Christabel in dizzy trance
Stumbling on the unsteady ground   590
Shuddered aloud, with a hissing sound;
And Geraldine again turned round,
And like a thing, that sought relief,
Full of wonder and full of grief,
She rolled her large bright eyes divine
Wildly on Sir Leoline.

The maid, alas! her thoughts are gone,
She nothing sees—no sight but one!
The maid, devoid of guile and sin,
I know not how, in fearful wise,   600
So deeply had she drunken in

That look, those shrunken serpent eyes,
That all her features were resigned
To this sole image in her mind:
And passively did imitate
That look of dull and treacherous hate!
And thus she stood, in dizzy trance,
Still picturing that look askance
With forced unconscious sympathy
Full before her father's view—   610
As far as such a look could be
In eyes so innocent and blue!

And when the trance was o'er, the maid
Paused awhile, and inly prayed:
Then falling at the Baron's feet,
"By my mother's soul do I entreat
That thou this woman send away!"
She said; and more she could not say:
For what she knew she could not tell,
O'er-mastered by the mighty spell.   620

Why is thy cheek so wan and wild,
Sir Leoline? Thy only child
Lies at thy feet, thy joy, thy pride,
So fair, so innocent, so mild;
The same, for whom thy lady died!
O, by the pangs of her dear mother
Think thou no evil of thy child!
For her, and thee, and for no other,
She prayed the moment ere she died:
Prayed that the babe for whom she died,   630
Might prove her dear lord's joy and pride!
    That prayer her deadly pangs beguiled,
        Sir Leoline!
    And wouldst thou wrong thy only child,
        Her child and thine?

Within the Baron's heart and brain
If thoughts, like these, had any share,
They only swelled his rage and pain,
And did but work confusion there.
His heart was cleft with pain and rage,   640
His cheeks they quivered, his eyes were wild,
Dishonoured thus in his old age;
Dishonoured by his only child,
And all his hospitality
To the wronged daughter of his friend
By more than woman's jealousy
Brought thus to a disgraceful end—
He rolled his eye with stern regard
Upon the gentle minstrel bard,
And said in tones abrupt, austere—   650
"Why, Bracy! dost thou loiter here?
I bade thee hence!" The bard obeyed;

And turning from his own sweet maid,
The agèd knight, Sir Leoline,
Led forth the lady Geraldine!

THE CONCLUSION TO PART THE SECOND

A little child, a limber elf,
Singing, dancing to itself,
A fairy thing with red round cheeks,
That always finds, and never seeks,
Makes such a vision to the sight   660
As fills a father's eyes with light;
And pleasures flow in so thick and fast
Upon his heart, that he at last
Must needs express his love's excess
With words of unmeant bitterness.
Perhaps 'tis pretty to force together
Thoughts so all unlike each other;
To mutter and mock a broken charm,
To dally with wrong that does no harm.
Perhaps 'tis tender too and pretty   670
At each wild word to feel within
A sweet recoil of love and pity.
And what, if in a world of sin
(O sorrow and shame should this be *true!*)
Such giddiness of heart and brain
Comes seldom save from rage and pain,
So talks as it's most used to do.

THE KNIGHT'S TOMB

Written probably in 1817, but included here with the other poems of "wonder." Sir Arthur lived in the North Country of "Christabel," Part the Second.

Where is the grave of Sir Arthur O'Kellyn?
Where may the grave of that good man be?—
By the side of a spring, on the breast of Helvellyn,
Under the twigs of a young birch tree!
The oak that in summer was sweet to hear,
And rustled its leaves in the fall of the year,
And whistled and roared in the winter alone,
Is gone,—and the birch in its stead is grown.—
The Knight's bones are dust,
And his good sword rust;—   10
His soul is with the saints, I trust.

KUBLA KHAN; OR, A VISION
IN A DREAM

A FRAGMENT

"The following fragment is here published at the request of a poet of great and deserved celebrity [Lord Byron], and, as far as the Author's own opinions are concerned, rather as a psychological curiosity, than on the ground of any supposed *poetic* merits.

"In the summer of the year 1797 [probably 1798], the Author, then in ill health, had retired to a lonely farmhouse between Porlock and Linton, on the Exmoor confines of Somerset and Devonshire. In consequence of a slight indisposition, an anodyne had been prescribed, from the effects of which he fell asleep in his chair at the moment he was reading the following sentence, or words of the same substance, in 'Purchas's Pilgrimage': 'Here the Khan Kubla commanded a palace to be built, and a stately garden thereunto. And thus ten miles of fertile ground were inclosed with a wall.' The Author continued for about three hours in a profound sleep, at least of the external senses, during which time he has the most vivid confidence, that he could not have composed less than from two to three hundred lines; if that indeed can be called composition in which all the images rose up before him as *things*, with a parallel production of the correspondent expressions, without any sensation or consciousness of effort. On awaking he appeared to himself to have a distinct recollection of the whole, and taking his pen, ink, and paper, instantly and eagerly wrote down the lines that are here preserved. At this moment he was unfortunately called out by a person on business from Porlock, and detained by him above an hour, and on his return to his room, found, to his no small surprise and mortification, that though he still retained some vague and dim recollection of the general purport of the vision, yet, with the exception of some eight or ten scattered lines and images, all the rest had passed away like the images on the surface of a stream into which a stone had been cast, but, alas! without the after restoration of the latter!

> "Then all the charm
> Is broken—all that phantom-world so fair
> Vanishes, and a thousand circlets spread,
> And each mis-shape[s] the other. Stay awhile,
> Poor youth! who scarcely dar'st lift up thine eyes—
> The stream will soon renew its smoothness, soon
> The visions will return! And lo, he stays,
> And soon the fragments dim of lovely forms
> Come trembling back, unite, and now once more
> The pool becomes a mirror.

"Yet from the still surviving recollections in his mind, the Author has frequently purposed to finish for himself what had been originally, as it were, given to him. Σαμερον αδιον ασω [Αὔριον ἄδιον ᾄσω 1834]: but the tomorrow is yet to come."—Coleridge

In Xanadu did Kubla Khan
A stately pleasure-dome decree:
Where Alph, the sacred river, ran

Introd. Σαμερον . . . ασω. To sing a sweeter song tomorrow. **1. Kubla Khan,** Kublai Khan (1214-1294) was the Mongol conqueror of China.

Through caverns measureless to man
  Down to a sunless sea.
So twice five miles of fertile ground
With walls and towers were girdled round:
And there were gardens bright with sinuous rills,
Where blossomed many an incense-bearing tree;
And here were forests ancient as the hills,   10
Enfolding sunny spots of greenery.

But oh! that deep romantic chasm which slanted
Down the green hill athwart a cedarn cover!
A savage place! as holy and enchanted
As e'er beneath a waning moon was haunted
By woman wailing for her demon-lover!
And from this chasm, with ceaseless turmoil seeth-
  ing,
As if this earth in fast thick pants were breathing,
A mighty fountain momently was forced:
Amid whose swift half-intermitted burst   20
Huge fragments vaulted like rebounding hail,
Or chaffy grain beneath the thresher's flail:
And 'mid these dancing rocks at once and ever
It flung up momently the sacred river.
Five miles meandering with a mazy motion
Through wood and dale the sacred river ran,
Then reached the caverns measureless to man,
And sank in tumult to a lifeless ocean:
And 'mid this tumult Kubla heard from far
Ancestral voices prophesying war!   30

    The shadow of the dome of pleasure
    Floated midway on the waves;
    Where was heard the mingled measure
    From the fountain and the caves.
It was a miracle of rare device,
A sunny pleasure-dome with caves of ice!

    A damsel with a dulcimer
    In a vision once I saw:
    It was an Abyssinian maid,
    And on her dulcimer she played,   40
    Singing of Mount Abora.
    Could I revive within me
    Her symphony and song,
    To such a deep delight 'twould win me,
That with music loud and long,
I would build that dome in air,
That sunny dome! those caves of ice!

14–16. **A savage place . . . demon-lover.** "In all the
millions permitted there are no more than five—five little
lines—of which one can say, 'These are the magic. These are
the vision. The rest is only poetry.' "—Kipling. The other
two are Keats's "Ode to a Nightingale," ll. 69–70.
17–24. **And from this chasm . . . sacred river,** suggested by the description of the Florida alligator hole in
William Bartram's *Travels*, 1791.

And all who heard should see them there,
And all should cry, Beware! Beware!
His flashing eyes, his floating hair!   50
Weave a circle round him thrice,
And close your eyes with holy dread,
For he on honey-dew hath fed,
And drunk the milk of Paradise.

FROST AT MIDNIGHT

The Frost performs its secret ministry,
Unhelped by any wind. The owlet's cry
Came loud—and hark, again! loud as before.
The inmates of my cottage, all at rest,
Have left me to that solitude, which suits
Abstruser musings: save that at my side
My cradled infant slumbers peacefully.
'Tis calm indeed! so calm, that it disturbs
And vexes meditation with its strange
And extreme silentness. Sea, hill, and wood,   10
This populous village! Sea, and hill, and wood,
With all the numberless goings-on of life,
Inaudible as dreams! the thin blue flame
Lies on my low-burnt fire, and quivers not;
Only that film, which fluttered on the grate,
Still flutters there, the sole unquiet thing.
Methinks, its motion in this hush of nature
Gives it dim sympathies with me who live,
Making it a companionable form,
Whose puny flaps and freaks the idling Spirit   20
By its own moods interprets, everywhere
Echo or mirror seeking of itself,
And makes a toy of Thought.

                              But O! how oft,
How oft, at school, with most believing mind,
Presageful, have I gazed upon the bars,
To watch that fluttering *stranger!* and as oft
With unclosed lids, already had I dreamt
Of my sweet birth-place, and the old church-tower,
Whose bells, the poor man's only music, rang
From morn to evening, all the hot Fair-day,   30
So sweetly, that they stirred and haunted me
With a wild pleasure, falling on mine ear
Most like articulate sounds of things to come!
So gazed I, till the soothing things, I dreamt,
Lulled me to sleep, and sleep prolonged my dreams!
And so I brooded all the following morn,
Awed by the stern preceptor's face, mine eye
Fixed with mock study on my swimming book:

26. **stranger!** "These [soot] films are called *strangers* and
are supposed to portend the arrival of some absent friend."
—*Poetical Register*—

Save if the door half opened, and I snatched
A hasty glance, and still my heart leaped up,   40
For still I hoped to see the *stranger's* face,
Townsman, or aunt, or sister more beloved,
My play-mate when we both were clothed alike!

Dear Babe, that sleepest cradled by my side,
Whose gentle breathings, heard in this deep calm,
Fill up the interspersèd vacancies
And momentary pauses of the thought!
My babe so beautiful! it thrills my heart
With tender gladness, thus to look at thee,
And think that thou shalt learn far other lore,   50
And in far other scenes! For I was reared
In the great city, pent 'mid cloisters dim,
And saw nought lovely but the sky and stars.
But *thou*, my babe! shalt wander like a breeze
By lakes and sandy shores, beneath the crags
Of ancient mountain, and beneath the clouds,
Which image in their bulk both lakes and shores
And mountain crags: so shalt thou see and hear
The lovely shapes and sounds intelligible
Of that eternal language, which thy God   60
Utters, who from eternity doth teach
Himself in all, and all things in himself.
Great universal Teacher! he shall mould
Thy spirit, and by giving make it ask.

Therefore all seasons shall be sweet to thee,
Whether the summer clothe the general earth
With greenness, or the redbreast sit and sing
Betwixt the tufts of snow on the bare branch
Of mossy apple-tree, while the nigh thatch   69
Smokes in the sun-thaw; whether the eve-drops fall
Heard only in the trances of the blast,
Or if the secret ministry of frost
Shall hang them up in silent icicles,
Quietly shining to the quiet Moon.

THE NIGHTINGALE

A CONVERSATION POEM, APRIL, 1798

No cloud, no relique of the sunken day
Distinguishes the West, no long thin slip
Of sullen light, no obscure trembling hues.
Come, we will rest on this old mossy bridge!
You see the glimmer of the stream beneath,
But hear no murmuring: it flows silently,
O'er its soft bed of verdure. All is still,
A balmy night! and though the stars be dim,
Yet let us think upon the vernal showers
That gladden the green earth, and we shall find   10
A pleasure in the dimness of the stars.

And hark! the Nightingale begins its song,
"Most musical, most melancholy" bird!
A melancholy bird? Oh! idle thought!
In Nature there is nothing melancholy.
But some night-wandering man whose heart was
        pierced
With the remembrance of a grievous wrong,
Or slow distemper, or neglected love,
(And so, poor wretch! filled all things with him-
        self,
And made all gentle sounds tell back the tale   20
Of his own sorrow) he, and such as he,
First named these notes a melancholy strain.
And many a poet echoes the conceit;
Poet who hath been building up the rhyme
When he had better far have stretched his limbs
Beside a brook in mossy forest-dell,
By sun or moon-light, to the influxes
Of shapes and sounds and shifting elements
Surrendering his whole spirit, of his song
And of his fame forgetful! so his fame   30
Should share in Nature's immortality,
A venerable thing! and so his song
Should make all Nature lovelier, and itself
Be loved like Nature! But 'twill not be so;
And youths and maidens most poetical,
Who lose the deepening twilights of the spring
In ball-rooms and hot theatres, they still
Full of meek sympathy must heave their sighs
O'er Philomela's pity-pleading strains.

My Friend, and thou, our Sister! we have learnt
A different lore: we may not thus profane   41
Nature's sweet voices, always full of love
And joyance! 'Tis the merry Nightingale
That crowds, and hurries, and precipitates
With fast thick warble his delicious notes,
As he were fearful that an April night
Would be too short for him to utter forth
His love-chant, and disburthen his full soul
Of all its music!

And I know a grove
Of large extent, hard by a castle huge,   50
Which the great lord inhabits not; and so
This grove is wild with tangling underwood,
And the trim walks are broken up, and grass,
Thin grass and king-cups grow within the paths.
But never elsewhere in one place I knew

13. **"Most musical . . . melancholy."** The quotation
is from Milton's "Il Penseroso," l. 62. **40. My Friend
and . . . our Sister,** William and Dorothy Wordsworth.
50–51. castle . . . lord, reference to Alfoxden manor
house, owned by the St. Albyns family, of which the Wordsworths were temporary tenants.

So many nightingales; and far and near,
In wood and thicket, over the wide grove,
They answer and provoke each other's songs,
With skirmish and capricious passagings,
And murmurs musical and swift jug jug,   60
And one low piping sound more sweet than all—
Stirring the air with such a harmony,
That should you close your eyes, you might almost
Forget it was not day! On moonlight bushes,
Whose dewy leaflets are but half-disclosed,
You may perchance behold them on the twigs,
Their bright, bright eyes, their eyes both bright and
      full,
Glistening, while many a glow-worm in the shade
Lights up her love-torch.

                              A most gentle Maid,
Who dwelleth in her hospitable home   70
Hard by the castle, and at latest eve
(Even like a Lady vowed and dedicate
To something more than Nature in the grove)
Glides through the pathways; she knows all their
      notes,
That gentle Maid! and oft, a moment's space,
What time the moon was lost behind a cloud,
Hath heard a pause of silence; till the moon
Emerging, hath awakened earth and sky
With one sensation, and those wakeful birds
Have all burst forth in choral minstrelsy,   80
As if some sudden gale had swept at once
A hundred airy harps! And she hath watched
Many a nightingale perch giddily
On blossomy twig still swinging from the breeze,
And to that motion tune his wanton song
Like tipsy-joy that reels with tossing head.

Farewell, O Warbler! till to-morrow eve,
And you, my friends! farewell, a short farewell!
We have been loitering long and pleasantly,
And now for our dear homes.—That strain
      again!   90
Full fain it would delay me! My dear babe,
Who, capable of no articulate sound,
Mars all things with his imitative lisp,
How he would place his hand beside his ear,
His little hand, the small forefinger up,
And bid us listen! And I deem it wise
To make him Nature's play-mate. He knows well
The evening-star; and once, when he awoke
In most distressful mood (some inward pain
Had made up that strange thing, an infant's
      dream),   100
I hurried with him to our orchard-plot,

69. Maid, Dorothy.

And he beheld the moon, and, hushed at once,
Suspends his sobs, and laughs most silently,
While his fair eyes, that swam with undropped
      tears,
Did glitter in the yellow moon-beam! Well!—
It is a father's tale: But if that Heaven
Should give me life, his childhood shall grow up
Familiar with these songs, that with the night
He may associate joy.—Once more, farewell,
Sweet Nightingale! once more, my friends! fare-
well.   110

FRANCE, AN ODE

Printed in the *Morning Post* in April, 1798, the poem
was preceded by a note beginning: "The following excellent Ode will be in unison with the feelings of every
friend to Liberty and foe to Oppression; of all who, admiring the French Revolution, detest and deplore the
conduct of France towards Switzerland."

I

Ye Clouds! that far above me float and pause,
  Whose pathless march no mortal may controul!
  Ye Ocean-Waves! that, wheresoe'er ye roll,
Yield homage only to eternal laws!
Ye Woods! that listen to the night-birds singing,
  Midway the smooth and perilous slope reclined,
Save when your own imperious branches swinging,
  Have made a solemn music of the wind!
Where, like a man beloved of God,
Through glooms, which never woodman trod,   10
  How oft, pursuing fancies holy,
My moonlight way o'er flowering weeds I wound,
  Inspired, beyond the guess of folly,
By each rude shape and wild unconquerable sound!
O ye loud Waves! and O ye Forests high!
  And O ye Clouds that far above me soared!
Thou rising Sun! thou blue rejoicing Sky!
  Yea, every thing that is and will be free!
Bear witness for me, wheresoe'er ye be,
  With what deep worship I have still adored   20
    The spirit of divinest Liberty.

2

When France in wrath her giant-limbs upreared,
  And with that oath, which smote air, earth, and
      sea,
  Stamped her strong foot and said she would be
      free,
Bear witness for me, how I hoped and feared!
With what a joy my lofty gratulation
  Unawed I sang, amid a slavish band:

And when to whelm the disenchanted nation,
  Like fiends embattled by a wizard's wand,
    The Monarchs marched in evil day,   30
    And Britain joined the dire array;
  Though dear her shores and circling ocean,
Though many friendships, many youthful loves
  Had swoln the patriot emotion
And flung a magic light o'er all her hills and groves;
  Yet still my voice, unaltered, sang defeat
    To all that braved the tyrant-quelling lance,
And shame too long delayed and vain retreat!
For ne'er, O Liberty! with partial aim
  I dimmed thy light or damped thy holy flame;   40
    But blessed the paeans of delivered France,
And hung my head and wept at Britain's name.

3

"And what," I said, "though Blasphemy's loud
    scream
  With that sweet music of deliverance strove!
Though all the fierce and drunken passions wove
A dance more wild than e'er was maniac's dream!
  Ye storms, that round the dawning east assem-
    bled,
The Sun was rising, though ye hid his light!"
  And when, to soothe my soul, that hoped and
    trembled,
The dissonance ceased, and all seemed calm and
    bright;   50
  When France her front deep-scarred and gory
  Concealed with clustering wreaths of glory;
    When, insupportably advancing,
  Her arm made mockery of the warrior's ramp;
    While timid looks of fury glancing,
  Domestic treason, crushed beneath her fatal
    stamp,
Writhed like a wounded dragon in his gore;
  Then I reproached my fears that would not flee;
"And soon," I said, "shall Wisdom teach her lore
In the low huts of them that toil and groan!   60
And, conquering by her happiness alone,
  Shall France compel the nations to be free,
Till Love and Joy look round, and call the Earth
    their own."

4

Forgive me, Freedom! O forgive those dreams!
  I hear thy voice, I hear thy loud lament,
  From bleak Helvetia's icy caverns sent—
I hear thy groans upon her blood-stained streams!
  Heroes, that for your peaceful country perished,
And ye that, fleeing, spot your mountain-snows
  With bleeding wounds; forgive me, that I
    cherished   70

One thought that ever blessed your cruel foes!
  To scatter rage, and traitorous guilt,
  Where Peace her jealous home had built;
    A patriot-race to disinherit
Of all that made their stormy wilds so dear;
  And with inexpiable spirit
To taint the bloodless freedom of the mountaineer—
O France, that mockest Heaven, adulterous, blind,
  And patriot only in pernicious toils!
Are these thy boasts, Champion of human kind?   80
  To mix with Kings in the low lust of sway,
  Yell in the hunt, and share the murderous prey;
To insult the shrine of Liberty with spoils
  From freemen torn; to tempt and to betray?

5

  The Sensual and the Dark rebel in vain,
  Slaves by their own compulsion! In mad game
  They burst their manacles and wear the name
    Of Freedom, graven on a heavier chain!
O Liberty! with profitless endeavour
Have I pursued thee, many a weary hour;   90
  But thou nor swell'st the victor's strain, nor ever
Didst breathe thy soul in forms of human power.
  Alike from all, howe'er they praise thee,
  (Nor prayer, nor boastful name delays thee)
    Alike from Priestcraft's harpy minions,
  And factious Blasphemy's obscener slaves,
    Thou speedest on thy subtle pinions,
The guide of homeless winds, and play-mate of the
    waves!
And there I felt thee!—on that sea-cliff's verge,
  Whose pines, scarce travelled by the breeze
    above,   100
Had made one murmur with the distant surge!
Yes, while I stood and gazed, my temples bare,
And shot my being through earth, sea, and air,
  Possessing all things with intensest love,
    O Liberty! my spirit felt thee there.

LINES

WRITTEN IN THE ALBUM AT ELBINGERODE, IN THE HARTZ FOREST

I stood on Brocken's sovran height, and saw
Woods crowding upon woods, hills over hills,
A surging scene, and only limited
By the blue distance. Heavily my way
Downward I dragged through fir-groves evermore,
Where bright green moss heaves in sepulchral
  forms

1. Brocken, the highest mountain in Germany as that
country was when Coleridge visited it in 1798–99.

Speckled with sunshine; and, but seldom heard,
The sweet bird's song became a hollow sound;
And the breeze, murmuring indivisibly,
Preserved its solemn murmur most distinct   10
From many a note of many a waterfall,
And the brook's chatter; 'mid whose islet-stones
The dingy kidling with its tinkling bell
Leaped frolicsome, or old romantic goat
Sat, his white beard slow waving. I moved on
In low and languid mood: for I had found
That outward forms, the loftiest, still receive
Their finer influence from the Life within;—
Fair cyphers else: fair, but of import vague
Or unconcerning, where the heart not finds   20
History or prophecy of friend, or child,
Or gentle maid, our first and early love,
Or father, or the venerable name
Of our adorèd country! O thou Queen,
Thou delegated Deity of Earth,
O dear, dear England! how my longing eye
Turned westward, shaping in the steady clouds
Thy sands and high white cliffs?

                                        My native Land!
Filled with the thought of thee this heart was
          proud,
Yea, mine eye swam with tears: that all the view   30
From sovran Brocken, woods and woody hills,
Floated away, like a departing dream,
Feeble and dim! Stranger, these impulses
Blame thou not lightly; nor will I profane,
With hasty judgment or injurious doubt,
That man's sublimer spirit, who can feel
That God is everywhere! the God who framed
Mankind to be one mighty family,
Himself our Father, and the World our Home.

LOVE

Professor T. M. Raysor (*Studies in Philology*, Vol. 26)
has shown that this poem records Coleridge's hopeless
love for Sarah Hutchinson, sister of Mary Hutchinson,
whom Coleridge met in 1799. Note the Gothic scenery,
the chivalric story, the Fiend in angel's guise (compare
"Christabel").

          All thoughts, all passions, all delights,
          Whatever stirs this mortal frame,
          All are but ministers of Love,
              And feed his sacred flame.

17–18. That outward forms . . . within. The passage
shows some lingering of Hartleian Associationism, but is a
step toward the philosophical outlook reached in "Dejection" (see stanzas 3–4). **24. adorèd country.** Compare the
patriotic sentiments of Wordsworth's 1802 sonnets.

          Oft in my waking dreams do I
          Live o'er again that happy hour,
          When midway on the mount I lay,
              Beside the ruined tower.

          The moonshine, stealing o'er the scene   10
          Had blended with the lights of eve;
          And she was there, my hope, my joy,
              My own dear Genevieve!

          She leant against the armèd man,
          The statue of the armèd knight;
          She stood and listened to my lay,
              Amid the lingering light.

          Few sorrows hath she of her own,
          My hope! my joy! my Genevieve!
          She loves me best, whene'er I sing
              The songs that make her grieve.   20

          I played a soft and doleful air,
          I sang an old and moving story—
          An old rude song, that suited well
              The ruin wild and hoary.

          She listened with a flitting blush,
          With downcast eyes and modest grace;
          For well she knew, I could not choose
              But gaze upon her face.

          I told her of the Knight that wore
          Upon his shield a burning brand;   30
          And that for ten long years he wooed
              The Lady of the Land.

          I told her how he pined: and ah!
          The deep, the low, the pleading tone
          With which I sang another's love,
              Interpreted my own.

          She listened with a flitting blush,
          With downcast eyes, and modest grace;
          And she forgave me, that I gazed
              Too fondly on her face!   40

          But when I told the cruel scorn
          That crazed that bold and lovely Knight,
          And that he crossed the mountain-woods,
              Nor rested day nor night;

          That sometimes from the savage den,
          And sometimes from the darksome shade,
          And sometimes starting up at once
              In green and sunny glade,—

There came and looked him in the face
An angel beautiful and bright;   50
And that he knew it was a Fiend,
    This miserable Knight!

And that unknowing what he did,
He leaped amid a murderous band,
And saved from outrage worse than death
    The Lady of the Land!

And how she wept, and clasped his knees;
And how she tended him in vain—
And ever strove to expiate
    The scorn that crazed his brain;—   60

And that she nursed him in a cave;
And how his madness went away,
When on the yellow forest-leaves
    A dying man he lay;—

His dying words—but when I reached
That tenderest strain of all the ditty,
My faltering voice and pausing harp
    Disturbed her soul with pity!

All impulses of soul and sense
Had thrilled my guileless Genevieve;   70
The music and the doleful tale,
    The rich and balmy eve;

And hopes, and fears that kindle hope,
An undistinguishable throng,
And gentle wishes long subdued,
    Subdued and cherished long!

She wept with pity and delight,
She blushed with love, and virgin-shame;
And like the murmur of a dream,
    I heard her breathe my name.   80

Her bosom heaved—she stepped aside,
As conscious of my look she stepped—
Then suddenly, with timorous eye
    She fled to me and wept.

She half enclosed me with her arms,
She pressed me with a meek embrace;
And bending back her head, looked up,
    And gazed upon my face.

'Twas partly love, and partly fear,
And partly 'twas a bashful art,   90
That I might rather feel, than see,
    The swelling of her heart.

I calmed her fears, and she was calm,
And told her love with virgin pride;
And so I won my Genevieve,
    My bright and beauteous Bride.

DEJECTION: AN ODE

See what is said about the critical importance of this
poem in the biographical-critical sketch of Coleridge;
also what is said in the general introduction about Transcendentalism. The poem was originally addressed to
Sarah Hutchinson (see "Love"), then to Wordsworth,
finally to "Lady." Wordsworth's "Resolution and Independence" and "Ode: Intimations of Immortality" are
in part answers to "Dejection." They treat the same
problem: What can the poet do when feeling loses its
vividness (and imagination consequently fades)?

> Late, late yestreen I saw the new Moon,
> With the old Moon in her arms;
> And I fear, I fear, my Master dear!
> We shall have a deadly storm.
> —*Ballad of Sir Patrick Spence*

I

Well! If the Bard was weather-wise, who made
    The grand old ballad of Sir Patrick Spence,
    This night, so tranquil now, will not go hence
Unroused by winds, that ply a busier trade
Than those which mould yon cloud in lazy flakes,
Or the dull sobbing draft, that moans and rakes
    Upon the strings of this Aeolian lute,
    Which better far were mute.
For lo! the New-moon winter-bright!
And overspread with phantom light,   10
(With swimming phantom light o'erspread
But rimmed and circled by a silver thread)
I see the old Moon in her lap, foretelling
    The coming-on of rain and squally blast.
And oh! that even now the gust were swelling,
    And the slant night-shower driving loud and fast!
Those sounds which oft have raised me, whilst they
    awed,
    And sent my soul abroad,
Might now perhaps their wonted impulse give,
Might startle this dull pain, and make it move and
    live!   20

2

A grief without a pang, void, dark, and drear,
    A stifled, drowsy, unimpassioned grief,
    Which finds no natural outlet, no relief,
        In word, or sigh, or tear—

95. so I won. Compare what was said about **sensibility,**
page 2; also, Othello's manner of winning Desdemona.

O Lady! in this wan and heartless mood,
To other thoughts by yonder throstle wooed,
  All this long eve, so balmy and serene,
Have I been gazing on the western sky,
  And its peculiar tint of yellow green:
And still I gaze—and with how blank an eye!   30
And those thin clouds above, in flakes and bars,
That give away their motion to the stars;
Those stars, that glide behind them or between,
Now sparkling, now bedimmed, but always seen:
Yon crescent Moon, as fixed as if it grew
In its own cloudless, starless lake of blue;
I see them all so excellently fair,
I see, not feel, how beautiful they are!

3

      My genial spirits fail;
      And what can these avail   40
To lift the smothering weight from off my breast?
      It were a vain endeavour,
      Though I should gaze for ever
On that green light that lingers in the west:
I may not hope from outward forms to win
The passion and the life, whose fountains are within.

4

O Lady! we receive but what we give,
And in our life alone does Nature live:
Ours is her wedding garment, ours her shroud!
      And would we aught behold, of higher worth,   50
Than that inanimate cold world allowed
To the poor loveless ever-anxious crowd,
      Ah! from the soul itself must issue forth
A light, a glory, a fair luminous cloud
      Enveloping the Earth—
And from the soul itself must there be sent
      A sweet and potent voice, of its own birth,
Of all sweet sounds the life and element!

5

O pure of heart! thou need'st not ask of me
What this strong music in the soul may be!   60
What, and wherein it doth exist,
This light, this glory, this fair luminous mist,
This beautiful and beauty-making power.
      Joy, virtuous Lady! Joy that ne'er was given,
Save to the pure, and in their purest hour,
Life, and Life's effluence, cloud at once and shower,
Joy, Lady! is the spirit and the power,
Which wedding Nature to us gives in dower
      A new Earth and new Heaven,

39. genial spirits. Compare Wordsworth's phrase, "genial sense of youth," in the ' Ode to Duty," written nearly
three years later.

Undreamt of by the sensual and the proud—   70
Joy is the sweet voice, Joy the luminous cloud—
      We in ourselves rejoice!
And thence flows all that charms or ear or sight,
      All melodies the echoes of that voice,
All colours a suffusion from that light.

6

There was a time when, though my path was rough,
      This joy within me dallied with distress,
And all misfortunes were but as the stuff
      Whence Fancy made me dreams of happiness:
For hope grew round me, like the twining vine,   80
And fruits, and foliage, not my own, seemed mine.
But now afflictions bow me down to earth:
Nor care I that they rob me of my mirth;
      But oh! each visitation
Suspends what nature gave me at my birth,
      My shaping spirit of Imagination.
For not to think of what I needs must feel,
      But to be still and patient, all I can;
And haply by abstruse research to steal
      From my own nature all the natural man—   90
This was my sole resource, my only plan:
Till that which suits a part infects the whole,
And now is almost grown the habit of my soul.

7

Hence, viper thoughts, that coil around my mind,
      Reality's dark dream!
I turn from you, and listen to the wind,
      Which long has raved unnoticed. What a scream
Of agony by torture lengthened out
That lute sent forth! Thou Wind, that rav'st with-
      out,
      Bare crag, or mountain-tairn, or blasted tree, 100
Or pine-grove whither woodman never clomb,
      Or lonely house, long held the witches' home,
      Methinks were fitter instruments for thee,
Mad Lutanist! who in this month of showers,
Of dark-brown gardens, and of peeping flowers,
Mak'st Devils' yule, with worse than wintry song,
The blossoms, buds, and timorous leaves among.
      Thou Actor, perfect in all tragic sounds!
Thou mighty Poet, e'en to frenzy bold!
      What tell'st thou now about?   110
      'Tis of the rushing of an host in rout,
      With groans, of trampled men, with smarting
         wounds—
At once they groan with pain, and shudder with the
      cold!
But hush! there is a pause of deepest silence!
      And all that noise, as of a rushing crowd,

With groans, and tremulous shudderings—all is
over—
   It tells another tale, with sounds less deep and
loud!
     A tale of less affright,
     And tempered with delight,
As Otway's self had framed the tender lay, —   120
     'Tis of a little child
     Upon a lonesome wild,
Not far from home, but she hath lost her way:
And now moans low in bitter grief and fear,
And now screams loud, and hopes to make her
mother hear.

8

'Tis midnight, but small thoughts have I of sleep:
Full seldom may my friend such vigils keep!
Visit her, gentle Sleep! with wings of healing,
   And may this storm be but a mountain-birth,   129
May all the stars hang bright above her dwelling,
  Silent as though they watched the sleeping Earth!
     With light heart may she rise,
     Gay fancy, cheerful eyes,
Joy lift her spirit, joy attune her voice;
To her may all things live, from pole to pole,
Their life the eddying of her living soul!
  O simple spirit, guided from above,
Dear Lady! friend devoutest of my choice,
Thus mayest thou ever, evermore rejoice.

THE PAINS OF SLEEP

Ere on my bed my limbs I lay,
It hath not been my use to pray
With moving lips or bended knees;
But silently, by slow degrees,
My spirit I to Love compose,
In humble trust mine eye-lids close,
With reverential resignation,
No wish conceived, no thought exprest,
Only a sense of supplication;
A sense o'er all my soul imprest   10
That I am weak, yet not unblest,
Since in me, round me, every where
Eternal Strength and Wisdom are.

But yester-night I prayed aloud
In anguish and in agony,

120. Otway's self. Thomas Otway was a seventeenth-century dramatist. The allusion is to his tragedy *The Orphan.* **121. 'Tis of a little child.** Compare Wordsworth's "Lucy Gray." **15. In anguish and in agony.** Coleridge was suffering at the time from the effects of overindulgence in opium. In a letter written to Southey and including the poem he says that while in Scotland he was arrested and temporarily imprisoned on suspicion that he was a spy.

Up-starting from the fiendish crowd
Of shapes and thoughts that tortured me:
A lurid light, a trampling throng,
Sense of intolerable wrong,
And whom I scorned, those only strong!   20
Thirst of revenge, the powerless will
Still baffled, and yet burning still!
Desire with loathing strangely mixed
On wild or hateful objects fixed.
Fantastic passions! maddening brawl!
And shame and terror over all!
Deeds to be hid which were not hid,
Which all confused I could not know
Whether I suffered, or I did:
For all seemed guilt, remorse or woe,   30
My own or others still the same
Life-stifling fear, soul-stifling shame!

So two nights passed: the night's dismay
Saddened and stunned the coming day.
Sleep, the wide blessing, seemed to me
Distemper's worst calamity.
The third night, when my own loud scream
Had waked me from the fiendish dream,
O'ercome with sufferings strange and wild,
I wept as I had been a child;   40
And having thus by tears subdued
My anguish to a milder mood,
Such punishments, I said, were due
To natures deepliest stained with sin:
For aye entempesting anew
The unfathomable hell within,
The horror of their deeds to view,
To know and loathe, yet wish and do!
Such griefs with such men well agree,
But wherefore, wherefore fall on me?   50
To be beloved is all I need,
And whom I love, I love indeed.

TO WILLIAM WORDSWORTH

COMPOSED ON THE NIGHT AFTER HIS RECITA-
TION OF A POEM ON THE GROWTH OF AN
INDIVIDUAL MIND

Friend of the wise! and Teacher of the Good!
Into my heart have I received that Lay
More than historic, that prophetic Lay
Wherein (high theme by thee first sung aright)
Of the foundations and the building up
Of a Human Spirit thou hast dared to tell

2. that Lay, *The Prelude,* which Wordsworth had completed in 1805, while Coleridge was in Malta.

What may be told, to the understanding mind
Revealable; and what within the mind
By vital breathings secret as the soul
Of vernal growth, oft quickens in the heart   10
Thoughts all too deep for words!—
                    Theme hard as high!
Of smiles spontaneous, and mysterious fears
(The first-born they of Reason and twin-birth),
Of tides obedient to external force,
And currents self-determined, as might seem,
Or by some inner Power; of moments awful,
Now in thy inner life, and now abroad,
When power streamed from thee, and thy soul re-
    ceived
The light reflected, as a light bestowed—
Of fancies fair, and milder hours of youth,   20
Hyblean murmurs of poetic thought
Industrious in its joy, in vales and glens
Native or outland, lakes and famous hills!
Or on the lonely high-road, when the stars
Were rising; or by secret mountain-streams,
The guides and the companions of thy way!
Of more than Fancy, of the Social Sense
Distending wide, and man beloved as man,
Where France in all her towns lay vibrating
Like some becalmèd bark beneath the burst   30
Of Heaven's immediate thunder, when no cloud
Is visible, or shadow on the main.
For thou wert there, thine own brows garlanded,
Amid the tremor of a realm aglow,
Amid a mighty nation jubilant,
When from the general heart of human kind
Hope sprang forth like a full-born Deity!
——Of that dear Hope afflicted and struck down,
So summoned homeward, thenceforth calm and
    sure   39
From the dread watch-tower of man's absolute self,
With light unwaning on her eyes, to look
Far on—herself a glory to behold,
The Angel of the vision! Then (last strain)
Of Duty, chosen Laws controlling choice,
Action and joy!—an Orphic song indeed,
A song divine of high and passionate thoughts
To their own music chaunted!

                    O great Bard!
Ere yet that last strain dying awed the air,
With stedfast eye I viewed thee in the choir
Of ever-enduring men. The truly great   50
Have all one age, and from one visible space
Shed influence! They, both in power and act,

21. **Hyblean,** mellifluous. Hybla was noted for its honey.
45. **Orphic song,** prophetic, mysterious. Orpheus was the
legendary Thracian hero who invented the lyre.

Are permanent, and Time is not with *them*,
Save as it worketh *for* them, they *in* it.
Nor less a sacred Roll, than those of old,
And to be placed, as they, with gradual fame
Among the archives of mankind, thy work
Makes audible a linkèd lay of Truth,
Of Truth profound a sweet continuous lay,
Not learnt, but native, her own natural notes!   60
Ah! as I listened with a heart forlorn,
The pulses of my being beat anew:
And even as Life returns upon the drowned,
Life's joy rekindling roused a throng of pains—
Keen pangs of Love, awakening as a babe
Turbulent, with an outcry in the heart;
And fears self-willed, that shunned the eye of hope;
And Hope that scarce would know itself from fear;
Sense of past youth, and manhood come in vain,
And genius given, and knowledge won in vain;   70
And all which I had culled in wood-walks wild,
And all which patient toil had reared, and all,
Commune with *thee* had opened out—but flowers
Strewed on my corse, and borne upon my bier
In the same coffin, for the self-same grave!

    That way no more! and ill beseems it me,
Who came a welcomer in herald's guise,
Singing of glory, and futurity,
To wander back on such unhealthful road,
Plucking the poisons of self-harm! And ill   80
Such intertwine beseems triumphal wreaths
Strewed before thy advancing!

                    Nor do thou,
Sage Bard! impair the memory of that hour
Of thy communion with my nobler mind
By pity or grief, already felt too long!
Nor let my words import more blame than needs.
The tumult rose and ceased: for Peace is nigh
Where wisdom's voice has found a listening heart.
Amid the howl of more than wintry storms,
The halcyon hears the voice of vernal hours   90
Already on the wing.

                    Eve following eve,
Dear tranquil time, when the sweet sense of Home
Is sweetest! moments for their own sake hailed
And more desired, more precious, for thy song,
In silence listening, like a devout child,
My soul lay passive, by thy various strain
Driven as in surges now beneath the stars,
With momentary stars of my own birth,
Fair constelled foam, still darting off
Into the darkness; now a tranquil sea,   100
Outspread and bright, yet swelling to the moon.

And when—O Friend! my comforter and guide!
Strong in thyself, and powerful to give strength!—
Thy long sustainèd Song finally closed,
And thy deep voice had ceased—yet thou thyself
Wert still before my eyes, and round us both
That happy vision of belovèd faces—
Scarce conscious, and yet conscious of its close
I sate, my being blended in one thought
(Thought was it? or aspiration? or resolve?)   110
Absorbed, yet hanging still upon the sound—
And when I rose, I found myself in prayer.

TIME, REAL AND IMAGINARY

AN ALLEGORY

On the wide level of a mountain's head,
(I knew not where, but 'twas some faery place)
Their pinions, ostrich-like, for sails out-spread,
Two lovely children run an endless race,
   A sister and a brother!
   This far outstript the other;
Yet ever runs she with reverted face,
And looks and listens for the boy behind:
   For he, alas! is blind!
O'er rough and smooth with even step he passed, 10
And knows not whether he be first or last.

YOUTH AND AGE

   Verse, a breeze mid blossoms straying,
   Where Hope clung feeding, like a bee—
   Both were mine! Life went a-maying
      With Nature, Hope, and Poesy,
         When I was young!

When I was young?—Ah, woful When!
Ah! for the change 'twixt Now and Then!
This breathing house not built with hands,
This body that does me grievous wrong,
O'er aery cliffs and glittering sands,   10
How lightly then it flashed along:—
Like those trim skiffs, unknown of yore,
On winding lakes and rivers wide,
That ask no aid of sail or oar,
That fear no spite of wind or tide!
Nought cared this body for wind or weather
When Youth and I lived in't together.

Flowers are lovely; Love is flower-like;
Friendship is a sheltering tree;
O! the joys, that came down shower-like,   20
Of Friendship, Love, and Liberty,
         Ere I was old!

Ere I was old? Ah woful Ere,
Which tells me, Youth's no longer here!
O Youth! for years so many and sweet,
'Tis known, that Thou and I were one,
I'll think it but a fond conceit—
It cannot be that Thou art gone!
Thy vesper-bell hath not yet tolled:—
And thou wert aye a masker bold!   30
What strange disguise hast now put on,
To make believe, that thou art gone?
I see these locks in silvery slips,
This drooping gait, this altered size:
But Spring-tide blossoms on thy lips,
And tears take sunshine from thine eyes!
Life is but thought: so think I will
That Youth and I are house-mates still.

Dew-drops are the gems of morning,
But the tears of mournful eve!   40
Where no hope is, life's a warning
That only serves to make us grieve,
        When we are old:
That only serves to make us grieve
With oft and tedious taking-leave,
Like some poor nigh-related guest,
That may not rudely be dismist;
Yet hath outstayed his welcome while,
And tells the jest without the smile.

WORK WITHOUT HOPE

LINES COMPOSED 21ST FEBRUARY 1825

All Nature seems at work. Slugs leave their lair—
The bees are stirring—birds are on the wing—
And Winter slumbering in the open air,
Wears on his smiling face a dream of Spring!
And I the while, the sole unbusy thing,
Nor honey make, nor pair, nor build, nor sing.

Yet well I ken the banks where amaranths blow,
Have traced the fount whence streams of nectar flow.
Bloom, O ye amaranths! bloom for whom ye may,
For me ye bloom not! Glide, rich streams, away!   10
With lips unbrightened, wreathless brow, I stroll:
And would you learn the spells that drowse my soul?
Work without Hope draws nectar in a sieve,
And Hope without an object cannot live.

EPITAPH

Stop, Christian passer-by!—Stop, child of God,
And read with gentle breast. Beneath this sod

A poet lies, or that which once seemed he.
O, lift one thought in prayer for S. T. C.;
That he who many a year with toil of breath
Found death in life, may here find life in death!
Mercy for praise—to be forgiven for fame
He asked, and hoped, through Christ. Do thou the
    same!

from BIOGRAPHIA LITERARIA

Several times Coleridge indicated that the original
critical ideas in the Preface to *Lyrical Ballads*, 1800, were
indistinguishably his own and Wordsworth's. When, in
1815-16, he wrote his *Biographia Literaria*, however, separation from Wordsworth and imperfectly reconciled
estrangement between the two gave him a detached
point of view toward the "Preface." His object, in the
following selections from *Biographia Literaria*, is to explain points of agreement and difference. But first he
must explain, as fundamental to his critical ideas, what
a poem is and what a poet is. In the paragraph on "The
poet, described in ideal perfection" (Chapter 14) is to be
found the heart of his critical theory. In Chapter 17 he
agrees with Wordsworth in the latter's attack on "poetic
diction" (meaning stereotyped "figures and metaphors"
from the older poetry that had become the slick coins of
poetic currency), but disagrees with Wordsworth's theory
"that the proper diction for poetry in general consists
altogether in a language taken, with due exceptions, from
the mouths of men in real life." This basic disagreement
also involves disagreement with Wordsworth's choice of
low and rustic life for his subjects—Wordsworth's own
best poems are inconsistent with his theory—and his
reasons therefor. Finally, in Chapter 18 Coleridge adversely criticizes Wordsworth's assertion that "there
neither is, nor can be, any *essential difference*" between
the language of prose and metrical composition. These
chapters from *Biographia Literaria* and the "Preface" to
which they refer are among the noblest expositions in
our language of the nature, the purpose, and the stuff of
poetry, and of the spirit and method of true literary
criticism.

CHAPTER 14 *(continued)* *

. . . Preface to the second edition [of *Lyrical Ballads*]—
The ensuing controversy, its causes and acrimony—
Philosophic definitions of a Poem and Poetry with
scholia. . . .

TO the second edition he [Wordsworth] added
a preface of considerable length; in which, notwithstanding some passages of apparently a contrary import, he was understood to contend for the

* Continued from page 77, where the beginning was
printed before Coleridge's "Renascence of Wonder" poems
as a statement of his aim in writing them.

extension of this style to poetry of all kinds, and to
reject as vicious and indefensible all phrases and
forms of speech that were not included in what he
(unfortunately, I think, adopting an equivocal expression) called the language of real life. From this
preface, prefixed to poems in which it was impossible to deny the presence of original genius, however
mistaken its direction might be deemed, arose the
whole long-continued controversy. For from the
conjunction of perceived power with supposed
heresy I explain the inveteracy and in some instances, I grieve to say, the acrimonious passions,
with which the controversy has been conducted by
the assailants.

Had Mr. Wordsworth's poems been the silly, the
childish things, which they were for a long time described as being: had they been really distinguished
from the compositions of other poets merely by
meanness of language and inanity of thought; had
they indeed contained nothing more than what is
found in the parodies and pretended imitations of
them; they must have sunk at once, a dead weight,
into the slough of oblivion, and have dragged the
preface along with them. But year after year increased the number of Mr. Wordsworth's admirers.
They were found too not in the lower classes of the
reading public, but chiefly among young men of
strong sensibility and meditative minds; and their
admiration (inflamed perhaps in some degree by
opposition) was distinguished by its intensity, I
might almost say, by its religious fervour. These
facts, and the intellectual energy of the author,
which was more or less consciously felt, where it was
outwardly and even boisterously denied, meeting
with sentiments of aversion to his opinions, and of
alarm at their consequences, produced an eddy of
criticism, which would of itself have borne up the
poems by the violence with which it whirled them
round and round. With many parts of this preface
in the sense attributed to them and which the words
undoubtedly seem to authorize, I never concurred;
but on the contrary objected to them as erroneous in
principle, and as contradictory (in appearance at
least) both to other parts of the same preface, and
to the author's own practice in the greater part of
the poems themselves. Mr. Wordsworth in his recent collection has, I find, degraded this prefatory
disquisition to the end of his second volume, to be
read or not at the reader's choice. But he has not, as
far as I can discover, announced any change in his
poetic creed. At all events, considering it as the
source of a controversy, in which I have been honoured more than I deserve by the frequent conjunction of my name with his, I think it expedient

to declare once for all, in what points I coincide with the opinions supported in that preface, and in what points I altogether differ. But in order to render myself intelligible I must previously, in as few words as possible, explain my views, first, of a Poem; and secondly, of Poetry itself, in kind, and in essence.

The office of philosophical disquisition consists in just distinction; while it is the privilege of the philosopher to preserve himself constantly aware, that distinction is not division. In order to obtain adequate notions of any truth, we must intellectually separate its distinguishable parts; and this is the technical process of philosophy. But having so done, we must then restore them in our conceptions to the unity, in which they actually co-exist; and this is the result of philosophy. A poem contains the same elements as a prose composition; the difference therefore must consist in a different combination of them, in consequence of a different object being proposed. According to the difference of the object will be the difference of the combination. It is possible, that the object may be merely to facilitate the recollection of any given facts or observations by artificial arrangement; and the composition will be a poem, merely because it is distinguished from prose by metre, or by rhyme, or by both conjointly. In this, the lowest sense, a man might attribute the name of a poem to the well-known enumeration of the days in the several months:

"Thirty days hath September,
April, June, and November," &c.

and others of the same class and purpose. And as a particular pleasure is found in anticipating the recurrence of sounds and quantities, all compositions that have this charm superadded, whatever be their contents, *may* be entitled poems.

So much for the superficial form. A difference of object and contents supplies an additional ground of distinction. The immediate purpose may be the communication of truths; either of truth absolute and demonstrable, as in works of science; or of facts experienced and recorded, as in history. Pleasure, and that of the highest and most permanent kind, may result from the attainment of the end; but it is not itself the immediate end. In other works the communication of pleasure may be the immediate purpose; and though truth, either moral or intellectual, ought to be the ultimate end, yet this will distinguish the character of the author, not the class to which the work belongs. Blest indeed is that state of society, in which the immediate purpose would be baffled by the perversion of the proper ultimate end;

in which no charm of diction or imagery could exempt the BATHYLLUS even of an Anacreon, or the ALEXIS of Virgil, from disgust and aversion!

But the communication of pleasure may be the immediate object of a work not metrically composed; and that object may have been in a high degree attained, as in novels and romances. Would then the mere superaddition of metre, with or without rhyme, entitle these to the name of poems? The answer is, that nothing can permanently please, which does not contain in itself the reason why it is so, and not otherwise. If metre be superadded, all other parts must be made consonant with it. They must be such, as to justify the perpetual and distinct attention to each part, which an exact correspondent recurrence of accent and sound are calculated to excite. The final definition then, so deduced, may be thus worded. A poem is that species of composition, which is opposed to works of science, by proposing for its *immediate* object pleasure, not truth; and from all other species—(having *this* object in common with it)—it is discriminated by proposing to itself such delight from the *whole*, as is compatible with a distinct gratification from each component *part*.

Controversy is not seldom excited in consequence of the disputants attaching each a different meaning to the same word; and in few instances has this been more striking, than in disputes concerning the present subject. If a man chooses to call every composition a poem, which is rhyme, or measure, or both, I must leave his opinion uncontroverted. The distinction is at least competent to characterize the writer's intention. If it were subjoined, that the whole is likewise entertaining or affecting, as a tale, or as a series of interesting reflections, I of course admit this as another fit ingredient of a poem, and an additional merit. But if the definition sought for be that of a *legitimate* poem, I answer, it must be one, the parts of which mutually support and explain each other; all in their proportion harmonizing with, and supporting the purpose and known influences of metrical arrangement. The philosophic critics of all ages coincide with the ultimate judgment of all countries, in equally denying the praises of a just poem, on the one hand, to a series of striking lines or distiches, each of which, absorbing the whole attention of the reader to itself, becomes disjoined from its context, and forms a separate whole, instead of a harmonizing part; and on the other hand, to an unsustained composition, from which the reader collects rapidly the general result unattracted by the component parts. The reader should be carried forward, not merely or chiefly by the mechanical impulse of curiosity, or by a restless desire to arrive at the final solution; but by the pleasurable activity of mind excited by the attractions of the journey itself. Like the motion of a serpent, which the Egyptians made the emblem of intellectual power; or like the path of sound through the air;—at every step he pauses and half recedes, and from the retrogressive movement collects the force which again carries him onward. *Praecipitandus est liber spiritus*, says Petronius most happily. The epithet, *liber*, here balances the preceding verb; and it is not easy to conceive more meaning condensed in fewer words.

But if this should be admitted as a satisfactory character of a poem, we have still to seek for a definition of poetry. The writings of Plato, and Jeremy Taylor, and Burnet's Theory of the Earth, furnish undeniable proofs that poetry of the highest kind may exist without metre, and even without the contradistinguishing objects of a poem. The first chapter of Isaiah—(indeed a very large portion of the whole book)—is poetry in the most emphatic sense; yet it would be not less irrational than strange to assert, that pleasure, and not truth was the immediate object of the prophet. In short, whatever specific import we attach to the word, Poetry, there will be found involved in it, as a necessary consequence, that a poem of any length neither can be, nor ought to be, all poetry. Yet if an harmonious whole is to be produced, the remaining parts must be preserved in keeping with the poetry; and this can be no otherwise effected than by such a studied selection and artificial arrangement, as will partake of one, though not a peculiar property of poetry. And this again can be no other than the property of exciting a more continuous and equal attention than the language of prose aims at, whether colloquial or written.

My own conclusions on the nature of poetry, in the strictest use of the word, have been in part anticipated in some of the remarks on the Fancy and Imagination in the early part of this work. What is poetry?—is so nearly the same question with, what is a poet?—that the answer to the one is involved in the solution of the other. For it is a distinction resulting from the poetic genius itself, which sustains and modifies the images, thoughts, and emotions of the poet's own mind.

The poet, described in ideal perfection, brings the whole soul of man into activity, with the subordina-

tion of its faculties to each other according to their relative worth and dignity. He diffuses a tone and spirit of unity, that blends, and (as it were) *fuses*, each into each, by that synthetic and magical power, to which I would exclusively appropriate the name of Imagination. This power, first put in action by the will and understanding, and retained under their irremissive, though gentle and unnoticed, control, *laxis effertur habenis*, reveals itself in the balance or reconcilement of opposite or discordant qualities: of sameness, with difference; of the general with the concrete; the idea with the image; the individual with the representative; the sense of novelty and freshness with old and familiar objects; a more than usual state of emotion with more than usual order; judgment ever awake and steady self-possession with enthusiasm and feeling profound or vehement; and while it blends and harmonizes the natural and the artificial, still subordinates art to nature; the manner to the matter; and our admiration of the poet to our sympathy with the poetry. Doubtless, as Sir John Davies observes of the soul—(and his words may with slight alteration be applied, and even more appropriately, to the poetic Imagination)—

"Doubtless this could not be, but that she turns
  Bodies to *spirit* by sublimation strange,
As fire converts to fire the things it burns,
  As we our food into our nature change.

"From their gross matter she abstracts *their* forms,
  And draws a kind of quintessence from things;
Which to her proper nature she transforms
  To bear them light on her celestial wings.

"*Thus* does she, when from *individual states*
  She doth abstract the universal kinds;
Which then re-clothed in divers names and fates
  Steal access through the senses to our minds."

Finally, Good Sense is the Body of poetic genius, Fancy its Drapery, Motion its Life, and Imagination the Soul that is everywhere, and in each; and forms all into one graceful and intelligent whole.

us a vision of life, not as it appeared to the understanding, but as it was revealed to reason." 2. The distinction between Fancy and Imagination, Understanding and Reason: (a) Fancy collects and combines particulars—corresponds to Understanding; (b) Imagination discovers the general and permanent—corresponds to Reason. 3. Imagination reveals itself in the balance or reconciliation of opposite or discordant qualities (see, for example, point 2 in "The Characteristics of Shakspere's Dramas," following). 4. "Imagination, so far from rejecting the actual, keeps in contact with it, but dissevers from its representation the accidental, the temporary, the contingent, and irregular, retaining only what disclosed its permanent nature and its essential relations to the universe." (See Ernest Bernbaum's *Guide through the Romantic Movement*, Thomas Nelson, 1933, pp. 104–05.) **9. laxis . . . habenis**, "carried along with loose reins."

9–10. Praecipitandus . . . spiritus. "The free spirit must be impelled forward." **49–50. The poet, described in ideal perfection . . . whole.** The paragraph contains the following ideas basic to Coleridge's theory of criticism: 1. The Aristotelian principle that "literature should give

CHAPTER 17

Examination of the tenets peculiar to Mr. Wordsworth—Rustic life (above all, low and rustic life) especially unfavourable to the formation of a human diction—The best parts of language the product of philosophers, not of clowns or shepherds—Poetry essentially ideal and generic—The language of Milton as much the language of real life, yea, incomparably more so than that of the cottager.

As far then as Mr. Wordsworth in his preface contended, and most ably contended, for a reformation in our poetic diction, as far as he has evinced the truth of passion, and the dramatic propriety of those figures and metaphors in the original poets, which, stripped of their justifying reasons, and converted into mere artifices of connection or ornament, constitute the characteristic falsity in the poetic style of the moderns; and as far as he has, with equal acuteness and clearness, pointed out the process by which this change was effected, and the resemblances between that state into which the reader's mind is thrown by the pleasurable confusion of thought from an unaccustomed train of words and images; and that state which is induced by the natural language of impassioned feeling; he undertook a useful task, and deserves all praise, both for the attempt and for the execution. The provocations to this remonstrance in behalf of truth and nature were still of perpetual recurrence before and after the publication of this preface. I cannot likewise but add, that the comparison of such poems of merit, as have been given to the public within the last ten or twelve years, with the majority of those produced previously to the appearance of that preface, leave[s] no doubt on my mind, that Mr. Wordsworth is fully justified in believing his efforts to have been by no means ineffectual. Not only in the verses of those who have professed their admiration of his genius, but even of those who have distinguished themselves by hostility to his theory, and depreciation of his writings, are the impressions of his principles plainly visible. It is possible, that with these principles others may have been blended, which are not equally evident; and some which are unsteady and subvertible from the narrowness or imperfection of their basis. But it is more than possible, that these errors of defect or exaggeration, by kindling and feeding the controversy, may have conduced

12. Mr. Wordsworth ff. Here, according to J. H. Shawcross, editor of *Biographia Literaria*, Coleridge is "indicating Wordsworth's true position; but he has not made it the basis of his criticism."

not only to the wider propagation of the accompanying truths, but that, by their frequent presentation to the mind in an excited state, they may have won for them a more permanent and practical result. A man will borrow a part from his opponent the more easily, if he feels himself justified in continuing to reject a part. While there remain important points in which he can still feel himself in the right, in which he still finds firm footing for continued resistance, he will gradually adopt those opinions, which were the least remote from his own convictions, as not less congruous with his own theory than with that which he reprobates. In like manner with a kind of instinctive prudence, he will abandon by little and little his weakest posts, till at length he seems to forget that they had ever belonged to him, or affects to consider them at most as accidental and "petty annexments," the removal of which leaves the citadel unhurt and unendangered.

My own differences from certain supposed parts of Mr. Wordsworth's theory ground themselves on the assumption, that his words had been rightly interpreted, as purporting that the proper diction for poetry in general consists altogether in a language taken, with due exceptions, from the mouths of men in real life, a language which actually constitutes the natural conversation of men under the influence of natural feelings. My objection is, first, that in any sense this rule is applicable only to certain classes of poetry; secondly, that even to these classes it is not applicable, except in such a sense, as hath never by any one (as far as I know or have read,) been denied or doubted; and lastly, that as far as, and in that degree in which, it is practicable, it is yet as a rule useless, if not injurious, and therefore either need not, or ought not to be practised. The poet informs his reader, that he had generally chosen low and rustic life; but not as low and rustic, or in order to repeat that pleasure of doubtful moral effect, which persons of elevated rank and of superior refinement oftentimes derive from a happy imitation of the rude unpolished manners and discourse of their inferiors. For the pleasure so derived may be traced to three exciting causes. The first is the naturalness, in fact, of the things represented. The second is the apparent naturalness of the representation, as raised and qualified by an imperceptible infusion of the author's own knowledge and talent, which infusion does, indeed, constitute it an imitation as distinguished from a mere copy. The third cause may be found in the reader's conscious feeling of his superiority awakened by the contrast presented to him; even as for the same purpose the kings and great barons of yore retained, sometimes actual clowns and fools, but more frequently shrewd and witty fellows in that character. These, however, were not Mr. Wordsworth's objects. *He* chose low and rustic life, "because in that condition the essential passions of the heart find a better soil, in which they can attain their maturity, are less under restraint, and speak a plainer and more emphatic language; because in that condition of life our elementary feelings co-exist in a state of greater simplicity, and consequently may be more accurately contemplated, and more forcibly communicated; because the manners of rural life germinate from those elementary feelings; and from the necessary character of rural occupations are more easily comprehended, and are more durable; and lastly, because in that condition the passions of men are incorporated with the beautiful and permanent forms of nature."

Now it is clear to me, that in the most interesting of the poems, in which the author is more or less dramatic, as THE BROTHERS, MICHAEL, RUTH, THE MAD MOTHER, and others, the persons introduced are by no means taken from low or rustic life in the common acceptation of those words! and it is not less clear, that the sentiments and language, as far as they can be conceived to have been really transferred from the minds and conversation of such persons, are attributable to causes and circumstances not necessarily connected with "their occupations and abode." The thoughts, feelings, language, and manners of the shepherd-farmers in the vales of Cumberland and Westmoreland, as far as they are actually adopted in those poems, may be accounted for from causes, which will and do produce the same results in every state of life, whether in town or country. As the two principal I rank that independence, which raises a man above servitude, or daily toil for the profit of others, yet not above the necessity of industry and a frugal simplicity of domestic life; and the accompanying unambitious, but solid and religious, education, which has rendered few books familiar, but the Bible, and the Liturgy or Hymn book. To this latter cause, indeed, which is so far accidental, that it is the blessing of particular countries and a particular age, not the product of particular places or employments, the poet owes the show of probability, that his personages might really feel, think, and talk with any tolerable resemblance to his representation. It is an excellent remark of Dr. Henry More's, that "a man of confined education, but of good parts, by constant reading of the Bible will naturally form a more winning and commanding rhetoric than those that are learned: the intermixture of tongues and of artificial phrases debasing *their* style."

It is, moreover, to be considered that to the formation of healthy feelings, and a reflecting mind, negations involve impediments not less formidable than sophistication and vicious intermixture. I am convinced, that for the human soul to prosper in rustic life a certain vantage-ground is prerequisite. It is not every man that is likely to be improved by a country life or by country labours. Education, or original sensibility, or both, must pre-exist, if the changes, forms, and incidents of nature are to prove a sufficient stimulant. And where these are not sufficient, the mind contracts and hardens by want of stimulants: and the man becomes selfish, sensual, gross, and hard-hearted. Let the management of the Poor Laws in Liverpool, Manchester, or Bristol be compared with the ordinary dispensation of the poor rates in agricultural villages, where the farmers are the overseers and guardians of the poor. If my own experience have not been particularly unfortunate, as well as that of the many respectable country clergymen with whom I have conversed on the subject, the result would engender more than scepticism concerning the desirable influences of low and rustic life in and for itself. Whatever may be concluded on the other side, from the stronger local attachments and enterprising spirit of the Swiss, and other mountaineers, applies to a particular mode of pastoral life, under forms of property that permit and beget manners truly republican, not to rustic life in general, or to the absence of artificial cultivation. On the contrary the mountaineers, whose manners have been so often eulogized, are in general better educated and greater readers than men of equal rank elsewhere. But where this is not the case, as among the peasantry of North Wales, the ancient mountains, with all their terrors and all their glories, are pictures to the blind, and music to the deaf.

I should not have entered so much into detail upon this passage, but here seems to be the point, to which all the lines of difference converge as to their source and centre;—I mean, as far as, and in whatever respect, my poetic creed *does* differ from the doctrines promulgated in this preface. I adopt with full faith the principle of Aristotle, that poetry, as poetry, is essentially ideal, that it avoids and excludes all accident; that its apparent individualities of rank, character, or occupation must be representative of a class; and that the persons of poetry must be clothed with generic attributes, with the common attributes of the class: not with such as one gifted individual might possibly possess, but such as from his situation it is most probable before-hand that he would possess. If my premises are right and my deductions legitimate, it follows that there can be no poetic medium between the swains of Theocritus and those of an imaginary golden age.

The characters of the vicar and the shepherd-mariner in the poem of THE BROTHERS, and that of the shepherd of Green-head Ghyll in the MICHAEL, have all the verisimilitude and representative quality, that the purposes of poetry can require. They are persons of a known and abiding class, and their manners and sentiments the natural product of circumstances common to the class. Take Michael for instance:

"An old man stout of heart, and strong of limb.
His bodily frame had been from youth to age
Of an unusual strength: his mind was keen,
Intense, and frugal, apt for all affairs,
And in his shepherd's calling he was prompt
And watchful more than ordinary men.
Hence he had learned the meaning of all winds,
Of blasts of every tone; and oftentimes
When others heeded not, He heard the South
Make subterraneous music, like the noise
Of bagpipers on distant Highland hills.
The Shepherd, at such warning, of his flock
Bethought him, and he to himself would say,
'The winds are now devising work for me!'
And truly, at all times, the storm, that drives
The traveller to a shelter, summoned him
Up to the mountains: he had been alone
Amid the heart of many thousand mists,
That came to him and left him on the heights.
So lived he, until his eightieth year was past.
And grossly that man errs, who should suppose
That the green valleys, and the streams and
      rocks,
Were things indifferent to the Shepherd's thoughts.
Fields, where with cheerful spirits he had breathed
The common air; the hills which he so oft
Had climbed with vigorous steps; which had im-
      pressed
So many incidents upon his mind
Of hardship, skill or courage, joy or fear;
Which, like a book, preserved the memory
Of the dumb animals, whom he had saved,
Had fed or sheltered, linking to such acts,
So grateful in themselves, the certainty
Of honourable gain; these fields, these hills
Which were his living Being, even more
Than his own blood—what could they less? had
      laid
Strong hold on his affections, were to him
A pleasurable feeling of blind love,
The pleasure which there is in life itself."

On the other hand, in the poems which are pitched in a lower key, as the HARRY GILL, and THE IDIOT BOY, the feelings are those of human nature in general; though the poet has judiciously laid the scene in the country, in order to place himself in the vicinity of interesting images, without the necessity of ascribing a sentimental perception of their beauty to the persons of his drama. IN THE IDIOT BOY, indeed, the mother's character is not so much the real and native product of a "situation where the essential passions of the heart find a better soil, in which they can attain their maturity and speak a plainer and more emphatic language," as it is an impersonation of an instinct abandoned by judgment. Hence the two following charges seem to me not wholly groundless: at least, they are the only plausible objections, which I have heard to that fine poem. The one is, that the author has not, in the poem itself, taken sufficient care to preclude from the reader's fancy the disgusting images of ordinary morbid idiocy, which yet it was by no means his intention to represent. He has even by the "burr, burr, burr," uncounteracted by any preceding description of the boy's beauty, assisted in recalling them. The other is, that the idiocy of the boy is so evenly balanced by the folly of the mother, as to present to the general reader rather a laughable burlesque on the blindness of anile dotage, than an analytic display of maternal affection in its ordinary workings.

In THE THORN, the poet himself acknowledges in a note the necessity of an introductory poem, in which he should have portrayed the character of the person from whom the words of the poem are supposed to proceed: a superstitious man moderately imaginative, of slow faculties and deep feelings, "a captain of a small trading vessel, for example, who, being past the middle age of life, had retired upon an annuity, or small independent income, to some village or country town of which he was not a native, or in which he had not been accustomed to live. Such men having nothing to do become credulous and talkative from indolence." But in a poem, still more in a lyric poem—and the Nurse in ROMEO AND JULIET alone prevents me from extending the remark even to dramatic poetry, if indeed even the Nurse can be deemed altogether a case in point—it is not possible to imitate truly a dull and garrulous discourser, without repeating the effects of dullness and garrulity. However this may be, I dare assert, that the parts—(and these form the far larger portion of the whole)—which might as well or still better have proceeded from the poet's own imagination, and have been spoken in his own character, are those which have given, and which will continue to give, universal delight; and that the passages exclusively appropriate to the supposed narrator, such as the last couplet of the third stanza; the seven last lines of the tenth; and the five following stanzas, with the exception of the four admirable lines at the commencement of the fourteenth, are felt by many unprejudiced and unsophisticated hearts, as sudden and unpleasant sinkings from the height to which the poet had previously lifted them, and to which he again re-elevates both himself and his reader.

If then I am compelled to doubt the theory, by which the choice of characters was to be directed, not only *a priori*, from grounds of reason, but both from the few instances in which the poet himself need be supposed to have been governed by it, and from the comparative inferiority of those instances; still more must I hesitate in my assent to the sentence which immediately follows the former citation; and which I can neither admit as particular fact, nor as general rule. "The language, too, of these men has been adopted (purified indeed from what appear to be its real defects, from all lasting and rational causes of dislike or disgust) because such men hourly communicate with the best objects from which the best part of language is originally derived; and because, from their rank in society and the sameness and narrow circle of their intercourse, being less under the action of social vanity, they convey their feelings and notions in simple and unelaborated expressions." To this I reply; that a rustic's language, purified from all provincialism and grossness, and so far reconstructed as to be made consistent with the rules of grammar— (which are in essence no other than the laws of universal logic, applied to psychological materials)— will not differ from the language of any other man of common sense, however learned or refined he may be, except as far as the notions, which the rustic has to convey, are fewer and more indiscriminate. This will become still clearer, if we add the consideration—(equally important though less obvious)— that the rustic, from the more imperfect development of his faculties, and from the lower state of their cultivation, aims almost solely to convey insulated facts, either those of his scanty experience or his traditional belief; while the educated man

15. **a priori,** from principles or definitions assumed to be true. 22. **"The language" ff.** Miss Marjorie Barstow, in *Wordsworth's Theory of Poetic Diction*, Yale University Press, 1917, thinks that Wordsworth and Coleridge use the word differently: To Coleridge "language" meant words considered in themselves, and especially in their syntactical relations; to Wordsworth, the whole imaginative expression of thought—in most cases, figures of speech.

chiefly seeks to discover and express those connections of things, or those relative bearings of fact to fact, from which some more or less general law is deducible. For facts are valuable to a wise man, chiefly as they lead to the discovery of the indwelling law, which is the true being of things, the sole solution of their modes of existence, and in the knowledge of which consists our dignity and our power.

As little can I agree with the assertion, that from the objects with which the rustic hourly communicates the best part of language is formed. For first, if to communicate with an object implies such a acquaintance with it, as renders it capable of being discriminately reflected on, the distinct knowledge of an uneducated rustic would furnish a very scanty vocabulary. The few things and modes of action requisite for his bodily conveniences would alone be individualized; while all the rest of nature would be expressed by a small number of confused general terms. Secondly, I deny that the words and combinations of words derived from the objects, with which the rustic is familiar, whether with distinct or confused knowledge, can be justly said to form the best part of language. It is more than probable, that many classes of the brute creation possess discriminating sounds, by which they can convey to each other notices of such objects as concern their food, shelter, or safety. Yet we hesitate to call the aggregate of such sounds a language, otherwise than metaphorically. The best part of human language, properly so called, is derived from reflection on the acts of the mind itself. It is formed by a voluntary appropriation of fixed symbols to internal acts, to processes and results of imagination, the greater part of which have no place in the consciousness of uneducated man; though in civilized society, by imitation and passive remembrance of what they hear from their religious instructors and other superiors, the most uneducated share in the harvest which they neither sowed, nor reaped. If the history of the phrases in hourly currency among our peasants were traced, a person not previously aware of the fact would be surprised at finding so large a number, which three or four centuries ago were the exclusive property of the universities and the schools; and, at the commencement of the Reformation, had been transferred from the school to the pulpit, and thus gradually passed into common life. The extreme difficulty, and often the impossibility, of finding words for the simplest moral and intellectual processes in the languages of uncivilized tribes has proved perhaps the weightiest obstacle to the progress of our most zealous and adroit missionaries. Yet these tribes are surrounded by the same nature as our peasants are; but in still more impressive forms; and they are, moreover, obliged to particularize many more of them. When, therefore, Mr. Wordsworth adds, "accordingly, such a language"—(meaning, as before, the language of rustic life purified from provincialism)—"arising out of repeated experience and regular feelings, is a more permanent, and a far more philosophical language, than that which is frequently substituted for it by 10 Poets, who think that they are conferring honour upon themselves and their art in proportion as they indulge in arbitrary and capricious habits of expression"; it may be answered, that the language, which he has in view, can be attributed to rustics with no greater right, than the style of Hooker or Bacon to Tom Brown or Sir Roger L'Estrange. Doubtless, if what is peculiar to each were omitted in each, the result must needs be the same. Further, that the poet, who uses an illogical diction, or a style fitted 20 to excite only the low and changeable pleasure of wonder by means of groundless novelty, substitutes a language of folly and vanity, not for that of the rustic, but for that of good sense and natural feeling.

Here let me be permitted to remind the reader, that the positions, which I controvert, are contained in the sentences—"a selection of the real language of men;"—"the language of these men" (that is, men in low and rustic life) "has been adopted; I have proposed to myself to imitate, and, as far as is 30 possible, to adopt the very language of men."

"Between the language of prose and that of metrical composition, there neither is, nor can be, any *essential difference*": it is against these exclusively that my opposition is directed.

I object, in the very first instance, to an equivocation in the use of the word "real." Every man's language varies, according to the extent of his knowledge, the activity of his faculties, and the depth or quickness of his feelings. Every man's language has, 40 first, its individualities; secondly, the common properties of the class to which he belongs; and thirdly, words and phrases of universal use. The language of Hooker, Bacon, Bishop Taylor, and Burke differs from the common language of the learned class only by the superior number and novelty of the thoughts and relations which they had to convey. The language of Algernon Sidney differs not at all from that, which every well-educated gentleman would wish to write, and (with due allowances for 50 the undeliberateness, and less connected train, of thinking natural and proper to conversation) such as he would wish to talk. Neither one nor the other differs half as much from the general language of

cultivated society, as the language of Mr. Wordsworth's homeliest composition differs from that of a common peasant. For "real" therefore, we must substitute ordinary, or *lingua communis*. And this, we have proved, is no more to be found in the phraseology of low and rustic life than in that of any other class. Omit the peculiarities of each and the result of course must be common to all. And assuredly the omissions and changes to be made in the language 10 of rustics, before it could be transferred to any species of poem, except the drama or other professed imitation, are at least as numerous and weighty, as would be required in adapting to the same purpose the ordinary language of tradesmen and manufacturers. Not to mention, that the language so highly extolled by Mr. Wordsworth varies in every county, nay in every village, according to the accidental character of the clergyman, the existence or non-existence of schools; or even, perhaps, as the 20 exciseman, publican, and barber happen to be, or not to be, zealous politicians, and readers of the weekly newspaper *pro bono publico*. Anterior to cultivation the *lingua communis* of every country, as Dante has well observed, exists every where in parts, and no where as a whole.

Neither is the case rendered at all more tenable by the addition of the words, "in a state of excitement." For the nature of a man's words, where he is strongly affected by joy, grief, or anger, must necessarily depend on the number and quality of the 30 essarily depend on the number and quality of the general truths, conceptions and images, and of the words expressing them, with which his mind had been previously stored. For the property of passion is not to create; but to set in increased activity. At least, whatever new connections of thoughts or images, or—(which is equally, if not more than equally, the appropriate effect of strong excitement)—whatever generalizations of truth or experience the heat of passion may produce; yet the terms 40 of their conveyance must have pre-existed in his former conversations, and are only collected and crowded together by the unusual stimulation. It is indeed very possible to adopt in a poem the unmeaning repetitions, habitual phrases, and other blank counters, which an unfurnished or confused understanding interposes at short intervals, in order to keep hold of his subject, which is still slipping

22. **pro bono publico,** for the public good. 28–33. **For the nature . . . previously stored.** "This is very true," comments Walter Raleigh in *Wordsworth*, Dutton, 1909, "and quite irrelevant. Wordsworth's allusion to the manner in which we associate words in a state of excitement was no part of his theory of diction. Men and women . . . were chosen . . . not as teachers of language but as unusually favorable subjects for the exhibition of the primary laws of our nature."

from him, and to give him time for recollection; or, in mere aid of vacancy, as in the scanty companies of a country stage the same player pops backwards and forwards, in order to prevent the appearance of empty spaces, in the procession of Macbeth, or Henry VIII. But what assistance to the poet, or ornament to the poem, these can supply, I am at a loss to conjecture. Nothing assuredly can differ either in origin or in mode more widely from the apparent tautologies of intense and turbulent feeling, in which the passion is greater and of longer endurance than to be exhausted or satisfied by a single representation of the image or incident exciting it. Such repetitions I admit to be a beauty of the highest kind; as illustrated by Mr. Wordsworth himself from the song of Deborah. *At her feet he bowed, he fell, he lay down: at her feet he bowed, he fell: where he bowed, there he fell down dead.* Judges v. 27.

CHAPTER 18

Language of metrical composition, why and wherein essentially different from that of prose—Origin and elements of metre—Its necessary consequences, and the conditions thereby imposed on the metrical writer in the choice of his diction.

I conclude, therefore, that the attempt is impracticable; and that, were it not impracticable, it would still be useless. For the very power of making the selection implies the previous possession of the language selected. Or where can the poet have lived? And by what rules could he direct his choice, which would not have enabled him to select and arrange his words by the light of his own judgment? We do not adopt the language of a class by the mere adoption of such words exclusively, as that class would use, or at least understand; but likewise by following the order, in which the words of such men are wont to succeed each other. Now this order, in the intercourse of uneducated men, is distinguished from the diction of their superiors in knowledge and power, by the greater disjunction and separation in the component parts of that, whatever it be, which they wish to communicate. There is a want of that prospectiveness of mind, that surview, which enables a man to foresee the whole of what he is to convey, appertaining to any one point; and by this means so to subordinate and arrange the different parts according to their relative importance, as to convey it at once, and as an organized whole.

Now I will take the first stanza, on which I have chanced to open, in the Lyrical Ballads. It is one of the most simple and the least peculiar in its language.

"In distant countries have I been,
    And yet I have not often seen
    A healthy man, a man full grown,
    Weep in the public roads, alone.
    But such a one, on English ground,
    And in the broad highway, I met;
    Along the broad highway he came,
    His cheeks with tears were wet:
    Sturdy he seemed, though he was sad;
    And in his arms a lamb he had."

The words here are doubtless such as are current in all ranks of life; and of course not less so in the hamlet and cottage than in the shop, manufactory, college, or palace. But is this the *order*, in which the rustic would have placed the words? I am grievously deceived, if the following less compact mode of commencing the same tale be not a far more faithful copy. "I have been in a many parts, far and near, and I don't know that I ever saw before a man crying by himself in the public road; a grown man I mean, that was neither sick nor hurt," etc., etc. But when I turn to the following stanza in The Thorn:

"At all times of the day and night
    This wretched woman thither goes;
    And she is known to every star,
    And every wind that blows:
    And there, beside the Thorn, she sits,
    When the blue day-light's in the skies,
    And when the whirlwind's on the hill,
    Or frosty air is keen and still,
    And to herself she cries,
    Oh misery! Oh misery!
    Oh woe is me! Oh misery!"

and compare this with the language of ordinary men; or with that which I can conceive at all likely to proceed, in real life, from such a narrator, as is supposed in the note to the poem; compare it either in the succession of the images or of the sentences; I am reminded of the sublime prayer and hymn of praise, which Milton, in opposition to an established liturgy, presents as a fair specimen of common extemporary devotion, and such as we might expect to hear from every self-inspired minister of a conventicle! And I reflect with delight, how little a mere theory, though of his own workmanship, interferes with the processes of genuine imagination in a man of true poetic genius, who possesses, as

Mr. Wordsworth, if ever man did, most assuredly does possess,

"The Vision and the Faculty divine."

CHARACTERISTICS OF SHAK–SPERE'S DRAMAS

For an account of Coleridge's Shakespearean criticism, see the biographical-critical sketch of him, page 74. For scholarly introduction, texts, and notes, see T. M. Raysor's *Coleridge's Shakespearean Criticism*, Harvard University Press, 1930.

IN lectures of which amusement forms a large part of the object, there are some peculiar difficulties. The architect places his foundation out of sight, and the musician tunes his instrument before he makes his appearance; but the lecturer has to try his chords in the presence of the assembly; an operation not likely, indeed, to produce much pleasure, but yet indispensably necessary to a right understanding of the subject to be developed.

Poetry in essence is as familiar to barbarous as to civilized nations. The Laplander and the savage Indian are cheered by it, as the inhabitants of London and Paris;—its spirit takes up and incorporates surrounding materials, as a plant clothes itself with soil and climate, whilst it exhibits the working of a vital principle within independent of all accidental circumstances. And to judge with fairness of an author's works, we ought to distinguish what is inward and essential from what is outward and circumstantial. It is essential to poetry that it be simple, and appeal to the elements and primary laws of our nature; that it be sensuous, and by its imagery elicit truth at a flash; that it be impassioned, and be able to move our feelings and awaken our affections. In comparing different poets with each other, we should inquire which have brought into the fullest play our imagination and our reason, or have created the greatest excitement and produced the completest harmony. If we consider great exquisiteness of language and sweetness of metre alone, it is impossible to deny to Pope the character of a delightful writer; but whether he be a poet, must depend upon our definition of the word; and, doubtless, if everything that pleases be poetry, Pope's satires and epistles must be poetry. This, I must say, that poetry, as distinguished from other modes of composition, does not rest in metre, and that it is not poetry, if it make no appeal to our passions or our imagination. One character belongs to all true poets, that they write from a principle within, not originating in any thing without; and that the true poet's work in its form, its shapings, and its modifications, is distinguished from all other works that assume to belong to the class of poetry, as a natural from an artificial flower, or as the mimic garden of a child from an enamelled meadow. In the former the flowers are broken from their stems and stuck into the ground; they are beautiful to the eye and fragrant to the sense, but their colours soon fade, and their odour is transient as the smile of the planter;—while the meadow may be visited again and again with renewed delight; its beauty is innate in the soil, and its bloom is of the freshness of nature.

The next ground of critical judgment, and point of comparison, will be as to how far a given poet has been influenced by accidental circumstances. As a living poet must surely write, not for the ages past, but for that in which he lives, and those which are to follow, it is on the one hand natural that he should not violate, and on the other necessary that he should not depend on, the mere manners and modes of his day. See how little does Shakspere leave us to regret that he was born in his particular age! The great era in modern times was what is called the Restoration of Letters;—the ages preceding it are called the dark ages; but it would be more wise, perhaps, to call them the ages in which we were in the dark. It is usually overlooked that the supposed dark period was not universal, but partial and successive, or alternate; that the dark age of England was not the dark age of Italy, but that one country was in its light and vigour, whilst another was in its gloom and bondage. But no sooner had the Reformation sounded through Europe like the blast of an archangel's trumpet, than from king to peasant there arose an enthusiasm for knowledge; the discovery of a manuscript became the subject of an embassy; Erasmus read by moonlight, because he could not afford a torch, and begged a penny, not for the love of charity, but for the love of learning. The three great points of attention were religion, morals, and taste; men of genius, as well as men of learning, who in this age need to be so widely distinguished, then alike became copyists of the ancients; and this, indeed, was the only way by which the taste of mankind could be improved, or their understandings informed. Whilst Dante imagined himself a humble follower of Virgil, and Ariosto of Homer, they were both unconscious of that greater power working within them, which in many points carried them beyond their supposed originals. All great discoveries bear the stamp of the age in which they are made;—hence we perceive the effects of the purer religion of the moderns visible for the most part in their lives; and in reading their works we should not content ourselves with the mere narratives of events long since passed, but should learn to apply their maxims and conduct to themselves.

Having intimated that times and manners lend their form and pressure to genius, let me once more draw a slight parallel between the ancient and modern stage,—the stages of Greece and of England. The Greeks were polytheists; their religion was local; almost the only object of all their knowledge, art, and taste, was their god; and, accordingly, their productions were, if the expression may be allowed, statuesque, whilst those of the moderns are picturesque. The Greeks reared a structure, which, in its parts, and as a whole, filled the mind with the calm and elevated impression of perfect beauty, and symmetrical proportion. The moderns also produced a whole—a more striking whole; but it was by blending materials, and fusing the parts together. And as the Pantheon is to York Minster or Westminster Abbey, so is Sophocles compared with Shakspere; in the one a completeness, a satisfaction, an excellence, on which the mind rests with complacency; in the other a multitude of interlaced materials, great and little, magnificent and mean, accompanied, indeed, with the sense of a falling short of perfection, and yet, at the same time, so promising of our social and individual progression, that we would not, if we could, exchange it for that repose of the mind which dwells on the forms of symmetry in the acquiescent admiration of grace. This general characteristic of the ancient and modern drama might be illustrated by a parallel of the ancient and modern music;—the one consisting of melody arising from a succession only of pleasing sounds,—the modern embracing harmony also, the result of combination, and the effect of a whole.

I have said, and I say it again, that great as was the genius of Shakspere, his judgment was at least equal to it. Of this any one will be convinced, who attentively considers those points in which the dramas of Greece and England differ, from the dissimilitude of circumstances by which each was modified and influenced. The Greek stage had its origin in the ceremonies of a sacrifice, such as of the goat to Bacchus, whom we most erroneously regard as merely the jolly god of wine;—for among the ancients he was venerable, as the symbol of that power which acts without our consciousness in the vital energies of nature—the *vinum mundi*—as Apollo was that of the conscious agency of our in-

52. **vinum mundi**, wine of the world.

tellectual being. The heroes of old, under the influences of this Bacchic enthusiasm, performed more than human actions; hence tales of the favourite champions soon passed into dialogue. On the Greek stage the chorus was always before the audience; the curtain was never dropped, as we should say; and change of place being therefore, in general, impossible, the absurd notion of condemning it merely as improbable in itself was never entertained by any one. If we can believe ourselves at Thebes in one act, we may believe ourselves at Athens in the next. If a story lasts twenty-four hours or twenty-four years, it is equally improbable. There seems to be no just boundary but what the feelings prescribe. But on the Greek stage, where the same persons were perpetually before the audience, great judgment was necessary in venturing on any such change. The poets never, therefore, attempted to impose on the senses by bringing places to men, but they did bring men to places, as in the well-known instance in the *Eumenides*, where, during an evident retirement of the chorus from the orchestra, the scene is changed to Athens, and Orestes is first introduced in the temple of Minerva, and the chorus of Furies come in afterwards in pursuit of him.

In the Greek drama there were no formal divisions into scenes and acts; there were no means, therefore, of allowing for the necessary lapse of time between one part of the dialogue and another, and unity of time in a strict sense was, of course, impossible. To overcome that difficulty of accounting for time, which is effected on the modern stage by dropping a curtain, the judgment and great genius of the ancients supplied music and measured motion, and with the lyric ode filled up the vacuity. In the story of the Agamemnon of Aeschylus, the capture of Troy is supposed to be announced by a fire lighted on the Asiatic shore, and the transmission of the signal by successive beacons to Mycenae. The signal is first seen at the 21st line, and the herald from Troy itself enters at the 486th, and Agamemnon himself at the 783rd line. But the practical absurdity of this was not felt by the audience, who, in imagination, stretched minutes into hours, while they listened to the lofty narrative odes of the chorus which almost entirely filled up the interspace. Another fact deserves attention here, namely, that regularly on the Greek stage a drama, or acted story, consisted in reality of three dramas, called together a trilogy, and performed consecutively in the course of one day. Now you may conceive a tragedy of Shakspere's as a trilogy connected in one single representation. Divide *Lear* into three parts, and each would be a play with the ancients;

or take the three Aeschylean dramas of *Agamemnon*, and divide them into, or call them, as many acts, and they together would be one play. The first act would comprise the usurpation of Aegisthus, and the murder of Agamemnon; the second, the revenge of Orestes, and the murder of his mother; and the third, the penance and absolution of Orestes;—occupying a period of twenty-two years.

The stage in Shakspere's time was a naked room with a blanket for a curtain; but he made it a field for monarchs. That law of unity, which has its foundations, not in the factitious necessity of custom, but in nature itself, the unity of feeling, is every where and at all times observed by Shakspere in his plays. Read *Romeo and Juliet;*—all is youth and spring;—youth with its follies, its virtues, its precipitancies;—youth with its odours, its flowers, and its transiency; it is one and the same feeling that commences, goes through, and ends the play. The old men, the Capulets and Montagues, are not common old men; they have an eagerness, a heartiness, a vehemence, the effect of spring; with Romeo, his change of passion, his sudden marriage, and his rash death, are all the effects of youth;—whilst in Juliet love has all that is tender and melancholy in the nightingale, all that is voluptuous in the rose, with whatever is sweet in the freshness of spring; but it ends with a long deep sigh like the last breeze of the Italian evening. This unity of feeling and character pervades every drama of Shakspere.

It seems to me that his plays are distinguished from those of all other dramatic poets by the following characteristics:—

1. Expectation in preference to surprise. It is like the true reading of the passage—"God said, Let there be light, and there was *light*";—not, "there *was* light." As the feeling with which we startle at a shooting star compared with that of watching the sunrise at the pre-established moment, such and so low is surprise compared with expectation.

2. Signal adherence to the great law of nature, that all opposites tend to attract and temper each other. Passion in Shakspere generally displays libertinism, but involves morality; and if there are exceptions to this, they are, independently of their intrinsic value, all of them indicative of individual character, and, like the farewell admonitions of a parent, have an end beyond the parental relation. Thus the Countess's beautiful precepts to Bertram,

by elevating her character, raise that of Helena her favourite, and soften down the point in her which Shakspere does not mean us not to see, but to see and to forgive, and at length to justify. And so it is in Polonius, who is the personified memory of wisdom no longer actually possessed. This admirable character is always misrepresented on the stage. Shakspere never intended to exhibit him as a buffoon; for although it was natural that Hamlet—a young man of fire and genius, detesting formality, and disliking Polonius on political grounds, as imagining that he had assisted his uncle in his usurpation—should express himself satirically, yet this must not be taken as exactly the poet's conception of him. In Polonius a certain induration of character had arisen from long habits of business; but take his advice to Laertes, and Ophelia's reverence for his memory, and we shall see that he was meant to be represented as a statesman somewhat past his faculties,—his recollections of life all full of wisdom, and showing a knowledge of human nature, whilst what immediately takes place before him and escapes from him, is indicative of weakness.

But as in Homer all the deities are in armour, even Venus, so in Shakspere all the characters are strong. Hence real folly and dulness are made by him the vehicles of wisdom. There is no difficulty for one being a fool to imitate a fool; but to be, remain, and speak like a wise man and a great wit, and yet so as to give a vivid representation of a veritable fool,—*hic labor, hoc opus est*. A drunken constable is not uncommon, nor hard to draw; but see and examine what goes to make up a Dogberry.

3. Keeping at all times in the high road of life. Shakspere has no innocent adulteries, no interesting incests, no virtuous vice; he never renders that amiable which religion and reason alike teach us to detest, or clothes impurity in the garb of virtue, like Beaumont and Fletcher, the Kotzebues of the day. Shakspere's fathers are roused by ingratitude, his husbands stung by unfaithfulness; in him, in short, the affections are wounded in those points in which all may, nay, must, feel. Let the morality of Shakspere be contrasted with that of the writers of his own, or the succeeding age, or of those of the present day, who boast their superiority in this respect. No one can dispute that the result of such a comparison is altogether in favour of Shakspere;—even the letters of women of high rank in his age

---

43. Signal adherence. Compare *Biographia Literaria*, chap. 14, next to last paragraph and note.   **51. Bertram**, in *All's Well That Ends Well*.

31. hic labor . . . est. This is the labor, this is the work.   **40. Kotzebues.** The German August Friedrich Ferdinand von Kotzebue (1761–1819) wrote over two hundred plays, as well as novels and historical works.

were often coarser than his writings. If he occasionally disgusts a keen sense of delicacy, he never injures the mind; he neither excites, nor flatters,
passion, in order to degrade the subject of it; he
does not use the faulty thing for a faulty purpose,
nor carries on warfare against virtue, by causing
wickedness to appear as no wickedness, through the
medium of a morbid sympathy with the unfortunate. In Shakspere vice never walks as in twilight;
nothing is purposely out of place;—he inverts
not the order of nature and propriety,—does not
make every magistrate a drunkard or glutton, nor
every poor man meek, humane, and temperate;
he has no benevolent butchers, or sentimental rat-
catchers.

4. Independence of the dramatic interest on the
plot. The interest in the plot is always in fact on account of the characters, not *vice versa*, as in almost
all other writers; the plot is a mere canvas and no
more. Hence arises the true justification of the
same stratagem being used in regard to Benedick
and Beatrice,—the vanity in each being alike. Take
away from the *Much Ado about Nothing* all that which
is not indispensable to the plot, either as having
little to do with it, or, at best, like Dogberry and his
comrades, forced into the service, when any other
less ingeniously absurd watchmen and night-
constables would have answered the mere necessities of the action;—take away Benedick, Beatrice,
Dogberry, and the reaction of the former on the
character of Hero,—and what will remain? In
other writers the main agent of the plot is always
the prominent character; in Shakspere it is so, or is
not so, as the character is in itself calculated, or not
calculated, to form the plot. Don John is the main-
spring of the plot of this play; but he is merely
shown and then withdrawn.

5. Independence of the interest on the story as
the ground-work of the plot. Hence Shakspere
never took the trouble of inventing stories. It was
enough for him to select from those that had been
already invented or recorded such as had one or
other, or both of two recommendations, namely,
suitableness to his particular purpose, and their
being parts of popular tradition,—names of which
we had often heard, and of their fortunes, and as to
which all we wanted was, to see the man himself.
So it is just the man himself—the Lear, the Shy-
lock, the Richard—that Shakspere makes us for the
first time acquainted with. Omit the first scene in
Lear, and yet everything will remain; so the first and
second scenes in *The Merchant of Venice*. Indeed it is
universally true.

6. Interfusion of the lyrical—that which in its

very essence is poetical—not only with the dramatic, as in the plays of Metastasio, where at the end
of the scene comes the *aria* as the *exit* speech of the
character,—but also in and through the dramatic.
Songs in Shakspere are introduced as songs only,
just as songs are in real life, beautifully as some of
them are characteristic of the person who had sung
or called for them, as Desdemona's "Willow," and
Ophelia's wild snatches, and the sweet carolings in
As You Like It. But the whole of the *Midsummer
Night's Dream* is one continued specimen of the
dramatized lyrical. And observe how exquisitely
the dramatic of Hotspur;—

"Marry, and I'm glad on't with all my heart;
    I'd rather be a kitten and cry mew," etc.

melts away into the lyric of Mortimer;—

"I understand thy looks; that pretty Welsh
Which thou pour'st down from these swelling
    heavens,
I am too perfect in," etc.

            Henry IV, part i, act iii, sc. i.

7. The characters of the *dramatis personae,* like
those in real life, are to be inferred by the reader;—
they are not told to him. And it is well worth remarking that Shakspere's characters, like those in
real life, are very commonly misunderstood, and
almost always understood by different persons in
different ways. The causes are the same in either
case. If you take only what the friends of the
character say, you may be deceived, and still more
so, if that which his enemies say; nay, even the
character himself sees himself through the medium
of his character, and not exactly as he is. Take all
together, not omitting a shrewd hint from the clown
or the fool, and perhaps your impression will be
right; and you may know whether you have in fact
discovered the poet's own idea, by all the speeches
receiving light from it, and attesting its reality by
reflecting it.

Lastly, in Shakspere the heterogeneous is united,
as it is in nature. You must not suppose a pressure
or passion always acting on or in the character:—
passion in Shakspere is that by which the individual
is distinguished from others, not that which makes
a different kind of him. Shakspere followed the
main march of the human affections. He entered
into no analysis of the passions or faiths of men, but

2. **Metastasio,** the adopted name of Pietro Antonio
Domenico Bonaventura (1698–1782), an Italian dramatist
and poet.

assured himself that such and such passions and faiths were grounded in our common nature, and not in the mere accidents of ignorance or disease.

This is an important consideration, and constitutes our Shakspere the morning star, the guide and the pioneer, of true philosophy.

Robert Southey
1774–1843

At Bristol on August 12, 1774, Robert Southey was born to a dry-goods merchant and his wife of that city. He was early half-adopted by his Aunt Tyler, who lived at the fashionable resort of Bath. This strong-minded maiden lady bought a copy of *Emile* and proceeded to bring up the boy in accordance with her interpretation of Rousseau's system of education. She indulged him in such books as *Goody Two Shoes* and encouraged him to do much precocious reading in Shakespeare, Beaumont and Fletcher, and, later, the Italian poets in translation. After much more of this sort of old-maidish and bookish training, the boy was entered at Westminster School. He remained four years, until his expulsion for writing an article in the school paper against overdiscipline. At Oxford one college refused him admission, but Balliol accepted him. His career there was radical and republican. He sympathized with the French Revolution, declaimed for freedom, and wrote an epic poem, *Joan of Arc*, emphasizing the liberating value of this French heroine of the people. From English history he selected Wat Tyler, leader of the fourteenth-century Peasants' Revolt, and dramatized his career. When, in 1794, he was visited by Coleridge, the two and their friend Robert Lovell formed the Pantisocracy scheme, collaborated in writing *The Fall of Robespierre*, and married sisters. Leaving his Edith at the church door of St. Mary Redcliffe, he went to Portugal to take a position with an uncle.

Between that event (1795) and 1803, Southey lived abroad for a while, wandered about, wrote poetry, and began his long *History of Portugal*. "The Battle of Blenheim," "The Well of St. Keyne," and "The Old Woman of Berkeley" belong to the ballad-writing phase of the 1790's. His most ambitious poems were long narratives—*Thalaba*, 1801, in unrhymed, irregular verse, about Arabian diabolism; *Madoc*, 1805, about a Welsh hero who goes to Florida, then to Aztec Mexico, in pre-Columbian times; and *The Curse of Kehama*, 1810, about a Brahmin who kills a Hindu crown prince for wronging his daughter and has a curse put upon him.

In 1803 Southey settled at Greta Hall, Keswick, in the Lake Country, as neighbor to Coleridge and Wordsworth. There he spent the remainder of his life quietly, toiling away at magazine articles and books, being a good neighbor and friend to such people as Scott and Wordsworth, and looking after his family and Coleridge's. His political ardor had cooled. He abandoned hope for the French Revolution, concluding that "the millennium would not come that bout," and associated himself with the conservatives, becoming one of the chief contributors to the Tory *Quarterly Review*. Long before 1813, when his friend Scott, declining the poet-laureateship for himself, helped to obtain the honor for Southey, Southey had been accused of being a turncoat and was derided by such liberals as Byron (*English Bards*). His enemies dug up his youthful *Wat Tyler* and gleefully published it. When, in 1821, he published his official poem on the death of George III, *A Vision of Judgment*, he brought upon his head the fiery burlesque bomb of Byron. By many serious and just people, however, Southey was esteemed as a man of pure motives and exemplary character, and his political changes seem less culpable to us today than they did to his contemporaries.

Southey was almost exclusively a professional man of letters—poet, critic, journalist, biographer, novelist, folklorist, historian—the author or editor of over one hundred volumes. Ambitious and prolific as he was, he is remembered only for a few good things. Such poems as "The Holly Tree," "My Days among the Dead Are Passed," and "How the Waters Come Down at Lodore," and the ballads mentioned above are memorable for a sincere, pungent homeliness or for their vivacity as jeux d'esprit. His *Ode Written during the Negotiations with Napoleon Buonaparte* (1813) has been characterized as "perhaps the loftiest chaunt of political invective, inspired by moral indignation." Southey's prose, admirable for its ease and lucidity, fares better than his poetry. His biographies of Nelson, John Wesley, Bunyan, and Cowper have been praised by em-

inent critics from Coleridge to George Saintsbury.
His rambling, folklore-crammed novel *The Doctor*
has been saved from oblivion by the nursery favorite "The Three Bears," which savors of the salt that
has preserved Southey's familiar verse. Perhaps one
reason why even his best work is little read today is
the one suggested by Byron—"A bard may chaunt
too often and too long."

THE WELL OF ST. KEYNE

A Well there is in the west country,
   And a clearer one never was seen;
There is not a wife in the west country
   But has heard of the Well of St. Keyne.

An oak and an elm tree stand beside,
   And behind does an ash-tree grow,
And a willow from the bank above
   Droops to the water below.

A traveller came to the Well of St. Keyne;
   Joyfully he drew nigh,   10
For from cock-crow he had been travelling,
   And there was not a cloud in the sky.

He drank of the water so cool and clear,
   For thirsty and hot was he,
And he sat down upon the bank,
   Under the willow-tree.

There came a man from the house hard by
   At the Well to fill his pail,
On the Well-side he rested it,
   And he bade the Stranger hail.   20

"Now art thou a bachelor, Stranger?" quoth he,
   "For an if thou hast a wife,
The happiest draught thou hast drank this day
   That ever thou didst in thy life.

"Or has thy good woman, if one thou hast,
   Ever here in Cornwall been?
For an if she have, I'll venture my life,
   She has drunk of the Well of St. Keyne."

"I have left a good woman who never was here,"
   The Stranger he made reply;   30
"But that my draught should be the better for that,
   I pray you answer me why."

"St. Keyne," quoth the Cornish-man, "many a
     time
   Drank of this crystal Well,

And before the Angel summoned her
   She laid on the water a spell.

"If the Husband of this gifted Well
   Shall drink before his Wife,
A happy man thenceforth is he,
   For he shall be Master for life.   40

"But if the Wife should drink of it first,
   God help the Husband then!"
The Stranger stoopt to the Well of St. Keyne,
   And drank of the waters again.

"You drank of the Well I warrant betimes?"
   He to the Cornish-man said:
But the Cornish-man smiled as the Stranger spake,
   And sheepishly shook his head.

"I hastened, as soon as the wedding was done,
   And left my Wife in the porch.   50
But i' faith, she had been wiser than me,
   For she took a bottle to Church."

THE OLD WOMAN OF BERKELEY

A BALLAD,
SHEWING HOW AN OLD WOMAN RODE DOUBLE,
AND WHO RODE BEFORE HER

The Raven croaked as she sate at her meal,
   And the Old Woman knew what he said,
And she grew pale at the Raven's tale,
   And sickened and went to her bed.

"Now fetch me my children, and fetch them with
     speed,"
   The Old Woman of Berkeley said,
"The Monk my son, and my daughter the Nun,
   Bid them hasten or I shall be dead."

The Monk her son, and her daughter the Nun,
   Their way to Berkeley went,   10
And they have brought with pious thought
   The holy sacrament.

The Old Woman shrieked as they entered her door,
   And she cried with a voice of despair,
"Now take away the sacrament,
   For its presence I cannot bear!"

Her lip it trembled with agony,
   The sweat ran down her brow,
"I have tortures in store for evermore,
   But spare me, my children, now!"   20

Away they sent the sacrament,
  The fit it left her weak,
She looked at her children with ghastly eyes,
  And faintly struggled to speak.

"All kind of sin I have rioted in,
  And the judgement now must be,
But I secured my children's souls,
  Oh! pray, my children, for me!

"I have 'nointed myself with infant's fat,
  The Fiends have been my slaves,   30
From sleeping babes I have sucked the breath,
And breaking by charms the sleep of death,
  I have called the dead from their graves.

"And the Devil will fetch me now in fire,
  My witchcrafts to atone;
And I who have troubled the dead man's grave
  Shall never have rest in my own.

"Bless, I entreat, my winding sheet,
  My children, I beg of you;
And with holy water sprinkle my shroud,   40
  And sprinkle my coffin too.

"And let me be chained in my coffin of stone,
  And fasten it strong, I implore,
With iron bars, and with three chains,
  Chain it to the church floor.

"And bless the chains and sprinkle them,
  And let fifty Priests stand round,
Who night and day the mass may say
  Where I lie on the ground.

"And see that fifty Choristers   50
  Beside the bier attend me,
And day and night by the tapers' light,
  With holy hymns defend me.

"Let the church bells all both great and small,
  Be tollèd by night and day,
To drive from thence the fiends who come
  To bear my body away.

"And ever have the church door barred
  After the even-song;
And I beseech you, children dear,   60
  Let the bars and bolts be strong.

"And let this be three days and nights
  My wretched corpse to save;
Till the fourth morning keep me safe,
  And then I may rest in my grave."

The Old Woman of Berkeley laid her down,
  And her eyes grew deadly dim,
Short came her breath, and the struggle of death
  Did loosen every limb.

They blest the old woman's winding sheet   70
  With rites and prayers due,
With holy water they sprinkled her shroud,
  And they sprinkled her coffin too.

And they chained her in her coffin of stone,
  And with iron barred it down,
And in the church with three strong chains
  They chained it to the ground.

And they blest the chains and sprinkled them,
  And fifty Priests stood round,
By night and day the mass to say   80
  Where she lay on the ground.

And fifty sacred Choristers
  Beside the bier attend her,
Who day and night by the tapers' light
  Should with holy hymns defend her.

To see the Priests and Choristers
  It was a goodly sight,
Each holding, as it were a staff,
  A taper burning bright.

And the church bells all both great and small,   90
  Did toll so loud and long;
And they have barred the church door hard,
  After the even-song.

And the first night the tapers' light
  Burnt steadily and clear,
But they without a hideous rout
  Of angry Fiends could hear;

A hideous roar at the church door
  Like a long thunder peal;   99
And the Priests they prayed, and the Choristers sung
  Louder in fearful zeal.

Loud tolled the bell, the Priests prayed well,
  The tapers they burnt bright,
The Monk her son, and her daughter the Nun,
  They told their beads all night.

The cock he crew, the Fiends they flew
  From the voice of the morning away;
Then undisturbed the Choristers sing,
  And the fifty Priests they pray;
As they had sung and prayed all night   110
  They prayed and sung all day.

The second night the tapers' light
  Burnt dismally and blue,
And every one saw his neighbour's face
  Like a dead man's face to view.

And yells and cries without arise
  That the stoutest heart might shock,
And a deafening roaring like a cataract pouring
  Over a mountain rock.

The Monk and Nun they told their beads   120
  As fast as they could tell,
And aye as louder grew the noise
  The faster went the bell.

Louder and louder the Choristers sung
  As they trembled more and more,
And the Priests as they prayed to heaven for aid,
  They smote their breasts full sore.

The cock he crew, the Fiends they flew
  From the voice of the morning away;
Then undisturbed the Choristers sing,   130
  And the fifty Priests they pray;
As they had sung and prayed all night
  They prayed and sung all day.

The third night came, and the tapers' flame
  A frightful stench did make,
And they burnt as though they had been dipt
  In the burning brimstone lake.

And the loud commotion, like the rushing of ocean,
  Grew momently more and more;
And strokes as of a battering ram,   140
  Did shake the strong church door.

The bellmen, they for very fear
  Could toll the bell no longer;
And still as louder grew the strokes,
  Their fear it grew the stronger.

The Monk and Nun forgot their beads,
  They fell on the ground in dismay;
There was not a single Saint in heaven
  To whom they did not pray.   149

And the Choristers' song, which late was so strong,
  Faltered with consternation,
For the church did rock as an earthquake shock
  Uplifted its foundation.

And a sound was heard like the trumpet's blast,
  That shall one day wake the dead;

The strong church door could bear no more,
  And the bolts and the bars they fled;

And the tapers' light was extinguished quite,
  And the Choristers faintly sung,
And the Priests dismayed, panted and prayed,   160
And on all Saints in heaven for aid
  They called with trembling tongue.

And in he came with eyes of flame,
  The Devil to fetch the dead,
And all the church with his presence glowed
  Like a fiery furnace red.

He laid his hand on the iron chains,
  And like flax they mouldered asunder,
And the coffin lid, which was barred so firm,
  He burst with his voice of thunder.   170

And he bade the Old Woman of Berkley rise,
  And come with her master away;
A cold sweat started on that cold corpse,
  At the voice she was forced to obey.

She rose on her feet in her winding sheet,
  Her dead flesh quivered with fear,
And a groan like that which the Old Woman gave
  Never did mortal hear.

She followed her Master to the church door,
  There stood a black horse there;   180
His breath was red like furnace smoke,
  His eyes like a meteor's glare.

The Devil he flung her on the horse,
  And he leapt up before,
And away like the lightning's speed they went,
  And she was seen no more.

They saw her no more, but her cries
  For four miles round they could hear,
And children at rest at their mothers' breast
  Started, and screamed with fear.   190

THE BATTLE OF BLENHEIM

I

It was a summer evening,
  Old Kaspar's work was done,
And he before his cottage door
  Was sitting in the sun,
And by him sported on the green
His little grandchild Wilhelmine.

2

She saw her brother Peterkin
  Roll something large and round,
Which he beside the rivulet
  In playing there had found;   10
He came to ask what he had found,
That was so large, and smooth, and round.

3

Old Kaspar took it from the boy,
  Who stood expectant by;
And then the old man shook his head,
  And with a natural sigh,
"'Tis some poor fellow's skull," said he,
"Who fell in the great victory.

4

"I find them in the garden,
  For there's many here about;   20
And often, when I go to plough,
  The ploughshare turns them out!
For many thousand men," said he,
"Were slain in that great victory."

5

"Now tell us what 'twas all about,"
  Young Peterkin he cries;
And little Wilhelmine looks up
  With wonder-waiting eyes;
"Now tell us all about the war,
And what they fought each other for.'   30

6

"It was the English," Kaspar cried,
  "Who put the French to rout;
But what they fought each other for,
  I could not well make out;
But every body said," quoth he,
"That 'twas a famous victory.

7

"My father lived at Blenheim then,
  Yon little stream hard by;
They burnt his dwelling to the ground,
  And he was forced to fly;   40
So with his wife and child he fled,
Nor had he where to rest his head.

8

"With fire and sword the country round
  Was wasted far and wide,

---

18. **great victory,** won in Bavaria, 1704, by the British
and Germans from the French and Bavarians.

And many a childing mother then,
  And new-born baby died;
But things like that, you know, must be
At every famous victory.

9

"They say it was a shocking sight
  After the field was won;   50
For may thousand bodies here
  Lay rotting in the sun;
But things like that, you know, must be
After a famous victory.

10

"Great praise the Duke of Marlbro' won,
  And our good Prince Eugene."
"Why, 'twas a very wicked thing!"
  Said little Wilhelmine.
"Nay—nay—my little girl," quoth he,
"It was a famous victory.   6o

11

"And every body praised the Duke,
  Who this great fight did win."
"But what good came of it at last?"
  Quoth little Peterkin.
"Why, that I cannot tell," said he;
"But 'twas a famous victory."

THE HOLLY TREE

I

O Reader! hast thou ever stood to see
  The Holly Tree?
The eye that contemplates it well perceives
  Its glossy leaves
Ordered by an intelligence so wise,
As might confound the Atheist's sophistries.

2

Below, a circling fence, its leaves are seen
  Wrinkled and keen;
No grazing cattle through their prickly round
  Can reach to wound;   10
But as they grow where nothing is to fear,
Smooth and unarmed the pointless leaves appear.

3

I love to view these things with curious eyes,
  And moralize;
And in this wisdom of the Holly Tree
  Can emblem see
Wherewith perchance to make a pleasant rhyme,
One which may profit in the after time.

4

Thus, though abroad perchance I might appear
  Harsh and austere,   20
To those who on my leisure would intrude
  Reserved and rude,
Gentle at home amid my friends I'd be
Like the high leaves upon the Holly Tree.

5

And should my youth, as youth is apt I know,
  Some harshness show,
All vain asperities I day by day
  Would wear away,
Till the smooth temper of my age should be
Like the high leaves upon the Holly Tree.   30

6

And as, when all the summer trees are seen
  So bright and green,
The Holly leaves a sober hue display
  Less bright than they;
But when the bare and wintry woods we see,
What then so cheerful as the Holly Tree?

7

So serious should my youth appear among
  The thoughtless throng,
So would I seem amid the young and gay
  More grave than they,   40
That in my age as cheerful I might be
As the green winter of the Holly Tree.

MY DAYS AMONG THE DEAD ARE PAST

My days among the dead are past;
  Around me I behold,
Where'er these casual eyes are cast,
  The mighty minds of old;
My never-failing friends are they,
With whom I converse day by day.

With them I take delight in weal,
  And seek relief in woe;
And while I understand and feel
  How much to them I owe,   10
My cheeks have often been bedewed
With tears of thoughtful gratitude.

My thoughts are with the dead, with them
  I live in long-past years,
Their virtues love, their faults condemn,
  Partake their hopes and fears,

And from their lessons seek and find
Instruction with an humble mind.

My hopes are with the dead, anon
  My place with them will be,   20
And I with them shall travel on
  Through all futurity;
Yet leaving here a name, I trust,
That will not perish in the dust.

from THE DOCTOR

Literary   Fair Tale.

THE STORY OF THE THREE BEARS

A tale which may content the minds
Of learned men and grave philosophers.—Gascoyne

ONCE upon a time there were Three Bears, who lived together in a house of their own, in a wood. One of them was a Little, Small, Wee Bear; and one was a Middle-sized Bear, and the other was a Great, Huge Bear. They had each a pot for their porridge, a little pot for the Little, Small, Wee Bear; and a middle-sized pot for the Middle Bear; and a great pot for the Great, Huge Bear. And they had each a chair to sit in; a little chair for the Little, Small, Wee Bear; and a middle-sized chair for the Middle Bear; and a great chair for the Great, Huge Bear. And they had each a bed to sleep in; a little bed for the Little, Small, Wee Bear; and a middle-sized bed for the Middle Bear; and a great bed for the Great, Huge Bear.

One day, after they had made the porridge for their breakfast, and poured it into their porridge-pots, they walked out into the wood while the porridge was cooling, that they might not burn their mouths, by beginning too soon to eat it. And while they were walking, a little old Woman came to the house. She could not have been a good, honest old Woman; for first she looked in at the window, and then she peeped in at the keyhole; and seeing nobody in the house, she lifted the latch. The door was not fastened, because the Bears were good Bears, who did nobody any harm, and never suspected that anybody would harm them. So the little old Woman opened the door, and went in; and well pleased she was when she saw the porridge on the table. If she had been a good little old Woman, she would have waited till the Bears came home, and then, perhaps, they would have asked her to breakfast; for they were good Bears,—a little rough or so, as the manner of Bears is, but for all that very good-natured and hospitable. But she was an impudent, bad old Woman, and set about helping herself.

So first she tasted the porridge of the Great, Huge Bear, and that was too hot for her; and she said a bad word about that. And then she tasted the porridge of the Middle Bear, and that was too cold for her; and she said a bad word about that, too. And then she went to the porridge of the Little, Small, Wee Bear, and tasted that; and that was neither too hot, nor too cold, but just right; and she liked it so well, that she ate it all up: but the naughty old Woman said a bad word about the little porridge- 10 pot, because it did not hold enough for her.

Then the little old Woman sate down in the chair of the Great, Huge Bear, and that was too hard for her. And then she sate down in the chair of the Middle Bear, and that was too soft for her. And then she sate down in the chair of the Little, Small, Wee Bear, and that was neither too hard, nor too soft, but just right. So she seated herself in it, and there she sate till the bottom of the chair came out, and down came hers, plump upon the ground. 20 And the naughty old Woman said a wicked word about that too.

Then the little old Woman went up stairs into the bed-chamber in which the three Bears slept. And first she lay down upon the bed of the Great, Huge Bear; but that was too high at the head for her. And next she lay down upon the bed of the Middle Bear; and that was too high at the foot for her. And then she lay down upon the bed of the Little, Small, Wee Bear; and that was neither too 30 high at the head, nor at the foot, but just right. So she covered herself up comfortably, and lay there till she fell fast asleep.

By this time the Three Bears thought their porridge would be cool enough; so they came home to breakfast. Now the little old Woman had left the spoon of the Great, Huge Bear, standing in his porridge.

"Somebody has been at my porridge!"

said the Great, Huge Bear, in his great, rough, gruff voice. And when the Middle Bear looked at his, he saw that the spoon was standing in it too. They were wooden spoons; if they had been silver ones, the naughty old Woman would have put them in her pocket.

"Somebody has been at my porridge!"

said the Middle Bear, in his middle voice.

Then the Little, Small, Wee Bear looked at his, 50 and there was the spoon in the porridge-pot, but the porridge was all gone.

"Somebody has been at my porridge, and has eaten it all up!"

said the Little, Small, Wee Bear, in his little, small, wee voice.

Upon this the Three Bears, seeing that some one had entered their house, and eaten up the Little, Small, Wee Bear's Breakfast, began to look about them. Now the little old Woman had not put the hard cushion straight when she rose from the chair of the Great, Huge Bear.

"Somebody has been sitting in my chair!"

said the Great, Huge Bear, in his great, rough, gruff voice.

And the little old Woman had squatted down the soft cushion of the Middle Bear.

"Somebody has been sitting in my chair!"

said the Middle Bear, in his middle voice.

And you know what the little old Woman had done to the third chair.

"Somebody has been sitting in my chair, and has sate the bottom of it out!"

said the Little, Small, Wee Bear, in his little, small, wee voice.

Then the Three Bears thought it necessary that they should make farther search; so they went up stairs into their bed-chamber. Now the little old Woman had pulled the pillow of the Great, Huge Bear, out of its place.

"Somebody has been lying in my bed!"

said the Great, Huge Bear, in his great, rough, gruff voice.

And the little old Woman had pulled the bolster of the Middle Bear out of its place.

"Somebody has been lying in my bed!"

said the Middle Bear, in his middle voice.

And when the Little, Small, Wee Bear came to 40 look at his bed, there was the bolster in its place; and the pillow in its place upon the bolster; and upon the pillow was the little old Woman's ugly, dirty head,—which was not in its place, for she had no business there.

"Somebody has been lying in my bed,—and here she is!"

said the Little, Small, Wee Bear, in his little, small, wee voice.

The little old Woman had heard in her sleep the great, rough, gruff voice of the Great, Huge Bear; but she was so fast asleep that it was no more to her than the roaring of wind, or the rumbling of thunder. And she had heard the middle voice of the Middle Bear, but it was only as if she had heard some one speaking in a dream. But when she heard the little, small, wee voice of the Little, Small, Wee Bear, it was so sharp, and so shrill, that it awakened her at once. Up she started; and when she saw the Three Bears on one side of the bed, she tumbled herself out at the other, and ran to the window. Now the window was open, because the Bears, like good, tidy Bears, as they were, always opened their bed-chamber window when they got up in the morning. Out the little old Woman jumped; and whether she broke her neck in the fall; or ran into the wood and was lost there; or found her way out of the wood, and was taken up by the constable and sent to the House of Correction for a vagrant as she was, I cannot tell. But the Three Bears never saw any thing more of her.

Charles Lamb
1775–1834

In the quiet seclusion of the Temple, a medieval quarter of the old city of London used by lawyers for their clubs and offices, Charles Lamb was born on February 10, 1775. His father was clerk to a lawyer named Samuel Salt, and possessed considerable literary cultivation. His mother was Elizabeth Field, of Blakesmore, Hertfordshire. One of Lamb's most memorable childhood experiences was a visit to his grandmother in Hertfordshire (see "Mackery End"). Two of the other children of the family lived to maturity—John, twelve years Charles's senior, and Mary, ten years older. Charles was educated at the neighboring Christ's Hospital school, where he was a schoolmate of Coleridge (see "Christ's Hospital"). Unable because of an impediment in speech to win a university scholarship, he went to work as a bookkeeper, first in the South Sea House, where John had a place, and then in the India House. In the latter he remained thirty-three years. An early love affair with Ann Simmons, whom he had met in Hertfordshire, was frustrated by family disaster. In 1796 his sister Mary suddenly became insane and killed their mother. Mary regained her sanity and in mental health retained her social charm, but remained subject to recurrent derangement. The care of her became Charles's labor of love.

As boy and man he had cultivated his literary tastes, and he and Mary made their home a gathering-place for many of the distinguished literati and artists about town. They numbered among their friends Southey, Coleridge, Wordsworth, Hazlitt, Leigh Hunt, and Haydon. Charles's letters to these and others are among the best of a period of fine letter-writers, and contain much brilliant informal literary criticism (for example "Letter to Wordsworth"). "I am a dab at prose; poetry I leave to my betters." After brief but moving poetic efforts of his own (for example, "The Old Familiar Faces"), Lamb began his major critical work by collaborating with Mary on *Tales from Shakespere*, 1807, one of the landmarks of nineteenth-century popular Shakespearean appreciation. After this he edited *Specimens of the Dramatic Poets Who Lived about the Time of Shakespere*, 1808, his selections and notes rediscovering dramatists like Heywood and Ford. In 1820, at the age of forty-five, he really found himself when he published in the *London Magazine* the first of his *Essays of Elia*. A few years later he was retired on a pension (see "The Superannuated Man"). He and Mary adopted an orphan girl, Emma Isola, who cheered their home until her marriage. More frequent recurrences of Mary's attacks darkened their last years together. Coleridge's death in July, 1834, shocked Lamb deeply. He followed on December 29, leaving behind him adequate provision for Mary.

Lamb was the prose poet of his native London, a stimulating and sympathetic friend of great writers of his age, an informal literary critic with swift and illuminating insight, but above all one of the greatest masters of the familiar essay. It is chiefly by his *Essays of Elia*, collected in 1833, that he lives and bids fair to live indefinitely. Like Wordsworth, he discovered that his greatest treasure was his memory of the past—of a past spent, however, not in country solitudes but in the teeming heart of a great city. Many of his best essays, such as "The South Sea House," "Christ's Hospital," and "Old China," are at the same time intimately autobiographical and descriptive of the old city that was passing away. "Old China" mentions most of his favorite themes—old books, old plays, old pictures, the theater, the society of Bridget (Mary). Most deeply personal, perhaps, are "Mackery End" and "Dream-Children," with their moods of faraway and long ago, their pathos of the past and the might-have-been. Character types whom Lamb knew are sketched in "Mrs. Battle's Opinions on Whist," "The South Sea House," and "Poor Relations." Lamb's criticism of everyday life and the art of living is well exemplified by "The Two Races of Men" and "Imperfect Sympathies." His best art and literary criticism outside his letters is found in such essays as "The Genius of Hogarth," "The Sanity of True Genius," and "On the Tragedies of Shakespere, Considered with Reference to Their Fitness for Stage Representation." The last-named is a witticism, like the more famous "Dissertation on Roast Pig." It was provoked by the epitaph on the actor David Garrick in Westminster Abbey:

SHAKESPEARE and GARRICK like twin stars shall shine
And earth irradiate with a beam divine.

Irritated by what he considered the impudence of this linking of names, Lamb maintained that Shakespeare's plays are more often than not spoiled by bad acting and, more seriously, that there is in them a flavor to be extracted only in quiet reading.

The charm of Lamb is a personal emanation from his writing. It is the result of a blend of humor and seriousness (never solemnity), willful whimsicality and sound sense, harmless malice (see "Imperfect Sympathies"), and tenderness, and a score more of the nuances of reconciled opposites, all conveyed by one of the most flexible and sensitive of prose styles. Of his writing, as Hazlitt said of his talk, it is true that "His jests scald like tears; and he probes a question with a play upon words." His charm exerts itself upon whoever opens and leisurely reads an essay here and there in any volume or collection of Elia. Blessed is he who finds Elia early, and equally blessed is he who finds Elia late. No literary source of pleasure will flow more satisfyingly from youth to old age. None can be less disappointing at any stage of the journey.

THE OLD FAMILIAR FACES

Where are they gone, the old familiar faces?

I had a mother, but she died, and left me,
Died prematurely in a day of horrors—
All, all are gone, the old familiar faces.

I have had playmates, I have had companions,
In my days of childhood, in my joyful school-days,
All, all are gone, the old familiar faces.

3. **Died prematurely,** in 1796, slain by Mary in a fit of insanity.   6. **school-days,** at Christ's Hospital.

I have been laughing, I have been carousing,
Drinking late, sitting late, with my bosom cronies,
All, all are gone, the old familiar faces.   10

I loved a love once, fairest among women.
Closed are her doors on me, I must not see her—
All, all are gone, the old familiar faces.

I have a friend, a kinder friend has no man.
Like an ingrate, I left my friend abruptly;
Left him, to muse on the old familiar faces.

Ghost-like, I paced round the haunts of my childhood.
Earth seemed a desert I was bound to traverse,
Seeking to find the old familiar faces—

Friend of my bosom, thou more than a brother,   20
Why wert not thou born in my father's dwelling?
So might we talk of the old familiar faces—

For some they have died, and some they have left me,
And some are taken from me; all are departed;
All, all are gone, the old familiar faces.

LETTER TO WORDSWORTH

January 30, 1801

THANKS for your Letter and Present. I had already borrowed your second volume. What most please me are, the Song of Lucy. . . . *Simon's sickly daughter* in the Sexton made me *cry*. Next to these are the description of the continuous Echoes in the story of Joanna's laugh, where the mountains and all the scenery absolutely seem alive—and that fine Shakesperian character of the Happy Man, in the Brothers,

"—that creeps about the fields,
Following his fancies by the hour, to bring
Tears down his cheek, or solitary smiles
Into his face, *until the Setting Sun
Write Fool upon his forehead.*"

I will mention one more: the delicate and curious feeling in the wish for the Cumberland Beggar, that he may have about him the melody of Birds, altho' he hear them not. Here the mind knowingly passes

11. **fairest among women,** Ann Simmons, "Alice W." (see "Dream-Children"). 14. **friend,** Charles Lloyd. 17. **haunts,** the Temple and perhaps Mackery End. 20. **Friend of my bosom,** Coleridge. 24. **taken from me,** Mary, sent to an asylum. 2. **second volume,** *Lyrical Ballads,* 2nd ed., 1800. 3. **Song of Lucy,** "Lucy Gray." 6. **Joanna,** "To Joanna," in *Poems on the Naming of Places,* 1800.

a fiction upon herself, first substituting her own feelings for the Beggar's, and, in the same breath detecting the fallacy, will not part with the wish. —The Poet's Epitaph is disfigured, to my taste by the vulgar satire upon parsons and lawyers in the beginning, and the coarse epithet of pin point in the 6th stanza. All the rest is eminently good, and your own. I will just add that it appears to me a fault in the Beggar, that the instructions conveyed in it are too direct and like a lecture: they don't slide into the mind of the reader, while he is imagining no such matter. An intelligent reader finds a sort of insult in being told, I will teach you how to think upon this subject. This fault, if I am right, is in a ten-thousandth worse degree to be found in Sterne and many many novelists & modern poets, who continually put a sign post up to show where you are to feel. They set out with assuming their readers to be stupid. Very different from Robinson Crusoe, The Vicar of Wakefield, Roderick Randon, and other beautiful bare narratives. There is implied an unwritten compact between Author and reader; I will tell you a story, and I suppose you will understand it. Modern novels "St. Leon's" and the like are full of such flowers as these "Let not my reader suppose," "Imagine, *if you can*"—modest!—&c.—I will here have done with praise and blame. I have written so much, only that you may not think I have passed over your book without observation.—I am sorry that Coleridge christened his Ancient Marinere "a poet's Reverie"—it is as bad as Bottom the Weaver's declaration that he is not a Lion but only the scenical representation of a Lion. What new idea is gained by this Title, but one subversive of all credit, which the tale should force upon us, of its truth? For me, I was never so affected with any human Tale. After first reading it, I was totally possessed with it for many days— I dislike all the miraculous part of it, but the feelings of the man dragged me along like Tom Piper's magic whistle. I totally differ from your idea that the Marinere should have had a character and profession. This is a Beauty in Gulliver's Travels, where the mind is kept in a placid state of little wonderments; but the Ancient Marinere undergoes such Trials, as overwhelm and bury all individuality or memory of what he was, like the state of a man in a Bad dream, one terrible peculiarity of which is: that all consciousness of personality is gone. Your other observation is I think as well a little un-

founded: the Marinere from being conversant in supernatural events *has* acquired a supernatural and strange cast of *phrase*, eye, appearance, &c. which frighten the wedding guest. You will excuse my remarks, because I am hurt and vexed that you should think it necessary, with a prose apology, to open the eyes of dead men that cannot see. To sum up a general opinion of the second vol.—I do not feel any one poem in it so forcibly as the Ancient Marinere, the Mad Mother, and the Lines at Tintern Abbey, in the first.—I could, too, have wished the Critical preface had appeared in a separate treatise. All its dogmas are true and just, and most of them new, *as* criticism. But they associate a *diminishing* idea with the Poems which follow, as having been written for *Experiment* on the public taste, more than having sprung (as they must have done) from living and daily circumstances.—I am prolix, because I am gratified in the opportunity of writing to you, and I don't well know when to leave off. I ought before this to have reply'd to your very kind invitation into Cumberland. With you and your Sister I could gang any where. But I am afraid whether I shall ever be able to afford so desperate a Journey. Separate from the pleasure of your company, I don't much care if I never see a mountain in my life. I have passed all my days in London, until I have formed as many and intense local attachments, as any of you mountaineers can have done with dead nature. The Lighted shops of the Strand and Fleet Street, the innumerable trades, tradesmen and customers, coaches, waggons, playhouses, all the bustle and wickedness round about Covent Garden, the very women of the Town, the Watchmen, drunken scenes, rattles,— life awake, if you awake, at all hours of the night, the impossibility of being dull in Fleet Street, the crowds, the very dirt & mud, the Sun shining upon houses and pavements, the print shops, the old book stalls, parsons cheap'ning books, coffee houses, steams of soups from kitchens, the pantomimes, London itself a pantomime and a masquerade,—all these things work themselves into my mind and feed me, without a power of satiating me. The wonder of these sights impels me into nightwalks about her crowded streets, and I often shed tears in the motley Strand from fulness of joy at so much Life.—All these emotions must be strange to you. So are your rural emotions to me. But consider, what must I have been doing all my life, not to have lent great portions of my heart with usury to such scenes?——

---

25. **St. Leon.** *St. Leon* was a novel by William Godwin. 32. **"a poet's Reverie."** The subtitle was omitted after the 1800 edition. 33–34. **Bottom . . . Lion,** in *A Midsummer Night's Dream.*

23. **gang,** go, used playfully, in reference to Wordsworth's Northern speech.

My attachments are all local, purely local. I have no passion (or have had none since I was in love, and then it was the spurious engendering of poetry & books) to groves and vallies. The rooms where I was born, the furniture which has been before my eyes all my life, a book case which has followed me about (like a faithful dog, only exceeding him in knowledge) wherever I have moved— old chairs, old tables, streets, squares, where I have sunned myself, my old school,—these are my mistresses. Have I not enough, without your mountains? I do not envy you. I should pity you, did I not know, that the Mind will make friends of any thing. Your sun & moon and skys and hills & lakes affect me no more, or scarcely come to me in more venerable characters, than as a gilded room with tapestry and tapers, where I might live with handsome visible objects. I consider the clouds above me but as a roof, beautifully painted but unable to satisfy my mind, and at last, like the pictures of the apartment of a connoisseur, unable to afford him any longer a pleasure. So fading upon me, from disuse, have been the Beauties of Nature, as they have been confinedly called; so ever fresh & green and warm are all the inventions of men, and assemblies of men in this great city. I should certainly have laughed with dear Joanna.

Give my kindest love, *and my sister's*, to D. & yourself and a kiss from me to little Barbara Lewthwaite.

Thank you for Liking my Play!!

C. Lamb

CHRIST'S HOSPITAL FIVE AND THIRTY YEARS AGO

IN Mr. Lamb's "works," published a year or two since, I find a magnificent eulogy on my old school, such as it was, or now appears to him to have been, between the years 1782 and 1789. It happens, very oddly, that my own standing at Christ's was nearly corresponding with his; and, with all gratitude to him for his enthusiasm for the cloisters, I think he has contrived to bring together whatever can be said in praise of them, dropping all the other side of the argument most ingeniously.

I remember L. at school; and can well recollect that he had some peculiar advantages, which I and others of his schoolfellows had not. His friends lived in town, and were near at hand; and he had the privilege of going to see them, almost as often as he wished, through some invidious distinction, which was denied to us. The present worthy sub-treasurer to the Inner Temple can explain how that happened. He had his tea and hot rolls in a morning, while we were battening upon our quarter of a penny loaf—our *crug*—moistened with attenuated small beer, in wooden piggins, smacking of the pitched leathern jack it was poured from. Our Monday's milk porritch, blue and tasteless, and the pease soup of Saturday, coarse and choking, were enriched for him with a slice of "extraordinary bread and butter," from the hot-loaf of the Temple. The Wednesday's mess of millet, somewhat less repugnant—(we had three banyan to four meat days in the week)—was endeared to his palate with a lump of double-refined, and a smack of ginger (to make it go down the more glibly) or the fragrant cinnamon. In lieu of our *half-pickled* Sundays, or *quite fresh* boiled beef on Thursdays (strong as *caro equina*), with detestable marigolds floating in the pail to poison the broth—our scanty mutton crags on Fridays—and rather more savoury, but grudging, portions of the same flesh, rotten-roasted or rare, on the Tuesdays (the only dish which excited our appetites, and disappointed our stomachs, in almost equal proportion)—he had his hot plate of roast veal, or the more tempting griskin (exotics unknown to our palates), cooked in the paternal kitchen (a great thing), and brought him daily by his maid or aunt! I remember the good old relative (in whom love forbade pride) squatting down upon some odd stone in a by-nook of the cloisters, disclosing the viands (of higher regale than those cates which the ravens ministered to the Tishbite); and the contending passions of L. at the unfolding. There was love for the bringer; shame for the thing brought, and the manner of its bringing; sympathy for those who were too many to share in it; and, at top of all, hunger (eldest, strongest of the passions!) predominant, breaking down the stony fences of shame, and awkwardness, and a troubling over-consciousness.

I was a poor friendless boy. My parents, and those who should care for me, were far away. Those few acquaintances of theirs, which they could reckon upon being kind to me in the great city, after a little forced notice, which they had the grace to take of me on my first arrival in town, soon grew

---

29–30. Barbara Lewthwaite, the little girl in Wordsworth's poem "The Pet Lamb." **31. Play,** *John Woodvil, a Tragedy.* Wordsworth was only "politely interested" in it. **39–40. eulogy . . . old school,** "Recollections of Christ's Hospital" (Lamb). Here and throughout the essay Lamb pretends to be somebody else (Coleridge), and thus is able to criticize his own point of view.

18. banyan, meatless (days), for sailors. **23–24. caro equina,** horse meat.

tired of my holiday visits. They seemed to them to recur too often, though I thought them few enough; and, one after another, they all failed me, and I felt myself alone among six hundred playmates.

O the cruelty of separating a poor lad from his early homestead! The yearnings which I used to have towards it in those unfledged years! How, in my dreams, would my native town (far in the west) come back, with its church, and trees, and faces! How I would wake weeping, and in the anguish of my heart exclaim upon sweet Calne in Wiltshire!

To this late hour of my life, I trace impressions left by the recollection of those friendless holidays. The long warm days of summer never return but they bring with them a gloom from the haunting memory of those *whole-day-leaves*, when, by some strange arrangement, we were turned out, for the live-long day, upon our own hands, whether we had friends to go to, or none. I remember those bathing-excursions to the New River, which L. recalls with such relish, better, I think, than he can—for he was a home-seeking lad, and did not much care for such water-pastimes:—How merrily we would sally forth into the fields; and strip under the first warmth of the sun; and wanton like young dace in the streams; getting us appetites for noon, which those of us that were pennyless (our scanty morning crust long since exhausted) had not the means of allaying—while the cattle, and the birds, and the fishes, were at feed about us, and we had nothing to satisfy our cravings—the very beauty of the day, and the exercise of the pastime, and the sense of liberty, setting a keener edge upon them! —How faint and languid, finally, we would return, towards nightfall, to our desired morsel, half-rejoicing, half-reluctant, that the hours of our uneasy liberty had expired!

It was worse in the days of winter, to go prowling about the streets objectless—shivering at cold windows of print-shops, to extract a little amusement; or haply, as a last resort, in the hope of a little novelty, to pay a fifty-times repeated visit (where our individual faces should be as well known to the warden as those of his own charges) to the Lions in the Tower—to whose levée, by courtesy immemorial, we had a prescriptive title to admission.

L.'s governor (so we called the patron who presented us to the foundation) lived in a manner under his paternal roof. Any complaint which he had to make was sure of being attended to. This was understood at Christ's, and was an effectual

screen to him against the severity of masters, or worse tyranny of the monitors. The oppressions of these young brutes are heart-sickening to call to recollection. I have been called out of my bed, and *waked for the purpose*, in the coldest winter nights— and this not once, but night after night—in my shirt, to receive the discipline of a leathern thong, with eleven other sufferers, because it pleased my callow overseer, when there has been any talking heard after we were gone to bed, to make the six last beds in the dormitory, where the youngest children of us slept, answerable for an offence they neither dared to commit, nor had the power to hinder.—The same execrable tyranny drove the younger part of us from the fires, when our feet were perishing with snow; and, under the cruelest penalties, forbade the indulgence of a drink of water, when we lay in sleepless summer nights, fevered with the season, and the day's sports.

There was one H——, who, I learned, in after days, was seen expiating some maturer offence in the hulks. (Do I flatter myself in fancying that this might be the planter of that name, who suffered— at Nevis, I think, or St. Kits,—some few years since? My friend Tobin was the benevolent instrument of bringing him to the gallows.) This petty Nero actually branded a boy, who had offended him, with a red hot iron; and nearly starved forty of us, with exacting contributions, to the one half of our bread, to pamper a young ass, which, incredible as it may seem, with the connivance of the nurse's daughter (a young flame of his) he had contrived to smuggle in, and keep upon the leads of the *ward*, as they called our dormitories. This game went on for better than a week, till the foolish beast, not able to fare well but he must cry roast meat—happier than Caligula's minion, could he have kept his own counsel—but, foolisher, alas! than any of his species in the fables—waxing fat, and kicking, in the fulness of bread, one unlucky minute would needs proclaim his good fortune to the world below; and, laying out his simple throat, blew such a ram's horn blast, as (toppling down the walls of his own Jericho) set concealment any longer at defiance. The client was dismissed, with certain attentions, to Smithfield; but I never understood that the patron underwent any censure on the occasion. This was in the stewardship of L.'s admired Perry.

Under the same *facile* administration, can L. have forgotten the cool impunity with which the nurses used to carry away openly, in open platters, for

---

48. **governor,** Samuel Salt, a lawyer, employed Lamb's father.

20. **H——,** Hodges, according to Lamb's own note. 37. **minion.** The Roman emperor Caligula appointed his horse first consul.

their own tables, one out of two of every hot joint, which the careful matron had been seeing scrupulously weighed out for our dinners? These things were daily practised in that magnificent apartment, which L. (grown connoisseur since, we presume) praises so highly for the grand paintings "by Verrio, and others," with which it is "hung round and adorned." But the sight of sleek, well-fed blue-coat boys in pictures was, at that time, I believe, little consolatory to him, or us, the living ones, who saw the better part of our provisions carried away before our faces by harpies; and ourselves reduced (with the Trojan in the hall of Dido)

"To feed our mind with idle portraiture."

L. has recorded the repugnance of the school to *gags*, or the fat of fresh beef boiled; and sets it down to some superstition. But these unctuous morsels are never grateful to young palates (children are universally fat-haters) and in strong, coarse, boiled meats, *unsalted*, are detestable. A *gag-eater* in our time was equivalent to a *ghoul*, and held in equal detestation. ———— suffered under the imputation.

"————'Twas said,
He ate strange flesh."

He was observed, after dinner, carefully to gather up the remnants left at his table (not many, nor very choice fragments, you may credit me)—and, in an especial manner, these disreputable morsels, which he would convey away, and secretly stow in the settle that stood at his bed-side. None saw when he ate them. It was rumoured that he privately devoured them in the night. He was watched, but no traces of such midnight practices were discoverable. Some reported, that, on leave-days, he had been seen to carry out of the bounds a large blue check handkerchief, full of something. This then must be the accursed thing. Conjecture next was at work to imagine how he could dispose of it. Some said he sold it to the beggars. This belief generally prevailed. He went about moping. None spake to him. No one would play with him. He was excommunicated; put out of the pale of the school. He was too powerful a boy to be beaten, but he underwent every mode of that negative punishment, which is more grievous than many stripes. Still he persevered. At length he was observed by two of his school-fellows, who were determined to get at the secret, and had traced him one leave-day for that purpose, to enter a large worn-out building, such as there exist specimens of in Chancery-lane, which are let out to various scales of pauperism with open door, and a common staircase. After him they silently slunk in, and followed by stealth up four flights, and saw him tap at a poor wicket, which was opened by an aged woman, meanly clad. Suspicion was now ripened into certainty. The informers had secured their victim. They had him in their toils. Accusation was formally preferred, and retribution most signal was looked for. Mr. Hathaway, the then steward (for this happened a little after my time), with that patient sagacity which tempered all his conduct, determined to investigate the matter, before he proceeded to sentence. The result was, that the supposed mendicants, the receivers or purchasers of the mysterious scraps, turned out to be the parents of ————, an honest couple come to decay,—whom this seasonable supply had, in all probability, saved from mendicancy; and that this young stork, at the expense of his own good name, had all this while been only feeding the old birds!—The governors on this occasion, much to their honour, voted a present relief to the family of ————, and presented him with a silver medal. The lesson which the steward read upon RASH JUDGMENT, on the occasion of publicly delivering the medal to ————, I believe, would not be lost upon his auditory.—I had left school then, but I well remember ————. He was a tall, shambling youth, with a cast in his eye, not at all calculated to conciliate hostile prejudices. I have since seen him carrying a baker's basket. I think I heard he did not do quite so well by himself, as he had done by the old folks.

I was a hypochondriac lad; and the sight of a boy in fetters, upon the day of my first putting on the blue clothes, was not exactly fitted to assuage the natural terrors of initiation. I was of tender years, barely turned of seven; and had only read of such things in books, or seen them but in dreams. I was told he had *run away*. This was the punishment for the first offence.—As a novice I was soon after taken to see the dungeons. These were little square, Bedlam cells, where a boy could just lie at his length upon straw and a blanket—a mattress, I think, was afterwards substituted—with a peep of light, let in askance, from a prison-orifice at top, barely enough to read by. Here the poor boy was locked in by himself all day, without sight of any but the porter who brought him his bread and water—who *might not speak to him;*—or of the beadle, who came twice a week to call him out to receive his periodical chastisement, which was almost welcome, because it separated him for a brief interval from solitude:—and here he was shut up by himself *of nights*, out of

41. Bedlam, from St. Mary of Bethlehem, a London asylum for the insane.

the reach of any sound, to suffer whatever horrors the weak nerves, and superstition incident to his time of life, might subject him to. This was the penalty for the second offence.—Wouldst thou like, reader, to see what became of him in the next degree?

The culprit, who had been a third time an offender, and whose expulsion was at this time deemed irreversible, was brought forth, as at some solemn *auto da fe*, arrayed in uncouth and most appalling attire—all trace of his late "watchet weeds" carefully effaced, he was exposed in a jacket, resembling those which London lamplighters formerly delighted in, with a cap of the same. The effect of this divestiture was such as the ingenious devisers of it could have anticipated. With his pale and frighted features, it was as if some of those disfigurements in Dante had seized upon him. In this disguisement he was brought into the hall (*L.'s favourite state-room*), where awaited him the whole number of his schoolfellows, whose joint lessons and sports he was thenceforth to share no more; the awful presence of the steward, to be seen for the last time; of the executioner beadle, clad in his state robe for the occasion; and of two faces more, of direr import, because never but in these extremities visible. These were governors; two of whom, by choice, or charter, were always accustomed to officiate at these *Ultima Supplicia;* not to mitigate (so at least we understood it), but to enforce the uttermost stripe. Old Bamber Gascoigne, and Peter Aubert, I remember, were colleagues on one occasion, when the beadle turning rather pale, a glass of brandy was ordered to prepare him for the mysteries. The scourging was, after the old Roman fashion, long and stately. The lictor accompanied the criminal quite round the hall. We were generally too faint with attending to the previous disgusting circumstances, to make accurate report with our eyes of the degree of corporal suffering inflicted. Report, of course, gave out the back knotty and livid. After scourging, he was made over, in his *San Benito*, to his friends, if he had any (but commonly such poor runagates were friendless), or to his parish officer, who, to enhance the effect of the scene, had his station allotted to him on the outside of the hall gate.

These solemn pageantries were not played off so often as to spoil the general mirth of the com-

munity. We had plenty of exercise and recreation *after* school hours; and, for myself, I must confess, that I was never happier, than *in* them. The Upper and Lower Grammar Schools were held in the same room; and an imaginary line only divided their bounds. Their character was as different as that of the inhabitants on the two sides of the Pyrenees. The Rev. James Boyer was the Upper Master: but the Rev. Matthew Field presided over that portion of the apartment, of which I had the good fortune to be a member. We lived a life as careless as birds. We talked and did just what we pleased, and nobody molested us. We carried an accidence, or a grammar, for form; but, for any trouble it gave us, we might take two years in getting through the verbs deponent, and another two in forgetting all that we had learned about them. There was now and then the formality of saying a lesson, but if you had not learned it, a brush across the shoulders (just enough to disturb a fly) was the sole remonstrance. Field never used the rod; and in truth he wielded the cane with no great good will—holding it "like a dancer." It looked in his hands rather like an emblem than an instrument of authority; and an emblem, too, he was ashamed of. He was a good easy man, that did not care to ruffle his own peace, nor perhaps set any great consideration upon the value of juvenile time. He came among us, now and then, but often stayed away whole days from us; and when he came, it made no difference to us—he had his private room to retire to, the short time he staid, to be out of the sound of our noise. Our mirth and uproar went on. We had classics of our own, without being beholden to "insolent Greece or haughty Rome," that passed current among us—Peter Wilkins—the Adventures of the Hon. Capt. Robert Boyle—the Fortunate Blue Coat Boy—and the like. Or we cultivated a turn for mechanic or scientific operations; making little sun-dials of paper; or weaving those ingenious parentheses, called *cat-cradles;* or making dry peas to dance upon the end of a tin pipe; or studying the art military over that laudable game "French and English," and a hundred other such devices to pass away the time—mixing the useful with the agreeable—as would have made the souls of Rousseau and John Locke chuckle to have seen us.

Matthew Field belonged to that class of modest divines who affect to mix in equal proportion the *gentleman,* the *scholar,* and the *Christian;* but, I know not how, the first ingredient is generally found to be the predominating dose in the composition. He was engaged in gay parties, or with his courtly bow at

---

10. auto da fe (Portuguese), act of faith, execution by the Inquisition.   **11. "watchet weeds,"** blue uniform worn by boys of Christ's.   **17–18. disfigurements in Dante,** *Inferno,* Cantos XXVIII–XXX.   **29. Ultima Supplicia,** extreme punishments.   **43. San Benito,** garment like those worn by the monks of the Benedictine order.

some episcopal levée, when he should have been attending upon us. He had had for many years the classical charge of a hundred children, during the four or five first years of their education; and his very highest form seldom proceeded further than two or three of the introductory fables of Phaedrus. How things were suffered to go on thus, I cannot guess. Boyer, who was the proper person to have remedied these abuses, always affected, perhaps felt, a delicacy in interfering in a province not 10 strictly his own. I have not been without my suspicions, that he was not altogether displeased at the contrast we presented to his end of the school. We were a sort of Helots to his young Spartans. He would sometimes, with ironic deference, send to borrow a rod of the Under Master, and then, with Sardonic grin, observe to one of his upper boys, "how neat and fresh the twigs looked." While his pale students were battering their brains over Xenophon and Plato, with a silence as deep as that 20 enjoined by the Samite, we were enjoying ourselves at our ease in our little Goshen. We saw a little into the secrets of his discipline, and the prospect did but the more reconcile us to our lot. His thunders rolled innocuous for us; his storms came near, but never touched us; contrary to Gideon's miracle, while all around were drenched, our fleece was dry. His boys turned out the better scholars; we, I suspect, have the advantage in temper. His pupils cannot speak of him without something of terror allay- 30 ing their gratitude; the remembrance of Field comes back with all the soothing images of indolence, and summer slumbers, and work like play, and innocent idleness, and Elysian exemptions, and life itself a "playing holiday."

Though sufficiently removed from the jurisdiction of Boyer, we were near enough (as I have said) to understand a little of his system. We occasionally heard sounds of the *Ululantes*, and caught glances of Tartarus. B. was a rabid pedant. His English style 40 was cramped to barbarism. His Easter anthems (for his duty obliged him to those periodical flights) were grating as scrannel pipes.—He would laugh, ay, and heartily, but then it must be at Flaccus's quibble about *Rex* —— or at the *tristis severitas in vultu*, or *inspicere in patinas*, of Terence—thin jests,

which at their first broaching could hardly have had *vis* enough to move a Roman muscle.—He had two wigs, both pedantic, but of different omen. The one serene, smiling, fresh powdered, betokening a mild day. The other, an old discoloured, unkempt, angry caxon, denoting frequent and bloody execution. Woe to the school, when he made his morning appearance in his *passy*, or *passionate wig*. No comet expounded surer.—J. B. had a heavy hand. I have known him double his knotty fist at a poor trembling child (the maternal milk hardly dry upon its lips) with a "Sirrah, do you presume to set your wits at me?"—Nothing was more common than to see him make a headlong entry into the schoolroom, from his inner recess, or library, and, with turbulent eye, singling out a lad, roar out, "Od's my life, Sirrah," (his favourite adjuration) "I have a great mind to whip you,"—then, with as sudden a retracting impulse, fling back into his chair—and, 20 after a cooling lapse of some minutes (during which all but the culprit had totally forgotten the context) drive headlong out again, piecing out his imperfect sense, as if it had been some Devil's Litany, with the expletory yell—"*and I* WILL, *too.*"—In his gentler moods, when the *rabidus furor* was assuaged, he had resort to an ingenious method, peculiar, for what I have heard, to himself, of whipping the boy, and reading the Debates, at the same time; a paragraph, and a lash between; which in those times, 30 when parliamentary oratory was most at a height and flourishing in these realms, was not calculated to impress the patient with a veneration for the diffuser graces of rhetoric.

Once, and but once, the uplifted rod was known to fall ineffectual from his hand—when droll squinting W—— having been caught putting the inside of the master's desk to a use for which the architect had clearly not designed it, to justify himself, with great simplicity averred, that *he did not* 40 *know that the thing had been forewarned*. This exquisite irrecognition of any law antecedent to the *oral* or *declaratory* struck so irresistibly upon the fancy of all who heard it (the pedagogue himself not excepted) that remission was unavoidable.

L. has given credit to B.'s great merits as an instructor. Coleridge, in his literary life, has pronounced a more intelligible and ample encomium on them. The author of the Country Spectator doubts not to compare him with the ablest teachers 50 of antiquity. Perhaps we cannot dismiss him better than with the pious ejaculation of C.——when he heard that his old master was on his death-bed—

21. **Samite**, Pythagoras, Greek philosopher (sixth century B.C.), who required his pupils to remain silent until they had listened to his lectures for five years. 26. **Gideon's miracle**. See Judges 6:36–38. 39. **Ululantes**, Howlers. 43. **scrannel pipes**, an allusion to Milton's "Lycidas," l. 124—dry, harsh. 45. **Rex**. See Horace, *Satires*, Book I, 7, l. 35. *Rex* is used in a double sense, as a man's name and in its ordinary meaning of King. 45–46. **tristis . . . vultu**, gloomy anxiety on the face. 46. **inspicere in patinas**, look into the stewpans.

2. **vis**, force, strength. 6. **caxon**, old name for a wig. 25. **rabidus furor**, raging madness.

"Poor J. B.!—may all his faults be forgiven; and may he be wafted to bliss by little cherub boys, all head and wings, with no *bottoms* to reproach his sublunary infirmities."

Under him were many good and sound scholars bred.—First Grecian of my time was Lancelot Pepys Stevens, kindest of boys and men, since Cogrammar-master (and inseparable companion) with Dr. T——e. What an edifying spectacle did this brace of friends present to those who remembered the anti-socialities of their predecessors! —You never met the one by chance in the street without a wonder, which was quickly dissipated by the almost immediate sub-appearance of the other. Generally arm in arm, these kindly coadjutors lightened for each other the toilsome duties of their profession, and when, in advanced age, one found it convenient to retire, the other was not long in discovering that it suited him to lay down the fasces also. Oh, it is pleasant, as it is rare, to find the same arm linked in yours at forty, which at thirteen helped it to turn over the *Cicero De Amicitia*, or some tale of Antique Friendship, which the young heart even then was burning to anticipate!—Co-Grecian with S. was Th——, who has since executed with ability various diplomatic functions at the Northern courts. Th—— was a tall, dark, saturnine youth, sparing of speech, with raven locks. —Thomas Fanshaw Middleton followed him (now Bishop of Calcutta) a scholar and a gentleman in his teens. He has the reputation of an excellent critic; and is author (besides the Country Spectator) of a Treatise on the Greek Article, against Sharpe.—M. is said to bear his mitre high in India, where the *regni novitas* (I dare say) sufficiently justifies the bearing. A humility quite as primitive as that of Jewel or Hooker might not be exactly fitted to impress the minds of those Anglo-Asiatic diocesans with a reverence for home institutions, and the church which those fathers watered. The manners of M. at school, though firm, were mild, and unassuming.—Next to M. (if not senior to him) was Richards, author of the Aboriginal Britons, the most spirited of the Oxford Prize Poems: a pale, studious Grecian.—Then followed poor S——, ill-fated M——! of these the Muse is silent,

> "Finding some of Edward's race
> Unhappy, pass their annals by."

Come back into memory, like as thou wert in the day-spring of thy fancies, with hope like a fiery column before thee—the dark pillar not yet turned —Samuel Taylor Coleridge—Logician, Metaphysician, Bard!—How have I seen the casual passer through the Cloisters stand still, intranced with admiration (while he weighed the disproportion between the *speech* and the *garb* of the young Mirandula), to hear thee unfold, in thy deep and sweet intonations, the mysteries of Jamblichus, or Plotinus (for even in those years thou waxedst not pale at such philosophic draughts), or reciting Homer in his Greek, or Pindar——while the walls of the old Grey Friars re-echoed to the accents of the *inspired charity-boy!* Many were the "witcombats," (to dally awhile with the words of old Fuller,) between him and C. V. Le G——, "which two I behold like a Spanish great gallion, and an English man-of-war; Master Coleridge, like the former, was built far higher in learning, solid, but slow in his performances. C. V. L., with the English man-of-war, lesser in bulk, but lighter in sailing, could turn with all tides, tack about, and take advantage of all winds, by the quickness of his wit and invention."

Nor shalt thou, their compeer, be quickly forgotten, Allen, with the cordial smile, and still more cordial laugh, with which thou wert wont to make the old Cloisters shake, in thy cognition of some poignant jest of theirs; or the anticipation of some more material, and, peradventure, practical one, of thine own. Extinct are those smiles, with that beautiful countenance, with which (for thou wert the *Nireus formosus* of the school), in the days of thy maturer waggery, thou didst disarm the wrath of infuriated town-damsel, who, incensed by provoking pinch, turning tigress-like round, suddenly converted by thy angel-look, exchanged the half-formed terrible "bl——," for a gentler greeting— *"bless a handsome face!"*

Next follow two, who ought to be now alive, and the friends of Elia—the junior Le G—— and F——; who impelled, the former by a roving temper, the latter by too quick a sense of neglect—ill capable of enduring the slights poor Sizars are sometimes subject to in our seats of learning—exchanged their Alma Mater for the camp; perishing, one by climate, and one on the plains of Salamanca:— Le G—— sanguine, volatile, sweet-natured; F—— dogged, faithful, anticipative of insult, warm-

6. Grecian, Greek scholar to Cambridge. **9. T——e,** Trollope, successor to Boyer. **25–27. Th——,** Thornton. **35. regni novitas,** newness of the rule. **46. S——,** Scott, who "died in Bedlam." (Lamb) **46. M——,** "Maunde, dismissed." (Lamb)

17. C. V. Le G——, C. V. Le Grice. **22–25. "man-of-war . . . invention,"** an allusion to Thomas Fuller's account of the wit combats between Shakespeare and Ben Jonson. **34. Nireus formosus,** handsome Nireus, Greek warrior in Homer. **42. F——,** Favell.

hearted, with something of the old Roman height about him.

Fine, frank-hearted Fr——, the present master of Hertford, with Marmaduke T——, mildest of Missionaries—and both my good friends still—close the catalogue of Grecians in my time.

THE TWO RACES OF MEN

THE human species, according to the best theory I can form of it, is composed of two distinct races, *the men who borrow*, and *the men who lend*. To these two original diversities may be reduced all those impertinent classifications of Gothic and Celtic tribes, white men, black men, red men. All the dwellers upon earth, "Parthians, and Medes, and Elamites," flock hither, and do naturally fall in with one or other of these primary distinctions. The infinite superiority of the former, which I choose to designate as the *great race*, is discernible in their figure, port, and a certain instinctive sovereignty. The latter are born degraded. "He shall serve his brethren." There is something in the air of one of this cast, lean and suspicious; contrasting with the open, trusting, generous manners of the other.

Observe who have been the greatest borrowers of all ages—Alcibiades—Falstaff—Sir Richard Steele—our late incomparable Brinsley—what a family likeness in all four!

What a careless, even deportment hath your borrower! what rosy gills! what a beautiful reliance on Providence doth he manifest,—taking no more thought than lilies! What contempt for money,—accounting it (yours and mine especially) no better than dross. What a liberal confounding of those pedantic distinctions of *meum* and *tuum*! or rather what a noble simplification of languages (beyond Tooke), resolving these supposed opposites into one clear, intelligible pronoun adjective!—What near approaches doth he make to the primitive *community*,—to the extent of one half of the principle at least!—

He is the true taxer who "calleth all the world up to be taxed"; and the distance is as vast between him and *one of us*, as subsisted betwixt the Augustan Majesty and the poorest obolary Jew that paid it tribute-pittance at Jerusalem!—His exactions, too, have such a cheerful, voluntary air! So far removed from your sour parochial or state-gatherers,—those

ink-horn varlets, who carry their want of welcome in their faces! He cometh to you with a smile, and troubleth you with no receipt; confining himself to no set season. Every day is his Candlemas, or his Feast of Holy Michael. He applieth the *lene tormentum* of a pleasant look to your purse,—which to that gentle warmth expands her silken leaves, as naturally as the cloak of the traveller, for which sun and wind contended! He is the true Propontic which never ebbeth! The sea which taketh handsomely at each man's hand. In vain the victim, whom he delighteth to honour, struggles with destiny; he is in the net. Lend therefore cheerfully, O man ordained to lend—that thou lose not in the end, with thy worldly penny, the reversion promised. Combine not preposterously in thine own person the penalties of Lazarus and of Dives!—but, when thou seest the proper authority coming, meet it smilingly, as it were half-way. Come, a handsome sacrifice! See how light *he* makes of it! Strain not courtesies with a noble enemy.

Reflections like the foregoing were forced upon my mind by the death of my old friend Ralph Bigod, Esq., who departed this life on Wednesday evening; dying, as he had lived, without much trouble. He boasted himself a descendant from mighty ancestors of that name, who heretofore held ducal dignities in this realm. In his actions and sentiments he belied not the stock to which he pretended. Early in life he found himself invested with ample revenues; which, with that noble disinterestedness which I have noticed as inherent in men of the *great race*, he took almost immediate measures entirely to dissipate and bring to nothing: for there is something revolting in the idea of a king holding a private purse; and the thoughts of Bigod were all regal. Thus furnished, by the very act of disfurnishment; getting rid of the cumbersome luggage of riches, more apt (as one sings)

"To slacken virtue, and abate her edge,
Than prompt her to do aught may merit praise";

he set forth, like some Alexander, upon his great enterprise, "borrowing and to borrow!"

In his periegesis, or triumphant progress throughout this island, it has been calculated that he laid a tythe part of the inhabitants under contribution. I reject this estimate as greatly exaggerated:—but having had the honour of accompanying my friend, divers times, in his perambulations about this vast

---

3. **Fr——**, Franklin. 29. **Brinsley**, Richard Brinsley Sheridan (1715–1816), dramatist and orator. 39. **Tooke**, Horne Tooke, English philologist. 47. **obolary**, having only small coins; impoverished.

5–6. **lene tormentum**, gentle stimulus. 9. **Propontic**, the Sea of Marmara. 17. **Lazarus and Dives**. See Luke 6:19–31. 41–42. **"To . . . praise,"** *Paradise Regained*, Book II, l. 455.

city, I own I was greatly struck at first with the prodigious number of faces we met who claimed a sort of respectful acquaintance with us. He was one day so obliging as to explain the phenomenon. It seems, these were his tributaries; feeders of his exchequer; gentlemen, his good friends (as he was pleased to express himself), to whom he had occasionally been beholden for a loan. Their multitudes did no way disconcert him. He rather took a pride in numbering them; and, with Comus, seemed pleased to be "stocked with so fair a herd."

With such sources, it was a wonder how he contrived to keep his treasury always empty. He did it by force of an aphorism, which he had often in his mouth, that "money kept longer than three days stinks." So he made use of it while it was fresh. A good part he drank away (for he was an excellent toss-pot), some he gave away, the rest he threw away, literally tossing and hurling it violently from him—as boys do burrs, or as if it had been infectious,—into ponds, or ditches, or deep holes,—inscrutable cavities of the earth;—or he would bury it (where he would never seek it again) by a river's side under some bank, which (he would facetiously observe) paid no interest—but out away from him it must go peremptorily, as Hagar's offspring into the wilderness, while it was sweet. He never missed it. The streams were perennial which fed his fisc. When new supplies became necessary, the first person that had the felicity to fall in with him, friend or stranger, was sure to contribute to the deficiency. For Bigod had an *undeniable* way with him. He had a cheerful, open exterior, a quick jovial eye, a bald forehead, just touched with grey (*cana fides*). He anticipated no excuse, and found none. And, waiving for a while my theory as to the *great race*, I would put it to the most untheorizing reader, who may at times have disposable coin in his pocket, whether it is not more repugnant to the kindliness of his nature to refuse such a one as I am describing, than to say *no* to a poor petitionary rogue (your bastard borrower) who, by his mumping visnomy, tells you, that he expects nothing better; and, therefore, whose preconceived notions and expectations you do in reality so much less shock in the refusal.

When I think of this man; his fiery glow of heart; his swell of feeling; how magnificent, how *ideal* he was; how great at the midnight hour; and when I compare with him the companions with whom I have associated since, I grudge the saving of a few

idle ducats, and think that I am fallen into the society of *lenders*, and *little men*.

To one like Elia, whose treasures are rather cased in leather covers than closed in iron coffers, there is a class of alienators more formidable than that which I have touched upon; I mean your *borrowers of books*—*those* mutilators of collections, spoilers of the symmetry of shelves, and creators of odd volumes. There is Comberbatch, matchless in his depredations!

That foul gap in the bottom shelf facing you, like a great eye-tooth knocked out—(you are now with me in my little back study in Bloomsbury, reader!)—with the huge Switzer-like tomes on each side (like the Guildhall giants, in their reformed posture, guardant of nothing) once held the tallest of my folios, *Opera Bonaventurae*, choice and massy divinity to which its two supporters (school divinity also, but of a lesser calibre,—Bellarmine, and Holy Thomas), showed but as dwarfs,—itself an Ascapart!—*that* Comberbatch abstracted upon the faith of a theory he holds, which is more easy, I confess, for me to suffer by than to refute, namely, that "the title to property in a book (my Bonaventure for instance), is in exact ratio to the claimant's powers of understanding and appreciating the same." Should he go on acting upon this theory, which of our shelves is safe?

The slight vacuum in the left-hand case—two shelves from the ceiling—scarcely distinguishable but by the quick eye of a loser—was whilom the commodious resting-place of Browne on Urn Burial. C. will hardly allege that he knows more about that treatise than I do, who introduced it to him, and was indeed the first (of the moderns) to discover its beauties—but so have I known a foolish lover to praise his mistress in the presence of a rival more qualified to carry her off than himself.—Just below, Dodsley's dramas want their fourth volume, where Vittoria Corombona is! The remainder nine are as distasteful as Priam's refuse sons, when the Fates *borrowed* Hector. Here stood the Anatomy of Melancholy, in sober state.—There loitered the Complete Angler; quiet as in life, by some stream side.—In

11. **"stocked . . . herd,"** Milton's *Comus*, l. 152. 26–27. **Hagar's offspring . . . wilderness,** Ishmael; see Genesis 16. 28. **fisc,** treasury—a pun. 34. **cana fides,** hoary fidelity. 42. **mumping visnomy,** mumbling physiognomy.

9. **Comberbatch,** resembles the name (Comberbacke) Coleridge assumed when he joined the cavalry. 17. **Opera Bonaventurae,** *Works* of Bonaventura, an Italian theologian. 19. **Bellarmine and Holy Thomas,** Italian theologians, the second being St. Thomas Aquinas. 20. **Ascapart,** a giant in the old romance *Bevis of Hampton.* 31. **Browne,** Sir Thomas Browne—one of Lamb's famous seventeenth-century prose models. 38. **Dodsley.** Robert Dodsley (1703–1764) published a famous collection of old plays. 39. **Vittoria Corombona,** a tragedy by John Webster. 41. **Hector,** an allusion to Priam's begging Achilles for the slain Hector (*Iliad*, Book XXIV, l. 486). 41–42. **Anatomy of Melancholy,** by Robert Burton. 42–43. **Complete Angler,** *The Compleat Angler* by Isaak Walton—another favorite of Lamb's.

yonder nook, John Buncle, a widower-volume, with "eyes closed," mourns his ravished mate.

One justice I must do my friend, that if he sometimes, like the sea, sweeps away a treasure, at another time, sea-like, he throws up as rich an equivalent to match it. I have a small under-collection of this nature (my friend's gatherings in his various calls), picked up, he has forgotten at what odd places, and deposited with as little memory at mine. I take in these orphans, the twice-deserted. These proselytes of the gate are welcome as the true Hebrews. There they stand in conjunction; natives, and naturalised. The latter seem as little disposed to inquire out their true lineage as I am.—I charge no warehouse-room for these deodands, nor shall ever put myself to the ungentlemanly trouble of advertising a sale of them to pay expenses.

To lose a volume to C. carries some sense and meaning in it. You are sure that he will make one hearty meal on your vianas, if he can give no account of the platter after it. But what moved thee, wayward, spiteful K., to be so importunate to carry off with thee, in spite of tears and adjurations to thee to forbear, the Letters of that princely woman, the thrice noble Margaret Newcastle?—knowing at the time, and knowing that I knew also, thou most assuredly wouldst never turn over one leaf of the illustrious folio:—what but the mere spirit of contradiction, and childish love of getting the better of thy friend?—Then, worst cut of all! to transport it with thee to the Gallican land—

"Unworthy land to harbour such a sweetness,
A virtue in which all ennobling thoughts dwelt,
Pure thoughts, kind thoughts, high thoughts, her sex's wonder!"

—hadst thou not thy play-books, and books of jests and fancies, about thee, to keep thee merry, even as thou keepest all companies with thy quips and mirthful tales?—Child of the Green-room, it was unkindly done of thee. Thy wife, too, that part-French, better-part Englishwoman!—that *she* could fix upon no other treatise to bear away, in kindly token of remembering us, than the works of Fulke Greville, Lord Brooke—of which no Frenchman, nor woman of France, Italy, or England, was ever by nature constituted to comprehend a tittle! *Was there not Zimmerman on Solitude?*

Reader, if haply thou art blessed with a moderate collection, be shy of showing it; or if thy heart over-floweth to lend them, lend thy books; but let it be to such a one as S. T. C.—he will return them (generally anticipating the time appointed) with usury; enriched with annotations, tripling their value. I have had experience. Many of these precious MSS. of his—(in *matter* oftentimes, and almost in quantity not unfrequently vying with the originals)—in no very clerkly hand—legible in my Daniel; in old Burton: in Sir Thomas Browne; and those abstruser cogitations of the Greville, now, alas! wandering in Pagan lands.—I counsel thee, shut not thy heart, not thy library, against S. T. C.

DREAM CHILDREN; A REVERIE

CHILDREN love to listen to stories about their elders, when *they* were children; to stretch their imagination to the conception of a traditionary great-uncle, or grandame, whom they never saw. It was in this spirit that my little ones crept about me the other evening to hear about their great-grandmother Field, who lived in a great house in Norfolk (a hundred times bigger than that in which they and papa lived) which had been the scene—so at least it was generally believed in that part of the country—of the tragic incidents which they had lately become familiar with from the ballad of the Children in the Wood. Certain it is that the whole story of the children and their cruel uncle was to be seen fairly carved out in wood upon the chimney-piece of the great hall, the whole story down to the Robin Redbreasts, till a foolish rich person pulled it down to set up a marble one of modern invention in its stead, with no story upon it. Here Alice put out one of her dear mother's looks, too tender to be called upbraiding. Then I went on to say, how religious and how good their great-grandmother Field was, how beloved and respected by every body, though she was not indeed the mistress of this great house, but had only the charge of it (and yet in some respects she might be said to be the mistress of it too) committed to her by the owner, who preferred living in a newer and more fashionable mansion which he had purchased somewhere in the adjoining county; but still she lived in it in a manner as if it had been her own, and kept up the dignity of the great house in a sort while she lived, which afterwards came to decay, and was nearly pulled down, and all its old ornaments stripped and carried away to the owner's other house, where they

1. **John Buncle,** a curious novel by Thomas Amory. 15. **deodands,** gifts to God, things forfeited to the Crown for pious uses. *32–35.* **"Unworthy land . . . wonder,"** authorship unidentified; it may be Lamb's own composition.

2. **S. T. C.,** Samuel Taylor Coleridge. **22–23. great-grandmother Field.** Mary Field was for fifty years housekeeper at Blakesware, Hertfordshire.

were set up, and looked as awkward as if some one were to carry away the old tombs they had seen lately at the Abbey, and stick them up in Lady C.'s tawdry gilt drawing-room. Here John smiled, as much as to say, "that would be foolish indeed." And then I told how, when she came to die, her funeral was attended by a concourse of all the poor, and some of the gentry too, of the neighbourhood for many miles round, to show their respect for her memory, because she had been such a good and re- 10 ligious woman; so good indeed that she knew all the Psaltery by heart, ay, and a great part of the Testament besides. Here little Alice spread her hands. Then I told what a tall, upright, graceful person their great-grandmother Field once was; and how in her youth she was esteemed the best dancer— here Alice's little right foot played an involuntary movement, till upon my looking grave, it desisted— the best dancer, I was saying, in the county, till a cruel disease, called a cancer, came, and bowed her 20 down with pain; but it could never bend her good spirits, or make them stoop, but they were still up-right, because she was so good and religious. Then I told how she was used to sleep by herself in a lone chamber of the great lone house; and how she be-lieved that an apparition of two infants was to be seen at midnight gliding up and down the great staircase near where she slept, but she said "those innocents would do her no harm"; and how fright-ened I used to be, though in those days I had my 30 maid to sleep with me, because I was never half so good or religious as she—and yet I never saw the infants. Here John expanded all his eye-brows and tried to look courageous. Then I told how good she was to all her grand-children, having us to the great house in the holydays, where I in particular used to spend many hours by myself, in gazing upon the old busts of the Twelve Caesars, that had been Em-perors of Rome, till the old marble heads would seem to live again, or I be turned into marble with 40 them; how I never could be tired with roaming about that huge mansion, with its vast empty rooms, with their worn-out hangings, fluttering tapestry, and carved oaken panels, with the gilding almost rubbed out—sometimes in the spacious old-fashioned gardens, which I had almost to myself, unless when now and then a solitary gardening man would cross me—and how the nectarines and peaches hung upon the walls, without my ever offer-ing to pluck them, because they were forbidden 50 fruit, unless now and then,—and because I had more pleasure in strolling about among the old melancholy-looking yew trees, or the firs, and pick-ing up the red berries, and the fir apples, which

were good for nothing but to look at—or in lying about upon the fresh grass, with all the fine garden smells around me—or basking in the orangery, till I could almost fancy myself ripening too along with the oranges and the limes in that grateful warmth— or in watching the dace that darted to and fro in the fish-pond, at the bottom of the garden, with here and there a great sulky pike hanging midway down the water in silent state, as if it mocked at their im- 10 pertinent friskings,—I had more pleasure in these busy-idle diversions than in all the sweet flavours of peaches, nectarines, oranges, and such like common baits of children. Here John slyly deposited back upon the plate a bunch of grapes, which, not unob-served by Alice, he had meditated dividing with her, and both seemed willing to relinquish them for the present as irrelevant. Then in somewhat a more heightened tone, I told how, though their great-grandmother Field loved all her grand-children, yet 20 in an especial manner she might be said to love their uncle, John L——, because he was so handsome and spirited a youth, and a king to the rest of us; and, instead of moping about in solitary corners, like some of us, he would mount the most mettle-some horse he could get, when but an imp no bigger than themselves, and make it carry him half over the county in a morning, and join the hunters when there were any out—and yet he loved the old great house and gardens too, but had too much spirit to 30 be always pent up within their boundaries—and how their uncle grew up to man's estate as brave as he was handsome, to the admiration of everybody, but of their great-grandmother Field most especially; and how he used to carry me upon his back when I was a lame-footed boy—for he was a good bit older than me—many a mile when I could not walk for pain;—and how in after life he became lame-footed too, and I did not always (I fear) make allowances enough for him when he was impatient, and in pain, 40 nor remember sufficiently how considerate he had been to me when I was lame-footed; and how when he died, though he had not been dead an hour, it seemed as if he had died a great while ago, such a distance there is betwixt life and death; and how I bore his death as I thought pretty well at first, but afterwards it haunted and haunted me; and though I did not cry or take it to heart as some do, and as I think he would have done if I had died, yet I missed him all day long, and knew not till then how much 50 I had loved him. I missed his kindness, and I missed his crossness, and wished him to be alive again, to

13. Here (p. 135, l. 35) . . . **John slyly deposited.** Note the responses of the children, here and elsewhere, to the un-folding of the story. **21. John L——,** John Lamb.

be quarrelling with him (for we quarrelled sometimes), rather than not have him again, and was as uneasy without him, as he their poor uncle must have been when the doctor took off his limb. Here the children fell a crying, and asked if their little mourning which they had on was not for uncle John, and they looked up, and prayed me not to go on about their uncle, but to tell them some stories about their pretty dead mother. Then I told how for seven long years, in hope sometimes, sometimes in despair, yet persisting ever, I courted the fair Alice W———n; and, as much as children could understand, I explained to them what coyness, and difficulty, and denial meant in maidens—when suddenly, turning to Alice, the soul of the first Alice looked out at her eyes with such a reality of representment, that I became in doubt which of them stood there before me, or whose that bright hair was; and while I stood gazing, both the children gradually grew fainter to my view, receding, and still receding till nothing at last but two mournful features were seen in the uttermost distance, which, without speech, strangely impressed upon me the effects of speech; "We are not of Alice, nor of thee, nor are we children at all. The children of Alice call Bartrum father. We are nothing; less than nothing, and dreams. We are only what might have been, and must wait upon the tedious shores of Lethe millions of ages before we have existence, and a name"—and immediately awaking, I found myself quietly seated in my bachelor arm-chair, where I had fallen asleep, with the faithful Bridget unchanged by my side—but John L. (or James Elia) was gone for ever.

OLD CHINA

I HAVE an almost feminine partiality for old china. When I go to see any great house, I inquire for the china-closet, and next for the picture gallery. I cannot defend the order of preference, but by saying, that we have all some taste or other, of too ancient a date to admit of our remembering distinctly that it was an acquired one. I can call to mind the first play, and the first exhibition, that I was taken to; but I am not conscious of a time when china jars and saucers were introduced into my imagination.

I had no repugnance then—why should I now have?—to those little, lawless, azure-tinctured grotesques, that under the notion of men and women, float about, uncircumscribed by any element, in that world before perspective—a china tea-cup.

12. **Alice W———n**, Ann Simmons.

I like to see my old friends—whom distance cannot diminish—figuring up in the air (so they appear to our optics), yet on *terra firma* still—for so we must in courtesy interpret that speck of deeper blue, which the decorous artist, to prevent absurdity, had made to spring up beneath their sandals.

I love the men with women's faces, and the women, if possible, with still more womanish expressions.

Here is a young and courtly Mandarin, handing tea to a lady from a salver—two miles off. See how distance seems to set off respect! And here the same lady, or another—for likeness is identity on teacups—is stepping into a little fairy boat, moored on the hither side of this calm garden river, with a dainty mincing foot, which in a right angle of incidence (as angles go in our world) must infallibly land her in the midst of a flowery mead—a furlong off on the other side of the same strange stream!

Farther on—if far or near can be predicted of their world—see horses, trees, pagodas, dancing the hays.

Here—a cow and rabbit couchant, and co-extensive—so objects show, seen through the lucid atmosphere of fine Cathay.

I was pointing out to my cousin last evening, over our Hyson (which we are old fashioned enough to drink unmixed still of an afternoon), some of these *speciosa miracula* upon a set of extraordinary old blue china (a recent purchase) which we were now for the first time using; and could not help remarking, how favourable circumstances had been to us of late years, that we could afford to please the eye sometimes with trifles of this sort—when a passing sentiment seemed to over-shade the brows of my companion. I am quick at detecting these summer clouds in Bridget.

"I wish the good old times would come again," she said, "when we were not quite so rich. I do not mean, that I want to be poor; but there was a middle state"—so she was pleased to ramble on,—"in which I am sure we were a great deal happier. A purchase is but a purchase, now that you have money enough and to spare. Formerly it used to be a triumph. When we coveted a cheap luxury (and, O! how much ado I had to get you to consent in those times!) we were used to have a debate two or three days before, and to weigh the *for* and *against*, and think what we might spare it out of, and what saving we could hit upon, that should be an equivalent. A thing was worth buying then, when we felt the money that we paid for it.

22. **hays**, country dance. 29. **speciosa miracula**, shining wonders. 37. **Bridget**, Mary Lamb.

"Do you remember the brown suit, which you made to hang upon you, till all your friends cried shame upon you, it grew so threadbare—and all because of that folio Beaumont and Fletcher, which you dragged home late at night from Barker's in Covent Garden? Do you remember how we eyed it for weeks before we could make up our minds to the purchase, and had not come to a determination till it was near ten o'clock of the Saturday night, when you set off from Islington, fearing you should be too late—and when the old bookseller with some grumbling opened his shop, and by the twinkling taper (for he was setting bedwards) lighted out the relic from his dusty treasures—and when you lugged it home, wishing it were twice as cumbersome—and when you presented it to me—and when we were exploring the perfectness of it (*collating*, you called it)—and while I was repairing some of the loose leaves with paste, which your impatience would not suffer to be left till day-break—was there no pleasure in being a poor man? or can those neat black clothes which you wear now, and are so careful to keep brushed, since we have become rich and finical—give you half the honest vanity with which you flaunted it about in that over-worn suit—your old corbeau—for four or five weeks longer than you should have done, to pacify your conscience for the mighty sum of fifteen—or sixteen shillings was it?—a great affair we thought it then—which you had lavished on the old folio. Now you can afford to buy any book that pleases you, but I do not see that you ever bring me home any nice old purchases now.

"When you came home with twenty apologies for laying out a less number of shillings upon that print after Lionardo, which we christened the 'Lady Blanch'; when you looked at the purchase, and thought of the money—and thought of the money, and looked again at the picture—was there no pleasure in being a poor man? Now, you have nothing to do but to walk into Colnaghi's, and buy a wilderness of Lionardos. Yet do you?

"Then, do you remember our pleasant walks to Enfield, and Potter's Bar, and Waltham, when we had a holyday—holydays and all other fun are gone now we are rich—and the little hand-basket in which I used to deposit our day's fare of savory cold lamb and salad—and how you would pry about at noon-tide for some decent house, where we might go in, and produce our store—only paying for the ale that you must call for—and speculate upon the looks of the landlady, and whether she was likely to allow us a table-cloth—and wish for such another honest hostess, as Izaak Walton has described many a one on the pleasant banks of the Lea, when he went a fishing—and sometimes they would prove obliging enough, and sometimes they would look grudgingly upon us—but we had cheerful looks still for one another, and would eat our plain food savorily, scarcely grudging Piscator his Trout Hall? Now—when we go out a day's pleasuring, which is seldom moreover, we *ride* part of the way—and go into a fine inn, and order the best of dinners, never debating the expense—which, after all, never has half the relish of those chance country snaps, when we were at the mercy of uncertain usage, and a precarious welcome.

"You are too proud to see a play anywhere now but in the pit. Do you remember where it was we used to sit, when we saw the battle of Hexham, and the Surrender of Calais, and Bannister and Mrs. Bland in the Children in the Wood—when we squeezed out our shillings a-piece to sit three or four times in a season in the one-shilling gallery—where you felt all the time that you ought not to have brought me—and more strongly I felt obligation to you for having brought me—and the pleasure was the better for a little shame—and when the curtain drew up, what cared we for our place in the house, or what mattered it where we were sitting, when our thoughts were with Rosalind in Arden, or with Viola at the Court of Illyria? You used to say, that the gallery was the best place of all for enjoying a play socially—that the relish of such exhibitions must be in proportion to the infrequency of going—that the company we met there, not being in general readers of plays, were obliged to attend the more, and did attend to what was going on, on the stage—because a word lost would have been a chasm, which it was impossible for them to fill up. With such reflections we consoled our pride then—and I appeal to you whether, as a woman, I met generally with less attention and accommodation than I have done since in more expensive situations in the house? The getting in indeed, and the crowding up those inconvenient staircases, was bad enough—but there was still a law of civility to woman recognised to quite as great an extent as we ever found in the other passages—and how a little difficulty overcome heightened the snug seat and the play, afterwards! Now we can only pay our money and walk in. You cannot see, you say, in the galleries now. I am sure we saw, and heard too, well enough then—but sight, and all, I think, is gone with our poverty.

---

4. Beaumont and Fletcher, Francis Beaumont and John Fletcher were dramatists of Shakespeare's time. **26. corbeau,** greenish, almost black, color.

29. Rosalind, in *As You Like It.* **29-30. Viola,** in *Twelfth Night.*

"There was pleasure in eating strawberries, before they became quite common—in the first dish of peas, while they were yet dear—to have them for a nice supper, a treat. What treat can we have now? If we were to treat ourselves now—that is, to have dainties a little above our means, it would be selfish and wicked. It is the very little more that we allow ourselves beyond what the actual poor can get at, that makes what I call a treat—when two people, living together, as we have done, now and then indulge themselves in a cheap luxury, which both like; while each apologises, and is willing to take both halves of the blame to his single share. I see no harm in people making much of themselves in that sense of the word. It may give them a hint how to make much of others. But now—what I mean by the word—we never do make much of ourselves. None but the poor can do it. I do not mean the veriest poor of all, but persons as we were, just above poverty.

"I know what you were going to say, that it is mighty pleasant at the end of the year to make all meet,—and much ado we used to have every Thirty-first Night of December to account for our exceedings—many a long face did you make over your puzzled accounts, and in contriving to make it out how we had spent so much—or that we had not spent so much—or that it was impossible we should spend so much next year—and still we found our slender capital decreasing—but then, betwixt ways, and projects, and compromises of one sort or another, and talk of curtailing this charge, and doing without that for the future—and the hope that youth brings, and laughing spirits (in which you were never poor till now) we pocketed up our loss, and in conclusion, with 'lusty brimmers' (as you used to quote it out of *hearty cheerful Mr. Cotton*, as you called him), we used to welcome in the 'coming guest.' Now we have no reckoning at all at the end of the old year—no flattering promises about the new year doing better for us."

Bridget is so sparing of her speech on most occasions, that when she gets into a rhetorical vein, I am careful how I interrupt it. I could not help, however, smiling at the phantom of wealth which her dear imagination had conjured up out of a clear income of poor—— hundred pounds a year. "It is true we were happier when we were poorer, but we were also younger, my cousin. I am afraid we must put up with the excess, for if we were to shake the superflux into the sea, we should not much mend ourselves. That we had much to struggle with, as we grew up together, we have reason to be most thankful. It strengthened, and knit our compact

closer. We could never have been what we have been to each other, if we had always had the sufficiency which you now complain of. The resisting power—those natural dilations of the youthful spirit, which circumstances cannot straiten—with us are long since passed away. Competence to age is supplementary youth, a sorry supplement indeed, but I fear the best that is to be had. We must ride where we formerly walked: live better, and lie softer—and shall be wise to do so—than we had means to do in those good old days you speak of. Yet could those days return—could you and I once more walk our thirty miles a day—could Bannister and Mrs. Bland again be young, and you and I be young to see them—could the good old one shilling gallery days return—they are dreams, my cousin, now—but could you and I at this moment, instead of this quiet argument, by our well-carpeted fireside, sitting on this luxurious sofa—be once more struggling up those inconvenient stair-cases, pushed about, and squeezed, and elbowed by the poorest rabble of poor gallery scramblers—could I once more hear those anxious shrieks of yours—and the delicious *Thank God, we are safe*, which always followed when the topmost stair, conquered, let in the first light of the whole cheerful theatre down beneath us—I know not the fathom line that ever touched a descent so deep as I would be willing to bury more wealth in than Croesus had, or the great Jew R—— is supposed to have, to purchase it. And now do just look at that merry little Chinese waiter holding an umbrella, big enough for a bed-tester, over the head of that pretty insipid half-Madonaish chit of a lady in that very blue summer-house."

POOR RELATIONS

A POOR Relation—is the most irrelevant thing in nature,—a piece of impertinent correspondency,—an odious approximation,—a haunting conscience,—a preposterous shadow, lengthening in the noontide of your prosperity,—an unwelcome remembrancer,—a perpetually recurring mortification,—a drain on your purse,—a more intolerable dun upon your pride,—a drawback upon success,—a rebuke to your rising,—a stain in your blood,—a blot on your scutcheon,—a rent in your garment,—a death's head at your banquet,—Agathocles' pot,—a Mordecai in your gate,—a

30. R——, Nathan Meyer Rothschild (1777–1836), founder of the great firm of international financiers. 32. **bed-tester,** canopy. 50. **Agathocles,** tyrant of Sicily. He was the son of a potter. 50. **Mordecai.** See Esther 3: 1–2; 5: 11–13.

Lazarus at your door,—a lion in your path,—a frog in your chamber,—a fly in your ointment,—a mote in your eye,—a triumph to your enemy, an apology to your friends,—the one thing not needful,—the hail in harvest,—the ounce of sour in a pound of sweet.

He is known by his knock. Your heart telleth you "That is Mr. ——." A rap, between familiarity and respect; that demands, and, at the same time, seems to despair of, entertainment. He entereth smiling and—embarrassed. He holdeth out his hand to you to shake, and—draweth it back again. He casually looketh in about dinner time—when the table is full. He offereth to go away, seeing you have company, but is induced to stay. He filleth a chair, and your visitor's two children are accommodated at a side table. He never cometh upon open days, when your wife says with some complacency, "My dear, perhaps Mr. —— will drop in to-day." He remembereth birthdays—and professeth he is fortunate to have stumbled upon one. He declareth against fish, the turbot being small—yet suffereth himself to be importuned into a slice against his first resolution. He sticketh by the port—yet will be prevailed upon to empty the remainder glass of claret, if a stranger press it upon him. He is a puzzle to the servants, who are fearful of being too obsequious, or not civil enough, to him. The guests think "they have seen him before." Every one speculateth upon his condition; and the most part take him to be—a tide-waiter. He calleth you by your Christian name, to imply that his other is the same with your own. He is too familiar by half, yet you wish he had less diffidence. With half the familiarity he might pass for a casual dependent; with more boldness he would be in no danger of being taken for what he is. He is too humble for a friend, yet taketh on him more state than befits a client. He is a worse guest than a country tenant, inasmuch as he bringeth up no rent—yet 'tis odds, from his garb and demeanour, that your guests take him for one. He is asked to make one at the whist table; refuseth on the score of poverty, and—resents being left out. When the company break up, he proffereth to go for a coach—and lets the servant go. He recollects your grandfather; and will thrust in some mean and quite unimportant anecdote of—the family. He knew it when it was not quite so flourishing as "he is blest in seeing it now." He reviveth past situations to institute what he calleth—favourable comparisons. With a reflecting sort of congratulation, he will inquire the price of your furniture: and insults you with a special commendation of your window-curtains. He is of

opinion that the urn is the more elegant shape, but, after all, there was something more comfortable about the old tea-kettle—which you must remember. He dare say you must find a great convenience in having a carriage of your own, and appealeth to your lady if it is not so. Inquireth if you have had your arms done on vellum yet; and did not know till lately, that such-and-such had been the crest of the family. His memory is unseasonable; his compliments perverse; his talk a trouble; his stay pertinacious; and when he goeth away, you dismiss his chair into a corner, as precipitately as possible, and feel fairly rid of two nuisances.

There is a worse evil under the sun, and that is—a female Poor Relation. You may do something with the other; you may pass him off tolerably well; but your indigent she-relative is hopeless. "He is an old humourist," you may say, "and affects to go threadbare. His circumstances are better than folks would take them to be. You are fond of having a Character at your table, and truly he is one." But in the indications of female poverty there can be no disguise. No woman dresses below herself from caprice. The truth must out without shuffling. "She is plainly related to the L——s; or what does she at their house?" She is, in all probability, your wife's cousin. Nine times out of ten, at least, this is the case. Her garb is something between a gentlewoman and a beggar, yet the former evidently predominates. She is most provokingly humble, and ostentatiously sensible to her inferiority. He may require to be repressed sometimes—*aliquando sufflaminandus erat*—but there is no raising her. You send her soup at dinner, and she begs to be helped—after the gentlemen. Mr. —— requests the honour of taking wine with her; she hesitates between Port and Madeira, and chooses the former—because he does. She calls the servant *Sir;* and insists on not troubling him to hold her plate. The housekeeper patronizes her. The children's governess takes upon her to correct her, when she has mistaken the piano for a harpsichord.

Richard Amlet, Esq., in the play, is a noticeable instance of the disadvantages, to which this chimerical notion of *affinity constituting a claim to an acquaintance*, may subject the spirit of a gentleman. A little foolish blood is all that is betwixt him and a lady of great estate. His stars are perpetually crossed by the malignant maternity of an old woman, who persists in calling him "her son Dick." But she has wherewithal in the end to recompense his indignities, and float him again upon the brilliant surface, under

1. **Lazarus.** See Luke 16: 20.

32–33. **aliquando . . . erat,** he even had to be squelched.
43. **play,** John Vanbrugh's *The Confederacy.*

which it had been her seeming business and pleasure all along to sink him. All men, besides, are not of Dick's temperament. I knew an Amlet in real life, who wanting Dick's buoyancy, sank indeed. Poor W—— was of my own standing at Christ's, a fine classic, and a youth of promise. If he had a blemish, it was too much pride; but its quality was inoffensive; it was not of that sort which hardens the heart, and serves to keep inferiors at a distance; it only sought to ward off derogation from itself. It was the principle of self-respect carried as far as it could go, without infringing upon that respect, which he would have every one else equally maintain for himself. He would have you to think alike with him on this topic. Many a quarrel have I had with him, when we were rather older boys, and our tallness made us more obnoxious to observation in the blue clothes, because I would not thread the alleys and blind ways of the town with him to elude notice, when we have been out together on a holiday in the streets of this sneering and prying metropolis. W—— went, sore with these notions, to Oxford, where the dignity and sweetness of a scholar's life, meeting with the alloy of a humble introduction, wrought in him a passionate devotion to the place, with a profound aversion from the society. The servitor's gown (worse than his school array) clung to him with Nessian venom. He thought himself ridiculous in a garb, under which Latimer must have walked erect; and in which Hooker, in his young days, possibly flaunted in a vein of no discommendable vanity. In the depths of college shades, or in his lonely chamber, the poor student shrunk from observation. He found shelter among books, which insult not; and studies, that ask no questions of a youth's finances. He was lord of his library, and seldom cared for looking out beyond his domains. The healing influence of studious pursuits was upon him, to soothe and to abstract. He was almost a healthy man; when the waywardness of his fate broke out against him with a second and worse malignity. The father of W—— had hitherto exercised the humble profession of house-painter at N——, near Oxford. A supposed interest with some of the heads of colleges had now induced him to take up his abode in that city, with the hope of being employed upon some public works which were talked of. From that moment I read in the countenance of the young man, the determination which at length tore him from academical pursuits for ever.

To a person unacquainted with our Universities, the distance between the gownsmen and the townsmen, as they are called—the trading part of the latter especially—is carried to an excess that would appear harsh and incredible. The temperament of W——'s father was diametrically the reverse of his own. Old W—— was a little, busy, cringing tradesman, who, with his son upon his arm, would stand bowing and scraping, cap in hand, to anything that wore the semblance of a gown—insensible to the winks and opener remonstrances of the young man, to whose chamber-fellow, or equal in standing, perhaps, he was thus obsequiously and gratuitously ducking. Such a state of things could not last. W—— must change the air of Oxford or be suffocated. He chose the former; and let the sturdy moralist, who strains the point of the filial duties as high as they can bear, censure the dereliction; he cannot estimate the struggle. I stood with W——, the last afternoon I ever saw him, under the eaves of his paternal dwelling. It was in the fine lane leading from the High-street to the back of —— college, where W—— kept his rooms. He seemed thoughtful, and more reconciled. I ventured to rally him—finding him in a better mood—upon a representation of the Artist Evangelist, which the old man, whose affairs were beginning to flourish, had caused to be set up in a splendid sort of frame over his really handsome shop, either as a token of prosperity, or badge of gratitude to his saint. W—— looked up at the Luke, and, like Satan, "knew his mounted sign—and fled." A letter on his father's table the next morning, announced that he had accepted a commission in a regiment about to embark for Portugal. He was among the first who perished before the walls of St. Sebastian.

I do not know how, upon a subject which I began with treating half seriously, I should have fallen upon a recital so eminently painful; but this theme of poor relationship is replete with so much matter for tragic as well as comic associations, that it is difficult to keep the account distinct without blending. The earliest impressions which I received on this matter, are certainly not attended with anything painful, or very humiliating, in the recalling. At my father's table (no very splendid one) was to be found, every Saturday, the mysterious figure of an aged gentleman, clothed in neat black, of a sad yet comely appearance. His deportment was of the essence of gravity; his words few or none; and I was not to make a noise in his presence. I had little inclination to have done so—for my cue was to admire in silence. A particular elbow chair was ap-

5. W——, Favell (mentioned in "Christ's Hospital") "left Cambridge because he was ashamed of his father, who had been a house-painter there." (Lamb) 28. Nessian venom. Hercules was poisoned by "the shirt of Nessus."

36. St. Sebastian, besieged by Wellington in 1813.

propriated to him, which was in no case to be violated. A peculiar sort of sweet pudding, which appeared on no other occasion, distinguished the days of his coming. I used to think him a prodigiously rich man. All I could make out of him was, that he and my father had been schoolfellows a world ago at Lincoln, and that he came from the Mint. The Mint I knew to be a place where all the money was coined—and I thought he was the owner of all that money. Awful ideas of the Tower twined themselves about his presence. He seemed above human infirmities and passions. A sort of melancholy grandeur invested him. From some inexplicable doom I fancied him obliged to go about in an eternal suit of mourning; a captive—a stately being, let out of the Tower on Saturdays. Often have I wondered at the temerity of my father, who, in spite of an habitual general respect which we all in common manifested towards him, would venture now and then to stand up against him in some argument, touching their youthful days. The houses of the ancient city of Lincoln are divided (as most of my readers know) between the dwellers on the hill, and in the valley. This marked distinction formed an obvious division between the boys who lived above (however brought together in a common school) and the boys whose paternal residence was on the plain; a sufficient cause of hostility in the code of these young Grotiuses. My father had been a leading Mountaineer; and would still maintain the general superiority, in skill and hardihood, of the *Above Boys* (his own faction) over the *Below Boys* (so were they called), of which party his contemporary had been a chieftain. Many and hot were the skirmishes on this topic—the only one upon which the old gentleman was ever brought out—and bad blood bred; even sometimes almost to the recommencement (so I expected) of actual hostilities. But my father, who scorned to insist upon advantages, generally contrived to turn the conversation upon some adroit by-commendation of the old Minster; in the general preference of which, before all other cathedrals in the island, the dweller on the hill, and the plain-born, could meet on a conciliating level, and lay down their less important differences. Once only I saw the old gentleman really ruffled, and I remembered with anguish the thought that came over me: "Perhaps he will never come here again." He had been pressed to take another plate of the viand, which I have already mentioned as the indispensable concomitant of his visits. He had refused with a resistance amounting to rigour—when my aunt, an old Lincolnian, but who had something of this in common with my cousin Bridget, that she would sometimes press civility out of season—uttered the following memorable application—"Do take another slice, Mr. Billet, for you do not get pudding every day." The old gentleman said nothing at the time—but he took occasion in the course of the evening, when some argument had intervened between them, to utter with an emphasis which chilled the company, and which chills me now as I write it—"Woman, you are superannuated." John Billet did not survive long, after the digesting of this affront; but he survived long enough to assure me that peace was actually restored! and, if I remember aright, another pudding was discreetly substituted in the place of that which had occasioned the offence. He died at the Mint (Anno 1781) where he had long held, what he accounted, a comfortable independence; and with five pounds, fourteen shillings, and a penny, which were found in his escritoire after his decease, left the world, blessing God that he had enough to bury him, and that he had never been obliged to any man for a six-pence. This was—a Poor Relation.

28–29. Grotiuses. Hugo Grotius (in Dutch, van Groot), the famous publicist and statesman, was very precocious as a child.

William Hazlitt
1778–1830 52.

William Hazlitt was born April 10, 1778, at Maidstone, Kent, where his father was a Unitarian minister. The Reverend William Hazlitt was a believer in the republican form of government and a friend of Benjamin Franklin. In 1783, in order to enjoy the freedom of the new American republic, he took his family to America. Here he preached to the New Jersey Assembly, lectured in the college that was to become the University of Pennsylvania, and founded the first Unitarian church in Boston. Since the younger William was only four years old at the time of the emigration, and the family did not remain long in America, this sojourn left few memories, the chief one being the taste of barberries that had hung all winter in the New England snow. At Wem, in Shropshire, his education began under his father, who destined him for the ministry. At fifteen he was sent to Hackney College, a Unitarian seminary. Between the ages of sixteen and twenty-one, Hazlitt tells us, he read novels by Fielding and Smollett; Burke's *Letter to a Noble Lord* and *Reflections on the French Revolution*, which impressed him as superb prose; Milton's *Paradise Lost;* and Rousseau's *La nouvelle Héloïse*, which touched the springs of emotion and imagination. He also saw the pictures at Burleigh House. But the greatest single event of his life was his "First Acquaintance with Poets" (the meeting with Coleridge and Wordsworth) in 1798. Of the walk with Coleridge toward Shrewsbury, Hazlitt wrote, twenty-five years later: "The light of his genius shone into my soul, like the sun's rays glittering in the puddles of the road. . . . that my understanding . . . did not remain dull and brutish, or at length found a language to express itself, I owe to Coleridge." His entrance into literature, however, was not immediate. Between 1799 and 1805 he undertook to master the art of painting, beginning under his brother John, who was a successful miniaturist, and studying at the Louvre in Paris. While in France he developed that loyalty to the cause of the French Revolution and that admiration for Napoleon which he never lost and which impelled him to undertake his *Life of Napoleon* as his last great enterprise. In 1805, as a result of matchmaking by Charles and Mary Lamb, he married Sarah Stoddart, who had a cottage at Winterslow and a small income. Convinced by now

that he would never make a great painter, he occupied himself by writing various essays on morals, philosophy, and economics.

The year 1812, when Hazlitt made his appearance as a public lecturer on the history of English philosophy, is regarded as a turning-point. Soon he was launched upon the journalistic, lecturing, and literary free-lancing career that was to engage him the rest of his life. He began to write dramatic criticism for the *Morning Chronicle*, at a time when Edmund Kean was the leading actor in a notable Shakespearean revival, and essays for Leigh Hunt's *Examiner*. He had rounded out his acquaintance with most of the literary lights of the period—Coleridge, Wordsworth, Lamb, Leigh Hunt, Keats, and Shelley. These friendships and the enmities he acquired, his journalistic connections, and his steadfast adherence to the principles of the French Revolution lined him up in the literary wars of the time. During 1818–20 he delivered a series of lectures, on *The English Poets*, on *English Comic Writers*, and on the *Dramatic Literature of the Age of Elizabeth*, which established him as a literary critic of the first rank. He was violently attacked by *Blackwood's* and the *Quarterly*, and got himself embroiled in the affair that resulted in the death in a duel of John Scott, editor of the *London Magazine*. About this time, his marriage was drifting toward the rocks because of an infatuation with Sarah Walker, decoy daughter of his London lodging-house. At his request, Sarah Stoddart Hazlitt divorced him; whereupon the other Sarah refused to marry him. Hazlitt reveals the whole story without reserve in his most imprudent book, *Liber Amoris*. Despite these fevered personal experiences, his writing went serenely on. In 1824 he again married, this time a widow who had an income sufficient for foreign travel for the two. Travel and his *Life of Napoleon* engaged his interest until his death in 1830.

This brief account of the life of Hazlitt suggests the salient features of his personality and character. He was moody, sensitive, and often difficult, even with his friends. Lacking the breeding and the formal education that most of his literary associates had, he suffered at times from an inferiority complex. He lived, loved, hated, talked, and wrote intensely. He quarreled, often to the point of final estrangement or enmity, with nearly every one of his friends except Lamb and Keats. The chief impression he gives of himself is that of an embittered, disillusioned man. Perhaps he was too uncompromising, made too many emotional demands on his friends. Yet his best and perhaps only lifelong friend, Charles Lamb, said of him, "I think William Hazlitt to be, in his natural and healthy state, one of the wisest and finest spirits breathing." Some of Hazlitt's observations of life and of human nature are among the noblest and most winsome in English essay-writing.

Hazlitt was a fighting literary critic, an art connoisseur with few rivals except Ruskin and Walter Pater, a master of the familiar essay, and the most comprehensive prose interpreter of the spirit of his age. His chief titles are *The Round Table*, 1817; *The Characters of Shakespear's Plays*, 1817; *Lectures on the English Poets*, 1818; *Lectures on the English Comic Writers*, 1819; *Lectures on the Dramatic Literature of the Age of Elizabeth*, 1820; *Liber Amoris*, 1823; *The Spirit of the Age*, 1825; *The Plain Speaker*, 1826; and *Life of Napoleon*, 1828–30. Except for the last, the twelve stout volumes in the Waller and Glover edition of his *Collected Works* are made up almost entirely of essays.

In the essay Hazlitt found the perfect medium for the expression of his many-sided genius. He was essentially a critic. Tasting, judging, and reporting his impressions he regarded as his chief function and delight. He was a critic of pictures, books, plays, men, and manners. He thought that the greatest quality in art was gusto, the power and passion defining an object. His literary criticism covers most of what is important from the Age of Elizabeth to the end of the Romantic Period. His criticisms of the stage and of painting are among the best written in English. Whatever his pen touched came to life: Coleridge, "shifting from one side of the foot-path to the other"; "that tenth of April, 1798, that I sat down to a volume of the *New Eloise*, at the inn at Llangollen, over a bottle of sherry and a cold chicken"; "The Pleasure of Painting" and "The Pleasure of Hating"; Bill Neate rolling along and superciliously sucking oranges; Tom Hickman, his back glistening in the sun like a panther's hide, and, later, "his face . . . like a human skull, a death's head, spouting blood." "My First Acquaintance with Poets" Mr. W. Somerset Maugham considers to be "not only the most thrilling piece he ever wrote but the finest essay in the English language." "We are all mighty fine fellows," said Robert Louis Stevenson, "but none of us can write like Hazlitt."

CHARACTERS OF SHAKESPEAR'S PLAYS

HAMLET

THIS is that Hamlet the Dane, whom we read of in our youth, and whom we may be said almost to remember in our after-years; he who made that famous soliloquy on life, who gave the advice to the players, who thought "this goodly frame, the earth, a steril promontory, and this brave o'er-hanging firmament, the air, this majestical roof fretted with golden fire, a foul and pestilent congregation of vapours"; whom "man delighted not, nor woman neither"; he who talked with the grave-diggers, and moralised on Yorick's skull; the school-fellow of Rosencrans and Guildenstern at Wittenberg; the friend of Horatio; the lover of Ophelia; he that was mad and sent to England; the slow avenger of his father's death; who lived at the court of Horwendillus five hundred years before we were born, but all those thoughts we seem to know as well as we do our own, because we have read them in Shakespear.

Hamlet is a name; his speeches and sayings but the idle coinage of the poet's brain. What then, are they not real? They are as real as our own thoughts. Their reality is in the reader's mind. It is *we* who are Hamlet. This play has a prophetic truth, which is above that of history. Whoever has become thoughtful and melancholy through his own mishaps or those of others; whoever has borne about with him the clouded brow of reflection, and thought himself "too much i' th' sun"; whoever has seen the golden lamp of day dimmed by envious mists rising in his own breast, and could find in the world before him only a dull blank with nothing left remarkable in it; whoever has known "the pangs of despised love, the insolence of office, or the spurns which patient merit of the unworthy takes"; he who has felt his mind sink within him, and sadness cling to his heart like a malady, who has had his hopes blighted and his youth staggered by the apparitions of strange things; who cannot be well at ease, while he sees evil hovering near him like a spectre; whose powers of action have been eaten up by thought, he to whom the universe seems infinite, and himself nothing; whose bitterness of soul makes him careless of consequences, and who goes to a play as his best resource to shove off, to a second re-

15–16. who lived . . . born, an allusion to the earliest form of the story, told by the Danish historian Saxo-Grammaticus c. 1200.

move, the evils of life by a mock representation of them—this is the true Hamlet.

We have been so used to this tragedy that we hardly know how to criticise it any more than we should know how to describe our own faces. But we must make such observations as we can. It is the one of Shakespear's plays that we think of the oftenest, because it abounds most in striking reflections on human life, and because the distresses of Hamlet are transferred, by the turn of his mind, to the general account of humanity. Whatever happens to him, we apply to ourselves, because he applied it so himself as a means of general reasoning. He is a great moraliser; and what makes him worth attending to is that he moralises on his own feelings and experience. He is not a common-place pedant. If *Lear* shows the greatest depth of passion, HAMLET is the most remarkable for the ingenuity, originality, and unstudied development of character. Shakespear had more magnanimity than any other poet, and he has shewn more of it in this play than in any other. There is no attempt to force an interest: every thing is left for time and circumstances to unfold. The attention is excited without effort, the incidents succeed each other as matters of course, the characters think and speak and act just as they might do, if left entirely to themselves. There is no set purpose, no straining at a point. The observations are suggested by the passing scene—the gusts of passion come and go like sounds of music borne on the wind. The whole play is an exact transcript of what might be supposed to have taken place at the court of Denmark, at the remote period of time fixed upon, before the modern refinements in morals and manners were heard of. It would have been interesting enough to have been admitted as a bystander in such a scene, at such a time, to have heard and seen something of what was going on. But here we are more than spectators. We have not only "the outward pageants and the signs of grief"; but "we have that within which passes shew." We read the thoughts of the heart, we catch the passions living as they rise. Other dramatic writers give us very fine versions and paraphrases of nature: but Shakespear, together with his own comments, gives us the original text, that we may judge for ourselves. This is a very great advantage.

The character of Hamlet stands quite by itself. It is not a character marked by strength of will or even of passion, but by refinement of thought and sentiment. Hamlet is as little of the hero as a man can well be: but he is a young and princely novice, full of high enthusiasm and quick sensibility—the sport of circumstances, questioning with fortune and refining on his own feelings, and forced from the natural bias of his disposition by the strangeness of his situation. He seems incapable of deliberate action, and is only hurried into extremities on the spur of the occasion, when he has no time to reflect, as in the scene where he kills Polonius, and again, where he alters the letters which Rosencrans and Guildenstern are taking with them to England, purporting his death. At other times, when he is most bound to act, he remains puzzled, undecided, and sceptical, dallies with his purposes, till the occasion is lost, and always finds some pretence to relapse into indolence and thoughtfulness again. For this reason he refuses to kill the King when he is at his prayers, and by a refinement in malice, which is in truth only an excuse for his own want of resolution, defers his revenge to some more fatal opportunity, when he shall be engaged in some act "that has no relish of salvation in it."

"He kneels and prays
And now I'll do 't, and so he goes to heaven,
And so am I revenged; *that would be scanned:*
He killed my father, and for that,
I, his sole son, send him to heaven.
Why this is reward, not revenge.
Up sword and know thou a more horrid time,
When he is drunk, asleep, or in a rage."

He is the prince of philosophical speculators, and because he cannot have his revenge perfect, according to the most refined idea his wish can form, he declines it altogether. So he scruples to trust the suggestions of the ghost, contrives the scene of the play to have surer proof of his uncle's guilt, and then rests satisfied with this confirmation of his suspicions, and the success of his experiment, instead of acting upon it. Yet he is sensible of his own weakness, taxes himself with it, and tries to reason himself out of it.

"How all occasions do inform against me,
And spur my dull revenge! What is a man,
If his chief good and market of his time
Be but to sleep and feed? A beast; no more.
Sure he that made us with such large discourse,
Looking before and after, gave us not
That capability and god-like reason
To rust in us unused: now whether it be
Bestial oblivion, or some craven scruple
Of thinking too precisely on th' event,—
A thought which quartered, hath but one part wisdom,
And ever three parts coward;—I do not know
Why yet I live to say, this thing's to do;

Sith I have cause, and will, and strength, and
   means
To do it. Examples gross as earth exhort me:
Witness this army of such mass and charge,
Led by a delicate and tender prince,
Whose spirit with divine ambition puffed,
Makes mouths at the invisible event,
Exposing what is mortal and unsure
To all that fortune, death and danger dare,
Even for an egg-shell. 'Tis not to be great
Never to stir without great argument;
But greatly to find quarrel in a straw,
When honour's at the stake. How stand I then,
That have a father killed, a mother stained,
Excitements of my reason and my blood,
And let all sleep, while to my shame I see
The imminent death of twenty thousand men,
That for a fantasy and trick of fame,
Go to their graves like beds, fight for a plot
Whereon the numbers cannot try the cause,
Which is not tomb enough, and continent
To hide the slain?—O, from this time forth,
My thoughts be bloody or be nothing worth."

Still he does nothing; and this very speculation on
his own infirmity only affords him another occasion for indulging it. It is not for any want of attachment to his father or abhorrence of his murder that
Hamlet is thus dilatory, but it is more to his taste to
indulge his imagination in reflecting upon the enormity of the crime and refining on his schemes of
vengeance, than to put them into immediate practice. His ruling passion is to think, not to act: and
any vague pretence that flatters this propensity instantly diverts him from his previous purposes.

   The moral perfection of this character has been
called in question, we think, by those who did not
understand it. It is more interesting than according to rules; amiable, though not faultless. The ethical delineations of "that noble and liberal casuist"
(as Shakespear has been called) do not exhibit the
drab-coloured quakerism of mortality. His plays are
not copied either from the Whole Duty of Man or
from The Academy of Compliments! We confess
we are a little shocked at the want of refinement in
those who are shocked at the want of refinement in
Hamlet. The neglect of punctilious exactness in his
behaviour either partakes of the "licence of the
time," or else belongs to the very excess of intellectual refinement in the character, which makes the

43. **Whole Duty of Man,** an ethical treatise of the seventeenth century, author unknown.   44. **The Academy of
Compliments,** another seventeenth-century treatise, on
courtship and manners.

common rules of life, as well as his own purposes,
sit loose upon him. He may be said to be amenable
only to the tribunal of his own thoughts, and is too
much taken up with the airy world of contemplation to lay as much stress as he ought on the practical consequences of things. His habitual principles
of action are unhinged and out of joint with the
time. His conduct to Ophelia is quite natural in his
circumstances. It is that of assumed severity only. It
10 is the effect of disappointed hope, of bitter regrets,
of affection suspended, not obliterated, by the distractions of the scenes around him! Amidst the natural and preternatural horrors of his situation, he
might be excused in delicacy from carrying on a
regular courtship. When "his father's spirit was in
arms," it was not a time for the son to make love in.
He could neither marry Ophelia, nor wound her
mind by explaining the cause of his alienation,
which he durst hardly trust himself to think of. It
20 would have taken him years to have come to a direct explanation on the point. In the harassed state
of his mind, he could not have done otherwise than
he did. His conduct does not contradict what he
says when he sees her funeral,

    "I loved Ophelia: forty thousand brothers
    Could not with all their quantity of love
    Make up my sum."

30 Nothing can be more affecting or beautiful than
the Queen's apostrophe to Ophelia on throwing the
flowers into the grave.

      —"Sweets to the sweet, farewell.
I hoped thou should'st have been my Hamlet's
    wife:
I thought thy bride-bed to have decked, sweet maid,
And not have strewed thy grave."

Shakespear was thoroughly a master of the mixed
motives of human character, and he here shews us
the Queen, who was so criminal in some respects,
not without sensibility and affection in other relations of life.—Ophelia is a character almost too exquisitely touching to be dwelt upon. Oh rose of
May, oh flower too soon faded! Her love, her madness, her death, are described with the truest
touches of tenderness and pathos. It is a character
which nobody but Shakespear could have drawn in
50 the way that he has done, and to the conception of
which there is not even the smallest approach, except in some of the old romantic ballads. Her
brother, Laertes, is a character we do not like so
well: he is too hot and choleric, and somewhat rho-

domontade. Polonius is a perfect character in its kind; nor is there any foundation for the objections which have been made to the consistency of this part. It is said that he acts very foolishly and talks very sensibly. There is no inconsistency in that. Again, that he talks wisely at one time and foolishly at another; that his advice to Laertes is very excellent, and his advice to the King and Queen on the subject of Hamlet's madness very ridiculous. But he gives the one as a father, and is sincere in it; he gives the other as a mere courtier, a busy-body, and is accordingly officious, garrulous, and impertinent. In short, Shakespear has been accused of inconsistency in this and other characters, only because he has kept up the distinction which there is in nature, between the understandings and moral habits of men, between the absurdity of their ideas and the absurdity of their motives. Polonius is not a fool, but he makes himself so. His folly, whether in his actions of speeches, comes under the head of impropriety of intention.

We do not like to see our author's plays acted, and least of all, HAMLET. There is no play that suffers so much in being transferred to the stage. Hamlet himself seems hardly capable of being acted. Mr. Kemble unavoidably fails in this character from a want of ease and variety. The character of Hamlet is made up of undulating lines; it has the yielding flexibility of "a wave o' th' sea." Mr. Kemble plays it like a man in armour, with a determined inveteracy of purpose, in one undeviating straight line, which is as remote from the natural grace and refined susceptibility of the character, as the sharp angles and abrupt starts which Mr. Kean introduces into the part. Mr. Kean's Hamlet is as much too splenetic and rash as Mr. Kemble's is too deliberate and formal. His manner is too strong and pointed. He throws severity, approaching to virulence, into the common observations and answers. There is nothing of this in Hamlet. He is, as it were, wrapped up in his reflections, and only *thinks aloud*. There should therefore be no attempt to impress what he says upon others by a studied exaggeration of emphasis or manner; no *talking at* his hearers. There should be as much of the gentleman and scholar as possible infused into the part, and as little of the actor. A pensive air of sadness should sit reluctantly upon his brow, but no appearance of fixed and sullen gloom. He is full of weakness and melancholy, but there is no harshness in his nature. He is the most amiable of misanthropes.

from THE FIGHT

The first part of the essay (omitted) tells how, on December 10, 1821, Hazlitt learns "by grapevine" where the fight the next day between Bill Neate and Tom Hickman is to be; how he luckily finds a way down to Hungerford by coach, exchanging fight lore and slang with the coachman and other passengers; how he sits up all night at a crowded inn in the neighborhood, enjoying the talk and the characters of his fellows; and how at last "The morning dawns . . . we saw the ring surrounded by covered carts, gigs, and carriages." The theme of the essay is best stated in the sentence commenting on the fortitude of the fighters, "This is the high and heroic state of man!"

READER, have you ever seen a fight? If not, you have a pleasure to come, at least if it is a fight like that between the Gas-man and Bill Neate. The crowd was very great when we arrived on the spot; open carriages were coming up, with streamers flying and music playing, and the country-people were pouring in over hedge and ditch in all directions, to see their hero beat or be beaten. The odds were still on Gas, but only about five to four. Gully had been down to try Neate, and had backed him considerably, which was a damper to the sanguine confidence of the adverse party. About two hundred thousand pounds were pending. The Gas says, he has lost 3000*l.* which were promised him by different gentlemen if he had won. He had presumed too much on himself, which had made others presume on him. This spirited and formidable young fellow seems to have taken for his motto the old maxim, that "there are three things necessary to success in life—*Impudence! Impudence! Impudence!*" It is so in matters of opinion, but not in the FANCY, which is the most practical of all things, though even here confidence is half the battle, but only half. Our friend had vapoured and swaggered too much, as if he wanted to grin and bully his adversary out of the fight. "Alas! the Bristol man was not so tamed!"— "This is *the grave-digger*" (would Tom Hickman exclaim in the moments of intoxication from gin and success, shewing his tremendous right hand), "this will send many of them to their long homes; I haven't done with them yet!" Why should he— though he had licked four of the best men within the hour, yet why should he threaten to inflict dishonourable chastisement on my old master Richmond, a veteran going off the stage, and who has borne his

---

1. **Polonius.** With these remarks on Polonius compare those by Coleridge in "Characteristics of Shakspere's Dramas," "2. Signal adherence . . ." **22–23. We do not like . . . Hamlet.** Lamb had argued similarly in "On the Tragedies of Shakspeare, Considered with Reference to Their Fitness for Stage Representation," 1811.

39. Fancy, slang term for prize fighting.

sable honours meekly? Magnanimity, my dear Tom, and bravery, should be inseparable. Or why should he go up to his antagonist, the first time he ever saw him at the Fives Court, and measuring him from head to foot with a glance of contempt, as Achilles surveyed Hector, say to him, "What, are you Bill Neate? I'll knock more blood out of that great carcase of thine, this day fortnight, than you ever knocked out of a bullock's!" It was not manly, 'twas not fighter-like. If he was sure of the victory 10 (as he was not), the less said about it the better. Modesty should accompany the FANCY as its shadow. The best men were always the best behaved. Jem Belcher, the Game Chicken (before whom the Gasman could not have lived) were civil, silent men. So is Cribb, so is Tom Belcher, the most elegant of sparrers, and not a man for every one to take by the nose. I enlarged on this topic in the mail (while Turtle was asleep), and said very wisely (as I thought) that impertinence was a part of no profes- 20 sion. A boxer was bound to beat his man, but not to thrust his fist, either actually or by implication, in every one's face. Even a highwayman, in the way of trade, may blow out your brains, but if he uses foul language at the same time, I should say he was no gentleman. A boxer, I would infer, need not be a blackguard or a coxcomb, more than another. Perhaps I pressed this point too much on a fallen man —Mr. Thomas Hickman has by this time learnt that first of all lessons, "That man was made to 30 mourn." He has lost nothing by the late fight but his presumption; and that every man may do as well without! By an over-display of this quality, however, the public had been prejudiced against him, and the *knowing-ones* were taken in. Few but those who had bet on him wished Gas to win. With my own prepossessions on the subject, the result of the 11th of December appeared to me as fine a piece of poetical justice as I had ever witnessed. The difference of weight between the two combatants 40 (14 stone to 12) was nothing to the sporting men. Great, heavy, clumsy, long-armed Bill Neate kicked the beam in the scale of the Gas-man's vanity. The amateurs were frightened at his big words, and thought that they would make up for the difference of six feet and five feet nine. Truly, the FANCY are not men of imagination. They judge of what has been, and cannot conceive of any thing that is to be. The Gas-man had won hitherto; therefore he must beat a man half as big again as himself—and that to 50 a certainty. Besides, there are as many feuds, factions, prejudices, pedantic notions in the FANCY as in the state or in the schools. Mr. Gully is almost

41. **stone.** A stone is 14 lbs.

the only cool, sensible man among them, who exercises an unbiassed discretion, and is not a slave to his passions in these matters. But enough of reflections, and to our tale. The day, as I have said, was fine for a December morning. The grass was wet, and the ground miry, and ploughed up with multitudinous feet, except that, within the ring itself, there was a spot of virgin-green closed in and unprofaned by vulgar tread, that shone with dazzling brightness in the mid-day sun. For it was now noon, and we had an hour to wait. This is the trying time. It is then the heart sickens, as you think what the two champions are about, and how short a time will determine their fate. After the first blow is struck, there is no opportunity for nervous apprehensions; you are swallowed up in the immediate interest of the scene—but

"Between the acting of a dreadful thing
And the first motion, all the interim is
Like a phantasma, or a hideous dream."

I found it so as I felt the sun's rays clinging to my back, and saw the white wintry clouds sink below the verge of the horizon. "So," I thought, "my fairest hopes have faded from my sight!—so will the Gasman's glory, or that of his adversary, vanish in an hour." The *swells* were parading in their white boxcoats, the outer ring was cleared with some bruises on the heads and shins of the rustic assembly (for the *cockneys* had been distanced by the sixty-six miles); the time drew near, I had got a good stand; a bustle, a buzz, ran through the crowd, and from the opposite side entered Neate, between his second and bottle-holder. He rolled along, swathed in his loose great coat, his knock-knees bending under his huge bulk; and, with a modest cheerful air, threw his hat into the ring. He then just looked round, and began quietly to undress; when from the other side there was a similar rush and an opening made, and the Gas-man came forward with a conscious air of anticipated triumph, too much like the cock-of-the-walk. He strutted about more than became a hero, sucked oranges with a supercilious air, and threw away the skin with a toss of his head, and went up and looked at Neate, which was an act of supererogation. The only sensible thing he did was, as he strode away from the modern Ajax, to fling out his arms, as if he wanted to try whether they would do their work that day. By this time they had stripped, and presented a strong contrast in appearance. If

19–21. "Between . . . dream." See *Julius Caesar*, Act II, sc. 1.   48. **Ajax,** one of the bravest of the Greek warriors in the siege of Troy. **Diomed,** mentioned six lines below, was another.

Neate was like Ajax, "with Atlantean shoulders, fit to bear" the pugilistic reputation of all Bristol, Hickman might be compared to Diomed, light, vigorous, elastic, and his back glistened in the sun, as he moved about, like a panther's hide. There was now a dead pause—attention was awe-struck. Who at that moment, big with a great event, did not draw his breath short—did not feel his heart throb? All was ready. They tossed up for the sun, and the Gas-man won. They were led up to the *scratch*—shook hands, and went at it.

In the first round every one thought it was all over. After making play a short time, the Gas-man flew at his adversary like a tiger, struck five blows in as many seconds, three first, and then following him as he staggered back, two more, right and left, and down he fell, a mighty ruin. There was a shout, and I said, "There is no standing this." Neate seemed like a lifeless lump of flesh and bone, round which the Gas-man's blows played with the rapidity of electricity or lightning, and you imagined he would only be lifted up to be knocked down again. It was as if Hickman held a sword or a fire in that right hand of his, and directed it against an unarmed body. They met again, and Neate seemed, not cowed, but particularly cautious. I saw his teeth clenched together and his brows knit close against the sun. He held out both his arms at full length straight before him, like two sledge-hammers, and raised his left an inch or two higher. The Gas-man could not get over this guard—they struck mutually and fell, but without advantage on either side. It was the same in the next round; but the balance of power was thus restored—the fate of the battle was suspended. No one could tell how it would end. This was the only moment in which opinion was divided; for, in the next, the Gas-man aiming a mortal blow at his adversary's neck, with his right hand, and failing from the length he had to reach, the other returned it with his left at full swing, planted a tremendous blow on his cheek-bone and eyebrow, and made a red ruin of that side of his face. The Gas-man went down, and there was another shout —a roar of triumph as the waves of fortune rolled tumultuously from side to side. This was a settler. Hickman got up, and "grinned horrible a ghastly smile," yet he was evidently dashed in his opinion of himself; it was the first time he had ever been so punished; all one side of his face was perfect scarlet, and his right eye was closed in dingy blackness, as he advanced to the fight, less confident, but still determined. After one or two rounds, not receiving another such remembrancer, he rallied and went at it with his former impetuosity. But in vain. His strength had been weakened,—his blows could not tell at such a distance,—he was obliged to fling himself at his adversary, and could not strike from his feet; and almost as regularly as he flew at him with his right hand, Neate warded the blow, or drew back out of its reach, and felled him with the return of his left. There was little cautious sparring—no half-hits—no tapping and trifling, none of the *petit-maitreship* of the art—they were almost all knock-down blows:—the fight was a good stand-up fight. The wonder was the half-minute time. If there had been a minute or more allowed between each round, it would have been intelligible how they should by degrees recover strength and resolution; but to see two men smashed to the ground, smeared with gore, stunned, senseless, the breath beaten out of their bodies; and then, before you recover from the shock, to see them rise up with new strength and courage, stand steady to inflict or receive mortal offence, and rush upon each other "like two clouds over the Caspian"—this is the most astonishing thing of all:—this is the high and heroic state of man! From this time forward the event became more certain every round; and about the twelfth it seemed as if it must have been over. Hickman generally stood with his back to me; but in the scuffle, he had changed positions, and Neate just then made a tremendous lunge at him, and hit him full in the face. It was doubtful whether he would fall backwards or forwards; he hung suspended for a second or two, and then fell back, throwing his hands in the air, and with his face lifted up to the sky. I never saw any thing more terrific than his aspect just before he fell. All traces of life, of natural expression, were gone from him. His face was like a human skull, a death's head, spouting blood. The eyes were filled with blood, the nose streamed with blood, the mouth gaped blood. He was not like an actual man, but like a preternatural, spectral appearance, or like one of the figures in Dante's *Inferno*. Yet he fought on after this for several rounds, still striking the first desperate blow, and Neate standing on the defensive, and using the same cautious guard to the last, as if he had still all his work to do; and it was not till the Gas-man was so stunned in the seven-

1. "with Atlantean shoulders." See *Paradise Lost*, Book II, l. 306. 46–47. "grinned horrible . . . smile." See *ibid.*, l. 816.

23–24. "like two clouds . . . Caspian." See *ibid.*, ll. 714–16. 25. high and heroic. "Scroggins said of the Gasman, that he thought he was a man of that courage, that if his hands were cut off, he would still fight on with the stumps—like that of Widrington,—

——'in doleful dumps,
Who, when his legs were smitten off
Still fought upon his stumps.'" (Hazlitt)

teenth or eighteenth round, that his senses forsook him, and he could not come to time, that the battle was declared over. Ye who despise the FANCY, do something to shew as much *pluck*, or as much self-possession as this, before you assume a superiority which you have never given a single proof of by any one action in the whole course of your lives!— When the Gas-man came to himself, the first words he uttered were, "Where am I? What is the matter?" "Nothing is the matter, Tom,—you have lost the battle, but you are the bravest man alive." And Jackson whispered to him, "I am collecting a purse for you, Tom."—Vain sounds, and unheard at that moment! Neate instantly went up and shook him cordially by the hand, and seeing some old acquaintance, began to flourish with his fists, calling out, "Ah you always said I couldn't fight—What do you think now?" But all in good humour, and without any appearance of arrogance; only it was evident Bill Neate was pleased that he had won the fight. When it was over, I asked Cribb if he did not think it was a good one? He said, "*Pretty well!*" The carrier-pigeons now mounted into the air, and one of them flew with the news of her husband's victory to the bosom of Mrs. Neate. Alas, for Mrs. Hickman! . . .

MY FIRST ACQUAINTANCE WITH POETS

MY father was a Dissenting Minister at W——m in Shropshire; and in the year 1798 (the figures that compose that date are to me like the "dreaded name of Demogorgon") Mr. Coleridge came to Shrewsbury, to succeed Mr. Rowe in the spiritual charge of a Unitarian Congregation there. He did not come till late on the Saturday afternoon before he was to preach; and Mr. Rowe, who himself went down to the coach in a state of anxiety and expectation, to look for the arrival of his successor, could find no one at all answering the description but a round-faced man in a short black coat (like a shooting jacket) which hardly seemed to have been made for him, but who seemed to be talking at a great rate to his fellow-passengers. Mr. Rowe had scarce returned to give an account of his disappointment, when the round-faced man in black entered, and dissipated all doubts on the subject, by beginning to talk. He did not cease while he staid; nor has

he since, that I know of. He held the good town of Shrewsbury in delightful suspense for three weeks that he remained there, "fluttering the *proud Salopians* like an eagle in a dove-cote"; and the Welch mountains that skirt the horizon with their tempestuous confusion, agree to have heard no such mystic sounds since the days of

"High-born Hoel's harp or soft Llewellyn's lay!"

As we passed along between W——m and Shrewsbury, and I eyed their blue tops seen through the wintry branches, or the red rustling leaves of the sturdy oak-trees by the road-side, a sound was in my ears as of a Siren's song; I was stunned, startled with it, as from deep sleep; but I had no notion then that I should ever be able to express my admiration to others in motley imagery or quaint allusion, till the light of his genius shone into my soul, like the sun's rays glittering in the puddles of the road. I was at that time dumb, inarticulate, helpless, like a worm by the way-side, crushed, bleeding, lifeless; but now, bursting from the deadly bands that "bound them,

"With Styx nine times round them,"

my ideas float on winged words, and as they expand their plumes, catch the golden light of other years. My soul has indeed remained in its original bondage, dark, obscure, with longings infinite and unsatisfied; my heart, shut up in the prison-house of this rude clay, has never found, nor will it ever find, a heart to speak to; but that my understanding also did not remain dumb and brutish, or at length found a language to express itself, I owe to Coleridge. But this is not to my purpose.

My father lived ten miles from Shrewsbury, and was in the habit of exchanging visits with Mr. Rowe, and with Mr. Jenkins of Whitchurch (nine miles farther on) according to the custom of Dissenting Ministers in each other's neighbourhood. A line of communication is thus established, by which the flame of civil and religious liberty is kept alive, and nourishes its smouldering fire unquenchable, like the fires in the Agamemnon of Aeschylus, placed at different stations, that waited for ten long years to announce with their blazing pyramids the destruction of Troy. Coleridge had agreed to come over to see my father, according to the courtesy of the country, as Mr. Rowe's probable successor; but in the meantime I had gone to hear him preach the Sun-

26. The remainder of the essay (omitted) describes the return to London, with good food and talk on the way. **32. W——m**, Wem. **35. "dreaded . . . Demogorgon."** See *Paradise Lost*, Book II, l. 964

3–4. "fluttering . . . dove-cote." See *Coriolanus*, Act V, sc. 6, l. *115.* **Salopians** is from Latin *Salopia* (**Shropshire**). **9. "High-born . . . lay."** See Thomas Gray's "The Bard," l. 28. **24. "With Styx . . . them."** See Pope's "Ode on St. Cecilia's Day," l. 90.

day after his arrival. A poet and a philosopher getting up into a Unitarian pulpit to preach the Gospel, was a romance in these degenerate days, a sort of revival of the primitive spirit of Christianity, which was not to be resisted.

It was in January, 1798, that I rose one morning before daylight, to walk ten miles in the mud, and went to hear this celebrated person preach. Never, the longest day I have to live, shall I have such another walk as this cold, raw, comfortless one, in the winter of the year 1798. *Il y a des impressions que ni le tems ni les circonstances peuvent effacer. Dusse-je vivre des siècles entiers, le doux tems de ma jeunesse ne peut renaître pour moi, ni s'effacer jamais dans ma mémoire.* When I got there, the organ was playing the 100th psalm, and, when it was done, Mr. Coleridge rose and gave out his text, "And he went up into the mountain to pray, HIMSELF, ALONE." As he gave out this text, his voice "rose like a steam of rich distilled perfumes," and when he came to the two last words, which he pronounced loud, deep, and distinct, it seemed to me, who was then young, as if the sounds had echoed from the bottom of the human heart, and as if that prayer might have floated in solemn silence through the universe. The idea of St. John came into mind, "of one crying in the wilderness, who had his loins girt about, and whose food was locusts and wild honey." The preacher then launched into his subject, like an eagle dallying with the wind. The sermon was upon peace and war; upon church and state—not their alliance, but their separation—on the spirit of the world and the spirit of Christianity, not as the same, but as opposed to one another. He talked of those who had "inscribed the cross of Christ on banners dripping with human gore." He made a poetical and pastoral excursion,—and to shew the fatal effects of war, drew a striking contrast between the simple shepherd boy, driving his team afield, or sitting under the hawthorn, piping to his flock, "as though he should never be old," and the same poor country-lad, crimped, kidnapped, brought into town, made drunk at an alehouse, turned into a wretched drummer-boy, with his hair sticking on end with powder and pomatum, a long cue at his back, and tricked out in the loathsome finery of the profession of blood.

"Such were the notes our once-loved poet sung."

And for myself, I could not have been more delighted if I had heard the music of the spheres. Poetry and Philosophy had met together. Truth and Genius had embraced, under the eye and with the sanction of Religion. This was even beyond my hopes. I returned home well satisfied. The sun that was still labouring pale and wan through the sky, obscured by thick mists, seemed an emblem of the *good cause;* and the cold dank drops of dew that hung half melted on the beard of the thistle, had something genial and refreshing in them; for there was a spirit of hope and youth in all nature, that turned every thing into good. The face of nature had not then the brand of JUS DIVINUM on it:

"Like to that sanguine flower inscribed with woe."

On the Tuesday following, the half-inspired speaker came. I was called down into the room where he was, and went half-hoping, half-afraid. He received me very graciously, and I listened for a long time without uttering a word. I did not suffer in his opinion by my silence. "For those two hours," he afterwards was pleased to say, "he was conversing with W. H.'s forehead!" His appearance was different from what I had anticipated from seeing him before. At a distance, and in the dim light of the chapel, there was to me a strange wildness in his aspect, a dusky obscurity, and I thought him pitted with the small-pox. His complexion was at that time clear, and even bright—

"As are the children of yon azure sheen."

His forehead was broad and high, light as if built of ivory, with large projecting eyebrows, and his eyes rolling beneath them like a sea with darkened lustre. "A certain tender bloom his face o'erspread," a purple tinge as we see it in the pale thoughtful complexions of the Spanish portrait-painters, Murillo and Velasquez. His mouth was gross, voluptuous, open, eloquent; his chin good-humoured and round; but his nose, the rudder of the face, the index of the will, was small, feeble, nothing—like what he has done. It might seem that the genius of his face as from a height surveyed and projected him (with sufficient capacity and huge aspiration) into the world unknown of thought and imagination, with nothing to support or guide his veering purpose, as if Columbus had launched his adventurous course for the New World in a scallop, without oars or compass. So at least I comment on it after the event.

11–14. **Il y a . . . mémoire.** There are impressions which neither time nor circumstances can efface. If I should live entire centuries, the sweet time of youth cannot return or efface itself from my memory.—Rousseau, *Confessions*, Part II, Book 7. 26–28. **"of one crying . . . wild honey."** See Mark 1:3, 6. 47. **"Such were . . . sung."** See Milton's *Comus*, 1. 556.

9. **good cause,** the French Revolution. 14. **Jus Divinum,** divine right (of kings). 15. **Like to . . . woe.** See Milton's *Lycidas*, 1. 106. 31. **As are . . . sheen.** See James Thomson's *The Castle of Indolence*, Book II, 1. 295.

Coleridge in his person was rather above the common size, inclining to the corpulent, or like Lord Hamlet, "somewhat fat and pursy." His hair (now, alas! grey) was then black and glossy as the raven's, and fell in smooth masses over his forehead. This long pendulous hair is peculiar to enthusiasts, to those whose minds tend heavenward; and is traditionally inseparable (though of a different colour) from the pictures of Christ. It ought to belong, as a character, to all who preach *Christ crucified*, and Coleridge was at that time one of those!

It was curious to observe the contrast between him and my father, who was a veteran in the cause, and then declining into the vale of years. He had been a poor Irish lad, carefully brought up by his parents, and sent to the University of Glasgow (where he studied under Adam Smith) to prepare him for his future destination. It was his mother's proudest wish to see her son a Dissenting Minister. So if we look back to past generations (as far as eye can reach) we see the same hopes, fears, wishes, followed by the same disappointments, throbbing in the human heart; and so we may see them (if we look forward) rising up for ever, and disappearing, like vapourish bubbles, in the human breast! After being tossed about from congregation to congregation in the heats of the Unitarian controversy, and squabbles about the American war, he had been relegated to an obscure village, where he was to spend the last thirty years of his life, far from the only converse that he loved, the talk about disputed texts of Scripture and the cause of civil and religious liberty. Here he passed his days, repining but resigned, in the study of the Bible, and the perusal of the Commentators,—huge folios, not easily got through, one of which would outlast a winter! Why did he pore on these from morn to night (with the exception of a walk in the fields or a turn in the garden to gather broccoli-plants or kidney-beans of his own rearing, with no small degree of pride and pleasure)? Here were "no figures nor no fantasies" —neither poetry nor philosophy—nothing to dazzle, nothing to excite modern curiosity; but to his lack-lustre eyes there appeared, within the pages of the ponderous, unwieldy, neglected tomes, the sacred name of JEHOVAH in Hebrew capitals: pressed down by the weight of the style, worn to the last fading thinness of the understanding, there were glimpses, glimmering notions of the patriarchal wanderings, with palm-trees hovering in the horizon, and processions of camels at the distance of three thousand years; there was Moses with the Burning Bush, the number of the Twelve Tribes,

17. **Adam Smith,** author of *The Wealth of Nations.*

types, shadows, glosses on the law and the prophets; there were discussions (dull enough) on the age of Methuselah, a mighty speculation! there were outlines, rude guesses at the shape of Noah's Ark and of the riches of Solomon's Temple; questions as to the date of the creation, predictions of the end of all things; the great lapses of time, the strange mutations of the globe were unfolded with the voluminous leaf, as it turned over; and though the soul might slumber with an hieroglyphic veil of inscrutable mysteries drawn over it, yet it was in a slumber ill-exchanged for all the sharpened realities of sense, wit, fancy, or reason. My father's life was comparatively a dream; but it was a dream of infinity and eternity, of death, the resurrection, and a judgment to come!

No two individuals were ever more unlike than were the host and his guest. A poet was to my father a sort of nondescript: yet whatever added grace to the Unitarian cause was to him welcome. He could hardly have been more surprised or pleased, if our visitor had worn wings. Indeed, his thoughts had wings; and as the silken sounds rustled round our little wainscoted parlour, my father threw back his spectacles over his forehead, his white hairs mixing with its sanguine hue; and a smile of delight beamed across his rugged cordial face, to think that Truth had found a new ally in Fancy! Besides, Coleridge seemed to take considerable notice of me, and that of itself was enough. He talked very familiarly, but agreeably, and glanced over a variety of subjects. At dinner-time he grew more animated, and dilated in a very edifying manner on Mary Wolstonecraft and Mackintosh. The last, he said, he considered (on my father's speaking of his *Vindiciae Galliciae* as a capital performance) as a clever scholastic man—a master of the topics,—or as the ready warehouseman of letters, who knew exactly where to lay his hand on what he wanted, though the goods were not his own. He thought him no match for Burke, either in style or matter. Burke was a metaphysician, Mackintosh a mere logician. Burke was an orator (almost a poet) who reasoned in figures, because he had an eye for nature: Mackintosh, on the other hand, was a rhetorician, who had only an eye to common-places. On this I ventured to say that I had always entertained a great opinion of Burke, and that (as far as I could find) the speaking of him with contempt might be made the test of a vulgar democratical mind. This was the first observation I

33. **Mary Wollstonecraft,** the author of *The Rights of Woman,* 1792, wife of William Godwin, and mother of Shelley's second wife. **Mackintosh,** Sir James Mackintosh, at the time also a sympathizer with the French Revolution.

ever made to Coleridge, and he said it was a very just and striking one. I remember the leg of Welsh mutton and the turnips on the table that day had the finest flavour imaginable. Coleridge added that Mackintosh and Tom Wedgwood (of whom, however, he spoke highly) had expressed a very indifferent opinion of his friend Mr. Wordsworth, on which he remarked to them—"He strides on so far before you, that he dwindles in the distance!" Godwin had once boasted to him of having carried on an argument with Mackintosh for three hours with dubious success; Coleridge told him—"If there had been a man of genius in the room, he would have settled the question in five minutes." He asked me if I had ever seen Mary Wolstonecraft, and I said, I had once for a few moments, and that she seemed to me to turn off Godwin's objections to something she advanced with quite a playful, easy air. He replied, that "this was only one instance of the ascendancy which people of imagination exercised over those of mere intellect." He did not rate Godwin very high (this was caprice or prejudice, real or affected) but he had a great idea of Mrs. Wolstonecraft's powers of conversation, none at all of her talent for book-making. We talked a little about Holcroft. He had been asked if he was not much struck *with* him, and he said, he thought himself in more danger of being struck *by* him. I complained that he would not let me get on at all, for he required a definition of every commonest word, exclaiming, "What do you mean by a *sensation*, Sir? What do you mean by an *idea*?" This, Coleridge said, was barricadoing the road to truth:—it was setting up a turnpike-gate at every step we took. I forget a great number of things, many more than I remember; but the day passed off pleasantly, and the next morning Mr. Coleridge was to return to Shrewsbury. When I came down to breakfast, I found that he had just received a letter from his friend T. Wedgwood, making him an offer of 150*l*. a-year if he chose to wave his present pursuit, and devote himself entirely to the study of poetry and philosophy. Coleridge seemed to make up his mind to close with this proposal in the act of tying on one of his shoes. It threw an additional damp on his departure. It took the wayward enthusiast quite from us to cast him into Deva's winding vales, or by the shores of old romance. Instead of living at ten miles distance, of being the pastor of a Dissenting congregation at Shrewsbury, he was henceforth to inhabit the Hill of Parnassus, to be a Shepherd on the Delectable Mountains. Alas! I

knew not the way thither, and felt very little gratitude for Mr. Wedgwood's bounty. I was presently relieved from the dilemma; for Mr. Coleridge, asking for a pen and ink, and going to a table to write something on a bit of card, advanced towards me with undulating step, and giving me the precious document, said that that was his address, *Mr. Coleridge, Nether Stowey, Somersetshire;* and that he should be glad to see me there in a few weeks' time, and, if I chose, would come half-way to meet me. I was not less surprised than the shepherd-boy (this simile is to be found in Cassandra) when he sees a thunderbolt fall close at his feet. I stammered out my acknowledgments and acceptance of this offer (I thought Mr. Wedgwood's annuity a trifle to it) as well as I could; and this mighty business being settled, the poet-preacher took leave, and I accompanied him six miles on the road. It was a fine morning in the middle of winter, and he talked the whole way. The scholar in Chaucer is described as going

——"Sounding on his way."

So Coleridge went on his. In digressing, in dilating, in passing from subject to subject, he appeared to me to float in air, to slide on ice. He told me in confidence (going along) that he should have preached two sermons before he accepted the situation at Shrewsbury, one on Infant Baptism, the other on the Lord's Supper, shewing that he could not administer either, which would have effectually disqualified him for the object in view. I observed that he continually crossed me on the way by shifting from one side of the foot-path to the other. This struck me as an odd movement; but I did not at that time connect it with any instability of purpose or involuntary change of principle, as I have done since. He seemed unable to keep on in a straight line. He spoke slightingly of Hume (whose Essay on Miracles he said was stolen from an objection started in one of South's sermons—*Credat Judaeus Apella!*). I was not very much pleased at this account of Hume, for I had just been reading, with infinite relish, that completest of all metaphysical *choke-pears*, his *Treatise on Human Nature*, to which the *Essays*, in point of scholastic subtlety and close reasoning, are mere elegant trifling, light summer-reading. Coleridge even denied the excellence of Hume's general style, which I think betrayed a want of taste or candour. He however made me amends by the manner in

9–10. **Godwin,** William Godwin, *Political Justice,* 1793. 25. **Holcroft.** Thomas Holcroft was a dramatist and novelist, also a radical.   **40. wave,** now spelled "waive."

22. **"Sounding on his way,"** a slight garbling of Chaucer's *Prologue to the Canterbury Tales,* l. 307, describing the Clerk of Oxford.   **41. Credat . . . Apella!** Let the Jew Apella believe it.

which he spoke of Berkeley. He dwelt particularly on his *Essay on Vision* as a masterpiece of analytical reasoning. So it undoubtedly is. He was exceedingly angry with Dr. Johnson for striking the stone with his foot, in allusion to this author's Theory of Matter and Spirit, and saying, "Thus I confute him, Sir." Coleridge drew a parallel (I don't know how he brought about the connection) between Bishop Berkeley and Tom Paine. He said the one was an instance of a subtle, the other of an acute mind, than which no two things could be more distinct. The one was a shop-boy's quality, the other the characteristic of a philosopher. He considered Bishop Butler as a true philosopher, a profound and conscientious thinker, a genuine reader of nature and of his own mind. He did not speak of his *Analogy*, but of his *Sermons at the Rolls' Chapel*, of which I had never heard. Coleridge somehow always contrived to prefer the *unknown* to the *known*. In this instance he was right. The *Analogy* is a tissue of sophistry, of wire-drawn, theological special-pleading; the *Sermons* (with the Preface to them) are in a fine vein of deep, matured reflection, a candid appeal to our observation of human nature, without pedantry and without bias. I told Coleridge I had written a few remarks, and was sometimes foolish enough to believe that I had made a discovery on the same subject (the *Natural Disinterestedness of the Human Mind*)—and I tried to explain my view of it to Coleridge, who listened with great willingness, but I did not succeed in making myself understood. I sat down to the task shortly afterwards for the twentieth time, got new pens and paper, determined to make clear work of it, wrote a few meagre sentences in the skeleton-style of a mathematical demonstration, stopped half-way down the second page; and, after trying in vain to pump up any words, images, notions, apprehensions, facts, or observations, from that gulph of abstraction in which I had plunged myself for four or five years preceding, gave up the attempt as labour in vain, and shed tears of helpless despondency on the blank unfinished paper. I can write fast enough now. Am I better than I was then? Oh no! One truth discovered, one pang of regret at not being able to express it, is better than all the fluency and flippancy in the world. Would that I could go back to what I then was! Why can we not revive past times as we can revisit old places? If I had the quaint Muse of Sir Philip Sidney to assist me, I would write a *Sonnet to the Road between W——m and Shrewsbury*, and immortalise every step of it by some fond enigmatical conceit. I would swear that the very milestones had ears, and that Harmer-hill stooped with all its pines, to listen to a poet, as he

passed! I remember but one other topic of discourse in this walk. He mentioned Paley, praised the naturalness and clearness of his style, but condemned his sentiments, thought him a mere time-serving casuist, and said that "the fact of his work on *Moral and Political Philosophy* being made a text-book in our Universities was a disgrace to the national character." We parted at the six-mile stone; and I returned homeward pensive but much pleased. I had met with unexpected notice from a person, whom I believed to have been prejudiced against me. "Kind and affable to me had been his condescension, and should be honoured ever with suitable regard." He was the first poet I had known, and he certainly answered to that inspired name. I had heard a great deal of his powers of conversation, and was not disappointed. In fact, I never met with any thing at all like them, either before or since. I could easily credit the accounts which were circulated of his holding forth to a large party of ladies and gentlemen, an evening or two before, on the Berkeleian Theory, when he made the whole material universe look like a transparency of fine words; and another story (which I believe he has somewhere told himself) of his being asked to a party at Birmingham, of his smoking tobacco and going to sleep after dinner on a sofa, where the company found him to their no small surprise, which was increased to wonder when he started up of a sudden, and rubbing his eyes, looked about him, and launched into a three-hours' description of the third heaven, of which he had had a dream, very different from Mr. Southey's Vision of Judgment, and also from that other Vision of Judgment, which Mr. Murray, the Secretary of the Bridge-street Junto, has taken into his especial keeping!

On my way back, I had a sound in my ears, it was the voice of Fancy: I had a light before me, it was the face of Poetry. The one still lingers there, the other has not quitted my side! Coleridge in truth met me half-way on the ground of philosophy, or I should not have been won over to his imaginative creed. I had an uneasy, pleasurable sensation all the time, till I was to visit him. During those months the chill breath of winter gave me a welcoming; the vernal air was balm and inspiration to me. The golden sun-sets, the silver star of evening, lighted me on my way to new hopes and prospects. *I was to visit Coleridge in the spring.* This circumstance was never absent from my thoughts, and mingled with all my feelings. I wrote to him at the time proposed, and received an answer postponing my intended visit for a week or two, but very cordially urging me to complete my promise then. This delay did not damp, but rather increased my ardour. In the meantime I went to Llangollen Vale, by way of initiating myself in the mysteries of natural scenery; and I must say I was enchanted with it. I had been reading Coleridge's description of England, in his fine *Ode on the Departing Year*, and I applied it, *con amore*, to the objects before me. That valley was to me (in a manner) the cradle of a new existence: in the river that winds through it, my spirit was baptised in the waters of Helicon!

I returned home, and soon after set out on my journey with unworn heart and untired feet. My way lay through Worcester and Gloucester, and by Upton, where I thought of Tom Jones and the adventure of the muff. I remember getting completely wet through one day, and stopping at an inn (I think it was at Tewkesbury) where I sat up all night to read Paul and Virginia. Sweet were the showers in early youth that drenched my body, and sweet the drops of pity that fell upon the books I read! I recollect a remark of Coleridge's upon this very book, that nothing could shew the gross indelicacy of French manners and the entire corruption of their imagination more strongly than the behaviour of the heroine in the last fatal scene, who turns away from a person on board the sinking vessel, that offers to save her life, because he has thrown off his clothes to assist him in swimming. Was this a time to think of such a circumstance? I once hinted to Wordsworth, as we were sailing in his boat on Grasmere lake, that I thought he had borrowed the idea of his *Poems on the Naming of Places* from the local inscriptions of the same kind in Paul and Virginia. He did not own the obligation, and stated some distinction without a difference, in defence of his claim to originality. Even the slightest variation would be sufficient for this purpose in his mind; for whatever *he* added or omitted would inevitably be worth all that any one else had done, and contain the marrow of the sentiment. I was still two days before the time fixed for my arrival, for I had taken care to set out early enough. I stopped these two days at Bridgewater, and when I was tired of sauntering on the banks of its muddy river, returned to the inn, and read Camilla. So have I loitered my life away, reading books, looking at pictures, going to plays, hearing, thinking, writing on what pleased me best. I

22. **Paul and Virginia.** *Paul et Virginie,* 1789, was a sentimental novel by Jacques Henri Bernardin de Saint-Pierre.
49. **Camilla,** a novel by Frances Burney, 1796.

have wanted only one thing to make me happy; but wanting that, have wanted everything!

I arrived, and was well received. The country about Nether Stowey is beautiful, green and hilly, and near the sea-shore. I saw it but the other day, after an interval of twenty years, from a hill near Taunton. How was the map of my life spread out before me, as the map of the country lay at my feet! In the afternoon Coleridge took me over to All-Foxden, a romantic old family-mansion of the St. Aubins, where Wordsworth lived. It was then in the possession of a friend of the poet's, who gave him the free use of it. Somehow that period (the time just after the French Revolution) was not a time when *nothing was given for nothing*. The mind opened, and a softness might be perceived coming over the heart of individuals, beneath "the scales that fence" our self-interest. Wordsworth himself was from home, but his sister kept house, and set before us a frugal repast; and we had free access to her brother's poems, the *Lyrical Ballads*, which were still in manuscript, or in the form of *Sybilline Leaves*. I dipped into a few of these with great satisfaction, and with the faith of a novice. I slept that night in an old room with blue hangings, and covered with the round-faced family-portraits of the age of George I. and II. and from the wooded declivity of the adjoining park that overlooked my window, at the dawn of day, could

"——hear the loud stag speak."

In the outset of life (and particularly at this time I felt it so) our imagination has a body to it. We are in a state between sleeping and waking, and have indistinct but glorious glimpses of strange shapes, and there is always something to come better than what we see. As in our dreams the fulness of the blood gives warmth and reality to the coinage of the brain, so in youth our ideas are clothed, and fed, and pampered with our good spirits; we breathe thick with thoughtless happiness, the weight of future years presses on the strong pulses of the heart, and we repose with undisturbed faith in truth and good. As we advance, we exhaust our fund of enjoyment and of hope. We are no longer wrapped in *lamb's-wool*, lulled in Elysium. As we taste the pleasures of life, their spirit evaporates, the sense palls; and nothing is left but the phantoms, the lifeless shadows of what *has been!*

That morning, as soon as breakfast was over, we strolled out into the park, and seating ourselves on the trunk of an old ash-tree that stretched along the

13. **free use of it.** Hazlitt was mistaken. Wordsworth paid £23 rent.

ground, Coleridge read aloud with a sonorous and musical voice the ballad of *Betty Foy*. I was not critically or sceptically inclined. I saw touches of truth and nature, and took the rest for granted. But in the *Thorn*, the *Mad Mother*, and the *Complaint of a Poor Indian Woman*, I felt that deeper power and pathos which have been since acknowledged,

"In spite of pride, in erring reason's spite,"

as the characteristics of this author; and the sense of a new style and a new spirit in poetry came over me. It had to me something of the effect that arises from the turning up of the fresh soil, or of the first welcome breath of Spring:

"While yet the trembling year is unconfirmed."

Coleridge and myself walked back to Stowey that evening, and his voice sounded high

"Of Providence, foreknowledge, will, and fate, Fixed fate, free-will, foreknowledge absolute,"

as we passed through echoing grove, by fairy stream or waterfall, gleaming in the summer moonlight! He lamented that Wordsworth was not prone enough to believe in the traditional superstitions of the place, and that there was a something corporeal, a *matter-of-fact-ness*, a clinging to the palpable, or often to the petty, in his poetry, in consequence. His genius was not a spirit that descended to him through the air; it sprung out of the ground like a flower, or unfolded itself from a green spray, on which the gold-finch sang. He said, however (if I remember right), that this objection must be confined to his descriptive pieces, that his philosophic poetry had a grand and comprehensive spirit in it, so that his soul seemed to inhabit the universe like a palace, and to discover truth by intuition, rather than by deduction. The next day Wordsworth arrived from Bristol at Coleridge's cottage. I think I see him now. He answered in some degree to his friend's description of him, but was more gaunt and Don Quixote-like. He was quaintly dressed (according to the costume of that unconstrained period) in a brown fustian jacket and striped pantaloons. There was something of a roll, a lounge in his gait, not unlike his own Peter Bell. There was a severe, worn pressure of thought about his temples, a fire in his eye (as if he saw something in objects more than the outward appearance), an intense high narrow forehead, a Roman nose, cheeks furrowed by strong purpose and feeling, and a convulsive inclination to laughter about the mouth, a good deal at variance

with the solemn, stately expression of the rest of his face. Chantry's bust wants the marking traits; but he was teazed into making it regular and heavy: Haydon's head of him, introduced into the *Entrance of Christ into Jerusalem*, is the most like his drooping weight of thought and expression. He sat down and talked very naturally and freely, with a mixture of clear gushing accents in his voice, a deep gutteral intonation, and a strong tincture of the northern burr, like the crust on wine. He instantly began to make havoc of the half of a Cheshire cheese on the table, and said triumphantly that "his marriage with experience had not been so unproductive as Mr. Southey's in teaching him a knowledge of the good things of this life." He had been to see the *Castle Spectre*, by Monk Lewis, while at Bristol, and described it very well. He said "it fitted the taste of the audience like a glove." This *ad captandum* merit was however by no means a recommendation of it, according to the severe principles of the new school, which reject rather than court popular effect. Wordsworth, looking out of the low, latticed window, said, "How beautifully the sun sets on that yellow bank!" I thought within myself, "With what eyes these poets see nature!" and ever after, when I saw the sun-set stream upon the objects facing it, conceived I had made a discovery, or thanked Mr. Wordsworth for having made one for me! We went over to All-Foxden again the day following, and Wordsworth read us the story of Peter Bell in the open air; and the comment made upon it by his face and voice was very different from that of some later critics! Whatever might be thought of the poem, "his face was a book where men might read strange matters," and he announced the fate of his hero in prophetic tones. There is a *chaunt* in the recitation both of Coleridge and Wordsworth, which acts as a spell upon the hearer, and disarms the judgment. Perhaps they have deceived themselves by making habitual use of this ambiguous accompaniment. Coleridge's manner is more full, animated, and varied; Wordsworth's more equable, sustained, and internal. The one might be termed more *dramatic*, the other more *lyrical*. Coleridge has told me that he himself liked to compose in walking over uneven ground, or breaking through the straggling branches of a copse-wood; whereas Wordsworth always wrote (if he could) walking up and down a straight gravel-walk, or in some spot where the continuity of his verse met with no collateral in-

46. **Peter Bell,** the hero of Wordsworth's poem by this name, published in 1819.

4-5. **Haydon's head . . . Jerusalem.** See page 368. 15-16. **Castle Spectre,** a Gothic drama. Compare the allusion to the spirit of Christabel's mother in Coleridge's "Christabel." 18. **ad captandum,** designed to captivate.

terruption. Returning that same evening, I got into a metaphysical argument with Wordsworth, while Coleridge was explaining the different notes of the nightingale to his sister, in which we neither of us succeeded in making ourselves perfectly clear and intelligible. Thus I passed three weeks at Nether Stowey and in the neighbourhood, generally devoting the afternoons to a delightful chat in an arbour made of bark by the poet's friend Tom Poole, sitting under two fine elm-trees, and listening to the bees humming round us, while we quaffed our *flip*. It was agreed, among other things, that we should make a jaunt down the Bristol-Channel, as far as Linton. We set off together on foot, Coleridge, John Chester, and I. This Chester was a native of Nether Stowey, one of those who were attracted to Coleridge's discourse as flies are to honey, or bees in swarming-time to the sound of a brass pan. He "followed in the chace like a dog who hunts, not like one that made up the cry." He had on a brown cloth coat, boots, and corduroy breeches, was low in stature, bow-legged, had a drag in his walk like a drover, which he assisted by a hazel switch, and kept on a sort of trot by the side of Coleridge, like a running footman by a state coach, that he might not lose a syllable or sound that fell from Coleridge's lips. He told me his private opinion, that Coleridge was a wonderful man. He scarcely opened his lips, much less offered an opinion the whole way: yet of the three, had I to chuse during that journey, I would be John Chester. He afterwards followed Coleridge into Germany, where the Kantean philosophers were puzzled how to bring him under any of their categories. When he sat down at table with his idol, John's felicity was complete; Sir Walter Scott's, or Mr. Blackwood's, when they sat down at the same table with the King, was not more so. We passed Dunster on our right, a small town between the brow of a hill and the sea. I remember eying it wistfully as it lay below us: contrasted with the woody scene around, it looked as clear, as pure, as *embrowned* and ideal as any landscape I have seen since, of Gaspar Poussin's or Domenichino's. We had a long day's march—(our feet kept time to the echoes of Coleridge's tongue)—through Minehead and by the Blue Anchor, and on to Linton, which we did not reach till near midnight, and where we had some difficulty in making a lodgment. We however knocked the people of the house up at last, and we were repaid for our apprehensions and fatigue by some excellent rashers of fried bacon and eggs. The view in coming along had been splendid. We walked for miles and miles on dark brown heaths

overlooking the Channel, with the Welsh hills beyond, and at times descended into little sheltered valleys close by the sea-side, with a smuggler's face scowling by us, and then had to ascend conical hills with a path winding up through a coppice to a barren top, like a monk's shaven crown, from one of which I pointed out to Coleridge's notice the bare masts of a vessel on the very edge of the horizon and within the red-orbed disk of the setting sun, like his own spectre-ship in the *Ancient Mariner*. At Linton the character of the sea-coast becomes more marked and rugged. There is a place called the *Valley of Rocks* (I suspect this was only the poetical name for it) bedded among precipices overhanging the sea, with rocky caverns beneath, into which the waves dash, and where the sea-gull for ever wheels its screaming flight. On the tops of these are huge stones thrown transverse, as if an earthquake had tossed them there, and behind these is a fretwork of perpendicular rocks, something like the *Giant's Causeway*. A thunder-storm came on while we were at the inn, and Coleridge was running out bareheaded to enjoy the commotion of the elements in the *Valley of Rocks*, but as if in spite, the clouds only muttered a few angry sounds, and let fall a few refreshing drops. Coleridge told me that he and Wordsworth were to have made this place the scene of a prose-tale, which was to have been in the manner of, but far superior to, the *Death of Abel*, but they had relinquished the design. In the morning of the second day, we breakfasted luxuriously in an old-fashioned parlour, on tea, toast, eggs, and honey, in the very sight of the bee-hives from which it had been taken, and a garden full of thyme and wild flowers that had produced it. On this occasion Coleridge spoke of Virgil's Georgics, but not well. I do not think he had much feeling for the classical or elegant. It was in this room that we found a little worn-out copy of the *Seasons*, lying in a window-seat, on which Coleridge exclaimed, "*That* is true fame!" He said Thomson was a great poet, rather than a good one; his style was as meretricious as his thoughts were natural. He spoke of Cowper as the best modern poet. He said the *Lyrical Ballads* were an experiment about to be tried by him and Wordsworth, to see how far the public taste would endure poetry written in a more natural and simple style than had hitherto been attempted; totally discarding the artifices of poetical diction, and making use only of such words as had probably been common in the most ordinary language since the days of Henry II. Some comparison was introduced between Shakespear and Milton. He said "he hardly

9. **Tom Poole,** who invited Coleridge to Nether Stowey.

29. **Death of Abel,** by Solomon Gessner, a Swiss poet.

knew which to prefer. Shakespear appeared to him a mere stripling in the art; he was as tall and as strong, with infinitely more activity than Milton, but he never appeared to have come to man's estate; or if he had, he would not have been a man, but a monster." He spoke with contempt of Gray, and with intolerance of Pope. He did not like the versification of the latter. He observed that "the ears of these couplet-writers might be charged with having short memories, that could not retain the harmony of whole passages." He thought little of Junius as a writer; he had a dislike of Dr. Johnson; and a much higher opinion of Burke as an orator and politician, than of Fox or Pitt. He however thought him very inferior in richness of style and imagery to some of our elder prose-writers, particularly Jeremy Taylor. He liked Richardson, but not Fielding; nor could I get him to enter into the merits of *Caleb Williams*. In short, he was profound and discriminating with respect to those authors whom he liked, and where he gave his judgment fair play; capricious, perverse, and prejudiced in his antipathies and distastes. We loitered on the "ribbed sea-sands," in such talk as this, a whole morning, and I recollect met with a curious seaweed, of which John Chester told us the country name! A fisherman gave Coleridge an account of a boy that had been drowned the day before, and that they had tried to save him at the risk of their own lives. He said "he did not know how it was that they ventured, but, Sir, we have a *nature* towards one another." This expression, Coleridge remarked to me, was a fine illustration of that theory of disinterestedness which I (in common with Butler) had adopted. I broached to him an argument of mine to prove that *likeness* was not mere association of ideas. I said that the mark in the sand put one in mind of a man's foot, not because it was part of a former impression of a man's foot (for it was quite new) but because it was like the shape of a man's foot. He assented to the justness of this distinction (which I have explained at length elsewhere, for the benefit of the curious) and John Chester listened; not from any interest in the subject, but because he was astonished that I should be able to suggest any thing to Coleridge that he did not already know. We returned on the third morning, and Coleridge remarked the silent cottage-smoke curling up the valleys where, a few evenings before, we had seen the lights gleaming through the dark.

In a day or two after we arrived at Stowey, we set out, I on my return home, and he for Germany. It was a Sunday morning, and he was to preach that day for Dr. Toulmin of Taunton. I asked him if he had prepared anything for the occasion? He said he had not even thought of the text, but should as soon as we parted. I did not go to hear him,—this was a fault,—but we met in the evening at Bridgewater. The next day we had a long day's walk to Bristol, and sat down, I recollect, by a well-side on the road, to cool ourselves and satisfy our thirst, when Coleridge repeated to me some descriptive lines from his tragedy of Remorse; which I must say became his mouth and that occasion better than they, some years after, did Mr. Elliston's and the Drury-lane boards,

"Oh memory! shield me from the world's poor strife,
And give those scenes thine everlasting life."

I saw no more of him for a year or two, during which period he had been wandering in the Hartz Forest in Germany; and his return was cometary, meteorous, unlike his setting out. It was not till some time after that I knew his friends Lamb and Southey. The last always appears to me (as I first saw him) with a common-place book under his arm, and the first with a *bon-mot* in his mouth. It was at Godwin's that I met him with Holcroft and Coleridge, where they were disputing fiercely which was the best—*Man as he was, or man as he is to be.* "Give me," says Lamb, "man as he is *not* to be." This saying was the beginning of a friendship between us, which I believe still continues.—Enough of this for the present.

"But there is matter for another rhyme,
And I to this may add a second tale."

19. **Caleb Williams,** a novel by William Godwin expounding in fictional form many of the ideas in *Political Justice.*

42–43. **"But . . . second tale."** See Wordsworth's "Hart-Leap Well," ll. 95–96.

Sir Walter Scott
1771–1832

Walter Scott was descended from a long line of swashbuckling freebooters with such picturesque nicknames as Auld Wat of Harden and Beardie. His father was the first of the family to settle down to town life, as a Writer to the Signet (attorney) in Edinburgh. Scott was born August 15, 1771, in a house at the head of the College Wynd (lane). His mother was the daughter of a professor in the University of Edinburgh. At the age of eighteen months he was stricken with infantile paralysis, which left his right leg withered. This physical misfortune probably determined his career as a writer, for otherwise he might have been a great man of action. In the belief that country life would be beneficial to him, his parents sent him to live with his grandparents at Sandy-Knowe, a farm with the old ruined tower of Smailholme standing on it. There, in the company of his grandmother, an aunt, an old shepherd, and the farm hands, who taught him the folklore of the countryside, the child became "healthy, high-spirited, and, lameness apart, sturdy." His early reading included Allan Ramsay's *Tea-Table Miscellany*, from which he learned ballads by heart. A visit to Bath, for the curative waters there, gave him his first sight of historic places in England and of a Shakespearean play. At the age of eight he resumed life with his family in Edinburgh and began attending the High School. More memorable to him than the classics which he studied or the schoolboy gang wars in which he fought was his discovery, at the age of thirteen, of Percy's *Reliques*. "To read and to remember," he wrote, "was in this instance the same thing, and henceforth I overwhelmed my school fellows and all who would listen to me, with tragical recitations from the ballads of Bishop Percy." At the University of Edinburgh a serious illness interrupted his study. Withdrawing, he apprenticed himself to his father for the study of law. (Many of his experiences as a law student are related in his novel *Redgauntlet*.) His passing the examination for license to practice law, in 1792, completed his formal education. Thus the chief components of his training were folklore, romance, and the law, with an intimate knowledge of the scenic and historic Scottish countryside—excellent preparation for the literary career awaiting him.

Already, while in the service of his father, he had started his ballad "raids" (expeditions to collect old ballads). In 1795 this interest was stimulated by his reading of German ballads. In the meantime, after an unhappy love-affair with Williamina Stuart, he fell in love with Charlotte Carpenter, daughter of a French royalist. Having joined the Edinburgh Light Dragoons, a cavalry company organized to resist French invasion, he courted Charlotte in uniform. His marriage to her followed shortly after the publication in 1796 of his first little volume of poetry, containing "William and Helen," a translation of Gottfried August Bürger's *"Lenore."* After making further translations of the sort and composing some original ballads for Monk Lewis's *Tales of Wonder*, he began work on his *Minstrelsy of the Scottish Border*. This magnificent collection of ballads and songs, most of them traditional, some of Scott's own composition, and some by other known authors, with its extensive introductions and notes, is the germinal work of Scott's literary career.

This career is a straightforward, expanding development. The phase of ballad collecting, editing, and imitation flowered in the *Minstrelsy*, 1802–03. From the *Minstrelsy* to metrical romances was the second step. This Scott took in *The Lay of the Last Minstrel*, 1805, a story in verse reminiscent of Coleridge's *Christabel* about two young lovers representing families at feud, with the mischievous dwarf Gilpin Horner and the doughty man-at-arms William of Deloraine playing important parts. *Marmion*, 1808, "a Tale of Flodden," relates the adventures of an English knight, culminating in the famous battle in which Scottish heroism shone in defeat. *The Lady of the Lake*, 1810, purest and sweetest of all Scott's romances, has its setting in the Trosachs country and recounts the tangled relations of James IV of Scotland, trying to pacify the Highland clans; the lovely Lady of the Lake, Ellen, and her fugitive father, Douglas; Roderick Dhu, the wild clan chieftain, and Malcolm Graeme, Ellen's lovers; and minor characters, such as Allanbane the minstrel. *Rokeby*, 1813, about the English civil wars of Charles I's time, and *The Lord of the Isles*, 1815, about Robert Bruce, complete the metrical romances. These made Scott the most popular British poet of the decade 1800–10.

While winning this literary success, Scott led a varied and energetic life in other fields. For a while he maintained an active law practice. Two years after his marriage he became sheriff of Selkirkshire. He drilled and roistered with his cavalry company. He was busy establishing an estate at Ashestiel on the Tweed and later at Abbotsford. But, most important activity of all, in its unfortunate consequences, he became a silent partner in the publishing firm of John Ballantyne and Company.

The final and widest phase of Scott's romancing began in 1814. Rummaging in a closet for fishing tackle, he turned up the manuscript of a novel that he had begun some years before. It seemed so promising that he finished it and published it anonymously as *Waverley*. This was the first of the great series of historical novels bearing the collective name Waverley. Taking Scotland of the seventeenth and eighteenth centuries for his settings, Scott wrote and published *Guy Mannering*, 1815; *Old Mortality* and *The Antiquary*, 1816; *The Heart of Midlothian* and *Rob Roy*, 1818; and *The Bride of Lammermoor*, 1819. Then he extended his field in space and time by writing *Ivanhoe*, 1820, treating England in the age of Richard Cœur-de-Lion; *The Abbot*, of the period of Mary Queen of Scots; *Kenilworth*, 1821, with its great scenes in the Age of Elizabeth; and *The Fortunes of Nigel*, 1822, concerned with Elizabeth's successor, James I. *Quentin Durward*, 1823, added France of the age of Louis XI, and *The Talisman*, 1825, added the Holy Land at the time of the Crusades to Scott's empire of romance. *Redgauntlet*, 1824, was a return to the native heath.

These literary conquests brought Scott world fame and wealth such as no writer before him had ever enjoyed from the products of his pen. He accepted the one modestly and shared the other generously. He built a beautiful estate at Abbotsford on the Tweed, established his family there in lordly splendor, and dispensed hospitality to visitors from all parts of the Western world (for example, Wordsworth and Washington Irving). In 1820 he was made a baronet. In 1825 Abbotsford celebrated brilliantly the engagement of his oldest son to a niece of one of the great families of Scotland. The following year brought financial ruin. The panic of the time and the bankruptcy of an English firm with which Ballantyne and Company had become involved broke the Scottish firm. As a silent partner, Scott could have escaped without utter loss. But he held himself to a gentleman's view of the business and accepted ultimate responsibility. He spent his fortune and the labors of his last years, often in

pain and sickness, clearing up the obligation. He died peacefully in 1832, admired and lamented by the world.

No brief sketch can fully suggest the amazing vitality and diversity of Scott as a human figure. Of all the Romanticists, he is perhaps the most admirable and attractive personally—the one we should most enjoy as friend and neighbor. His very faults—easy optimism, reckless generosity, overworldliness—are the excesses of his virtues. There is in the conduct of his life as of his art a richness akin to the careless opulence of Nature in her kindly moods. His open-handedness, his kindliness, his delight in men, women, and children of all walks of life, disarm those who would condemn him as a political Tory, an opponent of the French Revolution, a defender of the feudal status quo that he knew and revered. The scores of great character creations in his poems and novels flock to his defense.

As a literary figure, Scott was the prince of romancers. He revived the past on a scale of unparalleled magnificence and with an aspect of reality scarcely equaled by any writer after him. He reclaimed old ballads, composed new ones almost as good, and got everybody to reading them. He made best-sellers out of metrical romances telling stories centuries old. He created the historical novel and conquered the reading world with it. By his own profound knowledge of past times and by the universality of his understanding heart, he was able to enter imaginatively into the scenes and the lives of bygone ages. Compelled by the tastes of his own day and the conditions that he depicted to plot most of his novels about the figures and movements of aristocrats, he was really most interested in plain or humble folk like Meg Merrilies, Old Elspeth, Cuddie Headrigg, Wandering Willie, Edie Ochiltree, Dandie Dinmont, and Jeanie Deans. These were the people he had known and loved, as ballad raider in Liddesdale, as sheriff of Selkirkshire, and as laird of Abbotsford. They are alive in the past because they were alive in Scott's own experience. In the variety and the number of his authentic character creations he is of the glorious company of Shakespeare and Dickens. He is one of the sweetest singing poets. The numerous ballads and songs scattered through the lays and the novels treat, usually in natural narrative or dramatic settings, the themes of hunting, lovemaking, bride-stealing, clan gatherings and coronachs (laments), drinking, greenwood and outlaw life, Jacobite loyalty, incantation, and like interests and situations associated with a primitive or feudal order of society. They are breath of his breath, blood of his blood, who as a Scotsman knew and loved every foot of his country and every phase of its history and traditions.[1]

from MINSTRELSY OF THE SCOTTISH BORDER

KINMONT WILLIE

O have ye na heard o' the fause Sakelde?
  O have ye na heard o' the keen Lord Scroope?
How they hae ta'en bauld Kinmont Willie,
  On Hairibee to hang him up?

Had Willie had but twenty men,
  But twenty men as stout as he,
Fause Sakelde had never the Kinmont ta'en,
  Wi' eight score in his cumpanie.

They band his legs beneath the steed,
  They tied his hands behind his back;   10
They guarded him, fivesome on each side,
  And they brought him ower the Liddel-rack.

They led him thro' the Liddel-rack,
  And also thro' the Carlisle sands:
They brought him to Carlisle castell,
  To be at my Lord Scroope's commands.

"My hands are tied, but my tongue is free,
  And whae will dare this deed avow?
Or answer by the Border law?
  Or answer to the bauld Buccleuch!"   20

"Now haud thy tongue, thou rank reiver!
  There's never a Scot shall set ye free;
Before ye cross my castle yate,
  I trow ye shall take farewell o' me."

"Fear na ye that, my lord," quo' Willie;
  "By the faith o' my bodie, Lord Scroope," he said,
"I never yet lodged in a hostelrie,
  But I paid my lawing before I gaed."

Now word is gane to the bauld Keeper,
  In Branksome Ha', where that he lay,   30
That Lord Scroope has ta'en the Kinmont Willie,
  Between the hours of night and day.

He has ta'en the table wi' his hand,
  He garr'd the red wine spring on hie—
"Now Christ's curse on my head," he said,
  "But avenged of Lord Scroope I'll be!

"O is my basnet a widow's curch?
  Or my lance a wand of the willow-tree?
Or my arm a ladye's lilye hand?
  That an English lord should lightly me!   40

"And have they ta'en him, Kinmont Willie,
  Against the truce of Border tide?
And forgotten that the bauld Buccleuch
  Is Keeper here on the Scottish side?

"And have they e'en ta'en him, Kinmont Willie,
  Withouten either dread or fear?
And forgotten that the bauld Buccleuch
  Can back a steed, or shake a spear?

"O were there war between the lands,
  As well I wot that there is none,   50
I would slight Carlisle castell high,
  Tho' it were builded of marble stone.

"I would set that castell in a low,
  And sloken it with English blood!
There's nevir a man in Cumberland,
  Should ken where Carlisle castell stood.

"But since nae war's between the lands,
  And there is peace, and peace should be;
I'll neither harm English lad or lass,
  And yet the Kinmont freed shall be!"   60

He has call'd him forty Marchmen bauld,
  I trow they were of his ain name,
Except Sir Gilbert Elliot, call'd
  The Laird of Stobs, I mean the same.

He has call'd his forty Marchmen bauld,
  Were kinsmen of the bauld Buccleuch;
With spur on heel, and splent on spauld,
  And gleuves of green, and feathers blue.

1. For an eloquent exposition, by a young man, of what young people who do not read Scott are missing, see Sir David Cecil's articles "Sir Walter Scott" in the *Atlantic Monthly*, September–October, 1932. **1–2. fause,** false. **Sakelde . . . Lord Scroope.** Both were English. **3. taen bauld,** taken bold. Kinmont Willie was a Scot. **14. Carlisle,** an English city across the Firth of Solway. **20. Buccleuch,** one of Scott's feudal forbears. **21. reiver,** freebooter. **28. lawing,** reckoning (bill).

33–48. He has ta'en . . . spear. Professor F. J. Child (*The English and Scottish Popular Ballads*) suspected that Scott composed these lines. **34. garr'd,** made. **37. basnet,** helmet. **curch,** head covering. **40. lightly,** insult. **51. slight, 53. low,** flame. **54. sloken,** quench. **56. ken,** know. **61. Marchmen,** borderers ("march" means boundary). **67. splent on spauld,** armor on shoulder. **68. gleuves,** gloves.

There were five and five before them a',
  Wi' hunting horns and bugles bright;   70
And five and five came wi' Buccleuch,
  Like warden's men, array'd for fight.

And five and five like a mason gang,
  That carried the ladders lang and hie,
And five and five like broken men;
  And so they reach'd the Woodhouselee.

And as we cross'd the Bateable land,
  When to the English side we held,
The first o' men that we met wi',
  Whae sould it be but fause Sakelde?   80

"Where be ye gaun, ye hunters keen?"
  Quo' fause Sakelde; "come tell to me!"
"We go to hunt an English stag,
  Has trespass'd on the Scots countrie."

"Where be ye gaun, ye marshal men?"
  Quo' fause Sakelde; "come tell me true!"
"We go to catch a rank reiver,
  Has broken faith wi' the bauld Buccleuch."

"Where are ye gaun, ye mason lads,
  Wi a' your ladders lang and hie?"   90
"We gang to herry a corbie's nest,
  That wons not far frae Woodhouselee."

"Where be ye gaun, ye broken men?"
  Quo' fause Sakelde; "come tell to me!"
Now Dickie of Dryhope led that band,
  And the never a word o' lear had he.

"Why trespass ye on the English side?
  Row-footed outlaws, stand!" quo' he;
The nevir a word had Dickie to say,
  Sae he thrust the lance thro' his fause bodie. 100

Then on we held for Carlisle toun,
  And at Staneshaw-bank the Eden we cross'd;
The water was great and meikle of spait,
  But the nevir a horse nor man we lost.

And when we reach'd the Staneshaw-bank,
  The wind was rising loud and hie;
And there the Laird garr'd leave our steeds,
  For fear that they should stamp and nie.

And when we left the Staneshaw-bank,
  The wind began full loud to blaw;   110
And 'twas wind and weet, and fire and sleet,
  When we came beneath the castel wa'.

We crept on knees, and held our breath,
  Till we placed the ladders against the wa';
And sae ready was Buccleuch himsell
  To mount the first before us a'.

He has ta'en the watchman by the throat,
  He flung him down upon the lead—
"Had there not been peace between our lands
  Upon the other side thou hadst gaed!   120

"Now sound out, trumpets!" quo' Buccleuch;
  "Let's waken Lord Scroope, right merrilie!"
Then loud the warden's trumpets blew—
  "O whae dare meddle wi' me?"

Then speedilie to work we gaed,
  And raised the slogan ane and a',
And cut a hole thro' a sheet of lead,
  And so we wan to the castle ha'.

They thought King James and a' his men
  Had won the house wi' bow and spear: 130
It was but twenty Scots and ten
  That put a thousand in sic a stear!

Wi' coulters and wi' fore-hammers,
  We garr'd the bars bang merrilie,
Untill we cam to the inner prison,
  Where Willie o' Kinmont he did lie.

And when we cam to the lower prison,
  Where Willie o' Kinmont he did lie—
"O sleep ye, wake ye, Kinmont Willie,
  Upon the morn that thou's to die?"   140

"O I sleep saft, and I wake aft;
  It's lang since sleeping was fleyed frae me!
Gie my service back to my wyfe and bairns,
  And a' gude fellows that spier for me."

Then Red Rowan has hente him up,
  The starkest men in Teviotdale—
"Abide, abide now, Red Rowan,
  Till of my Lord Scroope I take farewell.

75. broken men, outlaws. 77. Bateable land, no man's land. 87. rank, bold, notorious. 91. herry a corbie's nest, rob a crow's nest. 92. wons, dwells. 96. lear, learning. 98. row-footed, rough-footed. 103. meikle of spait, in flood.

118. lead, roof (of lead). 128. wan, won. 132. sic a stear, such a fright. 142. fleyed, scared. 143. service, respects. 144. spier, inquire. 145. hente, seized. 146. starkest, strongest.

"Farewell, farewell, my gude Lord Scroope!
　My gude Lord Scroope, farewell!" he cried— 150
"I'll pay you for my lodging maill,
　When first we meet on the Border side."

Then shoulder high, with shout and cry,
　We bore him down the ladder lang;
At every stride Red Rowan made,
　I wot the Kinmont's airns played clang

"O mony a time," quo' Kinmont Willie,
　I have ridden horse baith wild and wood;
But a rougher beast than Red Rowan,
　I ween my legs have ne'er bestrode. 160

"And mony a time," quo' Kinmont Willie,
　"I've pricked a horse out oure the furs;
But since the day I backed a steed
　I nevir wore sic cumbrous spurs!"

We scarce had won the Staneshaw-bank,
　When a' the Carlisle bells were rung,
And a thousand men, in horse and foot,
　Cam wi' the keen Lord Scroope along.

Buccleuch has turn'd to Eden water,
　Even where it flow'd frae bank to brim, 170
And he has plunged in wi a' his band,
　And safely swam them through the stream.

He turn'd him on the other side,
　And at Lord Scroope his glove flung he—
"If ye like na my visit in merry England,
　In fair Scotland come visit me!"

All sore astonish'd stood Lord Scroope,
　He stood as still as rock of stane;
He scarcely dared to trew his eyes
　When through the water they had gane. 180

"He is either himsell a devil frae hell,
　Or else his mother a witch maun be;
I wad na have ridden that wan water,
　For a' the gowd in Christentie."

from MARMION

LOCHINVAR

O, young Lochinvar is come out of the west,
Through all the wide Border his steed was the best;

151. **lodging maill**, hotel bill.　158. **wood**, crazy.
160. **ween**, think.　162. **pricked . . . furs**, spurred over
the furrows.　179. **trew**, trust.　182. **maun**, must.

And save his good broadsword, he weapons had
　none,
He rode all unarmed, and he rode all alone.
So faithful in love, and so dauntless in war,
There never was knight like the young Lochinvar.
He staid not for brake, and he stopped not for stone,
He swam the Eske river where ford there was none;
But ere he alighted at Netherby gate,
The bride had consented, the gallant came late: 10
For a laggard in love, and a dastard in war,
Was to wed the fair Ellen of brave Lochinvar.

So boldly he entered the Netherby Hall,
Among bride's-men, and kinsmen, and brothers,
　and all:
Then spoke the bride's father, his hand on his
　sword,
(For the poor craven bridegroom said never a
　word,)
"O come ye in peace here, or come ye in war,
Or to dance at our bridal, young Lord Lochin-
　var?"—

"I long wooed your daughter, my suit you denied;—
Love swells like the Solway, but ebbs like its
　tide— 20
And now am I come, with this lost love of mine,
To lead but one measure, drink one cup of wine.
There are maidens in Scotland, more lovely by far,
That would gladly be bride to the young Lochin-
　var."

The bride kissed the goblet; the knight took it up,
He quaffed off the wine, and he threw down the
　cup.
She looked down to blush, and she looked up to sigh,
With a smile on her lips, and a tear in her eye.
He took her soft hand, ere her mother could bar,—
"Now tread we a measure!" said young Lochin-
　var. 30

So stately his form, and so lovely her face,
That never a hall such a galliard did grace:
While her mother did fret, and her father did fume,
And the bridegroom stood dangling his bonnet and
　plume;
And the bride-maidens whispered, "'Twere better
　by far
To have matched our fair cousin with young Loch-
　invar."

One touch to her hand, and one word in her ear,
When they reached the hall-door, and the charger
　stood near;

32. **galliard**, brisk dance.

So light to the croupe the fair lady he swung,
So light to the saddle before her he sprung!   40
"She is won! we are gone, over bank, bush, and
     scaur;
They'll have fleet steeds that follow," quoth young
     Lochinvar.

There was mounting 'mong Graemes of the Neth-
     erby clan;
Forsters, Fenwicks, and Musgraves, they rode and
     they ran;
There was racing and chasing, on Cannobie Lee,
But the lost bride of Netherby ne'er did they see.
So daring in love, and so dauntless in war.
Have ye e'er heard of gallant like young Lochinvar?

from THE LADY OF THE LAKE

CANTO I: THE CHASE

Harp of the North! that mouldering long hast hung
     On the witch-elm that shades Saint Fillan's spring,
And down the fitful breeze thy numbers flung,
     Till envious ivy did around thee cling,
Muffling with verdant ringlet every string,—
     O minstrel Harp! still must thine accents sleep?
'Mid rustling leaves and fountains murmuring,
     Still must thy sweeter sounds their silence keep,
Nor bid a warrior smile, nor teach a maid to weep?

Not thus, in ancient days of Caledon,   10
     Was thy voice mute amid the festal crowd,
When lay of hopeless love, or glory won,
     Aroused the fearful, or subdued the proud.
At each according pause, was heard aloud
     Thine ardent symphony sublime and high!
Fair dames and crested chiefs attention bowed;
     For still the burden of thy minstrelsy
Was Knighthood's dauntless deed, and Beauty's
     matchless eye.

O wake once more! how rude soe'er the hand
     That ventures o'er thy magic maze to stray;   20
O wake once more! though scarce my skill command
     Some feeble echoing of thine earlier lay:
Though harsh and faint, and soon to die away,
     And all unworthy of thy nobler strain,
Yet is one heart throb higher at its sway,
     The wizard note has not been touched in vain.
Then silent be no more! Enchantress, wake again!

1. **Harp of the North,** symbolical of the minstrelsy
of Scotland. The first twenty-seven lines are the invocation, in Spenserian stanzas. The body of the poem is pre-
vailingly in four-beat couplets, like Coleridge's "Christabel."

1

The stag at eve had drunk his fill,
Where danced the moon on Monan's rill,
And deep his midnight lair had made   30
In lone Glenartney's hazel shade;
But, when the sun his beacon red
Had kindled on Benvoirlich's head,
The deep-mouthed bloodhound's heavy bay
Resounded up the rocky way,
And faint, from farther distance borne,
Were heard the clanging hoof and horn.

2

As Chief, who hears his warder call,
"To arms! the foemen storm the wall,"
The antlered monarch of the waste   40
Sprung from his heathery couch in haste.
But, ere his fleet career he took,
The dew-drops from his flanks he shook;
Like crested leader proud and high,
Tossed his beamed frontlet to the sky;
A moment gazed adown the dale,
A moment snuffed the tainted gale,
A moment listened to the cry,
That thickened as the chase drew nigh;
Then, as the headmost foes appeared,   50
With one brave bound the copse he cleared,
And, stretching forward free and far,
Sought the wild heaths of Uam-Var.

3

Yelled on the view the opening pack;
Rock, glen, and cavern, paid them back;
To many a mingled sound at once
The awakened mountain gave response.
A hundred dogs bayed deep and strong,
Clattered a hundred steeds along,
Their peal the merry horns rung out,   60
A hundred voices joined the shout;
With hark and whoop and wild halloo,
No rest Benvoirlich's echoes knew.
Far from the tumult fled the roe,
Close in her covert cowered the doe;
The falcon, from her cairn on high,
Cast on the rout a wondering eye,
Till far beyond her piercing ken
The hurricane had swept the glen.
Faint and more faint, its failing din   70
Returned from cavern, cliff, and linn,
And silence settled, wide and still,
On the lone wood and mighty hill.

29. **Monan's rill.** The scene is the Highlands of Scotland, around Loch Lomond and the Trosachs. **71. linn,**
ravine.

4

Less loud the sounds of silvan war
Disturbed the heights of Uam-Var,
And roused the cavern, where, 'tis told,
A giant made his den of old;
For ere that steep ascent was won,
High in his pathway hung the sun,
And many a gallant, stayed perforce,   80
Was fain to breathe his faltering horse,
And of the trackers of the deer,
Scarce half the lessening pack was near;
So shrewdly on the mountain side
Had the bold burst their mettle tried.

5

The noble stag was pausing now,
Upon the mountain's southern brow,
Where broad extended, far beneath,
The varied realms of fair Menteith.
With anxious eye he wandered o'er   90
Mountain and meadow, moss and moor,
And pondered refuge from his toil,
By far Lochard or Aberfoyle.
But nearer was the copsewood grey,
That waved and wept on Loch-Achray,
And mingled with the pine-trees blue
On the bold cliffs of Benvenue.
Fresh vigour with the hope returned;
With flying foot the heath he spurned,
Held westward with unwearied race,   100
And left behind the panting chase.

6

'Twere long to tell what steeds gave o'er,
As swept the hunt through Cambus-more;
What reins were tightened in despair,
When rose Benledi's ridge in air;
Who flagged upon Bochastle's heath,
Who shunned to stem the flooded Teith,—
For twice that day, from shore to shore,
The gallant stag swam stoutly o'er.
Few were the stragglers, following far,   110
That reached the lake of Vennachar;
And when the Brigg of Turk was won,
The headmost horseman rode alone.

7

Alone, but with unbated zeal,
That horseman plied the scourge and steel;
For jaded now, and spent with toil,
Embossed with foam, and dark with soil,
While every gasp with sobs he drew,
The labouring stag strained full in view.

Two dogs of black Saint Hubert's breed,   120
Unmatched for courage, breath, and speed,
Fast on his flying traces came,
And all but won that desperate game;
For, scarce a spear's length from his haunch,
Vindictive toiled the bloodhounds stanch;
Nor nearer might the dogs attain,
Nor farther might the quarry strain.
Thus up the margin of the lake,
Between the precipice and brake,
O'er stock and rock their race they take.   130

8

The Hunter marked that mountain high,
The lone lake's western boundary,
And deemed the stag must turn to bay,
Where that huge rampart barred the way;
Already glorying in the prize,
Measured his antlers with his eyes;
For the death-wound and death-halloo,
Mustered his breath, his whinyard drew;—
But thundering as he came prepared,
With ready arm and weapon bared,   140
The wily quarry shunned the shock,
And turned him from the opposing rock;
Then, dashing down a darksome glen,
Soon lost to hound and hunter's ken,
In the deep Trosachs' wildest nook
His solitary refuge took.
There, while close couched, the thicket shed
Cold dews and wild-flowers on his head,
He heard the baffled dogs in vain
Rave through the hollow pass amain,   150
Chiding the rocks that yelled again.

9

Close on the hounds the hunter came,
To cheer them on the vanished game;
But, stumbling in the rugged dell,
The gallant horse exhausted fell.
The impatient rider strove in vain
To rouse him with the spur and rein,
For the good steed, his labours o'er,
Stretched his stiff limbs, to rise no more;
Then touched with pity and remorse,   160
He sorrowed o'er the expiring horse.
"I little thought, when first thy rein
I slacked upon the banks of Seine,
That Highland eagle e'er should feed
On thy fleet limbs, my matchless steed!
Woe worth the chase, woe worth the day,
That costs thy life, my gallant grey!"

138. whinyard, a short sword.   **166. worth,** be, become.

10

Then through the dell his horn resounds,
From vain pursuit to call the hounds.
Back limped, with slow and crippled pace,   170
The sulky leaders of the chase;
Close to their master's side they pressed,
With drooping tail and humbled crest;
But still the dingle's hollow throat
Prolonged the swelling bugle-note.
The owlets started from their dream,
The eagles answered with their scream,
Round and around the sounds were cast,
Till echo seemed an answering blast;
And on the hunter hied his way,   180
To join some comrades of the day;
Yet often paused, so strange the road,
So wondrous were the scenes it showed. . . .

from ROKEBY: Canto III

SONG

O, Brignall banks are wild and fair,
　　And Greta woods are green,
And you may gather garlands there,
　　Would grace a summer queen.
And as I rode by Dalton-hall,
　　Beneath the turrets high,
A Maiden on the castle wall
　　Was singing merrily,—
"O, Brignall banks are fresh and fair,
　　And Greta woods are green;   10
I'd rather rove with Edmund there,
　　Than reign our English queen."—

"If, Maiden, thou wouldst wend with me,
　　To leave both tower and town,
Thou first must guess what life lead we,
　　That dwell by dale and down?
And if thou canst that riddle read,
　　As read full well you may,
Then to the greenwood shalt thou speed,
　　As blithe as Queen of May."—   20
Yet sung she, "Brignall banks are fair,
　　And Greta woods are green;
I'd rather rove with Edmund there,
　　Than reign our English queen.

"I read you, by your bugle-horn,
　　And by your palfrey good,
I read you for a ranger sworn,
　　To keep the king's greenwood."—
"A Ranger, lady, winds his horn,
　　And 'tis at peep of light;   30

His blast is heard at merry morn,
　　And mine at dead of night."
Yet sung she, "Brignall banks are fair,
　　And Greta woods are gay;
I would I were with Edmund there,
　　To reign his Queen of May!

"With burnished brand and musketoon,
　　So gallantly you come,
I read you for a bold Dragoon,
　　That lists the tuck of drum."—   40
"I list no more the tuck of drum,
　　No more the trumpet hear;
But when the beetle sounds his hum,
　　My comrades take the spear.
"And O! though Brignall banks be fair,
　　And Greta woods be gay,
Yet mickle must the maiden dare,
　　Would reign my Queen of May!

"Maiden! a nameless life I lead,
　　A nameless death I'll die!   50
The fiend, whose lantern lights the mead,
　　Were better mate than I!
And when I'm with my comrades met
　　Beneath the greenwood bough,
What once we were we all forget,
　　Nor think what we are now.
"Yet Brignall banks are fresh and fair,
　　And Greta woods are green,
And you may gather garlands there
　　Would grace a summer queen."   60

ALLEN-A-DALE

Allen-a-Dale has no fagot for burning,
Allen-a-Dale has no furrow for turning,
Allen-a-Dale has no fleece for the spinning,
Yet Allen-a-Dale has red gold for the winning.
Come, read me my riddle! come, hearken my tale!
And tell me the craft of bold Allen-a-Dale.

The Baron of Ravensworth prances in pride,
And he views his domains upon Arkindale side.
The mere for his net, and the land for his game,
The chase for the wild, and the park for the tame: 10
Yet the fish of the lake, and the deer of the vale,
Are less free to Lord Dacre than Allen-a-Dale!

Allen-a-Dale was ne'er belted a knight,
Though his spur be as sharp, and his blade be as
　　bright;

47. mickle, much.

Allen-a-Dale is no baron or lord,
Yet twenty tall yeomen will draw at his word;
And the best of our nobles his bonnet will vail,
Who at Rere-cross on Stanmore meets Allen-a-Dale.

Allen-a-Dale to his wooing is come;
The mother, she asked of his household and
    home: 20
"Though the castle of Richmond stand fair on the
    hill,
My hall," quoth bold Allen, "shows gallanter still;
'Tis the blue vault of heaven, with its crescent so
    pale,
And with all its bright spangles!" said Allen-a-Dale.

The father was steel, and the mother was stone;
They lifted the latch, and they bade him be gone:
But loud, on the morrow, their wail and their cry:
He had laughed on the lass with his bonny black eye,
And she fled to the forest to hear a love-tale,
And the youth it was told by was Allen-a-Dale!   30

JOCK OF HAZELDEAN

"Why weep ye by the tide, ladie?
    Why weep ye by the tide?
I'll wed ye to my youngest son,
    And ye sall be his bride;
And ye sall be his bride, ladie,
    Sae comely to be seen"—
But aye she loot the tears down fa'
    For Jock of Hazeldean.

"Now let this wilfu' grief be done,
    And dry that cheek so pale;   10
Young Frank is chief of Errington,
    And Lord of Langley-dale;
His step is first in peaceful ha',
    His sword in battle keen"—
But aye she loot the tears down fa'
    For Jock of Hazeldean.

"A chain of gold ye sall not lack,
    Nor braid to bind your hair;
Nor mettled hound, nor managed hawk,
    Nor palfrey fresh and fair;   20
And you, the foremost o' them a',
    Shall ride our forest queen"—
But aye she loot the tears down fa'
    For Jock of Hazeldean.

The kirk was decked at morning-tide,
    The tapers glimmered fair;

The priest and bridegroom wait the bride,
    And dame and knight are there.
They sought her baith by bower and ha';
    The ladie was not seen!   30
She's o'er the Border, and awa'
    Wi' Jock of Hazeldean.

from THE ANTIQUARY

TIME

"Why sit'st thou by that ruined hall,
    Thou aged carle so stern and grey?
Dost thou its former pride recall,
    Or ponder how it passed away?"—

"Know'st thou not me?" the Deep Voice cried;
    "So long enjoyed, so oft misused—
Alternate, in thy fickle pride,
    Desired, neglected, and accused!

"Before my breath, like blazing flax,
    Man and his marvels pass away!   10
And changing empires wane and wax,
    Are founded, flourish, and decay.

"Redeem mine hours—the space is brief—
    While in my glass the sand-grains shiver,
And measureless thy joy or grief,
    When TIME and thou shalt part for ever!"

THE SUN UPON THE WEIRDLAW
HILL

The sun upon the Weirdlaw Hill,
    In Ettrick's vale, is sinking sweet;
The westland wind is hush and still,
    The lake lies sleeping at my feet.
Yet not the landscape to mine eye
    Bears those bright hues that once it bore,
Though evening, with her richest dye,
    Flames o'er the hills of Ettrick's shore.

With listless look along the plain,
    I see Tweed's silver current glide,   10
And coldly mark the holy fane
    Of Melrose rise in ruined pride.
The quiet lake, the balmy air,
    The hill, the stream, the tower, the tree,—
Are they still such as once they were?
    Or is the dreary change in me?

Time. **2. carle,** churl, peasant.

Alas, the warped and broken board,
  How can it bear the painter's dye!
The harp of strained and tuneless chord,
  How to the minstrel's skill reply!   20
To aching eyes each landscape lowers,
  To feverish pulse each gale blows chill;
And Araby's or Eden's bowers
  Were barren as this moorland hill.

from THE HEART OF MIDLOTHIAN

PROUD MAISIE

Sung by Madge Wildfire, the insane woman, as she
lies dying; one of the most exquisite literary ballads in
English. It "gives in its sixteen lines the essence of all
that needs to be said about the dying of a young girl."
                                    —Oliver Elton

Proud Maisie is in the wood,
  Walking so early;
Sweet Robin sits on the bush,
  Singing so rarely.

"Tell me, thou bonny bird,
  When shall I marry me?"—
"When six braw gentlemen
  Kirkward shall carry ye."

"Who makes the bridal bed,
  Birdie, say truly?"—   10
"The grey-headed sexton
  That delves the grave duly.

"The glow-worm o'er grave and stone
  Shall light thee steady;
The owl from the steeple sing,
  'Welcome, proud lady.' "

FAREWELL TO THE MUSE

Enchantress, farewell, who so oft hast decoyed me,
  At the close of the evening through woodlands to
    roam,
Where the forester, lated, with wonder espied me
  Explore the wild scenes he was quitting for home.
Farewell, and take with thee thy numbers wild
    speaking
  The language alternate of rapture and woe:
Oh! none but some lover, whose heart-strings are
    breaking,
  The pang that I feel at our parting can know.

Proud Maisie. 7. **braw,** fine.   *Farewell.* 3. **lated,** belated.

Each joy thou couldst double,—and when there
    came sorrow,
  Or pale disappointment, to darken my way,   10
What voice was like thine, that could sing of to-
    morrow,
  Till forgot in the strain was the grief of to-day!
But when friends drop around us in life's weary
    waning,
  The grief, Queen of Numbers, thou canst not
    assuage;
Nor the gradual estrangement of those yet remain-
    ing,
  The languor of pain, and the chillness of age.

'Twas thou that once taught me, in accents bewail-
    ing,
  To sing how a warrior lay stretched on the
    plain,
And a maiden hung o'er him with aid unavailing,
  And held to his lips the cold goblet in vain;   20
As vain thy enchantment, O Queen of wild Num-
    bers,
  To a bard when the reign of his fancy is o'er
And the quick pulse of feeling in apathy slum-
    bers—
  Farewell, then, Enchantress! I meet thee no
    more!

from QUENTIN DURWARD

COUNTY GUY

Ah! County Guy, the hour is nigh,
  The sun has left the lea,
The orange flower perfumes the bower,
  The breeze is on the sea.
The lark, his lay who thrilled all day,
  Sits hushed his partner nigh;
Breeze, bird, and flower, confess the hour,
  But where is County Guy?

The village maid steals through the shade,
  Her shepherd's suit to hear;   10
To beauty shy, by lattice high,
  Sings high-born Cavalier.
The star of Love, all stars above,
  Now reigns o'er earth and sky;
And high and low the influence know—
  But where is County Guy?

22. when the reign of his fancy is o'er. Compare Coleridge's "Dejection" and Wordsworth's "Resolution and
Independence." **1. County,** Earl or Count. The song is
sung by a little veiled maid in a tower. The music rather
than the sense is significant.

from REDGAUNTLET

WANDERING WILLIE'S TALE

Redgauntlet, 1824, is a historical novel relating to the Jacobite Plot of 1763. The Jacobites, from Latin *Jacobus*, James, were supporters of James II and his descendants against the Hanoverians, after the Revolution of 1688. The titular character is a descendant of the Redgauntlet in "Wandering Willie's Tale." The hero of *Redgauntlet*, Darsey Latimer, is, unknown to himself, also a descendant of the family. Wandering Willie, a blind fiddler, ballad-singer, and storyteller, tells his tale to Darsey as the two tramp across a lea to the ancestral castle. Since the Steenie Steenson of the tale is Willie's grandfather, the events relate to the families of both men.

"Wandering Willie's Tale" is perhaps Scott's best story of the supernatural, and one of the best of its kind in the world. A. W. Verrall, in his *Collected Literary Essays*, 1913, has shown that Scott shrewdly makes Willie tell his tale in such a way that it can be either accepted as supernatural or rationalized as a product of Steenie's drunken and excited imagining. In order to provide these alternatives, the story of the last interview with Sir Robert Redgauntlet is told twice, with slight differences between the two versions. By close observation, with the help of the notes, the student may be able to work out this problem of narrative psychology for himself.

YE maun have heard of Sir Robert Redgauntlet of that Ilk, who lived in these parts before the dear years. The country will lang mind him; and our fathers used to draw breath thick if ever they heard him named. He was out wi' the Hielandmen in Montrose's time; and again he was in the hills wi' Glencairn in the saxteen hundred and fifty-twa; and sae when King Charles the Second came in, wha was in sic favour as the Laird of Redgauntlet? He was knighted at Lonon court, wi' the King's ain sword; and being a redhot prelatist, he came down here, rampauging like a lion, with commissions of lieutenancy, (and of lunacy, for what I ken,) to put down a' the Whigs and Covenanters in the country. Wild wark they made of it; for the Whigs were as dour as the Cavaliers were fierce, and it was which should first tire the other. Redgauntlet was aye for the strong hand, and his name is kend as wide in the country as Claverhouse's or Tam Dalyell's. Glen, nor dargle, nor mountain, nor cave, could hide the puir hill-folk when Redgauntlet was out with bugle and bloodhound after them, as if they

had been sae mony deer. And troth, when they fand them, they didna mak muckle mair ceremony than a Hielandman wi' a roebuck—It was just, "Will ye tak the test?"—if not, "Make ready—present—fire!"—and there lay the recusant.

Far and wide was Sir Robert hated and feared. Men thought he had a direct compact with Satan—that he was proof against steel—and that bullets happed aff his buff-coat like hailstanes from a hearth—that he had a mear that would turn a hare on the side of Carrifra-gawns—and muckle to the same purpose, of whilk mair anon. The best blessing they wared on him was, "Deil scowp wi' Redgauntlet!" He wasna a bad master to his ain folk though, and was weel aneugh liked by his tenants; and as for the lackies and troopers that raid out wi' him to the persecutions, as the Whigs caa'd those killing times, they wad hae drunken themsells blind to his health at ony time.

Now you are to ken that my gudesire lived on Redgauntlet's grund—they ca' the place Primrose-Knowe. We had lived on the grund, and under the Redgauntlets, since the riding days, and lang before. It was a pleasant bit; and I think the air is callerer and fresher there than ony where else in the country. It's a' deserted now; and I sat on the broken door-cheek three days since, and was glad I couldna see the plight the place was in; but that's a' wide o' the mark. There dwelt my gudesire, Steenie Steenson, a rambling, rattling chiel' he had been in his young days, and could play weel on the pipes; he was famous at "Hoopers and Girders"—a' Cumberland couldna touch him at "Jockie Lattin"—and he had the finest finger for the back-lilt between Berwick and Carlisle. The like o' Steenie wasna the sort that they made Whigs o'. And so he became a Tory, as they ca' it, which we now ca' Jacobites, just out of a kind of needcessity, that he might belang to some side or other. He had nae ill-will to the Whig bodies, and liked little to see the blude rin, though, being obliged to follow Sir Robert in hunting and hosting, watching and warding, he saw muckle mischief, and maybe did some, that he couldna avoid.

Now Steenie was a kind of favourite with his master, and kend a' the folks about the castle, and was often sent for to play the pipes when they were

2. **muckle**, much.   5. **recusant,** one who refuses to conform (dissenter).   11. **Carrifra-gawns,** "A precipitous side of a mountain in Moffatdale." (Scott)   12. **whilk,** which.   13. **scowp,** make away.   16. **lackies,** camp followers.   17. **Whigs,** nonconformists.   23. **riding days,** persecution expeditions.   25. **callerer,** cooler.   30. **chiel',** fellow.   42. **hosting,** military mustering. Note Willie's fondness for alliterative phrases—"hunting and hosting, watching and warding," and the like.

28. **maun,** must.   29. **Ilk,** same name.   29–30. **dear years,** hard times.   38. **prelatist,** Catholic.   43. **dour,** stubborn.   45. **kend,** known.   46. **Claverhouse's,** Col. John Graham of Claverhouse (in Scott's *Old Mortality*), afterwards Viscount Dundee ("Bonny Dundee"). He is described later in Willie's tale.   47. **dargle,** dell.

at their merriment. Auld Dougal MacCallum, the butler, that had followed Sir Robert through gude and ill, thick and thin, pool and stream, was specially fond of the pipes, and aye gae my gudesire his gude word wi' the Laird; for Dougal could turn his master round his finger.

Weel, round came the Revolution, and it had like to have broken the hearts baith of Dougal and his master. But the change was not a'thegether sae great as they feared, and other folk thought for. The Whigs made an unco crawing what they wad do with their auld enemies, and in special wi' Sir Robert Redgauntlet. But there were ower mony great folks dipped in the same doings, to make a spick and span new warld. So Parliament passed it a' ower easy; and Sir Robert, bating that he was held to hunting foxes instead of Covenanters, remained just the man he was. His revel was as loud, and his hall as weel lighted, as ever it had been, though maybe he lacked the fines of the noncon- 20 formists, that used to come to stock his larder and cellar; for it is certain he began to be keener about the rents than his tenants used to find him before, and they behoved to be prompt to the rent-day, or else the Laird wasna pleased. And he was sic an awsome body that naebody cared to anger him; for the oaths he swore, and the rage that he used to get into, and the looks that he put on, made men sometimes think him a devil incarnate.

Weel, my gudesire was nae manager—no that 30 he was a very great misguider,—but he hadna the saving gift, and he got twa terms' rent in arrear. He got the first brash at Whitsunday put ower wi' fair word and piping; but when Martinmas came, there was a summons from the grund-officer to come wi' the rent on a day preceese, or else Steenie behoved to flit. Sair wark he had to get the siller; but he was weel-freended, and at last he got the haill scraped thegither—a thousand merks—the maist of it was from a neighbour they caa'd Laurie Lapraik—a sly 40 tod. Laurie had walth o' gear—could hunt wi' the hound and rin wi' the hare—and be Whig or Tory,

saunt or sinner, as the wind stood. He was a professor in this Revolution warld; but he liked an orra sough of this warld, and a tune on the pipes weel aneugh at a by time; and abune a', he thought he had gude security for the siller he lent my gudesire ower the stocking at Primrose-Knowe.

Away trots my gudesire to Redgauntlet Castle wi' a heavy purse and a light heart, glad to be out of the Laird's danger. Weel, the first thing he learned at the Castle was, that Sir Robert had fretted himsell into a fit of the gout, because he did not appear before twelve o'clock. It wasna a'thegether for sake of the money, Dougal thought, but because he didna like to part wi' my gudesire aff the grund. Dougal was glad to see Steenie, and brought him into the great oak parlour, and there sat the Laird his leesome lane, excepting that he had beside him a great, ill-favoured jackanape, that was a special pet of his; a cankered beast it was, and mony an ill-natured trick it played—ill to please it was, and easily angered—ran about the haill castle, chattering and yowling, and pinching, and biting folk, specially before ill-weather or disturbances in the state. Sir Robert caa'd it Major Weir, after the warlock that was burnt; and few folk liked either the name or the conditions of the creature—they thought there was something in it by ordinar—and my gudesire was not just easy in his mind when the door shut on him, and he saw himself in the room wi' naebody but the Laird, Dougal MacCallum, and the Major, a thing that hadna chanced to him before.

Sir Robert sat, or, I should say, lay, in a great armed chair, wi' his grand velvet gown, and his feet on a cradle; for he had baith gout and gravel, and his face looked as gash and ghastly as Satan's. Major Weir sat opposite to him, in a red laced coat, and the Laird's wig on his head; and aye as Sir Robert girned wi' pain, the jackanape girned too, like a sheep's-head between a pair of tangs—an ill-faur'd, fearsome couple they were. The Laird's buff-coat was hung on a pin behind him, and his broadsword and his pistols within reach; for he keepit up the auld fashion of having the weapons ready, and a horse saddled day and night, just as he used to do when he was able to loup on horse-

4. **aye gae,** always gave.   11. **unco crawing,** uncommon crowing, boast.   16. **bating,** except.   29. **devil incarnate.** "The caution and moderation of King William III., and his principles of unlimited toleration, deprived the Cameronians of the opportunity they ardently desired, to retaliate the injuries which they had received during the reign of prelacy, and purify the land, as they called it, from the pollution of blood. They esteemed the Revolution, therefore, only a half measure, which neither comprehended the rebuilding the Kirk in its full splendor, nor the revenge of the death of the Saints on their persecutors." (Scott) 33. **brash,** outburst (of anger).   35. **grund-officer,** overseer.   39. **merks,** marks. The mark was originally worth 13*s.* 4*d.*, but had greatly depreciated by Steenie's time. 41. **gear,** property.

1-2. **professor,** that is, of Catholic faith.   3. **orra sough,** other tune.   4. **aneugh,** enough. **by time,** one not given over to routine. **abune a',** above all.   14. **part wi'** . . . **grund,** dispossess.   17. **leesome lane,** all alone.   18. **jackanape,** monkey.   19. **cankered,** malignant.   25. **was burnt.** "A celebrated wizard, executed at Edinburgh for sorcery and other crimes." (Scott)   27. **by ordinar,** out of the ordinary.   35. **cradle,** a supporting framework. 36. **gash,** dismal-looking.   39. **girned,** showed his teeth, snarled.   41. **ill-faur'd,** ill-favored.   46. **loup,** leap.

back, and away after ony of the hill-folk he could get speerings of. Some said it was for fear of the Whigs taking vengeance, but I judge it was just his auld custom—he wasna gien to fear ony thing. The rental-book, wi' its black cover and brass clasps, was lying beside him; and a book of sculduddry sangs was put betwixt the leaves, to keep it open at the place where it bore evidence against the Good-man of Primrose-Knowe, as behind the hand with his mails and duties. Sir Robert gave my gudesire a look, as if he would have withered his heart in his bosom. Ye maun ken he had a way of bending his brows, that men saw the visible mark of a horse-shoe in his forehead, deep-dinted, as if it had been stamped there.

"Are ye come light-handed, ye son of a toom whistle?" said Sir Robert. "Zounds! if you are——"

My gudesire, with as gude a countenance as he could put on, made a leg, and placed the bag of money on the table wi' a dash, like a man that does something clever. The Laird drew it to him hastily —"Is it all here, Steenie, man?"

"Your honour will find it right," said my gudesire.

"Here, Dougal," said the Laird, "gie Steenie a tass of brandy downstairs, till I count the siller and write the receipt."

But they werena weel out of the room, when Sir Robert gied a yelloch that garr'd the Castle rock. Back ran Dougal—in flew the livery-men—yell on yell gied the Laird, ilk ane mair awfu' than the ither. My gudesire knew not whether to stand or flee, but he ventured back into the parlour, where a' was gaun hirdy-girdie—naebody to say "come in" or "gae out." Terribly the Laird roared for cauld water to his feet, and wine to cool his throat; and Hell, hell, hell, and its flames, was aye the word in his mouth. They brought him water, and when they plunged his swoln feet into the tub, he cried out it was burning; and folk said that it *did* bubble and sparkle like a seething caldron. He flung the cup at Dougal's head, and said he had given him blood instead of burgundy; and, sure aneugh, the lass washed clotted blood aff the carpet the neist day. The jackanape they caa'd Major Weir, it jibbered and cried as if it was mocking its master; my gudesire's head was like to turn—he forgot baith siller and receipt, and downstairs he banged; but as he ran, the shrieks came faint and

fainter; there was a deep-drawn shivering groan; and word gaed through the Castle that the Laird was dead.

Weel, away came my gudesire, wi' his finger in his mouth, and his best hope was, that Dougal had seen the money-bag, and heard the Laird speak of writing the receipt. The young Laird, now Sir John, came from Edinburgh, to see things put to rights. Sir John and his father never gree'd weel. Sir John had been bred an advocate, and afterwards sat in the last Scots Parliament and voted for the Union, having gotten, it was thought, a rug of the com-pensations—if his father could have come out of his grave, he would have brained him for it on his awn hearthstane. Some thought it was easier counting with the auld rough Knight than the fair-spoken young ane—but mair of that anon.

Dougal MacCallum, poor body, neither grat nor graned, but gaed about the house looking like a corpse, but directing, as was his duty, a' the order of the grand funeral. Now, Dougal looked aye waur and waur when night was coming, and was aye the last to gang to his bed, whilk was in a little round just opposite the chamber of dais, whilk his master occupied while he was living, and where he now lay in state, as they caa'd it, weel-a-day! The night be-fore the funeral, Dougal could keep his awn counsel nae langer; he came doun with his proud spirit, and fairly asked auld Hutcheon to sit in his room with him for an hour. When they were in the round, Dougal took ae tass of brandy to himsell, and gave another to Hutcheon, and wished him all health and lang life, and said that, for himsell, he wasna lang for this world; for that, every night since Sir Robert's death, his silver call had sounded from the state chamber, just as it used to do at nights in his lifetime, to call Dougal to help to turn him in his bed. Dougal said, that being alone with the dead on that floor of the tower, (for naebody cared to wake Sir Robert Redgauntlet like another corpse,) he had never daured to answer the call, but that now his conscience checked him for neglecting his duty; for, "though death breaks service," said MacCallum, "it shall never break my service to Sir Robert; and I will answer his next whistle, so be you will stand by me, Hutcheon."

Hutcheon had nae will to the wark, but he had stood by Dougal in battle and broil, and he wad not fail him at this pinch; so down the carles sat ower a stoup of brandy, and Hutcheon, who was some-

---

2. **speerings,** tidings. 6-7. **sculduddry sangs,** ribald songs. 10. **mails,** rents. 13. **horse-shoe.** Note this image in the rest of the story. 16. **toom,** empty. 19. **made a leg,** bowed. This is the first version of the interview. Note all cir-cumstances carefully. Could the receipt have been written? Could Steenie have carried it away unawares? 25. **tass,** drinking cup. 28. **gied . . . garr'd,** gave a yell that made. 44. **neist,** next.

10. **advocate,** lawyer. 12. **rug,** share. 18-19. **grat nor . . . graned,** wept nor groaned. 22. **waur,** worse. 24. **dais,** room of state. 39. **wake,** watch over the dead. 50. **stoup,** flagon.

thing of a clerk, would have read a chapter of the Bible; but Dougal would hear naething but a blaud of Davie Lindsay, whilk was the waur preparation.

When midnight came, and the house was quiet as the grave, sure enough the silver whistle sounded as sharp and shrill as if Sir Robert was blowing it, and up got the twa auld serving-men, and tottered into the room where the dead man lay. Hutcheon saw aneugh at the first glance; for there were torches in the room, which shewed him the foul fiend, in his ain shape, sitting on the Laird's coffin! Ower he cowped as if he had been dead. He could not tell how lang he lay in a trance at the door, but when he gathered himself, he cried on his neighbour, and getting nae answer, raised the house, when Dougal was found lying dead within twa steps of the bed where his master's coffin was placed. As for the whistle, it was gaen anes and aye; but mony a time was it heard at the top of the house on the bartizan, and amang the auld chimneys and turrets where the howlets have their nests. Sir John hushed the matter up, and the funeral passed over without mair bogle-work.

But when a' was ower, and the Laird was beginning to settle his affairs, every tenant was called up for his arrears, and my gudesire for the full sum that stood against him in the rental-book. Weel, away he trots to the Castle, to tell his story, and there he is introduced to Sir John, sitting in his father's chair, in deep mourning, with weepers and hanging cravat, and a small walking rapier by his side, instead of the auld broadsword that had a hundred-weight of steel about it, what with blade, chape, and basket-hilt. I have heard their communing so often tauld ower that I almost think I was there mysell, though I couldna be born at the time. (In fact, Alan, my companion mimicked, with a good deal of humour, the flattering, conciliating tone of the tenant's address, and the hypocritical melancholy of the Laird's reply. His grandfather, he said, had, while he spoke, his eye fixed on the rental-book, as if it were a mastiff-dog that he was afraid would spring up and bite him.)

"I wuss ye joy, sir, of the head seat, and the white loaf, and the braid lairdship. Your father was a kind man to friends and followers; muckle grace to you, Sir John, to fill his shoon—his boots, I suld

say, for he seldom wore shoon, unless it were muils when he had the gout."

"Ay, Steenie," quoth the laird, sighing deeply, and putting his napkin to his een, "his was a sudden call, and he will be missed in the country; no time to set his house in order—weel prepared Godward, no doubt, which is the root of the matter—but left us behind a tangled hesp to wind, Steenie.—Hem! hem! We maun go to business, Steenie; much to do, and little time to do it in."

Here he opened the fatal volume. I have heard of a thing they call Doomsday-book—I am clear it has been a rental of back-ganging tenants.

"Stephen," said Sir John, still in the same soft, sleekit tone of voice—"Stephen Stevenson, or Steenson, ye are down here for a year's rent behind the hand—due at last term."

Stephen. "Please your honour, Sir John, I paid it to your father."

Sir John. "Ye took a receipt then, doubtless, Stephen, and can produce it?"

Stephen. "Indeed I hadna time, an it like your honour; for nae sooner had I set doun the siller, and just as his honour Sir Robert, that's gaen, drew it till him to count it, and write out the receipt, he was ta'en wi' the pains that removed him."

"That was unlucky," said Sir John, after a pause. "But ye maybe paid it in the presence of somebody. I want but a *talis qualis* evidence, Stephen. I would go ower strictly to work with no poor man."

Stephen. "Troth, Sir John, there was naebody in the room but Dougal MacCallum the butler. But, as your honour kens, he has e'en followed his auld master."

"Very unlucky again, Stephen," said Sir John, without altering his voice a single note. "The man to whom ye paid the money is dead—and the man who witnessed the payment is dead too—and the siller, which should have been to the fore, is neither seen nor heard tell of in the repositories. How am I to believe a' this?"

Stephen. "I dinna ken, your honour; but there is a bit memorandum note of the very coins; for, God help me! I had to borrow out of twenty purses; and I am sure that ilka man there set down will take his grit oath for what purpose I borrowed the money."

Sir John. "I have little doubt ye *borrowed* the

---

2. **blaud**, ballad. 3. **waur**, worse. 11. **fiend**, the Devil. 12. **cowped**, fell. 18. **anes and aye**, once for all. 20. **bartizan**, small overhanging tower. 21. **howlets**, owls. 23. **bogle-work**, ghost work. 34–35. **communing**. Note that in this second version of the interview Steenie describes it *as if he had been there*. In the parenthesis that follows Scott directs attention to the fact. Why? 44. **wuss**, wish. 47. **shoon**, shoes.

1. **muils**, slippers (compare the modern English "mules"). 8. **hesp**, hank, of yarn. 15. **sleekit**, smooth. 25. **write out the receipt**. Compare the earlier version of the interview. Could the receipt have been written, by this account of circumstances? Verrall thinks that Scott deliberately planned the discrepancy. 29. **talis qualis**, such as it is, acceptable. 45. **ilka**, every.

money, Steenie. It is the *payment* to my father that I want to have some proof of.''

Stephen. ''The siller maun be about the house, Sir John. And since your honour never got it, and his honour that was canna have taen it wi' him, maybe some of the family may have seen it.''

Sir John. ''We will examine the servants, Stephen; that is but reasonable.''

But lackey and lass, and page and groom, all denied stoutly that they had ever seen such a bag of money as my gudesire described. What was waur, he had unluckily not mentioned to any living soul of them his purpose of paying his rent. Ae quean had noticed something under his arm, but she took it for the pipes.

Sir John Redgauntlet ordered the servants out of the room, and then said to my gudesire, ''Now, Steenie, ye see ye have fair play; and, as I have little doubt ye ken better where to find the siller than ony other body, I beg, in fair terms, and for your own sake, that you will end this fasherie; for, Stephen, ye maun pay or flit.''

''The Lord forgie your opinion,'' said Stephen, driven almost to his wit's end—''I am an honest man.''

''So am I, Stephen,'' said his honour; ''and so are all the folks in the house, I hope. But if there be a knave amongst us, it must be he that tells the story he cannot prove.'' He paused, and then added, mair sternly, ''If I understand your trick, sir, you want to take advantage of some malicious reports concerning things in this family, and particularly respecting my father's sudden death, thereby to cheat me out of the money, and perhaps take away my character, by insinuating that I have received the rent I am demanding.—Where do you suppose this money to be?—I insist upon knowing.''

My gudesire saw every thing look so muckle against him, that he grew nearly desperate—however, he shifted from one foot to another, looked to every corner of the room, and made no answer.

''Speak out, sirrah,'' said the Laird, assuming a look of his father's, a very particular ane, which he had when he was angry—it seemed as if the wrinkles of his frown made that self-same fearful shape of a horse's shoe in the middle of his brow;—''Speak out, sir! I *will* know your thoughts;—do you suppose that I have this money?''

''Far be it frae me to say so,'' said Stephen.

''Do you charge any of my people with having taken it?''

''I wad be laith to charge them that may be inno-

cent,'' said my gudesire; ''and if there be any one that is guilty, I have nae proof.''

''Some where the money must be, if there is a word of truth in your story,'' said Sir John. ''I ask where you think it is—and demand a correct answer?''

''In hell, if you *will* have my thoughts of it,'' said my gudesire, driven to extremity,—''in hell! with your father, his jackanape, and his silver whistle.''

Down the stairs he ran, (for the parlour was nae place for him after such a word,) and he heard the Laird swearing blood and wounds, behind him, as fast as ever did Sir Robert, and roaring for the bailie and the baron-officer.

Away rode my gudesire to his chief creditor, (him they caa'd Laurie Lapraik,) to try if he could make ony thing out of him; but when he tauld his story, he got but the worst word in his wame—thief, beggar, and dyvour, were the saftest terms; and to the boot of these hard terms, Laurie brought up the auld story of his dipping his hand in the blood of God's saunts, just as if a tenant could have helped riding with the Laird, and that a laird like Sir Robert Redgauntlet. My gudesire was by this time far beyond the bounds of patience, and, while he and Laurie were at deil speed the liars, he was wanchancie aneugh to abuse Lapraik's doctrine as weel as the man, and said things that garr'd folks' flesh grue that heard them;—he wasna just himsell, and he had lived wi' a wild set in his day.

At last they parted, and my gudesire was to ride hame through the wood of Pitmurkie, that is a' fou of black firs, as they say.—I ken the wood, but the firs may be black or white for what I can tell.—At the entry of the wood there is a wild common, and on the edge of the common, a little lonely changehouse, that was keepit then by an ostler-wife, they suld hae caa'd her Tibbie Faw, and there puir Steenie cried for a mutchkin of brandy, for he had had no refreshment the haill day. Tibbie was earnest wi' him to take a bite of meat, but he couldna think o't, nor would he take his foot out of the stirrup, and took off the brandy wholely at twa draughts, and named a toast at each:—the first was, the memory of Sir Robert Redgauntlet, and might he never lie quiet in his grave till he had righted his poor bond-tenant; and the second was, a health to Man's Enemy, if he would but get him back the

13. **quean,** young woman. 21. **fasherie,** foolishness. 52. **laith,** loath, reluctant.

18. **wame,** belly. 19. **dyvour,** bankrupt. 19–20. **to the boot of,** in addition to. 22. **saunts,** saints, that is, covenanter martyrs. 27. **wanchancie,** unlucky. 29. **grue,** creep. 34. **can tell.** Remember that Willie was blind. 36–37. **change-house,** small alehouse. 38. **suld hae,** are said to have. 39. **mutchkin,** a measure holding nearly a pint. Note that the brandy was taken on an empty stomach!

pock of siller, or tell him what came o't, for he saw the haill world was like to regard him as a thief and a cheat, and he took that waur than even the ruin of his house and hauld.

On he rode, little caring where. It was a dark night turned, and the trees made it yet darker, and he let the beast take its ain road through the wood; when all of a sudden, from tired and wearied that it was before, the nag began to spring, and flee, and stend, that my gudesire could hardly keep the sad- 10 dle.—Upon the whilk, a horseman, suddenly riding up beside him, said, "That's a mettle beast of yours, freend; will you sell him?"—So saying, he touched the horse's neck with his riding-wand, and it fell into its auld heigh-ho of a stumbling trot. "But his spunk's soon out of him, I think," continued the stranger, "and that is like mony a man's courage, that thinks he wad do great things till he come to the proof."

My gudesire scarce listened to this, but spurred 20 his horse, with "Gude e'en to you, freend."

But it's like the stranger was ane that doesna lightly yield his point; for, ride as Steenie liked, he was aye beside him at the self-same pace. At last my gudesire, Steenie Steenson, grew half angry; and, to say the truth, half feared.

"What is it that ye want with me, freend?" he said. "If ye be a robber, I have nae money; if ye be a leal man, wanting company, I have nae heart to mirth or speaking; and if ye want to ken the 30 road, I scarce ken it mysell."

"If you will tell me your grief," said the stranger, "I am one that, though I have been sair miscaa'd in the world, am the only hand for helping my freends."

So my gudesire, to ease his ain heart, mair than from any hope of help, told him the story from beginning to end.

"It's a hard pinch," said the stranger; "but I think I can help you."

"If you could lend the money, sir, and take a lang day—I ken nae other help on earth," said my gudesire.

"But there may be some under the earth," said the stranger. "Come, I'll be frank wi' you; I could lend you the money on bond, but you would maybe scruple my terms. Now, I can tell you that your auld Laird is disturbed in his grave by your curses, and the wailing of your family, and if ye

daur venture to go to see him, he will give you the receipt."

My gudesire's hair stood on end at this proposal, but he thought his companion might be some humorsome chield that was trying to frighten him, and might end with lending him the money. Besides, he was bauld wi' brandy, and desperate wi' distress, and he said he had courage to go to the gate of hell, and a step farther, for that receipt.— 10 The stranger laughed.

Weel, they rode on through the thickest of the wood, when, all of a sudden, the horse stopped at the door of a great house; and, but that he knew the place was ten miles off, my father would have thought he was at Redgauntlet Castle. They rode into the outer court-yard, through the muckle faulding yetts, and aneath the auld portcullis; and the whole front of the house was lighted, and there were pipes and fiddles, and as much dancing and 20 deray within as used to be in Sir Robert's house at Pace and Yule, and such high seasons. They lap off, and my gudesire, as seemed to him, fastened his horse to the very ring he had tied him to that morning, when he gaed to wait on the young Sir John.

"God!" said my gudesire, "if Sir Robert's death be but a dream!"

He knocked at the ha' door just as he was wont, and his auld acquaintance, Dougal MacCallum, just after his wont, too—came to open the door, and 30 said, "Piper Steenie, are ye there, lad? Sir Robert has been crying for you."

My gudesire was like a man in a dream—he looked for the stranger, but he was gane for the time. At last he just tried to say, "Ha! Dougal Driveower, are ye living? I thought ye had been dead."

"Never fash yoursell wi' me," said Dougal, "but look to yoursell; and see ye tak naething frae ony body here, neither meat, drink, or siller, except just 40 the receipt that is your ain."

So saying, he led the way out through halls and trances that were weel kend to my gudesire, and into the auld oak parlour; and there was as much singing of profane sangs, and birling of red wine, and speaking blasphemy and sculduddry, as had ever been in Redgauntlet Castle when it was at the blithest.

But, Lord take us in keeping, what a set of

---

1. **pock**, bag.   2. **haill**, whole.   4. **hauld**, tenure. 10. **stend**, rear up.   29. **leal**, honest.   46. **on bond**. With the compact between Steenie and the stranger, compare the similar one in Stephen Vincent Benét's story "The Devil and Daniel Webster," in *Thirteen o'Clock*, Farrar and Rinehart, 1937.

17. **faulding yetts**, folding gates.   20. **deray**, disorderly merrymaking.   21. **Pace and Yule**, Easter and Christmas. 37. **fash**, bother.   39–40. **neither . . . siller**, the usual taboo on entering supernatural regions. Acceptance would put the mortal visitor forever under supernatural power. 42. **trances**, passageways.   44. **birling**, drinking. 45. **sculduddry**, blasphemy.

ghastly revellers they were that sat around that table!—My gudesire kend mony that had long before gane to their place, for often had he piped to the most part in the hall of Redgauntlet. There was the fierce Middleton, and the dissolute Rothes, and the crafty Lauderdale; and Dalyell, with his bald head and a beard to his girdle; and Earlshall, with Cameron's blude on his hand; and wild Bonshaw, that tied blessed Mr. Cargill's limbs till the blude sprung; and Dunbarton Douglas, the twice-turned 10 traitor baith to country and king. There was the Bluidy Advocate MacKenyie, who, for his worldly wit and wisdom, had been to the rest as a god. And there was Claverhouse, as beautiful as when he lived, with his long, dark, curled locks streaming down over his laced buff-coat, and his left hand always on his right spule-blade, to hide the wound that the silver bullet had made. He sat apart from them all, and looked at them with a melancholy, haughty countenance; while the rest hallooed, and 20 sung, and laughed, that the room rang. But their smiles were fearfully contorted from time to time; and their laugh passed into such wild sounds, as made my gudesire's very nails grow blue, and chilled the marrow in his banes.

They that waited at the table were just the wicked serving-men and troopers, that had done their work and cruel bidding on earth. There was the Lang Lad of the Nethertown, that helped to take Argyle; and the Bishop's summoner, that they called the 30 Deil's Rattle-bag; and the wicked guardsmen in their laced coats; and the savage Highland Amorites, that shed blood like water; and many a proud serving-man, haughty of heart and bloody of hand, cringing to the rich, and making them wickeder than they would be; grinding the poor to powder, when the rich had broken them to fragments. And mony, mony mair were coming and ganging, a' as busy in their vocation as if they had been alive.

Sir Robert Redgauntlet, in the midst of a' this 40 fearful riot, cried, wi' a voice like thunder, on Steenie Piper to come to the board-head where he was sitting; his legs stretched out before him, and swathed up with flannel, with his holster pistols aside him, while the great broadsword rested against his chair, just as my gudesire had seen him the last time upon earth. The very cushion for the

jackanape was close to him, but the creature itsell was not there—it wasna its hour, it's likely; for he heard them say as he came forward, "Is not the Major come yet?" And another answered, "The jackanape will be here betimes the morn." And when my gudesire came forward, Sir Robert, or his ghaist, or the deevil in his likeness, said, "Weel, piper, hae ye settled wi' my son for the year's rent?"

With much ado my father gat breath to say, that Sir John would not settle without his honour's receipt.

"Ye shall hae that for a tune of the pipes, Steenie," said the appearance of Sir Robert.— "Play us up 'Weel hoddled, Luckie.' "

Now this was a tune my gudesire learned frae a warlock, that heard it when they were worshipping Satan at their meetings; and my gudesire had sometimes played it at the ranting suppers in Redgauntlet Castle, but never very willingly; and now he grew cauld at the very name of it, and said, for excuse, he hadna his pipes wi' him.

"MacCallum, ye limb of Beezlebub," said the fearfu' Sir Robert, "bring Steenie the pipes that I am keeping for him!"

MacCallum brought a pair of pipes might have served the piper of Donald of the Isles. But he gave my gudesire a nudge as he offered them; and looking secretly and closely, Steenie saw that the chanter was of steel, and heated to a white heat; so he had fair warning not to trust his fingers with it. So he excused himself again, and said, he was faint and frightened, and had not wind aneugh to fill the bag.

"Then ye maun eat and drink, Steenie," said the figure; "for we do little else here, and it's ill speaking between a fou man and a fasting."

Now these were the very words that the bloody Earl of Douglas said to keep the king's messenger in hand, while he cut the head off MacLellan of Bombie, at the Threave Castle; and that put Steenie mair and mair on his guard. So he spoke up like a man, and said he came neither to eat, or drink, or make minstrelsy; but simply for his ain—to ken what was come o' the money he had paid, and to get a discharge for it; and he was so stout-hearted by this time that he charged Sir Robert for conscience-sake—(he had no power to say the holy Name) and—as he hoped for peace and rest, to spread no snares for him, but just to give him 50 his ain.

1–2. around that table, one of Scott's greatest descriptive passages—"unsurpassable in apt and graphic phraseology" (T. F. Henderson); "nothing in the Odyssean Tartarus to equal it" (J. C. Shairp).   14. Claverhouse. Scott, who was sentimentally a Jacobite, is said to have kept a portrait of Claverhouse over his desk.   17. spule-blade, shoulder blade.   18. silver bullet. At Killiecrankie Claverhouse was shot with a silver bullet, as this was believed to have the power of killing witches and wizards.

14. 'Weel hoddled, Luckie,' a dance tune supposed to have been composed by the Devil.   29. chanter, finger pipe. 36. fou man, madman.   40. Threave Castle. "The reader is referred for particulars to Pitscottie's History of Scotland." (Scott)

The appearance gnashed its teeth and laughed, but it took from a large pocket-book the receipt, and handed it to Steenie. "There is your receipt, ye pitiful cur; and for the money, my dog-whelp of a son may go look for it in the Cat's Cradle."

My gudesire uttered mony thanks, and was about to retire, when Sir Robert roared aloud, "Stop though, thou sack-doudling son of a whore! I am not done with thee. HERE we do nothing for nothing; and you must return on this very day twelvemonth, to pay your master the homage that you owe me for my protection."

My father's tongue was loosed of a suddenty, and he said aloud, "I refer mysell to God's pleasure, and not to yours."

He had no sooner uttered the word than all was dark around him; and he sunk on the earth with such a sudden shock, that he lost both breath and sense.

How lang Steenie lay there, he could not tell, but when he came to himsell, he was lying in the auld kirkyard of Redgauntlet parochine just at the door of the family aisle, and the skutcheon of the auld knight, Sir Robert, hanging over his head. There was a deep morning fog on grass and gravestane around him, and his horse was feeding quietly beside the minister's twa cows. Steenie would have thought the whole was a dream, but he had the receipt in his hand, fairly written and signed by the auld Laird; only the last letters of his name were a little disorderly, written like one seized with sudden pain.

Sorely troubled in his mind, he left that dreary place, rode through the mist to Redgauntlet Castle, and with much ado he got speech of the Laird.

"Well, you dyvour bankrupt," was the first word, "have you brought me my rent?"

"No," answered my gudesire, "I have not; but I have brought your honour Sir Robert's receipt for it."

"How, sirrah?—Sir Robert's receipt!—You told me he had not given you one."

"Will your honour please to see if that bit line is right?"

Sir John looked at every line, and at every letter, with much attention; and at last at the date, which my gudesire had not observed. "*From my appointed place*," he read, "*this twenty-fifth of November*." "What—That is yesterday!—Villain, thou must have gone to hell for this!"

"I got it from your honour's father—whether he be in heaven or hell, I know not," said Steenie.

"I will delate you for a warlock to the Privy Council!" said Sir John. "I will send you to your master, the devil, with the help of a tar-barrel and a torch!"

"I intend to delate mysell to the Presbytery," said Steenie, "and tell them all I have seen last night, whilk are things fitter for them to judge of than a borrel man like me."

Sir John paused, composed himself, and desired to hear the full history; and my gudesire told it him from point to point, as I have told it you—word for word, neither more nor less.

Sir John was silent again for a long time, and at last he said, very composedly, "Steenie, this story of yours concerns the honour of many a noble family besides mine; and if it be a leasing-making, to keep yourself out of my danger, the least you can expect is to have a redhot iron driven through your tongue, and that will be as bad as scauding your fingers wi' a redhot chanter. But yet it may be true, Steenie; and if the money cast up, I shall not know what to think of it.—But where shall we find the Cat's Cradle? There are cats enough about the old house, but I think they kitten without the ceremony of bed or cradle."

"We were best ask Hutcheon," said my gudesire; "he kens a' the odd corners about as weel as—another serving-man that is now gane, and that I wad not like to name."

Aweel, Hutcheon, when he was asked, told them that a ruinous turret, lang disused, next to the clock-house, only accessible by a ladder, for the opening was on the outside, and far above the battlements, was called of old the Cat's Cradle.

"There will I go immediately," said Sir John; and he took (with what purpose Heaven kens) one of his father's pistols from the hall-table, where they had lain since the night he died, and hastened to the battlements.

It was a dangerous place to climb, for the ladder was auld and frail, and wanted ane or two rounds. However, up got Sir John, and entered at the turret door, where his body stopped the only little light that was in the bit turret. Something flees at him wi' a vengeance, maist dang him back ower—bang gaed the knight's pistol, and Hutcheon, that held the ladder, and my gudesire that stood beside him, hears a loud skelloch. A minute after, Sir John flings the body of the jackanape down to them, and cries that the siller is fund, and that they should come up and help him. And there was the bag of siller sure aneugh, and mony orra things besides,

---

8. **sack-doudling,** bagpipe-playing.   22. **kirkyard,** churchyard.   22. **parochine,** parish.

8. **borrel,** rough, unlearned.   16. **leasing-making,** lying. 45. **dang,** knocked.   48. **skelloch,** screech.

that had been missing for mony a day. And Sir John, when he had riped the turret weel, led my gudesire into the dining-parlour, and took him by the hand, and spoke kindly to him, and said he was sorry he should have doubted his word, and that he would hereafter be a good master to him, to make amends.

"And now, Steenie," said Sir John, "although this vision of yours tends, on the whole, to my father's credit, as an honest man, that he should, even after his death, desire to see justice done to a poor man like you, yet you are sensible that ill-dispositioned men might make bad constructions upon it, concerning his soul's health. So, I think, we had better lay the haill dirdum on that ill-deedie creature, Major Weir, and say naething about your dream in the wood of Pitmurkie. You had taken ower muckle brandy to be very certain about ony thing; and, Steenie, this receipt," (his hand shook while he held it out,)—"it's but a queer kind of document, and we will do best, I think, to put it quietly in the fire."

"Od, but for as queer as it is, it's a' the voucher I have for my rent" said my gudesire, who was afraid, it may be, of losing the benefit of Sir Robert's discharge.

"I will bear the contents to your credit in the rental-book, and give you a discharge under my own hand," said Sir John, "and that on the spot. And, Steenie, if you can hold your tongue about this matter, you shall sit, from this term downward, at an easier rent."

"Mony thanks to your honour," said Steenie, who saw easily in what corner the wind was; "doubtless I will be conformable to all your honour's commands; only I would willingly speak wi' some powerful minister on the subject, for I do not like the sort of soumons of appointment whilk your honour's father——"

"Do not call the phantom my father!" said Sir John, interrupting him.

"Weel, then, the thing that was so like him," said my gudesire; "he spoke of my coming back to see him this time twelvemonth, and it's a weight on my conscience."

2. riped, searched. 15. dirdum, hullabaloo.

"Aweel, then," said Sir John, "if you be so much distressed in mind, you may speak to our minister of the parish. He is a douce man, regards the honour of our family, and the mair that he may look for some patronage from me."

Wi' that, my gudesire readily agreed that the receipt should be burnt, and the Laird threw it into the chimney with his ain hand. Burn it would not for them, though; but away it flew up the lum, wi' a lang train of sparks at its tail, and a hissing noise like a squib.

My gudesire gaed down to the Manse, and the minister, when he had heard the story, said it was his real opinion that, though my gudesire had gaen very far in tampering with dangerous matters, yet, as he had refused the devil's arles, (for such was the offer of meat and drink,) and had refused to do homage by piping at his bidding, he hoped, that if he held a circumspect walk hereafter, Satan could take little advantage by what was come and gane. And, indeed, my gudesire, of his ain accord, lang foreswore baith the pipes and the brandy—it was not even till the year was out, and the fatal day past, that he would so much as take the fiddle, or drink usquebaugh or tippenny.

Sir John made up his story about the jackanape as he liked himsell; and some believe till this day there was no more in the matter than the filching nature of the brute. Indeed, ye'll no hinder some to threap, that it was nane o' the auld Enemy that Dougal and my gudesire saw in the Laird's room, but only that wanchancy creature, the Major, capering on the coffin; and that, as to the blawing on the Laird's whistle that was heard after he was dead, the filthy brute could do that as well as the Laird himsell, if no better. But Heaven kens the truth, whilk first came out by the minister's wife, after Sir John and her ain gudeman were baith in the moulds. And then my gudesire, wha was failed in his limbs, but not in his judgment or memory—at least nothing to speak of—was obliged to tell the real narrative to his freends, for the credit of his good name. He might else have been charged for a warlock.

3. douce, sensible, prudent. 9. lum, chimney. 16. arles, earnest money. 25. usquebaugh or tippenny, whisky or twopenny ale. 30. threap, hint.

Walter Savage Landor
1775–1864

Walter Savage Landor was born January 30, 1775, heir to the lands of an old Staffordshire and Warwickshire family. He spent his early childhood in the Shakespeare country. His way to school led him past the home of Joseph Addison's daughter. Of his school days at Rugby he boasted to a friend, seventy years later,

> "you remember that I fought
> Never with any but an older lad,
> And never lost but two fights in thirteen."

He was dismissed from Rugby as the result of a violent quarrel, in which he was right at first, with a teacher over a Latin quantity. At Oxford he wore his hair unpowdered, in defiance of custom, and was known as "a mad Jacobin." His university career was terminated by an incident in which he fired a shotgun at the window of a Tory undergraduate who had taunted him. Despite these disciplinary irregularities, Landor was recognized as a brilliant student and a promising poet. In 1795 he brought out his first volume, *Poems*. Having settled the Oxford business with his family, he went to live in South Wales. In that romantic region he met Rose Aylmer, who lent him a history of romance from which he got the plot for his first ambitious poem, an epic in Miltonic blank verse, entitled *Gebir*. This poem, about the love of the Spanish prince Gebir and the Egyptian princess Charoba, was published in 1798, and because of its stylistic splendor almost rivals *Lyrical Ballads* in marking the triumph of the Romantic Movement. Political controversy in London, a brief military experience in Spain, a disastrous experiment in social improvement on his estate of Llanthony in Wales, an imprudent marriage with a charming girl much younger than he, attempts at drama (*Count Julian*), and wanderings over the Continent occupied Landor, more or less futilely, until he settled down in Florence, Italy, in 1821. Living in the Medici palace, he began the most famous of his works, *Imaginary Conversations*. The rest of his life was made up of literary activity, friendships, and quarrels. "I never did a single wise thing in the whole course of my existence, although I have written many which have been thought such," he confessed in his last

years. His friendships with such men as Ralph Waldo Emerson, Wordsworth, Southey, and Robert Browning minimize our impression of his folly and violence. Before he died, on September 17, 1864, he took "a momentary pleasure and interest in the visit of the young English poet, Mr. Swinburne . . . who had made a pilgrimage to Florence on purpose to see the old man's face before he died."

Three features distinguish Landor's literary character and career. The first is the longevity and vitality of his genius. His first volume, *Poems*, was published in 1795, three years before *Lyrical Ballads;* his last, *Heroic Idyls*, in 1863, long after Tennyson, Browning, and the other great Victorians had become famous. Comparing the poems written during this period of sixty-eight years, we find that those composed in his old age, such as "The Hamadryad" (published when he was seventy-one), are as fresh as those of his young manhood, such as "Rose Aylmer" (published at thirty-one). Landor's second distinction is a sort of double ambidexterity. He wrote in Latin as easily as in English; he is equally good in poetry and in prose. The main difference between one of the poetical *Hellenics*, such as "Iphigeneia," and one of the prose *Imaginary Conversations*, such as "Tiberius and Vipsania," is the meter. The same qualities of "passionless feeling and impassioned thinking," of calm and stately strength, of control and repose, are in both. Finally, Landor is celebrated for the "strange fashion in which romantic and classic were blended in his work." He has been called "a classic writing in the Romantic age." The classic manner, explains Sir Sidney Colvin, is sharp outlines in a white light, naked and distinct; the romantic is a colored and iridescent atmosphere, glow of spirit, and magic and richness of suggestion.

To an age of ballyhoo Landor's stoic aloofness and serene indifference should be attractive by sheer contrast. "I shall dine late," he wrote; "but the dining-room will be well lighted, the guests few but select." To the elect guest he offers the company of famous men and women of the past, the epigrammatic utterance of such deathless emotions as that recorded in "Rose Aylmer," the quiet, haunting beauty of such pictures as that in "The Death of Artemidora."

ROSE AYLMER

Ah what avails the sceptred race,
  Ah what the form divine!
What every virtue, every grace!
  Rose Aylmer, all were thine.
Rose Aylmer, whom these wakeful eyes
  May weep, but never see,
A night of memories and of sighs
  I consecrate to thee.

PAST RUINED ILION

Past ruined Ilion Helen lives,
  Alcestis rises from the shades;
Verse calls them forth; 'tis verse that gives
  Immortal youth to mortal maids.

Soon shall Oblivion's deepening veil
  Hide all the peopled hills you see,
The gay, the proud, while lovers hail
  In distant ages you and me.

The tear for fading beauty check,
  For passing glory cease to sigh;   10
One form shall rise above the wreck,
  One name, Ianthe, shall not die.

WELL I REMEMBER HOW
YOU SMILED

Well I remember how you smiled
  To see me write your name upon
The soft sea-sand. "*O! what a child!
  You think you're writing upon stone!*"
I have since written what no tide
  Shall ever wash away, what men
Unborn shall read o'er ocean wide
  And find Ianthe's name again.

THE DEATH OF ARTEMIDORA

"Artemidora! Gods invisible,
  While thou art lying faint along the couch,

Past Ruined Ilion. **1. Ilion,** Troy. **2. Alcestis,** who died to save the life of her husband, King Admetus of Thessaly, and was brought back from Hades by Hercules. **12. Ianthe.** Southey addressed many poems (including the one that follows) to this name, supposed to represent Jane Sophia Swifte.

Have tied the sandal to thy veinèd feet
And stand beside thee, ready to convey
Thy weary steps where other rivers flow.
Refreshing shades will waft thy weariness
Away, and voices like thy own come nigh
Soliciting, nor vainly, thy embrace."
  Artemidora sighed, and would have pressed
The hand now pressing hers, but was too weak.   10
Fate's shears were over her dark hair unseen
While thus Elpenor spake: he looked into
Eyes that had given light and life erewhile
To those above them, those now dim with tears
And watchfulness. Again he spake of joy
Eternal. At that word, that sad word, *joy,*
Faithful and fond her bosom heaved once more:
Her head fell back; one sob, one loud deep sob
Swelled through the darkened chamber; 'twas not
  hers:
With her that old boat incorruptible,   20
Unwearied, undiverted in its course,
Had plashed the water up the farther strand.

ON SEEING A HAIR
OF LUCRETIA BORGIA

Borgia, thou once wert almost too august
And high for adoration;—now thou'rt dust;
All that remains of thee these plaits infold,
Calm hair, meandering with pellucid gold!

TO WORDSWORTH

Those who have laid the harp aside
  And turned to idler things,
From very restlessness have tried
  The loose and dusty strings;
And, catching back some favourite strain,
Run with it o'er the chords again.

But Memory is not a Muse,
  O Wordsworth!—though 'tis said
They all descend from her, and use
  To haunt her fountain-head: 10

12–17. he looked into . . . once more. Note the indirect way of indicating the relationship between the two—characteristic of Landor's technique. **19. 'twas not hers,** indirection again. **20. old boat,** Charon's. Charon ferried souls across the Styx. He could not be bribed. **7. But Memory is not a Muse.** Note in the following passage Landor's tactful treatment of the point that Wordsworth had possibly been relying too much on his memories and that his poetic powers were waning. Compare Wordsworth's treatment of the problem in "Resolution and Independence" and "Ode: Intimations."

That other men should work for me
In the rich mines of Poesie,
Pleases me better than the toil
   Of smoothing under hardened hand
With attic emery and oil,
   The shining point for Wisdom's wand;
Like those thou temperest 'mid the rills
Descending from thy native hills.

Without his governance, in vain
   Manhood is strong, and youth is bold.   20
If oftentimes the o'er-piled strain
   Clogs in the furnace, and grows cold,
Beneath his pinions deep and frore,
And swells, and melts, and flows no more,
That is because the heat beneath,
   Pants in its cavern poorly fed.
Life springs not from the couch of Death,
   Nor Muse nor Grace can raise the dead;
Unturned then let the mass remain,
Intractable to sun or rain.   30

A marsh, where only flat leaves lie,
And showing but the broken sky,
Too surely is the sweetest lay
That wins the ear and wastes the day;
Where youthful Fancy pouts alone
And lets not Wisdom touch her zone.
He who would build his fame up high,
The rule and plummet must apply,
Nor say—"I'll do what I have planned,"
Before he try if loam or sand   40
Be still remaining in the place
Delved for each polished pillar's base.
With skilful eye and fit device
Thou raisest every edifice:
Whether in sheltered vale it stand,
Or overlook the Dardan strand,
Amid the cypresses that mourn
Laodamia's love forlorn.

We both have run o'er half the space,
Listed for mortals' earthly race;   50
We both have crossed life's fervid line,
And other stars before us shine:
May they be bright and prosperous
As those that have been stars for us!
Our course by Milton's light was sped,
And Shakspeare shining overhead:
Chatting on deck was Dryden too,
The Bacon of the rhyming crew;

None ever crossed our mystic sea,
More richly stored with thought than he;   60
Though never tender nor sublime,
He wrestles with and conquers Time.
To learn my lore on Chaucer's knee,
I left much prouder company.
Thee, gentle Spenser fondly led;
But me he mostly sent to bed.

I wish them every joy above
That highly blessed spirits prove,
Save one: and that too shall be theirs,
But after many rolling years,   70
When 'mid their light, thy light appears.

TWENTY YEARS HENCE

Twenty years hence my eyes may grow
If not quite dim, yet rather so,
Still yours from others they shall know
    Twenty years hence.

Twenty years hence though it may hap
That I be called to take a nap
In a cool cell where thunder-clap
    Was never heard,

There breathe but o'er my arch of grass
A not too sadly sighed *Alas*,   10
And I shall catch, ere you can pass,
    That wingèd word.

TO ROBERT BROWNING

There is delight in singing, though none hear
Beside the singer; and there is delight
In praising, though the praiser sit alone
And see the praised far off him, far above.
   Shakspeare is not our poet, but the world's,
   Therefore on him no speech; and short for thee,
Browning! Since Chaucer was alive and hale,
No man hath walked along our roads with step
So active, so inquiring eye, or tongue
So varied in discourse. But warmer climes   10
Give brighter plumage, strong wing: the breeze
Of Alpine heights thou playest with, borne on
Beyond Sorrento and Amalfi, where
The Siren waits thee, singing song for song.

15. **attic,** refined. 23. **frore,** frozen. 36. **zone,** girdle.
46. **Dardan,** Trojan. 48. **Laodamia's love,** an allusion
to Wordsworth's poem "Laodamia."

Twenty Years Hence. 9. **arch of grass.** Compare Tennyson's "Maud," ll. 357 ff. 13. **Sorrento and Amalfi,** in Italy.

from THE HELLENICS

THRASYMEDES AND EUNÖE

Who will away to Athens with me? who
Loves choral songs and maidens crowned with
    flowers,
Unenvious? mount the pinnace; hoist the sail.
I promise ye, as many as are here,
Ye shall not, while ye tarry with me, taste
From unrinsed barrel the diluted wine
Of a low vineyard or a plant ill-pruned,
But such as anciently the Aegean isles
Poured in libation at their solemn feasts:
And the same goblets shall ye grasp, embossed   10
With no vile figures of loose languid boors,
But such as Gods have lived with, and have led.

The sea smiles bright before us. What white sail
Plays yonder? What pursues it? Like two hawks
Away they fly. Let us away in time
To overtake them. Are they menaces
We hear? And shall the strong repulse the weak,
Enraged at her defender? Hippias!
Art thou the man? 'Twas Hippias. He had found
His sister borne from the Cecropian port   20
By Thrasymedes. And reluctantly?
Ask, ask the maiden; I have no reply.
"Brother! O brother Hippias! O, if love,
If pity, ever toucht thy breast, forbear!
Strike not the brave, the gentle, the beloved,
My Thrasymedes, with his cloak alone
Protecting his own head and mine from harm."
"Didst thou not once before," cried Hippias,
Regardless of his sister, hoarse with wrath
At Thrasymedes, "didst not thou, dog-eyed,   30
Dare, as she walkt up to the Parthenon,
On the most holy of all holy days,
In sight of all the city, dare to kiss
Her maiden cheek?"
                    "Aye, before all the Gods,
Aye, before Pallas, before Artemis,
Aye, before Aphrodite, before Hera,
I dared; and dare again. Arise, my spouse!
Arise! and let my lips quaff purity
From thy fair open brow."
                        The sword was up,
And yet he kisst her twice. Some God withheld   40
The arm of Hippias; his proud blood seethed slower
And smote his breast less angrily; he laid
His hand on the white shoulder, and spake thus:
"Ye must return with me. A second time
Offended, will our sire Pisistratos

20. **Cecropian port**, Athens.   45. **Pisistratos**, tyrant of
Athens (605-527 B.C.).

Pardon the affront? Thou shouldst have askt thy-
    self
This question ere the sail first flapt the mast."
"Already thou hast taken life from me;
Put up thy sword," said the sad youth, his eyes
Sparkling; but whether love or rage or grief   50
They sparkled with, the Gods alone could see.
Piraeus they re-entered, and their ship
Drove up the little waves against the quay,
Whence was thrown out a rope from one above,
And Hippias caught it. From the virgin's waist
Her lover dropt his arm, and blusht to think
He had retained it there in sight of rude
Irreverent men: he led her forth, nor spake;
Hippias walkt silent too, until they reacht
The mansion of Pisistratos her sire.   60
Serenely in his sternness did the prince
Look on them both awhile: they saw not him,
For both had cast their eyes upon the ground.
"Are these the pirates thou hast taken, son?"
Said he. "Worse, father! worse than pirates they,
Who thus abuse thy patience, thus abuse
Thy pardon, thus abuse the holy rites
Twice over."
            "Well hast thou performed thy duty,"
Firmly and gravely said Pisistratos.
"Nothing then, rash young man! could turn thy
    heart   70
From Eunöe, my daughter?"
                        "Nothing, sir,
Shall ever turn it. I can die but once
And love but once. O Eunöe! farewell!"
"Nay, she shall see what thou canst bear for her."
"O father! shut me in my chamber, shut me
In my poor mother's tomb, dead or alive,
But never let me see what he can bear;
I know how much that is, when borne for me."
"Not yet: come on. And lag not thou behind,
Pirate of virgin and of princely hearts!   80
Before the people and before the Goddess
Thou hadst evinced the madness of thy passion,
And now wouldst bear from home and plenteous-
    ness
To poverty and exile, this my child."
Then shuddered Thrasymedes, and exclaimed,
"I see my crime; I saw it not before.
The daughter of Pisistratos was born
Neither for exile nor for poverty,
Ah! nor for me!" He would have wept, but one
Might see him, and weep worse. The prince un-
    moved   90
Strode on, and said, "To-morrow shall the people,
All who beheld thy trespasses, behold

52. **Piraeus,** the port of Athens.

The justice of Pisistratos, the love
He bears his daughter, and the reverence
In which he holds the highest law of God."
   He spake; and on the morrow they were one.

IPHIGENEIA AND AGAMEMNON

Iphigeneia, when she heard her doom
At Aulis, and when all beside the king
Had gone away, took his right-hand, and said,
"O father! I am young and very happy.
I do not think the pious Calchas heard
Distinctly what the Goddess spake. Old-age
Obscures the senses. If my nurse, who knew
My voice so well, sometimes misunderstood,
While I was resting on her knee both arms
And hitting it to make her mind my words,   10
And looking in her face, and she in mine,
Might he not also hear one word amiss,
Spoken from so far off, even from Olympus?"
The father placed his cheek upon her head,
And tears dropt down it, but the king of men
Replied not. Then the maiden spake once more.
"O father! sayst thou nothing? Hear'st thou not
Me, whom thou ever hast, until this hour,
Listened to fondly, and awakened me
To hear my voice amid the voice of birds,   20
When it was inarticulate as theirs,
And the down deadened it within the nest?"
He moved her gently from him, silent still,
And this, and this alone, brought tears from her,
Although she saw fate nearer: then with sighs,
"I thought to have laid down my hair before
Benignant Artemis, and not have dimmed
Her polisht altar with my virgin blood;
I thought to have selected the white flowers
To please the Nymphs, and to have askt of each   30
By name, and with no sorrowful regret,
Whether, since both my parents willed the change,
I might at Hymen's feet bend my clipt brow;
And (after those who mind us girls the most)
Adore our own Athena, that she would
Regard me mildly with her azure eyes.
But, father! to see you no more, and see
Your love, O father! go ere I am gone!"—
Gently he moved her off, and drew her back,
Bending his lofty head far over hers,   40
And the dark depths of nature heaved and burst.

He turned away; not far, but silent still.
She now first shuddered; for in him, so nigh,
So long a silence seemed the approach of death,
And like it. Once again she raised her voice.
"O father! if the ships are now detained,
And all your vows move not the Gods above,
When the knife strikes me there will be one prayer
The less to them: and purer can there be
Any, or more fervent than the daughter's prayer   50
For her dear father's safety and success?"
A groan that shook him shook not his resolve.
An aged man now entered, and without
One word, stept slowly on, and took the wrist
Of the pale maiden. She lookt up, and saw
The fillet of the priest and calm cold eyes.
Then turned she where her parent stood, and cried
"O father! grieve no more: the ships can sail."

DEATH STANDS ABOVE ME

Death stands above me, whispering low
   I know not what into my ear:
Of his strange language all I know
   Is, there is not a word of fear.

ON HIS SEVENTY-FIFTH
BIRTHDAY

I strove with none, for none was worth my strife:
   Nature I loved, and, next to Nature, Art:
I warmed both hands before the fire of Life;
   It sinks; and I am ready to depart.

THE THREE ROSES

When the buds began to burst,
Long ago, with Rose the First,
I was walking; joyous then
Far above all other men,
Till before us up there stood
Britonferry's oaken wood,
Whispering, "*Happy as thou art,
Happiness and thou must part.*"
Many summers have gone by
Since a Second Rose and I   10
(Rose from that same stem) have told
This and other tales of old.
She upon her wedding-day

---

96. they were one. Again, the oblique way of saying
—what? **1. her doom.** Agamemnon had killed a deer in
the sacred grove of Artemis. In punishment, Artemis had
becalmed the Greek fleet, on its way to Troy. The oracle had
declared that the fleet would not sail unless Agamemnon
sacrificed his daughter to Artemis.

The Three Roses. **2. Rose the First,** Rose Aylmer. **6.
Britonferry,** Briton Ferry in Wales. **10. Second Rose,** the
daughter of Rose Aylmer's half-sister.

Carried home my tenderest lay:
From her lap I now have heard
Gleeful, chirping, Rose the Third,
Not for *her* this hand of mine
Rhyme with nuptial wreath shall twine;
Cold and torpid it must lie,
Mute the tongue, and closed the eye.   20

TO MY NINTH DECADE

To my ninth decade I have tottered on,
  And no soft arm bends now my steps to steady;
She, who once led me where she would, is gone,
  So when he calls me, Death shall find me ready.

from IMAGINARY CONVERSATIONS

There are two classes of *Imaginary Conversations:* those which treat short and stirring scenes, and are full of action and emotion; and those which treat long and quiet scenes, and are full of discussion and reflection. Our following selections are of the first class. In writing the *Conversations,* Landor observed two rules: first, there was to be no direct narrative, and the stage directions were to be as few as possible; second, the speakers were to be real persons, living or dead. As a result of the first rule for dramatic presentation, the reader is compelled, for clear understanding, to notice closely all suggestions of setting, situation, stage direction, and dress, mood, and gesture of the characters. Close attention to details is rewarded by the glow of satisfaction that comes from co-operating with a skillful dramatic writer. The careful reader will enjoy nuances of indirection and suggestion like those which have been partially noted in Landor's poems.

MARCELLUS AND HANNIBAL

The time is the Second Punic War, between Rome and Carthage, for the mastery of the world. After the overwhelming defeat of the Romans at Cannae, in a skirmish at Venusia (208 B.C.), Marcellus, the young Roman general, has been mortally wounded and captured by the Gaulish forces of Hannibal, the Carthaginian commander. Hannibal arrives on the scene, at first excited and exultant. Note how his mood softens as he magnanimously realizes that he is facing a dying man. Note, too, the Roman serenity of Marcellus, concerned first about his country, then about his son.

Hannibal. Could a Numidian horseman ride **no** faster? Marcellus! oh! Marcellus! He moves not —he is dead. Did he not stir his fingers? Stand wide, soldiers—wide, forty paces—give him air— bring water—halt! Gather those broad leaves, and all the rest, growing under the brushwood—unbrace his armour. Loose the helmet first—his breast rises. I fancied his eyes were fixed on me—they have rolled back again. Who presumed to touch my shoulder? This horse? It was surely the horse of Marcellus! Let no man mount him. Ha! ha! the Romans, too, sink into luxury: here is gold about the charger.

Gaulish Chieftain. Execrable thief! The golden chain of our king under a beast's grinders! The vengeance of the gods hath overtaken the impure——

Hannibal. We will talk about vengeance when we have entered Rome, and about purity among the priests, if they will hear us. Sound for the surgeon. That arrow may be extracted from the side, deep as it is.—The conqueror of Syracuse lies before me.— Send a vessel off to Carthage. Say Hannibal is at the gates of Rome.—Marcellus, who stood alone between us, fallen. Brave man! I would rejoice and cannot.—How awfully serene a countenance! Such as we hear are in the islands of the Blessed. And how glorious a form and stature! Such too was theirs! They also once lay thus upon the earth wet with their blood—few other enter there. And what plain armour!

Gaulish Chieftain. My party slew him—indeed I think I slew him myself. I claim the chain: it belongs to my king; the glory of Gaul requires it. Never will she endure to see another take it.

Hannibal. My friend, the glory of Marcellus did not require him to wear it. When he suspended the arms of your brave king in the temple, he thought such a trinket unworthy of himself and of Jupiter. The shield he battered down, the breast-plate he pierced with his sword—these he showed to the people and to the gods; hardly his wife and little children saw this, ere his horse wore it.

Gaulish Chieftain. Hear me, O Hannibal!

Hannibal. What! when Marcellus lies before me? when his life may perhaps be recalled? when I may lead him in triumph to Carthage? when Italy, Sicily, Greece, Asia, wait to obey me? Content thee! I will give thee mine own bridle, worth ten such.

Gaulish Chieftain. For myself?

Hannibal. For thyself.

Gaulish Chieftain. And these rubies and emeralds, and that scarlet——

Hannibal. Yes, yes.

Gaulish Chieftain. O glorious Hannibal! unconquerable hero! O my happy country! to have such

The Three Roses. **14. lay,** "To a Bride." **16. Rose the Third,** Rose Aylmer's grand-niece. **48. no faster.** Note Hannibal's breathless sentences.

10. Gaulish Chieftain. What dramatic use is made of him? **21. serene a countenance!** Hannibal begins to think of Marcellus as a human being, not merely a fallen foe.

an ally and defender. I swear eternal gratitude—yes, gratitude, love, devotion, beyond eternity.

Hannibal. In all treaties we fix the time: I could hardly ask a longer. Go back to thy station.—I would see what the surgeon is about, and hear what he thinks. The life of Marcellus! the triumph of Hannibal! what else has the world in it? Only Rome and Carthage: these follow.

Marcellus. I must die then? The gods be praised! The commander of a Roman army is no captive.

Hannibal (to the Surgeon). Could not he bear a sea-voyage? Extract the arrow.

Surgeon. He expires that moment.

Marcellus. It pains me: extract it.

Hannibal. Marcellus, I see no expression of pain on your countenance, and never will I consent to hasten the death of an enemy in my power. Since your recovery is hopeless, you say truly you are no captive.

(*To the Surgeon.*) Is there nothing, man, that can assuage the mortal pain? for, suppress the signs of it as he may, he must feel it. Is there nothing to alleviate and allay it?

Marcellus. Hannibal, give me thy hand—thou hast found it and brought it me, compassion.

(*To the Surgeon.*) Go, friend; others want thy aid; several fell around me.

Hannibal. Recommend to your country, O Marcellus, while time permits it, reconciliation and peace with me, informing the Senate of my superiority in force, and the impossibility of resistance. The tablet is ready: let me take off this ring—try to write, to sign it, at least. Oh, what satisfaction I feel at seeing you able to rest upon the elbow, and even to smile!

Marcellus. Within an hour or less, with how severe a brow would Minos say to me, "Marcellus, is this thy writing?"

Rome loses one man: she hath lost many such, 40 and she still hath many left.

Hannibal. Afraid as you are of falsehood, say you this? I confess in shame the ferocity of my country-men. Unfortunately, too, the nearer posts are occupied by Gauls, infinitely more cruel. The Numidians are so in revenge; the Gauls both in revenge and in sport. My presence is required at a distance, and I apprehend the barbarity of one or other, learning, as they must do, your refusal to execute my wishes for the common good, and feeling that by this refusal you deprive them of their country, after so long an absence.

Marcellus. Hannibal, thou art not dying.

40–41. Rome loses . . . left. Note the old Roman spirit.

Hannibal. What then? What mean you?

Marcellus. That thou mayest, and very justly, have many things yet to apprehend: I can have none. The barbarity of thy soldiers is nothing to me: mine would not dare be cruel. Hannibal is forced to be absent; and his authority goes away with his horse. On this turf lies defaced the semblance of a general; but Marcellus is yet the regulator of his 10 army. Dost thou abdicate a power conferred on thee by thy nation? Or wouldst thou acknowledge it to have become, by thy own sole fault, less plenary than thy adversary's?

I have spoken too much: let me rest; this mantle oppresses me.

Hannibal. I placed my mantle on your head when the helmet was first removed, and while you were lying in the sun. Let me fold it under, and then replace the ring.

Marcellus. Take it, Hannibal. It was given me by 20 a poor woman who flew to me at Syracuse, and who covered it with her hair, torn off in desperation that she had no other gift to offer. Little thought I that her gift and her words should be mine. How suddenly may the most powerful be in the situation of the most helpless! Let that ring and the mantle under my head be the exchange of guests at parting. The time may come, Hannibal, when thou (and the gods alone know whether as conqueror or conquered) mayest sit under the roof of my children, 30 and in either case it shall serve thee. In thy adverse fortune, they will remember on whose pillow their father breathed his last; in thy prosperous (Heaven grant it may shine upon thee in some other country!) it will rejoice thee to protect them. We feel ourselves the most exempt from affliction when we relieve it, although we are then the most conscious that it may befall us.

There is one thing here which is not at the disposal of either.

Hannibal. What?

Marcellus. This body.

Hannibal. Whither would you be lifted? Men are ready.

Marcellus. I meant not so. My strength is failing. I seem to hear rather what is within than what is without. My sight and my other senses are in confusion. I would have said—This body, when a few bubbles of air shall have left it, is no more worthy of thy notice than of mine; but thy glory will not 50 let thee refuse it to the piety of my family.

Hannibal. You would ask something else. I perceive an inquietude not visible till now.

8. yet the regulator, Roman discipline. Note the Latinity of the style.

Marcellus. Duty and Death make us think of home sometimes.

Hannibal. Thitherward the thoughts of the conqueror and of the conquered fly together.

Marcellus. Hast thou any prisoners from my escort?

Hannibal. A few dying lie about—and let them lie—they are Tuscans. The remainder I saw at a distance, flying, and but one brave man among them—he appeared a Roman—a youth who turned back, though wounded. They surrounded and dragged him away, spurring his horse with their swords. These Etrurians measure their courage carefully, and tack it well together before they put it on, but throw it off again with lordly ease.

Marcellus, why think about them? or does aught else disquiet your thoughts?

Marcellus. I have suppressed it long enough. My son—my beloved son!

Hannibal. Where is he? Can it be? Was he with you?

Marcellus. He would have shared my fate—and has not. Gods of my country! beneficent throughout life to me, in death surpassingly beneficent: I render you, for the last time, thanks.

LEOFRIC AND GODIVA

According to legend, Leofric and Godiva lived, about 1040, in the Anglo-Saxon Kingdom of Mercia, where Leofric was Earl, and Lord of the city of Coventry. The two are riding into Coventry after the honeymoon, Leofric in a bad temper because his poverty-stricken vassals will not pay their feudal dues, Godiva moved by pity for her people. Note the dramatic use of the Bishop, to irritate Leofric further and, as a result of his bride's (to him) unseemly behavior, to provoke his rash oath.

Godiva. There is a dearth in the land, my sweet Leofric! Remember how many weeks of drought we have had, even in the deep pastures of Leicestershire; and how many Sundays we have heard the same prayers for rain, and supplications that it would please the Lord in his mercy to turn aside his anger from the poor, pining cattle. You, my dear husband, have imprisoned more than one malefactor for leaving his dead ox in the public way; and other hinds have fled before you out of the traces, in which they, and their sons and their daughters, and haply their old fathers and mothers, were dragging the abandoned wain homeward.

Although we were accompanied by many brave spearmen and skilful archers, it was perilous to pass the creatures which the farm-yard dogs, driven from the hearth by the poverty of their masters, were tearing and devouring; while others, bitten and lamed, filled the air either with long and deep howls or sharp and quick barkings, as they struggled with hunger and feebleness, or were exasperated by heat and pain. Nor could the thyme from the heath, nor the bruised branches of the fir-tree, extinguish or abate the foul odour.

Leofric. And now, Godiva, my darling, thou art afraid we should be eaten up before we enter the gates of Coventry; or perchance that in the gardens there are no roses to greet thee, no sweet herbs for thy mat and pillow.

Godiva. Leofric, I have no such fears. This is the month of roses: I find them everywhere since my blessed marriage. They, and all other sweet herbs, I know not why, seem to greet me wherever I look at them, as though they knew and expected me. Surely they cannot feel that I am fond of them.

Leofric. O light, laughing simpleton! But what wouldst thou? I came not hither to pray; and yet if praying would satisfy thee, or remove the drought, I would ride up straightway to Saint Michael's and pray until morning.

Godiva. I would do the same, O Leofric! but God hath turned away his ear from holier lips than mine. Would my own dear husband hear me, if I implored him for what is easier to accomplish,—what he can do like God?

Leofric. How! what is it?

Godiva. I would not, in the first hurry of your wrath, appeal to you, my loving Lord, in behalf of these unhappy men who have offended you.

Leofric. Unhappy! is that all?

Godiva. Unhappy they must surely be, to have offended you so grievously. What a soft air breathes over us! how quiet and serene and still an evening! how calm the heavens and the earth!—Shall none enjoy them; not even we, my Leofric? The sun is ready to set: let it never set, O Leofric, on your anger. These are not my words: they are better than mine. Should they lose their virtue from my unworthiness in uttering them?

Leofric. Godiva, wouldst thou plead to me for rebels?

Godiva. They have, then, drawn the sword against you? Indeed, I knew it not.

Leofric. They have omitted to send me my dues, established by my ancestors, well knowing of our nuptials, and of the charges and festivities they re-

---

25. thanks. Why? **39. dearth in the land.** Compare the technique of exposition here with that used in "Marcellus and Hannibal."

quire, and that in a season of such scarcity my own lands are insufficient.

Godiva. If they were starving, as they said they were——

Leofric. Must I starve too? Is it not enough to lose my vassals?

Godiva. Enough! O God! too much! too much! May you never lose them! Give them life, peace, comfort, contentment. There are those among them who kissed me in my infancy, and who blessed me at the baptismal font. Leofric, Leofric! the first old man I meet I shall think is one of those; and I shall think on the blessing he gave, and (ah me!) on the blessing I bring back to him. My heart will bleed, will burst; and he will weep at it! he will weep, poor soul, for the wife of a cruel lord who denounces vengeance on him, who carries death into his family!

Leofric. We must hold solemn festivals.

Godiva. We must, indeed.

Leofric. Well, then?

Godiva. Is the clamorousness that succeeds the death of God's dumb creatures, are crowded halls, are slaughtered cattle, festivals?—are maddening songs, and giddy dances, and hireling praises from parti-colored coats? Can the voice of a minstrel tell us better things of ourselves than our own internal one might tell us; or can his breath make our breath softer in sleep? O my beloved! let everything be a joyance to us: it will, if we will. Sad is the day, and worse must follow, when we hear the blackbird in the garden, and do not throb with joy. But, Leofric, the high festival is strown by the servant of God upon the heart of man. It is gladness, it is thanksgiving; it is the orphan, the starveling, pressed to the bosom, and bidden as its first commandment to remember its benefactor. We will hold this festival; the guests are ready: we may keep it up for weeks, and months, and years together, and always be the happier and the richer for it. The beverage of this feast, O Leofric, is sweeter than bee or flower or vine can give us: it flows from heaven; and in heaven will it abundantly be poured out again to him who pours it out here abundantly.

Leofric. Thou art wild.

Godiva. I have, indeed, lost myself. Some Power, some good kind Power, melts me (body and soul and voice) into tenderness and love. O my husband, we must obey it. Look upon me! look upon me! lift your sweet eyes from the ground! I will not cease to supplicate; I dare not.

Leofric. We may think upon it.

Godiva. O never say that! What! think upon goodness when you can be good? Let not the infants cry for sustenance! The mother of our blessed Lord will hear them; us never, never afterward.

Leofric. Here comes the Bishop: we are but one mile from the walls. Why dismountest thou? no bishop can expect it. Godiva! my honour and rank among men are humbled by this. Earl Godwin will hear of it. Up! up! the Bishop hath seen it: he urgeth his horse onward. Dost thou not hear him now upon the solid turf behind thee?

Godiva. Never, no, never will I rise, O Leofric, until you remit this most impious task—this tax on hard labour, on hard life.

Leofric. Turn round: look how the fat nag canters, as to the tune of a sinner's psalm, slow and hard-breathing. What reason or right can the people have to complain, while their bishop's steed is so sleek and well caparisoned? Inclination to change, desire to abolish old usages.—Up! up! for shame! They shall smart for it, idlers! Sir Bishop, I must blush for my young bride.

Godiva. My husband, my husband! will you pardon the city?

Leofric. Sir Bishop! I could not think you would have seen her in this plight. Will I pardon? Yea, Godiva, by the holy rood, will I pardon the city, when thou ridest naked at noontide through the streets!

Godiva. O my dear, cruel Leofric, where is the heart you gave me? It was not so: can mine have hardened it?

Bishop. Earl, thou abashest thy spouse; she turneth pale, and weepeth. Lady Godiva, peace be with thee.

Godiva. Thanks, holy man! peace will be with me when peace is with your city. Did you hear my Lord's cruel word?

Bishop. I did, lady.

Godiva. Will you remember it, and pray against it?

Bishop. Wilt *thou* forget it, daughter?

Godiva. I am not offended.

Bishop. Angel of peace and purity!

Godiva. But treasure it up in your heart: deem it an incense, good only when it is consumed and spent, ascending with prayer and sacrifice. And, now, what was it?

Bishop. Christ save us! that he will pardon the city when thou ridest naked through the streets at noon.

Godiva. Did he swear an oath?

Bishop. He sware by the holy rood.

Godiva. My Reedemer, thou hast heard it! save the city!

Leofric. We are now upon the beginning of the pavement: these are the suburbs. Let us think of feasting: we may pray afterward; to-morrow we shall rest.

Godiva. No judgments, then, to-morrow, Leofric?

Leofric. None: we will carouse.

Godiva. The saints of heaven have given me strength and confidence; my prayers are heard; the heart of my beloved is now softened.

Leofric. Ay, ay.

Godiva. Say, dearest Leofric, is there indeed no other hope, no other mediation?

Leofric. I have sworn. Beside, thou hast made me redden and turn my face away from thee, and all the knaves have seen it: this adds to the city's crime.

Godiva. I have blushed too, Leofric, and was not rash nor obdurate.

Leofric. But thou, my sweetest, art given to blushing: there is no conquering it in thee. I wish thou hadst not alighted so hastily and roughly: it hath shaken down a sheaf of thy hair. Take heed thou sit not upon it, lest it anguish thee. Well done! 20 it mingleth now sweetly with the cloth of gold upon the saddle, running here and there, as if it had life and faculties and business, and were working there-upon some newer and cunninger device. O my beauteous Eve! there is a Paradise about thee! the world is refreshed as thou movest and breathest on it. I cannot see or think of evil where thou art. I could throw my arms even here about thee. No signs for me! no shaking of sunbeams! no reproof or frown of wonderment.—I *will* say it—now, then, for 30 worse—I could close with my kisses thy half-open lips, ay, and those lovely and loving eyes, before the people.

Godiva. To-morrow you shall kiss me, and they shall bless you for it. I shall be very pale, for to-night I must fast and pray.

Leofric. I do not hear thee; the voices of the folk are so loud under this archway.

Godiva (to herself). God help them! good kind souls! I hope they will not crowd about me so to- 40 morrow. O Leofric! could my name be forgotten, and yours alone remembered! But perhaps my in-nocence may save me from reproach; and how many as innocent are in fear and famine! No eye will open on me but fresh from tears. What a young mother for so large a family! Shall my youth harm me? Under God's hand it gives me courage. Ah! when will the morning come? Ah! when will the noon be over?

"The story of Godiva, at one of whose festivals or fairs I 50 was present in my boyhood, has always much interested me; and I wrote a poem on it, sitting, I remember, by the *square pool* at Rugby. When I showed it to the friend in whom I had most confidence, he began to scoff at the subject; and, on his reaching the last line, his laughter was loud and immod-

erate. This conversation has brought both laughter and stanza back to me, and the earnestness with which I en-treated and implored my friend *not to tell the lads*, so heart-strickenly and desperately was I ashamed. The verses are these, if any one else should wish another laugh at me:

> In every hour, in every mood,
> O lady, it is sweet and good
> To bathe the soul in prayer;
> When we have ceased to bless and pray,
> To dream on thy long hair.

May the peppermint be still growing on the bank in that 10 place!" (Landor)

from THE PENTAMERON

Pentameron means five days (note Boccaccio's *Decam-eron*, tales told during ten days). The scene is Florence, Italy, in the fourteenth century. The famous storyteller and his friend the poet Petrarch are discussing Boccac-cio's love for Fiammetta. Their ideas of love are similar to those expressed by Petrarch in his sonnets to Laura. Es-sentially they are Neo-Platonic (see the discussion of Platonism and Neo-Platonism in the general introduc-tion). The "crystal vase" symbolizes the idea of the ne-cessity for the purgation of sensuous love. Before he can love Fiammetta perfectly, Boccaccio must drink away even the evoked memory of the first kiss.

This selection from the fifth day's interview of *The Pentameron* resembles the second class of *Imaginary Conver-sations* described in the introductory note to that work.

from THE DREAM OF BOCCACCIO

Boccaccio. In vain had I determined not only to mend in future, but to correct the past; in vain had I prayed most fervently for grace to accomplish it, with a final aspiration to Fiammetta that she would unite with your beloved Laura, and that, gentle and beatified spirits as they are, they would breathe together their purer prayers on mine. See what follows.

Petraca. Sigh not at it. Before we can see all that follows from their intercession, we must join them again. But let me hear anything in which they are concerned.

Boccaccio. I prayed; and my breast, after some few tears, grew calmer. Yet sleep did not ensue un-til the break of morning, when the dropping of soft rain on the leaves of the fig-tree at the window, and the chirping of a little bird, to tell another there was shelter under them, brought me repose and slumber. Scarcely had I closed my eyes, if indeed 50 time can be reckoned any more in sleep than in heaven, when my Fiammetta seemed to have led me into the meadow. You will see it below you: turn away that branch: gently! gently! do not break it; for the little bird sat there.

Petraca. I think, Giovanni, I can divine the place. Although this fig-tree, growing out of the wall between the cellar and us, is fantastic enough in its branches, yet that other which I see yonder, bent down and forced to crawl along the grass by the prepotency of the young shapely walnut-tree, is much more so. It forms a seat, about a cubit above the ground, level and long enough for several.

Boccaccio. Ha! you fancy it must be a favourite spot with me, because of the two strong forked stakes wherewith it is propped and supported!

Petraca. Poets know the haunts of poets at first sight; and he who loved Laura—O Laura! did I say he who *loved* thee?—hath whisperings where those feet would wander which have been restless after Fiammetta.

Boccaccio. It is true, my imagination has often conducted her thither; but here in this chamber she appeared to me more visibly in a dream.

"Thy prayers have been heard, O Giovanni," said she.

I sprang to embrace her.

"Do not spill the water! Ah! you have spilt a part of it."

I then observed in her hand a crystal vase. A few drops were sparkling on the sides and running down the rim: a few were trickling from the base and from the hand that held it.

"I must go down to the brook," said she, "and fill it again as it was filled before."

What a moment of agony was this to me! Could I be certain how long might be her absence? She went: I was following: she made a sign for me to turn back; I disobeyed her only an instant: yet my sense of disobedience, increasing my feebleness and confusion, made me lose sight of her. In the next moment she was again at my side, with the cup quite full. I stood motionless: I feared my breath might shake the water over. I looked her in the face for her commands—and to see it—to see it so calm, so beneficent, so beautiful. I was forgetting what I had prayed for, when she lowered her head, tasted of the cup, and gave it me. I drank; and suddenly sprang forth before me, many groves and palaces and gardens, and their statues and their avenues, and their labyrinths of alaternus and bay, and alcoves of citron, and watchful loopholes in the retirements of impenetrable pomegranate. Farther off, just below where the fountain slipt away from its marble hall and guardian gods, arose, from their beds of moss and drosera and darkest grass, the sisterhood of oleanders, fond of

46–47. **alaternus,** an ornamental evergreen buckthorn.
51. **drosera,** a bog plant, the sundew.

tantalising with their bosomed flowers and their moist and pouting blossoms the little shy rivulet, and of covering its face with all the colours of the dawn. My dream expanded and moved forward. I trod again the dust of Posilipo, soft as the feathers in the wings of Sleep. I emerged on Baia; I crossed her innumerable arches; I loitered in the breezy sunshine of her mole; I trusted the faithful seclusion of her caverns, the keepers of so many secrets; and I reposed on the buoyancy of her tepid sea. Then Naples, and her theatres and her churches, and grottoes and dells and forts and promontories, rushed forward in confusion, now among soft whispers, now among sweetest sounds, and subsided, and sank, and disappeared. Yet a memory seemed to come fresh from every one: each had time enough for its sale, for its pleasure, for its reflection, for its pang. As I mounted with silent steps the narrow staircase of the old palace, how distinctly did I feel against the palm of my hand the coldness of that smooth stone-work, and the greater of the cramps of iron in it!

"Ah me! is this forgetting?" cried I anxiously to Fiammetta.

"We must recall these scenes before us," she replied: "such is the punishment of them. Let us hope and believe that the apparition, and the compunction which must follow it, will be accepted as the full penalty, and that both will pass away almost together."

I feared to lose anything attendant on her presence: I feared to approach her forehead with my lips: I feared to touch the lily on its long wavy leaf in her hair, which filled my whole heart with fragrance. Venerating, adoring, I bowed my head at last to kiss her snow-white robe, and trembled at my presumption. And yet the effulgence of her countenance vivified while it chastened me. I loved her—I must not say *more* than ever—*better* than ever; it was Fiammetta who had inhabited the skies. As my hand opened toward her,

"Beware!" said she, faintly smiling; "beware, Giovanni! Take only the crystal; take it, and drink again."

"Must all be then forgotten?" said I sorrowfully.

"Remember your prayer and mine, Giovanni. Shall both have been granted—O how much worse than in vain?"

I drank instantly; I drank largely. How cool my bosom grew; how could it grow so cool before her! But it was not to remain in its quiescency; its trials were not yet over. I will not, Francesco! no, I may not commemorate the incidents she related to me, nor which of us said, "I blush for having loved *first*"; nor which of us replied, "Say *least*, and blush again."

The charm of the words (for I felt not the encumbrance of the body nor the acuteness of the spirit) seemed to possess me wholly. Although the water gave me strength and comfort, and somewhat of celestial pleasure, many tears fell around the border of the vase as she held it up before me, exhorting me to take courage, and inviting me with more than exhortation to accomplish my deliverance. She 10 came nearer, more tenderly, more earnestly; she held the dewy globe with both hands, leaning forward, and sighed and shook her head, drooping at my pusillanimity. It was only when a ringlet had touched the rim, and perhaps the water (for a sunbeam on the surface could never have given it such a golden hue) that I took courage, clasped it, and exhausted it. Sweet as was the water, sweet as was the serenity it gave me—alas! that also which it moved away from me was sweet!

"This time you can trust me alone," said she, and parted my hair, and kissed my brow. Again she went toward the brook: again my agitation, my weakness, my doubt, came over me: nor could I see her while she raised the water, nor knew I whence she drew it. When she returned, she was close to me at once: she smiled: her smile pierced me to the bones: it seemed an angel's. She sprinkled the pure water on me; she looked most fondly; she took my hand; she suffered me to press hers to my bosom; but, whether by design I can not tell, she let fall a few drops of the chilly element between.

"And now, O my beloved!" said she, "we have consigned to the bosom of God our earthly joys and sorrows. The joys can not return, let not the sorrows. These alone would trouble my repose among the blessed."

"Trouble thy repose! Fiammetta! Give me the chalice!" cried I—"not a drop will I leave in it, not a drop."

"Take it!" said that soft voice. "O now most dear Giovanni! I know thou hast strength enough; and there is but little—at the bottom lies our first kiss."

"Mine! didst thou say, beloved one! and is that left thee still?"

"*Mine*," said she, pensively; and as she abased her head, the broad leaf of the lily hid her brow and 20 her eyes; the light of heaven shone through the flower.

"O Fiammetta! Fiammetta!" cried I in agony, "God is the God of mercy, God is the God of love . . . can I, can I ever?" I struck the chalice against my head, unmindful that I held it; the water covered my face and my feet. I started up, not yet awake, and I heard the name of Fiammetta in the curtains.

Petraca. Love, O Giovanni, and life itself, are but dreams at best.

Thomas Moore
1779–1852

In Dublin, Ireland, above the grocery store which his father managed, Thomas Moore was born May 28, 1779. He spent his babyhood and early boyhood "surrounded by an atmosphere of music, love, poetry, and patriotism."[1] At the age of six he won a school prize for reading history. Later, in the English Grammar School he came under the influence of Samuel Whyte, who interested him in music, poetry, and acting. After graduating "first boy in his class," he entered Trinity College, Dublin, participated in undergraduate conspiracies against British oppression, contributed an imitation of Ossian to a United Irishmen newspaper, distinguished himself as a linguist, and began his translations of the Greek lyric poet Anacreon. After taking his degree in 1799, he set out for London with money "carefully sewed up by [his] mother in the waistband of [his] pantaloons."

Enrolling at the Middle Temple for the study of law, he soon forgot his original purpose and embarked upon one of the most triumphant charm careers on record. Besides possessing extraordinary personal magnetism, Moore was a pleasing parlor singer. The publication of timely newspaper verse and of his *Odes of Anacreon*, 1800, with their praise of wine, women, and song, confirmed his popularity. Political friends procured him a government position in Bermuda. This he left in the hands of a deputy, and he traveled in the United States, going as far west as Niagara Falls, where he was "all rapture and amazement." In 1807 the publication of the first of his *Irish Melodies*, a songbook with music

[1] Howard Mumford Jones, *The Harp That Once*, Henry Holt, 1937.

by Sir John Stevenson, made Moore the national bard of Ireland. In Dublin a theater audience rose to its feet and shouted for him. On a rough sea voyage elderly ladies invaded his cabin for a kiss. In England Moore was the Englishman's idea of what an Irishman should be. He sang his way into English hearts, making them enjoy the pathos of his country's fate without angering them by reminding them of their responsibility for it. In 1811, after a near-duel with him, Moore met Byron. Moore's *Lalla Rookh*, 1817, an idyllic Oriental romance, won him great popularity in Europe. In America, a generation ago, limp-leather copies of the poem occupied a prominent place on marble-topped tables.

Forced to flee from England as a result of the defalcation of his Bermuda deputy, Moore went to Italy and resumed his friendship with Byron. Before they separated, Byron gave his memoirs to Moore, thus designating him his official biographer. When Moore set about writing the biography, however, at the request of Lady Byron and her friends he destroyed the memoirs. Nevertheless, his biography of Byron remains the greatest single source of information about Byron's life. Besides this, published in 1830, Moore's important titles include: *Poems by the Late Thomas Little*, 1801, alluded to in Byron's *English Bards and Scotch Reviewers; Odes and Epistles*, 1806; *National Airs*, 1816; *The Fudge Family in Paris*, 1818; *Fables for the Holy Alliance*, 1823; and *The History of Ireland*, 1846. He died February 25, 1852.

Moore is remembered today as a genial friend of distinguished literary men, as the biographer of one of the most eminent poets, as a drawing-room romancer, and as an interpreter of Irish song to Englishmen. Because of the skill with which he married music and words, he is one of the true lyrists of the Romantic Period. His songs of Ireland's woes and past glories are no unworthy prelude to the nobler music of William Butler Yeats and the other poets of the Irish Renaissance.

THE LAKE OF THE DISMAL SWAMP

WRITTEN AT NORFOLK, IN VIRGINIA

"They made her a grave, too cold and damp
  For a soul so warm and true:
And she's gone to the Lake of the Dismal Swamp,
Where, all night long, by a fire-fly lamp,
  She paddles her white canoe.

3. Lake of the Dismal Swamp. The Great Dismal Swamp extends from a point ten or twelve miles south of Norfolk into North Carolina. The lake in the middle of it is called Drummond's Pond.

"And her fire-fly lamp I soon shall see,
  And her paddle I soon shall hear;
Long and loving our life shall be,
And I'll hide the maid in a cypress tree,
  When the footstep of death is near."   10

Away to the Dismal Swamp he speeds—
  His path was rugged and sore,
Through tangled juniper, beds of reeds,
Through many a fen, where the serpent feeds,
  And man never trod before.

And, when on the earth he sunk to sleep,
  If slumber his eyelids knew,
He lay where the deadly vine doth weep
Its venomous tear and nightly steep
  The flesh with blistering dew!   20

And near him the she-wolf stirred the brake,
  And the copper-snake breathed in his ear,
Till he starting cried, from his dream awake,
"Oh! when shall I see the dusky Lake,
  And the white canoe of my dear?"

He saw the Lake, and a meteor bright
  Quick over its surface played—
"Welcome," he said, "my dear one's light!"
And the dim shore echoed, for many a night,
  The name of the death-cold maid.   30

Till he hollowed a boat of the birchen bark,
  Which carried him off from shore;
Far, far he followed the meteor spark,
The wind was high and the clouds were dark,
  And the boat returned no more.

But oft, from the Indian hunter's camp,
  This lover and maid so true
Are seen at the hour of midnight damp
To cross the Lake by a fire-fly lamp,
  And paddle their white canoe!   40

from IRISH MELODIES

OH! BREATHE NOT HIS NAME

Oh! breathe not his name, let it sleep in the shade,
Where cold and unhonoured his relics are laid:
Sad, silent, and dark, be the tears that we shed,
As the night-dew that falls on the grass o'er his head.

1. his name, that of Robert Emmet, Irish revolutionist executed in 1803 at Dublin.

But the night-dew that falls, though in silence it
 weeps,
Shall brighten with verdure the grave where he
 sleeps;
And the tear that we shed, though in secret it rolls,
Shall long keep his memory green in our souls.

THE HARP THAT ONCE THROUGH
TARA'S HALLS

The harp that once through Tara's halls
  The soul of music shed,
Now hangs as mute on Tara's walls,
  As if that soul were fled.—
So sleeps the pride of former days,
  So glory's thrill is o'er,
And hearts, that once beat high for praise,
  Now feel that pulse no more.

No more to chiefs and ladies bright
  The harp of Tara swells;   10
The chord alone, that breaks at night,
  Its tale of ruin tells.
Thus Freedom now so seldom wakes,
  The only throb she gives,
Is when some heart indignant breaks,
  To show that still she lives

THE YOUNG MAY MOON

The young May moon is beaming, love,
The glow-worm's lamp is gleaming, love,
  How sweet to rove
  Through Morna's grove,
When the drowsy world is dreaming, love!
Then awake!—the heavens look bright, my dear,
'Tis never too late for delight, my dear,
  And the best of all ways
  To lengthen our days,
Is to steal a few hours from the night, my dear!   10

Now all the world is sleeping, love,
But the Sage, his star-watch keeping, love,
  And I, whose star,
  More glorious far,
Is the eye from that casement peeping, love.

Then awake!—till rise of sun, my dear,
The Sage's glass we'll shun, my dear,
  Or, in watching the flight
  Of bodies of light,
He might happen to take thee for one, my dear.   20

OH! HAD WE SOME BRIGHT LITTLE ISLE OF
OUR OWN

Oh! had we some bright little isle of our own,
In a blue summer ocean, far off and alone,
Where a leaf never dies in the still blooming
  bowers,
And the bee banquets on through a whole year of
  flowers;
  Where the sun loves to pause
  With so fond a delay,
  That the night only draws
  A thin veil o'er the day;
Where simply to feel that we breathe, that we
  live,
Is worth the best joy that life elsewhere can give.   10

There, with souls ever ardent and pure as the
  clime,
We should love, as they loved in the first golden
  time;
The glow of the sunshine, the balm of the air,
Would steal to our hearts, and make all summer
  there.
  With affection as free
  From decline as the bowers,
  And, with hope, like the bee,
  Living always on flowers,
Our life should resemble a long day of light,
And our death come on, holy and calm as the
  night.   20

THE TIME I'VE LOST IN WOOING

The time I've lost in wooing,
  In watching and pursuing
    The light, that lies
    In woman's eyes,
Has been my heart's undoing.
Though Wisdom oft has sought me,
I scorned the lore she brought me.
    My only books
    Were woman's looks,
And folly's all they've taught me.   10

The Harp. **1. Tara's.** Tara, near Dublin, was the capital
of Ireland during that country's glorious medieval period.
The Harp That Once is the title of the biography of Moore by
Howard Mumford Jones already referred to.
  "Moore prattled of 'the harp,' etc.; but the harp to which
his ears really listened was modern and gilded, and played
by a young lady in a drawing room."—Arthur Symons,
The Romantic Movement in English Poetry, Dutton, 1909.

1. some bright little isle. To measure Moore as a lyric
poet, compare this with William Butler Yeats's "The Lake
Isle of Innisfree" ("I will arise and go now, and go to
Innisfree"), page 998.

Her smile when Beauty granted,
I hung with gaze enchanted,
   Like him, the sprite,
   Whom maids by night
Oft meet in glen that's haunted.
Like him, too, Beauty won me,
But while her eyes were on me,
   If once their ray
   Was turned away,
O! winds could not outrun me.   20

And are those follies going?
And is my proud heart growing
   Too cold or wise
   For brilliant eyes
Again to set it glowing?
No, vain, alas! the endeavour
From bonds so sweet to sever;
   Poor Wisdom's chance
   Against a glance
Is now as weak as ever.   30

DEAR HARP OF MY COUNTRY

Dear Harp of my Country! in darkness I found
   thee,
   The cold chain of silence had hung o'er thee
   long,
When proudly, my own Island Harp, I unbound
   thee,
   And gave all thy chords to light, freedom, and
   song!
The warm lay of love and the light note of gladness
   Have wakened thy fondest, thy liveliest thrill;
But, so oft hast thou echoed the deep sigh of sadness,
   That ev'n in thy mirth it will steal from thee
   still.

Dear Harp of my Country! farewell to thy num-
   bers,
   This sweet wreath of song is the last we shall
   twine!   10
Go, sleep with the sunshine of Fame on thy slumbers,
   Till touched by some hand less unworthy than
   mine;
If the pulse of the patriot, soldier, or lover,
   Have throbbed at our lay, 'tis thy glory alone;
I was *but* as the wind, passing heedlessly over,
   And all the wild sweetness I waked was thy own.

The Time I've Lost. **13. sprite,** an Irish fairy, seen in the
fields at dusk. **2. chain of silence,** "a practical figure of
rhetoric among the ancient Irish." (Moore)

from NATIONAL AIRS

OFT, IN THE STILLY NIGHT

Scotch Air

Oft, in the stilly night,
   Ere Slumber's chain has bound me,
Fond Memory brings the light
   Of other days around me;
     The smiles, the tears,
     Of boyhood's years,
   The words of love then spoken;
     The eyes that shone,
     Now dimmed and gone,
   The cheerful hearts now broken!   10
Thus, in the stilly night,
   Ere Slumber's chain hath bound me,
Sad Memory brings the light
   Of other days around me.

When I remember all
   The friends, so linked together,
I've seen around me fall,
   Like leaves in wintry weather;
     I feel like one
     Who treads alone   20
   Some banquet-hall deserted,
     Whose lights are fled,
     Whose garlands dead,
   And all but he departed!
Thus, in the stilly night,
   Ere Slumber's chain has bound me,
Sad Memory brings the light
   Of other days around me.

A LETTER FROM NIAGARA FALLS

My dearest Mother,—

   I have seen the Falls, and am all rapture and
amazement, I cannot give you a better idea of what
I felt than by transcribing what I wrote off hastily
in my journal on returning. "Arrived at Chippewa,
within three miles of the Falls, on Saturday, July 21,
to dinner. That evening walked towards the Falls,
but got no farther than the rapids, which gave us a
prelibation of the grandeur we had to expect. Next
day, July 22, went to visit the Falls. Never shall I
forget the impression I felt at the first glimpse of
them which we got as the carriage passed over the

A Letter. **9. prelibation,** foretaste.

hill that overlooks them. We were not near enough to be agitated by the terrific effects of the scene; but saw through the trees this mighty flow of waters descending with calm magnificence, and received enough of its grandeur to set imagination on the wing; imagination which, even at Niagara, can outrun reality. I felt as if approaching the very residence of the Deity; the tears started into my eyes; and I remained, for moments after we had lost sight of the scene, in that delicious absorption which pious enthusiasm alone can produce. We arrived at the New Ladder and descended to the bottom. Here all its awful sublimities rushed full upon me. But the former exquisite sensation was gone. I now saw all. The string that had been touched by the first impulse, and which *fancy* would have kept for ever in vibration, now rested at *reality*. Yet though there was no more to imagine, there was much to feel. My whole heart and soul ascended towards the Divinity in a swell of devout admiration, which I never before experienced. Oh! bring the atheist here, and he cannot return an atheist! I pity the man who can coldly sit down to write a description of these ineffable wonders: much more do I pity him who can submit them to the admeasurement of gallons and yards. It is impossible by pen or pencil to convey even a faint idea of their magnificence. Painting is lifeless, and the most burning words of poetry have all been lavished upon inferior and ordinary subjects. We must have new combinations of language to describe the Falls of Niagara."

24 July, 1804.

George Gordon, Lord Byron
1788–1824

"Wildfire leaped about his cradle."[1] Byron was descended from high-strung, passionate men and women, many of whom led violent and reckless lives and came to sudden ends. His paternal grandfather, Admiral John Byron, was known by his mates as "Foulweather Jack." "He had no rest at sea, nor I on shore," Byron wrote of him. The great-uncle from whom Byron inherited his title killed a man in a duel across a candle-lighted table in an inn. Byron's father, Captain John Byron, a handsome and dissipated guardsman, known as "Mad Jack," eloped with the wife of the Marquis of Carmarthen, later married her, and spent her money before her early death. From this union was born Augusta, who was to be fateful for the poet. Captain Byron's second marriage was to Miss Catherine Gordon of Gight, an heiress descended from the royal house of Scotland, "a hot-headed, hasty-handed race." George Gordon, their only child, was born on January 22, 1788, in London. Important circumstances of his childhood were the natal affliction of a twisted foot, the uncongeniality of his parents, his father's death in 1791, the poverty of his early years, his mother's violence of affection and abuse (she taunted him with the epithet "lame brat"), and the scenery of Scotland, where he lived from the age of two to ten. In 1798 the death of the "wicked" Lord Byron gave him title to the barony of Newstead, and his mother took him to the family

[1] Ethel Colburn Mayne, *Byron*, 2 vols., Scribner, 1912.

seat, Newstead Abbey, an ancient Gothic priory in the Robin Hood country which Henry VIII had granted to a Sir John Byron in 1540.

After three years of torture from unsuccessful remedies for his lameness, Byron was sent to Harrow. Under the sympathetic headmastership of Dr. Drury, he was a brilliant but irregular pupil, led in boyish sports, and formed numerous friendships. Quarrels with Dr. Drury and the succeeding master clouded his last months there. A love affair with his cousin, Mary Chaworth, broken off by her marriage to a country squire, left him with memories that were to embitter much of his poetry (for example, "The Dream"). At Cambridge, which he entered when seventeen, he took the college curriculum lightly but read widely, dissipated freely, became proficient as a boxer and a fencer, and versified. His little volume of college verse, *Hours of Idleness*, 1807, was pounced upon by the *Edinburgh Review* and mercilessly ridiculed. Following his boxing master Captain Jackson's advice for a free-for-all, Byron did not take time to pick out his friends but struck out right and left in *English Bards and Scotch Reviewers*, 1809, a brilliant satire modeled on Pope's *Dunciad* and other poems written in the Popean manner. He had received his M.A. degree in July, 1808. In March, 1809, he took his seat in the House of Lords.

In June, Byron and his college friend John Cam Hobhouse set out on a tour of the Mediterranean and the Near East. Landing at Lisbon, they rode horseback nearly five hundred miles across Portugal and Spain while those countries were still in dangerous disorder from the Peninsular Wars with Napoleon. Scenery, battlefields, bullfights, banditti, and memories of the historic past excited them all the way to Seville and Cadiz. At Gibraltar they embarked and proceeded across the Mediterranean, enjoying its moonlit beauty and romance, to Albania, Greece, and Constantinople, visiting historical and scenic spots and encountering numerous adventures, especially in the wild mountain country of the Albanian Ali Pasha. These observations and experiences Byron wrote up in the Spenserian stanzas of *Childe Harold I and II*. The poem was published in 1812, two years after Byron's return to England. "I awoke one morning and found myself famous," he says of the effect of the poem. His Turkish Tales (*The Giaour*, *The Bride of Abydos*, *The Corsair*, and others) drew from the same sources as *Childe Harold* and confirmed his popularity. For nearly four years he was the social lion of London, the most famous young man in Europe.

Intrigues with women, some of them great ladies, a brief political career in the House of Lords, and poetry imperfectly absorbed his energies for a while. He began to think of settling down. In 1815 he was married to Anna Isabella Milbanke, an intellectual and highly proper young lady who thought she might reform him, even as he thought marriage might stabilize him. Both were wrong in their calculations. They were temperamentally ill-adapted to each other. As a husband, Byron was from the first brutal and unreasonable. Lady Byron insisted on an examination to determine his sanity. But there was a more serious cause of alienation growing out of Byron's incestuous relations with his half-sister, Augusta, now the wife of a Colonel Leigh.[1] Shortly after the birth of a daughter, Ada, Lord and Lady Byron agreed to a formal separation. The scandal of the separation, stirred by such imprudences as Byron's "Fare Thee Well," was enormous. From having been its spoiled darling, Byron became the scapegoat of the rotten Regency society. On April 25, 1816, he left England for what proved to be forever, a morally banished man. The separation and the exile were the crux of his life.

In Matthew Arnold's phrase, "Making a public show of a very genuine misery, he swept across Europe the pageant of his bleeding heart." His travel itinerary was to give the occasion, the material, and the plan for the third canto of *Childe*

Harold. Crossing the English Channel, he passed through the Low Countries, pausing at Waterloo, where the battle burial mound was still fresh and the red rain had made the harvest grow; ascended the Rhine (Drachenfels, Coblentz, Ehrenbreitstein); and on May 25 arrived at Geneva, Switzerland (Lake Leman, Clarens, Lausanne, Ferney), where he rented the Villa Diodati. Shelley, Mary Godwin, and Mary's stepsister Clara Jane Clairmont were neighbors. With Miss Clairmont he half-cynically accepted the status of an affair begun in London; she was to bear him a daughter, Allegra, the following January. With Shelley and such visitors as Monk Lewis he heard readings from Wordsworth and Goethe, talked about history, literature, and philosophy, and made boating and sight-seeing excursions in the neighborhood. "Half mad during the time . . . between metaphysics, mountains, lakes, love unextinguishable, thoughts unutterable, and the nightmare of my [his] own delinquencies," he composed *Childe Harold*, Canto the Third, *The Prisoner of Chillon*, "Stanzas to Augusta" (two poems with that title), and "The Epistle to Augusta," and began *Manfred: A Dramatic Poem*. Miss Clairmont copied the *Childe Harold* canto, and Shelley took it and the poems for *The Prisoner of Chillon* volume back to England in August for publication there.

By January, 1817, Byron was living in Venice, sunk in its dissipations, but finishing *Manfred* and writing other poems. Poetry had now become his greatest reality and occupation (see *Childe Harold*, Canto the Third, stanzas 4–7). He composed the fourth canto of *Childe Harold*, then made a new departure in the light, mocking vein of *Beppo*, 1818, bubbling up out of his Venetian dissipations. A visit from the Shelleys, trouble with Miss Clairmont and her baby, wilder profligacy, and the beginning of *Don Juan* (I and II completed and published in 1819) occupied him in 1818. From his "devilish deal of wear and tear of mind and body" he was rescued by a meeting with Teresa, the young wife of old Count Guiccioli. The ensuing liaison, regularized so far as it could be by custom, after a Papal decree had separated the Guicciolis, proved to be the most stabilizing single influence in Byron's life. He followed the Countess Guiccioli to Ravenna and lived there with her for nearly two years. During this time he composed poems (for example, *The Prophecy of Dante*) and dramas (for example, *Marino Faliero*) on Italian subjects, wrote and published the third to fifth cantos of *Don Juan*, resumed relations with the Shelley circle, now at Pisa, and interested himself in the Carbonari activities of

---

[1] The curious student is referred to Sir John C. Fox, *The Byron Mystery*, London, 1924.

Pietro Gamba, brother of the Countess. Trouble resulting from his political affiliations caused Byron's removal to Genoa in 1822.

In the meantime, Byron and Shelley had invited Leigh Hunt to Italy, to found and edit the *Liberal*. E.J. Trelawny, a fantastic adventurer who was to become one of Byron's and Shelley's biographers, joined the group. These associations were broken up in July by the drowning of Shelley. Byron participated in the burning of Shelley's body on the beach near Via Reggio. At Genoa, where he took up residence in September, 1822, Byron wrote *The Vision of Judgment* (published in the *Liberal*), the sixth to eighth cantos of *Don Juan*, and other poems.

In January, 1823, Byron actively interested himself in the cause of Greek independence. By August he was in Greece with Trelawny and other friends. Before the end of the year he had published the ninth to fourteenth cantos of *Don Juan*, had given his financial support and his personal leadership to a company of Greek soldiers, and had suffered a decline of health. "On This Day I Complete My Thirty-sixth Year," he wrote, January 22, 1824, as a record of fact and as title of a noble following poem. On April 19, at Missolonghi, in "The land of honorable death," he died of epilepsy or meningitis. The Greeks wished to give him "A soldier's grave" in the country for which he had spent his money and his life; but other wishes prevailed, and he was buried in Hucknall Torkard Church, near Newstead, on July 16.

From this brief story of his career, Byron's personality and character can be inferred only in part. He was far more than a literary man, far more than a notoriety who happened to be a great artist. In the old Goethe's view, he was "a personality in eminence such as never had been and is not likely to come again; a fiery mass of living valor hurling itself on life." A creature of extremes, of contradictions and paradoxes, Byron was a great lord and (in most of his relations with women) a thorough cad, a sentimentalist and a cynic, a revolutionist and a conservative, a dandified lady-killer and a man's man, an aristocrat and a republican, a frank sensualist and a conventionalist. But certain traits are admirably constant—his downright sincerity, his hatred of hypocrisy, his rugged intellectual honesty, his fidelity to the truth about himself as well as about others. Perhaps the chief quality that sets him apart as a man and as a poet was his power of dramatizing himself, of making himself vivid in an image, striking in a posture, memorable in a phrase. He is a wanderer o'er eternity, a weed flung from the rock but also one whom the waves know as a rider. He embodies and unbosoms that which was most within him—lightning. He stands in the ruined Colosseum and apostrophizes the Eternal City without appearing absurd. He is Manfred eating his heart out in remorse for a nameless and fearful crime but fearlessly rejecting the offices of religion and defying the powers of darkness and evil. He is Juan, passing in tears and scornful laughter along the highways of a world essentially like the world we know today.

The dominant themes and moods of Byron's poetry are readily recognizable. He is, with Scott, a describer and an interpreter of European history. His approach, however, is direct, personal, often dramatic: He visits Waterloo, the Castle of Chillon, Marathon, the Colosseum, recreates the historical events, the personalities, and the emotional associations which these places call up in his imagination, and panoplies all in his splendid rhetoric. Frequently, as in the Waterloo passage (*Childe Harold*, Canto the Third), he dramatizes a striking scene (the agony of lovers saying good-by on the eve of battle, the Scottish regiments swinging by with their skirling bagpipes).

The historic places most interesting and inspiring to Byron were those associated with man's agelong struggle for liberty. Emancipation is one of the greatest notes in Byron's poetry, as in *The Prisoner of Chillon*, the third and fourth cantos of *Childe Harold*, and "The Isles of Greece" song (*Don Juan*, Canto the Third).

Closely associated with this passion for liberty, as has been suggested, are his hatred of tyranny and his contempt for chicanery and hypocrisy. The satirical spirit, manifest early in *English Bards and Scotch Reviewers*, became his master bias in later life, as in *Don Juan* and *The Vision of Judgment*. He is the greatest satirical poet since Pope. His field of satire embraces nearly every aspect of modern life—the rottenness and decadence of high society, injustice and oppression in government and commerce, hypocrisy in religion, conventional but hollow morality, venality and weakness and cheapness in literature, power politics, and war.

Another side of Byron, often at war with his comic spirit, sometimes the ultimate motive of it (as when he laughs to keep from weeping), is his melancholy. Early satiety, disillusionment from having anticipated life, and the resulting bitter despondency, expressed in the first two cantos of *Childe Harold* and the personal lyrics (such as "There's Not a Joy the World Can Give"), deepen into the *Weltschmerz* of the third canto of *Childe Harold* and *Manfred*. He often suggests or expresses a predestinarian or fatalistic explanation: "Thyself to be thy proper hell," "a power upon me . . . which . . . makes it my fatality to live," "Fatal and fated in thy sufferings" (*Manfred*). This melancholy colors the poet's view of historical places and natural scenery. It shapes the unifying theme of such poems as the third canto of *Childe Harold* and those addressed to Augusta, namely, that a sick and alienated soul can find refuge and solace in nature. Hence, Byron's nature poetry differs from Wordsworth's in the point of view and spirit of approach, even when (as in the poems just named and in *The Prisoner of Chillon*) it is under Wordsworthian influence. "The secret of Wordsworth," said Coleridge, "is acquiescence; Byron is in revolt. To him Nature and humanity are antagonists, and he cleaves to Nature, yea, he would take her by violence to mark his alienation and severance from man." Byron's melancholy is not to be dismissed with the cheap flippancy of the undergraduate whom Mr. Herbert Agar tells about: "'What's the matter with this Byron?' asked one student of another. The other, a girl, answered, 'Oh, he just couldn't take it.'" [1] It was Byron's very capacity to take with tragic seriousness not only his own fate but the plight of a world out of joint that explains the bitterness of his poetry. If he took the world despairingly, he also knew how to face it with laughing courage or mocking gaiety, and to live and die gallantly. "My pangs shall find a voice," he asserted. This prophecy and a kindred one have been fulfilled—

"There is that within me which shall tire
Torture and Time, and breathe when I expire."

WHEN WE TWO PARTED

When we two parted
    In silence and tears,
Half broken-hearted
    To sever for years,
Pale grew thy cheek and cold,
    Colder thy kiss;
Truly that hour foretold
    Sorrow to this.

The dew of the morning
    Sunk chill on my brow—   10
It felt like the warning
    Of what I feel now.
Thy vows are all broken,
    And light is thy fame:
I hear thy name spoken,
    And share in its shame.

[1] *Land of the Free*, Houghton Mifflin, 1935, p. 44.

They name thee before me,
    A knell to mine ear;
A shudder comes o'er me—
    Why wert thou so dear?   20
They know not I knew thee,
    Who knew thee too well:—
Long, long shall I rue thee,
    Too deeply to tell.

In secret we met—
    In silence I grieve,
That thy heart could forget,
    Thy spirit deceive.
If I should meet thee
    After long years,   30
How should I greet thee?—
    With silence and tears.

from ENGLISH BARDS AND SCOTCH REVIEWERS

Behold! in various throngs the scribbling
    crew,   143
For notice eager, pass in long review:
Each spurs his jaded Pegasus apace,
And Rhyme and Blank maintain an equal race;
Sonnets on sonnets crowd, and ode on ode;
And Tales of Terror jostle on the road;
Immeasurable measures move along;
For simpering Folly loves a varied song,   150
To strange mysterious Dulness still the friend,
Admires the strain she cannot comprehend.
Thus Lays of Minstrels—may they be the last!—
On half-strung harps whine mournful to the
    blast,
While mountain spirits prate to river sprites,
That dames may listen to the sound at nights;
And goblin brats, of Gilpin Horner's brood,
Decoy young Border-nobles through the wood,
And skip at every step, Lord knows how high,
And frighten foolish babes, the Lord knows
    why;   160
While high-born ladies in their magic cell,
Forbidding Knights to read who cannot spell,
Despatch a courier to a wizard's grave,
And fight with honest men to shield a knave.

Next view in state, proud prancing on his roan,
The golden-crested haughty Marmion,
Now forging scrolls, now foremost in the fight,
Not quite a Felon, yet but half a Knight,
The gibbet or the field prepared to grace—
A mighty mixture of the great and base.   170

And think'st thou, SCOTT! by vain conceit perchance,
On public taste to foist thy stale romance,
Though MURRAY with his MILLER may combine
To yield thy muse just half-a-crown per line?
No! when the sons of song descend to trade,
Their bays are sear, their former laurels fade.
Let such forego the poet's sacred name,
Who rack their brains for lucre, not for fame:
Still for stern Mammon may they toil in vain!
And sadly gaze on gold they cannot gain!   180
Such be their meed, such still the just reward
Of prostituted Muse and hireling bard!
For this we spurn Apollo's venal son,
And bid a long "good night to Marmion."

These are the themes that claim our plaudits now;
These are the Bards to whom the Muse must bow;
While MILTON, DRYDEN, POPE, alike forgot,
Resign their hallowed Bays to WALTER SCOTT. . . .

With eagle pinion soaring to the skies,   201
Behold the Ballad-monger SOUTHEY rise!
To him let CAMOËNS, MILTON, TASSO yield,
Whose annual strains, like armies, take the field.
First in the ranks see Joan of Arc advance,
The scourge of England and the boast of France!
Though burnt by wicked BEDFORD for a witch,
Behold her statue placed in Glory's niche;
Her fetters burst, and just released from prison,
A virgin Phoenix from her ashes risen.   210
Next see tremendous Thalaba come on,
Arabia's monstrous, wild, and wond'rous son;
Domdaniel's dread destroyer, who o'erthrew
More mad magicians than the world e'er knew.
Immortal Hero! all thy foes o'ercome,
For ever reign—the rival of Tom Thumb!
Since startled Metre fled before thy face,
Well wert thou doomed the last of all thy race!
Well might triumphant Genii bear thee hence,
Illustrious conqueror of common sense!   220
Now, last and greatest, Madoc spreads his sails,
Cacique in Mexico, and Prince in Wales;
Tells us strange tales, as other travellers do,
More old than Mandeville's, and not so true.
Oh! SOUTHEY! SOUTHEY! cease thy varied song!
A bard may chaunt too often and too long:
As thou art strong in verse, in mercy spare!
A fourth, alas! were more than we could bear.
But if, in spite of all the world can say,
Thou still wilt verseward plod thy weary way;   230
If still in Berkeley-Ballads most uncivil,
Thou wilt devote old women to the devil,
The babe unborn thy dread intent may rue:
"God help thee," SOUTHEY, and thy readers too.

Next comes the dull disciple of thy school,
That mild apostate from poetic rule,
The simple WORDSWORTH, framer of a lay
As soft as evening in his favourite May,
Who warns his friend "to shake off toil and
    trouble,
And quit his books, for fear of growing double";   240
Who, both by precept and example, shows
That prose is verse, and verse is merely prose;
Convincing all, by demonstration plain,
Poetic souls delight in prose insane;
And Christmas stories tortured into rhyme
Contain the essence of the true sublime.
Thus, when he tells the tale of Betty Foy,
The idiot mother of "an idiot Boy";
A moon-struck, silly lad, who lost his way,
And, like his bard, confounded night with day;   250
So close on each pathetic part he dwells,
And each adventure so sublimely tells,
That all who view the "idiot in his glory"
Conceive the Bard the hero of the story.

Shall gentle COLERIDGE pass unnoticed here,
To turgid ode and tumid stanza dear?
Though themes of innocence amuse him best,
Yet still Obscurity's a welcome guest.
If Inspiration should her aid refuse
To him who takes a Pixy for a muse,   260
Yet none in lofty numbers can surpass
The bard who soars to elegize an ass.
So well the subject suits his noble mind,
He brays, the Laureate of the long-eared kind.

SHE WALKS IN BEAUTY

1

She walks in Beauty, like the night
    Of cloudless climes and starry skies;
And all that's best of dark and bright
    Meet in her aspect and her eyes:
Thus mellowed to that tender light
    Which Heaven to gaudy day denies.

2

One shade the more, one ray the less,
    Had half impaired the nameless grace
Which waves in every raven tress,
    Or softly lightens o'er her face;   10
Where thoughts serenely sweet express
    How pure, how dear their dwelling-place.

1. **She,** Byron's cousin, Lady Wilmot Horton, whom he
met in June, 1814, at a ball. She was in mourning, with
silver spangles on her dress.

3

And on that cheek, and o'er that brow,
   So soft, so calm, yet eloquent,
The smiles that win, the tints that glow,
   But tell of days in goodness spent,
A mind at peace with all below,
   A heart whose love is innocent!

THE DESTRUCTION OF SENNACHERIB

"And it came to pass that night, that the angel of the Lord went out, and smote in the camp of the Assyrians an hundred and fourscore and five thousand: and when they arose early in the morning, behold, they were all dead corpses."—II Kings 19:35. Byron wrote the poem for *Hebrew Melodies*, a songbook by a young Jewish musician named Nathan. The verse is anapestic tetrameter.

I

The Assyrian came down like the wolf on the fold,
And his cohorts were gleaming in purple and gold;
And the sheen of their spears was like stars on the sea,
When the blue wave rolls nightly on deep Galilee.

2

Like the leaves of the forest when Summer is green,
That host with their banners at sunset were seen:
Like the leaves of the forest when Autumn hath blown,
That host on the morrow lay withered and strown.

3

For the angel of Death spread his wings on the blast,
And breathed in the face of the foe as he passed; 10
And the eyes of the sleepers waxed deadly and chill,
And their hearts but once heaved, and for ever grew still!

4

And there lay the steed with his nostril all wide,
But through it there rolled not the breath of his pride;
And the foam of his gasping lay white on the turf,
And cold as the spray of the rock-beating surf.

5

And there lay the rider distorted and pale,
With the dew on his brow, and the rust on his mail:
And the tents were all silent—the banners alone—
The lances unlifted—the trumpet unblown. 20

6

And the widows of Ashur are loud in their wail,
And the idols are broke in the temple of Baal;
And the might of the Gentile, unsmote by the sword,
Hath melted like snow in the glance of the Lord!

STANZAS FOR MUSIC

(There's Not a Joy)

There's not a joy the world can give like that it takes away,
When the glow of early thought declines in Feeling's dull decay;
'Tis not on Youth's smooth cheek the blush alone, which fades so fast,
But the tender bloom of heart is gone, ere Youth itself be past.

Then the few whose spirits float above the wreck of happiness
Are driven o'er the shoals of guilt or ocean of excess:
The magnet of their course is gone, or only points in vain
The shore to which their shivered sail shall never stretch again.

Then the mortal coldness of the soul like Death itself comes down;
It cannot feel for others' woes, it dare not dream its own; 10
That heavy chill has frozen o'er the fountain of our tears,
And though the eye may sparkle still, 'tis where the ice appears.

Though wit may flash from fluent lips, and mirth distract the breast,
Through midnight hours that yield no more their former hope of rest;
'Tis but as ivy-leaves around the ruined turret wreath,
All green and wildly fresh without, but worn and grey beneath.

Oh could I feel as I have felt,—or be what I have been,
Or weep as I could once have wept, o'er many a vanished scene;

2. Feeling's dull decay. "My passions," wrote Byron, "were developed very early. . . . Perhaps this was one of the reasons which caused the anticipated melancholy of my thoughts,—having anticipated life." The poem was written in March, 1815, shortly after the death of a friend, the Earl of Dorset.

As springs, in deserts found, seem sweet, all brackish though they be,
So, midst the withered waste of life, those tears
  would flow to me.   20

FARE THEE WELL

Fare thee well! and if for ever,
  Still for ever, fare *thee well:*
Even though unforgiving, never
  'Gainst thee shall my heart rebel.

Would that breast were bared before thee
  Where thy head so oft hath lain,
While that placid sleep came o'er thee
  Which thou ne'er canst know again:

Would that breast, by thee glanced over,
  Every inmost thought could show!   10
Then thou wouldst at last discover
  'Twas not well to spurn it so.

Though the world for this commend thee—
  Though it smile upon the blow,
Even its praises must offend thee,
  Founded on another's woe:

Though my many faults defaced me,
  Could no other arm be found,
Than the one which once embraced me,
  To inflict a cureless wound?   20

Yet, oh yet, thyself deceive not—
  Love may sink by slow decay,
But by sudden wrench, believe not
  Hearts can thus be torn away:

Still thine own its life retaineth—
  Still must mine, though bleeding, beat;
And the undying thought which paineth
  Is—that we no more may meet.

These are words of deeper sorrow
  Than the wail above the dead;   30
Both shall live—but every morrow
  Wake us from a widowed bed.

And when thou wouldst solace gather—
  When our child's first accents flow—

Wilt thou teach her to say "Father!"
  Though his care she must forego?

When her little hands shall press thee—
  When her lip to thine is pressed—
Think of him whose prayer shall bless thee—
  Think of him thy love *had* blessed!   40

Should her lineaments resemble
  Those thou never more may'st see,
Then thy heart will softly tremble
  With a pulse yet true to me.

All my faults perchance thou knowest,
  All my madness—none can know;
All my hopes—where'er thou goest—
  Wither—yet with *thee* they go.

Every feeling hath been shaken;
  Pride—which not a world could bow—   50
Bows to thee—by thee forsaken,
  Even my soul forsakes me now:

But 'tis done—all words are idle—
  Words from me are vainer still;
But the thoughts we cannot bridle
  Force their way without the will.

Fare thee well! thus disunited—
  Torn from every nearer tie—
Seared in heart—and lone—and blighted—
  More than this I scarce can die.   60

STANZAS FOR MUSIC

(There Be None of Beauty's Daughters)

There be none of Beauty's daughters
  With a magic like thee;
And like music on the waters
  Is thy sweet voice to me:
When, as if its sound were causing
The charmèd Ocean's pausing
The waves lie still and gleaming,
And the lulled winds seem dreaming:

And the Midnight Moon is weaving
  Her bright chain o'er the deep;   10
Whose breast is gently heaving,
  As an infant's asleep:
So the spirit bows before thee,
To listen and adore thee;
With a full but soft emotion,
Like the swell of Summer's ocean.

1. thee, Lady Byron. The poem was written during the
scandal of the separation, in 1816, with ll. 408–13 and
419–26 of "Christabel" as a motto. As originally published,
there was no division into stanzas.

THE PRISONER OF CHILLON

A FABLE

The two following poems were written during the first summer of Byron's exile, after a boating tour of Lake Geneva with Shelley, and were published in *The Prisoner of Chillon* volume, 1816. They express one of Byron's greatest themes—human emancipation—the "Sonnet" explicitly, "The Prisoner" dramatically (it is a dramatic monologue). The subject, François de Bonnivard (1496–1570), was a Swiss patriot who twice suffered imprisonment for his political and religious opinions, under Charles III of Savoy. At the time he wrote the poems Byron "was not sufficiently aware of the history of Bonnivard." This fact may explain several liberties he took with the story: No brothers shared Bonnivard's fate; he was imprisoned twice, for two and six years; the dungeon was not below the level of the lake; imprisonment did not break his spirit, for he lived to a ripe old age, endowing a college in Geneva and marrying four times. The changes in the story, however, greatly enhance the pathos of the Prisoner's fate, Byron's artistic theme (see lines 8–10 and 134–37, which state that the Prisoner's fate was typical of all the martyrs of political and religious opinion). The student should note especially the circumstances of imprisonment, the dramatic use made of the other two brothers (the death of the younger being the emotional climax of the poem at line 210); the powerful description of the Prisoner's insensibility (ll. 231–50); the Wordsworthian and Coleridgean treatment of the restorative influences of free nature (ll. 251–365); and the subdued, diminuendo account of the Prisoner's liberation, with its Wordsworthian and Coleridgean idea of the inculcation of sympathy through suffering (ll. 366–92). The Bonnivard of the poem is really an idealized Byron, but Byron in one of his most attractive moods, open to the influences of his fellow Romanticists (Coleridge and Wordsworth, as indicated; Shelley, through personal association; Scott, in the form and spirit of much of the poem).

SONNET ON CHILLON

Eternal Spirit of the chainless Mind!
  Brightest in dungeons, Liberty! thou art,
  For there thy habitation is the heart—
The heart which love of thee alone can bind;
And when thy sons to fetters are consigned—
  To fetters, and the damp vault's dayless gloom,
  Their country conquers with their martyrdom,
And Freedom's fame finds wings on every wind.
Chillon! thy prison is a holy place,
  And thy sad floor an altar—for 'twas trod,   10
Until his very steps have left a trace
  Worn, as if thy cold pavement were a sod,
By Bonnivard!—May none those marks efface!
  For they appeal from tyranny to God.

THE PRISONER OF CHILLON

1

My hair is grey, but not with years,
Nor grew it white
    In a single night,
As men's have grown from sudden fears:
My limbs are bowed, though not with toil,
  But rusted with a vile repose,
For they have been a dungeon's spoil,
  And mine has been the fate of those
To whom the goodly earth and air
Are banned, and barred—forbidden fare;   10
But this was for my father's faith
I suffered chains and courted death;
That father perished at the stake
For tenets he would not forsake;
And for the same his lineal race
In darkness found a dwelling-place;
We were seven—who now are one,
  Six in youth, and one in age,
Finished as they had begun,
  Proud of Persecution's rage;   20
One in fire, and two in field,
Their belief with blood have sealed,
Dying as their father died,
For the God their foes denied;
Three were in a dungeon cast,
Of whom this wreck is left the last.

2

There are seven pillars of Gothic mould,
In Chillon's dungeons deep and old,
There are seven columns, massy and grey,
Dim with a dull imprisoned ray,   30
A sunbeam which hath lost its way,
And through the crevice and the cleft
Of the thick wall is fallen and left;
Creeping o'er the floor so damp,
Like a marsh's meteor lamp:
And in each pillar there is a ring,
  And in each ring there is a chain;
That iron is a cankering thing,
  For in these limbs its teeth remain,
With marks that will not wear away,   40
Till I have done with this new day,
Which now is painful to these eyes,
Which have not seen the sun so rise
For years—I cannot count them o'er,
I lost their long and heavy score,
When my last brother drooped and died,
And I lay living by his side.

3

They chained us each to a column stone,
And we were three—yet, each alone;
We could not move a single pace,   50
We could not see each other's face,
But with that pale and livid light
That made us strangers in our sight:
And thus together—yet apart,
Fettered in hand, but joined in heart,
'Twas still some solace, in the dearth
Of the pure elements of earth,
To hearken to each other's speech,
And each turn comforter to each
With some new hope, or legend old,   60
Or song heroically bold;
But even these at length grew cold.
Our voices took a dreary tone,
An echo of the dungeon stone,
  A grating sound, not full and free,
  As they of yore were wont to be:
  It might be fancy—but to me
They never sounded like our own.

4

I was the eldest of the three,
  And to uphold and cheer the rest   70
  I ought to do—and did my best—
And each did well in his degree.
  The youngest, whom my father loved,
Because our mother's brow was given
To him, with eyes as blue as heaven—
  For him my soul was sorely moved:
And truly might it be distressed
To see such bird in such a nest;
For he was beautiful as day—
  (When day was beautiful to me   80
  As to young eagles, being free)—
  A polar day, which will not see
A sunset till its summer's gone,
  Its sleepless summer of long light,
The snow-clad offspring of the sun:
  And thus he was as pure and bright,
And in his natural spirit gay,
With tears for naught but others' ills;
And then they flowed like mountain rills,
Unless he could assuage the woe   90
Which he abhorred to view below.

5

The other was as pure of mind,
But formed to combat with his kind;
Strong in his frame, and of a mood
Which 'gainst the world in war had stood,
And perished in the foremost rank
  With joy:—but not in chains to pine:
His spirit withered with their clank,
  I saw it silently decline—
  And so perchance in sooth did mine: 100
But yet I forced it on to cheer
Those relics of a home so dear.
He was a hunter of the hills,
  Had followed there the deer and wolf;
  To him his dungeon was a gulf,
And fettered feet the worst of ills.

6

Lake Leman lies by Chillon's walls:
A thousand feet in depth below
Its massy waters meet and flow;
Thus much the fathom-line was sent   110
From Chillon's snow-white battlement,
  Which round about the wave inthralls:
A double dungeon wall and wave
Have made—and like a living grave.
Below the surface of the lake
The dark vault lies wherein we lay:
We heard it ripple night and day;
  Sounding o'er our heads it knocked;
And I have felt the winter's spray   119
Wash through the bars when winds were high
And wanton in the happy sky;
  And then the very rock hath rocked,
  And I have felt it shake, unshocked,
Because I could have smiled to see
The death that would have set me free.

7

I said my nearer brother pined,
I said his mighty heart declined,
He loathed and put away his food;
It was not that 'twas coarse and rude,
For we were used to hunter's fare,   130
And for the like had little care:
The milk drawn from the mountain goat
Was changed for water from the moat,
Our bread was such as captives' tears
Have moistened many a thousand years,
Since man first pent his fellow men
Like brutes within an iron den;
But what were these to us or him?
These wasted not his heart or limb;
My brother's soul was of that mould   140
Which in a palace had grown cold,
Had his free breathing been denied
The range of the steep mountain's side;
But why delay the truth?—he died.
I saw, and could not hold his head,

Nor reach his dying hand—nor dead,—
Though hard I strove, but strove in vain,
To rend and gnash my bonds in twain.
He died—and they unlocked his chain,
And scooped for him a shallow grave   150
Even from the cold earth of our cave.
I begged them, as a boon, to lay
His corse in dust whereon the day
Might shine—it was a foolish thought,
But then within my brain it wrought,
That even in death his freeborn breast
In such a dungeon could not rest.
I might have spared my idle prayer—
They coldly laughed—and laid him there:
The flat and turfless earth above   160
The being we so much did love;
His empty chain above it leant,
Such Murder's fitting monument!

8

But he, the favourite and the flower,
Most cherished since his natal hour
His mother's image in fair face,
The infant love of all his race,
His martyred father's dearest thought,
My latest care, for whom I sought
To hoard my life, that his might be   170
Less wretched now, and one day free;
He, too, who yet had held untired
A spirit natural or inspired—
He, too, was struck, and day by day
Was withered on the stalk away.
Oh, God! it is a fearful thing
To see the human soul take wing
In any shape, in any mood:
I've seen it rushing forth in blood,
I've seen it on the breaking ocean   180
Strive with a swoln convulsive motion,
I've seen the sick and ghastly bed
Of Sin delirious with its dread:
But these were horrors—this was woe
Unmixed with such—but sure and slow:
He faded, and so calm and meek,
So softly worn, so sweetly weak,
So tearless, yet so tender—kind,
And grieved for those he left behind;
With all the while a cheek whose bloom   190
Was as a mockery of the tomb,
Whose tints as gently sunk away
As a departing rainbow's ray;
An eye of most transparent light
That almost made the dungeon bright;
And not a word of murmur—not
A groan o'er his untimely lot,—

A little talk of better days,
A little hope my own to raise,
For I was sunk in silence—lost   200
In this last loss, of all the most;
And then the sighs he would suppress
Of fainting Nature's feebleness,
More slowly drawn, grew less and less:
I listened, but I could not hear;
I called, for I was wild with fear;
I knew 'twas hopeless, but my dread
Would not be thus admonishèd;
I called, and thought I heard a sound—
I burst my chain with one strong bound,   210
And rushed to him:—I found him not,
I only stirred in this black spot,
I only lived, *I* only drew
The accursèd breath of dungeon-dew;
The last, the sole, the dearest link
Between me and the eternal brink,
Which bound me to my failing race,
Was broken in this fatal place.
One on the earth, and one beneath—
My brothers—both had ceased to breathe!   220
I took that hand which lay so still,
Alas! my own was full as chill;
I had not strength to stir, or strive,
But felt that I was still alive—
A frantic feeling, when we know
That what we love shall ne'er be so.
  I know not why
  I could not die,
I had no earthly hope—but faith,
And that forbade a selfish death.   230

9

What next befell me then and there
  I know not well—I never knew—
First came the loss of light, and air,
  And then of darkness too:
I had no thought, no feeling—none—
Among the stones I stood a stone,
And was, scarce conscious what I wist,
As shrubless crags within the mist;
For all was blank, and bleak, and grey;
It was not night—it was not day;   240
It was not even the dungeon-light,
So hateful to my heavy sight,
But vacancy absorbing space,
And fixedness—without a place;
There were no stars—no earth—no time—
No check—no change—no good—no crime—
But silence, and a stirless breath
Which neither was of life nor death;

A sea of stagnant idleness,
Blind, boundless, mute, and motionless!   250

10

A light broke in upon my brain,—
   It was the carol of a bird;
It ceased, and then it came again,
   The sweetest song ear ever heard,
And mine was thankful till my eyes
Ran over with the glad surprise,
And they that moment could not see
I was the mate of misery;
But then by dull degrees came back
My senses to their wonted track;   260
I saw the dungeon walls and floor
Close slowly round me as before,
I saw the glimmer of the sun
Creeping as it before had done,
But through the crevice where it came
That bird was perched, as fond and tame,
   And tamer than upon the tree;
A lovely bird, with azure wings,
And song that said a thousand things,
   And seemed to say them all for me!   270
I never saw its like before,
I ne'er shall see its likeness more:
It seemed like me to want a mate,
But was not half so desolate,
And it was come to love me when
None lived to love me so again,
And cheering from my dungeon's brink,
Had brought me back to feel and think.
I know not if it late were free,
   Or broke its cage to perch on mine,   280
But knowing well captivity,
   Sweet bird! I could not wish for thine!
Or if it were, in wingèd guise,
   A visitant from Paradise;
For—Heaven forgive that thought! the while
Which made me both to weep and smile—
I sometimes deemed that it might be
My brother's soul come down to me;
But then at last away it flew,
And then 'twas mortal well I knew,   290
For he would never thus have flown—
And left me twice so doubly lone,—
Lone—as the corse within its shroud,

Lone—as a solitary cloud,
   A single cloud on a sunny day,
While all the rest of heaven is clear,
A frown upon the atmosphere,
That hath no business to appear
   When skies are blue, and earth is gay.

11

A kind of change came in my fate,   300
My keepers grew compassionate;
I know not what had made them so,
They were inured to sights of woe,
But so it was:—my broken chain
With links unfastened did remain,
And it was liberty to stride
Along my cell from side to side,
And up and down, and then athwart,
And tread it over every part;
And round the pillars one by one   310
Returning where my walk begun,
Avoiding only, as I trod,
My brothers' graves without a sod;
For if I thought with heedless tread
My step profaned their lowly bed,
My breath came gaspingly and thick,
And my crushed heart fell blind and sick.

12

I made a footing in the wall,
   It was not therefrom to escape,
For I had buried one and all   320
   Who loved me in a human shape;
And the whole earth would henceforth be
A wider prison unto me:
No child—no sire—no kin had I,
No partner in my misery;
I thought of this, and I was glad,
For thought of them had made me mad;
But I was curious to ascend
To my barred windows, and to bend
Once more, upon the mountains high,   330
The quiet of a loving eye.

13

I saw them—and they were the same,
They were not changed like me in frame;
I saw their thousand years of snow
On high—their wide long lake below,
And the blue Rhone in fullest flow;
I heard the torrents leap and gush
O'er channelled rock and broken bush;

268. a lovely bird. Compare "The Ancient Mariner": the Mariner's mental state (ll. 244 ff.) and his redemption through the influence of the water-snakes (272 ff.) and the skylark's song (359 ff.). **292. twice so doubly lone,** because (1) he had lost the bird's companionship, and (2) this desertion proved that the bird was not his brother's spirit, thus depriving him of his comforting illusion.

294. Lone—as a solitary cloud. Compare Wordsworth's "I Wandered Lonely as a Cloud." **331. The quiet of a loving eye.** Compare Wordsworth's "The harvest of a loving eye" ("A Poet's Epitaph," l. 51).

I saw the white-walled distant town.
And whiter sails go skimming down;   340
And then there was a little isle,
Which in my very face did smile,
    The only one in view;
A small green isle, it seemed no more,
Scarce broader than my dungeon floor,
But in it there were three tall trees,
And o'er it blew the mountain breeze,
And by it there were waters flowing,
And on it there were young flowers growing,
    Of gentle breath and hue.   350
The fish swam by the castle wall,
And they seemed joyous each and all;
The eagle rode the rising blast,
Methought he never flew so fast
As then to me he seemed to fly;
And then new tears came in my eye,
And I felt troubled—and would fain
I had not felt my recent chain;
And when I did descend again,
The darkness of my dim abode   360
Fell on me as a heavy load;
It was as is a new-dug grave,
Closing o'er one we sought to save,—
And yet my glance, too much opprest,
Had almost need of such a rest.

14

It might be months, or years, or days—
    I kept no count, I took no note—
I had no hope my eyes to raise,
    And clear them of their dreary mote;
At last men came to set me free;   370
    I asked not why, and recked not where:
It was at length the same to me,
Fettered or fetterless to be,
    I learned to love despair.
And thus when they appeared at last,
And all my bonds aside were cast,
These heavy walls to me had grown
A hermitage—and all my own!
And half I felt as they were come
To tear me from a second home: 380
With spiders I had friendship made,
And watched them in their sullen trade,
Had seen the mice by moonlight play,
And why should I feel less than they?
We were all inmates of one place,
And I, the monarch of each race,
Had power to kill—yet, strange to tell!
In quiet we had learned to dwell;
My very chains and I grew friends,
So much a long communion tends   390

To make us what we are:—even I
Regained my freedom with a sigh.

STANZAS TO AUGUSTA

1

Though the day of my Destiny's over,
    And the star of my Fate hath declined,
Thy soft heart refused to discover
    The faults which so many could find;
Though thy Soul with my grief was acquainted,
    It shrunk not to share it with me,
And the Love which my Spirit hath painted
    It never hath found but in *Thee*.

2

Then when Nature around me is smiling,
    The last smile which answers to mine,   10
I do not believe it beguiling,
    Because it reminds me of thine;
And when winds are at war with the ocean,
    As the breasts I believed in with me,
If their billows excite an emotion,
    It is that they bear me from *Thee*.

3

Though the rock of my last Hope is shivered,
    And its fragments are sunk in the wave,
Though I feel that my soul is delivered
    To Pain—it shall not be its slave.   20
There is many a pang to pursue me:
    They may crush, but they shall not contemn—
They may torture, but shall not subdue me—
    'Tis of *Thee* that I think—not of them.

4

Though human, thou didst not deceive me,
    Though woman, thou didst not forsake,
Though loved, thou forborest to grieve me,
    Though slandered, thou never couldst shake,—
Though trusted, thou didst not disclaim me,
    Though parted, it was not to fly,   30
Though watchful, 'twas not to defame me,
    Nor, mute, that the world might belie.

5

Yet I blame not the World, nor despise it,
    Nor the war of the many with one;
If my Soul was not fitted to prize it,
    'Twas folly not sooner to shun:
And if dearly that error hath cost me,
    And more than I once could foresee,
I have found that, whatever it lost me,
    It could not deprive me of *Thee*.   40

6

From the wreck of the past, which hath perished,
  Thus much I at least may recall,
It hath taught me that what I most cherished
  Deserved to be dearest of all:
In the Desert a fountain is springing,
  In the wide waste there still is a tree,
And a bird in the solitude singing,
  Which speaks to my spirit of *Thee*.

STANZAS FOR MUSIC

(They Say That Hope Is Happiness)

1

They say that Hope is happiness;
  But genuine Love must prize the past,
And Memory wakes the thoughts that bless:
  They rose the first—they set the last;

2

And all that Memory loves the most
  Was once our only Hope to be,
And all that Hope adored and lost
  Hath melted into Memory.

3

Alas! it is delusion all:
  The future cheats us from afar,   10
Nor can we be what we recall,
  Nor dare we think on what we are.

from CHILDE HAROLD'S PILGRIMAGE

CANTO THE THIRD

"Afin que cette application vous forçât de penser à autre chose; il n'y a en vérité de remède que celui-là et le temps." *
Lettre du Roi de Prusse à D'Alembert, Sept. 7, 1776.

The student should review what has been said about the autobiographical implications of the poem, about its form, and about its plan, on pages 193–96 of the preceding biographical-critical sketch. (A rough sketch map or a line showing Byron's itinerary on any accessible map of Europe will be helpful in following Byron's movements and the topics treated.) The main topics are the poet's own personal history, nature, European history and pol-

* *"Afin que . . . le temps."* In order that this employment may force you to think of something else; there is indeed no remedy but that and time.

itics relating to man's struggle for freedom: really one theme—the poet himself; everything is viewed through the medium of his own personality, profoundly stirred by his recent experiences. The dominant sentiment is "the recourse of a socially alienated mind to an all-tolerant, all-seeing nature" (see especially stanzas 12–13, 46–47, 62, 67–68, 72, 75, 88–90, 93, 96–97, 109).

1

Is thy face like thy mother's, my fair child!
ADA! sole daughter of my house and heart?
When last I saw thy young blue eyes they smiled,
And then we parted,—not as now we part,
But with a hope.—
                  Awaking with a start,
The waters heave around me; and on high
The winds lift up their voices: I depart,
Whither I know not; but the hour's gone by,
When Albion's lessening shores could grieve or glad
  mine eye.

2

Once more upon the waters! yet once more!   10
And the waves bound beneath me as a steed
That knows his rider. Welcome to their roar!
Swift be their guidance, whereso'er it lead!
Though the strained mast should quiver as a reed,
And the rent canvas fluttering strew the gale,
Still must I on; for I am as a weed,
Flung from the rock, on Ocean's foam to sail
Where'er the surge may sweep, the tempest's breath
  prevail.

3

In my youth's summer I did sing of One,
The wandering outlaw of his own dark mind;   20
Again I seize the theme, then but begun,
And bear it with me, as the rushing wind
Bears the cloud onwards: in that Tale I find
The furrows of long thought, and dried-up tears,
Which, ebbing, leave a sterile track behind,
O'er which all heavily the journeying years
Plod the last sands of life,—where not a flower ap-
  pears.

5. Awaking with a start. Note the dramatic opening—the poet, aboard ship in mid-channel, dreaming about his child, is suddenly awakened by the waves to the reality of his exile. The break in the stanza and the line is called "rhetorical shock," a favorite device of Byron's (see stanzas 17, 99, 105, 110). **11–16. steed . . . rider . . . weed.** Note the two superb similes of self-characterization. **19. One.** Childe Harold (in the first and second cantos). ("Childe" means a young gentleman, usually the elder son of a nobleman.) Here begins a review of Byron's life between the end of the first tour and the beginning of his present exile (stanzas 3–15). Note the idea of satiety and disillusionment. Stanza 5 contains the germ of *Manfred, a Dramatic Poem*, written later.

4

Since my young days of passion—joy or pain—
Perchance my heart and harp have lost a string,
And both may jar: it may be that in vain   30
I would essay, as I have sung, to sing:
Yet, though a dreary strain, to this I cling;
So that it wean me from the weary dream
Of selfish grief or gladness—so it fling
Forgetfulness around me—it shall seem
To me, though to none else, a not ungrateful theme.

5

He, who grown agèd in this world of woe,
In deeds, not years, piercing the depths of life,
So that no wonder waits him—nor below
Can Love or Sorrow, Fame, Ambition, Strife,   40
Cut to his heart again with the keen knife
Of silent, sharp endurance—he can tell
Why Thought seeks refuge in lone caves, yet rife
With airy images, and shapes which dwell
Still unimpaired, though old, in the soul's haunted
    cell.

6

'Tis to create, and in creating live
A being more intense, that we endow
With form our fancy, gaining as we give
The life we image, even as I do now—
What am I? Nothing: but not so art thou,   50
Soul of my thought! with whom I traverse earth,
Invisible but gazing, as I glow
Mixed with thy spirit, blended with thy birth,
And feeling still with thee in my crushed feelings'
    dearth.

7

Yet must I think less wildly:—I *have* thought
Too long and darkly, till my brain became,
In its own eddy boiling and o'erwrought,
A whirling gulf of phantasy and flame:
And thus, untaught in youth my heart to tame,
My springs of life were poisoned. 'Tis too late!   60
Yet am I changed; though still enough the same
In strength to bear what Time can not abate,
And feed on bitter fruits without accusing Fate.

8

Something too much of this:—but now 'tis past,
And the spell closes with its silent seal.
Long absent HAROLD re-appears at last—
He of the breast which fain no more would feel,

46. **'Tis to create.** Here follows a poetic essay on poetry—
why Byron writes it.   66. **Long absent Harold re-appears.**
Note that in this Canto Byron identifies himself with his
hero; he had not done so in the first and second.

Wrung with the wounds which kill not, but ne'er
    heal;
Yet Time, who changes all, had altered him
In soul and aspect as in age: years steal   70
Fire from the mind as vigour from the limb;
And Life's enchanted cup but sparkles near the
    brim.

9

His had been quaffed too quickly, and he found
The dregs were wormwood; but he filled again,
And from a purer fount, on holier ground,
And deemed its spring perpetual!—but in vain!
Still round him clung invisibly a chain
Which galled for ever, fettering though unseen,
And heavy though it clanked not; worn with
    pain,
Which pined although it spoke not, and grew
    keen,   80
Entering with every step he took through many a
    scene.

10

Secure in guarded coldness, he had mixed
Again in fancied safety with his kind,
And deemed his spirit now so firmly fixed
And sheathed with an invulnerable mind,
That, if no joy, no sorrow lurked behind;
And he, as one, might 'midst the many stand
Unheeded, searching through the crowd to find
Fit speculation—such as in strange land
He found in wonder-works of God and Nature's
    hand.   90

11

But who can view the ripened rose, nor seek
To wear it? who can curiously behold
The smoothness and the sheen of Beauty's cheek,
Nor feel the heart can never all grow old?
Who can contemplate Fame through clouds un-
    fold
The star which rises o'er her steep, nor climb?
Harold, once more within the vortex, rolled
On with the giddy circle, chasing Time,
Yet with a nobler aim than in his Youth's fond
    prime.

12

But soon he knew himself the most unfit   100
Of men to herd with Man; with whom he held
Little in common; untaught to submit
His thoughts to others, though his soul was quelled
In youth by his own thoughts; still uncompelled,
He would not yield dominion of his mind

To Spirits against whom his own rebelled,
Proud though in desolation—which could find
A life within itself, to breathe without mankind.

13

Where rose the mountains, there to him were
    friends;
Where rolled the Ocean, thereon was his
    home; 110
Where a blue sky, and glowing clime, extends,
He had the passion and the power to roam;
The desert, forest, cavern, breaker's foam,
Were unto him companionship; they spake
A mutual language, clearer than the tome
Of his land's tongue, which he would oft forsake
For Nature's pages glassed by sunbeams on the
    lake.

14

Like the Chaldean, he could watch the stars,
Till he had peopled them with beings bright
As their own beams; and earth, and earth-born
    jars, 120
And human frailties, were forgotten quite:
Could he have kept his spirit to that flight
He had been happy; but this clay will sink
Its spark immortal, envying it the light
To which it mounts, as if to break the link
That keeps us from yon heaven which woos us to its
    brink.

15

But in Man's dwellings he became a thing
Restless and worn, and stern and wearisome,
Drooped as a wild-born falcon with clipt wing,
To whom the boundless air alone were home: 130
Then came his fit again, which to o'er-come,
As eagerly the barred-up bird will beat
His breast and beak against his wiry dome
Till the blood tinge his plumage—so the heat
Of his impeded Soul would through his bosom
    eat.

16

Self-exiled Harold wanders forth again,
With nought of Hope left, but with less of gloom;
The very knowledge that he lived in vain,
That all was over on this side the tomb,
Had made Despair a smilingness assume, 140
Which, though 'twere wild,—as on the plundered
    wreck
When mariners would madly meet their doom
With draughts intemperate on the sinking deck,—
Did yet inspire a cheer, which he forbore to check.

17

Stop!—for thy tread is on an Empire's dust!
An Earthquake's spoil is sepulchred below!
Is the spot marked with no colossal bust?
Nor column trophied for triumphal show?
None; but *the moral's truth* tells simpler so,
As the ground was before, thus let it be;— 150
How that red rain hath made the harvest grow!
And is this all the world has gained by thee,
Thou first and last of Fields! king-making Victory?

18

And Harold stands upon this place of skulls,
The grave of France, the deadly Waterloo!
How in an hour the Power which gave annuls
Its gifts, transferring fame as fleeting too!—
In "pride of place" here last the Eagle flew,
Then tore with bloody talon the rent plain,
Pierced by the shaft of banded nations
    through; 160
Ambition's life and labours all were vain—
He wears the shattered links of the World's broken
    chain.

19

Fit retribution! Gaul may champ the bit
And foam in fetters;—but is Earth more free?
Did nations combat to make *One* submit;
Or league to teach all Kings true Sovereignty?
What! shall reviving Thraldom again be
The patched-up Idol of enlightened days?
Shall we, who struck the Lion down, shall we
Pay the Wolf homage? proffering lowly gaze 170
And servile knees to Thrones? No; *prove* before ye
    praise!

20

If not, o'er one fallen Despot boast no more!
In vain fair cheeks were furrowed with hot tears
For Europe's flowers long rooted up before
The trampler of her vineyards; in vain, years
Of death, depopulation, bondage, fears,
Have all been borne, and broken by the accord
Of roused-up millions; all that most endears
Glory, is when the myrtle wreathes a Sword
Such as Harmodius drew on Athens' tyrant
    Lord. 180

21

There was a sound of revelry by night,
And Belgium's Capital had gathered then

145. **Empire's dust,** Napoleon's empire (and France's).
Byron visited Waterloo almost exactly a year after the battle.
181 ff. There was a sound of revelry . . . With this famous account of the Duchess of Richmond's ball, and of
Waterloo, compare Thackeray's in *Vanity Fair*, chaps. 29–32.

Her Beauty and her Chivalry, and bright
The lamps shone o'er fair women and brave men;
A thousand hearts beat happily; and when
Music arose with its voluptuous swell,
Soft eyes looked love to eyes which spake again,
And all went merry as a marriage bell;
But hush! hark! a deep sound strikes like a rising
 knell!

22

Did ye not hear it?—No—'twas but the
 Wind,   190
Or the car rattling o'er the stony street;
On with the dance! let joy be unconfined;
No sleep till morn, when Youth and Pleasure
 meet
To chase the glowing Hours with flying feet—
But hark!—that heavy sound breaks in once
 more,
As if the clouds its echo would repeat;
And nearer, clearer, deadlier than before!
Arm! Arm! it is—it is—the cannon's opening roar!

23

Within a windowed niche of that high hall
Sate Brunswick's fated Chieftain; he did hear 200
That sound the first amidst the festival,
And caught its tone with Death's prophetic ear;
And when they smiled because he deemed it near,
His heart more truly knew that peal too well
Which stretched his father on a bloody bier,
And roused the vengeance blood alone could
 quell;
He rushed into the field, and, foremost fighting, fell.

24

Ah! then and there was hurrying to and fro—
And gathering tears, and tremblings of distress,
And cheeks all pale, which but an hour ago 210
Blushed at the praise of their own loveliness—
And there were sudden partings, such as press
The life from out young hearts, and choking sighs
Which ne'er might be repeated; who could guess
If ever more should meet those mutual eyes,
Since upon night so sweet such awful morn could
 rise!

25

And there was mounting in hot haste—the steed,
The mustering squadron, and the clattering car,
Went pouring forward with impetuous speed,
And swiftly forming in the ranks of war— 220
And deep the thunder peal on peal afar;
And near, the beat of the alarming drum

Roused up the soldier ere the Morning Star;
While thronged the citizens with terror dumb,
Or whispering, with white lips—"The foe! They
 come! they come!"

26

And wild and high the "Cameron's gathering"
 rose!
The war-note of Lochiel, which Albyn's hills
Have heard, and heard, too, have her Saxon
 foes:—
How in the noon of night that pibroch thrills,
Savage and shrill! But with the breath which
 fills   230
Their mountain pipe, so fill the mountaineers
With the fierce native daring which instils
The stirring memory of a thousand years,
And Evan's—Donald's—fame rings in each clans-
 man's ears!

27

And Ardennes waves above them her green
 leaves,
Dewy with Nature's tear-drops, as they pass—
Grieving, if aught inanimate e'er grieves,
Over the unreturning brave,—alas!
Ere evening to be trodden like the grass
Which *now* beneath them, but *above* shall
 grow   240
In its next verdure, when this fiery mass
Of living Valour, rolling on the foe
And burning with high Hope, shall moulder cold
 and low.

28

Last noon beheld them full of lusty life;—
Last eve in Beauty's circle proudly gay,
The Midnight brought the signal-sound of strife,
The Morn the marshalling in arms,—the Day
Battle's magnificently-stern array!
The thunder-clouds close o'er it, which when rent
The earth is covered thick with other clay, 250
Which her own clay shall cover, heaped and pent,
Rider and horse,—friend, foe,—in one red burial
 blent!

29

Their praise is hymned by loftier harps than
 mine:
Yet one I would select from that proud throng,
Partly because they blend me with his line,
And partly that I did his Sire some wrong,
And partly that bright names will hallow song;
And his was of the bravest, and when showered

The death-bolts deadliest the thinned files along,
Even where the thickest of War's tempest
    lowered, 260
They reached no nobler breast than thine, young,
    gallant Howard!

30

There have been tears and breaking hearts for
    thee,
And mine were nothing, had I such to give;
But when I stood beneath the fresh green tree,
Which living waves where thou didst cease to live,
And saw around me the wide field revive
With fruits and fertile promise, and the Spring
Came forth her work of gladness to contrive,
With all her reckless birds upon the wing,
I turned from all she brought to those she could not
    bring. 270

31

I turned to thee, to thousands, of whom each
And one as all a ghastly gap did make
In his own kind and kindred, whom to teach
Forgetfulness were mercy for their sake;
The Archangel's trump, not Glory's, must awake
Those whom they thirst for; though the sound of
    Fame
May for a moment soothe, it cannot slake
The fever of vain longing, and the name
So honoured but assumes a stronger, bitterer claim.

32

They mourn, but smile at length—and, smiling,
    mourn: 280
The tree will wither long before it fall;
The hull drives on, though mast and sail be torn;
The roof-tree sinks, but moulders on the hall
In massy hoariness; the ruined wall
Stands when its wind-worn battlements are gone;
The bars survive the captive they enthral;
The day drags through though storms keep out
    the sun;
And thus the heart will break, yet brokenly live on:

33

Even as a broken Mirror, which the glass
In every fragment multiplies—and makes 290
A thousand images of one that was
The same—and still the more, the more it breaks;
And thus the heart will do which not forsakes,
Living in shattered guise; and still, and cold,
And bloodless, with its sleepless sorrow aches,
Yet withers on till all without is old,
Showing no visible sign, for such things are untold.

34

There is a very life in our despair,
Vitality of poison,—a quick root
Which feeds these deadly branches; for it
    were 300
As nothing did we die; but Life will suit
Itself to Sorrow's most detested fruit,
Like to the apples on the Dead Sea's shore,
All ashes to the taste: Did man compute
Existence by enjoyment, and count o'er
Such hours 'gainst years of life,—say, would **he**
    name threescore?

35

The Psalmist numbered out the years of man:
They are enough; and if thy tale be *true*,
Thou, who didst grudge him even that fleeting
    span,
More than enough, thou fatal Waterloo! 310
Millions of tongues record thee, and anew
Their children's lips shall echo them, and say—
"Here, where the sword united nations drew,
Our countrymen were warring on that day!"
And this is much—and all—which will not **pass**
    away.

36

There sunk the greatest, nor the worst of men,
Whose Spirit, antithetically mixed,
One moment of the mightiest, and again
On little objects with like firmness fixed;
Extreme in all things! hadst thou been be-
    twixt, 320
Thy throne had still been thine, or never been;
For Daring made thy rise as fall: thou seek'st
Even now to re-assume the imperial mien,
And shake again the world, the Thunderer of **the**
    scene!

37

Conqueror and Captive of the Earth art thou!
She trembles at thee still, and thy wild name
Was ne'er more bruited in men's minds than **now**
That thou art nothing, save the jest of Fame,
Who wooed thee once, thy Vassal, and became
The flatterer of thy fierceness—till thou wert 330
A God unto thyself; nor less the same
To the astounded kingdoms all inert,
Who deemed thee for a time whate'er thou didst
    assert.

38

Oh, more or less than man—in high or low—
Battling with nations, flying from the field;

Now making monarchs' necks thy footstool, now
More than thy meanest soldier taught to yield;
An Empire thou couldst crush, command, re-
     build,
But govern not thy pettiest passion, nor,
However deeply in men's spirits skilled,   340
Look through thine own, nor curb the lust of
     War,
Nor learn that tempted Fate will leave the loftiest
     Star.

39

Yet well thy soul hath brooked the turning tide
With that untaught innate philosophy,
Which, be it Wisdom, Coldness, or deep Pride,
Is gall and wormwood to an enemy.
When the whole host of hatred stood hard by,
To watch and mock thee shrinking, thou hast
     smiled
With a sedate and all-enduring eye;—
When Fortune fled her spoiled and favourite
     child,   350
He stood unbowed beneath the ills upon him piled.

40

Sager than in thy fortunes; for in them
Ambition steeled thee on too far to show
That just habitual scorn, which could contemn
Men and their thoughts; 'twas wise to feel, not so
To wear it ever on thy lip and brow,
And spurn the instruments thou wert to use
Till they were turned unto thine overthrow:
'Tis but a worthless world to win or lose;
So hath it proved to thee, and all such lot who
     choose.   360

41

If, like a tower upon a headland rock,
Thou hadst been made to stand or fall alone,
Such scorn of man had helped to brave the shock;
But men's thoughts were the steps which paved
     thy throne,
Their admiration thy best weapon shone;
The part of Philip's son was thine—not then
(Unless aside thy Purple had been thrown)
Like stern Diogenes to mock at men;
For sceptred Cynics Earth were far too wide a den.

42

But Quiet to quick bosoms is a Hell,   370
And *there* hath been thy bane; there is a fire
And motion of the Soul which will not dwell
In its own narrow being, but aspire
Beyond the fitting medium of desire;

And, but once kindled, quenchless evermore,
Preys upon high adventure, nor can tire
Of aught but rest; a fever at the core,
Fatal to him who bears, to all who ever bore.

43

This makes the madmen who have made men
     mad
By their contagion; Conquerors and Kings,   380
Founders of sects and systems, to whom add
Sophists, Bards, Statesmen, all unquiet things
Which stir too strongly the soul's secret springs,
And are themselves the fools to those they fool;
Envied, yet how unenviable! what stings
Are theirs! One breast laid open were a school
Which would unteach Mankind the lust to shine or
     rule:

44

Their breath is agitation, and their life
A storm whereon they ride, to sink at last,
And yet so nursed and bigoted to strife,   390
That should their days, surviving perils past,
Melt to calm twilight, they feel overcast
With sorrow and supineness, and so die;
Even as a flame unfed, which runs to waste
With its own flickering, or a sword laid by,
Which eats into itself, and rusts ingloriously.

45

He who ascends to mountain tops, shall find
The loftiest peaks most wrapt in clouds and snow;
He who surpasses or subdues mankind,
Must look down on the hate of those below.   400
Though high *above* the Sun of Glory glow,
And far *beneath* the Earth and Ocean spread,
Round him are icy rocks, and loudly blow
Contending tempests on his naked head,
And thus reward the toils which to those summits
     led.

46

Away with these! true Wisdom's world will be
Within its own creation, or in thine,
Maternal Nature! for who teems like thee,
Thus on the banks of thy majestic Rhine?
There Harold gazes on a work divine,   410
A blending of all beauties; streams and dells,
Fruit, foliage, crag, wood, cornfield, mountain,
     vine,
And chiefless castles breathing stern farewells
From gray but leafy walls, where Ruin greenly
     dwells.

409. majestic Rhine. Note the transition.

47

And there they stand, as stands a lofty mind,
Worn, but unstooping to the baser crowd,
All tenantless, save to the crannying Wind,
Or holding dark communion with the Cloud.
There was a day when they were young and
    proud;
Banners on high, and battles passed below;   420
But they who fought are in a bloody shroud,
And those which waved are shredless dust ere
    now,
And the bleak battlements shall bear no future blow.

48

Beneath those battlements, within those walls,
Power dwelt amidst her passions; in proud state
Each robber chief upheld his armèd halls,
Doing his evil will, nor less elate
Than mightier heroes of a longer date.
What want these outlaws conquerors should have
But History's purchased page to call them
    great?   430
A wider space—an ornamented grave?
Their hopes were not less warm, their souls were
    full as brave.

49

In their baronial feuds and single fields,
What deeds of prowess unrecorded died?
And Love, which lent a blazon to their shields,
With emblems well devised by amorous pride,
Through all the mail of iron hearts would glide;
But still their flame was fierceness, and drew on
Keen contest and destruction near allied,
And many a tower for some fair mischief won, 440
Saw the discoloured Rhine beneath its ruin run.

50

But Thou, exulting and abounding river!
Making thy waves a blessing as they flow
Through banks whose beauty would endure for
    ever
Could man but leave thy bright creation so,
Nor its fair promise from the surface mow
With the sharp scythe of conflict,—then to see
Thy valley of sweet waters, were to know
Earth paved like Heaven—and to seem such to
    me,
Even now what wants thy stream?—that it should
    Lethe be.   450

51

A thousand battles have assailed thy banks,
But these and half their fame have passed away,

And Slaughter heaped on high his weltering
    ranks;
Their very graves are gone, and what are they?
Thy tide washed down the blood of yesterday,
And all was stainless, and on thy clear stream
Glassed, with its dancing light, the sunny ray;
But o'er the blackened Memory's blighting dream
Thy waves would vainly roll, all sweeping as they
    seem.

52

Thus Harold inly said, and passed along,   460
Yet not insensible to all which here
Awoke the jocund birds to early song
In glens which might have made even exile dear:
Though on his brow were graven lines austere,
And tranquil sternness, which had ta'en the place
Of feelings fiercer far but less severe—
Joy was not always absent from his face
But o'er it in such scenes would steal with transient
    trace.

53

Nor was all Love shut from him, though his days
Of Passion had consumed themselves to dust. 470
It is in vain that we would coldly gaze
On such as smile upon us; the heart must
Leap kindly back to kindness, though Disgust
Hath weaned it from all worldings: thus he felt,
For there was soft Remembrance, and sweet Trust
In one fond breast, to which his own would melt,
And in its tenderer hour on that his bosom dwelt.

54

And he had learned to love,—I know not why,
For this in such as him seems strange of mood,—
The helpless looks of blooming Infancy,   480
Even in its earliest nurture; what subdued,
To change like this, a mind so far inbued
With scorn of man, it little boots to know;
But thus it was; and though in solitude
Small power the nipped affections have to grow,
In him this glowed when all beside had ceased to
    glow.

55

And there was one soft breast, as hath been said,
Which unto his was bound by stronger ties
Than the church links withal; and,—though un-
    wed,
That love was pure—and, far above disguise, 490
Had stood the test of mortal enmities,
Still undivided, and cemented more

476. one fond breast, Augusta's.

By peril, dreaded most in female eyes;
But this was firm, and from a foreign shore
Well to that heart might his these absent greetings
    pour!

1

The castled crag of Drachenfels
Frowns o'er the wide and winding Rhine,
Whose breast of waters broadly swells
Between the banks which bear the vine;
And hills all rich with blossomed trees,   500
And fields which promise corn and wine,
And scattered cities crowning these,
Whose far white walls along them shine,
Have strewed a scene, which I should see
With double joy wert *thou* with me.

2

And peasant girls, with deep blue eyes,
And hands which offer early flowers,
Walk smiling o'er this Paradise;
Above, the frequent feudal towers
Through green leaves lift their walls of
    gray;   510
And many a rock which steeply lowers,
And noble arch in proud decay,
Look o'er this vale of vintage-bowers;
But one thing want these banks of Rhine,—
Thy gentle hand to clasp in mine!

3

I send the lilies given to me—
Though long before thy hand they touch,
I know that they must withered be,
But yet reject them not as such;
For I have cherished them as dear,   520
Because they yet may meet thine eye,
And guide thy soul to mine even here,—
When thou behold'st them drooping nigh,
And know'st them gathered by the Rhine,
And offered from my heart to thine!

4

The river nobly foams and flows—
The charm of this enchanted ground,
And all its thousand turns disclose
Some fresher beauty's varying round:
The haughtiest breast its wish might bound   530
Through life to dwell delighted here;
Nor could on earth a spot be found

516. **I send the lilies.** When the poem appeared in 1816, while the scandal was still fresh, Augusta wished the lilies and the poem at the bottom of the Red Sea.

To nature and to me so dear—
Could thy dear eyes in following mine
Still sweeten more these banks of Rhine!

56

By Coblentz, on a rise of gentle ground,
There is a small and simple Pyramid,
Crowning the summit of the verdant mound;
Beneath its base are Heroes' ashes hid,
Our enemy's—but let not that forbid   540
Honour to Marceau! o'er whose early tomb
Tears, big tears, gushed from the rough soldier's
    lid,
Lamenting and yet envying such a doom,
Falling for France, whose rights he battled to re-
    sume.

57

Brief, brave, and glorious was his young career,—
His mourners were two hosts, his friends and foes;
And fitly may the stranger lingering here
Pray for his gallant Spirit's bright repose;
For he was Freedom's Champion, one of those,
The few in number, who had not o'erstept   550
The charter to chastise which she bestows
On such as wield her weapons; he had kept
The whiteness of his soul—and thus men o'er him
    wept.

58

Here Ehrenbreitstein, with her shattered wall
Black with the miner's blast, upon her height
Yet shows of what she was, when shell and ball
Rebounding idly on her strength did light:—
A Tower of Victory! from whence the flight
Of baffled foes was watched along the plain:
But Peace destroyed what War could never
    blight,   560
And laid those proud roofs bare to Summer's
    rain—
On which the iron shower for years had poured in
    vain.

59

Adieu to thee, fair Rhine! How long delighted
The stranger fain would linger on his way!
Thine is a scene alike where souls united,
Or lonely Contemplation thus might stray;
And could the ceaseless vultures cease to prey
On self-condemning bosoms, it were here,
Where Nature, nor too sombre nor too gay,
Wild but not rude, awful yet not austere,   570
Is to the mellow Earth as Autumn to the year.

60

Adieu to thee again! a vain adieu!
There can be no farewell to scene like thine;
The mind is coloured by thy every hue;
And if reluctantly the eyes resign
Their cherished gaze upon thee, lovely Rhine!
'Tis with the thankful heart of parting praise;
More mighty spots may rise, more glaring shine,
But none unite, in one attaching maze,
The brilliant, fair, and soft,—the glories of old
    days,   580

61

The negligently grand, the fruitful bloom
Of coming ripeness, the white city's sheen,
The rolling stream, the precipice's gloom,
The forest's growth, and Gothic walls between,
The wild rocks shaped as they had turrets been,
In mockery of man's art; and these withal
A race of faces happy as the scene,
Whose fertile bounties here extend to all,
Still springing o'er thy banks, though Empires near
    them fall.

62

But these recede. Above me are the Alps,   590
The Palaces of Nature, whose vast walls
Have pinnacled in clouds their snowy scalps,
And throned Eternity in icy halls
Of cold Sublimity, where forms and falls
The Avalanche—the thunderbolt of snow!
All that expands the spirit, yet appals,
Gather around these summits, as to show
How Earth may pierce to Heaven, yet leave vain
    man below.

63

But ere these matchless heights I dare to scan,
There is a spot should not be passed in
    vain,—   600
Morat! the proud, the patriot field! where man
May gaze on ghastly trophies of the slain,
Nor blush for those who conquered on that plain;
Here Burgundy bequeathed his tombless host,
A bony heap, through ages to remain,
Themselves their monument;—the Stygian coast
Unsepulchred they roamed, and shrieked each
    wandering ghost.

64

While Waterloo with Cannae's carnage vies,
Morat and Marathon twin names shall stand;
They were true Glory's stainless victories,   610
Won by the unambitious heart and hand
Of a proud, brotherly, and civic band,
All unbought champions in no princely cause
Of vice-entailed Corruption; they no land
Doomed to bewail the blasphemy of laws
Making Kings' rights divine, by some Draconic
    clause.

65

By a lone wall a lonelier column rears
A gray and grief-worn aspect of old days;
'Tis the last remnant of the wreck of years,
And looks as with the wild-bewildered gaze   620
Of one to stone converted by amaze,
Yet still with consciousness; and there it stands
Making a marvel that it not decays,
When the coeval pride of human hands,
Levelled Aventicum, hath strewed her subject lands.

66

And there—oh! sweet and sacred be the name!
Julia—the daughter—the devoted—gave
Her youth to Heaven; her heart, beneath a claim
Nearest to Heaven's, broke o'er a father's grave.
Justice is sworn 'gainst tears, and hers would
    crave   630
The life she lived in—but the Judge was just—
And then she died on him she could not save.
Their tomb was simple, and without a bust,
And held within their urn one mind—one heart—
    one dust.

67

But these are deeds which should not pass away,
And names that must not wither, though the
    Earth
Forgets her empires with a just decay,
The enslavers and the enslaved—their death and
    birth;
This high, the mountain-majesty of Worth
Should be—and shall, survivor of its woe,   640
And from its immortality, look forth
In the Sun's face, like yonder Alpine snow,
Imperishably pure beyond all things below.

68

Lake Leman woos me with its crystal face,
The mirror where the stars and mountains view
The stillness of their aspect in each trace
Its clear depth yields of their far height and hue:
There is too much of Man here, to look through

627–34. **Julia . . . one dust.** Byron's interest in the story
of Julia Alpinula, the young Aventian priestess who died
vainly to save her father, was stimulated by a forged
epitaph.

With a fit mind the might which I behold;
But soon in me shall Loneliness renew   650
Thoughts hid, but not less cherished than of old,
Ere mingling with the herd had penned me in their
    fold.

69

To fly from, need not be to hate, mankind:
All are not fit with them to stir and toil,
Nor is it discontent to keep the mind
Deep in its fountain, lest it overboil
In the hot throng, where we become the spoil
Of our infection, till too late and long
We may deplore and struggle with the coil,
In wretched interchange of wrong for wrong   660
Midst a contentious world, striving where none are
    strong.

70

There, in a moment we may plunge our years
In fatal penitence, and in the blight
Of our own Soul turn all our blood to tears,
And colour things to come with hues of Night;
The race of life becomes a hopeless flight
To those that walk in darkness: on the sea
The boldest steer but where their ports invite—
But there are wanderers o'er Eternity
Whose bark drives on and on, and anchored ne'er
    shall be.   670

71

Is it not better, then, to be alone,
And love Earth only for its earthly sake?
By the blue rushing of the arrowy Rhone,
Or the pure bosom of its nursing Lake,
Which feeds it as a mother who doth make
A fair but froward infant her own care,
Kissing its cries away as these awake;—
Is it not better thus our lives to wear,
Than join the crushing crowd, doomed to inflict or
    bear?

72

I live not in myself, but I become   680
Portion of that around me; and to me
High mountains are a feeling, but the hum
Of human cities torture: I can see
Nothing to loathe in Nature, save to be
A link reluctant in a fleshly chain,
Classed among creatures, when the soul can flee,
And with the sky—the peak—the heaving plain
Of ocean, or the stars, mingle—and not in vain.

680. I live not in myself. Compare Wordsworth's ideas
about nature, especially in "Tintern Abbey."

73

And thus I am absorbed, and this is life:—
I look upon the peopled desert past,   690
As on a place of agony and strife,
Where, for some sin, to Sorrow I was cast,
To act and suffer, but remount at last
With a fresh pinion; which I feel to spring,
Though young, yet waxing vigorous as the Blast
Which it would cope with, on delighted wing,
Spurning the clay-cold bonds which round our
    being cling.

74

And when, at length, the mind shall be all free
From what it hates in this degraded form,
Reft of its carnal life, save what shall be   700
Existent happier in the fly and worm,—
When Elements to Elements conform,
And dust is as it should be, shall I not
Feel all I see less dazzling but more warm?
The bodiless thought? the Spirit of each spot?
Of which, even now, I share at times the immortal
    lot?

75

Are not the mountains, waves, and skies, a part
Of me and of my Soul, as I of them?
Is not the love of these deep in my heart
With a pure passion? should I not contemn   710
All objects, if compared with these? and stem
A tide of suffering, rather than forego
Such feelings for the hard and worldly phlegm
Of those whose eyes are only turned below,
Gazing upon the ground, with thoughts which dare
    not glow?

76

But this is not my theme; and I return
To that which is immediate, and require
Those who find contemplation in the urn,
To look on One, whose dust was once all fire,—
A native of the land where I respire   720
The clear air for a while—a passing guest,
Where he became a being,—whose desire
Was to be glorious; 'twas a foolish quest,
The which to gain and keep, he sacrificed all rest.

77

Here the self-torturing sophist, wild Rousseau,
The apostle of Affliction, he who threw
Enchantment over Passion, and from Woe
Wrung overwhelming eloquence, first drew

698. And when, at length. Study this pantheistic conception of immortality.

The breath which made him wretched; yet he
   knew
How to make Madness beautiful, and cast   730
O'er erring deeds and thoughts, a heavenly hue
Of words, like sunbeams, dazzling as they past
The eyes, which o'er them shed tears feelingly and
   fast.

78

His love was Passion's essence—as a tree
On fire by lightning; with ethereal flame
Kindled he was, and blasted; for to be
Thus, and enamoured, were in him the same.
But his was not the love of living dame,
Nor of the dead who rise upon our dreams,
But of ideal Beauty, which became   740
In him existence, and o'erflowing teems
Along his burning page, distempered though it
   seems.

79

This breathed itself to life in Julie, *this*
Invested her with all that's wild and sweet;
This hallowed, too, the memorable kiss
Which every morn his fevered lip would greet,
From hers, who but with friendship his would
   meet;
But to that gentle touch, through brain and breast
Flashed the thrilled Spirit's love-devouring heat;
In that absorbing sigh perchance more blest   750
Than vulgar minds may be with all they seek
   possest.

80

His life was one long war with self-sought foes,
Or friends by him self-banished; for his mind
Had grown Suspicion's sanctuary, and chose,
For its own cruel sacrifice, the kind,
'Gainst whom he raged with fury strange and
   blind.
But he was phrensied,—wherefore, who may
   know?
Since cause might be which Skill could never
   find;
But he was phrensied by disease or woe,
To that worst pitch of all, which wears a reasoning
   show.   760

81

For then he was inspired, and from him came,
As from the Pythian's mystic cave of yore,
Those oracles which set the world in flame,
Nor ceased to burn till kingdoms were no more:

743. Julie, in Rousseau's novel *Julie, ou la nouvelle
Héloïse,* 1760.

Did he not this for France? which lay before
Bowed to the inborn tyranny of years,
Broken and trembling to the yoke she bore,
Till by the voice of him and his compeers,
Roused up to too much wrath, which follows o'er-
   grown fears?

82

They made themselves a fearful monument!   770
The wreck of old opinions—things which grew,
Breathed from the birth of Time: the veil they
   rent,
And what behind it lay, all earth shall view;
But good with ill they also overthrew,
Leaving but ruins, wherewith to rebuild
Upon the same foundation, and renew
Dungeons and thrones, which the same hour
   re-filled,
As heretofore, because Ambition was self-willed.

83

But this will not endure, nor be endured!
Mankind have felt their strength, and made it
   felt.   780
They might have used it better, but, allured
By their new vigour, sternly have they dealt
On one another; Pity ceased to melt
With her once natural charities. But they,
Who in Oppression's darkness caved had dwelt,
They were not eagles, nourished with the day;
What marvel then, at times, if they mistook their
   prey?

84

What deep wounds ever closed without a scar?
The heart's bleed longest, and but heal to wear
That which disfigures it; and they who war   790
With their own hopes, and have been vanquished,
   bear
Silence, but not submission: in his lair
Fixed Passion holds his breath, until the hour
Which shall atone for years; none need despair:
It came—it cometh—and will come,—the power
To punish or forgive—in *one* we shall be slower.

85

Clear, placid Leman! thy contrasted lake,
With the wild world I dwelt in, is a thing
Which warns me, with its stillness, to forsake
Earth's troubled waters for a purer spring.   800

797. Clear, placid Leman! Note that the famous description of Lake Geneva, the summit of the poem, is in three
scenes: (1) evening (idyllic peace), (2) night (storm, the
climax—in the poet's breast), and (3) morning (the earth
fresh and joyous).

This quiet sail is as a noiseless wing
To waft me from distraction; once I loved
Torn Ocean's roar, but thy soft murmuring
Sounds sweet as if a Sister's voice reproved,
That I with stern delights should e'er have been so
    moved.

86

It is the hush of night, and all between
Thy margin and the mountains, dusk, yet clear,
Mellowed and mingling, yet distinctly seen,
Save darkened Jura, whose capt heights appear
Precipitously steep; and drawing near,   810
There breathes a living fragrance from the shore,
Of flowers yet fresh with childhood; on the
    ear
Drops the light drip of the suspended oar,
Or chirps the grasshopper one good-night carol
    more.

87

He is an evening reveller, who makes
His life an infancy, and sings his fill;
At intervals, some bird from out the brakes
Starts into voice a moment, then is still.
There seems a floating whisper on the hill,
But that is fancy, for the Starlight dews   820
All silently their tears of Love instil,
Weeping themselves away, till they infuse
Deep into Nature's breast the spirit of her hues.

88

Ye Stars! which are the poetry of Heaven!
If in your bright leaves we would read the fate
Of men and empires,—'tis to be forgiven,
That in our aspirations to be great,
Our destinies o'erleap their mortal state,
And claim a kindred with you; for ye are
A Beauty and a Mystery, and create   830
In us such love and reverence from afar,
That Fortune,—Fame,—Power,—Life, have named
    themselves a Star.

89

All Heaven and Earth are still—though not in
    sleep,
But breathless, as we grow when feeling most;
And silent, as we stand in thoughts too deep:—
All Heaven and Earth are still: From the high
    host
Of stars to the lulled lake and mountain-coast,
All is concentered in a life intense,
Where not a beam, nor air, nor leaf is lost,

But hath a part of Being, and a sense   840
Of that which is of all Creator and Defence.

90

Then stirs the feeling infinite, so felt
In solitude, where we are *least* alone;
A truth, which through our being then doth
    melt,
And purifies from self: it is a tone,
The soul and source of Music, which makes
    known
Eternal harmony, and sheds a charm
Like to the fabled Cytherea's zone,
Binding all things with beauty;—'twould disarm
The spectre Death, had he substantial power to
    harm.   850

91

Not vainly did the early Persian make
His altar the high places, and the peak
Of earth-o'ergazing mountains, and thus take
A fit and unwalled temple, there to seek
The Spirit, in whose honour shrines are weak,
Upreared by human hands. Come and compare
Columns and idol-dwellings—Goth or Greek—
With Nature's realms of worship, earth and
    air—
Nor fix on fond abodes to circumscribe thy prayer!

92

The sky is changed!—and such a change! Oh
    Night,   860
And Storm, and Darkness, ye are wondrous
    strong,
Yet lovely in your strength, as is the light
Of a dark eye in Woman! Far along,
From peak to peak, the rattling crags among
Leaps the live thunder! Not from one lone cloud,
But every mountain now hath found a tongue,
And Jura answers, through her misty shroud,
Back to the joyous Alps, who call to her aloud!

93

And this is in the Night:—Most glorious Night!
Thou wert not sent for slumber! let me be   870
A sharer in thy fierce and far delight,—
A portion of the tempest and of thee!
How the lit lake shines, a phosphoric sea,
And the big rain comes dancing to the earth!
And now again 'tis black,—and now, the glee
Of the loud hills shakes with its mountain-mirth,
As if they did rejoice o'er a young Earthquake's
    birth.

94

Now, where the swift Rhone cleaves his way
  between
Heights which appear as lovers who have parted
In hate, whose mining depths so intervene,   880
That they can meet no more, though broken-
  hearted;
Though in their souls, which thus each other
  thwarted,
Love was the very root of the fond rage
Which blighted their life's bloom, and then de-
  parted:—
Itself expired, but leaving them an age
Of years all winters,—war within themselves to
  wage:

95

Now, where the quick Rhone thus hath cleft his
  way,
The mightiest of the storms hath taken his stand:
For here, not one, but many, make their play,
And fling their thunder-bolts from hand to hand,
Flashing and cast around: of all the band,   891
The brightest through these parted hills hath
  forked
His lightnings,—as if he did understand,
That in such gaps as Desolation worked,
There the hot shaft should blast whatever therein
  lurked.

96

Sky—Mountains—River—Winds—Lake—light-
  nings! ye!
With night, and clouds, and thunder, and a Soul
To make these felt and feeling, well may be
Things that have made me watchful; the far roll
Of your departing voices, is the knoll   900
Of what in me is sleepless,—if I rest.
But where of ye, O Tempests! is the goal?
Are ye like those within the human breast?
Or do ye find, at length, like eagles, some high
  nest?

97

Could I embody and unbosom now
That which is most within me,—could I wreak
My thoughts upon expression, and thus throw
Soul—heart—mind—passions—feelings—strong
  or weak—
All that I would have sought, and all I seek,

879. **Heights which appear.** Compare Coleridge's "Christabel," ll. 419–26.   900. **knoll,** knell (archaic). 905. **Could I embody,** the climax of the Lake Leman description and of the poem—in the poet's breast; another little essay on Byronic poetry.

Bear, know, feel—and yet breathe—into *one*
  word,   910
And that one word were Lightning, I would
  speak;
But as it is, I live and die unheard,
With a most voiceless thought, sheathing it as a
  sword.

98

The Morn is up again, the dewy Morn,
With breath all incense, and with cheek all
  bloom—
Laughing the clouds away with playful scorn,
And living as if earth contained no tomb,—
And glowing into day: we may resume
The march of our existence: and thus I,
Still on thy shores, fair Leman! may find room
And food for meditation, nor pass by   921
Much, that may give us pause, if pondered fittingly.

99

Clarens! sweet Clarens, birthplace of deep Love!
Thine air is the young breath of passionate
  Thought;
Thy trees take root in Love; the snows above
The very Glaciers have his colours caught,
And Sun-set into rose-hues sees them wrought
By rays which sleep there lovingly: the rocks,
The permanent crags, tell here of Love, who
  sought
In them a refuge from the worldly shocks,   930
Which stir and sting the Soul with Hope that woos,
  then mocks.

100

Clarens! by heavenly feet thy paths are trod,—
Undying Love's, who here ascends a throne
To which the steps are mountains; where the God
Is a pervading Life and Light,—so shown
Not on those summits solely, nor alone
In the still cave and forest; o'er the flower
His eye is sparkling, and his breath hath blown,
His soft and summer breath, whose tender power
Passes the strength of storms in their most desolate
  hour.   940

101

All things are here of *Him;* from the black pines,
Which are his shade on high, and the loud roar
Of torrents, where he listeneth, to the vines
Which slope his green path downward to the
  shore,

923. **Clarens!** Back to Rousseau of the *Confessions* and of *Julie, ou la nouvelle Héloïse.*

Where the bowed Waters meet him, and adore,
Kissing his feet with murmurs; and the Wood,
The covert of old trees, with trunks all hoar,
But light leaves, young as joy, stands where it
    stood,
Offering to him, and his, a populous solitude,—

102

A populous solitude of bees and birds,   950
And fairy-formed and many-coloured things,
Who worship him with notes more sweet than
    words,
And innocently open their glad wings,
Fearless and full of life: the gush of springs,
And fall of lofty fountains, and the bend
Of stirring branches, and the bud which brings
The swiftest thought of Beauty, here extend,
Mingling—and made by Love—unto one mighty
    end.

103

He who hath loved not, here would learn that
    lore,
And make his heart a spirit; he who knows   960
That tender mystery, will love the more;
For this is Love's recess, where vain men's woes,
And the world's waste, have driven him far from
    those,
For 'tis his nature to advance or die;
He stands not still, but or decays, or grows
Into a boundless blessing, which may vie.
With the immortal lights, in its eternity!

104

'Twas not for fiction chose Rousseau this spot,
Peopling it with affections; but he found
It was the scene which Passion must allot   970
To the mind's purified beings; 'twas the ground
Where early Love his Psyche's zone unbound,
And hallowed it with loveliness: 'tis lone,
And wonderful, and deep, and hath a sound,
And sense, and sight of sweetness; here the Rhone
Hath spread himself a couch, the Alps have reared
    a throne.

105

Lausanne! and Ferney! ye have been the abodes
Of Names which unto you bequeathed a name;
Mortals, who sought and found, by dangerous
    roads,

977. **Lausanne! and Ferney!** where Voltaire and Gibbon, respectively, lived for a time. Gibbon completed *The
Decline and Fall of the Roman Empire* at Ferney. Gibbon's
method and the point of view of his history are compactly
summarized.

A path to perpetuity of Fame: 980
They were gigantic minds, and their steep aim
Was, Titan-like, on daring doubts to pile
Thoughts which should call down thunder, and
    the flame
Of Heaven again assailed, if Heaven, the while,
On man and man's research could deign do more
    than smile.

106

The one was fire and fickleness, a child
Most mutable in wishes, but in mind
A wit as various,—gay, grave, sage, or wild,—
Historian, bard, philosopher, combined;
He multiplied himself among mankind,   990
The Proteus of their talents: But his own
Breathed most in ridicule,—which, as the wind,
Blew where it listed, laying all things prone,—
Now to o'erthrow a fool, and now to shake a throne.

107

The other, deep and slow, exhausting thought,
And hiving wisdom with each studious year,
In meditation dwelt—with learning wrought,
And shaped his weapon with an edge severe,
Sapping a solemn creed with solemn sneer;
The lord of irony,—that master spell,   1000
Which stung his foes to wrath, which grew from
    fear,
And doomed him to the zealot's ready Hell,
Which answers to all doubts so eloquently well.

108

Yet, peace be with their ashes,—for by them,
If merited, the penalty is paid;
It is not ours to judge,—far less condemn;
The hour must come when such things shall be
    made
Known unto all,—or hope and dread allayed
By slumber, on one pillow, in the dust,
Which, thus much we are sure, must lie decayed;
And when it shall revive, as is our trust,   1011
'Twill be to be forgiven—or suffer what is just.

109

But let me quit Man's works, again to read
His Maker's, spread around me, and suspend
This page, which from my reveries I feed,
Until it seems prolonging without end.
The clouds above me to the white Alps tend,
And I must pierce them, and survey whate'er
May be permitted, as my steps I bend   1019
To their most great and growing region, where
The earth to her embrace compels the powers of air.

110

Italia! too, Italia! looking on thee,
Full flashes on the Soul the light of ages,
Since the fierce Carthaginian almost won thee,
To the last halo of the Chiefs and Sages
Who glorify thy consecrated pages;
Thou wert the throne and grave of empires—still,
The fount at which the panting Mind assuages
Her thirst of knowledge, quaffing there her fill,
Flows from the eternal source of Rome's imperial
    hill.   1030

111

Thus far have I proceeded in a theme
Renewed with no kind auspices:—to feel
We are not what we have been, and to deem
We are not what we should be,—and to steel
The heart against itself; and to conceal,
With a proud caution, love, or hate, or aught,—
Passion or feeling, purpose, grief or zeal,—
Which is the tyrant Spirit of our thought,—
Is a stern task of soul:—No matter,—it is taught.

112

And for these words, thus woven into song,   1040
It may be that they are a harmless wile,—
The colouring of the scenes which fleet along,
Which I would seize, in passing, to beguile
My breast, or that of others, for a while.
Fame is the thirst of youth,—but I am not
So young as to regard men's frown or smile,
As loss or guerdon of a glorious lot;
I stood and stand alone,—remembered or forgot.

113

I have not loved the World, nor the World me;
I have not flattered its rank breath, nor bowed
To its idolatries a patient knee,   1051
Nor coined my cheek to smiles,—nor cried aloud
In worship of an echo; in the crowd
They could not deem me one of such—I stood
Among them, but not of them—in a shroud
Of thoughts which were not their thoughts, and
    still could,
Had I not filed my mind, which thus itself subdued.

114

I have not loved the World, nor the World me,—
But let us part fair foes; I do believe,   1059
Though I have found them not, that there may be
Words which are things,—hopes which will not
    deceive,
And Virtues which are merciful, nor weave
Snares for the failing; I would also deem

O'er others' griefs that some sincerely grieve—
That two, or one, are almost what they seem,—
That Goodness is no name—and Happiness no
    dream.

115

My daughter! with thy name this song begun;
My daughter! with thy name thus much shall
    end!—
I see thee not—I hear thee not—but none
Can be so wrapt in thee; Thou art the Friend 1070
To whom the shadows of far years extend:
Albeit my brow thou never should'st behold,
My voice shall with thy future visions blend,
And reach into thy heart,—when mine is cold,—
A token and a tone, even from thy father's mould.

116

To aid thy mind's development,—to watch
Thy dawn of little joys,—to sit and see
Almost thy very growth,—to view thee catch
Knowledge of objects,—wonders yet to thee!
To hold thee lightly on a gentle knee,   1080
And print on thy soft cheek a parent's kiss,—
This, it should seem, was not reserved for me—
Yet this was in my nature:—as it is,
I know not what is there, yet something like to this.

117

Yet, though dull Hate as duty should be taught,
I know that thou wilt love me,—though my name
Should be shut from thee, as a spell still fraught
With desolation, and a broken claim;
Though the grave closed between us,—'twere the
    same—
I know that thou wilt love me—though to drain
My blood from out thy being were an aim,   1091
And an attainment,—all would be in vain,—
Still thou would'st love me, still that more than life
    retain.

118

The child of Love, though born in bitterness,
And nurtured in Convulsion! Of thy sire
These were the elements,—and thine no less.
As yet such are around thee,—but thy fire
Shall be more tempered, and thy hope far higher.
Sweet be thy cradled slumbers! O'er the sea
And from the mountains where I now respire,
Fain would I waft such blessing upon thee, 1101
As—with a sigh—I deem thou might'st have been
    to me!

1094. **child of Love.** The poem ends on the same theme
and note on which it began.

SO, WE'LL GO NO MORE A-ROVING

So, we'll go no more a-roving
   So late into the night,
Though the heart be still as loving,
   And the moon be still as bright.

For the sword outwears its sheath,
   And the soul wears out the breast,
And the heart must pause to breathe,
   And Love itself have rest.

Though the night was made for loving,
   And the day returns too soon,   10
Yet we'll go no more a-roving
   By the light of the moon.

WHAT ARE YOU DOING NOW

What are you doing now,
   Oh Thomas Moore?
What are you doing now,
   Oh Thomas Moore?
Sighing or suing now,
Rhyming or wooing now,
Billing or cooing now,
   Which, Thomas Moore?

But the Carnival's coming,
   Oh Thomas Moore!   10
The Carnival's coming,
   Oh Thomas Moore!
Masking and humming,
Fifing and drumming,
Guitarring and strumming,
   Oh Thomas Moore!

MY BOAT IS ON THE SHORE

1

My boat is on the shore,
   And my bark is on the sea;
But, before I go, Tom Moore,
   Here's a double health to thee!

2

Here's a sigh to those who love me,
   And a smile to those who hate;
And, whatever sky's above me,
   Here's a heart for every fate.

3

Though the Ocean roar around me,
   Yet it still shall bear me on;   10
Though a desert should surround me,
   It hath springs that may be won.

4

Were't the last drop in the well,
   As I gasped upon the brink,
Ere my fainting spirit fell,
   'Tis to thee that I would drink.

5

With that water, as this wine,
   The libation I would pour
Should be—peace with thine and mine,
   And a health to thee, Tom Moore.   20

from DON JUAN

"Difficile est propriè communia dicere." *
    —Horace

"Dost thou think, because thou art virtuous, there shall be no more cakes and ale? Yes, by Saint Anne, and ginger shall be hot i' the mouth, too!"— Shakespeare, *Twelfth Night, or What You Will*.

Don Juan was begun in the summer of 1818 and occupied Byron intermittently the remainder of his life. The first and second cantos were published in 1819, the third to the fifth in 1821, the other completed cantos in 1823 and 1824, a fragment of the seventeenth in 1903. *Don Juan* is Byron's masterpiece and includes about one-fourth of all the poetry he wrote. In form, it is a romance of roguery (not high adventure but low), written in ottava rima (an eight-line stanza in iambic pentameter rhyming abababcc, humorous passages often having double or even triple rhymes, as "laureate . . . Tory at" in I, i). Because of its jocular references to epic conventions (I, 6), its mocking tone, its exaltation of low things and its irreverent treatment of high things, it is sometimes called a mock epic, the greatest of its class. A favorite mock-epic device is anticlimax (for example, the lament in Canto the First, stanzas 214–17; the scene in Canto the Second, stanzas 17–20, in which Juan reads Julia's letter; the passage in Canto the Second, stanzas 186–89, describing Juan and Haidée's first kiss). "I *have* no plan; I *had* no plan; but I have materials," Byron wrote to his friend and publisher Murray. He also said that he "meant to be a little quietly facetious upon everything." The poem, then, is "a satire on the abuses of society, not an eulogy of vice," taking its topics from the wanderings of its disreputable hero, Don Juan, who touches aspects of experience in a world not

* **"Difficile est . . . dicere."** It is difficult to speak properly about common things.

essentially different from the one we live in today. "It is," wrote Paul Elmer More, "the epic of modern life." In a sense, it is an immature poem. "Byron did not reach manhood in this world, but he was drawing toward it when he wrote *Don Juan*." He got rid of sentimentalism, changing it for mockery; but this is only a halfway position. Byron's evolution was toward "a stoical acceptance of life and the attainment of the comic vision." (On this point, see Professor G. R. Elliott's article in *Publications of the Modern Language Association*, Vol. XXXIX, and Professor C. J. Fuess's *Lord Byron as a Satirist in Verse*, Columbia University Press, 1912.)

FRAGMENT

On the back of the Poet's MS. of Canto I

I would to Heaven that I were so much clay,
    As I am blood, bone, marrow, passion, feeling—
Because at least the past were passed away—
    And for the future—(but I write this reeling,
Having got drunk exceedingly to-day,
    So that I seem to stand upon the ceiling)
I say—the future is a serious matter—
And so—for God's sake—hock and soda-water!

DEDICATION

1

Bob Southey! You're a poet—Poet-laureate,
    And representative of all the race;
Although 'tis true that you turned out a Tory at
    Last,—yours has lately been a common case;
And now, my Epic Renegade! what are ye at?
    With all the Lakers, in and out of place?
A nest of tuneful persons, to my eye
Like "four and twenty Blackbirds in a pye;

2

"Which pye being opened they began to sing,"
    (This old song and new simile holds good),   10
"A dainty dish to set before the King,"
    Or Regent, who admires such kind of food;—
And Coleridge, too, has lately taken wing,
    But like a hawk encumbered with his hood,—
Explaining Metaphysics to the nation—
I wish he would explain his Explanation.

3

You, Bob! are rather insolent, you know,
    At being disappointed in your wish
To supersede all warblers here below,
    And be the only Blackbird in the dish;   20
And then you overstrain yourself, or so,
    And tumble downward like the flying fish

16. **Explanation,** *Biographia Literaria,* perhaps.

Gasping on deck, because you soar too high, Bob,
And fall, for lack of moisture quite a-dry, Bob!

4

And Wordsworth, in a rather long "Excursion"
    (I think the quarto holds five hundred pages),
Has given a sample from the vasty version
    Of his new system to perplex the sages;
'Tis poetry—at least by his assertion,
    And may appear so when the dog-star rages—   30
And he who understands it would be able
To add a story to the Tower of Babel.

5

You—Gentlemen! by dint of long seclusion
    From better company, have kept your own
At Keswick, and, through still continued fusion
    Of one another's minds, at last have grown
To deem as a most logical conclusion,
    That poesy has wreaths for you alone:
There is a narrowness in such a notion,
Which makes me wish you'd change your lakes for
    Ocean.   40

6

I would not imitate the petty thought,
    Nor coin my self-love to so base a vice,
For all the glory your conversion brought,
    Since gold alone should not have been its price.
You have your salary: was't for that you wrought?
    And Wordsworth has his place in the Excise.
You're shabby fellows—true—but poets still,
And duly seated on the Immortal Hill.

7

Your bays may hide the baldness of your brows—
    Perhaps some virtuous blushes;—let them go—
To you I envy neither fruit nor boughs—   51
    And for the fame you would engross below,
The field is universal, and allows
    Scope to all such as feel the inherent glow:
Scott, Rogers, Campbell, Moore, and Crabbe, will
    try
'Gainst you the question with posterity.

8

For me, who, wandering with pedestrian Muses,
    Contend not with you on the wingèd steed,
I wish your fate may yield ye, when she chooses,
    The fame you envy, and the skill you need;   60
And, recollect, a poet nothing loses
    In giving to his brethen their full meed
Of merit—and complaint of present days
Is not the certain path to future praise.

9

He that reserves his laurels for posterity
   (Who does not often claim the bright reversion)
Has generally no great crop to spare it, he
   Being only injured by his own assertion;
And although here and there some glorious rarity
   Arise like Titan from the sea's immersion,   70
The major part of such appellants go
To—God knows where—for no one else can know.

10

If, fallen in evil days on evil tongues,
   Milton appealed to the Avenger, Time,
If Time, the Avenger, execrates his wrongs,
   And makes the word "Miltonic" mean "*Sublime*,"
He deigned not to belie his soul in songs,
   Nor turn his very talent to a crime;
He did not loathe the Sire to laud the Son,
But closed the tyrant-hater he begun.   80

11

Think'st thou, could he—the blind Old Man—
     arise,
   Like Samuel from the grave, to freeze once more
The blood of monarchs with his prophecies,
   Or be alive again—again all hoar
With time and trials, and those helpless eyes,
   And heartless daughters—worn—and pale—and
     poor;
Would *he* adore a sultan? *he* obey
The intellectual eunuch Castlereagh?

12

Cold-blooded, smooth-faced, placid miscreant!
   Dabbling its sleek young hands in Erin's gore,
And thus for wider carnage taught to pant,   91
   Transferred to gorge upon a sister shore,
The vulgarest tool that Tyranny could want,
   With just enough of talent, and no more,
To lengthen fetters by another fixed,
And offer poison long already mixed.

13

An orator of such set trash of phrase
   Ineffably—legitimately vile,
That even its grossest flatterers dare not praise,
   Nor foes—all nations—condescend to smile;   100
Not even a sprightly blunder's spark can blaze
   From that Ixion grindstone's ceaseless toil,
That turns and turns to give the world a notion
Of endless torments and perpetual motion.

102. Ixion . . . toil. For insulting the goddess Hera, King Ixion was condemned to turn a wheel perpetually.

14

A bungler even in its disgusting trade,
   And botching, patching, leaving still behind
Something of which its masters are afraid—
   States to be curbed, and thoughts to be confined,
Conspiracy or Congress to be made—
   Cobbling at manacles for all mankind—   110
A tinkering slave-maker, who mends old chains,
With God and Man's abhorrence for its gains.

15

If we may judge of matter by the mind,
   Emasculated to the marrow *It*
Hath but two objects, how to serve, and bind,
   Deeming the chain it wears even men may fit,
Eutropius of its many masters,—blind
   To worth as freedom, wisdom as to wit.
Fearless—because *no* feeling dwells in ice,
Its very courage stagnates to a vice.   120

16

Where shall I turn me not to *view* its bonds,
   For I will never *feel* them?—Italy!
Thy late reviving Roman soul desponds
   Beneath the lie this State-thing breathed o'er
     thee—
Thy clanking chain, and Erin's yet green wounds,
   Have voices—tongues to cry aloud for me.
Europe has slaves—allies—kings—armies still—
And Southey lives to sing them very ill.

17

Meantime, Sir Laureate, I proceed to dedicate,
   In honest simple verse, this song to you.   130
And, if in flattering strains I do not predicate,
   'Tis that I still retain my "buff and blue";
My politics as yet are all to educate:
   Apostasy's so fashionable, too,
To keep *one* creed's a task grown quite Herculean:
Is it not so, my Tory, ultra-Julian?

CANTO THE FIRST

1

I want a hero: an uncommon want,
   When every year and month sends forth a new
     one,
Till, after cloying the gazettes with cant,
   The age discovers he is not the true one:
Of such as these I should not care to vaunt,
   I'll therefore take our ancient friend Don Juan—

117. Eutropius, a eunuch, described by Gibbon.
136. ultra-Julian, Julian the Apostate, also mentioned by Gibbon.

We all have seen him, in the pantomime,
Sent to the Devil somewhat ere his time. . . .

5

Brave men were living before Agamemnon
    And since, exceeding valorous and sage,
A good deal like him too, though quite the same
        none;
    But then they shone not on the poet's page,
And so have been forgotten:—I condemn none,
    But can't find any in the present age
Fit for my poem (that is, for my new one);
So, as I said, I'll take my friend Don Juan.   40

6

Most epic poets plunge *"in medias res"*
    (Horace makes this the heroic turnpike road),
And then your hero tells, whene'er you please,
    What went before—by way of episode,
While seated after dinner at his ease,
    Beside his mistress in some soft abode,
Palace, or garden, paradise, or cavern,
Which serves the happy couple for a tavern.

7

That is the usual method, but not mine—
    My way is to begin with the beginning;   50
The regularity of my design
    Forbids all wandering as the worst of sinning,
And therefore I shall open with a line
    (Although it cost me half an hour in spinning)
Narrating somewhat of Don Juan's father,
And also of his mother, if you'd rather.

8

In Seville was he born, a pleasant city,
    Famous for oranges and women—he
Who has not seen it will be much to pity,
    So says the proverb—and I quite agree;   60
Of all the Spanish towns is none more pretty,
    Cadiz perhaps—but that you soon may see;—
Don Juan's parents lived beside the river,
A noble stream, and called the Guadalquivir.

9

His father's name was Jóse—*Don*, of course,
    A true Hidalgo, free from every stain
Of Moor or Hebrew blood, he traced his source
    Through the most Gothic gentlemen of Spain;
A better cavalier ne'er mounted horse,
    Or being mounted, e'er got down again,   70

Than Jóse, who begot our hero, who
Begot—but that's to come—Well, to renew:

10

His mother was a learnèd lady, famed
    For every branch of every science known—
In every Christian language ever named,
    With virtues equalled by her wit alone:
She made the cleverest people quite ashamed,
    And even the good with inward envy groan,
Finding themselves so very much exceeded,   79
In their own way, by all the things that she did. . . .

26

Don Jóse and the Donna Inez led
    For some time an unhappy sort of life,
Wishing each other, not divorced, but dead;
    They lived respectably as man and wife,
Their conduct was exceedingly well-bred,
    And gave no outward signs of inward strife,
Until at length the smothered fire broke out,
And put the business past all kind of doubt.

27

For Inez called some druggists and physicians,
    And tried to prove her loving lord was *mad*,   210
But as he had some lucid intermissions,
    She next decided he was only *bad*;
Yet when they asked her for her depositions,
    No sort of explanation could be had,
Save that her duty both to man and God
Required this conduct—which seemed very odd. . . .

32

Their friends had tried at reconciliation,
    Then their relations, who made matters worse,
('Twere hard to tell upon a like occasion   251
    To whom it may be best to have recourse—
I can't say much for friend or yet relation):
    The lawyers did their utmost for divorce,
But scarce a fee was paid on either side
Before, unluckily, Don Jóse died. . . .

38

Sagest of women, even of widows, she
    Resolved that Juan should be quite a paragon
And worthy of the noblest pedigree:
    (His Sire was of Castile, his Dam from Aragon):
Then for accomplishments of chivalry,   301
    In case our Lord the King should go to war
    again,

41. **"in medias res,"** into the middle of the action, an epic convention (compare *Paradise Lost*). **65. Jóse.** The name is of course properly José; Byron changes the accent for the sake of the meter.

73. **His mother.** The following stanza (with twelve more, omitted here) is a satirical portrait of Lady Byron. **209. called some druggists and physicians,** an allusion to Lady Byron's action with reference to Byron.

He learned the arts of riding, fencing, gunnery,
And how to scale a fortress—or a nunnery.

39

But that which Donna Inez most desired,
   And saw into herself each day before all
The learnèd tutors whom for him she hired,
   Was, that his breeding should be strictly moral:
Much into all his studies she inquired,
   And so they were submitted first to her, all,   310
Arts, sciences—no branch was made a mystery
To Juan's eyes, excepting natural history.

40

The languages, especially the dead,
   The sciences, and most of all the abstruse,
The arts, at least all such as could be said
   To be the most remote from common use,
In all these he was much and deeply read:
   But not a page of anything that's loose,
Or hints continuation of the species,   319
Was ever suffered, lest he should grow vicious. . . .

44

Juan was taught from out the best edition,
   Expurgated by learnèd men, who place,
Judiciously, from out the schoolboy's vision,
   The grosser parts; but, fearful to deface
Too much their modest bard by this omission,
   And pitying sore this mutilated case,   350
They only add them all in an appendix,
Which saves, in fact, the trouble of an index. . . .

50

At six, I said, he was a charming child,
   At twelve he was a fine, but quiet boy;
Although in infancy a little wild,
   They tamed him down amongst them: to destroy
His natural spirit not in vain they toiled,
   At least it seemed so; and his mother's joy
Was to declare how sage, and still, and steady,
Her young philosopher was grown already. . . .400

52

For my part I say nothing—nothing—but
   This I will say—my reasons are my own—   410
That if I had an only son to put
   To school (as God be praised that I have none),
'Tis not with Donna Inez I would shut
   Him up to learn his catechism alone,
No—no—I'd send him out betimes to college,
For there it was I picked up my own knowledge.

53

For there one learns—'tis not for me to boast,
   Though I acquired—but I pass over *that*,
As well as all the Greek I since have lost:—
   I say that there's the place—but "*Verbum sat*,"
I think I picked up too, as well as most,   421
   Knowledge of matters—but no matter *what*—
I never married—but, I think, I know
That sons should not be educated so.

54

Young Juan now was sixteen years of age,
   Tall, handsome, slender, but well knit: he seemed
Active, though not so sprightly, as a page;
   And everybody but his mother deemed
Him almost man; but she flew in a rage
   And bit her lips (for else she might have screamed)
If any said so, for to be precocious   431
Was in her eyes a thing the most atrocious.

55

Amongst her numerous acquaintance, all
   Selected for discretion and devotion,
There was the Donna Julia, whom to call
   Pretty were but to give a feeble notion
Of many charms in her as natural
   As sweetness to the flower, or salt to ocean,
Her zone to Venus, or his bow to Cupid,
(But this last simile is trite and stupid).   440

56

The darkness of her Oriental eye
   Accorded with her Moorish origin;
(Her blood was not all Spanish, by the by;
   In Spain, you know, this is a sort of sin;)
When proud Granada fell, and, forced to fly,
   Boabdil wept: of Donna Julia's kin
Some went to Africa, some stayed in Spain—
Her great great grandmamma chose to remain.

57

She married (I forget the pedigree)
   With an Hidalgo, who transmitted down   450
His blood less noble than such blood should be;
   At such alliances his sires would frown,
In that point so precise in each degree
   That they bred *in and in*, as might be shown,
Marrying their cousins—nay, their aunts, and nieces,
Which always spoils the breed, if it increases. . . .

420. "**Verbum sat**," A word to the wise is sufficient.

62

Wedded she was some years, and to a man
    Of fifty, and such husbands are in plenty;   490
And yet, I think, instead of such a ONE
    'Twere better to have TWO of five-and-twenty,
Especially in countries near the sun:
    And now I think on't, "*mi vien in mente*,"
Ladies even of the most uneasy virtue
Prefer a spouse whose age is short of thirty.

63

'Tis a sad thing, I cannot choose but say,
    And all the fault of that indecent sun,
Who cannot leave alone our helpless clay,
    But will keep baking, broiling, burning on,   500
That howsoever people fast and pray,
    The flesh is frail, and so the soul undone:
What men call gallantry, and gods adultery,
Is much more common where the climate's
    sultry. . . .

65

Alfonso was the name of Julia's lord,
    A man well looking for his years, and who
Was neither much beloved nor yet abhorred:
    They lived together as most people do,
Suffering each other's foibles by accord,
    And not exactly either *one* or *two;*
Yet he was jealous, though he did not show it,
For Jealousy dislikes the world to know it. . . .   520

69

Juan she saw, and, as a pretty child,
    Caressed him often—such a thing might be
Quite innocently done, and harmless styled,
    When she had twenty years, and thirteen he;
But I am not so sure I should have smiled
    When he was sixteen, Julia twenty-three;   550
These few short years make wondrous alterations,
Particularly amongst sun-burnt nations.

70

Whate'er the cause might be, they had become
    Changed; for the dame grew distant, the youth
      shy,
Their looks cast down, their greetings almost dumb,
    And much embarrassment in either eye;
There surely will be little doubt with some
    That Donna Julia knew the reason why,
But as for Juan, he had no more notion
Than he who never saw the sea or Ocean.   560

494. "mi vien in mente," it comes into my mind.

71

Yet Julia's very coldness still was kind,
    And tremulously gentle her small hand
Withdrew itself from his, but left behind
    A little pressure, thrilling, and so bland
And slight, so very slight, that to the mind
    'Twas but a doubt; but ne'er magician's wand
Wrought change with all Armida's fairy art
Like what this light touch left on Juan's heart.

72

And if she met him, though she smiled no more,
    She looked a sadness sweeter than her smile,   570
As if her heart had deeper thoughts in store
    She must not own, but cherished more the while
For that compression in its burning core;
    Even Innocence itself has many a wile,
And will not dare to trust itself with truth,
And Love is taught hypocrisy from youth. . . .

81

Love, then, but Love within its proper limits   641
    Was Julia's innocent determination
In young Don Juan's favour, and to him its
    Exertion might be useful on occasion;
And, lighted at too pure a shrine to dim its
    Ethereal lustre, with what sweet persuasion
He might be taught, by Love and her together—
I really don't know what, nor Julia either.

82

Fraught with this fine intention, and well fenced
    In mail of proof—her purity of soul—   650
She, for the future, of her strength convinced,
    And that her honour was a rock, or mole,
Exceeding sagely from that hour dispensed
    With any kind of troublesome control;
But whether Julia to the task was equal
Is that which must be mentioned in the sequel. . . .

86

So much for Julia. Now we'll turn to Juan.
    Poor little fellow! he had no idea
Of his own case, and never hit the true one;
    In feelings quick as Ovid's Miss Medea,   684
He puzzled over what he found a new one,
    But not as yet imagined it could be a
Thing quite in course, and not at all alarming,
Which, with a little patience, might grow charm-
    ing. . . .

567. **Armida's.** Armida is a character in Tasso's *Gerusa-
lemme liberata*. 684. **Medea,** sister of Circe. She eloped with
Jason.

104

'Twas on the sixth of June, about the hour
    Of half-past six—perhaps still nearer seven—
When Julia sate within as pretty a bower
    As e'er held houri in that heathenish heaven
Described by Mahomet, and Anacreon Moore,
    To whom the lyre and laurels have been given,
With all the trophies of triumphant song—   831
He won them well, and may he wear them long!

105

She sate, but not alone; I know not well
    How this same interview had taken place,
And even if I knew, I should not tell—
    People should hold their tongues in any case;
No matter how or why the thing befell,
    But there were she and Juan, face to face—
When two such faces are so, 'twould be wise,
But very difficult, to shut their eyes.   840

106

How beautiful she looked! her conscious heart
    Glowed in her cheek, and yet she felt no wrong.
Oh Love! how perfect is thy mystic art,
    Strengthening the weak, and trampling on the
        strong!
How self-deceitful is the sagest part
    Of mortals whom thy lure hath led along!—
The precipice she stood on was immense,
So was her creed in her own innocence. . . .

115

And Julia sate with Juan, half embraced
    And half retiring from the glowing arm,
Which trembled like the bosom where 'twas placed;
    Yet still she must have thought there was no
        harm,
Or else 'twere easy to withdraw her waist;
    But then the situation had its charm,
And then—God knows what next—I can't go on;
I'm almost sorry that I e'er begun. . . .   920

134

What then?—I do not know, no more do you—
    And so good night.—Return we to our story:
'Twas in November, when fine days are few,
    And the far mountains wax a little hoary,
And clap a white cape on their mantles blue;
    And the sea dashes round the promontory,   1070
And the loud breaker boils against the rock,
And sober suns must set at five o'clock.

829. Anacreon Moore, an allusion to Thomas Moore,
who translated the Greek *Odes of Anacreon*. **848. creed,**
belief.

135

'Twas, as the watchmen say, a cloudy night;
    No moon, no stars, the wind was low or loud
By gusts, and many a sparkling hearth was bright
    With the piled wood, round which the family
        crowd;
There's something cheerful in that sort of light,
    Even as a summer sky's without a cloud:
I'm fond of fire, and crickets, and all that,
A lobster salad, and champagne, and chat.   1080

136

'Twas midnight—Donna Julia was in bed,
    Sleeping, most probably,—when at her door
Arose a clatter might awake the dead,
    If they had never been awoke before,
And that they have been so we all have read,
    And are to be so, at the least, once more;—
The door was fastened, but with voice and fist
First knocks were heard, then "Madam—Madam
    —hist!

137

"For God's sake, Madam—Madam—here's my
        master,
    With more than half the city at his back—   1090
Was ever heard of such a curst disaster!
    'Tis not my fault—I kept good watch—Alack!
Do pray undo the bolt a little faster—
    They're on the stair just now, and in a crack
Will all be here; perhaps he yet may fly—
Surely the window's not so *very* high!" . . .

142

Now Julia found at length a voice, and cried,
    "In heaven's name, Don Alfonso, what d'ye
        mean?   1130
Has madness seized you? would that I had died
    Ere such a monster's victim I had been!
What may this midnight violence betide,
    A sudden fit of drunkenness or spleen?
Dare you suspect me, whom the thought would kill?
Search, then, the room!"—Alfonso said, "I will."

143

He searched, *they* searched, and rummaged every-
        where,
    Closet and clothes' press, chest and window-seat,
And found much linen, lace, and several pair
    Of stockings, slippers, brushes, combs, complete,
With other articles of ladies fair,   1141
    To keep them beautiful, or leave them neat:
Arras they pricked and curtains with their swords,
And wounded several shutters, and some boards.

144

Under the bed they searched, and there they
      found—
   No matter what—it was not that they sought;
They opened windows, gazing if the ground
   Had signs or footmarks, but the earth said
      nought;
And then they stared each other's faces round:
   'Tis odd, not one of all these seekers thought,   1150
And seems to me almost a sort of blunder,
Of looking *in* the bed as well as under.

145

During this inquisition Julia's tongue
   Was not asleep—"Yes, search and search," she
      cried,
"Insult on insult heap, and wrong on wrong!
   It was for this that I became a bride!
For this in silence I have suffered long
   A husband like Alfonso at my side;
But now I'll bear no more, nor here remain,
If there be law or lawyers in all Spain.   1160

146

"Yes, Don Alfonso! husband now no more,
   If ever you indeed deserved the name,
Is't worthy of your years?—you have three score—
   Fifty, or sixty, it is all the same—
Is't wise or fitting, causeless to explore
   For facts against a virtuous woman's fame?
Ungrateful, perjured, barbarous Don Alfonso,
How dare you think your lady would go on so?". . .

164

With him retired his *"posse comitatus,"*
   The attorney last, who lingered near the door
Reluctantly, still tarrying there as late as
   Antonia let him—not a little sore
At this most strange and unexplained *"hiatus"*
   In Don Alfonso's facts, which just now wore   1310
An awkward look; as he revolved the case,
The door was fastened in his legal face.

165

No sooner was it bolted, than—Oh Shame!
   Oh Sin! Oh Sorrow! and Oh Womankind!
How can you do such things and keep your fame,
   Unless this world, and t'other too, be blind?
Nothing so dear as an unfilched good name!
   But to proceed—for there is more behind:

1305. "posse comitatus," an armed force made up by a
sheriff or other peace officer to quell a riot or catch a criminal.

With much heartfelt reluctance be it said,
Young Juan slipped, half-smothered, from the
   bed.   1320

166

He had been hid—I don't pretend to say
   How, nor can I indeed describe the where—
Young, slender, and packed easily, he lay,
   No doubt, in little compass, round or square;
But pity him I neither must nor may
   His suffocation by that pretty pair;
'Twere better, sure, to die so, than be shut
With maudlin Clarence in his Malmsey butt. . . .

173

Now, Don Alfonso entering, but alone,
   Closed the oration of the trusty maid:
She loitered, and he told her to be gone,
   An order somewhat sullenly obeyed;   1380
However, present remedy was none,
   And no great good seemed answered if she staid;
Regarding both with slow and sidelong view,
She snuffed the candle, curtsied, and withdrew. . . .

180

Alfonso closed his speech, and begged her pardon,
   Which Julia half withheld, and then half granted,
And laid conditions, he thought very hard on,
   Denying several little things he wanted:
He stood like Adam lingering near his garden,
   With useless penitence perplexed and haunted,
Beseeching she no further would refuse,
When, lo! he stumbled o'er a pair of shoes.   1440

181

A pair of shoes!—what then? not much, if they
   Are such as fit with ladies' feet, but these
(No one can tell how much I grieve to say)
   Were masculine; to see them, and to seize,
Was but a moment's act.—Ah! well-a-day!
   My teeth begin to chatter, my veins freeze—
Alfonso first examined well their fashion,
And then flew out into another passion.

182

He left the room for his relinquished sword,
   And Julia instant to the closet flew.   1450
"Fly, Juan, fly! for heaven's sake—not a word—
   The door is open—you may yet slip through
The passage you so often have explored—
   Here is the garden-key—Fly—fly—Adieu!
Haste—haste! I hear Alfonso's hurrying feet—
Day has not broke—there's no one in the street."

1328. Clarence . . . Malmsey. In *Richard III* Clarence
is drowned in a cask of wine.

183

None can say that this was not good advice,
    The only mischief was, it came too late;
Of all experience 'tis the usual price,
    A sort of income-tax laid on by fate: 1460
Juan had reached the room-door in a trice,
    And might have done so by the garden-gate,
But met Alfonso in his dressing-gown,
    Who threatened death—so Juan knocked him
        down.

184

Dire was the scuffle, and out went the light;
    Antonia cried out "Rape!" and Julia "Fire!"
But not a servant stirred to aid the fight.
    Alfonso, pommelled to his heart's desire,
Swore lustily he'd be revenged this night;   1469
    And Juan, too, blasphemed an octave higher;
His blood was up: though young, he was a Tartar,
And not at all disposed to prove a martyr.

185

Alfonso's sword had dropped ere he could draw it,
    And they continued battling hand to hand,
For Juan very luckily ne'er saw it;
    His temper not being under great command,
If at that moment he had chanced to claw it,
    Alfonso's days had not been in the land
Much longer.—Think of husbands', lovers' lives!
And how ye may be doubly widows—wives!   1480

186

Alfonso grappled to detain the foe,
    And Juan throttled him to get away,
And blood ('twas from the nose) began to flow;
    At last, as they more faintly wrestling lay,
Juan contrived to give an awkward blow,
    And then his only garment quite gave way;
He fled, like Joseph, leaving it; but there,
I doubt, all likeness ends between the pair.

187

Lights came at length, and men, and maids, who
        found
    An awkward spectacle their eyes before;   1490
Antonia in hysterics, Julia swooned,
    Alfonso leaning, breathless by the door;
Some half-torn drapery scattered on the ground,
    Some blood, and several footsteps, but no more:
Juan the gate gained, turned the key about,
And liking not the inside, locked the out.

1487. **He fled, like Joseph.** See Genesis 39.

188

Here ends this canto.—Need I sing, or say,
    How Juan, naked, favoured by the night,
Who favours what she should not, found his way,
    And reached his home in an unseemly plight? 1500
The pleasant scandal which arose next day,
    The nine days' wonder which was brought to
        light,
And how Alfonso sued for a divorce,
Were in the English newspapers, of course. . . .

190

But Donna Inez, to divert the train
    Of one of the most circulating scandals
That had for centuries been known in Spain,
    At least since the retirement of the Vandals,
First vowed (and never had she vowed in vain)
    To Virgin Mary several pounds of candles;
And then, by the advice of some old ladies,
She sent her son to be shipped off from Cadiz. 1520

191

She had resolved that he should travel through
    All European climes, by land or sea,
To mend his former morals, and get new,
    Especially in France and Italy—
(At least this is the thing most people do).
    Julia was sent into a convent—she
Grieved—but, perhaps, her feelings may be better
Shown in the following copy of her Letter:—

192

"They tell me 'tis decided you depart:
    'Tis wise—'tis well, but not the less a pain; 1530
I have no further claim on your young heart,
    Mine is the victim, and would be again:
To love too much has been the only art
    I used;—I write in haste, and if a stain
Be on this sheet, 'tis not what it appears;
My eyeballs burn and throb, but have no tears." . . .

198

This note was written upon gilt-edge paper
    With a neat little crow-quill, slight and new;
Her small white hand could hardly reach the taper,
    It trembled as magnetic needles do,   1580
And yet she did not let one tear escape her;
    The seal a sun-flower; "*Elle vous suit partout*,"
The motto, cut upon a white cornelian;
The wax was superfine, its hue vermilion.

1582. **Elle vous suit partout.** "She follows you every-where."

199

This was Don Juan's earliest scrape; but whether
 I shall proceed with his adventures is
Dependent on the public altogether;
 We'll see, however, what they say to this:
Their favour in an author's cap's a feather,
 And no great mischief's done by their caprice;
And if their approbation we experience,   1591
Perhaps they'll have some more about a year
 hence.

200

My poem's epic, and is meant to be
 Divided in twelve books; each book containing,
With Love, and War, a heavy gale at sea,
 A list of ships, and captains, and kings reigning,
New characters; the episodes are three:
 A panoramic view of Hell's in training,
After the style of Virgil and of Homer,
So that my name of Epic's no misnomer.   1600

201

All these things will be specified in time,
 With strict regard to Aristotle's rules,
The *Vade Mecum* of the true sublime,
 Which makes so many poets and some fools:
Prose poets like blank-verse, I'm fond of rhyme,
 Good workmen never quarrel with their tools;
I've got new mythological machinery,
And very handsome supernatural scenery.

202

There's only one slight difference between
 Me and my epic brethren gone before,   1610
And here the advantage is my own, I ween
 (Not that I have not several merits more,
But this will more peculiarly be seen);
 They so embellish, that 'tis quite a bore
Their labyrinth of fables to thread through,
Whereas this story's actually true. . . .

204

If ever I should condescend to prose,
 I'll write poetical commandments, which
Shall supersede beyond all doubt all those
 That went before; in these I shall enrich
My text with many things that no one knows,
 And carry precept to the highest pitch: 1630
I'll call the work "Longinus o'er a Bottle,
Or, Every Poet his *own* Aristotle."

205

Thou shalt believe in Milton, Dryden, Pope;
 Thou shalt not set up Wordsworth, Coleridge,
 Southey;

Because the first is crazed beyond all hope,
 The second drunk, the third so quaint and
 mouthy:
With Crabbe it may be difficult to cope,
 And Campbell's Hippocrene is somewhat
 drouthy:
Thou shalt not steal from Samuel Rogers, nor
Commit—flirtation with the muse of Moore.   1640

206

Thou shalt not covet Mr. Sotheby's Muse,
 His Pegasus, nor anything that's his;
Thou shalt not bear false witness like "the Blues"—
 (There's one, at least, is very fond of this);
Thou shalt not write, in short, but what I choose;
 This is true criticism, and you may kiss—
Exactly as you please, or not,—the rod;
But if you don't, I'll lay it on, by G—d!

207

If any person should presume to assert
 This story is not moral, first, I pray,   1650
That they will not cry out before they're hurt,
 Then that they'll read it o'er again, and say
(But, doubtless, nobody will be so pert),
 That this is not a moral tale, though gay;
Besides, in Canto Twelfth, I mean to show
The very place where wicked people go. . . .

214

No more—no more—Oh! never more on me
 The freshness of the heart can fall like dew,
Which out of all the lovely things we see
 Extracts emotions beautiful and new;
Hived in our bosoms like the bag o' the bee.
 Think'st thou the honey with those objects grew?
Alas! 'twas not in them, but in thy power   1711
To double even the sweetness of a flower.

215

No more—no more—Oh! never more, my heart,
 Canst thou be my sole world, my universe!
Once all in all, but now a thing apart,
 Thou canst not be my blessing or my curse:
The illusion's gone for ever, and thou art
 Insensible, I trust, but none the worse,
And in thy stead I've got a deal of judgment,
Though Heaven knows how it ever found a lodg-
 ment.   1720

216

My days of love are over; me no more
 The charms of maid, wife, and still less of widow,

Can make the fool of which they made before,—
   In short, I must not lead the life I did do;
The credulous hope of mutual minds is o'er,
   The copious use of claret is forbid too,
So for a good old-gentlemanly vice,
I think I must take up with avarice.

217

Ambition was my idol, which was broken
   Before the shrines of Sorrow, and of Pleasure;
And the two last have left me many a token   1731
   O'er which reflection may be made at leisure;
Now, like Friar Bacon's Brazen Head, I've spoken,
   "Time is, Time was, Time's past":—a chymic treasure
Is glittering Youth, which I have spent betimes—
My heart in passion, and my head on rhymes. . . .

221

But for the present, gentle reader! and
   Still gentler purchaser! the Bard—that's I—
Must, with permission, shake you by the hand,
   And so—your humble servant, and Good-bye!
We meet again, if we should understand
   Each other; and if not, I shall not try
Your patience further than by this short sample—
'Twere well if others followed my example.

222

"Go, little Book, from this my solitude!
   I cast thee on the waters—go thy ways!   1770
And if—as I believe, thy vein be good,
   The World will find thee after many days."
When Southey's read, and Wordsworth understood,
   I can't help putting in my claim to praise—
The four first rhymes are Southey's, every line:
For God's sake, reader! take them not for mine.

from CANTO THE SECOND

8

But to our tale: the Donna Inez sent
   Her son to Cadiz only to embark;
To stay there had not answered her intent,
   But why?—we leave the reader in the dark—   60
'Twas for a voyage the young man was meant,
   As if a Spanish ship were Noah's ark,
To wean him from the wickedness of earth,
And send him like a Dove of Promise forth.

9

Don Juan bade his valet pack his things
   According to direction, then received

1769 ff. "Go, little Book, . . ." a parody of Southey's
"'The Lay of the Laureate, L'Envoy."

A lecture and some money: for four springs
   He was to travel; and though Inez grieved
(As every kind of parting has its stings),
   She hoped he would improve—perhaps believed:
A letter, too, she gave (he never read it)   71
Of good advice—and two or three of credit. . . .

11

Juan embarked—the ship got under way,
   The wind was fair, the water passing rough;
A devil of a sea rolls in that bay,
   As I, who've crossed it oft, know well enough;
And, standing upon deck, the dashing spray
   Flies in one's face, and makes it weather-tough:
And there he stood to take, and take again,
His first—perhaps his last—farewell of Spain.

12

I can't but say it is an awkward sight
   To see one's native land receding through   90
The growing waters; it unmans one quite,
   Especially when life is rather new:
I recollect Great Britain's coast looks white,
   But almost every other country's blue,
When gazing on them, mystified by distance,
We enter on our nautical existence. . . .

17

And Juan wept, and much he sighed and thought,
   While his salt tears dropped into the salt sea,   130
"Sweets to the sweet"; (I like so much to quote;
   You must excuse this extract,—'tis where she,
The Queen of Denmark, for Ophelia brought
   Flowers to the grave;) and, sobbing often, he
Reflected on his present situation,
And seriously resolved on reformation.

18

"Farewell, my Spain! a long farewell!" he cried,
   "Perhaps I may revisit thee no more,
But die, as many an exiled heart hath died,
   Of its own thirst to see again thy shore: 140
Farewell, where Guadalquivir's waters glide!
   Farewell, my mother! and, since all is o'er,
Farewell, too, dearest Julia!—(here he drew
Her letter out again, and read it through.)

19

"And oh! if e'er I should forget, I swear—
   But that's impossible, and cannot be—
Sooner shall this blue Ocean melt to air,
   Sooner shall Earth resolve itself to sea,
Than I resign thine image, oh, my fair!
   Or think of anything, excepting thee;   150

A mind diseased no remedy can physic—
(Here the ship gave a lurch, and he grew sea-sick.)

20

"Sooner shall Heaven kiss earth—(here he fell
 sicker)
 Oh, Julia! what is every other woe?—
(For God's sake let me have a glass of liquor;
 Pedro, Battista, help me down below.)
Julia, my love—(you rascal, Pedro, quicker)—
 Oh, Julia!—(this curst vessel pitches so)—
Belovèd Julia, hear me still beseeching!"
(Here he grew inarticulate with retching.) . . . 160

24

The ship, called the most holy "Trinidada,"
 Was steering duly for the port Leghorn;
For there the Spanish family Moncada
 Were settled long ere Juan's sire was born:
They were relations, and for them he had a
 Letter of introduction, which the morn 190
Of his departure had been sent him by
His Spanish friends for those in Italy.

25

His suite consisted of three servants and
 A tutor, the licentiate Pedrillo,
Who several languages did understand,
 But now lay sick and speechless on his pillow,
And, rocking in his hammock, longed for land,
 His headache being increased by every billow;
And the waves oozing through the port-hole made
His berth a little damp, and him afraid. . . . 200

49

'Twas twilight, and the sunless day went down
 Over the waste of waters; like a veil,
Which, if withdrawn, would but disclose the frown
 Of one whose hate is masked but to assail.
Thus to their hopeless eyes the night was shown,
 And grimly darkled o'er the faces pale, 390
And the dim desolate deep: twelve days had Fear
Been their familiar, and now Death was here.

50

Some trial had been making at a raft,
 With little hope in such a rolling sea,
A sort of thing at which one would have laughed,
 If any laughter at such times could be,
Unless with people who too much have quaffed,
 And have a kind of wild and horrid glee,
Half epileptical, and half hysterical:—
Their preservation would have been a miracle. 400

51

At half-past eight o'clock, booms, hencoops, spars,
 And all things, for a chance, had been cast
  loose,
That still could keep afloat the struggling tars,
 For yet they strove, although of no great use:
There was no light in heaven but a few stars,
 The boats put off o'ercrowded with their
  crews;
She gave a heel, and then a lurch to port,
And, going down head foremost—sunk, in short.

52

Then rose from sea to sky the wild farewell—
 Then shrieked the timid, and stood still the
  brave,— 410
Then some leaped overboard with dreadful yell,
 As eager to anticipate their grave;
And the sea yawned around her like a hell,
 And down she sucked with her the whirling
  wave,
Like one who grapples with his enemy,
And strives to strangle him before he die.

53

And first one universal shriek there rushed,
 Louder than the loud Ocean, like a crash
Of echoing thunder; and then all was hushed,
 Save the wild wind and the remorseless dash 420
Of billows; but at intervals there gushed,
 Accompanied by a convulsive splash,
A solitary shriek, the bubbling cry
Of some strong swimmer in his agony. . . .

56

Juan got into the long-boat, and there
 Contrived to help Pedrillo to a place;
It seemed as if they had exchanged their care,
 For Juan wore the magisterial face
Which courage gives, while poor Pedrillo's pair
 Of eyes were crying for their owner's case:
Battista, though (a name called shortly Tita),
Was lost by getting at some aqua-vita.

57

Pedro, his valet, too, he tried to save,
 But the same cause, conducive to his loss, 450
Left him so drunk, he jumped into the wave,
 As o'er the cutter's edge he tried to cross,
And so he found a wine-and-watery grave;
 They could not rescue him although so close,
Because the sea ran higher every minute,
And for the boat—the crew kept crowding in it.

58

A small old spaniel—which had been Don Jóse's,
  His father's, whom he loved, as ye may think,
For on such things the memory reposes
  With tenderness—stood howling on the brink,
Knowing, (dogs have such intellectual noses!)   461
  No doubt the vessel was about to sink;
And Juan caught him up, and ere he stepped
Off threw him in, then after him he leaped.

59

He also stuffed his money where he could
  About his person, and Pedrillo's too,
Who let him do, in fact, whate'er he would,
  Not knowing what himself to say, or do,
As every rising wave his dread renewed;
  But Juan, trusting they might still get through,
And deeming there were remedies for any ill,   471
Thus re-embarked his tutor and his spaniel.

60

'Twas a rough night, and blew so stiffly yet,
  That the sail was becalmed between the seas,
Though on the wave's high top too much to set,
  They dared not take it in for all the breeze: 476
Each sea curled o'er the stern, and kept them wet,
  And made them bale without a moment's ease,
So that themselves as well as hopes were damped,
And the poor little cutter quickly swamped. . . .

66

'Tis thus with people in an open boat,
  They live upon the love of Life, and bear
More than can be believed, or even thought,
  And stand like rocks the tempest's wear and tear;
And hardship still has been the sailor's lot,
  Since Noah's ark went cruising here and there;
She had a curious crew as well as cargo,
Like the first old Greek privateer, the Argo.

67

But man is a carnivorous production,
  And must have meals, at least one meal a day;
He cannot live, like woodcocks, upon suction,   531
  But, like the shark and tiger, must have prey;
Although his anatomical construction
  Bears vegetables, in a grumbling way,
Your labouring people think beyond all question
Beef, veal, and mutton, better for digestion.

68

And thus it was with this our hapless crew;
  For on the third day there came on a calm,

And though at first their strength it might renew,
  And lying on their weariness like balm,   540
Lulled them like turtles sleeping on the blue
  Of Ocean, when they woke they felt a qualm,
And fell all ravenously on their provision,
Instead of hoarding it with due precision.

69

The consequence was easily foreseen—
  They ate up all they had, and drank their wine,
In spite of all remonstrances, and then
  On what, in fact, next day were they to dine?
They hoped the wind would rise, these foolish men!
  And carry them to shore; these hopes were fine,
But as they had but one oar, and that brittle,   551
It would have been more wise to save their victual.

70

The fourth day came, but not a breath of air,
  And Ocean slumbered like an unweaned child:
The fifth day, and their boat lay floating there,
  The sea and sky were blue, and clear, and mild—
With their one oar (I wish they had had a pair)
  What could they do? and Hunger's rage grew
    wild:
So Juan's spaniel, spite of his entreating,
Was killed, and portioned out for present eating. 560

71

On the sixth day they fed upon his hide,
  And Juan, who had still refused, because
The creature was his father's dog that died,
  Now feeling all the vulture in his jaws,
With some remorse received (though first denied)
  As a great favour one of the fore-paws,
Which he divided with Pedrillo, who
Devoured it, longing for the other too. . . .

100

The land appeared a high and rocky coast,
  And higher grew the mountains as they drew,
Set by a current, toward it: they were lost
  In various conjectures, for none knew
To what part of the earth they had been tost,
  So changeable had been the winds that blew;
Some thought it was Mount Aetna, some the high-
    lands   799
Of Candia, Cyprus, Rhodes, or other islands. . . .

103

As they drew nigh the land, which now was seen
  Unequal in its aspect here and there,

799–800. Aetna . . . islands. The places named stretch
from the Ionian Sea to the Aegean Sea.

They felt the freshness of its growing green,
  That waved in forest-tops, and smoothed the air,
And fell upon their glazed eyes like a screen   821
  From glistening waves, and skies so hot and
    bare—
Lovely seemed any object that should sweep
Away the vast, salt, dread, eternal Deep.

104

The shore looked wild, without a trace of man,
  And girt by formidable waves; but they
Were mad for land, and thus their course they ran,
  Though right ahead the roaring breakers lay:
A reef between them also now began
  To show its boiling surf and bounding spray,   830
But finding no place for their landing better,
They ran the boat for shore,—and overset her.

105

But in his native stream, the Guadalquivir,
  Juan to lave his youthful limbs was wont;
And having learnt to swim in that sweet river,
  Had often turned the art to some account:
A better swimmer you could scarce see ever,
  He could, perhaps, have passed the Hellespont,
As once (a feat on which ourselves we prided)
Leander, Mr. Ekenhead, and I did.   840

106

So here, though faint, emaciated, and stark,
  He buoyed his boyish limbs, and strove to ply
With the quick wave, and gain, ere it was dark,
  The beach which lay before him, high and dry:
The greatest danger here was from a shark,
  That carried off his neighbour by the thigh;
As for the other two, they could not swim,
So nobody arrived on shore but him.

107

Nor yet had he arrived but for the oar,
  Which, providentially for him, was washed   850
Just as his feeble arms could strike no more,
  And the hard wave o'erwhelmed him as 'twas
    dashed
Within his grasp; he clung to it, and sore
  The waters beat while he thereto was lashed;
At last, with swimming, wading, scrambling, he
Rolled on the beach, half-senseless, from the sea:

108

There, breathless, with his digging nails he clung
  Fast to the sand, lest the returning wave,
From whose reluctant roar his life he wrung,
  Should suck him back to her insatiate grave: 860

And there he lay, full length, where he was flung,
  Before the entrance of a cliff-worn cave,
With just enough of life to feel its pain,
And deem that it was saved, perhaps in vain.

109

With slow and staggering effort he arose,
  But sunk again upon his bleeding knee
And quivering hand; and then he looked for those
  Who long had been his mates upon the sea;
But none of them appeared to share his woes,
  Save one, a corpse, from out the famished three,
Who died two days before, and now had found   871
An unknown barren beach for burial ground.

110

And as he gazed, his dizzy brain spun fast,
  And down he sunk; and as he sunk, the sand
Swam round and round, and all his senses passed:
  He fell upon his side, and his stretched hand
Drooped dripping on the oar (their jury-mast),
  And, like a withered lily, on the land
His slender frame and pallid aspect lay,
As fair a thing as e'er was formed of clay.   880

111

How long in his damp trance young Juan lay
  He knew not, for the earth was gone for him,
And Time had nothing more of night nor day
  For his congealing blood, and senses dim;
And how this heavy faintness passed away
  He knew not, till each painful pulse and limb,
And tingling vein, seemed throbbing back to life,
For Death, though vanquished, still retired with
    strife.

112

His eyes he opened, shut, again unclosed,
  For all was doubt and dizziness; he thought   890
He still was in the boat, and had but dozed,
  And felt again with his despair o'erwrought,
And wished it Death in which he had reposed,
  And then once more his feelings back were
    brought,
And slowly by his swimming eyes was seen
A lovely female face of seventeen.

113

'Twas bending close o'er his, and the small mouth
  Seemed almost prying into his for breath;
And chafing him, the soft warm hand of youth
  Recalled his answering spirits back from Death;
And, bathing his chill temples, tried to soothe   901
  Each pulse to animation, till beneath

Its gentle touch and trembling care, a sigh
To these kind efforts made a low reply.

114

Then was the cordial poured, and mantle flung
    Around his scarce-clad limbs; and the fair arm
Raised higher the faint head which o'er it hung;
    And her transparent cheek, all pure and warm,
Pillowed his death-like forehead; then she wrung
    His dewy curls, long drenched by every storm; 910
And watched with eagerness each throb that drew
A sigh from his heaved bosom—and hers, too.

115

And lifting him with care into the cave,
    The gentle girl, and her attendant,—one
Young, yet her elder, and of brow less grave,
    And more robust of figure—then begun
To kindle fire, and as the new flames gave
    Light to the rocks that roofed them, which the sun
Had never seen, the maid, or whatsoe'er
She was, appeared distinct, and tall, and fair.   920

116

Her brow was overhung with coins of gold,
    That sparkled o'er the auburn of her hair—
Her clustering hair, whose longer locks were rolled
    In braids behind; and though her stature were
Even of the highest for a female mould,
    They nearly reached her heel; and in her air
There was a something which bespoke command,
As one who was a Lady in the land.

117

Her hair, I said, was auburn; but her eyes
    Were black as Death, their lashes the same hue,
Of downcast length, in whose silk shadow lies   931
    Deepest attraction; for when to the view
Forth from its raven fringe the full glance flies,
    Ne'er with such force the swiftest arrow flew;
'Tis as the snake late coiled, who pours his length,
And hurls at once his venom and his strength.

118

Her brow was white and low, her cheek's pure dye
    Like twilight rosy still with the set sun;
Short upper lip—sweet lips! that make us sigh
    Ever to have seen such; for she was one   940
Fit for the model of a statuary
    (A race of mere impostors, when all's done—
I've seen much finer women, ripe and real,
Than all the nonsense of their stone ideal). . . .

124

I'll tell you who they were, this female pair,
    Lest they should seem Princesses in disguise;
Besides, I hate all mystery, and that air
    Of clap-trap, which your recent poets prize;
And so, in short, the girls they really were
    They shall appear before your curious eyes,   990
Mistress and maid; the first was only daughter
Of an old man, who lived upon the water.

125

A fisherman he had been in his youth,
    And still a sort of fisherman was he;
But other speculations were, in sooth,
    Added to his connexion with the sea,
Perhaps not so respectable, in truth:
    A little smuggling, and some piracy,
Left him, at last, the sole of many masters
Of an ill-gotten million of piastres.   1000

126

A fisher, therefore, was he,—though of men,
    Like Peter the Apostle, and he fished
For wandering merchant-vessels, now and then,
    And sometimes caught as many as he wished;
The cargoes he confiscated, and gain
    He sought in the slave-market too, and dished
Full many a morsel for that Turkish trade,
By which, no doubt, a good deal may be made.

127

He was a Greek, and on his isle had built
    (One of the wild and smaller Cyclades)   1010
A very handsome house from out his guilt,
    And there he lived exceedingly at ease;
Heaven knows what cash he got, or blood he spilt,
    A sad old fellow was he, if you please;
But this I know, it was a spacious building,
Full of barbaric carving, paint, and gilding.

128

He had an only daughter, called Haidée,
    The greatest heiress of the Eastern Isles;
Besides, so very beautiful was she,
    Her dowry was as nothing to her smiles: 1020
Still in her teens, and like a lovely tree
    She grew to womanhood, and between whiles
Rejected several suitors, just to learn
How to accept a better in his turn.

    1000. piastres, Turkish money.   **1010. Cyclades,** a great cluster of islands in the Aegean, east of Greece.

129

And walking out upon the beach, below
  The cliff, towards sunset, on that day she found,
Insensible,—not dead, but nearly so,—
  Don Juan, almost famished, and half drowned;
But being naked, she was shocked, you know,
  Yet deemed herself in common pity bound,   1030
As far as in her lay, "to take him in,
A stranger" dying, with so white a skin.

130

But taking him into her father's house
  Was not exactly the best way to save,
But like conveying to the cat the mouse,
  Or people in a trance into their grave;
Because the good old man had so much "νοῦς,"
  Unlike the honest Arab thieves so brave,
He would have hospitably cured the stranger
And sold him instantly when out of danger.   1040

131

And therefore, with her maid, she thought it best
  (A virgin always on her maid relies)
To place him in the cave for present rest:
  And when, at last, he opened his black eyes,
Their charity increased about their guest;
  And their compassion grew to such a size,
It opened half the turnpike-gates to Heaven—
(St. Paul says, 'tis the toll which must be given). . . .

142

And down the cliff the island virgin came,   1129
  And near the cave her quick light footsteps drew,
While the Sun smiled on her with his first flame,
  And young Aurora kissed her lips with dew,
Taking her for a sister; just the same
  Mistake you would have made on seeing the
    two,
Although the mortal, quite as fresh and fair,
Had all the advantage, too, of not being air.

143

And when into the cavern Haidée stepped
  All timidly, yet rapidly, she saw
That like an infant Juan sweetly slept;
  And then she stopped, and stood as if in awe 1140
(For sleep is awful), and on tiptoe crept
  And wrapped him closer, lest the air, too raw,
Should reach his blood, then o'er him still as Death
Bent, with hushed lips, that drank his scarce-drawn
  breath.

1037. "νοῦς," nous—mind (Greek).

144

And thus like to an Angel o'er the dying
  Who die in righteousness, she leaned; and there
All tranquilly the shipwrecked boy was lying,
  As o'er him lay the calm and stirless air:
But Zoe the meantime some eggs was frying,
  Since, after all, no doubt the youthful pair   1150
Must breakfast, and betimes—lest they should ask
    it,
She drew out her provision from the basket. . . .

174

And thus a moon rolled on, and fair Haidée
  Paid daily visits to her boy, and took
Such plentiful precautions, that still he
  Remained unknown within his craggy nook;
At last her father's prows put out to sea,
  For certain merchantmen upon the look,   1390
Not as of yore to carry off an Io,
But three Ragusan vessels, bound for Scio.

175

Then came her freedom, for she had no mother,
  So that, her father being at sea, she was
Free as a married woman, or such other
  Female, as where she likes may freely pass,
Without even the encumbrance of a brother,
  The freest she that ever gazed on glass:
I speak of Christian lands in this comparison,
Where wives, at least, are seldom kept in garri-
    son.   1400

176

Now she prolonged her visits and her talk
  (For they must talk), and he had learnt to
    say
So much as to propose to take a walk,—
  For little had he wandered since the day
On which, like a young flower snapped from the
    stalk,
  Drooping and dewy on the beach he lay,—
And thus they walked out in the afternoon,
And saw the sun set opposite the moon.

177

It was a wild and breaker-beaten coast,
  With cliffs above, and a broad sandy shore,   1410
Guarded by shoals and rocks as by an host,
  With here and there a creek, whose aspect wore
A better welcome to the tempest-tost;
  And rarely ceased the haughty billow's roar,
Save on the dead long summer days, which make
The outstretched Ocean glitter like a lake.

178

And the small ripple spilt upon the beach
   Scarcely o'erpassed the cream of your cham-
      pagne,
When o'er the brim the sparkling bumpers reach,
   That spring-dew of the spirit! the heart's rain! 1420
Few things surpass old wine; and they may preach
   Who please,—the more because they preach in
      vain,—
Let us have Wine and Women, Mirth and Laugh-
   ter,
Sermons and soda-water the day after.

179

Man, being reasonable, must get drunk;
   The best of Life is but intoxication:
Glory, the Grape, Love, Gold, in these are sunk
   The hopes of all men, and of every nation;
Without their sap, how branchless were the trunk
   Of Life's strange tree, so fruitful on occasion!
But to return,—Get very drunk; and when   1431
You wake with headache, you shall see what
   then.

180

Ring for your valet—bid him quickly bring
   Some hock and soda-water, then you'll know
A pleasure worthy Xerxes the great king;
   For not the blest sherbet, sublimed with snow,
Nor the first sparkle of the desert-spring,
   Nor Burgundy in all its sunset glow,
After long travel, Ennui, Love, or Slaughter,
Vie with that draught of hock and soda-water! 1440

181

The coast—I think it was the coast that I
   Was just describing—Yes, it *was* the coast—
Lay at this period quiet as the sky,
   The sands untumbled, the blue waves untossed,
And all was stillness, save the sea-bird's cry,
   And dolphin's leap, and little billow crossed
By some low rock or shelve, that made it fret
Against the boundary it scarcely wet.

182

And forth they wandered, her sire being gone,
   As I have said, upon an expedition;   1450
And mother, brother, guardian, she had none,
   Save Zoe, who, although with due precision
She waited on her lady with the Sun,
   Thought daily service was her only mission,
Bringing warm water, wreathing her long tresses,
And asking now and then for cast-off dresses.

183

It was the cooling hour, just when the rounded
   Red sun sinks down behind the azure hill,
Which then seems as if the whole earth it bounded,
   Circling all Nature, hushed, and dim, and still, 1460
With the far mountain-crescent half surrounded
   On one side, and the deep sea calm and chill
Upon the other, and the rosy sky,
With one star sparkling through it like an eye.

184

And thus they wandered forth, and hand in hand,
   Over the shining pebbles and the shells,
Glided along the smooth and hardened sand,
   And in the worn and wild receptacles
Worked by the storms, yet worked as it were
     planned—
   In hollow halls, with sparry roofs and cells,   1470
They turned to rest; and, each clasped by an arm,
Yielded to the deep Twilight's purple charm.

185

They looked up to the sky, whose floating glow
   Spread like a rosy Ocean, vast and bright;
They gazed upon the glittering sea below,
   Whence the broad Moon rose circling into sight;
They heard the waves splash, and the wind so low,
   And saw each other's dark eyes darting light
Into each other—and, beholding this,
Their lips drew near, and clung into a kiss;   1480

186

A long, long kiss, a kiss of Youth, and Love,
   And Beauty, all concentrating like rays
Into one focus, kindled from above;
   Such kisses as belong to early days,
Where Heart, and Soul, and Sense, in concert move,
   And the blood's lava, and the pulse a blaze,
Each kiss a heart-quake,—for a kiss's strength,
I think, it must be reckoned by its length.

187

By length I mean duration; theirs endured
   Heaven knows how long—no doubt they never
     reckoned;   1490
And if they had, they could not have secured
   The sum of their sensations to a second:
They had not spoken; but they felt allured,
   As if their souls and lips each other beckoned,
Which, being joined, like swarming bees they
     clung—
Their hearts the flowers from whence the honey
     sprung.

188

They were alone, but not alone as they
  Who shut in chambers think it loneliness;
The silent Ocean, and the starlight bay,
  The twilight glow, which momently grew less, 1500
The voiceless sands, and dropping caves, that lay
  Around them, made them to each other press,
As if there were no life beneath the sky
Save theirs, and that their life could never die.

189

They feared no eyes nor ears on that lone beach,
  They felt no terrors from the night; they were
All in all to each other; though their speech
  Was broken words, they *thought* a language
    there,—
And all the burning tongues the Passions teach
  Found in one sigh the best interpreter 1510
Of Nature's oracle—first love,—that all
Which Eve has left her daughters since her fall.

190

Haidée spoke not of scruples, asked no vows,
  Nor offered any; she had never heard
Of plight and promises to be a spouse,
  Or perils by a loving maid incurred;
She was all which pure Ignorance allows,
  And flew to her young mate like a young bird;
And, never having dreamt of falsehood, she
Had not one word to say of constancy. 1520

191

She loved, and was belovèd—she adored,
  And she was worshipped; after Nature's fashion,
Their intense souls, into each other poured,
  If souls could die, had perished in that passion,—
But by degrees their senses were restored,
  Again to be o'ercome, again to dash on;
And, beating 'gainst *his* bosom, Haidée's heart
Felt as if never more to beat apart.

192

Alas! they were so young, so beautiful,
  So lonely, loving, helpless, and the hour 1530
Was that in which the Heart is always full,
  And, having o'er itself no further power,
Prompts deeds Eternity can not annul,
  But pays off moments in an endless shower
Of hell-fire—all prepared for people giving
Pleasure or pain to one another living.

1521. **She loved, and was belovèd.** In its Romantic
aspects the love story of Juan and Haidée is a good example
of primitivism. But note that Byron flouts his own sentimentality.

193

Alas! for Juan and Haidée! they were
  So loving and so lovely—till then never,
Excepting our first parents, such a pair
  Had run the risk of being damned for ever; 1540
And Haidée, being devout as well as fair,
  Had, doubtless, heard about the Stygian river,
And Hell and Purgatory—but forgot
Just in the very crisis she should not.

194

They look upon each other, and their eyes
  Gleam in the moonlight; and her white arm
    clasps
Round Juan's head, and his around her lies
  Half buried in the tresses which it grasps;
She sits upon his knee, and drinks his sighs,
  He hers, until they end in broken gasps; 1550
And thus they form a group that's quite antique,
Half naked, loving, natural, and Greek. . . .

199

Alas! the love of Women! it is known
  To be a lovely and a fearful thing;
For all of theirs upon that die is thrown,
  And if 'tis lost, Life hath no more to bring
To them but mockeries of the past alone,
  And their revenge is as the tiger's spring, 1590
Deadly, and quick, and crushing; yet, as real
Torture is theirs—what they inflict they feel.

200

They are right; for man, to Man so oft unjust,
  Is always so to Women; one sole bond
Awaits them, treachery is all their trust;
  Taught to conceal, their bursting hearts de-
    spond
Over their idol, till some wealthier lust
  Buys them in marriage—and what rests beyond?
A thankless husband—next a faithless lover— 1599
Then dressing, nursing, praying—and all's over.

201

Some take a lover, some take drams or prayers,
  Some mind their household, others dissipation,
Some run away, and but exchange their cares,
  Losing the advantage of a virtuous station;
Few changes e'er can better their affairs,
  Theirs being an unnatural situation,
From the dull palace to the dirty hovel:
Some play the devil, and then write a novel.

202

Haidée was Nature's bride, and knew not this:
  Haidée was Passion's child, born where the
    sun   1610
Showers triple light, and scorches even the kiss
  Of his gazelle-eyed daughters; she was one
Made but to love, to feel that she was his
  Who was her chosen: what was said or done
Elsewhere was nothing. She had nought to fear,
Hope, care, nor love beyond,—her heart beat *here*.

203

And oh! that quickening of the heart, that beat!
  How much it costs us! yet each rising throb
Is in its cause as its effect so sweet,
  That Wisdom, ever on the watch to rob   1620
Joy of its alchemy, and to repeat
  Fine truths; even Conscience, too, has a tough
    job
To make us understand each good old maxim,
So good—I wonder Castlereagh don't tax 'em.

204

And now 'twas done—on the lone shore were
    plighted
  Their hearts; the stars, their nuptial torches, shed
Beauty upon the beautiful they lighted:
  Ocean their witness, and the cave their bed,
By their own feelings hallowed and united,
  Their priest was Solitude, and they were wed:
And they were happy, for to their young eyes   1631
Each was an angel, and earth paradise. . . .

from CANTO THE THIRD

12

Haidée and Juan were not married, but
  The fault was theirs, not mine; it is not fair,   90
Chaste reader, then, in any way to put
  The blame on me, unless you wish they were;
Then if you'd have them wedded, please to shut
  The book which treats of this erroneous pair,
Before the consequences grow too awful;
'Tis dangerous to read of loves unlawful.

13

Yet they were happy,—happy in the illicit
  Indulgence of their innocent desires;
But more imprudent grown with every visit,
  Haidée forgot the island was her Sire's;   100
When we have what we like 'tis hard to miss it,
  At least in the beginning, ere one tires;
Thus she came often, not a moment losing,
Whilst her piratical papa was cruising.

14

Let not his mode of raising cash seem strange,
  Although he fleeced the flags of every nation,
For into a Prime Minister but change
  His title, and 'tis nothing but taxation;
But he, more modest, took an humbler range
  Of Life, and in an honester vocation   110
Pursued o'er the high seas his watery journey,
And merely practised as a sea-attorney.

15

The good old gentleman had been detained
  By winds and waves, and some important cap-
    tures;
And, in the hope of more, at sea remained,
  Although a squall or two had damped his rap-
    tures,
By swamping one of the prizes; he had chained
  His prisoners, dividing them like chapters
In numbered lots; they all had cuffs and collars,
And average each from ten to a hundred dol-
    lars. . . .   120

19

Then having settled his marine affairs,
  Despatching single cruisers here and there,
His vessel having need of some repairs,
  He shaped his course to where his daughter fair
Continued still her hospitable cares;
  But that part of the coast being shoal and
    bare,   150
And rough with reefs which ran out many a mile,
His port lay on the other side o' the isle. . . .

27

He saw his white walls shining in the sun,
  His garden trees all shadowy and green;   210
He heard his rivulet's light bubbling run,
  The distant dog-bark; and perceived between
The umbrage of the wood so cool and dun,
  The moving figures, and the sparkling sheen
Of arms (in the East all arm)—and various dyes
Of coloured garbs, as bright as butterflies. . . .

40

Perhaps you think in stumbling on this feast   313
  He flew into a passion, and in fact
There was no mighty reason to be pleased;
  Perhaps you prophesy some sudden act,
The whip, the rack, or dungeon at the least,
  To teach his people to be more exact,
And that, proceeding at a very high rate,
He showed the royal *penchants* of a pirate.

41

You're wrong.—He was the mildest mannered man
  That ever scuttled ship or cut a throat: 322
With such true breeding of a gentleman,
  You never could divine his real thought;
No courtier could, and scarcely woman can
  Gird more deceit within a petticoat;
Pity he loved adventurous life's variety,
He was so great a loss to good society. . . .

51

He entered in the house no more his home,   401
  A thing to human feelings the most trying,
And harder for the heart to overcome,
  Perhaps, than even the mental pangs of dying;
To find our hearthstone turned into a tomb,
  And round its once warm precincts palely lying
The ashes of our hopes, is a deep grief,
Beyond a *single gentleman's* belief. . . .

78

And now they were diverted by their suite,
  Dwarfs, dancing girls, black eunuchs, and a
    poet,
Which made their new establishment complete;
  The last was of great fame, and liked to show it:
His verses rarely wanted their due feet—   621
  And for his theme—he seldom sung below it,
He being paid to satirise or flatter,
As the Psalm says, "inditing a good matter.". . .

84

He had travelled 'mongst Arabs, Turks, and Franks,
  And knew the self-loves of the different nations;
And having lived with people of all ranks,
  Had something ready upon most occasions—
Which got him a few presents and some thanks.
  He varied with some skill his adulations;   670
To "do at Rome as Romans do," a piece
Of conduct was which *he* observed in Greece.

85

Thus, usually, when *he* was asked to sing,
  He gave the different nations something national;
'Twas all the same to him—"God save the king,"
  Or "Ça Ira," according to the fashion all:
His Muse made increment of anything,
  From the high lyric down to the low rational;
If Pindar sang horse-races, what should hinder
Himself from being as pliable as Pindar?   680

676. "Ça Ira," "It will succeed," a song of the French
Revolution.

86

In France, for instance, he would write a chanson;
  In England, a six canto quarto tale;
In Spain he'd make a ballad or romance on
  The last war—much the same in Portugal;
In Germany, the Pegasus he'd prance on
  Would be old Goethe's—(see what says De Staël);
In Italy, he'd ape the "Trecentisti";
In Greece, he'd sing some sort of hymn like this
    t'ye:

I

The isles of Greece, the isles of Greece!
  Where burning Sappho loved and sung,   690
Where grew the arts of War and Peace,—
  Where Delos rose, and Phoebus sprung!
Eternal summer gilds them yet,
But all, except their Sun, is set.

2

The Scian and the Teian muse,
  The Hero's harp, the Lover's lute,
Have found the fame your shores refuse:
  Their place of birth alone is mute
To sounds which echo further west
Than your Sires' "Islands of the Blest."   700

3

The mountains look on Marathon—
  And Marathon looks on the sea;
And musing there an hour alone,
  I dreamed that Greece might still be free;
For standing on the Persians' grave,
I could not deem myself a slave.

4

A King sate on the rocky brow
  Which looks o'er sea-born Salamis;
And ships, by thousands, lay below,
  And men in nations;—all were his!   710
He counted them at break of day—
And when the Sun set, where were they?

5

And where are they? and where art thou,
  My country? On thy voiceless shore
The heroic lay is tuneless now—
  The heroic bosom beats no more!

686. **what says De Staël,** that Goethe represented all
German literature.   687. **"Trecentisti,"** imitators of
fourteenth-century Italian literature.   695. **Scian and
. . . Teian,** Homer and Anacreon.   700. **"Islands of the
Blest,"** islands in the Atlantic where heroes were said to
dwell after death.

And must thy Lyre, so long divine,
Degenerate into hands like mine?

6

'Tis something, in the dearth of Fame,
    Though linked among a fettered race,   720
To feel at least a patriot's shame,
    Even as I sing, suffuse my face;
For what is left the poet here?
For Greeks a blush—for Greece a tear.

7

Must *we* but weep o'er days more blest?
    Must *we* but blush?—Our fathers bled.
Earth! render back from out thy breast
    A remnant of our Spartan dead!
Of the three hundred grant but three.
To make a new Thermopylae!   730

8

What, silent still? and silent all?
    Ah! no;—the voices of the dead
Sound like a distant torrent's fall,
    And answer, "Let one living head,
But one arise,—we come, we come!"
'Tis but the living who are dumb.

9

In vain—in vain: strike other chords:
    Fill high the cup with Samian wine!
Leave battles to the Turkish hordes,
    And shed the blood of Scio's vine!   740
Hark! rising to the ignoble call—
How answers each bold Bacchanal!

10

You have the Pyrrhic dance as yet:
    Where is the Pyrrhic phalanx gone?
Of two such lessons, why forget
    The nobler and the manlier one?
You have the letters Cadmus gave—
Think ye he meant them for a slave?

11

Fill high the bowl with Samian wine!
    We will not think of themes like these!   750
It made Anacreon's song divine:
    He served—but served Polycrates—
A Tyrant; but our masters then
Were still, at least, our countrymen.

743–44. Pyrrhic dance . . . Pyrrhic phalanx. The
Greeks kept the sensuous dance but forgot the world-
conquering military formation that Philip and Alexander of
Macedon had taught them. These facts and the "Samian
wine" help explain their present enslavement.

12

The Tyrant of the Chersonese
    Was Freedom's best and bravest friend;
That tyrant was Miltiades!
    Oh! that the present hour would lend
Another despot of the kind!
Such chains as his were sure to bind.   760

13

Fill high the bowl with Samian wine!
    On Suli's rock, and Parga's shore,
Exists the remnant of a line
    Such as the Doric mothers bore;
And there, perhaps, some seed is sown,
The Heracleidan blood might own.

14

Trust not for freedom to the Franks—
    They have a king who buys and sells;
In native swords and native ranks,
    The only hope of courage dwells;   770
But Turkish force, and Latin fraud,
Would break your shield, however broad.

15

Fill high the bowl with Samian wine!
    Our virgins dance beneath the shade—
I see their glorious black eyes shine;
    But gazing on each glowing maid,
My own the burning tear-drop laves,
To think such breasts must suckle slaves.

16

Place me on Sunium's marbled steep,
    Where nothing, save the waves and I,   780
May hear our mutual murmurs sweep;
    There, swan-like, let me sing and die:
A land of slaves shall ne'er be mine—
Dash down yon cup of Samian wine!

87

Thus sung, or would, or could, or should have sung,
    The modern Greek, in tolerable verse:
If not like Orpheus quite, when Greece was young,
    Yet in these times he might have done much
        worse:
His strain displayed some feeling—right or wrong;
    And feeling, in a poet is the source   790
Of others' feeling; but they are such liars,
And take all colours—like the hands of dyers. . . .

101

T' our tale.—The feast was over, the slaves gone,
    The dwarfs and dancing girls had all retired;

The Arab lore and Poet's song were done,
   And every sound of revelry expired;   900
The lady and her lover, left alone,
   The rosy flood of Twilight's sky admired;—
Ave Maria! o'er the earth and sea,
That heavenliest hour of Heaven is worthiest thee!

102

Ave Maria! blessèd be the hour!
   The time, the clime, the spot, where I so oft
Have felt that moment in its fullest power
   Sink o'er the earth—so beautiful and soft—
While swung the deep bell in the distant tower,
   Or the faint dying day-hymn stole aloft,   910
And not a breath crept through the rosy air,
And yet the forest leaves seemed stirred with prayer.

103

Ave Maria! 'tis the hour of prayer!
   Ave Maria! 'tis the hour of Love!
Ave Maria! may our spirits dare
   Look up to thine and to thy Son's above!
Ave Maria! oh that face so fair!
   Those downcast eyes beneath the Almighty Dove—
What though 'tis but a pictured image?—strike—
That painting is no idol,—'tis too like.   920

104

Some kinder casuists are pleased to say,
   In nameless print—that I have no devotion;
But set those persons down with me to pray,
   And you shall see who has the properest notion
Of getting into Heaven the shortest way;
   My altars are the mountains and the Ocean,
Earth, air, stars,—all that springs from the great Whole,
Who hath produced, and will receive the Soul.

105

Sweet Hour of Twilight!—in the solitude
   Of the pine forest, and the silent shore   930
Which bounds Ravenna's immemorial wood,
   Rooted where once the Adrian wave flowed o'er,
To where the last Caesarean fortress stood,
   Evergreen forest! which Boccaccio's lore
And Dryden's lay made haunted ground to me,
How have I loved the twilight hour and thee!

106

The shrill cicalas, people of the pine,
   Making their summer lives one ceaseless song,
Were the sole echoes, save my steed's and mine,
   And Vesper bell's that rose the boughs along;   940

The spectre huntsman of Onesti's line,
   His hell-dogs, and their chase, and the fair throng
Which learned from this example not to fly
From a true lover,—shadowed my mind's eye.

107

Oh, Hesperus! thou bringest all good things—
   Home to the weary, to the hungry cheer,
To the young bird the parent's brooding wings,
   The welcome stall to the o'erlaboured steer;
Whate'er of peace about our hearth stone clings,
   Whate'er our household gods protect of dear,   950
Are gathered round us by thy look of rest;
Thou bring'st the child, too, to the mother's breast.

108

Soft Hour! which wakes the wish and melts the heart
   Of those who sail the seas, on the first day
When they from their sweet friends are torn apart;
   Or fills with love the pilgrim on his way
As the far bell of Vesper makes him start,
   Seeming to weep the dying day's decay;
Is this a fancy which our reason scorns?
Ah! surely Nothing dies but something mourns! . . .   960

from CANTO THE FOURTH

29

Now pillowed cheek to cheek, in loving sleep,   225
   Haidée and Juan their siesta took,
A gentle slumber, but it was not deep,
   For ever and anon a something shook
Juan, and shuddering o'er his frame would creep;
   And Haidée's sweet lips murmured like a brook
A wordless music, and her face so fair
Stirred with her dream, as rose-leaves with the air. . . .

31

She dreamed of being alone on the sea-shore,   241
   Chained to a rock; she knew not how, but stir
She could not from the spot, and the loud roar
   Grew, and each wave rose roughly, threatening her;
And o'er her upper lip they seemed to pour,
   Until she sobbed for breath, and soon they were
Foaming o'er her lone head, so fierce and high—
Each broke to drown her, yet she could not die.

32

Anon—she was released, and then she strayed
   O'er the sharp shingles with her bleeding feet,   250

And stumbled almost every step she made:
    And something rolled before her in a sheet,
Which she must still pursue howe'er afraid:
    'Twas white and indistinct, nor stopped to meet
Her glance nor grasp, for still she gazed and
    grasped,
And ran, but it escaped her as she clasped.

33

The dream changed:—in a cave she stood,—its
    walls
    Were hung with marble icicles; the work
Of ages on its water-fretted halls,
    Where waves might wash, and seals might breed
        and lurk;   260
Her hair was dripping, and the very balls
    Of her black eyes seemed turned to tears, and
        mirk
The sharp rocks looked below each drop they
        caught,
    Which froze to marble as it fell,—she thought.

34

And wet, and cold, and lifeless at her feet,
    Pale as the foam that frothed on his dead brow,
Which she essayed in vain to clear, (how sweet
    Were once her cares, how idle seemed they
        now!)
Lay Juan, nor could aught renew the beat
    Of his quenched heart: and the sea dirges low   270
Rang in her sad ears like a Mermaid's song,
And that brief dream appeared a life too long.

35

And gazing on the dead, she thought his face
    Faded, or altered into something new—
Like to her Father's features, till each trace
    More like and like to Lambro's aspect grew—
With all his keen worn look and Grecian grace;
    And starting, she awoke, and what to view?
Oh! Powers of Heaven! what dark eye meets she
        there?
'Tis—'tis her Father's—fixed upon the pair!   280

36

Then shrieking, she arose, and shrieking fell,
    With joy and sorrow, hope and fear, to see
Him whom she deemed a habitant where dwell
    The ocean-buried, risen from death, to be
Perchance the death of one she loved too well:
    Dear as her father had been to Haidée
It was a moment of that awful kind—
I have seen such—but must not call to mind.

37

Up Juan sprung to Haidée's bitter shriek,
    And caught her falling, and from off the wall   290
Snatched down his sabre, in hot haste to wreak
    Vengeance on him who was the cause of all:
Then Lambro, who till now forbore to speak,
    Smiled scornfully, and said, "Within my call,
A thousand scimitars await the word;
Put up, young man, put up your silly sword."

38

And Haidée clung around him; "Juan, 'tis—
    'Tis Lambro—'tis my father! Kneel with me—
He will forgive us—yes—it must be—yes.
    Oh! dearest father, in this agony   300
Of pleasure and of pain—even while I kiss
    Thy garment's hem with transport, can it be
That doubt should mingle with my filial joy?
Deal with me as thou wilt, but spare this boy."

39

High and inscrutable the old man stood,
    Calm in his voice, and calm within his eye—
Not always signs with him of calmest mood:
    He looked upon her, but gave no reply;
Then turned to Juan, in whose cheek the blood
    Oft came and went, as there resolved to die;   310
In arms, at least, he stood, in act to spring
On the first foe whom Lambro's call might bring.

40

"Young man, your sword"; so Lambro once more
        said:
    Juan replied, "Not while this arm is free."
The old man's cheek grew pale, but not with dread,
    And drawing from his belt a pistol, he
Replied, "Your blood be then on your own head."
    Then looked close at the flint, as if to see
'Twas fresh—for he had lately used the lock—
And next proceeded quietly to cock.   320

41

It has a strange quick jar upon the ear,
    That cocking of a pistol, when you know
A moment more will bring the sight to bear
    Upon your person, twelve yards off or so;
A gentlemanly distance, not too near,
    If you have got a former friend for foe;
But after being fired at once or twice,
The ear becomes more Irish, and less nice.

42

Lambro presented, and one instant more
    Had stopped this Canto, and Don Juan's breath,

When Haidée threw herself her boy before;   331
  Stern as her sire: "On me," she cried, "let Death
Descend—the fault is mine; this fatal shore
  He found—but sought not. I have pledged my
    faith;
I love him—I will die with him; I knew
Your nature's firmness—know your daughter's
  too." . . .

47

"Let him disarm; or, by my father's head,
  His own shall roll before you like a ball!"   370
He raised his whistle, as the word he said,
  And blew; another answered to the call,
And rushing in disorderly, though led,
  And armed from boot to turban, one and all,
Some twenty of his train came, rank on rank;
He gave the word,—"Arrest or slay the Frank."

48

Then, with a sudden movement, he withdrew
  His daughter; while compressed within his clasp,
'Twixt her and Juan interposed the crew;
  In vain she struggled in her father's grasp—   380
His arms were like a serpent's coil: then flew
  Upon their prey, as darts an angry asp,
The file of pirates; save the foremost, who
Had fallen, with his right shoulder half cut
  through.

49

The second had his cheek laid open; but
  The third, a wary, cool old sworder, took
The blows upon his cutlass, and then put
  His own well in; so well, ere you could look,
His man was floored, and helpless at his foot,
  With the blood running like a little brook   390
From two smart sabre gashes, deep and red—
One on the arm, the other on the head.

50

And then they bound him where he fell, and bore
  Juan from the apartment: with a sign
Old Lambro bade them take him to the shore,
  Where lay some ships which were to sail at nine.
They laid him in a boat, and plied the oar
  Until they reached some galliots, placed in line;
On board one of these, and under hatches,
They stowed him, with strict orders to the
  watches. . . .   400

376. **Frank,** Greek or Turkish term for any Western
European. 398. **galliots,** small boats propelled by sails and
oars.

58

The last sight which she saw was Juan's gore,   457
  And he himself o'ermastered and cut down;
His blood was running on the very floor
  Where late he trod, her beautiful, her own;
Thus much she viewed an instant and no more,—
  Her struggles ceased with one convulsive groan;
On her Sire's arm, which until now scarce held
Her writhing, fell she like a cedar felled.

59

A vein had burst, and her sweet lips' pure dyes
  Were dabbled with the deep blood which ran
    o'er;
And her head drooped as when the lily lies
  O'ercharged with rain: her summoned hand-
    maids bore
Their lady to her couch with gushing eyes;
  Of herbs and cordials they produced their
    store,   470
But she defied all means they could employ,
Like one Life could not hold, nor Death destroy.

60

Days lay she in that state unchanged, though chill—
  With nothing livid, still her lips were red;
She had no pulse, but Death seemed absent still;
  No hideous sign proclaimed her surely dead;
Corruption came not in each mind to kill
  All hope; to look upon her sweet face bred
New thoughts of Life, for it seemed full of soul—
She had so much, Earth could not claim the
  whole.   480

61

The ruling passion, such as marble shows
  When exquisitely chiselled, still lay there,
But fixed as marble's unchanged aspect throws
  O'er the fair Venus, but for ever fair;
O'er the Laocoon's all eternal throes,
  And ever-dying Gladiator's air,
Their energy like life forms all their fame,
Yet looks not life, for they are still the same. . . .

69

Twelve days and nights she withered thus; at
  last,   545
  Without a groan, or sigh, or glance, to show
A parting pang, the spirit from her passed:
  And they who watched her nearest could not
  know

484. **but for ever fair.** Note the effect of "but." Compare
Keats's "Ode on a Grecian Urn." stanza 5, page 335.

The very instant, till the change that cast
  Her sweet face into shadow, dull and slow,
Glazed o'er her eyes—the beautiful, the black—
Oh! to possess such lustre—and then lack! . . .

71

Thus lived—thus died she; never more on her   561
  Shall Sorrow light, or Shame. She was not made
Through years or moons the inner weight to bear,
  Which colder hearts endure till they are laid
By age in earth: her days and pleasures were
  Brief, but delightful—such as had not staid
Long with her destiny; but she sleeps well
By the sea-shore, whereon she loved to dwell.

72

That isle is now all desolate and bare,
  Its dwellings down, its tenant passed away;   570
None but her own and Father's grave is there,
  And nothing outward tells of human clay;
Ye could not know where lies a thing so fair,
  No stone is there to show, no tongue to say
What was; no dirge, except the hollow sea's,
Mourns o'er the Beauty of the Cyclades. . . .

EPIGRAMS

WHEN A MAN HATH NO FREEDOM TO FIGHT FOR AT HOME

When a man hath no freedom to fight for at home,
  Let him combat for that of his neighbours;
Let him think of the glories of Greece and of Rome,
  And get knocked on the head for his labours.

To do good to Mankind is the chivalrous plan,
  And is always as nobly requited;
Then battle for Freedom wherever you can,
  And, if not shot or hanged, you'll get knighted.

THE WORLD IS A BUNDLE OF HAY

The world is a bundle of hay,
  Mankind are the asses who pull,
Each tugs it a different way,—
  And the greatest of all is John Bull!

WHO KILLED JOHN KEATS?

"Who killed John Keats?"
  "I," says the *Quarterly*,
  So savage and Tartarly;
"'Twas one of my feats."

"Who shot the arrow?"
  "The poet-priest Milman
  (So ready to kill man),
Or Southey or Barrow."

STANZAS WRITTEN ON THE ROAD BETWEEN FLORENCE AND PISA

Oh talk not to me of a name great in story—
The days of our Youth are the days of our glory;
And the myrtle and ivy of sweet two-and-twenty
Are worth all your laurels, though ever so plenty.

What are garlands and crowns to the brow that is
  wrinkled?
'Tis but as a dead flower with May-dew be-
  sprinkled:
Then away with all such from the head that is
  hoary,
What care I for the wreaths that can *only* give
  glory?

Oh, FAME!—if I e'er took delight in thy praises,
'Twas less for the sake of thy high-sounding
  phrases,   10
Than to see the bright eyes of the dear One dis-
  cover,
She thought that I was not unworthy to love her.

There chiefly I sought thee, *there* only I found thee;
Her Glance was the best of the rays that surround
  thee;
When it sparkled o'er aught that was bright in my
  story,
I knew it was Love, and I felt it was Glory.

ON THIS DAY I COMPLETE MY THIRTY-SIXTH YEAR

I

'Tis time this heart should be unmoved,
  Since others it hath ceased to move:
Yet, though I cannot be beloved,
  Still let me love!

2

My days are in the yellow leaf;
  The flowers and fruits of Love are gone;
The worm, the canker, and the grief
  Are mine alone!

3

The fire that on my bosom preys
  Is lone as some Volcanic isle;   10
No torch is kindled at its blaze—
  A funeral pile.

4

The hope, the fear, the zealous care,
  The exalted portion of the pain
And power of love, I cannot share,
  But wear the chain.

5

But 'tis not *thus*—and 'tis not *here*—
  Such thoughts should shake my soul, nor *now*,
Where Glory decks the hero's bier,
  Or binds his brow.   20

6

The Sword, the Banner, and the Field,
  Glory and Greece, around me see!
The Spartan, borne upon his shield,
  Was not more free.

7

Awake! (not Greece—she *is* awake!)
  Awake, my spirit! Think through *whom*
Thy life-blood tracks its parent lake,
  And then strike home!

8

Tread those reviving passions down,
  Unworthy manhood!—unto thee   30
Indifferent should the smile or frown
  Of Beauty be.

9

If thou regret'st thy youth, *why live?*
  The land of honourable death
Is here:—up to the Field, and give
  Away thy breath!

10

Seek out—less often sought than found—
  A soldier's grave, for thee the best;
Then look around, and choose thy ground,
  And take thy Rest.   40

Missolonghi, Jan. 22, 1824.

Percy Bysshe Shelley
1792–1822

Born August 4, 1792, at Field Place, near Horsham, Sussex, Percy Bysshe Shelley was the first child of Timothy and Elizabeth Pilfold Shelley. The family was an old one, of country squires, and Field Place was a charming eighteenth-century mansion overlooking the lovely Sussex countryside. The other children close enough to be Shelley's companions were girls. Too exclusively, perhaps, in their society, he led his sisters in childish adventures about the house and neighborhood, making up stories about a gray-bearded alchemist who inhabited a garret and about the "Great Tortoise" and the "Great Old Snake" that lived in the woods near by. His interest in the marvelous was fed by fairy tales, Gothic novels, and other thrillers. Early, too, he began to dabble with the explosive and spectacular properties of chemical and physical materials.

At Sion House Academy, which he attended for two years with his cousin Thomas Medwin, and later at Eton, where he was a pupil to the age of eighteen, his interest in science and in Gothic tales continued. In both schools the boy ran afoul of the "oppressors of mankind"—hazing, the school discipline, the authority of Church and State, customs that he regarded as outworn—and in both places he was rebellious and miserable much of the time. Often the butt of his schoolfellows' pranks and derision, he sometimes defended himself furiously; once his revenge consisted in his blowing up his enemies' desks with gunpowder. At Eton, besides solacing himself with Gothic thrillers and scientific fooling, he began reading such radical literature as Godwin's *Political Justice*. The resulting unorthodox political and religious opinions that he formed brought about the termination by parental authority of a love affair with his cousin Harriet Grove. At the end of his schooling, he was the published author of a book of verse and a Gothic romance, *Zastrozzi*.

Shelley's Oxford sojourn was of a piece with his schooling, only briefer. With his friends, among them Thomas Jefferson Hogg, he read such skeptics as Locke, Hume, and Voltaire. Exhilarated by his skepticism, he amused himself by writing prominent bishops that he was an honest doubter, a soul seeking the light, then demolishing their evidences of Christianity by arguments cribbed from his books. In March of his freshman year he was expelled, and with him his friend Hogg, for "contumaciously refusing to answer [official] questions" about a pamphlet, *The Necessity of Atheism*, which he had written and published at his own expense.

Going to London, where his sisters, then in school, were able to help him, he refused to conciliate his father or seek reinstatement at Oxford. There he met Harriet Westbrook, a schoolmate of his sisters, impressed her with his political and religious views, and assumed the responsibility of enlightening her. He may also have impressed Harriet's sister as a very eligible prospective husband for Harriet. When, some months later, he learned that Harriet was in disgrace with her parents for having associated with an atheist and a rebel, he rescued her, like one of his Gothic knights, by running away with her to Edinburgh and marrying her, she being sixteen, he nineteen. Harriet's father and (later) Shelley's made some allowance for the support of the young couple. An apostle of Godwin and the new freedom, Shelley took his bride to Ireland on a honeymoon crusade of writing and speechmaking for the reform of government in that oppressed and miserable country. They are said to have distributed Shelley's sensible pamphlet *Declaration of Rights* by slipping copies into the pockets of unsuspecting Paddies on the streets, sending some up in balloons, and setting others adrift at sea in bottles. Returning to England, they wandered about in that country and in Wales, Shelley engaging in a Platonic friendship with Elizabeth Hitchener, a schoolmistress, experimenting in vegetarianism, and engaging in humanitarian activities. Early in 1813 Shelley published his first important poem, *Queen Mab*, expressing his Necessitarian ideas on the ruling principle of the universe, his denunciation of religion, his socialistic criticism of human society past and present, and his idealistic hopes for the future. Shortly afterward, he became personally acquainted with William Godwin, fell into financial distress, and began to feel that Harriet was not intellectually compatible. Meanwhile, he read incessantly, for the most part in materialistic philosophy. In 1814, he met seventeen-year-old Mary Wollstonecraft Godwin. Their mutual attraction was electric. In July they eloped to Switzerland. The will of Shelley's grandfather, who died early in 1815, left him with an income of about £5,000. This he divided fairly with Harriet, who was now the mother of two children. The summer of 1816 Shelley, Mary, and her stepsister Clara Jane Clairmont spent in

Switzerland, on intimate terms with Byron. Soon after their return to England Harriet drowned herself in the Serpentine River. When Shelley petitioned the Lord Chancellor Eldon for the custody of his children by Harriet, he was denied, on evidence, partly contained in *Queen Mab*, that he was not morally fit to rear them. Shelley regarded the verdict as a stigma and a virtual sentence of exile. For this reason, and also on account of his poor health, in March, 1818, he and his family left England for Italy. Like Byron, Shelley had come under "the Genius of Pain." His career as an intellectual playboy was at an end.

During this period of unsuccessful efforts for social reform and of domestic tragedy, Shelley was steadily acquiring intellectual and poetical power. *Alastor*, 1816, a blank-verse spiritual autobiography in its story of a young poet's quest for ideal beauty, shows new strength of thought and poetic style. "Hymn to Intellectual Beauty," 1817, inspired by Alpine scenery and the philosophy of Plato, realizes a truth that the young poet in *Alastor* had disregarded: ideal beauty, which "Gives grace and truth to life's unquiet dream," cannot be fully incorporated in earthly form or clasped in human shape. *The Revolt of Islam*, 1818, a long narrative poem in Spenserian stanzas about Laon and Cythna, lovers and leaders of a revolution, shows the revival of Shelley's hopes for mankind. Its "Dedication" is one of his most winsome and revealing autobiographical poems. "Lines Written among the Euganean Hills," 1818, describes the state of mind in which he first came to Italy. The same year that saw the composition of this poem saw the beginning of his masterpiece, *Prometheus Unbound*. His attainment of gigantic poetic stature had been swift.

Coming to Italy in 1818, the Shelleys spent part of the autumn at Byron's villa near Venice. Shelley's sense of humiliation, his remorse perhaps, his spiritual loneliness, and his grief over the death of his little daughter Clara are poignantly expressed in "Lines Written among the Euganean Hills." They are the personal undertone of *Prometheus Unbound*, begun at Byron's villa and completed in Rome and Florence. By this time, however, Shelley had begun to transcend personal sorrow and pain in his contemplation of the wrongs of the world and of mankind's happy deliverance. At Rome he became interested in a Roman murder story of the sixteenth century and dramatized it in *The Cenci*, the tragedy of Beatrice, a young girl violated by her own father and convicted and executed for killing him in revenge. At Florence, where *Prometheus Unbound* was finished and a son, Percy Florence, was born, he felt in the seasonal phenomena the symbol of that ultimate cosmic redemption which he suggests in the last stanza of "Ode to the West Wind." In 1819 he was grieved and angered by news of economic misery and political oppression coming out of England. His "Masque of Anarchy," "Song to the Men of England," and "England in 1819" voice his anger and pity and come nearest of all his poems to advocacy of direct action.

Shelley's last three years were spent in or near Pisa. His and Mary's capacity for making friends is one of the pleasing features of this last phase. They were the center of a circle that included John and Maria Gisborne, Sophia Stacey, Thomas Medwin, and Edward and Jane Williams. Toward the last, Edward Trelawny joined them, and Byron exchanged visits with them. All of these people are significant in one way or another to Shelley's poetry, as in the charming "Letter to Maria Gisborne" and "To Jane, with a Guitar." Acquaintance with the Greek Prince Mavrocordato deepened Shelley's interest in the cause of Greek independence, and he wrote his last long completed poem on the theme, *Hellas, a Lyrical Drama*, published in 1822. A short but intense infatuation with Emilia Viviani produced one of Shelley's greatest love poems. Emilia, a beautiful young Italian girl, was destined by her family to be the bride of an old nobleman, and when she objected to the match was immured in a convent. Shelley's championship of her cause and of love itself is proclaimed in *Epipsychidion*. News of the death of John Keats at Rome in February, 1821, moved Shelley to compose *Adonais*, one of the three greatest pastoral elegies in English poetry. Occasioned by a slight friendship with Keats and by Shelley's feeling that he himself "in another's fate now wept his own," *Adonais* is really a vindication of all poets and a triumphant assertion of their immortality. In the same year with *Epipsychidion*, vindication of love, and with *Adonais*, vindication of the poet, Shelley wrote his noble prose *Defence of Poetry*, in reply to an attack made by his friend Peacock.

Shelley's *Alastor* (ll. 304 ff.), his "Stanzas Written in Dejection near Naples," and *Adonais* contain passages descriptive of death by drowning. Their prophetic import was confirmed by events of the spring and early summer of 1822. In May the Shelleys moved to Casa Magni, near Lerici, on the Gulf of Spezzia. In June Leigh Hunt arrived at Leghorn, ready to begin editing the *Liberal*, sponsored by Byron and Shelley. On July 8, after a meeting with Byron to make arrangements for settling the Hunts, Shelley and Williams sailed from Leghorn for home in the *Ariel* (or, as Byron had insisted, the *Don Juan*). Somewhere off Via Reggio a sudden and violent squall arose. The young Englishmen did not arrive at their destination. Nearly two weeks later their bodies were found washed ashore, Shelley's with a volume of Keats in one pocket and a volume of Sophocles in another. Italian sanitary laws required cremation; and Byron, Hunt, Trelawny, and others burned the bodies on the beach. At the last moment Trelawny snatched Shelley's heart from the flames. Mary received the heart. Shelley's ashes were buried in the Protestant cemetery at Rome, which he had described in *Adonais* (stanzas 49–50) as the last resting-place of Keats.

In his "Julian and Maddalo," a delightful "conversation" poem about himself and Byron, Shelley describes himself:

> "*Me*—who am as a nerve o'er which do creep
> The else unfelt oppressions of this earth."

He is the poet of protest against man's inhumanity to man, of assault against tyranny entrenched in the Church, the State, formalized education, the political and economic order, custom and convention. His passion for justice and for human sympathy throbs in everything he wrote, from *Queen Mab* to *Hellas*. "I have," he wrote in his "Preface to *Prometheus Unbound*," "a passion for reforming the world." He is the greatest English prophet of human perfectibility, and his *Prometheus Unbound* is the most ambitious poetic treatment of that theme. Like most idealistic reformers, he is much clearer in his analysis and denunciation of evils than in his plan for correcting them. But far more than his satirist friend Byron, he is positive and constructive in his social thought. He believed that social regeneration could begin only with men's willing themselves to be free and good. "Gentleness, Virtue, Wisdom, and Endurance," he asserts, "bar the pit over Destruction's strength." Patience, forgiveness, defiance of unjust power, love, and hope bring "Life, Joy, Empire, and Victory." Practical means and measures, about which he was clearer than he is often represented to have been, would follow spiritual regeneration. His great function as a poet was "to familiarize the highly refined imagination of the most select classes of poetical readers with beautiful idealisms of moral excellence."

"The great secret of morals is love," he wrote; "the great instrument of moral good is the imagination." Shelley is the poet of ideal love and beauty informing all things, binding all things together, and offering in their fullness the satisfaction of man's physical needs, his moral desires, and his spiritual aspirations. "The essential thought of Shelley's creed," declares Symonds, "was that the universe is penetrated, vitalized, made real by a spirit, which he sometimes calls the Spirit of Nature [as in *Queen Mab*], but which is always conceived as more than Life, as that which gives its actuality to Life, and lastly Love and Beauty [as in *Adonais*]. To adore this spirit, to clasp it with affection, and to blend with it, is, he thought, the true object of man."[1] Thus Shelley's idealism motivates his attack on the world as he knew it and inspires his program and his hopes for the world as it was to be. In its broad principles, Shelley's is as practical as any other system which seeks causes and remedies in the heart of man. Those who deplore the vagueness of his poetic expression of the system should read his prose. The quiet, clear, reasonable thinking characteristic of his essays, prefaces, and letters creates a strong presumption that his poetry may be more sensible than it seems, and raises a question whether it may not be we who are lost in stormy visions, not he.

In Shelley's lyric poetry (and most of the best of his poetry is lyrical) appear the ideas and the convictions just described and several controlling moods and emotions related to them. Shelley is the poet of the free elements and forces of nature, which he conceives with the vividness of a primitive mythmaker, yet often with the fidelity to fact of a man of science. They are living, sentient, like himself, and capable of hearing him, sympathizing with him, and aiding him. "Be thou me, impetuous one," he cries to the West Wind. He *becomes* the Cloud. Self-pity, personal despondency, a sense of his own fraility, weakness, and bondage are often the burden of his song to them. But they are symbols of a spirit of liberation and regeneration that must ultimately triumph. He would be an instrument, with them, for bringing about the happy deliverance. That deliverance will come! The mighty Wind that blows through the world, Destroyer and Preserver, both sweeps away the dead leaves and brings the seeds of Spring.

> "A creature of impetuous breath,
>   Our torpor deadlier than death
> He knew not; whatsoe'er he saith
>   Flashes with life;
> He spurreth men, he quickeneth
>   To splendid strife."[2]

[1] John Addington Symonds, *Shelley*, English Men of Letters Series, Macmillan, 1909, p. 123.
[2] Sir William Watson, "Shelley's Centenary," in *Selected Poems*, Nelson, 1934.

from QUEEN MAB

A PHILOSOPHICAL POEM, WITH NOTES

ECRASEZ L'INFAME!—*Correspondance de Voltaire.*

". . . *Primum quod magnis doceo de rebus; et arctis Religionum animos nodis exsolvere pergo.*"

Lucret. lib. iv.

Δός ποῦ στῶ, καὶ κόσμον κινήσω.—Archimedes

Though *Queen Mab* (published before Shelley was twenty-one) is a relatively crude and immature poem, it is significant because it contains most of the themes, ideas, situations, and motivating passions which characterize Shelley's greatest poetry. The simple framework of the poem affords one of the clearest organizations of his thoughts and feelings that he ever achieved: The fairy Queen Mab descends to earth and takes the spirit of the sleeping Ianthe to her ethereal palace in the interstellar spaces. From the battlements of the palace she expounds the Necessitarian government of the universe (especially, section 6, ll. 146–219) and points out and explains a threefold vision—the Past (*Sic transit gloria mundi*—Thus passes away the glory of the world, because of "wealth, that curse of man"); the Present (the world as it is, cursed by war, tyranny, corruption, injustice, misery); and the Future (the world redeemed by faith in "perfection's germ" and in Necessity, which requires no prayers). The ideas are much more numerous, complex, and philosophical than this simplified statement would indicate; with the help suggested they should be studied in some detail as preparation for an understanding of Shelley's greater poems, where they appear in far less simple form. For purposes of future comparison, note especially Shelley's ideas on the government of the universe, on religion and priestcraft, on economic and social problems, and on history.

TO HARRIET

Whose is the love that gleaming through the world,
Wards off the poisonous arrow of its scorn?
    Whose is the warm and partial praise,
    Virtue's most sweet reward?

Beneath whose looks did my reviving soul
Riper in truth and virtuous daring grow?
    Whose eyes have I gazed fondly on,
    And loved mankind the more?

HARRIET! on thine:—thou wert my purer mind;
Thou wert the inspiration of my song;   10
    Thine are these early wilding flowers,
    Though garlanded by me.

Mottoes: Voltaire, "Crush the wretch" (meaning the Church). Lucretius, six lines from *De Rerum Natura*, of which the last two are the most significant—"First of all, I teach of great things; and seek to loose minds from the tight bonds of religion." Archimedes, "Give me a place to stand on and I will move the world."

Then press into thy breast this pledge of love;
And know, though time may change and years may
    roll,
  Each floweret gathered in my heart
    It consecrates to thine.

QUEEN MAB

I

  How wonderful is Death,
  Death and his brother Sleep!
One, pale as yonder waning moon
  With lips of lurid blue;
The other, rosy as the morn
  When throned on ocean's wave
It blushes o'er the world:
Yet both so passing wonderful!

  Hath then the gloomy Power
Whose reign is in the tainted sepulchres   10
  Seized on her sinless soul?
  Must then that peerless form
Which love and admiration cannot view
Without a beating heart, those azure veins
Which steal like streams along a field of snow,
  That lovely outline, which is fair
    As breathing marble, perish?
    Must putrefaction's breath
  Leave nothing of this heavenly sight
    But loathsomeness and ruin?   20
  Spare nothing but a gloomy theme,
On which the lightest heart might moralize?
    Or is it only a sweet slumber
    Stealing o'er sensation,
  Which the breath of roseate morning
    Chaseth into darkness?
    Will Ianthe wake again,
  And give that faithful bosom joy
  Whose sleepless spirit waits to catch
  Light, life and rapture from her smile?   30

  Yes! she will wake again,
Although her glowing limbs are motionless,
    And silent those sweet lips,
    Once breathing eloquence,
  That might have soothed a tyger's rage,
Or thawed the cold heart of a conqueror.
    Her dewy eyes are closed,
  And on their lids, whose texture fine
Scarce hides the dark blue orbs beneath,
    The baby Sleep is pillowed: 40
    Her golden tresses shade
    The bosom's stainless pride,
  Curling like tendrils of the parasite
    Around a marble column.

Hark! whence that rushing sound?
  'Tis like the wondrous strain
That round a lonely ruin swells,
  Which, wandering on the echoing shore,
    The enthusiast hears at evening:
'Tis softer than the west wind's sigh;   50
'Tis wilder than the unmeasured notes
  Of that strange lyre whose strings
  The genii of the breezes sweep:
    Those lines of rainbow light
Are like the moonbeams when they fall
Through some cathedral window, but the tints
    Are such as may not find
    Comparison on earth.

Behold the chariot of the Fairy Queen!
Celestial coursers paw the unyielding air;   60
Their filmy pennons at her word they furl,
And stop obedient to the reins of light:
  These the Queen of Spells drew in,
  She spread a charm around the spot,
And leaning graceful from the ethereal car,
    Long did she gaze, and silently,
    Upon the slumbering maid.

Oh! not the visioned poet in his dreams,
When silvery clouds float through the wildered brain,
  When every sight of lovely, wild and grand   70
    Astonishes, enraptures, elevates,
    When fancy at a glance combines
    The wond'rous and the beautiful,—
  So bright, so fair, so wild a shape
    Hath ever yet beheld,
As that which reined the coursers of the air,
  And poured the magic of her gaze
    Upon the maiden's sleep.

  The broad and yellow moon
  Shone dimly through her form—   80
That form of faultless symmetry;
  The pearly and pellucid car
    Moved not the moonlight's line:
    'Twas not an earthly pageant;
Those who had looked upon the sight,
    Passing all human glory,
    Saw not the yellow moon,
    Saw not the mortal scene,
    Heard not the night-wind's rush,
    Heard not an earthly sound,   90
    Saw but the fairy pageant,
    Heard but the heavenly strains
    That filled the lonely dwelling.

The Fairy's frame was slight; yon fibrous cloud,
  That catches but the palest tinge of even,

And which the straining eye can hardly seize
When melting into eastern twilight's shadow,
Were scarce so thin, so slight; but the fair star
That gems the glittering coronet of morn,
Sheds not a light so mild, so powerful,   100
As that which, bursting from the Fairy's form,
Spread a purpureal halo round the scene,
  Yet with an undulating motion,
  Swayed to her outline gracefully.

  From her celestial car
  The Fairy Queen descended,
  And thrice she waved her wand
  Circled with wreaths of amaranth:
  Her thin and misty form
  Moved with the moving air,   110
  And the clear silver tones,
  As thus she spoke, were such
As are unheard by all but gifted ear.

   Fairy

Stars! your balmiest influence shed!
Elements! your wrath suspend!
Sleep, Ocean, in the rocky bounds
  That circle thy domain!
Let not a breath be seen to stir
Around yon grass-grown ruin's height,
  Let even the restless gossamer   120
  Sleep on the moveless air!
  Soul of Ianthe! thou,
Judged alone worthy of the envied boon,
That waits the good and the sincere; that waits
Those who have struggled, and with resolute will
Vanquished earth's pride and meanness, burst
 the chains,
The icy chains of custom, and have shone
The day-stars of their age;—Soul of Ianthe!
  Awake! arise!

  Sudden arose   130
  Ianthe's Soul; it stood
  All beautiful in naked purity,
The perfect semblance of its bodily frame.
Instinct with inexpressible beauty and grace,
  Each stain of earthliness
  Had passed away, it reassumed
  Its native dignity, and stood
  Immortal amid ruin.

  Upon the couch the body lay,
  Wrapped in the depth of slumber;   140
Its features were fixed and meaningless,
  Yet animal life was there,

And every organ yet performed
  Its natural functions: 'twas a sight
Of wonder to behold the body and the soul.
  The self-same lineaments, the same
  Marks of identity were there:
Yet, oh how different! One aspires to Heaven,
Pants for its sempiternal heritage,
And ever changing, ever rising still,   150
  Wantons in endless being.
The other, for a time the unwilling sport
Of circumstance and passion, struggles on;
Fleets through its sad duration rapidly;
Then, like an useless and worn-out machine,
  Rots, perishes, and passes.

   Fairy

Spirit! who hast dived so deep;
Spirit! who hast soared so high;
Thou the fearless, thou the mild,
Accept the boon thy worth hath earned,   160
  Ascend the car with me.

   Spirit

Do I dream? Is this new feeling
But a visioned ghost of slumber?
  If indeed I am a soul,
A free, a disembodied soul,
  Speak again to me.

   Fairy

I am the Fairy MAB: to me 'tis given
The wonders of the human world to keep:
The secrets of the immeasurable past,
In the unfailing consciences of men,   170
Those stern, unflattering chroniclers, I find:
The future, from the causes which arise
In each event, I gather: not the sting
Which retributive memory implants
In the hard bosom of the selfish man;
Nor that extatic and exulting throb
Which virtue's votary feels when he sums up
The thoughts and actions of a well-spent day,
Are unforeseen, unregistered by me:
And it is yet permitted me, to rend   180
The veil of mortal frailty, that the spirit,
Clothed in its changeless purity, may know
How soonest to accomplish the great end
For which it hath its being, and may taste
That peace, which in the end all life will share.
This is the meed of virtue; happy Soul,
  Ascend the car with me!

The chains of earth's immurement
    Fell from Ianthe's spirit;
They shrank and brake like bandages of straw 190
    Beneath a wakened giant's strength.
        She knew her glorious change,
    And felt in apprehension uncontrolled
        New raptures opening round;
    Each day-dream of her mortal life,
    Each frenzied vision of the slumbers
        That closed each well-spent day,
        Seemed now to meet reality.

    The Fairy and the Soul proceeded;
        The silver clouds disparted;   200
    And as the car of magic they ascended,
    Again the speechless music swelled,
    Again the coursers of the air
Unfurled their azure pennons, and the Queen,
        Shaking the beamy reins,
        Bade them pursue their way.

        The magic car moved on.
    The night was fair, and countless stars
    Studded heaven's dark blue vault,—
        Just o'er the eastern wave   210
    Peeped the first faint smile of morn:—
        The magic car moved on—
        From the celestial hoofs
    The atmosphere in flaming sparkles flew,
        And where the burning wheels
    Eddied above the mountain's loftiest peak,
        Was traced a line of lightning.
    Now it flew far above a rock,
        The utmost verge of earth,
    The rival of the Andes, whose dark brow   220
        Lowered o'er the silver sea.

    Far, far below the chariot's path,
        Calm as a slumbering babe,
        Tremendous Ocean lay.
    The mirror of its stillness showed
        The pale and waning stars,
        The chariot's fiery track,
        And the grey light of morn
        Tinging those fleecy clouds
        That canopied the dawn.   230
    Seemed it, that the chariot's way
Lay through the midst of an immense concave,
    Radiant with million constellations, tinged
        With shades of infinite colour,
        And semicircled with a belt
        Flashing incessant meteors.

    The magic car moved on.
    As they approached their goal,

        The coursers seemed to gather speed;
    The sea no longer was distinguished; earth   240
        Appeared a vast and shadowy sphere;
        The sun's unclouded orb
        Rolled through the black concave;
        Its rays of rapid light
    Parted around the chariot's swifter course,
        And fell, like ocean's feathery spray
        Dashed from the boiling surge
        Before a vessel's prow.

        The magic car moved on.
        Earth's distant orb appeared   250
    The smallest light that twinkles in the heaven;
        Whilst round the chariot's way
        Innumerable systems rolled,
        And countless spheres diffused
        An ever-varying glory.
    It was a sight of wonder: some
    Were hornèd like the crescent moon;
    Some shed a mild and silver beam
    Like Hesperus o'er the western sea;
    Some dashed athwart with trains of flame,
    Like worlds to death and ruin driven;   261
Some shone like suns, and, as the chariot passed,
        Eclipsed all other light.

        Spirit of Nature! here!
    In this interminable wilderness
    Of worlds, at whose immensity
        Even soaring fancy staggers,
        Here is thy fitting temple.
            Yet not the lightest leaf
    That quivers to the passing breeze   270
        Is less instinct with thee:
        Yet not the meanest worm
That lurks in graves and fattens on the dead
    Less shares thy eternal breath.
        Spirit of Nature! thou!
    Imperishable as this scene,
        Here is thy fitting temple.

                2
    If solitude hath ever led thy steps
    To the wild ocean's echoing shore,
        And thou hast lingered there,
        Until the sun's broad orb
    Seemed resting on the burnished wave,
        Thou must have marked the lines
    Of purple gold, that motionless
        Hung o'er the sinking sphere:
    Thou must have marked the billowy clouds
    Edged with intolerable radiancy   10
        Towering like rocks of jet

Crowned with a diamond wreath.
And yet there is a moment,
When the sun's highest point
Peeps like a star o'er ocean's western edge,
When those far clouds of feathery gold,
  Shaded with deepest purple, gleam
  Like islands on a dark blue sea;
Then has thy fancy soared above the earth,
  And furled its wearied wing   20
  Within the Fairy's fane.

  Yet not the golden islands
  Gleaming in yon flood of light,
    Nor the feathery curtains
  Stretching o'er the sun's bright couch,
  Nor the burnished ocean waves
    Paving that gorgeous dome,
  So fair, so wonderful a sight
As Mab's ethereal palace could afford.
Yet likest evening's vault, that faery Hall!   30
As Heaven, low resting on the wave, it spread
  Its floors of flashing light,
  Its vast and azure dome,
  Its fertile golden islands
  Floating on a silver sea;
Whilst suns their mingling beamings darted
Through clouds of circumambient darkness,
  And pearly battlements around
  Looked o'er the immense of Heaven.

The magic car no longer moved.   40
  The Fairy and the Spirit
  Entered the Hall of Spells:
    Those golden clouds
  That rolled in glittering billows
  Beneath the azure canopy
With the etheral footsteps trembled not:
  The light and crimson mists,
Floating to strains of thrilling melody
  Through that unearthly dwelling,
Yielded to every movement of the will.   50
Upon their passive swell the Spirit leaned,
And, for the varied bliss that pressed around,
  Used not the glorious privilege
  Of virtue and of wisdom.

    Spirit! the Fairy said,
And pointed to the gorgeous dome,
  This is a wondrous sight
  And mocks all human grandeur;
But, were it virtue's only meed, to dwell
In a celestial palace, all resigned   60
To pleasurable impulses, immured
Within the prison of itself, the will

Of changeless Nature would be unfulfilled.
Learn to make others happy. Spirit, come!
This is thine high reward:—the past shall rise;
Thou shalt behold the present; I will teach
  The secrets of the future! . . .

    Behold, the Fairy cried,
  Palmyra's ruined palaces!—   110
  Behold! where grandeur frowned;
  Behold! where pleasure smiled;
What now remains?—the memory
  Of senselessness and shame—
  What is immortal there?
  Nothing—it stands to tell
  A melancholy tale, to give
  An awful warning: soon
Oblivion will steal silently
  The remnant of its fame.   120
  Monarchs and conquerors there
Proud o'er prostrate millions trod—
The earthquakes of the human race;
  Like them, forgotten when the ruin
  That marks their shock is past.

    Beside the eternal Nile,
  The Pyramids have risen.
Nile shall pursue his changeless way;
  Those pyramids shall fall;
Yea! not a stone shall stand to tell   130
  The spot whereon they stood;
  Their very site shall be forgotten,
  As is their builder's name!

    Behold yon sterile spot;
  Where now the wandering Arab's tent
    Flaps in the desert-blast.
  There once old Salem's haughty fane
Reared high to Heaven its thousand golden domes,
  And in the blushing face of day
    Exposed its shameful glory.   140
Oh! many a widow, many an orphan cursed
The building of that fane; and many a father,
Worn out with toil and slavery, implored
The poor man's God to sweep it from the earth,
And spare his children the detested task
Of piling stone on stone, and poisoning
    The choicest days of life,
    To soothe a dotard's vanity.
There an inhuman and uncultured race
Howled hideous praises to their Demon-God;   150
They rushed to war, tore from the mother's womb
The unborn child,—old age and infancy
Promiscuous perished; their victorious arms
Left not a soul to breathe. Oh! they were fiends:

But what was he who taught them that the God
Of nature and benevolence had given
A special sanction to the trade of blood?
His name and theirs are fading, and the tales
Of this barbarian nation, which imposture
Recites till terror credits, are pursuing   160
    Itself into forgetfulness.

    Where Athens, Rome, and Sparta stood,
    There is a moral desert now:
    The mean and miserable huts,
    The yet more wretched palaces,
    Contrasted with those ancient fanes,
    Now crumbling to oblivion;
    The long and lonely colonnades,
    Through which the ghost of Freedom stalks,
        Seem like a well-known tune,   170
Which, in some dear scene we have loved to hear,
        Remembered now in sadness.
        But, oh! how much more changed,
        How gloomier is the contrast
        Of human nature there!
Where Socrates expired, a tyrant's slave,
A coward and a fool, spreads death around—
        Then, shuddering, meets his own.
Where Cicero and Antoninus lived,
    A cowled and hypocritical monk   180
        Prays, curses and deceives.

    Spirit! ten thousand years
    Have scarcely passed away,
Since, in the waste where now the savage drinks
His enemy's blood, and aping Europe's sons,
    Wakes the unholy song of war,
    Arose a stately city,
Metropolis of the western continent:
    There, now, the mossy column-stone,
Indented by time's unrelaxing grasp,   190
    Which once appeared to brave
    All, save its country's ruin;
    There the wide forest scene,
Rude in the uncultivated loveliness
    Of gardens long run wild,
Seems, to the unwilling sojourner, whose steps
    Chance in that desert has delayed,
Thus to have stood since earth was what it is.
    Yet once it was the busiest haunt,
Whither, as to a common centre, flocked   200
    Strangers, and ships, and merchandize:
        Once peace and freedom blessed
        The cultivated plain:
        But wealth, that curse of man,
Blighted the bud of its prosperity:
Virtue and wisdom, truth and liberty,

Fled, to return not, until man shall know
    That they alone can give the bliss
        Worthy a soul that claims
        Its kindred with eternity. . . .   210

4
        Ah! whence yon glare   33
That fires the arch of heaven?—that dark red
    smoke
Blotting the silver moon? The stars are quenched
In darkness, and the pure and spangling snow
Gleams faintly through the gloom that gathers
    round!
Hark to that roar, whose swift and deaf'ning peals
In countless echoes through the mountains ring,
Startling pale midnight on her starry throne!   40
Now swells the intermingling din; the jar
Frequent and frightful of the bursting bomb;
The falling beam, the shriek, the groan, the shout,
The ceaseless clangor, and the rush of men
Inebriate with rage:—loud, and more loud
The discord grows; till pale death shuts the scene,
And o'er the conqueror and the conquered draws
His cold and bloody shroud.—Of all the men
Whom day's departing beam saw blooming there,
In proud and vigorous health; of all the hearts   50
That beat with anxious life at sun-set there;
How few survive, how few are beating now!
All is deep silence, like the fearful calm
That slumbers in the storm's portentous pause;
Save when the frantic wail of widowed love
Comes shuddering on the blast, or the faint moan
With which some soul bursts from the frame of clay
Wrapped round its struggling powers.
                The grey morn
Dawns on the mournful scene; the sulphurous
    smoke
Before the icy wind slow rolls away,   60
And the bright beams of frosty morning dance
Along the spangling snow. There tracks of blood
Even to the forest's depth, and scattered arms,
And lifeless warriors, whose hard lineaments
Death's self could change not, mark the dreadful
    path
Of the outsallying victors: far behind,
Black ashes note where their proud city stood.
Within yon forest is a gloomy glen—
Each tree which guards its darkness from the day,
Waves o'er a warrior's tomb.
             I see thee shrink,   70
Surpassing Spirit!—wert thou human else?
I see a shade of doubt and horror fleet
Across thy stainless features: yet fear not;

This is no unconnected misery,
Nor stands uncaused and irretrievable.
Man's evil nature, that apology
Which kings who rule, and cowards who crouch,
    set up
For their unnumbered crimes, sheds not the blood
Which desolates the discord-wasted land.
From kings, and priests, and statesmen, war arose,
Whose safety is man's deep unbettered woe,   81
Whose grandeur his debasement. Let the axe
Strike at the root, the poison-tree will fall;
And where its venomed exhalations spread
Ruin, and death, and woe, where millions lay
Quenching the serpent's famine, and their bones
Bleaching unburied in the putrid blast,
A garden shall arise, in loveliness
Surpassing fabled Eden.

                    Hath Nature's soul,
That formed this world so beautiful, that spread 90
Earth's lap with plenty, and life's smallest chord
Strung to unchanging unison, that gave
The happy birds their dwelling in the grove,
That yielded to the wanderers of the deep
The lovely silence of the unfathomed main,
And filled the meanest worm that crawls in dust
With spirit, thought, and love; on Man alone,
Partial in causeless malice, wantonly
Heaped ruin, vice, and slavery; his soul
Blasted with withering curses; placed afar   100
The meteor-happiness, that shuns his grasp,
But serving on the frightful gulf to glare,
Rent wide beneath his footsteps?

                    Nature!—no!
Kings, priests, and statesmen, blast the human
    flower
Even in its tender bud; their influence darts
Like subtle poison through the bloodless veins
Of desolate society. The child,
Ere he can lisp his mother's sacred name,
Swells with the unnatural pride of crime, and
    lifts
His baby-sword even in a hero's mood.   110
This infant-arm becomes the bloodiest scourge
Of devastated earth; whilst specious names,
Learned in soft childhood's unsuspecting hour,
Serve as the sophisms with which manhood dims
Bright reason's ray, and sanctifies the sword
Upraised to shed a brother's innocent blood.
Let priest-led slaves cease to proclaim that man
Inherits vice and misery, when force
And falsehood hang even o'er the cradled babe,
Stifling with rudest grasp all natural good.   120

Ah! to the stranger-soul, when first it peeps
From its new tenement, and looks abroad
For happiness and sympathy, how stern
And desolate a tract is this wide world!
How withered all the buds of natural good!
No shade, no shelter from the sweeping storms
Of pitiless power! On its wretched frame,
Poisoned, perchance, by the disease and woe
Heaped on the wretched parent whence it sprung
By morals, law, and custom, the pure winds   130
Of heaven, that renovate the insect tribes,
May breathe not. The untainting light of day
May visit not its longings. It is bound
Ere it has life: yea, all the chains are forged
Long ere its being; all liberty and love
And peace is torn from its defencelessness;
Cursed from its birth, even from its cradle doomed
To abjectness and bondage!

Throughout this varied and eternal world
Soul is the only element, the block   140
That for uncounted ages has remained.
The moveless pillar of a mountain's weight
Is active, living spirit. Every grain
Is sentient both in unity and part,
And the minutest atom comprehends
A world of loves and hatreds; these beget
Evil and good: hence truth and falsehood spring;
Hence will, and thought, and action, all the germs
Of pain or pleasure, sympathy or hate,
That variegate the eternal universe.   150
Soul is not more polluted than the beams
Of heaven's pure orb, ere round their rapid lines
The taint of earth-born atmospheres arise.

Man is of soul and body, formed for deeds
Of high resolve; on fancy's boldest wing
To soar unwearied, fearlessly to turn
The keenest pangs to peacefulness, and taste
The joys which mingled sense and spirit yield.
Or he is formed for abjectness and woe,
To grovel on the dunghill of his fears,   160
To shrink at every sound, to quench the flame
Of natural love in sensualism, to know
That hour as blest when on his worthless days
The frozen hand of death shall set its seal,
Yet fear the cure, though hating the disease.
The one is man that shall hereafter be;
The other, man as vice has made him now.

War is the statesman's game, the priest's delight,
The lawyer's jest, the hired assassin's trade,
And, to those royal murderers, whose mean thrones
Are bought by crimes of treachery and gore,   171

The bread they eat, the staff on which they
   lean.
Guards, garbed in blood-red livery, surround
Their palaces, participate the crimes
That force defends, and from a nation's rage
Secure the crown, which all the curses reach
That famine, frenzy, woe and penury breathe.
These are the hired bravos who defend
The tyrant's throne—the bullies of his fear;
These are the sinks and channels of worse vice, 180
The refuse of society, the dregs
Of all that is most vile: their cold hearts blend
Deceit with sternness, ignorance with pride,
All that is mean and villainous, with rage
Which hopelessness of good, and self-contempt,
Alone might kindle; they are decked in wealth,
Honour and power, then are sent abroad
To do their work. The pestilence that stalks
In gloomy triumph through some eastern land
Is less destroying. They cajole with gold,   190
And promises of fame, the thoughtless youth
Already crushed with servitude; he knows
His wretchedness too late, and cherishes
Repentance for his ruin, when his doom
Is sealed in gold and blood!
Those too the tyrant serve, who, skilled to
   snare
The feet of justice in the toils of law,
Stand, ready to oppress the weaker still;
And right or wrong will vindicate for gold,
Sneering at public virtue, which beneath   200
Their pitiless tread lies torn and trampled, where
Honour sits smiling at the sale of truth.

Then grave and hoary-headed hypocrites,
Without a hope, a passion, or a love,
Who, through a life of luxury and lies,
Have crept by flattery to the seats of power,
Support the system whence their honours flow. . .
They have three words:—well tyrants know their
   use,
Well pay them for the loan, with usury
Torn from a bleeding world!—God, Hell and
   Heaven.   210
A vengeful, pityless, and almighty fiend,
Whose mercy is a nick-name for the rage
Of tameless tygers hungering for blood.
Hell, a red gulf of everlasting fire,
Where poisonous and undying worms prolong
Eternal misery to those hapless slaves
Whose life has been a penance for its crimes.
And Heaven, a meed for those who dare belie
Their human nature, quake, believe, and cringe
Before the mockeries of earthly power.   220

These tools the tyrant tempers to his work,
Wields in his wrath, and as he wills, destroys,
Omnipotent in wickedness: the while
Youth springs, age moulders, manhood tamely does
His bidding, bribed by short-lived joys to lend
Force to the weakness of his trembling arm. . . .

6

. . . Throughout these infinite orbs of mingling
   light,   146
Of which yon earth is one, is wide diffused
A spirit of activity and life,
That knows no term, cessation, or decay;
That fades not when the lamp of earthly life,   150
Extinguished in the dampness of the grave,
Awhile there slumbers, more than when the babe
In the dim newness of its being feels
The impulses of sublunary things,
And all is wonder to unpractised sense:
But active, stedfast, and eternal, still
Guides the fierce whirlwind, in the tempest roars,
Cheers in the day, breathes in the balmy groves,
Strengthens in health, and poisons in disease;
And in the storm of change, that ceaselessly   160
Rolls round the eternal universe, and shakes
Its undecaying battlement, presides,
Apportioning with irresistible law
The place each spring of its machine shall fill;
So that when waves on waves tumultuous heap
Confusion to the clouds, and fiercely driven
Heaven's lightnings scorch the uprooted ocean-
   fords
Whilst, to the eye of shipwrecked mariner,
Lone sitting on the bare and shuddering rock,
All seems unlinked contingency and chance: 170
No atom of this turbulence fulfils
A vague and unnecessitated task,
Or acts but as it must and ought to act. . . .

Spirit of Nature! all-sufficing Power,   197
Necessity! thou mother of the world!
Unlike the God of human error, thou
Requirest no prayers or praises. . . .

8

The Fairy

The present and the past thou hast beheld:
It was a desolate sight. Now, Spirit, learn
   The secrets of the future.—Time!
Unfold the brooding pinion of thy gloom,
Render thou up thy half-devoured babes,
And from the cradles of eternity,
Where millions lie lulled to their portioned sleep

By the deep murmuring stream of passing things,
Tear thou that gloomy shroud.—Spirit, behold
    Thy glorious destiny! . . .   10

The habitable earth is full of bliss;
Those wastes of frozen billows that were hurled
By everlasting snow-storms round the poles,   60
Where matter dared not vegetate or live,
But ceaseless frost round the vast solitude
Bound its broad zone of stillness, are unloosed;
And fragrant zephyrs there from spicy isles
Ruffle the placid ocean-deep, that rolls
Its broad, bright surges to the sloping sand,
Whose roar is wakened into echoings sweet
To murmur through the heaven-breathing groves
And melodize with man's blest nature there. . . .

Here now the human being stands adorning
This loveliest earth with taintless body and mind;
Blessed from his birth with all bland impulses,   200
Which gently in his noble bosom wake
All kindly passions and all pure desires.
Him, still from hope to hope the bliss pursuing,
Which from the exhaustless lore of human weal
Draws on the virtuous mind, the thoughts that rise
In time-destroying infiniteness, gift
With self-enshrined eternity, that mocks
The unprevailing hoariness of age,
And man, once fleeting o'er the transient scene
Swift as an unremembered vision, stands   210
Immortal upon earth: no longer now
He slays the lamb that looks him in the face,
And horribly devours his mangled flesh,
Which, still avenging nature's broken law,
Kindled all putrid humours in his frame,
All evil passions, and all vain belief,
Hatred, despair, and loathing in his mind,
The germs of misery, death, disease, and crime.
No longer now the wingèd habitants,
That in the woods their sweet lives sing away,   220
Flee from the form of man; but gather round,
And prune their sunny feathers on the hands
Which little children stretch in friendly sport
Towards these dreadless partners of their play.
All things are void of terror: man has lost
His terrible prerogative, and stands
An equal amidst equals: happiness
And science dawn though late upon the earth;
Peace cheers the mind, health renovates the frame;
Disease and pleasure cease to mingle here,   230
Reason and passion cease to combat there;
Whilst each unfettered o'er the earth extend
Their all-subduing energies, and wield
The sceptre of a vast dominion there;

Whilst every shape and mode of matter lends
Its force to the omnipotence of mind,
Which from its dark mine drags the gem of truth
To decorate its paradise of peace. . . .

9

. . . The Body and the Soul united then;
A gentle start convulsed Ianthe's frame:
Her veiny eyelids quietly unclosed;
Moveless awhile the dark blue orbs remained:
She looked around in wonder, and beheld
Henry, who kneeled in silence by her couch,
Watching her sleep with looks of speechless love,
    And the bright beaming stars
    That through the casement shone.   240

from ALASTOR;

OR, THE SPIRIT OF SOLITUDE

*Nondum amabam, et amare amabam, quaerebam quid
amarem, amans amare.—Confess. St. August.*

When Shelley wrote *Alastor*, in 1815, his reform
schemes had failed, and he believed that he was soon to
die. The poem expresses his despair over the exhaustion
of his revolutionary ideals and aspirations. "A cruel demon, an Alastor [note that this is not the name of the poet
in the poem], a spirit of evil, a spirit which isolated him
from the interests and hopes of men—had seized on him,
and drove him far away in the wilderness to die."[1] In an
eloquent preface (with which the poem does not exactly
jibe), he condemns the selfish idealist, but condemns even
more sternly those who have no ideal at all. The motto
says, "Not yet did I love, and I loved to love; I sought
what I should love, loving to love." Perhaps in it lies the
deeper meaning of the poem: the vain hope for the mortal realization of ideal love—a mistake which Shelley
often made. A recent study, H. L. Hoffman's *An Odyssey
of the Soul: Shelley's "Alastor,"* Columbia University Press,
1933, treats the poem as profoundly autobiographical.
Much of the scenery of the poem Shelley got from his
tour of the Alps with Mary the summer before and
from a boating trip up the Thames just before he wrote it.

Earth, ocean, air, belovèd brotherhood!
If our great Mother has imbued my soul
With aught of natural piety to feel
Your love, and recompense the boon with mine;
If dewy morn, and odorous noon, and even,
With sunset and its gorgeous ministers,
And solemn midnight's tingling silentness;
If autumn's hollow sighs in the sere wood,

[1] Stopford Brooke, *Naturalism in English Poetry*, Dutton, 1920.
2. great Mother, Nature. Compare *Queen Mab*, sec. 6, ll.
146 ff. What is the difference in conception and attitude?

And winter robing with pure snow and crowns
Of starry ice the grey grass and bare boughs; 10
If spring's voluptuous pantings when she breathes
Her first sweet kisses, have been dear to me;
If no bright bird, insect, or gentle beast
I consciously have injured, but still loved
And cherished these my kindred; then forgive
This boast, belovèd brethren, and withdraw
No portion of your wonted favour now!

Mother of this unfathomable world!
Favour my solemn song, for I have loved
Thee ever, and thee only; I have watched 20
Thy shadow, and the darkness of thy steps,
And my heart ever gazes on the depth
Of thy deep mysteries. I have made my bed
In charnels and on coffins, where black death
Keeps record of the trophies won from thee,
Hoping to still these obstinate questionings
Of thee and thine, by forcing some lone ghost
Thy messenger, to render up the tale
Of what we are. In lone and silent hours,
When night makes a weird sound of its own stillness,
Like an inspired and desperate alchymist 31
Staking his very life on some dark hope,
Have I mixed awful talk and asking looks
With my most innocent love, until strange tears
Uniting with those breathless kisses, made
Such magic as compels the charmèd night
To render up thy charge: . . . and, though ne'er
  yet
Thou hast unveiled thy inmost sanctuary,
Enough from incommunicable dream,
And twilight phantasms, and deep noonday
  thought, 40
Has shone within me, that serenely now
And moveless, as a long-forgotten lyre
Suspended in the solitary dome
Of some mysterious and deserted fane,
I wait thy breath, Great Parent, that my strain
May modulate with murmurs of the air,
And motions of the forests and the sea,
And voice of living beings, and woven hymns
Of night and day, and the deep heart of man.

There was a Poet whose untimely tomb 50
No human hands with pious reverence reared,
But the charmed eddies of autumnal winds
Built o'er his mouldering bones a pyramid
Of mouldering leaves in the waste wilderness;—
A lovely youth,—no mourning maiden decked
With weeping flowers, or votive cypress wreath,
The lone couch of his everlasting sleep:—
Gentle, and brave, and generous,—no lorn bard

Breathed o'er his dark fate one melodious sigh:
He lived, he died, he sung, in solitude. 60
Strangers have wept to hear his passionate notes,
And virgins, as unknown he passed, have pined
And wasted for fond love of his wild eyes.
The fire of those soft orbs has ceased to burn,
And Silence, too enamoured of that voice,
Locks its mute music in her rugged cell.

By solemn vision and bright silver dream,
His infancy was nurtured. Every sight
And sound from the vast earth and ambient air,
Sent to his heart its choicest impulses. 70
The fountains of divine philosophy
Fled not his thirsting lips, and all of great,
Or good, or lovely, which the sacred past
In truth or fable consecrates, he felt
And knew. When early youth had passed, he left
His cold fireside and alienated home
To seek strange truths in undiscovered lands.
Many a wide waste and tangled wilderness
Has lured his fearless steps; and he has bought
With his sweet voice and eyes, from savage men,
His rest and food. Nature's most secret steps 81
He like her shadow has pursued, where'er
The red volcano overcanopies
Its fields of snow and pinnacles of ice
With burning smoke, or where bitumen lakes
On black bare pointed islets ever beat
With sluggish surge, or where the secret caves
Rugged and dark, winding among the springs
Of fire and poison, inaccessible
To avarice or pride, their starry domes 90
Of diamond and of gold expand above
Numberless and immeasurable halls,
Frequent with crystal column, and clear shrines
Of pearl, and thrones radiant with chrysolite.
Nor had that scene of ampler majesty
Than gems or gold, the varying roof of heaven
And the green earth lost in his heart its claims
To love and wonder; he would linger long
In lonesome vales, making the wild his home,
Until the doves and squirrels would partake 100
From his innocuous hand his bloodless food,
Lured by the gentle meaning of his looks,
And the wild antelope, that starts whene'er
The dry leaf rustles in the brake, suspend
Her timid steps to gaze upon a form
More graceful than her own. His wandering step
Obedient to high thoughts, has visited
The awful ruins of the days of old:

76. cold fireside and alienated home. Note Shelley's
trouble with his family after his expulsion from Oxford.

Athens, and Tyre, and Balbec, and the waste
Where stood Jerusalem, the fallen towers   110
Of Babylon, the eternal pyramids,
Memphis and Thebes, and whatsoe'er of strange
Sculptured on alabaster obelisk,
Or jasper tomb, or mutilated sphinx,
Dark Ethiopia in her desert hills
Conceals. Among the ruined temples there,
Stupendous columns, and wild images
Of more than man, where marble daemons watch
The Zodiac's brazen mystery, and dead men
Hang their mute thoughts on the mute walls
    around,   120
He lingered, poring on memorials
Of the world's youth; through the long burning day
Gazed on those speechless shapes, nor, when the
    moon
Filled the mysterious halls with floating shades
Suspended he that task, but ever gazed
And gazed, till meaning on his vacant mind
Flashed like strong inspiration, and he saw
The thrilling secrets of the birth of time.

Meanwhile an Arab maiden brought his food,
Her daily portion, from her father's tent,   130
And spread her matting for his couch, and stole
From duties and repose to tend his steps:—
Enamoured, yet not daring for deep awe
To speak her love:—and watched his nightly sleep,
Sleepless herself, to gaze upon his lips
Parted in slumber, whence the regular breath
Of innocent dreams arose: then, when red morn
Made paler the pale moon, to her cold home
Wildered, and wan, and panting, she returned.

The Poet wandering on, through Arabie   140
And Persia, and the wild Carmanian waste,
And o'er the aërial mountains which pour down
Indus and Oxus from their icy caves,
In joy and exultation held his way;
Till in the vale of Cashmire, far within
Its loneliest dell, where odorous plants entwine
Beneath the hollow rocks a natural bower,
Beside a sparkling rivulet he stretched
His languid limbs. A vision on his sleep
There came, a dream of hopes that never yet   150
Had flushed his cheek. He dreamed a veilèd maid
Sate near him, talking in low solemn tones.
Her voice was like the voice of his own soul
Heard in the calm of thought; its music long,

Like woven sounds of streams and breezes, held
His inmost sense suspended in its web
Of many-coloured woof and shifting hues.
Knowledge and truth and virtue were her theme,
And lofty hopes of divine liberty,
Thoughts the most dear to him, and poesy,   160
Herself a poet. Soon the solemn mood
Of her pure mind kindled through all her frame
A permeating fire: wild numbers then
She raised, with voice stifled in tremulous sobs
Subdued by its own pathos: her fair hands
Were bare alone, sweeping from some strange harp
Strange symphony, and in their branching veins
The eloquent blood told an ineffable tale.
The beating of her heart was heard to fill
The pauses of her music, and her breath,   170
Tumultuously accorded with those fits
Of intermitted song. Sudden she rose,
As if her heart impatiently endured
Its bursting burthen: at the sound he turned,
And saw by the warm light of their own life
Her glowing limbs beneath the sinuous veil
Of woven wind, her outspread arms now bare,
Her dark locks floating in the breath of night,
Her beamy bending eyes, her parted lips
Outstretched, and pale, and quivering eagerly.   180
His strong heart sunk and sickened with excess
Of love. He reared his shuddering limbs and quelled
His gasping breath, and spread his arms to meet
Her panting bosom; . . . she drew back a while,
Then, yielding to the irresistible joy,
With frantic gesture and short breathless cry
Folded his frame in her dissolving arms.
Now blackness veiled his dizzy eyes, and night
Involved and swallowed up the vision; sleep,
Like a dark flood suspended in its course,   190
Rolled back its impulse on his vacant brain.

Roused by the shock he started from his trance—
The cold white light of morning, the blue moon
Low in the west, the clear and garish hills,
The distinct valley and the vacant woods,
Spread round him where he stood. Whither have
    fled
The hues of heaven that canopied his bower,
Of yesternight? The sounds that soothed his sleep,
The mystery and the majesty of Earth,
The joy, the exultation? His wan eyes   200
Gaze on the empty scene as vacantly
As ocean's moon looks on the moon in heaven.
The spirit of sweet human love has sent
A vision to the sleep of him who spurned
Her choicest gifts. He eagerly pursues
Beyond the realms of dream that fleeting shade;

129. Arab maiden. Note carefully the poet's attitude to
human love.   **149. A vision on his sleep.** Note the "spurious Platonism" (confusion of sensuous and ideal love) in
what follows.

He overleaps the bounds. Alas! Alas!
Were limbs and breath and being interwined
Thus treacherously? Lost, lost, for ever lost,
In the wide pathless desert of dim sleep,   210
That beautiful shape! Does the dark gate of death
Conduct to thy mysterious paradise,
O Sleep? Does the bright arch of rainbow clouds,
And pendent mountains seen in the calm lake,
Lead only to a black and watery depth,
While death's blue vault, with loathliest vapours
   hung,
Where every shade which the foul grave exhales
Hides its dead eye from the detested day,
Conduct, O Sleep, to thy delightful realms?
This doubt with sudden tide flowed on his heart,
The insatiate hope which it awakened, stung   221
His brain even like despair. . . .

              •   The boat pursued
The windings of the cavern. Daylight shone   370
At length upon that gloomy river's flow;
Now, where the fiercest war among the waves
Is calm, on the unfathomable stream
The boat moved slowly. Where the mountain,
   riven,
Exposed those black depths to the azure sky,
Ere yet the flood's enormous volume fell
Even to the base of Caucasus, with sound
That shook the everlasting rocks, the mass
Filled with one whirlpool all that ample chasm:
Stair above stair the eddying waters rose,   380
Circling immeasurably fast, and laved
With alternating dash the knarlèd roots
Of mighty trees, that stretched their giant arms
In darkness over it. I' the midst was left,
Reflecting, yet distorting every cloud,
A pool of treacherous and tremendous calm.
Seized by the sway of the ascending stream,
With dizzy swiftness, round, and round, and round,
Ridge after ridge the straining boat arose,
Till on the verge of the extremest curve,   390
Where, through an opening of the rocky bank,
The waters overflow, and a smooth spot
Of glassy quiet mid those battling tides
Is left, the boat paused shuddering. Shall it sink—
Down the abyss? Shall the reverting stress
Of that resistless gulf embosom it?
Now shall it fall?—A wandering stream of wind,

369. **The boat pursued.** In the preceding portion of the
poem, omitted, the poet has wandered through the Near
East far into the interior of Asia, where "upon the lone
Chorasmian shore" he finds a little boat, launches it, and is
swept on by a whirlwind over "the multitudinous streams
of ocean's mountainous waste" into a cavern in the cliffs of
Caucasus.

Breathed from the west, has caught the expanded
   sail,
And, lo! with gentle motion, between banks
Of mossy slope, and on a placid stream,   400
Beneath a woven grove, it sails, and, hark!
The ghastly torrent mingles its far roar,
With the breeze murmuring in the musical woods.
Where the embowering trees recede, and leave
A little space of green expanse, the cove
Is closed by meeting banks, whose yellow flowers
For ever gaze on their own drooping eyes,
Reflected in the crystal calm. The wave
Of the boat's motion marred their pensive task,
Which nought but vagrant bird, or wanton wind,
Of falling spear-grass, or their own decay   411
Had e'er disturbed before. The Poet longed
To deck with their bright hues his withered hair,
But on his heart its solitude returned,
And he forbore. Not the strong impulse hid
In those flushed cheeks, bent eyes, and shadowy
   frame
Had yet performed its ministry: it hung
Upon his life, as lightning in a cloud
Gleams, hovering ere it vanish, ere the floods
Of night close over it. . . .

   When on the threshold of the green recess
The wanderer's footsteps fell, he knew that death
Was on him. Yet a little, ere it fled,
Did he resign his high and holy soul
To images of the majestic past,
That paused within his passive being now,   630
Like winds that bear sweet music, when they
   breathe
Through some dim latticed chamber. He did place
His pale lean hand upon the rugged trunk
Of the old pine. Upon an ivied stone
Reclined his languid head, his limbs did rest,
Diffused and motionless, on the smooth brink
Of that obscurest chasm;—and thus he lay,
Surrendering to their final impulses
The hovering powers of life. Hope and despair,
The torturers, slept; no mortal pain or fear   640
Marred his repose, the influxes of sense,
And his own being unalloyed by pain,
Yet feebler and more feeble, calmly fed
The stream of thought, till he lay breathing there
At peace, and faintly smiling:—his last sight
Was the great moon, which o'er the western line
Of the wide world her mighty horn suspended,
With whose dun beams inwoven darkness seemed
To mingle. Now upon the jaggèd hills

625. **threshold of the green recess.** The maelstrom has
thrown the boat up on the bank.

It rests, and still as the divided frame 650
Of the vast meteor sunk, the Poet's blood,
That ever beat in mystic sympathy
With nature's ebb and flow, grew feebler still:
And when two lessening points of light alone
Gleamed through the darkness, the alternate gasp
Of his faint respiration scarce did stir
The stagnate night:—till the minutest ray
Was quenched, the pulse yet lingered in his heart.
It paused—it fluttered. But when heaven remained
Utterly black, the murky shades involved 660
An image, silent, cold, and motionless,
As their own voiceless earth and vacant air.
Even as a vapour fed with golden beams
That ministered on sunlight, ere the west
Eclipses it, was now that wondrous frame—
No sense, no motion, no divinity—
A fragile lute, on whose harmonious strings
The breath of heaven did wander—a bright stream
Once fed with many-voicèd waves—a dream
Of youth, which night and time have quenched
     for ever, 670
Still, dark, and dry, and unremembered now.

O, for Medea's wondrous alchymy,
Which wheresoe'er it fell made the earth gleam
With bright flowers, and the wintry boughs exhale
From vernal blooms fresh fragrance! O, that God,
Profuse of poisons, would concede the chalice
Which but one living man has drained, who now,
Vessel of deathless wrath, a slave that feels
No proud exemption in the blighting curse
He bears, over the world wanders for ever, 680
Lone as incarnate death! O, that the dream
Of dark magician in his visioned cave,
Raking the cinders of a crucible
For life and power, even when his feeble hand
Shakes in its last decay, were the true law
Of this so lovely world! But thou art fled
Like some frail exhalation, which the dawn
Robes in its golden beams,—ah! thou hast fled!
The brave, the gentle, and the beautiful,
The child of grace and genius. Heartless things 690
Are done and said i' the world, and many worms
And beasts and men live on, and mighty Earth
From sea and mountain, city and wilderness,
In vesper low or joyous orison,
Lifts still its solemn voice:—but thou art fled—
Thou canst no longer know or love the shapes
Of this phantasmal scene, who have to thee

Been purest ministers, who are, alas!
Now thou art not. Upon those pallid lips
So sweet even in their silence, on those eyes 700
That image sleep in death, upon that form
Yet safe from the worm's outrage, let no tear
Be shed—not even in thought. Nor, when those
     hues
Are gone, and those divinest lineaments,
Worn by the senseless wind, shall live alone
In the frail pauses of this simple strain,
Let not high verse, mourning the memory
Of that which is no more, or painting's woe
Or sculpture, speak in feeble imagery
Their own cold powers. Art and eloquence, 710
And all the shows o' the world, are frail and vain
To weep a loss that turns their lights to shade.
It is a woe "too deep for tears," when all
Is reft at once, when some surpassing Spirit,
Whose light adorned the world around it, leaves
Those who remain behind, not sobs or groans,
The passionate tumult of a clinging hope;
But pale despair and cold tranquillity,
Nature's vast frame, the web of human things,
Birth and the grave, that are not as they were. 720

HYMN TO INTELLECTUAL
BEAUTY

The awful shadow of some unseen Power
     Floats though unseen among us; visiting
     This various world with as inconstant wing
As summer winds that creep from flower to flower;
Like moonbeams that behind some piny mountain
     shower,
     It visits with inconstant glance
     Each human heart and countenance;
Like hues and harmonies of evening,
     Like clouds in starlight widely spread,
     Like memory of music fled, 10
     Like aught that for its grace may be
Dear, and yet dearer for its mystery.

Spirit of BEAUTY, that dost consecrate
     With thine own hues all thou dost shine upon
     Of human thought or form, where art thou
          gone?
Why dost thou pass away and leave our state,
This dim vast vale of tears, vacant and desolate?
     Ask why the sunlight not for ever

---

677. **one living man,** Ahasuerus, the wandering Jew. He refused Jesus a resting-place on the Via Dolorosa and was condemned to wander over the earth until the second coming. He appears in *Queen Mab* and other Shelley poems.

713. **"too deep for tears."** See Wordsworth's "Ode: Intimations," l. 203.   **1. unseen Power.** Compare the discussion of Platonism in the general introduction; also, *Alastor*, ll. 1 ff.

Weaves rainbows o'er yon mountain river,
Why aught should fail and fade that once is shown;
    Why fear and dream and death and birth   21
    Cast on the daylight of this earth
    Such gloom, why man has such a scope
For love and hate, despondency and hope?

No voice from some sublimer world hath ever
    To sage or poet these responses given:
    Therefore the names of Demon, Ghost, and
        Heaven,
Remain the records of their vain endeavour:
Frail spells, whose uttered charm might not avail
    to sever,
    From all we hear and all we see,   30
    Doubt, chance, and mutability.
Thy light alone—like mist o'er mountains driven,
    Or music by the night wind sent
    Through strings of some still instrument,
    Or moonlight on a midnight stream,
Gives grace and truth to life's unquiet dream.

Love, Hope, and Self-esteem, like clouds depart
    And come, for some uncertain moments lent.
    Man were immortal, and omnipotent,
Didst thou, unknown and awful as thou art,   40
Keep with thy glorious train firm state within his
    heart.
    Thou messenger of sympathies,
    That wax and wane in lovers' eyes;
Thou, that to human thought art nourishment,
    Like darkness to a dying flame!
    Depart not as thy shadow came:
    Depart not, lest the grave should be,
Like life and fear, a dark reality.

While yet a boy I sought for ghosts, and sped
    Through many a listening chamber, cave, and
        ruin,   50
    And starlight wood, with fearful steps pursuing
Hopes of high talk with the departed dead.
I called on poisonous names with which our youth
    is fed;
    I was not heard—I saw them not—
    When musing deeply on the lot
Of life, at that sweet time when winds are wooing
    All vital things that wake to bring
    News of birds and blossoming,
    Sudden, thy shadow fell on me;
I shrieked, and clasped my hands in extacy!   60

I vowed that I would dedicate my powers
    To thee and thine: have I not kept the vow?

61. I vowed. See the last paragraph of the biographical-critical sketch of Shelley.

With beating heart and streaming eyes, even now
I call the phantoms of a thousand hours
Each from his voiceless grave: they have in visioned
    bowers
    Of studious zeal or love's delight
    Outwatched with me the envious night:
They know that never joy illumed my brow
    Unlinked with hope that thou wouldst free
    This world from its dark slavery,   70
    That thou, O awful LOVELINESS,
Wouldst give whate'er these words cannot express.

The day becomes more solemn and serene
    When noon is past: there is a harmony
    In autumn, and a lustre in its sky,
Which through the summer is not heard or seen,
As if it could not be, as if it had not been!
    Thus let thy power, which like the truth
    Of nature on my passive youth
Descended, to my onward life supply   80
    Its calm, to one who worships thee,
    And every form containing thee,
    Whom, SPIRIT fair, thy spells did bind
To fear himself, and love all human kind.

from THE REVOLT OF ISLAM

DEDICATION

There is no danger to a Man, that knows
What life and death is: there's not any law
Exceeds his knowledge: neither is it lawful
That he should stoop to any other law.—Chapman

TO MARY *

1

So now my summer task is ended, Mary,
And I return to thee, mine own heart's home;
As to his Queen some victor Knight of Faëry,
Earning bright spoils for her inchanted dome;
Nor thou disdain, that ere my fame become
A star among the stars of mortal night,
If it indeed may cleave its natal gloom,
Its doubtful promise thus I would unite
With thy belovèd name, thou Child of love and light.

2

The toil which stole from thee so many an hour   10
Is ended,—and the fruit is at thy feet!

* "Mary" is Mary Godwin. For comment on *The Revolt of Islam*, see the biographical-critical sketch of Shelley. **3. Queen . . . Knight.** Shelley and Mary read Spenser's *The Faërie Queene* together at Marlow. Note the Spenserian stanza.

No longer where the woods to frame a bower
With interlacèd branches mix and meet,
Or where, with sounds like many voices sweet,
Water-falls leap among wild islands green,
Which framed for my lone boat a lone retreat
Of moss-grown trees and weeds, shall I be seen:
But beside thee, where still my heart has ever been.

3

Thoughts of great deeds were mine, dear Friend, when first
The clouds which wrap this world from youth did pass.   20
I do remember well the hour which burst
My spirit's sleep; a fresh May-dawn it was,
When I walked forth upon the glittering grass,
And wept, I knew not why; until there rose
From the near school-room voices that, alas!
Were but one echo from a world of woes—
The harsh and grating strife of tyrants and of foes.

4

And then I clasped my hands, and looked around,—
—But none was near to mock my streaming eyes,
Which poured their warm drops on the sunny ground—   30
So without shame, I spake:—"I will be wise,
And just, and free, and mild, if in me lies
Such power, for I grow weary to behold
The selfish and the strong still tyrannise
Without reproach or check." I then controuled
My tears, my heart grew calm, and I was meek and bold.

5

And from that hour did I with earnest thought
Heap knowledge from forbidden mines of lore,
Yet nothing that my tyrants knew or taught
I cared to learn, but from that secret store   40
Wrought linkèd armour for my soul, before
It might walk forth to war among mankind;
Thus power and hope were strengthened more and more
Within me, till there came upon my mind
A sense of loneliness, a thirst with which I pined.

6

Alas that love should be a blight and snare
To those who seek all sympathies in one!—

Such once I sought in vain; then black despair,
The shadow of a starless night, was thrown
Over the world in which I moved alone:—   50
Yet never found I one not false to me,
Hard hearts, and cold, like weights of icy stone
Which crushed and withered mine, but could not be
Aught but a lifeless clog, until revived by thee.

7

Thou Friend, whose presence on my wintry heart
Fell, like bright Spring upon some herbless plain,
How beautiful and calm and free thou wert
In thy young wisdom, when the mortal chain
Of Custom thou didst burst and rend in twain,
And walk as free as light the clouds among,   60
Which many an envious slave then breathed in vain
From his dim dungeon, and my spirit sprung
To meet thee from the woes which had begirt it long.

8

No more alone through the world's wilderness,
Although I trod the paths of high intent,
I journeyed now: no more companionless,
Where solitude is like despair, I went.—
There is the wisdom of a stern content
When Poverty can blight the just and good,
When Infamy dares mock the innocent,   70
And cherished friends turn with the multitude
To trample: this was ours, and we unshaken stood!

9

Now has descended a serener hour,
And with inconstant fortune, friends return;
Though suffering leaves the knowledge and the power
Which says:—Let scorn be not repaid with scorn.
And from thy side two gentle babes are born
To fill our home with smiles, and thus are we
Most fortunate beneath life's beaming morn:
And these delights, and thou, have been to me   80
The parents of the Song I consecrate to thee.

10

Is it, that now my inexperienced fingers
But strike the prelude of a loftier strain!
Or must the lyre on which my spirit lingers
Soon pause in silence, ne'er to sound again,

---

21. **I do remember well the hour.** Compare "Hymn to Intellectual Beauty," ll. 61 ff. The experience is supposed to have occurred at Eton. Compare Wordsworth's similar experience, *Prelude*, Book IV, ll. 309 ff.

48. **then black despair,** over the ruin of his life with Harriet. 59. **Of Custom . . . burst.** Shelley and Mary eloped on July 28, 1814.

Though it might shake the Anarch Custom's
reign,
And charm the minds of men to Truth's own
sway,
Holier than was Amphion's? I would fain
Reply in hope—but I am worn away,
And Death and Love are yet contending for their
prey.   90

11

And what art thou? I know, but dare not speak:
Time may interpret to his silent years.
Yet in the paleness of thy thoughtful cheek,
And in the light thine ample forehead wears,
And in thy sweetest smiles, and in thy tears,
And in thy gentle speech, a prophecy
Is whispered, to subdue my fondest fears:
And through thine eyes, even in thy soul I see
A lamp of vestal fire burning internally.

12

They say that thou wert lovely from thy birth, 100
Of glorious parents, thou aspiring Child!
I wonder not—for One then left this earth
Whose life was like a setting planet mild,
Which clothed thee in the radiance undefiled
Of its departing glory; still her fame
Shines on thee, through the tempests dark and
wild
Which shake these latter days; and thou canst
claim
The shelter, from thy Sire, of an immortal name.

13

One voice came forth from many a mighty spirit,
Which was the echo of three thousand years;   110
And the tumultuous world stood mute to hear it,
As some lone man who in a desert hears
The music of his home:—unwonted fears
Fell on the pale oppressors of our race,
And Faith, and Custom, and low-thoughted
cares,
Like thunder-stricken dragons, for a space
Left the torn human heart, their food and dwelling-
place.

14

Truth's deathless voice pauses among mankind!
If there must be no response to my cry—
If men must rise and stamp with fury blind   120
On his pure name who loves them,—thou and I,
Sweet friend! can look from our tranquillity

102. **for One,** Mary Wollstonecraft. 108. **Sire,** William
Godwin. 109. **voice,** that of Truth.

Like lamps into the world's tempestuous night,—
Two tranquil stars, while clouds are passing by
Which wrap them from the foundering seaman's
sight,
That burn from year to year with unextinguished
light.

OZYMANDIAS

I met a traveller from an antique land
Who said: Two vast and trunkless legs of stone
Stand in the desert. Near them, on the sand,
Half sunk, a shattered visage lies, whose frown,
And wrinkled lip, and sneer of cold command,
Tell that its sculptor well those passions read
Which yet survive, stamped on these lifeless things,
The hand that mocked them, and the heart that fed;
And on the pedestal these words appear:
"My name is Ozymandias, king of kings;   10
Look on my works, ye Mighty, and despair!"
Nothing beside remains. Round the decay
Of that colossal wreck, boundless and bare
The lone and level sands stretch far away.

from JULIAN AND MADDALO

A CONVERSATION

Preface

Count Maddalo is a Venetian nobleman of ancient family and
of great fortune, who, without mixing much in the society of his
countrymen, resides chiefly at his magnificent palace in that city.
He is a person of the most consummate genius, and capable, if he
would direct his energies to such an end, of becoming the redeemer
of his degraded country. But it is his weakness to be proud: he
derives, from a comparison of his own extraordinary mind with
the dwarfish intellects that surround him, an intense apprehension
of the nothingness of human life. His passions and his powers are*
10 *incomparably greater than those of other men; and, instead of the
latter having been employed in curbing the former, they have mutually lent each other strength. His ambition preys upon itself, for
want of objects which it can consider worthy of exertion. I say
that Maddalo is proud, because I can find no other word to express the concentered and impatient feelings which consume him;
but it is on his own hopes and affections only that he seems to
trample, for in social life no human being can be more gentle,
patient, and unassuming than Maddalo. He is cheerful, frank,
and witty. His more serious conversation is a sort of intoxication;*
20 *men are held by it as by a spell. He has travelled much; and
there is an inexpressible charm in his relation of his adventures in
different countries.*

8. **hand . . . heart,** the sculptor's . . . the king's.
10. **Ozymandias,** Rameses II, the Egyptian pharaoh who
oppressed the children of Israel. The statue of him was at
Thebes. *** Count Maddalo,** Lord Byron.

Julian* is an Englishman of good family, passionately attached to those philosophical notions which assert the power of man over his own mind, and the immense improvements of which, by the extinction of certain moral superstitions, human society may be yet susceptible. Without concealing the evil in the world, he is for ever speculating how good may be made superior. He is a complete infidel, and a scoffer at all things reputed holy; and Maddalo takes a wicked pleasure in drawing out his taunts against religion. What Maddalo thinks on these matters is not exactly known. Julian, in spite of his heterodox opinions, is conjectured by his friends to possess some good qualities. How far this is possible the pious reader will determine. Julian is rather serious.

Of the Maniac I can give no information. He seems, by his own account, to have been disappointed in love. He was evidently a very cultivated and amiable person when in his right senses. His story, told at length, might be like many other stories of the same kind: the unconnected exclamations of his agony will perhaps be found a sufficient comment for the text of every heart.

I rode one evening with Count Maddalo
Upon the bank of land which breaks the flow
Of Adria towards Venice—a bare Strand
Of hillocks, heaped from ever-shifting sand,
Matted with thistle and amphibious weeds,
Such as from earth's embrace the salt ooze breeds,
Is this; an uninhabitable sea-side,
Which the lone fisher, when his nets are dried,
Abandons; and no other object breaks
The waste, but one dwarf tree and some few   10
    stakes
Broken and unrepaired, and the tide makes
A narrow space of level sand thereon,—
Where 'twas our wont to ride, while day went
    down.—
This ride was my delight.—I love all waste
And solitary places; where we taste
The pleasure of believing what we see
Is boundless, as we wish our souls to be:
And such was this wide ocean, and this shore
More barren than its billows;—and yet more
Than all, with a remembered friend I love   20
To ride as then I rode;—for the winds drove
The living spray along the sunny air
Into our faces; the blue Heavens were bare,
Stripped to their depths by the awakening north;
And from the waves, sound like delight broke forth
Harmonizing with solitude, and sent
Into our hearts aërial merriment.
So, as we rode, we talked; and the swift thought,
Winging itself with laughter, lingered not—
But flew from brain to brain;—such glee was
    ours—   30
Charged with light memories of remembered hours,
None slow enough for sadness; till we came

Homeward, which always makes the spirit tame,
This day had been cheerful but cold, and now
The sun was sinking, and the wind also.
Our talk grew somewhat serious, as may be
Talk interrupted with such raillery
As mocks itself, because it cannot scorn
The thoughts it would extinguish:—'twas forlorn
Yet pleasing; such as once, so poets tell,   40
The devils held within the dales of Hell,
Concerning God, freewill and destiny.
Of all that earth has been, or yet may be,
All that vain men imagine or believe,
Or hope can paint, or suffering may achieve,
We descanted; and I (for ever still
Is it not wise to make the best of ill?)
Argued against despondency, but pride
Made my companion take the darker side.
The sense that he was greater than his kind   50
Had struck, methinks, his eagle spirit blind
By gazing on its own exceeding light.
—Meanwhile the sun paused ere it should alight,
Over the horizon of the mountains—Oh
How beautiful is sunset, when the glow
Of Heaven descends upon a land like thee,
Thou Paradise of exiles, Italy!
Thy mountains, seas, and vineyards, and the towers
Of cities they encircle!—it was ours
To stand on thee, beholding it: and then,   60
Just where we had dismounted, the Count's men
Were waiting for us with the gondola.—
As those who pause on some delightful way
Though bent on pleasant pilgrimage, we stood
Looking upon the evening and the flood
Which lay between the city and the shore,
Paved with the image of the sky. . . . The hoar
And aëry Alps towards the North appeared
Through mist, an heaven-sustaining bulwark,
    reared
Between the East and West; and half the sky   70
Was roofed with clouds of rich emblazonry,
Dark purple at the zenith, which still grew
Down the steep West into a wondrous hue
Brighter than burning gold, even to the rent
Where the swift sun yet paused in his descent
Among the many folded hills: they were
Those famous Euganean hills, which bear,
As seen from Lido through the harbour piles,
The likeness of a clump of peakèd isles—
And then—as if the Earth and Sea had been   80
Dissolved into one lake of fire, were seen
Those mountains towering as from waves of flame
Around the vaporous sun, from which there came
The inmost purple spirit of light, and made
Their peaks transparent. "Ere it fade,"

Said my companion, "I will shew you soon
A better station—" so, o'er the lagune
We glided, and from that funereal bark
I leaned, and saw the city, and could mark
How from their many isles, in evening's gleam,   90
Its temples and its palaces did seem
Like fabrics of enchantment piled to Heaven.
I was about to speak, when—"We are even
Now at the point I meant," said Maddalo,
And bade the gondolieri cease to row.
"Look, Julian, on the West, and listen well
If you hear not a deep and heavy bell."
I looked, and saw between us and the sun
A building on an island; such a one
As age to age might add, for uses vile—   100
A windowless, deformed and dreary pile;
And on the top an open tower, where hung
A bell, which in the radiance swayed and swung;
We could just hear its hoarse and iron tongue:
The broad sun sunk behind it, and it tolled
In strong and black relief.—"What we behold
Shall be the madhouse and its belfry tower,"—
Said Maddalo; "and ever at this hour
Those who may cross the water, hear that bell,
Which calls the maniacs each one from his cell   110
To vespers."—"As much skill as need to pray
In thanks or hope for their dark lot have they
To their stern maker," I replied. "O ho!
You talk as in years past," said Maddalo.
"'Tis strange men change not. You were ever still
Among Christ's flock a perilous infidel,
A wolf for the meek lambs—if you can't swim,
Beware of Providence." I looked on him,
But the gay smile had faded in his eye.
"And such," he cried, "is our mortality;   120
And this must be the emblem and the sign
Of what should be eternal and divine.—
And like that black and dreary bell, the soul
Hung in a heaven-illumined tower, must toll
Our thoughts and our desires to meet below
Round the rent heart, and pray—as madmen do
For what? they know not, till the night of death,
As sunset that strange vision, severeth
Our memory from itself, and us from all
We sought, and yet were baffled!" I recall   130
The sense of what he said, although I mar
The force of his expressions. The broad star
Of day meanwhile had sunk behind the hill,
And the black bell became invisible,
And the red tower looked grey, and all between,
The churches, ships and palaces were seen

Huddled in gloom; into the purple sea
The orange hues of heaven sunk silently.
We hardly spoke, and soon the gondola
Conveyed me to my lodgings by the way.   140

The following morn was rainy, cold, and dim:
Ere Maddalo arose, I called on him,
And whilst I waited, with his child I played;
A lovelier toy sweet Nature never made;
A serious, subtle, wild, yet gentle being,
Graceful without design, and unforeseeing;
With eyes—Oh speak not of her eyes!—which seem
Twin mirrors of Italian Heaven, yet gleam
With such deep meaning, as we never see
But in the human countenance. With me   150
She was a special favourite: I had nursed
Her fine and feeble limbs when she came first
To this bleak world; and she yet seemed to know
On second sight her antient playfellow,
Less changed than she was by six months or so;
For after her first shyness was worn out
We sate there, rolling billiard balls about,
When the Count entered. Salutations past—
"The words you spoke last night might well have
    cast
A darkness on my spirit:—if man be   160
The passive thing you say, I should not see
Much harm in the religions and old saws,
(Though I may never own such leaden laws)
Which break a teachless nature to the yoke:
Mine is another faith"—thus much I spoke,
And noting he replied not, added—"See
This lovely child, blithe, innocent, and free;
She spends a happy time, with little care,
While we to such sick thoughts subjected are
As came on you last night—it is our will   170
That thus enchains us to permitted ill—
We might be otherwise—we might be all
We dream of happy, high, majestical.
Where is the love, beauty and truth we seek,
But in our mind? and if we were not weak,
Should we be less in deed than in desire?"
"Aye if we were not weak—and we aspire
How vainly to be strong!" said Maddalo;
"You talk Utopia."

                    "It remains to know,"
I then rejoined, "and those who try may find   180
How strong the chains are which our spirit bind:

106–30. "What we behold . . . baffled." Compare the two characteristic views of human life here expressed. The argument is resumed in ll. 159 ff.

143. his child, Allegra, natural daughter of Byron and Clara Jane Clairmont. Allegra was then about a year and a half old.   161. The passive thing you say. Maddalo's (Byron's) view of human life is mechanistic (Necessitarian, Predestinarian, denying freedom of will).   170. it is our will. Julian's (Shelley's) is vitalistic and idealistic (man has freedom of will; will is all-important).

Brittle perchance as straw. . . . We are assured
Much may be conquered, much may be endured
Of what degrades and crushes us. We know
That we have power over ourselves to do
And suffer—what, we know not till we try;
But something nobler than to live and die—
So taught those kings of old philosophy,
Who reigned before Religion made men blind;
And those who suffer with their suffering kind   190
Yet feel their faith, religion."
                                        "My dear friend,"
Said Maddalo, "my judgment will not bend
To your opinion, though I think you might
Make such a system refutation-tight,
As far as words go. I knew one like you,
Who to this city came some months ago,
With whom I argued in this sort, and he
Is now gone mad,—and so he answered me,—
Poor fellow! But if you would like to go,
We'll visit him, and his wild talk will shew   200
How vain are such aspiring theories."

"I hope to prove the induction otherwise,
And that a want of that true theory, still,
Which seeks a 'soul of goodness' in things ill,
Or in himself or others, has thus bowed
His being—there are some by nature proud,
Who patient in all else demand but this—
To love and be beloved with gentleness;
And being scorned, what wonder if they die
Some living death? this is not destiny,   210
But man's own wilful ill." . . .

LINES WRITTEN AMONG THE EUGANEAN HILLS

Shelley wrote that the poem "was written after a day's
excursion among those lovely mountains which surround
what was once the retreat, and where is now the sepulchre, of Petrarch. If any one is inclined to condemn the
insertion of the introductory lines, which image forth the
sudden relief of a state of deep despondency by the radiant visions disclosed by the sudden burst of an Italian
sunrise in autumn, on the highest peak of those delightful
mountains, I can only offer as my excuse, that they were
not erased at the request of a dear friend, with whom
added years of intercourse only add to my apprehension
of its value, and who would have had more right than
any one to complain, that she has not been able to extinguish in me the very power of delineating sadness."

200. **We'll visit him.** The remainder of the poem, about
four hundred lines, relates the visit with the madman and
continues the argument.

Many a green isle needs must be
In the deep wide sea of misery,
Or the mariner, worn and wan,
Never thus could voyage on
Day and night, and night and day,
Drifting on his dreary way,
With the solid darkness black
Closing round his vessel's track;
Whilst above the sunless sky,
Big with clouds, hangs heavily,   10
And behind the tempest fleet
Hurries on with lightning feet,
Riving sail, and cord, and plank,
Till the ship has almost drank
Death from the o'er-brimming deep,
And sinks down, down, like that sleep
When the dreamer seems to be
Weltering through eternity;
And the dim low line before
Of a dark and distant shore   20
Still recedes, as ever still,
Longing with divided will,
But no power to seek or shun,
He is ever drifted on
O'er the unreposing wave
To the haven of the grave.
What, if there no friends will greet?
What, if there no heart will meet
His with love's impatient beat?
Wander wheresoe'er he may,   30
Can he dream before that day
To find refuge from distress
In friendship's smile, in love's caress?
Then 'twill wreak him little woe
Whether such there be or no:
Senseless is the breast, and cold,
Which relenting love would fold;
Bloodless are the veins and chill
Which the pulse of pain did fill;
Every little living nerve   40
That from bitter words did swerve
Round the tortured lips and brow,
Are like sapless leaflets now
Frozen upon December's bough.

On the beach of a northern sea
Which tempests shake eternally,
As once the wretch there lay to sleep,
Lies a solitary heap,
One white skull and seven dry bones,
On the margin of the stones,   50
Where a few grey rushes stand,
Boundaries of the sea and land:
Nor is heard one voice of wail

But the sea-mews, as they sail
O'er the billows of the gale;
Or the whirlwind up and down
Howling, like a slaughtered town,
When a king in glory rides
Through the pomp of fratricides:
Those unburied bones around   60
There is many a mournful sound;
There is no lament for him,
Like a sunless vapour, dim,
Who once clothed with life and thought
What now moves nor murmurs not.

Ay, many flowering islands lie
In the waters of wide Agony:
To such a one this morn was led
My bark by soft winds piloted:
Mid the mountains Euganean   70
I stood listening to the paean
With which the legioned rooks did hail
The sun's uprise majestical;
Gathering round with wings all hoar,
Through the dewy mist they soar
Like grey shades, till the eastern heaven
Bursts, and then, as clouds of even,
Flecked with fire and azure, lie
In the unfathomable sky,
So their plumes of purple grain,   80
Starred with drops of golden rain,
Gleam above the sunlight woods,
As in silent multitudes
On the morning's fitful gale
Through the broken mist they sail,
And the vapours cloven and gleaming
Follow down the dark steep streaming,
Till all is bright, and clear, and still,
Round the solitary hill.

Beneath is spread like a green sea   90
The waveless plain of Lombardy,
Bounded by the vaporous air,
Islanded by cities fair;
Underneath day's azure eyes
Ocean's nursling, Venice lies,
A peopled labyrinth of walls,
Amphitrite's destined halls,
Which her hoary sire now paves
With his blue and beaming waves.
Lo! the sun upsprings behind,   100
Broad, red, radiant, half-reclined

On the level quivering line
Of the waters crystalline;
And before that chasm of light,
As within a furnace bright,
Column, tower, and dome, and spire,
Shine like obelisks of fire,
Pointing with inconstant motion
From the altar of dark ocean
To the sapphire-tinted skies;   110
As the flames of sacrifice
From the marble shrines did rise
As to pierce the dome of gold
Where Apollo spoke of old.

Sun-girt City! thou hast been
Ocean's child, and then his queen;
Now is come a darker day,
And thou soon must be his prey,
If the power that raised thee here
Hallow so thy watery bier.   120
A less dread ruin then than now,
With thy conquest-branded brow
Stooping to the slave of slaves
From thy throne among the waves,
Wilt thou be, when the sea-mew
Flies, as once before it flew,
O'er thine isles depopulate,
And all is in its ancient state,
Save where many a palace gate
With green sea-flowers overgrown   130
Like a rock of ocean's own,
Topples o'er the abandoned sea
As the tides change sullenly.
The fisher on his watery way,
Wandering at the close of day,
Will spread his sail and seize his oar,
Till he pass the gloomy shore,
Lest thy dead should, from their sleep
Bursting o'er the starlight deep,
Lead a rapid masque of death   140
O'er the waters of his path.

Those who alone thy towers behold
Quivering through aërial gold,
As I now behold them here,
Would imagine not they were
Sepulchres, where human forms,
Like pollution-nourished worms,
To the corpse of greatness cling,
Murdered and now mouldering:

---

73. **The sun's uprise.** Compare ll. 100, 206, 285, 320, noting that the plan of development is temporal (following the sun) and spatial (going from point to point in the panorama). 80. **grain,** dye. 97. **Amphitrite's,** of the goddess of the sea. 98. **sire,** Nereus, sea god of the Aegean.

116. **queen,** an allusion to the annual ceremony in which the Doge of Venice threw a ring into the sea, wedding it to his city. Compare Wordsworth's sonnet "On the Extinction of the Venetian Republic." 117. **darker day.** Austria then held the cities of northern Italy.

But if Freedom should awake   150
In her omnipotence, and shake
From the Celtic Anarch's hold
All the keys of dungeons cold,
Where a hundred cities lie
Chained like thee, ingloriously,
Thou and all thy sister band
Might adorn this sunny land,
Twining memories of old time
With new virtues more sublime;
If not, perish thou and they,   160
Clouds which stain truth's rising day
By her sun consumed away,
Earth can spare ye: while like flowers,
In the waste of years and hours,
From your dust new nations spring
With more kindly blossoming.

Perish! let there only be
Floating o'er thy heartless sea,
As the garment of thy sky
Clothes the world immortally,   170
One remembrance, more sublime
Than the tattered pall of time,
Which scarce hides thy visage wan;
That a tempest-cleaving swan
Of the songs of Albion,
Driven from his ancestral streams,
By the might of evil dreams,
Found a nest in thee; and Ocean
Welcomed him with such emotion
That its joy grew his, and sprung   180
From his lips like music flung
O'er a mighty thunder-fit,
Chastening terror: what though yet
Poesy's unfailing river,
Which through Albion winds for ever,
Lashing with melodious wave
Many a sacred poet's grave,
Mourn its latest nursling fled!
What though thou with all thy dead
Scarce can for this fame repay   190
Aught thine own,—oh, rather say,
Though thy sins and slaveries foul
Overcloud a sunlike soul!
As the ghost of Homer clings
Round Scamander's wasting springs;
As divinest Shakespeare's might
Fills Avon and the world with light
Like omniscient power, which he

Imaged 'mid mortality;
As the love from Petrarch's urn,   200
Yet amid yon hills doth burn,
A quenchless lamp by which the heart
Sees things unearthly; so thou art,
Mighty spirit: so shall be
The city that did refuge thee.

Lo, the sun floats up the sky
Like thought-wingèd Liberty,
Till the universal light
Seems to level plain and height;
From the sea a mist has spread,   210
And the beams of morn lie dead
On the towers of Venice now,
Like its glory long ago.
By the skirts of that grey cloud
Many-domèd Padua proud
Stands, a peopled solitude,
'Mid the harvest-shining plain,
Where the peasant heaps his grain
In the garner of his foe,
And the milk-white oxen slow   220
With the purple vintage strain,
Heaped upon the creaking wain,
That the brutal Celt may swill
Drunken sleep with savage will;
And the sickle to the sword
Lies unchanged, though many a lord,
Like a weed whose shade is poison,
Overgrows this region's foizon,
Sheaves of whom are ripe to come
To destruction's harvest-home: 230
Men must reap the things they sow,
Force from force must ever flow,
Or worse; but 'tis a bitter woe
That love or reason cannot change
The despot's rage, the slave's revenge.

Padua, thou within whose walls
Those mute guests at festivals,
Son and Mother, Death and Sin,
Played at dice for Ezzelin,
Till Death cried, "I win, I win!"   240
And Sin cursed to lose the wager,
But Death promised, to assuage her,
That he would petition for
Her to be made Vice-Emperor,
When the destined years were o'er,
Over all between the Po
And the eastern Alpine snow,
Under the mighty Austrian.
Sin smiled so as Sin only can,

152. **Celtic Anarch's,** Austria's. "Celtic" is used in the general sense of "northern." **167–205. Perish! . . . thee.** These lines, alluding to Lord Byron ("tempest-cleaving swan"), were interpolated after the rest of the poem had been written.

228. **foizon,** foison, abundance.

And since that time, ay, long before,   250
Both have ruled from shore to shore,
That incestuous pair, who follow
Tyrants as the sun the swallow,
As Repentance follows Crime,
And as changes follow Time.

In thine halls the lamp of learning,
Padua, now no more is burning;
Like a meteor, whose wild way
Is lost over the grave of day,
It gleams betrayed and to betray;   260
Once remotest nations came
To adore that sacred flame,
When it lit not many a hearth
On this cold and gloomy earth:
Now new fires from antique light
Spring beneath the wide world's might;
But their spark lies dead in thee,
Trampled out by tyranny.
As the Norway woodman quells,
In the depth of piny dells,   270
One light flame among the brakes
While the boundless forest shakes,
And its mighty trunks are torn
By the fire thus lowly born:
The spark beneath his feet is dead,
He starts to see the flames it fed
Howling through the darkened sky
With myriad tongues victoriously,
And sinks down in fear: so thou,
O tyranny, beholdest now   280
Light around thee, and thou hearest
The loud flames ascend, and fearest:
Grovel on the earth: aye, hide
In the dust thy purple pride!

Noon descends around me now;
'Tis the noon of autumn's glow,
When a soft and purple mist
Like a vaporous amethyst,
Or an air-dissolvèd star
Mingling light and fragrance, far   290
From the curved horizon's bound
To the point of heaven's profound,
Fills the overflowing sky;
And the plains that silent lie
Underneath; the leaves unsodden
Where the infant frost has trodden
With his morning-wingèd feet,
Whose bright print is gleaming yet;

285–334. Noon descends . . . again. This passage is
an excellent example of Shelley's mysticism (fusion of his
spirit with that of the universe).

And the red and golden vines,
Piercing with their trellised lines   300
The rough, dark-skirted wilderness;
The dun and bladed grass no less,
Pointing from this hoary tower
In the windless air; the flower
Glimmering at my feet; the line
Of the olive-sandalled Apennine
In the south dimly islanded;
And the Alps, whose snows are spread
High between the clouds and sun;
And of living things each one;   310
And my spirit, which so long
Darkened this swift stream of song,
Interpenetrated lie
By the glory of the sky:
Be it love, light, harmony,
Odour, or the soul of all
Which from heaven like dew doth fall,
Or the mind which feeds this verse
Peopling the lone universe.
Noon descends, and after noon   320
Autumn's evening meets me soon,
Leading the infantine moon,
And that one star, which to her
Almost seems to minister
Half the crimson light she brings
From the sunset's radiant springs:
And the soft dreams of the morn
(Which like wingèd winds had borne
To that silent isle, which lies
'Mid remembered agonies,   330
The frail bark of this lone being),
Pass, to other sufferers fleeing,
And its ancient pilot, Pain,
Sits beside the helm again.

Other flowering isles must be
In the sea of life and agony:
Other spirits float and flee
O'er that gulf: even now, perhaps,
On some rock the wild wave wraps,
With folding wings they waiting sit   340
For my bark, to pilot it
To some calm and blooming cove,
Where for me, and those I love,
May a windless bower be built,
Far from passion, pain, and guilt,
In a dell 'mid lawny hills,
Which the wild sea-murmur fills,
And soft sunshine, and the sound
Of old forests echoing round,
And the light and smell divine   350
Of all flowers that breathe and shine:

We may live so happy there,
That the spirits of the air,
Envying us, may even entice
To our healing paradise
The polluting multitude;
But their rage would be subdued
By that clime divine and calm,
And the winds whose wings rain balm
On the uplifted soul, and leaves   360
Under which the bright sea heaves:
While each breathless interval
In their whisperings musical
The inspired soul supplies
With its own deep melodies,
And the love which heals all strife
Circling, like the breath of life,
All things in that sweet abode
With its own mild brotherhood:
They, not it, would change; and soon   370
Every sprite beneath the moon
Would repent its envy vain,
And the earth grow young again.

STANZAS

WRITTEN IN DEJECTION, NEAR NAPLES

1

The sun is warm, the sky is clear,
    The waves are dancing fast and bright;
Blue isles and snowy mountains wear
    The purple noon's transparent might:
The breath of the moist air is light
    Around its unexpanded buds;
Like many a voice of one delight,
    The winds, the birds, the ocean floods,
The City's voice itself is soft like Solitude's.

2

I see the Deep's untrampled floor   10
    With green and purple sea-weeds strown;
I see the waves upon the shore,
    Like light dissolved in star-showers, thrown:
I sit upon the sands alone,
    The lightning of the noon-tide ocean
Is flashing round me, and a tone
    Arises from its measured motion,
How sweet! did any heart now share in my emotion.

3

Alas! I have nor hope nor health,
    Nor peace within nor calm around,   20

19. **Alas!** Note Shelley's characteristic self-pity.

Nor that content surpassing wealth
    The sage in meditation found,
And walked with inward glory crowned—
    Nor fame, nor power, nor love, nor leisure.
Others I see whom these surround—
    Smiling they live, and call life pleasure;
To me that cup has been dealt in another measure.

4

Yet now despair itself is mild,
    Even as the winds and waters are;
I could lie down like a tired child,   30
    And weep away the life of care
Which I have borne, and yet must bear,
    Till death like sleep might steal on me,
And I might feel in the warm air
    My cheek grow cold, and hear the sea
Breathe o'er my dying brain its last monotony.

5

Some might lament that I were cold,
    As I, when this sweet day is gone,
Which my lost heart, too soon grown old,
    Insults with this untimely moan;   40
They might lament—for I am one
    Whom men love not,—and yet regret,
Unlike this day, which, when the sun
    Shall on its stainless glory set,
Will linger, though enjoyed, like joy in memory yet.

SONG TO THE MEN OF ENGLAND

1

Men of England, wherefore plough
For the lords who lay ye low?
Wherefore weave with toil and care
The rich robes your tyrants wear?

2

Wherefore feed, and clothe, and save,
From the cradle to the grave,
Those ungrateful drones who would
Drain your sweat—nay, drink your blood!

27. **To me that cup.** The irregular "measure" of the line (probably intentional) emphasizes the different "measure" of the cup. **30–36. I could lie down . . . monotony.** With this picture of death by drowning, compare *Adonais*, stanza 55, l. 5. There is a similar one in *Alastor*, ll. 304 ff., omitted from our selection. **37. Some might lament.** When I am dead, some people may lament me as I lament this day (thus insulting its beauty). But the regrets will be different: Because I am unpopular, when people grieve for my death they will also regret mistakes in my life; whereas my memory of the passing of this day of perfect beauty will be untinged with regret for any defect.

3

Wherefore, Bees of England, forge
Many a weapon, chain, and scourge, 10
That these stingless drones may spoil
The forced produce of your toil?

4

Have ye leisure, comfort, calm,
Shelter, food, love's gentle balm?
Or what is it ye buy so dear
With your pain and with your fear?

5

The seed ye sow, another reaps;
The wealth ye find, another keeps;
The robes ye weave, another wears;
The arms ye forge, another bears. 20

6

Sow seed,—but let no tyrant reap;
Find wealth,—let no imposter heap;
Weave robes,—let not the idle wear;
Forge arms,—in your defence to bear.

7

Shrink to your cellars, holes, and cells;
In halls ye deck, another dwells.
Why shake the chains ye wrought? Ye see
The steel ye tempered glance on ye.

8

With plough and spade, and hoe and loom,
Trace your grave, and build your tomb, 30
And weave your winding-sheet, till fair
England be your sepulchre.

SONNET: ENGLAND IN 1819

An old, mad, blind, despised, and dying king,—
Princes, the dregs of their dull race, who flow
Through public scorn—mud from a muddy spring;
Rulers, who neither see, nor feel, nor know,
But leech-like to their fainting country cling,
Till they drop, blind in blood, without a blow;
A people starved and stabbed in the untilled field,—
An army, which liberticide and prey
Makes as a two-edged sword to all who wield—
Golden and sanguine laws which tempt and slay,
Religion Christless, Godless—a book sealed; 11
A Senate,—Time's worst statute unrepealed,—
Are graves, from which a glorious Phantom may
Burst, to illumine our tempestuous day.

1. **king,** George III.

ODE TO THE WEST WIND

The poem is a superb example of Shelley's mythmaking power in the treatment of natural phenomena, of the controlling moods and emotions of his lyrical poetry, and of his command of poetic structure when he was at his best. It is a modification of terza rima (interlinked iambic pentameter trimeters riming aba, bcb, cdc, ded, followed by a couplet, ff, the modification, to round out a strophe). Note the perfect structure: (1) the power and freedom of the wind manifested upon the leaves (stanza 1), the clouds (stanza 2), and the waves (stanza 3); (2) these manifestations summed up in "leaf," "cloud," and "wave" (stanza 4, ll. 43-45), in contrast with the poet's weakness and bondage (stanza 4, ll. 46-56); (3) the poet's prayer for such freedom and power to "Drive his dead thoughts over the universe" for the awakening of mankind (stanza 5, ll. 57-68), and his faith in the wind as a symbol of universal regeneration (stanza 5, ll. 69-70). Note the management of long, sustained sentences and clauses, and the pauses, to suggest the streaming, volleying, and relative lulling of the wind.

1

O wild West Wind, thou breath of Autumn's being,
Thou, from whose unseen presence the leaves dead
Are driven, like ghosts from an enchanter fleeing,

Yellow, and black, and pale, and hectic red,
Pestilence-stricken multitudes: O thou,
Who chariotest to their dark wintry bed

The wingèd seeds, where they lie cold and low,
Each like a corpse within its grave, until
Thine azure sister of the spring shall blow

Her clarion o'er the dreaming earth, and fill 10
(Driving sweet buds like flocks to feed in air)
With living hues and odours plain and hill:

Wild Spirit, which art moving every where;
Destroyer and preserver; hear, O, hear!

2

Thou on whose stream, 'mid the steep sky's commotion,
Loose clouds like earth's decaying leaves are shed,
Shook from the tangled boughs of Heaven and Ocean,

Angels of rain and lightning: there are spread
On the blue surface of thine airy surge,
Like the bright hair uplifted from the head 20

Of some fierce Maenad, even from the dim verge
Of the horizon to the zenith's height,
The locks of the approaching storm. Thou dirge

Of the dying year, to which this closing night
Will be the dome of a vast sepulchre,
Vaulted with all thy congregated might

Of vapours, from whose solid atmosphere
Black rain, and fire, and hail will burst: O, hear!

3

Thou who didst waken from his summer dreams
The blue Mediterranean, where he lay,   30
Lulled by the coil of his crystalline streams,

Beside a pumice isle in Baiae's bay,
And saw in sleep old palaces and towers
Quivering within the wave's intenser day,

All overgrown with azure moss and flowers
So sweet, the sense faints picturing them! Thou
For whose path the Atlantic's level powers

Cleave themselves into chasms, while far below
The sea-blooms and the oozy woods which wear
The sapless foliage of the ocean, know   40

Thy voice, and suddenly grow grey with fear,
And tremble and despoil themselves: O, hear!

4

If I were a dead leaf thou mightest bear;
If I were a swift cloud to fly with thee;
A wave to pant beneath thy power, and share

The impulse of thy strength, only less free
Than thou, O uncontroullable! If even
I were as in my boyhood, and could be

The comrade of thy wanderings over heaven,
As then, when to outstrip thy skiey speed   50
Scarce seemed a vision; I would ne'er have striven

As thus with thee in prayer in my sore need.
Oh! lift me as a wave, a leaf, a cloud!
I fall upon the thorns of life! I bleed!

A heavy weight of hours has chained and bowed
One too like thee: tameless, and swift, and proud.

5

Make me thy lyre, even as the forest is:
What if my leaves are falling like its own!
The tumult of thy mighty harmonies

Will take from both a deep, autumnal tone,   60
Sweet though in sadness. Be thou, spirit fierce,
My spirit! Be thou me, impetuous one!

Drive my dead thoughts over the universe
Like withered leaves to quicken a new birth!
And, by the incantation of this verse,

Scatter, as from an unextinguished hearth
Ashes and sparks, my words among mankind!
Be through my lips to unawakened earth

The trumpet of a prophecy! O, wind,
If Winter comes, can Spring be far behind?   70

THE INDIAN SERENADE

1

I arise from dreams of thee
In the first sweet sleep of night,
When the winds are breathing low,
And the stars are shining bright:
I arise from dreams of thee,
And a spirit in my feet
Hath led me—who knows how?
To thy chamber window—Sweet!

2

The wandering airs they faint
On the dark, the silent stream—   10
The Champak odours fail
Like sweet thoughts in a dream;
The Nightingale's complaint—
It dies upon her heart
As I must die on thine,
Oh belovèd as thou art!

3

Oh! lift me from the grass!
I die! I faint! I fail!
Let thy love in kisses rain
On my lips and eyelids pale.   20
My cheek is cold and white, alas!
My heart beats loud and fast,
Oh! press it close to thine again,
Where it will break at last.

LOVE'S PHILOSOPHY

1

The fountains mingle with the river,
     And the rivers with the ocean,

11. Champak, a sacred tree of India. The scene and the sentiments are supposed to be Oriental.

The winds of Heaven mix for ever
    With a sweet emotion;
Nothing in the world is single;
    All things by a law divine
In one another's being mingle—
    Why not I with thine?

2

See the mountains kiss high Heaven,
    And the waves clasp one another; 10
No sister flower would be forgiven
    If it disdained its brother;
And the sunlight clasps the earth,
    And the moonbeams kiss the sea:
What are all these kissings worth,
    If thou kiss not me?

POLITICAL GREATNESS *

Nor happiness, nor majesty, nor fame,
Nor peace, nor strength, nor skill in arms or arts,
Shepherd those herds whom tyranny makes tame;
Verse echoes not one beating of their hearts,
History is but the shadow of their shame;
Art veils her glass, or from the pageant starts
As to oblivion their blind millions fleet,
Staining that Heaven with obscene imagery
Of their own likeness. What are numbers knit
By force or custom? Man who would be man, 10
Must rule the empire of himself; in it
Must be supreme, establishing his throne
On vanquished will, quelling the anarchy
Of hopes and fears, being himself alone.

from PROMETHEUS UNBOUND

A LYRICAL DRAMA IN FOUR ACTS

The poem was begun at Este (Byron's villa) in September, 1818; the first act finished in October; Acts II and III composed near Rome (in the ruins of the Baths of Caracalla) in the spring of 1819; Act IV, an afterthought, written at Florence by December 15; the whole published by Ollier, in a volume including, besides the title poem, "Ode to the West Wind," "The Cloud," "To a Skylark," and "The Sensitive Plant." "I think," wrote Shelley, "if I can judge by its merits, the *Prometheus* cannot sell beyond twenty copies." Only a few magazines (for example, the *London*) reviewed the poem favorably; most (for example, the *Quarterly*) condemned it on the ground that it was immoral, blasphemous, and obscure. One reviewer remarked, "It was well that the author specified *Unbound; it will never be bound.*"

Prometheus Unbound was meant to be one of the great poems of the world. Its subject is: what was wrong with the world in Shelley's post-Revolutionary time, what sort of miracle was needed to redeem mankind, and what mankind and the world would be like if such a miracle took place (as Shelley believed it would). It is, then, like Dante's *Divine Comedy*, Milton's *Paradise Lost*, Goethe's *Faust*, and Thomas Hardy's *The Dynasts*, a great cosmic poem, in the universality of its theme, in the grandeur of its characters, in the vastness of its setting and action, in the sublimity of its philosophy (a Platonic conception of life and a faith in the perfectibility of man), and in the beauty of its form.

The fable of the poem combines two world-wide myths, that of the Fire-Bringer (Civilizer), and that of the Defier of the Gods or Savior of Mankind. Shelley's treatment of it was in part suggested by the *Prometheus Unbound* of Aeschylus, but he characteristically rejected Aeschylus' reconciliation of Prometheus and Jupiter. This fable is but a frame for objectifying *a drama within the soul of man.* The characters are all projections of elements in Pro-

metheus' nature; the actions are really all internal—what takes place in the soul of Prometheus (Mankind). In writing the poem Shelley's purpose was "to familiarize the highly refined imagination of the more select classes of poetical readers with beautiful idealisms of moral excellence."

Most critics (Professor N. I. White in the *Publications of the Modern Language Association*, Vol. XL, is the most notable exception) have regarded the poem as allegorical. Whether it is an allegory or not, the characters and the action have symbolical, representative significance. The following are at least working identifications: *Prometheus*— Humanity, the Genius of Man, Spirit of Mankind, Man's deathless aspiration and unconquerable will; *Jupiter*— the Principle of Evil, especially evil formed and fortified by man's religious, political, and social institutions, which have lost their original power for good and have hardened into the tyranny of custom and law; *Demogorgon*—Fate, the Eternal Principle of Change and Progress, Nemesis, Unalterable Law; *Asia*—Nature, the Creative Spirit, Intellectual Beauty, the Divine Principle of Sex; *Ione*— Hope, the Seer; *Panthea*—Faith, the Understander and Believer (the last two are Oceanides, sisters of Asia); *Hercules*—Strength.

Action: Prometheus speaks in agony from the icy rock to which he has been chained for three thousand years. Watching and waiting with him are Panthea and Ione. Purified by suffering, he calls on the Phantasm (subconscious self) of Jupiter to repeat the curse which he has pronounced on Jupiter; he would recall it. His doing so is the first step in self-regeneration and self-redemption. Mercury arrives and asks him to reveal a secret important to Jupiter and to submit to Jupiter—the price of peace. He refuses. The Furies torture him (with internal agonies

* *Political Greatness.* Also titled "Sonnet: To the Republic of Benevento."

and fears); the Spirits comfort him with accounts of human unselfishness and hope of good to be; Panthea reminds him of Asia's love. Act II in the Indian Caucasus
shows Asia, lover of Prometheus, and her sisters, Panthea
and Ione, mourning for Prometheus. Panthea tells Asia
of two dreams, one of Prometheus redeemed and the other
of a voice that cries "Follow!" The three follow to the
Cave of Demogorgon. Here Demogorgon describes Jupiter, prophesies his overthrow, and gives veiled answers
to questions about evil, fate, free will, and the like. The
Spirit of the Hour (of Jupiter's overthrow) appears and
drives off in her car. Another Hour transports the sisters
to Jupiter's court in Heaven. A voice in the Air sings
"Life of Life" (Act II, sc. 5, l. 48) and Asia sings "My
soul is an enchanted boat" (*ibid.*, l. 72)—the emotional
climax. In Act III Jupiter exults on his throne, he and his
queen, Thetis, expecting news of the incarnation of their
child. When the Car of the Hour arrives, Jupiter hails it
with joy. Ironically, the "child," Demogorgon, descends,
describes himself as the son of Jupiter and as Eternity,
and commands Jupiter to follow him to the abyss. Jupiter
at first defies him, then begs for mercy, and follows. This
is the objective climax of the poem (Act III, sc. 1,
ll. 52 ff.). In Scene 2 Apollo describes to Ocean the fall
of Jupiter, and Ocean says she will never again be vexed
by tempests (Prometheus' liberation liberates the physical
universe). In Scene 3 Hercules unbinds Prometheus in the
presence of Asia, Panthea, Ione, the Earth, and the other
Spirits. Prometheus, identifying Asia with "Life of Life,"
tells her how he will be happy with her, orders the Spirit
of the Hour to drive her car round the world with the
glad tidings of deliverance, and repairs with Asia to a
cave. In Scene 4, the Spirit of the Hour returns and tells
of the change that has come over the world. Act IV, an
afterthought, is a great symphony expressing the rapture
of the delivered universe and faith in the human virtues
that will redeem it ("This is the day").

DRAMATIS PERSONAE

PROMETHEUS	MERCURY
DEMOGORGON	HERCULES
JUPITER	ASIA
THE EARTH	PANTHEA } Oceanides
OCEAN	IONE
APOLLO	

THE PHANTASM OF JUPITER
THE SPIRIT OF THE EARTH
THE SPIRIT OF THE MOON
SPIRITS OF THE HOURS
SPIRITS. ECHOES. FAUNS. FURIES

from ACT I

SCENE. *A Ravine of Icy Rocks in the Indian Caucasus.*
PROMETHEUS *is discovered bound to the Precipice.*
PANTHEA *and* IONE *are seated at his feet. Time,*
Night. During the Scene, Morning slowly breaks.

Prometheus. Monarch of Gods and Daemons, and
  all Spirits
But One, who throng those bright and rolling worlds
Which Thou and I alone of living things
Behold with sleepless eyes! regard this Earth
Made multitudinous with thy slaves, whom thou
Requitest for knee-worship, prayer, and praise,
And toil, and hecatombs of broken hearts,
With fear and self-contempt and barren hope.
Whilst me, who am thy foe, eyeless in hate,
Hast thou made reign and triumph, to thy scorn,   10
O'er mine own misery and thy vain revenge.
Three thousand years of sleep-unsheltered hours,
And moments aye divided by keen pangs
Till they seemed years, torture and solitude,
Scorn and despair,—these are mine empire.
More glorious far than that which thou surveyest
From thine unenvied throne, O, Mighty God!
Almighty, had I deigned to share the shame
Of thine ill tyranny, and hung not here
Nailed to this wall of eagle-baffling mountain,   20
Black, wintry, dead, unmeasured; without herb,
Insect, or beast, or shape or sound of life.
Ah me! alas, pain, pain ever, for ever!

No change, no pause, no hope! Yet I endure.
I ask the Earth, have not the mountains felt?
I ask yon Heaven, the all-beholding Sun,
Has it not seen? The Sea, in storm or calm,
Heaven's ever-changing Shadow, spread below,
Have its deaf waves not heard my agony?
Ah me! alas, pain, pain ever, for ever!   30

The crawling glaciers pierce me with the spears
Of their moon-freezing crystals, the bright chains
Eat with their burning cold into my bones.
Heaven's wingèd hound, polluting from thy lips
His beak in poison not his own, tears up
My heart; and shapeless sights come wandering by,
The ghastly people of the realm of dream,
Mocking me: and the Earthquake-fiends are
  charged
To wrench the rivets from my quivering wounds
When the rocks split and close again behind: 40
While from their loud abysses howling throng
The genii of the storm, urging the rage
Of whirlwind, and afflict me with keen hail.
And yet to me welcome is day and night,
Whether one breaks the hoar frost of the morn,
Or starry, dim, and slow, the other climbs
The leaden-coloured east; for then they lead
The wingless, crawling hours, one among whom
—As some dark Priest hales the reluctant victim—
Shall drag thee, cruel King, to kiss the blood   50

From these pale feet, which then might trample
   thee
If they disdained not such a prostrate slave.
Disdain! Ah no! I pity thee. What ruin
Will hunt thee undefended through wide Heaven!
How will thy soul, cloven to its depth with terror,
Gape like a hell within! I speak in grief,
Not exultation, for I hate no more,
As then ere misery made me wise. The curse
Once breathed on thee I would recall. Ye Moun-
   tains,
Whose many-voicèd Echoes, through the mist   60
Of cataracts, flung the thunder of that spell!
Ye icy Springs, stagnant with wrinkling frost,
Which vibrated to hear me, and then crept
Shuddering through India! Thou serenest Air,
Through which the Sun walks burning without
   beams!
And ye swift Whirlwinds, who on poisèd wings
Hung mute and moveless o'er yon hushed abyss,
As thunder, louder than your own, made rock
The orbèd world! If then my words had power,
Though I am changed so that aught evil wish   70
Is dead within; although no memory be
Of what is hate, let them not lose it now!
What was that curse? for ye all heard me
   speak. . . .

Phantasm [of Jupiter]

Fiend, I defy thee! with a calm, fixed mind,
   All that thou canst inflict I bid thee do;
Foul Tyrant both of Gods and Human-kind,
   Only one being shalt thou not subdue.
Rain then thy plagues upon me here,
Ghastly disease, and frenzying fear;
And let alternate frost and fire
Eat into me, and be thine ire
Lightning, and cutting hail, and legioned forms   270
Of furies, driving by upon the wounding storms.

Aye, do thy worst. Thou art omnipotent.
   O'er all things but thyself I gave thee power,
And my own will. Be thy swift mischiefs sent
   To blast mankind, from yon ethereal tower.
Let thy malignant spirit move
In darkness over those I love:
On me and mine I imprecate
The utmost torture of thy hate;
And thus devote to sleepless agony,   280
This undeclining head while thou must reign on
   high.

262. **Fiend, I defy thee.** The Phantasm of Jupiter here
repeats the curse Prometheus had pronounced upon Jupiter.

But thou, who art the God and Lord: O, thou
   Who fillest with thy soul this world of woe,
To whom all things of Earth and Heaven do bow
   In fear and worship: all-prevailing foe!
I curse thee! let a sufferer's curse
Clasp thee, his torturer, like remorse!
Till thine Infinity shall be
A robe of envenomed agony;
And thine Omnipotence a crown of pain,   290
To cling like burning gold round thy dissolving
   brain!

Heap on thy soul, by virtue of this Curse,
   Ill deeds, then be thou damned, beholding
   good;
Both infinite as is the universe,
   And thou, and thy self-torturing solitude.
An awful image of calm power
Though now thou sittest, let the hour
Come, when thou must appear to be
That which thou art internally.
And after many a false and fruitless crime   300
Scorn track thy lagging fall through boundless space
   and time.

Prometheus. Were these my words, O Parent?
The Earth.   They were thine.
Prometheus. It doth repent me: words are quick
   and vain;
Grief for a while is blind, and so was mine.
I wish no living thing to suffer pain. . . .

Mercury. . . . Awful Sufferer!
To thee unwilling, most unwillingly
I come, by the great Father's will driven down,
To execute a doom of new revenge.
Alas! I pity thee, and hate myself
That I can do no more: aye from thy sight
Returning, for a season, heaven seems hell,
So thy worn form pursues me night and day,
Smiling reproach. Wise art thou, firm and good,   360
But vainly wouldst stand forth alone in strife
Against the Omnipotent; as yon clear lamps
That measure and divide the weary years
From which there is no refuge, long have taught
And long must teach. Even now thy Torturer arms
With the strange might of unimagined pains
The powers who scheme slow agonies in Hell,
And my commission is to lead them here,
Or what more subtle, foul, or savage fiends
People the abyss, and leave them to their task.   370
Be it not so! there is a secret known
To thee, and to none else of living things,
Which may transfer the sceptre of wide Heaven,

The fear of which perplexes the Supreme:
Clothe it in words, and bid it clasp his throne
In intercession; bend thy soul in prayer,
And like a suppliant in some gorgeous fane,
Let the will kneel within thy haughty heart:
For benefits and meek submission tame
The fiercest and the mightiest.

    Prometheus.   Evil minds   380
Change good to their own nature. I gave all
He has; and in return he chains me here
Years, ages, night and day: whether the Sun
Split my parched skin, or in the moony night
The crystal-wingèd snow cling round my hair:
Whilst my belovèd race is trampled down
By his thought-executing ministers.
Such is the tyrant's recompense: 'tis just:
He who is evil can receive no good;
And for a world bestowed, or a friend lost,   390
He can feel hate, fear, shame; not gratitude:
He but requites me for his own misdeed.
Kindness to such is keen reproach, which breaks
With bitter stings the light sleep of Revenge.
Submission, thou dost know I cannot try;
For what submission but that fatal word,
The death-seal of mankind's captivity,
Like the Sicilian's hair-suspended sword,
Which trembles o'er his crown, would he accept,
Or could I yield? Which yet I will not yield.   400
Let others flatter Crime, where it sits throned
In brief Omnipotence: secure are they:
For Justice, when triumphant, will weep down
Pity, not punishment, on her own wrongs,
Too much avenged by those who err. I wait,
Enduring thus, the retributive hour
Which since we spake is even nearer now.
But hark, the hell-hounds clamour: fear delay:
Behold! Heaven lowers under thy Father's frown.

    Mercury. Oh, that we might be spared: I to inflict
And thou to suffer! once more answer me: 411
Thou knowest not the period of Jove's power?

    Prometheus. I know but this, that it must come.

    Mercury.   Alas!
Thou canst not count thy years to come of pain?

    Prometheus. They last while Jove must reign: nor
    more, nor less
Do I desire or fear.

    Mercury.   Yet pause, and plunge
Into Eternity, where recorded time,
Even all that we imagine, age on age,
Seems but a point, and the reluctant mind
Flags wearily in its unending flight,   420
Till it sink, dizzy, blind, lost, shelterless;
Perchance it has not numbered the slow years
Which thou must spend in torture, unreprieved?

    Prometheus. Perchance no thought can count them,
    yet they pass.

    Mercury. If thou might'st dwell among the Gods
    the while,
Lapped in voluptuous joy?

    Prometheus.   I would not quit
This bleak ravine, these unrepentant pains.

    Mercury. Alas! I wonder at, yet pity thee.

    Prometheus. Pity the self-despising slaves of
    Heaven,
Not me, within whose mind sits peace serene,   430
As light in the sun, throned: how vain is talk!
Call up the fiends. . . .

from ACT II

from SCENE 3. *A Pinnacle of Rock among*
Mountains. ASIA *and* PANTHEA

    Panthea. Hither the sound has borne us—to the
    realm
Of Demogorgon, and the mighty portal,
Like a volcano's meteor-breathing chasm,
Whence the oracular vapour is hurled up
Which lonely men drink wandering in their youth,
And call truth, virtue, love, genius, or joy,
That maddening wine of life, whose dregs they drain
To deep intoxication; and uplift,
Like Maenads who cry loud, Evoe! Evoe!
The voice which is contagion to the world. . . .   10

from SCENE 4. *The Cave of* DEMOGORGON.

ASIA *and* PANTHEA

    Panthea. What veilèd form sits on that ebon
    throne?

    Asia. The veil has fallen.

    Panthea.   I see a mighty darkness
Filling the seat of power, and rays of gloom
Dart round, as light from the meridian sun.
Ungazed upon and shapeless; neither limb,
Nor form, nor outline; yet we feel it is
A living Spirit.

    Demogorgon. Ask what thou wouldst know.

    Asia. What canst thou tell?

    Demogorgon. All things thou dar'st demand.

    Asia. Who made the living world?

    Demogorgon.   God.

    Asia.   Who made all
That it contains? thought, passion, reason, will,   10
Imagination?

    Demogorgon. God: Almighty God.

    Asia. Who made that sense which, when the winds
    of spring
In rarest visitation, or the voice

Of one belovèd heard in youth alone,
Fills the faint eyes with falling tears which dim
The radiant looks of unbewailing flowers,
And leaves this peopled earth a solitude
When it returns no more?
   Demogorgon.   Merciful God.
   Asia. And who made terror, madness, crime, re-
    morse,
Which from the links of the great chain of things, 20
To every thought within the mind of man
Sway and drag heavily, and each one reels
Under the load towards the pit of death;
Abandoned hope, and love that turns to hate;
And self-contempt, bitterer to drink than blood;
Pain, whose unheeded and familiar speech
Is howling, and keen shrieks, day after day;
And Hell, or the sharp fear of Hell?
   Demogorgon.   He reigns.
   Asia. Utter his name: a world pining in pain
Asks but his name: curses shall drag him down. 30
   Demogorgon. He reigns.
   Asia.   I feel, I know it: who?
   Demogorgon.   He reigns.
   Asia. Who reigns? There was the Heaven and
    Earth at first,
And Light and Love; then Saturn, from whose
    throne
Time fell, an envious shadow: such the state
Of the earth's primal spirits beneath his sway,
As the calm joy of flowers and living leaves
Before the wind or sun has withered them
And semivital worms; but he refused
The birthright of their being, knowledge, power,
The skill which wields the elements, the thought 40
Which pierces this dim universe like light,
Self-empire, and the majesty of love;
For thirst of which they fainted. Then Prometheus
Gave wisdom, which is strength, to Jupiter,
And with this law alone, "Let man be free,"
Clothed him with the dominion of wide Heaven.
To know nor faith, nor love, nor law; to be
Omnipotent but friendless is to reign;
And Jove now reigned; for on the race of man
First famine, and then toil, and then disease, 50
Strife, wounds, and ghastly death unseen before,
Fell; and the unseasonable seasons drove
With alternating shafts of frost and fire,
Their shelterless, pale tribes to mountain caves:
And in their desert hearts fierce wants he sent,
And mad disquietudes, and shadows idle
Of unreal good, which levied mutual war,
So ruining the lair wherein they raged.
Prometheus saw, and waked the legioned hopes
Which sleep within folded Elysian flowers, 60

Nepenthe, Moly, Amaranth, fadeless blooms,
That they might hide with thin and rainbow wings
The shape of Death; and Love he sent to bind
The disunited tendrils of that vine
Which bears the wine of life, the human heart;
And he tamed fire which, like some beast of prey,
Most terrible, but lovely, played beneath
The frown of man; and tortured to his will
Iron and gold, the slaves and signs of power,
And gems and poisons, and all subtlest forms 70
Hidden beneath the mountains and the waves.
He gave man speech, and speech created thought,
Which is the measure of the universe;
And Science struck the thrones of earth and heaven,
Which shook, but fell not; and the harmonious
    mind
Poured itself forth in all-prophetic song;
And music lifted up the listening spirit
Until it walked, exempt form mortal care,
Godlike, o'er the clear billows of sweet sound;
And human hands first mimicked and then
    mocked, 80
With moulded limbs more lovely than its own,
The human form, till marble grew divine,
And mothers, gazing, drank the love men see
Reflected in their race, behold, and perish.
He told the hidden power of herbs and springs,
And Disease drank and slept. Death grew like sleep.
He taught the implicated orbits woven
Of the wide-wandering stars; and how the sun
Changes his lair, and by what secret spell
The pale moon is transformed, when her broad
    eye 90
Gazes not on the interlunar sea:
He taught to rule, as life directs the limbs,
The tempest-wingèd chariots of the Ocean,
And the Celt knew the Indian. Cities then
Were built, and through their snow-like columns
    flowed
The warm winds, and the azure aether shone,
And the blue sea and shadowy hills were seen.
Such, the alleviations of his state,
Prometheus gave to man, for which he hangs
Withering in destined pain: but who rains down 100
Evil, the immedicable plague, which, while
Man looks on his creation like a God
And sees that it is glorious, drives him on
The wreck of his own will, the scorn of earth,
The outcast, the abandoned, the alone?
Not Jove: while yet his frown shook heaven, aye
    when
His adversary from adamantine chains
Cursed him, he trembled like a slave. Declare
Who is his master? Is he too a slave?

Demogorgon. All spirits are enslaved which serve
  things evil: 110
Thou knowest if Jupiter be such or no.
  Asia. Whom called'st thou God?
  Demogorgon.   I spoke but as ye speak,
For Jove is the supreme of living things.
  Asia. Who is the master of the slave?
  Demogorgon.   If the abysm
Could vomit forth its secrets. But a voice
Is wanting, the deep truth is imageless;
For what would it avail to bid thee gaze
On the revolving world? What to bid speak
Fate, Time, Occasion, Chance and Change? To
  these
All things are subject but eternal Love.   120
  Asia. So much I asked before, and my heart gave
The response thou hast given; and of such truths
Each to itself must be the oracle.
One more demand; and do thou answer me
As mine own soul would answer, did it know
That which I ask. Prometheus shall arise
Henceforth the sun of this rejoicing world:
When shall the destined hour arrive?
  Demogorgon.   Behold!
  Asia. The rocks are cloven, and through the pur-
  ple night
I see cars drawn by rainbow-wingèd steeds   130
Which trample the dim winds: in each there stands
A wild-eyed charioteer urging their flight.
Some look behind, as fiends pursued them there,
And yet I see no shapes but the keen stars:
Others, with burning eyes, lean forth, and drink
With eager lips the wind of their own speed,
As if the thing they loved fled on before,
And now, even now, they clasped it. Their bright
  locks
Stream like a comet's flashing hair: they all sweep
  onward.
  Demogorgon. These are the immortal Hours,   140
Of whom thou didst demand. One waits for thee.
  Asia. A spirit with a dreadful countenance
Checks its dark chariot by the craggy gulf.
Unlike thy brethren, ghastly charioteer,
Who art thou? Whither wouldst thou bear me?
  Speak!
  Spirit. I am the shadow of a destiny
More dread than is my aspect: ere yon planet
Has set, the darkness which ascends with me
Shall wrap in lasting night heaven's kingless throne.
  Asia. What meanest thou?
  Panthea.   That terrible shadow floats
Up from its throne, as may the lurid smoke   151
Of earthquake-ruined cities o'er the sea.
Lo! it ascends the car; the coursers fly

Terrified: watch its path among the stars
Blackening the night!
  Asia.   Thus I am answered: strange!
  Panthea. See, near the verge, another chariot stays;
An ivory shell inlaid with crimson fire,
Which comes and goes within its sculptured rim
Of delicate strange tracery; the young spirit
That guides it has the dove-like eyes of hope;   160
How its soft smiles attract the soul! as light
Lures wingèd insects through the lampless air.

Spirit

My coursers are fed with the lightning,
  They drink of the whirlwind's stream,
And when the red morning is brightning
  They bathe in the fresh sunbeam;
  They have strength for their swiftness I deem,
Then ascend with me, daughter of Ocean.

I desire: and their speed makes night kindle;
  I fear: they outstrip the Typhoon;   170
Ere the cloud piled on Atlas can dwindle
  We encircle the earth and the moon:
  We shall rest from long labours at noon:
Then ascend with me, daughter of Ocean. . . .

from SCENE 5. *The Car pauses within a Cloud on the Top
  of a snowy Mountain.* ASIA, PANTHEA, *and the*
  SPIRIT OF THE HOUR.

Voice (*in the air, singing*)

Life of Life! thy lips enkindle
  With their love the breath between them;
And thy smiles before they dwindle   50
  Make the cold air fire; then screen them
In those looks, where whoso gazes
Faints, entangled in their mazes.

Child of Light! thy limbs are burning
  Through the vest which seems to hide them;
As the radiant lines of morning
  Through the clouds ere they divide them;
And this atmosphere divinest
Shrouds thee wheresoe'er thou shinest.

Fair are others; none beholds thee,   60
  But thy voice sounds low and tender
Like the fairest, for it folds thee
  From the sight, that liquid splendour,
And all feel, yet see thee never,
As I feel now, lost for ever!

Lamp of Earth! where'er thou movest
  Its dim shapes are clad with brightness,

And the souls of whom thou lovest
  Walk upon the winds with lightness,
Till they fail, as I am failing,   70
Dizzy, lost, yet unbewailing!

Asia

My soul is an enchanted boat,
  Which, like a sleeping swan, doth float
Upon the silver waves of thy sweet singing;
  And thine doth like an angel sit
  Beside a helm conducting it,
Whilst all the winds with melody are ringing.
  It seems to float ever, for ever,
  Upon that many-winding river,
  Between mountains, woods, abysses,   80
  A paradise of wildernesses!
Till, like one in slumber bound,
Borne to the ocean, I float down, around,
Into a sea profound, of ever-spreading sound:

  Meanwhile thy spirit lifts its pinions
  In music's most serene dominions;
Catching the winds that fan that happy heaven.
  And we sail on, away, afar,
  Without a course, without a star,
But, by the instinct of sweet music driven;   90
  Till through Elysian garden islets
  By thee, most beautiful of pilots,
  Where never mortal pinnace glided,
  The boat of my desire is guided:
Realms where the air we breathe is love,
Which in the winds and on the waves doth move,
Harmonizing this earth with what we feel above.

  We have passed Age's icy caves,
  And Manhood's dark and tossing waves,
And Youth's smooth ocean, smiling to betray: 100
  Beyond the glassy gulphs we flee
  Of shadow-peopled Infancy,
Through Death and Birth, to a diviner day;
  A paradise of vaulted bowers,
  Lit by downward-gazing flowers,
  And watery paths that wind between
  Wildernesses calm and green,
Peopled by shapes too bright to see,
And rest, having beheld: somewhat like thee;   109
Which walk upon the sea, and chant melodiously!

from ACT III

SCENE 1. *Heaven.* JUPITER *on his Throne;* THETIS *and the
other Deities assembled*

  Jupiter. Ye congregated powers of heaven, who
    share
The glory and the strength of him ye serve,

Rejoice! henceforth I am omnipotent,
All else had been subdued to me; alone
The soul of man, like unextinguished fire,
Yet burns towards heaven with fierce reproach, and
    doubt,
And lamentation, and reluctant prayer,
Hurling up insurrection, which might make
Our antique empire insecure, though built
On eldest faith, and hell's coeval, fear;   10
And though my curses through the pendulous air,
Like snow on herbless peaks, fall flake by flake,
And cling to it; though under my wrath's night
It climb the crags of life, step after step,
Which wound it, as ice wounds unsandalled feet,
It yet remains supreme o'er misery,
Aspiring, unrepressed, yet soon to fall:
Even now have I begotten a strange wonder,
That fatal child, the terror of the earth,
Who waits but till the destined hour arrive,   20
Bearing from Demogorgon's vacant throne
The dreadful might of ever-living limbs
Which clothed that awful spirit unbeheld,
To redescend, and trample out the spark.

Pour forth heaven's wine, Idaean Ganymede,
And let it fill the Daedal cups like fire,
And from the flower-inwoven soil divine
Ye all-triumphant harmonies arise,
As dew from earth under the twilight stars:
Drink! be the nectar circling through your veins
The soul of joy, ye ever-living Gods,   31
Till exultation burst in one wide voice
Like music from Elysian winds.

                         And thou
Ascend beside me, veilèd in the light
Of the desire which makes thee one with me,
Thetis, bright image of eternity!
When thou didst cry, "Insufferable might!
God! Spare me! I sustain not the quick flames,
The penetrating presence; all my being,
Like him whom the Numidian seps did thaw   40
Into a dew with poison, is dissolved,
Sinking through its foundations": even then
Two mighty spirits, mingling, made a third
Mightier than either, which, unbodied now,
Between us floats, felt, although unbeheld,
Waiting the incarnation, which ascends,
(Hear ye the thunder of the fiery wheels
Griding the winds?) from Demogorgon's throne.
Victory! victory! Feel'st thou not, O world!
The earthquake of his chariot thundering up   50
Olympus?

40. seps, venomous serpent.   **48. Griding,** piercing with
a harsh sound.

[*The Car of the* HOUR *arrives.* DEMOGORGON *descends and
moves towards the Throne of* JUPITER.]
                    Awful shape, what art thou? Speak!
Demogorgon. Eternity. Demand no direr name.
Descend, and follow me down the abyss.
I am thy child, as thou wert Saturn's child;
Mightier than thee: and we must dwell together
Henceforth in darkness. Lift thy lightnings not.
The tyranny of heaven none may retain,
Or reassume, or hold, succeeding thee:
Yet if thou wilt, as 'tis the destiny
Of trodden worms to writhe till they are dead,   60
Put forth thy might.
       Jupiter.   Detested prodigy!
Even thus beneath the deep Titanian prisons
I trample thee! thou lingerest?
                              Mercy! mercy!
No pity, no release, no respite! Oh,
That thou wouldst make mine enemy my judge,
Even where he hangs, seared by my long revenge,
On Caucasus! he would not doom me thus.
Gentle, and just, and dreadless, is he not
The monarch of the world? What then art thou?
No refuge! no appeal!
                    Sink with me then,   70
We two will sink on the wide waves of ruin,
Even as a vulture and a snake outspent
Drop, twisted in inextricable fight,
Into a shoreless sea. Let hell unlock
Its mounded oceans of tempestuous fire,
And whelm on them into the bottomless void
This desolated world, and thee, and me,
The conqueror and the conquered, and the wreck
Of that for which they combated.
                              Ai! Ai!
The elements obey me not. I sink   80
Dizzily down, ever, for ever, down.
And, like a cloud, mine enemy above
Darkens my fall with victory! Ai, Ai!

from SCENE 3. *Caucasus.* PROMETHEUS, HERCULES,
    IONE, *the* EARTH, SPIRITS, ASIA, *and* PANTHEA,
    borne in the Car with the SPIRIT OF THE HOUR.
    HERCULES *unbinds* PROMETHEUS, *who descends.*

    Hercules. Most glorious among spirits, thus doth
       strength
To wisdom, courage, and long-suffering love,
And thee, who art the form they animate,
Minister like a slave.
    Prometheus.   Thy gentle words
Are sweeter even than freedom long desired
And long delayed.
                    Asia, thou light of life,

Shadow of beauty unbeheld: and ye,
Fair sister nymphs, who made long years of pain
Sweet to remember, through your love and care:
Henceforth we will not part. There is a cave,   10
All overgrown with trailing odorous plants,
Which curtain out the day with leaves and flowers,
And paved with veinèd emerald, and a fountain
Leaps in the midst with an awakening sound.
From its curved roof the mountain's frozen tears,
Like snow, or silver, or long diamond spires,
Hang downward, raining forth a doubtful light:
And there is heard the ever-moving air,
Whispering without from tree to tree, and birds,
And bees; and all around are mossy seats,   20
And the rough walls are clothed with long soft grass;
A simple dwelling, which shall be our own;
Where we will sit and talk of time and change,
As the world ebbs and flows, ourselves unchanged.
What can hide man from mutability?
And if ye sigh, then I will smile; and thou,
Ione, shalt chaunt fragments of sea-music,
Until I weep, when ye shall smile away
The tears she brought, which yet were sweet to
       shed.
We will entangle buds and flowers and beams   30
Which twinkle on the fountain's brim, and make
Strange combinations out of common things,
Like human babes in their brief innocence;
And we will search, with looks and words of love,
For hidden thoughts, each lovelier than the last,
Our unexhausted spirits; and like lutes
Touched by the skill of the enamoured wind,
Weave harmonies divine, yet ever new,
From difference sweet where discord cannot be;
And hither come, sped on the charmèd winds,   40
Which meet from all the points of heaven, as bees
From every flower aëreal Enna feeds,
At their known island-homes in Himera,
The echoes of the human world, which tell
Of the low voice of love, almost unheard,
And dove-eyed pity's murmured pain, and music,
Itself the echo of the heart, and all
That tempers or improves man's life, now free;
And lovely apparitions, dim at first,
Then radiant, as the mind, arising bright   50
From the embrace of beauty, whence the forms
Of which these are the phantoms, casts on them
The gathered rays which are reality,
Shall visit us, the progeny immortal
Of Painting, Sculpture, and rapt Poesy,
And arts, though unimagined, yet to be.
The wandering voices and the shadows these
Of all that man becomes, the mediators
Of that best worship love, by him and us

Given and returned; swift shapes and sounds, which grow 60
More fair and soft as man grows wise and kind,
And, veil by veil, evil and error fall.
Such virtue has the cave and place around. . . .

from SCENE 4. *A Forest. In the Back-ground a Cave.* PRO-
METHEUS, ASIA, PANTHEA, IONE, *and the* SPIRIT
OF THE EARTH

The SPIRIT OF THE HOUR *enters.*

Spirit of the Hour. Soon as the sound had ceased
whose thunder filled
The abysses of the sky and the wide earth,
There was a change: the impalpable thin air
And the all-circling sunlight were transformed,
As if the sense of love dissolved in them 102
Had folded itself round the sphered world.
My vision then grew clear, and I could see
Into the mysteries of the universe: . . .

As I have said, I floated to the earth:
It was, as it is still, the pain of bliss
To move, to breathe, to be; I wandering went
Among the haunts and dwellings of mankind,
And first was disappointed not to see
Such mighty change as I had felt within
Expressed in outward things; but soon I looked, 130
And behold, thrones were kingless, and men walked
One with the other even as spirits do,
None fawned, none trampled; hate, disdain, or fear,
Self-love or self-contempt, on human brows
No more inscribed, as o'er the gate of hell,
"All hope abandon ye who enter here";
None frowned, none trembled, none with eager
fear
Gazed on another's eye of cold command,
Until the subject of a tyrant's will
Became, worse fate, the abject of his own, 140
Which spurred him, like an outspent horse, to death.
None wrought his lips in truth-entangling lines
Which smiled the lie his tongue disdained to speak;
None, with firm sneer, trod out in his own heart
The sparks of love and hope till these remained
Those bitter ashes, a soul self-consumed,
And the wretch crept a vampire among men,
Infecting all with his own hideous ill;
None talked that common, false, cold, hollow talk
Which makes the heart deny the *yes* it breathes, 150
Yet question that unmeant hypocrisy
With such a self-mistrust as has no name.
And women, too, frank, beautiful, and kind
As the free heaven which rains fresh light and dew
On the wide earth, past; gentle radiant forms,

From custom's evil taint exempt and pure;
Speaking the wisdom once they could not think,
Looking emotions once they feared to feel,
And changed to all which once they dared not be,
Yet being now, made earth like heaven; nor pride,
Nor jealousy, nor envy, nor ill-shame, 161
The bitterest of those drops of treasured gall,
Spoilt the sweet taste of the nepenthe, love.

Thrones, altars, judgment-seats, and prisons;
wherein,
And beside which, by wretched men were borne
Sceptres, tiaras, swords, and chains, and tomes
Of reasoned wrong, glozed on by ignorance,
Were like those monstrous and barbaric shapes,
The ghosts of a no more remembered fame,
Which, from their unworn obelisks, look forth 170
In triumph o'er the palaces and tombs
Of those who were their conquerors: mouldering
round,
Those imaged to the pride of kings and priests
A dark yet mighty faith, a power as wide
As is the world it wasted, and are now
But an astonishment; even so the tools
And emblems of its last captivity,
Amid the dwellings of the peopled earth,
Stand, not o'erthrown, but unregarded now.
And those foul shapes, abhorred by god and man,
Which, under many a name and many a form 181
Strange, savage, ghastly, dark, and execrable,
Were Jupiter, the tyrant of the world;
And which the nations, panic-stricken, served
With blood, and hearts broken by long hope, and
love
Dragged to his altars soiled and garlandless,
And slain amid men's unreclaiming tears,
Flattering the thing they feared, which fear was hate,
Frown, mouldering fast, o'er their abandoned
shrines:
The painted veil, by those who were, called life,
Which mimicked, as with colours idly spread, 191
All men believed or hoped, is torn aside;
The loathsome mask has fallen, the Man remains,—
Sceptreless, free, uncircumscribed,—but man:
Equal, unclassed, tribeless, and nationless,
Exempt from awe, worship, degree, the King
Over himself; just, gentle, wise,—but man:
Passionless? no; yet free from guilt or pain,
Which were, for his will made, or suffered them;
Nor yet exempt, though ruling them like slaves, 200
From chance, and death, and mutability,
The clogs of that which else might oversoar
The loftiest star of unascended heaven,
Pinnacled dim in the intense inane.

from ACT IV

Demogorgon

This is the day, which down the void abysm   554
At the Earth-born's spell yawns for Heaven's des-
    potism,
   And Conquest is dragged captive through the
    deep:
Love, from its awful throne of patient power
In the wise heart, from the last giddy hour
   Of dread endurance, from the slippery, steep,
And narrow verge of crag-like agony, springs   560
And folds over the world its healing wings.

Gentleness, Virtue, Wisdom, and Endurance,
These are the seals of that most firm assurance
   Which bars the pit over Destruction's strength;
And if, with infirm hand, Eternity,
Mother of many acts and hours, should free
   The serpent that would clasp her with his length;
These are the spells by which to re-assume
An empire o'er the disentangled doom.

To suffer woes which Hope thinks infinite;   570
To forgive wrongs darker than death or night;
   To defy Power, which seems omnipotent;
To love, and bear; to hope till Hope creates
From its own wreck the thing it contemplates:
   Neither to change, nor falter, nor repent;
This, like thy glory, Titan! is to be
Good, great and joyous, beautiful and free;
This is alone Life, Joy, Empire, and Victory!

THE CLOUD

1

I bring fresh showers for the thirsting flowers,
   From the seas and the streams;
I bear light shade for the leaves when laid
   In their noon-day dreams.
From my wings are shaken the dews that waken
   The sweet buds every one,
When rocked to rest on their mother's breast,
   As she dances about the sun.
I wield the flail of the lashing hail,
   And whiten the green plains under,   10
And then again I dissolve it in rain,
   And laugh as I pass in thunder.

2

I sift the snow on the mountains below,
   And their great pines groan aghast;
And all the night 'tis my pillow white,
   While I sleep in the arms of the blast.

Sublime on the towers of my skiey bowers,
   Lightning my pilot sits;
In a cavern under is fettered the thunder,
   It struggles and howls at fits;   20
Over earth and ocean, with gentle motion,
   This pilot is guiding me,
Lured by the love of the genii that move
   In the depths of the purple sea;
Over the rills, and the crags, and the hills,
   Over the lakes and the plains,
Wherever he dream, under mountain or stream,
   The Spirit he loves remains;
And I all the while bask in heaven's blue smile,
   Whilst he is dissolving in rains.   30

3

The sanguine sunrise, with his meteor eyes,
   And his burning plumes outspread,
Leaps on the back of my sailing rack,
   When the morning star shines dead;
As on the jag of a mountain crag,
   Which an earthquake rocks and swings,
An eagle alit one moment may sit
   In the light of its golden wings.
And when sunset may breathe, from the lit sea
   beneath,
   Its ardours of rest and of love,   40
And the crimson pall of eve may fall
   From the depth of heaven above,
With wings folded I rest, on mine airy nest,
   As still as a brooding dove.

4

That orbèd maiden with white fire laden,
   Whom mortals call the moon,
Glides glimmering o'er my fleece-like floor,
   By the midnight breezes strewn;
And wherever the beat of her unseen feet,
   Which only the angels hear,   50
May have broken the woof of my tent's thin
   roof,
   The stars peep behind her and peer;
And I laugh to see them whirl and flee,
   Like a swarm of golden bees,
When I widen the rent in my wind-built tent,
   Till the calm rivers, lakes, and seas,
Like strips of the sky fallen through me on high,
   Are each paved with the moon and these.

5

I bind the sun's throne with a burning zone,
   And the moon's with a girdle of pearl;   60
The volcanoes are dim, and the stars reel and swim,
   When the whirlwinds my banner unfurl.

From cape to cape, with a bridge-like shape,
  Over a torrent sea,
Sunbeam-proof, I hang like a roof,
  The mountains its columns be.
The triumphal arch through which I march
  With hurricane, fire, and snow,
When the powers of the air are chained to my
    chair,
  Is the million-coloured bow;   70
The sphere-fire above its soft colours wove,
  While the moist earth was laughing below.

I am the daughter of earth and water,
  And the nursling of the sky;
I pass through the pores of the ocean and shores;
  I change, but I cannot die.
For after the rain when with never a stain
  The pavilion of heaven is bare,
And the winds and sunbeams with their convex
    gleams,
  Build up the blue dome of air,   80
I silently laugh at my own cenotaph,
  And out of the caverns of rain,
Like a child from the womb, like a ghost from the
    tomb,
I arise and unbuild it again.

TO A SKYLARK

"It was on a beautiful summer evening while wandering [near Leghorn, Italy] among the lanes, whose myrtle
hedges were the bowers of the fireflies, that we heard the
caroling of the skylark, which inspired one of the most
beautiful of his poems."—Mrs. Shelley

1

Hail to thee, blithe Spirit!
  Bird thou never wert,
That from Heaven, or near it,
  Pourest thy full heart
In profuse strains of unpremeditated art.

2

Higher still and higher
  From the earth thou springest
Like a cloud of fire;
  The blue deep thou wingest,
And singing still dost soar, and soaring ever singest.

1. blithe Spirit, the key idea of the poem (the joyous,
soaring spirit of poetry). See following notes for suggestions
concerning method of development. **6–35. Higher . . .
melody,** direct description of qualities of the lark's songs
(aspiration, invisibility, poignancy, compass, mystery).

3

In the golden lightning   11
  Of the sunken Sun,
O'er which clouds are bright'ning,
  Thou dost float and run;
Like an unbodied joy whose race is just begun.

4

The pale purple even
  Melts around thy flight;
Like a star of Heaven,
  In the broad day-light
Thou art unseen, but yet I hear thy shrill delight,

5

Keen as are the arrows   21
  Of that silver sphere,
Whose intense lamp narrows
  In the white dawn clear,
Until we hardly see, we feel that it is there.

6

All the earth and air
  With thy voice is loud,
As, when Night is bare,
  From one lonely cloud
The moon rains out her beams, and Heaven is
    overflowed.   30

7

What thou art we know not;
  What is most like thee?
From rainbow clouds there flow not
  Drops so bright to see,
As from thy presence showers a rain of melody.

8

Like a poet hidden
  In the light of thought,
Singing hymns unbidden,
  Till the world is wrought
To sympathy with hopes and fears it heeded not:

9

Like a high-born maiden   41
  In a palace-tower,
Soothing her love-laden
  Soul in secret hour
With music sweet as love, which overflows her
    bower:

36–60. Like a poet . . . surpass, further description by
a series of radiant comparisons and analogies (note that all
the similes have one idea in common with the bird's song—
"hidden").

10

Like a glow-worm golden
    In a dell of dew,
Scattering unbeholden
    Its aërial hue
Among the flowers and grass, which screen it from
    the view: 50

11

Like a rose embowered
    In its own green leaves,
By warm winds deflowered,
    Till the scent it gives
Makes faint with too much sweet those heavy-
    wingèd thieves:

12

Sound of vernal showers
    On the twinkling grass,
Rain-awakened flowers,
    All that ever was
Joyous, and clear, and fresh, thy music doth sur-
    pass.   60

13

Teach us, Sprite or Bird,
    What sweet thoughts are thine:
I have never heard
    Praise of love or wine
That panted forth a flood of rapture so divine.

14

Chorus Hymeneal,
    Or triumphant chaunt,
Matched with thine, would be all
    But an empty vaunt,
A thing wherein we feel there is some hidden want.

15

What objects are the fountains   71
    Of thy happy strain?
What fields, or waves, or mountains?
    What shapes of sky or plain?
What love of thine own kind? what ignorance of
    pain?

16

With thy clear keen joyance
    Languor cannot be:
Shadow of annoyance
    Never came near thee:
Thou lovest—but ne'er knew love's sad satiety.   80

61–85. **Teach us . . . stream?** What thoughts can provoke such music, such happiness? Compare l. 80, "Thou
lovest—but ne'er knew love's sad satiety," with ll. 11–30 of
Keats's "Ode on a Grecian Urn."

17

Waking or asleep,
    Thou of death must deem
Things more true and deep
    Than we mortals dream,
Or how could thy notes flow in such a crystal
    stream?

18

We look before and after,
    And pine for what is not:
Our sincerest laughter
    With some pain is fraught;
Our sweetest songs are those that tell of saddest
    thought.   90

19

Yet if we could scorn
    Hate, and pride, and fear;
If we were things born
    Not to shed a tear,
I know not how thy joy we ever should come near.

20

Better than all measures
    Of delightful sound,
Better than all treasures
    That in books are found,
Thy skill to poet were, thou scorner of the ground!

21

Teach me half the gladness   101
    That thy brain must know,
Such harmonious madness
    From my lips would flow
The world should listen then, as I am listening
    now.

TO ——

1

I fear thy kisses, gentle maiden,
    Thou needest not fear mine;
My spirit is too deeply laden
    Ever to burthen thine.

86–100. **We look before and after . . . ground,** contrast between the bird's song and the desires, highest music,
and poetry of man. Note "Yet if we could scorn Hate" . . .
the condition in Shelley's formula for happiness. Compare
Prometheus' recalling the curse, and the last song of *Prometheus Unbound.* 101–05. **Teach me . . . now.** The prayer
to the bird is the consequence from, the climax to, the
preceding. Compare the last stanza of "Ode to the West
Wind." On what note does the poem end—hope or despair? Compare the ending of "The Indian Serenade."

2

I fear thy mien, thy tones, thy motion,
   Thou needest not fear mine;
Innocent is the heart's devotion
   With which I worship thine.

HYMN OF PAN

1

From the forests and highlands
   We come, we come;
From the river-girt islands,
   Where loud waves are dumb
     Listening my sweet pipings.
The wind in the reeds and the rushes,
   The bees on the bells of thyme,
The birds on the myrtle bushes,
   The cicale above in the lime
And the lizards below in the grass,   10
Were as silent as ever old Tmolus was,
     Listening my sweet pipings.

2

Liquid Penëus was flowing,
   And all dark Tempe lay
In Pelion's shadow, outgrowing
   The light of the dying day,
     Speeded by my sweet pipings.
The Sileni, and Sylvans, and Fauns,
   And the Nymphs of the woods and the waves,
To the edge of the moist river-lawns,   20
   And the brink of the dewy caves,
And all that did then attend and follow,
Were silent with love, as you now, Apollo,
   With envy of my sweet pipings.

3

I sang of the dancing stars,
   I sang of the daedal Earth,
And of Heaven—and the giant wars,
   And Love, and Death, and Birth,—
     And then I changed my pipings,—
Singing how down the vale of Maenalus   30
   I pursued a maiden and clasped a reed.
Gods and men, we are all deluded thus!
   It breaks in our bosom and then we bleed:
All wept, as I think both ye now would,
If envy or age had not frozen your blood,
   At the sorrow of my sweet pipings.

26. daedal, curiously made. One of Shelley's favorite words.

THE QUESTION

1

I dreamed that, as I wandered by the way,
   Bare winter suddenly was changed to spring,
And gentle odours led my steps astray,
   Mixed with a sound of waters murmuring
Along a shelving bank of turf, which lay
   Under a copse, and hardly dared to fling
Its green arms round the bosom of the stream,
But kissed it and then fled, as thou mightest in dream.

2

There grew pied wind-flowers and violets,
   Daisies, those pearled Arcturi of the earth—   10
The constellated flower that never sets;
   Faint oxlips—tender blue bells, at whose birth
The sod scarce heaved, and that tall flower that wets—
   Like a child, half in tenderness and mirth—
Its mother's face with Heaven's collected tears,
When the low wind, its playmate's voice, it hears.

3

And in the warm hedge grew lush eglantine,
   Green cow-bind and the moonlight-coloured May,
And cherry blossoms, and white cups whose wine
   Was the bright dew yet drained not by the day;
And wild roses, and ivy serpentine,   21
   With its dark buds and leaves, wandering astray;
And flowers azure, black, and streaked with gold,
Fairer than any wakened eyes behold.

4

And nearer to the river's trembling edge
   There grew broad flag-flowers, purple prankt with white,
And starry river buds among the sedge,
   And floating water-lilies broad and bright,
Which lit the oak that overhung the hedge
   With moonlight beams of their own watery light;   30
And bulrushes, and reeds of such deep green
As soothed the dazzled eye with sober sheen.

5

Methought that of these visionary flowers
   I made a nosegay, bound in such a way
That the same hues, which in their natural bowers
   Were mingled or opposed, the like array

10. Arcturi, Arcturus is one of the fixed stars.

Kept these imprisoned children of the Hours
  Within my hand . . . and then elate and gay
I hastened to the spot whence I had come,
That I might there present it!—oh! to whom?   40

THE WORLD'S WANDERERS

This was left unfinished. The MS. adds two lines
and the beginning of a third.

1

Tell me, thou star, whose wings of light
Speed thee in thy fiery flight,
In what cavern of the night
  Will thy pinions close now?
Tell me, moon, thou pale and grey
Pilgrim of heaven's homeless way,
In what depth of night or day
  Seekest thou repose now?

2

Weary wind, who wanderest
Like the world's rejected guest,   10
Hast thou still some secret nest
  On the tree or billow—

ADONAIS

Adonais was written in June, 1821, at Pisa, and printed
there in July. In the three months that had elapsed
after the death of Keats at Rome, Shelley seems not
to have made inquiries about the causes and circumstances of Keats's death (in his preface to the poem, he
even leaves blank the date of death). He was under the
impression that the harsh treatment accorded Keats by
the reviewers hastened, if it did not actually cause, that
untimely end. His motives were therefore three: (1) regret
that Keats should thus early have been "hooted off the
stage of life"; (2) indignation at the reviewers—from his
view Keats was a victim of oppression, the Romantic
symbol of the poet hounded by the world's brutality;
(3) identification of his own fate with the fate of Keats.
The last was undoubtedly the strongest motive. The
poem, then, combines two persistent and dominant elements in Shelley's life and thought—his warfare against
the oppressors of mankind, and his worship of the ideal
over the actual. Shelley's so-called sources had a great
deal to do with his treatment of the theme. The poem is a
pastoral elegy, in Spenserian stanzas, modeled on two
Greek pastoral elegies of the third century B.C.—Bion's
Lament for Adonis (which suggested the title, the general
idea, the lament refrain, the machinery of the loves,
echoes, and so on, the grief of nature, the picture of cor-

37. **Hours,** goddesses of law and order in nature.

ruption and physical death, the reabsorption into nature,
horror at the brutality of the slaughter); and Moschus'
Lament for Bion (which suggested the additional feature of
the grief of brother poets, "the mountain shepherds,"
Byron, Moore, Shelley himself, and Leigh Hunt). Besides
these Greek models, Shelley drew upon Keats's poetry,
and from his own ideas about the nature of reality and
immortality. In its structure the poem, like Milton's
"Lycidas," follows the old traditional machinery of the
pastoral elegy: invocation, inquiry into causes of death,
sympathy of nature, procession of mourners, personal digression, lament, climax, change of mood, and final consolation; but Shelley etherealizes the old framework. The
two main movements are these: (1) grief over the death
of the poet, indignation at the reviewers, sorrowful questioning of the meaning of life; turn (stanza 38) and (2) rejoicing over the immortality of the poet, triumphant assertion of the superiority of the ideal over the actual
(stanzas 39–55). *Adonais* is a great art poem; comprehension and enjoyment of it is one of the tests and one of the
rewards of a liberal education.

1

I weep for Adonais—he is dead!
Oh, weep for Adonais! though our tears
Thaw not the frost which binds so dear a head!
And thou, sad Hour, selected from all years
To mourn our loss, rouse thy obscure compeers,
And teach them thine own sorrow, say: with me
Died Adonais; till the Future dares
Forget the Past, his fate and fame shall be
An echo and a light unto eternity!

2

Where wert thou, mighty Mother, when he
    lay,   10
When thy Son lay, pierced by the shaft which flies
In darkness? where was lorn Urania
When Adonais died? With veilèd eyes,
'Mid listening Echoes, in her Paradise
She sate, while one, with soft enamoured breath,
Rekindled all the fading melodies,
With which, like flowers that mock the corse be-
    neath,
He had adorned and hid the coming bulk of death.

3

Oh, weep for Adonais—he is dead!
Wake, melancholy Mother, wake and weep!   20
Yet wherefore? Quench within their burning bed
Thy fiery tears, and let thy loud heart keep

1. **I weep,** keynote of stanzas 1–37.   10. **mighty Mother.**
Mythologically, Urania is goddess of Heavenly Love and
Poetry; philosophically, she is the Single Absolute Energy
or, in the Platonic sense, the parent of all goodness, truth,
and love. Note that the first lament issues from her lips.

Like his, a mute and uncomplaining sleep;
For he is gone, where all things wise and fair
Descend:—oh, dream not that the amorous Deep
Will yet restore him to the vital air;
Death feeds on his mute voice, and laughs at our
    despair.

4

Most musical of mourners, weep again!
Lament anew, Urania!—He died,
Who was the Sire of an immortal strain,   30
Blind, old, and lonely, when his country's pride,
The priest, the slave, and the liberticide,
Trampled and mocked with many a loathèd rite
Of lust and blood; he went, unterrified,
Into the gulf of death; but his clear Sprite
Yet reigns o'er earth; the third among the sons of
    light.

5

Most musical of mourners, weep anew!
Not all to that bright station dared to climb;
And happier they their happiness who knew,
Whose tapers yet burn through that night of
    time   40
In which suns perished; others more sublime,
Struck by the envious wrath of man or God,
Have sunk, extinct in their refulgent prime;
And some yet live, treading the thorny road,
Which leads, through toil and hate, to Fame's serene
    abode.

6

But now, thy youngest, dearest one, has perished,
The nursling of thy widowhood, who grew,
Like a pale flower by some sad maiden cherished,
And fed with true love tears, instead of dew;
Most musical of mourners, weep anew!   50
Thy extreme hope, the loveliest and the last,
The bloom, whose petals nipped before they blew
Died on the promise of the fruit, is waste;
The broken lily lies—the storm is overpast.

7

To that high Capital, where kingly Death
Keeps his pale court in beauty and decay,
He came; and bought, with price of purest breath,
A grave among the eternal.—Come away!
Haste, while the vault of blue Italian day
Is yet his fitting charnel-roof! while still   60
He lies, as if in dewy sleep he lay;
Awake him not! surely he takes his fill
Of deep and liquid rest, forgetful of all ill.

29. He, Milton. 55. high Capital, Rome, where Keats
died and was buried.

8

He will awake no more, oh, never more!—
Within the twilight chamber spreads apace
The shadow of white Death, and at the door
Invisible Corruption waits to trace
His extreme way to her dim dwelling-place;
The eternal Hunger sits, but pity and awe
Soothe her pale rage, nor dares she to deface   70
So fair a prey, till darkness and the law
Of change, shall o'er his sleep the mortal curtain
    draw.

9

Oh, weep for Adonais!—The quick Dreams,
The passion-wingèd Ministers of thought,
Who were his flocks, whom near the living
    streams
Of his young spirit he fed, and whom he taught
The love which was its music, wander not,—
Wander no more, from kindling brain to brain,
But droop there, whence they sprung; and
    mourn their lot
Round the cold heart, where, after their sweet
    pain,   80
They ne'er will gather strength, or find a home
    again.

10

And one with trembling hands clasps his cold
    head,
And fans him with her moonlight wings, and
    cries,
"Our love, our hope, our sorrow, is not dead;
See, on the silken fringe of his faint eyes,
Like dew upon a sleeping flower, there lies
A tear some Dream has loosened from his brain."
Lost Angel of a ruined Paradise!
She knew not 'twas her own; as with no stain
She faded, like a cloud which had outwept its
    rain.   90

11

One from a lucid urn of starry dew
Washed his light limbs as if embalming them;
Another clipped her profuse locks, and threw
The wreath upon him, like an anadem,
Which frozen tears instead of pearls begem;
Another in her wilful grief would break
Her bow and wingèd reeds, as if to stem
A greater loss with one which was more weak;
And dull the barbèd fire against his frozen cheek.

73–117. The quick Dreams, . . . stream. The personified abstractions are of Shelley's own imagining. They are
preparing the body for burial.

12

Another Splendour on his mouth alit,   100
That mouth, whence it was wont to draw the
  breath
Which gave it strength to pierce the guarded wit,
And pass into the panting heart beneath
With lightning and with music: the damp death
Quenched its caress upon its icy lips;
And, as a dying meteor stains a wreath
Of moonlight vapour, which the cold night clips,
It flushed through his pale limbs, and passed to its
  eclipse.

13

And others came . . . . Desires and Adorations,
Wingèd Persuasions and veiled Destinies,   110
Splendours, and Glooms, and glimmering Incar-
  nations
Of hopes and fears, and twilight Phantasies;
And Sorrow, with her family of Sighs,
And Pleasure, blind with tears, led by the gleam
Of her own dying smile instead of eyes,
Came in slow pomp;—the moving pomp might
  seem
Like pageantry of mist on an autumnal stream.

14

All he had loved, and moulded into thought,
From shape, and hue, and odour, and sweet
  sound,
Lamented Adonais. Morning sought   120
Her eastern watch-tower, and her hair unbound,
Wet with the tears which should adorn the
  ground,
Dimmed the aërial eyes that kindle day;
Afar the melancholy thunder moaned,
Pale Ocean in unquiet slumber lay,
And the wild winds flew round, sobbing in their
  dismay.

15

Lost Echo sits amid the voiceless mountains,
And feeds her grief with his remembered lay,
And will no more reply to winds or fountains,
Or amorous birds perched on the young green
  spray,   130
Or herdsman's horn, or bell at closing day;
Since she can mimic not his lips, more dear
Than those for whose disdain she pined away
Into a shadow of all sounds:—a drear
Murmur, between their songs, is all the woodmen
  hear.

16

Grief made the young Spring wild, and she threw
  down
Her kindling buds, as if she Autumn were,
Or they dead leaves; since her delight is flown,
For whom should she have waked the sullen year?
To Phoebus was not Hyacinth so dear,   140
Nor to himself Narcissus, as to both
Thou Adonais; wan they stand and sere
Amid the faint companions of their youth,
With dew all turned to tears; odour, to sighing ruth.

17

Thy spirit's sister, the lorn nightingale,
Mourns not her mate with such melodious pain;
Not so the eagle, who like thee could scale
Heaven, and could nourish in the sun's domain
Her mighty youth, with morning, doth complain,
Soaring and screaming round her empty nest,   150
As Albion wails for thee: the curse of Cain
Light on his head who pierced thy innocent
  breast,
And scared the angel soul that was its earthly guest!

18

Ah woe is me! Winter is come and gone,
But grief returns with the revolving year;
The airs and streams renew their joyous tone;
The ants, the bees, the swallows reappear;
Fresh leaves and flowers deck the dead Seasons'
  bier;
The amorous birds now pair in every brake,
And build their mossy homes in field and
  brere;   160
And the green lizard, and the golden snake,
Like unimprisoned flames, out of their trance
  awake.

19

Through wood and stream and field and hill and
  Ocean
A quickening life from the Earth's heart has burst
As it has ever done, with change and motion,
From the great morning of the world when first
God dawned on Chaos; in its stream immersed,
The lamps of Heaven flash with a softer light;
All baser things pant with life's sacred thirst;
Diffuse themselves; and spend in love's de-
  light,   170
The beauty and the joy of their renewèd might.

118–50. All he had loved, . . . nest, the grief of Nature,
personified in myths, some of which (for example, **the
lorn nightingale,** l. 145) Keats himself had created or used.

152. his head, the reviewer's.   **154–89. Winter is come
and gone . . . sorrow.** The return of physical life in spring
makes the fact of human death all the more unbearable and
mysterious.   **160. brere,** brier.

20

The leprous corpse touched by this spirit tender
Exhales itself in flowers of gentle breath;
Like incarnations of the stars, when splendour
Is changed to fragrance, they illumine death
And mock the merry worm that wakes beneath;
Nought we know, dies. Shall that alone which
    knows
Be as a sword consumed before the sheath
By sightless lightning?—th' intense atom glows
A moment, then is quenched in a most cold re-
    pose.   180

21

Alas! that all we loved of him should be,
But for our grief, as if it had not been,
And grief itself be mortal! Woe is me!
Whence are we, and why are we? of what scene
The actors or spectators? Great and mean
Meet massed in death, who lends what life must
    borrow.
As long as skies are blue, and fields are green,
Evening must usher night, night urge the mor-
    row,
Month follow month with woe, and year wake year
    to sorrow.

22

He will awake no more, oh, never more!   190
"Wake thou," cried Misery, "childless Mother,
    rise
Out of thy sleep, and slake, in thy heart's core,
A wound more fierce than his with tears and
    sighs."
And all the Dreams that watched Urania's eyes,
And all the Echoes whom their sister's song
Had held in holy silence, cried, "Arise!"
Swift as a Thought by the snake Memory stung,
From her ambrosial rest the fading Splendour
    sprung.

23

She rose like an autumnal Night, that springs
Out of the East, and follows wild and drear   200
The golden Day, which, on eternal wings,
Even as a ghost abandoning a bier,

Had left the Earth a corpse. Sorrow and fear
So struck, so roused, so rapt Urania;
So saddened round her like an atmosphere
Of stormy mist; so swept her on her way
Even to the mournful place where Adonais lay.

24

Out of her secret Paradise she sped,
Through camps and cities rough with stone, and
    steel,
And human hearts, which to her aery tread   210
Yielding not, wounded the invisible
Palms of her tender feet where'er they fell:
And barbèd tongues, and thoughts more sharp
    than they
Rent the soft Form they never could repel,
Whose sacred blood, like the young tears of May,
Paved with eternal flowers that undeserving way.

25

In the death-chamber for a moment Death,
Shamed by the presence of that living Might,
Blushed to annihilation, and the breath
Revisited those lips, and life's pale light   220
Flashed through those limbs, so late her dear
    delight.
"Leave me not wild and drear and comfortless,
As silent lightning leaves the starless night!
Leave me not!" cried Urania: her distress
Roused Death: Death rose and smiled, and met her
    vain caress.

26

"Stay yet awhile! speak to me once again;
Kiss me, so long but as a kiss may live;
And in my heartless breast and burning brain
That word, that kiss, shall all thoughts else sur-
    vive,
With food of saddest memory kept alive,   230
Now thou art dead, as if it were a part
Of thee, my Adonais! I would give
All that I am to be as thou now art,
But I am chained to Time, and cannot thence de-
    part!

27

"O gentle child, beautiful as thou wert,
Why didst thou leave the trodden paths of men
Too soon, and with weak hands though mighty
    heart
Dare the unpastured dragon in his den?
Defenceless as thou wert, oh! where was then

177. Nought we know, dies, that is, matter: Shelley's
statement of the theory of the conservation of energy: energy can neither be created nor destroyed. Is it not strange
that the mind, "that alone which knows," seems to go out,
while what is known, matter, is imperishable? It is as strange
as if a bolt of lightning should burn out the blade of the
sword (mind) and leave the sheath (the body) unconsumed.
The lowest depth of grief and despair in the poem.
186. lends what life must borrow, that is, plant and animal
life feed on dead things.

209 ff. Through camps and cities . . . the world as it
was in Shelley's time, and as it is today.

Wisdom the mirrored shield, or scorn the
    spear?   240
Or hadst thou waited the full cycle, when
Thy spirit should have filled its crescent sphere,
The monsters of life's waste had fled from thee like
    deer.

28

"The herded wolves, bold only to pursue;
The obscene ravens, clamorous o'er the dead;
The vultures, to the conqueror's banner true,
Who feed where Desolation first has fed,
And whose wings rain contagion;—how they
    fled,
When, like Apollo, from his golden bow
The Pythian of the age one arrow sped   250
And smiled!—The spoilers tempt no second
    blow,
They fawn on the proud feet that spurn them lying
    low.

29

"The sun comes forth, and many reptiles spawn;
He sets, and each ephemeral insect then
Is gathered into death without a dawn,
And the immortal stars awake again;
So is it in the world of living men:
A godlike mind soars forth, in its delight
Making earth bare and veiling heaven, and
    when
It sinks, the swarms that dimmed or shared its
    light   260
Leave to its kindred lamps the spirit's awful night."

30

Thus ceased she: and the mountain shepherds
    came,
Their garlands sere, their magic mantles rent;
The Pilgrim of Eternity, whose fame
Over his living head like Heaven is bent,
An early but enduring monument,
Came, veiling all the lightnings of his song
In sorrow; from her wilds Ierne sent
The sweetest lyrist of her saddest wrong,
And love taught grief to fall like music from his
    tongue.   270

250. The Pythian of the age . . . sped, Apollo slew the
snakes. Similarly, Lord Byron, in *English Bards and Scotch Reviewers,* had castigated the reviewers. A pity that Keats
could not have attained the maturity to cope with them!
264. The Pilgrim of Eternity, Byron. Compare *Childe
Harold's Pilgrimage,* Canto the Third, ll. 669-70. This is the
beginning of another "procession" of mourners—brother
poets—"mountain shepherds"—another specific "pastoral"
feature. **268. Ierne,** Ireland. Compare Moore's *Irish
Melodies.* **269. The sweetest lyrist,** Moore.

31

Midst others of less note, came one frail Form,
A phantom among men; companionless
As the last cloud of an expiring storm
Whose thunder is its knell; he, as I guess,
Had gazed on Nature's naked loveliness,
Actaeon-like, and now he fled astray
With feeble steps o'er the world's wilderness,
And his own thoughts, along that rugged way,
Pursued, like raging hounds, their father and their
    prey.

32

A pardlike Spirit beautiful and swift—   280
A Love in desolation masked;—a Power
Girt round with weakness;—it can scarce uplift
The weight of the superincumbent hour;
It is a dying lamp, a falling shower,
A breaking billow;—even whilst we speak
Is it not broken? On the withering flower
The killing sun smiles brightly: on a cheek
The life can burn in blood, even while the heart
    may break.

33

His head was bound with pansies overblown,
And faded violets, white, and pied, and blue;   290
And a light spear topped with a cypress cone,
Round whose rude shaft dark ivy-tresses grew
Yet dripping with the forest's noon-day dew,
Vibrated, as the ever-beating heart
Shook the weak hand that grasped it; of that crew
He came the last, neglected and apart;
A herd-abandoned deer struck by the hunter's dart.

34

All stood aloof, and at his partial moan
Smiled through their tears; well knew that gentle
    band
Who in another's fate now wept his own;   300
As in the accents of an unknown land,
He sung new sorrow; sad Urania scanned
The Stranger's mien, and murmured: "Who art
    thou?"
He answered not, but with a sudden hand
Made bare his branded and ensanguined brow,
Which was like Cain's or Christ's.—Oh! that it
    should be so!

271. one frail Form, Shelley's. Note the disproportion
between this characterization and those accorded to the
other poets (four stanzas to part of 30 and all of 35 for the
others). Note, too, l. 300, "Who in another's fate now wept
his own," and the characteristic self-pity of the whole passage. **276. Actaeon-like.** Actaeon surprised Diana in her
bath and was torn to pieces by her hounds. Thus the glimpse
of Immortal Beauty forever haunts the beholder.

35

What softer voice is hushed over the dead?
Athwart what brow is that dark mantle thrown?
What form leans sadly o'er the white death-bed,
In mockery of monumental stone,   310
The heavy heart heaving without a moan?
If it be He, who, gentlest of the wise,
Taught, soothed, loved, honoured the departed
   one,
Let me not vex, with inharmonious sighs,
The silence of that heart's accepted sacrifice.

36

Our Adonais has drunk poison—oh!
What deaf and viperous murderer could crown
Life's early cup with such a draught of woe?
The nameless worm would now itself disown:
It felt, yet could escape, the magic tone   320
Whose prelude held all envy, hate, and wrong,
But what was howling in one breast alone,
Silent with expectation of the song,
Whose master's hand is cold, whose silver lyre un-
   strung.

37

Live thou, whose infamy is not thy fame!
Live! fear no heavier chastisement from me,
Thou noteless blot on a remembered name!
But be thyself, and know thyself to be!
And ever at thy season be thou free
To spill the venom when thy fangs o'erflow;   330
Remorse and Self-contempt shall cling to thee;
Hot Shame shall burn upon thy secret brow,
And like a beaten hound tremble thou shalt—as now.

38

Nor let us weep that our delight is fled
Far from these carrion kites that scream below;
He wakes or sleeps with the enduring dead;
Thou canst not soar where he is sitting now.—
Dust to the dust! but the pure spirit shall flow
Back to the burning fountain whence it came,
A portion of the Eternal, which must glow   340
Through time and change, unquenchably the
   same,
Whilst thy cold embers choke the sordid hearth of
   shame.

39

Peace, peace! he is not dead, he doth not sleep—
He hath awakened from the dream of life—
'Tis we, who lost in stormy visions, keep
With phantoms an unprofitable strife,
And in mad trance strike with our spirit's knife
Invulnerable nothings—We decay
Like corpses in a charnel; fear and grief
Convulse us and consume us day by day,   350
And cold hopes swarm like worms within our living
   clay.

40

He has outsoared the shadow of our night;
Envy and calumny and hate and pain,
And that unrest which men miscall delight,
Can touch him not and torture not again;
From the contagion of the world's slow stain
He is secure, and now can never mourn
A heart grown cold, a head grown grey in vain;
Nor, when the spirit's self has ceased to burn,
With sparkless ashes load an unlamented urn.   360

41

He lives, he wakes—'tis Death is dead, not he;
Mourn not for Adonais.—Thou young Dawn,
Turn all thy dew to splendour, for from thee
The spirit thou lamentest is not gone;
Ye caverns and ye forests, cease to moan!
Cease, ye faint flowers and fountains, and thou
   Air,
Which like a morning veil thy scarf hadst thrown
O'er the abandoned Earth, now leave it bare
Even to the joyous stars which smile on its despair!

42

He is made one with Nature: there is heard   370
His voice in all her music, from the moan
Of thunder, to the song of night's sweet bird;
He is a presence to be felt and known
In darkness and in light, from herb and stone,

343–96. Peace, peace! he is not dead . . . stormy air.
In the following passage Shelley, as usual, reverses the ordinary conceptions of life and death. "Death is the veil which
those who live call life; They sleep, and it is lifted." (*Prometheus Unbound*, Act III, sc. 3, l. 113.) **370–414. He is
made one . . . our throng.** The conception of immortality involves several ideas, not always entirely consistent
with one another: (1) The spirit of Adonais is pantheistically
reabsorbed into the cycle of nature and continues to manifest itself in all that is lovely in nature; (2) it is similarly
reabsorbed into the Platonic essence of creative power
("Spirit's plastic stress") and is to be felt by the young and
generous for all time; (3) it is invited by the other "inheritors of unfulfilled renown" (poets who had died untimely and tragically) to ascend the seat reserved for it on
another star—the closest the poem comes to the Christian
notion of individual and conscious survival.

307. softer voice, Leigh Hunt's. If Shelley had known
more about the circumstances of Keats's death, he might
have included Joseph Severn, the young artist who came to
Italy with Keats and nursed the poet. **334–42. Nor let us
weep . . . shame.** This is the turn. In his indignation at
the reviewer, Shelley soars so high that he seems suddenly to
realize that the reviewer had not hurt that which was permanent in Keats; hence the following view of immortality
and the consequent change from mourning to rejoicing.

Spreading itself where'er that Power may move,
Which has withdrawn his being to its own;
Which wields the world with never wearied love,
Sustains it from beneath, and kindles it above.

43

He is a portion of the loveliness
Which once he made more lovely: he doth bear
His part, while the one Spirit's plastic stress   381
Sweeps through the dull dense world, compelling
    there,
All new successions to the forms they wear;
Torturing the unwilling dross that checks its flight
To its own likeness, as each mass may bear;
And bursting in its beauty and its might
From trees and beasts and men into the Heaven's
    light.

44

The splendours of the firmament of time
May be eclipsed, but are extinguished not;
Like stars to their appointed height they
    climb,   390
And death is a low mist which cannot blot
The brightness it may veil. When lofty thought
Lifts a young heart above its mortal lair,
And love and life contend in it, for what
Shall be its earthly doom, the dead live there
And move like winds of light on dark and stormy
    air.

45

The inheritors of unfulfilled renown
Rose from their thrones, built beyond mortal
    thought,
Far in the Unapparent. Chatterton
Rose pale, his solemn agony had not   400
Yet faded from him; Sidney, as he fought
And as he fell and as he lived and loved
Sublimely mild, a Spirit without spot,
Arose; and Lucan, by his death approved:
Oblivion as they rose shrank like a thing reproved.

46

And many more, whose names on Earth are dark,
But whose transmitted effluence cannot die
So long as fire outlives the parent spark,
Rose, robed in dazzling immortality.
"Thou art become as one of us," they cry;   410
"It was for thee yon kingless sphere has long
Swung blind in unascended majesty;
Silent alone amid an Heaven of Song.
Assume thy wingèd throne, thou Vesper of our
    throng!"

47

Who mourns for Adonais? oh come forth,
Fond wretch! and know thyself and him aright.
Clasp with thy panting soul the pendulous
    Earth;
As from a centre, dart thy spirit's light
Beyond all worlds, until its spacious might
Satiate the void circumference: then shrink   420
Even to a point within our day and night;
And keep thy heart light lest it make thee sink
When hope has kindled hope, and lured thee to the
    brink.

48

Or go to Rome, which is the sepulchre,
Oh, not of him, but of our joy: 'tis nought
That ages, empires, and religions there
Lie buried in the ravage they have wrought;
For such as he can lend,—they borrow not
Glory from those who made the world their prey;
And he is gathered to the kings of thought   430
Who waged contention with their time's decay,
And of the past are all that cannot pass away.

49

Go thou to Rome,—at once the Paradise,
The grave, the city, and the wilderness;
And where its wrecks like shattered mountains
    rise,
And flowering weeds, and fragrant copses dress
The bones of Desolation's nakedness
Pass, till the Spirit of the spot shall lead
Thy footsteps to a slope of green access
Where, like an infant's smile, over the dead   440
A light of laughing flowers along the grass is spread;

50

And grey walls moulder round, on which dull
    Time
Feeds, like slow fire upon a hoary brand;
And one keen pyramid with wedge sublime,
Pavilioning the dust of him who planned
This refuge for his memory, doth stand
Like flame transformed to marble; and beneath,

415–23. come forth . . . the brink. Let him who still
doubts the immortality of Adonais imagine he is at the center
of the universe and take a universal view; then, so far from
mourning Adonais, he will have to restrain himself from
leaping into eternity. **424–69. Or go to Rome . . . Heart.**
Or, if he is still a doubting Thomas, let him go to Rome
and see that, unlike others, who are distinguished by being
buried in Rome, Adonais *confers distinction* on the Eternal
City for being his last resting-place. The following description is of the Protestant cemetery in Rome, where,
in the shadow of the marble tomb of the ancient Roman
Emperor Cestius, Keats was buried, and where Shelley's
own ashes were to rest in a little more than a year.

A field is spread, on which a newer band
Have pitched in Heaven's smile their camp of
    death,
Welcoming him we lose with scarce extinguished
    breath. 450

51

Here pause: these graves are all too young as yet
To have outgrown the sorrow which consigned
Its charge to each; and if the seal is set,
Here, on one fountain of a mourning mind,
Break it not thou! too surely shalt thou find
Thine own well full, if thou returnest home,
Of tears and gall. From the world's bitter wind
Seek shelter in the shadow of the tomb.
What Adonais is, why fear we to become?

52

The One remains, the many change and pass; 460
Heaven's light forever shines, Earth's shadows
    fly;
Life, like a dome of many-coloured glass,
Stains the white radiance of Eternity,
Until Death tramples it to fragments.—Die,
If thou wouldst be with that which thou dost
    seek!
Follow where all is fled!—Rome's azure sky,
Flowers, ruins, statues, music, words, are weak
The glory they transfuse with fitting truth to speak.

53

Why linger, why turn back, why shrink, my
    Heart?
Thy hopes are gone before: from all things
    here 470
They have departed; thou shouldst now depart!
A light is passed from the revolving year,
And man, and woman; and what still is dear
Attracts to crush, repels to make thee wither.
The soft sky smiles,—the low wind whispers
    near:
'Tis Adonais calls! oh, hasten thither,
No more let life divide what Death can join to-
    gether.

460–86. The One . . . mortality. Shelley's most beautiful statement of the nature of Ultimate Reality. "The One"
is the Platonic Idea or Essence. In three figures "The One"
is contrasted with the individual and temporal ("One" and
"many," "Heaven's light" and "Earth's shadows," "dome
of many-coloured glass" and the white sunlight of "Eternity"). Just as, under a dome of colored glass, which breaks
up light into its primary colors, we should never see white
sunlight until the dome was broken, so we, covered by the
refracting dome of life, shall never know Ultimate Reality
until Death shatters the dome.

54

That Light whose smile kindles the Universe,
That Beauty in which all things work and move,
That Benediction which the eclipsing Curse 480
Of birth can quench not, that sustaining Love
Which through the web of being blindly wove
By man and beast and earth and air and sea,
Burns bright or dim, as each are mirrors of
The fire for which all thirst; now beams on me,
Consuming the last clouds of cold mortality.

55

The breath whose might I have invoked in song
Descends on me; my spirit's bark is driven,
Far from the shore, far from the trembling throng
Whose sails were never to the tempest given; 490
The massy earth and spherèd skies are riven!
I am borne darkly, fearfully, afar;
Whilst, burning through the inmost veil of
    Heaven,
The soul of Adonais, like a star,
Beacons from the abode where the Eternal are.

MUSIC, WHEN SOFT VOICES DIE

TO ——

Music, when soft voices die,
Vibrates in the memory—;
Odours, when sweet violets sicken,
Live within the sense they quicken.

Rose leaves, when the rose is dead,
Are heaped for the belovèd's bed;
And so thy thoughts, when thou art gone,
Love itself shall slumber on.

TO NIGHT

I

Swiftly walk o'er the western Wave,
    Spirit of Night!

478. That Light. Note the climax of ideas about the nature of Ultimate Reality. It runs the gamut from *Queen Mab*
through *Prometheus*. This is a higher conception than that the
Universe is Thought alone. Shelley transfers his conception
from the realm of intellect to the realm of emotion. Love, and
Love only, is the Universe. "Shelley's God was the Universe,
conceived as conscious and active love, and the worship he
gave it was love."—Stopford Brooke, *Naturalism in English
Poetry*, Dutton, 1920, p. 207. **487–95. The breath . . .
Eternal are.** Perhaps the passage tells as much as any poet
ever told about the way he felt when he had completed a
great poem. Compare the conclusion to Robert Browning's
"Saul." The stanza is also a final assertion of the deathless-
ness of the poet and of poetry—the larger theme of *Adonais*.
2. Spirit of Night! Another original and vivid myth. Compare "Ode to the West Wind," "The Cloud," and other
poems.

Out of the misty eastern cave,
Where, all the long and lone daylight,
Thou wovest dreams of joy and fear,
Which make thee terrible and dear,—
    Swift be thy flight!

2

Wrap thy form in a mantle grey,
    Star-inwrought!
Blind with thine hair the eyes of Day;   10
Kiss her until she be wearied out,
Then wander o'er city, and sea, and land,
Touching all with thine opiate wand—
    Come, long-sought!

3

When I arose and saw the dawn,
    I sighed for thee;
When Light rode high, and the dew was gone,
And noon lay heavy on flower and tree,
And the weary Day turned to his rest,
Lingering like an unloved guest,   20
    I sighed for thee.

4

Thy brother Death came, and cried,
    Wouldst thou me?
Thy sweet child Sleep, the filmy-eyed,
Murmured like a noon-tide bee,
Shall I nestle near thy side?
Wouldst thou me?—and I replied,
    No, . . . not thee!

5

Death will come when thou art dead,
    Soon, too soon—   30
Sleep will come when thou art fled;
Of neither would I ask the boon
I ask of thee, belovèd Night—
Swift be thine approaching flight,
    Come soon, soon!

A LAMENT

I

O world! O life! O time!
    On whose last steps I climb,
    Trembling at that where I had stood before;
When will return the glory of your prime?
    No more—Oh, never more!

32. **boon,** perhaps release from the distractions of the day, so that imagination will have free play.

2

Out of the day and night
A joy has taken flight:
    Fresh spring, and summer, and winter hoar,
Move my faint heart with grief, but with delight
    No more—Oh, never more!   10

LINES: WHEN THE LAMP IS SHATTERED

I

When the lamp is shattered,
The light in the dust lies dead—
    When the cloud is scattered,
The rainbow's glory is shed.
    When the lute is broken,
Sweet tones are remembered not;
    When the lips have spoken,
Loved accents are soon forgot.

2

    As music and splendour
Survive not the lamp and the lute,   10
    The heart's echoes render
No song when the spirit is mute:—
    No song but sad dirges,
Like the wind through a ruined cell,
    Or the mournful surges
That ring the dead seaman's knell.

3

    When hearts have once mingled,
Love first leaves the well-built nest;
    The weak one is singled
To endure what it once possest.   20
    O Love! who bewailest
The frailty of all things here,
    Why choose you the frailest
For your cradle, your home, and your bier?

4

    Its passions will rock thee,
As the storms rock the ravens on high:
    Bright reason will mock thee,
Like the sun from a wintry sky.
    From thy nest every rafter
Will rot, and thine eagle home   30
    Leave thee naked to laughter,
When leaves fall and cold winds come.

WITH A GUITAR; TO JANE

ARIEL to MIRANDA.—Take
This slave of music, for the sake
Of him, who is the slave of thee;
And teach it all the harmony
In which thou canst, and only thou,
Make the delighted spirit glow.
Till joy denies itself again,
And, too intense, is turned to pain;
For by permission and command
Of thine own Prince Ferdinand,　　　　10
Poor Ariel sends this silent token
Of more than ever can be spoken;
Your guardian spirit, Ariel, who,
From life to life, must still pursue
Your happiness, for thus alone
Can Ariel ever find his own.
From Prospero's enchanted cell,
As the mighty verses tell,
To the throne of Naples he
Lit you o'er the trackless sea,　　　　20
Flitting on, your prow before,
Like a living meteor.
When you die, the silent Moon,
In her interlunar swoon,
Is not sadder in her cell
Than deserted Ariel.
When you live again on Earth,
Like an unseen Star of birth,
Ariel guides you o'er the sea
Of life from your nativity;　　　　30
Many changes have been run
Since Ferdinand and you begun
Your course of love, and Ariel still
Has tracked your steps, and served your will.
Now, in humbler, happier lot,
This is all remembered not;
And now, alas! the poor sprite is
Imprisoned, for some fault of his,
In a body like a grave.
From you he only dares to crave,　　　　40
For his service and his sorrow,
A smile to day, a song to morrow.

The artist who this idol wrought,
To echo all harmonious thought,

Felled a tree, while on the steep
The woods were in their winter sleep,
Rocked in that repose divine
On the wind-swept Apennine;
And dreaming, some of autumn past,
And some of spring approaching fast,　　　　50
And some of April buds and showers,
And some of songs in July bowers,
And all of love,—and so this tree—
O that such our death may be—
Died in sleep, and felt no pain,
To live in happier form again,
From which, beneath Heaven's fairest star,
The artist wrought this loved guitar,
And taught it justly to reply,
To all who question skilfully,　　　　60
In language gentle as thine own;
Whispering in enamoured tone
Sweet oracles of woods and dells,
And summer winds in sylvan cells;
For it had learnt all harmonies
Of the plains and of the skies,
Of the forests and the mountains,
And the many-voicèd fountains;
The clearest echoes of the hills,
The softest notes of falling rills,　　　　70
The melodies of birds and bees,
The murmuring of summer seas,
And pattering rain, and breathing dew,
And airs of evening; and it knew
That seldom-heard mysterious sound,
Which, driven on its diurnal round,
As it floats through boundless day,
Our world enkindles on its way—
All this it knows, but will not tell
To those who cannot question well　　　　80
The spirit that inhabits it:
It talks according to the wit
Of its companions, and no more
Is heard than has been felt before
By those who tempt it to betray
These secrets of an elder day.—
But, sweetly as its answers will
Flatter hands of perfect skill,
It keeps its highest, holiest tone
For our belovèd Jane alone.—　　　　90

A DIRGE ✓

Rough wind, that moanest loud
　Grief too sad for song;
Wild wind, when sullen cloud
　Knells all the night long;

---

1. Ariel . . . Miranda. The inspiration and basic idea of this charming bit of vers de société (itself a pretty myth) is Shakespeare's *The Tempest*. Ariel (here Shelley) is the sprite imprisoned in the cloven pine, which speaks to Miranda (here Jane Williams), the daughter of Ariel's master, and Miranda's father, Duke Prospero. **10. Ferdinand,** Miranda's (here Jane's) husband (Edward Ellerker Williams).

Sad storm, whose tears are vain,
Bare woods, whose branches strain,
Deep caves and dreary main,—
    Wail, for the world's wrong!

MUTABILITY

We are as clouds that veil the midnight moon;
  How restlessly they speed, and gleam, and
     quiver,
Streaking the darkness radiantly!—yet soon
Night closes round, and they are lost for ever:

Or like forgotten lyres, whose dissonant strings
  Give various response to each varying blast,
To whose frail frame no second motion brings
  One mood or modulation like the last.

We rest.—A dream has power to poison sleep;
  We rise,—One wandering thought pollutes the
    day;   10
We feel, conceive or reason, laugh or weep;
  Embrace fond woe, or cast our cares away:

It is the same!—For, be it joy or sorrow,
  The path of its departure still is free;
Man's yesterday may ne'er be like his morrow;
  Naught may endure but Mutability.

from HELLAS

For an account of *Hellas*, see the biographical-critical
sketch. The "Semichoruses" express the main theme of
this dramatic poem. The "Chorus" sets forth a theory of
the great historical religions of the world.

Semichorus I

Life may change, but it may fly not;
Hope may vanish, but can die not;
Truth be veiled, but still it burneth;
Love repulsed,—but it returneth!

Semichorus II

Yet were life a charnel where
Hope lay coffined with Despair;
Yet were truth a sacred lie,   40
Love were lust—

Semichorus I

          If Liberty
Lent not life its soul of light,
Hope its iris of delight,
Truth its prophet's robe to wear,
Love its power to give and bear. . . .   45

Chorus

Worlds on worlds are rolling ever
  From creation to decay,
Like the bubbles on a river,
  Sparkling, bursting, borne away.   **200**
But they are still immortal
Who, through birth's orient portal
And death's dark chasm hurrying to and fro,
  Clothe their unceasing flight
  In the brief dust and light
Gathered around their chariots as they go;
  New shapes they still may weave,
  New Gods, new laws receive,
Bright or dim are they, as the robes they last
    On Death's bare ribs had cast.   **210**

A power from the unknown God,
  A Promethean conqueror came;
Like a triumphal path he trod
  The thorns of death and shame.
  A mortal shape to him
  Was like the vapour dim
Which the orient planet animates with light;
  Hell, Sin, and Slavery came,
  Like blood-hounds mild and tame,
Nor preyed until their lord had taken flight;   **220**
  The moon of Mahomet
  Arose, and it shall set:
While blazoned as on heaven's immortal noon
  The cross leads generations on.

Swift as the radiant shapes of sleep
  From one, whose dreams are Paradise,
Fly, when the fond wretch wakes to weep,
  And day peers forth with her blank eyes;
  So fleet, so faint, so fair,
  The Powers of earth and air   **230**
Fled from the folding star of Bethlehem;
  Apollo, Pan, and Love,
  And even Olympian Jove,
Grew weak, for killing Truth had glared on them;
  Our hills and seas and streams,
  Dispeopled of their dreams,
Their waters turned to blood, their dew to tears,
  Wailed for the golden years.

from A DEFENCE OF POETRY

In spirit and thought, *A Defence of Poetry* is close to the
idealism of *Adonais* and *Epipsychidion*, written the same
year. It is a "defence" against the attack made by Shelley's friend Thomas Love Peacock, in *The Four Ages of
Poetry*, 1820, on Romantic poetry. It was never completed. The two main topics of the part written are stated

by Shelley in his transitional tenth paragraph: (1) "what is poetry, and who are poets"; and (2) "its effects on society." The most original and significant portion of the essay belongs to the second topic, though understanding of Shelley's ideas on the first topic is an indispensable preliminary. The main points to be mastered are these: 1. Poetry, a product of the imagination set to metrical language, reveals the order and beauty of the universe; it is the direct expression of perfection ("the very image of life expressed in its eternal truth"). 2. If, then, poetry expresses ideal perfection, should the poet embody in his poems his beliefs about perfection and the way to it? The answer is no. As poetry is directly due to imaginative inspiration, not to reasoning, its true moral effect is produced through imagination, not through doctrine. The student should master Shelley's explanation of all these terms, reasons, and so on. Shelley's account of the moral efficacy of poetry, with his reasons, goes further than that of any of the other Romantics, with the possible exception of Keats. In his discussion of these topics Shelley makes some of the noblest claims ever put forth for poetry: "Poetry is the record of the best and happiest moments of the happiest and best minds." "Poetry redeems from decay the visitations of the divinity in man." "Poets are the unacknowledged legislators of the world," and so forth. (A. S. Cook's edition, *A Defence of Poetry*, Ginn, 1891, including Peacock's essay, and M. T. Solve's *Shelley, His Theory of Poetry*, University of Chicago Press, 1927, are valuable aids to study.)

PART I [1]

ACCORDING to one mode of regarding those two classes of mental action, which are called reason and imagination, the former may be considered as mind contemplating the relations borne by one thought to another, however produced, and the latter, as mind acting upon those thoughts so as to colour them with its own light, and composing from them, as from elements, other thoughts, each containing within itself the principle of its own integrity. The one is the τὸ ποιεῖν, or the principle of synthesis, and has for its objects those forms which are common to universal nature and existence itself; the other is the τὸ λογίζειν, or principle of analysis, and its action regards the relations of things, simply as relations; considering thoughts, not in their integral unity, but as the algebraical representations which conduct to certain general results. Reason is the enumeration of quantities already known; imagination is the perception of the value of those quantities, both separately and as a whole. Reason respects the differences, and imagination the similitudes of things. Reason is to imagination as the instrument to the agent, as the body to the spirit, as the shadow to the substance.

[1] The projected second and third parts were never written.

Poetry, in a general sense, may be defined to be "the expression of the imagination": and poetry is connate with the origin of man. Man is an instrument over which a series of external and internal impressions are driven, like the alternations of an ever-changing wind over an Aeolian lyre, which move it by their motion to ever-changing melody. But there is a principle within the human being, and perhaps within all sentient beings, which acts otherwise than in the lyre, and produces not melody, alone, but harmony, by an internal adjustment of the sounds or motions thus excited to the impressions which excite them. It is as if the lyre could accommodate its chords to the motions of that which strikes them, in a determined proportion of sound; even as the musician can accommodate his voice to the sound of the lyre. A child at play by itself will express its delight by its voice and motions; and every inflexion of tone and every gesture will bear exact relation to a corresponding antitype in the pleasurable impressions which awakened it; it will be the reflected image of that impression; and as the lyre trembles and sounds after the wind has died away, so the child seeks, by prolonging in its voice and motions the duration of the effect, to prolong also a consciousness of the cause. In relation to the objects which delight a child, these expressions are, what poetry is to higher objects. The savage (for the savage is to ages what the child is to years) expresses the emotions produced in him by surrounding objects in a similar manner; and language and gesture, together with plastic or pictorial imitation, become the image of the combined effect of those objects, and of his apprehension of them. Man in society, with all his passions and his pleasures, next becomes the object of the passions and pleasures of man; an additional class of emotions produces an augmented treasure of expressions; and language, gesture, and the imitative arts, become at once the representation and the medium, the pencil and the picture, the chisel and the statue, the chord and the harmony. The social sympathies, or those laws from which, as from its elements, society results, begin to develop themselves from the moment that two human beings coexist; the future is contained within the present, as the plant within the seed; and equality, diversity, unity, contrast, mutual dependence, become the principles alone capable of affording the motives according to which the will of a social being is determined to action, inasmuch as he is social; and constitute pleasure in sensation, virtue in sentiment, beauty in art, truth in reasoning, and love in the intercourse of kind. Hence men, even in the infancy of society, observe a certain order in their words and actions, distinct from that of the objects and the impressions represented by them, all expression being subject to the laws of that from which it proceeds. But let us dismiss those more general considerations which might involve an inquiry into the principles of society itself, and restrict our view to the manner in which the imagination is expressed upon its forms.

In the youth of the world, men dance and sing and imitate natural objects, observing in these actions, as in all others, a certain rhythm or order. And, although all men observe a similar, they observe not the same order, in the motions of the dance, in the melody of the song, in the combinations of language, in the series of their imitations of natural objects. For there is a certain order or rhythm belonging to each of these classes of mimetic representation, from which the hearer and the spectator receive an intenser and purer pleasure than from any other; the sense of an approximation to this order has been called taste by modern writers. Every man in the infancy of art, observes an order which approximates more or less closely to that from which this highest delight results: but the diversity is not sufficiently marked, as that its gradations should be sensible, except in those instances where the predominance of this faculty of approximation to the beautiful (for so we may be permitted to name the relation between this highest pleasure and its cause) is very great. Those in whom it exists in excess are poets, in the most universal sense of the word; and the pleasure resulting from the manner in which they express the influence of society or nature upon their own minds, communicates itself to others, and gathers a sort of reduplication from that community. Their language is vitally metaphorical; that is, it marks the before unapprehended relations of things and perpetuates their apprehension, until the words which represent them, become, through time, signs for portions or classes of thoughts instead of pictures of integral thoughts; and then if no new poets should arise to create afresh the associations which have been thus disorganised, language will be dead to all the nobler purposes of human intercourse. These similitudes or relations are finely said by Lord Bacon to be "the same footsteps of nature impressed upon the various subjects of the world"—and he considers the faculty which perceives them as the storehouse of axioms common to all knowledge. In the infancy of society every author is necessarily a poet, because language itself is poetry; and to be a poet is to apprehend the true and the beautiful, in a word, the good which exists in the relation, subsisting,

first between existence and perception, and secondly between perception and expression. Every original language near to its source is in itself the chaos of a cyclic poem: the copiousness of lexicography and the distinctions of grammar are the works of a later age, and are merely the catalogue and the form of the creations of poetry.

But poets, or those who imagine and express this indestructible order, are not only the authors of language and of music, of the dance, and architecture, and statuary, and painting; they are the institutors of laws, and the founders of civil society, and the inventors of the arts of life, and the teachers, who draw into a certain propinquity with the beautiful and the true, that partial apprehension of the agencies of the invisible world which is called religion. Hence all original religions are allegorical, or susceptible of allegory, and, like Janus, have a double face of false and true. Poets, according to the circumstances of the age and nation in which they appeared, were called, in the earlier epochs of the world, legislators, or prophets: a poet essentially comprises and unites both these characters. For he not only beholds intensely the present as it is, and discovers those laws according to which present things ought to be ordered, but he beholds the future in the present, and his thoughts are the germs of the flower and the fruit of latest time. Not that I assert poets to be prophets in the gross sense of the word, or that they can foretell the form as surely as they foreknow the spirit of events: such is the pretence of superstition, which would make poetry an attribute of prophecy, rather than prophecy an attribute of poetry. A poet participates in the eternal, the infinite, and the one; as far as relates to his conceptions, time and place and number are not. The grammatical forms which express the moods of time, and the difference of persons, and the distinction of place, are convertible with respect to the highest poetry without injuring it as poetry; and the choruses of Aeschylus, and the book of Job, and Dante's Paradise, would afford, more than any other writings, examples of this fact, if the limits of this essay did not forbid citation. The creations of sculpture, painting, and music, are illustrations still more decisive.

Language, colour, form, and religious and civil habits of action, are all the instruments and materials of poetry; they may be called poetry by that figure of speech which considers the effect as a synonym of the cause. But poetry in a more restricted sense expresses those arrangements of language, and especially metrical language, which are created by that imperial faculty, whose throne is curtained within the invisible nature of man. And this springs from the nature itself of language, which is a more direct representation of the actions and passions of our internal being, and is susceptible of more various and delicate combinations, than colour, form, or motion, and is more plastic and obedient to the control of that faculty of which it is the creation. For language is arbitrarily produced by the imagination, and has relation to thoughts alone; but all other materials, instruments, and conditions of art, have relations among each other, which limit and interpose between conception and expression. The former is as a mirror which reflects, the latter as a cloud which enfeebles, the light of which both are mediums of communication. Hence the fame of sculptors, painters, and musicians, although the intrinsic powers of the great masters of these arts may yield in no degree to that of those who have employed language as the hieroglyphic of their thoughts, has never equalled that of poets in the restricted sense of the term; as two performers of equal skill will produce unequal effects from a guitar and a harp. The fame of legislators and founders of religions, so long as their institutions last, alone seems to exceed that of poets in the restricted sense; but it can scarcely be a question, whether, if we deduct the celebrity which their flattery of the gross opinions of the vulgar usually conciliates, together with that which belonged to them in their higher character of poets, any excess will remain.

We have thus circumscribed the word Poetry within the limits of that art which is the most familiar and the most perfect expression of the faculty itself. It is necessary, however, to make the circle still narrower, and to determine the distinction between measured and unmeasured language; for the popular division into prose and verse is inadmissible in accurate philosophy.

Sounds as well as thoughts have relation both between each other and towards that which they represent, and a perception of the order of those relations has always been found connected with a perception of the order of the relations of thoughts. Hence the language of poets has ever affected a certain uniform and harmonious recurrence of sound, without which it were not poetry, and which is scarcely less indispensable to the communication of its actions, than the words themselves, without reference to that peculiar order. Hence the vanity of translation; it were as wise to cast a violet into a crucible that you might discover the formal principle of its colour and odour, as seek to transfuse from one language into another the creations of a poet. The plant must spring again from its seed, or it will bear no flower—and this is the burthen of the curse of Babel.

An observation of the regular mode of the recurrence of harmony in the language of poetical minds, together with its relation to music, produced metre, or a certain system of traditional forms of harmony of language. Yet it is by no means essential that a poet should accommodate his language to this traditional form, so that the harmony, which is its spirit, be observed. The practice is indeed convenient and popular, and to be preferred, especially in such composition as includes much action; but every great poet must inevitably innovate upon the example of his predecessors in the exact structure of his peculiar versification. The distinction between poets and prose writers is a vulgar error. The distinction between philosophers and poets has been anticipated. Plato was essentially a poet—the truth and splendour of his imagery, and the melody of his language, is [are] the most intense that it is possible to conceive. He rejected the measure of the epic, dramatic, and lyrical forms, because he sought to kindle a harmony in thoughts divested of shape and action, and he forbore to invent any regular plan of rhythm which would include, under determinate forms, the varied pauses of his style. Cicero sought to imitate the cadence of his periods, but with little success. Lord Bacon was a poet. His language has a sweet and majestic rhythm, which satisfies the sense, no less than the almost superhuman wisdom of his philosophy satisfies the intellect; it is a strain which distends, and then bursts the circumference of the reader's mind, and pours itself forth together with it into the universal element with which it has perpetual sympathy. All the authors of revolutions in opinion are not only necessarily poets as they are inventors, nor even as their words unveil the permanent analogy of things by images which participate in the life of truth; but as their periods are harmonious and rhythmical, and contain in themselves the elements of verse; being the echo of the eternal music. Nor are those supreme poets, who have employed traditional forms of rhythm on account of the form and action of their subjects, less capable of perceiving and teaching the truth of things, than those who have omitted that form. Shakespeare, Dante, and Milton (to confine ourselves to modern writers) are philosophers of the very loftiest power.

A poem is the very image of life expressed in its eternal truth. There is this difference between a story and a poem, that a story is a catalogue of detached facts, which have no other bond of connexion than time, place, circumstance, cause and effect; the other is the creation of actions according to the unchangeable forms of human nature, as existing in the mind of the creator, which is itself the image of all other minds. The one is partial, and applies only to a definite period of time, and a certain combination of events which can never again recur; the other is universal, and contains within itself the germ of a relation to whatever motives or actions have place in the possible varieties of human nature. Time, which destroys the beauty and the use of the story of particular facts, stript of the poetry which should invest them, augments that of Poetry, and for ever develops new and wonderful applications of the eternal truth which it contains. Hence epitomes have been called the moths of just history; they eat out the poetry of it. A story of particular facts is as a mirror which obscures and distorts that which should be beautiful: Poetry is a mirror which makes beautiful that which is distorted.

The parts of a composition may be poetical, without the composition as a whole being a poem. A single sentence may be considered as a whole, though it may be found in the midst of a series of unassimilated portions; a single word even may be a spark of inextinguishable thought. And thus all the great historians, Herodotus, Plutarch, Livy, were poets; and although the plan of these writers, especially that of Livy, restrained them from developing this faculty in its highest degree, they made copious and ample amends for their subjection, by filling all the interstices of their subjects with living images.

Having determined what is poetry, and who are poets, let us proceed to estimate its effects upon society.

Poetry is ever accompanied with pleasure: all spirits on which it falls open themselves to receive the wisdom which is mingled with its delight. In the infancy of the world, neither poets themselves nor their auditors are fully aware of the excellence of poetry: for it acts in a divine and unapprehended manner, beyond and above consciousness; and it is reserved for future generations to contemplate and measure the mighty cause and effect in all the strength and splendour of their union. Even in modern times, no living poet ever arrived at the fulness of his fame; the jury which sits in judgment upon a poet, belonging as he does to all time, must be composed of his peers: it must be impaneled by Time from the selectest of the wise of many generations. A Poet is a nightingale, who sits in darkness and sings to cheer its own solitude with sweet

sounds; his auditors are as men entranced by the melody of an unseen musician, who feel that they are moved and softened, yet know not whence or why. The poems of Homer and his contemporaries were the delight of infant Greece; they were the elements of that social system which is the column upon which all succeeding civilization has reposed. Homer embodied the ideal perfection of his age in human character; nor can we doubt that those who read his verses were awakened to an ambition of becoming like to Achilles, Hector, and Ulysses: the truth and beauty of friendship, patriotism, and persevering devotion to an object, were unveiled to the depths in these immortal creations: the sentiments of the auditors must have been refined and enlarged by a sympathy with such great and lovely impersonations, until from admiring they imitated, and from imitation they identified themselves with the objects of their admiration. Nor let it be objected, that these characters are remote from moral perfection, and that they can by no means be considered as edifying patterns for general imitation. Every epoch, under names more or less specious, has deified its peculiar errors; Revenge is the naked Idol of the worship of a semi-barbarous age; and Self-deceit is the veiled Image of unknown evil, before which luxury and satiety lie prostrate. But a poet considers the vices of his contemporaries as the temporary dress in which his creations must be arrayed, and which cover without concealing the eternal proportions of their beauty. An epic or dramatic personage is understood to wear them around his soul, as he may the antient armour or the modern uniform around his body; whilst it is easy to conceive a dress more graceful than either. The beauty of the internal nature cannot be so far concealed by its accidental vesture, but that the spirit of its form shall communicate itself to the very disguise, and indicate the shape it hides from the manner in which it is worn. A majestic form and graceful motions will express themselves through the most barbarous and tasteless costume. Few poets of the highest class have chosen to exhibit the beauty of their conceptions in its naked truth and splendour; and it is doubtful whether the alloy of costume, habit, &c., be not necessary to temper this planetary music for mortal ears.

The whole objection, however, of the immorality of poetry rests upon a misconception of the manner in which poetry acts to produce the moral improvement of man. Ethical science arranges the elements which poetry has created, and propounds schemes and proposes examples of civil and domestic life: nor is it for want of admirable doctrines that men hate, and despise, and censure, and deceive, and subjugate one another. But Poetry acts in another and diviner manner. It awakens and enlarges the mind itself by rendering it the receptacle of a thousand unapprehended combinations of thought. Poetry lifts the veil from the hidden beauty of the world, and makes familiar objects be as if they were not familiar; it reproduces all that it represents, and the impersonations clothed in its Elysian light stand thenceforward in the minds of those who have once contemplated them, as memorials of that gentle and exalted content which extends itself over all thoughts and actions with which its coexists. The great secret of morals is love; or a going out of our own nature, and an identification of ourselves with the beautiful which exists in thought, action, or person, not our own. A man, to be greatly good, must imagine intensely and comprehensively; he must put himself in the place of another and of many others; the pains and pleasures of his species must become his own. The great instrument of moral good is the imagination; and poetry administers to the effect by acting upon the cause. Poetry enlarges the circumference of the imagination by replenishing it with thoughts of ever new delight, which have the power of attracting and assimilating to their own nature all other thoughts, and which form new intervals and interstices whose void for ever craves fresh food. Poetry strengthens the faculty which is the organ of the moral nature of man, in the same manner as exercise strengthens a limb. A Poet therefore would do ill to embody his own conceptions of right and wrong, which are usually those of his place and time, in his poetical creations, which participate in neither. By this assumption of the inferior office of interpreting the effect, in which perhaps after all he might acquit himself but imperfectly, he would resign a glory in a participation in the cause. There was little danger that Homer, or any of the eternal Poets, should have so far misunderstood themselves as to have abdicated this throne of their widest dominion. Those in whom the poetical faculty, though great, is less intense, as Euripides, Lucan, Tasso, Spenser, have frequently affected a moral aim, and the effect of their poetry is diminished in exact proportion to the degree in which they compel us to advert to this purpose. . . .

The functions of the poetical faculty are twofold; by one it creates new materials for knowledge, and power and pleasure; by the other it engenders in the mind a desire to reproduce and arrange them according to a certain rhythm and order which may be called the beautiful and the good. The cultivation of poetry is never more to be desired than at periods when, from an excess of the selfish and calculating principle, the accumulation of the materials of external life exceed[s] the quantity of the power of assimilating them to the internal laws of human nature. The body has then become too unwieldy for that which animates it.

Poetry is indeed something divine. It is at once the centre and circumference of knowledge; it is that which comprehends all science, and that to which all science must be referred. It is at the same time the root and blossom of all other systems of thought; it is that from which all spring, and that which adorns all; and that which, if blighted, denies the fruit and the seed, and withholds from the barren world the nourishment and the succession of the scions of the tree of life. It is the perfect and consummate surface and bloom of all things; it is as the odour and the colour of the rose to the texture of the elements which compose it, as the form and splendour of unfaded beauty to the secrets of anatomy and corruption. What were Virtue, Love, Patriotism, Friendship—what were the scenery of this beautiful Universe which we inhabit; what were our consolations on this side of the grave, and what were our aspirations beyond it, if Poetry did not ascend to bring light and fire from those eternal regions where the owl-winged faculty of calculation dare not ever soar? Poetry is not like reasoning, a power to be exerted according to the determination of the will. A man cannot say, "I will compose poetry." The greatest poet even cannot say it: for the mind in creation is as a fading coal, which some invisible influence, like an inconstant wind, awakens to transitory brightness: this power arises from within, like the colour of a flower which fades and changes as it is developed, and the conscious portions of our natures are unprophetic either of its approach or its departure. Could this influence be durable in its original purity and force, it is impossible to predict the greatness of the results; but when composition begins, inspiration is already on the decline, and the most glorious poetry that has ever been communicated to the world is probably a feeble shadow of the original conceptions of the Poet. I appeal to the great poets of the present day, whether it be not an error to assert that the finest passages of poetry are produced by labour and study. The toil and the delay recommended by critics, can be justly interpreted to mean no more than a careful observation of the inspired moments, and an artificial connexion of the spaces between their suggestions by the intertexture of conventional expressions; a necessity only imposed by the limitedness of the poetical faculty itself; for Milton conceived the Paradise Lost as a whole before he executed it in portions. We have his own authority also for the Muse having "dictated" to him the "unpremeditated song," and let this be an answer to those who would allege the fifty-six various readings of the first line of the Orlando Furioso. Compositions so produced are to poetry what mosaic is to painting. This instinct and intuition of the poetical faculty is still more observable in the plastic and pictorial arts; a great statue or picture grows under the power of the artist as a child in the mother's womb; and the very mind which directs the hands in formation is incapable of accounting to itself for the origin, the gradations, or the media of the process.

Poetry is the record of the best and happiest moments of the happiest and best minds. We are aware of evanescent visitations of thought and feeling sometimes associated with place or person, sometimes regarding our own mind alone, and always arising unforeseen and departing unbidden, but elevating and delightful beyond all expression: so that even in the desire and the regret they leave, there cannot but be pleasure, participating as it does in the nature of its object. It is as it were the interpenetration of a diviner nature through our own; but its footsteps are like those of a wind over a sea, which the coming calm erases, and whose traces remain only, as on the wrinkled sand which paves it. These and corresponding conditions of being are experienced principally by those of the most delicate sensibility and the most enlarged imagination; and the state of mind produced by them is at war with every base desire. The enthusiasm of virtue, love, patriotism, and friendship, is essentially linked with such emotions; and whilst they last, self appears as what it is, an atom to a Universe. Poets are not only subject to these experiences as spirits of the most refined organization, but they can colour all that they combine with the evanescent hues of this ethereal world; a word, or a trait in the representation of a scene or a passion, will touch the enchanted chord, and reanimate, in those who have ever experienced these emotions, the sleeping, the cold, the buried image of the past. Poetry thus makes immortal all that is best and most beautiful in the world; it arrests the vanishing apparitions which haunt the interlunations of life, and veiling them, or in language or in form, sends them forth among mankind, bearing sweet news of kindred joy to those with whom their sisters abide—abide, because there is no portal of expression from

the caverns of the spirit which they inhabit into the universe of things. Poetry redeems from decay the visitations of the divinity in Man.

Poetry turns all things to loveliness; it exalts the beauty of that which is most beautiful, and it adds beauty to that which is most deformed; it marries exultation and horror, grief and pleasure, eternity and change; it subdues to union under its light yoke, all irreconcilable things. It transmutes all that it touches, and every form moving within the radiance of its presence is changed by wondrous sympathy to an incarnation of the spirit which it breathes; its secret alchemy turns to potable gold the poisonous waters which flow from death through life; it strips the veil of familiarity from the world, and lays bare the naked and sleeping beauty, which is the spirit of its forms.

All things exist as they are perceived; at least in relation to the percipient. "The mind is its own place, and of itself can make a Heaven of Hell, a Hell of Heaven." But poetry defeats the curse which binds us to be subjected to the accident of surrounding impressions. And whether it spreads its own figured curtain, or withdraws life's dark veil from before the scene of things, it equally creates for us a being within our being. It makes us the inhabitants of a world to which the familiar world is a chaos. It reproduces the common Universe of which we are portions and percipients, and it purges from our inward sight the film of familiarity which obscures from us the wonder of our being. It compels us to feel that which we perceive, and to imagine that which we know. It creates anew the universe, after it has been annihilated in our minds by the recurrence of impressions blunted by reiteration. It justifies the bold and true words of Tasso: *Non merita nome di creatore, se non Iddio ed il Poeta.*

A poet, as he is the author to others of the highest wisdom, pleasure, virtue and glory, so he ought personally to be the happiest, the best, the wisest, and the most illustrious of men. As to his glory, let Time be challenged to declare whether the fame of any other institutor of human life be comparable to that of a poet. That he is the wisest, the happiest, and the best, inasmuch as he is a poet, is equally incontrovertible: the greatest Poets have been men of the most spotless virtue, of the most consummate prudence, and, if we could look into the interior of their lives, the most fortunate of men: and the exceptions, as they regard those who possessed the poetic faculty in a high yet inferior degree, will be found on consideration to confirm rather than de-

37. Non merita . . . Poeta. "No one deserves the name of creator except God and the poet."

stroy the rule. Let us for a moment stoop to the arbitration of popular breath, and usurping and uniting in our own persons the incompatible characters of accuser, witness, judge, and executioner, let us without trial, testimony, or form, determine that certain motives of those who are "there sitting where we dare not soar," are reprehensible. Let us assume that Homer was a drunkard, that Virgil was a flatterer, that Horace was a coward, that Tasso was a madman, that Lord Bacon was a peculator, that Raphael was a libertine, that Spenser was a poet laureate. It is inconsistent with this division of our subject to cite living poets, but Posterity has done ample justice to the great names now referred to. Their errors have been weighed and found to have been dust in the balance; if their sins "were as scarlet, they are now white as snow": they have been washed in the blood of the mediator and the redeemer, Time. Observe in what a ludicrous chaos the imputations of real or fictitious crime have been confused in the contemporary calumnies against poetry and poets; consider how little is, as it appears—or appears, as it is; look to your own motives, and judge not, lest ye be judged.

Poetry, as has been said, differs in this respect from logic, that it is not subject to the control of the active powers of the mind, and that its birth and recurrence has [have] no necessary connexion with consciousness or will. It is presumptuous to determine that these are the necessary conditions of all mental causation, when mental effects are experienced insusceptible of being referred to them. The frequent recurrence of the poetical power, it is obvious to suppose, may produce in the mind an habit of order and harmony correlative with its own nature and with its effects upon other minds. But in the intervals of inspiration, and they may be frequent without being durable, a Poet becomes a man, and is abandoned to the sudden reflux of the influences under which others habitually live. But as he is more delicately organized than other men, and sensible to pain and pleasure, both his own and that of others, in a degree unknown to them, he will avoid the one and pursue the other with an ardour proportioned to this difference. And he renders himself obnoxious to calumny, when he neglects to observe the circumstances under which these objects of universal pursuit and flight have disguised themselves in one another's garments.

But there is nothing necessarily evil in this error, and thus cruelty, envy, revenge, avarice, and the passions purely evil, have never formed any portion of the popular imputations on the lives of poets.

I have thought it most favourable to the cause of truth to set down these remarks according to the order in which they were suggested to my mind, by a consideration of the subject itself, instead of following that of the treatise that excited me to make them public. Thus altogether devoid of the formality of a polemical reply; if the view they contain be just, they will be found to involve a refutation of the doctrines of the Four Ages of Poetry, so far at least as regards the first division of the subject. I can readily conjecture what should have moved the gall of the learned and intelligent author of that paper; I confess myself, like him, unwilling to be stunned by the Theseids of the hoarse Codri of the day. Bavius and Maevius undoubtedly are, as they ever were, insufferable persons. But it belongs to a philosophical critic to distinguish rather than confound.

The first part of these remarks has related to Poetry in its elements and principles; and it has been shewn, as well as the narrow limits assigned them would permit, that what is called poetry, in a restricted sense, has a common source with all other forms of order and of beauty, according to which the materials of human life are susceptible of being arranged, and which is Poetry in a universal sense.

The second part will have for its object an application of these principles to the present state of the cultivation of Poetry, and a defence of the attempt to idealize the modern forms of manners and opinions, and compel them into a subordination to the imaginative and creative faculty. For the literature of England, an energetic development of which has ever preceded or accompanied a great and free development of the national will, has arisen as it were from a new birth. In spite of the low-thoughted envy which would undervalue contemporary merit, our own will be a memorable age in intellectual achievements, and we live among such philosophers and poets as surpass beyond comparison any who have appeared since the last national struggle for civil and religious liberty. The most unfailing herald, companion, and follower of the awakening of a great people to work a beneficial change in opinion or institution, is Poetry. At such periods there is an accumulation of the power of communicating and receiving intense and impassioned conceptions respecting man and nature. The persons in whom this power resides, may often as far as regards many portions of their nature, have little apparent correspondence with that spirit of good of which they are the ministers. But even whilst they deny and abjure, they are yet compelled to serve, the Power which is seated on the throne of their own soul. It is impossible to read the compositions of the most celebrated writers of the present day without being startled with the electric life which burns within their words. They measure the circumference and sound the depths of human nature with a comprehensive and all-penetrating spirit, and they are themselves perhaps the most sincerely astonished at its manifestations; for it is less their spirit than the spirit of the age. Poets are the hierophants of an unapprehended inspiration; the mirrors of the gigantic shadows which futurity casts upon the present; the words which express what they understand not; the trumpets which sing to battle, and feel not what they inspire; the influence which is moved not, but moves. Poets are the unacknowledged legislators of the world.

LETTERS

Though his output was very large, Shelley was not the most charming letter-writer of the Romantic Period. He was usually too self-conscious to reveal himself as Keats or Lamb does. But he was capable of writing interestingly and charmingly. Of the following letters, the first was chosen to illustrate Shelley's Gothic-novel, horseplay youth; the second and third, to show how he reacted to the exile that produced his greatest poetry; and the fourth to suggest what he was thinking about just before the fatal sea voyage in July, 1822.

"AN EVENTFUL AND TERRIFIC MYSTERY"

To Edward Fergus Graham, London

Field Place [Horsham],
Monday [April 23, 1810]

My dear Graham,

At half after twelve do you be walking up and down the avenue of trees near Clapham Church, and when you see a Post Chaise stop at Mrs. Fenning's door, do you advance towards it, and without observing who are inside of it speak to them— An eventful and terrific mystery hangs over it—you are to change your name from Edward Fergus Graham to William Grove—prepare therefore for something extraordinary. There is more in a cucumber than you are aware of—in two cucumbers indeed; they are almost 2s. 6d. a piece—reflect well upon that!!!—All this is to be done on Tuesday [April 24], neither Elisbh, or myself cares what else you have to do.

36. Graham, an inmate of Shelley's household at Field Place, where his father was a factotum. He was educated in music. **39–40. Mrs. Fenning's door.** Church House School was attended by Shelley's younger sisters, Mary and Hellen. **49. Elisbh.** Elizabeth Shelley, the poet's eldest sister.

If Satan had never fallen
Hell had been made for thee!

Send two "Zastrozzis" to Sir J. Dashwood in Harley Street, directed to F. Dashwood, Esq.— Send one to Ransom Morland's to be directed to Mr. Chenevix.

I remain,
Yours devotedly,
P. B. Shelley.

N.B.—The avenue is composed of vegetable substances moulded in the form of trees called by the multitude Elm trees. Elisabeth calls them so, but they all lean as if the wind had given them a box on the ear, you therefore will know them— Stalk along the road towards them—and mind and keep yourself concealed as my Mother brings a blood-stained stiletto which she purposes to make you bathe in the life-blood of her enemy.

Never mind the Death-demons, and skeletons dripping with the putrefaction of the grave, that occasionally may blast your straining eyeball.— Persevere even though Hell and destruction should yawn beneath your feet.

Think of all this at the frightful hour of midnight, when the Hell-demon leans over your sleeping form and inspires those thoughts which eventually will lead you to the gates of destruction.

[signed by] Elisabeth Shelley.

Dear Graham,
Eliza. Shelley
the fiend of the Sussex solitudes shrieked in the wilderness at midnight—he thirsts for thy detestable gore, impious Fergus.—But the day of retribution will arrive.

H + D + means Hell Devil.

"THE ROMANS PLEASE ME MUCH"

To Thomas Love Peacock

Rome,
April 6, 1819.

My dear Peacock,

I sent you yesterday a long letter, all about antique Rome, which you had better keep for some leisure day. I received yours, and one of Hunt's

3. Zastrozzi, Shelley's Gothic novel. **45. Peacock,** one of Shelley's "unromantic" friends. He first met Shelley in Wales, and spent much time with him in travel and at Great Marlow, where they read Plato together; wrote *The Four Ages of Poetry,* which provoked *A Defence of Poetry;* gently satirized Shelley as Scythrop in his novel *Nightmare Abbey,* 1818; contributed valuable memoirs of Shelley.

yesterday.—So, you know the Boinvilles? I could not help considering Mrs. B., when I knew her, as the most admirable specimen of a human being I had ever seen. Nothing earthly ever appeared to be more perfect than her character and manners. It is improbable that I shall ever meet again the person whom I so much esteemed, and still admire. I wish however that when you see her, you would tell her that I have not forgotten her, nor any of the amiable circle once assembled round her; and that I desire such remembrances to her as an exile and a *Pariah* may be permitted to address to an acknowledged member of the community of mankind. I hear they dined at your lodgings. But no mention of A—— and his wife—where were they? Cornelia although so young when I saw her, gave indications of her mother's excellences; and, certainly less fascinating, is I doubt not, equally amiable and more sincere. It was hardly possible for a person of the extreme subtlety and delicacy of Mrs. Boinville's understanding and affections, to be quite sincere and constant.

I am all anxiety about your I. H. affair. There are few who will feel more hearty satisfaction at your success in this or any other enterprise than I shall. Pray let me have the earliest intelligence.

When shall I return to England? The Pythia has ascended the tripod, but she replies not. Our present plans—and I know not what can induce us to alter them—lead us back to Naples in a month or six weeks where it is almost decided that we should remain until the commencement of 1820. You may imagine, when we receive such letters as yours and Hunt's, what this resolution costs us—but these are not our only communications from England. My health is materially better. My spirits not the most brilliant in the world; but that we attribute to our solitary situation, and, though happy, how should I be lively? We see something of Italian society indeed: the Romans please me much, especially the women: who though totally devoid of every kind of information or culture of the imagination or affections or understanding, and, in this respect a kind of gentle savage—yet contrive to be interesting. Their extreme innocence and naïveté, the freedom and gentleness of their manners; the total absence of affectation makes an intercourse with them very like an intercourse with uncorrupted children, whom

1. **Boinvilles,** a charming family Shelley met in 1812, when he was cultivating vegetarianism under John Frank Newton, whose wife was Mrs. Boinville's sister. **14. A**——, probably Alfred, son of Mrs. Boinville. **15. Cornelia,** Turner, a daughter of Mrs. Boinville. Shelley was intimate with the two and their families at Bracknell. **22. I. H. affair.** Peacock was an applicant for a position with the East India House. **26. Pythia,** priestess and prophetess of Apollo at Delphi. She sat on the tripod to deliver her oracles.

they resemble in loveliness as well as simplicity. I have seen two women in society here of the highest beauty; their brows and lips, and the moulding of the face modelled with sculptural exactness, and the dark luxuriance of their hair floating over their fine complexions—and the lips—you must hear the commonplaces which escape from them before they cease to be dangerous. The only inferior part are the eyes, which though good and gentle, want the mazy depth of colour behind colour, with which the intellectual women of England and Germany entangle the heart in soul-inwoven labyrinths.

This is holy-week, and Rome is quite full. The Emperor of Austria is here, and Maria Louisa is coming. On their journey thro the other cities of Italy she was greeted with loud acclamations, and vivas of Napoleon. Idiots and slaves! Like the frogs in the fable because they are discontented with the log they call upon the Stork who devours them. Great festas and magnificent funzioni here, for which we can get no tickets; there are 5000 strangers in Rome, and only room for 500 at the celebration of the famous Miserere in the Sixtine Chapel, the only thing I regret we shall not be present at. After all, Rome is eternal; and were all that *is* extinguished, that which *has been*, the ruins and the sculptures, would remain, and Raffael and Guido be alone regretted of all that Christianity had suffered to spring forth from its dark and pernicious Chaos.

In the Square of St. Peter's there are about 300 fettered criminals at work, hoeing out the weeds that grow between the stones of the pavement. Their legs are heavily ironed, and some are chained two by two. They sit in long rows, hoeing out the weeds, dressed in party coloured clothes. Near them sit or saunter, groupes of soldiers, armed with loaded muskets. The iron discord of those innumerable chains clanks up into the sonorous air, and produces, contrasted with the musical dashing of the fountains, and the deep azure beauty of the sky, and the magnificence of the architecture around, a conflict of sensations allied to madness. It is the emblem of Italy: moral degradation contrasted with the glory of nature and the arts.

We see no English society here; it is not probable that we could if we desired it, and I am certain that we should find it insupportable. The manners of the rich English are wholly insupportable, and they assume pretensions which they would not venture upon in their own country. I am yet ignorant of the event of Hobhouse's election. I saw the last numbers were Lamb 4200; and Hobhouse, 3900—14th day. There is little hope. That mischievous Cobbet[t] has divided and weakened the interests of the popular party so that the factions who prey upon our country have been able to coalesce to its exclusion. The Newtons you have not seen. I am curious to know what kind of a girl Octavia becomes; she promised well. Tell H—— his Melpomene is in the Vatican, and that her attitude and drapery surpass if possible, the graces of her countenance.

My Prometheus Unbound is just finished, and in a month or two I shall send it. It is a drama with characters and mechanism of a kind yet unattempted; and I think the execution is better than any of my former attempts. By the bye have you seen Ollier? I never hear from him, and am ignorant whether some verses I sent him from Naples, entitled, I think, Lines on the Euganean hills, have reached him in safety or not. As to the Reviews, I suppose there is nothing but abuse; and this is not hearty or sincere enough to amuse me. As to the poem now printing, I lay no stress on it one way or the other. The concluding lines are natural.

I believe my dear Peacock that you wish us to come back to England. How is it possible? Health, competence, tranquillity—all these Italy permits, and England takes away. I am regarded by all who know or hear of me, except, I think, on the whole, five individuals as a rare prodigy of crime and pollution, whose look even might infect. This [is] a large computation, and I don't think I could mention more than you and Hogg and Hunt. Such is the spirit of the English abroad, as well as at home. These few compensate indeed, for all the rest, and if I were *alone* I should laugh, or if I were rich enough to do all things, which I shall never be. Pity me for my absence from those social enjoyments which England might afford me, and which I know so well how to appreciate. Still I shall return some fine morning, out of pure weakness of heart. . . .

My dear Peacock, most faithfully yours,
P. B. Shelley.

"ITALY IS . . . THE PARADISE OF EXILES"

To Thomas Medwin, Geneva

Florence,
Jan. 17, 1820.

My dear Medwin,
The winter at Florence has been, for the climate, unusually severe, and yet I imagine you must have suffered enough in Switzerland to make you regret

5. H——, Thomas Jefferson Hogg.   13. Ollier. Charles Ollier was Shelley's publisher.   19. poem now printing, "Rosalind and Helen."   48. Medwin was Shelley's cousin. The two were at Sion House Academy together.

that you did not come further South—At least I confidently expect that we shall see you in the Spring. We are fixed for the ensuing year in Tuscany, and you will always find me by addressing me at Leghorn—

Perhaps you belong to the tribe of the hopeless, and nothing shocks or surprises you in politics—I have enough of unrebuked hope remaining to be struck with horror at the proceedings in England. Yet I reflect, as a last consolation, that oppression which authorizes, often produces resistance—These are not times in which one has much spirit for writing Poetry, although there is a keen air in them that sharpens the wits of men and makes them imagine vividly even in the midst of despondence.

I daresay the lake before you is a plain of solid ice, bounded by the snowy hills, whose white mantles contrast with the aerial rose colour of the eternal glaciers—a scene more grand, yet like the recesses of the Antarctic circle—If your health allows you to skate, this plain is the floor of your Paradise, and the white world seems spinning backwards as you fly—The thaw may have arrived, or you may have departed, and this letter reach you in a very different scene—

This Italy, believe me, is a pleasant place, especially Rome and Naples. Tuscany is delightful eight months of the year; but nothing reconciles me to the slightest indication of winter: much less such infernal cold as my nerves have been racked upon for the last ten days—At Naples, all the worst is over in three weeks.—When you come hither, you must take up your abode with me, and I will give you all the experience which I have bought, at the usual market price, during the last year and an half residence in Italy.—

You used, I remember, to paint very well, and you were remarkable, if I do not mistake, for a peculiar taste in and knowledge of the *belle arti*—Italy is the place for you—the very place—the Paradise of exiles, the retreat of Pariahs—but I am thinking of myself rather than of you—

If you will be glad to see an old friend, who will be very glad to see you—if this is an inducement—come to Italy.

"THAT WILL BE DECIDED TOMORROW"

To Mary Wollstonecraft Shelley, Casa Magni

Pisa,
July 4, 1822.

My dearest Mary,
I have received both your letters, and shall attend to the instructions they convey. I did not think of

buying the *Bolivar;* Lord B. wishes to sell her, but I imagine would prefer ready money. I have as yet made no inquiries about houses near Pugnano—I have no moment of time to spare from Hunt's affairs; I am detained unwillingly here, and you will probably see Williams in the boat before me,—but that will be decided tomorrow.

Things are in the worst possible situation with respect to poor Hunt. I find Marianne in a desperate state of health, and on our arrival at Pisa sent for Vaccà. He decides that her case is hopeless, and that although it will be lingering, must inevitably end fatally. This decision he thought proper to communicate to Hunt; indicating at the same time, with great judgment and precision, the treatment necessary to be observed for availing himself of the chance of his being deceived. This intelligence has extinguished the last spark of poor Hunt's spirits, low enough before. The children are all well and much improved.

Lord Byron is at this moment on the point of leaving Tuscany. The Gambas have been exiled, and he declares his intention of following their fortunes. His first idea was to sail to America, which has been changed to Switzerland, then to Genoa, and last to Lucca.—Every body is in despair and every thing in confusion. Trelawny was on the point of sailing to Genoa for the purpose of transporting the *Bolivar* overland to the lake of Geneva, and had

already whispered in my ear his desire that I should not influence Lord Byron against this terrestrial navigation. He next received *orders* to weigh anchor and set sail for *Lerici.* He is now without instruction moody and disappointed. But it is the worst for poor Hunt, unless the present storm should blow over. He places his whole dependence upon this scheme of a Journal, for which every arrangement has been made and arrived with no other remnant of his £4[oo] than a debt of 60 crowns. Lord Byron must of course furnish the requisite funds at present, as I cannot; but he seems inclined to depart without the necessary explanations and arrangements due to such a situation as Hunt's. These, in spite of delicacy, I must procure; he offers him the copyright of the "Vision of Judgment" for the first number. This offer if sincere is *more* than enough to set up the journal, and, if sincere, will set everything right.

How are you, my best Mary? Write especially how is your health and how your spirits are, and whether you are not more reconciled to staying at Lerici, at least during the summer.

You have no idea how I am hurried and occupied; I have not a moment's leisure, but will write by next post. Ever, dearest Mary, Yours affectionately,

S.

I have found the translation of the "Symposium."

James Henry Leigh Hunt
1784-1859

When Isaac Hunt, a young Englishman sent to America to be educated, spoke the farewell oration on leaving college at Philadelphia, two young ladies fell in love with him. One of these, Mary Shewell, he afterward married. To the couple was born, at Southgate, near London, on October 19, 1784, a child whom they named James Henry Leigh Hunt, in honor of a young nobleman to whom the father had been tutor. The boy was sent to Christ's Hospital School some years after Lamb and Coleridge had left it but not too late to have two of their teachers. He rebelled against fagging, disliked the classics, and found surcease in the *Arabian Nights*, Chaucer, Spenser, Shakespeare, Milton, Thomson, and Gray. Like Lamb, he was prevented by his habit of stammering from winning a university scholarship, and he left school at the same age Lamb

had. Desultory reading, love-making, poetizing, and playgoing occupied him for a number of years.

At the age of twenty Hunt began his career as a prose writer by contributing a series of papers called "The Traveller" to a newspaper of the same name. Soon afterward, he began writing dramatic criticism and political articles for his brother John's paper, the *News.* At twenty-four he became editor of the *Examiner*, and for four years he conducted it successfully as a liberal journal. Meanwhile, he started a magazine, the *Reflector,* which during its short life published several of Lamb's essays. In 1812 he and his brother John were fined about $2,500 each and sentenced to jail for two years for publishing an article personally derogatory to the Prince Regent. Leigh Hunt bore his rather mild imprisonment cheerfully, with consolations from the society of some of the chief literary men of the age (Byron, Thomas Moore, Lamb, Hazlitt and others), spending much of his time reading Italian literature. His release was celebrated in a sonnet by John Keats (see page 315). In 1816 Hunt published *The Story of Rimini*, telling in fluent iambic pentameter couplets the story of Paolo and Francesca, from Dante. This poem, *The Feast of the Poets*, and several others were published in 1819 as *Poetical Works*. By this date Hunt had become the friend of four great poets— Wordsworth, Byron, Keats, and Shelley. Partly on account of these literary affiliations and partly on account of his politics, he was derided by the great reviews as chief of the Cockney School of Poetry. In his *Examiner* he had defended Shelley against the *Quarterly*. His *Indicator*, a periodical begun in 1819, was the first to recognize the genius of Keats. It published, too, some of Hunt's own charming light essays.

In 1822, as has already been noted, Hunt went to Italy to edit the *Liberal* for Byron and Shelley. After that unhappy venture, he returned in 1825 to England. His *Lord Byron and His Contemporaries*, 1828, with its unfavorable view of Byron's life and character, aroused the indignation of many people who thought Hunt showed bad taste in making revelations gained from Byron's confidence. Journalism, the writing of familiar essays, and criticism chiefly engaged his labors during the long remainder of his life. He died in 1859. Among his later publications were *Christianism (The Religion of the Heart)*, 1832; *Leigh Hunt's Journal*, 1834; *Imagination and Fancy*, 1844; *Wit and Humour*, 1846; *Men, Women, and Books*, 1847; *Autobiography*, 1850 and 1860; and *Table-Talk*, 1857.

Leigh Hunt is remembered today for four main reasons. First, he was a friend of poets greater than himself, encouraging them and defending them. Second, in *The Story of Rimini* he introduced a modified poetic form which Keats and others were to find splendidly adapted to storytelling. His short, simpler poems, such as "Abou ben Adhem," "Rondeau" (which is not really a rondeau), and "The Fish, the Man, and the Spirit," have "a personal accent" which still makes itself felt. In the third place, his familiar essays, though they did not achieve the distinction of Lamb's and Hazlitt's, are graceful and lively, and make good reading today. Finally, as a critic Hunt was almost unerring in his recognition of true poetical genius and extraordinarily felicitous in selecting passages illustrative of characteristic excellences. "Taste," he wrote, "is the maker of judgment." His own taste was supported by a fine capacity for clear and persuasive

exposition of critical principles. His "What Is Poetry?" remains one of the most attractive and understandable treatments of the Romantic theory of poetry. His friend Charles Lamb epitomized Hunt in a doggerel couplet:

"Wit, poet, prose-man, party-man, translator,
Hunt, your best title yet is *Indicator*."

from THE STORY OF RIMINI

Hunt's poem is founded on a passage in Dante's *Inferno*, where the tragic love of Paulo (as Hunt spells the name) and Francesca is "treated with imperial and immortal brevity." Hunt's telling of the story runs to over fifteen hundred lines of loosened iambic pentameter couplets varied by occasional triplets. The young Keats admired the poem.

Giovanni, the cold and haughty Lord of Rimini, sends his younger brother Paulo as his proxy to Ravenna, to marry the Princess Francesca for him and bring her back to Rimini. Together on their journey and afterward, Paulo and Francesca fall in love with each other, the climax of their passion occurring in the following passage, in which they read *Launcelot of the Lake* together in a vine-covered marble pavilion on the palace grounds. (In the sequel, Giovanni discovers their infatuation and forces Paulo to fight a duel with him. Unwilling to defend himself, Paulo throws himself on his brother's sword and is killed. Francesca dies of grief.)

from CANTO III

One day,—'twas on a summer afternoon,
When airs and gurgling brooks are best in tune,
And grasshoppers are loud, and day-work done,
And shades have heavy outlines in the sun,—
The princess came to her accustomed bower
To get her, if she could, a soothing hour;
Trying, as she was used, to leave her cares   510
Without, and slumberously enjoy the airs,
And the low-talking leaves, and that cool light
The vines let in, and all that hushing sight
Of closing wood seen through the opening door,
And distant plash of waters tumbling o'er,
And smell of citron blooms, and fifty luxuries more.

508. bower. Note that this rhyme word and three more ("cares," "light," and "sight") in the first ten lines have no punctuation mark or heavy pause after them. Note, too, that the sense runs on from one couplet to the next; in other words, that the couplet is not the mold of the thought. This is what is meant by loose or "run-on" couplet. Chaucer had written heroic couplet this way. From about the middle of the seventeenth century until the Romantic Period, however, poets who used heroic couplet tended to make the couplet the mold of the thought—one thought, one couplet. Hunt was among the first to loosen it up. Keats followed his example. **513. hushing,** an example of the liberties Hunt took with words.

She tried, as usual, for the trial's sake,
For even that diminished her heart-ache;
And never yet, how ill soe'er at ease,
Came she for nothing 'midst the flowers and
    trees. 520
Yet somehow or another, on that day
She seemed to feel too lightly borne away,—
Too much relieved,—too much inclined to draw
A careless joy from everything she saw,
And looking round her with a new-born eye,
As if some tree of knowledge had been nigh,
To taste of nature primitive and free,
And bask at ease in her heart's liberty.

Painfully clear those rising thoughts appeared,
With something dark at bottom that she feared; 530
And snatching from the fields her thoughtful look,
She reached o'er-head, and took her down a
    book,
And fell to reading with as fixed an air,
As though she had been wrapt since morning there.

'Twas Launcelot of the Lake, a bright romance,
That like a trumpet made young pulses dance. . . .

Ready she sat with one hand to turn o'er 571
The leaf, to which her thoughts ran on before,
The other propping her white brow, and throwing
Its ringlets out, under the skylight glowing.
So sat she fixed, and so observed was she
Of one, who at the door stood tenderly,—
Paulo,—who from a window seeing her
Go straight across the lawn, and guessing where,
Had thought she was in tears, and found, that
    day,
His usual efforts vain to keep away. 580
"May I come in?" said he;—it made her start,—
That smiling voice;—she coloured, pressed her
    heart
A moment, as for breath, and then with free
And usual tone said, "O yes,—certainly."
There's apt to be, at conscious times like these,
An affectation of a bright-eyed ease,
An air of something quite serene and sure,
As if to seem so, was to be, secure.
With this the lovers met, with this they spoke,
With this they sat down to the self-same book, 590

And Paulo, by degrees, gently embraced
With one permitted arm her lovely waist;
And both their cheeks, like peaches on a tree,
Leaned with a touch together, thrillingly;
And o'er the book they hung, and nothing said,
And every lingering page grew longer as they
    read.

As thus they sat, and felt with leaps of heart
Their colour change, they came upon the part
Where fond Geneura, with her flame long nurst,
Smiled upon Launcelot when he kissed her
    first:— 600
That touch, at last, through every fibre slid;
And Paulo turned, scarce knowing what he did,
Only he felt he could no more dissemble,
And kissed her, mouth to mouth, all in a tremble.
Sad were those hearts, and sweet was that long
    kiss:
Sacred be love from sight, whate'er it is.
The world was all forgot, the struggle o'er,
Desperate the joy.—That day they read no more.

SONNETS

THE NILE

In February, 1808, Hunt, Keats, and Shelley engaged in a sonnet competition on the subject of the Nile. This was Hunt's entry.

It flows through old hushed Egypt and its sands,
  Like some grave mighty thought threading a
    dream,
  And times and things, as in that vision, seem
Keeping along it their eternal stands,—
Caves, pillars, pyramids, the shepherd bands
  That roamed through the young world, the glory
    extreme
  Of high Sesostris, and that southern beam,
The laughing queen that caught the world's great
    hands.

Then comes a mightier silence, stern and strong,
As of a world left empty of its throng, 10
  And the void weighs on us; and then we wake,
And hear the fruitful stream lapsing along
  'Twixt villages, and think how we shall take
  Our own calm journey on for human sake.

---

521. **Yet somehow or another,** an example of Hunt's colloquial diction. Note "May I come in?" (l. 581), the reply, "O yes,—certainly" (l. 584), and "There's apt to be" (l. 585). Such expressions as these and "both their cheeks, like peaches on a tree" let Hunt in for the ridicule of the reviewers. They were imitated by Keats in his early poetry. What is the present-day attitude toward colloquialisms in poetry?

599. **Geneura,** Guinevere. 7. **Sesostris,** a mythical king of Egypt. 8. **queen,** Cleopatra. "Leigh Hunt's finest and most famous line."—Arthur Symons. "A re-discovery of a cadence lost for centuries."—Saintsbury. **world's great hands.** For a time Cleopatra was Julius Caesar's mistress.

ON A LOCK OF MILTON'S HAIR

It lies before me there, and my own breath
   Stirs its thin outer threads, as though beside
   The living head I stood in honoured pride,
Talking of lovely things that conquer death.
Perhaps he pressed it once, or underneath
   Ran his fine fingers, when he leant, blank-eyed,
   And saw, in fancy, Adam and his bride
With their rich locks, or his own Delphic wreath.

There seems a love in hair, though it be dead.
It is the gentlest, yet the strongest thread   10
   Of our frail plant,—a blossom from the tree
Surviving the proud trunk:—as though it said,
   Patience and Gentleness is Power. In me
Behold affectionate eternity.

ABOU BEN ADHEM

Abou Ben Adhem (may his tribe increase!)
Awoke one night from a deep dream of peace,
And saw, within the moonlight in his room,
Making it rich, and like a lily in bloom,
An angel writing in a book of gold:—
Exceeding peace had made Ben Adhem bold,
And to the presence in the room he said,
"What writest thou?"—The vision raised its head,
And with a look made of all sweet accord,
Answered, "The names of those who love the
   Lord."   10
"And is mine one?" said Abou. "Nay, not so,"
Replied the angel. Abou spoke more low,
But cheerly still; and said, "I pray thee then,
Write me as one that loves his fellow-men."

    The angel wrote, and vanished. The next night
It came again with a great wakening light,
And showed the names whom love of God had
   blessed,
And lo! Ben Adhem's name led all the rest.

THE GLOVE AND THE LIONS

King Francis was a hearty king, and loved a royal
   sport,
And one day, as his lions fought, sat looking on the
   court;
The nobles filled the benches, and the ladies in
   their pride,

8. **Delphic wreath,** the poet's fame (from Delphos, whence came Apollo, god of poetry). 1. **King Francis,** Francis I, King of France, 1515–47.

And 'mongst them sat the Count de Lorge, with
   one for whom he sighed:
And truly 'twas a gallant thing to see that crowning show,
Valour and love, and a king above, and the royal
   beasts below.

Ramped and roared the lions, with horrid laughing
   jaws;
They bit, they glared, gave blows like beams, a
   wind went with their paws;
With wallowing might and stifled roar they rolled
   on one another,
Till all the pit with sand and mane was in a thunderous smother;   10
The bloody foam above the bars came whisking
   through the air;
Said Francis then, "Faith, gentlemen, we're better
   here than there."

De Lorge's love o'erheard the King, a beauteous
   lively dame
With smiling lips and sharp bright eyes, which
   always seemed the same;
She thought, the Count my lover is brave as brave
   can be;
He surely would do wondrous things to show his
   love of me;
King, ladies, lovers, all look on; the occasion is
   divine;
I'll drop my glove, to prove his love; great glory
   will be mine.

She dropped her glove, to prove his love, then
   looked at him and smiled;
He bowed, and in a moment leaped among the
   lions wild;   20
The leap was quick, return was quick, he has regained his place,
Then threw the glove, but not with love, right in
   the lady's face.
"By God," said Francis, "rightly done!" and he
   rose from where he sat:
"No love," quoth he, "but vanity, sets love a task
   like that."

RONDEAU

One story of the occasion of the poem is that it was inspired by Jane Welch Carlyle's kissing Hunt when he
brought news that her husband's *Frederick the Great* had
been accepted for publication; another, that it "was in-

23. **"rightly done!"** Compare Browning's treatment of the lady's motive in "The Glove."

spired by Mrs. Carlyle, who was herself inspired to the act by hearing his [Hunt's] sonnet 'On a Lock of Milton's Hair.' " The poem is not really a rondeau, which is supposed to have fifteen lines (the ninth and fifteenth being a short refrain), rhyming aabba, aabc, aabbac.

Jenny kissed me when we met,
 Jumping from the chair she sat in;
Time, you thief, who love to get
 Sweets into your list, put that in:
Say I'm weary, say I'm sad,
Say that health and wealth have missed me,
Say I'm growing old, but add,
 Jenny kissed me.

THE FISH, THE MAN, AND
THE SPIRIT

The poem reminds one of the "flyting" in *Beowulf*. It "seems to touch and seize and communicate a strange, cold, inhuman imagination, as if the very element of water entered into communion with the mind . . . the poetry, which begins with a strange familiarity, ends with a strangeness wholly of elemental wonder. There Leigh Hunt speaks the language of poetry and with a personal accent."—Arthur Symons, *The Romantic Movement in English Poetry*, Dutton, 1909.

To a Fish

You strange, astonished-looking, angle-faced,
 Dreary-mouthed, gaping wretches of the sea,
 Gulping salt-water everlastingly,
Cold-blooded, though with red your blood be graced,
And mute, though dwellers in the roaring waste;
 And you, all shapes beside, that fishy be,—
 Some round, some flat, some long, all devilry,
Legless, unloving, infamously chaste:—

O scaly, slippery, wet, swift, staring wights,
 What is't ye do? What life lead? eh, dull goggles?
How do ye vary your vile days and nights?   11
 How pass your Sundays? Are ye still but joggles
In ceaseless wash? Still nought but gapes and bites, 10
 And drinks, and stares, diversified with boggles?

A Fish Answers

Amazing monster! that, for aught I know,
 With the first sight of thee didst make our race
 For ever stare! O flat and shocking face,
Grimly divided from the breast below!
Thou that on dry land horribly dost go
 With a split body and most ridiculous pace,   20
 Prong after prong, disgracer of all grace,
Long-useless-finned, haired, upright, unwet, slow!

O breather of the unbreathable, sword-sharp air,
 How canst exist? How bear thyself, thou dry
And dreary sloth? What particle canst share
 Of the only blessèd life, the watery?
I sometimes see of ye an actual *pair*
 Go by! linked fin by fin! most odiously.

The Fish Turns into a Man, and Then into a Spirit, and Again Speaks

Indulge thy smiling scorn, if smiling still,
 O man! and loathe, but a sort of love;   30
 For difference must its use by difference prove,
And, in sweet clang, the spheres with music fill.
One of the spirits am I, that at his will
 Live in what'er has life—fish, eagle, dove—
 No hate, no pride, beneath nought, nor above,
A visitor of the rounds of God's sweet skill.

Man's life is warm, glad, sad, 'twixt loves and graves,
 Boundless in hope, honoured with pangs austere,
Heaven-gazing; and his angel-wings he craves:—
 The fish is swift, small-needing, vague yet clear,
A cold, sweet silver life, wrapped in round waves,
 Quickened with touches of transporting fear.   42

PROEM TO SELECTION FROM
KEATS'S POETRY

KEATS was a born poet of the most poetical kind. All his feelings came to him through a poetical medium, or were speedily coloured by it. He enjoyed a jest as heartily as any one, and sympathized with the lowliest commonplace; but the next minute his thoughts were in a garden of enchantment, with nymphs, and fauns, and shapes of exalted humanity;

"Elysian beauty, melancholy grace."

It might be said of him, that he never beheld an oak-tree without seeing the Dryad. His fame may now forgive the critics who disliked his politics, and did not understand his poetry. Repeated editions of him in England, France, and America, attest its triumphant survival of all obloquy; and there can be no doubt that he has taken a permanent station among the British poets, of a very high, if not thoroughly mature, description.

Keats's early poetry, indeed, partook plentifully of the exuberance of youth; and even in most of his

8. "Elysian . . . grace." See Wordsworth's "Laodamia," l. 91.

later, his sensibility, sharpened by mortal illness, tended to a morbid excess. His region is "a wilderness of sweets"—flowers of all hue, and "weeds of glorious feature,"—where, as he says, the luxuriant soil brings

"The pipy hemlock to strange overgrowth."

But there also is the "rain-scented eglantine," and bushes of May-flowers, with bees, and myrtle, and bay,—and endless paths into forests haunted with the loveliest as well as gentlest beings; and the gods live in the distance, amid notes of majestic thunder. I do not need to say that no "surfeit" is ever there; but I do, that there is no end to the "nectared sweets." In what other English poet (however superior to him in other respects) are you so *certain* of never opening a page without lighting upon the loveliest imagery and the most eloquent expressions? Name one. Compare any succession of their pages at random, and see if the young poet is not sure to present his stock of beauty; crude it may be, in many instances; too indiscriminate in general; never, perhaps, thoroughly perfect in cultivation; but there it is, exquisite of its kind, and filling envy with despair. He died at five-and-twenty; he had not revised his earlier works, nor given his genius its last pruning. His Endymion, in resolving to be free from all critical trammels, had no versification; and his last noble fragment, Hyperion, is not faultless,—but it is nearly so. The Eve of St. Agnes betrays morbidity only in one instance (noticed in the comment). Even in his earliest productions, which are to be considered as those of youth just emerging from boyhood, are to be found passages of as masculine a beauty as ever were written. Witness the *Sonnet on reading Chapman's Homer*,—epical in the splendour and dignity of its images, and terminating with the noblest Greek simplicity. Among his finished productions, however, of any length, the *Eve of St. Agnes* still appears to me the most delightful and complete specimen of his genius. It stands mid-way between his most sensitive ones (which, though of rare beauty, occasionally sink into feebleness) and the less generally characteristic majesty of the fragment of *Hyperion*. Doubtless his greatest poetry is to be found in Hyperion; and had he lived, there is as little doubt he would have written chiefly in that strain; rising superior to those languishments of love which made the critics so angry, and which they might so easily have pardoned at his time of life. But the Eve of St. Agnes had already bid most of them adieu,—exquisitely loving as it is. It is young, but full-grown poetry of the rarest description;

31-32. in the comment. See stanza 25, l. 8.

graceful as the beardless Apollo; glowing and gorgeous with the colours of romance. I have therefore reprinted the whoe of it in the present volume, together with the comment alluded to in the Preface; especially as, in addition to felicity of treatment, its subject is in every respect a happy one, and helps to "paint" this our bower of "poetry with delight." Melancholy, it is true, will "break in" when the reader thinks of the early death of such a writer; but it is one of the benevolent provisions of nature, that all good things tend to pleasure in the recollection; when the bitterness of their loss is past, their own sweetness embalms them.

"A thing of beauty is a joy for ever."

While writing this paragraph, a hand-organ out-of-doors has been playing one of the mournfullest and loveliest airs of Bellini—another genius who died young. The sound of music always gives a feeling either of triumph or tenderness to the state of mind in which it is heard: in this instance it seemed like one departed spirit come to bear testimony to another, and to say how true indeed may be the union of sorrowful and sweet recollections.

Keats knew the youthful faults of his poetry as well as any man, as the reader may see by the preface to Endymion, and its touching though manly acknowledgement of them to critical candour. I have this moment read it again, after a lapse of years, and have been astonished to think how anybody could answer such an appeal to the mercy of strength, with the cruelty of weakness. All the good for which Mr. Gifford pretended to be zealous, he might have effected with pain to no one, and glory to himself; and therefore all the evil he mixed with it was of his own making. But the secret at the bottom of such unprovoked censure is exasperated inferiority. Young poets, upon the whole,—at least very young poets,—had better not publish at all. They are pretty sure to have faults; and jealousy and envy are as sure to find them out, and wreak upon them their own disappointments. The critic is often an unsuccessful author, almost always an inferior one to a man of genius, and possesses his sensibility neither to beauty nor to pain. If he does,—if by any chance he is a man of genius himself (and such things have been), sure and certain will be his regret, some day, for having given pains which he might have turned into noble pleasures; and nothing will console him but that very charity towards himself, the grace of which can only be secured to us by our having denied it to no one.

Let the student of poetry observe, that in all the luxury of the Eve of St. Agnes there is nothing of the conventional craft of artificial writers; no heaping up of words or similes for their own sakes or the rhyme's sake; no gaudy common-places; no borrowed airs of earnestness; no tricks of inversion; no substitution of reading or of ingenious thoughts for feeling or spontaneity; no irrelevancy or unfitness of any sort. All flows out of sincerity and passion. The writer is as much in love with the heroine as his hero is; his description of the painted window, however gorgeous, has not an untrue or superfluous word; and the only speck of fault in the whole poem arises from an excess of emotion.

John Keats
1795–1821

The facts about John Keats's early life illustrate the truism that Fortune often lavishes the gift of genius without regard for social circumstances. His father, Thomas Keats, had come from the Land's End country of Cornwall to London, got a job in the livery stable of the Swan and Hoop Inn, and married the daughter of the innkeeper, Frances Jennings. John, the first child, was born on October 29 (or 30), 1795. Three other children—George, Thomas, and Frances (Fanny)—were to be happily associated with him and to be affectionately recorded in his poems and letters, as was Georgiana, George's wife. At the age of eight John was sent to school at Enfield, a suburb ten miles north of London. About a year later, his father, while returning from a visit to the school, was killed by a fall from his horse. The death of the mother, from tuberculosis, terminated the boy's schooling when he was fifteen.

The school at Enfield, though obscure, was sound and thorough. The master, the Reverend John Clarke, and his son and assistant, Charles Cowden Clarke, were competent and sympathetic. The latter, only eight years Keats's senior, was young enough to become a stimulating and affectionate friend as well as teacher. Charles Cowden Clarke's *Autobiography* gives a charming account of their relations and of the boy's mind and character. Keats was, says Clarke, a favorite in the school. He was bright and studious, fond of history, music, and literature, and fascinated by classical mythology, which he read in such books as Tooke's *Pantheon* and Lemprière's *Classical Dictionary*. "Not the less beloved was he," adds Clarke, "for having a highly pugnacious spirit. . . . His passions at times were almost ungovernable . . . not merely [was he] the 'favourite of all,' like a pet prize-fighter, for his terrier courage; but his high-mindedness, his utter unconsciousness of a mean motive, his placability, his generosity, wrought so general a feeling in his behalf, that I never heard a word of disapproval from anyone who had known him." Clarke and others describe Keats as small in stature (even when grown he was little more than five feet in height), but well-knit, agile, and vigorous. His sister-in-law, Georgiana, wrote: "His eyes were dark brown, large, soft, and expressive, and his hair a golden red." As boy and man, he had a keen sense of humor. Once, attending a bearbaiting, he relished the antics of the low-life spectators. On another occasion he described with Hazlittean gusto the knockout punch of a lightweight prize fight.

Soon after his mother's death, Keats was taken out of school by his guardian, Mr. Richard Abbey, and apprenticed to the apothecary-surgeon Mr. Thomas Hammond, who lived at Edmonton, two miles from Enfield. Keats continued his medical studies at Guy's and St. Thomas's hospitals in London and passed his examinations for license to practice.

Both while at Edmonton and in London, he kept up his friendship with Charles Cowden Clarke, and began to explore those realms of gold which he had skirted in school. He had learned to love Virgil. When he was fifteen, Clarke read Spenser's *Epithalamion* to him one day in an old arbor. "That night," says Clarke, "he took away with him the *Faery Queen* and went through it . . . as a young horse would through a spring meadow—ramping . . . singled out epithets . . . hoisted himself up and looked burly and dominant, as he said—'What an image that is—"Sea-shouldering whales."'" His first known poem was "Imitation of Spenser." In 1816 he published his first sonnet, on Leigh Hunt's release from prison. Not long afterward, he visited Hunt and there met Shelley and another young man who was to be one of his best friends, John Hamilton Reynolds, poet and lawyer. During the same period he formed literary acquaintanceships with Hazlitt and Lamb. Early one morning, after he and Clarke had sat up all night reading the Elizabethan poet Chapman's translation of Homer, he left on Clarke's breakfast table the great sonnet recording that adventure. Under Hunt's influence he composed two fairly long poems, "I Stood Tip-Toe" and "Sleep and Poetry," expressing his ideas on the nature of poetry, its themes, its aim, and its function in human life. In 1817, with Shelley's help, he published these and others in a little volume entitled *Poems*.

In 1817, too, his artist friends Joseph Severn and B. R. Haydon showed him the Elgin Marbles, fragments of ancient Greek sculpture, and he wrote two sonnets expressing the sensations of that experience. Plastic art and his study of Wordsworth, Shakespeare, and Milton and other seventeenth-century poets were working upon his imagination. Going down to the Isle of Wight in the spring, he began *Endymion*, a long metrical romance in the free-running couplets he had learned from Hunt, treating the love of a shepherd prince for Diana, the moon goddess, as a type of the soul's search for ideal beauty. Unlike Shelley, who had treated a similar theme in *Alastor*, Keats showed that in order to succeed the hero must sympathize with others along his way and approach ideal beauty through love of a human being. While *Endymion* was still in progress, he wrote *Isabella*, another romance, relating in ottava rima a Boccaccian story of the death of love and beauty. Late in December he met Wordsworth, to whom he had owed much for the ethics of *Endymion*, and was with him frequently for a while thereafter. In April, 1818, he published *Endymion*. Continuing his study of the poets, with the addition of Dante, he began a summer walking tour of northern England, Scotland, and Ireland. A severe cold forced him to return sooner than he had expected. In August *Endymion* and its author were brutally attacked by *Blackwood's Magazine;* in September, they were ridiculed by the *Quarterly Review*. Contrary to popular belief, Keats was not snuffed out by an article. He took the attacks sensibly and bravely, and set about writing a greater poem, *Hyperion*. Toward the end of the year he underwent two profound emotional experiences—watching his brother Tom die of tuberculosis, and falling desperately in love with Fanny Brawne.

Though he was harassed by symptoms of tuberculosis, by poverty, and by despair in his love, the first nine months of 1819 were the period of Keats's noblest work. Besides his great odes, he composed his most beautiful verse romances. These were published, with the romance of 1818, in *Lamia, Isabella, The Eve of St. Agnes and Other Poems,* 1820, his third

and last volume. Throughout the remainder of 1819 and the spring and summer of 1820, Keats was steadily losing his fight with disease. In September, with his faithful friend Severn, he began a sorrowful search for health in Italy. They stopped at Rome. There, in the house by the Old Spanish Stairs, he died on February 23, 1821, aged twenty-five years, three months, and twenty-six days. He was buried in the Protestant cemetery near the pyramidal tomb of the ancient Roman emperor Cestius. For his epitaph he had dictated: "Here lies one whose name was writ in water." But he had also said, simply and proudly, that he would be "among the English poets."

Keats's poetical development is like the unrolling of one of those pageants of the seasons—pictures and music—that he and his master Spenser loved to describe. "I Stood Tip-Toe" shyly pipes the coming year, "Sleep and Poetry" paints the tender immaturity of April, and *Endymion* revels in the luxuries of late spring. *Isabella* is "languid June." "The Eve of St. Agnes," for all the bone-piercing cold of its chapel scene and fairy storm, is the ripe midsummer of the poet's art. "La Belle Dame sans Merci" and "Lamia" are fevered August, bright and hard and searing. Last is "Autumn," mellow Autumn, an untroubled recording of a moment of serene and perfect beauty, a complete surrender to Nature's mood, an acquiescent sigh in answer to the whisper of death. "Music wrung from the transience of lovely things runs like a monotone through the 1820 volume, but in different keys." [1] It runs through the great odes—"Psyche," "Indolence," "Grecian Urn," "To a Nightingale," "Melancholy," and "Autumn." It is present in many of the sixty-one sonnets, as in "Bright Star." It is dominant in the three romances written between April, 1818, and September, 1819. Behind these story-poems lies the great tradition of romantic storytelling, from Boccaccio, Spenser, and Shakespeare to Coleridge, Scott, and Byron. Each poem is in a different verse form, mood, and musical key. Each is the essence of romance in its peculiar kind. *Isabella*, 1818, in ottava rima, moans syllables of woe over frustrated love. "The Eve of St. Agnes," January, 1819, in Spenserian stanzas, sings a paean of youthful love triumphant in a world of heartless pomp, hate, cruelty, and death. The ballad "La Belle Dame sans Merci," treating the "wasting power of love" and the bareness of life after Romance has fled, introduces the mood and the theme of "Lamia," July-August, 1819. In the bright, nervous couplets

[1] Ernest de Sélincourt, Introduction to *The Poems of John Keats*, London, 1926.

suggested by a rereading of Dryden, "Lamia" is a sorrowful, disillusioned questioning of passion and romance, a troubled searching after truth.

Several of Keats's best poems and letters, scattered through his writing career, are mainly about poetry itself. In "I Stood Tip-Toe," "Sleep and Poetry," *Endymion* (I, ll. 777 ff.), incidentally in the odes, and, finally, in *The Vision of Hyperion* (a reworking of *Hyperion*), he gives a progressively maturing account of the themes of poetry and of its part in human life. First is nature, maker of poets, "the realm of Flora and old Pan," the inexhaustible source of sensations. The poet is one "whose strenuous tongue can burst Joy's grape against his palate fine." Closely related to the delights of nature that he may experience are ancient myths and lovely tales, "a flowery band to bind us to the earth." These are among the earliest forms of man's poetic response to the beauty of nature. Higher than these are "the agonies, the strife Of human hearts"— passion, heroic endeavor, tragedy, "the fierce dispute Betwixt damnation and impassioned clay." But beyond these there is an "ever-fleeting music." The "crown of life" is love and friendship; yet human love and friendship, like the beauty of nature, are but types of a higher reality. For the apprehension and enjoyment of these delights not merely fine senses are requisite, but imagination is indispensable. Imagination works upon the harvest of the senses and transmutes it. The imaginative vision, though based on realities sensuously experienced, is superior to material actuality. "What the imagination seizes as beauty must be truth—whether it existed before or not." Poetry, a blend of sensuous enjoyments transmuted by imagination, should "sooth the cares, and lift the thoughts of man." The true poet "pours out a balm upon the world."

Thus, often concealed by its rich and easily perceived sensuousness, there is a serious intellectual content in Keats's best poetry. "I Stood Tip-Toe" is more than a "posey," "Sleep and Poetry" more than a "Silent entangler of a beauty's tresses," *Endymion* more than a lovely tale, "The Eve of St. Agnes" more than an opulent romance of young love. The "Ode to Psyche" makes us feel that in the beauty of an old myth there is a refuge, "a rosy sanctuary" of the soul from a troubled world. The "Ode on a Grecian Urn" leads us to a perception of the truth, represented by the antique scenes depicted, that the eternal miracle of great art lies in its power to capture beauty and fix it in forms that will forever stir the beholder's or the hearer's imagination in the way the original experience stirred the artist's. In the half-sorrowful, half-glad words of consolation to the youth who will never kiss the girl, to the trees that will never come to fruit, to the piper whose melody will never be sounded, the poet suggests the superiority of art to life because of its changeless record of life's lovely moments. Yet in his recognition of the coldness of this changeless perfection, of the everlasting desolation of that little Greek town whose inhabitants will never return home from the sacrifice, he honestly admits a limitation in response to art that we all feel. Similarly, in "Ode to a Nightingale," though the bird's song, type of all poetry, may lift us for a little while out of this sad and transitory life, may bring us for a moment under the spell of beauty that was not born for death, yet it sinks at last to the word "Forlorn," which sorrowfully tolls us back to our sole selves. It is this search among transient human joys and fading earthly beauties for something that endures, even though we do not, this thrill of triumph in finding it in ideal beauty, this honest admission of our incompleteness in accepting the consolations of ideal beauty, but this dauntless faith in ideal beauty as the greatest good men can know—it is these that make Keats's thought as great as the music and the imagery that convey it.

EARLY SONNETS

Like this and the following five, Keats's early sonnets (1817 volume) were written in the Petrarchan (Italian) form; most of the later, beginning with "When I Have Fears," coming some pages after this group, in the Shakespearean (English) form.

WRITTEN ON THE DAY THAT MR. LEIGH HUNT LEFT PRISON

What though, for showing truth to flattered state,
  Kind Hunt was shut in prison, yet has he,
  In his immortal spirit, been as free
As the sky-searching lark, and as elate.
Minion of grandeur! think you he did wait?
  Think you he naught but prison walls did see,
  Till, so unwilling, thou unturn'dst the key?
Ah, no! far happier, nobler was his fate!
In Spenser's halls he strayed, and bowers fair,
  Culling enchanted flowers; and he flew   10
With daring Milton through the fields of air:
  To regions of his own genius true
Took happy flights. Who shall his fame impair
  When thou art dead, and all thy wretched crew?

KEEN, FITFUL GUSTS ARE WHISPERING HERE
AND THERE

Keen, fitful gusts are whispering here and there
   Among the bushes half leafless, and dry;
   The stars look very cold about the sky,
And I have many miles on foot to fare.
Yet feel I little of the cool bleak air,
   Or of the dead leaves rustling drearily,
   Or of those silver lamps that burn on high,
Or of the distance from home's pleasant lair:
For I am brimfull of the friendliness
   That in a little cottage I have found;   10
Of fair-haired Milton's eloquent distress,
   And all his love for gentle Lycid drowned;
Of lovely Laura in her light green dress,
   And faithful Petrarch gloriously crowned.

TO ONE WHO HAS BEEN LONG IN CITY PENT

To one who has been long in city pent,
   'Tis very sweet to look into the fair
   And open face of heaven,—to breathe a prayer
Full in the smile of the blue firmament.
Who is more happy, when, with heart's content,
   Fatigued he sinks into some pleasant lair
   Of wavy grass, and reads a debonair
And gentle tale of love and languishment?
Returning home at evening, with an ear
   Catching the notes of Philomel,—an eye   10
Watching the sailing cloudlet's bright career,
   He mourns that day so soon has glided by:
E'en like the passage of an angel's tear
   That falls through the clear ether silently.

ON FIRST LOOKING INTO CHAPMAN'S HOMER

Note the images of immensity with which Keats interprets his experience of discovering Homer: the heavens
and a new planet, the ocean and the sky (Cortez silhou-
etted against both).

Much have I travelled in the realms of gold,
   And many goodly states and kingdoms seen;
   Round many western islands have I been
Which bards in fealty to Apollo hold.
Oft of one wide expanse had I been told
   That deep-browed Homer ruled as his demesne;
   Yet did I never breathe its pure serene
Till I heard Chapman speak out loud and bold:

Then felt I like some watcher of the skies
   When a new planet swims into his ken;   10
Or like stout Cortez when with eagle eyes
   He stared at the Pacific—and all his men
Looked at each other with a wild surmise—
   Silent, upon a peak in Darien.

ADDRESSED TO HAYDON

Keats met Haydon late in 1816. See Haydon's "The
Immortal Dinner," page 368.

Great spirits now on earth are sojourning;
   He of the cloud, the cataract, the lake,
   Who on Helvellyn's summit, wide awake,
Catches his freshness from Archangel's wing:
He of the rose, the violet, the spring,
   The social smile, the chain for Freedom's sake:
   And lo!—whose stedfastness would never take
A meaner sound than Raphael's whispering.
And other spirits there are standing apart
   Upon the forehead of the age to come;   10
These, these will give the world another heart,
   And other pulses. Hear ye not the hum
Of mighty workings?—
   Listen awhile ye nations, and be dumb.

ON THE GRASSHOPPER AND CRICKET

This sonnet was written as the result of a challenge
from Leigh Hunt. It is anticipative of "Ode to a Nightingale" (compare stanza 7).

The poetry of earth is never dead:
   When all the birds are faint with the hot sun,
   And hide in cooling trees, a voice will run
From hedge to hedge about the new-mown mead;
That is the Grasshopper's—he takes the lead
   In summer luxury,—he has never done
   With his delights; for when tired out with fun
He rests at ease beneath some pleasant weed.
The poetry of earth is ceasing never:
   On a lone winter evening, when the frost   10
   Has wrought a silence, from the stove there
      shrills
The Cricket's song, in warmth increasing ever,
   And seems to one in drowsiness half lost,
   The Grasshopper's among some grassy hills.

from SLEEP AND POETRY

Composed (autumn and winter of 1816) in large part
at Hunt's house, the poem is an exemplification and a

---

4. many miles. Keats was living in London at the time,
frequently visiting Hunt in the Vale of Health, Hampstead.
11–14. Milton . . . Petrarch, other adventures in reading.
To One Who . . . **10. Philomel,** the nightingale. *On First
. . .* **1. realms of gold,** classical literature. **3. western islands,** European literature of a later date than the classical
age. **6. demesne,** possession. **8. Chapman.** George Chapman's *Iliad* was published in 1611, his *Odyssey* in 1614.

11. Cortez, a mistake for Balboa. Keats had seen Titian's
picture of Cortez "with eagle eyes." *Addressed . . . .* **2–4.
He of the cloud . . . wing,** Wordsworth. **5–8. He of the
rose . . . whispering,** Leigh Hunt.

defense of Hunt's new theory of diction and versification (see the notes on *The Story of Rimini*). The most significant portions, here included, contain Keats's "Ten years" poetic program (ll. 96–162), his adverse criticism of tendencies in English poetry during the Neoclassical period (ll. 162–206), and his plea for the return to nature and imaginative freedom that Wordsworth and others (Byron excepted) had begun (ll. 206–47). Note Keats's conception of the function of poetry (ll. 246–47).

O Poesy! for thee I hold my pen
That am not yet a glorious denizen
Of thy wide heaven—Should I rather kneel
Upon some mountain-top until I feel   50
A glowing splendour round about me hung,
And echo back the voice of thine own tongue?
O Poesy! for thee I grasp my pen
That am not yet a glorious denizen
Of thy wide heaven; yet, to my ardent prayer,
Yield from thy sanctuary some clear air,
Smoothed for intoxication by the breath
Of flowering bays, that I may die a death
Of luxury, and my young spirit follow
The morning sun-beams to the great Apollo   60
Like a fresh sacrifice; or, if I can hear
The o'erwhelming sweets, 'twill bring to me the fair
Visions of all places: a bowery nook
Will be elysium—an eternal book
Whence I may copy many a lovely saying
About the leaves, and flowers—about the playing
Of nymphs in woods, and fountains; and the shade
Keeping a silence round a sleeping maid;
And many a verse from so strange influence
That we must ever wonder how, and whence   70
It came. Also imaginings will hover
Round my fire-side, and haply there discover
Vistas of solemn beauty, where I'd wander
In happy silence, like the clear Meander
Through its lone vales; and where I found a spot
Of awfuller shade, or an enchanted grot,
Or a green hill o'erspread with chequered dress
Of flowers, and fearful from its loveliness,
Write on my tablets all that was permitted,
All that was for our human senses fitted.   80
Then the events of this wide world I'd seize
Like a strong giant, and my spirit teaze
Till at its shoulders it should proudly see
Wings to find out an immortality.

Stop and consider! life is but a day;
A fragile dew-drop on its perilous way
From a tree's summit; a poor Indian's sleep
While his boat hastens to the monstrous steep
Of Montmorenci. Why so sad a moan?
Life is the rose's hope while yet unblown;   90

The reading of an ever-changing tale;
The light uplifting of a maiden's veil;
A pigeon tumbling in clear summer air;
A laughing school-boy, without grief or care,
Riding the springy branches of an elm.

O for ten years, that I may overwhelm
Myself in poesy; so I may do the deed
That my own soul has to itself decreed.
Then will I pass the countries that I see
In long perspective, and continually   100
Taste their pure fountains. First the realm I'll pass
Of Flora, and old Pan: sleep in the grass,
Feed upon apples red, and strawberries,
And choose each pleasure that my fancy sees;
Catch the white-handed nymphs in shady places,
To woo sweet kisses from averted faces,—
Play with their fingers, touch their shoulders white
Into a pretty shrinking with a bite
As hard as lips can make it: till agreed,
A lovely tale of human life we'll read.   110
And one will teach a tame dove how it best
May fan the cool air gently o'er my rest;
Another, bending o'er her nimble tread,
Will set a green robe floating round her head,
And still will dance with ever varied ease,
Smiling upon the flowers and the trees:
Another will entice me on, and on
Through almond blossoms and rich cinnamon;
Till in the bosom of a leafy world
We rest in silence, like two gems upcurled   120
In the recesses of a pearly shell.

And can I ever bid these joys farewell?
Yes, I must pass them for a nobler life,
Where I may find the agonies, the strife
Of human hearts: for lo! I see afar,
O'ersailing the blue cragginess, a car
And steeds with streamy manes—the charioteer
Looks out upon the winds with glorious fear:
And now the numerous tramplings quiver lightly
Along a huge cloud's ridge; and now with sprightly
Wheel downward come they into fresher skies,   131
Tipt round with silver from the sun's bright eyes.
Still downward with capacious whirl they glide;
And now I see them on a green-hill's side
In breezy rest among the nodding stalks.
The charioteer with wond'rous gesture talks
To the trees and mountains; and there soon appear
Shapes of delight, of mystery, and fear,
Passing along before a dusky space
Made by some mighty oaks: as they would chase

96. ten years. Actually he was to have only about three.
101. First the realm. See page 315.

Some ever-fleeting music on they sweep.   141
Lo! how they murmur, laugh, and smile, and
    weep:
Some with upholden hand and mouth severe;
Some with their faces muffled to the ear
Between their arms; some, clear in youthful
    bloom,
Go glad and smilingly athwart the gloom;
Some looking back, and some with upward gaze;
Yes, thousands in a thousand different ways
Flit onward—now a lovely wreath of girls
Dancing their sleek hair into tangled curls;   150
And now broad wings. Most awfully intent
The driver of those steeds is forward bent,
And seems to listen: O that I might know
All that he writes with such a hurrying glow.

The visions all are fled—the car is fled
Into the light of heaven, and in their stead
A sense of real things comes doubly strong,
And, like a muddy stream, would bear along
My soul to nothingness: but I will strive
Against all doubtings, and will keep alive   160
The thought of that same chariot, and the strange
Journey it went.

           Is there so small a range
In the present strength of manhood, that the high
Imagination cannot freely fly
As she was wont of old? prepare her steeds,
Paw up against the light, and do strange deeds
Upon the clouds? Has she not shown us all?
From the clear space of ether, to the small
Breath of new buds unfolding? From the meaning
Of Jove's large eye-brow, to the tender greening
Of April meadows? Here her altar shone,   171
E'en in this isle; and who could paragon
The fervid choir that lifted up a noise
Of harmony, to where it aye will poise
Its mighty self of convoluting sound,
Huge as a planet, and like that roll round,
Eternally around a dizzy void?
Ay, in those days the Muses were nigh cloyed
With honours; nor had any other care
Than to sing out and sooth their wavy hair.   180

Could all this be forgotten? Yes, a schism
Nurtured by foppery and barbarism,
Made great Apollo blush for this his land.
Men were thought wise who could not understand

His glories: with a puling infant's force
They swayed about upon a rocking horse,
And thought it Pegasus. Ah dismal souled!
The winds of heaven blew, the ocean rolled
Its gathering waves—ye felt it not. The blue
Bared its eternal bosom, and the dew   190
Of summer nights collected still to make
The morning precious: beauty was awake!
Why were ye not awake? But ye were dead
To things ye knew not of,—were closely wed
To musty laws lined out with wretched rule
And compass vile: so that ye taught a school
Of dolts to smooth, inlay, and clip, and fit,
Till, like the certain wands of Jacob's wit,
Their verses tallied. Easy was the task:
A thousand handicraftsmen wore the mask   200
Of Poesy. Ill-fated, impious race!
That blasphemed the bright Lyrist to his face,
And did not know it,—no, they went about,
Holding a poor, decrepid standard out
Marked with most flimsy mottos, and in large
The name of one Boileau!

              O ye whose charge
It is to hover round our pleasant hills!
Whose congregated majesty so fills
My boundly reverence, that I cannot trace
Your hallowed names, in this unholy place,   210
So near those common folk; did not their shames
Affright you? Did our old lamenting Thames
Delight you? Did ye never cluster round
Delicious Avon, with a mournful sound,
And weep? or did ye wholly bid adieu
To regions where no more the laurel grew?
Or did ye stay to give a welcoming
To some lone spirits who could proudly sing
Their youth away, and die? 'Twas even so:
But let me think away those times of woe: 220
Now 'tis a fairer season; ye have breathed
Rich benedictions o'er us; ye have wreathed
Fresh garlands: for sweet music had been heard
In many places;—some has been upstirred
From out its crystal dwelling in a lake,
By a swan's ebon bill; from a thick brake,
Nested and quiet in a valley mild,
Bubbles a pipe; fine sounds are floating wild
About the earth: happy are ye and glad.

These things are doubtless; yet in truth we've
    had
Strange thunders from the potency of song;   231
Mingled indeed with what is sweet and strong,
From majesty: but in clear truth the themes

---

181. schism, the Neoclassical (seventeenth and eighteenth centuries) departure from the traditions of English
poetry, under foreign influence (Boileau, the French critic,
named in l. 206).

186. rocking horse, closed heroic couplet.

Are ugly clubs, the Poets Polyphemes
Disturbing the grand sea. A drainless shower
Of light is poesy; 'tis the supreme of power;
'Tis might half slumbering on its own right arm.
The very archings of her eye-lids charm
A thousand willing agents to obey,
And still she governs with the mildest sway: 240
But strength alone though of the Muses born
Is like a fallen angel: trees uptorn,
Darkness, and worms, and shrouds, and sepulchres
Delight it; for it feeds upon the burrs,
And thorns of life; forgetting the great end
Of poesy, that it should be a friend,
To sooth the cares, and lift the thoughts of man.

from ENDYMION

A POETIC ROMANCE

The general theme of *Endymion*, with its modifying ideas, has been stated in the biographical-critical sketch of Keats, page 314. The story opens with a description of the annual sacrificial feast of Pan in Latmos ("Hymn to Pan"). Endymion, young prince of Latmos, comes to the feast melancholy and distraught. Withdrawing with his sister Peona to a little island in a river near by, he tells her of his love for Diana and of three meetings he has already had with the goddess. Peona reproaches him for his madness and for his dreamy, inactive life. Several days later (Book II), wandering brainsick in the forest, Endymion sees a golden butterfly, follows it, and loses it. A wood nymph bids him wander on. From a cavern an airy voice bids him descend into "The silent mysteries of the earth" (in part, a symbol of poetry). He wanders among the enchantments of the subterranean world, encountering many wonders. There he meets two lovers, Alpheus and Arethusa, learns of the curse that had been put upon them, feels sympathy for them, and prays Diana to assist him in releasing them. Then he goes under the sea. In the depths of the sea (Book III), he recognizes other claims upon his benevolence and humanitarianism—another pair of lovers, the sea god Glaucus and the nymph Scylla, enchanted by the jealous Circe (queen of the senses). His sympathetic intercession for these and for Alpheus and Arethusa takes him a further step in his pursuit of divine essence. With the Indian Maiden (Book IV), he passes through the fourth and final stage of his ascent to fellowship with divine essence. He falls in love with her, first because he pities her (see her "Roundelay to Sorrow"). At the end of a voyage through the air with her, he decides to abandon the quest of Diana for her, a human lover, but at this point loses her. At the end, the Indian Maiden reveals herself as Diana, tells him that through sympathy for others and love for a human being he has passed his probation, and gives herself to him.

234. **Poets Polyphemes,** Byron, for example, whose turbulence Keats had come to dislike.

from BOOK I

[Credo]

A thing of beauty is a joy for ever:
Its loveliness increases; it will never
Pass into nothingness; but still will keep
A bower quiet for us, and a sleep
Full of sweet dreams, and health, and quiet breath-
      ing.
Therefore, on every morrow, are we wreathing
A flowery band to bind us to the earth,
Spite of despondence, of the inhuman dearth
Of noble natures, of the gloomy days,
Of all the unhealthy and o'er-darkened ways   10
Made for our searching: yes, in spite of all,
Some shape of beauty moves away the pall
From our dark spirits. Such the sun, the moon,
Trees old, and young, sprouting a shady boon
For simple sheep; and such are daffodils
With the green world they live in; and clear rills
That for themselves a cooling covert make
'Gainst the hot season; the mid forest brake,
Rich with a sprinkling of fair musk-rose blooms:
And such too is the grandeur of the dooms   20
We have imagined for the mighty dead;
All lovely tales that we have heard or read:
An endless fountain of immortal drink,
Pouring unto us from the heaven's brink.

Nor do we merely feel these essences
For one short hour; no, even as the trees
That whisper round a temple become soon
Dear as the temple's self, so does the moon,
The passion poesy, glories infinite,
Haunt us till they become a cheering light   30
Unto our souls, and bound to us so fast,
That, whether there be shine, or gloom o'ercast,
They always must be with us, or we die.

[Schedule]

Therefore, 'tis with full happiness that I
Will trace the story of Endymion.
The very music of the name has gone
Into my being, and each pleasant scene
Is growing fresh before me as the green
Of our own vallies: so I will begin
Now while I cannot hear the city's din;   40
Now while the early budders are just new,
And run in mazes of the youngest hue

34. **Therefore.** Believing as he does, he traces the story of Endymion, one of the "lovely tales," a "flowery band to bind us to the earth." 39. **so I will begin.** What follows is the poet's calendar of his present work. Note that every month and season is presented sensuously.

About old forests; while the willow trails
Its delicate amber; and the dairy pails
Bring home increase of milk. And, as the year
Grows lush in juicy stalks, I'll smoothly steer
My little boat, for many quiet hours,
With streams that deepen freshly into bowers.
Many and many a verse I hope to write,
Before the daisies, vermeil rimmed and white,   50
Hide in deep herbage; and ere yet the bees
Hum about globes of clover and sweet peas,
I must be near the middle of my story.
O may no wintry season, bare and hoary,
See it half finished: but let Autumn bold,
With universal tinge of sober gold,
Be all about me when I make an end.
And now at once, adventuresome, I send
My herald thought into a wilderness:
There let its trumpet blow, and quickly dress   60
My uncertain path with green, that I may speed
Easily onward, thorough flowers and weed. . . .

[Hymn to Pan]

"O thou, whose mighty palace roof doth hang
From jagged trunks, and overshadoweth
Eternal whispers, glooms, the birth, life, death
Of unseen flowers in heavy peacefulness;
Who lov'st to see the hamadryads dress
Their ruffled locks where meeting hazels darken;
And through whole solemn hours dost sit, and
     hearken
The dreary melody of bedded reeds—
In desolate places, where dank moisture breeds   240
In pipy hemlock to strange overgrowth;
Bethinking thee, how melancholy loth
Thou wast to lose fair Syrinx—do thou now,
By thy love's milky brow!
By all the trembling mazes that she ran,
Hear us, great Pan!

"O thou, for whose soul-soothing quiet, turtles
Passion their voices cooingly 'mong myrtles,
What time thou wanderest at eventide
Through sunny meadows, that outskirt the side
Of thine enmossèd realms: O thou, to whom   251
Broad leavèd fig trees even now foredoom
Their ripened fruitage; yellow girted bees
Their golden honeycombs; our village leas
Their fairest blossomed beans and poppied corn;
The chuckling linnet its five young unborn,
To sing for thee; low creeping strawberries
Their summer coolness; pent up butterflies
Their freckled wings; yea, the fresh budding year
All its completions—be quickly near,   260

By every wind that nods the mountain pine,
O forester divine!

"Thou, to whom every faun and satyr flies
For willing service; whether to surprise
The squatted hare while in half sleeping fit;
Or upward ragged precipices flit
To save poor lambkins from the eagle's maw;
Or by mysterious enticement draw
Bewildered shepherds to their path again;
Or to tread breathless round the frothy main,   270
And gather up all fancifullest shells
For thee to tumble into Naiads' cells,
And, being hidden, laugh at their out-peeping;
Or to delight thee with fantastic leaping,
The while they pelt each other on the crown
With silvery oak apples, and fir cones brown—
By all the echoes that about thee ring,
Hear us, O satyr king!

"O Hearkener to the loud clapping shears,
While ever and anon to his shorn peers   280
A ram goes bleating: Winder of the horn,
When snouted wild-boars routing tender corn
Anger our huntsmen: Breather round our farms,
To keep off mildews, and all weather harms:
Strange ministrant of undescribèd sounds,
That come a swooning over hollow grounds,
And wither drearily on barren moors:
Dread opener of the mysterious doors
Leading to universal knowledge—see,
Great son of Dryope,   290
The many that are come to pay their vows
With leaves about their brows!

"Be still the unimaginable lodge
For solitary thinking; such as dodge
Conception to the very bourne of heaven,
Then leave the naked brain: be still the leaven,
That spreading in this dull and clodded earth
Gives it a touch ethereal—a new birth:
Be still a symbol of immensity;
A firmament reflected in a sea;   300
An element filling the space between;
An unknown—but no more: we humbly screen
With uplift hands our foreheads, lowly bend-
     ing,
And giving out a shout most heaven rend-
     ing,
Conjure thee to receive our humble Paean,
Upon thy Mount Lycean!" . . .

293. the unimaginable lodge. Note the Neo-Platonic interpretation of nature beginning here. Compare Shelley's
"Adonais," stanza 43.

[Pleasure Thermometer]

"Wherein lies happiness? In that which becks
Our ready minds to fellowship divine,
A fellowship with essence; till we shine,
Full alchemized, and free of space. Behold   780
The clear religion of heaven! Fold
A rose leaf round thy finger's taperness,
And soothe thy lips: hist, when the airy stress
Of music's kiss impregnates the free winds,
And with a sympathetic touch unbinds
Aeolian magic from their lucid wombs:
Then old songs waken from enclouded tombs;
Old ditties sigh above their father's grave;
Ghosts of melodious prophesyings rave
Round every spot where trod Apollo's foot;   790
Bronze clarions awake, and faintly bruit,
Where long ago a giant battle was;
And, from the turf, a lullaby doth pass
In every place where infant Orpheus slept.
Feel we these things?—that moment have we stept
Into a sort of oneness, and our state
Is like a floating spirit's. But there are
Richer entanglements, enthralments far
More self-destroying, leading, by degrees,
To the chief intensity: the crown of these   800
Is made of love and friendship, and sits high
Upon the forehead of humanity.
All its more ponderous and bulky worth
Is friendship, whence there ever issues forth
A steady splendour; but at the tip-top,
There hangs by unseen film, an orbèd drop
Of light, and that is love: its influence,
Thrown in our eyes, genders a novel sense,
At which we start and fret; till in the end,
Melting into its radiance, we blend,   810
Mingle, and so become a part of it,—
Nor with aught else can our souls interknit
So wingedly: when we combine therewith,
Life's self is nourished by its proper pith,
And we are nurtured like a pelican brood.
Aye, so delicious is the unsating food,
That men, who might have towered in the van
Of all the congregated world, to fan
And winnow from the coming step of time
All chaff of custom, wipe away all slime   820
Left by men-slugs and human serpentry,
Have been content to let occasion die,

---

777. **Wherein lies happiness?** These lines (part of Endymion's defense of himself for dreaming and loving) were
inserted while the poem was in press. Keats called them his
"pleasure thermometer," that is, a graduated arrangement
of the themes of poetry. (Compare this statement with the
less mature one in "Sleep and Poetry," ll. 101 ff.) The lines
are also, of course, a justification of his telling the story of
Endymion, and a suggestion of his Neo-Platonic theme.

Whilst they did sleep in love's elysium.
And, truly, I would rather be struck dumb,
Than speak against this ardent listlessness:
For I have ever thought that it might bless
The world with benefits unknowingly;
As does the nightingale, upperchèd high,
And cloistered among cool and bunchèd leaves—
She sings but to her love, nor e'er conceives   830
How tiptoe Night holds back her dark-grey
    hood.
Just so may love, although 'tis understood
The mere commingling of passionate breath,
Produce more than our searching witnesseth:
What I know not: but who, of men, can tell
That flowers would bloom, or that green fruit
    would swell
To melting pulp, that fish would have bright
    mail,
The earth its dower of river, wood, and vale,
The meadows runnels, runnels pebble-stones,
The seed its harvest, or the lute its tones,   840
Tones ravishment, or ravishment its sweet
If human souls did never kiss and greet?

"Now, if this earthly love has power to make
Men's being mortal, immortal; to shake
Ambition from their memories, and brim
Their measure of content; what merest whim,
Seems all this poor endeavour after fame,
To one, who keeps within his stedfast aim
A love immortal, an immortal too." . . .

from BOOK IV

[Roundelay to Sorrow]

[Sung by the Indian Maiden to Endymion. It
wins his pity, which leads to love.]

"O Sorrow,
    Why dost borrow
The natural hue of health, from vermeil lips?—
    To give maiden blushes
    To the white rose bushes?   150
Or is't thy dewy hand the daisy tips?

"O Sorrow,
    Why dost borrow
The lustrous passion from a falcon-eye?—
    To give the glow-worm light?
    Or, on a moonless night,
To tinge, on syren shores, the salt sea-spry?

"O Sorrow,
    Why dost borrow

The mellow ditties from a mourning tongue?—
　　To give at evening pale   161
　　Unto the nightingale,
That thou mayst listen the cold dews among?

　　"O Sorrow,
　　Why dost borrow
Heart's lightness from the merriment of May?—
　　A lover would not tread
　　A cowslip on the head,
Though he should dance from eve till peep of
　　　　day—
　　Nor any drooping flower   170
　　Held sacred for thy bower,
Wherever he may sport himself and play.

　　"To Sorrow,
　　I bade good-morrow,
And thought to leave her far away behind;
　　But cheerly, cheerly,
　　She loves me dearly;
She is so constant to me, and so kind:
　　I would deceive her,
　　And so leave her,   180
But ah! she is so constant and so kind." . . .

SONNETS

ON THE SEA

It keeps eternal whisperings around
　　Desolate shores, and with its mighty swell
　　Gluts twice ten thousand Caverns, till the spell
Of Hecate leaves them their old shadowy sound.
Often 'tis in such gentle temper found,
　　That scarcely will the very smallest shell
　　Be moved for days from where it sometime fell,
When last the winds of Heaven were unbound.
Oh ye! who have your eye-balls vexed and tired,
　　Feast them upon the wideness of the Sea;   10
　　Oh ye! whose ears are dinned with uproar
　　　　rude,
　　Or fed too much with cloying melody—
　　Sit ye near some old Cavern's Mouth, and
　　　　brood
Until ye start, as if the sea-nymphs quired!

ON SEEING THE ELGIN MARBLES

My spirit is too weak—mortality
　　Weighs heavily on me like unwilling sleep,
　　And each imagined pinnacle and steep

Of godlike hardship, tells me I must die
Like a sick Eagle looking at the sky.
　　Yet 'tis a gentle luxury to weep
　　That I have not the cloudy winds to keep,
Fresh for the opening of the morning's eye.
Such dim-conceivèd glories of the brain
　　Bring round the heart an undescribable feud;
So do these wonders a most dizzy pain,   11
　　That mingles Grecian grandeur with the rude
Wasting of old Time—with a billowy main—
　　A sun—a shadow of a magnitude.

ON SITTING DOWN TO READ KING LEAR
ONCE AGAIN

O golden tongued romance, with serene lute!
　　Fair-plumèd Syren, Queen of far-away!
　　Leave melodizing on this wintry day,
Shut up thine olden pages, and be mute:
Adieu! for, once again, the fierce dispute
　　Betwixt damnation and impassioned clay
　　Must I burn through; once more humbly assay
The bitter-sweet of this Shakespearian fruit:
Chief poet! and ye clouds of Albion,
　　Begetters of our deep eternal theme!   10
When through the old oak Forest I am gone,
　　Let me not wander in a barren dream,
But, when I am consumèd in the fire,
Give me new Phoenix wings to fly at my desire.

WHEN I HAVE FEARS THAT I MAY
CEASE TO BE

　　This sonnet tells how the poet feels under the shadow
of *two* fears of death—that he may die before he writes
himself out, and also before he may consummate his love.
　　Note that this and all the other following sonnets of
Keats here reprinted are in the Shakespearean form.

When I have fears that I may cease to be
　　Before my pen has gleaned my teeming brain,
Before high-pilèd books, in charactery,
　　Hold like rich garners the full ripened grain;
When I behold, upon the night's starred face,
　　Huge cloudy symbols of a high romance,
And think that I may never live to trace
　　Their shadows, with the magic hand of chance;
And when I feel, fair creature of an hour,
　　That I shall never look upon thee more,   10

173–81. "To Sorrow . . . so kind." These nine lines are
the motto of Thomas Hardy's great novel *The Return of the
Native.* 4. Hecate, the dark goddess of magic and witchcraft,
usually associated with the underworld.

On Sitting . . . 6. Betwixt damnation and impassioned
clay, between Fate and human desires and aspirations. *King
Lear* is a fate drama of sorts. Compare "As flies to wanton
boys, are we to the gods," Act IV, sc. 1, l. 38.

Never have relish in the faery power
Of unreflecting love;—then on the shore
Of the wide world I stand alone, and think
Till love and fame to nothingness do sink.

THE HUMAN SEASONS

Four seasons fill the measure of the year;
There are four seasons in the mind of man;
He has his lusty Spring, when fancy clear
Takes in all beauty with an easy span:
He has his Summer, when luxuriously
Spring's honied cud of youthful thought he loves
To ruminate, and by such dreaming high
Is nearest unto heaven: quiet coves
His soul has in its Autumn, when his wings
He furleth close; contented so to look   10
On mists in idleness—to let fair things
Pass by unheeded as a threshold brook.
He has his Winter too of pale misfeature,
Or else he would forego his mortal nature.

STANZAS

IN A DREAR-NIGHTED DECEMBER

An early (1818) statement of one of Keats's chief lyrical themes—the transiency of joy and beauty. Happiness belongs only to childhood and early youth, the unreflective period of life; "to think is to be full of sorrow" ("Ode to a Nightingale," l. 27).

I

In a drear-nighted December,
      Too happy, happy tree,
Thy branches ne'er remember
      Their green felicity:
The north cannot undo them,
With a sleety whistle through them;
Nor frozen thawings glue them
      From budding at the prime.

2

In a drear-nighted December,
      Too happy, happy brook,   10
Thy bubblings ne'er remember
      Apollo's summer look;
But with a sweet forgetting,
They stay their crystal fretting,
Never, never petting
      About the frozen time.

Stanzas. **15. petting,** fretting.

3

Ah! would 'twere so with many
      A gentle girl and boy!
But were there ever any
      Writhed not at passed joy?   20
To know the change and feel it,
When there is none to heal it,
Nor numbèd sense to steel it,
      Was never said in rhyme.

LINES ON THE MERMAID TAVERN

Souls of Poets dead and gone,
What Elysium have ye known,
Happy field or mossy cavern,
Choicer than the Mermaid Tavern?
Have ye tippled drink more fine
Than mine host's Canary wine?
Or are fruits of Paradise
Sweeter than those dainty pies
Of venison? O generous food!
Drest as though bold Robin Hood   10
Would, with his Maid Marian,
Sup and bowse from horn and can.

      I have heard that on a day
Mine host's sign-board flew away,
Nobody knew whither, till
An astrolger's old quill
To a sheepskin gave the story,
Said he saw you in your glory,
Underneath a new-old sign
Sipping beverage divine,   20
And pledging with contented smack
The Mermaid in the Zodiac.

      Souls of Poets dead and gone,
What Elysium have ye known,
Happy field or mossy cavern,
Choicer than the Mermaid Tavern?

ODE

Written on the blank page before Beaumont and Fletcher's tragi-comedy, *The Fair Maid of the Inn.*

Bards of Passion and of Mirth,
Ye have left your souls on earth!

21. To know the change and feel it. Professor J. M. Murry and other scholars prefer a variant reading, "The feel of *not* to feel it." **4. Mermaid Tavern.** Here, according to tradition, Ben Jonson and Shakespeare and their cronies had their combats of wit. Keats is notable for his return to the Elizabethans. **12. bowse,** variant of "booze."

Have ye souls in heaven too,
Double-lived in regions new?
Yes, and those of heaven commune
With the spheres of sun and moon;
With the noise of fountains wond'rous
And the parle of voices thund'rous;
With the whisper of heaven's trees
And one another, in soft ease   10
Seated on Elysian lawns
Browsed by none but Dian's fawns;
Underneath large blue-bells tented,
Where the daisies are rose-scented,
And the rose herself has got
Perfume which on earth is not;
Where the nightingale doth sing
Not a senseless, trancèd thing,
But divine melodious truth;
Philosophic numbers smooth;
Tales and golden histories
Of heaven and its mysteries.

Thus ye live on high, and then
On the earth ye live again;
And the souls ye left behind you
Teach us, here, the way to find you,
Where your other souls are joying,
Never slumbered, never cloying.
Here, your earth-born souls still speak
To mortals, of their little week;   30
Of their sorrows and delights;
Of their passions and their spites;
Of their glory and their shame;
What doth strengthen and what maim.
Thus ye teach us, every day,
Wisdom, though fled far away.

Bards of Passion and of Mirth,
Ye have left your souls on earth!
Ye have souls in heaven too,
Double-lived in regions new!   40

ROBIN HOOD

To a Friend

No! those days are gone away,
And their hours are old and gray,
And their minutes buried all
Under the down-trodden pall
Of the leaves of many years:
Many times have winter's shears,

Frozen North, and chilling East,
Sounded tempests to the feast
Of the forest's whispering fleeces,
Since men knew nor rent nor leases.   10

No, the bugle sounds no more,
And the twanging bow no more;
Silent is the ivory shrill
Past the heath and up the hill;
There is no mid-forest laugh,
Where lone Echo gives the half
To some wight, amazed to hear
Jesting, deep in forest drear.

On the fairest time of June
You may go, with sun or moon,   20
Or the seven stars to light you,
Or the polar ray to right you;
But you never may behold
Little John, or Robin bold;
Never one, of all the clan,
Thrumming on an empty can
Some old hunting ditty, while
He doth his green way beguile
To fair hostess Merriment,
Down beside the pasture Trent;   30
For he left the merry tale
Messenger for spicy ale.

Gone, the merry morris din;
Gone, the song of Gamelyn;
Gone, the tough-belted outlaw
Idling in the "grenè shawe";
All are gone away and past!
And if Robin should be cast
Sudden from his turfèd grave,
And if Marian should have   40
Once again her forest days,
She would weep, and he would craze:
He would swear, for all his oaks,
Fall'n beneath the dockyard strokes,
Have rotted on the briny sea,
She would weep that her wild bees
Sang not to her—strange! that honey
Can't be got without hard money!

So it is: yet let us sing,
Honour to the old bow-string!   50
Honour to the bugle-horn!

Ode. **4. Double-lived.** With the following half-playful notion of poetic immortality, compare Shelley's in *Adonais*, stanzas 42–46.

43. for all his oaks. This and other concrete facts—for example, **rent** and **leases** (l. 10), **hard money** (l. 48) suggest what industrialization and a money economy did to the good old days and the good old ways. Keats is at one with the older Romanticists in revering the early traditions of the English folk.

Honour to the woods unshorn!
Honour to the Lincoln green!
Honour to the archer keen!
Honour to tight little John,
And the horse he rode upon!
Honour to bold Robin Hood,
Sleeping in the underwood!
Honour to maid Marian,
And to all the Sherwood-clan!   60
Though their days have hurried by
Let us two a burden try.

FANCY

Ever let the fancy roam,
Pleasure never is at home:
At a touch sweet Pleasure melteth,
Like to bubbles when rain pelteth;
Then let wingèd Fancy wander
Through the thought still spread beyond her:
Open wide the mind's cage-door,
She'll dart forth, and cloudward soar.
O sweet Fancy! let her loose;
Summer's joys are spoilt by use,   10
And the enjoying of the Spring
Fades as does its blossoming;
Autumn's red-lipped fruitage too,
Blushing through the mist and dew,
Cloys with tasting: What do then?
Sit thee by the ingle, when
The sear fagot blazes bright,
Spirit of a winter's night;
When the soundless earth is muffled,
And the cakèd snow is shuffled   20
From the ploughboy's heavy shoon;
When the Night doth meet the Noon
In a dark conspiracy
To banish Even from her sky.
Sit thee there, and send abroad,
With a mind self-overawed,
Fancy, high-commissioned:—send her!
She has vassals to attend her:
She will bring, in spite of frost,
Beauties that the earth hath lost;   30
She will bring thee, all together,
All delights of summer weather;
All the buds and bells of May,
From dewy sward or thorny spray;
All the heapèd Autumn's wealth,
With a still, mysterious stealth:
She will mix these pleasures up
Like three fit wines in a cup,

16. ingle, fireside.   21. shoon, shoes (archaic).

And thou shalt quaff it:—thou shalt hear
Distant harvest-carols clear;   40
Rustle of the reapèd corn;
Sweet birds antheming the morn:
And, in the same moment—hark!
'Tis the early April lark,
Or the rooks, with busy caw,
Foraging for sticks and straw.
Thou shalt, at one glance, behold
The daisy and the marigold;
White-plumed lilies, and the first
Hedge-grown primrose that hath burst;   50
Shaded hyacinth, alway
Sapphire queen of the mid-May;
And every leaf, and every flower
Pearlèd with the self-same shower.
Thou shalt see the field-mouse peep
Meagre from its cellèd sleep;
And the snake all winter-thin
Cast on sunny bank its skin;
Freckled nest-eggs thou shalt see
Hatching in the hawthorn-tree,   60
When the hen-bird's wing doth rest
Quiet on her mossy nest;
Then the hurry and alarm
When the bee-hive casts its swarm;
Acorns ripe down-pattering,
While the autumn breezes sing.

Oh, sweet Fancy! let her loose;
Every thing is spoilt by use:
Where's the cheek that doth not fade,
Too much gazed at? Where's the maid   70
Whose lip mature is ever new?
Where's the eye, however blue,
Doth not weary? Where's the face
One would meet in every place?
Where's the voice, however soft,
One would hear so very oft?
At a touch sweet Pleasure melteth
Like to bubbles when rain pelteth.
Let, then, wingèd Fancy find
Thee a mistress to thy mind: 80
Dulcet-eyed as Ceres' daughter,
Ere the God of Torment taught her
How to frown and how to chide;
With a waist and with a side
White as Hebe's, when her zone
Slipt its golden clasp, and down
Fell her kirtle to her feet.

69. the cheek that doth not fade. Compare "Ode to a Nightingale," l. 29.   81. Ceres' daughter, Prosperpine. Ceres was goddess of the harvest. Pluto carried Proserpine to the underworld.   82. God of Torment, Pluto.
85. Hebe's . . . zone, the girdle of the goddess of youth.

While she held the goblet sweet,
And Jove grew languid.—Break the mesh
Of the Fancy's silken leash;   90
Quickly break her prison-string
And such joys as these she'll bring.—
Let the wingèd Fancy roam,
Pleasure never is at home.

THE EVE OF ST. AGNES

In January, 1819, after his meeting with Fanny
Brawne, Keats visited old Mr. Dilke at Chichester and a
Mr. Snook at Bedhampton. He wrote his brother and
sister: "Nothing worth speaking of happened at either
place I took down some thin paper and wrote on it a
little poem called St. Agnes Eve."

To what has already been said (page 314) about the
poem, the following general suggestions for studying it
are added. Note carefully the chief elements: (1) The
framework—setting (including cultural age, Gothic castle,
the ascetic devotion of the Beadsman contrasted with the
"argent revelry" of the ball in the great castle hall, the
superstition about St. Agnes' Eve which makes the action
possible, the weather, and so on); (2) the *central picture* of
Madeline (stanzas 24 ff.); (3) the *story proper*—a rather
slight one of elopement, made possible by Madeline's belief in the superstition and the old nurse's complicity, the
confusion of the ball and its aftermath, and the state of the
weather. Observe closely the details and the significance
of contrasts; for example, the difference between the spectral old age of the Beadsman and Angela and the blooming youth of Madeline and Porphyro, between the ballroom and Madeline's room, between the music of the ball
and the music of Porphyro's lute, between the interior of
Madeline's room and the outside storm. Do not miss the
suggested meaning of the last scene—at the castle gate
(and what lies behind it) and in the storm the young
lovers face—or of the comment on the Baron, the Beadsman, and Angela at the end.

1

St. Agnes' Eve—Ah, bitter chill it was!
The owl, for all his feathers, was a-cold;
The hare limped trembling through the frozen
    grass,
And silent was the flock in woolly fold:
Numb were the Beadsman's fingers, while he told
His rosary, and while his frosted breath,
Like pious incense from a censer old,
Seemed taking flight for heaven, without a death,
Past the sweet Virgin's picture, while his prayer he
    saith.

1. St. Agnes' Eve, January 20, supposed to be the coldest
day of the year.   **5. Beadsman's.** A beadsman was, literally,
a *praying* man.

2

His prayer he saith, this patient, holy man;   10
Then takes his lamp, and riseth from his knees,
And back returneth, meagre, barefoot, wan,
Along the chapel aisle by slow degrees:
The sculptured dead, on each side, seem to
    freeze,
Emprisoned in black, purgatorial rails:
Knights, ladies, praying in dumb orat'ries,
He passeth by; and his weak spirit fails
To think how they may ache in icy hoods and mails.

3

Northward he turneth through a little door,
And scarce three steps, ere Music's golden tongue
Flattered to tears this aged man and poor;   21
But no—already had his deathbell rung;
The joys of all his life were said and sung:
His was harsh penance on St. Agnes' Eve:
Another way he went, and soon among
Rough ashes sat he for his soul's reprieve,
And all night kept awake, for sinners' sake to grieve.

4

That ancient Beadsman heard the prelude soft;
And so it chanced, for many a door was wide,
From hurry to and fro. Soon, up aloft,   30
The silver, snarling trumpets 'gan to chide:
The level chambers, ready with their pride,
Were glowing to receive a thousand guests:
The carvèd angels, ever eager-eyed,
Stared, where upon their heads the cornice rests,
With hair blown back, and wings put cross-wise on
    their breasts.

5

At length burst in the argent revelry,
With plume, tiara, and all rich array,
Numerous as shadows haunting faerily
The brain, new stuffed, in youth, with triumphs
    gay   40
Of old romance. These let us wish away,
And turn, sole-thoughted, to one Lady there,
Whose heart had brooded, all that wintry day,
On love, and winged St. Agnes' saintly care,
As she had heard old dames full many times
    declare.

15. black, purgatorial rails. Most editors assume that
"rails" means *railings*—"black, purgatorial" because the
sculptured dead are in Purgatory. But "rails" may mean
robes (from O. E. *hrægl*). If so, the dead are sculptured in garments appropriate for Purgatory.   **16. dumb orat'ries.** An
oratory is a small chapel for prayer; **dumb** because occupied
by the sculptured figures of the knights and ladies buried
there.

6

They told her how, upon St. Agnes' Eve,
Young virgins might have visions of delight,
And soft adorings from their loves receive
Upon the honeyed middle of the night,
If ceremonies due they did aright;   50
As, supperless to bed they must retire,
And couch supine their beauties, lilly white;
Nor look behind, nor sideways, but require
Of Heaven with upward eyes for all that they
    desire.

7

Full of this whim was thoughtful Madeline:
The music, yearning like a God in pain,
She scarcely heard: her maiden eyes divine,
Fixed on the floor, saw many a sweeping train
Pass by—she heeded not at all: in vain
Came many a tiptoe, amorous cavalier,   60
And back retired; not cooled by high disdain,
But she saw not: her heart was otherwhere:
She sighed for Agnes' dreams, the sweetest of the
    year.

8

She danced along with vague, regardless eyes,
Anxious her lips, her breathing quick and short:
The hallowed hour was near at hand: she sighs
Amid the timbrels, and the thronged resort
Of whisperers in anger, or in sport;
'Mid looks of love, defiance, hate, and scorn,
Hoodwinked with faery fancy; all amort,   70
Save to St. Agnes and her lambs unshorn,
And all the bliss to be before to-morrow morn.

9

So, purposing each moment to retire,
She lingered still. Meantime, across the moors,
Had come young Porphyro, with heart on
    fire
For Madeline. Beside the portal doors,
Buttressed from moonlight, stands he, and im-
    plores
All saints to give him sight of Madeline,
But for one moment in the tedious hours,
That he might gaze and worship all unseen;   80
Perchance speak, kneel, touch, kiss—in sooth such
    things have been.

60. tiptoe, amorous cavalier. Note how this characterization sets off Porphyro when he enters. **70. amort,** as if
lifeless. **71. lambs.** Unshorn lambs offered on St. Agnes'
day were later shorn, and the nuns wove the wool into cloth.
(Compare ll. 115–17.) **77. Buttressed from moonlight.**
Note the evocative power of the image—suggesting the loom
of the Gothic castle. Compare Scott's "Lochinvar."

10

He ventures in: let no buzzed whisper tell:
All eyes be muffled, or a hundred swords
Will storm his heart, Love's fev'rous citadel:
For him, those chambers held barbarian hordes,
Hyena foemen, and hot-blooded lords,
Whose very dogs would execrations howl
Against his lineage: not one breast affords
Him any mercy, in that mansion foul,
Save one old beldame, weak in body and in soul. 90

11

Ah, happy chance! the agèd creature came,
Shuffling along with ivory-headed wand,
To where he stood, hid from the torch's flame,
Behind a broad hall-pillar, far beyond
The sound of merriment and chorus bland:
He startled her; but soon she knew his face,
And grasped his fingers in her palsied hand,
Saying, "Mercy, Porphyro! hie thee from this
    place!
They are all here to-night, the whole blood-thirsty
    race!

12

"Get hence! get hence! there's dwarfish Hilde-
    brand;   100
He had a fever late, and in the fit
He cursèd thee and thine, both house and land:
Then there's that old Lord Maurice, not a whit
More tame for his gray hairs—Alas me! flit!
Flit like a ghost away."—"Ah, Gossip dear,
We're safe enough; here in this arm-chair sit,
And tell me how"—"Good Saints! not here, not
    here;
Follow me, child, or else these stones will be thy
    bier."

13

He followed through a lowly archèd way,
Brushing the cobwebs with his lofty plume;   110
And as she muttered "Well-a—well-a-day!"
He found him in a little moonlight room,
Pale, latticed, chill, and silent as a tomb.
"Now tell me where is Madeline," said he,
"O tell me, Angela, by the holy loom
Which none but secret sisterhood may see,
When they St. Agnes' wool are weaving, piously."

14

"St. Agnes! Ah! it is St. Agnes' Eve—
Yet men will murder upon holy days:

99. the whole blood-thirsty race. Compare the situation in *Romeo and Juliet.* **105. Gossip,** godmother—no disrespect.

Thou must hold water in a witch's sieve,   120
And be liege-lord of all the Elves and Fays,
To venture so: it fills me with amaze
To see thee, Porphyro!—St. Agnes' Eve!
God's help! my lady fair the conjuror plays
This very night: good angels her deceive!
But let me laugh awhile, I've mickle time to
    grieve."

15

Feebly she laugheth in the languid moon,
While Porphyro upon her face doth look,
Like puzzled urchin on an aged crone
Who keepeth closed a wond'rous riddle-book,   130
As spectacled she sits in chimney nook.
But soon his eyes grew brilliant, when she told
His lady's purpose; and he scarce could brook
Tears, at the thought of those enchantments
    cold,
And Madeline asleep in lap of legends old.

16

Sudden a thought came like a full-blown rose,
Flushing his brow, and in his painèd heart
Made purple riot: then doth he propose
A stratagem, that makes the beldame start:
"A cruel man and impious thou art: 140
Sweet lady, let her pray, and sleep, and dream
Alone with her good angels, far apart
From wicked men like thee. Go, go! I deem
Thou canst not surely be the same that thou didst
    seem."

17

"I will not harm her, by all saints I swear,"
Quoth Porphyro: "O may I ne'er find grace
When my weak voice shall whisper its last prayer,
If one of her soft ringlets I displace,
Or look with ruffian passion in her face:
Good Angela, believe me by these tears;   150
Or I will, even in a moment's space,
Awake, with horrid shout, my foemen's ears,
And beard them, though they be more fanged than
    wolves and bears."

18

"Ah! why wilt thou affright a feeble soul?
A poor, weak, palsy-stricken, churchyard thing,
Whose passing-bell may ere the midnight toll;
Whose prayers for thee, each morn and evening,

Were never missed."—Thus plaining, doth she
    bring
A gentler speech from burning Porphyro;
So woful, and of such deep sorrowing,   160
That Angela gives promise she will do
Whatever he shall wish, betide her weal or woe.

19

Which was, to lead him, in close secrecy,
Even to Madeline's chamber, and there hide
Him in a closet, of such privacy
That he might see her beauty unespied,
And win perhaps that night a peerless bride,
While legioned faeries paced the coverlet,
And pale enchantment held her sleepy-eyed.
Never on such a night have lovers met,   170
Since Merlin paid his Demon all the monstrous
    debt.

20

"It shall be as thou wishest," said the Dame:
"All cates and dainties shall be storèd there
Quickly on this feast-night: by the tambour frame
Her own lute thou wilt see: no time to spare,
For I am slow and feeble, and scarce dare
On such a catering trust my dizzy head.
Wait here, my child, with patience; kneel in
    prayer
The while: Ah! thou must needs the lady wed,
Or may I never leave my grave among the dead."

21

So saying, she hobbled off with busy fear.   181
The lover's endless minutes slowly passed;
The dame returned, and whispered in his ear
To follow her; with agèd eyes aghast
From fright of dim espial. Safe at last,
Through many a dusky gallery, they gain
The maiden's chamber, silken, hushed, and
    chaste;
Where Porphyro took covert, pleased amain.
His poor guide hurried back with agues in her
    brain.

22

Her falt'ring hand upon the balustrade,   190
Old Angela was feeling for the stair,
When Madeline, St. Agnes' charmèd maid,
Rose, like a missioned spirit, unaware:
With silver taper's light, and pious care,

---

126. mickle, much. **133. brook,** endure. **135. And
Madeline asleep in lap of legends old,** one of the notably
beautiful one-line pictures in the Alexandrine (the hexameter
line of a Spenserian stanza). Note others. **171. Demon,** his legendary father. **173. cates,** dainty
viands. The old Nurse realizes that Madeline, who has
gone to bed supperless (l. 51), will need refreshment for the
hard journey before her. **174. tambour frame,** embroidery
frame.

She turned, and down the aged gossip led
To a safe level matting. Now prepare,
Young Porphyro, for gazing on that bed;
She comes, she comes again, like ring-dove frayed
    and fled.

23

Out went the taper as she hurried in;
Its little smoke, in pallid moonshine, died: 200
She closed the door, she panted, all akin
To spirits of the air, and visions wide:
No uttered syllable, or, woe betide!
But to her heart, her heart was voluble,
Paining with eloquence her balmy side;
As though a tongueless nightingale should swell
Her throat in vain, and die, heart-stifled, in her
    dell.

24

A casement high and triple-arched there was,
All garlanded with carven imag'ries
Of fruits, and flowers, and bunches of knot-grass,
And diamonded with panes of quaint device, 211
Innumerable of stains and splendid dyes,
As are the tiger-moth's deep-damasked wings;
And in the midst, 'mong thousand heraldries,
And twilight saints, and dim emblazonings,
A shielded scutcheon blushed with blood of queens
    and kings.

25

Full on this casement shone the wintry moon,
And threw warm gules on Madeline's fair breast,
As down she knelt for heaven's grace and boon;
Rose-bloom fell on her hands, together prest, 220
And on her silver cross soft amethyst,
And on her hair a glory, like a saint:
She seemed a splendid angel, newly drest,
Save wings, for heaven:—Porphyro grew faint:
She knelt, so pure a thing, so free from mortal taint.

26

Anon his heart revives: her vespers done,
Of all its wreathèd pearls her hair she frees;
Unclasps her warmèd jewels one by one;
Loosens her fragrant boddice; by degrees

Her rich attire creeps rustling to her knees: 230
Half-hidden, like a mermaid in sea-weed,
Pensive awhile she dreams awake, and sees,
In fancy, fair St. Agnes in her bed,
But dares not look behind, or all the charm is fled.

27

Soon, trembling in her soft and chilly nest,
In sort of wakeful swoon, perplexed she lay,
Until the poppied warmth of sleep oppressed
Her soothèd limbs, and soul fatigued away;
Flown, like a thought, until the morrow-day;
Blissfully havened both from joy and pain;   240
Clasped like a missal where swart Paynims pray;
Blinded alike from sunshine and from rain,
As though a rose should shut, and be a bud again.

28

Stol'n to this paradise, and so entranced,
Porphyro gazed upon her empty dress,
And listened to her breathing, if it chanced
To wake into a slumberous tenderness;
Which when he heard, that minute did he bless,
And breathed himself: then from the closet crept,
Noiseless as fear in a wide wilderness,   250
And over the hushed carpet, silent, stept,
And 'tween the curtains peeped, where, lo!—how
    fast she slept.

29

Then by the bed-side, where the faded moon
Made a dim, silver twilight, soft he set
A table, and, half anguished, threw thereon
A cloth of woven crimson, gold, and jet:—
O for some drowsy Morphean amulet!
The boisterous, midnight, festive clarion,
The kettle-drum, and far-heard clarinet,
Affray his ears, though but in dying tone:—   260
The hall-door shuts again, and all the noise is gone.

30

And still she slept an azure-lidded sleep,
In blanchèd linen, smooth, and lavendered,
While he from forth the closet brought a heap
Of candied apple, quince, and plum, and gourd;
With jellies soother than the creamy curd,
And lucent syrops, tinct with cinnamon;
Manna and dates, in argosy transferred
From Fez; and spicèd dainties, every one,
From silken Samarcand to cedared Lebanon.   270

---

198. frayed, frightened.   **208. A casement high, ff.** A glance at photographic reproductions of the original MS. of the poem (in Amy Lowell's *John Keats*, 2 vols., Houghton Mifflin, 1925, Vol. II, between pp. 168–69) will show that such poetry is the result of revision after revision until the right images and words are found. Compare, also, the similar reproduction of stanzas 30–38 in M. R. Ridley's *Keats' Craftsmanship*, Oxford Press, 1933, pp. 162–63.   **218. gules,** heraldic term for red—the exactly right word for the *center* of the central picture.

241. clasped . . . pray, shut (as with clasps) like a prayer book where pagans (heathen) pray—hence secreted. **257. Morphean amulet,** sleep-producing charm (Morpheus was god of sleep).   **266. soother,** smoother.

31

These delicates he heaped with glowing hand
On golden dishes and in baskets bright
Of wreathèd silver: sumptuous they stand
In the retired quiet of the night,
Filling the chilly room with perfume light.—
"And now, my love, my seraph fair, awake!
Thou art my heaven, and I thine eremite:
Open thine eyes, for meek St. Agnes' sake,
Or I shall drowse beside thee, so my soul doth
      ache."

32

Thus whispering, his warm, unnervèd arm   280
Sank in her pillow. Shaded was her dream
By the dusk curtains:—'twas a midnight charm
Impossible to melt as icèd stream:
The lustrous salvers in the moonlight gleam;
Broad golden fringe upon the carpet lies:
It seemed he never, never could redeem
From such a stedfast spell his lady's eyes;
So mused awhile, entoiled in woofèd phantasies.

33

Awakening up, he took her hollow lute,—
Tumultuous,—and, in chords that tenderest be,
He played an ancient ditty, long since mute,   291
In Provence called "La belle dame sans mercy":
Close to her ear touching the melody;—
Wherewith disturbed, she uttered a soft moan:
He ceased—she panted quick—and suddenly
Her blue affrayèd eyes wide open shone:
Upon his knees he sank, pale as smooth-sculptured
      stone.

34

Her eyes were open, but she still beheld,
Now wide awake, the vision of her sleep:
There was a painful change, that nigh expelled
The blisses of her dream so pure and deep   301
At which fair Madeline began to weep,
And moan forth witless words with many a sigh;
While still her gaze on Porphyro would keep;
Who knelt, with joinèd hands and piteous eye,
Fearing to move or speak, she looked so dreamingly.

35

"Ah, Porphyro!" said she, "but even now
Thy voice was at sweet tremble in mine ear,

36

Beyond a mortal man impassioned far
At these voluptuous accents, he arose,
Ethereal, flushed, and like a throbbing star
Seen mid the sapphire heaven's deep repose;
Into her dream he melted, as the rose   320
Blendeth its odour with the violet,—
Solution sweet: meantime the frost-wind blows
Like Love's alarum pattering the sharp sleet
Against the window-panes; St. Agnes' moon hath
      set.

Made tunable with every sweetest vow;
And those sad eyes were spiritual and clear: 310
How changed thou art! how pallid, chill, and
      drear!
Give me that voice again, my Porphyro,
Those looks immortal, those complainings dear!
Oh leave me not in this eternal woe,
For if thou diest, my Love, I know not where to go."

37

'Tis dark: quick pattereth the flaw-blown sleet:
"This is no dream, my bride, my Madeline!"
'Tis dark: the icèd gusts still rave and beat:
"No dream, alas! alas! and woe is mine!
Porphyro will leave me here to fade and pine.—
Cruel! what traitor could thee hither bring?   330
I curse not, for my heart is lost in thine,
Though thou forsakest a deceivèd thing;—
A dove forlorn and lost with sick unprunèd wing."

38

"My Madeline! sweet dreamer! lovely bride!
Say, may I be for aye thy vassal blest?
Thy beauty's shield, heart-shaped and vermeil
      dyed?
Ah, silver shrine, here will I take my rest
After so many hours of toil and quest,
A famished pilgrim,—saved by miracle.
Though I have found, I will not rob thy nest   340
Saving of thy sweet self; if thou think'st well
To trust, fair Madeline, to no rude infidel.

39

"Hark! 'tis an elfin-storm from faery land,
Of haggard seeming, but a boon indeed:
Arise—arise! the morning is at hand;—
The bloated wassaillers will never heed:—
Let us away, my love, with happy speed;
There are no ears to hear, or eyes to see,—
Drowned all in Rhenish and the sleepy mead:

277. eremite, hermit (religious).   **292. In Provence
called . . . mercy.**" Alain Chartier, a medieval French
poet of Provence (one of the old kingdoms of France), wrote
a poem with this title. Keats got no more from it than the
title. Compare his ballad of the same title. The phrase
means "The beautiful lady without mercy."

325. flaw-blown, wind-blown.   **344. seeming**, appearance. Compare "haggard" in "La Belle Dame sans Merci."

Awake! arise! my love, and fearless be,   350
For o'er the southern moors I have a home for
  thee."

40

She hurried at his words, beset with fear,
For there were sleeping dragons all around,
At glaring watch, perhaps, with ready spears—
Down the wide stairs a darkling way they
  found.—
In all the house was heard no human sound.
A chain-drooped lamp was flickering by each
  door;
The arras, rich with horseman, hawk, and hound,
Fluttered in the besieging wind's uproar;
And the long carpets rose along the gusty floor.   360

41

They glide, like phantoms, into the wide hall,
Like phantoms, to the iron porch, they glide;
Where lay the Porter, in uneasy sprawl,
With a huge empty flaggon by his side:
The wakeful bloodhound rose, and shook his
  hide,
But his sagacious eye an inmate owns:
By one, and one, the bolts full easy slide:—
The chains lie silent on the footworn stones;—
The key turns, and the door upon its hinges groans.

42

And they are gone: aye, ages long ago   370
These lovers fled away into the storm.
That night the Baron dreamt of many a woe,
And all his warrior-guests, with shade and form
Of witch, and demon, and large coffin-worm,
Were long be-nightmared. Angela the old
Died palsy-twitched, with meagre face deform;
The Beadsman after thousand aves told,
For aye unsought-for slept among his ashes cold.

THE EVE OF SAINT MARK

A Fragment

Keats wrote the poem a little later than "The Eve of
St. Agnes," after a visit at Winchester, where he saw the
ancient cathedral. After describing the old city in a letter
to George and Georgiana, he said: "The great beauty of
poetry is that it makes everything, every place interesting.
The palatine Venice and the abbotine Winchester are
equally interesting." (His poem refers, of course, to the
Venetian cathedral.)

358. **arras,** a fabric (usually for hangings) with interwoven figures.

The story, of which only the opening situation was
written, was apparently meant to be a metrical romance
treating a superstition. If a person placed himself at twilight on St. Mark's Eve near the church porch, he would
see the apparitions of persons in the parish who were to
suffer from disease. If they remained on the porch, they
were to die; if they went away, they were to recover. It
was over this story that Bertha, in the "fragment," was
musing. The description of her and her surroundings is
notable for its quiet beauty, the pictorial charm of its
medievalism.

Upon a Sabbath-day it fell;
Twice holy was the Sabbath-bell,
That called the folk to evening prayer;
The city streets were clean and fair
From wholesome drench of April rains;
And, on the western window panes,
The chilly sunset faintly told
Of unmatured green vallies cold,
Of the green thorny bloomless hedge,
Of rivers new with spring-tide sedge,   10
Of primroses by sheltered rills,
And daisies on the aguish hills.
Twice holy was the Sabbath-bell:
The silent streets were crowded well
With staid and pious companies,
Warm from their fireside orat'ries;
And moving, with demurest air,
To even-song, and vesper prayer.
Each archèd porch, and entry low,
Was filled with patient folk and slow,   20
With whispers hush, and shuffling feet,
While played the organ loud and sweet.

The bells had ceased, the prayers begun,
And Bertha had not yet half done
A curious volume, patched and torn,
That all day long, from earliest morn,
Had taken captive her two eyes,
Among its golden broideries;
Perplexed her with a thousand things,—
The stars of Heaven, and angels' wings,   30
Martyrs in a fiery blaze,
Azure saints and silver rays,
Moses' breastplate, and the seven
Candlesticks John saw in Heaven,
The wingèd Lion of Saint Mark,
And the Covenantal Ark,
With its many mysteries,
Cherubim and golden mice.

Bertha was a maiden fair,
Dwelling in the old Minster-square;   40
From her fireside she could see,

Sidelong, its rich antiquity,
Far as the Bishop's garden-wall;
Where sycamores and elm-trees tall,
Full-leaved, the forest had outstript,
By no sharp north-wind ever nipt,
So sheltered by the mighty pile.
Bertha arose, and read awhile,
With forehead 'gainst the window-pane.
Again she tried, and then again,   50
Until the dusk eve left her dark
Upon the legend of St. Mark.
From plaited lawn-frill, fine and thin,
She lifted up her soft warm chin,
With aching neck and swimming eyes,
And dazed with saintly imageries.

All was gloom, and silent all,
Save now and then the still foot-fall
Of one returning homewards late,
Past the echoing minster-gate.   60

The clamorous daws, that all the day
Above tree-tops and towers play,
Pair by pair had gone to rest,
Each in its ancient belfry-nest,
Where asleep they fall betimes,
To music and the drowsy chimes.

All was silent, all was gloom,
Abroad and in the homely room:
Down she sat, poor cheated soul!
And struck a lamp from the dismal coal;   70
Leaned forward, with bright drooping hair
And slant book, full against the glare.
Her shadow, in uneasy guise,
Hovered about, a giant size,
On ceiling-beam and old oak chair,
The parrot's cage, and panel square;
And the warm angled winter screen,
On which were many monsters seen,
Called doves of Siam, Lima mice,
And legless birds of Paradise,
Macaw, and tender Avadavat,   80
And silken-furred Angora cat.
Untired she read, her shadow still
Glowered about, as it would fill
The room with wildest forms and shades,
As though some ghostly queen of spades
Had come to mock behind her back,
And dance, and ruffle her garments black.
Untired she read the legend page,
Of holy Mark, from youth to age,   90

81. **Avadavat,** a corruption of "amadavat," a songbird of India.

On land, on sea, in pagan chains,
Rejoicing for his many pains.
Sometimes the learned eremite,
With golden star, or dagger bright,
Referred to pious poesies
Written in smallest crow-quill size
Beneath the text; and thus the rhyme
Was parcelled out from time to time:
——"Als writith he of swevenis,
Men han beforne they wake in bliss,   100
Whanne that hir friendes thinke him bound
In crimpèd shroude farre under grounde;
And how a litling child mote be
A saint er its nativitie,
Gif that the modre (God her blesse!)
Kepen in solitarinesse,
And kissen devoute the holy croce.
Of Goddes love, and Sathan's force,—
He writith; and thinges many mo
Of swiche thinges I may not show.   110
Bot I must tellen verilie
Somdel of Saintè Cicilie,
And chieflie what he auctorethe
Of Saintè Markis life and dethe:"

At length her constant eyelids come
Upon the fervent martyrdom;
Then lastly to his holy shrine,
Exalt amid the tapers' shine
At Venice,—

LA BELLE DAME SANS MERCI

For a suggested interpretation, see page 314. See, also, the note on "The Eve of St. Agnes," l. 292. Sidney Colvin (*John Keats*, Scribner, 1917, p. 350) points out that the "metrical secret" of the poem is the shortening of the last line in each stanza from four beats to two, the two to take in reading the full time of four, making the movement one of "awed and bodeful slowness." There is another version of the poem, but according to Colvin this is the "right" one. It is here reprinted with Keats's punctuation and spelling.

O what can ail thee Knight at arms
    Alone and palely loitering?
The sedge has withered from the Lake
    And no birds sing!

O what can ail thee Knight at arms
    So haggard and so woe begone?

99. **swevenis,** dreams. In the next fifteen lines Keats is imitating Chaucerian English; his story is medieval. Compare Chatterton. 103. **mote,** must. 112. **Somdel,** some part, a bit.

The Squirrel's granary is full
    And the harvest's done.

I see a lilly on thy brow
    With anguish moist and fever dew   10
And on thy cheek a fading rose
    Fast withereth too.

I met a Lady in the Meads
    Full beautiful, a faery's child
Her hair was long, her foot was light
    And her eyes were wild—

I made a garland for her head,
    And bracelets too, and fragrant zone
She looked at me as she did love
    And made sweet moan—   20

I set her on my pacing steed—
    And nothing else saw all day long
For sidelong would she bend and sing
    A faerys song—

She found me roots of relish sweet
    And honey wild and manna dew
And sure in language strange she said
    I love thee true.

She took me to her elfin grot
    And there she wept and sighed full sore,   30
And there I shut her wild wild eyes
    With Kisses four.

And there she lullèd me asleep
    And there I dreamed. Ah Woe betide!
The latest dream I ever dreamt
    On the cold hill side

I saw pale Kings, and Princes too
    Pale warriors death pale were they all
They cried La belle dame sans merci
    Thee hath in thrall.   40

I saw their starved lips in the gloam
    With horrid warning gapèd wide
And I awoke, and found me here
    On the cold hill's side.

13. **Lady,** as in the old ballad of "Thomas Rymer and Queen of Elfland" (Child, No. 37). **29. elfin grot,** fairy cave. **32. Kisses four.** "Why four Kisses—you will say— why four because . . . I was obliged to choose an even number that both eyes might have fair play. . . . I think two a piece quite sufficient. Suppose I had seven; there would have been three and a half a piece—a very awkward affair." (Keats, in the jesting letter to George and Georgiana enclosing the poem)

And this is why I sojourn here
    Alone and palely loitering;
Though the sedge is withered from the Lake
    And no birds sing— . . .

ODE TO PSYCHE

For this and the following odes, the student is referred to the general discussion of them on page 315.

According to Colvin, the "Ode to Psyche" is the first of the spring, 1819, odes; according to De Sélincourt, the last. The development is as follows: the poet's delight in the story of Cupid and Psyche (stanza 1) and the emotional virtue of the flowers among which he saw them lying (stanza 2); his sense of the meaning of the old Greek nature religion, his joyous imagining of the beauty of its shrines and rituals, his regret that Cupid and Psyche came into the hierarchy "too late for antique vows" (stanzas 3–4); and his determination to build them "a rosy sanctuary" and be their priest. In imagery and phrasing "Psyche" is linked with three of the other great odes (see the footnotes).

The myth of Cupid and Psyche, too long to be detailed here, tells how Venus, jealous of the princess Psyche, sends Cupid to inspire her with an unworthy love, how Cupid himself falls genuinely in love with her, and how their devotion is tested and Psyche finally wins immortality.

O Goddess! hear these tuneless numbers, wrung
    By sweet enforcement and remembrance dear,
And pardon that thy secrets should be sung
    Even into thine own soft-conchèd ear:
Surely I dreamt to-day, or did I see
    The wingèd Psyche with awakened eyes?
I wandered in a forest thoughtlessly,
    And, on the sudden, fainting with surprise,
Saw two fair creatures, couchèd side by side
    In deepest grass, beneath the whispering roof   10
Of leaves and trembled blossoms, where there ran
        A brooklet, scarce espied:

'Mid hushed, cool-rooted flowers, fragrant-eyed,
    Blue, silver-white, and budded Tyrian,
They lay calm-breathing on the bedded grass;
    Their arms embracèd, and their pinions too;
    Their lips touched not, but had not bade adieu,
As if disjoinèd by soft-handed slumber,
And ready still past kisses to outnumber
    At tender eye-dawn of aurorean love: 20
        The winged boy I knew;

4. **soft-conchèd,** like a soft sea shell. **14. Tyrian,** Tyrian purple or crimson. **17. had not bade adieu.** Compare "Ode on a Grecian Urn," ll. 17–20; "Ode on Melancholy," ll. 22–23. See also l. 66, below.

But who wast thou, O happy, happy dove?
    His Psyche true!

O latest born and loveliest vision far
    Of all Olympus' faded hierarchy!
Fairer than Phoebe's sapphire-regioned star,
    Or Vesper, amorous glow-worm of the sky;
Fairer than these, though temple thou hast none,
    Nor altar heaped with flowers;
Nor virgin-choir to make delicious moan   30
    Upon the midnight hours;
No voice, no lute, no pipe, no incense sweet
    From chain-swung censer teeming;
No shrine, no grove, no oracle, no heat
    Of pale-mouthed prophet dreaming.

O brightest! though too late for antique vows,
    Too, too late for the fond believing lyre,
When holy were the haunted forest boughs,
    Holy the air, the water, and the fire;
Yet even in these days so far retired   40
    From happy pieties, thy lucent fans,
    Fluttering among the faint Olympians,
I see, and sing, by my own eyes inspired.
So let me be thy choir, and make a moan
    Upon the midnight hours;
Thy voice, thy lute, thy pipe, thy incense sweet
    From swingèd censer teeming;
Thy shrine, thy grove, thy oracle, thy heat
    Of pale-mouthed prophet dreaming.

Yes, I will be thy priest, and build a fane   50
    In some untrodden region of my mind,
Where branchèd thoughts, new grown with pleas-
      ant pain,
    Instead of pines shall murmur in the wind:
Far, far around shall those dark-clustered trees
    Fledge the wild-ridged mountains steep by steep;
And there by zephyrs, streams, and birds, and
    bees,
    The moss-lain Dryads shall be lulled to sleep;
And in the midst of this wide quietness
A rosy sanctuary will I dress
With the wreathed trellis of a working brain,   60
    With buds, and bells, and stars without a name,
With all the gardener Fancy e'er could feign,
    Who breeding flowers, will never breed the
    same:
And there shall be for thee all soft delight
    That shadowy thought can win,
A bright torch, and a casement ope at night,
    To let the warm Love in!

26. Phoebe's, Diana's (the moon goddess').   **66. casement ope at night.** Compare "Ode to a Nightingale," l. 70.

ODE ON A GRECIAN URN

Perhaps the first step toward understanding and enjoyment of this ode is visual recognition of the little picture groups connected with the "flowery tale" and "leaf-fringed legend" sculptured on the urn: (1) a marriage ceremony or procession ("pursuit" of the bride is a common feature of primitive ceremonies); (2) a piper under the trees; (3) a youth making love to a maiden under the trees; (4) a religious procession led by a priest with a heifer. The first conclusion suggested by these pictures is in stanzas 2–3: "the supremacy of ideal art over nature, because of its unchanging perfection" (Bridges). Stanza 4, with its tone of sadness, suggests another aspect of this conclusion: such art arrests the villagers and cuts them off from the rest of life as if they had been enchanted into eternal immobility. The last stanza expresses a generalization ("Beauty is truth, truth beauty") of which the urn itself and the poem about it are examples: Beauty and truth are aspects of the same ultimate reality. "These two are reached, apprehended, and expressed in different ways; beauty in or through sense or imagination, truth in or by 'thought,' 'knowledge,' or 'philosophy.' But the two are none the less one and the same; so that whatever is felt, perceived, imagined as beautiful, would, if adequately expressed in an intellectual form, be found a reality truly conceived; and truth, adequately transformed into the shape of 'sensation' or imagination, would have turned into beauty."—A. C. Bradley, "Keats and 'Philosophy,'" *The John Keats Memorial Volume*, Lane, 1924, p. 45. (See also Keats's letter to Bailey, November 22, 1817, below.)

I

Thou still unravished bride of quietness,
    Thou foster-child of silence and slow time,
Sylvan historian, who canst thus express
    A flowery tale more sweetly than our rhyme:
What leaf-fringed legend haunts about thy shape
    Of deities or mortals, or of both,
      In Tempe or the dales of Arcady?
    What men or gods are these? What maidens
    loth?
What mad pursuit? What struggle to escape?
    What pipes and timbrels? What wild ec-
    stasy?   10

2

Heard melodies are sweet, but those unheard
    Are sweeter; therefore, ye soft pipes, play on;
Not to the sensual ear, but, more endeared,
    Pipe to the spirit ditties of no tone:
Fair youth, beneath the trees, thou canst not leave
    Thy song, nor ever can those trees be bare;
      Bold Lover, never, never canst thou kiss,

13. sensual, sensuous.

Though winning near the goal—yet, do not grieve;
　　She cannot fade, though thou hast not thy bliss,
　　For ever wilt thou love, and she be fair!　　20

3

Ah, happy, happy boughs! that cannot shed
　　Your leaves, nor ever bid the Spring adieu;
And, happy melodist, unwearièd,
　　For ever piping songs for ever new;
More happy love! more happy, happy love!
　　For ever warm and still to be enjoyed,
　　For ever panting, and for ever young;
All breathing human passion far above,
　　That leaves a heart high-sorrowful and cloyed,
　　A burning forehead, and a parching tongue.　30

4

Who are these coming to the sacrifice?
　　To what green altar, O mysterious priest,
Lead'st thou that heifer lowing at the skies,
　　And all her silken flanks with garlands drest?
What little town by river or sea shore,
　　Or mountain-built with peaceful citadel,
　　Is emptied of this folk, this pious morn?
And, little town, thy streets for evermore
　　Will silent be; and not a soul to tell
　　Why thou art desolate, can e'er return.　　40

5

O Attic shape! Fair attitude! with brede
　　Of marble men and maidens overwrought,
With forest branches and the trodden weed;
　　Thou, silent form, dost tease us out of thought
As doth eternity: Cold Pastoral!
　　When old age shall this generation waste,
　　Thou shalt remain, in midst of other woe
Than ours, a friend to man, to whom thou say'st,
　　"Beauty is truth, truth beauty,"—that is all
　　Ye know on earth, and all ye need to know.　50

ODE TO A NIGHTINGALE

As in the "Ode on a Grecian Urn," the fundamental idea is the superiority of beauty and joy expressed in great art to beauty and joy as we know them in actual life, because in art they are eternal and unfading, in nature and life, transitory. In "Grecian Urn," plastic art is the subject; in "Nightingale," poetry (the bird's *song*, not

41. **brede,** embroidery. The word has been read as an unintentional and awkward pun—"brede [breed] of marble men and maidens"! 45. **Cold Pastoral,** "Pastoral" because the pictures pertain to country life; "Cold" because the urn is of marble and, perhaps, also because its unchanging perfection makes us sad. Compare Byron's *Don Juan*, Canto IV, stanza 61.

the song *bird*). Moreover, "Nightingale" is tragically personal (see biographical facts). The poem is developed in two scenes: (1) the poet sitting in his garden (Brown's Wentworth Place, Hampstead), in the *morning* (l. 9), listening to the nightingale's song, brooding over the difference between life as the bird knows it and life as he knows it, wishing for an escape (wine at first, then poetry, which he takes); and (2) the poet in the imagined world, at *night*, to which the nightingale's song has transported him, glimpsing the immortality which the song suggests, and being brought back at last forlornly to his "sole self."

1

My heart aches, and a drowsy numbness pains
　　My sense, as though of hemlock I had drunk,
Or emptied some dull opiate to the drains
　　One minute past, and Lethe-wards had sunk:
'Tis not through envy of thy happy lot,
　　But being too happy in thine happiness,—
　　　　That thou, light wingèd Dryad of the trees,
　　　　　　In some melodious plot
　　Of beechen green, and shadows numberless,
　　　　Singest of summer in full-throated ease.　　10

2

O, for a draught of vintage! that hath been
　　Cooled a long age in the deep-delvèd earth,
Tasting of Flora and the country green,
　　Dance, and Provençal song, and sunburnt mirth!
O for a beaker full of the warm South,
　　Full of the true, the blushful Hippocrene,
　　　　With beaded bubbles winking at the brim,
　　　　　　And purple-stainèd mouth;
　　That I might drink, and leave the world unseen,
　　　　And with thee fade away into the forest dim:　20

3

Fade far away, dissolve, and quite forget
　　What thou among the leaves hast never known,
The weariness, the fever, and the fret
　　Here, where men sit and hear each other groan;
Where palsy shakes a few, sad, last gray hairs,
　　Where youth grows pale, and spectre-thin, and dies;
　　　　Where but to think is to be full of sorrow
　　　　　　And leaden-eyed despairs,
　　Where Beauty cannot keep her lustrous eyes,
　　　　Or new Love pine at them beyond to-morrow.　　30

2. **hemlock,** poison (Socrates died of it). 4. **Lethe-wards.** Lethe was the river of forgetfulness. 13. **Flora,** goddess of flowers. 14. **Provençal.** Provence was the kingdom of medieval France from which the troubadours and modern lyric poetry came. 16. **Hippocrene,** the Muses' fountain in Helicon.

4

Away! away! for I will fly to thee,
  Not charioted by Bacchus and his pards,
But on the viewless wings of Poesy,
  Though the dull brain perplexes and retards:
Already with thee! tender is the night,
  And haply the Queen-Moon is on her throne,
    Clustered around by all her starry Fays;
      But here there is no light;
Save what from heaven is with the breezes blown
  Through verdurous glooms and winding mossy
    ways.   40

5

I cannot see what flowers are at my feet,
  Nor what soft incense hangs upon the boughs,
But, in embalmèd darkness, guess each sweet
  Wherewith the seasonable month endows
The grass, the thicket, and the fruit-tree wild;
  White hawthorn, and the pastoral eglantine;
    Fast fading violets covered up in leaves;
      And Mid-May's eldest child,
The coming musk-rose, full of dewy wine,
  The murmurous haunt of flies on summer
    eves.   50

6

Darkling I listen; and, for many a time
  I have been half in love with easeful Death,
Called him soft names in many a musèd rhyme,
  To take into the air my quiet breath;
Now more than ever seems it rich to die,
  To cease upon the midnight with no pain,
    While thou art pouring forth thy soul abroad
      In such an ecstasy!
Still wouldst thou sing, and I have ears in vain—
  To thy high requiem become a sod.   60

7

Thou wast not born for death, immortal Bird!
  No hungry generations tread thee down;
The voice I hear this passing night was heard
  In ancient days by emperor and clown:
Perhaps the self-same song that found a path
  Through the sad heart of Ruth, when, sick for
    home,
    She stood in tears amid the alien corn;
      The same that oft-times hath
Charmed magic casements, opening on the foam
  Of perilous seas, in faery lands forlorn.   70

32. **pards,** leopards. They were supposed to accompany
Bacchus, god of wine. **33. viewless,** invisible.
43. embalmèd, sweet-smelling. **66. Ruth.** See Ruth 2.
69. Charmed magic casements. Compare the note on
Coleridge's "Kubla Khan," ll. 14–16.

8

Forlorn! the very word is like a bell
  To toll me back from thee to my sole self!
Adieu! the fancy cannot cheat so well
  As she is famed to do, deceiving elf.
Adieu! adieu! thy plaintive anthem fades
  Past the near meadows, over the still stream,
    Up the hill-side; and now 'tis buried deep
      In the next valley-glades:
Was it a vision or a waking dream?
  Fled is that music:—Do I wake or sleep?   80

ODE ON MELANCHOLY

As in the "Ode on a Grecian Urn" and the "Ode to a
Nightingale," imagination carries the poet to a perception of truth that kills the fear of death. In the very act of
beholding the paradox ("She dwells with Beauty—
Beauty that must die") the imagination triumphs; it
wrings beauty out of transiency; it perceives that Melancholy, too, must die.

1

No, no, go not to Lethe, neither twist
  Wolf's-bane, tight-rooted, for its poisonous wine;
Nor suffer thy pale forehead to be kissed
  By nightshade, ruby grape of Proserpine;
Make not your rosary of yew-berries,
  Nor let the beetle, nor the death-moth be
    Your mournful Psyche, nor the downy owl
A partner in your sorrow's mysteries;
  For shade to shade will come too drowsily,
    And drown the wakeful anguish of the soul.   10

2

But when the melancholy fit shall fall
  Sudden from heaven like a weeping cloud,
That fosters the droop-headed flowers all,
  And hides the green hill in an April shroud;
Then glut thy sorrow on a morning rose,
  Or on the rainbow of the salt sand-wave,
    Or on the wealth of globèd peonies;
Or if thy mistress some rich anger shows,
  Emprison her soft hand, and let her rave,
    And feed deep, deep upon her peerless eyes. 20

3

She dwells with Beauty—Beauty that must die;
  And Joy, whose hand is ever at his lips

**1–10. Lethe . . . Wolf's-bane . . . nightshade . . . the
soul,** the traditional means to induce melancholy. The poet
rejects these for the one in stanza 2. The poem is the distilla-
tion of a century or more of Romantic musings on the theme.
See Amy Reed's *The Background of Gray's Elegy,* Columbia
University Press, 1924. **13. droop-headed flowers all,** "all
the flowers only sacred to sorrow."—Bridges.

Bidding adieu; and aching Pleasure nigh,
 Turning to Poison while the bee-mouth sips:
Ay, in the very temple of Delight
 Veiled Melancholy has her sovran shrine,
  Though seen of none save him whose strenuous
   tongue
Can burst Joy's grape against his palate fine;
His soul shall taste the sadness of her might,
 And be among her cloudy trophies hung. 30

TO AUTUMN

The last of the 1819 odes; written at Winchester in September, after the poet had seen the harvest fields. The poem is purely objective; the poet surrenders himself to nature's mood; there is no melancholy brooding. The method is purely delineative. "Every line is like a bough . . . weighed down with fruit to the breaking-point"—Oliver Elton, *A Survey of English Literature, 1780–1830*, London, 1912. First is "the scented landscape" (stanza 1); then the season is humanized by the pictures of universal human occupations (these should be clearly recognized and visualized); finally, there is the symphony of natural autumnal sounds. "Nature has never spoken more truly in the human tongue."—H. I'A. Fausset, *Keats*, London, 1922.

1

Season of mists and mellow fruitfulness,
 Close bosom-friend of the maturing sun;
Conspiring with him how to load and bless
 With fruit the vines that round the thatch-eaves
  run;
To bend with apples the mossed cottage-trees,
 And fill all fruit with ripeness to the core;
  To swell the gourd, and plump the hazel shells
 With a sweet kernel; to set budding more,
And still more, later flowers for the bees,
Until they think warm days will never cease, 10
 For Summer has o'er-brimmed their clammy
  cells.

2

Who hath not seen thee oft amid thy store?
 Sometimes whoever seeks abroad may find
Thee sitting careless on a granary floor,
 Thy hair soft-lifted by the winnowing wind;
Or on a half-reaped furrow sound asleep,
 Drowsed with the fume of poppies, while thy
  hook
Spares the next swath and all its twinèd flowers:
And sometimes like a gleaner thou dost keep
 Steady thy laden head across a brook; 20
 Or by a cider-press, with patient look,
  Thou watchest the last oozings hours by hours.

3

Where are the songs of Spring? Ay, where are they?
 Think not of them, thou hast thy music too,—
While barred clouds bloom the soft-dying day,
 And touch the stubble-plains with rosy hue;
Then in a wailful choir the small gnats mourn
 Among the river sallows, borne aloft
  Or sinking as the light wind lives or dies;
And full-grown lambs loud bleat from hilly bourn;
 Hedge-crickets sing; and now with treble soft 31
  The red-breast whistles from a garden-croft;
   And gathering swallows twitter in the skies.

SONNETS

TO FANNY

I cry your mercy—pity—love!—aye, love!
 Merciful love that tantalizes not,
One-thoughted, never-wandering, guileless love,
 Unmasked, and being seen—without a blot!
O! let me have thee whole,—all—all—be mine!
 That shape, that fairness, that sweet minor zest
Of love, your kiss,—those hands, those eyes divine,
 That warm, white, lucent, million-pleasured
  breast,—
Yourself—your soul—in pity give me all,
 Withhold no atom's atom or I die, 10
Or living on perhaps, your wretched thrall,
 Forget, in the mist of idle misery,
Life's purposes,—the palate of my mind
Losing its gust, and my ambition blind!

BRIGHT STAR! WOULD I WERE STEDFAST
AS THOU ART

Often called Keats's "last sonnet." When the ship that was taking him to Italy in September, 1820, encountered storms in the Channel and had to turn back for repairs, Keats went ashore and wrote the sonnet in a volume of Shakespeare's poems, facing "The Lover's Complaint." For an excellent critical article taking its title from the first line, see Leonard Bacon's "A Poet Steadfast as His Star," *Saturday Review of Literature*, Sept. 1, 1934.

Bright star! would I were stedfast as thou art—
 Not in lone splendour hung aloft the night
And watching, with eternal lids apart,
 Like Nature's patient, sleepless Eremite,
The moving waters at their priestlike task
 Of pure ablution round earth's human shores,

28. **sallows,** willows. 30. **bourn,** domain. Keats uses the word somewhat erroneously. 14. **gust.** taste.

Or gazing on the new soft-fallen mask
   Of snow upon the mountains and the moors—
No—yet still stedfast, still unchangeable,
   Pillowed upon my fair love's ripening breast,
To feel forever its soft fall and swell,   11
   Awake forever in a sweet unrest,
Still, still to hear her tender-taken breath,
And so live ever—or else swoon to death.

LETTERS

In a period of great letter-writers, Keats's letters are remarkable. Their spontaneity, naturalness, and complete sincerity, the wide range of interests they express, and the experiences they record make them fascinating for themselves and indispensable for an understanding of his personality and art. The first of those which follow chats charmingly to his little sister Fanny about her reading, about her travel, and about some of his poetic employments. The second sets forth his idea of happiness and of the attitude of mind and mood necessary to attain it; it is also (in the statement about the sparrow) an excellent description of what he meant by Shakespeare's "negative capability," one of the secrets of highest poetic power. The one to Reynolds is an eloquent interpretation of a passage in Wordsworth's "Tintern Abbey" and a tribute to the philosophic vision and understanding of the older poet; it also touches lightly Keats's friendships and his grief. The letter to Tom is one of the best of his fine travel letters—on Highland scenery and people. The famous "Vale of Soul-making" passage from his letter to George and Georgiana is one of his noblest utterances on human life. The last reprinted here is a love letter to Fanny Brawne.

Keats's letters, in three volumes, have been edited by H. B. Forman (London, 1895) and M. B. Forman (2d ed., Oxford Press, 1935). In 1933 Mr. Earle V. Weller published *Autobiography of John Keats* (Stanford University Press), an arrangement of Keats's letters and essays, prefaced by Charles Cowden Clarke's account of the poet's boyhood, which makes Keats tell the story of his own life. Keats used few paragraphs in his letters; others are indicated here to make reading easier.

"SCRIBBLINGS TO YOUR PLEASURE"

To Fanny Keats

Oxford, Sept 10th [1817]

My dear Fanny,

Let us now begin a regular question and answer—a little pro and con; letting it interfere as a pleasant method of my coming at your favorite little wants and enjoyments, that I may meet them in a way befitting a brother.

We have been so little together since you have been able to reflect on things that I know not whether you prefer the History of King Pepin to Bunyan's Pilgrim's Progress—or Cinderella and her glass slipper to Moor's Almanack. However in a few Letters I hope I shall be able to come at that and adapt my scribblings to your Pleasure. You must tell me about all you read if it be only six Pages in a Week—and this transmitted to me every now and then will procure you full sheets of Writing from me pretty frequently.—This I feel as a necessity for we ought to become intimately acquainted, in order that I may not only, as you grow up love you as my only Sister, but confide in you as my dearest friend. When I saw you last I told you of my intention of going to Oxford and 'tis now a Week since I disembark'd from his Whipship's Coach the Defiance in this place. I am living in Magdalen Hall on a visit to a young Man with whom I have not been long acquainted, but whom I like very much—we lead very industrious lives—he in general Studies and I in proceeding at a pretty good rate with a Poem which I hope you will see early in the next year.—Perhaps you might like to know what I am writing about. I will tell you.

Many Years ago there was a young handsome Shepherd who fed his flocks on a Mountain's Side called Latmus—he was a very contemplative sort of a Person and lived solitary among the trees and Plains little thinking that such a beautiful Creature as the Moon was growing mad in Love with him.—However so it was; and when he was asleep on the Grass she used to come down from heaven and admire him excessively for a long time; and at last could not refrain from carrying him away in her arms to the top of that high Mountain Latmus while he was a dreaming—but I dare say [you] have read this and all the other beautiful Tales which have come down from the ancient times of that beautiful Greece. If you have not let me know and I will tell you more at large of others quite as delightful.

This Oxford I have no doubt is the finest City in the world—it is full of old Gothic buildings—Spires—towers—Quadrangles—Cloisters—Groves &c. and is surrounded with more clear streams than ever I saw together. I take a Walk by the Side of one of them every Evening and, thank God, we have not had a drop of rain these many days.

I had a long and interesting Letter from George, cross lines by a short one from Tom yesterday dated Paris. They both send their loves to you. Like most Englishmen they feel a mighty preference for every

17. **young Man**, Benjamin Bailey. 26. **Shepherd**, Endymion.

thing English—the French Meadows, the trees, the yours—and thus in the course of time we shall each
People, the Towns, the Churches, the Books, the of us have a good Bundle—which, hereafter, when
every thing—although they may be in themselves things may have strangely altered and god knows
good: yet when put in comparison with our green what happened, we may read over together and
Island they all vanish like Swallows in October. look with pleasure on times past—that now are to
They have seen Cathedrals, Manuscripts, Foun- come. Give my Respects to the Ladies—and so my
tains, Pictures, Tragedy, Comedy,—with other dear Fanny I am ever
things you may by chance meet with in this Coun-
try such a[s] Washerwomen, Lamplighters, Turn- Your most affectionate Brother
pikemen, Fishkettles, Dancing Masters, Kettle 10 John
drums, Sentry Boxes, Rocking Horses &c.—and, If you direct—Post Office, Oxford—your Letter
now they have taken them over a set of boxing will be brought to me.—
gloves. I have written to George and requested
him, as you wish I should, to write to you.

I have been writing very hard lately, even till an
utter incapacity came on, and I feel it now about from "O FOR A LIFE OF SENSATIONS!"
my head: so you must not mind a little out of the
way sayings—though by the bye were my brain as To Benjamin Bailey
clear as a bell I think I should have a little pro-
pensity thereto. I shall stop here till I have finished 20 [Burford Bridge, November 22, 1817]
the 3rd Book of my Story; which I hope will be My dear Bailey,
accomplish'd in at most three Weeks from to day— . . . What the Imagination seizes as Beauty must
about which time you shall see me. be truth—whether it existed before or not,—for I

How do you like Miss Taylor's essays in Rhyme have the same idea of all our passions as of Love: they
—I just look'd into the Book and it appeared to me are all, in their sublime, creative of essential Beauty.
suitable to you—especially since I remember your In a Word, you may know my favourite speculation
liking for those pleasant little things the Original by my first Book, and the little Song I sent in my
Poems—the essays are the more mature production last, which is a representation from the fancy of the
of the same hand. While I was speaking about probable mode of operating in these Matters.
France it occurred to me to speak a few Words on 30 The Imagination may be compared to Adam's
their Language—it is perhaps the poorest one ever dream,—he awoke and found it truth:—I am more
spoken since the jabbering in the Tower of Babel, zealous in this affair, because I have never yet been
and when you come to know that the real use and able to perceive how anything can be known for
greatness of a Tongue is to be referred to its Litera- truth by consecutive reasoning—and yet it must be.
ture—you will be astonished to find how very in- Can it be that even the greatest Philosopher ever
ferior it is to our native Speech.—I wish the Italian arrived at his Goal without putting aside numerous
would supersede French in every school throughout objections?
the Country, for that is full of real Poetry and Ro- However it may be, O for a life of Sensations
mance of a kind more fitted for the Pleasure of La- rather than of Thoughts! It is "a Vision in the form
dies than perhaps our own.—It seems that the 40 of Youth," a shadow of reality to come—and this
only end to be gained in acquiring French is the im- consideration has further convinced me,—for it
mense accomplishment of speaking it—it is none at has come as auxiliary to another favourite specula-
all—a most lamentable mistake indeed. Italian tion of mine,—that we shall enjoy ourselves here-
indeed would sound most musically from Lips after by having what we called happiness on Earth
which began to pronounce it as early as the French repeated in a finer tone. And yet such a fate can
is crammed down our Mouths, as if we were young only befall those who delight in Sensation, rather
Jackdaws at the mercy of an overfeeding School- than hunger as you do after Truth. Adam's dream
boy. will do here, and seems to be a Conviction that

Now Fanny you must write soon—and write all Imagination and its empyreal reflexion, is the same
you think about, never mind what—only let me 50 as human life and its spiritual repetition. But, as I
have a good deal of your writing—You need not was saying, the simple imaginative Mind may have
do it all at once—be two or three or four day[s] its rewards in the repetition of its own silent Work-
about it, and let it be a diary of your little Life. ing coming continually on the Spirit with a fine
You will preserve all my Letters and I will secure Suddenness.

To compare great things with small, have you
never by being surprised with an old Melody, in a
delicious place by a delicious voice, *felt* over again

your very speculations and surmises at the time it first operated on your soul? do you not remember forming to yourself the Singer's face—more beautiful than it was possible, and yet, with the elevation of the Moment, you did not think so? Even then you were mounted on the Wings of Imagination, so high that the prototype must be hereafter—that delicious face you will see. What a time! I am continually running away from the subject. Sure this cannot be exactly the Case with a complex mind—one that is imaginative, and at the same time careful of its fruits,—who would exist partly on Sensation, partly on thought—to whom it is necessary that "years should bring the philosophic Mind"? Such a one I consider yours, and therefore it is necessary to your eternal happiness that you not only drink this old Wine of Heaven, which I shall call the redigestion of our most ethereal Musings upon Earth, but also increase in knowledge and know all things. I am glad to hear that you are in a fair way for Easter. You will soon get through your unpleasant reading, and then!—but the world is full of troubles, and I have not much reason to think myself pestered with many.

I think Jane or Marianne has a better opinion of me than I deserve: for, really and truly, I do not think my Brother's illness connected with mine—you know more of the real Cause than they do; nor have I any chance of being rack'd as you have been. You perhaps at one time thought there was such a thing as worldly happiness to be arrived at, at certain periods of time marked out,—you have of necessity from your disposition been thus led away—I scarcely remember counting upon any happiness—I look not for it if it be not in the present hour,—nothing startles me beyond the moment. The Setting Sun will always set me to rights, or if a Sparrow come before my Window, I take part in its existence and pick about the gravel. The first thing that strikes me on hearing a misfortune having befallen another is this—"Well, it cannot be helped: he will have the pleasure of trying the resources of his Spirit"—and I beg now, my dear Bailey, that hereafter should you observe anything cold in me not to put it to the account of heartlessness, but abstraction—for I assure you I sometimes feel not the influence of a passion or affection during a whole Week—and so long this sometimes continues, I begin to suspect myself, and the genuineness of my feelings at other times—thinking them a few barren Tragedy Tears.

My brother Tom is much improved—he is going to Devonshire—whither I shall follow him. At present, I am just arrived at Dorking—to change

the Scene—change the Air, and give me a spur to wind up my Poem, of which there are wanting 500 lines. I should have been here a day sooner, but the Reynoldses persuaded me to stop in Town to meet your friend Christie. There were Rice and Martin—we talked about Ghosts. I will have some Talk with Taylor and let you know,—when please God I come down at Christmas. I will find that Examiner if possible. My best regards to Gleig, my Brothers' to you and Mrs. Bentley.

> Your affectionate Friend
> John Keats.

I want to say much more to you—a few hints will set me going. Direct Burford Bridge near Dorking.

from "A MANSION OF MANY APARTMENTS"

To John Hamilton Reynolds

Teignmouth, 3 May [1818]

My dear Reynolds,

. . . With your patience, I will return to Wordsworth—whether or no he has an extended vision or a circumscribed grandeur—whether he is an eagle in his nest or on the wing. And to be more explicit and to show you how tall I stand by the giant, I will put down a simile of human life as far as I now perceive it; that is, to the point to which I say we both have arrived at—

Well—I compare human life to a large Mansion of Many apartments, two of which I can only describe, the doors of the rest being as yet shut upon me—The first we step into we call the Infant or Thoughtless Chamber, in which we remain as long as we do not think. We remain there a long while, and notwithstanding the doors of the second Chamber remain wide open, showing a bright appearance, we care not to hasten to it; but are at length imperceptibly impelled by the awakening of the thinking principle within us—we no sooner get into the second Chamber, which I shall call the Chamber of Maiden-Thought, than we become intoxicated with the light and the atmosphere, we see nothing but pleasant wonders, and think of delaying there for ever in delight. However among the effects this breathing is father of is that tremendous one of sharpening one's vision into the heart and nature of Man—of convincing one's nerves that the world is full of Misery and Heartbreak, Pain, Sickness, and oppression—whereby this Chamber of Maiden-Thought becomes gradually darkened, and at the same time, on all sides of it, many doors are set open—but all dark—all leading to dark pas-

2. **Poem**, *Endymion*.

sages. We see not the balance of good and evil; we are in a mist, *we* are now in that state—We feel the "burden of the Mystery."

To this point was Wordsworth come, as far as I can conceive, when he wrote "Tintern Abbey," and it seems to me that his Genius is explorative of those dark Passages. Now if we live, and go on thinking, we too shall explore them. . . . He is a genius and superior to us, in so far as he can, more than we, make discoveries, and shed a light in them. Here I must think Wordsworth is deeper than Milton, though I think it has depended more upon the general and gregarious advance of intellect, than individual greatness of Mind. From the Paradise Lost and the other Works of Milton, I hope it is not too presuming, even between ourselves, to say, that his Philosophy, human and divine, may be tolerably understood by one not much advanced in years. In his time Englishmen were just emancipated from a great superstition, and Men had got hold of certain points and resting-places in reasoning which were too newly born to be doubted, and too much opposed by the Mass of Europe not to be thought ethereal and authentically divine—Who could gainsay his ideas on virtue, vice, and Chastity in Comus just at the time of the dismissal of Cod-pieces and a hundred other disgraces? who would not rest satisfied with his hintings at good and evil in the Paradise Lost, when just free from the Inquisition and burning in Smithfield? The Reformation produced such immediate and great benefits, that Protestantism was considered under the immediate eye of heaven, and its own remaining dogmas and superstitions then, as it were, regenerated, constituted those resting-places and seeming sure points of Reasoning—from that I have mentioned, Milton, whatever he may have thought in the sequel, appears to have been content with these of his writings. He did not think into the human heart as Wordsworth has done. Yet Milton as a Philosopher had sure as great Powers as Wordsworth.

What is then to be inferred? O many things. It proves there is a really grand march of intellect; it proves that a mighty Providence subdues the mightiest minds to the service of the time being, whether it be in human Knowledge or Religion. I have often pitied a tutor who has to hear "Nom: Musa" so often dinn'd into his ears—I hope you may not have the same pain in this scribbling—I may have read these things before, but I never had even a thus dim perception of them; and moreover I like to say my lesson to one who will endure my tediousness, for my own sake.

After all there is certainly something real in the world—Moore's present to Hazlitt is real—I like that Moore, and am glad I saw him at the Theatre just before I left Town. Tom has spit a *leetle* blood this afternoon, and that is rather a damper—but I know—the truth is, there is something real in the World. Your third Chamber of Life shall be a lucky and a gentle one—stored with the wine of Love—and the Bread of Friendship.

When you see George, if he should not have received a letter from me tell him he will find one at home most likely—tell Bailey I hope soon to see him. Remember me to all. The leaves have been out here for many a day. I have written to George for the first stanzas of my "Isabel,"—I shall have them soon, and will copy the whole out for you.

Your affectionate friend
John Keats

"FLY CRAWLING UP A WAINSCOAT"

To Thomas Keats

Letter Findlay, August 3rd
[Postmark, Inverness, 6 August 1818]
Ah mio Ben.

My dear Tom,

We have made but poor progress lately, chiefly from bad weather, for my throat is in a fair way of getting quite well, so I have had nothing of consequence to tell you till yesterday when we went up Ben Nevis, the highest Mountain in Great Britain. On that account I will never ascend another in this empire—Skiddaw is nothing to it either in height or in difficulty. It is above 4,300 feet from the Sea level, and Fortwilliam stands at the head of a Salt water Lake, consequently we took it completely from that level. I am heartily glad it is done—it is almost like a fly crawling up a wainscoat. Imagine the task of mounting ten Saint Pauls without the convenience of Staircases.

We set out about five in the morning with a Guide in the Tartan and Cap, and soon arrived at the foot of the first ascent which we immediately began upon—after much fag and tug and a rest and a glass of whiskey apiece we gained the top of the first rise and saw then a tremendous chap above us, which the guide said was still far from the top. After the first Rise our way lay along a heath valley in which there was a Loch—after about a Mile in this

28. **progress.** Professor N. S. Bushnell's *A Walk after John Keats*, Oxford Press, 1936, recounts his experiences a few years ago while following in Keats's steps on this Northern tour.

Valley we began upon the next ascent, more formidable by far than the last, and kept mounting with short intervals of rest until we got above all vegetation, among nothing but loose Stones which lasted us to the very top—the Guide said we had three Miles of a stony ascent—we gained the first tolerable level after the valley to the height of what in the Valley we had thought the top and saw still above us another huge crag which still the Guide said was not the top—to that we made with an obstinate fag, and having gained it there came on a Mist, so that from that part to the very top we walked in a Mist.

The whole immense head of the Mountain is composed of large loose stones—thousands of acres. Before we had got halfway up we passed large patches of snow and near the top there is a chasm some hundred feet deep completely glutted with it.—Talking of chasms they are the finest wonder of the whole—they appear great rents in the very heart of the mountain though they are not, being at the side of it, but other huge crags arising round it give the appearance to Nevis of a shattered heart or Core in itself. These Chasms are 1500 feet in depth and are the most tremendous places I have ever seen—they turn one giddy if you choose to give way to it. We tumbled in large stones and set the echoes at work in fine style. Sometimes these chasms are tolerably clear, sometimes there is a misty cloud which seems to steam up and sometimes they are entirely smothered with clouds.

After a little time the Mist cleared away but still there were large Clouds about attracted by old Ben to a certain distance so as to form as it appeared large dome curtains which kept sailing about, opening and shutting at intervals here and there and everywhere: so that although we did not see one vast wide extent of prospect all round we saw something perhaps finer—these cloud-veils opening with a dissolving motion and showing us the mountainous region beneath as through a loophole— these cloudy loopholes ever varying and discovering fresh prospect east, west, north and south. Then it was misty again, and again it was fair—then puff came a cold breeze of wind and bared a craggy chap we had not yet seen though in close neighbourhood. Every now and then we had overhead blue Sky clear and the sun pretty warm.

I do not know whether I can give you an Idea of the prospect from a large Mountain top. You are on a stony plain which of course makes you forget you are on any but low ground—the horizon or rather edges of this plain being above 4000 feet above the Sea hide all the Country immediately beneath you, so that the next object[s] you see all round next to the edges of the flat top are the Summits of Mountains of some distance off. As you move about on all sides you see more or less of the near neighbour country according as the Mountain you stand upon is in different parts steep or rounded—but the most new thing of all is the sudden leap of the eye from the extremity of what appears a plain into so vast a distance.

On one part of the top there is a handsome pile of Stones done pointedly by some soldiers of artillery; I climbed onto them and so got a little higher than old Ben himself. It was not so cold as I expected—yet cold enough for a glass of Whiskey now and then. There is not a more fickle thing than the top of a Mountain—what would a Lady give to change her head-dress as often and with as little trouble!—There are a good many red deer upon Ben Nevis—we did not see one—the dog we had with us kept a very sharp look out and really languished for a bit of a worry.

I have said nothing yet of our getting on among the loose stones large and small sometimes on two, sometimes on three, sometimes four legs—sometimes two and stick, sometimes three and stick, then four again, then two, then a jump, so that we kept on ringing changes on foot, hand, stick, jump, boggle, stumble, foot, hand, foot (very gingerly), stick again, and then again a game at all fours.

After all there was one Mrs. Cameron of 50 years of age and the fattest woman in all Invernesshire who got up this Mountain some few years ago— true she had her servants—but then she had her self. She ought to have hired Sysyphus—"Up the high hill he leaves a huge round—Mrs. Cameron." 'Tis said a little conversation took place between the mountain and the Lady. After taking a glass of Whiskey as she was tolerably seated at ease she thus began— . . .

[Here he copies the "Lines on Ben Nevis."]

But what surprises me above all is how this Lady got down again. I felt it horribly. 'Twas the most vile descent—shook me all to pieces. Over leaf you will find a Sonnet I wrote on the top of Ben Nevis. We have just entered Inverness. I have three Letters from you and one [from] Fanny—and one from Dilke. I would set about crossing this all over for you but I will first write to Fanny and Mrs. Wylie. Then I will begin another to you and not before because I think it better you should have this as soon as possible. My Sore throat is not quite well and I intend stopping here a few days. . . .

[He copies the sonnet "Ben Nevis."]

Good bye till to-morrow.

Your most affectionate Brother
John—

from "VALE OF SOUL-MAKING"

To George and Georgiana Keats

[April 15, 1819]

My Dear Brother and Sister:

. . . The common cognomen of this world among the misguided and superstitious is "a vale of tears" from which we are to be redeemed by a certain arbitrary interposition of God and taken to Heaven—What a little circumscribed straightened notion! Call the world if you please "The vale of Soul-making." Then you will find out the use of the world (I am speaking now in the highest terms for human nature admitting it to be immortal which I will here take for granted for the purpose of showing a thought which has struck me concerning it) I say "*Soul-making*"—Soul as distinguished from an Intelligence. There may be intelligences or sparks of the divinity in millions—but they are not Souls till they acquire identities, till each one is personally itself. Intelligences are atoms of perception—they know and they see and they are pure, in short they are God.—How then are the Souls to be made? How then are these sparks which are God to have identity given them—so as ever to possess a bliss peculiar to each one's individual existence? How but by the medium of a world like this? . . .

Do you not see how necessary a World of Pains and troubles is to school an Intelligence and make it a Soul? . . . Seriously I think it probable that this system of Soul-making may have been the Parent of all the more palpable and personal schemes of Redemption among the Zoroastrians, the Christians and the Hindoos. For as one part of the human species must have their carved Jupiter; so another part must have the palpable and named Mediator and Saviour, their Christ, their Oromanes, and their Vishnu.

If what I have said should not be plain enough, as I fear it may not be, I will put you in the place where I began in this series of thoughts—I mean I began by seeing how man was formed by circumstances—and what are circumstances but touchstones of his heart? and what are touchstones but provings of his heart, but fortifiers or alterers of his nature? and what is his altered nature but his Soul?—and what was his Soul before it came into the world and had these provings and alterations and perfectionings?—An intelligence without Identity—and how is this Identity to be made? Through the medium of the Heart? and how is the heart to become this Medium but in a world of Circumstances?

There now I think what with Poetry and Theology you may thank your stars that my pen is not very long winded. Yesterday I received two Letters from your Mother and Henry, which I shall send by young Birkbeck with this.

Friday, April 30

Brown has been here rummaging up some of my old sins—that is to say sonnets. I do not think you remember them, so I will copy them out as well as two or three lately written. I have just written one on Fame—which Brown is transcribing and he has his book and mine. I must employ myself perhaps in a sonnet on the same subject.— . . .

[Here are given the two sonnets on "Fame," and the one "To Sleep."]

The following Poem—the last I have written—is the first and the only one with which I have taken even moderate pains. I have for the most part dash'd off my lines in a hurry. This I have done leisurely—I think it reads the more richly for it, and will I hope encourage me to write other things in even a more peaceable and healthy spirit. You must recollect that Psyche was not embodied as a goddess before the time of Apuleius the Platonist who lived after the Augustan age, and consequently the Goddess was never worshipped or sacrificed to with any of the ancient fervour—and perhaps never thought of in the old religion—I am more orthodox than to let a heathen Goddess be so neglected— . . .

[The "Ode to Psyche" follows here.]

I have been endeavouring to discover a better Sonnet Stanza than we have. The legitimate does not suit the language over well from the pouncing rhymes—the other kind appears too elegiac—and the couplet at the end of it has seldom a pleasing effect—I do not pretend to have succeeded—it will explain itself.

[Sonnet, "If by Dull Rhymes."]

[May 3]

This is the third of May, and everything is in delightful forwardness; the violets are not withered before the peeping of the first rose. You must let me know everything—how parcels go and come, what papers you have, and what newspapers you want, and other things. God bless you, my dear brother and sister,

Your ever affectionate Brother

John Keats.

"so let me speak of your beauty"

To Fanny Brawne

July 8th.

[Postmark, Newport, 10 July 1819.]

My sweet Girl,

Your Letter gave me more delight than anything in the world but yourself could do; indeed I am almost astonished that any absent one should have that luxurious power over my senses which I feel. Even when I am not thinking of you I receive your influence and a tenderer nature stealing upon me. All my thoughts, my unhappiest days and nights, have I find not at all cured me of my love of Beauty, but made it so intense that I am miserable that you are not with me: or rather breathe in that dull sort of patience that cannot be called Life. I never knew before, what such a love as you have made me feel, was; I did not believe in it; my Fancy was afraid of it, lest it should burn me up. But if you will fully love me, though there may be some fire, 'twill not be more than we can bear when moistened and bedewed with Pleasures. You mention "horrid people" and ask me whether it depend upon them whether I see you again. Do understand me, my love, in this. I have so much of you in my heart that I must turn Mentor when I see a chance of harm befalling you. I would never see any thing but Pleasure in your eyes, love on your lips, and Happiness in your steps. I would wish to see you among those amusements suitable to your inclinations and spirits; so that our loves might be a delight in the midst of Pleasures agreeable enough, rather than a resource from vexations and cares. But I doubt much, in case of the worst, whether I shall be philosopher enough to follow my own Lessons: if I saw my resolution give you a pain I could not.

Why may I not speak of your Beauty, since without that I could never have lov'd you?—I cannot conceive any beginning of such love as I have for you but Beauty. There may be a sort of love for which, without the least sneer at it, I have the highest respect and can admire it in others: but it has not the richness, the bloom, the full form, the enchantment of love after my own heart. So let me speak of your Beauty, though to my own endangering; if you could be so cruel to me as to try elsewhere its Power.

You say you are afraid I shall think you do not love me—in saying this you make me ache the more to be near you. I am at the diligent use of my faculties here, I do not pass a day without sprawling some blank verse or tagging some rhymes; and here I must confess, that (since I am on that subject) I love you the more in that I believe you have liked me for my own sake and for nothing else. I have met with women whom I really think would like to be married to a Poem and to be given away by a Novel.

I have seen your Comet, and only wish it was a sign that poor Rice would get well whose illness makes him rather a melancholy companion: and the more so as to conquer his feelings and hide them from me, with a forc'd Pun. I kiss'd your writing over in the hope you had indulg'd me by leaving a trace of honey. What was your dream? Tell it me and I will tell you that interpretation thereof.

Ever yours, my love!

John Keats

Do not accuse me of delay—we have not here an opportunity of sending letters every day. Write speedily.

18–19. liked me for my own sake. For a long time the legend persisted that Fanny Brawne was, to say the least, a shallow, flirtatious young woman, unworthy of the love Keats gave her. Amy Lowell attacked the legend. Recently Mr. Fred Edgcumbe's edition of *Letters from Fanny Brawne to Fanny Keats, 1820–24*, Oxford University Press, 1936, has been regarded as a complete refutation of it. Her own letters show that "When their love was young she may have been a rattle and a tease," but that "In its maturity she knew the worth of her lover . . . and she loved him as he deserved."

Thomas De Quincey
1785–1859

Thomas De Quincey was born August 15, 1785, at Manchester. His father was a successful merchant who had some literary taste and cultivation. His mother was a righteous, humorless woman with a vigorous intellect. The children of the family were precocious and high-strung. Two of them died of brain fever, one lived for years in a fantastic world of his own creation, and another, Pink, ran away to sea and encountered adventures rivaling those of one of Stevenson's heroes. A sickly, petted child, too soon acquainted with grief, an omnivorous reader, Thomas spent his early years at The Farm and at Greenhay, near Manchester. He attended schools at Bath, Winkfield, and Manchester. Before he was eleven, he was a skillful Latinist; at thirteen, he wrote Greek with ease and conversed in it. Mr. Morgan, his teacher, said of him, "That boy could harangue an Athenian mob better than you or I could address an English one." In 1802, while he was at Manchester Grammar School, he "was quoting from Wordsworth." Unhappy in his school life, he ran away, in the amusing manner related in his *Confessions of an English Opium-Eater.* Imperfectly reconciled with his family, he embarked upon travels in Wales. There he cut himself loose from the family and wandered at will until his money gave out and winter overtook him. In London, he lived precariously, companion of waif children and streetwalkers (Ann of Oxford Street). After a second reconciliation, he lived for a while at Everton, reading novels, projecting literary works, and keeping a diary.

Partly on Wordsworth's advice, in 1803 he entered Oxford. Here he lived a lonely life, "immersed in metaphysics, psychology, and moral Philosophy," reading Greek daily. His real passion, however, was for the new Romantic literature of Coleridge, Wordsworth, Southey, Lamb, and Landor. At Oxford he formed the opium habit, at first as a palliative for neuralgia brought on by the exposure of his *Wanderjahre*, and had some of the dreams that he was to describe in *Suspiria de Profundis.* He left Oxford in May, 1808, in the midst of his final examinations and therefore without his degree.

By 1807 De Quincey had formed an acquaintance with Lamb, and in that year he met Coleridge "in a muse beneath a gateway at Bridgewater." As the result of an exchange of confidences, De Quincey arranged to give Coleridge the sum of £300. The vividly remembered meeting with Wordsworth followed soon after, and an intimate friendship developed. In 1809 De Quincey succeeded Wordsworth as the tenant of Dove Cottage, Grasmere. He lived there for twenty-one years, in 1816 marrying Margaret Simpson, a farmer's daughter, and enjoying a happy domestic life, in spite of the snobbish attitude of the Wordsworths and others toward his wife. Opium, German philosophy, and writing made up his larger world. His last years he spent in Edinburgh, whither he went in 1830 because of his literary connections. He died peacefully there December 8, 1859.

De Quincey possessed extraordinary gifts—a marvelous memory, power of subtle analysis, sensitiveness to beauty, and sympathy for the weak and suffering. Next to Coleridge's, his conversation seems to have been the most brilliant of the period; his manners were exquisite; his bearing was winsome. His will, when he chose to exercise it, was strong. But he was impractical, a dreamer, an introvert. It is said that while he was in Edinburgh writing an essay on the theory of money he walked the streets one day trying to negotiate a loan of £1 on the security of a £10 Bank of England note. His opium habit seems to have been both a boon, in freeing and heightening his imaginative processes, and a bane, in cutting him off from reality and often defeating his practical purposes.

Very few of De Quincey's writings were originally planned or published as books. Most of them first appeared in such periodicals as the *London Magazine, Blackwood's*, and *Tait's Magazine*, from which they were collected into book form. Like Hazlitt's, most of them are in essay form. The chief titles as they are known today are: *Confessions of an English Opium-Eater,* 1821; *On the Knocking at the Gate in Macbeth,* 1823; *Essays on Kant,* 1824–33; *Murder as One of the Fine Arts,* 1827; *Autobiography,* 1834–53; *Revolt of the Tartars,* 1837; *Suspiria de Profundis,* 1845; *Joan of Arc,* 1847; *The Literature of Knowledge and the Literature of Power,* 1848; and *The English Mail-Coach,* 1849. This list falls into three groups—reminiscences; literary, historical, and social criticism; and imaginative or fantastic creations.

De Quincey has been called "the psychologist of style." The term was perhaps meant to describe his extraordinary subtlety in adjusting connotations of words, and sentence patterns and rhythms, to ideas and emotions, as well as in discovering the nuances of ideas and emotions. His polyphonic prose, exemplified by passages in the *Confessions, Suspiria, Joan of Arc,* and *The English Mail-Coach,* is as famous for its own distinctive organ splendor as Sir Thomas Browne's and Ruskin's are for theirs. Judged, however, by the present-day test of economy of the reader's attention, it has been shown to have serious faults—lack of conciseness, a tendency to digress, unseasonable levity, willfulness in handling quotations. But in his best writings, as Samuel Butler said of Homer, De Quincey struck oil, even though he succeeds only in boring us elsewhere. So long as there are lovers of grand and poetic prose, of sensitive and highly imaginative treatments of strange themes, of the splendid stuffs and dyes of dreams, De Quincey will be read by a few.

from ON THE KNOCKING AT THE GATE IN *MACBETH*

FROM my boyish days I had always felt a great perplexity on one point in *Macbeth.* It was this: —the knocking at the gate which succeeds to the murder of Duncan produced to my feelings an effect for which I never could account. The effect was that it reflected back upon the murderer a peculiar awfulness and a depth of solemnity; yet, however obstinately I endeavoured with my understanding to comprehend this, for many years I never could see *why* it should produce such an effect. . . .

In fact, my understanding said positively that it could *not* produce any effect. But I knew better; I felt that it did; and I waited and clung to the problem until further knowledge should enable me to solve it. At length, in 1812, Mr. Williams made his *début* on the stage of Ratcliffe Highway, and executed those unparalleled murders which have procured for him such a brilliant and undying reputation. On which murders, by the way, I must observe that in one respect they have had an ill effect, by making the connoisseur in murder very fastidious in his taste, and dissatisfied with anything that has been since done in that line. All other murders look pale by the deep crimson of his; and, as an amateur once said to me in a querulous tone,

50. in that line. De Quincey later wrote his extravaganza *Murder Considered as One of the Fine Arts* on the subject.

"There has been absolutely nothing *doing* since his time, or nothing that's worth speaking of." But this is wrong, for it is unreasonable to expect all men to be great artists, and born with the genius of Mr. Williams. Now, it will be remembered that in the first of these murders (that of the Marrs) the same incident (of a knocking at the door soon after the work of extermination was complete) did actually occur which the genius of Shakspeare has invented; and all good judges, and the most eminent dilettanti, acknowledged the felicity of Shakspeare's suggestion as soon as it was actually realized. Here, then, was a fresh proof that I was right in relying on my own feeling in opposition to my understanding; and again I set myself to study the problem. At length I solved it to my own satisfaction; and my solution is this:—Murder, in ordinary cases, where the sympathy is wholly directed to the case of the murdered person, is an incident of coarse and vulgar horror; and for this reason,—that it flings the interest exclusively upon the natural but ignoble instinct by which we cleave to life: an instance which, as being indispensable to the primal law of self-preservation, is the same in kind (though different in degree) amongst all living creatures. This instinct, therefore, because it annihilates all distinctions, and degrades the greatest of men to the level of "the poor beetle that we tread on," exhibits human nature in its most abject and humiliating attitude. Such an attitude would little suit the purposes of the poet. What then must he do? He must throw the interest on the murderer. Our sympathy must be with *him* (of course I mean a sympathy of comprehension, a sympathy by which we enter into his feelings, and are made to understand them,— not a sympathy of pity or approbation). In the murdered person, all strife of thought, all flux and reflux of passion and of purpose, are crushed by one overwhelming panic; the fear of instant death smites him "with its petrific mace." But in the murderer, such a murderer as a poet will condescend to, there must be raging some great storm of passion,— jealousy, ambition, vengeance, hatred,—which will create a hell within him; and into this hell we are to look.

In *Macbeth,* for the sake of gratifying his own enormous and teeming faculty of creation, Shakspeare has introduced two murderers: and, as usual in his hands, they are remarkably discriminated: but,— though in Macbeth the strife of mind is greater than in his wife, the tiger spirit not so awake, and his feelings caught chiefly by contagion from her,—yet, as both were finally involved in the guilt of murder, the murderous mind of necessity is finally to be presumed in both. This was to be expressed; and, on its own account, as well as to make it a more proportionable antagonist to the unoffending nature of their victim, "the gracious Duncan," and adequately to expound "the deep damnation of his taking off," this was to be expressed with peculiar energy. We were to be made to feel that the human nature,—*i.e.* the divine nature of love and mercy, spread through the hearts of all creatures, and seldom utterly withdrawn from man,—was gone, vanished, extinct, and that the fiendish nature had taken its place. And, as this effect is marvellously accomplished in the *dialogues* and *soliloquies* themselves, so it is finally consummated by the expedient under consideration; and it is to this that I now solicit the reader's attention. If the reader has ever witnessed a wife, daughter, or sister in a fainting fit, he may chance to have observed that the most affecting moment in such a spectacle is *that* in which a sigh and a stirring announce the recommencement of suspended life. Or, if the reader has ever been present in a vast metropolis on the day when some great national idol was carried in funeral pomp to his grave, and, chancing to walk near the course through which it passed, has felt powerfully, in the silence and desertion of the streets and in the stagnation of ordinary business, the deep interest which at that moment was possessing the heart of man,—if all at once he should hear the death-like stillness broken up by the sound of wheels rattling away from the scene, and making known that the transitory vision was dissolved, he will be aware that at no moment was his sense of the complete suspension and pause in ordinary human concerns so full and affecting as at that moment when the suspension ceases, and the goings-on of human life are suddenly resumed. All action in any direction is best expounded, measured, and made apprehensible, by reaction. Now, apply this to the case in *Macbeth*. Here, as I have said, the retiring of the human heart and the entrance of the fiendish heart was to be expressed and made sensible. Another world has stept in; and the murderers are taken out of the region of human things, human purposes, human desires. They are transfigured: Lady Macbeth is "unsexed"; Macbeth has forgot that he was born of woman; both are conformed to the image of devils; and the world of devils is suddenly revealed. But how shall this be conveyed and made palpable? In order that a new world may step in, this world must for a time disappear. The murderers and the murder must be insulated—cut off by an immeasurable gulf from the ordinary tide and succession of human affairs—locked up and sequestered in some deep recess; we

must be made sensible that the world of ordinary life is suddenly arrested, laid asleep, tranced, racked into a dread armistice; time must be annihilated, relation to things without abolished; and all must pass self-withdrawn into a deep syncope and suspension of earthly passion. Hence it is that, when the deed is done, when the work of darkness is perfect, then the world of darkness passes away like a pageantry in the clouds: the knocking at the gate is heard, and it makes known audibly that the reaction has commenced; the human has made its reflux upon the fiendish: the pulses of life are beginning to beat again; and the re-establishment of the goings-on of the world in which we live first makes us profoundly sensible of the awful parenthesis that has suspended them.

O mighty poet! Thy works are not as those of other men, simply and merely great works of art, but are also like the phenomena of nature, like the sun and the sea, the stars and the flowers, like frost and snow, rain and dew, hail-storm and thunder, which are to be studied with entire submission of our own faculties, and in the perfect faith that in them there can be no too much or too little, nothing useless or inert, but that, the farther we press in our discoveries, the more we shall see proofs of design and self-supporting arrangement where the careless eye had seen nothing but accident!

from SUSPIRIA DE PROFUNDIS

In 1845 De Quincey contributed to *Blackwood's Magazine* a series of three articles entitled "Suspiria de Profundis [Sighs from the Depths]: Being a Sequel to the *Confessions of an English Opium-Eater*." These were in "that species of prose-phantasy . . . of which his *Confessions* . . . had been, as he believed, the first example set in English literature." The following selection is regarded as "furnishing a key to the whole scheme," and as being "perhaps the finest thing that De Quincey ever wrote . . . the most perfect specimen of his . . . prose-poetry . . . and also one of the most magnificent pieces of prose in English or any other language."—David Masson, editor of De Quincey's *Works*.

LEVANA AND OUR LADIES OF SORROW

OFTENTIMES at Oxford I saw Levana in my dreams. I knew her by her Roman symbols. Who is Levana? Reader, that do not pretend to have leisure for very much scholarship, you will not be angry with me for telling you. Levana was the Roman goddess that performed for the new-born infant the earliest office of ennobling kindness,—typical, by its mode, of that grandeur which belongs to man everywhere, and of that benignity in powers invisible which even in Pagan worlds sometimes descends to sustain it. At the very moment of birth, just as the infant tasted for the first time the atmosphere of our troubled planet, it was laid on the ground. *That* might bear different interpretations. But immediately, lest so grand a creature should grovel there for more than one instant, either the paternal hand, as proxy for the goddess Levana, or some near kinsman, as proxy for the father, raised it upright, bade it look erect as the king of all this world, and presented its forehead to the stars, saying, perhaps, in his heart, "Behold what is greater than yourselves!" This symbolic act represented the function of Levana. And that mysterious lady, who never revealed her face (except to me in dreams), but always acted by delegation, had her name from the Latin verb (as still it is the Italian verb) *levare*, to raise aloft.

This is the explanation of Levana. And hence it has arisen that some people have understood by Levana the tutelary power that controls the education of the nursery. She, that would not suffer at his birth even a prefigurative or mimic degradation for her awful ward, far less could be supposed to suffer the real degradation attaching to the non-development of his powers. She therefore watches over human education. Now, the word *edŭco*, with the penultimate short, was derived (by a process often exemplified in the crystallisation of languages) from the word *edūco*, with the penultimate long. Whatsoever *edūces*, or develops, *educates*. By the education of Levana, therefore, is meant,—not the poor machinery that moves by spelling-books and grammars, but by that mighty system of central forces hidden in the deep bosom of human life, which by passion, by strife, by temptation, by the energies of resistance, works for ever upon children,—resting not day or night, any more than the mighty wheel of day and night themselves, whose moments, like restless spokes, are glimmering for ever as they revolve.

If, then, *these* are the ministries by which Levana works, how profoundly must she reverence the agencies of grief! But you, reader, think that children generally are not liable to grief such as mine. There are two senses in the word *generally*,—the sense of Euclid, where it means *universally* (or in the whole extent of the *genus*), and a foolish sense of this world, where it means *usually*. Now, I am far from saying that children universally are capable of grief like mine. But there are more than you ever heard of who die of grief in this island of ours. I will tell you a common case. The rules of Eton require that a

boy on the *foundation* should be there twelve years: he is superannuated at eighteen; consequently he must come at six. Children torn away from mothers and sisters at that age not unfrequently die. I speak of what I know. The complaint is not entered by the registrar as grief; but *that* it is. Grief of that sort, and at that age, has killed more than ever have been counted amongst its martyrs.

Therefore it is that Levana often communes with the powers that shake man's heart; therefore it is that she dotes upon grief. "These ladies," said I softly to myself, on seeing the ministers with whom Levana was conversing, "these are the Sorrows; and they are three in number: as the *Graces* are three, who dress man's life with beauty; the *Parcae* are three, who weave the dark arras of man's life in their mysterious loom always with colours sad in part, sometimes angry with tragic crimson and black; the *Furies* are three, who visit with retributions called from the other side of the grave offences that walk upon this; and once even the *Muses* were but three, who fit the harp, the trumpet, or the lute, to the great burdens of man's impassioned creations. These are the Sorrows, all three of whom I know." The last words I say *now;* but in Oxford I said, "one of whom I know, and the others too surely I *shall* know." For already, in my fervent youth, I saw (dimly relieved upon the dark background of my dreams) the imperfect lineaments of the awful Sisters.

These Sisters—by what name shall we call them? If I say simply "The Sorrows," there will be a chance of mistaking the term; it might be understood of individual sorrow,—separate cases of sorrow,—whereas I want a term expressing the mighty abstractions that incarnate themselves in all individual sufferings of man's heart; and I wish to have these abstractions presented as impersonations,—that is, as clothed with human attributes of life, and with functions pointing to flesh. Let us call them, therefore, *Our Ladies of Sorrow.*

I know them thoroughly, and have walked in all their kingdoms. Three sisters they are, of one mysterious household; and their paths are wide apart; but of their dominion there is no end. Them I saw often conversing with Levana, and sometimes about myself. Do they talk, then? Oh, no! Mighty phantoms like these disdain the infirmities of language. They may utter voices through the organs of man when they dwell in human hearts, but amongst themselves is no voice nor sound; eternal silence reigns in *their* kingdoms. They spoke not as they talked with Levana; they whispered not; they sang not; though oftentimes methought they *might* have sung: for I upon earth had heard their mysteries oftentimes deciphered by harp and timbrel, by dulcimer and organ. Like God, whose servants they are, they utter their pleasure not by sounds that perish, or by words that go astray, but by signs in heaven, by changes on earth, by pulses in secret rivers, heraldries painted on darkness, and hieroglyphics written on the tablets of the brain. *They* wheeled in mazes; *I* spelled the steps. *They* telegraphed from afar; *I* read the signals. *They* conspired together; and on the mirrors of darkness *my* eye traced the plots. *Theirs* were the symbols; *mine* are the words.

What is it the Sisters are? What is it that they do? Let me describe their form and their presence, if form it were that still fluctuated in its outline, or presence it were that for ever advanced to the front or for ever receded amongst shades.

The eldest of the three is named *Mater Lachrymarum*, Our Lady of Tears. She it is that night and day raves and moans, calling for vanished faces. She stood in Rama, when a voice was heard of lamentation,—Rachel weeping for her children, and refusing to be comforted. She it was that stood in Bethlehem on the night when Herod's sword swept its nurseries of Innocents, and the little feet were stiffened for ever which, heard at times as they tottered along floors overhead, woke pulses of love in household hearts that were not unmarked in heaven. Her eyes are sweet and subtle, wild and sleepy, by turns; oftentimes rising to the clouds, oftentimes challenging the heavens. She wears a diadem round her head. And I knew by childish memories that she could go abroad upon the winds, when she heard the sobbing of litanies, or the thundering of organs, and when she beheld the mustering of summer clouds. This Sister, the elder, it is that carries keys more than papal at her girdle, which open every cottage and every palace. She, to my knowledge, sat all last summer by the bedside of the blind beggar, him that so often and so gladly I talked with, whose pious daughter, eight years old, with the sunny countenance, resisted the temptations of play and village mirth, to travel all day long on dusty roads with her afflicted father. For this did God send her a great reward. In the spring time of the year, and whilst yet her own spring was budding, He recalled her to himself. But her blind father mourns for ever over *her:* still he dreams at midnight that the little guiding hand is locked within his own; and still he wakens to a darkness that is *now* within a second and a deeper darkness. This *Mater Lachrymarum* also has been sitting all this winter of 1844–5 within the bedchamber of the Czar, bringing before his eyes a daughter (not less pious) that vanished to God not less suddenly, and left behind her a darkness not less profound. By the power of her keys it is that Our Lady of Tears glides, a ghostly intruder, into the chambers of sleepless men, sleepless women, sleepless children, from Ganges to the Nile, from Nile to Mississippi. And her, because she is the first-born of her house, and has the widest empire, let us honour with the title of "Madonna."

The second Sister is called *Mater Suspiriorum*, Our Lady of Sighs. She never scales the clouds, nor walks abroad upon the winds. She wears no diadem. And her eyes, if they were ever seen, would be neither sweet nor subtle; no man could read their story; they would be found filled with perishing dreams, and with wrecks of forgotten delirium. But she raises not her eyes; her head, on which sits a dilapidated turban, droops for ever, for ever fastens on the dust. She weeps not. She groans not. But she sighs inaudibly at intervals. Her sister, Madonna, is oftentimes stormy and frantic; raging in the highest against heaven, and demanding back her darlings. But Our Lady of Sighs never clamours, never defies, dreams not of rebellious aspirations. She is humble to abjectness. Hers is the meekness that belongs to the hopeless. Murmur she may, but it is in her sleep. Whisper she may, but it is to herself in the twilight. Mutter she does at times, but it is in solitary places that are desolate as she is desolate, in ruined cities, and when the sun has gone down to his rest. This Sister is the visitor of the Pariah, of the Jew, of the bondsman to the oar in Mediterranean galleys; of the English criminal in Norfolk Island, blotted out from the books of remembrance in sweet far-off England; of the baffled penitent reverting his eyes for ever upon a solitary grave, which to him seems the altar overthrown of some past and bloody sacrifice, on which altar no oblations can now be availing, whether towards pardon that he might implore, or towards reparation that he might attempt. Every slave that at noonday looks up to the tropical sun with timid reproach, as he points with one hand to the earth, our general mother, but for *him* a stepmother, as he points with the other hand to the Bible, our general teacher, but against *him* sealed and sequestered; every woman sitting in darkness, without love to shelter her head, or hope to illumine her solitude, because the heaven-born instincts kindling in her nature germs of holy affections, which God implanted in her womanly bosom, hav-

41–47. Every slave . . . sequestered. "This . . . applies chiefly to the cotton and tobacco states of North America." (De Quincey)

ing been stifled by social necessities, now burn sullenly to waste, like sepulchral lamps amongst the ancients; every nun defrauded of her unreturning May-time by wicked kinsmen, whom God will judge; every captive in every dungeon; all that are betrayed, and all that are rejected; outcasts by traditionary law, and children of *hereditary* disgrace: all these walk with Our Lady of Sighs. She also carries a key; but she needs it little. For her kingdom is chiefly amongst the tents of Shem, and the houseless vagrant of every clime. Yet in the very highest ranks of man she finds chapels of her own; and even in glorious England there are some that, to the world, carry their heads as proudly as the reindeer, who yet secretly have received her mark upon their foreheads.

But the third Sister, who is also the youngest——! Hush! whisper, whilst we talk of *her!* Her kingdom is not large, or else no flesh should live; but within that kingdom all power is hers. Her head, turreted like that of Cybele, rises almost beyond the reach of sight. She droops not; and her eyes, rising so high, *might* be hidden by distance. But, being what they are, they cannot be hidden: through the treble veil of crape which she wears the fierce light of a blazing misery, that rests not for matins or for vespers, for noon of day or noon of night, for ebbing or for flowing tide, may be read from the very ground. She is the defier of God. She also is the mother of lunacies, and the suggestress of suicides. Deep lie the roots of her power; but narrow is the nation that she rules. For she can approach only those in whom a profound nature has been upheaved by central convulsions; in whom the heart trembles and the brain rocks under conspiracies of tempest from without and tempest from within. Madonna moves with uncertain steps, fast or slow, but still with tragic grace. Our Lady of Sighs creeps timidly and stealthily. But this youngest Sister moves with incalculable motions, bounding, and with tiger's leaps. She carries no key; for, though coming rarely amongst men, she storms all doors at which she is permitted to enter at all. And *her* name is *Mater Tenebrarum*—Our Lady of Darkness.

These were the *Semnai Theai* or Sublime Goddesses, these were the *Eumenides*, or Gracious Ladies (so called by antiquity in shuddering propitiation), of my Oxford dreams. Madonna spoke. She spoke by her mysterious hand. Touching my head, she beckoned to Our Lady of Sighs; and *what* she spoke, translated out of the signs which (except in dreams) no man reads, was this:—

"Lo! here is he, whom in childhood I dedicated to my altars. This is he that once I made my darling.

Him I led astray, him I beguiled; and from heaven I stole away his young heart to mine. Through me did he become idolatrous; and through me it was, by languishing desires, that he worshipped the worm, and prayed to the wormy grave. Holy was the grave to him; lovely was its darkness; saintly its corruption. Him, this young idolater, I have seasoned for thee, dear gentle Sister of Sighs! Do thou take him now to *thy* heart, and season him for our dreadful sister. And thou,"—turning to the *Mater Tenebrarum*, she said,—"wicked sister, that temptest and hatest, do thou take him from *her*. See that thy sceptre lie heavy on his head. Suffer not woman and her tenderness to sit near him in his darkness. Banish the frailties of hope; wither the relenting of love; scorch the fountains of tears; curse him as only thou canst curse. So shall he be accomplished in the furnace; so shall he see the things that ought *not* to be seen, sights that are abominable, and secrets that are unutterable. So shall he read elder truths, sad truths, grand truths, fearful truths. So shall he rise again *before* he dies. And so shall our commission be accomplished which from God we had,—to plague his heart until we had unfolded the capacities of his spirit."

from MEETING THE WORDSWORTHS

The event occurred in 1807, after De Quincey, through awe of the great man, had missed opportunities of meeting Wordsworth. On the eve of the meeting here related, he had escorted Mrs. Coleridge and her children in a post chaise from London to the Lake Country. The following account was first published in *Tait's Magazine* in 1839. Compare Hazlitt's similar "My First Acquaintance with Poets." Note the stress both writers give to Wordsworth's "animal passions."

I SAW sufficiently to be aware of two ladies just entering the room, through a doorway opening upon a little staircase. The foremost, a tallish young woman, with the most winning expression of benignity upon her features, advanced to me, presenting her hand with so frank an air that all embarrassment must have fled in a moment before the native goodness of her manner. This was Mrs. Wordsworth, cousin of the poet, and, for the last five years or more, his wife. . . .

Immediately behind her moved a lady, shorter, slighter, and perhaps, in all other respects, as different from her in personal characteristics as could have been wished for the most effective contrast. "Her face was of Egyptian brown"; rarely, in a woman of English birth, had I seen a more determinate gipsy tan. Her eyes were not soft, as Mrs. Wordsworth's, nor were they fierce or bold; but they were wild and startling, and hurried in their motion. Her manner was warm and even ardent; her sensibilities seemed constitutionally deep; and some subtle fire of impassioned intellect apparently burned within her, which, being alternately pushed forward into a conspicuous expression by the irrepressible instincts of her temperament, and then immediately checked, in obedience to the decorum of her sex and age, and her maidenly condition, gave to her whole demeanour, and to her conversation, an air of embarrassment, and even of self-conflict, that was almost distressing to witness. Even her very utterance and enunciation often suffered, in point of clearness and steadiness, from the agitation of her excessive organic sensibility. At times, the self-counteraction and self-baffling of her feelings caused her even to stammer, and so determinately to stammer that a stranger who should have seen her and quitted her in that state of feeling would certainly set her down for one plagued with that infirmity of speech as distressingly as Charles Lamb himself. This was Miss Wordsworth, the only sister of the poet—his "Dorothy"; who naturally owed so much to the lifelong intercourse with her great brother in his most solitary and sequestered years; but, on the other hand, to whom he has acknowledged obligations of the profoundest nature; and, in particular, this mighty one, through which we also, the admirers and the worshippers of this great poet, are become equally her debtors—that, whereas the intellect of Wordsworth was, by its original tendency, too stern, too austere, too much enamoured of an ascetic harsh sublimity, she it was—the lady who paced by his side continually through sylvan and mountain tracks, in Highland glens, and in the dim recesses of German charcoal-burners—that first *couched* his eye to the sense of beauty, humanized him by the gentler charities, and engrafted, with her delicate female touch, those graces upon the ruder growths of his nature which have since clothed the forest of his genius with a foliage corresponding in loveliness and beauty to the strength of its boughs and the massiness of its trunks. The greatest deductions from Miss Wordsworth's attractions, and from the exceeding interest which surrounded her in right of her character, of her history, and of the relation which she fulfilled towards her brother, were the glancing quickness of her motions, and other circumstances in her deportment (such as her stooping attitude when walking), which gave an ungraceful, and even an unsex-

ual character to her appearance when out-of-doors. She did not cultivate the graces which preside over the person and its carriage. But, on the other hand, she was a person of very remarkable endowments intellectually; and, in addition to the other great services which she rendered to her brother, this I may mention, as greater than all the rest, and it was one which equally operated to the benefit of every casual companion in a walk—viz. the exceeding sympathy, always ready and always profound, by which she made all that one could tell her, all that one could describe, all that one could quote from a foreign author, reverberate, as it were, *à plusieurs reprises*, to one's own feelings, by the manifest impression it made upon *hers*. The pulses of light are not more quick or more inevitable in their flow and undulation, than were the answering and echoing movements of her sympathizing attention. Her knowledge of literature was irregular, and thoroughly unsystematic. She was content to be ignorant of many things; but what she knew and had really mastered lay where it could not be disturbed—in the temple of her own most fervid heart. . . .

And "*what-like*"—to use a Westmoreland as well as a Scottish expression—"*what-like*" was Wordsworth? A reviewer in "Tait's Magazine," noticing some recent collection of literary portraits, gives it as his opinion that Charles Lamb's head was the finest among them. This remark may have been justified by the engraved portraits; but, certainly, the critic would have cancelled it, had he seen the original heads—at least, had he seen them in youth or in maturity; for Charles Lamb bore age with less disadvantage to the intellectual expression of his appearance than Wordsworth, to whom a sanguine complexion had, of late years, usurped upon the original bronze tint; and this change of hue, and change in the quality of skin, had been made fourfold more conspicuous, and more unfavourable in its general effect, by the harsh contrast of grizzled hair which had displaced the original brown. No change in personal appearance ever can have been so unfortunate; for, generally speaking, whatever other disadvantages old age may bring along with it, one effect, at least, in male subjects, has a compensating tendency—that it removes any tone of vigour too harsh, and mitigates the expression of power too unsubdued. But, in Wordsworth, the effect of the change has been to substitute an air of animal vigour, or, at least, hardiness, as if derived from constant exposure to the wind and weather, for the fine sombre complexion which he

13–14. **à plusieurs reprises,** repeatedly.

once wore, resembling that of a Venetian senator or a Spanish monk.

Here, however, in describing the personal appearance of Wordsworth, I go back, of course, to the point of time at which I am speaking. He was, upon the whole, not a well-made man. His legs were pointedly condemned by all female connoisseurs in legs; not that they were bad in any way which *would* force itself upon your notice—there was no absolute deformity about them; and undoubtedly they had been serviceable legs beyond the average standard of human requisition; for I calculate, upon good data, that with these identical legs Wordsworth must have traversed a distance of 175,000 to 180,000 English miles—a mode of exertion which, to him, stood in the stead of alcohol and all other stimulants whatsoever to the animal spirits; to which, indeed, he was indebted for a life of unclouded happiness, and we for much of what is most excellent in his writings. But, useful as they have proved themselves, the Wordsworthian legs were certainly not ornamental; and it was really a pity, as I agreed with a lady in thinking, that he had not another pair for evening dress parties—when no boots lend their friendly aid to mask our imperfections from the eyes of female rigorists—those *elegantes formarum spectatrices*. A sculptor would certainly have disapproved of their contour. But the worst part of Wordsworth's person was the bust; there was a narrowness and a droop about the shoulders which became striking, and had an effect of meanness, when brought into close juxtaposition with a figure of a more statuesque build. Once on a summer evening, walking in the Vale of Langdale with Wordsworth, his sister, and Mr. J——, a native Westmoreland clergyman, I remember that Miss Wordsworth was positively mortified by the peculiar illustration which settled upon this defective conformation. Mr. J——, a fine towering figure, six feet high, massy and columnar in his proportions, happened to be walking, a little in advance, with Wordsworth; Miss Wordsworth and myself being in the rear; and from the nature of the conversation which then prevailed in our front rank, something or other about money, devises, buying and selling, we of the rear-guard thought it requisite to preserve this arrangement for a space of three miles or more; during which time, at intervals, Miss Wordsworth would exclaim, in a tone of vexation, "Is it possible, can that be William? How very mean he looks!" And she did not conceal a mortification that seemed really painful, until I, for my part, could not forbear laughing

outright at the serious interest which she carried into this trifle. She was, however, right, as regarded the mere visual judgment. Wordsworth's figure, with all its defects, was brought into powerful relief by one which had been cast in a more square and massy mould; and in such a case it impressed a spectator with a sense of absolute meanness, more especially when viewed from behind and not counteracted by his countenance; and yet Wordsworth was of a good height (five feet ten), and not a slender man; on the contrary, by the side of Southey, his limbs looked thick, almost in a disproportionate degree. But the total effect of Wordsworth's person was always worst in a state of motion. Meantime, his face—that was one which would have made amends for greater defects of figure. . . .

Haydon, in his great picture of "Christ's Entry into Jerusalem," has introduced Wordsworth in the character of a disciple attending his Divine Master, and Voltaire in the character of a sneering Jewish elder. This fact is well known; and, as the picture itself is tolerably well known to the public eye, there are multitudes now living who will have seen a very impressive likeness of Wordsworth—some consciously, some not suspecting it. There will, however, always be many who have *not* seen any portrait at all of Wordsworth; and therefore I will describe its general outline and effect. It was a face of the long order, often falsely classed as oval. . . . The head was well filled out; and there, to begin with, was a great advantage over the head of Charles Lamb, which was absolutely truncated in the posterior region—sawn off, as it were, by no timid sawyer. . . . Wordsworth's forehead is also liable to caricature misrepresentations in these days of phrenology: but, whatever it may appear to be in any man's fanciful portrait, the real living forehead, as I have been in the habit of seeing it for more than five-and-twenty years, is not remarkable for its height; but it *is*, perhaps, remarkable for its breadth and expansive development. Neither are the eyes of Wordsworth "large," as is erroneously stated somewhere in "Peter's Letters"; on the contrary, they are (I think) rather small; but *that* does not interfere with their effect, which at times is fine, and suitable to his intellectual character. . . . I have seen Wordsworth's eyes oftentimes affected powerfully . . . [by a few weeks' walking]; his eyes are not, under any circumstances, bright, lustrous, or piercing; but, after a long day's toil in walking, I

26–27. **elegantes . . . spectatrices,** elegant viewers of beauty; that is, critics.

19–20. **"Christ's Entry into Jerusalem."** See Benjamin Robert Haydon, page 368.   45. **"Peter's Letters,"** by J. G. Lockhart.

have seen them assume an appearance the most solemn and spiritual that it is possible for the human eye to wear. The light which resides in them is at no time a superficial light; but, under favourable accidents, it is a light which seems to come from unfathomed depths: in fact, it is more truly entitled to be held "the light that never was on land or sea," a light radiating from some far spiritual world, than any the most idealizing that ever yet a painter's hand created. The nose, a little arched, is large; which, by the way (according to a natural phrenology, existing centuries ago amongst some of the lowest amongst the human species), has always been accounted an unequivocal expression of animal appetites organically strong. And that expressed the simple truth: Wordsworth's intellectual passions were fervent and strong: but they rested upon a basis of preternatural animal sensibility diffused through *all* the animal passions (or appetites); and something of that will be found to hold of all poets who have been great by original force and power, not (as Virgil) by means of fine management and exquisite artifice of composition applied to their conceptions. The mouth, and the whole circumjacencies of the mouth, composed the strongest feature in Wordsworth's face. . . . .

from THE ENGLISH MAIL–COACH

In the October 1849 number of *Blackwood's Magazine* De Quincey published anonymously an article entitled "The Glory of Motion," relating his coaching experiences, especially one ride in which the coach bore to various parts of England the news of the Battle of Waterloo. This article and two more he gave the title "The English Mail-Coach." His original intention was to make the series a part of his *Suspiria de Profundis*, but misunderstanding of its connection with *Suspiria* caused him to detach it. "Thirty-seven years ago," he wrote, "accident made me, in the dead of night, and of a night memorably solemn, the solitary witness of an appalling scene, which threatened instant death . . . to two young people" riding along the coach road in a light gig. Out of this incident as his motif, as in a musical fugue, he weaves the prose-poetry of his "Dream-Fugue." (In the July, 1938, *Musical Quarterly* Calvin S. Brown, III, has shown that De Quincey knew the fugue form and made it the pattern of this and several of his other essays.)

> *"Whence the sound*
> *Of instruments, that made melodious chime,*
> *Was heard, of harp and organ; and who moved*
> *Their stops and chords was seen; his volant touch*
> *Instinct through all proportions, low and high,*
> *Fled and pursued transverse the resonant fugue."*
>
> *Paradise Lost,* Bk. XI.

SECTION 3—DREAM-FUGUE

FOUNDED ON THE PRECEDING THEME OF
SUDDEN DEATH

Tumultuosissimamente

PASSION of sudden death! that once in youth I read and interpreted by the shadows of thy averted signs!—rapture of panic taking the shape (which amongst tombs in churches I have seen) of woman bursting her sepulchral bonds—of woman's Ionic form bending forward from the ruins of her grave with arching foot, with eyes upraised, with clasped adoring hands—waiting, watching, trembling, praying for the trumpet's call to rise from dust for ever! Ah, vision too fearful of shuddering humanity on the brink of almighty abysses!—vision that didst start back, that didst reel away, like a shrivelling scroll from before the wrath of fire racing on the wings of the wind! Epilepsy so brief of horror, wherefore is it that thou canst not die? Passing so suddenly into darkness, wherefore is it that still thou sheddest thy sad funeral blights upon the gorgeous mosaics of dreams? Fragment of music too passionate, heard once, and heard no more, what aileth thee, that thy deep rolling chords come up at intervals through all the worlds of sleep, and after forty years have lost no element of horror?

I

Lo, it is summer—almighty summer! The everlasting gates of life and summer are thrown open wide; and on the ocean, tranquil and verdant as a savannah, the unknown lady from the dreadful vision and I myself are floating—she upon a fairy pinnace, and I upon an English three-decker. Both of us are wooing gales of festal happiness within the domain of our common country, within that ancient watery park, within the pathless chase of ocean, where England takes her pleasure as a huntress through winter and summer, from the rising to the setting sun. Ah, what a wilderness of floral beauty was hidden, or was suddenly revealed, upon the tropic islands through which the pinnace moved! And upon her deck what a bevy of human flowers: young women how lovely, young men how noble, that were dancing together, and slowly drifting towards *us* amidst music and incense, amidst blossoms from forests and gorgeous corymbi from vin-

9. averted signs. "I read the course and changes of the lady's agony in the succession of her involuntary gestures; but it must be remembered that I read all this from the rear, never once catching the lady's full face, and even her profile imperfectly." (De Quincey) 49. corymbi, clusters of fruit or flowers.

tages, amidst natural carolling, and the echoes of sweet girlish laughter. Slowly the pinnace nears us, gaily she hails us, and silently she disappears beneath the shadow of our mighty bows. But then, as at some signal from heaven, the music, and the carols, and the sweet echoing of girlish laughter—all are hushed. What evil has smitten the pinnace, meeting or overtaking her? Did ruin to our friends couch within our own dreadful shadow? Was our shadow the shadow of death? I looked over the bow for an answer, and, behold! the pinnace was dismantled; the revel and the revellers were found no more; the glory of the vintage was dust; and the forests with their beauty were left without a witness upon the seas. "But where," and I turned to our crew—"where are the lovely women that danced beneath the awning of flowers and clustering corymbi? Whither have fled the noble young men that danced with *them?*" Answer there was none. But suddenly the man at the mast-head, whose countenance darkened with alarm, cried out, "Sail on the weather beam! Down she comes upon us: in seventy seconds she also will founder."

2

I looked to the weather side, and the summer had departed. The sea was rocking, and shaken with gathering wrath. Upon its surface sat mighty mists, which grouped themselves into arches and long cathedral aisles. Down one of these, with the fiery pace of a quarrel from a cross-bow, ran a frigate right athwart our course. "Are they mad?" some voice exclaimed from our deck. "Do they woo their ruin?" But in a moment, as she was close upon us, some impulse of a heady current or local vortex gave a wheeling bias to her course, and off she forged without a shock. As she ran past us, high aloft amongst the shrouds stood the lady of the pinnace. The deeps opened ahead in malice to receive her, towering surges of foam ran after her, the billows were fierce to catch her. But far away she was borne into desert spaces of the sea: whilst still by sight I followed her, as she ran before the howling gale, chased by angry sea-birds and by maddening billows; still I saw her, at the moment when she ran past us, standing amongst the shrouds, with her white draperies streaming before the wind. There she stood, with hair dishevelled, one hand clutched amongst the tackling—rising, sinking, fluttering, trembling, praying; there for leagues I saw her as she stood, raising at intervals one hand to heaven, amidst the fiery crests of the pursuing waves and the raving of the storm; until at last, upon a sound from

31. **quarrel,** bolt, of a crossbow.

afar of malicious laughter and mockery, all was hidden for ever in driving showers; and afterwards, but when I knew not, nor how.

3

Sweet funeral bells from some incalculable distance, wailing over the dead that die before the dawn, awakened me as I slept in a boat moored to some familiar shore. The morning twilight even then was breaking; and, by the dusky revelations which it spread, I saw a girl, adorned with a garland of white roses about her head for some great festival, running along the solitary strand in extremity of haste. Her running was the running of panic; and often she looked back as to some dreadful enemy in the rear. But, when I leaped ashore, and followed on her steps to warn her of a peril in front, alas! from me she fled as from another peril, and vainly I shouted to her of quicksands that lay ahead. Faster and faster she ran; round a promontory of rocks she wheeled out of sight; in an instant I also wheeled round it, but only to see the treacherous sands gathering above her head. Already her person was buried; only the fair young head and the diadem of white roses around it were still visible to the pitying heavens; and, last of all, was visible one white marble arm. I saw by the early twilight this fair young head, as it was sinking, down to darkness—saw this marble arm, as it rose above her head and her treacherous grave, tossing, faltering, rising, clutching, as at some false deceiving hand stretched out from the clouds—saw this marble arm uttering her dying hope, and then uttering her dying despair. The head, the diadem, the arm—these all had sunk; at last over these also the cruel quicksand had closed; and no memorial of the fair young girl remained on earth, except my own solitary tears, and the funeral bells from the desert seas, that, rising again more softly, sang a requiem over the grave of the buried child, and over her blighted dawn.

I sat, and wept in secret the tears that men have ever given to the memory of those that died before the dawn, and by the treachery of earth, our mother. But suddenly the tears and funeral bells were hushed by a shout as of many nations, and by a roar as from some great king's artillery, advancing rapidly along the valleys, and heard afar by echoes from the mountains. "Hush!" I said, as I bent my ear earthwards to listen—"hush!—this either is the very anarchy of strife, or else"—and then I listened more profoundly, and whispered as I raised my head—"or else, oh heavens! it is *victory* that is **final, victory that swallows up all strife.**"

4

Immediately, in trance, I was carried over land and sea to some distant kingdom, and placed upon a triumphal car, amongst companions crowned with laurel. The darkness of gathering midnight, brooding over all the land, hid from us the mighty crowds that were weaving restlessly about ourselves as a centre: we heard them, but saw them not. Tidings had arrived, within an hour, of a grandeur that measured itself against centuries; too full of pathos they were, too full of joy, to utter themselves by other language than by tears, by restless anthems, and *Te Deums* reverberated from the choirs and orchestras of earth. These tidings we that sat upon the laurelled car had it for our privilege to publish amongst all nations. And already, by signs audible through the darkness, by snortings and tramplings, our angry horses, that knew no fear of fleshly weariness, upbraided us with delay. Wherefore *was* it that we delayed? We waited for a secret word, that should bear witness to the hope of nations as now accomplished for ever. At midnight the secret word arrived; which word was—*Waterloo and Recovered Christendom!* The dreadful word shone by its own light; before us it went; high above our leaders' heads it rode, and spread a golden light over the paths which we traversed. Every city, at the presence of the secret word, threw open its gates. The rivers were conscious as we crossed. All the forests, as we ran along their margins, shivered in homage to the secret word. And the darkness comprehended it.

Two hours after midnight we approached a mighty Minster. Its gates, which rose to the clouds, were closed. But, when the dreadful word that rode before us reached them with its golden light, silently they moved back upon their hinges; and at a flying gallop our equipage entered the grand aisle of the cathedral. Headlong was our pace; and at every altar, in the little chapels and oratories to the right hand and left of our course, the lamps, dying or sickening, kindled anew in sympathy with the secret word that was flying past. Forty leagues we might have run in the cathedral, and as yet no strength of morning light had reached us, when before us we saw the aerial galleries of organ and choir. Every pinnacle of the fretwork, every station of advantage amongst the traceries, was crested by white-robed choristers that sang deliverance; that wept no more tears, as once their fathers had wept; but at intervals that sang together to the generations, saying,

"Chant the deliverer's praise in every tongue,"

and receiving answers from afar,

"Such as once in heaven and earth were sung."

And of their chanting was no end; of our headlong pace was neither pause nor slackening.

Thus as we ran like torrents—thus as we swept with bridal rapture over the Campo Santo of the cathedral graves—suddenly we became aware of a vast necropolis rising upon the far-off horizon—a city of sepulchres, built within the saintly cathedral for the warrior dead that rested from their feuds on earth. Of purple granite was the necropolis; yet, in the first minute, it lay like a purple stain upon the horizon, so mighty was the distance. In the second minute it trembled through many changes, growing into terraces and towers of wondrous altitude, so mighty was the pace. In the third minute already, with our dreadful gallop, we were entering its suburbs. Vast sarcophagi rose on every side, having towers and turrets that, upon the limits of the central aisle, strode forward with haughty intrusion, that ran back with mighty shadows into answering recesses. Every sarcophagus showed many bas-reliefs—bas-reliefs of battles and of battle-fields; battles from forgotten ages, battles from yesterday; battle-fields that, long since, nature had healed and reconciled to herself with the sweet oblivion of flowers; battle-fields that were yet angry and crimson with carnage. Where the terraces ran, there did *we* run; where the towers curved, there did *we* curve. With the flight of swallows our horses swept round every angle. Like rivers in flood wheeling round headlands, like hurricanes that ride into the secrets of forests, faster than ever light unwove the mazes of darkness, our flying equipage carried earthly passions, kindled warrior instincts, amongst the dust that lay around us—dust oftentimes of our noble fathers that had slept in God from Créci to Trafalgar. And now had we reached the last sarcophagus, now were we abreast of the last bas-relief, already had we recovered the arrow-like flight of the illimitable central aisle, when coming up this aisle to meet us we beheld afar off a female child, that rode in a carriage as frail as flowers. The mists which went before her hid the fawns that drew her, but could not hide the shells and tropic flowers with which she played—but could not hide the lovely smiles by which she uttered her trust in the mighty cathedral, and in the cherubim that looked down

8. Campo Santo, "(or cemetery) at Pisa, composed of earth brought from Jerusalem from a bed of sanctity as the highest prize which the noble piety of crusaders could ask or imagine." (De Quincey)

upon her from the mighty shafts of its pillars. Face to face she was meeting us; face to face she rode, as if danger there were none. "Oh, baby!" I exclaimed, "shalt thou be the ransom for Waterloo? Must we, that carry tidings of great joy to every people, be messengers of ruin to thee!" In horror I rose at the thought; but then also, in horror at the thought, rose one that was sculptured on a bas-relief—a Dying Trumpeter. Solemnly from the field of battle he rose to his feet; and, unslinging his stony trumpet, carried it, in his dying anguish, to his stony lips—sounding once, and yet once again; proclamation that, in *thy* ears, oh baby! spoke from the battlements of death. Immediately deep shadows fell between us, and aboriginal silence. The choir had ceased to sing. The hoofs of our horses, the dreadful rattle of our harness, the groaning of our wheels, alarmed the graves no more. By horror the bas-relief had been unlocked unto life. By horror we, that were so full of life, we men and our horses, with their fiery fore-legs rising in mid air to their everlasting gallop, were frozen to a bas-relief. Then a third time the trumpet sounded; the seals were taken off all pulses; life, and the frenzy of life, tore into their channels again; again the choir burst forth in sunny grandeur, as from the muffling of storms and darkness; again the thunderings of our horses carried temptation into the graves. One cry burst from our lips, as the clouds, drawing off from the aisle, showed it empty before us.—"Whither has the infant fled?—is the young child caught up to God?" Lo! afar off, in a vast recess, rose three mighty windows to the clouds; and on a level with their summits, at height insuperable to man, rose an altar of purest alabaster. On its eastern face was trembling a crimson glory. A glory was it from the reddening dawn that now streamed *through* the windows? Was it from the crimson robes of the martyrs painted *on* the windows? Was it from the bloody bas-reliefs of earth? There, suddenly, within that crimson radiance, rose the apparition of a woman's head, and then of a woman's figure. The child it was—grown up to woman's height. Clinging to the horns of the altar, voiceless she stood—sinking, rising, raving, despairing; and behind the volume of incense that, night and day, streamed upwards from the altar, dimly was seen the fiery font, and the shadow of that dreadful being who should have baptized her with the baptism of death. But by her side was kneeling her better angel, that hid his face with wings; that wept and pleaded for *her;* that prayed when *she* could *not;* that fought with Heaven by tears for *her* deliverance; which also, as he raised his immortal countenance from his wings, I saw, by the glory in his eye, that from Heaven he had won at last.

5

Then was completed the passion of the mighty fugue. The golden tubes of the organ, which as yet had but muttered at intervals—gleaming amongst clouds and surges of incense—threw up, as from fountains unfathomable, columns of heart-shattering music. Choir and anti-choir were filling fast with unknown voices. Thou also, Dying Trumpeter, with thy love that was victorious, and thy anguish that was finishing, didst enter the tumult; trumpet and echo—farewell love, and farewell anguish—rang through the dreadful *sanctus*. Oh, darkness of the grave! that from the crimson altar and from the fiery font wert visited and searched by the effulgence in the angel's eye—were these indeed thy children? Pomps of life, that, from the burials of centuries, rose again to the voice of perfect joy, did ye indeed mingle with the festivals of Death? Lo! as I looked back for seventy leagues through the mighty cathedral, I saw the quick and the dead that sang together to God, together that sang to the generations of man. All the hosts of jubilation, like armies that ride in pursuit, moved with one step. Us, that, with laurelled heads, were passing from the cathedral, they overtook, and, as with a garment, they wrapped us round with thunders greater than our own. As brothers we moved together; to the dawn that advanced, to the stars that fled; rendering thanks to God in the highest—that, having hid His face through one generation behind thick clouds of War, once again was ascending, from the Campo Santo of Waterloo was ascending, in the visions of Peace; rendering thanks for thee, young girl! whom having overshadowed with His ineffable passion of death, suddenly did God relent, suffered thy angel to turn aside His arm, and even in thee, sister unknown! shown to me for a moment only to be hidden for ever, found an occasion to glorify His goodness. A thousand times, amongst the phantoms of sleep, have I seen thee entering the gates of the golden dawn, with the secret word riding before thee, with the armies of the grave behind thee,—seen thee sinking, rising, raving, despairing; a thousand times in the worlds of sleep have seen thee followed by God's angel through storms, through desert seas, through the darkness of quicksands, through dreams and the dreadful revelations that are in dreams; only that at the last, with one sling of His victorious arm, He might snatch thee back from ruin, and might emblazon in thy deliverance the endless resurrections of His love!

LITERATURE OF KNOWLEDGE
AND LITERATURE OF POWER

The main idea of the following passage was first expressed in a series of articles, "Letters to a Young Man Whose Education Has Been Neglected," published in the *London Magazine* in 1823. Later De Quincey expanded the idea in "The Poetry of Pope," first published in the *North British Review*, August, 1848.

The thought and the argument developed in this essay constitute one of the best defenses ever written of the kind of education to which courses in literature contribute. Some critics of De Quincey have asserted that he did not go far enough in his distinction: he ought to have denied the name of literature altogether to those works which lack the dynamic element which he calls "power" (meaning emotion). On the point about emotional power, compare Shelley's in *A Defence of Poetry* (especially the second division of his essay—"Poetry is ever accompanied with pleasure" . . .).

WHAT is it that we mean by *literature?* Popularly, and amongst the thoughtless, it is held to include everything that is printed in a book. Little logic is required to disturb *that* definition. The most thoughtless person is easily made aware that in the idea of *literature* one essential element is some relation to a general and common interest of man,—so that what applies only to a local, or professional, or merely personal interest, even though presenting itself in the shape of a book, will not belong to Literature. So far the definition is easily narrowed; and it is as easily expanded. For not only is much that takes a station in books not literature; but inversely, much that really *is* literature never reaches a station in books. The weekly sermons of Christendom, that vast pulpit literature which acts so extensively upon the popular mind—to warn, to uphold, to renew, to comfort, to alarm—does not attain the sanctuary of libraries in the ten-thousandth part of its extent. The Drama again,—as, for instance, the finest part of Shakspeare's plays in England, and all leading Athenian plays in the noontide of the Attic stage,—operated as a literature on the public mind, and were (according to the strictest letter of that term) *published* through the audiences that witnessed their representation some time before they were published as things to be read; and they were published in this scenical mode of publication with much more effect than they could have had as books during ages of costly copying or of costly printing.

Books, therefore, do not suggest an idea coextensive and interchangeable with the idea of Literature; since much literature, scenic, forensic, or didactic (as from lecturers and public orators), may never come into books, and much that does come into books may connect itself with no literary interest. But a far more important correction, applicable to the common vague idea of literature, is to be sought not so much in a better definition of literature as in a sharper distinction of the two functions which it fulfils. In that great social organ which, collectively, we call literature, there may be distinguished two separate offices that may blend and often *do* so, but capable, severally, of a severe insulation, and naturally fitted for reciprocal repulsion. There is, first, the literature of *knowledge;* and, secondly, the literature of *power*. The function of the first is—to *teach;* the function of the second is—to *move:* the first is a rudder; the second, an oar or a sail. The first speaks to the *mere* discursive understanding; the second speaks ultimately, it may happen, to the higher understanding or reason, but always *through* affections of pleasure and sympathy. Remotely, it may travel towards an object seated in what Lord Bacon calls *dry* light; but, proximately, it does and must operate,—else it ceases to be a literature of *power*,—on and through that *humid* light which clothes itself in the mists and glittering *iris* of human passions, desires, and genial emotions.

Men have so little reflected on the higher functions of literature as to find it a paradox if one should describe it as a mean or subordinate purpose of books to give information. But this is a paradox only in the sense which makes it honourable to be paradoxical. Whenever we talk in ordinary language of seeking information or gaining knowledge, we understand the words as connected with something of absolute novelty. But it is the grandeur of all truth which *can* occupy a very high place in human interests that it is never absolutely novel to the meanest of minds: it exists eternally by way of germ or latent principle in the lowest as in the highest, needing to be developed, but never to be planted. To be capable of transplantation is the immediate criterion of a truth that ranges on a lower scale. Besides which, there is a rarer thing than truth,—namely, *power*, or deep sympathy with truth. What is the effect, for instance, upon society, of children? By the pity, by the tenderness, and by the peculiar modes of admiration which connect themselves with the helplessness, with the innocence, and with the simplicity of children, not only are the primal affections strengthened and continually renewed, but the qualities which are dearest in the sight of heaven,—the frailty, for instance, which appeals to forbearance, the innocence which symbolises the heavenly, and the simplicity which is most alien from the worldly,—are kept up in perpetual remembrance, and their ideals are continually re-freshed. A purpose of the same nature is answered by the higher literature, viz. the literature of power. What do you learn from "Paradise Lost"? Nothing at all. What do you learn from a cookery-book? Something new, something that you did not know before, in every paragraph. But would you there-fore put the wretched cookery-book on a higher level of estimation than the divine poem? What you owe to Milton is not any knowledge, of which a million separate items are still but a million of advancing steps on the same earthly level; what you owe is *power*,—that is, exercise and expansion to your own latent capacity of sympathy with the infinite, where every pulse and each separate influx is a step up-wards, a step ascending as upon a Jacob's ladder from earth to mysterious altitudes above the earth. *All* the steps of knowledge, from first to last, carry you further on the same plane, but could never raise you one foot above your ancient level of earth: whereas the very *first* step in power is a flight—is an ascending movement into another element where earth is forgotten.

Were it not that human sensibilities are venti-lated and continually called out into exercise by the great phenomena of infancy, or of real life as it moves through chance and change, or of literature as it recombines these elements in the mimicries of poetry, romance, &c., it is certain that, like any animal power or muscular energy falling into disuse, all such sensibilities would gradually droop and dwindle. It is in relation to these great *moral* capaci-ties of man that the literature of power, as contradis-tinguished from that of knowledge, lives and has its field of action. It is concerned with what is highest in man; for the Scriptures themselves never conde-scended to deal by suggestion or co-operation with the mere discursive understanding: when speaking of man in his intellectual capacity, the Scriptures speak not of the understanding, but of "*the under-standing heart*,"—making the heart, *i.e.* the great *in-tuitive* (or non-discursive) organ, to be the inter-changeable formula for man in his highest state of capacity for the infinite. Tragedy, romance, fairy tale, or epopee, all alike restore to man's mind the ideals of justice, of hope, of truth, of mercy, of retri-bution, which else (left to the support of daily life in its realities) would languish for want of sufficient illustration. What is meant, for instance, by poetic justice?—It does not mean a justice that differs by its object from the ordinary justice of human juris-prudence; for then it must be confessedly a very bad kind of justice; but it means a justice that differs

from common forensic justice by the degree in which it *attains* its object, a justice that is more omnipo-tent over its own ends, as dealing, not with the re-fractory elements of earthly life, but with the elements of its own creation, and with materials flexible to its own purest preconceptions. It is cer-tain that, were it not for the Literature of Power, these ideals would often remain amongst us as mere arid notional forms; whereas, by the creative forces of man put forth in literature, they gain a vernal life of restoration, and germinate into vital activities.

The commonest novel, by moving in alliance with human fears and hopes, with human instincts of wrong and right, sustains and quickens those af-fections. Calling them into action, it rescues them from torpor. And hence the pre-eminence over all authors that merely *teach*, of the meanest that *moves*, or that teaches, if at all, indirectly *by* moving. The very highest work that has ever existed in the Litera-ture of Knowledge is but a *provisional* work,—a book upon trial and sufferance, and *quamdiu bene se gesserit*. Let its teaching be even partially revised, let it be but expanded,—nay, even let its teaching be but placed in a better order,—and instantly it is super-seded. Whereas the feeblest works in the Literature of Power, surviving at all, survive as finished and unalterable amongst men. For instance, the *Principia* of Sir Isaac Newton was a book *militant* on earth from the first. In all stages of its progress it would have to fight for its existence; 1st, as regards abso-lute truth; 2dly, when that combat was over, as re-gards its form or mode of presenting the truth. And as soon as a La Place, or anybody else, builds higher upon the foundations laid by this book, effectually he throws it out of the sunshine into decay and dark-ness; by weapons won from this book he superan-nuates and destroys this book, so that soon the name of Newton remains as a mere *nominis umbra*, but his book, as a living power, has transmigrated into other forms. Now, on the contrary, the Iliad, the Prometheus of Aeschylus, the Othello or King Lear, the Hamlet or Macbeth, and the Paradise Lost, are not militant, but triumphant for ever as long as the languages exist in which they speak or can be taught to speak. They never *can* transmigrate into new in-carnations. To reproduce *these* in new forms, or vari-ations, even if in some things they should be im-proved, would be to plagiarise. A good steam-engine is properly superseded by a better. But one lovely pastoral valley is not superseded by another, nor a statue of Praxiteles by a statue of Michelangelo.

---

21. quamdiu . . . se gesserit, so long as it behaves itself well.   **33. La Place,** the astronomer Laplace. See page 8. **38. nominis umbra,** shadow of a name.

45. epopee, epic.

These things are separated not by imparity, but by disparity. They are not thought of as unequal under the same standard, but as different in *kind*, and, if otherwise equal, as equal under a different standard. Human works of immortal beauty and works of nature in one respect stand on the same footing: they never absolutely repeat each other, never approach so near as not to differ, and they differ not as better and worse, or simply by more and less: they differ by undecipherable and incommunicable differences, that cannot be caught by mimicries, that cannot be reflected in the mirror of copies, that cannot become ponderable in the scales of vulgar comparison. . . .

All the literature of knowledge builds only ground-nests, that are swept away by floods, or confounded by the plough; but the literature of power builds nests in aërial altitudes of temples sacred from violation, or of forests inaccessible to fraud. *This* is a great prerogative of the *power* literature; and it is a greater which lies in the mode of its influence. The *knowledge* literature, like the fashion of this world, passeth away. An Encyclopedia is its abstract; and,

in this respect, it may be taken for its speaking symbol—that before one generation has passed an Encyclopedia is superannuated; for it speaks through the dead memory and unimpassioned understanding, which have not the repose of higher faculties, but are continually enlarging and varying their phylacteries. But all literature properly so called—literature, κατ' ἐξοχην,—for the very reason that it is so much more durable than the literature of knowledge, is (and by the very same proportion it is) more intense and electrically searching in its impressions. The directions in which the tragedy of this planet has trained our human feelings to play, and the combinations into which the poetry of this planet has thrown our human passions of love and hatred, of admiration and contempt, exercise a power for bad or good over human life that cannot be contemplated, when stretching through many generations, without a sentiment allied to awe. And of this let every one be assured—that he owes to the impassioned books which he has read many a thousand more of emotions than he can consciously trace back to them. Dim by their origination, these emotions yet arise in him, and mould him through life, like forgotten incidents of his childhood. . . .

Francis Jeffrey
1773–1850

Francis Jeffrey, who became Lord Jeffrey before he died, spent a long life judging men, causes, and books, using much the same methods on all three. Educated at the High School of Edinburgh and at the universities of Glasgow, Edinburgh, and Oxford, he was admitted to the Scots bar in 1794. Because he was a whig and because Scottish litigants took their politics seriously, he got off to a slow start in the practice of his profession. In 1802 he, two other young lawyers with plenty of time on their hands, and a young clergyman without a curacy met in a garret and founded the most famous literary periodical of their time, the *Edinburgh Review*. Taking for its motto the Latin sentence translating into "The judge is condemned when the guilty is acquitted," and professing to be independent and nonpartisan politically, the *Edinburgh* haled before its bar the books and authors of the time. The independence of the *Edinburgh* was a long step forward in reviewing and in literary criticism, even if its critical standards looked backward to older,

neoclassical conceptions of life and art; and its influence was often salutary, though many of its judgments on men and letters were to be reversed by posterity. Despite its professed nonpartisanship, the *Edinburgh* exhibited such a strong Whig flavor that it provoked the establishment, by Scott and others, of the *Quarterly Review* in 1809. Jeffrey's review of Thomas Moore's *Epistles, Odes, and Other Poems* in 1806 brought a challenge from the author that resulted in the comic-opera duel at Chalk Farm, interrupted by officers and leading ultimately to friendship between the principals. But this was only a skirmish. Jeffrey's main war was waged against Wordsworth and the whole *Lyrical Ballads* theory of poetry. "This will never do," he wrote of *The Excursion* in 1814; and, "This, we think, has the merit of being the very worst poem we ever saw imprinted in a quarto volume," of *The White Doe of Rylstone*, a

6. **phylacteries,** small boxes containing scriptural passages and worn by orthodox Jews on their persons. 7. **κατ' ἐξοχην,** of highest excellence.

year later. Jeffrey lived to be personally acquainted with Wordsworth, to see the old poet acclaimed by the English-speaking world, and to become a prominent judge, but never to change his opinion of Wordsworth's poetry. The two died in the same year, 1850.

from *THE EXCURSION.* BY WILLIAM WORDSWORTH

THIS will never do. It bears no doubt the stamp of the author's heart and fancy; but unfortunately not half so visibly as that of his peculiar system. His former poems were intended to recommend that system, and to bespeak favour for it by their individual merit;—but this, we suspect, must be recommended by the system—and can only expect to succeed where it has been previously established. It is longer, weaker, and tamer, than any of Mr. Wordsworth's other productions; with less boldness of originality, and less even of that extreme simplicity and lowliness of tone which wavered so prettily, in the *Lyrical Ballads*, between silliness and pathos. We have imitations of Cowper, and even of Milton here, engrafted on the natural drawl of the Lakers—and all diluted into harmony by that profuse and irrepressible wordiness which deluges all the blank verse of this school of poetry, and lubricates and weakens the whole structure of their style.

Though it fairly fills four hundred and twenty good quarto pages, without note, vignette, or any sort of extraneous assistance, it is stated in the title—with something of an imprudent candour—to be but "a portion" of a larger work; and in the preface, where an attempt is rather unsuccessfully made to explain the whole design, it is still more rashly disclosed that it is but "a part of the second part, of a *long* and laborious work"—which is to consist of three parts!

What Mr. Wordsworth's ideas of length are, we have no means of accurately judging. But we cannot help suspecting that they are liberal, to a degree that will alarm the weakness of most modern readers. As far as we can gather from the preface, the entire poem—or one of them, for we really are not sure whether there is to be one or two—is of a biographical nature; and is to contain the history of the author's mind, and of the origin and progress of his poetical powers, up to the period when they were sufficiently matured to qualify him for the great work on which he has been so long employed. Now, the quarto before us contains an account of one of his youthful rambles in the vales of Cumberland, and occupies precisely the period of three days; so that, by the use of a very powerful *calculus*, some estimate may be formed of the probable extent of the entire biography.

This small specimen, however, and the statements with which it is prefaced, have been sufficient to set our minds at rest in one particular. The case of Mr. Wordsworth, we perceive, is now manifestly hopeless; and we give him up as altogether incurable, and beyond the power of criticism. We cannot indeed altogether omit taking precautions now and then against the spreading of the malady;—but for himself, though we shall watch the progress of his symptoms as a matter of professional curiosity and instruction, we really think it right not to harass him any longer with nauseous remedies,—but rather to throw in cordials and lenitives, and wait in patience for the natural termination of the disorder. In order to justify this desertion of our patient, however, it is proper to state why we despair of the success of a more active practice.

A man who has been for twenty years at work on such matter as is now before us, and who comes complacently forward with a whole quarto of it after all the admonitions he has received, cannot reasonably be expected to "change his hand, or check his pride," upon the suggestion of far weightier monitors than we can pretend to be. Inveterate habits must now have given a kind of sanctity to the errors of early taste; and the very powers of which we lament the perversion, have probably become incapable of any other application. The very quantity, too, that he has written, and is at this moment working up for publication upon the old pattern, makes it almost hopeless to look for any change of it. All this is so much capital already sunk in the concern, which must be sacrificed if it be abandoned: and no man likes to give up for lost the time and talent and labour which he has embodied in any permanent production. We were not previously aware of these obstacles to Mr. Wordsworth's conversion; and, considering the peculiarities of his former writings merely as the result of certain wanton and capricious experiments on public taste and indulgence, conceived it to be our duty to discour-

41. **three parts,** alluding to Wordsworth's plan for *The Recluse*, his "philosophical poem" which was to be his magnum opus—to include (1) *The Prelude* (introduction like "the ante-chapel to . . . a gothic church"—completed), (2) *The Recluse* proper (like "the body of a gothic church"—only a few hundred lines written), and (3) *The Excursion* (completed).

51. **experiments.** See "Preface to *Lyrical Ballads*," page 29.

age their repetition by all the means in our power. We now see clearly, however, how the case stands; —and, making up our minds, though with the most sincere pain and reluctance, to consider him as finally lost to the good cause of poetry, shall endeavour to be thankful for the occasional gleams of tenderness and beauty which the natural force of his imagination and affections must still shed over all his productions,—and to which we shall ever turn with delight, in spite of the affectation and mysticism and prolixity, with which they are so abundantly contrasted.

Long habits of seclusion, and an excessive ambition of originality, can alone account for the disproportion which seems to exist between this author's taste and his genius; or for the devotion with which he has sacrificed so many precious gifts at the shrine of those paltry idols which he has set up for himself among his lakes and his mountains. Solitary musings, amidst such scenes, might no doubt be expected to nurse up the mind to the majesty of poetical conception,—(though it is remarkable, that all the greater poets lived, or had lived, in the full current of society);—But the collision of equal minds,—the admonition of prevailing impressions—seems necessary to reduce its redundancies, and repress that tendency to extravagance or puerility, into which the self-indulgence and self-admiration of genius is so apt to be betrayed, when it is allowed to wanton, without awe or restraint, in the triumph and delight of its own intoxication. That its flights should be graceful and glorious in the eyes of men, it seems almost to be necessary that they should be made in the consciousness that men's eyes are to behold them,— and that the inward transport and vigour by which they are inspired, should be tempered by an occasional reference to what will be thought of them by those ultimate dispensers of glory. An habitual and general knowledge of the few settled and permanent maxims, which form the canon of general taste in all large and polished societies—a certain tact, which informs us at once that many things, which we still love, and are moved by in secret, must necessarily be despised as childish, or derided as absurd, in all such societies—though it will not stand in the place of genius, seems necessary to the success of its exertions; and though it will never enable any one to produce the higher beauties of art, can alone secure the talent which does produce them, from errors that must render it useless. Those who have most of the talent, however, commonly

acquire this knowledge with the greatest facility;— and if Mr. Wordsworth, instead of confining himself almost entirely to the society of the dalesmen and cottagers, and little children, who form the subjects of his book, had condescended to mingle a little more with the people that were to read and judge of it, we cannot help thinking, that its texture might have been considerably improved. At least it appears to us to be absolutely impossible, that any one who had lived or mixed familiarly with men of literature and ordinary judgment in poetry, (of course we exclude the coadjutors and disciples of his own school), could ever have fallen into such gross faults, or so long mistaken them for beauties. His first essays we looked upon in a good degree as poetical paradoxes,—maintained experimentally, in order to display talent, and court notoriety;— and so maintained, with no more serious belief in their truth than is usually generated by an ingenious and animated defence of other paradoxes. But when we find, that he has been for twenty years exclusively employed upon articles of this very fabric, and that he has still enough of raw material on hand to keep him so employed for twenty years to come, we cannot refuse him the justice of believing that he is a sincere convert to his own system, and must ascribe the peculiarities of his composition, not to any transient affectation, or accidental caprice of imagination, but to a settled perversity of taste or understanding, which has been fostered, if not altogether created, by the circumstances to which we have already alluded.

The volume before us, if we were to describe it very shortly, we should characterize as a tissue of moral and devotional ravings, in which innumerable changes are rung upon a very few simple and familiar ideas:—but with such an accompaniment of long words, long sentences, and unwieldy phrases —and such a hubbub of strained raptures and fantastical sublimities, that it is often difficult for the most skilful and attentive student to obtain a glimpse of the author's meaning—and altogether impossible for an ordinary reader to conjecture what he is about. Moral and religious enthusiasm, though undoubtedly poetical emotions, are at the same time but dangerous inspirers of poetry, nothing being so apt to run into interminable dulness or mellifluous extravagance, without giving the unfortunate author the slightest intimation of his danger. His laudable zeal for the efficacy of his preachments, he very naturally mistakes for the ardour of poetical inspiration;—and, while dealing out the high words and glowing phrases which are so readily supplied by themes of this description,

41. maxims. What follows is a good brief statement of Jeffrey's critical point of view.

can scarcely avoid believing that he is eminently original and impressive:—All sorts of commonplace notions and expressions are sanctified in his eyes, by the sublime ends for which they are employed; and the mystical verbiage of the methodist pulpit is repeated, till the speaker entertains no doubt that he is the chosen organ of divine truth and persuasion. But if such be the common hazards of seeking inspiration from those potent fountains, it may easily be conceived what chance Mr. Wordsworth 10 had of escaping their enchantment,—with his natural propensities to wordiness, and his unlucky habit of debasing pathos with vulgarity. The fact accordingly is, that in this production he is more obscure than a Pindaric poet of the seventeenth century; and more verbose "than even himself of yore"; while the wilfulness with which he persists in choosing his examples of intellectual dignity and tenderness exclusively from the lowest ranks of society, will be sufficiently apparent, from the cir- 20 cumstance of his having thought fit to make his chief prolocutor in this poetical dialogue, and chief advocate of Providence and Virtue, *an old Scotch Pedlar*— retired indeed from business—but still rambling about in his former haunts, and gossiping among his old customers, without his pack on his shoulders. The other persons of the drama are, a retired military chaplain, who has grown half an atheist and half a misanthrope—the wife of an unprosperous weaver—a servant girl with her infant—a parish 30 pauper, and one or two other personages of equal rank and dignity.

The character of the work is decidedly didactic; and more than nine tenths of it are occupied with a species of dialogue, or rather a series of long sermons or harangues which pass between the pedlar, the author, the old chaplain, and a worthy vicar, who entertains the whole party at dinner on the last day of their excursion. The incidents which occur in the course of it are as few and trifling as can 40 well be imagined;—and those which the different speakers narrate in the course of their discourses, are introduced rather to illustrate their arguments or opinions, than for any interest they are supposed to possess of their own.—The doctrine which the work is intended to enforce, we are by no means certain that we have discovered. In so far as we can collect, however, it seems to be neither more nor less than the old familiar one, that a firm belief in the providence of a wise and beneficent Being must be 50 our great stay and support under all afflictions and perplexities upon earth—and that there are indications of his power and goodness in all the aspects of the visible universe, whether living or inanimate—

every part of which should therefore be regarded with love and reverence, as exponents of those great attributes. We can testify, at least, that these salutary and important truths are inculcated at far greater lengths, and with more repetitions, than in any ten volumes of sermons that we ever perused. It is also maintained, with equal conciseness and originality, that there is frequently much good sense, as well as much enjoyment, in the humbler conditions of life; and that, in spite of great vices and abuses, there is a reasonable allowance both of happiness and goodness in society at large. If there be any deeper or more recondite doctrines in Mr. Wordsworth's book, we must confess that they have escaped us;—and, convinced as we are of the truth and soundness of those to which we have alluded, we cannot help thinking that they might have been better enforced with less parade and prolixity. His effusions on what may be called the physiognomy of external nature, or its moral and theological expression, are eminently fantastic, obscure, and affected.—It is quite time, however, that we should give the reader a more particular account of this singular performance.

It opens with a picture of the author toiling across a bare common in a hot summer day, and reaching at last a ruined hut surrounded with tall trees, where he meets by appointment with a hale old man, with an iron-pointed staff lying beside him. Then follows a retrospective account of their first acquaintance—formed, it seems, when the author was at a village school; and his aged friend occupied "one room—the fifth part of a house" in the neighbourhood. After this, we have the history of this reverend person at no small length. He was born, we are happy to find, in Scotland—among the hills of Athol; and his mother, after his father's death, married the parish schoolmaster—so that he was taught his letters betimes! But then, as it is here set forth with much solemnity,

"From his sixth year, the boy of whom I speak,
    In summer, tended cattle on the hills!"

And again, a few pages after, that there may be no risk of mistake as to a point of such essential importance—

"From early childhood, even, as hath been said,
From his *sixth year*, he had been sent abroad,
In summer, to tend herds: Such was his task!"

25. It opens. Here follows Jeffrey's summary of the setting and the action of the story of Margaret, referred to on page 7. This part of the poem Wordsworth had begun at Racedown in 1795, when he was living there with Dorothy, and before he developed the social and moral theories which Jeffrey laments.

in the course of this occupation, it is next recorded, that he acquired such a taste for rural scenery and open air, that when he was sent to teach a school in a neighbouring village, he found it "a misery to him," and determined to embrace the more romantic occupation of a Pedlar—or, as Mr. Wordsworth more musically expresses it,

"A vagrant merchant, bent beneath his load";

—and in the course of his peregrinations had acquired a very large acquaintance, which, after he had given up dealing, he frequently took a summer ramble to visit.

The author, on coming up to this interesting personage, finds him sitting with his eyes half shut;—and, not being quite sure whether he is asleep or awake, stands "some minutes space" in silence beside him. "At length," says he, with his own delightful simplicity—

"At length I hailed him—*seeing that his hat*
Was moist with water-drops, as if the brim
Had newly scoop'd a running stream!—
        . . . "'Tis," said I, "a burning day;
My lips are parched with thirst;—but you, I guess,
Have somewhere found relief."

Upon this, the benevolent old man points him out a well in a corner, to which the author repairs, and after minutely describing its situation, beyond a broken wall, and between two alders that "grew in a cold damp nook," he thus faithfully chronicles the process of his return.

"My thirst was slaked—and from the cheerless spot
Withdrawing, straightway to the shade returned
Where sate the old man on the cottage bench."

The Pedlar then gives an account of the last inhabitants of the deserted cottage beside them. These were, a good industrious weaver and his wife and children. They were very happy for awhile; till sickness and want of work came upon them; and then the father enlisted as a soldier, and the wife pined in the lonely cottage—growing every year more careless and desponding, as her anxiety and fears for her absent husband, of whom no tidings ever reached her, accumulated. Her children died, and left her cheerless and alone; and at last she died also; and the cottage fell to decay. We must say, that there is very considerable pathos in the telling of this simple story; and that they who can get over the repugnance excited by the triteness of its inci-

dents, and the lowness of its objects, will not fail to be struck with the author's knowledge of the human heart, and the power he possesses of stirring up its deepest and gentlest sympathies. His prolixity, indeed, it is not so easy to get over. This little story fills about twenty five quarto pages, and abounds, of course, with mawkish sentiment, and details of preposterous minuteness. When the tale is told, the travellers take their staffs, and end their first day's journey, without further adventure, at a little inn. . . .

If any one should doubt of the existence of such a perversion, or be disposed to dispute about the instances we have hastily brought forward, we would just beg leave to refer him to the general plan and character of the poem now before us.—Why should Mr. Wordsworth have made his hero a superannuated Pedlar? What but the most wretched and provoking perversity of taste and judgment, could induce any one to place his chosen advocate of wisdom and virtue in so absurd and fantastic a condition? Did Mr. Wordsworth really imagine, that his favourite doctrines were likely to gain anything in point of effect or authority by being put into the mouth of a person accustomed to higgle about tape, or brass sleeve-buttons? Or is it not plain that, independent of the ridicule and disgust which such a personification must excite in many of his readers, its adoption exposes his work throughout to the charge of revolting incongruity and utter disregard of probability or nature? For, after he has thus wilfully debased his moral teacher by a low occupation, is there one word that he puts into his mouth, or one sentiment of which he makes him the organ, that has the most remote reference to that occupation? Is there anything in his learned, abstracted, and logical harangues, that savours of the calling that is ascribed to him? Are any of their materials such as a pedlar could possibly have dealt in? Are the manners, the diction, the sentiments, in any, the very smallest degree, accommodated to a person in that condition? or are they not eminently and conspicuously such as could not by possibility belong to it? A man who went about selling flannel and pocket-handkerchiefs in this lofty diction, would soon frighten away all his customers; and would infallibly pass either for a madman, or for some

8. tale is told. In the following part of the review, here omitted, Jeffrey lays "some specimens of the work itself before . . . readers." Most of these exemplify "that rapturous mysticism which eludes all comprehension." Then, in fairness, he quotes samples of "a very great number of single lines and images, that sparkle like gems in the desert" among "the rubbish heaped . . . around them." This duty done, he resumes his exposition of Wordsworth's "perversion."

learned and affected gentleman, who, in a frolic, had taken up a character which he was peculiarly ill qualified for supporting.

The absurdity in this case, we think, is palpable and glaring; but it is exactly of the same nature with that which infects the whole substance of the work, a puerile ambition of singularity engrafted on an unlucky predilection for truisms, and an affected passion for simplicity and humble life, most awkwardly combined with a taste for mystical refine- 10 ments, and all the gorgeousness of obscure phraseology. His taste for simplicity is evinced, by sprinkling up and down his interminable declamations, a few descriptions of baby-houses, and of old hats with wet brims; and his amiable partiality for humble life, by assuring us, that a wordy rhetorician, who talks about Thebes, and allegorizes all the heathen mythology, was once a pedlar—and making him break in upon his magnificent orations with two or three awkward notices of something that he had 20 seen when selling winter raiment about the country —or of the changes in the state of society, which had almost annihilated his former calling.

from *THE WHITE DOE OF RYLSTONE.* BY WILLIAM WORDSWORTH

THIS, we think, has the merit of being the very worst poem we ever saw imprinted in a quarto volume; and though it was scarcely to be expected, we confess that Mr. Wordsworth, with all his ambition, should so soon have attained to that distinction, the wonder may perhaps be diminished, when we state, that it seems to us to consist of a happy union of all the faults, without any of the beauties, which belong to his school of poetry. It is just such a work, in short, as some wicked enemy 40 of that school might be supposed to have devised, on purpose to make it ridiculous; and when we first took it up, we could not help fancying that some ill-natured critic had taken this harsh method of instructing Mr. Wordsworth, by example, in the nature of those errors, against which our precepts had been so often directed in vain. We had not gone far, however, till we felt intimately, that nothing in the nature of a joke could be so insupportably dull;— and that this must be the work of one who earnestly 50 believed it to be a pattern of pathetic simplicity, and gave it out as such to the admiration of all in-

telligent readers. In this point of view, the work may be regarded as curious at least, if not in some degree interesting; and, at all events, it must be instructive to be made aware of the excesses into which superior understandings may be betrayed, by long self-indulgence, and the strange extravagances into which they may run, when under the influence of that intoxication which is produced by unrestrained admiration of themselves. This poetical in- 10 toxication, indeed, to pursue the figure a little farther, seems capable of assuming as many forms as the vulgar one which arises from wine; and it appears to require as delicate a management to make a man a good poet by the help of the one, as to make him a good companion by means of the other. In both cases, a little mistake as to the dose or the quality of the inspiring fluid may make him absolutely outrageous, or lull him over into the most profound stupidity, instead of brightening up the 20 hidden stores of his genius: And truly we are concerned to say, that Mr. Wordsworth seems hitherto to have been unlucky in the choice of his liquor— or of his bottle holder. In some of his odes and ethic exhortations, he was exposed to the public in a state of incoherent rapture and glorious delirium, to which we think we have seen a parallel among the humbler lovers of jollity. In the Lyrical Ballads, he was exhibited, on the whole, in a vein of very pretty deliration; but in the poem before us, he appears in 30 a state of low and maudlin imbecility, which would not have misbecome Master Silence himself, in the close of a social day. Whether this unhappy result is to be ascribed to any adulteration of his Castalian cups, or to the unlucky choice of his company over them, we cannot presume to say. It may be, that he has dashed his Hippocrene with too large an infusion of lake water, or assisted its operation too exclusively by the study of the ancient historical ballads of "the north countrie." That there are 40 palpable imitations of the style and manner of those venerable compositions in the work before us is indeed undeniable; but it unfortunately happens, that while the hobbling versification, the mean diction, and flat stupidity of these models are very exactly copied, and even improved upon, in this imitation, their rude energy, manly simplicity, and occasional felicity of expression, have totally disappeared; and, instead of them, a large allowance of the author's own metaphysical sensibility, and mys- 50 tical wordiness, is forced into an unnatural combination with the borrowed beauties which have just been mentioned.

The story of the poem, though not capable of furnishing out matter for a quarto volume, might yet

---

46. precepts. This review was published in 1815; that of the *Excursion*, the year before.

have made an interesting ballad; and, in the hands of Mr. Scott, or Lord Byron, would probably have supplied many images to be loved, and descriptions to be remembered. The incidents arise out of the short-lived Catholic insurrection of the Northern counties, in the reign of Elizabeth, which was supposed to be connected with the project of marrying the Queen of Scots to the Duke of Norfolk; and terminated in the ruin of the Earls of Northumberland and Westmoreland, by whom it was chiefly 10 abetted. Among the victims of this rash enterprize was Richard Norton of Rylstone, who comes to the array with a splendid banner, at the head of eight tall sons, but against the will and advice of a ninth, who, though he refused to join the host, yet follows unarmed in its rear, out of anxiety for the fate of his family; and, when the father and his gallant progeny are made prisoners, and led to execution, at York, recovers the fatal banner, and is slain by a party of the Queen's horse near Bolton priory, in 20 which place he had been ordered to deposit it by the dying voice of his father. The stately halls and pleasant bowers of Rylstone are then wasted and fall into desolation; while the heroic daughter, and only survivor of the house, is sheltered among its faithful retainers, and wanders about for many years in its neighbourhood, accompanied by a beautiful white doe, which had formerly been a pet in the family; and continues, long after the death of this sad survivor, to repair every Sunday to the 30 church-yard of Bolton priory, and there to feed and wander among the graves, to the wonder and delight of the rustic congregation that came there to worship.

This, we think, is a pretty subject for a ballad; and, in the author's better day, might have made a lyrical one of considerable interest: Let us see, however, how he deals with it since he has bethought him of publishing in quarto.

The First Canto merely contains the description 40 of the doe coming into the church-yard on Sunday, and of the congregation wondering at her. She is described as being as white as a lily,—or the moon, —or a ship in the sunshine; and this is the style in which Mr. Wordsworth marvels and moralizes about her through ten quarto pages. . . .

The Seventh and last canto contains the history of the desolated Emily and her faithful doe; but so very discreetly and cautiously written, that the 50 most tender-hearted reader may peruse it without the least risk of any excessive emotion. The poor lady runs about indeed for some years in a very disconsolate way in a worsted gown and flannel night-cap; but at last the old white doe finds her out, and takes again to following her—whereupon Mr. Wordsworth breaks out into this fine and natural rapture.

> "Oh, moment ever blest! O Pair!
> Beloved of Heaven, Heaven's choicest care!
> This was for you a precious greeting,
> For both a bounteous, fruitful meeting.
> Joined are they, and the sylvan Doe
> Can she depart? Can she forego
> The Lady, once her playful Peer? . . .
> "That day, the first of a reunion
> Which was to teem with high communion,
> That day of balmy April weather,
> They tarried in the wood together."

What follows is not quite so intelligible.

> "When Emily by morning light
> Went forth, the Doe was there in sight.
> She shrunk: with one frail shock of pain,
> Received and followed by a prayer,
> Did she behold—saw once again;
> Shun will she not, she feels, will bear;—
> But wheresoever she looked round
> All now was trouble-haunted ground."

But we make out that the lady's loneliness was cheered by this mute associate; and that the doe, in return, found a certain comfort in the lady's company—

> "Communication, like the ray
> Of a new morning, to the nature
> And prospects of the inferior Creature!"

In due time the poor lady dies, and is buried beside her mother; and the doe continues to haunt the places which they had frequented together, and especially to come and pasture every Sunday upon the fine grass in Bolton churchyard, the gate of which is never opened but on occasion of the weekly service.—In consequence of all which, we are assured by Mr. Wordsworth, that she "is approved by Earth and Sky, in their benignity"; and moreover, that the old Priory itself takes her for a daughter of the Eternal Prime—which we have no doubt is a very great compliment, though we have not the good luck to understand what it means.

> "And aye, methinks, this hoary Pile,
> Subdued by outrage and decay,
> Looks down upon her with a smile,
> A gracious smile that seems to say,
> 'Thou, thou are not a Child of Time,
> But Daughter of the Eternal Prime!'"

John Wilson Croker
1780–1857

John Wilson Croker, whose name has been infamously preserved to posterity chiefly by his having struck perhaps the cruelest blow ever inflicted on a young writer, was respected and noted in his own times as a statesman and an orator. Born in Galway, Ireland, and educated at Trinity College, Dublin, he entered upon a career as lawyer and writer. He was elected to Parliament, won the friendship of the Duke of Wellington, whom he served as secretary, and distinguished himself as an orator and a public official. For years he was one of the leading contributors to the *Quarterly Review*. His attack on Keats, "So savage and Tartarly," was inspired in part by political rancor, in part by hostility to the new poetry of his day. Keats's own reaction hardly occasioned Shelley's in *Adonais*. Now that the bitterness of such treatment has been sweetened by Keats's fame, the irony of posterity's reversal of Croker's verdict makes his review almost amusing reading.

ENDYMION: A POETIC ROMANCE.
BY JOHN KEATS

REVIEWERS have been sometimes accused of not reading the works which they affected to criticise. On the present occasion we shall anticipate the author's complaint, and honestly confess that we have not read his work. Not that we have been wanting in our duty—far from it—indeed, we have made efforts almost as superhuman as the story itself appears to be, to get through it; but with the fullest stretch of our perseverance, we are forced to confess that we have not been able to struggle beyond the first of the four books of which this Poetic Romance consists. We should extremely lament this want of energy, or whatever it may be, on our parts, were it not for one consolation—namely, that we are no better acquainted with the meaning of the book through which we have so painfully toiled, than we are with that of the three which we have not looked into.

It is not that Mr. Keats, (if this be his real name, for we almost doubt that any man in his senses would put his real name to such a rhapsody,) it is not, we say, that the author has not powers of language, rays of fancy, and gleams of genius—he has all these; but he is unhappily a disciple of the new school of what has been somewhere called Cockney poetry; which may be defined to consist of the most incongruous ideas in the most uncouth language.

Of this school, Mr. Leigh Hunt, as we observed in a former Number, aspires to be the hierophant. Our readers will recollect the pleasant recipes for harmonious and sublime poetry which he gave us in his preface to "Rimini," and the still more facetious instances of his harmony and sublimity in the verses themselves; and they will recollect above all the contempt of Pope, Johnson, and such poetasters and pseudo-critics, which so forcibly contrasted itself with Mr. Leigh Hunt's self-complacent approbation of

". . . all the things itself had wrote,
Of special merit though of little note."

This author is a copyist of Mr. Hunt; but he is more unintelligible, almost as rugged, twice as diffuse, and ten times more tiresome and absurd than his prototype, who, though he impudently presumed to seat himself in the chair of criticism, and to measure his own poetry by his own standard, yet generally had a meaning. But Mr. Keats had advanced no dogmas which he was bound to support by examples; his nonsense therefore is quite gratuitous; he writes it for its own sake; and, being bitten by Mr. Leigh Hunt's insane criticism, more than rivals the insanity of his poetry.

Mr. Keats's preface hints that his poem was produced under peculiar circumstances.

"Knowing within myself (he says) the manner in which this Poem has been produced, it is not without a feeling of regret that I make it public.— What manner I mean, will be *quite clear* to the reader, who must soon perceive great inexperience, immaturity, and every error denoting a feverish attempt, rather than a deed accomplished."

We humbly beg his pardon, but this does not appear to us to be *quite so clear*—we really do not know

4. Cockney poetry (compare Lake School), because it had its center in London and most of its members were residents of London. John Wilson ("Christopher North") probably invented the term in *Blackwood's*.

what he means—but the next passage is more intelligible.

"The first books, and indeed the two last, I feel sensible are not of such completion as to warrant their passing the press."

Thus "the two first books" are, even in his own judgment, unfit to appear, and "the two last" are, it seems, in the same condition—and as two and two make four, and as that is the whole number of books, we have a clear and, we believe, a very just estimate of the entire work.

Mr. Keats, however, deprecates criticism of this "immature and feverish work" in terms which are themselves sufficiently feverish; and we confess that we should have abstained from inflicting upon him any of the tortures of the "*fierce hell*" of criticism, which terrify his imagination, if he had not begged to be spared in order that he might write more; if we had not observed in him a certain degree of talent which deserves to be put in the right way, or which, at least, ought to be warned of the wrong; and if, finally, he had not told us that he is of an age and temper which imperiously require mental discipline.

Of the story we have been able to make out but little; it seems to be mythological, and probably relates to the loves of Diana and Endymion; but of this, as the scope of the work has altogether escaped us, we cannot speak with any degree of certainty; and must therefore content ourselves with giving some instances of its diction and versification; and here again we are perplexed and puzzled.—At first it appeared to us, that Mr. Keats had been amusing himself and wearying his readers with an immeasurable game of *bouts-rimés;* but, if we recollect rightly, it is an indispensable condition at this play, that the rhymes when filled up shall have a meaning; and our author, as we have already hinted, has no meaning. He seems to us to write a line at random, and then he follows not the thought excited by this line, but that suggested by the *rhyme* with which it concludes. There is hardly a complete couplet inclosing a complete idea in the whole book. He wanders from one subject to another, from the association, not of ideas but of sounds, and the work is composed of hemistichs which, it is quite evident, have forced themselves upon the author by the mere force of the catchwords on which they turn.

We shall select, not as the most striking instance, but as that least liable to suspicion, a passage from the opening of the poem.

". . . Such the sun, the moon,
Trees old and young, sprouting a shady boon

For simple sheep; and such are daffodils
With the green world they live in; and clear rills
That for themselves a cooling covert make
'Gainst the hot season; the mid-forest brake,
Rich with a sprinkling of fair musk-rose blooms;
And such, too, is the grandeur of the dooms
We have imagined for the mighty dead; &c. &c."

Here it is clear that the word, and not the idea, *moon* produces the simple sheep and their shady *boon*, and that "the *dooms* of the mighty dead" would never have intruded themselves but for the "*fair musk-rose blooms.*"

Again

"For 'twas the morn: Apollo's upward fire
Made every eastern cloud a silvery pyre
Of brightness so unsullied, that therein
A melancholy spirit well might win
Oblivion, and melt out his essence fine
Into the winds: rain-scented eglantine
Gave temperate sweets to the well-wooing sun;
The lark was lost in him; cold springs had run
To warm their chilliest bubbles in the grass;
Man's voice was on the mountains; and the mass
Of nature's lives and wonders pulsed tenfold,
To feel this sun-rise and its glories old."

Here Apollo's *fire* produces a *pyre*, a silvery pyre of clouds, *wherein* a spirit might *win* oblivion and melt his essence *fine*, and scented *eglantine* gives sweets to the *sun*, and cold springs had *run* into the *grass*, and then the pulse of the *mass* pulsed *tenfold* to feel the glories *old* of the new-born day, &c.

One example more.

"Be still the unimaginable lodge
For solitary thinkings, such as dodge
Conception to the very bourne of heaven,
Then leave the naked brain: be still the leaven,
That spreading in this dull and clodded earth
Gives it a touch ethereal—a new birth."

Lodge, dodge—heaven, leaven—earth, birth; such, in six words, is the sum and substance of six lines.

We come now to the author's taste in versification. He cannot indeed write a sentence, but perhaps he may be able to spin a line. Let us see. The following are specimens of his prosodial notions of our English heroic metre.

"Dear as the temple's self, so does the moon
The passion poesy, glories infinite."

"So plenteously all weed-hidden roots."

"Of some strange history, potent to send."

"Before the deep intoxication."

"Her scarf into a fluttering pavilion."

"The stubborn canvass for my voyage prepared."

"Endymion! the cave is secreter
Than the isle of Delos. Echo hence shall stir
No sighs but sigh-warm kisses, or light noise
Of thy combing hand, the while it travelling cloys
And trembles through my labyrinthine hair."

By this time our readers must be pretty well satisfied as to the meaning of his sentences and the structure of his lines. We now present them with some of the new words with which, in imitation of Mr. Leigh Hunt, he adorns our language.

We are told that "turtles *passion* their voices"; that an "arbor was *nested*"; and a lady's locks "*gordianed up*"; and to supply the place of the nouns thus verbalized Mr. Keats with great fecundity, spawns new ones; such as "men-slugs and human *serpentry*"; the "*honey-feel of bliss*"; "wives prepare *needments*"—and so forth.

Then he has formed new verbs by the process of cutting off their natural tails, the adverbs, and affixing them to their foreheads; thus, "the wine out-sparkled"; the "multitude up-followed"; and "night up-took." "The wind up-blows"; and the "hours are down-sunken."

But if he sinks some adverbs in the verbs, he compensates the language with adverbs and adjectives which he separates from the parent stock. Thus, a lady "whispers *pantingly* and close," makes "*hushing* signs," and steers her skiff into a "*ripply* cove"; a shower falls "*refreshfully*"; and a vulture has a "*spreaded* tail."

But enough of Mr. Leigh Hunt and his simple neophyte.—If any one should be bold enough to purchase this "Poetic Romance," and so much more patient, than ourselves, as to get beyond the first book, and so much more fortunate as to find a meaning, we entreat him to make us acquainted with his success; we shall then return to the task which we now abandon in despair, and endeavour to make all due amends to Mr. Keats and to our readers.

Benjamin Robert Haydon
1786–1846

Benjamin Robert Haydon was born at Plymouth, January 26, 1786. On a ceiling of Plympton St. Mary School, which he attended, was a sketch in burnt cork made by Sir Joshua Reynolds when that famous painter was a pupil there. Determined to be a painter himself, Haydon went up to London and studied under Fuseli at the Royal Academy. He early achieved some prominence for his paintings of Biblical, historical, and literary subjects, such as "The Repose in Egypt," "Dentatus," "Macbeth," and "The Judgment of Solomon." After studying at the Louvre in Paris, he returned to England and began work on his masterpiece, "Christ's Entry into Jerusalem." Wordsworth, Lamb, Keats, and other friends sat for the heads of the various figures in the picture. Meanwhile, Haydon had pleaded for recognition of the priceless value of the Elgin Marbles, introducing the young Keats to them, quarreled with Wordsworth's painter friend and patron Sir George Beaumont, and been imprisoned for debt. His lectures on painting and design, begun in 1835, exercised a beneficial influence on English artistic taste and architecture. But his violence and

self-assertiveness earned for him the epithet "the mad painter Haydon."

Haydon's *Autobiography*, published in 1853, has been described as "one of the most natural books ever written." The following selection from it, a famous anecdote of the period, illustrates both this quality of the book and the conviviality and high spirits of the Romanticists in their lighter moments. A recent play, Mr. Laurence Housman's *Charles! Charles!* is based on it. "Christ's Entry into Jerusalem," described as the background of the anecdote, was the nucleus of the American Gallery of Painting founded by Haydon's cousin, John Haviland of Philadelphia. It is said to be now in the Art Museum of Cincinnati, Ohio.

from AUTOBIOGRAPHY

THE IMMORTAL DINNER

IN December Wordsworth was in town, and as Keats wished to know him I made up a party to dinner of Charles Lamb, Wordsworth, Keats, and Monkhouse, his friend, and a very pleasant party we had.

I wrote to Lamb, and told him the address was "22, Lisson Grove North, at Rossi's, half way up, right-hand corner." I received his characteristic reply:

"My dear Haydon,
"I will come with pleasure to 22. Lisson Grove North, at Rossi's, half-way up, right-hand side, if I can find it.
　　　　　"Yours,
　　　　　"C. Lamb.
"20. Russel Court,
　　Covent Garden East,
　　　half-way up, next the corner,
　　　　left-hand side."

On 28th December, the immortal dinner came off in my painting-room, with "Jerusalem" towering up behind us as a background. Wordsworth was a fine cue, and we had a glorious set-to,—on Homer, Shakespeare, Milton, and Virgil. Lamb got exceedingly merry and exquisitely witty; and his fun in the midst of Wordsworth's solemn intonations of oratory was like the sarcasm and wit of the fool in the intervals of Lear's passion. Lamb soon got delightfully merry. He made a speech and voted me absent, and made them drink my health. "Now," said Lamb, "you old lake poet, you rascally poet, why do you call Voltaire dull?" We all defended Wordsworth, and affirmed there was a state of mind when Voltaire would be dull. "Well," said Lamb, "here's Voltaire—the Messiah of the French nation, and a very proper one too."

He then, in a strain of humour beyond description, abused me for putting Newton's head into my picture,—"a fellow," said he, "who believed nothing unless it was as clear as the three sides of a triangle." And then he and Keats agreed he had destroyed all the poetry of the rainbow, by reducing it to the prismatic colours. It was impossible to resist him, and we all drank "Newton's health, and confusion to mathematics." It was delightful to see the good-humour of Wordsworth in giving in to all our frolics without affectation, and laughing as heartily as the best of us.

By this time other friends joined, amongst them poor Ritchie, who was going to penetrate by Fezzan to Timbuctoo. I introduced him to all as "a gentleman going to Africa." Lamb seemed to take no notice; but all of a sudden he roared out, "Which is the gentleman we are going to lose?" We then drank the victim's health, in which Ritchie joined.

In the morning of this delightful day, a gentle-man, a perfect stranger, had called on me. He said he knew my friends, had an enthusiasm for Wordsworth, and begged I would procure him the happiness of an introduction. He told me he was a comptroller of stamps, and often had correspondence with the poet. I thought it a liberty; but still, as he seemed a gentleman, I told him he might come.

When we retired to tea we found the comptroller. In introducing him to Wordsworth I forgot to say who he was. After a little time the comptroller looked down, looked up, and said to Wordsworth, "Don't you think, sir, Milton was a great genius?" Keats looked at me, Wordsworth looked at the comptroller. Lamb, who was dozing by the fire, turned round and said, "Pray, sir, did you say Milton was a great genius?" "No, sir, I asked Mr. Wordsworth if he were not." "Oh," said Lamb, "then you are a silly fellow." "Charles, my dear Charles," said Wordsworth; but Lamb, perfectly innocent of the confusion he had created, was off again by the fire.

After an awful pause the comptroller said, "Don't you think Newton a great genius?" I could not stand it any longer. Keats put his head into my books. Ritchie squeezed in a laugh. Wordsworth seemed asking himself, "Who is this?" Lamb got up, and, taking a candle, said, "Sir, will you allow me to look at your phrenological development?" He then turned his back on the poor man, and at every question of the comptroller he chaunted:

"Diddle diddle dumpling, my son John
　Went to bed with his breeches on."

The man in office, finding Wordsworth did not know who he was, said in a spasmodic and half-chuckling anticipation of assured victory, "I have had the honour of some correspondence with you, Mr. Wordsworth." "With me, sir?" said Wordsworth. "Not that I remember." "Don't you, sir? I am a comptroller of stamps." There was a dead silence; the comptroller evidently thinking that was enough. While we were waiting for Wordsworth's reply, Lamb sung out:

"Hey diddle diddle,
　The cat and the fiddle."

"My dear Charles," said Wordsworth.

"Diddle diddle dumpling, my son John,"

chaunted Lamb; and then rising, exclaimed, "Do let me have another look at that gentleman's organs." Keats and I hurried Lamb into the painting-room, shut the door, and gave way to inextinguishable laughter. We went back, but the comptroller was irreconcilable. We soothed and smiled, and asked him to supper. He stayed, though his dignity was sorely affected. However, being a good-natured man, we parted all in good humour, and no ill effects followed.

All the while, until Monkhouse succeeded, we could hear Lamb struggling in the painting-room, and calling at intervals, "Who is that fellow? Allow me to see his organs once more."

It was indeed an immortal evening. Words- 10 worth's fine intonation as he quoted Milton and Virgil, Keats' eager inspired look, Lamb's quaint sparkle of lambent humour, so speeded the stream of conversation, that in my life I never passed a more delightful time. All our fun was within bounds. Not a word passed that an apostle might

not have listened to. It was a night worthy of the Elizabethan age, and my solemn "Jerusalem" flashing up by the flame of the fire, with Christ hanging over us like a vision, all made up a picture which will long glow upon

> "that inward eye
> Which is the bliss of solitude."

Keats made Ritchie promise he would carry his "Endymion" to the great desert of Sahara, and fling it in the midst.

Poor Ritchie went to Africa, and died, as Lamb foresaw, in 1819. Keats died in 1821, at Rome. C. Lamb is gone, joking to the last. Monkhouse is dead, and Wordsworth and I are the only two now living (1841) of that glorious party.

Thomas Hood
1799–1845

The son of a London bookseller, Thomas Hood fortunately had a teacher who, he said, "made him feel it impossible not to take an interest in learning while he [the teacher] seemed so interested in teaching." After his schooling, Hood relieved the tedium of several years as a bookkeeper by literary exercises, overtaxed himself, and recovered his health in outdoor life at Dundee, Scotland. In 1821, after the death of the editor John Scott in a duel, Hood became a subeditor of the *London Magazine*. This connection threw him into the society of Lamb, De Quincey, and others of their circle. His *Odes and Addresses*, 1825, and *Plea of the Midsummer Fairies*, 1827, were written under the influence of Keats, partly as a result of Hood's having married a sister of Keats's friend John Hamilton Reynolds. Thereafter Hood acquired great popularity as a writer on romantic, humorous, and social subjects in a series of annuals and miscellanies. His most famous poem, "The Song of the Shirt," was first published in the Christmas, 1843, number of *Punch*. After 1828, he was a regular contributor to the *Athenaeum*. He died May 3, 1845, one of the most popular writers of his time, especially honored by working people for his sympathetic and eloquent treatment of their hardships and tragedies. Hood's work and career show how imperceptibly the later Romanticists merge into the early Victorians.

FAITHLESS NELLY GRAY

A PATHETIC BALLAD

Ben Battle was a soldier bold,
    And used to war's alarms;
But a cannon-ball took off his legs,
    So he laid down his arms!

Now as they bore him off the field,
    Said he, "Let others shoot,
For here I leave my second leg,
    And the Forty-second Foot!"

The army-surgeons made him limbs:
    Said he,—"They're only pegs: 10
But there's as wooden members quite,
    As represent my legs!"

Now Ben he loved a pretty maid,
    Her name was Nelly Gray;
So he went to pay her his devours,
    When he'd devoured his pay!

But when he called on Nelly Gray,
    She made him quite a scoff;
And when she saw his wooden legs,
    Began to take them off!   20

"O, Nelly Gray! O, Nelly Gray!
    Is this your love so warm?

The love that loves a scarlet coat
  Should be more uniform!"

Said she, "I loved a soldier once,
  For he was blithe and brave;
But I will never have a man
  With both legs in the grave!

"Before you had those timber toes,
  Your love I did allow,   30
But then, you know, you stand upon
  Another footing now!"

"O, Nelly Gray! O, Nelly Gray!
  For all your jeering speeches,
At duty's call, I left my legs
  In Badajos's *breaches!*"

"Why, then," said she, "you've lost the feet
  Of legs in war's alarms,
And now you cannot wear your shoes
  Upon your feats of arms!"   40

"O, false and fickle Nelly Gray!
  I know why you refuse:—
Though I've no feet—some other man
  Is standing in my shoes!

"I wish I ne'er had seen your face;
  But, now, a long farewell!
For you will be my death:—alas!
  You will not be my *Nell!*"

Now when he went from Nelly Gray,
  His heart so heavy got—   50
And life was such a burthen grown,
  It made him take a knot!

So round his melancholy neck,
  A rope he did entwine,
And, for his second time in life,
  Enlisted in the Line!

One end he tied around a beam,
  And then removed his pegs,
And, as his legs were off,—of course,
  He soon was off his legs!   60

And there he hung, till he was dead
  As any nail in town,—
For though distress had cut him up,
  It could not cut him down!

A dozen men sat on his corpse,
  To find out why he died—

36. **Badajos's breaches.** The city of Badajos, Spain, was besieged during the Peninsular War.

And they buried Ben in four cross-roads,
  With a *stake* in his inside!

I REMEMBER, I REMEMBER

1

I remember, I remember,
  The house where I was born,
The little window where the sun
  Came peeping in at morn;
He never came a wink too soon,
  Nor brought too long a day,
But now, I often wish the night
  Had borne my breath away!

2

I remember, I remember,
  The roses, red and white,   10
The violets, and the lily-cups,
  Those flowers made of light!
The lilacs where the robin built,
  And where my brother set
The laburnum on his birthday,—
  The tree is living yet!

3

I remember, I remember,
  Where I was used to swing,
And thought the air must rush as fresh
  To swallows on the wing;   20
My spirit flew in feathers then,
  That is so heavy now,
And summer pools could hardly cool
  The fever on my brow!

4

I remember, I remember,
  The fir trees dark and high;
I used to think their slender tops
  Were close against the sky:
It was a childish ignorance,
  But now 'tis little joy   30
To know I'm farther off from Heaven
  Than when I was a boy.

THE SONG OF THE SHIRT

With fingers weary and worn,
  With eyelids heavy and red,

68. **With a stake,** formerly customary in the burial of suicides. The stake was to keep them from wandering around as vampires.

A woman sat, in unwomanly rags,
　　Plying her needle and thread—
　　　Stitch! stitch! stitch!
In poverty, hunger, and dirt,
　　And still with a voice of dolorous pitch
She sang the "Song of the Shirt."

"Work! work! work!
　　While the cock is crowing aloof!　　　10
And work—work—work,
　　Till the stars shine through the roof!
It's Oh! to be a slave
　　Along with the barbarous Turk,
Where woman has never a soul to save,
　　If this is Christian work!

"Work—work—work
　　Till the brain begins to swim;
Work—work—work
　　Till the eyes are heavy and dim!　　20
Seam, and gusset, and band,
　　Band, and gusset, and seam,
Till over the buttons I fall asleep,
　　And sew them on in a dream!

"O! Men with Sisters dear!
　　O! Men with Mothers and Wives!
It is not linen you're wearing out,
　　But human creatures' lives!
Stitch—stitch—stitch,
　　In poverty, hunger, and dirt,　　　30
Sewing at once, with a double thread,
　　A Shroud as well as a Shirt.

"But why do I talk of Death?
　　That Phantom of grisly bone,
I hardly fear his terrible shape,
　　It seems so like my own—
It seems so like my own,
　　Because of the fasts I keep;
Oh, God! that bread should be so dear,
　　And flesh and blood so cheap!　　　40

"Work—work—work!
　　My labour never flags;
And what are its wages? A bed of straw,
　　A crust of bread—and rags.
That shattered roof—and this naked floor—
　　A table—a broken chair—
And a wall so blank, my shadow I thank
　　For sometimes falling there!

"Work—work—work!
　　From weary chime to chime,　　　50

Work—work—work—
　　As prisoners work for crime!
Band, and gusset, and seam,
　　Seam, and gusset, and band,
Till the heart is sick, and the brain benumbed,
　　As well as the weary hand.

"Work—work—work,
　　In the dull December light,
And work—work—work,
　　When the weather is warm and bright—　　60
While underneath the eaves
　　The brooding swallows cling
As if to show me their sunny backs
　　And twit me with the spring.

"Oh! but to breathe the breath
　　Of the cowslip and primrose sweet—
With the sky above my head,
　　And the grass beneath my feet,
For only one short hour
　　To feel as I used to feel,　　　70
Before I knew the woes of want
　　And the walk that costs a meal!

"Oh! but for one short hour!
　　A respite however brief!
No blessed leisure for Love or Hope,
　　But only time for Grief!
A little weeping would ease my heart,
　　But in their briny bed
My tears must stop, for every drop
　　Hinders needle and thread!　　　80

Seam, and gusset, and band,
　　Band, and gusset, and seam,
Work, work, work,
　　Like the Engine that works by Steam!
A mere machine of iron and wood
　　That toils for Mammon's sake—
Without a brain to ponder and craze,
　　Or a heart to feel—and break!

With fingers weary and worn,
　　With eyelids heavy and red,　　　90
A woman sat in unwomanly rags,
　　Plying her needle and thread—
　　　Stitch! stitch! stitch!
In poverty, hunger, and dirt,
And still with a voice of dolorous pitch,—
　　Would that its tone could reach the rich!—
　　She sang this "Song of the Shirt!"

SUGGESTIONS FOR FURTHER READING

GENERAL LITERARY HISTORY AND CRITICISM

The following works are additional to those cited in the Introduction in biographical and critical sketches, and in notes.

Brooke, Stopford A., *Naturalism in English Poetry*, Dutton, 1920. Excellent exposition of ideas of the Romantics; good interpretations of important works.

The Cambridge History of English Literature, ed. by A. W. Ward and A. R. Waller, 14 vols., Putnam, 1907–17, Vols. XI–XII. Standard encyclopedic work.

Cazamian, Louis, and Legouis, Emile, *A History of English Literature*, revised and reset, 2 vols. in 1, Macmillan, 1929. Mature criticism by two eminent French scholars.

Elton, Oliver, *A Survey of English Literature, 1780–1830*, 2 vols., Longmans, 1912. Perhaps the best detailed survey.

Gingerich, Solomon Francis, *Essays in the Romantic Poets*, Macmillan, 1924. Excellent interpretations.

Pierce, F. E., *Currents and Eddies of the English Romantic Generation*, Yale University Press, 1918. One of the best accounts of personal relations, "schools," and group interests.

Raleigh, Sir Walter A., *Romance: Two Lectures*, Princeton University Press, 1916. Interesting and stimulating treatments of characteristic traits.

THE NOVEL

Lovett, Robert Morss, and Hughes, Helen Sard, *The History of the Novel in England*, Houghton Mifflin, 1932. Chaps. VI–VIII are the best brief treatment for the period.

Jane Austen, *Pride and Prejudice*, 1813

Maria Edgeworth, *Castle Rackrent*, 1800

Sir Walter Scott, *Guy Mannering*, 1815

These and the principal other works of the three chief novelists of the period are obtainable in Everyman's Library, Dutton; Pocket Classics, Macmillan; World's Classics, Oxford; and the like inexpensive editions.

HISTORY, SOCIAL CONDITIONS

Bushnell, Nelson S., *The Historical Background of English Literature*, Holt, 1930, chaps. XI–XIII. Perhaps the best brief treatment of the subject. Inexpensive.

Dowden, Edward, *The French Revolution and English Literature*, Scribner, 1914. A classic work.

Somervell, D. C., *English Thought in the Nineteenth Century*, Longmans, 1936. Chap. I, especially "IV: Five Poets," is excellent.

MUSIC AND ART

Whitley, William Thomas, *Art in England, 1800–1820*, Macmillan, 1928

——*Art in England, 1821–1837*, Cambridge University Press, 1930. Both volumes are richly illustrated.

Dannreather, Edward, *The Romantic Period, Oxford History of Music*, Vol. VI, Oxford, 1937

McKinney, Howard D., and Anderson, W. R., *Music in History, the Evolution of an Art*, American Book Co., 1940. Illustrated. The chapter "Music Becomes More Personal" describes "The Romantic Ideal in Art."

PHONOGRAPH RECORDS

Columbia Masterworks Set M-375* (The Voice of Poetry), Vol. I, has readings by Edith Evans: 17151-D, Wordsworth's "A Slumber Did My Spirit Seal" and Keats's "La Belle Dame sans Merci"; 17152-D, Blake's "The Tiger," Byron's "She Walks in Beauty," Wordsworth's "Upon Westminster Bridge," Scott's "Allan-a-Dale"; 17153-D, Wordsworth's "The Highland Reaper." Vol. II has readings by John Gielgud: 17208-D, Shelley's "Ode to the West Wind"; 17209-D, Shelley's "Ozymandias "and Byron's "So We'll Go No More a-Roving." See, also, *Masterpieces of Literature*, 3 vols.

RCA Victor has: Songs by Thomas Moore: 1238, "Believe Me, If All Those Endearing Young Charms," by Lawrence Tibbett; 1553, "The Harp That Once through Tara's Hall," by John McCormack; 1355, "The Last Rose of Summer," by Amelita Galli-Curci; 14611, "She Far Is from the Land," by John McCormack; 15858, "Bendemeer's Stream," by John Charles Thomas; 24537, "Has Sorrow Thy Young Days Shaded?" by Ruth Carhart. Sir Walter Scott's "Ave Maria" from *The Lady of the Lake*: 15752, by Dorothy Maynor; 14210, by Marian Anderson; 8423, by Elizabeth Schumann; 7778, by Hulda Laschanska; 8033, by John McCormack.

BYRON

Complete Poetical Works, ed. by P. E. More, Student's Cambridge Edition, Houghton Mifflin, 1906. In many ways the best 1-vol. edition.

Lord Byron in His Letters, ed. by V. H. Collins, London: Murray, 1927. A good substitute for complete editions of the letters, which are expensive.

The Best of Byron, ed. by R. A. Rice, Nelson, 1933. Excellent introduction and notes; good selections.

Drinkwater, John, *The Pilgrim of Eternity—A Conflict*, Doran, 1926. Animated and sympathetic.

Maurois, André, *Byron*, trans. by Harriet Miles, Appleton, 1930. Byron from the French point of view.

Nicolson, Harold G., *Byron: The Last Journey, April 1823–April 1824*, Houghton Mifflin, 1924. An absorbing narrative.

COLERIDGE

Complete Poems, ed. by E. H. Coleridge, Standard Authors, Oxford, 1927. The most satisfactory inexpensive edition.

Biographia Literaria, Everyman's Library, Dutton. Not so good as Shawcross's ed., Oxford Press, but cheaper, and satisfactory for ordinary purposes.

Lectures on Shakespere, Everyman's Library, Dutton. Not so good as T. M. Raysor's ed., Oxford Press, but less expensive.

Fausset, H. I'A., *Samuel Taylor Coleridge*, Harcourt, Brace, 1926

Hanson, Lawrence, *The Life of Samuel Taylor Coleridge, The Early Years*, Oxford Press, 1939. A very readable account of the most interesting period.

Lowes, John Livingston, *The Road to Xanadu*, Houghton Mifflin, new ed., 1930. One of the most exciting pieces of literary detective work and criticism ever written.

DE QUINCEY

Selections from De Quincey, ed. by M. H. Turk, Ginn, 1902

Winchester, C. T., *A Group of English Essayists*, Macmillan, 1910

Eaton, Horace A., *Thomas De Quincey: A Biographical Narrative*, Oxford Press, 1936. Sound and humanly interesting.

HAZLITT

Essays, selected and ed. with introd. by Percy V. D. Shelley, Modern Student's Library, Scribner, 1924.

Birrell, Augustine, *William Hazlitt*, English Men of Letters Series, Macmillan, 1902. The best inexpensive life; P. P. Howe's, Doran, the standard full-length biography, is expensive.

Zeitlin, Jacob, ed., *Hazlitt on English Literature: An Introduction to the Appreciation of Literature*, Oxford Press, 1913. Best brief analysis of Hazlitt's critical principles and ideas.

KEATS

Complete Poetical Works and Letters, ed. by H. E. Scudder, Student's Cambridge Edition, Houghton Mifflin, 1899. Perhaps the best inexpensive edition of the scope indicated. (Compare the Shelley list.)

Complete Poems and Selected Letters, ed. by C. D. Thorpe, Series in Literature, Doubleday, Doran, 1935. Very satisfactory introduction and notes; 58 of the most important and interesting letters.

Autobiography of John Keats, compiled by E. V. Weller, Stanford University Press, 1934. An arrangement of Keats's letters, prefaced by C. C. Clarke's account of his early boyhood, makes Keats tell the story of his own life.

Colvin, Sidney, *John Keats: His Life and Poetry*, Scribner, 1925. There is little to choose between this and Amy Lowell's biography, Houghton Mifflin, 1925; they are the standard biographies. Both contain excellent criticism.

Garrod, H. W., *Keats*, Oxford Press, 1926. Excellent criticism.

Thorpe, C. D., *The Mind of John Keats*, Oxford Press, 1926. Thoroughly useful.

LAMB

Complete Works and Letters, Modern Library. The only inexpensive complete 1-vol. edition.

Blunden, E. C., *Charles Lamb and His Contemporaries*, Cambridge University Press, 1937. Lively treatment of Lamb and his friends.

SCOTT

Complete Poems, Standard Authors, Oxford Press. The least expensive of the standard complete editions.

The Waverley Pageant: The Best Passages from [Scott's] Novels, selected with critical introductions by Hugh Walpole, Harper, 1932. The best short cut to acquaintance with the great novels.

Gwynn, Stephen, *Life of Sir Walter Scott*, Little, Brown, 1930. One of the most readable of the recent biographies.

Novels. See THE NOVEL, above.

SHELLEY

Complete Poetical Works, ed. by Thomas Hutchinson, Standard Authors, Oxford Press. Little except difference of cost to choose between this and the Student's Cambridge, Houghton Mifflin, and the Globe, Macmillan. The Modern Library offers *The Complete Poems of Keats and Shelley* in one inexpensive volume.

The Letters of Percy Bysshe Shelley, ed. by Roger Ingpen, 2 vols., Scribner, 1909. The best; no complete inexpensive edition.

Clarke, Isabel C., *Shelley and Byron*, Ryerson Press, 1934

Maurois, André, *Ariel: A Shelley Romance*, Appleton, 1924. Sound factually; enthralling as fiction.

Winwar, Frances, *The Romantic Rebels*, Little, Brown, 1935. A biographical story and study of Byron, Shelley, and Keats.

Clutton-Brock, Arthur, *Shelley the Man and the Poet*, Dutton, 1912. Perhaps the best 1-vol. critical study of Shelley.

White, Newman Ivey, *Shelley*, 2 vols., Knopf, 1940. Will be recognized, perhaps, as the definitive biography.

WORDSWORTH

Complete Poems, ed. by Thomas Hutchinson and with introduction and notes by G. M. Harper, Oxford Standard Authors, Oxford Press, 1933. Lacks a few features found in Student's Cambridge Edition, Houghton Mifflin, but less expensive.

The Prelude . . . (*Text of 1805*), ed. by Ernest de Sélincourt, Oxford Standard Authors, Oxford Press, 1933. The poem as Wordsworth the young man wrote it.

Harper, George McLean, *William Wordsworth: His Life, Works, and Influences*, 2 vols., Scribner. The standard biography. The best inexpensive brief one is F. W. H. Meyers's in the English Men of Letters Series, Macmillan.

Garrod, H. W., *Wordsworth: Lectures and Essays*, Oxford Press, 1923. Sound and illuminating criticism.

The Victorian Period

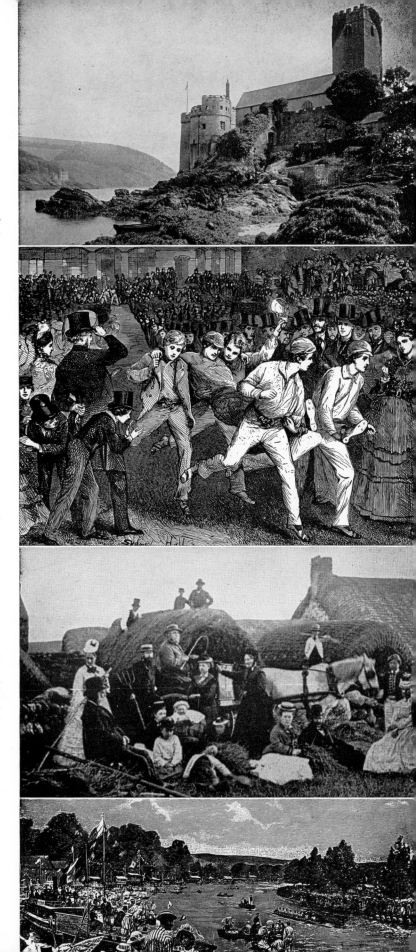

The castle at Dartmouth, Devonshire. Such a castle inspired Tennyson's *Locksley Hall* and many other poems in Victorian days. (Ewing Galloway)

Cricket at Lord's — Eton vs. Harrow, 1870. The fashionable crowd watches the victor being borne triumphantly away. The cricket fields have been held responsible for much English courage and sportsmanship. (Culver Service)

A West County Harvest Gathering, 1869. The rarity of photographs in the sixties probably accounts for the self-conscious postures and expressions. The picture is also interesting as evidence of Victorian England's habit of making country labors an excuse for social gatherings. (Messrs. Gibson, of Penzance)

Thames Regatta, 1884. The Thames, of great commercial importance, also continued to furnish, during the Victorian Age, a background for pleasure boating and boat racing. (Culver Service)

Afternoon in Hyde Park, 1889. When London was in full season, riding in Rotten Row presented a spectacle of pomp and magnificence rarely equalled. Even the horses were sleek, well-groomed, and decorated with heraldic devices. (Culver Service)

Mrs. Langtry's London residence — a fashionable interior of the nineties. (Rischgitz Agency)

Below left. A Flower-girl in Cheapside, 1892. (General Photographic Agency)

Below. A winter evening in London, about 1859. While there was only one Rotten Row, there were many Huxton Streets. As the cold wind swept down drab lanes, ladies' maids on their way to church or laborers returning from work would pass homeless sweeps, beggars, and others warming icy fingers at street braziers. (Culver Service)

Below right. A London Coffee-stall, about 1861. (Culver Service)

Victoria and Albert leaving Windsor Castle to start their afternoon drive (about 1856). Not only because of her acts, throughout the sixty-four years of her reign, but because her character expressed the dominant trends Victoria played an important part in shaping the age. (Culver Service)

The Crystal Palace and the Great Exhibition of 1851. *Above,* the north transept; *below,* a view of the interior. This Exhibition, coming at the end of the troubled days that opened Victoria's reign, forecast the golden age of prosperity which England's expanding industrial civilization promised. (Culver Service)

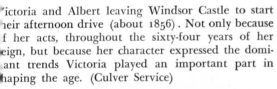

William Morris's colophon for *News from Nowhere.* After looking at the appalling ugliness and the heavy stuffiness of the whole Exhibition, the young Morris determined to reform Victorian artistic taste. Besides other activities, he designed type and raised the standards of printing. (Bettmann)

The British Museum's new reading room, 1857. From a contemporary lithograph. (Bettmann Archive)

Gladstone defending his First Home Rule Bill before Parliament. From a woodcut of 1868. (Bettmann Archive)

TENNYSON
From an engraving by
Samuel Laurence

BROWNING
From a portrait by
Samuel Laurence

CARLYLE
From a daguerreotype

ARNOLD
From a contemporary pho-
tograph (Culver Service)

RUSKIN
From a contemporary pho-
tograph (Culver Service)

THE VICTORIAN PERIOD

1830 - 1900.

The General Character of the Period

EVERY fresh generation among men finds it necessary to rebel against its elders. The generation that began to write books twenty years ago remembered the Victorians very well—had, in fact, grown up in the Victorian shadow—and in its struggle to throw off that yoke gloried in "debunking" the Victorians. Add to this the fact that the Victorians were not "picturesque" in the sense that time and costume films have made the Elizabethans picturesque, and it is not strange that young people have come to regard the Victorians as moral snobs, hypocrites, and stuffy prudes.

No period in history could be disposed of so cavalierly as that, least of all the extraordinarily complicated one we name Victorian. Probably the very idea of "periods" is only a concession to the limitations of the human mind. "Nothing is so hard to deal with as a period," says Agnes Repplier. "Nothing is so unmanageable as a date. People will be born a few years too early; they will live a few years too long." Yet the Age of Pericles or the Age of Elizabeth has a degree of unity that we do not find in the last three-quarters of the nineteenth century in England. Victoria held the throne from 1837 to 1901. But the first part of her reign inherited the problems and continued many of the tendencies of the post-Napoleonic period,

and the last was already busy preparing the holocaust of 1914. Had two or three monarchs reigned during her time, probably no historian would ever have attempted to crowd them all into the chronicle under a single heading.

A TIME OF POLITICAL CHANGE. Moderns who derive their impressions of the Victorians from the novels of Anthony Trollope may easily become discouraged over their own problems and sigh for the good old days. And the middle years of the long reign were well worth sighing for. What we now call the proletariat were uncomfortable enough, but with Karl Marx still only an exiled German Jew reading obscurely in the British Museum, nobody was much concerned about the proletariat. For a little while the middle class lived at ease in "the best of all possible worlds."

Yet it is always very easy to underestimate the seriousness of *that* crisis and to get unduly excited over *this* one. Whatever else life may have seemed to the Victorians, it never seemed a quiet affair; on the contrary, they thought of themselves as moving with breakneck speed "down the ringing grooves of change." And they were right about it, and we are wrong, for in many ways 1901 was farther away from 1837 than 1837 had been from 1066.

It has now become fashionable to berate the Victorians for their tendency to compromise. We have a just grievance here, for if they had gone to the root of their difficulties, instead of just trying to patch things up and "muddle through," they would not have handed so many of their still unsolved problems on to us. But may not one reason for their compromises have been that life had now grown too complex for the out-and-out solutions that might have served, and were sometimes found, in earlier days?

A TIME OF INTELLECTUAL CONFLICT. There was conflict in society, and there was conflict within the individual. Even the great Victorians were, in general, badly puzzled men. Victorian literature reflects this bewilderment. Tennyson, the representative poet of the age, embraced a much wider range than any of his predecessors, but compare him with Milton, Dryden, or even Wordsworth, and you will find that he creates a scattered effect. He is not anything in particular, as these writers were—each in his own way—something in particular.

Paradox possessed the Victorians. In theory they committed themselves to a "hard-boiled" utilitarianism, yet their literature was idealistic and decorously romantic. They were respectable even when they were not moral, pious even when they were not religious, but they destroyed the Christian faith as the men of the past had understood it, and their scientists were in many ways far more materialistic in outlook than our scientists are today. Not even in politics were the issues clear-cut. The Whigs prepared the way for the great economic reform of the age, the repeal of the Corn Laws, but it was a Tory leader, Peel, who finally put it over.

Political Backgrounds

The first great "Victorian" reform actually antedated Victoria by five years. Until 1832 the old Tudor list of boroughs was still in use. Many large towns of recent growth were quite unrepresented in Parliament; some of the localities which sent "representatives" were unpopulated. The lords who controlled these "rotten boroughs," as they were called, sold seats to the highest bidder.

The Reform Bill of 1832 abolished all boroughs having less than 2,000 inhabitants, and decreased by 50 per cent the number of representatives admitted from towns having between 2,000 and 4,000. In urban districts the vote was given to all who paid an annual rental of £10 or more for their houses; in the country a comparable property qualification was set up.

Fear alone put the bill through. The first time the Commons passed it, the House of Lords rejected it. Rioting broke out, and civil war seemed imminent. King William IV cast the deciding vote when he recalled Lord Grey, the Prime Minister, and promised that if necessary he would create enough new Whig peers to outvote the Tory enemies of the measure in the upper house.

Yet the Reform Bill was less revolutionary than it seemed. It was not a genuinely democratic measure; it gave the vote neither to factory workers nor to agricultural laborers. Furthermore, the conservatism of the new voters themselves made its effects less sensational than its enemies had feared. It was the thriving middle classes—the merchants and the bankers and the manufacturers—who had worked for it, and it was their interests that were served. A new commercial aristocracy was remaking England and preparing to take control of the Government, always with a decent respect for picturesque, time-hallowed forms and ceremonies.

THE WHIGS AND THE TORIES. It was inevitable that the Whigs (Liberals) should support the measure and the Tories (Conservatives) oppose it. The Whigs were the middle-class party as early as there was a middle class. Spiritually they were descended from the Parliamentarians of Oliver Cromwell's day. By this time they had attracted some radicals of whom Oliver would not have approved; on the other hand, their old alliance with capitalism had only been strengthened. The Tories, on the other hand, had a sentimental, even a mystical, reverence for the old aristocratic ways. They had been influenced by Burke and the nebulous German philosophy of transcendentalism brought into England by Coleridge; their ideas were working like leaven in the Oriental imagination of a young novelist-politician named Benjamin Disraeli. To Disraeli the state was not a mechanism but an organism; his "Young England" party planned to save the country by restoring feudal ideals. In later years, when he became Prime Minister, Disraeli did not restore feudalism, but both his mysticism and his Hebrew romanticism contributed importantly to the building of the Empire, and they survive today in the half-mystical ideal that pervades the British Commonwealth of Nations. Disraeli was never a democrat in the sense in which his great rival, William Ewart Gladstone, was a democrat; at all costs, he sought to avoid breaking the line of historic continuity. For Gladstone, on the other hand, the voice of the people was the voice of God; they were the rulers of England, and he was prepared to carry out their mandates.

THE CHARTIST MOVEMENT. The undemocratic character of the Reform Bill was less apparent in

1832 than it is today. But the Poor Law of 1834 must have jarred many trustful souls who believed that the millennium had dawned.

Up to this time, indigent persons in England had been entitled to the dole. They might live where and as they pleased, and they might supplement the assistance the Government saw fit to grant them in any way they liked. Now all this was changed. Partial aid came to an end; it must be all or nothing. Paupers must live in the workhouse—"the Bastille of the Poor"—and permit creatures like Oliver Twist's Mr. Bumble to rule them body and soul, or else they must starve.

The Chartist Movement of the forties testified eloquently to the disillusionment that followed. Hard times accentuated the problem, and a rising birth rate or a declining death rate made the condition of the poor worse than it need otherwise have been. The Chartist demands were six in number: (1) the abolition of property qualifications for members of Parliament; (2) a salary for members of Parliament; (3) annual election of Parliament; (4) equal electoral districts; (5) equal manhood suffrage; (6) voting by secret ballot. To the conservatives all this seemed very dangerous indeed.

The Chartists circulated monster petitions and secured thousands of signatures; in 1848 they undertook an abortive march on London. Chartism failed as a movement, though ultimately most of its ends were achieved, because, unlike the advocates of the Reform Bill, and unlike those who brought about the repeal of the Corn Laws, the Chartists found no way to identify their cause with the special interests of any influential class. Improved economic conditions caused some of them to become lukewarm, and the Corn Law struggle itself, which set up one single definite goal, seduced others.

A HALF-UNDERSTOOD IMPERIALISM. The Victorians as a whole were not a political-minded people, and foreign affairs as such did not interest them very much. Both Palmerston and Disraeli were truculent in their foreign policy; good luck played a larger role than wisdom in keeping the peace. Relations with America thrice approached the breaking-point: first in 1844, when James K. Polk was elected President on a platform which demanded that latitude 54° 40′ N. be established as the northern boundary of the United States; next during the Civil War, when the Union blockade of Confederate ports cut off England's supply of cotton; finally in Cleveland's administration, when the Venezuela boundary dispute threatened the Monroe Doctrine. These crises were fortunately resolved, but the Victorian peace cracked in the Crimean War of 1854–56 and in the struggle against the Boers in South Africa, which lapped over the end of the old Queen's reign. The Crimean adventure, which resulted from Britain's policy of protecting Turkey as a buffer against Russia, was badly mismanaged; the charge of the Light Brigade, which Tennyson celebrated with bitter, unconscious irony, might well symbolize the conflict as a whole. The Boer War was definitely an imperialistic conflict. The issue was created by private patrioteers rather than by the Government; once it had arisen, the Government, as is the unhappy way of governments in such matters, proceeded to man the guns.

Through it all nobody seemed to understand any too well the play being presented in the international theater. Nobody understood what Bismarck was doing in Germany, for example. When the Reich threatened Schleswig and Holstein in 1863, Britain promised to aid Denmark in retaining them. But the man of blood and iron stood firm, Britain backed down, and the little duchies were swallowed by Prussia. Nobody had thought through the problem of war; nobody was prepared to pay the price of peace. It is true that Gladstone would have sympathized with Sir Esmé Wingfield-Stratford's brave question, "What is there more necessarily lovable in Empire than in elephantiasis?" But even Gladstone served English imperialism. Despite his Christian idealism, despite his "Little England" principles, it was Gladstone who took Britain into Egypt, crushing Arabi's national insurrection for no better reason than that some 17,000 Englishmen had invested their money in the Khedive Ismail's bonds.

The Economic Background

The political life of the Victorian period, in its domestic aspects at least, is intimately tied up with its economic theory. The Poor Law, for example, was framed by the Utilitarians Edwin Chadwick and Nassau William Senior, who believed that the way to abolish poverty was to refuse to relieve it.

The laissez-faire doctrine, as it is called, goes back to Adam Smith's *Wealth of Nations*, 1776, but it was afterwards elaborated by Jeremy Bentham, T. R. Malthus, David Ricardo, and James Mill. These men tested right and wrong by "the tendency of actions to produce pleasure or pain." To Bentham pleasure was pleasure, and that was all there was to say about it; he found it impossible to distinguish between the kind of pleasure that comes from listening to a concert of sacred music and that which results from indulgence in drink or drugs. But he did clearly hold that the purpose of organized society is to secure the greatest happiness of the greatest number, and in the economic sphere this meant to him that the function of government is not to govern. Just leave things alone, was his implication, and the situation will adjust itself automatically. Wages and profits are fixed by the automatic laws of supply and demand. If a man makes £1,000,000, there is no help for it. If he starves to death in the gutter, there is no help for that either. Assist a beggar and you upset the sacred laws of economics; you are, in fact, a kind of economic pervert who has committed an outrage against nature. The good clergyman Malthus made his special contribution to the political economy of his time in 1798 by figuring out that while the population of a country increases in geometrical proportions (2, 4, 16, 256, and so on), the food supply can increase only in arithmetical proportions (2, 4, 8, 16, 32, and so on). Though Malthus was quick to add that "moral restraint" could hold the population in check, nobody had much faith in moral restraint; the specter of coming starvation haunted men's minds for generations. In 1817 Ricardo, a Jewish banker, worked out the connection between wages and variations in the laboring population.

This is the "dismal science," as Carlyle called it. Dickens, who derived so many of his ideas from Carlyle, castigated it again and again, never more effectively than in *The Chimes*, where Mr. Filer and Alderman Cute break Toby's faith in life by proving conclusively that being long past the average age, he has no right to exist at all, and that whenever he eats tripe—notoriously the most extravagant food that a man can eat—he takes every bite he swallows out of the mouths of widows and orphans. And if it be objected that Dickens was a caricaturist, let us remember that the *Westminster Review*, organ of the Utilitarians, had found Scrooge's presentation of a turkey to Bob Cratchit, in *A Christmas Carol*, quite incompatible with the principles of political economy!

Yet the Utilitarians were not monsters. On one side of him, indeed, Bentham (himself an eccentric good enough for any novel of Dickens) was an apostle of human liberty. He believed in free speech and free assembly; he accepted most of the ideas of the Chartists; he championed labor's right to organize; he would educate poor children and abolish cruel punishments.

It was the Utilitarians who brought about the repeal of the Corn Laws in 1846.[1] Such a reform

---

[1] Corn, in England, means grain, specifically wheat. The Corn Laws were protective tariffs that favored the English farmers.

was wholly in line with laissez-faire principles, for customs duties interfere with trade between nations quite as definitely as, let us say, factory legislation or child-labor legislation represents an intrusion of government into the business of money-making at home. When the farmers declared that the repeal of protective tariffs would make it impossible to raise crops in England, the free traders were not in the least dismayed. England would simply have to buy her food beyond the seas and pay for it with manufactured articles that she could produce better and cheaper than other nations. As it turned out, English agriculture was not destroyed, though its importance declined. The time was close at hand when neither free trade nor protection could make it possible for the little island to feed her expanding population without help from overseas. From that time on she had to sell enough goods abroad to buy the food she needed, and she had to keep the sea lanes open to bring it in.

UNPARALLELED PROSPERITY. The fifties faced the future with confidence. J. A. Roebuck, M.P., who thanked God for "our unrivalled happiness" and prayed that it might last, was far more typical of his time than the hypercritical Matthew Arnold who ridiculed him. God would seem to have done pretty well in the way of answering Roebuck's prayer, for one does not hear of "depression" again before the seventies, and then it is only a comparatively mild variety which appears. Yet to some God had very little to do with it. During those golden mid-Victorian days one might send a pious genuflection His way—that was only seemly—but one knew that the real blessing was free trade.

Actually, of course, free trade was powerfully supplemented by other forces. It is not difficult for a nation to be prosperous at a time when war and civil strife have put most of its potential rivals out of the running, and made it, almost in spite of itself, the commercial center of the world. Coal, steel, steam, railroads—these were the magic watchwords. The rapid industrialization of the country was creating new jobs right and left. So was the increasing centralization of the Government, for while the Benthamites insisted on leaving things alone, they found in practice that in their complicated age it took a great deal of machinery to do even that.

An Age of Reform

As time went on, the Utilitarians found themselves obliged to accept even a good many reforms that did not square with their theory. Moreover, not all Englishmen were Utilitarians. The influence of Rousseau was not dead, Evangelicalism was a powerful force in the nation, and the seeds of many of the reforms that flowered in the Victorian period had been well planted before the start of the nineteenth century.

THE ABOLITION OF SLAVERY. The Evangelicals could not always be depended upon to back the reformers. Sometimes they were so much preoccupied with personal salvation that they neglected mundane affairs altogether. One of the first reviewers of *Jane Eyre* found in the book "a murmuring against the comforts of the rich and against the privations of the poor, which, so far as each individual is concerned, is a murmuring against God's appointment." But when it came to slavery, the Evangelicals were clear that there was "neither bond nor free in Christ Jesus." The black man was a brother, and (especially if he was a Christian) they could see no justification for holding him in chains.

The wealth of many great English families rested on a West Indian foundation. As far back as 1772, West Indian planters who had brought slaves to England found themselves deprived by Lord Mansfield's decision that, under common law, no human being could be held in bondage in the British Isles. This decision was followed in 1807 by the abolition of the slave trade, after a strenuous campaign under Wilberforce and others with Quaker and Methodist backing. The process was completed in 1833 when slavery was ended in the colonies themselves.

THE CALL FOR INDUSTRIAL REFORM. But if chattel slavery was gone, industrial slavery continued. Much sentimentality was evoked by the pitiful figure of the chimney sweep. The Victorians did not invent the chimney sweep, but it was not until 1864 that they succeeded in doing away with him. There was an organization of master sweeps, and ugly stories of kidnapping were told. The boys crawled through narrow, dirty chimneys, rubbing their knees raw in climbing, brushing soot down upon themselves. Some of the chimneys were so narrow that only a naked child could get through, and burning and suffocating were sometimes reported. The plight of the chimney sweep appealed to the imagination and inflamed the conscience, but other less picturesque sufferers were quite as unhappy. Women and children sometimes worked from fourteen to sixteen hours a day in the coal mines, dragging loaded carts behind them on their hands and knees.

The seventh Earl of Shaftesbury was the great hero of factory-reform legislation. In 1833 the first important Factory Law regulated child labor in the textile industries. Its provisions were conservative.

Night work was prohibited for young people under eighteen, but even children under eleven might still work nine hours every day. The important thing was to have made a beginning. In 1842 the employment of women and children in the coal mines was ended; in 1850 women in industry were limited to a ten-hour day. In 1850, also, the textile industry accepted a Saturday half-holiday. The press had its share in bringing about these reforms. *Blackwood's Magazine* opened its columns to Mrs. Browning's passionate poem, "The Cry of the Children," and Thomas Hood's indictment of sweated labor, "The Song of the Shirt," appeared in the great British magazine of humor, *Punch*, which was often surprisingly valiant in championing the cause of the underprivileged.

But the masses were no longer depending helplessly on the aid they might receive from fairminded individuals among the upper classes. Gradually they were winning the right to help themselves. Trade-unionism was legalized in 1864; twenty years later the first successful co-operative appeared. In 1859 the right to strike was won.

Karl Marx founded the first International Workingmen's Association in London in 1864; three years later he published the Bible of modern Communism, *Das Kapital*. But there was no real interest in Communism (or Socialism, for that matter) in England before the eighties. William Morris's Socialism was less revolutionary than it appeared. It rested on his love of beauty; he simply could not endure the ugliness that modern capitalism had created. But he never found a party that satisfied him, and he was himself one of the most uncompromising individualists who ever lived. In 1884 the Fabian Society appeared, headed by Beatrice and Sidney Webb, Bernard Shaw, and other uppermiddle-class intellectuals. The Fabians set themselves steadily against violent revolution. As they saw it, Socialism could only come gradually, through a steady widening of the functions of the state.

WIDENING SOCIAL REFORMS. It is not fair to the Victorians to permit ourselves to be impressed by the amount of suffering they tolerated without remembering also what an enormous quantity of historic debris they succeeded in carting away. When Victoria ascended the throne, four hundred and thirty-eight offenses were still punishable by death in England! Long after the death penalty had been limited to murderers, executions were still held in public, and when Charles Dickens (who opposed capital punishment itself) and others began to agitate against this, they were often regarded as highly eccentric. Since it was the purpose of capital punishment to discourage murder, why not inflict the punishment in public and thus impress as many people as possible? But at last the objectors got their way. When penalties were softened, crime decreased instead of increasing, as the die-hards had predicted it would. The unarmed police force of our day came into being, and the swift, sure, efficient administration of justice that characterizes contemporary England was in a fair way to be developed.

Once the rights of women and children had been recognized in industry, it was inevitable that they should be recognized elsewhere as well. There was the right to an education, for example. In 1870, for the first time in English history, the Elementary Education Bill was designed to provide sufficient schools for everybody. (In 1891 a common-school education became compulsory.) After 1867 women were admitted to examinations in the University of London. Girton College for the higher education of women was incorporated at Cambridge in 1872.

Modern women do not often recall such names as Frances Power Cobbe, Sophia Jex-Blake, Octavia Hill, Emma Cons, Emily Davies, and Barbara Leigh-Smith, but these women and others like them did a great deal to win for women the privileges they enjoy today. So, directly or indirectly, did the great women novelists, and so did Florence Nightingale, whose contribution to modern nursing was the only good thing to come out of the Crimean War. Moreover there were men like George Meredith and John Stuart Mill who worked as hard for "female emancipation" as any woman.

Science and Religion

But politics and economics do not make up the whole of a people's life. In Victorian times, at least, both science and religion touched experience at least as closely; for literature they were much more important. Religion was, of course, an inheritance from the long past, but the scope of science was broadening with a rush. Logically there was no reason why the two should ever clash, for religion deals with values while science is concerned with processes. But since both scientists and religionists were human beings, there were any number of good practical reasons for conflict.

The rapid expansion of Victorian industry was in itself the result of the application of new scientific processes to age-old methods of getting a living. Even aside from industrialism, scientific invention

modified, recharactered, mechanized, and enriched life in many ways. It is hard to realize that Queen Victoria was the first British sovereign to be photographed. Before her reign was over she had been photographed in motion. She had also spoken through the telephone, and she had heard her voice recorded on wax cylinders.

During these years, for the first time in human history, surgical progress was made possible by the use of anesthetics—which were even used in childbirth, over the protests of fools who cried out against the impiety of attempting to alleviate the curse that a vengeful Deity had placed upon His disobedient Eve.

THE EVOLUTIONARY HYPOTHESIS. But it was not only in this practical manner that science affected Victorian lives. Applications are obvious; ideas are fundamental. When one thinks of Victorian scientists one thinks, first of all, of Charles Darwin and his self-appointed bulldog, Thomas Henry Huxley, whose great gifts as writer and lecturer did so much to popularize Darwin's work. Darwin's *Origin of Species*, 1859, maintained that all living creatures had developed, through infinite differentiation, from a single source; his special emphasis on the idea of survival of the fittest through "natural selection" caught the popular imagination. But Darwin was by no means the only great Victorian scientist. Faraday the physicist impressed the public with his discoveries; so did Galton, who did pioneer work in heredity. And it would be hard to overemphasize the importance of Sir Charles Lyell's *Principles of Geology*, 1830–33, which prepared the way for Darwinism by establishing a continuous history for life on this planet.

Darwin was not even the first evolutionist. *The Development Hypothesis* by Herbert Spencer appeared in 1852. Eight years before that, Robert Chambers, the indefatigable proprietor of *Chambers's Journal*, had startled the English public with the suggestion that man had descended from a monkey or both from some common ancestor. Scientists did not take Chambers's *Vestiges of the Natural History of Creation* seriously, but it had a considerable influence on the popular mind. Disraeli burlesqued it in his novel *Tancred;* as late as 1861, *Punch* referred to it familiarly, along with Darwin's own work:

> The *Vestiges* taught
> That all came from naught
> By "development" so called "progressive,"
> That insects and worms
> Assume higher forms
> By modification excessive.

Then Darwin set forth
In a book of much worth
The importance of "Nature's selection,"
How the struggle for life
Is a laudable strife
And results in "specific distinction."

Am I satyr or man?
Pray tell me who can,
And settle my place in the scale,
A man in ape's shape,
An anthropoid ape,
Or a monkey deprived of its tail?

EVOLUTION AND RELIGION. It was obvious that if the evolutionists were right, the Church could no longer maintain the historicity of the Book of Genesis, nor could she continue to believe, in terms of Archbishop Ussher's chronology, that God had created the world in the year 4004 B.C.

Darwinism divided the religious world into three camps:

1. There were those who saw the evolutionary hypothesis as an unconfirmed theory. They did not believe that the evidence Darwin had accumulated justified the conclusions he had drawn. Substantially the whole Roman Catholic Church was in this camp.

2. There were those who—regretfully or enthusiastically, according to their temperament—felt not only that Darwin had established his hypothesis, but that having done so, he had left no room for God in the universe. They, therefore, were compelled to reorient all their thinking and living on a naturalistic basis.

3. Finally, there were the leaders of the "Broad Church" and others—men like Frederick Denison Maurice, Arthur Penrhyn Stanley, Benjamin Jowett, Thomas and Matthew Arnold, Charles Kingsley, and Alfred Tennyson—who felt that evolution was simply "God's way of doing things." They embraced the new hypothesis eagerly; it seemed to them that they had a greater God to worship than they had ever known before.

The term "Broad Church" needs definition. At the beginning of Victoria's reign, the Church of England was divided into two wings—the "High and Dry" Church and the Evangelicals. The Evangelicals had more in common with the Dissenters—followers of the Wesleys, George Fox, and others—than they had with the "High and Dry" Church.

The clergy of the "High and Dry" Church are well portrayed for us in Jane Austen's novels. They were nearly as coldhearted as the Deists of the eighteenth century. Almost to a man they favored state supremacy in ecclesiastical affairs; for them the Church was a means of finding a comfortable living for younger sons rather than an agency for advancing the kingdom of God.

In so far as the "High and Dry" Church was reclaimable, it was reclaimed by the Oxford Movement, a sacramentarian crusade, which will be described in this volume in the introduction to the selections from John Henry Newman. But some men were not moved by sacramentalism; neither could they relish the ardent emotionalism of such great Dissenting preachers as Charles Haddon Spurgeon, nor the mystical Transcendentalism that Samuel Taylor Coleridge had found in the German philosophers. What were they to do?

The "Broad Church" was the answer to their problem. The leaders of this movement had a truly national vision; they wanted a genuine English Church; they were willing to lower the barriers far enough so that the Dissenters themselves might come in. They tried to reconcile science and religion; they also perceived the necessity of applying Christianity to social problems.

Why, then, was not the movement more successful? It would seem to have suited the spirit of the age. Religious barriers were falling everywhere. Roman Catholic emancipation came in 1829. Jews were admitted to Parliament at the end of the fifties. Oxford and Cambridge opened their doors to Dissenters in 1871. Perhaps it is not quite fair to speak of the "Broad Church" as unsuccessful. For the Christian religion still lives in this world, and in English-speaking countries the "Broad Church" leaders have had a considerable influence upon it. Their difficulty was that they were themselves influenced by the uncertainty, the shallow rationalism, of the age, corrupted by the compromising spirit of the age. A creed that is too general to offend anybody generally ends by holding nobody. Religion succeeds best with men when it makes absolute claims.

Not all the problems that disturbed the religious mind of England were posed by natural science. The scientific spirit invaded the Church itself when the "higher criticism"—which was largely a German importation—insisted on applying the same criteria to the literary study of the Bible that were being applied to Homer and to Shakespeare. George Eliot translated David Strauss's rationalistic, but by no means atheistic, *Life of Jesus* in 1846, and found herself obliged to give up the Christian religion as she had understood it.

Even liberals like Kingsley and Maurice were shocked when Jowett, Temple, Mark Pattison, and others attempted a thoroughgoing discussion of some of the critical problems of Biblical scholarship in *Essays and Reviews*, 1860. Two years later, Bishop Colenso of Natal created a tremendous sensation when he denied not only the Mosaic authorship of the Pentateuch but the historical character of much of it. In South Africa his fellow bishops excommunicated him; in England only Bishop Thirlwall took his part.

THE FUNDAMENTAL QUESTION: IS THIS A SPIRITUAL WORLD? All these battles were skirmishes; they did not touch the real problem. The fundamental question was not whether Moses wrote the Pentateuch nor even whether men had descended from monkeys. The fundamental question was whether man was a machine or a spiritual entity. Could the spirit of religion survive in a mechanized world?

Such men as Lightfoot, Westcott, Hort, and Gore seemed to answer triumphantly in the affirmative. They were great scholars, they were men of God, they had a blazing passion for social righteousness. But they were not all England. People like Harriet Martineau and Charles Bradlaugh did not hesitate to propagandize in behalf of out-and-out atheism. Even more dangerous to established religion were those who did recognize spiritual values but who felt that the time had now come to transfer values from heaven to earth. Phenomena were the legitimate concern of the human mind; noumena might well be left to take care of themselves.

For some, the evolutionary process itself had taken on religious significance, and this was all the religion they needed or could accept. "Progress," said Herbert Spencer, "is not an accident but a necessity. What we call evil and immorality must disappear. It is certain that man must become perfect." One cannot entertain such an idea without having all his other beliefs affected. One reason why David Strauss found it impossible to accept the Jesus of the New Testament was that as an evolutionist he could not believe that the perfect man had appeared so early in human history.

Many Victorian religionists were too hidebound to be able to accept new ideas. Thus and so had religion always been conceived. One must continue to conceive it thus and so; otherwise one must scrap religion altogether. On the other hand, many of the scientists, though theoretically taking their whole stand on the principle of free experimentation, were quite as dogmatic as the narrowest among the theologians.

A revealing illustration lies to hand in the matter of psychical research. The investigation of psychic phenomena under laboratory conditions began in Victorian times. And it is true that two of the greatest Victorian scientists—Crookes and Wallace—were convinced by scientific experimentation of the truth of spiritualism. But since most of their colleagues refused even to investigate such matters, the inevitable result was that the whole vital business was largely consigned to the quacks. Wingfield-Stratford says aptly: "Had the problem been approached with an honest determination to sift the true from the false and to follow the truth wherever it might have led, the conclusion might have emerged, not, perhaps, that the claims of the spiritualists were to be accepted at their face value, but that the universe was a far less simple affair than a mere working hypothesis would lead one to suppose, and that science, even towards the close of the nineteenth century, might be only scratching at the surface of reality." [1]

RELIGION IN VICTORIAN LITERATURE. The importance of religion and the religious struggle for Victorian literature appears clearly in the fact that one can classify the poets of the time in terms of their religious attitudes. Tennyson and Browning are, of course, the great poets of faith. Tennyson conducted his spiritual ablutions in public; at one period or another of his life he faced all the problems of his time; he helped his contemporaries because he made it possible for them to think his thoughts after him. Browning doubted and struggled only in the early, anonymous, and uncharacteristic *Pauline;* if he had any doubts thereafter, he kept them strictly to himself; his published work is one vigorous, unceasing affirmation. Matthew Arnold and Arthur Hugh Clough stand over against Tennyson and Browning as the poets of doubt. They were quite as deeply interested in religion and, though they failed to find the same certainty, quite as religious in spirit. The Roman Catholic poets—Coventry Patmore, Gerard Manley Hopkins, Francis Thompson, and Alice Meynell—made up a special group; Catholics are always less at the mercy of the beating winds and storms of doctrine than their Protestant brethren. Christina Rossetti was not a Roman Catholic, but she had much of the Catholic devotional spirit. Emily Brontë, the mystic, was not a Victorian except in time, and time is an illusion that held no meaning for her.

[1] In *The Victorian Sunset* from the omnibus volume, *The Victorian Cycle*, William Morrow & Company. Reprinted by permission.

With the later Victorians, however, the attitude toward religion changed. The change appears not so much in Swinburne, whose very hostility to Christianity had much of evangelical fervor about it; certainly not in Hardy, with all his devastating irony, for Hardy's heart, like George Eliot's, clung passionately to the old God, whatever may be said of his head. It appeared rather in men like Meredith, Rossetti, and Morris. Meredith was not irreligious, but no trace of otherworldliness ever appeared in him. Rossetti was a mystic, but his mysticism concerned itself with man and woman rather than with man and God. William Morris began as a Tractarian, but so far as religious dogma was concerned, he ended a pronounced nothingarian.

Perhaps the reaction was inevitable. Tennyson's *In Memoriam*, for all its greatness, is no doubt a painfully introspective work, and a series of weak imitations of *In Memoriam* must have been intolerable. Yet the reaction was unfortunate. Bernard Shaw may or may not be right when he contends that art has never been great except when providing the iconography for a live religion. But even among the minor Victorians, it was the men of faith who best succeeded in realizing their full potentialities.

The Greatness of Victorian Literature

The greatness of Victorian literature is all the more impressive when we consider the comparatively slight achievements of the Victorians in the other arts. Their painting and their music were not impressive. English music had been negligible since the seventeenth century, though there were signs of hope toward the end of the period—Sir Edward Elgar's setting for John Henry Newman's poem *The Dream of Gerontius*, for example, and, in lighter vein, the enchanting comic operas of Gilbert and Sullivan.

THE FAILURE OF VICTORIAN DRAMA. Like Elizabethan literature, Victorian literature is remarkable as having touched a high level in many different fields. It is interesting, therefore, that the Victorians should have been weakest just where the Elizabethans were so wonderfully strong—in the drama. They had, to be sure, their great actors—Macready, Irving, Ellen Terry—but when these great artists wished to appear in fine plays, they were obliged to choose the plays of the past. The "star system" and the long "run" are often blamed for this condition. It is true that for many years the "legitimate" drama in London was legally confined to two theaters—Covent Garden and Drury Lane; as the population of the city increased, both auditoriums were so greatly enlarged that at last only spectacular effects could hope to "carry." It is not correct to say that the great writers of the period were not interested in the drama; they were, but they had not mastered playwrighting in the technical sense. Lesser writers such as Bulwer, Tom Taylor, and Dion Boucicault turned out many interesting plays. One may even feel that their unabashed "hokum" deserves praise for holding fast to one element in the theater's magic that twentieth-century playwrights—with their queer idea that the theater is a clinic—have often lost. But when all is said and done, one can hardly take them very seriously as dramatists. *Society, Caste,* and other plays by T. W. Robertson constituted an important pioneering service. As we read them today they seem curiously old-fashioned; in their own time they were daring experiments in the direction of naturalism. The real dramatic revival, however, did not begin until the nineties, when Oscar Wilde, Henry Arthur Jones, and Arthur Wing Pinero got to work. These "society" playwrights were followed soon by the exponents of the drama of purpose, which had its fountainhead in Ibsen and whose most distinguished representative in England is Bernard Shaw.

THE VICTORIAN NOVEL: DICKENS AND HIS SCHOOL. But if the Victorians failed with the drama, they more than atoned in their remarkable development of a type of literature that was only modestly beginning in Queen Elizabeth's time, and which has now become the outstanding "modern" type—the novel. And since, unlike other forms of Victorian literature, the novel cannot be illustrated in such a book as this, it seems fitting to offer here a brief outline of its development.

The eighteenth century had already contributed importantly to prose fiction with Richardson, Fielding, Smollett, and Sterne; the Georgians had Jane Austen and "the Prince, the King, the Emperor, the God Almighty of novelists" (as Wilkie Collins called him), Sir Walter Scott. The Victorians nearly matched Scott in the person of Charles Dickens, whose marvellous creative fertility gave him a place beside the older master; in this aspect, indeed, he is surpassed in England only by Shakespeare himself. Dickens did not idealize the past as Scott had done. He was a romanticist, but it was the romance of the here and now that enthralled him; he is the only modern novelist whose contact with his audience is as intimate as that of the primitive folk-bard. Yet on one side he leaned toward naturalism; allow for the picturesque exaggeration characteristic of Mr. Shaw, and the statement that *Little Dorrit* is a more seditious book than *Das Kapital* is not without point.

Dickens's sensationalism and his didacticism were taken up by Wilkie Collins and Charles Reade, and if any writers have ever succeeded in destroying the things they hated and bringing about the reforms they desired, these men did it. Charles Kingsley and Mrs. Gaskell belong to the Dickens school by an extension of the term on the didactic side, though Mrs. Gaskell's best work was done not in sociological novels like *Mary Barton* and *North and South*, where she actually anticipated Dickens and Reade in applying the novel to the study of labor problems, but in *Cranford* and *Wives and Daughters*, which concern themselves with more personal, more feminine interests. The somewhat muddled Kingsley was always in the thick of the fight for human betterment. *Yeast* and *Alton Locke* reflect the Chartist movement directly, and even when he wrote historical novels—*Hypatia* or *Westward Ho!*—he carried all the problems of the present along with him.

THACKERAY; TROLLOPE; THE BRONTËS. Over against the Dickens school stands William Makepeace Thackeray. The difference between Dickens and Thackeray can easily be exaggerated. Both men inherited the eighteenth-century tradition, Dickens from Smollett, Thackeray from Fielding. Both evoked their characters rather than constructed them. But not until he reached the beautiful novel he did not live to finish, *Denis Duval*, did Thackeray surrender to romance. He is an upperclass man, a snob, and a cynic at the same time that he is a sentimentalist and an innocent. Dickens's strenuous idealism was beyond him. It has often been pointed out that *Vanity Fair* is the most comprehensive picture and the most serious criticism of English society that fiction had thus far achieved.

Anthony Trollope, the most prolific of all the great Victorian novelists, was, like Thackeray, a realist. The six Barsetshire novels, which describe life in and about a cathedral town, are his most popular books, but equally good work went into the political novels and into many others quite unconnected with any series. Trollope is frequently reproached for his lack of subtlety. He was sufficiently subtle to deceive most of the people who have written about him. As Michael Sadleir has pointed out, he honored all the conventions of his time, yet he made it clear to the really discerning reader that there was not much about men and women that he did not know.

Charlotte Brontë greatly admired Thackeray, but neither she nor her sister Emily belonged to any school. They were outstanding individualists in a great age of individualism; in them romanticism and subjectivity took full possession of the English novel. In its own time, Emily's *Wuthering Heights* was generally considered a strange, chaotic book. We know now that it was as deliberately "built" as a symphony of Mozart's, and Lord David Cecil is by no means alone in considering it the greatest of all Victorian novels.

THE "NEW" NOVEL: GEORGE ELIOT, MEREDITH, HARDY. The apparent outward similarities between George Eliot's novels and those of her predecessors may easily blind us to the revolutionary character of her work. She turned away from the novel of Dickens and Thackeray toward what we understand as the novel today. George Eliot brought mature intellectuality and a carefully formulated philosophy of life to her fiction. Of creative power in the Scott-Dickens sense she had little—none after she had used up the memories of her youth in such books as *Adam Bede* and *The Mill on the Floss*. She was not so much interested in telling a story as in expounding a theme; her books are not entertainment, but serious criticism of life. The Victorians gave her a place among the great writers of all time; Herbert Spencer wanted no novels admitted to the London Library "except, of course, those of George Eliot."

George Meredith may be compared and contrasted with both George Eliot and Thomas Hardy. Like George Eliot, he is a moralist; like her, he finds selfishness the cause of our human ills. But unlike George Eliot, he works through comedy, not tragedy, and he attempts in his books no actual reconstruction of human society. Meredith holds a mirror up to his times, but he is careful not to get an accurate reflection; this, we feel, is what human life might have been like if Meredith, not God, had made the world. His style is willful, highly elliptical, and deliberately difficult; he asks more of the reader than any novelist had asked since Sterne.

Hardy's methods were old-fashioned compared to Meredith's, but his ideas were devastating, revolutionary. Both men accepted the teachings of modern science, but Meredith was an optimist and Hardy was a pessimist. Nature is friendly to man in Meredith; in Hardy it crushes him, not malevolently but through sheer indifference. His characters inhabit that world of shrinking values which was all that science had left the unhappy intellectuals of Victoria's last years.

THE "ARTISTIC" NOVEL: STEVENSON AND HENRY JAMES. George Eliot, Meredith, and Hardy brought modern thought into the novel; it remained for Robert Louis Stevenson and Henry James (who, though an American by birth, did much of his best work in England, and died a British subject) to establish it as an art form. Different as they were in temperament and in subject matter, Stevenson and James stand together in their intense preoccupation with their medium, as well as in their tendency to reject the old Fielding convention of the omniscient author and to tell their story from the point of view of, preferably, some semidetached participant. Stevenson asserted a neo-Christian, neo-Stoic optimism against the pessimism of Schopenhauer, the *Rubáiyát*, and Thomas Hardy; against the delicate esthetic despair of Walter Pater and the decadents. Realism he rejected because he considered it unreal; his frankly subjective romanticism dedicated itself to the task of describing life as it appears to the man who lives it. Henry James was, par excellence, the novelist of the inner life. Nothing much happened in his books or in his life, yet he could declare: "Of course, for myself I live, live intensely and am fed by life, and my value, whatever it be, lies in my own kind of expression of that." James traced processes of development as no one else since Richardson had cared to trace them in English fiction, and he was, of course, far more sensitive and intelligent than Richardson. His influence on modern fiction has been great.

SUGGESTIONS FOR FURTHER READING. Esmé Wingfield-Stratford's *The Victorian Cycle* (Morrow, 1935)—an omnibus comprising *Those Earnest Victorians*, *The Victorian Sunset*, and *The Victorian Aftermath*—is a brilliant survey of the period. Lytton Strachey's *Queen Victoria* (Harcourt, Brace, 1921) is a fine work of art, but the author's anti-Victorian bias must be allowed for; Edith Sitwell's *Victoria of England* (Houghton Mifflin, 1936) is a fairer-minded book. Much of the color of Victorian life has been caught by Rita Wellman in *Victoria Royal* (Scribners, 1939) and by Peter Quennell in *Victorian Panorama* (Scribners, 1937); the latter contains an excellent collection of Victorian photographs. Probably the most delightful of all books about the Victorians is *The Victorians and Their Reading*, by Amy Cruse (Houghton Mifflin, 1935).

For a selected list of additional reading about the Victorians, see page 937, at the end of this section.

Thomas Babington Macaulay
1800–1859

[handwritten marginalia: 1. writer to popularize history / easy to read / style—very clear and fluent / forthright utterance of opinion / historical unit / politician]

Macaulay—Lytton Strachey's Philistine who reached Parnassus—was the advance herald of the millennium, mid-Victorian style. "The history of our country during the past hundred and sixty years," he wrote, "is eminently the history of physical, of moral, and of intellectual improvement." It was from this point of view that he approached the problem when he came to write that history, and the definitely Whiggish interpretation he presented ruled the public mind without too serious challenge at least until the war of 1914–18.

Macaulay was born in Leicestershire, October 25, 1800; his father, an Evangelical philanthropist and religious editor, saw no contradiction between risking his fortune for his antislavery principles and urging the Government to take a strong line against restive English workmen. Tom was an amazing but unpretentious infant prodigy. During his residence at Trinity College, Cambridge, where he distinguished himself as a classicist but ignored mathematics, and of which he became a fellow in 1824, he abandoned his inherited Tory standards and became a Whig.

The future historian was no writer merely; he was a man of large affairs. In 1826 he was called to the bar; in 1829 he was appointed Commissioner of Bankruptcy; in 1830 he was elected to Parliament. In 1832 he became a member of the Board of Control concerned with Indian affairs; for several years he was stationed in India, where he earned a large fortune and made an enviably humane and able record as administrator. In 1839 he became Secretary at War in Lord Melbourne's Cabinet; in 1846 he was Paymaster General. The next year he practically retired from public life to devote himself to literature.

He had, of course, been writing for many years. His first essay, "Milton," was published in 1825 in the *Edinburgh Review*, and Macaulay was the mainstay of the popularity of the review for twenty years.

Most of his famous "brief lives in the manner of Plutarch" were "book reviews" in the *Edinburgh* or articles for the *Encyclopaedia Britannica*. The *Lays of Ancient Rome*, heroic narrative poetry, once known to "every schoolboy" (to use a favorite phrase of Macaulay's own) were published in 1842, the first two volumes of the *History* in 1848. Macaulay had hoped to continue the history down to the Reform Bill, but it took him twenty years to write the five volumes which covered the years 1688–1702, and the last of these did not appear until after his own death, December 28, 1859. Meanwhile, among many other honors, he had been raised to the peer- 10 age (in 1857) as Baron Macaulay of Rothley.

Macaulay was the first writer to "popularize" history, which he caused to displace the latest novel in milady's boudoir and to take its place beside Shakespeare and the Bible on the pioneer's narrow bookshelf, without resort to any of the cheap and feeble tricks in which so many later popularizers have indulged. But because he was so definitely a "typical" Victorian (if there is such a thing), be- cause, at any rate, he perfectly exemplifies the 20 limitations of Victorian insight, and because he did not rise to the frozen heights of mystic insight and serene artistic achievement where a writer may sit securely disdainful of changing literary fashions, he has, in our own time, served as a target of the anti-Victorians. It is not enough, they feel, to condemn his ideas; his style must be condemned also. So we find Edith Batho and Bonamy Dobrée (in *The Victorians and After 1830–1914*, McBride, 1938) telling us that "his prose, for all its skill, is a machine-made 30 product of the industrial revolution; it works beautifully, like a well-oiled engine; it glitters magnificently as the pistons work smoothly and relentlessly up and down." If this is not wholly just, there is still enough truth in it to carry a sting. Macaulay was terribly at ease in Zion; whether we are to despise him for it or envy him—that is another question. In any event, his superb gift for narrative remains; that, at least, cannot be denied.

from THE HISTORY OF ENGLAND FROM THE ACCESSION OF JAMES II

from Chapter 3

[England in 1685]

A great many notes, particularly of a geographical character, which might have been added to this selection have been omitted on the ground that they are not necessary to the understanding of an allusive but very clear piece of writing. Macaulay's own notes, mainly of a documentary character, have been omitted also.

IN the seventeenth century the City was the merchant's residence. Those mansions of the great old burghers which still exist have been turned into counting houses and warehouses: but it is evident that they were originally not inferior in magnificence to the dwellings which were then inhabited by the nobility. They sometimes stand in retired and gloomy courts, and are accessible only by inconvenient passages: but their dimensions are ample, and their aspect stately. The entrances are decorated with richly carved pillars and canopies. The staircases and landing places are not wanting in grandeur. The floors are sometimes of wood, tessellated after the fashion of France. The palace of Sir Robert Clayton, in the Old Jewry, contained a superb banqueting room wainscoted with cedar, and adorned with battles of gods and giants in fresco. Sir Dudley North expended four thousand pounds, a sum which would then have been important to a Duke, on the rich furniture of his reception rooms in Basinghall Street. In such abodes, under the last Stuarts, the heads of the great firms lived splendidly and hospitably. To their dwelling place they were bound by the strongest ties of interest and affection. There they had passed their youth, had made their friendships, had courted their wives, had seen their children grow up, had laid the remains of their parents in the earth, and expected that their own remains would be laid. That intense patriotism which is peculiar to the members of societies congregated within a narrow space was, in such circumstances, strongly developed. London was, to the Londoner, what Athens was to the Athenian of the age of Pericles, what Florence was to the Florentine of the fifteenth century. The citizen was proud of the grandeur of his city, punctilious about her claims to respect, ambitious of her offices, and zealous for her franchises. . . .

We should greatly err if we were to suppose that any of the streets and squares then bore the same aspect as at present. The great majority of the houses, indeed, have, since that time, been wholly, or in great part, rebuilt. If the most fashionable parts of the capital could be placed before us such as they then were, we should be disgusted by their squalid appearance, and poisoned by their noisome atmosphere. In Covent Garden a filthy and noisy

15. **Old Jewry,** a street near Mercer's Hall, so called from the fact that the Jews lived there in medieval times.

market was held close to the dwellings of the great. Fruit women screamed, carters fought, cabbage stalks and rotten apples accumulated in heaps at the thresholds of the Countess of Berkshire and of the Bishop of Durham.

The centre of Lincoln's Inn Fields was an open space where the rabble congregated every evening, within a few yards of Cardigan House and Winchester House, to hear mountebanks harangue, to see bears dance, and to set dogs at oxen. Rubbish was shot in every part of the area. Horses were exercised there. The beggars were as noisy and importunate as in the worst governed cities of the Continent. A Lincoln's Inn mumper was a proverb. The whole fraternity knew the arms and liveries of every charitably disposed grandee in the neighbourhood, and, as soon as his lordship's coach and six appeared, came hopping and crawling in crowds to persecute him. These disorders lasted, in spite of many accidents, and of some legal proceedings, till, in the reign of George the Second, Sir Joseph Jekyll, Master of the Rolls, was knocked down and nearly killed in the middle of the square. Then at length palisades were set up, and a pleasant garden laid out.

Saint James's Square was a receptacle for all the offal and cinders, for all the dead cats and dead dogs of Westminster. At one time a cudgel player kept the ring there. At another time an impudent squatter settled himself there, and built a shed for rubbish under the windows of the gilded saloons in which the first magnates of the realm, Norfolk, Ormond, Kent, and Pembroke, gave banquets and balls. It was not till these nuisances had lasted through a whole generation, and till much had been written about them, that the inhabitants applied to Parliament for permission to put up rails, and to plant trees.

When such was the state of the region inhabited by the most luxurious portion of society, we may easily believe that the great body of the population suffered what would now be considered as insupportable grievances. The pavement was detestable; all foreigners cried shame upon it. The drainage was so bad that in rainy weather the gutters soon became torrents. Several facetious poets have commemorated the fury with which these black rivulets roared down Snow Hill and Ludgate Hill, bearing to Fleet Ditch a vast tribute of animal and vegetable filth from the stalls of butchers and greengrocers. This flood was profusely thrown to right and left by coaches and carts. To keep as far from the car-riage road as possible was therefore the wish of every pedestrian. The mild and timid gave the wall. The bold and athletic took it. If two roisterers met, they cocked their hats in each other's faces, and pushed each other about till the weaker was shoved towards the kennel. If he was a mere bully he sneaked off, muttering that he should find a time. If he was pugnacious, the encounter probably ended in a duel behind Montague House.

The houses were not numbered. There would indeed have been little advantage in numbering them; for of the coachmen, chairmen, porters, and errand boys of London, a very small proportion could read. It was necessary to use marks which the most ignorant could understand. The shops were therefore distinguished by painted or sculptured signs, which gave a gay and grotesque aspect to the streets. The walk from Charing Cross to Whitechapel lay through an endless succession of Saracens' Heads, Royal Oaks, Blue Bears, and Golden Lambs, which disappeared when they were no longer required for the direction of the common people.

When the evening closed in, the difficulty and danger of walking about London became serious indeed. The garret windows were opened, and pails were emptied, with little regard to those who were passing below. Falls, bruises, and broken bones were of constant occurrence. For, till the last year of the reign of Charles the Second, most of the streets were left in profound darkness. Thieves and robbers plied their trade with impunity: yet they were hardly so terrible to peaceable citizens as another class of ruffians. It was a favourite amusement of dissolute young gentlemen to swagger by night about the town, breaking windows, upsetting sedans, beating quiet men, and offering rude caresses to pretty women. Several dynasties of these tyrants had, since the Restoration, domineered over the streets. The Muns and Tityre Tus had given place to the Hectors, and the Hectors had been recently succeeded by the Scourers. At a later period arose the Nicker, the Hawcubite, and the yet more dreaded name of Mohawk. The machinery for keeping the peace was utterly contemptible. There was an Act of Common Council which provided that more than a thousand watchmen should be constantly on the alert in the city, from sunset to sunrise, and that every inhabitant should take his turn of duty. But this Act was negligently executed. Few of those who were summoned left their homes; and those few generally found it more agree-

---

14. mumper, beggar. 21. the reign of George the Second, 1727–60.

6. kennel, gutter. 30. the reign of Charles the Second, 1660–85.

able to tipple in alehouses than to pace the streets.

It ought to be noticed that, in the last year of the reign of Charles the Second, began a great change in the police of London, a change which has perhaps added as much to the happiness of the body of the people as revolutions of much greater fame. An ingenious projector, named Edward Heming, obtained letters patent conveying to him, for a term of years, the exclusive right of lighting up London. He undertook, for a moderate consideration, to place a light before every tenth door, on moonless nights, from Michaelmas to Lady Day, and from six to twelve of the clock. Those who now see the capital all the year round, from dusk to dawn, blazing with a splendour beside which the illuminations for La Hogue and Blenheim would have looked pale, may perhaps smile to think of Heming's lanterns, which glimmered feebly before one house in ten during a small part of one night in three. But such was not the feeling of his contemporaries. His scheme was enthusiastically applauded, and furiously attacked. The friends of improvement extolled him as the greatest of all the benefactors of his city. What, they asked, were the boasted inventions of Archimedes, when compared with the achievement of the man who had turned the nocturnal shades into noon day? In spite of these eloquent eulogies the cause of darkness was not left undefended. There were fools in that age who opposed the introduction of what was called the new light as strenuously as fools in our age have opposed the introduction of vaccination and railroads, as strenuously as the fools of an age anterior to the dawn of history doubtless opposed the introduction of the plough and of alphabetical writing. Many years after the date of Heming's patent there were extensive districts in which no lamp was seen.

We may easily imagine what, in such times, must have been the state of the quarters of London which were peopled by the outcasts of society. Among those quarters one had attained a scandalous preeminence. On the confines of the City and the Temple had been founded, in the thirteenth century, a House of Carmelite Friars, distinguished by their white hoods. The precinct of this house had, before the Reformation, been a sanctuary for criminals, and still retained the privilege of protecting debtors from arrest. Insolvents consequently were to be found in every dwelling, from cellar to garret. Of these a large proportion were knaves and libertines, and were followed to their asylum by women more abandoned than themselves. The civil power was unable to keep order in a district swarming with such inhabitants; and thus Whitefriars became the favourite resort of all who wished to be emancipated from the restraints of the law. Though the immunities legally belonging to the place extended only to cases of debt, cheats, false witnesses, forgers, and highwaymen found refuge there. For amidst a rabble so desperate no peace officer's life was in safety. At the cry of "Rescue," bullies with swords and cudgels, and termagant hags with spits and broomsticks, poured forth by hundreds; and the intruder was fortunate if he escaped back into Fleet Street, hustled, stripped, and pumped upon. Even the warrant of the Chief Justice of England could not be executed without the help of a company of musketeers. Such relics of the barbarism of the darkest ages were to be found within a short walk of the chambers where Somers was studying history and law, of the chapel where Tillotson was preaching, of the coffee house where Dryden was passing judgment on poems and plays, and of the hall where the Royal Society was examining the astronomical system of Isaac Newton.

Each of the two cities which made up the capital of England had its own centre of attraction. In the metropolis of commerce the point of convergence was the Exchange; in the metropolis of fashion the Palace. But the Palace did not retain its influence so long as the Exchange. The Revolution completely altered the relations between the Court and the higher classes of society. It was by degrees discovered that the King, in his individual capacity, had very little to give; that coronets and garters, bishoprics and embassies, lordships of the Treasury and tellerships of the Exchequer, nay, even charges in the royal stud and bedchamber, were really bestowed, not by him, but by his advisers. Every ambitious and covetous man perceived that he would consult his own interest far better by acquiring the dominion of a Cornish borough, and by rendering good service to the ministry during a critical session, than by becoming the companion, or even the minion, of his prince. It was therefore in the antechambers, not of George the First and of George

---

12. **from Michaelmas to Lady Day,** from September 29 (the feast of the Archangel Michael) to March 25 (the feast of the Annunciation of the Virgin Mary). 16. **La Hogue,** a roadstead in Normandy, off which Admiral Russell defeated the French fleet, 1692. **Blenheim,** a village in Bavaria, near which Marlborough defeated the French, 1704. 25. **Archimedes,** Greek mathematician (c. 287–212 B.C.). 46–47. **a sanctuary for criminals,** because civil law was inoperative within sacred precincts.

23. **Somers,** John, Baron Somers (1651–1716), Lord Chancellor. 24. **Tillotson,** John Tillotson (1630–1694), Archbishop of Canterbury. 28. **Isaac Newton,** mathematician and philosopher (1642–1727), who discovered the law of universal gravitation. 49. **George the First,** reigned 1714–27.

the Second, but of Walpole and of Pelham, that the daily crowd of courtiers was to be found. It is also to be remarked that the same Revolution, which made it impossible that our Kings should use the patronage of the state, merely for the purpose of gratifying their personal predilections, gave us several Kings unfitted by their education and habits to be gracious and affable hosts. They had been born and bred on the Continent. They never felt themselves at home in our island. If they spoke our language, they spoke it inelegantly and with effort. Our national character they never fully understood. Our national manners they hardly attempted to acquire. The most important part of their duty they performed better than any ruler who had preceded them: for they governed strictly according to law: but they could not be the first gentlemen of the realm, the heads of polite society. If ever they unbent, it was in a very small circle where hardly an English face was to be seen; and they were never so happy as when they could escape for a summer to their native land. They had indeed their days of reception for our nobility and gentry; but the reception was mere matter of form, and became at last as solemn a ceremony as a funeral.

Not such was the court of Charles the Second. Whitehall, when he dwelt there, was the focus of political intrigue and of fashionable gaiety. Half the jobbing and half the flirting of the metropolis went on under his roof. Whoever could make himself agreeable to the prince, or could secure the good offices of the mistress, might hope to rise in the world without rendering any service to the government, without being even known by sight to any minister of state. This courtier got a frigate, and that a company; a third, the pardon of a rich offender; a fourth, a lease of crown land on easy terms. If the King notified his pleasure that a briefless lawyer should be made a judge, or that a libertine baronet should be made a peer, the gravest counsellors, after a little murmuring, submitted. Interest, therefore, drew a constant press of suitors to the gates of the palace; and those gates always stood wide. The King kept open house every day, and all day long, for the good society of London, the extreme Whigs only excepted. Hardly any gentleman had any difficulty in making his way to the royal presence. The levee was exactly what the word imports. Some men of quality came every morning to stand round their master, to chat with him while his wig was combed and his cravat tied, and to accompany him on his early walk through the Park. All persons who had been properly introduced might, without any special invitation, go to see him dine, sup, dance, and play at hazard, and might have the pleasure of hearing him tell stories, which indeed he told remarkably well, about his flight from Worcester, and about the misery which he had endured when he was a state prisoner in the hands of the canting meddling preachers of Scotland. Bystanders whom His Majesty recognised often came in for a courteous word. This proved a far more successful kingcraft than any that his father or grandfather had practised. It was not easy for the most austere republican of the school of Marvel to resist the fascination of so much good humour and affability: and many a veteran Cavalier, in whose heart the remembrance of unrequited sacrifices and services had been festering during twenty years, was compensated in one moment for wounds and sequestrations by his sovereign's kind nod, and "God bless you, my old friend!"

Whitehall naturally became the chief staple of news. Whenever there was a rumour that anything important had happened or was about to happen, people hastened thither to obtain intelligence from the fountain head. The galleries presented the appearance of a modern club room at an anxious time. They were full of people enquiring whether the Dutch mail was in, what tidings the express from France had brought, whether John Sobiesky had beaten the Turks, whether the Doge of Genoa was really at Paris. These were matters about which it was safe to talk aloud. But there were subjects concerning which information was asked and given in whispers. Had Halifax got the better of Rochester? Was there to be a Parliament? Was the Duke of York really going to Scotland? Had Monmouth really been summoned from the Hague? Men tried to read the countenance of every minister as he went through the throng to and from the royal closet. All sorts of auguries were drawn from the tone in which His Majesty spoke to the Lord President, or from the laugh with which His Majesty honoured a jest of the Lord Privy Seal; and in a few hours the hopes and fears inspired by such

1. **Walpole,** Sir Robert Walpole (1676–1745), Prime Minister and Chancellor of the Exchequer. **Pelham,** Sir Thomas Pelham-Hobbes (1693–1768), who opposed Walpole. 3–8. **the same Revolution . . . hosts.** The kings who followed James II, banished from England by the "Bloodless Revolution" of 1688, were unable to speak English.

9. **Worcester,** where Cromwell defeated the royalist Scotch army, September 3, 1651. 17. **Marvel,** Andrew Marvell (1621–1678), poet and friend of Milton. 32. **John Sobiesky,** John III, King of Poland, 1674–96. 39. **Monmouth,** James, Duke of Monmouth (1649–1685), illegitimate son of Charles II, who was backed by Shaftesbury and a Protestant party as his father's successor. He was beheaded for treason in 1685. See Dryden's poem "Absalom and Achitophel."

slight indications had spread to all the coffee houses from St. James's to the Tower.

The coffee house must not be dismissed with a cursory mention. It might indeed at that time have been not improperly called a most important political institution. No Parliament had sat for years. The municipal council of the City had ceased to speak the sense of the citizens. Public meetings, harangues, resolutions, and the rest of the modern machinery of agitation had not yet come into fashion. Nothing resembling the modern newspaper existed. In such circumstances the coffee houses were the chief organs through which the public opinion of the metropolis vented itself.

The first of these establishments had been set up, in the time of the Commonwealth, by a Turkey merchant, who had acquired among the Mahometans a taste for their favourite beverage. The convenience of being able to make appointments in any part of the town, and of being able to pass evenings socially at a very small charge, was so great that the fashion spread fast. Every man of the upper or middle class went daily to his coffee house to learn the news and to discuss it. Every coffee house had one or more orators to whose eloquence the crowd listened with admiration, and who soon became, what the journalists of our own time have been called, a fourth Estate of the realm. The Court had long seen with uneasiness the growth of this new power in the state. An attempt had been made, during Danby's administration, to close the coffee houses. But men of all parties missed their usual places of resort so much that there was an universal outcry. The government did not venture, in opposition to a feeling so strong and general, to enforce a regulation of which the legality might well be questioned. Since that time ten years had elapsed, and during those years the number and influence of the coffee houses had been constantly increasing. Foreigners remarked that the coffee house was that which especially distinguished London from all other cities; that the coffee house was the Londoner's home, and that those who wished to find a gentleman commonly asked, not whether he lived in Fleet Street or Chancery Lane, but whether he frequented the Grecian or the Rainbow. Nobody was excluded from these places who laid down his penny at the bar. Yet every rank and profession, and every shade of religious and political opinion, had its own head quarters. There were houses near St. James's

Park where fops congregated, their heads and shoulders covered with black or flaxen wigs, not less ample than those which are now worn by the Chancellor and by the Speaker of the House of Commons. The wig came from Paris; and so did the rest of the fine gentleman's ornaments, his embroidered coat, his fringed gloves, and the tassel which upheld his pantaloons. The conversation was in that dialect which, long after it had ceased to be spoken in fashionable circles, continued, in the mouth of Lord Foppington, to excite the mirth of theatres. The atmosphere was like that of a perfumer's shop. Tobacco in any other form than that of richly scented snuff was held in abomination. If any clown, ignorant of the usages of the house, called for a pipe, the sneers of the whole assembly and the short answers of the waiters soon convinced him that he had better go somewhere else. Nor, indeed, would he have had far to go. For, in general, the coffee rooms reeked with tobacco like a guardroom; and strangers sometimes expressed their surprise that so many people should leave their own firesides to sit in the midst of eternal fog and stench. Nowhere was the smoking more constant than at Will's. That celebrated house, situated between Covent Garden and Bow Street, was sacred to polite letters. There the talk was about poetical justice and the unities of place and time. There was a faction for Perrault and the moderns, a faction for Boileau and the ancients. One group debated whether Paradise Lost ought not to have been in rhyme. To another an envious poetaster demonstrated that Venice Preserved ought to have been hooted from the stage. Under no roof was a greater variety of figures to be seen, Earls in stars and garters, clergymen in cassocks and bands, pert Templars, sheepish lads from the Universities, translators and indexmakers in ragged coats of frieze. The great press was to get near the chair where John Dryden sate. In winter that chair was always in the warmest nook by the fire; in summer it stood in the balcony. To bow to the Laureate, and to hear his opinion of Racine's last tragedy or of Bossu's treatise on epic poetry, was thought a privilege. A pinch from his snuff box was an honour sufficient to turn

11. Lord Foppington, in *The Relapse* by Sir John Vanbrugh, 1696.   **29. Perrault and the moderns.** Charles Perrault (1628–1703), French poet and critic, championed the modern writers as against the ancients. His chief claim to fame is now his *Mother Goose Stories,* 1697, in which such famous tales as "Cinderella," "Little Red Riding Hood," "The Sleeping Beauty," and "Puss in Boots" were first printed. **30. Boileau and the ancients.** Nicolas Boileau-Despréaux (1636–1711) contested Perrault's position. **33. Venice Preserved,** Thomas Otway's famous tragedy, 1682.   **43. Racine,** Jean Baptiste Racine (1639–1699), French dramatist. **43. Bossu,** René Le Bossu (1631–1680), French critic.

28. a fourth Estate, added to the clergy, the nobles, and the commons.   **31. Danby's administration.** Sir Thomas Osborne, Earl of Danby (1631–1712) was Lord Treasurer from 1673 to 1678.

the head of a young enthusiast. There were coffee houses where the first medical men might be consulted. Doctor John Radcliffe, who, in the year 1685, rose to the largest practice in London, came daily, at the hour when the Exchange was full, from his house in Bow Street, then a fashionable part of the capital, to Garraway's, and was to be found, surrounded by surgeons and apothecaries, at a particular table. There were Puritan coffee houses where no oath was heard, and where lankhaired men discussed election and reprobation through their noses; Jew coffee houses where darkeyed money changers from Venice and from Amsterdam greeted each other; and Popish coffee houses where, as good Protestants believed, Jesuits planned, over their cups, another great fire, and cast silver bullets to shoot the King.

These gregarious habits had no small share in forming the character of the Londoner of that age. He was, indeed, a different being from the rustic Englishman. There was not then the intercourse which now exists between the two classes. Only very great men were in the habit of dividing the year between town and country. Few esquires came to the capital thrice in their lives. Nor was it yet the practice of all citizens in easy circumstances to breathe the fresh air of the fields and woods during some weeks of every summer. A cockney, in a rural village, was stared at as much as if he had intruded into a Kraal of Hottentots. On the other hand, when the lord of a Lincolnshire or Shropshire manor appeared in Fleet Street, he was as easily distinguished from the resident population as a Turk or a Lascar. His dress, his gait, his accent, the manner in which he stared at the shops, stumbled into the gutters, ran against the porters, and stood under the waterspouts, marked him out as an excellent subject for the operations of swindlers and banterers. Bullies jostled him into the kennel. Hackney coachmen splashed him from head to foot. Thieves explored with perfect security the huge pockets of his horseman's coat, while he stood entranced by the splendour of the Lord Mayor's show. Moneydroppers, sore from the cart's tail, introduced themselves to him, and appeared to him the most honest friendly gentlemen that he had ever seen. Painted women, the refuse of Lewkner Lane and Whetstone Park, passed themselves on him for countesses and maids of honour. If he asked his way to Saint James's, his informants sent him to Mile End. If he went into a shop, he was instantly discerned to be a fit purchaser of everything that nobody else would buy, of secondhand embroidery, copper rings, and watches that would not go. If he rambled into any fashionable coffee house, he became a mark for the insolent derision of fops and the grave waggery of Templars. Enraged and mortified, he soon returned to his mansion, and there, in the homage of his tenants and the conversation of his boon companions, found consolation for the vexations and humiliations which he had undergone. There he once more felt himself a great man; and he saw nothing above him except when at the assizes he took his seat on the bench near the Judge, or when at the muster of the militia he saluted the Lord Lieutenant.

The chief cause which made the fusion of the different elements of society so imperfect was the extreme difficulty which our ancestors found in passing from place to place. . . .

It was by the highways that both travellers and goods generally passed from place to place; and those highways appear to have been far worse than might have been expected from the degree of wealth and civilisation which the nation had even then attained. On the best lines of communication the ruts were deep, the descents precipitous, and the way often such as it was hardly possible to distinguish, in the dusk, from the unenclosed heath and fen which lay on both sides. . . .

People, in the time of Charles the Second, travelled with six horses, because with a smaller number there was great danger of sticking fast in the mire. Nor were even six horses always sufficient. Vanbrugh, in the succeeding generation, described with great humour the way in which a country gentleman, newly chosen a member of Parliament, went up to London. On that occasion all the exertions of six beasts, two of which had been taken from the plough, could not save the family coach from being imbedded in a quagmire.

Public carriages had recently been much improved. During the years which immediately followed the Restoration, a diligence ran between London and Oxford in two days. The passengers slept at Beaconsfield. At length, in the spring of 1669, a great and daring innovation was attempted. It was announced that a vehicle, described as the Flying Coach, would perform the whole journey

44. Moneydroppers, criminals who made the acquaintance of unsuspecting strangers by pretending to restore to them coins they had dropped. **sore from the cart's tail,** having been whipped through the streets at the tail of a cart.

36–38. Vanbrugh . . . described with great humour, in his unfinished play *A Journey to London*, completed by Colley Cibber as *The Provoked Husband,* 1728.

between sunrise and sunset. This spirited undertaking was solemnly considered and sanctioned by the Heads of the University, and appears to have excited the same sort of interest which is excited in our own time by the opening of a new railway. The Vicechancellor, by a notice affixed in all public places, prescribed the hour and place of departure. The success of the experiment was complete. At six in the morning the carriage began to move from before the ancient front of All Souls College: and at seven in the evening the adventurous gentlemen who had run the first risk were safely deposited at their inn in London. The emulation of the sister University was moved; and soon a diligence was set up which in one day carried passengers from Cambridge to the capital. At the close of the reign of Charles the Second, flying carriages ran thrice a week from London to the chief towns. But no stage coach, indeed no stage waggon, appears to have proceeded further north than York, or further west than Exeter. The ordinary day's journey of a flying coach was about fifty miles in the summer; but in winter, when the ways were bad and the nights long, little more than thirty. The Chester coach, the York coach, and the Exeter coach generally reached London in four days during the fine season, but at Christmas not till the sixth day. The passengers, six in number, were all seated in the carriage. For accidents were so frequent that it would have been most perilous to mount the roof. The ordinary fare was about twopence halfpenny a mile in summer, and somewhat more in winter.

This mode of travelling, which by Englishmen of the present day would be regarded as insufferably slow, seemed to our ancestors wonderfully and indeed alarmingly rapid. In a work published a few months before the death of Charles the Second, the flying coaches are extolled as far superior to any similar vehicles ever known in the world. . . .

In spite of the attractions of the flying coaches, it was still usual for men who enjoyed health and vigour, and who were not encumbered by much baggage, to perform long journeys on horseback. If the traveller wished to move expeditiously he rode post. Fresh saddle horses and guides were to be procured at convenient distances along all the great lines of road. The charge was threepence a mile for each horse, and fourpence a stage for the guide. In this manner, when the ways were good, it was possible to travel, for a considerable time, as rapidly as by any conveyance known in England, till vehicles were propelled by steam. . . .

Whatever might be the way in which a journey was performed, the travellers, unless they were numerous and well armed, ran considerable risk of being stopped and plundered. The mounted highwayman, a marauder known to our generation only from books, was to be found on every main road. The waste tracts which lay on the great routes near London were especially haunted by plunderers of this class. Hounslow Heath, on the Great Western Road, and Finchley Common, on the Great Northern Road, were perhaps the most celebrated of these spots. The Cambridge scholars trembled when they approached Epping Forest, even in broad daylight. Seamen who had just been paid off at Chatham were often compelled to deliver their purses on Gadshill, celebrated near a hundred years earlier by the greatest of poets as the scene of the depredations of Falstaff. The public authorities seem to have been often at a loss how to deal with the plunderers. . . .

It was necessary to the success and even to the safety of the highwayman that he should be a bold and skilful rider, and that his manners and appearance should be such as suited the master of a fine horse. He therefore held an aristocratical position in the community of thieves, appeared at fashionable coffee houses and gaming houses, and betted with men of quality on the race ground. Sometimes, indeed, he was a man of good family and education. A romantic interest therefore attached, and perhaps still attaches, to the names of freebooters of this class. The vulgar eagerly drank in tales of their ferocity and audacity, of their occasional acts of generosity and good nature, of their amours, of their miraculous escapes, of their desperate struggles, and of their manly bearing at the bar and in the cart. Thus it was related of William Nevison, the great robber of Yorkshire, that he levied a quarterly tribute on all the northern drovers, and, in return, not only spared them himself, but protected them against all other thieves; that he demanded purses in the most courteous manner; that he gave largely to the poor what he had taken from the rich; that his life was once spared by the royal clemency, but that he again tempted his fate, and at length died, in 1685, on the gallows of York. It was related how Claude Duval, the French page of the Duke of Richmond, took to the road, became captain of a formidable gang, and had the honour to be named first in a royal proclamation against notorious offenders; how at the head of his troop he stopped a lady's coach, in which there was a booty of four hundred pounds; how he took only one hundred, and suffered the fair owner to ransom the rest by dancing a coranto with him on the heath; how his vivacious gallantry stole away the hearts of all women; how his dexterity at sword and pistol made him a terror to all men; how, at length, in the year 1670, he was seized when overcome by wine; how dames of high rank visited him in prison, and with tears interceded for his life; how the King would have granted a pardon, but for the interference of Judge Morton, the terror of highwaymen, who threatened to resign his office unless the law were carried into full effect; and how, after the execution, the corpse lay in state with all the pomp of scutcheons, wax lights, black hangings and mutes, till the same cruel Judge, who had intercepted the mercy of the crown, sent officers to disturb the obsequies. In these anecdotes there is doubtless a large mixture of fable; but they are not on that account unworthy of being recorded; for it is both an authentic and an important fact that such tales, whether false or true, were heard by our ancestors with eagerness and faith. . . .

In the capital the coffee houses supplied in some measure the place of a journal. Thither the Londoners flocked, as the Athenians of old flocked to the market place, to hear whether there was any news. There men might learn how brutally a Whig had been treated the day before in Westminster Hall, what horrible accounts the letters from Edinburgh gave of the torturing of Covenanters, how grossly the Navy Board had cheated the crown in the victualling of the fleet, and what grave charges the Lord Privy Seal had brought against the Treasury in the matter of the hearth money. But people who lived at a distance from the great theatre of political contention could be kept regularly informed of what was passing there only by means of newsletters. To prepare such letters became a calling in London, as it now is among the natives of India. The newswriter rambled from coffee room to coffee room, collecting reports, squeezed himself into the Sessions House at the Old Bailey if there was an interesting trial, nay, perhaps obtained admission to the gallery of Whitehall, and noticed how the King and Duke looked. In this way he gathered materials for weekly epistles destined to enlighten some county town or some bench of rustic magistrates. Such were the sources from which the inhabitants of the largest provincial cities, and the

great body of the gentry and clergy, learned almost all that they knew of the history of their own time. We must suppose that at Cambridge there were as many persons curious to know what was passing in the world as at almost any place in the kingdom, out of London. Yet at Cambridge, during a great part of the reign of Charles the Second, the Doctors of Laws and the Masters of Arts had no regular supply of news except through the London Gazette. At length the services of one of the collectors of intelligence in the capital were employed. That was a memorable day on which the first newsletter from London was laid on the table of the only coffee room in Cambridge. At the seat of a man of fortune in the country the newsletter was impatiently expected. Within a week after it had arrived it had been thumbed by twenty families. It furnished the neighbouring squires with matter for talk over their October, and the neighbouring rectors with topics for sharp sermons against Whiggery or Popery. . . .

It is scarcely necessary to say that there were then no provincial newspapers. Indeed, except in the capital and at the two Universities, there was scarcely a printer in the kingdom. The only press in England north of Trent appears to have been at York.

It was not only by means of the London Gazette that the government undertook to furnish political instruction to the people. That journal contained a scanty supply of news without comment. Another journal, published under the patronage of the court, consisted of comment without news. This paper, called the Observator, was edited by an old Tory pamphleteer named Roger Lestrange. Lestrange was by no means deficient in readiness and shrewdness; and his diction, though coarse, and disfigured by a mean and flippant jargon which then passed for wit in the green room and the tavern, was not without keenness and vigour. But his nature, at once ferocious and ignoble, showed itself in every line that he penned. When the first Observators appeared there was some excuse for his acrimony. For the Whigs were then powerful; and he had to contend against numerous adversaries, whose unscrupulous violence might seem to justify unsparing retaliation. But in 1685 all opposition had been crushed. A generous spirit would have disdained to insult a party which could not reply, and to aggravate the misery of prisoners, of exiles, of bereaved families: but from the malice of Lestrange the grave was no hiding place, and the house of mourning no

31. Covenanters, Scotch Presbyterians; see an encyclopedia for details. Sir Walter Scott's *Old Mortality* concerns their insurrection under Charles II. **43. Old Bailey,** the central criminal court in London.

19. October, ale brewed in October.

sanctuary. In the last month of the reign of Charles the Second, William Jenkyn, an aged dissenting pastor of great note, who had been cruelly persecuted for no crime but that of worshipping God according to the fashion generally followed throughout Protestant Europe, died of hardships and privations in Newgate. The outbreak of popular sympathy could not be repressed. The corpse was followed to the grave by a train of a hundred and fifty coaches. Even courtiers looked sad. Even the unthinking King showed some signs of concern. Lestrange alone set up a howl of savage exultation, laughed at the weak compassion of the Trimmers, proclaimed that the blasphemous old impostor had met with a most righteous punishment, and vowed to wage war, not only to the death, but after death, with all the mock saints and martyrs. Such was the spirit of the paper which was at this time the oracle of the Tory party, and especially of the parochial clergy.

Literature which could be carried by the post bag then formed the greater part of the intellectual nutriment ruminated by the country divines and country justices. The difficulty and expense of conveying large packets from place to place was so great, that an extensive work was longer in making its way from Paternoster Row to Devonshire or Lancashire than it now is in reaching Kentucky. How scantily a rural parsonage was then furnished, even with books the most necessary to a theologian, has already been remarked. The houses of the gentry were not more plentifully supplied. Few knights of the shire had libraries so good as may now perpetually be found in a servants' hall, or in the back parlour of a small shopkeeper. An esquire passed among his neighbours for a great scholar, if Hudibras and Baker's Chronicle, Tarlton's Jests and the Seven Champions of Christendom, lay in his hall window among the fishing rods and fowling pieces. No circulating library, no book society, then existed even in the capital: but in the capital those students who could not afford to purchase largely had a resource. The shops of the great booksellers, near Saint Paul's Churchyard, were crowded every day and all day long with readers; and a known customer was often permitted to carry a volume home. In the country there was no such accommodation; and every man was under the necessity of buying whatever he wished to read.

As to the lady of the manor and her daughters, their literary stores generally consisted of a prayer book and a receipt book. But in truth they lost little by living in rural seclusion. For, even in the highest ranks, and in those situations which afforded the greatest facilities for mental improvement, the English women of that generation were decidedly worse educated than they have been at any other time since the revival of learning. At an earlier period they had studied the masterpieces of ancient genius. In the present day they seldom bestow much attention on the dead languages; but they are familiar with the tongue of Pascal and Molière, with the tongue of Dante and Tasso, with the tongue of Goethe and Schiller; nor is there any purer or more graceful English than that which accomplished women now speak and write. But, during the latter part of the seventeenth century, the culture of the female mind seems to have been almost entirely neglected. If a damsel had the least smattering of literature she was regarded as a prodigy. Ladies highly born, highly bred, and naturally quick witted, were unable to write a line in their mother tongue without solecisms and faults of spelling such as a charity girl would now be ashamed to commit.

The explanation may easily be found. Extravagant licentiousness, the natural effect of extravagant austerity, was now the mode: and licentiousness had produced its ordinary effect, the moral and intellectual degradation of women. To their personal beauty, it was the fashion to pay rude and impudent homage. But the admiration and desire which they inspired were seldom mingled with respect, with affection, or with any chivalrous sentiment. The qualities which fit them to be companions, advisers, confidential friends, rather repelled than attracted the libertines of Whitehall. In that court a maid of honour, who dressed in such a manner as to do full justice to a white bosom, who ogled significantly, who danced voluptuously, who excelled in pert repartee, who was not ashamed to romp

---

13. **Trimmers,** moderates.   27. **Paternoster Row,** the center of English publishing activity.   36–38. **Hudibras,** by Samuel Butler, 1663, 1664, 1678, a savage satire on the Puritans, said to have been Charles II's favorite poem. **Baker's Chronicle,** of the kings of England from the Roman period to Charles II, written by Sir Richard Baker in 1643. **Tarlton's Jests,** attributed to Richard Tarlton, the Charlie Chaplin of Shakespeare's time and one of the most famous clowns of all time. **The Seven Champions of Christendom,** a famous romance by Richard Johnson, published about 1597.

17. **Pascal,** Blaise Pascal (1623–1662), French philosopher. **Molière** (Jean Baptiste Poquelin, 1622–1673), the most famous of all French comic dramatists.   18. **Dante and Tasso,** Dante Alighieri (1265–1321), author of *The Divine Comedy,* greatest of Italian poets, and one of the three or four greatest names in world literature. Torquato Tasso (1544–1595), great Italian poet, author of *Jerusalem Delivered.*   19. **Goethe and Schiller,** Johann Wolfgang von Goethe (1749–1832), the greatest of German poets, author of *Faust.* Friedrich Schiller (1759–1805), famous German poet and dramatist.

with Lords of the Bedchamber and Captains of the Guards, to sing sly verses with sly expression, or to put on a page's dress for a frolic, was more likely to be followed and admired, more likely to be honoured with royal attentions, more likely to win a rich and noble husband than Jane Grey or Lucy Hutchinson would have been. In such circumstances the standard of female attainments was necessarily low; and it was more dangerous to be above that standard than to be beneath it. Extreme ignorance and frivolity were thought less unbecoming in a lady than the slightest tincture of pedantry. Of the too celebrated women whose faces we still admire on the walls of Hampton Court, few indeed were in the habit of reading anything more valuable than acrostics, lampoons, and translations of the Clelia and the Grand Cyrus.

The literary acquirements, even of the accomplished gentlemen of that generation, seem to have been somewhat less solid and profound than at an earlier or a later period. Greek learning, at least, did not flourish among us in the days of Charles the Second, as it had flourished before the civil war, or as it again flourished long after the Revolution. There were undoubtedly scholars to whom the whole Greek literature, from Homer to Photius, was familiar: but such scholars were to be found almost exclusively among the clergy resident at the Universities, and even at the Universities were few, and were not fully appreciated. At Cambridge it was not thought by any means necessary that a divine should be able to read the Gospels in the original. Nor was the standard at Oxford higher. When, in the reign of William the Third, Christ Church rose up as one man to defend the genuineness of the Epistles of Phalaris, that great college, then considered as the first seat of philology in the kingdom, could not muster such a stock of Attic learning as is now possessed by several youths at every great public school.

from LORD CLIVE

[The Conquest of Bengal]

This passage from Macaulay's essay on Lord Clive tells the story of perhaps the most spectacular chapter in

the history of Britain's conquest of India. Robert Clive (1725–1774), later Baron Clive of Plassey, went to India as representative of the East India Company. His life ended in tragedy. He was tried by Parliament for alleged maladministration of Indian affairs, and secured only a qualified acquittal. Broken in health and spirit, he committed suicide, November 22, 1774.

Macaulay's essay was published in the *Edinburgh Review* in 1840 as a review of *The Life of Robert Lord Clive; Collected from the Family Papers, communicated by the Earl of Powis*, by Major-General Sir John Malcolm, K.C.B., 3 vols., 1836.

OF the provinces which had been subject to the house of Tamerlane, the wealthiest was Bengal. No part of India possessed such natural advantages both for agriculture and for commerce. The Ganges, rushing through a hundred channels to the sea, has formed a vast plain of rich mould which, even under the tropical sky, rivals the verdure of an English April. The rice fields yield an increase such as is elsewhere unknown. Spices, sugar, vegetable oils, are produced with marvellous exuberance. The rivers afford an inexhaustible supply of fish. The desolate islands along the sea-coast, overgrown by noxious vegetation, and swarming with deer and tigers, supply the cultivated districts with abundance of salt. The great stream which fertilises the soil is, at the same time, the chief highway of Eastern commerce. On its banks, and on those of its tributary waters, are the wealthiest marts, the most splendid capitals, and the most sacred shrines of India. The tyranny of man had for ages struggled in vain against the overflowing bounty of nature. In spite of the Mussulman despot, and of the Mahratta freebooter, Bengal was known through the East as the garden of Eden, as the rich kingdom. Its population multiplied exceedingly. Distant provinces were nourished from the overflowing of its granaries; and the noble ladies of London and Paris were clothed in the delicate produce of its looms. The race by whom this rich tract was peopled, enervated by a soft climate and accustomed to peaceful employments, bore the same relation to other Asiatics which the Asiatics generally bear to the bold and energetic children of Europe. The Castilians have a proverb, that in Valencia the earth is water and the men women; and the description is at least equally applicable to the vast plain of the Lower Ganges. Whatever the Bengalee does he does languidly. His favourite pursuits are sedentary.

6. **Jane Grey,** queen of England for nine days as the dupe of the Protestant party after the death of Edward VI in 1553, and who was beheaded after Mary I had come into power. **Lucy Hutchinson** (b. 1620), wife and biographer of the Puritan soldier Colonel John Hutchinson. 17. **Clelia and the Grand Cyrus,** French romances by Madeleine de Scudéry (1607–1701), long popular in England. 26. **Photius,** patriarch of Constantinople and one of the great scholars of the Greek Church (c. 820–891). 34. **The reign of William the Third,** 1689–1702. 35–36. **Epistles of Phalaris,** spurious letters, purportedly of the sixth century B.C. They were discredited by Richard Bentley (1662–1742).

14. **Tamerlane,** Mongol conqueror of India (c. 1333–1405). 34. **Mussulman despot.** The head of the Empire of India, a Mohammedan, was regarded as a despot by his Hindu subjects. 35. **Mahratta freebooter,** one living in the Deccan or Bombay region.

He shrinks from bodily exertion; and, though voluble in dispute, and singularly pertinacious in the war of chicane, he seldom engages in a personal conflict, and scarcely ever enlists as a soldier. We doubt whether there be a hundred genuine Bengalees in the whole army of the East India Company. There never, perhaps, existed a people so thoroughly fitted by nature and by habit for a foreign yoke.

The great commercial companies of Europe had 10 long possessed factories in Bengal. The French were settled, as they still are, at Chandernagore on the Hoogley. Higher up the stream the Dutch held Chinsurah. Nearer to the sea the English had built Fort William. A church and ample warehouses rose in the vicinity. A row of spacious houses, belonging to the chief factors of the East India Company, lined the banks of the river; and in the neighbourhood had sprung up a large and busy native town, where some Hindoo merchants of great opulence 20 had fixed their abode. But the tract now covered by the palaces of Chowringhee contained only a few miserable huts thatched with straw. A jungle, abandoned to water-fowl and alligators, covered the site of the present Citadel, and the Course, which is now daily crowded at sunset with the gayest equipages of Calcutta. For the ground on which the settlement stood, the English, like other great landholders, paid rent to the government; and they were, like other great landholders, permitted to 30 exercise a certain jurisdiction within their domain.

The great province of Bengal, together with Orissa and Bahar, had long been governed by a viceroy, whom the English called Aliverdy Khan, and who, like the other viceroys of the Mogul, had become virtually independent. He died in 1756, and the sovereignty descended to his grandson, a youth under twenty years of age, who bore the name of Surajah Dowlah. Oriental despots are perhaps the worst class of human beings; and this unhappy 40 boy was one of the worst specimens of his class. His understanding was naturally feeble, and his temper naturally unamiable. His education had been such as would have enervated even a vigorous intellect and perverted even a generous disposition. He was unreasonable, because nobody ever dared to reason with him, and selfish, because he had never been made to feel himself dependent on the good will of others. Early debauchery had unnerved his body and his mind. He indulged immoderately in the use 50 of ardent spirits, which inflamed his weak brain almost to madness. His chosen companions were flatterers, sprung from the dregs of the people, and recommended by nothing but buffoonery and servility. It is said that he had arrived at the last stage of human depravity, when cruelty becomes pleasing for its own sake, when the sight of pain, as pain, where no advantage is to be gained, no offence punished, no danger averted, is an agreeable excitement. It had early been his amusement to torture beasts and birds; and, when he grew up, he enjoyed with still keener relish the misery of his fellow-creatures.

From a child Surajah Dowlah had hated the English. It was his whim to do so; and his whims were never opposed. He had also formed a very exaggerated notion of the wealth which might be obtained by plundering them; and his feeble and uncultivated mind was incapable of perceiving that the riches of Calcutta, had they been even greater than he imagined, would not compensate him for what he must lose, if the European trade, of which Bengal was a chief seat, should be driven by his violence to some other quarter. Pretexts for a quarrel were readily found. The English, in expectation of a war with France, had begun to fortify their settlement without special permission from the Nabob. A rich native, whom he longed to plunder, had taken refuge at Calcutta, and had not been delivered up. On such grounds as these Surajah Dowlah marched with a great army against Fort William.

The servants of the Company at Madras had been forced by Dupleix to become statesmen and soldiers. Those in Bengal were still mere traders, and were terrified and bewildered by the approaching danger. The governor, who had heard much of Surajah Dowlah's cruelty, was frightened out of his wits, jumped into a boat, and took refuge in the nearest ship. The military commandant thought that he could not do better than follow so good an example. The fort was taken after a feeble resistance; and great numbers of the English fell into the hands of the conquerors. The Nabob seated himself with regal pomp in the principal hall of the factory, and ordered Mr. Holwell, the first in rank among the prisoners, to be brought before him. His Highness talked about the insolence of the English, and grumbled at the smallness of the treasure which he had found, but promised to spare their lives, and retired to rest.

Then was committed that great crime, memo-

---

17. factor, an East India Company employee of middle grade.   **22. Chowringhee,** a suburb of Calcutta, containing the Governor's palace and other public buildings.

32. Madras, a seaport on the east coast of India.   **33. Dupleix,** Joseph François Dupleix (1697–1763), a French general.   **51. Then,** June 20, 1756.

rable for its singular atrocity, memorable for the tremendous retribution by which it was followed. The English captives were left to the mercy of the guards, and the guards determined to secure them for the night in the prison of the garrison, a chamber known by the fearful name of the Black Hole. Even for a single European malefactor, that dungeon would, in such a climate, have been too close and narrow. The space was only twenty feet square. The air-holes were small and obstructed. It was the summer solstice, the season when the fierce heat of Bengal can scarcely be rendered tolerable to natives of England by lofty halls and by the constant waving of fans. The number of the prisoners was one hundred and forty-six. When they were ordered to enter the cell, they imagined that the soldiers were joking; and, being in high spirits on account of the promise of the Nabob to spare their lives, they laughed and jested at the absurdity of the notion. They soon discovered their mistake. They expostulated; they entreated; but in vain. The guards threatened to cut down all who hesitated. The captives were driven into the cell at the point of the sword, and the door was instantly shut and locked upon them.

Nothing in history or fiction, not even the story which Ugolino told in the sea of everlasting ice, after he had wiped his bloody lips on the scalp of his murderer, approaches the horrors which were recounted by the few survivors of that night. They cried for mercy. They strove to burst the door. Holwell who, even in that extremity, retained some presence of mind, offered large bribes to the gaolers. But the answer was that nothing could be done without the Nabob's orders, that the Nabob was asleep, and that he would be angry if anybody woke him. Then the prisoners went mad with despair. They trampled each other down, fought for the places at the windows, fought for the pittance of water with which the cruel mercy of the murderers mocked their agonies, raved, prayed, blasphemed, implored the guards to fire among them. The gaolers in the meantime held lights to the bars, and shouted with laughter at the frantic struggles of their victims. At length the tumult died away in low gaspings and moanings. The day broke. The Nabob had slept off his debauch, and permitted the door to be opened. But it was some time before the soldiers could make a lane for the survivors, by piling up on each side the heaps of corpses on which

the burning climate had already begun to do its loathsome work. When at length a passage was made, twenty-three ghastly figures, such as their own mothers would not have known, staggered one by one out of the charnel-house. A pit was instantly dug. The dead bodies, a hundred and twenty-three in number, were flung into it promiscuously, and covered up.

But these things—which, after the lapse of more than eighty years, cannot be told or read without horror—awakened neither remorse nor pity in the bosom of the savage Nabob. He inflicted no punishment on the murderers. He showed no tenderness to the survivors. Some of them, indeed, from whom nothing was to be got, were suffered to depart; but those from whom it was thought that anything could be extorted were treated with execrable cruelty. Holwell, unable to walk, was carried before the tyrant, who reproached him, threatened him, and sent him up the country in irons, together with some other gentlemen who were suspected of knowing more than they chose to tell about the treasures of the Company. These persons, still bowed down by the sufferings of that great agony, were lodged in miserable sheds, and fed only with grain and water, till at length the intercessions of the female relations of the Nabob procured their release. One Englishwoman had survived that night. She was placed in the harem of the Prince at Moorshedabad.

Surajah Dowlah, in the meantime, sent letters to his nominal sovereign at Delhi, describing the late conquest in the most pompous language. He placed a garrison in Fort William, forbade Englishmen to dwell in the neighbourhood, and directed that, in memory of his great actions, Calcutta should thenceforward be called Alinagore, that is to say, the Port of God.

In August the news of the fall of Calcutta reached Madras, and excited the fiercest and bitterest resentment. The cry of the whole settlement was for vengeance. Within forty-eight hours after the arrival of the intelligence it was determined that an expedition should be sent to the Hoogley, and that Clive should be at the head of the land forces. The naval armament was under the command of Admiral Watson. Nine hundred English infantry, fine troops and full of spirit, and fifteen hundred sepoys, composed the army which sailed to punish a Prince who had more subjects than Lewis the Fifteenth or the Empress Maria Theresa. In October the expedi-

---

26–29. not even the story . . . murderer, one of the most powerful passages in Dante's *Divine Comedy, Inferno,* Cantos XXII–XXIII. See "The Monk's Tale," in Chaucer's *Canterbury Tales.*

49. Lewis the Fifteenth, Louis XV, king of France 1715–74. **50. Maria Theresa** (1717–1780), Queen of Hungary and Bohemia, Archduchess of Austria, and wife of the German Emperor Francis I.

tion sailed; but it had to make its way against adverse winds and did not reach Bengal till December.

The Nabob was revelling in fancied security at Moorshedabad. He was so profoundly ignorant of the state of foreign countries that he often used to say that there were not ten thousand men in all Europe; and it had never occurred to him as possible that the English would dare to invade his dominions. But, though undisturbed by any fear of 10 their military power, he began to miss them greatly. His revenues fell off; and his ministers succeeded in making him understand that a ruler may sometimes find it more profitable to protect traders in the open enjoyment of their gains than to put them to the torture for the purpose of discovering hidden chests of gold and jewels. He was already disposed to permit the Company to resume its mercantile operations in his country, when he received the news that an English armament was in the Hoog- 20 ley. He instantly ordered all his troops to assemble at Moorshedabad, and marched towards Calcutta.

Clive had commenced operations with his usual vigour. He took Budgebudge, routed the garrison of Fort William, recovered Calcutta, stormed and sacked Hoogley. The Nabob, already disposed to make some concessions to the English, was confirmed in his pacific disposition by these proofs of their power and spirit. He accordingly made overtures to the chiefs of the invading armament, and 30 offered to restore the factory, and to give compensation to those whom he had despoiled.

Clive's profession was war; and he felt that there was something discreditable in an accommodation with Surajah Dowlah. But his power was limited. A committee, chiefly composed of servants of the Company who had fled from Calcutta, had the principal direction of affairs; and these persons were eager to be restored to their posts and compensated for their losses. The government of Ma- 40 dras, apprised that war had commenced in Europe, and apprehensive of an attack from the French, became impatient for the return of the armament. The promises of the Nabob were large, the chances of a contest doubtful; and Clive consented to treat, though he expressed his regret that things should not be concluded in so glorious a manner as he could have wished.

With this negotiation commences a new chapter in the life of Clive. Hitherto he had been merely a 50 soldier carrying into effect, with eminent ability and valour, the plans of others. Henceforth he is to be chiefly regarded as a statesman; and his military movements are to be considered as subordinate to

his political designs. That in his new capacity he displayed great ability, and obtained great success, is unquestionable. But it is also unquestionable that the transactions in which he now began to take a part have left a stain on his moral character.

We can by no means agree with Sir John Malcolm, who is obstinately resolved to see nothing but honour and integrity in the conduct of his hero. But we can as little agree with Mr. Mill, who has gone so far as to say that Clive was a man "to whom deception, when it suited his purpose, never cost a pang." Clive seems to us to have been constitutionally the very opposite of a knave, bold even to temerity, sincere even to indiscretion, hearty in friendship, open in enmity. Neither in his private life, nor in those parts of his public life in which he had to do with his countrymen, do we find any signs of a propensity to cunning. On the contrary, in all the disputes in which he was engaged as an Englishman against Englishmen, from his boxing-matches at school to those stormy altercations at the India House and in Parliament amidst which his later years were passed, his very faults were those of a high and magnanimous spirit. The truth seems to have been that he considered Oriental politics as a game in which nothing was unfair. He knew that the standard of morality among the natives of India differed widely from that established in England. He knew that he had to deal with men destitute of what in Europe is called honour, with men who would give any promise without hesitation and break any promise without shame, with men who would unscrupulously employ corruption, perjury, forgery, to compass their ends. His letters show that the great difference between Asiatic and European morality was constantly in his thoughts. He seems to have imagined, most erroneously in our opinion, that he could effect nothing against such adversaries, if he was content to be bound by ties from which they were free, if he went on telling truth, and hearing none, if he fulfilled, to his own hurt, all his engagements with confederates who never kept an engagement that was not to their advantage. Accordingly this man, in the other parts of his life an honourable English gentleman and soldier, was no sooner matched against an Indian intriguer, than he became himself an Indian intriguer, and descended, without scruple, to falsehood, to hypocritical caresses, to the substitution of documents, and to the counterfeiting of hands.

The negotiations between the English and the

6–7. **Sir John Malcolm,** whose book Macaulay is reviewing. See the introductory note.   **9. Mr. Mill,** James Mill (1773–1836), in his *The History of British India*, 1817–18.

Nabob were carried on chiefly by two agents, Mr. Watts, a servant of the Company, and a Bengalee of the name of Omichund. This Omichund had been one of the wealthiest native merchants resident at Calcutta, and had sustained great losses in consequence of the Nabob's expedition against that place. In the course of his commercial transactions, he had seen much of the English, and was peculiarly qualified to serve as a medium of communication between them and a native court. He possessed great influence with his own race, and had in large measure the Hindoo talents, quick observation, tact, dexterity, perseverance, and the Hindoo vices, servility, greediness, and treachery.

The Nabob behaved with all the faithlessness of an Indian statesman, and with all the levity of a boy whose mind had been enfeebled by power and self-indulgence. He promised, retracted, hesitated, evaded. At one time he advanced with his army in a threatening manner towards Calcutta; but when he saw the resolute front which the English presented, he fell back in alarm, and consented to make peace with them on their own terms. The treaty was no sooner concluded than he formed new designs against them. He intrigued with the French authorities at Chandernagore. He invited Bussy to march from the Deccan to the Hoogley, and to drive the English out of Bengal. All this was well known to Clive and Watson. They determined accordingly to strike a decisive blow, and to attack Chandernagore, before the force there could be strengthened by new arrivals, either from the south of India, or from Europe. Watson directed the expedition by water, Clive by land. The success of the combined movements was rapid and complete. The fort, the garrison, the artillery, the military stores, all fell into the hands of the English. Near five hundred European troops were among the prisoners.

The Nabob had feared and hated the English, even while he was still able to oppose to them their French rivals. The French were now vanquished; and he began to regard the English with still greater fear and still greater hatred. His weak and unprincipled mind oscillated between servility and insolence. One day he sent a large sum to Calcutta, as part of the compensation due for the wrongs which he had committed. The next day he sent a present of jewels to Bussy, exhorting that distinguished officer to hasten to protect Bengal "against Clive, the daring in war, on whom," says his Highness, "may all bad fortune attend." He ordered his

army to march against the English. He countermanded his orders. He tore Clive's letters. He then sent answers in the most florid language of compliment. He ordered Watts out of his presence, and threatened to impale him. He again sent for Watts, and begged pardon for the insult. In the meantime, his wretched maladministration, his folly, his dissolute manners, and his love of the lowest company, had disgusted all classes of his subjects, soldiers, traders, civil functionaries, the proud and ostentatious Mahommedans, the timid, supple, and parsimonious Hindoos. A formidable confederacy was formed against him, in which were included Roydullub, the minister of finance, Meer Jaffier, the principal commander of the troops, and Jugget Seit, the richest banker in India. The plot was confided to the English agents, and a communication was opened between the malcontents at Moorshedabad and the committee at Calcutta.

In the committee there was much hesitation; but Clive's voice was given in favour of the conspirators, and his vigour and firmness bore down all opposition. It was determined that the English should lend their powerful assistance to depose Surajah Dowlah, and to place Meer Jaffier on the throne of Bengal. In return, Meer Jaffier promised ample compensation to the Company and its servants, and a liberal donative to the army, the navy, and the committee. The odious vices of Surajah Dowlah, the wrongs which the English had suffered at his hands, the dangers to which our trade must have been exposed had he continued to reign, appear to us fully to justify the resolution of deposing him. But nothing can justify the dissimulation which Clive stooped to practise. He wrote to Surajah Dowlah in terms so affectionate that they for a time lulled that weak prince into perfect security. The same courier who carried this "soothing letter," as Clive calls it, to the Nabob, carried to Mr. Watts a letter in the following terms: "Tell Meer Jaffier to fear nothing. I will join him with five thousand men who never turned their backs. Assure him I will march night and day to his assistance, and stand by him as long as I have a man left."

It was impossible that a plot which had so many ramifications should long remain entirely concealed. Enough reached the ears of the Nabob to arouse his suspicions. But he was soon quieted by the fictions and artifices which the inventive genius of Omichund produced with miraculous readiness. All was going well; the plot was nearly ripe; when Clive learned that Omichund was likely to play false. The artful Bengalee had been promised a liberal compensation for all that he had lost at Cal-

3. **Omichund,** Amir Chand (d. 1767), was a Sikh, not a Bengali.   27. **Bussy,** the Marquis de Bussy-Castlenau, who had succeeded Dupleix as French commander.

cutta. But this would not satisfy him. His services had been great. He held the thread of the whole intrigue. By one word breathed in the ear of Surajah Dowlah, he could undo all that he had done. The lives of Watts, of Meer Jaffier, of all the conspirators, were at his mercy; and he determined to take advantage of his situation and to make his own terms. He demanded three hundred thousand pounds sterling as the price of his secrecy and of his assistance. The committee, incensed by the treachery and appalled by the danger, knew not what course to take. But Clive was more than Omichund's match in Omichund's own arts. The man, he said, was a villain. Any artifice which would defeat such knavery was justifiable. The best course would be to promise what was asked. Omichund would soon be at their mercy; and then they might punish him by withholding from him, not only the bribe which he now demanded, but also the compensation which all the other sufferers of Calcutta were to receive.

His advice was taken. But how was the wary and sagacious Hindoo to be deceived? He had demanded that an article touching his claims should be inserted in the treaty between Meer Jaffier and the English, and he would not be satisfied unless he saw it with his own eyes. Clive had an expedient ready. Two treaties were drawn up, one on white paper, the other on red, the former real, the latter fictitious. In the former Omichund's name was not mentioned; the latter, which was to be shown to him, contained a stipulation in his favour.

But another difficulty arose. Admiral Watson had scruples about signing the red treaty. Omichund's vigilance and acuteness were such that the absence of so important a name would probably awaken his suspicions. But Clive was not a man to do anything by halves. We almost blush to write it. He forged Admiral Watson's name.

All was now ready for action. Mr. Watts fled secretly from Moorshedabad. Clive put his troops in motion, and wrote to the Nabob in a tone very different from that of his previous letters. He set forth all the wrongs which the British had suffered, offered to submit the points in dispute to the arbitration of Meer Jaffier, and concluded by announcing that, as the rains were about to set in, he and his men would do themselves the honour of waiting on his Highness for an answer.

Surajah Dowlah instantly assembled his whole force, and marched to encounter the English. It had been agreed that Meer Jaffier should separate himself from the Nabob, and carry over his division to Clive. But, as the decisive moment approached, the fears of the conspirator overpowered his ambition. Clive had advanced to Cossimbuzar; the Nabob lay with a mighty power a few miles off at Plassey; and still Meer Jaffier delayed to fulfil his engagements, and returned evasive answers to the earnest remonstrances of the English general.

Clive was in a painfully anxious situation. He could place no confidence in the sincerity or in the courage of his confederate; and, whatever confidence he might place in his own military talents, and in the valour and discipline of his troops, it was no light thing to engage an army twenty times as numerous as his own. Before him lay a river over which it was easy to advance, but over which, if things went ill, not one of his little band would ever return. On this occasion, for the first and for the last time, his dauntless spirit, during a few hours, shrank from the fearful responsibility of making a decision. He called a council of war. The majority pronounced against fighting; and Clive declared his concurrence with the majority. Long afterwards, he said that he had never called but one council of war, and that, if he had taken the advice of that council, the British would never have been masters of Bengal. But scarcely had the meeting broken up when he was himself again. He retired alone under the shade of some trees, and passed near an hour there in thought. He came back determined to put everything to the hazard, and gave orders that all should be in readiness for passing the river on the morrow.

The river was passed; and, at the close of a toilsome day's march, the army, long after sunset, took up its quarters in a grove of mango-trees near Plassey, within a mile of the enemy. Clive was unable to sleep; he heard, through the whole night, the sound of drums and cymbals from the vast camp of the Nabob. It is not strange that even his stout heart should now and then have sunk, when he reflected against what odds, and for what a prize, he was in a few hours to contend.

Nor was the rest of Surajah Dowlah more peaceful. His mind, at once weak and stormy, was distracted by wild and horrible apprehensions. Appalled by the greatness and nearness of the crisis, distrusting his captains, dreading every one who approached him, dreading to be left alone, he sat gloomily in his tent, haunted, a Greek poet would have said, by the furies of those who had cursed him with their last breath in the Black Hole.

The day broke, the day which was to decide the fate of India. At sunrise the army of the Nabob, pouring through many openings of the camp, began to move towards the grove where the English lay. Forty thousand infantry, armed with firelocks, pikes, swords, bows and arrows, covered the plain. They were accompanied by fifty pieces of ordnance of the largest size, each tugged by a long team of white oxen, and each pushed on from behind by an elephant. Some smaller guns, under the direction of a few French auxiliaries, were perhaps more formidable. The cavalry were fifteen thousand, drawn, not from the effeminate population of Bengal, but from the bolder race which inhabits the northern provinces; and the practised eye of Clive could perceive that both the men and the horses were more powerful than those of the Carnatic. The force which he had to oppose to this great multitude consisted of only three thousand men. But of these nearly a thousand were English; and all were led by English officers, and trained in the English discipline. Conspicuous in the ranks of the little army were the men of the Thirty-Ninth Regiment, which still bears on its colours, amidst many honourable additions won under Wellington in Spain and Gascony, the name of Plassey, and the proud motto, *Primus in Indis*.

The battle commenced with a cannonade in which the artillery of the Nabob did scarcely any execution, while the few field-pieces of the English produced great effect. Several of the most distinguished officers in Surajah Dowlah's service fell. Disorder began to spread through his ranks. His own terror increased every moment. One of the conspirators urged on him the expediency of retreating. The insidious advice, agreeing as it did with what his own terrors suggested, was readily received. He ordered his army to fall back, and this order decided his fate. Clive snatched the moment, and ordered his troops to advance. The confused and dispirited multitude gave way before the onset of disciplined valour. No mob attacked by regular soldiers was ever more completely routed. The little band of Frenchmen, who alone ventured to confront the English, were swept down the stream of fugitives. In an hour the forces of Surajah Dowlah were dispersed, never to reassemble. Only five hundred of the vanquished were slain. But their camp, their guns, their baggage, innumerable waggons, innumerable cattle, remained in the power of the conquerors. With the loss of twenty-two soldiers killed and fifty wounded, Clive had scattered an army of near sixty thousand men, and subdued an empire larger and more populous than Great Britain.

Meer Jaffier had given no assistance to the English during the action. But as soon as he saw

13. **Carnatic,** a section of India along the eastern coast.

that the fate of the day was decided, he drew off his division of the army, and, when the battle was over, sent his congratulations to his ally. The next morning he repaired to the English quarters, not a little uneasy as to the reception which awaited him there. He gave evident signs of alarm when a guard was drawn out to receive him with the honours due to his rank. But his apprehensions were speedily removed, Clive came forward to meet him, embraced him, saluted him as Nabob of the three great provinces of Bengal, Bahar, and Orissa, listened graciously to his apologies, and advised him to march without delay to Moorshedabad.

Surajah Dowlah had fled from the field of battle with all the speed with which a fleet camel could carry him, and arrived at Moorshedabad in little more than twenty-four hours. There he called his counsellors round him. The wisest advised him to put himself into the hands of the English, from whom he had nothing worse to fear than deposition and confinement. But he attributed this suggestion to treachery. Others urged him to try the chance of war again. He approved the advice, and issued orders accordingly. But he wanted spirit to adhere even during one day to a manly resolution. He learned that Meer Jaffier had arrived, and his terrors became insupportable. Disguised in a mean dress, with a casket of jewels in his hand, he let himself down at night from a window of his palace, and, accompanied by only two attendants, embarked on the river for Patna.

In a few days Clive arrived at Moorshedabad, escorted by two hundred English soldiers and three hundred sepoys. For his residence had been assigned a palace, which was surrounded by a garden so spacious that all the troops who accompanied him could conveniently encamp within it. The ceremony of the installation of Meer Jaffier was instantly performed. Clive led the new Nabob to the seat of honour, placed him on it, presented to him, after the immemorial fashion of the East, an offering of gold, and then, turning to the natives who filled the hall, congratulated them on the good fortune which had freed them from a tyrant. He was compelled on this occasion to use the services of an interpreter; for it is remarkable that, long as he resided in India, intimately acquainted as he was with Indian politics and with the Indian character, and adored as he was by his Indian soldiery, he never learned to express himself with facility in any Indian language. He is said indeed to have been sometimes under the necessity of employing, in his intercourse with natives of India, the smattering of Portuguese which he had acquired, when a lad in Brazil.

The new sovereign was now called upon to fulfil the engagements into which he had entered with his allies. A conference was held at the house of Jugget Seit, the great banker, for the purpose of making the necessary arrangements. Omichund came thither, fully believing himself to stand high in the favour of Clive who, with dissimulation surpassing even the dissimulation of Bengal, had up to that day treated him with undiminished kindness. The white treaty was produced and read. Clive then turned to Mr. Scrafton, one of the servants of the Company, and said in English, "It is now time to undeceive Omichund." "Omichund," said Mr. Scrafton in Hindostanee, "the red treaty is a trick. You are to have nothing." Omichund fell back insensible into the arms of his attendants. He revived; but his mind was irreparably ruined. Clive, who, though little troubled by scruples of conscience in his dealings with Indian politicians, was not inhuman, seems to have been touched. He saw Omichund a few days later, spoke to him kindly, advised him to make a pilgrimage to one of the great temples of India, in the hope that change of scene might restore his health, and was even disposed, notwithstanding all that had passed, again to employ him in the public service. But, from the moment of that sudden shock, the unhappy man sank gradually into idiocy. He, who had formerly been distinguished by the strength of his understanding and the simplicity of his habits, now squandered the remains of his fortune on childish trinkets, and loved to exhibit himself dressed in rich garments, and hung with precious stones. In this abject state he languished a few months, and then died.

We should not think it necessary to offer any remarks for the purpose of directing the judgment of our readers with respect to this transaction, had not Sir John Malcolm undertaken to defend it in all its parts. He regrets, indeed, that it was necessary to employ means so liable to abuse as forgery; but he will not admit that any blame attaches to those who deceived the deceiver. He thinks that the English were not bound to keep faith with one who kept no faith with them, and that, if they had fulfilled their engagements with the wily Bengalee, so signal an example of successful treason would have produced a crowd of imitators. Now, we will not discuss this point on any rigid principles of morality. Indeed, it is quite unnecessary to do so: for, looking at the question as a question of expediency in the lowest sense of the word, and using no arguments but such as Machiavelli might have employed in his conferences with Borgia, we are convinced that Clive

52-53. Machiavelli . . . Borgia, Niccolo Machiavelli

was altogether in the wrong, and that he committed, not merely a crime, but a blunder. That honesty is the best policy is a maxim which we firmly believe to be generally correct, even with respect to the temporal interest of individuals; but with respect to societies, the rule is subject to still fewer exceptions, and that for this reason, that the life of societies is longer than the life of individuals. It is possible to mention men who have owed great worldly prosperity to breaches of private faith. But we doubt whether it be possible to mention a state which has on the whole been a gainer by a breach of public faith. The entire history of British India is an illustration of the great truth, that it is not prudent to oppose perfidy to perfidy, and that the most efficient weapon with which men can encounter falsehood is truth. During a long course of years, the English rulers of India, surrounded by allies and enemies whom no engagement could bind, have generally acted with sincerity and uprightness; and the event has proved that sincerity and uprightness are wisdom. English valour and English intelligence have done less to extend and to preserve our Oriental empire than English veracity. All that we could have gained by imitating the doublings, the evasions, the fictions, the perjuries which have been employed against us, is as nothing, when compared with what we have gained by being the one power in India on whose word reliance can be placed. No oath which superstition can devise, no hostage however precious, inspires a hundredth part of the confidence which is produced by the "yea, yea," and "nay, nay," of a British envoy. No fastness, however strong by art or nature, gives to its inmates a security like that enjoyed by the chief who, passing through the territories of powerful and deadly enemies, is armed with the British guarantee. The mightiest princes of the East can scarcely, by the offer of enormous usury, draw forth any portion of the wealth which is concealed under the hearths of their subjects. The British Government offers little more than four per cent.; and avarice hastens to bring forth tens of millions of rupees from its most secret repositories. A hostile monarch may promise mountains of gold to our sepoys, on condition that they will desert the standard of the Company. The Company promises only a moderate pension after a long service. But every sepoy knows that the promise of the Company will be kept; he knows that if he lives a hundred years

(1469-1527), author of an influential political treatise, *The Prince.* His name has become synonomous with the idea that the state is not bound by the principles of morality. He served Cesare Borgia (1476-1507), ruler of Florence.

his rice and salt are as secure as the salary of the Governor-General: and he knows that there is not another state in India which would not, in spite of the most solemn vows, leave him to die of hunger in a ditch as soon as he had ceased to be useful. The greatest advantage which a government can possess is to be the one trustworthy government in the midst of governments which nobody can trust. This advantage we enjoy in Asia. Had we acted during the last two generations on the principles which Sir John Malcolm appears to have considered as sound, had we as often as we had to deal with people like Omichund, retaliated by lying and forging, and breaking faith, after their fashion, it is our firm belief that no courage or capacity could have upheld our empire.

Sir John Malcolm admits that Clive's breach of faith could be justified only by the strongest necessity. As we think that breach of faith not only unnecessary, but most inexpedient, we need hardly say that we altogether condemn it.

Omichund was not the only victim of the revolution. Surajah Dowlah was taken a few days after his flight, and was brought before Meer Jaffier. There he flung himself on the ground in convulsions of fear, and with tears and loud cries implored the mercy which he had never shown. Meer Jaffier hesitated; but his son Meeran, a youth of seventeen, who in feebleness of brain and savageness of nature greatly resembled the wretched captive, was implacable. Surajah Dowlah was led into a secret chamber, to which in a short time the ministers of death were sent. In this act the English bore no part; and Meer Jaffier understood so much of their feelings, that he thought it necessary to apologise to them for having avenged them on their most malignant enemy.

The shower of wealth now fell copiously on the Company and its servants. A sum of eight hundred thousand pounds sterling, in coined silver, was sent down the river from Moorshedabad to Fort William. The fleet which conveyed this treasure consisted of more than a hundred boats, and performed its triumphal voyage with flags flying and music playing. Calcutta, which a few months before had been desolate, was now more prosperous than ever. Trade revived; and the signs of affluence appeared in every English house. As to Clive, there was no limit to his acquisitions but his own moderation. The treasury of Bengal was thrown open to him. There were piled up, after the usage of Indian princes, immense masses of coin, among which might not seldom be detected the florins and byzants with which, before any European ship had turned the Cape of Good Hope, the Venetians purchased the stuffs and spices of the East. Clive walked between heaps of gold and silver, crowned with rubies and diamonds, and was at liberty to help himself. He accepted between two and three hundred thousand pounds. . . .

Thomas Carlyle
1795-1881

Carlyle was the Hebrew prophet among Victorian writers; if both Ruskin and Matthew Arnold understood the social malady as well as he did (and prescribed for it more clearly), none other attained his apocalyptic splendor. Like all great writers, he owed at least as much to his style as to his ideas:

"He exhibited, in an extraordinary degree," says Bliss Perry in *Thomas Carlyle* (Bobbs-Merrill, 1915),[1] "a combination of what are known as the 'visual,' the 'audile' and the 'motor' types of imagination. If his sensitiveness to visual impressions resembles that of Dickens . . . in his nervous response to stimuli of sound he is like Walt Whitman, and in

[1] Used by special permission of The Bobbs-Merrill Company.

his motor type of imaginative energy he is another Tolstoi. Artists of this motor type think with their whole body. Their nerve centers compel them, whether they will or no, to a perpetual dynamic activity. They can not help creating a 'Private Theater under their own Hat' and turning actors in it. They write in terms of bodily sensation."

Carlyle was born, of peasant stock, in Ecclefechan, Dumfrieshire, Scotland, December 4, 1795. He rejected the dogmas of his inherited Calvinism, but he never escaped its integrity, its harshness, its respect for authority, its indifference to the fine arts and the spirit of good nature, its worship of work. Though he attended Edinburgh University from 1809 to 1814, he left without taking a degree;

he rejected the ministry, he rejected, after brief experiments, both schoolteaching and the law. Four years, from 1818 to 1822, he spent in an agonized self-searching of one of the most turbulent souls God ever gave a man; he studied mathematics, chemistry, physics, and mineralogy, but he found himself at last through the German Transcendentalists, and to make them known in England was his first self-appointed task. In 1826 he married Jane Welsh, who was quite as thin-skinned and high-spirited as he was himself, and who made him one of the most fascinating, one of the most fiercely loyal, but by no means one of the most comfortable, wives a man of letters ever had. "Mr. and Mrs. Carlyle on the whole enjoyed life together," said Tennyson, "else they would not have chaffed one another so heartily."

From 1828 to 1834 the Carlyles lived on Jane's farm at Craigenputtock, where sometimes, for three months running, not so much as a beggar came to the door. Here, among other things, Carlyle wrote his greatest book, *Sartor Resartus* (see below), and hence he removed to 24 Cheyne Row, Chelsea, London, where he continued to reside until his death, February 5, 1881.

The first great work Carlyle produced in London was *The French Revolution*, 1837 (see page 418), which established his fame, though *Sartor Resartus* had failed to do so. *Heroes and Hero-Worship* (see page 425) was the text of a series of lectures delivered in 1840. Later Carlyle studied two heroes at greater length. Mrs. Carlyle lived for years "in the valley of the shadow of Cromwell," and when her husband's book about him came out in 1845, it turned out to be *Oliver Cromwell's Letters and Speeches: with Elucidations*, rather than a complete biography. It established a favorable view of the great dictator, however, against the judgments of earlier historians, a view which has only recently been seriously questioned. *The History of Friedrich II of Prussia, called Frederick the Great*, published in six volumes between 1858 and 1865, dealt with an even more dubious hero; today it is the most neglected of all Carlyle's books. *The Life of John Sterling*, 1851—to complete the record on its biographical side—was a gracious tribute to a personal friend.

Meanwhile Carlyle had continued his direct discussion of contemporary problems, notably in *Chartism*, 1840; *Past and Present*, 1843 (see page 429); and *Latter-Day Pamphlets*, 1850.

In 1866 Carlyle experienced his greatest triumph and his greatest sorrow; while he was in Edinburgh to deliver his inaugural address as Lord Rector of the university, Mrs. Carlyle died. With her, Carlyle himself largely died; despite the homage of many great men, he lived his last years in bleak loneliness. His *Reminiscences* were posthumously published in 1881.

Carlyle's anti-Semitism, his hatred of democracy, his praise of "the beneficient whip," his adoration of the man on horseback, do not help his fame today in English-speaking countries; it was no accident that he should have championed Germany against France in 1870, and it is no accident that he should be widely read in the Third Reich. (As early as 1933, H. J. C. Grierson published a little book called *Carlyle and Hitler*, Cambridge University Press.) But later world-conditions must not be permitted to prejudice us against the vital elements in Carlyle's work. Prescriptions were never his forte; like Emerson, who was so closely connected with him, he had essentially a seminal mind. It is true that he volubly proclaimed the cult of silence through many volumes, and it is true that, while perpetually urging the value of the deed, he forgot, as Matthew Arnold, for one, never forgot, that the value of a man's doing is wholly dependent on what he does. But when all allowances are made, Carlyle is still the archenemy of Victorian materialism— "Nature is no longer dead hostile Matter, but the veil and mysterious garment of the unseen"—and in this aspect many a great Victorian marches under his banner.

from SARTOR RESARTUS

Sartor Resartus (*The Tailor Retailored*) takes its point of departure from an extended metaphor in Section 3 of Swift's *Tale of a Tub*, where God is conceived of as a tailor and the universe as a huge suit of clothes. Not only is the material world clothing, but man's body is clothing, social institutions are clothing, Time and Space themselves are clothing. This idea is developed in Books I and III. Carlyle's purpose was not to advocate either a physical or a spiritual nudism, but to teach men the necessity of differentiating between the essential and the nonessential, to establish the fundamentally spiritual character of Reality, and to bring men face to face with this Reality.

The method of development is fantastic. Part II purports to contain autobiographical fragments from the writings of Diogenes Teufelsdröckh (God-begotten Devil's Dung), Professor of Things in General at the University of Weissnichtwo (Don't-Know-Where). By presenting himself as editor, not author, Carlyle achieves almost absolute expositorial license in setting forth his own ideas and experiences.

The present reprint presents most of the three chapters

from Book II in which the great spiritual crisis of Teufels-dröckh's life is set forth. To this is added an important passage from Book III.

The editor of *Fraser's Magazine* was bold enough to serialize *Sartor* in 1833–34, but his readers were not amused. Emerson got the book published in America in 1836, but it did not appear in England until two years later.

BOOK II: Chapter 7

The Everlasting No

UNDER the strange nebulous envelopment, wherein our Professor has now shrouded himself, no doubt but his spiritual nature is nevertheless progressive, and growing: for how can the "Son of Time," in any case, stand still? We behold him, through those dim years, in a state of crisis, of transition: his mad Pilgrimings, and general solution into aimless Discontinuity, what is all this but a mad Fermentation; wherefrom, the fiercer it is, the clearer product will one day evolve itself?

Such transitions are ever full of pain: thus the Eagle when he moults is sickly; and, to attain his new beak, must harshly dash-off the old one upon rocks. What Stoicism soever our Wanderer, in his individual acts and motions, may affect, it is clear that there is a hot fever of anarchy and misery raging within; coruscations of which flash out: as, indeed, how could there be other? Have we not seen him disappointed, bemocked of Destiny, through long years? All that the young heart might desire and pray for has been denied; nay, as in the last worst instance, offered and then snatched away. Ever an "excellent Passivity"; but of useful, reasonable Activity, essential to the former as Food to Hunger, nothing granted: till at length, in this wild Pilgrimage, he must forcibly seize for himself an Activity, though useless, unreasonable. Alas, his cup of bitterness, which had been filling drop by drop, ever since that first "ruddy morning" in the Hinterschlag Gymnasium, was at the very lip; and then with that poison-drop, of the Towgood-and-Blumine business, it runs over, and even hisses over in a deluge of foam.

He himself says once, with more justice than originality: "Man is, properly speaking, based upon Hope, he has no other possession but Hope; this world of his is emphatically the Place of Hope." What, then, was our Professor's possession? We see

him, for the present, quite shut-out from Hope; looking not into the golden orient, but vaguely all round into a dim copper firmament, pregnant with earthquake and tornado.

Alas, shut-out from Hope, in a deeper sense than we yet dream of! For, as he wanders wearisomely through this world, he has now lost all tidings of another and higher. Full of religion, or at least of religiosity, as our Friend has since exhibited himself, he hides not that, in those days, he was wholly irreligious: "Doubt had darkened into Unbelief," says he; "shade after shade goes grimly over your soul, till you have the fixed, starless, Tartarean black." To such readers as have reflected, what can be called reflecting, on man's life, and happily discovered, in contradiction to much Profit-and-loss Philosophy, speculative and practical, that Soul is *not* synonymous with Stomach; who understand, therefore, in our Friend's words, "that, for man's well-being, Faith is properly the one thing needful; how, with it, Martyrs, otherwise weak, can cheerfully endure the shame and the cross; and without it, Worldlings puke-up their sick existence, by suicide, in the midst of luxury": to such it will be clear that, for a pure moral nature, the loss of his religious Belief was the loss of everything. Unhappy young man! All wounds, the crush of long-continued Destitution, the stab of false Friendship and of false Love, all wounds in thy so genial heart, would have healed again, had not its life-warmth been withdrawn. Well might he exclaim, in his wild way: "Is there no God, then; but at best an absentee God, sitting idle, ever since the first Sabbath, at the outside of his Universe, and *seeing* it go? Has the word Duty no meaning; is what we call Duty no divine Messenger and Guide, but a false earthly Fantasm, made-up of Desire and Fear, of emanations from the Gallows and from Dr. Graham's Celestial-Bed? Happiness of an approving Conscience! Did not Paul of Tarsus, whom admiring men have since named Saint, feel that *he* was 'the chief of sinners'; and Nero of Rome, jocund in spirit (*wohlgemuth*), spend much of his time in fiddling?

13. **Tartarean,** infernal. Tartarus is described in the *Iliad* as situated as far below Hades as heaven is high above the earth. **16–17. Profit-and-loss Philosophy,** Utilitarianism; see pages 377–78. **20. the one thing needful.** See Luke 10:42. **22. endure the shame and the cross.** See Hebrews 12:2. **32–34. Is there . . . go.** Eighteenth-century Deists thought of God as transcendent rather than immanent; He made the world and then went off and left it. **38–39. Dr. Graham's Celestial-Bed,** an elaborate contraption, supposed to cure sterility in married persons, invented by a quack named James Graham (1745–1794). **41–42. the chief of sinners.** See 1 Timothy 1:15. **42–43. Nero . . . fiddling,** according to Tacitus and Suetonius. He is popularly believed to have "fiddled" while Rome burned.

16–17. **Son of Time,** a phrase from Goethe's poem *"Gott, Gemüth, und Welt."* 41–42. **Hinterschlag,** Smite-Behind. **Gymnasium,** the German high school. Carlyle is thinking of an experience of his own at Annan Academy; the passage refers to Book II, chap. 3.

Foolish Word-monger and Motive-grinder, who in thy Logic-mill hast an earthly mechanism for the Godlike itself, and wouldst fain grind me out Virtue from the husks of Pleasure,—I tell thee, Nay! To the unregenerate Prometheus Vinctus of a man, it is ever the bitterest aggravation of his wretchedness that he is conscious of Virtue, that he feels himself the victim not of suffering only, but of injustice. What then? Is the heroic inspiration we name Virtue but some Passion; some bubble of the blood, bubbling in the direction others *profit* by? I know not: only this I know, If what thou namest Happiness be our true aim, then are we all astray. With Stupidity and sound Digestion man may front much. But what, in these dull unimaginative days, are the terrors of Conscience to the diseases of the Liver! Not on Morality, but on Cookery, let us build our stronghold: there brandishing our frying-pan, as censer, let us offer sweet incense to the Devil, and live at ease on the fat things *he* has provided for his Elect!"

Thus has the bewildered Wanderer to stand, as so many have done, shouting question after question into the Sibyl-cave of Destiny, and receive no Answer but an Echo. It is all a grim Desert, this once-fair world of his; wherein is heard only the howling of wild-beasts, or the shrieks of despairing, hate-filled men; and no Pillar of Cloud by day, and no Pillar of Fire by night, any longer guides the Pilgrim. To such length has the spirit of Inquiry carried him. "But what boots it (*was thut's*)?" cries he: "it is but the common lot in this era. Not having come to spiritual majority prior to the *Siècle de Louis Quinze*, and not being born purely a Loghead (*Dummkopf*), thou hast no other outlook. The whole world is, like thee, sold to Unbelief; their old Temples of the Godhead, which for long have not been rainproof, crumble down; and men ask now: Where is the Godhead; our eyes never saw him?"

Pitiful enough were it, for all these wild utterances, to call our Diogenes wicked. Unprofitable servants as we all are, perhaps at no era of his life was he more decisively the Servant of Goodness, the Servant of God, than even now when doubting God's existence. "One circumstance I note," says

he: "after all the nameless woe that Inquiry, which for me, what it is not always, was genuine Love of Truth, had wrought me, I nevertheless still loved Truth, and would bate no jot of my allegiance to her. 'Truth!' I cried, 'though the Heavens crush me for following her: no Falsehood! though a whole celestial Lubberland were the price of Apostasy.' In conduct it was the same. Had a divine Messenger from the clouds, or miraculous Handwriting on the wall, convincingly proclaimed to me *This thou shalt do*, with what passionate readiness, as I often thought, would I have done it, had it been leaping into the infernal Fire. Thus, in spite of all Motive-grinders, and Mechanical Profit-and-Loss Philosophies, with the sick ophthalmia and hallucination they had brought on, was the Infinite nature of Duty still dimly present to me: living without God in the world, of God's light I was not utterly bereft; if my as yet sealed eyes, with their unspeakable longing, could nowhere see Him, nevertheless in my heart He was present, and His heaven-written Law still stood legible and sacred there."

Meanwhile, under all these tribulations, and temporal and spiritual destitutions, what must the Wanderer, in his silent soul, have endured! "The painfullest feeling," writes he, "is that of your own Feebleness (*Unkraft*); ever, as the English Milton says, to be weak is the true misery. And yet of your Strength there is and can be no clear feeling, save by what you have prospered in, by what you have done. Between vague wavering Capability and fixed indubitable Performance, what a difference! A certain inarticulate Self-consciousness dwells dimly in us; which only our Works can render articulate and decisively discernible. Our Works are the mirror wherein the spirit first sees its natural lineaments. Hence, too, the folly of that impossible Precept, *Know thyself*; till it be translated into this partially possible one, *Know what thou canst work-at*.

"But for me, so strangely unprosperous had I been, the net-result of my Workings amounted as yet simply to—Nothing. How then could I believe in my Strength, when there was as yet no mirror to see it in? Ever did this agitating, yet, as I now perceive, quite frivolous question, remain to me insoluble: Hast thou a certain Faculty, a certain Worth, such even as the most have not; or art thou the completest Dullard of these modern times? Alas! the fearful Unbelief is unbelief in yourself; and how could I believe? Had not my first, last Faith in

5. Prometheus Vinctus, a drama by Aeschylus. Because he stole fire from heaven for men, Prometheus was chained to a rock in the Caucasus, with a vulture gnawing his vitals. **21. his Elect,** who, according to the Calvinistic theology by which Carlyle was deeply influenced, and against which he rebelled, have been foreordained to salvation. **23–24. shouting . . . Destiny.** See *Aeneid*, Book VI, ll. 36 ff. **28–29. Pillar of Cloud . . . by night.** See Exodus 13:21–22. **33–34. Siècle de Louis Quinze,** Voltaire's *Précis du siècle de Louis XV* (*The Age of Louis XV*), which Carlyle disliked. **41–42. Unprofitable servants . . . are.** See Luke 17:10.

7. Lubberland, land of sluggards. **9–10. miraculous . . . wall,** as in Daniel 5:5–28. **17–18. living . . . world.** See Ephesians 2:12. **27–28. as the English . . . misery.** See *Paradise Lost*, Book I, ll. 157 ff. **38. Know thyself,** the motto on the temple at Delphi.

myself, when even to me the Heavens seemed laid open, and I dared to love, been all-too cruelly belied? The speculative Mystery of Life grew ever more mysterious to me: neither in the practical Mystery had I made the slightest progress, but been everywhere buffeted, foiled, and contemptuously cast-out. A feeble unit in the middle of a threatening Infinitude, I seemed to have nothing given me but eyes, whereby to discern my own wretchedness. Invisible yet impenetrable walls, as of Enchant- 10 ment, divided me from all living: was there, in the wide world, any true bosom I could press trustfully to mine? O Heaven, No, there was none! I kept a lock upon my lips: why should I speak much with that shifting variety of so-called Friends, in whose withered, vain and too-hungry souls Friendship was but an incredible tradition? In such cases, your resource is to talk little, and that little mostly from the Newspapers. Now when I look back, it was a strange isolation I then lived in. The men and 20 women around me, even speaking with me, were but Figures; I had, practically, forgotten that they were alive, that they were not merely automatic. In midst of their crowded streets and assemblages, I walked solitary; and (except as it was my own heart, not another's, that I kept devouring) savage also, as the tiger in his jungle. Some comfort it would have been, could I, like a Faust, have fancied myself tempted and tormented of the Devil; for a Hell, as I imagine, without Life, though only diabolic 30 Life, were more frightful: but in our age of Downpulling and Disbelief, the very Devil has been pulled down, you cannot so much as believe in a Devil. To me the Universe was all void of Life, of Purpose, of Volition, even of Hostility: it was one huge, dead, immeasurable Steam-engine, rolling on, in its dead indifference, to grind me limb from limb. O, the vast, gloomy, solitary Golgotha, and Mill of Death! Why was the Living banished thither companionless, conscious? Why, if there is no Devil; 40 nay, unless the Devil is your God?"

A prey incessantly to such corrosions, might not, moreover, as the worst aggravation to them, the iron constitution even of a Teufelsdröckh threaten to fail? We conjecture that he has known sickness; and, in spite of his locomotive habits, perhaps sickness of the chronic sort. Hear this, for example: "How beautiful to die of broken-heart, on Paper!

28–29. like a Faust . . . Devil. In the old German legend, which reached its apogee in Goethe's *Faust* (1808, 1832), Faust sold his soul to the Devil for a life of pleasure of the senses.   38. Golgotha, the Place of Skulls, where Jesus was crucified.   46–47. perhaps . . . sort, an autobiographical reference to Carlyle's own dyspepsia.   48. How beautiful . . . on Paper! Like the romantic poets—Byron, or Goethe in *Wilhelm Meister*.

Quite another thing in practice; every window of your Feeling, even of your Intellect, as it were, begrimed and mud-bespattered, so that no pure ray can enter; a whole Drugshop in your inwards; the fordone soul drowning slowly in quagmires of Disgust!"

Putting all which external and internal miseries together, may we not find in the following sentences, quite in our Professor's still vein, signifi- 10 cance enough? "From Suicide a certain aftershine (*Nachschein*) of Christianity withheld me: perhaps also a certain indolence of character; for, was not that a remedy I had at any time within reach? Often, however, was there a question present to me: Should some one now, at the turning of that corner, blow thee suddenly out of Space, into the other World, or other No-World, by pistol-shot,— how were it? On which ground, too, I have often, in sea-storms and sieged cities and other death- 20 scenes, exhibited an imperturbability, which passed, falsely enough, for courage.

"So had it lasted," concludes the Wanderer, "so had it lasted, as in bitter protracted Death-agony, through long years. The heart within me, unvisited by any heavenly dewdrop, was smouldering in sulphurous, slow-consuming fire. Almost since earliest memory I had shed no tear; or once only when I, murmuring half-audibly, recited Faust's Deathsong, that wild *Selig der den er im Siegesglanze* 30 *findet* (Happy whom *he* finds in Battle's splendour), and thought that of this last Friend even I was not forsaken, that Destiny itself could not doom me not to die. Having no hope, neither had I any definite fear, were it of Man or of Devil: nay, I often felt as if it might be solacing, could the Arch-Devil himself, though in Tartarean terrors, but rise to me, that I might tell him a little of my mind. And yet, strangely enough, I lived in a continual indefinite, pining fear; tremulous, pusillanimous, apprehen- 40 sive of I knew not what: it seemed as if all things in the Heavens above and the Earth beneath would hurt me; as if the Heavens and the Earth were but boundless jaws of a devouring monster, wherein I, palpitating, waited to be devoured.

"Full of such humour, and perhaps the miserablest man in the whole French Capital or Suburbs, was I, one sultry Dogday, after much perambulation, toiling along the dirty little *Rue Saint-Thomas de l'Enfer*, among civic rubbish enough, in a close

10–13. From Suicide . . . within reach. For Carlyle's own experience, see his *Journal*, December 31, 1823.   29–30. Selig . . . splendour, inaccurately quoted from Goethe's *Faust*, Part I, sc. 4, ll. 1572–76.   48–49. Rue Saint-Thomas de l'Enfer, St.-Thomas-of-Hell Street. Carlyle had the experience described in Leith Walk, Edinburgh, in June, 1821.

atmosphere, and over pavements hot as Nebuchadnezzar's Furnace; whereby doubtless my spirits
were little cheered; when, all at once, there rose a
Thought in me, and I asked myself: 'What *art* thou
afraid of? Wherefore, like a coward, dost thou forever pip and whimper, and go cowering and trembling? Despicable biped! what is the sum-total of
the worst that lies before thee? Death? Well, Death;
and say the pangs of Tophet too, and all that the
Devil and Man may, will or can do against thee!
Hast thou not a heart; canst thou not suffer whatsoever it be; and, as a Child of Freedom, though outcast, trample Tophet itself under thy feet, while it
consumes thee? Let it come, then; I will meet it
and defy it!' And as I so thought, there rushed like
a stream of fire over my whole soul; and I shook
base Fear away from me forever. I was strong, of
unknown strength; a spirit, almost a god. Ever
from that time, the temper of my misery was
changed: not Fear or whining Sorrow was it, but
Indignation and grim fire-eyed Defiance.

"Thus had the Everlasting No (*das ewige Nein*)
pealed authoritatively through all the recesses of
my Being, of my Me; and then was it that my
whole Me stood up, in native God-created majesty,
and with emphasis recorded its Protest. Such a
Protest, the most important transaction in Life,
may that same Indignation and Defiance, in a psychological point of view, be fitly called. The Everlasting No had said: 'Behold, thou art fatherless,
outcast, and the Universe is mine (the Devil's)'; to
which my whole Me now made answer: '*I* am not
thine, but Free, and forever hate thee!'

"It is from this hour that I incline to date my
Spiritual New-birth, or Baphometic Fire-baptism;
perhaps I directly thereupon began to be a Man.''

from Chapter 8

Centre of Indifference

Though, after this "Baphometic Fire-baptism"
of his, our Wanderer signifies that his Unrest was
but increased; as, indeed, "Indignation and Defiance," especially against things in general, are not
the most peaceable inmates; yet can the Psychologist surmise that it was no longer a quite hopeless
Unrest; that henceforth it had at least a fixed

centre to revolve round. For the fire-baptised soul,
long so scathed and thunder-riven, here feels its
own Freedom, which feeling is its Baphometic Baptism: the citadel of its whole kingdom it has thus
gained by assault, and will keep inexpugnable; out-
wards from which the remaining dominions, not
indeed without hard battling, will doubtless by
degrees be conquered and pacificated. Under
another figure, we might say, if in that great moment, in the *Rue Saint-Thomas de l'Enfer*, the old
inward Satanic School was not yet thrown out of
doors, it received peremptory judicial notice to
quit;—whereby, for the rest, its howl-chantings,
Ernulphus-cursings, and rebellious gnashings of
teeth, might, in the meanwhile, become only the
more tumultuous, and difficult to keep secret.

Accordingly, if we scrutinise these Pilgrimings
well, there is perhaps discernible henceforth a certain incipient method in their madness. Not wholly
as a Spectre does Teufelsdröckh now storm through
the world; at worst as a spectre-fighting Man, nay
who will one day be a Spectre-queller. If pilgriming
restlessly to so many "Saints' Wells," and ever
without quenching of his thirst, he nevertheless
finds little secular wells, whereby from time to time
some alleviation is ministered. In a word, he is now,
if not ceasing, yet intermitting to "eat his own
heart"; and clutches round him outwardly on the
Not-Me for wholesomer food. Does not the following glimpse exhibit him in a much more natural
state?

"Towns also and Cities, especially the ancient, I
failed not to look upon with interest. How beautiful to see thereby, as through a long vista, into the
remote Time; to have, as it were, an actual section
of almost the earliest Past brought safe into the
Present, and set before your eyes! There, in that
old City, was a live ember of Culinary Fire put
down, say only two thousand years ago; and there,
burning more or less triumphantly, with such fuel
as the region yielded, it has burnt, and still burns,
and thou thyself seest the very smoke thereof. Ah!
and the far more mysterious live ember of Vital
Fire was then also put down there; and still miraculously burns and spreads; and the smoke and ashes
thereof (in these Judgment-Halls and Church-
yards), and its bellows-engines (in these Churches),
thou still seest; and its flame, looking out from

1–2. Nebuchadnezzar's Furnace. See Daniel 3. 9. Tophet, an Old Testament word of uncertain etymology, indicating originally a place where human sacrifices were
performed, later used loosely (as here) for hell. 35. Baphometic, from Baphomet, a corruption of the word *Mahomet*, an idol or symbol which the Templars were accused
of worshiping. 41. Centre of Indifference, the point midway between the two extremes of the magnet.

14. Ernulphus-cursings. The curse of Ernulphus (1040–
1124), Bishop of Rochester, is one of the most elaborate on
record. It may be read in Sterne's *Tristram Shandy*, Vol. 3,
chap. 11. 18–19. a certain . . . madness. See *Hamlet*,
Act II, sc. 2, ll. 211–12. 28–29. the Not-Me, a philosophical term for the objective world, existing outside one's
own personality.

every kind countenance, and every hateful one, still warms thee or scorches thee.

"Of Man's Activity and Attainment the chief results are aeriform, mystic, and preserved in Tradition only: such are his Forms of Government, with the Authority they rest on; his Customs, or Fashions both of Cloth-habits and of Soul-habits; much more his collective stock of Handicrafts, the whole Faculty he has acquired of manipulating Nature: all these things, as indispensable and price- 10 less as they are, cannot in any way be fixed under lock and key, but must flit, spirit-like, on impalpable vehicles, from Father to Son; if you demand sight of them, they are nowhere to be met with. Visible Ploughmen and Hammermen there have been, ever from Cain and Tubalcain downwards: but where does your accumulated Agricultural, Metallurgic, and other Manufacturing SKILL lie warehoused? It transmits itself on the atmospheric air, on the sun's rays (by Hearing and by Vision); 20 it is a thing aeriform, impalpable, of quite spiritual sort. In like manner, ask me not, Where are the LAWS; where is the GOVERNMENT? In vain wilt thou go to Schönbrunn, to Downing Street, to the Palais Bourbon: thou findest nothing there but brick or stone houses, and some bundles of Papers tied with tape. Where, then, is that same cunningly-devised almighty GOVERNMENT of theirs to be laid hands on? Everywhere, yet nowhere: seen only in its works, this too is a thing aeriform, invisible; or 30 if you will, mystic and miraculous. So spiritual (*geistig*) is our whole daily Life: all that we do springs out of Mystery, Spirit, invisible Force; only like a little Cloud-image, or Armida's Palace, air-built, does the Actual body itself forth from the great mystic Deep.

"Visible and tangible products of the Past, again, I reckon-up to the extent of three: Cities, with their Cabinets and Arsenals; then tilled Fields, to either or to both of which divisions Roads with their 40 Bridges may belong; and thirdly—Books. In which third truly, the last invented, lies a worth far surpassing that of the two others. Wondrous indeed is the virtue of a true Book. Not like a dead city of stones, yearly crumbling, yearly needing repair; more like a tilled field, but then a spiritual field: like a spiritual tree, let me rather say, it stands from year to year, and from age to age (we have Books that already number some hundred-and-fifty human ages); and yearly comes its new produce of 50 leaves (Commentaries, Deductions, Philosophical, Political Systems; or were it only Sermons, Pamphlets, Journalistic Essays), every one of which is talismanic and thaumaturgic, for it can persuade men. O thou who art able to write a Book, which once in the two centuries or oftener there is a man gifted to do, envy not him whom they name City-builder, and inexpressibly pity him whom they name Conqueror or City-burner! Thou too art a Conqueror and Victor: but of the true sort, namely over the Devil: thou too hast built what will outlast all marble and metal, and be a wonder-bringing City of the Mind, a Temple and Seminary and Prophetic Mount, whereto all kindreds of the Earth will pilgrim.—Fool! why journeyest thou wearisomely, in thy antiquarian fervour, to gaze on the stone pyramids of Geeza, or the clay ones of Sacchara? These stand there, as I can tell thee, idle and inert, looking over the Desert, foolishly enough, for the last three-thousand years: but canst thou not open thy Hebrew BIBLE, then, or even Luther's Version thereof?"

No less satisfactory is his sudden appearance not in Battle, yet on some Battle-field; which, we soon gather, must be that of Wagram; so that here, for once, is a certain approximation to distinctness of date. Omitting much, let us impart what follows:

"Horrible enough! A whole Marchfeld strewed with shell-splinters, cannon-shot, ruined tumbrils, and dead men and horses; stragglers still remaining not so much as buried. And those red mould heaps: ay, there lie the Shells of Men, out of which all the Life and Virtue has been blown; and now are they swept together, and crammed-down out of sight, like blown Egg-shells!—Did Nature, when she bade the Donau bring down his mould-cargoes from the Carinthian and Carpathian Heights, and spread them out here into the softest, richest level,—intend thee, O Marchfeld, for a corn-bearing Nursery, whereon her children might be nursed; or for a Cockpit, wherein they might the more commodiously be throttled and tattered? Were thy three broad Highways, meeting here from the ends of Europe, made for Ammunition-wagons, then? Were thy Wagrams and Stillfrieds but so many ready-

16. **Cain and Tubalcain.** See Genesis 4:19–22. 24–25. **Schönbrunn . . . Downing Street . . . Palais Bourbon,** centers of government in Vienna, London, Paris. 34. **Armida's Palace,** in Tasso's *Jerusalem Delivered,* 1580.

17–18. **Geeza . . . Sacchara,** Ghizeh, Sakkara, near Cairo. 21–22. **Luther's Version,** a famous and influential translation of the Bible into German (1534–35) by Martin Luther. 25. **Wagram,** a village near Vienna where Napoleon defeated the Austrians, July 5–6, 1809. 28. **Marchfeld,** the plain in the midst of which Wagram lies; here, at Stillfried, Ottokar II, King of Bohemia, defeated the Hungarians in 1260, and was himself defeated and slain by Rodolf of Hapsburg in 1278; here Napoleon won the victory alluded to in the last note. 36. **Donau,** Danube.

built Case-mates, wherein the house of Hapsburg might batter with artillery, and with artillery be battered? König Ottokar, amid yonder hillocks, dies under Rodolf's truncheon; here Kaiser Franz falls a-swoon under Napoleon's: within which five centuries, to omit the others, how has thy breast, fair Plain, been defaced and defiled! The greensward is torn-up and trampled-down; man's fond care of it, his fruit-trees, hedgerow, and pleasant dwellings, blown-away with gunpowder; and the kind seedfield lies a desolate, hideous Place of Sculls.—Nevertheless, Nature is at work; neither shall these Powder-Devilkins with their utmost devilry gainsay her: but all that gore and carnage will be shrouded-in, absorbed into manure; and next year the Marchfeld will be green, nay greener. Thrifty unwearied Nature, ever out of our great waste educing some little profit of thy own,—how dost thou, from the very carcass of the Killer, bring Life for the Living!

"What, speaking in quite unofficial language, is the net-purport and upshot of war? To my own knowledge, for example, there dwell and toil, in the British village of Dumdrudge, usually some five-hundred souls. From these, by certain 'Natural Enemies' of the French, there are successively selected, during the French war, say thirty able-bodied men: Dumdrudge, at her own expense, has suckled and nursed them: she has, not without difficulty and sorrow, fed them up to manhood, and even trained them to crafts, so that one can weave, another build, another hammer, and the weakest can stand under thirty stone avoirdupois. Nevertheless, amid much weeping and swearing, they are selected; all dressed in red; and shipped away, at the public charges, some two-thousand miles, or say only to the south of Spain; and fed there till wanted. And now to that same spot, in the south of Spain, are thirty similar French artisans, from a French Dumdrudge, in like manner wending: till at length, after infinite effort, the two parties come into actual juxtaposition; and Thirty stands fronting Thirty, each with a gun in his hand. Straightway the word 'Fire!' is given: and they blow the souls out of one another; and in place of sixty brisk useful craftsmen, the world has sixty dead carcasses,

which it must bury, and anew shed tears for. Had these men any quarrel? Busy as the Devil is, not the smallest! They lived far enough apart; were the entirest strangers; nay, in so wide a Universe, there was even, unconsciously, by Commerce, some mutual helpfulness between them. How then? Simpleton! their Governors had fallen-out; and, instead of shooting one another, had the cunning to make these poor blockheads shoot.—Alas, so is it in Deutschland, and hitherto in all other lands; still as of old, 'what devilry soever Kings do, the Greeks must pay the piper!'—In that fiction of the English Smollet, it is true, the final Cessation of War is perhaps prophetically shadowed forth; where the two Natural Enemies, in person, take each a Tobacco-pipe, filled with Brimstone; light the same, and smoke in one another's faces, till the weaker gives in: but from such predicted Peace-Era, what blood-filled trenches, and contentious centuries, may still divide us!"

Thus can the Professor, at least in lucid intervals, look away from his own sorrows, over the many-coloured world, and pertinently enough note what is passing there. . . .

But amid these specialties, let us not forget the great generality, which is our chief quest here: How prospered the inner man of Teufelsdröckh under so much outward shifting? Does Legion still lurk in him, though repressed; or has he exorcised that Devil's Brood? We can answer that the symptoms continue promising. Experience is the grand spiritual Doctor; and with him Teufelsdröckh has now been long a patient, swallowing many a bitter bolus. Unless our poor Friend belong to the numerous class of Incurables, which seems not likely, some cure will doubtless be effected. We should rather say that Legion, or the Satanic Scheol, was now pretty well extirpated and cast out, but next to nothing introduced in its room; whereby the heart remains, for the while, in a quiet but no comfortable state.

"At length, after so much roasting," thus writes our Autobiographer, "I was what you might name calcined. Pray only that it be not rather, as is the more frequent issue, reduced to a *caput-mortuum*! But in any case, by mere dint of practice, I had grown familiar with many things. Wretchedness was still wretched; but I could now partly see

1. house of Hapsburg, one of the great royal families of Europe, embracing many Holy Roman Emperors, rulers of Spain from 1516 to 1700, rulers of Austria from 1276 to 1918. 4. Kaiser Franz, Francis I of Austria, who ruled from 1792 to 1835. 19-20. from the very . . . Living. Carlyle may have been thinking of Samson's experience, Judges 14. 24. Dumdrudge, a coined name intended to suggest "dumb drudgery." 25-26. 'Natural Enemies,' a term applied to the French by the English during the Napoleonic Wars.

10. Deutschland, Germany. 11-12. what devilry . . . the piper. See Horace, *Epistles*, Book I, 2, 1. 14. 12-13. that fiction . . . Smollet, *The Adventures of Ferdinand Count Fathom* by Tobias Smollett (1721-1771). 29. Legion. See Mark 5:9. 46. caput-mortuum, death's-head, worthless residue.

through it, and despise it. Which highest mortal, in this inane Existence, had I not found a Shadow-hunter, or Shadow-hunted; and, when I looked through his brave garnitures, miserable enough? Thy wishes have all been sniffed aside, thought I: but what, had they even been all granted! Did not the Boy Alexander weep because he had not two Planets to conquer; or a whole Solar System; or after that, a whole Universe? *Ach Gott*, when I gazed into these Stars, have they not looked down on me as if with pity, from their serene spaces; like Eyes glistening with heavenly tears over the little lot of man! Thousands of human generations, all as noisy as our own, have been swallowed-up of Time, and there remains no wreck of them any more; and Arcturus and Orion and Sirius and the Pleiades are still shining in their courses, clear and young, as when the Shepherd first noted them in the plain of Shinar. Pshaw! what is this paltry little Dog-cage of an Earth; what art thou that sittest whining there? Thou art still Nothing, Nobody: true; but who, then, is Something, Somebody? For thee the Family of Man has no use; it rejects thee; thou art wholly as a dissevered limb: so be it; perhaps it is better so!"

Too-heavy-laden Teufelsdröckh! Yet surely his bands are loosening; one day he will hurl the burden far from him, and bound forth free and with a second youth.

"This," says our Professor, "was the CENTRE OF INDIFFERENCE I had now reached; through which whoso travels from the Negative Pole to the Positive must necessarily pass."

from Chapter 9

The Everlasting Yea

"Temptations in the Wilderness!" exclaims Teufelsdröckh: "Have we not all to be tried with such? Not so easily can the old Adam, lodged in us by birth, be dispossessed. Our Life is compassed round with Necessity; yet is the meaning of Life itself no other than Freedom, than Voluntary Force: thus have we a warfare; in the beginning, especially, a hard-fought battle. For the God-given mandate, *Work thou in Welldoing*, lies mysteriously written, in Promethean Prophetic Characters, in our hearts;

6-8. Did not . . . conquer, Alexander the Great (356–323 B.C.). 18-19. the plain of Shinar, where the Tower of Babel was built; see Genesis 11:1–9. 39. Temptations in the Wilderness. For Jesus' temptation in the wilderness, to which Carlyle refers in this paragraph and the next, see Matthew 4 and Luke 4. 41. the old Adam, man's sinful nature; see Colossians 3:9. 47. Work thou in Welldoing. See 2 Thessalonians 3:13.

and leaves us no rest, night or day, till it be deciphered and obeyed; till it burn forth, in our conduct, a visible, acted Gospel of Freedom. And as the clay-given mandate, *Eat thou and be filled*, at the same time persuasively proclaims itself through every nerve,—must not there be a confusion, a contest, before the better Influence can become the upper?

"To me nothing seems more natural than that the Son of Man, when such God-given mandate first prophetically stirs within him, and the Clay must now be vanquished, or vanquish,—should be carried of the spirit into grim Solitudes, and there fronting the Tempter do grimmest battle with him; defiantly setting him at naught, till he yield and fly. Name it as we choose: with or without visible Devil, whether in the natural Desert of rocks and sands, or in the populous moral Desert of selfishness and baseness,—to such Temptation are we all called. Unhappy if we are not! Unhappy if we are but Half-men, in whom that divine handwriting has never blazed forth, all-subduing, in true sun-splendour; but quivers dubiously amid meaner lights: or smoulders, in dull pain, in darkness, under earthly vapours!—Our Wilderness is the wide World in an Atheistic Century; our Forty Days are long years of suffering and fasting: nevertheless, to these also comes an end. Yes, to me also was given, if not Victory, yet the consciousness of Battle, and the resolve to persevere therein while life or faculty is left. To me also, entangled in the enchanted forests, demon-peopled, doleful of sight and of sound, it was given, after weariest wanderings, to work out my way into the higher sunlit slopes—of that Mountain which has no summit, or whose summit is in Heaven only!" . . .

So that, for Teufelsdröckh also, there has been a "glorious revolution": these mad shadow-hunting and shadow-hunted Pilgrimings of his were but some purifying "Temptation in the Wilderness," before his Apostolic work (such as it was) could begin; which Temptation is now happily over, and the Devil once more worsted! Was "that high moment in the *Rue de l'Enfer*," then, properly the turning-point of the battle; when the Fiend said, *Worship me or be torn in shreds*; and was answered valiantly with an *Apage Satana?*—Singular Teufelsdröckh, would thou hadst told thy singular story in plain words! But it is fruitless to look there, in those Paper-bags, for such. Nothing but innuendoes,

48. Apage Satana, Get thee hence, Satan! See Matthew 4:10; Luke 4:8. 51. Paper-bags, into which Teufelsdröckh's manuscripts were alleged to have been thrust.

figurative crotchets: a typical Shadow, fitfully wavering, prophetico-satiric; no clear logical Picture. "How paint to the sensual eye," asks he once, "what passes in the Holy-of-Holies of Man's Soul; in what words, known to these profane times, speak even afar-off of the unspeakable?" We ask in turn: Why perplex these times, profane as they are, with needless obscurity, by omission and by commission? Not mystical only is our Professor, but whimsical; and involves himself, now more than ever in eye-bewildering *chiaroscuro.* Successive glimpses, here faithfully imparted, our more gifted readers must endeavour to combine for their own behoof.

He says: "The hot Harmattan wind had raged itself out; its howl went silent within me; and the long-deafened soul could now hear. I paused in my wild wanderings; and sat me down to wait, and consider; for it was as if the hour of change drew nigh. I seemed to surrender, to renounce utterly, and say: Fly, then, false shadows of Hope; I will chase you no more, I will believe you no more. And ye too, haggard spectres of Fear, I care not for you; ye too are all shadows and a lie. Let me rest here: for I am way-weary and life-weary; I will rest here, were it but to die: to die or to live is alike to me; alike insignificant."—And again: "Here, then, as I lay in that CENTRE OF INDIFFERENCE; cast, doubtless by benignant upper Influence, into a healing sleep, the heavy dreams rolled gradually away, and I awoke to a new Heaven and a new Earth. The first preliminary moral Act, Annihilation of Self (*Selbsttödtung*), had been happily accomplished; and my mind's eyes were now unsealed, and its hands ungyved."

Might we not also conjecture that the following passage refers to his Locality, during this same "healing sleep"; that his Pilgrim-staff lies cast aside here, on "the high table-land"; and indeed that the repose is already taking wholesome effect on him? If it were not that the tone, in some parts, has more of riancy, even of levity, than we could have expected! However, in Teufelsdröckh, there is always the strangest Dualism: light dancing, with guitar-music, will be going on in the fore-court, while by fits from within comes the faint whimpering of woe and wail. We transcribe the piece entire!

"Beautiful it was to sit there, as in my skyey Tent, musing and meditating; on the high table-land, in front of the Mountains; over me, as roof, the azure Dome, and around me, for walls, four azure-flowing curtains,—namely, of the Four azure winds, on

whose bottom-fringes also I have seen gilding. And then to fancy the fair Castles that stood sheltered in these Mountain hollows; with their green flower-lawns, and white dames and damosels, lovely enough: or better still, the straw-roofed Cottages, wherein stood many a Mother baking bread, with her children round her:—all hidden and protectingly folded-up in the valley-folds; yet there and alive, as sure as if I beheld them. Or to see, as well as fancy, the nine Towns and Villages, that lay round my mountain-seat, which, in still weather, were wont to speak to me (by their steeple-bells) with metal tongue; and, in almost all weather, proclaimed their vitality by repeated Smoke-clouds; whereon, as on a culinary horologe, I might read the hour of the day. For it was the smoke of cookery, as kind housewives at morning, midday, eventide, were boiling their husbands' kettles; and ever a blue pillar rose up into the air, successively or simultaneously, from each of the nine, saying, as plainly as smoke could say: Such and such a meal is getting ready here. Not uninteresting! For you have the whole Borough, with all its love-makings and scandal-mongeries, contentions and contentments, as in miniature, and could cover it all with your hat.— If, in my wide Wayfarings, I had learned to look into the business of the World in its details, here perhaps was the place for combining it into general propositions, and deducing inferences therefrom.

"Often also could I see the black Tempest marching in anger through the Distance: round some Schreckhorn, as yet grim-blue, would the eddying vapour gather, and there tumultuously eddy, and flow down like a mad witch's hair; till, after a space, it vanished, and, in the clear sunbeam, your Schreckhorn stood smiling grim-white, for the vapour had held snow. How thou fermentest and elaboratest, in thy great fermenting-vat and laboratory of an Atmosphere, of a World, O Nature!— Or what is Nature? Ha! why do I not name thee GOD? Art not thou the 'Living Garment of God'? O Heavens, is it, in very deed, HE, then, that ever speaks through thee; that lives and loves in thee, that lives and loves in me?

"Fore-shadows, call them rather fore-splendours, of that Truth, and Beginning of Truths, fell mysteriously over my soul. Sweeter than Dayspring to the Shipwrecked in Nova Zembla; ah, like the mother's voice to her little child that strays bewil-

14. **Harmattan wind,** a wind which blows from the interior of Africa to the Atlantic coast. **30. new Heaven and a new Earth.** See Revelation 21:1.

32. Schreckhorn, Peak of Terror. Several in the Bernese Alps are so named. **41. 'Living Garment of God.'** See Goethe's *Faust,* Part I, sc. 1, ll. 501-09. **48. Nova Zembla,** an arctic archipelago, separating the Kara and Barents seas. Carlyle refers to an ill-starred Dutch expedition thither in May, 1596.

dered, weeping, in unknown tumults; like soft streamings of celestial music to my too-exasperated heart, came that Evangel. The Universe is not dead and demoniacal, a charnel-house with spectres; but godlike, and my Father's!

"With other eyes, too, could I now look upon my fellow man; with an infinite Love, an infinite Pity. Poor, wandering, wayward man! Art thou not tired, and beaten with stripes, even as I am? Ever, whether thou bear the royal mantle or the beggar's gabardine, art thou not so weary, so heavy-laden; and thy Bed of Rest is but a Grave. O my Brother, my Brother, why cannot I shelter thee in my bosom, and wipe away all tears from thy eyes! Truly, the din of many-voiced Life, which, in this solitude, with the mind's organ, I could hear, was no longer a maddening discord, but a melting one; like inarticulate cries, and sobbings of a dumb creature, which in the ear of Heaven are prayers. The poor Earth, with her poor joys, was now my needy Mother, not my cruel Stepdame; man, with his so mad Wants and so mean Endeavours, had become the dearer to me; and even for his sufferings and his sins, I now first named him Brother. Thus I was standing in the porch of that 'Sanctuary of Sorrow'; by strange, steep ways had I too been guided thither; and ere long its sacred gates would open, and the 'Divine Depth of Sorrow' lie disclosed to me."

The Professor says, he here first got eye on the Knot that had been strangling him, and straightway could unfasten it, and was free. "A vain interminable controversy," writes he, "touching what is at present called Origin of Evil, or some such thing, arises in every soul, since the beginning of the world; and in every soul, that would pass from idle Suffering into actual Endeavouring, must first be put an end to. The most, in our time, have to go content with a simple, incomplete enough Suppression of this controversy; to a few some Solution of it is indispensable. In every new era, too, such Solution comes-out in different terms; and ever the Solution of the last era has become obsolete, and is found unserviceable. For it is man's nature to change his Dialect from century to century; he cannot help it though he would. The authentic *Church-Catechism* of our present century has not yet fallen into my hands: meanwhile, for my own private behoof, I attempt to elucidate the matter so. Man's Unhappiness, as I construe, comes of his Greatness; it is because there is an Infinite in him, which with all his cunning he cannot quite bury

under the Finite. Will the whole Finance Ministers and Upholsterers and Confectioners of modern Europe undertake, in joint-stock company, to make one Shoeblack HAPPY? They cannot accomplish it, above an hour or two; for the Shoeblack also has a Soul quite other than his Stomach; and would require, if you consider it, for his permanent satisfaction and saturation, simply this allotment, no more, and no less: *God's infinite Universe altogether to himself*, therein to enjoy infinitely, and fill every wish as fast as it rose. Oceans of Hochheimer, a Throat like that of Ophiuchus: speak not of them; to the infinite Shoeblack they are as nothing. No sooner is your ocean filled, than he grumbles that it might have been of better vintage. Try him with half of a Universe, of an Omnipotence, he sets to quarrelling with the proprietor of the other half, and declares himself the most maltreated of men.—Always there is a black spot in our sunshine: it is even as I said, the *Shadow of Ourselves*.

"But the whim we have of Happiness is somewhat thus. By certain valuations, and averages, of our own striking, we come upon some sort of average terrestrial lot; this we fancy belongs to us by nature, and of indefeasible right. It is simple payment of our wages, of our deserts; requires neither thanks nor complaint; only such *overplus* as there may be do we account Happiness; any *deficit* again is Misery. Now consider that we have the valuation of our own deserts ourselves, and what a fund of Self-conceit there is in each of us,—do you wonder that the balance should so often dip the wrong way, and many a Blockhead cry: See there, what a payment; was ever worthy gentleman so used!—I tell thee, Blockhead, it all comes of thy Vanity; of what thou *fanciest* those same deserts of thine to be. Fancy that thou deservest to be hanged (as is most likely), thou wilt feel it happiness to be only shot: fancy that thou deservest to be hanged in a hair-halter, it will be a luxury to die in hemp.

"So true is it, what I then say, that *the Fraction of Life can be increased in value not so much by increasing your Numerator as by lessening your Denominator*. Nay, unless my Algebra deceive me, *Unity* itself divided by *Zero* will give *Infinity*. Make thy claim of wages a zero, then; thou hast the world under thy feet. Well did the Wisest of our time write: 'It is only with Renunciation (*Entsagen*) that Life, properly speaking, can be said to begin.'

"I asked myself: What is this that, ever since earliest years, thou hast been fretting and fuming,

---

14. and wipe . . . eyes. See Revelation 21:4. 25–28. 'Sanctuary of Sorrow' . . . 'Divine Depth of Sorrow,' Goethean phrases from *Wilhelm Meister*.

11. **Hochheimer**, a German wine. 12. **Ophiuchus**, the constellation Serpentarius; see *Paradise Lost*, Book II, l. 708. 47. **the Wisest of our time**, Goethe.

and lamenting and self-tormenting, on account of? Say it in a word: is it not because thou art not HAPPY? Because the THOU (sweet gentleman) is not sufficiently honoured, nourished, soft-bedded, and lovingly cared for? Foolish soul! What Act of Legislature was there that *thou* shouldst be Happy? A little while ago thou hadst no right to *be* at all. What if thou wert born and predestined not to be Happy, but to be Unhappy! Art thou nothing other than a Vulture, then, that fliest through the Universe seeking after somewhat to *eat*; and shrieking dolefully because carrion enough is not given thee? Close thy *Byron*; open thy *Goethe*."

"*Es leuchtet mir ein,* I see a glimpse of it!" cries he elsewhere: "there is in man a HIGHER than Love of Happiness: he can do without Happiness, and instead thereof find Blessedness! Was it not to preach-forth this same HIGHER that sages and martyrs, the Poet and the Priest, in all times, have spoken and suffered; bearing testimony, through life and through death, of the Godlike that is in Man, and how in the Godlike only has he Strength and Freedom? Which God-inspired Doctrine art thou also honoured to be taught; O Heavens! and broken with manifold merciful Afflictions, even till thou become contrite, and learn it! O, thank thy Destiny for these; thankfully bear what yet remain: thou hadst need of them; the Self in thee needed to be annihilated. By benignant fever-paroxysms is Life rooting out the deep-seated chronic Diseases, and triumphs over Death. On the roaring billows of Time, thou art not engulfed, but borne aloft into the azure of Eternity. Love not Pleasure; love God. This is the EVERLASTING YEA, wherein all contradiction is solved: wherein whoso walks and works, it is well with him."

And again: "Small is it that thou canst trample the Earth with its injuries under thy feet, as old Greek Zeno trained thee: thou canst love the Earth while it injures thee, and even because it injures thee; for this a Greater than Zeno was needed, and he too was sent. Knowest thou that '*Worship of Sorrow*'? The Temple thereof, founded some eighteen centuries ago, now lies in ruins, overgrown with jungle, the habitation of doleful creatures: nevertheless, venture forward; in a low crypt, arched out of falling fragments, thou findest the Altar still there, and its sacred Lamp perennially burning."

Without pretending to comment on which strange utterances, the Editor will only remark, that there lies beside them much of a still more questionable character; unsuited to the general apprehension; nay wherein he himself does not see his way. Nebulous disquisitions on Religion, yet not without bursts of splendour; on the "perennial continuance of Inspiration"; on Prophecy; that there are "true Priests, as well as Baal-Priests, in our own day": with more of the like sort. We select some fractions, by way of finish to this farrago.

"Cease, my much-respected Herr von Voltaire," thus apostrophises the Professor: "shut thy sweet voice; for the task appointed thee seems finished. Sufficiently hast thou demonstrated this proposition, considerable or otherwise: That the Mythus of the Christian Religion looks not in the eighteenth century as it did in the eighth. Alas, were thy six-and-thirty quartos, and the six-and-thirty thousand other quartos and folios, and flying sheets or reams, printed before and since on the same subject, all needed to convince us of so little! But what next? Wilt thou help us to embody the divine Spirit of that Religion in a new Mythus, in a new vehicle and vesture, that our Souls, otherwise too like perishing, may live? What! thou hast no faculty in that kind? Only a torch for burning, no hammer for building? Take our thanks, then, and——thyself away.

"Meanwhile what are antiquated Mythuses to me? Or is the God present, felt in my own heart, a thing which Herr von Voltaire will dispute out of me; or dispute into me? To the '*Worship of Sorrow*' ascribe what origin and genesis thou pleasest, *has* not that Worship originated, and been generated; is it not *here*? Feel it in thy heart, and then say whether it is of God! This is Belief; all else is Opinion,—for which latter whoso will let him worry and be worried."

"Neither," observes he elsewhere, "shall ye tear-out one another's eyes, struggling over 'Plenary Inspiration,' and suchlike: try rather to get a little even Partial Inspiration, each of you for himself. One BIBLE I know, of whose Plenary Inspiration doubt is not so much as possible; nay with my own eyes I saw the God's-Hand writing it: thereof all other Bibles are but leaves,—say, in Picture-Writing to assist the weaker faculty."

Or, to give the wearied reader relief, and bring it to an end, let him take the following perhaps more intelligible passage:

8–9. What if thou . . . Unhappy, an interesting survival of Carlyle's Calvinistic background. **16. he,** Wilhelm Meister. **33. Love . . . God.** See 2 Timothy 3:4. **39. Zeno,** Greek Stoic philosopher of the third century B.C., who taught that virtue, not pleasure, is the end of life. **41. Greater than Zeno,** Christ. **45. the habitation . . . creatures.** See Isaiah 13:21.

9. Baal-Priests, the priests who, in Israel in Elijah's time, served not Jehovah but Baal of Canaan; see, especially, 1 Kings 18. **40–41. 'Plenary Inspiration,'** the doctrine that the Bible is completely inspired.

"To me, in this our life," says the Professor, "which is an internecine warfare with the Time-spirit, other warfare seems questionable. Hast thou in any way a Contention with thy brother, I advise thee, think well what the meaning thereof is. If thou gauge it to the bottom, it is simply this: 'Fellow, see! thou art taking more than thy share of Happiness in the world, something from *my* share: which, by the Heavens, thou shalt not; nay I will fight thee rather.'—Alas, and the whole lot to be 10 divided is such a beggarly matter, truly a 'feast of shells,' for the substance has been spilled out: not enough to quench one Appetite; and the collective human species clutching at them!—Can we not, in all such cases, rather say: 'Take it, thou too-ravenous individual; take that pitiful additional fraction of a share, which I reckoned mine, but which thou so wantest; take it with a blessing: would to Heaven I had enough for thee!'—If Fichte's *Wissenschaftslehre* be, 'to a certain extent, 20 Applied Christianity,' surely to a still greater extent, so is this. We have here not a Whole Duty of Man, yet a Half Duty, namely the Passive half: could we but do it, as we can demonstrate it!

"But indeed Conviction, were it never so excellent, is worthless till it convert itself into Conduct. Nay properly Conviction is not possible till then; inasmuch as all Speculation is by nature endless, formless, a vortex amid vortices: only by a felt indubitable certainty of Experience does it find any 30 centre to revolve round, and so fashion itself into a system. Most true is it, as a wise man teaches us, that 'Doubt of any sort cannot be removed except by Action.' On which ground, too, let him who gropes painfully in darkness or uncertain light, and prays vehemently that the dawn may ripen into day, lay this other precept well to heart, which to me was of invaluable service: '*Do the Duty which lies nearest thee*,' which thou knowest to be a Duty! Thy second Duty will already have become clearer. 40

"May we not say, however, that the hour of Spiritual Enfranchisement is even this: When your Ideal World, wherein the whole man has been dimly struggling and inexpressibly languishing to work, becomes revealed, and thrown open; and you discover, with amazement enough, like the Lothario in *Wilhelm Meister*, that your 'America is here or nowhere'? The Situation that has not its

Duty, its Ideal, was never yet occupied by man. Yes here, in this poor, miserable, hampered, despicable Actual, wherein thou even now standest, here or nowhere is thy Ideal: work it out therefrom; and working, believe, live, be free. Fool! the Ideal is in thyself, the impediment too is in thyself: thy Condition is but the stuff thou art to shape that same Ideal out of: what matters whether such stuff be of this sort or that, so the Form thou give it be heroic, 10 be poetic? O thou that pinest in the imprisonment of the Actual, and criest bitterly to the gods for a kingdom wherein to rule and create, know this of a truth: the thing thou seekest is already with thee, 'here or nowhere,' couldst thou only see!

"But it is with man's Soul as it was with Nature: the beginning of Creation is—Light. Till the eye have vision, the whole members are in bonds. Divine moment, when over the tempest-tost Soul, as once over the wild-weltering Chaos, it is spoken: 20 Let there be Light! Ever to the greatest that has felt such moment, is it not miraculous and God-announcing; even as, under simpler figures, to the simplest and least. The mad primeval Discord is hushed; the rudely-jumbled conflicting elements bind themselves into separate Firmaments: deep silent rock-foundations are built beneath; and the skyey vault with its everlasting Luminaries above: instead of a dark wasteful Chaos, we have a blooming, fertile, heaven-encompassed World.

"I too could now say to myself: Be no longer a Chaos, but a World, or even Worldkin. Produce! Produce! Were it but the pitifullest infinitesimal fraction of a Product, produce it, in God's name! 'Tis the utmost thou hast in thee: out with it, then. Up, up! Whatsoever thy hand findeth to do, do it with thy whole might. Work while it is called Today; for the Night cometh, wherein no man can work."

from BOOK III: Chapter 8

Natural Supernaturalism

"But deepest of all illusory Appearances, for hiding Wonder, as for many other ends, are your two grand fundamental world-enveloping Appearances, SPACE and TIME. These, as spun and woven for us from before Birth itself, to clothe our celestial ME for dwelling here, and yet to blind it,—lie all em-50 bracing, as the universal canvas, or warp and woof,

20–21. Fichte's . . . Christianity. *Wissenschaftslehre* (*The Doctrine of Knowledge*) was published in 1794 by Johann Gottlieb Fichte, an eminent philosopher of the school of Kant. The quotation in this passage is from Novalis. **22–23. Whole Duty of Man**, the title of a famous devotional book, of unknown authorship, published in 1659. **33–34. 'Doubt . . . Action,'** from *Wilhelm Meister*.

16. the beginning . . . Light. See Genesis 1:3. **16–17. Till the eye . . . bonds.** See Matthew 6:22–23. **35–38. Whatsoever . . . work.** See Ecclesiastes 9:10; John 9:4.

whereby all minor Illusions, in this Phantasm Existence, weave and paint themselves. In vain, while here on Earth, shall you endeavour to strip them off; you can, at best, but rend them asunder for moments, and look through.

"Fortunatus had a wishing Hat, which when he put on, and wished himself Anywhere, behold he was There. By this means had Fortunatus triumphed over Space, he had annihilated Space; for him there was no Where, but all was Here. Were a Hatter to establish himself, in the Wahngasse of Weissnichtwo, and make felts of this sort for all mankind, what a world we should have of it! Still stranger, should, on the opposite side of the street, another Hatter establish himself; and as his fellow-craftsman made Space-annihilating Hats, make Time-annihilating! Of both would I purchase, were it with my last groschen; but chiefly of this latter. To clap-on your felt, and, simply by wishing that you were Any*where*, straightway to be *There*! Next to clap-on your other felt, and, simply by wishing that you were Any*when*, straightway to be *Then*! This were indeed the grander: shooting at will from the Fire-Creation of the World to its Fire-Consummation; here historically present in the First Century, conversing face to face with Paul and Seneca; there prophetically in the Thirty-first, conversing also face to face with other Pauls and Senecas, who as yet stand hidden in the depth of that late Time!

"Or thinkest thou it were impossible, unimaginable? Is the Past annihilated, then, or only past; is the Future non-extant, or only future? Those mystic faculties of thine, Memory and Hope, already answer: already through those mystic avenues, thou the Earth-blinded summonest both Past and Future, and communest with them, though as yet darkly, and with mute beckonings. The curtains of Yesterday drop down, the curtains of Tomorrow roll up; but Yesterday and Tomorrow both *are*. Pierce through the Time-element, glance into the Eternal. Believe what thou findest written in the sanctuaries of Man's Soul, even as all Thinkers, in all ages, have devoutly read it there: that Time and Space are not God, but creations of God; that with God as it is a universal HERE, so is it an everlasting Now.

"And seest thou therein any glimpse of IMMORTALITY?—O Heaven! Is the white Tomb of our Loved One, who died from our arms, and had to be left behind us there, which rises in the distance, like a pale, mournfully receding Milestone, to tell how many toilsome uncheered miles we have journeyed on alone,—but a pale spectral Illusion! Is the lost Friend still mysteriously Here, even as we are Here mysteriously, with God!—Know of a truth that only the Time-shadows have perished, or are perishable; that the real Being of whatever was, and whatever is, and whatever will be, *is* even now and forever. This, should it unhappily seem new, thou mayest ponder at thy leisure; for the next twenty years, or the next twenty centuries: believe it thou must; understand it thou canst not.

"That the Thought-forms, Space and Time, wherein, once for all, we are sent into this Earth to live, should condition and determine our whole Practical reasonings, conceptions, and imagings or imaginings,—seems altogether fit, just, and unavoidable. But that they should, furthermore, usurp such sway over pure spiritual Meditation, and blind us to the wonder everywhere lying close on us, seems nowise so. Admit Space and Time to their due rank as Forms of Thought; nay even, if thou wilt, to their quite undue rank of Realities: and consider, then, with thyself how their thin disguises hide from us the brightest God-effulgences! Thus, were it not miraculous, could I stretch forth my hand and clutch the Sun? Yet thou seest me daily stretch forth my hand and therewith clutch many a thing, and swing it hither and thither. Art thou a grown baby, then, to fancy that the Miracle lies in miles of distance, or in pounds avoirdupois of weight; and not to see that the true inexplicable God-revealing Miracle lies in this, that I can stretch forth my hand at all; that I have free Force to clutch aught therewith? Innumerable other of this sort are the deceptions, and wonder-hiding stupefactions, which Space practises on us.

"Still worse is it with regard to Time. Your grand anti-magician, and universal wonder hider, is this same lying Time. Had we but the Time-annihilating Hat, to put on for once only, we should see ourselves in a World of Miracles, wherein all fabled or authentic Thaumaturgy, and feats of Magic, were outdone. But unhappily we have not such a Hat; and man, poor fool that he is, can seldom and scantily help himself without one.

---

6. Fortunatus, a famous old story, which appears in English literature in Thomas Dekker's play *Old Fortunatus*, 1599. **11. Wahngasse,** Illusion Street. **18. groschen,** a German coin worth about 2 cents. **21–23. Next . . . Then.** A contemporary thinker, J. W. Dunne, claims to have achieved something of this. See *An Experiment with Time* (Macmillan, 1927), *This Serial Universe* (Macmillan, 1938), *The New Immortality* (Harper, 1939). The idea has also appealed powerfully to a large number of creative writers, including H. G. Wells, in *The Time Machine* (Holt, 1895) and John Balderston, in *Berkeley Square* (Macmillan, 1930). **28–29. Paul and Seneca.** Legend says St. Paul had some contact with Seneca, Roman Stoic philosopher of the first century.

"Were it not wonderful, for instance, had Orpheus, or Amphion, built the walls of Thebes by the mere sound of his Lyre? Yet tell me, Who built these walls of Weissnichtwo; summoning-out all the sandstone rocks, to dance along from the *Steinbruch* (now a huge Troglodyte Chasm, with frightful green-mantled pools); and shape themselves into Doric and Ionic pillars, squared ashlar houses and noble streets? Was it not the still higher Orpheus, or Orpheuses, who, in past centuries, by the divine Music of Wisdom, succeeded in civilising Man? Our highest Orpheus walked in Judea, eighteen hundred years ago: his sphere-melody, flowing in wild native tones, took captive the ravished souls of men; and, being of a true sphere-melody, still flows and sounds, though now with thousandfold accompaniments, and rich symphonies, through all our hearts; and modulates, and divinely leads them. Is that a wonder, which happens in two hours; and does it cease to be wonderful if happening in two million? Not only was Thebes built by the music of an Orpheus; but without the music of some inspired Orpheus was no city ever built, no work that man glories-in ever done.

"Sweep away the Illusion of Time; glance, if thou hast eyes, from the near moving-cause to its far-distant Mover: The stroke that came transmitted through a whole galaxy of elastic balls, was it less a stroke than if the last ball only had been struck, and sent flying? O, could I (with the Time-annihilating Hat) transport thee direct from the Beginnings to the Endings, how were thy eyesight unsealed, and thy heart set flaming in the Light-sea of celestial wonder! Then sawest thou that this fair Universe, were it in the meanest province thereof, is in very deed the star-domed City of God; that through every star, through every grass-blade, and most through every Living Soul, the glory of a present God still beams. But Nature, which is the Time-vesture of God, and reveals Him to the wise, hides Him from the foolish.

"Again, could anything be more miraculous than an actual authentic Ghost? The English Johnson longed, all his life, to see one; but could not, though he went to Cock Lane, and thence to the church-vaults, and tapped on coffins. Foolish Doctor! Did he never, with the mind's eye as well as with the body's, look round him into that full tide of human Life he so loved; did he never so much as look into Himself? The good Doctor was a Ghost, as actual and authentic as heart could wish; well-nigh a million of Ghosts were travelling the streets by his side. Once more I say, sweep away the illusion of Time; compress the threescore years into three minutes: what else was he, what else are we? Are we not Spirits, that are shaped into a body, into an Appearance; and that fade-away again into air and Invisibility? This is no metaphor, it is a simple scientific *fact*: we start out of Nothingness, take figure, and are Apparitions; round us, as round the veriest spectre, is Eternity; and to Eternity minutes are as years and aeons. Come there not tones of Love and Faith, as from celestial harp-strings, like the Song of beatified Souls? And again, do not we squeak and jibber (in our discordant, screech-owlish debatings and recriminatings); and glide bodeful, and feeble, and fearful; or uproar (*poltern*), and revel in our mad Dance of the Dead,—till the scent of the morning air summons us to our still Home; and dreamy Night becomes awake and Day? Where now is Alexander of Macedon: does the steel Host, that yelled in fierce battle-shouts at Issus and Arbela, remain behind him; or have they all vanished utterly, even as perturbed Goblins must? Napoleon too, and his Moscow Retreats and Austerlitz Campaigns! Was it all other than the veriest Spectre-hunt; which has now, with its howling tumult that made Night hideous, flitted away?— Ghosts! There are nigh a thousand-million walking the Earth openly at noontide; some half-hundred have vanished from it, some half-hundred have arisen in it, ere thy watch ticks once.

"O Heaven, it is mysterious, it is awful to consider that we not only carry each a future Ghost within him; but are, in very deed, Ghosts! These Limbs, whence had we them; this stormy Force; this life-blood with its burning Passion? They are dust and shadow; a Shadow-system gathered round our ME; wherein, through some moments or years, the Divine Essence is to be revealed in the Flesh. That warrior on his strong war-horse, fire flashes

---

1-2. **Orpheus, or Amphion.** It was Amphion who built the walls of Thebes by charming the stones into place with his music. Orpheus, best known for his invasion of Hades in search of his wife Eurydice, charmed wild beasts. **5. Steinbruch,** quarry. **36. City of God,** the title of a famous book by St. Augustine. **43-46. The English Johnson . . . coffins.** The Cock Lane Ghost was a famous hoax, cleared up in 1762. A pamphlet on the subject, *The Mystery Revealed*, attributed to Oliver Goldsmith, was reprinted by Richard W. Ellis at the Georgian Press in 1928.

18-19. squeak and jibber, squeak and gibber, *Hamlet,* Act I, sc. 1, l. 116. **22-23. till . . . Home,** *Hamlet,* Act I, sc. 5, l. 58. **26-27. Issus and Arbela,** in Cilicia and Assyria, where Alexander the Great defeated the Persians, 333 and 331 B.C. **29-30. Moscow Retreats.** Napoleon's retreat from Moscow in 1812 practically destroyed the French army. **Austerlitz Campaigns.** In December, 1805, at Austerlitz, Napoleon defeated the Austrians. **32. made Night hideous.** See *Hamlet,* Act I, sc. 4, l. 54. **42. dust and shadow,** *pulvis et umbra.* The phrase is from Horace's *Odes.* See Stevenson's essay of that title in this volume.

through his eyes; force dwells in his arm and heart: but warrior and war-horse are a vision; a revealed Force, nothing more. Stately they tread the Earth, as if it were a firm substance: fool! the earth is but a film; it cracks in twain, and warrior and war-horse sink beyond plummet's sounding. Plummet's? Fantasy herself will not follow them. A little while ago, they were not; a little while, and they are not, their very ashes are not.

"So has it been from the beginning, so will it be to the end. Generation after generation takes to itself the Form of a Body; and forth-issuing from Cimmerian Night, on Heaven's mission APPEARS. What Force and Fire is in each he expends: one grinding in the mill of Industry; one hunter-like climbing the giddy Alpine heights of Science; one madly dashed in pieces on the rocks of Strife, in war with his fellow:—and then the Heaven-sent is recalled; his earthly Vesture falls away, and soon even to Sense becomes a vanished Shadow. Thus, like some wild-flaming, wild-thundering train of Heaven's Artillery, does this mysterious MANKIND thunder and flame, in long-drawn, quick-succeeding grandeur, through the unknown Deep. Thus, like a God-created, fire-breathing Spirit-host, we emerge from the Inane; haste stormfully across the astonished Earth; then plunge again into the Inane. Earth's mountains are levelled, and her seas filled up, in our passage: can the Earth, which is but dead and a vision, resist Spirits which have reality and are alive? On the hardest adamant some foot-print of us is stamped-in; the last Rear of the host will read traces of the earliest Van. But whence?—O Heaven, whither? Sense knows not; Faith knows not; only that it is through Mystery to Mystery, from God and to God.

> 'We *are such stuff*
> As Dreams are made of, and our little Life
> Is rounded with a sleep!' "

from THE FRENCH REVOLUTION

To Carlyle the French Revolution was a gigantic sermon on the text "Be not deceived; God is not mocked." His method was to flash thousands of living pictures before the eye—panoramas, close-ups, long shots—in a method astonishingly suggestive of some great motion picture in the classical tradition; for example, Mr. D. W. Griffith's *Intolerance*.

The book is not impartial history (if there is such a thing). It is history seen through the eyes of a great writer who was at once literary artist and pamphleteer. In many passages, Carlyle chooses, combines, and interprets his material in the manner of a conscientious historical novelist. Without this book, Dickens's *Tale of Two Cities* would never have been written.

One of Carlyle's greatest "mob scenes" and two more intimate "sequences" are here reprinted. The fall of the Bastille on July 14, 1789, was the first great success of the revolution. King Louis XVI was guillotined January 21, 1793. Jean Paul Marat, one of the bloodiest of the revolutionary tyrants, was slain by Charlotte Corday (1768–1793) on July 13, 1793.

In this reprint the editor has not thought it necessary to explain all geographical references or to identify minor revolutionary leaders.

from BOOK V: The Third Estate

Chapter 6: *Storm and Victory*

[The Fall of the Bastille]

TO describe this Siege of the Bastille (thought to be one of the most important in History) perhaps transcends the talent of mortals. Could one but, after infinite reading, get to understand so much as the plan of the building! But there is open Esplanade, at the end of the Rue Saint-Antoine; there are such Forecourts, *Cour Avancé, Cour de l'Orme*, arched Gateway (where Louis Tournay now fights); then new drawbridges, dormant-bridges, rampart-bastions, and the grim Eight Towers: a labyrinthic Mass, high-frowning there, of all ages from twenty years to four hundred and twenty;—beleaguered, in this its last hour, as we said, by mere Chaos come again! Ordnance of all calibres; throats of all capacities; men of all plans, every man his own engineer: seldom since the war of Pygmies and Cranes was there seen so anomalous a thing. Half-pay Elie is home for a suit of regimentals; no one would heed him in coloured clothes: half-pay Hulin is haranguing Gardes Françaises in the Place de Grève. Frantic Patriots pick up the grapeshots; bear them, still hot (or seemingly so), to the Hôtel-de-Ville:—Paris, you perceive, is to be burnt! Flesselles is "pale to the very lips," for the roar of the multitude grows deep. Paris wholly has got to the acme of its frenzy; whirled, all ways, by panic

---

6. **beyond plummet's sounding.** See *The Tempest*, Act V, sc. 1, l. 56.   13. **Cimmerian.** According to the *Odyssey* (Book XI, l. 14), the mist-filled country of the Cimmerians lay far in the western ocean. See Milton's "L'Allegro," l. 10. 26–27. **haste . . . Earth,** phrasing borrowed from Schiller's *Death of Wallenstein*, Act III, sc. 15, ll. 1928–30. 38–40. **We are . . . sleep.** *The Tempest*, Act IV, sc. 1, ll. 156–58. Shakespeare has "on," not "of."

32–33. **Cour Avancé, Cour de l'Orme,** Forecourt, Elm Court.   41–42. **the war . . . Cranes,** referred to in Book III of the *Iliad*.

madness. At every street-barricade, there whirls simmering a minor whirlpool,—strengthening the barricade, since God knows what is coming; and all minor whirlpools play distractedly into that grand Fire-Mahlstrom which is lashing round the Bastille.

And so it lashes and it roars. Cholat the wine-merchant has become an impromptu cannoneer. See Georget, of the Marine Service, fresh from Brest, ply the King of Siam's cannon. Singular (if we were not used to the like): Georget lay, last night, taking his ease at his inn; the King of Siam's cannon also lay, knowing nothing of *him*, for a hundred years. Yet now, at the right instant, they have got together, and discourse eloquent music. For, hearing what was toward, Georget sprang from the Brest Diligence, and ran. Gardes Françaises also will be here, with real artillery: were not the walls so thick!—Upwards from the Esplanade, horizontally from all neighbouring roofs and windows, flashes one irregular deluge of musketry, without effect. The Invalides lie flat, firing comparatively at their ease from behind stone; hardly through portholes, show the tip of a nose. We fall, shot; and make no impression!

Let conflagration rage; of whatsoever is combustible! Guard-rooms are burnt, Invalides mess-rooms. A distracted "Peruke-maker with two fiery torches" is for burning "the saltpetres of the Arsenal";—had not a woman run screaming; had not a Patriot, with some tincture of Natural Philosophy, instantly struck the wind out of him (butt of musket on pit of stomach), overturned barrels, and stayed the devouring element. A young beautiful lady, seized escaping in these Outer Courts, and thought falsely to be De Launay's daughter, shall be burnt in De Launay's sight; she lies swooned on a paillasse: but again a Patriot, it is brave Aubin Bonne-mère the old soldier, dashes in, and rescues her. Straw is burnt; three cartloads of it, hauled thither, go up in white smoke: almost to the choking of Patriotism itself; so that Elie had, with singed brows, to drag back one cart; and Réole the "gigantic haberdasher" another. Smoke as of Tophet; confusion as of Babel; noise as of the Crack of Doom!

Blood flows; the aliment of new madness. The wounded are carried into houses of the Rue Cerisaie; the dying leave their last mandate not to yield till the accursed Stronghold fall. And yet, alas, how fall? The walls are so thick! Deputations, three in number, arrive from the Hôtel-de-Ville; Abbé

Fauchet (who was of one) can say, with what almost superhuman courage of benevolence. These wave their Town-flag in the arched Gateway; and stand, rolling their drum; but to no purpose. In such Crack of Doom, De Launay cannot hear them, dare not believe them: they return, with justified rage, the whew of lead still singing in their ears. What to do? The Firemen are here, squirting with their fire-pumps on the Invalides cannon, to wet the touchholes; they unfortunately cannot squirt so high; but produce only clouds of spray. Individuals of classical knowledge propose *catapults*. Santerre, the sonorous Brewer of the Suburb Saint-Antoine, advises rather that the place be fired, by a "mixture of phosphorus and oil-of-turpentine spouted up through forcing pumps": O Spinola-Santerre, hast thou the mixture *ready*? Every man his own engineer! And still the fire-deluge abates not: even women are firing, and Turks; at least one woman (with her sweetheart), and one Turk. Gardes Françaises have come: real cannon, real cannoneers. Usher Maillard is busy; half-pay Elie, half-pay Hulin rage in the midst of thousands.

How the great Bastille Clock ticks (inaudible) in its Inner Court there, at its ease, hour after hour; as if nothing special, for it or the world, were passing! It tolled One when the firing began; and is now pointing towards Five, and still the firing slakes not.—Far down, in their vaults, the seven Prisoners hear muffled din as of earthquakes; their Turnkeys answer vaguely.

Woe to thee, De Launay, with thy poor hundred Invalides! Broglie is distant, and his ears heavy: Besenval hears, but can send no help. One poor troop of Hussars has crept, reconnoitring, cautiously along the Quais, as far as the Pont Neuf. "We are come to join you," said the Captain; for the crowd seems shoreless. A large-headed dwarfish individual, of smoke-bleared aspect, shambles forward, opening his blue lips, for there is sense in him; and croaks: "Alight then, and give up your arms!" The Hussar-Captain is too happy to be escorted to the Barriers, and dismissed on parole. Who the squat individual was? Men answer, It is M. Marat, author of the excellent pacific *Avis au Peuple*! Great truly, O thou remarkable Dogleech, is this thy day of emergence and new-birth: and yet this same day come four years——!—But let the curtains of the Future hang.

What shall De Launay do? One thing only De Launay could have done: what he said he would do.

5. Fire-Mahlstrom, maelstrom of fire.   16. Diligence, stagecoach.   36–37. paillasse, straw mattress.   43. Tophet. See Note on "The Everlasting No," page 408, col. 1, l. 9. 44. Babel. See Genesis 11:1–9.

45–46. Avis au Peuple. Advice to the People. Jean Paul Marat (1744–1793). See page 422 ff.   46. Dogleech. Marat, who had practiced medicine, was often scoffed at as a quack.

Fancy him sitting, from the first, with lighted taper, within arm's length of the Powder-Magazine; motionless, like old Roman Senator, or Bronze Lamp-holder; coldly apprising Thuriot, and all men, by a slight motion of his eye, what his resolution was:—Harmless he sat there, while unharmed; but the King's Fortress, meanwhile, could, might, would, or should, in nowise be surrendered, save to the King's Messenger: one old man's life is worthless, so it be lost with honour; but think, ye brawling 10 *canaille*, how will it be when a whole Bastille springs skyward!—In such statuesque, taper-holding attitude, one fancies De Launay might have left Thuriot, the red Clerks of the Basoche, Curé of Saint-Stephen and all the tag-rag-and-bobtail of the world, to work their will.

And yet, withal, he could not do it. Hast thou considered how each man's heart is so tremulously responsive to the hearts of all men; hast thou noted how omnipotent is the very sound of many men? 20 How their shriek of indignation palsies the strong soul; their howl of contumely withers with unfelt pangs? The Ritter Gluck confessed that the ground-tone of the noblest passage, in one of his noblest Operas, was the voice of the Populace he had heard at Vienna, crying to their Kaiser: Bread! Bread! Great is the combined voice of men; the utterance of their *instincts*, which are truer than their *thoughts*: it is the greatest a man encounters, among the sounds and shadows which make up this World of 30 Time. He who can resist that, has his footing somewhere *beyond* Time. De Launay could not do it. Distracted, he hovers between two; hopes in the middle of despair; surrenders not his Fortress; declares that he will blow it up, seizes torches to blow it up, and does not blow it. Unhappy old De Launay, it is the death-agony of thy Bastille and thee! Jail, Jailoring and Jailor, all three, such as they may have been, must finish.

For four hours now has the World-Bedlam 40 roared: call it the World-Chimera, blowing fire! The poor Invalides have sunk under their battle-ments, or rise only with reversed muskets: they have made a white flag of napkins: go beating the *chamade*, or seeming to beat, for one can hear nothing. The very Swiss at the Portcullis look weary of firing; disheartened in the fire-deluge: a porthole at the drawbridge is opened, as by one that would speak. See Huissier Maillard, the shifty man! On his plank, swinging over the abyss of that stone 50 Ditch; plank resting on parapet, balanced by weight of Patriots,—he hovers perilous: such a Dove towards such an Ark! Deftly, thou shifty Usher: one man already fell; and lies smashed, far down there, against the masonry! Usher Maillard falls not: deftly, unerring he walks, with out-spread palm. The Swiss holds a paper through his port-hole; the shifty Usher snatches it, and returns. Terms of surrender: Pardon, immunity to all! Are they accepted?—"*Foi d'officier*, On the word of an officer," answers half-pay Hulin,—or half-pay Elie, for men do not agree on it, "they are!" Sinks the drawbridge,—Usher Maillard bolting it when down; rushes-in the living deluge: the Bastille is fallen! *Victoire*! *La Bastille est prise*!

from BOOK XV: Regicide

Chapter 8: *Place de la Révolution*

[The Execution of Louis XVI]

To this conclusion, then, hast thou come, O hapless Louis! The Son of Sixty Kings is to die on the Scaffold by form of Law. Under Sixty Kings this same form of Law, form of Society, has been fashioning itself together these thousand years; and has become, one way and other, a most strange Machine. Surely, if needful, it is also frightful, this Machine; dead, blind; not what it should be; which, with swift stroke, or by cold slow torture, has wasted the lives and souls of innumerable men. And behold now a King himself, or say rather Kinghood in his person, is to expire here in cruel tortures;—like a Phalaris shut in the belly of his own red-heated Brazen Bull! It is ever so; and thou shouldst know it, O haughty tyrannous man: injustice breeds injustice; curses and falsehoods do verily return "always *home*," wide as they may wander. Innocent Louis bears the sins of many generations: he too experiences that man's tribunal is not in this Earth; that if he had no Higher one, it were not well with him.

A King dying by such violence appeals impressively to the imagination; as the like must do, and ought to do. And yet at bottom it is not the King dying, but the man! Kingship is a coat: the grand loss is of the skin. The man from whom you take his Life, to him can the whole combined world do *more*? Lally went on his hurdle; his mouth filled with a gag. Miserablest mortals, doomed for pick-

---

23. **Ritter,** Knight. **Gluck,** Christoph Willibald Gluck (1714–1787), composer of *Orfeo ed Euridice, Orfeo,* and other operas. 45. **chamade,** sign of surrender.

2. **Dove . . . Ark.** See Genesis 8:6–12. 14. **Victoire! La Bastille est prise!** Victory! The Bastille is taken! 34. **Phalaris,** ruler of Sicily (sixth century B.C.), whom Pindar accuses of having roasted his victims alive in a brazen bull.

ing pockets, have a whole five-act Tragedy in them, in that dumb pain, as they go to the gallows, unregarded; they consume the cup of trembling down to the lees. For Kings and for Beggars, for the justly doomed and the unjustly, it is a hard thing to die. Pity them all: thy utmost pity, with all aids and appliances and throne-and-scaffold contrasts, how far short is it of the thing pitied!

A Confessor has come; Abbé Edgeworth, of Irish extraction, whom the King knew by good report, has come promptly on this solemn mission. Leave the Earth alone, then, thou hapless King; it with its malice will go its way, thou also canst go thine. A hard scene yet remains: the parting with our loved ones. Kind hearts, environed in the same grim peril with us; to be left *here!* Let the Reader look with the eyes of Valet Cléry through these glass-doors, where also the Municipality watches; and see the cruelest of scenes:

"At half-past eight, the door of the anteroom opened: the Queen appeared first, leading her Son by the hand; then Madame Royale and Madame Elizabeth: they all flung themselves into the arms of the King. Silence reigned for some minutes; interrupted only by sobs. The Queen made a movement to lead his Majesty towards the inner room, where M. Edgeworth was waiting unknown to them: 'No,' said the King, 'let us go into the dining-room; it is there only that I can see you.' They entered there; I shut the door of it, which was of glass. The King sat down, the Queen on his left hand, Madame Elizabeth on his right, Madame Royale almost in front; the young Prince remained standing between his Father's legs. They all leaned toward him, and often held him embraced. This scene of woe lasted an hour and three quarters; during which we could hear nothing; we could see only that always when the King spoke, the sobbings of the Princesses redoubled, continued for some minutes; and that then the King began again to speak."—And so our meetings and our partings do now end! The sorrows we gave each other; the poor joys we faithfully shared, and all our lovings and our sufferings, and confused toilings under the earthly Sun, are over. Thou good soul, I shall never, never through all ages of Time, see thee any

more!—*Never!* O Reader, knowest thou that hard word?

For nearly two hours this agony lasts; then they tear themselves asunder. "Promise that you will see us on the morrow." He promises:—Ah yes, yes; yet once; and go now, ye loved ones; cry to God for yourselves and me!—It was a hard scene, but it is over. He will not see them on the morrow. The Queen, in passing through the ante-room, glanced at the Cerberus Municipals; and, with woman's vehemence, said through her tears, "*Vous êtes tous des scélérats.*"

King Louis slept sound, till five in the morning, when Cléry, as he had been ordered, awoke him. Cléry dressed his hair: while this went forward, Louis took a ring from his watch, and kept trying it on his finger; it was his wedding-ring, which he is now to return to the Queen as a mute farewell. At half-past six, he took the Sacrament; and continued in devotion, and conference with Abbé Edgeworth. He will not see his Family: it were too hard to bear.

At eight, the Municipals enter: the King gives them his Will, and messages and effects; which they, at first, brutally refuse to take charge of: he gives them a roll of gold pieces, a hundred and twenty-five louis; these are to be returned to Malesherbes, who had lent them. At nine, Santerre says the hour is come. The King begs to retire for three minutes. At the end of three minutes, Santerre again says the hour is come. "Stamping on the ground with his right-foot, Louis answers: '*Partons*, Let us go.' "—How the rolling of those drums comes in, through the Temple bastions and bulwarks, on the heart of a queenly wife; soon to be a widow! He is gone, then, and has not seen us? A Queen weeps bitterly; a King's Sister and Children. Over all these Four does Death also hover: all shall perish miserably save one; she, as Duchesse d'Angoulême, will live,—not happily.

At the Temple Gate were some faint cries, perhaps from voices of pitiful women: "*Grâce! Grâce!*" Through the rest of the streets there is silence as of the grave. No man not armed is allowed to be there: the armed, did any even pity, dare not express it, each man overawed by all his neighbours. All windows are down, none seen looking through them. All shops are shut. No wheel-carriage rolls, this morning, in these streets but one only. Eighty-thousand armed men stand ranked, like armed statues of men; cannons bristle, cannoneers with match burning, but no word or movement: it is as

---

18. **Cléry,** who attended the king in his captivity, and afterwards published a journal.   23–24. **the Queen,** Marie Antoinette. **her Son,** Louis XVII, titular King of France after the execution of his father until his own death in 1795. **Madame Royale,** the king's daughter, the Duchesse d'Angoulême. **Madame Elizabeth,** sister of Louis XVI, executed in 1794.

11–12. **"Vous . . . scélérats."** "You are all scoundrels." 42. **"Grâce! Grâce!"** a plea for mercy.

a city enchanted into silence and stone: one carriage with its escort, slowly rumbling, is the only sound. Louis reads, in his Book of Devotion, the Prayers of the Dying: clatter of this death-march falls sharp on the ear, in the great silence; but the thought would fain struggle heavenward, and forget the Earth.

As the clocks strike ten, behold the Place de la Révolution, once Place de Louis Quinze: the Guillotine, mounted near the old Pedestal where once stood the Statue of that Louis! Far round, all bristles with cannons and armed men: spectators crowding in the rear; D'Orléans Egalité there in cabriolet. Swift messengers, *hoquetons*, speed to the Townhall, every three minutes: near by is the Convention sitting,—vengeful for Lepelletier. Heedless of all, Louis reads his Prayers of the Dying; not till five minutes yet has he finished; then the Carriage opens. What temper he is in? Ten different witnesses will give ten different accounts of it. He is in the collision of all tempers; arrived now at the black Mahlstrom and descent of Death: in sorrow, in indignation, in resignation struggling to be resigned. "Take care of M. Edgeworth," he straitly charges the Lieutenant who is sitting with them: then they two descend.

The drums are beating: "*Taisez-vous*, Silence!" he cries "in a terrible voice, *d'une voix terrible*." He mounts the scaffold, not without delay; he is in puce coat, breeches of grey, white stockings. He strips off the coat; stands disclosed in a sleeve-waistcoat of white flannel. The Executioners approach to bind him: he spurns, resists; Abbé Edgeworth has to remind him how the Saviour, in whom men trust, submitted to be bound. His hands are tied, his head bare; the fatal moment is come. He advances to the edge of the Scaffold, "his face very red," and says: "Frenchmen, I die innocent: it is from the Scaffold and near appearing before God that I tell you so. I pardon my enemies; I desire that France—" A General on horseback, Santerre or another, prances out, with uplifted hands: "*Tambours!*" The drums drown the voice. "Executioners, do your duty!" The Executioners, desperate lest themselves be murdered (for Santerre and his Armed Ranks will strike, if they do not), seize the hapless Louis: six of them desperate, him singly desperate, struggling there; and bind him to their plank. Abbé Edgeworth, stooping, bespeaks him: "Son of Saint Louis, ascend to Heaven." The Axe

clanks down; a King's Life is shorn away. It is Monday the 21st of January 1793. He was aged Thirty-eight years four months and twenty-eight days.

Executioner Samson shows the Head: fierce shout of *Vive la République* rises, and swells; caps raised on bayonets, hats waving: students of the College of Four Nations take it up, on the far Quais; fling it over Paris. D'Orléans drives off in his cabriolet: the Townhall Councillors rub their hands, saying, "It is done, It is done." There is dipping of handkerchiefs, of pike-points in the blood. Headsman Samson, though he afterwards denied it, sells locks of the hair: fractions of the puce coat are long after worn in rings.—And so, in some half-hour it is done; and the multitude has all departed. Pastrycooks, coffee-sellers, milkmen sing out their trivial quotidian cries: the world wags on, as if this were a common day. In the coffeehouses that evening, says Prudhomme, Patriot shook hands with Patriot in a more cordial manner than usual. Not till some days after, according to Mercier, did public men see what a grave thing it was. . . .

from BOOK XVII: Chapter 1

Charlotte Corday

. . . Amid which dim ferment of Caen and the World, History specially notices one thing: in the lobby of the Mansion *de l'Intendance*, where busy Deputies are coming and going, a young Lady with an aged valet, taking grave graceful leave of Deputy Barbaroux. She is of stately Norman figure; in her twenty-fifth year; of beautiful still countenance: her name is Charlotte Corday, heretofore styled D'Armans, while Nobility still was. Barbaroux has given her a Note to Deputy Duperret,—him who once drew his sword in the effervescence. Apparently she will to Paris on some errand? "She was a Republican before the Revolution, and never wanted energy." A completeness, a decision is in this fair female Figure: "by energy she means the spirit that will prompt one to sacrifice himself for his country." What if she, this fair young Charlotte, had emerged from her secluded stillness, suddenly like a Star; cruel-lovely, with half-angelic, half-daemonic splendour; to gleam for a moment, and in a moment be extinguished: to be held in memory, so bright-complete was she, through long

13. **D'Orléans Egalité,** Louis Philippe Joseph, fifth Duke of Orléans, born 1747, executed 1793.   14. **hoquetons,** yeomen of the guard.   34–35. **the Saviour . . . bound.** See Matthew 27:2.   50. **Saint Louis,** Louis IX, King of France, 1226 to 1270.

6. **Vive la République,** Long live the Republic. 20. **Prudhomme,** a revolutionary writer.   33. **Mansion de l'Intendance,** house of administration.

centuries!—Quitting Cimmerian Coalitions without, and the dim-simmering Twenty-five millions within, History will look fixedly at this one fair Apparition of a Charlotte Corday; will note whither Charlotte moves, how the little Life burns forth so radiant, then vanishes swallowed of the Night.

With Barbaroux's Note of Introduction, and slight stock of luggage, we see Charlotte on Tuesday the 9th of July seated in the Caen Diligence, with a place for Paris. None takes farewell of her, wishes her Good-journey: her Father will find a line left, signifying that she is gone to England, that he must pardon her, and forget her. The drowsy Diligence lumbers along; amid drowsy talk of Politics, and praise of the Mountain; in which she mingles not: all night, all day, and again all night. On Thursday, not long before noon, we are at the bridge of Neuilly; here is Paris with her thousand black domes, the goal and purpose of thy journey! Arrived at the Inn de la Providence in the Rue des Vieux Augustins, Charlotte demands a room; hastens to bed; sleeps all afternoon and night, till the morrow morning.

On the morrow morning, she delivers her Note to Duperret. It relates to certain Family Papers which are in the Minister of the Interior's hands; which a Nun at Caen, an old Convent-friend of Charlotte's, has need of; which Duperret shall assist her in getting: this then was Charlotte's errand to Paris? She has finished this, in the course of Friday; —yet says nothing of returning. She has seen and silently investigated several things. The Convention, in bodily reality, she has seen; what the Mountain is like. The living physiognomy of Marat she could not see; he is sick at present, and confined to home.

About eight on the Saturday morning, she purchases a large sheath-knife in the Palais Royal; then straightway, in the Place des Victoires, takes a hackney-coach: "To the Rue de l'Ecole de Médicine, No. 44." It is the residence of the Citoyen Marat!—The Citoyen Marat is ill, and cannot be seen; which seems to disappoint her much. Her business is with Marat, then? Hapless beautiful Charlotte; hapless squalid Marat! From Caen in the utmost West, from Neuchâtel in the utmost East, they two are drawing nigh each other; they two have, very strangely, business together.— Charlotte, returning to her Inn, despatches a short Note to Marat; signifying that she is from Caen, the seat of rebellion; that she desires earnestly to see him, and "will put it in his power to do France a great service." No answer. Charlotte writes another Note, still more pressing; sets out with it by coach, about seven in the evening, herself. Tired day-labourers have again finished their Week; huge Paris is circling and simmering, manifold, according to its vague wont: this one fair Figure has decision in it; drives straight,—towards a purpose.

It is yellow July evening, we say, the thirteenth of the month; eve of the Bastille day,—when "M. Marat," four years ago, in the crowd of the Pont Neuf, shrewdly required of that Besenval Hussar-party, which had such friendly dispositions, "to dismount, and give up their arms, then"; and became notable among Patriot men. Four years: what a road he has travelled;—and sits now, about half-past seven of the clock, stewing in slipper-bath; sore afflicted; ill of Revolution Fever,—of what other malady this History had rather not name. Excessively sick and worn, poor man: with precisely eleven-pence-halfpenny of ready-money, in paper; with slipper-bath; strong three-footed stool for writing on, the while; and a squalid—Washerwoman one may call her: that is her civic establishment in Medical-School Street; thither and not elsewhither has this road led him. Not to the reign of Brotherhood and Perfect Felicity; yet surely on the way towards that?—Hark, a rap again! A musical woman's voice, refusing to be rejected: it is the Citoyenne who would do France a service. Marat, recognising from within, cries, Admit her. Charlotte Corday is admitted.

Citoyen Marat, I am from Caen the seat of rebellion, and wished to speak with you.—Be seated, mon enfant. Now what are the Traitors doing at Caen? What Deputies are at Caen?—Charlotte names some Deputies. "Their heads shall fall within a fortnight," croaks the eager People's-friend, clutching his tablets to write: Barbaroux, Pétion, writes he with bare shrunk arm, turning aside in the bath: Pétion, and Louvet, and—Charlotte has drawn her knife from the sheath; plunges it, with one sure stroke, into the writer's heart. "A moi, chère amie. Help, dear!" no more could the Death-choked say or shriek. The helpful Washerwoman running in, there is no Friend of the People, or Friend of the Washerwoman left; but his life with a groan gushes out, indignant, to the shades below.

And so Marat People's-friend is ended; the lone Stylites has got hurled down suddenly from his

1. Cimmerian. See Note 13 on "Natural Supernaturalism," page 418.   16. the Mountain, a political faction.   43. Citoyen, citizen.   47. Neuchâtel, Marat's birthplace.

31. Citoyenne, citizeness.   36. mon enfant, my child.   51. Stylites, St. Simeon Stylites, a Syrian monk of the fourth century, who lived many years on top of a pillar.

Pillar,—*whitherward* He that made him knows. Patriot Paris may sound triple and tenfold, in dole and wail; reëchoed by Patriot France; and the Convention, "Chabot pale with terror, declaring that they are to be all assassinated," may decree him Pantheon Honours, Public Funeral, Mirabeau's dust making way for him; and Jacobin Societies, in lamentable oratory, summing up his character, parallel him to One, whom they think it honour to call "the good Sansculotte,"—whom we name not here; also a Chapel may be made, for the urn that holds his Heart, in the Place du Carrousel; and new-born children be named Marat; and Lago-di-Como Hawkers bake mountains of stucco into unbeautiful Busts; and David paint his Picture, or Death-Scene; and such other Apotheosis take place as the human genius, in these circumstances, can devise: but Marat returns no more to the light of this Sun. One sole circumstance we have read with clear sympathy, in the old *Moniteur* Newspaper: how Marat's Brother comes from Neuchâtel to ask of the Convention, "that the deceased Jean-Paul Marat's musket be given him." For Marat too had a brother and natural affections; and was wrapped once in swaddling-clothes, and slept safe in a cradle like the rest of us. Ye children of men!—A sister of his, they say, lives still to this day in Paris.

As for Charlotte Corday, her work is accomplished; the recompense of it is near and sure. The *chère amie*, and neighbours of the house, flying at her, she "overturns some movables," entrenches herself till the gendarmes arrive; then quietly surrenders; goes quietly to the Abbaye Prison: she alone quiet, all Paris sounding, in wonder, in rage or admiration, round her. Duperret is put in arrest, on account of her; his Papers sealed,—which may lead to consequences. Fauchet, in like manner; though Fauchet had not so much as heard of her. Charlotte, confronted with these two Deputies, praises the grave firmness of Duperret, censures the dejection of Fauchet.

On Wednesday morning, the thronged Palais de Justice and Revolutionary Tribunal can see her face; beautiful and calm: she dates it "fourth day of the Preparation of Peace." A strange murmur ran through the Hall, at sight of her; you could not say of what character. Tinville has his indictments and tape-papers: the cutler of the Palais Royal will testify that he sold her the sheath-knife; "All these details are needless," interrupted Charlotte; "it is I that killed Marat." By whose instigation?—"By no one's." What tempted you, then? His crimes. "I killed one man," added she, raising her voice extremely (*extrêmement*), as they went on with their questions, "I killed one man to save a hundred thousand; a villain to save innocents; a savage wild-beast to give repose to my country. I was a Republican before the Revolution; I never wanted energy." There is therefore nothing to be said. The public gazes astonished: the hasty limners sketch her features, Charlotte not disapproving: the men of law proceed with their formalities. The doom is Death as a murderess. To her Advocate she gives thanks; in gentle phrase, in high-flown classical spirit. To the Priest they send her she gives thanks; but needs not any shriving, any ghostly or other aid from him.

On this same evening therefore, about half-past seven o'clock, from the gate of the Conciergerie, to a City all on tiptoe, the fatal Cart issues; seated on it a fair young creature, sheeted in red smock of Murderess; so beautiful, serene, so full of life; journeying towards death,—alone amid the World. Many take off their hats, saluting reverently; for what heart but must be touched? Others growl and howl. Adam Lux, of Mentz, declares that she is greater than Brutus; that it were beautiful to die with her: the head of this young man seems turned. At the Place de la Révolution, the countenance of Charlotte wears the same still smile. The executioners proceed to bind her feet; she resists, thinking it meant as an insult; on a word of explanation, she submits with cheerful apology. As the last act, all being now ready, they take the neckerchief from her neck; a blush of maidenly shame overspreads that fair face and neck; the cheeks were still tinged with it when the executioner lifted the severed head, to show it to the people. "It is most true," says Forster, "that he struck the cheek insultingly; for I saw it with my eyes: the Police imprisoned him for it."

In this manner have the Beautifulest and the Squalidest come in collision, and extinguished one another. Jean-Paul Marat and Marie-Anne Charlotte Corday both, suddenly, are no more. "Day of Preparation of Peace"? Alas, how were peace possible or preparable, while, for example, the hearts of lovely Maidens, in their convent-stillness, are dreaming, not of Love-paradises and the light of

---

6–7. **Mirabeau,** revolutionary leader who died in 1791.
7–8. **Jacobin Societies,** radical clubs that exercised a great influence in the Revolution.   10. **Sansculotte,** radical revolutionary (literally "without breeches"). Chabot (1759–1794), revolutionary leader, called Jesus the first sansculotte.
15. **David,** Louis David (1748–1825), French painter.
31. **chère amie,** dear friend or love, the "washerwoman" whom Marat called in his death agony.

31. **Brutus,** who killed Julius Caesar.

Life, but of Codrus'-sacrifices and Death well-earned? That Twenty-five million hearts have got to such temper, this *is* the Anarchy; the soul of it lies in this: whereof not peace can be the embodiment! The death of Marat, whetting old animosities tenfold, will be worse than any life. O ye hapless Two, mutually extinctive, the Beautiful and the Squalid, sleep ye well,—in the Mother's bosom that bore you both!

This is the History of Charlotte Corday; most definite, most complete; angelic-daemonic: like a Star! Adam Lux goes home, half-delirious; to pour forth his Apotheosis of her, in paper and print; to propose that she have a statue with this inscription, *Greater than Brutus.* Friends represent his danger; Lux is reckless; thinks it were beautiful to die with her.

from ON HEROES, HERO–WORSHIP AND THE HEROIC IN HISTORY

Carlyle's philosophy of history as essentially the biography of great leaders is best set forth in the lectures generally known as *Heroes and Hero-Worship.* The hero is considered as divinity (Odin), as prophet (Mahomet), as poet (Dante, Shakespeare), as priest (Luther, Knox), as man of letters (Johnson, Rousseau, Burns), as king (Cromwell, Napoleon). The first part of Lecture 1, which sets forth Carlyle's general ideas on the subject, is reprinted here.

from Lecture 1

The Hero as Divinity . . .

WE have undertaken to discourse here for a little on Great Men, their manner of appearance in our world's business, how they have shaped themselves in the world's history, what ideas men formed of them, what work they did;—on Heroes, namely, and on their reception and performance; what I call Hero-worship and the Heroic in human affairs. Too evidently this is a large topic; deserving quite other treatment than we can expect to give it at present. A large topic; indeed, an illimitable one; wide as Universal History itself. For, as I take it, Universal History, the history of what man has accomplished in this world, is at bottom the History of the Great Men who have worked here. They were the leaders of men, these great ones; the modellers, patterns, and in a wide

sense creators, of whatsoever the general mass of men contrived to do or to attain; all things that we see standing accomplished in the world are properly the outer material result, the practical realisation and embodiment, of Thoughts that dwelt in the Great Men sent into the world: the soul of the whole world's history, it may justly be considered, were the history of these. Too clearly it is a topic we shall do no justice to in this place!

One comfort is, that Great Men, taken up in any way, are profitable company. We cannot look, however imperfectly, upon a great man, without gaining something by him. He is the living light-fountain, which it is good and pleasant to be near. The light which enlightens, which has enlightened the darkness of the world; and this not as a kindled lamp only, but rather as a natural luminary shining by the gift of Heaven; a flowing light-fountain, as I say, of native original insight, of manhood and heroic nobleness;—in whose radiance all souls feel that it is well with them. On any terms whatsoever, you will not grudge to wander in such neighbourhood for a while. These Six classes of Heroes, chosen out of widely-distant countries and epochs, and in mere external figure differing altogether, ought, if we look faithfully at them, to illustrate several things for us. Could we see *them* well, we should get some glimpses into the very marrow of the world's history. How happy, could I but, in any measure, in such times as these, make manifest to you the meanings of Heroism; the divine relation (for I may well call it such) which in all times unites a Great Man to other men; and thus, as it were, not exhaust my subject, but so much as break ground on it! At all events, I must make the attempt.

It is well said, in every sense, that a man's religion is the chief fact with regard to him. A man's, or a nation of men's. By religion I do not mean here the church-creed which he professes, the articles of faith which he will sign and, in words or otherwise, assert; not this wholly, in many cases not this at all. We see men of all kinds of professed creeds attain to almost all degrees of worth or worthlessness under each or any of them. This is not what I call religion, this profession and assertion; which is often only a profession and assertion from the outworks of the man, from the mere argumentative region of him, if even so deep as that. But the thing a man does practically believe (and this is often enough

---

1. Codrus, a reputed king of Athens (c. 1060 B.C.), who disguised himself as a peasant and met the invader, because the oracle had told him that Athens would be saved if her king should be struck down by the enemy.

23. Six classes of Heroes, as Divinity (Odin); as Prophet (Mahomet); as Poet (Dante, Shakespeare); as Priest (Luther, Knox); as Man of Letters (Johnson, Rousseau, Burns); as King (Cromwell, Napoleon), as noted above.

without asserting it even to himself, much less to others); the thing a man does practically lay to heart, and know for certain, concerning his vital relations to this mysterious Universe, and his duty and destiny there, that is in all cases the primary thing for him, and creatively determines all the rest. That is his *religion*; or, it may be, his mere scepticism and *no-religion*: the manner it is in which he feels himself to be spiritually related to the Unseen World or No-World; and I say, if you tell me 10 what that is, you tell me to a very great extent what the man is, what the kind of things he will do is. Of a man or of a nation we inquire, therefore, first of all, What religion they had? Was it Heathenism,— plurality of gods, mere sensuous representation of this Mystery of Life, and for chief recognised element therein Physical Force? Was it Christianism; faith in an Invisible, not as real only, but as the only reality; Time, through every meanest moment of it, resting on Eternity; Pagan empire of Force 20 displaced by a nobler supremacy, that of Holiness? Was it Scepticism, uncertainty and inquiry whether there was an Unseen World, any Mystery of Life except a mad one;—doubt as to all this, or perhaps unbelief and flat denial? Answering of this question is giving us the soul of the history of the man or nation. The thoughts they had were the parents of the actions they did; their feelings were parents of their thoughts: it was the unseen and spiritual in them that determined the outward and actual;—their 30 religion, as I say, was the great fact about them. In these Discourses, limited as we are, it will be good to direct our survey chiefly to that religious phasis of the matter. That once known well, all is known. We have chosen as the first Hero in our series, Odin the central figure of Scandinavian Paganism; an emblem to us of a most extensive province of things. Let us look for a little at the Hero as Divinity, the oldest primary form of Heroism.

Surely it seems a very strange-looking thing this 40 Paganism; almost inconceivable to us in these days. A bewildering, inextricable jungle of delusions, confusions, falsehoods, and absurdities, covering the whole field of Life! A thing that fills us with astonishment, almost, if it were possible, with incredulity,—for truly it is not easy to understand that sane men could ever calmly, with their eyes open, believe and live by such a set of doctrines. That men should have worshipped their poor fellow-man as a God, and not him only, but stocks and stones, and 50 all manner of animate and inanimate objects; and fashioned for themselves such a distracted chaos of hallucinations by way of Theory of the Universe: all this looks like an incredible fable. Nevertheless,

it is a clear fact that they did it. Such hideous inextricable jungle of misworships, misbeliefs, men, made as we are, did actually hold by, and live at home in. This is strange. Yes, we may pause in sorrow and silence over the depths of darkness that are in man; if we rejoice in the heights of purer vision he has attained to. Such things were and are in man; in all men; in us too.

Some speculators have a short way of accounting for the Pagan religion: mere quackery, priestcraft, and dupery, say they; no sane man ever did believe it,—merely contrived to persuade other men, not worthy of the name of sane, to believe it! It will be often our duty to protest against this sort of hypothesis about men's doings and history; and I here, on the very threshold, protest against it in reference to Paganism, and to all other *isms* by which man has ever for a length of time striven to walk in this world. They have all had a truth in them, or men 20 would not have taken them up. Quackery and dupery do abound; in religions, above all in the more advanced decaying stages of religions, they have fearfully abounded; but quackery was never the originating influence in such things; it was not the health and life of such things, but their disease, the sure precursor of their being about to die! Let us never forget this. It seems to me a most mournful hypothesis, that of quackery giving birth to any faith even in savage men. Quackery gives birth to 30 nothing; gives death to all things. We shall not see into the true heart of anything, if we look merely at the quackeries of it; if we do not reject the quackeries altogether; as mere diseases, corruptions, with which our and all men's sole duty is to have done with them, to sweep them out of our thoughts as out of our practice. Man everywhere is the born enemy of lies.——We shall begin to have a chance of understanding Paganism, when we first admit that to its followers it was, at one time, earnestly true. Let 40 us consider it very certain that men did believe in Paganism; men with open eyes, sound senses, men made altogether like ourselves; that we, had we been there, should have believed in it. Ask now, What Paganism could have been?

Another theory, somewhat more respectable, attributes such things to Allegory. It was a play of poetic minds, say these theorists; a shadowing-forth, in allegorical fable, in personification and visual form, of what such poetic minds had known 50 and felt of this Universe. Which agrees, add they, with a primary law of human nature, still everywhere observably at work, though in less important things. That what a man feels intensely, he struggles to speak-out of him, to see represented before him in visual shape, and as if with a kind of life and historical reality in it. Now doubtless there is such a law, and it is one of the deepest in human nature; neither need we doubt that it did operate fundamentally in this business. The hypothesis which ascribes Paganism wholly or mostly to this agency, I call a little more respectable; but I cannot yet call it the true hypothesis. Think, would *we* believe, and take with us as our life-guidance, an allegory, a poetic sport? Not sport but earnest is what we should require. It is a most earnest thing to be alive in this world; to die is not sport for a man. Man's life never was a sport to him; it was a stern reality, altogether a serious matter to be alive! . . .

You remember that fancy of Plato's, of a man who had grown to maturity in some dark distance, and was brought on a sudden into the upper air to see the sun rise. What would his wonder be, his rapt astonishment at the sight we daily witness with indifference! With the free open sense of a child, yet with the ripe faculty of a man, his whole heart would be kindled by that sight, he would discern it well to be Godlike, his soul would fall down in worship before it. Now, just such a childlike greatness was in the primitive nations. The first Pagan Thinker among rude men, the first man that began to think, was precisely this child-man of Plato's. Simple, open as a child, yet with the depth and strength of a man. Nature had as yet no name to him; he had not yet united under a name the infinite variety of sights, sounds, shapes and motions, which we now collectively name Universe, Nature, or the like,—and so with a name dismiss it from us. To the wild deep-hearted man all was yet new, not veiled under names or formulas; it stood naked, flashing-in on him there, beautiful, awful, unspeakable. Nature was to this man, what to the Thinker and Prophet it for ever is, *preter*natural. This green flowery rock-built earth, the trees, the mountains, rivers, many-sounding seas;—that great deep sea of azure that swims overhead; the winds sweeping through it; the black cloud fashioning itself together, now pouring out fire, now hail and rain; what *is* it? Ay, what? At bottom we do not yet know; we can never know at all. It is not by our superior insight that we escape the difficulty; it is by our superior levity, our inattention, our *want* of insight. It is by *not* thinking that we cease to wonder at it. Hardened round us, encasing wholly every notion we form, is a wrappage of traditions, hearsays, mere *words*. We call that fire of the black

16. **that fancy of Plato's.** See *Phaedo*, 109; *Republic*, Book VII.

thunder-cloud "electricity," and lecture learnedly about it, and grind the like of it out of glass and silk: but *what* is it? What made it? Whence comes it? Whither goes it? Science has done much for us; but it is a poor science that would hide from us the great deep sacred infinitude of Nescience, whither we can never penetrate, on which all science swims as a mere superficial film. This world, after all our science and sciences, is still a miracle; wonderful, inscrutable, *magical* and more, to whosoever will *think* of it.

That great mystery of TIME, were there no other; the illimitable, silent, never-resting thing called Time, rolling, rushing on, swift, silent, like an all-embracing ocean-tide, on which we and all the Universe swim like exhalations, like apparitions which *are*, and then *are not*: this is for ever very literally a miracle; a thing to strike us dumb,—for we have no word to speak about it. This Universe, ah me—what could the wild man know of it; what can we yet know? That it is a Force, and thousandfold Complexity of Forces; a Force which is *not we*. That is all; it is not we, it is altogether different from *us*. Force, Force, everywhere Force; we ourselves a mysterious Force in the centre of that. "There is not a leaf rotting on the highway but has Force in it: how else could it rot?" Nay surely, to the Atheistic Thinker, if such a one were possible, it must be a miracle too, this huge illimitable whirlwind of Force, which envelops us here; never-resting whirlwind, high as Immensity, old as Eternity. What is it? God's creation, the religious people answer; it is the Almighty God's! Atheistic science babbles poorly of it, with scientific nomenclatures, experiments and what-not, as if it were a poor dead thing, to be bottled-up in Leyden jars and sold over counters: but the natural sense of man, in all times, if he will honestly apply his sense, proclaims it to be a living thing,—ah, an unspeakable, godlike thing; towards which the best attitude for us, after never so much science, is awe, devout prostration and humility of soul; worship if not in words, then in silence. . . .

Worship is transcendent wonder; wonder for which there is now no limit or measure; that is worship. To these primeval men, all things and everything they saw exist beside them were an emblem of the Godlike, of some God.

And look what perennial fibre of truth was in that. To us also, through every star, through every blade of grass, is not a God made visible, if we will open our minds and eyes? We do not worship in that way now: but is it not reckoned still a merit, proof of what we call a "poetic nature," that we recognise how every object has a divine beauty in it; how every object still verily is "a window through which we may look into Infinitude itself"? He that can discern the loveliness of things, we call him Poet, Painter, Man of Genius, gifted, lovable. These poor Sabeans did even what he does,—in their own fashion. That they did it, in what fashion soever, was a merit: better than what the entirely stupid man did, what the horse and camel did,— namely, nothing!

But now if all things whatsoever that we look upon are emblems to us of the Highest God, I add that more so than any of them is man such an emblem. You have heard of St. Chrysostom's celebrated saying in reference to the Shekinah, or Ark of Testimony, visible Revelation of God, among the Hebrews: "The true Shekinah is Man!" Yes, it is even so: this is no vain phrase; it is veritably so. The essence of our being, the mystery in us that calls itself "I,"—ah, what words have we for such things?—is a breath of Heaven; the Highest Being reveals himself in man. This body, these faculties, this life of ours, is it not all as a vesture for that Unnamed? "There is but one Temple in the Universe," says the devout Novalis, "and that is the Body of Man. Nothing is holier than that high form. Bending before men is a reverence done to this Revelation in the Flesh. We touch Heaven when we lay our hand on a human body!" This sounds much like a mere flourish of rhetoric; but it is not so. If well meditated, it will turn out to be a scientific fact; the expression, in such words as can be had, of the actual truth of the thing. *We* are the miracle of miracles,—the great inscrutable mystery of God. We cannot understand it, we know not how to speak of it; but we may feel and know, if we like, that it is verily so.

Well; these truths were once more readily felt than now. The young generations of the world, who had in them the freshness of young children, and yet the depth of earnest men, who did not think they had finished-off all things in Heaven and Earth by merely giving them scientific names, but had to gaze direct at them there, with awe and wonder: they felt better what of divinity is in **man** and Nature;—they, without being mad, could *worship* Nature, and man more than anything else in Nature. Worship, that is, as I said above, admire without limit: this, in the full use of their faculties,

with all sincerity of heart, they could do. I consider Hero-worship to be the grand modifying element in that ancient system of thought. What I called the perplexed jungle of Paganism sprang, we may say, out of many roots: every admiration, adoration of a star or natural object, was a root or fibre of a root; but Hero-worship is the deepest root of all; the taproot, from which in a great degree all the rest were nourished and grown.

And now if worship even of a star had some meaning in it, how much more might that of a Hero! Worship of a Hero is transcendent admiration of a Great Man. I say great men are still admirable! I say there is, at the bottom, nothing else admirable! No nobler feeling than this of admiration for one higher than himself dwells in the breast of man. It is to this hour, and at all hours, the vivifying influence in man's life. Religion I find stand upon it; not Paganism only, but far higher and truer religions,—all religion hitherto known. Hero-worship, heartfelt prostrate admiration, submission, burning, boundless, for a noblest godlike Form of Man,—is not that the germ of Christianity itself? The greatest of all Heroes in One—whom we do not name here! Let sacred silence meditate that sacred matter; you will find it the ultimate perfection of a principle extant throughout man's whole history on earth.

Or coming into lower, less *un*speakable provinces, is not all Loyalty akin to religious Faith also? Faith is loyalty to some inspired Teacher, some spiritual Hero. And what therefore is loyalty proper, the life-breath of all society, but an effluence of Hero-worship, submissive admiration for the truly great? Society is founded on Hero-worship. All dignities of rank, on which human association rests, are what we may call a *Hero*-archy (Government of Heroes),—or a Hierarchy, for it is "sacred" enough withal! The Duke means *Dux*, Leader; King is *Kön-ning*, *Kan-ning*, Man that *knows* or *cans*. Society everywhere is some representation, not *in*supportably inaccurate, of a graduated Worship of Heroes —reverence and obedience done to men really great and wise. Not *in*supportably inaccurate, I say! They are all as bank-notes, these social dignitaries, all representing gold;—and several of them, alas, always are *forged* notes. . . .

I am well aware that in these days Hero-worship, the thing I call Hero-worship, professes to have

---

7. **Sabeans**, Syrian inhabitants of Mesopotamia.   15. **St. Chrysostom**, celebrated Father and preacher of the Greek Church (c. 347–407).   26. **Novalis**, pseud. of Friedrich von Hardenberg (1772–1801), German writer, much loved by Carlyle.

23–24. **the germ of Christianity itself.** Carlyle is, no doubt, thinking of the doctrine of the Incarnation. See Browning, "Saul," ll. 308–12.   39–40. **King . . . cans.** Carlyle's etymology, here as frequently elsewhere, is incorrect.

gone out, and finally ceased. This, for reasons which it will be worth while some time to inquire into, is an age that as it were denies the existence of great men; denies the desirableness of great men. Show our critics a great man, a Luther for example, they begin to what they call "account" for him; not to worship him, but take the dimensions of him,—and bring him out to be a little kind of man! He was the "creature of the Time," they say; the Time called him forth, the Time did everything, 10 he nothing—but what we the little critic could have done too! This seems to me but melancholy work. The Time call forth? Alas, we have known Times *call* loudly enough for their great man; but not find him when they called! He was not there; Providence had not sent him; the Time, *calling* its loudest, had to go down to confusion and wreck because he would not come when called.

For if we will think of it, no Time need have gone 20 to ruin, could it have *found* a man great enough, a man wise and good enough: wisdom to discern truly what the Time wanted, valour to lead it on the right road thither; these are the salvation of any Time. But I liken common languid Times, with their unbelief, distress, perplexity, with their languid doubting characters and embarrassed circumstances, impotently crumbling down into ever worse distress towards final ruin;—all this I liken to dry dead fuel, waiting for the lightning out of 30 Heaven that shall kindle it. The great man, with his free force direct out of God's own hand, is the lightning. His word is the wise healing word which all can believe in. All blazes round him now, when he has once struck on it, into fire like his own. The dry mouldering sticks are thought to have called him forth. They did want him greatly; but as to calling him forth—!—Those are critics of small vision, I think, who cry: "See, is it not the sticks that made the fire?" No sadder proof can be given 40 by a man of his own littleness than disbelief in great men. There is no sadder symptom of a generation than such general blindness to the spiritual lightning, with faith only in the heap of barren dead fuel. It is the last consummation of unbelief. In all epochs of the world's history, we shall find the Great Man to have been the indispensable saviour of his epoch;—the lightning, without which the fuel never would have burnt. The History of the World, I said already, was the Biography of Great 50 Men. . . .

5. **Luther,** Martin Luther, the leader of the Reformation in Germany. See note 21–22 on page 409.

from PAST AND PRESENT

Past and Present was described by its author as "a somewhat fiery and questionable 'Tract for the Times,' *not* by a Puseyite, which the terrible aspect of things here has forced from me." Breaking in upon his work on Oliver Cromwell, it got itself written during the first two months of 1843, and it constitutes probably Carlyle's most important public service.

It is divided into four books: Proem, The Ancient Monk, The Modern Worker, and Horoscope. The second part is based on *The Chronica Jocelini de Brakelonda*, which had just been published by the Camden Society, and describes, by way of contrast to modern conditions, the life of a twelfth-century abbey under Abbot Samson, "a man worth looking at," in a day when reverence for God, respect for authority and authorized leaders, and unselfish devotion to work created a stable world. Carlyle did not believe in the possibility of organizing life in nineteenth-century England on the feudal plan, but he did maintain the necessity of reviving the ideals to which Abbot Samson and his contemporaries gave their allegiance; especially did he insist upon modern "Captains of Industry" assuming the responsibilities which rulers under the feudal system had once assumed. Strangely combining bitter hatred of the democratic system with a burning sympathy for the poor, *Past and Present* became one of the strong Victorian influences in the direction of social amelioration.

from BOOK III: Chapter 5

The English

AND yet, with all thy theoretic platitudes, what a depth of practical sense in thee, great England! A depth of sense, of justice, and courage; in which, under all emergencies and world-bewilderments, and under this most complex of emergencies we now live in, there is still hope, there is still assurance!

The English are a dumb people. They can do great acts, but not describe them. Like the old Romans, and some few others, *their* Epic Poem is written on the Earth's surface: England her Mark! It is complained that they have no artists: one Shakespeare indeed; but for Raphael only a Reynolds; for Mozart nothing but a Mr. Bishop: not a picture, not a song. And yet they did produce one Shakespeare: consider how the element of Shakespearean melody does lie imprisoned in their nature;

44–45. but for Raphael . . . Mr. Bishop. Raphael, one of the most famous of all Italian painters (1483–1520). **Reynolds,** Sir Joshua Reynolds (1723–1792), English portrait-painter. **Mozart,** Wolfgang Amadeus Mozart (1756–1791), Austrian composer, one of the greatest. **Bishop,** Sir Henry R. Bishop (1786–1855), English composer, teacher, and musical director.

reduced to unfold itself in mere Cottonmills, Constitutional Governments, and such like;—all the more interesting when it does become visible, as even in such unexpected shapes it succeeds in doing! Goethe spoke of the Horse, how impressive, almost affecting it was that an animal of such qualities should stand obstructed so; its speech nothing but an inarticulate neighing, its handiness mere *hoof*iness, the fingers all constricted, tied together, the finger-nails coagulated into a mere hoof, shod with iron. The more significant, thinks he, are those eye-lashings of the generous noble quadruped; those prancings, curvings of the neck clothed with thunder. . . .

The spoken Word, the written Poem, is said to be an epitome of the man; how much more the done Work. Whatsoever of morality and of intelligence; what of patience, perseverance, faithfulness, or method, insight, ingenuity, energy; in a word, whatsoever of Strength the man had in him will lie written in the Work he does. To work: why, it is to try himself against Nature, and her everlasting unerring Laws; these will tell a true verdict as to the man. So much of virtue and of faculty did *we* find in him; so much and no more! He had such capacity of harmonising himself with *me* and my unalterable ever-veracious Laws; of coöperating and working as *I* bade him;—and has prospered, and has not prospered, as you see! . . .

How one loves to see the burly figure of him, this thick-skinned, seemingly opaque, perhaps sulky, almost stupid Man of Practice, pitted against some light adroit Man of Theory, all equipped with clear logic, and able anywhere to give you Why for Wherefore! The adroit Man of Theory, so light of movement, clear of utterance, with his bow full-bent and quiver full of arrow-arguments,—surely he will strike down the game, transfix everywhere the heart of the matter; triumph everywhere, as he proves that he shall and must do? To your astonishment, it turns out oftenest No. The cloudy-browed, thick-soled, opaque Practicality, with no logic utterance, in silence mainly, with here and there a low grunt or growl, has in him what transcends all logic-utterance: a Congruity with the Unuttered. The Speakable, which lies atop, as a superficial film, or outer skin, is his or is not his: but the Doable, which reaches down to the World's centre, you find him there! . . .

Of all the Nations in the world at present the English are the stupidest in speech, the wisest in action. As good as a "dumb" Nation, I say, who cannot speak, and have never yet spoken,—spite of the Shakespeares and Miltons who show us what possibilities there are!—O Mr. Bull, I look in that surly face of thine with a mixture of pity and laughter, yet also with wonder and veneration. Thou complainest not, my illustrious friend; and yet I believe the heart of thee is full of sorrow, of unspoken sadness, seriousness,—profound melancholy (as some have said) the basis of thy being. Unconsciously, for thou speakest of nothing, this great Universe is great to thee. Not by levity of floating, but by stubborn force of swimming, shalt thou make thy way. The Fates sing of thee that thou shalt many times be thought an ass and a dull ox, and shalt with a godlike indifference believe it. My friend,—and it is all untrue, nothing ever falser in point of fact! Thou art of those great ones whose greatness the small passer-by does not discern. Thy very stupidity is wiser than their wisdom. A grand *vis inertiae* is in thee; how many grand qualities unknown to small men! Nature alone knows thee, acknowledges the bulk and strength of thee: thy Epic, unsung in words, is written in huge characters on the face of this Planet,—sea-moles, cotton-trades, railways, fleets and cities, Indian Empires, Americas, New-Hollands; legible throughout the Solar System! . . .

Ask Bull his spoken opinion of any matter,— oftentimes the force of dullness can no farther go. You stand silent, incredulous, as over a platitude that borders on the Infinite. The man's Churchisms, Dissenterisms, Puseyisms, Benthamisms, College Philosophies, Fashionable Literatures, are unexampled in this world. Fate's prophecy is fulfilled; you call the man an ox and an ass. But set him once to work,—respectable man! His spoken sense is next to nothing, nine-tenths of it palpable *non*sense: but his unspoken sense, his inner silent feeling of what is true, what does agree with fact, what is doable and what is not doable,—this seeks its fellow in the world. A terrible worker; irresistible against marshes, mountains, impediments, disorder, incivilization; everywhere vanquishing disorder, leaving it behind him as method and order. . . .

Nay withal, stupid as he is, our dear John,—ever,

4. Mr. Bull, John Bull, who typifies England, as Uncle Sam typifies America.   **21. vis inertiae,** force of inertia. **33. Churchisms,** referring to the Established Church and possibly to the Oxford Movement. **Dissenterisms** refers to Methodists, Congregationalists, Quakers, and so on. **Puseyisms** refers to the Oxford Movement; see introduction and notes to selections from Cardinal Newman in this volume. **Benthamisms** refers to Utilitarianism; see pages 377–78 and introduction to selections from John Stuart Mill.

after infinite tumblings, and spoken platitudes in-numerable from barrel-heads and parliament-benches, he does settle down somewhere about the just conclusion; you are certain that his jumblings and tumblings will end, after years or centuries, in the stable equilibrium. Stable equilibrium, I say; centre-of-gravity lowest;—not the unstable, with centre-of-gravity highest, as I have known it done by quicker people! For indeed, do but jumble and tumble sufficiently, you avoid that worse fault, of settling with your centre-of-gravity highest; your centre-of-gravity is certain to come lowest, and to stay there. If slowness, what we in our impatience call "stupidity," be the price of stable equilibrium over unstable, shall we grudge a little slowness? Not the least admirable quality of Bull is, after all, that of remaining insensible to logic; holding out for considerable periods, ten years or more, as in this of the Corn-Laws, after all arguments and shadow of arguments have faded away from him, till the very urchins on the street titter at the argu-ments he brings. Logic,—Λογική, the "Art of Speech,"—does indeed speak so and so; clear enough: nevertheless Bull still shakes his head; will see whether nothing else *illogical*, not yet "spoken," not yet able to be "spoken," do not lie in the business, as there so often does!—My firm belief is, that, finding himself now enchanted, hand-shackled, foot-shackled, in Poor-Law Bastilles and elsewhere, he will retire three days to his bed, and *arrive* at a conclusion or two! His three-years "total stagna-tion of trade," alas, is not that a painful enough "lying in bed to consider himself"? Poor Bull!

Bull is a born Conservative; for this too I inex-pressibly honour him. All great Peoples are con-servative; slow to believe in novelties; patient of much error in actualities; deeply and for ever cer-tain of the greatness that is in LAW, in Custom once solemnly established, and now long recognised as just and final.—True, O Radical Reformer, there is no Custom that can, properly speaking, be final; none. And yet thou seest *Customs* which, in all civilised countries, are accounted final; nay, under the Old-Roman name of *Mores*, are accounted *Morality*, Virtue, Laws of God Himself. Such, I assure thee, not a few of them are; such almost all of them once were. And greatly do I respect the solid character,—a blockhead, thou wilt say; yes, but a well-conditioned blockhead, and the best-conditioned,—who esteems all "Customs once solemnly acknowledged" to be ultimate, divine, and the rule of a man to walk by, nothing doubt-ing, not inquiring farther. What a time of it had we, were all men's life and trade still, in all parts of it, a problem, a hypothetic seeking, to be settled by painful Logics and Baconian Inductions! The Clerk in Eastcheap cannot spend the day in verifying his Ready-Reckoner; he must take it as verified, true and indisputable; or his Bookkeeping by Double Entry will stand still. "Where is your Posted Ledger?" asks the Master at night.—"Sir," answers the other, "I was verifying my Ready-Reckoner, and find some errors. The Ledger is—!"—Fancy such a thing! . . .

O my Conservative friends, who still specially name and struggle to approve yourselves "Con-servative," would to Heaven I could persuade you of this world-old fact, than which Fate is not surer, That Truth and Justice alone are *capable* of being "conserved" and preserved! The thing which is unjust, which is *not* according to God's Law, will you, in a God's Universe, try to conserve that? It is so old, say you? Yes, and the hotter haste ought *you*, of all others, to be in to let it grow no older! If but the faintest whisper in your hearts intimate to you that it is not fair,—hasten, for the sake of Con-servatism itself, to probe it rigorously, to cast it forth at once and forever if guilty. How will or can you preserve *it*, the thing that is not fair? "Impossi-bility" a thousandfold is marked on that. And ye call yourselves Conservatives, Aristocracies:—ought not honour and nobleness of mind, if they had de-parted from all the Earth elsewhere, to find their last refuge with you? Ye unfortunate!

The bough that is dead shall be cut away, for the sake of the tree itself. Old? Yes, it is too old. Many a weary winter has it swung and creaked there, and gnawed and fretted, with its dead wood, the organic substance and still living fibre of this good tree; many a long summer has its ugly naked brown de-faced the fair green umbrage; every day it has done mischief, and that only: off with it, for the tree's sake, if for nothing more; let the Conservatism that would preserve cut *it* away. Did no wood-forester apprise you that a dead bough with its dead root left sticking there is extraneous, poisonous; is as a dead iron spike, some horrid rusty ploughshare driven into the living substance;—nay is far worse;

19. Corn-Laws. See page 378.   **29. Poor-Law Bas-tilles,** workhouses; see pages 376–77.   **30–31. he will retire . . . or two,** as was the custom of the famous engi-neer James Brindley (1716–1772), to whom Carlyle paid his tribute in a portion of this essay not included in the present reprint.

7. Baconian Inductions. Sir Francis Bacon set forth the inductive method of reasoning (as opposed to the deductive method employed by the Scholastic philosophers) in his *Novum Organum*, 1620.   **8. Eastcheap,** a street in London's financial district.

for in every windstorm ("commercial crisis" or the like), it frets and creaks, jolts itself to and fro, and cannot lie quiet as your dead iron spike would.

If I were the Conservative Party of England (which is another bold figure of speech), I would not for a hundred thousand pounds an hour allow those Corn-Laws to continue! Potosi and Golconda put together would not purchase my assent to them. Do you count what treasuries of bitter indignation they are laying up for you in every just English heart? Do you know what questions, not as to Corn-prices and Sliding-scales alone, they are *forcing* every reflective Englishman to ask himself? Questions insoluble, or hitherto unsolved; deeper than any of our Logic-plummets hitherto will sound: questions deep enough,—which it were better that we did not name even in thought! You are forcing us to think of them, to begin uttering them. The utterance of them is begun; and where will it be ended, think you? When two millions of one's brother-men sit in Workhouses, and five millions, as is insolently said, "rejoice in potatoes," there are various things that must be begun, let them end where they can.

from Chapter 11

Labour

For there is a perennial nobleness, and even sacredness, in Work. Were he never so benighted, forgetful of his high calling, there is always hope in a man that actually and earnestly works: in Idleness alone is there perpetual despair. Work, never so Mammonish, mean, *is* in communication with Nature; the real desire to get Work done will itself lead one more and more to truth, to Nature's appointments and regulations which are truth.

The latest Gospel in this world is, Know thy work and do it. "Know thyself": long enough has that poor "self" of thine tormented thee; thou wilt never get to "know" it, I believe! Think it not thy business, this of knowing thyself; thou art an unknowable individual: know what thou canst work at; and work at it, like a Hercules! That will be thy better plan.

It has been written, "an endless significance lies in Work"; a man perfects himself by working. Foul jungles are cleared away, fair seed-fields rise in-

stead, and stately cities; and withal the man himself first ceases to be a jungle and foul unwholesome desert thereby. Consider how, even in the meanest sorts of Labour, the whole soul of a man is composed into a kind of real harmony, the instant he sets himself to work! Doubt, Desire, Sorrow, Remorse, Indignation, Despair itself, all these like helldogs lie beleaguering the soul of the poor day-worker, as of every man: but he bends himself with free valour against his task, and all these are stilled, all these shrink murmuring far off into their caves. The man is now a man. The blessed glow of Labour in him, is it not as purifying fire, wherein all poison is burnt up, and of sour smoke itself there is made bright blessed flame!

Destiny, on the whole, has no other way of cultivating us. A formless Chaos, once set it *revolving*, grows round and ever rounder; ranges itself, by mere force of gravity, into strata, spherical courses; is no longer a Chaos, but a round compacted World. What would become of the Earth, did she cease to revolve? In the poor old Earth, so long as she revolves, all inequalities, irregularities disperse themselves; all irregularities are incessantly becoming regular. Hast thou looked on the Potter's wheel, one of the venerablest objects; old as the Prophet Ezekiel and far older? Rude lumps of clay, how they spin themselves up, by mere quick whirling, into beautiful circular dishes. And fancy the most assiduous Potter, but without his wheel; reduced to make dishes, or rather amorphous botches, by mere kneading and baking! Even such a Potter were Destiny, with a human soul that would rest and lie at ease, that would not work and spin! Of an idle unrevolving man the kindest Destiny, like the most assiduous Potter without wheel, can bake and knead nothing other than a botch; let her spend on him what expensive colouring, what gilding and enamelling she will, he is but a botch. Not a dish; no, a bulging, kneaded, crooked, shambling, squint-cornered, amorphous botch,—a mere enamelled vessel of dishonour! Let the idle think of this.

Blessed is he who has found his work; let him ask no other blessedness. He has a work, a life-purpose; he has found it, and will follow it! How, as a free-flowing channel, dug and torn by noble force through the sour mud-swamp of one's existence, like an ever-deepening river there, it runs and flows;—draining-off the sour festering water, gradually from the root of the remotest grass-blade; making, instead of pestilential swamp, a green

---

7. Potosi, a department of Bolivia, rich in ore. **Golconda,** a fortress and ruined city in India, known for its diamonds. **34. Mammonish.** In the New Testament, mammon is either riches (Luke 16:9–11) or the god of riches (Matthew 6:24; Luke 16:13). See *Paradise Lost*, Book II, ll. 226 ff. **39. "Know thyself."** See note 38, page 406—a favorite quotation with Carlyle.

25. Potter's wheel. See, in this volume, Browning's "Rabbi Ben Ezra" and FitzGerald's "Rubáiyát of Omar Khayyám," with notes.

fruitful meadow with its clear-flowing stream. How blessed for the meadow itself, let the stream and *its* value be great or small! Labour is Life: from the inmost heart of the Worker rises his god-given Force, the sacred celestial Life-essence breathed into him by Almighty God; from his inmost heart awakens him to all nobleness,—to all knowledge, "self-knowledge" and much else, so soon as Work fitly begins. Knowledge? The knowledge that will hold good in working, cleave thou to that; for Nature herself accredits that, says Yea to that. Properly thou hast no other knowledge but what thou hast got by working: the rest is yet all a hypothesis of knowledge; a thing to be argued of in schools, a thing floating in the clouds, in endless logic-vortices, till we try it and fix it. "Doubt, of whatever kind, can be ended by Action alone." . . .

Brave Sea-captain, Norse Sea-king,—Columbus, my hero, royallest Sea-king of all! it is no friendly environment this of thine, in the waste deep waters; around thee mutinous discouraged souls, behind thee disgrace and ruin, before thee the unpenetrated veil of Night. Brother, these wild water-mountains, bounding from their deep bases (ten miles deep, I am told), are not entirely there on thy behalf! Meseems *they* have other work than floating thee forward:—and the huge Winds, that sweep from Ursa Major to the Tropics and Equators, dancing their giant-waltz through the kingdoms of Chaos and Immensity, they care little about filling rightly or filling wrongly the small shoulder-of-mutton sails in this cockle-skiff of thine! Thou art not among articulate-speaking friends, my brother; thou art among immeasurable dumb monsters, tumbling, howling wide as the world here. Secret, far off, invisible to all hearts but thine, there lies a help in them: see how thou wilt get at that. Patiently thou wilt wait till the mad South-wester spend itself, saving thyself by dextrous science of defence, the while: valiantly, with swift decision, wilt thou strike in, when the favouring East, the Possible, springs up. Mutiny of men thou wilt sternly repress; weakness, despondency, thou wilt cheerily encourage: thou wilt swallow down complaint, unreason, weariness, weakness of others and thyself;—how much wilt thou swallow down! There shall be a depth of Silence in thee, deeper than this Sea, which is but ten miles deep: a Silence unsoundable; known to God only. Thou shalt be a Great Man. Yes, my World-Soldier, thou of the World Marine-service,—thou wilt have to be *greater* than this tumultuous unmeasured World here round thee is: thou, in thy strong soul, as with wrestler's arms, shalt embrace it, harness it down; and make it bear thee on,—to new Americas, or whither God wills!

from Chapter 13

Democracy

If the Serene Highnesses and Majesties do not take note of that, then, as I perceive, *that* will take note of itself! The time for levity, insincerity, and idle babble and play-acting, in all kinds, is gone by; it is a serious, grave time. Old long-vexed questions, not yet solved in logical words or parliamentary laws, are fast solving themselves in facts, somewhat unblessed to behold! This largest of questions, this question of Work and Wages, which ought, had we heeded Heaven's voice, to have begun two generations ago or more, cannot be delayed longer without hearing Earth's voice. "Labour" will verily need to be somewhat "organised," as they say,— God knows with what difficulty. Man will actually need to have his debts and earnings a little better paid by man; which, let Parliaments speak of them, or be silent of them, are eternally his due from man, and cannot, without penalty and at length not without death-penalty, be withheld. How much ought to cease among us straightway; how much ought to begin straightway, while the hours yet are! . . .

Life was never a May-game for men: in all times the lot of the dumb millions born to toil was defaced with manifold sufferings, injustices, heavy burdens, avoidable and unavoidable; not play at all, but hard work that made the sinews sore and the heart sore. As bond slaves, *villani, bordarii, sochemanni,* nay indeed as dukes, earls and kings, men were oftentimes made weary of their life; and had to say, in the sweat of their brow and of their soul, Behold, it is not sport, it is grim earnest, and our back can bear no more! Who knows not what massacrings and harryings there have been; grinding, long-continuing, unbearable injustices,—till the heart had to rise in madness, and some "*Eu Sachsen, nimith euer sachses,* You Saxons, out with your gully-knives, then!" You Saxons, some "arrestment," partial "arrestment of the Knaves and Dastards" has become indispensable!—The page of Dryasdust is heavy with such details.

And yet I will venture to believe that in no time,

9. **that,** that "Tools and the Man" is now our epic.
36. **villani,** free peasants. **bordarii,** cottage tenants bound to menial service. **sochemanni,** socmen, having tenure by service. 38–39. **in the sweat of their brow.** See Genesis 3:19.

since the beginnings of Society, was the lot of those same dumb millions of toilers so entirely unbearable as it is even in the days now passing over us. It is not to die, or even to die of hunger, that makes a man wretched; many men have died; all men must die, —the last exit of us all is in a Fire-Chariot of Pain. But it is to live miserable we know not why; to work sore and yet gain nothing; to be heart-worn, weary, yet isolated, unrelated, girt-in with a cold universal Laissez-faire: it is to die slowly all our life long, im- prisoned in a deaf, dead, Infinite Injustice, as in the accursed iron belly of a Phalaris' Bull! . . .

Gurth, born thrall of Cedric the Saxon, has been greatly pitied by Dryasdust and others. Gurth, with the brass collar round his neck, tending Cedric's pigs in the glades of the wood, is not what I call an exemplar of human felicity: but Gurth, with the sky above him, with the free air and tinted boscage and umbrage round him, and in him at least the cer- tainty of supper and social lodging when he came home; Gurth to me seems happy, in comparison with many a Lancashire and Buckinghamshire man of these days, not born thrall of anybody! Gurth's brass collar did not gall him: Cedric *de-served* to be his Master. The pigs were Cedric's, but Gurth too would get his parings of them. Gurth had the inexpressible satisfaction of feeling himself related indissolubly, though in a rude brass-collar way, to his fellow-mortals in this Earth. He had superiors, inferiors, equals.—Gurth is now "eman-cipated" long since; has what we call "Liberty." Liberty, I am told, is a Divine thing. Liberty when it becomes the "Liberty to die by starvation" is not so divine!

Liberty? The true liberty of a man, you would say, consisted in his finding out, or being forced to find out, the right path, and to walk thereon. To learn, or to be taught, what work he actually was able for; and then by permission, persuasion, and even compulsion, to set about doing of the same! That is his true blessedness, honour, "liberty" and maximum of wellbeing: if liberty be not that, I for one have small care about liberty. You do not allow a palpable madman to leap over precipices; you violate his liberty, you that are wise; and keep him, were it in strait-waistcoats, away from the preci-pices! Every stupid, every cowardly and foolish man is but a less palpable madman: his true liberty were that a wiser man, that any and every wiser

man, could, by brass collars, or in whatever milder or sharper way, lay hold of him when he was going wrong, and order and compel him to go a little righter. O, if thou really art my *Senior*, Seigneur, my *Elder*, Presbyter or Priest,—if thou art in very deed my *Wiser*, may a beneficent instinct lead and impel thee to "conquer" me, to command me! If thou do know better than I what is good and right, I con-jure thee in the name of God, force me to do it; were it by never such brass collars, whips and handcuffs, leave me not to walk over precipices! That I have been called, by all the Newspapers, a "free man" will avail me little, if my pilgrimage have ended in death and wreck. O that the Newspapers had called me slave, coward, fool, or what it pleased their sweet voices to name me, and I had attained not death, but life!—Liberty requires new definitions.

A conscious abhorrence and intolerance of Folly, of Baseness, Stupidity, Poltroonery and all that brood of things, dwells deep in some men: still deeper in others an *unconscious* abhorrence and in-tolerance, clothed moreover by the beneficent Su-preme Powers in what stout appetites, energies, egoisms so-called, are suitable to it;—these latter are your Conquerors, Romans, Normans, Russians, Indo-English; Founders of what we call Aristoc-racies. Which indeed have they not the most "di-vine right" to found;—being themselves very Ἄριστοι, BRAVEST, BEST; and conquering generally a confused rabble of WORST, or at lowest, clearly enough, of WORSE? I think their divine right, tried, with affirmatory verdict, in the greatest Law-Court known to me, was good! A class of men who are dreadfully exclaimed against by Dryasdust, of whom nevertheless beneficent Nature has often-times had need; and may, alas, again have need.

When, across the hundredfold poor scepticisms, trivialisms, and constitutional cobwebberies of Dryasdust, you catch any glimpse of a William the Conqueror, a Tancred of Hauteville or such like,— do you not discern veritably some rude outline of a true God-made King; whom not the Champion of England cased in tin, but all Nature and the Uni-verse were calling to the throne? It is absolutely necessary that he get thither. Nature does not mean her poor Saxon children to perish, of obesity, stupor or other malady, as yet: a stern Ruler and Line of Rulers therefore is called in,—a stern but most beneficent *perpetual House-Surgeon* is by Nature her-

6. a Fire-Chariot of Pain. See 2 Kings 2:11–12. 10. Laissez-faire. See pages 377–78 in this volume. 12. Pharlaris' Bull. See note 34 on "The Execution of Louis XVI," page 420. 14. Gurth . . . Saxon, in Scott's *Ivanhoe*.

34. Dryasdust, an imaginary pedant, addressed by Sir Walter Scott in several prefaces of his novels. 39–40. Wil-liam the Conqueror, William of Normandy, who con-quered the Anglo-Saxons in the battle of Hastings and became William I (reigned 1066–87). Tancred of Haute-ville, a Norman hero of the First Crusade.

self called in, and even the appropriate *fees* are provided for him! Dryasdust talks lamentably about Hereward and the Fen Counties; fate of Earl Waltheof; Yorkshire and the North reduced to ashes; all of which is undoubtedly lamentable. But even Dryasdust apprises me of one fact: "A child, in this William's reign, might have carried a purse of gold from end to end of England." My erudite friend, it is a fact which outweighs a thousand! Sweep away thy constitutional, sentimental, and other cobwebberies; look eye to eye, if thou still have any eye, in the face of this big burly William Bastard: thou wilt see a fellow of most flashing discernment, of most strong lion-heart;—in whom, as it were, within a frame of oak and iron, the gods have planted the soul of "a man of genius"! Dost thou call that nothing? I call it an immense thing! —Rage enough was in this Willelmus Conquaestor, rage enough for his occasions;—and yet the essential element of him, as of all such men, is not scorching *fire*, but shining illuminative *light*. Fire and light are strangely interchangeable; nay, at bottom, I have found them different forms of the same most godlike "elementary substance" in our world: a thing worth stating in these days. The essential element of this Conquaestor is, first of all, the most sun-eyed perception of what *is* really what on this God's-Earth;—which, thou wilt find, does mean at bottom "Justice," and "Virtues" not a few: *Conformity* to what the Maker has seen good to make; that, I suppose, will mean Justice and a Virtue or two?—

Dost thou think Willelmus Conquaestor would have tolerated ten years' jargon, one hour's jargon, on the propriety of killing Cotton-manufactures by partridge Corn-Laws? I fancy, this was not the man to knock out of his night's-rest with nothing but a noisy bedlamism in your mouth! "Assist us still better to bush the partridges; strangle Plugson who spins the shirts?"—*"Par la Splendeur de Dieu!"*—— Dost thou think Willelmus Conquaestor, in this new time, with Steam-engine Captains of Industry on one hand of him, and Joe-Manton Captains of Idleness on the other, would have doubted which *was* really the BEST; which did deserve strangling, and which not?

I have a certain indestructible regard for Willelmus Conquaestor. A resident House-Surgeon, provided by Nature for her beloved English People, and even furnished with the requisite fees, as I said; for he by no means felt himself doing Nature's work, this Willelmus, but his own work exclusively! And his own work withal it was; informed *"par la Splendeur de Dieu."*—I say, it is necessary to get the work out of such a man, however harsh that be! When a world, not yet doomed for death, is rushing down to ever-deeper Baseness and Confusion, it is a dire necessity of Nature's to bring in her ARISTOCRACIES, her BEST, even by forcible methods. When their descendants or representatives cease entirely to *be* the Best, Nature's poor world will very soon rush down again to Baseness; and it becomes a dire necessity of Nature's to cast them out. Hence French Revolutions, Five-point Charters, Democracies, and a mournful list of *Etceteras*, in these our afflicted times. . . .

But truly, as I had to remark in the meanwhile, "the liberty of not being oppressed by your fellow man" is an indispensable, yet one of the most insignificant fractional parts of Human Liberty. No man oppresses thee, can bid thee fetch or carry, come or go, without reason shown. True; from all men thou art emancipated: but from Thyself and from the Devil—? No man, wiser, unwiser, can make thee come or go: but thy own futilities, bewilderments, thy false appetites for Money, Windsor Georges and such like? No man oppresses thee, O free and independent Franchiser: but does not this stupid Porter-pot oppress thee? No Son of Adam can bid thee come or go; but this absurd Pot of Heavy-wet, this can and does! Thou art the thrall not of Cedric the Saxon, but of thy own brutal appetites, and this scoured dish of liquor. And thou pratest of thy "liberty"? Thou entire blockhead!

Heavy-wet and gin: alas, these are not the only kinds of thraldom. Thou who walkest in a vain show, looking out with ornamental dilettante sniff, and serene supremacy, at all Life and all Death; and amblest jauntily; perking up thy poor talk into crotchets, thy poor conduct into fatuous somnambulisms;—and *art* as an "enchanted Ape" under God's sky, where thou mightest have been a man, had proper Schoolmasters and Conquerors, and Constables with cat-o'-nine tails, been vouchsafed thee: dost thou call that "liberty"? Or your unreposing Mammon-worshipper, again, driven, as if by Galvanisms, by Devils and Fixed-Ideas, who

3. **Hereward,** a Saxon outlaw who opposed William the Conqueror; see Charles Kingsley's novel *Hereward the Last of the English,* 1866. **3–4. Earl Waltheof,** Earl of Northumberland, executed by William the Conqueror, 1076. **12–13. William Bastard,** William the Conqueror, who was of illegitimate birth. **18. Willelmus Conquaestor,** William the Conqueror. **39. "Par . . . Dieu!"** By the splendor of God! one of William's oaths. **42–43. Joe-Manton . . . Idleness,** aristocrats fiddling away their time hunting with guns made by a famous London gunsmith, Joseph Manton (c. 1766–1835).

32. **Windsor Georges,** pomp and splendor, as in royal processions. **36. Heavy-wet,** malt liquor.

rises early and sits late, chasing the impossible; straining every faculty to "fill himself with the east wind,"—how merciful were it, could you, by mild persuasion or by the severest tyranny so-called, check him in his mad path, and turn him into a wiser one! All painful tyranny, in that case again, were but mild "surgery"; the pain of it cheap, as health and life, instead of galvanism and fixed-idea, are cheap at any price.

Sure enough, of all paths a man could strike into, there *is*, at any given moment, a *best path* for every man; a thing which, here and now, it were of all things *wisest* for him to do;—which could he be but led or driven to do, he were then doing "like a man," as we phrase it; all men and gods agreeing with him, the whole Universe virtually exclaiming Well-done to him! His success, in such case, were complete; his felicity a maximum. This path, to find this path and walk in it, is the one thing needful for him. Whatsoever forwards him in that, let it come to him even in the shape of blows and spurnings, is liberty: whatsoever hinders him, were it wardmotes, open-vestries, poll-booths, tremendous cheers, rivers of heavy-wet, is slavery. . . .

from BOOK IV: Chapter I

Aristocracies

. . . If the convulsive struggles of the last Half-Century have taught poor struggling convulsed Europe any truth, it may perhaps be this as the essence of innumerable others: That Europe requires a real Aristocracy, a real Priesthood, or it cannot continue to exist. Huge French Revolutions, Napoleonisms, then Bourbonisms with their corollary of Three Days, finishing in very unfinal Louis-Philippisms: all this ought to be didactic! All this may have taught us, That False Aristocracies are insupportable; that No-Aristocracies, Liberty-and-Equalities are impossible; that true Aristocracies are at once indispensable and not easily attained.

Aristocracy and Priesthood, a Governing Class and a Teaching Class: these two, sometimes separate, and endeavouring to harmonise themselves, sometimes conjoined as one, and the King a Pontiff-King:—there did no Society exist without these two vital elements, there will none exist. It lies in the very nature of man: you will visit no remotest village in the most republican country of the world, where virtually or actually you do not find these two powers at work. Man, little as he may suppose it, is necessitated to obey superiors. He is a social being in virtue of this necessity; nay he could not be gregarious otherwise. He obeys those whom he esteems better than himself, wiser, braver; and will forever obey such; and even be ready and delighted to do it.

The Wiser, Braver: these, a Virtual Aristocracy everywhere and everywhen, do in all Societies that reach any articulate shape, develop themselves into a ruling class, an Actual Aristocracy, with settled modes of operating, what are called laws and even *private-laws* or privileges, and so forth; very notable to look upon in this world.—Aristocracy and Priesthood, we say, are sometimes united. For indeed the Wiser and the Braver are properly but one class; no wise man but needed first of all to be a brave man, or he never had been wise. The noble Priest was always a noble *Aristos* to begin with, and something more to end with. Your Luther, your Knox, your Anselm, Becket, Abbot Samson, Samuel Johnson, if they had not been brave enough, by what possibility could they ever have been wise?—If, from accident or forethought, this your Actual Aristocracy have got discriminated into Two Classes, there can be no doubt but the Priest Class is the more dignified; supreme over the other, as governing head is over active hand. And yet in practice again, it is likeliest the reverse will be found arranged;—a sign that the arrangement is already vitiated; that a split is introduced into it, which will widen and widen till the whole be rent asunder.

In England, in Europe generally, we may say that these two Virtualities have unfolded themselves into Actualities, in by far the noblest and richest manner any region of the world ever saw. A spiritual Guideship, a practical Governorship, fruit of the grand conscious endeavours, say rather of the immeasurable unconscious instincts and necessities of men, have established themselves; very

2-3. "fill . . . wind." See Job 15:2.   **34-37. Huge French Revolutions . . . Louis-Philippisms.** The French Revolution began in 1789. Napoleon came into power in 1799 and was crushed at Waterloo in 1815. The Bourbons were restored to the throne of France after Napoleon lost it. Three days of disorder (February 22-24, 1848) led to the abdication of Louis Philippe.

22-23. Knox, John Knox (c. 1505-1572), leader of the Reformation in Scotland. **Anselm,** Archbishop of Canterbury, author of the "substitutionary theory" of the Atonement (1033-1109). **Becket,** Thomas à Becket (c. 1118-1170), who engaged in a bitter controversy with Henry II over the respective rights of Church and State in England (as Anselm, before him, had contested with William II—William Rufus), and who, after his murder in Canterbury Cathedral, became the great English ecclesiastical martyr (see Chaucer's *Canterbury Tales*). **Abbot Samson,** head of the Abbey of St. Edmund's Bury, at the close of the twelfth century, who plays a large role in *Past and Present*. **Samuel Johnson,** the "Grand Cham" of eighteenth-century English letters (1709-1784); see selections from his work and Boswell's in Vol. I of this work.

strange to behold. Everywhere, while so much has been forgotten, you find the King's Palace, and the Viceking's Castle, Mansion, Manorhouse; till there is not an inch of ground from sea to sea but has both its King and Viceking, long due series of Vicekings, its Squire, Earl, Duke or whatever the title of him,—to whom you have given the land, that he may govern you in it.

More touching still, there is not a hamlet where poor peasants congregate, but, by one means and another, a Church-Apparatus has been got together,—roofed edifice, with revenues and belfries; pulpit, reading-desk, with Books and Methods: possibility, in short, and strict prescription, That a man stand there and speak of spiritual things to men. It is beautiful;—even in its great obscuration and decadence, it is among the beautifulest, most touching objects one sees on the Earth. This Speaking Man has indeed, in these times, wandered terribly from the point; has, alas, as it were, totally lost sight of the point: yet, at bottom, whom have we to compare with him? Of all public functionaries boarded and lodged on the Industry of Modern Europe, is there one worthier of the board he has? A man even professing, and never so languidly making still some endeavour, to save the souls of men: contrast him with a man professing to do little but shoot the partridges of men! I wish he could find the point again, this Speaking One; and stick to it with tenacity, with deadly energy; for there is need of him yet! The Speaking Function, this of Truth coming to us with a living voice, nay in a living shape, and as a concrete practical exemplar: this, with all our Writing and Printing Functions, has a perennial place. Could he but find the point again,—take the old spectacles off his nose, and looking up discover, almost in contact with him, what the *real* Satanas, and soul-devouring, world-devouring *Devil*, now is! Original Sin and suchlike are bad enough, I doubt not: but distilled Gin, dark Ignorance, Stupidity, dark Corn-Law, Bastille and Company, what are they! *Will* he discover our new real Satan, whom he has to fight; or go on droning through his old nose-spectacles about old extinct Satans; and never see the real one, till he *feel* him at his own throat and ours? That is a question, for the world! Let us not intermeddle with it here.

Sorrowful, phantasmal as this same Double Aristocracy of Teachers and Governors now looks, it is worth all men's while to know that the purport of it is and remains noble and most real. Dryasdust,

looking merely at the surface, is greatly in error as to those ancient Kings. William Conqueror, William Rufus or Redbeard, Stephen Curthose himself, much more Henry Beauclerc and our brave Plantagenet Henry: the life of these men was not a vulturous Fighting; it was a valorous Governing,—to which occasionally Fighting did, and alas must yet, though far seldomer now, superadd itself as an accident, a distressing impedimental adjunct. The fighting too was indispensable, for ascertaining who had the might over whom, the right over whom. By much hard fighting, as we once said, "the unrealities, beaten into dust, flew gradually off"; and left the plain reality and fact, "Thou stronger than I; thou wiser than I; thou king, and subject I," in a somewhat clearer condition. . . .

Old Anselm, exiled Archbishop of Canterbury, one of the purest-minded "men of genius," was travelling to make his appeal to Rome against King Rufus,—a man of rough ways, in whom the "inner Lightbeam" shone very fitfully. It is beautiful to read, in Monk Eadmer, how the Continental populations welcomed and venerated this Anselm, as no French population now venerates Jean-Jacques or giant-killing Voltaire; as not even an American population now venerates a Schnüspel the distinguished Novelist! They had, by phantasy and true insight, the intensest conviction that a God's-Blessing dwelt in this Anselm,—as is my conviction too. They crowded round, with bent knees and enkindled hearts, to receive his blessing, to hear his voice, to see the light of his face. My blessings on them and on him!—But the notablest was a certain necessitous or covetous Duke of Burgundy, in straitened circumstances we shall hope,—who reflected that in all likelihood this English Archbishop, going towards Rome to appeal, must have taken store of cash with him to bribe the Cardinals. Wherefore he of Burgundy, for his part, decided to lie in wait and rob him. "In an open space of a wood," some "wood" then green and growing, eight centuries ago, in Burgundian Land,—this fierce Duke, with fierce steel followers, shaggy, savage, as the Russian bear, dashes out on the weak old Anselm; who is riding along there, on his small quiet-going pony; escorted only by Eadmer and

2–5. William Rufus or Redbeard, William II, reigned 1087–1100. **Stephen Curthose,** reigned 1135–54. **Henry Beauclerc** (fine scholar), Henry I, reigned 1100–35. **Plantagenet Henry,** Henry II, reigned 1154–89. **23. Monk Eadmer,** of Canterbury, a chronicler of the early twelfth century. **25–26. Jean-Jacques,** Jean Jacques Rousseau (1712–1778). **Voltaire,** François Marie Arouet (1694–1778). French writers who helped prepare the public mind for the revolution. **27. Schnüspel,** a made name.

39. Original Sin, according to Calvin and other theologians the taint inherited by human nature from Adam and Eve.

another poor Monk on ponies; and, except small modicum of roadmoney, not a gold coin in his possession. The steelclad Russian bear emerges, glaring: the old white-bearded man starts not,—paces on unmoved, looking into him with those clear old earnest eyes, with that venerable sorrowful time-worn face; of whom no man or thing need be afraid, and who also is afraid of no created man or thing. The fire-eyes of his Burgundian Grace meet these clear eye-glances, convey them swift to his heart: he 10 bethinks him that probably this feeble, fearless, hoary Figure has in it something of the Most High God; that probably he shall be damned if he meddle with it,—that, on the whole, he had better not. He plunges, the rough savage, from his war-horse, down to his knees; embraces the feet of old Anselm: he too begs his blessing; orders men to escort him, guard him from being robbed, and under dread penalties see him safe on his way. *Per os Dei*, as his Majesty was wont to ejaculate!   20

Neither is this quarrel of Rufus and Anselm, of Henry and Becket, uninstructive to us. It was, at bottom, a great quarrel. For, admitting that Anselm was full of divine blessing, he by no means included in him all forms of divine blessing:—there were far other forms withal, which he little dreamed of; and William Redbeard was unconsciously the representative and spokesman of these. In truth, could your divine Anselm, your divine Pope Gregory have had their way, the results had been very notable. Our 30 Western World had all become a European Thibet, with one Grand Lama sitting at Rome; our one honourable business that of singing mass, all day and all night. Which would not in the least have suited us. The Supreme Powers willed it not so.

It was as if King Redbeard unconsciously, addressing Anselm, Becket and the others, had said: "Right Reverend, your Theory of the Universe is indisputable by man or devil. To the core of our heart we feel that this divine thing, which you call 40 Mother Church, does fill the whole world hitherto known, and is and shall be all our salvation and all our desire. And yet—and yet—Behold, though it is an unspoken secret, the world is *wider* than any of us think, Right Reverend! Behold, there are yet other immeasurable Sacrednesses in this that you call Heathenism, Secularity! On the whole, I, in an obscure but most rooted manner, feel that I cannot comply with you. Western Thibet and perpetual mass-chanting,—No. I am, so to speak, in the 50 family-way; with child, of I know not what,—cer-

tainly of something far different from this! I have— *Per os Dei*, I have Manchester Cotton-trades, Bromwicham Iron-trades, American Commonwealths, Indian Empires, Steam Mechanisms, and Shakespeare Dramas, in my belly; and cannot do it, Right Reverend!"—So accordingly it was decided: and Saxon Becket spilt his life in Canterbury Cathedral, as Scottish Wallace did on Tower-hill, and as generally a noble man and martyr has to do,—not 10 for nothing; no, but for a divine something other than *he* had altogether calculated. We will now quit this of the hard, organic, but limited Feudal Ages; and glance timidly into the immense Industrial Ages, as yet all inorganic, and in a quite pulpy condition, requiring desperately to harden themselves into some organism!

Our Epic having now become *Tools and the Man*, it is more than usually impossible to prophesy the Future. The boundless Future does lie there, pre-20 destined, nay already extant though unseen; hiding, in its Continents of Darkness, "gladness and sorrow": but the supremest intelligence of man cannot prefigure much of it:—the united intelligence and effort of All Men in all coming generations, this alone will gradually prefigure it, and figure and form it into a seen fact! Straining our eyes hitherto, the utmost effort of intelligence sheds but some most glimmering dawn, a little way into its dark enormous Deeps: only huge outlines loom uncer-30 tain on the sight; and the ray of prophecy, at a short distance, expires. But may we not say, here as always, Sufficient for the day is the evil thereof! To shape the whole Future is not our problem; but only to shape faithfully a small part of it, according to rules already known. It is perhaps possible for each of us, who will with due earnestness inquire, to ascertain clearly what he, for his own part, ought to do: this let him, with true heart, do, and continue doing. The general issue will, as it has always done, 40 rest well with a Higher Intelligence than ours.

One grand "outline," or even two, many earnest readers may perhaps, at this stage of the business, be able to prefigure for themselves,—and draw some guidance from. One prediction, or even two, are already possible. For the Life-tree Igdrasil, in all its new developments, is the selfsame world-old Life-tree: having found an element or elements there, running from the very roots of it in Hela's Realms, in the Well of Mimer and of the Three

---

19. Per os Dei, by the mouth of God.   **22. Henry and Becket.** See note 22, page 436.   **29. Pope Gregory**, Gregory VII, pope from 1073 to 1085.

7–8. **Saxon Becket.** See note 22 on page 436. **Wallace**, Sir William Wallace (c. 1270–1305), Scottish patriot.   **32. Sufficient . . . thereof.** See Matthew 6:34.   **45. For the Life-tree Igdrasil**, Yggdrasill, in Norse mythology the great ash tree symbolizing the universe.   **48–49. Hela's Realms**, the underworld; Hela is the goddess of the dead. **Well**

Nornas or TIMES, up to this present hour of it in our hearts, we conclude that such will have to continue. A man has, in his own soul, an Eternal; can read something of the Eternal there, if he will look! He already knows what will continue; what cannot, by any means or appliance whatsoever, be made to continue!

One wide and widest "outline" ought really, in all ways, to be becoming clear to us; this namely: That a "Splendour of God," in one form or other, will have to unfold itself from the heart of these our Industrial Ages too; or they will never get themselves "organised"; but continue chaotic, distressed, distracted evermore, and have to perish in frantic suicidal dissolution. A second "outline" or prophecy, narrower, but also wide enough, seems not less certain: That there will again *be* a King in Israel; a system of Order and Government; and every man shall, in some measure, see himself constrained to do that which is right in the King's eyes. This too we may call a sure element of the Future; for this too is of the Eternal;—this too is of the Present, though hidden from most; and without it no fiber of the Past ever was. An actual new Sovereignty, Industrial Aristocracy, real not imaginary Aristocracy, is indispensable and indubitable for us.

But what an Aristocracy; on what new, far more complex and cunningly devised conditions than that old Feudal fighting one! For we are to bethink us that the Epic verily is not *Arms and the Man*, but *Tools and the Man*,—an infinitely wider kind of Epic. And again we are to bethink us that men cannot now be bound to men by *brass-collars*, not at all: that this brass-collar method, in all figures of it, has vanished out of Europe forevermore! Huge Democracy, walking the streets everywhere in its Sack Coat, has asserted so much; irrevocably, brooking no reply! True enough, man *is* forever the "born

of Mimer, a spring flowing from the roots of Yggdrasill, the abode of a giant, Mimir. **Three Nornas or Times,** the Scandinavian Fates: Urth (the Past), Verthandi (the Present), Skuld (the Future). **19–20. see himself . . . eyes.** See Judges 17:1; 18:1; 19:1; 21:25. **30. Arms and the Man,** as in ancient times; note the first line of Virgil's *Aeneid*. **33. brass-collars,** like Gurth's; see note 14, page 434.

thrall" of certain men, born master of certain other men, born equal of certain others, let him acknowledge the fact or not. It is unblessed for him when he cannot acknowledge this fact; he is in the chaotic state, ready to perish, till he do get the fact acknowledged. But no man is, or can henceforth be, the brass-collar thrall of any man; you will have to bind him by other, far nobler and cunninger methods. Once for all, he is to be loose of the brass-collar, to have a scope *as* wide as his faculties now are:—will he not be all the usefuler to you in that new state? Let him go abroad as a trusted one, as a free one; and return home to you with rich earnings at night! Gurth could only tend pigs; this one will build cities, conquer waste worlds.—How, in conjunction with inevitable Democracy, indispensable Sovereignty is to exist: certainly it is the hugest question ever heretofore propounded to Mankind! The solution of which is work for long years and centuries. Years and centuries, of one knows not what complexion;—blessed or unblessed, according as they shall, with earnest valiant effort, make progress therein, or, in slothful unveracity and dilettantism, only talk of making progress. For either progress therein, or swift and ever swifter progress towards dissolution, is henceforth a necessity.

It is of importance that this grand reformation were begun; that Corn-Law Debatings and other jargon, little less than delirious in such a time, had fled far away, and left us room to begin! For the evil has grown practical, extremely conspicuous; if it be not seen and provided for, the blindest fool will have to feel it ere long. There is much that can wait; but there is something also that cannot wait. With millions of eager Working Men imprisoned in "Impossibility" and Poor-Law Bastilles, it is time that some means of dealing with them were trying to become "possible"! Of the Government of England, of all articulate-speaking functionaries, real and imaginary Aristocracies, of me and of thee, it is imperatively demanded, "How do you mean to manage these men? Where are they to find a supportable existence? What is to become of them, —and of you!"

greek purity and urbanity, success and honesty
everything is centered around religion

John Henry, Cardinal Newman
1801–1890

John Henry Newman was born in London, February 21, 1801. His father was a banker; his mother had French Huguenot blood. Even as a child he manifested an imaginative, spiritual nature; it seemed natural to him to think of the world as filled with angels. He expressed this view later in one of his sermons:

"And yet in spite of the universal world which we see, there is another world, quite as far-spreading, quite as close to us, and more wonderful; another world all around us, though we see it not, and more wonderful than the world we see, for this reason if for no other, that we do not see it. All around us are numberless objects, coming and going, watching, working, or waiting, which we see not: this is that other world, which the eyes reach not unto, but faith only."

In 1816 Newman experienced an inner conversion and dedicated himself to the religious life, his conception of which already included celibacy. In 1822 he became a fellow of Oriel College, Oxford; in 1824 he was ordained a deacon in the Anglican Church, in 1825 a priest; in 1826 he became a tutor at Oriel. In 1828 he was appointed vicar of St. Mary's Church at Oxford. In 1832 he toured southern Europe and made up his mind that it was his mission to redeem the English Church.

The Oxford Movement, sometimes called by its contemporaries Tractarianism or Puseyism, gave Newman his opportunity. This movement began July 14, 1833, with a sermon on "National Apostasy" in which John Keble protested against the abolition by Parliament of a number of Anglican bishoprics in Ireland. The bishoprics themselves were, in a Roman Catholic country, of no particular importance; the real issue was the old, old problem of the relationship between Church and State. The Oxford Movement was romantic in its feeling for the past, its desire to restore something of the fervor and color of medievalism to the modern Church—Newman's love for Scott's novels was no accident—but it had no truck with the revolutionary spirit of Romanticism. Its conception of religion was the sacramentarian conception; it took its stand on the basis of authority. The Church was

God's representative on earth; to her the truth had been entrusted. On the whole the movement was more classic than romantic. Newman reasoned his position closely every step of the way; if he used intuition also, this was because he was always reasonable enough to understand that reason is not all of human life.

Newman and his associates wished to appeal to the authority of the undivided Church. They recognized the need of reform, but they hoped to bring this about not through introducing new elements but by re-emphasizing the neglected Catholic elements already present. For Protestantism, liberalism, rationalism—"the doctrine that there is no positive truth in religion, but that one creed is as good as another"—Newman had no sympathy.

Newman, Keble, Froude, Pusey, and their associates carried on their propaganda through many sermons and through a series of ninety *Tracts for the Times*, 1833–41. Tract 90, in which Newman himself argued for a Catholic interpretation of the Thirty-nine Articles (the authoritative statement of Anglican faith, adopted in 1562), marked the end of the first stage of the movement and an important crisis in his own career. The storm of protest awakened proved clearly that the Anglican Church rejected the Catholic view; unless Newman were either to surrender his logic or betray his principles, he must, therefore, set his feet on the road to Rome. In 1842 he resigned from St. Mary's, and went with a few close followers into a semimonastic retreat at Littlemore; in 1845 he became a Roman Catholic; in 1846 he was ordained a priest.

The last half of Newman's life was, in general, much quieter than the first. He lived near Birmingham at the head of the Oratory at Egbaston, and his efforts were now necessarily largely confined to his own coreligionists. In his Catholic faith he found perfect peace and confidence, but his relations with the hierarchy were not always happy. The thwarting of his attempt to establish a Catholic University in Dublin (see page 441) was typical of many sad experiences; there were times when he asked himself whether his years as a Catholic had been wasted. In 1864, however, his *Apologia pro Vita Sua* brought him once more before the public as prominently as ever in his Oxford days; his saintly char-

Defend Church of England against protestantism
was rejected about his writing by the authority of
anglicanism.

acter came at last to be appreciated; Englishmen of all shades of belief began to realize that here was a great man whose apprehension of life, though importantly different from their own, might still possess validity. In 1877 the aging man became an honorary fellow of Trinity College, Oxford; in 1879 Pope Leo XIII made him a cardinal; he died August 11, 1890.

Newman was always the churchman; except for his poems—*Lyra Apostolica*, 1834; *The Dream of Gerontius*, 1865, and others—and two novels mediocre as fiction but extremely interesting on the ideational side—*Loss and Gain*, 1848, and *Callista*, 1856—his mode and method were never "literary." Yet he belongs to English literature by virtue of his style, and surely few men have been more importantly concerned with English civilization. Through his Tractarian years he lived in the eyes of the nation; the fate of religion itself seemed to hang on his decisions. As a Catholic, though a less representative figure, he was no less challenging and revealing.

The Oxford Movement touched literature at many points: we see it in such poets as Coventry Patmore and Christina Rossetti; the early William Morris shows traces of it; so does Tennyson. Joseph Ellis Baker has devoted a whole book to *The Novel and the Oxford Movement* (Princeton University Press, 1932). Charlotte M. Yonge (*The Heir of Redclyffe*, 1853) was the great Church of England novelist, but the finest monument of the movement in fiction is that glorious novel by Joseph Henry Shorthouse, *John Inglesant*, 1880.

THE SIGN OF THE CROSS

Whene'er across this sinful flesh of mine
   I draw the Holy Sign,
All good thoughts stir within me, and renew
   Their slumbering strength divine;
Till there springs up a courage high and true
   To suffer and to do.

And who shall say, but hateful spirits around,
   For their brief hour unbound,
Shudder to see, and wail their overthrow?
   While on far heathen ground   10
Some lonely Saint hails the fresh odour, though
   Its source he cannot know.

THE PILLAR OF THE CLOUD

Set to music by J. W. Dykes, these lines, universally known as "Lead, Kindly Light," have become one of the great hymns of the Christian Church. For the circumstances of Newman's composition of this poem, see his own account on page 458 of this volume. For the origin of the title, see Exodus 13.

Lead, Kindly Light, amid the encircling gloom,
   Lead Thou me on!
The night is dark, and I am far from home—
   Lead Thou me on!
Keep Thou my feet; I do not ask to see
The distant scene,—one step enough for me.

I was not ever thus, nor prayed that Thou
   Shouldst lead me on.
I loved to choose and see my path; but now
   Lead Thou me on!   10
I loved the garish day, and, spite of fears,
Pride ruled my will: remember not past years.

So long Thy power hath blest me, sure it still
   Will lead me on,
O'er moor and fen, o'er crag and torrent, till
   The night is gone;
And with the morn those angel faces smile
Which I have loved long since, and lost awhile.

from THE IDEA OF A UNIVERSITY

The series of lectures looking toward the establishment of a Catholic university which Newman, the rector elect, delivered in Dublin in 1852 as "The Scope and Nature of University Education" still remains one of our best statements of the liberal ideal. In practice Newman was to find that the Irish bishops did not share his views; his tenure of office was brief. The lectures, published as *The Idea of a University*, are now conveniently available, together with other papers on kindred themes, in "Everyman's Library" under the title *Essays on University Subjects*. Newman's views on education should be compared and contrasted with those of Arnold and Huxley, as given elsewhere in this volume.

from Discourse V

Knowledge Its Own End

I

I HAVE said that all branches of knowledge are connected together, because the subject-matter of knowledge is intimately united in itself, as being the acts and the work of the Creator. Hence it is that the Sciences, into which our knowledge may be said to be cast, have multiplied bearings one on another, and an internal sympathy, and admit, or rather demand, comparison and adjustment. They complete, correct, balance each other. This consideration, if well-founded, must be taken into account, not only as regards the attainment of truth, which is their common end, but as regards the influence which they exercise upon those whose education consists in the study of them. I have said already, that to give undue prominence to one is to be unjust to another; to neglect or supersede these is to divert those from their proper object. It is to unsettle the boundary lines between science and science, to disturb their action, to destroy the harmony which binds them together. Such a proceeding will have a correspond-ing effect when introduced into a place of educa-tion. There is no science but tells a different tale, when viewed as a portion of a whole, from what it is likely to suggest when taken by itself, without the safeguard, as I may call it, of others. . . .

It is a great point then to enlarge the range of studies which a University professes, even for the sake of the students; and, though they cannot pur-sue every subject which is open to them, they will be the gainers by living among those and under those who represent the whole circle. This I conceive to be the advantage of a seat of universal learning, considered as a place of education. An assemblage of learned men, zealous for their own sciences, and rivals of each other, are brought, by familiar inter-course and for the sake of intellectual peace, to ad-just together the claims and relations of their respec-tive subjects of investigation. They learn to respect, to consult, to aid each other. Thus is created a pure and clear atmosphere of thought, which the student also breathes, though in his own case he only pur-sues a few sciences out of the multitude. He profits by an intellectual tradition, which is independent of particular teachers, which guides him in his choice of subjects, and duly interprets for him those which he chooses. He apprehends the great outlines of knowledge, the principles on which it rests, the scale of its parts, its lights and its shades, its great points and its little, as he otherwise cannot apprehend them. Hence it is that his education is called "Lib-eral." A habit of mind is formed which lasts through life, of which the attributes are, freedom, equitable-ness, calmness, moderation, and wisdom; or what in a former Discourse I have ventured to call a philo-sophical habit. This then I would assign as the spe-cial fruit of the education furnished at a University, as contrasted with other places of teaching or modes of teaching. This is the main purpose of a Univer-sity in its treatment of its students.

And now the question is asked me, What is the *use*

of it? and my answer will constitute the main sub-ject of the Discourses which are to follow.

2

Cautious and practical thinkers, I say, will ask of me, what, after all, is the gain of this Philosophy, of which I make such account, and from which I promise so much. Even supposing it to enable us to exercise the degree of trust exactly due to every sci-ence respectively, and to estimate precisely the value of every truth which is anywhere to be found, how are we better for this master view of things, which I have been extolling? Does it not reverse the principle of the division of labour? will practical ob-jects be obtained better or worse by its cultivation? to what then does it lead? where does it end? what does it do? how does it profit? what does it promise? Particular sciences are respectively the basis of def-inite arts, which carry on to results tangible and beneficial the truths which are the subjects of the knowledge attained; what is the Art of this science of sciences? what is the fruit of such a Philosophy? what are we proposing to effect, what inducements do we hold out to the Catholic community, when we set about the enterprise of founding a University?

I am asked what is the end of University Educa-tion, and of the Liberal or Philosophical Knowledge which I conceive it to impart: I answer, that what I have already said has been sufficient to show that it has a very tangible, real, and sufficient end, though the end cannot be divided from that knowl-edge itself. Knowledge is capable of being its own end. Such is the constitution of the human mind, that any kind of knowledge, if it be really such, is its own reward. And if this is true of all knowledge, it is true also of that special Philosophy, which I have made to consist in a comprehensive view of truth in all its branches, of the relations of science to science, of their mutual bearings, and their re-spective values. What the worth of such an acquire-ment is, compared with other objects which we seek,—wealth or power or honour or the conven-iences and comforts of life, I do not profess here to discuss; but I would maintain, and mean to show, that it is an object, in its own nature so really and undeniably good, as to be the compensation of a great deal of thought in the compassing, and a great deal of trouble in the attaining. . . .

4

Things, which can bear to be cut off from every-thing else and yet persist in living, must have life in themselves; pursuits, which issue in nothing, and still maintain their ground for ages, which are regarded as admirable, though they have not as yet proved themselves to be useful, must have their sufficient end in themselves, whatever it turn out to be. And we are brought to the same conclusion by considering the force of the epithet, by which the knowledge under consideration is popularly designated. It is common to speak of "*liberal* knowledge," of the "*liberal* arts and studies," and of a "*liberal* education," as the especial characteristic or property of a University and of a gentleman; what is really meant by the word? Now, first, in its grammatical sense it is opposed to *servile;* and by "servile work" is understood, as our catechisms inform us, bodily labour, mechanical employment, and the like, in which the mind has little or no part. Parallel to such servile works are those arts, if they deserve the name, of which the poet speaks, which owe their origin and their method to hazard, not to skill; as, for instance, the practice and operations of an empiric. As far as this contrast may be considered as a guide into the meaning of the word, liberal education and liberal pursuits are exercises of mind, of reason, of reflection.

But we want something more for its explanation, for there are bodily exercises which are liberal, and mental exercises which are not so. For instance, in ancient times the practitioners in medicine were commonly slaves; yet it was an art as intellectual in its nature, in spite of the pretence, fraud, and quackery with which it might then, as now, be debased, as it was heavenly in its aim. And so in like manner, we contrast a liberal education with a commercial education or a professional; yet no one can deny that commerce and the professions afford scope for the highest and most diversified powers of mind. There is then a great variety of intellectual exercises, which are not technically called "liberal"; on the other hand, I say, there are exercises of the body which do receive that appellation. Such, for instance, was the palaestra, in ancient times; such the Olympic games, in which strength and dexterity of body as well as of mind gained the prize. In Xenophon we read of the young Persian nobility being taught to ride on horseback and to speak the truth; both being among the accomplishments of a gentleman. War, too, however rough a profession, has ever been accounted liberal, unless in cases when it becomes heroic, which would introduce us to another subject.

Now comparing these instances together, we shall have no difficulty in determining the principle of this apparent variation in the application of the term which I am examining. Manly games, or games of skill, or military prowess, though bodily, are, it seems, accounted liberal; on the other hand, what is merely professional, though highly intellectual, nay, though liberal in comparison of trade and manual labour, is not simply called liberal, and mercantile occupations are not liberal at all. Why this distinction? because that alone is liberal knowledge, which stands on its own pretensions, which is independent of sequel, expects no complement, refuses to be *informed* (as it is called) by any end, or absorbed into any art, in order duly to present itself to our contemplation. The most ordinary pursuits have this specific character, if they are self-sufficient and complete; the highest lose it, when they minister to something beyond them. It is absurd to balance, in point of worth and importance, a treatise on reducing fractures with a game of cricket or a fox-chase; yet of the two the bodily exercise has that quality which we call "liberal," and the intellectual has not. And so of the learned professions altogether, considered merely as professions; although one of them be the most popularly beneficial, and another the most politically important, and the third the most intimately divine of all human pursuits, yet the very greatness of their end, the health of the body, or of the commonwealth, or of the soul, diminishes, not increases, their claim to the appellation "liberal," and that still more, if they are cut down to the strict exigencies of that end. If, for instance, Theology, instead of being cultivated as a contemplation, be limited to the purposes of the pulpit or be represented by the catechism, it loses, —not its usefulness, not its divine character, not its meritoriousness, (rather it gains a claim upon these titles by such charitable condescension),—but it does lose the particular attribute which I am illustrating; just as a face worn by tears and fasting loses its beauty, or a labourer's hand loses its delicateness;—for Theology thus exercised is not simple knowledge, but rather is an art or a business making use of Theology. And thus it appears that even what is supernatural need not be liberal, nor need a hero be a gentleman, for the plain reason that one idea is not another idea. And in like manner the Baconian Philosophy, by using its physical sciences in the service of man, does thereby transfer them from the order of Liberal Pursuits to, I do not say the inferior, but the distinct class of the Useful. And, to take a different instance, hence again, as is evident, whenever personal gain is the motive, still more distinctive an effect has it upon the character of a given pursuit; thus racing, which was a liberal exercise in

17. the poet speaks. Newman's own note refers to Aristotle's *Nichomachean Ethics,* VI—Τέχνη τύχην ἔστερξε καὶ τύχη τέχνην.—"Art loves fate, and fate loves art." 40. palaestra, wrestling school. 42. Xenophon, Athenian soldier and historian (c. 434–c. 355 B.C.).

X - greek philosopher, historian
400 B.C.

Greece, forfeits its rank in times like these, so far as it is made the occasion of gambling.

All that I have been now saying is summed up in a few characteristic words of the great Philosopher. "Of possessions," he says, "those rather are useful, which bear fruit; those *liberal, which tend to enjoyment.* By fruitful, I mean, which yield revenue; by enjoyable, where *nothing accrues of consequence beyond the using.*" . . . .

6

Now bear with me, Gentlemen, if what I am about to say, has at first sight a fanciful appearance. Philosophy, then, or Science, is related to Knowledge in this way:—Knowledge is called by the name of Science or Philosophy, when it is acted upon, informed, or if I may use a strong figure, impregnated by Reason. Reason is the principle of that intrinsic fecundity of Knowledge, which, to those who possess it, is its especial value, and which ₂₀ dispenses with the necessity of their looking abroad for any end to rest upon external to itself. Knowledge, indeed, when thus exalted into a scientific form, is also power; not only is it excellent in itself, but whatever such excellence may be, it is something more, it has a result beyond itself. Doubtless; but that is a further consideration, with which I am not concerned. I only say that, prior to its being a power, it is a good; that it is, not only an instrument, but an end. I know well it may resolve itself ₃₀ into an art, and terminate in a mechanical process, and in tangible fruit; but it also may fall back upon that Reason which informs it, and resolve itself into Philosophy. In one case it is called Useful Knowledge, in the other Liberal. The same person may cultivate it in both ways at once; but this again is a matter foreign to my subject; here I do but say that there are two ways of using Knowledge, and in matter of fact those who use it in one way are not likely to use it in the other, or at least in a very lim-₄₀ ited measure. You see, then, here are two methods of Education; the end of the one is to be philosophical, of the other to be mechanical; the one rises towards general ideas, the other is exhausted upon what is particular and external. Let me not be thought to deny the necessity, or to decry the benefit, of such attention to what is particular and practical, as belongs to the useful or mechanical arts; life could not go on without them; we owe our daily welfare to them; their exercise is the duty of the ₅₀ many, and we owe to the many a debt of gratitude for fulfilling that duty. I only say that Knowledge,

in proportion as it tends more and more to be particular, ceases to be Knowledge. . . . When I speak of Knowledge, I mean something intellectual, something which grasps what it perceives through the senses; something which takes a view of things; which sees more than the senses convey; which reasons upon what it sees, and while it sees; which invests it with an idea. It expresses itself, not in a mere enunciation, but by an enthymeme: it is of the na-₁₀ ture of science from the first, and in this consists its dignity. The principle of real dignity in Knowledge, its worth, its desirableness, considered irrespectively of its results, is this germ within it of a scientific or a philosophical process. This is how it comes to be an end in itself; this is why it admits of being called Liberal. Not to know the relative disposition of things is the state of slaves or children; to have mapped out the Universe is the boast, or at least the ambition, of Philosophy.

Moreover, such knowledge is not a mere extrinsic ₂₀ or accidental advantage, which is ours to-day and another's to-morrow, which may be got up from a book, and easily forgotten again, which we can command or communicate at our pleasure, which we can borrow for the occasion, carry about in our hand, and take into the market; it is an acquired illumination, it is a habit, a personal possession, and an inward endowment. And this is the reason, why it is more correct, as well as more usual, to speak of a University as a place of education, than of instruc-₃₀ tion, though, when knowledge is concerned, instruction would at first sight have seemed the more appropriate word. . . . When, then, we speak of the communication of Knowledge as being Education, we thereby really imply that that Knowledge is a state or condition of mind; and since cultivation of mind is surely worth seeking for its own sake, we are thus brought once more to the conclusion, which the word "Liberal" and the word "Philosophy" have already suggested, that there is a Knowledge, ₄₀ which is desirable, though nothing come of it, as being of itself a treasure, and a sufficient remuneration of years of labour.

7

. . . It may be objected . . . that, when we profess to seek Knowledge for some end or other beyond itself, whatever it be, we speak intelligibly; but that, whatever men may have said, however obstinately the idea may have kept its ground from ₅₀ age to age, still it is simply unmeaning to say that we seek Knowledge for its own sake, and for noth-

---

5–9. "Of possessions . . . the using." "Aristotle, *Rhetoric*, I, 5." (Newman)

9. enthymeme: an argument with the premise understood; or with only two propositions.

ing else; for that it ever leads to something beyond itself, which therefore is its end, and the cause why it is desirable;—moreover, that this end is two-fold, either of this world or of the next; that all knowledge is cultivated either for secular objects or for eternal; that if it is directed to secular objects, it is called Useful Knowledge, if to eternal, Religious or Christian Knowledge;—in consequence, that if, as I have allowed, this Liberal Knowledge does not benefit the body or estate, it ought to benefit the soul; but if the fact be really so, that it is neither a physical or a secular good on the one hand, nor a moral good on the other, it cannot be a good at all, and is not worth the trouble which is necessary for its acquisition.

And then I may be reminded that the professors of this Liberal or Philosophical Knowledge have themselves, in every age, recognized this exposition of the matter, and have submitted to the issue in which it terminates; for they have ever been attempting to make men virtuous; or, if not, at least have assumed that refinement of mind was virtue, and that they themselves were the virtuous portion of mankind. This they have professed on the one hand; and on the other, they have utterly failed in their professions, so as ever to make themselves a proverb among men, and a laughing-stock both to the grave and the dissipated portion of mankind, in consequence of them. Thus they have furnished against themselves both the ground and the means of their own exposure, without any trouble at all to anyone else. In a word, from the time that Athens was the University of the world, what has Philosophy taught men, but to promise without practising, and to aspire without attaining? What has the deep and lofty thought of its disciples ended in but eloquent words? Nay, what has its teaching ever meditated, when it was boldest in its remedies for human ill, beyond charming us to sleep by its lessons, that we might feel nothing at all? like some melodious air, or rather like those strong and transporting perfumes, which at first spread their sweetness over everything they touch, but in a little while do but offend in proportion as they once pleased us. Did Philosophy support Cicero under the disfavour of the fickle populace, or nerve Seneca to oppose an imperial tyrant? It abandoned Brutus, as he sorrowfully confessed, in his greatest need, and it forced Cato, as his panegyrist strangely boasts, into the false

position of defying heaven. How few can be counted among its professors, who, like Polemo, were thereby converted from a profligate course, or like Anaxagoras, thought the world well lost in exchange for its possession? The philosopher in *Rasselas* taught a superhuman doctrine, and then succumbed without an effort to a trial of human affection.

"He discoursed," we are told, "with great energy on the government of the passions. His look was venerable, his action graceful, his pronunciation clear, and his diction elegant. He showed, with great strength of sentiment and variety of illustration, that human nature is degraded and debased, when the lower faculties predominate over the higher. He communicated the various precepts given, from time to time, for the conquest of passion, and displayed the happiness of those who had obtained the important victory, after which man is no longer the slave of fear, nor the fool of hope. . . . He enumerated many examples of heroes immovable by pain or pleasure, who looked with indifference on those modes or accidents to which the vulgar give the names of good and evil."

Rasselas in a few days found the philosopher in a room half darkened, with his eyes misty, and his face pale. "Sir," said he, "you have come at a time when all human friendship is useless; what I suffer cannot be remedied, what I have lost cannot be supplied. My daughter, my only daughter, from whose tenderness I expected all the comforts of my age, died last night of a fever." "Sir," said the prince, "mortality is an event by which a wise man can never be surprised; we know that death is always near, and it should therefore always be expected." "Young man," answered the philosopher, "you speak like one who has never felt the pangs of separation." "Have you, then, forgot the precept," said Rasselas, "which you so powerfully enforced? . . . consider that external things are naturally variable, but truth and reason are always the same." "What comfort," said the mourner, "can truth and reason afford me? Of what effect are they now, but to tell me that my daughter will not be restored?"

8

Better, far better, to make no professions, you will say, than to cheat others with what we are not, and to scandalize them with what we are. The sensualist, or the man of the world, at any rate, is not the

44–48. **Cicero . . . Seneca . . . Brutus . . . Cato.** Possibly Newman refers to Cicero's compromising course during the contest between Pompey and Julius Caesar. Seneca, Brutus, and Marcus Cato the Younger all committed suicide, Seneca in 65 A.D. when accused of conspiring against Nero, Brutus in 42 B.C. after his defeat by Octavius, following the assassination of Julius Caesar (as in Shakespeare's play), Cato in

46 B.C. to avoid being conquered by Julius Caesar. Cato was praised by Cicero and by Lucan (compare Addison's tragedy, 1713). 2. **Polemo,** Greek philosopher of the third century B.C. 3–4. **Anaxagoras,** Greek philosopher of the fifth century B.C., who preferred exile to recantation. 5. **Rasselas,** Dr. Samuel Johnson's novel of that title, 1759, chap. 18.

victim of fine words, but pursues a reality and gains it. The Philosophy of Utility, you will say, Gentlemen, has at least done its work; and I grant it,—it aimed low, but it has fulfilled its aim. If that man of great intellect who has been its Prophet in the conduct of life played false to his own professions, he was not bound by his philosophy to be true to his friend or faithful in his trust. Moral virtue was not the line in which he undertook to instruct men; and though, as the poet calls him, he were the "mean- 10 est" of mankind, he was so in what may be called his private capacity and without any prejudice to the theory of induction. He had a right to be so, if he chose, for anything that the Idols of the den or the theatre had to say to the contrary. His mission was the increase of physical enjoyment and social comfort; and most wonderfully, most awfully has he fulfilled his conception and his design. Almost day by day have we fresh and fresh shoots, and buds, and blossoms, which are to ripen into fruit, on that 20 magical tree of Knowledge which he planted, and to which none of us perhaps, except the very poor, but owes, if not his present life, at least his daily food, his health, and general well-being. He was the divinely provided minister of temporal benefits to all of us so great, that, whatever I am forced to think of him as a man, I have not the heart, from mere gratitude, to speak of him severely. And, in spite of the tendencies of his philosophy, which are, as we see at this day, to depreciate, or to trample on 30 Theology, he has himself, in his writings, gone out of his way, as if with a prophetic misgiving of those tendencies, to insist on it as the instrument of that beneficent Father, who, when He came on earth in visible form, took on Him first and most prominently the office of assuaging the bodily wounds of human nature. And truly, like the old mediciner in the tale, "he sat diligently at his work, and hummed, with cheerful countenance, a pious song"; and then in turn "went out singing into the mead- 40 ows so gaily, that those who had seen him from afar might well have thought it was a youth gathering flowers for his beloved, instead of an old physician gathering healing herbs in the morning dew."

5. **Prophet,** Sir Francis Bacon. See his life and selections from his writings in Vol. I of the present work.   **10. poet,** Alexander Pope, in "An Essay on Man," Ep. IV, ll. 281–82. **14. Idols.** Bacon classifies the false notions to which the mind is subject as idols of the tribe, of the cave, of the market place, and of the theater (*Novum Organum,* I). **31–34. he has himself . . . of that beneficent Father.** Bacon definitely commits himself to belief in God in his essay "Of Atheism," and in many other passages of his writings.   **37–44. And truly . . . morning dew."** "Fouqué's *Unknown Patient.*" (Newman) Baron de la Motte Fouqué (1777–1843) was a German poet and novelist best known today by his *Undine,* 1811.

Alas, that men, in the action of life or in their heart of hearts, are not what they seem to be in their moments of excitement, or in their trances or intoxications of genius,—so good, so noble, so serene! Alas, that Bacon too in his own way should after all be but the fellow of those heathen philosophers who in their disadvantages had some excuse for their inconsistency, and who surprise us rather in what they did say than in what they did not do! Alas, that he too, like Socrates or Seneca, must be 10 stripped of his holy-day coat, which looks so fair, and should be but a mockery amid his most majestic gravity of phrase; and, for all his vast abilities, should, in the littleness of his own moral being, but typify the intellectual narrowness of his school! However, granting all this, heroism after all was not his philosophy:—I cannot deny he has abundantly achieved what he proposed. His is simply a Method whereby bodily discomforts and temporal wants are to be most effectually removed from the greatest 20 number; and already, before it has shown any signs of exhaustion, the gifts of nature, in their most artificial shapes and luxurious profusion and diversity, from all quarters of the earth, are, it is undeniable, by its means brought even to our doors, and we rejoice in them.

9

Useful Knowledge then, I grant, has done its work; and Liberal Knowledge as certainly has not done its work,—that is, supposing, as the objectors 30 assume, its direct end, like Religious Knowledge, is to make men better; but this, I will not for an instant allow, and, unless I allow it, those objectors have said nothing to the purpose. I admit, rather I maintain, what they have been urging, for I consider Knowledge to have its end in itself. For all its friends, or its enemies, may say, I insist upon it, that it is as real a mistake to burden it with virtue or religion as with the mechanical arts. Its direct business is not to steel the soul against temptation or to 40 console it in affliction, any more than to set the loom in motion, or to direct the steam carriage; be it ever so much the means or the condition of both material and moral advancement, still, taken by and in itself, it as little mends our hearts as it improves out temporal circumstances. And if its eulogists claim for it such a power, they commit the very same kind of encroachment on a province not their own as the political economist who should maintain 50 that his science educated him for casuistry or diplomacy. Knowledge is one thing, virtue is another; good sense is not conscience, refinement is not humility, nor is largeness and justness of view faith.

Philosophy, however enlightened, however profound, gives no command over the passions, no influential motives, no vivifying principles. Liberal Education makes not the Christian, not the Catholic, but the gentleman. It is well to be a gentleman, it is well to have a cultivated intellect, a delicate taste, a candid, equitable, dispassionate mind, a noble and courteous bearing in the conduct of life; —these are the connatural qualities of a large knowledge; they are the objects of a University; I [10] am advocating, I shall illustrate and insist upon them; but still, I repeat, they are no guarantee for sanctity or even for conscientiousness, they may attach to the man of the world, to the profligate, to the heartless,—pleasant, alas, and attractive as he shows when decked out in them. Taken by themselves, they do but seem to be what they are not; they look like virtue at a distance, but they are detected by close observers, and on the long run; and hence it is that they are popularly accused of pre- [20] tence and hypocrisy, not, I repeat, from their own fault, but because their professors and their admirers persist in taking them for what they are not, and are officious in arrogating for them a praise to which they have no claim. Quarry the granite rock with razors, or moor the vessel with a thread of silk; then may you hope with such keen and delicate instruments as human knowledge and human reason to contend against those giants, the passion and the pride of man.

Surely we are not driven to theories of this kind, in order to vindicate the value and dignity of Liberal Knowledge. Surely the real grounds on which its pretensions rest are not so very subtle or abstruse, so very strange or improbable. Surely it is very intelligible to say, and that is what I say here, that Liberal Education, viewed in itself, is simply the cultivation of the intellect, as such, and its object is nothing more or less than intellectual excellence. Every thing has its own perfection, be it [40] higher or lower in the scale of things; and the perfection of one is not the perfection of another. Things animate, inanimate, visible, invisible, all are good in their kind, and have a *best* of themselves, which is an object of pursuit. Why do you take such pains with your garden or your park? You see to your walks and turf and shrubberies; to your trees and drives; not as if you meant to make an orchard of the one, or corn or pasture land of the other, but because there is a special beauty in all that is goodly [50] in wood, water, plain, and slope, brought all together by art into one shape, and grouped into one whole. Your cities are beautiful, your palaces, your public buildings, your territorial mansions, your churches; and their beauty leads to nothing beyond itself. There is a physical beauty and a moral: there is a beauty of person, there is a beauty of our moral being, which is natural virtue; and in like manner there is a beauty, there is a perfection, of the intellect. There is an ideal perfection in these various subject-matters, towards which individual instances are seen to rise, and which are the standards for all instances whatever. The Greek divinities and demi- [10] gods, as the statuary has moulded them, with their symmetry of figure and their high forehead and their regular features, are the perfection of physical beauty. The heroes, of whom history tells, Alexander, or Caesar, or Scipio, or Saladin, are the representatives of that magnanimity or self-mastery which is the greatness of human nature. Christianity too has its heroes, and in the supernatural order, and we call them Saints. The artist puts before him beauty of feature and form; the poet, beauty of mind; the preacher, the beauty of grace: then intel- [20] lect too, I repeat, has its beauty, and it has those who aim at it. To open the mind, to correct it, to refine it, to enable it to know, and to digest, master, rule, and use its knowledge, to give it power over its own faculties, application, flexibility, method, critical exactness, sagacity, resource, address, eloquent expression, is an object as intelligible (for here we are inquiring, not what the object of a Liberal Education is worth, nor what use the Church makes [30] of it, but what it is in itself), I say, an object as intelligible as the cultivation of virtue, while, at the same time, it is absolutely distinct from it.

10

This indeed is but a temporal object, and a transitory possession: but so are other things in themselves which we make much of and pursue. The moralist will tell us that man, in all his functions, is but a flower which blossoms and fades, except so far [40] as a higher principle breathes upon him, and makes him and what he is immortal. Body and mind are carried on into an eternal state of being by the gifts of Divine Munificence; but at first they do but fail in a failing world; and if the powers of intellect decay, the powers of the body have decayed before them, and, as an Hospital or an Almshouse, though its end be ephemeral, may be sanctified to the service of religion, so surely may a University, even were it nothing more than I have as yet described it. [50] We attain to heaven by using this world well,

14. **Scipio,** the conqueror of Hannibal (c. 237–c. 183 B.C.). **Saladin,** Sultan of Egypt (1137–1193), who opposed the Christians in the Third Crusade. See Scott's novel *The Talisman.*

though it is to pass away; we perfect our nature, not by undoing it, but by adding to it what is more than nature, and directing it towards aims higher than its own. . . .

from Discourse VIII

Knowledge Viewed in Relation to Religion

[Definition of a Gentleman]

It is . . . almost a definition of a gentleman to say he is one who never inflicts pain. This description is both refined and, as far as it goes, accurate. He is mainly occupied in merely removing the obstacles which hinder the free and unembarrassed action of those about him; and he concurs with their movements rather than takes the initiative himself. His benefits may be considered as parallel to what are called comforts or conveniences in arrangements of a personal nature: like an easy chair or a good fire, which do their part in dispelling cold and fatigue, though nature provides both means of rest and animal heat without them. The true gentleman in like manner carefully avoids whatever may cause a jar or a jolt in the minds of those with whom he is cast;—all clashing of opinion, or collision of feeling, all restraint, or suspicion, or gloom, or resentment; his great concern being to make every one at their ease and at home. He has his eyes on all his company; he is tender towards the bashful, gentle towards the distant, and merciful towards the absurd; he can recollect to whom he is speaking; he guards against unseasonable allusions, or topics which may irritate; he is seldom prominent in conversation, and never wearisome. He makes light of favours while he does them, and seems to be receiving when he is conferring. He never speaks of himself except when compelled, never defends himself by a mere retort, he has no ears for slander or gossip, is scrupulous in imputing motives to those who interfere with him, and interprets everything for the best. He is never mean or little in his disputes, never takes unfair advantage, never mistakes personalities or sharp sayings for arguments, or insinuates evil which he dare not say out. From a long-sighted prudence, he observes the maxim of the ancient sage, that we should ever conduct ourselves towards our enemy as if he were one day to be our friend. He has too much good sense to be affronted at insults, he is too well employed to remember injuries, and too indolent to bear malice. He is patient, forbearing, and resigned, on philosophical principles; he submits to pain, because it is inevitable, to bereavement, because it is irreparable, and to death, be-

cause it is his destiny. If he engages in controversy of any kind, his disciplined intellect preserves him from the blundering discourtesy of better, though less educated minds; who, like blunt weapons, tear and hack instead of cutting clean, who mistake the point in argument, waste their strength on trifles, misconceive their adversary, and leave the question more involved than they find it. He may be right or wrong in his opinion, but he is too clear-headed to be unjust; he is as simple as he is forcible, and as brief as he is decisive. Nowhere shall we find greater candour, consideration, indulgence: he throws himself into the minds of his opponents, he accounts for their mistakes. He knows the weakness of human reason as well as its strength, its province and its limits. If he be an unbeliever, he will be too profound and large-minded to ridicule religion or to act against it; he is too wise to be a dogmatist or fanatic in his infidelity. He respects piety and devotion; he even supports institutions as venerable, beautiful, or useful, to which he does not assent; he honours the ministers of religion, and he is contented to decline its mysteries without assailing or denouncing them. He is a friend of religious toleration, and that, not only because his philosophy has taught him to look on all forms of faith with an impartial eye, but also from the gentleness and effeminacy of feeling, which is the attendant on civilization.

Not that he may not hold a religion too, in his own way, even when he is not a Christian. In that case his religion is one of imagination and sentiment; it is the embodiment of those ideas of the sublime, majestic, and beautiful, without which there can be no large philosophy. Sometimes he acknowledges the being of God, sometimes he invests an unknown principle or quality with the attributes of perfection. And this deduction of his reason, or creation of his fancy, he makes the occasion of such excellent thoughts, and the starting-point of so varied and systematic a teaching, that he even seems like a disciple of Christianity itself. From the very accuracy and steadiness of his logical powers, he is able to see what sentiments are consistent in those who hold any religious doctrine at all, and he appears to others to feel and to hold a whole circle of theological truths which exist in his mind no otherwise than as a number of deductions.

Such are some of the lineaments of the ethical character, which the cultivated intellect will form, apart from religious principle. They are seen within the pale of the Church and without it, in holy men and in profligate; they form the *beau-idéal* of the world; they partly assist and partly distort the development of the Catholic. They may subserve the education of a St. Francis de Sales or a Cardinal Pole; they may be the limits of the virtue of a Shaftesbury or a Gibbon. Basil and Julian were fellow-students at the schools of Athens; and one became the Saint and Doctor of the Church, the other her scoffer and relentless foe.

from APOLOGIA PRO VITA SUA

Cardinal Newman's autobiography, *Apologia pro Vita Sua* (*Justification for His Life*) was occasioned by a controversy with Charles Kingsley (1819–1875), novelist and Anglican divine, who had accused him, and the Roman clergy in general, of little respect for truthtelling. Since not only his honor but the honor of his church was involved, Newman felt bound to reply; the result was both a brilliant piece of controversial writing and a great piece of spiritual autobiography.

Kingsley's attack on Newman is usually regarded as his worst failure; the *Apologia* itself was the means of re-establishing its author, after many years of comparative neglect, in the hearts of his countrymen. Years afterward Newman wrote: "As to Mr. Kingsley, much less could I feel any resentment against him, when he was accidentally the instrument, in the good Providence of God, by whom I had an opportunity given me, which otherwise I should not have had, of vindicating my character and conduct. . . . I heard, too, a few years back from a friend that she chanced to go into Chester Cathedral and found Mr. Kingsley preaching about me, kindly, though, of course, with criticisms on me. . . . I have always hoped that by good luck I might meet him, feeling sure that there would be no embarrassment on my part, and I said Mass for his soul as soon as I heard of his death."

from PART III

History of My Religious Opinions

I WAS brought up from a child to take great delight in reading the Bible; but I had no formed religious convictions till I was fifteen. Of course I had perfect knowledge of my Catechism.

After I was grown up, I put on paper such recollections as I had of my thoughts and feelings on religious subjects, at the time that I was a child and a boy. Out of these I select two, which are at once the most definite among them, and also have a bearing on my later convictions.

In the paper to which I have referred, written either in the Long Vacation of 1820, or in October, 1823, the following notices of my school days were sufficiently prominent in my memory for me to consider them worth recording:—"I used to wish the Arabian Tales were true: my imagination ran on unknown influences, on magical powers, and talismans. . . . I thought life might be a dream, or I an Angel, and all this world a deception, my fellow-angels by a playful device concealing themselves from me, and deceiving me with the semblance of a material world." . . .

The other remark is this: "I was very superstitious, and for some time previous to my conversion" [when I was fifteen] "used constantly to cross myself on going into the dark." . . .

When I was fourteen, I read Paine's Tracts against the Old Testament, and found pleasure in thinking of the objections which were contained in them. Also, I read some of Hume's Essays; and perhaps that on Miracles. So at least I gave my father to understand; but perhaps it was a brag. Also, I recollect copying out some French verses, perhaps Voltaire's, against the immortality of the soul, and saying to myself something like "How dreadful, but how plausible!"

When I was fifteen, a great change of thought took place in me. I fell under the influences of a definite Creed, and received into my intellect impressions of dogma, which, through God's mercy, have never been effaced or obscured. Above and beyond the conversations and sermons of the excellent man, long dead, who was the human means of this beginning of divine faith in me, was the effect of the books which he put into my hands, all of the school of Calvin. One of the first books I read was a work of Romaine's; I neither recollect the title nor the contents, except one doctrine, which of course I do not include among those which I believe to have come from a divine source, viz. the

2–4. **St. Francis de Sales,** Bishop of Geneva (1567–1622). **Cardinal Pole** (1500–1558), Archbishop of Canterbury under Queen Mary (Tudor). **Shaftesbury,** Anthony Ashley Cooper, third Earl of Shaftesbury (1671–1713), English Deistic philosopher. **Gibbon,** Edward Gibbon (1737–1794), English historian and sceptic, whose hostility to Christianity appears clearly in his *Decline and Fall of the Roman Empire.* **Basil,** one of the great Fathers of the Greek Church (c. 329–379). **Julian,** the Apostate, the Roman emperor who tried to restore paganism (331–363). 42. **Catechism,** the Anglican Catechism, which is contained in the *Book of Common Prayer.*

22–23. **Paine's Tracts against the Old Testament,** in *The Age of Reason* (1794–1807), by the Deistic and revolutionary philosopher Thomas Paine, whose *Common Sense* so importantly affected the cause of the American Revolution. 25–26. **Hume's Essays . . . Miracles.** The essay "Of Miracles" by David Hume, philosopher, historian, and sceptic, is in his *Enquiry Concerning Human Understanding,* 1748. 41. **Calvin,** John Calvin (1509–1564), the French Protestant leader of the Reformation, whose *Institutes of the Christian Religion* had a very important influence on theology. 42. **Romaine's,** of William Romaine (1714–1795), an English clergyman and writer of the Calvinistic school.

doctrine of final perseverance. I received it at once, and believed that the inward conversion of which I was conscious (and of which I still am more certain than that I have hands and feet,) would last into the next life, and that I was elected to eternal glory. I have no consciousness that this belief had any tendency whatever to lead me to be careless about pleasing God. I retained it till the age of twenty-one, when it gradually faded away; but I believe that it had some influence on my opinions, in the direction of those childish imaginations which I have already mentioned, viz. in isolating me from the objects which surrounded me, in confirming me in my mistrust of the reality of material phenomena, and making me rest in the thought of two and two only supreme and luminously self-evident beings, myself and my Creator;—for while I considered myself predestined to salvation, I thought others simply passed over, not predestined to eternal death. I only thought of the mercy to myself.

The detestable doctrine last mentioned is simply denied and abjured, unless my memory strangely deceives me, by the writer who made a deeper impression on my mind than any other, and to whom I almost owe my soul,—Thomas Scott of Aston Sandford. I so admired and delighted in his writings, that, when I was an Undergraduate, I thought of making a visit to his Parsonage, in order to see a man whom I so deeply revered. I hardly think I could have given up the idea of this expedition, even after I had taken my degree; for the news of his death in 1821 came upon me as a disappointment as well as a sorrow. I hung upon the lips of Daniel Wilson, afterwards Bishop of Calcutta, as in two sermons at St. John's Chapel he gave the history of Scott's life and death. I had been possessed of his Essays from a boy; his Commentary I bought when I was an undergraduate. . . .

Calvinists make a sharp separation between the elect and the world; there is much in this that is parallel or cognate to the Catholic doctrine; but they go on to say, as I understand them, very differently from Catholicism,—that the converted and the unconverted can be discriminated by man, that the justified are conscious of their state of justifica-

tion, and that the regenerate cannot fall away. Catholics on the other hand shade and soften the awful antagonism between good and evil, which is one of their dogmas, by holding that there are different degrees of justification, that there is a great difference in point of gravity between sin and sin, that there is the possibility and the danger of falling away, and that there is no certain knowledge given to any one that he is simply in a state of grace, and much less that he is to persevere to the end. . . .

Now I come to two other works, which produced a deep impression on me in the same autumn of 1816, when I was fifteen years old, each contrary to each, and planting in me the seeds of an intellectual inconsistency which disabled me for a long course of years. I read Joseph Milner's Church History, and was nothing short of enamoured of the long extracts from St. Augustine and the other Fathers which I found there. I read them as being the religion of the primitive Christians: but simultaneously with Milner I read Newton on the Prophecies, and in consequence became most firmly convinced that the Pope was the Antichrist predicted by Daniel, St. Paul, and St. John. My imagination was stained by the effects of this doctrine up to the year 1843; it had been obliterated from my reason and judgment at an earlier date; but the thought remained upon me as a sort of false conscience. Hence came that conflict of mind, which so many have felt besides myself;—leading some men to make a compromise between two ideas, so inconsistent with each other,—driving others to beat out the one idea or the other from their minds,—and ending in my own case, after many years of intellectual unrest, in the gradual decay and extinction of one of them,—I do not say in its violent death, for why should I not have murdered it sooner, if I murdered it at all?

I am obliged to mention, though I do it with great reluctance, another deep imagination, which at this time, the autumn of 1816, took possession of me,—there can be no mistake about the fact;—viz.

17. Joseph Milner's Church History, *History of the Church of Christ,* 1794–97.   **19. St. Augustine,** Bishop of Hippo (354–430), one of the most influential of the **Fathers** (that is, early Christian writers accepted as authorities) of the Latin Church.   **22. Newton on the Prophecies,** *Dissertation on the Prophecies,* 1754, by Thomas Newton, Bishop of Bristol.   **24–25. Antichrist predicted by Daniel, St. Paul, and St. John.** The Antichrist is the great antagonist to be conquered by Christ at his Second Coming. The term is used only in 1 John 2:18–22, 4:3; 2 John 7. But see also 2 Thessalonians 2:1–12; 2 Corinthians 6:15; Revelation 11:4–13, 13:1–18, 17, 19:11–21; and, in the Old Testament, Daniel 11:36. See further art. "Antichrist" in Hastings, *Dictionary of the Bible,* and S. J. Case, *The Millennial Hope* (University of Chicago Press, 1918).

1. final perseverance, continuance in a state of grace until it is succeeded by a state of glory, one of the cardinal doctrines of Calvinism.   **5. elected to eternal glory.** Calvinists believed in predestination or election, the doctrine that God had of His own volition chosen some persons for heaven and others for hell.   **25–26. Thomas Scott of Aston Sandford,** an English Anglican divine (1747–1821), whose commentary on the Bible, published in weekly parts, 1788–92, had an enormous influence.   **34. Daniel Wilson** (1778–1858).   **35. St. John's Chapel,** at Oxford.

that it was the will of God that I should lead a single life. This anticipation, which has held its ground almost continuously ever since,—with the break of a month now and a month then, up to 1829, and, after that date, without any break at all,—was more or less connected, in my mind, with the notion that my calling in life would require such a sacrifice as celibacy involved; as, for instance, missionary work among the heathen, to which I had a great drawing for some years. It also strengthened my feeling of separation from the visible world, of which I have spoken above.

In 1822 I came under very different influences from those to which I had hitherto been subjected. At that time, Mr. Whately, as he was then, afterwards Archbishop of Dublin, for the few months he remained in Oxford, which he was leaving for good, showed great kindness to me. He renewed it in 1825, when he became Principal of Alban Hall, making me his Vice-Principal and Tutor. . . . From 1822 to 1825 I saw most of the present Provost of Oriel, Dr. Hawkins, at that time Vicar of St. Mary's; and, when I took orders in 1824 and had a curacy at Oxford, then, during the Long Vacations, I was especially thrown into his company. I can say with a full heart that I love him, and have never ceased to love him; and I thus preface what otherwise might sound rude, that in the course of the many years in which we were together afterwards, he provoked me very much from time to time, though I am perfectly certain that I have provoked him a great deal more. Moreover, in me such provocation was unbecoming, both because he was the head of my College, and because in the first years that I knew him, he had been in many ways of great service to my mind. . . .

It was Dr. Hawkins too who taught me to anticipate that, before many years were over, there would be an attack made upon the books and the canon of Scripture. I was brought to the same belief by the conversation of Mr. Blanco White, who also led me to have freer views on the subject of inspiration than were usual in the Church of England at the time.

There is one other principle, which I gained from Dr. Hawkins, more directly bearing upon Catholicism, than any that I have mentioned; and that is the doctrine of Tradition. When I was an Undergraduate, I heard him preach in the University Pulpit his celebrated sermon on the subject, and recollect how long it appeared to me, though he was at that time a very striking preacher; but, when I read it and studied it as his gift, it made a most serious impression upon me. He does not go one step, I think, beyond the high Anglican doctrine, nay he does not reach it; but he does his work thoroughly, and his view was original with him, and his subject was a novel one at the time. He lays down a proposition, self-evident as soon as stated, to those who have at all examined the structure of Scripture, viz. that the sacred text was never intended to teach doctrine, but only to prove it, and that, if we would learn doctrine, we must have recourse to the formularies of the Church; for instance to the Catechism, and to the Creeds. He considers, that, after learning from them the doctrines of Christianity, the inquirer must verify them by Scripture. This view, most true in its outline, most fruitful in its consequences, opened upon me a large field of thought. Dr. Whately held it too. . . .

It is with pleasure that I pay here a tribute to the memory of the Rev. William James, then Fellow of Oriel; who, about the year 1823, taught me the doctrine of Apostolical Succession, in the course of a walk, I think, round Christ Church meadow: I recollect being somewhat impatient on the subject at the time.

It was at about this date, I suppose, that I read Bishop Butler's Analogy; the study of which has been to so many, as it was to me, an era in their religious opinions. Its inculcation of a visible Church, the oracle of truth and a pattern of sanctity, of the duties of external religion, and of the historical character of Revelation, are characteristics of this great work which strike the reader at once; for myself, if I may attempt to determine what I most gained from it, it lay in two points, which I shall have an opportunity of dwelling on in the sequel; they are the underlying principles of a great portion of my teaching. First, the very idea of an analogy between the separate works of God leads to the conclusion that the system which is of less importance is economically or sacramentally connected with the more momentous system, and of this conclusion the theory, to which I was inclined as a boy, viz. the unreality of material phe-

16. Mr. Whately, Richard Whately (1787–1863). 23. Dr. Hawkins, Edward Hawkins (1789–1882). 24. St. Mary's, the Oxford University church. 41–42. an attack . . . Scripture. See pages 381–82 of this volume. 43. Mr. Blanco White, Joseph Blanco White (1775–1841).

25–26. the doctrine of Apostolical Succession, the belief that a clergyman's ordination has no validity unless it can be traced back, through the laying on of hands, to the Apostles. 31. Bishop Butler's Analogy, The Analogy of Religion, 1736, by Joseph Butler, a famous and influential work. See E. C. Mossner, Bishop Butler and the Age of Reason, Macmillan, 1936.

nomena, is an ultimate resolution. At this time I did not make the distinction between matter itself and its phenomena, which is so necessary and so obvious in discussing the subject. Secondly, Butler's doctrine that Probability is the guide of life, led me, at least under the teaching to which a few years later I was introduced, to the question of the logical cogency of faith, on which I have written so much. Thus to Butler I trace those two principles of my teaching, which have led to a charge against me both of fancifulness and of scepticism. . . .

Dr. Whately attributed my leaving his *clientela* to a wish on my part to be the head of a party myself. I do not think that it was deserved. My habitual feeling then and since has been, that it was not I who sought friends, but friends who sought me. Never man had kinder or more indulgent friends than I have had, but I expressed my own feeling as to the mode in which I gained them, in this very year 1829, in the course of a copy of verses. Speaking of my blessings, I said, "Blessings of friends, which to my door, *unasked*, *unhoped*, have come." They have come, they have gone; they came to my great joy, they went to my great grief. He who gave, took away. Dr. Whately's impression about me, however, admits of this explanation:—

During the first years of my residence at Oriel, though proud of my College, I was not at home there. I was very much alone, and I used often to take my daily walk by myself. . . . At that time indeed I had the intimacy of my dear and true friend Dr. Pusey, and could not fail to admire and revere a soul so devoted to the cause of religion, so full of good works, so faithful in his affections; but he left residence when I was getting to know him well. As to Dr. Whately himself, he was too much my superior to allow of my being at my ease with him; and to no one in Oxford at this time did I open my heart fully and familiarly. But things changed in 1826. At that time I became one of the Tutors of my College, and this gave me position; besides, I had written one or two Essays which had been well received. I began to be known. I preached my first University Sermon. Next year I was one of the Public Examiners for the B.A. degree. It was to me like the feeling of spring weather after winter; and, if I may so speak, I came out of my shell; I remained out of it till 1841.

The two persons who knew me best at that time are still alive, beneficed clergymen, no longer my friends. They could tell better than any one else what I was in those years. . . . It was at this time that I began to have influence, which steadily increased for a course of years. I gained upon my pupils, and was in particular intimate and affectionate with two of our probationer fellows, Robert I. Wilberforce and Richard Hurrell Froude. Whately then, an acute man, perhaps saw around me the signs of an incipient party of which I was not conscious myself. And thus we discern the first elements of that movement afterwards called Tractarian.

The true and primary author of it, however, as is usual with great motive-powers, was out of sight. Having carried off as a mere boy the highest honours of the University, he had turned from the admiration which haunted his steps, and sought for a better and holier satisfaction in pastoral work in the country. Need I say that I am speaking of John Keble? The first time that I was in a room with him was on occasion of my election to a fellowship at Oriel, when I was sent for into the Tower, to shake hands with the Provost and Fellows. How is that hour fixed in my memory after the changes of forty-two years, forty-two this very day on which I write! I have lately had a letter in my hands, which I sent at the time to my great friend, John Bowden, with whom I passed almost exclusively my Undergraduate years. "I had to hasten to the Tower," I say to him, "to receive the congratulations of all the Fellows. I bore it till Keble took my hand, and then felt so abashed and unworthy of the honour done me, that I seemed desirous of quite sinking into the ground." His had been the first name which I had heard spoken of, with reverence rather than admiration, when I came up to Oxford. When one day I was walking in High Street with my dear earliest friend just mentioned, with what eagerness did he cry out, "There's Keble!" and with what awe did I look at him! Then at another time I heard a Master of Arts of my college give an account how he had just then had occasion to introduce himself on some business to Keble, and how gentle, courteous, and unaffected Keble had been, so as almost to put him out of countenance. Then too it was reported, truly or falsely, how a rising man of brilliant reputation, the present Dean of St. Paul's, Dr. Milman, admired and loved him, adding, that somehow he

---

33. **Dr. Pusey**, Edward Bouverie Pusey (1800–1882), Regius professor of Hebrew at Oxford, and Canon of Christ Church; a leader of the Oxford Movement.

6–7. **Robert I. Wilberforce** (1802–1857), a son of William Wilberforce. **Richard Hurrell Froude**, fellow of Oriel College (1803–1836). 19–20. **John Keble**, professor of poetry at Oxford (1792–1866). 27. **John Bowden** (1798–1844). 47. **Dr. Milman**, Henry Hart Milman (1791–1868), professor of poetry at Oxford from 1821 to 1831.

was unlike any one else. However, at the time when I was elected Fellow of Oriel he was not in residence, and he was shy of me for years in consequence of the marks which I bore upon me of the evangelical and liberal schools. At least so I have ever thought. Hurrell Froude brought us together about 1828: it is one of the sayings preserved in his "Remains,"—"Do you know the story of the murderer who had done one good thing in his life? Well; if I was ever asked what good deed I had ever done, 10 I should say that I had brought Keble and Newman to understand each other."

The Christian Year made its appearance in 1827. It is not necessary, and scarcely becoming, to praise a book which has already become one of the classics of the language. When the general tone of religious literature was so nerveless and impotent, as it was at that time, Keble struck an original note and woke up in the hearts of thousands a new music, the music of a school, long unknown in England. Nor 20 can I pretend to analyze, in my own instance, the effect of religious teaching so deep, so pure, so beautiful. I have never till now tried to do so; yet I think I am not wrong in saying, that the two main intellectual truths which it brought home to me, were the same two, which I had learned from Butler, though recast in the creative mind of my new master. The first of these was what may be called, in a large sense of the word, the Sacramental system; that is, the doctrine that material phenomena are 30 both the types and the instruments of real things unseen,—a doctrine, which embraces, not only what Anglicans, as well as Catholics, believe about Sacraments properly so called; but also the article of "the Communion of Saints" in its fulness; and likewise the Mysteries of the faith. . . .

On the second intellectual principle which I gained from Mr. Keble, I could say a great deal; if this were the place for it. It runs through very much 40 that I have written, and has gained for me many hard names. Butler teaches us that probability is the guide of life. The danger of this doctrine, in the case of many minds, is, its tendency to destroy in them absolute certainty, leading them to consider every conclusion as doubtful, and resolving truth into an opinion, which it is safe to obey or to profess, but not possible to embrace with full internal

13. **The Christian Year,** a very influential collection of sacred poetry which supplied a poem for every Sunday and holy 50 day observed by the Church of England.   **35. "the Communion of Saints,"** "the spiritual solidarity which binds together the faithful on earth, the souls in purgatory, and the saints in heaven in the organic unity of the same mystical body under Christ its head, and in constant interchange of supernatural offices." (*Catholic Encyclopaedia*)

assent. If this were to be allowed, then the celebrated saying, "O God, if there be a God, save my soul, if I have a soul!" would be the highest measure of devotion:—but who can really pray to a Being, about whose existence he is seriously in doubt?

I considered that Mr. Keble met this difficulty by ascribing the firmness of assent which we give to religious doctrine, not to the probabilities which 10 introduced it, but to the living power of faith and love which accepted it. In matters of religion, he seemed to say, it is not merely probability which makes us intellectually certain, but probability as it is put to account by faith and love. It is faith and love which give to probability a force which it has not in itself. Faith and love are directed towards an Object; in the vision of that Object they live; it is that Object, received in faith and love, which renders it reasonable to take probability as sufficient 20 for internal conviction. Thus the argument about Probability, in the matter of religion, became an argument from Personality, which in fact is one form of the argument from Authority. . . . .

Hurrell Froude was a pupil of Keble's, formed by him, and in turn reacting upon him. I knew him first in 1826, and was in the closest and most affectionate friendship with him from about 1829 till his death in 1836. He was a man of the highest gifts,— 30 so truly many-sided, that it would be presumptuous in me to attempt to describe him, except under those aspects, in which he came before me. Nor have I here to speak of the gentleness and tenderness of nature, the playfulness, the free elastic force and graceful versatility of mind, and the patient winning considerateness in discussion, which endeared him to those to whom he opened his heart; for I am all along engaged upon matters of belief and opinion, and am introducing others into my 40 narrative, not for their own sake, or because I love and have loved them, so much as because, and so far as, they have influenced my theological views. In this respect then, I speak of Hurrell Froude,—in his intellectual aspect,—as a man of high genius, brimful and overflowing with ideas and views, in him original, which were too many and strong even for his bodily strength, and which crowded and jostled against each other in their effort after distinct shape and expression. And he had an intellect 50 as critical and logical as it was speculative and bold. Dying prematurely, as he did, and in the conflict and transition-state of opinion, his religious views never reached their ultimate conclusion, by the very reason of their multitude and their depth. His opinions arrested and influenced me, even when they did not gain my assent. He professed openly his admiration of the Church of Rome, and his hatred of the Reformers. He delighted in the notion of an hierarchical system, of sacerdotal power and of full ecclesiastical liberty. He felt scorn of the maxim, "The Bible and the Bible only is the religion of Protestants"; and he gloried in accepting Tradition as a main instrument of religious teaching. He had a high severe idea of the intrinsic excellence of Virginity; and he considered the Blessed Virgin its great Pattern. He delighted in thinking of the Saints; he had a keen appreciation of the idea of sanctity, its possibility and its heights; and he was more than inclined to believe a large amount of miraculous interference as occurring in the early and middle ages. He embraced the principle of penance and mortification. He had a deep devotion to the Real Presence, in which he had a firm faith. He was powerfully drawn to the Medieval Church, but not to the Primitive.

He had a keen insight into abstract truth; but he was an Englishman to the backbone in his severe adherence to the real and the concrete. He had a most classical taste, and a genius for philosophy and art; and he was fond of historical inquiry, and the politics of religion. He had no turn for theology as such. He had no appreciation of the writings of the Fathers, of the detail or development of doctrine, of the definite traditions of the Church viewed in their matter, of the teaching of the Ecumenical Councils, or of the controversies out of which they arose. He took an eager, courageous view of things on the whole. I should say that his power of entering into the minds of others did not equal his other gifts; he could not believe, for instance, that I really held the Roman Church to be Antichristian. On many points he would not believe but that I agreed with him, when I did not. He seemed not to understand my difficulties. His were of a different kind, the contrariety between theory and fact. He was a high Tory of the Cavalier stamp, and was disgusted with the Toryism of the opponents of the Reform Bill. He was smitten with the love of the Theocratic Church; he went abroad and was shocked by the degeneracy which he thought he saw in the Catholics of Italy.

It is difficult to enumerate the precise additions to my theological creed which I derived from a friend to whom I owe so much. He made me look with admiration towards the Church of Rome, and in the same degree to dislike the Reformation. He fixed deep in me the idea of devotion to the Blessed Virgin, and he led me gradually to believe in the Real Presence.

There is one remaining source of my opinions to be mentioned, and that far from the least important. In proportion as I moved out of the shadow of liberalism which had hung over my course, my early devotion towards the Fathers returned; and in the Long Vacation of 1828 I set about to read them chronologically, beginning with St. Ignatius and St. Justin. About 1830 a proposal was made to me by Mr. Hugh Rose, who with Mr. Lyall was providing writers for a Theological Library, to furnish them with a History of the Principal Councils. I accepted it, and at once set to work on the Council of Nicaea. It was launching myself on an ocean with currents innumerable; and I was drifted back first to the ante-Nicene history, and then to the Church of Alexandria. The work at last appeared under the title of "The Arians of the Fourth Century"; and of its 422 pages, the first 117 consisted of introductory matter, and the Council of Nicaea did not appear till the 254th, and then occupied at most twenty pages.

I do not know when I first learnt to consider that Antiquity was the true exponent of the doctrines of Christianity and the basis of the Church of England; but I take it for granted that Bishop Bull, whose works at this time I read, was my chief introduction to this principle. The course of reading which I pursued in the composition of my work was directly adapted to develope it in my mind. What principally attracted me in the ante-Nicene period was the great Church of Alexandria, the historical centre of teaching in those times. Of Rome for some centuries comparatively little is known. The battle of Arianism was first fought in Alexandria; Athanasius, the champion of the truth, was Bishop of

11–12. **the Blessed Virgin,** Mary the mother of Jesus. See art. "Virgin Birth of Christ," *Catholic Encyclopaedia.* **19. the Real Presence,** the dogma that Jesus Christ is truly present in the Eucharist under the appearances of bread and wine.   **44. Reform Bill,** of 1832. See page 376 of this volume.

14. **St. Ignatius,** Bishop of Antioch in the second century. 15. **St. Justin,** Justin Martyr, Palestinian Church Father in the second century. 16. **Mr. Hugh Rose,** a clergyman (1795–1838) important in the opening stages of the Oxford Movement. **Mr. Lyall,** William Rose Lyall (1788–1857). 19–20. **Council of Nicaea,** which met in 325 at the call of the Emperor Constantine, and which put down Arianism. 32. **Bishop Bull,** George Bull (1634–1710). 41–42. **Arianism,** the view championed at Nicaea by Arius (c. 280–336), Greek patriarch of Alexandria, who maintained that Christ was the first of all created beings, and therefore not co-eternal with, and of the same substance as, God the Father. **Athanasius, the champion of the truth,** that is, champion of the Trinitarian view which put down Arianism (c. 296–373).

Alexandria; and in his writings he refers to the great religious names of an earlier date, to Origen, Dionysius, and others who were the glory of its see, or of its school. The broad philosophy of Clement and Origen carried me away; the philosophy, not the theological doctrine; and I have drawn out some features of it in my volume, with the zeal and freshness, but with the partiality of a neophyte. Some portions of their teaching, magnificent in themselves, came like music to my inward ear, as if the response to ideas, which, with little external to encourage them, I had cherished so long. These were based on the mystical or sacramental principle, and spoke of the various Economies or Dispensations of the Eternal. I understood them to mean that the exterior world, physical and historical, was but the outward manifestation of realities greater than itself. Nature was a parable: Scripture was an allegory: pagan literature, philosophy, and mythology, properly understood, were but a preparation for the Gospel. The Greek poets and sages were in a certain sense prophets; for "thoughts beyond their thought to those high bards were given." There had been a divine dispensation granted to the Jews; there had been in some sense a dispensation carried on in favour of the Gentiles. He who had taken the seed of Jacob for His elect people, had not therefore cast the rest of mankind out of His sight. In the fulness of time both Judaism and Paganism had come to nought; the outward framework, which concealed yet suggested the Living Truth, had never been intended to last, and it was dissolving under the beams of the sun of justice behind it and through it. The process of change had been slow; it had been done not rashly, but by rule, and measure, "at sundry times and in divers manners," first one disclosure and then another, till the whole was brought into full manifestation. And thus room was made for the anticipation of further and deeper disclosures, of truths still under the veil of the letter, and in their season to be revealed. The visible world still remains without its divine interpretation; Holy Church in her sacraments and her hierarchical appointments, will remain even to the end of the world, only a symbol of those heavenly facts which fill eternity. Her mysteries are but the expressions in human language of truths to which the human mind is unequal. It is evident how much there was in all this in correspondence with the thoughts which had attracted me when I was

young, and with the doctrine which I have already connected with the Analogy and the Christian Year.

I suppose it was to the Alexandrian school and to the early church that I owe in particular what I definitely held about the Angels. I viewed them, not only as the ministers employed by the Creator in the Jewish and Christian dispensations, as we find on the face of Scripture, but as carrying on, as Scripture also implies, the Economy of the Visible World. I considered them as the real causes of motion, light, and life, and of those elementary principles of the physical universe, which, when offered in their developments to our senses, suggest to us the notion of cause and effect, and of what are called the laws of nature. I have drawn out this doctrine in my Sermon for Michaelmas day, written not later than 1834. I say of the Angels, "Every breath of air and ray of light and heat, every beautiful prospect is, as it were, the skirts of their garments, the waving of the robes of those whose faces see God." Again, I ask what would be the thoughts of a man who, "when examining a flower, or a herb, or a pebble, or a ray of light, which he treats as something so beneath him in the scale of existence, suddenly discovered that he was in the presence of some powerful being who was hidden behind the visible things he was inspecting, who, though concealing his wise hand, was giving them their beauty, grace, and perfection, as being God's instrument for the purpose, nay, whose robe and ornaments those objects were, which he was so eager to analyze?" and I therefore remark that "we may say with grateful and simple hearts with the Three Holy Children, 'O all ye works of the Lord, &c., &c., bless ye the Lord, praise Him, and magnify Him for ever.' "

Also, besides the hosts of evil spirits, I considered there was a middle race, δαιμόνια, neither in heaven, nor in hell; partially fallen, capricious, wayward; noble or crafty, benevolent or malicious, as the case might be. They gave a sort of inspiration or intelligence to races, nations, and classes of men. Hence the action of bodies politic and associations, which is so different often from that of the individuals who compose them. Hence the character and the instinct of states and governments, of religious communities and communions. I thought they were inhabited by unseen intelligences. My preference of the Personal to the Abstract would naturally lead

2. **Origen,** of Alexandria (c. 185–254), one of the great Greek Fathers. **Dionysius** (c. 190–265), Bishop of Alexandria.   4. **Clement,** of Alexandria (c. 150–c. 220). 26–27. **the seed of Jacob,** the Jews.   36. **"at sundry times and in divers manners."** See Hebrews 1:1.

17. **Michaelmas day,** September 29, the feast of the Archangel Michael.   34–35. **Three Holy Children.** See Daniel 3.   39. δαιμόνια, demons, spirits intermediate between God and man (not devils).

me to this view. I thought it countenanced by the mention of "the Prince of Persia" in the Prophet Daniel; and I think I considered that it was of such intermediate beings that the Apocalypse spoke, when it introduced "the Angels of the Seven Churches."

In 1837 I made a further development of this doctrine. I said to my great friend, Samuel Francis Wood, in a letter which came into my hands on his death, "I have an idea. The mass of the Fathers (Justin, Athenagoras, Irenaeus, Clement, Tertullian, Origen, Lactantius, Sulpicius, Ambrose, Nazianzen,) hold that, though Satan fell from the beginning, the Angels fell before the deluge, falling in love with the daughters of men. This has lately come across me as a remarkable solution of a notion which I cannot help holding. Daniel speaks as if each nation had its guardian Angel. I cannot but think that there are beings with a great deal of good in them, yet with great defects, who are the animating principles of certain institutions, &c., &c. . . . Take England, with many high virtues, and yet a low Catholicism. It seems to me that John Bull is a spirit neither of heaven nor hell. . . . Has not the Christian Church, in its parts, surrendered itself to one or other of these simulations of the truth? . . . How are we to avoid Scylla and Charybdis and go straight on to the very image of Christ?" &c., &c.

I am aware that what I have been saying will, with many men, be doing credit to my imagination at the expense of my judgment—"Hippoclides doesn't care"; I am not setting myself up as a pattern of good sense or of anything else: I am but vindicating myself from the charge of dishonesty.— There is indeed another view of the Economy brought out, in the course of the same dissertation on the subject, in my History of the Arians, which has afforded matter for the latter imputation;

but I reserve it for the concluding portion of my Reply.

While I was engaged in writing my work upon the Arians, great events were happening at home and abroad, which brought out into form and passionate expression the various beliefs which had so gradually been winning their way into my mind. Shortly before, there had been a Revolution in France; the Bourbons had been dismissed: and I believed that it was unchristian for nations to cast off their governors, and, much more, sovereigns who had the divine right of inheritance. Again, the great Reform Agitation was going on around me as I wrote. The Whigs had come into power; Lord Grey had told the bishops to set their house in order, and some of the Prelates had been insulted and threatened in the streets of London. The vital question was how were we to keep the Church from being liberalized? there was such apathy on the subject in some quarters, such imbecile alarm in others; the true principles of Churchmanship seemed so radically decayed, and there was such distraction in the Councils of the Clergy. The Bishop of London of the day, an active and open-hearted man, had been for years engaged in diluting the high orthodoxy of the Church by the introduction of the Evangelical body into places of influence and trust. He had deeply offended men who agreed with myself, by an off-hand saying (as it was reported) to the effect that belief in the Apostolical succession had gone out with the Non-jurors. "We can count you," he said to some of the gravest and most venerated persons of the old school. And the Evangelical party itself seemed, with their late successes, to have lost that simplicity and unworldliness which I admired so much in Milner and Scott. . . . With the Establishment thus divided and threatened, thus ignorant of its true strength, I compared that fresh vigorous power of which I was reading in the first centuries. In her triumphant zeal on behalf of that Primeval Mystery, to which I had had so great a devotion from my youth, I recognized the movement of my Spiritual Mother. "Incessu patuit Dea." The self-conquest of her Ascetics, the patience of her Martyrs, the irresistible determination of her Bishops, the joyous swing of her advance, both exalted and abashed me. I said to myself,

1–3. the mention . . . Daniel. See Daniel 10:13. 4–6. the Apocalypse . . . Churches." See Revelation 1. 11–13. Athenagoras, one of the oldest Christian apologetic writers, who worked in the second century in Athens and Alexandria. Irenaeus, Bishop of Lyons (c. 130–c. 202). Tertullian, one of the most famous and influential Fathers of the Latin Church (c. 155–c. 222). Lactantius, a Christian writer of the fourth century, who did much of his work in Gaul. Sulpicius, Christian historian (c. 363–c. 410), likewise of Gaul. Ambrose, Bishop of Milan (c. 340–397). Nazianzen, St. Gregory of Nazianzus (c. 329–c. 389), one of the great Fathers of the Eastern Church. 14–15. the Angels . . . men. See Genesis 6:1–4. 24. John Bull, England. The term was first used by John Arbuthnot (1667–1735). 27–28. Scylla and Charybdis, a monster and a whirlpool separated only by a narrow passage, in Homer's Odyssey, Book XII. 32–33. "Hippoclides doesn't care," as reported by Herodotus, History, Book VI, sec. 129, after his prospective father-in-law had eliminated him as a suitor for his daughter's hand.

9–10. there had been . . . dismissed, the revolution of 1830, which dethroned Charles X. 15. Lord Grey, Charles, Earl Grey, Prime Minister 1830–34. 32. Nonjurors, the four hundred clergymen who, in 1688, refused to take the oath of allegiance to William and Mary. 44–45. "Incessu patuit Dea." "She is proved a goddess by her walk." (Virgil, Aeneid, Book I, l. 405)

"Look on this picture and on that"; I felt affection for my own Church, but not tenderness; I felt dismay at her prospects, anger and scorn at her do-nothing perplexity. I thought that if Liberalism once got a footing within her, it was sure of the victory in the event. I saw that Reformation principles were powerless to rescue her. As to leaving her, the thought never crossed my imagination; still I ever kept before me that there was something greater than the Established Church, and that that was the Church Catholic and Apostolic, set up from the beginning, of which she was but the local presence and organ. She was nothing, unless she was this. She must be dealt with strongly, or she would be lost. There was need of a second Reformation.

At this time I was disengaged from College duties, and my health had suffered from the labour involved in the composition of my Volume. It was ready for the Press in July 1832, though not published till the end of 1833. I was easily persuaded to join Hurrell Froude and his father, who were going to the south of Europe for the health of the former.

We set out in December, 1832. It was during this expedition that my Verses which are in the Lyra Apostolica were written;—a few indeed before it, but not more than one or two of them after it. Exchanging, as I was, definite Tutorial labours, and the literary quiet and pleasant friendships of the last six years, for foreign countries and an unknown future, I naturally was led to think that some inward changes, as well as some larger course of action, was coming upon me. At Whitchurch, while waiting for the down mail to Falmouth, I wrote the verses about my Guardian Angel, which begin with these words: "Are these the tracks of some unearthly Friend?" and go on to speak of "the vision" which haunted me:—that vision is more or less brought out in the whole series of these compositions.

I went to various coasts of the Mediterranean, parted with my friends at Rome; went down for the second time to Sicily, at the end of April, and got back to England by Palermo in the early part of July. The strangeness of foreign life threw me back into myself; I found pleasure in historical sites and beautiful scenes, not in men and manners. . . .

It was the success of the Liberal cause which fretted me inwardly. I became fierce against its instruments and its manifestations. A French vessel was at Algiers; I would not even look at the tri-colour. On my return, though forced to stop a day at Paris, I kept indoors the whole time, and all that I saw of that beautiful city, was what I saw from the Diligence. . . . At this time I was specially annoyed with Dr. Arnold, though it did not last into later years. Some one, I think, asked in conversation at Rome, whether a certain interpretation of Scripture was Christian? it was answered that Dr. Arnold took it; I interposed, "But is *he* a Christian?" The subject went out of my head at once; when afterwards I was taxed with it I could say no more in explanation, than that I thought I must have been alluding to some free views of Dr. Arnold about the Old Testament:—I thought I must have meant, "But who is to answer for Arnold?" . . .

Especially when I was left by myself, the thought came upon me that deliverance is wrought, not by the many but by the few, not by bodies but by persons. Now it was, I think, that I repeated to myself the words, which had ever been dear to me from my school days, "Exoriare aliquis!"—now too, that Southey's beautiful poem of Thalaba, for which I had an immense liking, came forcibly to my mind. I began to think that I had a mission. There are sentences of my letters to my friends to this effect, if they are not destroyed. When we took leave of Monsignore Wiseman, he had courteously expressed a wish that we might make a second visit to Rome; I said with great gravity, "We have a work to do in England." I went down at once to Sicily, and the presentiment grew stronger. I struck into the middle of the island, and fell ill of a fever at Leonforte. My servant thought that I was dying, and begged for my last directions. I gave them, as he wished; but I said, "I shall not die." I repeated, "I shall not die, for I have not sinned against light, I have not sinned against light." I never have been able to make out at all what I meant.

I got to Castro-Giovanni, and was laid up there for nearly three weeks. Towards the end of May I set off for Palermo, taking three days for the journey. Before starting from my inn in the morning of May 26th or 27th, I sat down on my bed, and began to sob bitterly. My servant, who had acted as my nurse, asked what ailed me. I could only answer, "I have a work to do in England."

I was aching to get home; yet for want of a vessel I was kept at Palermo for three weeks. I began to visit the churches, and they calmed my impatience,

1. **"Look . . . that."** See *Hamlet*, Act III, sc. 4, l. 53.
24–25. **Lyra Apostolica**, 1836, a collection of poems by Keble, Newman, Froude, and others.   42. **Palermo**, in Sicily.

5. **Dr. Arnold**, Thomas Arnold (1795–1842), Matthew Arnold's father, headmaster of Rugby, and a leader in the Broad Church movement (see page 381 of this volume).
22. **"Exoriare aliquis!"** "May someone arise!"

though I did not attend any services. I knew nothing of the Presence of the Blessed Sacrament there.
At last I got off in an orange boat, bound for Marseilles. We were becalmed a whole week in the
Straits of Bonifacio. Then it was that I wrote the
lines, "Lead, kindly light," which have since become
well known. I was writing verses the whole time of
my passage. At length I got to Marseilles, and set
off for England. The fatigue of travelling was too
much for me, and I was laid up for several days at
Lyons. At last I got off again, and did not stop
night or day till I reached England, and my
mother's house. My brother had arrived from
Persia only a few hours before. This was on the
Tuesday. The following Sunday, July 14th,
Mr. Keble preached the Assize Sermon in the University Pulpit. It was published under the title of
"National Apostasy." I have ever considered and
kept the day, as the start of the religious movement
of 1833.

from PART VII

General Answer to Mr. Kingsley

From the time that I became a Catholic, of
course I have no further history of my religious
opinions to narrate. In saying this, I do not mean to
say that my mind has been idle, or that I have given
up thinking on theological subjects; but that I have
had no changes to record, and have had no anxiety
of heart whatever. I have been in perfect peace and
contentment. I never have had one doubt. I was
not conscious to myself, on my conversion, of any
difference of thought or of temper from what I had
before. I was not conscious of firmer faith in the
fundamental truths of revelation, or of more self-
command; I had not more fervour; but it was like
coming into port after a rough sea; and my happiness on that score remains to this day without
interruption.
     Nor had I any trouble about receiving those ad-
ditional articles which are not found in the Anglican Creed. Some of them I believed already, but
not any one of them was a trial to me. I made a
profession of them upon my reception with the
greatest ease, and I have the same ease in believing
them now. I am far of course from denying that
every article of the Christian Creed, whether as
held by Catholics or by Protestants, is beset with
intellectual difficulties; and it is simple fact that,
for myself, I cannot answer those difficulties. Many
persons are very sensitive of the difficulties of religion; I am as sensitive as any one; but I have never

5. **Straits of Bonifacio,** between Corsica and Sardinia.

been able to see a connexion between apprehending
those difficulties, however keenly, and multiplying
them to any extent, and doubting the doctrines to
which they are attached. Ten thousand difficulties
do not make one doubt, as I understand the subject; difficulty and doubt are incommensurate. . . .

     But I am going to take upon myself the responsi-
bility of more than the mere Creed of the Church;
as the parties accusing me are determined I shall
do. They say, that now, in that I am a Catholic,
though I may not have offences of my own against
honesty to answer for, yet, at least, I am answerable
for the offences of others, of my co-religionists, of
my brother priests, of the Church herself. I am quite
willing to accept the responsibility; and, as I have
been able, as I trust, by means of a few words, to
dissipate, in the minds of all those who do not begin
with disbelieving me, the suspicion with which so
many Protestants start, in forming their judgment
of Catholics, viz. that our Creed is actually set up in
inevitable superstition and hypocrisy, as the original sin of Catholicism; so now I will go on, as
before, identifying myself with the Church and
vindicating it,—not of course denying the enormous mass of sin and ignorance which exists of
necessity in that world-wide multiform Communion,—but going to the proof of this one point, that
its system is in no sense dishonest, and that therefore the upholders and teachers of that system, as
such, have a claim to be acquitted in their own
persons of that odious imputation.

     Starting then with the being of a God (which, as
I have said, is as certain to me as the certainty of
my own existence, though when I try to put the
grounds of that certainty into logical shape I find a
difficulty in doing so in mood and figure to my
satisfaction), I look out of myself into the world of
men, and there I see a sight which fills me with unspeakable distress. The world seems simply to give
the lie to that great truth, of which my whole being
is so full; and the effect upon me is, in consequence,
as a matter of necessity, as confusing as if it denied
that I am in existence myself. If I looked into a
mirror, and did not see my face, I should have the
sort of feeling which actually comes upon me, when
I look into this living busy world, and see no reflexion of its Creator. This is, to me, one of the great
difficulties of this absolute primary truth, to which
I referred just now. Were it not for this voice, speaking so clearly in my conscience and my heart, I
should be an atheist, or a pantheist, or a polytheist
when I looked into the world. . . .

To consider the world in its length and breadth, its various history, the many races of man, their starts, their fortunes, their mutual alienation, their conflicts; and then their ways, habits, governments, forms of worship; their enterprises, their aimless courses, their random achievements and acquirements, the impotent conclusion of long-standing facts, the tokens so faint and broken, of a superintending design, the blind evolution of what turn out to be great powers or truth, the progress of things, as if from unreasoning elements, not towards final causes, the greatness and littleness of man, his far-reaching aims, his short duration, the curtain hung over his futurity, the disappointments of life, the defeat of good, the success of evil, physical pain, mental anguish, the prevalence and intensity of sin, the pervading idolatries, the corruptions, the dreary hopeless irreligion, that condition of the whole race, so fearfully yet exactly described in the Apostle's words, "having no hope and without God in the world,"—all this is a vision to dizzy and appal; and inflicts upon the mind the sense of a profound mystery, which is absolutely beyond human solution.

What shall be said to this heart-piercing, reason-bewildering fact? I can only answer, that either there is no Creator, or this living society of men is in a true sense discarded from His presence. Did I see a boy of good make and mind, with the tokens on him of a refined nature, cast upon the world without provision, unable to say whence he came, his birth-place or his family connexions, I should conclude that there was some mystery connected with his history, and that he was one, of whom, from one cause or other, his parents were ashamed. Thus only should I be able to account for the contrast between the promise and condition of his being. And so I argue about the world;—*if* there be a God, *since* there is a God, the human race is implicated in some terrible aboriginal calamity. It is out of joint with the purposes of its Creator. This is a fact, a fact as true as the fact of its existence; and thus the doctrine of what is theologically called original sin becomes to me almost as certain as that the world exists, and as the existence of God.

And now, supposing it were the blessed and loving will of the Creator to interfere in this anarchical condition of things, what are we to suppose would be the methods which might be necessarily or naturally involved in His object of mercy? Since the world is in so abnormal a state, surely it would be no surprise to me, if the interposition were of necessity equally extraordinary—or what is called miraculous. But that subject does not directly come into the scope of my present remarks. Miracles as evidence, involve an argument; and of course I am thinking of some means which does not immediately run into argument. I am rather asking what must be the face-to-face antagonist, by which to withstand and baffle the fierce energy of passion and the all-corroding, all-dissolving scepticism of the intellect in religious inquiries? I have no intention at all to deny, that truth is the real object of our reason, and that, if it does not attain to truth, either the premiss or the process is in fault; but I am not speaking of right reason, but of reason as it acts in fact and concretely in fallen man. I know that even the unaided reason, when correctly exercised, leads to a belief in God, in the immortality of the soul, and in a future retribution; but I am considering it actually and historically; and in this point of view, I do not think I am wrong in saying that its tendency is towards a simple unbelief in matters of religion. No truth, however sacred, can stand against it, in the long run; and hence it is that in the pagan world, when our Lord came, the last traces of the religious knowledge of former times were all but disappearing from those portions of the world in which the intellect had been active and had had a career.

And in these latter days, in like manner, outside the Catholic Church things are tending, with far greater rapidity than in that old time from the circumstance of the age, to atheism in one shape or other. What a scene, what a prospect, does the whole of Europe present at this day! and not only Europe, but every government and every civilization through the world which is under the influence of the European mind! Especially, for it most concerns us, how sorrowful, in the view of religion, even taken in its most elementary, most attenuated form, is the spectacle presented to us by the educated intellect of England, France, and Germany! Lovers of their country and of their race, religious men, external to the Catholic Church, have attempted various expedients to arrest fierce wilful human nature in its onward course, and to bring it into subjection. The necessity of some form of religion for the interests of humanity, has been generally acknowledged: but where was the concrete representative of things invisible, which would have the force and the toughness necessary to be a breakwater against the deluge? Three centuries ago the establishment of religion, material, legal, and social, was generally adopted as the best expedient for the purpose, in those countries which separated

20–21. "having . . . world," St. Paul, in Ephesians 2:12.
43. original sin, the hereditary stain inherited by all mankind from Adam.

from the Catholic Church; and for a long time it was successful; but now the crevices of those establishments are admitting the enemy. Thirty years ago, education was relied upon: ten years ago there was a hope that wars would cease for ever, under the influence of commercial enterprise and the reign of the useful and fine arts; but will any one venture to say that there is any thing any where on this earth, which will afford a fulcrum for us, whereby to keep the earth from moving onwards?

The judgment, which experience passes on establishments or education, as a means of maintaining religious truth in this anarchical world, must be extended even to Scripture, though Scripture be divine. Experience proves surely that the Bible does not answer a purpose for which it was never intended. It may be accidentally the means of the conversion of individuals; but a book, after all, cannot make a stand against the wild living intellect of man, and in this day it begins to testify, as regards its own structure and contents, to the power of that universal solvent, which is so successfully acting upon religious establishments.

Supposing then it to be the Will of the Creator to interfere in human affairs, and to make provisions for retaining in the world a knowledge of Himself, so definite and distinct as to be proof against the energy of human scepticism, in such a case,—I am far from saying that there was no other way,—but there is nothing to surprise the mind, if He should think fit to introduce a power into the world, invested with the prerogative of infallibility in religious matters. Such a provision would be a direct, immediate, active, and prompt means of withstanding the difficulty; it would be an instrument suited to the need; and, when I find that this is the very claim of the Catholic Church, not only do I feel no difficulty in admitting the idea, but there is a fitness in it, which recommends it to my mind. And thus I am brought to speak of the Church's infallibility, as a provision, adapted by the mercy of the Creator, to preserve religion in the world, and to restrain that freedom of thought, which of course in itself is one of the greatest of our natural gifts, and to rescue it from its own suicidal excesses. And let it be observed that, neither here nor in what follows, shall I have occasion to speak directly of the revealed body of truths, but only as they bear upon the defence of natural religion. I say, that a power, possessed of infallibility in religious teaching, is happily adapted to be a working instrument, in the course of human affairs, for smiting hard and

throwing back the immense energy of the aggressive intellect:—and in saying this, as in the other things that I have to say, it must still be recollected that I am all along bearing in mind my main purpose, which is a defence of myself.

I am defending myself here from a plausible charge brought against Catholics, as will be seen better as I proceed. The charge is this:—that I, as a Catholic, not only make profession to hold doctrines which I cannot possibly believe in my heart, but that I also believe in the existence of a power on earth, which at its own will imposes upon men any new set of *credenda*, when it pleases, by a claim to infallibility; in consequence, that my own thoughts are not my own property; that I cannot tell that to-morrow I may not have to give up what I hold to-day, and that the necessary effect of such a condition of mind must be a degrading bondage, or a bitter inward rebellion relieving itself in secret infidelity, or the necessity of ignoring the whole subject of religion in a sort of disgust, and of mechanically saying every thing that the Church says, and leaving to others the defence of it. As then I have above spoken of the relation of my mind towards the Catholic Creed, so now I shall speak of the attitude which it takes up in the view of the Church's infallibility.

And first, the initial doctrine of the infallible teacher must be an emphatic protest against the existing state of mankind. Man had rebelled against his Maker. It was this that caused the divine interposition: and the first act of the divinely accredited messenger must be to proclaim it. The Church must denounce rebellion as of all possible evils the greatest. She must have no terms with it; if she would be true to her Master, she must ban and anathematize it. This is the meaning of a statement which has furnished matter for one of those special accusations to which I am at present replying: I have, however, no fault at all to confess in regard to it; I have nothing to withdraw, and in consequence I here deliberately repeat it. I said, "The Catholic Church holds it better for the sun and moon to drop from heaven, for the earth to fail, and for all the many millions on it to die of starvation in extremest agony, as far as temporal affliction goes, than that one soul, I will not say, should be lost, but should commit one single venial sin, should tell one wilful untruth, or should steal one poor farthing without excuse." I think the principle here enunciated to be the mere preamble in the formal credentials of the Catholic Church, as an Act of Parliament might begin with a "*Whereas*." It is because of

5–7. **that wars would cease . . . fine arts,** as manifested in the Great Exhibition at the Crystal Palace in 1851.

13. **credenda,** articles of faith.

the intensity of the evil which has possession of mankind, that a suitable antagonist has been provided against it; and the initial act of that divinely-commissioned power is of course to deliver her challenge and to defy the enemy. Such a preamble then gives a meaning to her position in the world, and an interpretation to her whole course of teaching and action.

In like manner she has ever put forth, with most energetic distinctness, those other great elementary truths, which either are an explanation of her mission or give a character to her work. She does not teach that human nature is irreclaimable, else wherefore should she be sent? not that it is to be shattered and reversed, but to be extricated, purified, and restored; not that it is a mere mass of evil, but that it has the promise of great things, and even now has a virtue and a praise proper to itself. But in the next place she knows and she preaches that such a restoration, as she aims at effecting in it, must be brought about, not simply through any outward provision of preaching and teaching, even though it be her own, but from a certain inward spiritual power or grace imparted directly from above, and which is in her keeping. She has it in charge to rescue human nature from its misery, but not simply by raising it upon its own level, but by lifting it up to a higher level than its own. She recognizes in it real moral excellence though degraded, but she cannot set it free from earth except by exalting it towards heaven. It was for this end that a renovating grace was put into her hands, and therefore from the nature of the gift, as well as from the reasonableness of the case, she goes on, as a further point, to insist, that all true conversion must begin with the first springs of thought, and to teach that each individual man must be in his own person one whole and perfect temple of God, while he is also one of the living stones which build up a visible religious community. And thus the distinctions between nature and grace, and between outward and inward religion, become two further articles in what I have called the preamble of her divine commission. . . .

Passing now from what I have called the preamble of that grant of power, with which the Church is invested, to that power itself, Infallibility, I make two brief remarks: on the one hand, I am not here determining anything about the essential seat of that power, because that is a question doctrinal, not historical and practical; nor, on the other hand, am I extending the direct subject-matter, over which that power has jurisdiction, beyond

religious opinion:—and now as to the power itself.

This power, viewed in its fulness, is as tremendous as the giant evil which has called for it. It claims, when brought into exercise in the legitimate manner, for otherwise of course it is but dormant, to have for itself a sure guidance into the very meaning of every portion of the Divine Message in detail, which was committed by our Lord to His Apostles. It claims to know its own limits, and to decide what it can determine absolutely and what it cannot. It claims, moreover, to have a hold upon statements not directly religious, so far as this, to determine whether they indirectly relate to religion, and, according to its own definitive judgment, to pronounce whether or not, in a particular case, they are consistent with revealed truth. It claims to decide magisterially, whether infallibly or not, that such and such statements are or are not prejudicial to the Apostolic *depositum* of faith, in their spirit or in their consequences, and to allow them, or condemn and forbid them, accordingly. It claims to impose silence at will on any matters, or controversies, of doctrine, which on its own *ipse dixit* it pronounces to be dangerous, or inexpedient, or inopportune. It claims that whatever may be the judgment of Catholics upon such acts, these acts should be received by them with those outward marks of reverence, submission, and loyalty, which Englishmen, for instance, pay to the presence of their sovereign, without public criticism on them, as being in their matter inexpedient, or in their manner violent or harsh. And lastly, it claims to have the right of inflicting spiritual punishment, of cutting off from the ordinary channels of the divine life, and of simply excommunicating, those who refuse to submit themselves to its formal declarations. Such is the infallibility lodged in the Catholic Church, viewed in the concrete, as clothed and surrounded by the appendages of its high sovereignty: it is, to repeat what I said above, a supereminent prodigious power sent upon earth to encounter and master a giant evil.

And now, having thus described it, I profess my own absolute submission to its claim. I believe the whole revealed dogma as taught by the Apostles, as committed by the Apostles to the Church, and as declared by the Church to me. I receive it, as it is infallibly interpreted by the authority to whom it is thus committed, and (implicitly) as it shall be, in like manner, further interpreted by that same authority till the end of time. I submit, moreover, to the universally received traditions of the Church, in which lies the matter of those new dogmatic

23–24. **ipse dixit**, assertion (without proof)

definitions which are from time to time made, and which in all times are the clothing and the illustration of the Catholic dogma as already defined. And I submit myself to those other decisions of the Holy See, theological or not, through the organs which it has itself appointed, which, waiving the question of their infallibility, on the lowest ground come to me with a claim to be accepted and obeyed. Also, I consider that, gradually and in the course of ages, Catholic inquiry has taken certain definite shapes, and has thrown itself into the form of a science, with a method and a phraseology of its own, under the intellectual handling of great minds, such as St. Athanasius, St. Augustine, and St. Thomas; and I feel no temptation at all to break in pieces the great legacy of thought thus committed to us for these latter days.

All this being considered to be a profession *ex animo*, as on my own part, so also on the part of the Catholic body, as far as I know it, it will at first sight be said that the restless intellect of our common humanity is utterly weighed down to the repression of all independent effort and action whatever, so that, if this is to be the mode of bringing it into order, it is brought into order only to be destroyed. But this is far from the result, far from what I conceive to be the intention of that high Providence who has provided a great remedy for a great evil,—far from borne out by the history of the conflict between Infallibility and Reason in the past, and the prospect of it in the future. The energy of the human intellect "does from opposition grow"; it thrives and is joyous, with a tough elastic strength, under the terrible blows of the divinely-fashioned weapon, and is never so much itself as when it has lately been overthrown. It is the custom with Protestant writers to consider that, whereas there are two great principles in action in the history of religion, Authority and Private Judgment, they have all the Private Judgment to themselves, and we have the full inheritance and the superincumbent oppression of Authority. But this is not so; it is the vast Catholic body itself, and it only, which affords an arena for both combatants in that awful, never-dying duel. It is necessary for the very life of religion, viewed in its large operations and its history, that the warfare should be incessantly carried on. Every exercise of Infallibility is brought out into act by an intense and varied operation of the Reason, from within and without, and provokes again a reaction of Reason against it; and, as in a civil polity the State exists and endures by means of the rivalry and collision, the encroachments and defeats of its constituent parts, so in like manner Catholic Christendom is no simple exhibition of religious absolutism, but it presents a continuous picture of Authority and Private Judgment alternately advancing and retreating as the ebb and flow of the tide;—it is a vast assemblage of human beings with wilful intellects and wild passions, brought together into one by the beauty and the majesty of a Superhuman Power—into what may be called a large reformatory or training-school, not to be sent to bed, not to be buried alive, but for the melting, refining, and moulding, as in some moral factory, by an incessant noisy process (if I may proceed to another metaphor), of the raw material of human nature, so excellent, so dangerous, so capable of divine purposes.

St. Paul says in one place that his Apostolical power is given him to edification, and not to destruction. There can be no better account of the Infallibility of the Church. It is a supply for a need, and it does not go beyond that need. Its object is, and its effect also, not to enfeeble the freedom or vigour of human thought in religious speculation, but to resist and control its extravagance. What have been its great works? All of them in the distinct province of theology:—to put down Arianism, Eutychianism, Pelagianism, Manichaeism, Lutheranism, Jansenism. Such is the broad result of its action in the past;—and now as to the securities which are given us that so it ever will act in time to come.

First, Infallibility cannot act outside of a definite circle of thought, and it must in all its decisions, or *definitions*, as they are called, profess to be keeping within it. The great truths of the moral law, of natural religion, and of Apostolical faith, are both its boundary and its foundation. It must not go beyond them, and it must ever appeal to them. Both its subject-matter, and its articles in that subject-matter, are fixed. Thus, in illustration, it does not

19. St. Paul says in one place, in 2 Corinthians 10:8. **29–30. Eutychianism**, from Eutyches, a monk of the Greek Church (fifth century), the essence of the view being that Christ had been one nature after the Incarnation. **Pelagianism**, from Pelagius, a British monk (fourth and fifth centuries), who taught a number of heresies, denying the doctrine of original sin, and maintaining the ability of men to save themselves through righteous living, though without the aid of the Gospel. **Manichaeism**, from Mani (c. 216–277), who introduced Persian dualism into Christianity, distinguishing between the spiritual Christ, as divine, and the historical Jesus, as evil. **Lutheranism**, the religious beliefs and ecclesiastical practices of Martin Luther (1483–1546), who headed the Protestant revolt in Germany. **Jansenism**, a many-sided heresy named from Cornelis Jansen (1585–1639), Bishop of Ypres. See art. "Jansenism" in *New International Encyclopaedia*.

14. St. Thomas, St. Thomas Aquinas (c. 1225–1274), whose *Sum of Theology* is the authoritative statement of Catholic doctrine. **19. ex animo**, from the heart.

extend to statements, however sound and evident, which are mere logical conclusions from the Articles of the Apostolic *Depositum;* again, it can pronounce nothing about the persons of heretics, whose works fall within its legitimate province. It must ever profess to be guided by Scripture and by tradition. It must refer to the particular Apostolic truth which it is enforcing, or (what is called) *defining.* Nothing, then, can be presented to me, in time to come, as part of the faith, but what I ought already to have received, and have not actually received, (if not) merely because it has not been told me. Nothing can be imposed upon me different in kind

from what I hold already,—much less contrary to it. The new truth which is promulgated, if it is to be called new, must be at least homogeneous, cognate, implicit, viewed relatively to the old truth. It must be what I may even have guessed, or wished, to be included in the Apostolic revelation; and at least it will be of such a character, that my thoughts readily concur in it or coalesce with it, as soon as I hear it. Perhaps I and others actually have always believed it, and the only question which is now decided in my behalf, is that I am henceforth to believe that I have only been holding what the Apostles held before me.

John Stuart Mill
1806–1873

By blood and training, John Stuart Mill inherited the Utilitarian point of view (see pages 377–78 of this volume). He himself is still popularly regarded as the great Victorian thinking machine, the high priest of Reason in his generation. As a matter of fact, however, Mill, while clinging in important particulars to the Positivist outlook, modified classical Utilitarianism in important particulars. His study of Wordsworth, Coleridge, and others led him to distinguish between kinds and qualities of pleasure after a fashion that his father, James Mill, had never known, and he found in practice that he could not continue to serve the Utilitarian ideal of "the greatest happiness of the greatest number" without so far abandoning the laissez-faire principle as virtually to advocate a form of State Socialism. The admirable vigor and clarity of his thinking appear in the stirring defense of freedom by which he is represented in this volume; the nobility and disinterested passion of his character are quite as obvious.

The facts of Mill's life are easily summarized. He was born in London, May 20, 1806, entered the service of the East India Company at seventeen, and continued in that service until the dissolution of the company thirty-five years later. He edited the *London and Westminster Review*; married in 1851 Mrs. Harriet Taylor, with whom he had long been intimate, and who had an important influence upon him; became a member of Parliament in 1865, but was defeated three years later. In 1866 he headed a committee to bring Governor Eyre, the Jamaica butcher, to justice, against the opposition of an

astonishing number of the great Victorians. He spent his last years in France, and died at Avignon, May 8, 1873.

Mill served many causes. He defended the French revolutionaries in 1830, and supported the Union cause in the Civil War. He supported Charles Bradlaugh's long-contested right to sit in Parliament despite his atheism. He opposed heavy armaments, and advocated a liberal policy toward Ireland. He favored woman suffrage and the extension of the franchise; to escape the rule of ignorance he suggested plural voting for educated persons. Co-operative production, profit-sharing, popular education, and religious toleration all found in him an ardent advocate.

Among Mill's important works are *A System of Logic*, 1843; *Principles of Political Economy*, 1848; *On Liberty*, 1859; *Considerations on Representative Government*, 1861; *Utilitarianism*, 1863; *The Subjection of Women*, 1869; *Autobiography*, 1873; *Nature, the Utility of Religion, and Theism*, 1874. *The Letters of John Stuart Mill* were edited by Hugh Elliott (Longmans, 1910).

from ON LIBERTY

from CHAPTER 2

Of the Liberty of Thought and Discussion

THE time, it is to be hoped, is gone by, when any defence would be necessary of the "liberty of the press," as one of the securities against corrupt or tyrannical government. No argument, we may suppose, can now be needed, against permitting a legislature or an executive, not identified in interest with the people, to prescribe opinions to them, and determine what doctrines or what arguments they shall be allowed to hear. This aspect of the question, besides, has been so often and so triumphantly enforced by preceding writers, that it needs not be specially insisted on in this place. Though the law of England, on the subject of the press, is as servile to this day as it was in the time of the Tudors, there is little danger of its being actually put in force against political discussion, except during some temporary panic, when fear of insurrection drives ministers and judges from their propriety; and, speaking generally, it is not, in constitutional countries, to be apprehended, that the government, whether completely responsible to the people or not, will often attempt to control the expression of opinion, except when in doing so it makes itself the organ of the general intolerance of the public. Let us suppose, therefore, that the government is entirely at one with the people, and never thinks of exerting any power of coercion unless in agreement with what it conceives to be their voice. But I deny the right of the people to exercise such coercion, either by themselves or by their government. The power itself is illegitimate. The best government has no more title to it than the worst. It is as noxious, or more noxious, when exerted in accordance with public opinion, than when in opposition to it. If all mankind minus one, were of one opinion, and only one person were of the contrary opinion, mankind would be no more justified in silencing that one person, than he, if he had the power, would be justified in silencing mankind. Were an opinion a personal possession of no value except to the owner; if to be obstructed in the enjoyment of it were simply a private injury, it would make some difference whether the injury was inflicted only on a few persons or on many. But the peculiar evil of silencing the expression of an opinion is, that it is robbing the human race; posterity as well as the existing generation; those who dissent from the opinion, still more than those who hold it. If the opinion is right, they are deprived of the opportunity of exchanging error for truth: if wrong, they lose, what is almost as great a benefit, the clearer perception and livelier impression of truth, produced by its collision with error.

It is necessary to consider separately these two

11. the time of the Tudors, Henry VII (1485–1509); Henry VIII (1509–47); Edward VI (1547–53); Mary (1553–58); Elizabeth (1558–1603).

hypotheses, each of which has a distinct branch of the argument corresponding to it. We can never be sure that the opinion we are endeavouring to stifle is a false opinion; and if we were sure, stifling it would be an evil still.

First: the opinion which it is attempted to suppress by authority may possibly be true. Those who desire to suppress it, of course deny its truth; but they are not infallible. They have no authority to decide the question for all mankind, and exclude every other person from the means of judging. To refuse a hearing to an opinion, because they are sure that it is false, is to assume that *their* certainty is the same thing as *absolute* certainty. All silencing of discussion is an assumption of infallibility. Its condemnation may be allowed to rest on this common argument, not the worse for being common.

Unfortunately for the good sense of mankind, the fact of their fallibility is far from carrying the weight in their practical judgment, which is always allowed to it in theory; for while every one well knows himself to be fallible, few think it necessary to take any precautions against their own fallibility, or admit the supposition that any opinion, of which they feel very certain, may be one of the examples of the error to which they acknowledge themselves to be liable. Absolute princes, or others who are accustomed to unlimited deference, usually feel this complete confidence in their own opinions on nearly all subjects. People more happily situated, who sometimes hear their opinions disputed, and are not wholly unused to be set right when they are wrong, place the same unbounded reliance only on such of their opinions as are shared by all who surround them, or to whom they habitually defer: for in proportion to a man's want of confidence in his own solitary judgment, does he usually repose, with implicit trust, on the infallibility of "the world" in general. And the world, to each individual, means the part of it with which he comes in contact; his party, his sect, his church, his class of society: the man may be called, by comparison, almost liberal and large-minded to whom it means anything so comprehensive as his own country or his own age. Nor is his faith in this collective authority at all shaken by his being aware that other ages, countries, sects, churches, classes, and parties have thought, and even now think, the exact reverse. He devolves upon his own world the responsibility of being in the right against the dissentient worlds of other people; and it never troubles him that mere accident has decided which of these numerous worlds is the object of his reliance, and that the same causes which make him a Churchman in London, would have made him a Buddhist or a Confucian in Pekin. Yet it is as evident in itself, as any amount of argument can make it, that ages are no more infallible than individuals; every age having held many opinions which subsequent ages have deemed not only false but absurd; and it is as certain that many opinions, now general, will be rejected by future ages, as it is that many, once general, are rejected by the present. . . .

When we consider either the history of opinion, or the ordinary conduct of human life, to what is it to be ascribed that the one and the other are no worse than they are? Not certainly to the inherent force of the human understanding; for, on any matter not self-evident, there are ninety-nine persons totally incapable of judging of it, for one who is capable; and the capacity of the hundredth person is only comparative; for the majority of the eminent men of every past generation held many opinions now known to be erroneous, and did or approved numerous things which no one will now justify. Why is it, then, that there is on the whole a preponderance among mankind of rational opinions and rational conduct? If there really is this preponderance—which there must be unless human affairs are, and have always been, in an almost desperate state—it is owing to a quality of the human mind, the source of everything respectable in man either as an intellectual or as a moral being, namely, that his errors are corrigible. He is capable of rectifying his mistakes, by discussion and experience. Not by experience alone. There must be discussion, to show how experience is to be interpreted. Wrong opinions and practices gradually yield to fact and argument: but facts and arguments, to produce any effect on the mind, must be brought before it. Very few facts are able to tell their own story, without comments to bring out their meaning. The whole strength and value, then, of human judgment, depending on the one property, that it can be set right when it is wrong, reliance can be placed on it only when the means of setting it right are kept constantly at hand. In the case of any person whose judgment is really deserving of confidence, how has it become so? Because he has kept his mind open to criticism of his opinions and conduct. Because it has been his practice to listen to all that could be said against him; to profit by as much of it as was just, and expound to himself, and upon occasion to others, the fallacy of what was fallacious. Because he has felt, that the

1. **Churchman,** a member of the Church of England.

only way in which a human being can make some approach to knowing the whole of a subject, is by hearing what can be said about it by persons of every variety of opinion, and studying all modes in which it can be looked at by every character of mind. No wise man ever acquired his wisdom in any mode but this; nor is it in the nature of human intellect to become wise in any other manner. The steady habit of correcting and completing his own opinion by collating it with those of others, so far from causing doubt and hesitation in carrying it into practice, is the only stable foundation for a just reliance on it: for, being cognisant of all that can, at least obviously, be said against him, and having taken up his position against all gainsayers —knowing that he has sought for objections and difficulties, instead of avoiding them, and has shut out no light which can be thrown upon the subject from any quarter—he has a right to think his judgment better than that of any person, or any multitude, who have not gone through a similar process.

It is not too much to require that what the wisest of mankind, those who are best entitled to trust their own judgment, find necessary to warrant their relying on it, should be submitted to by that miscellaneous collection of a few wise and many foolish individuals, called the public. The most intolerant of churches, the Roman Catholic Church, even at the canonization of a saint, admits, and listens patiently to, a "devil's advocate." The holiest of men, it appears, cannot be admitted to posthumous honours, until all that the devil could say against him is known and weighed. If even the Newtonian philosophy were not permitted to be questioned, mankind could not feel as complete assurance of its truth as they now do. The beliefs which we have most warrant for, have no safeguard to rest on, but a standing invitation to the whole world to prove them unfounded. If the challenge is not accepted, or is accepted and the attempt fails, we are far enough from certainty still; but we have done the best that the existing state of human reason admits of; we have neglected nothing that could give the truth a chance of reaching us: if the lists are kept open, we may hope that if there be a better truth, it will be found when the human mind is capable of receiving it; and in the meantime we may rely on having attained such approach to truth, as is possible in our own day. This is the amount of certainty attainable

34–35. **Newtonian philosophy,** as set forth in the *Principia* of Sir Isaac Newton (1642–1727). Not being able to foresee Einstein, Mill had no idea, when he wrote these words, how seriously the Newtonian philosophy was to be questioned in the future!

by a fallible being, and this the sole way of attaining it.

Strange it is, that men should admit the validity of the arguments for free discussion, but object to their being "pushed to an extreme"; not seeing that unless the reasons are good for an extreme case, they are not good for any case. Strange that they should imagine that they are not assuming infallibility, when they acknowledge that there should be free discussion on all subjects which can possibly be doubtful, but think that some particular principle or doctrine should be forbidden to be questioned because it is so *certain*, that is, because *they are certain* that it is certain. To call any proposition certain, while there is any one who would deny its certainty if permitted, but who is not permitted, is to assume that we ourselves, and those who agree with us, are the judges of certainty, and judges without hearing the other side.

In the present age—which has been described as "destitute of faith, but terrified at scepticism"—in which people feel sure, not so much that their opinions are true, as that they should not know what to do without them—the claims of an opinion to be protected from public attack are rested not so much on its truth, as on its importance to society. There are, it is alleged, certain beliefs, so useful, not to say indispensable to well-being, that it is as much the duty of governments to uphold those beliefs, as to protect any other of the interests of society. In a case of such necessity, and so directly in the line of their duty, something less than infallibility may, it is maintained, warrant, and even bind, governments, to act on their own opinion, confirmed by the general opinion of mankind. It is also often argued, and still oftener thought, that none but bad men would desire to weaken these salutary beliefs; and there can be nothing wrong, it is thought, in restraining bad men, and prohibiting what only such men would wish to practise. This mode of thinking makes the justification of restraints on discussion not a question of the truth of doctrines, but of their usefulness; and flatters itself by that means to escape the responsibility of claiming to be an infallible judge of opinions. But those who thus satisfy themselves, do not perceive that the assumption of infallibility is merely shifted from one point to another. The usefulness of an opinion is itself matter of opinion: as disputable, as open to discussion, and requiring discussion as much, as the opinion itself. There is the same need of an infallible judge of opinions to decide an opinion to be noxious, as to decide it to be false, unless the opinion condemned has full opportunity of defending itself. And it will

not do to say that the heretic may be allowed to maintain the utility or harmlessness of his opinion, though forbidden to maintain its truth. The truth of an opinion is part of its utility. If we would know whether or not it is desirable that a proposition should be believed, is it possible to exclude the consideration of whether or not it is true? In the opinion, not of bad men, but of the best men, no belief which is contrary to truth can be really useful: and can you prevent such men from urging that plea, when they are charged with culpability for denying some doctrine which they are told is useful, but which they believe to be false? Those who are on the side of received opinions, never fail to take all possible advantage of this plea; you do not find *them* handling the question of utility as if it could be completely abstracted from that of truth: on the contrary, it is, above all, because their doctrine is the "truth," that the knowledge or the belief of it is held to be so indispensable. There can be no fair discussion of the question of usefulness, when an argument so vital may be employed on one side, but not on the other. And in point of fact, when law or public feeling do not permit the truth of an opinion to be disputed, they are just as little tolerant of a denial of its usefulness. The utmost they allow is an extenuation of its absolute necessity, or of the positive guilt of rejecting it. . . .

Mankind can hardly be too often reminded that there was once a man named Socrates, between whom and the legal authorities and public opinion of his time there took place a memorable collision. Born in an age and country abounding in individual greatness, this man has been handed down to us by those who best knew both him and the age, as the most virtuous man in it; while *we* know him as the head and prototype of all subsequent teachers of virtue, the source equally of the lofty inspiration of Plato and the judicious utilitarianism of Aristotle, "*i maëstri di color che sanno*," the two headsprings of ethical as of all other philosophy. This acknowledged master of all the eminent thinkers who have since lived—whose fame, still growing after more than two thousand years, all but outweighs the whole remainder of the names which make his native city illustrious—was put to death by his countrymen, after a judicial conviction, for impiety and

31. **Socrates,** Athenian philosopher (469–399 B.C.). 40. **Plato** (c. 427–347 B.C.), the principal disciple of Socrates, and author of the *Apologia*, in which the story of his death is told. **Aristotle,** Greek philosopher (384–322 B.C.), one of the most important influences on the thinking of western Europe. 41. "**i maëstri di color che sanno,**" "the teachers of those who know." See Dante, *The Divine Comedy, Inferno,* Canto IV, l. 131.

immorality. Impiety, in denying the gods recognised by the State; indeed his accuser asserted (see the "Apologia") that he believed in no gods at all. Immorality in being, by his doctrines and instructions, a "corruptor of youth." Of these charges the tribunal, there is every ground for believing, honestly found him guilty, and condemned the man who probably of all then born had deserved best of mankind, to be put to death as a criminal.

To pass from this to the only other instance of judicial iniquity, the mention of which, after the condemnation of Socrates, would not be an anticlimax: the event which took place on Calvary rather more than eighteen hundred years ago. The man who left on the memory of those who witnessed his life and conversation, such an impression of his moral grandeur, that eighteen subsequent centuries have done homage to him as the Almighty in person, was ignominiously put to death, as what? As a blasphemer. Men did not merely mistake their benefactor; they mistook him for the exact contrary of what he was, and treated him as that prodigy of impiety, which they themselves are now held to be, for their treatment of him. The feelings with which mankind now regard these lamentable transactions, especially the later of the two, render them extremely unjust in their judgment of the unhappy actors. These were, to all appearance, not bad men —not worse than men commonly are, but rather the contrary; men who possessed in a full, or somewhat more than a full measure, the religious, moral, and patriotic feelings of their time and people: the very kind of men who, in all times, our own included, have every chance of passing through life blameless and respected. The high-priest who rent his garments when the words were pronounced, which, according to all the ideas of his country, constituted the blackest guilt, was in all probability quite as sincere in his horror and indignation, as the generality of respectable and pious men now are in the religious and moral sentiments they profess; and most of those who now shudder at his conduct, if they had lived in his time, and been born Jews, would have acted precisely as he did. Orthodox Christians who are tempted to think that those who stoned to death the first martyrs must have been worse men than they themselves are, ought to remember that one of those persecutors was Saint Paul.

Let us add one more example, the most striking of all, if the impressiveness of an error is measured by the wisdom and virtue of him who falls into it. If ever any one, possessed of power, had grounds for thinking himself the best and most enlightened among his contemporaries, it was the Emperor Marcus Aurelius. Absolute monarch of the whole civilized world, he preserved through life not only the most unblemished justice, but what was less to be expected from his Stoical breeding, the tenderest heart. The few failings which are attributed to him, were all on the side of indulgence: while his writings, the highest ethical product of the ancient mind, differ scarcely perceptibly, if they differ at all, from the most characteristic teachings of Christ. This man, a better Christian in all but the dogmatic sense of the word, than almost any of the ostensibly Christian sovereigns who have since reigned, persecuted Christianity. Placed at the summit of all the previous attainments of humanity, with an open, unfettered intellect, and a character which led him of himself to embody in his moral writings the Christian ideal, he yet failed to see that Christianity was to be a good and not an evil to the world, with his duties to which he was so deeply penetrated. Existing society he knew to be in a deplorable state. But such as it was, he saw, or thought he saw, that it was held together, and prevented from being worse, by belief and reverence of the received divinities. As a ruler of mankind, he deemed it his duty not to suffer society to fall in pieces; and saw not how, if its existing ties were removed, any others could be formed which could again knit it together. The new religion openly aimed at dissolving these ties: unless, therefore, it was his duty to adopt that religion, it seemed to be his duty to put it down. Inasmuch then as the theology of Christianity did not appear to him true or of divine origin; inasmuch as this strange history of a crucified God was not credible to him, and a system which purported to rest entirely upon a foundation to him so wholly unbelievable, could not be foreseen by him to be that renovating agency which, after all abatements, it has in fact proved to be; the gentlest and most amiable of philosophers and rulers, under a solemn sense of duty, authorized the persecution of Christianity. To my mind this is one of the most tragical facts in all history. It is a bitter thought, how different a thing the Christianity of the world might have been, if the Christian faith had been adopted as the religion of the empire under the auspices of Marcus Aurelius instead of those of Constantine. But

---

35-36. **The high priest . . . garments.** See Mark 14:63.
48-49. **Saint Paul,** or Saul (as he was then) guarded the clothes of those who stoned Stephen, the first Christian martyr (Acts 6-7).

5-6. **Emperor Marcus Aurelius,** reigned 161-180 A.D., author of the famous *Meditations*. 51. **Constantine.** When Constantine made Christianity the official religion of the

it would be equally unjust to him and false to truth, to deny, that no one plea which can be urged for punishing anti-Christian teaching, was wanting to Marcus Aurelius for punishing, as he did, the propagation of Christianity. No Christian more firmly believes that Atheism is false, and tends to the dissolution of society, than Marcus Aurelius believed the same things of Christianity; he who, of all men then living, might have been thought the most capable of appreciating it. Unless any one who approves of punishment for the promulgation of opinions, flatters himself that he is a wiser and better man than Marcus Aurelius—more deeply versed in the wisdom of his time, more elevated in his intellect above it—more earnest in his search for truth, or more single-minded in his devotion to it when found;—let him abstain from that assumption of the joint infallibility of himself and the multitude, which the great Antoninus made with so unfortunate a result. . . .

Let us now pass to the second division of the argument, and dismissing the supposition that any of the received opinions may be false, let us assume them to be true, and examine into the worth of the manner in which they are likely to be held, when their truth is not freely and openly canvassed. However unwillingly a person who has a strong opinion may admit the possibility that his opinion may be false, he ought to be moved by the consideration that however true it may be, if it is not fully, frequently, and fearlessly discussed, it will be held as a dead dogma, not a living truth.

There is a class of persons (happily not quite so numerous as formerly) who think it enough if a person assents undoubtingly to what they think true, though he has no knowledge whatever of the grounds of the opinion, and could not make a tenable defence of it against the most superficial objections. Such persons, if they can once get their creed taught from authority, naturally think that no good, and some harm, comes of its being allowed to be questioned. Where their influence prevails, they make it nearly impossible for the received opinion to be rejected wisely and considerately, though it may still be rejected rashly and ignorantly; for to shut out discussion entirely is seldom possible, and when it once gets in, beliefs not grounded on conviction are apt to give way before the slightest semblance of an argument. Waiving,

however, this possibility—assuming that the true opinion abides in the mind, but abides as a prejudice, a belief independent of, and proof against, argument—this is not the way in which truth ought to be held by a rational being. This is not knowing the truth. Truth, thus held, is but one superstition the more, accidentally clinging to the words which enunciate a truth.

If the intellect and judgment of mankind ought to be cultivated, a thing which Protestants at least do not deny, on what can these faculties be more appropriately exercised by any one, than on the things which concern him so much that it is considered necessary for him to hold opinions on them? If the cultivation of the understanding consists in one thing more than in another, it is surely in learning the grounds of one's own opinions. Whatever people believe, on subjects on which it is of the first importance to believe rightly, they ought to be able to defend against at least the common objections. But, some one may say, "Let them be *taught* the grounds of their opinions. It does not follow that opinions must be merely parroted because they are never heard controverted. Persons who learn geometry do not simply commit the theorems to memory, but understand and learn likewise the demonstrations; and it would be absurd to say that they remain ignorant of the grounds of geometrical truths, because they never hear any one deny, and attempt to disprove them." Undoubtedly: and such teaching suffices on a subject like mathematics, where there is nothing at all to be said on the wrong side of the question. The peculiarity of the evidence of mathematical truths is, that all the argument is on one side. There are no objections, and no answers to objections. But on every subject on which difference of opinion is possible, the truth depends on a balance to be struck between two sets of conflicting reasons. Even in natural philosophy, there is always some other explanation possible of the same facts; some geocentric theory instead of heliocentric, some phlogiston instead of oxygen; and it has to be shown why that other theory cannot be the true one: and until this is shown, and until we know how it is shown, we do not understand the grounds of our opinion. But when we turn to subjects infinitely more complicated, to morals, religion, politics, social relations, and the business of life, three-fourths of the arguments for every disputed opinion consist in dispelling the appearances which favour some opinion different from it. The greatest orator, save one, of antiquity, has left it on record that he always studied his adversary's case with as great, if not with still greater, intensity than even his own. What Cicero practised as the means of forensic success, requires to be imitated by all who study any subject in order to arrive at the truth. He who knows only his own side of the case, knows little of that. His reasons may be good, and no one may have been able to refute them. But if he is equally unable to refute the reasons on the opposite side; if he does not so much as know what they are, he has no ground for preferring either opinion. The rational position for him would be suspension of judgment, and unless he contents himself with that, he is either led by authority, or adopts, like the generality of the world, the side to which he feels most inclination. Nor is it enough that he should hear the arguments of adversaries from his own teachers, presented as they state them, and accompanied by what they offer as refutations. That is not the way to do justice to the arguments, or bring them into real contact with his own mind. He must be able to hear them from persons who actually believe them; who defend them in earnest, and do their very utmost for them. He must know them in their most plausible and persuasive form; he must feel the whole force of the difficulty which the true view of the subject has to encounter and dispose of; else he will never really possess himself of the portion of truth which meets and removes that difficulty. Ninety-nine in a hundred of what are called educated men are in this condition; even of those who can argue fluently for their opinions. Their conclusion may be true, but it might be false for anything they know: they have never thrown themselves into the mental position of those who think differently from them, and considered what such persons may have to say; and consequently they do not, in any proper sense of the word, know the doctrine which they themselves profess. They do not know those parts of it which explain and justify the remainder; the considerations which show that a fact which seemingly conflicts with another is reconcilable with it, or that, of two apparently strong reasons, one and not the other ought to be preferred. All that part of the truth which turns the scale, and decides the judgment of a completely informed mind, they are strangers to; nor is it ever really known, but to those who have attended equally and impartially to both sides, and endeavoured to see the reasons of both in the strongest light. So essential is this discipline to a real understanding of moral and human subjects, that if opponents of all important truths do not exist, it is indispensable to imagine them, and supply them with the strongest arguments which the most skilful devil's advocate can conjure up. . . .

If . . . the mischievous operation of the absence of free discussion, when the received opinions are true, were confined to leaving men ignorant of the grounds of those opinions, it might be thought that this, if an intellectual, is no moral evil, and does not affect the worth of the opinions, regarded in their influence on the character. The fact, however, is, that not only the grounds of the opinion are forgotten in the absence of discussion, but too often the meaning of the opinion itself. The words which convey it, cease to suggest ideas, or suggest only a small portion of those they were originally employed to communicate. Instead of a vivid conception and a living belief, there remain only a few phrases retained by rote; or, if any part, the shell and husk only of the meaning is retained, the finer essence being lost. The great chapter in human history which this fact occupies and fills, cannot be too earnestly studied and meditated on.

It is illustrated in the experience of almost all ethical doctrines and religious creeds. They are all full of meaning and vitality to those who originate them, and to the direct disciples of the originators. Their meaning continues to be felt in undiminished strength, and is perhaps brought out into even fuller consciousness, so long as the struggle lasts to give the doctrine or creed an ascendancy over other creeds. At last it either prevails, and becomes the general opinion, or its progress stops; it keeps possession of the ground it has gained, but ceases to spread further. When either of these results has become apparent, controversy on the subject flags, and gradually dies away. The doctrine has taken its place, if not as a received opinion, as one of the admitted sects or divisions of opinion: those who hold it have generally inherited, not adopted it; and conversion from one of these doctrines to another, being now an exceptional fact, occupies little place in the thoughts of their professors. Instead of being, as at first, constantly on the alert either to defend themselves against the world, or to bring the world over to them, they have subsided into acquiescence, and neither listen, when they can help it, to arguments against their creed, nor trouble dissentients (if there be such) with arguments in its favour. From this time may usually be dated the decline in the living power of the doctrine. We often hear the teachers of all creeds lamenting the difficulty of keeping up in the minds of believers a lively apprehension of the truth which they nominally recognise, so that it may penetrate the feelings, and acquire a real mas-

1. Cicero, Roman orator, statesman, and writer (106–43 B.C.).

tery over the conduct. No such difficulty is complained of while the creed is still fighting for its existence: even the weaker combatants then know and feel what they are fighting for, and the difference between it and other doctrines; and in that period of every creed's existence, not a few persons may be found, who have realized its fundamental principles in all the forms of thought, have weighed and considered them in all their important bearings, and have experienced the full effect on the character, which belief in that creed ought to produce in a mind thoroughly imbued with it. But when it has come to be an hereditary creed, and to be received passively, not actively—when the mind is no longer compelled, in the same degree as at first, to exercise its vital powers on the questions which its belief presents to it, there is a progressive tendency to forget all of the belief except the formularies, or to give it a dull and torpid assent, as if accepting it on trust dispensed with the necessity of realizing it in consciousness, or testing it by personal experience; until it almost ceases to connect itself at all with the inner life of the human being. Then are seen the cases, so frequent in this age of the world as almost to form the majority, in which the creed remains as it were outside the mind, encrusting and petrifying it against all other influences addressed to the higher parts of our nature; manifesting its power by not suffering any fresh and living conviction to get in, but itself doing nothing for the mind or heart, except standing sentinel over them to keep them vacant.

To what an extent doctrines intrinsically fitted to make the deepest impression upon the mind may remain in it as dead beliefs, without being ever realized in the imagination, the feelings, or the understanding, is exemplified by the manner in which the majority of believers hold the doctrines of Christianity. By Christianity I here mean what is accounted such by all churches and sects—the maxims and precepts contained in the New Testament. These are considered sacred, and accepted as laws, by all professing Christians. Yet it is scarcely too much to say that not one Christian in a thousand guides or tests his individual conduct by reference to those laws. The standard to which he does refer it, is the custom of his nation, his class, or his religious profession. He has thus, on the one hand, a collection of ethical maxims, which he believes to have been vouchsafed to him by infallible wisdom as rules for his government; and on the other, a set of every-day judgments and practices, which go a certain length with some of those maxims, not so great a length with others, stand in direct opposition to some, and are, on the whole, a compromise between the Christian creed and the interests and suggestions of worldly life. To the first of these standards he gives his homage; to the other his real allegiance. All Christians believe that the blessed are the poor and humble, and those who are ill-used by the world; that it is easier for a camel to pass through the eye of a needle than for a rich man to enter the kingdom of heaven; that they should judge not, lest they be judged; that they should swear not at all; that they should love their neighbour as themselves; that if one take their cloak, they should give him their coat also; that they should take no thought for the morrow; that if they would be perfect they should sell all that they have and give it to the poor. They are not insincere when they say that they believe these things. They do believe them, as people believe what they have always heard lauded and never discussed. But in the sense of that living belief which regulates conduct, they believe these doctrines just up to the point to which it is usual to act upon them. The doctrines in their integrity are serviceable to pelt adversaries with; and it is understood that they are to be put forward (when possible) as the reasons for whatever people do that they think laudable. But any one who reminded them that the maxims require an infinity of things which they never even think of doing, would gain nothing but to be classed among those very unpopular characters who affect to be better than other people. The doctrines have no hold on ordinary believers—are not a power in their minds. They have an habitual respect for the sound of them, but no feeling which spreads from the words to the things signified, and forces the mind to take *them* in, and make them conform to the formula. Whenever conduct is concerned, they look round for Mr. A and B to direct them how far to go in obeying Christ.

Now we may be well assured that the case was not thus, but far otherwise, with the early Christians. Had it been thus, Christianity never would have expanded from an obscure sect of the despised Hebrews into the religion of the Roman empire. When their enemies said, "See how these Christians love one another" (a remark not likely to be made by anybody now), they assuredly had a much livelier feeling of the meaning of their creed that they have ever had since. And to this cause, probably, it is chiefly owing that Christianity now makes so little

5-6. **All Christians believe . . . the poor.** See the Sermon on the Mount, Matthew 5–7, and other passages in that Gospel. 44–46. **When their enemies . . . one another,"** quoted from the Latin Church Father Tertullian (c. 160–c. 220 A.D.).

progress in extending its domain, and, after eighteen centuries, is still nearly confined to Europeans and the descendants of Europeans. Even with the strictly religious, who are much in earnest about their doctrines, and attach a greater amount of meaning to many of them than people in general, it commonly happens that the part which is thus comparatively active in their minds is that which was made by Calvin, or Knox, or some such person much nearer in character to themselves. The sayings of Christ coexist passively in their minds, producing hardly any effect beyond what is caused by mere listening to words so amiable and bland. There are many reasons, doubtless, why doctrines which are the badge of a sect retain more of their vitality than those common to all recognised sects, and why more pains are taken by teachers to keep their meaning alive; but one reason certainly is, that the peculiar doctrines are more questioned, and have to be oftener defended against open gainsayers. Both teachers and learners go to sleep at their post, as soon as there is no enemy in the field. . . .

It still remains to speak of one of the principal causes which make diversity of opinion advantageous, and will continue to do so until mankind shall have entered a stage of intellectual advancement which at present seems at an incalculable distance. We have hitherto considered only two possibilities: that the received opinion may be false, and some other opinion, consequently, true; or that, the received opinion being true, a conflict with the opposite error is essential to a clear apprehension and deep feeling of its truth. But there is a commoner case than either of these; when the conflicting doctrines, instead of being one true and the other false, share the truth between them; and the nonconforming opinion is needed to supply the remainder of the truth, of which the received doctrine embodies only a part. Popular opinions, on subjects not palpable to sense, are often true, but seldom or never the whole truth. They are a part of the truth; sometimes a greater, sometimes a smaller part, but exaggerated, distorted, and disjoined from the truths by which they ought to be accompanied and limited. Heretical opinions, on the other hand, are generally some of these suppressed and neglected truths, bursting the bonds which kept them down, and either seeking reconciliation with the truth contained in the common opinion, or fronting it as enemies, and setting themselves up, with similar exclusiveness, as the whole truth. The latter case is hitherto the most frequent, as, in the human mind,

one-sidedness has always been the rule, and many-sidedness the exception. Hence, even in revolutions of opinion, one part of the truth usually sets while another rises. Even progress, which ought to superadd, for the most part only substitutes, one partial and incomplete truth for another; improvement consisting chiefly in this, that the new fragment of truth is more wanted, more adapted to the needs of the time, than that which it displaces. Such being the partial character of prevailing opinions, even when resting on a true foundation, every opinion which embodies somewhat of the portion of truth which the common opinion omits, ought to be considered precious, with whatever amount of error and confusion that truth may be blended. No sober judge of human affairs will feel bound to be indignant because those who force on our notice truths which we should otherwise have overlooked, overlook some of those which we see. Rather, he will think that so long as popular truth is one-sided, it is more desirable than otherwise that unpopular truth should have one-sided asserters too; such being usually the most energetic, and the most likely to compel reluctant attention to the fragment of wisdom which they proclaim as if it were the whole.

Thus, in the eighteenth century, when nearly all the instructed, and all those of the uninstructed who were led by them, were lost in admiration of what is called civilization, and of the marvels of modern science, literature, and philosophy, and while greatly overrating the amount of unlikeness between the men of modern and those of ancient times, indulged the belief that the whole of the difference was in their own favour; with what a salutary shock did the paradoxes of Rousseau explode like bombshells in the midst, dislocating the compact mass of one-sided opinion, and forcing its elements to recombine in a better form and with additional ingredients. Not that the current opinions were on the whole farther from the truth than Rousseau's were; on the contrary, they were nearer to it; they contained more of positive truth, and very much less of error. Nevertheless there lay in Rousseau's doctrine, and has floated down the stream of opinion along with it, a considerable amount of exactly those truths which the popular opinion wanted; and these are the deposit which was left behind when the flood subsided. The superior worth of simplicity of life, the enervating and demoralizing effect of the trammels and hypocrisies of artificial society, are ideas which have never been

10. **nearer,** than Christ.

35. Rousseau. Rousseau's primitivistic ideas had a tremendous influence on both political and educational theory, and on English literature.

entirely absent from cultivated minds since Rousseau wrote; and they will in time produce their due effect, though at present needing to be asserted as much as ever, and to be asserted by deeds, for words, on this subject, have nearly exhausted their power.

In politics, again, it is almost a commonplace, that a party of order or stability, and a party of progress or reform, are both necessary elements of a healthy state of political life; until the one or the other shall have so enlarged its mental grasp as to be a party equally of order and of progress, knowing and distinguishing what is fit to be preserved from what ought to be swept away. Each of these modes of thinking derives its utility from the deficiencies of the other; but it is in a great measure the opposition of the other that keeps each within the limits of reason and sanity. Unless opinions favourable to democracy and to aristocracy, to property and to equality, to co-operation and to competition, to luxury and to abstinence, to sociality and to individuality, to liberty and to discipline, and all the other standing antagonisms of practical life, are expressed with equal freedom, and enforced and defended with equal talent and energy, there is no chance of both elements obtaining their due; one scale is sure to go up, and the other down. Truth, in the great practical concerns of life, is so much a question of the reconciling and combining of opposites, that very few have minds sufficiently capacious and impartial to make the adjustment with an approach to correctness, and it has to be made by the rough process of a struggle between combatants fighting under hostile banners. On any of the great open questions just enumerated, if either of the two opinions has a better claim than the other, not merely to be tolerated, but to be encouraged and countenanced, it is the one which happens at the particular time and place to be in a minority. That is the opinion which, for the time being, represents the neglected interests, the side of human well-being which is in danger of obtaining less than its share. I am aware that there is not, in this country, any intolerance of differences of opinion on most of these topics. They are adduced to show, by admitted and multiplied examples, the universality of the fact, that only through diversity of opinion is there, in the existing state of human intellect, a chance of fair play to all sides of the truth. When there are persons to be found, who form an exception to the apparent unanimity of the world on any subject, even if the world is in the right, it is always probable that dissentients have something worth hearing to say for themselves,

and that truth would lose something by their silence. . . .

I do not pretend that the most unlimited use of the freedom of enunciating all possible opinions would put an end to the evils of religious or philosophical sectarianism. Every truth which men of narrow capacity are in earnest about, is sure to be asserted, inculcated, and in many ways even acted on, as if no other truth existed in the world, or at all events none that could limit or qualify the first. I acknowledge that the tendency of all opinions to become sectarian is not cured by the freest discussion, but is often heightened and exacerbated thereby; the truth which ought to have been, but was not, seen, being rejected all the more violently because proclaimed by persons regarded as opponents. But it is not on the impassioned partisan, it is on the calmer and more disinterested bystander, that this collision of opinions works its salutary effect. Not the violent conflict between parts of the truth, but the quiet suppression of half of it, is the formidable evil; there is always hope when people are forced to listen to both sides; it is when they attend only to one that errors harden into prejudices, and truth itself ceases to have the effect of truth, by being exaggerated into falsehood. And since there are few mental attributes more rare than that judicial faculty which can sit in intelligent judgment between two sides of a question, of which only one is represented by an advocate before it, truth has no chance but in proportion as every side of it, every opinion which embodies any fraction of the truth, not only finds advocates, but is so advocated as to be listened to.

We have now recognised the necessity to the mental well-being of mankind (on which all their other well-being depends) of freedom of opinion, and freedom of the expression of opinion, on four distinct grounds; which we will now briefly recapitulate.

First, if any opinion is compelled to silence, that opinion may, for aught we can certainly know, be true. To deny this is to assume our own infallibility.

Secondly, though the silenced opinion be an error, it may, and very commonly does, contain a portion of truth; and since the general or prevailing opinion on any subject is rarely or never the whole truth, it is only by the collision of adverse opinions that the remainder of the truth has any chance of being supplied.

Thirdly, even if the received opinion be not only true, but the whole truth; unless it is suffered to be, and actually is, vigorously and earnestly contested, it will, by most of those who receive it, be held in the manner of a prejudice, with little comprehension or feeling of its rational grounds. And not only this, but, fourthly, the meaning of the doctrine itself will be in danger of being lost, or enfeebled, and deprived of its vital effect on the character and conduct: the dogma becoming a mere formal profession, inefficacious for good, but cumbering the ground, and preventing the growth of any real and heartfelt conviction, from reason or personal experience.

Before quitting the subject of freedom of opinion, it is fit to take some notice of those who say, that the free expression of all opinions should be permitted, on condition that the manner be temperate, and do not pass the bounds of fair discussion. Much might be said on the impossibility of fixing where these supposed bounds are to be placed; for if the test be offence to those whose opinion is attacked, I think experience testifies that this offence is given whenever the attack is telling and powerful, and that every opponent who pushes them hard, and whom they find it difficult to answer, appears to them, if he shows any strong feeling on the subject, an intemperate opponent. But this, though an important consideration in a practical point of view, merges in a more fundamental objection. Undoubtedly the manner of asserting an opinion, even though it be a true one, may be very objectionable, and may justly incur severe censure. But the principal offences of the kind are such as it is mostly impossible, unless by accidental self-betrayal, to bring home to conviction. The gravest of them is, to argue sophistically, to suppress facts or arguments, to misstate the elements of the case, or misrepresent the opposite opinion. But all this, even to the most aggravated degree, is so continually done in perfect good faith, by persons who are not considered, and in many other respects may not deserve to be considered, ignorant or incompetent, that it is rarely possible on adequate grounds conscientiously to stamp the misrepresentation as morally culpable; and still less could law presume to interfere with this kind of controversial misconduct. With regard to what is commonly meant by intemperate discussion, namely invective, sarcasm, personality, and the like, the denunciation of these weapons would deserve more sympathy if it were ever proposed to interdict them equally to both sides; but it is only desired to restrain the employment of them against the prevailing opinion: against the unprevailing they may not only be used without general disapproval, but will be likely to obtain for him who uses them

the praise of honest zeal and righteous indignation. Yet whatever mischief arises from their use, is greatest when they are employed against the comparatively defenceless; and whatever unfair advantage can be derived by any opinion from this mode of asserting it, accrues almost exclusively to received opinions. The worst offence of this kind which can be committed by a polemic, is to stigmatize those who hold the contrary opinion as bad and immoral men. To calumny of this sort, those who hold any unpopular opinion are peculiarly exposed, because they are in general few and uninfluential, and nobody but themselves feels much interested in seeing justice done them; but this weapon is, from the nature of the case, denied to those who attack a prevailing opinion: they can neither use it with safety to themselves, nor, if they could, would it do anything but recoil on their own cause. In general, opinions contrary to those commonly received can only obtain a hearing by studied moderation of language, and the most cautious avoidance of unnecessary offence, from which they hardly ever deviate even in a slight degree without losing ground: while unmeasured vituperation employed on the side of the prevailing opinion, really does deter people from professing contrary opinions, and from listening to those who profess them. For the interest, therefore, of truth and justice, it is far more important to restrain this employment of vituperative language than the other; and, for example, if it were necessary to choose, there would be much more need to discourage offensive attacks on infidelity, than on religion. It is, however, obvious that law and authority have no business with restraining either, while opinion ought, in every instance, to determine its verdict by the circumstances of the individual case; condemning every one, on whichever side of the argument he places himself, in whose mode of advocacy either want of candour, or malignity, bigotry, or intolerance of feeling manifest themselves; but not inferring these vices from the side which a person takes, though it be the contrary side of the question to our own: and giving merited honour to every one, whatever opinion he may hold, who has calmness to see and honesty to state what his opponents and their opinions really are, exaggerating nothing to their discredit, keeping nothing back which tells, or can be supposed to tell, in their favour. This is the real morality of public discussion: and if often violated, I am happy to think that there are many controversialists who to a great extent observe it, and a still greater number who conscientiously strive towards it.

Alfred, Lord Tennyson
1809–1892

Tennyson was Victoria's poet laureate. During his lifetime his supreme greatness was generally taken for granted, though it is true that he struggled long against public neglect, and that there never was a time when somebody was not saying about him much what those who dislike him are saying to-day. In the inevitable reaction against all things Victorian which came upon us some years ago it was inevitable that he should suffer somewhat. Yet if we were to meet Tennyson in some ghostly visitation, he might not at all approximate our idea of what a Victorian poet ought to be. He was a great, gruff, black, shaggy man, with a canine flash about his upper lip. When he was a student at Cambridge he kept a pet snake in his room. He drank in his time a vast quantity of port wine, and he reeked of tobacco through his ribs. In general social intercourse he was notoriously shy and ungracious.

Nobody has ever denied that on the technical side Tennyson is one of the greatest poets. Those who attack him attack his thought—his pale proprieties, his sentimentality, his shallow optimism. Sometimes these judgments are made unfairly, from the point of view of a later time. Among his contemporaries, Huxley, who was anything but pious, considered Tennyson the modern Lucretius. In a sense he sums up all English poetry. He had no single contribution to make so original as those of Wordsworth, Coleridge, Byron, Shelley, or Keats, but he had a vastly wider range than any of them.

Tennyson was born at Somersby rectory, Lincolnshire, on August 6, 1809. When he was eight years old, he was sent to school at Louth, where the master banged his scholars' heads with a book to assist their memories—a method which evidently failed in Tennyson's case, for he afterward declared that he retained nothing of what he had been taught at Louth except one Latin tag. Probably his lifelong shyness was partly determined by this unhappy experience. Later he was tutored at home by his father, and in 1828 he went to Trinity College, Cambridge, but he was not distinguished as a student and never took a degree. The important thing Cambridge did for him was to bring him in contact with the "Twelve Apostles," a company of students which included Richard Monckton Milnes, later Lord Houghton, Frederick Denison Maurice, and Arthur Henry Hallam. As a group they helped to impress him with a sense of the sacredness of his poetic calling; Hallam individually brought him one of the great experiences of his life (see the introductory note to *In Memoriam*).

Tennyson had been writing poetry since he was five years old. In 1827 he and his brother Charles had collaborated in *Poems by Two Brothers* (with a few contributions from a third brother, Frederick). In 1829 he won the Chancellor's medal for poetry at Cambridge. His first proper book, *Poems Chiefly Lyrical*, 1830, was extravagantly puffed by Hallam and his friends, and quite as extravagantly damned by the influential critic "Christopher North" (John Wilson) in *Blackwood's*. Tennyson had the bad judgment to make a rather insolent reply, and this circumstance may have added to the venom of John Gibson Lockhart's review of the 1832 volume, *Poems*, in the *Quarterly Review*. Lockhart's review was, in any event, diabolically effective; it destroyed Tennyson's reputation and made him for years an object of derision and a joke. No wonder that when Hallam's death followed hard upon this crushing disappointment, Tennyson should almost have despaired.

He did not quite despair, however, for he spent the next ten years industriously perfecting his art; when he reappeared in 1842 with *Poems*, in two volumes, he had won his public. In 1846 he was granted a small pension; in 1847 he published *The Princess*.

The year 1850 was a crowning year in Tennyson's life. In the spring he published *In Memoriam;* in June he married Emily Sellwood, to whom he had been engaged through fourteen years of poverty; in November he was appointed poet laureate. In 1853 he built a house at Farringford on the Isle of Wight, in 1868 another at Aldworth in Surrey.

Once he had found his stride, Tennyson's industry never slackened. *Maud, and Other Poems* came out in 1855; *Idylls of the King* in 1859, and subsequently; *Idylls of the Hearth* (*Enoch Arden, and Other Poems*) in 1864. After 1875 he turned his attention to the drama and wrote a number of plays, including *Queen Mary, Harold*, and *Becket*. Both *Becket* and *The Cup* were produced by Sir Henry Irving; the latter ran more than one hundred and thirty nights.

The most important publications of Tennyson's last years were *Ballads, and Other Poems*, 1880; *Tiresias, and Other Poems*, 1885; *Demeter, and Other Poems*, 1889; *The Death of Oenone, Akbar's Death, and Other Poems*, 1892. He died October 6, 1892, with his Shakespeare on the moonlight-drenched bed beside him, open to the boatman's song in *Cymbeline*.

THE POET

This poem expresses Tennyson's essentially prophetic conception of the poet's function, a point of view greatly encouraged by his contacts with the "Twelve Apostles" at Cambridge. Though he says nothing in these lines concerning the esthetic aspect of poetry, he never neglected this in practice.

The poet in a golden clime was born,
  With golden stars above;
Dowered with the hate of hate, the scorn of scorn,
  The love of love.

He saw through life and death, through good and
  ill,
  He saw through his own soul.
The marvel of the everlasting will,
  An open scroll,

Before him lay: with echoing feet he threaded
  The secretest walks of fame: 10
The viewless arrows of his thoughts were headed
  And winged with flame,

Like Indian reeds blown from his silver tongue,
  And of so fierce a flight,
From Calpe unto Caucasus they sung,
  Filling with light

And vagrant melodies the winds which bore
  Them earthward till they lit;
Then, like the arrow-seeds of the field flower,
  The fruitful wit   20

Cleaving, took root, and springing forth anew
  Where'er they fell, behold,
Like to the mother plant in semblance, grew
  A flower all gold,

And bravely furnished all abroad to fling
  The wingèd shafts of truth,
To throng with stately blooms the breathing spring
  Of Hope and Youth.

13. **Indian reeds,** evidently used as blowpipes for the distribution of the poet's metaphorical arrows. 15. **Calpe,** Gibraltar. 19. **field flower,** the dandelion. 25. **bravely,** brilliantly.

So many minds did gird their orbs with beams,
  Though one did fling the fire.   30
Heaven flowed upon the soul in many dreams
  Of high desire.

Thus truth was multiplied on truth, the world
  Like one great garden showed,
And through the wreaths of floating dark upcurled,
  Rare sunrise flowed.

And Freedom reared in that august sunrise
  Her beautiful bold brow,
When rites and forms before his burning eyes
  Melted like snow.   40

There was no blood upon her maiden robes
  Sunned by those orient skies;
But round about the circles of the globes
  Of her keen eyes

And in her raiment's hem was traced in flame
  WISDOM, a name to shake
All evil dreams of power—a sacred name.
  And when she spake,

Her words did gather thunder as they ran,
  And as the lightning to the thunder   50
Which follows it, riving the spirit of man,
  Making earth wonder,

So was their meaning to her words. No sword
  Of wrath her right arm whirled,
But one poor poet's scroll, and with *his* word
  She shook the world.

THE LADY OF SHALOTT

According to Tennyson, the key to the meaning of this, his first Arthurian poem, is to be found in the last four lines of Part II. He explains: "The new-born love for something, for some one in the wide world from which she has been so long secluded, takes her out of the region of shadows into that of realities."

PART I

On either side the river lie
Long fields of barley and of rye,
That clothe the wold and meet the sky;
And through the field the road runs by
  To many-towered Camelot;
And up and down the people go,
Gazing where the lilies blow

3. **wold,** forest. 5. **Camelot,** King Arthur's city, in Cornwall. 7. **blow,** bloom.

Round an island there below,
　The island of Shalott.

Willows whiten, aspens quiver,　　　　10
Little breezes dusk and shiver
Through the wave that runs for ever
By the island in the river
　Flowing down to Camelot.
Four gray walls, and four gray towers,
Overlook a space of flowers,
And the silent isle imbowers
　The Lady of Shalott.

By the margin, willow-veiled,
Slide the heavy barges trailed　　　　20
By slow horses; and unhailed
The shallop flitteth silken-sailed
　Skimming down to Camelot:
But who hath seen her wave her hand?
Or at the casement seen her stand?
Or is she known in all the land,
　The Lady of Shalott?

Only reapers, reaping early
In among the bearded barley,
Hear a song that echoes cheerly　　　　30
From the river winding clearly,
　Down to towered Camelot:
And by the moon the reaper weary,
Piling sheaves in uplands airy,
Listening, whispers "'Tis the fairy
　Lady of Shalott."

PART II

There she weaves by night and day
A magic web with colours gay.
She has heard a whisper say,
A curse is on her if she stay　　　　40
　To look down to Camelot.
She knows not what the curse may be,
And so she weaveth steadily,
And little other care hath she,
　The Lady of Shalott.

And moving through a mirror clear
That hangs before her all the year,
Shadows of the world appear.
There she sees the highway near
　Winding down to Camelot:　　　　50

There the river eddy whirls,
And there the surly village-churls,
And the red cloaks of market girls,
　Pass onward from Shalott.

Sometimes a troop of damsels glad,
An abbot on an ambling pad,
Sometimes a curly shepherd-lad,
Or long-haired page in crimson clad,
　Goes by to towered Camelot;
And sometimes through the mirror blue　　　　60
The knights come riding two and two:
She hath no loyal knight and true,
　The Lady of Shalott.

But in her web she still delights
To weave the mirror's magic sights,
For often through the silent nights
A funeral, with plumes and lights
　And music, went to Camelot:
Or when the moon was overhead,
Came two young lovers lately wed;　　　　70
"I am half sick of shadows," said
　The Lady of Shalott.

PART III

A bow-shot from her bower-eaves,
He rode between the barley-sheaves,
The sun came dazzling through the leaves,
And flamed upon the brazen greaves
　Of bold Sir Lancelot.
A red-cross knight for ever kneeled
To a lady in his shield,
That sparkled on the yellow field,　　　　80
　Beside remote Shalott.

The gemmy bridle glittered free,
Like to some branch of stars we see
Hung in the golden Galaxy.
The bridle bells rang merrily
　As he rode down to Camelot:
And from his blazoned baldric slung
A mighty silver bugle hung,
And as he rode his armour rung,
　Beside remote Shalott.　　　　90

All in the blue unclouded weather
Thick-jewelled shone the saddle-leather,
The helmet and the helmet-feather
Burned like one burning flame together,
　As he rode down to Camelot.
As often through the purple night,
Below the starry clusters bright,

9. Shalott, from Tennyson's source, the Italian romance *Donna di Scalotta.* Shalott and Astolat, Malory's name for Elaine's home, are the same word. See Tennyson's "Lancelot and Elaine," *Idylls of the King.* **10. Willows whiten.** The white undersides of the leaves are turned up by the wind.

84. Galaxy, the Milky Way.

Some bearded meteor, trailing light,
　　Moves over still Shalott.

His broad clear brow in sunlight glowed;　100
On burnished hooves his war-horse trode;
From underneath his helmet flowed
His coal-black curls as on he rode,
　　As he rode down to Camelot.
From the bank and from the river
He flashed into the crystal mirror,
"Tirra lirra," by the river
　　Sang Sir Lancelot.

She left the web, she left the loom,
She made three paces through the room,　110
She saw the water-lily bloom,
She saw the helmet and the plume,
　　She looked down to Camelot.
Out flew the web and floated wide;
The mirror cracked from side to side;
"The curse is come upon me," cried
　　The Lady of Shalott.

PART IV

In the stormy east-wind straining,
The pale yellow woods were waning,
The broad stream in his banks complaining,
Heavily the low sky raining　121
　　Over towered Camelot;
Down she came and found a boat
Beneath a willow left afloat,
And round about the prow she wrote
　　The Lady of Shalott.

And down the river's dim expanse
Like some bold seër in a trance,
Seeing all his own mischance—
With a glassy countenance　130
　　Did she look to Camelot.
And at the closing of the day
She loosed the chain, and down she lay;
The broad stream bore her far away,
　　The Lady of Shalott.

Lying, robed in snowy white
That loosely flew to left and right—
The leaves upon her falling light—
Through the noises of the night
　　She floated down to Camelot:　140
And as the boat-head wound along
The willowy hills and fields among,
They heard her singing her last song,
　　The Lady of Shalott.

Heard a carol, mournful, holy,
Chanted loudly, chanted lowly,
Till her blood was frozen slowly,
And her eyes were darkened wholly,
　　Turned to towered Camelot.
For ere she reached upon the tide　150
The first house by the water-side,
Singing in her song she died,
　　The Lady of Shalott.

Under tower and balcony,
By garden-wall and gallery,
A gleaming shape she floated by,
Dead-pale between the houses high,
　　Silent into Camelot.
Out upon the wharfs they came,
Knight and burgher, lord and dame,　160
And round the prow they read her name,
　　The Lady of Shalott.

Who is this? and what is here?
And in the lighted palace near
Died the sound of royal cheer;
And they crossed themselves for fear,
　　All the knights at Camelot:
But Lancelot mused a little space;
He said, "She has a lovely face;
God in his mercy lend her grace,　170
　　The Lady of Shalott."

THE PALACE OF ART

"Trench said to me, when we were at Trinity together, 'Tennyson, we cannot live in art.'" Be it noted that the "Soul" in the poem is not an artist—artistic creation demands a high discipline of its own; she simply enjoys the art that others have created. None of her pleasures are ignoble in themselves; she fails because she uses them selfishly (see ll. 293–96). Tennyson said that the poem embodied his "own belief that the Godlike life is with man and for man, that

> " 'Beauty, Good and Knowledge are three sisters . . .
> That never can be sundered without tears.
> And he that shuts out Love, in turn shall be
> Shut out from Love, and on her threshold lie,
> Howling in outer darkness.' "

Comparing the poem as it appears here (1842) with the version Lockhart ridiculed (1832), one sees how much Tennyson's taste had improved in the intervening ten years. To take but one example, in the original version the collection of portraits in the palace is so extensive that the effect is ridiculous. It seems as if the poet has determined to slight nobody. In the revised version there are but four portraits—Milton, Shakespeare, Dante,

Homer—and the poet has added the mosaic depicting
the struggles of humanity over which the soul treads
haughtily on her way to the throne.

I built my soul a lordly pleasure-house,
   Wherein at ease for aye to dwell.
I said, "O Soul, make merry and carouse,
   Dear soul, for all is well."

A huge crag-platform, smooth as burnished brass
   I chose. The rangèd ramparts bright
From level meadow-bases of deep grass
   Suddenly scaled the light.

Thereon I built it firm. Of ledge or shelf
   The rock rose clear, or winding stair.   10
My soul would live alone unto herself
   In her high palace there.

And "while the world runs round and round," I
   said,
   "Reign thou apart, a quiet king,
Still as, while Saturn whirls, his stedfast shade
   Sleeps on his luminous ring."

To which my soul made answer readily:
   "Trust me, in bliss I shall abide
In this great mansion, that is built for me,
   So royal-rich and wide."   20

*   *   *

Four courts I made, East, West and South and
   North,
   In each a squared lawn, wherefrom
The golden gorge of dragons spouted forth
   A flood of fountain-foam.

And round the cool green courts there ran a row
   Of cloisters, branched like mighty woods,
Echoing all night to that sonorous flow
   Of spouted fountain-floods.

And round the roofs a gilded gallery
   That lent broad verge to distant lands,   30
Far as the wild swan wings, to where the sky
   Dipt down to sea and sands.

From those four jets four currents in one swell
   Across the mountain streamed below
In misty folds, that floating as they fell
   Lit up a torrent-bow.

1–4. **I built . . . well,"** probably an echo of the parable
of the rich fool, Luke 12:16–21. **30. lent . . . verge,**
brought (as it were) to the verge of, that is, made visible.

And high on every peak a statue seemed
   To hang on tiptoe, tossing up
A cloud of incense of all odour steamed
   From out a golden cup.   40

So that she thought, "And who shall gaze upon
   My palace with unblinded eyes,
While this great bow will waver in the sun,
   And that sweet incense rise?"

For that sweet incense rose and never failed,
   And, while day sank or mounted higher,
The light aërial gallery, golden-railed,
   Burnt like a fringe of fire.

Likewise the deep-set windows, stained and traced,
   Would seem slow-flaming crimson fires   50
From shadowed grots of arches interlaced,
   And tipt with frost-like spires.

*   *   *

Full of long-sounding corridors it was,
   That over-vaulted grateful gloom,
Through which the livelong day my soul did pass,
   Well-pleased, from room to room.

Full of great rooms and small the palace stood,
   All various, each a perfect whole
From living Nature, fit for every mood
   And change of my still soul.   60

For some were hung with arras green and blue,
   Showing a gaudy summer-morn,
Where with puffed cheek the belted hunter blew
   His wreathèd bugle-horn.

One seemed all dark and red—a tract of sand,
   And some one pacing there alone,
Who paced for ever in a glimmering land,
   Lit with a low large moon.

One showed an iron coast and angry waves.
   You seemed to hear them climb and fall   70
And roar rock-thwarted under bellowing caves,
   Beneath the windy wall.

And one, a full-fed river winding slow
   By herds upon an endless plain,
The ragged rims of thunder brooding low,
   With shadow-streaks of rain.

And one, the reapers at their sultry toil.
   In front they bound the sheaves. Behind

Were realms of upland, prodigal in oil,
　　And hoary to the wind. 80

And one a foreground black with stones and slags,
　　Beyond, a line of heights, and higher
All barred with long white cloud the scornful crags,
　　And highest, snow and fire.

And one, an English home—gray twilight poured
　　On dewy pastures, dewy trees,
Softer than sleep—all things in order stored,
　　A haunt of ancient Peace.

Nor these alone, but every landscape fair,
　　As fit for every mood of mind, 90
Or gay, or grave, or sweet, or stern, was there
　　Not less than truth designed.

*　　　　　*　　　　　*

Or the maid-mother by a crucifix,
　　In tracts of pasture sunny-warm,
Beneath branch-work of costly sardonyx
　　Sat smiling, babe in arm.

Or in a clear-walled city on the sea,
　　Near gilded organ-pipes, her hair
Wound with white roses, slept St. Cecily;
　　An angel looked at her. 100

Or thronging all one porch of Paradise
　　A group of Houris bowed to see
The dying Islamite, with hands and eyes
　　That said, We wait for thee.

Or mythic Uther's deeply-wounded son
　　In some fair space of sloping greens
Lay, dozing in the vale of Avalon,
　　And watched by weeping queens.

Or hollowing one hand against his ear,
　　To list a foot-fall, ere he saw 110
The wood-nymph, stayed the Ausonian king to hear
　　Of wisdom and of law.

Or over hills with peaky tops engrailed,
　　And many a tract of palm and rice,

The throne of Indian Cama slowly sailed
　　A summer fanned with spice.

Or sweet Europa's mantle blew unclasped,
　　From off her shoulder backward borne:
From one hand drooped a crocus: one hand grasped
　　The mild bull's golden horn. 120

Or else flushed Ganymede, his rosy thigh
　　Half-buried in the Eagle's down,
Sole as a flying star shot through the sky
　　Above the pillared town.

Nor these alone: but every legend fair
　　Which the supreme Caucasian mind
Carved out of Nature for itself, was there,
　　Not less than life, designed.

*　　　　　*　　　　　*

Then in the towers I placed great bells that swung,
　　Moved of themselves, with silver sound; 130
And with choice paintings of wise men I hung
　　The royal dais round.

For there was Milton like a seraph strong,
　　Beside him Shakespeare bland and mild;
And there the world-worn Dante grasped his song,
　　And somewhat grimly smiled.

And there the Ionian father of the rest;
　　A million wrinkles carved his skin;
A hundred winters snowed upon his breast,
　　From cheek and throat and chin. 140

Above, the fair hall-ceiling stately-set
　　Many an arch high up did lift,
And angels rising and descending met
　　With interchange of gift.

Below was all mosaic choicely planned
　　With cycles of the human tale
Of this wide world, the times of every land
　　So wrought, they will not fail.

The people here, a beast of burden slow,
　　Toiled onward, pricked with goads and stings;
Here played, a tiger, rolling to and fro 151
　　The heads and crowns of kings;

80. hoary to the wind. The undersides of the olive leaves are a whitish gray. **99. St. Cecily.** St. Cecilia, patron saint of music, was regarded as the inventor of the organ. She was martyred at Rome about 230 A.D. **102. Houris,** beautiful girls in the Mohammedan (Islamite) paradise. **105. Uther's . . . son.** King Arthur. For the story referred to, see Tennyson's "The Passing of Arthur," page 521 in this volume. **107. Avalon,** an island in the western seas, the paradise of Celtic mythology. **111. Ausonian king.** Ausonian means Italian. Egeria, a wood nymph, instructed Numa Pompilius.

115. Cama, Hindu god of love. **117. Europa,** Phoenician princess whom Zeus, in the form of a bull, spirited away from the field where she was sporting among the flowers. **121. Ganymede,** a Trojan boy abducted by Zeus in the form of an eagle and made cupbearer to the gods, supplanting Hebe. **137. Ionian father,** Homer. **149–56. The people . . . cure** (on page 480), references to French history of the Revolutionary period.

Here rose, an athlete, strong to break or bind
  All force in bonds that might endure,
And here once more like some sick man declined,
    And trusted any cure.

But over these she trod: and those great bells
  Began to chime. She took her throne:
She sat betwixt the shining Oriels,
    To sing her songs alone.   160

And through the topmost Oriels' coloured flame
  Two godlike faces gazed below;
Plato the wise, and large-browed Verulam,
    The first of those who know.

And all those names, that in their motion were
  Full-welling fountain-heads of change,
Betwixt the slender shafts were blazoned fair
    In diverse raiment strange:

Through which the lights, rose, amber, emerald, blue,
  Flushed in her temples and her eyes,   170
And from her lips, as morn from Memnon, drew
    Rivers of melodies.

No nightingale delighteth to prolong
  Her low preamble all alone,
More than my soul to hear her echoed song
    Throb through the ribbèd stone;

Singing and murmuring in her feastful mirth,
  Joying to feel herself alive,
Lord over Nature, Lord of the visible earth,
    Lord of the senses five;   180

Communing with herself: "All these are mine,
  And let the world have peace or wars,
'Tis one to me." She—when young night divine
    Crowned dying day with stars,

Making sweet close of his delicious toils—
  Lit light in wreaths and anadems,
And pure quintessences of precious oils
    In hollowed moons of gems,

To mimic heaven; and clapt her hands and cried,
  "I marvel if my still delight   190
In this great house so royal-rich, and wide,
    Be flattered to the height.

"O all things fair to sate my various eyes!
  O shapes and hues that please me well!
O silent faces of the Great and Wise,
    My Gods, with whom I dwell!

"O God-like isolation which art mine,
  I can but count thee perfect gain,
What time I watch the darkening droves of swine
    That range on yonder plain.   200

"In filthy sloughs they roll a prurient skin,
  They graze and wallow, breed and sleep;
And oft some brainless devil enters in,
    And drives them to the deep."

Then of the moral instinct would she prate
  And of the rising from the dead,
As hers by right of full-accomplished Fate;
    And at the last she said:

"I take possession of man's mind and deed.
  I care not what the sects may brawl.   210
I sit as God holding no form of creed,
    But contemplating all."

       *   *   *

Full oft the riddle of the painful earth
  Flashed through her as she sat alone,
Yet not the less held she her solemn mirth,
    And intellectual throne.

And so she throve and prospered: so three years
  She prospered: on the fourth she fell,
Like Herod, when the shout was in his ears,
    Struck through with pangs of hell.   220

Lest she should fail and perish utterly,
  God, before whom ever lie bare
The abysmal deeps of Personality,
    Plagued her with sore despair.

When she would think, where'er she turned her sight
  The airy hand confusion wrought,
Wrote, "Mene, mene," and divided quite
    The kingdom of her thought.

Deep dread and loathing of her solitude
  Fell on her, from which mood was born   230

163. **Verulam**, Sir Francis Bacon.   171–72. **Memnon . . . melodies.** The statue of King Amenophis III, near Thebes, was believed to sound like a harp at sunrise. The Greeks identified it with Memnon, king of Ethiopia, killed by Achilles.

199–204. **swine . . . deep."** In Matthew 8:28–34 the evil spirits expelled from the Gadarenian demoniac take refuge in a herd of swine, causing them to rush into the sea. 219–20. **Herod . . . hell.** See Acts 12:21–23. 227. **"Mene, mene,"** the handwriting on the wall, indicating that God has rejected Belshazzar's kingdom (see Daniel 5:1–31).

Scorn of herself; again, from out that mood
    Laughter at her self-scorn.

"What! is not this my place of strength," she
    said,
    "My spacious mansion built for me,
Whereof the strong foundation-stones were laid
    Since my first memory?"

But in dark corners of her palace stood
    Uncertain shapes; and unawares
On white-eyed phantasms weeping tears of blood,
    And horrible nightmares,   240

And hollow shades enclosing hearts of flame,
    And, with dim fretted foreheads all,
On corpses three-months-old at noon she came,
    That stood against the wall.

A spot of dull stagnation, without light
    Or power of movement, seemed my soul,
'Mid onward-sloping motions infinite
    Making for one sure goal.

A still salt pool, locked in with bars of sand,
    Left on the shore; that hears all night   250
The plunging seas draw backward from the land
    Their moon-led waters white.

A star that with the choral starry dance
    Joined not, but stood, and standing saw
The hollow orb of moving Circumstance
    Rolled round by one fixed law.

Back on herself her serpent pride had curled.
    "No voice," she shrieked in that lone hall,
"No voice breaks through the stillness of this world:
    One deep, deep silence all!"   260

She, mouldering with the dull earth's mouldering
    sod,
    Inwrapt tenfold in slothful shame,
Lay there exiled from eternal God,
    Lost to her place and name;

And death and life she hated equally,
    And nothing saw, for her despair,
But dreadful time, dreadful eternity,
    No comfort anywhere;

Remaining utterly confused with fears,
    And ever worse with growing time,   270
And ever unrelieved by dismal tears,
    And all alone in crime:

Shut up as in a crumbling tomb, girt round
    With blackness as a solid wall,
Far off she seemed to hear the dully sound
    Of human footsteps fall.

As in strange lands a traveller walking slow,
    In doubt and great perplexity,
A little before moon-rise hears the low
    Moan of an unknown sea;   280

And knows not if it be thunder, or a sound
    Of rocks thrown down, or one deep cry
Of great wild beasts; then thinketh, "I have found
    A new land, but I die."

She howled aloud, "I am on fire within.
    There comes no murmur of reply.
What is it that will take away my sin,
    And save me lest I die?"

So when four years were wholly finishèd,
    She threw her royal robes away.   290
"Make me a cottage in the vale," she said,
    "Where I may mourn and pray.

"Yet pull not down my palace towers, that are
    So lightly, beautifully built:
Perchance I may return with others there
    When I have purged my guilt."

THE LOTOS-EATERS

In the course of their wanderings, Ulysses and his companions come to the land of the lotus-eaters, where they
are possessed by the lethargy of their hosts. See *Odyssey*,
Book IX, ll. 82 ff. and, in this book, the note to "Ulysses,"
page 490. In mood and style "The Lotos-Eaters" shows
the influence of Spenser and his followers; for example,
Thomson's *Castle of Indolence*.

"Courage!" he said, and pointed toward the land,
"This mounting wave will roll us shoreward soon."
In the afternoon they came unto a land
In which it seemèd always afternoon.
All round the coast the languid air did swoon,
Breathing like one that hath a weary dream.
Full-faced above the valley stood the moon;
And like a downward smoke, the slender stream
Along the cliff to fall and pause and fall did seem.

A land of streams! some, like a downward smoke, 10
Slow-dropping veils of thinnest lawn, did go;
And some through wavering lights and shadows
    broke.

Rolling a slumbrous sheet of foam below.
They saw the gleaming river seaward flow
From the inner land: far off, three mountain-tops,
Three silent pinnacles of aged snow,
Stood sunset-flushed: and, dewed with showery
    drops,
Up-clomb the shadowy pine above the woven copse.

The charmèd sunset lingered low adown
In the red West: through mountain clefts the dale
Was seen far inland, and the yellow down   21
Bordered with palm, and many a winding vale
And meadow, set with slender galingale;
A land where all things always seemed the same!
And round about the keel with faces pale,
Dark faces pale against that rosy flame,
The mild-eyed melancholy Lotos-eaters came.

Branches they bore of that enchanted stem,
Laden with flower and fruit, whereof they gave
To each, but whoso did receive of them,   30
And taste, to him the gushing of the wave
Far far away did seem to mourn and rave
On alien shores; and if his fellow spake,
His voice was thin, as voices from the grave;
And deep-asleep he seemed, yet all awake,
And music in his ears his beating heart did make.

They sat them down upon the yellow sand,
Between the sun and moon upon the shore;
And sweet it was to dream of Fatherland,
Of child, and wife, and slave; but evermore   40
Most weary seemed the sea, weary the oar,
Weary the wandering fields of barren foam.
Then some one said, "We will return no more";
And all at once they sang, "Our island home
Is far beyond the wave; we will no longer roam."

CHORIC SONG

1

There is sweet music here that softer falls
Than petals from blown roses on the grass,
Or night-dews on still waters between walls
Of shadowy granite, in a gleaming pass;
Music that gentlier on the spirit lies,   50
Than tired eyelids upon tired eyes;
Music that brings sweet sleep down from the blissful
    skies.
Here are cool mosses deep,
And through the moss the ivies creep,
And in the stream the long-leaved flowers weep,
And from the craggy ledge the poppy hangs in sleep.

23. **galingale,** cypress.

2

Why are we weighed upon with heaviness,
And utterly consumed with sharp distress,
While all things else have rest from weariness?
All things have rest: why should we toil alone,   60
We only toil, who are the first of things,
And make perpetual moan,
Still from one sorrow to another thrown:
Nor ever fold our wings,
And cease from wanderings,
Nor steep our brows in slumber's holy balm;
Nor harken what the inner spirit sings,
"There is no joy but calm!"
Why should we only toil, the roof and crown of
    things?

3

Lo! in the middle of the wood,   70
The folded leaf is wooed from out the bud
With winds upon the branch, and there
Grows green and broad, and takes no care,
Sun-steeped at noon, and in the moon
Nightly dew-fed; and turning yellow
Falls, and floats adown the air.
Lo! sweetened with the summer light,
The full-juiced apple, waxing over-mellow,
Drops in a silent autumn night.
All its allotted length of days,   80
The flower ripens in its place,
Ripens and fades, and falls, and hath no toil,
Fast-rooted in the fruitful soil.

4

Hateful is the dark-blue sky,
Vaulted o'er the dark-blue sea.
Death is the end of life; ah, why
Should life all labour be?
Let us alone. Time driveth onward fast,
And in a little while our lips are dumb.
Let us alone. What is it that will last?   90
All things are taken from us, and become
Portions and parcels of the dreadful Past.
Let us alone. What pleasure can we have
To war with evil? Is there any peace
In ever climbing up the climbing wave?
All things have rest, and ripen toward the grave
In silence; ripen, fall and cease:
Give us long rest or death, dark death, or dreamful
    ease.

5

How sweet it were, hearing the downward stream,
With half-shut eyes ever to seem   100
Falling asleep in a half-dream!

To dream and dream, like yonder amber light,
Which will not leave the myrrh-bush on the height;
To hear each other's whispered speech;
Eating the Lotos day by day,
To watch the crisping ripples on the beach,
And tender curving lines of creamy spray;
To lend our hearts and spirits wholly
To the influence of mild-minded melancholy;
To muse and brood and live again in memory,   110
With those old faces of our infancy
Heaped over with a mound of grass,
Two handfuls of white dust, shut in an urn of brass!

6

Dear is the memory of our wedded lives,
And dear the last embraces of our wives
And their warm tears: but all hath suffered change:
For surely now our household hearths are cold:
Our sons inherit us: our looks are strange:
And we should come like ghosts to trouble joy.
Or else the island princes over-bold   120
Have eat our substance, and the minstrel sings
Before them of the ten years' war in Troy,
And our great deeds, as half-forgotten things.
Is there confusion in the little isle?
Let what is broken so remain.
The Gods are hard to reconcile:
'Tis hard to settle order once again.
There *is* confusion worse than death,
Trouble on trouble, pain on pain,
Long labour unto agèd breath,   130
Sore task to hearts worn out by many wars
And eyes grown dim with gazing on the pilot-stars.

7

But, propt on beds of amaranth and moly,
How sweet (while warm airs lull us, blowing lowly)
With half-dropt eyelid still,
Beneath a heaven dark and holy,
To watch the long bright river drawing slowly
His waters from the purple hill—
To hear the dewy echoes calling
From cave to cave through the thick-twinèd vine—
To watch the emerald-coloured water falling   141
Through many a woven acanthus-wreath divine!
Only to hear and see the far-off sparkling brine,
Only to hear were sweet, stretched out beneath the
  pine.

8

The Lotos blooms below the barren peak:
The Lotos blows by every winding creek:

All day the wind breathes low with mellower
  tone:
Through every hollow cave and alley lone
Round and round the spicy downs the yellow
  Lotos-dust is blown.
We have had enough of action, and of motion
  we,
Rolled to starboard, rolled to larboard, when the
  surge was seething free,   151
Where the wallowing monster spouted his foam-
  fountains in the sea.
Let us swear an oath, and keep it with an equal
  mind,
In the hollow Lotos-land to live and lie reclined
On the hills like Gods together, careless of man-
  kind.
For they lie beside their nectar, and the bolts are
  hurled
Far below them in the valleys, and the clouds are
  lightly curled
Round their golden houses, girdled with the gleam-
  ing world:
Where they smile in secret, looking over wasted
  lands,
Blight and famine, plague and earthquake, roaring
  deeps and fiery sands,   160
Clanging fights, and flaming towns, and sinking
  ships, and praying hands.
But they smile, they find a music centred in a doleful song
Steaming up, a lamentation and an ancient tale of
  wrong,
Like a tale of little meaning though the words are
  strong;
Chanted from an ill-used race of men that cleave
  the soil,
Sow the seed, and reap the harvest with enduring
  toil,
Storing yearly little dues of wheat, and wine and
  oil;
Till they perish and they suffer—some, 'tis whispered—down in hell
Suffer endless anguish, others in Elysian valleys
  dwell,
Resting weary limbs at last on beds of asphodel.   170
Surely, surely, slumber is more sweet than toil, the
  shore
Than labour in the deep mid-ocean, wind and wave
  and oar;
Oh rest ye, brother mariners, we will not wander
  more.

120. island princes, Penelope's suitors. 133. amaranth,
an imaginary never-fading flower. moly, a fabulous herb
named by Homer as defeating the magic of Circe.

169. Elysian valleys, the Greek paradise. 170. asphodel, daffodil.

A DREAM OF FAIR WOMEN

Tennyson owes his dream "frame," but not his subject matter, to Chaucer. As he himself points out, Cleopatra is the only woman who appears both in this poem and in the *Legend*. The piece has been much revised; in 1832 it began "with some stanzas about a man sailing in a balloon"!

I read, before my eyelids dropt their shade,
   "*The Legend of Good Women*," long ago
Sung by the morning star of song, who made
   His music heard below;

Dan Chaucer, the first warbler, whose sweet breath
   Preluded those melodious bursts that fill
The spacious times of great Elizabeth
   With sounds that echo still.

And, for a while, the knowledge of his art
   Held me above the subject, as strong gales   10
Hold swollen clouds from raining, though my heart,
   Brimful of those wild tales,

Charged both mine eyes with tears. In every land
   I saw, wherever light illumineth,
Beauty and anguish walking hand in hand
   The downward slope to death.

Those far-renownèd brides of ancient song
   Peopled the hollow dark, like burning stars,
And I heard sounds of insult, shame, and wrong,
   And trumpets blown for wars;   20

And clattering flints battered with clanging hoofs;
   And I saw crowds in columned sanctuaries;
And forms that passed at windows and on roofs
   Of marble palaces;

Corpses across the threshold; heroes tall
   Dislodging pinnacle and parapet
Upon the tortoise creeping to the wall;
   Lances in ambush set;

And high shrine-doors burst through with heated
    blasts
   That run before the fluttering tongues of fire;   30
White surf wind-scattered over sails and masts,
   And ever climbing higher;

5. Dan, a Middle English title of honor, equivalent to "master" or "sir".   **9. knowledge,** in the sense of cognizance or recognition. The poet means that, for the time being, he was so much preoccupied with his admiration for Chaucer's art that a direct, overwhelming response to the emotional appeal of the woeful subject matter of the *Legend* was inhibited.   **27. tortoise . . . wall,** soldiers creeping to the wall of a besieged city under the protection of their shields.

Squadrons and squares of men in brazen plates,
   Scaffolds, still sheets of water, divers woes,
Ranges of glimmering vaults with iron grates,
   And hushed seraglios.

So shape chased shape as swift as, when to land
   Bluster the winds and tides the self-same way,
Crisp foam-flakes scud along the level sand,
   Torn from the fringe of spray.   40

I started once, or seemed to start in pain,
   Resolved on noble things, and strove to speak,
As when a great thought strikes along the brain,
   And flushes all the cheek.

And once my arm was lifted to hew down
   A cavalier from off his saddle-bow,
That bore a lady from a leaguered town;
   And then, I know not how,

All those sharp fancies, by down-lapsing thought
   Streamed onward, lost their edges, and did creep
Rolled on each other, rounded, smoothed, and
    brought   51
   Into the gulfs of sleep.

At last methought that I had wandered far
   In an old wood: fresh-washed in coolest dew
The maiden splendours of the morning star
   Shook in the stedfast blue.

Enormous elm-tree-boles did stoop and lean
   Upon the dusky brushwood underneath
Their broad curved branches, fledged with clearest
    green,
   New from its silken sheath.   60

The dim red morn had died, her journey done,
   And with dead lips smiled at the twilight plain,
Half-fallen across the threshold of the sun,
   Never to rise again.

There was no motion in the dumb dead air,
   Not any song of bird or sound of rill;
Gross darkness of the inner sepulchre
   Is not so deadly still

As that wide forest. Growths of jasmine turned
   Their humid arms festooning tree to tree,   70
And at the root through lush green grasses burned
   The red anemone.

45. And once my arm, etc. The reader, now thoroughly aroused, projects himself imaginatively into the story, like the unsophisticated theatergoer who cries out to warn the heroine of a melodrama.   **49. down-lapsing.** See l. 52.

I knew the flowers, I knew the leaves, I knew
   The tearful glimmer of the languid dawn
On those long, rank, dark wood-walks drenched in
     dew,
   Leading from lawn to lawn.

The smell of violets, hidden in the green,
   Poured back into my empty soul and frame
The times when I remember to have been
   Joyful and free from blame.   80

And from within me a clear under-tone
   Thrilled through mine ears in that unblissful
     clime,
"Pass freely through: the wood is all thine own,
   Until the end of time."

At length I saw a lady within call,
   Stiller than chiselled marble, standing there;
A daughter of the gods, divinely tall,
   And most divinely fair.

Her loveliness with shame and with surprise
   Froze my swift speech: she turning on my face 90
The star-like sorrows of immortal eyes,
   Spoke slowly in her place.

"I had great beauty: ask thou not my name:
   No one can be more wise than destiny.
Many drew swords and died. Where'er I came
   I brought calamity."

"No marvel, sovereign lady: in fair field
   Myself for such a face had boldly died,"
I answered free; and turning I appealed
   To one that stood beside.   100

But she, with sick and scornful looks averse,
   To her full height her stately stature draws;
"My youth," she said, "was blasted with a curse:
   This woman was the cause.

"I was cut off from hope in that sad place,
   Which men called Aulis in those iron years:
My father held his hand upon his face;
   I, blinded with my tears,

"Still strove to speak: my voice was thick with
    sighs
   As in a dream. Dimly I could descry   110
The stern black-bearded kings with wolfish eyes,
   Waiting to see me die.

"The high masts flickered as they lay afloat;
   The crowds, the temples, wavered, and the shore;
The bright death quivered at the victim's throat;
   Touched; and I knew no more."

Whereto the other with a downward brow:
   "I would the white cold heavy-plunging foam,
Whirled by the wind, had rolled me deep below,
   Then when I left my home."   120

Her slow full words sank through the silence drear,
   As thunder-drops fall on a sleeping sea:
Sudden I heard a voice that cried, "Come here,
   That I may look on thee."

I turning saw, throned on a flowery rise,
   One sitting on a crimson scarf unrolled;
A queen, with swarthy cheeks and bold black
    eyes,
   Brow-bound with burning gold.

She, flashing forth a haughty smile, began:
   "I governed men by change, and so I swayed 130
All moods. 'Tis long since I have seen a man.
   Once, like the moon, I made

"The ever-shifting currents of the blood
   According to my humour ebb and flow.
I have no men to govern in this wood:
   That makes my only woe.

"Nay—yet it chafes me that I could not bend
   One will; nor tame and tutor with mine eye
That dull cold-blooded Caesar. Prythee, friend,
   Where is Mark Antony?   140

"The man, my lover, with whom I rode sublime
   On Fortune's neck: we sat as God by God:
The Nilus would have risen before his time
   And flooded at our nod.

76. lawn, glade. **85–96. a lady . . . calamity."** Helen's
flight from her husband, Menelaus, king of Sparta, with
Paris, a prince of Troy, was the cause of the Trojan War.
100. one, Iphigenia, daughter of Agamemnon. The Greek
host was becalmed at Aulis because her father had had the
misfortune to kill a stag sacred to Diana. Only the sacrifice of
the girl could appease the goddess, but at the last moment
Diana was moved to pity and snatched her victim from the
altar.

127–76. A queen . . . kings (on page 486), Cleopatra
(69–30 B.C.) last of the Ptolemies, queen of Egypt. Tennyson
is indebted to Shakespeare's *Antony and Cleopatra* for her
swarthiness (ll. 127–28), her volatility (ll. 130–34), and the
masculine vigor suggested in ll. 145–46. **Libyan** means
African. **Canopus** is a star. **That dull cold-blooded Caesar**
(l. 139) is Octavius. After the defeat of Antony in 31 B.C., and
his subsequent death, Cleopatra killed herself with an asp
(**worm**) to avoid being taken to Rome by Octavius to grace
his triumph.

"We drank the Libyan Sun to sleep, and lit
　Lamps which out-burned Canopus. O my life
In Egypt! O the dalliance and the wit,
　The flattery and the strife,

"And the wild kiss, when fresh from war's alarms,
　My Hercules, my Roman Antony,　　　　　　150
My mailèd Bacchus leapt into my arms,
　Contented there to die!

"And there he died: and when I heard my name
　Sighed forth with life I would not brook my fear
Of the other: with a worm I balked his fame.
　What else was left? look here!"

(With that she tore her robe apart, and half
　The polished argent of her breast to sight
Laid bare. Thereto she pointed with a laugh,
　Showing the aspick's bite.)　　　　　　　160

"I died a Queen. The Roman soldier found
　Me lying dead, my crown about my brows,
A name for ever!—lying robed and crowned,
　Worthy a Roman spouse."

Her warbling voice, a lyre of widest range
　Struck by all passion, did fall down and glance
From tone to tone, and glided through all change
　Of liveliest utterance.

When she made pause I knew not for delight;
　Because with sudden motion from the ground　170
She raised her piercing orbs, and filled with light
　The interval of sound.

Still with their fires Love tipt his keenest darts;
　As once they drew into two burning rings
All beams of Love, melting the mighty hearts
　Of captains and of kings.

Slowly my sense undazzled. Then I heard
　A noise of some one coming through the lawn,
And singing clearer than the crested bird
　That claps his wings at dawn.　　　　　　180

"The torrent brooks of hallowed Israel
　From craggy hollows pouring, late and soon,
Sound all night long, in falling through the dell,
　Far-heard beneath the moon.

178. some one, Jephthah's daughter, whom he was compelled to sacrifice, having rashly vowed in battle that if the Lord would deliver the children of Ammon into his hand, he would make a burnt offering of "whatsoever cometh forth of the doors of my house [at **Mizpeh**] to meet me, when I return." —Judges 11:29–40

"The balmy moon of blessèd Israel
　Floods all the deep-blue gloom with beams divine:
All night the splintered crags that wall the dell
　With spires of silver shine."

As one that museth where broad sunshine laves
　The lawn by some cathedral, through the door
Hearing the holy organ rolling waves　　　　191
　Of sound on roof and floor

Within, and anthem sung, is charmed and tied
　To where he stands,—so stood I, when that flow
Of music left the lips of her that died
　To save her father's vow;

The daughter of the warrior Gileadite,
　A maiden pure; as when she went along
From Mizpeh's towered gate with welcome light,
　With timbrel and with song.　　　　　　200

My words leapt forth: "Heaven heads the count of crimes
　With that wild oath." She rendered answer high:
"Not so, nor once alone; a thousand times
　I would be born and die.

"Single I grew, like some green plant, whose root
　Creeps to the garden water-pipes beneath,
Feeding the flower; but ere my flower to fruit
　Changed, I was ripe for death.

"My God, my land, my father—these did move
　Me from my bliss of life, that Nature gave,　210
Lowered softly with a threefold cord of love
　Down to a silent grave.

"And I went mourning, 'No fair Hebrew boy
　Shall smile away my maiden blame among
The Hebrew mothers'—emptied of all joy,
　Leaving the dance and song,

"Leaving the olive-gardens far below,
　Leaving the promise of my bridal bower,
The valleys of grape-loaded vines that glow
　Beneath the battled tower.　　　　　　220

205–07. like some green plant . . . flower. Tennyson's accuracy sometimes deteriorated to pedantry. Knowing that in a garden the roots of plants would gravitate toward the water pipes, he could not avoid noting that totally irrelevant (and quite unpoetic) fact. In Mrs. Gaskell's *Cranford* there is a countryman who decided that Tennyson was a great poet because he knew that ash buds were black in March. Paul Elmer More points out that it would have been more sensible had he decided that Tennyson was a good botanist! **213. "And I went mourning.** Woman's function in Israel was to bear children; failing in this, she failed in the whole purpose of her life. See Judges 11:37.

"The light white cloud swam over us. Anon
We heard the lion roaring from his den;
We saw the large white stars rise one by one,
   Or, from the darkened glen,

"Saw God divide the night with flying flame,
   And thunder on the everlasting hills.
I heard Him, for He spake, and grief became
   A solemn scorn of ills.

"When the next moon was rolled into the sky,
   Strength came to me that equalled my desire. 230
How beautiful a thing it was to die
   For God and for my sire!

"It comforts me in this one thought to dwell,
   That I subdued me to my father's will;
Because the kiss he gave me, ere I fell,
   Sweetens the spirit still.

"Moreover it is written that my race
   Hewed Ammon, hip and thigh, from Aroer
On Arnon unto Minneth." Here her face
   Glowed, as I looked at her.   240

She locked her lips: she left me where I stood:
   "Glory to God," she sang, and past afar,
Thridding the sombre boskage of the wood,
   Toward the morning-star.

Losing her carol I stood pensively,
   As one that from a casement leans his head,
When midnight bells cease ringing suddenly,
   And the old year is dead.

"Alas! alas!" a low voice, full of care,
   Murmured beside me: "Turn and look on me:
I am that Rosamond, whom men call fair,   251
   If what I was I be.

"Would I had been some maiden coarse and
   poor!
O me, that I should ever see the light!
Those dragon eyes of angered Eleanor
   Do hunt me, day and night."

She ceased in tears, fallen from hope and trust:
   To whom the Egyptian: "O, you tamely died!
You should have clung to Fulvia's waist, and thrust
   The dagger through her side."   260

243. **Thridding . . . boskage,** threading her way through the thickets.   **251. Rosamond,** Rosamond Clifford, mistress of Henry II, said to have been murdered by his wife, Eleanor of Aquitaine.   **258. Egyptian,** Cleopatra. **259. Fulvia's,** that is, Eleanor's. Fulvia was Antony's wife.

With that sharp sound the white dawn's creeping
   beams,
   Stol'n to my brain, dissolved the mystery
Of folded sleep. The captain of my dreams
   Ruled in the eastern sky.

Morn broadened on the borders of the dark,
   Ere I saw her, who clasped in her last trance
Her murdered father's head, or Joan of Arc,
   A light of ancient France;

Or her who knew that Love can vanquish Death,
   Who kneeling, with one arm about her king,   270
Drew forth the poison with her balmy breath,
   Sweet as new buds in Spring.

No memory labours longer from the deep
   Gold-mines of thought to lift the hidden ore
That glimpses, moving up, than I from sleep
   To gather and tell o'er

Each little sound and sight. With what dull pain
   Compassed, how eagerly I sought to strike
Into that wondrous track of dreams again!
   But no two dreams are like.   280

As when a soul laments, which hath been blest,
   Desiring what is mingled with past years,
In yearnings that can never be exprest
   By signs or groans or tears;

Because all words, though culled with choicest art,
   Failing to give the bitter of the sweet,
Wither beneath the palate, and the heart
   Faints, faded by its heat.

YOU ASK ME, WHY, THOUGH ILL
AT EASE

You ask me, why, though ill at ease,
   Within this region I subsist,
   Whose spirits falter in the mist,
And languish for the purple seas.

It is the land that freemen till,
   That sober-suited Freedom chose,
   The land, where girt with friends or foes
A man may speak the thing he will;

263. **captain of my dreams,** Venus, the morning star. 266. **her,** Margaret Roper, daughter of Sir Thomas More, martyred under Henry VIII, who kept her father's head after his execution, and was buried embracing it.   267. **Joan of Arc,** the national heroine of France (1412-1431), who turned the tide of the Hundred Years' War.   269. **her,** Eleanor of Castile, wife of Edward I, who sucked the blood from his wound after he had been stabbed by a poisoned dagger.

A land of settled government,
  A land of just and old renown,   10
  Where Freedom slowly broadens down
From precedent to precedent:

Where faction seldom gathers head,
  But by degrees to fullness wrought,
  The strength of some diffusive thought
Hath time and space to work and spread.

Should banded unions persecute
  Opinion, and induce a time
  When single thought is civil crime,
And individual freedom mute;   20

Though Power should make from land to land
  The name of Britain trebly great—
  Though every channel of the State
Should fill and choke with golden sand—

Yet waft me from the harbour-mouth,
  Wild wind! I seek a warmer sky,
  And I will see before I die
The palms and temples of the South.

OF OLD SAT FREEDOM ON THE HEIGHTS

Of old sat Freedom on the heights,
  The thunders breaking at her feet:
  Above her shook the starry lights:
She heard the torrents meet.

There in her place she did rejoice,
  Self-gathered in her prophet-mind,
  But fragments of her mighty voice
Came rolling on the wind.

Then stept she down through town and field
  To mingle with the human race,   10
  And part by part to men revealed
The fullness of her face—

Grave mother of majestic works,
  From her isle-altar gazing down,
  Who, God-like, grasps the triple forks,
And, King-like, wears the crown:

Her open eyes desire the truth.
  The wisdom of a thousand years

Of Old Sat Freedom on the Heights. **14. isle-altar,** England.
15. triple forks, trident, Neptune's symbol of authority,
indicating England's control of the seas.

Is in them. May perpetual youth
  Keep dry their light from tears;   20

That her fair form may stand and shine,
  Make bright our days and light our dreams,
Turning to scorn with lips divine
  The falsehood of extremes!

DORA

Tennyson found "Dora" very difficult to write; it was
hard for him to subdue his natural luxuriance to the
Spartan simplicity the subject seemed to demand. He had
his reward when Wordsworth told him he had been trying unsuccessfully all his life to write such a pastoral.
Without Wordsworth's example the poem would never
have been written, but the immediate source was the
sketch of Dora Creswell in *Our Village*, by Miss Mitford.

With farmer Allan at the farm abode
William and Dora. William was his son,
And she his niece. He often looked at them,
And often thought, "I'll make them man and wife."
Now Dora felt her uncle's will in all,
And yearned toward William; but the youth, be-
  cause
He had been always with her in the house,
Thought not of Dora.
                        Then there came a day
When Allan called his son, and said, "My son:
I married late, but I would wish to see   10
My grandchild on my knees before I die:
And I have set my heart upon a match.
Now therefore look to Dora; she is well
To look to; thrifty too beyond her age.
She is my brother's daughter: he and I
Had once hard words, and parted, and he died
In foreign lands; but for his sake I bred
His daughter Dora: take her for your wife;
For I have wished this marriage, night and day,
For many years." But William answered short;   20
"I cannot marry Dora; by my life,
I will not marry Dora." Then the old man
Was wroth, and doubled up his hands, and said:
"You will not, boy! you dare to answer thus!
But in my time a father's word was law,
And so it shall be now for me. Look to it;
Consider, William: take a month to think,
And let me have an answer to my wish;
Or, by the Lord that made me, you shall pack,
And never more darken my doors again."   30
But William answered madly; bit his lips,
And broke away. The more he looked at her
The less he liked her; and his ways were harsh;

But Dora bore them meekly. Then before
The month was out he left his father's house,
And hired himself to work within the fields;
And half in love, half spite, he wooed and wed
A labourer's daughter, Mary Morrison.

    Then, when the bells were ringing, Allan called
His niece and said: "My girl, I love you well;   40
But if you speak with him that was my son,
Or change a word with her he calls his wife,
My home is none of yours. My will is law."
And Dora promised, being meek. She thought,
"It cannot be: my uncle's mind will change!"

    And days went on, and there was born a boy
To William; then distresses came on him;
And day by day he passed his father's gate,
Heart-broken, and his father helped him not.
But Dora stored what little she could save,   50
And sent it them by stealth, nor did they know
Who sent it; till at last a fever seized
On William, and in harvest time he died.

    Then Dora went to Mary. Mary sat
And looked with tears upon her boy, and thought
Hard things of Dora. Dora came and said:
"I have obeyed my uncle until now,
And I have sinned, for it was all through me
This evil came on William at the first.
But, Mary, for the sake of him that's gone,   60
And for your sake, the woman that he chose,
And for this orphan, I am come to you:
You know there has not been for these five years
So full a harvest: let me take the boy,
And I will set him in my uncle's eye
Among the wheat; that when his heart is glad
Of the full harvest, he may see the boy,
And bless him for the sake of him that's gone."

    And Dora took the child, and went her way
Across the wheat, and sat upon a mound   70
That was unsown, where many poppies grew.
Far off the farmer came into the field
And spied her not; for none of all his men
Dare tell him Dora waited with the child;
And Dora would have risen and gone to him,
But her heart failed her; and the reapers reaped,
And the sun fell, and all the land was dark.

    But when the morrow came, she rose and took
The child once more, and sat upon the mound;
And made a little wreath of all the flowers   80
That grew about, and tied it round his hat
To make him pleasing in her uncle's eye.
Then when the farmer passed into the field
He spied her, and he left his men at work,
And came and said: "Where were you yesterday?

---

74. Dare, not a shift to the present tense. *Dare* is an original past form, older than *durst.*

Whose child is that? What are you doing here?"
So Dora cast her eyes upon the ground,
And answered softly, "This is William's child!"
"And did I not," said Allan, "did I not
Forbid you, Dora?" Dora said again: 90
"Do with me as you will, but take the child,
And bless him for the sake of him that's gone!"
And Allan said, "I see it is a trick
Got up betwixt you and the woman there.
I must be taught my duty, and by you!
You knew my word was law, and yet you dared
To slight it. Well—for I will take the boy;
But go you hence, and never see me more."

    So saying, he took the boy that cried aloud
And struggled hard. The wreath of flowers fell   100
At Dora's feet. She bowed upon her hands,
And the boy's cry came to her from the field,
More and more distant. She bowed down her head,
Remembering the day when first she came,
And all the things that had been. She bowed down
And wept in secret; and the reapers reaped,
And the sun fell, and all the land was dark.

    Then Dora went to Mary's house, and stood
Upon the threshold. Mary saw the boy
Was not with Dora. She broke out in praise   110
To God, that helped her in her widowhood.
And Dora said, "My uncle took the boy;
But, Mary, let me live and work with you:
He says that he will never see me more."
Then answered Mary, "This shall never be,
That thou shouldst take my trouble on thyself:
And, now I think, he shall not have the boy,
For he will teach him hardness, and to slight
His mother; therefore thou and I will go,
And I will have my boy, and bring him home;   120
And I will beg of him to take thee back:
But if he will not take thee back again,
Then thou and I will live within one house,
And work for William's child, until he grows
Of age to help us."

               So the women kissed
Each other, and set out, and reached the farm.
The door was off the latch: they peeped, and saw
The boy set up betwixt his grandsire's knees,
Who thrust him in the hollows of his arm,
And clapt him on the hands and on the cheeks,   130
Like one that loved him: and the lad stretched out
And babbled for the golden seal, that hung
From Allan's watch, and sparkled by the fire.
Then they came in: but when the boy beheld
His mother, he cried out to come to her:
And Allan set him down, and Mary said:

    "O Father!—if you let me call you so—
I never came a-begging for myself,

Or William, or this child; but now I come
For Dora: take her back; she loves you well.   140
O Sir, when William died, he died at peace
With all men; for I asked him, and he said,
He could not ever rue his marrying me—
I had been a patient wife: but, Sir, he said
That he was wrong to cross his father thus:
'God bless him!' he said, 'and may he never know
The troubles I have gone through!' Then he turned
His face and passed—unhappy that I am!
But now, Sir, let me have my boy, for you
Will make him hard, and he will learn to slight   150
His father's memory; and take Dora back,
And let all this be as it was before."

    So Mary said, and Dora hid her face
By Mary. There was silence in the room;
And all at once the old man burst in sobs:—
    "I have been to blame—to blame. I have killed
        my son.
I have killed him—but I loved him—my dear son.
May God forgive me!—I have been to blame.
Kiss me, my children."
                        Then they clung about
The old man's neck, and kissed him many times.   160
And all the man was broken with remorse;
And all his love came back a hundredfold;
And for three hours he sobbed o'er William's child
Thinking of William.
                    So those four abode
Within one house together; and as years
Went forward, Mary took another mate;
But Dora lived unmarried till her death.

ULYSSES

Ulysses is the hero of Homer's *Odyssey*, which relates
the ten years' wandering that intervened between his departure from Troy, at the end of the war, and his return
to Ithaca, where he slew the insolent suitors of his faithful
wife, Penelope, and re-established himself as king. The
Greeks were familiar with further wanderings of Ulysses
to appease the god Poseidon, whom he had offended.
Dante's *Divine Comedy*, Canto XXVI, had already endowed
him with what we should call the pioneer spirit. But the
conception of his departure from Ithaca, inspired by an
irresistible desire for new experiences, is original with
Tennyson, for whom the poem had definitely an autobiographical significance. He wrote it soon after the
death of Hallam, and he himself said of it that it gave
"the feeling about the need of going forward and braving
the struggle of life perhaps more simply than anything in
In Memoriam." It has always been regarded as one of his
great achievements; it is interesting, also, to study his use
of a form which Browning is often thought of as having

made distinctly his own, the dramatic monologue. The
speaker is, of course, Ulysses himself.

It little profits that an idle king,
By this still hearth, among these barren crags,
Matched with an agèd wife, I mete and dole
Unequal laws unto a savage race,
That hoard, and sleep, and feed, and know not me.
I cannot rest from travel: I will drink
Life to the lees: all times I have enjoyed
Greatly, have suffered greatly, both with those
That loved me, and alone; on shore, and when
Through scudding drifts the rainy Hyades   10
Vext the dim sea: I am become a name;
For always roaming with a hungry heart
Much have I seen and known; cities of men
And manners, climates, councils, governments,
Myself not least, but honoured of them all;
And drunk delight of battle with my peers,
Far on the ringing plains of windy Troy.
I am a part of all that I have met;
Yet all experience is an arch wherethrough
Gleams that untravelled world, whose margin fades
For ever and for ever when I move.   21
How dull it is to pause, to make an end,
To rust unburnished, not to shine in use!
As though to breathe were life. Life piled on life
Were all too little, and of one to me
Little remains: but every hour is saved
From that eternal silence, something more,
A bringer of new things; and vile it were
For some three suns to store and hoard myself,
And this gray spirit yearning in desire   30
To follow knowledge like a sinking star,
Beyond the utmost bound of human thought.

    This is my son, mine own Telemachus,
To whom I leave the sceptre and the isle—
Well-loved of me, discerning to fulfil
This labour, by slow prudence to make mild
A rugged people, and through soft degrees
Subdue them to the useful and the good.
Most blameless is he, centred in the sphere
Of common duties, decent not to fail   40
In offices of tenderness, and pay
Meet adoration to my household gods,
When I am gone. He works his work, I mine.

    There lies the port; the vessel puffs her sail:
There gloom the dark broad seas. My mariners,
Souls that have toiled, and wrought, and thought
        with me—
That ever with a frolic welcome took
The thunder and the sunshine, and opposed

10. rainy Hyades, a cluster of stars in the constellation
Taurus, believed to cause rainy weather.

Free hearts, free foreheads—you and I are old;
Old age hath yet his honour and his toil; 50
Death closes all: but something ere the end,
Some work of noble note, may yet be done,
Not unbecoming men that strove with Gods.
The lights begin to twinkle from the rocks:
The long day wanes: the slow moon climbs: the
   deep
Moans round with many voices. Come, my friends,
'Tis not too late to seek a newer world.
Push off, and sitting well in order smite
The sounding furrows; for my purpose holds
To sail beyond the sunset, and the baths 60
Of all the western stars, until I die.
It may be that the gulfs will wash us down:
It may be we shall touch the Happy Isles,
And see the great Achilles, whom we knew.
Though much is taken, much abides; and though
We are not now that strength which in old days
Moved earth and heaven; that which we are, we
   are;
One equal temper of heroic hearts,
Made weak by time and fate, but strong in will
To strive, to seek, to find, and not to yield. 70

LOCKSLEY HALL

"Locksley Hall" is a monologue, expressing a young
man's grief and disgust over the loss of his sweetheart, his
cousin Amy, who has been induced by her parents to
marry a fox-hunting squire, a much wealthier man. The
speaker is not an attractive character, and Tennyson is
well within his rights when he insists that he has not
painted a self-portrait. He was, nevertheless, much preoccupied with this kind of man—who recurs notably in
Maud—and the preoccupation indicates a somewhat
morbid strain in his genius. In "Locksley Hall Sixty
Years After" the hero of the present poem is reintroduced
so that we may see what life has taught him. "Locksley
Hall" is almost invariably included in anthologies, not so
much for its poetic merit, which is considerable, as because of the many interesting references it contains not

51–53. Death closes all . . . Gods. Not being a Christian, Ulysses does not believe in immortality; his hunger for
life is desperate, for he must soon go down into the darkness.
One of Dante's most effective symbols of experience in *The
Divine Comedy* is his conception of the heretics who denied
immortality, who are enclosed in red-hot tombs upon which
the lids are slowly closing. The reference to **the Happy Isles**
(l. 63), where Ulysses hopes to see the great hero Achilles,
who was slain in the war, must not be taken to contradict
any of this. The Islands of the Blessed, described by Hesiod,
Pindar, and others as lying toward the edge of the westward
ocean, are the abiding-place of certain specially favored
mortals who have been rescued by the gods from the common doom of men. **55–56. The long day wanes . . .
many voices.** Note the sympathetic nature background.
Being an old man, Ulysses sails out into the twilight.

only to the events of Tennyson's time but, as in ll. 119–30,
by anticipation to our own.

Comrades, leave me here a little, while as yet 'tis
   early morn:
Leave me here, and when you want me, sound upon
   the bugle-horn.

'Tis the place, and all around it, as of old, the cur-
   lews call,
Dreary gleams about the moorland flying over
   Locksley Hall;

Locksley Hall, that in the distance overlooks the
   sandy tracts,
And the hollow ocean-ridges roaring into cataracts.

Many a night from yonder ivied casement, ere I
   went to rest,
Did I look on great Orion sloping slowly to the
   West.

Many a night I saw the Pleiads, rising through the
   mellow shade,
Glitter like a swarm of fire-flies tangled in a silver
   braid. 10

Here about the beach I wandered, nourishing a
   youth sublime
With the fairy tales of science, and the long result of
   Time;

When the centuries behind me like a fruitful land
   reposed;
When I clung to all the present for the promise that
   it closed:

When I dipt into the future far as human eye could
   see;
Saw the Vision of the world, and all the wonder that
   would be.—

In the Spring a fuller crimson comes upon the robin's breast;
In the Spring the wanton lapwing gets himself another crest;

In the Spring a livelier iris changes on the burnished dove;
In the Spring a young man's fancy lightly turns to
   thoughts of love. 20

4. Dreary . . . Hall. An absolute construction, Tennyson told Dr. Furness, not an assertion concerning the cur-
lews.

Then her cheek was pale and thinner than should
    be for one so young,
And her eyes on all my motions with a mute observ-
    ance hung.

And I said, "My cousin Amy, speak, and speak the
    truth to me,
Trust me, cousin, all the current of my being sets to
    thee."

On her pallid cheek and forehead came a colour
    and a light,
As I have seen the rosy red flushing in the northern
    night.

And she turned—her bosom shaken with a sudden
    storm of sighs—
All the spirit deeply dawning in the dark of hazel
    eyes—

Saying, "I have hid my feelings, fearing they should
    do me wrong";
Saying, "Dost thou love me, cousin?" weeping, "I
    have loved thee long."   30

Love took up the glass of Time, and turned it in his
    glowing hands;
Every moment, lightly shaken, ran itself in golden
    sands.

Love took up the harp of Life, and smote on all the
    chords with might;
Smote the chord of Self, that, trembling, passed in
    music out of sight.

Many a morning on the moorland did we hear the
    copses ring,
And her whisper thronged my pulses with the ful-
    ness of the Spring.

Many an evening by the waters did we watch the
    stately ships,
And our spirits rushed together at the touching of
    the lips.

O my cousin, shallow-hearted! O my Amy, mine no
    more!
O the dreary, dreary moorland! O the barren, bar-
    ren shore!   40

Falser than all fancy fathoms, falser than all songs
    have sung,
Puppet to a father's threat, and servile to a shrewish
    tongue!

24. **sets,** flows.

Is it well to wish thee happy?—having known me—
    to decline
On a range of lower feelings and a narrower heart
    than mine!

Yet it shall be: thou shalt lower to his level day by
    day,
What is fine within thee growing coarse to sym-
    pathise with clay.

As the husband is, the wife is: thou art mated with a
    clown,
And the grossness of his nature will have weight to
    drag thee down.

He will hold thee, when his passion shall have spent
    its novel force,
Something better than his dog, a little dearer than
    his horse.   50

What is this? his eyes are heavy: think not they are
    glazed with wine.
Go to him: it is thy duty: kiss him: take his hand in
    thine.

It may be my lord is weary, that his brain is over-
    wrought:
Soothe him with thy finer fancies, touch him with
    thy lighter thought.

He will answer to the purpose, easy things to under-
    stand—
Better thou wert dead before me, though I slew thee
    with my hand!

Better thou and I were lying, hidden from the
    heart's disgrace,
Rolled in one another's arms, and silent in a last
    embrace.

Cursed be the social wants that sin against the
    strength of youth!
Cursed be the social lies that warp us from the living
    truth!   60

Cursed be the sickly forms that err from honest Na-
    ture's rule!
Cursed be the gold that gilds the straitened fore-
    head of the fool!

Well—'tis well that I should bluster!—Hadst thou
    less unworthy proved—
Would to God—for I had loved thee more than ever
    wife was loved.

Am I mad, that I should cherish that which bears
but bitter fruit?
I will pluck it from my bosom, though my heart be
at the root.

Never, though my mortal summers to such length of
years should come
As the many-wintered crow that leads the clanging
rookery home.

Where is comfort? in division of the records of the
mind?
Can I part her from herself, and love her, as I knew
her, kind?   70

I remember one that perished: sweetly did she speak
and move:
Such a one do I remember, whom to look at was to
love.

Can I think of her as dead, and love her for the love
she bore?
No—she never loved me truly: love is love for evermore.

Comfort? comfort scorned of devils! this is truth the
poet sings,
That a sorrow's crown of sorrow is remembering
happier things.

Drug thy memories, lest thou learn it, lest thy heart
be put to proof,
In the dead unhappy night, and when the rain is on
the roof.

Like a dog, he hunts in dreams, and thou art staring
at the wall,
Where the dying night-lamp flickers, and the shad-
ows rise and fall.   80

Then a hand shall pass before thee, pointing to his
drunken sleep,
To thy widowed marriage-pillows, to the tears that
thou wilt weep.

Thou shalt hear the "Never, never," whispered by
the phantom years,
And a song from out the distance in the ringing of
thine ears;

And an eye shall vex thee, looking ancient kindness
on thy pain.
Turn thee, turn thee on thy pillow: get thee to thy
rest again.

Nay, but Nature brings thee solace; for a tender
voice will cry.
'Tis a purer life than thine; a lip to drain thy trouble dry.

Baby lips will laugh me down: my latest rival brings
thee rest.
Baby fingers, waxen touches, press me from the
mother's breast.   90

O, the child too clothes the father with a dearness
not his due.
Half is thine and half is his: it will be worthy of the
two.

O, I see thee old and formal, fitted to thy petty
part,
With a little hoard of maxims preaching down a
daughter's heart.

"They were dangerous guides the feelings—she herself was not exempt—
Truly, she herself had suffered"—Perish in thy self-
contempt!

Overlive it—lower yet—be happy! wherefore
should I care?
I myself must mix with action, lest I wither by despair.

What is that which I should turn to, lighting upon
days like these?
Every door is barred with gold, and opens but to
golden keys.   100

Every gate is thronged with suitors, all the markets
overflow.
I have but an angry fancy: what is that which I
should do?

I had been content to perish, falling on the foeman's
ground,
When the ranks are rolled in vapour, and the winds
are laid with sound.

---

76. That . . . things. A paraphrase of Dante, *Inferno*,
Canto V, ll. 121–23.   **79. he,** Amy's husband, who cries out
the language of the hunt in his drunken stupor.

95–96. "They . . . suffered." The quotation is given
indirectly.   **104. winds are laid,** the supposed effect of cannon fire.

But the jingling of the guinea helps the hurt that
    Honour feels,
And the nations do but murmur, snarling at each
    other's heels.

Can I but relive in sadness? I will turn that earlier
    page.
Hide me from my deep emotion, O thou wondrous
    Mother-Age!

Make me feel the wild pulsation that I felt before
    the strife,
When I heard my days before me, and the tumult of
    my life;   110

Yearning for the large excitement that the coming
    years would yield,
Eager-hearted as a boy when first he leaves his
    father's field,

And at night along the dusky highway near and
    nearer drawn,
Sees in heaven the light of London flaring like a
    dreary dawn;

And his spirit leaps within him to be gone before
    him then,
Underneath the light he looks at, in among the
    throngs of men:

Men, my brothers, men the workers, ever reaping
    something new:
That which they have done but earnest of the things
    that they shall do:

For I dipt into the future, far as human eye could
    see,
Saw the Vision of the world, and all the wonder that
    would be;   120

Saw the heavens fill with commerce, argosies of
    magic sails,
Pilots of the purple twilight, dropping down with
    costly bales;

Heard the heavens fill with shouting, and there
    rained a ghastly dew
From the nations' airy navies grappling in the cen-
    tral blue;

Far along the world-wide whisper of the south-wind
    rushing warm,
With the standards of the peoples plunging through
    the thunder-storm;

Till the war-drum throbbed no longer, and the
    battle-flags were furled
In the Parliament of man, the Federation of the
    world.

There the common sense of most shall hold a fretful
    realm in awe,
And the kindly earth shall slumber, lapt in univer-
    sal law.   130

So I triumphed ere my passion sweeping through
    me left me dry,
Left me with the palsied heart, and left me with the
    jaundiced eye;

Eye, to which all order festers, all things here are
    out of joint:
Science moves, but slowly slowly, creeping on from
    point to point:

Slowly comes a hungry people, as a lion creeping
    nigher,
Glares at one that nods and winks behind a slowly-
    dying fire.

Yet I doubt not through the ages one increasing
    purpose runs,
And the thoughts of men are widened with the proc-
    ess of the suns.

What is that to him that reaps not harvest of his
    youthful joys,
Though the deep heart of existence beat for ever
    like a boy's?   140

Knowledge comes, but wisdom lingers, and I linger
    on the shore,
And the individual withers, and the world is more
    and more.

Knowledge comes, but wisdom lingers, and he bears
    a laden breast,
Full of sad experience, moving toward the stillness
    of his rest.

Hark, my merry comrades call me, sounding on the
    bugle-horn,
They to whom my foolish passion were a target for
    their scorn:

135. **hungry people,** a reference either to contemporary
revolutionary activities or to Malthus's theory of population
(see page 378).

Shall it not be scorn to me to harp on such a mouldered string?
I am shamed through all my nature to have loved so
slight a thing.

Weakness to be wroth with weakness! woman's
pleasure, woman's pain—
Nature made them blinder motions bounded in a
shallower brain: 150

Woman is the lesser man, and all thy passions,
matched with mine,
Are as moonlight unto sunlight, and as water unto
wine—

Here at least, where nature sickens, nothing. Ah, for
some retreat
Deep in yonder shining Orient, where my life began
to beat;

Where in wild Mahratta-battle fell my father evil-
starred;—
I was left a trampled orphan, and a selfish uncle's
ward.

Or to burst all links of habit—there to wander far
away,
On from island unto island at the gateways of the
day.

Larger constellations burning, mellow moons and
happy skies,
Breadths of tropic shade and palms in cluster, knots
of Paradise.   160

Never comes the trader, never floats an European
flag,
Slides the bird o'er lustrous woodland, swings the
trailer from the crag;

Droops the heavy-blossomed bower, hangs the
heavy-fruited tree—
Summer isles of Eden lying in dark-purple spheres
of sea.

There methinks would be enjoyment more than in
this march of mind,
In the steamship, in the railway, in the thoughts
that shake mankind.

There the passions cramped no longer shall have
scope and breathing space;
I will take some savage woman, she shall rear my
dusky race.

153-56. Ah, . . . ward. The hero was born in India,
where his father died fighting the Mahrattas.

Iron jointed, supple-sinewed, they shall dive, and
they shall run,
Catch the wild goat by the hair, and hurl their
lances in the sun;   170

Whistle back the parrot's call, and leap the rainbows of the brooks,
Not with blinded eyesight poring over miserable
books—

Fool, again the dream, the fancy! but I *know* my
words are wild,
But I count the gray barbarian lower than the
Christian child.

I, to herd with narrow foreheads, vacant of our
glorious gains,
Like a beast with lower pleasures, like a beast with
lower pains!

Mated with a squalid savage—what to me were sun
or clime?
I the heir of all the ages, in the foremost files of
time—

I that rather held it better men should perish one by
one,
Than that earth should stand at gaze like Joshua's
moon in Ajalon!   180

Not in vain the distance beacons. Forward, forward
let us range,
Let the great world spin for ever down the ringing
grooves of change.

Through the shadow of the globe we sweep into the
younger day:
Better fifty years of Europe than a cycle of Cathay.

Mother-Age (for mine I knew not) help me as when
life begun:
Rift the hills, and roll the waters, flash the lightnings, weigh the Sun.

O, I see the crescent promise of my spirit hath not
set.
Ancient founts of inspiration well through all my
fancy yet.

180. **Joshua's moon in Ajalon.** Joshua commanded the
moon to stand still in the valley of Ajalon until the Israelites
had avenged themselves upon their enemies (see Joshua 10:
12–13).   182. **grooves.** Having traveled only once on the
railroad, Tennyson was under the impression that the
wheels turned in grooves.   184. **Cathay,** China.

Howsoever these things be, a long farewell to Locksley Hall!

Now for me the woods may wither, now for me the roof-tree fall.   190

Comes a vapour from the margin, blackening over heath and holt,

Cramming all the blast before it, in its breast a thunderbolt.

Let it fall on Locksley Hall, with rain or hail, or fire or snow;

For the mighty wind arises, roaring seaward, and I go.

ST. AGNES' EVE

On St. Agnes' Eve (January 21) girls tried to envision their future husbands (see Keats's "The Eve of St. Agnes"). Tennyson has worked the theme out in religious terms; the nun is the bride of Christ.

> Deep on the convent-roof the snows
>   Are sparkling to the moon:
> My breath to heaven like vapour goes:
>   May my soul follow soon!
> The shadows of the convent-towers
>   Slant down the snowy sward,
> Still creeping with the creeping hours
>   That lead me to my Lord:
> Make Thou my spirit pure and clear
>   As are the frosty skies,   10
> Or this first snowdrop of the year
>   That in my bosom lies.
>
> As these white robes are soiled and dark,
>   To yonder shining ground;
> As this pale taper's earthly spark,
>   To yonder argent round;
> So shows my soul before the Lamb,
>   My spirit before Thee;
> So in mine earthly house I am,
>   To that I hope to be.   20
> Break up the heavens, O Lord! and far,
>   Through all yon starlight keen,
> Draw me, thy bride, a glittering star,
>   In raiment white and clean.
>
> He lifts me to the golden doors;
>   The flashes come and go;
> All heaven bursts her starry floors,
>   And strows her lights below,

16. **yonder argent round,** the full moon.

And deepens on and up! the gates
    Roll back, and far within   30
For me the Heavenly Bridegroom waits,
    To make me pure of sin.
The sabbaths of Eternity,
    One sabbath deep and wide—
A light upon the shining sea—
    The Bridegroom with his bride!

BREAK, BREAK, BREAK

> Break, break, break,
>   On thy cold gray stones, O Sea!
> And I would that my tongue could utter
>   The thoughts that arise in me.
>
> O well for the fisherman's boy,
>   That he shouts with his sister at play!
> O well for the sailor lad,
>   That he sings in his boat on the bay!
>
> And the stately ships go on
>   To their haven under the hill;   10
> But O for the touch of a vanished hand,
>   And the sound of a voice that is still!
>
> Break, break, break,
>   At the foot of thy crags, O Sea!
> But the tender grace of a day that is dead
>   Will never come back to me.

Songs from THE PRINCESS

The Princess, 1847, the story of an abortive attempt to "emancipate" women by educating them completely apart from men, is Tennyson's discussion of the "woman question." The action involves both battle and comic-opera disguises, and the conclusion is that the natural affections must not be repressed. The story is definitely "dated"; Gilbert and Sullivan, indeed, burlesqued it in *Princess Ida* as early as 1884. But the lyrics Tennyson used as interludes are among the most glorious in English literature. "Sweet and low" was set to music by Barnby, "Now sleeps the crimson petal" by Quilter (see John McCormack's recording, Victor 1307).

I. AS THROUGH THE LAND

> As through the land at eve we went,
>   And plucked the ripened ears,
> We fell out, my wife and I,

11–12. hand . . . voice. Hallam's. See notes to "Ulysses" and *In Memoriam*.

O we fell out, I know not why,
   And kissed again with tears.
And blessings on the falling out
   That all the more endears,
When we fall out with those we love
   And kiss again with tears!
For when we came where lies the child   10
   We lost in other years,
There above the little grave,
O there above the little grave,
   We kissed again with tears.

2. SWEET AND LOW

Sweet and low, sweet and low,
   Wind of the western sea,
Low, low, breathe and blow,
   Wind of the western sea!
Over the rolling waters go,
Come from the dying moon, and blow,
   Blow him again to me;
While my little one, while my pretty one, sleeps.

Sleep and rest, sleep and rest,
   Father will come to thee soon;   10
Rest, rest, on mother's breast,
   Father will come to thee soon;
Father will come to his babe in the nest,
Silver sails all out of the west
   Under the silver moon:
Sleep, my little one, sleep, my pretty one, sleep.

3. THE SPLENDOUR FALLS

The splendour falls on castle walls
   And snowy summits old in story:
The long light shakes across the lakes,
   And the wild cataract leaps in glory.
Blow, bugle, blow, set the wild echoes flying,
Blow, bugle; answer, echoes, dying, dying, dying.

O hark, O hear! how thin and clear,
   And thinner, clearer, farther going!
O sweet and far from cliff and scar
   The horns of Elfland faintly blowing!   10
Blow, let us hear the purple glens replying:
Blow, bugle; answer, echoes, dying, dying, dying.

O love, they die in yon rich sky,
   They faint on hill or field or river:
Our echoes roll from soul to soul,
   And grow for ever and for ever.
Blow, bugle, blow, set the wild echoes flying,
And answer, echoes, answer, dying, dying, dying.

4. TEARS, IDLE TEARS

Tears, idle tears, I know not what they mean,
Tears from the depth of some divine despair
Rise in the heart, and gather to the eyes,
In looking on the happy Autumn-fields,
And thinking of the days that are no more.

Fresh as the first beam glittering on a sail,
That brings our friends up from the underworld,
Sad as the last which reddens over one
That sinks with all we love below the verge;
So sad, so fresh, the days that are no more.   10

Ah, sad and strange as in dark summer dawns
The earliest pipe of half-awakened birds
To dying ears, when unto dying eyes
The casement slowly grows a glimmering square;
So sad, so strange, the days that are no more.

Dear as remembered kisses after death,
And sweet as those by hopeless fancy feigned
On lips that are for others; deep as love,
Deep as first love, and wild with all regret;
O Death in Life, the days that are no more.   20

5. HOME THEY BROUGHT

Home they brought her warrior dead:
   She nor swooned, nor uttered cry:
All her maidens, watching, said,
   "She must weep or she will die."

Then they praised him, soft and low,
   Called him worthy to be loved,
Truest friend and noblest foe;
   Yet she neither spoke nor moved.

Stole a maiden from her place,
   Lightly to the warrior stept,   10
Took the face-cloth from the face;
   Yet she neither moved nor wept.

Rose a nurse of ninety years,
   Set his child upon her knee—
Like summer tempest came her tears—
   "Sweet my child, I live for thee."

6. ASK ME NO MORE

Ask me no more: the moon may draw the sea;
   The cloud may stoop from heaven and take the
      shape
With fold to fold, of mountain or of cape;
But O too fond, when have I answered thee?
   Ask me no more.

Ask me no more: what answer should I give?
　I love not hollow cheek or faded eye:
　Yet, O my friend, I will not have thee die!
Ask me no more, lest I should bid thee live;
　　　　Ask me no more.　　　10

Ask me no more: thy fate and mine are seaied:
　I strove against the stream and all in vain:
　Let the great river take me to the main:
No more, dear love, for at a touch I yield;
　　　　Ask me no more.

7. NOW SLEEPS THE CRIMSON PETAL

Now sleeps the crimson petal, now the white;
　Nor waves the cypress in the palace walk;

Nor winks the gold fin in the porphyry font:
　The fire-fly wakens: waken thou with me.

Now droops the milkwhite peacock like a ghost,
　And like a ghost she glimmers on to me.

Now lies the Earth all Danaë to the stars,
　And all thy heart lies open unto me.

Now slides the silent meteor on, and leaves
　A shining furrow, as thy thoughts in me.　　10

Now folds the lily all her sweetness up,
　And slips into the bosom of the lake:
So fold thyself, my dearest, thou, and slip
Into my bosom and be lost in me.

from IN MEMORIAM A. H. H.

Obiit MDCCCXXXIII

Elegy

Arthur Henry Hallam, Tennyson's most intimate friend and prospective brother-in-law, died suddenly in Vienna, September 15, 1833. For Tennyson this death marked the beginning of a long period of spiritual struggle; he could never believe in life again until he had explained to himself how, in a world ruled by a good God, such a man could be cut off at the very beginning of his usefulness. He worked on this problem for seventeen years. The result was *In Memoriam*, which is probably his masterpiece and certainly one of the most important of all theological poems.

Milton saw Edward King ("Lycidas"), Shelley saw Keats ("Adonais"), Matthew Arnold saw Clough ("Thyrsis"), less as individuals than as types of unfulfilment. But Alfred Tennyson loved Arthur Henry Hallam. It was natural, therefore, that instead of expressing himself, as these other poets did, in the pastoral elegy (which is a highly artificial form of literature), he should rather, after a long period of gestation, have cast his utterance into a freer and more spacious form. He is careful, to be sure, to prevent our assuming that there has been no artistic rearrangement of materials in his spiritual autobiography. "It must be remembered that this is a poem, *not* an actual biography. . . . The different moods of sorrow as in a drama are dramatically given, and my conviction that fear, doubts, and suffering will find answer and relief only through Faith in a God of Love. 'I' is not always the author speaking of himself, but the voice of the human race speaking through him." It is clear that Tennyson wrote the poem for himself, to serve his own needs; but because the problem with which he grapples must be faced, in some form, by all who lose a

loved one, and because, disdaining all factitious comfort, he frankly faced every difficulty in the way of faith that the age presented to his typically Victorian mind, the results he achieved were valuable not only for him but for tens of thousands of his contemporaries. To know *In Memoriam*, consequently, with all its implications, is to know Victorian England.

Though the "*In Memoriam* quatrain" had been used inconspicuously in English poetry before Tennyson, the poet was not aware of this; he consequently invented it anew. In his *Tennyson's "In Memoriam," Its Purpose and Its Structure* (Houghton Mifflin, 1884), John F. Genung outlines suggestively as follows:

PROLOGUE
INTRODUCTORY STAGE, 1–27

Prospect	1–6
Defining-Point—Beginning	7
Arrival and Burial of the Dead	17–20

FIRST CYCLE—28–77

Christmas-Tide	28–30
Springtide	38–39
First Anniversary	72

SECOND CYCLE—78–103

Christmas-Tide	78
New Year	83
Second Anniversary	99

---

7. **hollow cheek or faded eye.** The battle has necessitated turning the college into a hospital. Pity draws the princess to love.

7. **Danaë,** a princess of Argos imprisoned by her father in a brazen tower. Here Zeus visited her in the form of a golden shower.

THIRD CYCLE—104–131

Genung calls the Prologue the period of overwhelming grief. The First Cycle he calls the cycle of the past. The Second Cycle is the cycle of the present. The Third Cycle is the cycle of the future. Note the use of seasons and anniversaries to mark stages and transitions.

PROLOGUE

Strong Son of God, immortal Love,
   Whom we, that have not seen thy face,
   By faith, and faith alone, embrace,
Believing where we cannot prove;

Thine are these orbs of light and shade;
   Thou madest Life in man and brute;
   Thou madest Death; and lo, thy foot
Is on the skull which thou hast made.

Thou wilt not leave us in the dust:
   Thou madest man, he knows not why,   10
   He thinks he was not made to die;
And thou hast made him: thou art just.

Thou seemest human and divine,
   The highest, holiest manhood, thou:
   Our wills are ours, we know not how;
Our wills are ours, to make them thine.

Our little systems have their day;
   They have their day and cease to be:
   They are but broken lights of thee,
And thou, O Lord, art more than they.   20

We have but faith: we cannot know;
   For knowledge is of things we see;
   And yet we trust it comes from thee,
A beam in darkness: let it grow.

Let knowledge grow from more to more,
   But more of reverence in us dwell;

1–4. Strong Son . . . cannot prove. See John 20:24–29. **5. orbs,** planets. **7–8. thy foot . . . hast made.** Since the Maker of Life made Death, Death cannot have the last word. The Son is not generally thought of as the Creator, but see John 1:3. **15–16. Our wills . . . to make them thine.** Tennyson maintains the freedom of the human will, without which there can be no morality, but perceives the necessity for a voluntary adjustment of the will of the individual to the universe. **25. Let knowledge grow.** Tennyson had no patience with religionists who opposed scientific investigation and experiment.

That mind and soul, according well,
May make one music as before,

But vaster. We are fools and slight;
   We mock thee when we do not fear: 30
   But help thy foolish ones to bear;
Help thy vain worlds to bear thy light.

Forgive what seemed my sin in me;
   What seemed my worth since I began;
   For merit lives from man to man,
And not from man, O Lord, to thee.

Forgive my grief for one removed,
   Thy creature, whom I found so fair.
   I trust he lives in thee, and there
I find him worthier to be loved.   40

Forgive these wild and wandering cries,
   Confusions of a wasted youth;
   Forgive them where they fail in truth,
And in thy wisdom make me wise.

1

I held it truth, with him who sings
   To one clear harp in divers tones,
   That men may rise on stepping-stones
Of their dead selves to higher things.

But who shall so forecast the years
   And find in loss a gain to match?
   Or reach a hand through time to catch
The far-off interest of tears?

Let Love clasp Grief lest both be drowned,
   Let darkness keep her raven gloss: 10
   Ah, sweeter to be drunk with loss,
To dance with death, to beat the ground,

Than that the victor Hours should scorn
   The long result of love, and boast,
   "Behold the man that loved and lost,
But all he was is overworn."

3

O Sorrow, cruel fellowship,
   O Priestess in the vaults of Death,
   O sweet and bitter in a breath,
What whispers from thy lying lip?

27. according, agreeing. **28. as before,** before modern science upset previously entertained beliefs. **35–36. merit lives . . . to thee.** Man can impute praise or blame to man, but not to God. **42. wasted,** desolated. *Sec. 1.* **1. him.** In 1891 Tennyson thought he had meant Goethe.

"The stars," she whispers, "blindly run;
A web is wov'n across the sky;
From out waste places comes a cry,
And murmurs from the dying sun:

"And all the phantom, Nature, stands—
With all the music in her tone,   10
A hollow echo of my own,—
A hollow form with empty hands."

And shall I take a thing so blind,
Embrace her as my natural good;
Or crush her, like a vice of blood,
Upon the threshold of the mind?

5

I sometimes hold it half a sin
To put in words the grief I feel;
For words, like Nature, half reveal
And half conceal the Soul within.

But, for the unquiet heart and brain,
A use in measured language lies;
The sad mechanic exercise,
Like dull narcotics, numbing pain.

In words, like weeds, I'll wrap me o'er,
Like coarsest clothes against the cold: 10
But that large grief which these enfold
Is given in outline and no more.

6

One writes, that "Other friends remain,"
That "Loss is common to the race"—
And common is the commonplace,
And vacant chaff well meant for grain.

That loss is common would not make
My own less bitter, rather more:
Too common! Never morning wore
To evening, but some heart did break.

O father, wheresoe'er thou be,
Who pledgest now thy gallant son;   10
A shot, ere half thy draught be done,
Hath stilled the life that beat from thee.

O mother, praying God will save
Thy sailor,—while thy head is bowed,

His heavy-shotted hammock-shroud
Drops in his vast and wandering grave.

Ye know no more than I who wrought
At that last hour to please him well;
Who mused on all I had to tell,
And something written, something thought;   20

Expecting still his advent home;
And ever met him on his way
With wishes, thinking, "here to-day,"
Or "here to-morrow will he come."

O somewhere, meek, unconscious dove,
That sittest ranging golden hair;
And glad to find thyself so fair,
Poor child, that waitest for thy love!

For now her father's chimney glows
In expectation of a guest;   30
And thinking "this will please him best,"
She takes a riband or a rose;

For he will see them on to-night;
And with the thought her colour burns;
And, having left the glass, she turns
Once more to set a ringlet right;

And, even when she turned, the curse
Had fallen, and her future Lord
Was drowned in passing through the ford,
Or killed in falling from his horse.   40

O what to her shall be the end?
And what to me remains of good?
To her, perpetual maidenhood,
And unto me no second friend.

7

Dark house, by which once more I stand
Here in the long unlovely street,
Doors, where my heart was used to beat
So quickly, waiting for a hand,

A hand that can be clasped no more—
Behold me, for I cannot sleep,
And like a guilty thing I creep
At earliest morning to the door.

He is not here; but far away
The noise of life begins again,   10
And ghastly through the drizzling rain
On the bald street breaks the blank day.

Sec. 5. **9. weeds**, garments, as in "widow's weeds." Sec. 6. **1–8. One . . . break.** See *Hamlet*, Act I, sc. 2. The Queen brings Hamlet the same shallow comfort of which Tennyson speaks here. The poet, like the prince, replies in effect that the universality of sorrow makes his own situation worse, not better. Through his own sufferings he enters into the experience of all who suffer; imaginatively he bears the burden of all the suffering of the world.

26. ranging, arranging. **1. Dark house**, where Hallam lived. **12. bald . . . breaks . . . blank.** Note the effective alliteration and tone color.

18

'Tis well; 'tis something; we may stand
    Where he in English earth is laid,
    And from his ashes may be made
The violet of his native land.

'Tis little; but it looks in truth
    As if the quiet bones were blest
    Among familiar names to rest
And in the places of his youth.

Come then, pure hands, and bear the head
    That sleeps or wears the mask of sleep,   10
    And come, whatever loves to weep,
And hear the ritual of the dead.

Ah yet, ev'n yet, if this might be,
    I, falling on his faithful heart,
    Would breathing through his lips impart
The life that almost dies in me;

That dies not, but endures with pain,
    And slowly forms the firmer mind,
    Treasuring the look it cannot find,
The words that are not heard again.   20

21

I sing to him that rests below,
    And, since the grasses round me wave,
    I take the grasses of the grave,
And make them pipes whereon to blow.

The traveller hears me now and then,
    And sometimes harshly will he speak:
    "This fellow would make weakness weak,
And melt the waxen hearts of men."

Another answers, "Let him be,
    He loves to make parade of pain,   10
    That with his piping he may gain
The praise that comes to constancy."

A third is wroth: "Is this an hour
    For private sorrow's barren song,
    When more and more the people throng
The chairs and thrones of civil power?

"A time to sicken and to swoon,
    When Science reaches forth her arms
    To feel from world to world, and charms
Her secret from the latest moon?"   20

Behold, ye speak an idle thing:
    Ye never knew the sacred dust:
    I do but sing because I must,
And pipe but as the linnets sing:

And one is glad; her note is gay,
    For now her little ones have ranged;
    And one is sad; her note is changed,
Because her brood is stolen away.

27

I envy not in any moods
    The captive void of noble rage,
    The linnet born within the cage,
That never knew the summer woods:

I envy not the beast that takes
    His license in the field of time,
    Unfettered by the sense of crime,
To whom a conscience never wakes;

Nor, what may count itself as blest,
    The heart that never plighted troth   10
    But stagnates in the weeds of sloth;
Nor any want-begotten rest.

I hold it true, whate'er befall;
    I feel it, when I sorrow most;
    'Tis better to have loved and lost
Than never to have loved at all.

28

The time draws near the birth of Christ:
    The moon is hid; the night is still;
    The Christmas bells from hill to hill
Answer each other in the mist.

Four voices of four hamlets round,
    From far and near, on mead and moor,
    Swell out and fail, as if a door
Were shut between me and the sound:

Each voice four changes on the wind,
    That now dilate, and now decrease,   10
    Peace and goodwill, goodwill and peace,
Peace and goodwill, to all mankind.

This year I slept and woke with pain,
    I almost wished no more to wake,
    And that my hold on life would break
Before I heard those bells again:

Sec. 18. **2. Where . . . laid.** Hallam's body was returned to England for burial. **14–16. I . . . me.** See Elisha's restoration of the Shunammite's son (2 Kings 4:32–37). *Sec. 21.* **13–16. an hour . . . power.** Probably a reference to the Chartist movement (see page 377 of this volume). **18–20. Science . . . moon.** Neptune was discovered in 1846; the eighth satellite of Saturn, two years later.

Sec. 27. **9–16. Nor . . . at all.** One of the most interesting points to observe about *In Memoriam* is the poet's consistent refusal to purchase peace at the cost of love, that is, by forgetfulness. *Sec. 28.* **1. The time . . . Christ,** the first Christmas after Hallam's death, 1833. **9. Each voice four changes.** Each church had four bells.

But they my troubled spirit rule,
 For they controlled me when a boy;
 They bring me sorrow touched with joy,
The merry merry bells of Yule.   20

30

With trembling fingers did we weave
 The holly round the Christmas hearth;
 A rainy cloud possessed the earth,
And sadly fell our Christmas-eve.

At our old pastimes in the hall
 We gamboled, making vain pretence
 Of gladness, with an awful sense
Of one mute Shadow watching all.

We paused: the winds were in the beech:
 We heard them sweep the winter land; 10
 And in a circle hand-in-hand
Sat silent, looking each at each.

Then echo-like our voices rang;
 We sung, though every eye was dim,
 A merry song we sang with him
Last year: impetuously we sang:

We ceased: a gentler feeling crept
 Upon us: surely rest is meet:
 "They rest," we said, "their sleep is sweet,"
And silence followed, and we wept. 20

Our voices took a higher range;
 Once more we sang: "They do not die
 Nor lose their mortal sympathy,
Nor change to us, although they change;

"Rapt from the fickle and the frail
 With gathered power, yet the same,
 Pierces the keen seraphic flame
From orb to orb, from veil to veil."

Rise, happy morn, rise, holy morn,
 Draw forth the cheerful day from night: 30
 O Father, touch the east, and light
The light that shone when Hope was born.

33

O thou that after toil and storm
 Mayst seem to have reached a purer air,

Whose faith has centre everywhere,
 Nor cares to fix itself to form,

Leave thou thy sister when she prays,
 Her early Heaven, her happy views;
 Nor thou with shadowed hint confuse
A life that leads melodious days.

Her faith through form is pure as thine,
 Her hands are quicker unto good: 10
 Oh, sacred be the flesh and blood
To which she links a truth divine!

See thou, that countest reason ripe
 In holding by the law within,
 Thou fail not in a world of sin,
And ev'n for want of such a type.

34

My own dim life should teach me this,
 That life shall live for evermore,
 Else earth is darkness at the core,
And dust and ashes all that is;

This round of green, this orb of flame,
 Fantastic beauty; such as lurks
 In some wild Poet, when he works
Without a conscience or an aim.

What then were God to such as I?
 'Twere hardly worth my while to choose 10
 Of things all mortal, or to use
A little patience ere I die;

'Twere best at once to sink to peace,
 Like birds the charming serpent draws,
 To drop head-foremost in the jaws
Of vacant darkness and to cease.

35

Yet if some voice that man could trust
 Should murmur from the narrow house,
 "The cheeks drop in; the body bows;
Man dies: nor is there hope in dust":

Might I not say? "Yet even here,
 But for one hour, O Love, I strive
 To keep so sweet a thing alive":
But I should turn mine ears and hear

---

4. sadly. See Sec. 78, l. 4; Sec. 105, l. 4. **32. when Hope was born,** with Christ, who brought the hope of immortality to men. *Sec. 33.* The poet warns those who have "emancipated" themselves from "narrow" creeds and ceremonies not to disturb the simple, adequate faith of others and not to hold themselves superior to these others.

Sec. 33. **9. form,** creeds, ritualistic observances, etc. **11. flesh and blood,** possibly the bread and wine of the sacrament, more probably any symbol that has a spiritual significance for the believer. Tennyson argues that the faith and purity of life fostered by such things makes them sacred, even if they have in themselves no absolute value. *Sec. 34.* **5. round . . . orb,** earth . . . sun.

The moanings of the homeless sea,
　The sound of streams that swift or slow　10
　Draw down Aeonian hills, and sow
The dust of continents to be;

And Love would answer with a sigh,
　"The sound of that forgetful shore
　Will change my sweetness more and more,
Half-dead to know that I shall die."

O me, what profits it to put
　An idle case? If Death were seen
　At first as Death, Love had not been,
Or been in narrowest working shut,　20

Mere fellowship of sluggish moods,
　Or in his coarsest Satyr-shape
　Had bruised the herb and crushed the grape,
And basked and battened in the woods.

36

Though truths in manhood darkly join,
　Deep-seated in our mystic frame,
　We yield all blessing to the name
Of Him that made them current coin;

For Wisdom dealt with mortal powers,
　Where truth in closest words shall fail,
　When truth embodied in a tale
Shall enter in at lowly doors.

And so the Word had breath, and wrought
　With human hands the creed of creeds　10
　In loveliness of perfect deeds,
More strong than all poetic thought;

Which he may read that binds the sheaf,
　Or builds the house, or digs the grave,
　And those wild eyes that watch the wave
In roarings round the coral reef.

38

With weary steps I loiter on,
　Though always under altered skies
　The purple from the distance dies,
My prospect and horizon gone.

Sec. 35. **11. Aeonian hills,** hills which have endured for ages. **22. Satyr-shape.** In Greek mythology, the satyrs— half human, half equine—were notably lustful. The poet is arguing that without immortality life has no meaning. On that basis love is possible only on the animal level. *Sec. 36.* **1–4. Though . . . coin.** The mature thinker may perceive the harmony of all religions, but we of the Western world owe our religion to Jesus Christ. **7–8. a tale . . . doors.** See the parables of Jesus. **9. the Word.** See John 1:1–18.

No joy the blowing season gives,
　The herald melodies of spring,
　But in the songs I love to sing
A doubtful gleam of solace lives.

If any care for what is here
　Survive in spirits rendered free,　10
　Then are these songs I sing of thee
Not all ungrateful to thine ear.

47

That each, who seems a separate whole,
　Should move his rounds, and fusing all
　The skirts of self again, should fall
Remerging in the general Soul,

Is faith as vague as all unsweet:
　Eternal form shall still divide
　The eternal soul from all beside;
And I shall know him when we meet:

And we shall sit at endless feast,
　Enjoying each the other's good:　10
　What vaster dream can hit the mood
Of Love on earth? He seeks at least

Upon the last and sharpest height,
　Before the spirits fade away,
　Some landing-place, to clasp and say,
"Farewell! We lose ourselves in light."

50

Be near me when my light is low,
　When the blood creeps, and the nerves prick
　And tingle; and the heart is sick,
And all the wheels of Being slow.

Be near me when the sensuous frame
　Is racked with pangs that conquer trust;
　And Time, a maniac scattering dust,
And Life, a Fury slinging flame.

Be near me when my faith is dry,
　And men the flies of latter spring,　10
　That lay their eggs, and sting and sing
And weave their petty cells and die.

Be near me when I fade away,
　To point the term of human strife,
　And on the low dark verge of life
The twilight of eternal day.

Sec. 47. Tennyson here considers a possible compromise between extinction and immortality: the soul survives, but loses its individual identity. He rejects this idea as unsatisfactory.

52

I cannot love thee as I ought,
  For love reflects the thing beloved;
  My words are only words, and moved
Upon the topmost froth of thought.

"Yet blame not thou thy plaintive song,"
  The Spirit of true love replied;
  "Thou canst not move me from thy side,
Nor human frailty do me wrong.

"What keeps a spirit wholly true
  To that ideal which he bears?   10
  What record? not the sinless years
That breathed beneath the Syrian blue:

"So fret not, like an idle girl,
  That life is dashed with flecks of sin.
  Abide: thy wealth is gathered in,
When Time hath sundered shell from pearl."

54

Oh yet we trust that somehow good
  Will be the final goal of ill,
  To pangs of nature, sins of will,
Defects of doubt, and taints of blood;

That nothing walks with aimless feet;
  That not one life shall be destroyed,
  Or cast as rubbish to the void,
When God hath made the pile complete;

That not a worm is cloven in vain;
  That not a moth with vain desire   10
  Is shrivelled in a fruitless fire,
Or but subserves another's gain.

Behold, we know not anything;
  I can but trust that good shall fall
  At last—far off—at last, to all,
And every winter change to spring.

So runs my dream: but what am I?
  An infant crying in the night:
  An infant crying for the light:
And with no language but a cry.   20

55

The wish, that of the living whole
  No life may fail beyond the grave,
  Derives it not from what we have
The likest God within the soul?

Are God and Nature then at strife,
  That Nature lends such evil dreams?
  So careful of the type she seems,
So careless of the single life;

That I, considering everywhere
  Her secret meaning in her deeds,   10
  And finding that of fifty seeds
She often brings but one to bear,

I falter where I firmly trod,
  And falling with my weight of cares
  Upon the great world's altar-stairs
That slope through darkness up to God,

I stretch lame hands of faith, and grope,
  And gather dust and chaff, and call
  To what I feel is Lord of all,
And faintly trust the larger hope.   20

56

"So careful of the type?" but no.
  From scarpèd cliff and quarried stone
  She cries, "A thousand types are gone:
I care for nothing, all shall go.

"Thou makest thine appeal to me:
  I bring to life, I bring to death:
  The spirit does but mean the breath:
I know no more." And he, shall he,

Man, her last work, who seemed so fair,
  Such splendid purpose in his eyes,   10
  Who rolled the psalm to wintry skies,
Who built him fanes of fruitless prayer,

Sec. 55. 1–6. The wish . . . dreams. Tennyson was no pantheist; "The Higher Pantheism" (page 519) is not pantheistic at all in the ordinary sense. For him the source of our religious convictions was "within ourselves," not in the world of nature. At Cambridge he voted no on the question "Is an intelligible First Cause deducible from the phenomena of the universe?" (See Sec. 124, ll. 5–8.) **20. the larger hope,** universal salvation, one of Tennyson's most earnest religious convictions. He said he "would rather know that he was to be lost eternally than not to know that the whole human race was to live eternally." When the Revised Version of the Bible was published, he was greatly disappointed that the revisers had kept the word *eternal* in the passage, "Depart from me, ye cursed, into the eternal fire" (Matthew 25:41). He had hoped that some such word as "Aeonian" might be employed. *Sec. 56. 3. She,* Nature. **12. fanes,** temples, churches.

Sec. 52. In this section the poet exhorts himself not to permit an oversensitive conscience (Chaucer's "spiced conscience") to deprive him of a sense of fellowship with his departed friend. **11. the sinless years,** the earthly life of Jesus. *Sec. 54.* This section and Secs. 55–56 are full of references to the evolutionary philosophy, though Darwin's *Origin of Species* was not published until 1859.

Who trusted God was love indeed
  And love Creation's final law—
  Though Nature, red in tooth and claw
With ravine, shrieked against his creed—

Who loved, who suffered countless ills,
  Who battled for the True, the Just,
  Be blown about the desert dust,
Or sealed within the iron hills?   20

No more? A monster then, a dream,
  A discord. Dragons of the prime,
  That tare each other in their slime,
Were mellow music matched with him.

O life as futile, then, as frail!
  O for thy voice to soothe and bless!
  What hope of answer, or redress?
Behind the veil, behind the veil.

72

Risest thou thus, dim dawn, again,
  And howlest, issuing out of night,
  With blasts that blow the poplar white,
And lash with storm the streaming pane?

Day, when my crowned estate begun
  To pine in that reverse of doom,
  Which sickened every living bloom,
And blurred the splendour of the sun;

Who usherest in the dolorous hour
  With thy quick tears that make the rose   10
  Pull sideways, and the daisy close
Her crimson fringes to the shower;

Who might'st have heaved a windless flame
  Up the deep East, or, whispering, played
  A chequer-work of beam and shade
Along the hills, yet looked the same.

As wan, as chill, as wild as now;
  Day, marked as with some hideous crime,
  When the dark hand struck down through time,
And cancelled nature's best: but thou,   20

22–24. **Dragons . . . with him.** If man's spiritual aspirations are doomed to disappointment, then the prehistoric monsters, who had no spiritual aspirations, were more harmoniously adjusted to their environment than he to his. **26. thy,** Hallam's. *Sec.* 72. This poem commemorates the anniversary of Hallam's death. **3. With blasts . . . white.** The white undersides of the poplar leaves are turned up by the wind. **5. crowned,** with happiness. **6. doom,** sentence.

Lift as thou may'st thy burthened brows
  Through clouds that drench the morning star,
  And whirl the ungarnered sheaf afar,
And sow the sky with flying boughs,

And up thy vault with roaring sound
  Climb thy thick noon, disastrous day;
  Touch thy dull goal of joyless gray,
And hide thy shame beneath the ground.

73

So many worlds, so much to do,
  So little done, such things to be,
  How know I what had need of thee,
For thou wert strong as thou wert true?

The fame is quenched that I foresaw,
  The head hath missed an earthly wreath:
  I curse not nature, no, nor death;
For nothing is that errs from law.

We pass; the path that each man trod
  Is dim, or will be dim, with weeds: 10
  What fame is left for human deeds
In endless age? It rests with God.

O hollow wraith of dying fame,
  Fade wholly, while the soul exults,
  And self-infolds the large results
Of force that would have forged a name.

78

Again at Christmas did we weave
  The holly round the Christmas hearth;
  The silent snow possessed the earth,
And calmly fell our Christmas-eve:

The yule-clog sparkled keen with frost,
  No wing of wind the region swept,
  But over all things brooding slept
The quiet sense of something lost.

As in the winters left behind,
  Again our ancient games had place,   10
  The mimic picture's breathing grace,
And dance and song and hoodman-blind.

Who showed a token of distress?
  No single tear, no mark of pain:
  O sorrow, then can sorrow wane?
O grief, can grief be changed to less?

Sec. 73. **3. thee,** Hallam. *Sec.* 78. **1. Christmas,** the second Christmas, 1834. **5. clog,** log (dial.).

O last regret, regret can die!
  No—mixt with all this mystic frame,
  Her deep relations are the same,
But with long use her tears are dry.   20

83

Dip down upon the northern shore,
  O sweet new-year delaying long;
  Thou doest expectant nature wrong;
Delaying long, delay no more.

What stays thee from the clouded noons,
  Thy sweetness from its proper place?
  Can trouble live with April days,
Or sadness in the summer moons?

Bring orchis, bring the foxglove spire,
  The little speedwell's darling blue,   10
  Deep tulips dashed with fiery dew,
Laburnums, dropping-wells of fire.

O thou, new-year, delaying long,
  Delayest the sorrow in my blood,
  That longs to burst a frozen bud
And flood a fresher throat with song.

85

This truth came borne with bier and pall,
  I felt it, when I sorrowed most,
  'Tis better to have loved and lost,
Than never to have loved at all——

O true in word, and tried in deed,
  Demanding, so to bring relief
  To this which is our common grief,
What kind of life is that I lead;

And whether trust in things above
  Be dimmed of sorrow, or sustained;   10
  And whether love for him have drained
My capabilities of love;

Your words have virtue such as draws
  A faithful answer from the breast,
  Through light reproaches, half exprest,
And loyal unto kindly laws.

My blood an even tenor kept,
  Till on mine ear this message falls,
  That in Vienna's fatal walls
God's finger touched him, and he slept.   20

Sec. 85. This poem was addressed to Edmund Law Lushington, who married Tennyson's sister Cecilia in 1842.

The great Intelligences fair
  That range above our mortal state,
  In circle round the blessed gate,
Received and gave him welcome there;

And led him through the blissful climes,
  And showed him in the fountain fresh
  All knowledge that the sons of flesh
Shall gather in the cycled times.

But I remained, whose hopes were dim,
  Whose life, whose thoughts were little worth,
  To wander on a darkened earth,   31
Where all things round me breathed of him.

O friendship, equal-poised control,
  O heart, with kindliest motion warm,
  O sacred essence, other form,
O solemn ghost, O crownèd soul!

Yet none could better know than I,
  How much of act at human hands
  The sense of human will demands
By which we dare to live or die.   40

Whatever way my days decline,
  I felt and feel, though left alone,
  His being working in mine own,
The footsteps of his life in mine;

A life that all the Muses decked
  With gifts of grace, that might express
  All-comprehensive tenderness,
All-subtilising intellect:

And so my passion hath not swerved
  To works of weakness, but I find   50
  An image comforting the mind,
And in my grief a strength reserved.

Likewise the imaginative woe,
  That loved to handle spiritual strife,
  Diffused the shock through all my life,
But in the present broke the blow.

My pulses therefore beat again
  For other friends that once I met;
  Nor can it suit me to forget
The mighty hopes that make us men.   60

I woo your love: I count it crime
  To mourn for any overmuch;
  I, the divided half of such
A friendship as had mastered Time;

Which masters Time indeed, and is
 Eternal, separate from fears:
 The all-assuming months and years
Can take no part away from this:

But Summer on the steaming floods,
 And Spring that swells the narrow brooks, 70
 And Autumn, with a noise of rooks,
That gather in the waning woods,

And every pulse of wind and wave
 Recalls, in change of light or gloom,
 My old affection of the tomb,
And my prime passion in the grave:

My old affection of the tomb,
 A part of stillness, yearns to speak:
 "Arise, and get thee forth and seek
A friendship for the years to come. 80

"I watch thee from the quiet shore;
 Thy spirit up to mine can reach;
 But in dear words of human speech
We two communicate no more."

And I, "Can clouds of nature stain
 The starry clearness of the free?
 How is it? Canst thou feel for me
Some painless sympathy with pain?"

And lightly does the whisper fall;
 "'Tis hard for thee to fathom this; 90
 I triumph in conclusive bliss,
And that serene result of all."

So hold I commerce with the dead;
 Or so methinks the dead would say;
 Or so shall grief with symbols play
And pining life be fancy-fed.

Now looking to some settled end,
 That these things pass, and I shall prove
 A meeting somewhere, love with love,
I crave your pardon, O my friend; 100

If not so fresh, with love as true,
 I, clasping brother-hands, aver
 I could not, if I would, transfer
The whole I felt for him to you.

For which be they that hold apart
 The promise of the golden hours?
 First love, first friendship, equal powers,
That marry with the virgin heart.

85. **nature,** life as we know it here. 86. **the free,** the dead.

Still mine, that cannot but deplore,
 That beats within a lonely place, 110
 That yet remembers his embrace,
But at his footstep leaps no more,

My heart, though widowed, may not rest
 Quite in the love of what is gone,
 But seeks to beat in time with one
That warms another living breast.

Ah, take the imperfect gift I bring,
 Knowing the primrose yet is dear,
 The primrose of the later year,
As not unlike to that of Spring. 120

94

How pure at heart and sound in head,
 With what divine affections bold
 Should be the man whose thought would hold
An hour's communion with the dead.

In vain shalt thou, or any, call
 The spirits from their golden day,
 Except, like them, thou too canst say,
My spirit is at peace with all.

They haunt the silence of the breast,
 Imaginations calm and fair, 10
 The memory like a cloudless air,
The conscience as a sea at rest:

But when the heart is full of din,
 And doubt beside the portal waits,
 They can but listen at the gates,
And hear the household jar within.

96

You say, but with no touch of scorn,
 Sweet-hearted, you, whose light-blue eyes
 Are tender over drowning flies,
You tell me, doubt is Devil-born.

I know not: one indeed I knew
 In many a subtle question versed,
 Who touched a jarring lyre at first,
But ever strove to make it true:

Perplext in faith, but pure in deeds,
 At last he beat his music out. 10
 There lives more faith in honest doubt,
Believe me, than in half the creeds.

Sec. 96. This section is addressed to a simple believer, evidently feminine, who does not understand the true significance of the poet's experience. 5. **one,** Hallam.

He fought his doubts and gathered strength,
　He would not make his judgment blind,
　He faced the spectres of the mind
And laid them: thus he came at length

To find a stronger faith his own;
　And Power was with him in the night,
　Which makes the darkness and the light,
And dwells not in the light alone,　20

But in the darkness and the cloud,
　As over Sinaï's peaks of old,
　While Israel made their gods of gold,
Although the trumpet blew so loud.

104

The time draws near the birth of Christ;
　The moon is hid, the night is still;
　A single church below the hill
Is pealing, folded in the mist.

A single peal of bells below,
　That wakens at this hour of rest
　A single murmur in the breast,
That these are not the bells I know.

Like strangers' voices here they sound,
　In lands where not a memory strays,　10
　Nor landmark breathes of other days,
But all is new unhallowed ground.

105

To-night ungathered let us leave
　This laurel, let this holly stand:
　We live within the stranger's land,
And strangely falls our Christmas-eve.

Our father's dust is left alone
　And silent under other snows:
　There in due time the woodbine blows,
The violet comes, but we are gone.

No more shall wayward grief abuse
　The genial hour with mask and mime;　10
　For change of place, like growth of time,
Has broke the bond of dying use.

Let cares that petty shadows cast,
　By which our lives are chiefly proved,
　A little spare the night I loved,
And hold it solemn to the past.

But let no footstep beat the floor,
　Nor bowl of wassail mantle warm;
　For who would keep an ancient form
Through which the spirit breathes no more?　20

Be neither song, nor game, nor feast;
　Nor harp be touched, nor flute be blown;
　No dance, no motion, save alone
What lightens in the lucid east

Of rising worlds by yonder wood.
　Long sleeps the summer in the seed;
　Run out your measured arcs, and lead
The closing cycle rich in good.

106

Ring out, wild bells, to the wild sky,
　The flying cloud, the frosty light:
　The year is dying in the night;
Ring out, wild bells, and let him die.

Ring out the old, ring in the new,
　Ring, happy bells, across the snow:
　The year is going, let him go;
Ring out the false, ring in the true.

Ring out the grief that saps the mind,
　For those that here we see no more;　10
　Ring out the feud of rich and poor,
Ring in redress to all mankind.

Ring out a slowly dying cause,
　And ancient forms of party strife;
　Ring in the nobler modes of life,
With sweeter manners, purer laws.

Ring out the want, the care, the sin,
　The faithless coldness of the times;
　Ring out, ring out my mournful rhymes,
But ring the fuller minstrel in.　20

Ring out false pride in place and blood,
　The civic slander and the spite;
　Ring in the love of truth and right,
Ring in the common love of good.

21–24. **But . . . loud.** The children of Israel made a
golden calf in the plains while Moses received the Ten Commandments from God on Mount Sinai. See Exodus ch. 32.
Sec. 104. **1. The time draws near,** Christmas of 1837.
3. church, Waltham Abbey, near which Tennyson was now
living. *Sec. 105.* **7. blows,** blooms.

Sec. 106. This famous New Year's song has been set to music
by Gounod.

Ring out old shapes of foul disease;
  Ring out the narrowing lust of gold;
  Ring out the thousand wars of old,
Ring in the thousand years of peace.

Ring in the valiant man and free,
  The larger heart, the kindlier hand;   30
  Ring out the darkness of the land,
Ring in the Christ that is to be.

107

It is the day when he was born,
  A bitter day that early sank
  Behind a purple-frosty bank
Of vapour, leaving night forlorn.

The time admits not flowers or leaves
  To deck the banquet. Fiercely flies
  The blast of North and East, and ice
Makes daggers at the sharpened eaves,

And bristles all the brakes and thorns
  To yon hard crescent, as she hangs   10
  Above the wood which grides and clangs
Its leafless ribs and iron horns

Together, in the drifts that pass
  To darken on the rolling brine
  That breaks the coast. But fetch the wine,
Arrange the board and brim the glass;

Bring in great logs and let them lie,
  To make a solid core of heat;
  Be cheerful-minded, talk and treat
Of all things ev'n as he were by;   20

We keep the day. With festal cheer,
  With books and music, surely we
  Will drink to him, whate'er he be,
And sing the songs he loved to hear.

108

I will not shut me from my kind,
  And, lest I stiffen into stone,
  I will not eat my heart alone,
Nor feed with sighs a passing wind:

What profit lies in barren faith,
  And vacant yearning, though with might
  To scale the heaven's highest height,
Or dive below the wells of Death?

What find I in the highest place,
  But mine own phantom chanting hymns?   10
  And on the depths of death there swims
The reflex of a human face.

I'll rather take what fruit may be
  Of sorrow under human skies:
  'Tis held that sorrow makes us wise,
Whatever wisdom sleep with thee.

113

'Tis held that sorrow makes us wise;
  Yet how much wisdom sleeps with thee
  Which not alone had guided me,
But served the seasons that may rise;

For can I doubt, who knew thee keen
  In intellect, with force and skill
  To strive, to fashion, to fulfil—
I doubt not what thou wouldst have been:

A life in civic action warm,
  A soul on highest mission sent,   10
  A potent voice of Parliament,
A pillar steadfast in the storm,

Should licensed boldness gather force,
  Becoming, when the time has birth,
  A lever to uplift the earth
And roll it in another course,

With thousand shocks that come and go,
  With agonies, with energies,
  With overthrowings, and with cries,
And undulations to and fro.   20

115

Now fades the last long streak of snow,
  Now burgeons every maze of quick
  About the flowering squares, and thick
By ashen roots the violets blow.

Now rings the woodland loud and long,
  The distance takes a lovelier hue,
  And drowned in yonder living blue
The lark becomes a sightless song.

Now dance the lights on lawn and lea,
  The flocks are whiter down the vale,   10
  And milkier every milky sail
On winding stream or distant sea;

28. thousand years of peace. See Revelation 20.
Sec. 107. **1. day,** February 1. Its brevity is symbolical of
Hallam's short life.   **11. grides,** scrapes raspingly.

Sec. 113. **13–16. Should licensed boldness . . . another
course,** a strong expression of Tennyson's political conservatism.

Where now the seamew pipes, or dives
    In yonder greening gleam, and fly
    The happy birds, that change their sky
To build and brood; that live their lives

From land to land; and in my breast
    Spring wakens too; and my regret
    Becomes an April violet,
And buds and blossoms like the rest.   20

118

Contemplate all this work of Time,
    The giant labouring in his youth;
    Nor dream of human love and truth,
As dying Nature's earth and lime;

But trust that those we call the dead
    Are breathers of an ampler day
    For ever nobler ends. They say,
The solid earth whereon we tread

In tracts of fluent heat began,
    And grew to seeming-random forms,   10
    The seeming prey of cyclic storms,
Till at the last arose the man;

Who throve and branched from clime to clime,
    The herald of a higher race,
    And of himself in higher place,
If so he type this work of time

Within himself, from more to more;
    Or, crowned with attributes of woe
    Like glories, move his course, and show
That life is not as idle ore,   20

But iron dug from central gloom,
    And heated hot with burning fears,
    And dipt in baths of hissing tears,
And battered with the shocks of doom

To shape and use. Arise and fly
    The reeling Faun, the sensual feast;
    Move upward, working out the beast,
And let the ape and tiger die.

123

There rolls the deep where grew the tree.
    O earth, what changes hast thou seen!
    There where the long street roars, hath been
The stillness of the central sea.

7–15. They say . . . place. Another interesting reference to nineteenth-century science.   **25–28. Arise and fly
. . . tiger die.** The evolutionary hypothesis itself seemed
to Tennyson to afford a sound scientific basis for morality.

The hills are shadows, and they flow
    From form to form, and nothing stands;
    They melt like mist, the solid lands,
Like clouds they shape themselves and go.

But in my spirit will I dwell,
    And dream my dream, and hold it true;   10
    For though my lips may breathe adieu,
I cannot think the thing farewell.

124

That which we dare invoke to bless;
    Our dearest faith; our ghastliest doubt;
    He, They, One, All; within, without;
The Power in darkness whom we guess;

I found Him not in world or sun,
    Or eagle's wing, or insect's eye;
    Nor through the questions men may try,
The petty cobwebs we have spun:

If e'er when faith had fall'n asleep,
    I heard a voice "believe no more"   10
    And heard an ever-breaking shore
That tumbled in the Godless deep;

A warmth within the breast would melt
    The freezing reason's colder part,
    And like a man in wrath the heart
Stood up and answered "I have felt."

No, like a child in doubt and fear:
    But that blind clamour made me wise;
    Then was I as a child that cries,
But, crying, knows his father near;   20

And what I am beheld again
    What is, and no man understands;
    And out of darkness came the hands
That reach through nature, moulding men.

125

Whatever I have said or sung,
    Some bitter notes my harp would give,
    Yea, though there often seemed to live
A contradiction on the tongue,

Yet Hope had never lost her youth;
    She did but look through dimmer eyes;
    Or Love but played with gracious lies,
Because he felt so fixed in truth:

16. "I have felt." To Tennyson, a mystic, man is more
than his mind.

And if the song were full of care,
  He breathed the spirit of the song;   10
  And if the words were sweet and strong
He set his royal signet there;

Abiding with me till I sail
  To seek thee on the mystic deeps,
  And this electric force, that keeps
A thousand pulses dancing, fail.

126

Love is and was my Lord and King,
  And in his presence I attend
  To hear the tidings of my friend,
Which every hour his couriers bring.

Love is and was my King and Lord,
  And will be, though as yet I keep
  Within his court on earth, and sleep
Encompassed by his faithful guard,

And hear at times a sentinel
  Who moves about from place to place,   10
  And whispers to the worlds of space,
In the deep night, that all is well.

127

And all is well, though faith and form
  Be sundered in the night of fear;
  Well roars the storm to those that hear
A deeper voice across the storm,

Proclaiming social truth shall spread,
  And justice, ev'n though thrice again
  The red fool-fury of the Seine
Should pile her barricades with dead.

But ill for him that wears a crown,
  And him, the lazar, in his rags: 10
  They tremble, the sustaining crags;
The spires of ice are toppled down,

And molten up, and roar in flood;
  The fortress crashes from on high,
  The brute earth lightens to the sky,
And the great Aeon sinks in blood,

And compassed by the fires of Hell;
  While thou, dear spirit, happy star,
  O'erlook'st the tumult from afar,
And smilest, knowing all is well.   20

Sec. 127. **6–8. thrice . . . dead.** There were revolutions
in France in 1789, 1830, and 1848.

128

The love that rose on stronger wings,
  Unpalsied when he met with Death,
  Is comrade of the lesser faith
That sees the course of human things.

No doubt vast eddies in the flood
  Of onward time shall yet be made,
  And throned races may degrade;
Yet O ye mysteries of good,

Wild Hours that fly with Hope and Fear,
  If all your office had to do   10
  With old results that look like new;
If this were all your mission here,

To draw, to sheathe a useless sword,
  To fool the crowd with glorious lies,
  To cleave a creed in sects and cries,
To change the bearing of a word,

To shift an arbitrary power,
  To cramp the student at his desk,
  To make old bareness picturesque
And tuft with grass a feudal tower;   20

Why then my scorn might well descend
  On you and yours. I see in part
  That all, as in some piece of art,
Is toil coöperant to an end.

129

Dear friend, far off, my lost desire,
  So far, so near in woe and weal;
  O loved the most, when most I feel
There is a lower and a higher;

Known and unknown; human, divine;
  Sweet human hand and lips and eye;
  Dear heavenly friend that canst not die,
Mine, mine, for ever, ever mine;

Strange friend, past, present, and to be;
  Loved deeplier, darklier understood;   10
  Behold, I dream a dream of good,
And mingle all the world with thee.

130

Thy voice is on the rolling air;
  I hear thee where the waters run;
  Thou standest in the rising sun,
And in the setting thou art fair.

What art thou then? I cannot guess;
    But though I seem in star and flower
    To feel thee some diffusive power,
I do not therefore love thee less:

My love involves the love before;
    My love is vaster passion now;   10
    Though mixed with God and Nature thou,
I seem to love thee more and more.

Far off thou art, but ever nigh;
    I have thee still, and I rejoice;
    I prosper, circled with thy voice;
I shall not lose thee though I die.

131

O living will that shalt endure
    When all that seems shall suffer shock,
    Rise in the spiritual rock,
Flow through our deeds and make them pure,

That we may lift from out of dust
    A voice as unto him that hears,
    A cry above the conquered years
To one that with us works, and trust,

With faith that comes of self-control,
    The truths that never can be proved   10
    Until we close with all we loved,
And all we flow from, soul in soul.

EPILOGUE

O true and tried, so well and long,
    Demand not thou a marriage lay;
    In that it is thy marriage day
Is music more than any song.

Nor have I felt so much of bliss
    Since first he told me that he loved
    A daughter of our house; nor proved
Since that dark day a day like this;

Though I since then have numbered o'er
    Some thrice three years: they went and came,   10
    Remade the blood and changed the frame,
And yet is love not less, but more;

Sec. 131. **1. living will,** free will.   **3. spiritual rock,** Christ.
See 1 Corinthians 10:4. *Epilogue.* This is a nuptial song for
Cecilia Tennyson and Edmund Low Lushington. Beginning
with a funeral, *In Memoriam* ends "cheerfully," as Tennyson intended, with a wedding. **6. he,** Hallam, who was engaged to Emily Tennyson. **8. that dark day,** Hallam's
death day.

No longer caring to embalm
    In dying songs a dead regret,
    But like a statue solid-set,
And moulded in colossal calm.

Regret is dead, but love is more
    Than in the summers that are flown,
    For I myself with these have grown
To something greater than before;   20

Which makes appear the songs I made
    As echoes out of weaker times,
    As half but idle brawling rhymes,
The sport of random sun and shade.

But where is she, the bridal flower,
    That must be made a wife ere noon?
    She enters, glowing like the moon
Of Eden on its bridal bower:

On me she bends her blissful eyes
    And then on thee; they meet thy look   30
    And brighten like the star that shook
Betwixt the palms of paradise.

O when her life was yet in bud,
    He too foretold the perfect rose.
    For thee she grew, for thee she grows
For ever, and as fair as good.

And thou art worthy; full of power;
    As gentle; liberal-minded, great,
    Consistent; wearing all that weight
Of learning lightly like a flower.   40

But now set out: the noon is near,
    And I must give away the bride;
    She fears not, or with thee beside
And me behind her, will not fear.

For I that danced her on my knee,
    That watched her on her nurse's arm,
    That shielded all her life from harm
At last must part with her to thee;

Now waiting to be made a wife,
    Her feet, my darling, on the dead;   50
    Their pensive tablets round her head,
And the most living words of life

31–32. brighten . . . paradise. An echo of Catullus,
Ode 64, l. 206.   **40. learning.** Lushington was a professor of
Greek.   **50. Her feet . . . on the dead.** In English
churches the dead are often buried beneath the pavement.

Breathed in her ear. The ring is on,
  The "wilt thou" answered, and again
  The "wilt thou" asked, till out of twain
Her sweet "I will" has made you one.

Now sign your names, which shall be read,
  Mute symbols of a joyful morn,
  By village eyes as yet unborn;
The names are signed, and overhead   60

Begins the clash and clang that tells
  The joy to every wandering breeze;
  The blind wall rocks, and on the trees
The dead leaf trembles to the bells.

O happy hour, and happier hours
  Await them. Many a merry face
  Salutes them—maidens of the place,
That pelt us in the porch with flowers.

O happy hour, behold the bride
  With him to whom her hand I gave.   70
  They leave the porch, they pass the grave
That has to-day its sunny side.

To-day the grave is bright for me,
  For them the light of life increased,
  Who stay to share the morning feast,
Who rest to-night beside the sea.

Let all my genial spirits advance
  To meet and greet a whiter sun;
  My drooping memory will not shun
The foaming grape of eastern France.   80

It circles round, and fancy plays,
  And hearts are warmed and faces bloom,
  As drinking health to bride and groom
We wish them store of happy days.

Nor count me all to blame if I
  Conjecture of a stiller guest,
  Perchance, perchance, among the rest,
And, though in silence, wishing joy.

But they must go, the time draws on,
  And those white-favoured horses wait;   90
  They rise, but linger; it is late;
Farewell, we kiss, and they are gone.

A shade falls on us like the dark
  From little cloudlets on the grass,
  But sweeps away as out we pass
To range the woods, to roam the park,

Discussing how their courtship grew,
  And talk of others that are wed,
  And how she looked, and what he said,
And back we come at fall of dew.   100

Again the feast, the speech, the glee,
  The shade of passing thought, the wealth
  Of words and wit, the double health,
The crowning cup, the three-times-three,

And last the dance;—till I retire:
  Dumb is that tower which spake so loud,
  And high in heaven the streaming cloud,
And on the downs a rising fire:

And rise, O moon, from yonder down,
  Till over down and over dale   110
  All night the shining vapour sail
And pass the silent-lighted town,

The white-faced halls, the glancing rills,
  And catch at every mountain head,
  And o'er the friths that branch and spread
Their sleeping silver through the hills;

And touch with shade the bridal doors,
  With tender gloom the roof, the wall;
  And breaking let the splendour fall
To spangle all the happy shores   120

By which they rest, and ocean sounds,
  And, star and system rolling past,
  A soul shall draw from out the vast
And strike his being into bounds,

And, moved through life of lower phase,
  Result in man, be born and think,
  And act and love, a closer link
Betwixt us and the crowning race

Of those that, eye to eye, shall look
  On knowledge; under whose command   130
  Is Earth and Earth's, and in their hand
Is Nature like an open book;

No longer half-akin to brute,
  For all we thought and loved and did,
  And hoped, and suffered, is but seed
Of what in them is flower and fruit;

Whereof the man, that with me trod
  This planet, was a noble type
  Appearing ere the times were ripe,
That friend of mine who lives in God,   140

That God, which ever lives and loves,
    One God, one law, one element,
    And one far-off divine event,
To which the whole creation moves.

THE EAGLE

FRAGMENT

He clasps the crag with crooked hands;
Close to the sun in lonely lands,
Ringed with the azure world, he stands.

The wrinkled sea beneath him crawls;
He watches from his mountain walls,
And like a thunderbolt he falls.

from MAUD

Maud, a Monodrama, 1855, was one of Tennyson's favorites among his poems; "a little *Hamlet*," he called it. He
loved to read aloud to his visitors—Henry James says that
when he read his poems he took more out of them that he
had put into them in writing—and *Maud* was the poem he
generally chose. Though the work has some astonishing
technical merits, it has never been generally liked. Its
morbidness, the role insanity plays in it, the jingoism of
the Crimean War episode, all make a wholly disinterested criticism difficult. But, as in the case of *The Princess*,
there can be no question as to the lyrics. "Come into the
garden, Maud" has been set to music by Balfe (see
John McCormack's recording, Victor 6202).

O LET THE SOLID GROUND

1

O let the solid ground
    Not fail beneath my feet
Before my life has found
    What some have found so sweet;
Then let come what come may,
What matter if I go mad,
I shall have had my day.

2

Let the sweet heavens endure,
    Not close and darken above me
Before I am quite quite sure   10
    That there is one to love me;
Then let come what come may
To a life that has been so sad,
I shall have had my day.

GO NOT, HAPPY DAY

Go not, happy day,
    From the shining fields,
Go not, happy day,
    Till the maiden yields.
Rosy is the West,
    Rosy is the South,
Roses are her cheeks,
    And a rose her mouth.
When the happy Yes
    Falters from her lips,   10
Pass and blush the news
    Over glowing ships;
Over blowing seas,
    Over seas at rest,
Pass the happy news,
    Blush it through the West;
Till the red man dance
    By his red cedar-tree,
And the red man's babe
    Leap, beyond the sea.   20
Blush from West to East,
    Blush from East to West,
Till the West is East,
    Blush it through the West.
Rosy is the West,
    Rosy is the South,
Roses are her cheeks,
    And a rose her mouth.

COME INTO THE GARDEN, MAUD

1

Come into the garden, Maud,
    For the black bat, night, has flown,
Come into the garden, Maud,
    I am here at the gate alone;
And the woodbine spices are wafted abroad,
    And the musk of the rose is blown.

2

For a breeze of morning moves,
    And the planet of Love is on high,
Beginning to faint in the light that she loves
    On a bed of daffodil sky,   10
To faint in the light of the sun she loves,
    To faint in his light, and to die.

3

All night have the roses heard
    The flute, violin, bassoon;
All night has the casement jessamine stirred
    To the dancers dancing in tune;
Till a silence fell with the waking bird,
    And a hush with the setting moon.

4

I said to the lily, "There is but one
  With whom she has heart to be gay.   20
When will the dancers leave her alone?
  She is weary of dance and play."
Now half to the setting moon are gone,
  And half to the rising day;
Low on the sand and loud on the stone
  The last wheel echoes away.

5

I said to the rose, "The brief night goes
  In babble and revel and wine.
O young lord-lover, what sighs are those,
  For one that will never be thine?   30
But mine, but mine," so I sware to the rose,
  "For ever and ever, mine."

6

And the soul of the rose went into my blood,
  As the music clashed in the hall;
And long by the garden lake I stood,
  For I heard your rivulet fall
From the lake to the meadow and on to the wood,
  Our wood, that is dearer than all;

7

From the meadow your walks have left so sweet
  That whenever a March-wind sighs   40
He sets the jewel-print of your feet
  In violets blue as your eyes,
To the woody hollows in which we meet
  And the valleys of Paradise.

8

The slender acacia would not shake
  One long milk-bloom on the tree;
The white lake-blossom fell into the lake
  As the pimpernel dozed on the lea;
But the rose was awake all night for your sake,
  Knowing your promise to me;   50
The lilies and roses were all awake,
  They sighed for the dawn and thee.

9

Queen rose of the rosebud garden of girls,
  Come hither, the dances are done,
In gloss of satin and glimmer of pearls,
  Queen lily and rose in one;
Shine out, little head, sunning over with curls,
  To the flowers, and be their sun.

10

There has fallen a splendid tear
  From the passion-flower at the gate.   60
She is coming, my dove, my dear;
  She is coming, my life, my fate;
The red rose cries, "She is near, she is near";
  And the white rose weeps, "She is late";
The larkspur listens, "I hear, I hear";
  And the lily whispers, "I wait."

11

She is coming, my own, my sweet;
  Were it ever so airy a tread,
My heart would hear her and beat,
  Were it earth in an earthy bed;   70
My dust would hear her and beat,
  Had I lain for a century dead;
Would start and tremble under her feet,
  And blossom in purple and red.

O THAT 'TWERE POSSIBLE

1

O that 'twere possible
After long grief and pain
To find the arms of my true love
Round me once again!

2

When I was wont to meet her
In the silent woody places
By the home that gave me birth,
We stood tranced in long embraces
Mixt with kisses sweeter sweeter
Than anything on earth.   10

3

A shadow flits before me,
Not thou, but like to thee:
Ah Christ, that it were possible
For one short hour to see
The souls we loved, that they might tell us
What and where they be.

4

It leads me forth at evening,
It lightly winds and steals
In a cold white robe before me,
When all my spirit reels   20
At the shouts, the leagues of lights,
And the roaring of the wheels.

5

Half the night I waste in sighs,
Half in dreams I sorrow after
The delight of early skies;
In a wakeful doze I sorrow
For the hand, the lips, the eyes,
For the meeting of the morrow,
The delight of happy laughter,
The delight of low replies.   30

6

'Tis a morning pure and sweet,
And a dewy splendour falls
On the little flower that clings
To the turrets and the walls;
'Tis a morning pure and sweet,
And the light and shadow fleet;
She is walking in the meadow,
And the woodland echo rings;
In a moment we shall meet;
She is singing in the meadow   40
And the rivulet at her feet
Ripples on in light and shadow
To the ballad that she sings.

7

Do I hear her sing as of old,
My bird with the shining head,
My own dove with the tender eye?
But there rings on a sudden a passionate cry,
There is some one dying or dead,
And a sullen thunder is rolled;
For a tumult shakes the city,   50
And I wake, my dream is fled;
In the shuddering dawn, behold,
Without knowledge, without pity,
By the curtains of my bed
That abiding phantom cold.

8

Get thee hence, nor come again,
Mix not memory with doubt,
Pass, thou deathlike type of pain,
Pass and cease to move about!
'Tis the blot upon the brain   60
That *will* show itself without.

9

Then I rise, the eavedrops fall,
And the yellow vapours choke
The great city sounding wide;
The day comes, a dull red ball
Wrapt in drifts of lurid smoke
On the misty river-tide.

10

Through the hubbub of the market
I steal, a wasted frame;
It crosses here, it crosses there,   70
Through all that crowd confused and loud,
The shadow still the same;
And on my heavy eyelids
My anguish hangs like shame.

11

Alas for her that met me,
That heard me softly call,
Came glimmering through the laurels
At the quiet evenfall,
In the garden by the turrets
Of the old manorial hall.   80

12

Would the happy spirit descend,
From the realms of light and song,
In the chamber or the street,
As she looks among the blest,
Should I fear to greet my friend
Or to say "Forgive the wrong,"
Or to ask her, "Take me, sweet,
To the regions of thy rest"?

13

But the broad light glares and beats,
And the shadow flits and fleets   90
And will not let me be;
And I loathe the squares and streets,
And the faces that one meets,
Hearts with no love for me:
Always I long to creep
Into some still cavern deep,
There to weep, and weep, and weep
My whole soul out to thee.

MILTON

Alcaics

One of Tennyson's several "experiments in quantity." This one is an English imitation of a form of prosody invented by the Greek Alcaeus. For Milton, see selections in Volume I of this work.

O mighty-mouthed inventor of harmonies,
O skilled to sing of Time or Eternity,
    God-gifted organ-voice of England,
        Milton, a name to resound for ages;
Whose Titan angels, Gabriel, Abdiel,

5. Gabriel, Abdiel, champions of God against Satan in Book V of *Paradise Lost.* Tennyson calls them Titans, after the giants of Greek mythology.

Starred from Jehovah's gorgeous armouries,
Tower, as the deep-domed empyrëan
Rings to the roar of an angel onset—
Me rather all that bowery loneliness,
The brooks of Eden mazily murmuring, 10
And bloom profuse and cedar arches
Charm, as a wanderer out in ocean,
Where some refulgent sunset of India
Streams o'er a rich ambrosial ocean isle,
And crimson-hued the stately palm-woods
Whisper in odorous heights of even.

NORTHERN FARMER

Old Style

This poem, in Lincolnshire dialect, developed out of
the reported words of a farm bailiff—"God A'mighty
little knows what He's about a-taking me. An' Squire
will be so mad an' all." It is one of Tennyson's few
humorous poems.

1

Wheer 'asta beän saw long and meä liggin' 'ere
aloän?
Noorse? thourt nowt o' a noorse: whoy, Doctor's
abeän an' agoän:
Says that I moänt 'a naw moor aäle: but I beänt a
fool:
Git ma my aäle, fur I beänt a-gawin' to breäk my
rule.

2

Doctors, they knaws nowt, fur a says what's naw-
ways true:
Naw soort o' koind o' use to saäy the things that a
do.
I've 'ed my point o' aäle ivry noight sin' I beän 'ere.
An' I've 'ed my quart ivry market-noight for foorty
year.

3

Parson's a beän loikewoise, an' a sittin' 'ere o' my
bed.
"The amoighty's a taäkin o' you to 'issén, my
friend," a said,   10
An' a towd ma my sins, an 's toithe were due, an' I
gied it in hond;
I done moy duty boy 'um, as I 'a done boy the
lond.

4

Larn'd a ma' beä. I reckons I 'annot sa mooch to
larn.
But a cast oop, thot a did, 'bout Bessy Marris's
barne.
Thaw a knaws I hallus voäted wi' Squoire an'
choorch an' staäte,
An' i' the woost o' toimes I wur niver agin the
raäte.

5

An' I hallus coom'd to 's chooch afoor moy Sally
wur deäd,
An' 'eärd 'um a bummin' awaäy loike a buzzard-
clock ower my 'eäd,
An' I niver knaw'd whot a meäned but I thowt a
'ad summut to saäy,
An' I thowt a said whot a owt to 'a said an' I
coom'd awaäy.   20

6

Bessy Marris's barne! tha knaws she laäid it to meä.
Mowt a beän, mayhap, for she wur a bad un, sheä.
'Siver, I kep 'um, I kep 'um, my lass, tha mun un-
derstond;
I done moy duty boy 'um, as I 'a done boy the lond.

7

But Parson a cooms an' a goäs, an' a says it eäsy an'
freeä:
"The amoighty's a taäkin o' you to 'issén, my
friend," says 'eä.
I weänt saäy men be loiars, thaw summun said it in
'aäste:
But 'e reäds wonn sarmin a weeäk, an' I 'a stubbed
Thurnaby waäste.

8

D'ya moind the waäste, my lass? naw, naw, tha was
not born then;
Theer wur a boggle in it, I often 'eärd 'um mysén;
Moäst loike a butter-bump, fur I 'eärd 'um about
an' about,   31
But I stubbed 'um oop wi' the lot, an' raäved an'
rembled 'um out.

1. Wheer . . . aloän? Where hast thou been so long and
me lying here alone? **2. Noorse? . . . noorse.** Nurse? thou
art a blockhead of a nurse. **abeän an' agoän,** been and
gone. **3. moänt 'a,** may not have. **5. a,** he. **10. 'issén,** himself. **11. towd,** told. **an 's toithe,** and his tithe. **gied,** gave.
12. moy, my. **boy 'um,** by him.

13. Larn'd a ma' beä. Learned he may be. **I 'annot sa
mooch to larn,** I'm not so much for learning. **14. a cast oop,**
he threw up (to me). **barne,** baby. **15. Thaw a knaws,**
though he knows. **hallus,** always. **16. raäte,** poor tax.
18. 'um, the clergyman. **a bummin',** buzzing. **buzzard-
clock,** cockchafer. **21. laäid it to meä,** accused me of being
its father. **22. Mowt a beän,** it may have been. **23. 'Siver,**
whatever the truth of the charge may be. **27. summun,** the psalmist. (Psalm 116:1). **28. stubbed,**
grubbed up the roots, prepared for cultivation. **29. moind,**
remember. **30. boggle,** ghost. **31. butter-bump,** bittern,
a variety of heron. **32. raäved an' rembled 'um out,**
plowed him up and threw him out.

9

Keäper's it wur; fo' they fun 'um theer a-laäid of
  'is faäce
Down i' the woild 'enemies afoor I coomed to the
  plaäce.
Noäks or Thimbleby—toäner 'ed shot 'um as deäd
  as a naäil.
Noäks wur 'anged for it oop at 'soize—but git ma
  my aäle.

10

Dubbut looök at the waäste: theer warn't not feeäd
  for a cow;
Nowt at all but bracken an' fuzz, an' looök at it
  now—
Warnt worth nowt a haäcre, an' now theer's lots
  o' feeäd,
Fourscoor yows upon it an' some on it down i'
  seeäd.   40

11

Nobbut a bit on it's left, an' I meän'd to 'a stubbed
  it at fall,
Done it ta-year I meäned, an' runned plow thruff it
  an' all,
If godamoighty an' parson 'ud nobbut let ma aloän,
Meä, wi' haäte hoonderd haäcre o' Squoire's, an'
  lond o' my oän.

12

Do godamoighty knaw what a's doing a-taäkin' o'
  meä?
I beänt wonn as saws 'ere a beän an' yonder a peä;
An' Squoire 'ull be sa mad an' all—a' dear a' dear!
And I 'a managed for Squoire coom Michaelmas
  thutty year.

13

A mowt 'a taäen owd Joänes, as 'ant not a 'aäpoth
  o' sense,
Or a mowt 'a taäen young Robins—a niver mended
  a fence: 50
But godamoighty a moost taäke meä an' taäke ma
  now
Wi' aäf the cows to cauve an' Thurnaby hoälms to
  plow!

33. Keäper's it wur. It was the ghost of the (former)
gamekeeper. fun, found.   34. 'enemies, anemones.
35. toäner, one or the other. 36. 'soize, assizes. 37. Dubbut, do but.   40. yows, ewes.   41. Nobbut, nothing but.
42. ta-year, this year. thruff, through.   44. haäte, eight.
46. wonn as saws, such a one as sows. 48. coom . . . year,
thirty years next Michaelmas (September 29).   49. A . . .
sense. He (God) might have taken old Jones who hasn't
a ha'penny worth of sense. 52. cauve, calve. hoälms, holms,
mounds of rising ground.

14

Looök 'ow quoloty smoiles when they seeäs ma a
  passin' boy,
Says to thessén, naw doubt, "what a man a beä
  sewer-loy!"
Fur they knaws what I beän to Squoire sin fust a
  coomed to the 'All;
I done moy duty by Squoire an' I done moy duty
  boy hall.

15

Squoire's i' Lunnon, an' summun I reckons 'ull 'a
  to wroite,
For whoä's to howd the lond ater meä thot muddles
  ma quoit;
Sartin-sewer I beä, thot a weänt niver give it to
  Joänes,
Naw, nor a moänt to Robins—a niver rembles the
  stoäns.   60

16

But summun 'ull come ater meä mayhap wi' 'is
  kittle o' steäm
Huzzin' an' maäzin' the blessed feälds wi' the
  Divil's oän teäm.
Sin' I mun doy I mun doy, thaw loife they says is
  sweet,
But sin' I mun doy I mun doy, for I couldn abeär to
  see it.

17

What atta stannin' theer fur, an' doesn bring ma
  the aäle?
Doctor's a 'toättler, lass, an a's hallus i' the owd
  taäle;
I weänt breäk rules fur Doctor, a knaws naw moor
  nor a floy;
Git ma my aäle I tell tha, an' if I mun doy I mun
  doy.

WAGES

Eighteen years after *In Memoriam*, immortality is still
central in Tennyson's creed. As he once put it: "There's a
something that watches over us; and our individuality
endures: that's my faith, and that's all my faith."

53. quoloty, quality.   54. thessén, themselves. sewer-loy,
surely. 55. fust, first. 57. 'ull 'a to wroite, will have
to write.   58. muddles, stumps. quoit, completely.
59. Sartin-sewer, certain-sure. weänt, won't. 61. kittle o'
steäm, steam thresher, which was just coming in. The dying
man does not hold with newfangled devices.   62. Huzzin'
an' maäzin', worrying and frightening.   63. mun doy,
must die. thaw, though.   66. 'toättler, teetotaler. a's . . .
taäle, he is always telling the same old tale, that is, you must
not drink.

Glory of warrior, glory of orator, glory of song,
  Paid with a voice flying by to be lost on an endless
    sea—
Glory of Virtue, to fight, to struggle, to right the
    wrong—
  Nay, but she aimed not at glory, no lover of glory
    she:
Give her the glory of going on, and still to be.

The wages of sin is death: if the wages of Virtue be
    dust,
  Would she have heart to endure for the life of the
    worm and the fly?
She desires no isles of the blest, no quiet seats of the
    just,
  To rest in a golden grove, or to bask in a summer
    sky:
Give her the wages of going on, and not to die.   10

THE HIGHER PANTHEISM

Tennyson here sees God in nature, but unlike the pantheist he does not permit his God to be swallowed up in nature; hence the title of this poem. See the note on *In Memoriam*, Sec. 55, and Swinburne's parody, "The High Pantheism in a Nutshell," page 859.

Tennyson was one of the founders of the Metaphysical Society of Great Britain. In his later years he was much interested in occult speculation.

The sun, the moon, the stars, the seas, the hills and
    the plains—
Are not these, O Soul, the Vision of Him who
    reigns?

Is not the Vision He? though He be not that which
    He seems?
Dreams are true while they last, and do we not live
    in dreams?

Earth, these solid stars, this weight of body and
    limb,
Are they not sign and symbol of thy division from
    Him?

Dark is the world to thee: thyself art the reason why;
For is He not all but that which has power to feel
    "I am I"?

Glory about thee, without thee; and thou fulfillest
    thy doom
Making Him broken gleams, and a stifled splendour
    and gloom.   10

Wages. **6. The wages . . . death.** See Romans 6:23.

Speak to Him thou for He hears, and Spirit with
    Spirit can meet—
Closer is He than breathing, and nearer than hands
    and feet.

God is law, say the wise; O Soul, and let us rejoice,
For if He thunder by law the thunder is yet His
    voice.

Law is God, say some: no God at all, says the
    fool;   15
For all we have power to see is a straight staff bent
    in a pool;

And the ear of man cannot hear, and the eye of man
    cannot see;
But if we could see and hear, this Vision—were it
    not He?

IN THE GARDEN AT SWAINSTON

The poem is a tribute to Tennyson's friend Sir John Simeon, who lived at Swainston. The two other friends who preceded him in death are Hallam and Henry Lushington.

Nightingales warbled without,
  Within was weeping for thee:
Shadows of three dead men
  Walked in the walks with me,
  Shadows of three dead men and thou wast one of
    the three.

Nightingales sang in his woods:
  The Master was far away:
Nightingales warbled and sang
  Of a passion that lasts but a day;
  Still in the house in his coffin the Prince of courtesy lay.   10

Two dead men have I known
  In courtesy like to thee:
Two dead men have I loved
  With a love that ever will be:
  Three dead men have I loved and thou art last of
    the three.

FLOWER IN THE CRANNIED WALL

Flower in the crannied wall,
I pluck you out of the crannies,

The Higher Pantheism. **15. says the fool.** See Psalm 14:1.

I hold you here, root and all, in my hand,
Little flower—but *if* I could understand
What you are, root and all, and all in all,
I should know what God and man is.

from THE IDYLLS OF THE KING

Tennyson's interest in King Arthur went back to his earliest years. "The Lady of Shalott" (page 475) was his first Arthurian poem; it was followed by "Sir Launcelot and Queen Guinevere," "Sir Galahad," and "Morte d'Arthur" (later taken up into "The Passing of Arthur"). At one time he seems to have planned an Arthurian drama. The general plan of the *Idylls* was first mapped out in 1855, and three poems appeared two years later. The other nine followed through the years until the last— "Balin and Balan"—came out in 1885. As they stand, the idylls are intended, in a general way, to trace the progress of the year from January to December.

Malory's *Morte d'Arthur* was the principal source, supplemented later by Lady Charlotte Guest's translation of the *Mabinogion*, a collection of Welsh tales.

The *Idylls* are allegorical, an

"old imperfect tale,
New-old, and shadowing Sense at war with Soul,"

only in a general way. In later years Tennyson complained of the critics: "They have taken my hobby, and ridden it too hard, and have explained some things too allegorically, although there is an allegorical or perhaps rather a parabolic drift in the poem."

Those who dislike Tennyson's Victorianism have generally little use for the *Idylls*. It is true that the inhabitants of Camelot as he presents them never convince us that they lived in the sixth century, but it is equally certain that he never intended them to. Seeing Arthur as the ideal Englishman, an inspiration to his countrymen in any age, the poet saw no reason why he should not present him as an incarnation of the particular ideals which appealed most strongly to Victorian gentlemen. What one thinks of the result must be determined by many factors, and one's particular attitude toward the validity of the Victorian ideal must certainly enter into it. But it would be difficult to maintain that the attempt in itself was illegitimate.

DEDICATION

These to His Memory—since he held them dear,
Perchance as finding there unconsciously
Some image of himself—I dedicate,
I dedicate, I consecrate with tears—
These Idylls.

6. is. The singular verb is used because the central idea of the poem is the unity of all life. **1. His,** of Prince Albert, consort of Queen Victoria.

And indeed He seems to me
Scarce other than my king's ideal knight,
"Who reverenced his conscience as his king;
Whose glory was, redressing human wrong;
Who spake no slander, no, nor listened to it;
Who loved one only and who clave to her—"   10
Her—over all whose realms to their last isle,
Commingled with the gloom of imminent war,
The shadow of His loss drew like eclipse,
Darkening the world. We have lost him; he is
   gone.
We know him now; all narrow jealousies
Are silent, and we see him as he moved,
How modest, kindly, all-accomplished, wise,
With what sublime repression of himself,
And in what limits, and how tenderly;
Not swaying to this faction or to that;   20
Not making his high place the lawless perch
Of winged ambitions, nor a vantage-ground
For pleasure; but through all this tract of years
Wearing the white flower of a blameless life,
Before a thousand peering littlenesses,
In that fierce light which beats upon a throne
And blackens every blot; for where is he
Who dares foreshadow for an only son
A lovelier life, a more unstained, than his?
Or how should England dreaming of *his* sons   30
Hope more for these than some inheritance
Of such a life, a heart, a mind as thine,
Thou noble Father of her Kings to be,
Laborious for her people and her poor—
Voice in the rich dawn of an ampler day—
Far-sighted summoner of War and Waste
To fruitful strifes and rivalries of peace—
Sweet nature gilded by the gracious gleam
Of letters, dear to Science, dear to Art,
Dear to thy land and ours, a Prince indeed,   40
Beyond all titles, and a household name,
Hereafter, through all times, Albert the Good.

    Break not, O woman's-heart, but still endure;
Break not, for thou art Royal, but endure,
Remembering all the beauty of that star
Which shone so close beside Thee that ye made
One light together, but has past and leaves
The Crown a lonely splendour.

6–10. Scarce other . . . to her." See "Guinevere" (*Idylls of the King*), ll. 464–79. **12. imminent war,** with the United States, 1862, averted largely through Prince Albert's efforts, one of his last public services. **15. jealousies.** There was considerable feeling against Prince Albert as a "foreigner." Only after his death was he appreciated cordially. **36–37. summoner . . . of peace.** Prince Albert was the inspiration of the Crystal Palace Exhibition of 1851. **40. thy land,** Saxe-Coburg-Gotha, Germany.

May all love,
His love, unseen but felt, o'ershadow thee,
The love of all Thy sons encompass thee,   50
The love of all Thy daughters cherish thee,
The love of all Thy people comfort thee,
Till God's love set Thee at his side again!

THE PASSING OF ARTHUR

That story which the bold Sir Bedivere,
First made and latest left of all the knights,
Told, when the man was no more than a voice
In the white winter of his age, to those
With whom he dwelt, new faces, other minds.

For on their march to westward, Bedivere,
Who slowly paced among the slumbering host,
Heard in his tent the moanings of the King:

"I found Him in the shining of the stars,
I marked Him in the flowering of His fields,   10
But in His ways with men I find Him not.
I waged His wars, and now I pass and die.
O me! for why is all around us here
As if some lesser god had made the world,
But had not force to shape it as he would,
Till the High God behold it from beyond,
And enter it, and make it beautiful?
Or else as if the world were wholly fair,
But that these eyes of men are dense and dim,
And have not power to see it as it is: 20
Perchance, because we see not to the close;—
For I, being simple, thought to work His will,
And have but stricken with the sword in vain;
And all whereon I leaned in wife and friend
Is traitor to my peace, and all my realm
Reels back into the beast, and is no more.
My God, thou hast forgotten me in my death:
Nay—God my Christ—I pass but shall not die."

Then, ere that last weird battle in the west,
There came on Arthur sleeping, Gawain killed   30
In Lancelot's war, the ghost of Gawain blown
Along a wandering wind, and past his ear
Went shrilling: "Hollow, hollow all delight!
Hail, King! to-morrow thou shalt pass away.
Farewell! there is an isle of rest for thee.
And I am blown along a wandering wind,
And hollow, hollow, hollow all delight."
And fainter onward, like wild birds that change

Their season in the night and wail their way
From cloud to cloud, down the long wind the dream
Shrilled; but in going mingled with dim cries   41
Far in the moonlit haze among the hills,
As of some lonely city sacked by night,
When all is lost, and wife and child with wail
Pass to new lords; and Arthur woke and called:
"Who spake? A dream. O light upon the wind,
Thine, Gawain, was the voice—are these dim cries
Thine? or doth all that haunts the waste and wild
Mourn, knowing it will go along with me?"

This heard the bold Sir Bedivere and spake: 50
"O me, my King, let pass whatever will,
Elves, and the harmless glamour of the field;
But in their stead thy name and glory cling
To all high places like a golden cloud
For ever; but as yet thou shalt not pass.
Light was Gawain in life, and light in death
Is Gawain, for the ghost is as the man;
And care not thou for dreams from him, but rise—
I hear the steps of Modred in the west,
And with him many of thy people, and knights   60
Once thine, whom thou hast loved, but grosser
         grown
Than heathen, spitting at their vows and thee.
Right well in heart they know thee for the King.
Arise, go forth and conquer as of old."

Then spake King Arthur to Sir Bedivere:
"Far other is this battle in the west
Whereto we move than when we strove in youth,
And brake the petty kings, and fought with Rome,
Or thrust the heathen from the Roman wall,
And shook him through the north. Ill doom is mine
To war against my people and my knights.   71
The king who fights his people fights himself.
And they my knights, who loved me once, the stroke
That strikes them dead is as my death to me.
Yet let us hence, and find or feel a way
Through this blind haze, which ever since I saw
One lying in the dust at Almesbury,
Hath folded in the passes of the world."

Then rose the King and moved his host by night,
And ever pushed Sir Modred, league by league,   80
Back to the sunset bound of Lyonnesse—
A land of old upheaven from the abyss
By fire, to sink into the abyss again;
Where fragments of forgotten peoples dwelt,

---

6. **westward,** to the battle against the rebel Modred.
24–26. **And all . . . is no more.** The end of the noble
fellowship of the Knights of the Round Table was marked by
Arthur's discovery that his queen, Guinevere, and his trusted
friend, Sir Lancelot, had betrayed him.   28. **I pass but shall
not die."** See ll. 191–92.

77. **Almesbury,** the nunnery where Guinevere had taken
refuge.   81. **Lyonnesse,** a fabled country supposed to have
embraced the Scilly Islands and part of what is now Cornwall.

And the long mountains ended in a coast
Of ever-shifting sand, and far away
The phantom circle of a moaning sea.
There the pursuer could pursue no more,
And he that fled no further fly the King;
And there, that day when the great light of heaven
Burned at his lowest in the rolling year,   91
On the waste sand by the waste sea they closed.
Nor ever yet had Arthur fought a fight
Like this last, dim, weird battle of the west.
A deathwhite mist slept over sand and sea:
Whereof the chill, to him who breathed it, drew
Down with his blood, till all his heart was cold
With formless fear; and ev'n on Arthur fell
Confusion, since he saw not whom he fought.
For friend and foe were shadows in the mist,   100
And friend slew friend not knowing whom he slew;
And some had visions out of golden youth,
And some beheld the faces of old ghosts
Look in upon the battle; and in the mist
Was many a noble deed, many a base,
And chance and craft and strength in single fights,
And ever and anon with host to host
Shocks, and the splintering spear, the hard mail
      hewn,
Shield-breakings, and the clash of brands, the crash
Of battleaxes on shattered helms, and shrieks   110
After the Christ, of those who falling down
Looked up for heaven, and only saw the mist;
And shouts of heathen and the traitor knights,
Oaths, insult, filth, and monstrous blasphemies,
Sweat, writhings, anguish, labouring of the lungs
In that close mist, and cryings for the light,
Moans of the dying, and voices of the dead.

Last, as by some one deathbed after wail
Of suffering, silence follows, or through death
Or deathlike swoon, thus over all that shore,   120
Save for some whisper of the seething seas,
A dead hush fell; but when the dolorous day
Grew drearier toward twilight falling, came
A bitter wind, clear from the North, and blew
The mist aside, and with that wind the tide
Rose, and the pale King glanced across the field
Of battle: but no man was moving there;
Nor any cry of Christian heard thereon,
Nor yet of heathen; only the wan wave
Brake in among dead faces, to and fro   130
Swaying the helpless hands, and up and down
Tumbling the hollow helmets of the fallen,
And shivered brands that once had fought with
      Rome,

90–91. when . . . lowest, at the winter solstice, about
December 22.

And rolling far along the gloomy shores
The voice of days of old and days to be.

Then spake King Arthur to Sir Bedivere,
And whiter than the mist that all day long
Had held the field of battle was the King:

"Hearest thou this great voice that shakes the
      world,
And wastes the narrow realm whereon we move,
And beats upon the faces of the dead,   141
My dead, as though they had not died for me?—
O Bedivere, for on my heart hath fall'n
Confusion, till I know not what I am,
Nor whence I am, nor whether I be king.
Behold, I seem but king among the dead."

Then spake the bold Sir Bedivere: "My King,
King everywhere! and so the dead have kings,
There also will I worship thee as King.
Yet still thy life is whole, and still I live   150
Who love thee; but who hates thee, he that brought
The heathen back among us, yonder stands,
Modred, unharmed, the traitor of thine house."

Then spake the King: "My house hath been my
      doom.
But call not thou this traitor of my house
Who hath but dwelt beneath one roof with me.
My house are rather they who sware my vows,
Yea, even while they brake them, owned me King.
And well for thee, saying in my dark hour,
When all the purport of my throne hath failed,   160
That quick or dead thou holdest me for King.
King am I, whatsoever be their cry;
And one last act of kinghood shalt thou see
Yet, ere I pass." And uttering this the King
Made at the man: then Modred smote his liege
Hard on that helm which many a heathen sword
Had beaten thin; while Arthur at one blow,
Striking the last stroke with Excalibur,
Slew him, and all but slain himself, he fell.

So all day long the noise of battle rolled   170
Among the mountains by the winter sea;
Until King Arthur's Table, man by man,
Had fall'n in Lyonnesse about their lord,
King Arthur. Then, because his wound was deep,
The bold Sir Bedivere uplifted him,
And bore him to a chapel nigh the field,
A broken chancel with a broken cross,
That stood on a dark strait of barren land:
On one side lay the Ocean, and on one
Lay a great water, and the moon was full.   180

Then spake King Arthur to Sir Bedivere:
"The sequel of to-day unsolders all
The goodliest fellowship of famous knights
Whereof this world holds record. Such a sleep
They sleep—the men I loved. I think that we
Shall never more, at any future time,
Delight our souls with talk of knightly deeds,
Walking about the gardens and the halls
Of Camelot, as in the days that were.
I perish by this people which I made,—　　　190
Though Merlin sware that I should come again
To rule once more—but, let what will be, be,
I am so deeply smitten through the helm
That without help I cannot last till morn.
Thou therefore take my brand Excalibur,
Which was my pride: for thou rememberest how
In those old days, one summer noon, an arm
Rose up from out the bosom of the lake,
Clothed in white samite, mystic, wonderful,
Holding the sword—and how I rowed across　　200
And took it, and have worn it, like a king;
And, wheresoever I am sung or told
In aftertime, this also shall be known:
But now delay not: take Excalibur,
And fling him far into the middle mere:
Watch what thou seest, and lightly bring me word."

To him replied the bold Sir Bedivere:
"It is not meet, Sir King, to leave thee thus,
Aidless, alone, and smitten through the helm—
A little thing may harm a wounded man;　　210
Yet I thy hest will all perform at full,
Watch what I see, and lightly bring thee word."

So saying, from the ruined shrine he stept,
And in the moon athwart the place of tombs,
Where lay the mighty bones of ancient men,
Old knights, and over them the sea-wind sang
Shrill, chill, with flakes of foam. He, stepping down
By zigzag paths, and juts of pointed rock,
Came on the shining levels of the lake.

There drew he forth the brand Excalibur,　　220
And o'er him, drawing it, the winter moon,
Brightening the skirts of a long cloud, ran forth
And sparkled keen with frost against the hilt;
For all the haft twinkled with diamond sparks,
Myriads of topaz-lights, and jacinth-work
Of subtlest jewellery. He gazed so long
That both his eyes were dazzled as he stood,
This way and that dividing the swift mind,
In act to throw: but at the last it seemed

Better to leave Excalibur concealed　　230
There in the many-knotted waterflags,
That whistled stiff and dry about the marge.
So strode he back slow to the wounded King.

Then spake King Arthur to Sir Bedivere:
"Hast thou performed my mission which I gave?
What is it thou hast seen? or what hast heard?"

And answer made the bold Sir Bedivere:
"I heard the ripple washing in the reeds,
And the wild water lapping on the crag."

To whom replied King Arthur, faint and pale:
"Thou hast betrayed thy nature and thy name,　241
Not rendering true answer, as beseemed
Thy fealty, nor like a noble knight;
For surer sign had followed, either hand,
Or voice, or else a motion of the mere.
This is a shameful thing for men to lie.
Yet now, I charge thee, quickly go again,
As thou art lief and dear, and do the thing
I bade thee, watch, and lightly bring me word."

Then went Sir Bedivere the second time　　250
Across the ridge, and paced beside the mere,
Counting the dewy pebbles, fixed in thought;
But when he saw the wonder of the hilt,
How curiously and strangely chased, he smote
His palms together, and he cried aloud:

"And if indeed I cast the brand away,
Surely a precious thing, one worthy note,
Should thus be lost for ever from the earth,
Which might have pleased the eyes of many men.
What good should follow this, if this were done?　260
What harm, undone? Deep harm to disobey,
Seeing obedience is the bond of rule.
Were it well to obey then, if a king demand
An act unprofitable, against himself?
The King is sick, and knows not what he does.
What record, or what relic of my lord
Should be to aftertime, but empty breath
And rumours of a doubt? But were this kept,
Stored in some treasure-house of mighty kings,
Some one might show it at a joust of arms,　　270
Saying: 'King Arthur's sword, Excalibur,
Wrought by the lonely maiden of the Lake.
Nine years she wrought it, sitting in the deeps
Upon the hidden bases of the hills.'
So might some old man speak in the aftertime
To all the people, winning reverence.
But now much honour and much fame were lost."

---

189. Camelot, the seat of Arthur's court.　**205. mere,** lake.　**211. hest,** command.

248. lief, beloved.

So spake he, clouded with his own conceit,
And hid Excalibur the second time,
And so strode back slow to the wounded King.   280

Then spoke King Arthur, breathing heavily:
"What is it thou hast seen? or what hast heard?"

And answer made the bold Sir Bedivere:
"I heard the water lapping on the crag,
And the long ripple washing in the reeds."

To whom replied King Arthur, much in wrath:
"Ah miserable and unkind, untrue,
Unknightly, traitor-hearted! Woe is me!
Authority forgets a dying king,
Laid widowed of the power in his eye   290
That bowed the will. I see thee what thou art,
For thou, the latest-left of all my knights,
In whom should meet the offices of all,
Thou wouldst betray me for the precious hilt;
Either from lust of gold, or like a girl
Valuing the giddy pleasure of the eyes.
Yet, for a man may fail in duty twice,
And the third time may prosper, get thee hence;
But, if thou spare to fling Excalibur,
I will arise and slay thee with my hands."   300

Then quickly rose Sir Bedivere, and ran,
And, leaping down the ridges lightly, plunged
Among the bulrush beds, and clutched the sword,
And strongly wheeled and threw it. The great
     brand
Made lightnings in the splendour of the moon,
And flashing round and round, and whirled in an
     arch,
Shot like a streamer of the northern morn,
Seen where the moving isles of winter shock
By night, with noises of the Northern Sea.
So flashed and fell the brand Excalibur: 310
But ere he dipt the surface, rose an arm
Clothed in white samite, mystic, wonderful,
And caught him by the hilt, and brandished him
Three times, and drew him under in the mere.
And lightly went the other to the King.

Then spoke King Arthur, drawing thicker
     breath:
"Now see I by thine eyes that this is done.
Speak out: what is it thou hast heard, or seen?"

And answer made the bold Sir Bedivere:
"Sir King, I closed mine eyelids, lest the gems   320

278. conceit, fancy.   307. streamer of the northern
morn, Aurora Borealis.   308. moving isles, icebergs.

Should blind my purpose, for I never saw,
Nor shall see, here or elsewhere, till I die,
Not though I live three lives of mortal men,
So great a miracle as yonder hilt.
Then with both hands I flung him, wheeling him;
But when I looked again, behold an arm,
Clothed in white samite, mystic, wonderful,
That caught him by the hilt, and brandished him
Three times, and drew him under in the mere."

And answer made King Arthur, breathing hard:
"My end draws nigh; 'tis time that I were gone.   331
Make broad thy shoulders to receive my weight,
And bear me to the margin; yet I fear
My wound hath taken cold, and I shall die."

So saying, from the pavement he half rose,
Slowly, with pain, reclining on his arm,
And looking wistfully with wide blue eyes
As in a picture. Him Sir Bedivere
Remorsefully regarded through his tears,
And would have spoken, but he found not words;
Then took with care, and kneeling on one knee,   341
O'er both his shoulders drew the languid hands,
And rising bore him through the place of tombs.

But, as he walked, King Arthur panted hard,
Like one that feels a nightmare on his bed
When all the house is mute. So sighed the King,
Muttering and murmuring at his ear, "Quick,
     quick!
I fear it is too late, and I shall die."
But the other swiftly strode from ridge to ridge,
Clothed with his breath, and looking, as he walked,
Larger than human on the frozen hills.   351
He heard the deep behind him, and a cry
Before. His own thought drove him like a goad.
Dry clashed his harness in the icy caves
And barren chasms, and all to left and right
The bare black cliff clanged round him, as he based
His feet on juts of slippery crag that rang
Sharp-smitten with the dint of armèd heels—
And on a sudden, lo, the level lake,
And the long glories of the winter moon!   360

Then saw they how there hove a dusky barge,
Dark as a funeral scarf from stem to stern,
Beneath them; and descending they were ware
That all the decks were dense with stately forms,
Black-stoled, black-hooded, like a dream—by these
Three Queens with crowns of gold: and from them
     rose.

366. Three Queens. Malory makes them King Arthur's
sister, Queen Morgen le Fay; the Queen of Northgales; the
Queen of the Waste Lands. When Tennyson was asked

A cry that shivered to the tingling stars,
And, as it were one voice, an agony
Of lamentation, like a wind that shrills
All night in a waste land, where no one comes,   370
Or hath come, since the making of the world.

   Then murmured Arthur, "Place me in the
      barge."
So to the barge they came. There those three
      Queens
Put forth their hands, and took the King, and wept.
But she that rose the tallest of them all
And fairest, laid his head upon her lap,
And loosed the shattered casque, and chafed his
      hands,
And called him by his name, complaining loud,
And dropping bitter tears against a brow
Striped with dark blood: for all his face was
      white
And colourless, and like the withered moon   381
Smote by the fresh beam of the springing east;
And all his greaves and cuisses dashed with drops
Of onset; and the light and lustrous curls—
That made his forehead like a rising sun
High from the dais-throne—were parched with
      dust;
Or, clotted into points and hanging loose,
Mixed with the knightly growth that fringed his
      lips.
So like a shattered column lay the King;
Not like that Arthur who, with lance in rest,   390
From spur to plume a star of tournament,
Shot through the lists at Camelot, and charged
Before the eyes of ladies and of kings.

   Then loudly cried the bold Sir Bedivere:
"Ah! my Lord Arthur, whither shall I go?
Where shall I hide my forehead and my eyes?
For now I see the true old times are dead,
When every morning brought a noble chance,
And every chance brought out a noble knight.
Such times have been not since the light that led   400
The holy Elders with the gift of myrrh.
But now the whole Round Table is dissolved
Which was an image of the mighty world;
And I, the last, go forth companionless,

whether, in the allegorical interpretation, the three queens
were to be identified as Faith, Hope, and Charity, he replied: "They mean that and they do not. They are also those
three Graces, but they are much more. I hate to be tied down
to say, 'This means that,' because the thought within the
image is much more than any one interpretation."—Hallam, Lord Tennyson, *Alfred, Lord Tennyson, a Memoir*, Macmillan, 1897.   **401. The holy Elders,** the Magi, who brought
gold and frankincense and myrrh to the infant Jesus (see
Matthew 2:1–12).

And the days darken round me, and the years,
Among new men, strange faces, other minds."

   And slowly answered Arthur from the barge:
"The old order changeth, yielding place to new,
And God fulfils himself in many ways,
Lest one good custom should corrupt the world.   410
Comfort thyself; what comfort is in me?
I have lived my life, and that which I have done
May He within himself make pure! but thou,
If thou shouldst never see my face again,
Pray for my soul. More things are wrought by
      prayer
Than this world dreams of. Wherefore, let thy voice
Rise like a fountain for me night and day.
For what are men better than sheep or goats
That nourish a blind life within the brain,
If, knowing God, they lift not hands of prayer   420
Both for themselves and those who call them friend?
For so the whole round earth is every way
Bound by gold chains about the feet of God.
But now farewell. I am going a long way
With these thou seest—if indeed I go
(For all my mind is clouded with a doubt)—
To the island-valley of Avilion;
Where falls not hail, or rain, or any snow,
Nor ever wind blows loudly; but it lies
Deep-meadowed, happy, fair with orchard lawns
And bowery hollows crowned with summer sea,   431
Where I will heal me of my grievous wound."

   So said he, and the barge with oar and sail
Moved from the brink, like some full-breasted
      swan
That, fluting a wild carol ere her death,
Ruffles her pure cold plume, and takes the flood
With swarthy webs. Long stood Sir Bedivere
Revolving many memories, till the hull
Looked one black dot against the verge of dawn,
And on the mere the wailing died away.   440

   But when that moan had passed for evermore,
The stillness of the dead world's winter dawn
Amazed him, and he groaned, "The King is gone."
And therewithal came on him the weird rhyme,
"From the great deep to the great deep he goes."

   Whereat he slowly turned and slowly clomb
The last hard footstep of that iron crag;

   408. "The old order . . . new. See "The Coming of
Arthur" (*Idylls of the King*), l. 508.   **427. Avilion,** Avalon.
435. wild carol, a reference to the old belief that the
swan sings just before her death.   **445. "From the great
deep . . . he goes."** See Merlin's prophecy, "The Coming
of Arthur," l. 410.

Thence marked the black hull moving yet, and
    cried,
"He passes to be King among the dead,
And after healing of his grievous wound   450
He comes again; but—if he come no more—
O me, be yon dark Queens in yon black boat,
Who shrieked and wailed, the three whereat we
    gazed
On that high day, when, clothed with living light,
They stood before his throne in silence, friends
Of Arthur, who should help him at his need?"

Then from the dawn it seemed there came, but
    faint
As from beyond the limit of the world,
Like the last echo born of a great cry,
Sounds, as if some fair city were one voice   460
Around a king returning from his wars.

Thereat once more he moved about, and clomb
Ev'n to the highest he could climb, and saw,
Straining his eyes beneath an arch of hand,
Or thought he saw, the speck that bare the King,
Down that long water opening on the deep
Somewhere far off, pass on and on, and go
From less to less and vanish into light.
And the new sun rose bringing the new year.

TO THE QUEEN

O loyal to the royal in thyself,
And loyal to thy land, as this to thee—
Bear witness, that rememberable day,
When, pale as yet and fever-worn, the Prince
Who scarce had plucked his flickering life again
From halfway down the shadow of the grave,
Past with thee through thy people and their love,
And London rolled one tide of joy through all
Her trebled millions, and loud leagues of man
And welcome! witness, too, the silent cry,   10
The prayer of many a race and creed, and clime—
Thunderless lightnings striking under sea
From sunset and sunrise of all thy realm,
And that true North, whereof we lately heard
A strain to shame us, "Keep you to yourselves;
So loyal is too costly! friends—your love
Is but a burthen: loose the bond, and go."
Is this the tone of empire? here the faith
That made us rulers? this, indeed, her voice

And meaning whom the roar of Hougoumont   20
Left mightiest of all peoples under heaven?
What shock has fooled her since, that she should
    speak
So feebly? wealthier—wealthier—hour by hour!
The voice of Britain, or a sinking land,
Some third-rate isle half-lost among her seas?
There rang her voice, when the full city pealed
Thee and thy Prince! The loyal to their crown
Are loyal to their own far sons, who love
Our ocean-empire with her boundless homes
For ever-broadening England, and her throne   30
In our vast Orient, and one isle, one isle,
That knows not her own greatness: if she knows
And dreads it we are fall'n.—But thou, my Queen,
Not for itself, but through thy living love
For one to whom I made it o'er his grave
Sacred, accept this old imperfect tale,
New-old, and shadowing Sense at war with Soul,
Ideal manhood closed in real man,
Rather than that gray king, whose name, a ghost,
Streams like a cloud, man-shaped, from mountain
    peak,   40
And cleaves to cairn and cromlech still; or him
Of Geoffrey's book, or him of Malleor's, one
Touched by the adulterous finger of a time
That hovered between war and wantonness,
And crownings and dethronements. Take withal
The poet's blessing, and his trust that Heaven
Will blow the tempest in the distance back
From thine and ours: for some are scared, who
    mark,
Or wisely or unwisely, signs of storm,
Waverings of every vane with every wind,   50
And wordy trucklings to the transient hour,
And fierce or careless looseners of the faith,
And Softness breeding scorn of simple life,
Or Cowardice, the child of lust for gold,
Or Labour, with a groan and not a voice,
Or Art with poisonous honey stol'n from France,
And that which knows, but careful for itself,
And that which knows not, ruling that which knows
To its own harm: the goal of this great world
Lies beyond sight: yet—if our slowly-grown   60
And crowned Republic's crowning common-sense
That saved her many times, not fail—their fears
Are morning shadows huger than the shapes

3. that rememberable day, February 27, 1872, when a
public service of thanksgiving was held at St. Paul's after the
recovery from typhoid fever of Prince Albert Edward (later
Edward VII). 12. Thunderless lightnings, cablegrams.
14–17. true North . . . and go." Some "Little England-
ers" opposed holding Canada after the addition of Manitoba
in 1869.

20. Hougoumont, Waterloo, from a château on the field.
35. one, the Prince Consort. See "Dedication," page 520.
39. gray king, King Arthur. 41. cairn . . . cromlech,
stones sacred to the Druids. 42. Geoffrey's book, *Historia
Regnum Brittaniae* by Geoffrey of Monmouth (twelfth century),
the earliest detailed story of King Arthur. Malleor's, Malory's *Morte d'Arthur*. 56. Art . . . France. A good expression of Tennyson's attitude toward contemporary French
literature.

That cast them, not those gloomier which forego
The darkness of that battle in the West,
Where all of high and holy dies away.

THE REVENGE

A Ballad of the Fleet

The sea fight commemorated in this poem took place in 1591; Tennyson's main source was Sir Walter Raleigh's *Report of the Truth of the Fight about the Isles of Azores This Last Summer.* For the hero, see A. L. Rowse, *Sir Richard Grenville of the Revenge* (Houghton Mifflin, 1937).

In *Alfred Tennyson, How To Know Him* (Bobbs-Merrill, 1917),[1] Raymond M. Alden has this interesting comment on the verse form of "The Revenge":

"At the height of Tennyson's rhythmical symphonies we should probably place the ballad of 'The Revenge.' No one, so far as I know, has ever instanced this poem under the head of 'free verse,' yet it would be very difficult to name its metrical type. Just as one is prepared to call it 'trochaic' it becomes clearly trisyllabic; just as we are sure it is 'anapaestic' it falls back into the rhythm of twos or fours which carries Sir Richard's final march:

And the stately Spanish men to their flagship bore him then,
Where they laid him by the mast, old Sir Richard caught at last.

Lovers of verse form may profitably study it in a hundred details,—the extraordinary effect produced by the sudden opening on a bold accent in stanza six:

Thousands of their soldiers looked down from their decks and laughed;

the change of movement, strikingly orchestral in effect, for the sunset scene of stanza nine:

And the sun went down, and the stars came out far over the summer sea;

the glorious emphasis obtained by the unexpected media pause and rhyme in the hero's last words,

'With a joyful spirit I, Sir Richard Grenville, die;'

and the hurrying, windy epilogue which dismisses the whole Armada to destruction. It is all a metrical *tour de force* (not to speak here of its more inward qualities) which defies both conventional critic and uncrafty imitator."

1

At Flores in the Azores Sir Richard Grenville lay,
And a pinnace, like a fluttered bird, came flying from far away:

[1] Used by special permission of The Bobbs-Merrill Company.

"Spanish ships of war at sea! we have sighted fifty-three!"
Then sware Lord Thomas Howard: "'Fore God I am no coward;
But I cannot meet them here, for my ships are out of gear,
And the half my men are sick. I must fly, but follow quick.
We are six ships of the line; can we fight with fifty-three?"

2

Then spake Sir Richard Grenville: "I know you are no coward;
You fly them for a moment to fight with them again.
But I've ninety men and more that are lying sick ashore.   10
I should count myself the coward if I left them, my Lord Howard,
To these Inquisition dogs and the devildoms of Spain."

3

So Lord Howard past away with five ships of war that day,
Till he melted like a cloud in the silent summer heaven;
But Sir Richard bore in hand all his sick men from the land
Very carefully and slow,
Men of Bideford in Devon,
And we laid them on the ballast down below;
For we brought them all aboard,
And they blest him in their pain, that they were not left to Spain,   20
To the thumbscrew and the stake, for the glory of the Lord.

4

He had only a hundred seamen to work the ship and to fight,
And he sailed away from Flores till the Spaniard came in sight,
With his huge sea-castles heaving upon the weather bow.
"Shall we fight or shall we fly?
Good Sir Richard, tell us now,
For to fight is but to die!
There'll be little of us left by the time this sun be set."

7. ships of the line, fighting ships. **12. Inquisition.** The special function of the "holy office" was to deal with cases of heresy. It was especially active in Spain. **17. Bideford,** Grenville's birthplace. It plays a considerable part in Kingsley's novel of the Elizabethan sea rovers, *Westward Ho!* **21. To . . . the Lord,** that is, to the Inquisition.

And Sir Richard said again: "We be all good English men.
Let us bang these dogs of Seville, the children of the
devil,   30
For I never turned my back upon Don or devil
yet."

5

Sir Richard spoke and he laughed, and we roared a
hurrah, and so
The little Revenge ran on sheer into the heart of the
foe,
With her hundred fighters on deck, and her ninety
sick below;
For half of their fleet to the right and half to the left
were seen,
And the little Revenge ran on through the long sea-
lane between.

6

Thousands of their soldiers looked down from their
decks and laughed,
Thousands of their seamen made mock at the mad
little craft
Running on and on, till delayed
By their mountain-like San Philip that, of fifteen
hundred tons,   40
And up-shadowing high above us with her yawning
tiers of guns,
Took the breath from our sails, and we stayed.

7

And while now the great San Philip hung above us
like a cloud
Whence the thunderbolt will fall
Long and loud,
Four galleons drew away
From the Spanish fleet that day,
And two upon the larboard and two upon the star-
board lay,
And the battle-thunder broke from them all.

8

But anon the great San Philip, she bethought herself
and went   50
Having that within her womb that had left her ill
content;
And the rest they came aboard us, and they fought
us hand to hand,
For a dozen times they came with their pikes and
musqueteers,
And a dozen times we shook 'em off as a dog that
shakes his ears
When he leaps from the water to the land.

9

And the sun went down, and the stars came out far
over the summer sea,
But never a moment ceased the fight of the one and
the fifty-three.
Ship after ship, the whole night long, their high-
built galleons came,
Ship after ship, the whole night long, with her
battle-thunder and flame;
Ship after ship, the whole night long, drew back
with her dead and her shame.   60
For some were sunk and many were shattered, and
so could fight us no more—
God of battles, was ever a battle like this in the
world before?

10

For he said "Fight on! fight on!"
Though his vessel was all but a wreck;
And it chanced that, when half of the short summer
night was gone,
With a grisly wound to be drest he had left the
deck,
But a bullet struck him that was dressing it suddenly
dead,
And himself he was wounded again in the side and
the head,
And he said "Fight on! fight on!"

11

And the night went down, and the sun smiled out
far over the summer sea,   70
And the Spanish fleet with broken sides lay round
us all in a ring;
But they dared not touch us again, for they feared
that we still could sting,
So they watched what the end would be.
And we had not fought them in vain,
But in perilous plight were we,
Seeing forty of our poor hundred were slain,
And half of the rest of us maimed for life
In the crash of the cannonades and the desperate
strife;
And the sick men down in the hold were most of
them stark and cold,
And the pikes were all broken or bent, and the
powder was all of it spent;   80
And the masts and the rigging were lying over the
side;
But Sir Richard cried in his English pride,
"We have fought such a fight for a day and a
night
As may never be fought again!
We have won great glory, my men!

And a day less or more
At sea or ashore,
We die—does it matter when?
Sink me the ship, Master Gunner—sink her, split
  her in twain!
Fall into the hands of God, not into the hands of
  Spain!"   90

12

And the gunner said "Ay, ay," but the seamen
  made reply:
"We have children, we have wives,
And the Lord hath spared our lives.
We will make the Spaniard promise, if we yield, to
  let us go;
We shall live to fight again and to strike another
  blow."
And the lion there lay dying, and they yielded to
  the foe.

13

And the stately Spanish men to their flagship bore
  him then,
Where they laid him by the mast, old Sir Richard
  caught at last,
And they praised him to his face with their courtly
  foreign grace;
But he rose upon their decks, and he cried: 100
"I have fought for Queen and Faith like a valiant
  man and true;
I have only done my duty as a man is bound to
  do:
With a joyful spirit I Sir Richard Grenville die!"
And he fell upon their decks, and he died.

14

And they stared at the dead that had been so valiant and true,
And had holden the power and glory of Spain so
  cheap
That he dared her with one little ship and his English few;
Was he devil or man? He was devil for aught they
  knew,
But they sank his body with honour down into the
  deep,
And they manned the Revenge with a swarthier
  alien crew,   110
And away she sailed with her loss and longed for
  her own;
When a wind from the lands they had ruined awoke
  from sleep,
And the water began to heave and the weather to
  moan,

And or ever that evening ended a great gale
  blew,
And a wave like the wave that is raised by an earthquake grew,
Till it smote on their hulls and their sails and their
  masts and their flags,
And the whole sea plunged and fell on the shot-
  shattered navy of Spain,
And the little Revenge herself went down by the
  island crags
To be lost evermore in the main.

RIZPAH

17—

In the Biblical story (2 Samuel 21:1–14), God indicates his disapproval of the wrong King Saul had done
the Gibeonites by sending famine upon Israel; David,
therefore, is compelled to deliver up the sons of Rizpah
to be slain as a sacrifice. "And Rizpah . . . took sack-
cloth, and spread it for her upon the rock, from the beginning of harvest until water dropped upon them from
heaven, and suffered neither the birds of the air to rest on
them by day, nor the beasts of the field by night." When
the rains fall, it is clear that God has accepted the sacrifice; Rizpah's sons may now be taken down and buried
and their souls may find rest in Sheol.

Tennyson sees Rizpah's spirit living again in an English mother of the eighteenth century who collects the
bones of her son as they fall from the gallows where he
has been hanged in chains for robbing the mail, because
she wants him to be able to rise up whole on the Judgment Day and also because she thinks it necessary for his
salvation that he should be buried in consecrated ground.
He took the suggestion from an incident reported in a
current magazine.

"Rizpah" is one of Tennyson's great achievements; it
convinced Swinburne that the laureate was a greater
poet than Alfred de Musset. The pathos of the situation
is deepened by having the heroic mother harassed upon
her deathbed by an unsympathetic parish visitor, a
fanatical Calvinist.

For another version of the Rizpah story, see Amy
Lowell, "Dried Marjoram," in *Legends*, 1921, written independently of Tennyson's poem, which the author did
not read until afterward.

I

Wailing, wailing, wailing, the wind over land and
  sea—
And Willy's voice in the wind, "O mother, come
  out to me."
Why should he call me to-night, when he knows
  that I cannot go?
For the downs are as bright as day, and the full
  moon stares at the snow.

2

We should be seen, my dear; they would spy us out
of the town.
The loud black nights for us, and the storm rushing
over the down,
When I cannot see my own hand, but am led by the
creak of the chain,
And grovel and grope for my son till I find myself
drenched with the rain.
Anything fallen again? nay—what was there left to
fall?
I have taken them home, I have numbered the
bones, I have hidden them all.   10
What am I saying? and what are *you?* do you come
as a spy?
Falls? what falls? who knows? As the tree falls so
must it lie.

4

Who let her in? how long has she been? you—what
have you heard?
Why did you sit so quiet? you never have spoken a
word.
O—to pray with me—yes—a lady—none of their
spies—
But the night has crept into my heart, and begun to
darken my eyes.

5

Ah—you, that have lived so soft, what should *you*
know of the night,
The blast and the burning shame and the bitter
frost and the fright?
I have done it, while you were asleep—you were
only made for the day.
I have gathered my baby together—and now you
may go your way.   20

6

Nay—for it's kind of you, Madam, to sit by an old
dying wife.
But say nothing hard of my boy, I have only an
hour of life.
I kissed my boy in the prison, before he went out to
die.
"They dared me to do it," he said, and he never has
told me a lie.
I whipt him for robbing an orchard once when he
was but a child—
"The farmer dared me to do it," he said; he was
always so wild—
And idle—and couldn't be idle—my Willy—he
never could rest.
The King should have made him a soldier, he
would have been one of his best.

7

But he lived with a lot of wild mates, and they never
would let him be good;
They swore that he dare not rob the mail, and he
swore that he would;   30
And he took no life, but he took one purse, and
when all was done
He flung it among his fellows—"I'll none of it,"
said my son.

8

I came into court to the Judge and the lawyers. I
told them my tale,
God's own truth—but they killed him, they killed
him for robbing the mail.
They hanged him in chains for a show—we had
always borne a good name—
To be hanged for a thief—and then put away—isn't
that enough shame?
Dust to dust—low down—let us hide! but they set
him so high
That all the ships of the world could stare at him,
passing by.
God 'ill pardon the hell-black raven and horrible
fowls of the air,
But not the black heart of the lawyer who killed him
and hanged him there.   40

9

And the jailer forced me away. I had bid him my
last good-bye;
They had fastened the door of his cell. "O mother!"
I heard him cry.
I couldn't get back though I tried, he had some-
thing further to say,
And now I never shall know it. The jailer forced me
away.

10

Then since I couldn't but hear that cry of my boy
that was dead,
They seized me and shut me up: they fastened me
down on my bed.
"Mother, O mother!"—he called in the dark to me
year after year—
They beat me for that, they beat me—you know
that I couldn't but hear;
And then at the last they found I had grown so
stupid and still
They let me abroad again—but the creatures had
worked their will.   50

11

Flesh of my flesh was gone, but bone of my bone was
  left—
I stole them all from the lawyers—and you, will you
  call it a theft?—
My baby, the bones that had sucked me, the bones
  that had laughed and had cried—
Theirs? O no! they are mine—not theirs—they had
  moved in my side.

12

Do you think I was scared by the bones? I kissed
  'em, I buried 'em all—
I can't dig deep, I am old—in the night by the
  churchyard wall.
My Willy 'ill rise up whole when the trumpet of
  judgment 'ill sound,
But I charge you never to say that I laid him in holy
  ground.

13

They would scratch him up—they would hang him
  again on the cursed tree.
Sin? O yes—we are sinners, I know—let all that
  be,   60
And read me a Bible verse of the Lord's good will
  toward men—
"Full of compassion and mercy, the Lord"—let me
  hear it again;
"Full of compassion and mercy—long-suffering."
  Yes, O yes!
For the lawyer is born but to murder—the Saviour
  lives but to bless.
He'll never put on the black cap except for the worst
  of the worst,
And the first may be last—I have heard it in church
  —and the last may be first.
Suffering—O long-suffering—yes, as the Lord must
  know,
Year after year in the mist and the wind and the
  shower and the snow.

14

Heard, have you? what? they have told you he
  never repented his sin.
How do they know it? are *they* his mother? are *you*
  of his kin?   70
Heard! have you ever heard, when the storm on the
  downs began,
The wind that 'ill wail like a child and the sea that
  'ill moan like a man?

62. "Full . . . the Lord." See Psalm 86:15. 65. black
cap, worn by English judges in pronouncing the death sentence. 66. And the first . . . may be first. See Matthew
19:30.

15

Election, Election and Reprobation—it's all very
  well.
But I go to-night to my boy, and I shall not find him
  in Hell.
For I cared so much for my boy that the Lord has
  looked into my care,
And He means me I'm sure to be happy with Willy,
  I know not where.

16

And if *he* be lost—but to save *my* soul, that is all
  your desire:
Do you think that I care for *my* soul if my boy be
  gone to the fire?
I have been with God in the dark—go, go, you may
  leave me alone—
You never have borne a child—you are just as hard
  as a stone.   80

17

Madam, I beg your pardon! I think that you mean
  to be kind,
But I cannot hear what you say for my Willy's
  voice in the wind—
The snow and the sky so bright—he used but to call
  in the dark,
And he calls to me now from the church and not
  from the gibbet—for hark!
Nay—you can hear it yourself—it is coming—
  shaking the walls—
Willy—the moon's in a cloud——Good-night. I am
  going. He calls.

"FRATER AVE ATQUE VALE"

Row us out from Desenzano, to your Sirmione row!
So they rowed, and there we landed—"O venusta
  Sirmio!"
There to me through all the groves of olive in the
  summer glow,
There beneath the Roman ruin where the purple
  flowers grow,
Came that "Ave atque Vale" of the Poet's hopeless
  woe,
Tenderest of Roman poets nineteen-hundred years
  ago,

73. Election . . . Reprobation, a reference to the Cal-
vinistic belief that some persons are foreordained to salvation
and others to damnation. *"Frater Ave Atque Vale,"* "Brother,
Hail and Farewell," quoted from Catullus, Ode 101,
l. 10, a lament for the poet's brother. 1. Desenzano . . .
Sirmione, a town and a peninsula on Lake Gardo in the
Catullus country. 2. "O venusta Sirmio!" "O beautiful
Sirmio," quoted from Catullus.

"Frater Ave atque Vale"—as we wandered to and
    fro
Gazing at the Lydian laughter of the Garda Lake
    below
Sweet Catullus's all-but-island, olive-silvery Sirmio!

TO VIRGIL

WRITTEN AT THE REQUEST OF THE MANTUANS FOR THE NINETEENTH CENTENARY OF VIRGIL'S DEATH

1

Roman Virgil, thou that singest
    Ilion's lofty temples robed in fire,
Ilion falling, Rome arising,
    wars, and filial faith, and Dido's pyre;

2

Landscape-lover, lord of language
    more than he that sang the Works and Days,
All the chosen coin of fancy
    flashing out from many a golden phrase;

3

Thou that singest wheat and woodland,
    tilth and vineyard, hive and horse and herd;   10
All the charm of all the Muses
    often flowering in a lonely word;

4

Poet of the happy Tityrus
    piping underneath his beechen bowers;
Poet of the poet-satyr
    whom the laughing shepherd bound with flowers;

5

Chanter of the Pollio, glorying
    in the blissful years again to be,
Summers of the snakeless meadow,
    unlaborious earth and oarless sea;   20

6

Thou that seëst Universal
    Nature moved by Universal Mind;
Thou majestic in thy sadness
    at the doubtful doom of human kind;

"*Frater Ave atque Vale*" **8. Lydian laughter.** The inhabitants of this region were supposed to have come from Lydia.
See Catullus's "*O Lydiae lacus undae, Ridete.*" **1–4. singest
. . . Dido's pyre.** The references are to the *Aeneid.* **6. he
that sang,** Hesiod. **9–12. singest . . . lonely word.** The
references are to Virgil as the poet of the *Georgics.*
13. Tityrus, in *Eclogues,* I. **15. poet-satyr,** in *Eclogues,* VI.
17. Pollio, in *Eclogues,* IV. **21–28. Thou that seëst . . .
rise no more.** The references are to the *Aeneid,* Book VI.

7

Light among the vanished ages;
    star that gildest yet this phantom shore;
Golden branch amid the shadows,
    kings and realms that pass to rise no more;

8

Now thy Forum roars no longer,
    fallen every purple Caesar's dome—   30
Though thine ocean-roll of rhythm
    sound for ever of Imperial Rome—

9

Now the Rome of slaves hath perished,
    and the Rome of freemen holds her place,
I, from out the Northern Island
    sundered once from all the human race,

10

I salute thee, Mantovano,
    I that loved thee since my day began,
Wielder of the stateliest measure
    ever moulded by the lips of man.   40

MERLIN AND THE GLEAM

Merlin, King Arthur's great magician, is here the
poet; The Gleam is "the higher poetic imagination." The
poem is a poetical autobiography. Among the clearest
references are those in stanza 3 to the unfavorable reception of Tennyson's early poems, in stanza 5 to the
"English Idyls," in stanza 6 to the Arthurian poems, and
in stanza 7 to the death of another Arthur, Hallam. For
purposes of climax Tennyson departs here from the actual
order; Hallam's death, of course, long antedated the
Idylls of the King.

1

O young Mariner,
You from the haven
Under the sea-cliff,
You that are watching
The gray Magician
With eyes of wonder,
I am Merlin,
And *I* am dying,
I am Merlin
Who follow The Gleam.   10

2

Mighty the Wizard
Who found me at sunrise

29. Forum, the Roman market place.   **37. Mantovano.**
Virgil was born in Mantua.

Sleeping, and woke me
And learned me Magic!
Great the Master,
And sweet the Magic,
When over the valley,
In early summers,
Over the mountain,
On human faces,   20
And all around me,
Moving to melody,
Floated The Gleam.

3

Once at the croak of a Raven who crost it,
A barbarous people,
Blind to the magic,
And deaf to the melody,
Snarled at and cursed me.
A demon vext me,
The light retreated,   30
The landskip darkened,
The melody deadened,
The Master whispered
"Follow The Gleam."

4

Then to the melody,
Over a wilderness
Gliding, and glancing at
Elf of the woodland,
Gnome of the cavern,
Griffin and Giant,   40
And dancing of Fairies
In desolate hollows,
And wraiths of the mountain,
And rolling of dragons
By warble of water,
Or cataract music
Of falling torrents,
Flitted The Gleam.

5

Down from the mountain
And over the level,   50
And streaming and shining on
Silent river,
Silvery willow,
Pasture and plowland,
Innocent maidens,
Garrulous children,
Homestead and harvest,
Reaper and gleaner,
And rough-ruddy faces

Of lowly labour,   60
Slided The Gleam—

6

Then, with a melody
Stronger and statelier,
Led me at length
To the city and palace
Of Arthur the king;
Touched at the golden
Cross of the churches,
Flashed on the Tournament,
Flickered and bickered   70
From helmet to helmet,
And last on the forehead
Of Arthur the blameless
Rested The Gleam.

7

Clouds and darkness
Closed upon Camelot;
Arthur had vanished
I knew not whither,
The king who loved me,
And cannot die;   80
For out of the darkness
Silent and slowly
The Gleam, that had waned to a wintry glimmer
On icy fallow
And faded forest,
Drew to the valley
Named of the shadow,
And slowly brightening
Out of the glimmer,
And slowly moving again to a melody   90
Yearningly tender,
Fell on the shadow,
No longer a shadow,
But clothed with The Gleam.

8

And broader and brighter
The Gleam flying onward,
Wed to the melody,
Sang through the world;
And slower and fainter,
Old and weary,   100
But eager to follow,
I saw, whenever
In passing it glanced upon
Hamlet or city,
That under the Crosses
The dead man's garden,

The mortal hillock,
Would break into blossom;
And so to the land's
Last limit I came——   110
And can no longer,
But die rejoicing,
For through the Magic
Of Him the Mighty,
Who taught me in childhood,
There on the border
Of boundless Ocean,
And all but in Heaven
Hovers The Gleam.

9

Not of the sunlight,   120
Not of the moonlight,
Not of the starlight!
O young Mariner,
Down to the haven,
Call your companions,
Launch your vessel,
And crowd your canvas,
And, ere it vanishes
Over the margin,
After it, follow it,   130
Follow The Gleam.

BY AN EVOLUTIONIST

The Lord let the house of a brute to the soul of a
    man,
    And the man said "Am I your debtor?"
And the Lord—"Not yet: but make it as clean as
    you can,
    And then I will let you a better."

I

If my body come from brutes, my soul uncertain, or
    a fable,
    Why not bask amid the senses while the sun of
    morning shines,
I, the finer brute rejoicing in my hounds, and in my
    stable,
    Youth and Health, and birth and wealth, and
    choice of women and of wines?

2

What hast thou done for me, grim Old Age, save
    breaking my bones on the rack?
    Would I had past in the morning that looks so
    bright from afar!   10

OLD AGE

Done for thee? starved the wild beast that was linkt
    with thee eighty years back.
    Less weight now for the ladder-of-heaven that
    hangs on a star.

I

If my body come from brutes, though somewhat
    finer than their own,
    I am heir, and this my kingdom. Shall the royal
    voice be mute?
No, but if the rebel subject seek to drag me from the
    throne,
    Hold the sceptre, Human Soul, and rule thy
    Province of the brute.

2

I have climbed to the snows of Age, and I gaze at a
    field in the Past,
    Where I sank with the body at times in the
    sloughs of a low desire,
But I hear no yelp of the beast, and the Man is quiet
    at last
    As he stands on the heights of his life with a
    glimpse of a height that is higher.   10

FAR—FAR—AWAY

(For Music)

What sight so lured him through the fields he knew
As where earth's green stole into heaven's own hue,
                    Far—far—away?

What sound was dearest in his native dells?
The mellow lin-lan-lone of evening bells
                    Far—far—away.

What vague world-whisper, mystic pain or joy,
Through those three words would haunt him when
    a boy,
                    Far—far—away?

A whisper from his dawn of life? a breath   10
From some fair dawn beyond the doors of death
                    Far—far—away?

Far, far, how far? from o'er the gates of Birth,
The faint horizons, all the bounds of earth,
                    Far—far—away?

What charm in words, a charm no words could
    give?
O dying words, can Music make you live
                    Far—far—away?

JUNE BRACKEN AND HEATHER[1]

To ———

There on the top of the down,
The wild heather round me and over me June's
  high blue,
When I looked at the bracken so bright and the
  heather so brown,
I thought to myself I would offer this book to you,
This, and my love together,
To you that are seventy-seven,
With a faith as clear as the heights of the June-blue
  heaven,
And a fancy as summer-new
As the green of the bracken amid the gloom of the
  heather.

CROSSING THE BAR

In this poem, which, at his own request, is placed at
the end of his collected poems, Tennyson describes death
in terms of a sea voyage. A bar is any bank of sand, gravel,
or the like across the mouth of a river; it is generally
advisable to take the bar when there is plenty of water
over it. The poet is embarking for the otherworld; the
tide is full, but is now ebbing back to the sea. After taking
the ship out across the bar the pilot drops off and returns
to his station on land; at this time, a passenger might well
expect to see him "face to face." Ordinarily no such desire would be felt very strongly, but Tennyson uses the
term to indicate "That Divine and Unseen Who is always
guiding us."

Sunset and evening star,
  And one clear call for me!
And may there be no moaning of the bar,
  When I put out to sea,

But such a tide as moving seems asleep,
  Too full for sound and foam,
When that which drew from out the boundless deep
  Turns again home.

Twilight and evening bell,
  And after that the dark!   10
And may there be no sadness of farewell,
  When I embark;

For though from out our bourne of Time and **Place**
  The flood may bear me far,
I hope to see my Pilot face to face
  When I have crost the bar.

Robert Browning
1812–1889

Robert Browning was born at Camberwell, just
across the Thames from London, May 7, 1812. His
relations with his father were much like Milton's
with his. His mother, who was of Scotch and German ancestry, influenced especially his love of
music, his interest in fauna and flora, and his religion. The elder Robert Browning, having displeased his family by objecting to the use of slave
labor on the family plantation in the West Indies,
had been left to make his own way in the Bank of
England. This did not prevent him from collecting
a library of six thousand well-chosen volumes in
many languages, almost all of which his son devoured at an early age. Though Browning had
many tutors in language, science, and music, he
attended school but seldom. Oxford and Cambridge were not open to Dissenters in his day, and
less than a year at the new University of London

was enough. "Italy was my university," he once
said, but he had another which was more important—his father's library. Browning never found it
possible to realize that he was a learned man, and
his celebrated obscurity is due largely to this inability. *Sordello* alienated English readers for many
years; even Mrs. Carlyle was not sure whether it
was the name of a man or of a city or of a book. Yet
it was inevitable that Browning should write *Sordello*. The intimate details of the Guelph-Ghibelline
struggles were as plain as the palm of his hand to
him; how should he know that they were not perfectly familiar to others also?

Browning's first poetic passion was for Byron, but
of the unpublished volume *Incondita*, which testifies
to this influence, little has survived. Byron was
superseded by Shelley, who appears clearly in
Pauline, 1833. In this extremely uncharacteristic
work, Browning manifests the very young man's
intense preoccupation with himself, conducting, as

[1] From *Death of Oenone*, reprinted by permission of The
Macmillan Company. *To* ———, to Mrs. Tennyson.

it were, his spiritual ablutions in public. This was a mistake he was never to make again. *Paracelsus*, 1835, marks the beginning of the true Browning.

In 1837, Browning's play, *Strafford*, was produced by W. C. Macready; five years later, the same great actor-manager brought out *A Blot in the 'Scutcheon*. The usual view with regard to Browning's plays is that they were mere preparation for his dramatic monologues, that while he had great skill in developing a situation, he could never have mastered the practical requirements of playwrighting. Yet even as the record stands Browning has not failed on the boards anything like so completely as is often assumed. The production of *In a Balcony* in New York in 1900 was successful enough so that it went on the road and played into the summer of 1901, and Julia Marlowe had some success with *Colombe's Birthday*. It is interesting also to note that in the early days of the motion picture D. W. Griffith made several films from Browning sources for the Biograph Company; *Pippa Passes* attracted much attention in 1909 as a pioneer attempt to develop an "artistic" film.

In 1841 Browning found himself with three plays on his hands—*Pippa Passes, King Victor and King Charles*, and *The Return of the Druses*. Edward Moxon agreed to publish these, as well as a series of poems, in cheap pamphlet form. The ensuing series of pamphlets was called *Bells and Pomegranates*, 1841–46. About the time publication was completed Browning married Elizabeth Barrett (see the introductory note to Mrs. Browning's poems) and went to live in Italy.

In 1849 the first edition of Browning's *Collected Poems* came out. This was followed in 1850 by *Christmas Eve and Easter Day*, in 1855 by *Men and Women*. Though *Men and Women* contained some of his very finest poems, Browning had not yet found his public; he did not publish another book for nine years. After the death of Mrs. Browning in 1861, he returned to London with their only child.

Now, after a period of painful readjustment to life, Browning entered upon his final phase as Henry James's "accomplished, saturated, sane, sound man of the London world and the world of culture." In 1864 he published *Dramatis Personae*. In 1868, the six-volume edition of his *Collected Poems* appeared, and at the same time he earned a wider hearing with *The Ring and the Book*, his greatest achievement.

Like Tennyson, Browning was immensely productive during his later years, but with the exception of the two series of *Dramatic Idyls*, 1879–80, few of the poems he wrote during this period are now

widely read. His work during these years was both increasingly obscure and increasingly addicted to metaphysical speculation. *Asolando*, 1889, was his last book.

By this time Browning had received the D.C.L. from Oxford, and Dr. Furnivall had founded the Browning Society. After long neglect, the poet was now a classic in his own lifetime; he carried his wrongs bravely and his honors lightly. The Browning Society became a veritable symbol of late nineteenth-century culture all over the English-speaking world. At the height of his fame, Browning died in Venice, December 12, 1889.

Although it took Browning longer to win his place among the Victorian giants than it took Tennyson, he now stands even more secure. To be sure, he would not approve of all his admirers. To value him merely for his cacophonies, his bold and skillful versification, his deliberate sacrifice of melody to drama, his tendency to stress psychology at the expense of sensuous beauty—this, he would feel, is to get it all but the point. Browning's real significance, like that of every really great writer, is a spiritual significance; he made one of the most exciting affirmations in the history of English poetry. A famous American singer once declared that if she could so live that those who came in touch with her felt encouragement and enrichment, that was all she asked of life. That was how Browning lived and wrote, and even those who are not fortunate enough to share his faith in all its aspects must respond in spite of themselves to his tremendous enthusiasm.

from PIPPA PASSES

The song of the little silk-weaver in the drama *Pippa Passes*, a study in unconscious influence, is generally taken as an expression of Browning's own optimism. Though it is unfair to take any dramatic utterance out of its context and attribute it to the poet personally, the spirit of these lines is not uncharacteristic of Browning. In its musical setting by Mrs. H. H. Beach, "The Year's at the Spring" has been sung by many distinguished singers, among them Madame Emma Eames (Victor record 88008).

> The year's at the spring
> And day's at the morn;
> Morning's at seven;
> The hill-side's dew-pearled;
> The lark's on the wing;
> The snail's on the thorn:
> God's in his heaven—
> All's right with the world!

CAVALIER TUNES

3. BOOT AND SADDLE

Browning wrote three dramatic lyrics from the point of view of King Charles I's supporters in the English Civil War. The speakers are imaginary characters.

Boot, saddle, to horse, and away!
Rescue my castle before the hot day
Brightens to blue from its silvery grey,
    CHORUS.—*Boot, saddle, to horse, and away!*

Ride past the suburbs, asleep as you'd say;
Many's the friend there, will listen and pray
"God's luck to gallants that strike up the lay—
    CHORUS.—*Boot, saddle, to horse, and away!*"

Forty miles off, like a roebuck at bay,
Flouts Castle Brancepeth the Roundheads' array:
Who laughs, "Good fellows ere this, by my fay,   11
    CHORUS.—*Boot, saddle, to horse, and away!*"

Who? My wife Gertrude; that, honest and gay,
Laughs when you talk of surrendering, "Nay!
I've better counsellors; what counsel they?
    CHORUS.—*Boot, saddle, to horse, and away!*"

SOLILOQUY OF THE SPANISH CLOISTER

In this shocking and amusing monologue we hear the voice of a man who has "fallen in hate." The easily contented, somewhat puttering, probably not too intelligent Brother Lawrence gets "on the nerves" of the speaker. Being cloistered, he cannot escape from the object of his detestation, and his hatred has poisoned his whole life. In stanza 4 he imputes his own sensuality to Lawrence; in stanza 5 he bolsters his own egoism with the reminder that he is a better formalist than the other man. In stanzas 7 and 8 he speculates on the possibility of tricking Lawrence out of his salvation; note the implicit admission that unless he is tricked, Lawrence is sure of it. Browning leaves the construction in both stanzas incomplete grammatically, the implication being "Do you suppose I could do that?" But by the time we reach stanza 9 our speaker is desperate. He is not playing for high stakes now; he would risk his own soul to be able to destroy a rosebush.

I

Gr-r-r—there go, my heart's abhorrence!
    Water your damned flower-pots, do!

10. Roundheads, the Parliamentarians, so called because they "bobbed" their hair, instead of wearing it in long curls like the Cavaliers.

If hate killed men, Brother Lawrence,
    God's blood, would not mine kill you!
What? your myrtle-bush wants trimming?
    Oh, that rose has prior claims—
Needs its leaden vase filled brimming?
    Hell dry you up with its flames!

2

At the meal we sit together:
    Salve tibi! I must hear   10
Wise talk of the kind of weather,
    Sort of season, time of year:
Not a plenteous cork-crop: scarcely
    Dare we hope oak-galls, I doubt:
What's the Latin name for "parsley"?
    What's the Greek name for Swine's Snout?

3

Whew! We'll have our platter burnished,
    Laid with care on our own shelf!
With a fire-new spoon we're furnished,
    And a goblet for ourself,   20
Rinsed like something sacrificial
    Ere 'tis fit to touch our chaps—
Marked with L for our initial!
    (He-he! There his lily snaps!)

4

Saint, forsooth! While brown Dolores
    Squats outside the Convent bank
With Sanchicha, telling stories,
    Steeping tresses in the tank,
Blue-black, lustrous, thick like horsehairs,
    —Can't I see his dead eye glow,   30
Bright as 'twere a Barbary corsair's?
    (That is, if he'd let it show!)

5

When he finishes refection,
    Knife and fork he never lays
Cross-wise, to my recollection,
    As do I, in Jesu's praise.
I the Trinity illustrate,
    Drinking watered orange-pulp—
In three sips the Arian frustrate;
    While he drains his at one gulp.   40

6

Oh, those melons? If he's able
    We're to have a feast! so nice!

10. Salve tibi, Hail to thee. **31. Barbary corsair,** a privateer or pirate of the Barbary coast (North Africa), not noted for sexual or any other virtues. **39. Arian.** Arius denied the equality of the Son with God the Father. The Council of Nicea (325 A.D.), where he was opposed by Athanasius, condemned his views.

One goes to the Abbot's table,
    All of us get each a slice.
How go on your flowers? None double?
    Not one fruit-sort can you spy?
Strange!—And I, too, at such trouble,
    Keep them close-nipped on the sly!

7

There's a great text in Galatians,
    Once you trip on it, entails   50
Twenty-nine distinct damnations,
    One sure, if another fails:
If I trip him just a-dying,
    Sure of heaven as sure can be,
Spin him round and send him flying
    Off to hell, a Manichee?

8

Or, my scrofulous French novel
    On grey paper with blunt type!
Simply glance at it, you grovel
    Hand and foot in Belial's gripe: 60
If I double down its pages
    At the woeful sixteenth print,
When he gathers his greengages,
    Ope a sieve and slip it in't?

9

Or, there's Satan!—one might venture
    Pledge one's soul to him, yet leave
Such a flaw in the indenture
    As he'd miss till, past retrieve,
Blasted lay that rose-acacia
    We're so proud of! *Hy, Zy, Hine* . . .   70
'St, there's Vespers! *Plena gratiâ*
    Ave, Virgo! Gr-r-r—you swine!

MY LAST DUCHESS

Ferrara

Browning varies the technique of his dramatic monologues: the Spanish monk soliloquizes, but the Duke of
Ferrara (a city near Venice) talks to the envoy with
whom he is negotiating for a bride and shows him the
portrait of his late wife.

49. text in Galatians. Galatians 3:10 (which in turn refers to Deuteronomy 28) and Galatians 5:19–21 have both
been suggested. The latter passage enumerates only seventeen sins, but one of them is heresy, the sin of which our
speaker plans to "get" Brother Lawrence. The Church
taught that the eternal state of the soul depends on its spiritual condition at the moment of death. (See Hamlet's reluctance to kill the King at prayer, *Hamlet*, Act III, sc. 3).
60. Belial's, used loosely as a synonym for Satan's. **70. Hy,
Zy, Hine,** probably indicating the sound of the vesper bells.
71–72. Plena . . . Virgo! Hail, Virgin, full of grace—a
formal prayer.

That's my last Duchess painted on the wall,
Looking as if she were alive. I call
That piece a wonder, now: Frà Pandolf's hands
Worked busily a day, and there she stands.
Will't please you sit and look at her? I said
"Frà Pandolf" by design, for never read
Strangers like you that pictured countenance,
The depth and passion of its earnest glance,
But to myself they turned (since none puts by
The curtain I have drawn for you, but I)   10
And seemed as they would ask me, if they durst,
How such a glance came there; so, not the first
Are you to turn and ask thus. Sir, 'twas not
Her husband's presence only, called that spot
Of joy into the Duchess' cheek: perhaps
Frà Pandolf chanced to say, "Her mantle laps
Over my lady's wrist too much," or "Paint
Must never hope to reproduce the faint
Half-flush that dies along her throat": such stuff
Was courtesy, she thought, and cause enough   20
For calling up that spot of joy. She had
A heart—how shall I say?—too soon made glad,
Too easily impressed: she liked whate'er
She looked on, and her looks went everywhere.
Sir, 'twas all one! My favour at her breast,
The dropping of the daylight in the West,
The bough of cherries some officious fool
Broke in the orchard for her, the white mule
She rode with round the terrace—all and each
Would draw from her alike the approving speech,
Or blush, at least. She thanked men,—good! but thanked   31
Somehow—I know not how—as if she ranked
My gift of a nine-hundred-years-old name
With anybody's gift. Who'd stoop to blame
This sort of trifling? Even had you skill
In speech—(which I have not)—to make your will
Quite clear to such an one, and say, "Just this
Or that in you disgusts me; here you miss,
Or there exceed the mark"—and if she let
Herself be lessoned so, nor plainly set   40
Her wits to yours, forsooth, and made excuse,
—E'en then would be some stooping; and I choose

3. Frà Pandolf, Brother Pandolf, an imaginary painter, a
monk.   **8. The depth . . . glance.** Spoken ironically.
9–10. since none . . . but I. The Duke is a "man of
property"; his art treasures are for him alone. Probably it
pleases him to know that he has the image of his dead wife—
as he never had the original—absolutely under his own control. The important thing is to understand that no sentiment
is indicated.   **33–34. My gift . . . anybody's gift.** Evidently the social position of the Duchess was inferior to that
of her husband.

Never to stoop. Oh sir, she smiled, no doubt,
Whene'er I passed her; but who passed without
Much the same smile? This grew; I gave com-
 mands;
Then all smiles stopped together. There she stands
As if alive. Will't please you rise? We'll meet
The company below, then. I repeat,
The Count your master's known munificence
Is ample warrant that no just pretence   50
Of mine for dowry will be disallowed;
Though his fair daughter's self, as I avowed
At starting, is my object. Nay, we'll go
Together down, sir. Notice Neptune, though,
Taming a sea-horse, thought a rarity,
Which Claus of Innsbruck cast in bronze for me!

MEETING AT NIGHT

The grey sea and the long black land;
And the yellow half-moon large and low;
And the startled little waves that leap
In fiery ringlets from their sleep,
As I gain the cove with pushing prow,
And quench its speed i' the slushy sand.

Then a mile of warm sea-scented beach;
Three fields to cross till a farm appears;
A tap at the pane, the quick sharp scratch
And blue spurt of a lighted match,   10
And a voice less loud, through its joys and
 fears,
Than the two hearts beating each to each!

PARTING AT MORNING

Round the cape of a sudden came the sea,
And the sun looked over the mountain's rim:
And straight was a path of gold for him,
And the need of a world of men for me.

45–46. I gave . . . together. When Hiram Corson asked Browning if this meant that the Duchess was put to death, he first replied affirmatively, then added, "or he might have had her shut up in a convent." In any event, he broke her heart and was responsible for her death. **53–54. Nay . . . down, sir.** Too cruel to be aware that his heartlessness has shocked the envoy, the Duke is most condescending. The two men descend the stairs side by side, as if they were equals. **54–56. Notice . . . for me. Neptune** is the god of the sea. **Claus** is an imaginary sculptor. **Innsbruck** in the Tyrol was famous for its statues. This touch completes the revelation of the Duke's character. He can turn without a qualm from one art treasure, the portrait of a woman whose life he ruined, to another which depicts a scene in mythology. **8. farm,** farmhouse, as often in British usage. *Parting at Morning.* **3. him,** the sun.

HOME–THOUGHTS, FROM ABROAD

Oh, to be in England
Now that April's there,
And whoever wakes in England
Sees, some morning, unaware,
That the lowest boughs and the brush-wood sheaf
Round the elm-tree bole are in tiny leaf,
While the chaffinch sings on the orchard bough
In England—now!

And after April, when May follows,   9
And the whitethroat builds, and all the swallows!
Hark, where my blossomed pear-tree in the hedge
Leans to the field and scatters on the clover
Blossoms and dewdrops—at the bent spray's edge—
That's the wise thrush; he sings each song twice
 over,
Lest you should think he never could recapture
The first fine careless rapture!
And though the fields look rough with hoary
 dew,
All will be gay when noontide wakes anew
The buttercups, the little children's dower
—Far brighter than this gaudy melon-flower!   20

HOME–THOUGHTS, FROM THE SEA

Nobly, nobly Cape Saint Vincent to the North-west
 died away;
Sunset ran, one glorious blood-red, reeking into
 Cadiz Bay;
Bluish 'mid the burning water, full in face Trafalgar
 lay;
In the dimmest North-east distance dawned Gibral-
 tar grand and grey;
"Here and here did England help me: how can I
 help England?"—say,
Whoso turns as I, this evening, turn to God to praise
 and pray,
While Jove's planet rises yonder, silent over Africa.

Home-thoughts, from the Sea. **1. Cape Saint Vincent,** the southwest point of Portugal, scene of an English naval victory over Spain, 1797. **2. Cadiz,** on the southwest coast of Spain, where England defeated the second Spanish Armada, 1596. **3. Trafalgar,** east of Cadiz Bay, the scene of Nelson's great victory, 1805. **4. Gibraltar,** the rock and fortress guarding the entrance to the Mediterranean, owned by England since 1713. **5. say.** Let us say, or suppose we say. Browning's argument is that true patriotism is inseparable from piety, which alone can make a nation great. **7. Jove's planet,** Jupiter.

THE BISHOP ORDERS HIS TOMB AT SAINT PRAXED'S CHURCH

Rome, 15—

"I know of no other piece of modern English, prose or poetry, in which there is so much told, as in these lines, of the Renaissance spirit,—its worldliness, inconsistency, pride, hypocrisy, ignorance of itself, love of art, of luxury, and of good Latin. It is nearly all that I have said of the central Renaissance in thirty pages of the *Stones of Venice*, put into as many lines, Browning's also being the antecedent work."—John Ruskin, *Modern Painters*, Vol. 4.

Vanity, saith the preacher, vanity!
Draw round my bed: is Anselm keeping back?
Nephews—sons mine . . . ah God, I know not!
  Well—
She, men would have to be your mother once,
Old Gandolf envied me, so fair she was!
What's done is done, and she is dead beside,
Dead long ago, and I am Bishop since,
And as she died so must we die ourselves,
And thence ye may perceive the world's a dream.
Life, how and what is it? As here I lie   10
In this state-chamber, dying by degrees,
Hours and long hours in the dead night, I ask
"Do I live, am I dead?" Peace, peace seems all.
Saint Praxed's ever was the church for peace;
And so, about this tomb of mine. I fought
With tooth and nail to save my niche, ye know:
—Old Gandolf cozened me, despite my care;
Shrewd was that snatch from out the corner South
He graced his carrion with, God curse the same!
Yet still my niche is not so cramped but thence   20
One sees the pulpit o' the epistle-side,
And somewhat of the choir, those silent seats,
And up into the aery dome where live
The angels, and a sunbeam's sure to lurk:
And I shall fill my slab of basalt there,
And 'neath my tabernacle take my rest,
With those nine columns round me, two and two,
The odd one at my feet where Anselm stands:
Peach-blossom marble all, the rare, the ripe
As fresh-poured red wine of a mighty pulse.   30
—Old Gandolf with his paltry onion-stone,
Put me where I may look at him! True peach,
Rosy and flawless: how I earned the prize!
Draw close: that conflagration of my church

—What then? So much was saved if aught were
  missed!
My sons, ye would not be my death? Go dig
The white-grape vineyard where the oil-press stood,
Drop water gently till the surface sink,
And if ye find . . . Ah God, I know not, I! . . .
Bedded in store of rotten fig-leaves soft,   40
And corded up in a tight olive-frail,
Some lump, ah God, of *lapis lazuli*,
Big as a Jew's head cut off at the nape,
Blue as a vein o'er the Madonna's breast . . .
Sons, all have I bequeathed you, villas, all,
That brave Frascati villa with its bath,
So, let the blue lump poise between my knees,
Like God the Father's globe on both his hands
Ye worship in the Jesu Church so gay,
For Gandolf shall not chose but see and burst!   50
Swift as a weaver's shuttle fleet our years:
Man goeth to the grave, and where is he?
Did I say basalt for my slab, sons? Black—
'Twas ever antique-black I meant! How else
Shall ye contrast my frieze to come beneath?
The bas-relief in bronze ye promised me,
Those Pans and Nymphs ye wot of, and perchance
Some tripod, thyrsus, with a vase or so,
The Saviour at his sermon on the mount,
Saint Praxed in a glory, and one Pan   60
Ready to twitch the Nymph's last garment off,
And Moses with the tables . . . but I know
Ye mark me not! What do they whisper thee,
Child of my bowels, Anselm? Ah, ye hope
To revel down my villas while I gasp
Bricked o'er with beggar's mouldy travertine
Which Gandolf from his tomb-top chuckles at!
Nay, boys, ye love me—all of jasper, then!
'Tis jasper ye stand pledged to, lest I grieve
My bath must needs be left behind, alas!   70
One block, pure green as a pistachio-nut,
There's plenty jasper somewhere in the world—
And have I not Saint Praxed's ear to pray
Horses for ye, and brown Greek manuscripts,
And mistresses with great smooth marbly limbs?

41. olive-frail, a basket to hold olives. **46. Frascati**, a fashionable district, near Rome. **49. Jesu Church.** There is or was such an image as the Bishop refers to in the Church of the Jesuits in Rome. With characteristic irreverence the Bishop would take upon himself the posture of God. **51. Swift . . . years.** See Job 7: 6. **56–62. The bas-relief . . . the tables.** The mingling of Christian and pagan symbolism is characteristic of the Renaissance (see Milton's "Lycidas"). Here it is also intended to show the Bishop's lack of respect for sacred things. **Pan** (l. 57) was the god of the fields. The priestess of Apollo at Delphi sat on a **tripod** (l. 58); the worshipers of Dionysos carried a **thyrsus** (l. 58). The **sermon on the mount** (l. 59) is recorded in Matthew 5–7. **Moses** gets **the tables** of the Law (l. 62) from Yahweh on Mount Sinai in Exodus 24 ff.

1. Vanity . . . vanity. See Ecclesiastes 1:2. **3. Nephews,** by a pious fiction, since, of course, they were his illegitimate children. **5. Gandolf,** the Bishop's hated predecessor and rival in love. **21. the epistle-side.** The epistles are read on the right-hand side of the pulpit as one faces the altar, the Gospels on the left. **26. tabernacle,** a canopy over the tomb.

—That's if ye carve my epitaph aright,
Choice Latin, picked phrase, Tully's every word,
No gaudy ware like Gandolf's second line—
Tully, my masters? Ulpian serves his need!
And then how I shall lie through centuries,   80
And hear the blessed mutter of the mass,
And see God made and eaten all day long,
And feel the steady candle-flame, and taste
Good strong thick stupefying incense-smoke!
For as I lie here, hours of the dead night,
Dying in state and by such slow degrees,
I fold my arms as if they clasped a crook,
And stretch my feet forth straight as stone can
     point,
And let the bedclothes, for a mortcloth, drop
Into great laps and folds of sculptor's-work: 90
And as yon tapers dwindle, and strange thoughts
Grow, with a certain humming in my ears,
About the life before I lived this life,
And this life too, popes, cardinals and priests,
Saint Praxed at his sermon on the mount,
Your tall pale mother with her talking eyes,
And new-found agate urns as fresh as day,
And marble's language, Latin pure, discreet,
—Aha, ELUCESCEBAT quoth our friend?
No Tully, said I, Ulpian at the best!   100
Evil and brief hath been my pilgrimage.
All *lapis*, all, sons! Else I give the Pope
My villas! Will ye ever eat my heart?
Ever your eyes were as a lizard's quick,
They glitter like your mother's for my soul,
Or ye would heighten my impoverished frieze,
Piece out its starved design, and fill my vase
With grapes, and add a vizor and a Term,
And to the tripod ye would tie a lynx
That in his struggle throws the thyrsus down,   110
To comfort me on my entablature
Whereon I am to lie till I must ask

"Do I live, am I dead?" There, leave me,
     there!
For ye have stabbed me with ingratitude
To death—ye wish it—God, ye wish it! Stone—
Gritstone, a-crumble! Clammy squares which
     sweat
As if the corpse they keep were oozing through—
And no more *lapis* to delight the world!
Well go! I bless ye. Fewer tapers there,
But in a row: and, going, turn your backs   120
—Ay, like departing altar-ministrants,
And leave me in my church, the church for
     peace,
That I may watch at leisure if he leers—
Old Gandolf—at me, from his onion-stone,
As still he envied me, so fair she was!

SAUL

"Saul" is possibly the greatest short poem in the language. It was suggested by 1 Samuel 16:14–23, which relates how David, the shepherd lad, was called to bring his music to cure King Saul, who was suffering from melancholia, and, as W. C. DeVane has shown, by Christopher Smart's preface to his "Ode to Musick on Saint Cecilia's Day." The poem has had an interesting history. Only the first nine divisions were published in 1845; the rest did not come out until ten years later. The meaning of the poem, as we know it today, inheres in the second part, but, as A. W. Crawford has pointed out, Browning could not achieve the great affirmation it comprises until he had first worked out his own theological problems.

The order of David's procedure is significant. He first appeals to the interests and enthusiasms which man shares with the other animals (stanzas 5–6), from which he passes, first, to what has been called "the help-tunes of the great epochs in human life" (7), then, by way of a transition through that paean in praise of "the wild joys of living" (9), to "songs of human aspiration." On the merely human level one cannot go beyond a great king's hope of deathless glory; at the end of stanza 15, therefore, David has reached an impasse. Deliverance comes through a fresh revelation of the character of God. What David cannot do for Saul can be achieved in God, who is love. Otherwise, the rule which prevails everywhere else in the universe is broken, and the Creator finds himself surpassed by the creature, which is unthinkable.

The ideas expressed in the poem are, of course, much too advanced for David's day. David lived late in the eleventh and early in the tenth century B.C., Hosea, the first prophet to think of God as love, in the eighth century B.C. Actually, Browning goes beyond the range of the Old Testament altogether, expressing, at the end of stanza 18, the Christian doctrine of the Incarnation.

77–79. Choice Latin . . . his need! The Bishop's love of pure Latin is one of the few sincere things about him. **Tully** is Cicero, whom the Bishop takes as setting the standard. He regards **Ulpian**, a Roman jurist (170–228) as far below Tully's level. **80–84. And then how . . . incense-smoke!** These lines contain a reference to the Roman Catholic doctrine of transubstantiation, the belief that every time the mass is celebrated a miracle occurs and the bread and wine on the altar become the body and blood of Christ. But Browning makes even this reference to a sacred mystery point the Bishop's sensuality; the passage is almost cannibalistic. The dying man has no interest in the spiritual significance of the service or of the sacrament, and probably no belief in it; on the other hand, it interests him tremendously as a colorful pageant. **87. crook**, the crosier, or shepherd's staff, symbol of the bishop's office. **95. Saint Praxed at his sermon.** Saint Praxed (Prassede) was a female saint of first-century Rome. This is one of several indications that the Bishop's mind is wandering. **99. Elucescebat**, he was famous. The Bishop prefers the pure classical form, *elucebat*. **108. Term**, a bust on a square block of stone.

1

Said Abner, "At last thou art come! Ere I tell, ere
thou speak,

Kiss my cheek, wish me well!" Then I wished it,
and did kiss his cheek.

And he: "Since the King, O my friend, for thy
countenance sent,

Neither drunken nor eaten have we; nor until from
his tent

Thou return with the joyful assurance the King liveth yet,

Shall our lip with the honey be bright, with the
water be wet.

For out of the black mid-tent's silence, a space of
three days,

Not a sound hath escaped to thy servants, of prayer
nor of praise,

To betoken that Saul and the Spirit have ended
their strife,

And that, faint in his triumph, the monarch sinks
back upon life.   10

2

"Yet now my heart leaps, O belovèd! God's child
with his dew

On thy gracious gold hair, and those lilies still living
and blue

Just broken to twine round thy harp-strings, as if no
wild heat

Were now raging to torture the desert!"

3

          Then I, as was meet,

Knelt down to the God of my fathers, and rose on
my feet,

And ran o'er the sand burnt to powder. The tent
was unlooped;

I pulled up the spear that obstructed, and under
I stooped;

Hands and knees on the slippery grass-patch, all
withered and gone,

That extends to the second enclosure, I groped my
way on

Till I felt where the foldskirts fly open. Then once
more I prayed,   20

And opened the foldskirts and entered, and was not
afraid

But spoke, "Here is David, thy servant!" And no
voice replied.

---

1. **Abner,** Saul's cousin and commander in chief. **thou,**
David.   9. **Spirit,** the "evil spirit" of 1 Samuel 16:14.
12. **gold hair.** The "ruddy" quality attributed to David in
1 Samuel 16:12 properly refers to skin but has always been
popularly applied to his hair.

At the first I saw nought but the blackness; but soon
I descried

A something more black than the blackness—the
vast, the upright

Main prop which sustains the pavilion: and slow
into sight

Grew a figure against it, gigantic and blackest of all.

Then a sunbeam, that burst through the tent-roof,
showed Saul.

4

He stood as erect as that tent-prop, both arms
stretched out wide

On the great cross-support in the centre, that goes
to each side;

He relaxed not a muscle, but hung there as, caught
in his pangs   30

And waiting his change, the king-serpent all heavily hangs,

Far away from his kind, in the pine, till deliverance
come

With the spring-time,—so agonised Saul, drear and
stark, blind and dumb.

5

Then I tuned my harp,—took off the lilies we
twine round its chords

Lest they snap 'neath the stress of the noontide—
those sunbeams like swords!

And I first played the tune all our sheep know, as,
one after one,

So docile they come to the pen-door till folding be
done.

They are white and untorn by the bushes, for lo,
they have fed

Where the long grasses stifle the water within the
stream's bed;

And now one after one seeks its lodging, as star follows star   40

Into eve and the blue far above us,—so blue and so
far!

6

—Then the tune, for which quails on the cornland
will each leave his mate

To fly after the player; then, what makes the crickets elate

Till for boldness they fight one another; and then,
what has weight

To set the quick jerboa a-musing outside his sand
house—

There are none such as he for a wonder, half bird
and half mouse!

---

31. **king-serpent,** a very large serpent. The particular variety is not specified.

God made all the creatures and gave them our love
and our fear,

To give sign, we and they are his children, one family here.

7

Then I played the help-tune of our reapers, their
wine-song, when hand

Grasps at hand, eye lights eye in good friendship,
and great hearts expand   50

And grow one in the sense of this world's life.—And
then, the last song

When the dead man is praised on his journey—
"Bear, bear him along,

With his few faults shut up like dead flowerets! Are
balm-seeds not here

To console us? The land has none left such as he on
the bier.

Oh, would we might keep thee, my brother!"—
And then, the glad chaunt

Of the marriage,—first go the young maidens, next,
she whom we vaunt

As the beauty, the pride of our dwelling.—And
then, the great march

Wherein man runs to man to assist him and buttress
an arch

Nought can break; who shall harm them, our
friends?—Then, the chorus intoned

As the Levites go up to the altar in glory enthroned.

But I stopped here: for here in the darkness Saul
groaned.   61

8

And I paused, held my breath in such silence, and
listened apart;

And the tent shook, for mighty Saul shuddered: and
sparkles 'gan dart

From the jewels that woke in his turban, at once
with a start,

All its lordly male-sapphires, and rubies courageous
at heart.

So the head: but the body still moved not, still hung
there erect.

And I bent once again to my playing, pursued it unchecked,

As I sang,—

9

"Oh, our manhood's prime vigour! No spirit feels
waste,

Not a muscle is stopped in its playing nor sinew un-
braced.

60. Levites, servants of the priests.

Oh, the wild joys of living! the leaping from rock up
to rock,   70

The strong rending of boughs from the fir-tree, the
cool silver shock

Of the plunge in a pool's living water, the hunt of
the bear,

And the sultriness showing the lion is couched in his
lair.

And the meal, the rich dates yellowed over with
gold dust divine,

And the locust-flesh steeped in the pitcher, the full
draught of wine,

And the sleep in the dried river-channel where bulrushes tell

That the water was wont to go warbling so softly
and well.

How good is man's life, the mere living! how fit to
employ

All the heart and the soul and the senses for ever in
joy!

Hast thou loved the white locks of thy father, whose
sword thou didst guard   80

When he trusted thee forth with the armies, for
glorious reward?

Didst thou see the thin hands of thy mother, held up
as men sung

The low song of the nearly-departed, and hear her
faint tongue

Joining in while it could to the witness, 'Let one
more attest,

I have lived, seen God's hand through a lifetime,
and all was for best'?

Then they sung through their tears in strong triumph, not much, but the rest.

And thy brothers, the help and the contest, the
working whence grew

Such result as, from seething grape-bundles, the
spirit strained true:

And the friends of thy boyhood—that boyhood of
wonder and hope,

Present promise and wealth of the future beyond
the eye's scope,—   90

Till lo, thou art grown to a monarch; a people is
thine;

And all gifts, which the world offers singly, on one
head combine!

On one head, all the beauty and strength, love and
rage (like the throe

That, a-work in the rock, helps its labour and lets
the gold go)

High ambition and deeds which surpass it, fame
crowning them,—all

Brought to blaze on the head of one creature—King
Saul!"

10

And lo, with that leap of my spirit,—heart, hand,
harp and voice,
Each lifting Saul's name out of sorrow, each bidding
rejoice
Saul's fame in the light it was made for—as when,
dare I say,
The Lord's army, in rapture of service, strains
through its array,   100
And upsoareth the cherubim-chariot—"Saul!"
cried I, and stopped,
And waited the thing that should follow. Then Saul,
who hung propped
By the tent's cross-support in the centre, was struck
by his name.
Have ye seen when Spring's arrowy summons goes
right to the aim,
And some mountain, the last to withstand her, that
held (he alone,
While the vale laughed in freedom and flowers) on a
broad bust of stone
A year's snow bound about for a breastplate,—
leaves grasp of the sheet?
Fold on fold all at once it crowds thunderously
down to his feet,
And there fronts you, stark, black, but alive yet,
your mountain of old,
With his rents, the successive bequeathings of ages
untold—   110
Yea, each harm got in fighting your battles, each
furrow and scar
Of his head thrust 'twixt you and the tempest—all
hail, there they are!
—Now again to be softened with verdure, again
hold the nest
Of the dove, tempt the goat and its young to the
green on his crest
For their food in the ardours of summer. One long
shudder thrilled
All the tent till the very air tingled, then sank and
was stilled
At the King's self left standing before me, released
and aware.
What was gone, what remained? All to traverse,
'twixt hope and despair,
Death was past, life not come: so he waited. Awhile
his right hand
Held the brow, helped the eyes left too vacant forth-
with to remand   120
To their place what new objects should enter: 'twas
Saul as before.
I looked up and dared gaze at those eyes, nor was
hurt any more

Than by slow pallid sunsets in autumn, ye watch
from the shore,
At their sad level gaze o'er the ocean—a sun's slow
decline
Over hills which, resolved in stern silence, o'erlap
and entwine
Base with base to knit strength more intensely: so,
arm folded arm
O'er the chest whose slow heavings subsided.

11

What spell or what charm,
(For, awhile there was trouble within me) what
next should I urge
To sustain him where song had restored him?—
Song filled to the verge
His cup with the wine of this life, pressing all that it
yields   130
Of mere fruitage, the strength and the beauty: be-
yond, on what fields,
Glean a vintage more potent and perfect to brighten
the eye
And bring blood to the lip, and commend them the
cup they put by?
He saith, "It is good"; still he drinks not: he lets me
praise life,
Gives assent, yet would die for his own part.

12

Then fancies grew rife
Which had come long ago on the pasture, when
round me the sheep
Fed in silence—above, the one eagle wheeled slow
as in sleep;
And I lay in my hollow and mused on the world
that might lie
'Neath his ken, though I saw but the strip 'twixt
the hill and the sky:
And I laughed—"Since my days are ordained to be
passed with my flocks,   140
Let me people at least, with my fancies, the plains
and the rocks,
Dream the life I am never to mix with, and image
the show
Of mankind as they live in those fashions I hardly
shall know!
Schemes of life, its best rules and right uses, the
courage that gains,
And the prudence that keeps what men strive for."
And now these old trains
Of vague thought came again; I grew surer; so,
once more the string
Of my harp made response to my spirit, as thus—

13

"Yea, my King,"

I began—"thou dost well in rejecting mere comforts that spring

From the mere mortal life held in common by man and by brute:

In our flesh grows the branch of this life, in our soul it bears fruit.   150

Thou hast marked the slow rise of the tree,—how its stem trembled first

Till it passed the kid's lip, the stag's antler; then safely outburst

The fan-branches all round; and thou mindest when these too, in turn,

Broke a-bloom and the palm-tree seemed perfect: yet more was to learn,

E'en the good that comes in with the palm-fruit. Our dates shall we slight,

When their juice brings a cure for all sorrow? or care for the plight

Of the palm's self whose slow growth produced them? Not so! stem and branch

Shall decay, nor be known in their place, while the palm-wine shall staunch

Every wound of man's spirit in winter. I pour thee such wine.

Leave the flesh to the fate it was fit for! the spirit be thine!   160

By the spirit, when age shall o'ercome thee, thou still shalt enjoy

More indeed, than at first when inconscious, the life of a boy.

Crush that life, and behold its wine running! Each deed thou hast done

Dies, revives, goes to work in the world; until e'en as the sun

Looking down on the earth, though clouds spoil him, though tempests efface,

Can find nothing his own deed produced not, must everywhere trace

The results of his past summer-prime,—so, each ray of thy will,

Every flash of thy passion and prowess, long over, shall thrill

Thy whole people, the countless, with ardour, till they too give forth

A like cheer to their sons, who in turn, fill the South and the North   170

With the radiance thy deed was the germ of. Carouse in the past!

But the license of age has its limit; thou diest at last:

As the lion when age dims his eyeball, the rose at her height,

So with man—so his power and his beauty for ever take flight.

No! Again a long draught of my soul-wine! Look forth o'er the years!

Thou hast done now with eyes for the actual; begin with the seer's!

Is Saul dead? In the depth of the vale make his tomb—bid arise

A grey mountain of marble heaped four-square till, built to the skies,

Let it mark where the great First King slumbers: whose fame would ye know?

Up above see the rock's naked face, where the record shall go   180

In great characters cut by the scribe,—Such was Saul, so he did;

With the sages directing the work, by the populace chid,—

For not half, they'll affirm, is comprised there! Which fault to amend,

In the grove with his kind grows the cedar, whereon they shall spend

(See, in tablets 'tis level before them) their praise, and record

With the gold of the graver, Saul's story,—the statesman's great word

Side by side with the poet's sweet comment. The river's a-wave

With smooth paper-reeds grazing each other when prophet-winds rave:

So the pen gives unborn generations their due and their part

In thy being! Then, first of the mighty, thank God that thou art!"   190

14

And behold while I sang . . . but O Thou who didst grant me that day,

And before it not seldom hast granted thy help to essay,

Carry on and complete an adventure,—my shield and my sword

In that act where my soul was thy servant, thy word was my word,—

Still be with me, who then at the summit of human endeavour

And scaling the highest, man's thought could, gazed hopeless as ever

On the new stretch of heaven above me—till, mighty to save,

Just one lift of thy hand cleared that distance— God's throne from man's grave!

188. paper-reeds, papyrus plants.

Let me tell out my tale to its ending—my voice to
  my heart
Which can scarce dare believe in what marvels last
  night I took part,   200
As this morning I gather the fragments, alone with
  my sheep,
And still fear lest the terrible glory evanish like
  sleep!
For I wake in the grey dewy covert, while Hebron
  upheaves
The dawn struggling with night on his shoulder,
  and Kidron retrieves
Slow the damage of yesterday's sunshine.

15

                          I say then,—my song
While I sang thus, assuring the monarch, and ever
  more strong
Made a proffer of good to console him—he slowly
  resumed
His old motions and habitudes kingly. The right-
  hand replumed
His black locks to their wonted composure, ad-
  justed the swathes
Of his turban, and see—the huge sweat that his
  countenance bathes,   210
He wipes off with the robe; and he girds now his
  loins as of yore,
And feels slow for the armlets of price, with the clasp
  set before.
He is Saul, ye remember in glory,—ere error had
  bent
The broad brow from the daily communion; and
  still, though much spent
Be the life and the bearing that front you, the same,
  God did choose,
To receive what a man may waste, desecrate, never
  quite lose.
So sank he along by the tent-prop till, stayed by the
  pile
Of his armour and war-cloak and garments, he
  leaned there awhile,

203. **Hebron,** a city.   204. **Kidron,** a brook near Jerusalem.   **213–14. ere error . . . communion.** The Old Testament contains two different stories concerning the rejection
of Saul by Samuel. In 1 Samuel 13, he is rejected because he
himself offered sacrifice before a battle instead of waiting for
Samuel to come to do it. In 1 Samuel 15, the difficulty is that
he spared Agag, king of the Amalekites, and some of the
booty, when they ought to have been "devoted." The truth
of the matter seems to have been that Saul was, generally
speaking, a disappointment to Samuel and the religious
party. He was apparently a man capable of great enthusiasm,
of a somewhat primitive variety, but his staying power seems
to have been weak. Whether his failure was the cause of his
melancholia or was itself caused by it, it is impossible to determine at this distance. In any case, the problem was, in
part at least, pathological.

And sat out my singing,—one arm round the tent-
  prop, to raise
His bent head, and the other hung slack—till I
  touched on the praise   220
I foresaw from all men in all time, to the man pa-
  tient there;
And thus ended, the harp falling forward. Then first
  I was 'ware
That he sat, as I say, with my head just above his
  vast knees
Which were thrust out on each side around me, like
  oak-roots which please
To encircle a lamb when it slumbers. I looked up to
  know
If the best I could do had brought solace: he spoke
  not, but slow
Lifted up the hand slack at his side, till he laid it
  with care
Soft and grave, but in mild settled will, on my brow:
  through my hair
The large fingers were pushed, and he bent back
  my head, with kind power—
All my face back, intent to peruse it, as men do a
  flower.   230
Thus held he me there with his great eyes that
  scrutinized mine—
And oh, all my heart how it loved him! but where
  was the sign?
I yearned—"Could I help thee, my father, inventing a bliss,
I would add, to that life of the past, both the future
  and this;
I would give thee new life altogether, as good, ages
  hence,
As this moment,—had love but the warrant, love's
  heart to dispense!"

16

Then the truth came upon me. No harp more—no
  song more! outbroke—

17

"I have gone the whole round of creation: I saw
  and I spoke:
I, a work of God's hand for that purpose, received
  in my brain
And pronounced on the rest of his handwork—returned him again   240
His creation's approval or censure: I spoke as I saw:
I report, as a man may of God's work—all's love,
  yet all's law.
Now I lay down the judgeship he lent me. Each
  faculty tasked

To perceive him, has gained an abyss, where a dew-
  drop was asked.
Have I knowledge? confounded it shrivels at Wis-
  dom laid bare.
Have I forethought? how purblind, how blank, to
  the Infinite Care!
Do I task my faculty highest, to image success?
I but open my eyes,—and perfection, no more and
  no less,
In the kind I imagined, full-fronts me, and God is
  seen God
In the star, in the stone, in the flesh, in the soul and
  the clod.   250
And thus looking within and around me, I ever re-
  new
(With that stoop of the soul which in bending up-
  raises it too)
The submission of man's nothing-perfect to God's
  all-complete,
As by each new obeisance in spirit, I climb to his feet.
Yet with all this abounding experience, this deity
  known,
I shall dare to discover some province, some gift of
  my own.
There's a faculty pleasant to exercise, hard to hood-
  wink,
I am fain to keep still in abeyance, (I laugh as I
  think)
Lest, insisting to claim and parade in it, wot ye, I
  worst
E'en the Giver in one gift.—Behold, I could love if
  I durst!   260
But I sink the pretension as fearing a man may o'er-
  take
God's own speed in the one way of love: I abstain
  for love's sake.
—What, my soul? see thus far and no farther? when
  doors great and small,
Nine-and-ninety flew ope at our touch, should the
  hundredth appal?
In the least things have faith, yet distrust in the
  greatest of all?
Do I find love so full in my nature, God's ultimate
  gift,
That I doubt his own love can compete with it?
  Here, the parts shift?
Here, the creature surpass the Creator,—the end,
  what Began?
Would I fain in my impotent yearning do all for this
  man,
And dare doubt he alone shall not help him, who
  yet alone can?   270
Would it ever have entered my mind, the bare will,
  much less power,

To bestow on this Saul what I sang of, the marvellous dower
Of the life he was gifted and filled with? to make
  such a soul,
Such a body, and then such an earth for insphering
  the whole?
And doth it not enter my mind (as my warm tears
  attest)
These good things being given, to go on, and give
  one more, the best?
Ay, to save and redeem and restore him, maintain
  at the height
This perfection,—succeed with life's day-spring,
  death's minute of night?
Interpose at the difficult minute, snatch Saul the
  mistake,
Saul the failure, the ruin he seems now,—and bid
  him awake   280
From the dream, the probation, the prelude, to find
  himself set
Clear and safe in new light and new life,—a new
  harmony yet
To be run, and continued, and ended—who knows?
  —or endure!
The man taught enough by life's dream, of the rest
  to make sure;
By the pain-throb, triumphantly winning intensified
  bliss,
And the next world's reward and repose, by the
  struggles in this.

18

"I believe it! 'Tis thou, God, that givest, 'tis I who
  receive:
In the first is the last, in thy will is my power to believe.
All's one gift: thou canst grant it moreover, as
  prompt to my prayer
As I breathe out this breath, as I open these arms to
  the air.   290
From thy will, stream the worlds, life and nature,
  thy dread Sabaoth:
I will?—the mere atoms despise me! Why am I not
  loth
To look that, even that in the face too? Why is it I
  dare
Think but lightly of such impuissance? What stops
  my despair?
This;—'tis not what man Does which exalts him,
  but what man Would do!

291. Sabaoth, a title applied to God in His manifestation
as "Lord of Hosts," first in a military sense, later with a
wider meaning.

See the King—I would help him but cannot, the
   wishes fall through.
Could I wrestle to raise him from sorrow, grow poor
   to enrich,
To fill up his life, starve my own out, I would—
   knowing which,
I know that my service is perfect. Oh, speak through
   me now!
Would I suffer for him that I love? So wouldst thou
   —so wilt thou!   300
So shall crown thee the topmost, ineffablest, uttermost crown—
And thy love fill infinitude wholly, nor leave up nor
   down
One spot for the creature to stand in! It is by no
   breath,
Turn of eye, wave of hand, that salvation joins issue
   with death!
As thy Love is discovered almighty, almighty be
   proved
Thy power, that exists with and for it, of being Beloved!
He who did most, shall bear most; the strongest
   shall stand the most weak.
'Tis the weakness in strength, that I cry for! my
   flesh, that I seek
In the Godhead! I seek and I find it. O Saul, it shall
   be
A Face like my face that receives thee; a Man like to
   me,   310
Thou shalt love and be loved by, for ever: a Hand
   like this hand
Shall throw open the gates of new life to thee! See
   the Christ stand!"

19

I know not too well how I found my way home in
   the night.
There were witnesses, cohorts about me, to left and
   to right,
Angels, powers, the unuttered, unseen, the alive, the
   aware:
I repressed, I got through them as hardly, as strug-
   gling there,
As a runner beset by the populace famished for
   news—
Life or death. The whole earth was awakened, hell
   loosed with her crews;
And the stars of night beat with emotion, and tin-
   gled and shot
Out in fire the strong pain of pent knowledge: but
   I fainted not,   320
For the Hand still impelled me at once and sup-
   ported, suppressed

All the tumult, and quenched it with quiet, and
   holy behest,
Till the rapture was shut in itself, and the earth sank
   to rest.
Anon at the dawn, all that trouble had withered
   from earth—
Not so much, but I saw it die out in the day's tender
   birth;
In the gathered intensity brought to the grey of the
   hills;
In the shuddering forests' held breath; in the sudden
   wind-thrills;
In the startled wild beasts that bore off, each with
   eye sidling still
Though averted with wonder and dread; in the
   birds stiff and chill
That rose heavily, as I approached them, made
   stupid with awe: 330
E'en the serpent that slid away silent,—he felt the
   new law.
The same stared in the white humid faces upturned
   by the flowers;
The same worked in the heart of the cedar and
   moved the vine-bowers:
And the little brooks witnessing murmured, persistent and low,
With their obstinate, all but hushed voices—"E'en
   so, it is so!"

A WOMAN'S LAST WORD

1

Let's contend no more, Love,
   Strive nor weep:
All be as before, Love,
   —Only sleep!

2

What so wild as words are?
   I and thou
In debate, as birds are,
   Hawk on bough!

3

See the creature stalking
   While we speak!   10
Hush and hide the talking,
   Cheek on cheek!

4

What so false as truth is,
   False to thee?

13–14. *What . . . thee?* What difference does it make
that what I have said is true? When truth works against our
love, it is itself the falsest of all false things.

Where the serpent's tooth is
  Shun the tree—

5

Where the apple reddens
  Never pry—
Lest we lose our Edens,
  Eve and I.   20

6

Be a god and hold me
  With a charm!
Be a man and fold me
  With thine arm!

7

Teach me, only teach, Love!
  As I ought
I will speak thy speech, Love,
  Think thy thought—

8

Meet, if thou require it,
  Both demands,   30
Laying flesh and spirit
  In thy hands.

9

That shall be to-morrow,
  Not to-night:
I must bury sorrow
  Out of sight:

10

—Must a little weep, Love,
  (Foolish me!)
And so fall asleep, Love,
  Loved by thee.   40

EVELYN HOPE

1

Beautiful Evelyn Hope is dead!
  Sit and watch by her side an hour.
That is her book-shelf, this her bed;
  She plucked that piece of geranium-flower,
Beginning to die too, in the glass;
  Little has yet been changed, I think:
The shutters are shut, no light may pass
  Save two long rays through the hinge's chink.

15–20. **Where . . . Eve and I.** Compare the story of the
Fall of Man in Genesis 3. For **serpent's tooth,** see *King Lear,*
Act I, sc. 4, l. 310.

2

Sixteen years old when she died!
  Perhaps she had scarcely heard my name;   10
It was not her time to love; beside,
  Her life had many a hope and aim,
Duties enough and little cares,
  And now was quiet, now astir,
Till God's hand beckoned unawares,—
  And the sweet white brow is all of her.

3

Is it too late then, Evelyn Hope?
  What, your soul was pure and true,
The good stars met in your horoscope,
  Made you of spirit, fire and dew—   20
And, just because I was thrice as old
  And our paths in the world diverged so wide,
Each was nought to each, must I be told?
  We were fellow mortals, nought beside?

4

No, indeed! for God above
  Is great to grant, as mighty to make,
And creates the love to reward the love:
  I claim you still, for my own love's sake!
Delayed it may be for more lives yet,
  Through worlds I shall traverse, not a few: 30
Much is to learn, much to forget
  Ere the time be come for taking you.

5

But the time will come,—at last it will,
  When, Evelyn Hope, what meant (I shall say)
In the lower earth, in the years long still,
  That body and soul so pure and gay?
Why your hair was amber, I shall divine,
  And your mouth of your own geranium's red—
And what you would do with me, in fine,
  In the new life come in the old one's stead. 40

6

I have lived (I shall say) so much since then,
  Given up myself so many times,
Gained me the gains of various men,
  Ransacked the ages, spoiled the climes;
Yet one thing, one, in my soul's full scope,
  Either I missed or itself missed me:
And I want and find you, Evelyn Hope!
  What is the issue? let us see!

7

I loved you, Evelyn, all the while!
  My heart seemed full as it could hold?   50

There was place and to spare for the frank young
    smile,
  And the red young mouth, and the hair's young
    gold.
So, hush,—I will give you this leaf to keep:
  See, I shut it inside the sweet cold hand!
There, that is our secret: go to sleep!
  You will wake, and remember, and understand.

LOVE AMONG THE RUINS

"Love among the Ruins," one of Browning's most beloved poems, proves that he could write as melodiously
as anyone else when he chose. There is a twofold contrast
in the poem: between the past and the present (note the
careful parallelism within each stanza); between love and
glory. The general opinion is that the landscape is
Italianate; for dissenting views, see Fehr, *Archiv*, Vol.
CXLII (1921), pp. 260–62 (Babylon) and Law, *Modern
Language Notes*, Vol. XXXVII (1922), p. 312 ("a com-
posite picture of Babylon and Jerusalem").

1

Where the quiet-coloured end of evening smiles
    Miles and miles
On the solitary pastures where our sheep
    Half-asleep
Tinkle homeward through the twilight, stray or
    stop
    As they crop—
Was the site once of a city great and gay,
    (So they say)
Of our country's very capital, its prince
    Ages since   10
Held his court in, gathered councils, wielding far
    Peace or war.

2

Now,—the country does not even boast a tree,
    As you see,
To distinguish slopes of verdure, certain rills
    From the hills
Intersect and give a name to, (else they run
    Into one)
Where the domed and daring palace shot its spires
    Up like fires   20
O'er the hundred-gated circuit of a wall
    Bounding all,
Made of marble, men might march on nor be
    pressed,
    Twelve abreast.

3

And such plenty and perfection, see, of grass
    Never was!

Such a carpet as, this summer-time, o'erspreads
    And embeds
Every vestige of the city, guessed alone,
    Stock or stone—   30
Where a multitude of men breathed joy and woe
    Long ago;
Lust of glory pricked their hearts up, dread of shame
    Struck them tame;
And that glory and that shame alike, the gold
    Bought and sold.

4

Now,—the single little turret that remains
    On the plains,
By the caper overrooted, by the gourd
    Overscored,   40
While the patching houseleek's head of blossom
    winks
    Through the chinks—
Marks the basement whence a tower in ancient time
    Sprang sublime,
And a burning ring, all round, the chariots traced
    As they raced,
And the monarch and his minions and his dames
    Viewed the games.

5

And I know, while thus the quiet-coloured eve
    Smiles to leave   50
To their folding, all our many-tinkling fleece
    In such peace.
And the slopes and rills in undistinguished grey
    Melt away—
That a girl with eager eyes and yellow hair
    Waits me there
In the turret whence the charioteers caught soul
    For the goal,
When the king looked, where she looks now, breath-
    less, dumb
    Till I come.   60

6

But he looked upon the city, every side,
    Far and wide,
All the mountains topped with temples, all the
    glades'
    Colonnades,
All the causeys, bridges, aqueducts,—and then,
    All the men!
When I do come, she will speak not, she will stand,
    Either hand
On my shoulder, give her eyes the first embrace
    Of my face,   70

65. causeys, causeways.

Ere we rush, ere we extinguish sight and speech
    Each on each.

7

In one year they sent a million fighters forth
    South and North,
And they built their gods a brazen pillar high
    As the sky,
Yet reserved a thousand chariots in full force—
    Gold, of course.
Oh heart! oh blood that freezes, blood that burns!
    Earth's returns   80
For whole centuries of folly, noise and sin!
    Shut them in,
With their triumphs and their glories and the rest!
    Love is best.

MEMORABILIA

   This poem, "Things Worth Remembering," relates an experience of Browning's own. The speaker, an enthusiast for Shelley, encounters a man who once had the privilege of meeting the poet, but who so little appreciated his good fortune that his present companion's interest and enthusiasm strikes him as a theme for laughter. The speaker implies that he himself could no more have forgotten such a stroke of luck than he could have forgotten finding an eagle-feather during an otherwise commonplace walk over a dull and lonely moor.

I

    Ah, did you once see Shelley plain,
      And did he stop and speak to you
    And did you speak to him again?
      How strange it seems and new!

2

    But you were living before that,
      And also you are living after;
    And the memory I started at—
      My starting moves your laughter!

3

    I crossed a moor, with a name of its own
      And a certain use in the world no doubt, 10
    Yet a hand's-breadth of it shines alone
      'Mid the blank miles round about:

4

    For there I picked up on the heather,
      And there I put inside my breast
    A moulted feather, an eagle-feather!
      Well, I forget the rest.

THE LAST RIDE TOGETHER

   This poem is one of Browning's great expressions of his favorite doctrines of success in failure and of the superiority of love not only to glory but to art—this last a somewhat unusual point of view for a poet. William Lyon Phelps (*Robert Browning*, new ed., Bobbs-Merrill, 1932) comments as follows on ll. 78–81:

   "I was once seated in the square room in the gallery at Dresden that holds the most famous picture in the world, Rafael's Sistine Madonna. A number of tourists were in the place, and we were all gazing steadfastly at the immortal Virgin, when a pretty, fresh-colored young American girl entered the room. Every man's head twisted away from the masterpiece of art, and every man's eyes stared at the commonplace stranger, because she was alive! I was much amused, and could not help thinking of Browning's lines."

I

I said—Then, dearest, since 'tis so,
Since now at length my fate I know,
Since nothing all my love avails,
Since all, my life seemed meant for, fails,
    Since this was written and needs must be—
My whole heart rises up to bless
Your name in pride and thankfulness!
Take back the hope you gave,—I claim
Only a memory of the same,
—And this beside, if you will not blame,   10
    Your leave for one more last ride with me.

2

My mistress bent that brow of hers;
Those deep dark eyes where pride demurs
When pity would be softening through,
Fixed me a breathing-while or two
    With life or death in the balance: right!
The blood replenished me again;
My last thought was at least not vain:
I and my mistress, side by side
Shall be together, breathe and ride,   20
So, one day more am I deified.
    Who knows but the world may end to-night?

3

Hush! if you saw some western cloud
All billowy-bosomed, over-bowed
By many benedictions—sun's
And moon's and evening-star's at once—
    And so, you, looking and loving best,
Conscious grew, your passion drew
Cloud, sunset, moonrise, star-shine too,
Down on you, near and yet more near,   30
Till flesh must fade for heaven was here!—

Thus leant she and lingered—joy and fear!
  Thus lay she a moment on my breast.

4

Then we began to ride. My soul
Smoothed itself out, a long-cramped scroll
Freshening and fluttering in the wind.
Past hopes already lay behind.
    What need to strive with a life awry?
Had I said that, had I done this,
So might I gain, so might I miss.   40
Might she have loved me? just as well
She might have hated, who can tell!
Where had I been now if the worst befell?
    And here we are riding, she and I.

5

Fail I alone, in words and deeds?
Why, all men strive, and who succeeds?
We rode; it seemed my spirit flew,
Saw other regions, cities new,
    As the world rushed by on either side.
I thought,—All labour, yet no less   50
Bear up beneath their unsuccess.
Look at the end of work, contrast
The petty done, the undone vast,
This present of theirs with the hopeful past!
    I hoped she would love me; here we ride.

6

What hand and brain went ever paired?
What heart alike conceived and dared?
What act proved all its thought had been?
What will but felt the fleshly screen?
    We ride and I see her bosom heave.   60
There's many a crown for who can reach.
Ten lines, a statesman's life in each!
The flag stuck on a heap of bones,
A soldier's doing! what atones?
    They scratch his name on the Abbey-stones.
    My riding is better, by their leave.

7

What does it all mean, poet? Well,
Your brains beat into rhythm, you tell
What we felt only; you expressed
You hold things beautiful the best,   70
    And pace them in rhyme so, side by side.
'Tis something, nay 'tis much: but then,
Have you yourself what's best for men?
Are you—poor, sick, old ere your time—
Nearer one whit your own sublime

33. Thus lay she . . . on my breast, as she mounted her horse.

Than we who never have turned a rhyme?
    Sing, riding's a joy! For me, I ride.

8

And you, great sculptor—so, you gave
A score of years to Art, her slave,
And that's your Venus, whence we turn   80
To yonder girl that fords the burn!
    You acquiesce, and shall I repine?
What, man of music, you grown grey
With notes and nothing else to say,
Is this your sole praise from a friend,
"Greatly his opera's strains intend,
    But in music we know how fashions end!"
    I gave my youth; but we ride, in fine.

9

Who knows what's fit for us? Had fate
Proposed bliss here should sublimate   90
My being—had I signed the bond—
Still one must lead some life beyond,
    Have a bliss to die with, dim-descried.
This foot once planted on the goal,
This glory-garland round my soul,
Could I descry such? Try and test!
    I sink back shuddering from the quest.
Earth being so good, would heaven seem best?
    Now, heaven and she are beyond this ride.

10

And yet—she has not spoke so long!   100
What if heaven be that, fair and strong
At life's best, with our eyes upturned
Whither life's flower is first discerned,
    We, fixed so, ever should so abide?
What if we still ride on, we two
With life for ever old yet new,
Changed not in kind but in degree,
The instant made eternity,—
    And heaven just prove that I and she
    Ride, ride together, for ever ride?   110

A GRAMMARIAN'S FUNERAL

SHORTLY AFTER THE REVIVAL OF LEARNING IN EUROPE

"A Grammarian's Funeral" is typical of Browning's
tendency to set himself the most difficult subject possible.
To a scholar he gives a funeral typical of an epic hero, a
scholar, moreover, of the kind the average layman finds
it most difficult to sympathize with, a grammarian, a man
who has spent his life grubbing about among Greek

81. burn, brook.

roots, yet a great hero because he set himself a task transcending the limits of a human lifetime. Many years after this poem was written, Robert Louis Stevenson was buried in much this fashion in Samoa.

Let us begin and carry up this corpse,
    Singing together.
Leave we the common crofts, the vulgar thorpes
    Each in its tether
Sleeping safe on the bosom of the plain,
    Cared-for till cock-crow:
Look out if yonder be not day again
    Rimming the rock-row!
That's the appropriate country; there, man's
    thought,
    Rarer, intenser,   10
Self-gathered for an outbreak, as it ought,
    Chafes in the censer.
Leave we the unlettered plain its herd and crop;
    Seek we sepulture
On a tall mountain, cited to the top,
    Crowded with culture!
All the peaks soar, but one the rest excels;
    Clouds overcome it;
No! yonder sparkle is the citadel's
    Circling its summit.   20
Thither our path lies; wind we up the heights;
    Wait ye the warning?
Our low life was the level's and the night's;
    He's for the morning.
Step to a tune, square chests, erect each head,
    'Ware the beholders!
This is our master, famous calm and dead,
    Borne on our shoulders.

Sleep, crop and herd! sleep, darkling thorpe and
    croft,
    Safe from the weather!   30
He, whom we convoy to his grave aloft,
    Singing together,
He was a man born with thy face and throat,
    Lyric Apollo!
Long he lived nameless: how should spring take
    note
    Winter would follow?
Till lo, the little touch, and youth was gone!
    Cramped and diminished,
Moaned he, "New measures, other feet anon!
    My dance is finished"?   40
No, that's the world's way: (keep the mountain-side,
    Make for the city!)

He knew the signal, and stepped on with pride
    Over men's pity;
Left play for work, and grappled with the world
    Bent on escaping:
"What's in the scroll," quoth he, "thou keepest
    furled?
    Show me their shaping,
Theirs who most studied man, the bard and sage,—
    Give!"—So, he gowned him,   50
Straight got by heart that book to its last page:
    Learnèd, we found him.
Yea, but we found him bald too, eyes like lead,
    Accents uncertain:
"Time to taste life," another would have said,
    "Up with the curtain!"
This man said rather, "Actual life comes next?
    Patience a moment!
Grant I have mastered learning's crabbed text,
    Still there's the comment.   60
Let me know all! Prate not of most or least,
    Painful or easy!
Even to the crumbs I'd fain eat up the feast,
    Ay, nor feel queasy."
Oh, such a life as he resolved to live,
    When he had learned it,
When he had gathered all books had to give!
    Sooner, he spurned it.
Image the whole, then execute the parts—
    Fancy the fabric   70
Quite, ere you build, ere steel strike fire from
    quartz,
    Ere mortar dab brick!

(Here's the town-gate reached: there's the market-
    place
    Gaping before us.)
Yea, this in him was the peculiar grace
    (Hearten our chorus!)
That before living he'd learn how to live—
    No end to learning:
Earn the means first—God surely will contrive
    Use for our earning.   80
Others mistrust and say, "But time escapes:
    Live now or never!"
He said, "What's time? Leave Now for dogs and
    apes!
    Man has Forever."
Back to his book then: deeper drooped his head:
    Calculus racked him:
Leaden before, his eyes grew dross of lead:
    Tussis attacked him.

7-8. Look out . . . rock-row! The sun is coming up over the mountains. **12. censer,** the crater of a volcano. **34. Apollo,** the Greek god of youth, beauty, poetry, music, and oracles.

47. scroll, manuscript. **50. gowned him,** put on the scholar's gown, that is, studied. **86. Calculus,** the stone. **88. Tussis,** a bronchial cough.

"Now, master, take a little rest!"—not he!
    (Caution redoubled,   90
Step two abreast, the way winds narrowly!)
    Not a whit troubled
Back to his studies, fresher than at first,
    Fierce as a dragon
He (soul-hydroptic with a sacred thirst)
    Sucked at the flagon.
Oh, if we draw a circle premature,
    Heedless of far gain,
Greedy for quick returns of profit, sure
    Bad is our bargain!   100
Was it not great? did not he throw on God,
    (He loves the burthen)—
God's task to make the heavenly period
    Perfect the earthen?
Did not he magnify the mind, show clear
    Just what it all meant?
He would not discount life, as fools do here,
    Paid by instalment.
He ventured neck or nothing—heaven's success
    Found, or earth's failure: 110
"Wilt thou trust death or not?" He answered "Yes!
    Hence with life's pale lure!"
That low man seeks a little thing to do,
    Sees it and does it:
This high man, with a great thing to pursue,
    Dies ere he knows it.
That low man goes on adding one to one,
    His hundred's soon hit:
This high man, aiming at a million,
    Misses an unit.   120
That, has the world here—should he need the
    next,
    Let the world mind him!
This, throws himself on God, and unperplexed
    Seeking shall find him.
So, with the throttling hands of death at strife,
    Ground he at grammar;
Still, through the rattle, parts of speech were rife:
    While he could stammer
He settled *Hoti's* business—let it be!—
    Properly based *Oun*—   130
Gave us the doctrine of the enclitic *De*,
    Dead from the waist down.
Well, here's the platform, here's the proper place:
    Hail to your purlieus,
All ye highfliers of the feathered race,
    Swallows and curlews!
Here's the top-peak; the multitude below
    Live, for they can, there:

This man decided not to Live but Know—
    Bury this man there?   140
Here—here's his place, where meteors shoot, clouds
    form,
    Lightnings are loosened,
Stars come and go! Let joy break with the
    storm,
    Peace let the dew send!
Lofty designs must close in like effects:
    Loftily lying,
Leave him—still loftier than the world suspects,
    Living and dying.

THE STATUE AND THE BUST

There's a palace in Florence, the world knows well,
And a statue watches it from the square,
And this story of both do our townsmen tell.

Ages ago, a lady there,
At the farthest window facing the East
Asked, "Who rides by with the royal air?"

The bridesmaids' prattle around her ceased;
She leaned forth, one on either hand;
They saw how the blush of the bride increased—

They felt by its beats her heart expand—   10
As one at each ear and both in a breath
Whispered, "The Great-Duke Ferdinand."

That self-same instant, underneath,
The Duke rode past in his idle way,
Empty and fine like a swordless sheath.

Gay he rode, with a friend as gay,
Till he threw his head back—"Who is she?"
—"A bride the Riccardi brings home to-day."

Hair in heaps lay heavily
Over a pale brow spirit-pure—   20
Carved like the heart of the coal-black tree,

Crisped like a war-steed's encolure—
And vainly sought to dissemble her eyes
Of the blackest black our eyes endure.

1. palace in Florence, Palazzo Antinori, the home of the Riccardi family at the time of the story. Florence was also the birthplace of Dante, whose *Divine Comedy* was written in terza rima, as is this poem.   **12. "The Great-Duke Ferdinand."** Ferdinand I became Grand Duke of Florence in 1587.   **15. Empty . . . sheath,** because he had no purpose in his life. Compare ll. 25–26.   **21–22. Carved . . . Crisped.** Both refer to the lady's hair. **encolure,** mane.   **23. dissemble,** in the sense of hide.

95. hydroptic, thirsty.   **129–31. Hoti's business . . . Oun . . . the enclitic De,** difficult points in Greek grammar.

And lo, a blade for a knight's emprise
Filled the fine empty sheath of a man,—
The Duke grew straightway brave and wise.

He looked at her, as a lover can;
She looked at him, as one who awakes:
The past was a sleep, and her life began.   30

Now, love so ordered for both their sakes,
A feast was held that selfsame night
In the pile which the mighty shadow makes.

(For Via Larga is three-parts light,
But the palace overshadows one,
Because of a crime which may God requite!

To Florence and God the wrong was done,
Through the first republic's murder there
By Cosimo and his cursèd son.)

The Duke (with the statue's face in the square)   40
Turned in the midst of his multitude
At the bright approach of the bridal pair.

Face to face the lovers stood
A single minute and no more,
While the bridegroom bent as a man subdued—

Bowed till his bonnet brushed the floor—
For the Duke on the lady a kiss conferred,
As the courtly custom was of yore.

In a minute can lovers exchange a word?
If a word did pass, which I do not think,   50
Only one out of the thousand heard.

That was the bridegroom. At day's brink
He and his bride were alone at last
In a bedchamber by a taper's blink.

Calmly he said that her lot was cast,
That the door she had passed was shut on her
Till the final catafalk repassed.

The world meanwhile, its noise and stir,
Through a certain window facing the East,
She could watch like a convent's chronicler.   60

Since passing the door might lead to a feast,
And a feast might lead to so much beside,
He, of many evils, chose the least.

"Freely I choose too," said the bride—
"Your window and its world suffice,"
Replied the tongue, while the heart replied—

"If I spend the night with that devil twice,
May his window serve as my loop of hell
Whence a damned soul looks on paradise!

"I fly to the Duke who loves me well,   70
Sit by his side and laugh at sorrow
Ere I count another ave-bell.

"'Tis only the coat of a page to borrow,
And tie my hair in a horse-boy's trim,
And I save my soul—but not to-morrow"—

(She checked herself and her eye grew dim)
"My father tarries to bless my state:
I must keep it one day more for him.

"Is one day more so long to wait?
Moreover the Duke rides past, I know;   80
We shall see each other, sure as fate."

She turned on her side and slept. Just so!
So we resolve on a thing and sleep:
So did the lady, ages ago.

That night the Duke said, "Dear or cheap
As the cost of this cup of bliss may prove
To body or soul, I will drain it deep."

And on the morrow, bold with love,
He beckoned the bridegroom (close on call,
As his duty bade, by the Duke's alcove)   90

And smiled "'Twas a very funeral,
Your lady will think, this feast of ours,—
A shame to efface, whate'er befall!

"What if we break from the Arno bowers,
And try if Petraja, cool and green,
Cure last night's fault with this morning's flowers?"

The bridegroom, not a thought to be seen
On his steady brow and quiet mouth,
Said, "Too much favour for me so mean!

"But, alas! my lady leaves the South   100
Each wind that comes from the Apennine
Is a menace to her tender youth:

"Nor a way exists, the wise opine,
If she quits her palace twice this year,
To avert the flower of life's decline."

Quoth the Duke, "A sage and a kindly fear.
Moreover Petraja is cold this spring:
Be our feast to-night as usual here!"

And then to himself—"Which night shall bring
Thy bride to her lover's embraces, fool—   110
Or I am the fool, and thou art the king!

"Yet my passion must wait a night, nor cool—
For to-night the Envoy arrives from France
Whose heart I unlock with thyself, my tool.

"I need thee still and might miss perchance.
To-day is not wholly lost, beside,
With its hope of my lady's countenance:

"For I ride—what should I do but ride?
And passing her palace, if I list,
May glance at its window—well betide!"   120

So said, so done: nor the lady missed
One ray that broke from the ardent brow,
Nor a curl of the lips where the spirit kissed.

Be sure that each renewed the vow,
No morrow's sun should arise and set
And leave them then as it left them now.

But next day passed, and next day yet,
With still fresh cause to wait one day more
Ere each leaped over the parapet.

And still, as love's brief morning wore,   130
With a gentle start, half smile, half sigh,
They found love not as it seemed before.

They thought it would work infallibly,
But not in despite of heaven and earth:
The rose would blow when the storm passed by.

Meantime they could profit in winter's dearth
By store of fruits that supplant the rose:
The world and its ways have a certain worth:

And to press a point while these oppose
Were simple policy; better wait: 140
We lose no friends and we gain no foes.

Meantime, worse fates than a lover's fate,
Who daily may ride and pass and look
Where his lady watches behind the grate!

And she—she watched the square like a book
Holding one picture and only one,
Which daily to find she undertook:

When the picture was reached the book was done,
And she turned from the picture at night to scheme
Of tearing it out for herself next sun.   150

So weeks grew months, years; gleam by gleam
The glory dropped from their youth and love,
And both perceived they had dreamed a dream;

Which hovered as dreams do, still above:
But who can take a dream for a truth?
Oh, hide our eyes from the next remove!

One day as the lady saw her youth
Depart, and the silver thread that streaked
Her hair, and, worn by the serpent's tooth,

The brow so puckered, the chin so peaked,—   160
And wondered who the woman was,
Hollow-eyed and haggard-cheeked,

Fronting her silent in the glass—
"Summon here," she suddenly said,
"Before the rest of my old self pass,

"Him, the Carver, a hand to aid,
Who fashions the clay no love will change,
And fixes a beauty never to fade.

"Let Robbia's craft so apt and strange
Arrest the remains of young and fair,   170
And rivet them while the seasons range.

"Make me a face on the window there,
Waiting as ever, mute the while,
My love to pass below in the square!

"And let me think that it may beguile
Dreary days which the dead must spend
Down in their darkness under the aisle,

100. **leaves the South,** that is, has come from the South.
101. **Apennine,** a mountain range near Florence.

159. **the serpent's tooth,** age, care, frustration.
169. **Robbia's craft.** The last of the Della Robbias, famous Florentine sculptors and ceramists, died in 1566, but their terra-cotta work continued to be manufactured by others.

"To say, 'What matters it at the end?
I did no more while my heart was warm
Than does that image, my pale-faced friend.'   180

"Where is the use of the lip's red charm,
The heaven of hair, the pride of the brow,
And the blood that blues the inside arm—

"Unless we turn, as the soul knows how,
The earthly gift to an end divine?
A lady of clay is as good, I trow."

But long ere Robbia's cornice, fine,
With flowers and fruits which leaves enlace,
Was set where now is the empty shrine—

(And, leaning out of a bright blue space,   190
As a ghost might lean from a chink of sky,
The passionate pale lady's face—

Eyeing ever, with earnest eye
And quick-turned neck at its breathless stretch,
Some one who ever is passing by—)

The Duke had sighed like the simplest wretch
In Florence, "Youth—my dream escapes!
Will its record stay?" And he bade them fetch

Some subtle moulder of brazen shapes—
"Can the soul, the will, die out of a man   200
Ere his body find the grave that gapes?

"John of Douay shall effect my plan,
Set me on horseback here aloft,
Alive, as the crafty sculptor can,

"In the very square I have crossed so oft:
That men may admire, when future suns
Shall touch the eyes to a purpose soft,

"While the mouth and the brow stay brave in
          bronze—
Admire and say, 'When he was alive
How he would take his pleasure once!'   210

"And it shall go hard but I contrive
To listen the while, and laugh in my tomb
At idleness which aspires to strive."

So! While these wait the trump of doom,
How do their spirits pass, I wonder,
Nights and days in the narrow room?

Still, I suppose, they sit and ponder
What a gift life was, ages ago,
Six steps out of the chapel yonder.

Only they see not God, I know,   220
Nor all that chivalry of his,
The soldier-saints who, row on row,

Burn upward each to his point of bliss—
Since. the end of life being manifest,
He had burned his way through the world to this.

I hear you reproach, "But delay was best,
For their end was a crime."—Oh, a crime will do
As well, I reply, to serve for a test,

As a virtue golden through and through,
Sufficient to vindicate itself   230
And prove its worth at a moment's view!

Must a game be played for the sake of pelf?
Where a button goes, 'twere an epigram
To offer the stamp of the very Guelph.

The true has no value beyond the sham:
As well the counter as coin, I submit,
When your table's a hat, and your prize, a dram.

Stake your counter as boldly every whit,
Venture as warily, use the same skill,
Do your best, whether winning or losing it,   240

If you choose to play!—is my principle.
Let a man contend to the uttermost
For his life's set prize, be it what it will!

The counter our lovers staked was lost
As surely as if it were lawful coin:
And the sin I impute to each frustrate ghost

189. empty shrine. The empty shrine is historical; the bust, unlike the Grand Duke's statue in the Piazza della Santa Annunziata, is not.   202. "John of Douay, Giovanni da Bologna (1525–1608).

216. narrow room, the grave.   227. crime, the contemplated elopement.   228. As well. Actually, in this instance, it serves better. Browning is trying to drive home, with the greatest possible emphasis, the idea that doing nothing is in itself a sin. Had the action the lovers were tempted to commit been a righteous action, this proposition must have been self-evident. test, of the afore-mentioned proposition. 233. 'twere an epigram, it would be absurd, a subject for jest. The epigram is often satirical in spirit.   234. the stamp of the very Guelph, real money, stamped with the insigne of the ruler.   236. counter, a worthless coin, used to represent money in a gambling game.

Is—the unlit lamp and the ungirt loin,
Though the end in sight was a vice, I say.
You of the virtue (we issue join)
How strive you? *De te, fabula!*   250

"CHILDE ROLAND TO THE DARK TOWER CAME"

(See Edgar's Song in "LEAR")

William Lyon Phelps (*Robert Browning*, new ed., Bobbs-Merrill, 1932)[1] has this masterly summary of interpretations:

"The poem *Childe Roland* is unique among Browning's monologues. His poetry usually is that of the noon-day and the market-place; but this might have been written by Coleridge, or Maeterlinck, or Edgar Allan Poe. It has indeed the 'wizard twilight Coleridge knew.' The atmosphere is uncanny and ghoul-haunted: the scenery is a series of sombre and horrible imaginings. No consistent allegory can be made of it, for which fact we should rejoice. It is a poem, not a sermon; it is intended to stimulate the imagination, rather than awaken the conscience. And as we accompany the knight on his lonely and fearful journey, we feel thrills caused only by works of genius.

"The poem is an example of the power of creative imagination. Out of one line from an old ballad quoted by Shakespeare, Browning has built up a marvellous succession of vivid pictures. The twilight deepens as Childe Roland advances; one can feel the darkness coming on.

　　　. . . hands unseen
Were hanging the night around us fast.

"Although the poem means nothing specifically except a triumphant close to a heart-shaking experience, the close is so solemnly splendid that it is difficult to repress a shout of physical exultation. One lonely man, in the presence of all the Powers of the Air, sends out an honest blast of defiance—the individual will against the malignant forces of the whole universe.

247. the unlit lamp and the ungirt loin. See Luke 12:35; also the parable of the wise and foolish virgins, Matthew 25:1–13.　**248. Though the end in sight was a vice.** It is not a fair interpretation of Browning's meaning to say that he teaches that the lovers would have "seen God" if they had committed adultery. The matter is much more complicated than that. In an article on "The Statue and the Bust" in *Poet-Lore*, Vol. X (1898), pp. 397–416, Prentiss Cummings reminds us that Guido, in *The Ring and the Book*, did carry out his purpose, but that Browning does not therefore commend him. "A commendable life involves two things: first, a right purpose; and second, corresponding action." In the present poem, "Browning has . . . knowingly suppressed the importance of a right purpose . . . in order to teach with great force the duty of carrying one's purpose out; and in considering the ethics of conduct as a whole his lesson is knowingly imperfect."　**250. De te, fabula!** The parable concerns you. The story has not been told for its own sake, but rather for its suggestive and symbolical value.

[1] Copyright, 1915, 1932. Used by special permission of the publishers, The Bobbs-Merrill Company.

"What happened when he blew his horn? Did the awful mountains in the blood-red sunset dissolve as the walls of Jericho fell to a similar sound? Did the round, squat Tower vanish like a dream-phantom? Or was the sound of the horn the last breath of the hero? If we believe the former, then Childe Roland is telling his experience to a listener; it is the song of the man 'who came whither he went.' If the latter, which seems to me more dramatic, and more like Browning, then the monologue is murmured by the solitary knight as he advances on his darkening path.

"Three entirely different interpretations may be made of the poem. First, the Tower is the quest, and Success is found only in the moment of Failure. Second, the Tower is the quest, and when found is worth nothing: the hero has spent his life searching something that in the end is seen to be only a round, squat, blind turret—for such things do men throw away their lives! Third, the Tower is not the quest at all—it is damnation, and when the knight turns *aside* from the true road to seek the Tower, he is a lost soul steadily slipping through increasing darkness to hell.

"Whilst I do not believe this third interpretation, for it seems to me contrary to the whole spirit of the piece, it is surprising that if one reads through the poem with that idea and none other in mind, how much support can be found for it. The hoary cripple is the devil, meant to lead us into temptation; and the third stanza seems for the moment to complete this thought.

　　　If at his counsel I should turn aside
　　　　Into that ominous tract, which, all agree
　　　　Hides the Dark Tower. Yet acquiescingly
　　　I did turn as he pointed:

If all knew that the ominous tract contained the Dark Tower, why was the knight outside of it, if the Tower were his quest? He turns aside, acquiescingly: he has given up a life of noble aspiration, and now hands over his despairing heart in surrender to the powers of darkness. He goes on his way a beaten man, only hoping that the end may not be long delayed.

"Much in the letter of the poem may support this view; but the whole spirit of it is opposed to such an interpretation, and the ringing close does not sound like spiritual failure. Nor do I believe in the second interpretation; for it is quite unlike Browning to write a magnificent poem with a cynical conclusion.

"No, I believe that once upon a time, Roland, Giles, Cuthbert, and other knights in solemn assembly took an oath to go on the quest of the Dark Tower: to find it or perish on the way. All but these three have apparently kept their word; they have never returned, and when Roland is on the last stages of his journey, he sees why; they have died a horrible death. The quest is indeed an unspeakably perilous thing: for all but Giles and Cuthbert are dead, and these two suffered a fate worse than death—the awful fear inspired by something hideous on the march changed these splendid specimens of manhood into craven traitors. Roland remembers with cruel agony the ruddy young face of Cuthbert, glowing under its yellow hair: was there ever such a magnificent fellow? But the path to the Tower had shaken his manhood, and disgraced him forever. How well Roland remembers the morning when Giles took the oath to find the Tower! That was ten years ago. The frank, manly young knight stepped forth, and declared proudly that he dared do all that might become a man. But he had some awful experience in the course of the quest that changed him from the soul of honor to a whimpering coward. His own companions spat upon him and cursed him.

"Roland alone is left. And he has experienced so many disappointments that now all hope of finding the Tower is dead in his breast. Just one spark of manhood remains. He can not succeed, but God grant that he may be fit to fail.

> . . . just to fail as they, seemed best,
> And all the doubt was now—should I be fit?

"As he advances the country becomes an abomination of desolation; then appear evidences of struggle, the marks of monsters: then the awful, boiling river, with the nerve-shattering shriek from its depths as he thrust in his spear. On the other bank, fresh evidences of fearful combats, followed farther along by the appearance of engines of torture. Those of his companions who had survived the beasts had there perished in this frightful manner. Nevertheless, Roland advances, his eyes on the ground. Suddenly the wide wing of some dreadful bird of the night brushes his cap, and he looks up—to his overwhelming amazement, *he sees the Tower!* He sees it as the sailor sees the rocks on a dark night, only when the ship is lost. He sees it in a sudden glare of hell; the air is full of mocking laughter, the scorn of fiends mingling with the sound of the names of their victims, his peers and comrades all lost! The ugly misshapen mountains look like sinister giants, lying chin upon hand, lazily awaiting his destruction. But this atom of humanity, in the presence of all the material forces of this world and the supernatural powers of darkness, places the horn to his lips, and sends out on the evening air a shrill blast of utter defiance. He that endureth to the end shall be saved. Not his possessions, not his happiness, not his bodily frame—they all succumb: but *he* shall be saved.

"Thus we may take this wholly romantic poem as one more noble illustration of Browning's favorite doctrine—Success in Failure."

1

My first thought was, he lied in every word,
That hoary cripple, with malicious eye
Askance to watch the working of his lie
On mine, and mouth scarce able to afford
Suppression of the glee, that pursed and scored
Its edge, at one more victim gained thereby.

2

What else should he be set for, with his staff?
What, save to waylay with his lies, ensnare

All travellers who might find him posted there,
And ask the road? I guessed what skull-like laugh 10
Would break, what crutch 'gin write my epitaph
For pastime in the dusty thoroughfare,

3

If at his counsel I should turn aside
Into that ominous tract which, all agree,
Hides the Dark Tower. Yet acquiescingly
I did turn as he pointed: neither pride
Nor hope rekindling at the end descried,
So much as gladness that some end might be.

4

For, what with my whole world-wide wandering,
What with my search drawn out through years,
my hope 20
Dwindled into a ghost not fit to cope
With that obstreperous joy success would bring,—
I hardly tried now to rebuke the spring
My heart made, finding failure in its scope.

5

As when a sick man very near to death
Seems dead indeed, and feels begin and end
The tears and takes the farewell of each friend,
And hears one bid the other go, draw breath
Freelier outside, ("since all is o'er," he saith,
"And the blow fallen no grieving can amend";)

6

While some discuss if near the other graves 31
Be room enough for this, and when a day
Suits best for carrying the corpse away,
With care about the banners, scarves and staves:
And still the man hears all, and only craves
He may not shame such tender love and stay.

7

Thus, I had so long suffered in this quest,
Heard failure prophesied so oft, been writ
So many times among "The Band"—to wit,
The knights who to the Dark Tower's search addressed
Their steps—that just to fail as they, seemed best, 40
And all the doubt was now—should I be fit?

8

So, quiet as despair, I turned from him,
That hateful cripple, out of his highway
Into the path he pointed. All the day
Had been a dreary one at best, and dim
Was settling to its close, yet shot one grim
Red leer to see the plain catch its estray.

48. estray, the one astray; that is, Childe Roland.

9

For mark! no sooner was I fairly found
    Pledged to the plain, after a pace or two,   50
    Than, pausing to throw backward a last view
O'er the safe road, 'twas gone; grey plain all round:
Nothing but plain to the horizon's bound.
    I might go on; nought else remained to do.

10

So, on I went. I think I never saw
    Such starved ignoble nature; nothing throve:
    For flowers—as well expect a cedar grove!
But cockle, spurge, according to their law
Might propagate their kind, with none to awe,
    You'd think; a burr had been a treasure trove. 60

11

No! penury, inertness and grimace,
    In some strange sort, were the land's portion.
    "See
Or shut your eyes," said Nature peevishly,
"It nothing skills: I cannot help my case:
'Tis the Last Judgment's fire must cure this place,
    Calcine its clods and set my prisoners free."

12

If there pushed any ragged thistle-stalk
    Above its mates, the head was chopped; the bents
    Were jealous else. What made those holes and
      rents
In the dock's harsh swarth leaves, bruised as to
    baulk   70
All hope of greenness? 'tis a brute must walk
    Pashing their life out, with a brute's intents.

13

As for the grass, it grew as scant as hair
    In leprosy; thin dry blades pricked the mud
    Which underneath looked kneaded up with
      blood.
One stiff blind horse, his every bone a-stare,
Stood stupefied, however he came there:
    Thrust out past service from the devil's stud!

14

Alive? he might be dead for aught I know,
    With that red gaunt and colloped neck a-strain,
    And shut eyes underneath the rusty mane;   81
Seldom went such grotesqueness with such woe;
I never saw a brute I hated so;
    He must be wicked to deserve such pain.

72. Pashing, throwing or striking violently.

15

I shut my eyes and turned them on my heart.
    As a man calls for wine before he fights,
    I asked one draught of earlier, happier sights,
Ere fitly I could hope to play my part.
Think first, fight afterwards—the soldier's art:
    One taste of the old time sets all to rights.   90

16

Not it! I fancied Cuthbert's reddening face
    Beneath its garniture of curly gold,
    Dear fellow, till I almost felt him fold
An arm in mine to fix me to the place,
That way he used. Alas, one night's disgrace!
    Out went my heart's new fire and left it cold.

17

Giles then, the soul of honour—there he stands
    Frank as ten years ago when knighted first.
    What honest man should dare (he said) he durst.
Good—but the scene shifts—faugh! what hangman
    hands   100
Pin to his breast a parchment? His own bands
    Read it. Poor traitor, spit upon and curst!

18

Better this present than a past like that;
    Back therefore to my darkening path again!
    No sound, no sight as far as eye could strain.
Will the night send a howlet or a bat?
I asked: when something on the dismal flat
    Came to arrest my thoughts and change their
    train.

19

A sudden little river crossed my path
    As unexpected as a serpent comes.   110
    No sluggish tide congenial to the glooms;
This, as it frothed by, might have been a bath
For the fiend's glowing hoof—to see the wrath
    Of its black eddy bespate with flakes and spumes.

20

So petty yet so spiteful! All along,
    Low scrubby alders kneeled down over it;
    Drenched willows flung them headlong in a fit
Of mute despair, a suicidal throng:
The river which had done them all the wrong,
    Whate'er that was, rolled by, deterred no whit.

21

Which, while I forded,—good saints, how I feared
    To set my foot upon a dead man's cheek,   122
    Each step, or feel the spear I thrust to seek
114. bespate, spattered.

For hollows, tangled in his hair or beard!
—It may have been a water-rat I speared,
   But, ugh! it sounded like a baby's shriek.

22

Glad was I when I reached the other bank.
   Now for a better country. Vain presage!
   Who were the strugglers, what war did they
      wage,
Whose savage trample thus could pad the dank 130
Soil to a plash? Toads in a poisoned tank,
   Or wild cats in a red-hot iron cage—

23

The fight must so have seemed in that fell cirque.
   What penned them there, with all the plain to
      choose?
   No foot-print leading to that horrid mews,
None out of it. Mad brewage set to work
Their brains, no doubt, like galley-slaves the Turk
   Pits for his pastime, Christians against Jews.

24

And more than that—a furlong on—why, there!
   What bad use was that engine for, that wheel, 140
   Or brake, not wheel—that harrow fit to reel
Men's bodies out like silk? with all the air
Of Tophet's tool, on earth left unaware,
   Or brought to sharpen its rusty teeth of steel.

25

Then came a bit of stubbed ground, once a wood,
   Next a marsh, it would seem, and now mere earth
   Desperate and done with; (so a fool finds mirth,
Makes a thing and then mars it, till his mood
Changes and off he goes!) within a rood—
   Bog, clay and rubble, sand and stark black
      dearth.   150

26

Now blotches rankling, coloured gay and grim,
   Now patches where some leanness of the soil's
   Broke into moss or substances like boils;
Then came some palsied oak, a cleft in him
Like a distorted mouth that splits its rim
   Gaping at death, and dies while it recoils.

27

And just as far as ever from the end!
   Nought in the distance but the evening, nought
To point my footstep further! At the thought,
A great black bird, Apollyon's bosom-friend,   160

143. **Tophet,** here, hell.   160. **Apollyon,** the devil. See
Revelation 9:11 and the famous scene in *The Pilgrim's Progress.*

Sailed past, nor beat his wide wing dragon-penned
   That brushed my cap—perchance the guide I
      sought.

28

For, looking up, aware I somehow grew,
   'Spite of the dusk, the plain had given place
   All round to mountains—with such name to
      grace
Mere ugly heights and heaps now stolen in view.
How thus they had surprised me,—solve it, you!
   How to get from them was no clearer case.

29

Yet half I seemed to recognize some trick
   Of mischief happened to me, God knows when—
   In a bad dream perhaps. Here ended, then,   171
Progress this way. When, in the very nick
Of giving up, one time more, came a click
   As when a trap shuts—you're inside the den!

30

Burningly it came on me all at once,
   This was the place! those two hills on the right,
   Crouched like two bulls locked horn in horn in
      fight;
While to the left, a tall scalped mountain . . .
      Dunce,
Dotard, a-dozing at the very nonce,
   After a life spent training for the sight!   180

31

What in the midst lay but the Tower itself?
   The round squat turret, blind as the fool's heart,
   Built of brown stone, without a counterpart
In the whole world. The tempest's mocking elf
Points to the shipman thus the unseen shelf
   He strikes on, only when the timbers start.

32

Not see? because of night perhaps?—why, day
   Came back again for that! before it left,
   The dying sunset kindled through a cleft:
The hills, like giants at a hunting, lay,   199
Chin upon hand, to see the game at bay,—
   "Now stab and end the creature—to the heft!"

33

Not hear? when noise was everywhere! it tolled
   Increasing like a bell. Names in my ears,
   Of all the lost adventurers my peers,—

161. **dragon-penned,** feathered like a dragon's wing.
184–86. **The tempest's mocking elf . . . the timbers
start,** as in "The Tale of Carmilhan," in Longfellow's *Tales
of a Wayside Inn.*

How such a one was strong, and such was bold,
And such was fortunate, yet each of old
   Lost, lost! one moment knelled the woe of years.

34

There they stood, ranged along the hillsides, met
   To view the last of me, a living frame   200
   For one more picture! in a sheet of flame
I saw them and I knew them all. And yet
Dauntless the slug-horn to my lips I set,
   And blew. *"Childe Roland to the Dark Tower came."*

FRA LIPPO LIPPI

Browning derived his information concerning Fra
Lippo Lippi (1406–1469) from Vasari and from Filippo
Baldinucci, who stresses the artist's break with the manner of his predecessors. In the poem the painter-monk is
returning to the house of his patron, Cosimo de Medici
(now the Palazzo Riccardi—see notes to "The Statue
and the Bust"), whence he had fled to join a gay carnival
crowd, when he is apprehended by the watch. In his
monologue he states, among other things, his artistic
creed. Art is its own justification; it is not necessary to use
it to preach a sermon or to teach a lesson. Nor need the
painter add "something more." If he simply employs his
skill to reproduce what already exists in nature, so that
those who carelessly passed it by at first hand may respond to its beauty on canvas, he has fulfilled his function. Both the "naturalists" and the "art for art's sake"
crowd have their points of affinity with Fra Lippo Lippi!

Browning himself was neither a naturalist nor an "art
for art's sake" man—nor was he a loose liver—yet it is
clear that Fra Lippo Lippi held all his sympathy, as he
holds ours also. He was a friar without vocation, and the
special circumstances under which he entered the cloister
cause us to judge his failings leniently. Browning did
think of himself as opposing a certain reality to the
febrile idealism of much Victorian poetry, and above
all he was an enthusiastic apostle of the strenuous life. He
could hardly have failed to admire a man who, whatever
other Biblical adjurations he may have disregarded, at
least obeyed the command "All that thy hand findeth
to do, do thou with thy might."

I am poor brother Lippo, by your leave!
You need not clap your torches to my face.
Zooks, what's to blame? you think you see a monk!
What, 'tis past midnight, and you go the rounds,
And here you catch me at an alley's end
Where sportive ladies leave their doors ajar?
The Carmine's my cloister: hunt it up,
Do,—harry out, if you must show your zeal,

Whatever rat, there, haps on his wrong hole,
And nip each softling of a wee white mouse, 10
Weke, weke, that's crept to keep him company!
Aha, you know your betters! Then, you'll take
Your hand away that's fiddling on my throat,
And please to know me likewise. Who am I?
Why, one, sir, who is lodging with a friend
Three streets off—he's a certain . . . how d'ye
   call?
Master—a . . . Cosimo of the Medici,
I' the house that caps the corner. Boh! you were
   best!
Remember and tell me, the day you're hanged,
How you affected such a gullet's-gripe! 20
But you, sir, it concerns you that your knaves
Pick up a manner nor discredit you:
Zooks, are we pilchards, that they sweep the streets
And count fair prize what comes into their net?
He's Judas to a tittle, that man is!
Just such a face! Why, sir, you make amends.
Lord, I'm not angry! Bid your hangdogs go
Drink out this quarter-florin to the health
Of the munificent House that harbours me
(And many more beside, lads! more beside!) 30
And all's come square again. I'd like his face—
His, elbowing on his comrade in the door
With the pike and lantern,—for the slave that holds
John Baptist's head a-dangle by the hair
With one hand ("Look you, now," as who should
   say)
And his weapon in the other, yet unwiped!
It's not your chance to have a bit of chalk,
A wood-coal or the like? or you should see!
Yes, I'm the painter, since you style me so.
What, brother Lippo's doings, up and down, 40
You know them and they take you? like enough!
I saw the proper twinkle in your eye—
'Tell you, I liked your looks at very first.
Let's sit and set things straight now, hip to haunch.
Here's spring come, and the nights one makes up
   bands
To roam the town and sing out carnival,
And I've been three weeks shut within my mew,
A-painting for the great man, saints and saints
And saints again. I could not paint all night—
Ouf! I leaned out of window for fresh air. 50
There came a hurry of feet and little feet,
A sweep of lute-strings, laughs, and whiffs of song,—

Flower o' the broom,
Take away love, and our earth is a tomb!
Flower o' the quince,
I let Lisa go, and what good in life since?
Flower o' the thyme—and so on. Round they went.
Scarce had they turned the corner when a titter
Like the skipping of rabbits by moonlight,—three
   slim shapes,
And a face that looked up . . . zooks, sir, flesh and
   blood,   60
That's all I'm made of! Into shreds it went,
Curtain and counterpane and coverlet,
All the bed-furniture—a dozen knots,
There was a ladder! Down I let myself,
Hands and feet, scrambling somehow, and so
   dropped,
And after them. I came up with the fun
Hard by Saint Laurence, hail fellow, well met,—
Flower o' the rose,
If I've been merry, what matter who knows?
And so as I was stealing back again   70
To get to bed and have a bit of sleep
Ere I rise up to-morrow and go work
On Jerome knocking at his poor old breast
With his great round stone to subdue the flesh,
You snap me of the sudden. Ah, I see!
Though your eye twinkles still, you shake your
   head—
Mine's shaved—a monk, you say—the sting's in
   that!
If Master Cosimo announced himself,
Mum's the word naturally; but a monk!
Come, what am I a beast for? tell us, now!   80
I was a baby when my mother died
And father died and left me in the street.
I starved there, God knows how, a year or two
On fig-skins, melon-parings, rinds and shucks,
Refuse and rubbish. One fine frosty day,
My stomach being empty as your hat,
The wind doubled me up and down I went.
Old Aunt Lapaccia trussed me with one hand,
(Its fellow was a stinger as I knew)
And so along the wall, over the bridge,   90
By the straight cut to the convent. Six words there,
While I stood munching my first bread that month:
"So, boy, you're minded," quoth the good fat
   father
Wiping his own mouth, 'twas refection-time,—
"To quit this very miserable world?
Will you renounce" . . . "the mouthful of bread?"
   thought I;

By no means! Brief, they made a monk of me;
I did renounce the world, its pride and greed,
Palace, farm, villa, shop and banking-house,
Trash, such as these poor devils of Medici   100
Have given their hearts to—all at eight years old.
Well, sir, I found in time, you may be sure,
'Twas not for nothing—the good bellyful,
The warm serge and the rope that goes all round,
And day-long blessed idleness beside!
"Let's see what the urchin's fit for"—that came
   next.
Not overmuch their way, I must confess.
Such a to-do! They tried me with their books:
Lord, they'd have taught me Latin in pure waste!
Flower o' the clove,   110
All the Latin I construe is "amo," I love!
But, mind you, when a boy starves in the streets
Eight years together, as my fortune was,
Watching folk's faces to know who will fling
The bit of half-stripped grape-bunch he desires,
And who will curse or kick him for his pains,—
Which gentleman processional and fine,
Holding a candle to the Sacrament,
Will wink and let him lift a plate and catch
The droppings of the wax to sell again,   120
Or holla for the Eight and have him whipped,—
How say I?—nay, which dog bites, which lets drop
His bone from the heap of offal in the street,—
Why, soul and sense of him grow sharp alike,
He learns the look of things, and none the less
For admonition from the hunger-pinch.
I had a store of such remarks, be sure,
Which, after I found leisure, turned to use.
I drew men's faces on my copy-books,
Scrawled them within the antiphonary's marge, 130
Joined legs and arms to the long music-notes,
Found eyes and nose and chin for A's and B's,
And made a string of pictures of the world
Betwixt the ins and outs of verb and noun,
On the wall, the bench, the door. The monks looked
   black.
"Nay," quoth the Prior, "turn him out, d'ye say?
In no wise. Lose a crow and catch a lark.
What if at last we get our man of parts,
We Carmelites, like those Camaldolese
And Preaching Friars, to do our church up fine 140
And put the front on it that ought to be!"

117. **gentleman processional and fine,** a gentleman
finely attired in churchly garb to march in a religious procession.   **120. wax,** of candles burned in churches.
121. the Eight, Florentine magistrates.   **127. remarks,**
things noticed.   **130. antiphonary's marge,** margins of the
choir book.   **139–40. Carmelites,** an order of friars which
derives its name from Mt. Carmel. **Camaldolese,** of the
convent of Camaldoli, near Florence. **Preaching Friars,**
Dominicans.

67. **Hard by Saint Laurence,** near the Church of San
Lorenzo.   73. **Jerome knocking,** St. Jerome (340?–420),
often so represented.

And hereupon he bade me daub away.
Thank you! my head being crammed, the walls a
    blank,
Never was such prompt disemburdening.
First, every sort of monk, the black and white,
I drew them, fat and lean: then, folk at church,
From good old gossips waiting to confess
Their cribs of barrel-droppings, candle-ends,—
To the breathless fellow at the altar-foot,
Fresh from his murder, safe and sitting there   150
With the little children round him in a row
Of admiration, half for his beard and half
For that white anger of his victim's son
Shaking a fist at him with one fierce arm,
Signing himself with the other because of Christ
(Whose sad face on the cross sees only this
After the passion of a thousand years)
Till some poor girl, her apron o'er her head,
(Which the intense eyes looked through) came at
    eve
On tiptoe, said a word, dropped in a loaf,   160
Her pair of earrings and a bunch of flowers
(The brute took growling), prayed, and so was
    gone.
I painted all, then cried "'Tis ask and have;
Choose, for more's ready!"—laid the ladder flat,
And showed my covered bit of cloister-wall.
The monks closed in a circle and praised loud
Till checked, taught what to see and not to see,
Being simple bodies,—"That's the very man!
Look at the boy who stoops to pat the dog!
That woman's like the Prior's niece who comes   170
To care about his asthma: it's the life!"
But there my triumph's straw-fire flared and
    funked;
Their betters took their turn to see and say:
The Prior and the learnèd pulled a face
And stopped all that in no time. "How? what's
    here?
Quite from the mark of painting, bless us all!
Faces, arms, legs and bodies like the true
As much as pea and pea! it's devil's-game!
Your business is not to catch men with show,
With homage to the perishable clay,   180
But lift them over it, ignore it all,
Make them forget there's such a thing as flesh.
Your business is to paint the souls of men—
Man's soul, and it's a fire, smoke . . . no, it's
    not . . .
It's vapour done up like a new-born babe—

(In that shape when you die it leaves your mouth)
It's . . . well, what matters talking, it's the soul!
Give us no more of body than shows soul!
Here's Giotto, with his Saint a-praising God,
That sets us praising,—why not stop with him?   190
Why put all thoughts of praise out of our head
With wonder at lines, colours, and what not?
Paint the soul, never mind the legs and arms!
Rub all out, try at it a second time.
Oh, that white smallish female with the breasts,
She's just my niece . . . Herodias, I would say,—
Who went and danced and got men's heads cut off!
Have it all out!" Now, is this sense, I ask?
A fine way to paint soul, by painting body
So ill, the eye can't stop there, must go further 200
And can't fare worse! Thus, yellow does for white
When what you put for yellow's simply black,
And any sort of meaning looks intense
When all beside itself means and looks nought.
Why can't a painter lift each foot in turn,
Left foot and right foot, go a double step,
Make his flesh liker and his soul more like,
Both in their order? Take the prettiest face,
The Prior's niece . . . patron-saint—is it so pretty
You can't discover if it means hope, fear,   210
Sorrow or joy? won't beauty go with these?
Suppose I've made her eyes all right and blue,
Can't I take breath and try to add life's flash,
And then add soul and heighten them threefold?
Or say there's beauty with no soul at all—
(I never saw it—put the case the same—)
If you get simple beauty and nought else,
You get about the best thing God invents:
That's somewhat: and you'll find the soul you have
    missed,
Within yourself, when you return him thanks.
"Rub all out!" Well, well, there's my life, in short,
And so the thing has gone on ever since.   221
I'm grown a man no doubt, I've broken bounds:
You should not take a fellow eight years old
And make him swear to never kiss the girls.
I'm my own master, paint now as I please—
Having a friend, you see, in the Corner-house!
Lord, it's fast holding by the rings in front—
Those great rings serve more purposes than just
To plant a flag in, or tie up a horse!   230
And yet the old schooling sticks, the old grave eyes
Are peeping o'er my shoulder as I work,
The heads shake still—"It's art's decline, my son!

189. Giotto, the great painter (1276–1337). His method
conformed to the notions of propriety entertained by Fra
Lippo Lippi's critics.   196–97. Herodias . . . cut off. It
was Salome, the daughter of Herodias, who danced. See
note on l. 34.   229. more purposes, climbing, in the
speaker's case.

148. cribs, thefts. barrel-droppings, wine. candle-ends,
see l. 120.   150. safe, because the civil law could not seize
him in a sacred place.   157. passion, suffering, as in Passion Play.

You're not of the true painters, great and old;
Brother Angelico's the man, you'll find;
Brother Lorenzo stands his single peer:
Fag on at flesh, you'll never make the third!"
Flower o' the pine,
You keep your mistr . . . manners, and I'll stick to mine!
I'm not the third, then: bless us, they must know!
Don't you think they're the likeliest to know,   241
They with their Latin? So, I swallow my rage,
Clench my teeth, suck my lips in tight, and paint
To please them—sometimes do and sometimes
        don't;
For, doing most, there's pretty sure to come
A turn, some warm eve finds me at my saints—
A laugh, a cry, the business of the world—
(*Flower o' the peach,*
Death for us all, and his own life for each!)
And my whole soul revolves, the cup runs over, 250
The world and life's too big to pass for a dream,
And I do these wild things in sheer despite,
And play the fooleries you catch me at,
In pure rage! The old mill-horse, out at grass
After hard years, throws up his stiff heels so,
Although the miller does not preach to him
The only good of grass is to make chaff.
What would men have? Do they like grass or no—
May they or mayn't they? all I want's the thing
Settled for ever one way. As it is,   260
You tell too many lies and hurt yourself:
You don't like what you only like too much,
You do like what, if given you at your word
You find abundantly detestable.
For me, I think I speak as I was taught;
I always see the garden and God there
A-making man's wife: and, my lesson learned,
The value and significance of flesh,
I can't unlearn ten minutes afterwards.

    You understand me: I'm a beast, I know.   270
But see, now—why, I see as certainly
As that the morning-star's about to shine,
What will hap some day. We've a youngster here
Comes to our convent, studies what I do,
Slouches and stares and lets no atom drop:
His name is Guidi—he'll not mind the monks—
They call him Hulking Tom, he lets them talk—
He picks my practice up—he'll paint apace,
I hope so—though I never live so long,
I know what's sure to follow. You be judge!   280
You speak no Latin more than I, belike;

However, you're my man, you've seen the world
—The beauty and the wonder and the power,
The shapes of things, their colours, lights and
        shades,
Changes, surprises,—and God made it all!
—For what? Do you feel thankful, ay or no,
For this fair town's face, yonder river's line,
The mountain round it and the sky above,
Much more the figures of man, woman, child,
These are the frame to? What's it all about?   290
To be passed over, despised? or dwelt upon,
Wondered at? oh, this last course!—you say.
But why not do as well as say,—paint these
Just as they are, careless what comes of it?
God's works—paint anyone, and count it crime
To let a truth slip. Don't object, "His works
Are here already; nature is complete:
Suppose you reproduce her—(which you can't
There's no advantage! you must beat her, then.)"
For, don't you mark? we're made so that we love
First when we see them painted, things we have
        passed   301
Perhaps a hundred times nor cared to see;
And so they are better, painted—better to us,
Which is the same thing. Art was given for that;
God uses us to help each other so,
Lending our minds out. Have you noticed, now,
Your cullion's hanging face? A bit of chalk,
And trust me but you should, though! How much
        more,
If I drew higher things with the same truth!
That were to take the Prior's pulpit-place,   310
Interpret God to all of you! Oh, oh,
It makes me mad to see what men shall do
And we in our graves! This world's no blot for us,
Nor blank; it means intensely, and means good:
To find its meaning is my meat and drink.
"Ay, but you don't so instigate to prayer!"
Strikes in the Prior: "when your meaning's plain
It does not say to folk—remember matins,
Or, mind you fast next Friday!" Why, for this
What need of art at all? A skull and bones,   320
Two bits of stick nailed crosswise, or, what's best,
A bell to chime the hour with, does as well.
I painted a Saint Laurence six months since
At Prato, splashed the fresco in fine style:
"How looks my painting, now the scaffold's down?"
I ask a brother: "Hugely," he returns—
Already not one phiz of your three slaves
Who turn the Deacon off his toasted side,

---

235. Brother Angelico, Fra Angelico, the noted painter
(1387-1455).   **236. Brother Lorenzo,** Lorenzo Monaco
(c. 1370-1425).   **276. Guidi,** Masaccio (1401-1428), actually Fra Lippo Lippi's predecessor, not his successor.

323-24. Saint Laurence . . . fine style. St. Lawrence
was martyred in 258 A.D. by being roasted on a gridiron. At
one point he asked his tormentors to turn him over; he was
"done on one side." **At Prato,** the cathedral at Prato, a
town near Florence.

But's scratched and prodded to our heart's content,
The pious people have so eased their own   330
With coming to say prayers there in a rage:
We get on fast to see the bricks beneath.
Expect another job this time next year,
For pity and religion grow i' the crowd—
Your painting serves its purpose!" Hang the fools!

—That is—you'll not mistake an idle word
Spoke in a huff by a poor monk, God wot,
Tasting the air this spicy night which turns
The unaccustomed head like Chianti wine!
Oh, the church knows! don't misreport me, now!
It's natural a poor monk out of bounds   341
Should have his apt word to excuse himself:
And hearken how I plot to make amends.
I have bethought me: I shall paint a piece
. . . There's for you! Give me six months, then go,
    see
Something in Sant' Ambrogio's! Bless the nuns!
They want a cast o' my office. I shall paint
God in the midst, Madonna and her babe,
Ringed by a bowery, flowery angel-brood,
Lilies and vestments and white faces, sweet   350
As puff on puff of grated orris-root
When ladies crowd to Church at midsummer.
And then i' the front, of course a saint or two—
Saint John, because he saves the Florentines,
Saint Ambrose, who puts down in black and white
The convent's friends and gives them a long day,
And Job, I must have him there past mistake,
The man of Uz (and Us without the z,
Painters who need his patience). Well, all these
Secured at their devotion, up shall come   360
Out of a corner when you least expect,
As one by a dark stair into a great light,
Music and talking, who but Lippo! I!—
Mazed, motionless, and moonstruck—I'm the man!
Back I shrink—what is this I see and hear?
I, caught up with my monk's-things by mistake,
My old serge gown and rope that goes all round,
I, in this presence, this pure company!
Where's a hole, where's a corner for escape?
Then steps a sweet angelic slip of a thing   370

Forward, puts out a soft palm—"Not so fast!"
—Addresses the celestial presence, "nay—
He made you and devised you, after all,
Though he's none of you! Could Saint John there
    draw—
His camel-hair make up a painting-brush?
We come to brother Lippo for all that,
Iste perfecit opus!" So, all smile—
I shuffle sideways with my blushing face
Under the cover of a hundred wings
Thrown like a spread of kirtles when you're gay 380
And play hot cockles, all the doors being shut,
Till, wholly unexpected, in there pops
The hothead husband! Thus I scuttle off
To some safe bench behind, not letting go
The palm of her, the little lily thing
That spoke the good word for me in the nick,
Like the Prior's niece . . . Saint Lucy, I would
    say.
And so all's saved for me, and for the church
A pretty picture gained. Go, six months hence! 389
Your hand, sir, and good-bye: no lights, no lights!
The street's hushed, and I know my own way back,
Don't fear me! There's the grey beginning. Zooks!

ANDREA DEL SARTO

(CALLED "THE FAULTLESS PAINTER")

John Kenyon asked for a photograph of Andrea del
Sarto's picture of his wife and himself in the Pitti Palace,
Florence; Browning, unable to secure one, sent this poem
instead. Andrea's pictures often give the impression of
something viewed through a kind of white mist; the poet
has been wonderfully successful in creating the same
effect in another medium. The silvery grayness of this
"twilight piece" makes a most interesting contrast with
the nervous vitality of "Fra Lippo Lippi." In both cases
the style is the man, not the man writing, but the man
portrayed.

Andrea d'Agnolo di Francesco di Luca (1486–1531)
was the son of a tailor, hence "del Sarto." Browning's
sources for the poem were the same as for "Fra Lippo
Lippi"—Vasari and Baldinucci. The apostle of the glory
of the imperfect could not sympathize with a man who
was able to achieve everything he wanted to do—

"Ah, but a man's reach should exceed his grasp,
    Or what's a heaven for?"

339. **Chianti wine,** wine from Chianti, a region south of
Florence.   345. **There's for you!** He gives him money.
346. **Sant' Ambrogio's,** St. Ambrose's Church in Florence.
347 ff. **I shall paint** . . . The picture described in "The
Coronation of the Virgin," which now hangs in the Academy
of Fine Arts, Florence.   354. **Saint John . . . Florentines.**
St. John the Baptist is the patron saint of Florence.
355–56. **Saint Ambrose . . . long day.** St. Ambrose is
to be shown writing down the names of those who have made
gifts to the convent. As long as these names can be read, the
fame of the donors will endure.   357. **Job,** the hero of the
Old Testament book which bears his name, popularly regarded as a type of patience.   258. **Uz,** where Job lived.

375. **camel-hair,** the raiment of John the Baptist, according to Mark 1:6.   377. **Iste perfecit opus!"** This one did
the work. A scroll attached to the artist's portrait in the
painting carries this legend.   380. **kirtles,** short skirts.
381. **hot cockles.** The blindfolded player in the old English game of cockles must guess who strikes him. But the reference to "The hothead husband" in l. 383 shows that the
monk is thinking also of a less innocent game!

Moreover no true artist ever stops working before he has reached his point of failure. Browning presents Andrea as enslaved to soulless beauty—the complaisant, subservient husband of a faithless wife. And since no man can create anything greater than his own soul, Andrea's pictures, for all their technical perfection, must be essentially meaningless. Some recent writers take a much more favorable view of both Andrea's character and his art.

But do not let us quarrel any more,
No, my Lucrezia; bear with me for once:
Sit down and all shall happen as you wish.
You turn your face, but does it bring your heart?
I'll work then for your friend's friend, never fear,
Treat his own subject after his own way,
Fix his own time, accept too his own price,
And shut the money into this small hand
When next it takes mine. Will it? tenderly?
Oh, I'll content him,—but to-morrow, Love!   10
I often am much wearier than you think,
This evening more than usual, and it seems
As if—forgive now—should you let me sit
Here by the window with your hand in mine
And look a half-hour forth on Fiesole,
Both of one mind, as married people use,
Quietly, quietly the evening through,
I might get up to-morrow to my work
Cheerful and fresh as ever. Let us try.
To-morrow, how you shall be glad for this!   20
Your soft hand is a woman of itself,
And mine the man's bared breast she curls inside.
Don't count the time lost, neither; you must serve
For each of the five pictures we require:
It saves a model. So! keep looking so—
My serpentining beauty, rounds on rounds!
—How could you ever prick those perfect ears,
Even to put the pearl there! oh, so sweet—
My face, my moon, my everybody's moon,
Which everybody looks on and calls his,   30
And, I suppose, is looked on by in turn,
While she looks—no one's: very dear, no less.
You smile? why, there's my picture ready made,
There's what we painters call our harmony!
A common greyness silvers everything,—
All in a twilight, you and I alike
—You, at the point of your first pride in me
(That's gone you know),—but I, at every point;
My youth, my hope, my art, being all toned down
To yonder sober pleasant Fiesole.   40
There's the bell clinking from the chapel-top;
That length of convent-wall across the way
Holds the trees safer, huddled more inside;
The last monk leaves the garden; days decrease,

And autumn grows, autumn in everything.
Eh? the whole seems to fall into a shape
As if I saw alike my work and self
And all that I was born to be and do,
A twilight-piece. Love, we are in God's hand.
How strange now looks the life he makes us lead;   50
So free we seem, so fettered fast we are!
I feel he laid the fetter: let it lie!
This chamber for example—turn your head—
All that's behind us! You don't understand
Nor care to understand about my art,
But you can hear at least when people speak:
And that cartoon, the second from the door
—It is the thing, Love! so such things should be—
Behold Madonna!—I am bold to say.
I can do with my pencil what I know,   60
What I see, what at bottom of my heart
I wish for, if I ever wish so deep—
Do easily, too—when I say, perfectly,
I do not boast, perhaps: yourself are judge,
Who listened to the Legate's talk last week,
And just as much they used to say in France.
At any rate 'tis easy, all of it!
No sketches first, no studies, that's long past:
I do what many dream of, all their lives,
—Dream? strive to do, and agonize to do,   70
And fail in doing. I could count twenty such
On twice your fingers, and not leave this town,
Who strive—you don't know how the others strive
To paint a little thing like that you smeared
Carelessly passing with your robes afloat,—
Yet do much less, so much less, Someone says,
(I know his name, no matter)—so much less!
Well, less is more, Lucrezia: I am judged.
There burns a truer light of God in them,
In their vexed beating stuffed and stopped-up brain,
Heart, or whate'er else, than goes on to prompt   81
This low-pulsed forthright craftsman's hand of mine.
Their works drop groundward, but themselves, I
    know,
Reach many a time a heaven that's shut to me,
Enter and take their place there sure enough,
Though they come back and cannot tell the world.
My works are nearer heaven, but I sit here.
The sudden blood of these men! at a word—
Praise them, it boils, or blame them, it boils too.
I, painting from myself and to myself,   90
Know what I do, am unmoved by men's blame
Or their praise either. Somebody remarks
Morello's outline there is wrongly traced,

15. **Fiesole,** a suburb of Florence.   16. **use,** are accustomed to do.

49–52. **Love . . . let it lie!** Andrea finds fatalism comforting. If God is responsible for his condition, then he need take no responsibility himself.   93. **Morello,** a mountain in the Apennines.

His hue mistaken; what of that? or else,
Rightly traced and well ordered; what of that?
Speak as they please, what does the mountain care?
Ah, but a man's reach should exceed his grasp,
Or what's a heaven for? All is silver-grey
Placid and perfect with my art: the worse!
I know both what I want and what might gain,   100
And yet how profitless to know, to sigh
"Had I been two, another and myself,
Our head would have o'erlooked the world!" No
    doubt.
Yonder's a work now, of that famous youth
The Urbinate who died five years ago.
('Tis copied, George Vasari sent it me.)
Well, I can fancy how he did it all,
Pouring his soul, with kings and popes to see,
Reaching, that heaven might so replenish him,
Above and through his art—for it gives way;   110
That arm is wrongly put—and there again—
A fault to pardon in the drawing's lines,
Its body, so to speak: its soul is right,
He means right—that, a child may understand.
Still, what an arm! and I could alter it:
But all the play, the insight and the stretch—
Out of me, out of me! And wherefore out?
Had you enjoined them on me, given me soul,
We might have risen to Rafael, I and you!
Nay, Love, you did give all I asked, I think—   120
More than I merit, yes, by many times.
But had you—oh, with the same perfect brow,
And perfect eyes, and more than perfect mouth,
And the low voice my soul hears, as a bird
The fowler's pipe, and follows to the snare—
Had you, with these the same, but brought a mind!
Some women do so. Had the mouth there urged
"God and the glory! never care for gain.
The present by the future, what is that?
Live for fame, side by side with Agnolo!   130
Rafael is waiting: up to God, all three!"
I might have done it for you. So it seems:
Perhaps not. All is as God over-rules.
Besides, incentives come from the soul's self;
The rest avail not. Why do I need you?
What wife had Rafael, or has Agnolo?
In this world, who can do a thing, will not;
And who would do it, cannot, I perceive:
Yet the will's somewhat—somewhat, too, the power—
And thus we half-men struggle. At the end,   140
God, I conclude, compensates, punishes.

'Tis safer for me, if the award be strict,
That I am something underrated here,
Poor this long while, despised, to speak the truth.
I dared not, do you know, leave home all day,
For fear of chancing on the Paris lords.
The best is when they pass and look aside;
But they speak sometimes; I must bear it all.
Well may they speak! That Francis, that first time,
And that long festal year at Fontainebleau!   150
I surely then could sometimes leave the ground,
Put on the glory, Rafael's daily wear,
In that humane great monarch's golden look,—
One finger in his beard or twisted curl
Over his mouth's good mark that made the smile,
One arm about my shoulder, round my neck,
The jingle of his gold chain in my ear,
I painting proudly with his breath on me,
All his court round him, seeing with his eyes,
Such frank French eyes, and such a fire of souls   160
Profuse, my hand kept plying by those hearts,—
And, best of all, this, this, this face beyond,
This in the background, waiting on my work,
To crown the issue with a last reward!
A good time, was it not, my kingly days?
And had you not grown restless . . . but I know—
'Tis done and past; 'twas right, my instinct said;
Too live the life grew, golden and not grey,
And I'm the weak-eyed bat no sun should tempt
Out of the grange whose four walls make his world.
How could it end in any other way?   171
You called me, and I came home to your heart.
The triumph was—to reach and stay there; since
I reached it ere the triumph, what is lost?
Let my hands frame your face in your hair's gold,
You beautiful Lucrezia that are mine!
"Rafael did this, Andrea painted that;
The Roman's is the better when you pray,
But still the other's Virgin was his wife—"
Men will excuse me. I am glad to judge   180
Both pictures in your presence; clearer grows
My better fortune, I resolve to think.
For, do you know, Lucrezia, as God lives,
Said one day Agnolo, his very self,
To Rafael . . . I have known it all these years . . .
(When the young man was flaming out his thoughts
Upon a palace-wall for Rome to see,
Too lifted up in heart because of it)
"Friend, there's a certain sorry little scrub

---

105. Urbinate, Raphael, a native of Urbino.
106. George Vasari, (1512–1574), who studied under Andrea, and wrote *The Lives of the Most Eminent Painters, Sculptors, and Architects,* an important source for this poem (see the introductory note).   **130. Agnolo,** Michelangelo (1475–1564).

149. That Francis, Francis I (1494–1547), king of France. According to the story Browning accepted, Andrea left the King's palace at Fontainebleau in obedience to Lucrezia's call, and bought her a house with the money Francis had entrusted to him for the purchase of art treasures. **178. The Roman's,** Raphael's. **186–88. When . . . it,** when Raphael was painting in the Vatican.

Goes up and down our Florence, none cares how, 190
Who, were he set to plan and execute
As you are, pricked on by your popes and kings,
Would bring the sweat into that brow of yours!"
To Rafael's!—And indeed the arm is wrong.
I hardly dare . . . yet, only you to see,
Give the chalk here—quick, thus the line should go!
Ay, but the soul! he's Rafael! rub it out!
Still, all I care for, if he spoke the truth,
(What he? why, who but Michel Agnolo?
Do you forget already words like those?) 200
If really there was such a chance, so lost,—
Is, whether you're—not grateful—but more pleased.
Well, let me think so. And you smile indeed!
This hour has been an hour! Another smile?
If you would sit thus by me every night
I should work better, do you comprehend?
I mean that I should earn more, give you more.
See, it is settled dusk now; there's a star;
Morello's gone, the watch-lights show the wall,
The cue-owls speak the name we call them by. 210
Come from the window, love,—come in, at last,
Inside the melancholy little house
We built to be so gay with. God is just.
King Francis may forgive me: oft at nights
When I look up from painting, eyes tired out,
The walls become illumined, brick from brick
Distinct, instead of mortar, fierce bright gold,
That gold of his I did cement them with!
Let us but love each other. Must you go?
That Cousin here again? he waits outside? 220
Must see you—you, and not with me? Those loans?
More gaming debts to pay? you smiled for that?
Well, let smiles buy me! have you more to spend?
While hand and eye and something of a heart
Are left me, work's my ware, and what's it worth?
I'll pay my fancy. Only let me sit
The grey remainder of the evening out,
Idle, you call it, and muse perfectly
How I could paint, were I but back in France,
One picture, just one more—the Virgin's face, 230
Not yours this time! I want you at my side
To hear them—that is, Michel Agnolo—
Judge all I do and tell you of its worth.
Will you? Tomorrow, satisfy your friend.
I take the subjects for his corridor,
Finish the portrait out of hand—there, there,
And throw him in another thing or two
If he demurs; the whole should prove enough
To pay for this same Cousin's freak. Beside,
What's better and what's all I care about, 240
Get you the thirteen scudi for the ruff!

220. Cousin, lover.   241. scudi. The scudo is an Italian coin.

Love, does that please you? Ah, but what does he,
The Cousin! what does he to please you more?

I am grown peaceful as old age to-night.
I regret little, I would change still less.
Since there my past life lies, why alter it?
The very wrong to Francis!—it is true
I took his coin, was tempted and complied,
And built this house and sinned, and all is said.
My father and my mother died of want. 250
Well, had I riches of my own? you see
How one gets rich! Let each one bear his lot.
They were born poor, lived poor, and poor they died:
And I have laboured somewhat in my time
And not been paid profusely. Some good son
Paint my two hundred pictures—let him try!
No doubt, there's something strikes a balance. Yes,
You loved me quite enough, it seems to-night.
This must suffice me here. What would one have?
In heaven, perhaps, new chances, one more chance— 260
Four great walls in the New Jerusalem,
Meted on each side by the angel's reed,
For Leonard, Rafael, Agnolo and me
To cover—the three first without a wife,
While I have mine! So—still they overcome
Because there's still Lucrezia,—as I choose.

Again the Cousin's whistle! Go, my Love.

ABT VOGLER

(AFTER HE HAS BEEN EXTEMPORISING UPON THE
MUSICAL INSTRUMENT OF HIS INVENTION)

The Abbé Georg Joseph Vogler (1749–1814) was master to Weber, Meyerbeer, and other musicians; among his less famous pupils, as DeVane has shown, was Browning's own teacher, John Relfe. The "musical instrument of his invention" was the orchestrion, a small portable organ. Vogler was noted for his extemporizing, though his compositional activities were not confined to it.

No other great English poet understood music better, or used it more effectively in his poetry, than Browning. Arthur Symons calls "Abt Vogler" "the richest, deepest, fullest poem on music in the language."

I

Would that the structure brave, the manifold music I build,
    Bidding my organ obey, calling its keys to their work,

250. My father . . . want. Andrea neglected his own family to lavish benefits on Lucrezia's.   261. New Jerusalem. See Revelation 21:10-21.   263. Leonard, Leonardo da Vinci (1452–1519).

Claiming each slave of the sound, at a touch, as
  when Solomon willed
  Armies of angels that soar, legions of demons that
    lurk,
Man, brute, reptile, fly,—alien of end and of aim,
  Adverse, each from the other heaven-high, hell-
    deep removed,—
Should rush into sight at once as he named the
  ineffable Name,
  And pile him a palace straight, to pleasure the
    princess he loved!

2

Would it might tarry like his, the beautiful building
  of mine,
  This which my keys in a crowd pressed and im-
    portuned to raise!   10
Ah, one and all, how they helped, would dispart
  now and now combine,
  Zealous to hasten the work, heighten their master
    his praise!
And one would bury his brow with a blind plunge
  down to hell,
  Burrow awhile and build, broad on the roots of
    things,
Then up again swim into sight, having based me
  my palace well,
  Founded it, fearless of flame, flat on the nether
    springs.

3

And another would mount and march, like the
  excellent minion he was,
  Ay, another and yet another, one crowd but with
    many a crest,
Raising my rampired walls of gold as transparent as
  glass,
  Eager to do and die, yield each his place to the
    rest: 20
For higher still and higher (as a runner tips with
  fire,
  When a great illumination surprises a festal
    night—
Outlining round and round Rome's dome from
  space to spire)
  Up, the pinnacled glory reached, and the pride of
    my soul was in sight.

3. Solomon willed. Jewish legend gave Solomon great
power over supernatural beings.   **7. the ineffable Name,**
the name of God, in English usually rendered Jahweh or
Yahweh (in popular books, Jehovah). In the later Israelitish
community it became the custom to substitute Adonai (Lord)
for "the ineffable Name."   **19. rampired,** furnished with
ramparts.   **21–23. as a runner tips . . . space to spire.**
The reference is to the illumination of the dome of St. Peter's
Cathedral on festival occasions.

4

In sight? Not half! for it seemed, it was certain, to
  match man's birth,
  Nature in turn conceived, obeying an impulse as
    I;
And the emulous heaven yearned down, made
  effort to reach the earth,
  As the earth had done her best, in my passion, to
    scale the sky:
Novel splendours burst forth, grew familiar and
  dwelt with mine,
  Not a point nor peak but found and fixed its wan-
    dering star;   30
Meteor-moons, balls of blaze: and they did not pale
  nor pine,
  For earth had attained to heaven, there was no
    more near nor far.

5

Nay more; for there wanted not who walked in the
  glare and glow,
  Presences plain in the place; or, fresh from the
    Protoplast,
Furnished for ages to come, when a kindlier wind
  should blow,
  Lured now to begin and live, in a house to their
    liking at last;
Or else the wonderful Dead who have passed
  through the body and gone,
  But were back once more to breathe in an old
    world worth their new:
What never had been, was now; what was, as it
  shall be anon;
  And what is,—shall I say, matched both? for I
    was made perfect too.   40

6

All through my keys that gave their sounds to a
  wish of my soul,
  All through my soul that praised as its wish
    flowed visibly forth,
All through music and me! For think, had I
  painted the whole,
  Why, there it had stood, to see, nor the process so
    wonder-worth:
Had I written the same, made verse—still, effect
  proceeds from cause,
  Ye know why the forms are fair, ye hear how the
    tale is told;
It is all triumphant art, but art in obedience to laws,
  Painter and poet are proud in the artist-list en-
    rolled:—

34. fresh from the Protoplast, that is, newly created.

7

But here is the finger of God, a flash of the will that
   can,
    Existent behind all laws, that made them and,
    lo, they are!   50
And I know not if, save in this, such gift be allowed
   to man,
    That out of three sounds he frame, not a fourth
    sound, but a star.
Consider it well: each tone of our scale in itself is
   nought;
    It is everywhere in the world—loud, soft, and all
    is said:
Give it to me to use! I mix it with two in my
   thought:
    And, there! Ye have heard and seen: consider
    and bow the head!

8

Well, it is gone at last, the palace of music I reared;
    Gone! and the good tears start, the praises that
    come too slow;
For one is assured at first, one scarce can say that
   he feared,
    That he even gave it a thought, the gone thing
    was to go.   60
Never to be again! But many more of the kind
    As good, nay, better perchance: is this your com-
    fort to me?
To me, who must be saved because I cling with my
   mind
    To the same, same self, same love, same God: ay,
    what was, shall be.

9

Therefore to whom turn I but to thee, the ineffable
   Name?
    Builder and maker, thou, of houses not made with
    hands!
What, have fear of change from thee who art ever
   the same?
    Doubt that thy power can fill the heart that thy
    power expands?
There shall never be one lost good! What was, shall
   live as before;

51–52. And I know not . . . but a star. Though the
architect, the painter, and the poet achieve a permanence
denied the musician (especially the extemporizer), they seem
to Abt Vogler less creative than he. In one form or another,
they recreate what already exists in nature, but his creation
comes into being as something without an original.
66. Builder . . . with hands. This line echoes two passages of Scripture: Hebrews 11:10, 2 Corinthians 5:1.
69–72. There shall never . . . a perfect round. These
lines, definitely Platonic in spirit, link up with Browning's
favorite doctrine of the glory of the imperfect, which is more
fully expressed in the next two sections. Abt Vogler's art is

The evil is null, is nought, is silence implying
   sound;   70
What was good shall be good, with, for evil, so
   much good more;
    On the earth the broken arcs; in the heaven, a
    perfect round.

10

All we have willed or hoped or dreamed of good
   shall exist;
    Not its semblance, but itself; no beauty, nor
    good, nor power
Whose voice has gone forth, but each survives for
   the melodist
When eternity affirms the conception of an hour.
The high that proved too high, the heroic for earth
   too hard,
    The passion that left the ground to lose itself in
    the sky,
Are music sent up to God by the lover and the bard;
    Enough that he heard it once: we shall hear it
    by and by.   80

11

And what is our failure here but a triumph's evidence
    For the fulness of the days? Have we withered or
    agonised?
Why else was the pause prolonged but that singing
   might issue thence?
    Why rushed the discords in but that harmony
    should be prized?
Sorrow is hard to bear, and doubt is slow to clear,
    Each sufferer says his say, his scheme of the
    weal and woe:
But God has a few of us whom he whispers in the
   ear;
    The rest may reason and welcome: 'tis we musi-
    cians know.

12

Well, it is earth with me; silence resumes her reign:
    I will be patient and proud, and soberly acqui-
    esce.   90
Give me the keys. I feel for the common chord
   again,
    Sliding by semitones, till I sink to the minor,—yes,
And I blunt it into a ninth, and I stand on alien
   ground,

very closely connected with his religion. As he sees it, evil, a
negative force, is to life what discord is to music.   **91. common chord,** a given tone with its third and fifth.   **93. ninth,**
(a) an interval containing an octave and a second; (b) a
chord consisting of the common chord with the eighth
advanced one note. See Berdoe, *The Browning Cyclopaedia,*
Macmillan, 1891.

Surveying awhile the heights I rolled from into
    the deep;
Which, hark, I have dared and done, for my resting-
    place is found,
  The C Major of this life: so, now I will try to
    sleep.

RABBI BEN EZRA

Abraham Ibn Ezra (1092–1157) was noted for his
learning in many fields, but his principal fame was as a
commentator on the Old Testament. The last part of his
life was happier than the first, and there are a good many
parallels between the ideas he held and those attributed
to him by Browning.

Poetry has a natural affinity with youth; it was like
Browning, with his delight in difficult subjects, to write
a poem in which the later years are glorified. Rabbi
Ben Ezra accepts the inevitable disappointments and
dissatisfactions of life as the very badge of human
greatness. This world, which contains the wherewithal
to satisfy the animals, does not satisfy us; by this we
know that we are the sons of God. The poem contains
also one of Browning's most famous statements of his
faith in the glory of the imperfect.

That the symbolism of the potter's wheel toward the
close may have been designed as a reply to FitzGerald's
deterministic use of the same figure in *The Rubáiyát of
Omar Khayyám* has been conjectured; compare also Isaiah
64:8 and Jeremiah 18:2–6. DeVane speculates reasonably: "It seems probable that when Browning read of
the potter and the pots in the *Rubáiyát* he thought at
once of Isaiah's words, 'But now, O Lord, thou art our
father; we are the clay, and thou our potter; and we all
are the work of thy hand'—and that he thought too of
Rabbi Ben Ezra's commentary on Isaiah. He then, remembering the fine robust spirit of Ben Ezra, used the
general ideas of the Jewish philosopher to combat Fitz-
Gerald and Omar."—*A Browning Handbook*, Crofts, 1935,
p. 260.

I

Grow old along with me!
  The best is yet to be,
The last of life, for which the first was made:
  Our times are in His hand
  Who saith, "A whole I planned,
Youth shows but half; trust God: see all, nor be
    afraid!"

2

Not that, amassing flowers,
  Youth sighed, "Which rose make ours,
Which lily leave and then as best recall?"

96. **C Major of this life.** The C Major is the natural scale,
without sharps or flats, a symbol of the common level of
everyday life.

Not that, admiring stars,   10
  It yearned "Nor Jove, nor Mars;
Mine be some figured flame which blends, tran-
    scends them all!"

3

Not for such hopes and fears
  Annulling youth's brief years,
Do I remonstrate: folly wide the mark!
  Rather I prize the doubt
  Low kinds exist without,
Finished and finite clods, untroubled by a spark.

4

Poor vaunt of life indeed,
  Were man but formed to feed   20
On joy, to solely seek and find and feast:
  Such feasting ended, then
  As sure an end to men;
Irks care the crop-full bird? Frets doubt the maw-
    crammed beast?

5

Rejoice we are allied
  To That which doth provide
And not partake, effect and not receive!
  A spark disturbs our clod;
  Nearer we hold of God
Who gives, than of His tribes that take, I must
    believe.   30

6

Then, welcome each rebuff
  That turns earth's smoothness rough,
Each sting that bids nor sit nor stand but go!
  Be our joys three-parts pain!
  Strive, and hold cheap the strain;
Learn, nor account the pang; dare, never grudge
    the throe!

7

For thence,—a paradox
  Which comforts while it mocks,—
Shall life succeed in that it seems to fail:
  What I aspired to be,   40
  And was not, comforts me:
A brute I might have been, but would not sink i'
    the scale.

8

What is he but a brute
  Whose flesh has soul to suit,
Whose spirit works lest arms and legs want play?

To man, propose this test—
Thy body at its best,
How far can that project thy soul on its lone way?

9

Yet gifts should prove their use:
I own the Past profuse   50
Of power each side, perfection every turn:
Eyes, ears took in their dole,
Brain treasured up the whole;
Should not the heart beat once "How good to live
    and learn"?

10

Not once beat "Praise be Thine!
I see the whole design,
I, who saw power, see now love perfect too:
Perfect I call Thy plan:
Thanks that I was a man!
Maker, remake, complete,—I trust what Thou
    shalt do!"   60

11

For pleasant is this flesh;
Our soul, in its rose-mesh
Pulled ever to the earth, still yearns for rest;
Would we some prize might hold
To match those manifold
Possessions of the brute,—gain most, as we did best!

12

Let us not always say
"Spite of this flesh to-day
I strove, made head, gained ground upon the
    whole!"
As the bird wings and sings,   70
Let us cry "All good things
Are ours, nor soul helps flesh more, now, than flesh
    helps soul!"

13

Therefore I summon age
To grant youth's heritage,
Life's struggle having so far reached its term:
Thence shall I pass, approved
A man, for aye removed
From the developed brute; a god though in the
    germ.

14

And I shall thereupon
Take rest, ere I be gone   80
Once more on my adventure brave and new:

81. Once more . . . new, in the next life.

Fearless and unperplexed,
When I wage battle next,
What weapons to select, what armour to indue.

15

Youth ended, I shall try
My gain or loss thereby;
Leave the fire ashes, what survives is gold:
And I shall weigh the same,
Give life its praise or blame:
Young, all lay in dispute; I shall know, being old. 90

16

For note, when evening shuts,
A certain moment cuts
The deed off, calls the glory from the grey:
A whisper from the west
Shoots—"Add this to the rest,
Take it and try its worth: here dies another day."

17

So, still within this life,
Though lifted o'er its strife,
Let me discern, compare, pronounce at last,
"This rage was right i' the main,   100
That acquiescence vain:
The Future I may face now I have proved the
    Past."

18

For more is not reserved
To man, with soul just nerved
To act to-morrow what he learns to-day:
Here, work enough to watch
The Master work, and catch
Hints of the proper craft, tricks of the tool's true
    play.

19

As it was better, youth
Should strive, through acts uncouth,   110
Toward making, than repose on aught found made:
So, better, age, exempt
From strife, should know, than tempt
Further. Thou waitedest age: wait death nor be
    afraid!

20

Enough now, if the Right
And Good and Infinite
Be named here, as thou callest thy hand thine own,
With knowledge absolute,
Subject to no dispute
From fools that crowded youth, nor let thee feel
    alone.   120

84. indue, put on.   102. proved, tested.

21

Be there, for once and all,
Severed great minds from small,
Announced to each his station in the Past!
    Was I, the world arraigned,
    Were they, my soul disdained,
Right? Let age speak the truth and give us peace at
    last!

22

Now, who shall arbitrate?
Ten men love what I hate,
Shun what I follow, slight what I receive;
    Ten, who in ears and eyes   130
    Match me: we all surmise,
They this thing, and I that: whom shall my soul
    believe?

23

Not on the vulgar mass
Called "work," must sentence pass,
Things done, that took the eye and had the price;
    O'er which, from level stand,
    The low world laid its hand,
Found straightway to its mind, could value in a
    trice:

24

But all, the world's course thumb
And finger failed to plumb,   140
So passed in making up the main account;
    All instincts immature,
    All purposes unsure,
That weighed not as his work, yet swelled the man's
    amount:

25

Thoughts hardly to be packed
Into a narrow act,
Fancies that broke through language and escaped;
    All I could never be,
    All, men ignored in me,
This, I was worth to God, whose wheel the pitcher
    shaped.   150

26

Ay, note that Potter's wheel,
That metaphor! and feel
Why time spins fast, why passive lies our clay,—
    Thou, to whom fools propound,
    When the wine makes its round,
"Since life fleets, all is change; the Past gone, seize
    to-day!"

    124–25. Was I . . . they. Supply "whom" following
"I" and "they."

27

Fool! All that is, at all,
Lasts ever, past recall;
Earth changes, but thy soul and God stand sure:
    What entered into thee,   160
    That was, is, and shall be:
Time's wheel runs back or stops: Potter and clay
    endure.

28

He fixed thee 'mid this dance
Of plastic circumstance,
This Present, thou, forsooth, wouldst fain arrest:
    Machinery just meant
    To give thy soul its bent,
Try thee and turn thee forth, sufficiently impressed.

29

What though the earlier grooves,
Which ran the laughing loves   170
Around thy base, no longer pause and press?
    What though, about thy rim,
    Skull-things in order grim
Grow out, in graver mood, obey the sterner stress?

30

Look not thou down but up!
To uses of a cup,
The festal board, lamp's flash and trumpet's peal,
    The new wine's foaming flow,
    The Master's lips aglow!
Thou, heaven's consummate cup, what need'st
    thou with earth's wheel?   180

31

But I need, now as then,
Thee, God, who mouldest men;
And since, not even while the whirl was worst,
    Did I,—to the wheel of life
    With shapes and colours rife,
Bound dizzily,—mistake my end, to slake Thy thirst:

32

So, take and use Thy work:
Amend what flaws may lurk,
What strain o' the stuff, what warpings past the
    aim!
    My times be in Thy hand!   190
    Perfect the cup as planned!
Let age approve of youth, and death complete the
    same!

CALIBAN UPON SETEBOS;
OR, NATURAL THEOLOGY IN THE ISLAND

"Thou thoughtest that I was altogether such a one as thyself."

Caliban is the monster in Shakespeare's play *The Tempest;* Sycorax, his mother; Setebos, the name of his god. The magician Prospero holds him in bondage. The action of the play takes place on an unnamed island.

The main title of Browning's poem is intentionally ironical. We read Darwin on evolution, Gibbon on the Roman Empire; why not, then, hear Caliban upon Setebos?

Natural theology—the religious beliefs deducible from the phenomena of nature—stands over against revealed theology, which presupposes that the Deity has taken the initiative to convey some special knowledge of the Truth to a particular group. (See the Bible, the Koran, the *Book of Mormon, Science and Health,* and so on.) In ll. 217–18 Caliban specifically denies the possibility of revelation.

The epigraph is from Psalm 50:21, where it is addressed by God to the wicked. Alexander Pope declared: "An honest man's the noblest work of God." Robert G. Ingersoll, the nineteenth-century American agnostic, cynically reversed the saying: "An honest god's the noblest work of man." Anthropomorphism, the well-known human tendency to frame God in our own image, is undoubtedly the object of some of Browning's shafts in this poem; there are passages, such as ll. 98–108, where he is clearly thinking particularly of the Calvinists, whose special faith in foreordination and election he abhorred. See C. R. Tracy, "Caliban upon Setebos," *Studies in Philology,* Vol. XXXV (1938), pp. 487–99.

Shakespeare's attitude toward Caliban is nearly as unsympathetic and unpsychological as Prospero's own; Browning, probably finding a suggestion in current speculations concerning the "missing link" of Darwinian evolution, takes us on a tour in Caliban's mind. It proves a very interesting mind.

Some aspects of the monster's life and thought are, indeed, quite revolting. His god is not a god of law but a god of caprice. (The difference between the two conceptions is well summarized in Lyman Abbott's saying: "The Ten Commandments are not right because God commanded them; God commanded them because they were right.") Setebos is a moon god; he made the world for spite and for sport; he wanted to escape from ennui; there is no suggestion of any higher motive. The only reason Caliban does not hate him is that he knows that if he were God he would behave quite as badly himself!

But this realization itself indicates capacity for development in Caliban, and it does not stand alone. The monster's joy in creative activity (l. 188) is significant; so is his feeling that Setebos could not possibly have made the stars. He is too sensitive to accept the consistent dualism of his mother, who believed that the Quiet made the world and Setebos vexed it; the world does not bear the signature of the Quiet! Nor can her son agree with Sycorax that more torture is to be looked for after death; Setebos, he feels sure, has done his worst and his all here. (To get the full force of this we must remember that though Browning's faith in immortality was absolute, he did not believe in eternal damnation; annihilation was, to his way of thinking, infinitely more humane than the Calvinistic view of eternity.)

Caliban's two gods and the relations between them suggests H. G. Wells's now abandoned theology in *God the Invisible King,* Macmillan, 1917. Of late years, a number of much more accomplished theologians than Mr. Wells have centered their thought around the conception of a finite God (see Edgar Sheffield Brightman, *The Problem of God,* Abingdon Press, 1930).

For other interesting treatments of Caliban in literature, see Ernest Renan's *Caliban,* 1878, and Percy MacKaye's Shakespeare tercentenary masque, *Caliban by the Yellow Sands,* Doubleday, Page, 1916.

It will save much trouble in reading this poem if certain matters are cleared up at the outset. In ll. 1–23, Browning sets his stage; Caliban does not "blossom into speech" before l. 24. Note the use of brackets to mark this passage off from the monologue, and compare ll. 284–95. The matter is slightly confusing because the second passage, especially, is more or less in Caliban's own style.

The use of an apostrophe before a verb indicates Caliban. He generally speaks of himself in the third person—to help conceal his identity should Setebos overhear him, Stopford Brooke conjectured—rather to indicate the rudimentary character of his own mind, thinks William Lyon Phelps. Caliban refers consistently to Setebos as "He" and to the Quiet as "it."

['Will sprawl, now that the heat of day is best,
Flat on his belly in the pit's much mire,
With elbows wide, fists clenched to prop his chin.
And, while he kicks both feet in the cool slush,
And feels about his spine small eft-things course,
Run in and out each arm, and make him laugh:
And while above his head a pompion-plant,
Coating the cave-top as a brow its eye,
Creeps down to touch and tickle hair and beard,
And now a flower drops with a bee inside,   10
And now a fruit to snap at, catch and crunch,—
He looks out o'er yon sea which sunbeams cross
And recross till they weave a spider-web,
(Meshes of fire, some great fish breaks at times)
And talks to his own self, howe'er he please,
Touching that other, whom his dam called God.
Because to talk about Him, vexes—ha,
Could He but know! and time to vex is now,
When talk is safer than in winter-time.

5. eft-things, newts.   7. pompion-plant, pumpkin. 19. When talk . . . winter-time. In winter Setebos stays closer to the island.

Moreover Prosper and Miranda sleep   20
In confidence he drudges at their task,
And it is good to cheat the pair, and gibe,
Letting the rank tongue blossom into speech.]

Setebos, Setebos, and Setebos!
'Thinketh, He dwelleth i' the cold o' the moon.

'Thinketh He made it, with the sun to match,
But not the stars; the stars came otherwise;
Only made clouds, winds, meteors, such as that:
Also this isle, what lives and grows thereon,
And snaky sea which rounds and ends the same.   30

'Thinketh, it came of being ill at ease:
He hated that He cannot change His cold,
Nor cure its ache. 'Hath spied an icy fish
That longed to 'scape the rock-stream where she
     lived,
And thaw herself within the lukewarm brine
O' the lazy sea her stream thrusts far amid,
A crystal spike 'twixt two warm walls of wave;
Only, she ever sickened, found repulse
At the other kind of water, not her life,
(Green-dense and dim-delicious, bred o' the sun,)
Flounced back from bliss she was not born to
     breathe,   41
And in her old bounds buried her despair,
Hating and loving warmth alike: so He.

'Thinketh, He made thereat the sun, this isle,
Trees and the fowls here, beast and creeping thing.
Yon otter, sleek-wet, black, lithe as a leech;
Yon auk, one fire-eye in a ball of foam,
That floats and feeds; a certain badger brown
He hath watched hunt with that slant white-
     wedge eye
By moonlight; and the pie with the long tongue   50
That pricks deep into oakwarts for a worm,
And says a plain word when she finds her prize,
But will not eat the ants; the ants themselves
That build a wall of seeds and settled stalks
About their hole—He made all these and more,
Made all we see, and us, in spite: how else?
He could not, Himself, make a second self
To be His mate; as well have made Himself:
He would not make what he mislikes or slights,
An eyesore to Him, or not worth His pains: 60
But did, in envy, listlessness or sport,
Make what Himself would fain, in a manner, be—
Weaker in most points, stronger in a few,
Worthy, and yet mere playthings all the while,
Things He admires and mocks too,—that is it.

    50. pie, magpie.

Because, so brave, so better though they be,
It nothing skills if He begin to plague.
Look now, I melt a gourd-fruit into mash,
And honeycomb and pods, I have perceived,
Which bite like finches when they bill and kiss,—   70
Then, when froth rises bladdery, drink up all,
Quick, quick, till maggots scamper through my
     brain;
Last, throw me on my back i' the seeded thyme,
And wanton, wishing I were born a bird.
Put case, unable to be what I wish,
I yet could make a live bird out of clay:
Would not I take clay, pinch my Caliban
Able to fly?—for, there, see, he hath wings,
And great comb like the hoopoe's to admire,
And there, a sting to do his foes offence,   80
There, and I will that he begin to live,
Fly to yon rock-top, nip me off the horns
Of grigs high up that make the merry din,
Saucy through their veined wings, and mind me
     not.
In which feat, if his leg snapped, brittle clay,
And he lay stupid-like,—why, I should laugh;
And if he, spying me, should fall to weep,
Beseech me to be good, repair his wrong,
Bid his poor leg smart less or grow again,—
Well, as the chance were, this might take or else   90
Not take my fancy: I might hear his cry,
And give the mankin three sound legs for one,
Or pluck the other off, leave him like an egg,
And lessoned he was mine and merely clay.
Were this no pleasure, lying in the thyme,
Drinking the mash, with brain become alive,
Making and marrying clay at will? So He.

'Thinketh, such shows nor right nor wrong in Him,
Nor kind, nor cruel: He is strong and Lord.
'Am strong myself compared to yonder crabs   100
That march now from the mountain to the sea;
'Let twenty pass, and stone the twenty-first,
Loving not, hating not, just choosing so.
'Say, the first straggler that boasts purple spots
Shall join the file, one pincer twisted off;
'Say, this bruised fellow shall receive a worm,
And two worms he whose nippers end in red;
As it likes me each time, I do: so He.

Well then, 'supposeth He is good i' the main,
Placable if His mind and ways were guessed,   110
But rougher than His handiwork, be sure!

67. skills, avails.   71. bladdery, in bubbles.   75. Put
case. Consider this hypothetical case.   82. nip me off, the
ethical dative, common in Shakespeare, sometimes found in
formal writing and frequently in popular speech to this day.
See l. 262.   83. grigs, crickets or grasshoppers.

Oh, He hath made things worthier than Himself,
And envieth that, so helped, such things do more
Than He who made them! What consoles but this?
That they, unless through Him, do nought at all,
And must submit: what other use in things?
'Hath cut a pipe of pithless elder-joint
That, blown through, gives exact the scream o' the
    jay
When from her wing you twitch the feathers blue:
Sound this, and little birds that hate the jay   120
Flock within stone's throw, glad their foe is hurt:
Put case such pipe could prattle and boast forsooth
"I catch the birds, I am the crafty thing,
I make the cry my maker cannot make
With his great round mouth; he must blow through
    mine!"
Would not I smash it with my foot? So He.

But wherefore rough, why cold and ill at ease?
Aha, that is a question! Ask, for that,
What knows,—the something over Setebos   129
That made Him, or He, may be, found and fought,
Worsted, drove off and did to nothing, perchance.
There may be something quiet o'er His head,
Out of His reach, that feels nor joy nor grief,
Since both derive from weakness in some way.
I joy because the quails come; would not joy
Could I bring quails here when I have a mind:
This Quiet, all it hath a mind to, doth.
'Esteemeth stars the outposts of its couch,
But never spends much thought nor care that way.
It may look up, work up,—the worse for those   140
It works on! 'Careth but for Setebos
The many-handed as a cuttle-fish,
Who, making Himself feared through what He does,
Looks up, first, and perceives he cannot soar
To what is quiet and hath happy life;
Next looks down here, and out of very spite
Makes this a bauble-world to ape yon real,
These good things to match those as hips do grapes.
'Tis solace making baubles, ay, and sport.
Himself peeped late, eyed Prosper at his books   150
Careless and lofty, lord now of the isle:
Vexed, 'stitched a book of broad leaves, arrow-
    shaped,
Wrote thereon, he knows what, prodigious words;
Has peeled a wand and called it by a name;
Weareth at whiles for an enchanter's robe

The eyed skin of a supple oncelot;
And hath an ounce sleeker than youngling mole,
A four-legged serpent he makes cower and couch,
Now snarl, now hold its breath and mind his eye,
And saith she is Miranda and my wife: 160
'Keeps for his Ariel a tall pouch-bill crane
He bids go wade for fish and straight disgorge;
Also a sea-beast, lumpish, which he snared,
Blinded the eyes of, and brought somewhat tame,
And split its toe-webs, and now pens the drudge
In a hole o' the rock and calls him Caliban;
A bitter heart that bides its time and bites.
'Plays thus at being Prosper in a way,
Taketh his mirth with make-believes: so He.

His dam held that the Quiet made all things   170
Which Setebos vexed only: 'holds not so.
Who made them weak, meant weakness He might
    vex.
Had He meant other, while His hand was in,
Why not make horny eyes no thorn could prick,
Or plate my scalp with bone against the snow,
Or overscale my flesh 'neath joint and joint,
Like an orc's armour? Ay,—so spoil His sport!
He is the One now: only He doth all.

'Saith, He may like, perchance, what profits Him.
Ay, himself loves what does him good; but why?   180
'Gets good no otherwise. This blinded beast
Loves whoso places flesh-meat on his nose,
But, had he eyes, would want no help, but hate
Or love, just as it liked him: He hath eyes.
Also it pleaseth Setebos to work,
Use all His hands, and exercise much craft,
By no means for the love of what is worked.
'Tasteth, himself, no finer good i' the world
When all goes right, in this safe summer-time,
And he wants little, hungers, aches not much,   190
Than trying what to do with wit and strength.
'Falls to make something: 'piled yon pile of turfs,
And squared and stuck there squares of soft white
    chalk,
And, with a fish-tooth, scratched a moon on each,
And set up endwise certain spikes of tree,
And crowned the whole with a sloth's skull a-top,
Found dead i' the woods, too hard for one to kill.
No use at all i' the work, for work's sole sake;
'Shall some day knock it down again: so He.

'Saith He is terrible: watch His feats in proof!   200
One hurricane will spoil six good months' hope.
He hath a spite against me, that I know,
Just as He favours Prosper, who knows why?
So it is, all the same, as well I find.
'Wove wattles half the winter, fenced them firm
With stone and stake to stop she-tortoises
Crawling to lay their eggs here: well, one wave,
Feeling the foot of Him upon its neck,
Gaped as a snake does, lolled out its large tongue,
And licked the whole labour flat: so much for spite.
Saw a ball flame down late (yonder it lies)   211
Where, half an hour before, I slept i' the shade:
Often they scatter sparkles: there is force!
'Dug up a newt He may have envied once
And turned to stone, shut up inside a stone.
Please Him and hinder this?—What Prosper does?
Aha, if He would tell me how! Not He!
There is the sport: discover how or die!
All need not die, for of the things o' the isle
Some flee afar, some dive, some run up trees;   220
Those at His mercy,—why, they please Him most
When . . . when . . . well, never try the same
       way twice!
Repeat what act has pleased, He may grow wroth.
You must not know His ways, and play Him off,
Sure of the issue. 'Doth the like himself:
'Spareth a squirrel that it nothing fears
But steals the nut from underneath my thumb,
And when I threat, bites stoutly in defence:
'Spareth an urchin that contrariwise,
Curls up into a ball, pretending death   230
For fright at my approach: the two ways please.
But what would move my choler more than this,
That either creature counted on its life
To-morrow and next day and all days to come,
Saying, forsooth, in the inmost of its heart,
"Because he did so yesterday with me,
And otherwise with such another brute,
So must he do henceforth and always."—Ay?
Would teach the reasoning couple what "must"
       means!
'Doth as he likes, or wherefore Lord? So He.   240

'Conceiveth all things will continue thus,
And we shall have to live in fear of Him
So long as He lives, keeps His strength: no change,
If He have done His best, make no new world
To please Him more, so leave off watching this,—
If He surprise not even the Quiet's self

216. **Please Him . . . does?** Shall I win his favor, as
Prospero does, so that he may not treat me as he treated, for
example, the newt? 226. **that,** so that. 244. **make,** if he
make.

Some strange day,—or, suppose, grow into it
As grubs grow butterflies: else, here are we,
And there is He, and nowhere help at all.

'Believeth with the life, the pain shall stop.   250
His dam held different, that after death
He both plagued enemies and feasted friends:
Idly! He doth His worst in this our life,
Giving just respite lest we die through pain,
Saving last pain for worst,—with which, an end.
Meanwhile, the best way to escape His ire
Is, not to seem too happy. 'Sees, himself,
Yonder two flies, with purple films and pink,
Bask on the pompion-bell above: kills both.
'Sees two black painful beetles roll their ball   260
On head and tail as if to save their lives:
Moves them the stick away they strive to clear.

Even so, 'would have Him misconceive, suppose
This Caliban strives hard and ails no less,
And always, above all else, envies Him;
Wherefore he mainly dances on dark nights,
Moans in the sun, gets under holes to laugh,
And never speaks his mind save housed as now:
Outside, 'groans, curses. If He caught me here,
O'erheard this speech, and asked "What chucklest
       at?"   270
'Would, to appease Him, cut a finger off,
Or of my three kid yearlings burn the best,
Or let the toothsome apples rot on tree,
Or push my tame beast for the orc to taste:
While myself lit a fire, and made a song
And sung it, "*What I hate, be consecrate
To celebrate Thee and Thy state, no mate
For Thee; what see for envy in poor me?*"
Hoping the while, since evils sometimes mend,
Warts rub away and sores are cured with slime,   280
That some strange day, will either the Quiet
       catch
And conquer Setebos, or likelier He
Decrepit may doze, doze, as good as die.

252. **He,** Setebos.   253. **Idly!** His dam held these ideas
idly; that is, they are wrong.   254. **just . . . pain,**
just enough respite so that we do not die under torture.
271 ff. **'Would, to appease him . . .** Browning is thinking of the primitive habit of sacrificing to the gods, also,
perhaps, of the idea still prevalent in his own time that God
is pleased to have people give up the things that make them
happy. See ll. 294–95. 276. **What I hate.** Setebos must not
suspect Caliban's own attachment to the offering; he is a
jealous god. 277–78. **no mate for Thee,** there is no mate
for Thee; that is, Setebos is unique and incomparable; why,
then, should he permit so insignificant a creature as Caliban
to rouse his wrath? 283. **Decrepit may doze . . . die.**
This contrasts interestingly with Hardy's hope, in *The
Dynasts* and elsewhere, that the Immanent Will behind
the universe, now blind, may some day come to wake and
understand.

[What, what? A curtain o'er the world at once!
Crickets stop hissing; not a bird—or, yes,
There scuds His raven that has told Him all!
It was fool's play, this prattling! Ha! The wind
Shoulders the pillared dust, death's house o' the
   move,
And fast invading fires begin! White blaze—
A tree's head snaps—and there, there, there, there,
   there,   290
His thunder follows! Fool to gibe at Him!
Lo! 'Lieth flat and loveth Setebos!
'Maketh his teeth meet through his upper lip,
Will let those quails fly, will not eat this month
One little mess of whelks, so he may 'scape!]

CONFESSIONS

1

What is he buzzing in my ears?
   "Now that I come to die,
Do I view the world as a vale of tears?"
   Ah, reverend sir, not I!

2

What I viewed there once, what I view again
   Where the physic bottles stand
On the table's edge,—is a suburb lane,
   With a wall to my bedside hand.

3

That lane sloped, much as the bottles do,
   From a house you could descry   10
O'er the garden-wall: is the curtain blue
   Or green to a healthy eye?

4

To mine, it serves for the old June weather
   Blue above lane and wall;
And that farthest bottle labelled "Ether"
   Is the house o'ertopping all.

5

At a terrace, somewhere near the stopper,
   There watched for me, one June,
A girl: I know, sir, it's improper,
   My poor mind's out of tune.   20

6

Only, there was a way . . . you crept
   Close by the side, to dodge
Eyes in the house, two eyes except:
   They styled their house "The Lodge."

7

What right had a lounger up their lane?
   But, by creeping very close,
With the good wall's help,—their eyes might strain
   And stretch themselves to Oes,

8

Yet never catch her and me together,
   As she left the attic, there,   30
By the rim of the bottle labelled "Ether,"
   And stole from stair to stair,

9

And stood by the rose-wreathed gate. Alas,
   We loved, sir—used to meet:
How sad and bad and mad it was—
   But then, how it was sweet!

PROSPICE

The title (Latin) means "Look Forward." The poem
was written shortly after the death of Mrs. Browning, who
is distinctly referred to at the close.

Fear death?—to feel the fog in my throat,
   The mist in my face,
When the snows begin, and the blasts denote
   I am nearing the place,
The power of the night, the press of the storm,
   The post of the foe;
Where he stands, the Arch Fear in a visible form,
   Yet the strong man must go:
For the journey is done and the summit attained,
   And the barriers fall,   10
Though a battle's to fight ere the guerdon be
   gained,
   The reward of it all.
I was ever a fighter, so—one fight more,
   The best and the last!
I would hate that death bandaged my eyes and for-
   bore,
   And bade me creep past.
No! let me taste the whole of it, fare like my peers
   The heroes of old,
Bear the brunt, in a minute pay glad life's arrears
   Of pain, darkness and cold.   20
For sudden the worst turns the best to the brave,
   The black minute's at end,
And the elements' rage, the fiend-voices that rave,
   Shall dwindle, shall blend,
Shall change, shall become first a peace out of pain.
   Then a light, then thy breast,
O thou soul of my soul! I shall clasp thee again,
   And with God be the rest!

APPARENT FAILURE

"We shall soon lose a celebrated building."
—*Paris Newspaper.*

I

No, for I'll save it! Seven years since,
   I passed through Paris, stopped a day
To see the baptism of your Prince;
   Saw, made my bow, and went my way:
Walking the heat and headache off,
   I took the Seine-side, you surmise,
Thought of the Congress, Gortschakoff,
   Cavour's appeal and Buol's replies,
So sauntered till—what met my eyes?

2

Only the Doric little Morgue!   10
   The dead-house where you show your drowned:
Petrarch's Vaucluse makes proud the Sorgue,
   Your Morgue has made the Seine renowned.
One pays one's debt in such a case;
   I plucked up heart and entered,—stalked,
Keeping a tolerable face
   Compared with some whose cheeks were chalked:
Let them! No Briton's to be baulked!

3

First came the silent gazers; next,
   A screen of glass, we're thankful for;   20
Last, the sight's self, the sermon's text,
   The three men who did most abhor
Their life in Paris yesterday,
   So killed themselves: and now, enthroned
Each on his copper couch, they lay
   Fronting me, waiting to be owned.
I thought, and think, their sin's atoned.

4

Poor men, God made, and all for that!
   The reverence struck me; o'er each head

1. **Seven years since**, in 1856.   **3. your Prince**, Prince
Louis Napoleon, son of Napoleon III.   **7. Congress**, the
Congress of Paris, 1856. **Gortschakoff**, Prince Alexander
Gortchakov, who represented Russia.   **8. Cavour's appeal**,
for the recognition of Piedmont in return for the aid she had
given France and Britain in the Crimea. **Buol**, Count von
Buol-Schauenstein, who represented Austria at the Congress.
12. Petrarch's . . . Sorgue. The great poet (1304–1374)
once lived at Vaucluse, near the source of the Sorgue River.

Religiously was hung its hat,   30
   Each coat dripped by the owner's bed
Sacred from touch: each had his berth,
   His bounds, his proper place of rest,
Who last night tenanted on earth
   Some arch, where twelve such slept abreast,—
Unless the plain asphalt seemed best.

5

How did it happen, my poor boy?
   You wanted to be Buonaparte
And have the Tuileries for toy,
   And could not, so it broke your heart?   40
You, old one by his side, I judge,
   Were, red as blood, a socialist,
A leveller! Does the Empire grudge
   You've gained what no Republic missed?
Be quiet, and unclench your fist!

6

And this—why, he was red in vain,
   Or black,—poor fellow that is blue!
What fancy was it turned your brain?
   Oh, women were the prize for you!
Money gets women, cards and dice   50
   Get money, and ill-luck gets just
The copper couch and one clear nice
   Cool squirt of water o'er your bust,
The right thing to extinguish lust!

7

It's wiser being good than bad;
   It's safer being meek than fierce:
It's fitter being sane than mad.
   My own hope is, a sun will pierce
The thickest cloud earth ever stretched;
   That, after Last, returns the First,   60
Though a wide compass round be fetched;
   That what began best, can't end worst,
Nor what God blessed once, prove accurst.

39. Tuileries, the royal palace in Paris.   **46–47. red . . .
black.** Browning refers to the gambling game of rouge-et-
noir. The "poor fellow that is blue" gambled his life and lost.
55–63. "It's wiser . . . prove accurst." "The first three
lines of the last stanza are meant ironically; the six concluding lines of the last stanza are Browning's faith, sincerely expressed."—DeVane, *The Browning Handbook*, p. 277.

from THE RING AND THE BOOK

The primary source of Browning's most elaborate poem was *The Old Yellow Book*, a collection of documents relating to an Italian murder case of 1698, which the poet purchased for eightpence at a Florentine bookstall, probably in June, 1860. The documents, mostly printed but partly in manuscript, had been bound together by a contemporary lawyer. The volume is now in the library of Balliol College, Oxford.

Browning is known to have been considering *The Old Yellow Book* as poetic material as early as 1862, but the elaborate plan finally developed does not seem to have been conceived before the summer of 1864. *The Ring and the Book* was published in four volumes, issued November and December, 1868, January and February, 1869.

The historical situation was, briefly, as follows. Guido Franceschini, a second-rate Florentine nobleman, married, at Rome, 1693, Pompilia, supposed daughter of Pietro and Violante Comparini. The marriage was very unhappy. In 1694 Violante revealed the fact that Pompilia was not her own daughter but had been purchased from a disreputable woman and brought up as a Comparini in order that her foster-parents might inherit a legacy which had been left to them on condition of their having a child. Litigation between Guido and the Comparinis followed. In April, 1697, Pompilia fled from her husband's house under the protection of a young canon, Giuseppe Caponsacchi. Guido overtook them at Castelnuovo and had them arrested. Caponsacchi was banished for three years; Pompilia was first sent to a convent, but, being about to have a child, was permitted to go to her foster-parents in Rome. On December 18, 1697, she gave birth to a son. On January 2, 1698, Guido and four henchmen murdered Comparini and left Pompilia with twenty-two wounds in her body; she died four days later. On February 18, 1698, Guido and his confederates were sentenced to death. Guido appealed to Pope Innocent XII for clemency, but His Holiness refused it. The executions took place on February 22, 1698. A subsequent court session cleared Pompilia's name.

Browning's poem, which runs to more than twenty thousand lines, is divided into twelve books. Book I, "The Ring and the Book," explains the title. The book is, of course, *The Old Yellow Book;* the ring belonged to Mrs. Browning. Browning's analogy between the making of a ring and the making of a poem is intricate and forced; his "fancy" was not, as he modestly termed it, the "alloy" added to the gold of his records, or, if it was, it was fortunately permitted to remain in the finished product. The glorious apostrophe to the soul of Mrs. Browning, which concludes Book I, and serves as a kind of dedication for the poem, follows this introduction. Book II, "Half Rome," gives the viewpoint of those who feel that Guido was justified in what he did; Pompilia was an unfaithful wife, and he struck to avenge his honor. The speaker in Book III, "The Other Half Rome," is no better informed, but being more chivalrous and more humane, he takes Pompilia's part. Book IV, "Tertium Quid," is the utterance of a detached spirit who weighs evidence pro and con but refuses to commit himself to a definite decision.

Book V, "Count Guido Franceschini," the criminal's defense before his judges, is the first major monologue. Guido is conciliatory, hypocritical, and diabolically clever; unless we are very careful we may almost be convinced. Guido is the only one among his dramatis personae whom Browning allows to speak twice; in Book XI, "Guido," after the Pope has finally condemned him the murderer shows his true savagery, the two monologues forming thus the most effective possible contrast. Book VI, "Giuseppe Caponsacchi," also contrasts effectively with what has preceded it. Instead of trying to ingratiate himself with his judges, the indignant priest boldly takes the offensive. He has served God and helpless innocence; it is those who quibble over technicalities while a woman lies dying who are on trial, not he! Book VII, "Pompilia," the young wife's testimony on her deathbed, is given complete in this book.

After "Pompilia," the first of the poem's two magnificent high points, Browning deliberately introduces anticlimax in Book VIII, "Dominus Hyacinthus de Archangelis" (Guido's lawyer) and Book IX, "Juris Doctor Johannes-Baptista Bottinius" (Pompilia's lawyer). Both are preoccupied with technicalities and their own selfish interests; the poet has no more respect for one than for the other.

Book X, "The Pope" (Innocent XII), is the second great climax. The first part of the Pope's speech is a review of the case, the second, an inquiry, more from Browning's point of view than from that of a seventeenth-century churchman, into the Christian faith. Then follows Guido's speech, in Book XI, referred to above.

In Book XII, "The Book and the Ring," Browning again speaks in his own person, tying up loose ends, introducing several fresh testimonies, and interpreting, finally, the significance of his material.

There has been much discussion as to the degree of Browning's faithfulness to history in *The Ring and the Book*. The poet seems, strangely, to have believed that he had made an accurate report of a historical event, but such misrepresentation is unfair to his genius. The major characters, as they live and breathe, are his, not the *Old Yellow Book's;* Pompilia, one of the few characters in modern literature who can, without extravagance, be compared to the great heroines of Shakespeare, was undoubtedly indebted to Elizabeth Barrett Browning. The Beatrice of *The Divine Comedy* may be the greatest tribute ever paid to a woman, but she is so etherealized and universalized that all the individual qualities of the human being have dropped out. Indeed Dante could have done nothing else, for he knew his Beatrice, even in this life, only as an ideal, never as a woman. It was very different with Browning and his love, and the difference shows in Pompilia's monologue.

In method, *The Ring and the Book* represents the ultimate development of Browning's genius for the dramatic monologue. Perhaps only Browning, with his well-known delight in difficulties, would have dared risk tiring his readers by telling the same story so many times. But it is no mere feat of skill that he achieves when he holds our interest, for we are not held by the story as such—that, with a fine disregard for the ordinary story-values, Browning had given us early in Book I. We are interested in the characters and the motives of the people who lived it. Like Dickens, like Meredith, Browning loved a murder trial, but we shall belie him grossly if, while admitting his art, we lament, as Carlyle was inclined to do, that he has lavished it upon so sordid, so unimportant a subject. Rather, as Dean Frederick Morgan Padelford has pointed out, the sensitive reader "experiences that enlarging sense, that emancipation, which attends the sudden realization that life is shot through with meaning, that there is no commonplace, that in the most obscure of lives are epitomized the very forces that struggle for the mastery of the universe" (Preface to *The Ring and the Book*, Modern Student's Library, Scribner, 1917, p. xvi).

The Ring and the Book is much less difficult reading than a great deal of Browning's work; it is not surprising that it should have attracted a wider public than many of his earlier poems. In 1927 Arthur Goodrich and Rose Palmer made a play of it—*Caponsacchi*—which furnished Walter Hampden with one of the great successes of his career.

from BOOK I: THE RING AND THE BOOK

O lyric Love, half angel and half bird,
And all a wonder and a wild desire,—
Boldest of hearts that ever braved the sun,
Took sanctuary within the holier blue,
And sang a kindred soul out to his face,—
Yet human at the red-ripe of the heart—
When the first summons from the darkling earth
Reached thee amid thy chambers, blanched their blue,
And bared them of the glory—to drop down,
To toil for man, to suffer or to die,—   1400
This is the same voice: can thy soul know change?
Hail then, and hearken from the realms of help!
Never may I commence my song, my due
To God who best taught song by gift of thee,
Except with bent head and beseeching hand—
That still, despite the distance and the dark,
What was, again may be; some interchange
Of grace, some splendour once thy very thought,
Some benediction anciently thy smile:
—Never conclude, but raising hand and head   1410
Thither where eyes, that cannot reach, yet yearn
For all hope, all sustainment, all reward,

Their utmost up and on,—so blessing back
In those thy realms of help, that heaven thy home,
Some whiteness which, I judge, thy face makes proud,
Some wanness where, I think, thy foot may fall!

BOOK VII: POMPILIA

I am just seventeen years and five months old,
And, if I lived one day more, three full weeks;
'Tis writ so in the church's register,
Lorenzo in Lucina, all my names
At length, so many names for one poor child,
—Francesca Camilla Vittoria Angela
Pompilia Comparini,—laughable!
Also 'tis writ that I was married there
Four years ago: and they will add, I hope,
When they insert my death, a word or two,—   10
Omitting all about the mode of death,—
This, in its place, this which one cares to know,
That I had been a mother of a son
Exactly two weeks. It will be through grace
O' the Curate, not through any claim I have;
Because the boy was born at, so baptized
Close to, the Villa, in the proper church:
A pretty church, I say no word against,
Yet stranger-like,—while this Lorenzo seems
My own particular place, I always say.   20
I used to wonder, when I stood scarce high
As the bed here, what the marble lion meant,
With half his body rushing from the wall,
Eating the figure of a prostrate man—
(To the right, it is, of entry by the door)—
An ominous sign to one baptized like me,
Married, and to be buried there, I hope.
And they should add, to have my life complete,
He is a boy and Gaetan by name—
Gaetano, for a reason,—if the friar   30
Don Celestine will ask this grace for me
Of Curate Ottoboni: he it was
Baptized me: he remembers my whole life
As I do his grey hair.

                        All these few things
I know are true,—will you remember them?
Because time flies. The surgeon cared for me,
To count my wounds,—twenty-two dagger-wounds,
Five deadly, but I do not suffer much—
Or too much pain,—and am to die to-night.

4. **Lorenzo in Lucina**, the Church of San Lorenzo-in-Lucina, in Rome, Pompilia's "own" church, the church in which she was brought up.   30. **Gaetano, for a reason.** See ll. 100–07.   31. **Don Celestine**, who heard her confession.

Oh how God good is that my babe was born,   40
—Better than born, baptized and hid away
Before this happened, safe from being hurt!
That had been sin God could not well forgive:
He was too young to smile and save himself.
When they took, two days after he was born,
My babe away from me to be baptized
And hidden awhile, for fear his foe should find,—
The country-woman, used to nursing babes,
Said "Why take on so? where is the great loss?
These next three weeks he will but sleep and feed,
Only begin to smile at the month's end;   51
He would not know you, if you kept him here,
Sooner than that; so, spend three merry weeks
Snug in the Villa, getting strong and stout,
And then I bring him back to be your own,
And both of you may steal to—we know where!"
The month—there wants of it two weeks this day!
Still, I half fancied when I heard the knock
At the Villa in the dusk, it might prove she—
Come to say "Since he smiles before the time,   60
Why should I cheat you out of one good hour?
Back I have brought him; speak to him and judge!"
Now I shall never see him; what is worse,
When he grows up and gets to be my age,
He will seem hardly more than great boy;
And if he asks "What was my mother like?"
People may answer "Like girls of seventeen"—
And how can he but think of this and that,
Lucias, Marias, Sofias, who titter or blush
When he regards them as such boys may do?   70
Therefore I wish someone will please to say
I looked already old though I was young;
Do I not . . . say, if you are by to speak . . .
Look nearer twenty? No more like, at least,
Girls who look arch or redden when boys laugh,
Than the poor Virgin that I used to know
At our street-corner in a lonely niche,—
The babe, that sat upon her knees, broke off,—
Thin white glazed clay, you pitied her the more:
She, not the gay ones, always got my rose.   80

How happy those are who know how to write!
Such could write what their son should read in time,
Had they a whole day to live out like me.
Also my name is not a common name,
"Pompilia," and may help to keep apart
A little the thing I am from what girls are.
But then how far away, how hard to find
Will anything about me have become,

Even if the boy bethink himself and ask!
No father that he ever knew at all,   90
Nor had ever—no, never had, I say!
That is the truth,—nor any mother left,
Out of the little two weeks that she lived,
Fit for such memory as might assist:
As good too as no family, no name,
Not even poor old Pietro's name, nor hers,
Poor kind unwise Violante, since it seems
They must not be my parents any more.
That is why something put it in my head
To call the boy "Gaetano"—no old name   100
For sorrow's sake; I looked up to the sky
And took a new saint to begin anew.
One who has only been made saint—how long?
Twenty-five years: so, carefuller, perhaps,
To guard a namesake than those old saints grow,
Tired out by this time,—see my own five saints!

On second thoughts, I hope he will regard
The history of me as what someone dreamed,
And get to disbelieve it at the last:
Since to myself it dwindles fast to that,   110
Sheer dreaming and impossibility,—
Just in four days too! All the seventeen years,
Not once did a suspicion visit me
How very different a lot is mine
From any other woman's in the world.
The reason must be, 'twas by step and step
It got to grow so terrible and strange.
These strange woes stole on tiptoe, as it were,
Into my neighbourhood and privacy,
Sat down where I sat, laid them where I lay;   120
And I was found familiarised with fear,
When friends broke in, held up a torch and cried
"Why, you Pompilia in the cavern thus,
How comes that arm of yours about a wolf?
And the soft length,—lies in and out your feet
And laps you round the knee,—a snake it is!"
And so on.

                      Well, and they are right enough,
By the torch they hold up now: for first, observe,
I never had a father,—no, nor yet
A mother: my own boy can say at least   130
"I had a mother whom I kept two weeks!"
Not I, who little used to doubt . . . I doubt
Good Pietro, kind Violante, gave me birth?
They loved me always as I love my babe
(—Nearly so, that is—quite so could not be—)
Did for me all I meant to do for him,

---

43. **That . . . forgive.** If Guido had killed his child, God himself could hardly have forgiven him. As it is, Pompilia still hopes that he may be forgiven. 78. **The babe . . . broke off.** Therefore she is a good symbol for Pompilia.

102. **a new saint.** St. Gaetan (1480–1547) was canonized in 1671. 106. **my own five saints,** for whom she was named. They had not taken very good care of her. See ll. 6–7.

Till one surprising day, three years ago,
They both declared, at Rome, before some judge
In some Court where the people flocked to hear,
That really I had never been their child,   140
Was a mere castaway, the careless crime
Of an unknown man, the crime and care too much
Of a woman known too well,—little to these,
Therefore, of whom I was the flesh and blood:
What then to Pietro and Violante, both
No more my relatives than you or you?
Nothing to them! You know what they declared.

So with my husband,—just such a surprise,
Such a mistake, in that relationship!
Everyone says that husbands love their wives,   150
Guard them and guide them, give them happiness;
'Tis duty, law, pleasure, religion: well,
You see how much of this comes true in mine!
People indeed would fain have somehow proved
He was no husband: but he did not hear,
Or would not wait, and so has killed us all.
Then there is . . . only let me name one more!
There is the friend,—men will not ask about,
But tell untruths of, and give nicknames to,
And think my lover, most surprise of all!   160
Do only hear, it is the priest they mean,
Giuseppe Caponsacchi: a priest—love,
And love me! Well, yet people think he did.
I am married, he has taken priestly vows,
They know that, and yet go on, say, the same,
"Yes, how he loves you!" "That was love"—they
    say,
When anything is answered that they ask:
Or else "No wonder you love him"—they say.
Then they shake heads, pity much, scarcely blame—
As if we neither of us lacked excuse,   170
And anyhow are punished to the full,
And downright love atones for everything!
Nay, I heard read out in the public Court
Before the judge, in presence of my friends,
Letters 'twas said the priest had sent to me,
And other letters sent him by myself,
We being lovers!

              Listen what this is like!
When I was a mere child, my mother . . . . that's
Violante, you must let me call her so,
Nor waste time, trying to unlearn the word . . . .
She brought a neighbour's child of my own age 181
To play with me of rainy afternoons;
And, since there hung a tapestry on the wall,

We two agreed to find each other out
Among the figures. "Tisbe, that is you,
With half-moon on your hair-knot, spear in hand,
Flying, but no wings, only the great scarf
Blown to a bluish rainbow at your back:
Call off your hound and leave the stag alone!"
"—And there are you, Pompilia, such green leaves
Flourishing out of your five finger-ends,   191
And all the rest of you so brown and rough:
Why is it you are turned a sort of tree?"
You know the figures never were ourselves
Though we nicknamed them so. Thus, all my life,—
As well what was, as what, like this, was not,—
Looks old, fantastic and impossible:
I touch a fairy thing that fades and fades.
—Even to my babe! I thought, when he was born,
Something began for once that would not end,   200
Nor change into a laugh at me, but stay
For evermore, eternally quite mine.
Well, so he is,—but yet they bore him off,
The third day, lest my husband should lay traps
And catch him, and by means of him catch me.
Since they have saved him so, it was well done:
Yet thence comes such confusion of what was
With what will be,—that late seems long ago,
And, what years should bring round, already come,
Till even he withdraws into a dream   210
As the rest do: I fancy him grown great,
Strong, stern, a tall young man who tutors me,
Frowns with the others "Poor imprudent child!
Why did you venture out of the safe street?
Why go so far from help to that lone house?
Why open at the whisper and the knock?"

Six days ago when it was New Year's-day,
We bent above the fire and talked of him,
What he should do when he was grown and great.
Violante, Pietro, each had given the arm   220
I leant on, to walk by, from couch to chair
And fireside,—laughed, as I lay safe at last,
"Pompilia's march from bed to board is made,
Pompilia back again and with a babe,
Shall one day lend his arm and help her walk!"
Then we all wished each other more New Years.
Pietro began to scheme—"Our cause is gained;
The law is stronger than a wicked man:
Let him henceforth go his way, leave us ours!
We will avoid the city, tempt no more   230
The greedy ones by feasting and parade,—
Live at the other villa, we know where,
Still farther off, and we can watch the babe

---

156. would not wait. A legal decision on the matter of
Pompilia's relationship to Guido was pending when he murdered her.

185. that, evidently a representation of Diana.
193. turned a sort of tree. The river god Peneus turned
his daughter Daphne to a laurel to save her from Apollo.

Grow fast in the good air; and wood is cheap
And wine sincere outside the city gate.
I still have two or three old friends will grope
Their way along the mere half-mile of road,
With staff and lantern on a moonless night
When one needs talk: they'll find me, never fear,
And I'll find them a flask of the old sort yet!"   240
Violante said "You chatter like a crow:
Pompilia tires o' the tattle, and shall to bed:
Do not too much the first day,—somewhat more
To-morrow, and, the next, begin the cape
And hood and coat! I have spun wool enough."
Oh what a happy friendly eve was that!

And, next day, about noon, out Pietro went—
He was so happy and would talk so much,
Until Violante pushed and laughed him forth
Sight-seeing in the cold,—"So much to see   250
I' the churches! Swathe your throat three times!"
    she cried,
"And, above all, beware the slippery ways,
And bring us all the news by supper-time!"
He came back late, laid by cloak, staff and hat,
Powdered so thick with snow it made us laugh,
Rolled a great log upon the ash o' the hearth,
And bade Violante treat us to a flask,
Because he had obeyed her faithfully,
Gone sight-see through the seven, and found no
    church
To his mind like San Giovanni—"There's the fold,
And all the sheep together, big as cats!   261
And such a shepherd, half the size of life,
Starts up and hears the angel"—when, at the door,
A tap: we started up: you know the rest.

Pietro at least had done no harm, I know;
Nor even Violante, so much harm as makes
Such revenge lawful. Certainly she erred—
Did wrong, how shall I dare say otherwise?—
In telling that first falsehood, buying me
From my poor faulty mother at a price,   270
To pass off upon Pietro as his child.
If one should take my babe, give him a name,
Say he was not Gaetano and my own,
But that some other woman made his mouth
And hands and feet,—how very false were that!
No good could come of that; and all harm did.
Yet if a stranger were to represent
"Needs must you either give your babe to me
And let me call him mine for evermore,

Or let your husband get him"—ah, my God,   280
That were a trial I refuse to face!
Well, just so here: it proved wrong but seemed right
To poor Violante—for there lay, she said,
My poor real dying mother in her rags,
Who put me from her with the life and all,
Poverty, pain, shame and disease at once,
To die the easier by what price I fetched—
Also (I hope) because I should be spared
Sorrow and sin,—why may not that have helped?
My father,—he was no one, any one,—   290
The worse, the likelier,—call him,—he who came,
Was wicked for his pleasure, went his way,
And left no trace to track by; there remained
Nothing but me, the unnecessary life,
To catch up or let fall,—and yet a thing
She could make happy, be made happy with,
This poor Violante,—who would frown thereat?

Well, God, you see! God plants us where we grow.
It is not that because a bud is born
At a wild briar's end, full i' the wild beast's way,
We ought to pluck and put it out of reach   301
On the oak-tree top,—say "There the bud be-
    longs!"
She thought, moreover, real lies were lies told
For harm's sake; whereas this had good at heart,
Good for my mother, good for me, and good
For Pietro who was meant to love a babe,
And needed one to make his life of use,
Receive his house and land when he should die.
Wrong, wrong and always wrong! how plainly
    wrong!
For see, this fault kept pricking, as faults do,   310
All the same at her heart: this falsehood hatched,
She could not let it go nor keep it fast.
She told me so,—the first time I was found
Locked in her arms once more after the pain,
When the nuns let me leave them and go home,
And both of us cried all the cares away,—
This it was set her on to make amends,
This brought about the marriage—simply this!
Do let me speak for her you blame so much!
When Paul, my husband's brother, found me out,
Heard there was wealth for who should marry me,
So, came and made a speech to ask my hand   322
For Guido,—she, instead of piercing straight
Through the pretence to the ignoble truth,
Fancied she saw God's very finger point,
Designate just the time for planting me
(The wild-briar slip she plucked to love and wear)
In soil where I could strike real root, and grow,

235. sincere, pure.   259. the seven, the seven hills of
Rome.   260–63. San Giovanni, the Lateran. "There's
the fold, . . ." a representation of the manger scene in
the church.

319. you, those gathered about her bed where she lies dying, and to whom her speech is addressed.

And get to be the thing I called myself:
For, wife and husband are one flesh, God says,   330
And I, whose parents seemed such and were none,
Should in a husband have a husband now,
Find nothing, this time, but was what it seemed,
—All truth and no confusion any more.
I know she meant all good to me, all pain
To herself,—since how could it be aught but pain,
To give me up, so, from her very breast,
The wilding flower-tree-branch that, all those
        years,
She had got used to feel for and find fixed?
She meant well: has it been so ill i' the main?   340
That is but fair to ask: one cannot judge
Of what has been the ill or well of life,
The day that one is dying,—sorrows change
Into not altogether sorrow-like;
I do see strangeness but scarce misery,
Now it is over, and no danger more.
My child is safe; there seems not so much pain.
It comes, most like, that I am just absolved,
Purged of the past, the foul in me, washed fair,—
One cannot both have and not have, you know,—
Being right now, I am happy and colour things.   351
Yes, everybody that leaves life sees all
Softened and bettered: so with other sights:
To me at least was never evening yet
But seemed far beautifuller than its day,
For past is past.

                    There was a fancy came,
When somewhere, in the journey with my friend,
We stepped into a hovel to get food;
And there began a yelp here, a bark there,—
Misunderstanding creatures that were wroth   360
And vexed themselves and us till we retired.
The hovel is life: no matter what dogs bit
Or cats scratched in the hovel I break from,
All outside is lone field, moon and such peace—
Flowing in, filling up as with a sea
Whereon comes Someone, walks fast on the white,
Jesus Christ's self, Don Celestine declares,
To meet me and calm all things back again.

Beside, up to my marriage, thirteen years
Were, each day, happy as the day was long: 370
This may have made the change too terrible.

330. **God says,** in Genesis 2:24.   348. **It,** death. **most like,** most likely. **that,** when. The Church teaches that the eternal condition of the soul depends upon its spiritual condition at the time of death. Pompilia, passing into eternity just after having made her confession and received absolution, would have no sins to purge in Purgatory. 351. **I . . . colour things,** see them not objectively but in the light of my own mood and spiritual condition. 366-67. **Whereon . . . self.** See Matthew 14:22-33.

I know that when Violante told me first
The cavalier—she meant to bring next morn,
Whom I must also let take, kiss my hand—
Would be at San Lorenzo the same eve
And marry me,—which over, we should go
Home both of us without him as before,
And, till she bade speak, I must hold my tongue,
Such being the correct way with girl-brides,
From whom one word would make a father
        blush,—   380
I know, I say, that when she told me this,
—Well, I no more saw sense in what she said
Than a lamb does in people clipping wool;
Only lay down and let myself be clipped.
And when next day the cavalier who came—
(Tisbe had told me that the slim young man
With wings at head, and wings at feet, and sword
Threatening a monster, in our tapestry,
Would eat a girl else,—was a cavalier)
When he proved Guido Franceschini,—old   390
And nothing like so tall as I myself,
Hook-nosed and yellow in a bush of beard,
Much like a thing I saw on a boy's wrist,
He called an owl and used for catching birds,—
And when he took my hand and made a smile—
Why, the uncomfortableness of it all
Seemed hardly more important in the case
Than,—when one gives you, say, a coin to spend,—
Its newness or its oldness; if the piece
Weigh properly and buy you what you wish,   400
No matter whether you get grime or glare!
Men take the coin, return you grapes and figs.
Here, marriage was the coin, a dirty piece
Would purchase me the praise of those I loved:
About what else should I concern myself?

So, hardly knowing what a husband meant,
I supposed this or any man would serve,
No whit the worse for being so uncouth:
For I was ill once and a doctor came
With a great ugly hat, no plume thereto,   410
Black jerkin and black buckles and black sword,
And white sharp beard over the ruff in front,
And oh so lean, so sour-faced and austere!—
Who felt my pulse, made me put out my tongue,
Then oped a phial, dripped a drop or two
Of a black bitter something,—I was cured!
What mattered the fierce beard or the grim face?
It was the physic beautified the man,
Master Malpichi,—never met his match
In Rome, they said,—so ugly all the same!   420

386. **slim young man,** probably Perseus, who saved Andromeda.   419. **Master Malpichi,** Marcello Malpighi (1628-1694), a great physician.

However, I was hurried through a storm,
Next dark eve of December's deadest day—
How it rained!—through our street and the Lion's-
mouth
And the bit of Corso,—cloaked round, covered
close,
I was like something strange or contraband,—
Into blank San Lorenzo, up the aisle,
My mother keeping hold of me so tight,
I fancied we were come to see a corpse
Before the altar which she pulled me toward.
There we found waiting an unpleasant priest   430
Who proved the brother, not our parish friend,
But one with mischief-making mouth and eye,
Paul, whom I know since to my cost. And then
I heard the heavy church-door lock out help
Behind us: for the customary warmth,
Two tapers shivered on the altar. "Quick—
Lose no time!"—cried the priest. And straightway
down
From . . . what's behind the altar where he hid—
Hawk-nose and yellowness and bush and all,   439
Stepped Guido, caught my hand, and there was I
O' the chancel, and the priest had opened book,
Read here and there, made me say that and this,
And after, told me I was now a wife,
Honoured indeed, since Christ thus weds the
Church,
And therefore turned he water into wine,
To show I should obey my spouse like Christ.
Then the two slipped aside and talked apart,
And I, silent and scared, got down again
And joined my mother who was weeping now.
Nobody seemed to mind us any more,   450
And both of us on tiptoe found our way
To the door which was unlocked by this, and wide.
When we were in the street, the rain had stopped,
All things looked better. At our own house-door,
Violante whispered "No one syllable
To Pietro! Girl-brides never breathe a word!"
"—Well treated to a wetting, draggle-tails!"
Laughed Pietro as he opened—"Very near
You made me brave the gutter's roaring sea
To carry off from roost old dove and young,   460
Trussed up in church, the cote, by me, the kite!
What do these priests mean, praying folk to death
On stormy afternoons, with Christmas close
To wash our sins off nor require the rain?"
Violante gave my hand a timely squeeze,
Madonna saved me from immodest speech,
I kissed him and was quiet, being a bride.

423–24. the Lion's-mouth . . . Corso, streets in Rome.
445. turned . . . wine. The incident is related in John
2:1-10. Paul interprets it as a parable.

When I saw nothing more, the next three weeks,
Of Guido—"Nor the Church sees Christ" thought I:
"Nothing is changed however, wine is wine   470
And water only water in our house.
Nor did I see that ugly doctor since
That cure of the illness: just as I was cured,
I am married,—neither scarecrow will return."

Three weeks, I chuckled—"How would Giulia
stare,
And Tecla smile and Tisbe laugh outright,
Were it not impudent for brides to talk!"—
Until one morning, as I sat and sang
At the broidery-frame alone i' the chamber,—loud
Voices, two, three together, sobbings too,   480
And my name, "Guido," "Paolo," flung like stones
From each to the other! In I ran to see.
There stood the very Guido and the priest
With sly face,—formal but nowise afraid,—
While Pietro seemed all red and angry, scarce
Able to stutter out his wrath in words;
And this it was that made my mother sob,
As he reproached her—"You have murdered us,
Me and yourself and this our child beside!"
Then Guido interposed "Murdered or not,   490
Be it enough your child is now my wife!
I claim and come to take her." Paul put in,
"Consider—kinsman, dare I term you so?—
What is the good of your sagacity
Except to counsel in a strait like this?
I guarantee the parties man and wife
Whether you like or loathe it, bless or ban.
May spilt milk be put back within the bowl—
The done thing, undone? You, it is, we look
For counsel to, you fitliest will advise!   500
Since milk, though spilt and spoilt, does marble
good,
Better we down on knees and scrub the floor,
Than sigh, 'the waste would make a syllabub!'
Help us so turn disaster to account,
So predispose the groom, he needs shall grace
The bride with favour from the very first,
Not begin marriage an embittered man!"
He smiled,—the game so wholly in his hands!
While fast and faster sobbed Violante—"Ay,
All of us murdered, past averting now   510
O my sin, O my secret!" and such like.

Then I began to half surmise the truth;
Something had happened, low, mean, underhand,
False, and my mother was to blame, and I
To pity, whom all spoke of, none addressed:
I was the chattel that had caused a crime.
I stood mute,—those who tangled must untie

The embroilment. Pietro cried "Withdraw, my
      child!
She is not helpful to the sacrifice
At this stage,—do you want the victim by   520
While you discuss the value of her blood?
For her sake, I consent to hear you talk:
Go, child, and pray God help the innocent!"

I did go and was praying God, when came
Violante, with eyes swollen and red enough,
But movement on her mouth for make-believe
Matters were somehow getting right again.
She bade me sit down by her side and hear.
"You are too young and cannot understand,
Nor did your father understand at first.   530
I wished to benefit all three of us,
And when he failed to take my meaning,—why,
I tried to have my way at unaware—
Obtained him the advantage he refused.
As if I put before him wholesome food
Instead of broken victual,—he finds change
I' the viands, never cares to reason why,
But falls to blaming me, would fling the plate
From window, scandalize the neighbourhood,
Even while he smacks his lips,—men's way, my
      child!   540
But either you have prayed him unperverse
Or I have talked him back into his wits:
And Paolo was a help in time of need,—
Guido, not much—my child, the way of men!
A priest is more a woman than a man,
And Paul did wonders to persuade. In short,
Yes, he was wrong, your father sees and says;
My scheme was worth attempting: and bears
      fruit,
Gives you a husband and a noble name,
A palace and no end of pleasant things.   550
What do you care about a handsome youth?
They are so volatile, and tease their wives!
This is the kind of man to keep the house.
We lose no daughter,—gain a son, that's all:
For 'tis arranged we never separate,
Nor miss, in our grey time of life, the tints
Of you that colour eve to match with morn.
In good or ill, we share and share alike,
And cast our lots into a common lap,
And all three die together as we lived!   560
Only, at Arezzo,—that's a Tuscan town,
Not so large as this noisy Rome, no doubt,
But older far and finer much, say folk,—
In a great palace where you will be queen,
Know the Archbishop and the Governor,
And we see homage done you ere we die.
Therefore, be good and pardon!"—"Pardon what?

You know things, I am very ignorant:
All is right if you only will not cry!"

And so an end! Because a blank begins   570
From when, at the word, she kissed me hard and
      hot,
And took me back to where my father leaned
Opposite Guido—who stood eyeing him,
As eyes the butcher the cast panting ox
That feels his fate is come, nor struggles more,—
While Paul looked archly on, pricked brow at whiles
With the pen-point as to punish triumph there,—
And said "Count Guido, take your lawful wife
Until death part you!"

                      All since is one blank,
Over and ended; a terrific dream.   580
It is the good of dreams—so soon they go!
Wake in a horror of heart-beats, you may—
Cry "The dread thing will never from my
      thoughts!"
Still, a few daylight doses of plain life,
Cock-crow and sparrow-chirp, or bleat and bell
Of goats that trot by, tinkling, to be milked;
And when you rub your eyes awake and wide,
Where is the harm o' the horror? Gone! So here.
I know I wake,—but from what? Blank, I say!
This is the note of evil: for good lasts.   590
Even when Don Celestine bade "Search and find!
For your soul's sake, remember what is past,
The better to forgive it,"—all in vain!
What was fast getting indistinct before,
Vanished outright. By special grace perhaps,
Between that first calm and this last, four years
Vanish,—one quarter of my life, you know.
I am held up, amid the nothingness,
By one or two truths only—thence I hang,
And there I live,—the rest is death or dream,   600
All but those points of my support. I think
Of what I saw at Rome once in the Square
O' the Spaniards, opposite the Spanish House:
There was a foreigner had trained a goat,
A shuddering white woman of a beast,
To climb up, stand straight on a pile of sticks
Put close, which gave the creature room enough:
When she was settled there he, one by one,
Took away all the sticks, left just the four
Whereon the little hoofs did really rest,   610
There she kept firm, all underneath was air.
So, what I hold by, are my prayer to God,
My hope, that came in answer to the prayer,
Some hand would interpose and save me—hand

602–03. **Square o' the Spaniards**, Piazza di Spagna. **the
Spanish house,** where the Spanish ambassador lived.

Which proved to be my friend's hand: and,—blest
bliss,—
That fancy which began so faint at first,
That thrill of dawn's suffusion through my dark,
Which I perceive was promise of my child,
The light his unborn face sent long before,—
God's way of breaking the good news to flesh.   620
That is all left now of those four bad years.
Don Celestine urged "But remember more!
Other men's faults may help me find your own.
I need the cruelty exposed, explained,
Or how can I advise you to forgive?"
He thought I could not properly forgive
Unless I ceased forgetting,—which is true:
For, bringing back reluctantly to mind
My husband's treatment of me,—by a light
That's later than my life-time, I review   630
And comprehend much and imagine more,
And have but little to forgive at last.
For now,—be fair and say,—is it not true
He was ill-used and cheated of his hope
To get enriched by marriage? Marriage gave
Me and no money, broke the compact so:
He had a right to ask me on those terms,
As Pietro and Violante to declare
They would not give me: so the bargain stood:
They broke it, and he felt himself aggrieved,   640
Became unkind with me to punish them.
They said 'twas he began deception first,
Nor, in one point whereto he pledged himself,
Kept promise: what of that, suppose it were?
Echoes die off, scarcely reverberate
For ever,—why should ill keep echoing ill,
And never let our ears have done with noise?
Then my poor parents took the violent way
To thwart him,—he must needs retaliate,—wrong,
Wrong, and all wrong,—better say, all blind!   650
As I myself was, that is sure, who else
Had understood the mystery: for his wife
Was bound in some sort to help somehow there.
It seems as if I might have interposed,
Blunted the edge of their resentment so,
Since he vexed me because they first vexed him;
"I will entreat them to desist, submit,
Give him the money and be poor in peace,—
Certainly not go tell the world: perhaps
He will grow quiet with his gains."
                          Yes, say   660
Something to this effect and you do well!
But then you have to see first: I was blind.

That is the fruit of all such wormy ways,
The indirect, the unapproved of God:
You cannot find their author's end and aim,
Not even to substitute your good for bad,
Your straight for the irregular; you stand
Stupefied, profitless, as cow or sheep
That miss a man's mind; anger him just twice
By trial at repairing the first fault.   670
Thus, when he blamed me, "You are a coquette,
A lure-owl posturing to attract birds,
You look love-lures at theatre and church,
In walk, at window!"—that, I knew, was false:
But why he charged me falsely, whither sought
To drive me by such charge,—how could I know?
So, unaware, I only made things worse.
I tried to soothe him by abjuring walk,
Window, church, theatre, for good and all,
As if he had been in earnest: that, you know,   680
Was nothing like the object of his charge.
Yes, when I got my maid to supplicate
The priest, whose name she read when she would
read
Those feigned false letters I was forced to hear
Though I could read no word of,—he should cease
Writing,—nay, if he minded prayer of mine,
Cease from so much as even pass the street
Whereon our house looked,—in my ignorance
I was just thwarting Guido's true intent;
Which was, to bring about a wicked change   690
Of sport to earnest, tempt a thoughtless man
To write indeed, and pass the house, and more,
Till both of us were taken in a crime.
He ought not to have wished me thus act lies,
Simulate folly: but,—wrong or right, the wish,—
I failed to apprehend its drift. How plain
It follows,—if I fell into such fault,
He also may have overreached the mark,
Made mistake, by perversity of brain,
I' the whole sad strange plot, the grotesque intrigue
To make me and my friend unself ourselves,   701
Be other man and woman than we were!
Think it out, you who have the time! for me,—
I cannot say less; more I will not say.
Leave it to God to cover and undo!
Only, my dulness should not prove too much!
—Not prove that in a certain other point
Wherein my husband blamed me,—and you
blame,
If I interpret smiles and shakes of head,—
I was dull too. Oh, if I dared but speak!   710
Must I speak? I am blamed that I forwent
A way to make my husband's favour come.
That is true: I was firm, withstood, refused . . .
—Women as you are, how can I find the words?

I felt there was just one thing Guido claimed
I had no right to give nor he to take;
We being in estrangement, soul from soul:
Till, when I sought help, the Archbishop smiled,
Inquiring into privacies of life,
—Said I was blameable—(he stands for God)   720
Nowise entitled to exemption there.
Then I obeyed,—as surely had obeyed
Were the injunction "Since your husband bids,
Swallow the burning coal he proffers you!"
But I did wrong, and he gave wrong advice
Though he were thrice Archbishop,—that, I
    know!—
Now I have got to die and see things clear.
Remember I was barely twelve years old—
A child at marriage: I was let alone
For weeks, I told you, lived my child-life still   730
Even at Arezzo, when I woke and found
First . . . but I need not think of that again—
Over and ended! Try and take the sense
Of what I signify, if it must be so.
After the first, my husband, for hate's sake,
Said one eve, when the simpler cruelty
Seemed somewhat dull at edge and fit to bear,
"We have been man and wife six months almost:
How long is this your comedy to last?
Go this night to my chamber, not your own!"   740
At which word, I did rush—most true the
    charge—
And gain the Archbishop's house—he stands for
    God—
And fall upon my knees and clasp his feet,
Praying him hinder what my estranged soul
Refused to bear, though patient of the rest:
"Place me within a convent," I implored—
"Let me henceforward lead the virgin life
You praise in Her you bid me imitate!"
What did he answer? "Folly of ignorance!
Know, daughter, circumstances make or mar   750
Virginity,—'tis virtue or 'tis vice.
That which was glory in the Mother of God
Had been, for instance, damnable in Eve
Created to be mother of mankind.
Had Eve, in answer to her Maker's speech
'Be fruitful, multiply, replenish earth'—
Pouted 'But I choose rather to remain
Single'—why, she had spared herself forthwith
Further probation by the apple and snake,
Been pushed straight out of Paradise! For see—   760
If motherhood be qualified impure,
I catch you making God command Eve sin!

748. **Her,** the Blessed Virgin, the Mother of Christ.
756. **'Be fruitful . . . earth.'** See Genesis 1 : 28.   759. **Further probation . . . snake.** See Genesis 3.

—A blasphemy so like these Molinists',
I must suspect you dip into their books."
Then he pursued " 'Twas in your covenant!"

No! There my husband never used deceit.
He never did by speech nor act imply
"Because of our souls' yearning that we meet
And mix in soul through flesh, which yours and
    mine
Wear and impress, and make their visible selves,
—All which means, for the love of you and me,   771
Let us become one flesh, being one soul!"
He only stipulated for the wealth;
Honest so far. But when he spoke as plain—
Dreadfully honest also—"Since our souls
Stand each from each, a whole world's width be-
    tween,
Give me the fleshy vesture I can reach
And rend and leave just fit for hell to burn!"—
Why, in God's name, for Guido's soul's own sake
Imperilled by polluting mine,—I say,   780
I did resist; would I had overcome!

My heart died out at the Archbishop's smile;
—It seemed so stale and worn a way o' the world,
As though 'twere nature frowning—"Here is
    Spring,
The sun shines as he shone at Adam's fall,
The earth requires that warmth reach everywhere:
What, must your patch of snow be saved forsooth
Because you rather fancy snow than flowers?"
Something in this style he began with me.
Last he said, savagely for a good man,   790
"This explains why you call your husband harsh,
Harsh to you, harsh to whom you love. God's
    Bread!
The poor Count has to manage a mere child
Whose parents leave untaught the simplest things
Their duty was and privilege to teach,—
Goodwives' instruction, gossips' lore: they laugh
And leave the Count the task,—or leave it me!"
Then I resolved to tell a frightful thing.
"I am not ignorant,—know what I say,
Declaring this is sought for hate, not love.   800
Sir, you may hear things like almighty God.
I tell you that my housemate, yes—the priest
My husband's brother, Canon Girolamo—
Has taught me what depraved and misnamed love
Means, and what outward signs denote the sin,

763. **Molinists,** followers of Miguel de Molinos (1640–1696), Spanish Quietist, whose teachings were condemned as heretical (see encyclopedia). The term Molinist is also applied to followers of Luis Molina, a Spanish theologian of the sixteenth century.   796. **Goodwives,** housewives. **gossips,** godparents.

For he solicits me and says he loves,
The idle young priest with nought else to do.
My husband sees this, knows this, and lets be.
Is it your counsel I bear this beside?"
"—More scandal, and against a priest this time! 810
What, 'tis the Canon now?"—less snappishly—
"Rise up, my child, for such a child you are,
The rod were too advanced a punishment!
Let's try the honeyed cake. A parable!
'Without a parable spake He not to them.'
There was a ripe round long black toothsome fruit,
Even a flower-fig, the prime boast of May:
And, to the tree, said . . . either the spirit o' the
     fig,
Or, if we bring in men, the gardener,
Archbishop of the orchard—had I time   820
To try o' the two which fits in best: indeed
It might be the Creator's self, but then
The tree should bear an apple, I suppose,—
Well, anyhow, one with authority said
'Ripe fig, burst skin, regale the fig-pecker—
The bird whereof thou art a perquisite!'
'Nay,' with a flounce, replied the restif fig,
'I much prefer to keep my pulp myself:
He may go breakfastless and dinnerless,
Supperless of one crimson seed, for me!'   830
So, back she flopped into her bunch of leaves.
He flew off, left her,—did the natural lord,—
And lo, three hundred thousand bees and wasps
Found her out, feasted on her to the shuck:
Such gain the fig's that gave its bird no bite!
The moral,—fools elude their proper lot,
Tempt other fools, get ruined all alike.
Therefore go home, embrace your husband quick!
Which if this Canon brother chance to see,
He will the sooner back to book again."   840

So, home I did go; so, the worst befell:
So, I had proof the Archbishop was just man,
And hardly that, and certainly no more.
For, miserable consequence to me,
My husband's hatred waxed nor waned at all,
His brother's boldness grew effrontery soon,
And my last stay and comfort in myself
Was forced from me: henceforth I looked to
     God
Only, nor cared my desecrated soul   849
Should have fair walls, gay windows for the
     world.
God's glimmer, that came through the ruin-top,
Was witness why all lights were quenched inside:
Henceforth I asked God counsel, not mankind.

815. 'Without . . . them.' So Matthew 13:34 records
of Christ's relation to the multitude. 827. restif, restive.

So, when I made the effort, freed myself,
They said—"No care to save appearance here!
How cynic,—when, how wanton, were enough!"
—Adding, it all came of my mother's life—
My own real mother, whom I never knew,
Who did wrong (if she needs must have done
     wrong)
Through being all her life, not my four years,   860
At mercy of the hateful: every beast
O' the field was wont to break that fountain-fence,
Trample the silver into mud so murk
Heaven could not find itself reflected there.
Now they cry "Out on her, who, plashy pool,
Bequeathed turbidity and bitterness
To the daughter-stream where Guido dipt and
     drank!"

Well, since she had to bear this brand—let me!
The rather do I understand her now,—
From my experience of what hate calls love,—   870
Much love might be in what their love called hate.
If she sold . . . what they call, sold . . . me her
     child—
I shall believe she hoped in her poor heart
That I at least might try be good and pure,
Begin to live untempted, not go doomed
And done with ere once found in fault, as she.
Oh and, my mother, it all came to this?
Why should I trust those that speak ill of you,
When I mistrust who speaks even well of them?
Why, since all bound to do me good, did harm,   880
May not you, seeming as you harmed me most,
Have meant to do most good—and feed your child
From bramble-bush, whom not one orchard-tree
But drew bough back from, nor let one fruit fall?
This it was for you sacrificed your babe?
Gained just this, giving your heart's hope away
As I might give mine, loving it as you,
If . . . but that never could be asked of me!

There, enough! I have my support again,
Again the knowledge that my babe was, is,   890
Will be mine only. Him, by death, I give
Outright to God, without a further care,—
But not to any parent in the world,—
So to be safe: why is it we repine?
What guardianship were safer could we choose?
All human plans and projects come to nought:
My life, and what I know of other lives,
Prove that: no plan nor project! God shall care!

And now you are not tired? How patient then
All of you,—Oh yes, patient this long while   900
Listening, and understanding, I am sure!

Four days ago, when I was sound and well
And like to live, no one would understand.
People were kind, but smiled "And what of him,
Your friend, whose tonsure the rich dark-brown
    hides?
There, there!—your lover, do we dream he was?
A priest too—never were such naughtiness!
Still, he thinks many a long think, never fear,
After the shy pale lady,—lay so light
For a moment in his arms, the lucky one!"   910
And so on: wherefore should I blame you much?
So we are made, such difference in minds,
Such difference too in eyes that see the minds!
That man, you misinterpret and misprise—
The glory of his nature, I had thought,
Shot itself out in white light, blazed the truth
Through every atom of his act with me:
Yet where I point you, through the crystal shrine,
Purity in quintessence, one dew-drop,
You all descry a spider in the midst.   920
One says "The head of it is plain to see,"
And one, "They are the feet by which I judge,"
All say, "Those films were spun by nothing else."

Then, I must lay my babe away with God,
Nor think of him again, for gratitude.
Yes, my last breath shall wholly spend itself
In one attempt more to disperse the stain,
The mist from other breath fond mouths have
    made,
About a lustrous and pellucid soul:
So that, when I am gone but sorrow stays,   930
And people need assurance in their doubt
If God yet have a servant, man a friend,
The weak a saviour and the vile a foe,—
Let him be present, by the name invoked,
Giuseppe-Maria Caponsacchi!

                      There,
Strength comes already with the utterance!
I will remember once more for his sake
The sorrow: for he lives and is belied.
Could he be here, how he would speak for me!

I had been miserable three drear years   940
In that dread palace and lay passive now,
When I first learned there could be such a man.
Thus it fell: I was at a public play,
In the last days of Carnival last March,
Brought there I knew not why, but now know well.
My husband put me where I sat, in front;
Then crouched down, breathed cold through me
    from behind,
Stationed i' the shadow,—none in front could see,—

I, it was, faced the stranger-throng beneath,
The crowd with upturned faces, eyes one stare,   950
Voices one buzz. I looked but to the stage,
Whereon two lovers sang and interchanged
"True life is only love, love only bliss:
I love thee—thee I love!" then they embraced.
I looked thence to the ceiling and the walls,—
Over the crowd, those voices and those eyes,—
My thoughts went through the roof and out, to
    Rome
On wings of music, waft of measured words,—
Set me down there, a happy child again,
Sure that to-morrow would be festa-day,   960
Hearing my parents praise past festas more,
And seeing they were old if I was young,
Yet wondering why they still would end dis-
    course
With "We must soon go, you abide your time,
And,—might we haply see the proper friend
Throw his arm over you and make you safe!"

Sudden I saw him; into my lap there fell
A foolish twist of comfits, broke my dream
And brought me from the air and laid me low,
As ruined as the soaring bee that's reached   970
(So Pietro told me at the Villa once)
By the dust-handful. There the comfits lay:
I looked to see who flung them, and I faced
This Caponsacchi, looking up in turn.
Ere I could reason out why, I felt sure,
Whoever flung them, his was not the hand,—
Up rose the round face and good-natured grin
Of him who, in effect, had played the prank,
From covert close beside the earnest face,—
Fat waggish Conti, friend of all the world.   980
He was my husband's cousin, privileged
To throw the thing: the other, silent, grave,
Solemn almost, saw me, as I saw him.

There is a psalm Don Celestine recites,
"Had I a dove's wings, how I fain would flee!"
The psalm runs not "I hope, I pray for wings,"—
Not "If wings fall from heaven, I fix them fast,"—
Simply "How good it were to fly and rest,
Have hope now, and one day expect content!
How well to do what I shall never do!"   990
So I said "Had there been a man like that,
To lift me with his strength out of all strife
Into the calm, how I could fly and rest!
I have a keeper in the garden here
Whose sole employment is to strike me low
If ever I, for solace, seek the sun.

    981. cousin, used loosely for relative, as in Shakespeare.
984. psalm, Psalm 55 : 6.

Life means with me successful feigning death,
Lying stone-like, eluding notice so,
Forgoing here the turf and there the sky.
Suppose that man had been instead of this!"   1000

Presently Conti laughed into my ear,
—Had tripped up to the raised place where I
      sat—
"Cousin, I flung them brutishly and hard!
Because you must be hurt, to look austere
As Caponsacchi yonder, my tall friend
A-gazing now. Ah, Guido, you so close?
Keep on your knees, do! Beg her to forgive!
My cornet battered like a cannon-ball.
Good-bye, I'm gone!"—nor waited the reply.

That night at supper, out my husband broke,   1010
"Why was that throwing, that buffoonery?
Do you think I am your dupe? What man would
      dare
Throw comfits in a stranger lady's lap?
'Twas knowledge of you bred such insolence
In Caponsacchi; he dared shoot the bolt,
Using that Conti for his stalking-horse.
How could you see him this once and no more,
When he is always haunting hereabout
At the street-corner or the palace-side,
Publishing my shame and your impudence?   1020
You are a wanton,—I a dupe, you think?
O Christ, what hinders that I kill her quick?"
Whereat he drew his sword and feigned a thrust.

All this, now,—being not so strange to me,
Used to such misconception day by day
And broken-in to bear,—I bore, this time,
More quietly than woman should perhaps:
Repeated the mere truth and held my tongue.

Then he said, "Since you play the ignorant,
I shall instruct you. This amour,—commenced   1030
Or finished or midway in act, all's one,
'Tis the town-talk; so my revenge shall be.
Does he presume because he is a priest?
I warn him that the sword I wear shall pink
His lily-scented cassock through and through,
Next time I catch him underneath your eaves!"
But he had threatened with the sword so oft
And, after all, not kept his promise. All
I said was, "Let God save the innocent!
Moreover, death is far from a bad fate.   1040
I shall go pray for you and me, not him;
And then I look to sleep, come death or, worse,
Life." So, I slept.

1008. cornet, a mock cornet, used for festival purposes.

                    There may have elapsed a week,
When Margherita,—called my waiting-maid,
Whom it is said my husband found too fair—
Who stood and heard the charge and the reply,
Who never once would let the matter rest
From that night forward, but rang changes still
On this the thrust and that the shame, and how
Good cause for jealousy cures jealous fools,   1050
And what a paragon was this same priest
She talked about until I stopped my ears,—
She said, "A week is gone; you comb your hair,
Then go mope in a corner, cheek on palm,
Till night comes round again,—so, waste a week
As if your husband menaced you in sport.
Have not I some acquaintance with his tricks?
Oh no, he did not stab the serving-man
Who made and sang the rhymes about me once!
For why? They sent him to the wars next day.   1060
Nor poisoned he the foreigner, my friend,
Who wagered on the whiteness of my breast,—
The swarth skins of our city in dispute:
For, though he paid me proper compliment,
The Count well knew he was besotted with
Somebody else, a skin as black as ink,
(As all the town knew save my foreigner)
He found and wedded presently,—'Why need
Better revenge?'—the Count asked. But what's
      here?
A priest, that does not fight, and cannot wed, 1070
Yet must be dealt with! If the Count took fire
For the poor pastime of a minute,—me—
What were the conflagration for yourself,
Countess and lady-wife and all the rest?
The priest will perish; you will grieve too late:
So shall the city-ladies' handsomest,
Frankest and liberalest gentleman
Die for you, to appease a scurvy dog
Hanging's too good for. Is there no escape?
Were it not simple Christian charity   1080
To warn the priest be on his guard,—save him
Assured death, save yourself from causing it?
I meet him in the street. Give me a glove,
A ring to show for token! Mum's the word!"

I answered, "If you were, as styled, my maid,
I would command you: as you are, you say,
My husband's intimate,—assist his wife
Who can do nothing but entreat 'Be still!'
Even if you speak truth and a crime is planned,
Leave help to God as I am forced to do!   1090
There is no other help, or we should craze,
Seeing such evil with no human cure.
Reflect that God, who makes the storm desist,
Can make an angry violent heart subside.

Why should we venture teach Him governance?
Never address me on this subject more!"

Next night she said "But I went, all the same,
—Ay, saw your Caponsacchi in his house,
And come back stuffed with news I must outpour.
I told him 'Sir, my mistress is a stone: 1100
Why should you harm her for no good you get?
For you do harm her—prowl about our place
With the Count never distant half the street,
Lurking at every corner, would you look!
'Tis certain she has witched you with a spell.
Are there not other beauties at your beck?
We all know, Donna This and Monna That
Die for a glance of yours, yet here you gaze!
Go make them grateful, leave the stone its cold!'
And he—oh, he turned first white and then red,
And then—'To her behest I bow myself,   1111
Whom I love with my body and my soul:
Only a word i' the bowing! See, I write
One little word, no harm to see or hear!
Then, fear no further!' This is what he wrote.
I know you cannot read,—therefore, let me!
'My idol!' " . . .

            But I took it from her hand
And tore it into shreds. "Why join the rest
Who harm me? Have I ever done you wrong?
People have told me 'tis you wrong myself: 1120
Let it suffice I either feel no wrong
Or else forgive it,—yet you turn my foe!
The others hunt me and you throw a noose!"

She muttered "Have your wilful way!" I slept.

Whereupon . . . no, I leave my husband out!
It is not to do him more hurt, I speak.
Let it suffice, when misery was most,
One day, I swooned and got a respite so.
She stooped as I was slowly coming to,
This Margherita, ever on my trace,   1130
And whispered—"Caponsacchi!"

                  If I drowned,
But woke afloat i' the wave with upturned eyes,
And found their first sight was a star! I turned—
For the first time, I let her have her will,
Heard passively,—"The imposthume at such head,
One touch, one lancet-puncture would relieve,—
And still no glance the good physician's way
Who rids you of the torment in a trice!
Still he writes letters you refuse to hear.
He may prevent your husband, kill himself,   1140

1140. prevent, anticipate.

So desperate and all fordone is he!
Just hear the pretty verse he made to-day!
A sonnet from Mirtillo. 'Peerless fair . . .'
All poetry is difficult to read,
—The sense of it is, anyhow, he seeks
Leave to contrive you an escape from hell,
And for that purpose asks an interview.
I can write, I can grant it in your name,
Or, what is better, lead you to his house.
Your husband dashes you against the stones;   1150
This man would place each fragment in a shrine:
You hate him, love your husband!"

                  I returned
"It is not true I love my husband,—no,
Nor hate this man. I listen while you speak,
—Assured that what you say is false, the same:
Much as when once, to me a little child,
A rough gaunt man in rags, with eyes on fire,
A crowd of boys and idlers at his heels,
Rushed as I crossed the Square, and held my head
In his two hands, 'Here's she will let me speak!   1160
You little girl, whose eyes do good to mine,
I am the Pope, am Sextus, now the Sixth;
And that Twelfth Innocent, proclaimed to-day,
Is Lucifer disguised in human flesh!
The angels, met in conclave, crowned me!'—thus
He gibbered and I listened; but I knew
All was delusion, ere folks interposed
'Unfasten him, the maniac!' Thus I know
All your report of Caponsacchi false,
Folly or dreaming; I have seen so much   1170
By that adventure at the spectacle,
The face I fronted that one first, last time:
He would belie it by such words and thoughts.
Therefore while you profess to show him me,
I ever see his own face. Get you gone!"

"—That will I, nor once open mouth again,—
No, by Saint Joseph and the Holy Ghost!
On your head be the damage, so adieu!"

And so more days, more deeds I must forget,
Till . . . what a strange thing now is to declare!
Since I say anything, say all if true!   1181
And how my life seems lengthened as to serve!
It may be idle or inopportune,
But, true?—why, what was all I said but truth,
Even when I found that such as are untrue
Could only take the truth in through a lie?
Now—I am speaking truth to the Truth's self:
God will lend credit to my words this time.

1143. Mirtillo, a familiar name in pastoral poetry.
1163. to-day, July 12, 1691. Pope Sextus VI existed only
in the madman's imagination.

It had got half through April. I arose
One vivid daybreak,—who had gone to bed   1190
In the old way my wont those last three years,
Careless until, the cup drained, I should die.
The last sound in my ear, the over-night,
Had been a something let drop on the sly
In prattle by Margherita, "Soon enough
Gaieties end, now Easter's past: a week,
And the Archbishop gets him back to Rome,—
Everyone leaves the town for Rome, this Spring,—
Even Caponsacchi, out of heart and hope,
Resigns himself and follows with the flock."   1200
I heard this drop and drop like rain outside
Fast-falling through the darkness while she spoke:
So had I heard with like indifference,
"And Michael's pair of wings will arrive first
At Rome to introduce the company,
Will bear him from our picture where he fights
Satan,—expect to have that dragon loose
And never a defender!"—my sole thought
Being still, as night came, "Done, another day!
How good to sleep and so get nearer death!"—   1210
When, what, first thing at daybreak, pierced the
     sleep
With a summons to me? Up I sprang alive,
Light in me, light without me, everywhere
Change! A broad yellow sunbeam was let fall
From heaven to earth,—a sudden drawbridge lay,
Along which marched a myriad merry motes,
Mocking the flies that crossed them and recrossed
In rival dance, companions new-born too.
On the house-eaves, a dripping shag of weed
Shook diamonds on each dull grey lattice-square,
As first one, then another bird leapt by,   1221
And light was off, and lo was back again,
Always with one voice,—where are two such joys?—
The blessed building-sparrow! I stepped forth,
Stood on the terrace,—o'er the roofs, such sky!
My heart sang, "I too am to go away,
I too have something I must care about,
Carry away with me to Rome, to Rome!
The bird brings hither sticks and hairs and wool,
And nowhere else i' the world; what fly breaks rank,
Falls out of the procession that befits,   1231
From window here to window there, with all
The world to choose,—so well he knows his course?
I have my purpose and my motive too,
My march to Rome, like any bird or fly!
Had I been dead! How right to be alive!
Last night I almost prayed for leave to die,
Wished Guido all his pleasure with the sword
Or the poison,—poison, sword, was but a trick,

Harmless, may God forgive him the poor jest!   1240
My life is charmed, will last till I reach Rome!
Yesterday, but for the sin,—ah, nameless be
The deed I could have dared against myself!
Now—see if I will touch an unripe fruit,
And risk the health I want to have and use!
Not to live, now, would be the wickedness,—
For life means to make haste and go to Rome
And leave Arezzo, leave all woes at once!"

Now, understand here, by no means mistake!
Long ago had I tried to leave that house   1250
When it seemed such procedure would stop sin;
And still failed more the more I tried—at first
The Archbishop, as I told you,—next, our lord
The Governor,—indeed I found my way,
I went to the great palace where he rules,
Though I knew well 'twas he who,—when I gave
A jewel or two, themselves had given me,
Back to my parents,—since they wanted bread,
They who had never let me want a nosegay,—he
Spoke of the jail for felons, if they kept   1260
What was first theirs, then mine, so doubly theirs,
Though all the while my husband's most of all!
I knew well who had spoke the word wrought this:
Yet, being in extremity, I fled
To the Governor, as I say,—scarce opened lip
When—the cold cruel snicker close behind—
Guido was on my trace, already there,
Exchanging nod and wink for shrug and smile,
And I—pushed back to him and, for my pains,
Paid with . . . but why remember what is past?
I sought out a poor friar the people call   1271
The Roman, and confessed my sin which came
Of their sin,—that fact could not be repressed,—
The frightfulness of my despair in God:
And, feeling, through the grate, his horror shake,
Implored him, "Write for me who cannot write,
Apprise my parents, make them rescue me!
You bid me be courageous and trust God:
Do you in turn dare somewhat, trust and write
'Dear friends, who used to be my parents once,   1280
And now declare you have no part in me,
This is some riddle I want wit to solve,
Since you must love me with no difference.
Even suppose you altered,—there's your hate,
To ask for: hate of you two dearest ones
I shall find liker love than love found here,
If husbands love their wives. Take me away
And hate me as you do the gnats and fleas,
Even the scorpions! How I shall rejoice!'
Write that and save me!" And he promised—wrote
Or did not write; things never changed at all: 1291

1206. our picture, in the Church of San Francesco in
Arezzo.

1263. who, Guido.

He was not like the Augustinian here!
Last, in a desperation I appealed
To friends, whoever wished me better days,
To Guillichini, that's of kin,—"What, I—
Travel to Rome with you? A flying gout
Bids me deny my heart and mind my leg!"
Then I tried Conti, used to brave—laugh back
The louring thunder when his cousin scowled
At me protected by his presence: "You—   1300
Who well know what you cannot save me from,—
Carry me off! What frightens you, a priest?"
He shook his head, looked grave—"Above my
    strength!
Guido has claws that scratch, shows feline teeth;
A formidabler foe than I dare fret:
Give me a dog to deal with, twice the size!
Of course I am a priest and Canon too,
But . . . by the bye . . . though both, not quite
    so bold
As he, my fellow-Canon, brother-priest,
The personage in such ill odour here   1310
Because of the reports—pure birth o' the brain—
Our Caponsacchi, he's your true Saint George
To slay the monster, set the Princess free,
And have the whole High-Altar to himself:
I always think so when I see that piece
I' the Pieve, that's his church and mine, you know:
Though you drop eyes at mention of his name!"

That name had got to take a half-grotesque
Half-ominous, wholly enigmatic sense,
Like any by-word, broken bit of song   1320
Born with a meaning, changed by mouth and
    mouth
That mix it in a sneer or smile, as chance
Bids, till it now means nought but ugliness
And perhaps shame.

                    —All this intends to say,
That, over-night, the notion of escape
Had seemed distemper, dreaming; and the name,—
Not the man, but the name of him, thus made
Into a mockery and disgrace,—why, she
Who uttered it persistently, had laughed,   1329
"I name his name, and there you start and wince
As criminal from the red tongs' touch!"—yet now,
Now, as I stood letting morn bathe me bright,
Choosing which butterfly should bear my news,—
The white, the brown one, or that tinier blue,—
The Margherita, I detested so,

In she came—"The fine day, the good Spring time!
What, up and out at window? That is best.
No thought of Caponsacchi?—who stood there
All night on one leg, like the sentry crane,
Under the pelting of your water-spout—   1340
Looked last look at your lattice ere he leave
Our city, bury his dead hope at Rome?
Ay, go to looking-glass and make you fine,
While he may die ere touch one least loose hair
You drag at with the comb in such a rage!"

I turned—"Tell Caponsacchi he may come!"

"Tell him to come? Ah, but, for charity,
A truce to fooling! Come? What,—come this eve?
Peter and Paul! But I see through the trick—
Yes, come, and take a flower-pot on his head   1350
Flung from your terrace! No joke, sincere truth?"

How plainly I perceived hell flash and fade
O' the face of her,—the doubt that first paled joy,
Then, final reassurance I indeed
Was caught now, never to be free again!
What did I care?—who felt myself of force
To play with the silk, and spurn the horsehair-
    springe.

"But—do you know that I have bade him come,
And in your own name? I presumed so much,
Knowing the thing you needed in your heart.   1360
But somehow—what had I to show in proof?
He would not come: half-promised, that was all,
And wrote the letters you refused to read.
What is the message that shall move him now?"

"After the Ave Maria, at first dark,
I will be standing on the terrace, say!"

"I would I had a good long lock of hair
Should prove I was not lying! Never mind!"

Off she went—"May he not refuse, that's all—
Fearing a trick!"

                    I answered, "He will come."
And, all day, I sent prayer like incense up   1371
To God the strong, God the beneficent,
God ever mindful in all strife and strait,
Who, for our own good, makes the need extreme,
Till at the last He puts forth might and saves.
An old rhyme came into my head and rang
Of how a virgin, for the faith of God,
Hid herself, from the Paynims that pursued,

1292. **the Augustinian,** Don Celestine.   **1295. of
kin,** to Guido.   **1315. that piece,** a painting by
Vasari, in the Church of Santa Maria della Pieve, Arezzo.
1321. changed, exchanged.

1349. Peter and Paul! An oath by Sts. Peter and Paul.

In a cave's heart; until a thunderstone,
Wrapped in a flame, revealed the couch and prey:
And they laughed—"Thanks to lightning, ours at
    last!" 1381
And she cried "Wrath of God, assert His love!
Servant of God, thou fire, befriend His child!"
And lo, the fire she grasped at, fixed its flash,
Lay in her hand a calm cold dreadful sword
She brandished till pursuers strewed the ground,
So did the souls within them die away,
As o'er the prostrate bodies, sworded, safe,
She walked forth to the solitudes and Christ:
So should I grasp the lightning and be saved! 1390

And still, as the day wore, the trouble grew
Whereby I guessed there would be born a star,
Until at an intense throe of the dusk,
I started up, was pushed, I dare to say,
Out on the terrace, leaned and looked at last
Where the deliverer waited me: the same
Silent and solemn face, I first descried
At the spectacle, confronted mine once more.

So was the minute twice vouchsafed me, so
The manhood, wasted then, was still at watch 1400
To save me yet a second time: no change
Here, though all else changed in the changing
    world!

I spoke on the instant, as my duty bade,
In some such sense as this, whatever the phrase.

"Friend, foolish words were borne from you to me;
Your soul behind them is the pure strong wind,
Not dust and feathers which its breath may bear:
These to the witless seem the wind itself,
Since proving thus the first of it they feel.
If by mischance you blew offence my way, 1410
The straws are dropt, the wind desists no whit,
And how such strays were caught up in the street
And took a motion from you, why inquire?
I speak to the strong soul, no weak disguise.
If it be truth,—why should I doubt it truth?—
You serve God specially, as priests are bound,
And care about me, stranger as I am,
So far as wish my good,—that miracle
I take to intimate He wills you serve
By saving me,—what else can He direct? 1420
Here is the service. Since a long while now,
I am in course of being put to death:
While death concerned nothing but me, I bowed
The head and bade, in heart, my husband strike.
Now I imperil something more, it seems,
Something that's trulier me than this myself,

Something I trust in God and you to save.
You go to Rome, they tell me: take me there,
Put me back with my people!"

                   He replied—
The first word I heard ever from his lips, 1430
All himself in it,—an eternity
Of speech, to match the immeasurable depths
O' the soul that then broke silence—"I am yours."

So did the star rise, soon to lead my step,
Lead on, nor pause before it should stand still
Above the House o' the Babe,—my babe to be,
That knew me first and thus made me know him,
That had his right of life and claim on mine,
And would not let me die till he was born,
But pricked me at the heart to save us both, 1440
Saying "Have you the will? Leave God the way!"
And the way was Caponsacchi—"mine," thank
    God!
He was mine, he is mine, he will be mine.

No pause i' the leading and the light! I know,
Next night there was a cloud came, and not he:
But I prayed through the darkness till it broke
And let him shine. The second night, he came.

"The plan is rash; the project desperate:
In such a flight needs must I risk your life,
Give food for falsehood, folly or mistake, 1450
Ground for your husband's rancour and revenge"—
So he began again, with the same face.
I felt that, the same loyalty—one star
Turning now red that was so white before—
One service apprehended newly: just
A word of mine and there the white was back!

"No, friend, for you will take me! 'Tis yourself
Risk all, not I,—who let you, for I trust
In the compensating great God: enough!
I know you: when is it that you will come?" 1460

"To-morrow at the day's dawn." Then I heard
What I should do: how to prepare for flight
And where to fly.

                That night my husband bade
"—You, whom I loathe, beware you break my sleep
This whole night! Couch beside me like the corpse
I would you were!" The rest you know, I think—
How I found Caponsacchi and escaped.

And this man, men call sinner? Jesus Christ!
Of whom men said, with mouths Thyself mad'st
    once,

"He hath a devil"—say he was Thy saint,   1470
My Caponsacchi! Shield and show—unshroud
In Thine own time the glory of the soul
If aught obscure,—if ink-spot, from vile pens
Scribbling a charge against him—(I was glad
Then, for the first time, that I could not write)—
Flirted his way, have flecked the blaze!

                                        For me,
'Tis otherwise: let men take, sift my thoughts
—Thoughts I throw like the flax for sun to bleach!
I did pray, do pray, in the prayer shall die,
"Oh, to have Caponsacchi for my guide!"   1480
Ever the face upturned to mine, the hand
Holding my hand across the world,—a sense
That reads, as only such can read, the mark
God sets on women, signifying so
She should—shall peradventure—be divine;
Yet 'ware, the while, how weakness mars the print
And makes confusion, leaves the thing men see,
—Not this man sees,—who from his soul, re-writes
The obliterated charter,—love and strength
Mending what's marred: "So kneels a votarist,   1490
Weeds some poor waste traditionary plot
Where shrine once was, where temple yet may be,
Purging the place but worshipping the while,
By faith and not by sight, sight clearest so,—
Such way the saints work,"—says Don Celestine.
But I, not privileged to see a saint
Of old when such walked earth with crown and
    palm,
If I call "saint" what saints call something else—
The saints must bear with me, impute the fault
To a soul i' the bud, so starved by ignorance,   1500
Stinted of warmth, it will not blow this year
Nor recognize the orb which Spring-flowers know.
But if meanwhile some insect with a heart
Worth floods of lazy music, spendthrift joy—
Some fire-fly renounced Spring for my dwarfed cup,
Crept close to me, brought lustre for the dark,
Comfort against the cold,—what though excess
Of comfort should miscall the creature—sun?
What did the sun to hinder while harsh hands
Petal by petal, crude and colourless,   1510
Tore me? This one heart gave me all the Spring!

Is all told? There's the journey: and where's time
To tell you how that heart burst out in shine?
Yet certain points do press on me too hard.
Each place must have a name, though I forget:
How strange it was—there where the plain begins
And the small river mitigates its flow—

When eve was fading fast, and my soul sank,
And he divined what surge of bitterness,
In overtaking me, would float me back   1520
Whence I was carried by the striding day—
So,—"This grey place was famous once," said he—
And he began that legend of the place
As if in answer to the unspoken fear,
And told me all about a brave man dead,
Which lifted me and let my soul go on!
How did he know too,—at that town's approach
By the rock-side,—that in coming near the signs
Of life, the house-roofs and the church and tower,
I saw the old boundary and wall o' the world   1530
Rise plain as ever round me, hard and cold,
As if the broken circlet joined again,
Tightened itself about me with no break,—
As if the town would turn Arezzo's self,—
The husband there,—the friends my enemies,
All ranged against me, not an avenue
To try, but would be blocked and drive me back
On him,—this other, . . . oh the heart in that!
Did not he find, bring, put into my arms
A new-born babe?—and I saw faces beam   1540
Of the young mother proud to teach me joy,
And gossips round expecting my surprise
At the sudden hole through earth that lets in
    heaven.
I could believe himself by his strong will
Had woven around me what I thought the world
We went along in, every circumstance,
Towns, flowers and faces, all things helped so well!
For, through the journey, was it natural
Such comfort should arise from first to last?
As I look back, all is one milky way;   1550
Still bettered more, the more remembered, so
Do new stars bud while I but search for old,
And fill all gaps i' the glory, and grow him—
Him I now see make the shine everywhere.
Even at the last when the bewildered flesh,
The cloud of weariness about my soul
Clogging too heavily, sucked down all sense,—
Still its last voice was, "He will watch and care;
Let the strength go, I am content: he stays!"
I doubt not he did stay and care for all—   1560
From that sick minute when the head swam round,
And the eyes looked their last and died on him,
As in his arms he caught me and, you say,
Carried me in, that tragical red eve,
And laid me where I next returned to life
In the other red of morning, two red plates
That crushed together, crushed the time between,
And are since then a solid fire to me,—
When in, my dreadful husband and the world
Broke,—and I saw him, master, by hell's right,   1570

And saw my angel helplessly held back
By guards that helped the malice—the lamb prone,
The serpent towering and triumphant—then
Came all the strength back in a sudden swell,
I did for once see right, do right, give tongue
The adequate protest: for a worm must turn
If it would have its wrong observed by God.
I did spring up, attempt to thrust aside
That ice-block 'twixt the sun and me, lay low
The neutralizer of all good and truth.   1580
If I sinned so,—never obey voice more
O' the Just and Terrible, who bids us—"Bear!"
Not—"Stand by, bear to see my angels bear!"
I am clear it was on impulse to serve God
Not save myself,—no—nor my child unborn!
Had I else waited patiently till now?—
Who saw my old kind parents, silly-sooth
And too much trustful, for their worst of faults,
Cheated, brow-beaten, stripped and starved, cast
    out
Into the kennel: I remonstrated,   1590
Then sank to silence, for,—their woes at end,
Themselves gone,—only I was left to plague.
If only I was threatened and belied,
What matter? I could bear it and did bear;
It was a comfort, still one lot for all:
They were not persecuted for my sake
And I, estranged, the single happy one.
But when at last, all by myself I stood
Obeying the clear voice which bade me rise,
Not for my own sake but my babe unborn,   1600
And take the angel's hand was sent to help—
And found the old adversary athwart the path—
Not my hand simply struck from the angel's, but
The very angel's self made foul i' the face
By the fiend who struck there,—that I would not
    bear,
That only I resisted! So, my first
And last resistance was invincible.
Prayers move God; threats, and nothing else, move
    men!
I must have prayed a man as he were God
When I implored the Governor to right   1610
My parents' wrongs: the answer was a smile.
The Archbishop,—did I clasp his feet enough,
Hide my face hotly on them, while I told
More than I dared make my own mother know?
The profit was—compassion and a jest.
This time, the foolish prayers were done with, right
Used might, and solemnized the sport at once.
All was against the combat: vantage, mine?

1587. **silly-sooth,** perhaps "simply true." See *Twelfth Night,* Act II, sc. 4, l. 47. **1618. vantage, mine?** what vantage was mine?

The runaway avowed, the accomplice-wife,
In company with the plan-contriving priest?   1620
Yet, shame thus rank and patent, I struck, bare,
At foe from head to foot in magic mail,
And off it withered, cobweb-armoury
Against the lightning! 'Twas truth singed the lies
And saved me, not the vain sword nor weak speech!

You see, I will not have the service fail!
I say, the angel saved me: I am safe!
Others may want and wish, I wish nor want
One point o' the circle plainer, where I stand
Traced round about with white to front the world.
What of the calumny I came across,   1631
What o' the way to the end?—the end crowns all.
The judges judged aright i' the main, gave me
The uttermost of my heart's desire, a truce
From torture and Arezzo, balm for hurt
With the quiet nuns,—God recompense the good!
Who said and sang away the ugly past.
And, when my final fortune was revealed,
What safety while, amid my parents' arms,
My babe was given me! Yes, he saved my babe:
It would not have peeped forth, the bird-like thing,
Through that Arezzo noise and trouble: back   1642
Had it returned nor ever let me see!
But the sweet peace cured all, and let me live
And give my bird the life among the leaves
God meant him! Weeks and months of quietude,
I could lie in such peace and learn so much—
Begin the task, I see how needful now,
Of understanding somewhat of my past,—
Know life a little, I should leave so soon.   1650
Therefore, because this man restored my soul,
All has been right; I have gained my gain, enjoyed
As well as suffered,—nay, got foretaste too
Of better life beginning where this ends—
All through the breathing-while allowed me thus,
Which let good premonitions reach my soul
Unthwarted, and benignant influence flow
And interpenetrate and change my heart,
Uncrossed by what was wicked,—nay, unkind.
For, as the weakness of my time drew nigh,   1660
Nobody did me one disservice more,
Spoke coldly or looked strangely, broke the love
I lay in the arms of, till my boy was born,
Born all in love, with nought to spoil the bliss
A whole long fortnight: in a life like mine
A fortnight filled with bliss is long and much.
All women are not mothers of a boy,
Though they live twice the length of my whole life,
And, as they fancy, happily all the same.
There I lay, then, all my great fortnight long,   1670
As if it would continue, broaden out

Happily more and more, and lead to heaven:
Christmas before me,—was not that a chance?
I never realized God's birth before—
How he grew likest God in being born.
This time I felt like Mary, had my babe
Lying a little on my breast like hers.
So all went on till, just four days ago—
The night and the tap.

           Oh it shall be success
To the whole of our poor family! My friends   1680
. . . Nay, father and mother,—give me back my
    word!
They have been rudely stripped of life, disgraced
Like children who must needs go clothed too fine,
Carry the garb of Carnival in Lent:
If they too much affected frippery,
They have been punished and submit themselves,
Say no word: all is over, they see God
Who will not be extreme to mark their fault
Or He had granted respite: they are safe.

For that most woeful man my husband once,   1690
Who, needing respite, still draws vital breath,
I—pardon him? So far as lies in me,
I give him for his good the life he takes,
Praying the world will therefore acquiesce.
Let him make God amends,—none, none to me
Who thank him rather that, whereas strange fate
Mockingly styled him husband and me wife,
Himself this way at least pronounced divorce,
Blotted the marriage-bond: this blood of mine
Flies forth exultingly at any door,   1700
Washes the parchment white, and thanks the blow.
We shall not meet in this world nor the next,
But where will God be absent? In His face
Is light, but in His shadow healing too:
Let Guido touch the shadow and be healed!
And as my presence was importunate,—
My earthly good, temptation and a snare,—
Nothing about me but drew somehow down
His hate upon me,—somewhat so excused
Therefore, since hate was thus the truth of him,—
May my evanishment for evermore   1711
Help further to relieve the heart that cast
Such object of its natural loathing forth!
So he was made; he nowise made himself:
I could not love him, but his mother did.
His soul has never lain beside my soul;

1673. a chance? that is, a happy chance. 1681. Nay
. . . word! She insists on still calling them father and
mother. 1687–89. God . . . respite. If God had intended
to judge their fault severely, He would have given them time
to prepare for death, would not have permitted them to be
cut off so suddenly as they were.

But for the unresisting body,—thanks!
He burned that garment spotted by the flesh.
Whatever he touched is rightly ruined: plague
It caught, and disinfection it had craved   1720
Still but for Guido; I am saved through him
So as by fire; to him—thanks and farewell!

Even for my babe, my boy, there's safety thence—
From the sudden death of me, I mean: we poor
Weak souls, how we endeavour to be strong!
I was already using up my life,—
This portion, now, should do him such a good,
This other go to keep off such an ill!
The great life; see, a breath and it is gone!
So is detached, so left all by itself   1730
The little life, the fact which means so much.
Shall not God stoop the kindlier to His work,
His marvel of creation, foot would crush,
Now that the hand He trusted to receive
And hold it, lets the treasure fall perforce?
The better; He shall have in orphanage
His own way all the clearlier: if my babe
Outlived the hour—and he has lived two weeks—
It is through God who knows I am not by.
Who is it makes the soft gold hair turn black,   1740
And sets the tongue, might lie so long at rest,
Trying to talk? Let us leave God alone!
Why should I doubt He will explain in time
What I feel now, but fail to find the words?
My babe nor was, nor is, nor yet shall be
Count Guido Franceschini's child at all—
Only his mother's, born of love not hate!
So shall I have my rights in after-time.
It seems absurd, impossible to-day;
So seems so much else, not explained but known!

Ah! Friends, I thank and bless you every one!   1751
No more now: I withdraw from earth and man
To my own soul, compose myself for God.

Well, and there is more! Yes, my end of breath
Shall bear away my soul in being true!
He is still here, not outside with the world,
Here, here, I have him in his rightful place!
'Tis now, when I am most upon the move,
I feel for what I verily find—again
The face, again the eyes, again, through all,   1760
The heart and its immeasurable love
Of my one friend, my only, all my own,
Who put his breast between the spears and me.
Ever with Caponsacchi! Otherwise
Here alone would be failure, loss to me—
How much more loss to him, with life debarred
From giving life, love locked from love's display,

The day-star stopped its task that makes night
  morn!
O lover of my life, O soldier-saint,
No work begun shall ever pause for death!   1770
Love will be helpful to me more and more
I' the coming course, the new path I must tread—
My weak hand in thy strong hand, strong for that!
Tell him that if I seem without him now,
That's the world's insight! Oh, he understands!
He is at Civita—do I once doubt
The world again is holding us apart?
He had been here, displayed in my behalf
The broad brow that reverberates the truth,
And flashed the word God gave him, back to man!
I know where the free soul is flown! My fate   1781
Will have been hard for even him to bear:
Let it confirm him in the trust of God,
Showing how holily he dared the deed!
And, for the rest,—say, from the deed, no touch
Of harm came, but all good, all happiness,
Not one faint fleck of failure! Why explain?
What I see, oh, he sees and how much more!
Tell him,—I know not wherefore the true word
Should fade and fall unuttered at the last—   1790
It was the name of him I sprang to meet
When came the knock, the summons and the end.
"My great heart, my strong hand are back again!"
I would have sprung to these, beckoning across
Murder and hell gigantic and distinct
O' the threshold, posted to exclude me heaven:
He is ordained to call and I to come!
Do not the dead wear flowers when dressed for God?
Say,—I am all in flowers from head to foot!
Say,—not one flower of all he said and did,   1800
Might seem to flit unnoticed, fade unknown,
But dropped a seed has grown a balsam-tree
Whereof the blossoming perfumes the place
At this supreme of moments! He is a priest;
He cannot marry therefore, which is right:
I think he would not marry if he could.
Marriage on earth seems such a counterfeit,
Mere imitation of the inimitable:
In heaven we have the real and true and sure.
'Tis there they neither marry nor are given   1810
In marriage but are as the angels: right,
Oh how right that is, how like Jesus Christ
To say that! Marriage-making for the earth,
With gold so much,—birth, power, repute so much,
Or beauty, youth so much, in lack of these!
Be as the angels rather, who, apart,
Know themselves into one, are found at length
Married, but marry never, no, nor give
In marriage; they are man and wife at once

1810–11. 'Tis there . . . angels. See Matthew 22:30.

When the true time is: here we have to wait   1820
Not so long neither! Could we by a wish
Have what we will and get the future now,
Would we wish ought done undone in the past?
So, let him wait God's instant men call years;
Meantime hold hard by truth and his great soul,
Do out the duty! Through such souls alone
God stooping shows sufficient of His light
For us i' the dark to rise by. And I rise.

HOUSE

This poem is very characteristic of Browning, who always insisted that his private life belonged to himself, that his poems were the "utterances of so many imaginary persons—not mine." In the quotation from Wordsworth's "Scorn Not the Sonnet" in the last stanza (with which compare l. 4) and in Browning's own rejoinder to it, we have juxtaposed not only two different interpretations of Shakespeare's sonnets but two different conceptions of the whole question of the poet's relation to his work. In these days, when what Irving Babbitt called "the Paul Pry school of criticism" flourishes, and so many persons are interested in the lives of poets while quite indifferent to their poetry, it is good to reread Browning's vigorous protest. Being himself a man whose life might have been written across the skies, he was in a very strong position to make it. For a recent, thorough discussion of the problems involved in this question, see C. S. Lewis and E. M. W. Tillyard, *The Personal Heresy*, Oxford Press, 1939.

1

Shall I sonnet-sing you about myself?
  Do I live in a house you would like to see?
Is it scant of gear, has it store of pelf?
  "Unlock my heart with a sonnet-key?"

2

Invite the world, as my betters have done?
  "Take notice: this building remains on view,
Its suites of reception every one,
  Its private apartment and bedroom too;

3

"For a ticket, apply to the Publisher."
  No: thanking the public, I must decline.   10
A peep through my window, if folk prefer;
  But, please you, no foot over threshold of mine!

4

I have mixed with a crowd and heard free talk
  In a foreign land where an earthquake chanced:
And a house stood gaping, nought to baulk
  Man's eye wherever he gazed or glanced.

5

The whole of the frontage shaven sheer,
    The inside gaped: exposed to day,
Right and wrong and common and queer,
    Bare, as the palm of your hand, it lay.   20

6

The owner? Oh, he had been crushed, no doubt!
    "Odd tables and chairs for a man of wealth!
What a parcel of musty old books about!
    He smoked,—no wonder he lost his health!

7

"I doubt if he bathed before he dressed.
    A brasier?—the pagan, he burned perfumes!
You see it is proved, what the neighbours guessed:
    His wife and himself had separate rooms."

8

Friends, the goodman of the house at least
    Kept house to himself till an earthquake came: 30
'Tis the fall of its frontage permits you feast
    On the inside arrangement you praise or blame.

9

Outside should suffice for evidence:
    And whoso desires to penetrate
Deeper, must dive by the spirit-sense—
    No optics like yours, at any rate!

10

"Hoity-toity! A street to explore,
    Your house the exception! '*With this same key
Shakespeare unlocked his heart,*' once more!"
    Did Shakespeare? If so, the less Shakespeare
    he!   40

NATURAL MAGIC

I

    All I can say is—I saw it!
The room was as bare as your hand.
I locked in the swarth little lady,—I swear,
    From the head to the foot of her—well, quite as
    bare!
"No Nautch shall cheat me," said I, "taking my
    stand

22–28. "Odd tables . . . separate rooms." These words
are spoken by some person exploring the ruined house.
37–39. "Hoity-toity . . . once more!" These lines are
spoken by some hypothetical objector to Browning's demand
for privacy. Why must he keep his house locked when all
other houses in the street, including Shakespeare's, are left
open? **5. Nautch,** a Hindu dancing girl, in this case either
herself a magician or working with one.

At this bolt which I draw!" And this bolt—I with-
    draw it,
And there laughs the lady, not bare, but embowered
With—who knows what verdure, o'erfruited, o'er-
    flowered?
        Impossible! Only—I saw it!

2

    All I can sing is—I feel it!   10
This life was as blank as that room;
I let you pass in here. Precaution, indeed?
Walls, ceiling and floor,—not a chance for a weed!
Wide opens the entrance: where's cold now, where's
    gloom?
No May to sow seed here, no June to reveal it,
Behold you enshrined in these blooms of your bring-
    ing,
These fruits of your bearing—nay, birds of your
    winging!
        A fairy-tale! Only—I feel it!

ADAM, LILITH AND EVE

According to the Talmud, Lilith was the first wife of
Adam; she was discarded when she became intractable.
The reference in l. 17 to the man whom Eve really loved
shows that Browning is merely using the old Hebrew
names to indicate perennial types of women; Eve, obviously, could have had no secret lover, for Adam was the
only man in the world. The confessions made under
duress are both true, but as soon as the women regain
self-possession they pretend they were only joking, and
the man, being a gentleman, pretends to believe them.

One day it thundered and lightened.
Two women, fairly frightened,
Sank to their knees, transformed, transfixed,
At the feet of the man who sat betwixt;
And "Mercy!" cried each—"if I tell the truth
Of a passage in my youth!"

Said This: "Do you mind the morning
I met your love with scorning?
As the worst of the venom left my lips,
I thought 'If, despite this lie, he strips   10
The mask from my soul with a kiss—I crawl
His slave,—soul, body and all!'"

Said That: "We stood to be married;
The priest, or someone, tarried;
'If Paradise-door prove locked?' smiled you.
I thought, as I nodded, smiling too,
'Did one, that's away, arrive—nor late
Nor soon should unlock Hell's gate!'"

It ceased to lighten and thunder.
Up started both in wonder, 20
Looked round and saw that the sky was clear,
Then laughed, "Confess you believed us, Dear!"
"I saw through the joke!" the man replied
They re-seated themselves beside.

NEVER THE TIME AND THE PLACE

Never the time and the place
And the loved one all together!
This path—how soft to pace!
This May—what magic weather!
Where is the loved one's face?
In a dream that loved one's face meets mine,
But the house is narrow, the place is bleak
Where, outside, rain and wind combine
With a furtive ear, if I strive to speak,
With a hostile eye at my flushing cheek, 10
With a malice that marks each word, each
sign!
O enemy sly and serpentine,
Uncoil thee from the waking man!
Do I hold the Past
Thus firm and fast
Yet doubt if the Future hold I can?
This path so soft to pace shall lead
Through the magic of May to herself indeed!
Or narrow if needs the house must be,
Outside are the storms and strangers: we— 20
Oh, close, safe, warm sleep I and she,
—I and she!

WHY I AM A LIBERAL

"Why?" Because all I haply can and do,
All that I am now, all I hope to be,—
Whence comes it save from fortune setting free
Body and soul the purpose to pursue,
God traced for both? If fetters, not a few,
Of prejudice, convention, fall from me,
These shall I bid men—each in his degree
Also God-guided—bear, and gaily too?

But little do or can the best of us:
That little is achieved through Liberty. 10
Who, then, dares hold, emancipated thus,
His fellow shall continue bound? Not I,
Who live, love, labour freely, nor discuss
A brother's right to freedom. That is "Why."

SUMMUM BONUM

All the breath and the bloom of the year in the bag
of one bee:
All the wonder and wealth of the mine in the
heart of one gem:
In the core of one pearl all the shade and the shine
of the sea:
Breath and bloom, shade and shine,—wonder,
wealth, and—how far above them—
Truth, that's brighter than gem,
Trust, that's purer than pearl,—
Brightest truth, purest trust in the universe—all
were for me
In the kiss of one girl.

A PEARL, A GIRL

A simple ring with a single stone
To the vulgar eye no stone of price:
Whisper the right word, that alone—
Forth starts a sprite, like fire from ice,
And lo, you are lord (says an Eastern scroll)
Of heaven and earth, lord whole and sole
Through the power in a pearl.

A woman ('tis I this time that say)
With little the world counts worthy praise:
Utter the true word—out and away 10
Escapes her soul: I am wrapt in blaze,
Creation's lord, of heaven and earth
Lord whole and sole—by a minute's birth—
Through the love in a girl!

MUCKLE-MOUTH MEG

In *Tales of a Grandfather*, Sir Walter Scott tells this
story of one of his Border ancestors whom he always
owned with pride. The situation, quite credible in the
days when Border raids were common, is historical, but
the development is Browning's own. The title of the
poem means "Big-mouthed Meg."

Frowned the Laird on the Lord: "So, red-handed I
catch thee?
Death-doomed by our Law of the Border!
We've a gallows outside and a chiel to dispatch
thee:
Who trespasses—hangs: all's in order."

Muckle-Mouth Meg. **1. Laird,** Sir Gideon Murray, of Eli-
bank, later Deputy Treasurer of Scotland. **Lord,** Sir William Scott, favorite of King James VI. **3. chiel,** youth.

He met frown with smile, did the young English
   gallant:
  Then the Laird's dame: "Nay, Husband, I beg!
He's comely: be merciful! Grace for the callant
  —If he marries our Muckle-mouth Meg!"

"No mile-wide-mouthed monster of yours do I
   marry:
  Grant rather the gallows!" laughed he.   10
"Foul fare kith and kin of you—why do you tarry?"
  "To tame your fierce temper!" quoth she.

"Shove him quick in the Hole, shut him fast for a
   week:
  Cold, darkness and hunger work wonders:
Who lion-like roars now, mouse-fashion will squeak,
  And 'it rains' soon succeed to 'it thunders.' "

A week did he bide in the cold and the dark
  —Not hunger: for duly at morning
In flitted a lass, and a voice like a lark
  Chirped "Muckle-mouth Meg still ye're
   scorning?   20

"Go hang, but here's parritch to hearten ye first!"
  "Did Meg's muckle-mouth boast within some
Such music as yours, mine should match it or
   burst:
  No frog-jaws! So tell folk, my Winsome!"

Soon week came to end, and, from Hole's door set
   wide,
  Out he marched, and there waited the lassie:
"Yon gallows, or Muckle-mouth Meg for a bride!
  Consider! Sky's blue and turf's grassy:

"Life's sweet: shall I say ye wed Muckle-mouth
   Meg?"
  "Not I," quoth the stout heart: "too eerie   30
The mouth that can swallow a bubblyjock's
   egg:
  Shall I let it munch mine? Never, Dearie!"

7. callant, lad.   21. parritch, porridge.   31. bubblyjock, turkey.

"Not Muckle-mouth Meg? Wow, the obstinate man!
  Perhaps he would rather wed me!"
"Ay, would he—with just for a dowry your can!"
  "I'm Muckle-mouth Meg," chirruped she.

"Then so—so—so—so—" as he kissed her apace—
  "Will I widen thee out till thou turnest
From Margaret Minnikin-mou', by God's grace,
  To Muckle-mouth Meg in good earnest!"   40

EPILOGUE

This is the last poem in Browning's last book *Asolando*,
published on the day of his death.

At the midnight in the silence of the sleep-time,
  When you set your fancies free,
Will they pass to where—by death, fools think, im-
   prisoned—
Low he lies who once so loved you, whom you loved
   so,
    —Pity me?

Oh to love so, be so loved, yet so mistaken!
  What had I on earth to do
With the slothful, with the mawkish, the unmanly?
Like the aimless, helpless, hopeless, did I drivel
    —Being—who?   10

One who never turned his back but marched breast
   forward,
  Never doubted clouds would break,
Never dreamed, though right were worsted, wrong
   would triumph,
Held we fall to rise, are baffled to fight better,
    Sleep to wake.

No, at noonday in the bustle of man's work-time
  Greet the unseen with a cheer!
Bid him forward, breast and back as either should
   be,
"Strive and thrive!" cry "Speed,—fight on, fare ever
   There as here!"   20

35. can, the vessel in which she has been bringing him
drink.   39. Minnikin-mou', small-mouthed.

Elizabeth Barrett Browning
1806–1861

Nowadays, as Virginia Woolf has amusingly and metaphorically remarked, "the only place in the mansion of literature . . . . assigned . . . . [Mrs. Browning] is downstairs in the servants' quarters, where, in company with Mrs. Hemans, Eliza Cook, Jean Ingelow, Alexander Smith, Edwin Arnold, and Robert Montgomery she bangs the crockery about and eats vast handfuls of peas on the point of her knife" (*The Second Common Reader*, Harcourt, Brace, 1932).

It was not always so. When her future husband met Mrs. Browning (through his admiration for her poetry) in 1845, her reputation was far greater than his, and as long as they lived together most of the money that literature made in that household came through her books. When Wordsworth died in 1850, she was suggested for the laureateship.

Her technical deficiencies only partly explain the reaction against her. Many of her themes were topical. We are no longer passionately interested in Italian unification, and if children are still being exploited in industry, we flatter ourselves that our approach to the problem is more "scientific," less "Victorian," than hers. Less Victorian, at least, it certainly is. Like Tennyson, Mrs. Browning was eminently of her time, and she lacked the positive genius to beat down our prejudices and compel us to accept her as we accept him, when he is at his best, on such terms as genius may elect.

But whatever may be said of the rest of her poems, if our recent publishing record affords any index *Sonnets from the Portuguese*, 1850, is safe. This is partly because the restraint and compression of the Italian sonnet form helped her to avoid some— not all—of her faults, but more because the sonnets stand, in a biographical-minded age, the one work which gives us their author in the aspect in which our contemporaries best like to think of her—as the love of Robert Browning.

"I love" were the words which began his first letter to her, in January, 1845—"I love your verses with all my heart, dear Miss Barrett." Later in the same letter he added, "I love you too." Having been born March 6, 1806, the woman who received this letter was nearly forty—six years older than the man who wrote it—and almost a helpless invalid. When he begged for a meeting, in May,

she yielded, somewhat in spite of her better judgment, for she knew there was nothing to see in her.

What happened constitutes, as everybody knows, one of the great romances in English literary history. To Browning the same test came that comes to Caponsacchi in *The Ring and the Book*. He was the Gallant Knight who literally, in unromantic nineteenth-century Wimpole Street, carried off the Fairy Princess from the Ogre's Castle. For a true picture of Edward Moulton-Barrett one must go to Jeannette Marks's book *The Family of the Barrett*, Macmillan, 1938; the lecherous monster of Rudolph Besier's play *The Barretts of Wimpole Street*, Little, Brown, 1931 never existed save in a playwright's imagination. Yet the real Barrett behaved almost as unreasonably as the monster in the play; having made up his mind that Death would be the next visitor to his daughter's sickroom, he could not bring himself to admit Life. For Elizabeth the choice soon presented itself as an alternative between death and elopement, and nobody who understands her hunger for "Life—Love— Italy" need be surprised at the choice she made. This was in September, 1846. Browning gave her fifteen happy years of wifehood and motherhood at the Casa Guidi, Florence, before, on June 29, 1861, she died in his arms.

The title of her anonymously published sonnets was, of course, a smoke screen. They were completed, apparently, before the marriage, but Browning, who had injudiciously expressed himself against making verse of one's love, did not see them until three years later. Mrs. Browning's other books included *Poems*, 1844; *Casa Guidi Windows* (which reflects her passion for Italy), 1851; *Aurora Leigh* (a novel in verse), 1857; *Poems before Congress*, 1860.

from SONNETS FROM THE PORTUGUESE

I

I thought once how Theocritus had sung
Of the sweet years, the dear and wished-for years,
Who each one in a gracious hand appears
To bear a gift for mortals, old or young:

1. **Theocritus,** Greek pastoral poet (third century B.C.).

And, as I mused it in his antique tongue,
I saw, in gradual vision through my tears,
The sweet, sad years, the melancholy years,
Those of my own life, who by turns had flung
A shadow across me. Straightway I was 'ware,   10
So weeping, how a mystic Shape did move
Behind me, and drew me backward by the hair,
And a voice said in mastery, while I strove, . . .
"Guess now who holds thee?"—"Death," I said.
  But, there,
The silver answer rang . . . . "Not Death, but
  Love."

3

Unlike are we, unlike, O princely Heart!
Unlike our uses and our destinies.
Our ministering two angels look surprise
On one another, as they strike athwart
Their wings in passing. Thou, bethink thee, art
A guest for queens to social pageantries,
With gages from a hundred brighter eyes
Than tears even can make mine, to play thy part
Of chief musician. What hast *thou* to do
With looking from the lattice-lights at me,   10
A poor, tired, wandering singer, . . . singing
  through
The dark, and leaning up a cypress-tree?
The chrism is on thine head,—on mine, the dew,—
And Death must dig the level where these agree.

4

Thou hast thy calling to some palace-floor,
Most gracious singer of high poems! where
The dancers will break footing, from the care
Of watching up thy pregnant lips for more.
And dost thou lift this house's latch too poor
For hand of thine? and canst thou think and bear
To let thy music drop here unaware
In folds of golden fulness at my door?
Look up and see the casement broken in,
The bats and owlets builders in the roof!   10
My cricket chirps against thy mandolin.
Hush, call no echo up in further proof
Of desolation! there's a voice within
That weeps . . . as thou must sing . . . alone,
  aloof.

6

Go from me. Yet I feel that I shall stand
Henceforward in thy shadow. Nevermore
Alone upon the threshold of my door
Of individual life, I shall command

Sec. 3. **12. cypress-tree,** traditionally associated with
death.

The uses of my soul, nor lift my hand
Serenely in the sunshine as before,
Without the sense of that which I forbore, . . .
Thy touch upon the palm. The widest land
Doom takes to part us, leaves thy heart in mine
With pulses that beat double. What I do   10
And what I dream include thee, as the wine
Must taste of its own grapes. And when I sue
God for myself, He hears that name of thine,
And sees within my eyes the tears of two.

7

The face of all the world is changed, I think,
Since first I heard the footsteps of thy soul
Move still, oh, still, beside me, as they stole
Betwixt me and the dreadful outer brink
Of obvious death, where I, who thought to sink,
Was caught up into love, and taught the whole
Of life in a new rhythm. The cup of dole
God gave for baptism, I am fain to drink,
And praise its sweetness, Sweet, with thee anear.
The names of country, heaven, are changed away
For where thou art or shalt be, there or here;   11
And this . . . . this lute and song . . . loved yes-
  terday,
(The singing angels know) are only dear
Because thy name moves right in what they say.

8

What can I give thee back, O liberal
And princely giver, who hast brought the gold
And purple of thine heart, unstained, untold,
And laid them on the outside of the wall
For such as I to take or leave withal,
In unexpected largesse? am I cold,
Ungrateful, that for these most manifold
High gifts, I render nothing back at all?
Not so; not cold,—but very poor instead.
Ask God who knows. For frequent tears have run
The colours from my life, and left so dead   11
And pale a stuff, it were not fitly done
To give the same as pillow to thy head.
Go farther! let it serve to trample on.

9

Can it be right to give what I can give?
To let thee sit beneath the fall of tears
As salt as mine, and hear the sighing years
Re-sighing on my lips renunciative
Through those infrequent smiles which fail to live
For all thy adjurations? O my fears,
That this can scarce be right! We are not peers,
So to be lovers; and I own, and grieve,
That givers of such gifts as mine are, must

Be counted with the ungenerous. Out, alas!   10
I will not soil thy purple with my dust,
Nor breathe my poison on thy Venice-glass,
Nor give thee any love . . . which were unjust.
Belovèd, I only love thee! let it pass.

14

If thou must love me, let it be for nought
Except for love's sake only. Do not say
"I love her for her smile . . . her look . . . her
    way
Of speaking gently, . . . for a trick of thought
That falls in well with mine, and certes brought
A sense of pleasant ease on such a day"—
For these things in themselves, Belovèd, may
Be changed, or change for thee,—and love, so
    wrought,
May be unwrought so. Neither love me for
Thine own dear pity's wiping my cheeks dry,—
A creature might forget to weep, who bore   11
Thy comfort long, and lose thy love thereby!
But love me for love's sake, that evermore
Thou may'st love on, through love's eternity.

18

I never gave a lock of hair away
To a man, dearest, except this to thee,
Which now upon my fingers thoughtfully
I ring out to the full brown length and say
"Take it." My day of youth went yesterday;
My hair no longer bounds to my foot's glee,
Nor plant I it from rose or myrtle-tree,
As girls do, any more. It only may
Now shade on two pale cheeks, the mark of tears,
Taught drooping from the head that hangs aside
Through sorrow's trick. I thought the funeral-
    shears   11
Would take this first, but Love is justified,—
Take it thou, . . . finding pure, from all those
    years,
The kiss my mother left here when she died.

20

Belovèd, my Belovèd, when I think
That thou wast in the world a year ago,
What time I sat alone here in the snow
And saw no footprint, heard the silence sink
No moment at thy voice, . . . but, link by link,
Went counting all my chains as if that so
They never could fall off at any blow

Sec. 9. **12. Venice-glass,** a fine, fragile drinking-glass; originally manufactured at Murano, near Venice.   *Sec. 18.*
7–8. Nor plant . . . any more. She no longer fixes leaves
or blossoms in her hair, as she did when she was younger.

Struck by thy possible hand . . . why, thus I
    drink
Of life's great cup of wonder! Wonderful,
Never to feel thee thrill the day or night   10
With personal act or speech,—nor ever cull
Some prescience of thee with the blossoms white
Thou sawest growing! Atheists are as dull,
Who cannot guess God's presence out of sight.

22

When our two souls stand up erect and strong,
Face to face, silent, drawing nigh and nigher,
Until the lengthening wings break into fire
At either curvèd point,—what bitter wrong
Can the earth do to us, that we should not long
Be here contented? Think. In mounting higher,
The angels would press on us, and aspire
To drop some golden orb of perfect song
Into our deep, dear silence. Let us stay
Rather on earth, Belovèd,—where the unfit,   10
Contrarious moods of men recoil away
And isolate pure spirits, and permit
A place to stand and love in for a day,
With darkness and the death-hour rounding it.

23

Is it indeed so? If I lay here dead,
Wouldst thou miss any life in losing mine?
And would the sun for thee more coldly shine
Because of grave-damps falling round my head?
I marvelled, my Belovèd, when I read
Thy thought so in the letter. I am thine—
But . . . *so* much to thee? Can I pour thy wine
While my hands tremble? Then my soul, instead
Of dreams of death, resumes life's lower range.
Then, love me, Love! look on me . . . breathe on
    me!   10
As brighter ladies do not count it strange,
For love, to give up acres and degree,
I yield the grave for thy sake, and exchange
My near sweet view of Heaven, for earth with thee!

24

Let the world's sharpness like a clasping knife
Shut in upon itself and do no harm
In this close hand of Love, now soft and warm,
And let us hear no sound of human strife
After the click of the shutting. Life to life—
I lean upon thee, dear, without alarm,
And feel as safe as guarded by a charm
Against the stab of worldlings, who if rife
Are weak to injure. Very whitely still
The lilies of our lives may reassure   10
Their blossoms from their roots, accessible

Alone to heavenly dews that drop not fewer;
Growing straight, out of man's reach, on the hill.
God only, who made us rich, can make us poor.

25

A heavy heart, Belovèd, have I borne
From year to year until I saw thy face,
And sorrow after sorrow took the place
Of all those natural joys as lightly worn
As the stringed pearls . . . each lifted in its turn
By a beating heart at dance-time. Hopes apace
Were changed to long despairs, till God's own grace
Could scarcely lift above the world forlorn
My heavy heart. Then *thou* didst bid me bring
And let it drop adown thy calmly great   10
Deep being! Fast it sinketh, as a thing
Which its own nature doth precipitate,
While thine doth close above it, mediating
Betwixt the stars and the unaccomplished fate.

26

I lived with visions for my company
Instead of men and women, years ago,
And found them gentle mates, nor thought to know
A sweeter music than they played to me.
But soon their trailing purple was not free
Of this world's dust,—their lutes did silent grow,
And I myself grew faint and blind below
Their vanishing eyes. Then THOU didst come . . .
    to be,
Belovèd, what they seemed. Their shining fronts,
Their songs, their splendours (better, yet the same,
As river-water hallowed into fonts)   11
Met in thee, and from out thee overcame
My soul with satisfaction of all wants—
Because God's gifts put man's best dreams to shame.

27

My own Belovèd, who hast lifted me
From this drear flat of earth where I was thrown,
And, in betwixt the languid ringlets, blown
A life-breath, till the forehead hopefully
Shines out again, as all the angels see,
Before thy saving kiss! My own, my own,
Who camest to me when the world was gone,
And I who looked for only God found *thee!*
I find thee; I am safe, and strong, and glad.
As one who stands in dewless asphodel,   10
Looks backward on the tedious time he had
In the upper life,—so I, with bosom-swell,
Make witness, here, between the good and bad,
That Love, as strong as Death, retrieves as well.

Sec. 27. **10. asphodel,** here, a flower in the Greek other-world.

28

My letters! all dead paper, . . . mute and white!—
And yet they seem alive and quivering
Against my tremulous hands which loose the string
And let them drop down on my knee to-night.
This said, . . . he wished to have me in his sight
Once, as a friend: this fixed a day in spring
To come and touch my hand . . . a simple thing,
Yet I wept for it!—this, . . . the paper's light . . .
Said, *Dear, I love thee;* and I sank and quailed
As if God's future thundered on my past.   10
This said, *I am thine*—and so its ink has paled
With lying at my heart that beat too fast.
And this . . . O Love, thy words have ill availed,
If, what this said, I dared repeat at last!

35

If I leave all for thee, wilt thou exchange
And be all to me? Shall I never miss
Home-talk and blessing and the common kiss
That comes to each in turn, nor count it strange,
When I look up, to drop on a new range
Of walls and floors . . . another home than this?
Nay, wilt thou fill that place by me which is
Filled by dead eyes too tender to know change?
That's hardest. If to conquer love, has tried,
To conquer grief, tries more . . . as all things
    prove;   10
For grief indeed is love and grief beside.
Alas, I have grieved so I am hard to love.
Yet love me—wilt thou? Open thine heart wide,
And fold within, the wet wings of thy dove.

36

When we met first and loved, I did not build
Upon the event with marble. Could it mean
To last, a love set pendulous between
Sorrow and sorrow? Nay, I rather thrilled,
Distrusting every light that seemed to gild
The onward path, and feared to overlean
A finger even. And, though I have grown serene
And strong since then, I think that God has willed
A still renewable fear . . . O love, O troth . . .
Lest these enclaspèd hands should never hold,   10
This mutual kiss drop down between us both
As an unowned thing, once the lips being cold.
And Love, be false! if *he*, to keep one oath,
Must lose one joy, by his life's star foretold.

38

First time he kissed me, he but only kissed
The fingers of this hand wherewith I write;

Sec. 35. **1. leave all.** Mrs. Browning's elopement closed her former home to her forever.

And, ever since, it grew more clean and white, ...
Slow to world-greetings . . . quick with its "Oh, list,"
When the angels speak. A ring of amethyst
I could not wear here, plainer to my sight,
Than that first kiss. The second passed in height
The first, and sought the forehead, and half missed,
Half falling on the hair. O beyond meed!
That was the chrism of love, which love's own crown,   10
With sanctifying sweetness, did precede.
The third upon my lips was folded down
In perfect, purple state; since when, indeed,
I have been proud and said, "My love, my own."

41

I thank all who have loved me in their hearts,
With thanks and love from mine. Deep thanks to all
Who paused a little near the prison-wall,
To hear my music in its louder parts,
Ere they went onward, each one to the mart's
Or temple's occupation, beyond call.
But thou, who, in my voice's sink and fall,
When the sob took it, thy divinest Art's
Own instrument didst drop down at thy foot,
To hearken what I said between my tears, . . .   10
Instruct me how to thank thee!—Oh, to shoot
My soul's full meaning into future years,
That *they* should lend it utterance, and salute
Love that endures, from Life that disappears!

43

How do I love thee? Let me count the ways.
I love thee to the depth and breadth and height
My soul can reach, when feeling out of sight
For the ends of Being and ideal Grace.
I love thee to the level of every day's
Most quiet need, by sun and candlelight.
I love thee freely, as men strive for Right;
I love thee purely, as they turn from Praise.
I love thee with the passion put to use
In my old griefs, and with my childhood's faith.
I love thee with a love I seemed to lose   11
With my lost saints,—I love thee with the breath,
Smiles, tears, of all my life!—and, if God choose,
I shall but love thee better after death.

44

Belovèd, thou hast brought me many flowers
Plucked in the garden, all the summer through
And winter, and it seemed as if they grew
In this close room, nor missed the sun and showers.
So, in the like name of that love of ours,
Take back these thoughts which here unfolded too,
And which on warm and cold days I withdrew
From my heart's ground. Indeed, those beds and bowers
Be overgrown with bitter weeds and rue,
And wait thy weeding: yet here's eglantine,   10
Here's ivy!—take them, as I used to do
Thy flowers, and keep them where they shall not pine.
Instruct thine eyes to keep their colours true,
And tell thy soul their roots are left in mine.

Emily Brontë
1818–1848

Poems by Currer, Ellis, and Acton Bell was published in 1846. Two persons are known to have purchased it; the bulk of the edition was used for trunk-lining. Today such copies as have survived are worth almost their weight in gold.

Three sisters wrote the poems in a lonely parsonage at Haworth, on the edge of the Yorkshire moors. It was a place that knew disease, eccentricity, and (in the person of Branwell, the son of the household) a life-destroying dissipation, but it knew also the glorifying power of the ideal. Two of the "Bells"—Currer (Charlotte Brontë) and Ellis (Emily Brontë)—won fame as novelists, the former with *Jane Eyre*, *Shirley*, and *Villette*, the latter with *Wuthering Heights*, the only English novel before Hardy to achieve a cosmic outlook. Acton (Anne Brontë) also published two novels, but probably nobody would read them today if they had not been written by the sister of Charlotte and Emily.

As a poet Emily is the only Brontë to deserve serious consideration. Her reputation has now advanced to such heights that Christina Rossetti is her only possible rival as England's most distinguished woman poet. There is nothing to tell of her life except what she herself told in her poems and her one superb novel, for, in the ordinary sense of the term, nothing ever happened to her. She did go with Charlotte to the Pensionnat Héger in Brussels, but Brussels did not impress her, and she did not impress Brussels. Almost completely independent of outward circumstance, she was one of the most self-sufficient women who ever lived; she died, of tuberculosis, in her thirtieth year, literally in her boots. One doubts that even that made any difference to her; as a mystic, she was quite at home in eternity.

Emily Brontë's mental and spiritual characteristics are revealed clearly enough in her poems—in "The Prisoner" she has given us one of the best descriptions we have of the mystical experience—but the reader must always allow for the fact that, unlike Charlotte's, her genius was not lyrical but dramatic. Much ink has been wasted in an attempt to identify the lover of "Remembrance"; we know now that the poem is Rosina's lament for King Julius in the Gondal saga. The Brontë children discovered a strong mythmaking faculty in themselves at an early age. Charlotte and Branwell wrote about an African kingdom called Angria; Emily and Anne chose an island in the Pacific which they named Gondal. The Angrian material has now been printed in part; the Gondal materials, unfortunately, no longer exist.

REMEMBRANCE

Cold in the earth—and the deep snow piled above
    thee,
Far, far removed, cold in the dreary grave!
Have I forgot, my only Love, to love thee,
Severed at last by Time's all-severing wave?

Now, when alone, do my thoughts no longer hover
Over the mountains, on that northern shore,
Resting their wings where heath and fern-leaves
    cover
Thy noble heart for ever, ever more?

Cold in the earth—and fifteen wild Decembers,
From those brown hills, have melted into spring: 10
Faithful, indeed, is the spirit that remembers
After such years of change and suffering!

Sweet Love of youth, forgive, if I forget thee,
While the world's tide is bearing me along;
Other desires and other hopes beset me,
Hopes which obscure, but cannot do thee wrong!

No later light has lightened up my heaven,
No second moon has ever shone for me;

All my life's bliss from thy dear life was given,
All my life's bliss is in the grave with thee. 20

But, when the days of golden dreams had perished,
And ev'n Despair was powerless to destroy;
Then did I learn how existence could be cherished,
Strengthened, and fed without the aid of joy.

Then did I check the tears of useless passion—
Weaned my young soul from yearning after thine;
Sternly denied its burning wish to hasten
Down to that tomb already more than mine.

And, even yet, I dare not let it languish,
Dare not indulge in memory's rapturous pain; 30
Once drinking deep of that divinest anguish,
How could I seek the empty world again?

SONG

The linnet in the rocky dells,
    The moor-lark in the air,
The bee among the heather bells
    That hide my lady fair:

The wild deer browse above her breast;
    The wild birds raise their brood;
And they, her smiles of love caressed,
    Have left her solitude!

I ween, that when the grave's dark wall
    Did first her form retain, 10
They thought their hearts could ne'er recall
    The light of joy again.

They thought the tide of grief would flow
    Unchecked through future years;
But where is all their anguish now,
    And where are all their tears?

Well, let them fight for honour's breath,
    Or pleasure's shade pursue—
The dweller in the land of death
    Is changed and careless too. 20

And, if their eyes should watch and weep
    Till sorrow's source were dry,
She would not, in her tranquil sleep,
    Return a single sigh!

Blow, west-wind, by the lonely mound,
    And murmur, summer-streams—
There is no need of other sound
    To soothe my lady's dreams.

THE PRISONER

A Fragment

In the dungeon-crypts idly did I stray,
Reckless of the lives wasting there away;
"Draw the ponderous bars! open, Warder stern!"
He dared not say me nay—the hinges harshly
    turn.

"Our guests are darkly lodged," I whispered, gazing
    through
The vault, whose grated eye showed heaven more
    grey than blue;
(This was when glad Spring laughed in awaking
    pride);
"Ay, darkly lodged enough!" returned my sullen
    guide.

Then, God forgive my youth; forgive my careless
    tongue;
I scoffed, as the chill chains on the damp flagstones
    rung: 10
"Confined in triple walls, art thou so much to fear,
That we must bind thee down and clench thy fetters
    here?"

The captive raised her face; it was as soft and mild
As sculptured marble saint, or slumbering un-
    weaned child;
It was so soft and mild, it was so sweet and fair,
Pain could not trace a line, nor grief a shadow there!

The captive raised her hand and pressed it to her
    brow:
"I have been struck," she said, "and I am suffering
    now;
Yet these are little worth, your bolts and irons
    strong;
And, were they forged in steel, they could not hold
    me long."   20

Hoarse laughed the jailor grim: "Shall I be won to
    hear;
Dost think, fond, dreaming wretch, that *I* shall
    grant thy prayer?
Or, better still, wilt melt my master's heart with
    groans?
Ah! sooner might the sun thaw down these granite
    stones.

"My master's voice is low, his aspect bland and
    kind,
But hard as hardest flint the soul that lurks behind;

And I am rough and rude, yet not more rough to see
Than is the hidden ghost that has its home in me."

About her lips there played a smile of almost scorn:
"My friend," she gently said, "you have not heard
    me mourn;   30
When you my kindred's lives, *my* lost life, can re-
    store,
Then may I weep and sue,—but never, friend,
    before!

"Still, let my tyrants know, I am not doomed to
    wear
Year after year in gloom, and desolate despair;
A messenger of Hope comes every night to me,
And offers for short life, eternal liberty.

"He comes with western winds, with evening's
    wandering airs,
With that clear dusk of heaven that brings the
    thickest stars.
Winds take a pensive tone, and stars a tender fire,
And visions rise, and change, that kill me with
    desire.   40

"Desire for nothing known in my maturer years,
When joy grew mad with awe, at counting future
    tears.
When, if my spirit's sky was full of flashes warm,
I knew not whence they came, from sun or thunder-
    storm.

"But, first, a hush of peace—a soundless calm de-
    scends;
The struggle of distress, and fierce impatience ends;
Mute music soothes my breast—unuttered har-
    mony,
That I could never dream, till Earth was lost to me.

"Then dawns the Invisible; the Unseen its truth
    reveals;
My outward sense is gone, my inward essence feels:
Its wings are almost free—its home, its harbour
    found,   51
Measuring the gulf, it stoops—and dares the final
    bound.

"Oh! dreadful is the check—intense the agony—
When the ear begins to hear, and the eye begins to
    see;
When the pulse begins to throb, the brain to think
    again;
The soul to feel the flesh, and the flesh to feel the
    chain.

"Yet I would lose no sting, would wish no torture
   less;
The more that anguish racks, the earlier it will
   bless;
And robed in fires of hell, or bright with heavenly
   shine,
If it but herald death, the vision is divine!"   60

She ceased to speak, and we, unanswering, turned
   to go—
We had no further power to work the captive woe:
Her cheek, her gleaming eye, declared that man
   had given
A sentence, unapproved, and overruled by Heaven.

Then like a tender child whose hand did just en-
   fold
Safe in its eager grasp a bird it wept to hold,
When pierced with one wild glance from the
   troubled hazel eye,
It gushes into tears and lets its treasure fly,

Thus ruth and selfish love, together striving, tore
The heart all newly taught to pity and adore;   70
If I should break the chain, I felt my bird would go;
Yet I must break the chain, or seal the prisoner's
   woe.

TO IMAGINATION

When weary with the long day's care,
   And earthly change from pain to pain,
And lost, and ready to despair,
   Thy kind voice calls me back again,
O my true friend! I am not lone,
While thou canst speak with such a tone!

So hopeless is the world without,
   The world within I doubly prize;
Thy world, where guile, and hate, and doubt
   And cold suspicion never rise;   10
Where thou, and I, and Liberty,
Have undisputed sovereignty.

What matters it, that all around
   Danger, and guilt, and darkness lie,
If but within our bosom's bound
   We hold a bright, untroubled sky,
Warm with ten thousand mingled rays
Of suns that know no winter days?

Reason, indeed, may oft complain
   For Nature's sad reality,   20

And tell the suffering heart how vain
   Its cherished dreams must always be;
And Truth may rudely trample down
   The flowers of Fancy, newly-blown:

But thou art ever there, to bring
   The hovering vision back, and breathe
New glories o'er the blighted spring,
   And call a lovelier Life from Death,
And whisper, with a voice divine,
Of real worlds, as bright as thine.   30

I trust not to thy phantom bliss,
   Yet, still, in evening's quiet hour,
With never-failing thankfulness,
   I welcome thee, Benignant Power,
Sure solacer of human cares,
And sweeter hope, when hope despairs!

THE OLD STOIC

Riches I hold in light esteem,
   And Love I laugh to scorn;
And lust of fame was but a dream,
   That vanished with the morn:

And if I pray, the only prayer
   That moves my lips for me
Is, "Leave the heart that now I bear,
   And give me liberty!"

Yes, as my swift days near their goal,
   'Tis all that I implore;—   10
In life and death a chainless soul,
   With courage to endure.

THE VISIONARY

Silent is the house: all are laid asleep:
One alone looks out o'er the snow-wreaths deep,
Watching every cloud, dreading every breeze
That whirls the 'wildering drift, and bends the
   groaning trees.

Cheerful is the hearth, soft the matted floor;
Not one shivering gust creeps through pane or door;
The little lamp burns straight, its rays shoot strong
   and far:
I trim it well, to be the wanderer's guiding-star.

Frown, my haughty sire! chide, my angry dame!
Set your slaves to spy; threaten me with shame: 10

But neither sire nor dame, nor prying serf shall know
What angel nightly tracks that waste of frozen snow.

What I love shall come like visitant of air,
Safe in secret power from lurking human snare;
Who loves me, no word of mine shall e'er betray,
Though for faith unstained my life must forfeit pay.

Burn then, little lamp; glimmer straight and clear—
Hush! a rustling wing stirs, methinks, the air:
He for whom I wait thus ever comes to me;
Strange Power! I trust thy might; trust thou my
    constancy.   · 20

STANZAS

Often rebuked, yet always back returning
    To those first feelings that were born with me,
And leaving busy chase of wealth and learning
    For idle dreams of things which cannot be:

To-day, I will seek not the shadowy region:
    Its unsustaining vastness waxes drear;
And visions rising, legion after legion,
    Bring the unreal world too strangely near.

I'll walk, but not in old heroic traces,
    And not in paths of high morality,   10
And not among the half-distinguished faces,
    The clouded forms of long-past history.

I'll walk where my own nature would be leading:
    It vexes me to choose another guide:
Where the grey flocks in ferny glens are feeding;
    Where the wild wind blows on the mountain-side.

What have those lonely mountains worth revealing?
    More glory and more grief than I can tell:
The earth that wakes *one* human heart to feeling 19
    Can centre both the worlds of Heaven and Hell.

I AM THE ONLY BEING

I am the only being whose doom
    No tongue would ask, no eye would mourn;
I've never caused a thought of gloom,
    A smile of joy, since I was born.

In secret pleasure, secret tears,
    This changeful life has slipped away,
As friendless after eighteen years,
    As lone as on my natal day.

There have been times I cannot hide,
    There have been times when this was drear, 10
When my sad soul forgot its pride
    And longed for one to love me here.

But those were in the early glow
    Of feelings, long subdued by care;
And they have died so long ago,
    I hardly now believe they were.

First melted off the hope of youth,
    Then fancy's rainbow fast withdrew;
And then experience told me truth
    In mortal bosoms never grew.   20

'Twas grief enough to think mankind
    All hollow, servile, insincere;
But worse to turn to my own mind,
    And find the same corruption there.

LINES BY CLAUDIA

I did not sleep; 'twas noon of day;
    I saw the burning sunshine fall,
The long grass bending where I lay,
    The blue sky brooding over all.

I heard the mellow hum of bees,
    And singing birds and sighing trees,
And, far away, in woody dell
    The music of the Sabbath-bell.

I did not dream: remembrance still
    Clasped round my heart its fetters chill; 10
    But I am sure the soul is free
To leave its clay a little while,
    Or how, in exile-misery,
    Could I have seen my country smile?

In English fields my limbs were laid,
    With English turf beneath my head;
My spirit wandered o'er that shore
    Where nought but it may wander more.

Yet if the soul can thus return,
    I need not, and I will not mourn;   20
    And vainly did you drive me far
With leagues of ocean stretched between:
    My mortal flesh you might debar,
    But not the eternal fire within.

My monarch died to rule for ever
    A heart that can forget him never;
    And dear to me, ay, doubly dear,

Though shut within the silent tomb,
  His name shall be for whoso bear
This long-sustained and hopeless doom.   30

And brighter in the hour of woe
  Than in the blaze of victory's pride,
That glory-shedding star shall glow,
  For which we fought and bled and died.

LAST LINES

No coward soul is mine,
No trembler in the world's storm-troubled sphere:
  I see Heaven's glories shine,
And Faith shines equal, arming me from Fear.

O God within my breast,
Almighty, ever-present Deity!
  Life—that in me has rest,
As I—undying Life—have power in Thee!

Vain are the thousand creeds
That move men's hearts: unutterably vain;   10

Worthless as withered weeds,
Or idlest froth amid the boundless main,

To waken doubt in one
Holding so fast by Thy infinity,
  So surely anchored on
The steadfast rock of Immortality.

With wide-embracing love
Thy Spirit animates eternal years,
  Pervades and broods above,
Changes, sustains, dissolves, creates, and rears.   20

Though earth and man were gone,
And suns and universes ceased to be,
  And Thou wert left alone,
Every existence would exist in Thee.

There is not room for Death,
Nor atom that his might could render void:
  Thou—THOU art Being and Breath,
And what THOU art may never be destroyed.

Edward FitzGerald
1809–1883

Of the life of Edward FitzGerald, beloved friend of Tennyson and Thackeray, there is little to tell. As Gamaliel Bradford puts it, he "was born in 1809, spent some years of his childhood in France, was educated at King Edward the Sixth's School at Bury St. Edmund's and at Cambridge. Then, until 1883, he walked a little, talked a little, thought a little, scribbled a little as he would have said himself, smoked a great deal, and died." (*Bare Souls*, Harper, 1924.)

The "scribbling" took the form of translations from Persian, Greek, and Spanish, of which all except the *Six Dramas from Calderon Freely Translated*, 1853, appeared anonymously. All FitzGerald's translations are "free." He himself said: "I suppose very few people have ever taken such pains in translation as I have: though certainly not to be literal. But at all costs a thing must *live:* with a trans-fusion of one's own worse life if one can't retain the original's better." To none of his works do his words apply better than to the one which gave him his fame, *The Rubáiyát of Omar Khayyám.*

Omar, called Khayyám (the tent-maker), prob-ably from his father's occupation, was a Persian poet, astronomer, mathematician, unsystematic philosopher, and free-liver who is said to have died in 1123 A.D. There are a hundred and fifty-eight of his multitudinous *rubā'īs* (quatrains) in the Bodleian manuscript FitzGerald used, "independent stanzas, consisting each of four lines of equal, though varied, prosody; sometimes *all* rhyming, but oftener (as here imitated) the third line a blank. Somewhat as in the Greek alcaic, where the penultimate line seems to lift and suspend the wave that falls over in the last. As usual with such kind of Oriental verse, the Rubáiyát follow one another according to al-phabetic rime—a strange succession of grave and gay" (FitzGerald). The translator combined and arranged to suit himself, imposing his own con-tinuity upon heterogeneous material.

Success was by no means instantaneous. Of the original paper-bound edition of 1859, which con-tained seventy-five quatrains, most of the copies were exposed for sale by a London bookseller at a penny each; fortunately Swinburne and Rossetti came upon them, and their enthusiasm helped to turn the tide. The revised edition of 1868 ran to one hundred and ten stanzas; later editions, 1872 and

1879, reduced the number to one hundred and one, and established a new order. (The fourth edition is reprinted here.) By the seventies, "advanced" spirits in England were already beginning to tire of moral earnestness. Consequently Omar's melancholy, his determination not to miss any of the pleasures of the senses, his agnostic materialism dashed with occasional vagrant gleams of mystic yearning, were destined to endear him to a very large public as the years went by. His vogue lasted at least until the war of 1914–18; in some respects, indeed, it is with us still. Important contributions to the *Rubáiyát* craze were made by Liza Lehmann's song cycle *In a Persian Garden* (1896) and, in the United States at least, by Elihu Vedder's famous illustrated edition (Houghton Mifflin, 1884).

FitzGerald himself described the mood of the Rubáiyát as "a desperate sort of thing, unfortunately at the bottom of all thinking men's minds, but made music of." It is to be feared that he would not quite have approved of all his admirers. He hated to go to London during the last years of his life. "The wickedness of London appals me; and yet I am no paragon." Perhaps he would more have relished the knowledge that Thomas Hardy on his deathbed asked to have stanza 81 read to him.

THE RUBÁIYÁT OF OMAR KHAYYÁM

1

Wake! For the Sun, who scattered into flight
The Stars before him from the Field of Night,
   Drives Night along with them from Heav'n, and strikes
The Sultàn's Turret with a Shaft of Light.

2

Before the phantom of False morning died,
Methought a Voice within the Tavern cried,
   "When all the Temple is prepared within,
Why nods the drowsy Worshipper outside?"

3

And, as the Cock crew, those who stood before
The Tavern shouted—"Open then the Door!   10
   You know how little while we have to stay,
And, once departed, may return no more."

4

Now the New Year reviving old Desires,
The thoughtful Soul to Solitude retires,
   Where the WHITE HAND OF MOSES on the Bough
Puts out, and Jesus from the Ground suspires.

5

Iram indeed is gone with all his Rose,
And Jamshyd's Sev'n-ringed Cup where no one knows;

5. False morning, "a transient light on the horizon about an hour before the . . . true dawn; a well-known phenomenon in the east." (FitzGerald)   **13. New Year,** beginning with the vernal equinox.   **15–16. White Hand . . . suspires.** "Exodus 4:6; where Moses draws forth his hand—not, according to the Persians, '*leprous as snow*'—but *white*, as our May-blossom in spring perhaps. According to them also the healing power of Jesus resided in his breath." (FitzGerald)   **17. Iram,** an ancient Persian garden.   **18. Jamshyd's Sev'n-ringed Cup.** Jamshyd was a legendary king of Persia. The seven rings on his divining cup typified the seven heavens, the seven planets, the seven seas, and so on.

But still a Ruby kindles in the Vine,
And many a Garden by the Water blows.   20

6

And David's lips are lockt; but in divine
High-piping Pehleví, with "Wine! Wine! Wine!
   Red Wine!"—the Nightingale cries to the Rose
That sallow cheek of hers to incarnadine.

7

Come, fill the Cup, and in the fire of Spring
Your Winter-garment of Repentance fling:
   The Bird of Time has but a little way
To flutter—and the Bird is on the Wing.

8

Whether at Naishápúr or Babylon,
Whether the Cup with sweet or bitter run,   30
   The Wine of Life keeps oozing drop by drop,
The Leaves of Life keep falling one by one.

9

Each Morn a thousand Roses brings, you say;
Yes, but where leaves the Rose of Yesterday?
   And this first Summer month that brings the Rose
Shall take Jamshyd and Kaikobád away.

10

Well, let it take them! What have we to do
With Kaikobád the Great, or Kaikhosrú?
   Let Zál and Rustum bluster as they will,
Or Hátim call to Supper—heed not you.   40

21. David, king of Judah and Israel (c. 1033–993 B.C.).   **22. Pehleví,** an ancient literary language of Persia.   **29. Naishápúr,** Omar's home city in Persia.   **36. Kaikobád,** another ancient legendary king.   **38. Kaikhosrú,** Cyrus the Great, who overthrew Belshazzar, King of Babylonia, and founded the Persian Empire, 538 B.C.   **39. Zál and Rustum.** For Rustum, see Matthew Arnold's poem, page 672. Zal was his father.   **40. Hátim** typifies Oriental hospitality.

11

With me along the strip of Herbage strown
That just divides the desert from the sown,
    Where name of Slave and Sultán is forgot-
And Peace to Mahmúd on his golden Throne!

12

A Book of Verses underneath the Bough,
A Jug of Wine, a Loaf of Bread—and Thou
    Beside me singing in the Wilderness—
Oh, Wilderness were Paradise enow!

13

Some for the Glories of This World; and some
Sigh for the Prophet's Paradise to come;   50
    Ah, take the Cash, and let the Credit go,
Nor heed the rumble of a distant Drum!

14

Look to the blowing Rose about us—"Lo,
Laughing," she says, "into the world I blow,
    At once the silken tassel of my Purse
Tear, and its Treasure on the Garden throw."

15

And those who husbanded the Golden grain,
And those who flung it to the winds like Rain,
    Alike to no such aureate Earth are turned
As, buried once, Men want dug up again.   60

16

The Worldly Hope men set their Hearts upon
Turns Ashes—or it prospers; and anon,
    Like Snow upon the Desert's dusty Face,
Lighting a little hour or two—is gone.

17

Think, in this battered Caravanserai
Whose Portals are alternate Night and Day,
    How Sultán after Sultán with his Pomp
Abode his destined Hour, and went his way.

18

They say the Lion and the Lizard keep
The Courts where Jamshyd gloried and drank deep:
    And Bahrám, the great Hunter—the Wild Ass   71
Stamps o'er his Head, but cannot break his Sleep.

19

I sometimes think that never blows so red
The Rose as where some buried Caesar bled;
    That every Hyacinth the Garden wears
Dropt in her Lap from some once lovely Head.

20

And this reviving Herb whose tender Green
Fledges the River-Lip on which we lean—
    Ah, lean upon it lightly! for who knows
From what once lovely Lip it springs unseen!   80

21

Ah, my Belovèd, fill the Cup that clears
To-day of past Regret and future Fears:
    To-morrow!—Why, To-morrow I may be
Myself with Yesterday's Sev'n thousand Years.

22

For some we loved, the loveliest and the best
That from his Vintage rolling Time hath prest,
    Have drunk their Cup a Round or two before,
And one by one crept silently to rest.

23

And we, that now make merry in the Room
They left, and Summer dresses in new bloom,   90
    Ourselves must we beneath the Couch of Earth
Descend—ourselves to make a Couch—for whom?

24

Ah, make the most of what we yet may spend,
Before we too into the Dust descend;
    Dust into Dust, and under Dust, to lie,
Sans Wine, sans Song, sans Singer, and—sans End!

25

Alike for those who for To-day prepare,
And those that after some To-morrow stare,
    A Muezzín from the Tower of Darkness cries,
"Fools, your Reward is neither Here nor There." 100

26

Why, all the Saints and Sages who discussed
Of the Two Worlds so wisely—they are thrust
    Like foolish Prophets forth; their Words to Scorn
Are scattered, and their Mouths are stopt with
        Dust.

44. **Mahmúd,** the sultan.   50. **Prophet's,** Mohammed's.
52. **Drum,** "beaten outside of palace." (FitzGerald)
56. **Treasure,** "the rose's golden center." (FitzGerald)
71. **Bahrám,** a ruler of Persia drowned in a swamp while
hunting a wild ass.

75. **Hyacinth.** The hyacinth sprang up from the ground
watered by the blood of Hyacinthus, who had been accidentally killed by Apollo.   84. **Sev'n thousand Years,** "a
thousand years to each planet." (FitzGerald)   96. **Sans,** without (French).   99. **Muezzín,** a crier who summons Mohammedans to prayer.

27

Myself when young did eagerly frequent
Doctor and Saint, and heard great argument
   About it and about: but evermore
Came out by the same door where in I went.

28

With them the seed of Wisdom did I sow,
And with mine own hand wrought to make it grow;
   And this was all the Harvest that I reaped— 111
"I came like Water, and like Wind I go."

29

Into this Universe, and *Why* not knowing
Nor *Whence*, like Water willy-nilly flowing;
   And out of it, as Wind along the Waste,
I know not *Whither*, willy-nilly blowing.

30

What, without asking, hither hurried *Whence?*
And, without asking, *Whither* hurried hence!
   Oh, many a Cup of this forbidden Wine
Must drown the memory of that insolence! 120

31

Up from Earth's Centre through the Seventh Gate
I rose, and on the Throne of Saturn sate,
   And many a Knot unravelled by the Road;
But not the Master-knot of Human Fate.

32

There was the Door to which I found no Key;
There was the Veil through which I might not see:
   Some little talk awhile of ME and THEE
There was—and then no more of THEE and ME.

33

Earth could not answer; nor the Seas that mourn
In flowing Purple, of their Lord forlorn; 130
   Nor rolling Heaven, with all his Signs revealed
And hidden by the sleeve of Night and Morn.

34

Then of the THEE IN ME who works behind
The Veil, I lifted up my hands to find
   A lamp amid the Darkness; and I heard,
As from Without—"THE ME WITHIN THEE BLIND!"

119. **forbidden,** by the Mohammedan religion. 122. **Saturn,** here, lord of the seventh heaven, enthroned in one of the nine concentric spheres which, according to the Ptolemaic system of astronomy, surrounded the earth. 131. **Signs,** of the zodiac.

35

Then to the Lip of this poor earthen Urn
I leaned, the Secret of my Life to learn:
   And Lip to Lip it murmured—"While you live,
Drink!—for, once dead, you never shall return."

36

I think the Vessel, that with fugitive 141
Articulation answered, once did live,
   And drink; and Ah! the passive Lip I kissed,
How many Kisses might it take—and give!

37

For I remember stopping by the way
To watch a Potter thumping his wet Clay;
   And with its all-obliterated Tongue
It murmured—"Gently, Brother, gently, pray!"

38

And has not such a Story from of Old
Down Man's successive generations rolled 150
   Of such a clod of saturated Earth
Cast by the Maker into Human mould?

39

And not a drop that from our Cups we throw
For Earth to drink of, but may steal below
   To quench the fire of Anguish in some Eye
There hidden—far beneath, and long ago.

40

As then the Tulip for her morning sup,
Of Heav'nly Vintage from the soil looks up,
   Do you devoutly do the like, till Heav'n
To Earth invert you—like an empty Cup. 160

41

Perplext no more with Human or Divine,
To-morrow's tangle to the winds resign,
   And lose your fingers in the tresses of
The Cypress-slender Minister of Wine.

145 ff. **For I remember . . .** "One of the Persian poets— Attar, I think—has a pretty story about this. A thirsty traveller dips his hand into a spring of water to drink from. By-and-by comes another and draws up and drinks from an earthen bowl, and then departs, leaving his bowl behind him. The first traveller takes it up for another draught; but is surprised to find that the same water which had tasted sweet from his own hand tastes bitter from the earthen bowl. But a voice—from heaven, I think—tells him the clay from which the bowl is made was once man, and, into whatever shape renewed, can never lose the bitter flavour of mortality." (FitzGerald) 153–54. **a drop . . . drink of,** a custom in the East, says FitzGerald. 164. **Cypress-slender . . . Wine,** the girl who passes the wine.

42

And if the Wine you drink, the Lip you press,
End in what All begins and ends in—Yes;
  Think that you are To-day what Yesterday
You were—To-morrow you shall not be less.

43

So when the Angel of the darker Drink
At last shall find you by the river-brink,   170
  And offering his Cup, invite your Soul
Forth to your Lips to quaff—you shall not shrink.

44

Why, if the Soul can fling the Dust aside,
And naked on the Air of Heaven ride,
  Were't not a Shame—were't not a Shame for him
In this clay carcase crippled to abide?

45

'Tis but a Tent where takes his one day's rest
A Sultán to the realm of Death addrest;
  The Sultán rises, and the dark Ferrásh
Strikes, and prepares it for another Guest.   180

46

And fear not lest Existence closing your
Account, and mine, should know the like no more;
  The Eternal Sákí from that Bowl has poured
Millions of Bubbles like us, and will pour.

47

When You and I behind the Veil are past,
Oh, but the long, long while the World shall last,
  Which of our Coming and Departure heeds
As the Sea's self should heed a pebble-cast.

48

A Moment's Halt—a momentary taste
Of Being from the Well amid the Waste—   190
  And Lo!—the phantom Caravan has reached
The Nothing it set out from—Oh, make haste!

49

Would you that spangle of Existence spend
About the secret—quick about it, Friend!
  A Hair perhaps divides the False and True—
And upon what, prithee, may life depend?

50

A Hair perhaps divides the False and True—
Yes; and a single Alif were the clue—
  Could you but find it—to the Treasure-house,
And peradventure to The Master too;   200

179. **Ferrásh,** the servant who takes down the tent.
183. **Sákí,** wine-bearer, here used symbolically. 198. **Alif,**
the first letter of the Arabic alphabet, a single vertical stroke.

51

Whose secret Presence, through Creation's veins
Running Quicksilver-like, eludes your pains;
  Taking all shapes from Máh to Máhi; and
They change and perish all—but He remains;

52

A moment guessed—then back behind the Fold
Immerst of Darkness round the Drama rolled
  Which, for the Pastime of Eternity,
He doth himself contrive, enact, behold.

53

But if in vain, down on the stubborn floor
Of Earth, and up to Heav'n's unopening Door,   210
  You gaze To-day, while You are You—how then
To-morrow, You when shall be You no more?

54

Waste not your Hour, nor in the vain pursuit
Of This and That endeavour and dispute;
  Better be jocund with the fruitful Grape
Than sadden after none, or bitter, Fruit.

55

You know, my Friends, with what a brave Carouse
I made a Second Marriage in my house;
  Divorced old barren Reason from my Bed,
And took the Daughter of the Vine to Spouse.   220

56

For "Is" and "Is-not" though with Rule and Line
And "Up-and-down" by Logic I define,
  Of all that one should care to fathom, I
Was never deep in anything but—Wine.

57

Ah, but my Computations, People say,
Reduced the Year to better reckoning?—Nay,
  'Twas only striking from the Calendar
Unborn To-morrow, and dead Yesterday.

58

And lately, by the Tavern Door agape,
Came shining through the Dusk an Angel Shape
  Bearing a Vessel on his Shoulder; and   231
He bid me taste of it; and 'twas—the Grape!

59

The Grape that can with Logic Absolute
The Two-and-Seventy jarring Sects confute:

203. **from Máh to Máhi,** from fish to moon. 225. **Com-**
putations, Omar, astronomer and mathematician, helped
reform the calendar. 234. **The Two-and-Seventy jarring**
Sects, "The seventy-two religions supposed to divide the
world." (FitzGerald)

The sovereign Alchemist that in a trice
Life's leaden metal into Gold transmute:

60

The mighty Mahmúd, Allah-breathing Lord,
That all the misbelieving and black Horde
   Of Fears and Sorrows that infest the Soul
Scatters before him with his whirlwind Sword.   240

61

Why, be this Juice the growth of God, who dare
Blaspheme the twisted tendril as a Snare?
   A Blessing, we should use it, should we not?
And if a Curse—why, then, Who set it there?

62

I must abjure the Balm of Life, I must,
Scared by some After-reckoning ta'en on trust,
   Or lured with Hope of some Diviner Drink,
To fill the Cup—when crumbled into Dust!

63

O threats of Hell and Hopes of Paradise!
One thing at least is certain—*This* Life flies;   250
   One thing is certain and the rest is Lies;
The Flower that once has blown for ever dies.

64

Strange, is it not? that of the myriads who
Before us passed the door of Darkness through,
   Not one returns to tell us of the Road,
Which to discover we must travel too.

65

The Revelations of Devout and Learned
Who rose before us, and as Prophets burned,
   Are all but Stories, which, awoke from Sleep
They told their comrades, and to Sleep returned.

66

I sent my Soul through the Invisible,   261
Some letter of that After-life to spell:
   And by and by my Soul returned to me,
And answered "I Myself am Heav'n and Hell:"

67

Heav'n but the Vision of fulfilled Desire,
And Hell the Shadow from a Soul on fire,
   Cast on the Darkness into which Ourselves,
So late emerged from, shall so soon expire.

237–40. The mighty . . . Sword. Mahmúd. See l. 44.
Allah-breathing, uttering the name of Allah in adoration.
The rest of the passage refers to the conquest of India by
Mahmud the Great.   **241. be this Juice,** since the wine is.
242. the twisted tendril, of the grapevine.

68

We are no other than a moving row
Of Magic Shadow-shapes that come and go   270
   Round with the Sun-illumined Lantern held
In Midnight by the Master of the Show;

69

But helpless Pieces of the Game He plays
Upon this Chequer-board of Nights and Days;
   Hither and thither moves, and checks, and slays,
And one by one back in the Closet lays.

70

The Ball no question makes of Ayes and Noes,
But Here or There as strikes the Player goes;
   And He that tossed you down into the Field,
He knows about it all—HE knows—HE knows!   280

71

The Moving Finger writes; and, having writ,
Moves on: nor all your Piety nor Wit
   Shall lure it back to cancel half a Line,
Nor all your Tears wash out a Word of it.

72

And that inverted Bowl they call the Sky,
Whereunder crawling cooped we live and die,
   Lift not your hands to *It* for help—for It
As impotently moves as you or I.

73

With Earth's first Clay They did the Last Man
   knead,
And there of the Last Harvest sowed the Seed: 290
   And the first Morning of Creation wrote
What the Last Dawn of Reckoning shall read.

74

YESTERDAY *This* Day's Madness did prepare;
TO-MORROW'S Silence, Triumph, or Despair:
   Drink! for you know not whence you came, nor
      why:
Drink! for you know not why you go, nor where.

75

I tell you this—When, started from the Goal,
Over the flaming shoulders of the Foal
   Of Heav'n Parwín and Mushtarí they flung,
In my predestined Plot of Dust and Soul   300

277. Ball, in the polo game.   **298–99. Foal of Heav'n,**
the constellation Equuleus, the Little Horse. **Parwín and
Mushtarí,** the Pleiades and Jupiter.

76

The Vine had struck a fibre: which about
If clings my Being—let the Dervish flout;
    Of my Base metal may be filed a Key,
That shall unlock the Door he howls without.

77

And this I know: whether the one True Light
Kindle to Love, or Wrath consume me quite,
    One Flash of It within the Tavern caught
Better than in the Temple lost outright.

78

What! out of senseless Nothing to provoke
A conscious Something to resent the yoke   310
    Of unpermitted Pleasure, under pain
Of Everlasting Penalties, if broke!

79

What! from his helpless Creature be repaid
Pure Gold for what he lent him dross-allayed—
    Sue for a Debt we never did contract,
And cannot answer—Oh, the sorry trade!

80

O Thou, who didst with Pitfall and with gin
Beset the Road I was to wander in,
    Thou wilt not with Predestined Evil round
Enmesh, and then impute my Fall to Sin!   320

81

O Thou, who Man of baser Earth didst make,
And ev'n with Paradise devise the Snake:
    For all the Sin wherewith the Face of Man
Is blackened—Man's forgiveness give—and take!

82

As under cover of departing Day
Slunk hunger-stricken Ramazán away,
    Once more within the Potter's house alone
I stood, surrounded by the Shapes of Clay.

83

Shapes of all Sorts and Sizes, great and small,
That stood along the floor and by the wall;   330
    And some loquacious Vessels were; and some
Listened perhaps, but never talked at all.

84

Said one among them—"Surely not in vain
My substance of the common Earth was ta'en

302. Dervish, a devotee. 326. Ramazán, the fasting month. 327 ff. Once more within the Potter's house . . . With Omar's references to the potter, compare Jeremiah's (18-19) and St. Paul's echo to the same (Romans 9:21 ff.); also Browning's in "Rabbi Ben Ezra," page 572 ff.

And to this Figure moulded, to be broke,
Or trampled back to shapeless Earth again."

85

Then said a Second—"Ne'er a peevish Boy
Would break the Bowl from which he drank in joy;
    And He that with his hand the Vessel made
Will surely not in after Wrath destroy."   340

86

After a momentary silence spake
Some Vessel of a more ungainly Make;
    "They sneer at me for leaning all awry:
What! did the Hand then of the Potter shake?"

87

Whereat some one of the loquacious Lot—
I think a Súfi pipkin—waxing hot—
    "All this of Pot and Potter—Tell me then,
Who is the Potter, pray, and who the Pot?"

88

"Why," said another, "Some there are who tell
Of one who threatens he will toss to Hell   350
    The luckless Pots he marred in making—Pish!
He's a Good Fellow, and 'twill all be well."

89

"Well," murmured one, "Let whoso make or buy,
My Clay with long Oblivion is gone dry:
    But fill me with the old familiar Juice,
Methinks I might recover by and by."

90

So while the Vessels one by one were speaking,
The little Moon looked in that all were seeking:
    And then they jogged each other, "Brother!
        Brother!
Now for the Porter's shoulder-knot a-creaking."   360

91

Ah, with the Grape my fading Life provide,
And wash the Body whence the Life has died,
    And lay me, shrouded in the living Leaf,
By some not unfrequented Garden-side.

92

That ev'n my buried Ashes such a snare
Of Vintage shall fling up into the Air
    As not a True-believer passing by
But shall be overtaken unaware.

346. Súfi, a Persian mystic. 358. Moon looked in, marking the end of the fast. 360. Porter's shoulder-knot a-creaking, as he carries the jars filled with wine.

93

Indeed the Idols I have loved so long
Have done my credit in this World much wrong:
Have drowned my Glory in a shallow Cup, 371
And sold my Reputation for a Song.

94

Indeed, indeed, Repentance oft before
I swore—but was I sober when I swore?
And then and then came Spring, and Rose-in-
hand
My thread-bare Penitence apieces tore.

95

And much as Wine has played the Infidel,
And robbed me of my Robe of Honour—Well,
I wonder often what the Vintners buy
One half so precious as the stuff they sell. 380

96

Yet Ah, that Spring should vanish with the Rose!
That Youth's sweet-scented manuscript should
close!
The Nightingale that in the branches sang,
Ah whence, and whither flown again, who knows!

97

Would but the Desert of the Fountain yield
One glimpse—if dimly, yet indeed, revealed,

To which the fainting Traveller might spring,
As springs the trampled herbage of the field!

98

Would but some wingèd Angel ere too late
Arrest the yet unfolded Roll of Fate, 390
And make the stern Recorder otherwise
Enregister, or quite obliterate!

99

Ah Love! could you and I with Him conspire
To grasp this sorry Scheme of Things entire,
Would not we shatter it to bits—and then
Re-mould it nearer to the Heart's Desire!

100

Yon rising Moon that looks for us again—
How oft hereafter will she wax and wane;
How oft hereafter rising look for us
Through this same Garden—and for *one* in vain! 400

101

And when like her, O Sákí, you shall pass
Among the Guests Star-scattered on the Grass,
And in your joyous errand reach the spot
Where I made One—turn down an empty Glass!

TAMÁM

John Ruskin
1819-1900

John Ruskin was born in London, February 8, 1819. His father was a Scotch Calvinist, a wine merchant, and a millionaire. The boy was educated by his mother and by private tutors, and he traveled widely with his parents, both in Great Britain and on the Continent, developing his passionate love of scenery and his great sensitiveness to beauty. His career at Oxford was broken by ill-health, but he was graduated in 1842, winning the Newdigate Prize for poetry.

Ruskin's first important book was Volume I of *Modern Painters*, 1843 (see page 628). *Modern Paint-ers, The Seven Lamps of Architecture,* 1849, and *The Stones of Venice,* 1851–53 (see page 631) contain his most important art criticism. In 1860 he turned to political economy in *Unto This Last,* and startled England with a furious attack upon Utilitarian

369. **Idols,** wine and the praise of wine.

economics (see page 377–78). *Unto This Last* was soon followed by *Sesame and Lilies,* 1865 (see page 645), *The Ethics of the Dust,* 1866, *The Crown of Wild Olive,* 1866, and *Time and Tide,* 1867. Many of his most important ideas in political economy were expressed also in *Fors Clavigera* (see page 663), a series of letters addressed to the workingmen of England over the years 1871 to 1884. The Slade Professorship of Art at Oxford, which Ruskin held for a number of years beginning in 1870, produced several books, including *Aratra Pentelici,* 1872, which deals with sculpture, and *Val d'Arno,* 1874, which concerns Florentine art of the thirteenth century.

393–96. Ah Love! . . . Desire. See O. Henry's story "The Rubaiyat of a Scotch Highball" (*The Trimmed Lamp*), which, among other things, illustrates the special popularity of the Rubáiyát among bohemians and would-be sophisticates of the late nineteenth and early twentieth centuries. **401. Sákí.** See note on l. 183. **Tamám.** The end.

In *The Queen of the Air*, 1869, he wrote of Greek myths of the cloud and storm; in *Love's Meinie*, 1873, 1881, of birds; in *Proserpina*, 1875–86, of wayside flowers; in *Deucalion*, 1875–83, of rocks. This by no means exhausts Ruskin's list; he was a very prolific writer, and his range was immense; he had well over fifty years of authorship.

Ruskin's private life was none too happy; there was a neurotic strain in him, despite all his greatness, and his emotional balance was perhaps adversely affected by the domination of his mother. His ill-advised marriage ended, after six years, in an annullment, and Mrs. Ruskin married the painter John Everett Millais. Later Ruskin had a very unhappy love affair with a girl named Rose LaTouche. During his last years, Ruskin's mind was partially deranged; much of his autobiography, *Praeterita*, 1885–89, had to be written during lucid intervals. He died January 20, 1900.

Many of Ruskin's most important ideas are expounded by himself in the selections printed here. His art criticism took hold of people partly because of his luxuriant style but more because of its vitality. He never concerned himself with mere technicalities. So far as he was concerned, technique was merely the language of art; the all-important question was what the man had to say about life. But as he saw it, a work of art was the product not merely of the artist but also of his times. Great art was national and social; a rotten society could not produce pure art. The art of the Renaissance was inferior to that of the Gothic Middle Ages because the life of the Renaissance had sunk to a lower level; as for contemporary England, capitalism had well-nigh finished art there. "It is the vainest of affectations to try and put beauty into shadows, while all real things that cast them are in deformity and pain. . . . *You cannot have a landscape by Turner without a country for him to paint; you cannot have a portrait by Titian without a man to be portrayed.* . . . The beginning of art *is in getting our country clean, and our people beautiful.* . . . Beautiful art can only be produced by people who have beautiful things about them, and leisure to look at them." The principle he finally arrived at was a simple one: "Life without industry is guilt, and industry without art is brutality."

It will be seen that Ruskin's shift of emphasis from the work of an art critic in his first phase to that of a reformer in his second startled his critics only because they had understood nothing he had said to them. Everything he finally stood for was implicit in his work from the beginning; it is not too much to say that his advocacy of the income tax, of

limitation of income, of shorter hours of labor, and of the responsibility of the state to care for the aged and destitute, all resulted, directly or indirectly, from his conception of the nature of beauty.

The importance of Ruskin's influence is difficult to evaluate; like Carlyle, like Dickens on his ideational side, he seemed, in his own time, a voice crying in the wilderness; in ours, many of his ideas have been quietly accepted. Carlyle's influence upon him was perhaps unfortunate; though he never embraced the hero cult in its complete brutality, he went farther than many of us today would have had him go; moreover, because, like Carlyle, he looked backward for his inspiration, he sought to solve social problems in terms of a modified feudalism—society organized into classes, with the rich and the gifted bearing the heavier burdens. This ideal expressed itself notably in the Guild of St. George, which Ruskin organized about himself as "Master" in 1871, and to which (together with various experiments in housing, education, and so on) he gave almost all his money. No more than Tolstoi did he consider the actual work of the world beneath him; he cleaned streets; on one occasion, he and a group of his students at Oxford built a road—not too well, it is said, but they got it built.

The surprising thing about Ruskin is not that he should have made mistakes—even absurd mistakes—but that he should so clearly have perceived and defined a need. It was unfortunate that the champion of the Pre-Raphaelites should have been so insensitive to Whistler as to provoke a lawsuit by condemning one of the artist's paintings, but in the light of his background it was not surprising. It does not now seem that we shall soon have achieved a state of society in which we shall find it safe to sneer at Ruskin, or possible not to admire him.

from PRAETERITA

Though Ruskin did not publish his autobiography, *Praeterita* (*The Past*) until comparatively late in his life, two selections are given here as providing an excellent introduction to his work.

from Chapter I: THE SPRINGS OF WANDEL *

I AM, and my father was before me, a violent Tory of the old school;—Walter Scott's school, that is to say, and Homer's. I name these two out of the numberless great Tory writers, because they were my own two masters. I had Walter Scott's

* *Wandel*, a stream near Croydon, in Surrey, where Ruskin played as a child.

novels, and the *Iliad* (Pope's translation), for constant reading when I was a child, on week-days: on Sunday, their effect was tempered by *Robinson Crusoe* and the *Pilgrim's Progress;* my mother having it deeply in her heart to make an evangelical clergyman of me. Fortunately, I had an aunt more evangelical than my mother; and my aunt gave me cold mutton for Sunday's dinner, which—as I much preferred it hot—greatly diminished the influence of the *Pilgrim's Progress;* and the end of the matter was, that I got all the noble imaginative teaching of Defoe and Bunyan, and yet—am not an evangelical clergyman. . . .

From my own chosen masters, then, Scott and Homer, I learned the Toryism which my best afterthought has only served to confirm.

That is to say, a most sincere love of kings, and dislike of everybody who attempted to disobey them. Only, both by Homer and Scott, I was taught strange ideas about kings, which I find for the present much obsolete; for, I perceived that both the author of the *Iliad* and the author of *Waverley* made their kings, or king-loving persons, do harder work than anybody else. Tydides or Idomeneus always killed twenty Trojans to other people's one, and Redgauntlet speared more salmon than any of the Solway fishermen; and—which was particularly a subject of admiration to me—I observed that they not only did more, but in proportion to their doings *got* less, than other people—nay, that the best of them were even ready to govern for nothing! and let their followers divide any quantity of spoil or profit. Of late it has seemed to me that the idea of a king has become exactly the contrary of this, and that it has been supposed the duty of superior persons generally to govern less, and get more, than anybody else. So that it was, perhaps, quite as well that in those early days my contemplation of existent kingship was a very distant one.

The aunt who gave me cold mutton on Sundays was my father's sister: she lived at Bridge-end, in the town of Perth, and had a garden full of gooseberry-bushes, sloping down to the Tay, with a door opening to the water, which ran past it, clear-brown over the pebbles three or four feet deep; swift-eddying,—an infinite thing for a child to look down into.

My father began business as a wine-merchant, with no capital, and a considerable amount of debts bequeathed him by my grandfather. He accepted the bequest, and paid them all before he began to lay by anything for himself,—for which his best friends called him a fool, and I, without expressing any opinion as to his wisdom, which I knew in such matters to be at least equal to mine, have written on a granite slab over his grave that he was "an entirely honest merchant." As days went on he was able to take a house in Hunter Street, Brunswick Square, No. 54 (the windows of it, fortunately for me, commanded a view of a marvellous iron post, out of which the water-carts were filled through beautiful little trap-doors, by pipes like boa-constrictors; and I was never weary of contemplating that mystery, and the delicious dripping consequent); and as years went on, and I came to be four or five years old, he could command a post-chaise and a pair for two months in the summer, by help of which, with my mother and me, he went the round of his country customers (who liked to see the principal of the house his own traveller); so that, at a jog-trot pace, and through the panoramic opening of the four windows of a postchaise, made more panoramic still to me because my seat was a little bracket in front, (for we used to hire the chaise regularly for the two months out of Long Acre, and so could have it bracketed and pocketed as we liked), I saw all the high-roads, and most of the cross ones, of England and Wales; and great part of lowland Scotland, as far as Perth, where every other year we spent the whole summer: and I used to read the *Abbot* at Kinross, and the *Monastery* in Glen Farg, which I confused with "Glendearg," and thought that the White Lady had as certainly lived by the streamlet in that glen of the Ochils, as the Queen of Scots in the island of Loch Leven.

To my farther great benefit, as I grew older, I thus saw nearly all the noblemen's houses in England; in reverent and healthy delight of uncovetous admiration,—perceiving, as soon as I could perceive any political truth at all, that it was probably much happier to live in a small house, and have Warwick Castle to be astonished at, than to live in Warwick Castle and have nothing to be astonished at; but that, at all events, it would not make Brunswick Square in the least more pleasantly habitable, to pull Warwick Castle down. And at this day, though I have kind invitations enough to visit America, I could not, even for a couple of months, live in a country so miserable as to possess no castles.

Nevertheless, having formed my notion of king-

23–24. **the author . . . Waverley,** Homer and Sir Walter Scott respectively. 27. **Redgauntlet,** in Scott's novel of that name, 1824.

33. **the White Lady,** in *The Monastery,* 1820. 35. **the Queen of Scots,** Mary Stuart, in *The Abbot,* 1820. Both novels are by Scott.

hood chiefly from the FitzJames of the *Lady of the Lake*, and a noblesse from the Douglas there, and the Douglas in *Marmion*, a painful wonder soon arose in my child-mind, why the castles should now be always empty. Tantallon was there; but no Archibald of Angus:—Stirling, but no Knight of Snowdoun. The galleries and gardens of England were beautiful to see—but his Lordship and her Ladyship were always in town, said the housekeepers and gardeners. Deep yearning took hold of me for a kind of "Restoration," which I began slowly to feel that Charles the Second had not altogether effected, though I always wore a gilded oak-apple very piously in my button-hole on the 29th of May. It seemed to me that Charles the Second's Restoration had been, as compared with the Restoration I wanted, much as that gilded oak-apple to a real apple. And as I grew wiser, the desire for sweet pippins instead of bitter ones, and Living Kings instead of dead ones, appeared to me rational as well as romantic; and gradually it has become the main purpose of my life to grow pippins, and its chief hope, to see Kings.

Chapter 2: HERNE-HILL ALMOND BLOSSOMS

WHEN I was about four years old my father found himself able to buy the lease of a house on Herne Hill, a rustic eminence four miles south of the "Standard in Cornhill"; of which the leafy seclusion remains, in all essential points of character, unchanged to this day: certain Gothic splendours, lately indulged in by our wealthier neighbours, being the only serious innovations; and these are so graciously concealed by the fine trees of their grounds, that the passing viator remains unappalled by them; and I can still walk up and down the piece of road between the Fox tavern and the Herne Hill station, imagining myself four years old.

Our house was the northernmost of a group which stand accurately on the top or dome of the hill, where the ground is for a small space level, as the snows are, (I understand,) on the dome of Mont Blanc; presently falling, however, in what may be, in the London clay formation, considered a precipitous slope, to our valley of Chamouni (or of Dulwich) on the east; and with a softer descent into Cold Harbour-lane on the west: on the south, no less beautifully declining to the dale of the Effra, (doubtless shortened from Effrena, signifying the

"Unbridled" river; recently, I regret to say, bricked over for the convenience of Mr. Biffin, chemist, and others); while on the north, prolonged indeed with slight depression some half mile or so, and receiving, in the parish of Lambeth, the chivalric title of "Champion Hill," it plunges down at last to efface itself in the plains of Peckham, and the rural barbarism of Goose Green.

The group, of which our house was the quarter, consisted of two precisely similar partner-couples of houses, gardens and all to match; still the two highest blocks of buildings seen from Norwood on the crest of the ridge; so that the house itself, three-storied, with garrets above, commanded, in those comparatively smokeless days, a very notable view from its garret windows, of the Norwood hills on one side, and the winter sunrise over them; and of the valley of the Thames on the other, with Windsor telescopically clear in the distance, and Harrow, conspicuous always in fine weather to open vision against the summer sunset. It had front and back garden in sufficient proportion to its size; the front, richly set with old evergreens, and well-grown lilac and laburnum; the back, seventy yards long by twenty wide, renowned over all the hill for its pears and apples, which had been chosen with extreme care by our predecessor, (shame on me to forget the name of a man to whom I owe so much!)—and possessing also a strong old mulberry tree, a tall white-heart cherry tree, a black Kentish one, and an almost unbroken hedge, all round, of alternate gooseberry and currant bush; decked, in due season, (for the ground was wholly beneficent) with magical splendour of abundant fruit: fresh green, soft amber, and rough-bristled crimson bending the spinous branches; clustered pearl and pendant ruby joyfully discoverable under the large leaves that looked like vine.

The differences of primal importance which I observed between the nature of this garden, and that of Eden, as I had imagined it, were, that, in this one, *all* the fruit was forbidden; and there were no companionable beasts: in other respects the little domain answered every purpose of Paradise to me; and the climate, in that cycle of our years, allowed me to pass most of my life in it. My mother never gave me more to learn than she knew I could easily get learnt, if I set myself honestly to work, by twelve o'clock. She never allowed anything to disturb me when my task was set; if it was not said rightly by twelve o'clock, I was kept in till I knew it, and in general, even when Latin Grammar came to supplement the Psalms, I was my own master for at

---

1–3. **the Lady of the Lake . . . Marmion,** narrative poems by Scott, 1810 and 1808 respectively. 44. **Mont Blanc,** in southeastern France, on the Italian border, the highest mountain in the Alps. 46. **valley of Chamouni,** or Chamonix, east of Mont Blanc.

41. **Eden.** See Genesis 2–3.

at least an hour before half-past one dinner, and for the rest of the afternoon.

My mother, herself finding her chief personal pleasure in her flowers, was often planting or pruning beside me, at least if I chose to stay beside *her*. I never thought of doing anything behind her back which I would not have done before her face; and her presence was therefore no restraint to me; but, also, no particular pleasure, for, from having always been left so much alone, I had generally my own little affairs to see after; and, on the whole, by the time I was seven years old, was already getting too independent, mentally, even of my father and mother; and, having nobody else to be dependent upon, began to lead a very small, perky, contented, conceited, Cock-Robinson-Crusoe sort of life, in the central point which it appeared to me, (as it must naturally appear to geometrical animals,) that I occupied in the universe.

This was partly the fault of my father's modesty; and partly of his pride. He had so much more confidence in my mother's judgment as to such matters than in his own, that he never ventured even to help, much less to cross her, in the conduct of my education; on the other hand, in the fixed purpose of making an ecclesiastical gentlemen of me, with the superfinest of manners, and access to the highest circles of fleshly and spiritual society, the visits to Croydon, where I entirely loved my aunt, and young baker-cousins, became rarer and more rare: the society of our neighbours on the hill could not be had without breaking up our regular and sweetly selfish manner of living; and on the whole, I had nothing animate to care for, in a childish way, but myself, some nests of ants, which the gardener would never leave undisturbed for me, and a sociable bird or two; though I never had the sense or perseverance to make one really tame. But that was partly because, if ever I managed to bring one to be the least trustful of me, the cats got it.

Under these circumstances, what powers of imagination I possessed, either fastened themselves on inanimate things—the sky, the leaves, and pebbles, observable within the walls of Eden,—or caught at any opportunity of flight into regions of romance, compatible with the objective realities of existence in the nineteenth century, within a mile and a quarter of Camberwell Green.

Herein my father, happily, though with no definite intention other than of pleasing me, when he found he could do so without infringing any of my mother's rules, became my guide. I was particularly fond of watching him shave; and was always allowed to come into his room in the morning (under the one in which I am now writing), to be the motionless witness of that operation. Over his dressing-table hung one of his own water-colour drawings, made under the teaching of the elder Nasmyth; I believe, at the High School of Edinburgh. It was done in the early manner of tinting, which, just about the time when my father was at the High School, Dr. Monro was teaching Turner; namely, in grey under-tints of Prussian blue and British ink, washed with warm colour afterward on the lights. It represented Conway Castle, with its Frith, and, in the foreground, a cottage, a fisherman, and a boat at the water's edge.

When my father had finished shaving, he always told me a story about this picture. The custom began without any initial purpose of his, in consequence of my troublesome curiosity whether the fisherman lived in the cottage, and where he was going to in the boat. It being settled, for peace' sake, that he *did* live in the cottage, and was going in the boat to fish near the castle, the plot of the drama afterwards gradually thickened; and became, I believe, involved with that of the tragedy of *Douglas*, and of the *Castle Spectre*, in both of which pieces my father had performed in private theatricals, before my mother, and a select Edinburgh audience, when he was a boy of sixteen, and she, at grave twenty, a model housekeeper, and very scornful and religiously suspicious of theatricals. But she was never weary of telling me, in later years, how beautiful my father looked in his Highland dress, with the high black feathers.

In the afternoons, when my father returned (always punctually) from his business, he dined, at half-past four, in the front parlour, my mother sitting beside him to hear the events of the day, and give counsel and encouragement with respect to the same;—chiefly the last, for my father was apt to be vexed if orders for sherry fell the least short of their due standard, even for a day or two. I was never present at this time, however, and only avouch what I relate by hearsay and probable conjecture; for between four and six it would have been a grave

7. **the elder Nasmyth**, Alexander Nasmyth (1758–1840), portrait and landscape painter. 11. **Dr. Monro was teaching Turner**, Thomas Monro (1759–1833), physician and connoisseur; J. M. W. Turner (1775–1851), English landscape painter, Ruskin's admiration for whom was the foundation of his career as an art critic; see, especially the introductory note to selections from *Modern Painters*, page 628 27. **Douglas and . . . Castle Spectre**, *Douglas*, 1757, a famous tragedy by John Home. *The Castle Spectre*, 1798, a play by M. G. Lewis, author of *The Monk*.

16. **Cock-Robinson-Crusoe**, Cock Robin, the bird hero of the nursery rhyme "Who Killed Cock Robin?" Robinson Crusoe, the hero of Defoe's novel, 1719.

misdemeanour in me if I so much as approached the parlour door. After that, in summer time, we were all in the garden as long as the day lasted; tea under the white-heart cherry tree; or in winter and rough weather, at six o'clock in the drawing-room,—I having my cup of milk, and slice of bread-and-butter, in a little recess, with a table in front of it, wholly sacred to me; and in which I remained in the evenings as an Idol in a niche, while my mother knitted, and my father read to her,—and to me, so far as I chose to listen.

The series of the Waverley novels, then drawing towards its close, was still the chief source of delight in all households caring for literature; and I can no more recollect the time when I did not know them than when I did not know the Bible; but I have still a vivid remembrance of my father's intense expression of sorrow mixed with scorn, as he threw down *Count Robert of Paris,* after reading three or four pages; and knew that the life of Scott was ended: the scorn being a very complex and bitter feeling in him,—partly, indeed, of the book itself, but chiefly of the wretches who were tormenting and selling the wrecked intellect, and not a little, deep down, of the subtle dishonesty which had essentially caused the ruin. My father never could forgive Scott his concealment of the Ballantyne partnership.

Such being the salutary pleasures of Herne Hill, I have next with deeper gratitude to chronicle what I owe to my mother for the resolutely consistent lessons which so exercised me in the Scriptures as to make every word of them familiar to my ear in habitual music,—yet in that familiarity reverenced, as transcending all thought, and ordaining all conduct.

This she effected, not by her own sayings or personal authority; but simply by compelling me to read the book thoroughly, for myself. As soon as I was able to read with fluency, she began a course of Bible work with me, which never ceased till I went to Oxford. She read alternate verses with me, watching, at first, every intonation of my voice, and correcting the false ones, till she made me understand the verse, if within my reach, rightly, and energetically. It might be beyond me altogether; that she did not care about; but she made sure that as soon as I got hold of it at all, I should get hold of it by the right end.

4–5. **winter and rough weather.** See *As You Like It,* Act II, sc. 5, l. 8.   26–27. **My father . . . partnership.** Scott was unwise in his business arrangements with Constable and the Ballantynes, but there was no intention of dishonesty. When they crashed in 1826, Scott voluntarily assumed a huge debt, and wrote himself to death to pay it off. **Count Robert of Paris,** much his poorest book, was written during this period.

In this way she began with the first verse of Genesis, and went straight through, to the last verse of the Apocalypse; hard names, numbers, Levitical law, and all; and began again at Genesis the next day. If a name was hard, the better the exercise in pronunciation,—if the chapter was tiresome, the better lesson in patience,—if loathsome, the better lesson in faith that there was some use in its being so outspoken. After our chapters, (from two to three a day, according to their length, the first thing after breakfast, and no interruption from servants allowed,—none from visitors, who either joined in the reading or had to stay upstairs,—and none from any visitings or excursions, except real travelling,) I had to learn a few verses by heart, or repeat, to make sure I had not lost, something of what was already known; and, with the chapters thus gradually possessed from the first word to the last, I had to learn the whole body of the fine old Scottish paraphrases, which are good, melodious, and forceful verse; and to which, together with the Bible itself, I owe the first cultivation of my ear in sound.

It is strange that of all the pieces of the Bible which my mother thus taught me, that which cost me most to learn, and which was, to my child's mind, chiefly repulsive—the 119th Psalm—has now become of all the most precious to me, in its overflowing and glorious passion of love for the Law of God, in opposition to the abuse of it by modern preachers of what they imagine to be His gospel.

But it is only by deliberate effort that I recall the long morning hours of toil, as regular as sunrise,—toil on both sides equal—by which, year after year, my mother forced me to learn these paraphrases, and chapters, (the eighth of 1st Kings being one—try it, good reader, in a leisure hour!) allowing not so much as a syllable to be missed or misplaced; while every sentence was required to be said over and over again till she was satisfied with the accent of it. I recollect a struggle between us of about three weeks, concerning the accent of the "of" in the lines

> "Shall any following spring revive
> The ashes of the urn?"—

I insisting, partly in childish obstinacy, and partly in true instinct for rhythm, (being wholly careless on the subject both of urns and their contents,) on reciting it with an accented *of*. It was not, I say, till after three weeks' labour, that my mother got the accent lightened on the "of" and laid on the ashes, to her mind. But had it taken three years she would have done it, having once undertaken to do it. And, assuredly, had she not done it,—well, there's no knowing what would have happened; but I'm very thankful she *did*. . . .

. . . It is perhaps already time to mark what advantage and mischief, by the chances of life up to seven years old, had been irrevocably determined for me.

I will first count my blessings (as a not unwise friend once recommended me to do, continually; whereas I have a bad trick of always numbering the thorns in my fingers and not the bones in them).

And for best and truest beginning of all blessings, I had been taught the perfect meaning of Peace, in thought, act, and word.

I never had heard my father's or mother's voice once raised in any question with each other; nor seen an angry or even slightly hurt or offended, glance in the eyes of either. I had never heard a servant scolded; nor even suddenly, passionately, or in any severe manner, blamed. I had never seen a moment's trouble or disorder in any household matter; nor anything whatever either done in a hurry, or undone in due time. I had no conception of such a feeling as anxiety; my father's occasional vexation in the afternoons, when he had only got an order for twelve butts after expecting one for fifteen, as I have just stated, was never manifested to *me;* and itself related only to the question whether his name would be a step higher or lower in the year's list of sherry exporters; for he never spent more than half his income, and therefore found himself little incommoded by occasional variations in the total of it. I had never done any wrong that I knew of—beyond occasionally delaying the commitment to heart of some improving sentence, that I might watch a wasp on the window pane, or a bird in the cherry tree; and I had never seen any grief.

Next to this quite priceless gift of Peace, I had received the perfect understanding of the natures of Obedience and Faith. I obeyed word, or lifted finger, of father or mother, simply as a ship her helm; not only without idea of resistance, but receiving the direction as a part of my own life and force, and helpful law, as necessary to me in every moral action as the law of gravity in leaping. And my practice in Faith was soon complete: nothing was ever promised me that was not given; nothing ever threatened me that was not inflicted, and nothing ever told me that was not true.

Peace, obedience, faith; these three for chief good; next to these, the habit of fixed attention with both eyes and mind—on which I will not further enlarge at this moment, this being the main practical faculty of my life, causing Mazzini to say of me, in conversation authentically reported, a year or two before his death, that I had "the most analytic mind in Europe." An opinion in which, so far as I am acquainted with Europe, I am myself entirely disposed to concur.

Lastly, an extreme perfection in palate and all other bodily senses, given by the utter prohibition of cake, wine, comfits, or, except in carefullest restriction, fruit; and by fine preparation of what food was given me. Such I esteem the main blessings of my childhood;—next, let me count the equally dominant calamities.

First, that I had nothing to love.

My parents were—in a sort—visible powers of nature to me, no more loved than the sun and the moon: only I should have been annoyed and puzzled if either of them had gone out; (how much, now, when both are darkened!)—still less did I love God; not that I had any quarrel with Him, or fear of Him; but simply found what people told me was His service, disagreeable; and what people told me was His book, not entertaining. I had no companions to quarrel with, neither; nobody to assist, and nobody to thank. Not a servant was ever allowed to do anything for me, but what it was their duty to do; and why should I have been grateful to the cook for cooking, or the gardener for gardening,—when the one dared not give me a baked potato without asking leave, and the other would not let my ants' nests alone, because they made the walks untidy? The evil consequence of all this was not, however, what might perhaps have been expected, that I grew up selfish or unaffectionate; but that, when affection did come, it came with violence utterly rampant and unmanageable, at least by me, who never before had anything to manage.

For (second of chief calamities) I had nothing to endure. Danger or pain of any kind I knew not: my strength was never exercised, my patience never tried, and my courage never fortified. Not that I was ever afraid of anything,—either ghosts, thunder, or beasts; and one of the nearest approaches to insubordination which I was ever tempted into as a child, was in passionate effort to get leave to play with the lion's cubs in Wombwell's menagerie.

Thirdly. I was taught no precision nor etiquette of manners; it was enough if, in the little society we saw, I remained unobtrusive, and replied to a question without shyness: but the shyness came later, and increased as I grew conscious of the rudeness arising from the want of social discipline, and

1. **Mazzini,** Giuseppe Mazzini (1805–1872), Italian liberator.

found it impossible to acquire, in advanced life, dexterity in any bodily exercise, skill in any pleasing accomplishment, or ease and tact in ordinary behaviour.

Lastly, and chief of evils. My judgment of right and wrong, and powers of independent action, were left entirely undeveloped; because the bridle and blinkers were never taken off me. Children should have their times of being off duty, like soldiers; and when once the obedience, if required, is certain, the little creature should be very early put for periods of practice in complete command of itself; set on the barebacked horse of its own will, and left to break it by its own strength. But the ceaseless authority exercised over my youth left me, when cast out at last into the world, unable for some time to do more than drift with its vortices.

My present verdict, therefore, on the general tenor of my education at that time, must be, that it was at once too formal and too luxurious; leaving my character, at the most important moment for its construction, cramped indeed, but not disciplined; and only by protection innocent, instead of by practice virtuous.

from MODERN PAINTERS

The book which Ruskin published in 1843 was originally planned as "Turner and the Ancients"; it appeared as *Modern Painters: Their Superiority in the Art of Landscape Painting to all the Ancient Masters Proved by Examples of the True, the Beautiful and the Intellectual, from the Works of Modern Artists, especially from Those of J. M. W. Turner, Esq., R.A.* It was followed by Volume 2 in 1843, by Volumes 3 and 4 in 1856, and by Volume 5 in 1880. Without ever forgetting his purpose of vindicating Turner, Ruskin widened his scope until he had expressed a whole theory of art.

from VOLUME 3: Chapter 1

Of the Received Opinions Touching the "Grand Style" *

IT seems to me, and may seem to the reader, strange that we should need to ask the question, "What is poetry?" Here is a word we have been using all our lives, and, I suppose, with a very distinct idea attached to it; and when I am now called upon to give a definition of this idea, I find myself at a pause. What is more singular, I do not at present recollect hearing the question often asked, though surely it is a very natural one; and I never recollect hearing it answered, or even attempted to be an-

* **Grand Style.** Compare Matthew Arnold's remarks on the Grand Style, page 696.

swered. In general, people shelter themselves under metaphors, and while we hear poetry described as an utterance of the soul, an effusion of Divinity, or voice of nature, or in other terms equally elevated and obscure, we never attain anything like a definite explanation of the character which actually distinguishes it from prose.

I come, after some embarrassment, to the conclusion, that poetry "is the suggestion, by the imagination, of noble grounds for the noble emotions." I mean, by the noble emotions, those four principal sacred passions—Love, Veneration, Admiration, and Joy (this latter especially, if unselfish); and their opposites—Hatred, Indignation (or Scorn), Horror, and Grief,—this last, when unselfish, becoming Compassion. These passions in their various combinations constitute what is called "poetical feeling," when they are felt on noble grounds, that is, on great and true grounds. Indignation, for instance, is a poetical feeling, if excited by serious injury; but it is not a poetical feeling if entertained on being cheated out of a small sum of money. It is very possible the manner of the cheat may have been such as to justify considerable indignation; but the feeling is nevertheless not poetical unless the grounds of it be large as well as just. In like manner, energetic admiration may be excited in certain minds by a display of fireworks, or a street of handsome shops; but the feeling is not poetical, because the grounds of it are false, and therefore ignoble. There is in reality nothing to deserve admiration either in the firing of packets of gunpowder, or in the display of the stocks of warehouses. But admiration excited by the budding of a flower is a poetical feeling, because it is impossible that this manifestation of spiritual power and vital beauty can ever be enough admired.

Farther, it is necessary to the existence of poetry that the grounds of these feelings should be *furnished by the imagination*. Poetical feeling, that is to say, mere noble emotion, is not poetry. It is happily inherent in all human nature deserving the name, and is found often to be purest in the least sophisticated. But the power of assembling, by *the help of the imagination*, such images as will excite these feelings, is the power of the poet or literally of the "Maker."

Now this power of exciting the emotions depends of course on the richness of the imagination, and on its choice of those images which, in combination, will be most effective, or, for the particular work to be done, most fit. And it is altogether impossible for a writer not endowed with invention to conceive what tools a true poet will make use of, or in what way he will apply them, or what unexpected results he will bring out by them; so that it is vain to say that the details of poetry ought to possess, or ever do possess, any *definite* character. Generally speaking, poetry runs into finer and more delicate details than prose; but the details are not poetical because they are more delicate, but because they are employed so as to bring out an affecting result. For instance, no one but a true poet would have thought of exciting our pity for a bereaved father by describing his way of locking the door of his house:

"Perhaps to himself at that moment he said,
'The key I must take, for my Ellen is dead.'
But of this in my ears not a word did he speak;
And he went to the chase with a tear on his cheek."

In like manner, in painting, it is altogether impossible to say beforehand what details a great painter may make poetical by his use of them to excite noble emotions: and we shall, therefore, find presently that a painting is to be classed in the great or inferior schools, not according to the kind of details which it represents, but according to the uses for which it employs them.

It is only farther to be noticed, that infinite confusion has been introduced into this subject by the careless and illogical custom of opposing painting to poetry, instead of regarding poetry as consisting in a noble use, whether of colours or words. Painting is properly to be opposed to *speaking* or *writing*, but not to *poetry*. Both painting and speaking are methods of expression. Poetry is the employment of either for the noblest purposes.

This question being thus far determined, we may proceed with our paper in the *Idler*.

"It is very difficult to determine the exact degree of enthusiasm that the arts of Painting and Poetry may admit. There may, perhaps, be too great indulgence as well as too great a restraint of imagination; if the one produces incoherent monsters, the other produces what is full as bad, lifeless insipidity. An intimate knowledge of the passions, and good sense, but not common sense, must at last determine its limits. It has been thought, and I believe with reason, that Michael Angelo sometimes transgressed those limits; and, I think, I have seen figures of him of which it was very difficult to determine whether they were in the highest degree sublime or extremely ridiculous. Such faults may be said to be the ebullitions of genius; but at least he had this merit, that he never was insipid; and whatever passion his

works may excite, they will always escape contempt.

"What I have had under consideration is the sublimest style, particularly that of Michael Angelo, the Homer of painting. Other kinds may admit of this naturalness, which of the lowest kind is the chief merit; but in painting, as in poetry, the highest style has the least of common nature."

From this passage we gather three important indications of the supposed nature of the Great Style. That it is the work of men in a state of enthusiasm. That it is like the writing of Homer; and that it has as little as possible of "common nature" in it.

First, it is produced by men in a state of enthusiasm. That is, by men who feel *strongly* and *nobly;* for we do not call a strong feeling of envy, jealousy, or ambition, "enthusiasm." That is, therefore, by men who feel poetically. This much we may admit, I think, with perfect safety. Great art is produced by men who feel acutely and nobly; and it is in some sort an expression of this personal feeling. We can easily conceive that there may be a sufficiently marked distinction between such art, and that which is produced by men who do not feel at all, but who reproduce, though ever so accurately, yet coldly, like human mirrors, the scenes which pass before their eyes.

Secondly, Great Art is like the writing of Homer, and this chiefly because it has little of "common nature" in it. We are not clearly informed what is meant by common nature in this passage. Homer seems to describe a great deal of what is common: —cookery, for instance, very carefully in all its processes. I suppose the passage in the *Iliad* which, on the whole, has excited most admiration, is that which describes a wife's sorrow at parting from her husband, and a child's fright at its father's helmet; and I hope, at least, the former feeling may be considered "common nature." But the true greatness of Homer's style is, doubtless, held by our author to consist in his imaginations of things not only uncommon but impossible (such as spirits in brazen armour, or monsters with heads of men and bodies of beasts), and in his occasional delineations of the human character and form in their utmost, or heroic, strength and beauty. We gather then on the whole, that a painter in the Great Style must be enthusiastic, or full of emotion, and must paint the human form in its utmost strength and beauty, and perhaps certain impossible forms besides, liable by persons not in an equally enthusiastic state of mind to be looked upon as in some degree absurd. This I presume to be Reynolds's meaning, and to be **all**

34. paper, an essay by Sir Joshua Reynolds, printed in the *Idler,* Oct. 20, 1759, from which Ruskin had already quoted in a part of the chapter not given here.

34–37. I suppose . . . helmet, in Book VI.

that he intends us to gather from his comparison of the Great Style with the writings of Homer. But if that comparison be a just one in all respects, surely two other corollaries ought to be drawn from it, namely,—first, that these Heroic or Impossible images are to be mingled with others very unheroic and very possible; and, secondly, that in the representation of the Heroic or Impossible forms, the greatest care must be taken in *finishing the details*, so that a painter must not be satisfied with painting well the countenance and the body of his hero, but ought to spend the greatest part of his time (as Homer the greatest number of verses) in elaborating the sculptured pattern on his shield. . . .

from VOLUME 3: Chapter 12

Of the Pathetic Fallacy

Now, therefore, putting these tiresome and absurd words quite out of our way, we may go on at our ease to examine the point in question,—namely, the difference between the ordinary, proper, and true appearances of things to us; and the extraordinary, or false appearances, when we are under the influence of emotion, or contemplative fancy; false appearances, I say, as being entirely unconnected with any real power or character in the object, and only imputed to it by us.

For instance—

"The spendthrift crocus, bursting through the mould
Naked and shivering, with his cup of gold."

This is very beautiful, and yet very untrue. The crocus is not a spendthrift, but a hardy plant; its yellow is not gold, but saffron. How is it that we enjoy so much the having it put into our heads that it is anything else than a plain crocus?

It is an important question. For, throughout our past reasonings about art, we have always found that nothing could be good or useful, or ultimately pleasurable, which was untrue. But here is something pleasurable in written poetry which is nevertheless *untrue*. And what is more, if we think over our favourite poetry, we shall find it full of this kind of fallacy, and that we like it all the more for being so.

It will appear also, on consideration of the matter, that this fallacy is of two principal kinds. Either, as in this case of the crocus, it is the fallacy of wilful fancy, which involves no real expectation that it will be believed; or else it is a fallacy caused by an excited state of the feelings, making us, for the time, more or less irrational. Of the cheating of the fancy we shall have to speak presently; but, in this chapter, I want to examine the nature of the other error, that which the mind admits when affected strongly by emotion. Thus, for instance, in *Alton Locke*,—

"They rowed her in across the rolling foam—
The cruel, crawling foam."

The foam is not cruel, neither does it crawl. The state of mind which attributes to it these characters of a living creature is one in which the reason is unhinged by grief. All violent feelings have the same effect. They produce in us a falseness in all our impressions of external things, which I would generally characterize as the "pathetic fallacy."

Now we are in the habit of considering this fallacy as eminently a character of poetical description, and the temper of mind in which we allow it, as one eminently poetical, because passionate. But, I believe, if we look well into the matter, that we shall find the greatest poets do not often admit this kind of falseness,—that it is only the second order of poets who much delight in it.

Thus, when Dante describes the spirits falling from the bank of Acheron "as dead leaves flutter from a bough," he gives the most perfect image possible of their utter lightness, feebleness, passiveness, and scattering agony of despair, without, however, for an instant losing his own clear perception that *these* are souls, and *those* are leaves: he makes no confusion of one with the other. But when Coleridge speaks of

"The one red leaf, the last of its clan,
That dances as often as dance it can,"

he has a morbid, that is to say, a so far false, idea about the leaf: he fancies a life in it, and will, which there are not; confuses its powerlessness with choice, its fading death with merriment, and the wind that shakes it with music. Here, however, there is some beauty, even in the morbid passage; but take an instance in Homer and Pope. Without the knowledge of Ulysses, Elpenor, his youngest follower, has fallen from an upper chamber in the Circean palace, and has been left dead, unmissed by his leader or companions, in the haste of their departure. They cross

---

13–14. **in elaborating . . . shield,** in Book XVIII, ll. 480 ff.—probably the most famous descriptive passage in literature.   31–33. **"The spendthrift . . . gold."** See Oliver Wendell Holmes, "Spring," ll. 13–14.

10–11. **"They rowed . . . foam."** See Charles Kingsley's novel, *Alton Locke*, 1850, chap. 26.   28–30. **Dante describes . . . bough.** See *Inferno*, Book III, ll. 112 ff.   37–38. **"The one . . . can."** See "Christabel," Part I, ll. 49–50.

to the Cimmerian land; and Ulysses sum-
he shades from Tartarus. The first which
is that of the lost Elpenor. Ulysses, amazed,
xactly the spirit of bitter and terrified light-
ich is seen in Hamlet, addresses the spirit
simple, startled words:—

nor! How camest thou under the Shadowy
s? Hast thou come faster on foot than I in
ck ship?"

ich Pope renders thus:—

"O, say, what angry power Elpenor led
To glide in shades, and wander with the dead?
How could thy soul, by realms and seas disjoined,
Outfly the nimble sail, and leave the lagging
    wind?"

I sincerely hope the reader finds no pleasure here,
either in the nimbleness of the sail, or the laziness of
the wind! And yet how is it that these conceits are
so painful now, when thy have been pleasant to us
in the other instances?

For a very simple reason. They are not a *pathetic*
fallacy at all, for they are put into the mouth of the
wrong passion—a passion which never could possibly have spoken them—agonized curiosity. Ulysses
wants to know the facts of the matter; and the very
last thing his mind could do at the moment would
be to pause, or suggest in anywise what was *not* a
fact. The delay in the first three lines, and conceit
in the last, jar upon us instantly, like the most frightful discord in music. No poet of true imaginative
power could possibly have written the passage.

from THE STONES OF VENICE

In *The Stones of Venice* (to which *The Seven Lamps of
Architecture* was something of an introduction), Ruskin
adumbrated his essentially religious conception of art.
His aim, he afterwards declared, was "to show that the
Gothic architecture of Venice had arisen out of, and indicated in all its features, a state of pure national faith,
and of domestic virtue; and that its Renaissance architecture had arisen out of, and in all its features indicated,
a state of concealed national infidelity, and of domestic
corruption."

The description of St. Mark's Cathedral in Venice is
given here as perhaps the most famous of all Ruskin's
"purple passages," and the discussion of the nature of
Gothic as the most important and influential statement
he ever made of the essential element in his creed expounded therein.

7–9. "Elpenor . . . ship." See *Odyssey*, Book XI, ll.
57–58.

from VOLUME 2: Chapter 4

St. Mark's

AND well may they fall back, for beyond those
troops of ordered arches there rises a vision out
of the earth, and all the great square seems to have
opened from it in a kind of awe, that we may see it
far away;—a multitude of pillars and white domes,
clustered into a long low pyramid of coloured light;
a treasure-heap, it seems, partly of gold, and partly
of opal and mother-of-pearl, hollowed beneath into
five great vaulted porches, ceiled with fair mosaic,
and beset with sculpture of alabaster, clear as amber
and delicate as ivory,—sculpture fantastic and involved, of palm leaves and lilies, and grapes and
pomegranates, and birds clinging and fluttering
among the branches, all twined together into an
endless network of buds and plumes; and, in the
midst of it, the solemn forms of angels, sceptred, and
robed to the feet, and leaning to each other across
the gates, their figures indistinct among the gleaming of the golden ground through the leaves beside
them, interrupted and dim, like the morning light
as it faded back among the branches of Eden, when
first its gates were angel-guarded long ago. And
round the walls of the porches there are set pillars of
variegated stones, jasper and porphyry, and deep-
green serpentine spotted with flakes of snow, and
marbles, that half refuse and half yield to the sunshine, Cleopatra-like, "their bluest veins to kiss"—
the shadow, as it steals back from them, revealing
line after line of azure undulation, as a receding tide
leaves the waved sand; their capitals rich with interwoven tracery, rooted knots of herbage, and drifting leaves of acanthus and vine, and mystical signs,
all beginning and ending in the Cross; and above
them, in the broad archivolts, a continuous chain
of language and of life—angels, and the signs of
heaven, and the labours of men, each in its appointed season upon the earth; and above these,
another range of glittering pinnacles, mixed with
white arches edged with scarlet flowers,—a confusion of delight, amidst which the breasts of the
Greek horses are seen blazing in their breadth of
golden strength, and the St. Mark's lion, lifted on a
blue field covered with stars, until at last, as if in
ecstasy, the crests of the arches break into a marble
foam, and toss themselves far into the blue sky in
flashes and wreaths of sculptured spray, as if the
breakers on the Lido shore had been frost-bound

30. "their . . . kiss." See Shakespeare's *Antony and Cleopatra*, Act II, sc. 5, l. 29.   45. the St. Mark's lion, the emblem
of St. Mark, the patron saint of Venice, whither his shrine
was removed from Alexandria in the ninth century.

before they fell, and the sea-nymphs had inlaid them with coral and amethyst.

Between that grim cathedral of England and this, what an interval! There is a type of it in the very birds that haunt them; for, instead of the restless crowd, hoarse-voiced and sable-winged, drifting on the bleak upper air, the St. Mark's porches are full of doves, that nestle among the marble foliage, and mingle the soft iridescence of their living plumes, changing at every motion, with the tints, hardly less lovely, that have stood unchanged for seven hundred years.

And what effect has this splendour on those who pass beneath it? You may walk from sunrise to sunset, to and fro, before the gateway of St. Mark's, and you will not see an eye lifted to it, nor a countenance brightened by it. Priest and layman, soldier and civilian, rich and poor, pass by it alike regardlessly. Up to the very recesses of the porches, the meanest tradesmen of the city push their counters; nay, the foundations of its pillars are themselves the seats— not "of them that sell doves" for sacrifice, but of the vendors of toys and caricatures. Round the whole square in front of the church there is almost a continuous line of cafés, where the idle Venetians of the middle classes lounge, and read empty journals; in its centre the Austrian bands play during the time of vespers, their martial music jarring with the organ notes,—the march drowning the miserere, and the sullen crowd thickening round them,—a crowd, which, if it had its will, would stiletto every soldier that pipes to it. And in the recesses of the porches, all day long, knots of men of the lowest classes, unemployed and listless, lie basking in the sun like lizards; and unregarded children,—every heavy glance of their young eyes full of desperation and stony depravity, and their throats hoarse with cursing,—gamble, and fight, and snarl, and sleep, hour after hour, clashing their bruised centesimi upon the marble ledges of the church porch. And the images of Christ and His angels look down upon it continually.

That we may not enter the church out of the midst of the horror of this, let us turn aside under the portico which looks across the sea, and passing round within the two massive pillars brought from St. Jean d'Acre, we shall find the gate of the Baptistery; let us enter there. The heavy door closes behind us instantly, and the light and the turbulence of the Piazzetta, are together shut out by it.

We are in a low vaulted room; vaulted, not with arches but with small cupolas starred with gold, and chequered with gloomy figures: in the centre is a bronze font charged with rich bas-reliefs, a small figure of the Baptist standing above it in a single ray of light that glances across the narrow room, dying as it falls from a window high in the wall, and the first thing that it strikes, and the only thing that it strikes brightly, is a tomb. We hardly know if it be a tomb indeed; for it is like a narrow couch set beside the window, low-roofed and curtained, so that it might seem, but that it is some height above the pavement, to have been drawn towards the window, that the sleeper might be wakened early;—only there are two angels, who have drawn the curtain back, and are looking down upon him. Let us look also, and thank that gentle light that rests upon his forehead for ever, and dies away upon his breast.

The face is of a man in middle life, but there are two deep furrows right across the forehead, dividing it like the foundations of a tower: the height of it above is bound by the fillet of the ducal cap. The rest of the features are singularly small and delicate, the lips sharp, perhaps the sharpness of death being added to that of the natural lines; but there is a sweet smile upon them, and a deep serenity upon the whole countenance. The roof of the canopy above has been blue, filled with stars; beneath, in the centre of the tomb on which the figure rests, is a seated figure of the Virgin, and the border of it all around is of flowers and soft leaves, growing rich and deep, as if in a field in summer.

It is the Doge Andrea Dandolo, a man early great among the great of Venice; and early lost. She chose him for her king in his 36th year; he died ten years later, leaving behind him that history to which we owe half of what we know of her former fortunes.

Look round at the room in which he lies. The floor of it is of rich mosaic, encompassed by a low seat of red marble, and its walls are of alabaster, but worn and shattered, and darkly stained with age, almost a ruin,—in places the slabs of marble have fallen away altogether, and the rugged brickwork is seen through the rents, but all beautiful; the ravaging fissures fretting their way among the islands and channelled zones of the alabaster, and the timestains on its translucent masses darkened into fields

---

3. that grim cathedral of England, in an English town, described earlier in the chapter.   22. "of them . . . doves." See Matthew 21:12; Mark 11:15; John 2:16.   26–32. in its centre . . . pipes to it. When this was written, Italy was under the domination of Austria.   39. centesimi, small Italian coins.   46–47. the two . . . St. Jean d'Acre, from the church of St. Saba at Acre, which the Venetians destroyed in 1256.   47. Baptistery, a separate building, used for baptismal services.

8. the Baptist, St. John the Baptist; see Matthew 3. 39–41. that history . . . fortunes, The Venetian Chronicle of Andrea Sandolo, doge of Venice from 1343 to 1354.

of rich golden brown, like the colour of seaweed when the sun strikes on it through deep sea. The light fades away into the recess of the chamber towards the altar, and the eye can hardly trace the lines of the bas-relief behind it of the baptism of Christ: but on the vaulting of the roof the figures are distinct, and there are seen upon it two great circles, one surrounded by the "Principalities and powers in heavenly places," of which Milton has expressed the ancient division in the single massy line,

"Thrones, Dominations, Princedoms, Virtues, Powers,"

and around the other, the Apostles; Christ the centre of both: and upon the walls, again and again repeated, the gaunt figure of the Baptist, in every circumstance of his life and death; and the streams of the Jordan running down between their cloven rocks; the axe laid to the root of a fruitless tree that springs up on their shore. "Every tree that bringeth not forth good fruit shall be hewn down, and cast into the fire." Yes, verily: to be baptized with fire, or to be cast therein; it is the choice set before all men. The march-notes still murmur through the grated window, and mingle with the sounding in our ears of the sentence of judgment, which the old Greek has written on the Baptistery wall. Venice has made her choice.

He who lies under that stony canopy would have taught her another choice, in his day, if she would have listened to him; but he and his counsels have long been forgotten by her, and the dust lies upon his lips.

Through the heavy door whose bronze network closes the place of his rest, let us enter the church itself. It is lost in still deeper twilight, to which the eye must be accustomed for some moments before the form of the building can be traced; and then there opens before us a vast cave, hewn out into the form of a Cross, and divided into shadowy aisles by many pillars. Round the domes of its roof the light enters only through narrow apertures like large stars; and here and there a ray or two from some far-away casement wanders into the darkness, and casts a narrow phosphoric stream upon the waves of marble that heave and fall in a thousand colours along the floor. What else there is of light is from torches, or silver lamps, burning ceaselessly in the recesses of the chapels; the roof sheeted with gold, and the polished walls covered with alabaster, give back at every curve and angle some feeble gleaming

to the flames; and the glories round the heads of the sculptured saints flash out upon us as we pass them, and sink again into the gloom. Under foot and over head, a continual succession of crowded imagery, one picture passing into another, as in a dream; forms beautiful and terrible mixed together; dragons and serpents, and ravening beasts of prey, and graceful birds that in the midst of them drink from running fountains and feed from vases of crystal; the passions and the pleasures of human life symbolized together, and the mystery of its redemption; for the mazes of interwoven lines and changeful pictures lead always at last to the Cross, lifted and carved in every place and upon every stone; sometimes with the serpent of eternity wrapt round it, sometimes with doves beneath its arms, and sweet herbage growing forth from its feet; but conspicuous most of all on the great rood that crosses the church before the altar, raised in bright blazonry against the shadow of the apse. And although in the recesses of the aisles and chapels, when the mist of the incense hangs heavily, we may see continually a figure traced in faint lines upon their marble, a woman standing with her eyes raised to heaven, and the inscription above her, "Mother of God," she is not here the presiding deity. It is the Cross that is first seen, and always, burning in the centre of the temple; and every dome and hollow of its roof has the figure of Christ in the utmost height of it, raised in power, or returning in judgment.

Nor is this interior without effect on the minds of the people. At every hour of the day there are groups collected before the various shrines, and solitary worshippers scattered through the darker places of the church, evidently in prayer both deep and reverent, and, for the most part, profoundly sorrowful. The devotees at the greater number of the renowned shrines of Romanism may be seen murmuring their appointed prayers with wandering eyes and unengaged gestures; but the step of the stranger does not disturb those who kneel on the pavement of St. Mark's; and hardly a moment passes, from early morning to sunset, in which we may not see some half-veiled figure enter beneath the Arabian porch, cast itself into long abasement on the floor of the temple, and then rising slowly with more confirmed step, and with a passionate kiss and clasp of the arms given to the feet of the crucifix, by which the lamps burn always in the northern aisle, leave the church, as if comforted.

But we must not hastily conclude from this that

8–9. "Principalities . . . places." See Ephesians 3:10. 11–12. "Thrones . . . Powers." See *Paradise Lost*, Book V, l. 601.   20–22. "Every tree . . . fire." See Matthew 3:10.

15. the serpent of eternity, that is, as a symbol of eternity.   25–26. she . . . deity, as she is at the church of San Donato in Murano, described in the preceding chapter.

the nobler characters of the building have at present any influence in fostering a devotional spirit. There is distress enough in Venice to bring many to their knees, without excitement from external imagery; and whatever there may be in the temper of the worship offered in St. Mark's more than can be accounted for by reference to the unhappy circumstances of the city, is assuredly not owing either to the beauty of its architecture or to the impressiveness of the Scripture histories embodied in its mosaics. That it has a peculiar effect, however slight, on the popular mind, may perhaps be safely conjectured from the number of worshippers which it attracts, while the churches of St. Paul and the Frari, larger in size and more central in position, are left comparatively empty. But this effect is altogether to be ascribed to its richer assemblage of those sources of influence which address themselves to the commonest instincts of the human mind, and which, in all ages and countries, have been more or less employed in the support of superstition. Darkness and mystery; confused recesses of building; artificial light employed in small quantity, but maintained with a constancy which seems to give it a kind of sacredness; preciousness of material easily comprehended by the vulgar eye; close air loaded with a sweet and peculiar odour associated only with religious services, solemn music, and tangible idols or images having popular legends attached to them,—these, the stage properties of superstition, which have been from the beginning of the world, and must be to the end of it, employed by all nations, whether openly savage or nominally civilized, to produce a false awe in minds incapable of apprehending the true nature of the Deity, are assembled in St. Mark's to a degree, as far as I know, unexampled in any other European church. The arts of the Magus and the Brahmin are exhausted in the animation of a paralyzed Christianity; and the popular sentiment which these arts excite is to be regarded by us with no more respect than we should have considered ourselves justified in rendering to the devotion of the worshippers at Eleusis, Ellora, or Edfou.

from Chapter 6: THE NATURE OF GOTHIC

. . . I shall endeavour . . . to give the reader in this chapter an idea, at once broad and definite, of the true nature of *Gothic* architecture, properly so called. . . .

44. **Eleusis, Ellora, or Edfou,** in Greece, India, and Egypt respectively.

I believe . . . that the characteristic or moral elements of Gothic are the following, placed in the order of their importance:

1. Savageness.   4. Grotesqueness.
2. Changefulness.   5. Rigidity.
3. Naturalism.   6. Redundance. . . .

I shall proceed to examine them in their order.

1. SAVAGENESS. I am not sure when the word "Gothic" was first generically applied to the architecture of the North; but I presume that, whatever the date of its original usage, it was intended to imply reproach, and express the barbaric character of the nations among whom that architecture arose. It never implied that they were literally of Gothic lineage, far less that their architecture had been originally invented by the Goths themselves; but it did imply that they and their buildings together exhibited a degree of sternness and rudeness, which, in contradistinction to the character of Southern and Eastern nations, appeared like a perpetual reflection of the contrast between the Goth and the Roman in their first encounter. And when that fallen Roman, in the utmost impotence of his luxury, and insolence of his guilt, became the model for the imitation of civilized Europe, at the close of the so-called Dark ages, the word Gothic became a term of unmitigated contempt, not unmixed with aversion. From that contempt, by the exertion of the antiquaries and architects of this century, Gothic architecture has been sufficiently vindicated. . . . It is true, greatly and deeply true, that the architecture of the North is rude and wild; but it is not true, that, for this reason, we are to condemn it, or despise. Far otherwise: I believe it is in this very character that it deserves our profoundest reverence.

The charts of the world which have been drawn up by modern science have thrown into a narrow space the expression of a vast amount of knowledge, but I have never yet seen any one pictorial enough to enable the spectator to imagine the kind of contrast in physical character which exists between Northern and Southern countries. We know the differences in detail, but we have not that broad glance and grasp which would enable us to feel them in their fulness. We know that gentians grow on the Alps, and olives on the Apennines; but we do not enough conceive for ourselves that variegated mosaic of the world's surface which a bird sees in its migration, that difference between the district of the gentian and of the olive which the stork and the swallow see far off, as they lean upon the sirocco wind. Let us, for a moment, try to raise ourselves even above the level of their flight, and imagine the Mediterranean lying beneath us like an irregular lake, and all its ancient promontories sleeping in the sun: here and there an angry spot of thunder, a grey stain of storm, moving upon the burning field; and here and there a fixed wreath of white volcano smoke, surrounded by its circle of ashes; but for the most part a great peacefulness of light, Syria and Greece, Italy and Spain, laid like pieces of a golden pavement into the sea-blue, chased, as we stoop 10 nearer to them, with bossy beaten work of mountain chains, and glowing softly with terraced gardens, and flowers heavy with frankincense, mixed among masses of laurel, and orange, and plumy palm, that abate with their grey-green shadows the burning of the marble rocks, and of the ledges of porphyry sloping under lucent sand. Then let us pass farther towards the north, until we see the orient colours change gradually into a vast belt of rainy green, where the pastures of Switzerland, and 20 poplar valleys of France, and dark forests of the Danube and Carpathians stretch from the mouths of the Loire to those of the Volga, seen through clefts in grey swirls of rain-cloud and flaky veils of the mist of the brooks, spreading low along the pasture lands: and then, farther north still, to see the earth heave into mighty masses of leaden rock and heathy moor, bordering with a broad waste of gloomy purple that belt of field and wood, and splintering into irregular and grisly islands amidst 30 the northern seas, beaten by storm, and chilled by ice-drift, and tormented by furious pulses of contending tide, until the roots of the last forests fail from among the hill ravines, and the hunger of the north wind bites their peaks into barrenness; and, at last, the wall of ice, durable like iron, sets, death-like, its white teeth against us out of the polar twilight. And, having once traversed in thought this gradation of the zoned iris of the earth in all its material vastness, let us go down nearer to it, and 40 watch the parallel change in the belt of animal life: the multitudes of swift and brilliant creatures that glance in the air and sea, or tread the sands of the southern zone; striped zebras and spotted leopards, glistening serpents, and birds arrayed in purple and scarlet. Let us contrast their delicacy and brilliancy of colour, and swiftness of motion, with the frost-cramped strength, and shaggy covering, and dusky plumage of the northern tribes; contrast the Arabian horse with the Shetland, the tiger and leopard 50 with the wolf and bear, the antelope with the elk, the bird of paradise with the osprey; and then, submissively acknowledging the great laws by which the earth and all that it bears are ruled throughout

their being, let us not condemn, but rejoice in the expression by man of his own rest in the statutes of the lands that gave him birth. Let us watch him with reverence as he sets side by side the burning gems, and smooths with soft sculpture the jasper pillars, that are to reflect a ceaseless sunshine, and rise into a cloudless sky: but not with less reverence let us stand by him, when, with rough strength and hurried stroke, he smites an uncouth animation out of the rocks which he has torn from among the moss of the moorland, and heaves into the darkened air the pile of iron buttress and rugged wall, instinct with work of an imagination as wild and wayward as the northern sea; creatures of ungainly shape and rigid limb, but full of wolfish life; fierce as the winds that beat, and changeful as the clouds that shade them.

There is, I repeat, no degradation, no reproach in this, but all dignity and honourableness: and we should err grievously in refusing either to recognize as an essential character of the existing architecture of the North, or to admit as a desirable character in that which it yet may be, this wildness of thought, and roughness of work; this look of mountain brotherhood between the cathedral and the Alp; this magnificence of sturdy power, put forth only the more energetically because the fine finger-touch was chilled away by the frosty wind, and the eye dimmed by the moor-mist, or blinded by the hail; this out-speaking of the strong spirit of men who may not gather redundant fruitage from the earth, nor bask in dreamy benignity of sunshine, but must break the rock for bread, and cleave the forest for fire, and show, even in what they did for their delight, some of the hard habits of the arm and heart that grew on them as they swung the axe or pressed the plough.

If, however, the savageness of Gothic architecture, merely as an expression of its origin among Northern nations, may be considered, in some sort, a noble character, it possesses a higher nobility still, when considered as an index, not of climate, but of religious principle.

In the 13th and 14th paragraphs of Chapter XXI. of the first volume of this work, it was noticed that the systems of architectural ornament, properly so called, might be divided into three:—
1. Servile ornament, in which the execution or power of the inferior workman is entirely subjected to the intellect of the higher;—2. Constitutional ornament, in which the executive inferior power is, to a certain point, emancipated and independent, having a will of its own, yet confessing its inferiority and rendering obedience to higher powers;—and

3. Revolutionary ornament, in which no executive inferiority is admitted at all. I must here explain the nature of these divisions at somewhat greater length.

Of Servile ornament, the principal schools are the Greek, Ninevite, and Egyptian; but their servility is of different kinds. The Greek master-workman was far advanced in knowledge and power above the Assyrian or Egyptian. Neither he nor those for whom he worked could endure the appearance of imperfection in anything; and, therefore, what or- 10 nament he appointed to be done by those beneath him was composed of mere geometrical forms,— balls, ridges, and perfectly symmetrical foliage,— which could be executed with absolute precision by line and rule, and were as perfect in their way, when completed, as his own figure sculpture. The Assyrian and Egyptian, on the contrary, less cognisant of accurate form in anything, were content to allow their figure sculpture to be executed by inferior workmen, but lowered the method of its treatment 20 to a standard which every workman could reach, and then trained him by discipline so rigid, that there was no chance of his falling beneath the standard appointed. The Greek gave to the lower workman no subject which he could not perfectly execute. The Assyrian gave him subjects which he could only execute imperfectly, but fixed a legal standard for his imperfection. The workman was, in both systems, a slave.

But in the mediaeval, or especially Christian, 30 system of ornament, this slavery is done away with altogether; Christianity having recognized, in small things as well as great, the individual value of every soul. But it not only recognizes its value; it confesses its imperfection, in only bestowing dignity upon the acknowledgment of unworthiness. That admission of lost power and fallen nature, which the Greek or Ninevite felt to be intensely painful, and, as far as might be, altogether refused, the Christian makes daily and hourly, contemplating the fact of it with- 40 out fear, as tending, in the end, to God's greater glory. Therefore, to every spirit which Christianity summons to her service, her exhortation is: Do what you can, and confess frankly what you are unable to do; neither let your effort be shortened for fear of failure, nor your confession silenced for fear of shame. And it is, perhaps, the principal admirableness of the Gothic schools of architecture, that they thus receive the results of the labour of inferior minds; and out of fragments full of imperfection, 50 and betraying that imperfection in every touch, indulgently raise up a stately and unaccusable whole.

But the modern English mind has this much in common with that of the Greek, that it intensely desires, in all things, the utmost completion or perfection compatible with their nature. This is a noble character in the abstract, but becomes ignoble when it causes us to forget the relative dignities of that nature itself, and to prefer the perfectness of the lower nature to the imperfection of the higher; not considering that as, judged by such a rule, all the brute animals would be preferable to man, because more perfect in their functions and kind, and yet are always held inferior to him, so also in the works of man, those which are more perfect in their kind are always inferior to those which are, in their nature, liable to more faults and shortcomings. . . .

And observe, you are put to stern choice in this matter. You must either make a tool of the creature, or a man of him. You cannot make both. Men were not intended to work with the accuracy of tools, to be precise and perfect in all their actions. If you will have that precision out of them, and make their fingers measure degrees like cog-wheels, and their arms strike curves like compasses, you must unhumanise them. All the energy of their spirits must must be given to make cogs and compasses of themselves. All their attention and strength must go to the accomplishment of the mean act. The eye of the soul must be bent upon the finger-point, and the soul's force must fill all the invisible nerves that guide it, ten hours a day, that it may not err from its steely precision, and so soul and sight be worn away, and the whole human being be lost at last— a heap of sawdust, so far as its intellectual work in this world is concerned; saved only by its Heart, which cannot go into the form of cogs and compasses, but expands, after the ten hours are over, into fireside humanity. On the other hand, if you will make a man of the working creature, you cannot make a tool. Let him but begin to imagine, to think, to try to do anything worth doing; and the engine-turned precision is lost at once. Out come all his roughness, all his dulness, all his incapability; shame upon shame, failure upon failure, pause after pause: but out comes the whole majesty of him also; and we know the height of it only when we see the clouds settling upon him. And, whether the clouds be bright or dark, there will be transfiguration behind and within them.

And now, reader, look round this English room of yours, about which you have been proud so often, because the work of it was so good and strong, and the ornaments of it so finished. Examine again all those accurate mouldings, and perfect polishings, and unerring adjustments of the seasoned wood and tempered steel. Many a time you have exulted over them, and thought how great England was, because her slightest work was done so thoroughly. Alas! if read rightly, these perfectnesses are signs of a slavery in our England a thousand times more bitter and more degrading than that of the scourged African, or helot Greek. Men may be beaten, chained, tormented, yoked like cattle, slaughtered like summer flies, and yet remain in one sense, and the best sense, free. But to smother their souls within them, to blight and hew into rotting pollards the suckling branches of their human intelligence, to make the flesh and skin which, after the worm's work on it, is to see God, into leathern thongs to yoke machinery with,—this it is to be slave-masters indeed; and there might be more freedom in England, though her feudal lords' lightest words were worth men's lives, and though the blood of the vexed husbandman dropped in the furrows of her fields, than there is while the animation of her multitudes is sent like fuel to feed the factory smoke, and the strength of them is given daily to be wasted into the fineness of a web, or racked into the exactness of a line.

And, on the other hand, go forth again to gaze upon the old cathedral front, where you have smiled so often at the fantastic ignorance of the old sculptors: examine once more those ugly goblins, and formless monsters, and stern statues, anatomiless and rigid; but do not mock at them, for they are signs of the life and liberty of every workman who struck the stone; a freedom of thought, and rank in scale of being, such as no laws, no charters, no charities can secure; but which it must be the first aim of all Europe at this day to regain for her children.

Let me not be thought to speak wildly or extravagantly. It is verily this degradation of the operative into a machine, which, more than any other evil of the times, is leading the mass of the nations everywhere into vain, incoherent, destructive struggling for a freedom of which they cannot explain the nature to themselves. Their universal outcry against wealth, and against nobility, is not forced from them either by the pressure of famine, or the sting of mortified pride. These do much, and have done much in all ages; but the foundations of society were never yet shaken as they are at this day. It is not that men are ill fed, but that they have no pleasure in the work by which they make their bread, and therefore look to wealth as the only means of pleasure. It is not that men are pained by the scorn of the upper classes, but they cannot endure their own; for they feel that the kind of labour to which they are condemned is verily a degrading one, and

makes them less than men. Never had the upper classes so much sympathy with the lower, or charity for them, as they have at this day, and yet never were they so much hated by them: for, of old, the separation between the noble and the poor was merely a wall built by law; now it is a veritable difference in level of standing, a precipice between upper and lower grounds in the field of humanity, and there is pestilential air at the bottom of it. I know not if a day is ever to come when the nature of right freedom will be understood, and when men will see that to obey another man, to labour for him, yield reverence to him or to his place, is not slavery. It is often the best kind of liberty,—liberty from care. The man who says to one, Go, and he goeth, and to another, Come, and he cometh, has, in most cases, more sense of restraint and difficulty than the man who obeys him. The movements of the one are hindered by the burden on his shoulder; of the other, by the bridle on his lips: there is no way by which the burden may be lightened; but we need not suffer from the bridle if we do not champ at it. To yield reverence to another, to hold ourselves and our lives at his disposal, is not slavery; often it is the noblest state in which a man can live in this world. There is, indeed, a reverence which is servile, that is to say irrational or selfish: but there is also noble reverence, that is to say, reasonable and loving; and a man is never so noble as when he is reverent in this kind; nay, even if the feeling pass the bounds of mere reason, so that it be loving, a man is raised by it. Which had, in reality, most of the serf nature in him,—the Irish peasant who was lying in wait yesterday for his landlord, with his musket muzzle thrust through the ragged hedge; or that old mountain servant, who, 200 years ago, at Inverkeithing, gave up his own life and the lives of his seven sons for his chief?—as each fell, calling forth his brother to the death, "Another for Hector!" And therefore, in all ages and all countries, reverence has been paid and sacrifice made by men to each other, not only without complaint, but rejoicingly; and famine, and peril, and sword, and all evil, and all shame, have been borne willingly in the causes of masters and kings; for all these gifts of the heart ennobled the men who gave, not less than the men who received them, and nature prompted,

---

6. helot, Spartan serf.

15–16. **The man . . . cometh.** See Matthew 8:9. 36–40. **that old . . . Hector."** "In the battle of Inverkeithing, between the Royalists and Oliver Cromwell's troops, a foster-father and seven brave sons are known to have . . . sacrificed themselves for Sir Hector Maclean of Duart; the old man, whenever one of his boys fell, thrusting forward another to fill his place at the right hand of the beloved chief, with the . . . words . . .—'Another for Hector!'"—Sir Walter Scott, *The Fair Maid of Perth*, Preface.

and God rewarded the sacrifice. But to feel their souls withering within them, unthanked, to find their whole being sunk into an unrecognized abyss, to be counted off into a heap of mechanism, numbered with its wheels, and weighed with its hammer strokes;—this nature bade not,—this God blesses not,—this, humanity for no long time is able to endure.

We have much studied and much perfected, of late, the great civilized invention of the division of labour; only we give it a false name. It is not, truly speaking, the labour that is divided; but the men:—Divided into mere segments of men—broken into small fragments and crumbs of life; so that all the little piece of intelligence that is left in a man is not enough to make a pin, or a nail, but exhausts itself in making the point of a pin, or the head of a nail. Now it is a good and desirable thing, truly, to make many pins in a day; but if we could only see with what crystal sand their points were polished,—sand of human soul, much to be magnified before it can be discerned for what it is,—we should think there might be some loss in it also. And the great cry that rises from all our manufacturing cities, louder than their furnace blast, is all in very deed for this,—that we manufacture everything there except men; we blanch cotton, and strengthen steel, and refine sugar, and shape pottery; but to brighten, to strengthen, to refine, or to form a single living spirit, never enters into our estimate of advantages. And all the evil to which that cry is urging our myriads can be met only in one way: not by teaching nor preaching, for to teach them is but to show them their misery, and to preach to them, if we do nothing more than preach, is to mock at it. It can be met only by a right understanding, on the part of all classes, of what kinds of labour are good for men, raising them, and making them happy; by a determined sacrifice of such convenience, or beauty, or cheapness as is to be got only by the degradation of the workman; and by equally determined demand for the products and results of healthy and ennobling labour. . . .

I should be led far from the matter in hand, if I were to pursue this interesting subject. Enough, I trust, has been said to show the reader that the rudeness or imperfection which at first rendered the term "Gothic" one of reproach is indeed, when rightly understood, one of the most noble characters of Christian architecture, and not only a noble but an *essential* one. It seems a fantastic paradox, but it is nevertheless a most important truth, that no architecture can be truly noble which is *not* imperfect. And this is easily demonstrable. For since the architect, whom we will suppose capable of doing all in perfection, cannot execute the whole with his own hands, he must either make slaves of his workmen in the old Greek, and present English fashion, and level his work to a slave's capacities, which is to degrade it; or else he must take his workmen as he finds them, and let them show their weaknesses together with their strength, which will involve the Gothic imperfection, but render the whole work as noble as the intellect of the age can make it.

But the principle may be stated more broadly still. I have confined the illustration of it to architecture, but I must not leave it as if true of architecture only. Hitherto I have used the words imperfect and perfect merely to distinguish between work grossly unskilful, and work executed with average precision and science; and I have been pleading that any degree of unskilfulness should be admitted, so only that the labourer's mind had room for expression. But, accurately speaking, no good work whatever can be perfect, and *the demand for perfection is always a sign of a misunderstanding of the ends of art.*

This for two reasons, both based on everlasting laws. The first, that no great man ever stops working till he has reached his point of failure: that is to say, his mind is always far in advance of his powers of execution, and the latter will now and then give way in trying to follow it; besides that he will always give to the inferior portions of his work only such inferior attention as they require; and according to his greatness he becomes so accustomed to the feeling of dissatisfaction with the best he can do, that in moments of lassitude or anger with himself he will not care though the beholder be dissatisfied also. I believe there has only been one man who would not acknowledge this necessity, and strove always to reach perfection, Leonardo; the end of his vain effort being merely that he would take ten years to a picture, and leave it unfinished. And therefore, if we are to have great men working at all, or less men doing their best, the work will be imperfect, however beautiful. Of human work none but what is bad can be perfect, in its own bad way.

The second reason is, that imperfection is in some sort essential to all that we know of life. It is the sign of life in a mortal body, that is to say, of a state of progress and change. Nothing that lives is, or can be, rigidly perfect; part of it is decaying, part nascent. The foxglove blossom,—a third part bud, a third part past, a third part in full bloom,—is a type of

39. Leonardo, Leonardo da Vinci, the great painter (1452–1519).

the life of this world. And in all things that live there are certain irregularities and deficiencies which are not only signs of life, but sources of beauty. No human face is exactly the same in its lines on each side, no leaf perfect in its lobes, no branch in its symmetry. All admit irregularity as they imply change; and to banish imperfection is to destroy expression, to check exertion, to paralyze vitality. All things are literally better, lovelier, and more beloved for the imperfections which have been divinely appointed, that the law of human life may be Effort, and the law of human judgment, Mercy.

Accept this then for a universal law, that neither architecture nor any other noble work of man can be good unless it be imperfect; and let us be prepared for the otherwise strange fact, which we shall discern clearly as we approach the period of the Renaissance, that the first cause of the fall of the arts of Europe was a relentless requirement of perfection, incapable alike either of being silenced by veneration for greatness, or softened into forgiveness of simplicity.

Thus far then of the Rudeness or Savageness, which is the first mental element of Gothic architecture. It is an element in many other healthy architectures also, as the Byzantine and Romanesque; but true Gothic cannot exist without it.

The second mental element above named was CHANGEFULNESS, or Variety.

I have already enforced the allowing independent operation to the inferior workman, simply as a duty *to him*, and as ennobling the architecture by rendering it more Christian. We have now to consider what reward we obtain for the performance of this duty, namely, the perpetual variety of every feature of the building.

Wherever the workman is utterly enslaved, the parts of the building must of course be absolutely like each other; for the perfection of his execution can only be reached by exercising him in doing one thing, and giving him nothing else to do. The degree in which the workman is degraded may be thus known at a glance, by observing whether the several parts of the building are similar or not; and if, as in Greek work, all the capitals are alike, and all the mouldings unvaried, then the degradation is complete; if, as in Egyptian or Ninevite work, though the manner of executing certain figures is always the same, the order of design is perpetually varied, the degradation is less total; if, as in Gothic work, there is perpetual change both in design and execution, the workman must have been altogether set free.

How much the beholder gains from the liberty of the labourer may perhaps be questioned in England, where one of the strongest instincts in nearly every mind is that Love of Order which makes us desire that our house windows should pair like our carriage horses, and allows us to yield our faith unhesitatingly to architectural theories which fix a form for everything, and forbid variation from it. I would not impeach love of order: it is one of the most useful elements of the English mind; it helps us in our commerce and in all purely practical matters; and it is in many cases one of the foundation stones of morality. Only do not let us suppose that love of order is love of art. It is true that order, in its highest sense, is one of the necessities of art, just as time is a necessity of music; but love of order has no more to do with our right enjoyment of architecture or painting, than love of punctuality with the appreciation of an opera. Experience, I fear, teaches us that accurate and methodical habits in daily life are seldom characteristic of those who either quickly perceive, or richly possess, the creative powers of art; there is, however, nothing inconsistent between the two instincts, and nothing to hinder us from retaining our business habits, and yet fully allowing and enjoying the noblest gifts of Invention. We already do so, in every other branch of art except architecture, and we only do *not* so there because we have been taught that it would be wrong. Our architects gravely inform us that, as there are four rules of arithmetic, there are five orders of architecture; we, in our simplicity, think that this sounds consistent, and believe them. They inform us also that there is one proper form for Corinthian capitals, another for Doric, and another for Ionic. We, considering that there is also a proper form for the letters A, B, and C, think that this also sounds consistent, and accept the proposition. Understanding, therefore, that one form of the said capitals is proper, and no other, and having a conscientious horror of all impropriety, we allow the architect to provide us with the said capitals, of the proper form, in such and such a quantity, and in all other points to take care that the legal forms are observed; which having done, we rest in forced confidence that we are well housed.

But our higher instincts are not deceived. We take no pleasure in the building provided for us, resembling that which we take in a new book or a new picture. We may be proud of its size, complacent in its correctness, and happy in its convenience. We may take the same pleasure in its symmetry and workmanship as in a well-ordered room, or a skilful piece of manufacture. And this we suppose to be all the pleasure that architecture was ever intended to give us. The idea of reading a building as we would read Milton or Dante, and getting the same kind of delight out of the stones as out of the stanzas, never enters our minds for a moment. And for good reason;—There is indeed rhythm in the verses, quite as strict as the symmetries or rhythm of the architecture, and a thousand times more beautiful, but there is something else than rhythm. The verses were neither made to order, nor to match, as the capitals were; and we have therefore a kind of 10 pleasure in them other than a sense of propriety. But it requires a strong effort of common sense to shake ourselves quit of all that we have been taught for the last two centuries, and wake to the perception of a truth just as simple and certain as it is new: that great art, whether expressing itself in words, colours, or stones, does *not* say the same thing over and over again; that the merit of architectural, as of every other art, consists in its saying new and different things; that to repeat itself is no more a charac- 20 teristic of genius in marble than it is of genius in print; and that we may, without offending any laws of good taste, require of an architect, as we do of a novelist, that he should be not only correct, but entertaining.

Yet all this is true, and self-evident; only hidden from us, as many other self-evident things are, by false teaching. Nothing is a great work of art, for the production of which either rules or models can be given. Exactly so far as architecture works on 30 known rules, and from given models, it is not an art, but a manufacture; and it is, of the two procedures, rather less rational (because more easy) to copy capitals or mouldings from Phidias, and call ourselves architects, than to copy heads and hands from Titian, and call ourselves painters.

Let us then understand at once that change or variety is as much a necessity to the human heart and brain in buildings as in books; that there is no merit, though there is some occasional use, in 40 monotony; and that we must no more expect to derive either pleasure or profit from an architecture whose ornaments are of one pattern, and whose pillars are of one proportion, than we should out of a universe in which the clouds were all of one shape, and the trees all of one size.

And this we confess in deeds, though not in words. All the pleasure which the people of the nineteenth century take in art, is in pictures, sculpture, minor objects of virtù, or mediaeval architec- 50 ture, which we enjoy under the term picturesque: no pleasure is taken anywhere in modern buildings,

34. **Phidias**, Greek sculptor (c. 500–c. 432 B.C.). 36. **Titian**, Venetian painter (1477–1576).

and we find all men of true feeling delighting to escape out of modern cities into natural scenery: hence, as I shall hereafter show, that peculiar love of landscape, which is characteristic of the age. It would be well, if in all other matters, we were as ready to put up with what we dislike, for the sake of compliance with established law, as we are in architecture.

How so debased a law ever came to be established, we shall see when we come to describe the Renaissance schools; here we have only to note, as the second most essential element of the Gothic spirit, that it broke through that law wherever it found it in existence; it not only dared, but delighted in, the infringement of every servile principle; and invented a series of forms of which the merit was, not merely that they were new, but that they were *capable of perpetual novelty*. The pointed arch was not merely a bold variation from the round, but it admitted of millions of variations in itself; for the proportions of a pointed arch are changeable to infinity, while a circular arch is always the same. The grouped shaft was not merely a bold variation from the single one, but it admitted of millions of variations in its grouping, and in the proportions resultant from its grouping. The introduction of tracery was not only a startling change in the treatment of window lights, but admitted endless changes in the interlacement of the tracery bars themselves. So that, while in all living Christian architecture the love of variety exists, the Gothic schools exhibited that love in culminating energy; and their influence, wherever it extended itself, may be sooner and farther traced by this character than by any other; the tendency to the adoption of Gothic types being always first shown by greater irregularity, and richer variation in the forms of the architecture it is about to supersede, long before the appearance of the pointed arch or of any other recognizable *outward* sign of the Gothic mind.

We must, however, herein note carefully what distinction there is between a healthy and a diseased love of change; for as it was in healthy love of change that the Gothic architecture rose, it was partly in consequence of diseased love of change that it was destroyed. In order to understand this clearly, it will be necessary to consider the different ways in which change and monotony are presented to us in nature; both having their use, like darkness and light, and the one incapable of being enjoyed without the other: change being most delightful after some prolongation of monotony, as light appears most brilliant after the eyes have been for some time closed. . . . .

. . . . The variety of the Gothic schools is the more healthy and beautiful, because in many cases it is entirely unstudied, and results, not from the mere love of change, but from practical necessities. For in one point of view Gothic is not only the best, but the *only rational* architecture, as being that which can fit itself most easily to all services, vulgar or noble. Undefined in its slope of roof, height of shaft, breadth of arch, or disposition of ground plan, it can shrink into a turret, expand into a hall, coil into a staircase, or spring into a spire, with undegraded grace and unexhausted energy; and whenever it finds occasion for change in its form or purpose, it submits to it without the slightest sense of loss either to its unity or majesty,—subtle and flexible like a fiery serpent, but ever attentive to the voice of the charmer. And it is one of the chief virtues of the Gothic builders, that they never suffered ideas of outside symmetries and consistencies to interfere with the real use and value of what they did. If they wanted a window, they opened one; a room, they added one; a buttress, they built one; utterly regardless of any established conventionalities of external appearance, knowing (as indeed it always happened) that such daring interruptions of the formal plan would rather give additional interest to its symmetry than injure it. So that, in the best times of Gothic, a useless window would rather have been opened in an unexpected place for the sake of the surprise, than a useful one forbidden for the sake of symmetry. Every successive architect, employed upon a great work, built the pieces he added in his own way, utterly regardless of the style adopted by his predecessors; and if two towers were raised in nominal correspondence at the sides of a cathedral front, one was nearly sure to be different from the other, and in each the style at the top to be different from the style at the bottom.

These marked variations were, however, only permitted as part of the great system of perpetual change which ran through every member of Gothic design, and rendered it as endless a field for the beholder's inquiry as for the builder's imagination: change, which in the best schools is subtle and delicate, and rendered more delightful by intermingling of a noble monotony; in the more barbaric schools is somewhat fantastic and redundant; but, in all, a necessary and constant condition of the life of the school. Sometimes the variety is in one feature, sometimes in another; it may be in the capitals or crockets, in the niches or the traceries, or in all together, but in some one or other of the features it will be found always. If the mouldings are constant, the surface sculpture will change; if the capitals are

of a fixed design, the traceries will change; if the traceries are monotonous, the capitals will change: and if even, as in some fine schools, the early English for example, there is the slightest approximation to an unvarying type of mouldings, capitals, and floral decoration, the variety is found in the disposition of the masses, and in the figure sculpture. . . .

The third constituent element of the Gothic mind was stated to be NATURALISM; that is to say, the love of natural objects for their own sake, and the effort to represent them frankly, unconstrained by artistical laws.

This characteristic of the style partly follows in necessary connection with those named above. For, so soon as the workman is left free to represent what subjects he chooses, he must look to the nature that is round him for material, and will endeavour to represent it as he sees it, with more or less accuracy according to the skill he possesses, and with much play of fancy, but with small respect for law. There is, however, a marked distinction between the imaginations of the Western and Eastern races, even when both are left free; the Western, or Gothic, delighting most in the representation of facts, and the Eastern (Arabian, Persian, and Chinese) in the harmony of colours and forms. Each of these intellectual dispositions has its particular forms of error and abuse, which, though I have often before stated, I must here again briefly explain; and this the rather, because the word Naturalism is, in one of its senses, justly used as a term of reproach, and the questions respecting the real relations of art and nature are so many and so confused throughout all the schools of Europe at this day, that I cannot clearly enunciate any single truth without appearing to admit, in fellowship with it, some kind of error, unless the reader will bear with me in entering into such an analysis of the subject as will serve us for general guidance.

We are to remember, in the first place, that the arrangement of colours and lines is an art analogous to the composition of music, and entirely independent of the representation of facts. Good colouring does not necessarily convey the image of anything but itself. It consists in certain proportions and arrangements of rays of light, but not in likenesses to anything. A few touches of certain greys and purples laid by a master's hand on white paper will be good colouring; as more touches are added beside them, we may find out that they were intended to represent a dove's neck, and we may praise, as the drawing advances, the perfect imitation of the dove's neck. But the good colouring does not consist in that imitation, but in the abstract qualities and relations of the grey and purple.

In like manner, as soon as a great sculptor begins to shape his work out of the block, we shall see that its lines are nobly arranged, and of noble character. We may not have the slightest idea for what the forms are intended, whether they are of man or beast, of vegetation or drapery. Their likeness to anything does not affect their nobleness. They are magnificent forms, and that is all we need care to know of them, in order to say whether the workman is a good or bad sculptor.

Now the noblest art is an exact unison of the abstract value, with the imitative power, of forms and colours. It is the noblest composition, used to express the noblest facts. But the human mind cannot in general unite the two perfections: it either pursues the fact to the neglect of the composition, or pursues the composition to the neglect of the fact.

And it is intended by the Deity that it *should* do this: the best art is not always wanted. Facts are often wanted without art, as in a geological diagram; and art often without facts, as in a Turkey carpet. And most men have been made capable of giving either one or the other, but not both; only one or two, the very highest, can give both.

Observe then. Men are universally divided, as respects their artistical qualifications, into three great classes; a right, a left, and a centre. On the right side are the men of facts, on the left the men of design, in the centre the men of both.

The three classes of course pass into each other by imperceptible gradations. The men of facts are hardly ever altogether without powers of design; the men of design are always in some measure cognizant of facts; and as each class possesses more or less of the powers of the opposite one, it approaches to the character of the central class. Few men, even in that central rank, are so exactly throned on the summit of the crest that they cannot be perceived to incline in the least one way or the other, embracing both horizons with their glance. Now each of these classes has, as I above said, a healthy function in the world, and correlative diseases or unhealthy functions; and, when the work of either of them is seen in its morbid condition, we are apt to find fault with the class of workmen, instead of finding fault only with the particular abuse which has perverted their action. . . .

There is, however, one direction in which the Naturalism of the Gothic workmen is peculiarly manifested; and this direction is even more characteristic of the school than the Naturalism itself; I mean their peculiar fondness for the forms of Vegetation. In rendering the various circumstances of daily life, Egyptian and Ninevite sculpture is as frank and as diffuse as the Gothic. From the highest pomps of state or triumphs of battle, to the most trivial domestic arts and amusements, all is taken advantage of to fill the field of granite with the perpetual interest of a crowded drama; and the early Lombardic and Romanesque sculpture is equally copious in its description of the familiar circumstances of war and the chase. But in all the scenes portrayed by the workmen of these nations, vegetation occurs only as an explanatory accessary; the reed is introduced to mark the course of the river, or the tree to mark the covert of the wild beast, or the ambush of the enemy, but there is no especial interest in the forms of the vegetation strong enough to induce them to make it a subject of separate and accurate study. Again, among the nations who followed the arts of design exclusively, the forms of foliage introduced were meagre and general, and their real intricacy and life were neither admired nor expressed. But to the Gothic workman the living foliage became a subject of intense affection, and he struggled to render all its characters with as much accuracy as was compatible with the laws of his design and the nature of his material, not unfrequently tempted in his enthusiasm to transgress the one and disguise the other.

There is a peculiar significance in this, indicative both of higher civilization and gentler temperament, than had before been manifested in architecture. Rudeness, and the love of change, which we have insisted upon as the first elements of Gothic, are also elements common to all healthy schools. But here is a softer element mingled with them, peculiar to the Gothic itself. The rudeness or ignorance which would have been painfully exposed in the treatment of the human form, are still not so great as to prevent the successful rendering of the wayside herbage; and the love of change, which becomes morbid and feverish in following the haste of the hunter and the rage of the combatant, is at once soothed and satisfied as it watches the wandering of the tendril, and the budding of the flower. Nor is this all: the new direction of mental interest marks an infinite change in the means and the habits of life. The nations whose chief support was in the chase, whose chief interest was in the battle, whose chief pleasure was in the banquet, would take small care respecting the shapes of leaves and flowers; and notice little in the forms of the forest trees which sheltered them, except the signs indicative of the wood which would make the toughest lance, the closest roof, or the clearest fire. The affectionate observation of the grace and outward character of vegetation is the sure sign of a more tranquil and gentle existence, sustained by the gifts, and gladdened by the splendour, of the earth. In that careful distinction of species, and richness of delicate and undisturbed organization, which characterize the Gothic design, there is the history of rural and thoughtful life, influenced by habitual tenderness, and devoted to subtle inquiry; and every discriminating and delicate touch of the chisel, as it rounds the petal or guides the branch, is a prophecy of the development of the entire body of the natural sciences, beginning with that of medicine, of the recovery of literature, and the establishment of the most necessary principles of domestic wisdom and national peace.

I have before alluded to the strange and vain supposition, that the original conception of Gothic architecture had been derived from vegetation,—from the symmetry of avenues, and the interlacing of branches. It is a supposition which never could have existed for a moment in the mind of any person acquainted with early Gothic; but, however idle as a theory, it is most valuable as a testimony to the character of the perfected style. It is precisely because the reverse of this theory is the fact, because the Gothic did not arise out of, but develope itself into, a resemblance to vegetation, that this resemblance is so instructive as an indication of the temper of the builders. It was no chance suggestion of the form of an arch from the bending of a bough, but a gradual and continual discovery of a beauty in natural forms which could be more and more perfectly transferred into those of stone, that influenced at once the heart of the people, and the form of the edifice. The Gothic architecture arose in massy and mountainous strength, axe-hewn, and iron-bound, block heaved upon block by the monk's enthusiasm and the soldier's force; and cramped and stanchioned into such weight of grisly wall, as might bury the anchoret in darkness, and beat back the utmost storm of battle, suffering but by the same narrow crosslet the passing of the sunbeam, or of the arrow. Gradually, as that monkish enthusiasm became more thoughtful, and as the sound of war became more and more intermittent beyond the gates of the convent or the keep, the stony pillar grew slender and the vaulted roof grew light, till they had wreathed themselves into the semblance of the summer woods at their fairest, and of the dead field-flowers, long trodden down in blood, sweet monumental statues were set to bloom for ever, beneath the porch of the temple, or the canopy of the tomb.

Nor is it only as a sign of greater gentleness or refinement of mind, but as a proof of the best possible direction of this refinement, that the tendency of the Gothic to the expression of vegetative life is to be admired. That sentence of Genesis, "I have given thee every green herb for meat," like all the rest of the book, has a profound symbolical as well as a literal meaning. It is not merely the nourishment of the body, but the food of the soul, that is intended. The green herb is, of all nature, that which is most essential to the healthy spiritual life of man. Most of us do not need fine scenery; the precipice and the mountain peak are not intended to be seen by all men,—perhaps their power is greatest over those who are unaccustomed to them. But trees, and fields, and flowers were made for all, and are necessary for all. God has connected the labour which is essential to the bodily sustenance, with the pleasures which are healthiest for the heart; and while He made the ground stubborn, He made its herbage fragrant, and its blossoms fair. The proudest architecture that man can build has no higher honour than to bear the image and recall the memory of that grass of the field which is, at once, the type and the support of his existence; the goodly building is then most glorious when it is sculptured into the likeness of the leaves of Paradise; and the great Gothic spirit, as we showed it to be noble in its disquietude, is also noble in its hold of nature; it is, indeed, like the dove of Noah, in that she found no rest upon the face of the waters,—but like her in this also, "Lo, IN HER MOUTH WAS AN OLIVE BRANCH, PLUCKED OFF."

The fourth essential element of the Gothic mind was above stated to be the sense of the GROTESQUE; but I shall defer the endeavour to define this most curious and subtle character until we have occasion to examine one of the divisions of the Renaissance schools, which was morbidly influenced by it. . . . It is the less necessary to insist upon it here, because every reader familiar with Gothic architecture must understand what I mean, and will, I believe, have no hesitation in admitting that the tendency to delight in fantastic and ludicrous, as well as in sublime, images, is a universal instinct of the Gothic imagination.

The fifth element above named was RIGIDITY; and this character I must endeavour carefully to define, for neither the word I have used, nor any other that I can think of, will express it accurately.

7–8. "I have . . . meat." See Genesis 1:30. 34–35. "Lo . . . off." See Genesis 8:11.

For I mean, not merely stable, but *active* rigidity; the peculiar energy which gives tension to movement, and stiffness to resistance, which makes the fiercest lightning forked rather than curved, and the stoutest oak-branch angular rather than bending, and is as much seen in the quivering of the lance as in the glittering of the icicle.

I have before had occasion . . . to note some manifestations of this energy or fixedness; but it must be still more attentively considered here, as it shows itself throughout the whole structure and decoration of Gothic work. Egyptian and Greek buildings stand, for the most part, by their own weight and mass, one stone passively incumbent on another: but in the Gothic vaults and traceries there is a stiffness analogous to that of the bones of a limb, or fibres of a tree; an elastic tension and communication of force from part to part, and also a studious expression of this throughout every visible line of the building. And, in like manner, the Greek and Egyptian ornament is either mere surface engraving, as if the face of the wall had been stamped with a seal, or its lines are flowing, lithe, and luxuriant; in either case, there is no expression of energy in the framework of the ornament itself. But the Gothic ornament stands out in prickly independence, and frosty fortitude, jutting into crockets, and freezing into pinnacles; here starting up into a monster, there germinating into a blossom; anon knitting itself into a branch, alternately thorny, bossy, and bristly, or writhed into every form of nervous entanglement; but, even when most graceful, never for an instant languid, always quickset: erring, if at all, ever on the side of brusquerie. . . .

Last, because the least essential, of the constituent elements of this noble school, was placed that of REDUNDANCE,—the uncalculating bestowal of the wealth of its labour. There is, indeed, much Gothic, and that of the best period, in which this element is hardly traceable, and which depends for its effect almost exclusively on loveliness of simple design and grace of uninvolved proportion; still, in the most characteristic buildings, a certain portion of their effect depends upon accumulation of ornament; and many of those which have most influence on the minds of men, have attained it by means of this attribute alone. And although, by careful study of the school, it is possible to arrive at a condition of taste which shall be better contended by a few perfect lines than by a whole façade covered with fretwork, the building which only satisfies such a taste is not to be considered the best. For the very first requirement of Gothic architecture being, as we saw above, that it shall both admit the aid, and appeal to the admiration, of the rudest as well as the most refined minds, the richness of the work is, paradoxical as the statement may appear, a part of its humility. No architecture is so haughty as that which is simple; which refuses to address the eye, except in a few clear and forceful lines; which implies, in offering so little to our regards, that all it has offered is perfect; and disdains, either by the complexity of the attractiveness of its features, to embarrass our investigation, or betray us into delight. That humility, which is the very life of the Gothic school, is shown not only in the imperfection, but in the accumulation, of ornament. The inferior rank of the workman is often shown as much in the richness, as the roughness, of his work; and if the co-operation of every hand, and the sympathy of every heart, are to be received, we must be content to allow the redundance which disguises the failure of the feeble, and wins the regard of the inattentive. There are, however, far nobler interests mingling, in the Gothic heart, with the rude love of decorative accumulation: a magnificent enthusiasm, which feels as if it never could do enough to reach the fulness of its ideal; and unselfishness of sacrifice, which would rather cast fruitless labour before the altar than stand idle in the market; and, finally, a profound sympathy with the fulness and wealth of the material universe, rising out of that Naturalism whose operation we have already endeavoured to define. The sculptor who sought for his models among the forest leaves, could not but quickly and deeply feel that complexity need not involve the loss of grace, nor richness that of repose; and every hour which he spent in the study of the minute and various work of Nature, made him feel more forcibly the barrenness of what was best in that of man: nor is it to be wondered at, that, seeing her perfect and exquisite creations poured forth in a profusion which conception could not grasp nor calculation sum, he should think that it ill became him to be niggardly of his own rude craftsmanship; and where he saw throughout the universe a faultless beauty lavished on measureless spaces of broidered field and blooming mountain, to grudge his poor and imperfect labour to the few stones that he had raised one upon another, for habitation or memorial. The years of his life passed away before his task was accomplished; but generation succeeded generation with unwearied enthusiasm, and the cathedral front was at last lost in the tapestry of its traceries, like a rock among the thickets and herbage of spring.

from SESAME AND LILIES

In 1864, Ruskin gave two lectures at Manchester: "Of King's Treasuries" (which deals largely with the problem of reading) and "Of Queen's Gardens" (which concerns mainly the sphere, duties, and education of women); these made up the first edition of *Sesame and Lilies*, 1865. The third lecture, here reprinted in part, was given at Dublin in 1868, and added to the book in 1871.

"Why *Sesame and Lilies* I have never been able to unriddle. He [Ruskin] introduces a quotation about a sesame (or oil seed) cake from Lucian, and a text from Isaiah about lilies blooming in the desert; but I fail to understand what 'Sesame' has to do with the Royal Treasury, or why a 'lily' in a desert is a royal garden—nor does it much signify."—Frederic Harrison, *John Ruskin*, English Men of Letters, Macmillan, 1902.

from Lecture 3
The Mystery of Life and Its Arts

WHEN I accepted the privilege of addressing you to-day, I was not aware of a restriction with respect to the topics of discussion which may be brought before this Society—a restriction which, though entirely wise and right under the circumstances contemplated in its introduction, would necessarily have disabled me, thinking as I think, from preparing any lecture for you on the subject of art in a form which might be permanently useful. Pardon me, therefore, in so far as I must transgress such limitation; for indeed my infringement will be of the letter—not of the spirit—of your commands. In whatever I may say touching the religion which has been the foundation of art, or the policy which has contributed to its power, if I offend one, I shall offend all; for I shall take no note of any separations in creeds, or antagonisms in parties: neither do I fear that ultimately I shall offend any, by proving—or at least stating as capable of positive proof—the connection of all that is best in the crafts and arts of man, with the simplicity of his faith, and the sincerity of his patriotism.

But I speak to you under another disadvantage, by which I am checked in frankness of utterance, not here only, but everywhere: namely, that I am never fully aware how far my audiences are disposed to give me credit for real knowledge of my subject, or how far they grant me attention only because I have been sometimes thought an ingenious or pleasant essayist upon it. For I have had what, in many respects, I boldly call the misfortune, to set

my words sometimes prettily together; not without a foolish vanity in the poor knack that I had of doing so: until I was heavily punished for this pride, by finding that many people thought of the words only, and cared nothing for their meaning. Happily, therefore, the power of using such pleasant language—if indeed it ever were mine—is passing away from me; and whatever I am now able to say at all, I find myself forced to say with great plainness. For my thoughts have changed also, as my words have; and whereas in earlier life, what little influence I obtained was due perhaps chiefly to the enthusiasm with which I was able to dwell on the beauty of the physical clouds, and of their colours in the sky; so all the influence I now desire to retain must be due to the earnestness with which I am endeavouring to trace the form and beauty of another kind of cloud than those; the bright cloud of which it is written—"What is your life? It is even as a vapour that appeareth for a little time, and then vanisheth away." . . .

I spent the ten strongest years of my life, (from twenty to thirty,) in endeavouring to show the excellence of the work of the man whom I believed, and rightly believed, to be the greatest painter of the schools of England since Reynolds. I had then perfect faith in the power of every great truth of beauty to prevail ultimately, and take its right place in usefulness and honour; and I strove to bring the painter's work into this due place, while the painter was yet alive. But he knew, better than I, the uselessness of talking about what people could not see for themselves. He always discouraged me scornfully, even when he thanked me—and he died before even the superficial effect of my work was visible. I went on, however, thinking I could at least be of use to the public, if not to him, in proving his power. My books got talked about a little. The prices of modern pictures, generally, rose, and I was beginning to take some pleasure in a sense of gradual victory, when, fortunately or unfortunately, an opportunity of perfect trial undeceived me at once, and for ever. The Trustees of the National Gallery commissioned me to arrange the Turner drawings there, and permitted me to prepare three hundred examples of his studies from nature, for exhibition at Kensington. At Kensington they were, and are, placed for exhibition; but they are not exhibited, for the room in which they hang is always empty.

Well—this showed me at once, that those ten

---

25. **this Society,** the Royal College of Science, Dublin, before whom this lecture was delivered, May 13, 1868.

19–21. "What . . . away." See James 4:14. **26–27. the greatest painter . . . since Reynolds,** Turner. Sir Joshua Reynolds (1723–1792).

years of my life had been, in their chief purpose, lost. For that, I did not so much care; I had, at least, learned my own business thoroughly, and should be able, as I fondly supposed, after such a lesson, now to use my knowledge, with better effect. But what I did care for was the—to me frightful—discovery, that the most splendid genius in the arts might be permitted by Providence to labour and perish uselessly; that in the very fineness of it there might be something rendering it invisible to ordinary eyes; 10 but that, with this strange excellence, faults might be mingled which would be as deadly as its virtues were vain; that the glory of it was perishable, as well as invisible, and the gift and grace of it might be to us as snow in summer and as rain in harvest.

That was the first mystery of life to me. But, while my best energy was given to the study of painting, I had put collateral effort, more prudent if less enthusiastic, into that of architecture; and in this I could not complain of meeting with no sym- 20 pathy. Among several personal reasons which caused me to desire that I might give this, my closing lecture on the subject of art here, in Ireland, one of the chief was, that in reading it, I should stand near the beautiful building,—the engineer's school of your college,—which was the first realization I had the joy to see, of the principles I had, until then, been endeavouring to teach! but which, alas, is now, to me, no more than the richly canopied monument of one of the most earnest souls that ever 30 gave itself to the arts, and one of my truest and most loving friends, Benjamin Woodward. Nor was it here in Ireland only that I received the help of Irish sympathy and genius. When to another friend, Sir Thomas Deane, with Mr. Woodward, was entrusted the building of the museum at Oxford, the best details of the work were executed by sculptors who had been born and trained here; and the first window of the façade of the building, in which was inaugurated the study of natural science in Eng- 40 land, in true fellowship with literature, was carved from my design by an Irish sculptor.

You may perhaps think that no man ought to speak of disappointment, to whom, even in one branch of labour, so much success was granted. Had Mr. Woodward now been beside me, I had not so spoken; but his gentle and passionate spirit was cut off from the fulfilment of its purposes, and the work we did together is now become vain. It may not be so in future; but the architecture we en- 50 deavoured to introduce is inconsistent alike with the reckless luxury, the deforming mechanism, and the

squalid misery of modern cities; among the formative fashions of the day, aided, especially in England, by ecclesiastical sentiment, it indeed obtained notoriety; and sometimes behind an engine furnace, or a railroad bank, you may detect the pathetic discord of its momentary grace, and, with toil, decipher its floral carvings choked with soot. I felt answerable to the schools I loved, only for their injury. I perceived that this new portion of my strength had also been spent in vain; and from amidst streets of iron, and palaces of crystal, shrank back at last to the carving of the mountain and colour of the flower.

And still I could tell of failure, and failure repeated, as years went on; but I have trespassed enough on your patience to show you, in part, the causes of my discouragement. Now let me more deliberately tell you its results. You know there is a tendency in the minds of many men, when they are heavily disappointed in the main purposes of their life, to feel, and perhaps in warning, perhaps in mockery, to declare, that life itself is a vanity. Because it has disappointed them, they think its nature is of disappointment always, or at best, of pleasure that can be grasped by imagination only; that the cloud of it has no strength nor fire within; but is a painted cloud only, to be delighted in, yet despised. . . .

But the effect of failure upon my own mind has been just the reverse of this. The more that my life disappointed me, the more solemn and wonderful it became to me. It seemed, contrarily to Pope's saying, that the vanity of it *was* indeed given in vain; but that there was something behind the veil of it, which was not vanity. It became to me not a painted cloud, but a terrible and impenetrable one: not a mirage, which vanished as I drew near, but a pillar of darkness, to which I was forbidden to draw near. For I saw that both my own failure, and such success in petty things as in its poor triumph seemed to me worse than failure, came from the want of sufficiently earnest effort to understand the whole law and meaning of existence, and to bring it to noble and due end; as, on the other hand, I saw more and more clearly that all enduring success in the arts, or in any other occupation, had come from the ruling of lower purposes, not by a conviction of their nothingness, but by a solemn faith in the advancing power of human nature, or in the promise, however

11. **palaces of crystal**, the Crystal Palace, built in Hyde Park, 1851, to house Prince Albert's Great Exhibition; see Christopher Hobhouse, *1851 and the Crystal Palace*, Dutton, 1937. 33–34. **Pope's saying**, in *An Essay on Man*, Part II, l. 290.

32. **Benjamin Woodward** (1815–1861).   34–35. **Sir Thomas Deane** (1792–1871).

dimly apprehended, that the mortal part of it would one day be swallowed up in immortality; and that, indeed, the arts themselves never had reached any vital strength or honour, but in the effort to proclaim this immortality, and in the service either of great and just religion, or of some unselfish patriotism, and law of such national life as must be the foundation of religion.

Nothing that I have ever said is more true or necessary—nothing has been more misunderstood or misapplied—than my strong assertion that the arts can never be right themselves, unless their motive is right. It is misunderstood this way: weak painters, who have never learned their business, and cannot lay a true line, continually come to me, crying out— "Look at this picture of mine; it *must* be good, I had such a lovely motive. I have put my whole heart into it, and taken years to think over its treatment." Well, the only answer for these people is—if one had the cruelty to make it—"Sir, you cannot think over *any*thing in any number of years,—you haven't the head to do it; and though you had fine motives, strong enough to make you burn yourself in a slow fire, if only first you could paint a picture, you can't paint one, nor half an inch of one; you haven't the hand to do it."

But, far more decisively we have to say to the men who *do* know their business, or may know it if they choose—"Sir, you have this gift, and a mighty one; see that you serve your nation faithfully with it. It is a greater trust than ships and armies: you might cast *them* away, if you were their captain, with less treason to your people than in casting your own glorious power away, and serving the devil with it instead of men. Ships and armies you may replace if they are lost, but a great intellect, once abused, is a curse to the earth for ever."

This, then, I meant by saying that the arts must have noble motive. This also I said respecting them, that they never had prospered, nor could prosper, but when they had such true purpose, and were devoted to the proclamation of divine truth or law. And yet I saw also that they had always failed in this proclamation—that poetry, and sculpture, and painting, though only great when they strove to teach us something about the gods, never had taught us anything trustworthy about the gods, but had always betrayed their trust in the crisis of it, and, with their powers at the full reach, became ministers to pride and to lust. And I felt also, with increasing amazement, the unconquerable apathy in ourselves and hearers, no less than in these the teachers; and that while the wisdom and rightness of every act and art of life could only be consistent with a right understanding of the ends of life, we were all plunged as in a languid dream—our hearts fat, and our eyes heavy, and our ears closed, lest the inspiration of hand or voice should reach us—lest we should see with our eyes, and understand with our hearts, and be healed.

This intense apathy in all of us is the first great mystery of life; it stands in the way of every perception, every virtue. There is no making ourselves feel enough astonishment at it. That the occupations or pastimes of life should have no motive, is understandable; but—That life itself should have no motive—that we neither care to find out what it may lead to, nor to guard against its being for ever taken away from us—here is a mystery indeed. For just suppose I were able to call at this moment to any one in this audience by name, and to tell him positively that I knew a large estate had been lately left to him on some curious conditions; but that though I knew it was large, I did not know how large, nor even where it was—whether in the East Indies or the West, or in England, or at the Antipodes. I only knew it was a vast estate, and that there was a chance of his losing it altogether if he did not soon find out on what terms it had been left to him. Suppose I were able to say this positively to any single man in this audience, and he knew that I did not speak without warrant, do you think that he would rest content with that vague knowledge, if it were anywise possible to obtain more? Would he not give every energy to find some trace of the facts, and never rest till he had ascertained where this place was, and what it was like? And suppose he were a young man, and all he could discover by his best endeavour was that the estate was never to be his at all, unless he persevered, during certain years of probation, in an orderly and industrious life; but that, according to the rightness of his conduct, the portion of the estate assigned to him would be greater or less, so that it literally depended on his behaviour from day to day whether he got ten thousand a year, or thirty thousand a year, or nothing whatever—would you not think it strange if the youth never troubled himself to satisfy the conditions in any way, nor ever to know what was required of him, but lived exactly as he chose, and never inquired whether his chances of the estate were increasing or passing away? Well, you know that this is actually and literally so with the greater number of the educated persons now living in Christian countries. Nearly every man and woman in any company such as this, outwardly professes to believe—and a large number unquestionably think they believe—much more than this; not only that a quite unlimited estate is in prospect for them if they please the Holder of it, but that the infinite contrary of such a possession—an estate of perpetual misery—is in store for them if they displease this great Land-Holder, this great Heaven-Holder. And yet there is not one in a thousand of these human souls that cares to think, for ten minutes of the day, where this estate is or how beautiful it is, or what kind of life they are to lead in it, or what kind of life they must lead to obtain it.

You fancy that you care to know this: so little do you care that, probably, at this moment many of you are displeased with me for talking of the matter! You came to hear about the Art of this world, not about the Life of the next, and you are provoked with me for talking of what you can hear any Sunday in church. But do not be afraid. I will tell you something before you go about pictures, and carvings, and pottery, and what else you would like better to hear of than the other world. Nay, perhaps you say, "We want you to talk of pictures and pottery, because we are sure that you know something of them, and you know nothing of the other world." Well—I don't. That is quite true. But the very strangeness and mystery of which I urge you to take notice, is in this—that I do not;—nor you either. Can you answer a single bold question unflinchingly about that other world?—Are you sure there is a heaven? Sure there is a hell? Sure that men are dropping before your faces through the pavements of these streets into eternal fire, or sure that they are not? Sure that at your own death you are going to be delivered from all sorrow, to be endowed with all virtue, to be gifted with all felicity, and raised into perpetual companionship with a King, compared to whom the kings of the earth are as grasshoppers, and the nations as the dust of His feet? Are you sure of this? or, if not sure, do any of us so much as care to make it sure? and, if not, how can anything that we do be right—how can anything we think be wise? what honour can there be in the arts that amuse us, or what profit in the possessions that please?

Is not this a mystery of life?

But farther, you may, perhaps, think it a beneficent ordinance for the generality of men that they do not, with earnestness or anxiety, dwell on such questions of the future because the business of the day could not be done if this kind of thought were taken by all of us for the morrow. Be it so: but at least we might anticipate that the greatest and wisest of us, who were evidently the appointed teachers of the rest, would set themselves apart to seek out

36–37. the kings . . . His feet? See Isaiah 40:22.

whatever could be surely known of the future destinies of their race; and to teach this in no rhetorical or ambiguous manner, but in the plainest and most severely earnest words.

Now, the highest representatives of men who have thus endeavoured, during the Christian era, to search out these deep things, and relate them, are Dante and Milton. There are none who for earnestness of thought, for mastery of word, can be classed with these. I am not at present, mind you, speaking of persons set apart in any priestly or pastoral office, to deliver creeds to us, or doctrines; but of men who try to discover and set forth, as far as by human intellect is possible, the facts of the other world. Divines may perhaps teach us how to arrive there, but only these two poets have in any powerful manner striven to discover, or in any definite words professed to tell, what we shall see and become there; or how those upper and nether worlds are, and have been, inhabited.

And what have they told us? Milton's account of the most important event in his whole system of the universe, the fall of the angels, is evidently unbelievable to himself; and the more so, that it is wholly founded on, and in a great part spoiled and degraded from, Hesiod's account of the decisive war of the younger gods with the Titans. The rest of his poem is a picturesque drama, in which every artifice of invention is visibly and consciously employed; not a single fact being, for an instant, conceived as tenable by any living faith. Dante's conception is far more intense, and, by himself, for the time, not to be escaped from; it is indeed a vision, but a vision only, and that one of the wildest that ever entranced a soul—a dream in which every grotesque type or phantasy of heathen tradition is renewed, and adorned; and the destinies of the Christian Church, under their most sacred symbols, become literally subordinate to the praise, and are only to be understood by the aid, of one dear Florentine maiden.

I tell you truly that, as I strive more with this strange lethargy and trance in myself, and awake to the meaning and power of life, it seems daily more amazing to me that men such as these should dare to play with the most precious truths, (or the most deadly untruths,) by which the whole human race listening to them could be informed, or deceived;— all the world their audiences for ever, with pleased

26–27. Hesiod's . . . Titans, in his *Theogony* (eighth century B.C.). The war ended in the overthrow of the Titans and the establishment of the Olympian pantheon. 40. one . . . maiden, Beatrice Portinari, whom Dante sought to honor by saying of her what had never been said of any woman, and whom he presents, in *The Divine Comedy*, as the symbol of revealed truth. See also his early sonnet sequence, *La Vita Nuova* (*The New Life*).

ear, and passionate heart;—and yet, to this submissive infinitude of souls, and evermore succeeding and succeeding multitude, hungry for bread of life, they do but play upon sweetly modulated pipes; with pompous nomenclature adorn the councils of hell; touch a troubadour's guitar to the courses of the sun; and fill the openings of eternity, before which prophets have veiled their faces, and which angels desire to look into, with idle puppets of their scholastic imagination, and melancholy lights of frantic faith in their lost mortal love.

Is not this a mystery of life? . . .

Be it so, then. About this human life that is to be, or that is, the wise religious men tell us nothing that we can trust; and the wise contemplative men, nothing that can give us peace. But there is yet a third class, to whom we may turn—the wise practical men. We have sat at the feet of the poets who sang of heaven, and they have told us their dreams. We have listened to the poets who sang of earth, and they have chanted to us dirges and words of despair. But there is one class of men more:—men, not capable of vision, nor sensitive to sorrow, but firm of purpose—practised in business; learned in all that can be, (by handling,) known. Men, whose hearts and hopes are wholly in this present world, from whom, therefore, we may surely learn, at least, how, at present, conveniently to live in it. What will *they* say to us, or show us by example? These kings—these councillors—these statesmen and builders of kingdoms—these capitalists and men of business, who weigh the earth, and the dust of it, in a balance. They know the world, surely; and what is the mystery of life to us, is none to them. They can surely show us how to live, while we live, and to gather out of the present world what is best.

I think I can best tell you their answer, by telling you a dream I had once. For though I am no poet, I have dreams sometimes:—I dreamed I was at a child's May-day party, in which every means of entertainment had been provided for them by a wise and kind host. It was in a stately house, with beautiful gardens attached to it; and the children had been set free in the rooms and gardens, with no care whatever but how to pass their afternoon rejoicingly. They did not, indeed, know much about what was to happen next day; and some of them, I thought, were a little frightened, because there was a chance of their being sent to a new school where there were examinations; but they kept the thoughts of that out of their heads as well as they could, and resolved to enjoy themselves. The house, I said, was

33–34. who weigh . . . balance. See Isaiah 40:12.

in a beautiful garden, and in the garden were all kinds of flowers; sweet, grassy banks for rest; and smooth lawns for play; and pleasant streams and woods; and rocky places for climbing. And the children were happy for a little while, but presently they separated themselves into parties; and then each party declared it would have a piece of the garden for its own, and that none of the others should have anything to do with that piece. Next, they quarrelled violently which pieces they would have; and at last the boys took up the thing, as boys should do, "practically," and fought in the flower-beds till there was hardly a flower left standing; then they trampled down each other's bits of the garden out of spite; and the girls cried till they could cry no more; and so they all lay down at last breathless in the ruin, and waited for the time when they were to be taken home in the evening.

Meanwhile, the children in the house had been making themselves happy also in their manner. For them, there had been provided every kind of indoor pleasure: there was music for them to dance to; and the library was open, with all manner of amusing books; and there was a museum full of the most curious shells, and animals, and birds; and there was a workshop, with lathes and carpenter's tools, for the ingenious boys; and there were pretty fantastic dresses, for the girls to dress in; and there were microscopes, and kaleidoscopes; and whatever toys a child could fancy; and a table, in the dining-room, loaded with everything nice to eat.

But, in the midst of all this, it struck two or three of the more "practical" children, that they would like some of the brass-headed nails that studded the chairs; and so they set to work to pull them out. Presently, the others, who were reading, or looking at shells, took a fancy to do the like; and, in a little while, all the children, nearly, were spraining their fingers, in pulling out brass-headed nails. With all that they could pull out, they were not satisfied; and then, everybody wanted some of somebody else's. And at last, the really practical and sensible ones declared, that nothing was of any real consequence, that afternoon, except to get plenty of brass-headed nails; and that the books, and the cakes, and the microscopes were of no use at all in themselves, but only, if they could be exchanged for nail-heads. And at last they began to fight for nail-heads, as the others fought for the bits of garden. Only here and there, a despised one shrank away into a corner, and tried to get a little quiet with a book, in the midst of the noise; but all the practical ones thought of nothing else but counting nail-heads all the afternoon—even though they knew they would not be allowed to carry so much as one brass knob away with them. But no—it was—"Who has most nails? I have a hundred, and you have fifty; or, I have a thousand, and you have two. I must have as many as you before I leave the house, or I cannot possibly go home in peace." At last, they made so much noise that I awoke, and thought to myself, "What a false dream that is, of *children!*" The child is the father of the man; and wiser. Children never do such foolish things. Only men do.

But there is yet one last class of persons to be interrogated. The wise religious men we have asked in vain; the wise contemplative men, in vain; the wise worldly men, in vain. But there is another group yet. In the midst of this vanity of empty religion—of tragic contemplation—of wrathful and wretched ambition, and dispute for dust, there is yet one great group of persons, by whom all these disputers live—the persons who have determined, or have had it by a beneficent Providence determined for them, that they will do something useful; that whatever may be prepared for them hereafter, or happen to them here, they will, at least, deserve the food that God gives them by winning it honourably: and that, however fallen from the purity, or far from the peace, of Eden, they will carry out the duty of human dominion, though they have lost its felicity; and dress and keep the wilderness, though they no more can dress or keep the garden.

These,—hewers of wood, and drawers of water,— these, bent under burdens, or torn of scourges— these, that dig and weave—that plant and build; workers in wood, and in marble, and in iron—by whom all food, clothing, habitation, furniture, and means of delight are produced, for themselves, and for all men beside; men, whose deeds are good, though their words may be few; men, whose lives are serviceable, be they never so short, and worthy of honour, be they never so humble;—from these, surely, at least, we may receive some clear message of teaching; and pierce, for an instant, into the mystery of life, and of its arts.

Yes; from these, at last, we do receive a lesson. But I grieve to say, or rather—for that is the deeper truth of the matter—I rejoice to say—this message of theirs can only be received by joining them—not by thinking about them.

You sent for me to talk to you of art; and I have obeyed you in coming. But the main thing I have to tell you is,—that art must not be talked about.

The fact that there is talk about it at all, signifies that it is ill done, or cannot be done. No true painter ever speaks, or ever has spoken, much of his art. The greatest speak nothing. Even Reynolds is no exception, for he wrote of all that he could not himself do, and was utterly silent respecting all that he himself did. . . .

. . . The more beautiful the art, the more it is essentially the work of people who *feel themselves wrong*;—who are striving for the fulfilment of a law, and the grasp of a loveliness, which they have not yet attained, which they feel even farther and farther from attaining the more they strive for it. And yet, in still deeper sense, it is the work of people who know also that they are right. The very sense of inevitable error from their purpose marks the perfectness of that purpose, and the continued sense of failure arises from the continued opening of the eyes more clearly to all the sacredest laws of truth.

This is one lesson. The second is a very plain, and greatly precious one: namely—that whenever the arts and labours of life are fulfilled in this spirit of striving against misrule, and doing whatever we have to do, honourably and perfectly, they invariably bring happiness, as much as seems possible to the nature of man. In all other paths by which that happiness is pursued there is disappointment, or destruction: for ambition and for passion there is no rest—no fruition; the fairest pleasures of youth perish in a darkness greater than their past light: and the loftiest and purest love too often does but inflame the cloud of life with endless fire of pain. But, ascending from lowest to highest, through every scale of human industry, that industry worthily followed, gives peace. Ask the labourer in the field, at the forge, or in the mine; ask the patient, delicate-fingered artisan, or the strong-armed, fiery-hearted worker in bronze, and in marble, and with the colours of light; and none of these, who are true workmen, will ever tell you, that they have found the law of heaven an unkind one—that in the sweat of their face they should eat bread, till they return to the ground; nor that they ever found it an unrewarded obedience, if, indeed, it was rendered faithfully to the command—"Whatsoever thy hand findeth to do—do it with thy might."

These are the two great and constant lessons which our labourers teach us of the mystery of life. But there is another, and a sadder one, which they

---

8–9. The child . . . man. See Wordsworth's "My Heart Leaps up When I Behold," page 57. **25–29. and that, however . . . garden.** See Genesis 2:8–17; 3:22–24. **30. hewers . . . water.** See Joshua 9:21.

4–7. Even Reynolds . . . himself did, a reference to Reynolds's *Discourses before the Royal Academy,* 1778. **42–44. that in . . . ground.** See Genesis 3:19. **46–47. "Whatsoever . . . might."** See Ecclesiastes 9:10.

cannot teach us, which we must read on their tomb-stones.

"Do it with thy might." There have been myriads upon myriads of human creatures who have obeyed this law—who have put every breath and nerve of their being into its toil—who have devoted every hour, and exhausted every faculty—who have bequeathed their unaccomplished thoughts at death—who, being dead, have yet spoken, by majesty of memory, and strength of example. And, at last, what has all this "Might" of humanity accomplished, in six thousand years of labour and sorrow? What has it *done*? Take the three chief occupations and arts of men, one by one, and count their achievements. Begin with the first—the lord of them all—Agriculture. Six thousand years have passed since we were set to till the ground, from which we were taken. How much of it is tilled? How much of that which is, wisely or well? In the very centre and chief garden of Europe—where the two forms of parent Christianity have had their fortresses—where the noble Catholics of the Forest Cantons, and the noble Protestants of the Vaudois valleys, have maintained, for dateless ages, their faiths and liberties—there the unchecked Alpine rivers yet run wild in devastation; and the marshes, which a few hundred men could redeem with a year's labour, still blast their helpless inhabitants into fevered idiotism. That is so, in the centre of Europe! While, on the near coast of Africa, once the Garden of the Hesperides, an Arab woman, but a few sunsets since, ate her child, for famine. And, with all the treasures of the East at our feet, we, in our own dominion, could not find a few grains of rice, for a people that asked of us no more; but stood by, and saw five hundred thousand of them perish of hunger.

Then, after agriculture, the art of kings, take the next head of human arts—Weaving; the art of queens, honoured of all noble Heathen women, in the person of their virgin goddess—honoured of all Hebrew women, by the word of their wisest king—"She layeth her hands to the spindle, and her hands hold the distaff; she stretcheth out her hand to the poor. She is not afraid of the snow for her house-hold, for all her houshold are clothed with scarlet. She maketh herself covering of tapestry; her clothing is silk and purple. She maketh fine linen, and selleth it, and delivereth girdles to the merchant." What have we done in all these thousands of years with this bright art of Greek maid and Christian matron? Six thousand years of weaving, and have we learned to weave? Might not every naked wall have been purple with tapestry, and every feeble breast fenced with sweet colours from the cold? What have we done? Our fingers are too few, it seems, to twist together some poor covering for our bodies. We set our streams to work for us, and choke the air with fire, to turn our spinning-wheels—and, —*are we yet clothed*? Are not the streets of the capitals of Europe foul with sale of cast clouts and rotten rags? Is not the beauty of your sweet children left in wretchedness of disgrace, while, with better honour, nature clothes the brood of the bird in its nest, and the suckling of the wolf in her den? And does not every winter's snow robe what you have not robed, and shroud what you have not shrouded; and every winter's wind bear up to heaven its wasted souls, to witness against you hereafter, by the voice of their Christ,—"I was naked, and ye clothed me not"?

Lastly—take the Art of Building—the strongest—proudest—most orderly—most enduring of the arts of man; that of which the produce is in the surest manner accumulative, and need not perish, or be replaced; but if once well done, will stand more strongly than the unbalanced rocks—more prevalently than the crumbling hills. The art which is associated with all civic pride and sacred principle; with which men record their power—satisfy their enthusiasm—make sure their defence—define and make dear their habitation. And in six thousand years of building, what have we done? Of the greater part of all that skill and strength, *no* vestige is left, but fallen stones, that encumber the fields and impede the streams. But, from this waste of disorder, and of time, and of rage, what *is* left to us? Constructive and progressive creatures that we are, with ruling brains, and forming hands, capable of fellowship, and thirsting for fame, can we not contend, in comfort, with the insects of the forest, or, in achievement, with the worm of the sea? The white surf rages in vain against the ramparts built by poor atoms of scarcely nascent life; but only ridges of formless ruin mark the places where once dwelt our noblest multitudes. The ant and the moth have cells for each of their young, but our little ones lie in festering heaps, in homes that con-

9. who . . . spoken. See Hebrews 11:4. 16–17. Six thousand years . . . taken. According to the chronology of Archbishop Ussher (1581–1656), the world was created in 4004 B.C. 21–23. where the noble Catholics . . . Vaudois valleys, in Switzerland. See Milton's sonnet "On the Late Massacre in Piedmont," in Volume I. 30. Garden of the Hesperides, where the golden apples were kept; in the older forms of the story, located on an island far in the west. See art. "Hesperides" in *New International Encyclopaedia*, or C. M. Gayley's *Classic Myths*, Ginn, 2d ed., 1911. 40. their virgin goddess, Athena, goddess, among other things, of weaving. 42. "She layeth . . . the merchant." (l. 4, next column). See Proverbs 31:10–31.

16–17. cast . . . rags. See Jeremiah 38:11. 25. "I was . . . not." See Matthew 25:43.

sume them like graves; and night by night, from the corners of our streets, rises up the cry of the homeless—"I was a stranger, and ye took me not in."

Must it be always thus? Is our life for ever to be without profit—without possession? Shall the strength of its generations be as barren as death; or cast away their labour, as the wild fig-tree casts her untimely figs? Is it all a dream then—the desire of the eyes and the pride of life—or, if it be, might we not live in nobler dream than this? The poets and prophets, the wise men, and the scribes, though they have told us nothing about a life to come, have told us much about the life that is now. They have had—they also,—their dreams, and we have laughed at them. They have dreamed of mercy, and of justice; they have dreamed of peace and goodwill; they have dreamed of labour undisappointed, and of rest undisturbed; they have dreamed of fulness in harvest, and overflowing in store; they have dreamed of wisdom in council, and of providence in law; of gladness of parents, and strength of children, and glory of grey hairs. And at these visions of theirs we have mocked, and held them for idle and vain, unreal and unaccomplishable. What have we accomplished with our realities? Is this what has come of our worldly wisdom, tried against their folly? this, our mightiest possible, against their impotent ideal? or, have we only wandered among the spectra of a baser felicity, and chased phantoms of the tombs, instead of visions of the Almighty; and walked after the imaginations of our evil hearts, instead of after the counsels of Eternity, until our lives—not in the likeness of the cloud of heaven, but of the smoke of hell—have become "as a vapour, that appeareth for a little time, and then vanisheth away"?

Does it vanish then? Are you sure of that?—sure, that the nothingness of the grave will be a rest from this troubled nothingness; and that the coiling shadow, which disquiets itself in vain, cannot change into the smoke of the torment that ascends for ever? Will any answer that they *are* sure of it, and that there is no fear, nor hope, nor desire, nor labour, whither they go? Be it so: will you not, then, make as sure of the Life that now is, as you are of the Death that is to come? Your hearts are wholly in this world—will you not give them to it wisely, as well as perfectly? And see, first of all, that you *have* hearts, and sound hearts, too, to give. Because you have no heaven to look for, is that any reason that you should remain ignorant of this wonderful and infinite earth, which is firmly and instantly given you in possession? Although your days are numbered, and the following darkness sure, is it necessary that you should share the degradation of the brute, because you are condemned to its mortality; or live the life of the moth, and of the worm, because you are to companion them in the dust? Not so; we may have but a few thousands of days to spend, perhaps hundreds only—perhaps tens; nay, the longest of our time and best, looked back on, will be but as a moment, as the twinkling of an eye; still we are men, not insects; we are living spirits, not passing clouds. "He maketh the winds His messengers; the momentary fire, His minister"; and shall we do less than *these*? Let us do the work of men while we bear the form of them; and, as we snatch our narrow portion of time out of Eternity, snatch also our narrow inheritance of passion out of Immortality—even though our lives *be* as a vapour, that appeareth for a little time, and then vanisheth away.

But there are some of you who believe not this—who think this cloud of life has no such close—that it is to float, revealed and illumined, upon the floor of heaven, in the day when He cometh with clouds, and every eye shall see Him. Some day, you believe, within these five, or ten, or twenty years, for every one of us the judgment will be set, and the books opened. If that be true, far more than that must be true. Is there but one day of judgment? Why, for us every day is a day of judgment—every day is a Dies Irae, and writes its irrevocable verdict in the flame of its West. Think you that judgment waits till the doors of the grave are opened? It waits at the doors of your houses—it waits at the corners of your streets; we are in the midst of judgment—the insects that we crush are our judges—the moments we fret away are our judges—the elements that feed us, judge, as they minister—and the pleasures that deceive us, judge, as they indulge. Let us, for our lives, do the work of Men while we bear the form of them, if indeed those lives are *Not* as a vapour, and do *Not* vanish away.

"The work of men"—and what is that? Well, we may any of us know very quickly, on the condition of being wholly ready to do it. But many of us are for the most part thinking, not of what we are to do, but of what we are to get; and the best of us are

3. "I was . . . in." See Matthew 25:43.   7–8. as the . . . figs? See Revelation 6:13.   30–31. walked . . . hearts. See Jeremiah 11:8.   34–35. "as a vapour . . . away." See James 4:14.   39–41. which disquiets itself . . . for ever? See Psalm 42:5; Revelation 14:11.   42–43. there is no . . . go? See Ecclesiastes 9:10.

14–15. "He maketh . . . minister." See Psalm 104:3–4. 25–26. He cometh . . . Him. See Revelation 1:7. 28–29. the judgment . . . opened. See Daniel 7:10. 31–32. Dies Irae, "Day of Wrath," one of the most famous pieces of sacred poetry in the world, attributed to Thomas of Celano (thirteenth century); see Scott's translation at the close of *The Lay of the Last Minstrel*.

sunk into the sin of Ananias, and it is a mortal one—we want to keep back part of the price; and we continually talk of taking up our cross, as if the only harm in a cross was the *weight* of it—as if it was only a thing to be carried, instead of to be—crucified upon. "They that are His have crucified the flesh, with the affections and lusts." Does that mean, think you, that in time of national distress, of religious trial, of crisis for every interest and hope of humanity—none of us will cease jesting, none cease idling, none put themselves to any wholesome work, none take so much as a tag of lace off their footmen's coats, to save the world? Or does it rather mean, that they are ready to leave houses, lands, and kindreds—yes, and life, if need be? Life!—some of us are ready enough to throw that away, joyless as we have made it. But "*station* in Life"—how many of us are ready to quit *that*? Is it not always the great objection, where there is question of finding something useful to do—"We cannot leave our stations in Life"?

Those of us who really cannot—that is to say, who can only maintain themselves by continuing in some business or salaried office, have already something to do; and all that they have to see to is, that they do it honestly and with all their might. But with most people who use that apology, "remaining in the station of life to which Providence has called them" means keeping all the carriages, and all the footmen and large houses they can possibly pay for; and, once for all, I say that if ever Providence *did* put them into stations of that sort—which is not at all a matter of certainty—Providence is just now very distinctly calling them out again. Levi's station in life was the receipt of custom; and Peter's, the shore of Galilee; and Paul's, the antechambers of the High Priest,—which "station in life" each had to leave, with brief notice.

And, whatever our station in life may be, at this crisis, those of us who mean to fulfil our duty ought first to live on as little as we can; and, secondly, to do all the wholesome work for it we can, and to spend all we can spare in doing all the sure good we can.

And sure good is, first in feeding people, then in dressing people, then in lodging people, and lastly in rightly pleasing people, with arts, or sciences, or any other subject of thought.

1. **the sin of Ananias.** See Acts 5:1–11. **6–7. "They . . . lusts."** See Galatians 5:24. **34–37. Levi's station . . . High Priest.** Levi was a tax-collector before he became a disciple of Jesus (see Mark 2:14); "Simon called Peter" was a Galilean fisherman (see Matthew 4:18–22); Paul (Saul, before his conversion) was a member of the Sanhedrim and "a Pharisee of the Pharisees" (see Acts 8:1–3; 9:1ff.).

I say first in feeding; and, once for all, do not let yourselves be deceived by any of the common talk of "indiscriminate charity." The order to us is not to feed the deserving hungry, nor the industrious hungry, nor the amiable and well-intentioned hungry, but simply to feed the hungry. It is quite true, infallibly true, that if any man will not work, neither should he eat—think of that, and every time you sit down to your dinner, ladies and gentlemen, say solemnly, before you ask a blessing, "How much work have I done to-day for my dinner?" But the proper way to enforce that order on those below you, as well as on yourselves, is not to leave vagabonds and honest people to starve together, but very distinctly to discern and seize your vagabond; and shut your vagabond up out of honest people's way, and very sternly then see that, until he has worked, he does *not* eat. But the first thing is to be sure you have the food to give; and, therefore, to enforce the organization of vast activities in agriculture and in commerce, for the production of the wholesomest food, and proper storing and distribution of it, so that no famine shall any more be possible among civilized beings. There is plenty of work in this business alone, and at once, for any number of people who like to engage in it.

Secondly, dressing people—that is to say, urging every one within reach of your influence to be always neat and clean, and giving them means of being so. In so far as they absolutely refuse, you must give up the effort with respect to them, only taking care that no children within your sphere of influence shall any more be brought up with such habits; and that every person who is willing to dress with propriety shall have encouragement to do so. And the first absolutely necessary step towards this is the gradual adoption of a consistent dress for different ranks of persons, so that their rank shall be known by their dress; and the restriction of the changes of fashion within certain limits. All which appears for the present quite impossible; but it is only so far even difficult as it is difficult to conquer our vanity, frivolity, and desire to appear what we are not. And it is not, nor ever shall be, creed of mine, that these mean and shallow vices are unconquerable by Christian women.

And then, thirdly, lodging people, which you may think should have been put first, but I put it third, because we must feed and clothe people where we find them, and lodge them afterward. And providing lodgment for them means a great deal of vigorous legislation, and cutting down of

3–4. **The order . . . hungry.** See Isaiah 58:7. 7–8. **that if any . . . eat.** See 2 Thessalonians 3:10.

vested interests that stand in the way, and after that, or before that, so far as we can get it, thorough sanitary and remedial action in the houses that we have; and then the building of more, strongly, beautifully, and in groups of limited extent, kept in proportion to their streams, and walled round, so that there may be no festering and wretched suburb anywhere, but clean and busy street within, and the open country without, with a belt of beautiful garden and orchard round the walls, so that from any part of the city perfectly fresh air and grass, and sight of far horizon, might be reachable in a few minutes' walk. This the final aim; but in immediate action every minor and possible good to be instantly done, when, and as, we can; roofs mended that have holes in them—fences patched that have gaps in them—walls buttressed that totter—and floors propped that shake; cleanliness and order enforced with our own hands and eyes, till we are breathless, every day. And all the fine arts will healthily follow. I myself have washed a flight of stone stairs all down, with bucket and broom, in a Savoy inn, where they hadn't washed their stairs since they first went up them; and I never made a better sketch than that afternoon.

These, then, are the three first needs of civilized life; and the law for every Christian man and woman is, that they shall be in direct service towards one of these three needs, as far as is consistent with their own special occupation, and if they have no special business, then wholly in one of these services. And out of such exertion in plain duty all other good will come; for in this direct contention with material evil, you will find out the real nature of all evil; you will discern by the various kinds of resistance, what is really the fault and main antagonism to good; also you will find the most unexpected helps and profound lessons given, and truths will come thus down to us which the speculation of all our lives would never have raised us up to. You will find nearly every educational problem solved, as soon as you truly want to do something; everybody will become of use in their own fittest way, and will learn what is best for them to know in that use. Competitive examination will then, and not till then, be wholesome, because it will be daily, and calm, and in practice; and on these familiar arts, and minute, but certain and serviceable knowledges, will be surely edified and sustained the greater arts and splendid theoretical sciences.

But much more than this. On such holy and simple practice will be founded, indeed, at last, an infallible religion. The greatest of all the mysteries of life, and the most terrible, is the corruption of even the sincerest religion, which is not daily founded on rational, effective, humble, and helpful action. Helpful action, observe! for there is just one law, which, obeyed, keeps all religions pure—forgotten, makes them all false. Whenever in any religious faith, dark or bright, we allow our minds to dwell upon the points in which we differ from other people, we are wrong, and in the devil's power. That is the essence of the Pharisee's thanksgiving—"Lord, I thank Thee that I am not as other men are." At every moment of our lives we should be trying to find out, not in what we differ from other people, but in what we agree with them; and the moment we find we can agree as to anything that should be done, kind or good, (and who but fools couldn't?) then do it; push at it together: you can't quarrel in a side-by-side push; but the moment that even the best men stop pushing, and begin talking, they mistake their pugnacity for piety, and it's all over. I will not speak of the crimes which in past times have been committed in the name of Christ, nor of the follies which are at this hour held to be consistent with obedience to Him; but I *will* speak of the morbid corruption and waste of vital power in religious sentiment, by which the pure strength of that which should be the guiding soul of every nation, the splendour of its youthful manhood, and spotless light of its maidenhood, is averted or cast away. You may see continually girls who have never been taught to do a single useful thing thoroughly; who cannot sew, who cannot cook, who cannot cast an account, nor prepare a medicine, whose whole life has been passed either in play or in pride; you will find girls like these, when they are earnest-hearted, cast all their innate passion of religious spirit, which was meant by God to support them through the irksomeness of daily toil, into grievous and vain meditation over the meaning of the great Book, of which no syllable was ever yet to be understood but through a deed; all the instinctive wisdom and mercy of their womanhood made vain, and the glory of their pure consciences warped into fruitless agony concerning questions which the laws of common serviceable life would have either solved for them in an instant, or kept out of their way. Give such a girl any true work that will make her active in the dawn, and weary at night, with the consciousness that her fellow-creatures have indeed been the better for her day, and the powerless sorrow of her enthusiasm will transform itself into a majesty of radiant and beneficent peace.

So with our youths. We once taught them to make Latin verses, and called them educated; now

9-10. **"Lord . . . are."** See Luke 18:9-14.

we teach them to leap and to row, to hit a ball with a bat, and call them educated. Can they plough, can they sow, can they plant at the right time, or build with a steady hand? Is it the effort of their lives to be chaste, knightly, faithful, holy in thought, lovely in word and deed? Indeed it is, with some, nay, with many, and the strength of England is in them, and the hope; but we have to turn their courage from the toil of war to the toil of mercy; and their intellect from dispute of words to discernment of things; and their knighthood from the errantry of adventure to the state and fidelity of a kingly power. And then, indeed, shall abide, for them and for us, an incorruptible felicity, and an infallible religion; shall abide for us Faith, no more to be assailed by temptation, no more to be defended by wrath and by fear;—shall abide with us Hope, no more to be quenched by the years that overwhelm, or made ashamed by the shadows that betray:— shall abide for us, and with us, the greatest of these; the abiding will, the abiding name of our Father. For the greatest of these is Charity.

from THE CROWN OF WILD OLIVE

The crown of wild olive was the only prize given to winners at the Olympic Games; Ruskin uses it to discourage runners in the race of life from working for material reward.

The four lectures contained in the book thus entitled (1866) were "War," "The Future of England," "Work," and "Traffic."

Lecture 2: TRAFFIC

YOU cannot have good architecture merely by asking people's advice on occasion. All good architecture is the expression of national life and character, and it is produced by a prevalent and eager national taste, or desire for beauty. And I want you to think a little of the deep significance of this word "taste"; for no statement of mine has been more earnestly or oftener controverted than that good taste is essentially a moral quality. "No," say many of my antagonists, "taste is one thing, morality is another. Tell us what is pretty: we shall be glad to know that; but we need no sermons—even were you able to preach them, which may be doubted."

Permit me, therefore, to fortify this old dogma of mine somewhat. Taste is not only a part and an index of morality;—it is the ONLY morality. The first,

and last, and closest trial question to any living creature is, "What do you like?" Tell me what you like, and I'll tell you what you are. Go out into the street, and ask the first man or woman you meet, what their "taste" is; and if they answer candidly, you know them, body and soul. "You, my friend in the rags, with the unsteady gait, what do *you* like?" "A pipe and a quatern of gin." I know you. "You, good woman, with the quick step and tidy bonnet, what do you like?" "A swept hearth, and a clean tea-table; and my husband opposite me, and a baby at my breast." Good, I know you also. "You, little girl with the golden hair and the soft eyes, what do you like?" "My canary, and a run among the wood hyacinths." "You, little boy with the dirty hands, and the low forehead, what do you like?" "A shy at the sparrows, and a game at pitch farthing." Good; we know them all now. What more need we ask?

"Nay," perhaps you answer; "we need rather to ask what these people and children do, than what they like. If they *do* right, it is no matter that they like what is wrong; and if they *do* wrong, it is no matter that they like what is right. Doing is the great thing; and it does not matter that the man likes drinking, so that he does not drink; nor that the little girl likes to be kind to her canary, if she will not learn her lessons; nor that the little boy likes throwing stones at the sparrows, if he goes to the Sunday school." Indeed, for a short time, and in a provisional sense, this is true. For if, resolutely, people do what is right, in time to come they like doing it. But they only are in a right moral state when they *have* come to like doing it; and as long as they don't like it, they are still in a vicious state. The man is not in health of body who is always thinking of the bottle in the cupboard, though he bravely bears his thirst; but the man who heartily enjoys water in the morning, and wine in the evening, each in its proper quantity and time. And the entire object of true education is to make people not merely *do* the right things, but *enjoy* the right things: —not merely industrious, but to love industry—not merely learned, but to love knowledge—not merely pure, but to love purity—not merely just, but to hunger and thirst after justice.

But you may answer or think, "Is the liking for outside ornaments,—for pictures, or statues, or furniture, or architecture, a moral quality?" Yes, most surely, if a rightly set liking. Taste for *any* pictures or statues is not a moral quality, but taste for good ones is. Only here again we have to define the word "good." I don't mean by "good," clever— or learned—or difficult in the doing. Take a picture

---

22. For the greatest . . . Charity. See 1 Corinthians 13:13.

44–45. but to hunger . . . justice, see Matthew 5:6.

by Teniers, of sots quarrelling over their dice; it is an entirely clever picture; so clever that nothing in its kind has ever been done equal to it; but it is also an entirely base and evil picture. It is an expression of delight in the prolonged contemplation of a vile thing, and delight in that is an "unmannered," or "immoral" quality. It is "bad taste" in the profoundest sense—it is the taste of the devils. On the other hand, a picture of Titian's, or a Greek statue, or a Greek coin, or a Turner landscape, expresses delight in the perpetual contemplation of a good and perfect thing. That is an entirely moral quality—it is the taste of the angels. And all delight in fine art, and all love of it, resolve themselves into simple love of that which deserves love. That deserving is the quality which we call "loveliness"—(we ought to have an opposite word, hateliness, to be said of the things which deserve to be hated); and it is not an indifferent nor optional thing whether we love this or that; but it is just the vital function of all our being. What we *like* determines what we *are*, and is the sign of what we are; and to teach taste is inevitably to form character. . . .

And so completely and unexceptionally is this so, that, if I had time to-night, I could show you that a nation cannot be affected by any vice, or weakness, without expressing it, legibly, and for ever, either in bad art, or by want of art; and that there is no national virtue, small or great, which is not manifestly expressed in all the art which circumstances enable the people possessing that virtue to produce. Take, for instance, your great English virtue of enduring and patient courage. You have at present in England only one art of any consequence—that is, iron-working. You know thoroughly well how to cast and hammer iron. Now, do you think, in those masses of lava which you build volcanic cones to melt, and which you forge at the mouths of the Infernos you have created; do you think, on those iron plates, your courage and endurance are not written for ever,—not merely with an iron pen, but on iron parchment? And take also your great English vice—European vice—vice of all the world— vice of all other worlds that roll or shine in heaven, bearing with them yet the atmosphere of hell—the vice of jealousy, which brings competition into your commerce, treachery into your councils, and dishonour into your wars—that vice which has rendered for you, and for your next neighbouring nation,

the daily occupations of existence no longer possible, but with the mail upon your breasts and the sword loose in its sheath; so that at last, you have realized for all the multitudes of the two great peoples who lead the so-called civilization of the earth, —you have realized for them all, I say, in person and in policy, what was once true only of the rough Border riders of your Cheviot hills—

"They carved at the meal
   With gloves of steel,
And they drank the red wine through the helmet
   barred";—

do you think that this national shame and dastardliness of heart are not written as legibly on every rivet of your iron armour as the strength of the right hands that forged it?

Friends, I know not whether this thing be the more ludicrous or the more melancholy. It is quite unspeakably both. Suppose, instead of being now sent for by you, I had been sent for by some private gentleman, living in a suburban house, with his garden separated only by a fruit wall from his next door neighbour's; and he had called me to consult with him on the furnishing of his drawing-room. I begin looking about me, and find the walls rather bare; I think such and such a paper might be desirable—perhaps a little fresco here and there on the ceiling—a damask curtain or so at the windows. "Ah," says my employer, "damask curtains, indeed! That's all very fine, but you know I can't afford that kind of thing just now!" "Yet the world credits you with a splendid income!" "Ah, yes," says my friend, "but do you know, at present I am obliged to spend it nearly all in steel-traps?" "Steel-traps! for whom?" "Why, for that fellow on the other side the wall, you know; we're very good friends, capital friends; but we are obliged to keep our traps set on both sides of the wall; we could not possibly keep on friendly terms without them, and our spring guns. The worst of it is, we are both clever fellows enough; and there's never a day passes that we don't find out a new trap, or a new gun-barrel, or something; we spend about fifteen millions a year each in our traps, take it altogether; and I don't see how we're to do with less." A highly comic state of life for two private gentlemen! but for two nations, it seems to me, not wholly comic. Bedlam would be comic, perhaps, if there were only one madman in it; and your Christmas pantomime is comic, when there is only one clown in it; but when the whole world

---

1. Teniers. There were two famous Dutch painters of this name—David Teniers, the elder (1582–1649) and David Teniers, the younger (1610–1690).

9–12. "They carved . . . barred," Scott, *Lay of the Last Minstrel*, I, 31 ff.   **48. Bedlam,** the hospital of St. Mary of Bethlehem, London, a lunatic asylum.

turns clown, and paints itself red with its own heart's blood instead of vermilion, it is something else than comic, I think.

Mind, I know a great deal of this is play, and willingly allow for that. You don't know what to do with yourselves for a sensation: fox-hunting and cricketing will not carry you through the whole of this unendurably long mortal life: you liked popguns when you were schoolboys, and rifles and Armstrongs are only the same things better made: but then the worst of it is, that what was play to you when boys, was not play to the sparrows; and what is play to you now, is not play to the small birds of State neither; and for the black eagles, you are somewhat shy of taking shots at them, if I mistake not.

I must get back to the matter in hand, however. Believe me, without farther instance, I could show you, in all time, that every nation's vice, or virtue, was written in its art: the soldiership of early Greece; the sensuality of late Italy; the visionary religion of Tuscany; the splendid human energy of Venice. I have no time to do this to-night (I have done it elsewhere before now); but I proceed to apply the principle to ourselves in a more searching manner.

I notice that among all the new buildings which cover your once wild hills, churches and schools are mixed in due, that is to say, in large proportion, with your mills and mansions; and I notice also that the churches and schools are almost always Gothic, and the mansions and mills are never Gothic. May I ask the meaning of this? for, remember, it is peculiarly a modern phenomenon. When Gothic was invented, houses were Gothic as well as churches; and when the Italian style superseded the Gothic, churches were Italian as well as houses. If there is a Gothic spire to the cathedral of Antwerp, there is a Gothic belfry to the Hôtel de Ville at Brussels; if Inigo Jones builds an Italian Whitehall, Sir Christopher Wren builds an Italian St. Paul's. But now you live under one school of architecture, and worship under another. What do you mean by doing this? Am I to understand that you are thinking of changing your architecture back to Gothic; and that you treat your churches experimentally, because it does not matter what mistakes you make in a church? Or am I to understand that you consider Gothic a pre-eminently sacred and beautiful mode of building, which you think, like the fine frankincense, should be mixed for the tabernacle only, and reserved for your religious services? For if this be the feeling, though it may seem at first as if it were graceful and reverent, at the root of the matter, it signifies neither more nor less than that you have separated your religion from your life.

For consider what a wide significance this fact has; and remember that it is not you only, but all the people of England, who are behaving thus, just now.

You have all got into the habit of calling the church "the house of God." I have seen, over the doors of many churches, the legend actually carved, "*This* is the house of God and this is the gate of heaven." Now, note where that legend comes from, and of what place it was first spoken. A boy leaves his father's house to go on a long journey on foot, to visit his uncle: he has to cross a wild hill-desert; just as if one of your own boys had to cross the wolds to visit an uncle at Carlisle. The second or third day your boy finds himself somewhere between Hawes and Brough, in the midst of the moors, at sunset. It is stony ground, and boggy; he cannot go one foot farther that night. Down he lies, to sleep, on Wharnside, where best he may, gathering a few of the stones together to put under his head;—so wild the place is, he cannot get anything but stones. And there, lying under the broad night, he has a dream; and he sees a ladder set up on the earth, and the top of it reaches to heaven, and the angels of God are seen ascending and descending upon it. And when he wakes out of his sleep, he says, "How dreadful is this place; surely this is none other than the house of God, and this is the gate of heaven." This PLACE, observe; not this church; not this city; not this stone, even, which he puts up for a memorial—the piece of flint on which his head was lain. But this *place;* this windy slope of Wharnside; this moorland hollow, torrent-bitten, snow-blighted! this *any* place where God lets down the ladder. And how are you to know where that will be? or how are you to determine where it may be, but by being ready for it always? Do you know where the lightning is to fall next? You *do* know that, partly; you can guide the lightning; but you cannot guide the going forth of the Spirit, which is as that lightning when it shines from the east to the west.

But the perpetual and insolent warping of that strong verse to serve a merely ecclesiastical purpose, is only one of the thousand instances in which we sink back into gross Judaism. We call our churches

10. **Armstrongs,** big guns, named from William George, Baron Armstrong.   14. **black eagles,** Austrian insigne. **40–41. if Inigo Jones . . . St. Paul's.** Inigo Jones (1573–1652) designed the banqueting house at Whitehall, 1619–22. **Sir Christopher Wren** (1632–1723) rebuilt St. Paul's Cathedral after the great fire of 1666.

12–35. You have all got . . . gate of heaven." See Genesis 28: 10–22.

"temples." Now, you know perfectly well they are *not* temples. They have never had, never can have, anything whatever to do with temples. They are "synagogues"—"gathering places—"where you gather yourselves together as an assembly; and by not calling them so, you again miss the force of another mighty text—"Thou, when thou prayest, shalt not be as the hypocrites are; for they love to pray standing in the *churches*" [we should translate it], "that they may be seen of men. But thou, when thou prayest, enter into thy closet, and when thou hast shut thy door, pray to thy Father,"—which is, not in chancel nor in aisle, but "in secret."

Now, you feel, as I say this to you—I know you feel—as if I were trying to take away the honour of your churches. Not so; I am trying to prove to you the honour of your houses and your hills; not that the Church is not sacred—but that the whole Earth is. I would have you feel what careless, what constant, what infectious sin there is in all modes of thought, whereby, in calling your churches only "holy," you call your hearths and homes "profane"; and have separated yourselves from the heathen by casting all your household gods to the ground, instead of recognizing, in the places of their many and feeble Lares, the presence of your One and Mighty Lord and Lar. . . .

In all my past work, my endeavour has been to show that good architecture is essentially religious—the production of a faithful and virtuous, not of an infidel and corrupted people. But in the course of doing this, I have had also to show that good architecture is not *ecclesiastical*. People are so apt to look upon religion as the business of the clergy, not their own, that the moment they hear of anything depending on "religion," they think it must also have depended on the priesthood; and I have had to take what place was to be occupied between these two errors, and fight both, often with seeming contradiction. Good architecture is the work of good and believing men; therefore, you say, at least some people say, "Good architecture must essentially have been the work of the clergy, not of the laity." No— a thousand times no; good architecture has always been the work of the commonalty, *not* of the clergy. "What," you say, "those glorious cathedrals—the pride of Europe—did their builders not form Gothic architecture?" No; they corrupted Gothic architecture. Gothic was formed in the baron's castle, and the burgher's street. It was formed by the thoughts, and hands, and powers of labouring citizens and warrior kings. By the monk it was used as an instrument for the aid of his superstition; when that superstition became a beautiful madness, and the best hearts of Europe vainly dreamed and pined in the cloister, and vainly raged and perished in the crusade,—through that fury of perverted faith and wasted war, the Gothic rose also to its loveliest, most fantastic, and, finally, most foolish dreams; and in those dreams was lost.

I hope, now, that there is no risk of your misunderstanding me when I come to the gist of what I want to say to-night;—when I repeat, that every great national architecture has been the result and exponent of a great national religion. You can't have bits of it here, bits there—you must have it everywhere or nowhere. It is not the monopoly of a clerical company—it is not the exponent of a theological dogma—it is not the hieroglyphic writing of an initiated priesthood; it is the manly language of a people inspired by resolute and common purpose, and rendering resolute and common fidelity to the legible laws of an undoubted God.

Now there have as yet been three distinct schools of European architecture. I say, European, because Asiatic and African architectures belong so entirely to other races and climates, that there is no question of them here; only, in passing, I will simply assure you that whatever is good or great in Egypt, and Syria, and India, is just as good or great for the same reasons as the buildings on our side of the Bosphorus. We Europeans, then, have had three great religions: the Greek, which was the worship of the God of Wisdom and Power; the Mediaeval, which was the worship of the God of Judgment and Consolation; the Renaissance, which was the worship of the God of Pride and Beauty: these three we have had—they are past,—and now, at last, we English have got a fourth religion, and a God of our own, about which I want to ask you. But I must explain these three old ones first.

I repeat, first, the Greeks essentially worshipped the God of Wisdom; so that whatever contended against their religion,—to the Jews a stumblingblock,—was, to the Greeks—*Foolishness.*

The first Greek idea of deity was that expressed in the word, of which we keep the remnant in our words "*Di*-urnal" and "*Di*-vine"—the god of *Day,* Jupiter the revealer. Athena is his daughter, but especially daughter of the Intellect, springing armed from the head. We are only with the help of recent investigation beginning to penetrate the depth of meaning couched under the Athenaic

---

7–13. "Thou, when thou prayest . . . in secret." See Matthew 6:5–6.   26. Lares, Roman household gods.

43–44. to the Jews . . . Foolishness. See 1 Corinthians 1:23.

symbols: but I may note rapidly, that her aegis, the mantle with the serpent fringes, in which she often, in the best statues, is represented as folding up her left hand, for better guard; and the Gorgon, on her shield, are both representative mainly of the chilling horror and sadness (turning men to stone, as it were,) of the outmost and superficial spheres of knowledge—that knowledge which separates, in bitterness, hardness, and sorrow, the heart of the full-grown man from the heart of the child. For out of imperfect knowledge spring terror, dissension, danger, and disdain; but from perfect knowledge, given by the full-revealed Athena, strength and peace, in sign of which she is crowned with the olive spray, and bears the resistless spear.

This, then, was the Greek conception of purest Deity; and every habit of life, and every form of his art developed themselves from the seeking this bright, serene, resistless wisdom; and setting himself, as a man, to do things evermore rightly and strongly; not with any ardent affection or ultimate hope; but with a resolute and continent energy of will, as knowing that for failure there was no consolation, and for sin there was no remission. And the Greek architecture rose unerring, bright, clearly defined, and self-contained.

Next followed in Europe the great Christian faith, which was essentially the religion of Comfort. Its great doctrine is the remission of sins; for which cause, it happens, too often, in certain phases of Christianity, that sin and sickness themselves are partly glorified, as if, the more you had to be healed of, the more divine was the healing. The practical result of this doctrine, in art, is a continual contemplation of sin and disease, and of imaginary states of purification from them; thus we have an architecture conceived in a mingled sentiment of melancholy and aspiration, partly severe, partly luxuriant, which will bend itself to every one of our needs, and every one of our fancies, and be strong or weak with us, as we are strong or weak ourselves. It is, of all architecture, the basest, when base people build it—of all, the noblest, when built by the noble.

And now note that both these religions—Greek and Mediaeval—perished by falsehood in their own main purpose. The Greek religion of Wisdom perished in a false philosophy—"Oppositions of science, falsely so called." The Mediaeval religion of Consolation perished in false comfort; in remission of sins given lyingly. It was the selling of absolution that ended the Mediaeval faith; and I can tell you more, it is the selling of absolution which, to the end of time, will mark false Christianity. Pure Christianity gives her remission of sins only by *ending* them; but false Christianity gets her remission of sins by *compounding for* them. And there are many ways of compounding for them. We English have beautiful little quiet ways of buying absolution, whether in low Church or high, far more cunning than any of Tetzel's trading.

Then, thirdly, there followed the religion of Pleasure, in which all Europe gave itself to luxury, ending in death. First, *bals masqués* in every saloon, and then guillotines in every square. And all these three worships issue in vast temple building. Your Greek worshipped Wisdom, and built you the Parthenon—the Virgin's temple. The Mediaeval worshipped Consolation, and built you Virgin temples also—but to our Lady of Salvation. Then the Revivalist worshipped beauty, of a sort, and built you Versailles and the Vatican. Now, lastly, will you tell me what *we* worship, and what *we* build?

You know we are speaking always of the real, active, continual, national worship; that by which men act, while they live; not that which they talk of, when they die. Now, we have, indeed, a nominal religion, to which we pay tithes of property and sevenths of time; but we have also a practical and earnest religion, to which we devote nine-tenths of our property and six-sevenths of our time. And we dispute a great deal about the nominal religion: but we are all unanimous about this practical one; of which I think you will admit that the ruling goddess may be best generally described as the "Goddess of Getting-on," or "Britannia of the Market." The Athenians had an "Athena Agoraia," or Athena of the Market; but she was a subordinate type of their goddess, while our Britannia Agoraia is the principal type of ours. And all your great architectural works are, of course, built to her. It is long since you built a great cathedral; and how you would laugh at me if I proposed building a cathedral on

4. **Gorgon,** in Greek mythology, three snaky-haired sisters whose aspect turned beholders to stone; the best-known, Medusa, was slain by Perseus.

9. **Tetzel's trading.** For the theory of indulgences (never "a selling of absolution"), see art. "Indulgences," *Catholic Encyclopaedia.* Indulgences were abused by unscrupulous men (like Chaucer's Pardoner). Johann Tetzel (c. 1460–1519), who sold indulgences in Germany, aroused Martin Luther, and thus contributed to the Reformation. 12. **bals masqués,** masked balls, masquerades. 16. **Parthenon,** built on the Acropolis, Athens, fifth century B.C. 16–18. **The Mediaeval . . . Salvation,** see Henry Adams's excellent description of Chartres Cathedral in *Mont Saint Michel and Chartres,* Houghton Mifflin, c. 1904, especially chaps. VI, X, XIII. 19. **Revivalist,** of classical architecture. 20. **Versailles and the Vatican.** The palace at Versailles dates chiefly from 1661; it was restored under Louis-Philippe (1830–48). The beginnings of the Vatican, as we know it today, go back at least to Nicholas V (1447–55).

the top of one of these hills of yours, to make it an Acropolis! But your railroad mounds, vaster than the walls of Babylon; your railroad stations, vaster than the temple of Ephesus, and innumerable; your chimneys, how much more mighty and costly than cathedral spires! your harbour-piers; your warehouses; your exchanges!—all these are built to your great Goddess of "Getting-on"; and she has formed, and will continue to form, your architecture, as long as you worship her; and it is quite vain to ask me to tell you how to build to *her*; you know far better than I.

There might, indeed, on some theories, be a conceivably good architecture for Exchanges—that is to say, if there were any heroism in the fact or deed of exchange, which might be typically carved on the outside of your building. For, you know, all beautiful architecture must be adorned with sculpture or painting; and for sculpture or painting, you must have a subject. And hitherto it has been a received opinion among the nations of the world that the only right subjects for either, were *heroisms* of some sort. Even on his pots and his flagons, the Greek put a Hercules slaying lions, or an Apollo slaying serpents, or Bacchus slaying melancholy giants, and earthborn despondencies. On his temples, the Greek put contests of great warriors in founding states, or of gods with evil spirits. On his houses and temples alike, the Christian put carvings of angels conquering devils; or of hero-martyrs exchanging this world for another; subject inappropriate, I think, to our direction of exchange here. And the Master of Christians not only left His followers without any orders as to the sculpture of affairs of exchange on the outside of buildings, but gave some strong evidence of His dislike of affairs of exchange within them. And yet there might surely be a heroism in such affairs; and all commerce become a kind of selling of doves, not impious. The wonder has always been great to me, that heroism has never been supposed to be in anywise consistent with the practice of supplying people with food, or clothes; but rather with that of quartering one's self upon them for food, and stripping them of their clothes. Spoiling of armour is an heroic deed in all ages; but the selling of clothes, old or new, has never taken any colour of

magnanimity. Yet one does not see why feeding the hungry and clothing the naked should ever become base businesses, even when engaged in on a large scale. If one could contrive to attach the notion of conquest to them anyhow! so that, supposing there were anywhere an obstinate race, who refused to be comforted, one might take some pride in giving them compulsory comfort! and, as it were, "*occupying* a country" with one's gifts, instead of one's armies? If one could only consider it as much a victory to get a barren field sown, as to get an eared field stripped; and contend who should build villages, instead of who should "carry" them! Are not all forms of heroism conceivable in doing these serviceable deeds? You doubt who is strongest? It might be ascertained by push of spade, as well as push of sword. Who is wisest? There are witty things to be thought of in planning other business than campaigns. Who is bravest? There are always the elements to fight with, stronger than men; and nearly as merciless.

The only absolutely and unapproachably heroic element in the soldier's work seems to be—that he is paid little for it—and regularly: while you traffickers, and exchangers, and others occupied in presumably benevolent business, like to be paid much for it—and by chance. I never can make out how it is that a *knight*-errant does not expect to be paid for his trouble, but a *pedlar*-errant always does;—that people are willing to take hard knocks for nothing, but never to sell ribands cheap; that they are ready to go on fervent crusades, to recover the tomb of a buried God, but never on any travels to fulfil the orders of a living one;—that they will go anywhere barefoot to preach their faith, but must be well bribed to practise it, and are perfectly ready to give the Gospel gratis, but never the loaves and fishes.

If you chose to take the matter up on any such soldierly principle; to do your commerce, and your feeding of nations, for fixed salaries; and to be as particular about giving people the best food, and the best cloth, as soldiers are about giving them the best gunpowder, I could carve something for you on your exchange worth looking at. But I can only at present suggest decorating its frieze with pendant purses; and making its pillars broad at the base, for the sticking of bills. And in the innermost chambers of it there might be a statue of Britannia of the Market, who may have, perhaps advisably, a partridge for her crest, typical at once of her courage

---

4. **temple of Ephesus,** in Asia Minor. The temple was sacred to Diana.   24. **Hercules,** the great, half-divine "strong man" of Greek mythology. **Apollo,** the god of manly beauty, poetry, music, etc. **Bacchus,** the god of wine. For the particular adventures referred to, see Gayley's *Classic Myths,* or some similar handbook of mythology. 36–37. **gave some strong evidence . . . them,** when he drove the money-changers out of the Temple; see Matthew 21:12–13.

32–33. **to go . . . God,** as western Europe did in the Crusades (11th, 12th, 13th centuries). 37–38. **the loaves and fishes.** See Matthew 14:19, 15:36.

in fighting for noble ideas, and of her interest in game; and round its neck, the inscription in golden letters, "Perdix fovit quae non peperit." Then, for her spear, she might have a weaver's beam; and on her shield, instead of St. George's Cross, the Milanese boar, semi-fleeced, with the town of Gennesaret proper, in the field; and the legend, "In the best market," and her corslet, of leather, folded over her heart in the shape of a purse, with thirty slits in it, for a piece of money to go in at, on each day of the month. And I doubt not but that the people would come to see your exchange, and its goddess, with applause.

Nevertheless, I want to point out to you certain strange characters in this goddess of yours. She differs from the great Greek and Mediaeval deities essentially in two things—first, as to the continuance of her presumed power; secondly, as to the extent of it.

First, as to the Continuance.

The Greek Goddess of Wisdom gave continual increase of wisdom, as the Christian Spirit of Comfort (or Comforter) continual increase of comfort. There was no question, with these, of any limit or cessation of function. But with your Agora Goddess, that is just the most important question. Getting on—but where to? Gathering together—but how much? Do you mean to gather always—never to spend? If so, I wish you joy of your goddess, for I am just as well off as you, without the trouble of worshipping her at all. But if you do not spend, somebody else will—somebody else must. And it is because of this (among many other such errors) that I have fearlessly declared your so-called science of Political Economy to be no science; because, namely, it has omitted the study of exactly the most important branch of the business—the study of *spending*. For spend you must, and as much as you make, ultimately. You gather corn:—will you bury England under a heap of grain; or will you, when you have gathered, finally eat? You gather gold:—will you make your house-roofs of it, or pave your streets with it? That is still one way of spending it. But if you keep it, that you may get more, I'll give you more; I'll give you all the gold you want—all you can imagine—if you can tell me what you'll do with it. You shall have thousands of gold pieces;—thousands of thousands—millions—mountains, of gold: where will you keep them? Will you put an Olympus of silver upon a golden Pelion—make Ossa like a wart? Do you think the rain and dew would then come down to you, in the streams from such mountains, more blessedly than they will down the mountains which God has made for you, of moss and whinstone? But it is not gold that you want to gather! What is it? greenbacks? No; not those neither. What is it then—is it ciphers after a capital I? Cannot you practise writing ciphers, and write as many as you want! Write ciphers for an hour every morning, in a big book, and say every evening, I am worth all those naughts more than I was yesterday. Won't that do? Well, what in the name of Plutus is it you want? Not gold, not greenbacks, not ciphers after a capital I? You will have to answer, after all, "No; we want, somehow or other, money's *worth*." Well, what is that? Let your Goddess of Getting-on discover it, and let her learn to stay therein.

But there is yet another question to be asked respecting this Goddess of Getting-on. The first was of the continuance of her power; the second is of its extent.

Pallas and the Madonna were supposed to be all the world's Pallas, and all the world's Madonna. They could teach all men, and they could comfort all men. But, look strictly into the nature of the power of your Goddess of Getting-on; and you will find she is the Goddess—not of everybody's getting on—but only of somebody's getting on. This is a vital, or rather deathful, distinction. Examine it in your own ideal of the state of national life which this Goddess is to evoke and maintain. I asked you what it was, when I was last here;—you have never told me. Now, shall I try to tell you?

Your ideal of human life then is, I think, that it should be passed in a pleasant undulating world, with iron and coal everywhere underneath it. On each pleasant bank of this world is to be a beautiful mansion, with two wings; and stables, and coach-houses; a moderately-sized park; a large garden and hot-houses; and pleasant carriage drives through the shrubberies. In this mansion are to live the favoured votaries of the Goddess; the English gentleman, with his gracious wife, and his

3. "Perdix . . . peperit." See Jeremiah 17:11—"As the partridge sitteth on eggs, and hatcheth them not; so he that getteth riches, and not by right, shall leave them in the midst of his days, and at his end shall be a fool." 5. St. George's Cross, worn by Knights of the Garter. 6. the town of Gennesaret. There is no "town of Gennesaret" in the New Testament. The "land of Gennesaret" is mentioned twice—in Matthew 14:34-36 and Mark 6:53-56. Neither passage throws any light on what Ruskin may have had in mind in this reference. 9. with thirty slits in it, possibly an allusion to the thirty pieces of silver Judas received for betraying Jesus; see Matthew 26:14-16.

5. Olympus, the mountain-home of the Greek pantheon. Pelion, Ossa, mountains piled one atop the other by the giants in trying to scale Olympus; see *Hamlet* Act V, sc. 1, l. 305. 18. Plutus, the god of riches. 28. Pallas, Athena, Minerva.

beautiful family; he always able to have the boudoir and the jewels for the wife, and the beautiful ball dresses for the daughters, and hunters for the sons, and a shooting in the Highlands for himself. At the bottom of the bank, is to be the mill; not less than a quarter of a mile long, with one steam engine at each end, and two in the middle, and a chimney three hundred feet high. In this mill are to be in constant employment from eight hundred to a thousand workers, who never drink, never strike, always go to church on Sunday, and always express themselves in respectful language.

Is not that, broadly, and in the main features, the kind of thing you propose to yourselves? It is very pretty indeed, seen from above; not at all so pretty, seen from below. For, observe, while to one family this deity is indeed the Goddess of Getting-on, to a thousand families she is the Goddess of *not* Getting-on. "Nay," you say, "they have all their chance." Yes, so has every one in a lottery, but there must always be the same number of blanks. "Ah! but in a lottery it is not skill and intelligence which take the lead, but blind chance." What then! do you think the old practice, that "they should take who have the power, and they should keep who can," is less iniquitous, when the power has become power of brains instead of fist? and that, though we may not take advantage of a child's or a woman's weakness, we may of a man's foolishness? "Nay, but finally, work must be done, and some one must be at the top, some one at the bottom." Granted, my friends. Work must always be, and captains of work must always be; and if you in the least remember the tone of any of my writings, you must know that they are thought unfit for this age, because they are always insisting on need of government, and speaking with scorn of liberty. But I beg you to observe that there is a wide difference between being captains or governors of work, and taking the profits of it. It does not follow, because you are general of an army, that you are to take all the treasure, or land, it wins; (if it fight for treasure or land); neither, because you are king of a nation, that you are to consume all the profits of the nation's work. Real kings, on the contrary, are known invariably by their doing quite the reverse of this—by their taking the least possible quantity of the nation's work for themselves. There is no test of real kinghood so infallible as that. Does the crowned creature live simply, bravely, unostentatiously? probably he *is* a King. Does he cover his body with jewels, and his table with delicates? in all probability he is *not* a King. It is possible he may be, as Solomon was; but that is when the nation shares his splendour with him. Solomon made gold, not only to be in his own palace as stones, but to be in Jerusalem as stones. But, even so, for the most part, these splendid kinghoods expire in ruin, and only the true kinghoods live, which are of royal labourers governing loyal labourers; who, both leading rough lives, establish the true dynasties. Conclusively you will find that because you are king of a nation, it does not follow that you are to gather for yourself all the wealth of that nation; neither, because you are king of a small part of the nation, and lord over the means of its maintenance—over field, or mill, or mine,—are you to take all the produce of that piece of the foundation of national existence for yourself.

You will tell me I need not preach against these things, for I cannot mend them. No, good friends, I cannot; but you can, and you will; or something else can and will. Even good things have no abiding power—and shall these evil things persist in victorious evil? All history shows, on the contrary, that to be the exact thing they never can do. Change *must* come; but it is ours to determine whether change of growth, or change of death. Shall the Parthenon be in ruins on its rock, and Bolton priory in its meadow, but these mills of yours be the consummation of the buildings of the earth, and their wheels be as the wheels of eternity? Think you that "men may come, and men may go," but—mills—go on for ever? Not so; out of these, better or worse shall come; and it is for you to choose which.

I know that none of this wrong is done with deliberate purpose. I know, on the contrary, that you wish your workmen well; that you do much for them, and that you desire to do more for them, if you saw your way to such benevolence safely. I know that even all this wrong and misery are brought about by a warped sense of duty, each of you striving to do his best; but, unhappily, not knowing for whom this best should be done. And all our hearts have been betrayed by the plausible impiety of the modern economist, telling us that, "To do the best for ourselves, is finally to do the best for others." Friends, our great Master said not so; and most absolutely we shall find this world is not made so. Indeed, to do the best for others, is finally to do the best for ourselves; but it will not do to have our eyes fixed on that issue. . . .

1. **Solomon**, King of Israel, 9th century B.C.; for his wealth, see 1 Kings 10:14–23.   **26. Bolton priory,** an abbey in Yorkshire.   **29–30. "men . . . for ever,** a reference to Tennyson's poem, "The Brook."

from FORS CLAVIGERA

In Letter 2 of *Fors Clavigera* (1871–84), Ruskin presented a detailed explanation of his title. Fors "is the best part of three good English words, Force, Fortitude, and Fortune." Clava means club; clavis, key; clavus, nail. "Clavigera may mean, therefore, either Club-bearer, Key-bearer, or Nail-bearer." Hence "Fors, the Club-bearer, means the strength of Hercules, or of Deed. Fors, the Key-bearer, means the strength of Ulysses, or of Patience. Fors, the Nail-bearer, means the strength of Lycurgus, or of Law."

Letter 58

The Catholic Prayer

"Deus, a quo sancta desideria, recta consilia, et justa sunt opera, da servis tuis illam quam mundus dare non potest pacem, ut et corda nostra mandatis tuis, et, hostium sublata formidine, tempora, sint tuâ protectione tranquilla."

"God, from whom are all holy desires, right counsels, and just works, give to Thy servants that peace which the world cannot, that both our hearts, in Thy commandments, and our times, the fear of enemies being taken away, may be calm under Thy guard."

THE adulteration of this great Catholic prayer in our English church-service (as needless as it was senseless, since the pure form of it contains nothing but absolutely Christian prayer, and is as fit for the most stammering Protestant lips as for Dante's), destroyed all the definite meaning of it, and left merely the vague expression of desire for peace, on quite unregarded terms. For of the millions of people who utter the prayer at least weekly, there is not one in a thousand who is ever taught, or can for themselves find out, either what a holy desire means, or a right counsel means, or a just work means,—or what the world is, or what the peace is which it cannot give. And half-an-hour after they have insulted God by praying to Him in this deadest of all dead languages, not understood of the people, they leave the church, themselves pacified in their perennial determination to put no check on their natural covetousness; to act on their own opinions, be they right or wrong; to do whatever they can make money by, be it just or unjust; and to thrust themselves, with the utmost of their soul and strength, to the highest, by them attainable, pinnacle of the most bedrummed and betrumpeted booth in the Fair of the World.

The prayer, in its pure text, is essentially, indeed, a monastic one; but it is written for the great Monastery of the Servants of God, whom the world hates. It cannot be uttered with honesty but by these; nor can it ever be answered but with the peace bequeathed to these, "not as the world giveth."

Of which peace, the nature is not to be without war, but undisturbed in the midst of war; and not without enemies, but without fear of them. It is a peace without pain, because desiring only what is holy; without anxiety, because it thinks only what is right; without disappointment, because a just work is always successful; without sorrow, because "great peace have they which love Thy Law, and nothing shall offend them"; and without terror, because the God of all battles is its Guard.

So far as any living souls in the England of this day can use, understandingly, the words of this collect, they are already, consciously or not, companions of all good labourers in the vineyard of God. For those who use it reverently, yet have never set themselves to find out what the commandments of God are, nor how lovable they are, nor how far, instead of those commandments, the laws of the world are the only code they care for, nor how far they still think their own thoughts and speak their own words, it is assuredly time to search out these things. And I believe that, after having searched them out, no sincerely good and religious person would find, whatever his own particular form of belief might be, anything which he could reasonably refuse, or which he ought in anywise to fear to profess before all men, in the following statement of creed and resolution, which must be written with their own hand, and signed, with the solemnity of a vow, by every person received into the St. George's Company.

   I. I trust in the Living God, Father Almighty, Maker of heaven and earth, and of all things and creatures visible and invisible.

    I trust in the kindness of His law, and the goodness of His work.

    And I will strive to love Him, and keep His law, and see His work, while I live.

   II. I trust in the nobleness of human nature, in the majesty of its faculties, the fulness of its mercy, and the joy of its love.

    And I will strive to love my neighbour as myself, and, even when I cannot, will act as if I did.

   III. I will labour, with such strength and oppor-

3–4. "not . . . giveth." See John 14:27. 12–13. "great . . . them." See Psalms 119:165. 35. St. George's Company, see general introduction to Ruskin, pages 621–622.

tunity as God gives me, for my own daily bread; and all that my hand finds to do, I will do with my might.

IV. I will not deceive, or cause to be deceived, any human being for my gain or pleasure; nor hurt, or cause to be hurt, any human being for my gain or pleasure; nor rob, or cause to be robbed, any human being for my gain or pleasure.

V. I will not kill nor hurt any living creature needlessly, nor destroy any beautiful thing, but will strive to save and comfort all gentle life, and guard and perfect all natural beauty, upon the earth.

VI. I will strive to raise my own body and soul daily into higher powers of duty and happiness; not in rivalship or contention with others, but for the help, delight, and honour of others, and for the joy and peace of my own life.

VII. I will obey all the laws of my country faithfully; and the orders of its monarch, and of all persons appointed to be in authority under its monarch, so far as such laws or commands are consistent with what I suppose to be the law of God; and when they are not, or seem in anywise to need change, I will oppose them loyally and deliberately, not with malicious, concealed, or disorderly violence.

VIII. And with the same faithfulness, and under the limits of the same obedience, which I render to the laws of my country, and the commands of its rulers, I will obey the laws of the Society called of St. George, into which I am this day received; and the orders of its masters, and of all persons appointed to be in authority under its masters, so long as I remain a Companion, called of St. George.

Matthew Arnold
1822–1888

"My poems represent, on the whole," so Matthew Arnold wrote his mother, "the main movement of mind of the last quarter of a century, and thus they will probably have their day as people become conscious to themselves of what that movement of mind is, and interested in the literary productions which reflect it. It might fairly be urged that I have less poetical sentiment than Tennyson, and less intellectual vigour and abundance than Browning; yet, because I have perhaps more of a fusion of the two than either of them, and have more regularly applied that fusion to the main line of modern development, I am likely enough to have my turn, as they have had theirs."

Matthew Arnold was born at Laleham, December 24, 1822, the son of Thomas Arnold, soon to become as headmaster of Rugby one of the great English teachers of his day. Matthew's own education included both Rugby and Oxford; he taught briefly at Rugby, and became a fellow of Oriel College, Oxford, in 1845. For four years he acted as secretary to Lord Landsdowne; in 1851 he married, and was appointed inspector of schools. This onerous position he held for many years, preparing elaborate reports on both English and continental schools with meticulous care. In 1883–84

he lectured in the United States. He died of heart failure at Liverpool, April 15, 1888.

Arnold's early poems appeared in The Strayed Reveller, 1849, and Empedocles on Etna, 1852, both "by A," and both withdrawn from circulation by the author. The first volume to which he put his name was Poems, 1853. Many reprints were included in Poems, Second Series, 1855, and in the inaccurately titled New Poems, 1867. Merope, a classical tragedy, appeared in 1858. After 1867 Arnold wrote only a few more poems, elegies on friends and pets. The elegiac is, indeed, a dominant note in Arnold's poetry; a wistful, nostalgic melancholy holds his muse in thrall; he celebrates, as someone has said, his lost friends and his lost faith. Yet he is never possessed by the conventional Victorian sentimentalism.

The well of poetry dried up in him very early; possibly the Oxford professorship to which he was appointed in 1857 helped to turn his mind toward criticism. He had already shown his fine discernment as a critic, not only in the Preface to the 1853 volume but in many of the poems themselves. His first volume of criticism, On Translating Homer, 1861, is comparatively unimportant, but he found his stride with Essays in Criticism, 1865 (Second

Series, 1888). Though *On the Study of Celtic Literature*, 1867, has often been scoffed at, it defined aspects of the Celtic temperament which are generally accepted to this day. (Arnold returned to this theme in *Irish Essays and Others*, 1882). With *Culture and Anarchy*, 1869, he turned to the criticism of society; *Friendship's Garland*, 1871, is also in this field. Between 1870 and 1877 he published four books on religious themes—*St. Paul and Protestantism*, 1870; *Literature and Dogma*, 1873; *God and the Bible*, 1875; *Last Essays on Church and Religion*, 1877. *Mixed Essays* appeared in 1879, while *Discourses in America*, 1885, and *Civilization in the United States*, 1888 (he didn't find much) came out of the American tour.

Stuart Sherman pointed out that as a critic Arnold is judicial rather than either historical or impressionistic. The study of backgrounds he considered mere dilettantism unless it resulted in clearer understanding and greater enjoyment of the literature itself. He derived his standards from the classics, keeping great passages of classical literature in mind to serve as a touchstone in estimating as yet untested work. Poetry was for him a "criticism of life," and the value of the poet could not be divorced from the soundness of the criticism he presented. He considered Wordsworth England's chief poet since Milton, but he refused to swallow Wordsworth's sentimental pantheism. Goethe's naturalism influenced him profoundly, and his critical method was importantly affected by Sainte-Beuve.

In his social criticism Arnold stakes everything upon culture; if we would save society in a day of crumbling standards, we must find the best that men have thought and known and make it prevail. Here, again he finds his ideal in Greece. The England of his day he saw divided between Barbarians, Philistines, and Populace, with no higher ideal than that of doing as one likes, and without any particular consideration of the value of the thing done. Though he never subscribed to Carlyle's worship of the hero, he felt the lack in England of the continental notion of the state. He found the ideal of equality more highly respected in France than in England, because the French have a genius for society. But though he found both security and happiness quite impossible in the midst of suffering, he rejected all socialistic and communistic schemes as too much concerned with mere material well-being.

Religion, for Arnold, was "morality touched by emotion," God, "a stream of tendency, not ourselves, that makes for righteousness." On this basis he hoped to bring religion within the scope of his Goethean naturalism. He was sure that men could neither do without the Christian religion nor do

with it as at present constituted; he tried, therefore, to desupernaturalize it. The result was a kind of Christian agnosticism, if there is such a thing, or, as Gladstone put it, "He combined a sincere devotion to the Christian religion with a faculty for presenting it in such a form as to be recognisable neither by friend or foe." Actually he expected many of the functions of religion to be taken over by poetry. "Our religion has materialized itself in the fact, in the supposed fact; it has attached its emotion to the fact, and now the fact is failing it."

As a man, Arnold had nearly all the virtues. In his youth he was considered rather fantastically frivolous, and even in later years, a gay light manner concealed his real seriousness; perhaps this is why he was so definitely a social success in French salons. Some persons perceived and resented in him an air of superior, aristocratic aloofness; when the worshipful young Gamaliel Bradford met him on his American lecture tour, Arnold dashed the boy's enthusiasm somewhat by placing his hand on his shoulder and asking "What is the age?" But he was a man who found it impossible to shirk a duty, however unpleasant, and equally impossible to regard himself as a martyr for having performed it.

QUIET WORK

One lesson, Nature, let me learn of thee,
One lesson which in every wind is blown,
One lesson of two duties kept at one
Though the loud world proclaim their enmity—

Of toil unsevered from tranquillity!
Of labour, that in lasting fruit outgrows
Far noisier schemes, accomplished in repose,
Too great for haste, too high for rivalry!

Yes, while on earth a thousand discords ring,
Man's fitful uproar mingling with his toil   10
Still do thy sleepless ministers move on,

Their glorious tasks in silence perfecting;
Still working, blaming still our vain turmoil,
Labourers that shall not fail, when man is gone.

TO A FRIEND

Who prop, thou ask'st, in these bad days, my mind?—
He much, the old man, who, clearest-souled of men,

To a Friend. C. B. Tinker and H. F. Lowry in *The Poetry of Matthew Arnold: A Commentary*, Oxford Press, 1940, conjecture Arthur Hugh Clough (1819–1861), a Victorian poet whose affinity of spirit with Arnold was very close.   **2. the old man.** Homer.

Saw The Wide Prospect, and the Asian Fen,
And Tmolus hill, and Smyrna bay, though blind.

Much he, whose friendship I not long since won,
That halting slave, who in Nicopolis
Taught Arrian, when Vespasian's brutal son
Cleared Rome of what most shamed him. But be
   his

My special thanks, whose even-balanced soul,
From first youth tested up to extreme old age,   10
Business could not make dull, nor passion wild;

Who saw life steadily, and saw it whole;
The mellow glory of the Attic stage,
Singer of sweet Colonus, and its child.

SHAKESPEARE

Others abide our question. Thou art free.
We ask and ask—Thou smilest and art still,
Out-topping knowledge. For the loftiest hill,
Who to the stars uncrowns his majesty,

Planting his steadfast footsteps in the sea,
Making the heaven of heavens his dwelling-place,
Spares but the cloudy border of his base
To the foiled searching of mortality;

And thou, who didst the stars and sunbeams know,
Self-schooled, self-scanned, self-honoured, self-
   secure,
Didst tread on earth unguessed at.—Better so!   11

All pains the immortal spirit must endure,
All weakness which impairs, all griefs which bow,
Find their sole speech in that victorious brow.

IN HARMONY WITH NATURE

TO A PREACHER

"In harmony with Nature?" Restless fool,
Who with such heat dost preach what were to thee,
When true, the last impossibility—
To be like Nature strong, like Nature cool!

To a Friend. **3. The Wide Prospect,** Europe, a literal translation of the Greek Εὐρώπη. **Asian Fen,** marshlands in Asia
Minor, in the northwest corner of which Troy was situated.
4. Tmolus hill . . . Smyrna bay, a mountain and a seaport in Asia Minor.   **6. That halting slave,** Epictetus, Stoic
philosopher (c. 60–c. 120).   **7. Arrian,** Greek philosopher
and historian, a pupil of Epictetus (d. c. 180).   **7–8. Vespasian's . . . him.** Domitian, Roman Emperor from 81 to
96, who banished Epictetus.   **8. his,** Sophocles', the great
Athenian dramatist (497–406 B.C.).   **14. Colonus,** the birth-
place of Sophocles.

Know, man hath all which Nature hath, but more,
And in that *more* lie all his hopes of good.
Nature is cruel, man is sick of blood;
Nature is stubborn, man would fain adore;

Nature is fickle, man hath need of rest;
Nature forgives no debt, and fears no grave;   10
Man would be mild, and with safe conscience blest.

Man must begin, know this, where Nature ends;
Nature and man can never be fast friends.
Fool, if thou canst not pass her, rest her slave!

THE FORSAKEN MERMAN

Marriage between a human and a creature of the sea
is a familiar situation in folklore, but generally it is the
female that comes from the sea. The human may lose a
soul or the sea-creature gain one through such a union.

Come, dear children, let us away;
Down and away below!
Now my brothers call from the bay,
Now the great winds shoreward blow,
Now the salt tides seaward flow;
Now the wild white horses play,
Champ and chafe and toss in the spray.
Children dear, let us away!
This way, this way!

Call her once before you go—   10
Call once yet!
In a voice that she will know:
"Margaret! Margaret!"
Children's voices should be dear
(Call once more) to a mother's ear;
Children's voices, wild with pain—
Surely she will come again!
Call her once and come away;
This way, this way!
"Mother dear, we cannot stay!   20
The wild white horses foam and fret."
Margaret! Margaret!

Come, dear children, come away down;
Call no more!
One last look at the white-walled town,
And the little grey church on the windy shore;
Then come down!
She will not come though you call all day;
Come away, come away!

Children dear, was it yesterday   30
We heard the sweet bells over the bay?

In the caverns where we lay,
Through the surf and through the swell,
The far-off sound of a silver bell?
Sand-strewn caverns, cool and deep,
Where the winds are all asleep;
Where the spent lights quiver and gleam,
Where the salt weed sways in the stream,
Where the sea-beasts, ranged all round,
Feed in the ooze of their pasture-ground;   40
Where the sea-snakes coil and twine,
Dry their mail and bask in the brine;
Where great whales come sailing by,
Sail and sail, with unshut eye,
Round the world for ever and aye?
When did music come this way?
Children dear, was it yesterday?

Children dear, was it yesterday
(Call yet once) that she went away?
Once she sate with you and me,   50
On a red gold throne in the heart of the sea,
And the youngest sate on her knee.
She combed its bright hair, and she tended it well,
When down swung the sound of a far-off bell.
She sighed, she looked up through the clear green
   sea;
She said: "I must go, for my kinsfolk pray
In the little grey church on the shore to-day.
'Twill be Easter-time in the world—ah me!
And I lose my poor soul, Merman! here with thee."
I said: "Go up, dear heart, through the waves;   60
Say thy prayer, and come back to the kind sea-
   caves!"
She smiled, she went up through the surf in the bay.
Children dear, was it yesterday?

Children dear, were we long alone?
"The sea grows stormy, the little ones moan;
Long prayers," I said, "in the world they say;
Come!" I said; and we rose through the surf in the
   bay.
We went up the beach, by the sandy down
Where the sea-stocks bloom, to the white-walled
   town;
Through the narrow paved streets, where all was
   still,   70
To the little grey church on the windy hill.
From the church came a murmur of folk at their
   prayers,
But we stood without in the cold blowing airs.
We climbed on the graves, on the stones worn with
   rains,
And we gazed up the aisle through the small leaded
   panes.

She sate by the pillar; we saw her clear:
"Margaret, hist! come quick, we are here!
Dear heart," I said, "we are long alone;
The sea grows stormy, the little ones moan."
But, ah, she gave me never a look,   80
For her eyes were sealed to the holy book!
Loud prays the priest; shut stands the door.
Come away, children, call no more!
Come away, come down, call no more!

   Down, down, down!
Down to the depths of the sea!
She sits at her wheel in the humming town,
Singing most joyfully.
Hark what she sings: "O joy, O joy,
For the humming street, and the child with its toy!
For the priest, and the bell, and the holy well;   91
For the wheel where I spun,
And the blessed light of the sun!"
And so she sings her fill,
Singing most joyfully,
Till the spindle drops from her hand,
And the whizzing wheel stands still.
She steals to the window, and looks at the sand,
And over the sand at the sea;
And her eyes are set in a stare;   100
And anon there breaks a sigh,
And anon there drops a tear,
From a sorrow-clouded eye,
And a heart sorrow-laden,
A long, long sigh;
For the cold strange eye of a little Mermaiden
And the gleam of her golden hair.

   Come away, away children;
Come children, come down!
The hoarse wind blows coldly;   110
Lights shine in the town.
She will start from her slumber
When gusts shake the door;
She will hear the winds howling,
Will hear the waves roar.
We shall see, while above us
The waves roar and whirl,
A ceiling of amber,
A pavement of pearl.
Singing: "Here came a mortal,   120
But faithless was she!
And alone dwell for ever
The kings of the sea."

But, children, at midnight,
When soft the winds blow,
When clear falls the moonlight,

When spring-tides are low;
When sweet airs come seaward
From heaths starred with broom,
And high rocks throw mildly   130
On the blanched sands a gloom;
Up the still, glistening beaches,
Up the creeks we will hie,
Over banks of bright seaweed
The ebb-tide leaves dry.
We will gaze, from the sand-hills,
At the white, sleeping town;
At the church on the hill-side—
And then come back down.
Singing: "There dwells a loved one,   140
But cruel is she!
She left lonely for ever
The kings of the sea."

MEMORIAL VERSES

April, 1850

Goethe in Weimar sleeps, and Greece,
Long since, saw Byron's struggle cease.
But one such death remained to come;
The last poetic voice is dumb—
We stand to-day by Wordsworth's tomb.

When Byron's eyes were shut in death,
We bowed our head and held our breath.
He taught us little; but our soul
Had *felt* him like the thunder's roll.
With shivering heart the strife we saw   10
Of passion with eternal law;
And yet with reverential awe
We watched the fount of fiery life
Which served for that Titanic strife.

When Goethe's death was told, we said:
Sunk, then, is Europe's sagest head.
Physician of the iron age,
Goethe has done his pilgrimage.
He took the suffering human race,
He read each wound, each weakness clear;   20
And struck his finger on the place,
And said: *Thou ailest here, and here!*

1. **Goethe,** Johann Wolfgang von Goethe (1749–1832), the greatest German poet and a prime influence on Arnold. 1–2. **Greece . . . cease.** See the life of Byron, page 193 of this volume. 5. **to-day,** April, 1850. 14. **Titanic,** from the Titans of Greek mythology, who were overthrown by the Olympian gods. 17. **iron age,** in classical mythology the fourth, last, and worst of the periods of world history (gold, silver, brass, iron), here applied to the years of war and revolution through which Goethe lived and whose turmoil he ignored to devote himself to art.

He looked on Europe's dying hour
Of fitful dream and feverish power;
His eye plunged down the weltering strife,
The turmoil of expiring life—
He said: *The end is everywhere,
Art still has truth, take refuge there!*
And he was happy, if to know
Causes of things, and far below   30
His feet to see the lurid flow
Of terror, and insane distress,
And headlong fate, be happiness.

And Wordsworth!—Ah, pale ghosts, rejoice!
For never has such soothing voice
Been to your shadowy world conveyed,
Since erst, at morn, some wandering shade
Heard the clear song of Orpheus come
Through Hades, and the mournful gloom.
Wordsworth has gone from us—and ye,   40
Ah, may ye feel his voice as we!
He too upon a wintry clime
Had fallen—on this iron time
Of doubts, disputes, distractions, fears.
He found us when the age had bound
Our souls in its benumbing round;
He spoke, and loosed our heart in tears.
He laid us as we lay at birth
On the cool flowery lap of earth,
Smiles broke from us and we had ease;   50
The hills were round us, and the breeze
Went o'er the sun-lit fields again;
Our foreheads felt the wind and rain.
Our youth returned; for there was shed
On spirits that had long been dead,
Spirits dried up and closely furled,
The freshness of the early world.

Ah! since dark days still bring to light
Man's prudence and man's fiery might,
Time may restore us in his course   60
Goethe's sage mind and Byron's force;
But where will Europe's latter hour
Again find Wordsworth's healing power?
Others will teach us how to dare,
And against fear our breast to steel;
Others will strengthen us to bear—
But who, ah! who, will make us feel?
The cloud of mortal destiny,
Others will front it fearlessly—
But who, like him, will put it by?   70

29–33. **And he . . . happiness.** See Virgil, *Georgics*, II, ll. 490–92. 38. **Orpheus,** the legendary Greek musician who invaded Hades in search of his wife Eurydice. See Frances E. Sabin, *Classical Myths That Live Today*, Silver, Burdett, 1927.

Keep fresh the grass upon his grave
O Rotha, with thy living wave!
Sing him thy best! for few or none
Hears thy voice right, now he is gone.

SELF–DEPENDENCE

Weary of myself, and sick of asking
What I am, and what I ought to be,
At this vessel's prow I stand, which bears me
Forwards, forwards, o'er the starlit sea.

And a look of passionate desire
O'er the sea and to the stars I send:
"Ye who from my childhood up have calmed me,
Calm me, ah, compose me to the end!

"Ah, once more," I cried, "ye stars, ye waters,
On my heart your mighty charm renew;   10
Still, still let me, as I gaze upon you,
Feel my soul becoming vast like you!"

From the intense, clear, star-sown vault of heaven,
Over the lit sea's unquiet way,
In the rustling night-air came the answer:
"Wouldst thou *be* as these are? *Live* as they.

"Unaffrighted by the silence round them,
Undistracted by the sights they see,
These demand not that the things without them
Yield them love, amusement, sympathy.   20

"And with joy the stars perform their shining,
And the sea its long moon-silvered roll;
For self-poised they live, nor pine with noting
All the fever of some differing soul.

"Bounded by themselves, and unregardful
In what state God's other works may be,
In their own tasks all their powers pouring,
These attain the mighty life you see."

O air-born voice! long since, severely clear,
A cry like thine in mine own heart I hear: 30
"Resolve to be thyself; and know that he,
Who finds himself, loses his misery!"

A SUMMER NIGHT

In the deserted, moon-blanched street,
How lonely rings the echo of my feet!

72. **Rotha**, a stream near Grasmere, where Wordsworth is
buried.

Those windows, which I gaze at, frown,
Silent and white, unopening down,
Repellent as the world;—but see,
A break between the housetops shows
The moon! and, lost behind her, fading dim
Into the dewy dark obscurity
Down at the far horizon's rim,
Doth a whole tract of heaven disclose!   10

And to my mind the thought
Is on a sudden brought
Of a past night, and a far different scene.
Headlands stood out into the moonlit deep
As clearly as at noon;
The spring-tide's brimming flow
Heaved dazzlingly between;
Houses, with long white sweep,
Girdled the glistening bay;
Behind, through the soft air,   20
The blue haze-cradled mountains spread away,
The night was far more fair—
But the same restless pacings to and fro,
And the same vainly throbbing heart was there,
And the same bright, calm moon.

And the calm moonlight seems to say:
Hast thou then still the old unquiet breast,
Which neither deadens into rest,
Nor ever feels the fiery glow
That whirls the spirit from itself away,   30
But fluctuates to and fro,
Never by passion quite possessed
And never quite benumbed by the world's sway?—
And I, I know not if to pray
Still to be what I am, or yield and be
Like all the other men I see.

For most men in a brazen prison live,
Where, in the sun's hot eye,
With heads bent o'er their toil, they languidly
Their lives to some unmeaning taskwork give,   40
Dreaming of nought beyond their prison-wall.
And as, year after year,
Fresh products of their barren labour fall
From their tired hands, and rest
Never yet comes more near,
Gloom settles slowly down over their breast;
And while they try to stem
The waves of mournful thought by which they are
          prest,
Death in their prison reaches them,
Unfreed, having seen nothing, still unblest.   50

And the rest, a few,
Escape their prison and depart

On the wide ocean of life anew.
There the freed prisoner, where'er his heart
Listeth, will sail;
Nor doth he know how there prevail,
Despotic on that sea,
Trade-winds which cross it from eternity.
Awhile he holds some false way, undebarred
By thwarting signs, and braves   60
The freshening wind and blackening waves.
And then the tempest strikes him; and between
The lightning-bursts is seen
Only a driving wreck,
And the pale master on his spar-strewn deck
With anguished face and flying hair
Grasping the rudder hard,
Still bent to make some port he knows not where,
Still standing for some false, impossible shore.
And sterner comes the roar   70
Of sea and wind, and through the deepening gloom
Fainter and fainter wreck and helmsman loom,
And he too disappears, and comes no more.

Is there no life, but these alone?
Madman or slave, must man be one?

Plainness and clearness without shadow of stain!
Clearness divine!
Ye heavens, whose pure dark regions have no sign
Of languor, though so calm, and, though so great,
Are yet untroubled and unpassionate;   80
Who, though so noble, share in the world's toil,
And, though so tasked, keep free from dust and soil!
I will not say that your mild deeps retain
A tinge, it may be, of their silent pain
Who have longed deeply once, and longed in vain—
But I will rather say that you remain
A world above man's head, to let him see
How boundless might his soul's horizons be,
How vast, yet of what clear transparency!
How it were good to abide there, and breathe free;
How fair a lot to fill   91
Is left to each man still!

THE BURIED LIFE

Light flows our war of mocking words, and yet,
Behold, with tears mine eyes are wet!
I feel a nameless sadness o'er me roll.
Yes, yes, we know that we can jest,
We know, we know that we can smile!
But there's a something in this breast,
To which thy light words bring no rest,
And thy gay smiles no anodyne.

Give me thy hand, and hush awhile,
And turn those limpid eyes on mine,   10
And let me read there, love! thy inmost soul.

Alas! is even love too weak
To unlock the heart, and let it speak?
Are even lovers powerless to reveal
To one another what indeed they feel?
I knew the mass of men concealed
Their thoughts, for fear that if revealed
They would by other men be met
With blank indifference, or with blame reproved;
I knew they lived and moved   20
Tricked in disguises, alien to the rest
Of men, and alien to themselves—and yet
The same heart beats in every human breast!

But we, my love!—doth a like spell benumb
Our hearts, our voices?—must we too be dumb?

Ah! well for us, if even we,
Even for a moment, can get free
Our heart, and have our lips unchained;
For that which seals them hath been deep-ordained!

Fate, which foresaw   30
How frivolous a baby man would be—
By what distractions he would be possessed,
How he would pour himself in every strife,
And well-nigh change his own identity—
That it might keep from his capricious play
His genuine self, and force him to obey
Even in his own despite his being's law,
Bade through the deep recesses of our breast
The unregarded river of our life
Pursue with indiscernible flow its way;   40
And that we should not see
The buried stream, and seem to be
Eddying at large in blind uncertainty,
Though driving on with it eternally.

But often, in the world's most crowded streets,
But often, in the din of strife,
There rises an unspeakable desire
After the knowledge of our buried life;
A thirst to spend our fire and restless force
In tracking out our true, original course;   50
A longing to inquire
Into the mystery of this heart which beats
So wild, so deep in us—to know
Whence our lives come and where they go.
And many a man in his own breast then delves,
But deep enough, alas! none ever mines.
And we have been on many thousand lines,

And we have shown, on each, spirit and power;
But hardly have we, for one little hour,
Been on our own line, have we been ourselves— 60
Hardly had skill to utter one of all
The nameless feelings that course through our
    breast,
But they course on for ever unexpressed.
And long we try in vain to speak and act
Our hidden self, and what we say and do
Is eloquent, is well—but 'tis not true!
And then we will no more be racked
With inward striving, and demand
Of all the thousand nothings of the hour
Their stupefying power;   70
Ah yes, and they benumb us at our call!
Yet still, from time to time, vague and forlorn,
From the soul's subterranean depth upborne
As from an infinitely distant land,
Come airs, and floating echoes, and convey
A melancholy into all our day.

Only—but this is rare—
When a belovèd hand is laid in ours,
When, jaded with the rush and glare
Of the interminable hours,   80
Our eyes can in another's eyes read clear,
When our world-deafened ear
Is by the tones of a loved voice caressed—
A bolt is shot back somewhere in our breast,
And a lost pulse of feeling stirs again.
The eye sinks inward, and the heart lies plain,
And what we mean, we say, and what we would, we
    know.
A man becomes aware of his life's flow,
And hears its winding murmur; and he sees
The meadows where it glides, the sun, the breeze. 90

And there arrives a lull in the hot race
Wherein he doth for ever chase
That flying and elusive shadow, rest.
An air of coolness plays upon his face,
And an unwonted calm pervades his breast.
And then he thinks he knows
The hills where his life rose,
And the sea where it goes.

MORALITY

We cannot kindle when we will
    The fire which in the heart resides;
The spirit bloweth and is still,
    In mystery our soul abides.

1–4. We . . . abides. See John 3:8.

But tasks in hours of insight willed
Can be through hours of gloom fulfilled.

With aching hands and bleeding feet
We dig and heap, lay stone on stone;
We bear the burden and the heat
Of the long day, and wish 'twere done.   10
    Not till the hours of light return,
    All we have built do we discern.

Then, when the clouds are off the soul,
When thou dost bask in Nature's eye,
Ask, how *she* viewed thy self-control,
Thy struggling, tasked morality—
    Nature, whose free, light, cheerful air,
    Oft made thee, in thy gloom, despair.

And she, whose censure thou dost dread,
Whose eye thou wast afraid to seek,   20
See, on her face a glow is spread,
A strong emotion on her cheek!
    "Ah, child!" she cries, "that strife divine,
    Whence was it, for it is not mine?

"There is no effort on *my* brow—
I do not strive, I do not weep;
I rush with the swift spheres and glow
In joy, and when I will, I sleep.
    Yet that severe, that earnest air,
    I saw, I felt it once—but where?   30

"I knew not yet the gauge of time,
Nor wore the manacles of space;
I felt it in some other clime,
I saw it in some other place.
    'Twas when the heavenly house I trod,
    And lay upon the breast of God."

THE FUTURE

A wanderer is man from his birth.
He was born in a ship
On the breast of the river of Time;
Brimming with wonder and joy
He spreads out his arms to the light,
Rivets his gaze on the banks of the stream.

As what he sees is, so have his thoughts been.
Whether he wakes,
Where the snowy mountainous pass,
Echoing the screams of the eagles,   10
Hems in its gorges the bed
Of the new-born clear-flowing stream;

Whether he first sees light
Where the river in gleaming rings
Sluggishly winds through the plain;
Whether in sound of the swallowing sea—
As is the world on the banks,
So is the mind of the man.

Vainly does each, as he glides,
Fable and dream   20
Of the lands which the river of Time
Had left ere he woke on its breast,
Or shall reach when his eyes have been closed.
Only the tract where he sails
He wots of; only the thoughts,
Raised by the objects he passes, are his.

Who can see the green earth any more
As she was by the sources of Time?
Who imagines her fields as they lay
In the sunshine, unworn by the plough?   30
Who thinks as they thought,
The tribes who then roamed on her breast,
Her vigorous, primitive sons?

What girl
Now reads in her bosom as clear
As Rebekah read, when she sate
At eve by the palm-shaded well?
Who guards in her breast
As deep, as pellucid a spring
Of feeling, as tranquil, as sure?   40

What bard,
At the height of his vision, can deem
Of God, of the world, of the soul,
With a plainness as near,
As flashing as Moses felt
When he lay in the night by his flock
On the starlit Arabian waste?
Can rise and obey
The beck of the Spirit like him?

This tract which the river of Time   50
Now flows through with us, is the plain.
Gone is the calm of its earlier shore.
Bordered by cities and hoarse
With a thousand cries is its stream.
And we on its breast, our minds
Are confused as the cries which we hear,
Changing and shot as the sights which we see.

And we say that repose has fled
For ever the course of the river of Time.

36. **Rebekah.** See Genesis 24.   45. **Moses.** See Exodus 3.

That cities will crowd to its edge   60
In a blacker, incessanter line;
That the din will be more on its banks,
Denser the trade on its stream,
Flatter the plain where it flows,
Fiercer the sun overhead.
That never will those on its breast
See an ennobling sight,
Drink of the feeling of quiet again.

But what was before us we know not,
And we know not what shall succeed.   70

Haply, the river of Time—
As it grows, as the towns on its marge
Fling their wavering lights
On a wider, statelier stream—
May acquire, if not the calm
Of its early mountainous shore,
Yet a solemn peace of its own.

And the width of the waters, the hush
Of the grey expanse where he floats,
Freshening its current and spotted with foam
As it draws to the Ocean, may strike   81
Peace to the soul of the man on its breast—
As the pale waste widens around him,
As the banks fade dimmer away,
As the stars come out, and the night-wind
Brings up the stream
Murmurs and scents of the infinite sea.

SOHRAB AND RUSTUM

An Episode

The ultimate source of this story is the Persian epic
Shah Namah (*Book of Kings*) by Firdausi (c. 940–c. 1020).
Arnold's immediate source was Sir John Malcolm's *History of Persia*, 1825.

And the first grey of morning filled the east,
And the fog rose out of the Oxus stream.
But all the Tartar camp along the stream
Was hushed, and still the men were plunged in
    sleep;
Sohrab alone, he slept not; all night long
He had lain wakeful, tossing on his bed;
But when the grey dawn stole into his tent,
He rose, and clad himself, and girt his sword,
And took his horseman's cloak, and left his tent,

1. **And.** The beginning emphasizes the episodic nature
of the poem.   2. **Oxus,** a great river of central Asia, now
known as Amu Darya.   3. **Tartar camp.** Sohrab, a Persian
by birth, is in military service with the Tartars.

And went abroad into the cold wet fog,   10
Through the dim camp to Peran-Wisa's tent.
  Through the black Tartar tents he passed, which stood
Clustering like bee-hives on the low flat strand
Of Oxus, where the summer-floods o'erflow
When the sun melts the snows in high Pamere;
Through the black tents he passed, o'er that low strand,
And to a hillock came, a little back
From the stream's brink—the spot where first a boat,
Crossing the stream in summer, scrapes the land.
The men of former times had crowned the top   20
With a clay fort; but that was fall'n, and now
The Tartars built there Peran-Wisa's tent,
A dome of laths, and o'er it felts were spread.
And Sohrab came there, and went in, and stood
Upon the thick-piled carpets in the tent,
And found the old man sleeping on his bed
Of rugs and felts, and near him lay his arms.
And Peran-Wisa heard him, though the step
Was dulled; for he slept light, an old man's sleep;
And he rose quickly on one arm, and said:—   30
  "Who art thou? for it is not yet clear dawn.
Speak! is there news, or any night alarm?"
  But Sohrab came to the bedside, and said:—
"Thou know'st me, Peran-Wisa! it is I.
The sun is not yet risen, and the foe
Sleep; but I sleep not; all night long I lie
Tossing and wakeful, and I come to thee.
For so did King Afrasiab bid me seek
Thy counsel, and to heed thee as thy son,
In Samarcand, before the army marched;   40
And I will tell thee what my heart desires.
Thou know'st if, since from Ader-baijan first
I came among the Tartars and bore arms,
I have still served Afrasiab well, and shown,
At my boy's years, the courage of a man.
This too thou know'st, that while I still bear on
The conquering Tartar ensigns through the world,
And beat the Persians back on every field,
I seek one man, one man, and one alone—
Rustum, my father; who I hoped should greet,   50
Should one day greet, upon some well-fought field,
His not unworthy, not inglorious son.
So I long hoped, but him I never find.
Come then, hear now, and grant me what I ask.
Let the two armies rest to-day; but I
Will challenge forth the bravest Persian lords

To meet me, man to man; if I prevail,
Rustum will surely hear it; if I fall—
Old man, the dead need no one, claim no kin.
Dim is the rumour of a common fight,   60
Where host meets host, and many names are sunk;
But of a single combat fame speaks clear."
  He spoke; and Peran-Wisa took the hand
Of the young man in his, and sighed, and said:—
  "O Sohrab, an unquiet heart is thine!
Canst thou not rest among the Tartar chiefs,
And share the battle's common chance with us
Who love thee, but must press for ever first,
In single fight incurring single risk,
To find a father thou hast never seen?   70
That were far best, my son, to stay with us
Unmurmuring; in our tents, while it is war,
And when 'tis truce, then in Afrasiab's towns.
But, if this one desire indeed rules all,
To seek out Rustum—seek him not through fight!
Seek him in peace, and carry to his arms,
O Sohrab, carry an unwounded son!
But far hence seek him, for he is not here.
For now it is not as when I was young,
When Rustum was in front of every fray;   80
But now he keeps apart, and sits at home,
In Seistan, with Zal, his father old.
Whether that his own mighty strength at last
Feels the abhorred approaches of old age,
Or in some quarrel with the Persian King.
There go!—Thou wilt not? Yet my heart forebodes
Danger or death awaits thee on this field.
Fain would I know thee safe and well, though lost
To us; fain therefore send thee hence, in peace
To seek thy father, not seek single fights   90
In vain;—but who can keep the lion's cub
From ravening, and who govern Rustum's son?
Go, I will grant thee what thy heart desires."
  So said he, and dropped Sohrab's hand, and left
His bed, and the warm rugs whereon he lay;
And o'er his chilly limbs his woollen coat
He passed, and tied his sandals on his feet,
And threw a white cloak round him, and he took
In his right hand a ruler's staff, no sword;
And on his head he set his sheep-skin cap,   100
Black, glossy, curled, the fleece of Kara-Kul;
And raised the curtain of his tent, and called
His herald to his side, and went abroad.
  The sun by this had risen, and cleared the fog
From the broad Oxus and the glittering sands.
And from their tents the Tartar horsemen filed
Into the open plain; so Haman bade—

---

11. **Peran-Wisa,** the Tartar leader.   15. **Pamere,** a plateau in central Asia.   25. **thick-piled,** heavy-napped.
38. **Afrasiab,** the Tartar king.   40. **Samarcand,** the old Tartar capital in Turkestan.   42. **Ader-baijan,** a province in Persia.

82. **Seistan,** a region bordering southwestern Afghanistan and eastern Persia.   101. **Kara-Kul.** Karakul sheep, from the province of Bokhara, are valued for their fur.

Haman, who next to Peran-Wisa ruled
The host, and still was in his lusty prime.
From their black tents, long files of horse, they
    streamed;   110
As when some grey November morn the files,
In marching order spread, of long-necked cranes
Stream over Casbin and the southern slopes
Of Elburz, from the Aralian estuaries,
Or some frore Caspian reed-bed, southward bound
For the warm Persian sea-board—so they streamed.
The Tartars of the Oxus, the King's guard,
First, with black sheep-skin caps and with long
    spears;
Large men, large steeds; who from Bokhara come
And Khiva, and ferment the milk of mares.   120
Next, the more temperate Toorkmuns of the
    south,
The Tukas, and the lances of Salore,
And those from Attruck and the Caspian sands;
Light men and on light steeds, who only drink
The acrid milk of camels, and their wells.
And then a swarm of wandering horse, who came
From far, and a more doubtful service owned;
The Tartars of Ferghana, from the banks
Of the Jaxartes, men with scanty beards
And close-set skull-caps; and those wilder hordes 130
Who roam o'er Kipchak and the northern waste,
Kalmucks and unkempt Kuzzaks, tribes who stray
Nearest the Pole, and wandering Kirghizzes,
Who come on shaggy ponies from Pamere;
These all filed out from camp into the plain.
And on the other side the Persians formed;—
First a light cloud of horse, Tartars they seemed,
The Ilyats of Khorassan; and behind,
The royal troops of Persia, horse and foot,
Marshalled battalions bright in burnished steel. 140
But Peran-Wisa with his herald came,
Threading the Tartar squadrons to the front,
And with his staff kept back the foremost ranks.
And when Ferood, who led the Persians, saw
That Peran-Wisa kept the Tartars back,
He took his spear, and to the front he came,
And checked his ranks, and fixed them where they
    stood.
And the old Tartar came upon the sand
Betwixt the silent hosts, and spake, and said:—
    "Ferood, and ye, Persians and Tartars, hear! 150
Let there be truce between the hosts to-day.
But choose a champion from the Persian lords
To fight our champion Sohrab, man to man."

111 ff. As when . . . This is the first of many examples of
the so-called epic, or Homeric, simile in "Sohrab and Rustum." Compare Homer's *Iliad*. The following lines contain
specific references to many localities and tribes, mostly of
central Asia.

As, in the country, on a morn in June,
When the dew glistens on the pearlèd ears,
A shiver runs through the deep corn for joy—
So, when they heard what Peran-Wisa said,
A thrill through all the Tartar squadrons ran
Of pride and hope for Sohrab, whom they loved.
    But as a troop of pedlars, from Cabool,   160
Cross underneath the Indian Caucasus,
That vast sky-neighbouring mountain of milk snow,
Crossing so high, that, as they mount, they pass
Long flocks of travelling birds dead on the snow,
Choked by the air, and scarce can they themselves
Slake their parched throats with sugared mul-
    berries—
In single file they move, and stop their breath,
For fear they should dislodge the o'erhanging
    snows—
So the pale Persians held their breath with fear.
    And to Ferood his brother chiefs came up   170
To counsel; Gudurz and Zoarrah came,
And Feraburz, who ruled the Persian host
Second, and was the uncle of the King;
These came and counselled, and then Gudurz
    said:—
    "Ferood, shame bids us take their challenge up,
Yet champion have we none to match this youth.
He has the wild stag's foot, the lion's heart.
But Rustum came last night; aloof he sits
And sullen, and has pitched his tents apart.
Him will I seek, and carry to his ear   180
The Tartar challenge, and this young man's name.
Haply he will forget his wrath, and fight.
Stand forth the while, and take their challenge
    up."
    So spake he; and Ferood stood forth and cried:—
"Old man, be it agreed as thou hast said!
Let Sohrab arm, and we will find a man."
    He spake: and Peran-Wisa turned, and strode
Back through the opening squadrons to his tent.
But through the anxious Persians Gudurz ran,
And crossed the camp which lay behind, and
    reached,   190
Out on the sands beyond it, Rustum's tents.
Of scarlet cloth they were, and glittering gay,
Just pitched; the high pavilion in the midst
Was Rustum's, and his men lay camped around.
And Gudurz entered Rustum's tent, and found
Rustum; his morning meal was done, but still
The table stood before him, charged with food—
A side of roasted sheep, and cakes of bread,
And dark green melons; and there Rustum sate

156. corn, grain, wheat.   160. Cabool, Kabul, a city in
northern Afghanistan.   161. Indian Caucasus, the mountains between Turkestan and Afghanistan.

Listless, and held a falcon on his wrist, 200
And played with it; but Gudurz came and stood
Before him; and he looked, and saw him stand,
And with a cry sprang up and dropped the bird,
And greeted Gudurz with both hands, and said:—
"Welcome! these eyes could see no better sight.
What news? but sit down first, and eat and drink."
But Gudurz stood in the tent-door, and said:—
"Not now! a time will come to eat and drink,
But not to-day; to-day has other needs.
The armies are drawn out, and stand at gaze; 210
For from the Tartars is a challenge brought
To pick a champion from the Persian lords
To fight their champion—and thou know'st his
name—
Sohrab men call him, but his birth is hid.
O Rustum, like thy might is this young man's!
He has the wild stag's foot, the lion's heart;
And he is young, and Iran's chiefs are old,
Or else too weak; and all eyes turn to thee.
Come down and help us, Rustum, or we lose!"
He spoke; but Rustum answered with a smile:—
"Go to! if Iran's chiefs are old, then I 221
Am older; if the young are weak, the King
Errs strangely; for the King, for Kai Khosroo,
Himself is young, and honours younger men,
And lets the agèd moulder to their graves.
Rustum he loves no more, but loves the young—
The young may rise at Sohrab's vaunts, not I.
For what care I, though all speak Sohrab's fame?
For would that I myself had such a son,
And not that one slight helpless girl I have— 230
A son so famed, so brave, to send to war,
And I to tarry with the snow-haired Zal,
My father, whom the robber Afghans vex,
And clip his borders short, and drive his herds,
And he has none to guard his weak old age.
There would I go, and hang my armour up,
And with my great name fence that weak old man,
And spend the goodly treasures I have got,
And rest my age, and hear of Sohrab's fame,
And leave to death the hosts of thankless kings, 240
And with these slaughterous hands draw sword no
more."
He spoke, and smiled; and Gudurz made
reply:—
"What then, O Rustum, will men say to this,
When Sohrab dares our bravest forth, and seeks
Thee most of all, and thou, whom most he seeks,
Hidest thy face? Take heed lest men should say:
Like some old miser, Rustum hoards his fame,
And shuns to peril it with younger men."

217. Iran, Persia.   223. Kai Khosroo, possibly Cyrus
the Great (sixth century B.C.).

And, greatly moved, then Rustum made reply:—
"O Gudurz, wherefore dost thou say such words?
Thou knowest better words than this to say. 251
What is one more, one less, obscure or famed,
Valiant or craven, young or old, to me?
Are not they mortal, am not I myself?
But who for men of nought would do great deeds?
Come, thou shalt see how Rustum hoards his fame!
But I will fight unknown, and in plain arms;
Let not men say of Rustum, he was matched
In single fight with any mortal man."
He spoke, and frowned; and Gudurz turned, and
ran 260
Back quickly through the camp in fear and joy—
Fear at his wrath, but joy that Rustum came.
But Rustum strode to his tent-door, and called
His followers in, and bade them bring his arms,
And clad himself in steel; the arms he chose
Were plain, and on his shield was no device,
Only his helm was rich, inlaid with gold,
And, from the fluted spine atop, a plume
Of horsehair waved, a scarlet horsehair plume.
So armed, he issued forth; and Ruksh, his horse, 270
Followed him like a faithful hound at heel—
Ruksh, whose renown was noised through all the
earth,
The horse, whom Rustum on a foray once
Did in Bokhara by the river find
A colt beneath its dam, and drove him home,
And reared him; a bright bay, with lofty crest,
Dight with a saddle-cloth of broidered green
Crusted with gold, and on the ground were worked
All beasts of chase, all beasts which hunters know.
So followed, Rustum left his tents, and crossed 280
The camp, and to the Persian host appeared.
And all the Persians knew him, and with shouts
Hailed; but the Tartars knew not who he was.
And dear as the wet diver to the eyes
Of his pale wife who waits and weeps on shore,
By sandy Bahrein, in the Persian Gulf,
Plunging all day in the blue waves, at night,
Having made up his tale of precious pearls,
Rejoins her in their hut upon the sands—
So dear to the pale Persians Rustum came. 290
And Rustum to the Persian front advanced,
And Sohrab armed in Haman's tent, and came.
And as afield the reapers cut a swath
Down through the middle of a rich man's corn,
And on each side are squares of standing corn,
And in the midst a stubble, short and bare—
So on each side were squares of men, with spears
Bristling, and in the midst, the open sand.

257. in plain arms, without the devices which would reveal his identity.   286. Bahrein, the Aval Islands.

And Rustum came upon the sand, and cast
His eyes toward the Tartar tents, and saw   300
Sohrab come forth, and eyed him as he came.

    As some rich woman, on a winter's morn,
Eyes through her silken curtains the poor drudge
Who with numb blackened fingers makes her fire—
At cock-crow, on a starlit winter's morn,
When the frost flowers the whitened window-
    panes—
And wonders how she lives, and what the thoughts
Of that poor drudge may be; so Rustum eyed
The unknown adventurous youth, who from afar
Came seeking Rustum, and defying forth   310
All the most valiant chiefs; long he perused
His spirited air, and wondered who he was.
For very young he seemed, tenderly reared;
Like some young cypress, tall, and dark, and
    straight,
Which in a queen's secluded garden throws
Its slight dark shadow on the moonlit turf,
By midnight, to a bubbling fountain's sound—
So slender Sohrab seemed, so softly reared.
And a deep pity entered Rustum's soul
As he beheld him coming; and he stood,   320
And beckoned to him with his hand, and said:—

    "O thou young man, the air of Heaven is soft,
And warm, and pleasant; but the grave is cold!
Heaven's air is better than the cold dead grave.
Behold me! I am vast, and clad in iron,
And tried; and I have stood on many a field
Of blood, and I have fought with many a foe—
Never was that field lost, or that foe saved.
O Sohrab, wherefore wilt thou rush on death?
Be governed! quit the Tartar host, and come   330
To Iran, and be as my son to me,
And fight beneath my banner till I die!
There are no youths in Iran brave as thou."

    So he spake, mildly; Sohrab heard his voice,
The mighty voice of Rustum, and he saw
His giant figure planted on the sand,
Sole, like some single tower, which a chief
Hath builded on the waste in former years
Against the robbers; and he saw that head,
Streaked with its first grey hairs;—hope filled his
    soul,   340
And he ran forward and embraced his knees,
And clasped his hand within his own, and said:—

    "O, by thy father's head! by thine own soul!
Art thou not Rustum? speak! art thou not he?"

    But Rustum eyed askance the kneeling youth,
And turned away, and spake to his own soul:—

    "Ah me, I muse what this young fox may mean!
False, wily, boastful, are these Tartar boys.
For if I now confess this thing he asks,

And hide it not, but say: *Rustum is here!*   350
He will not yield indeed, nor quit our foes,
But he will find some pretext not to fight,
And praise my fame, and proffer courteous gifts,
A belt or sword perhaps, and go his way.
And on a feast-tide, in Afrasiab's hall,
In Samarcand, he will arise and cry:
'I challenged once, when the two armies camped
Beside the Oxus, all the Persian lords
To cope with me in single fight; but they
Shrank, only Rustum dared; then he and I   360
Changed gifts, and went on equal terms away.'
So will he speak, perhaps, while men applaud;
Then were the chiefs of Iran shamed through me."

    And then he turned, and sternly spake aloud:—
"Rise! wherefore dost thou vainly question thus
Of Rustum? I am here, whom thou hast called
By challenge forth; make good thy vaunt, or yield!
Is it with Rustum only thou wouldst fight?
Rash boy, men look on Rustum's face and flee!
For well I know, that did great Rustum stand   370
Before thy face this day, and were revealed,
There would be then no talk of fighting more.
But being what I am, I tell thee this—
Do thou record it in thine inmost soul:
Either thou shalt renounce thy vaunt and yield,
Or else thy bones shall strew this sand, till winds
Bleach them, or Oxus with his summer-floods,
Oxus in summer wash them all away."

    He spoke; and Sohrab answered, on his feet:—
"Art thou so fierce? Thou wilt not fright me so!   380
I am no girl, to be made pale by words.
Yet this thou hast said well, did Rustum stand
Here on this field, there were no fighting then.
But Rustum is far hence, and we stand here.
Begin! thou art more vast, more dread than I,
And thou art proved, I know, and I am young—
But yet success sways with the breath of Heaven.
And though thou thinkest that thou knowest sure
Thy victory, yet thou canst not surely know.
For we are all, like swimmers in the sea,   390
Poised on the top of a huge wave of fate,
Which hangs uncertain to which side to fall.
And whether it will heave us up to land,
Or whether it will roll us out to sea,
Back out to sea, to the deep waves of death,
We know not, and no search will make us know;
Only the event will teach us in its hour."

    He spoke, and Rustum answered not, but hurled
His spear; down from the shoulder, down it came,
As on some partridge in the corn a hawk,   400
That long has towered in the airy clouds,

400 ff. As on some partridge . . . This simile is an excellent example of epic glorification.

Drops like a plummet; Sohrab saw it come,
And sprang aside, quick as a flash; the spear
Hissed, and went quivering down into the sand,
Which it sent flying wide;—then Sohrab threw
In turn, and full struck Rustum's shield; sharp rang,
The iron plates rang sharp, but turned the spear.
And Rustum seized his club, which none but he
Could wield; an unlopped trunk it was, and huge,
Still rough—like those which men in treeless plains
To build them boats fish from the flooded rivers,
Hyphasis or Hydaspes, when, high up   412
By their dark springs, the wind in winter-time
Hath made in Himalayan forests wrack,
And strewn the channels with torn boughs—so huge
The club which Rustum lifted now, and struck
One stroke; but again Sohrab sprang aside,
Lithe as the glancing snake, and the club came
Thundering to earth, and leapt from Rustum's
     hand.
And Rustum followed his own blow, and fell   420
To his knees, and with his fingers clutched the sand;
And now might Sohrab have unsheathed his sword,
And pierced the mighty Rustum while he lay
Dizzy, and on his knees, and choked with sand;
But he looked on, and smiled, nor bared his sword,
But courteously drew back, and spoke, and said:—
     "Thou strik'st too hard! that club of thine will
          float
Upon the summer-floods, and not my bones.
But rise, and be not wroth! not wroth am I;
No, when I see thee, wrath forsakes my soul.   430
Thou say'st, thou art not Rustum; be it so!
Who art thou then, that canst so touch my soul?
Boy as I am, I have seen battles too—
Have waded foremost in their bloody waves,
And heard their hollow roar of dying men;
But never was my heart thus touched before.
Are they from Heaven, these softenings of the heart?
O thou old warrior, let us yield to Heaven!
Come, plant we here in earth our angry spears,
And make a truce, and sit upon this sand,   440
And pledge each other in red wine, like friends,
And thou shalt talk to me of Rustum's deeds.
There are enough foes in the Persian host,
Whom I may meet, and strike, and feel no pang;
Champions enough Afrasiab has, whom thou
Mayst fight; fight *them*, when they confront thy
     spear!
But oh, let there be peace 'twixt thee and me!"
     He ceased, but while he spake, Rustum had risen,
And stood erect, trembling with rage; his club
He left to lie, but had regained his spear,   450
Whose fiery point now in his mailed right-hand

412. **Hyphasis or Hydaspes**, rivers in northern India.

Blazed bright and baleful, like that autumn-star,
The baleful sign of fevers; dust had soiled
His stately crest, and dimmed his glittering arms.
His breast heaved, his lips foamed, and twice his
     voice
Was choked with rage; at last these words broke
     way:—
     "Girl! nimble with thy feet, not with thy hands!
Curled minion, dancer, coiner of sweet words!
Fight, let me hear thy hateful voice no more!
Thou art not in Afrasiab's gardens now   460
With Tartar girls, with whom thou art wont to
     dance;
But on the Oxus-sands, and in the dance
Of battle, and with me, who make no play
Of war; I fight it out, and hand to hand.
Speak not to me of truce, and pledge, and wine!
Remember all thy valour; try thy feints
And cunning! all the pity I had is gone;
Because thou hast shamed me before both the hosts
With thy light skipping tricks, and thy girl's wiles."
     He spoke, and Sohrab kindled at his taunts,   470
And he too drew his sword; at once they rushed
Together, as two eagles on one prey
Come rushing down together from the clouds,
One from the east, one from the west; their shields
Dashed with a clang together, and a din
Rose, such as that the sinewy woodcutters
Make often in the forest's heart at morn,
Of hewing axes, crashing trees—such blows
Rustum and Sohrab on each other hailed.
And you would say that sun and stars took part   480
In that unnatural conflict; for a cloud
Grew suddenly in Heaven, and darked the sun
Over the fighters' heads; and a wind rose
Under their feet, and moaning swept the plain,
And in a sandy whirlwind wrapped the pair.
In gloom they twain were wrapped, and they alone;
For both the on-looking hosts on either hand
Stood in broad daylight, and the sky was pure,
And the sun sparkled on the Oxus stream.
But in the gloom they fought, with bloodshot eyes
And labouring breath; first Rustum struck the
     shield   491
Which Sohrab held stiff out; the steel-spiked spear
Rent the tough plates, but failed to reach the skin,
And Rustum plucked it back with angry groan.
Then Sohrab with his sword smote Rustum's helm,
Nor clove its steel quite through; but all the crest
He shore away, and that proud horsehair plume,
Never till now defiled, sank to the dust;
And Rustum bowed his head; but then the gloom

452. **that autumn-star,** Sirius, to which the ancients attached many superstitions.

Grew blacker, thunder rumbled in the air,   500
And lightnings rent the cloud; and Ruksh, the
    horse,
Who stood at hand, uttered a dreadful cry;—
No horse's cry was that, most like the roar
Of some pained desert-lion, who all day
Hath trailed the hunter's javelin in his side,
And comes at night to die upon the sand.
The two hosts heard that cry, and quaked for fear,
And Oxus curdled as it crossed his stream.
But Sohrab heard, and quailed not, but rushed on,
And struck again; and again Rustum bowed   510
His head; but this time all the blade, like glass,
Sprang in a thousand shivers on the helm,
And in the hand the hilt remained alone.
Then Rustum raised his head; his dreadful eyes
Glared, and he shook on high his menacing spear,
And shouted: *Rustum!*—Sohrab heard that shout,
And shrank amazed; back he recoiled one step,
And scanned with blinking eyes the advancing
    form;
And then he stood bewildered; and he dropped 519
His covering shield, and the spear pierced his side.
He reeled, and staggering back, sank to the ground;
And then the gloom dispersed, and the wind fell,
And the bright sun broke forth, and melted all
The cloud; and the two armies saw the pair—
Saw Rustum standing, safe upon his feet,
And Sohrab, wounded, on the bloody sand.

    Then, with a bitter smile, Rustum began:—
"Sohrab, thou thoughtest in thy mind to kill
A Persian lord this day, and strip his corpse,
And bear thy trophies to Afrasiab's tent.   530
Or else that the great Rustum would come down
Himself to fight, and that thy wiles would move
His heart to take a gift, and let thee go.
And then that all the Tartar host would praise
Thy courage or thy craft, and spread thy fame,
To glad thy father in his weak old age.
Fool, thou art slain, and by an unknown man!
Dearer to the red jackals shalt thou be
Than to thy friends, and to thy father old."

    And, with a fearless mien, Sohrab replied:— 540
"Unknown thou art; yet thy fierce vaunt is vain.
Thou dost not slay me, proud and boastful man!
No! Rustum slays me, and this filial heart.
For were I matched with ten such men as thee,
And I were that which till to-day I was,
They should be lying here, I standing there.
But that belovèd name unnerved my arm—
That name, and something, I confess, in thee,
Which troubles all my heart, and made my shield
Fall; and thy spear transfixed an unarmed foe.   550
And now thou boastest, and insult'st my fate.

But hear thou this, fierce man, tremble to hear:
The mighty Rustum shall avenge my death!
My father, whom I seek through all the world,
He shall avenge my death, and punish thee!"

    As when some hunter in the spring hath found
A breeding eagle sitting on her nest,
Upon the craggy isle of a hill-lake,
And pierced her with an arrow as she rose,
And followed her to find her where she fell   560
Far off;—anon her mate comes winging back
From hunting, and a great way off descries
His huddling young left sole; at that, he checks
His pinion, and with short uneasy sweeps
Circles above his eyry, with loud screams
Chiding his mate back to her nest; but she
Lies dying, with the arrow in her side,
In some far stony gorge out of his ken,
A heap of fluttering feathers—never more
Shall the lake glass her, flying over it;   570
Never the black and dripping precipices
Echo her stormy scream as she sails by—
As that poor bird flies home, nor knows his loss,
So Rustum knew not his own loss, but stood
Over his dying son, and knew him not.

    But, with a cold incredulous voice, he said:—
"What prate is this of fathers and revenge?
The mighty Rustum never had a son."

    And, with a failing voice, Sohrab replied:—
"Ah yes, he had! and that lost son am I.   580
Surely the news will one day reach his ear,
Reach Rustum, where he sits, and tarries long,
Somewhere, I know not where, but far from here;
And pierce him like a stab, and make him leap
To arms, and cry for vengeance upon thee.
Fierce man, bethink thee, for an only son!
What will that grief, what will that vengeance be?
Oh, could I live, till I that grief had seen!
Yet him I pity not so much, but her,
My mother, who in Ader-baijan dwells   590
With that old king, her father, who grows grey
With age, and rules over the valiant Koords.
Her most I pity, who no more will see
Sohrab returning from the Tartar camp,
With spoils and honour, when the war is done.
But a dark rumour will be bruited up,
From tribe to tribe, until it reach her ear;
And then will that defenceless woman learn
That Sohrab will rejoice her sight no more,
But that in battle with a nameless foe,   600
By the far-distant Oxus, he is slain."

    He spoke; and as he ceased, he wept aloud,
Thinking of her he left, and his own death.
He spoke; but Rustum listened, plunged in thought.

592. **Koords,** Curds, of northwestern Persia.

Nor did he yet believe it was his son
Who spoke, although he called back names he
    knew;
For he had had sure tidings that the babe,
Which was in Ader-baijan born to him,
Had been a puny girl, no boy at all—
So that sad mother sent him word, for fear   610
Rustum should seek the boy, to train in arms
And so he deemed that either Sohrab took,
By a false boast, the style of Rustum's son;
Or that men gave it him, to swell his fame.
So deemed he; yet he listened, plunged in thought
And his soul set to grief, as the vast tide
Of the bright rocking Ocean sets to shore
At the full moon; tears gathered in his eyes;
For he remembered his own early youth,
And all its bounding rapture; as, at dawn,   620
The shepherd from his mountain-lodge descries
A far, bright city, smitten by the sun,
Through many rolling clouds—so Rustum saw
His youth; saw Sohrab's mother, in her bloom;
And that old king, her father, who loved well
His wandering guest, and gave him his fair child
With joy; and all the pleasant life they led,
They three, in that long-distant summer-time—
The castle, and the dewy woods, and hunt
And hound, and morn on those delightful hills   630
In Ader-baijan. And he saw that Youth,
Of age and looks to be his own dear son,
Piteous and lovely, lying on the sand,
Like some rich hyacinth which by the scythe
Of an unskilful gardener has been cut,
Mowing the garden grass-plots near its bed,
And lies, a fragrant tower of purple bloom,
On the mown, dying grass—so Sohrab lay,
Lovely in death, upon the common sand.
And Rustum gazed on him with grief, and said:—
    "O Sohrab, thou indeed art such a son   641
Whom Rustum, wert thou his, might well have
    loved.
Yet here thou errest, Sohrab, or else men
Have told thee false—thou art not Rustum's son.
For Rustum had no son; one child he had—
But one—a girl; who with her mother now
Plies some light female task, nor dreams of us—
Of us she dreams not, nor of wounds, nor war."
    But Sohrab answered him in wrath; for now
The anguish of the deep-fixed spear grew fierce,
And he desired to draw forth the steel,   651
And let the blood flow free, and so to die—
But first he would convince his stubborn foe;
And, rising sternly on one arm, he said:—
    "Man, who art thou who dost deny my words?
Truth sits upon the lips of dying men,

And falsehood, while I lived, was far from mine.
I tell thee, pricked upon this arm I bear
That seal which Rustum to my mother gave,
That she might prick it on the babe she bore."   660
    He spoke; and all the blood left Rustum's cheeks,
And his knees tottered, and he smote his hand
Against his breast, his heavy mailèd hand,
That the hard iron corslet clanked aloud;
And to his heart he pressed the other hand,
And in a hollow voice he spake, and said:—
    "Sohrab, that were a proof which could not lie!
If thou show this, then art thou Rustum's son."
    Then, with weak hasty fingers, Sohrab loosed
His belt, and near the shoulder bared his arm,   670
And showed a sign in faint vermilion points
Pricked; as a cunning workman, in Pekin,
Pricks with vermilion some clear porcelain vase,
An emperor's gift—at early morn he paints,
And all day long, and, when night comes, the lamp
Lights up his studious forehead and thin hands—
So delicately pricked the sign appeared
On Sohrab's arm, the sign of Rustum's seal.
It was that griffin, which of old reared Zal,
Rustum's great father, whom they left to die,   680
A helpless babe, among the mountain-rocks;
Him that kind creature found, and reared, and
    loved—
Then Rustum took it for his glorious sign.
And Sohrab bared that image on his arm,
And himself scanned it long with mournful eyes,
And then he touched it with his hand and said:—
    "How say'st thou? Is that sign the proper sign
Of Rustum's son, or of some other man's?"
    He spoke; but Rustum gazed, and gazed, and
    stood
Speechless; and then he uttered one sharp cry: 690
O boy—thy father!—and his voice choked there.
And then a dark cloud passed before his eyes,
And his head swam, and he sank down to earth.
But Sohrab crawled to where he lay, and cast
His arms about his neck, and kissed his lips,
And with fond faltering fingers stroked his cheeks,
Trying to call him back to life; and life
Came back to Rustum, and he oped his eyes,
And they stood wide with horror; and he seized
In both his hands the dust which lay around,   700
And threw it on his head, and smirched his hair,—
His hair, and face, and beard, and glittering arms;
And strong convulsive groanings shook his breast,
And his sobs choked him; and he clutched his
    sword,
To draw it, and for ever let life out.
But Sohrab saw his thought, and held his hands,
And with a soothing voice he spake, and said:—

"Father, forbear! for I but meet to-day
The doom which at my birth was written down
In Heaven, and thou art Heaven's unconscious
    hand.   710
Surely my heart cried out that it was thou,
When first I saw thee; and thy heart spoke too,
I know it! but fate trod those promptings down
Under its iron heel; fate, fate engaged
The strife, and hurled me on my father's spear.
But let us speak no more of this! I find
My father; let me feel that I have found!
Come, sit beside me on this sand, and take
My head betwixt thy hands, and kiss my cheeks,
And wash them with thy tears, and say: *My son!*   720
Quick! quick! for numbered are my sands of life,
And swift; for like the lightning to this field
I came, and like the wind I go away—
Sudden, and swift, and like a passing wind.
But it was writ in Heaven that this should be."

So said he, and his voice released the heart
Of Rustum, and his tears broke forth; he cast
His arms round his son's neck, and wept aloud,
And kissed him. And awe fell on both the hosts,
When they saw Rustum's grief; and Ruksh, the
    horse,   730
With his head bowing to the ground and mane
Sweeping the dust, came near, and in mute woe
First to the one then to the other moved
His head, as if inquiring what their grief
Might mean; and from his dark, compassionate
    eyes,
The big warm tears rolled down, and caked the
    sand.
But Rustum chid him with stern voice, and said:—

"Ruksh, now thou grievest; but, O Ruksh, thy
    feet
Should first have rotted on their nimble joints,
Or ere they brought thy master to this field!"   740
But Sohrab looked upon the horse and said:—
"Is this, then, Ruksh? How often, in past days,
My mother told me of thee, thou brave steed,
My terrible father's terrible horse! and said,
That I should one day find thy lord and thee.
Come, let me lay my hand upon thy mane!
O Ruksh, thou art more fortunate than I;
For thou hast gone where I shall never go,
And snuffed the breezes of my father's home.
And thou hast trod the sands of Seistan,   750
And seen the River of Helmund, and the Lake
Of Zirrah; and the aged Zal himself
Has often stroked thy neck, and given thee food,
Corn in a golden platter soaked with wine,
And said; *O Ruksh! bear Rustum well!*—but I
Have never known my grandsire's furrowed face,

Nor seen his lofty house in Seistan,
Nor slaked my thirst at the clear Helmund stream;
But lodged among my father's foes, and seen
Afrasiab's cities only, Samarcand,   760
Bokhara, and lone Khiva in the waste,
And the black Toorkmun tents; and only drunk
The desert rivers, Moorghab and Tejend,
Kohik, and where the Kalmuks feed their sheep,
The northern Sir; and this great Oxus stream,
The yellow Oxus, by whose brink I die."

Then, with a heavy groan, Rustum bewailed:—
"Oh, that its waves were flowing over me!
Oh, that I saw its grains of yellow silt
Roll tumbling in the current o'er my head!"   770
But, with a grave mild voice, Sohrab replied:—
"Desire not that, my father! thou must live.
For some are born to do great deeds, and live,
As some are born to be obscured, and die.
Do thou the deeds I die too young to do,
And reap a second glory in thine age;
Thou art my father, and thy gain is mine.
But come! thou seest this great host of men
Which follow me; I pray thee, slay not these!
Let me entreat for them; what have they done?   780
They followed me, my hope, my fame, my star.
Let them all cross the Oxus back in peace.
But me thou must bear hence, not send with them,
But carry me with thee to Seistan,
And place me on a bed, and mourn for me,
Thou, and the snow-haired Zal, and all thy friends.
And thou must lay me in that lovely earth,
And heap a stately mound above my bones,
And plant a far-seen pillar over all.
That so the passing horseman on the waste   790
May see my tomb a great way off, and cry:
*Sohrab, the mighty Rustum's son, lies there,
Whom his great father did in ignorance kill!*
And I be not forgotten in my grave."

And, with a mournful voice, Rustum replied:—
"Fear not! as thou hast said, Sohrab, my son,
So shall it be; for I will burn my tents,
And quit the host, and bear thee hence with me,
And carry thee away to Seistan,
And place thee on a bed, and mourn for thee,   800
With the snow-headed Zal, and all my friends.
And I will lay thee in that lovely earth,
And heap a stately mound above thy bones,
And plant a far-seen pillar over all,
And men shall not forget thee in thy grave.
And I will spare thy host; yea, let them go!
Let them all cross the Oxus back in peace!

762. **Toorkmun,** Turks living in central Asia.   764. **Kalmuks,** Mongols of western China.   765. **Sir,** the Jaxartes
River in Turkestan.

What should I do with slaying any more?
For would that all that I have ever slain
Might be once more alive; my bitterest foes,   810
And they who were called champions in their time,
And through whose death I won that fame I have—
And I were nothing but a common man,
A poor, mean soldier, and without renown,
So thou mightest live too, my son, my son!
Or rather would that I, even I myself,
Might now be lying on this bloody sand,
Near death, and by an ignorant stroke of thine,
Not thou of mine! and I might die, not thou;
And I, not thou, be borne to Seistan;   820
And Zal might weep above my grave, not thine;
And say: *O son, I weep thee not too sore,*
For willingly, I know, thou met'st thine end!
But now in blood and battles was my youth,
And full of blood and battles is my age,
And I shall never end this life of blood."

Then, at the point of death, Sohrab replied:—
"A life of blood indeed, thou dreadful man!
But thou shalt yet have peace; only not now,
Not yet! but thou shalt have it on that day,   830
When thou shalt sail in a high-masted ship,
Thou and the other peers of Kai Khosroo,
Returning home over the salt blue sea,
From laying thy dear master in his grave."

And Rustum gazed in Sohrab's face, and said:—
"Soon be that day, my son, and deep that sea!
Till then, if fate so wills, let me endure."

He spoke; and Sohrab smiled on him, and took
The spear, and drew it from his side, and eased
His wound's imperious anguish; but the blood   840
Came welling from the open gash, and life
Flowed with the stream;—all down his cold white
    side
The crimson torrent ran, dim now and soiled,
Like the soiled tissue of white violets
Left, freshly gathered, on their native bank,
By children whom their nurses call with haste
Indoors from the sun's eye; his head drooped low,
His limbs grew slack; motionless, white, he lay—
White, with eyes closed; only when heavy gasps,
Deep heavy gasps quivering through all his frame,
Convulsed him back to life, he opened them,   851
And fixed them feebly on his father's face;
Till now all strength was ebbed, and from his limbs
Unwillingly the spirit fled away,
Regretting the warm mansion which it left,
And youth, and bloom, and this delightful world.

So, on the bloody sand, Sohrab lay dead;
And the great Rustum drew his horseman's cloak
Down o'er his face, and sate by his dead son.
As those black granite pillars, once high-reared   860

By Jemshid in Persepolis, to bear
His house, now 'mid their broken flights of steps
Lie prone, enormous, down the mountain side—
So in the sand lay Rustum by his son.

And night came down over the solemn waste,
And the two gazing hosts, and that sole pair,
And darkened all; and a cold fog, with night,
Crept from the Oxus. Soon a hum arose,
As of a great assembly loosed, and fires
Began to twinkle through the fog; for now   870
Both armies moved to camp, and took their meal;
The Persians took it on the open sands
Southward, the Tartars by the river marge;
And Rustum and his son were left alone.

But the majestic river floated on,
Out of the mist and hum of that low land,
Into the frosty starlight, and there moved,
Rejoicing, through the hushed Chorasmian waste,
Under the solitary moon;—he flowed
Right for the polar star, past Orgunjè,   880
Brimming, and bright, and large; then sands begin
To hem his watery march, and dam his streams,
And split his currents; that for many a league
The shorn and parcelled Oxus strains along
Through beds of sand and matted rushy isles—
Oxus, forgetting the bright speed he had
In his high mountain-cradle in Pamere,
A foiled circuitous wanderer—till at last
The longed-for dash of waves is heard, and wide
His luminous home of waters opens, bright   890
And tranquil, from whose floor the new-bathed
    stars
Emerge, and shine upon the Aral Sea.

PHILOMELA

"Pandion (son of Erichthonius, special ward to Minerva) had two daughters, Procne and Philomela, of whom he gave the former in marriage to Tereus, king of Thrace (or of Daulis in Phocis). This ruler, after his wife had borne him a son, Itys (or Itylus), wearied of her, plucked out her tongue by the roots to insure her silence, and, pretending that she was dead, took in marriage the other sister, Philomela. Procne, by means of a web, into which she wove her story, informed Philomela of the horrible truth. In revenge upon Tereus, the sisters killed Itylus, and served up the child as food to his father; but the gods, in indignation, transformed Procne into a swallow, Philomela into a nightingale, forever bemoaning the murdered Itylus, and Tereus into a hawk, forever pursuing the sisters."—Charles M. Gayley, *Classic Myths*, Ginn, 1911.

861. Jemshid, a legendary king of Persia (see *The Rubáiyát of Omar Khayyám*, l. 18). **Persepolis,** his capital. **878. Chorasmian waste,** Khiva, in Turkestan. **880. Orgunjè,** a village on the Oxus.

Hark! ah, the nightingale—
The tawny-throated!
Hark, from that moonlit cedar what a burst!
What triumph! hark!—what pain!

O wanderer from a Grecian shore,
Still, after many years, in distant lands,
Still nourishing in thy bewildered brain
That wild, unquenched, deep-sunken, old-world
    pain—
Say, will it never heal?
And can this fragrant lawn   10
With its cool trees, and night,
And the sweet, tranquil Thames,
And moonshine, and the dew,
To thy racked heart and brain
Afford no balm?

Dost thou to-night behold,
Here, through the moonlight on this English grass,
The unfriendly palace in the Thracian wild?
Dost thou again peruse
With hot cheeks and seared eyes   20
The too clear web, and thy dumb sister's shame?
Dost thou once more assay
Thy flight, and feel come over thee,
Poor fugitive, the feathery change
Once more, and once more seem to make resound
With love and hate, triumph and agony,
Lone Daulis, and the high Cephissian vale?
Listen, Eugenia—
How thick the bursts come crowding through the
    leaves!
Again—thou hearest?   30
Eternal passion!
Eternal pain!

REQUIESCAT

The person commemorated in this poem, if not imaginary, is unknown. The title is Latin for "May she rest [in peace]."

    Strew on her roses, roses,
      And never a spray of yew!
    In quiet she reposes;
      Ah, would that I did too!

    Her mirth the world required;
      She bathed it in smiles of glee.
    But her heart was tired, tired,
      And now they let her be.

27. **Daulis,** in Phocis, Greece, where Philomela lived. **Cephissian.** Cephissus is a river in Phocis. 28. **Eugenia,** an imaginary companion. *Requiescat.* 2. **yew,** a tree common in graveyards, often used as a symbol of death.

    Her life was turning, turning,
      In mazes of heat and sound.   10
    But for peace her soul was yearning,
      And now peace laps her round.

    Her cabined, ample spirit,
      It fluttered and failed for breath.
    To-night it doth inherit
      The vasty hall of death.

THE SCHOLAR-GIPSY

Go, for they call you, shepherd, from the hill;
    Go, shepherd, and untie the wattled cotes!
      No longer leave thy wistful flock unfed,
    Nor let thy bawling fellows rack their throats,
      Nor the cropped herbage shoot another head.
        But when the fields are still,
    And the tired men and dogs all gone to rest,
      And only the white sheep are sometimes
        seen
    Cross and recross the strips of moon-blanched
      green,
    Come, shepherd, and again begin the quest!   10

Here, where the reaper was at work of late—
    In this high field's dark corner, where he leaves
      His coat, his basket, and his earthen cruse,
    And in the sun all morning binds the sheaves,
      Then here, at noon, comes back his stores to
        use—
        Here will I sit and wait,
    While to my ear from uplands far away
      The bleating of the folded flocks is borne,
      With distant cries of reapers in the corn—
    All the live murmur of a summer's day.   20

Screened is this nook o'er the high, half-reaped
      field,
    And here till sun-down, shepherd! will I be.
      Through the thick corn the scarlet poppies
        peep,

1. **shepherd.** Tinker and Lowry (*op. cit.*, pp. 208–09) point out that the function of the shepherd is not quite clear. "What is the quest [l. 10] which is to be renewed by moonlight? Is it the same quest as that of the scholar-gipsy, or merely emblematic of the spiritual quest of the thoughtful soul? And who is the companion that is to share it? 'Thyrsis,' very probably, for Clough and Arnold are naturally associated in the reader's mind with the spiritual and philosophical 'quests' of their time." "Thyrsis" (see page 686) is an elegy for Arthur Hugh Clough, Victorian poet who gave up much for his spiritual and intellectual integrity. The spirit of the scholar-gipsy is not wholly unlike Clough's. 2. **wattled cotes,** sheepfolds made of twigs or withes. 19. **corn,** grain, wheat.

And round green roots and yellowing stalks I see
  Pale pink convolvulus in tendrils creep;
    And air-swept lindens yield
Their scent, and rustle down their perfumed
    showers
  Of bloom on the bent grass where I am laid,
  And bower me from the August sun with shade;
And the eye travels down to Oxford's towers. 30

And near me on the grass lies Glanvil's book—
  Come, let me read the oft-read tale again!
    The story of the Oxford scholar poor,
  Of pregnant parts and quick inventive brain,
    Who, tired of knocking at preferment's door,
      One summer-morn forsook
  His friends, and went to learn the gipsy-lore,
  And roamed the world with that wild brother-
    hood,
  And came, as most men deemed, to little good,
But came to Oxford and his friends no more. 40

But once, years after, in the country-lanes,
  Two scholars, whom at college erst he knew,
    Met him, and of his way of life enquired;
  Whereat he answered, that the gipsy-crew,
    His mates, had arts to rule as they desired
      The workings of men's brains,
  And they can bind them to what thoughts they
    will.
    "And I," he said, "the secret of their art,
  When fully learned, will to the world impart;
But it needs heaven-sent moments for this skill."

This said, he left them, and returned no more.—
  But rumours hung about the country-side, 52
    That the lost Scholar long was seen to stray,
  Seen by rare glimpses, pensive and tongue-tied,
    In hat of antique shape, and cloak of grey,
      The same the gipsies wore.
  Shepherds had met him on the Hurst in spring;
  At some lone alehouse in the Berkshire moors,
  On the warm ingle-bench, the smock-frocked
    boors
Had found him seated at their entering, 60

But, 'mid their drink and clatter, he would fly.
  And I myself seem half to know thy looks,
    And put the shepherds, wanderer! on thy
    trace;

And boys who in lone wheatfields scare the rooks
  I ask if thou hast passed their quiet place;
    Or in my boat I lie
Moored to the cool bank in the summer-heats,
  'Mid wide grass meadows which the sunshine
    fills,
  And watch the warm, green-muffled Cumner
    hills,
And wonder if thou haunt'st their shy retreats. 70

For most, I know, thou lov'st retired ground!
  Thee at the ferry Oxford riders blithe,
    Returning home on summer-nights, have met
  Crossing the stripling Thames at Bab-lock-hithe,
    Trailing in the cool stream thy fingers wet,
      As the punt's rope chops round;
  And leaning backward in a pensive dream,
  And fostering in thy lap a heap of flowers
    Plucked in shy fields and distant Wychwood
    bowers,
And thine eyes resting on the moonlit stream. 80

And then they land, and thou art seen no more!—
  Maidens, who from the distant hamlets come
    To dance around the Fyfield elm in May,
  Oft through the darkening fields have seen thee
    roam,
  Or cross a stile into the public way.
    Oft thou hast given them store
  Of flowers—the frail-leafed, white anemony,
  Dark bluebells drenched with dews of summer
    eves,
  And purple orchises with spotted leaves—
But none hath words she can report of thee. 90

And, above Godstow Bridge, when hay-time's here
  In June, and many a scythe in sunshine flames,
    Men who through those wide fields of breezy
    grass
  Where black-winged swallows haunt the glitter-
    ing Thames,
    To bathe in the abandoned lasher pass,
      Have often passed thee near
  Sitting upon the river bank o'ergrown;
  Marked thine outlandish garb, thy figure
    spare,
  Thy dark vague eyes, and soft abstracted air—
But, when they came from bathing, thou wast
    gone! 100

31. Glanvil's book, *The Vanity of Dogmatizing,* 1661, by Joseph Glanvill, in which the story of the scholar who left Oxford to live with the gypsies is told. (See Tinker and Lowry, *op. cit.,* pp. 205–06.) **57. Hurst,** Cumner Hurst, in the parish of Cumner, near Oxford. **58. Berkshire, the** county south of Oxford.

74. Bab-lock-hithe, a ferry near Cumner village. **79. Wychwood,** a forest northwest of Oxford. **83. To dance . . . May,** a reference to the Maypole dance in the village of **Fyfield,** near Oxford. **91. Godstow Bridge,** about two miles up the Thames from Oxford. **95. lasher pass,** a pool fed by water from a weir.

At some lone homestead in the Cumner hills,
    Where at her open door the housewife darns,
        Thou hast been seen, or hanging on a gate
    To watch the threshers in the mossy barns.
        Children, who early range these slopes and
            late
            For cresses from the rills,
    Have known thee eying, all an April-day,
        The springing pastures and the feeding kine;
        And marked thee, when the stars come out and
            shine,
    Through the long dewy grass move slow away.

In autumn, on the skirts of Bagley Wood—   111
    Where most the gipsies by the turf-edged way
        Pitch their smoked tents, and every bush you
            see
    With scarlet patches tagged and shreds of grey,
        Above the forest-ground called Thessaly—
            The blackbird, picking food,
    Sees thee, nor stops his meal, nor fears at all;
        So often has he known thee past him stray,
        Rapt, twirling in thy hand a withered spray,
    And waiting for the spark from heaven to fall.   120

And once, in winter, on the causeway chill
    Where home through flooded fields foot-travellers
        go,
        Have I not passed thee on the wooden bridge,
    Wrapt in thy cloak and battling with the snow,
        Thy face toward Hinksey and its wintry ridge?
            And thou hast climbed the hill,
    And gained the white brow of the Cumner
        range;
        Turned once to watch, while thick the snow-
            flakes fall,
        The line of festal light in Christ-Church hall—
    Then sought thy straw in some sequestered
        grange.   130

But what—I dream! Two hundred years are
    flown
    Since first thy story ran through Oxford halls,
        And the grave Glanvil did the tale inscribe
    That thou wert wandered from the studious
        walls
        To learn strange arts, and join a gipsy-tribe;
            And thou from earth art gone

111. **Bagley Wood,** southwest of Oxford.   114. **With
scarlet . . grey,** hung with the clothes of the gypsies.
115. **Thessaly,** near Bagley Wood.   120. **spark,** of inspiration.   125. **Hinksey.** See note on "Thyrsis," l. 2 (page 686).
129. **Christ-Church hall,** the dining-hall of Christ
Church College, Oxford.

Long since, and in some quiet churchyard laid—
    Some country-nook, where o'er thy unknown
        grave
    Tall grasses and white flowering nettles wave,
    Under a dark, red-fruited yew-tree's shade.   140

—No, no, thou hast not felt the lapse of hours!
    For what wears out the life of mortal men?
        'Tis that from change to change their being
            rolls;
    'Tis that repeated shocks, again, again,
        Exhaust the energy of strongest souls
            And numb the elastic powers.
    Till having used our nerves with bliss and teen,
        And tired upon a thousand schemes our wit,
        To the just-pausing Genius we remit   149
    Our worn-out life, and are—what we have been.

Thou hast not lived, why should'st thou perish,
    so?
    Thou hadst *one* aim, *one* business, *one* desire;
        Else wert thou long since numbered with the
            dead!
    Else hadst thou spent, like other men, thy fire!
        The generations of thy peers are fled,
            And we ourselves shall go;
    But thou possessest an immortal lot,
        And we imagine thee exempt from age
        And living as thou liv'st on Glanvil's page,
    Because thou hadst—what we, alas! have not.   160

For early didst thou leave the world, with powers
    Fresh, undiverted to the world without,
        Firm to their mark, not spent on other things;
    Free from the sick fatigue, the languid doubt,
        Which much to have tried, in much been
            baffled, brings.
            O life unlike to ours!
    Who fluctuate idly without term or scope,
        Of whom each strives, nor knows for what he
            strives,
        And each half lives a hundred different lives;
    Who wait like thee, but not, like thee, in hope.

Thou waitest for the spark from heaven! and we,
    Light half-believers of our casual creeds,   172
        Who never deeply felt, nor clearly willed,
        Whose insight never has borne fruit in deeds,
            Whose vague resolves never have been fulfilled;
            For whom each year we see

149–50. **To the . . . been.** A Genius is a tutelary deity
or guiding spirit. The general sense of the passage is not
clear.

Breeds new beginnings, disappointments new;
  Who hesitate and falter life away,
  And lose to-morrow the ground won to-day—
Ah! do not we, wanderer! await it too?   180

Yes, we await it!—but it still delays,
  And then we suffer! and amongst us one,
  Who most has suffered, takes dejectedly
His seat upon the intellectual throne;
  And all his store of sad experience he
  Lays bare of wretched days;
Tells us his misery's birth and growth and signs,
  And how the dying spark of hope was fed,
  And how the breast was soothed, and how the
      head,
And all his hourly varied anodynes.   190

This for our wisest! and we others pine,
  And wish the long unhappy dream would end,
  And waive all claim to bliss, and try to bear;
With close-lipped patience for our only friend,
  Sad patience, too near neighbour to despair—
  But none has hope like thine!
Thou through the fields and through the woods
      dost stray,
  Roaming the country-side, a truant boy,
  Nursing thy project in unclouded joy,
And every doubt long blown by time away.   200

O born in days when wits were fresh and clear,
  And life ran gaily as the sparkling Thames;
  Before this strange disease of modern life,
With its sick hurry, its divided aims,
  Its heads o'ertaxed, its palsied hearts, was
      rife—
  Fly hence, our contact fear!
Still fly, plunge deeper in the bowering wood!
  Averse, as Dido did with gesture stern
  From her false friend's approach in Hades turn,
Wave us away, and keep thy solitude!   210

Still nursing the unconquerable hope,
  Still clutching the inviolable shade,
  With a free, onward impulse brushing through,
By night, the silvered branches of the glade—

Far on the forest-skirts, where none pursue,
  On some mild pastoral slope
Emerge, and resting on the moonlit pales
Freshen thy flowers as in former years
With dew, or listen with enchanted ears,
  From the dark dingles, to the nightingales!   220

But fly our paths, our feverish contact fly!
  For strong the infection of our mental strife,
  Which, though it gives no bliss, yet spoils for
      rest;
And we should win thee from thy own fair life,
  Like us distracted, and like us unblest.
  Soon, soon thy cheer would die,
Thy hopes grow timorous, and unfixed thy
      powers,
  And thy clear aims be cross and shifting made;
  And then thy glad perennial youth would
      fade,
Fade, and grow old at last, and die like ours.   230

Then fly our greetings, fly our speech and smiles!
  —As some grave Tyrian trader, from the sea,
  Descried at sunrise an emerging prow
Lifting the cool-haired creepers stealthily,
  The fringes of a southward-facing brow
  Among the Aegaean isles;
And saw the merry Grecian coaster come,
  Freighted with amber grapes, and Chian wine,
  Green, bursting figs, and tunnies steeped in
      brine—
And knew the intruders on his ancient home,   240

The young light-hearted masters of the waves—
  And snatched his rudder, and shook out more
      sail;
  And day and night held on indignantly
O'er the blue Midland waters with the gale,
  Betwixt the Syrtes and soft Sicily,
  To where the Atlantic raves
Outside the western straits; and unbent sails
  There, where down cloudy cliffs, through
      sheets of foam,
  Shy traffickers, the dark Iberians come;
And on the beach undid his corded bales.   250

182–90. one. Arnold once declared the reference was to
Goethe. Tinker and Lowry (*op. cit.*, pp. 209–11) suggest a
number of reasons for believing that he may rather have had
Tennyson in mind. If this identification be accepted, the
suffering would refer to the death of Hallam; **the intellectual throne** (see Tennyson's "The Palace of Art," l. 216)
would have some reference to the laureateship; the **hourly
varied anodynes** would be the many poems which make
up *In Memoriam*.   **208–10. as Dido . . . solitude!** When
Aeneas passed through Hades he was spurned by the shade
of Dido, who had killed herself for love of him (*Aeneid*, Book
VI, ll. 450–71).

232. Tyrian, Phoenician of Tyre. The Phoenicians were
the great traders of the Mediterranean area until displaced
by the Greeks. For the controversy concerning the suitableness of this figure, see Tinker and Lowry, *op. cit.*, pp. 212–14.
234. cool-haired creepers, evidently foliage overhanging
the entrance to some waterway.   **237. come,** a past participle, say Tinker and Lowry.   **238. Chian,** from Chios,
an island in the Aegean.   **244. Midland,** Mediterranean.
245. Syrtes, Gulf of Sidra, on the northern coast of Africa.
249. Iberians, inhabitants of the Spanish peninsula,
where the Tyrian hopes to find a new market.

THYRSIS

A MONODY, *to commemorate the author's friend,*
ARTHUR HUGH CLOUGH, *who died at Florence, 1861.*

"Thyrsis" ranks with Milton's "Lycidas" and Shelley's
"Adonais" among the great pastoral elegies of English
literature. The tradition traces back to Theocritus, Bion,
and Moschus in late Greek literature (more particularly
to Theocritus in Arnold's case, though his poem owes
more to observation than to reading), and the identification of the poet and his friends with shepherds is conventional. Thyrsis (Clough—see note on l. 1 of "The Scholar-
Gypsy," page 682) and Corydon (Arnold) are traditional
names.

How changed is here each spot man makes or
    fills!
  In the two Hinkseys nothing keeps the same;
    The village street its haunted mansion lacks,
  And from the sign is gone Sibylla's name,
    And from the roofs the twisted chimney-
      stacks—
    Are ye too changed, ye hills?
  See, 'tis no foot of unfamiliar men
    To-night from Oxford up your pathway strays!
  Here came I often, often, in old days—
  Thyrsis and I; we still had Thyrsis then.   10

Runs it not here, the track by Childsworth Farm,
  Past the high wood, to where the elm-tree crowns
    The hill behind whose ridge the sunset flames?
  The signal-elm, that looks on Ilsley Downs,
    The Vale, the three lone weirs, the youthful
      Thames?—
    This winter-eve is warm,
  Humid the air! leafless, yet soft as spring,
    The tender purple spray on copse and briers!
  And that sweet city with her dreaming spires,
  She needs not June for beauty's heightening, 20

Lovely all times she lies, lovely to-night!—
  Only, methinks, some loss of habit's power
    Befalls me wandering through this upland
    dim.
  Once passed I blindfold here, at any hour;
    Now seldom come I, since I came with him.
    That single elm-tree bright

Against the west—I miss it! is it gone?
  We prized it dearly; while it stood, we said,
  Our friend, the Gipsy-Scholar, was not dead;
  While the tree lived, he in these fields lived on.

Too rare, too rare, grow now my visits here,   30
  But once I knew each field, each flower, each
    stick;
    And with the country-folk acquaintance made
  By barn in threshing-time, by new-built rick.
    Here, too, our shepherd-pipes we first assayed.
    Ah me! this many a year
  My pipe is lost, my shepherd's holiday!
    Needs must I lose them, needs with heavy
    heart
    Into the world and wave of men depart;
  But Thyrsis of his own will went away.   40

It irked him to be here, he could not rest.
  He loved each simple joy the country yields,
    He loved his mates; but yet he could not
    keep,
  For that a shadow loured on the fields,
    Here with the shepherds and the silly sheep.
    Some life of men unblest
  He knew, which made him droop, and filled his
    head.
  He went; his piping took a troubled sound
    Of storms that rage outside our happy ground;
  He could not wait their passing, he is dead.   50

So, some tempestuous morn in early June,
  When the year's primal burst of bloom is o'er,
    Before the roses and the longest day—
  When garden-walks and all the grassy floor
    With blossoms red and white of fallen May
    And chestnut-flowers are strewn—
  So have I heard the cuckoo's parting cry,
    From the wet field, through the vext garden-
    trees,
    Come with the volleying rain and tossing
    breeze:
  The bloom is gone, and with the bloom go I!   60

Too quick despairer, wherefore wilt thou go?
  Soon will the high Midsummer pomps come on,
    Soon will the musk carnations break and swell,

2. two Hinkseys, villages southwest of Oxford. 4. Sib-
ylla, Greek or Roman prophetess, possibly used on the sign
of an inn. 11. Childsworth Farm, Chiswell Farm, near
Oxford. 14. signal-elm. Topographers are not agreed
as to the location of this tree. Ilsley Downs, in western
Berkshire, the county south of Oxford.   15. youthful
Thames, because not yet far from its source. 19. sweet city,
Oxford.

29. the Gipsy-Scholar. Compare the preceding poem.
35. our shepherd-pipes we first assayed, first attempted
poetry. 37. My pipe is lost. Arnold was writing very little
poetry as he grew older. 40. Thyrsis . . . went away.
Clough resigned his Oriel fellowship in 1848 because he could
no longer profess faith in the Thirty-nine Articles. 45. silly,
simple. 48–50. his piping . . . dead. Clough's poetry
reflects the religious, intellectual, and even political struggles
of his time.

Soon shall we have gold-dusted snapdragon,
  Sweet-William with his homely cottage-smell,
    And stocks in fragrant blow;
  Roses that down the alleys shine afar,
  And open, jasmine-muffled lattices,
  And groups under the dreaming garden-trees,
And the full moon, and the white evening-star. 70

He hearkens not! light comer, he is flown!
  What matters it? next year he will return,
    And we shall have him in the sweet spring-
      days,
  With whitening hedges, and uncrumpling fern,
  And blue-bells trembling by the forest-ways,
    And scent of hay new-mown.
  But Thyrsis never more we swains shall see;
    See him come back, and cut a smoother reed,
    And blow a strain the world at last shall heed—
For Time, not Corydon, hath conquered thee! 80

Alack, for Corydon no rival now!—
  But when Sicilian shepherds lost a mate,
    Some good survivor with his flute would go,
  Piping a ditty sad for Bion's fate;
    And cross the unpermitted ferry's flow,
      And relax Pluto's brow,
  And make leap up with joy the beauteous head
  Of Proserpine, among whose crownèd hair
  Are flowers first opened on Sicilian air,
And flute his friend, like Orpheus, from the dead.

O easy access to the hearer's grace   91
  When Dorian shepherds sang to Proserpine!
    For she herself had trod Sicilian fields,
  She knew the Dorian water's gush divine,
    She knew each lily white which Enna yields,
      Each rose with blushing face;
  She loved the Dorian pipe, the Dorian strain.
    But ah, of our poor Thames she never heard!
    Her foot the Cumner cowslips never stirred;
And we should tease her with our plaint in vain!

Well! wind-dispersed and vain the words will be,
  Yet, Thyrsis, let me give my grief its hour 102
    In the old haunt, and find our tree-topped
      hill!

80. **Time . . . thee!** Competitive singing-matches are common in pastoral poetry. 85. **unpermitted ferry,** the river Styx in Hades, crossed only by the spirits of the dead. 86. **Pluto,** god of the underworld. 88. **Proserpine,** queen of the underworld, originally a girl of Sicily, whom Pluto carried off while she was gathering flowers in the vale of Enna. 90. **Orpheus.** Orpheus, Greek musician, invaded Hades in search of his dead wife Eurydice. 92. **Dorian,** Sicilian. 99. **Cumner.** See the note on "The Scholar-Gipsy," l. 57 (page 683).

Who, if not I, for questing here hath power?
  I know the wood which hides the daffodil,
    I know the Fyfield tree,
  I know what white, what purple fritillaries
    The grassy harvest of the river-fields,
    Above by Ensham, down by Sandford, yields,
  And what sedged brooks are Thames's tribu-
    taries;   110

I know these slopes; who knows them if not I?—
  But many a dingle on the loved hill-side,
    With thorns once studded, old, white-blossomed
      trees,
  Where thick the cowslips grew, and far descried
    High towered the spikes of purple orchises,
      Hath since our day put by
  The coronals of that forgotten time;
    Down each green bank hath gone the plough-
      boy's team,
    And only in the hidden brookside gleam
Primroses, orphans of the flowery prime.   120

Where is the girl, who by the boatman's door,
  Above the locks, above the boating throng,
    Unmoored our skiff when through the Wy-
      tham flats,
  Red loosestrife and blond meadow-sweet among
    And darting swallows and light water-gnats,
      We tracked the shy Thames shore?
  Where are the mowers, who, as the tiny swell
    Of our boat passing heaved the river-grass,
    Stood with suspended scythe to see us pass?—
They all are gone, and thou art gone as well! 130

Yes, thou art gone! and round me too the night
  In ever-nearing circle weaves her shade.
    I see her veil draw soft across the day,
  I feel her slowly chilling breath invade
    The cheek grown thin, the brown hair sprent
      with grey;
      I feel her finger light
  Laid pausefully upon life's headlong train;—
    The foot less prompt to meet the morning dew,
    The heart less bounding at emotion new,
And hope, once crushed, less quick to spring
  again.   140

And long the way appears, which seemed so short
  To the less practised eye of sanguine youth;
    And high the mountain-tops, in cloudy air,

106. **Fyfield tree.** See "The Scholar-Gipsy," l. 83 (page 683). 109. **Ensham,** Eynsham, northwest of Oxford. **Sandford,** south of Oxford. 123. **Wytham flats,** northwest of Oxford. 135. **sprent,** sprinkled. 137. **pausefully, so as** to occasion a pause.

The mountain-tops where is the throne of Truth,
 Tops in life's morning-sun so bright and bare!
  Unbreachable the fort
Of the long-battered world uplifts its wall;
 And strange and vain the earthly turmoil
   grows,
 And near and real the charm of thy repose,
And night as welcome as a friend would fall. 150

But hush! the upland hath a sudden loss
 Of quiet!—Look, adown the dusk hill-side,
 A troop of Oxford hunters going home,
 As in old days, jovial and talking, ride!
  From hunting with the Berkshire hounds they
   come.
  Quick! let me fly, and cross
Into yon farther field!—'Tis done; and see,
 Backed by the sunset, which doth glorify
 The orange and pale violet evening-sky,
Bare on its lonely ridge, the Tree! the Tree! 160

I take the omen! Eve lets down her veil,
 The white fog creeps from bush to bush about,
 The west unflushes, the high stars grow bright,
 And in the scattered farms the lights come out.
  I cannot reach the signal-tree to-night,
   Yet, happy omen, hail!
Hear it from thy broad lucent Arno-vale
 (For there thine earth-forgetting eyelids keep
 The morningless and unawakening sleep
Under the flowery oleanders pale), 170

Hear it, O Thyrsis, still our tree is there!—
 Ah, vain! These English fields, this upland dim,
 These brambles pale with mist engarlanded,
 That lone, sky-pointing tree, are not for him;
  To a boon southern country he is fled,
   And now in happier air,
Wandering with the great Mother's train divine
 (And purer or more subtle soul than thee,
 I trow, the mighty Mother doth not see)
Within a folding of the Apennine, 180

Thou hearest the immortal chants of old!—
 Putting his sickle to the perilous grain
 In the hot cornfield of the Phrygian king,
 For thee the Lityerses-song again
  Young Daphnis with his silver voice doth sing;
   Sings his Sicilian fold,

His sheep, his hapless love, his blinded eyes—
 And how a call celestial round him rang,
 And heavenward from the fountain-brink he
   sprang,
And all the marvel of the golden skies. 190

There thou art gone, and me thou leavest here
 Sole in these fields! yet will I not despair.
  Despair I will not, while I yet descry
Neath the mild canopy of English air
 That lonely tree against the western sky.
  Still, still these slopes, 'tis clear,
Our Gipsy-Scholar haunts, outliving thee!
 Fields where soft sheep from cages pull the hay,
 Woods with anemonies in flower till May,
Know him a wanderer still; then why not me? 200

A fugitive and gracious light he seeks,
 Shy to illumine; and I seek it too.
  This does not come with houses or with gold,
With place, with honour, and a flattering crew;
 'Tis not in the world's market bought and
   sold—
  But the smooth-slipping weeks
Drop by, and leave its seeker still untired;
 Out of the heed of mortals he is gone,
 He wends unfollowed, he must house alone;
Yet on he fares, by his own heart inspired. 210

Thou too, O Thyrsis, on like quest wast bound;
 Thou wanderedst with me for a little hour!
  Men gave thee nothing; but this happy quest,
If men esteemed thee feeble, gave thee power,
 If men procured thee trouble, gave thee rest.
  And this rude Cumner ground,
Its fir-topped Hurst, its farms, its quiet fields,
 Here cam'st thou in thy jocund youthful time,
 Here was thine height of strength, thy golden
   prime!
And still the haunt beloved a virtue yields. 220

What though the music of thy rustic flute
 Kept not for long its happy, country tone;
  Lost it too soon, and learnt a stormy note
Of men contention-tost, of men who groan,
 Which tasked thy pipe too sore, and tired thy
   throat—
  It failed, and thou wast mute!

---

167. **Arno-vale.** Florence, where Clough died, is on the
Arno.   177. **great Mother,** Cybele, goddess of nature.
183–84. **Phrygian king . . . Lityerses,** who compelled
strangers to compete with him in reaping, cut off the heads of
the vanquished, and sang as he disposed of their bodies.
Daphnis, the ideal Sicilian shepherd, entered into this perilous contest to deliver his sweetheart, Piplea, from **Lityerses'**
power; he was overcome but delivered by Hercules.

217. **Hurst.** See the note on "The Scholar-Gipsy," l. 57
(page 683). 221–26. **What . . . mute!** Tinker and Lowry
(*op. cit.*, p. 217) point out that this statement is not literally
true, "for the verse composed at Oxford had its own note of
perplexity and melancholy which reflected the religious
stirring and controversy within the university. Moreover,
in 'The Bothie,' 'Amours de Voyage,' and some of his later
satires, Clough's humour and gaiety were at their best."

Yet hadst thou alway visions of our light,
　And long with men of care thou couldst not
　　　stay,
　And soon thy foot resumed its wandering
　　　way,
　Left human haunt, and on alone till night.　230

Too rare, too rare, grow now my visits here!
　'Mid city-noise, not, as with thee of yore,
　　Thyrsis! in reach of sheep-bells is my home.
　—Then through the great town's harsh, heart-
　　　wearying roar,
　Let in thy voice a whisper often come,
　　To chase fatigue and fear:
　Why faintest thou? I wandered till I died.
　Roam on! The light we sought is shining still.
　Dost thou ask proof? Our tree yet crowns the hill,
　Our Scholar travels yet the loved hill-side.　240

DOVER BEACH

This poem has been given an elaborate musical setting by the young American composer Samuel Barber (Victor record 8998).

The sea is calm to-night.
The tide is full, the moon lies fair
Upon the straits;—on the French coast the light
Gleams and is gone; the cliffs of England stand,
Glimmering and vast, out in the tranquil bay.
Come to the window, sweet is the night-air!
Only, from the long line of spray
Where the sea meets the moon-blanched land,
Listen! you hear the grating roar
Of pebbles which the waves draw back, and
　fling,
At their return, up the high strand,　　　　　　11
Begin, and cease, and then again begin,
With tremulous cadence slow, and bring
The eternal note of sadness in.

Sophocles long ago
Heard it on the Aegaean, and it brought
Into his mind the turbid ebb and flow
Of human misery; we
Find also in the sound a thought,
Hearing it by this distant northern sea.　　　20

Dover Beach. Dover is in Kent at the eastern end of the English Channel, where England is separated from the continent by only twenty miles.　**4–5. the cliffs . . . bay,** a reference to the white chalk cliffs of Dover.　**15–18. Sophocles . . . misery.** Arnold is generally believed to have been thinking of the *Antigone*, ll. 583 ff. Tinker and Lowry (*op. cit.*, pp. 177–78) suggest other possibilities.

The Sea of Faith
Was once, too, at the full, and round earth's shore
Lay like the folds of a bright girdle furled.
But now I only hear
Its melancholy, long, withdrawing roar,
Retreating, to the breath
Of the night-wind, down the vast edges drear
And naked shingles of the world.

Ah, love, let us be true
To one another! for the world, which seems　30
To lie before us like a land of dreams,
So various, so beautiful, so new,
Hath really neither joy, nor love, nor light,
Nor certitude, nor peace, nor help for pain;
And we are here as on a darkling plain
Swept with confused alarms of struggle and flight,
Where ignorant armies clash by night.

THE LAST WORD

Creep into thy narrow bed,
Creep, and let no more be said!
Vain thy onset! all stands fast.
Thou thyself must break at last.

Let the long contention cease!
Geese are swans, and swans are geese.
Let them have it how they will!
Thou art tired; best be still.

They out-talked thee, hissed thee, tore thee?
Better men fared thus before thee;　　　　　10
Fired their ringing shot and passed,
Hotly charged—and sank at last.

Charge once more, then, and be dumb!
Let the victors, when they come,
When the forts of folly fall,
Find thy body by the wall!

RUGBY CHAPEL

November, 1857

The poet's father, Dr. Thomas Arnold, headmaster of Rugby, died of heart failure in 1842, and was buried in the college chapel.

29–37. Ah, love . . . night. Tinker and Lowry (*op. cit.*, pp. 175–76) point out reasons for believing that these lines were written before the rest of the poem. They contain "no reference to the sea or the tides," and may have been suggested by Thucydides' history of the Peloponnesian War, Book VII, Chaps. 43–44.

Coldly, sadly descends
The autumn-evening. The field
Strewn with its dank yellow drifts
Of withered leaves, and the elms,
Fade into dimness apace,
Silent;—hardly a shout
From a few boys late at their play!
The lights come out in the street,
In the school-room windows;—but cold,
Solemn, unlighted, austere,   10
Through the gathering darkness, arise
The chapel-walls, in whose bound
Thou, my father! art laid.

There thou dost lie, in the gloom
Of the autumn evening. But ah!
That word, *gloom*, to my mind
Brings thee back, in the light
Of thy radiant vigour, again;
In the gloom of November we passed
Days not dark at thy side;   20
Seasons impaired not the ray
Of thy buoyant cheerfulness clear.
Such thou wast! and I stand
In the autumn evening, and think
Of bygone autumns with thee.

Fifteen years have gone round
Since thou arosest to tread,
In the summer-morning, the road
Of death, at a call unforeseen,
Sudden. For fifteen years,   30
We who till then in thy shade
Rested as under the boughs
Of a mighty oak, have endured
Sunshine and rain as we might,
Bare, unshaded, alone,
Lacking the shelter of thee.

O strong soul, by what shore
Tarriest thou now? For that force,
Surely, has not been left vain!
Somewhere, surely, afar,   40
In the sounding labour-house vast
Of being, is practised that strength,
Zealous, beneficent, firm!

Yes, in some far-shining sphere,
Conscious or not of the past,
Still thou performest the word
Of the Spirit in whom thou dost live—
Prompt, unwearied, as here!
Still thou upraisest with zeal
The humble good from the ground,   50

Sternly repressest the bad!
Still, like a trumpet, dost rouse
Those who with half-open eyes
Tread the border-land dim
’Twixt vice and virtue; revivest,
Succourest!—this was thy work,
This was thy life upon earth.

What is the course of the life
Of mortal men on the earth?—
Most men eddy about   60
Here and there—eat and drink,
Chatter and love and hate,
Gather and squander, are raised
Aloft, are hurled in the dust,
Striving blindly, achieving
Nothing; and then they die—
Perish;—and no one asks
Who or what they have been,
More than he asks what waves,
In the moonlit solitudes mild   70
Of the midmost Ocean, have swelled,
Foamed for a moment, and gone.

And there are some, whom a thirst
Ardent, unquenchable, fires,
Not with the crowd to be spent,
Not without aim to go round
In an eddy of purposeless dust,
Effort unmeaning and vain.
Ah yes! some of us strive
Not without action to die   80
Fruitless, but something to snatch
From dull oblivion, nor all
Glut the devouring grave!
We, we have chosen our path—
Path to a clear-purposed goal,
Path of advance!—but it leads
A long, steep journey, through sunk
Gorges, o’er mountains in snow.
Cheerful, with friends, we set forth—
Then, on the height, comes the storm.   90
Thunder crashes from rock
To rock, the cataracts reply,
Lightnings dazzle our eyes.
Roaring torrents have breached
The track, the stream-bed descends
In the place where the wayfarer once
Planted his footstep—the spray
Boils o’er its borders! aloft
The unseen snow-beds dislodge
Their hanging ruin; alas,   100
Havoc is made in our train!
Friends, who set forth at our side,

Falter, are lost in the storm.
We, we only are left!
With frowning foreheads, with lips
Sternly compressed, we strain on,
On—and at nightfall at last
Come to the end of our way,
To the lonely inn 'mid the rocks;
Where the gaunt and taciturn host   110
Stands on the threshold, the wind
Shaking his thin white hairs—
Holds his lantern to scan
Our storm-beat figures, and asks:
Whom in our party we bring?
Whom we have left in the snow?

Sadly we answer: We bring
Only ourselves! we lost
Sight of the rest in the storm.
Hardly ourselves we fought through,   120
Stripped, without friends, as we are.
Friends, companions, and train,
The avalanche swept from our side.

But thou would'st not *alone*
Be saved, my father! *alone*
Conquer and come to thy goal,
Leaving the rest in the wild.
We were weary, and we
Fearful, and we in our march
Fain to drop down and to die.   130
Still thou turnedst, and still
Beckonedst the trembler, and still
Gavest the weary thy hand.

If, in the paths of the world,
Stones might have wounded thy feet,
Toil or dejection have tried
Thy spirit, of that we saw
Nothing—to us thou wast still
Cheerful, and helpful, and firm!
Therefore to thee it was given   140
Many to save with thyself;
And, at the end of thy day,
O faithful shepherd! to come,
Bringing thy sheep in thy hand.
And through thee I believe
In the noble and great who are gone;
Pure souls honoured and blest
By former ages, who else—
Such, so soulless, so poor,
Is the race of men whom I see—   150
Seemed but a dream of the heart,
Seemed but a cry of desire.

110. gaunt . . . host, Death.

Yes! I believe that there lived
Others like thee in the past,
Not like the men of the crowd
Who all round me to-day
Bluster or cringe, and make life
Hideous, and arid, and vile;
But souls tempered with fire,
Fervent, heroic, and good,   160
Helpers and friends of mankind.

Servants of God!—or sons
Shall I not call you? because
Not as servants ye knew
Your Father's innermost mind,
His, who unwillingly sees
One of his little ones lost—
Yours is the praise, if mankind
Hath not as yet in its march
Fainted, and fallen, and died!   170

See! In the rocks of the world
Marches the host of mankind,
A feeble, wavering line.
Where are they tending?—A God
Marshalled them, gave them their goal.
Ah, but the way is so long!
Years they have been in the wild!
Sore thirst plagues them, the rocks,
Rising all round, overawe;
Factions divide them, their host   180
Threatens to break, to dissolve.
—Ah, keep, keep them combined!
Else, of the myriads who fill
That army, not one shall arrive;
Sole they shall stray; in the rocks
Stagger for ever in vain,
Die one by one in the waste.

Then, in such hour of need
Of your fainting, dispirited race,
Ye, like angels, appear,   190
Radiant with ardour divine!
Beacons of hope, ye appear!
Languor is not in your heart,
Weakness is not in your word,
Weariness not on your brow.
Ye alight in our van! at your voice,
Panic, despair, flee away.
Ye move through the ranks, recall
The stragglers, refresh the outworn,
Praise, re-inspire the brave!   200

162–65. Servants . . . mind, see John 15:15. 166–
67. His . . . lost, see Matthew 18:6, 12. 190. Ye, the servants of God.

Order, courage, return.
Eyes rekindling, and prayers,
Follow your steps as ye go.
Ye fill up the gaps in our files,
Strengthen the wavering line,
Stablish, continue our march,
On, to the bound of the waste,
On, to the City of God.

GEIST'S GRAVE

Arnold's three last poems were elegies for pets—
"Geist's Grave," for a dachshund belonging to the poet's
son, Richard; "Poor Matthias," for a canary; "Kaiser
Dead," for "our dear dear mongrel."

Four years!—and didst thou stay above
The ground, which hides thee now, but four?
And all that life, and all that love,
Were crowded, Geist! into no more?

Only four years those winning ways,
Which make me for thy presence yearn,
Called us to pet thee or to praise,
Dear little friend! at every turn?

That loving heart, that patient soul,
Had they indeed no longer span,   10
To run their course, and reach their goal,
And read their homily to man?

That liquid, melancholy eye,
From whose pathetic, soul-fed springs
Seemed surging the Virgilian cry,
The sense of tears in mortal things—

That steadfast, mournful strain, consoled
By spirits gloriously gay,
And temper of heroic mould—
What, was four years their whole short day?   20

Yes, only four!—and not the course
Of all the centuries yet to come,
And not the infinite resource
Of Nature, with her countless sum

Of figures, with her fulness vast
Of new creation evermore,
Can ever quite repeat the past,
Or just thy little self restore.

15. Virgilian cry, *Sunt lacrimae rerum* (*Aeneid*, Book I,
l. 462).

Stern law of every mortal lot!
Which man, proud man, finds hard to bear,   30
And builds himself I know not what
Of second life I know not where.

But thou, when struck thine hour to go,
On us, who stood despondent by,
A meek last glance of love didst throw,
And humbly lay thee down to die.

Yet would we keep thee in our heart—
Would fix our favourite on the scene,
Nor let thee utterly depart
And be as if thou ne'er hadst been.   40

And so there rise these lines of verse
On lips that rarely form them now;
While to each other we rehearse:
Such ways, such arts, such looks hadst thou!

We stroke thy broad brown paws again,
We bid thee to thy vacant chair,
We greet thee by the window-pane,
We hear thy scuffle on the stair.

We see the flaps of thy large ears
Quick raised to ask which way we go;   50
Crossing the frozen lake, appears
Thy small black figure on the snow!

Nor to us only art thou dear
Who mourn thee in thine English home;
Thou hast thine absent master's tear,
Dropped by the far Australian foam.

Thy memory lasts both here and there,
And thou shalt live as long as we.
And after that—thou dost not care!
In us was all the world to thee.   60

Yet, fondly zealous for thy fame,
Even to a date beyond our own
We strive to carry down thy name,
By mounded turf, and graven stone.

We lay thee, close within our reach,
Here, where the grass is smooth and warm,
Between the holly and the beech,
Where oft we watched thy couchant form,

55. absent master. Richard Arnold died in Australia

Asleep, yet lending half an ear
To travellers on the Portsmouth road—   70
There build we thee, O guardian dear,
Marked with a stone, thy last abode!

Then some, who through this garden pass,
When we too, like thyself, are clay,
Shall see thy grave upon the grass,
And stop before the stone, and say:

People who lived here long ago
Did by this stone, it seems, intend
To name for future times to know
The dachs-hund, Geist, their little friend.   80

from POEMS

from PREFACE TO THE FIRST EDITION, 1853

WE . . . naturally take pleasure, says Aristotle, in any imitation or representation whatever: this is the basis of our love of Poetry: and we take pleasure in them, he adds, because all knowledge is naturally agreeable to us; not to the philosopher only, but to mankind at large. Every representation therefore which is consistently drawn may be supposed to be interesting, inasmuch as it gratifies this natural interest in knowledge of all kinds. . . . .

Any accurate representation may therefore be expected to be interesting; but, if the representation be a poetical one, more than this is demanded. It is demanded, not only that it shall interest, but also that it shall inspirit and rejoice the reader: that it shall convey a charm, and infuse delight. . . .

A poetical work, therefore, is not yet justified when it has been shown to be an accurate, and therefore interesting representation; it has to be shown also that it is a representation from which men can derive enjoyment. In presence of the most tragic circumstances represented in a work of Art, the feeling of enjoyment, as is well known, may still subsist: the representation of the most utter calamity, of the liveliest anguish, is not sufficient to destroy it: the more tragic the situation, the deeper becomes the enjoyment; and the situation is more tragic in proportion as it becomes more terrible.

What then are the situations, from the representation of which, though accurate, no poetical enjoyment can be derived? They are those in which the suffering finds no vent in action; in which a continuous state of mental distress is prolonged, unrelieved by incident, hope, or resistance; in which there is everything to be endured, nothing to be done. In such situations there is inevitably something morbid, in the description of them something monotonous. When they occur in actual life, they are painful, not tragic; the representation of them in poetry is painful also. . . .

What are the eternal objects of Poetry, among all nations and at all times? They are actions; human actions; possessing an inherent interest in themselves, and which are to be communicated in an interesting manner by the art of the Poet. . . .

The Poet, then, has in the first place to select an excellent action; and what actions are the most excellent? Those, certainly, which most powerfully appeal to the great primary human affections: to those elementary feelings which subsist permanently in the race, and which are independent of time. These feelings are permanent and the same; that which interests them is permanent and the same also. The modernness or antiquity of an action, therefore, has nothing to do with its fitness for poetical representation; this depends upon its inherent qualities. To the elementary part of our nature, to our passions, that which is great and passionate is eternally interesting; and interesting solely in proportion to its greatness and to its passion. A great human action of a thousand years ago is more interesting to it than a smaller human action of to-day, even though upon the representation of this last the most consummate skill may have been expended, and though it has the advantage of appealing by its modern language, familiar manners, and contemporary allusions, to all our transient feelings and interests. . . .

It may be urged, however, that past actions may be interesting in themselves, but that they are not to be adopted by the modern Poet, because it is impossible for him to have them clearly present to his own mind, and he cannot therefore feel them deeply, nor represent them forcibly. But this is not necessarily the case. The externals of a past action, indeed, he cannot know with the precision of a contemporary; but his business is with its essentials. The outward man of Oedipus or of Macbeth, the houses in which they lived, the ceremonies of their

---

70. Portsmouth road, near Arnold's house at Cobham, Surrey.   **18–19. Aristotle,** in his *Poetics,* Book IV, 2–5.

48. Oedipus, king of Thebes, a famous hero of Greek legend. See three plays by Sophocles—*Oedipus Tyrannus, Oedipus Coloneus,* and *Antigone.*

courts, he cannot accurately figure to himself; but neither do they essentially concern him. His business is with their inward man; with their feelings and behaviour in certain tragic situations, which engage their passions as men; these have in them nothing local and casual; they are as accessible to the modern Poet as to a contemporary.

The date of an action, then, signifies nothing: the action itself, its selection and construction, this is what is all-important. This the Greeks understood far more clearly than we do. The radical difference between their poetical theory and ours consists, as it appears to me, in this: that, with them, the poetical character of the action in itself, and the conduct of it, was the first consideration; with us, attention is fixed mainly on the value of the separate thoughts and images which occur in the treatment of an action. They regarded the whole; we regard the parts. With them, the action predominated over the expression of it; with us, the expression predominates over the action. Not that they failed in expression, or were inattentive to it; on the contrary, they are the highest models of expression, the unapproached masters of the *grand style:* but their expression is so excellent because it is so admirably kept in its right degree of prominence; because it is so simple and so well subordinated; because it draws its force directly from the pregnancy of the matter which it conveys. For what reason was the Greek tragic poet confined to so limited a range of subjects? Because there are so few actions which united in themselves, in the highest degree, the conditions of excellence: and it was not thought that on any but an excellent subject could an excellent Poem be constructed. A few actions, therefore, eminently adapted for tragedy, maintained almost exclusive possession of the Greek tragic stage. Their significance appeared inexhaustible; they were as permanent problems, perpetually offered to the genius of every fresh poet. This too is the reason of what appears to us moderns a certain baldness of expression in Greek tragedy; of the triviality with which we often reproach the remarks of the chorus, where it takes part in the dialogue: that the action itself, the situation of Orestes, or Merope, or Alcmaeon, was to stand the central point of interest, unforgotten, absorbing, principal; that no accessories were for a moment to distract the

spectator's attention from this, that the tone of the parts was to be perpetually kept down, in order not to impair the grandiose effect of the whole. The terrible old mythic story on which the drama was founded stood, before he entered the theatre, traced in its bare outlines upon the spectator's mind; it stood in his memory, as a group of statuary, faintly seen, at the end of a long and dark vista: then came the Poet, embodying outlines, developing situations, not a word wasted, not a sentiment capriciously thrown in: stroke upon stroke, the drama proceeded: the light deepened upon the group; more and more it revealed itself to the rivetted gaze of the spectator: until at last, when the final words were spoken, it stood before him in broad sunlight, a model of immortal beauty. . . .

. . . We can hardly at the present day understand what Menander meant, when he told a man who inquired as to the progress of his comedy that he had finished it, not having yet written a single line, because he had constructed the action of it in his mind. A modern critic would have assured him that the merit of his piece depended on the brilliant things which arose under his pen as he went along. We have poems which seem to exist merely for the sake of single lines and passages; not for the sake of producing any total impression. We have critics who seem to direct their attention merely to detached expressions, to the language about the action, not to the action itself. I verily think that the majority of them do not in their hearts believe that there is such a thing as a total-impression to be derived from a poem at all, or to be demanded from a poet; they think the term a commonplace of metaphysical criticism. They will permit the Poet to select any action he pleases, and to suffer that action to go as it will, provided he gratifies them with occasional bursts of fine writing, and with a shower of isolated thoughts and images. . . .

But the modern critic not only permits a false practice; he absolutely prescribes false aims.—"A true allegory of the state of one's own mind in a representative history," the Poet is told, "is perhaps the highest thing that one can attempt in the way of poetry."—And accordingly he attempts it. An allegory of the state of one's own mind, the highest problem of an art which imitates actions! No assuredly, it is not, it never can be so: no great poetical work has ever been produced with such an aim. Faust itself, in which something of the kind is attempted, wonderful passages as it contains, and in

44-45. Orestes, the son of Agamemnon, who avenged his father's murder upon his mother Clytemnestra, a hero to all three of the great Greek tragic dramatists—Aeschylus, Sophocles, Euripides. **Merope,** a Greek queen who avenged the murder of her husband, and who appears in plays by Euripides, Voltaire, and Arnold himself. **Alcmaeon,** a Greek legendary hero, in some aspects resembling Orestes; the plays in which he figures are no longer extant.

19. Menander, Greek comic dramatist (343-291 B.C.).

spite of the unsurpassed beauty of the scenes which relate to Margaret, Faust itself, judged as a whole, and judged strictly as a poetical work, is defective: its illustrious author, the greatest poet of modern times, the greatest critic of all times, would have been the first to acknowledge it; he only defended his work, indeed, by asserting it to be "something incommensurable."

The confusion of the present times is great, the multitude of voices counselling different things bewildering, the number of existing works capable of attracting a young writer's attention and of becoming his models, immense: what he wants is a hand to guide him through the confusion, a voice to prescribe to him the aim which he should keep in view, and to explain to him that the value of the literary works which offer themselves to his attention is relative to their power of helping him forward on his road towards this aim. Such a guide the English writer at the present day will nowhere find. Failing this, all that can be looked for, all indeed that can be desired, is, that his attention should be fixed on excellent models; that he may reproduce, at any rate, something of their excellence, by penetrating himself with their works and by catching their spirit, if he cannot be taught to produce what is excellent independently.

Foremost among these models for the English writer stands Shakespeare: a name the greatest perhaps of all poetical names; a name never to be mentioned without reverence. I will venture, however, to express a doubt, whether the influence of his works, excellent and fruitful for the readers of poetry, for the great majority, has been an unmixed advantage to the writers of it. Shakespeare indeed chose excellent subjects; the world could afford no better than Macbeth, or Romeo and Juliet, or Othello: he had no theory respecting the necessity of choosing subjects of present import, or the paramount interest attaching to allegories of the state of one's own mind; like all great poets, he knew well what constituted a poetical action; like them, wherever he found such an action, he took it; like them, too, he found his best in past times. But to these general characteristics of all great poets he added a special one of his own; a gift, namely, of happy, abundant, and ingenious expression, eminent and unrivalled: so eminent as irresistibly to strike the attention first in him, and even to throw into comparative shade his other excellences as a poet. Here has been the mischief. These other excellences were his funda-

mental excellences *as a poet;* what distinguishes the artist from the mere amateur, says Goethe, is *Architectonicè* in the highest sense; that power of execution, which creates, forms, and constitutes: not the profoundness of single thoughts, not the richness of imagery, not the abundance of illustration. But these attractive accessories of a poetical work being more easily seized than the spirit of the whole, and these accessories being possessed by Shakespeare in an unequalled degree, a young writer having recourse to Shakespeare as his model runs great risk of being vanquished and absorbed by them, and, in consequence, of reproducing, according to the measure of his power, these, and these alone. Of this preponding quality of Shakespeare's genius, accordingly, almost the whole of modern English poetry has, it appears to me, felt the influence. To the exclusive attention on the part of his imitators to this, it is in a great degree owing that of the majority of modern poetical works the details alone are valuable, the composition worthless. . . .

Let me give an instance of what I mean. I will take it from the works of the very chief among those who seem to have been formed in the school of Shakespeare; of one whose exquisite genius and pathetic death render him for ever interesting. I will take the poem of Isabella, or the Pot of Basil, by Keats. I choose this rather than the Endymion, because the latter work (which a modern critic has classed with the Fairy Queen!), although undoubtedly there blows through it the breath of genius, is yet as a whole so utterly incoherent, as not strictly to merit the name of a poem at all. The poem of Isabella, then, is a perfect treasure-house of graceful and felicitous words and images: almost in every stanza there occurs one of those vivid and picturesque turns of expression, by which the object is made to flash upon the eye of the mind, and which thrill the reader with a sudden delight. This one short poem contains, perhaps, a greater number of happy single expressions which one could quote than all the extant tragedies of Sophocles. But the action, the story? The action in itself is an excellent one; but so feebly is it conceived by the Poet, so loosely constructed, that the effect produced by it, in and for itself, is absolutely null. Let the reader, after he has finished the poem of Keats, turn to the same story in the Decameron: he will then feel how pregnant and interesting the same action has become in the hands of a great artist, who above all things delineates his

---

6–8. he only . . . incommensurable." Arnold quotes Goethe's judgment of his *Faust* from Eckermann's report of his *Conversations with Goethe,* Jan. 3, 1830.

2. says Goethe, in his discussion of dilettantism in *Ferneres über Kunst.* **48–49. the same story in the Decameron,** by Giovanni Boccaccio, fourth day, fifth novel.

object; who subordinates expression to that which it is designed to express. . . .

What, then, it will be asked, are the ancients to be our sole models? the ancients with their comparatively narrow range of experience, and their widely different circumstances? Not, certainly, that which is narrow in the ancients, nor that in which we can no longer sympathize. An action like the action of the Antigone of Sophocles, which turns upon the conflict between the heroine's duty to her brother's corpse and that to the laws of her country, is no longer one in which it is possible that we should feel a deep interest. I am speaking too, it will be remembered, not of the best sources of intellectual stimulus for the general reader, but of the best models of instruction for the individual writer. This last may certainly learn of the ancients, better than anywhere else, three things which it is vitally important for him to know:—the all-importance of the choice of a subject; the necessity of accurate construction; and the subordinate character of expression. He will learn from them how unspeakably superior is the effect of the one moral impression left by a great action treated as a whole, to the effect produced by the most striking single thought or by the happiest image. As he penetrates into the spirit of the great classical works, as he becomes gradually aware of their intense significance, their noble simplicity, and their calm pathos, he will be convinced that it is this effect, unity and profoundness of moral impression, at which the ancient Poets aimed; that it is this which constitutes the grandeur of their works, and which makes them immortal. He will desire to direct his own efforts towards producing the same effect. Above all, he will deliver himself from the jargon of modern criticism, and escape the danger of producing poetical works conceived in the spirit of the passing time, and which partake of its transitoriness. . . .

A host of voices will indignantly rejoin that the present age is inferior to the past neither in moral grandeur nor in spiritual health. He who possesses the discipline I speak of will content himself with remembering the judgements passed upon the present age, in this respect, by the two men, the one of strongest head and the other of widest culture, whom it has produced; by Goethe and by Niebuhr. It will be sufficient for him that he knows the opinions held by these two great men respecting the present age and its literature; and

48–49. **Niebuhr**, Barthold Georg Niebuhr (1776–1831), the great German historian.

that he feels assured in his own mind that their aims and demands upon life were such as he would wish, at any rate, his own to be; and their judgement as to what is impeding and disabling such as he may safely follow. He will not, however, maintain a hostile attitude towards the false pretensions of his age; he will content himself with not being overwhelmed by them. He will esteem himself fortunate if he can succeed in banishing from his mind all feelings of contradiction, and irritation, and impatience; in order to delight himself with the contemplation of some noble action of a heroic time, and to enable others, through his representation of it, to delight in it also. . . .

Two kinds of *dilettanti*, says Goethe, there are in poetry: he who neglects the indispensable mechanical part, and thinks he has done enough if he shows spirituality and feeling; and he who seeks to arrive at poetry merely by mechanism, in which he can acquire an artisan's readiness, and is without soul and matter. And he adds, that the first does most harm to Art, and the last to himself. If we must be *dilettanti*: if it is impossible for us, under the circumstances amidst which we live, to think clearly, to feel nobly, and to delineate firmly: if we cannot attain to the mastery of the great artists—let us, at least, have so much respect for our Art as to prefer it to ourselves: let us not bewilder our successors: let us transmit to them the practice of Poetry, with its boundaries and wholesome regulative laws, under which excellent works may again, perhaps, at some future time, be produced, not yet fallen into oblivion through our neglect, not yet condemned and cancelled by the influence of their eternal enemy, Caprice.

from ON TRANSLATING HOMER
LAST WORDS

[The Grand Style]

Compare Ruskin's "Of the Received Opinions Touching the 'Grand Style,'" (page 628).

NOTHING has raised more questioning among my critics than these words,—*noble, the grand style*. People complain that I do not define these words sufficiently, that I do not tell them enough about them. "The grand style,—but what *is* the grand style?"—they cry; some with an inclination to believe in it, but puzzled; others mockingly and with incredulity. Alas! the grand style is the last

16. **says Goethe.** See note on l. 2, page 695.

matter in the world for verbal definition to deal with adequately. One may say of it as is said of faith: "One must feel it in order to know what it is." But, as of faith, so too one may say of nobleness, of the grand style: "Woe to those who know it not!" Yet this expression, though indefinable, has a charm; one is the better for considering it; *bonum est, nos hic esse;* nay, one loves to try to explain it, though one knows that one must speak imperfectly. For those, then, who ask the question,—What is the grand style?—with sincerity, I will try to make some answer, inadequate as it must be. For those who ask it mockingly I have no answer, except to repeat to them, with compassionate sorrow, the Gospel words: *Moriemini in peccatis vestris,*—Ye shall die in your sins.

But let me, at any rate, have the pleasure of again giving, before I begin to try and define the grand style, a specimen of what it *is*.

"Standing on earth, not wrapt above the pole,
More safe I sing with mortal voice, unchanged
To hoarse or mute, though fall'n on evil days,
On evil days though fall'n, and evil tongues." . . .

There is the grand style in perfection; and anyone who has a sense for it, will feel it a thousand times better from repeating those lines than from hearing anything I can say about it.

Let us try, however, what *can* be said, controlling what we say by examples. I think it will be found that the grand style arises in poetry, *when a noble nature, poetically gifted, treats with simplicity or with severity a serious subject.* . . .

The best model of the grand style simple is Homer; perhaps the best model of the grand style severe is Milton. But Dante is remarkable for affording admirable examples of both styles; he has the grand style which arises from simplicity, and he has the grand style which arises from severity; and from him I will illustrate them both. In a former lecture I pointed out what that severity of poetical style is, which comes from saying a thing with a kind of intense compression, or in an illusive, brief, almost haughty way, as if the poet's mind were charged

with so many and such grave matters, that he would not deign to treat any one of them explicitly. Of this severity the last line of the following stanza of the *Purgatory* is a good example. Dante has been telling Forese that Virgil had guided him through Hell, and he goes on:

> "Indi m' han tratto su gli suoi conforti,
> Salendo e rigirando la Montagna
> *Che drizza voi che il mondo fece torti.*"

"Thence hath his comforting aid led me up, climbing and circling the Mountain, *which straightens you whom the world made crooked.*" These last words, "la Montagna *che drizza voi che il mondo fece torti,*"—"the Mountain *which straightens you whom the world made crooked,*"—for the Mountain of Purgatory, I call an excellent specimen of the grand style in severity, where the poet's mind is too full charged to suffer him to speak more explicitly. But the very next stanza is a beautiful specimen of the grand style in simplicity, where a noble nature and a poetical gift unite to utter a thing with the most limpid plainness and clearness:

> "Tanto dice di farmi sua compagna
> Ch' io sarò là dove fia Beatrice;
> Quivi convien che senza lui rimagna."

"So long," Dante continues, "so long he (Virgil) saith he will bear me company, until I shall be there where Beatrice is; there it behoves that without him I remain." But the noble simplicity of that in the Italian no words of mine can render.

Both these styles, the simple and the severe, are truly grand; the severe seems, perhaps, the grandest, so long as we attend most to the great personality, to the noble nature, in the poet its author; the simple seems the grandest when we attend most to the exquisite faculty, to the poetical gift. But the simple is no doubt to be preferred. It is the more *magical:* in the other there is something intellectual, something which gives scope for a play of thought which may exist where the poetical gift is either wanting or present in only inferior degree: the severe is much more imitable, and this a little spoils its charm. A kind of semblance of this style keeps Young going, one may say, through all the nine parts of that most indifferent production, the *Night Thoughts.* But the grand style in simplicity is

7-8. bonum est, nos hic esse. See Matthew 17:4 (Vulgate). 15. Moriemini in peccatis vestris. See John 8:24 (Vulgate). 20-23. "Standing . . . tongues." See Milton's *Paradise Lost,* Book VII, ll. 23-26. 36. Dante, Dante Alighieri (1265-1321), the greatest Italian poet. 40. form r lecture. The three lectures which comprise *On Translating Homer,* 1860, were read at Oxford in 1860. *On Translating Homer: Last Words,* from which the excerpt in this anthology is taken, was published separately in 1862, as a reply to Professor Francis William Newman (1805–1897), who had objected to Arnold's criticism in his Oxford lectures of Newman's translation of the *Iliad.*

5. Forese, Forese Donati, Dante's brother-in-law and friend, wh m he finds being purged of the sin of gluttony in purgatory. 31. no words of mine can render. Both quotations from *The Divine Comedy* are taken from *Purgatory,* Canto 23, ll. 124-29. 47. Night Thoughts, by Edward Young, one of the most famous poems of the "graveyard school," published in 1742.

inimitable:

αἰὼν ἀσφαλὴς
οὐκ ἔγεντ' οὔτ' Αἰακίδᾳ παρὰ Πηλεῖ,
οὔτε παρ' ἀντιθέῳ Κάδμῳ· λέγονται μὰν βροτῶν
ὄλβον ὑπέρτατον οἱ σχεῖν, οἵ τε καὶ χρυσαμπύκων
μελπομενᾶν ἐν ὄρει Μοισᾶν, καὶ ἐν ἑπταπύλοις
ἄϊον Θήβαις . . .

There is a limpidness in that, a want of salient points to seize and transfer, which makes imitation impossible, except by a genius akin to the genius which produced it.

from ESSAYS IN CRITICISM, FIRST SERIES

from Chapter 1: THE FUNCTION OF CRITICISM AT THE PRESENT TIME

MANY objections have been made to a proposition which, in some remarks of mine on translating Homer, I ventured to put forth; a proposition about criticism, and its importance at the present day. I said: "Of the literature of France and Germany, as of the intellect of Europe in general, the main effort, for now many years, has been a critical effort; the endeavour, in all branches of knowledge, theology, philosophy, history, art, science, to see the object as in itself it really is." I added, that owing to the operation in English literature of certain causes, "almost the last thing for which one would come to English literature is just that very thing which now Europe most desires,—criticism"; and that the power and value of English literature was thereby impaired. More than one rejoinder declared that the importance I here assigned to criticism was excessive, and asserted the inherent superiority of the creative effort of the human spirit over its critical effort. . . .

. . . It is undeniable that the exercise of a creative power, that a free creative activity, is the highest function of man; it is proved to be so by man's finding in it his true happiness. But it is undeniable, also, that men may have the sense of exercising this free creative activity in other ways than in producing great works of literature or art; if it were not so, all but a very few men would be shut out from the

2–7. αἰὼν . . . Θήβαις. "A secure time fell to the lot neither of Peleus the son of Aeacus, nor of the godlike Cadmus; howbeit these are said to have had, of all mortals, the supreme of happiness, who heard the golden-snooded Muses sing, one of them on the mountain (Pelion), the other in seven-gated Thebus." (Arnold) The quotation is from the *Pythian Odes* of Pindar.   21–22. in some remarks . . . Homer, at the end of Lecture 2 of *On Translating Homer*.

true happiness of all men. They may have it in well-doing, they may have it in learning, they may have it even in criticising. This is one thing to be kept in mind. Another is, that the exercise of the creative power in the production of great works of literature or art, however high this exercise of it may rank, is not at all epochs and under all conditions possible; and that therefore labour may be vainly spent in attempting it, which might with more fruit be used in preparing for it, in rendering it possible. This creative power works with elements, with materials; what if it has not those materials, those elements, ready for its use? In that case it must surely wait till they are ready. Now, in literature,—I will limit myself to literature, for it is about literature that the question arises,—the elements with which the creative power works are ideas; the best ideas on every matter which literature touches, current at the time. At any rate we may lay it down as certain that in modern literature no manifestation of the creative power not working with these can be very important or fruitful. And I say *current* at the time, not merely accessible at the time; for creative literary genius does not principally show itself in discovering new ideas, that is rather the business of the philosopher. The grand work of literary genius is a work of synthesis and exposition, not of analysis and discovery; its gift lies in the faculty of being happily inspired by a certain intellectual and spiritual atmosphere, by a certain order of ideas, when it finds itself in them; of dealing divinely with these ideas, presenting them in the most effective and attractive combinations,—making beautiful works with them, in short. But it must have the atmosphere, it must find itself amidst the order of ideas, in order to work freely; and these it is not so easy to command. This is why great creative epochs in literature are so rare, this is why there is so much that is unsatisfactory in the productions of many men of real genius; because, for the creation of a master-work of literature two powers must concur, the power of the man and the power of the moment, and the man is not enough without the moment; the creative power has, for its happy exercise, appointed elements, and those elements are not in its own control.

Nay, they are more within the control of the critical power. It is the business of the critical power, as I said in the words already quoted, "in all branches of knowledge, theology, philosophy, history, art, science, to see the object as in itself it really is." Thus it tends, at last, to make an intellectual situation of which the creative power can profitably avail itself. It tends to establish an order of ideas, if not absolutely true, yet true by comparison with that which it displaces; to make the best ideas prevail. Presently these new ideas reach society, the touch of truth is the touch of life, and there is a stir and growth everywhere; out of this stir and growth come the creative epochs of literature.

Or, to narrow our range, and quit these considerations of the general march of genius and of society,—considerations which are apt to become too abstract and impalpable,—every one can see that a poet, for instance, ought to know life and the world before dealing with them in poetry; and life and the world being in modern times very complex things, the creation of a modern poet, to be worth much, implies a great critical effort behind it; else it must be a comparatively poor, barren, and short-lived affair. This is why Byron's poetry had so little endurance in it, and Goethe's so much; both Byron and Goethe had a great productive power, but Goethe's was nourished by a great critical effort providing the true materials for it, and Byron's was not; Goethe knew life and the world, the poet's necessary subjects, much more comprehensively and thoroughly than Byron. . . .

It has long seemed to me that the burst of creative activity in our literature, through the first quarter of this century, had about it in fact something premature; and that from this cause its productions are doomed, most of them, in spite of the sanguine hopes which accompanied and do still accompany them, to prove hardly more lasting than the productions of far less splendid epochs. And this prematureness comes from its having proceeded without having its proper data, without sufficient materials to work with. In other words, the English poetry of the first quarter of this century, with plenty of energy, plenty of creative force, did not know enough. This makes Byron so empty of matter, Shelley so incoherent, Wordsworth even, profound as he is, yet so wanting in completeness and variety. Wordsworth cared little for books, and disparaged Goethe. . . .

But to speak of books and reading may easily lead to a misunderstanding here. It was not really books and reading that lacked to our poetry at this epoch: Shelley had plenty of reading, Coleridge had immense reading. Pindar and Sophocles—as we all say so glibly, and often with so little discernment of the real import of what we are saying—had not many books; Shakspeare was no deep reader. True; but in the Greece of Pindar and Sophocles, in the England of Shakspeare, the poet lived in a current

48. Pindar, Greek lyric poet (522–c. 448 B.C.).

of ideas in the highest degree animating and nourishing to the creative power; society was, in the fullest measure, permeated by fresh thought, intelligent and alive. And this state of things is the true basis for the creative power's exercise, in this it finds its data, its materials, truly ready for its hand; all the books and reading in the world are only valuable as they are helps to this. Even when this does not actually exist, books and reading may enable a man to construct a kind of semblance of it in his own mind, a world of knowledge and intelligence in which he may live and work. This is by no means an equivalent to the artist for the nationally diffused life and thought of the epochs of Sophocles or Shakspeare; but, besides that it may be a means of preparation for such epochs, it does really constitute, if many share in it, a quickening and sustaining atmosphere of great value. Such an atmosphere the many-sided learning and the long and widely combined critical effort of Germany formed for Goethe, when he lived and worked. There was no national glow of life and thought there as in the Athens of Pericles or the England of Elizabeth. That was the poet's weakness. But there was a sort of equivalent for it in the complete culture and unfettered thinking of a large body of Germans. That was his strength. In the England of the first quarter of this century there was neither a national glow of life and thought, such as we had in the age of Elizabeth, nor yet a culture and a force of learning and criticism such as were to be found in Germany. Therefore the creative power of poetry wanted, for success in the highest sense, materials and a basis; a thorough interpretation of the world was necessarily denied to it. . . .

It is of the last importance that English criticism should clearly discern what rule for its course, in order to avail itself of the field now opening to it, and to produce fruit for the future, it ought to take. The rule may be summed up in one word,—*disinterestedness*. And how is criticism to show disinterestedness? By keeping aloof from what is called "the practical view of things"; by resolutely following the law of its own nature, which is to be a free play of the mind on all subjects which it touches. By steadily refusing to lend itself to any of those ulterior, political, practical considerations about ideas, which plenty of people will be sure to attach to them, which perhaps ought often to be attached to them, which in this country at any rate are certain to be attached to them quite sufficiently, but which

22–23. Pericles, Athenian statesman (c. 495–429 B.C.). **Elizabeth,** Queen of England from 1558 to 1603.

criticism has really nothing to do with. Its business is, as I have said, simply to know the best that is known and thought in the world, and by in its turn making this known, to create a current of true and fresh ideas. Its business is to do this with inflexible honesty, with due ability; but its business is to do no more, and to leave alone all questions of practical consequences and applications, questions which will never fail to have due prominence given to them. Else criticism, besides being really false to [10] its own nature, merely continues in the old rut which it has hitherto followed in this country, and will certainly miss the chance now given to it. For what is at present the bane of criticism in this country? It is that practical considerations cling to it and stifle it. It subserves interests not its own. Our organs of criticism are organs of men and parties having practical ends to serve, and with them those practical ends are the first thing and the play of mind the second; so much play of mind as is com- [20] patible with the prosecution of those practical ends is all that is wanted. An organ like the *Revue des Deux Mondes*, having for its main function to understand and utter the best that is known and thought in the world, existing, it may be said, as just an organ for a free play of the mind, we have not. But we have the *Edinburgh Review*, existing as an organ of the old Whigs, and for as much play of mind as may suit its being that; we have the *Quarterly Review*, existing as an organ of the Tories, and for as much [30] play of mind as may suit its being that; we have the *British Quarterly Review*, existing as an organ of the political Dissenters, and for as much play of mind as may suit its being that; we have the *Times*, existing as an organ of the common, satisfied, well-to-do Englishman, and for as much play of mind as may suit its being that. And so on through all the various fractions, political and religious, of our society; every fraction has, as such, its organ of criticism, but the notion of combining all fractions in the com- [40] mon pleasure of a free disinterested play of mind meets with no favour. Directly this play of mind wants to have more scope, and to forget the pressure of practical considerations a little, it is checked, it is made to feel the chain. We saw this the other day in the extinction, so much to be regretted, of the *Home and Foreign Review*. Perhaps in no organ of criticism in this country was there so much knowl-

edge, so much play of mind; but these could not save it. The *Dublin Review* subordinates play of mind to the practical business of English and Irish Catholicism, and lives. . . .

It is because criticism has so little kept in the pure intellectual sphere, has so little detached itself from practice, has been so directly polemical and controversial, that it has so ill accomplished, in this [10] country, its best spiritual work; which is to keep man from a self-satisfaction which is retarding and vulgarising, to lead him towards perfection, by making his mind dwell upon what is excellent in itself, and the absolute beauty and fitness of things. A polemical practical criticism makes men blind even to the ideal imperfection of their practice, makes them willingly assert its ideal perfection, in order the better to secure it against attack; and clearly this is narrowing and baneful for them. If [20] they were reassured on the practical side, speculative considerations of ideal perfection they might be brought to entertain, and their spiritual horizon would thus gradually widen. Sir Charles Adderley says to the Warwickshire farmers:—

"Talk of the improvement of breed! Why, the race we ourselves represent, the men and women, the old Anglo-Saxon race, are the best breed in the whole world. . . . The absence of a too enervating climate, too unclouded skies, and a too luxurious [30] nature, has produced so vigorous a race of people, and has rendered us so superior to all the world."

Mr. Roebuck says to the Sheffield cutlers:—

"I look around me and ask what is the state of England? Is not property safe? Is not every man able to say what he likes? Can you not walk from one end of England to the other in perfect security? I ask you whether, the world over or in past history, there is anything like it? Nothing. I pray that our unrivalled happiness may last."

[40] Now obviously there is a peril for poor human nature in words and thoughts of such exuberant self-satisfaction, until we find ourselves safe in the streets of the Celestial City.

"Das wenige verschwindet leicht dem Blicke
Der vorwärts sieht, wie viel noch übrig bleibt—"

says Goethe; "the little that is done seems nothing when we look forward and see how much we have yet to do." Clearly this is a better line of reflection

22–23. **Revue des Deux Mondes,** Paris, established 1831; still current.   27. **Edinburgh Review,** established 1802; still current.   29. **Quarterly Review,** London, established 1809; still current.   32. **British Quarterly Review,** London, 1845–86.   34. **Times,** London, established 1788; still current.   47. **Home and Foreign Review,** London, 1862–64.

2. **Dublin Review,** established 1836; still current. 23. **Sir Charles Adderley,** first Baron Norton (1814–1905). 32. **Mr. Roebuck,** John Arthur Roebuck, M.P. (1801–1879), radical politician, one of Arnold's favorite targets. 47. **says Goethe,** in *Iphigenia in Tauris,* Act I, sc. 2, ll. 91–92.

for weak humanity, so long as it remains on this earthly field of labour and trial.

But neither Sir Charles Adderley nor Mr. Roebuck is by nature inaccessible to considerations of this sort. They only lose sight of them owing to the controversial life we all lead, and the practical form which all speculation takes with us. They have in view opponents whose aim is not ideal, but practical; and in their zeal to uphold their own practice against these innovators, they go so far as even to attribute to this practice an ideal perfection. Somebody has been wanting to introduce a six-pound franchise, or to abolish church-rates, or to collect agricultural statistics by force, or to diminish local self-government. How natural, in reply to such proposals, very likely improper or ill-timed, to go a little beyond the mark and to say stoutly, "Such a race of people as we stand, so superior to all the world! The old Anglo-Saxon race, the best breed in the whole world! I pray that our unrivalled happiness may last! I ask you whether, the world over or in past history, there is anything like it?" And so long as criticism answers this dithyramb by insisting that the old Anglo-Saxon race would be still more superior to all others if it had no church-rates, or that our unrivalled happiness would last yet longer with a six-pound franchise, so long will the strain, "The best breed in the whole world!" swell louder and louder, everything ideal and refining will be lost out of sight, and both the assailed and their critics will remain in a sphere, to say the truth, perfectly unvital, a sphere in which spiritual progression is impossible, But let criticism leave church-rates and the franchise alone, and in the most candid spirit, without a single lurking thought of practical innovation, confront with our dithyramb this paragraph on which I stumbled in a newspaper immediately after reading Mr. Roebuck:—

"A shocking child murder has just been committed at Nottingham. A girl named Wragg left the workhouse there on Saturday morning with her young illegitimate child. The child was soon afterwards found dead on Mapperly Hills, having been strangled. Wragg is in custody."

Nothing but that; but, in juxtaposition with the absolute eulogies of Sir Charles Adderley and Mr. Roebuck, how eloquent, how suggestive are those few lines! "Our old Anglo-Saxon breed, the best in the whole world!"—how much that is harsh and ill-favoured there is in this best! Wragg! If we are to talk of ideal perfection, of "the best in the whole world," has any one reflected what a touch of grossness in our race, what an original shortcoming in the more delicate spiritual perceptions, is shown by the natural growth amongst us of such hideous names,—Higginbottom, Stiggins, Bugg! In Ionia and Attica they were luckier in this respect than "the best race in the world"; by the Ilissus there was no Wragg, poor thing! And "our unrivalled happiness";—what an element of grimness, bareness, and hideousness mixes with it and blurs it; the workhouse, the dismal Mapperly Hills,—how dismal those who have seen them will remember;—the gloom, the smoke, the cold, the strangled illegitimate child! "I ask you whether, the world over or in past history, there is anything like it?" Perhaps not, one is inclined to answer; but at any rate, in that case, the world is very much to be pitied. And the final touch,—short, bleak, and inhuman: Wragg is in custody. The sex lost in the confusion of our unrivalled happiness; or (shall I say?) the superfluous Christian name lopped off by the straightforward vigour of our old Anglo-Saxon breed! There is profit for the spirit in such contrasts as this; criticism serves the cause of perfection by establishing them. By eluding sterile conflict, by refusing to remain in the sphere where alone narrow and relative conceptions have any worth and validity, criticism may diminish its momentary importance, but only in this way has it a chance of gaining admittance for those wider and more perfect conceptions to which all its duty is really owed. Mr. Roebuck will have a poor opinion of an adversary who replies to his defiant songs of triumph only by murmuring under his breath, Wragg is in custody; but in no other way will these songs of triumph be induced gradually to moderate themselves, to get rid of what in them is excessive and offensive, and to fall into a softer and truer key.

It will be said that it is a very subtle and indirect action which I am thus prescribing for criticism, and that, by embracing in this manner the Indian virtue of detachment and abandoning the sphere of practical life, it condemns itself to a slow and obscure work. Slow and obscure it may be, but it is the only proper work of criticism. The mass of mankind will never have any ardent zeal for seeing things as they are; very inadequate ideas will always satisfy them. On these inadequate ideas reposes, and must repose, the general practice of the world. That is as much as saying that whoever sets himself to see things as they are will find himself one

---

12–13. six-pound franchise, a bill to grant the right to vote to all persons owning property worth £6 (instead of £10) per year. church-rates, taxes for the support of the Church of England.

6–7. Ionia . . . Attica, districts in ancient Greece. 8. Ilissus, a river near Athens. 42. Indian, Hindu, Buddhist.

of a very small circle; but it is only by this small circle resolutely doing its own work that adequate ideas will ever get current at all. The rush and roar of practical life will always have a dizzying and attracting effect upon the most collected spectator, and tend to draw him into its vortex; most of all will this be the case where that life is so powerful as it is in England. But it is only by remaining collected, and refusing to lend himself to the point of view of the practical man, that the critic can do the practical man any service; and it is only by the greatest sincerity in pursuing his own course, and by at last convincing even the practical man of his sincerity, that he can escape misunderstandings which perpetually threaten him. . . .

Do what he will, . . . the critic will still remain exposed to frequent misunderstandings, and nowhere so much as in this country. For here people are particularly indisposed even to comprehend that without this free disinterested treatment of things, truth and the highest culture are out of the question. So immersed are they in practical life, so accustomed to take all their notions from this life and its processes, that they are apt to think that truth and culture themselves can be reached by the processes of this life, and that it is an impertinent singularity to think of reaching them in any other. We are all *terrae filii*," cries their eloquent advocate; "all Philistines together. Away with the notion of proceeding by any other course than the course dear to the Philistines; let us have a social movement, let us organise and combine a party to pursue truth and new thought, let us call it *the liberal party*, and let us all stick to each other, and back each other up. Let us have no nonsense about independent criticism, and intellectual delicacy, and the few and the many. Don't let us trouble ourselves about foreign thought; we shall invent the whole thing for ourselves as we go along. If one of us speaks well, applaud him; if one of us speaks ill, applaud him too; we are all in the same movement, we are all liberals, we are all in pursuit of truth." In this way the pursuit of truth becomes really a social, practical, pleasurable affair, almost requiring a chairman, a secretary, and advertisements; with the excitement of an occasional scandal, with a little resistance to give the happy sense of difficulty overcome; but, in general, plenty of bustle and very little thought. To act is so easy, as Goethe says; to think is so hard! It is true that the critic has many temptations to go with the stream, to make one of the party movement, one of these *terrae filii*; it seems ungracious to refuse to be a *terrae filius*, when so many excellent people are; but the critic's duty is to refuse, or, if resistance is vain, at least to cry with Obermann, *Périssons en résistant.* . . .

I lately heard a man of thought and energy contrasting the want of ardour and movement which he now found amongst young men in this country with what he remembered in his own youth, twenty years ago. "What reformers we were then!" he exclaimed; "What a zeal we had! how we canvassed every institution in Church and State, and were prepared to remodel them all on first principles!" He was inclined to regret, as a spiritual flagging, the lull which he saw. I am disposed rather to regard it as a pause in which the turn to a new mode of spiritual progress is being accomplished. Everything was long seen, by the young and ardent amongst us, in inseparable connection with politics and practical life. We have pretty well exhausted the benefits of seeing things in this connection, we have got all that can be got by so seeing them. Let us try a more disinterested mode of seeing them; let us betake ourselves more to the serener life of the mind and spirit. This life, too, may have its excesses and dangers; but they are not for us at present. Let us think of quietly enlarging our stock of true and fresh ideas, and not, as soon as we get an idea or half an idea, be running out with it into the street, and trying to make it rule there. Our ideas will, in the end, shape the world all the better for maturing a little. . . .

If I have insisted so much on the course which criticism must take where politics and religion are concerned, it is because, where these burning matters are in question, it is most likely to go astray. I have wished, above all, to insist on the attitude which criticism should adopt towards things in general; on its right tone and temper of mind. But then comes another question as to the subject-matter which literary criticism should most seek. Here, in general, its course is determined for it by the idea which is the law of its being; the idea of a disinterested endeavour to learn and propagate the best

<hr />

29. terrae filii," sons of the earth. **30. Philistines,** one of Arnold's most famous words, used first in "Heinrich Heine" (*Essays in Criticism*), most elaborately in "Barbarians, Philistines, Populace" (*Culture and Anarchy*). By it he indicates an uncultured member of the middle class. Historically, the Philistines were a non-Semitic people in Palestine with whom the Hebrews had considerable friction. They play a considerable part in the story of Samson (Book of Judges).

9. Périssons en résistant. Let us die resisting. See Etienne Pivert de Senancour (1770–1846), *Obermann*, Letter 90. **39–41. If . . . concerned.** Much of this discussion has been omitted from the present reprint.

hat is known and thought in the world, and thus to establish a current of fresh and true ideas. By the very nature of things, as England is not all the world, much of the best that is known and thought n the world cannot be of English growth, must be oreign; by the nature of things, again, it is just this hat we are least likely to know, while English hought is streaming in upon us from all sides, and akes excellent care that we shall not be ignorant of its existence. The English critic of literature, therefore, must dwell much on foreign thought, and with particular heed on any part of it, which, while significant and fruitful in itself, is for any reason pecially likely to escape him. . . .

But stop, some one will say; all this talk is of no practical use to us whatever; this criticism of yours is not what we have in our minds when we speak of criticism; when we speak of critics and criticism, we mean critics and criticism of the current English iterature of the day; when you offer to tell criticism ts function, it is to this criticism that we expect you o address yourself. I am sorry for it, for I am afraid I must disappoint these expectations. I am bound by my own definition of criticism: *a disinterested endeavour to learn and propagate the best that is known and thought in the world.* How much of current English iterature comes into this "best that is known and thought in the world"? Not very much, I fear; certainly less, at this moment, than of the current literature of France or Germany. Well, then, am I to alter my definition of criticism, in order to meet the requirements of a number of practising English critics, who, after all, are free in their choice of a business? That would be making criticism lend itself just to one of those alien practical considerations, which, I have said, are so fatal to it. One may say, indeed, to those who have to deal with the mass—so much better disregarded—of current English literature, that they may at all events endeavour, in dealing with this, to try it, so far as they can, by the standard of the best that is known and thought in the world; one may say, that to get anywhere near this standard, every critic should try and possess one great literature, at least, besides his own; and the more unlike his own, the better. But, after all, the criticism I am really concerned with, —the criticism which alone can much help us for the future, the criticism which, throughout Europe, is at the present day meant, when so much stress is laid on the importance of criticism and the critical spirit,—is a criticism which regards Europe as being, for intellectual and spiritual purposes, one great confederation, bound to a joint action and work-ing to a common result; and whose members have, for their proper outfit, a knowledge of Greek, Roman, and Eastern antiquity, and of one another. . . .

I conclude with what I said at the beginning: to have the sense of creative activity is the great happiness and the great proof of being alive, and it is not denied to criticism to have it; but then criticism must be sincere, simple, flexible, ardent, ever widening its knowledge. Then it may have, in no contemptible measure, a joyful sense of creative activity; a sense which a man of insight and conscience will prefer to what he might derive from a poor, starved, fragmentary, inadequate creation. And at some epochs no other creation is possible.

Still, in full measure, the sense of creative activity belongs only to genuine creation; in literature we must never forget that. But what true man of letters ever can forget it? It is no such common matter for a gifted nature to come into possession of a current of true and living ideas, and to produce amidst the inspiration of them, that we are likely to underrate it. The epochs of Aeschylus and Shakspeare make us feel their pre-eminence. In an epoch like those is, no doubt, the true life of literature; there is the promised land, towards which criticism can only beckon. That promised land it will not be ours to enter, and we shall die in the wilderness: but to have desired to enter it, to have saluted it from afar, is already, perhaps, the best distinction among contemporaries; it will certainly be the best title to esteem with posterity.

from CULTURE AND ANARCHY

from Chapter I: SWEETNESS AND LIGHT

THE disparagers of culture make its motive curiosity; sometimes, indeed, they make its motive mere exclusiveness and vanity. The culture which is supposed to plume itself on a smattering of Greek and Latin is a culture which is begotten by nothing so intellectual as curiosity; it is valued either out of sheer vanity and ignorance or else as an engine of social and class distinction, separating its holder, like a badge or title, from other people who have not got it. No serious man would call this *culture*, or attach any value to it, as culture, at all. To find the real ground for the very different estimate which serious people will set upon culture, we must find some motive for culture in the terms of which

24. **Aeschylus,** Greek tragic dramatist (525-456 B.C.).

may lie a real ambiguity; and such a motive the word *curiosity* gives us.

I have before now pointed out that we English do not, like the foreigners, use this word in a good sense as well as in a bad sense. With us the word is always used in a somewhat disapproving sense. A liberal and intelligent eagerness about the things of the mind may be meant by a foreigner when he speaks of curiosity, but with us the word always conveys a certain notion of frivolous and unedifying 10 activity. In the *Quarterly Review*, some little time ago, was an estimate of the celebrated French critic, M. Sainte-Beuve, and a very inadequate estimate it in my judgment was. And its inadequacy consisted chiefly in this: that in our English way it left out of sight the double sense really involved in the word *curiosity*, thinking enough was said to stamp M. Sainte-Beuve with blame if it was said that he was impelled in his operations as a critic by curiosity, and omitting either to perceive that M. Sainte- 20 Beuve himself, and many other people with him, would consider that this was praiseworthy and not blameworthy, or to point out why it ought really to be accounted worthy of blame and not of praise. For as there is a curiosity about intellectual matters which is futile, and merely a disease, so there is certainly a curiosity,—a desire after the things of the mind simply for their own sakes and for the pleasure of seeing them as they are,—which is, in an intelligent being, natural and laudable. Nay, 30 and the very desire to see things as they are implies a balance and regulation of mind which is not often attained without fruitful effort, and which is the very opposite of the blind and diseased impulse of mind which is what we mean to blame when we blame curiosity. . . .

But there is of culture another view, in which not solely the scientific passion, the sheer desire to see things as they are, natural and proper in an intelli- 40 gent being, appears as the ground of it. There is a view in which all the love of our neighbour, the impulses towards action, help, and beneficence, the desire for removing human error, clearing human confusion, and diminishing human misery, the noble aspiration to leave the world better and happier than we found it,—motives eminently such as are called social,—come in as part of the grounds of culture, and the main and pre-eminent part. Culture is then properly described not as having its 50 origin in curiosity, but as having its origin in the love of perfection; it is *a study of perfection*. . . . As,

13. **M. Sainte-Beuve,** Charles Augustin Sainte-Beuve (1804–1869).

in the first view of it, we took for its worthy motto Montesquieu's words: "To render an intelligent being yet more intelligent!" so, in the second view of it, there is no better motto which it can have than these words of Bishop Wilson: "To make reason and the will of God prevail!"

Only, whereas the passion for doing good is apt to be overhasty in determining what reason and the will of God say, because its turn is for acting rather than thinking and it wants to be beginning to act; and whereas it is apt to take its own conceptions, which proceed from its own state of development and share in all the imperfections and immaturities of this, for a basis of action; what distinguishes culture is, that it is possessed by the scientific passion as well as by the passion of doing good; that it demands worthy notions of reason and the will of God, and does not readily suffer its own crude conceptions to substitute themselves for them. And knowing that no action or institution can be salutary and stable which is not based on reason and the will of God, it is not so bent on acting and instituting, even with the great aim of diminishing human error and misery ever before its thoughts, but that it can remember that acting and instituting are of little use, unless we know how and what we ought to act and to institute. . . .

The moment this view of culture is seized, the moment it is regarded not solely as the endeavour to see things as they are, to draw towards a knowledge of the universal order which seems to be intended and aimed at in the world, and which it is a man's happiness to go along with or his misery to go counter to,—to learn, in short, the will of God,— the moment, I say, culture is considered not merely as the endeavour to *see* and *learn* this, but as the endeavour, also, to make it *prevail*, the moral, social, and beneficent character of culture becomes manifest. . . .

And religion, the greatest and most important of the efforts by which the human race has manifested its impulse to perfect itself,—religion, that voice of the deepest human experience,—does not only enjoin and sanction the aim which is the great aim of culture, the aim of setting ourselves to ascertain what perfection is and to make it prevail; but also, in determining generally in what human perfection consists, religion comes to a conclusion iden-

2. **Montesquieu,** Charles de Secondat, Baron de la Brède et de Montesquieu (1689–1755), French political philosopher. 5. **Bishop Wilson,** Thomas Wilson (1663–1755), Bishop of Sodor and Man.

his philosophy

ical with that which culture,—culture seeking the determination of this question through *all* the voices of human experience which have been heard upon it, of art, science, poetry, philosophy, history, as well as of religion, in order to give a greater fulness and certainty to its solution,—likewise reaches. Religion says: *The kingdom of God is within you;* and culture, in like manner, places human perfection in an *internal* condition, in the growth and predominance of our humanity proper, as distinguished from our animality. It places it in the ever-increasing efficacy and in the general harmonious expansion of those gifts of thought and feeling, which make the peculiar dignity, wealth, and happiness of human nature. As I have said on a former occasion: 'It is in making endless additions to itself, in the endless expansion of its powers, in endless growth in wisdom and beauty, that the spirit of the human race finds its ideal. To reach this ideal, culture is an indispensable aid, and that is the true value of culture." Not a having and a resting, but a growing and a becoming, is the character of perfection as culture conceives it; and here, too, it coincides with religion.

And because men are all members of one great whole, and the sympathy which is in human nature will not allow one member to be indifferent to the rest or to have a perfect welfare independent of the rest, the expansion of our humanity, to suit the idea of perfection which culture forms, must be a *general* expansion. Perfection, as culture conceives it, is not possible while the individual remains isolated. The individual is required, under pain of being stunted and enfeebled in his own development if he disobeys, to carry others along with him in his march towards perfection, to be continually doing all he can to enlarge and increase the volume of the human stream sweeping thitherward. And here, once more, culture lays on us the same obligation as religion which says, as Bishop Wilson has admirably put it, that "to promote the kingdom of God is to increase and hasten one's own happiness."

But, finally, perfection,—as culture from a thorough disinterested study of human nature and human experience learns to conceive it,—is a harmonious expansion of *all* the powers which make the beauty and worth of human nature, and is not consistent with the over-development of any one power at the expense of the rest. Here culture goes beyond religion, as religion is generally conceived by us.

If culture, then, is a study of perfection, and of harmonious perfection, general perfection, and perfection which consists in becoming something rather than in having something, in an inward condition of the mind and spirit, not in an outward set of circumstances,—it is clear that culture, instead of being the frivolous and useless thing which Mr. Bright, and Mr. Frederic Harrison, and many other Liberals are apt to call it, has a very important function to fulfil for mankind. And this function is particularly important in our modern world, of which the whole civilisation is, to a much greater degree than the civilisation of Greece and Rome, mechanical and external, and tends constantly to become more so. But above all in our own country has culture a weighty part to perform, because here that mechanical character, which civilisation tends to take everywhere, is shown in the most eminent degree. Indeed nearly all the characters of perfection, as culture teaches us to fix them, meet in this country with some powerful tendency which thwarts them and sets them at defiance. The idea of perfection as an *inward* condition of the mind and spirit is at variance with the mechanical and material civilisation in esteem with us, and nowhere, as I have said, so much in esteem as with us. The idea of perfection as a *general* expansion of the human family is at variance with our strong individualism, our hatred of all limits to the unrestrained swing of the individual's personality, our maxim of "every man for himself." Above all, the idea of perfection as a *harmonious* expansion of human nature is at variance with our want of flexibility, with our inaptitude for seeing more than one side of a thing, with our intense energetic absorption in the particular pursuit we happen to be following. So culture has a rough task to achieve in this country. Its preachers have, and are likely long to have, a hard time of it, and they will much oftener be regarded, for a great while to come, as elegant or spurious Jeremiahs than as friends and benefactors. That, however, will not prevent their doing in the end good service if they persevere. And, meanwhile, the mode of action they have to pursue, and the sort of habits they must fight against, ought to be made quite clear for

7. **The kingdom . . . you.** See Luke 17:21. The meaning of the passage is disputed; see any good Bible commentary.

7. **Mr. Bright,** John Bright (1811–1889), famous Victorian statesman. 8. **Mr. Frederic Harrison** (1831–1923), a prominent Victorian writer in varied fields, known especially as a leader of the Positivist movement. 40. **elegant or spurious Jeremiahs.** Jeremiah (seventh century B.C.) was probably the greatest of the Hebrew prophets (see Stefan Zweig's play *Jeremiah*, Viking Press, 1923, and Franz Werfel's novel *Hearken to the Voice*, Viking Press, 1938), but from the popular attribution to him of the Book of Lamentations he enjoys an undeserved reputation as "the weeping prophet." Note the word "jeremiad," a lamenting and denunciatory complaint.

individual is required
bishop

every one to see, who may be willing to look at the matter attentively and dispassionately.

Faith in machinery, is, I said, our besetting danger; often in machinery most absurdly disproportioned to the end which this machinery, if it is to do any good at all, is to serve; but always in machinery, as if it had a value in and for itself. What is freedom but machinery? what is population but machinery? what is coal but machinery? what are railroads but machinery? what is wealth but machinery? what are, even, religious organisations but machinery? Now almost every voice in England is accustomed to speak of these things as if they were precious ends in themselves, and therefore had some of the characters of perfection indisputably joined to them. . . .

. . . Every one must have observed the strange language current during the late discussions as to the possible failures of our supplies of coal. Our coal, thousands of people were saying, is the real basis of our national greatness; if our coal runs short, there is an end of the greatness of England. But what *is* greatness?—culture makes us ask. Greatness is a spiritual condition worthy to excite love, interest, and admiration; and the outward proof of possessing greatness is that we excite love, interest, and admiration. If England were swallowed up by the sea to-morrow, which of the two, a hundred years hence, would most excite the love, interest, and admiration of mankind,—would most, therefore, show the evidences of having possessed greatness,—the England of the last twenty years, or the England of Elizabeth, of a time of splendid spiritual effort, but when our coal, and our industrial operations depending on coal, were very little developed? Well, then, what an unsound habit of mind it must be which makes us talk of things like coal or iron as constituting the greatness of England, and how salutary a friend is culture, bent on seeing things as they are, and thus dissipating delusions of this kind and fixing standards of perfection that are real!

Wealth, again, that end to which our prodigious works for material advantage are directed,—the commonest of commonplaces tells us how men are always apt to regard wealth as a precious end in itself; and certainly they have never been so apt thus to regard it as they are in England at the present time. Never did people believe anything more firmly than nine Englishmen out of ten at the present day believe that our greatness and welfare are proved by our being so very rich. Now, the use of culture is that it helps us, by means of its spiritual standard of perfection, to regard wealth as but machinery, and not only to say as a matter of words that we regard wealth as but machinery, but really to perceive and feel that it is so. If it were not for this purging effect wrought upon our minds by culture, the whole world, the future as well as the present, would inevitably belong to the Philistines. The people who believe most that our greatness and welfare are proved by our being very rich, and who most give their lives and thoughts to becoming rich, are just the very people whom we call Philistines. Culture says: "Consider these people, then, their way of life, their habits, their manners, the very tones of their voice; look at them attentively; observe the literature they read, the things which give them pleasure, the words which come forth out of their mouths, the thoughts which make the furniture of their minds; would any amount of wealth be worth having with the condition that one was to become just like these people by having it?" . . .

Population, again, and bodily health and vigour, are things which are nowhere treated in such an unintelligent, misleading, exaggerated way as in England. Both are really machinery; yet how many people all around us do we see rest in them and fail to look beyond them! Why, one has heard people, fresh from reading certain articles of the *Times* on the Registrar-General's returns of marriages and births in this country, who would talk of our large English families in quite a solemn strain, as if they had something in itself beautiful, elevating, and meritorious in them; as if the British Philistine would have only to present himself before the Great Judge with his twelve children, in order to be received among the sheep as a matter of right!

But bodily health and vigour, it may be said, are not to be classed with wealth and population as mere machinery; they have a more real and essential value. True; but only as they are more intimately connected with a perfect spiritual condition than wealth or population are. The moment we disjoin them from the idea of a perfect spiritual condition, and pursue them, as we do pursue them, for their own sake and as ends in themselves, our worship of them becomes as mere worship of machinery, as our worship of wealth or population, and as unintelligent and vulgarising a worship as that is. Every one with anything like an adequate idea of human perfection has distinctly marked this subordination to higher and spiritual ends of the

7. **Philistines.** See note on page 702.

cultivation of bodily vigour and activity. "Bodily exercise profiteth little; but godliness is profitable unto all things," says the author of the Epistle to Timothy. And the utilitarian Franklin says just as explicitly:—"Eat and drink such an exact quantity as suits the constitution of thy body, *in reference to the services of the mind.*" But the point of view of culture, keeping the mark of human perfection simply and broadly in view, and not assigning to this perfection, as religion or utilitarianism assigns to it, a special and limited character, this point of view, I say, of culture is best given by these words of Epictetus:—"It is a sign of ἀφυΐα," says he,—that is, of a nature not finely tempered,—"to give yourselves up to things which relate to the body; to make, for instance, a great fuss about exercise, a great fuss about eating, a great fuss about drinking, a great fuss about walking, a great fuss about riding. All these things ought to be done merely by the way: the formation of the spirit and character must be our real concern." This is admirable; and, indeed, the Greek word εὐφυΐα, a finely tempered nature, gives exactly the notion of perfection as culture brings us to conceive it: a harmonious perfection, a perfection in which the characters of beauty and intelligence are both present, which unites "the two noblest of things,"—as Swift, who of one of the two, at any rate, had himself all too little, most happily calls them in his *Battle of the Books,*—"the two noblest of things, *sweetness and light.*" The εὐφυής is the man who tends towards sweetness and light; the ἀφυής, on the other hand, is our Philistine. The immense spiritual significance of the Greeks is due to their having been inspired with this central and happy idea of the essential character of human perfection; and Mr. Bright's misconception of culture, as a smattering of Greek and Latin, comes itself, after all, from this wonderful significance of the Greeks having affected the very machinery of our education, and is in itself a kind of homage to it.

In thus making sweetness and light to be characters of perfection, culture is of like spirit with poetry, follows one law with poetry. Far more than on our freedom, our population, and our industrialism, many amongst us rely upon our religious organisations to save us. I have called religion a yet more important manifestation of human nature than poetry, because it has worked on a broader scale for perfection, and with greater masses of men. But the idea of beauty and of a human nature perfect on all its sides, which is the dominant idea of poetry, is a true and invaluable idea, though it has not yet had the success that the idea of conquering the obvious faults of our animality, and of a human nature perfect on the moral side,—which is the dominant idea of religion,—has been enabled to have; and it is destined, adding to itself the religious idea of a devout energy, to transform and govern the other.

The best art and poetry of the Greeks, in which religion and poetry are one, in which the idea of beauty and of a human nature perfect on all sides adds to itself a religious and devout energy, and works in the strength of that, is on this account of such surpassing interest and instructiveness for us, though it was,—as, having regard to the human race in general, and, indeed, having regard to the Greeks themselves, we must own,—a premature attempt, an attempt which for success needed the moral and religious fibre in humanity to be more braced and developed than it had yet been. But Greece did not err in having the idea of beauty, harmony, and complete human perfection, so present and paramount. It is impossible to have this idea too present and paramount; only, the moral fibre must be braced too. And we, because we have braced the moral fibre, are not on that account in the right way, if at the same time the idea of beauty, harmony, and complete human perfection, is wanting or misapprehended amongst us; and evidently it *is* wanting or misapprehended at present. And when we rely as we do on our religious organisations, which in themselves do not and cannot give us this idea, and think we have done enough if we make them spread and prevail, then, I say, we fall into our common fault of overvaluing machinery.

Nothing is more common than for people to confound the inward peace and satisfaction which follows the subduing of the obvious faults of our animality with what I may call absolute inward peace and satisfaction,—the peace and satisfaction which are reached as we draw near to complete spiritual perfection, and not merely to moral perfection, or rather to relative moral perfection. No people in the world have done more and struggled more to attain this relative moral perfection than our English race has. For no people in the world has the command to *resist the devil,* to *overcome the wicked one,* in the nearest and most obvious sense of those words, had such a pressing force and reality. And we have had our reward, not only in the great worldly prosperity which our obedience to this

1–3. "Bodily . . . things." See 1 Timothy, 4:8. The author is St. Paul. 5–7. "Eat . . . mind." Inaccurately quoted from *Poor Richard's Almanack.* 13–21. "It is . . . concern." Freely translated from the *Encheiridion.* **Epictetus.** See note on page 666. **29. Battle of the Books,** published 1704. From it, as the context shows, Arnold derived the title of this essay.

49. resist . . . one. See James 4:7.

command has brought us, but also, and far more, in great inward peace and satisfaction. But to me few things are more pathetic than to see people, on the strength of the inward peace and satisfaction which their rudimentary efforts towards perfection have brought them, employ, concerning their incomplete perfection and the religious organisations within which they have found it, language which properly applies only to complete perfection, and is a far-off echo of the human soul's prophecy of it. Religion itself, I need hardly say, supplies them in abundance with this grand language. And very freely do they use it; yet it is really the severest possible criticism of such an incomplete perfection as alone we have yet reached through our religious organisations. . . .

But men of culture and poetry, it will be said, are again and again failing, and failing conspicuously, in the necessary first stage to a harmonious perfection, in the subduing of the great obvious faults of our animality, which it is the glory of these religious organisations to have helped us to subdue. True, they do often so fail. They have often been without the virtues as well as the faults of the Puritan; it has been one of their dangers that they so felt the Puritan's faults that they too much neglected the practice of his virtues. I will not, however, exculpate them at the Puritan's expense. They have often failed in morality, and morality is indispensable. And they have been punished for their failure, as the Puritan has been rewarded for his performance. They have been punished wherein they erred; but their ideal of beauty, of sweetness and light, and a human nature complete on all its sides, remains the true ideal of perfection still; just as the Puritan's ideal of perfection remains narrow and inadequate, although for what he did well he has been richly rewarded. Notwithstanding the mighty results of the Pilgrim Fathers' voyage, they and their standard of perfection are rightly judged when we figure to ourselves Shakspeare or Virgil,—souls in whom sweetness and light, and all that in human nature is most humane, were eminent,—accompanying them on their voyage, and think what intolerable company Shakspeare and Virgil would have found them! . . .

Culture, however, shows its single-minded love of perfection, its desire simply to make reason and the will of God prevail, its freedom from fanaticism, by its attitude towards all this machinery, even while it insists that it is machinery. Fanatics, seeing the mischief men do themselves by their blind belief in some machinery or other,—whether it is wealth and industrialism, or whether it is the cultivation of bodily strength and activity, or whether it is a political organisation,—or whether it is a religious organisation,—oppose with might and main the tendency to this or that political and religious organisation, or to games and athletic exercises, or to wealth and industrialism, and try violently to stop it. But the flexibility which sweetness and light give, and which is one of the rewards of culture pursued in good faith, enables a man to see that a tendency may be necessary, and even, as a preparation for something in the future, salutary, and yet that the generations or individuals who obey this tendency are sacrificed to it, that they fall short of the hope of perfection by following it; and that its mischiefs are to be criticised, lest it should take too firm a hold and last after it has served its purpose. . . .

I remember, when I was under the influence of a mind to which I feel the greatest obligations, the mind of a man who was the very incarnation of sanity and clear sense, a man the most considerable, it seems to me, whom America has yet produced,—Benjamin Franklin,—I remember the relief with which, after long feeling the sway of Franklin's imperturbable common-sense, I came upon a project of his for a new version of the Book of Job, to replace the old version, the style of which, says Franklin, has become obsolete, and thence less agreeable. "I give," he continues, "a few verses, which may serve as a sample of the kind of version I would recommend." We all recollect the famous verse in our translation: "Then Satan answered the Lord and said: 'Doth Job fear God for nought?'" Franklin makes this: "Does your Majesty imagine that Job's good conduct is the effect of mere personal attachment and affection?" I well remember how, when first I read that, I drew a deep breath of relief, and said to myself: "After all, there is a stretch of humanity beyond Franklin's victorious good sense!" So, after hearing Bentham cried loudly up as the renovator of modern society, and Bentham's mind and ideas proposed as the rulers of our future, I open the *Deontology*. There I read: "While Xenophon was writing his history and Euclid teaching geometry, Socrates and Plato were talking nonsense under pretence of talking wisdom

41–42. **Franklin's victorious good sense!"** Harrold and Templeman (*English Prose of the Victorian Era*, Oxford Press, 1938), have pointed out that since Franklin's discussion of the Book of Job is included among his *Bagatelles*, it can hardly have been intended seriously. 45. **Deontology**, *Deontology, or, The Science of Morality*, by Jeremy Bentham, edited and arranged for the press, after Bentham's death, by John Bowring, 1834.

nd morality. This morality of theirs consisted in words; this wisdom of theirs was the denial of maters known to every man's experience." From the moment of reading that, I am delivered from the bondage of Bentham! the fanaticism of his adhernts can touch me no longer. I feel the inadequacy of his mind and ideas for supplying the rule of human society, for perfection.

Culture tends always thus to deal with the men of a system, of disciples, of a school; with men like Comte, or the late Mr. Buckle, or Mr. Mill. However much it may find to admire in these personages, or in some of them, it nevertheless remembers the text: "Be not ye called Rabbi!" and it soon passes on from any Rabbi. But Jacobinism loves a Rabbi; it does not want to pass on from its Rabbi in pursuit of a future and still unreached perfection; it wants its Rabbi and his ideas to stand for perfection, that they may with the more authority recast the world; and for Jacobinism, therefore, culture,— eternally passing onwards and seeking,—is an impertinence and an offence. But culture, just because it resists this tendency of Jacobinism to impose on us a man with limitations and errors of his own along with the true ideas of which he is the organ, really does the world and Jacobinism itself a service.

So, too, Jacobinism, in its fierce hatred of the past and of those whom it makes liable for the sins of the past, cannot away with the inexhaustible indulgence proper to culture, the consideration of circumstances, the severe judgment of actions joined to the merciful judgment of persons. "The man of culture is in politics," cries Mr. Frederic Harrison, "one of the poorest mortals alive!" Mr. Frederic Harrison wants to be doing business, and he complains that the man of culture stops him with a "turn for small fault-finding, love of selfish ease, and indecision in action." Of what use is culture, he asks, except for "a critic of new books or a professor of *belles-lettres*"? Why, it is of use because, in presence of the fierce exasperation which breathes, or rather, I may say, hisses through the whole production in which Mr. Frederic Harrison asks that question, it reminds us that the perfection of human nature is sweetness and light. It is of use because, like religion,—that other effort after perfection,—it testifies, that, where bitter envying and strife are, there is confusion and every evil work.

The pursuit of perfection, then, is the pursuit of sweetness and light. He who works for sweetness and light, works to make reason and the will of God prevail. He who works for machinery, he who works for hatred, works only for confusion. Culture looks beyond machinery, culture hates hatred; culture has one great passion, the passion for sweetness and light. It has one even yet greater!—the passion for making them *prevail*. It is not satisfied till we *all* come to a perfect man; it knows that the sweetness and light of the few must be imperfect until the raw and unkindled masses of humanity are touched with sweetness and light. If I have not shrunk from saying that we must work for sweetness and light, so neither have I shrunk from saying that we must have a broad basis, must have sweetness and light for as many as possible. Again and again I have insisted how those are the happy moments of humanity, how those are the marking epochs of a people's life, how those are the flowering times for literature and art and all the creative power of genius, when there is a *national* glow of life and thought, when the whole of society is in the fullest measure permeated by thought, sensible to beauty, intelligent and alive. Only it must be *real* thought and *real* beauty; *real* sweetness and *real* light. Plenty of people will try to give the masses, as they call them, an intellectual food prepared and adapted in the way they think proper for the actual condition of the masses. The ordinary popular literature is an example of this way of working on the masses. Plenty of people will try to indoctrinate the masses with the set of ideas and judgments constituting the creed of their own profession or party. Our religious and political organisations give an example of this way of working on the masses. I condemn neither way; but culture works differently. It does not try to teach down to the level of inferior classes; it does not try to win them for this or that sect of its own, with ready-made judgments and watchwords. It seeks to do away with classes; to make the best that has been thought and known in the world current everywhere; to make all men live in an atmosphere of sweetness and light, where they may use ideas, as it uses them itself, freely,—nourished, and not bound by them.

This is the *social idea;* and the men of culture are the true apostles of equality. The great men of cul-

---

11. Comte, Auguste Comte (1798–1857), French philosopher, whose religion was Positivism, or "the religion of humanity." **Mr. Buckle,** Henry Thomas Buckle (1821–1862), who tried to write the history of English civilization scientifically. **Mr. Mill.** See pages 463–73 in this volume. **14. "Be not ye . . . Rabbi!"** See Matthew 23:8. "Rabbi" means "master." **15. Jacobinism.** Literally the Jacobins were a political club in France prominently concerned in the French Revolution. Arnold takes "fierceness" and "addiction to an abstract system" as "the signal marks" of Jacobinism, as he uses the term, while its "ways" are "violent indignation with the past, abstract systems of renovation applied wholesale, [and] a new doctrine drawn up in black and white for elaborating down to the very smallest details a rational society for the future."

ture are those who have had a passion for diffusing, for making prevail, for carrying from one end of society to the other, the best knowledge, the best ideas of their time; who have laboured to divest knowledge of all that was harsh, uncouth, difficult, abstract, professional, exclusive; to humanise it, to make it efficient outside the clique of the cultivated and learned, yet still remaining the *best* knowledge and thought of the time, and a true source, therefore, of sweetness and light. Such a man was Abelard in the Middle Ages, in spite of all his imperfections; and thence the boundless emotion and enthusiasm which Abelard excited. Such were Lessing and Herder in Germany, at the end of the last century; and their services to Germany were in this way inestimably precious. Generations will pass, and literary monuments will accumulate, and works far more perfect than the works of Lessing and Herder will be produced in Germany; and yet the names of these two men will fill a German with a reverence and enthusiasm such as the names of the most gifted masters will hardly awaken. And why? Because they *humanised* knowledge; because they broadened the basis of life and intelligence; because they worked powerfully to diffuse sweetness and light, to make reason and the will of God prevail. With Saint Augustine they said: "Let us not leave thee alone to make in the secret of thy knowledge, as thou didst before the creation of the firmament, the division of light from darkness; let the children of thy spirit, placed in their firmament, make their light shine upon the earth, mark the division of night and day, and announce the revolution of the times; for the old order is passed, and the new arises; the night is spent, the day is come forth; and thou shalt crown the year with thy blessing, when thou shalt send forth labourers into thy harvest sown by other hands than theirs; when thou shalt send forth new labourers to new seed-times, whereof the harvest shall be not yet."

from Chapter 4: HEBRAISM AND HELLENISM

THE fundamental ground . . . [of] our [English] preference of doing to thinking . . . is a main element in our nature, and as we study it we find ourselves opening up a number of large questions on every side.

Let me go back for a moment to Bishop Wilson who says: "First, never go against the best light you have; secondly, take care that your light be not darkness." We show, as a nation, laudable energy and persistence in walking according to the best light we have, but are not quite careful enough perhaps, to see that our light be not darkness. This is only another version of the old story that energy is our strong point and favourable characteristic rather than intelligence. But we may give to this idea a more general form still, in which it will have a yet larger range of application. We may regard this energy driving at practice, this paramount sense of the obligation of duty, self-control, and work, this earnestness in going manfully with the best light we have, as one force. And we may regard the intelligence driving at those ideas which are, after all the basis of right practice, the ardent sense for all the new and changing combinations of them which man's development brings with it, the indomitable impulse to know and adjust them perfectly, as another force. And these two forces we may regard as in some sense rivals,—rivals not by the necessity of their own nature, but as exhibited in man and his history,—and rivals dividing the empire of the world between them. And to give these forces names from the two races of men who have supplied the most signal and splendid manifestations of them, we may call them respectively the forces of Hebraism and Hellenism. Hebraism and Hellenism,—between these two points of influence moves our world. At one time it feels more powerfully the attraction of one of them, at another time of the other; and it ought to be, though it never is, evenly and happily balanced between them.

The final aim of both Hellenism and Hebraism, as of all great spiritual disciplines, is no doubt the same: man's perfection or salvation. The very language which they both of them use in schooling us to reach this aim is often identical. Even when their language indicates by variation,—sometimes a broad variation, often a but slight and subtle variation,—the different courses of thought which are uppermost in each discipline, even then the unity of the final end and aim is still apparent. To employ the actual words of that discipline with which we ourselves are all of us most familiar, and the words of which, therefore, come most home to us, that final end and aim is "that we might be partakers of the divine nature." These are the words of a He-

---

10–11. Abelard, Pierre Abelard (1079–1142), famous French philosopher, known to modern theologians as the first noteworthy proponent of the "moral influence" theory of the Atonement, and to the general reader for *The Love-Letters of Abelard and Héloïse.* **13. Lessing,** Gotthold Ephraim Lessing (1729–1781). **14. Herder,** Johann Gottfried von Herder (1744–1803). **27–40. "Let . . . yet."** Quoted from the famous *Confessions* by St. Augustine.

1. Bishop Wilson. See note on page 704. **29–30. Hebraism and Hellenism.** The two great sources of Western civilization are the Graeco-Roman and the Hebrew-Christian. Arnold may have found a suggestion for the use of these terms in Heine. **49–50. "that . . . nature."** See 2 Peter 1:4.

rew apostle, but of Hellenism and Hebraism alike his is, I say, the aim. When the two are confronted, s they very often are confronted, it is nearly always ith what I may call a rhetorical purpose; the eaker's whole design is to exalt and enthrone one f the two, and he uses the other only as a foil and enable him the better to give effect to his purpose. Obviously, with us, it is usually Hellenism which is ius reduced to minister to the triumph of Hebraism. There is a sermon on Greece and the Greek 10 pirit by a man never to be mentioned without interest and respect, Frederick Robertson, in which his rhetorical use of Greece and the Greek spirit, nd the inadequate exhibition of them necessarily onsequent upon this, is almost ludicrous, and ould be censurable if it were not to be explained y the exigencies of a sermon. On the other hand, Ieinrich Heine, and other writers of his sort, give s the spectacle of the tables completely turned, and f Hebraism brought in just as a foil and contrast to 20 Iellenism, and to make the superiority of Hellenism nore manifest. In both these cases there is injustice nd misrepresentation. The aim and end of both Iebraism and Hellenism is, as I have said, one and he same, and this aim and end is august and admirable.

Still, they pursue this aim by very different ourses. The uppermost idea with Hellenism is to ee things as they really are; the uppermost idea ith Hebraism is conduct and obedience. Nothing 30 an do away with this ineffaceable difference. The Greek quarrel with the body and its desires is, that hey hinder right thinking; the Hebrew quarrel ith them is, that they hinder right acting. "He hat keepeth the law, happy is he"; "Blessed is the nan that feareth the Eternal, that delighteth greatly n his commandments";—that is the Hebrew notion of felicity; and, pursued with passion and tenacity, this notion would not let the Hebrew rest till, s is well known, he had at last got out of the law a 40 ietwork of prescriptions to enwrap his whole life, o govern every moment of it, every impulse, every ction. The Greek notion of felicity, on the other and, is perfectly conveyed in these words of a great rench moralist: *"C'est le bonheur des hommes,"*— vhen? when they abhor that which is evil?—no; vhen they exercise themselves in the law of the Lord lay and night?—no; when they die daily?—no;

when they walk about the New Jerusalem with palms in their hands?—no; but when they think aright, when their thought hits: *"quand ils pensent juste."* At the bottom of both the Greek and the Hebrew notion is the desire, native in man, for reason and the will of God, the feeling after the universal order,—in a word, the love of God. But, while Hebraism seizes upon certain plain, capital intimations of the universal order, and rivets itself, one may say, with unequalled grandeur of earnestness and intensity on the study and observance of them, the bent of Hellenism is to follow, with flexible activity, the whole play of the universal order, to be apprehensive of missing any part of it, of sacrificing one part to another, to slip away from resting in this or that intimation of it, however capital. An unclouded clearness of mind, an unimpeded play of thought, is what this bent drives at. The governing idea of Hellenism is *spontaneity of consciousness;* that of Hebraism, *strictness of conscience.*

Christianity changed nothing in this essential bent of Hebraism to set doing above knowing. Self-conquest, self-devotion, the following not our own individual will, but the will of God, *obedience,* is the fundamental idea of this form, also, of the discipline to which we have attached the general name of Hebraism. Only, as the old law and the network of prescriptions with which it enveloped human life were evidently a motive-power not driving and searching enough to produce the result aimed at,— patient continuance in well-doing, self-conquest,— Christianity substituted for them boundless devotion to that inspiring and affecting pattern of self-conquest offered by Jesus Christ; and by the new motive-power, of which the essence was this, though the love and admiration of Christian churches have for centuries been employed in varying, amplifying, and adoring the plain description of it, Christianity, as St. Paul truly says, "establishes the law," and in the strength of the ampler power which she has thus supplied to fulfil it, has accomplished the miracles, which we all see, of her history.

So long as we do not forget that both Hellenism and Hebraism are profound and admirable manifestations of man's life, tendencies, and powers, and that both of them aim at a like final result, we can hardly insist too strongly on the divergence of line 50 and of operation with which they proceed. It is a divergence so great that it most truly, as the prophet

---

12. **Frederick Robertson** (1816–1853), one of the reatest preachers of Arnold's time. **18. Heinrich Heine,** great German lyric poet, of Hebrew extraction (1797– 856). **34–35.** "He . . . he." See Proverbs 29:18. 5–37. "Blessed . . . commandments." See Psalm 112:1. 5. "C'est le bonheur . . . juste" (*line 4, next column*). Iuman felicity is to think rightly. **46. abhor . . . evil?** ee Romans 12:9. **48. die daily?** See 1 Corinthians 15:31.

1–2. walk . . . hands? See Revelation 7:9. For description of the New Jerusalem, see chaps. 19–22. **40–41. "establishes the law."** See Romans 3:31.

Zechariah says, "has raised up thy sons, O Zion, against thy sons, O Greece!" The difference whether it is by doing or by knowing that we set most store, and the practical consequences which follow from this difference, leave their mark on all the history of our race and of its development. Language may be abundantly quoted from both Hellenism and Hebraism to make it seem that one follows the same current as the other towards the same goal. They are, truly, borne towards the same goal; but the currents which bear them are infinitely different. It is true, Solomon will praise knowing: "Understanding is a well-spring of life unto him that hath it." And in the New Testament, again, Jesus Christ is a "light," and "truth makes us free." It is true, Aristotle will undervalue knowing: "In what concerns virtue," says he, "three things are necessary—knowledge, deliberate will and perseverance; but, whereas the two last are all-important, the first is a matter of little importance." It is true that with the same impatience with which St. James enjoins a man to be not a forgetful hearer, but a *doer of the work*, Epictetus exhorts us to *do* what we have demonstrated to ourselves we ought to do; or he taunts us with futility, for being armed at all points to prove that lying is wrong, yet all the time continuing to lie. It is true, Plato, in words which are almost the words of the New Testament or the *Imitation*, calls life a learning to die. But underneath the superficial agreement the fundamental divergence still subsists. The understanding of Solomon is "the walking in the way of the commandments"; this is "the way of peace," and it is of this that blessedness comes. In the New Testament, the truth which gives us the peace of God and makes us free, is the love of Christ constraining us to crucify, as he did, and with a like purpose of moral regeneration, the flesh with its affections and lusts, and thus establishing, as we have seen, the law. The moral virtues, on the other hand, are with Aristotle but the porch and access to the intellectual, and with these last is blessedness. That partaking of the divine life, which both Hellenism and Hebraism, as we have said, fix as their crowning aim, Plato expressly denies to the man of practical virtue merely,

of self-conquest with any other motive than that of perfect intellectual vision. He reserves it for the lover of pure knowledge, of seeing things as they really are,—the φιλομαθής.

Both Hellenism and Hebraism arise out of the wants of human nature, and address themselves to satisfying those wants. But their methods are so different, they lay stress on such different points and call into being by their respective disciplines such different activities, that the face which human nature presents when it passes from the hands of one of them to those of the other, is no longer the same. To get rid of one's ignorance, to see things as they are, and by seeing them as they are to see them in their beauty, is the simple and attractive idea which Hellenism holds out before human nature; and from the simplicity and charm of this ideal, Hellenism, and human life in the hands of Hellenism, is invested with a kind of aërial ease, clearness, and radiancy; they are full of what we call sweetness and light. Difficulties are kept out of view, and the beauty and rationalness of the ideal have all our thoughts. "The best man is he who most tries to perfect himself, and the happiest man is he who most feels that he *is* perfecting himself,"—this account of the matter by Socrates, the true Socrates of the *Memorabilia*, has something so simple, spontaneous, and unsophisticated about it, that it seems to fill us with clearness and hope when we hear it. But there is a saying which I have heard attributed to Mr. Carlyle about Socrates,—a very happy saying, whether it is really Mr. Carlyle's or not,—which excellently marks the essential point in which Hebraism differs from Hellenism. "Socrates," this saying goes, "is terribly *at ease in Zion*." Hebraism—and here is the source of its wonderful strength,—has always been severely preoccupied with an awful sense of the impossibility of being at ease in Zion; of the difficulties which oppose themselves to man's pursuit or attainment of that perfection of which Socrates talks so hopefully, and, as from this point of view one might almost say, so glibly. It is all very well to talk of getting rid of one's ignorance, of seeing things in their reality, seeing them in their beauty; but how is this to be done when there is something which thwarts and spoils all our efforts?

This something is *sin;* and the space which sin fills in Hebraism, as compared with Hellenism, is indeed prodigious. This obstacle to perfection fills the whole scene, and perfection appears remote and rising away from earth, in the background. Under

1–2. "has raised . . . Greece!" See Zechariah 9:13. **13–14. "Understanding . . . it."** See Proverbs 16:22. Solomon was traditionally regarded as the author of Proverbs. **15. "light,"** a favorite designation of Christ in the Gospel According to St. John. **15–20. "truth makes us free."** See John 8:32. **It is true . . . importance."** Quoted from the *Nichomachean Ethics* of Aristotle. **22–23. not . . . work.** See James 1:25. **Epictetus.** See note on page 666. **27. Plato,** in his *Phaedo.* **29. Imitation,** *The Imitation of Christ,* one of the devotional classics of Christian literature, attributed to Thomas à Kempis (1380–1471). **32–33. "the walking . . . peace."** See Proverbs 1–3.

23–25. "The best man . . . himself." Quoted from the *Memorabilia* of Xenophon (c. 434–c. 355 B.C.). **35. "at ease in Zion."** See Amos 6:1.

e name of sin, the difficulties of knowing oneself nd conquering oneself which impede man's pas- ge to perfection, become, for Hebraism, a positive, ctive entity hostile to man, a mysterious power hich I heard Dr. Pusey the other day, in one of his npressive sermons, compare to a hideous hunch- ack seated on our shoulders, and which it is the ain business of our lives to hate and oppose. The iscipline of the Old Testament may be summed up s a discipline teaching us to abhor and flee from n; the discipline of the New Testament, as a dis- ipline teaching us to die to it. As Hellenism speaks f thinking clearly, seeing things in their essence and eauty, as a grand and precious feat for man to chieve, so Hebraism speaks of becoming conscious f sin, of wakening to a sense of sin, as a feat of this ind. It is obvious to what wide divergence these dif- ering tendencies, actively followed, must lead. As ne passes and repasses from Hellenism to Hebraism, om Plato to St. Paul, one feels inclined to rub ne's eyes and ask oneself whether man is indeed a entle and simple being, showing the traces of a oble and divine nature; or an unhappy chained aptive, labouring with groanings that cannot be ttered to free himself from the body of this death.

Apparently it was the Hellenic conception of uman nature which was unsound, for the world ould not live by it. Absolutely to call it unsound, owever, is to fall into the common error of its Iebraising enemies; but it was unsound at that articular moment of man's development, it was remature. The indispensable basis of conduct and elf-control, the platform upon which alone the per- ection aimed at by Greece can come into bloom, vas not to be reached by our race so easily; cen- uries of probation and discipline were needed to ring us to it. Therefore the bright promise of Iellenism faded, and Hebraism ruled the world. hen was seen that astonishing spectacle, so well arked by the often-quoted words of the prophet Zechariah, when men of all languages and nations ook hold of the skirt of him that was a Jew, saying: -"*We will go with you, for we have heard that God is ith you.*" And the Hebraism which thus received nd ruled a world all gone out of the way and alto- ether become unprofitable, was, and could not ut be, the later, the more spiritual, the more at- ractive development of Hebraism. It was Christian- ty; that is to say, Hebraism aiming at self-conquest nd rescue from the thrall of vile affections, not by bedience to the letter of a law, but by conformity

to the image of a self-sacrificing example. To a world stricken with moral enervation Christianity offered its spectacle of an inspired self-sacrifice; to men who refused themselves nothing, it showed one who refused himself everything;—"*my Saviour ban- ished joy!*" says George Herbert. When the *alma Venus*, the life-giving and joy-giving power of na- ture, so fondly cherished by the Pagan world, could not save her followers from self-dissatisfaction and ennui, the severe words of the apostle came brac- ingly and refreshingly: "Let no man deceive you with vain words, for because of these things cometh the wrath of God upon the children of disobedi- ence." Through age after age and generation after generation, our race, or all that part of our race which was most living and progressive, was *bap- tized into a death;* and endeavoured, by suffering in the flesh, to cease from sin. Of this endeavour, the animating labours and afflictions of early Christian- ity, the touching asceticism of mediaeval Christian- ity, are the great historical manifestations. Literary monuments of it, each in its own way incomparable, remain in the Epistles of St. Paul, in St. Augustine's Confessions, and in the two original and simplest books of the Imitation.

Of two disciplines laying their main stress, the one, on clear intelligence, the other, on firm obedi- ence; the one, on comprehensively knowing the grounds of one's duty, the other, on diligently prac- tising it; the one, on taking all possible care (to use Bishop Wilson's words again) that the light we have be not darkness, the other, that according to the best light we have we diligently walk,—the priority naturally belongs to that discipline which braces all man's moral powers, and founds for him an in- dispensable basis of character. And, therefore, it is justly said of the Jewish people, who were charged with setting powerfully forth that side of the divine order to which the words *conscience* and *self-conquest* point, that they were "entrusted with the oracles of God"; as it is justly said of Christianity, which followed Judaism and which set forth this side with a much deeper effectiveness and a much wider in- fluence, that the wisdom of the old Pagan world was foolishness compared to it. No words of devo- tion and admiration can be too strong to render thanks to these beneficent forces which have so borne forward humanity in its appointed work of

6. **says George Herbert,** in his poem "The Size." 6– 7. **alma Venus.** *Alma* (nourishing, cherishing) is a favorite epithet of Ceres, Venus, and other deities. 11–14. "**Let no man . . . disobedience.**" See Ephesians 5:6. 16–17. **bap- tized into a death.** See Romans 6:3. 40–41. "**entrusted . . . God.**" See Romans 3:2. 44–45. **that the wisdom . . . foolishness.** See 1 Corinthians 3:19.

5. **Dr. Pusey.** See note on page 452. 23–25. **or an un- appy . . . death.** See Romans 7–8. 43–44. "**We will . . with you.**" See Zechariah 8:23.

coming to the knowledge and possession of itself; above all, in those great moments when their action was the wholesomest and the most necessary.

But the evolution of these forces, separately and in themselves, is not the whole evolution of humanity,—their single history is not the whole history of man; whereas their admirers are always apt to make it stand for the whole history. Hebraism and Hellenism are, neither of them, the *law* of human development, as their admirers are prone to make them; they are, each of them, *contributions* to human development,—august contributions, invaluable contributions; and each showing itself to us more august, more invaluable, more preponderant over the other, according to the moment in which we take them, and the relation in which we stand to them. The nations of our modern world, children of that immense and salutary movement which broke up the Pagan world, inevitably stand to Hellenism in a relation which dwarfs it, and to Hebraism in a relation which magnifies it. They are inevitably prone to take Hebraism as the law of human development, and not as simply a contribution to it, however precious. And yet the lesson must perforce be learned, that the human spirit is wider than the most priceless of the forces which bear it onward, and that to the whole development of man Hebraism itself is, like Hellenism, but a contribution. . . .

But meanwhile, by alternations of Hebraism and Hellenism, of a man's intellectual and moral impulses, of the effort to see things as they really are, and the effort to win peace by self-conquest, the human spirit proceeds; and each of these two forces has its appointed hours of culmination and seasons of rule. As the great movement of Christianity was a triumph of Hebraism and man's moral impulses, so the great movement which goes by the name of the Renascence was an uprising and reinstatement of man's intellectual impulses and of Hellenism. We in England, the devoted children of Protestantism, chiefly know the Renascence by its subordinate and secondary side of the Reformation. The Reformation has been often called a Hebraising revival, a return to the ardour and sincereness of

primitive Christianity. No one, however, can stud the development of Protestantism and of Protesta churches without feeling that into the Reformatio too,—Hebraising child of the Renascence and o spring of its fervour, rather than its intelligence, it undoubtedly was,—the subtle Hellenic leaven the Renascence found its way, and that the exa respective parts, in the Reformation, of Hebrais and of Hellenism, are not easy to separate. B what we may with truth say is, that all whic Protestantism was to itself clearly conscious of, a which it succeeded in clearly setting forth in word had the characters of Hebraism rather than Hellenism. The Reformation was strong, in tha it was an earnest return to the Bible and to doin from the heart the will of God as there writte It was weak, in that it never consciously graspe or applied the central idea of the Renascence,— the Hellenic idea of pursuing, in all lines of acti ity, the law and science, to use Plato's words, things as they really are. Whatever direct super ority, therefore, Protestantism had over Cathol cism was a moral superiority, a superiority arisin out of its greater sincerity and earnestness,—at th moment of its apparition at any rate,—in dealin with the heart and conscience. Its pretensions an intellectual superiority are in general qui illusory. For Hellenism, for the thinking side i man as distinguished from the acting side, th attitude of mind of Protestantism towards the Bibl in no respect differs from the attitude of mind o Catholicism towards the Church. The mental hab of him who imagines that Balaam's ass spoke, i no respect differs from the mental habit of him wh imagines that a Madonna of wood or stone winke and the one, who says that God's Church make him believe what he believes, and the other, wh says that God's Word makes him believe what h believes, are for the philosopher perfectly alike i not really and truly knowing, when they say *God' Church* and *God's Word*, what it is they say, or wherec they affirm.

In the sixteenth century, therefore, Hellenism re entered the world, and again stood in presence o Hebraism,—a Hebraism renewed and purged Now, it has not been enough observed, how, in th seventeenth century, a fate befell Hellenism in som respects analogous to that which befell it at th commencement of our era. The Renascence, tha great re-awakening of Hellenism, that irresistibl return of humanity to nature and to seeing thing as they are, which in art, in literature, and i physics, produced such splendid fruits, had, like th

41. Renascence. "I have ventured to give the foreign *Renaissance*—destined to become of more common use amongst us as the movement which it denotes comes, as it will come, increasingly to interest us—an English form." (Arnold) The English form has not generally established itself. Some writers make a distinction between Renaissance (rĕn'ĕ̇-säns' or rē-nā'säns), to indicate the historic movement, and renascence (rē-năs'ĕns), revival.

33. Balaam's ass spoke. See Numbers 22.

nterior Hellenism of the Pagan world, a side of moral weakness and of relaxation or insensibility of the moral fibre, which in Italy showed itself with the most startling plainness, but which in France, England, and other countries was very apparent too. Again this loss of spiritual balance, this exclusive preponderance given to man's perceiving and knowing side, this unnatural defect of his feeling and acting side, provoked a reaction. Let us trace that reaction where it most nearly concerns us.

Science has now made visible to everybody the great and pregnant elements of difference which lie in race, and in how signal a manner they make the genius and history of an Indo-European people vary from those of a Semitic people. Hellenism is of Indo-European growth, Hebraism is of Semitic growth; and we English, a nation of Indo-European stock, seem to belong naturally to the movement of Hellenism. But nothing more strongly marks the essential unity of man, than the affinities we can perceive, in this point or that, between members of one family of peoples and members of another. And no affinity of this kind is more strongly marked than that likeness in the strength and prominence of the moral fibre, which, notwithstanding immense elements of difference, knits in some special sort the genius and history of us English, and our American descendants across the Atlantic, to the genius and history of the Hebrew people. Puritanism, which has been so great a power in the English nation, and in the strongest part of the English nation, was originally the reaction in the seventeenth century of the conscience and moral sense of our race, against the moral indifference and lax rule of conduct which in the sixteenth century came in with the Renascence. It was a reaction of Hebraism against Hellenism; and it powerfully manifested itself, as was natural, in a people with much of what we call a Hebraising turn, with a signal affinity for the bent which was the master-bent of Hebrew life. Eminently Indo-European by its *humour*, by the power it shows, through this gift, of imaginatively acknowledging the multiform aspects of the problem of life, and of thus getting itself unfixed from its own over-certainty, of smiling at its own over-tenacity, our race has yet (and a great part of its strength lies here), in matters of practical life and moral conduct, a strong share of the assuredness, the tenacity, the intensity of the Hebrews. This turn manifested itself in Puritanism, and has had a great part in shaping our history for the last two hundred years. Undoubtedly it checked and changed amongst us that movement of the Renascence which we see producing in the reign of Elizabeth such wonderful fruits. Undoubtedly it stopped the prominent rule and direct development of that order of ideas which we call by the name of Hellenism, and gave the first rank to a different order of ideas. Apparently, too, as we said of the former defeat of Hellenism, if Hellenism was defeated, this shows that Hellenism was imperfect, and that its ascendency at that moment would not have been for the world's good.

Yet there is a very important difference between the defeat inflicted on Hellenism by Christianity eighteen hundred years ago, and the check given to the Renascence by Puritanism. The greatness of the difference is well measured by the difference in force, beauty, significance, and usefulness, between primitive Christianity and Protestantism. Eighteen hundred years ago it was altogether the hour of Hebraism. Primitive Christianity was legitimately and truly the ascendant force in the world at that time, and the way of mankind's progress lay through its full development. Another hour in man's development began in the fifteenth century, and the main road of his progress then lay for a time through Hellenism. Puritanism was no longer the central current of the world's progress, it was a side stream crossing the central current and checking it. The cross and the check may have been necessary and salutary, but that does not do away with the essential difference between the main stream of man's advance and a cross or side stream. For more than two hundred years the main stream of man's advance has moved towards knowing himself and the world, seeing things as they are, spontaneity of consciousness; the main impulse of a great part, and that the strongest part, of our nation has been towards strictness of conscience. They have made the secondary the principal at the wrong moment, and the principal they have at the wrong moment treated as secondary. This contravention of the natural order has produced, as such contravention always must produce, a certain confusion and false movement, of which we are now beginning to feel, in almost every direction, the inconvenience. In all directions our habitual courses of action seem to be losing efficaciousness, credit, and control, both with others and even with ourselves. Everywhere we see the beginnings of confusion, and we want a clue to some sound order and authority. This we can only get by going back upon the actual instincts and forces which rule our life, seeing them as they really are, connecting them with other instincts and forces, and enlarging our whole view and rule of life.

from LITERATURE AND DOGMA

from Chapter 12: THE TRUE GREATNESS OF CHRISTIANITY

NO; the *mystery* hidden from ages and generations, which none of the rulers of this world knew, the mystery revealed finally by Jesus Christ and rejected by the Jews, was not the doctrine of the Trinity, nor anything speculative. It was the method and the secret of Jesus. Jesus did not change the object for men,—righteousness. He made clear what it was, and that it was this:—his *method* and his *secret*.

This was the *mystery*, and the Apostles had still the consciousness that it was. To "learn Christ," to "be taught the truth as it is in Jesus," was not, with them, to acquire certain tenets about One God in Trinity and Trinity in Unity. It was *"to be renewed in the spirit of your mind, and to put on the new man which after God is created in righteousness and true holiness."* And this exactly amounts to the method and secret of Jesus.

For Catholic and for Protestant theology alike, this consciousness, which the Apostles had still preserved, was lost. For Catholic and Protestant theology alike, the truth as it is in Jesus, the mystery revealed in Christ, meant something totally different from his method and secret. But they recognised, and indeed the thing was so plain that they could not well miss it, they recognised that on all Christians the method and secret of Jesus were enjoined. So to this extent the method and secret of Jesus were preached and had their effect. To this extent true Christianity has been known, and to the extent before stated it has been neglected. . . .

2

Few things are more melancholy than to observe Christian apologists taunting the Jews with the failure of Hebraism to fulfil the splendid promises of prophecy, and Jewish apologists taunting Christendom with the like failure on the part of Christianity. Neither has yet fulfilled them, or could yet have fulfilled them. Certainly the restoration by Cyrus, the Second Temple, the Maccabean victories, are hardly more than the shadows of a fulfilment of the magnificent words: "The sons of them that afflicted thee shall come bending unto thee, and all they that despised thee shall bow themselves down at the soles of thy feet; thy gates shall not be shut day nor night, that men may bring unto thee the treasure of the Gentiles, and that their kings may be brought." The Christianisation of all the leading nations of the world is, it is said, a much better fulfilment of that promise. Be it so. Yet does Christendom, let us ask, offer more than a shadow of the fulfilment of *this:* "Violence shall no more be heard in thy land; the vile person shall no more be called liberal, nor the churl bountiful; thy people shall be all righteous; they shall *all* know me, from the least to the greatest; I will put my law in their inward parts, and write it in their hearts; the Eternal shall be thine everlasting light, and the days of thy mourning shall be ended"? Manifestly it does not. Yet the two promises hang together; one of them is not truly fulfilled unless the other is.

The promises were made to *righteousness*, with all which the idea of righteousness involves. And it involves Christianity. They were made on the immediate prospect of a small triumph for righteousness, the restoration of the Jews after the captivity in Babylon; but they are not satisfied by that triumph. The prevalence of the profession of Christianity is a larger triumph; yet in itself it hardly satisfies them any better. What satisfies them is the prevailing of that which righteousness really is, and nothing else satisfies them. Now, Christianity is that which righteousness really is. Therefore, if something called Christianity prevails, and yet the promises are not satisfied, the inference is that this *something* is not that which righteousness really is, and therefore not really Christianity. And as the course of the world is perpetually establishing the pre-eminence of righteousness, and confounding whatever denies this pre-eminence, so, too, the course of the world is for ever establishing what righteousness really is,— that is to say, true Christianity,—and confounding whatever pretends to be true Christianity and is not.

Now, just as the constitution of things turned out to be against the great unrighteous kingdoms of the

5–6. the mystery . . . generations. "Colossians 1:26." (Arnold)   6–7. which . . . knew. "1 Corinthians 2:18." (Arnold)   8–9. the doctrine . . . Trinity, the doctrine that the one God exists in three persons—Father, Son, and Holy Spirit.   15–20. "learn . . . holiness." For these three quotations, see Ephesians 4:20–24.   44–45. the restoration . . . Maccabean victories. Nebuchadnezzar (properly Nebuchadrezzar), King of Babylonia, carried the Jews into captivity, 597 and 586 B.C. After Cyrus the Persian conquered Babylonia in 538 B.C. the Jews were permitted to return to Palestine, for the Persians did not use deportation of subject peoples as an element in imperial policy. The **Second Temple** was completed under the governor Zerubbabel, urged on by the prophets Haggai and Zechariah, by 516 B.C. The Maccabees were a Jewish family who headed a revolt against Antiochus Epiphanes, a fanatical Hellenist, one of Alexander's successors in Syria, in the second century B.C., and thus inaugurated a new heroic age in Hebrew history.   2–8. "The sons . . . may be brought." "Isaiah 60:4, 11." (Arnold)   12–19. "Violence . . . ended?" "Isaiah 60:18; 32:5; 60:21; Jeremiah 31:34, 33; Isaiah 60:20." (Arnold)

heathen world, and against all the brilliant Ishmaels we have seen since, so the constitution of things turns out to be against all false presentations of Christianity, such as the theology of the Fathers or Protestant theology. They do not work successfully, they do not reach the aim, they do not bring the world to the fruition of the promises made to righteousness. And the reason is, because they substitute for what is really righteousness something else. Catholic dogma or Lutheran justification by faith they substitute for the method and secret of Jesus.

Nevertheless, as all Christian Churches do recommend the method and the secret of Jesus, though not in the right way or in the right eminency, still the world is made partially acquainted with what righteousness really is, and the doctrine produces some effect, although the full effect is much thwarted and deadened by the false way in which the doctrine is presented. Still, the effect produced is great. For instance, the sum of individual happiness that has been caused by Christianity is, any one can see, enormous. But let us take the effect of Christianity on the world. And if we look at the thing closely, we shall find that its effect has been this: Christianity has brought the world, or at any rate all the leading part of the world, *to regard righteousness as only the Jews regarded it before the coming of Christ.* The world has accepted, so far as profession goes, that original revelation made to Israel: *the pre-eminence of righteousness.* The infinite truth and attractiveness of the method and secret and character of Jesus, however falsely surrounded, have prevailed with the world so far as this. And this is an immense gain, and a signal witness to Christianity. The world does homage to the pre-eminence of righteousness; and here we have one of those fulfilments of prophecy which are so real and so glorious. "Glorious things are spoken of thee, O City of God! I will make mention of Rahab and Babylon as of them that know me! behold, the Philistines also, and Tyre, with the Ethiopians,—these were born *there!* And of Zion it shall be reported: This and that man was born in *her!*—and the Most High shall stablish her. The Eternal shall count, when he writeth up the people: This man was born *there!*" That

prophecy is at the present day abundantly fulfilled. The world's chief nations have now all come, we see, to reckon and profess themselves *born in Zion,*—born, that is, in the religion of Zion, *the city of righteousness.*

But there remains the question: *what* righteousness really is. The method and secret and sweet reasonableness of Jesus. But the world does not see this; for it puts, as righteousness, something else first and this second. So that here, too, as to seeing what righteousness really is, the world now is much in the same position in which the Jews, when Jesus Christ came, were. It is often said: If Jesus Christ came now, his religion would be rejected. And this is only another way of saying that the world now, as the Jewish people formerly, has something which thwarts and confuses its perception of what righteousness really is. It is so; and the thwarting cause is the same now as then:—the dogmatic system current, the so-called orthodox theology. This prevents now, as it did then, that which righteousness really is, the method and secret of Jesus, from being rightly received, from operating fully, and from accomplishing its due effect.

So true is this, that we have only to look at our own community to see the almost precise parallel, so far as religion is concerned, to the state of things presented in Judaea when Jesus Christ came. The multitudes are the same everywhere. The chief priests and elders of the people, and the scribes, are our bishops and dogmatists, with their pseudo-science of learned theology blinding their eyes, and always,—whenever simple souls are disposed to think that the method and secret of Jesus is true religion, and that the Great Personal First Cause and the Godhead of the Eternal Son have nothing to do with it,—eager to cry out: *This people that knoweth not the law are cursed!* The Pharisees, with their genuine concern for religion, but total want of perception of what religion really is, and by their temper, attitude, and aims doing their best to make religion impossible, are the Protestant Dissenters. The Sadducees are our friends the philosophical Liberals, who believe neither in angel nor spirit but in Mr. Herbert Spencer. Even the Roman governor

---

1–2. **Ishmael,** Abraham's son by Hagar, contrasted with Isaac, his son "of the promise," by Sarai (see Genesis 16, 17). 4. **Fathers.** See note on page 450. 10. **Lutheran justification by faith.** Justification by faith, as opposed to good works, was the cornerstone of Martin Luther's theology. Luther was combating the view that man may purchase his own salvation. Extremists later deduced the conclusion that if good works do not buy salvation, evil works cannot prevent it. This is Antinomianism, often referred to in English literature. 38–45. **"Glorious things . . . there!"** "Psalms 87: 3, 6." (Arnold) **Zion** is Jerusalem.

37–38. **This people . . . cursed.** "John 7: 49." (Arnold) **Pharisees,** the Puritans of New Testament Jewry, a sect distinguished for their strict observance of law and tradition. 43. **Sadducees,** the aristocratic rationalists of New Testament Jewry, who recognized only the authority of the canonical Scriptures (that is, the Law and the Prophets), and consequently rejected the Resurrection, angels, and other late ideas in Israel. 45. **Mr. Herbert Spencer,** a very influential rationalistic philosopher (1820–1903). **the Roman governor,** Pontius Pilate, who condemned Jesus to death, upon the insistence of his Jewish enemies, though he himself could find no fault in him.

has his close parallel in our celebrated aristocracy, with its superficial good sense and good nature, its complete inaptitude for ideas, its profound helplessness in presence of all great spiritual movements. And the result is, that the splendid promises to righteousness made by the Hebrew prophets, claimed by the Jews as the property of Judaism, claimed by us as the property of Christianity, are almost as ludicrously inapplicable to our religious state now, as to theirs then.

And this, we say, is again a signal witness to Christianity. Jesus Christ came to reveal what righteousness, to which the promises belong, really is; and so long as this, though shown by Jesus, is not recognised by us, we may call ourselves Christendom as much as we please, the true character of a Christendom will be wanting to us, because the great promises of prophecy will be still without their fulfilment. Nothing will do except righteousness; and no other conception of righteousness will do, except Jesus Christ's conception of it:—his *method* and his *secret*. . . .

3

. . . The more we trace the real law of Christianity's action, the grander it will seem. Certainly in the Gospels there is plenty of matter to call out our feelings. But perhaps this has been somewhat over-used and mis-used. . . . And perhaps, too, we do wrong, and inevitably fall into what is artificial and unnatural, in labouring so much to produce in ourselves now, as the one impulse determining us to use the method and secret of Jesus, that conscious ardent sensation of personal love to him, which we find the first generation of Christians feeling and professing, and which was the natural motor for those who were with him or near him, and, so to speak, touched him; and in making this our first object. At any rate, misemployed as this motor has often been, it might be well to forego or at least suspend its use for ourselves and others for a time, and to fix our minds exclusively on the recommendation given to the method and secret of Jesus by their being *true*, and by the whole course of things proving this.

Now, just as the best recommendation of the oracle committed to Israel, *Righteousness is salvation*, is found in our more and more discovering, in our own history and in the whole history of the world, that it *is* so, so we shall find it to be with the method and secret of Jesus. That this *is* the righteousness which is salvation, that the method and secret of Jesus, that is to say, conscience and self-renouncement, *are* righteousness, bring about the kingdom of God or

the reign of righteousness,—this, which is the Christian revelation and what Jesus came to establish, is best impressed, for the present at any rate, by experiencing and showing again and again, in ourselves and in the course of the world, that it *is* so; that this is the righteousness which is saving, and that there is none other. Let us but well observe what comes, in ourselves or the world, of trying any other, of not being convinced that this is righteousness, and this only; and we shall find ourselves more and more, as by irresistible viewless hands, caught and drawn towards the Christian revelation, and made to desire more and more to serve it. No proof can be so solid as this experimental proof; and none again, can be so grand, so fitted to fill us with awe, admiration, and gratitude. So that feeling and emotion will now well come in after it, though not before it. For the whole course of human things is really, according to this experience, leading up to the fulfilment of Jesus Christ's promise to his disciples: *Fear not, little flock! for it is your Father's good pleasure to give you the kingdom.* . . . The kingdom of the Lord the world is already become, by its chief nations professing the religion of righteousness. The kingdom of Christ the world will have to become, it is on its way to become, because the profession of righteousness, except as Jesus Christ interpreted righteousness, is vain. . . .

4

Let us keep hold of this same experimental process in dealing with the promise of immortality; although here, if anywhere, *Aberglaube*, extra-belief, hope, anticipation, may well be permitted to come in. Still, what we need for our foundation is not *Aberglaube*, but *Glaube;* not extra-belief in what is beyond the range of possible experience, but belief in what can and should be known to be true. . . .

Here, again, it is far best to take what is experimentally true, and nothing else, as our foundation, and afterwards to let hope and aspiration grow, if so it may be, out of this. Israel had said: "In the way of righteousness is life, and in the pathway thereof there is no death." He had said: "The righteous hath hope in his death." He had cried to his *Eternal that loveth righteousness:* "Thou wilt not leave my soul in the grave, neither wilt thou suffer thy

---

21–22. Fear not . . . kingdom. See Luke 12:32.
33. Aberglaube. The dictionary definition is "superstition." **44–46. "In . . . death."** "Proverbs 12:28." (Arnold) **46–47. "The righteous . . . death."** "Proverbs 14:32." (Arnold) **48. "Thou . . . life."** (*page 719, line 2*) "Psalms 16:10–11." (Arnold)

faithful servant to see corruption! thou wilt show me the path of life!" And by a kind of short cut to the conclusion thus laid down, the Jews constructed their fairy-tale of an advent, judgment, and resurrection, as we find it in the Book of Daniel. Jesus, again, had said: "If a man keep my word, he shall never see death." And by a kind of short cut to the conclusion thus laid down, Christians constructed their fairy-tale of the second advent, the resurrection of the body, the New Jerusalem. But instead of fairy-tales, let us begin, at least, with certainties.

And a certainty is the sense of *life*, of being truly *alive*, which accompanies righteousness. If this experimental sense does not rise to be stronger in us, does not rise to the sense of being inextinguishable, that is probably because our experience of righteousness is really so very small. Here, therefore, we may well permit ourselves to trust Jesus, whose practice and intuition both of them went, in these matters, so far deeper than ours. At any rate, we have in our experience this strong sense of *life from righteousness* to start with; capable of being developed, apparently, by progress in righteousness into something immeasurably stronger. Here is the true basis for all religious aspiration after immortality. And it is an experimental basis; and therefore, as to grandeur, it is again, when compared with the popular *Aberglaube*, grand with all the superior grandeur, on a subject of the highest seriousness, of reality over fantasy.

At present, the fantasy hides the grandeur of the reality. But when all the *Aberglaube* of the second advent, with its signs in the sky, sounding trumpets and opening graves, is cleared away, then and not till then will come out the profound truth and grandeur of words of Jesus like these: "The hour is coming, when they that are in the graves shall hear the voice of the Son of God; and they that hear shall *live*."

5. **the Book of Daniel.** The Book of Daniel, now generally dated in the Maccabean period, is the first important Jewish apocalypse, that is, an attempt to describe what will happen when God intervenes directly to overthrow the present world-order and set up his kingdom on earth. Apocalyptics flourishes during periods of stress and strain; it is pessimistic concerning the ordinary remedial processes of life and puts its trust in sheer supernaturalism. From the Maccabean period on down to New Testament times, apocalypticism was very popular in Israel (see the Apocrypha). For a brilliant argument (not generally accepted by New Testament scholars) that Jesus' own view of the future was the apocalyptic view, see Albert Schweitzer, *The Quest of the Historical Jesus*, Macmillan, 1910. For a general survey of apocalypticism, see Shirley Jackson Case, *The Millennial Hope*, University of Chicago Press, 1918.   6-7. **"If . . . death."** "John 8:51." (Arnold)   10. **New Jerusalem.** See Revelation 19–22. The Book of Revelation is the great New Testament apocalypse.   36–39. **"The hour . . . live."** See John 5:25.

Finally, and above all. As, for the right inculcation of righteousness, we need the inspiring words of Israel's love for it, that is, we need the Bible; so, for the right inculcation of the method and secret of Jesus, we need the *epieikeia*, the sweet reasonableness, of Jesus. That is, in other words again, we need the *Bible;* for only through the Bible-records of Jesus can we get at his *epieikeia*. Even in these records, it is and can be presented but imperfectly; but only by reading and re-reading the Bible can we get at it at all.

Now, greatly as the failure, from the stress laid upon the pseudo-science of Church-dogma, to lay enough stress upon the method and secret of Jesus, has kept Christianity back from showing itself in its full power, it is probable that the failure to apply to the method and secret of Jesus, so far as these have at any rate been used, his sweet reasonableness or *epieikeia*, has kept it back even more. And the *infinite* of the religion of Jesus,—its immense capacity for ceaseless progress and farther development,— lies principally, perhaps, in the line of extricating more and more his sweet reasonableness, and applying it to his method and secret. For it is obvious from experience, how much our use of Christ's method and secret requires to be guided and governed by his *epieikeia*. Indeed, without this, his method and secret seem often of no use at all. The Flagellants imagined that they were employing his secret; and the Dissenters, with their "spirit of watchful jealousy," imagine that they are employing his method. To be sure, Mr. Bradlaugh imagines that the method and the secret of Jesus, nay, and Jesus himself too, are all baneful, and that the sooner we get rid of them all, the better. So far, then, the Flagellants and the Dissenters are in advance of Mr. Bradlaugh: they value Christianity, and they profess the method and secret of Jesus. But they employ them so ill, that one is tempted to say they might nearly as well be without them. And this is because they are wholly without his sweet reasonableness, or *epieikeia*. Now this can only be got, first, by knowing that it is in the Bible, and looking for it there; and then, by reading and re-reading the Gospels continually, until we catch something of it.

This, again, is an experimental process. That the *epieikeia* or sweet reasonableness of Jesus may be

31. **Flagellants,** religious enthusiasts who served God by scourging themselves; see an encyclopedia.   34. **Mr. Bradlaugh,** Charles Bradlaugh (1833–1891), politician and reformer, whose right to sit in the House of Commons was long contested on account of his atheism.

brought to govern our use of his method and secret, and that it can and will make our use of his method and secret quite a different thing, is proved by our actually finding this to be so when we try. So that the culmination of Christian righteousness in the applying, to guide our use of the method and secret of Jesus, his sweet reasonableness or *epieikeia*, is proved from experience. We end, therefore, as we began,—by experience. And the whole series of experiences, of which the survey is thus completed, rests primarily, upon one fundamental fact,—itself, eminently, a fact of experience: *the necessity of righteousness*. . . .

from DISCOURSES IN AMERICA

from Lecture 2: LITERATURE AND SCIENCE

THE question is raised whether, to meet the needs of our modern life, the predominance ought not now to pass from letters to science; and naturally the question is nowhere raised with more energy than here in the United States. The design of abasing what is called "mere literary instruction and education," and of exalting what is called "sound, extensive, and practical scientific knowledge," is, in this intensely modern world of the United States, even more perhaps than in Europe, a very popular design, and makes great and rapid progress.

I am going to ask whether the present movement for ousting letters from their old predominance in education, and for transferring the predominance in education to the natural sciences, whether this brisk and flourishing movement ought to prevail, and whether it is likely that in the end it really will prevail. . . .

Some of you may possibly remember a phrase of mine which has been the object of a good deal of comment; an observation to the effect that in our culture, the aim being *to know ourselves and the world*, we have, as the means to this end, *to know the best which has been thought and said in the world*. A man of science, who is also an excellent writer and the very prince of debaters, Professor Huxley, in a discourse at the opending of Sir Josiah Mason's college at Birmingham, laying hold of this phrase, expanded it by quoting some more words of mine, which are these: "The civilised world is to be regarded as now

being, for intellectual and spiritual purposes, one great confederation, bound to a joint action and working to a common result; and whose members have for their proper outfit a knowledge of Greek, Roman, and Eastern antiquity, and of one another. Special local and temporary advantages being put out of account, that modern nation will in the intellectual and spiritual sphere make most progress, which most thoroughly carries out this programme."

Now on my phrase, thus enlarged, Professor Huxley remarks that when I speak of the above-mentioned knowledge as enabling us to know ourselves and the world, I assert *literature* to contain the materials which suffice for thus making us know ourselves and the world. But it is not by any means clear, says he, that after having learnt all which ancient and modern literatures have to tell us, we have laid a sufficiently broad and deep foundation for that criticism of life, that knowledge of ourselves and the world, which constitutes culture. On the contrary, Professor Huxley declares that he finds himself "wholly unable to admit that either nations or individuals will really advance, if their outfit draws nothing from the stores of physical science. An army without weapons of precision, and with no particular base of operations, might more hopefully enter upon a campaign on the Rhine, than a man, devoid of a knowledge of what physical science has done in the last century, upon a criticism of life." . . .

But when we talk of knowing Greek and Roman antiquity, for instance, which is the knowledge people have called the humanities, I for my part mean a knowledge which is something more than a superficial humanism, mainly decorative. . . .

When I speak of knowing Greek and Roman antiquity . . . as a help to knowing ourselves and the world, I mean more than a knowledge of so much vocabulary, so much grammar, so many portions of authors in the Greek and Latin languages, I mean knowing the Greeks and Romans, and their life and genius, and what they were and did in the world; what we get from them, and what is its value. . . .

The same also as to knowing our own and other modern nations. . . . To know the best that has been thought and said by the modern nations, is to know, says Professor Huxley, "only what modern *literatures* have to tell us; it is the criticism of life contained in modern literature." And yet "the distinc-

---

41–44. to know ourselves . . . the world. See Arnold's essay on "The Function of Criticism," page 698. **46–48. Professor Huxley . . . Birmingham.** See pages 733–39 in this volume.

tive character of our times," he urges, "lies in the vast and constantly increasing part which is played by natural knowledge." And how, therefore, can a man, devoid of knowledge of what physical science has done in the last century, enter hopefully upon a criticism of modern life?

Let us, I say, be agreed about the meaning of the terms we are using. I talk of knowing the best which has been thought and uttered in the world; Professor Huxley says this means knowing *literature*. Literature is a large word; it may mean everything written with letters or printed in a book. Euclid's *Elements* and Newton's *Principia* are thus literature. All knowledge that reaches us through books is literature. But by literature Professor Huxley means *belles lettres*. He means to make me say, that knowing the best which has been thought and said by the modern nations is knowing their *belles lettres* and no more. And this is no sufficient equipment, he argues, for a criticism of modern life. But as I do not mean, by knowing ancient Rome, knowing merely more or less of Latin *belles lettres*, and taking no account of Rome's military, and political, and legal, and administrative work in the world; and as, by knowing ancient Greece, I understand knowing her as the giver of Greek art, and the guide to a free and right use of reason and to scientific method, and the founder of our mathematics and physics and astronomy and biology,—I understand knowing her as all this, and not merely knowing certain Greek poems, and histories, and treatises, and speeches,—so as to the knowledge of modern nations also. By knowing modern nations, I mean not merely knowing their *belles lettres*, but knowing also what has been done by such men as Copernicus, Galileo, Newton, Darwin. . . .

There is, therefore, really no question between Professor Huxley and me as to whether knowing the great results of the modern scientific study of nature is not required as a part of our culture, as well as knowing the products of literature and art. But to follow the processes by which those results are reached, ought, say the friends of physical science, to be made the staple of education for the bulk of mankind. And here there does arise a question between those whom Professor Huxley calls with playful sarcasm "the Levites of culture," and those whom the poor humanist is sometimes apt to regard as its Nebuchadnezzars.

The great results of the scientific investigation of nature we are agreed upon knowing, but how much of our study are we bound to give to the processes by which those results are reached? The results have their visible bearing on human life. But all the processes, too, all the items of fact, by which those results are reached and established, are interesting. All knowledge is interesting to a wise man, and the knowledge of nature is interesting to all men. It is very interesting to know, that, from the albuminous white of the egg, the chick in the egg gets the materials for its flesh, bones, blood, and feathers; while, from the fatty yolk of the egg, it gets the heat and energy which enable it at length to break its shell and begin the world. It is less interesting, perhaps, but still it is interesting, to know that when a taper burns, the wax is converted into carbonic acid and water. Moreover, it is quite true that the habit of dealing with facts, which is given by the study of nature, is, as the friends of physical science praise it for being, an excellent discipline. The appeal, in the study of nature, is constantly to observation and experiment; not only is it said that the thing is so, but we can be made to see that it is so. Not only does a man tell us that when a taper burns the wax is converted into carbonic acid and water, as a man may tell us, if he likes, that Charon is punting his ferry-boat on the river Styx, or that Victor Hugo is a sublime poet, or Mr. Gladstone the most admirable of statesmen; but we are made to see that the conversion into carbonic acid and water does actually happen. This reality of natural knowledge it is, which makes the friends of physical science contrast it, as a knowledge of things, with the humanist's knowledge, which is, say they, a knowledge of words. And hence Professor Huxley is moved to lay it down that, "for the purpose of attaining real culture, an exclusively scientific education is at least as effectual as an exclusively literary education." And a certain President of the Section for Mechanical Science in the British Association is, in Scripture phrase, "very bold," and declares that if a man, in his mental training, "has substituted literature and history for natural science, he has chosen the less useful alternative." But whether we go these lengths or not, we must all admit that in natural science the habit gained of dealing with facts is a

the study of the humanities, sometimes especially the Greek and Latin classics, and who opposes the doctrinaire. **27. Charon,** in classical mythology the ferryman who carries the souls of the dead across the River Styx. **28. Victor Hugo,** one of the giant figures in French literature (1802–1885). **29. Mr. Gladstone,** William Ewart Gladstone (1809–1898), the most eminent Liberal leader of Victorian England.

12–13. Euclid's Elements, of geometry. **13. Newton's Principia,** *Philosophiae Naturalis Principia Mathematica,* 1687, by Sir Isaac Newton. **48. "the Levites,** a subordinate rank of the priesthood in ancient Israel **50. Nebuchadnezzar.** See note on page 716. **49. A humanist** is one who believes in

most valuable discipline, and that every one should have some experience of it.

More than this, however, is demanded by the reformers. It is proposed to make the training in natural science the main part of education, for the great majority of mankind at any rate. And here, I confess, I part company with the friends of physical science, with whom up to this point I have been agreeing. . . .

All knowledge is, as I said just now, interesting; and even items of knowledge which from the nature of the case cannot well be related, but must stand isolated in our thoughts, have their interest. Even lists of exceptions have their interest. If we are studying Greek accents, it is interesting to know that *pais* and *pas*, and some other monosyllables of the same form of declension, do not take the circumflex upon the last syllable of the genitive plural, but vary, in this respect, from the common rule. If we are studying physiology, it is interesting to know that the pulmonary artery carries dark blood and the pulmonary vein carries bright blood, departing in this respect from the common rule for the division of labour between the veins and the arteries. But every one knows how we seek naturally to combine the pieces of our knowledge together, to bring them under general rules, to relate them to principles; and how unsatisfactory and tiresome it would be to go on for ever learning lists of exceptions, or accumulating items of fact which must stand isolated.

Well, that same need of relating our knowledge, which operates here within the sphere of our knowledge itself, we shall find operating, also, outside that sphere. We experience, as we go on learning and knowing,—the vast majority of us experience,—the need of relating what we have learnt and known to the sense which we have in us for conduct, to the sense which we have in us for beauty. . . .

But, no doubt, some kinds of knowledge cannot be made to directly serve the instinct in question, cannot be directly related to the sense for beauty, to the sense for conduct. These are instrument-knowledges; they lead on to other knowledges, which can. A man who passes his life in instrument-knowledges is a specialist. They may be invaluable as instruments to something beyond, for those who have the gift thus to employ them; and they may be disciplines in themselves wherein it is useful for every one to have some schooling. But it is inconceivable that the generality of men should pass all their mental life with Greek accents or with formal logic. My friend Professor Sylvester, who is one of the first mathematicians in the world, holds transcendental doctrines as to the virtue of mathematics, but those doctrines are not for common men. In the very Senate House and heart of our English Cambridge I once ventured, though not without an apology for my profaneness, to hazard the opinion that for the majority of mankind a little of mathematics, even, goes a long way. Of course this is quite consistent with their being of immense importance as an instrument to something else; but it is the few who have the aptitude for thus using them, not the bulk of mankind.

The natural sciences do not, however, stand on the same footing with these instrument-knowledges. Experience shows us that the generality of men will find more interest in learning that, when a taper burns, the wax is converted into carbonic acid and water, or in learning the explanation of the phenomenon of dew, or in learning how the circulation of the blood is carried on, than they find in learning that the genitive plural of *pais* and *pas* does not take the circumflex on the termination. And one piece of natural knowledge is added to another, and others are added to that, and at last we come to propositions so interesting as Mr. Darwin's famous proposition that "our ancestor was a hairy quadruped furnished with a tail and pointed ears, probably arboreal in his habits." . . .

Interesting, indeed, these results of science are, important they are, and we should all of us be acquainted with them. But what I now wish you to mark is, that we are still, when they are propounded to us and we receive them, we are still in the sphere of intellect and knowledge. And for the generality of men there will be found, I say, to arise, when they have duly taken in the proposition that their ancestor was "a hairy quadruped furnished with a tail and pointed ears, probably arboreal in his habits," there will be found to arise an invincible desire to relate this proposition to the sense in us for conduct, and to the sense in us for beauty. But this the men of science will not do for us, and will hardly even profess to do. They will give us other pieces of knowledge, other facts, about other animals and their ancestors, or about plants, or about stones, or about stars; and they may finally bring us to those great "general conceptions of the universe, which are forced upon us all," says Professor Huxley, "by the progress of physical science." But still it will be *knowledge* only which they give us; knowledge not

1. **Professor Sylvester**, James Joseph Sylvester (1814–1897), English mathematician.

put for us into relation with our sense for conduct, our sense for beauty, and touched with emotion by being so put; not thus put for us, and therefore, to the majority of mankind, after a certain while, unsatisfying, wearying.

Not to the born naturalist, I admit. But what do we mean by a born naturalist? We mean a man in whom the zeal for observing nature is so uncommonly strong and eminent, that it marks him off from the bulk of mankind. Such a man will pass his life happily in collecting natural knowledge and reasoning upon it, and will ask for nothing, or hardly anything, more. I have heard it said that the sagacious and admirable naturalist whom we lost not very long ago, Mr. Darwin, once owned to a friend that for his part he did not experience the necessity for two things which most men find so necessary to them,—religion and poetry; science and the domestic affections, he thought, were enough. To a born naturalist, I can well understand that this should seem so. So absorbing is his occupation with nature, so strong his love for his occupation, that he goes on acquiring natural knowledge and reasoning upon it, and has little time or inclination for thinking about getting it related to the desire in man for conduct, the desire in man for beauty. He relates it to them for himself as he goes along, so far as he feels the need; and he draws from the domestic affections all the additional solace necessary. But then Darwins are extremely rare. Another great and admirable master of natural knowledge, Faraday, was a Sandemanian. That is to say, he related his knowledge to his instinct for conduct and to his instinct for beauty, by the aid of that respectable Scottish sectary, Robert Sandeman. And so strong, in general, is the demand of religion and poetry to have their share in a man, to associate themselves with his knowing, and to relieve and rejoice it, that, probably, for one man amongst us with the disposition to do as Darwin did in this respect, there are at least fifty with the disposition to do as Faraday.

Education lays hold upon us, in fact, by satisfying this demand. Professor Huxley holds up to scorn mediaeval education, with its neglect of the knowledge of nature, its poverty even of literary studies, its formal logic devoted to "showing how and why that which the Church said was true and must be true." But the great mediaeval Universities were not brought into being, we may be sure, by the zeal for giving a jejune and contemptible education. Kings

have been their nursing fathers, and queens have been their nursing mothers, but not for this. The mediaeval Universities came into being, because the supposed knowledge, delivered by Scripture and the Church, so deeply engaged men's hearts, by so simply, easily, and powerfully relating itself to their desire for conduct, their desire for beauty. All other knowledge was dominated by this supposed knowledge and was subordinated to it, because of the surpassing strength of the hold which it gained upon the affections of men, by allying itself profoundly with their sense for conduct, their sense for beauty.

But now, says Professor Huxley, conceptions of the universe fatal to the notions held by our forefathers have been forced upon us by physical science. Grant to him that they are thus fatal, that the new conceptions must and will soon become current everywhere, and that every one will finally perceive them to be fatal to the beliefs of our forefathers. The need of humane letters, as they are truly called, because they serve the paramount desire in men that good should be for ever present to them,—the need of humane letters, to establish a relation between the new conceptions, and our instinct for beauty, our instinct for conduct, is only the more visible. The Middle Age could do without humane letters, as it could do without the study of nature, because its supposed knowledge was made to engage its emotions so powerfully. Grant that the supposed knowledge disappears, its power of being made to engage the emotions will of course disappear along with it,—but the emotions themselves, and their claim to be engaged and satisfied, will remain. Now if we find by experience that humane letters have an undeniable power of engaging the emotions, the importance of humane letters in a man's training becomes not less, but greater, in proportion to the success of modern science in extirpating what it calls "mediaeval thinking."

Have humane letters, then, have poetry and eloquence, the power here attributed to them of engaging the emotions, and do they exercise it? And if they have it and exercise it, *how* do they exercise it, so as to exert an influence upon man's sense for conduct, his sense for beauty? Finally, even if they both can and do exert an influence upon the senses in question, how are they to relate to them the results,—the modern results,—of natural science? All these questions may be asked. First, have poetry and eloquence the power of calling out the emotions? The appeal is to experience. Experience shows that for the vast majority of men, for mankind in general, they have the power. Next, do they

31. Faraday, Michael Faraday (1791–1867), great physicist and chemist.   **32. Sandemanian,** a follower of Robert Sandeman (1718–1771); see arts. "Sandeman, Robert" and "Sandemanians, or Glassites," in *New International Encyclopaedia.*

exercise it? They do. But then, *how* do they exercise it so as to affect man's sense for conduct, his sense for beauty? And this is perhaps a case for applying the Preacher's words: "Though a man labour to seek it out, yet he shall not find it; yea, farther, though a wise man think to know it, yet shall he not be able to find it." Why should it be one thing, in its effect upon the emotions, to say, "Patience is a virtue," and quite another thing, in its effect upon the emotions, to say with Homer,

τλητὸν γὰρ Μοῖραι θυμὸν θέσαν ἀνθρώποισιν.—

"for an enduring heart have the destinies appointed to the children of men"! Why should it be one thing, in its effect upon the emotions, to say with the philosopher Spinoza, *Felicitas in eo consistit quod homo suum esse conservare potest*—"Man's happiness consists in his being able to preserve his own essence," and quite another thing, in its effect upon the emotions, to say with the Gospel, "What is a man advantaged, if he gain the whole world, and lose himself, forfeit himself?" How does this difference of effect arise? I cannot tell, and I am not much concerned to know; the important thing is that it does arise, and that we can profit by it. But how, finally, are poetry and eloquence to exercise the power of relating the modern results of natural science to man's instinct for conduct, his instinct for beauty? And here again I answer that I do not know *how* they will exercise it, but that they can and will exercise it I am sure. I do not mean that modern philosophical poets and modern philosophical moralists are to come and relate for us, in express terms, the results of modern scientific research to our instinct for conduct, our instinct for beauty. But I mean that we shall find, as a matter of experience, if we know the best that has been thought and uttered in the world, we shall find that the art and poetry and eloquence of men who lived, perhaps, long ago, who had the most limited natural knowledge, who had the most erroneous conceptions about many important matters, we shall find that this art, and poetry, and eloquence, have in fact not only the power of refreshing and delighting us, they have also the power,—such is the strength and worth, in essentials, of their authors' criticism of life,—they have a fortifying, and elevating, and quickening, and suggestive power, capable of wonderfully helping us to relate the results of modern science to our need for conduct, our need for beauty.

Homer's conceptions of the physical universe were, I imagine, grotesque; but really, under the shock of hearing from modern science that "the world is not subordinated to man's use, and that man is not the cynosure of things terrestrial," I could, for my own part, desire no better comfort than Homer's line which I quoted just now,

τλητὸν γὰρ Μοῖραι θυμὸν θέσαν ἀνθρώποισιν.—

"for an enduring heart have the destinies appointed to the children of men"!

And the more that men's minds are cleared, the more that the results of science are frankly accepted, the more that poetry and eloquence come to be received and studied as what in truth they really are,—the criticism of life by gifted men, alive and active with extraordinary power at an unusual number of points;—so much the more will the value of humane letters, and of art also, which is an utterance having a like kind of power with theirs, be felt and acknowledged, and their place in education be secured.

Let us therefore, all of us, avoid indeed as much as possible any invidious comparison between the merits of humane letters, as means of education, and the merits of the natural sciences. But when some President of a Section for Mechanical Science insists on making the comparison, and tells us that "he who in his training has substituted literature and history for natural science has chosen the less useful alternative," let us make answer to him that the student of humane letters only, will, at least, know also the great general conceptions brought in by modern physical science; for science, as Professor Huxley says, forces them upon us all. But the student of the natural sciences only, will, by our very hypothesis, know nothing of humane letters; not to mention that in setting himself to be perpetually accumulating natural knowledge, he sets himself to do what only specialists have in general the gift for doing genially. And so he will probably be unsatisfied, or at any rate incomplete, and even more incomplete than the student of humane letters only. . . .

If then there is to be separation and option between humane letters on the one hand, and the natural sciences on the other, the great majority of mankind, all who have not exceptional and overpowering aptitudes for the study of nature, would do well, I cannot but think, to choose to be educated in humane letters rather than in the natural sciences. Letters will call out their being at more points, will make them live more. . . .

4–7. "Though . . . it." "Ecclesiastes, 8:17." (Arnold) 12. τλητὸν . . . ἀνθρώποισιν. "Iliad, xxiv, 49." (Arnold) 17–18. "Man's . . . essence," quoted from the *Ethics* of Benedict Spinoza (1632–1677). 20–22. "What . . . self?" See Luke 9:25.

Thomas Henry Huxley
1825–1895

Thomas Henry Huxley was born at Ealing, May 4, 1825. He studied medicine; went to Australia in 1846 as assistant surgeon on the British naval vessel *Rattlesnake*, and laid the foundation of his fame by his researches on marine animals during this cruise. Not until 1855, however, did the brilliant young scientist find sufficient economic security to make it possible for him to marry Miss Henrietta Heathorn, whom he had met in Sydney.

It would be tedious to enumerate the positions Huxley held as a teacher, the learned societies with which he was connected, the scientific and scholastic honors which came to him, the royal commissions upon which he sat. When *The Origin of Species* appeared in 1859, he was one of the three men upon whose judgment Darwin offered to rest his case. From then on he was "Darwin's Bulldog," devoting much of his energy to defending Darwinism against its opponents, and often carrying the war into the enemy's country. One of the severest of his recent critics, Professor Robert Shafer, feels that Huxley's success as a controversialist was unfortunate, if only because it led to his investing most of his literary energies in occasional writing, and consequently never thinking out all the implications of his position with entire consistency. "While he supposed he was taking the path to knowledge," Professor Shafer adds, "with entirely open and unprejudiced mind, he was in reality swearing allegiance to a particular, specialized kind of knowledge. He was undertaking to accept only one kind of evidence, to take a sectarian view of reality, to see life in terms of its external, sensible forms."—*Christianity and Naturalism*, Yale University Press, 1932.

Huxley championed a scientific as against a classical education (compare Newman, Arnold), yet did not dislike literature and the classics; he accepted some basic materialistic assumptions, but refused to call himself an infidel; he championed evolution, but, unlike Herbert Spencer, could discern no ethical trend in it. He believed "that a deep sense of religion was compatible with the entire absence of theology," and that "the ethical progress of society depends not on imitating the cosmic process, still less in running away from it, but in combating it." He was interested in many "causes," always on the liberal side; like Mill, he was a feminist, and like

him he opposed English imperialism as represented by Governor Eyre in Jamaica.

In 1876 Huxley came to the United States to deliver an address at the opening of the Johns Hopkins University in Baltimore. He died, a Privy Councilor, June 29, 1895.

Among Huxley's works are *Evidence as to Man's Place in Nature*, 1863; *Lay Sermons, Addresses, and Reviews*, 1870; *Science and Culture*, 1881; *Science and Morals*, 1886; *Ethics and Evolution*, 1893; and his *Autobiography*, 1889. The three papers included in this anthology give (1) a basic statement of his scientific attitude, (2) one of his most significant utterances on education, (3) a note on his own interpretation of some of the religious implications of his work.

from METHOD AND RESULTS[1]

ON THE PHYSICAL BASIS OF LIFE

IN order to make the title of this discourse generally intelligible, I have translated the term "Protoplasm," which is the scientific name of the substance of which I am about to speak, by the words "the physical basis of life." I suppose that, to many, the idea that there is such a thing as a physical basis, or matter, of life may be novel—so widely spread is the conception of life as a something which works through matter, but is independent of it; and even those who are aware that matter and life are inseparably connected, may not be prepared for the conclusion plainly suggested by the phrase, "*the* physical basis or matter of life," that there is some one kind of matter which is common to all living beings, and that their endless diversities are bound together by a physical, as well as an ideal, unity. In fact, when first apprehended, such a doctrine as this appears almost shocking to common sense.

What, truly, can seem to be more obviously different from one another, in faculty, in form, and in substance, than the various kinds of living beings? What community of faculty can there be between

[1] By Thomas Henry Huxley, reprinted by permission of D. Appleton-Century Company, Inc.

the brightly-coloured lichen, which so nearly resembles a mere mineral incrustation of the bare rock on which it grows, and the painter, to whom it is instinct with beauty, or the botanist, whom it feeds with knowledge?

Again, think of the microscopic fungus—a mere infinitesimal ovoid particle, which finds space and duration enough to multiply into countless millions in the body of a living fly; and then of the wealth of foliage, the luxuriance of flower and fruit, which 10 lies between this bald sketch of a plant and the giant pine of California, towering to the dimensions of a cathedral spire, or the Indian fig, which covers acres with its profound shadow, and endures while nations and empires come and go around its vast circumference. Or, turning to the other half of the world of life, picture to yourselves the great Finner whale, hugest of beasts that live, or have lived, disporting his eighty or ninety feet of bone, muscle, and blubber, with easy roll, among waves in which the 20 stoutest ship that ever left dockyard would flounder hopelessly; and contrast him with the invisible animalcules—mere gelatinous specks, multitudes of which could, in fact, dance upon the point of a needle with the same ease as the angels of the Schoolmen could, in imagination. With these images before your minds, you may well ask, what community of form, or structure, is there between the animalcule and the whale; or between the fungus and the fig-tree? And, à fortiori, between all 30 four?

Finally, if we regard substance, or material composition, what hidden bond can connect the flower which a girl wears in her hair and the blood which courses through her youthful veins; or, what is there in common between the dense and resisting mass of the oak, or the strong fabric of the tortoise, and those broad disks of glassy jelly which may be seen pulsating through the waters of a calm sea, but which drain away to mere films in the hand which 40 raises them out of their element?

Such objections as these must, I think, arise in the mind of every one who ponders, for the first time, upon the conception of a single physical basis of life underlying all the diversities of vital existence; but I propose to demonstrate to you that, notwithstanding these apparent difficulties, a threefold unity—namely, a unity of power or faculty, a unity of form, and a unity of substantial composition—does pervade the whole living world.

No very abstruse argumentation is needed, in the first place to prove that the powers, or faculties, of all kinds of living matter, diverse as they may be in degree, are substantially similar in kind.

Goethe has condensed a survey of all powers of mankind into the well-known epigram:—

"Warum treibt sich das Volk so und schreit? Es will
    sich ernähren
Kinder zeugen, und die nähren so gut es vermag.

*   *   *

Weiter bringt es kein Mensch, stell' er sich wie
    er auch will."

In physiological language this means, that all the multifarious and complicated activities of man are comprehensible under three categories. Either they are immediately directed towards the maintenance and development of the body, or they effect transitory changes in the relative positions of parts of the body, or they tend towards the continuance of the species. Even those manifestations of intellect, of feeling, and of will, which we rightly name the higher faculties, are not excluded from this classification, inasmuch as to every one but the subject of them, they are known only as transitory changes in the relative positions of parts of the body. Speech, gesture, and every other form of human action are, in the long run, resolvable into muscular contraction, and muscular contraction is but a transitory change in the relative positions of the parts of a muscle. But the scheme which is large enough to embrace the activities of the highest form of life, covers all those of the lower creatures. The lowest plant, or animalcule, feeds, grows, and reproduces its kind. In addition, all animals manifest those transitory changes of form which we class under irritability and contractility; and, it is more than probable, that when the vegetable world is thoroughly explored, we shall find all plants in possession of the same powers, at one time or other of their existence.

I am not now alluding to such phaenomena, at once rare and conspicuous, as those exhibited by the leaflets of the sensitive plants, or the stamens of the barberry, but to much more widely spread, and at the same time, more subtle and hidden, manifestations of vegetable contractility. You are doubtless aware that the common nettle owes its stinging 50 property to the innumerable stiff and needle-like,

---

though exquisitely delicate, hairs which cover its surface. Each stinging-needle tapers from a broad base to a slender summit, which, though rounded at the end, is of such microscopic fineness that it readily penetrates, and breaks off in, the skin. The whole hair consists of a very delicate outer case of wood, closely applied to the inner surface of which is a layer of semi-fluid matter, full of innumerable granules of extreme minuteness. This semi-fluid lining is protoplasm, which thus constitutes a kind of bag, full of a limpid liquid, and roughly corresponding in form with the interior of the hair which it fills. When viewed with a sufficiently high magnifying power, the protoplasmic layer of the nettle hair is seen to be in a condition of unceasing activity. Local contractions of the whole thickness of its substance pass slowly and gradually from point to point, and give rise to the appearance of progressive waves, just as the bending of successive stalks of corn by a breeze produces the apparent billows of a corn-field.

But, in addition to these movements, and independently of them, the granules are driven, in relatively rapid streams, through channels in the protoplasm which seem to have a considerable amount of persistence. Most commonly, the currents in adjacent parts of the protoplasm take similar directions; and, thus, there is a general stream up one side of the hair and down the other. But this does not prevent the existence of partial currents which take different routes; and sometimes trains of granules may be seen coursing swiftly in opposite directions within a twenty-thousandth of an inch of one another; while, occasionally, opposite streams come into direct collision, and, after a longer or shorter struggle, one predominates. The cause of these currents seems to lie in contractions of the protoplasm which bounds the channels in which they flow, but which are so minute that the best microscopes show only their effects, and not themselves.

The spectacle afforded by the wonderful energies prisoned within the compass of the microscopic hair of a plant, which we commonly regard as a merely passive organism, is not easily forgotten by one who has watched its display, continued hour after hour, without pause or sign of weakening. The possible complexity of many other organic forms, seemingly as simple as the protoplasm of the nettle, dawns upon one; and the comparison of such a protoplasm to a body with an internal circulation, which has been put forward by an eminent physiologist, loses much of its startling character. Currents similar to those of the hairs of the nettle have been observed in a great multitude of very different plants, and weighty authorities have suggested that they probably occur, in more or less perfection, in all young vegetable cells. If such be the case, the wonderful noonday silence of a tropical forest is, after all, due only to the dulness of our hearing; and could our ears catch the murmur of these tiny Maelstroms, as they whirl in the innumerable myriads of living cells which constitute each tree, we should be stunned, as with the roar of a great city.

Among the lower plants, it is the rule rather than the exception, that contractility should be still more openly manifested at some periods of their existence. The protoplasm of *Algae* and *Fungi* becomes, under many circumstances, partially, or completely, freed from its woody case, and exhibits movements of its whole mass, or is propelled by the contractility of one, or more, hair-like prolongations of its body, which are called vibratile cilia. And, so far as the conditions of the manifestation of the phaenomena of contractility have yet been studied, they are the same for the plant as for the animal. Heat and electric shocks influence both, and in the same way, though it may be in different degrees. It is by no means my intention to suggest that there is no difference in faculty between the lowest plant and the highest, or between plants and animals. But the difference between the powers of the lowest plant, or animal, and those of the highest, is one of degree, not of kind, and depends, as Milne-Edwards long ago so well pointed out, upon the extent to which the principle of the division of labour is carried out in the living economy. In the lowest organism all parts are competent to perform all functions, and one and the same portion of protoplasm may successfully take on the function of feeding, moving, or reproducing apparatus. In the highest, on the contrary, a great number of parts combine to perform each function, each part doing its allotted share of the work with great accuracy and efficiency, but being useless for any other purpose.

On the other hand, notwithstanding all the fundamental resemblances which exist between the powers of the protoplasm in plants and in animals, they present a striking difference (to which I shall advert more at length presently), in the fact that plants can manufacture fresh protoplasm out of mineral compounds, whereas animals are obliged to procure it ready made, and hence, in the long run, depend upon plants. Upon what condition this difference in the powers of the two great divisions of the world of life depends, nothing is at present known.

With such qualifications as arise out of the last-

29. **Milne-Edwards,** Henry Milne-Edwards (1800–1885).

mentioned fact, it may be truly said that the acts of all living things are fundamentally one. Is any such unity predicable of their forms? Let us seek in easily verified facts for a reply to this question. If a drop of blood be drawn by pricking one's finger, and viewed with proper precautions, and under a sufficiently high microscopic power, there will be seen, among the innumerable multitude of little, circular, discoidal bodies, or corpuscles, which float in it and give it its colour, a comparatively small number of 10 colourless corpuscles, of somewhat larger size and very irregular shape. If the drop of blood be kept at the temperature of the body, these colourless corpuscles will be seen to exhibit a marvellous activity, changing their forms with great rapidity, drawing in and thrusting out prolongations of their substance, and creeping about as if they were independent organisms.

The substance which is thus active is a mass of protoplasm, and its activity differs in detail, rather 20 than in principle, from that of the protoplasm of the nettle. Under sundry circumstances the corpuscle dies and becomes distended into a round mass, in the midst of which is seen a smaller spherical body, which existed, but was more or less hidden, in the living corpuscle, and is called its *nucleus*. Corpuscles of essentially similar structure are to be found in the skin, in the lining of the mouth, and scattered through the whole framework of the body. Nay, more; in the earliest condition of the human 30 organism, in that state in which it has but just become distinguishable from the egg in which it arises, it is nothing but an aggregation of such corpuscles, and every organ of the body was, once, no more than such an aggregation.

Thus a nucleated mass of protoplasm turns out to be what may be termed the structural unit of the human body. As a matter of fact, the body, in its earliest state, is a mere multiple of such units; and in its perfect condition, it is a multiple of such units, 40 variously modified.

But does the formula which expresses the essential structural character of the highest animal cover all the rest, as the statement of its powers and faculties covered that of all others? Very nearly. Beast and fowl, reptile and fish, mollusk, worm, and polype, are all composed of structural units of the same character, namely, masses of protoplasm with a nucleus. There are sundry very low animals, each of which, structurally, is a mere colourless blood- 50 corpuscle, leading an independent life. But, at the very bottom of the animal scale, even this simplicity becomes simplified, and all the phaenomena of life are manifested by a particle of protoplasm with-

out a nucleus. Nor are such organisms insignificant by reason of their want of complexity. It is a fair question whether the protoplasm of those simplest forms of life, which people an immense extent of the bottom of the sea, would not outweigh that of all the higher living beings which inhabit the land put together. And in ancient times, no less than at the present day, such living beings as these have been the greatest of rock builders.

What has been said of the animal world is no less true of plants. Imbedded in the protoplasm at the broad, or attached, end of the nettle hair, there lies a spheroidal nucleus. Careful examination further proves that the whole substance of the nettle is made up of a repetition of such masses of nucleated protoplasm, each contained in a wooden case, which is modified in form, sometimes into a woody fibre, sometimes into a duct or spiral vessel, sometimes into a pollen grain, or an ovule. Traced back 20 to its earliest state, the nettle arises as the man does, in a particle of nucleated protoplasm. And in the lowest plants, as in the lowest animals, a single mass of such protoplasm may constitute the whole plant, or the protoplasm may exist without a nucleus.

Under these circumstances it may well be asked, how is one mass of non-nucleated protoplasm to be distinguished from another? why call one "plant" and the other "animal"?

The only reply is that, so far as form is concerned, plants and animals are not separable, and that, in many cases, it is a mere matter of convention whether we call a given organism an animal or a plant. There is a living body called *Aethalium septicum*, which appears upon decaying vegetable substances, and, in one of its forms, is common upon the surfaces of tan-pits. In this condition it is, to all intents and purposes, a fungus, and formerly was always regarded as such; but the remarkable in- 40 vestigations of De Bary have shown that, in another condition, the *Aethalium* is an actively locomotive creature, and takes in solid matters, upon which, apparently, it feeds, thus exhibiting the most characteristic feature of animality. Is this a plant; or is it an animal? Is it both; or is it neither? Some decide in favour of the last supposition, and establish an intermediate kingdom, a sort of biological No Man's Land for all these questionable forms. But, as it is admittedly impossible to draw any distinct 50 boundary line between this no man's land and the vegetable world on the one hand, or the animal, on the other, it appears to me that this proceeding

40. **De Bary,** Heinrich Anton De Bary (1831–1888), German botanist.

merely doubles the difficulty which, before, was single.

Protoplasm, simple or nucleated, is the formal basis of all life. It is the clay of the potter: which, bake it and paint it as he will, remains clay, separated by artifice, and not by nature, from the commonest brick or sun-dried clod.

Thus it becomes clear that all living powers are cognate, and that all living forms are fundamentally of one character. The researches of the chemist have revealed a no less striking uniformity of material composition in living matter.

In perfect strictness, it is true that chemical investigation can tell us little or nothing, directly, of the composition of living matter, inasmuch as such matter must needs die in the act of analysis,—and upon this very obvious ground, objections, which I confess seem to me to be somewhat frivolous, have been raised to the drawing of any conclusions whatever respecting the composition of actually living matter, from that of the dead matter of life, which alone is accessible to us. But objectors of this class do not seem to reflect that it is also, in strictness, true that we know nothing about the composition of any body whatever, as it is. The statement that a crystal of calc-spar consists of carbonate of lime, is quite true, if we only mean that, by appropriate processes, it may be resolved into carbonic acid and quicklime. If you pass the same carbonic acid over the very quicklime thus obtained, you will obtain carbonate of lime again; but it will not be calc-spar, nor anything like it. Can it, therefore, be said that chemical analysis teaches nothing about the chemical composition of calc-spar? Such a statement would be absurd; but it is hardly more so than the talk one occasionally hears about the uselessness of applying the results of chemical analysis to the living bodies which have yielded them.

One fact, at any rate, is out of reach of such refinements, and this is, that all the forms of protoplasm which have yet been examined contain the four elements, carbon, hydrogen, oxygen, and nitrogen, in very complex union, and that they behave similarly towards several reagents. To this complex combination, the nature of which has never been determined with exactness, the name of Protein has been applied. And if we use this term with such caution as may properly arise out of our comparative ignorance of the things for which it stands, it may be truly said, that all protoplasm is proteinaceous, or, as the white, or albumen, of an egg is one of the commonest examples of a nearly pure protein matter, we may say that all living matter is more or less albuminoid.

Perhaps it would not yet be safe to say that all forms of protoplasm are affected by the direct action of electric shocks; and yet the number of cases in which the contraction of protoplasm is shown to be affected by this agency increases every day.

Nor can it be affirmed with perfect confidence, that all forms of protoplasm are liable to undergo that peculiar coagulation at a temperature of 40°–50° centigrade, which has been called "heat-stiffening," though Kühne's beautiful researches have proved this occurrence to take place in so many and such diverse living beings, that it is hardly rash to expect that the law holds good for all.

Enough has, perhaps, been said to prove the existence of a general uniformity in the character of the protoplasm, or physical basis, of life, in whatever group of living beings it may be studied. But it will be understood that this general uniformity by no means excludes any amount of special modifications of the fundamental substance. The mineral, carbonate of lime, assumes an immense diversity of characters, though no one doubts that, under all these Protean changes, it is one and the same thing.

And now, what is the ultimate fate, and what the origin, of the matter of life?

Is it, as some of the older naturalists supposed, diffused throughout the universe in molecules, which are indestructible and unchangeable in themselves; but, in endless transmigration, unite in innumerable permutations, into the diversified forms of life we know? Or, is the matter of life composed of ordinary matter, differing from it only in the manner in which its atoms are aggregated? Is it built up of ordinary matter, and again resolved into ordinary matter when its work is done?

Modern science does not hesitate a moment between these alternatives. Physiology writes over the portals of life—

"Debemur morti nos nostraque,"

with a profounder meaning than the Roman poet attached to that melancholy line. Under whatever disguise it takes refuge, whether fungus or oak, worm or man, the living protoplasm not only ultimately dies and is resolved into its mineral and lifeless constituents, but is always dying, and, strange as the paradox may sound, could not live unless it died.

10. **Kühne,** Willy Kühne (1837–1900), German physiologist. 41. **"Debemur . . . nostraque."** "We owe ourselves, and all we have, to death." The Roman poet is Horace (65–8 B.C.), in *Ars Poetica*, l. 63.

In the wonderful story of the "Peau de Chagrin," the hero becomes possessed of a magical wild ass' skin, which yields him the means of gratifying all his wishes. But its surface represents the duration of the proprietor's life; and for every satisfied desire the skin shrinks in proportion to the intensity of fruition, until at length life and the last handbreadth of the *peau de chagrin*, disappear with the gratification of a last wish.

Balzac's studies had led him over a wide range of [10] thought and speculation, and his shadowing forth of physiological truth in this strange story may have been intentional. At any rate, the matter of life is a veritable *peau de chagrin*, and for every vital act it is somewhat the smaller. All work implies waste, and the work of life results, directly or indirectly, in the waste of protoplasm.

Every word uttered by a speaker costs him some physical loss; and, in the strictest sense, he burns that others may have light—so much eloquence, so [20] much of his body resolved into carbonic acid, water, and urea. It is clear that this process of expenditure cannot go on for ever. But, happily, the protoplasmic *peau de chagrin* differs from Balzac's in its capacity of being repaired, and brought back to its full size, after every exertion.

For example, this present lecture, whatever its intellectual worth to you, has a certain physical value to me, which is, conceivably, expressible by the number of grains of protoplasm and other bod- [30] ily substance wasted in maintaining my vital processes during its delivery. My *peau de chagrin* will be distinctly smaller at the end of the discourse than it was at the beginning. By and by, I shall probably have recourse to the substance commonly called mutton, for the purpose of stretching it back to its original size. Now this mutton was once the living protoplasm, more or less modified, of another animal—a sheep. As I shall eat it, it is the same matter altered, not only by death, but by exposure to sun- [40] dry artificial operations in the process of cooking.

But these changes, whatever be their extent, have not rendered it incompetent to resume its old functions as matter of life. A singular inward laboratory, which I possess, will dissolve a certain portion of the modified protoplasm; the solution so formed will pass into my veins; and the subtle influences to which it will then be subjected will convert the dead protoplasm into living protoplasm, and transubstantiate sheep into man.

Nor is this all. If digestion were a thing to be trifled with, I might sup upon lobster, and the matter of life of the crustacean would undergo the same wonderful metamorphosis into humanity. And were I to return to my own place by sea, and undergo shipwreck, the crustacean might, and probably would, return the compliment, and demonstrate our common nature by turning my protoplasm into living lobster. Or, if nothing better were to be had, I might supply my wants with mere bread, and I should find the protoplasm of the wheat-plant to be convertible into man, with no more trouble than that of the sheep, and with far less, I fancy, than that of the lobster.

Hence it appears to be a matter of no great moment what animal, or what plant, I lay under contribution for protoplasm, and the fact speaks volumes for the general identity of that substance in all living beings. I share this catholicity of assimilation with other animals, all of which, so far as we know, could thrive equally well on the protoplasm of any of their fellows, or of any plant; but here the assimilative powers of the animal world cease. A solution of smelling-salts in water, with an infinitesimal proportion of some other saline matters, contains all the elementary bodies which enter into the composition of protoplasm; but, as I need hardly say, a hogshead of that fluid would not keep a hungry man from starving, nor would it save any animal whatever from a like fate. An animal cannot make protoplasm, but must take it ready-made [30] from some other animal, or some plant—the animal's highest feat of constructive chemistry being to convert dead protoplasm into that living matter of life which is appropriate to itself.

Therefore, in seeking for the origin of protoplasm, we must eventually turn to the vegetable world. A fluid containing carbonic acid, water, and nitrogenous salts, which offers such a Barmecide feast to the animal, is a table richly spread to multitudes of plants; and, with a due supply of only such [40] materials, many a plant will not only maintain itself in vigour, but grow and multiply until it has increased a million-fold, or a million million-fold, the quantity of protoplasm which it originally possessed; in this way building up the matter of life, to an indefinite extent, from the common matter of the universe.

Thus, the animal can only raise the complex substance of dead protoplasm to the higher power, as one may say, of living protoplasm; while the plant [50] can raise the less complex substances—carbonic acid, water, and nitrogenous salts—to the same

---

1. **"Peau de Chagrin,"** by Honoré de Balzac, 1834. The title means "Skin of a Wild Ass."

37–38. **Barmecide feast,** a feast of imaginary food, from "The Story of the Barber's Sixth Brother," in *The Arabian Nights' Entertainments.*

stage of living protoplasm, if not to the same level. But the plant also has its limitations. Some of the fungi, for example, appear to need higher compounds to start with; and no known plant can live upon the uncompounded elements of protoplasm. A plant supplied with pure carbon, hydrogen, oxygen, and nitrogen, phosphorus, sulphur, and the like, would as infallibly die as the animal in his bath of smelling-salts, though it would be surrounded by all the constituents of protoplasm. Nor, indeed, need the process of simplification of vegetable food be carried so far as this, in order to arrive at the limit of the plant's thaumaturgy. Let water, carbonic acid, and all the other needful constituents be supplied except nitrogenous salts, and an ordinary plant will still be unable to manufacture protoplasm.

Thus the matter of life, so far as we know it (and we have no right to speculate on any other), breaks up, in consequence of that continual death which is the condition of its manifesting vitality, into carbonic acid, water, and nitrogenous compounds, which certainly possess no properties but those of ordinary matter. And out of these same forms of ordinary matter, and from none which are simpler, the vegetable world builds up all the protoplasm which keeps the animal world a-going. Plants are the accumulators of the power which animals distribute and disperse.

But it will be observed, that the existence of the matter of life depends on the pre-existence of certain compounds; namely, carbonic acid, water, and certain nitrogenous bodies. Withdraw any one of these three from the world, and all vital phaenomena come to an end. They are as necessary to the protoplasm of the plant, as the protoplasm of the plant is to that of the animal. Carbon, hydrogen, oxygen, and nitrogen are all lifeless bodies. Of these, carbon and oxygen unite in certain proportions and under certain conditions, to give rise to carbonic acid; hydrogen and oxygen produce water; nitrogen and other elements give rise to nitrogenous salts. These new compounds, like the elementary bodies of which they are composed, are lifeless. But when they are brought together, under certain conditions, they give rise to the still more complex body, protoplasm, and this protoplasm exhibits the phaenomena of life.

I see no break in this series of steps in molecular complication, and I am unable to understand why the language which is applicable to any one term of the series may not be used to any of the others. We think fit to call different kinds of matter carbon, oxygen, hydrogen, and nitrogen, and to speak of

the various powers and activities of these substances as the properties of the matter of which they are composed.

When hydrogen and oxygen are mixed in a certain proportion, and an electric spark is passed through them, they disappear, and a quantity of water, equal in weight to the sum of their weights, appears in their place. There is not the slightest parity between the passive and active powers of the water and those of the oxygen and hydrogen which have given rise to it. At 32° Fahrenheit, and far below that temperature, oxygen and hydrogen are elastic gaseous bodies, whose particles tend to rush away from one another with great force. Water, at the same temperature, is a strong though brittle solid whose particles tend to cohere into definite geometrical shapes, and sometimes build up frosty imitations of the most complex forms of vegetable foliage.

Nevertheless we call these, and many other strange phaenomena, the properties of the water, and we do not hesitate to believe that, in some way or another, they result from the properties of the component elements of the water. We do not assume that a something called "aquosity" entered into and took possession of the oxidated hydrogen as soon as it was formed, and then guided the aqueous particles to their places in the facets of the crystal, or amongst the leaflets of the hoar-frost. On the contrary, we live in the hope and in the faith that, by the advance of molecular physics, we shall by and by be able to see our way as clearly from the constituents of water to the properties of water, as we are now able to deduce the operations of a watch from the form of its parts and the manner in which they are put together.

Is the case in any way changed when carbonic acid, water, and nitrogenous salts disappear, and in their place, under the influence of pre-existing living protoplasm, an equivalent weight of the matter of life makes its appearance?

It is true that there is no sort of parity between the properties of the components and the properties of the resultant, but neither was there in the case of the water. It is also true that what I have spoken of as the influence of pre-existing living matter is something quite unintelligible; but does anybody quite comprehend the *modus operandi* of an electric spark, which traverses a mixture of oxygen and hydrogen?

What justification is there, then, for the assumption of the existence in the living matter of a something which has no representative, or correla-

48. **modus operandi,** method of working.

tive, in the not living matter which gave rise to it? What better philosophical status has "vitality" than "aquosity"? And why should "vitality" hope for a better fate than the other "itys" which have disappeared since Martinus Scriblerus accounted for the operation of the meat-jack by its inherent "meat-roasting quality," and scorned the "materialism" of those who explained the turning of the spit by a certain mechanism worked by the draught of the chimney.

If scientific language is to possess a definite and constant signification whenever it is employed, it seems to me that we are logically bound to apply to the protoplasm, or physical basis of life, the same conceptions as those which are held to be legitimate elsewhere. If the phaenomena exhibited by water are its properties, so are those presented by protoplasm, living or dead, its properties.

If the properties of water may be properly said to result from the nature and disposition of its component molecules, I can find no intelligible ground for refusing to say that the properties of protoplasm result from the nature and disposition of its molecules.

But I bid you beware that, in accepting these conclusions, you are placing your feet on the first rung of a ladder which, in most people's estimation, is the reverse of Jacob's, and leads to the antipodes of heaven. It may seem a small thing to admit that the dull vital actions of a fungus, or a foraminifer, are the properties of their protoplasm, and are the direct results of the nature of the matter of which they are composed. But if, as I have endeavoured to prove to you, their protoplasm is essentially identical with, and most readily converted into, that of any animal, I can discover no logical halting-place between the admission that such is the case, and the further concession that all vital action may, with equal propriety, be said to be the result of the molecular forces of the protoplasm which displays it. And if so, it must be true, in the same sense and to the same extent, that the thoughts to which I am now giving utterance, and your thoughts regarding them, are the expression of molecular changes in that matter of life which is the source of our other vital phaenomena.

Past experience leads me to be tolerably certain that, when the propositions I have just placed before you are accessible to public comment and

5-10. since Martinus Scriblerus . . . chimney. Martin Scriblerus is a fictitious character spoken of by Arbuthnot, Pope, and Swift. The reference here is to Swift. **28. Jacob's.** Add "ladder." See Genesis 28.

criticism, they will be condemned by many zealous persons, and perhaps by some few of the wise and thoughtful. I should not wonder if "gross and brutal materialism" were the mildest phrase applied to them in certain quarters. And, most undoubtedly, the terms of the propositions are distinctly materialistic. Nevertheless two things are certain; the one, that I hold the statements to be substantially true; the other, that I, individually, am no materialist, but, on the contrary, believe materialism to involve grave philosophical error.

This union of materialistic terminology with the repudiation of materialistic philosophy I share with some of the most thoughtful men with whom I am acquainted. . . .

. . . Why trouble ourselves about matters of which, however important they may be, we do know nothing, and can know nothing? We live in a world which is full of misery and ignorance, and the plain duty of each and all of us is to try to make the little corner he can influence somewhat less miserable and somewhat less ignorant than it was before he entered it. To do this effectually it is necessary to be fully possessed of only two beliefs: the first, that the order of Nature is ascertainable by our faculties to an extent which is practically unlimited; the second, that our volition counts for something as a condition of the course of events.

Each of these beliefs can be verified experimentally, as often as we like to try. Each, therefore, stands upon the strongest foundation upon which any belief can rest, and forms one of our highest truths. If we find that the ascertainment of the order of nature is facilitated by using one terminology, or one set of symbols, rather than another, it is our clear duty to use the former; and no harm can accrue, so long as we bear in mind, that we are dealing merely with terms and symbols.

In itself it is of little moment whether we express the phaenomena of matter in terms of spirit; or the phaenomena of spirit in terms of matter: matter may be regarded as a form of thought, thought may be regarded as a property of matter—each statement has a certain relative truth. But with a view to the progress of science, the materialistic terminology is in every way to be preferred. For it connects thought with the other phaenomena of the universe, and suggests inquiry into the nature of those physical conditions, or concomitants of thought, which are more or less accessible to us, and a knowledge of which may, in future, help us to exercise the same kind of control over the world of thought, as we already possess in respect of the material world;

whereas, the alternative, or spiritualistic, terminology is utterly barren, and leads to nothing but obscurity and confusion of ideas.

Thus there can be little doubt, that the further science advances, the more extensively and consistently will all the phaenomena of Nature be represented by materialistic formulae and symbols.

But the man of science, who, forgetting the limits of philosophical inquiry, slides from these formulae and symbols into what is commonly understood by materialism, seems to me to place himself on a level with the mathematician, who should mistake the x's and y's with which he works his problems, for real entities—and with this further disadvantage, as compared with the mathematician, that the blunders of the latter are of no practical consequence, while the errors of systematic materialism may paralyse the energies and destroy the beauty of a life.

from SCIENCE AND EDUCATION[1]

SCIENCE AND CULTURE

FROM the time that the first suggestion to introduce physical science into ordinary education was timidly whispered, until now, the advocates of scientific education have met with opposition of two kinds. On the one hand, they have been pooh-poohed by the men of business who pride themselves on being the representatives of practicality; while, on the other hand, they have been excommunicated by the classical scholars, in their capacity of Levites in charge of the ark of culture and monopolists of liberal education.

The practical men believed that the idol whom they worship—rule of thumb—has been the source of the past prosperity, and will suffice for the future welfare of the arts and manufactures. They are of opinion that science is speculative rubbish; that theory and practice have nothing to do with one another; and that the scientific habit of mind is an impediment, rather than an aid, in the conduct of ordinary affairs.

I have used the past tense in speaking of the practical men—for although they were very formidable thirty years ago, I am not sure that the pure species has not been extirpated. In fact, so far as mere argument goes, they have been subjected to such a *feu d'enfer* that it is a miracle if any have escaped. But I have remarked that your typical practical man has an unexpected resemblance to one of Milton's angels. His spiritual wounds, such as are inflicted by logical weapons, may be as deep as a well and as wide as a church door, but beyond shedding a few drops of ichor, celestial or otherwise, he is no whit the worse. So, if any of these opponents be left, I will not waste time in vain repetition of the demonstrative evidence of the practical value of science; but knowing that a parable will sometimes penetrate where syllogisms fail to effect an entrance, I will offer a story for their consideration.

Once upon a time, a boy, with nothing to depend upon but his own vigorous nature, was thrown into the thick of the struggle for existence in the midst of a great manufacturing population. He seems to have had a hard fight, inasmuch as, by the time he was thirty years of age, his total disposable funds amounted to twenty pounds. Nevertheless, middle life found him giving proof of his comprehension of the practical problems he had been roughly called upon to solve, by a career of remarkable prosperity.

Finally, having reached old age with its well-earned surroundings of "honour, troops of friends," the hero of my story bethought himself of those who were making a like start in life, and how he could stretch out a helping hand to them.

After long and anxious reflection this successful practical man of business could devise nothing better than to provide them with the means of obtaining "sound, extensive, and practical scientific knowledge." And he devoted a large part of his wealth and five years of incessant work to this end.

I need not point the moral of a tale which, as the solid and spacious fabric of the Scientific College assures us, is no fable, nor can anything which I could say intensify the force of this practical answer to practical objections.

We may take it for granted then, that, in the opinion of those best qualified to judge, the diffusion of thorough scientific education is an absolutely essential condition of industrial progress; and that the College which has been opened today will confer an inestimable boon upon those whose livelihood is to be gained by the practice of the arts and manufactures of the district.

The only question worth discussion is, whether the conditions, under which the work of the College

---

[1] By Thomas Henry Huxley, reprinted by permission of D. Appleton-Century Company, Inc.

33. Levites in charge of the ark of culture. Huxley's reference is to Matthew Arnold; see Arnold's "Literature and Science" in this volume. For the Biblical reference, see Joshua 6 and art. "Priests and Levites" in Hastings's *Dictionary of the Bible.*

1. feu d'enfer, scathing fire. **4–8. His spiritual wounds . . . the worse.** See *Paradise Lost,* Book VI, ll. 327–53. **14. a boy,** Josiah Mason (1795–1881), founder of the Scientific College in Birmingham at whose opening **Huxley** delivered this address.

is to be carried out, are such as to give it the best possible chance of achieving permanent success.

Sir Josiah Mason, without doubt most wisely, has left very large freedom of action to the trustees, to whom he proposes ultimately to commit the administration of the College, so that they may be able to adjust its arrangements in accordance with the changing conditions of the future. But, with respect to three points, he has laid most explicit injunctions upon both administrators and teachers.

Party politics are forbidden to enter into the minds of either, so far as the work of the College is concerned; theology is as sternly banished from its precincts; and finally, it is especially declared that the College shall make no provision for "mere literary instruction and education."

It does not concern me at present to dwell upon the first two injunctions any longer than may be needful to express my full conviction of their wisdom. But the third prohibition brings us face to face with those other opponents of scientific education, who are by no means in the moribund condition of the practical man, but alive, alert, and formidable.

It is not impossible that we shall hear this express exclusion of "literary instruction and education" from a College which, nevertheless, professes to give a high and efficient education, sharply criticised. Certainly the time was that the Levites of culture would have sounded their trumpets against its walls as against an educational Jericho.

How often have we not been told that the study of physical science is incompetent to confer culture; that it touches none of the higher problems of life; and, what is worse, that the continual devotion to scientific studies tends to generate a narrow and bigoted belief in the applicability of scientific methods to the search after truth of all kinds? How frequently one has reason to observe that no reply to a troublesome argument tells so well as calling its author a "mere scientific specialist." And, as I am afraid it is not permissible to speak of this form of opposition to scientific education in the past tense; may we not expect to be told that this, not only omission, but prohibition, of "mere literary instruction and education" is a patent example of scientific narrow-mindedness?

I am not acquainted with Sir Josiah Mason's reasons for the action which he has taken; but if, as I apprehend is the case, he refers to the ordinary classical course of our schools and universities by the name of "mere literary instruction and education," I venture to offer sundry reasons of my own in support of that action.

30. Jericho. See Judges 6.

For I hold very strongly by two convictions:— The first is, that neither the discipline nor the subject-matter of classical education is of such direct value to the student of physical science as to justify the expenditure of valuable time upon either; and the second is, that for the purpose of attaining real culture, an exclusively scientific education is at least as effectual as an exclusively literary education.

I need hardly point out to you that these opinions, especially the latter, are diametrically opposed to those of the great majority of educated Englishmen, influenced as they are by school and university traditions. In their belief, culture is obtainable only by a liberal education; and a liberal education is synonymous, not merely with education and instruction in literature, but in one particular form of literature, namely, that of Greek and Roman antiquity. They hold that the man who has learned Latin and Greek, however little, is educated; while he who is versed in other branches of knowledge, however deeply, is a more or less respectable specialist, not admissible into the cultured caste. The stamp of the educated man, the University degree, is not for him.

I am too well acquainted with the generous catholicity of spirit, the true sympathy with scientific thought, which pervades the writings of our chief apostle of culture to identify him with these opinions; and yet one may cull from one and another of those epistles to the Philistines, which so much delight all who do not answer to that name, sentences which lend them some support.

Mr. Arnold tells us that the meaning of culture is "to know the best that has been thought and said in the world." It is the criticism of life contained in literature. That criticism regards "Europe as being, for intellectual and spiritual purposes, one great confederation, bound to a joint action and working to a common result; and whose members have, for their common outfit, a knowledge of Greek, Roman, and Eastern antiquity, and of one another. Special, local, and temporary advantages being put out of account, that modern nation will in the intellectual and spiritual sphere make most progress, which most thoroughly carries out this programme. And what is that but saying that we too, all of us, as individuals, the more thoroughly we carry it out, shall make the more progress?"

We have here to deal with two distinct propositions. The first, that a criticism of life is the essence

33–48. Mr. Arnold . . . progress?" Both the quotations in this paragraph are from Arnold's essay on "The Function of Criticism at the Present Time," which is included in this volume.

of culture; the second, that literature contains the materials which suffice for the construction of such criticism.

I think that we must all assent to the first proposition. For culture certainly means something quite different from learning or technical skill. It implies the possession of an ideal, and the habit of critically estimating the value of things by comparison with a theoretic standard. Perfect culture should supply a complete theory of life, based upon a clear knowledge alike of its possibilities and of its limitations.

But we may agree to all this, and yet strongly dissent from the assumption that literature alone is competent to supply this knowledge. After having learnt all that Greek, Roman, and Eastern antiquity have thought and said, and all that modern literature have to tell us, it is not self-evident that we have laid a sufficiently broad and deep foundation for that criticism of life, which constitutes culture.

Indeed, to any one acquainted with the scope of physical science, it is not at all evident. Considering progress only in the "intellectual and spiritual sphere," I find myself wholly unable to admit that either nations or individuals will really advance, if their common outfit draws nothing from the stores of physical science. I should say that an army, without weapons of precision and with no particular base of operations, might more hopefully enter upon a campaign on the Rhine, than a man, devoid of a knowledge of what physical science has done in the last century, upon a criticism of life.

When a biologist meets with an anomaly, he instinctively turns to the study of development to clear it up. The rationale of contradictory opinions may with equal confidence be sought in history.

It is, happily, no new thing that Englishmen should employ their wealth in building and endowing institutions for educational purposes. But, five or six hundred years ago, deeds of foundation expressed or implied conditions as nearly as possible contrary to those which have been thought expedient by Sir Josiah Mason. That is to say, physical science was practically ignored, while a certain literary training was enjoined as a means to the acquirement of knowledge which was essentially theological.

The reason of this singular contradiction between the actions of men alike animated by a strong and disinterested desire to promote the welfare of their fellows, is easily discovered.

At that time, in fact, if any one desired knowledge beyond such as could be obtained by his own observation, or by common conversation, his first necessity was to learn the Latin language, inasmuch as all the higher knowledge of the western world was contained in works written in that language. Hence, Latin grammar, with logic and rhetoric, studied through Latin, were the fundamentals of education. With respect to the substance of the knowledge imparted through this channel, the Jewish and Christian Scriptures, as interpreted and supplemented by the Romish Church, were held to contain a complete and infallibly true body of information.

Theological dicta were, to the thinkers of those days, that which the axioms and definitions of Euclid are to the geometers of these. The business of the philosophers of the middle ages was to deduce from the data furnished by the theologians, conclusions in accordance with ecclesiastical decrees. They were allowed the high privilege of showing, by logical process, how and why that which the Church said was true, must be true. And if their demonstrations fell short of or exceeded this limit, the Church was maternally ready to check their aberrations; if need were by the help of the secular arm.

Between the two, our ancestors were furnished with a compact and complete criticism of life. They were told how the world began and how it would end; they learned that all material existence was but a base and insignificant blot upon the fair face of the spiritual world, and that nature was, to all intents and purposes, the play-ground of the devil; they learned that the earth is the centre of the visible universe, and that man is the cynosure of things terrestrial, and more especially was it inculcated that the course of nature had no fixed order, but that it could be, and constantly was, altered by the agency of innumerable spiritual beings, good and bad, according as they were moved by the deeds and prayers of men. The sum and substance of the whole doctrine was to produce the conviction that the only thing really worth knowing in this world was how to secure that place in a better which, under certain conditions, the Church promised.

Our ancestors had a living belief in this theory of life, and acted upon it in their dealings with education, as in all other matters. Culture meant saintliness—after the fashion of the saints of those days; the education that led to it was, of necessity, theological; and the way to theology lay through Latin.

That the study of nature—further than was requisite for the satisfaction of everyday wants—should have any bearing on human life was far from the thoughts of men thus trained. Indeed, as nature had been cursed for man's sake, it was an obvious conclusion that those who meddled with nature were likely to come into pretty close contact with Satan. And, if any born scientific investigator followed his instincts, he might safely reckon upon earning the reputation, and probably upon suffering the fate, of a sorcerer.

Had the western world been left to itself in Chinese isolation, there is no saying how long this state of things might have endured. But, happily, it was not left to itself. Even earlier than the thirteenth century, the development of Moorish civilisation in Spain and the great movement of the Crusades had introduced the leaven which, from that day to this, has never ceased to work. At first, through the intermediation of Arabic translations, afterwards by the study of the originals, the western nations of Europe became acquainted with the writings of the ancient philosophers and poets, and, in time, with the whole of the vast literature of antiquity.

Whatever there was of high intellectual aspiration or dominant capacity in Italy, France, Germany, and England, spent itself for centuries in taking possession of the rich inheritance left by the dead civilisations of Greece and Rome. Marvellously aided by the invention of printing, classical learning spread and flourished. Those who possessed it prided themselves on having attained the highest culture then within the reach of mankind.

And justly. For, saving Dante on his solitary pinnacle, there was no figure in modern literature at the time of the Renascence to compare with the men of antiquity; there was no art to compete with their sculpture; there was no physical science but that which Greece had created. Above all, there was no other example of perfect intellectual freedom— of the unhesitating acceptance of reason as the sole guide to truth and the supreme arbiter of conduct.

The new learning necessarily soon exerted a profound influence upon education. The language of the monks and schoolmen seemed little better than gibberish to scholars fresh from Virgil and Cicero, and the study of Latin was placed upon a new foundation. Moreover, Latin itself ceased to afford the sole key to knowledge. The student who sought the highest thought of antiquity, found only a second-hand reflection of it in Roman literature, and turned his face to the full light of the Greeks. And after a battle, not altogether dissimilar to that which is at present being fought over the teaching of physical science, the study of Greek was recog-

nised as an essential element of all higher education.

Then the Humanists, as they were called, won the day; and the great reform which they effected was of incalculable service to mankind. But the Nemesis of all reformers is finality; and the reformers of education, like those of religion, fell into the profound, however common, error of mistaking the beginning for the end of the work of reformation.

The representatives of the Humanists, in the nineteenth century, take their stand upon classical education as the sole avenue to culture, as firmly as if we were still in the age of Renascence. Yet, surely, the present intellectual relations of the modern and the ancient worlds are profoundly different from those which obtained three centuries ago. Leaving aside the existence of a great and characteristically modern literature, of modern painting, and, especially, of modern music, there is one feature of the present state of the civilised world which separates it more widely from the Renascence, than the Renascence was separated from the middle ages.

This distinctive character of our own times lies in the vast and constantly increasing part which is played by natural knowledge. Not only is our daily life shaped by it, not only does the prosperity of millions of men depend upon it, but our whole theory of life has long been influenced, consciously or unconsciously, by the general conceptions of the universe, which have been forced upon us by physical science.

In fact, the most elementary acquaintance with the results of scientific investigation shows us that they offer a broad and striking contradiction to the opinion so implicitly credited and taught in the middle ages.

The notions of the beginning and the end of the world entertained by our forefathers are no longer credible. It is very certain that the earth is not the chief body in the material universe, and that the world is not subordinated to man's use. It is even more certain that nature is the expression of a definite order with which nothing interferes, and that the chief business of mankind is to learn that order and govern themselves accordingly. Moreover this scientific "criticism of life" presents itself to us with different credentials from any other. It appeals not to authority, nor to what anybody may have thought or said, but to nature. It admits that all our interpretations of natural fact are more or less imperfect and symbolic, and bids the learner seek for truth not among words but among things. It warns us that the assertion which outstrips evidence is not only a blunder but a crime.

1. **as nature . . . sake.** See Genesis 3:17.   **42. Virgil,** author of the *Aeneid*, one of the greatest Roman poets (70–19 B.C.).

The purely classical education advocated by the representatives of the Humanists in our day, gives no inkling of all this. A man may be a better scholar than Erasmus, and know no more of the chief causes of the present intellectual fermentation than Erasmus did. Scholarly and pious persons, worthy of all respect, favour us with allocutions upon the sadness of the antagonism of science to their mediaeval way of thinking, which betray an ignorance of the first principles of scientific investigation, an incapacity for understanding what a man of science means by veracity, and an unconsciousness of the weight of established scientific truths, which is almost comical.

There is no great force in the *tu quoque* argument, or else the advocates of scientific education might fairly enough retort upon the modern Humanists that they may be learned specialists, but that they possess no such sound foundation for a criticism of life as deserves the name of culture. And, indeed, if we were disposed to be cruel, we might urge that the Humanists have brought this reproach upon themselves, not because they are too full of the spirit of the ancient Greek, but because they lack it.

The period of the Renascence is commonly called that of the "Revival of Letters," as if the influences then brought to bear upon the mind of Western Europe had been wholly exhausted in the field of literature. I think it is very commonly forgotten that the revival of science, effected by the same agency, although less conspicuous, was not less momentous.

In fact, the few and scattered students of nature of that day picked up the clue to her secrets exactly as it fell from the hands of the Greeks a thousand years before. The foundations of mathematics were so well laid by them, that our children learn their geometry from a book written for the schools of Alexandria two thousand years ago. Modern astronomy is the natural continuation and development of the work of Hipparchus and of Ptolemy; modern physics of that of Democritus and of Archimedes; it was long before modern biological science outgrew the knowledge bequeathed to us by Aristotle, by Theophrastus, and by Galen.

4. Erasmus, the great Dutch scholar (c. 1466–1536), author of *The Praise of Folly*, a reformer who refused to leave the Church with the Protestants. **15. tu quoque.** "So are you!" **38–39. a book . . . ago.** Euclid's *Élements* (of geometry). **41. Hipparchus,** Greek astronomer (c. 160–c. 125 B.C.). **Ptolemy,** Greco-Egyptian astronomer (second century A.D.). **42–43. Democritus,** Greek natural philosopher (c. 460–c. 362 B.C.). **Archimedes,** Greek mathematician (c. 287–212 B.C.). **45. Theophrastus,** Greek philosopher and botanist (died c. 287 B.C.). **Galen,** Greek physician (130–c.200), long recognized as an authority on medicine.

We cannot know all the best thoughts and saying of the Greeks unless we know what they thought about natural phenomena. We cannot fully apprehend their criticism of life unless we understand the extent to which that criticism was affected by scientific conceptions. We falsely pretend to be the inheritors of their culture, unless we are penetrated, as the best minds among them were, with an unhesitating faith that the free employment of reason, in accordance with scientific method, is the sole method of reaching truth.

Thus I venture to think that the pretensions of our modern Humanists to the possession of the monopoly of culture and to the exclusive inheritance of the spirit of antiquity must be abated, if not abandoned. But I should be very sorry that anything I have said should be taken to imply a desire on my part to depreciate the value of classical education, as it might be and as it sometimes is. The native capacities of mankind vary no less than their opportunities; and while culture is one, the road by which one man may best reach it is widely different from that which is most advantageous to another. Again, while scientific education is yet inchoate and tentative, classical education is thoroughly well organised upon the practical experience of generations of teachers. So that, given ample time for learning and estimation for ordinary life, or for a literary career, I do not think that a young Englishman in search of culture can do better than follow the course usually marked out for him, supplementing its deficiencies by his own efforts.

But for those who mean to make science their serious occupation; or who intend to follow the profession of medicine; or who have to enter early upon the business of life; for all these, in my opinion, classical education is a mistake; and it is for this reason that I am glad to see "mere literary education and instruction" shut out from the curriculum of Sir Josiah Mason's College, seeing that its inclusion would probably lead to the introduction of the ordinary smattering of Latin and Greek.

Nevertheless, I am the last person to question the importance of genuine literary education, or to suppose that intellectual culture can be complete without it. An exclusively scientific training will bring about a mental twist as surely as an exclusively literary training. The value of the cargo does not compensate for a ship's being out of trim; and I should be very sorry to think that the Scientific College would turn out none but lop-sided men.

There is no need, however, that such a catastrophe should happen. Instruction in English, French, and German is provided, and thus the three greatest literatures of the modern world are made accessible to the student.

French and German, and especially the latter language, are absolutely indispensable to those who desire full knowledge in any department of science. But even supposing that the knowledge of these languages acquired is not more than sufficient for purely scientific purposes, every Englishman has, in his native tongue, an almost perfect instrument of literary expression; and, in his own literature, mod- [10] els of every kind of literary excellence. If an Englishman cannot get literary culture out of his Bible, his Shakespeare, his Milton, neither, in my belief, will the profoundest study of Homer and Sophocles, Virgil and Horace, give it to him.

Thus, since the constitution of the College makes sufficient provision for literary as well as for scientific education, and since artistic instruction is also contemplated, it seems to me that a fairly complete culture is offered to all who are willing to take [20] advantage of it.

But I am not sure that at this point the "practical" man, scotched but not slain, may ask what all this talk about culture has to do with an Institution, the object of which is defined to be "to promote the prosperity of the manufactures and the industry of the country." He may suggest that what is wanted for this end is not culture, nor even a purely scientific discipline, but simply a knowledge of applied science.

I often wish that this phrase, "applied science," had never been invented. For it suggests that there is a sort of scientific knowledge of direct practical use, which can be studied apart from another sort of scientific knowledge, which is of no practical utility, and which is termed "pure science." But there is no more complete fallacy than this. What people call applied science is nothing but the application of pure science to particular classes of problems. It consists of deductions from those gen- [40] eral principles, established by reasoning and observation, which constitute pure science. No one can safely make these deductions until he has a firm grasp of the principles; and he can obtain that grasp only by personal experience of the operations of observation and of reasoning on which they are founded.

Almost all the processes employed in the arts and manufactures fall within the range either of physics or of chemistry. In order to improve them, one must [50] thoroughly understand them; and no one has a

chance of really understanding them, unless he has obtained that mastery of principles and that habit of dealing with facts, which is given by long-continued and well-directed purely scientific training in the physical and the chemical laboratory. So that there really is no question as to the necessity of purely scientific discipline, even if the work of the College were limited by the narrowest interpretation of its stated aims.

And, as to the desirableness of a wider culture than that yielded by science alone, it is to be recollected that the improvement of manufacturing processes is only one of the conditions which contribute to the prosperity of industry. Industry is a means and not an end; and mankind work only to get something which they want. What that something is depends partly on their innate, and partly on their acquired, desires.

If the wealth resulting from prosperous industry is to be spent upon the gratification of unworthy desires, if the increasing perfection of manufacturing processes is to be accompanied by an increasing debasement of those who carry them on, I do not see the good of industry and prosperity,

Now it is perfectly true that men's views of what is desirable depend upon their characters; and that the innate proclivities to which we give that name are not touched by any amount of instruction. But it does not follow that even mere intellectual educa- [30] tion may not, to an indefinite extent, modify the practical manifestation of the characters of men in their actions, by supplying them with motives unknown to the ignorant. A pleasure-loving character will have pleasure of some sort; but, if you give him the choice, he may prefer pleasures which do not degrade him to those which do. And this choice is offered to every man, who possesses in literary or artistic culture a never-failing source of pleasures, which are neither withered by age, nor staled by [40] custom, nor embittered in the recollection by the pangs of self-reproach.

If the Institution opened today fulfils the intention of its founder, the picked intelligences among all classes of the population of this district will pass through it. No child born in Birmingham, henceforward, if he have the capacity to profit by the opportunities offered to him, first in the primary and other schools, and afterwards in the Scientific College, need fail to obtain, not merely the instruction, [50] but the culture most appropriate to the conditions of his life.

Within these walls, the future employer and the

---

14. Homer, the alleged father of Greek literature, to whom the *Iliad* and the *Odyssey* are attributed. **Sophocles,** one of the greatest Greek dramatists (c. 496–406 B.C.).

39–40. neither . . . custom. See Shakespeare's *Antony and Cleopatra,* Act II, sc. 2, ll. 240–41.

future artisan may sojourn together for a while, and carry, through all their lives, the stamp of the influences then brought to bear upon them. Hence, it is not beside the mark to remind you, that the prosperity of industry depends not merely upon the improvement of manufacturing processes, not merely upon the ennobling of the individual character, but upon a third condition, namely, a clear understanding of the conditions of social life, on the part of both the capitalist and the operative, and their agreement upon common principles of social action. They must learn that social phenomena are as much the expression of natural laws as any others; that no social arrangements can be permanent unless they harmonise with the requirements of social statics and dynamics; and that, in the nature of things, there is an arbiter whose decisions execute themselves.

But this knowledge is only to be obtained by the application of the methods of investigation adopted in physical researches to the investigation of the phaenomena of society. Hence, I confess, I should like to see one addition made to the excellent scheme of education propounded for the College, in the shape of provision for the teaching of Sociology. For though we are all agreed that party politics are to have no place in the instruction of the College; yet in this country, practically governed as it is now by universal suffrage, every man who does his duty must exercise political functions. And, if the evils which are inseparable from the good of political liberty are to be checked, if the perpetual oscillation of nations between anarchy and despotism is to be replaced by the steady march of self-restraining freedom; it will be because men will gradually bring themselves to deal with political, as they now deal with scientific questions; to be as ashamed of undue haste and partisan prejudice in the one case as in the other; and to believe that the machinery of society is at least as delicate as that of a spinning-jenny, and as little likely to be improved by the meddling of those who have not taken the trouble to master the principles of its action.

In conclusion, I am sure that I make myself the mouthpiece of all present in offering to the venerable founder of the Institution, which now commences its beneficent career, our congratulations on the completion of his work; and in expressing the conviction, that the remotest posterity will point to it as a crucial instance of the wisdom which natural piety leads all men to ascribe to their ancestors.

from SCIENCE AND CHRISTIAN TRADITION[1]

AGNOSTICISM AND CHRISTIANITY

NEMO ergo ex me scire quaerat, quod me nescire scio, nisi forte ut nescire discat.—Augustinus, *De Civ. Dei*, xii. 7.

THE present discussion has arisen out of the use, which has become general in the last few years, of the terms "Agnostic" and "Agnosticism."

The people who call themselves "Agnostics" have been charged with doing so because they have not the courage to declare themselves "Infidels." It has been insinuated that they have adopted a new name in order to escape the unpleasantness which attaches to their proper denomination. To this wholly erroneous imputation, I have replied by showing that the term "Agnostic" did, as a matter of fact, arise in a manner which negatives it; and my statement has not been, and cannot be, refuted. Moreover, speaking for myself, and without impugning the right of any other person to use the term in another sense, I further say that Agnosticism is not properly described as a "negative" creed, nor indeed as a creed of any kind, except in so far as it expresses absolute faith in the validity of a principle, which is as much ethical as intellectual. This principle may be stated in various ways, but they all amount to this: that it is wrong for a man to say that he is certain of the objective truth of any proposition unless he can produce evidence which logically justifies that certainty. This is what Agnosticism asserts; and, in my opinion, it is all that is essential to Agnosticism. That which Agnostics deny and repudiate, as immoral, is the contrary doctrine, that there are propositions which men ought to believe, without logically satisfactory evidence; and that reprobation ought to attach to the profession of disbelief in such inadequately supported propositions. The justification of the Agnostic principle lies in the success which follows upon its application, whether in the field of natural, or in that of civil, history; and in the fact that, so far as these topics are concerned, no sane man thinks of denying its validity.

Still speaking for myself, I add, that though Agnosticism is not, and cannot be, a creed, except in so far as its general principle is concerned; yet that the application of that principle results in the

[1] By Thomas Henry Huxley, reprinted by permission of D. Appleton-Century Company, Inc.

6-8. Nemo . . . discat. "No one, therefore, should seek to learn knowledge from me, for I know that I do not know, unless indeed he wishes to learn that he does not know."—Augustine, *City of God*.

denial of, or the suspension of judgment concerning, a number of propositions respecting which our contemporary ecclesiastical "gnostics" profess entire certainty. And, in so far as these ecclesiastical persons can be justified in their old-established custom (which many nowadays think more honoured in the breach than the observance) of using opprobrious names to those who differ from them, I fully admit their right to call me and those who think with me "Infidels"; all I have ventured to urge is that they must not expect us to speak of ourselves by that title.

The extent of the region of the uncertain, the number of the problems the investigation of which ends in a verdict of not proven, will vary according to the knowledge and the intellectual habits of the individual Agnostic. I do not very much care to speak of anything as "unknowable." What I am sure about is that there are many topics about which I know nothing; and which, so far as I can see, are out of reach of my faculties. But whether these things are knowable by any one else is exactly one of those matters which is beyond my knowledge, though I may have a tolerably strong opinion as to the probabilities of the case. Relatively to myself, I am quite sure that the region of uncertainty—the nebulous country in which words play the part of realities—is far more extensive than I could wish. Materialism and Idealism; Theism and Atheism; the doctrine of the soul and its mortality or immortality—appear in the history of philosophy like the shades of Scandinavian heroes, eternally slaying one another and eternally coming to life again in a metaphysical "Nifelheim." It is getting on for twenty-five centuries, at least, since mankind began seriously to give their minds to these topics. Generation after generation, philosophy has been doomed to roll the stone uphill; and, just as all the world swore it was at the top, down it has rolled to the bottom again. All this is written in innumerable books; and he who will toil through them will discover that the stone is just where it was when the work began. Hume saw this; Kant saw it; since their time, more and more eyes have been cleansed of the films which prevented them from seeing it; until now the weight and number of those who refuse to be the prey of verbal mystifications has begun to tell in practical life.

It was inevitable that a conflict should arise be-

tween Agnosticism and Theology; or rather, I ought to say, between Agnosticism and Ecclesiasticism. For Theology, the science, is one thing; and Ecclesiasticism, the championship of a foregone conclusion as to the truth of a particular form of Theology, is another. With scientific Theology, Agnosticism has no quarrel. On the contrary, the Agnostic, knowing too well the influence of prejudice and idiosyncrasy, even on those who desire most earnestly to be impartial, can wish for nothing more urgently than that the scientific theologian should not only be at perfect liberty to thresh out the matter in his own fashion; but that he should, if he can, find flaws in the Agnostic position; and, even if demonstration is not to be had, that he should put, in their full force, the grounds of the conclusions he thinks probable. The scientific theologian admits the Agnostic principle, however widely his results may differ from those reached by the majority of Agnostics.

But, as between Agnosticism and Ecclesiasticism, or, as our neighbours across the Channel call it, Clericalism, there can be neither peace nor truce. The Cleric asserts that it is morally wrong not to believe certain propositions, whatever the results of a strict scientific investigation of the evidence of these propositions. He tell us "that religious error is, in itself, of an immoral nature." He declares that he has prejudged certain conclusions, and looks upon those who show cause for arrest of judgment as emissaries of Satan. It necessarily follows that, for him, the attainment of faith, not the ascertainment of truth, is the highest aim of mental life. And, on careful analysis of the nature of this faith, it will too often be found to be, not the mystic process of unity with the Divine, understood by the religious enthusiast; but that which the candid simplicity of a Sunday scholar once defined it to be. "Faith," said this unconscious plagiarist of Tertullian, "is the power of saying you believe things which are incredible."

Now I, and many other Agnostics, believe that faith, in this sense, is an abomination; and though we do not indulge in the luxury of self-righteousness so far as to call those who are not of our way of thinking hard names, we do feel that the disagreement between ourselves and those who hold this doctrine is even more moral than intellectual. It is desirable there should be an end of any mistakes on this topic. If our clerical opponents were clearly aware of the real state of the case, there would be

5–7. **custom . . . observance.** See *Hamlet*, Act I, sc. 4:15–16.   33. **"Nifelheim,"** the kingdom of cold and darkness, in Norse mythology the place of punishment.   36–39. **philosophy . . . again.** In Greek mythology this task was imposed, in Hades, upon Sisyphus, evil king of Corinth.   42. **Hume,** David Hume (1711–1776), Scotch historian and philosopher. **Kant,** Immanuel Kant (1724–1804), German philosopher.

26–27. **"that religious error . . . nature."** Huxley's note indicates that he is quoting here from Cardinal Newman's "Essay on Development." 37–40. **"Faith . . . incredible."** Huxley refers to a passage in the treatise on baptism by Tertullian.

an end of the curious delusion, which often appears between the lines of their writings, that those whom they are so fond of calling "Infidels" are people who not only ought to be, but in their hearts are, ashamed of themselves. It would be discourteous to do more than hint the antipodal opposition of this pleasant dream of theirs to facts.

The clerics and their lay allies commonly tell us, that if we refuse to admit that there is good ground for expressing definite convictions about certain topics, the bonds of human society will dissolve and mankind lapse into savagery. There are several answers to this assertion. One is that the bonds of human society were formed without the aid of their theology; and, in the opinion of not a few competent judges, have been weakened rather than strengthened by a good deal of it. Greek science, Greek art, the ethics of old Israel, the social organisation of old Rome, contrived to come into being, without the help of any one who believed in a single distinctive article of the simplest of the Christian creeds. The science, the art, the jurisprudence, the chief political and social theories, of the modern world have grown out of those of Greece and Rome—not by favour of, but in the teeth of, the fundamental teachings of early Christianity, to which science, art, and any serious occupation with the things of this world, were alike despicable.

Again, all that is best in the ethics of the modern world, in so far as it has not grown out of Greek thought, or Barbarian manhood, is the direct development of the ethics of old Israel. There is no code of legislation, ancient or modern, at once so just and so merciful, so tender to the weak and poor, as the Jewish law; and, if the Gospels are to be trusted, Jesus of Nazareth himself declared that he taught nothing but that which lay implicitly, or explicitly, in the religious and ethical system of his people.

"And the scribe said unto him, Of a truth, Teacher, thou hast well said that he is one; and there is none other but he and to love him with all the heart, and with all the understanding, and with all the strength, and to love his neighbour as himself, is much more than all whole burnt offerings and sacrifices." (Mark xii. 32, 33.)

Here is the briefest of summaries of the teaching of the prophets of Israel of the eighth century; does the Teacher, whose doctrine is thus set forth in his presence, repudiate the exposition? Nay; we are told, on the contrary, that Jesus saw that he "answered discreetly," and replied, "Thou art not far from the kingdom of God."

So that I think that even if the creeds, from the so-called "Apostles'" to the so-called "Athanasian," were swept into oblivion; and even if the human race should arrive at the conclusion that, whether a bishop washes a cup or leaves it unwashed, is not a matter of the least consequence, it will get on very well. The causes which have led to the development of morality in mankind, which have guided or impelled us all the way from the savage to the civilised state, will not cease to operate because a number of ecclesiastical hypotheses turn out to be baseless. And, even if the absurd notion that morality is more the child of speculation than of practical necessity and inherited instinct, had any foundation; if all the world is going to thieve, murder, and otherwise misconduct itself as soon as it discovers that certain portions of ancient history are mythical; what is the relevance of such arguments to any one who holds by the Agnostic principle?

Surely, the attempt to cast out Beelzebub by the aid of Beelzebub is a hopeful procedure as compared to that of preserving morality by the aid of immorality. For I suppose it is admitted that an Agnostic may be perfectly sincere, may be competent, and may have studied the question at issue with as much care as his clerical opponents. But, if the Agnostic really believes what he says, the "dreadful consequence" argufier (consistently, I admit, with his own principles) virtually asks him to abstain from telling the truth, or to say what he believes to be untrue, because of the supposed injurious consequences to morality. "Beloved brethren, that we may be spotlessly moral, before all things let us lie," is the sum total of many an exhortation addressed to the "Infidel." Now, as I have already pointed out, we cannot oblige our exhorters. We leave the practical application of the convenient doctrines of "Reserve" and "Non-natural interpretation" to those who invented them.

I trust that I have now made amends for any ambiguity, or want of fulness, in my previous exposition of that which I hold to be the essence of the Agnostic doctrine. Henceforward, I might hope to hear no more of the assertion that we are necessarily Materialists, Idealists, Atheists, Theists, or

31. **Barbarian.** From the point of view of the ancient Greeks all non-Greeks were barbarians.

2–3. **"Thou . . . God."** See Mark 12 : 34. 5. **"Apostles',"** the earliest and best-known Christian creed (beginning "I believe in God, the Father Almighty, Maker of Heaven and Earth"). It is of unknown origin. **"Athanasian,"** a famous creed, attributed by tradition to Athanasius (see notes to Newman's *Apologia pro Vita Sua*). 23–24. **the attempt . . . Beelzebub.** See Matthew 12 : 22–30. Beelzebub is (here) the prince of devils.

any other ists, if experience had led me to think that the proved falsity of a statement was any guarantee against its repetition. And those who appreciate the nature of our position will see, at once, that when Ecclesiasticism declares that we ought to believe this, that, and the other, and are very wicked if we don't, it is impossible for us to give any answer but this: We have not the slightest objection to believe anything you like, if you will give us good

grounds for belief; but, if you cannot, we must respectfully refuse, even if that refusal should wreck morality and insure our own damnation several times over. We are quite content to leave that to the decision of the future. The course of the past has impressed us with the firm conviction that no good ever comes of falsehood, and we feel warranted in refusing even to experiment in that direction. . . .

Victorian Humor

Charles Stuart Calverley
1831–1884

Charles Stuart Calverley was a Cambridge fellow, a barrister, and a gifted classicist, noted for his felicitous translations from the Latin as well as for his humorous verse. A skating accident made him an invalid for almost the last twenty years of his life.

BALLAD

PART I

The auld wife sat at her ivied door,
  (*Butter and eggs and a pound of cheese*)
A thing she had frequently done before;
  And her spectacles lay on her aproned knees.

The piper he piped on the hill-top high,
  (*Butter and eggs and a pound of cheese*)
Till the cow said "I die" and the goose asked "Why?"
  And the dog said nothing, but searched for fleas.

The farmer he strode through the square farmyard;
  (*Butter and eggs and a pound of cheese*)   10
His last brew of ale was a trifle hard—
  The connexion of which with the plot one sees.

The farmer's daughter hath frank blue eyes;
  (*Butter and eggs and a pound of cheese*)
She hears the rooks caw in the windy skies,
  As she sits at her lattice and shells her peas.

The farmer's daughter hath ripe red lips;
  (*Butter and eggs and a pound of cheese*)

If you try to approach her, away she skips
  Over tables and chairs with apparent ease.   20

The farmer's daughter hath soft brown hair
  (*Butter and eggs and a pound of cheese*)
And I met with a ballad, I can't say where,
  Which wholly consisted of lines like these.

PART II

She sat with her hands 'neath her dimpled cheeks,
  (*Butter and eggs and a pound of cheese*)
And spake not a word. While a lady speaks
  There is hope, but she didn't even sneeze.

She sat with her hands 'neath her crimson cheeks;
  (*Butter and eggs and a pound of cheese*)   30
She gave up mending her father's breeks,
  And let the cat roll in her best chemise.

She sat with her hands 'neath her burning cheeks
  (*Butter and eggs and a pound of cheese*)
And gazed at the piper for thirteen weeks;
  Then she followed him out o'er the misty leas.

Her sheep followed her, as their tails did them.
  (*Butter and eggs and a pound of cheese*)
And this song is considered a perfect gem,
  And as to the meaning, it's what you please.   40

COMPANIONS

A Tale of a Grandfather

I know not what we pondered
  Or made pretty pretence to talk,
As, her hand within mine, we wandered
  Toward the pool by the lime-tree walk,

While the dew fell in showers from the passion
    flowers
    And the blush-rose bent on her stalk.

I cannot recall her figure:
    Was it regal as Juno's own?
Or only a trifle bigger
    Than the elves who surround the throne   10
Of the Faëry Queen, and are seen, I ween,
    By mortals in dreams alone?

What her eyes were like, I know not:
    Perhaps they were blurred with tears;
And perhaps in yon skies there glow not
    (On the contrary) clearer spheres.
No! as to her eyes I am just as wise
    As you or the cat, my dears.

Her teeth, I presume, were "pearly":
    But which was she, brunette or blonde?   20
Her hair, was it quaintly curly,
    Or as straight as a beadle's wand?
That I failed to remark;—it was rather dark
    And shadowy round the pond.

Then the hand that reposed so snugly
    In mine—was it plump or spare?
Was the countenance fair or ugly?
    Nay, children, you have me there!
My eyes were p'raps blurred; and besides I'd heard
    That it's horribly rude to stare.   30

And I—was I brusque and surly?
    Or oppressively bland and fond?
Was I partial to rising early?
    Or why did we twain abscond,
All breakfastless too, from the public view
    To prowl by a misty pond?

What passed, what was felt or spoken—
    Whether anything passed at all—
And whether the heart was broken
    That beat under that shelt'ring shawl—   40
(If shawl she had on, which I doubt)—has gone,
    Yes, gone from me past recall.

Was I haply the lady's suitor?
    Or her uncle? I can't make out—
Ask your governess, dears, or tutor.
    For myself, I'm in hopeless doubt
As to why we were there, who on earth we were,
    And what this is all about.

8. Juno, queen of the gods in Roman religion.

Edward Lear
1812–1888

Edward Lear, "the laureate of all nonsense poets," was a painter. His first *Book of Nonsense*, 1846, grew out of the verses he made to amuse the children on the estate of the Earl of Derby, where he was engaged to paint pictures of the birds and animals in His Lordship's collection. As a landscape painter, Lear traveled extensively, finally settling, because of ill-health, at San Remo, Italy.

Lear's books were literally read to pieces during his own time—in a two-year search Bertha Coolidge could find only one copy of the first edition of the *Book of Nonsense.* Since his death he has been much less popular than Lewis Carroll, though his admirers give him special acclaim as the fabricator of pure nonsense, without overtones or extraneous elements. He was a burly, kindly, rather lonely man, who was warmly admired by the Tennysons and many other distinguished contemporaries.

THE JUMBLIES[1]

1

They went to sea in a sieve, they did;
    In a sieve they went to sea:
In spite of all their friends could say,
On a winter's morn, on a stormy day,
    In a sieve they went to sea.
And when the sieve turned round and round,
And every one cried, "You'll be drowned!"
They called aloud, "Our sieve ain't big,
But we don't care a button; we don't care a fig:
    In a sieve we'll go to sea!"   10
      Far and few, far and few,
        Are the lands where the Jumblies live:
      Their heads are green, and their hands are
        blue;
        And they went to sea in a sieve.

2

They sailed away in a sieve, they did,
    In a sieve they sailed so fast,
With only a beautiful pea-green veil
Tied with a ribbon, by way of a sail,
    To a small tobacco-pipe mast.

[1] Courtesy of Frederick Warne & Company, Inc., original publishers of Edward Lear.

11–14. Far . . . sieve. This refrain is repeated at the end of each stanza, but is disregarded in the numbering here.

And every one said who saw them go,   20
"Oh! won't they be soon upset, you know?
For the sky is dark, and the voyage is long;
And, happen what may, it's extremely wrong
    In a sieve to sail so fast."

3

The water it soon came in, it did;
    The water it soon came in:
So, to keep them dry, they wrapped their feet
In a pinky paper all folded neat;
    And they fastened it down with a pin.
And they passed the night in a crockery-jar;   30
And each of them said, "How wise we are!
Though the sky be dark, and the voyage be long,
Yet we never can think we were rash or wrong
    While round in our sieve we spin."

4

And all night long they sailed away;
    And, when the sun went down,
They whistled and warbled a moony song
To the echoing sound of a coppery gong,
    In the shade of the mountains brown,
"O Timballoo! how happy we are   40
When we live in a sieve and a crockery-jar!
And all night long, in the moonlight pale,
We sail away with a pea-green sail
    In the shade of the mountains brown."

5

They sailed to the Western Sea, they did,—
    To a land all covered with trees:
And they bought an owl, and a useful cart,
And a pound of rice, and a cranberry-tart,
    And a hive of silvery bees;
And they bought a pig, and some green jackdaws, 50
And a lovely monkey with lollipop paws,
And forty bottles of ring-bo-ree,
    And no end of Stilton cheese.

6

And in twenty years they all came back,—
    In twenty years or more;
And every one said, "How tall they've grown!
For they've been to the Lakes, and the Torrible
    Zone,
    And the hills of Chankly Bore."
And they drank their health, and gave them a feast
Of dumplings made of beautiful yeast;   60
And every one said, "If we only live,
We, too, will go to sea in a sieve,
    To the hills of the Chankly Bore."

Far and few, far and few,
    Are the lands where the Jumblies live.
Their heads are green, and their hands are
    blue;
    And they went to sea in a sieve.

THE POBBLE WHO HAS NO TOES

1

The Pobble who has no toes
    Had once as many as we;
When they said, "Some day you may lose them
    all";
    He replied, "Fish fiddle de-dee!"
And his Aunt Jobiska made him drink
Lavender water tinged with pink;
For she said, "The World in general knows
There's nothing so good for a Pobble's toes!"

2

The Pobble who has no toes,
    Swam across the Bristol Channel;   10
But before he set out he wrapped his nose
    In a piece of scarlet flannel.
For his Aunt Jobiska said, "No harm
Can come to his toes if his nose is warm;
And it's perfectly known that a Pobble's toes
Are safe—provided he minds his nose."

3

The Pobble swam fast and well,
    And when boats or ships came near him,
He tinkledy-blinkledy-winkled a bell
    So that all the world could hear him.   20
And all the Sailors and Admirals cried,
When they saw him nearing the further side,—
"He has gone to fish, for his Aunt Jobiska's
Runcible Cat with crimson whiskers!"

4

But before he touched the shore,—
    The shore of the Bristol Channel,
A sea-green Porpoise carried away
    His wrapper of scarlet flannel.
And when he came to observe his feet,
Formerly garnished with toes so neat,   30
His face at once became forlorn
On perceiving that all his toes were gone!

5

And nobody ever knew,
    From that dark day to the present,
Whoso had taken the Pobble's toes,
    In a manner so far from pleasant.

Whether the shrimps or crawfish gray,
Or crafty Mermaids stole them away,
Nobody knew; and nobody knows
How the Pobble was robbed of his twice five toes! 40

6

The Pobble who has no toes
  Was placed in a friendly Bark,
And they rowed him back, and carried him up
  To his Aunt Jobiska's Park.
And she made him a feast, at his earnest wish,
Of eggs and buttercups fried with fish;
And she said, "It's a fact the whole world knows,
That Pobbles are happier without their toes."

Lewis Carroll
1832–1898

Lewis Carroll's experience has been just the opposite of Jonathan Swift's. Swift wrote *Gulliver's Travels*, the bitterest book in English literature, which, so far as the "general reader" is concerned, has now been relegated to the quite special eminence of a nursery classic. Lewis Carroll told the story which became *Alice's Adventures in Wonderland*, 1865, to amuse a little girl, and it has become one of the most universally beloved of all English books, as great a favorite with philosophers as with infants. *Through the Looking-Glass*, 1871, is one of the few sequels that are not inferior to the books they followed.

In private life, Lewis Carroll was the Reverend Charles Lutwidge Dodgson, a mathematical lecturer at Oxford, where he lived a secluded life, brightened by his many friendships with children. It is true that he tried to keep Lewis Carroll and C. L. Dodgson apart from each other, but the story that Queen Victoria asked for his books only to receive *The Condensation of Determinants* and *A Syllabus of Plane Algebraical Geometry* is apocryphal.

from ALICE'S ADVENTURES IN WONDERLAND

THE CROCODILE

These lines are a parody of a poem by Isaac Watts, "Against Idleness and Mischief."

  How doth the little crocodile
    Improve his shining tail,
  And pour the waters of the Nile
    On every shining scale!

  How cheerfully he seems to grin,
    How neatly spreads his claws,
  And welcomes little fishes in
    With gently smiling jaws!

FATHER WILLIAM

This poem is a parody of "The Old Man's Comforts" by Robert Southey.

"You are old, Father William," the young man said,
  "And your hair has become very white;
And yet you incessantly stand on your head—
  Do you think, at your age, it is right?"

"In my youth," Father William replied to his son,
  "I feared it might injure the brain;
But now that I'm perfectly sure I have none,
  Why, I do it again and again."

"You are old," said the youth, "as I mentioned before,
  And have grown most uncommonly fat; 10
Yet you turned a back-somersault in at the door—
  Pray, what is the reason of that?"

"In my youth," said the sage, as he shook his grey locks,
  "I kept all my limbs very supple
By the use of this ointment—one shilling the box—
  Allow me to sell you a couple?"

"You are old," said the youth, "and your jaws are too weak
  For anything tougher than suet;
Yet you finished the goose, with the bones and the beak—
  Pray, how did you manage to do it?" 20

"In my youth," said his father, "I took to the law,
  And argued each case with my wife;
And the muscular strength which it gave to my jaw
  Has lasted the rest of my life."

"You are old," said the youth, "one would hardly suppose
  That your eye was as steady as ever;
Yet you balanced an eel on the end of your nose—
  What made you so awfully clever?"

"I have answered three questions, and that is enough,"
  Said his father, "Don't give yourself airs! 30
Do you think I can listen all day to such stuff?
  Be off, or I'll kick you down-stairs!"

from THROUGH THE LOOKING–
GLASS

JABBERWOCKY

This jingle is full of what Lewis Carroll called "port-
manteau words"; for example, "slithy" combines "slimy"
and "lithe."

'Twas brillig, and the slithy toves
    Did gyre and gimble in the wabe;
All mimsy were the borogoves,
    And the mome raths outgrabe.

"Beware the Jabberwock, my son!
    The jaws that bite, the claws that catch!
Beware the Jubjub bird, and shun
    The frumious Bandersnatch!"

He took his vorpal sword in hand:
    Long time the manxome foe he sought—   10
So rested he by the Tumtum tree,
    And stood awhile in thought.

And, as in uffish thought he stood,
    The Jabberwock, with eyes of flame,
Came whiffling through the tulgey wood,
    And burbled as it came!

One, two! One, two! And through and through
    The vorpal blade went snicker-snack!
He left it dead, and with its head
    He went galumphing back.   20

"And hast thou slain the Jabberwock?
    Come to my arms, my beamish boy!
O frabjous day! Callooh! Callay!"
    He chortled in his joy.

'Twas brillig, and the slithy toves
    Did gyre and gimble in the wabe;
All mimsy were the borogoves,
    And the mome raths outgrabe.

THE WALRUS AND THE CARPENTER

The sun was shining on the sea,
    Shining with all his might;
He did his very best to make
    The billows smooth and bright—
And this was odd, because it was
    The middle of the night.

The moon was shining sulkily,
    Because she thought the sun

Had got no business to be there
    After the day was done—   10
"It's very rude of him," she said,
    "To come and spoil the fun!"

The sea was wet as wet could be,
    The sands were dry as dry.
You could not see a cloud, because
    No cloud was in the sky;
No birds were flying overhead—
    There were no birds to fly.

The Walrus and the Carpenter
    Were walking close at hand;   20
They wept like anything to see
    Such quantities of sand—
"If this were only cleared away,"
    They said, "it would be grand!"

"If seven maids with seven mops
    Swept it for half a year,
Do you suppose," the Walrus said,
    "That they could get it clear?"
"I doubt it," said the Carpenter,
    And shed a bitter tear.   30

"O Oysters, come and walk with us!"
    The Walrus did beseech.
"A pleasant walk, a pleasant talk,
    Along the briny beach;
We cannot do with more than four,
    To give a hand to each."

The eldest Oyster looked at him,
    But never a word he said;
The eldest Oyster winked his eye,
    And shook his heavy head—   40
Meaning to say he did not choose
    To leave the oyster-bed.

But four young Oysters hurried up,
    All eager for the treat;
Their coats were brushed, their faces washed,
    Their shoes were clean and neat—
And this was odd, because, you know,
    They hadn't any feet.

Four other Oysters followed them,
    And yet another four;   50
And thick and fast they came at last,
    And more, and more, and more—
All hopping through the frothy waves,
    And scrambling to the shore.

The Walrus and the Carpenter
　　Walked on a mile or so,
And then they rested on a rock
　　Conveniently low—
And all the little Oysters stood
　　And waited in a row. 60

"The time has come," the Walrus said,
　　"To talk of many things:
Of shoes—and ships—and sealing-wax—
　　Of cabbages—and kings—
And why the sea is boiling hot—
　　And whether pigs have wings."

"But wait a bit," the Oysters cried,
　　"Before we have our chat;
For some of us are out of breath,
　　And all of us are fat!" 70
"No hurry!" said the Carpenter.
　　They thanked him much for that.

"A loaf of bread," the Walrus said,
　　"Is what we chiefly need;
Pepper and vinegar besides
　　Are very good indeed—
Now, if you're ready, Oysters dear,
　　We can begin to feed."

"But not on us!" the Oysters cried,
　　Turning a little blue. 80
"After such kindness, that would be
　　A dismal thing to do!"
"The night is fine," the Walrus said
　　"Do you admire the view?

"It was so kind of you to come!
　　And you are very nice!"
The Carpenter said nothing but,
　　"Cut us another slice.
I wish you were not quite so deaf—
　　I've had to ask you twice!" 90

"It seems a shame," the Walrus said,
　　"To play them such a trick,
After we've brought them out so far,
　　And made them trot so quick!"
The Carpenter said nothing but,
　　"The butter's spread too thick!"

"I weep for you," the Walrus said;
　　"I deeply sympathize."
With sobs and tears he sorted out
　　Those of the largest size, 100
Holding his pocket-handkerchief
　　Before his streaming eyes.

"O Oysters," said the Carpenter,
　　"You've had a pleasant run!
Shall we be trotting home again?"
　　But answer came there none—
And this was scarcely odd, because
　　They'd eaten every one.

W. S. Gilbert
1836–1911

A practicing barrister, William Schwenck Gilbert (later Sir William) made his first success in literature with the *Bab Ballads*, 1869, 1873, illustrated by himself. He wrote a number of plays in prose (*Tom Cobb, Engaged*, and others) and in verse (*The Palace of Truth, Pygmalion and Galatea*, and so on), but it was not until he formed his partnership with the musician Sir Arthur Sullivan (1842–1900) that he became a world figure. *H.M.S. Pinafore*, 1878, which pokes fun at Italian opera and the British Navy, was their first "smash hit," *The Mikado*, 1885, no doubt their greatest. A man feared all his life for his caustic tongue, Gilbert died gallantly in 1911, when, at the age of seventy-five, he tried to save a girl from drowning.

An amazing combination of gaiety, stinging satire, and haunting melody, the Gilbert and Sullivan operas are probably as sure of immortality as anything that has come out of the English theater since Shakespeare. The Rupert D'Oyly Carte company, which still gives the operas exactly as they were given in Gilbert's time, has now made complete recordings of all of them, which are released in this country through the Victor Company.

THE YARN OF THE *NANCY BELL*

'Twas on the shores that round our coast
　　From Deal to Ramsgate span,
That I found alone on a piece of stone
　　An elderly naval man.

His hair was weedy, his beard was long
　　And weedy and long was he,
And I heard this wight on the shore recite
　　In a singular minor key:

"Oh, I am a cook and a captain bold,
　　And the mate of the *Nancy* brig, 10
And a bo'sun tight, and a midshipmite,
　　And the crew of the captain's gig."

2. **Deal to Ramsgate,** watering-places in Kent.

And he shook his fists, and he tore his hair,
    Till I really felt afraid,
For I couldn't help thinking the man had been
        drinking,
    And so I simply said:

"Oh, elderly man, it's little I know
    Of the duties of men of the sea,
And I'll eat my hand if I understand
    However you can be   20

"At once a cook, and a captain bold,
    And the mate of the *Nancy* brig,
And a bo'sun tight, and a midshipmite,
    And the crew of the captain's gig."

Then he gave a hitch to his trousers, which
    Is a trick all seamen larn,
And having got rid of a thumping quid,
    He spun this painful yarn:

"'Twas in the good ship *Nancy Bell*
    That we sailed to the Indian Sea,   30
And there on a reef we come to grief
    Which has often occurred to me.

"And pretty nigh all the crew was drowned
    (There was seventy-seven o' soul),
And only ten of the *Nancy's* men
    Said 'Here!' to the muster-roll.

"There was me and the cook and the captain bold,
    And the mate of the *Nancy* brig,
And the bo'sun tight, and a midshipmite,
    And the crew of the captain's gig.   40

"For a month we'd neither wittles nor drink,
    Till a-hungry we did feel,
So we drawed a lot, and, accordin' shot
    The captain for our meal.

"The next lot fell to the *Nancy's* mate,
    And a delicate dish he made;
Then our appetite with the midshipmite
    We seven survivors stayed.

"And then we murdered the bo'sun tight,
    And he much resembled pig;   50
Then we wittled free, did the cook and me,
    On the crew of the captain's gig.

"Then only the cook and me was left,
    And the delicate question, 'Which
Of us two goes to the kettle?' arose,
    And we argued it out as sich.

"For I loved that cook as a brother, I did,
    And the cook he worshipped me;
But we'd both be blowed if we'd either be stowed
    In the other chap's hold, you see.   60

"'I'll be eat if you dines off me,' says TOM;
    'Yes, that,' says I, 'you'll be,—'
'I'm boiled if I die, my friend,' quoth I,
    And 'Exactly so,' quoth he.

"Says he, 'Dear JAMES, to murder me
    Were a foolish thing to do,
For don't you see that you can't cook *me*,
    While I can—and will—cook *you*?'

"So he boils the water, and takes the salt
    And the pepper in portions true   70
(Which he never forgot) and some chopped shalot,
    And some sage and parsley too.

"'Come here,' says he, with a proper pride
    Which his smiling features tell,
''Twill soothing be if I let you see
    How extremely nice you'll smell.'

"And he stirred it round and round and round,
    And he sniffed at the foaming froth;
When I ups with his heels, and smothers his squeals
    In the scum of the boiling broth.   80

"And I eat that cook in a week or less,
    And —as I eating be
The last of his chops, why, I almost drops,
    For a wessel in sight I see!

"And I never grin, and I never smile,
    And I never larf nor play,
But sit and croak, and a single joke
    I have—which is to say:

"Oh, I am a cook and captain bold,
    And the mate of the *Nancy* brig,   90
And a bo'sun tight, *and* a midshipmite,
    And the crew of the captain's gig!'"

from PATIENCE:

OR, BUNTHORNE'S BRIDE

Am I Alone?

Bunthorne, the "Fleshly Poet" who sings this song, was
originally intended as a take-off on Swinburne. But by

71. **shalot,** a kind of onion (usually shallot).

the time the opera was produced Swinburne had abandoned much of his early flamboyance, and George Grossmith, Jr., made up the part to resemble Oscar Wilde. When Wilde went to the United States in 1882, his lecture tour was sponsored, though he himself did not know it, by those who wished him to advertise the forthcoming production of *Patience!*

Recitative

Am I alone,
    And unobserved? I am!
Then let me own
    I'm an aesthetic sham!

This air severe
    Is but a mere
           Veneer!
This cynic smile
    Is but a wile
           Of guile!   10
This costume chaste
    Is but good taste
           Misplaced!
Let me confess!

A languid love for lilies does *not* blight me!
Lank limbs and haggard cheeks do *not* delight me!
    I do *not* care for dirty greens
        By any means.
    I do *not* long for all one sees
        That's Japanese.   20
I am *not* fond of uttering platitudes
    In stained-glass attitudes.
In short my mediaevalism's affectation,
Born of a morbid love of admiration!

Song

If you're anxious for to shine in the high aesthetic
    line as a man of culture rare,
You must get up all the germs of the transcendental
    terms, and plant them everywhere.
You must lie upon the daisies, and discourse in
    novel phrases of your complicated state of mind,
The meaning doesn't matter if it's only idle chatter
    of a transcendental kind.
        And every one will say,
        As you walk your mystic way,
"If this young man expresses himself in terms too
    deep for *me*,
Why, what a very singularly deep young man this
    deep young man must be!"

Be eloquent in praise of the very dull old days
    which have long since passed away,
And convince 'em, if you can, that the reign of good
    Queen Anne was Culture's palmiest day.   10
Of course you will pooh-pooh whatever's fresh and
    new, and declare it's crude and mean,
For Art stopped short in the cultivated court of the
    Empress Josephine.
        And every one will say,
        As you walk your mystic way,
"If that's not good enough for him which is good
    enough for *me*,
Why, what a very cultivated kind of youth this
    kind of youth must be!"

Then a sentimental passion of a vegetable fashion
    must excite your languid spleen,
An attachment *à la* Plato for a bashful young
    potato, or a not-too-French French bean!
Though the Philistines may jostle, you will rank as
    an apostle in the high aesthetic band,
If you walk down Piccadilly with a poppy or a lily
    in your mediaeval hand.   20
        And every one will say,
        As you walk your flowery way,
"If he's content with a vegetable love, which would
    certainly not suit *me*,
Why, what a most particularly pure young man
    this pure young man must be!"

from IOLANTHE;

OR, THE PEER AND THE PERI

The Law Is the True Embodiment

Minors left without parents or guardians come under the jurisdiction of the Court of Chancery. Phyllis, the heroine of *Iolanthe,* is so attractive that the Lords have appealed to the Chancellor in a body to bestow her upon whichever one of them she may select. But the Chancellor himself has "the misfortune to be singularly attracted by this young lady," and if he could reconcile it with his duty he would unhesitatingly bestow her upon himself. "The feelings of a Lord Chancellor who is in love with a Ward of Court are not to be envied. What is his position? Can he give his own consent to his own marriage with his own Ward? Can he marry his own Ward without his own consent? And if he marries his own Ward without his own consent, can he commit himself for contempt of his own Court? And if he commit himself for contempt of

10. **the reign of Good Queen Anne,** 1702–14, when classical ideals prevailed in English letters.   **12. Empress Josephine,** the wife of Napoleon.   **18. attachment à la Plato,** Platonic affection.   **19. Philistines,** in Matthew Arnold's sense of the term, as uncultured persons.   **20. Piccadilly,** a street in London.

his Court, can he appear by counsel before himself, to move for arrest of his own judgment? Ah, my Lords, it is indeed painful to have to sit upon a woolsack which is stuffed with such thorns as these!''

    The Law is the true embodiment
    Of everything that's excellent.
    It has no kind of fault or flaw,
    And I, my Lords, embody the Law.
    The constitutional guardian I
    Of pretty young Wards in Chancery,
    All very agreeable girls, and none
    Are over the age of twenty-one.
      A pleasant occupation for
      A rather susceptible Chancellor!   10

    But though the compliment implied
    Inflates me with legitimate pride,
    It nevertheless can't be denied
    That it has its inconvenient side.
    For I'm not so old and not so plain,
    And I'm quite prepared to marry again;
    But there'd be the deuce to pay in the Lords
    If I fell in love with one of my Wards;
      Which rather tries my temper, for
      I'm *such* a susceptible Chancellor!   20

    And every one who'd marry a Ward
    Must come to me for my accord,
    And in my court I sit all day,
    Giving agreeable girls away,
    With one for him—and one for he—
    And one for you—and one for ye—
    And one for thou—and one for thee—
    But never, oh, never, a one for me!
      Which is exasperating for
      A highly susceptible Chancellor!   30

When I Went to the Bar

    Strephon, who has dared to love Phyllis without the consent of the Court, seeks to justify himself on the plea that he is governed by "Nature's Acts of Parliament." The Chancellor admits that he has no jurisdiction over nature, but he can find no evidence that "Nature has interested herself in the matter." Strephon's unsupported word is not evidence. "An affidavit from a thunderstorm, or a few words on oath from a heavy shower" would be another matter, but neither is forthcoming. So the Chancellor determines regretfully "to apply the prosaic rules of evidence to a case which bubbles over with poetical emotion."

When I went to the Bar as a very young man,
    (Said I to myself, said I),

I'll work on a new and original plan
    (Said I to myself, said I),
I'll never assume that a rogue or a thief
Is a gentlemen worthy implicit belief
Because his attorney has sent me a brief
    (Said I to myself, said I!).

Ere I go into court I will read my brief through
    (Said I to myself, said I).   10
And I'll never take work I'm unable to do
    (Said I to myself, said I),
My learned profession I'll never disgrace
By taking a fee with a grin on my face
When I haven't been there to attend to the case
    (Said I to myself, said I!).

I'll never throw dust in a juryman's eyes
    (Said I to myself, said I),
Or hoodwink a judge who is not over-wise
    (Said I to myself, said I),   20
Or assume that the witnesses summoned in force
In Exchequer, Queen's Bench, Common Pleas, or Divorce
Have perjured themselves as a matter of course
    (Said I to myself, said I!).

In other professions in which men engage
    (Said I to myself, said I),
The Army, the Navy, the Church, and the State
    (Said I to myself, said I),
Professional license, if carried too far,
Your chance of promotion will certainly mar—   30
And I fancy the rule might apply to the Bar
    (Said I to myself, said I!).

from THE MIKADO;
OR, THE TOWN OF TITIPU

As Some Day It May Happen

    Ko-Ko, a tailor, became Lord High Executioner of the town of Titipu under remarkable circumstances. He had been condemned to death for flirting, but the authorities humanely decided to put an end to all executions by releasing him from prison and elevating him to the executioner's office; being himself under sentence, he could not (they reasoned) cut off anyone else's head until he had first cut off his own. In the following song, Ko-Ko nominates a list of prospective victims. As a matter of fact, however, Ko-Ko couldn't kill anybody, Ko-Ko couldn't even kill a bluebottle—a fact which leads to troublesome complications for him later in the opera.

22. Exchequer . . . Divorce, branches of the High Court of Justice. For details, see a dictionary.

As some day it may happen that a victim must be
  found,
  I've got a little list—I've got a little list
Of society offenders who might well be under-
  ground,
  And who never would be missed—who never
  would be missed!
There's the pestilential nuisances who write for
  autographs—
All people who have flabby hands and irritating
  laughs—
All children who are up in dates, and floor you with
  'em flat—
All persons who in shaking hands, shake hands with
  you like *that*—
And all third persons who on spoiling *tête-à-têtes*
  insist—
  They'd none of 'em be missed—they'd none of
  'em be missed!   10

Chorus
  He's got 'em on the list—he's got 'em on the list;
  And they'll none of 'em be missed—they'll none
  of 'em be missed.

There's the nigger serenader, and the others of his
  race,
  And the piano-organist—I've got him on the list!
And the people who eat peppermint and puff it in
  your face,
  They never would be missed—they never would
  be missed!
Then the idiot who praises, with enthusiastic tone,
All centuries but this, and every country but his
  own;
And the lady from the provinces who dresses like a
  guy,

And who "doesn't think she waltzes, but would
  rather like to try";   20
And that singular anomaly, the lady novelist—
  I don't think she'd be missed—I'm *sure* she'd not
  be missed!

Chorus
  He's got her on the list—he's got her on the list;
  And I don't think she'll be missed—I'm *sure* she'll
  not be missed!

And that *Nisi Prius* nuisance, who just now is rather
  rife,
  The Judicial humourist—I've got *him* on the list!
All funny fellows, comic men, and clowns of private
  life—
  They'd none of 'em be missed—they'd none of
  'em be missed!
And apologetic statesmen of a compromising kind,
Such as—What d'ye call him—Thing'em-bob, and
  likewise—Never-mind,   30
And 'St—'st—'st—and What's-his-name, and also
  You-know-who—
The task of filling up the blanks I'd rather leave to
  you.
But it really doesn't matter whom you put upon the
  list,
  For they'd none of 'em be missed—they'd none of
  'em be missed!

Chorus
  You may put 'em on the list—you may put 'em
  on the list;
  And they'll none of 'em be missed—they'll none
  of 'em be missed!

25. Nisi Prius, a legal term for a case triable at assizes, the
literal meaning of which is "unless before."

Charles Dickens
1812–1870

Charles Dickens, represented here as a humorist, was, as all the world knows, much else besides. He was one of the greatest of the Victorians; he was also one of the greatest of novelists. His contemporary popularity was enormous, and he still retains it; there has never been a time when his critical reputation stood higher than it does today.

Dickens was born at Landport, February 7, 1812. After an impecunious childhood, reflected directly in the blacking-warehouse episode of *David Copperfield*, he gained his first foothold in the world as a parliamentary reporter. With *The Pickwick Papers* he found himself and his public; the book was followed, in order, by *Oliver Twist*, *Nicholas Nickleby*, *The Old Curiosity Shop*, *Barnaby Rudge*, *Martin Chuzzlewit*, *Dombey and Son*, *David Copperfield*, *Bleak House*, *Hard Times*, *Little Dorrit*, *A Tale of Two Cities*, *Great Expectations*, and *Our Mutual Friend*. In addition there was the series of *Christmas Books*, of which *A Christmas Carol* was the first and the greatest, and a considerable number of other short pieces. Dickens edited two magazines—*Household Words* and *All the Year Round*—and did an enormous amount of philanthropic work. A gifted actor, he produced many plays for charity; in later life he gave professional readings from his novels. His American tour in 1868 —he had first visited America, nonprofessionally, in 1842—was as successful as Jenny Lind's; people actually stood in line all night to buy tickets. Dickens was a restless man of phenomenal nervous energy; the incomplete collection of his "Letters" in the Nonesuch Dickens comprises some seven thousand items. He died June 8, 1870.

There is much melodrama and sentimentality in Dickens's novels, but there is no insincerity. He believed passionately in his work, and he never wrote down to his audience. His contact with it was very personal; he was the voice of a people in a sense in which this can be said of no other modern writer. His characters, sometimes called caricatures, though not always true to life, are often truer than life; they have the superactual reality of primitive legend.

The early, exuberant, undisillusioned Dickens is seen at his best in *Pickwick* and *Nickleby*. Social purpose first intrudes notably in *Oliver Twist*, an attack on the poor law and on crime-breeding conditions in the slums. In *Martin Chuzzlewit*, he used his American experiences, and also created his greatest character, Mrs. Gamp, an all-too-true picture of what the English nurse was sometimes like before Florence Nightingale made nursing a respectable profession for women; Mrs. Gamp has the vitality of Falstaff or the Wife of Bath. With *Dombey and Son* he began to turn toward a more realistic type of fiction, but he could not yet bring it off with complete success. In *Bleak House* he first achieved a pervasive plot; the book is an attack on the Court of Chancery, and every one of the long list of characters is brought into contact with the great chancery suit. Up to this time, some of Dickens's best characters— such as Pecksniff, Cap'n Cuttle, and Micawber— had had hardly anything to do with the plot of the books in which they appeared, or when contact was made, it was perfunctory and unconvincing. *Hard Times* and *A Tale of Two Cities* show Dickens's sympathy for Carlyle; the former presents Carlyle's ideas on economics, while the latter "dramatizes" *The French Revolution*. *Great Expectations* is a more sophisticated *Copperfield*. A satisfactory solution to *The Mystery of Edwin Drood*, which Dickens left unfinished at his death, is still to be found.

from THE POSTHUMOUS PAPERS OF THE PICKWICK CLUB

The Pickwick Papers, as the book published in 1837 commonly called, is farcical in tone beyond any later publication of Dickens, and there is nothing more amusing in it than the story of Mr. Pickwick's trial for breach of promise, which is here given in part. It was suggested by an episode ("Surrey Shooting: Mr. Jorrocks in Trouble") in *Jorrocks' Jaunts and Jollities* by R. S. Surtees, which had been serialized in the *New Sporting Magazine*, 1831–34. When *Jorrocks* came out in book form in 1838, poor Surtees was accused of having "cribbed" from Dickens!

[BARDELL VS. PICKWICK]

from Chapter 12

MR. PICKWICK'S apartments in Goswell Street, although on a limited scale, were not only of a very neat and comfortable description, but peculiarly adapted for the residence of a man of his genius and observation. . . . His landlady, Mrs. Bardell—the relict and sole executrix of a deceased custom-house officer—was a comely woman of bustling manners and agreeable appearance, with a natural genius for cooking, improved by study and long practice into an exquisite talent. . . .

To any one acquainted with . . . the admirable regulation of Mr. Pickwick's mind, his appearance and behaviour on the morning previous to that which had been fixed upon for the journey to Eatanswill, would have been most mysterious and unaccountable. He paced the room to and fro with hurried steps, popped his head out of the window at intervals of about three minutes each, constantly referred to his watch, and exhibited many other manifestations of impatience very unusual with him.

"Mrs. Bardell," said Mr. Pickwick, at last, as that amiable female approached the termination of a prolonged dusting of the apartment—

"Sir," said Mrs. Bardell. . . .

"Do you think it's a much greater expense to keep two people, than to keep one?"

"La, Mr. Pickwick," said Mrs. Bardell, colouring up to the very border of her cap, as she fancied she observed a species of matrimonial twinkle in the eyes of her lodger; "La, Mr. Pickwick, what a question!"

"Well, but do you?" inquired Mr. Pickwick.

"That depends . . . that depends a good deal upon the person, you know, Mr. Pickwick; and whether it's a saving and careful person, sir."

"That's very true," said Mr. Pickwick, "but the person I have in my eye . . . I think possesses these qualities; and has, moreover, a considerable knowledge of the world, and a great deal of sharpness, Mrs. Bardell; which may be of material use to me."

"La, Mr. Pickwick," said Mrs. Bardell; the crimson rising to her cap-border again.

"I do," said Mr. Pickwick . . . "I do, indeed; and to tell you the truth, Mrs. Bardell, I have made up my mind."

"Dear me, sir," exclaimed Mrs. Bardell.

"You'll think it very strange now," said the amiable Mr. Pickwick, with a good-humoured glance at his companion, "that I never consulted you about this matter, and never even mentioned it, till I sent your little boy out this morning—eh?"

Mrs. Bardell could only reply by a look. . . .

"Well," said Mr. Pickwick, "what do you think?"

"Oh, Mr. Pickwick," said Mrs. Bardell, trembling with agitation, "you're very kind, sir."

"It'll save you a good deal of trouble, won't it?" said Mr. Pickwick.

"Oh, I never thought anything of the trouble, sir," replied Mrs. Bardell; "and, of course, I should take more trouble to please you then, than ever; but it is so kind of you, Mr. Pickwick, to have so much consideration for my loneliness."

"Ah, to be sure," said Mr. Pickwick; "I never thought of that. When I am in town, you'll always have somebody to sit with you. To be sure, so you will."

"I'm sure I ought to be a very happy woman," said Mrs. Bardell.

"And your little boy——" . . .

"Bless his heart!" . . .

"He, too, will have a companion . . . a lively one, who'll teach him, I'll be bound, more tricks in a week than he would ever learn in a year." And Mr. Pickwick smiled placidly.

"Oh, you dear——" said Mrs. Bardell.

Mr. Pickwick started.

"Oh you kind, good, playful dear," said Mrs. Bardell; and without more ado, she rose from her chair, and flung her arms round Mr. Pickwick's neck, with a cataract of tears and a chorus of sobs.

"Bless my soul," cried the astonished Mr. Pickwick;—"Mrs. Bardell, my good woman—dear me, what a situation—pray consider—Mrs. Bardell, don't—if anybody should come——"

"Oh, let them come," exclaimed Mrs. Bardell frantically; "I'll never leave you—dear, kind, good soul!" and with these words Mrs. Bardell clung the tighter.

"Mercy upon me," said Mr. Pickwick, struggling violently, "I hear somebody coming up the stairs. Don't, don't, there's a good creature, don't." But entreaty and remonstrance were alike unavailing: for Mrs. Bardell had fainted in Mr. Pickwick's arms; and before he could gain time to deposit her on a chair, Master Bardell entered the room, ushering in Mr. Tupman, Mr. Winkle, and Mr. Snodgrass.

Mr. Pickwick was struck motionless and speechless. He stood with his lovely burden in his arms, gazing vacantly on the countenances of his friends, without the slightest attempt at recognition or explanation. They, in their turn, stared at him; and Master Bardell, in his turn, stared at everybody. . . .

"What is the matter?" said [at length] the three tongue-tied Pickwickians.

"I don't know," replied Mr. Pickwick pettishly. . . . "Now, help me, lead this woman down stairs."

"Oh, I am better now," said Mrs. Bardell faintly.

"Let me lead you down stairs," said the ever gallant Mr. Tupman.

"Thank you, sir—thank you," exclaimed Mrs. Bardell, hysterically. And down stairs she was led accordingly. . . .

"I cannot conceive—" said Mr. Pickwick, when his friend returned—"I cannot conceive what has been the matter with that woman. I had merely announced to her my intention of keeping a man servant, when she fell into the extraordinary paroxysm in which you found her. Very extraordinary thing."

"Very," said his three friends.

"Placed me in such an extremely awkward situation," continued Mr. Pickwick.

"Very," was the reply of his followers, as they coughed slightly, and looked dubiously at each other.

This behaviour was not lost upon Mr. Pickwick. He remarked their incredulity. They evidently suspected him. . . .

[Suspect him they did, and so did others; and suspicion was not lessened when Mrs. Bardell, through Messrs. Dodson and Fogg, a precious pair of legal scoundrels, brought suit for breach of promise of marriage.]

from Chapter 34

. . . "Bardell and Pickwick," cried the gentleman in black, calling on the case. . . .

"I am for the plaintiff, my Lord," said Mr. Serjeant Buzfuz.

"Who is with you, brother Buzfuz?" said the judge. Mr. Skimpin bowed, to intimate that he was.

"I appear for the defendant, my Lord," said Mr. Serjeant Snubbin.

"Anybody with you, brother Snubbin?" inquired the court.

"Mr. Phunky, my Lord," replied Serjeant Snubbin.

"Serjeant Buzfuz and Mr. Skimpin for the plaintiff," said the judge, writing down the names in his note-book, and reading as he wrote; "for the defendant, Serjeant Snubbin and Mr. Monkey."

"Beg your Lordship's pardon, Phunky."

"Oh, very good," said the judge; "I never had the pleasure of hearing the gentleman's name before." Here Mr. Phunky bowed and smiled, and the judge bowed and smiled too, and then Mr. Phunky, blushing into the very whites of his eyes, tried to look as if he didn't know that everybody was gazing at him: a thing which no man ever succeeded in doing yet, or in all reasonable probability, ever will.

"Go on," said the judge.

The ushers again called silence, and Mr. Skimpin proceeded to "open the case"; and the case appeared to have very little inside it when he had opened it, for he kept such particulars as he knew, completely to himself, and sat down, after a lapse of three minutes, leaving the jury in precisely the same advanced stage of wisdom as they were in before.

Serjeant Buzfuz then rose with all the majesty and dignity which the grave nature of the proceedings demanded, and having whispered to Dodson, and conferred briefly with Fogg, pulled his gown over his shoulders, settled his wig, and addressed the jury.

Serjeant Buzfuz began by saying, that never, in the whole course of his professional experience—never, from the very first moment of his applying himself to the study and practice of the law—had he approached a case with feelings of such deep emotion, or with such a heavy sense of the responsibility imposed upon him—a responsibility, he would say, which he could never have supported, were he not buoyed up and sustained by a conviction so strong, that it amounted to positive certainty that the cause of truth and justice, or, in other words, the cause of his much-injured and most oppressed client, must prevail with the high-minded and intelligent dozen of men whom he now saw in that box before him. . . .

A visible effect was produced immediately; several jurymen beginning to take voluminous notes with the utmost eagerness.

"You have heard from my learned friend, gentlemen," continued Serjeant Buzfuz . . . "that this is an action for a breach of promise of marriage, in which the damages are laid at £1,500. But you have not heard from my learned friend, inasmuch as it did not come within my learned friend's province to tell you, what are the facts and circumstances of the case. Those facts and circumstances, gentlemen, you shall hear detailed by me. . . .

"The plaintiff, gentlemen, . . . is a widow; yes, gentlemen, a widow. The late Mr. Bardell, after enjoying, for many years, the esteem and confidence of his sovereign, as one of the guardians of his royal revenues, glided almost imperceptibly from the world, to seek elsewhere for that repose and peace which a custom-house can never afford."

At this pathetic description of the decease of

Mr. Bardell, who had been knocked on the head with a quart-pot in a public-house cellar, the learned serjeant's voice faltered, and he proceeded with emotion:

"Some time before his death, he had stamped his likeness upon a little boy. With this little boy, the only pledge of her departed exciseman, Mrs. Bardell shrunk from the world, and courted the retirement and tranquillity of Goswell Street; and here she placed in her front-parlour window a written placard, bearing this inscription—'Apartments furnished for a single gentleman. Inquire within.'" Here Serjeant Buzfuz paused, while several gentlemen of the jury took a note of the document.

"There is no date to that, is there, sir?" inquired a juror.

"There is no date, gentlemen," replied Serjeant Buzfuz; "but I am instructed to say that it was put in the plaintiff's parlour-window just this time three years. I intreat the attention of the jury to the wording of this document. 'Apartments furnished for a single gentleman'! Mrs. Bardell's opinions of the opposite sex, gentlemen, were derived from a long contemplation of the inestimable qualities of her lost husband. She had no fear, she had no distrust, she had no suspicion, all was confidence and reliance. 'Mr. Bardell,' said the widow; 'Mr. Bardell was a man of honour, Mr. Bardell was a man of his word, Mr. Bardell was no deceiver, Mr. Bardell was once a single gentleman himself; *to* single gentlemen I look for protection, for assistance, for comfort, and for consolation; *in* single gentlemen I shall perpetually see something to remind me of what Mr. Bardell was, when he first won my young and untried affections; to a single gentleman, then, shall my lodgings be let.' Actuated by this beautiful and touching impulse (among the best impulses of our imperfect nature, gentlemen,) the lonely and desolate widow dried her tears, furnished her first floor, caught the innocent boy to her maternal bosom, and put the bill up in her parlour-window. Did it remain there long? No. The serpent was on the watch, the train was laid, the mine was preparing, the sapper and miner was at work. Before the bill had been in the parlour-window three days—three days—gentlemen—a Being, erect upon two legs, and bearing all the outward semblance of a man, and not of a monster, knocked at the door of Mrs. Bardell's house. He inquired within; he took the lodgings; and on the very next day he entered into possession of them. This man was Pickwick—Pickwick, the defendant."

Serjeant Buzfuz, who had proceeded with such volubility that his face was perfectly crimson, here paused for breath. The silence awoke Mr. Justice Stareleigh, who immediately wrote down something with a pen without any ink in it, and looked unusually profound, to impress the jury with the belief that he always thought most deeply with his eyes shut. Serjeant Buzfuz proceeded.

"Of this man Pickwick I will say little; the subject presents but few attractions; and I, gentlemen, am not the man, nor are you, gentlemen, the men, to delight in the contemplation of revolting heartlessness, and of systematic villainy."

Here Mr. Pickwick, who had been writhing in silence for some time, gave a violent start, as if some vague idea of assaulting Serjeant Buzfuz, in the august presence of justice and law, suggested itself to his mind. . . .

"I say systematic villainy, gentlemen," said Serjeant Buzfuz, looking through Mr. Pickwick, and talking *at* him; "and when I say systematic villainy, let me tell the defendant Pickwick, if he be in court, as I am informed he is, that it would have been more decent in him, more becoming, in better judgment, and in better taste, if he had stopped away. Let me tell him, gentlemen, that any gestures of dissent or disapprobation in which he may indulge in this court will not go down with you; that you will know how to value and how to appreciate them; and let me tell him further, as my lord will tell you, gentlemen, that a counsel, in the discharge of his duty to his client, is neither to be intimidated, nor bullied, nor put down; and that any attempt to do either the one or the other, or the first, or the last, will recoil on the head of the attempter, be he plaintiff or be he defendant, be his name Pickwick, or Noakes, or Stoakes, or Stiles, or Brown, or Thompson."

This little divergence from the subject in hand, had, of course, the intended effect of turning all eyes to Mr. Pickwick. Serjeant Buzfuz, having partially recovered from the state of moral elevation into which he had lashed himself, resumed:

"I shall show you, gentlemen, that for two years Pickwick continued to reside constantly, and without interruption or intermission, at Mrs. Bardell's house. I shall show you that Mrs. Bardell, during the whole of that time waited on him, attended to his comforts, cooked his meals, looked out his linen for the washer-woman when it went abroad, darned, aired, and prepared it for wear, when it came home, and, in short, enjoyed his fullest trust and confidence. I shall show you that, on many occasions, he gave halfpence, and on some occasions even sixpences, to her little boy; and I shall prove to you, by a witness whose testimony it will be impossible for my learned friend to weaken or controvert, that on one occasion he patted the boy on the head, and, after inquiring whether he had won any *alley tors* or *commoneys* lately (both of which I understand to be a particular species of marbles much prized by the youth of this town), made use of this remarkable expression: 'How should you like to have another father?' I shall prove to you, gentlemen, that about a year ago, Pickwick suddenly began to absent himself from home, during long intervals, as if with the intention of gradually breaking off from my client; but I shall show you also, that his resolution was not at that time sufficiently strong, or that his better feelings conquered, if better feelings he has, or that the charms and accomplishments of my client prevailed against his unmanly intentions; by proving to you, that on one occasion, when he returned from the country, he distinctly and in terms, offered her marriage: previously, however, taking special care that there should be no witness to their solemn contract; and I am in a situation to prove to you, on the testimony of three of his own friends,—most unwilling witnesses, gentlemen—most unwilling witnesses—that on that morning he was discovered by them holding the plaintiff in his arms, and soothing her agitation by his caresses and endearments."

A visible impression was produced upon the auditors by this part of the learned serjeant's address. Drawing forth two very small scraps of paper, he proceeded:

"And now, gentlemen, but one word more. Two letters have passed between these parties, letters which are admitted to be in the hand-writing of the defendant, and which speak volumes indeed. These letters, too, bespeak the character of the man. They are not open, fervent, eloquent epistles, breathing nothing but the language of affectionate attachment. They are covert, sly, underhanded communications, but, fortunately, far more conclusive than if couched in the most glowing language and the most poetic imagery—letters that must be viewed with a cautious and suspicious eye—letters that were evidently intended at the time, by Pickwick, to mislead and delude any third parties into whose hands they might fall. Let me read the first:—'Garraway's, twelve o'clock. Dear Mrs. B.—Chops and Tomata sauce. Yours, PICKWICK.' Gentlemen, what does this mean? Chops and Tomata sauce! Yours, Pickwick! Chops! Gracious heavens! and Tomata sauce! Gentlemen, is the happiness of a sensitive and confiding female to be trifled away, by such shallow artifices as these? The next has no date

whatever, which in itself is suspicious. 'Dear Mrs. B., I shall not be at home till to-morrow. Slow coach.' And then follows this very remarkable expression. 'Don't trouble yourself about the warming-pan.' The warming-pan! Why, gentlemen, who *does* trouble himself about a warming-pan? When was the peace of mind of man or woman broken or disturbed by a warming-pan, which is in itself a harmless, a useful, and I will add, gentlemen, a comforting article of domestic furniture? Why is Mrs. Bardell so earnestly entreated not to agitate herself about this warming-pan, unless (as is no doubt the case) it is a mere cover for hidden fire—a mere substitute for some endearing word or promise, agreeably to a preconcerted system of correspondence, artfully contrived by Pickwick with a view to his contemplated desertion, and which I am not in a condition to explain? And what does this allusion to the slow coach mean? For aught I know, it may be a reference to Pickwick himself, who has most unquestionably been a criminally slow coach during the whole of this transaction, but whose speed will now be very unexpectedly accelerated, and whose wheels, gentlemen, as he will find to his cost, will very soon be greased by you! . . .

"But enough of this, gentlemen," said Mr. Serjeant Buzfuz, "it is difficult to smile with an aching heart; it is ill jesting when our deepest sympathies are awakened. My client's hopes and prospects are ruined, and it is no figure of speech to say that her occupation is gone indeed. The bill is down—but there is no tenant. Eligible single gentlemen pass and repass—but there is no invitation for them to inquire within or without. All is gloom and silence in the house; even the voice of the child is hushed; his infant sports are disregarded when his mother weeps; his 'alley tors' and his 'commoneys' are alike neglected; he forgets the long familiar cry of 'knuckle down,' and at tip-cheese, or odd and even, his hand is out. But Pickwick, gentlemen, Pickwick, the ruthless destroyer of this domestic oasis in the desert of Goswell Street—Pickwick, who has choked up the well, and thrown ashes on the sward—Pickwick, who comes before you to-day with his heartless Tomata sauce and warming-pans—Pickwick still rears his head with unblushing effrontery, and gazes without a sigh on the ruin he has made. Damages, gentlemen—heavy damages—is the only punishment with which you can visit him; the only recompense you can award to my client. And for those damages she now appeals to an enlightened, a high-minded, a right-feeling, a conscientious, a dispassionate, a sympathising, a contemplative jury of her civilised countrymen." With this beautiful peroration, Mr. Serjeant Buzfuz sat down, and Mr. Justice Stareleigh woke up. . . .

"Nathaniel Winkle!" said Mr. Skimpin.

"Here!" replied a feeble voice. Mr. Winkle entered the witness-box, and having been duly sworn, bowed to the judge with considerable deference.

"Don't look at me, sir," said the judge, sharply, in acknowledgment of the salute; "look at the jury."

Mr. Winkle obeyed the mandate, and looked at the place where he thought it most probable the jury might be; for seeing anything in his then state of intellectual complication was wholly out of the question.

Mr. Winkle was then examined by Mr. Skimpin, who, being a promising young man of two or three and forty, was of course anxious to confuse a witness who was notoriously predisposed in favour of the other side, as much as he could.

"Now, sir," said Mr. Skimpin, "have the goodness to let his Lordship and the jury know what your name is, will you?" and Mr. Skimpin inclined his head on one side to listen with great sharpness to the answer, and glanced at the jury meanwhile, as if to imply that he rather expected Mr. Winkle's natural taste for perjury would induce him to give some name which did not belong to him.

"Winkle," replied the witness.

"What's your Christian name, sir?" angrily inquired the little judge.

"Nathaniel, sir."

"Daniel,—any other name?"

"Nathaniel, sir—my Lord, I mean."

"Nathaniel Daniel, or Daniel Nathaniel?"

"No, my Lord, only Nathaniel; not Daniel at all."

"What did you tell me it was Daniel for, then, sir?" inquired the judge.

"I didn't, my Lord," replied Mr. Winkle.

"You did, sir," replied the judge, with a severe frown. "How could I have got Daniel on my notes, unless you told me so, sir?"

This argument was, of course, unanswerable.

"Mr. Winkle has rather a short memory, my Lord," interposed Mr. Skimpin, with another glance at the jury. "We shall find means to refresh it before we have quite done with him, I dare say."

"You had better be careful, sir," said the little judge, with a sinister look at the witness.

Poor Mr. Winkle bowed, and endeavoured to feign an easiness of manner, which, in his then state of confusion, gave him rather the air of a disconcerted pickpocket.

"Now, Mr. Winkle," said Mr. Skimpin, "attend to me, if you please, sir; and let me recommend you, for your own sake, to bear in mind his Lordship's injunction to be careful. I believe you are a particular friend of Pickwick, the defendant, are you not?"

"I have known Mr. Pickwick now, as well as I recollect at this moment, nearly——"

"Pray, Mr. Winkle, do not evade the question. Are you, or are you not, a particular friend of the defendant's?"

"I was just about to say, that——"

"Will you, or will you not, answer my question, sir?"

"If you don't answer the question you'll be committed, sir," interposed the little judge, looking over his note-book.

"Come, sir," said Mr. Skimpin, "yes or not, if you please."

"Yes, I am," replied Mr. Winkle.

"Yes, you are. And why couldn't you say that at once, sir? Perhaps you know the plaintiff, too? Eh, Mr. Winkle?"

"I don't know her; I've seen her."

"Oh, you don't know her, but you've seen her? Now, have the goodness to tell the gentlemen of the jury what you mean by *that*, Mr. Winkle."

"I mean that I am not intimate with her, but I have seen her when I went to call on Mr. Pickwick in Goswell Street."

"How often have you seen her, sir?"

"How often?"

"Yes, Mr. Winkle, how often? I'll repeat the question for you a dozen times, if you require it, sir." And the learned gentleman, with a firm and steady frown, placed his hands on his hips, and smiled suspiciously at the jury.

On this question there arose the edifying browbeating, customary on such points. First of all, Mr. Winkle said it was quite impossible for him to say how many times he had seen Mrs. Bardell. Then he was asked if he had seen her twenty times, to which he replied, "Certainly,—more than that." Then he was asked whether he hadn't seen her a hundred times—whether he couldn't swear that he had seen her more than fifty times—whether he didn't know that he had seen her at least seventy-five times—and so forth; the satisfactory confusion which was arrived at, at last, being, that he had better take care of himself, and mind what he was about. The witness having been by these means reduced to the requisite ebb of nervous perplexity, the examination was continued as follows:

"Pray, Mr. Winkle, do you remember calling on the defendant Pickwick at these apartments in the plaintiff's house in Goswell Street, on one particular morning, in the month of July last?"

"Yes, I do."

"Were you accompanied on that occasion by a friend of the name of Tupman, and another of the name of Snodgrass?"

"Yes, I was." . . .

"Now, sir, tell the gentlemen of the jury what you saw on entering the defendant's room, on this particular morning. Come; out with it, sir; we must have it, sooner or later."

"The defendant, Mr. Pickwick, was holding the plaintiff in his arms, with his hands clasping her waist," replied Mr. Winkle with natural hesitation, "and the plaintiff appeared to have fainted away."

"Did you hear the defendant say anything?"

"I heard him call Mrs. Bardell a good creature, and I heard him ask her to compose herself, for what a situation it was, if anybody should come, or words to that effect."

"Now, Mr. Winkle, I have only one more question to ask you, and I beg you to bear in mind his Lordship's caution. Will you undertake to swear that Pickwick, the defendant, did not say on the occasion in question, 'My dear Mrs. Bardell, you're a good creature; compose yourself to this situation, for to this situation you must come,' or words to *that* effect?"

"I—I didn't understand him so, certainly," said Mr. Winkle, astounded at this ingenious dove-tailing of the few words he had heard, "I was on the staircase, and couldn't hear distinctly; the impression on my mind is——"

"The gentlemen of the jury want none of the impressions on your mind, Mr. Winkle, which I fear would be of little service to honest, straightforward men," interposed Mr. Skimpin. "You were on the staircase, and didn't distinctly hear; but you will not swear that Pickwick did not make use of the expressions I have quoted? Do I understand that?"

"No, I will not," replied Mr. Winkle; and down sat Mr. Skimpin with a triumphant countenance. . . .

Serjeant Buzfuz now rose with more importance that he had yet exhibited, if that were possible, and vociferated: "Call Samuel Weller."

It was quite unnecessary to call Samuel Weller; for Samuel Weller stepped briskly into the box the instant his name was pronounced; and placing his hat on the floor, and his arms on the rail, took a bird's-eye view of the bar, and a comprehensive survey of the bench, with a remarkably cheerful and lively aspect.

"What's your name, sir?" inquired the judge.

"Sam Weller, my lord," replied that gentleman.

"Do you spell it with a 'V' or a 'W'?" inquired the judge.

"That depends upon the taste and fancy of the speller, my lord," replied Sam; "I never had occasion to spell it more than once or twice in my life, but I spells it with a 'V.' "

Here a voice in the gallery exclaimed aloud, "Quite right too, Samivel, quite right. Put it down a we, my lord, put it down a we."

"Who is that, who dares to address the court?" said the little judge, looking up. "Usher."

"Yes, my lord."

"Bring that person here instantly."

"Yes, my lord."

But as the usher didn't find the person, he didn't bring him; and, after a great commotion, all the people who had got up to look for the culprit sat down again. The little judge turned to the witness as soon as his indignation would allow him to speak, and said,

"Do you know who that was, sir?"

"I rayther suspect it was my father, my lord," replied Sam.

"Do you see him here now?" said the judge.

"No, I don't, my lord," replied Sam, staring right up into the lantern in the roof of the court.

"If you could have pointed him out, I would have committed him instantly," said the judge.

Sam bowed his acknowledgments and turned, with unimpaired cheerfulness of countenance, towards Serjeant Buzfuz.

"Now, Mr. Weller," said Serjeant Buzfuz.

"Now, sir," replied Sam.

"I believe you are in the service of Mr. Pickwick, the defendant in this case. Speak up, if you please, Mr. Weller."

"I mean to speak up, sir," replied Sam; "I am in the service o' that 'ere gen'l'man, and a wery good service it is."

"Little to do, and plenty to get, I suppose?" said Serjeant Buzfuz, with jocularity.

"Oh, quite enough to get, sir, as the soldier said ven they ordered him three hundred and fifty lashes," replied Sam.

"You must not tell us what the soldier, or any other man, said, sir," interposed the judge; "it's not evidence."

"Wery good, my lord," replied Sam.

"Do you recollect anything particular happening

on the morning when you were first engaged by the defendant; eh, Mr. Weller?" said Serjeant Buzfuz.

"Yes, I do, sir," replied Sam.

"Have the goodness to tell the jury what it was."

"I had a reg'lar new fit out o' clothes that mornin', gen'l'men of the jury," said Sam, "and that was a wery partickler and uncommon circumstance vith me in those days."

Hereupon there was a general laugh; and the little judge, looking with an angry countenance over his desk, said, "You had better be careful, sir."

"So Mr. Pickwick said at the time, my lord," replied Sam; "and I was wery careful o' that 'ere suit o' clothes; wery careful indeed, my lord."

The judge looked sternly at Sam for full two minutes, but Sam's features were so perfectly calm and serene that the judge said nothing, and motioned Serjeant Buzfuz to proceed.

"Do you mean to tell me, Mr. Weller," said Serjeant Buzfuz, folding his arms emphatically, and turning half-round to the jury, as if in mute assurance that he would bother the witness yet: "Do you mean to tell me, Mr. Weller, that you saw nothing of this fainting on the part of the plaintiff in the arms of the defendant, which you have heard described by the witnesses?"

"Certainly not," replied Sam. "I was in the passage 'till they called me up, and then the old lady was not there."

"Now, attend, Mr. Weller," said Serjeant Buzfuz, dipping a large pen into the inkstand before him, for the purpose of frightening Sam with a show of taking down his answer. "You were in the passage, and yet saw nothing of what was going forward. Have you a pair of eyes, Mr. Weller?"

"Yes, I have a pair of eyes," replied Sam, "and that's just it. If they wos a pair o' patent double million magnifyin' gas microscopes of hextra power, p'raps I might be able to see through a flight o' stairs and a deal door; but bein' only eyes, you see, my wision's limited."

At this answer, which was delivered without the slightest appearance of irritation, and with the most complete simplicity and equanimity of manner, the spectators tittered, the little judge smiled, and Serjeant Buzfuz looked particularly foolish. After a short consultation with Dodson and Fogg, the learned Serjeant again turned towards Sam, and said, with a painful effort to conceal his vexation, "Now, Mr. Weller, I'll ask you a question on another point, if you please."

"If you please, sir," rejoined Sam, with the utmost good-humour.

"Do you remember going up to Mrs. Bardell's house, one night in November last?"

"Oh yes, very well."

"Oh, you do remember that, Mr. Weller," said Serjeant Buzfuz, recovering his spirits; "I thought we should get at something at last."

"I rayther thought that, too, sir," replied Sam. . . .

"Well; I suppose you went up to have a little talk about this trial—eh, Mr. Weller?" said Serjeant Buzfuz, looking knowingly at the jury.

"I went up to pay the rent; but we did get a talkin' about the trial," replied Sam.

"Oh, you did get a talking about the trial," said Serjeant Buzfuz, brightening up with the anticipation of some important discovery. "Now what passed about the trial; will you have the goodness to tell us, Mr. Weller?"

"Vith all the pleasure in life, sir," replied Sam. "Arter a few unimportant obserwations . . . the ladies gets into a very great state o' admiration at the honourable conduct of Mr. Dodson and Fogg—them two gen'l'men as is settin' near you now." This, of course, drew general attention to Dodson and Fogg, who looked as virtuous as possible.

"The attorneys for the plaintiff," said Mr. Serjeant Buzfuz. "Well! They spoke in high praise of the honourable conduct of Messrs. Dodson and Fogg, the attorneys for the plaintiff, did they?"

"Yes," said Sam, "they said what a wery gen'rous thing it was o' them to have taken up the case on spec, and to charge nothing at all for costs, unless they got 'em out of Mr. Pickwick."

At this very unexpected reply, the spectators tittered again, and Dodson and Fogg, turning very red, leant over to Sergeant Buzfuz, and in a hurried manner whispered something in his ear.

"You are quite right," said Serjeant Buzfuz aloud, with affected composure. "It's perfectly useless, my lord, attempting to get at any evidence through the impenetrable stupidity of this witness. I will not trouble the court by asking him any more questions. Stand down, sir."

"Would any other gen'l'man like to ask me anythin'?" inquired Sam, taking up his hat, and looking round most deliberately.

"Not I, Mr. Weller, thank you," said Serjeant Snubbin, laughing.

"You may go down, sir," said Serjeant Buzfuz, waving his hand impatiently. Sam went down accordingly, after doing Messrs. Dodson and Fogg's case as much harm as he conveniently could, and saying just as little respecting Mr. Pickwick as might be, which was precisely the object he had had in view all along.

"I have no objection to admit, my lord," said Serjeant Snubbin, "if it will save the examination of another witness, that Mr. Pickwick has retired from business, and is a gentleman of considerable independent property."

"Very well," said Serjeant Buzfuz, putting in the two letters to be read. "Then that's my case, my lord."

Serjeant Snubbin then addressed the jury on behalf of the defendant; and a very long and a very emphatic address he delivered, in which he bestowed the highest possible eulogiums on the conduct and character of Mr. Pickwick. . . . It is sufficient to add in general terms, that he did the best he could for Mr. Pickwick; and the best, as everybody knows, on the infallible authority of the old adage, could do no more.

Mr. Justice Stareleigh summed up, in the old-established and most approved form. He read as much of his notes to the jury as he could decipher on so short a notice, and made running comments on the evidence as he went along. If Mrs. Bardell were right, it was perfectly clear that Mr. Pickwick was wrong, and if they thought the evidence . . . worthy of credence they would believe it, and, if they didn't, why, they wouldn't. If they were satisfied that a breach of promise of marriage had been committed, they would find for the plaintiff with such damages as they thought proper; and if, on the other hand, it appeared to them that no promise of marriage had ever been given, they would find for the defendant with no damages at all. The jury then retired to their private room to talk the matter over, and the judge retired to *his* private room, to refresh himself with a mutton chop and a glass of sherry.

An anxious quarter of an hour elapsed; the jury came back; the judge was fetched in. Mr. Pickwick put on his spectacles, and gazed at the foreman with an agitated countenance and a quickly beating heart.

"Gentlemen," said the individual in black, "are you all agreed upon your verdict?"

"We are," replied the foreman.

"Do you find for the plaintiff, gentlemen, or for the defendant?"

"For the plaintiff."

"With what damages, gentlemen?"

"Seven hundred and fifty pounds."

Mr. Pickwick took off his spectacles, carefully wiped the glasses, folded them into their case, and put them in his pocket; then having drawn on his gloves with great nicety; and stared at the foreman all the while, he mechanically . . . [left the court].

They stopped in a side room while Perker paid the court fees; and here, Mr. Pickwick was joined by his friends. Here, too, he encountered Messrs. Dodson and Fogg, rubbing their hands with every token of outward satisfaction. . . .

"You imagine you'll get your costs, don't you, gentlemen?" said Mr. Pickwick.

Fogg said they thought it rather probable. Dodson smiled, and said they'd try.

"You may try, and try, and try again, Messrs. Dodson and Fogg," said Mr. Pickwick vehemently, "but not one farthing of costs or damages do you ever get from me, if I spend the rest of my existence in a debtor's prison." . . .

. . . Mr. Pickwick allowed himself to be led by his solicitor and friends to the door, and there assisted into a hackney-coach, which had been fetched for the purpose, by the ever watchful Sam Weller.

Sam had put up the steps, and was preparing to jump upon the box, when he felt himself gently touched on the shoulder; and looking round, his father stood before him. The old gentleman's countenance wore a mournful expression, as he shook his head gravely, and said, in warning accents:

"I know'd what 'ud come o' this here mode o' doin' bisness. Oh Sammy, Sammy, vy worn't there a alleybi!"

William Makepeace Thackeray
1811–1863

Thackeray, here represented by two of his *Roundabout Papers*, was Dickens's great rival among the Victorian novelists. He was born in India July 18, 1811, and educated at the Charterhouse and at Cambridge. He began his writing career as a staff contributor to *Fraser's Magazine*, by burlesquing Bulwer, Lever, Fenimore Cooper, and many other leading novelists of the day. *Catherine* burlesqued the crime story, which he considered a vicious thing. A more ambitious undertaking was *Barry Lyndon*, the story of a scoundrel, a sustained piece of irony in the manner of Fielding's *Jonathan Wild*. This book did not attract the public, however; Thackeray had to wait for real recognition until he published *Vanity Fair* in 1847.

Five years later he wrote *Henry Esmond*, which is universally regarded as one of the great English historical novels. *Pendennis*, *The Newcomes*, and *The Virginians* complete the list of his major works—for *Philip* is hardly major in anything but length. Lacking Dickens's energy, Thackeray shrank from large undertakings; more than half the bulk of his collected works consists of sketches, burlesques, and other miscellanea. His position in English literature is secure, though it rests on a very few works and on his always elegant but unpretentious style.

Thackeray's private life was clouded by the insanity of his dearly loved wife, but he was charming in his relations with his daughters. He was a clubman, with a clubman's geniality and a clubman's limitations of sympathy and understanding. Toward the end of his life he became editor of the *Cornhill Magazine* and, like Dickens, toured the United States. He died suddenly on December 24, 1863.

ON BEING FOUND OUT

AT the close (let us say) of Queen Anne's reign, when I was a boy at a private and preparatory school for young gentlemen, I remember the wiseacre of a master ordering us all, one night, to march into a little garden at the back of the house, and thence to proceed one by one into a tool or henhouse, (I was but a tender little thing just put into short clothes, and can't exactly say whether the house was for tools or hens,) and in that house to put our hands into a sack which stood on a bench, a candle burning beside it. I put my hand into the sack. My hand came out quite black. I went and joined the other boys in the schoolroom; and all their hands were black too.

By reason of my tender age (and there are some critics who, I hope, will be satisfied by my acknowledging that I am a hundred and fifty-six next birthday) I could not understand what was the meaning of this night excursion—this candle, this tool-house, this bag of soot. I think we little boys were taken out of our sleep to be brought to the ordeal. We came, then, and showed our little hands to the master; washed them or not—most probably, I should say, not—and so went bewildered back to bed.

Something had been stolen in the school that day; and Mr. Wiseacre having read in a book of an ingenious method of finding out a thief by making him put his hand into a sack (which, if guilty, the rogue would shirk from doing), all we boys were subjected to the trial. Goodness knows what the lost object was, or who stole it. We all had black hands to show the master. And the thief, whoever he was, was not Found Out that time.

I wonder if the rascal is alive—an elderly scoundrel he must be by this time; and a hoary old hypocrite, to whom an old schoolfellow presents his kindest regards—parenthetically remarking what a dreadful place that private school was; cold, chilblains, bad dinners, not enough victuals, and caning awful!—Are you alive still, I say, you nameless villain, who escaped discovery on that day of crime? I hope you have escaped often since, old sinner. Ah, what a lucky thing it is, for you and me, my man, that we are *not* found out in all our peccadilloes; and that our backs can slip away from the master and the cane!

Just consider what life would be, if every rogue was found out, and flogged *coram populo*! What a butchery, what an indecency, what an endless swishing of the rod! Don't cry out about my misanthropy. My good friend Mealymouth, I will trouble you to tell me, do you go to church? When there, do you say, or do you not, that you are a miserable sinner? and saying so, do you believe or disbelieve

40. coram populo! in public.

it? If you are a M. S., don't you deserve correction, and aren't you grateful if you are to be let off? I say again, what a blessed thing it is that we are not all found out!

Just picture to yourself everybody who does wrong being found out, and punished accordingly. Fancy all the boys in all the school being whipped; and then the assistants, and then the head master (Dr. Badford let us call him). Fancy the provost-marshal being tied up, having previously superin-tended the correction of the whole army. After the young gentlemen have had their turn for the faulty exercises, fancy Dr. Lincolnsinn being taken up for certain faults in *his* Essay and Review. After the clergyman has cried his peccavi, suppose we hoist up a bishop, and give him a couple of dozen! (I see my Lord Bishop of Double-Gloucester sitting in a very uneasy posture on his right reverend bench.) After we have cast off the bishop, what are we to say to the Minister who appointed him? My Lord Cinqwarden, it is painful to have to use personal correction to a boy of your age; but really . . . *Siste tandem, carnifex!* The butchery is too horrible. The hand drops powerless, appalled at the quantity of birch which it must cut and brandish. I am glad we are not all found out, I say again; and protest, my dear brethren, against our having our deserts.

To fancy all men found out and punished is bad enough; but imagine all women found out in the distinguished social circle in which you and I have the honour to move. Is it not a mercy that a many of these fair criminals remain unpunished and un-discovered? There is Mrs. Longbow, who is for ever practising, and who shoots poisoned arrows, too; when you meet her you don't call her liar, and charge her with the wickedness she has done, and is doing. There is Mrs. Painter, who passes for a most respectable woman, and a model in society. There is no use in saying what you really know regarding her and her goings on. There is Diana Hunter—what a little haughty prude it is; and yet *we* know stories about her which are not altogether edifying. I say it is best, for the sake of the good, that the bad should not all be found out. You don't want your children to know the history of that lady in the next box, who is so handsome, and whom they admire so. Ah me, what would life be if we were all found out, and punished for all our faults? Jack Ketch would be in permanence; and then who would hang Jack Ketch?

They talk of murderers being pretty certainly found out. Psha! I have heard an authority awfully competent vow and declare that scores and hundreds of murders are committed, and nobody is the wiser. That terrible man mentioned one or two ways of committing murder, which he maintained were quite common, and were scarcely ever found out. A man, for instance, comes home to his wife, and . . . but I pause—I know that this Magazine has a very large circulation. Hundreds and hundreds of thousands—why not say a million of people at once?—well, say a million, read it. And amongst these countless readers, I might be teaching some monster how to make away with his wife without being found out, some fiend of a woman how to destroy her dear husband. I will *not* then tell this easy and simple way of murder, as communicated to me by a most respectable party in the confidence of private intercourse. Suppose some gentle reader were to try this most simple and easy receipt—it seems to me almost infallible—and come to grief in consequence, and be found out and hanged? Should I ever pardon myself for having been the means of doing injury to a single one of our es-teemed subscribers? The prescription whereof I speak—that is to say, whereof I *don't* speak—shall be buried in this bosom. No, I am a humane man. I am not one of your Bluebeards to go and say to my wife, "My dear! I am going away for a few days to Brighton. Here are all the keys of the house. You may open every door and closet, except the one at the end of the oak-room opposite the fire-place, with the little bronze Shakespeare on the mantelpiece (or what not)." I don't say this to a woman—unless, to be sure, I want to get rid of her—because, after such a caution, I know she'll peep into the closet. I say nothing about the closet at all. I keep the key in my pocket, and a being whom I love, but who, as I know, has many weaknesses, out of harm's way. You toss up your head, dear angel, drub on the ground with your lovely little feet, on the table with your sweet rosy fingers, and cry, "Oh, sneerer! You don't know the depth of woman's feeling, the lofty scorn of all deceit, the entire absence of mean curiosity in the sex, or never, never would you libel us so!" Ah, Delia! dear, dear Delia! It is because I fancy I *do* know something about you (not all, mind—no, no; no man knows that)—Ah, my bride, my ringdove, my rose, my poppet—choose, in fact, whatever name you like—bulbul of my grove, fountain of my desert, sunshine of my darkling life, and joy of my dungeoned existence, it is be-

---

14. **Essay and Review.** See page 382.   15. **peccavi,** I have sinned.   23. **Siste tandem, carnifex!** But hold, executioner!   49. **Jack Ketch,** the hangman.

9. **this Magazine,** the *Cornhill Magazine,* in which this es-say first appeared.

cause I *do* know a little about you that I conclude to say nothing of that private closet, and keep my key in my pocket. You take away that closet-key then, and the house-key. You lock Delia in. You keep her out of harm's way and gadding, and so she never *can* be found out.

And yet by little strange accidents and coincidents how we are being found out every day. You remember that old story of the Abbé Kakatoes, who told the company at supper one night how the first confession he ever received was—from a murderer let us say. Presently enters to supper the Marquis de Croquemitaine. "Palsambleu, abbé!" says the brilliant marquis, taking a pinch of snuff, "are you here? Gentlemen and ladies! I was the abbé's first penitent, and I made him a confession which I promise you astonished him."

To be sure how queerly things are found out! Here is an instance. Only the other day I was writing in these Roundabout Papers about a certain man, whom I facetiously called Baggs, and who had abused me to my friends, who of course told me. Shortly after that paper was published another friend—Sacks let us call him—scowls fiercely at me as I am sitting in perfect good-humour at the club, and passes on without speaking. A cut. A quarrel. Sacks thinks it is about him that I was writing: whereas, upon my honour and conscience, I never had him once in my mind, and was pointing my moral from quite another man. But don't you see, by this wrath of the guilty-conscienced Sacks, that he had been abusing me too? He has owned himself guilty, never having been accused. He has winced when nobody thought of hitting him. I did but put the cap out, and madly butting and chafing, behold my friend rushes out to put his head into it! Never mind, Sacks, you are found out; but I bear you no malice, my man.

And yet to be found out, I know from my own experience, must be painful and odious, and cruelly mortifying to the inward vanity. Suppose I am a poltroon, let us say. With fierce moustache, loud talk, plentiful oaths, and an immense stick, I keep up nevertheless a character for courage. I swear fearfully at cabmen and women; brandish my bludgeon, and perhaps knock down a little man or two with it: brag of the images which I break at the shooting-gallery, and pass amongst my friends for a whiskery fire-eater, afraid of neither man nor dragon. Ah me! Suppose some brisk little chap steps up and gives me a caning in St. James's Street, with all the heads of my friends looking out of all the club windows. My reputation is gone. I

frighten no man more. My nose is pulled by whipper-snappers, who jump up on a chair to reach it. I am found out. And in the days of my triumphs, when people were yet afraid of me, and were taken in by my swagger, I always knew that I was a lily-liver, and expected that I should be found out some day.

That certainty of being found out must haunt and depress many a bold braggadocio spirit. Let us say it is a clergyman, who can pump copious floods of tears out of his own eyes and those of his audience. He thinks to himself, "I am but a poor swindling, chattering rogue. My bills are unpaid. I have jilted several women whom I have promised to marry. I don't know whether I believe what I preach, and I know I have stolen the very sermon over which I have been snivelling. Have they found me out?" says he, as his head drops down on the cushion.

Then your writer, poet, historian, novelist, or what not? The *Beacon* says that "Jones's work is one of the first order." The *Lamp* declares that "Jones's tragedy surpasses every work since the days of Him of Avon." The *Comet* asserts that "J's 'Life of Goody Twoshoes' is κτῆμα ἐς ἀεί, a noble and enduring monument to the fame of that admirable Englishwoman," and so forth. But then Jones knows that he has lent the critic of the *Beacon* five pounds; that his publisher has a half-share in the *Lamp;* and that the *Comet* comes repeatedly to dine with him. It is all very well. Jones is immortal until he is found out; and then down comes the extinguisher, and the immortal is dead and buried. The idea (*dies irae!*) of discovery must haunt many a man, and make him uneasy, as the trumpets are puffing in his triumph. Brown, who has a higher place than he deserves, cowers before Smith, who has found him out. What is a chorus of critics shouting "Bravo"?— a public clapping hands and flinging garlands? Brown knows that Smith has found him out. Puff, trumpets! Wave, banners! Huzza, boys, for the immortal Brown! "This is all very well," B. thinks (bowing the while, smiling, laying his hand to his heart); "but there stands Smith at the window: *he* has measured me; and some day the others will find me out too." It is a very curious sensation to sit by a man who has found you out, and who, as you know, has found you out; or, *vice versâ*, to sit with a man whom *you* have found out. His talent? Bah! His virtue? We know a little story or two about his virtue, and he knows we know it. We are thinking over friend Robinson's antecedents, as we grin, bow

13. "Palsambleu," Zounds!

22-23. **Goody Twoshoes.** *The History of Goody Twoshoes*, a famous nursery tale published in 1765, is often ascribed to Oliver Goldsmith. 23. κτῆμα ἐς ἀεί, a possession forever. 31-32. dies irae! See note 31-32 on page 652.

and talk; and we are both humbugs together. Robinson a good fellow, is he? You know how he behaved to Hicks? A good-natured man, is he? Pray do you remember that little story of Mrs. Robinson's black eye? How men have to work, to talk, to smile, to go to bed, and try and sleep, with this dread of being found out on their consciences! Bardolph, who has robbed a church, and Nym, who has taken a purse, go to their usual haunts, and smoke their pipes with their companions. Mr. De-10 tective Bullseye appears, and says, "Oh, Bardolph! I want you about that there pyx business!" Mr. Bardolph knocks the ashes out of his pipe, puts out his hands to the little steel cuffs, and walks away quite meekly. He is found out. He must go. "Good-by, Doll Tearsheet! Good-by, Mrs. Quickly, ma'am!" The other gentlemen and ladies *de la société* look on and exchange mute adieux with the departing friends. And an assured time will come when the other gentlemen and ladies will be found out too. 20

What a wonderful and beautiful provision of nature it has been that, for the most part, our womankind are not endowed with the faculty of finding us out! *They* don't doubt, and probe, and weigh, and take your measure. Lay down this paper, my benevolent friend and reader, go into your drawing-room now, and utter a joke ever so old, and I wager sixpence the ladies there will all begin to laugh. Go to Brown's house, and tell Mrs. Brown and the young ladies what you think of him, and see what a 30 welcome you will get! In like manner, let him come to your house, and tell *your* good lady his candid opinion of you, and fancy how she will receive him! Would you have your wife and children know you exactly for what you are, and esteem you precisely at your worth? If so, my friend, you will live in a dreary house, and you will have but a chilly fireside. Do you suppose the people round it don't see your homely face as under a glamour, and, as it were, with a halo of love round it? You don't fancy 40 you *are*, as you seem to them? No such thing, my man. Put away that monstrous conceit, and be thankful that *they* have not found you out.

OGRES

I DARE say the reader has remarked that the upright and independent vowel, which stands in the vowel-list between E and O, has formed the 50

8–16. Bardolph . . . Nym . . . Doll Tearsheet . . . Mrs. Quickly, characters in Shakespeare's *King Henry IV*. For that there pyx business see *King Henry V*, Act III, sc. 6, ll. 36 ff.

subject of the main part of these essays. How does that vowel feel this morning?—fresh, good-humoured, and lively? The Roundabout lines, which fall from this pen, are correspondingly brisk and cheerful. Has anything, on the contrary, disagreed with the vowel? Has its rest been disturbed, or was yesterday's dinner too good, or yesterday's wine not good enough? Under such circumstances, a darkling, misanthropic tinge, no doubt, is cast upon the paper. The jokes, if attempted, are elaborate and dreary. The bitter temper breaks out. That sneering manner is adopted, which you know, and which exhibits itself so especially when the writer is speaking about women. A moody carelessness comes over him. He sees no good in anybody or thing: and treats gentlemen, ladies, history, and things in general, with a like gloomy flippancy. Agreed. When the vowel in question is in that mood, if you like airy gaiety and tender gushing benevolence—if you want to be satisfied with yourself and the rest of your fellow-beings; I recommend you, my dear creature, to go to some other shop in Cornhill, or turn to some other article. There are moods in the mind of the vowel of which we are speaking, when it is ill conditioned and captious. Who always keeps good health, and good humour? Do not philosophers grumble? Are not sages sometimes out of temper? and do not angel-women go off in tantrums? To-day my mood is dark. I scowl as I dip my pen in the inkstand.

Here is the day come round—for everything here is done with the utmost regularity:—intellectual labor, sixteen hours; meals, thirty-two minutes; exercise, a hundred and forty-eight minutes; conversation with the family, chiefly literary, and about the housekeeping, one hour and four minutes; sleep, three hours and fifteen minutes (at the end of the month, when the Magazine is complete, I own I take eight minutes more); and the rest for the toilette and the world. Well, I say, the *Roundabout Paper Day* being come, and the subject long since settled in my mind, an excellent subject—a most telling, lively, and popular subject—I go to breakfast determined to finish that meal in $9\frac{3}{4}$ minutes, as usual, and then retire to my desk and work, when —oh, provoking!—here in the paper is the very subject treated, on which I was going to write! Yesterday another paper which I saw treated it— and of course, as I need not tell you, spoiled it. Last Saturday, another paper had an article on the subject; perhaps you may guess what it was—but I won't tell you. Only this is true, my favourite subject, which was about to make the best paper we have had for a long time: my bird, my game that I was going to shoot and serve up with such a delicate sauce, has been found by other sportsmen; and pop, pop, pop, a half-dozen of guns have banged at it, mangled it, and brought it down.

"And can't you take some other text?" say you. All this is mighty well. But if you have set your heart on a certain dish for dinner, be it cold boiled veal, or what you will, and they bring you turtle and venison, don't you feel disappointed? During your walk you have been making up your mind that that cold meat, with moderation and a pickle, will be a very sufficient dinner: you have accustomed your thoughts to it; and here, in place of it, is a turkey, surrounded by coarse sausages, or a reeking pigeon-pie or a fulsome roast-pig. I have known many a good and kind man made furiously angry by such a *contretemps*. I have known him lose his temper, call his wife and servants names, and a whole household made miserable. If, then, as is notoriously the case, it is too dangerous to baulk a man about his dinner, how much more about his article? I came to my meal with an ogre-like appetite and gusto. Fee, faw, fum! Wife, where is that tender little Prince-kin? Have you trussed him, and did you stuff him nicely, and have you taken care to baste him and do him, not too brown, as I told you? Quick! I am hungry! I begin to whet my knife, to roll my eyes about, and roar and clap my huge chest like a gorilla; and then my poor Ogrina has to tell me that the little princes have all run away, whilst she was in the kitchen, making the paste to bake them in! I pause in the description. I won't condescend to report the bad language, which you know must ensue, when an ogre, whose mind is ill regulated, and whose habits of self-indulgence are notorious, finds himself disappointed of his greedy hopes. What treatment of his wife, what abuse and brutal behaviour to his children, who, though ogrillons, are children! My dears, you may fancy, and need not ask my delicate pen to describe, the language and behaviour of a vulgar, coarse, greedy, large man with an immense mouth and teeth, which are too frequently employed in the gobbling and crunching of raw man's meat.

And in this circuitous way you see I have reached my present subject, which is, Ogres. You fancy they are dead or only fictitious characters—myth-ical representatives of strength, cruelty, stupidity, and lust for blood? Though they had seven-leagued boots, you remember all sorts of little whipping-snapping Tom Thumbs used to elude and outrun them. They were so stupid that they gave into the most shallow ambuscades and artifices: witness

that well-known ogre, who, because Jack cut open the hasty-pudding, instantly ripped open his own stupid waistcoat and interior. They were cruel, brutal, disgusting, with their sharpened teeth, im-mense knives, and roaring voices! but they always ended by being overcome by little Tom Thumbkins, or some other smart little champion.

Yes; they were conquered in the end there is no doubt. They plunged headlong (and uttering the most frightful bad language) into some pit where Jack came with his smart *couteau de chasse* and whipped their brutal heads off. They would be go-ing to devour maidens,

> "But ever when it seemed
> Their need was at the sorest,
> A knight, in armour bright,
> Came riding through the forest."

And down, after a combat, would go the brutal persecutor, with a lance through his midriff. Yes, I say, this is very true and well. But you remember that round the ogre's cave the ground was covered, for hundreds and hundreds of yards, *with the bones of the victims* whom he had lured into the castle. Many knights and maids came to him and perished under his knife and teeth. Were dragons the same as ogres? monsters dwelling in caverns, whence they rushed, attired in plate armour, wielding pikes and torches, and destroying stray passengers who passed by their lair? Monsters, brutes, rapacious tyrants, ruffians, as they were, doubtless they ended by be-ing overcome. But, before they were destroyed, they did a deal of mischief. The bones round their caves were countless. They had sent many brave souls to Hades, before their own fled, howling out of their rascal carcasses, to the same place of gloom.

There is no greater mistake than to suppose that fairies, champions, distressed damsels, and by con-sequence ogres, have ceased to exist. It may not be *ogreable* to them (pardon the horrible pleasantry, but as I am writing in the solitude of my chamber, I am grinding my teeth—yelling, roaring, and curs-ing—brandishing my scissors and paper-cutter, and as it were, have become an ogre). I say there is no greater mistake than to suppose that ogres have ceased to exist. We all *know* ogres. Their caverns are round us, and about us. There are the castles of several ogres within a mile of the spot where I write. I think some of them suspect I am an ogre myself. I am not: but I know they are. I visit them. I don't mean to say that they take a cold roast prince out of

---

1–3. **that well-known ogre . . . interior,** in the fairy story of "Jack the Giant-Killer." 11. **couteau de chasse,** hunting knife.

the cupboard, and have a cannibal feast before *me*. But I see the bones lying about the roads to their houses, and in the areas and gardens. Politeness, of course, prevents me from making any remarks; but I know them well enough. One of the ways to know 'em is to watch the scared looks of the ogres' wives and children. They lead an awful life. They are present at dreadful cruelties. In their excesses those ogres will stab about, and kill not only strangers who happen to call in and ask a night's lodging, but 10 they will outrage, murder, and chop up their own kin. We all know ogres, I say, and have been in their dens often. It is not necessary that ogres who ask you to dine should offer their guests the *peculiar dish* which they like. They cannot always get a Tom Thumb family. They eat mutton and beef too; and I dare say even go out to tea, and invite you to drink it. But I tell you there are numbers of them going about in the world. And now you have my word for it, and this little hint, it is quite curious 20 what an interest society may be made to have for you, by your determining to find out the ogres you meet there.

"What does the man mean?" says Mrs. Downright, to whom a joke is a very grave thing. I mean, madam, that in the company assembled in your genteel drawing-room, who bow here and there and smirk in white neck-cloths, you receive men who elbow through life successfully enough, but who are ogres in private: men wicked, false, rapacious, flat- 30 tering; cruel hectors at home, smiling courtiers abroad; causing wives, children, servants, parents, to tremble before them, and smiling and bowing as they bid strangers welcome into their castles. I say, there are men who have crunched the bones of victim after victim; in whose closets lie skeletons picked frightfully clean. When these ogres come out into the world, you don't suppose they show their knives, and their great teeth? A neat simple white neck-cloth, a merry rather obsequious manner, a cadav- 40 erous look, perhaps, now and again, and a rather dreadful grin; but I know ogres very considerably respected: and when you hint to such and such a man, "My dear sir, Mr. Sharpus, whom you appear to like, is, I assure you, a most dreadful cannibal"; the gentleman cries, "Oh, psha, nonsense! Dare say not so black as he is painted. Dare say not worse than his neighbours." We condone everything in this country—private treason, falsehood, flattery, cruelty at home, roguery, and double dealing. 50 What! Do you mean to say in your acquaintance you don't know ogres guilty of countless crimes of fraud and force, and that knowing them you don't shake hands with them; dine with them at your table; and meet them at their own? Depend upon it, in the time when there were real live ogres in real caverns or castles, gobbling up real knights and virgins, when they went into the world—the neighbouring market-town, let us say, or earl's castle—though their nature and reputation were pretty well known, their notorious foibles were never alluded to. You would say, "What, Blunderbore, my boy! How do you do? How well and fresh you look! What's the receipt you have for keeping so young and rosy?" And your wife would softly ask after Mrs. Blunderbore and the dear children. Or it would be, "My dear Humguffin! try that pork. It is home-bred, home-fed, and, I promise you, tender. Tell me if you think it is as good as yours? John, a glass of Burgundy to Colonel Humguffin!" You don't suppose there would be any unpleasant allusions to disagreeable home-reports regarding Humguffin's manner of furnishing his larder? I say we all of us know ogres. We shake hands and dine with ogres. And if inconvenient moralists tell us we are cowards for our pains, we turn round with a *tu quoque*, or say that we don't meddle with other folk's affairs; that people are much less black than they are painted, and so on. What! Won't half the county go to Ogreham Castle? Won't some of the clergy say grace at dinner? Won't the mothers bring their daughters to dance with the young Rawheads? And if Lady Ogreham happens to die—I won't say to go the way of all flesh, that is too revolting—I say if Ogreham is a widower, do you aver, on your conscience and honour, that mothers will not be found to offer their young girls to supply the lamented lady's place? How stale this misanthropy is! Something must have disagreed with this cynic. Yes, my good woman. I dare say you would like to call another subject. Yes, my fine fellow; ogre at home, supple as a dancing-master abroad, and shaking in thy pumps, and wearing a horrible grin of sham gaiety to conceal thy terror, lest I should point thee out:—thou art prosperous and honoured, art thou? I say thou hast been a tyrant and a robber. Thou hast plundered the poor. Thou hast bullied the weak. Thou hast laid violent hands on the goods of the innocent and confiding. Thou hast made a prey of the meek and gentle who asked for thy protection. Thou hast been hard to thy kinsfolk, and cruel to thy family. Go, monster! Ah, when shall little Jack come and drill daylight through thy wicked cannibal carcass? I see the ogre pass on, bowing right and left to the company; and he gives a dreadful sidelong glance of suspicion as he is talking to my lord bishop in the corner there.

22–23. tu quoque, thou also.

Ogres in our days need not be giants at all. In former times, and in children's books, where it is necessary to paint your moral in such large letters that there can be no mistake about it, ogres are made with that enormous mouth and *ratelier* which you know of, and with which they can swallow down a baby, almost without using that great knife which they always carry. They are too cunning now-a-days. They go about in society, slim, small, quietly dressed, and showing no especially great appetite. In my own young days there used to be play ogres—men who would devour a young fellow in one sitting, and leave him without a bit of flesh on his bones. They were quiet gentlemanlike-looking people. They got the young fellow into their cave. Champagne, pâté-de-foie-gras, and numberless good things, were handed about; and then, having eaten, the young man was devoured in his turn. I believe these card and dice ogres have died away almost as entirely as the hasty-pudding giants whom Tom Thumb overcame. Now, there are ogres in City courts who lure you into their dens. About our Cornish mines I am told there are many most plausible ogres, who tempt you into their caverns and pick your bones there. In a certain newspaper there used to be lately a whole column of advertisements from ogres who would put on the most plausible, nay, piteous appearance, in order to inveigle their victims. You would read, "A tradesman, established for seventy years in the City, and known, and much respected by Messrs. N. M. Rothschild and Baring Brothers, has pressing need for three pounds until next Saturday. He can give security for half a million, and forty thousand pounds will be given for the use of the loan," and so on; or, "An influential body of capitalists are about to establish a company, of which the business will be enormous and the profits proportionately prodigious. They will require A SECRETARY, of good address and appearance, at a salary of two thousand per annum. He need not be able to write, but address and manners are absolutely necessary. As a mark of confidence in the company, he will have to deposit," &c.; or, "A young widow (of pleasing manners and appearance) who has a pressing necessity for four pounds ten for three weeks, offers her Erard's grand piano, valued at three hundred guineas; a diamond cross of eight hundred pounds; and board and lodging in her elegant villa near Banbury Cross, with the best references and society, in return for the loan." I suspect these people are ogres. There are ogres and ogres. Polyphemus was a great, tall, one-eyed, notorious ogre, fetching his victims out of a hole, and gobbling them one after another. There could be no mistake about him. But so were the Sirens ogres—pretty blue-eyed things, peeping at you coaxingly from out of the water, and singing their melodious wheedles. And the bones round their caves were more numerous than the ribs, skulls, and thigh-bones round the cavern of hulking Polypheme.

To the castle-gates of some of these monsters up rides the dapper champion of the pen; puffs boldly upon the horn which hangs by the chain; enters the hall resolutely, and challenges the big tyrant sulking within. We defy him to combat, the enormous roaring ruffian! We give him a meeting on the green plain before his castle. Green? No wonder it should be green: it is manured with human bones. After a few graceful wheels and curvets, we take our ground. We stoop over our saddle. 'Tis but to kiss the locket of our lady-love's hair. And now the vizor is up: the lance is in rest (Gillott's iron is the point for me). A touch of the spur in the gallant sides of Pegasus, and we gallop at the great brute.

"Cut off his ugly head, Flibbertygibbet, my squire!" And who are these who pour out of the castle? the imprisoned maidens, the maltreated widows, the poor old hoary grandfathers, who have been locked up in the dungeons these scores and scores of years, writhing under the tyranny of that ruffian! Ah ye knights of the pen! May honour be your shield, and truth tip your lances! Be gentle to all gentle people. Be modest to women. Be tender to children. And as for the Ogre Humbug, out sword, and have at him.

---

5. **ratelier,** set of teeth. **31-32. N. M. Rothschild,** Nathan Mayer Rothschild, first Lord Rothschild (1840–1915), the great English banker. **Baring Brothers,** one of the great English banking houses, founded in 1770.

8. **Polyphemus.** See Homer's *Odyssey*, Book IX. **11. Sirens.** See the *Odyssey*, Book XI. **29–30. Gillott's . . . me.** Joseph Gillot (1799–1873) was the first great English manufacturer of steel pens. **31. Pegasus,** the winged horse of Greek mythology, who has become a symbol of poetic inspiration.

Dante Gabriel Rossetti
1828–1882

Dante Gabriel Rossetti was born in London, May 12, 1828, the son of an exiled Italian poet and patriot who married the high-minded young daughter of an English mother and an Italian father, and finally became a professor in King's College. His son William Michael Rossetti described the father as an intense lover of liberty and an undogmatic, intensely antipapal Christian.

Dante Gabriel's talents budded early. As a small child he wrote a drama and made pictures for *King Henry VI* and the *Iliad; Hamlet* and Scott's novels were among his literary passions. But he was impatient of formal instruction. At King's College School he disliked both the "moral" atmosphere and the rough games. In 1848 he became a pupil of the artist Ford Madox Brown, who put him to work painting pickle jars. Brown, Holman Hunt, John Everett Millais, and Rossetti were the original Pre-Raphaelites; later, Morris, Swinburne, Ruskin, and Edward Burne-Jones were all connected, in one way or another, with the movement.

As a painter, Rossetti is distinguished for his use of color, his abundant symbolism, and the unearthly beauty (half spiritual, half sensual) which he casts over his work. But the aim of the Pre-Raphaelite Brotherhood was "to divest art of conventionality, to work with sincerity of purpose, to reproduce with fidelity." They took their name from the conviction that painting had declined since Raphael; to achieve sincerity and spontaneity one must stop imitating Raphael and return to the painters who preceded him, the men who created the beautiful frescoes at the Campo Santo in Pisa, and who went to life itself for their inspiration.

Most Englishmen quite failed to perceive any gleams of mystical idealism in all this. Charles Dickens attacked the Brotherhood furiously; all he expected to find in their pictures was "that every brick in the house will be a portrait; that the man's boots will be copied with the utmost fidelity from a pair of Bluchers sent up out of Northamptonshire for that purpose; and that the texture of his hands (including four chilblains, a whitlow, and ten dirty nails) will be a triumph of the painter's art." Yet the Pre-Raphaelites were never interested in "realism" for its own sake. Ruskin rushed to their defense; the battle was one of the hottest waged on any artistic front during Victoria's time. As a matter of fact, Hunt was the only member of the group who remained permanently loyal to the original program; in 1853 Millais himself became a member of the hated Academy.

In 1850 Rossetti fell in love with Elizabeth Siddal, a milliner's assistant who had become the favorite model of the Pre-Raphaelites, a girl of some talent both in painting and in writing. Elizabeth had tubercular tendencies, but this alone does not explain the long engagement. Rossetti seems both to have wanted to marry "Guggum," as he called her, and not to marry her; he may not have been entirely faithful to her. In any case, he never brought her happiness, either before or after their union in 1860.

In 1861, Mrs. Rossetti was delivered of a stillborn child, and her frail health was permanently shattered. Financial worries did not help her through a difficult period; neither did her husband's vagaries. Laudanum was the only thing she could find that did, and she used it freely. One night in 1862 Rossetti found her unconscious in her bed with an empty vial beside her. She died early the next morning, whether a suicide or the victim of an accident will never be known.

Rossetti blamed himself, and began attending séances in a vain effort to get a message from "Guggum." He buried the manuscript of his unpublished poems with her; nine years later he had them exhumed. He began to suffer hallucinations, encountering his wronged wife's spirit at every turn, and finding her reincarnated in birds and animals. Rossetti declined rapidly from then on, though still able, on occasion, to do magnificent work. Failing eyesight, hypochondria, the persecution "complex," insomnia, the use of chloral to control the insomnia, followed by whisky to take away the nausea left by the chloral—these melancholy milestones mark his descent toward paranoia. In 1872 he attempted suicide. He died April 9, 1882.

As a poet there can be no question that Rossetti belongs with the immortals. He represents a rebellion against the dominant preoccupations of the great early Victorians: he is no moralist; he is moving toward the "art for art's sake" position which was formulated by Pater and overdramatized by Oscar Wilde. But despite all the errors of his tragic life, he is not himself among the immoralists. His dominant note has been happily defined as a kind of "fleshly mysticism"; his confessed inability to draw a clean-cut distinction between the soul's beauty and the body's beauty left him open to Robert Buchanan's attack ("The Fleshly School of Poetry," 1872), but nobody has ever believed that Buchanan's criticism was fair. The passionate directness of Rossetti's poetry, its brave reaffirmation of the validity of the individual experience, and its intellectualized passion—these qualities were precious contributions to the development of English poetry. As Albert Edmund Trombly has observed, Rossetti is matchless in his combination of melody, sonority, color, and virility.

Rossetti's early poems—"The Blessed Damozel" and others—were first published in *The Germ*, a magazine which he and his colleagues established in 1850 and which ran for four numbers. His collected *Poems* appeared in 1870, *Ballads and Sonnets* in 1881.

THE BLESSED DAMOZEL

One of the most glorious mystical poems in any language, "The Blessed Damozel" was suggested by Edgar Allan Poe's "The Raven." "I saw," said Rossetti, "that Poe had done the utmost it was possible to do with the grief of the lover on earth, and I determined to reverse the conditions, and give utterance to the yearning of the loved one in heaven." O. Henry's powerful story "The Furnished Room" (*The Four Million*) affords, at one point, an interesting comparison. See Debussy's setting of "The Blessed Damozel" for female voices and orchestra, after the French text by Gabriel Sarrazin.

The blessed damozel leaned out
    From the gold bar of Heaven;
Her eyes were deeper than the depth
    Of waters stilled at even;
She had three lilies in her hand,
    And the stars in her hair were seven.

Her robe, ungirt from clasp to hem,
    No wrought flowers did adorn,
But a white rose of Mary's gift,
    For service meetly worn;   10
Her hair that lay along her back
    Was yellow like ripe corn.

Herseemed she scarce had been a day
    One of God's choristers;
The wonder was not yet quite gone
    From that still look of hers;

10. For . . . worn, suitably worn while serving the Blessed Virgin

Albeit, to them she left, her day
    Had counted as ten years.

(To one, it is ten years of years.
    . . . Yet now, and in this place,   20
Surely she leaned o'er me—her hair
    Fell all about my face. . . .
Nothing: the autumn fall of leaves.
    The whole year sets apace.)

It was the rampart of God's house
    That she was standing on;
By God built over the sheer depth
    The which is Space begun;
So high, that looking downward thence
    She scarce could see the sun.   30

It lies in Heaven, across the flood
    Of ether, as a bridge.
Beneath, the tides of day and night
    With flame and darkness ridge
The void, as low as where this earth
    Spins like a fretful midge.

Around her, lovers, newly met
    'Mid deathless love's acclaims,
Spoke evermore among themselves
    Their heart-remembered names;   40
And the souls mounting up to God
    Went by her like thin flames.

And still she bowed herself and stooped
    Out of the circling charm;
Until her bosom must have made
    The bar she leaned on warm,
And the lilies lay as if asleep
    Along her bended arm.

From the fixed place of Heaven she saw
    Time like a pulse shake fierce   50
Through all the worlds. Her gaze still strove
    Within the gulf to pierce
Its path; and now she spoke as when
    The stars sang in their spheres.

The sun was gone now; the curled moon
    Was like a little feather

19-24. (To . . . apace.) Here, and elsewhere in the poem, parentheses are used to indicate the shift to the viewpoint of the lover on earth.   54. The stars . . . spheres. According to the Ptolemaic astronomy, the stars and planets make music as they move about the earth in their concentric spheres. See Job 38: 7; *The Merchant of Venice*, Act V, sc. 1, ll. 60–65.

Fluttering far down the gulf; and now
   She spoke through the still weather.
Her voice was like the voice the stars
   Had when they sang together.   60

(Ah sweet! Even now, in that bird's song,
   Strove not her accents there,
Fain to be hearkened? When those bells
   Possessed the mid-day air,
Strove not her steps to reach my side
   Down all the echoing stair?)

"I wish that he were come to me,
   For he will come," she said.
"Have I not prayed in Heaven?—on earth,
   Lord, Lord, has he not prayed?   70
Are not two prayers a perfect strength.
   And shall I feel afraid?

"When round his head the aureole clings,
   And he is clothed in white,
I'll take his hand and go with him
   To the deep wells of light;
We will step down as to a stream,
   And bathe there in God's sight.

"We two will stand beside that shrine,
   Occult, withheld, untrod,   80
Whose lamps are stirred continually
   With prayer sent up to God;
And see our old prayers, granted, melt
   Each like a little cloud.

"We two will lie i' the shadow of
   That living mystic tree
Within whose secret growth the Dove
   Is sometimes felt to be,
While every leaf that His plumes touch
   Saith His Name audibly.   90

"And I myself will teach to him,
   I myself, lying so,
The songs I sing here; which his voice
   Shall pause in, hushed and slow,
And find some knowledge at each pause.
   Or some new thing to know."

(Alas! We two, we two, thou say'st!
   Yea, one wast thou with me
That once of old. But shall God lift
   To endless unity   100

The soul whose likeness with thy soul
   Was but its love for thee?)

"We two," she said, "will seek the groves
   Where the lady Mary is,
With her five handmaidens, whose names
   Are five sweet symphonies,
Cecily, Gertrude, Magdalen,
   Margaret and Rosalys.

"Circlewise sit they, with bound locks
   And foreheads garlanded;   110
Into the fine cloth white like flame
   Weaving the golden thread,
To fashion the birth-robes for them
   Who are just born, being dead.

"He shall fear, haply, and be dumb:
   Then will I lay my cheek
To his, and tell about our love,
   Not once abashed or weak:
And the dear Mother will approve
   My pride, and let me speak.   120

"Herself shall bring us, hand in hand,
   To Him round whom all souls
Kneel, the clear-ranged unnumbered heads
   Bowed with their aureoles:
And angels meeting us shall sing
   To their citherns and citoles.

"There will I ask of Christ the Lord
   Thus much for him and me:—
Only to live as once on earth
   With Love,—only to be,   130
As then awhile, for ever now
   Together, I and he."

She gazed and listened and then said,
   Less sad of speech than mild,—
"All this is when he comes." She ceased.
   The light thrilled towards her, filled
With angels in strong level flight.
   Her eyes prayed, and she smiled.

(I saw her smile.) But soon their path
   Was vague in distant spheres: 140
And then she cast her arms along
   The golden barriers,
And laid her face between her hands,
   And wept. (I heard her tears.)

86. That living mystic tree. See Revelation 22 : 2.
87. Dove, the Holy Spirit. See Luke 3 : 22.

107–08. Cecily . . . Rosalys, five saints. **112. golden thread,** used in weaving in England as far back as Anglo-Saxon times. Rossetti gives it symbolic religious significance.

MY SISTER'S SLEEP

This poem is not autobiographical.

She fell asleep on Christmas Eve:
　　At length the long-ungranted shade
　　Of weary eyelids overweighed
The pain nought else might yet relieve.

Our mother, who had leaned all day
　　Over the bed from chime to chime,
　　Then raised herself for the first time,
And as she sat her down, did pray.

Her little work-table was spread
　　With work to finish. For the glare　　10
　　Made by her candle, she had care
To work some distance from the bed.

Without, there was a cold moon up,
　　Of winter radiance sheer and thin;
　　The hollow halo it was in
Was like an icy crystal cup.

Through the small room, with subtle sound
　　Of flame, by vents the fireshine drove
　　And reddened. In its dim alcove
The mirror shed a clearness round.　　20

I had been sitting up some nights,
　　And my tired mind felt weak and blank;
　　Like a sharp strengthening wine it drank
The stillness and the broken lights.

Twelve struck. That sound, by dwindling years
　　Heard in each hour, crept off; and then
　　The ruffled silence spread again,
Like water that a pebble stirs.

Our mother rose from where she sat:
　　Her needles, as she laid them down,　　30
　　Met lightly, and her silken gown
Settled: no other noise than that.

' Glory unto the Newly Born!'
　　So, as said angels, she did say;
　　Because we were in Christmas Day,
Though it would still be long till morn.

Just then in the room over us
　　There was a pushing back of chairs,
　　As some who had sat unawares
So late, now heard the hour, and rose.　　40

With anxious softly-stepping haste
　　Our mother went where Margaret lay,
　　Fearing the sounds o'erhead—should they
Have broken her long watched-for rest!

She stooped an instant, calm, and turned;
　　But suddenly turned back again;
　　And all her features seemed in pain
With woe, and her eyes gazed and yearned.

For my part, I but hid my face,
　　And held my breath, and spoke no word:　　50
　　There was none spoken; but I heard
The silence for a little space.

Our mother bowed herself and wept:
　　And both my arms fell, and I said,
　　"God knows I knew that she was dead."
And there, all white, my sister slept.

Then kneeling, upon Christmas morn
　　A little after twelve o'clock,
　　We said, ere the first quarter struck,
"Christ's blessing on the newly born!"　　60

ON REFUSAL OF AID BETWEEN NATIONS

This poem is a protest against what Rossetti considered the shameful indifference of other nations toward the struggle of Italy and Hungary against Austria.

Not that the earth is changing, O my God!
　　Nor that the seasons totter in their walk,—
　　Not that the virulent ill of act and talk
Seethes ever as a winepress ever trod,—
Not therefore are we certain that the rod
　　Weighs in thine hand to smite thy world; though now
Beneath thine hand so many nations bow,
So many kings:—not therefore, O my God!—

But because Man is parcelled out in men
　　Today; because, for any wrongful blow,　　10
　　No man not stricken asks, "I would be told
Why thou dost strike"; but his heart whispers then,
　　"He is he, I am I." By this we know
　　That our earth falls asunder, being old.

60. "Christ's . . . newly born!" See "The Blessed Damozel," l. 114.

SISTER HELEN

This story of black magic is based on the old belief that a person may be injured by what is done to his image. The custom of hanging in effigy originated in this belief, and the primitive fear of having one's features copied or photographed is closely connected with it. For an interesting literary parallel, see Susan Nunsuch's treatment of Eustacia Vye in *The Return of the Native* by Thomas Hardy.

"Why did you melt your waxen man,
    Sister Helen?
To-day is the third since you began."
"The time was long, yet the time ran,
    Little brother."
  (*O Mother, Mary Mother,*
Three days to-day, between Hell and Heaven!)

"But if you have done your work aright,
    Sister Helen,
You'll let me play, for you said I might." 10
"Be very still in your play to-night,
    Little brother."
  (*O Mother, Mary Mother,*
Third night, to-night, between Hell and Heaven!)

"You said it must melt ere vesper-bell,
    Sister Helen;
If now it be molten, all is well."
"Even so,—nay, peace! you cannot tell,
    Little brother."
  (*O Mother, Mary Mother,* 20
O what is this, between Hell and Heaven?)

"Oh the waxen knave was plump to-day,
    Sister Helen;
How like dead folk he has dropped away!"
"Nay now, of the dead what can you say,
    Little brother?"
  (*O Mother, Mary Mother,*
What of the dead, between Hell and Heaven?)

"See, see, the sunken pile of wood,
    Sister Helen, 30
Shines through the thinned wax red as blood!"
"Nay now, when looked you yet on blood,
    Little brother?"
  (*O Mother, Mary Mother,*
How pale she is, between Hell and Heaven!)

"Now close your eyes, for they're sick and sore,
    Sister Helen,
And I'll play without the gallery door."

"Aye, let me rest,—I'll lie on the floor,
    Little brother." 40
  (*O Mother, Mary Mother,*
What rest to-night, between Hell and Heaven?)

"Here high up in the balcony,
    Sister Helen,
The moon flies face to face with me."
"Aye, look and say whatever you see,
    Little brother."
  (*O Mother, Mary Mother,*
What sight to-night, between Hell and Heaven?)

"Outside it's merry in the wind's wake, 50
    Sister Helen;
In the shaken trees the chill stars shake."
"Hush, heard you a horse-tread as you spake,
    Little brother?"
  (*O Mother, Mary Mother,*
What sound to-night between Hell and Heaven?)

"I hear a horse-tread, and I see,
    Sister Helen,
Three horsemen that ride terribly."
"Little brother, whence come the three, 60
    Little brother?"
  (*O Mother, Mary Mother,*
Whence should they come, between Hell and Heaven?)

"They come by the hill-verge from Boyne Bar,
    Sister Helen,
And one draws nigh, but two are afar."
"Look, look, do you know them who they are,
    Little brother?"
  (*O Mother, Mary Mother,*
Who should they be, between Hell and Heaven?) 70

"Oh, it's Keith of Eastholm rides so fast,
    Sister Helen,
For I know the white mane on the blast."
"The hour has come, has come at last,
    Little brother!"
  (*O Mother, Mary Mother,*
Her hour at last, between Hell and Heaven!)

"He has made a sign and called Halloo!
    Sister Helen,
And he says that he would speak with you." 80
"Oh tell him I fear the frozen dew,
    Little brother."
  (*O Mother, Mary Mother,*
Why laughs she thus, between Hell and Heaven?)

64. Boyne Bar, at the mouth of the Boyne River, Leinster, Ireland

"The wind is loud, but I hear him cry,
            Sister Helen,
That Keith of Ewern's like to die."
"And he and thou, and thou and I,
            Little brother."
            (*O Mother, Mary Mother,*   90
And they and we, between Hell and Heaven!)

"Three days ago, on his marriage-morn,
            Sister Helen,
He sickened, and lies since then forlorn."
"For bridegroom's side is the bride a thorn,
            Little brother?"
            (*O Mother, Mary Mother,*
Cold bridal cheer, between Hell and Heaven!)

"Three days and nights he has lain abed,
            Sister Helen,   100
And he prays in torment to be dead."
"The thing may chance, if he have prayed,
            Little brother!"
            (*O Mother, Mary Mother,*
If ye have prayed, between Hell and Heaven!)

"But he has not ceased to cry to-day,
            Sister Helen,
That you should take your curse away."
"*My* prayer was heard,—he need but pray,
            Little brother!"   110
            (*O Mother, Mary Mother,*
Shall God not hear, between Hell and Heaven?)

"But he says, till you take back your ban,
            Sister Helen,
His soul would pass, yet never can."
"Nay then, shall I slay a living man,
            Little brother?"
            (*O Mother, Mary Mother,*
A living soul, between Hell and Heaven!)

"But he calls for ever on your name,   120
            Sister Helen,
And says that he melts before a flame."
"My heart for his pleasure fared the same,
            Little brother."
            (*O Mother, Mary Mother,*
Fire at the heart, between Hell and Heaven!)

"Here's Keith of Westholm riding fast,
            Sister Helen,
For I know the white plume on the blast."
"The hour, the sweet hour I forecast,   130
            Little brother!"

87. **Keith of Ewern**, the false lover whom Sister Helen is
destroying.

            (*O Mother, Mary Mother,*
Is the hour sweet, between Hell and Heaven?)

"He stops to speak, and he stills his horse,
            Sister Helen;
But his words are drowned in the wind's course."
"Nay hear, nay hear, you must hear perforce,
            Little brother!"
            (*O Mother, Mary Mother,*
What word now heard, between Hell and Heaven!)   140

"Oh he says that Keith of Ewern's cry,
            Sister Helen,
Is ever to see you ere he die."
"In all that his soul sees, there am I,
            Little brother!"
            (*O Mother, Mary Mother,*
The soul's one sight, between Hell and Heaven!)

"He sends a ring and a broken coin,
            Sister Helen,
And bids you mind the banks of Boyne."   150
"What else he broke will he ever join,
            Little brother?"
            (*O Mother, Mary Mother,*
No, never joined, between Hell and Heaven!)

"He yields you these and craves full fain,
            Sister Helen,
You pardon him in his mortal pain."
"What else he took will he give again,
            Little brother?"
            (*O Mother, Mary Mother,*   160
Not twice to give, between Hell and Heaven!)

"He calls your name in an agony,
            Sister Helen,
That even dead Love must weep to see."
"Hate, born of Love, is blind as he,
            Little brother!"
            (*O Mother, Mary Mother,*
Love turned to hate, between Hell and Heaven!)

"Oh, it's Keith of Keith now that rides fast,
            Sister Helen,   170
For I know the white hair on the blast."
"The short short hour will soon be past,
            Little brother!"
            (*O Mother, Mary Mother,*
Will soon be past, between Hell and Heaven!)

148. **a broken coin**, Keith of Ewern's half of the coin that
he and Helen broke together when they plighted their troth
by the banks of the Boyne.

"He looks at me and he tries to speak,
      Sister Helen,
But oh! his voice is sad and weak!"
"What here should the mighty Baron seek,
      Little brother?"   180
    (*O Mother, Mary Mother,*
Is this the end, between Hell and Heaven?)

"Oh his son still cries, if you forgive,
      Sister Helen,
The body dies but the soul shall live."
"Fire shall forgive me as I forgive,
      Little brother!"
    (*O Mother, Mary Mother,*
As she forgives, between Hell and Heaven!)

"Oh he prays you, as his heart would rive,   190
      Sister Helen,
To save his dear son's soul alive."
"Fire cannot slay it, it shall thrive,
      Little brother!"
    (*O Mother, Mary Mother,*
Alas, alas, between Hell and Heaven!)

"He cries to you, kneeling in the road,
      Sister Helen,
To go with him for the love of God!"
"The way is long to his son's abode,   200
      Little brother."
    (*O Mother, Mary Mother,*
The way is long, between Hell and Heaven!)

"A lady's here, by a dark steed brought,
      Sister Helen,
So darkly clad, I saw her not."
"See her now or never see aught,
      Little brother!"
    (*O Mother, Mary Mother,*
What more to see, between Hell and Heaven?)   210

"Her hood falls back, and the moon shines fair,
      Sister Helen,
On the Lady of Ewern's golden hair."
"Blest hour of my power and her despair,
      Little brother!"
    (*O Mother, Mary Mother,*
Hour blest and banned, between Hell and Heaven!)

"Pale, pale her cheeks, that in pride did glow,
      Sister Helen,
Neath the bridal wreath three days ago."   220

186. "**Fire shall forgive me**, probably when she is burned
for witchcraft.

"One morn for pride and three days for woe,
      Little brother!"
    (*O Mother, Mary Mother,*
Three days, three nights, between Hell and Heaven!)

"Her clasped hands stretch from her bending head,
      Sister Helen;
With the loud wind's wail her sobs are wed."
"What wedding-strains hath her bridal-bed,
      Little brother?"
    (*O Mother, Mary Mother,*   230
What strain but death's, between Hell and Heaven?)

"She may not speak, she sinks in a swoon,
      Sister Helen,—
She lifts her lips and gasps on the moon."
"Oh! might I but hear her soul's blithe tune,
      Little brother!"
    (*O Mother, Mary Mother,*
Her woe's dumb cry, between Hell and Heaven!)

"They've caught her to Westholm's saddle-bow,
      Sister Helen,   240
And her moonlit hair gleams white in its flow."
"Let it turn whiter than winter snow,
      Little brother!"
    (*O Mother, Mary Mother,*
Woe-withered gold, between Hell and Heaven!)

"O Sister Helen, you heard the bell,
      Sister Helen!
More loud than the vesper-chime it fell."
"No vesper-chime, but a dying knell,
      Little brother!"   250
    (*O Mother, Mary Mother,*
His dying knell, between Hell and Heaven!)

"Alas! but I fear the heavy sound,
      Sister Helen;
Is it in the sky or in the ground?"
"Say, have they turned their horses round,
      Little brother?"
    (*O Mother, Mary Mother,*
What would she more, between Hell and Heaven?)

"They have raised the old man from his knee,   260
      Sister Helen,
And they ride in silence hastily."
"More fast the naked soul doth flee,
      Little brother!"
    (*O Mother, Mary Mother,*
The naked soul, between Hell and Heaven!)

Flank to flank are the three steeds gone,
    Sister Helen,
But the lady's dark steed goes alone."
And lonely her bridegroom's soul hath flown,   270
    Little brother."
    (*O Mother, Mary Mother,*
The lonely ghost, between Hell and Heaven!)

Oh the wind is sad in the iron chill,
    Sister Helen,
And weary sad they look by the hill."
But he and I are sadder still,
    Little brother!"
    (*O Mother, Mary Mother,*
Most sad of all, between Hell and Heaven!)   280

See, see, the wax has dropped from its place,
    Sister Helen,
And the flames are winning up apace!"
Yet here they burn but for a space,
    Little brother!"
    (*O Mother, Mary Mother,*
Here for a space, between Hell and Heaven!)

Ah! what white thing at the door has crossed,
    Sister Helen?
Ah! what is this that sighs in the frost?"   290
A soul that's lost as mine is lost,
    Little brother!"
    (*O Mother, Mary Mother,*
Lost, lost, all lost, between Hell and Heaven!)

FIRST LOVE REMEMBERED

Peace in her chamber, wheresoe'er
    It be, a holy place:
The thought still brings my soul such grace
    As morning meadows wear.

Whether it still be small and light,
    A maid's who dreams alone,
As from her orchard-gate the moon
    Its ceiling showed at night:

Or whether, in a shadow dense
    As nuptial hymns invoke,   10
Innocent maidenhood awoke
    To married innocence:

There still the thanks unheard await
    The unconscious gift bequeathed;
For there my soul this hour has breathed
    An air inviolate.

SUDDEN LIGHT

I have been here before,
    But when or how I cannot tell:
I know the grass beyond the door,
    The sweet keen smell,
The sighing sound, the lights around the shore.

You have been mine before,—
    How long ago I may not know:
But just when at that swallow's soar
    Your neck turned so,
Some veil did fall,—I knew it all of yore.   10

Has this been thus before?
    And shall not thus time's eddying flight
Still with our lives our loves restore
    In death's despite,
And day and night yield one delight once more?

THE BALLAD OF DEAD LADIES

from FRANÇOIS VILLON

The vagabond François Villon (1431–1463?) was the first and one of the greatest of French lyric poets. Stevenson has both a famous essay (in *Familiar Studies of Men and Books*) and a famous short story ("A Lodging for the Night") about him, and he has been the hero of many romances, one of which, Justin Huntly McCarthy's *If I Were King*, achieved great popularity in this country through the famous actor E. H. Sothern (1859–1933). "The Ballad of Dead Ladies" is a translation of Villon's *Ballade des dames du temps jadis*. See Swinburne's "A Ballad of François Villon," page 855.

Tell me now in what hidden way is
    Lady Flora the lovely Roman?
Where's Hipparchia, and where is Thaïs,
    Neither of them the fairer woman?
    Where is Echo, beheld of no man,
Only heard on river and mere,—
    She whose beauty was more than human? . . .
But where are the snows of yester-year?

Where's Héloïse, the learnèd nun,
    For whose sake Abeillard, I ween,   10

The Ballad of Dead Ladies. **2. Lady Flora,** either the Roman goddess of flowers or any one of several well-known Roman courtesans. **3. Hipparchia,** wife of Crates, Greek philosopher, 3d century B.C. **Thaïs,** either the Athenian courtesan associated with Alexander the Great (see Dryden's "Alexander's Feast") or the Egyptian courtesan turned saint who is the heroine of the novel by Anatole France. **5. Echo,** in Greek mythology a nymph who wasted away for love of Narcissus until only her voice was left. **9. Héloïse.** Héloïse and Abélard (1079–1142), famous scholastic philosopher, are among the most famous lovers of history. Canon Fulbert, uncle of Héloïse, caused Abélard to be emasculated. Abélard became a monk, Héloïse a nun.

Lost manhood and put priesthood on?
  (From Love he won such dule and teen!)
  And where, I pray you, is the Queen
Who willed that Buridan should steer
  Sewed in a sack's mouth down the Seine? . . .
But where are the snows of yester-year?

White Queen Blanche, like a queen of lilies,
  With a voice like any mermaiden,—
Bertha Broadfoot, Beatrice, Alice,
  And Ermengarde the lady of Maine,—   20
  And that good Joan whom Englishmen
At Rouen doomed and burned her there,—
  Mother of God, where are they then? . . .
But where are the snows of yester-year?

Nay, never ask this week, fair lord,
  Where they are gone, nor yet this year,
Except with this for an overword,—
  "But where are the snows of yester-year?"

from THE HOUSE OF LIFE

"The House of Life," which is probably Rossetti's
most important single work, is a monument of his erotic
mysticism. It is not exactly a sonnet sequence, for it does
not tell a connected story; it is rather a series of sonnets
on different aspects of life as love. About half the poems
were recovered from Mrs. Rossetti's coffin in 1869; in
1881 the series was completed in *Ballads and Sonnets*. The
title has astrological significance.

THE SONNET

A sonnet is a moment's monument—
  Memorial from the Soul's eternity
  To one dead deathless hour. Look that it be,
Whether for lustral rite or dire portent,
Of its own arduous fullness reverent.
  Carve it in ivory or in ebony,
  As Day or Night may rule; and let Time see
Its flowering crest impearled and orient.

A sonnet is a coin; its face reveals
  The Soul—its converse, to what Power 'tis due:— 10

12. **dule and teen,** grief and sorrow. 13. **the Queen.**
Marguerite de Bourgogne (14th century) had her lovers
thrown into the Seine; Jean Buridan was one who escaped
this doom. 17. **Queen Blanche,** Blanche of Castille, mother
of King Louis IX of France. 19. **Bertha Broadfoot,** mother
of Charlemagne. **Beatrice, Alice,** any one of a number of
well-known ladies in medieval history or legend. Beatrice
may be Dante's Beatrice, the heroine of *The Divine Comedy.*
20. **Ermengarde,** a twelfth-century lady, daughter of
d'Hélie, Count of Maine, and wife of Foulques V, Count of
Anjou. 21. **Joan,** Joan of Arc.

Whether for tribute to the august appeals
  Of Life, or dower in Love's high retinue,
It serve; or 'mid the dark wharf's cavernous breath,
In Charon's palm it pay the toll to Death.

Part I. Youth and Change

I. LOVE ENTHRONED

I marked all kindred Powers the heart finds fair:—
  Truth, with awed lips; and Hope, with eye
    upcast;
  And Fame, whose loud wings fan the ashen Past
To signal-fires, Oblivion's flight to scare;
And Youth, with still some single golden hair
  Unto his shoulder clinging, since the last
  Embrace wherein two sweet arms held him fast;
And Life, still wreathing flowers for Death to wear.

Love's throne was not with these; but far above
  All passionate wind of welcome and farewell   1
He sat in breathless bowers they dream not of;
  Though Truth foreknow Love's heart, and Hope
    foretell,
  And Fame be for Love's sake desirable,
And Youth be dear, and Life be sweet to Love.

2. BRIDAL BIRTH

As when desire, long darkling, dawns, and first
  The mother looks upon the newborn child,
  Even so my Lady stood at gaze and smiled
When her soul knew at length the Love it nursed.
Born with her life, creature of poignant thirst
  And exquisite hunger, at her heart Love lay
  Quickening in darkness, till a voice that day
Cried on him, and the bonds of birth were burst.

Now, shielded in his wings, our faces yearn
  Together, as his full-grown feet now range   10
    The grove, and his warm hands our couch
      prepare:
Till to his song our bodiless souls in turn
  Be born his children, when Death's nuptial
    change
    Leaves us for light the halo of his hair.

4. LOVESIGHT

When do I see thee most, belovèd one?
  When in the light the spirits of mine eyes
  Before thy face, their altar, solemnize
The worship of that Love through thee made
  known?
Or when in the dusk hours, (we two alone,)
  Close-kissed and eloquent of still replies
  Thy twilight-hidden glimmering visage lies,

d my soul only sees thy soul its own?
love, my love! if I no more should see
yself, nor on the earth the shadow of thee,   10
Nor image of thine eyes in any spring,—
ow then should sound upon Life's darkening
  slope
he ground-whirl of the perished leaves of Hope,
  The wind of Death's imperishable wing?

5. HEART'S HOPE

y what word's power, the keys of paths untrod,
  Shall I the difficult deeps of Love explore,
  Till parted waves of Song yield up the shore
ven as that sea which Israel crossed dryshod?
r lo! in some poor rhythmic period,
  Lady, I fain would tell how evermore
  Thy soul I know not from thy body, nor
hee from myself, neither our love from God.

ea, in God's name, and Love's, and thine, would I
  Draw from one loving heart such evidence   10
s to all hearts all things shall signify;
  Tender as dawn's first hill-fire, and intense
  As instantaneous penetrating sense,
n Spring's birth-hour, of other Springs gone by.

18. GENIUS IN BEAUTY

eauty like hers is genuis. Not the call
  Of Homer's or of Dante's heart sublime,—
  Not Michael's hand furrowing the zones of
    time,—
s more with compassed mysteries musical;
ay, not in Spring's or Summer's sweet footfall
  More gathered gifts exuberant Life bequeaths
  Than does this sovereign face, whose love-spell
    breathes
ven from its shadowed contour on the wall.

s many men are poets in their youth,
  But for one sweet-strung soul the wires prolong 10
  Even through all change the indominable song;
o in likewise the envenomed years, whose tooth
ends shallower grace with ruin void of ruth,
  Upon this beauty's power shall wreck no wrong.

19. SILENT NOON

our hands lie open in the long, fresh grass,—
  The finger-points look through like rosy blooms:
  Your eyes smile peace. The pasture gleams and
    glooms
Neath billowing skies that scatter and amass.

Sec. 5. Heart's Hope. **4. sea . . . dryshod?** The story is in
xodus 14.   *Sec. 18. Genius in Beauty.* **3. Michael,** Michel-
ngelo.

All round our nest, far as the eye can pass,
  Are golden kingcup-fields with silver edge
  Where the cow-parsley skirts the hawthorn-
    hedge.
'Tis visible silence, still as the hour-glass.

Deep in the sun-searched growths the dragon-fly
Hangs like a blue thread loosened from the sky:— 10
  So this winged hour is dropt to us from above.
Oh! clasp we to our hearts, for deathless dower,
This close-companioned inarticulate hour
  When twofold silence was the song of love.

24. PRIDE OF YOUTH

Even as a child, of sorrow that we give
The dead, but little in his heart can find,
Since without need of thought to his clear mind
Their turn it is to die and his to live:—
Even so the wingèd New Love smiles to receive
Along his eddying plumes the auroral wind,
Nor, forward glorying, casts one look behind
Where night-rack shrouds the Old Love fugitive.

There is a change in every hour's recall,
  And the last cowslip in the fields we see   10
  On the same day with the first corn-poppy.
Alas for hourly change! Alas for all
The loves that from his hand proud Youth lets fall,
  Even as the beads of a told rosary!

28. SOUL-LIGHT

What other woman could be loved like you,
  Or how of you should love possess his fill?
  After the fulness of all rapture, still,—
As at the end of some deep avenue
A tender glamour of the day,—there comes to view
  Far in your eyes a yet more hungering thrill,—
  Such fire as Love's soul-winnowing hands distil
Even from his inmost ark of light and dew.

And as the traveller triumphs with the sun,
  Glorying in heat's mid-height, yet star tide brings
  Wonder new-born, and still fresh transport
    springs   11
From limpid lambent hours of day begun;—
  Even so, through eyes and voice, your soul doth
    move
  My soul with changeful light of infinite love.

34. THE DARK GLASS

Not I myself know all my love for thee:
  How should I reach so far, who cannot weigh
  To-morrow's dower by gage of yesterday?

Shall birth and death, and all dark names that
    be
As doors and windows bared to some loud sea,
    Lash deaf mine ears and blind my face with
        spray;
    And shall my sense pierce love,—the last relay
And ultimate outpost of eternity?

Lo! what am I to Love, the lord of all?
    One murmuring shell he gathers from the sand,—
    One little heart-flame sheltered in his hand.   11
Yet through thine eyes he grants me clearest call
And veriest touch of powers primordial
    That any hour-girt life may understand.

53. WITHOUT HER

What of her glass without her? The blank grey
    There where the pool is blind of the moon's
        face.
    Her dress without her? The tossed empty space
Of cloud-rack whence the moon has passed away.
Her paths without her? Day's appointed sway
    Usurped by desolate night. Her pillowed place
    Without her? Tears, ah me! for love's good
        grace,
And cold forgetfulness of night or day.

What of the heart without her? Nay, poor heart,
    Of thee what word remains ere speech be still?   10
    A wayfarer by barren ways and chill,
Steep ways and weary, without her thou art.
Where the long cloud, the long wood's counterpart,
    Sheds double darkness up the labouring hill.

Part II. Change and Fate

69. AUTUMN IDLENESS

This sunlight shames November where he grieves
    In dead red leaves, and will not let him shun
    The day, though bough with bough be over-run.
But with a blessing every glade receives
High salutation; while from hillock-eaves
    The deer gaze calling, dappled white and dun,
    As if, being foresters of old, the sun
Had marked them with the shade of forest-leaves.

Here dawn to-day unveiled her magic glass;
    Here noon now gives the thirst and takes the
        dew;   10
Till eve bring rest when other good things pass.
    And here the lost hours the lost hours renew
While I still lead my shadow o'er the grass,
    Nor know, for longing, that which I should do.

77. SOUL'S BEAUTY

(Sibylla Palmifera)

Under the arch of Life, where love and death,
    Terror and mystery, guard her shrine, I saw
    Beauty enthroned; and though her gaze struck
        awe,
I drew it in as simply as my breath.
Hers are the eyes which, over and beneath,
    The sky and sea bend on thee,—which can draw,
    By sea or sky or woman, to one law,
The allotted bondman of her palm and wreath.

That is that Lady Bounty, in whose praise
    Thy voice and hand shake still,—long known to
        thee   1
    By flying hair and fluttering hem,—the beat
Following her daily of thy heart and feet,
    How passionately and irretrievably,
In what fond flight, how many ways and days!

78. BODY'S BEAUTY

Of Adam's first wife, Lilith, it is told
    (The witch he loved before the gift of Eve,)
    That, ere the snake's, her sweet tongue could
        deceive,
And her enchanted hair was the first gold.
And still she sits, young while the earth is old,
    And, subtly of herself contemplative,
    Draws men to watch the bright net she can
        weave,
Till heart and body and life are in its hold.

The rose and poppy are her flowers; for where
    Is he not found, O Lilith, whom shed scent   10
And soft-shed kisses and soft sleep shall snare?
    Lo! as that youth's eyes burned at thine, so went
    Thy spell through him, and left his straight neck
        bent,
And round his heart one strangling golden hair.

83. BARREN SPRING

Once more the changed year's turning wheel re-
    turns:
    And as a girl sails balanced in the wind,
    And now before and now again behind
Stoops as it swoops, with cheek that laughs and
    burns,—
So Spring comes merry towards me now, but earns
    No answering smile from me, whose life is twined

Sec. 77. Soul's Beauty. **Sibylla Palmifera**, the palm-bearing
Sibyl. This sonnet and the next were originally written for
paintings. *Sec. 78. Body's Beauty.* **1. Lilith.** See note on
Browning's "Adam, Lilith, and Eve," page 602.

With the dead boughs that winter still must bind,
nd whom to-day the Spring no more concerns.

ehold, this crocus is a withering flame;
 This snowdrop, snow; this apple-blossom's part 10
To breed the fruit that breeds the serpent's art.
ay, for these Spring-flowers, turn thy face from
  them,
or gaze till on the year's last lily-stem
 The white cup shrivels round the golden heart.

101. THE ONE HOPE

When vain desire at last and vain regret
 Go hand in hand to death, and all is vain,
 What shall assuage the unforgotten pain
nd teach the unforgetful to forget?
hall Peace be still a sunk stream long unmet,—
 Or may the soul at once in a green plain
 Stoop through the spray of some sweet life-
  fountain
nd cull the dew-drenched flowering amulet?

h! when the wan soul in that golden air
 Between the scriptured petals softly blown   10
 Peers breathless for the gift of grace unknown,—
h! let none other written spell soe'er
 But only the one Hope's one name be there,—
 Not less nor more, but even that word alone.

ALAS, SO LONG!

Ah! dear one, we were young so long,
 It seemed that youth would never go,
For skies and trees were ever in song
 And water in singing flow
In the days we never again shall know.
   Alas, so long!
 Ah! then was it all Spring weather?
 Nay, but we were young and together.

Ah! dear one, I've been old so long,
 It seems that age is loath to part,   10
Though days and years have never a song,
 And oh! have they still the art
That warmed the pulses of heart to heart?
   Alas, so long!
 Ah, then was it all Spring weather?
 Nay, but we were young and together.

Ah, dear one, you've been dead so long,—
 How long until we meet again,

Sec. 83. Barren Spring. **11. To breed . . . art,** a reference
to the Hebrew story of the fall of man in Genesis 3.

Where hours may never lose their song
 Nor flowers forget the rain   20
In glad moonlight that never shall wane?
   Alas, so long!
 Ah! shall it be then Spring weather,
 And ah! shall we be young together?

THE KING'S TRAGEDY

James I of Scots.—20th February, 1437

This remarkable ballad was Rossetti's last great
achievement; he himself said that it was as if his own life
ebbed out with it.

King James I of Scotland (1394–1437) was one of the
ablest and most attractive of the Stuart kings. As a young
prince he was captured at sea by the English and imprisoned for nearly twenty years. When he was released in
1424, he married the daughter of the Earl of Somerset,
Joan Beaufort, whom he is said to have fallen in love with
when he saw her through the windows at Windsor
Castle, thus duplicating the experience of Palamon and
Arcite with Emelye in "The Knight's Tale." James and
his bride were crowned king and queen of Scotland at
Scone, May 21, 1424. The royal poet told the story of
his romance in *The King's Quair* [book], written in the
seven-line stanza which his master, Chaucer, had already
used in *Troilus and Criseyde*, but which has always since
been known as rime royal. King James I met his death in
the manner Rossetti has described. Evan John's *Crippled
Splendour* (Dutton, 1938) is an exciting historical novel
about him.

Like the other characters, the narrator of "The King's
Tragedy" is historical. The Barlas family still carries a
broken arm on its crest.

I Catherine am a Douglas born,
 A name to all Scots dear;
And Kate Barlass they've called me now
 Through many a waning year.

This old arm's withered now. 'Twas once
 Most deft 'mong maidens all
To rein the steed, to wing the shaft,
 To smite the palm-play ball.

In hall adown the close-linked dance
 It has shone most white and fair;   10
It has been the rest for a true lord's head,
And many a sweet babe's nursing-bed,
 And the bar to a King's chambère.

Aye, lasses, draw round Kate Barlass,
 And hark with bated breath

8. palm-play ball, a game resembling tennis in which the
ball is struck with the palm of the hand.

How good King James, King Robert's son,
  Was foully done to death.

Through all the days of his gallant youth
  The princely James was pent,
By his friends at first and then by his foes,   20
  In long imprisonment.

For the elder Prince, the kingdom's heir,
  By treason's murderous brood
Was slain; and the father quaked for the child
  With the royal mortal blood.

I' the Bass Rock fort, by his father's care,
  Was his childhood's life assured;
And Henry the subtle Bolingbroke,
Proud England's King, 'neath the southron yoke
  His youth for long years immured.   30

Yet in all things meet for a kingly man
  Himself did he approve;
And the nightingale through his prison-wall
  Taught him both lore and love.

For once, when the bird's song drew him close
  To the opened window-pane,
In her bowers beneath a lady stood,
A light of life to his sorrowful mood,
  Like a lily amid the rain.

And for her sake, to the sweet bird's note,   40
  He framed a sweeter Song,
More sweet than ever a poet's heart
  Gave yet to the English tongue.

She was a lady of royal blood;
  And when, past sorrow and teen,
He stood where still through his crownless years
  His Scotish realm had been,
At Scone were the happy lovers crowned,
  A heart-wed King and Queen.

But the bird may fall from the bough of youth,   50
  And song be turned to moan,
And Love's storm-cloud be the shadow of Hate,
When the tempest-waves of a troubled State
  Are beating against a throne.

Yet well they loved; and the god of Love,
  Whom well the King had sung,

Might find on the earth no truer hearts
  His lowliest swains among.

From the days when first she rode abroad
  With Scotish maids in her train,   6
I Catherine Douglas won the trust
  Of my mistress sweet Queen Jane.

And oft she sighed, "To be born a King!"
  And oft along the way
When she saw the homely lovers pass
  She has said, "Alack the day!"

Years waned,—the loving and toiling years:
  Till England's wrong renewed
Drove James, by outrage cast on his crown,
  To the open field of feud.   7

'Twas when the King and his host were met
  At the leaguer of Roxbro' hold,
The Queen o' the sudden sought his camp
  With a tale of dread to be told.

And she showed him a secret letter writ
  That spoke of treasonous strife,
And how a band of his noblest lords
  Were sworn to take his life.

"And it may be here or it may be there,
  In the camp or the court," she said;   8
"But for my sake come to your people's arms
  And guard your royal head."

Quoth he, "'Tis the fifteenth day of the siege,
  And the castle's nigh to yield."
"O face your foes on your throne," she cried,
  "And show the power you wield;
And under your Scotish people's love
  You shall sit as under your shield."

At the fair Queen's side I stood that day
  When he bade them raise the siege,   90
And back to his Court he sped to know
  How the lords would meet their Liege.

But when he summoned his Parliament,
  The louring brows hung round,
Like clouds that circle the mountain-head
  Ere the first low thunders sound.

16. King Robert, Robert III (1390–1424). **26. Bass Rock,** an island in the Firth of Forth. **28. Henry,** King Henry IV of England (1399–1413).

62. Jane, the Scotch equivalent of Joan. **65. homely,** humble. **68–70. Till England's wrong . . . feud.** English border raids and an attempt to capture James's daughter led the Scottish king to attack Roxburgh Castle in 1436.

For he had tamed the nobles' lust
   And curbed their power and pride,
And reached out an arm to right the poor
   Through Scotland far and wide;   100
And many a lordly wrong-doer
   By the headsman's axe had died.

'Twas then upspoke Sir Robert Graeme,
   The bold o'ermastering man:—
"O King, in the name of your Three Estates
   I set you under their ban!

"For, as your lords made oath to you
   Of service and fealty,
Even in likewise you pledged your oath
   Their faithful sire to be:—   110

"Yet all we here that are nobly sprung
   Have mourned dear kith and kin
Since first for the Scottish Barons' curse
   Did your bloody rule begin."

With that he laid his hands on his King—
   "Is this not so, my lords?"
But of all who had sworn to league with him
   Not one spake back to his words.

Quoth the King:—"Thou speak'st but for one
   Estate,
   Nor doth it avow thy gage.   120
Let my liege lords hale this traitor hence!"
   The Graeme fired dark with rage:—
"Who works for lesser men than himself,
   He earns but a witless wage!"

But soon from the dungeon where he lay
   He won by privy plots,
And forth he fled with a price on his head
   To the country of the Wild Scots.

And word there came from Sir Robert Graeme
   To the King at Edinbro':—   130
"No Liege of mine thou art; but I see
From this day forth alone in thee
   God's creature, my mortal foe.

"Through thee are my wife and children lost,
   My heritage and lands;
And when my God shall show me a way,
Thyself my mortal foe will I slay
   With these my proper hands."

105. **Three Estates,** the nobility, the clergy, the common
people.   **128. country of the Wild Scots,** the Highlands.

Against the coming of Christmastide
   That year the King bade call   140
I' the Black Friars' Charterhouse of Perth
   A solemn festival.

And we of his household rode with him
   In a close-ranked company;
But not till the sun had sunk from his throne
   Did we reach the Scotish Sea.

That eve was clenched for a boding storm,
   'Neath a toilsome moon half seen;
The cloud stooped low and the surf rose high;
And where there was a line of the sky,   150
   Wild wings loomed dark between.

And on a rock of the black beach-side
   By the veiled moon dimly lit,
There was something seemed to heave with life
   As the King drew nigh to it.

And was it only the tossing furze
   Or brake of the waste sea-wold?
Or was it an eagle bent to the blast?
When near we came, we knew it at last
   For a woman tattered and old.   160

But it seemed as though by a fire within
   Her writhen limbs were wrung;
And as soon as the King was close to her,
   She stood up gaunt and strong.

'Twas then the moon sailed clear of the rack
   On high in her hollow dome;
And still as aloft with hoary crest
   Each clamorous wave rang home,
Like fire in snow the moonlight blazed
   Amid the champing foam.   170

And the woman held his eyes with her eyes:—
   "O King, thou art come at last;
But thy wraith has haunted the Scotish Sea
   To my sight for four years past.

"Four years it is since first I met,
   'Twixt the Duchray and the Dhu,
A shape whose feet clung close in a shroud,
   And that shape for thine I knew.

"A year again, and on Inchkeith Isle
   I saw thee pass in the breeze,   180
141. Black Friars' Charterhouse, a monastery. **Perth,** a
city in Perthshire.   **176. Duchray,** a stream in Dumbarton.
Dhu, a lake in Aberdeen.   **179. Inchkeith Isle,** in the
Firth of Forth.

With the cerecloth risen above thy feet
  And wound about thy knees.

"And yet a year, in the Links of Forth,
  As a wanderer without rest,
Thou cam'st with both thine arms i' the shroud
  That clung high up thy breast.

"And in this hour I find thee here,
  And well mine eyes may note
That the winding-sheet hath passed thy breast
  And risen around thy throat.   190

"And when I meet thee again, O King,
  That of death hast such sore drouth,—
Except thou turn again on this shore,—
The winding-sheet shall have moved once more
  And covered thine eyes and mouth.

"O King, whom poor men bless for their King,
  Of thy fate be not so fain;
But these my words for God's message take,
And turn thy steed, O King, for her sake
  Who rides beside thy rein!"   200

While the woman spoke, the King's horse reared
  As if it would breast the sea,
And the Queen turned pale as she heard on the gale
  The voice die dolorously.

When the woman ceased, the steed was still,
  But the King gazed on her yet,
And in silence save for the wail of the sea
  His eyes and her eyes met.

At last he said, "God's ways are His own;
  Man is but shadow and dust.   210
Last night I prayed by His altar-stone;
Tonight I wend to the Feast of His Son;
  And in Him I set my trust.

"I have held my people in sacred charge,
  And have not feared the sting
Of proud men's hate,—to His will resigned
Who has but one same death for a hind
  And one same death for a King.

"And if God in His wisdom have brought close
  The day when I must die,   220
That day by water or fire or air
My feet shall fall in the destined snare
  Wherever my road may lie.

   192. That of death . . . drouth, since he is now going to
meet death.

"What man can say but the Fiend hath set
  Thy sorcery on my path,
My heart with the fear of death to fill,
And turn me against God's very will
  To sink in His burning wrath?"

The woman stood as the train rode past,
  And moved nor limb nor eye;   230
And when we were shipped, we saw her there
  Still standing against the sky.

As the ship made way, the moon once more
  Sank slow in her rising pall;
And I thought of the shrouded wraith of the King,
  And I said, "The Heavens know all."

And now, ye lasses, must ye hear
  How my name is Kate Barlass—
But a little thing, when all the tale
  Is told of the weary mass   240
Of crime and woe which in Scotland's realm
  God's will let come to pass.

'Twas in the Charterhouse of Perth
  That the King and all his Court
Were met, the Christmas Feast being done,
  For solace and disport.

'Twas a wind-wild eve in February,
  And against the casement-pane
The branches smote like summoning hands,
  And muttered the driving rain.   250

And when the wind swooped over the lift
  And made the whole heaven frown,
It seemed a grip was laid on the walls
  To tug the housetop down.

And the Queen was there, more stately fair
  Than a lily in garden set;
And the King was loath to stir from her side,
For as on the day when she was his bride,
  Even so he loved her yet.

And the Earl of Athole, the King's false friend, 26c
  Sat with him at the board;
And Robert Stuart the chamberlain
  Who had sold his sovereign Lord.

Yet the traitor Christopher Chaumber there
  Would fain have told him all,
And vainly four times that night he strove
  To reach the King through the hall.

But the wine is bright at the goblet's brim
  Though the poison lurk beneath;
And the apples still are red on the tree   270
Within whose shade may the adder be
  That shall turn thy life to death.

There was a knight of the King's fast friends
  Whom he called the King of Love;
And to such bright cheer and courtesy
  That name might best behove.

And the King and Queen both loved him well
  For his gentle knightliness;
And with him the King, as that eve wore on,
  Was playing at the chess.   280

And the King said (for he thought to jest
  And soothe the Queen thereby;)—
"In a book 'tis writ that this same year
  A King shall in Scotland die.

"And I have pondered the matter o'er,
  And this have I found, Sir Hugh,—
There are but two Kings on Scotish ground,
  And those Kings are I and you.

"And I have a wife and a newborn heir,
  And you are yourself alone;   290
So stand you stark at my side with me
  To guard our double throne.

"For here sit I and my wife and child,
  As well your heart shall approve,
In full surrender and soothfastness,
  Beneath your Kingdom of Love."

And the Knight laughed, and the Queen too smiled;
  But I knew her heavy thought,
And I strove to find in the good King's jest
  What cheer might thence be wrought.   300

And I said, "My Liege, for the Queen's dear love
  Now sing the song that of old
You made, when a captive Prince you lay,
And the nightingale sang sweet on the spray,
  In Windsor's castle-hold."

Then he smiled the smile I knew so well
  When he thought to please the Queen;
The smile which under all bitter frowns
  Of hate that rose between,
Forever dwelt at the poet's heart   310
  Like the bird of love unseen.

And he kissed her hand and took his harp,
  And the music sweetly rang;
And when the song burst forth, it seemed
  'Twas the nightingale that sang.

"*Worship, ye lovers, on this May:*
  Of bliss your kalends are begun.
Sing with us, Away, Winter, away!
  Come, Summer, the sweet season and sun!
  Awake for shame,—your heaven is won,—   320
And amorously your heads lift all:
Thank Love, that you to his grace doth call!"

But when he bent to the Queen, and sang
  The speech whose praise was hers,
It seemed his voice was the voice of the Spring
  And the voice of the bygone years.

"*The fairest and the freshest flower*
That ever I saw before that hour,
The which o' the sudden made to start
The blood of my body to my heart.   330

* * *

Ah sweet, are ye a worldly creature
Or heavenly thing in form of nature?"

And the song was long, and richly stored
  With wonder and beauteous things;
And the harp was tuned to every change
  Of minstrel ministerings;
But when he spoke of the Queen at the last,
  Its strings were his own heart-strings.

"*Unworthy but only of her grace,*
  Upon Love's rock that's easy and sure,   340
In guerdon of all my love's space
  She took me her humble creäture.
  Thus fell my blissful aventure
In youth of love that from day to day
Flowereth aye new, and further I say.

"*To reckon all the circumstance*
  As happed when lessen gan my sore,
Of my rancour and woeful chance,
  It were too long,—I have done therefor.
  And of this flower I say no more,   350
But unto my help her heart hath tended
And even from death her man defended."

316 ff. "Worship, ye lovers . . . Rossetti apologized for
the necessity of reducing his quotations from *The King's
Quair* from ten- to eight-syllabled lines "in order that they
might harmonize with the ballad meter." **kalends,** the first
day of the Roman month. **343. aventure,** fortune or chance.

"Aye, even from death," to myself I said;
　　For I thought of the day when she
Had borne him the news, at Roxbro' siege,
　　Of the fell confederacy.

But Death even then took aim as he sang
　　With an arrow deadly bright;
And the grinning skull lurked grimly aloof,
And the wings were spread far over the roof　　360
　　More dark than the winter night.

Yet truly along the amorous song
　　Of Love's high pomp and state,
There were words of Fortune's trackless doom
　　And the dreadful face of Fate.

And oft have I heard again in dreams
　　The voice of dire appeal
In which the King then sang of the pit
　　That is under Fortune's wheel.

"*And under the wheel beheld I there*　　370
　　An ugly Pit as deep as hell,
That to behold I quaked for fear.
　　And this I heard, that who therein fell
　　Came no more up, tidings to tell:
Whereat, astound of the fearful sight,
I wist not what to do for fright,"

And oft has my thought called up again
　　These words of the changeful song:
"*Wist thou thy pain and thy travail*
To come, well might'st thou weep and wail!"　　380
　　And our wail, O God! is long.

But the song's end was all of his love;
　　And well his heart was graced
With her smiling lips and her tear-bright eyes
　　As his arm went round her waist.

And on the swell of her long fair throat
　　Close clung the necklet-chain
As he bent her pearl-tired head aside,
And in the warmth of his love and pride
　　He kissed her lips full fain.　　390

And her true face was a rosy red,
　　The very red of the rose
That, couched on the happy garden-bed,
　　In the summer sunlight glows.

And all the wondrous things of love
　　That sang so sweet through the song
388. tired, bedecked.

Were in the look that met in their eyes,
　　And the look was deep and long.

'Twas then a knock came at the outer gate,
　　And the usher sought the King.　　400
"The woman you met by the Scotish Sea,
　　My Liege, would tell you a thing;
And she says that her present need for speech
　　Will bear no gainsaying."

And the King said: "The hour is late;
　　To-morrow will serve, I ween."
Then he charged the usher strictly, and said:
　　"No word of this to the Queen."

But the usher came again to the King.
　　"Shall I call her back?" quoth he;　　410
"For as she went on her way, she cried,
　　'Woe! Woe! then the thing must be!'"

And the King paused, but he did not speak.
　　Then he called for the Voidee-cup:
And as we heard the twelfth hour strike,
There by true lips and false lips alike
　　Was the draft of trust drained up.

So with reverence meet to King and Queen,
　　To bed went all from the board;
And the last to leave of the courtly train　　420
Was Robert Stuart the chamberlain
　　Who had sold his sovereign lord.

And all the locks of the chamber door
　　Had the traitor riven and brast;
And that Fate might win sure way from afar
He had drawn out every bolt and bar
　　That made the entrance fast.

And now at midnight he stole his way
　　To the moat of the outer wall,
And laid strong hurdles closely across　　430
　　Where the traitors' tread should fall.

But we that were the Queen's bower-maids
　　Alone were left behind;
And with heed we drew the curtains close
　　Against the winter wind.

And now that all was still through the hall,
　　More clearly we heard the rain
That clamoured ever against the glass
　　And the boughs that beat on the pane.

414. Voidee-cup, a drink of spiced wine, served before
bedtime.　　**424. brast,** broken (Scotch).

But the fire was bright in the ingle-nook,   440
  And through empty space around
The shadows cast on the arrased wall
'Mid the pictured kings stood sudden and tall
  Like spectres sprung from the ground.

And the bed was dight in a deep alcove;
  And as he stood by the fire
The King was still in talk with the Queen
  While he doffed his goodly attire.

And the song had brought the image back
  Of many a bygone year;   450
And many a loving word they said
With hand in hand and head laid to head;
  And none of us went anear.

But Love was weeping outside the house,
  A child in the piteous rain;
And as he watched the arrow of Death,
He wailed for his own shafts close in the sheath
  That never should fly again.

And now beneath the window arose
  A wild voice suddenly: 460
And the King reared straight, but the Queen fell
    back
  As for bitter dule to dree;
And all of us knew the woman's voice
  Who spoke by the Scotish Sea.

"O King," she cried, "in an evil hour
  They drove me from thy gate;
And yet my voice must rise to thine ears;
  But alas! it comes too late!

"Last night at mid-watch, by Aberdour,
  When the moon was dead in the skies,   470
O King, in a death-light of thine own
  I saw thy shape arise.

"And in full season, as erst I said,
  The doom had gained its growth;
And the shroud had risen above thy neck
  And covered thine eyes and mouth.

"And no moon woke, but the pale dawn broke,
  And still thy soul stood there;
And I thought its silence cried to my soul
  As the first rays crowned its hair.   480

445. **dight,** prepared.   462. **dule to dree,** sorrow to
suffer (Scotch).   469. **Aberdour,** a town on the north
shore of the Firth of Forth.

"Since then have I journeyed fast and fain
  In very despite of Fate,
Lest Hope might still be found in God's will;
  But they drove me from thy gate.

"For every man on God's ground, O King,
  His death grows up from his birth
In a shadow-plant perpetually;
And thine towers high, a black yew-tree,
  O'er the Charterhouse of Perth!"

That room was built far out from the house;   490
  And none but we in the room
Might hear the voice that rose beneath,
  Nor the tread of the coming doom.

For now there came a torchlight-glare,
  And a clang of arms there came;
And not a soul in that space but thought
  Of the foe Sir Robert Graeme.

Yea, from the country of the wild Scots,
  O'er mountain, valley, and glen,
He had brought with him in murderous league   500
  Three hundred armèd men.

The King knew all in an instant's flash,
  And like a King did he stand;
But there was no armour in all the room,
  Nor weapon lay to his hand.

And all we women flew to the door
  And thought to have made it fast;
But the bolts were gone and the bars were gone
  And the locks were riven and brast.

And he caught the pale pale Queen in his arms
  As the iron footsteps fell,—   511
Then loosed her, standing alone, and said,
  "Our bliss was our farewell!"

And 'twixt his lips he murmured a prayer,
  And he crossed his brow and breast;
And proudly in royal hardihood
Even so with folded arms he stood,—
  The prize of the bloody quest.

Then on me leaped the Queen like a deer:—
  "O Catherine, help!" she cried.   520
And low at his feet we clasped his knees
  Together side by side.
"Oh! even a King, for his people's sake,
  From treasonous death must hide!"

"For *her* sake most!" I cried, and I marked
   The pang that my words could wring.
And the iron tongs from the chimmey-nook
   I snatched and held to the King—
"Wrench up the plank! and the vault beneath
   Shall yield safe harbouring." 530

With brows low-bent, from my eager hand
   The heavy heft did he take;
And the plank at his feet he wrenched and tore;
And as he frowned through the open floor,
   Again I said, "For her sake!"

Then he cried to the Queen, "God's will be done!"
   For her hands were clasped in prayer.
And down he sprang to the inner crypt;
And straight we closed the plank he had ripped
   And toiled to smooth it fair. 540

(Alas! in that vault a gap once was
   Wherethrough the King might have fled;
But three days since close-walled had it been
By his will; for the ball would roll therein
   When without at the palm he played.)

Then the Queen cried, "Catherine, keep the door,
   And I to this will suffice!"
At her word I rose all dazed to my feet,
   And my heart was fire and ice.

And louder ever the voices grew, 550
   And the tramp of men in mail;
Until to my brain it seemed to be
As though I tossed on a ship at sea
   In the teeth of a crashing gale.

Then back I flew to the rest; and hard
   We strove with sinews knit
To force the table against the door;
   But we might not compass it.

Then my wild gaze sped far down the hall
   To the place of the hearthstone-sill; 560
And the Queen bent ever above the floor,
   For the plank was rising still.

And now the rush was heard on the stair,
   And "God, what help?" was our cry.
And was I frenzied or was I bold?
I looked at each empty stanchion-hold,
   And no bar but my arm had I!

Like iron felt my arm, as through
   The staple I made it pass—

Alack! it was flesh and bone—no more! 570
'Twas Catherine Douglas sprang to the door,
   But I fell back Kate Barlass.

With that they all thronged into the hall,
   Half dim to my failing ken;
And the space that was but a void before
   Was a crowd of wrathful men.

Behind the door I had fall'n and lay,
   Yet my sense was wildly aware,
And for all the pain of my shattered arm
   I never fainted there. 580

Even as I fell, my eyes were cast
   Where the King leaped down to the pit;
And lo! the plank was smooth in its place,
   And the Queen stood far from it.

And under the litters and through the bed
   And within the presses all
The traitors sought for the King, and pierced
   The arras around the wall.

And through the chamber they ramped and stormed
   Like lions loose in the lair, 590
And scarce could trust to their very eyes—
   For behold! no King was there.

Then one of them seized the Queen, and cried,
   "Now tell us, where is thy lord?"
And he held the sharp point over her heart.
She drooped not her eyes nor did she start,
   But she answered never a word.

Then the sword half pierced the true true breast;
   But it was the Graeme's own son
Cried, "This is a woman,—we seek a man!" 600
   And away from her girdle zone
He struck the point of the murderous steel;
   And that foul deed was not done.

And forth flowed all the throng like a sea,
   And 'twas empty space once more;
And my eyes sought out the wounded Queen
   As I lay behind the door.

And I said, "Dear Lady, leave me here,
   For I cannot help you now;
But fly while you may, and none shall reck 610
   Of my place here lying low."

And she said, "My Catherine, God help thee!"
   Then she looked to the distant floor,

And clasping her hands, "O God help *him*,"
She sobbed, "for we can no more!"

But God He knows what help may mean,
If it mean to live or to die;
And what sore sorrow and mighty moan
On earth it may cost ere yet a throne
Be filled in His house on high.   620

And now the ladies fled with the Queen;
And through the open door
The night-wind wailed round the empty room
And the rushes shook on the floor.

And the bed drooped low in the dark recess
Whence the arras was rent away;
And the firelight still shone over the space
Where our hidden secret lay.

And the rain had ceased, and the moonbeams lit
The window high in the wall,—   630
Bright beams that on the plank that I knew
Through the painted pane did fall
And gleamed with the splendour of Scotland's crown
And shield armorial.

But then a great wind swept up the skies,
And the climbing moon fell back;
And the royal blazon fled from the floor,
And naught remained on its track;
And high in the darkened window-pane
The shield and the crown were black.   640

And what I say next I partly saw
And partly I heard in sooth,
And partly since from the murderers' lips
The torture wrung the truth.

For now again came the armèd tread,
And fast through the hall it fell;
But the throng was less; and ere I saw,
By the voice without I could tell
That Robert Stuart had come with them
Who knew that chamber well.   650

And over the space the Graeme strode dark
With his mantle round him flung;
And in his eye was a flaming light
But not a word on his tongue.

And Stuart held a torch to the floor,
And he found the thing he sought;
And they slashed the plank away with their swords;
And O God! I fainted not!

And the traitor held his torch in the gap,
All smoking and smouldering;   660
And through the vapour and fire, beneath
In the dark crypt's narrow ring,
With a shout that pealed to the room's high roof
They saw their naked King.

Half naked he stood, but stood as one
Who yet could do and dare;
With the crown, the King was stript away,—
The Knight was reft of his battle-array,—
But still the Man was there.

From the rout then stepped a villain forth:—   670
Sir John Hall was his name;
With a knife unsheathed he leapt to the vault
Beneath the torchlight-flame.

Of his person and stature was the King
A man right manly strong,
And mightily by the shoulder-blades
His foe to his feet he flung.

Then the traitor's brother, Sir Thomas Hall,
Sprang down to work his worst;
And the King caught the second man by the neck
And flung him above the first.   681

And he smote and trampled them under him;
And a long month thence they bare
All black their throats with the grip of his hands
When the hangman's hand came there.

And sore he strove to have had their knives,
But the sharp blades gashed his hands.
Oh, James! so armed, thou hadst battled there
Till help had come of thy bands;
And oh! once more thou hadst held our throne   690
And ruled thy Scotish lands!

But while the King o'er his foes still raged
With a heart that nought could tame,
Another man sprang down to the crypt;
And with his sword in his hand hard-gripped,
There stood Sir Robert Graeme.

(Now shame on the recreant traitor's heart
Who durst not face his King
Till the body unarmed was wearied out
With two-fold combating!   700

Ah! well might the people sing and say,
As oft ye have heard aright:—
664. naked, unarmed.

"*O Robert Graeme, O Robert Graeme,*
Who slew our King, God give thee shame!"
        For he slew him not as a knight.)

And the naked King turned round at bay,
        But his strength had passed the goal,
And he could but gasp:—"Mine hour is come;
But oh! to succour thine own soul's doom,
        Let a priest now shrive my soul!"   710

And the traitor looked on the King's spent strength,
        And said:—"Have I kept my word?—
Yea, King, the mortal pledge that I gave?
No black friar's shrift thy soul shall save,
        But the shrift of this red sword!"

With that he smote his King through the breast;
        And all they three in the pen
Fell on him and stabbed and stabbed him there
        Like merciless murderous men.

Yet seemed it now that Sir Robert Graeme,   720
        Ere the King's last breath was o'er,
Turned sick at heart with the deadly sight
        And would have done no more.

But a cry came from the troop above:
        "If him thou do not slay,
The price of his life that thou dost spare
        Thy forfeit life shall pay!"

O God! what more did I hear or see,
        Or how should I tell the rest?
But there at length our King lay slain   730
        With sixteen wounds in his breast.

O God! and now did a bell boom forth,
        And the murderers turned and fled;—
Too late, too late, O God, did it sound!—
And I heard the true men mustering round,
        And the cries and the coming read.

But ere they came, to the black death-gap
        Somewise did I creep and steal;
And lo! or ever I swooned away,
Through the dusk I saw where the white face lay
        In the Pit of Fortune's Wheel.   741

And now, ye Scotish maids who have heard
        Dread things of the days grown old,—
Even at the last, of true Queen Jane
        May somewhat yet be told,
And how she dealt for her dear lord's sake
        Dire vengeance manifold.

'Twas in the Charterhouse of Perth,
        In the fair-lit Death-chapelle,
That the slain King's corpse on bier was laid   750
        With chaunt and requiem-knell.

And all with royal wealth of balm
        Was the body purified;
And none could trace on the brow and lips
        The death that he had died.

In his robes of state he lay asleep
        With orb and sceptre in hand;
And by the crown he wore on his throne
        Was his kingly forehead spanned.

And, girls, 'twas a sweet sad thing to see   760
        How the curling golden hair,
As in the day of the poet's youth,
        From the King's crown clustered there.

And if all had come to pass in the brain
        That throbbed beneath those curls,
Then Scots had said in the days to come
That this their soil was a different home
        And a different Scotland, girls!

And the Queen sat by him night and day,
        And oft she knelt in prayer,   770
All wan and pale in the widow's veil
        That shrouded her shining hair.

And I had got good help of my hurt.
        And only to me some sign
She made; and save the priests that were there
        No face would she see but mine.

And the month of March wore on apace;
        And now fresh couriers fared
Still from the country of the Wild Scots
        With news of the traitors snared.   780

And still as I told her day by day,
        Her pallor changed to sight,
And the frost grew to a furnace-flame
        That burnt her visage white.

And evermore as I brought her word,
        She bent to her dead King James,
And in the cold ear with fire-drawn breath
        She spoke the traitors' names.

But when the name of Sir Robert Graeme
        Was the one she had to give,   790
I ran to hold her up from the floor;

For the froth was on her lips, and sore
  I feared that she could not live.

And the month of March wore nigh to its end,
  And still was the death-pall spread;
For she would not bury her slaughtered lord
  Till his slayers all were dead.

And now of their dooms dread tidings came,
  And of torments fierce and dire;
And naught she spake,—she had ceased to speak,—
  But her eyes were a soul on fire.   801

But when I told her the bitter end
  Of the stern and just award,
She leaned o'er the bier, and thrice three times
  She kissed the lips of her lord.

And then she said, "My King, they are dead!"
  And she knelt on the chapel-floor,
And whispered low with a strange proud smile,—
  "James, James, they suffered more!"

Last she stood up to her queenly height,   810
  But she shook like an autumn leaf,
As though the fire wherein she burned
Then left her body, and all were turned
  To winter of life-long grief.

And "O James!" she said—"My James!" she said,—
  "Alas for the woful thing,
That a poet true and a friend of man,
In desperate days of bale and ban,
  Should needs be born a King!"

Christina Rossetti
1830–1894

Christina Georgina, the youngest of the four Rossetti children, was born in London on December 5, 1830. She was closely involved in the beginnings of Pre-Raphaelitism—served as a model for her brother's pictures and tried her own hand at drawing. But while she shared Dante Gabriel's marvelous sensitiveness to the sights and sounds of the sensual world, this side of her nature was balanced (or overbalanced) by a spirit of intense devoutness in harmony with the tenets and standards of that part of the Church of England which had been regenerated by the Oxford Movement. "I cannot possibly use the word happy without meaning something beyond this present life," she wrote. No Freudian is needed to discern a conflict between her intensely feminine preoccupation with loving and being loved and her tendency toward asceticism; her passionate Italian nature responded to the lure of the flesh only to crucify it. James Collinson, her first sweetheart, she dismissed because he was a Roman Catholic; Charles Cayley, her second, whom she loved as long as life remained in her, she refused on account of the uncertainty of his religious views. There was physical, as well as mental, suffering in her life, for she was cursed both with Graves' disease and with cancer, but in spite of all her melancholy and all her trials, in spite, also, of what, even in her day, were coming to be regarded as very narrow views, she never lost her gift for charming nonsense. The austerities of her faith she kept for herself; it flowed out toward others in Christian love and an unceasing, unpretentious search for ways of doing good. She died December 29, 1894.

Christina Rossetti's first book was published when she was only seventeen years old. In 1861 she contributed some poems to *Macmillan's Magazine;* the next year, *Goblin Market and Other Poems* became the first literary success of the Pre-Raphaelite Movement. This was followed by *The Prince's Progress*, 1866, *Sing-Song*, 1872, and other volumes, all of which have now been collected in her *Poetical Works*, edited by W. M. Rossetti (Macmillan, 1924). She also wrote short stories, tracts, and books for children.

Her poems, unpretentious like herself, are more highly regarded today than they have ever been. "She accepted the conditions which are at the very root of mortal and earthly life," says Walter De La Mare; "and in that acceptance triumphed." But their quality is easier to feel than to define. Most of her critics agree despairingly with the late Sir Walter Raleigh that "you cannot lecture on really pure poetry any more than you can talk about the ingredients of pure water—it is adulterated, methylated, sanded poetry that makes the best lectures. . . . The only thing that Christina makes me want to do is cry, not lecture."

GOBLIN MARKET[1]

J. A. Noble interpreted "Goblin Market" as "a little spiritual drama of love's vicarious redemption, in which the child redeemer goes into the wilderness to be tempted of the devil, that by her painful conquest she may succor and save the sister who has been vanquished and all but slain." The author herself denied any allegorical intent. But it is also true that her original title was "A Peep at the Goblins—To M. F. R." (her sister, Maria Francesca Rossetti), and this can hardly be entirely without significance. It is not necessary—it may not even be possible—to make a consistent allegory out of the poem, but neither can one fail to discern moral and religious overtones in the fairy-tale situation, nor believe that such a devout mind as Christina's would be quite unaware of them.

In the story itself the central idea is that the goblins never appear to give the second healing taste to one who has partaken of their wares. Forbidden fruit has been used to symbolize transgression at least as far back as the Eden story, and there are other points of similarity to many old tales. Christina Rossetti shared a passion for animals with her brother, Dante Gabriel, who gave the poem its final title, and who furnished two illustrations for the first edition.

Morning and evening
Maids heard the goblins cry:
"Come buy our orchard fruits,
Come buy, come buy:
Apples and quinces,
Lemons and oranges,
Plump unpecked cherries,
Melons and raspberries,
Bloom-down-cheeked peaches,
Swart-headed mulberries,   10
Wild free-born cranberries,
Crab-apples, dewberries,
Pine-apples, blackberries,
Apricots, strawberries;—
All ripe together
In summer weather,—
Morns that pass by,
Fair eves that fly;
Come buy, come buy:
Our grapes fresh from the vine,   20
Pomegranates full and fine,
Dates and sharp bullaces,
Rare pears and greengages,
Damsons and bilberries,
Taste them and try:
Currants and gooseberries,
Bright-fire-like barberries,

Figs to fill your mouth,
Citrons from the South,
Sweet to tongue and sound to eye;   30
Come buy, come buy."

Evening by evening
Among the brookside rushes,
Laura bowed her head to hear,
Lizzie veiled her blushes:
Crouching close together
In the cooling weather,
With clasping arms and cautioning lips,
With tingling cheeks and finger tips.
"Lie close," Laura said,   40
Pricking up her golden head:
"We must not look at goblin men,
We must not buy their fruits:
Who knows upon what soil they fed
Their hungry thirsty roots?"
"Come buy," call the goblins
Hobbling down the glen.
"O," cried Lizzie, "Laura, Laura,
You should not peep at goblin men."
Lizzie covered up her eyes,   50
Covered close lest they should look;
Laura reared her glossy head,
And whispered like the restless brook:
"Look, Lizzie, look, Lizzie,
Down the glen tramp little men.
One hauls a basket,
One bears a plate,
One lugs a golden dish
Of many pounds' weight.
How fair the vine must grow   60
Whose grapes are so luscious;
How warm the wind must blow
Through those fruit bushes."
"No," said Lizzie: "No, no, no;
Their offers should not charm us,
Their evil gifts would harm us."
She thrust a dimpled finger
In each ear, shut eyes and ran:
Curious Laura chose to linger
Wondering at each merchant man.   70
One had a cat's face,
One whisked a tail,
One tramped at a rat's pace,
One crawled like a snail,
One like a wombat prowled obtuse and furry,
One like a ratel tumbled hurry-skurry.
She heard a voice like voice of doves
Cooing all together:
They sounded kind and full of loves
In the pleasant weather.   80

[1] This and the other poems by Christinia Rossetti are from the *Poetical Works*, published by The Macmillan Company and used by permission.   **22. bullaces**, small plums.

Laura stretched her gleaming neck
Like a rush-imbedded swan,
Like a lily from the beck,
Like a moonlit poplar branch,
Like a vessel at the launch
When its last restraint is gone.

Backwards up the mossy glen
Turned and trooped the goblin men,
With their shrill repeated cry,
"Come buy, come buy."   90
When they reached where Laura was
They stood stock still upon the moss,
Leering at each other,
Brother with queer brother;
Signalling each other,
Brother with sly brother.
One set his basket down,
One reared his plate;
One began to weave a crown
Of tendrils, leaves, and rough nuts brown   100
(Men sell not such in any town);
One heaved the golden weight
Of dish and fruit to offer her:
"Come buy, come buy," was still their cry.
Laura stared but did not stir,
Longed but had no money.
The whisk-tailed merchant bade her taste
In tones as smooth as honey,
The cat-faced purred,
The rat-paced spoke a word   110
Of welcome, and the snail-paced even was heard;
One parrot-voiced and jolly
Cried "Pretty Goblin" still for "Pretty Polly";—
One whistled like a bird.

But sweet-tooth Laura spoke in haste:
"Good Folk, I have no coin;
To take were to purloin:
I have no copper in my purse,
I have no silver either,
And all my gold is on the furze   120
That shakes in windy weather
Above the rusty heather."
"You have much gold upon your head,"
They answered altogether:
"Buy from us with a golden curl."
She clipped a precious golden lock,
She dropped a tear more rare than pearl,
Then sucked their fruit globes fair or red.
Sweeter than honey from the rock,
Stronger than man-rejoicing wine,   130
Clearer than water flowed that juice;
She never tasted such before,

How should it cloy with length of use?
She sucked and sucked and sucked the more
Fruits which that unknown orchard bore;
She sucked until her lips were sore;
Then flung the emptied rinds away,
But gathered up one kernel stone,
And knew not was it night or day
As she turned home alone.   140

Lizzie met her at the gate
Full of wise upbraidings:
"Dear, you should not stay so late,
Twilight is not good for maidens;
Should not loiter in the glen
In the haunts of goblin men.
Do you not remember Jeanie,
How she met them in the moonlight,
Took their gifts both choice and many,
Ate their fruits and wore their flowers   150
Plucked from bowers
Where summer ripens at all hours?
But ever in the noonlight
She pined and pined away;
Sought them by night and day,
Found them no more, but dwindled and grew
    grey;
Then fell with the first snow,
While to this day no grass will grow
Where she lies low:
I planted daisies there a year ago   160
That never blow.
You should not loiter so."
"Nay, hush," said Laura:
"Nay, hush, my sister:
I ate and ate my fill,
Yet my mouth waters still;
To-morrow night I will
Buy more";—and kissed her.
"Have done with sorrow;
I'll bring you plums to-morrow   170
Fresh on their mother twigs,
Cherries worth getting;
You cannot think what figs
My teeth have met in,
What melons icy-cold
Piled on a dish of gold
Too huge for me to hold,
What peaches with a velvet nap,
Pellucid grapes without one seed:
Odorous indeed must be the mead   180
Whereon they grow, and pure the wave they
    drink
With lilies at the brink,
And sugar-sweet their sap."

Golden head by golden head,
Like two pigeons in one nest
Folded in each other's wings,
They lay down in their curtained bed:
Like two blossoms on one stem,
Like two flakes of new-fall'n snow,
Like two wands of ivory   190
Tipped with gold for awful kings.
Moon and stars gazed in at them,
Wind sang to them lullaby,
Lumbering owls forbore to fly,
Not a bat flapped to and fro
Round their nest:
Cheek to cheek and breast to breast
Locked together in one nest.

Early in the morning
When the first cock crowed his warning,   200
Neat like bees, as sweet and busy,
Laura rose with Lizzie:
Fetched in honey, milked the cows,
Aired and set to rights the house,
Kneaded cakes of whitest wheat,
Cakes for dainty mouths to eat,
Next churned butter, whipped up cream,
Fed their poultry, sat and sewed;
Talked as modest maidens should:
Lizzie with an open heart,   210
Laura in an absent dream,
One content, one sick in part;
One warbling for the mere bright day's delight,
One longing for the night.

At length slow evening came:
They went with pitchers to the reedy brook;
Lizzie most placid in her look,
Laura most like a leaping flame.
They drew the gurgling water from its deep.
Lizzie plucked purple and rich golden flags,   220
Then turning homeward said: "The sunset flushes
Those furthest loftiest crags;
Come, Laura, not another maiden lags,
No wilful squirrel wags,
The beasts and birds are fast asleep."
But Laura loitered still among the rushes,
And said the bank was steep.

And said the hour was early still,
The dew not fall'n, the wind not chill;
Listening ever, but not catching   230
The customary cry,
"Come buy, come buy,"
With its iterated jingle
Of sugar-baited words;

Not for all her watching
Once discerning even one goblin
Racing, whisking, tumbling, hobbling—
Let alone the herds
That used to tramp along the glen,
In groups or single,   240
Of brisk fruit-merchant men.

Till Lizzie urged: "O Laura, come;
I hear the fruit-call, but I dare not look:
You should not loiter longer at this brook:
Come with me home.
The stars rise, the moon bends her arc,
Each glow-worm winks her spark,
Let us get home before the night grows dark:
For clouds may gather
Though this is summer weather,   250
Put out the lights and drench us through;
Then if we lost our way what should we do?"

Laura turned cold as stone
To find her sister heard that cry alone,
That goblin cry,
"Come buy our fruits, come buy."
Must she then buy no more such dainty fruit?
Must she no more such succous pasture find,
Gone deaf and blind?
Her tree of life drooped from the root: 260
She said not one word in her heart's sore ache;
But peering through the dimness nought discerning,
Trudged home, her pitcher dripping all the way;
So crept to bed, and lay
Silent till Lizzie slept;
Then sat up in passionate yearning,
And gnashed her teeth for balked desire, and wept
As if her heart would break.

Day after day, night after night,
Laura kept watch in vain,   270
In sullen silence of exceeding pain.
She never caught again the goblin cry:
"Come buy, come buy";—
She never spied the goblin men
Hawking their fruits along the glen:
But when the noon waxed bright
Her hair grew thin and grey;
She dwindled, as the fair full moon doth turn
To swift decay, and burn
Her fire away.   280

One day remembering her kernel-stone
She set it by a wall that faced the south;
Dewed it with tears, hoped for a root,

258. **succous**, juicy.

Watched for a waxing shoot,
But there came none.
It never saw the sun,
It never felt the trickling moisture run:
While with sunk eyes and faded mouth
She dreamed of melons, as a traveller sees
False waves in desert drouth   290
With shade of leaf-crowned trees,
And burns the thirstier in the sandful breeze.

She no more swept the house,
Tended the fowls or cows,
Fetched honey, kneaded cakes of wheat,
Brought water from the brook:
But sat down listless in the chimney-nook
And would not eat.

Tender Lizzie could not bear
To watch her sister's cankerous care,   300
Yet not to share.
She night and morning
Caught the goblins' cry:
"Come buy our orchard fruits,
Come buy, come buy":—
Beside the brook, along the glen,
She heard the tramp of goblin men,
The voice and stir
Poor Laura could not hear;
Longed to buy fruit to comfort her,   310
But feared to pay too dear.
She thought of Jeanie in her grave,
Who should have been a bride;
But who for joys brides hope to have
Fell sick and died
In her gay prime,
In earliest winter-time,
With the first glazing rime,
With the first snow-fall of crisp winter-time.

Till Laura dwindling   320
Seemed knocking at Death's door.
Then Lizzie weighed no more
Better and worse;
But put a silver penny in her purse,
Kissed Laura, crossed the heath with clumps of
        furze
At twilight, halted by the brook;
And for the first time in her life
Began to listen and look.

Laughed every goblin
When they spied her peeping: 330
Came towards her hobbling,
Flying, running, leaping,

Puffing and blowing,
Chuckling, clapping, crowing,
Clucking and gobbling,
Mopping and mowing,
Full of airs and graces,
Pulling wry faces,
Demure grimaces,
Cat-like and rat-like,   340
Ratel- and wombat-like,
Snail-paced in a hurry,
Parrot-voiced and whistler,
Helter skelter, hurry skurry,
Chattering like magpies,
Fluttering like pigeons,
Gliding like fishes,—
Hugged her and kissed her:
Squeezed and caressed her:
Stretched up their dishes,   350
Panniers, and plates:
"Look at our apples
Russet and dun,
Bob at our cherries,
Bite at our peaches,
Citrons and dates,
Grapes for the asking,
Pears red with basking
Out in the sun,
Plums on their twigs;   360
Pluck them and suck them,—
Pomegranates, figs."

"Good folk," said Lizzie,
Mindful of Jeanie,
"Give me much and many":—
Held out her apron,
Tossed them her penny.
"Nay, take a seat with us,
Honour and eat with us,"
They answered grinning: 370
"Our feast is but beginning.
Night yet is early,
Warm and dew-pearly,
Wakeful and starry:
Such fruits as these
No man can carry;
Half their bloom would fly,
Half their dew would dry,
Half their flavour would pass by.
Sit down and feast with us,   380
Be welcome guest with us,
Cheer you and rest with us."
"Thank you," said Lizzie; "but one waits
At home alone for me:
So, without further parleying,

If you will not sell me any
Of your fruits though much and many,
Give me back my silver penny
I tossed you for a fee."—
They began to scratch their pates,   390
No longer wagging, purring,
But visibly demurring,
Grunting and snarling.
One called her proud,
Cross-grained, uncivil;
Their tones waxed loud,
Their looks were evil.
Lashing their tails
They trod and hustled her,
Elbowed and jostled her,   400
Clawed with their nails,
Barking, mewing, hissing, mocking,
Tore her gown and soiled her stocking,
Twitched her hair out by the roots,
Stamped upon her tender feet,
Held her hands and squeezed their fruits
Against her mouth to make her eat.

White and golden Lizzie stood,
Like a lily in a flood,—
Like a rock of blue-veined stone   410
Lashed by tides obstreperously,—
Like a beacon left alone
In a hoary roaring sea,
Sending up a golden fire,—
Like a fruit-crowned orange-tree
White with blossoms honey-sweet
Sore beset by wasp and bee,—
Like a royal virgin town
Topped with gilded dome and spire
Close beleaguered by a fleet   420
Mad to tug her standard down.

One may lead a horse to water,
Twenty cannot make him drink.
Though the goblins cuffed and caught her,
Coaxed and fought her,
Bullied and besought her,
Scratched her, pinched her black as ink,
Kicked and knocked her,
Mauled and mocked her,
Lizzie uttered not a word;   430
Would not open lip from lip
Lest they should cram a mouthful in:
But laughed in heart to feel the drip
Of juice that syrupped all her face
And lodged in dimples of her chin,
And streaked her neck which quaked like curd.
At last the evil people,

Worn out by her resistance,
Flung back her penny, kicked their fruit
Along whichever road they took,   440
Not leaving root or stone or shoot;
Some writhed into the ground,
Some dived into the brook
With ring and ripple,
Some scudded on the gale without a sound,
Some vanished in the distance.

In a smart, ache, tingle,
Lizzie went her way;
Knew not was it night or day;
Sprang up the bank, tore through the furze,   450
Threaded copse and dingle,
And heard her penny jingle
Bouncing in her purse,—
Its bounce was music to her ear.
She ran and ran
As if she feared some goblin man
Dogged her with gibe or curse
Or something worse:
But not one goblin skurried after,
Nor was she pricked by fear;   460
The kind heart made her windy-paced
That urged her home quite out of breath with haste
And inward laughter.

She cried "Laura," up the garden,
"Did you miss me?
Come and kiss me.
Never mind my bruises,
Hug me, kiss me, suck my juices
Squeezed from goblin fruits for you,
Goblin pulp and goblin dew.   470
Eat me, drink me, love me;
Laura, make much of me:
For your sake I have braved the glen
And had to do with goblin merchant men."

Laura started from her chair,
Flung her arms up in the air,
Clutched her hair:
"Lizzie, Lizzie, have you tasted
For my sake the fruit forbidden?
Must your light like mine be hidden,   480
Your young life like mine be wasted,
Undone in mine undoing
And ruined in my ruin,
Thirsty, cankered, goblin-ridden?"
She clung about her sister,
Kissed and kissed and kissed her:
Tears once again
Refreshed her shrunken eyes,

Dropping like rain
After long sultry drouth;   490
Shaking with aguish fear, and pain,
She kissed and kissed her with a hungry mouth.

Her lips began to scorch,
That juice was wormwood to her tongue,
She loathed the feast:
Writhing as one possessed she leaped and sung,
Rent all her robe, and wrung
Her hands in lamentable haste,
And beat her breast.
Her locks streamed like the torch   500
Borne by a racer at full speed,
Or like the mane of horses in their flight,
Or like an eagle when she stems the light
Straight toward the sun,
Or like a caged thing freed,
Or like a flying flag when armies run.

Swift fire spread through her veins, knocked at her
    heart,
Met the fire smouldering there
And overbore its lesser flame;
She gorged on bitterness without a name: 510
Ah! fool, to choose such part
Of soul-consuming care!
Sense failed in the mortal strife:
Like the watch-tower of a town
Which an earthquake shatters down,
Like a lightning-striken mast,
Like a wind-uprooted tree
Spun about,
Like a foam-topped waterspout
Cast down headlong in the sea,   520
She fell at last;
Pleasure past and anguish past,
Is it death or is it life?

Life out of death.
That night long Lizzie watched by her,
Counted her pulse's flagging stir,
Felt for her breath,
Held water to her lips, and cooled her face
With tears and fanning leaves.
But when the first birds chirped about their eaves,
And early reapers plodded to the place   531
Of golden sheaves,
And dew-wet grass
Bowed in the morning winds so brisk to pass,
And new buds with new day
Opened of cup-like lilies on the stream,
Laura awoke as from a dream,
Laughed in the innocent old way,

Hugged Lizzie but not twice or thrice;
Her gleaming locks showed not one thread of grey,
Her breath was sweet as May,   541
And light danced in her eyes.

Days, weeks, months, years
Afterwards, when both were wives
With children of their own;
Their mother-hearts beset with fears,
Their lives bound up in tender lives;
Laura would call the little ones
And tell them of her early prime,
Those pleasant days long gone   550
Of not-returning time:
Would talk about the haunted glen,
The wicked quaint fruit-merchant men,
Their fruits like honey to the throat,
But poison in the blood
(Men sell not such in any town):
Would tell them how her sister stood
In deadly peril to do her good,
And win the fiery antidote:
Then joining hands to little hands   560
Would bid them cling together,—
"For there is no friend like a sister,
In calm or stormy weather,
To cheer one on the tedious way,
To fetch one if one goes astray,
To lift one if one totters down,
To strengthen whilst one stands."

AT HOME

When I was dead, my spirit turned
    To seek the much-frequented house.
I passed the door, and saw my friends
    Feasting beneath green orange-boughs;
From hand to hand they pushed the wine,
    They sucked the pulp of plum and peach;
They sang, they jested, and they laughed,
    For each was loved of each.

I listened to their honest chat.
    Said one: "To-morrow we shall be   10
Plod plod along the featureless sands,
    And coasting miles and miles of sea."
Said one: "Before the turn of tide
    We will achieve the eyrie-seat."
Said one: "To-morrow shall be like
    To-day, but much more sweet."

"To-morrow," said they, strong with hope,
    And dwelt upon the pleasant way:

"To-morrow," cried they one and all,
   While no one spoke of yesterday.   20
Their life stood full at blessed noon;
   I, only I, had passed away:
"To-morrow and to-day," they cried;
   I was of yesterday.

I shivered comfortless, but cast
   No chill across the tablecloth;
I all-forgotten shivered, sad
   To stay, and yet to part how loth:
I passed from the familiar room,
   I who from love had passed away,   30
Like the remembrance of a guest
   That tarrieth but a day.

A DIRGE

Why were you born when the snow was falling?
You should have come to the cuckoo's calling,
Or when grapes are green in the cluster,
Or, at least, when lithe swallows muster
   For their far off flying
   From summer dying.

Why did you die when the lambs were cropping?
You should have died at the apples' dropping,
When the grasshopper comes to trouble,
And the wheat-fields are sodden stubble,   10
   And all winds go sighing
   For sweet things dying.

NOBLE SISTERS

"Now did you mark a falcon,
   Sister dear, sister dear,
Flying toward my window
   In the morning cool and clear?
With jingling bells about her neck,
   But what beneath her wing?
It may have been a ribbon,
   Or it may have been a ring."—
     "I marked a falcon swooping
      At the break of day: 10
     And for your love, my sister dove,
      I 'frayed the thief away."—

"Or did you spy a ruddy hound,
   Sister fair and tall,
Went snuffing round my garden bound,
   Or crouched by my bower wall?

With a silken leash about his neck;
   But in his mouth may be
A chain of gold and silver links,
   Or a letter writ to me."—   26
     "I heard a hound, highborn sister,
      Stood baying at the moon:
     I rose and drove him from your wall
      Lest you should wake too soon."—

"Or did you meet a pretty page
   Sat swinging on the gate?
Sat whistling, whistling like a bird,
   Or may be slept too late:
With eaglets broidered on his cap,
   And eaglets on his glove.   30
If you had turned his pockets out,
   You had found some pledge of love."—
     "I met him at this daybreak,
      Scarce the east was red:
     Lest the creaking gate should anger you,
      I packed him home to bed."—

"O patience, sister! Did you see
   A young man tall and strong,
Swift-footed to uphold the right
   And to uproot the wrong,   40
Come home across the desolate sea
   To woo me for his wife?
And in his heart my heart is locked,
   And in his life my life."—
     "I met a nameless man, sister,
      Who loitered round our door:
     I said: Her husband loves her much
      And yet she loves him more."—

"Fie, sister, fie, a wicked lie,
   A lie, a wicked lie!   50
I have none other love but him,
   Nor will have till I die.
And you have turned him from our door,
   And stabbed him with a lie:
I will go seek him through the world
   In sorrow till I die."—
     "Go seek in sorrow, sister,
      And find in sorrow too:
     If thus you shame our father's name
      My curse go forth with you."   60

A BIRTHDAY

My heart is like a singing bird
   Whose nest is in a watered shoot;
My heart is like an apple-tree
   Whose boughs are bent with thickset fruit;

My heart is like a rainbow shell
   That paddles in a halcyon sea;
My heart is gladder than all these
   Because my love is come to me.

Raise me a dais of silk and down;
   Hang it with vair and purple dyes;   10
Carve it in doves and pomegranates,
   And peacocks with a hundred eyes;
Work it in gold and silver grapes,
   In leaves and silver fleurs-de-lys;
Because the birthday of my life
   Is come, my love is come to me.

REMEMBER

Remember me when I am gone away,
   Gone far away into the silent land;
   When you can no more hold me by the hand,
Nor I half turn to go yet turning stay.
Remember me when no more day by day
   You tell me of our future that you planned:
   Only remember me; you understand
It will be late to counsel then or pray.
Yet if you should forget me for a while
   And afterwards remember, do not grieve: 10
   For if the darkness and corruption leave
A vestige of the thoughts that once I had,
Better by far you should forget and smile
   Than that you should remember and be sad.

AFTER DEATH

The curtains were half drawn, the floor was swept
   And strewn with rushes, rosemary and may
   Lay thick upon the bed on which I lay,
Where through the lattice ivy-shadows crept.
He leaned above me, thinking that I slept
   And could not hear him; but I heard him say:
   "Poor child, poor child": and as he turned
      away
Came a deep silence, and I knew he wept.
He did not touch the shroud, or raise the fold
   That hid my face, or take my hand in his,   10
     Or ruffle the smooth pillows for my head:
     He did not love me living; but once dead
He pitied me; and very sweet it is
To know he still is warm though I am cold.

After Death. **2. rosemary.** Compare Ophelia's "There's rosemary, that's for remembrance." (*Hamlet*, Act IV, sc. 5, l. 175)

SONG

When I am dead, my dearest,
   Sing no sad songs for me;
Plant thou no roses at my head,
   Nor shady cypress tree:
Be the green grass above me
   With showers and dewdrops wet;
And if thou wilt, remember,
   And if thou wilt, forget.

I shall not see the shadows,
   I shall not feel the rain;   10
I shall not hear the nightingale
   Sing on as if in pain:
And dreaming through the twilight
   That doth not rise nor set,
Haply I may remember,
   And haply may forget.

UP–HILL

Does the road wind up-hill all the way?
   Yes, to the very end.
Will the day's journey take the whole long day?
   From morn to night, my friend.

But is there for the night a resting-place?
   A roof for when the slow dark hours begin.
May not the darkness hide it from my face?
   You cannot miss that inn.

Shall I meet other wayfarers at night?
   Those who have gone before.   10
Then must I knock, or call when just in sight?
   They will not keep you standing at that door.

Shall I find comfort, travel-sore and weak?
   Of labour you shall find the sum.
Will there be beds for me and all who seek?
   Yea, beds for all who come.

A BETTER RESURRECTION

I have no wit, no words, no tears;
   My heart within me like a stone
Is numbed too much for hopes or fears.
   Look right, look left, I dwell alone;
I lift mine eyes, but dimmed with grief
   No everlasting hills I see;

Song. **4. cypress tree,** emblem of mourning.   *Up-Hill*
12. standing at that door. See Revelation 3:20.

My life is in the falling leaf:
    O Jesus, quicken me!

My life is like a faded leaf,
    My harvest dwindled to a husk;   10
Truly my life is void and brief
    And tedious in the barren dusk;
My life is like a frozen thing,
    No bud nor greenness can I see:
Yet rise it shall,—the sap of Spring;
    O Jesus, rise in me!

My life is like a broken bowl,
    A broken bowl that cannot hold
One drop of water for my soul
    Or cordial in the searching cold;   20
Cast in the fire the perished thing;
    Melt and remould it, till it be
A royal cup for Him, my King:
    O Jesus, drink of me!

THE THREE ENEMIES

THE FLESH

"Sweet, thou art pale."
             "More pale to see,
Christ hung upon the cruel tree
And bore His Father's wrath for me."

"Sweet, thou art sad."
             "Beneath a rod
More heavy, Christ for my sake trod
The winepress of the wrath of God."

"Sweet, thou art weary."
             "Not so Christ;
Whose mighty love of me sufficed
For Strength, Salvation, Eucharist."

"Sweet, thou art footsore."
             "If I bleed,   10
His feet have bled: yea in my need
His Heart once bled for mine indeed."

THE WORLD

"Sweet, thou art young."
             "So He was young
Who for my sake in silence hung
Upon the Cross with Passion wrung."

"Look, thou art fair."
             "He was more fair
Than men, Who deigned for me to wear
A visage marred beyond compare."

6. **winepress . . . God."** See Isaiah 63:2–3.

"And thou hast riches."
             "Daily bread:
All else is His; Who living, dead,   20
For me lacked where to lay His Head."

"And life is sweet."
             "It was not so
To Him, Whose Cup did overflow
With mine unutterable woe."

THE DEVIL

"Thou drinkest deep."
             "When Christ would sup
He drained the dregs from out my cup:
So how should I be lifted up?"

"Thou shalt win Glory."
             "In the skies,
Lord Jesus, cover up mine eyes
Lest they should look on vanities."   30

"Thou shalt have Knowledge."
             "Helpless dust!
In Thee, O Lord, I put my trust:
Answer Thou for me, Wise and Just."

"And Might."
             "Get thee behind me. Lord,
Who has redeemed and not abhorred
My soul, oh keep it by Thy Word."

A PORTRAIT

The first section, originally entitled "Saint Elisabeth of Hungary," was later combined with the second, inspired by the death of Lady Elizabeth Howard.

I

She gave up beauty in her tender youth,
    Gave all her hope and joy and pleasant ways;
    She covered up her eyes lest they should gaze
On vanity, and chose the bitter truth.
Harsh towards herself, towards others full of ruth,
    Servant of servants, little known to praise,
    Long prayers and fasts trenched on her nights
        and days:
She schooled herself to sights and sounds uncouth,
That with the poor and stricken she might make
    A home, until the least of all sufficed   10
Her wants; her own self learned she to forsake,
Counting all earthly gain but hurt and loss.

21. For me . . . Head." See Matthew 8:20. **34. "Get thee behind me.** See Luke 4:8.

So with calm will she chose and bore the cross,
    And hated all for love of Jesus Christ.

2

They knelt in silent anguish by her bed,
    And could not weep; but calmly there she lay.
    All pain had left her; and the sun's last ray
Shone through upon her, warming into red
The shady curtains. In her heart she said:
    "Heaven opens; I leave these and go away: 20
    The Bridegroom calls,—shall the Bride seek to
        stay?"
Then low upon her breast she bowed her head.
O lily-flower, O gem of priceless worth,
    O dove with patient voice and patient eyes,
O fruitful vine amid a land of dearth,
    O maid replete with loving purities,
Thou bowedst down thy head with friends on earth
    To raise it with the saints in Paradise.

BEAUTY IS VAIN

While roses are so red,
While lilies are so white,
Shall a woman exalt her face
Because it gives delight?
She's not so sweet as a rose,
A lily's straighter than she,
And if she were as red or white
She'd be but one of three.

Whether she flush in love's summer
    Or in its winter grow pale,   10
Whether she flaunt her beauty
Or hide it away in a veil,
Be she red or white,
And stand she erect or bowed,
Time will win the race he runs with her
And hide her away in a shroud.

PARADISE

This poem is full of references to the description of the
City of God in Revelation 21–22.

Once in a dream I saw the flowers
    That bud and bloom in Paradise;
    More fair they are than waking eyes
Have seen in all this world of ours.

And faint the perfume-bearing rose,
    And faint the lily on its stem,
    And faint the perfect violet,
        Compared with them.

I heard the songs of Paradise;
    Each bird sat singing in his place;   10
    A tender song so full of grace
It soared like incense to the skies.
Each bird sat singing to his mate
    Soft cooing notes among the trees:
    The nightingale herself were cold
        To such as these.

I saw the fourfold River flow,
    And deep it was, with golden sand;
    It flowed between a mossy land
With murmured music grave and low.   20
It hath refreshment for all thirst,
    For fainting spirits strength and rest;
    Earth holds not such a draught as this
        From east to west.

The Tree of Life stood budding there,
    Abundant with its twelvefold fruits;
    Eternal sap sustains its roots,
Its shadowing branches fill the air.
Its leaves are healing for the world,
    Its fruit the hungry world can feed,   30
    Sweeter than honey to the taste
        And balm indeed.

I saw the Gate called Beautiful,
    And looked, but scarce could look within;
    I saw the golden streets begin,
And outskirts of the glassy pool.
Oh harps, oh crowns of plenteous stars,
    Oh green palm branches many-leaved—
    Eye hath not seen, nor ear hath heard,
        Nor heart conceived!   40

I hope to see these things again,
    But not as once in dreams by night;
    To see them with my very sight,
And touch and handle and attain:
To have all Heaven beneath my feet
    For narrow way that once they trod;
    To have my part with all the saints,
        And with my God.

A Portrait. **14. hated all . . . Christ.** See Luke 14:26.
21. The Bridegroom . . . stay." There are many passages in the New Testament in which Christ is spoken of as
the bridegroom and the Christian as the bride. Look up these
words in any good concordance.

39–40. Eye . . . conceived!" See 1 Corinthians 2:9.
46. For . . . trod, by way of recompense for having traveled the narrow path here. See Matthew 7:14.

WEARY IN WELL–DOING

I would have gone; God bade me stay:
   I would have worked; God bade me rest.
He broke my will from day to day,
   He read my yearnings unexprest,
     And said them nay.

Now I would stay; God bids me go:
   Now I would rest; God bids me work.
He breaks my heart tost to and fro;
   My soul is wrung with doubts that lurk
     And vex it so.   10

I go, Lord, where Thou sendest me;
   Day after day I plod and moil:
But, Christ my God, when will it be
   That I may let alone my toil
     And rest with Thee?

from SING–SONG

If I were a Queen,
   What would I do?
I'd make you King,
   And I'd wait on you.

If I were a King,
   What would I do?
I'd make you Queen,
   For I'd marry you.

—————

Mother shake the cherry-tree,
   Susan catch a cherry;
Oh how funny that will be,
   Let's be merry!

One for brother, one for sister,
   Two for mother more,
Six for father, hot and tired,
   Knocking at the door.

—————

The wind has such a rainy sound
   Moaning through the town,
The sea has such a windy sound,—
   Will the ships go down?

The apples in the orchard
   Tumble from their tree.—
Oh, will the ships go down, go down,
   In the windy sea?

—————

Fly away, fly away over the sea,
   Sun-loving swallow, for summer is done;
Come again, come again, come back to me,
   Bringing the summer and bringing the sun.

—————

Who has seen the wind?
   Neither I nor you:
But when the leaves hang trembling
   The wind is passing through.

Who has seen the wind?
   Neither you nor I:
But when the trees bow down their heads
   The wind is passing by.

—————

Boats sail on the rivers,
   And ships sail on the seas;
But clouds that sail across the sky
   Are prettier far than these.

There are bridges on the rivers,
   As pretty as you please;
But the bow that bridges heaven,
   And overtops the trees,
And builds a road from earth to sky,
   Is prettier far than these.   10

from MONNA INNOMINATA

"Monna Innominata" (My Nameless Lady), a series
of fourteen sonnets, is supposed to be spoken by one of
the unknown ladies praised by the Italian poets who preceded Dante and Petrarch. W. M. Rossetti is the authority for regarding the poem as autobiographical, an expression of his sister's own love for Charles Cayley.

SONNET 11

"Vien dietro a me e lascia dir le genti."
                  —Dante
"Contando i casi della vita nostra."
                —Petrarca

Many in aftertimes will say of you
   "He loved her"—while of me what will they say?
   Not that I loved you more than just in play,
For fashion's sake as idle women do.
Even let them prate; who know not what we knew
   Of love and parting in exceeding pain,
   Of parting hopeless here to meet again,

Sing-Song (last selection). **1. Boats . . . rivers.** Compare
the musical setting by the American composer Sidney Homer,
sung by Madame Louise Homer (Victor record 87205).
Monna Innominata. **"Vien . . . genti."** Come after me and
let the people talk (*Purgatory* Cantos 5, 13). **"Contando . . .
nostra."** Pointing the dangers of life below (Sonnet 244).

Hopeless on earth, and heaven is out of view.
But by my heart of love laid bare to you,
   My love that you can make not void nor vain,   10
Love that foregoes you but to claim anew
Beyond this passage of the gate of death,
   I charge you at the Judgment make it plain
   My love of you was life and not a breath.

SLEEPING AT LAST

This is believed to be the last poem Christina Rossetti
wrote.

Sleeping at last, the trouble and tumult over,
   Sleeping at last, the struggle and horror past,

Cold and white, out of sight of friend and of
      lover,
            Sleeping at last.

   No more a tired heart downcast or overcast,
No more pangs that wring or shifting fears that
      hover,
   Sleeping at last in a dreamless sleep locked
      fast.

Fast asleep. Singing birds in their leafy cover
   Cannot wake her, nor shake her the gusty
      blast.
Under the purple thyme and the purple clover   10
      Sleeping at last.

William Morris
1834–1896

Poet, craftsman, and publicist, William Morris
lived perhaps the fullest life of all the great nineteenth-century poets. The three phases of his work
were closely connected; like Ruskin, who influenced
him, he perceived that it is futile to achieve beauty
in one's dream life while the world of actuality that
hems one in on every side is overwhelmingly ugly;
later he came to believe that the only way to get rid
of this ugliness was to destroy the present economic
order.

Morris was born of a well-to-do commercial family, at Walthamstow, March 24, 1834. He was
brought up on the edge of Epping Forest, which
tremendously stimulated his imagination; in art as
well as in nature, the glamour of the past soon
powerfully enthralled him. One of his great early
passions was for Scott's novels, but he could not
remember ever having learned to read.

When Morris went to Oxford in 1853 he was
thinking of taking holy orders. Partly as the result of
an association with Rossetti and Burne-Jones, his interests shifted from religion to art. He tried architecture, then painting. In the *Oxford and Cambridge
Magazine*, which he financed, he published the
stories now reprinted in "Everyman's Library" as
The Early Romances of William Morris. In 1858 he published *The Defence of Guinevere and Other Poems*. The
general public did not relish the Pre-Raphaelitish,
un-Tennysonian spirit of this volume; a more
romantic, less psychological, and less obscure
treatment of medievalism was still in vogue. In

1859 Morris married Jane Burden, a beautiful
girl who had served as a Pre-Raphaelite model.
   For her he built the beautiful "Red House" in
Kent, and it was out of his inability to buy the
things he wanted for it in the open market that the
firm of Morris, Marshall, Faulkner, and Company
was formed. Among other articles this firm produced furniture, tapestries, embroideries, carpets,
tiles, designs for wallpaper and chintzes, and
stained-glass windows. Thorough research everywhere was Morris's rule—he studied dyes for two
years—and he gave prizes not for designs but for
finished articles. "Have nothing in your houses,"he
cried, "that you do not know to be useful or believe
to be beautiful." Actually he made the useful articles beautiful. His employees were not wage slaves
but creative artists, and his business was very successful.

Toward the close of his life Morris took up his
last craft, printing, and established the Kelmscott
Press. Here again everything was made to order—
ink, paper, everything was built from the bottom.
The Kelmscott Chaucer is one of the most famous
of printed books. Morris raced against time to complete it, and its appearance only briefly antedated
his death.

Morris's most elaborate poems were *The Earthly
Paradise, The Life and Death of Jason* (see notes on
pages 810–11), and *The Story of Sigurd the Volsung
and the Fall of the Niblungs*, 1877, which Bernard
Shaw thinks the greatest epic since Homer. Before

he finished *The Earthly Paradise*, Morris had become tremendously interested in Northern myth; two trips to Iceland (1871 and 1873) did much to increase this interest. In 1873 he published *Love Is Enough*, a morality play based on the *Mabinogion*. He made extensive translations from Scandinavian sources, from the *Odyssey* and the *Aeneid*, *Beowulf*, and so forth. His last great literary enterprise was a series of gloriously titled Northern romances—*The House of the Wolfings*, 1889; *The Roots of the Mountains*, 1890; *The Story of the Glittering Plain*, 1890; *The Wood beyond the World*, 1894; *Child Christopher and Goldilind the Fair*, 1895; *The Well at the World's End*, 1896; *The Water of the Wondrous Isles*, 1897; *The Sundering Flood*, 1898.

Morris's public service was in two fields, as a member of the Society for the Protection of Ancient Buildings and as a Socialist. From 1883 to 1890 he gave his energies largely to Socialist propaganda. He did not take up this work primarily because he pitied the unfortunate—"Do you notice," asked Rossetti, "that Topsy never gives a penny to a beggar?"—but because he was convinced that the heroic race he liked to write about could never breed in England under modern conditions. His Socialistic views are set forth directly in *The Aims of Art*, 1887, in *Signs of Change*, 1888; and artistically in his beautiful story of the Peasant's Revolt of 1381, *A Dream of John Ball*, 1888, in his Utopia, *News from Nowhere*, 1891, and in *Poems By the Way*, 1891. "Yes, surely! and if others can see it as I have seen it, then it may be called a vision rather than a dream." Morris died (of trying to live ten men's lives, as somebody has said) October 3, 1896.

Morris was a shaggy, full-bodied man, of abounding vitality. He was restless, impatient, and of violent temper, and he inspired both enthusiasm and repulsion. He hated conventional society and conventional ways—he hated the "modern" both in literature and in life—and it was said of him that he had a great capacity for producing and annexing dirt. He wrote very rapidly, sometimes as much as seven hundred lines of poetry in a day, and he disliked revision; when changes were necessary, he rewrote. His work is the bread of poetry, not its appetizers; he has few magical lines; but, as John Drinkwater has observed, the complaint of languidness which some persons make against his long poems indicates a lack in them rather than in him; he lived intensely every moment of his life, and he did not need prodding to keep him alive. Above all, he is an interesting example of a man whose zealous service of the present flowed directly from his idealization of the past.

THE DEFENCE OF GUENEVERE

Guinevere, King Arthur's queen, on trial for adultery, addresses her judges while she waits for Lancelot to come and deliver her. He had been found in her chamber by a company of knights, all save one of whom he slew.

The poem contains references also to a previous occasion upon which Guinevere had been under sentence. This had followed her imprisonment by Sir Meliagraunce in his castle, la Fausse Garde, from which Lancelot rescued her. Coming into her chamber, he cut his arm on the window bars, and his blood was found on her bed. Lancelot saved Guinevere from the stake on this occasion by slaying Meliagraunce in judicial combat.

Malory's *Morte d'Arthur*, Books 19-20, is Morris's source for this poem. Three other Arthurian poems were published with this one—"King Arthur's Tomb," "Sir Galahad, a Christmas Mystery," and "The Chapel in Lyoness."

But, knowing now that they would have her speak,
She threw her wet hair backward from her brow,
Her hand close to her mouth touching her cheek,

As though she had had there a shameful blow,
And feeling it shameful to feel aught but shame
All through her heart, yet felt her cheek burned so,

She must a little touch it; like one lame
She walked away from Gauwaine, with her head
Still lifted up; and on her cheek of flame

The tears dried quick; she stopped at last and said:
"O knights and lords, it seems but little skill   11
To talk of well-known things past now and dead.

"God wot I ought to say, I have done ill,
And pray you all forgiveness heartily!
Because you must be right, such great lords—still

"Listen, suppose your time were come to die,
And you were quite alone and very weak;
Yea, laid a dying while very mightily

"The wind was ruffling up the narrow streak
Of river through your broad lands running well: 20
Suppose a hush should come, then some one speak:

" 'One of these cloths is heaven, and one is hell,
Now choose one cloth for ever; which they be,
I will not tell you, you must somehow tell

" 'Of your own strength and mightiness; here, see!'
Yea, yea, my lord, and you to ope your eyes,
At foot of your familiar bed to see

"A great God's angel standing, with such dyes,
Not known on earth, on his great wings, and hands,
Held out two ways, light from the inner skies   30

"Showing him well, and making his commands
Seem to be God's commands, moreover, too,
Holding within his hands the cloths on wands;

"And one of these strange choosing cloths was blue,
Wavy and long, and one cut short and red;
No man could tell the better of the two.

"After a shivering half-hour you said,
'God help! heaven's colour, the blue'; and he said:
    'hell.'
Perhaps you then would roll upon your bed,

"And cry to all good men that loved you well,   40
'Ah Christ! if only I had known, known, known';
Launcelot went away, then I could tell,

"Like wisest man how all things would be, moan,
And roll and hurt myself, and long to die,
And yet fear much to die for what was sown.

"Nevertheless you, O Sir Gauwaine, lie,
Whatever may have happened through these years,
God knows I speak truth, saying that you lie."

Her voice was low at first, being full of tears,
But as it cleared, it grew full loud and shrill,   50
Growing a windy shriek in all men's ears,

A ringing in their startled brains, until
She said that Gauwaine lied, then her voice sunk,
And her great eyes began again to fill,

Though still she stood right up, and never shrunk,
But spoke on bravely, glorious lady fair!
Whatever tears her full lips may have drunk,

She stood, and seemed to think, and wrung her
    hair,
Spoke out at last with no more trace of shame,
With passionate twisting of her body there: 60

"It chanced upon a day that Launcelot came
To dwell at Arthur's court: at Christmas-time
This happened; when the heralds sung his name,

' 'Son of King Ban of Benwick,' seemed to chime
Along with all the bells that rang that day,
O'er the white roofs, with little change of rhyme.

"Christmas and whitened winter passed away,
And over me the April sunshine came,
Made very awful with black hail-clouds, yea,

"And in the Summer I grew white with flame,   70
And bowed my head down—Autumn, and the
    sick
Sure knowledge things would never be the same,

"However often Spring might be most thick
Of blossoms and buds, smote on me, and I grew
Careless of most things, let the clock tick, tick,

"To my unhappy pulse, that beat right through
My eager body; while I laughed out loud,
And let my lips curl up at false or true,

"Seemed cold and shallow without any cloud.
Behold my judges, then the cloths were brought;   80
While I was dizzied thus, old thoughts would
    crowd,

"Belonging to the time ere I was bought
By Arthur's great name and his little love;
Must I give up for ever then, I thought,

"That which I deemed would ever round me move
Glorifying all things; for a little word,
Scarce ever meant at all, must I now prove

"Stone-cold for ever? Pray you, does the Lord
Will that all folks should be quite happy and good?
I love God now a little, if this cord   90

"Were broken, once for all what striving could
Make me love anything in earth or heaven?
So day by day it grew, as if one should

"Slip slowly down some path worn smooth and even,
Down to a cool sea on a summer day;
Yet still in slipping there was some small leaven

"Of stretched hands catching small stones by the
    way,
Until one surely reached the sea at last,
And felt strange new joy as the worn head lay

---

46. **"Nevertheless. . . . lie.** For some unexplained reason, Morris made Gawain Guinevere's accuser. In Malory he is her defender.

70. **I grew white with flame,** that is, fell in love with Lancelot. **75. clock,** of course an anachronism. **80. the cloths were brought.** This symbolism harks back to her parable in ll. 21 ff. **86. a little word,** her marriage vow.

"Back, with the hair like sea-weed; yea all past   100
Sweat of the forehead, dryness of the lips,
Washed utterly out by the dear waves o'ercast,

"In the lone sea, far off from any ships!
Do I not know now of a day in Spring?
No minute of that wild day ever slips

"From out my memory; I hear thrushes sing,
And wheresoever I may be, straightway
Thoughts of it all come up with most fresh sting:

"I was half mad with beauty on that day,
And went without my ladies all alone,   110
In a quiet garden walled round every way;

"I was right joyful of that wall of stone,
That shut the flowers and trees up with the sky,
And trebled all the beauty: to the bone,

"Yea right through to my heart, grown very shy
With weary thoughts, it pierced, and made me
    glad;
Exceedingly glad, and I knew verily,

"A little thing just then had made me mad;
I dared not think, as I was wont to do,
Sometimes, upon my beauty; if I had   120

"Held out my long hand up against the blue,
And, looking on the tenderly darkened fingers,
Thought that by rights one ought to see quite
    through,

"There, see you, where the soft still light yet lingers,
Round by the edges; what should I have done,
If this had joined with yellow spotted singers,

"And startling green drawn upward by the sun?
But shouting, loosed out, see now! all my hair,
And trancedly stood watching the west wind run

"With faintest half-heard breathing sound; why
    there   130
I lose my head e'en now in doing this;
But shortly listen: In that garden fair

"Came Launcelot walking; this is true, the kiss
Wherewith we kissed in meeting that spring day,
I scarce dare talk of the remembered bliss,

"When both our mouths went wandering in one way,
And aching sorely, met among the leaves;
Our hands being left behind strained far away.

"Never within a yard of my bright sleeves
Had Launcelot come before: and now, so nigh!   140
After that day why is it Guenevere grieves?

"Nevertheless you, O Sir Gauwaine, lie,
Whatever happened on through all those years,
God knows I speak truth, saying that you lie.

"Being such a lady could I weep these tears
If this were true? A great queen such as I
Having sinned this way, straight her conscience
    sears;

"And afterwards she liveth hatefully,
Slaying and poisoning, certes never weeps,—
Gauwaine be friends now, speak me lovingly.   150

"Do I not see how God's dear pity creeps
All through your frame, and trembles in your
    mouth?
Remember in what grave your mother sleeps,

"Buried in some place far down in the south,
Men are forgetting as I speak to you;
By her head severed in that awful drouth

"Of pity that drew Agravaine's fell blow,
I pray your pity! let me not scream out
For ever after, when the shrill winds blow

"Through half your castle-locks! let me not shout   160
For ever after in the winter night
When you ride out alone! in battle-rout

"Let not my rusting tears make your sword light!
Ah! God of mercy, how he turns away!
So, ever must I dress me to the fight,

"So: let God's justice work! Gauwaine, I say,
See me hew down your proofs: yea all men know
Even as you said how Mellyagraunce one day,

"One bitter day in *la Fausse Garde*, for so
All good knights held it after, saw: 170
Yea, sirs, by cursed unknightly outrage; though

142-44. **"Nevertheless . . . lie.** The repetition at this point would seem to indicate that Morris did not think Guinevere guilty of any more serious infidelity than her kiss. In his "King Arthur's Tomb," however, her sin is deeper. **153. your mother,** Morgause, Arthur's sister, was slain by her son, Sir Gaheris, not by Agravaine (l. 157), when he found her faithless to his father (Malory, Book X). **171. unknightly outrage,** the entrance of Meliagraunce into Guinevere's chamber and his thrusting aside the curtains of her bed before she was up.

"You, Gauwaine, held his word without a flaw,
This Mellyagraunce saw blood upon my bed—
Whose blood then pray you? is there any law

"To make a queen say why some spots of red
Lie on her coverlet? or will you say:
'Your hands are white, lady, as when you wed,

" 'Where did you bleed?' and must I stammer out,
        'Nay,
I blush indeed, fair lord, only to rend
My sleeve up to my shoulder, where there lay   180

" 'A knife-point last night': so must I defend
The honour of the Lady Guenevere?
Not so, fair lords, even if the world should end

"This very day, and you were judges here
Instead of God. Did you see Mellyagraunce
When Launcelot stood by him? what white fear

"Curdled his blood, and how his teeth did dance,
His side sink in? as my knight cried and said,
'Slayer of unarmed men, here is a chance!

" 'Setter of traps, I pray you guard your head,   190
By God, I am so glad to fight with you,
Stripper of ladies, that my hand feels lead

" 'For driving weight; hurrah now! draw and do,
For all my wounds are moving in my breast,
And I am getting mad with waiting so.'

"He struck his hands together o'er the beast,
Who fell down flat, and grovelled at his feet,
And groaned at being slain so young—'at least.'

"My knight said: 'Rise you, sir, who are so fleet
At catching ladies, half-armed will I fight,   200
My left side all uncovered!' then I weet,

"Up sprang Sir Mellyagraunce with great delight
Upon his knave's face; not until just then
Did I quite hate him, as I saw my knight

"Along the lists look to my stake and pen
With such a joyous smile, it made me sigh
From agony beneath my waist-chain, when

190. "Setter of traps. Lancelot had fallen into a trap while
being shown about the castle of Meliagraunce. 201. uncovered, unprotected.

"The fight began, and to me they drew nigh;
Ever Sir Launcelot kept him on the right,
And traversed warily, and ever high   210

"And fast leapt caitiff's sword, until my knight
Sudden threw up his sword to his left hand,
Caught it, and swung it; that was all the fight,

"Except a spout of blood on the hot land;
For it was hottest summer; and I know
I wondered how the fire, while I should stand,

"And burn, against the heat, would quiver so,
Yards above my head; thus these matters went;
Which things were only warnings of the woe

"That fell on me. Yet Mellyagraunce was shent,   220
For Mellyagraunce had fought against the Lord;
Therefore, my lords, take heed lest you be blent

"With all this wickedness; say no rash word
Against me, being so beautiful; my eyes,
Wept all away to grey, may bring some sword

"To drown you in your blood; see my breast rise,
Like waves of purple sea, as here I stand;
And how my arms are moved in wonderful wise,

"Yea also at my full heart's strong command,
See through my long throat how the words go up
In ripples to my mouth; how in my hand   231

"The shadow lies like wine within a cup
Of marvellously coloured gold; yea now
This little wind is rising, look you up,

"And wonder how the light is falling so
Within my moving tresses: will you dare,
When you have looked a little on my brow,

"To say this thing is vile? or will you care
For any plausible lies of cunning woof,
When you can see my face with no lie there   240

"For ever? am I not a gracious proof—
'But in your chamber Launcelot was found'—
Is there a good knight then would stand aloof,

'When a queen says with gentle queenly sound:
'O true as steel come now and talk with me,
I love to see your step upon the ground

220. shent, destroyed.   222. blent, blinded.

" 'Unwavering, also well I love to see
That gracious smile light up your face, and hear
Your wonderful words, that all mean verily

" 'The thing they seem to mean: good friend, so dear
To me in everything, come here to-night,   251
Or else the hours will pass most dull and drear;

" 'If you come not, I fear this time I might
Get thinking over much of times gone by,
When I was young, and green hope was in sight:

" 'For no man cares now to know why I sigh;
And no man comes to sing me pleasant songs,
Nor any brings me the sweet flowers that lie

" 'So thick in the gardens; therefore one so longs
To see you, Launcelot; that we may be   260
Like children once again, free from all wrongs

" 'Just for one night.' Did he not come to me?
What thing could keep true Launcelot away
If I said 'Come'? There was one less than three

"In my quiet room that night, and we were gay;
Till sudden I rose up, weak, pale, and sick,
Because a bawling broke our dream up, yea

"I looked at Launcelot's face and could not speak,
For he looked helpless too, for a little while;
Then I remember how I tried to shriek,   270

"And could not, but fell down; from tile to tile
The stones they threw up rattled o'er my head
And made me dizzier; till within awhile

"My maids were all about me, and my head
On Launcelot's breast was being soothed away
From its white chattering, until Launcelot said—

"By God! I will not tell you more to-day,
Judge any way you will— what matters it?
You know quite well the story of that fray,

"How Launcelot stilled their bawling, the mad fit 280
That caught up Gauwaine— all, all, verily,
But just that which would save me; these things flit.

"Nevertheless you, O Sir Gauwaine, lie;
Whatever may have happened these long years,
God knows I speak truth, saying that you lie!

267. **bawling,** the coming of the knights with their accusations.

"All I have said is truth, by Christ's dear tears."
She would not speak another word, but stood
Turned sideways; listening, like a man who hears

His brother's trumpet sounding through the wood
Of his foes' lances. She leaned eagerly,   290
And gave a slight spring sometimes, as she could

At last hear something really; joyfully
Her cheek grew crimson, as the headlong speed
Of the roan charger drew all men to see,
The knight who came was Launcelot at good need.

SHAMEFUL DEATH[1]

There were four of us about that bed;
   The mass-priest knelt at the side,
I and his mother stood at the head,
   Over his feet lay the bride;
We were quite sure that he was dead,
   Though his eyes were open wide.

He did not die in the night,
   He did not die in the day,
But in the morning twilight
   His spirit passed away,   10
When neither sun nor moon was bright,
   And the trees were merely grey.

He was not slain with the sword,
   Knight's axe, or the knightly spear,
Yet spoke he never a word
   After he came in here;
I cut away the cord
   From the neck of my brother dear.

He did not strike one blow,
   For the recreants came behind,   20
In a place where the hornbeams grow,
   A path right hard to find,
For the hornbeam boughs swing so,
   That the twilight makes it blind.

They lighted a great torch then,
   When his arms were pinioned fast,
Sir John the knight of the Fen,
   Sir Guy of the Dolorous Blast,

2. **mass-priest,** a priest employed in a special chapel (in this case, no doubt, the family chapel) to celebrate masses only.

With knights threescore and ten,
Hung brave Lord Hugh at last.   30

I am threescore and ten,
And my hair is all turned grey,
But I met Sir John of the Fen
Long ago on a summer day,
And am glad to think of the moment when
I took his life away.

I am threescore and ten,
And my strength is mostly passed,
But long ago I and my men,
When the sky was overcast,   40
And the smoke rolled over the reeds of the fen,
Slew Guy of the Dolorous Blast.

And now, knights all of you,
I pray you pray for Sir Hugh,
A good knight and a true,
And for Alice, his wife, pray too.

THE EVE OF CRECY

The speaker is Sir Lambert of the Wood, a French
knight, musing on the eve of the battle of Crécy, 1346,
one of the great English victories of the Hundred Years'
War.

Gold on her head, and gold on her feet,
And gold where the hems of her kirtle meet,
And a golden girdle round my sweet;—
Ah! qu'elle est belle La Marguerite.

Margaret's maids are fair to see,
Freshly dressed and pleasantly;
Margaret's hair falls down to her knee;—
Ah! qu'elle est belle La Marguerite.

If I were rich I would kiss her feet,
I would kiss the place where the gold hems meet,   10
And the golden girdle round my sweet—
Ah! qu'elle est belle La Marguerite.

Ah me! I have never touched her hand;
When the arriere-ban goes through the land,
Six basnets under my pennon stand;—
Ah! qu'elle est belle La Marguerite.

And many an one grins under his hood:
Sir Lambert du Bois, with all his men good,

Has neither food nor firewood.—
Ah! qu'elle est belle La Marguerite.   20

If I were rich I would kiss her feet,
And the golden girdle of my sweet,
And thereabouts where the gold hems meet;
Ah! qu'elle est belle La Marguerite.

Yet even now it is good to think,
While my few poor varlets grumble and drink
In my desolate hall, where the fires sink,—
Ah! qu'elle est belle La Marguerite.

Of Margaret sitting glorious there,
In glory of gold and glory of hair,   30
And glory of glorious face most fair;—
Ah! qu'elle est belle La Marguerite.

Likewise to-night I made good cheer,
Because this battle draweth near:
For what have I to lose or fear?—
Ah! qu'elle est belle La Marguerite.

For, look you, my horse is good to prance
A right fair measure in this war-dance,
Before the eyes of Philip of France;—
Ah! qu'elle est belle La Marguerite.   40

And sometime it may hap, perdie,
While my new towers stand up three and three,
And my hall gets painted fair to see—
Ah! qu'elle est belle La Marguerite.

That folks may say: "Times change, by the
rood,
For Lambert, banneret of the wood,
Has heaps of food and firewood;—
Ah! qu'elle est belle La Marguerite;

"And wonderful eyes, too, under the hood
Of a damsel of right noble blood."   50
St. Ives, for Lambert of the Wood!
Ah! qu'elle est belle La Marguerite.

THE HAYSTACK IN THE FLOODS

Had she come all the way for this,
To part at last without a kiss?

4. qu'elle . . . Marguerite! how beautiful is Marguerite!   14. arriere-ban, the call to arms.   15. basnets,
helmets. pennon, banner.

39. Philip of France, Philip VI (reigned 1320–50).
41. perdie, par Dieu, literally, by God.   46. banneret,
a knight who leads vassals under his own banner, ranking
next below a baron.

Yea, had she borne the dirt and rain
That her own eyes might see him slain
Beside the haystack in the floods?

Along the dripping leafless woods,
The stirrup touching either shoe,
She rode astride as troopers do;
With kirtle kilted to her knee,
To which the mud splashed wretchedly;   10
And the wet dripped from every tree
Upon her head and heavy hair,
And on her eyelids broad and fair;
The tears and rain ran down her face.
By fits and starts they rode apace,
And very often was his place
Far off from her; he had to ride
Ahead, to see what might betide
When the roads crossed; and sometimes, when
There rose a murmuring from his men,   20
Had to turn back with promises;
Ah me! she had but little ease;
And often for pure doubt and dread
She sobbed, made giddy in the head
By the swift riding; while, for cold,
Her slender fingers scarce could hold
The wet reins; yea, and scarcely, too,
She felt the foot within her shoe
Against the stirrup: all for this,
To part at last without a kiss   30
Beside the haystack in the floods.

For when they neared that old soaked hay,
They saw across the only way
That Judas, Godmar, and the three
Red running lions dismally
Grinned from his pennon, under which
In one straight line along the ditch,
They counted thirty heads.

                    So then,
While Robert turned round to his men,
She saw at once the wretched end,   40
And, stooping down, tried hard to rend
Her coif the wrong way from her head,
And hid her eyes; while Robert said:
"Nay, love, 'tis scarcely two to one;
At Poictiers where we made them run
So fast: why, sweet my love, good cheer,
The Gascon frontier is so near,
Nought after this."

But: "O!" she said,
"My God! my God! I have to tread
The long way back without you; then   50
The court at Paris; those six men;
The gratings of the Chatelet;
The swift Seine on some rainy day
Like this, and people standing by,
And laughing, while my weak hands try
To recollect how strong men swim.
All this, or else a life with him,
For which I should be damned at last.
Would God that this next hour were past!"

He answered not, but cried his cry,   60
"St. George for Marny!" cheerily;
And laid his hand upon her rein.
Alas! no man of all his train
Gave back that cheery cry again;
And, while for rage his thumb beat fast
Upon his sword-hilt, some one cast
About his neck a kerchief long,
And bound him.

                    Then they went along
To Godmar; who said: "Now, Jehane,
Your lover's life is on the wane   70
So fast, that, if this very hour
You yield not as my paramour,
He will not see the rain leave off—
Nay, keep your tongue from gibe and scoff
Sir Robert, or I slay you now."

She laid her hand upon her brow,
Then gazed upon the palm, as though
She thought her forehead bled, and—"No!"
She said, and turned her head away,
As there were nothing else to say,   80
And everything were settled: red
Grew Godmar's face from chin to head:
"Jehane, on yonder hill there stands
My castle, guarding well my lands:
What hinders me from taking you,
And doing that I list to do
To your fair wilful body, while
Your knight lies dead?"

                    A wicked smile
Wrinkled her face, her lips grew thin,
A long way out she thrust her chin: 90

45. **Poictiers.** At the battle of Poictiers, 1356, the English defeated the French against five-to-one odds. 47. **Gascon frontier.** Gascony was English territory.

50–56. **then . . . swim.** Jehane, accused of witchcraft, would be imprisoned at Paris in the Chatelet, and finally flung into the Seine. If she sank she would be judged innocent, the theory being that the water would not take a witch to its bosom. 61. **"St. George for Marny!"** The name of the hero of the poem is Sir Robert de Marny. St. George is the patron saint of England.

"You know that I should strangle you
While you were sleeping; or bite through
Your throat, by God's help: ah!" she said,
"Lord Jesus, pity your poor maid!
For in such wise they hem me in,
I cannot choose but sin and sin,
Whatever happens: yet I think
They could not make me eat or drink,
And so should I just reach my rest."
"Nay, if you do not my behest,   100
O Jehane! though I love you well,"
Said Godmar, "would I fail to tell
All that I know?" "Foul lies," she said.
"Eh! lies, my Jehane? by God's head,
At Paris folks would deem them true!
Do you know, Jehane, they cry for you:
'Jehane the brown! Jehane the brown!
Give us Jehane to burn or drown!'—
Eh— gag me Robert!— sweet my friend,
This were indeed a piteous end   110
For those long fingers, and long feet,
And long neck, and smooth shoulders sweet;
An end that few men would forget
That saw it.— So, an hour yet:
Consider, Jehane, which to take
Of life or death!"

        So, scarce awake,
Dismounting, did she leave that place,
And totter some yards: with her face
Turned upward to the sky she lay,
Her head on a wet heap of hay,   120
And fell asleep: and while she slept,
And did not dream, the minutes crept
Round to the twelve again; but she,
Being waked at last, sighed quietly,
And strangely childlike came, and said:
"I will not." Straightway Godmar's head,
As though it hung on strong wires, turned
Most sharply round, and his face burned.

For Robert— both his eyes were dry,
He could not weep, but gloomily   130
He seemed to watch the rain; yea, too,
His lips were firm; he tried once more
To touch her lips; she reached out, sore
And vain desire so tortured them,
The poor grey lips, and now the hem
Of his sleeve brushed them.

        With a start
Up Godmar rose, thrust them apart;
From Robert's throat he loosed the bands
Of silk and mail; with empty hands

Held out, she stood and gazed, and saw   140
The long bright blade without a flaw
Glide out from Godmar's sheath, his hand
In Robert's hair; she saw him bend
Back Robert's head; she saw him send
The thin steel down; the blow told well,
Right backward the knight Robert fell,
And moaned as dogs do, being half dead,
Unwitting, as I deem: so then
Godmar turned grinning to his men,
Who ran, some five or six, and beat   150
His head to pieces at their feet.

Then Godmar turned again and said:
"So, Jehane, the first fitte is read!
Take note, my lady, that your way
Lies backward to the Chatelet!"
She shook her head and gazed awhile
At her cold hands with a rueful smile,
As though this thing had made her mad.

This was the parting that they had
Beside the haystack in the floods.   160

SUMMER DAWN

Pray but one prayer for me 'twixt thy closed
    lips,
  Think but one thought of me up in the stars.
The summer night waneth, the morning light
    slips,
  Faint and grey 'twixt the leaves of the aspen, be-
    twixt the cloud-bars,
That are patiently waiting there for the dawn:
  Patient and colourless, though Heaven's gold
Waits to float through them along with the sun.
Far out in the meadows, above the young corn,
  The heavy elms wait, and restless and cold
The uneasy wind rises; the roses are dun;   10
Through the long twilight they pray for the dawn.
Round the lone house in the midst of the corn.
  Speak but one word to me over the corn,
  Over the tender, bowed locks of the corn.

TWO RED ROSES ACROSS THE
MOON

There was a lady lived in a hall,
Large of her eyes, and slim and tall;
And ever she sung from noon to noon,
  Two red roses across the moon.

153. fitte, canto, division, as of a poem.

There was a knight came riding by
In early spring, when the roads were dry;
And he heard that lady sing at the noon,
Two red roses across the moon.

Yet none the more he stopped at all,
But he rode a-gallop past the hall;   10
And left that lady singing at noon,
Two red roses across the moon.

Because, forsooth, the battle was set,
And the scarlet and blue had got to be met,
He rode on the spur till the next warm noon:—
Two red roses across the moon.

But the battle was scattered from hill to hill,
From the windmill to the watermill;
And he said to himself, as it neared the noon,
Two red roses across the moon.   20

You scarce could see for the scarlet and blue,
A golden helm or a golden shoe:
So he cried, as the fight grew thick at the noon,
Two red roses across the moon!

Verily then the gold bore through
The huddled spears of the scarlet and blue;
And they cried, as they cut them down at the noon,
Two red roses across the moon!

I trow he stopped when he rode again
By the hall, though draggled sore with the rain;   30
And his lips were pinched to kiss at the noon
Two red roses across the moon.

Under the may she stooped to the crown,
All was gold, there was nothing of brown;
And the horns blew up in the hall at noon,
Two red roses across the moon.

from THE LIFE AND DEATH OF JASON

The story of Jason's quest for the Golden Fleece was originally intended by Morris for inclusion in *The Earthly Paradise*. It grew into an independent, impressive work, however, which was published in 1867.

from BOOK IV

I Know a Little Garden-close

With this song the water nymph sings young Hylas asleep.

I know a little garden-close,
Set thick with lily and red rose,

1. **garden-close,** an enclosed garden.

Where I would wander if I might
From dewy morn to dewy night,
And have one with me wandering.
  And though within it no birds sing,
And though no pillared house is there,
And though the apple boughs are bare
Of fruit and blossom, would to God,
Her feet upon the green grass trod,   10
And I beheld them as before.
  There comes a murmur from the shore,
And in the place two fair streams are,
Drawn from the purple hills afar,
Drawn down unto the restless sea:
Dark hills whose flowers ne'er feed the bee,
The shore no ship has ever seen,
Tormented by the billows green,
Whose murmur comes unceasingly
Unto the place for which I cry.   20
  For which I cry both day and night,
For which I let slip all delight,
That maketh me both deaf and blind,
Careless to win, unskilled to find,
And quick to lose what all men seek.
  Yet tottering as I am and weak,
Still have I left a little breath
To seek within the jaws of death
An entrance to that happy place,
To seek the unforgotten face,   30
Once seen, once kissed, once reft from me
Anigh the murmuring of the sea.

from BOOK XII

O Death, That Maketh Life so Sweet

Orpheus sings this song to encourage his companions on their homeward journey.

O death, that maketh life so sweet,
O fear, with mirth before thy feet,
What have ye yet in store for us,
The conquerors, the glorious?
  Men say: "For fear that thou shouldst die
To-morrow, let to-day pass by
Flower-crowned and singing"; yet have we
Passed our to-day upon the sea,
Or in a poisonous unknown land,
With fear and death on either hand,   10
And listless when the day was done
Have scarcely hoped to see the sun
Dawn on the morrow of the earth,
Nor in our hearts have thought of mirth.
And while the world lasts, scarce again
Shall any sons of men bear pain
Like we have borne, yet be alive.

So surely not in vain we strive
Like other men for our reward;
Sweet peace and deep, the chequered sward
Beneath the ancient mulberry-trees,   21
The smooth-paved gilded palaces,
Where the shy thin-clad damsels sweet
Make music with their gold-ringed feet.
The fountain court amidst of it,
Where the short-haired slave maidens sit,
While on the veinèd pavement lie
The honied things and spicery
Their arms have borne from out the town.

   The dancers on the thymy down   30
In summer twilight, when the earth
Is still of all things but their mirth,
And echoes borne upon the wind
Of others in like way entwined:
   The merchant-town's fair market-place,
Where over many a changing face
The pigeons of the temple flit,
And still the outland merchants sit
Like kings above their merchandise,
Lying to foolish men and wise.   40
   Ah! if they heard that we were come
Into the bay, and bringing home
That which all men have talked about,
Some men with rage, and some with doubt,
Some with desire, and some with praise;
Then would the people throng the ways,
Nor heed the outland merchandise,
Nor any talk, from fools or wise,
But tales of our accomplished quest.
   What soul within the house shall rest   50
When we come home? The wily king
Shall leave his throne to see the thing;
No man shall keep the landward gate,
The hurried traveller shall wait
Until our bulwarks graze the quay,
Unslain the milk-white bull shall be
Beside the quivering altar-flame;
Scarce shall the maiden clasp for shame
Over her breast the raiment thin
The morn that Argo cometh in.   60
   Then cometh happy life again
That payeth well our toil and pain
In that sweet hour, when all our woe
But as a pensive tale we know,
Nor yet remember deadly fear,
For surely now if death be near
Unthought-of is it, and unseen
When sweet is, that hath bitter been.

30. **thymy down,** a tract of open upland, covered with thyme.   43. **That . . . about,** the Golden Fleece.

from THE EARTHLY PARADISE

The general plan of Morris's most elaborate work (1868–70) was indebted to Chaucer. Driven from their native Norway by the Black Death, a group of fourteenth-century wanderers start out in search of the Earthly Paradise. They find their haven at last in a "Western land" whose inhabitants are descendants of the ancient Greeks. Two solemn feasts a month are ordained, and at each feast two tales are told, one by the hosts and one by the visitors. This gives Morris a chance to use both classical and later European material. Among the twenty-four stories presented are "Atalanta's Race," "The Man Born to Be King," "The Story of Cupid and Psyche," "The Love of Alcestis," "Pygmalion and the Image," "The Story of Rhodope," and "The Hill of Venus." Most of the tales are in the romantic vein, though some, like "The Lovers of Gudrun" and the Bellerophon stories (derived from Book VI of the *Iliad*) are in the epic manner.

AN APOLOGY

Of Heaven or Hell I have no power to sing,
I cannot ease the burden of your fears,
Or make quick-coming death a little thing,
Or bring again the pleasure of past years,
Nor for my words shall ye forget your tears,
Or hope again, for aught that I can say,
The idle singer of an empty day.

But rather, when aweary of your mirth,
From full hearts still unsatisfied ye sigh,
And, feeling kindly unto all the earth,   10
Grudge every minute as it passes by,
Made the more mindful that the sweet days die—
Remember me a little then, I pray,
The idle singer of an empty day.

The heavy trouble, the bewildering care
That weighs us down who live and earn our bread,
These idle verses have no power to bear;
So let me sing of names rememberèd,
Because they, living not, can ne'er be dead,
Or long time take their memory quite away   20
From us poor singers of an empty day.

Dreamer of dreams, born out of my due time,
Why should I strive to set the crooked straight?
Let it suffice me that my murmuring rhyme
Beats with light wing against the ivory gate,
Telling a tale not too importunate
To those who in the sleepy region stay,
Lulled by the singer of an empty day.

25. **the ivory gate,** the egress through which true dreams issue from the house of Morpheus, god of sleep. False dreams pass through a gate of horn.

Folk say, a wizard to a northern king   29
At Christmas-tide such wondrous things did show,
That through one window men beheld the spring,
And through another saw the summer glow,
And through a third the fruited vines a-row,
While still, unheard, but in its wonted way,
Piped the drear wind of that December day.

So with this Earthly Paradise it is,
If ye will read aright, and pardon me,
Who strive to build a shadowy isle of bliss
Midmost the beating of the steely sea,
Where tossed about all hearts of men must be;   40
Whose ravening monsters mighty men shall slay,
Not the poor singer of an empty day.

THE LADY OF THE LAND

Morris prefixed the following argument to this tale: "A
certain man, having landed on an island in the Greek
Sea, found there a beautiful damsel, whom he fain would
have delivered from a strange and dreadful doom, but
failing herein, he died soon afterwards."

The spell of enchantment that can be broken only by
love is a very common theme in folklore. See "The Wife
of Bath's Tale" in Chaucer's *Canterbury Tales* and "The
Tale of Florent" in Gower's *Confessio Amantis;* among the
ballads, "The Wedding of Sir Gawain and Dame Rag-
nell," "The Marriage of Sir Gawain," "King Henry,"
and "Kemp Owyne"; among our standard fairy tales,
"The Frog Prince," "The Sleeping Beauty," "Beauty
and the Beast," and "Ricky of the Tuft." Sometimes the
man is transformed, sometimes the woman; in Sir Arthur
Wing Pinero's play *The Enchanted Cottage,* "a Fable,"
1922, the situation is doubled, and both persons are
transformed. Browning's "Muckle-Mouth Meg" (page
803) is a rationalization of the old folklore theme.

It happened once, some men of Italy
Midst the Greek Islands went a sea-roving,
And much good fortune had they on the sea:
Of many a man they had the ransoming,
And many a chain they gat, and goodly thing;
And midst their voyage to an isle they came,
Whereof my story keepeth not the name.

Now though but little was there left to gain,
Because the richer folk had gone away,
Yet since by this of water they were fain,   10
They came to anchor in a land-locked bay,
Whence in a while some went ashore to play,
Going but lightly armed in twos or threes,
For midst that folk they feared no enemies.

10. **by this,** by this time.

And of these fellows that thus went ashore,
One was there who left all his friends behind;
Who going inland ever more and more,
And being left quite alone, at last did find
A lonely valley sheltered from the wind,
Wherein, amidst an ancient cypress wood,   20
A long-deserted ruined castle stood.

The wood, once ordered in fair grove and glade,
With gardens overlooked by terraces,
And marble-pavèd pools for pleasure made,
Was tangled now, and choked with fallen trees;
And he who went there, with but little ease
Must stumble by the stream's side, once made meet
For tender women's dainty wandering feet.

The raven's croak, the low wind choked and
        drear,
The baffled stream, the grey wolf's doleful cry,   30
Were all the sounds that mariner could hear,
As through the wood he wandered painfully;
But as unto the house he drew anigh,
The pillars of a ruined shrine he saw,
The once fair temple of a fallen law.

No image was there left behind to tell
Before whose face the knees of men had bowed;
An altar of black stone, of old wrought well,
Alone beneath a ruined roof now showed
The goal whereto the folk were wont to crowd,   40
Seeking for things forgotten long ago,
Praying for heads long ages laid a-low.

Close to the temple was the castle-gate,
Doorless and crumbling; there our fellow turned,
Trembling indeed at what might chance to wait
The prey entrapped, yet with a heart that burned
To know the most of what might there be learned,
And hoping somewhat too, amid his fear,
To light on such things as all men hold dear.

Noble the house was, nor seemed built for war,
But rather like the work of other days,   51
When men, in better peace than now they are,
Had leisure on the world around to gaze,
And noted well the past times' changing ways;
And fair with sculptured stories it was wrought,
By lapse of time unto dim ruin brought.

Now as he looked about on all these things,
And strove to read the mouldering histories,
Above the door an image with wise wings,
Whose unclad limbs a serpent seemed to seize,   60
He dimly saw, although the western breeze,

And years of biting frost and washing rain,
Had made the carver's labour well-nigh vain.

But this, though perished sore, and worn away,
He noted well, because it seemed to be,
After the fashion of another day,
Some great man's badge of war, or armoury,
And round it a carved wreath he seemed to see:
But taking note of these things, at the last
The mariner beneath the gateway passed.   70

And there a lovely cloistered court he found,
A fountain in the midst o'erthrown and dry,
And in the cloister briers twining round
The slender shafts; the wondrous imagery
Outworn by more than many years gone by;
Because the country people, in their fear
Of wizardry, had wrought destruction here;

And piteously these fair things had been maimed;
There stood great Jove, lacking his head of might;
Here was the archer, swift Apollo, lamed;   80
The shapely limbs of Venus hid from sight
By weeds and shards; Diana's ankles light
Bound with the cable of some coasting ship;
And rusty nails through Helen's maddening lip.

Therefrom unto the chambers did he pass,
And found them fair still, midst of their decay,
Though in them now no sign of man there was,
And everything but stone had passed away
That made them lovely in that vanished day;   89
Nay, the mere walls themselves would soon be gone
And nought be left but heaps of mouldering stone.

But he, when all the place he had gone o'er,
And with much trouble clomb the broken stair,
And from the topmost turret seen the shore
And his good ship drawn up at anchor there,
Came down again, and found a crypt most fair
Built wonderfully beneath the greatest hall;
And there he saw a door within the wall,

Well-hinged, close shut; nor was there in that place
Another on its hinges, therefore he   100
Stood there and pondered for a little space,
And thought, "Perchance some marvel I shall see,
For surely here some dweller there must be,

79. **Jove**, ruler of the gods in the Roman Pantheon.
81. **Venus**, goddess of love. 82. **Diana**, goddess, among other things, of the moon, the chase, and (as Hecate) of the lower world. 84. **Helen**, wife of Menelaus, king of Sparta, whose abduction by the Trojan prince Paris was the cause of the Trojan War.

Because this door seems whole, and new, and sound,
While nought but ruin I can see around."

So with that word, moved by a strong desire,
He tried the hasp, that yielded to his hand,
And in a strange place, lit as by a fire
Unseen but near, he presently did stand;
And by an odorous breeze his face was fanned,   110
As though in some Arabian plain he stood,
Anigh the border of a spice-tree wood.

He moved not for a while, but looking round,
He wondered much to see the place so fair,
Because, unlike the castle above ground,
No pillager or wrecker had been there;
It seemed that time had passed on otherwhere,
Nor laid a finger on this hidden place,
Rich with the wealth of some forgotten race.

With hangings, fresh as when they left the loom,
The walls were hung a space above the head;   121
Slim ivory chairs were set about the room,
And in one corner was a dainty bed,
That seemed for some fair queen apparelèd;
And marble was the worst stone of the floor
That with rich Indian webs was covered o'er.

The wanderer trembled when he saw all this,
Because he deemed by magic it was wrought;
Yet in his heart a longing for some bliss,
Whereof the hard and changing world knows nought,   130
Arose and urged him on, and dimmed the thought
That there perchance some devil lurked to slay
The heedless wanderer from the light of day.

Over against him was another door
Set in the wall; so, casting fear aside,
With hurried steps he crossed the varied floor,
And there again the silver latch he tried
And with no pain the door he opened wide,
And entering the new chamber cautiously
The glory of great heaps of gold could see.   140

Upon the floor uncounted medals lay,
Like things of little value; here and there
Stood golden caldrons, that might well outweigh
The biggest midst an emperor's copper-ware,
And golden cups were set on tables fair,
Themselves of gold; and in all hollow things
Were stored great gems, worthy the crowns of kings.

The walls and roof with gold were overlaid,
And precious raiment from the wall hung down:

The fall of kings that treasure might have stayed, 150
Or gained some longing conqueror great renown,
Or built again some god-destroyed old town;
What wonder, if this plunderer of the sea
Stood gazing at it long and dizzily?

But at the last his troubled eyes and dazed
He lifted from the glory of that gold,
And then the image, that wellnigh erased
Over the castle-gate he did behold,
Above a door well wrought in coloured gold
Again he saw—a naked girl with wings   160
Enfolded in a serpent's scaly rings.

And even as his eyes were fixed on it
A woman's voice came from the other side,
And through his heart strange hopes began to flit
That in some wondrous land he might abide
Not dying, master of a deathless bride,
So o'er the gold which now he scarce could see
He went, and passed this last door eagerly.

Then in a room he stood wherein there was
A marble bath, whose brimming water yet   170
Was scarcely still; a vessel of green glass
Half full of odorous ointment was there set
Upon the topmost step that still was wet,
And jewelled shoes and women's dainty gear,
Lay cast upon the varied pavement near.

In one quick glance these things his eyes did
       see,
But speedily they turned round to behold
Another sight, for throned on ivory
There sat a woman, whose wet tresses rolled
On to the floor in waves of gleaming gold,   180
Cast back from such a form as, erewhile shown
To one poor shepherd, lighted up Troy town.

Naked she was, the kisses of her feet
Upon the floor a dying path had made
From the full bath unto her ivory seat;
In her right hand, upon her bosom laid,
She held a golden comb, a mirror weighed
Her left hand down, aback her fair head lay
Dreaming awake of some long vanished day.   189

Her eyes were shut, but she seemed not to sleep,
Her lips were murmuring things unheard and low,
Or sometimes twitched as though she needs must
       weep

181–82. such a form . . . Troy town. Venus promised
Helen to Paris if he would award the golden apple ("for the
fairest") to her rather than to Juno or Minerva.

Though from her eyes the tears refused to flow,
And oft with heavenly red her cheek did glow,
As if remembrance of some half-sweet shame
Across the web of many memories came.

There stood the man, scarce daring to draw
       breath
For fear the lovely sight should fade away;
Forgetting heaven, forgetting life and death,
Trembling for fear lest something he should say   200
Unwitting, lest some sob should yet betray
His presence there, for to his eager eyes
Already did the tears begin to rise.

But as he gazed, she moved, and with a sigh
Bent forward, dropping down her golden head;
"Alas, alas! another day gone by,
Another day and no soul come," she said;
"Another year, and still I am not dead!"
And with that word once more her head she raised,
And on the trembling man with great eyes gazed.

Then he imploring hands to her did reach,   211
And toward her very slowly 'gan to move
And with wet eyes her pity did beseech,
And seeing her about to speak, he strove
From trembling lips to utter words of love;
And with a look she stayed his doubtful feet,
And made sweet music as their eyes did meet.

For now she spoke in gentle voice and clear,
Using the Greek tongue that he knew full well;
"What man art thou, that thus hast wandered
       here,
And found this lonely chamber where I dwell?   221
Beware, beware! for I have many a spell;
If greed of power and gold have led thee on,
Not lightly shall this untold wealth be won.

"But if thou com'st here, knowing of my tale,
In hope to bear away my body fair,
Stout must thine heart be, nor shall that avail
If thou a wicked heart in thee dost bear;
So once again I bid thee to beware,
Because no base man things like this may see,   230
And live thereafter long and happily."

"Lady," he said, " in Florence is my home,
And in my city noble is my name;
Neither on peddling voyage am I come,
But, like my fathers, bent to gather fame;
And though thy face has set my heart a-flame
Yet of thy story nothing do I know,
But here have wandered heedlessly enow.

"But since the sight of thee mine eyes did bless,
What can I be but thine? what wouldst thou have?
From those thy words, I deem from some distress
By deeds of mine thy dear life I might save;   242
Oh, then, delay not! if one ever gave
His life to any, mine I give to thee;
Come, tell me what the price of love must be?

"Swift death, to be with thee a day and night
And with the earliest dawning to be slain?
Or better, a long year of great delight,
And many years of misery and pain?
Or worse, and this poor hour for all my gain?   250
A sorry merchant am I on this day,
E'en as thou willest, so must I obey."

She said, "What brave words! Nought divine am
     I,
But an unhappy and unheard-of maid
Compelled by evil fate and destiny
To live, who long ago should have been laid
Under the earth within the cypress shade.
Hearken awhile, and quickly shalt thou know
What deed I pray thee to accomplish now.

"God grant indeed thy words are not for nought!
Then shalt thou save me, since for many a day   261
To such a dreadful life I have been brought:
Nor will I spare with all my heart to pay
What man soever takes my grief away;
Ah! I will love thee, if thou lovest me
But well enough my saviour now to be.

"My father lived a many years agone,
Lord of this land, master of all cunning,
Who ruddy gold could draw from out grey stone,
And gather wealth from many an uncouth thing;
He made the wilderness rejoice and sing,   271
And such a leech he was that none could say
Without his word what soul should pass away.

"Unto Diana such a gift he gave,
Goddess above, below, and on the earth,
That I should be her virgin and her slave
From the first hour of my most wretched birth;
Therefore my life had known but little mirth
When I had come unto my twentieth year
And the last time of hallowing drew anear.   280

"So in her temple had I lived and died
And all would long ago have passed away,
But ere that time came, did strange things betide,
Whereby I am alive unto this day;

280. **hallowing**, consecration.

Alas, the bitter words that I must say!
Ah! can I bring my wretched tongue to tell
How I was brought unto this fearful hell.

"A queen I was, what gods I knew I loved,
And nothing evil was there in my thought,
And yet by love my wretched heart was moved   290
Until to utter ruin I was brought!
Alas! thou sayest our gods were vain and nought·
Wait, wait, till thou hast heard this tale of mine
Then shalt thou think them devilish or divine.

"Hearken! in spite of father and of vow,
I loved a man; but for that sin I think
Men had forgiven me—yea, yea, even thou;
But from the gods the full cup must I drink,
And into misery unheard of sink,
Tormented, when their own names are forgot,   300
And men must doubt e'er if they lived or not.

"Glorious my lover was unto my sight,
Most beautiful,—of love we grew so fain
That we at last agreed, that on a night
We should be happy, but that he were slain
Or shut in hold; and neither joy nor pain
Should else forbid that hoped-for time to be;
So came the night that made a wretch of me.

"Ah! well do I remember all that night,
When through the window shone the orb of June,
And by the bed flickered the taper's light,   311
Whereby I trembled, gazing at the moon;
Ah me! the meeting that we had, when soon
Into his strong, well-trusted arms I fell,
And many a sorrow we began to tell.

"Ah me! what parting on that night we had!
I think the story of my great despair
A little while might merry folk make sad;
For, as he swept away my yellow hair
To make my shoulder and my bosom bare,   320
I raised mine eyes, and shuddering could behold
A shadow cast upon the bed of gold:

"Then suddenly was quenched my hot desire
And he untwined his arms; the moon so pale
A while ago, seemed changed to blood and fire,
And yet my limbs beneath me did not fail,
And neither had I strength to cry or wail,
But stood there helpless, bare, and shivering,
With staring eyes still fixed upon the thing.

"Because the shade that on the bed of gold   330
The changed and dreadful moon was throwing down

Was of Diana, whom I did behold,
With knotted hair, and shining girt-up gown,
And on the high white brow, a deadly frown
Bent upon us, who stood scarce drawing breath,
Striving to meet the horrible sure death.

"No word at all the dreadful goddess said,
But soon across my feet my lover lay,
And well indeed I knew that he was dead;
And would that I had died on that same day!   340
For in a while the image turned away,
And without words my doom I understood,
And felt a horror change my human blood.

"And there I fell, and on the floor I lay
By the dead man, till daylight came on me,
And not a word thenceforward could I say
For three years; till of grief and misery,
The lingering pest, the cruel enemy,
My father and his folk were dead and gone,
And in this castle I was left alone: 350

"And then the doom foreseen upon me fell,
For Queen Diana did my body change
Into a fork-tongued dragon flesh and fell,
And through the island nightly do I range,
Or in the green sea mate with monsters strange,
When in the middle of the moonlit night
The sleepy mariner I do affright.

"But all day long upon this gold I lie
Within this place, where never mason's hand
Smote trowel on the marble noisily;   360
Drowsy I lie, no folk at my command,
Who once was called the Lady of the Land;
Who might have bought a kingdom with a kiss,
Yea, half the world with such a sight as this."

And therewithal, with rosy fingers light,
Backward her heavy-hanging hair she threw,
To give her naked beauty more to sight;
But when, forgetting all the things he knew,
Maddened with love unto the prize he drew,
She cried, "Nay, wait! for wherefore wilt thou
        die,
Why should we not be happy, thou and I?   371

"Wilt thou not save me? Once in every year
This rightful form of mine that thou dost see
By favour of the goddess have I here
From sunrise unto sunset given me,
That some brave man may end my misery.
And thou—art thou not brave? can thy heart fail,
Whose eyes e'en now are weeping at my tale?

"Then listen! when this day is overpast,
A fearful monster shall I be again,   380
And thou mayst be my saviour at the last;
Unless, once more, thy words are nought and vain.
If thou of love and sovereignty art fain,
Come thou next morn, and when thou seest here
A hideous dragon, have thereof no fear.

"But take the loathsome head up in thine hands,
And kiss it, and be master presently
Of twice the wealth that is in all the lands,
From Cathay to the head of Italy;
And master also, if it pleaseth thee,   390
Of all thou praisest as so fresh and bright,
Of what thou callest crown of all delight.

"Ah! with what joy then shall I see again
The sunlight on the green grass and the trees,
And hear the clatter of the summer rain,
And see the joyous folk beyond the seas.
Ah, me! to hold my child upon my knees,
After the weeping of unkindly tears,
And all the wrongs of these four hundred years.

"Go now, go quick! leave this grey heap of stone;
And from thy glad heart think upon thy way,   401
How I shall love thee—yea, love thee alone,
That bringest me from dark death unto day;
For this shall be thy wages and thy pay;
Unheard-of wealth, unheard-of love is near,
If thou hast heart a little dread to bear."

Therewith she turned to go; but he cried out,
"Ah! wilt thou leave me then without one kiss,
To slay the very seeds of fear and doubt,
That glad tomorrow may bring certain bliss?   410
Hast thou forgotten how love lives by this,
The memory of some hopeful close embrace,
Low whispered words within some lonely place?"

But she, when his bright glittering eyes she saw,
And burning cheeks, cried out, "Alas, alas!
Must I be quite undone, and wilt thou draw
A worse fate on me than the first one was?
O haste thee from this fatal place to pass!
Yet, ere thou goest, take this, lest thou shouldst
        deem
Thou hast been fooled by some midday dream."   420

So saying, blushing like a new-kissed maid,
From off her neck a little gem she drew,
That, 'twixt those snowy rose-tinged hillocks laid,
The secrets of her glorious beauty knew;
And ere he well perceived what she would do,

She touched his hand, the gem within it lay,
And, turning, from his sight she fled away.

Then at the doorway where her rosy heel
Had glanced and vanished, he awhile did stare,
And still upon his hand he seemed to feel   430
The varying kisses of her fingers fair;
Then turned he toward the dreary crypt and bare,
And dizzily throughout the castle passed,
Till by the ruined fane he stood at last.

Then weighing still the gem within his hand,
He stumbled backward through the cypress wood,
Thinking the while of some strange lovely land,
Where all his life should be most fair and good
Till on the valley's wall of hills he stood,
And slowly thence passed down unto the bay   440
Red with the death of that bewildering day.

The next day came, and he, who all the night
Had ceaselessly been turning in his bed,
Arose and clad himself in armour bright,
And many a danger he remembered;
Storming of towns, lone sieges full of dread,
That with renown his heart had borne him through
And this thing seemed a little thing to do.

So on he went, and on the way he thought
Of all the glorious things of yesterday,   450
Nought of the price whereat they must be bought,
But ever to himself did softly say,
"No roaming now, my wars are passed away;
No long dull days devoid of happiness,
When such a love my yearning heart shall bless."

Thus to the castle did he come at last,
But when unto the gateway he drew near,
And underneath its ruined archway passed
Into the court, a strange noise did he hear,
And through his heart there shot a pang of fear;   460
Trembling, he gat his sword into his hand,
And midmost of the cloisters took his stand.

But for a while that unknown noise increased,
A rattling, that with strident roars did blend,
And whining moans; but suddenly it ceased,
A fearful thing stood at the cloister's end,
And eyed him for a while, then 'gan to wend
Adown the cloisters, and began again
That rattling, and the moan like fiends in pain.

And as it came on towards him, with its teeth   470
The body of a slain goat did it tear,
The blood whereof in its hot jaws did seethe,

And on its tongue he saw the smoking hair;
Then his heart sank, and standing trembling there,
Throughout his mind wild thoughts and fearful ran,
"Some fiend she was," he said, "the bane of man."

Yet he abode her still, although his blood
Curdled within him: the thing dropped the goat,
And creeping on, came close to where he stood,
And raised its head to him, and wrinkled throat,   480
Then he cried out and wildly at her smote,
Shutting his eyes, and turned and from the place
Ran swiftly, with a white and ghastly face.

But little things rough stones and tree-trunks
    seemed,
And if he fell, he rose and ran on still;
No more he felt his hurts than if he dreamed,
He made no stay for valley or steep hill,
Heedless, he dashed through many a foaming rill,
Until he came unto the ship at last,
And with no word into the deep hold passed.   490

Meanwhile the dragon, seeing him clean gone,
Followed him not, but crying horribly,
Caught up within her jaws a block of stone
And ground it into powder, then turned she,
With cries that folk could hear far out at sea,
And reached the treasure set apart of old,
To brood above the hidden heaps of gold.

Yet was she seen again on many a day
By some half-waking mariner, or herd,
Playing amid the ripples of the bay,   500
Or on the hills making all things afeard,
Or in the wood, that did that castle gird,
But never any man again durst go
To seek her woman's form, and end her woe.

As for the man, who knows what things he bore?
What mournful faces peopled the sad night,
What wailings vexed him with reproaches sore,
What images of that nigh-gained delight!
What dreamed caresses from soft hands and white,
Turning to horrors ere they reached the best: 510
What struggles vain, what shame, what huge un-
    rest?

No man he knew; three days he lay and raved,
And cried for death, until a lethargy
Fell on him, and his fellows thought him saved;
But on the third night he awoke to die;
And at Byzantium doth his body lie

516. Byzantium, Constantinople, now Istanbul.

Between two blossoming pomegranate trees,
Within the churchyard of the Genoese.

L'ENVOI

Here are we for the last time face to face,
Thou and I, Book, before I bid thee speed
Upon thy perilous journey to that place
For which I have done on thee pilgrim's weed,
Striving to get thee all things for thy need—
I love thee, whatso time or men may say
Of the poor singer of an empty day.

Good reason why I love thee, e'en if thou
Be mocked or clean forgot as time wears on;
For ever as thy fashioning did grow,   10
Kind word and praise because of thee I won
From those without whom were my world all gone,
My hope fallen dead, my singing cast away,
And I set soothly in an empty day.

I love thee; yet this last time must it be
That thou must hold thy peace and I must speak,
Lest if thou babble I begin to see
Thy gear too thin, thy limbs and heart too weak,
To find the land thou goest forth to seek—
—Though what harm if thou die upon the way,   20
Thou idle singer of an empty day?

But though this land desired thou never reach,
Yet folk who know it mayst thou meet or death;
Therefore a word unto thee would I teach
To answer these, who, noting thy weak breath,
Thy wandering eyes, thy heart of little faith,
May make thy fond desire a sport and play,
Mocking the singer of an empty day.

That land's name, say'st thou? and the road
    thereto?
Nay, Book, thou mockest, saying thou know'st it not;
Surely no book of verse I ever knew   31
But ever was the heart within him hot
To gain the Land of Matters Unforgot—
—There, now we both laugh—as the whole world
    may,
At us poor singers of an empty day.

Nay, let it pass, and harken! Hast thou heard
That therein I believe I have a friend,
Of whom for love I may not be afeard?
It is to him indeed I bid thee wend;
Yea, he perchance may meet thee ere thou end, 40
Dying so far off from the hedge of bay,
Thou idle singer of an empty day!

Well, think of him, I bid thee, on the road,
And if it hap that midst of thy defeat,
Fainting beneath thy follies' heavy load,
My Master, GEOFFREY CHAUCER, thou do meet,
Then shalt thou win a space of rest full sweet;
Then be thou bold and speak the words I say,
The idle singer of an empty day!

"O Master, O thou great of heart and tongue,   50
Thou well mayst ask me why I wander here,
In raiment rent of stories oft besung!
But of thy gentleness draw thou anear,
And then the heart of one who held thee dear
Mayst thou behold! So near as that I lay
Unto the singer of an empty day.

"For this he ever said, who sent me forth
To seek a place amid thy company;
That howsoever little was my worth,
Yet was he worth e'en just so much as I;   60
He said that rhyme hath little skill to lie;
Nor feigned to cast his worser part away;
In idle singing for an empty day.

"I have beheld him tremble oft enough
At things he could not choose but trust to me,
Although he knew the world was wise and rough:
And never did he fail to let me see
His love,—his folly and faithlessness, maybe;
And still in turn I gave him voice to pray
Such prayers as cling about an empty day.   70

"Thou, keen-eyed, reading me, mayst read him
    through,
For surely little is there left behind;
No power great deeds unnameable to do;
No knowledge for which words he may not find,
No love of things as vague as autumn wind—
—Earth of the earth lies hidden by my clay,
The idle singer of an empty day!

"Children we twain are, saith he, late made wise
In love, but in all else most childish still,
And seeking still the pleasure of our eyes,   80
And what our ears with sweetest sounds may fill;
Not fearing Love, lest these things he should kill;
Howe'er his pain by pleasure doth he lay,
Making a strange tale of an empty day.

"Death have we hated, knowing not what it
    meant;
Life had we loved, through green leaf and through
    sere,
Though still the less we knew of its intent;

The Earth and Heaven through countless year on
    year,
Slow changing, were to us but curtains fair,
Hung round about a little room, where play   90
Weeping and laughter of man's empty day.

"O Master, if thine heart could love us yet,
Spite of things left undone, and wrongly done,
Some place in loving hearts then should we get,
For thou, sweet-souled, didst never stand alone,
But knew'st the joy and woe of many an one—
—By lovers dead, who live through thee, we pray,
Help thou us singers of an empty day!"

Fearest thou, Book, what answer thou mayst gain
Lest he should scorn thee, and thereof thou die?   100
Nay, it shall not be.—Thou mayst toil in vain,
And never draw the House of Fame anigh;
Yet he and his shall know whereof we cry,
Shall call it not ill done to strive to lay
The ghosts that crowd about life's empty day.

Then let the others go! and if indeed
In some old garden thou and I have wrought,
And made fresh flowers spring up from hoarded
    seed,
And fragrance of old days and deeds have brought
Back to folk weary, all was not for nought.   110
—No little part it was for me to play—
The idle singer of an empty day.

WRITTEN IN A COPY OF
THE EARTHLY PARADISE

Dec. 25, 1870

So many stories written here
And none among them but doth bear
Its weight of trouble and of woe!
Well may you ask why it is so;
For surely neither sour nor dull
In such a world, of fair things full,
Should folk be.
          Ah, my dears, indeed
My wisdom fails me at my need
To tell why tales that move the earth   10
Are seldom of content and mirth.
Yet think if it may come of this—
That lives fulfilled of ease and bliss
Crave not for aught that we can give,
And scorn the broken lives we live;
Unlike to us they pass us by,
A dying laugh their history.

But those that struggled sore, and failed
Had one thing left them, that availed
When all things else were nought—   20
              E'en Love—
Whose sweet voice, crying as they strove,
Begat sweet pity, and more love still,
Waste places with sweet tales to fill;
Whereby we, living here, may learn
Our eyes toward very Love to turn,
And all the pain it bringeth meet
As nothing strange amid the sweet:
Whereby we too may hope to be
Grains in the great world's memory   30
Of pain endured, and nobleness
That life ill-understood doth bless.

NO MASTER

Saith man to man, We've heard and known
    That we no master need
To live upon this earth, our own,
    In fair and manly deed.
The grief of slaves long passed away
    For us hath forged the chain,
Till now each worker's patient day
    Builds up the House of Pain.

And we, shall we too crouch and quail,
    Ashamed, afraid of strife,   10
And lest our lives untimely fail
    Embrace the Death in Life?
Nay, cry aloud, and have no fear,
    We few against the world;
Awake, arise! the hope we bear
    Against the curse is hurled.

It grows and grows—are we the same,
    The feeble band, the few?
Or what are these with eyes aflame,
    And hands to deal and do?   20
This is the host that bears the word,
    "No Master high or low"—
A lightning flame, a shearing sword,
    A storm to overthrow.

A DEATH SONG

On November 13, 1887, the London police attacked a
Socialist parade in which Morris was marching, and the
poet's friend Alfred Linnell died from the injuries he
received. Proceeds from the sale of "A Death Song" in
penny-pamphlet form were dedicated to the relief of
Linnell's children.

What cometh here from west to east awending?
And who are these, the marchers stern and slow?
We bear the message that the rich are sending
Aback to those who bade them wake and know.
Not one, not one, nor thousands must they slay,
But one and all if they would dusk the day.

We asked them for a life of toilsome earning,
They bade us bide their leisure for our bread;
We crave to speak to tell our woeful learning:
We come back speechless, bearing back our dead.
Not one, not one, nor thousands must they slay,   11
But one and all if they would dusk the day.

They will not learn; they have no ears to hearken.
They turn their faces from the eyes of fate;
Their gay-lit halls shut out the skies that darken.
But, lo! this dead man knocking at the gate.
Not one, not one, nor thousands must they slay,
But one and all if they would dusk the day.

Here lies the sign that we shall break our prison;
Amidst the storm he won a prisoner's rest;   20
But in the cloudy dawn the sun arisen
Brings us our day of work to win the best.
Not one, not one, nor thousands must they slay,
But one and all if they would dusk the day.

TO THE MUSE OF THE NORTH

O muse that swayest the sad Northern Song,
Thy right hand full of smiting of wrong,
Thy left hand holding pity; thy breast
Heaving with hope of that so certain rest:
Thou, with the grey eyes kind and unafraid,
The soft lips trembling not, though they have said
The doom of the World and those that dwell
    therein,
The lips that smile not though thy children win
The fated Love that draws the fated Death.
O, borne adown the fresh stream of thy breath,   10
Let some word reach my ears and touch my heart,
That, if it may be, I may have a part
In that great sorrow of thy children dead
That vexed the brow, and bowed adown the
    head,
Whitened the hair, made life a wondrous dream,
And death the murmur of a restful stream,
But left no stain upon those souls of thine
Whose greatness through the tangled world doth
    shine.
O Mother, and Love and Sister all in one,
Come thou; for sure I am enough alone   20

That thou thine arms about my heart shouldst
    throw,
And wrap me in the grief of long ago.

KNIGHT AAGEN & MAIDEN ELSE

Translated from the Danish

It was the fair knight Aagen
To an isle he went his way,
And plighted troth to Else,
Who was so fair a may.

He plighted troth to Else
All with the ruddy gold,
But or ere that day's moon came again
Low he lay in the black, black mould.

It was the maiden Else,
She was fulfilled of woe   10
When she heard how the fair knight Aagen
In the black mould lay alow.

Uprose the fair knight Aagen,
Coffin on back took he,
And he's away to her bower,
Sore hard as the work might be.

With that same chest on door he smote,
For the lack of flesh and skin;
"O hearken, maiden Else,
And let thy true-love in!"   20

Then answered maiden Else,
"Never open I my door,
But and if thou namest Jesu's name
As thou hadst might before."

"O hearken, maiden Else,
And open thou thy door,
For Jesu's name I well may name
As I had might before!"

Then uprose maiden Else,
O'er her cheek the salt tears ran,   30
Nor spared she into her very bower
To welcome that dead man.

O, she's taken up her comb of gold
And combed adown her hair,
And for every hair she combed adown
There fell a weary tear.

4. may, maid.

"Hearken thou, knight Aagen,
Hearken, true-love, and tell,
If down-adown in the black, black earth
Thou farest ever well?"   40

"O whenso thou art joyous,
And the heart is glad in thee,
Then fares it with my coffin
That red roses are with me.

"But whenso thou art sorrowful
And weary is thy mood,
Then all within my coffin
Is it dreadful with dark blood.

"Now is the red cock a-crowing,
To the earth adown must I;   50
Down to the earth wend all dead folk,
And I wend in company.

"Now is the black cock a-crowing,
To the earth must I a-down,
For the gates of Heaven are opening now,
Thereto must I begone."

Uprose the fair knight Aagen,
Coffin on back took he.
And he's away to the churchyard now,
Sore hard as the work might be.   60

But so wrought maiden Else,
Because of her weary mood,
That she followed after her own true love
All through the mirk wild wood.

But when the wood was well passed through,
And in the churchyard they were,
Then was the fair knight Aagen
Waxen wan of his golden hair.

And when therefrom they wended
And were the church within,   70
Then was the fair knight Aagen
Waxen wan of cheek and chin.

"Hearken thou, maiden Else,
Hearken, true-love, to me,
Weep no more for thine own troth-plight,
However it shall be!

"Look thou up to the heavens aloft,
To the little stars and bright,
And thou shalt see how sweetly
It fareth with the night!"   80

She looked up to the heavens aloft,
To the little stars bright above.
The dead man sank into his grave,
Ne'er again she saw her love.

Home then went the maiden Else,
Mid sorrow manifold,
And ere that night's moon came again
She lay alow in the mould.

FOR THE BED AT KELMSCOTT

Kelmscott Manor was Morris's home in Lechdale.
The bed itself is the speaker.

The wind's on the wold
And the night is a-cold,
And Thames runs chill
Twixt mead and hill,
But kind and dear
Is the old house here,
And my heart is warm
Midst winter's harm.
Rest, then and rest,
And think of the best   10
Twixt summer and spring
When all birds sing
In the town of the tree,
And ye lie in me
And scarce dare move
Lest earth and its love
Should fade away
Ere the full of the day.

I am old and have seen
Many things that have been,   20
Both grief and peace,
And wane and increase.
No tale I tell
Of ill or well,
But this I say,
Night treadeth on day,
And for the worst and best
Right good is rest.

THE SOCIALIST IDEAL

I. ART

Written for the "New Review," January 1891

This paper was followed by a second on Politics, by
G. Bernard Shaw, and a third on Literature, by H. S.
Salt.

SOME people will perhaps not be prepared to hear that Socialism has any ideal of art, for in the first place it is so obviously founded on the necessity for dealing with the bare economy of life that many, and even some Socialists, can see nothing save that economic basis; and moreover, many who might be disposed to admit the necessity of an economic change in the direction of Socialism believe quite sincerely that art is fostered by the inequalities of condition which it is the first business of Socialism to do away with, and indeed that it cannot exist without them. Nevertheless, in the teeth of these opinions I assert first that Socialism is an all-embracing theory of life, and that as it has an ethic and a religion of its own, so also it has an aesthetic: so that to every one who wishes to study Socialism duly it is necessary to look on it from the aesthetic point of view. And, secondly, I assert that inequality of condition, whatever may have been the case in former ages of the world, has now become incompatible with the existence of a healthy art.

But before I go further I must explain that I use the word *art* in a wider sense than is commonly used amongst us today; for convenience' sake, indeed, I will exclude all appeals to the intellect and emotions that are not addressed to the eyesight, though, properly speaking, music and all literature that deals with style should be considered as portions of art; but I can exclude from consideration as a possible vehicle of art no production of man which can be looked at. And here at once becomes obvious the sundering of the ways between the Socialist and the commercial view of art. To the Socialist a house, a knife, a cup, a steam engine, or what not, anything, I repeat, that is made by man and has form, must either be a work of art or destructive to art. The Commercialist, on the other hand, divides "manufactured articles" into those which are prepensely works of art, and are offered for sale in the market as such, and those which have no pretence and could have no pretence to artistic qualities. The one side asserts indifference, the other denies it. The Commercialist sees that in the great mass of civilized human labour there is no pretence to art, and thinks that this is natural, inevitable, and on the whole desirable. The Socialist, on the contrary, sees in this obvious lack of art a *disease* peculiar to modern civilization and hurtful to humanity; and furthermore believes it to be a disease which can be remedied.

This disease and injury to humanity, also, he thinks is no trifling matter, but a grievous deduction from the happiness of man; for he knows that the all-pervading art of which I have been speaking, and to the possibility of which the Commercialist is blind, is *the expression of pleasure in the labour of production;* and that, since all persons who are not mere burdens on the community must produce, in some form or another, it follows that under our present system most *honest* men must lead unhappy lives, since their work, which is the most important part of their lives, is devoid of pleasure.

Or, to put it very bluntly and shortly, under the present state of society happiness is only possible to artists and thieves.

It will at once be seen from this statement how necessary it is for Socialists to consider the due relation of art to society; for it is their aim to realize a reasonable, logical, and stable society; and of the two groups above-named it must be said that the artists (using the word in its present narrow meaning) are few, and are too busy over their special work (small blame to them) to pay much heed to public matters; and that the thieves (of all classes) form a disturbing element in society.

Now, the Socialist not only sees this disease in the body politic, but also thinks that he knows the cause of it, and consequently can conceive of a remedy; and that all the more because the disease is in the main peculiar, as above-said, to modern civilization. Art was once the common possession of the whole people; it was the rule in the Middle Ages that the produce of handicraft was beautiful. Doubtless, there were eyesores in the palmy days of mediaeval art, but these were caused by destruction of wares, not as now by the making of them: it was the act of war and devastation that grieved the eye of the artist then; the sacked town, the burned village, the deserted fields. Ruin bore on its face the tokens of its essential hideousness; to-day, it is prosperity that is externally ugly.

The story of the Lancashire manufacturer who, coming back from Italy, that sad museum of the nations, rejoiced to see the smoke, with which he was poisoning the beauty of the earth, pouring out of his chimney, gives us a genuine type of the active rich man of the Commercial Period, degraded into incapacity of even wishing for decent surroundings. In those past days the wounds of war were grievous indeed, but peace would bring back pleasure to men, and the hope of peace was at least conceivable; but now, peace can no longer help us and has no hope for us; the prosperity of the country, by whatever "leaps and bounds" it may advance, will but make everything more and more ugly about us; it will become more a definitely established axiom that the longing for beauty, the interest in history, the intelligence of the whole nation, shall be of no power to stop one rich man from injuring the whole nation to the full extent of his riches, that is, of his privilege of taxing other people; it will be proved to demonstration, at least to all lovers of beauty and a decent life, that private property is public robbery.

Nor, however much we may suffer from this if we happen to be artists, should we Socialists at least complain of it. For, in fact, the "peace" of Commercialism is not peace, but bitter war, and the ghastly waste of Lancashire and the ever-spreading squalor of London are at least object-lessons to teach us that this is so, that there is war in the land which quells all our efforts to live wholesomely and happily. The *necessity* of the time, I say, is to feed the commercial war which we are all of us waging in some way or another; if, while we are doing this, we can manage, some of us, to adorn our lives with some little pleasure of the eyes, it is well, but it is no *necessity*, it is a luxury, the lack of which we must endure.

Thus, in this matter also does the artificial famine of inequality, felt in so many other ways, impoverish us despite of our riches; and we sit starving amidst our gold, the Midas of the ages.

Let me state bluntly a few facts about the present condition of the arts before I try to lay before my readers the definite Socialist ideal which I have been asked to state. It is necessary to do this because no ideal for the future can be conceived of unless we proceed by way of contrast; it is the desire to escape from the present failure which forces us into what are called "ideals": in fact, they are mostly attempts by persons of strong hope to embody their discontent with the present.

It will scarcely be denied, I suppose, that at present art is only enjoyed, or indeed thought of, by comparatively a few persons, broadly speaking, by the rich and the parasites that minister to them directly. The poor can only afford to have what art is given to them in charity; which is of the inferior quality inherent in all such gifts—not worth picking up except by starving people.

Now, having eliminated the poor (that is, almost the whole mass of those that make anything that has *form*, which, as before-said, must either be helpful to life or destructive of it), as not sharing in art from any side, let us see how the rich, who do share in it to a certain extent, get on with it. But poorly, I think, although they are rich. By abstracting themselves from the general life of man that surrounds them, they can get some pleasure from a few works of art; whether they be part of the wreckage of times past, or produced by the individual labour, intelligence, and patience of a few men of genius of to-day fighting desperately against all the tend-

encies of the age. But they can do no more than surround themselves with a little circle of hot-house atmosphere of art hopelessly at odds with the common air of day. A rich man may have a house full of pictures, and beautiful books, and furniture and so forth; but as soon as he steps out into the streets he is again in the midst of ugliness to which he must blunt his senses, or be miserable if he really cares about art. Even when he is in the country, amidst the beauty of trees and fields, he cannot prevent some neighbouring landowner making the landscape hideous with utilitarian agriculture; nay, it is almost certain that his own steward or agent will force him into doing the like on his own lands; he cannot even rescue his parish church from the hands of the restoring parson. He can go where he likes and do what he likes outside the realm of art, but there he is helpless. Why is this? Simply because the great mass of effective art, that which pervades all life, *must* be the result of the harmonious co-operation of neighbours. And a rich man has no neighbours—nothing but rivals and parasites.

Now the outcome of this is that though the educated classes (as we call them) have theoretically some share in art, or might have, as a matter of fact they have very little. Outside the circle of the artists themselves there are very few even of the educated classes who care about art. Art is kept alive by a small group of artists working in a spirit quite antagonistic to the spirit of the time; and they also suffer from the lack of co-operation which is an essential lack in the art of our epoch. They are limited, therefore, to the production of a few individualistic works, which are looked upon by almost everybody as curiosities to be examined, and not as pieces of beauty to be enjoyed. Nor have they any position or power of helping the public in general matters of taste (to use a somewhat ugly word). For example, in laying out all the parks and pleasure grounds which have lately been acquired for the public, as far as I know, no artist has been consulted; whereas they ought to have been laid out by a committee of artists; and I will venture to say that even a badly chosen committee (and it might easily be well chosen) would have saved the public from most of the disasters which have resulted from handing them over to the tender mercies of the landscape gardener.

This, then, is the position of art in this epoch. It is helpless and crippled amidst the sea of utilitarian brutality. It cannot perform the most necessary functions: it cannot build a decent house, or ornament a book, or lay out a garden, or prevent the ladies of the time from dressing in a way that caricatures the body and degrades it. On the one hand it is cut off from the traditions of the past, on the other from the life of the present. It is the art of a clique and not of the people. The people are too poor to have any share of it.

As an artist I *know* this, because I can *see* it. As a Socialist I know that it can never be bettered as long as we are living in that special condition of inequality which is produced by the direct and intimate exploitation of the makers of wares, the workmen, at the hands of those who are not producers in any, even the widest, acceptation of the word.

The first point, therefore, in the Socialist ideal of art is that it should be common to the whole people; and this can only be the case if it comes to be recognized that art should be an integral part of all manufactured wares that have definite form and are intended for any endurance. In other words, instead of looking upon art as a luxury incidental to a certain privileged position, the Socialist claims art as a necessity of human life which society has no right to withhold from any one of the citizens; and he claims also that in order that this claim may be established people shall have every opportunity of taking to the work which each is best fitted for; not only that there may be the least possible waste of human effort, but also that that effort may be exercised pleasurably. For I must here repeat what I have often had to say, that the pleasurable exercise of our energies is at once the source of all art and the cause of all happiness: that is to say, it is the end of life. So that once again the society which does not give a due opportunity to all its members to exercise their energies pleasurably has forgotten the end of life, is not fulfilling its functions, and therefore is a mere tyranny to be resisted at all points.

Furthermore, in the making of wares there should be some of the spirit of the handicraftsman, whether the goods be made by hand, or by a machine that helps the hand, or by one that supersedes it. Now the essential part of the spirit of the handicraftsman is the instinct for looking at the wares in themselves and their essential use as the object of his work. Their secondary uses, the exigencies of the market, are nothing to him; it does not matter to him whether the goods he makes are for the use of a slave or a king, his business is to make them as excellent as may be; if he does otherwise he is making wares for rogues to sell to fools, and he is himself a rogue by reason of his complicity. All this means that he is making the goods for *himself;* for his own pleasure in making them and using them. But to do this he requires reciprocity, or else he will be ill-found, except in the goods that he himself makes.

His neighbours must make goods in the same spirit that he does; and each, being a good workman after his kind, will be ready to recognize excellence in the others, or to note defects; because the primary purpose of the goods, their *use* in fact, will never be lost sight of. Thus the market of neighbours, the interchange of mutual good services, will be established, and will take the place of the present gambling-market, and its bond-slave the modern factory system. But the wording in this fashion, with the unforced and instinctive reciprocity of service, clearly implies the existence of something more than a mere gregarious collection of workmen. It implies a consciousness of the existence of a society of neighbours, that is of equals; of men who do indeed expect to be made use of by others, but only so far as the services they give are pleasing to themselves; so far as they are services the performance of which is necessary to their own well-being and happiness.

Now, as on the one hand I *know* that no worthy popular art can grow out of any other soil than this of freedom and mutual respect, so on the other I feel sure both that this opportunity will be given to art and also that it will avail itself of it, and that, once again, nothing which is made by man will be ugly, but will have its due form, and its due ornament, will tell the tale of its making and the tale of its use, even where it tells no other tale. And this because when people once more take pleasure in their work, when the pleasure rises to a certain point, the expression of it will become irresistible, and that expression of pleasure is art, whatever form it may take. As to that form, do not let us trouble ourselves about it; remembering that after all the earliest art which we have record of is still art to us; that Homer is no more out of date than Browning; that the most scientifically-minded of people (I had almost said the most utilitarian), the ancient Greeks, are still thought to have produced good artists; that the most superstitious epoch of the world, the early Middle Ages, produced the freest art; though there is reason enough for that if I had time to go into it.

For in fact, considering the relation of the modern world to art, our business is now, and for long will be, not so much attempting to produce definite art, as rather clearing the ground to give art its opportunity. We have been such slaves to the modern practice of the unlimited manufacture of makeshifts for real wares, that we run a serious risk of destroying the very material of art; of making it necessary that men, in order to have any artistic perception, should be born blind, and should get their ideas of beauty from the hearsay of books. This degradation is surely the first thing which we should deal with;

and certainly Socialists must deal with it at the first opportunity; *they* at least must see, however much others may shut their eyes: for they cannot help reflecting that to condemn a vast population to live in South Lancashire while art and education are being furthered in decent places, is like feasting within earshot of a patient on the rack.

Anyhow, the first step toward the fresh new-birth of art *must* interfere with the privilege of private persons to destroy the beauty of the earth for their private advantage, and thereby to rob the community. The day when some company of enemies of the community are forbidden, for example, to turn the fields of Kent into another collection of cinder heaps in order that they may extract wealth, unearned by them, from a mass of half-paid labourers; the day when some hitherto all powerful "pigskin stuffed with money" is told that he shall not pull down some ancient building in order that he may force his fellow citizens to pay him additional rack-rent for land which is not his (save as the newly acquired watch of the highwayman is)—that day will be the beginning of the fresh new-birth of art in modern times.

But that day will also be one of the memorable days of Socialism; for this very privilege, which is but the privilege of the robber by force of arms, is 10 just the thing which it is the aim and end of our present organisation to uphold; and all the formidable executive at the back of it, army, police, law courts, presided over by the judge as representing the executive, is directed towards this one end—to take care that the richest shall rule, and shall have full licence to injure the commonwealth to the full extent of his riches.

George Meredith
1828–1909

Meredith and Hardy are the only two Victorians who won front rank both as novelist and as poet. Meredith was born in Portsmouth, February 12, 1828, the son of a tailor. His education was unsystematic, two years at a Moravian school in Austria being probably the most significant part of it. He attempted to study law; he did editorial work alike in the newspaper and the periodical fields; he served in Italy as a war correspondent (see his novels, *Sandra Belloni* and *Vittoria*); for thirty-five years he earned his living as a publisher's reader. In 1849 he was married, most unhappily, to Thomas Love Peacock's daughter, who deserted him in 1858; in 1864 he married Marie Vulliamy. His first book was a collection of *Poems*, 1851; his first real novel was *The Ordeal of Richard Feverel*, 1859. *Evan Harrington, Rhoda Fleming, Beauchamp's Career,* and *The Egoist* followed, but Meredith did not find a large public until *Diana of the Crossways* appeared in 1885. About the same time he lost both his wife and his health; during his later years he was crippled by paralysis. By this time, however, he was at the height of his reputation, and his home at Box Hill, Surrey, had become a literary shrine. In 1892 he became president of the British Society of Authors; in 1905 he received the Order of Merit. He died May 18, 1909.

Though Meredith does not disdain to use the term "God" freely, he was basically a nature-worshiper. He was a romanticist, but he based his romanticism on science; he hated both asceticism and sensuality, and he hated sentimentalism, which he regarded as merely an inverted sensuality. He accepted the evolutionary hypothesis, but he interpreted it optimistically, not pessimistically, as Hardy did. But he did not share Spencer's or Macaulay's faith in automatic progress; he believed that to serve the needs of life men must give themselves unselfishly to the purposes of life. Like George Eliot, he saw egoism at the root of all human difficulties.

Disdaining a supernatural solution of the human problem, Meredith found comedy—"sword of the common sense"—a powerful weapon against sentimentalism, egoism, and all their breed. What George Eliot develops through tragedy, he develops through comedy; as Stuart Sherman observes, the comic spirit is for him "a fine celestial sunlight in the mind, answering to the theological Grace of God in the heart."

Meredith was a feminist, and most of his later novels deal with some form of the "woman question." He believed that men need women to keep them sane, to prevent ill-balanced, inflated idealism. He needed women in his novels because the particular kind of intellectual comedy through which he worked out his ideas can exist only in a society in which men and women mingle on terms of at least approximate equality. Being less muscular than man, woman could not maintain her position by brute force; her humor, however, places her in a very strong position.

As a novelist Meredith never reached anything like his potential audience because of the difficulties and eccentricities of his style. *The Ordeal of Richard Feverel* is not difficult reading, but many of the later books are; after *Diana*, when he had won a hearing, Meredith seemed perversely determined to wreak vengeance upon the public for its long neglect of him by making his novels as difficult to read as possible. He would labor what seems a trifling point for pages upon pages, then pass over an important climax in a phrase.

His poetry, fortunately, is less difficult. He was a poet by nature, and his attitude toward life is that of a poet even when he is writing prose. Poetry freed him from the exigencies of narrative, which he never mastered, and in writing it he was not betrayed by his temperamental shying at the obvious. Among his titles in this field are *Poems and Lyrics of the Joy of Earth, Ballads and Poems of Tragic Life, A Reading of Earth*, and *A Reading of Life*.

JUGGLING JERRY[1]

1

Pitch here the tent, while the old horse grazes:
  By the old hedge-side we'll halt a stage.
It's nigh my last above the daisies:
  My next leaf'll be man's blank page.
Yes, my old girl! and it's no use crying:
  Juggler, constable, king, must bow.
One that outjuggles all's been spying
  Long to have me, and he has me now.

2

We've travelled times to this old common:
  Often we've hung our pots in the gorse.   10
We've had a stirring life, old woman,
  You, and I, and the old grey horse.
Races, and fairs, and royal occasions,
  Found us coming to their call:
Now they'll miss us at our stations:
  There's a Juggler outjuggles all!

3

Up goes the lark, as if all were jolly!
  Over the duck-pond the willow shakes.
Easy to think that grieving's folly,
  When the hand's firm as driven stakes!   20
Ay, when we're strong, and braced, and manful,
  Life's a sweet fiddle: but we're a batch
Born to become the Great Juggler's han'ful:
  Balls he shies up, and is safe to catch.

4

Here's where the lads of the village cricket:
  I was a lad not wide from here:
Couldn't I whip off the bail from the wicket?
  Like an old world those days appear!
Donkey, sheep, geese, and thatched ale-house—I
    know them!
  They are old friends of my halts, and seem,   30
Somehow, as if kind thanks I owe them:
  Juggling don't hinder the heart's esteem.

5

Juggling's no sin, for we must have victual:
  Nature allows us to bait for the fool.
Holding one's own makes us juggle no little;
  But, to increase it, hard juggling's the rule.
You that are sneering at my profession,
  Haven't you juggled a vast amount?
There's the Prime Minister, in one Session,
  Juggles more games than my sins'll count.   40

6

I've murdered insects with mock thunder:
  Conscience, for that, in men don't quail.
I've made bread from the bump of wonder:
  That's my business, and there's my tale.
Fashion and rank all praised the professor:
  Ay! and I've had my smile from the Queen:
Bravo, Jerry! she meant: God bless her!
  Ain't this a sermon on that scene?

7

I've studied men from my topsy-turvy
  Close, and, I reckon, rather true.   50
Some are fine fellows: some, right scurvy:
  Most, a dash between the two.
But it's a woman, old girl, that makes me
  Think more kindly of the race:
And it's a woman, old girl, that shakes me
  When the Great Juggler I must face.

[1] This and the following selections are from *The Poetical Works of George Meredith*, Charles Scribner's Sons. Reprinted by permission.

25. cricket, play cricket.   53-54. But it's . . . race, a characteristically Meredithian point of view, as all readers of his novels will recognize.

8

We two were married, due and legal:
   Honest we've lived since we've been one.
Lord! I could then jump like an eagle:
   You danced bright as a bit o' the sun. 60
Birds in a May-bush we were! right merry!
   All night we kissed, we juggled all day.
Joy was the heart of Juggling Jerry!
   Now from his old girl he's juggled away.

9

It's past parsons to console us:
   No, nor no doctor fetch for me:
I can die without my bolus;
   Two of a trade, lass, never agree!
Parson and Doctor!—don't they love rarely
   Fighting the devil in other men's fields! 70
Stand up yourself and match him fairly:
   Then see how the rascal yields!

10

I, lass, have lived no gipsy, flaunting
   Finery while this poor helpmate grubs:
Coin I've stored, and you won't be wanting:
   You shan't beg from the troughs and tubs.
Nobly you've stuck to me, though in his kitchen
   Many a Marquis would hail you Cook!
Palaces you could have ruled and grown rich in,
   But your old Jerry you never forsook. 80

11

Hand up the chirper! ripe ale winks in it;
   Let's have comfort and be at peace.
Once a stout draught made me light as a linnet.
   Cheer up! the Lord must have his lease.
May be—for none see in that black hollow—
   It's just a place where we're held in pawn,
And, when the Great Juggler makes as to swallow,
   It's just the sword-trick—I ain't quite gone!

12

Yonder came smells of the gorse, so nutty,
   Gold-like and warm: it's the prime of May. 90
Better than mortar, brick and putty,
   Is God's house on a blowing day.
Lean me more up the mound; now I feel it:
   All the old heath-smells! Ain't it strange?
There's the world laughing, as if to conceal it,
   But He's by us, juggling the change.

81. chirper, chirper cup (that is, producing merriment),
"the cup that cheers."

13

I mind it well, by the sea-beach lying,
   Once—it's long gone—when two gulls we beheld,
Which, as the moon got up, were flying
   Down a big wave that sparked and swelled. 100
Crack, went a gun: one fell: the second
   Wheeled round him twice, and was off for new
      luck:
There in the dark her white wing beckoned:—
   Drop me a kiss—I'm the bird dead-struck!

from MODERN LOVE

Modern Love is often spoken of as a sonnet sequence;
actually each stanza is sixteen lines in length. The situation described has some points in common with that in
which Meredith found himself after his unfortunate
marriage to the daughter of Thomas Love Peacock.

I

By this he knew she wept with waking eyes:
That, at his hand's light quiver by her head,
The strange low sobs that shook their common bed
Were called into her with a sharp surprise,
And strangled mute, like little gaping snakes,
Dreadfully venomous to him. She lay
Stone-still, and the long darkness flowed away
With muffled pulses. Then, as midnight makes
Her giant heart of Memory and Tears
Drink the pale drug of silence, and so beat 10
Sleep's heavy measure, they from head to feet
Were moveless, looking through their dead black
      years,
By vain regret scrawled over the blank wall.
Like sculptured effigies they might be seen
Upon their marriage-tomb, the sword between;
Each wishing for the sword that severs all.

13

"I play for Seasons, not Eternities!"
Says Nature, laughing on her way. "So must
All those whose stake is nothing more than dust!"
And lo, she wins, and of her harmonies
She is full sure! Upon her dying rose
She drops a look of fondness, and goes by,
Scarce any retrospection in her eye;
For she the laws of growth most deeply knows,
Whose hands bear, here, a seed-bag—there, an urn.
Pledged she herself to aught, 'twould mark her end!
This lesson of our only visible friend 11
Can we not teach our foolish hearts to learn?

15. the sword between, a reference to the sword **often**
placed between chaste lovers in the medieval romances.

Yes! yes!—but, oh, our human rose is fair
Surpassingly! Lose calmly Love's great bliss,
When the renewed for ever of a kiss
Whirls life within the shower of loosened hair!

16

In our old shipwrecked days there was an hour,
When in the firelight steadily aglow,
Joined slackly, we beheld the red chasm grow
Among the clicking coals. Our library-bower
That eve was left to us; and hushed we sat
As lovers to whom Time is whispering.
From sudden-opened doors we heard them sing;
The nodding elders mixed good wine with chat.
Well knew we that Life's greatest treasure lay
With us, and of it was our talk. "Ah, yes!   10
Love dies!" I said: I never thought it less.
She yearned to me that sentence to unsay.
Then when the fire domed blackening, I found
Her cheek was salt against my kiss, and swift
Up the sharp scale of sobs her breast did lift:—
Now am I haunted by that taste! that sound!

17

At dinner, she is hostess, I am host.
Went the feast ever cheerfuller? She keeps
The Topic over intellectual deeps
In buoyancy afloat. They see no ghost.
With sparkling surface-eyes we ply the ball:
It is in truth a most contagious game:
HIDING THE SKELETON shall be its name.
Such play as this the devils might appal!
But here's the greater wonder: in that we,
Enamoured of an acting naught can tire,   10
Each other, like true hypocrites, admire;
Warm-lighted looks, Love's ephemeridae,
Shoot gaily o'er the dishes and the wine.
We waken envy of our happy lot.
Fast, sweet, and golden, shows the marriage-knot.
Dear guests, you now have seen Love's corpse-light
    shine.

29

Am I failing? For no longer can I cast
A glory round about this head of gold.
Glory she wears, but springing from the mould;
Not like the consecration of the Past!
Is my soul beggared? Something more than earth
I cry for still: I cannot be at peace
In having Love upon a mortal lease.

Sec. 17. 3. The Topic, of conversation.   4. They, the
guests.   16. corpse-light, a light like the flame of a candle,
sometimes seen in graveyards and damp places, and believed to portend death.

I cannot take the woman at her worth!
Where is the ancient wealth wherewith I clothed
Our human nakedness, and could endow   10
With spiritual splendour a white brow
That else had grinned at me the fact I loathed?
A kiss is but a kiss now! and no wave
Of a great flood that whirls me to the sea.
But, as you will! we'll sit contentedly,
And eat our pot of honey on the grave.

43

Mark where the pressing wind shoots javelin-like
Its skeleton shadow on the broad-backed wave!
Here is a fitting spot to dig Love's grave;
Here where the ponderous breakers plunge and
    strike,
And dart their hissing tongues high up the sand:
In hearing of the ocean, and in sight
Of those ribbed wind-streaks running into white.
If I the death of Love had deeply planned,
I never could have made it half so sure,
As by the unblest kisses which upbraid   10
The full-waked sense; or failing that, degrade!
'Tis morning; but no morning can restore
What we have forfeited. I see no sin;
The wrong is mixed. In tragic life, God wot,
No villain need be! Passions spin the plot;
We are betrayed by what is false within.

44

They say that Pity in Love's service dwells,
A porter at the rosy temple's gate.
I missed him going: but it is my fate
To come upon him now beside his wells;
Whereby I know that I Love's temple leave,
And that the purple doors have closed behind.
Poor soul! if, in those early days unkind,
Thy power to sting had been but power to grieve,
We now might with an equal spirit meet,
And not be matched like innocence and vice.   10
She for the Temple's worship has paid price,
And takes the coin of Pity as a cheat.
She sees through simulation to the bone:
What's best in her impels her to the worst:
Never, she cries, shall Pity soothe Love's thirst,
Or foul hypocrisy for truth atone!

47

We saw the swallows gathering in the sky,
And in the osier-isle we heard them noise.
We had not to look back on summer joys,
Or forward to a summer of bright dye:
But in the largeness of the evening earth

Sec. 43. 14. wot, knows.

Our spirits grew as we went side by side.
The hour became her husband and my bride.
Love, that had robbed us so, thus blessed our
    dearth!
The pilgrims of the years waxed very loud
In multitudinous chatterings, as the flood   10
Full brown came from the West, and like pale
    blood
Expanded to the upper crimson cloud.
Love, that had robbed us of immortal things,
This little moment mercifully gave,
Where I have seen across the twilight wave
The swan sail with her young beneath her wings.

50

Thus piteously Love closed what he begat:
The union of this ever-diverse pair!
These two were rapid falcons in a snare,
Condemned to do the flitting of the bat.
Lovers beneath the singing sky of May,
They wandered once, clear as the dew on flowers,
But they fed not on the advancing hours:
Their hearts held cravings for the buried day.
Then each applied to each that fatal knife,
Deep questioning, which probes to endless dole.   10
Ah, what a dusty answer gets the soul
When hot for certainties in this our life!—
In tragic hints here see what evermore
Moves dark as yonder midnight ocean's force,
Thundering like ramping hosts of warrior horse,
To throw that faint thin line upon the shore!

LOVE IN THE VALLEY

This beautiful poem is notable for the way in which
the rhythm itself is used "to give Meredith's feeling for
the exquisite light-hearted, light-footed girl whose nature
he is trying to recapture and set in words for us." In the
nineteenth stanza we get the impression of "a hot, drowsy,
summer noon"; there are actually nineteen extra stresses
in this stanza. See Elsa Chapin and Russell Thomas, *A
New Approach to Poetry*, University of Chicago Press, 1929,
pp. 38 ff.

Under yonder beech-tree single on the green-
    sward,
    Couched with her arms behind her golden head,
Knees and tresses folded to slip and ripple idly,
    Lies my young love sleeping in the shade.
Had I the heart to slide an arm beneath her,
    Press her parting lips as her waist I gather slow,
Waking in amazement she could not but embrace
    me:
    Then would she hold me and never let me go?

Shy as the squirrel and wayward as the swallow,
    Swift as the swallow along the river's light   10
Circleting the surface to meet his mirrored wing-
    lets,
    Fleeter she seems in her stay than in her flight.
Shy as the squirrel that leaps among the pine-tops,
    Wayward as the swallow overhead at set of sun,
She whom I love is hard to catch and conquer,
    Hard, but O the glory of the winning were she
    won!

When her mother tends her before the laughing
    mirror,
    Tying up her laces, looping up her hair,
Often she thinks, were this wild thing wedded,
    More love should I have, and much less care.   20
When her mother tends her before the lighted
    mirror,
    Loosening her laces, combing down her curls,
Often she thinks, were this wild thing wedded,
    I should miss but one for many boys and girls.

Heartless she is as the shadow in the meadows
    Flying to the hills on a blue and breezy noon.
No, she is athirst and drinking up her wonder:
    Earth to her is young as the slip of the new moon.
Deals she an unkindness, 'tis but her rapid measure,
    Even as in a dance; and her smile can heal no
    less: 30
Like the swinging May-cloud that pelts the flowers
    with hailstones
    Off a sunny border, she was made to bruise and
    bless.

Lovely are the curves of the white owl sweeping
    Wavy in the dusk lit by one large star.
Lone on the fir-branch, his rattle-note unvaried,
    Brooding o'er the gloom, spins the brown eve-jar.
Darker grows the valley, more and more forgetting:
    So were it with me if forgetting could be willed.
Tell the grassy hollow that holds the bubbling well-
    spring,
    Tell it to forget the source that keeps it filled.   40

Stepping down the hill with her fair companions,
    Arm in arm, all against the raying West,
Boldly she sings, to the merry tune she marches,
    Brave in her shape, and sweeter unpossessed.
Sweeter, for she is what my heart first awaking
    Whispered the world was; morning light is she.
Love that so desires would fain keep her change-
    less;
    Fain would fling the net, and fain have her free.

36. eve-jar, nightjar.

Happy happy time, when the white star hovers
    Low over dim fields fresh with bloomy dew,   50
Near the face of dawn, that draws athwart the
    darkness,
    Threading it with colour, like yewberries the
    yew.
Thicker crowd the shades as the grave East deepens
    Glowing, and with crimson a long cloud swells.
Maiden still the morn is; and strange she is, and
    secret;
    Strange her eyes; her cheeks are cold as cold sea-
    shells.

Sunrays, leaning on our southern hills and lighting
    Wild cloud-mountains that drag the hills along,
Oft ends the day of your shifting brilliant laugh-
    ter
    Chill as a dull face frowning on a song.   60
Ay, but shows the South-west a ripple-feathered
    bosom
    Blown to silver while the clouds are shaken and
    ascend
Scaling the mid-heavens as they stream, there
    comes a sunset
    Rich, deep like love in beauty without end.

When at dawn she sighs, and like an infant to the
    window
    Turns grave eyes craving light, released from
    dreams,
Beautiful she looks, like a white water-lily
    Bursting out of bud in havens of the streams.
When from bed she rises clothed from neck to
    ankle
    In her long nightgown sweet as boughs of May, 70
Beautiful she looks, like a tall garden lily
    Pure from the night, and splendid for the day.

Mother of the dews, dark eye-lashed twilight,
    Low-lidded twilight, o'er the valley's brim,
Rounding on thy breast sings the dew-delighted
    skylark,
    Clear as though the dewdrops had their voice in
    him.
Hidden where the rose-flush drinks the rayless
    planet,
    Fountain-full he pours the spraying fountain-
    showers.
Let me hear her laughter, I would have her ever
    Cool as dew in twilight, the lark above the
    flowers.   80

77. **rayless planet,** the morning star, whose rays have
been quenched by the rising sun.

All the girls are out with their baskets for the prim-
rose;
    Up lanes, woods through, they troop in joyful
    bands.
My sweet leads: she knows not why, but now she
    loiters,
    Eyes the bent anemones, and hangs her hands.
Such a look will tell that the violets are peeping,
    Coming the rose: and unaware a cry
Springs in her bosom for odours and for colour,
    Covert and the nightingale; she knows not why.

Kerchiefed head and chin she darts between her
    tulips,
    Streaming like a willow grey in arrowy rain: 90
Some bend beaten cheek to gravel, and their angel
    She will be; she lifts them, and on she speeds
    again.
Black the driving raincloud breasts the iron gate-
    way:
    She is forth to cheer a neighbour lacking mirth.
So when sky and grass met rolling dumb for thunder
    Saw I once a white dove, sole light of earth.

Prim little scholars are the flowers of her garden,
    Trained to stand in rows, and asking if they
    please.
I might love them well but for loving more the wild
    ones:
    O my wild ones! they tell me more than these. 100
You, my wild one, you tell of honied field-rose,
    Violet, blushing eglantine in life; and even as
    they,
They by the wayside are earnest of your goodness,
    You are of life's, on the banks that line the way.

Peering at her chamber the white crowns the red
    rose,
    Jasmine winds the porch with stars two and three.
Parted is the window; she sleeps; the starry jasmine
    Breathes a falling breath that carries thoughts of
    me.
Sweeter unpossessed, have I said of her my sweetest?
    Not while she sleeps: while she sleeps the jasmine
    breathes,   110
Luring her to love; she sleeps; the starry jasmine
    Bears me to her pillow under white rose-wreaths.

Yellow with birdfoot-trefoil are the grass-glades;
    Yellow with cinquefoil of the dew-grey leaf;
Yellow with stonecrop; the moss-mounds are
    yellow;

113. **birdfoot-trefoil,** a clover-shaped leaf or flower, suggesting the spreading foot of a bird.

Blue-necked the wheat sways, yellowing to the
   sheaf.
Green-yellow bursts from the copse the laughing
   yaffle:
   Sharp as a sickle is the edge of shade and shine:
Earth in her heart laughs looking at the heavens,
   Thinking of the harvest: I look and think of
   mine.   120

This I may know: her dressing and undressing
   Such a change of light shows as when the skies in
   sport
Shift from cloud to moonlight; or edging over
   thunder
   Slips a ray of sun; or sweeping into port
White sails furl; or on the ocean borders
   White sails lean along the waves leaping green.
Visions of her shower before me, but from eyesight
   Guarded she would be like the sun were she seen.

Front door and back of the mossed old farmhouse
   Open with the morn, and in a breezy link   130
Freshly sparkles garden to stripe-shadowed orchard,
   Green across a rill where on sand the minnows
   wink.
Busy in the grass the early sun of summer
   Swarms, and the blackbird's mellow fluting notes
Call my darling up with round and roguish chal-
   lenge:
   Quaintest, richest carol of all the singing throats!

Cool was the woodside; cool as her white dairy
   Keeping sweet the cream-pan; and there the boys
   from school,
Cricketing below, rushed brown and red with sun-
   shine;   139
   O the dark translucence of the deep-eyed cool!
Spying from the farm, herself she fetched a pitcher
   Full of milk, and tilted for each in turn the beak.
Then a little fellow, mouth up and on tiptoe,
   Said, "I will kiss you": she laughed and leaned
   her cheek.

Doves of the fir-wood walling high our red roof
   Through the long noon coo, crooning through the
   coo.
Loose droop the leaves, and down the sleepy road-
   way
   Sometimes pipes a chaffinch; loose droops the
   blue.
Cows flap a slow tail knee-deep in the river,
   Breathless, given up to sun and gnat and fly. 150

117. **yaffle,** the green woodpecker.   130. **link,** land adjacent to a bend in a stream.

Nowhere is she seen; and if I see her nowhere,
   Lightning may come, straight rains and tiger sky.

O the golden sheaf, the rustling treasure-armful!
   O the nutbrown tresses nodding interlaced!
O the treasure-tresses one another over
   Nodding! O the girdle slack about the waist!
Slain are the poppies that shot their random scarlet
   Quick amid the wheatears: wound about the
   waist,
Gathered, see these brides of Earth one blush of
   ripeness!
   O the nutbrown tresses nodding interlaced! 160

Large and smoky red the sun's cold disk drops,
   Clipped by naked hills, on violet shaded snow:
Eastward large and still lights up a bower of moon-
   rise,
   Whence at her leisure steps the moon aglow.
Nightlong on black print-branches our beech-tree
   Gazes in this whiteness: nightlong could I.
Here may life on death or death on life be painted.
   Let me clasp her soul to know she cannot die!

Gossips count her faults; they scour a narrow cham-
   ber
   Where there is no window, read not heaven or
   her.   170
"When she was a tiny," one aged woman quavers,
   Plucks at my heart and leads me by the ear.
Faults she had once as she learnt to run and tum-
   bled:
   Faults of feature some see, beauty not complete.
Yet, good gossips, beauty that makes holy
   Earth and air, may have faults from head to feet.

Hither she comes; she comes to me; she lingers,
   Deepens her brown eyebrows, while in new sur-
   prise
High rise the lashes in wonder of a stranger;
   Yet am I the light and living of her eyes. 180
Something friends have told her fills her heart to
   brimming,
   Nets her in her blushes, and wounds her, and
   tames.—
Sure of her haven, O like a dove alighting,
   Arms up, she dropped: our souls were in our
   names.

Soon will she lie like a white-frost sunrise.
   Yellow oats and brown wheat, barley pale as rye,
Long since your sheaves have yielded to the
   thresher,
   165. **print-branches,** shadows.

Felt the girdle loosened, seen the tresses fly.
Soon will she lie like a blood-red sunset.
  Swift   with   the   to-morrow,   green-winged
    Spring!   190
Sing from the South-West, bring her back the
    truants,
  Nightingale and swallow, song and dipping wing.

Soft new beech-leaves, up to beamy April
  Spreading bough on bough a primrose moun-
    tain, you,
Lucid in the moon, raise lilies to the skyfields,
  Youngest green transfused in silver shining
    through:
Fairer than the lily, than the wild white cherry:
  Fair as in image my seraph love appears
Borne to me by dreams when dawn is at my eye-
    lids:
  Fair as in the flesh she swims to me on tears.   200

Could I find a place to be alone with heaven,
  I would speak my heart out: heaven is my need.
Every woodland tree is flushing like the dogwood,
  Flashing like the whitebeam, swaying like the
    reed.
Flushing like the dogwood crimson in October;
  Streaming like the flag-reed South-West blown;
Flashing as in gusts the sudden-lighted white-
    beam:
  All seem to know what is for heaven alone.

THE LARK ASCENDING

He rises and begins to round,
He drops the silver chain of sound,
Of many links without a break,
In chirrup, whistle, slur and shake,
All intervolved and spreading wide,
Like water-dimples down a tide
Where ripple ripple overcurls
And eddy into eddy whirls;
A press of hurried notes that run
So fleet they scarce are more than one,   10
Yet changeingly the trills repeat
And linger ringing while they fleet,
Sweet to the quick o' the ear, and dear
To her beyond the handmaid ear,
Who sits beside our inner springs,
Too often dry for this he brings,
Which seems the very jet of earth
At sight of sun, her music's mirth,

14. her, the spirit of Nature within us, which hears that
which her handmaid, the ear of clay, cannot hear.

As up he wings the spiral stair,
A song of light, and pierces air   20
With fountain ardour, fountain play,
To reach the shining tops of day,
And drink in everything discerned
An ecstasy to music turned,
Impelled by what his happy bill
Disperses; drinking, showering still,
Unthinking save that he may give
His voice the outlet, there to live
Renewed in endless notes of glee,
So thirsty of his voice is he,   30
For all to hear and all to know
That he is joy, awake, aglow,
The tumult of the heart to hear
Through pureness filtered crystal-clear,
And know the pleasure sprinkled bright
By simple singing of delight,
Shrill, irreflective, unrestrained,
Rapt, ringing, on the jet sustained
Without a break, without a fall,
Sweet-silvery, sheer lyrical,   40
Perennial, quavering up the chord
Like myriad dews of sunny sward
That trembling into fulness shine,
And sparkle dropping argentine;
Such wooing as the ear receives
From zephyr caught in choric leaves
Of aspens when their chattering net
Is flushed to white with shivers wet;
And such the water-spirit's chime
On mountain heights in morning's prime,   50
Too freshly sweet to seem excess,
Too animate to need a stress;
But wider over many heads
The starry voice ascending spreads,
Awakening, as it waxes thin,
The best in us to him akin;
And every face to watch him raised
Puts on the light of children praised,
So rich our human pleasure ripes
When sweetness on sincereness pipes,   60
Though nought be promised from the seas,
But only a soft-ruffling breeze
Sweep glittering on a still content,
Serenity in ravishment.

For singing till his heaven fills,
'Tis love of earth that he instils,
And ever winging up and up,
Our valley is his golden cup,
And he the wine which overflows
To lift us with him as he goes:
The woods and brooks, the sheep and kine,

He is, the hills, the human line,
The meadows green, the fallows brown,
The dreams of labour in the town;
He sings the sap, the quickened veins;
The wedding song of sun and rains
He is, the dance of children, thanks
Of sowers, shout of primrose-banks,
And eye of violets while they breathe;
All these the circling song will wreathe,   80
And you shall hear the herb and tree,
The better heart of men shall see,
Shall feel celestially, as long
As you crave nothing save the song.

Was never voice of ours could say
Our inmost in the sweetest way,
Like yonder voice aloft, and link
All hearers in the song they drink.
Our wisdom speaks from failing blood,
Our passion is too full in flood,   90
We want the key of his wild note
Of truthful in a tuneful throat,
The song seraphically free
Of taint of personality,
So pure that it salutes the suns,
The voice of one for millions,
In whom the millions rejoice
For giving their one spirit voice.

Yet men have we, whom we revere,
Now names, and men still housing here,   100
Whose lives, by many a battle-dint
Defaced, and grinding wheels on flint,
Yield substance, though they sing not, sweet
For song our highest heaven to greet:
Whom heavenly singing gives us new,
Enspheres them brilliant in our blue,
From firmest base to farthest leap,
Because their love of Earth is deep,
And they are warriors in accord
With life to serve, and pass reward,   110
So touching purest and so heard
In the brain's reflex of yon bird:
Wherefore their soul in me, or mine,
Through self-forgetfulness divine,
In them, that song aloft maintains,
To fill the sky and thrill the plains
With showerings drawn from human stores,
As he to silence nearer soars,
Extends the world at wings and dome,
More spacious making more our home,   120
Till lost on his aërial rings
In light, and then the fancy sings.

91. **want**, lack.   110. **pass**, pass up, disdain.

LUCIFER IN STARLIGHT

On a starred night Prince Lucifer uprose.
Tired of his dark dominion swung the fiend
Above the rolling ball in cloud part screened,
Where sinners hugged their spectre of repose.
Poor prey to his hot fit of pride were those.
And now upon his western wing he leaned,
Now his huge bulk o'er Afric's sands careened,
Now the black planet shadowed Arctic snows.
Soaring through wider zones that pricked his scars
With memory of the old revolt from Awe,   10
He reached the middle height, and at the stars,
Which are the brain of heaven, he looked, and sank.
Around the ancient track marched, rank on rank,
The army of unalterable law.

ON THE DANGER OF WAR

Avert, High Wisdom, never vainly wooed,
This threat of War, that shows a land brain-sick.
When nations gain the pitch where rhetoric
Seems reason they are ripe for cannon's food.
Dark looms the issue though the cause be good.
But with the doubt 'tis our old devil's trick.
O now the down-slope of the lunatic
Illumine lest we redden of that brood.
For not since man in his first view of thee
Ascended to the heavens giving sign   10
Within him of deep sky and sounded sea,
Did he unforfeiting thy laws transgress;
In peril of his blood his ears incline
To drums whose loudness is their emptiness.

HARD WEATHER

Bursts from a rending East in flaws
The young green leaflet's harrier, sworn
To strew the garden, strip the shaws,
And show our Spring with banner torn.
Was ever such virago morn?
The wind has teeth, the wind has claws.
All the wind's wolves through woods are loose,
The wild wind's falconry aloft.
Shrill underfoot the grassblade shrews,
At gallop, clumped, and down the croft   10

Lucifer in Starlight. **1. Prince Lucifer.** Lucifer is the planet Venus, the morning star. On the basis of Isaiah 14:12—"How art thou fallen from heaven, O Lucifer, son of the morning!" —Lucifer has been popularly identified (as in *Paradise Lost*) with the rebel archangel.   **2. his dark dominion,** hell. **3. the rolling ball,** the earth.   **5. Poor prey . . . those.** If Lucifer had not fallen through pride, he would never have corrupted humanity.   **9. scars,** of battle against the heavenly hosts.   *Hard Weather.* **9. shrews,** curses.

Bestrid by shadows, beaten, tossed;
It seems a scythe, it seems a rod.
The howl is up at the howl's accost;
The shivers greet and the shivers nod.

Is the land ship? we are rolled, we drive
Tritonly, cleaving hiss and hum;
Whirl with the dead, or mount or dive,
Or down in dregs, or on in scum.
And drums the distant, pipes the near,
And vale and hill are grey in grey,   20
As when the surge is crumbling sheer,
And sea-mews wing the haze of spray.
Clouds—are they bony witches?—swarms,
Darting swift on the robber's flight,
Hurry an infant sky in arms:
It peeps, it becks; 'tis day, 'tis night.
Black while over the loop of blue
The swathe is closed, like shroud on corse.
Lo, as if swift the Furies flew,
The Fates at heel at a cry to horse!   30

Interpret me the savage whirr:
And is it Nature scourged, or she,
Her offspring's executioner,
Reducing land to barren sea?
But is there meaning in a day
When this fierce angel of the air,
Intent to throw, and haply slay,
Can for what breath of life we bear
Exact the wrestle? Call to mind
The many meanings glistening up   40
When Nature, to her nurslings kind,
Hands them the fruitage and the cup!
And seek we rich significance
Not otherwother than with those tides
Of pleasure on the sunned expanse,
Whose flow deludes, whose ebb derides?

Look in the face of men who fare
Lock-mouthed, a match in lungs and thews
For this fierce angel of the air,
To twist with him and take his bruise.   50
That is the face beloved of old
Of Earth, young mother of her brood:
Nor broken for us shows the mould
When muscle is in mind renewed:
Though farther from her nature rude,

16. **Tritonly,** like Triton, a demigod of the sea. 29. **Furies,** the Erinyes of Greek mythology, who pursue the sinner in this world and the next. After Euripides they are three in number—Alecto, Megaera, Tisiphone. 30. **Fates,** in Greek mythology, Clotho (Spinner), who draws out the thread of human life, Lachesis (Disposer of Lots), who determines its length, Atropos (Inflexible), who cuts it off.

Yet nearer to her spirit's hold:
And though of gentler mood serene,
Still forceful of her fountain-jet.
So shall her blows be shrewdly met,
Be luminously read the scene   60
Where Life is at her grindstone set,
That she may give us edging keen,
String us for battle, till as play
The common strokes of fortune shower.
Such meaning in a dagger-day
Our wits may clasp to wax in power.
Yea, feel us warmer at her breast,
By spin of blood in lusty drill,
Than when her honeyed hands caressed,
And Pleasure, sapping, seemed to fill.   70

Behold the life at ease; it drifts.
The sharpened life commands its course.
She winnows, winnows roughly; sifts,
To dip her chosen in her source:
Contention is the vital force,
Whence pluck they brain, her prize of gifts,
Sky of the senses! on which height,
Not disconnected, yet released,
They see how spirit comes to light,
Through conquest of the inner beast,   80
Which Measure tames to movement sane,
In harmony with what is fair.
Never is Earth misread by brain:
That is the welling of her, there
The mirror: with one step beyond,
For likewise is it voice; and more,
Benignest kinship bids respond,
When wail the weak, and them restore
Whom days as fell as this may rive,
While Earth sits ebon in her gloom,   90
Us atomies of life alive
Unheeding, bent on life to come.
Her children of the labouring brain,
These are the champions of the race,
True parents, and the sole humane,
With understanding for their base.
Earth yields the milk, but all her mind
Is vowed to thresh for stouter stock.
Her passion for old giantkind,
That scaled the mount, uphurled the rock,   100
Devolves on them who read aright
Her meaning and devoutly serve;
Nor in her starlessness of night
Peruse her with the craven nerve:
But even as she from grass to corn,
To eagle high from grubbing mole,
Prove in strong brain her noblest born,
The station for the flight of soul.

MEDITATION UNDER STARS

What links are ours with orbs that are
    So resolutely far:
The solitary asks, and they
Give radiance as from a shield:
    Still at the death of day,
    The seen, the unrevealed.
Implacable they shine
To us who would of Life obtain
An answer for the life we strain
    To nourish with one sign.   10
Nor can imagination throw
The penetrative shaft: we pass
The breath of thought, who would divine
    If haply they may grow
As Earth; have our desire to know;
If life comes there to grain from grass,
And flowers like ours of toil and pain;
    Has passion to beat bar,
    Win space from cleaving brain;
    The mystic link attain,   20
    Whereby star holds on star.

Those visible immortals beam
    Allurement to the dream:
Ireful at human hungers brook
    No question in the look.
For ever virgin to our sense,
Remote they wane to gaze intense:
Prolong it, and in ruthlessness they smite
The beating heart behind the ball of sight
    Till we conceive their heavens hoar,   30
    Those lights they raise but sparkles frore,
And Earth, our blood-warm Earth, a shuddering
    prey
To that frigidity of brainless ray.

Yet space is given for breath of thought
Beyond our bounds when musing: more,
When to that musing love is brought,
And love is asked of love's wherefore.
'Tis Earth's, her gift; else have we nought:
Her gift, her secret, here our tie.
And not with her and yonder sky?   40
Bethink you: were it Earth alone
Breeds love, would not her region be
    The sole delight and throne
    Of generous Deity?

To deeper than this ball of sight
  Appeal the lustrous people of the night.

Fronting yon shoreless, sown with fiery sails,
    It is our ravenous that quails,
Flesh by its craven thirsts and fears distraught.
    The spirit leaps alight,   50
    Doubts not in them is he,
The binder of his sheaves, the sane, the right:
Of magnitude to magnitude is wrought,
To feel it large of the great life they hold:
In them to come, or vaster intervolved,
The issues known in us, our unsolved solved:
That there with toil Life climbs the self-same Tree,
Whose roots enrichment have from ripeness
    dropped.
So may we read and little find them cold:
Let it but be the lord of Mind to guide   60
Our eyes; no branch of Reason's growing lopped;
Nor dreaming on a dream; but fortified
By day to penetrate black midnight; see,
Hear, feel, outside the senses; even that we,
The specks of dust upon a mound of mould,
We who reflect those rays, though low our place,
    To them are lastingly allied.

So may we read, and little find them cold:
Not frosty lamps illumining dead space,
Not distant aliens, not senseless powers.   70
The fire is in them whereof we are born;
The music of their motion may be ours.
Spirit shall deem them beckoning Earth and voiced
Sisterly to her, in her beams rejoiced.
Of love, the grand impulsion, we behold
    The love that lends her grace
    Among the starry fold.
Then at new flood of customary morn,
    Look at her through her showers,
    Her mists, her streaming gold,   80
A wonder edges the familiar face:
She wears no more that robe of printed hours;
Half strange seems Earth, and sweeter than her
    flowers.

from ESSAY: ON THE IDEA OF COMEDY AND THE USES OF THE COMIC SPIRIT[1]

The essay from which the following passages are extracted—and which is generally called, for short, *An Essay on Comedy*—was a lecture delivered before the London Institution for the Advancement of Literature and the Diffusion of Useful Knowledge, February 1, 1877. It is the most elaborate statement Meredith ever

[1] Published by Charles Scribner's Sons. Reprinted by permission.

made of what might almost be called his Gospel of Comedy—it is also, no doubt, the most famous discussion of comedy in the English language—but it should be compared with the prelude to *The Egoist* and with the poem "Ode to the Comic Spirit." For the general significance of comedy in Meredith's philosophy see also the discussion of his life and work on pages 825–26 of this volume.

Professor Lane Cooper made an elaborate edition of this essay for "The Modern Student's Library," Scribner, 1918; the present editor has found Professor Cooper's annotations very helpful.

GOOD Comedies are such rare productions that, notwithstanding the wealth of our literature in the Comic element, it would not occupy us long to run over the English list. If they are brought to the test I shall propose, very reputable Comedies will be found unworthy of their station, like the ladies of Arthur's Court when they were reduced to the ordeal of the mantle.

There are plain reasons why the Comic poet is not a frequent apparition; and why the great Comic poet remains without a fellow. A society of cultivated men and women is required, wherein ideas are current, and the perceptions quick, that he may be supplied with matter and an audience. The semi-barbarism of merely giddy communities, and feverish emotional periods, repel him; and also a state of marked social inequality of the sexes; nor can he whose business is to address the mind be understood where there is not a moderate degree of intellectual activity.

Moreover, to touch and kindle the mind through laughter, demands, more than sprightliness, a most subtle delicacy. That must be a natal gift in the Comic poet. The substance he deals with will show him a startling exhibition of the dyer's hand, if he is without it. People are ready to surrender themselves to witty thumps on the back, breast, and sides; all except the head: and it is there that he aims. He must be subtle to penetrate. A corresponding acuteness must exist to welcome him. The necessity for the two conditions will explain how it is that we count him during centuries in the singular number. . . .

Shakespeare is a well-spring of characters which are saturated with the comic spirit; with more of what we will call blood-life than is to be found anywhere out of Shakespeare; and they are of this world, but they are of the world enlarged to our embrace by imagination, and by great poetic imagination. They are, as it were—I put it to suit my present comparison—creatures of the woods and wilds, not in walled towns, not grouped and toned to pursue a comic exhibition of the narrower world of society. Jaques, Falstaff and his regiment, the varied troop of Clowns, Malvolio, Sir Hugh Evans and Fluellen—marvelous Welshmen!—Benedick and Beatrice, Dogberry, and the rest, are subjects of a special study in the poetically comic.

His Comedy of incredible imbroglio belongs to the literary section. One may conceive that there was a natural resemblance between him and Menander, both in the scheme and style of his lighter plays. Had Shakespeare lived in a later and less emotional, less heroical, period of our history, he might have turned to the painting of manners as well as humanity. Euripides would probably, in the time of Menander, when Athens was enslaved but prosperous, have lent his hand to the composition of romantic comedy. He certainly inspired that fine genius.

Politically, it is accounted a misfortune for France that her nobles thronged to the Court of Louis Quatorze. It was a boon to the comic poet. He had that lively quicksilver world of the animalcule passions, the huge pretensions, the placid absurdities, under his eyes in full activity; vociferous quacks and snapping dupes, hypocrites, posturers, extravagants, pedants, rose-pink ladies and mad grammarians, sonnetteering marquises, high-flying mistresses, plain-minded maids, inter-threading as in a loom, noisy as at a fair. A simply bourgeois circle will not furnish it, for the middle class must have the brilliant, flippant, independent upper for a spur and a pattern; otherwise it is likely to be inwardly dull, as well as outwardly correct. Yet, though the King was benevolent toward Molière, it is not to the French Court that we are indebted for his unrivalled studies of mankind in society. For the amusement of the Court the ballets and farces were written, which are dearer to the rabble upper, as to the rabble lower, class than intellectual comedy. The French bourgeoisie of Paris were sufficiently

7–10. **Jaques,** in *As You Like It.* **Falstaff and his regiment,** in *King Henry IV.* **Malvolio,** in *Twelfth Night.* **Sir Hugh Evans,** in *The Merry Wives of Windsor.* **Fluellen,** in *King Henry V.* **Benedick and Beatrice, Dogberry,** in *Much Ado about Nothing.* 13. **His Comedy of incredible imbroglio,** *The Comedy of Errors,* which is indebted to the Roman dramatist Plautus (c. 254–184 B.C.) not to the Greek **Menander.** 20. **Euripides,** Greek dramatist (480–406 B.C.). 26–27. **Louis Quatorze,** Louis XIV (reigned 1643–1715). 40. **Molière,** French dramatist (1622–1673).

18–20. **like the ladies . . . mantle.** Compare the ballad of "The Boy and the Mantle" (F. J. Child, *English and Scottish Popular Ballads,* No. 29). The mantle tested marital fidelity. 37. **a startling . . . hand.** See Shakespeare's Sonnet

quick-witted and enlightened by education to welcome great works like Le Tartuffe, Les Femmes Savantes, and Le Misanthrope, works that were perilous ventures on the popular intelligence, big vessels to launch on streams running to shallows. The Tartuffe hove into view as an enemy's vessel; it offended, not *"Dieu, mais . . . les dévots,"* as the Prince de Condé explained the cabal raised against it to the King. . . .

The Misanthrope was yet more frigidly received. Molière thought it dead. "I cannot improve on it, and assuredly never shall," he said. It is one of the French titles to honour that this quintessential comedy of the opposition of Alceste and Célimène was ultimately understood and applauded. In all countries the middle class presents the public which, fighting the world, and with a good footing in the fight, knows the world best. It may be the most selfish, but that is a question leading us into sophistries. Cultivated men and women who do not skim the cream of life, and are attached to the duties, yet escape the harsher blows, make acute and balanced observers. Molière is their poet.

Of this class in England, a large body, neither Puritan nor Bacchanalian, have a sentimental objection to face the study of the actual world. They take up disdain of it, when its truths appear humiliating; when the facts are not immediately forced on them, they take up the pride of incredulity. They live in a hazy atmosphere that they suppose an ideal one. Humorous writing they will endure, perhaps approve, if it mingles with pathos to shake and elevate the feelings. They approve of Satire, because, like the beak of the vulture, it smells of carrion, which they are not. But of Comedy they have a shivering dread, for Comedy enfolds them with the wretched host of the world, huddles them with us all in an ignoble assimilation, and cannot be used by any exalted variety as a scourge and a broom. Nay, to be an exalted variety is to come under the calm, curious eye of the Comic spirit, and be probed for what you are. Men are seen among them, and very many cultivated women. You may distinguish them by a favourite phrase: "Surely we are not so bad!" and the remark: "If that is human nature, save us from it!" as if it could be done: but in the peculiar Paradise of the wilful people who will not see, the exclamation assumes the saving grace. . . .

Congreve's Way of the World is an exception to our other comedies, his own among them, by virtue of the remarkable brilliancy of the writing, and the figure of Millamant. The comedy has no idea in it, beyond the stale one that so the world goes; and it concludes with the jaded discovery of a document at a convenient season for the descent of the curtain. A plot was an afterthought with Congreve. By the help of a wooden villain (Maskwell), marked Gallows to the flattest eye, he gets a sort of plot in The Double-Dealer. His Way of the World might be called The Conquest of a Town Coquette, and Millamant is a perfect portrait of a coquette, both in her resistance to Mirabel and the manner of her surrender, and also in her tongue. The wit here is not so salient as in certain passages of Love for Love, where Valentine feigns madness, or retorts on his father, or Mrs. Frail rejoices in the harmlessness of wounds to a woman's virtue, if she "keeps them from air." In The Way of the World, it appears less prepared in the smartness, and is more diffused in the more characteristic style of the speakers. Here, however, as elsewhere, his famous wit is like a bully-fencer, not ashamed to lay traps for its exhibition, transparently petulant for the train between certain ordinary words and the powder-magazine of the improprieties to be fired. Contrast the wit of Congreve with Molière's. That of the first is a Toledo blade, sharp, and wonderfully supple for steel; cast for duelling, restless in the scabbard, being so pretty when out of it. To shine, it must have an adversary. Molière's wit is like a running brook, with innumerable fresh lights on it at every turn of the wood through which its business is to find a way. It does not run in search of obstructions, to be noisy over them; but when dead leaves and viler substances are heaped along the course, its natural song is heightened. Without effort, and with no dazzling flashes of achievement, it is full of healing, the wit of good breeding, the wit of wisdom. . . .

German attempts at Comedy remind one vividly of Heine's image of his country in the dancing of Atta Troll. Lessing tried his hand at it, with a sobering effect upon readers. The intention to produce the reverse effect is just visible, and therein, like the portly graces of the poor old Pyrenean Bear poising

7. not **"Dieu, mais . . . les dévots,"** not "God but the devout." 7–8. **the Prince de Condé,** Louis II de Bourbon, prince, duc d'Enghien (1621–1686).

1. **Congreve's Way of the World.** *The Way of the World*, 1700, by William Congreve, is perhaps the finest flower of the brilliant and scandalous Restoration comedy. **44–48. Heine's image . . . Pyrenean Bear.** Atta Troll is a bear dancing in the Pyrenees in the poem of that title (1846) by the German poet Heinrich Heine. Not all critics will accept Meredith's condemnation of the comedies of **Lessing.**

and twirling on his right hind-leg and his left, consists the fun. Jean Paul Richter gives the best edition of the German Comic in the contrast of Siebenkäs with his Lenette. A light of the Comic is in Goethe; enough to complete the splendid figure of the man, but no more.

The German literary laugh, like the timed awakenings of their Barbarossa in the hollows of the Untersberg, is infrequent, and rather monstrous—never a laugh of men and women in concert. It comes of unrefined abstract fancy, grotesque or grim, or gross, like the peculiar humours of their little earthmen. Spiritual laughter they have not yet attained to: sentimentalism waylays them in the flight. Here and there a Volkslied or Märchen shows a national aptitude for stout animal laughter; and we see that the literature is built on it, which is hopeful so far; but to enjoy it, to enter into the philosophy of the Broad Grin, that seems to hesitate between the skull and the embryo, and reaches its perfection in breadth from the pulling of two square fingers at the corners of the mouth, one must have aid of "the good Rhine wine," and be of German blood unmixed besides. This treble-Dutch lumbersomeness of the Comic spirit is of itself exclusive of the idea of Comedy, and the poor voice allowed to women in German domestic life will account for the absence of comic dialogues reflecting upon life in that land. I shall speak of it again in the second section of this lecture.

Eastward you have total silence of Comedy among a people intensely susceptible to laughter, as the *Arabian Nights* will testify. Where the veil is over women's faces, you cannot have society, without which the senses are barbarous and the Comic Spirit is driven to the gutters of grossness to slake its thirst. Arabs in this respect are worse than Italians—much worse than Germans; just in the degree that their system of treating women is worse. . . .

There has been fun in Bagdad. But there never will be civilization where Comedy is not possible; and that comes of some degree of social equality of the sexes. I am not quoting the Arab to exhort and disturb the somnolent East; rather for cultivated women to recognize that the Comic Muse is one of their best friends. They are blind to their interests in swelling the ranks of the sentimentalists. Let them look with their clearest vision abroad and at home. They will see that where they have no social freedom, Comedy is absent; where they are household drudges, the form of Comedy is primitive: where they are tolerably independent, but uncultivated, exciting melodrama takes its place, and a sentimental version of them. Yet the Comic will out, as they would know if they listened to some of the private conversations of men whose minds are undirected by the Comic Muse: as the sentimental man, to his astonishment, would know likewise, if he in similar fashion could receive a lesson. But where women are on the road to an equal footing with men, in attainments and in liberty—in what they have won for themselves, and what has been granted them by a fair civilization—there, and only waiting to be transplanted from life to the stage, or the novel, or the poem, pure Comedy flourishes, and is, as it would help them to be, the sweetest of diversions, the wisest of delightful companions.

Now, to look about us in the present time, I think it will be acknowledged that in neglecting the cultivation of the Comic idea, we are losing the aid of a powerful auxiliar. You see Folly perpetually sliding into new shapes in a society possessed of wealth and leisure, with many whims, many strange ailments and strange doctors. Plenty of common-sense is in the world to thrust her back when she pretends to empire. But the first-born of common-sense, the vigilant Comic, which is the genius of thoughtful laughter, which would readily extinguish her at the outset, is not serving as a public advocate. . . .

Taking them generally, the English public are most in sympathy with [the] primitive Aristophanic comedy, wherein the comic is capped by the grotesque, irony tips the wit, and satire is a naked sword. They have the basis of the Comic in them: an esteem for common-sense. They cordially dislike the reverse of it. They have a rich laugh, though it is not the *gros rire* of the Gaul tossing *gros sel*, nor the polished Frenchman's mentally digestive laugh. And if they have now, like a monarch with a troop of dwarfs, too many jesters kicking the dictionary about, to let them *reflect* that they are dull, occasionally like the pensive monarch surprising himself with an idea of an idea of his own, they look so. And they are given to looking in the glass. They

2. **Jean Paul Richter**, German humorist (1763–1825). **Siebenkäs** and **Lenette** are a mismated husband and wife in a work he published in 1796.   **8–9. Barbarossa . . . Untersberg.** Frederick Barbarossa (c. 1123–1190), emperor of the Holy Roman Empire, was long thought of as sleeping in the Untersberg (near Salzburg), from which he was expected to return and restore the glories of the German race.   **15. Volkslied**, folk song. **Märchen**, fairy tale or traditional popular tale.

38–39. Aristophanic comedy, of Aristophanes, Greek comic dramatist (c. 448–c. 380 B.C.).   **44–45. gros rire**, rough loud laughter. **gros sel**, coarse or obscene wit.

must see that something ails them. How much even the better order of them will endure, without a thought of the defensive, when the person afflicting them is protected from satire, we read in Memoirs of a Preceding Age, where the vulgarly tyrannous hostess of a great house of reception shuffled the guests and played them like a pack of cards, with her exact estimate of the strength of each one printed on them: and still this house continued to be the most popular in England; nor did the lady ever [10] appear in print or on the boards as the comic type that she was.

It has been suggested that they have not yet spiritually comprehended the signification of living in society; for who are cheerfuller, brisker of wit, in the fields, and as explorers, colonizers, backwoodsmen? They are happy in rough exercise, and also in complete repose. The intermediate condition, when they are called upon to talk to one another, upon other than affairs of business or their hobbies, re- [20] veals them wearing a curious look of vacancy, as it were the socket of an eye wanting. The Comic is perpetually springing up in social life, and it oppresses them from not being perceived.

Thus, at a dinner-party, one of the guests, who happens to have enrolled himself in a Burial Company, politely entreats the others to inscribe their names as shareholders, expatiating on the advantages accruing to them in the event of their very possible speedy death, the salubrity of the site, the [30] aptitude of the soil for a quick consumption of their remains, etc.; and they drink sadness from the incongruous man, and conceive indigestion, not seeing him in a sharply defined light, that would bid them taste the comic of him. Or it is mentioned that a newly elected member of our Parliament celebrates his arrival at eminence by the publication of a book on cab-fares, dedicated to a beloved female relative deceased, and the comment on it is the word "Indeed." But, merely for a contrast, turn to a [40] not uncommon scene of yesterday in the hunting-field, where a brilliant young rider, having broken his collar-bone, trots away very soon after, against medical interdict, half put together in splinters, to the most distant meet of his neighbourhood, sure of escaping his doctor, who is the first person he encounters. "I came here purposely to avoid you," says the patient. "I came here purposely to take care of you," says the doctor. Off they go, and come to a swollen brook. The patient clears it hand- [50]

somely: the doctor tumbles in. All the field are alive with the heartiest relish of every incident and every cross-light on it; and dull would the man have been thought who had not his word to say about it when riding home.

In our prose literature we have had delightful Comic writers. Besides Fielding and Goldsmith, there is Miss Austen, whose Emma and Mr. Elton might walk straight into a comedy, were the plot arranged for them. Galt's neglected novels have some characters and strokes of shrewd comedy. In our poetic literature the comic is delicate and graceful above the touch of Italian and French. Generally, however, the English elect excel in satire, and they are noble humourists. The national disposition is for hard-hitting, with a moral purpose to sanction it; or for a rosy, sometimes a larmoyant, geniality, not unmanly in its verging upon tenderness, and with a singular attraction for thick-headedness, to decorate it with asses' ears and the most beautiful sylvan haloes. But the Comic is a different spirit.

You may estimate your capacity for Comic perception by being able to detect the ridicule of them you love, without loving them less: and more by being able to see yourself somewhat ridiculous in dear eyes, and accepting the correction their image of you proposes.

Each one of an affectionate couple may be willing, as we say, to die for the other, yet unwilling to utter the agreeable word at the right moment; but if the wits were sufficiently quick for them to perceive that they are in a comic situation, as affectionate couples must be when they quarrel, they would not wait for the moon or the almanac, or a Dorine, to bring back the flood-tide of tender feelings, that they should join hands and lips.

If you detect the ridicule, and your kindliness is chilled by it, you are slipping into the grasp of Satire.

If, instead of falling foul of the ridiculous person with a satiric rod, to make him writhe and shriek aloud, you prefer to sting him under a semi-caress, by which he shall in his anguish be rendered dubious whether indeed anything has hurt him, you are an engine of Irony.

If you laugh all round him, tumble him, roll him about, deal him a smack, and drop a tear on him,

---

4-12. we read in Memoirs . . . that she was. A. W. Pollard identified the hostess for Lane Cooper as Elizabeth Vassall Fox, Lady Holland (1770-1845). For details see Lane Cooper's note in his edition of *An Essay on Comedy*, pages 268-69.

7. **Fielding,** Henry Fielding (1707-1754), author of *Tom Jones*, rated by some critics as the greatest English novel. **Goldsmith,** Oliver Goldsmith, author of *The Vicar of Wakefield* (1728-1774). **8. Miss Austen,** Jane Austen, author of *Pride and Prejudice* (1775-1817). **whose Emma and Mr. Elton,** in her novel *Emma*, 1816. **10. Galt,** John Galt (1779-1839), a Scotch realistic novelist, author of *The Ayrshire Legatees* and *The Annals of the Parish*. **34. Dorine,** a character in Molière's *Tartuffe*.

own his likeness to you and yours to your neighbour, spare him as little as you shun, pity him as much as you expose, it is a spirit of Humour that is moving you.

The Comic, which is the perceptive, is the governing spirit, awakening and giving aim to these powers of laughter, but it is not to be confounded with them: it enfolds a thinner form of them, differing from satire, in not sharply driving into the quivering sensibilities, and from humour, in not comforting them and tucking them up, or indicating a broader than the range of this bustling world to them.

Fielding's Jonathan Wild presents a case of this peculiar distinction, when that man of eminent greatness remarks upon the unfairness of a trial in which the condemnation has been brought about by twelve men of the opposite party; for it is not satiric, it is not humorous; yet it is immensely comic to hear a guilty villain protesting that his own "party" should have a voice in the Law. It opens an avenue into villains' ratiocination. And the Comic is not cancelled though we should suppose Jonathan to be giving play to his humour.

Apply the case to the man of deep wit, who is ever certain of his condemnation by the opposite party, and then it ceases to be comic, and will be satiric.

The look of Fielding upon Richardson is essentially comic. His method of correcting the sentimental writer is a mixture of the comic and the humourous. Parson Adams is a creation of humour. But both the conception and the presentation of Alceste and of Tartuffe, of Célimène and Philaminte, are purely comic, addressed to the intellect: there is no humour in them, and they refresh the intellect they quicken to detect their comedy, by force of the contrast they offer between themselves and the wiser world about them; that is to say, society, or that assemblage of minds whereof the Comic spirit has its origin.

Byron had splendid powers of humour, and the most poetic satire that we have example of, fusing at times to hard irony. He had no strong comic sense, or he would not have taken an anti-social position, which is directly opposed to the Comic; and in his philosophy, judged by philosophers, he is

a comic figure, by reason of this deficiency. "Sobald er reflectirt ist er ein Kind," Goethe says of him. Carlyle sees him in this comic light, treats him in the humorous manner.

The Satirist is a moral agent, often a social scavenger, working on a storage of bile.

The Ironist is one thing or another, according to his caprice. Irony is the humour of satire; it may be savage as in Swift, with a moral object, or sedate, as in Gibbon, with a malicious. The foppish irony fretting to be seen, and the irony which leers, that you shall not mistake its intention, are failures in satiric effort pretending to the treasures of ambiguity.

The Humourist of mean order is a refreshing laugher, giving tone to the feelings, and sometimes allowing the feelings to be too much for him; but the humourist of high has an embrace of contrasts beyond the scope of the Comic poet.

Heart and mind laugh out at Don Quixote, and still you brood on him. The juxtaposition of the knight and squire is a Comic conception, the opposition of their natures most humorous. They are as different as the two hemispheres in the time of Columbus, yet they touch and are bound in one by laughter. The knight's great aims and constant mishaps, his chivalrous valiancy exercise on absurd objects, his good sense along the highroad of the craziest of expeditions; the compassion he plucks out of derision, and the admirable figure he preserves while stalking through the frantically grotesque and burlesque assailing him, are in the loftiest moods of humour, fusing the Tragic sentiment with the Comic narrative.

The stroke of the great humourist is world-wide, with lights of Tragedy in his laughter. . . .

If you believe that our civilization is founded in common-sense (and it is the first condition of sanity to believe it), you will, when contemplating men, discern a Spirit overhead; not more heavenly than the light flashed upward from glassy surfaces, but luminous and watchful; never shooting beyond them, nor lagging in the rear; so closely attached to them that it may be taken for a slavish reflex, until its features are studied. It has the sage's brows, and the sunny malice of a faun lurks at the

---

14. Fielding's Jonathan Wild, 1743, one of the most sustained pieces of irony in the language, the history of a criminal in a style of pretended admiration.   29–30. The look . . . comic. Fielding's *Joseph Andrews*, 1742, began as a burlesque of *Pamela*, 1740, the first novel of Samuel Richardson (1689–1761), which Fielding regarded as both ridiculous and immoral.   32. Parson Adams, in Fielding's *Joseph Andrews*.   34. Alceste, in Molière's *Le misanthrope*.   34. Tartuffe, in Molière's *Tartuffe*.   34. Célimène, in *Le misanthrope*. 34–35. Philaminte, in Molière's *Les femmes savantes*.

2–3. "Sobald . . . ein Kind." As soon as he begins to think he is a child.   9–10. it may be savage . . . object, as in "A Modest Proposal." See Volume I.   11. Gibbon, Edward Gibbon. See note in page 449.   22–23. the knight and squire, the idealistic Don Quixote and the unidealistic Sancho Panza, in the great novel *Don Quixote* by Miguel de Cervantes Saavedra, known as Cervantes (1547–1616).

corners of the half-closed lips drawn in an idle wari-
ness of half-tension. That slim feasting smile, shaped
like the long-bow, was once a big round satyr's
laugh, that flung up the brows like a fortress lifted
by gunpowder. The laugh will come again, but it
will be of the order of the smile, finely tempered,
showing sunlight of the mind, mental richness
rather than noisy enormity. Its common aspect is
one of unsolicitous observation, as if surveying a
full field and having leisure to dart on its chosen 10
morsels, without any fluttering eagerness. Men's
future upon earth does not attract it; their honesty
and shapeliness in the present does; and whenever
they wax out of proportion, overblown, affected,
pretentious, bombastical, hypocritical, pedantic,
fantastically delicate; whenever it sees them self-
deceived or hoodwinked, given to run riot in idolatries, drifting into vanities, congregating in absurdities, planning short-sightedly, plotting dementedly;
whenever they are at variance with their professions, 20
and violate the unwritten but perceptible laws binding them in consideration one to another; whenever
they offend sound reason, fair justice; are false in
humility or mined with conceit, individually, or in
the bulk—the Spirit overhead will look humanely
malign and cast an oblique light on them, followed
by volleys of silvery laughter. That is the Comic
Spirit.

Not to distinguish it is to be bull-blind to the
spiritual, and to deny the existence of a mind of 30
man where minds of men are in working conjunction.

You must, as I have said, believe that our state of
society is founded in common-sense, otherwise you
will not be struck by the contrasts the Comic Spirit
perceives, or have it to look to for your consolation.
You will, in fact, be standing in that peculiar
oblique beam of light, yourself illuminated to the
general eye as the very object of chase and doomed
quarry of the thing obscure to you. But to feel its 40
presence and to see it is your assurance that many
sane and solid minds are with you in what you are
experiencing: and this of itself spares you the pain
of satirical heat, and the bitter craving to strike
heavy blows. You share the sublime of wrath, that
would not have hurt the foolish, but merely demonstrate their foolishness. Molière was contented to
revenge himself on the critics of the École des
Femmes by writing the Critique de l'École des
Femmes, one of the wisest as well as the playfullest 50
of studies in criticism. A perception of the Comic
Spirit gives high fellowship. You become a citizen of
the selecter world, the highest we know of in connection with our old world, which is not super-

mundane. Look there for your unchallengeable
upper class! You feel that you are one of this our
civilized community, that you cannot escape from
it, and would not if you could. Good hope sustains
you: weariness does not overwhelm you; in isolation
you see no charms for vanity; personal pride is
greatly moderated. Nor shall your title of citizen-
ship exclude you from worlds of imagination or of
devotion. The Comic spirit is not hostile to the
sweetest songfully poetic. Chaucer bubbles with it:
Shakespeare overflows: there is a mild moon's ray
of it (pale with super-refinement through distance
from our flesh and blood planet) in *Comus*. Pope has
it, and it is the daylight side of the night half ob-
scuring Cowper. It is only hostile to the priestly element, when that, by baleful swelling, transcends
and overlaps the bounds of its office: and then, in
extreme cases, it is too true to itself to speak, and
veils the lamp: as, for example, the spectacle of
Bossuet over the dead body of Molière, at which the
dark angels may, but men do not, laugh. . . .

The laughter heard in circles not pervaded by
the Comic idea will sound harsh and soul-less, like
versified prose, if you step into them with a sense of
the distinction. You will fancy you have changed
your habitation to a planet remoter from the sun.
You may be among powerful brains too. You will
not find poets—or but a stray one, over-worshipped.
You will find learned men undoubtedly, professors,
reputed philosophers, and illustrious dilettanti.
They have in them, perhaps, every element composing light, except the Comic. They read verse,
they discourse of art; but their eminent faculties are
not under that vigilant sense of a collective supervi-
sion, spiritual and present, which we have taken
note of. They build a temple of arrogance; they
speak much in the voice of oracles; their hilarity, if
it does not dip in grossness, is usually a form of pugnacity.

Insufficiency of sight in the eye looking outward
has deprived them of the eye that should look inward. They have never weighed themselves in the
delicate balance of the Comic idea so as to obtain a
suspicion of the rights and dues of the world; and
they have, in consequence, an irritable personality.
A very learned English professor crushed an argument in a political discussion, by asking his adver-

13. **Comus,** by John Milton, 1637.   14–15. **the night
half-obscuring Cowper.** Meredith refers to such poems as
"The Castaway" in which Cowper speaks of his belief that
God had condemned him to hell. See Gamaliel Bradford's
portrait of Cowper in *Bare Souls* (Harper, 1924).   19–
20. **the spectacle . . . Molière.** Jacques Bénigne **Bossuet**
(1627–1704), famous French preacher, condemned Molière's
plays.

sary angrily: "Are you aware, sir, that I am a philologer?"

The practice of polite society will help in training them, and the professor on a sofa, with beautiful ladies on each side of him, may become their pupil and a scholar in manners without knowing it: he is at least a fair and pleasing spectacle to the Comic Muse. But the society named polite is volatile in its adorations, and to-morrow will be petting a bronzed soldier, or a black African, or a prince, or a spiritualist: ideas cannot take root in its ever-shifting soil. It is besides addicted in self-defence to gabble exclusively of the affairs of its rapidly revolving world, as children on a whirligoround bestow their attention on the wooden horse or cradle ahead of them, to escape from giddiness and preserve a notion of identity. The professor is better out of a circle that often confounds by lionizing, sometimes annoys by abandoning, and always confuses. The school that teaches gently what peril there is lest a cultivated head should still be coxcomb's, and the collisions which may befall high-soaring minds, empty or full, is more to be recommended than the sphere of incessant motion supplying it with material.

Lands where the Comic spirit is obscure overhead are rank with raw crops of matter. The traveller accustomed to smooth highways and people not covered with burrs and prickles is amazed, amid so much that is fair and cherishable, to come upon such curious barbarism. An Englishman paid a visit of admiration to a professor in the Land of Culture, and was introduced by him to another distinguished professor, to whom he took so cordially as to walk out with him alone one afternoon. The first professor, an erudite entirely worthy of the sentiment of scholarly esteem prompting the visit, behaved (if we exclude the dagger) with the vindictive jealousy of an injured Spanish beauty. After a short prelude of gloom and obscure explosions, he discharged upon his faithless admirer the bolts of passionate logic familiar to the ears of flighty caballeros:—"Either I am a fit object of your admiration, or I am not. Of these things, one—either you are competent to judge, in which case I stand condemned by you; or you are incompetent, and therefore impertinent, and you may betake yourself to your country again, hypocrite!" The admirer was for persuading the wounded scholar that it is given to us to be able to admire two professors at a time. He was driven forth.

Perhaps this might have occurred in any country, and a comedy of The Pedant, discovering the greedy humanity within the dusty scholar, would not bring it home to one in particular. I am mindful that it was in Germany, when I observe that the Germans have gone through no comic training to warn them of the sly, wise emanation eyeing them from aloft, nor much of satirical. Heinrich Heine has not been enough to cause them to smart and meditate. Nationally, as well as individually, when they are excited they are in danger of the grotesque; as when, for instance, they decline to listen to evidence, and raise a national outcry because one of German blood has been convicted of crime in a foreign country. They are acute critics, yet they still wield clubs in controversy. Compare them in this respect with the people schooled in La Bruyère, La Fontaine, Molière; with the people who have the figures of a Trissotin and a Vadius before them for a comic warning of the personal vanities of the caressed professor. It is more than difference of race. It is the difference of traditions, temper, and style, which comes of schooling.

The French controversialist is a polished swordsman, to be dreaded in his graces and courtesies. The German is Orson, or the mob, or a marching army, in defence of a good case or a bad—a big or a little. His irony is a missile of terrific tonnage: sarcasm he emits like a blast from a dragon's mouth. He must and will be Titan. He stamps his foe underfoot, and is astonished that the creature is not dead, but stinging; for, in truth, the Titan is contending, by comparison, with a god.

When the Germans lie on their arms, looking across the Alsatian frontier at the crowds of Frenchmen rushing to applaud L'Ami Fritz at the Théâtre Français, looking and considering the meaning of that applause, which is grimly comic in its political response to the domestic moral of the play—when the Germans watch and are silent, their force of character tells. They are kings in music, we may say princes in poetry, good speculators in philosophy, and our leaders in scholarship. That so gifted a race, possessed moreover of the stern good sense which collects the waters of laughter to make the wells, should show at a disadvantage, I hold for a proof, instructive to us, that the discipline of the Comic spirit is needful to their growth. We see what they can reach to in that great figure of modern manhood, Goethe. They are a growing people; they are conversable as well; and when their men, as in

14. **La Bruyère, La Fontaine,** French authors (1645-1696) and (1621-1695).   16. **Trissotin . . . Vadius,** characters in Molière's *Les femmes savantes*.   23. **Orson,** the uncouth one in the old French story of *Valentine and Orson*.   27. **Titan,** possibly Hyperion.   33. **L'Ami Fritz,** a comedy by Erckmann-Chatrian, produced December 4, 1876. Its presentation aroused passions connected with Germany's conquest of Alsace.

France, and at intervals at Berlin tea-tables, consent to talk on equal terms with their women, and to listen to them, their growth will be accelerated and be shapelier. Comedy, or, in any form, the Comic spirit, will then come to them to cut some figures out of the block, show them the mirror, enliven and irradiate the social intelligence.

Modern French comedy is commendable for the directness of the study of actual life, as far as that, which is but the early step in such a scholarship, can be of service in composing and colouring the picture. A consequence of this crude, though well-meant, realism is the collision of the writers in their scenes and incidents, and in their characters. The Muse of most of them is an *Aventurière*. She is clever, and a certain diversion exists in the united scheme for confounding her. The object of this person is to reinstate herself in the decorous world; and either, having accomplished this purpose through deceit, she has a *nostalgie de la boue*, that eventually casts her back into it, or she is exposed in her course of deception when she is about to gain her end. A very good, innocent young man is her victim, or a very astute, goodish young man obstructs her path. This latter is enabled to be the champion of the decorous world by knowing the indecorous well. He has assisted in the progress of *Aventurières* downward; he will not help them to ascend. The world is with him; and certainly it is not much of an ascension they aspire to; but what sort of a figure is he? The triumph of a candid realism is to show him no hero. You are to admire him (for it must be supposed that realism pretends to waken some admiration) as a credibly living young man; no better, only a little firmer and shrewder, than the rest. If, however, you think at all, after the curtain has fallen, you are likely to think that the Aventurières have a case to plead against him. True, and the author has not said any-

thing to the contrary; he has but painted from the life; he leaves his audience to the reflections of unphilosophic minds upon life, from the specimen he has presented in the bright and narrow circle of a spy-glass.

I do not know that the fly in amber is of any particular use, but the Comic idea enclosed in a comedy makes it more generally perceptible and portable, and that is an advantage. There is a benefit to men in taking the lessons of Comedy in congregations, for it enlivens the wits; and to writers it is beneficial, for they must have a clear scheme, and even if they have no idea to present, they must prove that they have made the public sit to them before the sitting to see the picture. And writing for the stage would be a corrective of a too-incrusted scholarly style, into which some great ones fall at times. It keeps minor writers to a definite plan, and to English. Many of them now swelling a plethoric market in the composition of novels, in pun-manufactories and in journalism; attached to the machinery forcing perishable matter on a public that swallows voraciously and groans; might, with encouragement, be attending to the study of art in literature. Our critics appear to be fascinated by the quaintness of our public, as the world is when our beast-garden has a new importation of magnitude, and the creature's appetite is reverently consulted. They stipulate for a writer's popularity before they will do much more than take the position of umpires to record his failure or success. Now the pig supplies the most popular of dishes, but it is not accounted the most honoured of animals, unless it be by the cottager. Our public might surely be led to try other, perhaps finer, meat. It has good taste in song. It might be taught as justly, on the whole, and the sooner when the cottager's view of the feast shall cease to be the humble one of our literary critics, to extend this capacity for delicate choosing in the direction of the matter arousing laughter.

15. **Aventurière**, adventuress. 20. **nostalgie de la boue**, nostalgia for the mud. The reference is to *Le mariage d'Olympe*, by Emile Augier (1820–1889).

Algernon Charles Swinburne
1837–1909

Swinburne was the "enfant terrible" of Victorian poetry. He was born in London on April 5, 1837, of a distinguished and aristocratic family; his early training was largely under his mother, the daughter of the Earl of Ashburnham, and his grandfather, Sir John Edward Swinburne, who in all his habits of thinking and living was a French gentleman of the old school. The boy distinguished himself at Eton and at Oxford by his encyclopedic reading in several languages, and also by his insubordination; he left both places, with the approval of the authorities, before having completed his course. For a time he lived with Meredith and Rossetti in London; he was regarded as sharing the ideals of the Pre-Raphaelite Brotherhood.

Swinburne's first publication—a volume containing two plays, *The Queen Mother* and *Rosamund*—was stillborn in 1860; but in 1865 *Atalanta in Calydon* attracted much attention; and in 1866 *Poems and Ballads* was both a poetic triumph and a rousing scandal. Christina Rossetti expunged the daring reference to God as "the supreme evil" from her copy of *Atalanta;* had she tried to remove from *Poems and Ballads* all the passages which indicated an interest in sexual abnormalities she must surely have gutted the book.

Swinburne's actual experience of sin, however, always lagged far behind his large imaginative comprehension of it. He was a frail, nervous creature, his small elflike body crowned by an amazing shock of red hair. It is not surprising, therefore, that he should almost have wrecked himself when he tried to travel the same pace with a giant like Richard Burton and a sybarite like Richard Monckton Milnes. His *Songs before Sunrise*, 1867, in which he spoke eagerly in behalf of Italian liberation, was the result of a friendly conspiracy among his friends, who sought to enlist in some cause the rebellious enthusiasm they saw him wasting in mere self-indulgence. "No more love frenzy," said Mazzini, and Swinburne, who had as great a capacity for hero worship as any man who ever lived, adored Mazzini. But the remedy had only a temporary effectiveness; by 1879 he had shown himself clearly incapable of driving himself in any other direction than toward the rocks. That was when Theodore Watts-Dunton took charge of him. For the last thirty years of Swinburne's life Watts-Dunton managed all his practical affairs and made most of his decisions for him. A steady stream of books flowed from Swinburne during these years; most of them are generally considered inferior to his earlier works. It must not be assumed, however, that without Watts-Dunton the aging Swinburne would have written better books. Without him he would have written nothing. He died at Putney on April 10, 1909.

Among Swinburne's poetic works, in addition to those already mentioned, are the second (1878) and the third (1889) series of *Poems and Ballads; Tristram of Lyonesse and Other Poems*, 1882; *A Century of Roundels*, 1883; *Astrophel and Other Poems*, 1894; *Rosamund, Queen of the Lombards*, 1899. His extensive critical writings include studies of Shakespeare, Blake, Victor Hugo, the Elizabethan dramatists, and several Victorian novelists.

The weaknesses of Swinburne's character are evident; the elements of strength included his sensitiveness to beauty, his enthusiasm for liberty (which he betrayed when he sanctioned British outrages in Ireland and South Africa), and his ability to find satisfaction in "the noble pleasure of praising." Unfortunately this last was balanced by his ability to find satisfaction in the ignoble pleasure of damning; his critical writing, consequently, veers between extravagant praise and equally extravagant censure—he was never pleased or displeased in moderation. Yet he has many sane, unspoiled passages, and many which evidence his capacity to achieve a fundamentally just assessment of life.

Established Victorian values crumble badly in Swinburne. The religious indifference of Morris and Rossetti becomes with him a positive hostility, though the very violence of his reaction probably indicates that the religious view of life had a stronger hold upon him that he would admit. Technically he is a great master of words and rhythms. There is a luscious quality, however, not only in his mind but in his style. It is not true that he lacks ideas, but it is sometimes hard to find the idea in the welter of words. Matthew Arnold complained that Swinburne used a hundred words where one would have expressed his meaning. For this reason primarily, now that the passions awakened by his eager rebellion have had time to cool, lovers of poetry will

probably always be divided between those who
love Swinburne and those who detest him.

from ATALANTA IN CALYDON

Atalanta in Calydon, 1865, was Swinburne's attempt "to
do something original in English which might in some degree reproduce for English readers the likeness of a Greek
tragedy with something of its true poetic life and charm."
Three beautiful choruses from the play are given here.

1. WHEN THE HOUNDS OF SPRING

When the hounds of spring are on winter's traces,
   The mother of months in meadow or plain
Fills the shadows and windy places
   With lisp of leaves and ripple of rain;
And the brown bright nightingale amorous
Is half assuaged for Itylus,
For the Thracian ships and the foreign faces,
   The tongueless vigil, and all the pain.

Come with bows bent and with emptying of quivers,
   Maiden most perfect, lady of light,   10
With a noise of winds and many rivers,
   With a clamour of waters, and with might;
Bind on thy sandals, O thou most fleet,
Over the splendour and speed of thy feet;
For the faint east quickens, the wan west shivers,
   Round the feet of the day and the feet of the
      night.

Where shall we find her, how shall we sing to her,
   Fold our hands round her knees, and cling?
O that man's heart were as fire and could spring to
      her,
   Fire, or the strength of the streams that spring!
For the stars and the winds are unto her   21
As raiment, as songs of the harp-player;
For the risen stars and the fallen cling to her,
   And the southwest-wind and the west-wind sing.

For winter's rains and ruins are over,
   And all the season of snows and sins;
The days dividing lover and lover,
   The light that loses, the night that wins;
And time remembered is grief forgotten,
And frosts are slain and flowers begotten,   30
And in green underwood and cover
   Blossom by blossom the spring begins.

2. **The mother of months,** the moon goddess, Artemis or
Diana.   5–8. **And the brown . . . pain.** See the note on
Arnold's "Philomela," page 681 of this volume.

The full streams feed on flower of rushes,
   Ripe grasses trammel a travelling foot,
The faint fresh flame of the young year flushes
   From leaf to flower and flower to fruit;
And fruit and leaf are as gold and fire,
And the oat is heard above the lyre,
And the hoofèd heel of a satyr crushes
   The chestnut-husk at the chestnut-root.   40

And Pan by noon and Bacchus by night,
   Fleeter of foot than the fleet-foot kid,
Follows with dancing and fills with delight
   The Maenad and the Bassarid;
And soft as lips that laugh and hide
The laughing leaves of the trees divide,
And screen from seeing and leave in sight
   The god pursuing, the maiden hid.

The ivy falls with the Bacchanal's hair
   Over her eyebrows hiding her eyes;   50
The wild vine slipping down leaves bare
   Her bright breast shortening into sighs;
The wild vine slips with the weight of its leaves,
But the berried ivy catches and cleaves
To the limbs that glitter, the feet that scare
   The wolf that follows, the fawn that flies.

2. BEFORE THE BEGINNING OF YEARS

Before the beginning of years,
   There came to the making of man
Time, with a gift of tears;
   Grief, with a glass that ran;
Pleasure, with pain for leaven;
   Summer, with flowers that fell;
Remembrance fallen from heaven,
   And madness risen from hell;
Strength without hands to smite;
   Love that endures for a breath;   10
Night, the shadow of light,
   And life, the shadow of death.

And the high gods took in hand
   Fire, and the falling of tears,
And a measure of sliding sand
   From under the feet of the years;
And froth and drift of the sea;
   And dust of the labouring earth;

38. **oat,** the shepherd's pipe, made of oat straw.   39. **satyr,**
in Greek mythology half man and half god. Satyrs were
often pictured as partly equine in appearance. They were
also noted for their lust.   41. **Pan,** god of woods and fields,
patron of shepherds and hunters. **Bacchus,** Dionysus, god of
wine.   44. **Maenad,** a female devotee of Bacchus. **Bassarid,**
a Thracian maenad.

And bodies of things to be
  In the houses of death and of birth;   20
And wrought with weeping and laughter,
  And fashioned with loathing and love,
With life before and after
  And death beneath and above,
For a day and a night and a morrow,
  That his strength might endure for a span
With travail and heavy sorrow,
  The holy spirit of man.

From the winds of the north and the south
  They gathered as unto strife;   30
They breathed upon his mouth,
  They filled his body with life;
Eyesight and speech they wrought
  For the veils of the soul therein,
A time for labour and thought,
  A time to serve and to sin;
They gave him light in his ways,
  And love, and a space for delight,
And beauty and length of days,
  And night, and sleep in the night.   40
His speech is a burning fire;
  With his lips he travaileth;
In his heart is a blind desire,
  In his eyes foreknowledge of death;
He weaves, and is clothed with derision;
  Sows, and he shall not reap;
His life is a watch or a vision
  Between a sleep and a sleep.

3. WE HAVE SEEN THEE, O LOVE

We have seen thee, O Love, thou art fair; thou art
  goodly, O Love;
Thy wings make light in the air as the wings of a
  dove.
Thy feet are as winds that divide the stream of the
  sea;
Earth is thy covering to hide thee, the garment of
  thee.
Thou art swift and subtle and blind as a flame of
  fire;
Before thee the laughter, behind thee the tears of
  desire;
And twain go forth beside thee, a man with a maid;
Her eyes are the eyes of a bride whom delight makes
  afraid;
As the breath in the buds that stir is her bridal
  breath:
But Fate is the name of her; and his name is
  Death.   10

1-2. **We have seen thee . . . of a dove.** See Song of
Solomon 4:1.

HYMN TO PROSERPINE

(After the Proclamation in Rome of the Christian Faith)

Vicisti, Galilaee

"After the proclamation in Rome of the **Christian**
faith," that is, after Constantine's Edict of Milan, 313, an
unconverted pagan laments the passing of the old gods.
Proserpine, originally a girl of Sicily, was carried off by
Pluto to become the queen of the lower world and therefore of death. "*Vicisti, Galilaee*" means "Thou hast conquered, Galilean," the Galilean being, of course, Jesus;
these are the traditional last words of the emperor Julian
the Apostate (331–363), who attempted to restore the
pagan gods.

The poem is not a dramatic utterance merely; it represents Swinburne's own point of view as well as the speaker's. Historically it is open to grave objection. It was the
pagan world that was sad at this time; abounding joy was
the distinctive note of Christian experience. The Resurrection, not the Crucifixion (see l. 44) was what particularly interested the early Christians; nor did they stress
the sorrows of the Virgin Mary more than her joys (see
l. 81). Line 110 prejudges the whole question at issue between paganism and Christianity; it is the very essence of
the Christian faith that there is a "God found stronger
than death." For a striking interpretation of early Christian experience in which all these points are brought out,
see Bernard Shaw's play *Androcles and the Lion.*

Swinburne might be defended, however, on the ground
that what really interested him was the religious problem
in his own day. He had many contemporaries who seriously presented the Christian religion in terms of the
travesty he here combats.

I have lived long enough, having seen one thing;
  that love hath an end;
Goddess and maiden and queen, be near me now
  and befriend.
Thou art more than the day or the morrow, the
  seasons that laugh or that weep;
For these give joy and sorrow; but thou, Proserpina,
  sleep.
Sweet is the treading of wine, and sweet the feet of
  the dove;
But a goodlier gift is thine than foam of the grapes
  or love.
Yea, is not even Apollo, with hair and harpstring of
  gold,
A bitter God to follow, a beautiful God to be-
  hold?
I am sick of singing; the bays burn deep and chafe:
  I am fain

5. **dove,** sacred to Venus. 9. **singing,** making **poems.**
bays, laurel, with which poets were crowned.

To rest a little from praise and grievous pleasure
and pain.   10
For the Gods we know not of, who give us our daily
breath,
We know they are cruel as love or life, and lovely as
death.
O Gods dethroned and deceased, cast forth, wiped
out in a day!
From your wrath is the world released, redeemed
from your chains, men say.
New Gods are crowned in the city, their flowers
have broken your rods;
They are merciful, clothed with pity, the young
compassionate Gods.
But for me their new device is barren, the days are
bare;
Things long past over suffice, and men forgotten
that were.
Time and the Gods are at strife: ye dwell in the
midst thereof,
Draining a little life from the barren breasts of
love.   20
I say to you, cease, take rest; yea, I say to you all, be
at peace,
Till the bitter milk of her breast and the barren
bosom shall cease.
Wilt thou yet take all, Galilean? but these thou
shalt not take,
The laurel, the palms and the paean, the breasts of
of the nymphs in the brake;
Breasts more soft than a dove's, that tremble with
tenderer breath;
And all the wings of the Loves, and all the joy before
death;
All the feet of the hours that sound as a single lyre,
Dropped and deep in the flowers, with strings that
flicker like fire.
More than these wilt thou give, things fairer than
all these things?
Nay, for a little we live, and life hath mutable
wings.   30
A little while and we die; shall life not thrive as it
may?
For no man under the sky lives twice, outliving his
day.
And grief is a grievous thing, and a man hath
enough of his fears;
Why should he labour, and bring fresh grief to
blacken his years?
Thou has conquered, O pale Galilean; the world
has grown grey from thy breath;
We have drunken of things Lethean, and fed on the
fulness of death.

36. Lethean. Lethe is the river of forgetfulness in Hades.

Laurel is green for a season, and love is sweet for a
day;
But love grows bitter with treason, and laurel out-
lives not May.
Sleep, shall we sleep after all? for the world is not
sweet in the end;
For the old faiths loosen and fall, the new years
ruin and rend.   40
Fate is a sea without shore, and the soul is a rock
that abides;
But her ears are vexed with the roar and her face
with the foam of the tides.
O lips that the live blood faints in, the leavings of
racks and rods!
O ghastly glories of saints, dead limbs of gibbeted
Gods!
Though all men abase them before you in spirit,
and all knees bend,
I kneel not neither adore you, but standing, look to
the end.
All delicate days and pleasant, all spirits and sor-
rows are cast
Far out with the foam of the present that sweeps to
the surf of the past:
Where beyond the extreme sea-wall, and between
the remote sea-gates,
Waste water washes, and tall ships founder, and
deep death waits: 50
Where, mighty with deepening sides, clad about
with the seas as with wings,
And impelled of invisible tides, and fulfilled of unspeakable things,
White-eyed and poisonous-finned, shark-toothed
and serpentine-curled,
Rolls, under the whitening wind of the future, the
wave of the world.
The depths stand naked in sunder behind it, the
storms flee away;
In the hollow before it the thunder is taken and
snared as a prey;
In its sides is the north-wind bound; and its salt is
of all men's tears;
With light of ruin, and sound of changes, and pulse
of years:
With travail of day after day, and with trouble of
hour upon hour;
And bitter as blood is the spray; and the crests are
as fangs that devour: 60
And its vapour and storm of its steam as the sighing
of spirits to be;
And its noise as the noise in a dream; and its depth
as the roots of the sea:
And the height of its heads as the height of the utmost stars of the air:

And the ends of the earth at the might thereof
    tremble, and time is made bare.
Will ye bridle the deep sea with reins, will ye
    chasten the high sea with rods?
Will ye take her to chain her with chains, who is
    older than all ye Gods?
All ye as a wind shall go by, as a fire shall ye pass
    and be past;
Ye are Gods, and behold ye shall die, and the waves
    be upon you at last.
In the darkness of time, in the deeps of the years, in
    the changes of things,
Ye shall sleep as a slain man sleeps, and the world
    shall forget you for kings.   70
Though the feet of thine high priests tread where
    thy lords and our forefathers trod,
Though these that were Gods are dead, and thou
    being dead art a God,
Though before thee the throned Cytherean be
    fallen, and hidden her head,
Yet thy kingdom shall pass, Galilean, thy dead shall
    go down to thee dead.
Of the maiden thy mother men sing as a goddess
    with grace clad around;
Thou art throned where another was king; where
    another was queen she is crowned.
Yea, once we had sight of another: but now she is
    queen, say these.
Not as thine, not as thine was our mother, a blossom
    of flowering seas,
Clothed round with the world's desire as with rai-
    ment, and fair as the foam,
And fleeter than kindled fire, and a goddess, and
    mother of Rome.   80
For thine came pale and a maiden, and sister to
    sorrow; but ours,
Her deep hair heavily laden with odour and colour
    of flowers,
White rose of the rose-white water, a silver splen-
    dour, a flame,
Bent down unto us that besought her, and earth
    grew sweet with her name.
For thine came weeping, a slave among slaves, and
    rejected; but she
Came flushed from the full-flushed wave, and im-
    perial, her foot on the sea,
And the wonderful waters knew her, the winds and
    the viewless ways,
And the roses grew rosier, and bluer the sea-blue
    stream of the bays.

73. Cytherean, Venus, who, according to Hesiod, was
formed of the foam of the sea gathering itself about the
mutilated body of Uranus, and came to land at Cythera, in
Cyprus. See Botticelli's famous painting "The Birth of
Venus."

Ye are fallen, our lords, by what token? we wist
    that ye should not fall.
Ye were all so fair that are broken; and one more
    fair than ye all.   90
But I turn to her still, having seen she shall surely
    abide in the end;
Goddess and maiden and queen, be near me now
    and befriend.
O daughter of earth, of my mother, her crown and
    blossom of birth,
I am also, I also, thy brother; I go as I came unto
    earth.
In the night where thine eyes are as moons are in
    heaven, the night where thou art,
Where the silence is more than all tunes, where
    sleep overflows from the heart,
Where the poppies are sweet as the rose in our
    world, and the red rose is white,
And the wind falls faint as it blows with the fume
    of the flowers of the night,
And the murmur of spirits that sleep in the shadow
    of Gods from afar
Grows dim in thine ears and deep as the deep dim
    soul of a star,   100
In the sweet low light of thy face, under heavens un-
    trod by the sun,
Let my soul with their souls find place, and forget
    what is done and undone.
Thou art more than the Gods who number the days
    of our temporal breath;
For these give labour and slumber; but thou, Proser-
    pina, death.
Therefore now at thy feet I abide for a season in
    silence. I know
I shall die as my fathers died, and sleep as they
    sleep; even so.
For the glass of the years is brittle wherein we gaze
    for a span;
A little soul for a little bears up this corpse which is
    man.
So long I endure, no longer; and laugh not again,
    neither weep.
For there is no God found stronger than death; and
    death is a sleep.   110

A MATCH

If love were what the rose is,
    And I were like the leaf,
Our lives would grow together

91. her, Proserpine.   **97. poppies,** sacred to Proserpine.
108. A little soul . . . man. Swinburne quotes Epictetus: "Thou art a little soul bearing up a corpse."

In sad or singing weather,
Blown fields or flowerful closes,
    Green pleasure or grey grief;
If love were what the rose is,
    And I were like the leaf.

If I were what the words are,
    And love were like the tune,   10
With double sound and single
Delight our lips would mingle,
With kisses glad as birds are
    That get sweet rain at noon;
If I were what the words are
    And love were like the tune.

If you were life, my darling,
    And I your love were death,
We'd shine and snow together
Ere March made sweet the weather   20
With daffodil and starling
    And hours of fruitful breath;
If you were life, my darling,
    And I your love were death.

If you were thrall to sorrow,
    And I were page to joy,
We'd play for lives and seasons
With loving looks and treasons
And tears of night and morrow
    And laughs of maid and boy;   30
If you were thrall to sorrow,
    And I were page to joy.

If you were April's lady,
    And I were lord in May,
We'd throw with leaves for hours
And draw for days with flowers,
Till day like night were shady
    And night were bright like day;
If you were April's lady,
    And I were lord in May.   40

If you were queen of pleasure,
    And I were king of pain,
We'd hunt down love together,
Pluck out his flying-feather,
And teach his feet a measure,
    And find his mouth a rein;
If you were queen of pleasure,
    And I were king of pain.

5. **closes,** enclosures, here gardens.

IN MEMORY OF
WALTER SAVAGE LANDOR

Back to the flower-town, side by side,
    The bright months bring,
New-born, the bridegroom and the bride,
    Freedom and spring.

The sweet land laughs from sea to sea,
    Filled full of sun;
All things come back to her, being free;
    All things but one.

In many a tender wheaten plot
    Flowers that were dead   10
Live, and old suns revive; but not
    That holier head.

By this white wandering waste of sea,
    Far north, I hear
One face shall never turn to me
    As once this year:

Shall never smile and turn and rest
    On mine as there,
Nor one most sacred hand be prest
    Upon my hair.   20

I came as one whose thoughts half linger,
    Half run before;
The youngest to the oldest singer
    That England bore.

I found him whom I shall not find
    Till all grief end,
In holiest age our mightiest mind,
    Father and friend.

But thou, if anything endure,
    If hope there be,   30
O spirit that man's life left pure,
    Man's death set free,

Not with disdain of days that were
    Look earthward now;
Let dreams revive the reverend hair,
    The imperial brow;

Walter Savage Landor. See pages 178–89.   **1. flower-
town,** Florence, where Landor died.   **4. Freedom.** Like
Swinburne, Landor sympathized with Italy in her struggle
for freedom.   **21. I came.** Swinburne visited Landor in
Florence in 1864.   **27. In holiest age.** For Swinburne the
Romantic Period was hallowed by its enthusiasm for liberty.

Come back in sleep, for in the life
  Where thou art not
We find none like thee. Time and strife
  And the world's lot   40

Move thee no more; but love at least
  And reverent heart
May move thee, royal and released,
  Soul, as thou art.

And thou, his Florence, to thy trust
  Receive and keep,
Keep safe his dedicated dust,
  His sacred sleep.

So shall thy lovers, come from far,
  Mix with thy name   50
As morning-star with evening-star
  His faultless fame.

THE GARDEN OF PROSERPINE

Here, where the world is quiet,
  Here, where all trouble seems
Dead winds's and pent waves' riot
  In doubtful dreams of dreams;
I watch the green field growing
For reaping folk and sowing,
For harvest time and mowing,
  A sleepy world of streams.

I am tired of tears and laughter,
  And men that laugh and weep;   10
Of what may come hereafter
  For men that sow to reap:
I am weary of days and hours,
Blown buds of barren flowers,
Desires and dreams and powers
  And everything but sleep.

Here life has death for neighbour,
  And far from eye or ear
Wan waves and wet winds labour,
  Weak ships and spirits steer;   20
They drive adrift, and whither
They wot not who make thither;
But no such winds blow hither,
  And no such things grow here.

No growth of moor or coppice,
  No heather-flower or vine,

Proserpine. See the introductory note to "Hymn to Proserpine," page 846 of this volume.

But bloomless buds of poppies,
  Green grapes of Proserpine,
Pale beds of blowing rushes
Where no leaf blooms or blushes,   30
Save this whereout she crushes
  For dead men deadly wine.

Pale, without name or number,
  In fruitless fields of corn,
They bow themselves and slumber
  All night till light is born;
And like a soul belated,
In hell and heaven unmated,
By cloud and mist abated
  Comes out of darkness morn.   40

Though one were strong as seven,
  He too with death shall dwell,
Nor wake with wings in heaven,
  Nor weep for pains in hell;
Though one were fair as roses,
His beauty clouds and closes;
And well though love reposes,
  In the end it is not well.

Pale, beyond porch and portal,
  Crowned with calm leaves, she stands   50
Who gathers all things mortal
  With cold immortal hands;
Her languid lips are sweeter
Than love's who fears to greet her
To men that mix and meet her
  From many times and lands.

She waits for each and other,
  She waits for all men born;
Forgets the earth her mother,
  The life of fruits and corn;   60
And spring and seed and swallow
Take wing for her and follow
Where summer song rings hollow
  And flowers are put to scorn.

There go the loves that wither,
  The old loves with wearier wings;
And all dead years draw thither,
  And all disastrous things;
Dead dreams of days forsaken,
Blind buds that snows have shaken,   70
Wild leaves that winds have taken,
  Red strays of ruined springs.

We are not sure of sorrow,
  And joy was never sure:

34. corn, grain.

To-day will die to-morrow;
  Time stoops to no man's lure;
And love, grown faint and fretful,
With lips but half regretful
Sighs, and with eyes forgetful
  Weeps that no loves endure.   80

From too much love of living,
  From hope and fear set free,
We thank with brief thanksgiving
  Whatever gods may be
That no life lives for ever;
That dead men rise up never;
That even the weariest river
  Winds somewhere safe to sea.

Then star nor sun shall waken,
  Nor any change of light: 90
Nor sound of waters shaken,
  Nor any sound or sight:
Nor wintry leaves nor vernal,
Nor days nor things diurnal;
Only the sleep eternal
  In an eternal night.

A CHRISTMAS CAROL

Three damsels in the queen's chamber,
  The queen's mouth was most fair;
She spake a word of God's mother
  As the combs went in her hair.
    Mary that is of might,
    Bring us to thy Son's sight.

They held the gold combs out from her,
  A span's length off her head;
She sang this song of God's mother
  And of her bearing-bed.   10
    Mary most full of grace,
    Bring us to thy Son's face.

When she sat at Joseph's hand,
  She looked against her side;
And either way from the short silk band
  Her girdle was all wried.
    Mary that all good may,
    Bring us to thy Son's way.

Mary had three women for her bed,
  The twain were maidens clean;   20
The first of them had white and red,

The third had riven green.
  Mary that is so sweet,
  Bring us to thy Son's feet.

She had three women for her hair,
  Two were gloved soft and shod;
The third had feet and fingers bare,
  She was the likest God.
    Mary that wieldeth land,
    Bring us to thy Son's hand.   30

She had three women for her ease,
  The twain were good women:
The first two were the two Maries,
  The third was Magdalen.
    Mary that perfect is,
    Bring us to thy Son's kiss.

Joseph had three workmen in his stall,
  To serve him well upon;
The first of them were Peter and Paul,
  The third of them was John.   40
    Mary, God's handmaiden,
    Bring us to thy Son's ken.

"If your child be none other man's,
  But if it be very mine,
The bedstead shall be gold two spans,
  The bedfoot silver fine."
    Mary that made God mirth,
    Bring us to thy Son's birth.

"If the child be some other man's,
  And if it be none of mine,   50
The manger shall be straw two spans,
  Betwixen kine and kine."
    Mary that made sin cease,
    Bring us to thy Son's peace.

33. two Maries. Mary the mother of James, for one;
the identification of the other is uncertain. See Hastings,
Dictionary of the Bible, art. "Mary."   34. Magdalen, Mary
Magdalen, one of the women who ministered to our Lord,
and from whom he cast out seven devils (Mark 16:9).
Traditionally (but unbiblically) she is identified with the
woman who was a sinner and who anointed the feet of
Jesus in the Pharisee's house (Luke 7:36 ff.). For her
legend, see Edith Olivier, *Mary Magdalen*, Appleton-
Century, 1934.   39–40. Peter . . . Paul . . . John.
Peter and John were disciples of Jesus; Paul, the Apostle
to the Gentiles, did not become a Christian until after
Jesus' death. No one of them, of course, ever worked for
Joseph.   43–46. "If your child . . . fine." According to
Matthew 1:18 ff., Joseph was suspicious of his betrothed
wife until the angel of the Lord explained to him that the
child "which is conceived of her is of the Holy Ghost."
51. The manger. According to Luke 2:7 (though not according to Matthew) the newborn Jesus was laid "in a
manger; because there was no room for them in the inn."

Christ was born upon this wise,
  It fell on such a night,
Neither with sounds of psalteries,
  Nor with fire for light.
    Mary that is God's spouse,
    Bring us to thy Son's house.   60

The star came out upon the east
  With a great sound and sweet:
Kings gave gold to make him feast
  And myrrh for him to eat.
    Mary, of thy sweet mood,
    Bring us to thy Son's good.

He had two handmaids at his head,
  One handmaid at his feet;
The twain of them were fair and red,
  The third one was right sweet.   70
    Mary that is most wise,
    Bring us to thy Son's eyes. Amen.

TO WALT WHITMAN IN AMERICA

Send but a song oversea for us,
  Heart of their hearts who are free,
Heart of their singer, to be for us
  More than our singing can be;
Ours, in the tempest at error,
With no light but the twilight of terror;
  Send us a song oversea!

Sweet-smelling of pine-leaves and grasses,
  And blown as a tree through and through
With the winds of the keen mountain-passes,   10
  And tender as sun-smitten dew;
Sharp-tongued as the winter that shakes
The wastes of your limitless lakes,
  Wide-eyed as the sea-line's blue.

O strong-winged soul with prophetic
  Lips hot with the bloodbeats of song,
With tremor of heartstrings magnetic,
  With thoughts as thunders in throng,
With consonant ardours of chords
That pierce men's souls as with swords   20
  And hale them hearing along,

61-64. **The star . . . eat.** See Matthew 2:1-12. *Walt Whitman,* the American poet (1819-1892), author of *Leaves of Grass,* was regarded by Swinburne, when he wrote this poem, as the voice of American democracy.

Make us too music, to be with us
  As a word from a world's heart warm,
To sail the dark as a sea with us,
  Full-sailed, outsinging the storm,
A song to put fire in our ears
Whose burning shall burn up tears,
  Whose sign bid battle reform;

A note in the ranks of a clarion,
  A word in the wind of cheer,   30
To consume as with lightning the carrion
  That makes time foul for us here;
In the air that our dead things infest
A blast of the breath of the west,
  Till east way as west way is clear.

Out of the sun beyond sunset,
  From the evening whence morning shall be,
With the rollers in measureless onset,
  With the van of the storming sea,
With the world-wide wind, with the breath   40
That breaks ships driven upon death,
  With the passion of all things free,

With the sea-steeds footless and frantic,
  White myriads for death to bestride
In the charge of the ruining Atlantic
  Where deaths by regiments ride,
With clouds and clamours of waters,
With a long note shriller than slaughter's
  On the furrowless fields world-wide,

With terror, with ardour and wonder,   50
  With the soul of the season that wakes
When the weight of a whole year's thunder
  In the tidestream of autumn breaks,
Let the flight of the wide-winged word
Come over, come in and be heard,
  Take form and fire for our sakes.

For a continent bloodless with travail
  Here toils and brawls as it can,
And the web of it who shall unravel
  Of all that peer on the plan;   60
Would fain grow men, but they grow not,
And fain be free, but they know not
  One name for freedom and man?

One name, not twain for division;
  One thing, not twain, from the birth;
Spirit and substance and vision,
  Worth more than worship is worth;

Unbeheld, unadored, undivined,
The cause, the centre, the mind,
   The secret and sense of the earth.   70

Here as a weakling in irons,
   Here as a weanling in bands,
As a prey that the stake-net environs,
   Our life that we looked for stands;
And the man-child naked and dear,
Democracy, turns on us here
   Eyes trembling with tremulous hands.

It sees not what season shall bring to it
   Sweet fruit of its bitter desire;
Few voices it hears yet sing to it,   80
   Few pulses of hearts reaspire;
Foresees not time, nor forehears
The noises of imminent years,
   Earthquake, and thunder, and fire:

When crowned and weaponed and curbless
   It shall walk without helm or shield
The bare burnt furrows and herbless
   Of war's last flame-stricken field,
Till godlike, equal with time,
It stand in the sun sublime,   90
   In the godhead of man revealed.

Round your people and over them
   Light like raiment is drawn,
Close as a garment to cover them
   Wrought not of mail nor of lawn;
Here, with hope hardly to wear,
Naked nations and bare
   Swim, sink, strike out for the dawn.

Chains are here, and a prison,
   Kings, and subjects, and shame;   100
If the God upon you be arisen,
   How should our songs be the same?
How, in confusion of change,
How shall we sing, in a strange
   Land, songs praising his name?

God is buried and dead to us,
   Even the spirit of earth,
Freedom; so have they said to us,
   Some with mocking and mirth,
Some with heartbreak and tears;   110
And a God without eyes, without ears,
   Who shall sing of him, dead in the birth?

73. **stake-net,** a fishing net fastened with stakes. **102–
05. How should . . . his name?** See Psalm 137.

The earth-god Freedom, the lonely
   Face lightening, the footprint unshod,
Not as one man crucified only
   Nor scourged with but one life's rod;
The soul that is substance of nations,
Reincarnate with fresh generations;
   The great god Man, which is God.

But in weariest of years and obscurest   120
   Doth it live not at heart of all things,
The one God and one spirit, a purest
   Life, fed from unstanchable springs?
Within love, within hatred it is,
And its seed in the stripe as the kiss,
   And in slaves is the germ, and in kings.

Freedom we call it, for holier
   Name of the soul's there is none;
Surelier it labours, if slowlier,
   Than the metres of star or of sun;   130
Slowlier than life into breath,
Surelier than time into death,
   It moves till its labour be done.

Till the motion be done and the measure
   Circling through season and clime,
Slumber and sorrow and pleasure,
   Vision of virtue and crime;
Till consummate with conquering eyes,
A soul disembodied, it rise
   From the body transfigured of time.   140

Till it rise and remain and take station
   With the stars of the world that rejoice;
Till the voice of its heart's exultation
   Be as theirs an invariable voice;
By no discord of evil estranged,
By no pause, by no breach in it changed,
   By no clash in the chord of its choice.

It is one with the world's generations,
   With the spirit, the star, and the sod;
With the kingless and king-stricken nations,   150
   With the cross, and the chain, and the rod;
The most high, the most secret, most lonely,
The earth-soul Freedom, that only
   Lives, and that only is God.

A FORSAKEN GARDEN

In a coign of the cliff between lowland and highland,
   At the sea-down's edge between windward and lee,
125. stripe, the mark of the lash.

Walled round with rocks as an inland island,
  The ghost of a garden fronts the sea.
A girdle of brushwood and thorn encloses
  The steep square slope of the blossomless bed
Where the weeds that grew green from the graves
        of its roses
    Now lie dead.

The fields fall southward, abrupt and broken,
  To the low last edge of the long lone land.   10
If a step should sound or a word be spoken,
  Would a ghost not rise at the strange guest's
        hand?
So long have the grey bare walks lain guestless,
  Through branches and briars if a man make way,
He shall find no life but the sea-wind's, restless
      Night and day.

The dense hard passage is blind and stifled
  That crawls by a track none turn to climb
To the strait waste place that the years have rifled
  Of all but the thorns that are touched not of
        time.   20
The thorns he spares when the rose is taken;
  The rocks are left when he wastes the plain.
The wind that wanders, the weeds wind-shaken,
      These remain.

Not a flower to be pressed of the foot that falls not;
  As the heart of a dead man the seed-plots are dry;
From the thicket of thorns whence the nightingale
        calls not,
  Could she call, there were never a rose to reply.
Over the meadows that blossom and wither
  Rings but the note of a sea-bird's song;   30
Only the sun and the rain come hither
      All year long.

The sun burns sere and the rain dishevels
  One gaunt bleak blossom of scentless breath.
Only the wind here hovers and revels
  In a round where life seems barren as death.
Here there was laughing of old, there was weeping,
  Haply, of lovers none ever will know,
Whose eyes went seaward a hundred sleeping
      Years ago.   40

Heart handfast in heart as they stood, "Look
        thither,"
  Did he whisper? "look forth from the flowers to
        the sea;
For the foam-flowers endure when the rose-blos-
        soms wither,
  And men that love lightly may die—but we?"

And the same wind sang and the same waves
        whitened,
  And or ever the garden's last petals were shed,
In the lips that had whispered, the eyes that had
        lightened,
    Love was dead.

Or they loved their life through, and then went
        whither?
  And were one to the end—but what end who
        knows?   50
Love deep as the sea as a rose must wither,
  As the rose-red seaweed that mocks the rose.
Shall the dead take thought for the dead to love
        them?
  What love was ever as deep as a grave?
They are loveless now as the grass above them
      Or the wave.

All are at one now, roses and lovers,
  Not known of the cliffs and the fields and the
        sea.
Not a breath of the time that has been hovers
  In the air now soft with a summer to be.   60
Not a breath shall there sweeten the seasons here-
        after
  Of the flowers or the lovers that laugh now or
        weep,
When as they that are free now of weeping and
        laughter
    We shall sleep.

Here death may deal not again for ever;
  Here change may come not till all change end.
From the graves they have made they shall rise up
        never,
  Who have left nought living to ravage and
        rend.
Earth, stones, and thorns of the wild ground
        growing,
  While the sun and the rain live, these shall be; 70
Till a last wind's breath upon all these blowing
      Roll the sea.

Till the slow sea rise and the sheer cliff crumble,
  Till terrace and meadow the deep gulfs drink,
Till the strength of the waves of the high tides
        humble
  The fields that lessen, the rocks that shrink,
Here now in his triumph where all things falter,
  Stretched out on the spoils that his own hand
        spread,
As a god self-slain on his own strange altar,
    Death lies dead.   80

CYRIL TOURNEUR

Tourneur (c. 1575–1626) was a late Elizabethan dramatist, of the spirit of whose plays—*The Atheist's Tragedy* and *The Revenger's Tragedy*—Swinburne has given a brilliant interpretation in the following sonnet.

A sea that heaves with horror of the night,
    As maddened by the moon that hangs aghast
    With strain and torment of the ravening blast,
Haggard as hell, a bleak blind bloody light;
No shore but one red reef of rock in sight,
    Whereon the waifs of many a wreck were cast
    And shattered in the fierce nights overpast
Wherein more souls toward hell than heaven took
    flight;
And 'twixt the shark-toothed rocks and swallowing
    shoals
A cry as out of hell from all these souls   10
    Sent through the sheer gorge of the slaughtering
    sea,
Whose thousand throats, full-fed with life by death,
Fill the black air with foam and furious breath;
    And over all these one star—Chastity.

TRIADS

1

The word of the sun to the sky,
    The word of the wind to the sea,
    The word of the moon to the night,
                        What may it be?

The sense to the flower of the fly,
    The sense of the bird to the tree,
    The sense to the cloud of the light,
                        Who can tell me?

The song of the fields to the kye,
    The song of the lime to the bee,   10
    The song of the depth to the height,
                        Who knows all three?

2

The message of April to May
    That May sends on into June
    And June gives out to July
                        For birthday boon;

The delight of the dawn in the day,
    The delight of the day in the noon,
    The delight of a song in a sigh
                        That breaks the tune;   20

The secret of passing away,
    The cost of the change of the moon,
    None knows it with ear or with eye,
                        But all will soon.

3

The live wave's love for the shore,
    The shore's for the wave as it dies,
    The love of the thunder-fire
                        That sears the skies,

We shall know not though life wax hoar,
    Till all life, spent into sighs,   30
    Burn out as consumed with desire
                        Of death's strange eyes:

Till the secret be secret no more
    In the light of one hour as it flies,
    Be the hour as of suns that expire
                        Or suns that rise.

A BALLAD OF FRANÇOIS VILLON

Prince of All Ballad-Makers

Bird of the bitter bright grey golden morn
    Scarce risen upon the dusk of dolorous years,
First of us all and sweetest singer born
    Whose far shrill note the world of new men hears
    Cleave the cold shuddering shade as twilight
    clears;
When song new-born put off the old world's attire
And felt its tune on her changed lips expire,
    Writ foremost on the roll of them that came
Fresh girt for service of the latter lyre,
    Villon, our sad bad glad mad brother's name!   10

Alas the joy, the sorrow, and the scorn,
    That clothed thy life with hopes and sins and
    fears,
And gave thee stones for bread and tares for corn
    And plume-plucked gaol-birds for thy starveling
    peers
    Till death clipt close their flight with shameful
    shears;
Till shifts came short and loves were hard to hire,
When lilt of song nor twitch of twangling wire
    Could buy thee bread or kisses; when light
    fame
Spurned like a ball and haled through brake and
    briar,
    Villon, our sad bad glad mad brother's name!   20

1. golden morn, the Renaissance.   **2. dolorous years,** the Middle Ages.   **13. stones for bread.** See Matthew 7:9.

Poor splendid wings so frayed and soiled and torn!
 Poor kind wild eyes so dashed with light quick
  tears!
Poor perfect voice, most blithe when most forlorn,
 That rings athwart the sea whence no man steers
 Like joy-bells crossed with death-bells in our
  ears!
What far delight has cooled the fierce desire
That like some ravenous bird was strong to tire
 On that frail flesh and soul consumed with
  flame,
But left more sweet than roses to respire,
 Villon, our sad bad glad mad brother's name? 30

ENVOI

Prince of sweet songs made out of tears and fire,
A harlot was thy nurse, a God thy sire;
 Shame soiled thy song, and song assoiled thy
  shame.
But from thy feet now death has washed the mire,
Love reads out first at head of all our quire,
 Villon, our sad bad glad mad brother's name.

NELL GWYN

Nell Gwyn (1650–1687), the only courtesan who ever won the heart of the English people, began life as an orange girl at the Theatre Royal, but became a distinguished Restoration comedienne and the mistress of King Charles II. She was witty, kindly, and greathearted, free from the vices generally attributed to the mistresses of kings. Her most recent biography is Clifford Bax, *Pretty Witty Nell* (Morrow, 1932).

Sweet heart, that no taint of the throne or the stage
 Could touch with unclean transformation, or
  alter
 To the likeness of courtiers whose consciences
  falter
At the smile or the frown, at the mirth or the rage,
Of a master whom chance could inflame or as-
 suage,
 Our Lady of Laughter, invoked in no psalter,
 Adored of no faithful that cringe and that palter,
Praise be with thee yet from a hag-ridden age.

Our Lady of Pity thou wast: and to thee
All England, whose sons are the sons of the sea, 10
 Gives thanks, and will hear not if history snarls
When the name of the friend of her sailors is
 spoken;

12. the friend of her sailors. Tradition credits Nell Gwyn with having persuaded the King to establish Chelsea Hospital.

And thy lover she cannot but love—by the token
 That thy name was the last on the lips of King
  Charles.

THE WINDS

O weary fa' the east wind,
 And weary fa' the west:
And gin I were under the wan waves wide
 I wot weel wad I rest.

O weary fa' the north wind,
 And weary fa' the south:
The sea went ower my good lord's head
 Or ever he kissed my mouth.

Weary fa' the windward rocks,
 And weary fa' the lee: 10
They might hae sunken sevenscore ships,
 And let my love's gang free.

And weary fa' ye, mariners a',
 And weary fa' the sea:
It might hae taken an hundred men,
 And let my ae love be.

A JACOBITE'S FAREWELL
1716

A Scottish Jacobite (sympathizer with the House of Stuart) takes leave of his love following the failure of the rising of 1716 in behalf of the "Old Pretender," son of King James II. See *Rob Roy* by Sir Walter Scott.

There's nae mair lands to tyne, my dear,
 And nae mair lives to gie;
Though a man think sair to live nae mair,
 There's but one day to die.

For a' things come and a' days gane,
 What needs ye rend your hair?
But kiss me till the morn's morrow,
 Then I'll kiss ye nae mair.

O lands are lost and life's losing,
 And what were they to gie? 10
Fu' mony a man gives all he can,
 But nae man else gives ye.

Nell Gwyn. **14. That thy name . . . King Charles.** "Let not poor Nelly starve" are said to have been King Charles's dying words. *The Winds.* **1. weary fa',** weary on, a curse befall (Scotch dialect). **3. gin,** if. **4. wot weel wad,** know well would. **12. gang,** go. **15. hae,** have. **16. ae,** one. *A Jacobite's Farewell.* **1. tyne,** lose. **2. gie,** give. **3. sair,** sore.

Our king wons ower the sea's water,
   And I in prison sair;
But I'll win out the morn's morrow
   And ye'll see me nae mair.

THE ROUNDEL

A roundel is wrought as a ring or a star-bright
   sphere,
With craft of delight and with cunning of sound
   unsought,
That the heart of the hearer may smile if to pleasure
     his ear
     A roundel is wrought.

Its jewel of music is carven of all or of aught—
Love, laughter, or mourning—remembrance of
   rapture or fear—
That fancy may fashion to hang in the ear of
   thought.

As a bird's quick song runs round, and the hearts in
   us hear
Pause answer to pause, and again the same strain
   caught,
So moves the device whence, round as a pearl or
   tear,   10
     A roundel is wrought.

WILLIAM SHAKESPEARE

Not if men's tongues and angels' all in one
   Spake, might the word be said that might speak
     Thee.
   Streams, winds, woods, flowers, fields, mountains,
     yea, the sea,
What power is in them all to praise the sun?
His praise is this,—he can be praised of none.
   Man, woman, child, praise God for him; but he
   Exults not to be worshipped, but to be.
He is; and, being, beholds his work well done.
All joy, all glory, all sorrow, all strength, all mirth,
Are his: without him, day were night on earth.   10
   Time knows not his from time's own period.
All lutes, all harps, all viols, all flutes, all lyres,

A Jacobite's Farewell. **13. wons,** lives (in France). The Jacobites never acknowledged the right of the house of Hanover
to hold the English throne. When they toasted "the King" at
banquets, each was careful to carry his wine glass over a tumbler of water.   *The Roundel.* **1. roundel,** a French lyric
form of which Swinburne was fond, and which he exemplifies
here and elsewhere.

Fall dumb before him ere one string suspires.
All stars are angels; but the sun is God.

ADIEUX A MARIE STUART

Mary Stuart's motto, "In my end is my beginning,"
had for her, no doubt, a religious meaning, but it has
come to apply even to her life on this earth. With the single exception of Cleopatra, probably no other woman
has longer enthralled the imagination of men than the
beautiful unfortunate who was queen of Scotland, nominally from 1542, actively from 1561, until 1568, and
who, after a long and illegal imprisonment in England,
was beheaded in 1587 by a court which had no jurisdiction over her, on the charge of having conspired against
Queen Elizabeth.

Mary's fascination is due in part to the fact that the
full truth about her will never be known; like a goddess
she brings her devotees the imperious demand for faith.
She has been presented by writers as everything from a
demon to a saint.

When Swinburne confronted Mary, his passionate re-
publicanism came into conflict with his romanticism
and his inclination toward hero worship, and his repub-
licanism went down and out. He had no patience, however, with those who believed the queen innocent (see
his "Note on the Character of Mary Queen of Scots"
in his *Miscellanies*). Swinburne's trilogy of poetic tragedies
—*Chastelard*, 1865; *Bothwell*, 1874; *Mary Stuart*, 1874—is
the most elaborate piece of literature ever written about
Mary Stuart.   She also appears in Schiller's *Maria Stuart*,
1800; Sir Walter Scott's novel *The Abbot*, 1820; and, more
recently, in two plays, one by John Drinkwater and one
by Maxwell Anderson—*Mary Stuart*, 1921, and *Mary of
Scotland*, 1933.

I

Queen, for whose house my fathers fought,
   With hopes that rose and fell,
Red star of boyhood's fiery thought,
   Farewell.

They gave their lives, and I, my queen,
   Have given you of my life,
Seeing your brave star burn high between
   Men's strife.

The strife that lightened round their spears
   Long since fell still: so long   10
Hardly may hope to last in years
   My song.

But still through strife of time and thought
   Your light on me too fell:
Queen, in whose name we sang or fought,
   Farewell.

2

There beats no heart on either border
  Wherethrough the north blasts blow
But keeps your memory as a warder
  His beacon-fire aglow.   20

Long since, it fired with love and wonder
  Mine, for whose April age
Blithe midsummer made banquet under
  The shade of Hermitage.

Soft sang the burn's blithe notes, that gather
  Strength to ring true;
And air and trees and sun and heather
  Remembered you.

Old border ghosts of fight or fairy
  Or love or teen,   30
These they forgot, remembering Mary
  The Queen.

3

Queen once of Scots and ever of ours
  Whose sires brought forth for you
Their lives to strew your way like flowers,
  Adieu.

Dead is full many a dead man's name
  Who died for you this long
Time past: shall this too fare the same,
  My song?   40

But surely, though it die or live,
  Your face was worth
All that a man may think to give
  On earth.

No darkness cast of years between
  Can darken you:
Man's love will never bid my queen
  Adieu.

4

Love hangs like light about your name
  As music round the shell: 50
No heart can take of you a tame
  Farewell.

Yet, when your very face was seen,
  Ill gifts were yours for giving:

17. **either border,** Scotland or England.   24. **Hermitage,** a castle on the Hermitage River, Roxborough, Scotland, scene of a romantic incident in the life of Queen Mary.
25. **burn,** brook.   30. **teen,** sorrow.

Love gat strange guerdons of my queen
  When living.

O diamond heart, unflawed and clear,
  The whole world's crowning jewel!
Was ever heart so deadly dear
  So cruel?   60

Yet none for you of all that bled
  Grudged once one drop that fell:
Not one to life reluctant said
  Farewell.

5

Strange love they have given you, love disloyal,
  Who mock with praise your name,
To leave a head so rare and royal
  Too low for praise or blame.

You could not love nor hate, they tell us,
  You had nor sense nor sting: 70
In God's name, then, what plague befell us
  To fight for such a thing?

"Some faults the gods will give," to fetter
  Man's highest intent:
But surely you were something better
  Than innocent!

No maid that strays with steps unwary
  Through snares unseen,
But one to live and die for; Mary,
  The Queen.   80

6

Forgive them all their praise, who blot
  Your fame with praise of you:
Then love may say, and falter not,
  Adieu.

Yet some you hardly would forgive
  Who did you much less wrong
Once; but resentment should not live
  Too long.

They never saw your lip's bright bow,
  Your swordbright eyes,   90
The bluest of heavenly things below
  The skies.

Clear eyes that love's self finds most like
  A swordblade's blue,
A swordblade's ever keen to strike,
  Adieu.

7

Though all things breathe or sound of fight
  That yet make up your spell,
To bid you were to bid the light
  Farewell.   100

Farewell the song says only, being
  A star whose race is run;
Farewell the soul says never, seeing
  The sun.

Yet, wellnigh as with flash of tears,
  The song must say but so
That took your praise up twenty years
  Ago.

More bright than stars or moons that vary,
  Sun kindling heaven and hell,
Here, after all these years, Queen Mary,   110
  Farewell.

THE HIGHER PANTHEISM
IN A NUTSHELL

This poem, one of Swinburne's most amusing parodies,
burlesques "The Higher Pantheism," by Tennyson
(page 519 of this volume).

One, who is not, we see: but one, whom we see not,
  is:
Surely this is not that: but that is assuredly this.

What, and wherefore, and whence? for under is
  over and under:
If thunder could be without lightning, lightning
  could be without thunder.

Doubt is faith in the main: but faith, on the whole,
  is doubt:
We cannot believe by proof: but could we believe
  without?

Why, and whither, and how? for barley and rye are
  not clover:
Neither are straight lines curves: yet over is under
  and over.

Two and two may be four: but four and four are not
  eight:
Fate and God may be twain: but God is the same
  thing as fate.   10

107–08. twenty years Ago, when he wrote *Chastelard.*

Ask a man what he thinks, and get from a man what
  he feels:
God, once caught in the fact, shows you a fair pair
  of heels.

Body and spirit are twins: God only knows which is
  which:
The soul squats down in the flesh, like a tinker
  drunk in a ditch.

More is the whole than a part: but half is more than
  the whole:
Clearly, the soul is the body: but is not the body the
  soul?

One and two are not one: but one and nothing is
  two:
Truth can hardly be false, if falsehood cannot be
  true.

Once the mastodon was: pterodactyls were common
  as cocks:
Then the mammoth was God: now is He a prize
  ox.   20

Parallels all things are: yet many of these are askew:
You are certainly I: but certainly I am not you.

Springs the rock from the plain, shoots the stream
  from the rock:
Cocks exist for the hen: but hens exist for the cock.

God, whom we see not, is: and God, who is not, we
  see:
Fiddle, we know, is diddle: and diddle, we take it, is
  dee.

NEPHELIDIA

Any possible reader who is offended by Swinburne's
burlesque of Tennyson (the preceding poem) ought surely
to forgive him after reading this consummate burlesque
of himself. The title means "Cloudlets."

From the depth of the dreamy decline of the dawn
    through a notable nimbus of nebulous noon-
    shine,
  Pallid and pink as the palm of the flag-flower
    that flickers with fear of the flies as they float,
Are the looks of our lovers that lustrously lean from
  a marvel of mystic miraculous moonshine,
  These that we feel in the blood of our blushes
    that thicken and threaten with throbs through
    the throat?

Thicken and thrill as a theatre thronged at appeal
    of an actor's appalled agitation,
  Fainter with fear of the fires of the future than
    pale with the promise of pride in the past;
Flushed with the famishing fullness of fever that red-
    dens with radiance of rathe recreation,
  Gaunt as the ghastliest of glimpses that gleam
    through the gloom of the gloaming when
    ghosts go aghast?
Nay, for the nick of the tick of the time is a tremu-
    lous touch on the temples of terror,
  Strained as the sinews yet strenuous with strife of
    the dead who is dumb as the dust-heaps of
    death: 10
Surely no soul is it, sweet as the spasm of erotic
    emotional exquisite error,
  Bathed in the balms of beatified bliss, beatific it-
    self by beatitude's breath.
Surely no spirit or sense of a soul that was soft to the
    spirit and soul of our senses
  Sweetens the stress of suspiring suspicion that
    sobs in the semblance and sound of a sigh;
Only this oracle opens Olympian, in mystical moods
    and triangular tenses—
  "Life is the lust of a lamp for the light that is
    dark till the dawn of the day when we die."
Mild is the mirk and monotonous music of memory,
    melodiously mute as it may be,
  While the hope in the heart of a hero is bruised by
    the breach of men's rapiers, resigned to the rod;
Made meed as a mother whose bosom-beats bound
    with the bliss-bringing bulk of a balm-breath-
    ing baby,
  As they grope through the grave-yard of creeds,
    under skies growing green at a groan for the
    grimness of God.   20
Blank is the book of his bounty beholden of old, and
    its binding is blacker than bluer:
  Out of blue into black is the scheme of the skies,
    and their dews are the wine of the bloodshed of
    things;
Till the darkling desire of delight shall be free as a
    fawn that is freed from the fangs that pursue
    her,
  Till the heart-beats of hell shall be hushed by a
    hymn from the hunt that has harried the ken-
    nel of kings.

TO A CAT

Among all the beautiful tributes that men of genius
have lavished upon the cat, none is more deservedly famous than this poem. See Carl Van Vechten's fascinating

encyclopedia of catlore, *The Tiger in the House* (Knopf,
1920).

I

Stately, kindly, lordly friend,
    Condescend
Here to sit by me, and turn
Glorious eyes that smile and burn,
Golden eyes, love's lustrous meed,
On the golden page I read.

All your wondrous wealth of hair,
    Dark and fair,
Silken-shaggy, soft and bright
As the clouds and beams of night,   10
Pays my reverent hand's caress
Back with friendlier gentleness.

Dogs may fawn on all and some
    As they come;
You, a friend of loftier mind,
Answer friends alone in kind.
Just your foot upon my hand
Softly bids it understand.

Morning round this silent sweet
    Garden-seat   20
Sheds its wealth of gathering light,
Thrills the gradual clouds with might,
Changes woodland, orchard, heath,
Lawn, and garden there beneath.

Fair and dim they gleamed below:
    Now they glow
Deep as even your sunbright eyes,
Fair as even the wakening skies.
Can it not or can it be
Now that you give thanks to see?   30

May not you rejoice as I,
    Seeing the sky
Change to heaven revealed, and bid
Earth reveal the heaven it hid
All night long from stars and moon,
Now the sun sets all in tune?

What within you wakes with day
    Who can say?
All too little may we tell,
Friends who like each other well,   40
What might haply, if we might.
Bid us read our lives aright.

2

Wild on woodland ways your sires
      Flashed like fires;
Fair as flame and fierce and fleet
As with wings on wingless feet
Shone and sprang your mother, free,
Bright and brave as wind or sea.

Free and proud and glad as they,
      Here to-day   50
Rests or roams their radiant child,
      Vanquished not, but reconciled,
Free from curb of aught above
Save the lovely curb of love.

Love through dreams of souls divine
      Fain would shine
Round a dawn whose light and song
Then should right our mutual wrong—
Speak, and seal the love-lit law
Sweet Assisi's seer foresaw.   60

Dreams were theirs; yet haply may
      Dawn a day
When such friends and fellows born,
Seeing our earth as fair at morn,
May for wiser love's sake see
More of heaven's deep heart than we.

THE SALT OF THE EARTH

One of the most striking (and most unexpected) developments of Swinburne's later years was a considerable number of poems expressing ecstatic appreciation of childhood. In 1918 these poems were collected by Sir Edmund Gosse in a book called *The Springtide of Life*, with illustrations by Arthur Rackham (Lippincott).

If childhood were not in the world,
      But only men and women grown;
No baby-locks in tendrils curled,
      No baby-blossoms blown;

Though men were stronger, women fairer,
      And nearer all delights in reach,
And verse and music uttered rarer
      Tones of more godlike speech;

Though the utmost life of life's best hours
      Found, as it cannot now find, words;   10

60. Sweet Assisi's seer, St. Francis of Assisi (1182–1226), founder of the Franciscan order, and possibly the most beloved of all the saints, who felt strongly the underlying mystic harmony of all created things.

Though desert sands were sweet as flowers
      And flowers could sing like birds,

But children never heard them, never
      They felt a child's foot leap and run—
This were a drearier star than ever
      Yet looked upon the sun.

A CHILD'S LAUGHTER

All the bells of heaven may ring,
All the birds of heaven may sing,
All the wells on earth may spring,
All the winds on earth may bring
      All sweet sounds together;
Sweeter far than all things heard,
Hand of harper, tone of bird,
Sound of woods at sundawn stirred,
Welling water's winsome word,
      Wind in warm wan weather,   10

One thing yet there is, that none
Hearing ere its chime be done
Knows not well the sweetest one
Heard of man beneath the sun,
      Hoped in heaven hereafter;
Soft and strong and loud and light,
Very sound of very light
Heard from morning's rosiest height,
When the soul of all delight
      Fills a child's clear laughter.   20

Golden bells of welcome rolled
Never forth such notes, nor told
Hours so blithe in tones so bold,
As the radiant mouth of gold
      Here that rings forth heaven.
If the golden-crested wren
Were a nightingale—why, then,
Something seen and heard of men
Might be half as sweet as when
      Laughs a child of seven.   30

CHILDREN

Of such is the kingdom of heaven.
      No glory that ever was shed
From the crowning star of the seven
      That crown the north world's head,

Children. **1. Of such . . . heaven,** the words of Jesus in Matthew 19:14. **3. crowning star,** the North Star. **the seven,** the constellation Ursa Minor.

No word that ever was spoken
  Of human or godlike tongue,
Gave ever such godlike token
  Since human harps were strung.

No sign that ever was given
  To faithful or faithless eyes   10
Showed ever beyond clouds riven
  So clear a Paradise.

Earth's creeds may be seventy times seven
  And blood have defiled each creed;
If of such be the kingdom of heaven,
  It must be heaven indeed.

ON THE DEATHS OF THOMAS CARLYLE AND GEORGE ELIOT

Two souls diverse out of our human sight
  Pass, followed one with love and each with
    wonder:
  The stormy sophist with his mouth of thunder,
Clothed with loud words and mantled in the might
Of darkness and magnificence of night;
  And one whose eye could smite the night in
    sunder,
  Searching if light or no light were thereunder,
And found in love of loving-kindness light.
Duty divine and Thought with eyes of fire
Still following Righteousness with deep desire   10
  Shone sole and stern before her and above,
Sure stars and sole to steer by; but more sweet
Shone lower the loveliest lamp for earthly feet,
  The light of little children, and their love.

DICKENS

Chief in thy generation born of men,
  Whom English praise acclaimed as English-
    born,

Thomas Carlyle. See pages 403–39 of this volume. *George Eliot*, Mary Ann Evans Cross (1819–1880), the great novelist. See page 384. *Dickens*. See pages 383–84, 752–60 of this volume.

With eyes that matched the worldwide eyes of
  morn
For gleam of tears or laughter, tenderest then
When thoughts of children warmed their light, or
  when
  Reverence of age with love and labour worn,
  Or godlike pity fired with godlike scorn,
Shot through them flame that winged thy swift live
  pen:
Where stars and suns that we behold not burn,
  Higher even than here, though highest was here
    thy place,   10
  Love sees thy spirit laugh and speak and shine
With Shakespeare and the soft bright soul of Sterne
  And Fielding's kindliest might and Goldsmith's
    grace;
  Scarce one more loved or worthier love than
    thine.

ON THE DEATH OF ROBERT BROWNING

This is the last of a series of seven sonnets inspired by the death of Browning (see pages 535–36 of this volume). Note how, in writing of Browning, Swinburne catches Browning's own strenuous faith and optimism; compare this poem with "The Garden of Proserpine," ll. 81–88 (page 851 of this volume).

He held no dream worth waking: so he said,
  He who stands now on death's triumphal steep,
  Awakened out of life wherein we sleep
And dream of what he knows and sees, being dead.
But never death for him was dark or dread:
  "Look forth," he bade the soul, and fear not.
    Weep,
  All ye that trust not in his truth, and keep
Vain memory's vision of a vanished head
As all that lives of all that once was he
Save that which lightens from his word: but we,   10
  Who, seeing the sunset-coloured waters roll,
Yet know the sun subdued not of the sea,
  Nor weep nor doubt that still the spirit is whole,
  And life and death but shadows of the soul.

Dickens. **12. Sterne,** Laurence Sterne (1713–1768), one of the great English humorists, author of *Tristram Shandy*.

[handwritten marginalia: Declaration + picturesque (360) / Divine Service — feeling / give very vivid picture — important / style / Conclusion / frankest expr / sensan of his / philosophy / Belief / Philoso phy]

Walter Pater
1839–1894

Walter Horatio Pater was born in East London, August 4, 1839, the son of Dr. Richard Glode Pater, a physician. Dr. Pater's early death was unfortunate for perhaps more than one reason; he left his son to be reared at Enfield under the exclusively feminine care of mother and grandmother, a fact which certainly did not tend to encourage the development of any of the robuster potentialities that may have existed as elements in his delicately-attuned genius.

Pater attended King's School, Canterbury, and Queen's College, Oxford; he became a fellow of Brasenose College in 1864. He knew the metropolis, and he traveled in Germany, Italy, and France. But for the most part he lived quietly, in modest college rooms, conscientious in the performance of his duties but indifferent to administrative affairs as such, always kindly and accessible, but always conveying the impression that his real life was passed in a world of his own. He died July 30, 1894.

As a writer, Pater concerned himself with the souls of individuals and of civilizations. His first book, *Studies in the History of the Renaissance* (later called simply *The Renaissance*) appeared in 1873. In his second, *Marius the Epicurean,* 1885, which concerns the spiritual life of a sensitive young man of Marcus Aurelius' time, he attempted a kind of novel, but he left *Gaston de Latour,* 1896, which might have been a companion volume to *Marius,* unfinished. The method of *Imaginary Portraits,* 1887, was possibly more congenial to him; in any case it established an individual type of writing ideally suited to his somewhat peculiar genius. In *Appreciations,* 1889, he collected various studies in literary criticism. *Plato and Platonism,* 1893, and *Greek Studies,* 1895, explore several Hellenic themes.

In the development of the Esthetic Movement, Pater stands midway between Ruskin and Arnold, on the one hand, and Wilde on the other. Neither of the older men could have countenanced the somewhat enervating philosophy he expressed in the famous "Conclusion" to his book on the Renaissance (page 869), but it is well to remember that Pater did not wholly countenance it either; he went so far as to remove it from the second edition of his book, for fear of the deleterious influence it might have on young men. There was nothing of Wilde's immoralism about him; for all his relativity, he dis-

liked being called a hedonist, and his simple, blameless life was about as close to asceticism as anybody has ever come outside a monastery. The growing uncertainty of a groping age is reflected in Pater, yet he would have carried out his youthful plan to enter the Church if his friends had not prevented him, and though Benjamin Jowett complained with some justice that he seemed to think religion was all ritual, in some aspects he was a more spiritual man than Jowett himself. His ideal of burning always "with a hard, gem-like flame" by no means ruled self-sacrifice out of his philosophy of life, and he felt idealistically that the function of all higher education was "to impart the art . . . of so relieving the ideal or poetic traits, the elements of distinction in our every-day life—of so exclusively living in them—that the unadorned remainder of it, the mere drift of *débris* of our days, comes to be as though it were not."

It was, no doubt, inevitable that such a man should see "a certain kind of temperament, the power of being deeply moved by the presence of beautiful objects" as more important for the critic than "a correct abstract definition of beauty"; that his own criticism should be what we call impressionistic, or what Anatole France defines as a record of the adventures of the soul among masterpieces. It is hard to separate his critical from his creative writing; there is as much Pater as Leonardo in the famous description of the smile of the Mona Lisa; the step from the *Renaissance* to "The Child in the House" and the *Imaginary Portraits* with which it is so closely allied was not a long one. But it was about as long a step as Pater could take. He could never have been a true novelist; the fastidiousness, the exclusiveness—even the morbidness—in his heroes all derive from himself.

He wrote slowly and deliberately; his carefully wrought periods are poetic prose, like De Quincey's, like Sir Thomas Browne's. Pater has always been the subject of considerable misunderstanding; the English temperament being what it is, his themes and his style alike must seem febrile, decadent, and bloodless to many readers. But he will always hold his place with those who, like him, love cats better than dogs, and enjoy Botticelli more rapturously than some greater painters.

[handwritten marginalia at bottom: belief — Beauty for beauty's sake]

from THE RENAISSANCE

In its original form, Pater's book on the Renaissance contained studies of "Aucassin and Nicolette," as representative of the early Renaissance; of Pico della Mirandola, Botticelli, Leonardo da Vinci, Luca della Robbia, and Michelangelo, as Renaissance philosophy, painting, sculpture, and poetry; of Du Bellay, as typical of the later Renaissance. To these an earlier essay on Winckelmann and a consideration of "Amis and Amile" were later added. The excerpts printed here are from the first edition.

The Preface is given here in part as important for the understanding of Pater's critical principles, the "Conclusion" as the frankest statement he ever made of his philosophy. The description of "La Gioconda" in the essay on Leonardo is probably the most famous of all Pater's purple passages, while the essay on Botticelli, which is given in full, is an altogether charming and thoroughly characteristic piece of work.

PREFACE

MANY attempts have been made by writers on art and poetry to define beauty in the abstract, to express it in the most general terms, to find some universal formula for it. The value of such attempts has most often been in the suggestive and penetrating things said by the way. Such discussions help us very little to enjoy what has been well done in art or poetry, to discriminate between what is more and what is less excellent in them, or to use words like beauty, excellence, art, poetry, with more meaning than they would otherwise have. Beauty, like all other qualities presented to human experience, is relative; and the definition of it becomes unmeaning and useless in proportion to its abstractness. To define beauty not in the most abstract, but in the most concrete terms possible, not to find a universal formula for it, but the formula which expresses most adequately this or that special manifestation of it, is the aim of the true student of aesthetics.

"To see the object as in itself it really is," has been justly said to be the aim of all true criticism whatever; and in aesthetic criticism the first step towards seeing one's object as it really is, is to know one's own impression as it really is, to discriminate it, to realise it distinctly. The objects with which aesthetic criticism deals, music, poetry, artistic and accomplished forms of human life, are indeed receptacles of so many powers or forces; they possess, like natural elements, so many virtues or qualities. What is this song or picture, this engaging personality presented in life or in a book, to *me?* What effect does it really produce on me? Does it give me pleasure? and if so, what sort or degree of pleasure? How is my nature modified by its presence and under its influence? The answers to these questions are the original facts with which the aesthetic critic has to do; and, as in the study of light, of morals, of number, one must realise such primary data for one's self or not at all. And he who experiences these impressions strongly, and drives directly at the analysis and discrimination of them, has no need to trouble himself with the abstract question what beauty is in itself, or its exact relation to truth or experience,—metaphysical questions, as unprofitable as metaphysical questions elsewhere. He may pass them all by as being, answerable or not, of no interest to him.

The aesthetic critic, then, regards all the objects with which he has to do, all works of art and the fairer forms of nature and human life, as powers or forces, producing pleasurable sensations, each of a more or less peculiar and unique kind. This influence he feels and wishes to explain, by analysing it, and reducing it to its elements. To him, the picture, the landscape, the engaging personality in life or in a book, La Gioconda, the hills of Carrara, Pico of Mirandula, are valuable for their virtues, as we say in speaking of a herb, a wine, a gem; for the property each has of affecting one with a special, unique impression of pleasure. Education grows in proportion as one's susceptibility to these impressions increases in depth and variety. And the function of the aesthetic critic is to distinguish, analyse, and separate from its adjuncts, the virtue by which a picture, a landscape, a fair personality in life or in a book, produces this special impression of beauty or pleasure, to indicate what the source of that impression is, and under what conditions it is experienced. His end is reached when he has disengaged that virtue, and noted it, as a chemist notes some natural element, for himself and others; and the rule for those who would reach this end is stated with great exactness in the words of a recent critic of Sainte-Beuve: "De se borner à connaître de près les belles choses, et à s'en nourrir en exquis amateurs, en humanistes accomplis."

What is important, then, is not that the critic should possess a correct abstract definition of

42–43. **has been justly said,** by Matthew Arnold, in *On Translating Homer.*

26–27. **La Gioconda.** See the next selection. **Carrara,** a city in northern Italy from whose surrounding hills Carrara marble is derived. **Pico of Mirandula,** Giovanni Pico, Count of Mirandola (1463–1494), Renaissance scholar and philosopher. 44–46. **"De se borner . . . accomplis."** "To limit themselves to understanding fine things intimately, and to steep themselves therein as perfect connoisseurs and accomplished humanists."

influence = had great influence on Oscar Wild — (Pre-Raphaelite's idea).
looked for beauty for its end.

beauty for the intellect, but a certain kind of temperament, the power of being deeply moved by the presence of beautiful objects. He will remember always that beauty exists in many forms. To him all periods, types, schools of taste, are in themselves equal. In all ages there have been some excellent workmen and some excellent work done. The question he asks is always, In whom did the stir, the genius, the sentiment of the period find itself? who was the receptacle of its refinement, its elevation, its taste? "The ages are all equal," says William Blake, "but genius is always above its age."

Often it will require great nicety to disengage this virtue from the commoner elements with which it may be found in combination. Few artists, not Goethe or Byron even, work quite cleanly, casting off all debris, and leaving us only what the heat of their imagination has wholly fused and transformed. Take, for instance, the writings of Wordsworth. The heat of his genius, entering into the substance of his work, has crystallised a part, but only a part, of it; and in that great mass of verse there is much which might well be forgotten. But scattered up and down it, sometimes fusing and transforming entire compositions, like the Stanzas on "Resolution and Independence," or the Ode on the "Recollections of Childhood," sometimes, as if at random, turning a fine crystal here and there, in a matter it does not wholly search through and transform, we trace the action of his unique incommunicable faculty, that strange mystical sense of a life in natural things, and of man's life as a part of nature, drawing strength and colour and character from local influences, from the hills and streams and natural sights and sounds. Well! that is the *virtue*, the active principle in Wordsworth's poetry; and then the function of the critic of Wordsworth is to follow up that active principle, to disengage it, to mark the degree in which it penetrates his verse. . . .

LEONARDO DA VINCI

. . . "La Gioconda" is, in the truest sense, Leonardo's masterpiece, the revealing instance of his mode of thought and work. In suggestiveness, only the Melancholia of Dürer is comparable to it; and no crude symbolism disturbs the effect of its subdued and graceful mystery. We all know the face and hands of the figure, set in its marble chair, in that cirque of fantastic rocks, as in some faint light under sea. Perhaps of all ancient pictures time has chilled it least. As often happens with works in which invention seems to reach its limit, there is an element in it given to, not invented by, the master. In that inestimable folio of drawings, once in the possession of Vasari, were certain designs by Verrocchio, faces of such impressive beauty that Leonardo in his boyhood copied them many times. It is hard not to connect with these designs of the elder by-past master, as with its germinal principle, the unfathomable smile, always with a touch of something sinister in it, which plays over all Leonardo's work. Besides, the picture is a portrait. From childhood we see this image defining itself on the fabric of his dreams; and but for express historical testimony, we might fancy that this was but his ideal lady, embodied and beheld at last. What was the relationship of a living Florentine to this creature of his thought? By what strange affinities had she and the dream grown thus apart, yet so closely together? Present from the first, incorporeal in Leonardo's thought, dimly traced in the designs of Verrocchio, she is found present at last in Il Giocondo's house. That there is much of mere portraiture in the picture is attested by the legend that by artificial means, the presence of mimes and flute-players, that subtle expression was protracted on the face. Again, was it in four years and by renewed labour never really completed, or in four months and as by stroke of magic, that the image was projected?

The presence that thus so strangely rose beside the waters is expressive of what in the ways of a thousand years man had come to desire. Hers is the head upon which all "the ends of the world are come," and the eyelids are a little weary. It is a beauty wrought out from within upon the flesh, the deposit, little cell by cell, of strange thoughts and fantastic reveries and exquisite passions. Set it for a moment beside one of those white Greek goddesses or beautiful women of antiquity, and how would they be troubled by this beauty, into which the soul with all its maladies has passed! All the thoughts and experience of the world have etched and moulded there in that which they have of power to refine and make expressive the outward form, the animalism of Greece, the lust of Rome, the reverie of the middle age with its spiritual ambition and imaginative loves, the return of the Pagan world, the sins of the Borgias. She is older than the rocks

26–27. **Ode on the "Recollections of Childhood."** Pater means "Ode on Intimations of Immortality from Recollections of Early Childhood." See page 67.   42. **"La Gioconda,"** the most famous portrait in the world, more generally known as the "Mona Lisa."   45. **Dürer,** Albrecht Dürer (1471–1528), one of the greatest of German painters and engravers.

7. **Vasari.** See note on page 568. **Verrocchio,** Andrea del Verrocchio (1435–1488), Italian sculptor and painter.   35–36. **"the ends . . . come."** See I Corinthians I:II.   50. **the Borgias,** a famous Italian family of the fifteenth century, important for politics, art, religion, and crime.

among which she sits; like the vampire, she has been dead many times, and learned the secrets of the grave; and has been a diver in deep seas, and keeps their fallen day about her; and trafficked for strange webs with Eastern merchants, and, as Leda, was the mother of Helen of Troy, and, as Saint Anne, the mother of Mary; and all this has been to her but as the sound of lyres and flutes, and lives only in the delicacy with which it has moulded the changing lineaments, and tinged the eyelids and the hands. The fancy of a perpetual life, sweeping together ten thousand experiences, is an old one; and modern philosophy has conceived the idea of humanity as wrought upon by, and summing up in itself, all modes of thought and life. Certainly Lady Lisa might stand as the embodiment of the old fancy, the symbol of the modern idea.

SANDRO BOTTICELLI

Alessandro Filipepi (c. 1444–1510) was called Botticelli ("small cask") from a nickname attached to his eldest brother. His fame has increased notably since Pater wrote of him, though there are still some critics who take a somewhat lofty attitude toward him. Yukio Yashiro's *Sandro Botticelli and the Italian Renaissance* (Hale, Cushman, and Flint, 1930) is a full biography, and James Cleugh has novelized the painter's life in his *Tuscan Spring* (Reynal and Hitchcock, 1939). *Botticelli* (Oxford Press, 1937) contains many excellent reproductions of his paintings.

In Leonardo's treatise on painting only one contemporary is mentioned by name—Sandro Botticelli. This pre-eminence may be due to chance only, but to some will rather appear a result of deliberate judgment; for people have begun to find out the charm of Botticelli's work, and his name, little known in the last century, is quietly becoming important. In the middle of the fifteenth century he had already anticipated much of that meditative subtlety which is sometimes supposed peculiar to the great imaginative workmen of its close. Leaving the simple religion which had occupied the followers of Giotto for a century, and the simple naturalism which had grown out of it, a thing of birds and flowers only, he sought inspiration in what to him were works of the modern world, the writings of

Dante and Boccaccio, and in new readings of his own of classical stories; or, if he painted religious incidents, painted them with an under-current of original sentiment which touches you as the real matter of the picture through the veil of its ostensible subject. What is the peculiar sensation, what is the peculiar quality of pleasure, which his work has the property of exciting in us, and which we cannot get elsewhere? For this, especially when he has to speak of a comparatively unknown artist, is always the chief question which a critic has to answer.

In an age when the lives of artists were full of adventure, his life is almost colourless. Criticism indeed has cleared away much of the gossip which Vasari accumulated, has touched the legend of Lippo and Lucrezia, and rehabilitated the character of Andrea del Castagno; but in Botticelli's case there is no legend to dissipate. He did not even go by his true name: Sandro is a nickname, and his true name is Filipepi, Botticelli being only the name of the goldsmith who first taught him art. Only two things happened to him, two things which he shared with other artists—he was invited to Rome to paint in the Sistine Chapel, and he fell in later life under the influence of Savonarola, passing apparently almost out of men's sight in a sort of religious melancholy which lasted till his death in 1515, according to the received date. Vasari says that he plunged into the study of Dante, and even wrote a comment on the "Divine Comedy." But it seems strange that he should have lived on inactive so long; and one almost wishes that some document might come to light which, fixing the date of his death earlier, might relieve one, in thinking of him, of his dejected old age.

He is before all things a poetical painter, blending the charm of story and sentiment, the medium of the art of poetry, with the charm of line and colour, the medium of abstract painting. So he becomes the illustrator of Dante. In a few rare examples of the edition of 1481, the blank spaces left at the beginning of every canto for the hand of the illuminator have been filled, as far as the nineteenth canto of the "Inferno," with impressions of engraved plates, seemingly by way of experiment, for

---

1. **vampire,** a dead human being which prolongs its earthly existence by sucking the blood of living mortals. See Montague Summers, *The Vampire, His Kith and Kin* and *The Vampire in Europe*, Dutton, 1928, 1929.   **5–6. Leda . . . Troy,** the wife of Tyndareus, King of Sparta, the mother of **Helen** (whose beauty caused the Trojan War) by Zeus, who visited her in the form of a swan. See *Iliad*, Book III, l. 426. **6–7. Saint Anne, the mother of Mary,** in "The Gospel of the Birth of Mary," in the Apocryphal New Testament. **43. Giotto.** See note on page 564.

1. **Boccaccio,** Giovanni Boccaccio (1313–1375), author of the *Decameron* and other famous works.   **16–17. Lippo . . . Lucrezia . . . Andrea del Castagno.** See Browning's "Fra Lippo Lippi" (page 562) and "Andrea del Sarto" (page 566), both based on Vasari's accounts.   **17–21. Botticelli . . . art.** This is a legend. See the introductory note.   **25. Savonarola,** Girolamo Savonarola (1452–1498), the great Florentine reformer; see George Eliot's *Romola*.   **28. the received date.** It is now 1510.   **44. "Inferno."** *The Divine Comedy* tells the story of Dante's journey through Hell (*Inferno*), Purgatory (*Purgatorio*), and Heaven (*Paradiso*).

in the copy in the Bodleian Library, one of the three impressions it contains has been printed upside down and much awry in the midst of the luxurious printed page. Giotto, and the followers of Giotto, with their almost childish religious aim, had not learned to put that weight of meaning into outward things, light, colour, every-day gesture, which the poetry of the "Divine Comedy" involves, and before the fifteenth century Dante could hardly have found an illustrator. Botticelli's illustrations are crowded with incident, blending with a naïve carelessness of pictorial propriety three phases of the same scene into one plate. The grotesques, so often a stumbling-block to painters who forget that the words of a poet, which only feebly present an image to the mind, must be lowered in key when translated into form, make one regret that he has not rather chosen for illustration the more subdued imagery of the "Purgatorio." Yet in the scene of those who "go down quick into hell" there is an invention about the fire taking hold on the upturned soles of the feet, which proves that the design is no mere translation of Dante's words, but a true painter's vision; while the scene of the Centaurs wins one at once, for, forgetful of the actual circumstances of their appearance, Botticelli has gone off with delight on the thought of the Centaurs themselves, bright small creatures of the woodland, with arch baby faces and mignon forms, drawing tiny bows.

Botticelli lived in a generation of naturalists, and he might have been a mere naturalist among them. There are traces enough in his work of that alert sense of outward things which, in the pictures of that period, fills the lawns with delicate living creatures, and the hill-sides with pools of water, and the pools of water with flowering reeds. But this was not enough for him; he is a visionary painter, and in his visionariness he resembles Dante. Giotto, the tried companion of Dante, Masaccio, Ghirlandaio even, do but transcribe with more or less refining the outward image; they are dramatic, not visionary, painters; they are almost impassive spectators of the action before them. But the genius of which Botticelli is the type usurps the data before it as the exponent of ideas, moods, visions of its own; with this interest it plays fast and loose with those data, rejecting some and isolating others, and always combining them anew. To him, as to Dante, the scene,

the colour, the outward image or gesture, comes with all its incisive and importunate reality; but awakes in him, moreover, by some subtle structure of his own, a mood which it awakes in no one else, of which it is the double or repetition, and which it clothes, that all may share it, with sensuous circumstances.

But he is far enough from accepting the conventional orthodoxy of Dante which, referring all human action to the easy formula of purgatory, heaven and hell, leaves an insoluble element of prose in the depths of Dante's poetry. One picture of his, with the portrait of the donor, Matteo Palmieri, below, had the credit or discredit of attracting some shadow of ecclesiastical censure. This Matteo Palmieri—two dim figures move under that name in contemporary history—was the reputed author of a poem, still unedited, "La Città Divina," which represented the human race as an incarnation of those angels who, in the revolt of Lucifer, were neither for God nor for his enemies, a fantasy of that earlier Alexandrian philosophy, about which the Florentine intellect in that century was so curious. Botticelli's picture may have been only one of those familiar compositions in which religious reverie has recorded its impressions of the various forms of beatified existence—*Glorias*, as they were called, like that in which Giotto painted the portrait of Dante; but somehow it was suspected of embodying in a picture the wayward dream of Palmieri, and the chapel where it hung was closed. Artists so entire as Botticelli are usually careless about philosophical theories, even when the philosopher is a Florentine of the fifteenth century, and his work a poem in *terza rima*. But Botticelli, who wrote a commentary on Dante, and became the disciple of Savonarola, may well have let such theories come and go across him. True or false, the story interprets much of the peculiar sentiment with which he infuses his profane and sacred persons, comely, and in a certain sense like angels, but with a sense of displacement or loss about them—the wistfulness of exiles, conscious of a passion and energy greater than any known issue of them explains, which runs through all his varied work with a sentiment of ineffable melancholy.

So just what Dante scorns as unworthy alike of heaven and hell, Botticelli accepts, that middle world in which men take no side in great conflicts, and decide no great causes, and make great refusals. He thus sets for himself the limits within which art, undisturbed by any moral ambition, does its most

---

1. **Bodleian Library,** at Oxford. **17–19. make one regret . . . "Purgatorio."** Botticelli illustrated the whole *Divine Comedy,* but Pater had not seen all his pictures. **19–22. Yet in the scene . . . feet.** See *Inferno,* Canto XIX, ll. 13–30. **24. the scene of the Centaurs,** *Inferno,* Canto XII, ll. 55 ff. **39. Masaccio.** See note on page 565. Florentine painter. **Ghirlandaio,** Domenico di Tommaso Curradi di Doffo Bigordi (1449–1494), Florentine painter.

18. "La Città Divina," "The Divine City." **19–21. those angels . . . his enemies.** See *The Divine Comedy, Inferno,* Canto III, ll. 34 ff.

sincere and surest work. His interest is neither in the untempered goodness of Angelico's saints, nor the untempered evil of Orcagna's "Inferno"; but with men and women, in their mixed and uncertain condition, always attractive, clothed sometimes by passion with a character of loveliness and energy, but saddened perpetually by the shadow upon them of the great things from which they shrink. His morality is all sympathy; and it is this sympathy, conveying into his work somewhat more than is usual of the true complexion of humanity, which makes him, visionary as he is, so forcible a realist.

It is this which gives to his Madonnas their unique expression and charm. He has worked out in them a distinct and peculiar type, definite enough in his own mind, for he has painted it over and over again, sometimes one might think almost mechanically, as a pastime during that dark period when his thoughts were so heavy upon him. Hardly any collection of note is without one of these circular pictures, into which the attendant angels depress their heads so naïvely. Perhaps you have sometimes wondered why those peevish-looking Madonnas, conformed to no acknowledged or obvious type of beauty, attract you more and more, and often come back to you when the Sistine Madonna and the virgins of Fra Angelico are forgotten. At first, contrasting them with those, you may have thought that there was even something in them mean or abject, for the abstract lines of the face have little nobleness, and the colour is wan. For with Botticelli she too, though she holds in her hands the "Desire of all nations," is one of those who are neither for God nor for his enemies; and her choice is on her face. The white light on it is cast up hard and cheerless from below, as when snow lies upon the ground, and the children look up with surprise at the strange whiteness of the ceiling. Her trouble is in the very caress of the mysterious child, whose gaze is always far from her, and who has already that sweet look of devotion which men have never been able altogether to love, and which still makes the born saint an object almost of suspicion to his earthly brethren. Once, indeed, he guides her hand to transcribe in a book the words of her exaltation, the *Ave*, and the *Magnificat*, and the *Gaude Maria*, and the young angels, glad to rouse her for a moment from her dejection, are eager to hold the inkhorn and to support the book; but the pen almost drops from her hand, and the high cold words have no meaning for her, and her true children are those others, in the midst of whom, in her rude home, the intolerable honour came to her, with that look of wistful inquiry on their irregular faces which you see in startled animals—gipsy children, such as those who, in Apennine villages, still hold out their long brown arms to beg of you, but on Sundays become *enfants du chœur*, with their thick black hair nicely combed, and fair white linen on their sun-burnt throats.

What is strangest is that he carries this sentiment into classical subjects, its most complete expression being a picture in the Uffizii, of Venus rising from the sea, in which the grotesque emblems of the middle age, and a landscape full of its peculiar feeling, and even its strange draperies powdered all over in the Gothic manner with a quaint conceit of daisies, frame a figure that reminds you of the faultless nude studies of Ingres. At first, perhaps, you are attracted only by a quaintness of design, which seems to recall all at once whatever you have read of Florence in the fifteenth century; afterwards you may think that this quaintness must be incongruous with the subject, and that the colour is cadaverous, or at least cold. And yet, the more you come to understand what imaginative colouring really is, that all colour is no mere delightful quality of natural things, but a spirit upon them by which they become expressive to the spirit, the better you will like this peculiar quality of colour; and you will find that quaint design of Botticelli's a more direct inlet into the Greek temper than the works of the Greeks themselves even of the finest period. Of the Greeks as they really were, of their difference from ourselves, of the aspects of their outward life, we know far more than Botticelli, or his most learned contemporaries; but for us, long familiarity has taken off the edge of the lesson, and we are hardly conscious of what we owe to the Hellenic spirit. But in pictures like this of Botticelli's you have a record of the first impression made by it on minds turned back towards it in almost painful aspiration from a world in which it had been ignored so long; and in the passion, the energy, the industry of realisation, with which Botticelli carries out his intention, is the

---

2. **Angelico.** See note on page 565.   3. **Orcagna,** Andrea di Cione (c. 1300–1368), great early Florentine painter. 26. **Sistine Madonna,** by Raphael, perhaps the most famous of all Madonna pictures.   32–33. **"Desire of all nations,"** the Christ child.   44. **Once,** in the picture called "The Magnificat," in the Uffizzi Gallery at Florence. 45–46. **Ave,** Ave Maria (Hail, Mary), a prayer to the Virgin as the Mother of God, from the salutations of Gabriel and Elizabeth in Luke 1:28, 42. **Magnificat** (Latin for "[my soul] magnifies"). See Luke 1:46–55. **Gaude Maria,** "Rejoice, Mary," a hymn used in the Christmas season.

11. **Apennine villages,** in central Italy.   12–13. **enfants du chœur,** choirboys.   17–18. **a picture . . . sea.** "The Birth of Venus" and the "Primavera" ("Spring") are probably Botticelli's two best-known paintings.   23. **Ingres,** Jean Auguste Dominique Ingres (1780–1867), great **French** painter.

exact measure of the legitimate influence over the human mind of the imaginative system of which this is the central myth. The light is, indeed, cold— mere sunless dawn; but a later painter would have cloyed you with sunshine; and you can see the better for that quietness in the morning air each long promontory, as it slopes down to the water's edge. Men go forth to their labours until the evening; but she is awake before them, and you might think that the sorrow in her face was at the thought of the 10 whole long day of love yet to come. An emblematical figure of the wind blows hard across the grey water, moving forward the dainty-lipped shell on which she sails, the sea "showing his teeth" as it moves in thin lines of foam, and sucking in one by one the falling roses, each severe in outline, plucked off short at the stalk, but embrowned a little, as Botticelli's flowers always are. Botticelli meant all that imagery to be altogether pleasurable; and it was partly an incompleteness of resources, insepa- 20 rable from the art of that time, that subdued and chilled it; but this predilection for minor tones counts also; and what is unmistakable is the sadness with which he has conceived the goddess of pleasure as the depositary of a great power over the lives of men.

I have said that the peculiar character of Botticelli is the result of a blending in him of a sympathy for humanity in its uncertain condition, its attractiveness, its investiture at rarer moments in a character 30 of loveliness and energy, with his consciousness of the shadow upon it of the great things from which it shrinks, and that this conveys into his work somewhat more than painting usually attains of the true complexion of humanity. He paints the story of the goddess of pleasure in other episodes besides that of her birth from the sea, but never without some shadow of death in the grey flesh and wan flowers. He paints Madonnas, but they shrink from the pressure of the divine child, and plead in unmistakable 40 undertones for a warmer, lower humanity. The same figure—tradition connects it with Simonetta, the mistress of Giuliano de' Medici—appears again as Judith returning home across the hill country when the great deed is over, and the moment of revulsion come, and the olive branch in her hand is becoming a burthen; as Justice, sitting on a throne, but with a fixed look of self-hatred which makes the sword in her hand seem that of a suicide; and again

43. **Giuliano de' Medici,** Giulio de' Medici (c. 1480–1534), who became Pope Clement VII.   45. **the great deed,** the slaying of the Assyrian general Holofernes, which raised the siege of Bethulia. The story is in the Apocrypha; see also Thomas Bailey Aldrich's play *Judith of Bethulia*, 1905.

as Veritas, in the allegorical picture of Calumnia, where one may note in passing the suggestiveness of an accident which identifies the image of Truth with the person of Venus. We might trace the same sentiment through his engravings; but his share in them is doubtful, and the object of this brief study has been attained if I have defined aright the temper in which he worked.

But, after all, it may be asked, is a painter like Botticelli, a second-rate painter, a proper subject for general criticism? There are a few great painters, like Michelangelo or Leonardo, whose work has become a force in general culture, partly for this very reason that they have absorbed into themselves all such workmen as Sandro Botticelli; and, over and above mere technical or antiquarian criticism, general criticism may be very well employed in that sort of interpretation which adjusts the position of these men to general culture, whereas smaller men can 20 be the proper subjects only of technical or antiquarian treatment. But, besides those great men, there is a certain number of artists who have a distinct faculty of their own by which they convey to us a peculiar quality of pleasure which we cannot get elsewhere, and these, too, have their place in general culture, and must be interpreted to it by those who have felt their charm strongly, and are often the objects of a special diligence and a consideration wholly affectionate, just because there is not about 30 them the stress of a great name and authority. Of this select number Botticelli is one; he has the freshness, the uncertain and diffident promise which belong to the earlier Renaissance itself, and make it perhaps the most interesting period in the history of the mind; in studying his work one begins to understand to how great a place in human culture the art of Italy had been called.

CONCLUSION

Δέγει που Ἡράκλειτος ὅτι πάντα χωρεῖ καὶ οὐδὲν μένει

To regard all things and principles of things as inconstant modes or fashions has more and more become the tendency of modern thought. Let us begin with that which is without—our physical life. Fix upon it in one of its more exquisite intervals, the moment, for instance, of delicious recoil from the flood of water in summer heat. What is the whole physical life in that moment but a combination of 50 natural elements to which science gives their names? But these elements, phosphorus and lime and delicate fibres, are present not in the human body alone:

41. Δέγι . . . μένει. "Heraclitus says, 'All things give way; nothing remaineth.'" (Pater's translation)

absolute gratitude to Beauty.

we detect them in places most remote from it. Our physical life is a perpetual motion of them—the passage of the blood, the waste and repairing of the lenses of the eye, the modification of the tissues of the brain under every ray of light and sound—processes which science reduces to simpler and more elementary forces. Like the elements of which we are composed, the action of these forces extends beyond us; it rusts iron and ripens corn. Far out on every side of us those elements are broadcast, driven by many forces; and birth and gesture and death and the springing of violets from the grave are but a few out of ten thousand resulting combinations. That clear perpetual outline of face and limb is but an image of ours under which we group them—a design in a web, the actual threads of which pass out beyond it. This at least of flame-like our life has, that it is but the concurrence, renewed from moment to moment, of forces parting sooner or later on their ways.

Or if we begin with the inward world of thought and feeling, the whirlpool is still more rapid, the flame more eager and devouring. There it is no longer the gradual darkening of the eye and fading of colour from the wall,—movements of the shore side, where the water flows down indeed, though in apparent rest,—but the race of the midstream, a drift of momentary acts of sight and passion and thought. At first sight experience seems to bury us under a flood of external objects, pressing upon us with a sharp and importunate reality, calling us out of ourselves in a thousand forms of action. But when reflection begins to act upon those objects they are dissipated under its influence; the cohesive force seems suspended like a trick of magic; each object is loosed into a group of impressions—colour, odour, texture,—in the mind of the observer. And if we continue to dwell on this world, not of objects in the solidity with which language invests them, but of impressions unstable, flickering, inconsistent, which burn and are extinguished with our consciousness of them, it contracts still further; the whole scope of observation is dwarfed into the narrow chamber of the individual mind. Experience, already reduced to a swarm of impressions, is ringed round for each one of us by that thick wall of personality through which no real voice has ever pierced on its way to us, or from us to that which we can only conjecture to be without. Every one of those impressions is the impression of the individual in his isolation, each mind keeping as a solitary prisoner its own dream of a world.

Analysis goes a step farther still, and assures us that those impressions of the individual mind to which, for each one of us, experience dwindles

down, are in perpetual flight; that each of them is limited by time, and that as time is infinitely divisible, each of them is infinitely divisible also; all that is actual in it being a single moment, gone while we try to apprehend it, of which it may ever be more truly said that it has ceased to be than that it is. To such a tremulous wisp constantly reforming itself on the stream, to a single sharp impression, with a sense in it, a relic more or less fleeting, of such moments gone by, what is *real* in our life fines itself down. It is with this movement, with the passage and dissolution of impressions, images, sensations, that analysis leaves off,—that continual vanishing away, that strange, perpetual weaving and unweaving of ourselves.

Philosophiren, says Novalis, *ist dephlegmatisiren, vivificiren.* The service of philosophy, of religion and culture as well, to the human spirit, is to rouse, to startle it to a sharp and eager observation. Every moment some form grows perfect in hand or face; some tone on the hills or the sea is choicer than the rest; some mood of passion or insight or intellectual excitement is irresistibly real and attractive to us,— for that moment only. Not the fruit of experience, but experience itself is the end. A counted number of pulses only is given to us of a variegated, dramatic life. How may we see in them all that is to be seen in them by the finest senses? How shall we pass most swiftly from point to point, and be present always at the focus where the greatest number of vital forces unite in their purest energy?

To burn always with this hard, gem-like flame, to maintain this ecstasy, is success in life. Failure is to form habits; for habit is relative to a stereotyped world, and meantime it is only the roughness of the eye that makes any two persons, things, situations, seem alike. While all melts under our feet, we may well catch at any exquisite passion, or any contribution to knowledge that seems, by a lifted horizon, to set the spirit free for a moment, or any stirring of the senses, strange dyes, strange flowers, and curious odours, or work of the artist's hands, or the face of one's friend. Not to discriminate every moment some passionate attitude in those about us, and in the very brilliance of their gifts some tragic dividing of forces on their ways is, on this short day of frost and sun, to sleep before evening. With this sense of the splendour of our experience and of its awful brevity, gathering all we are into one desperate effort to see and touch, we shall hardly have time to

16–17. **Philosophiren** . . . **vivificiren.** To philosophize is to cast off inertia, to animate oneself. Novalis (pseud. of Friedrich von Hardenberg; 1772–1801) was one of the German romantics.

make theories about the things we see and touch. What we have to do is to be for ever curiously testing new opinions and courting new impressions, never acquiescing in a facile orthodoxy of Comte or of Hegel, or of our own. Theories, religious or philosophical ideas, as points of view, instruments of criticism, may help us to gather up what might otherwise pass unregarded by us. *La philosophie, c'est la microscope de la pensée.* The theory or idea, or system, which requires of us the sacrifice of any part of this experience, in consideration of some interest into which we cannot enter, or some abstract morality we have not identified with ourselves, or what is only conventional, has no real claim upon us.

One of the most beautiful passages of Rousseau is that in the sixth book of the "Confessions," where he describes the awakening in him of the literary sense. An undefinable taint of death had always clung about him, and now in early manhood he believed himself stricken by mortal disease. He asked himself how he might make as much as possible of the interval that remained; and he was not biassed by anything in his previous life when he decided that it must be by intellectual excitement, which he found just then in the clear, fresh writings of Voltaire. Well, we are all *condamnés*, as Victor Hugo says: *les hommes sont tous condamnés à morte avec des sursis indéfinis:* we have an interval, and then our place knows us no more. Some spend this interval in listlessness, some in high passions, the wisest in art and song. For our one chance is in expanding that interval, in getting as many pulsations as possible into the given time. Great passions may give us this quickened sense of life, ecstasy and sorrow of love, political or religious enthusiasm, or the "enthusiasm of humanity." Only, be sure it is passion, that it does yield you this fruit of a quickened, multiplied consciousness. Of this wisdom, the poetic passion, the desire of beauty, the love of art for art's sake has most; for art comes to you professing frankly to give nothing but the highest quality to your moments as they pass, and simply for those moments' sake.

THE CHILD IN THE HOUSE[1]

This beautiful piece of writing, almost indefinable as to genre, was subtitled "An Imaginary Portrait" when it first appeared in *Macmillan's Magazine* in 1878, thus anticipating the title of the book with whose contents it has much in common. It is generally regarded as containing autobiographical elements.

AS Florian Deleal walked, one hot afternoon, he overtook by the wayside a poor aged man, and, as he seemed weary with the road, helped him on with the burden which he carried, a certain distance. And as the man told his story, it chanced that he named the place, a little place in the neighbourhood of a great city, where Florian had passed his earliest years, but which he had never since seen, and, the story told, went forward on his journey comforted. And that night, like a reward for his pity, a dream of that place came to Florian, a dream which did for him the office of the finer sort of memory, bringing its object to mind with a great clearness, yet, as sometimes happens in dreams, raised a little above itself, and above ordinary retrospect. The true aspect of the place, especially of the house there in which he had lived as a child, the fashion of its doors, its hearths, its windows, the very scent upon the air of it, was with him in sleep for a season; only, with tints more musically blent on wall and floor, and some finer light and shadow running in and out along its curves and angles, and with all its little carvings daintier. He awoke with a sigh at the thought of almost thirty years which lay between him and that place, yet with a flutter of pleasure still within him at the fair light, as if it were a smile, upon it. And it happened that this accident of his dream was just the thing needed for the beginning of a certain design he then had in view, the noting, namely, of some things in the story of his spirit—in that process of brain-building by which we are, each one of us, what we are. With the image of the place so clear and favourable upon him, he fell to thinking of himself therein, and how his thoughts had grown up to him. In that half-spiritualised house he could watch the better, over again, the gradual expansion of the soul which had come to be there—of which indeed, through the law which makes the material objects about them so large an element in children's lives, it had actually become a part; inward and outward being woven through and through each other into one inextricable texture—half, tint and trace and accident of homely colour and form, from the wood and the bricks; half, mere soul-stuff, floated thither from who knows how far. In the house and garden of his dream he saw a child moving, and could divide the main streams at least of the winds that had played on him, and study so the first stage in that mental journey.

8–9. La philosophie . . . pensée. Philosophy is the microscope of thought.   27–28. les hommes . . . indéfinis. Men are all under sentence of death, with indefinite reprieves.   [1] From *Imaginary Portraits*, The Macmillan Company, 1887. Reprinted by permission.

The *old house*, as when Florian talked of it afterwards he always called it, (as all children do, who can recollect a change of home, soon enough but not too soon to mark a period in their lives) really was an old house; and an element of French descent in its inmates—descent from Watteau, the old court-painter, one of whose gallant pieces still hung in one of the rooms—might explain, together with some other things, a noticeable trimness and comely whiteness about everything there—the curtains, the 10 couches, the paint on the walls with which the light and shadow played so delicately; might explain also the tolerance of the great poplar in the garden, a tree most often despised by English people, but which French people love, having observed a certain fresh way its leaves have of dealing with the wind, making it sound, in never so slight a stirring of the air, like running water.

The old-fashioned, low wainscoting went round the rooms, and up the staircase with carved balus- 20 ters and shadowy angles, landing half-way up at a broad window, with a swallow's nest below the sill, and the blossom of an old pear-tree showing across it in late April, against the blue, below which the perfumed juice of the find of fallen fruit in autumn was so fresh. At the next turning came the closet which held on its deep shelves the best china. Little angel faces and reedy flutings stood out round the fireplace of the children's room. And on the top of the house, above the large attic, where the white 30 mice ran in the twilight—an infinite, unexplored wonderland of childish treasures, glass beads, empty scent-bottles still sweet, thrum of coloured silks, among its lumber—a flat space of roof, railed round, gave a view of the neighbouring steeples; for the house, as I said, stood near a great city, which sent up heavenwards, over the twisting weather-vanes, not seldom, its beds of rolling cloud and smoke, touched with storm or sunshine. But the child of whom I am writing did not hate the fog 40 because of the crimson lights which fell from it sometimes upon the chimneys, and the whites which gleamed through its openings, on summer mornings, on turret or pavement. For it is false to suppose that a child's sense of beauty is dependent on any choiceness or special fineness, in the objects which present themselves to it, though this indeed comes to be the rule with most of us in later life; earlier, in some degree, we see inwardly; and the child finds for itself, and with unstinted delight, a 50

difference for the sense, in those whites and reds through the smoke on very homely buildings, and in the gold of the dandelions at the roadside, just beyond the houses, where not a handful of earth is virgin and untouched, in the lack of better ministries to its desire of beauty.

This house then stood not far beyond the gloom and rumours of the town, among high garden-walls, bright all summer-time with Golden-rod and brown-and-golden Wall-flower—*Flos Parietis*, as the children's Latin-reading father taught them to call it, while he was with them. Tracing back the threads of his complex spiritual habit, as he was used in after years to do, Florian found that he owed to the place many tones of sentiment afterwards customary with him, certain inward lights under which things most naturally presented themselves to him. The coming and going of travellers to the town along the way, the shadow of the streets, the sudden breath of the neighbouring gardens, the singular brightness of bright weather there, its singular darknesses which linked themselves in his mind to certain engraved illustrations in the old big Bible at home, the coolness of the dark, cavernous shops round the great church, with its giddy winding stair up to the pigeons and the bells—a citadel of peace in the heart of the trouble—all this acted on his childish fancy, so that ever afterwards the like aspects and incidents never failed to throw him into a well-recognised imaginative mood, seeming actually to have become a part of the texture of his mind. Also, Florian could trace home to this point a pervading preference in himself for a kind of comeliness and dignity, an *urbanity* literally, in modes of life, which he connected with the pale people of towns, and which made him susceptible to a kind of exquisite satisfaction in the trimness and well-considered grace of certain things and persons he afterwards met with, here and there, in his way through the world.

So the child of whom I am writing lived on there quietly; things without ministering to him, as he sat daily at the window with the birdcage hanging below it, and his mother taught him to read, wondering at the ease with which he learned, and at the quickness of his memory. The perfume of the little flowers of the lime-tree fell through the air upon them like rain; while time seemed to move ever more slowly to the murmur of the bees in it, till it almost stood still on June afternoons. How insignificant, at the moment, seem the influences of the sensible things which are tossed and fall and lie about us, so, or so, in the environment of early

---

6. **Watteau,** Jean Antoine Watteau (1684–1721); see "A Prince of Court Painters," in *Imaginary Portraits.* But Pater was really thinking of his possible relative, Jean Baptiste Pater (1696–1736), who, as Jean Baptiste, also appears in "A Prince of Court Painters."

34. **urbanity.** Note the etymology of the word.

childhood. How indelibly, as we afterwards discover, they affect us; with what capricious attractions and associations they figure themselves on the white paper, the smooth wax, of our ingenuous souls, as "with lead in the rock for ever," giving form and feature, and as it were assigned houseroom in our memory, to early experiences of feeling and thought, which abide with us ever afterwards, thus, and not otherwise. The realities and passions, the rumours of the greater world without, steal in upon us, each by its own special little passage-way, through the wall of custom about us; and never afterwards quite detach themselves from this or that accident, or trick, in the mode of their first entrance to us. Our susceptibilities, the discovery of our powers, manifold experiences—our various experiences of the coming and going of bodily pain, for instance—belong to this or the other well-remembered place in the material habitation—that little white room with the window across which the heavy blossoms could beat so peevishly in the wind, with just that particular catch or throb, such a sense of teasing in it, on gusty mornings; and the early habitation thus gradually becomes a sort of material shrine or sanctuary of sentiment; a system of visible symbolism interweaves itself through all our thoughts and passions; and irresistibly, little shapes, voices, accidents—the angle at which the sun in the morning fell on the pillow—become parts of the great chain wherewith we are bound.

Thus far, for Florian, what all this had determined was a peculiarly strong sense of home—so forcible a motive with all of us—prompting to us our customary love of the earth, and the larger part of our fear of death, that revulsion we have from it, as from something strange, untried, unfriendly; though life-long imprisonment, they tell you, and final banishment from home is a thing bitterer still; the looking forward to but a short space, a mere childish *goûter* and dessert of it, before the end, being so great a resource of effort to pilgrims and wayfarers, and the soldier in distant quarters, and lending, in lack of that, some power of solace to the thought of sleep in the home churchyard, at least— dead cheek by dead cheek, and with the rain soaking in upon one from above.

So powerful is this instinct, and yet accidents like those I have been speaking of so mechanically determine it; its essence being indeed the early familiar, as constituting our ideal, or typical conception, of rest and security. Out of so many possible conditions, just this for you and that for me, brings ever the unmistakeable realisation of the delightful *chez soi;* this for the Englishman, for me and you, with the closely-drawn white curtain and the shaded lamp; that, quite other, for the wandering Arab, who folds his tent every morning, and makes his sleeping-place among haunted ruins, or in old tombs.

With Florian then the sense of home became singularly intense, his good fortune being that the special character of his home was in itself so essentially home-like. As after many wanderings I have come to fancy that some parts of Surrey and Kent are, for Englishmen, the true landscape, true home-counties, by right, partly, of a certain earthy warmth in the yellow of the sand below their gorse-bushes, and of a certain grey-blue mist after rain, in the hollows of the hills there, welcome to fatigued eyes, and never seen farther south; so I think that the sort of house I have described, with precisely those proportions of red-brick and green, and with a just perceptible monotony in the subdued order of it, for its distinguishing note, is for Englishmen at least typically home-like. And so for Florian that general human instinct was reinforced by this special home-likeness in the place his wandering soul had happened to light on, as, in the second degree, its body and earthly tabernacle; the sense of harmony between his soul and its physical environment became, for a time at least, like perfectly played music, and the life led there singularly tranquil and filled with a curious sense of self-possession. The love of security, of an habitually undisputed standing-ground or sleeping-place, came to count for much in the generation and correcting of his thoughts, and afterwards as a salutary principle of restraint in all his wanderings of spirit. The wistful yearning towards home, in absence from it, as the shadows of evening deepened, and he followed in thought what was doing there from hour to hour, interpreted to him much of a yearning and regret he experienced afterwards, towards he knew not what, out of strange ways of feeling and thought in which, from time to time, his spirit found itself alone; and in the tears shed in such absences there seemed always to be some soul-subduing foretaste of what his last tears might be.

And the sense of security could hardly have been deeper, the quiet of the child's soul being one with the quiet of its home, a place "inclosed" and "sealed." But upon this assured place, upon the child's assured soul which resembled it, there came floating in from the larger world without, as at

1–5. **How indelibly . . . for ever.''** The **white paper** echoes Locke, the **smooth wax,** Aristotle; the quotation is from Job 19:23, 24.   40. **goûter,** lunch, snack.

3. **chez soi,** at home.

windows left ajar unknowingly, or over the high garden walls, two streams of impressions, the sentiments of beauty and pain—recognitions of the visible, tangible, audible loveliness of things, as a very real and somewhat tyrannous element in them—and of the sorrow of the world, of grown people and children and animals, as a thing not to be put by in them. From this point he could trace two predominant processes of mental change in him—the growth of an almost diseased sensibility to the spectacle of suffering, and, parallel with this, the rapid growth of a certain capacity of fascination by bright colour and choice form—the sweet curvings, for instance, of the lips of those who seemed to him comely persons, modulated in such delicate unison to the things they said or sang,—marking early the activity in him of a more than customary sensuousness, "the lust of the eye," as the Preacher says, which might lead him, one day, how far! Could he have foreseen the weariness of the way! In music sometimes the two sorts of impressions came together, and he would weep, to the surprise of older people. Tears of joy too the child knew, also to older people's surprise; real tears, once, of relief from long-strung, childish expectation, when he found returned at evening, with new roses in her cheeks, the little sister who had been to a place where there was a wood, and brought back for him a treasure of fallen acorns, and black crow's feathers, and his peace at finding her again near him mingled all night with some intimate sense of the distant forest, the rumour of its breezes, with the glossy blackbirds aslant and the branches lifted in them, and of the perfect nicety of the little cups that fell. So those two elementary apprehensions of the tenderness and of the colour in things grew apace in him, and were seen by him afterwards to send their roots back into the beginnings of life.

Let me note first some of the occasions of his recognition of the element of pain in things—incidents, now and again, which seemed suddenly to awake in him the whole force of that sentiment which Goethe has called the *Weltschmerz*, and in which the concentrated sorrow of the world seemed suddenly to lie heavy upon him. A book lay in an old book-case, of which he cared to remember one picture—a woman sitting, with hands bound behind her, the dress, the cap, the hair, folded with a simplicity which touched him strangely, as if not by her own hands, but with some ambiguous care at the hands of others—Queen Marie Antoinette, on her way to execution—we all remember David's drawing, meant merely to make her ridiculous. The face that had been so high had learned to be mute and resistless; but out of its very resistlessness, seemed now to call on men to have pity, and forbear; and he took note of that, as he closed the book, as a thing to look at again, if he should at any time find himself tempted to be cruel. Again, he would never quite forget the appeal in the small sister's face, in the garden under the lilacs, terrified at a spider lighted on her sleeve. He could trace back to the look then noted a certain mercy he conceived always for people in fear, even of little things, which seemed to make him, though but for a moment, capable of almost any sacrifice of himself. Impressible, susceptible persons, indeed, who had had their sorrows, lived about him; and this sensibility was due in part to the tacit influence of their presence, enforcing upon him habitually the fact that there are those who pass their days, as a matter of course, in a sort of "going quietly." Most poignantly of all he could recall, in unfading minutest circumstance, the cry on the stair, sounding bitterly through the house, and struck into his soul for ever, of an aged woman, his father's sister, come now to announce his death in distant India; how it seemed to make the aged woman like a child again; and, he knew not why, but this fancy was full of pity to him. There were the little sorrows of the dumb animals too—of the white angora, with a dark tail like an ermine's, and a face like a flower, who fell into a lingering sickness, and became quite delicately human in its valetudinarianism, and came to have a hundred different expressions of voice—how it grew worse and worse, till it began to feel the light too much for it, and at last, after one wild morning of pain, the little soul flickered away from the body, quite worn to death already, and now but feebly retaining it.

So he wanted another pet; and as there were starlings about the place, which could be taught to speak, one of them was caught, and he meant to treat it kindly; but in the night its young ones could be heard crying after it, and the responsive cry of the mother-bird towards them; and at last, with the first light, though not till after some debate with himself, he went down and opened the cage, and saw a sharp bound of the prisoner up to her nestlings; and therewith came the sense of remorse,— that he too was become an accomplice in moving, to the limit of his small power, the springs and handles

---

18–19. **as the Preacher says,** not Ecclesiastes, but 1 John 2:16.   **43. Weltschmerz,** an expansive, sentimental world-weariness, which often afflicts young people in too comfortable circumstances.

2. **David.** See note on page 424. The picture may be seen in Stefan Zweig's *Marie Antoinette*, Viking Press, 1933.

of that great machine in things, constructed so ingeniously to play pain-fugues on the delicate nerve-work of living creatures.

I have remarked how, in the process of our brain-building, as the house of thought in which we live gets itself together, like some airy bird's-nest of floating thistle-down and chance straws, compact at last, little accidents have their consequence; and thus it happened that, as he walked one evening, a garden gate, usually closed, stood open; and lo! within, a great red hawthorn in full flower, embossing heavily the bleached and twisted trunk and branches, so aged that there were but few green leaves thereon—a plumage of tender, crimson fire out of the heart of the dry wood. The perfume of the tree had now and again reached him, in the currents of the wind, over the wall, and he had wondered what might be behind it, and was now allowed to fill his arms with the flowers—flowers enough for all the old blue-china pots along the chimney-piece, making *fête* in the children's room. Was it some periodic moment in the expansion of soul within him, or mere trick of heat in the heavily-laden summer air? But the beauty of the thing struck home to him feverishly; and in dreams at night he loitered along a magic roadway of crimson flowers, which seemed to open ruddily in thick, fresh masses about his feet, and fill softly all the little hollows in the banks on either side. Always afterwards, summer by summer, as the flowers came on, the blossom of the red hawthorn still seemed to him absolutely the reddest of all things; and the goodly crimson, still alive in the works of old Venetian masters or old Flemish tapestries, called out always from afar the recollection of the flame in those perishing little petals, as it pulsed gradually out of them, kept long in the drawers of an old cabinet. Also then, for the first time, he seemed to experience a passionateness in his relation to fair outward objects, an inexplicable excitement in their presence, which disturbed him, and from which he half longed to be free. A touch of regret or desire mingled all night with the remembered presence of the red flowers, and their perfume in the darkness about him: and the longing for some undivined, entire possession of them was the beginning of a revelation to him, growing ever clearer, with the coming of the gracious summer guise of fields and trees and persons in each succeeding year, of a certain, at times seemingly exclusive, predominance in his interests, of beautiful physical things, a kind of tyranny of the senses over him.

In later years he came upon philosophies which occupied him much in the estimate of the proportion of the sensuous and the ideal elements in human knowledge, the relative parts they bear in it; and, in his intellectual scheme, was led to assign very little to the abstract thought, and much to its sensible vehicle or occasion. Such metaphysical speculation did but reinforce what was instinctive in his way of receiving the world, and for him, everywhere, that sensible vehicle or occasion became, perhaps only too surely, the necessary concomitant of any perception of things, real enough to be of any weight or reckoning, in his house of thought. There were times when he could think of the necessity he was under of associating all thoughts to touch and sight, as a sympathetic link between himself and actual, feeling, living objects; a protest in favour of real men and women against mere grey, unreal abstractions; and he remembered gratefully how the Christian religion, hardly less than the religion of the ancient Greeks, translating so much of its spiritual verity into things that may be seen, condescends in part to sanction this infirmity, if so it be, of our human existence, wherein the world of sense is so much with us, and welcomed this thought as a kind of keeper and sentinel over his soul therein. But certainly, he came more and more to be unable to care for, or think of soul but as in an actual body, or of any world but that wherein are water and trees, and where men and women look so or so, and press actual hands. It was the trick even his pity learned, fastening those who suffered in anywise to his affections by a kind of sensible attachments. He would think of Julian, fallen into incurable sickness, as spoiled in the sweet blossom of his skin like pale amber, and his honey-like hair; of Cecil, early dead, as cut off from the lilies, from golden summer days, from women's voices; and then what comforted him a little was the thought of the turning of the child's flesh to violets in the turf above him. And thinking of the very poor, it was not the things which most men care most for that he yearned to give them; but fairer roses, perhaps, and power to taste quite as they will, at their ease and not task-burdened, a certain desirable, clear light in the new morning, through which sometimes he had noticed them, quite unconscious of it, on their way to their early toil.

So he yielded himself to these things, to be played upon by them like a musical instrument, and began to note with deepening watchfulness, but always with some puzzled, unutterable longing in his enjoyment, the phases of the seasons and of the growing or waning day, down even to the shadowy

22–23. **the world . . . us,** almost certainly an echo of Wordsworth's famous sonnet; see page 67.

changes wrought on bare wall or ceiling—the light cast up from the snow, bringing out their darkest angles; the brown light in the cloud, which meant rain; that almost too austere clearness, in the protracted light of the lengthening day, before warm weather began, as if it lingered but to make a severer workday, with the school-books opened earlier and later; that beam of June sunshine, at last, as he lay awake before the time, a way of gold-dust across the darkness; all the humming, the freshness, the perfume of the garden seemed to lie upon it— and coming in one afternoon in September, along the red gravel walk, to look for a basket of yellow crab-apples left in the cool, old parlour, he remembered it the more, and how the colours struck upon him, because a wasp on one bitten apple stung him, and he felt the passion of sudden, severe pain. For this too brought its curious reflexions; and, in relief from it, he would wonder over it—how it had then been with him—puzzled at the depth of the charm or spell over him, which lay, for a little while at least, in the mere absence of pain; once, especially, when an older boy taught him to make flowers of sealing-wax, and he had burnt his hand badly at the lighted taper, and been unable to sleep. He remembered that also afterwards, as a sort of typical thing —a white vision of heat about him, clinging closely, through the languid scent of the ointments put upon the place to make it well.

Also, as he felt this pressure upon him of the sensible world, then, as often afterwards, there would come another sort of curious questioning how the last impressions of eye and ear might happen to him, how they would find him—the scent of the last flower, the soft yellowness of the last morning, the last recognition of some object of affection, hand or voice; it could not be but that the latest look of the eyes, before their final closing, would be strangely vivid; one would go with the hot tears, the cry, the touch of the wistful bystander, impressed how deeply on one! or would it be, perhaps, a mere frail retiring of all things, great or little, away from one, into a level distance?

For with this desire of physical beauty mingled itself early the fear of death—the fear of death intensified by the desire of beauty. Hitherto he had never gazed upon dead faces, as sometimes, afterwards, at the *Morgue* in Paris, or in that fair cemetery at Munich, where all the dead must go and lie in state before burial, behind glass windows, among the flowers and incense and holy candles—the aged clergy with their sacred ornaments, the young men in their dancing-shoes and spotless white linen— after which visits, those waxen, resistless faces

would always live with him for many days, making the broadest sunshine sickly. The child had heard indeed of the death of his father, and how, in the Indian station, a fever had taken him, so that though not in action he had yet died as a soldier; and hearing of the "resurrection of the just," he could think of him as still abroad in the world, somehow, for his protection—a grand, though perhaps rather terrible figure, in beautiful soldier's things, like the figure in the picture of Joshua's Vision in the Bible —and of that, round which the mourners moved so softly, and afterwards with such solemn singing, as but a worn-out garment left at a deserted lodging. So it was, until on a summer day he walked with his mother through a fair churchyard. In a bright dress he rambled among the graves, in the gay weather, and so came, in one corner, upon an open grave for a child—a dark space on the brilliant grass—the black mould heaped up round it, weighing down the little jewelled branches of the dwarf rose-bushes in flower. And therewith came, full-grown, never wholly to leave him, with the certainty that even children do sometimes die, the physical horror of death, with its wholly selfish recoil from the association of lower forms of life, and the suffocating weight above. No benign, grave figure in beautiful soldier's things any longer abroad in the world for his protection! only a few poor, piteous bones; and above them, possibly, a certain sort of figure he hoped not to see. For sitting one day in the garden below an open window, he heard people talking, and could not but listen, how, in a sleepless hour, a sick woman had seen one of the dead sitting beside her, come to call her hence; and from the broken talk evolved with much clearness the notion that not all those dead people had really departed to the churchyard, nor were quite so motionless as they looked, but led a secret, half-fugitive life in their old homes, quite free by night, though sometimes visible in the day, dodging from room to room, with no great goodwill towards those who shared the place with them. All night the figure sat beside him in the reveries of his broken sleep, and was not quite gone in the morning—an odd, irreconcileable new member of the household, making the sweet familiar chambers unfriendly and suspect by its uncertain presence. He could have hated the dead he had pitied so, for being thus. Afterwards he came to think of those poor, home-returning ghosts, which all men have fancied to themselves—the *revenants*— pathetically, as crying, or beating with vain hands

6. **"resurrection of the just."** See Luke 14:14.   **10. Joshua's Vision.** See Joshua 6:13–15.   **50. revenants,** returners (from the dead).

Hopkins (Oxford University Press, 1931) is now standard. A two-volume edition of his correspondence—Vol. I. *Letters to Robert Bridges;* Vol. II. *Correspondence with Richard Watson Dixon*—was issued by the same house in 1935; in 1938 this was supplemented by *Further Letters*, which includes the correspondence with Coventry Patmore.

HEAVEN–HAVEN[1]

A NUN TAKES THE VEIL

I have desired to go
    Where springs not fail,
To fields where flies no sharp and sided hail
    And a few lilies blow.

And I have asked to be
    Where no storms come,
Where the green swell is in the havens dumb,
    And out of the swing of the sea.

THE HABIT OF PERFECTION

Elected Silence, sing to me
And beat upon my whorlèd ear,
Pipe me to pastures still and be
The music that I care to hear.

Shape nothing, lips; be lovely-dumb:
It is the shut, the curfew sent
From there where all surrenders come
Which only makes you eloquent.

Be shellèd, eyes, with double dark
And find the uncreated light: 10
This ruck and reel which you remark
Coils, keeps, and teases simple sight.

Palate, the hutch of tasty lust,
Desire not to be rinsed with wine:
The can must be so sweet, the crust
So fresh that come in fasts divine!

Nostrils, your careless breath that spend
Upon the stir and keep of pride,
What relish shall the censers send
Along the sanctuary side!   20

O feel-of-primrose hands, O feet
That want the yield of plushy sward,
But you shall walk the golden street
And you unhouse and house the Lord.

And, Poverty, be thou the bride
And now the marriage feast begun,
And lily-coloured clothes provide
Your spouse not laboured-at nor spun.

THE SEA AND THE SKYLARK

On ear and ear two noises too old to end
    Trench—right, the tide that ramps against the
        shore;
    With a flood or a fall, low lull-off or all roar,
Frequenting there while moon shall wear and wend.

Left hand, off land, I hear the lark ascend,
    His rash-fresh re-winded new-skeinèd score
    In crisps of curl off wild winch whirl, and pour
And pelt music, till none's to spill nor spend.

How these two shame this shallow and frail town!
    How ring right out our sordid turbid time,   10
Being pure! We, life's pride and cared-for crown,

    Have lost that cheer and charm of earth's past
        prime:
Our make and making break, are breaking, down
    To man's last dust, drain fast towards man's first
        slime.

GOD'S GRANDEUR

The world is charged with the grandeur of God.
    It will flame out, like shining from shook foil;
    It gathers to a greatness, like the ooze of oil
Crushed. Why do men then now not reck his rod?
Generations have trod, have trod, have trod;
    And all is seared with trade; bleared, smeared
        with toil;
    And wears man's smudge and shares man's smell:
        the soil
Is bare now, nor can foot feel, being shod.

And for all this, nature is never spent;
    There lives the dearest freshness deep down
        things;   10
And though the last lights off the black West went
    Oh, morning, at the brown brink eastward,
        springs—

[1] This and the following selections are from the *Poems of Gerard Manley Hopkins*, Oxford University Press. They are reprinted by permission of the Press and the poet's family. **11. ruck and reel,** the confusion of the world.

23. you, his feet. **the golden street,** in heaven. **27–28. lily-coloured . . . spun.** See Matthew 6:28–29. *God's Grandeur.* **3–4. oil Crushed,** from olives.

Because the Holy Ghost over the bent
  World broods with warm breast and with ah!
  bright wings.

HURRAHING IN THE HARVEST

Summer ends now; now, barbarous in beauty, the
  stooks arise
  Around; up above, what wind-walks! what
  lovely behaviour
  Of silk-sack clouds! has wilder, wilful-wavier
Meal-drift moulded ever and melted across
  skies?

I walk, I lift up, I lift up heart, eyes,
  Down all that glory in the heavens to glean our
  Saviour;
  And, éyes, heárt, what looks, what lips yet gave
  you a
Rapturous love's greeting of realer, of rounder re-
  plies?

And the azurous hung hills are his world-wielding
  shoulder
  Majestic—as a stallion stalwart, very-violet-
  sweet!—   10
These things, these things were here and but the be-
  holder
  Wanting; which two when they once meet,
The heart rears wings bold and bolder
  And hurls for him, O half hurls earth for him off
  under his feet.

THE WINDHOVER

To Christ Our Lord

I caught this morning morning's minion, kingdom
  of daylight's dauphin, dapple-dawn-drawn
  Falcon, in his riding
Of the rolling level underneath him steady air,
  and striding
High there, how he rung upon the rein of a wim-
  pling wing
In his ecstasy! then off, off forth on swing,
  As a skate's heel sweeps smooth on a bow-bend:
  the hurl and gliding

Hurrahing in the Harvest. **1. stooks,** shocks of corn. *Wind-*
hover, sparrow hawk.   *To Christ Our Lord.* Possibly because Hopkins considered this his best poem. **1. kingdom**
of daylight's dauphin, miniature sun. **2. rolling level un-**
derneath him steady air, the steady air rolling level underneath him.   **3. rung upon the rein.** A horse is rung upon
the rein when caused to walk around its trainer on a long
rein. **wimpling,** rippling.

Rebuffed the big wind. My heart in hiding
Stirred for a bird,—the achieve of, the mastery of
  the thing!

Brute beauty and valour and act, oh, air, pride,
  plume, here
  Buckle! AND the fire that breaks from thee then, a
  billion
Times told lovelier, more dangerous, O my chevalier!

No wonder of it: shéer plód makes plough down
  sillion
Shine, and blue-bleak embers, ah my dear,
  Fall, gall themselves, and gash gold-vermilion.

PIED BEAUTY

Glory be to God for dappled things—
  For skies of couple-colour as a brinded cow;
    For rose-moles all in stipple upon trout that
    swim;
Fresh-firecoal chestnut-falls; finches' wings;
  Landscape plotted and pieced—fold, fallow, and
    plough;
    And áll trádes, their gear and tackle and trim.

All things counter, original, spare, strange;
  Whatever is fickle, freckled (who knows how?)
    With swift, slow; sweet, sour; adazzle, dim;
He fathers-forth whose beauty is past change:
                Praise him.   10

The Windhover. **6. My heart in hiding.** "Why in hiding?
Hiding from what? Does this link up with 'a billion times told
lovelier, more dangerous, O my chevalier!'? What is the
greater danger and what the less? I should say the poet's heart
is in hiding from Life, has chosen a safer way, and that the
greater danger is the greater exposure to temptation and error
than a more adventurous, less sheltered course (sheltered by
Faith?) brings with it. Another, equally plausible reading
would be this: Renouncing the glamour of the outer life of
adventure the poet transfers its qualities of audacity to the
inner life. (*Here* is the bosom, the inner consciousness.)
The greater danger is that to which the moral hero is exposed. Both readings may be combined, but pages of prose
would be required for a paraphrase of the result. The last
three lines carry the thought of the achievement possible
through renunciation further, and explain, with the image of
the ash-covered fire, why the dangers of the inner life are
greater." (I. A. Richards, "Gerard Hopkins," *Dial*, Vol.
LXXXI (1926), pp. 195–203. This article has been very
useful in glossing "The Windhover.") **10. O my cheva-**
lier! Richards conjectures that it refers not to Christ but
"only to the poet, though the moral ideal, embodied of course
for Hopkins in Christ, is before the mind." **11. plough**
down sillion, sillion (the ridge between two furrows) turned
down by a plough. *Pied Beauty.* **2. couple-colour.** 2
colors. **3. rose-moles all in stipple.** The rose-colored dots
look as if they had been stippled in.   **4. chestnut-falls,**
chestnuts stripped of their husks.   **6. trim,** equipment.
7. counter, in opposition. **spare,** rare.

THE CAGED SKYLARK

As a dare-gale skylark scanted in a dull cage
   Man's mounting spirit in his bone-house, mean
      house, dwells—
   That bird beyond the remembering his free fells;
This in drudgery, day-labouring-out life's age.

Though aloft on turf or perch or poor low stage,
   Both sing sometímes the sweetest, sweetest spells,
   Yet both droop deadly sómetimes in their cells
Or wring their barriers in bursts of fear or rage.

Not that sweet-fowl, the song-fowl, needs no rest—
Why, hear him, hear him babble and drop down to
      his nest,   10
   But his own nest, wild nest, no prison.

Man's spirit will be flesh-bound when found at best,
But uncumbered: meadow-down is not distressed
   For a rainbow footing it nor he for his bónes rísen.

SONNETS

MY OWN HEART LET ME MORE HAVE PITY ON

My own heart let me have more pity on; let
   Me live to my sad self hereafter kind,
   Charitable; not live this tormented mind
With this tormented mind tormenting yet.
   I cast for comfort I can no more get

By groping round my comfortless, than blind
Eyes in their dark can day or thirst can find
Thirst's all-in-all in all a world of wet.

Soul, self; come, poor Jackself, I do advise
You, jaded, let be; call off thoughts awhile   10
Elsewhere; leave comfort root-room; let joy size
At God knows when to God knows what; whose
   smile
's not wrung, see you; unforeseen time rather—as
   skies
Betweenpie mountains—lights a lovely mile.

THOU ART INDEED JUST, LORD

*Justus quidem tu es, Domine, si disputem tecum: verum-
tamen justa loquar ad te: Quare via impiorum prosperatur?
&c.*

Thou art indeed just, Lord, if I contend
With thee; but, sir, so what I plead is just.
Why do sinners' ways prosper? and why must
Disappointment all I endeavour end?
   Wert thou my enemy, O thou my friend,
How wouldst thou worse, I wonder, than thou dost
Defeat, thwart me? Oh, the sots and thralls of lust
Do in spare hours more thrive than I that spend,
Sir, life upon thy cause. See, banks and brakes
Now, leavèd how thick! lacèd they are again   10
With fretty chervil, look, and fresh wind shakes
Them; birds build—but not I build; no, but strain,
Time's eunuch, and not breed one work that wakes.
Mine, O thou lord of life, send my roots rain.

Robert Louis Stevenson
1850–1894

Robert Louis Stevenson was one of the most versatile writers of his time; beginning with his own experiences in living (*An Inland Voyage,* 1878; *Travels with a Donkey,* 1879) and in reading (*Virginibus Puerisque,* 1881; *Familiar Studies of Men and Books,* 1882), he worked his way out and back (into the past) until he had written almost every kind of book that a man can write. His first long fiction was *Treasure Island,* 1883, written ostensibly for the amusement of his stepson, Lloyd Osbourne, and still the finest example in English literature of the "penny dreadful" raised to the level of fine art. R.L.S. won his popularity slowly; *Strange Case of Dr. Jekyll and Mr. Hyde,* 1886, which is half

pseudo-science and half supernaturalism, was the earliest book to enjoy a huge sale. The same year produced *Kidnapped,* a story of adventure in the Highlands and elsewhere; the boy hero, David Bal-

My Own Heart Let Me More Have Pity On. **6. comfortless.**
"I have added the comma after *comfortless;* that word has
the same grammatical value as *dark* in the following line.
'I cast for comfort, (which) I can no more find in my comfortless (world) than a blind man in his dark world. . . .'"
(Bridges) **14. betweenpie,** "a strange word, in which *pie*
apparently makes a compound verb with *between,* meaning
'as the sky seen between dark mountains is brightly
dappled,' the grammar such as *intervariegates* would make.
This word might have delighted William Barnes, if the
verb 'to pie' existed." (Bridges). *Thou Art Indeed Just,
Lord.* **Justus quidem . . .** Jeremiah 12:1, quoted from the
Vulgate.

four, is somewhat overshadowed by Alan Breck, who contends with the pirate John Silver, of *Treasure Island*, as Stevenson's most famous character. David's adventures were later continued into early manhood in *David Balfour* (entitled *Catriona* in England), which R.L.S. published the year of his death. *The Master of Ballantrae*, 1889, is the most ambitious of his completed novels, but it would probably have been surpassed by *Weir of Hermiston*, 1896, if Stevenson had lived to finish it; as it stands, *Weir* is a magnificent fragment. Less successful experiments included *Prince Otto*, 1885, an imitation of Meredith's *Adventures of Harry Richmond*, and *The Black Arrow*, 1888, a romance of the Wars of the Roses, which is merely a good story for adolescents.

Stevenson's was a personality of extraordinary complexity and charm, at once Puritan and bohemian. The boy who loved harlots in the slums of his native Edinburgh lived to write the beautiful *Vailima Prayers*. He had been expected to follow the ancestral profession of lighthouse engineer, but ill-health combined with a rebellious spirit to prevent this. His apprenticeship to the law was only half-hearted; he had the writing urge if any man ever had it, and he began to write before he had anything to say, training himself by careful imitation of his favorite authors. Like many consumptives, he had a vast hunger for life. He never coddled himself, but his illness drove him to cross the world in search of a favorable climate, and finally landed him at Samoa, where he was well enough to plant a small wilderness and make himself persona non grata to the nations which cherished imperialistic interests in the South Seas. No doubt his dauntless courage was an important element in the spell R.L.S. cast over thousands of readers who, though they never looked upon his face, yet came to think of him less as an author than as a friend.

Like his friend Henry James, Stevenson helped English readers to begin to take the novel seriously as a work of art, but unlike Henry James, he was a romanticist. His critical essays achieved a stirring restatement of the case for romanticism in terms which his contemporaries could understand; this was his most important critical service. He had an important affinity not only with the Scottish "Kailyard school" of which J. M. Barrie was the most distinguished member but with many other romancers. (See the introductory note to "A Gossip on Romance," page 889.) Stevenson's romanticism was closely associated with his general philosophical attitude. (See the introductory note to "Pulvis et Umbra," page 895.)

THE CELESTIAL SURGEON[1]

If I have faltered more or less
In my great task of happiness;
If I have moved among my race
And shown no glorious morning face;
If beams from happy human eyes
Have moved me not; if morning skies,
Books, and my food, and summer rain
Knocked on my sullen heart in vain:—
Lord, Thy most pointed pleasure take
And stab my spirit broad awake;   10
Or, Lord, if too obdurate I,
Choose Thou, before that spirit die,
A piercing pain, a killing sin,
And to my dead heart run them in!

IN THE STATES

With half a heart I wander here
    As from an age gone by,
A brother—yet though young in years,
    An elder brother, I.

You speak another tongue than mine,
    Though both were English born.
I towards the night of time decline,
    You mount into the morn.

Youth shall grow great and strong and free,
    But age must still decay: 10
To-morrow for the States,—for me,
    England and Yesterday.

THE SPAEWIFE

O, I wad like to ken—to the beggar-wife says I—
Why chops are guid to brander and nane sae guid to fry,
An' siller, that's sae braw to keep, is brawer still to gi'e.
—*It's gey an' easy speirin'*, says the beggar-wife to me.

O, I wad like to ken—to the beggar-wife says I—
Hoo a' things come to be whaur we find them when we try,

[1] This and the following selections by Robert Louis Stevenson are reprinted by permission of Charles Scribner's Sons. *Spaewife*, fortune-teller.   2. **brander**, broil on a gridiron. 3. **siller**, money.   **braw**, good.   4. It's . . . **speirin'**. It's easy enough to ask.

The lasses in their claes an' the fishes in the sea.
—*It's gey an' easy speirin'*, says the beggar-wife to
me.

O, I wad like to ken—to the beggar-wife says I—
Why lads are a' to sell an' lasses a' to buy;   10
An' naebody for dacency but barely twa or three.
—*It's gey an' easy speirin'*, says the beggar-wife to
me.

O, I wad like to ken—to the beggar-wife says I—
Gin death's as shüre to men as killin' is to kye,
Why God has filled the yearth sae fu' o' tasty
things to pree.
—*It's gey an' easy speirin'*, says the beggar-wife to
me.

O, I wad like to ken—to the beggar-wife says I—
The reason o' the cause an' the wherefore o' the
why,
Wi' mony anither riddle brings the tear into my
e'e.   19
—*It's gey an' easy speirin'*, says the beggar-wife to
me.

MY WIFE

Stevenson met Fanny Van de Grift Osbourne, an
American woman living apart from her husband, in
France in 1876; she was later divorced, and they were
married in San Francisco in 1880. Between these two
dates fell some of Stevenson's saddest experiences; he
broke with his family to go to Mrs. Osbourne, and he almost starved to death in San Francisco before their problem was finally worked out (see *The Amateur Emigrant*,
1895; *Across the Plains*, 1892).

Mrs. Stevenson was a vivid, forceful personality, and
her influence on her husband was great. As to its nature
and quality there has been much controversy among recent writers on Stevenson, and not all the evidence is in
yet. With her he wrote *More Arabian Nights*, 1885; with
her son, Lloyd, *The Wrong Box*, 1889, *The Wrecker*, 1892,
The Ebb-Tide, 1894.

Trusty, dusky, vivid, true,
With eyes of gold and bramble-dew,
Steel-true and blade-straight,
The great artificer
Made my mate.

Honour, anger, valour, fire;
A love that life could never tire,
Death quench or evil stir,
The mighty master
Gave to her.   10

The Spaewife. **7. claes,** clothes. **14. Gin,** if. **15. pree,**
taste.

Teacher, tender, comrade, wife,
A fellow-farer true through life,
Heart-whole and soul-free
The august father
Gave to me.

BRIGHT IS THE RING OF WORDS

Bright is the ring of words
When the right man rings them,
Fair the fall of songs
When the singer sings them.
Still they are carolled and said—
On wings they are carrièd—
After the singer is dead
And the maker buried.

Low as the singer lies
In the field of heather,   10
Songs of his fashion bring
The swains together.
And when the west is red
With the sunset embers,
The lover lingers and sings
And the maid remembers.

SING ME A SONG

Sing me a song of a lad that is gone,
Say, could that lad be I?
Merry of soul he sailed on a day
Over the sea to Skye.

Mull was astern, Rum on the port,
Egg on the starboard bow;
Glory of youth glowed in his soul:
Where is that glory now?

Sing me a song of a lad that is gone,
Say, could that lad be I?   10
Merry of soul he sailed on a day
Over the sea to Skye.

Give me again all that was there,
Give me the sun that shone!
Give me the eyes, give me the soul,
Give me the lad that's gone!

Sing me a song of a lad that is gone,
Say, could that lad be I?

Sing Me A Song. **5–6. Mull . . . Egg,** islands off the western coast of Scotland.

Merry of soul he sailed on a day
  Over the sea to Skye.   20

Billow and breeze, islands and seas,
  Mountains of rain and sun,
All that was good, all that was fair,
  All that was me is gone.

REQUIEM

Under the wide and starry sky,
  Dig the grave and let me lie.
Glad did I live and gladly die,
  And I laid me down with a will.

This be the verse you grave for me:
  Here he lies where he longed to be;
Home is the sailor, home from sea,
  And the hunter home from the hill.

THRAWN JANET

"Thrawn Janet," written in Lowland Scots, is in the classic tradition of Scottish diablerie, and Janet is "by far the most common of names for witch-wives." Moreover, "There are several cases recorded of warlocks awaiting execution in their cells, who were found with their necks 'thrawn,' hanging by the thinnest of tapes, and with other circumstances that demonstrated beyond a doubt that the Devil had done the deed, either to preclude all possible confessions from the victim or to punish him for confessions or renunciations already made." See Douglas Percy Bliss, *The Devil in Scotland*, Macmillan, 1934, which, alongside the essay on "The Devil and His Folk in Scottish Life and Literature," from which the foregoing quotations have been made, reprints, with handsome woodcut illustrations by Mr. Bliss, Burns's "Tam o' Shanter," Scott's "Wandering Willie's Tale," and two stories by Stevenson, "Thrawn Janet" and "The Tale of Tod Lapraik" (from *David Balfour*).

Stevenson has recorded that when he wrote "Thrawn Janet" it "frightened him to death," and he generally considered it one of his finest achievements. His critics seem nearly unanimous in placing it first among his achievements in the short story.

THE REVEREND MURDOCH SOULIS was long minister of the moorland parish of Balweary, in the vale of Dule. A severe, bleak-faced old man, dreadful to his hearers, he dwelt in the last years of his life, without relative or servant or any human company, in the small and lonely manse under the Hanging Shaw. In spite of the iron composure of his

53. **Shaw,** wood.

features, his eye was wild, scared, and uncertain; and when he dwelt, in private admonitions, on the future of the impenitent, it seemed as if his eye pierced through the storms of time to the terrors of eternity. Many young persons, coming to prepare themselves against the season of the Holy Communion, were dreadfully affected by his talk. He had a sermon on 1st Peter, v. and 8th, "The devil as a roaring lion," on the Sunday after every seventeenth of August, 10 and he was accustomed to surpass himself upon that text both by the appalling nature of the matter and the terror of his bearing in the pulpit. The children were frightened into fits, and the old looked more than usually oracular, and were, all that day, full of those hints that Hamlet deprecated. The manse itself, where it stood by the water of Dule among some thick trees, with the Shaw overhanging it on the one side, and on the other many cold, moorish hilltops rising towards the sky, had begun, at a very early 20 period of Mr. Soulis's ministry, to be avoided in the dusk hours by all who valued themselves upon their prudence; and guidmen sitting at the clachan alehouse shook their heads together at the thought of passing late by that uncanny neighbourhood. There was one spot, to be more particular, which was regarded with especial awe. The manse stood between the high-road and the water of Dule, with a gable to each; its back was towards the kirktown of Balweary, nearly half a mile away; in front of it, a bare 30 garden, hedged with thorn, occupied the land between the river and the road. The house was two stories high, with two large rooms on each. It opened not directly on the garden, but on a causewayed path, or passage, giving on the road on the one hand, and closed on the other by the tall willows and elders that bordered on the stream. And it was this strip of causeway that enjoyed among the young parishioners of Balweary so infamous a reputation. The minister walked there often after dark, 40 sometimes groaning aloud in the instancy of his unspoken prayers; and when he was far from home, and the manse door was locked, the more daring schoolboys ventured, with beating hearts, to "follow my leader" across that legendary spot.

This atmosphere of terror, surrounding, as it did, a man of God of spotless character and orthodoxy, was a common cause of wonder and subject of inquiry among the few strangers who were led by chance or business into that unknown, outlying 50 country. But many even of the people of the parish

15. **hints that Hamlet deprecated,** an obscure reference. The word "hint" does not occur in *Hamlet*. I do not know what passage Stevenson had in mind.   22. **clachan,** a small village around a church, a hamlet.

were ignorant of the strange events which had marked the first year of Mr. Soulis's ministrations; and among those who were better informed, some were naturally reticent, and others shy of that particular topic. Now and again, only, one of the older folk would warm into courage over his third tumbler, and recount the cause of the minister's strange looks and solitary life.

Fifty years syne, when Mr. Soulis cam' first into Ba'weary, he was still a young man—a callant, the folk said—fu' o' book-learnin' and grand at the exposition, but, as was natural in sae young a man, wi' nae leevin' experience in religion. The younger sort were greatly taken wi' his gifts and his gab; but auld, concerned, serious men and women were moved even to prayer for the young man, whom they took to be a self-deceiver, and the parish that was like to be sae ill-supplied. It was before the days o' the Moderates—weary fa' them; but ill things are like guid—they baith come bit by bit, a pickle at a time; and there were folk even then that said the Lord had left the college professors to their ain devices, an' the lads that went to study wi' them wad hae done mair and better sittin' in a peat-bog, like their forebears of the persecution, wi' a Bible under their oxter and a speerit o' prayer in their heart. There was nae doubt, onyway, but that Mr. Soulis had been ower lang at the college. He was careful and troubled for many things besides the ae thing needful. He had a feck o' books wi' him—mair than had ever been seen before in a' that presbytery; and a sair wark the carrier had wi' them, for they were a' like to have smoored in the De'il's Hag between this and Kilmackerlie. They were books o' divinity, to be sure, or so they ca'd them; but the serious were o' opinion there was little service for sae mony, when the hail o' God's Word would gang in the neuk of a plaid. Then he wad sit half the day, an' half the nicht forbye, which was scant decent—writin', nae less; an' first, they were feared he wad read his sermons; and syne it proved he was writin' a book himsel', which was surely no fittin' for ane of his years an' sma' experience.

Onyway it behoved him to get an auld, decent wife to keep the manse for him an' see to his bit denners; an' he was recommended to an auld limmer—Janet M'Clour, they ca'd her—an' sae far left to himsel' as to be ower persuaded. There was mony advised him to the contrar, for Janet was mair than suspeckit by the best folk in Ba'weary. Lang or that, she had had a wean to a dragoon; she hadnae come forrit for maybe thretty year; and bairns had seen her mumblin' to hersel' up on Key's Loan in the gloamin', whilk was an unco time an' place for a God-fearin' woman. Howsoever, it was the laird himsel' that had first tauld the minister o' Janet; and in thae days he wad have gane a far gate to pleesure the laird. When folk tauld him that Janet was sib to the de'il, it was a' superstition by his way o' it; an' when they cast up the Bible to him an' the witch o' Endor, he wad threep it doun their thrapples that thir days were a' gane by, an' the de'il was mercifully restrained.

Weel, when it got about the clachan that Janet M'Clour was to be servant at the manse, the folk were fair mad wi' her an' him thegither; an' some o' the guidwives had nae better to dae than get round her door-cheeks and chairge her wi' a' that was ken't again' her, frae the sodger's bairn to John Tamson's twa kye. She was nae great speaker; folk usually let her gang her ain gate, an' she let them gang theirs, wi' neither Fair-guid-een nor Fair-guid-day; but when she buckled to, she had a tongue to deave the miller. Up she got, an' there wasna an auld story in Ba'weary but she gart somebody lowp for it that day; they couldnae say ae thing but she could say twa to it; till, at the hinder end, the guidwives up and claught haud of her, and clawed the coats aff her back, and pu'd her doun the clachan to the water o' Dule, to see if she were a witch or no, soum or droun. The carline skirled till ye could hear her at the Hangin' Shaw, and she focht like ten; there was mony a guidwife bure the mark of her neist day an' mony a lang day after; and just in the

10. **syne**, ago.   11. **callant**, stripling.   12–13. **exposition**, of the Scriptures.   20. **Moderates**, a party in the Church of Scotland inclined to look somewhat tolerantly upon beliefs and practices violating strict Calvinistic doctrine and discipline.   20. **weary fa' them**, woe befall them.   21. **a pickle**, a little.   26. **of the persecution**, Calvinists oppressed by non-Calvinists in control of the government.   26–27. **under their oxter**, under their armpit.   29–31. **He was . . . needful**, an echo of Jesus' rebuke to Martha in Luke 10:41–42.   31. **feck**, quantity.   34. **smoored**, smothered.   34. **Hag**, a pit in moss ground.   38. **neuk**, corner (nook).   40. **forbye**, besides.   42. **syne**, here, then.

1. **wife**, woman, not a wife for himself.   2–3. **limmer**, hussy, jade, a rather loose term of reproach.   7. **Lang or that**, long before that.   7. **wean**, baby.   8. **come forrit**, "to offer oneself as a communicant." (Stevenson)   9. **bairns**, children.   10. **whilk**, which.   10. **unco**, strange, remarkable.   13. **he wad have gane a far gate**, he would have gone a great distance.   15. **sib to the de'il**, kin to the devil.   17. **witch o' Endor**. See 1 Samuel 28:7–25.   17–18. **threep it doun their thrapples**, vehemently affirm it and thrust it down their throats.   18. **thir days**, that is, of the Old Testament dispensation.   24. **cheeks**, sides.   25–26. **John Tamson's twa kye**, upon which Janet, being suspected of witchcraft, was no doubt accused of having cast a spell.   27. **gang her ain gate**, go her own way.   30. **deave**, deafen.   31. **gart**, caused.   31. **lowp**, jump.   37. **soum or droun**. If she "soumed" (swam), she was a witch, the belief being that the water would not receive such a creature unto itself.   37. **carline**, beldam.   37. **skirled**, screeched.

hettest o' the collieshangie, wha suld come up (for his sins) but the new minister!

"Women," said he (and he had a grand voice), "I charge you in the Lord's name to let her go."

Janet ran to him—she was fair wud wi' terror—an' clang to him, an' prayed him, for Christ's sake, save her frae the cummers; an' they, for their pairt, tauld him a' that was ken't, and maybe mair.

"Woman," says he to Janet, "is this true?"

"As the Lord sees me," says she, "as the Lord 10 made me, no a word o't. Forbye the bairn," says she, "I've been a decent woman a' my days."

"Will you," says Mr. Soulis, "in the name of God, and before me, His unworthy minister, renounce the devil and his works?"

Weel, it wad appear that when he askit that, she gave a girn that fairly frichtit them that saw her, an' they could hear her teeth play dirl thegither in her chafts; but there was naething for't but the ae way or the ither; an' Janet lifted up her hand and re- 20 nounced the de'il before them a'.

"And now," says Mr. Soulis to the guidwives, "home with ye, one and all, and pray to God for His forgiveness."

An' he gied Janet his arm, though she had little on her but a sark, and took her up the clachan to her ain door like a leddy of the land; an' her screighin' and laughin' as was a scandal to be heard.

There were mony grave folk lang ower their pray- 30 ers that nicht; but when the morn cam' there was sic a fear fell upon a' Ba'weary that the bairns hid theirsels, and even the men-folk stood and keekit frae their doors. For there was Janet comin' doun the clachan—her or her likeness, nane could tell—wi' her neck thrawn, and her heid on ae side, like a body that has been hangit, and a girn on her face like an unstreakit corp. By an' by they got used wi' it, and even speered at her to ken what was wrang; but frae that day forth she couldna speak like a 40 Christian woman, but slavered and played click wi' her teeth like a pair o' shears; and frae that day forth the name o' God cam' never on her lips. Whiles she wad try to say it, but it michtna be. Them that kenned best said least; but they never gied that Thing the name o' Janet M'Clour; for the auld Janet, by their way o't, was in muckle hell that day. But the minister was neither to haud nor to bind; he

preached about naething but the folk's cruelty that had gi'en her a stroke of the palsy; he skelpit the bairns that meddled her; an' he had her up to the manse that same nicht, and dwalled there a' his lane wi' her under the Hangin' Shaw.

Weel, time gaed by: and the idler sort commenced to think mair lichtly o' that black business. The minister was weel thocht o'; he was aye late at the writing, folk wad see his can'le doon by the Dule water after twal' at e'en; an' he seemed pleased wi' himsel' and upsitten as at first, though a'body could see that he was dwining. As for Janet she cam' an' she gaed; if she didna speak muckle afore, it was reason she should speak less then; she meddled naebody; but she was an eldritch thing to see, an' nane wad hae mistrysted wi' her for Ba'weary glebe.

About the end o' July there cam' a spell o' weather, the like o't never was in that countryside; it was lown an' het an' heartless; the herds couldna win up the Black Hill, the bairns were ower weariet to play; an' yet it was gousty too, wi' claps o' het wund that rumm'led in the glens, and bits o' shouers that slockened naething. We aye thocht it büt to thun'er on the morn; but the morn cam', an' the morn's morning, and it was aye the same uncanny weather, sair on folks and bestial. O' a' that were the waur, nane suffered like Mr. Soulis; he could neither sleep nor eat, he tauld his elders; an' when he wasna writin' at his weary book, he wad be stravaguin' ower a' the countryside like a man possessed, when a'body else was blythe to keep caller ben the house.

Abune Hangin' Shaw, in the bield o' the Black Hill, there's a bit enclosed grund wi' an iron yett; an' it seems, in the auld days, that was the kirkyaird o' Ba'weary, an' consecrated by the Papists before the blessed licht shone upon the kingdom. It was a great howff o' Mr. Soulis's, onyway; there he would sit an' consider his sermons; and indeed it's a bieldy bit. Weel, as he cam' ower the wast end o' the Black Hill ae day, he saw first twa, an' syne fower, an' syne seeven corbie craws fleein' round an' round abune the auld kirkyaird. They flew laigh and heavy, an' squawked to ither as they gaed; and it was clear to Mr. Soulis that something had put them frae their ordinar'. He wasna easy fleyed, an' gaed straucht up to the wa's; an' what suld he find there but a man, or the appearance o' a man, sittin'

---

1. **collieshangie,** squabble.   5. **wud,** mad.   7. **cummers,** women, often used in an uncomplimentary sense. 17. **girn,** grin—showing the teeth in pain or rage, not joy. 18. **play dirl,** vibrate.   19. **chafts,** jaws.   25. **gied,** gave. 26. **sark,** shift.   28. **screighin',** screeching.   33. **keekit,** peeped.   36. **thrawn,** turned, twisted.   38. **unstreakit,** not laid out (unstretched).   39. **speered,** asked.   43. **Whiles,** at times.   47. **muckle,** much.   48. **haud.** hold.

2. **skelpit,** spanked.   12. **dwining,** wasting.   15. **eldritch,** unearthly.   16. **mistrysted,** broken an engagement. 20. **lown,** calm.   24. **slockened,** slaked.   31. **stravaguin',** wandering.   34. **bield,** shelter.   35. **yett,** gate.   39. **howff,** haunt.   43. **corbie,** raven.   44. **laigh,** low.   47. **fleyed,** frightened.

in the inside upon a grave. He was of a great stature, an' black as hell, and his e'en were singular to see. Mr. Soulis had heard tell o' black men, mony's the time; but there was something unco about this black man that daunted him. Het as he was, he took a kind o' cauld grue in the marrow o' his banes; but up he spak for a' that; an' says he: "My friend, are you a stranger in this place?" The black man answered never a word; he got upon his feet, an' begoud to hirsle to the wa' on the far side; but he aye lookit at the minister; an' the minister stood an' lookit back; till a' in a meenit the black man was ower the wa' an' rinnin' for the bield o' the trees. Mr. Soulis, he hardly kenned why, ran after him; but he was sair forjeskit wi' his walk an' the het, unhalesome weather; and rin as he likit, he got nae mair than a glisk o' the black man amang the birks, till he won doun to the foot o' the hillside, an' there he saw him ance mair, gaun, hap-step-an'-lowp ower Dule water to the manse.

Mr. Soulis wasna weel pleased that this fearsome gangrel suld mak' sae free wi' Ba'weary manse; an' he ran the harder, an', wet shoon, ower the burn, an' up the walk; but the deil a black man was there to see. He stepped out upon the road, but there was naebody there; he gaed a' ower the gairden, but na, nae black man. At the hinder end, and a bit feared as was but natural, he lifted the hasp an' into the manse; and there was Janet M'Clour before his een, wi' her thrawn craig, and nane sae pleased to see him. And he aye minded sinsyne, when first he set his een upon her, he had the same cauld and deidly grue.

"Janet," says he, "have you seen a black man?"

"A black man?" quo' she. "Save us a'! Ye're no wise, minister. There's nae black man in a' Ba'weary."

But she didna speak plain, ye maun understand; but yam-yammered, like a powney wi' the bit in its moo.

"Weel," says he, "Janet, if there was nae black man, I have spoken with the Accuser of the Brethren."

And he sat doun like ane wi' a fever, an' his teeth chittered in his heid.

"Hoots," says she, "think shame to yoursel', minister"; an' gied him a drap brandy that she keepit aye by her.

Syne Mr. Soulis gaed into his study amang a' his books. It's a lang, laigh, mirk chalmer, perishin' cauld in winter, an' no' very dry even in the tap o' the simmer, for the manse stands near the burn. Sae doun he sat, and thocht o' a' that had come an' gane since he was in Ba'weary, an' his hame, an' the days when he was a bairn an' ran daffin' on the braes; and that black man aye ran in his heid like the owercome o' a sang. Aye the mair he thocht, the mair he thocht o' the black man. He tried the prayer, an' the words wadna come to him; an' he tried, they say, to write at his book, but he couldna mak' nae mair o' that. There was whiles he thocht the black man was at his oxter, an' the swat stood upon him cauld as well-water; and there was other whiles, when he cam' to himsel' like a christened bairn an' minded naething.

The upshot was that he gaed to the window an' stood glowrin' at Dule water. The trees are unco thick, an' the water lies deep an' black under the manse; an' there was Janet washin' the cla'es wi' her coats kilted. She had her back to the minister, an' he, for his pairt, hardly kenned what he was lookin' at. Syne she turned round, an' shawed her face; Mr. Soulis had the same cauld grue as twice that day afore, an' it was borne in upon him what folk said, that Janet was deid lang syne, an' this was a bogle in her clay-cauld flesh. He drew back a pickle and he scanned her narrowly. She was tramp-trampin' in the cla'es, croonin' to hersel'; and eh! Gude guide us, but it was a fearsome face. Whiles she sang louder, but there was nae man born o' woman that could tell the words o' her sang; an' whiles she lookit side-lang doun, but there was naething there for her to look at. There gaed a scunner through the flesh upon his banes; and that was Heeven's advertisement. But Mr. Soulis just blamed himsel', he said, to think sae ill o' a puir, auld afflicted wife that hadna a freend forbye himsel'; an' he put up a bit prayer for him an' her, an' drank a little caller water—for his heart rose again' the meat—an' gaed up to his naked bed in the gloamin'.

That was a nicht that has never been forgotten in Ba'weary, the nicht o' the seventeenth o' August, seventeen hun'er' an' twal'. It had been het afore, as I hae said, but that nicht it was hetter than ever. The sun gaed doun amang unco-lookin' clouds; it fell as mirk as the pit; no' a star, no' a breath o' wund;

1–3. He was . . . to see. "It was a common belief in Scotland that the devil appeared as a black man. This appears in several witch trials and I think in Law's *Memorials*, that delightful store-house of the quaint and grisly." (Stevenson)   6. grue, goose flesh.   9–10. begoud, began.   10. hirsle, rustle.   15. forjeskit, tired out.   17. glisk, glance.   17. birks, birches.   19. gaun, hap-step-an'-lowp, going hop, step, and jump.   22. gangrel, vagrant.   23. burn, brook.   30. craig, throat.   31. sinsyne, since then, afterward.

9. daffin', larking.   10. braes, small hills.   24. coats kilted, skirts turned up.   37. scunner, shudder of loathing.   43. caller, cool.

ye couldna see your han' afore your face, and even the auld folk cuist the covers frae their beds and lay pechin' for their breath. Wi' a' that he had upon his mind, it was geyan unlikely Mr. Soulis wad get muckle sleep. He lay an' he tummled; the gude, caller bed that he got into brunt his very banes; whiles he slept, and whiles he waukened; whiles he heard the time o' nicht, and whiles a tyke yowlin' up the muir, as if somebody was deid; whiles he thocht he heard bogles claverin' in his lug, an' whiles he 10 saw spunkies in the room. He behoved, he judged, to be sick; an' sick he was—little he jaloosed the sickness.

At the hinder end he got a clearness in his mind, sat up in his sark on the bed-side, and fell thinkin' ance mair o' the black man an' Janet. He couldna weel tell how—maybe it was the cauld to his feet—but it cam' in upon him wi' a spate that there was some connection between thir twa, an' that either or baith o' them were bogles. An' just 20 at that moment, in Janet's room, which was neist to his, there cam' a stramp o' feet as if men were wars'lin', an' then a loud bang; an' then a wund gaed reishling round the fower quarters of the house; an' then a' was ance mair as seelent as the grave.

Mr. Soulis was feared for neither man nor deevil. He got his tinder-box, an' lit a can'le, an' made three steps o't ower to Janet's door. It was on the hasp, an' he pushed it open, an' keekit bauldly in. 30 It was a big room, as big as the minister's ain, an' plenished wi' grand, auld, solid gear, for he had naething else. There was a fower-posted bed wi' auld tapestry; and a braw cabinet o' aik, that was fu' o' the minister's divinity books, an' put there to be out o' the gate; an' a wheen duds o' Janet's lying here and there about the floor. But nae Janet could Mr. Soulis see; nor ony sign o' a contention. In he gaed (an' there's few that wad hae followed him) an' lookit a' round, an' listened. But there was nae- 40 thing to be heard, neither inside the manse nor in a' Ba'weary parish, an' naething to be seen but the muckle shadows turnin' round the can'le. An' then a' at aince the minister's heart played dunt an' stood stock-still; an' a cauld wund blew amang the hairs o' his heid. Whaten a weary sicht was that for the puir man's een! For there was Janet hangin' frae a nail beside the auld aik cabinet: her heid aye lay on her shouther, her een were steekit, the

tongue projected frae her mouth, an' her heels were twa feet clear abune the floor.

"God forgive us all!" thocht Mr. Soulis; "poor Janet's dead."

He cam' a step nearer to the corp; an' then his heart fair whammled in his inside. For, by what cantrip it wad ill beseem a man to judge, she was hingin' frae a single nail an' by a single wursted thread for darnin' hose.

It's an awfu' thing to be your lane at nicht wi' siccan prodigies o' darkness; but Mr. Soulis was strong in the Lord. He turned an' gaed his ways oot o' that room, and lockit the door ahint him; and step by step, doon the stairs, as heavy as leed; and set doon the can'le on the table at the stairfoot. He couldna pray, he couldna think, he was dreepin' wi' caul' swat, an' naething could he hear but the dunt-dunt-duntin' o' his ain heart. He micht maybe hae stood there an hour, or maybe twa, he minded sae little; when a' o' a sudden, he heard a laigh, uncanny steer upstairs; a foot gaed to an' fro in the chalmer whaur the corp was hingin'; syne the door was opened, though he minded weel that he had lockit it; an' syne there was a step upon the landin', an' it seemed to him as if the corp was lookin' ower the rail and doun upon him whaur he stood.

He took up the can'le again (for he couldna want the licht), an' as saftly as ever he could, gaed straucht oot o' the manse an' to the far end o' the causeway. It was aye pit-mirk; the flame o' the can'le, when he set it on the grund, brunt steedy and clear as in a room; naething moved, but the Dule water seepin' and sabbin' doon the glen, an' yon unhaly footstep than cam' ploddin' doon the stairs inside the manse. He kenned the foot ower weel, for it was Janet's; and at ilka step that cam' a wee thing nearer, the cauld got deeper in his vitals. He commended his soul to Him that made an' keepit him; "and, O Lord," said he, "give me strength this night to war against the powers of evil."

By this time the foot was comin' through the passage for the door; he could hear a hand skirt alang the wa', as if the fearsome thing was feelin' for its way. The saughs tossed an' maned thegither, a long sigh cam' ower the hills, the flame o' the can'le was blawn aboot; an' there stood the corp o' Thrawn Janet, wi' her grogram goun an' her black mutch, wi' the heid aye upon the shouther, an' the girn still 50 upon the face o't—leevin', ye wad hae said—deid,

3. **pechin'**, panting. 4. **geyan unlikely**, very unlikely. 8. **tyke**, dog. 10. **claverin'**, gossiping. 10. **lug**, ear. 11. **spunkies**, will-o'-the-wisps 12. **jaloosed**, suspected. 18. **spate**, flood. 36. **out o' the gate**, out of the way. 36. **wheen duds**, quantity of clothes. 44. **played dunt**, beat hard. 49. **steekit**, shut

6. **whammled**, turned upside down. 11. **siccan**, such. 21. **steer**, stir. 45. **saughs**, willows. 48. **grogram**, a coarse fabric of silk, mohair, and wool. 48. **mutch**, cap or coif.

as Mr. Soulis weel kenned—upon the threshold o' the manse.

It's a strange thing that the saul o' man should be that thirled into his perishable body; but the minister saw that, an' his heart didna break.

She didna stand there lang; she began to move again an' cam' slowly towards Mr. Soulis whaur he stood under the saughs. A' the life o' his body, a' the strength o' his speerit, were glowerin' frae his een. It seemed she was gaun to speak, but wanted words, an' made a sign wi' the left hand. There cam' a clap o' wund, like a cat's fuff; oot gaed the can'le, the saughs skreighed like folk; an' Mr. Soulis kenned that, live or die, this was the end o't.

"Witch, beldame, devil!" he cried, "I charge you, by the power of God, be gone—if you be dead, to the grave—if you be damned, to hell."

An' at that moment the Lord's ain hand out o' the Heevens struck the Horror whaur it stood; the auld, deid, desecrated corp o' the witch-wife, sae lang keepit frae the grave an' hirsled round by de'ils, lowed up like a brunstane spunk an' fell in ashes to the grund; the thunder followed, peal on dirlin' peal, the rairin' rain upon the back o' that; an' Mr. Soulis lowped through the garden hedge, an' ran, wi' skelloch upon skelloch, for the clachan.

That same mornin', John Christie saw the Black Man pass the Muckle Cairn as it was chappin' six; before eicht he gaed by the change-house at Knockdow; an' no' lang after, Sandy M'Lellan saw him gaun linkin' doun the braes frae Kilmackerlie. There's little doubt but it was him that dwalled sae lang in Janet's body; but he was awa' at last; and sinsyne the de'il has never fashed us in Ba'weary.

But it was a sair dispensation for the minister; lang, lang he lay ravin' in his bed; and frae that hour to this he was the man ye ken the day.

A GOSSIP ON ROMANCE

"The Lantern-Bearers" (in *Across the Plains*), "A Gossip on Romance," and "A Humble Remonstrance" (both in *Memories and Portraits*) are Stevenson's most important attempts as a critic to vindicate his love for romance. This was determined partly by his love of colorful and adventurous materials, but that was not the basic thing. He did not believe it possible for fiction to present life directly; it could only describe how somebody reacts to life. He hated "realism" and "naturalism" because they were based on the assumption that the business of the artist was to de-

scribe human experience without passion or prejudice from the outside. Since no life can be lived in this manner, it must necessarily follow that "realism" and "naturalism" are fundamentally and basically untrue.

This reasoned defense of romanticism has had considerable influence upon modern fiction. Stevenson helped make it possible for the romanticist to continue to take himself seriously as a literary artist. He showed that the assumptions at the root of the modern attack on romanticism are basically hostile to all imaginative writing, and helped prevent the theorizers from acquiring a stranglehold on the novel.

IN anything fit to be called by the name of reading, the process itself should be absorbing and voluptuous; we should gloat over a book, be rapt clean out of ourselves, and rise from the perusal, our mind filled with the busiest, kaleidoscopic dance of images, incapable of sleep or of continuous thought. The words, if the book be eloquent, should run thenceforward in our ears like the noise of breakers, and the story, if it be a story, repeat itself in a thousand coloured pictures to the eye. It was for this last pleasure that we read so closely, and loved our books so dearly, in the bright, troubled period of boyhood. Eloquence and thought, character and conversation, were but obstacles to brush aside as we dug blithely after a certain sort of incident, like a pig for truffles. For my part, I liked a story to begin with an old wayside inn where, "towards the close of the year 17—," several gentlemen in three-cocked hats were playing bowls. A friend of mine preferred the Malabar coast in a storm, with a ship beating to windward, and a scowling fellow of Herculean proportions striding along the beach; he, to be sure, was a pirate. This was further afield than my homekeeping fancy loved to travel, and designed altogether for a larger canvas than the tales that I affected. Give me a highwayman and I was full to the brim; a Jacobite would do, but the highwayman was my favourite dish. I can still hear that merry clatter of the hoofs along the moonlit lane; night and the coming of day are still related in my mind with the doings of John Rann or Jerry Abershaw; and the words "post-chaise," the "great North road,"

4. **thirled into,** drilled into, hence difficult to separate from. 12. **fuff,** puff. 22. **lowed,** flamed. 26. **skelloch,** shrill cry. 28. **chappin',** striking. 29. **change-house,** an inn where horses were changed. 31. **linkin',** tripping. 34. **fashed,** troubled.

32–33. **Malabar coast,** southwestern coast of India. 40. **Jacobite,** one loyal to the Stuarts after the revolution of 1688. The Jacobite rebellions of 1715 and 1745 in behalf of the Old Pretender (James III and VIII) and the Young Pretender (Bonnie Prince Charlie) respectively have been the favorite themes of Scotch romancers from Scott to John Buchan.   44. **John Rann or Jerry Abershaw,** well-known criminals, executed in 1774 and 1795 respectively. 45. **"great North road,"** a road leading out of London. Stevenson tried to catch the magic the phrase had for him in a novel, *The Great North Road*, which remained a fragment.

"ostler," and "nag" still sound in my ears like poetry. One and all, at least, and each with his particular fancy, we read story-books in childhood, not for eloquence or character or thought, but for some quality of the brute incident. That quality was not mere bloodshed or wonder. Although each of these was welcome in its place, the charm for the sake of which we read depended on something different from either. My elders used to read novels aloud; and I can still remember four different passages which I heard, before I was ten, with the same keen and lasting pleasure. One I discovered long afterwards to be the admirable opening of *What will He Do with It?*: it was no wonder that I was pleased with that. The other three still remain unidentified. One is a little vague; it was about a dark, tall house at night, and people groping on the stairs by the light that escaped from the open door of a sickroom. In another, a lover left a ball, and went walking in a cool, dewy park, whence he could watch the lighted windows and the figures of the dancers as they moved. This was the most sentimental impression I think I had yet received, for a child is somewhat deaf to the sentimental. In the last, a poet, who had been tragically wrangling with his wife, walked forth on the sea-beach on a tempestuous night and witnessed the horrors of a wreck. Different as they are, all these early favourites have a common note—they have all a touch of the romantic.

Drama is the poetry of conduct, romance the poetry of circumstance. The pleasure that we take in life is of two sorts—the active and the passive. Now we are conscious of a great command over our destiny; anon we are lifted up by circumstance, as by a breaking wave, and dashed we know not how into the future. Now we are pleased by our conduct, anon merely pleased by our surroundings. It would be hard to say which of these modes of satisfaction is the more effective, but the latter is surely the more constant. Conduct is three parts of life, they say; but I think they put it high. There is a vast deal in life and letters both which is not immoral, but simply non-moral; which either does not regard the human will at all, or deals with it in obvious and healthy relations; where the interest turns, not upon what a man shall choose to do, but on how he manages to do it; not on the passionate slips and hesitations of the conscience, but on the

problems of the body and of the practical intelligence, in clean, open-air adventure, the shock of arms or the diplomacy of life. With such material as this it is impossible to build a play, for the serious theatre exists solely on moral grounds, and is a standing proof of the dissemination of the human conscience. But it is possible to build, upon this ground, the most joyous of verses, and the most lively, beautiful, and buoyant tales.

One thing in life calls for another; there is a fitness in events and places. The sight of a pleasant arbour puts it in our mind to sit there. One place suggests work, another idleness, a third early rising and long rambles in the dew. The effect of night, of any flowing water, of lighted cities, of the peep of day, of ships, of the open ocean, calls up in the mind an army of anonymous desires and pleasures. Something, we feel, should happen; we know not what, yet we proceed in quest of it. And many of the happiest hours of life fleet by us in this vain attendance on the genius of the place and moment. It is thus that tracts of young fir, and low rocks that reach into deep soundings, particularly torture and delight me. Something must have happened in such places, and perhaps ages back, to members of my race; and when I was a child I tried in vain to invent appropriate games for them, as I still try, just as vainly, to fit them with the proper story. Some places speak distinctly. Certain dank gardens cry aloud for a murder; certain old houses demand to be haunted; certain coasts are set apart for shipwreck. Other spots again seem to abide their destiny, suggestive and impenetrable, "miching mallecho." The inn at Burford Bridge, with its arbours and green garden and silent, eddying river—though it is known already as the place where Keats wrote some of his *Endymion* and Nelson parted from his Emma—still seems to wait the coming of the appropriate legend. Within these ivied walls, behind these old green shutters, some further business smoulders, waiting for its hour. The old Hawes Inn at the Queen's Ferry makes a similar call upon my fancy. There it stands, apart from the town, beside the pier, in a climate of its own, half inland, half marine—in front, the ferry bubbling with the tide and the guardship swinging to her anchor; behind, the old garden with the trees. Americans seek it already for the sake of Lovel and Oldbuck, who

13–14. **What will He Do with It?** by Sir Edward Bulwer-Lytton, 1858.   24–28. **In the last . . . a wreck.** "Since traced by many obliging correspondents to the gallery of Charles Kingsley." (Stevenson) The novel is *Two Years Ago*, 1857.   42. **they.** See Matthew Arnold, *Literature and Dogma*, chap. 1.

34–35. **"miching mallecho,"** hidden mischief. See *Hamlet*, Act III, sc. 2, l. 147.   38–39. **Nelson parted from his Emma.** Horatio Nelson (1758–1805) loved Lady Hamilton (1761?–1815). See Marjorie Bowen, *Patriotic Lady*, Appleton-Century, 1936.

dined there at the beginning of the *Antiquary*. But you need not tell me—that is not all; there is some story, unrecorded or not yet complete, which must express the meaning of that inn more fully. So it is with names and faces; so it is with incidents that are idle and inconclusive in themselves; and yet seem like the beginning of some quaint romance, which the all-careless author leaves untold. How many of these romances have we not seen determine at their birth; how many people have met us with a look of meaning in their eye, and sunk at once into trivial acquaintances; to how many places have we not drawn near, with express intimations—"here my destiny awaits me"—and we have but dined there and passed on! I have lived both at the Hawes and Burford in a perpetual flutter, on the heels, as it seemed, of some adventure that should justify the place; but though the feeling had me to bed at night and called me again at morning in one unbroken round of pleasure and suspense, nothing befell me in either worth remark. The man or the hour had not yet come; but some day, I think, a boat shall put off from the Queen's Ferry, fraught with a dear cargo, and some frosty night a horseman, on a tragic errand, rattle with his whip upon the green shutters of the inn at Burford.

Now this is one of the natural appetites with which any lively literature has to count. The desire for knowledge, I had almost added the desire for meat, is not more deeply seated than this demand for fit and striking incident. The dullest of clowns tells, or tries to tell, himself a story, as the feeblest of children uses invention in his play; and even as the imaginative grown person, joining in the game, at once enriches it with many delightful circumstances, the great creative writer shows us the realisation and the apotheosis of the day-dreams of common men. His stories may be nourished with the realities of life, but their true mark is to satisfy the nameless longings of the reader, and to obey the ideal laws of the day-dream. The right kind of thing should fall out in the right kind of place; the right kind of thing should follow; and not only the characters talk aptly and think naturally, but all the circumstances in a tale answer one to another like notes in music. The threads of a story come from time to time together and make a picture in the web; the characters fall from time to time into some attitude to each other or to nature,

which stamps the story home like an illustration. Crusoe recoiling from the footprint, Achilles shouting over against the Trojans, Ulysses bending the great bow, Christian running with his fingers in his ears,— these are each culminating moments in the legend, and each has been printed on the mind's eye for ever. Other things we may forget; we may forget the words, although they are beautiful; we may forget the author's comment, although perhaps it was ingenious and true; but these epoch-making scenes, which put the last mark of truth upon a story, and fill up, at one blow, our capacity for sympathetic pleasure, we so adopt into the very bosom of our mind that neither time nor tide can efface or weaken the impression. This, then, is the plastic part of literature: to embody character, thought, or emotion in some act or attitude that shall be remarkably striking to the mind's eye. This is the highest and hardest thing to do in words; the thing which, once accomplished, equally delights the schoolboy and the sage, and makes, in its own right, the quality of epics. Compared with this, all other purposes in literature, except the purely lyrical or the purely philosophic, are bastard in nature, facile of execution, and feeble in result. It is one thing to write about the inn at Burford, or to describe scenery with the word-painters; it is quite another to seize on the heart of the suggestion and make a country famous with a legend. It is one thing to remark and to dissect, with the most cutting logic, the complications of life, and of the human spirit; it is quite another to give them body and blood in the story of Ajax or of Hamlet. The first is literature, but the second is something besides, for it is likewise art.

English people of the present day are apt, I know not why, to look somewhat down on incident, and reserve their admiration for the clink of teaspoons and the accents of the curate. It is thought clever to write a novel with no story at all, or at least with a very dull one. Reduced even to the lowest terms, a certain interest can be communicated by the art of narrative; a sense of human kinship stirred; and a kind of monotonous fitness, comparable to the words and air of *Sandy's Mull*, preserved among the infinitesimal occurrences recorded. Some people work, in this manner, with even a strong touch. Mr. Trollope's inimitable clergymen naturally arise to the mind in this connection. But even Mr. Trollope does not confine himself to chronicling

---

1. the **Antiquary,** by Sir Walter Scott, 1816. 22–27. **The man . . . Burford.** "Since the above was written I have tried to launch the boat with my own hand in *Kidnapped*. Some day, perhaps, I may try a rattle at the shutters." (Stevenson)

2–7. **Crusoe . . . for ever.** Famous moments in Defoe's *Robinson Crusoe,* Homer's *Iliad* and *Odyssey,* Bunyan's *The Pilgrim's Progress.* 33. **the story of Ajax,** in the *Iliad.* 50. **Mr. Trollope,** Anthony Trollope (1815–1882). See page 384.

small beer. Mr. Crawley's collision with the Bishop's wife, Mr. Melnotte dallying in the deserted banquet-room, are typical incidents, epically conceived, fitly embodying a crisis. Or again look at Thackeray. If Rawdon Crawley's blow were not delivered, *Vanity Fair* would cease to be a work of art. That scene is the chief ganglion of the tale; and the discharge of energy from Rawdon's fist is the reward and consolation of the reader. The end of *Esmond* is a yet wider excursion from the author's customary fields; the scene at Castlewood is pure Dumas; the great and wily English borrower has here borrowed from the great, unblushing French thief; as usual, he has borrowed admirably well, and the breaking of the sword rounds off the best of all his books with a manly, martial note. But perhaps nothing can more strongly illustrate the necessity for marking incident than to compare the living fame of *Robinson Crusoe* with the discredit of *Clarissa Harlowe*. *Clarissa* is a book of a far more startling import, worked out, on a great canvas, with inimitable courage and unflagging art. It contains wit, character, passion, plot, conversations full of spirit and insight, letters sparkling with unstrained humanity; and if the death of the heroine be somewhat frigid and artificial, the last days of the hero strike the only note of what we now call Byronism, between the Elizabethans and Byron himself. And yet a little story of a shipwrecked sailor, with not a tenth part of the style nor a thousandth part of the wisdom, exploring none of the arcana of humanity and deprived of the perennial interest of love, goes on from edition to edition, while *Clarissa* lies upon the shelves unread. A friend of mine, a Welsh blacksmith, was twenty-five years old and could neither read nor write, when he heard a chapter of *Robinson* read aloud in a farm kitchen. Up to that moment he had sat content, huddled in his ignorance, but he left that farm another man. There were daydreams, it appeared, divine day-dreams, written and printed and bound, and to be bought for money and enjoyed at pleasure. Down he sat that day, painfully learned to read Welsh, and returned to borrow the book. It had been lost, nor could he find another copy but one that was in English. Down he sat once more, learned English, and at length, and with entire delight, read *Robinson*. It is like the story of a love-chase. If he had heard a letter from *Clarissa*, would he have been fired with the same chivalrous ardour? I wonder. Yet *Clarissa* has every quality that can be shown in prose, one alone excepted—pictorial or picture-making romance. While *Robinson* depends, for the most part and with the overwhelming majority of its readers, on the charm of circumstance.

In the highest achievements of the art of words, the dramatic and the pictorial, the moral and romantic interest, rise and fall together by a common and organic law. Situation is animated with passion, passion clothed upon with situation. Neither exists for itself, but each inheres indissolubly with the other. This is high art; and not only the highest art possible in words, but the highest art of all, since it combines the greatest mass and diversity of the elements of truth and pleasure. Such are epics, and the few prose tales that have the epic weight. But as from a school of works, aping the creative, incident and romance are ruthlessly discarded, so may character and drama be omitted or subordinated to romance. There is one book, for example, more generally loved than Shakespeare, that captivates in childhood, and still delights in age—I mean the *Arabian Nights*—where you shall look in vain for moral or for intellectual interest. No human face or voice greets us among that wooden crowd of kings and genies, sorcerers and beggarmen. Adventure, in the most naked terms, furnishes forth the entertainment and is found enough. Dumas approaches perhaps nearest of any modern to these Arabian authors in the purely material charm of some of his romances. The early part of *Monte Cristo*, down to the finding of the treasure, is a piece of perfect story-telling; the man never breathed who shared these moving incidents without a tremor; and yet Faria is a thing of packthread and Dantès little more than a name. The sequel is one longdrawn error, gloomy, bloody, unnatural, and dull; but as for these early chapters, I do not believe there is another volume extant where you can breathe the same unmingled atmosphere of romance. It is very thin and light, to be sure, as on a high mountain; but it is brisk and clear and sunny in proportion. I saw the other day, with envy, an old and very clever lady setting forth on a second or third voyage into *Monte Cristo*. Here are stories which powerfully affect the reader, which can be reperused at any age, and where the characters are no more than puppets. The bony fist of the showman visibly propels them; their springs are an open secret; their faces are of wood, their bellies filled with bran; and yet we thrillingly partake of their adventures. And

---

1–3. **Mr. Crawley's . . . banquet-room.** The incidents referred to occur in *The Last Chronicle of Barset*, 1867, and *The Way We Live Now*, 1875, respectively. The second name is properly Melmotte. **19–20. Clarissa Harlowe,** 1747–48, by Samuel Richardson, the longest, and one of the greatest, novels in the English language, but not one of the liveliest. **26–28. the only note . . . Byron himself.** Stevenson's statement is, of course, not true. There is much "Byronism" in the Gothic novels, to adduce no further examples.

the point may be illustrated still further. The last interview between Lucy and Richard Feverel is pure drama; more than that, it is the strongest scene, since Shakespeare, in the English tongue. Their first meeting by the river, on the other hand, is pure romance; it has nothing to do with character; it might happen to any other boy and maiden, and be none the less delightful for the change. And yet I think he would be a bold man who should choose between these passages. Thus in the same book we may have two scenes, each capital in its order: in the one, human passion, deep calling unto deep, shall utter its genuine voice; in the second, according circumstances, like instruments in tune, shall build up a trivial but desirable incident, such as we love to prefigure for ourselves; and in the end, in spite of the critics, we may hesitate to give the preference to either. The one may ask more genius—I do not say it does; but at least the other dwells as clearly in the memory.

True romantic art, again, makes a romance of all things. It reaches into the highest abstraction of the ideal; it does not refuse the most pedestrian realism. *Robinson Crusoe* is as realistic as it is romantic; both qualities are pushed to an extreme, and neither suffers. Nor does romance depend upon the material importance of the incidents. To deal with strong and deadly elements, banditti, pirates, war and murder, is to conjure with great names, and, in the event of failure, to double the disgrace. The arrival of Haydn and Consuelo at the Canon's villa is a very trifling incident; yet we may read a dozen boisterous stories from beginning to end, and not receive so fresh and stirring an impression of adventure. It was the scene of Crusoe at the wreck, if I remember rightly, that so bewitched my blacksmith. Nor is the fact surprising. Every single article the castaway recovers from the hulk is "a joy for ever" to the man who reads of them. They are the things that should be found, and the bare enumeration stirs the blood. I found a glimmer of the same interest the other day in a new book, *The Sailor's Sweetheart*, by Mr. Clark Russell. The whole business of the brig *Morning Star* is very rightly felt and spiritedly written; but the clothes, the books, and the money satisfy the reader's mind like things to eat. We are dealing here with the old cut-and-dry, legitimate interest of treasure-trove. But even treasure-trove can be made dull. There are few people who have not groaned under the plethora of goods that fell to the lot of the *Swiss Family Robinson*, that dreary family. They found article after article, creature after creature, from milk-kine to pieces of ordnance, a whole consignment; but no informing taste had presided over the selection, there was no smack or relish in the invoice; and these riches left the fancy cold. The box of goods in Verne's *Mysterious Island* is another case in point: there was no gusto and no glamour about that; it might have come from a shop. But the two hundred and seventy-eight Australian sovereigns on board the *Morning Star* fell upon me like a surprise that I had expected; whole vistas of secondary stories, besides the one in hand, radiated forth from that discovery, as they radiate from a striking particular in life; and I was made for the moment as happy as a reader has the right to be.

To come at all at the nature of this quality of romance, we must bear in mind the peculiarity of our attitude to any art. No art produces illusion; in the theatre we never forget that we are in the theatre; and while we read a story, we sit wavering between two minds, now merely clapping our hands at the merit of the performance, now condescending to take an active part in fancy with the characters. This last is the triumph of romantic story-telling: when the reader consciously plays at being the hero, the scene is a good scene. Now in character-studies the pleasure that we take is critical; we watch, we approve, we smile at incongruities, we are moved to sudden heats of sympathy for courage, suffering, or virtue. But the characters are still themselves, they are not us; the more clearly they are depicted, the more widely do they stand away from us, the more imperiously do they thrust us back into our place as a spectator. I cannot identify myself with Rawdon Crawley or with Eugène de Rastignac, for I have scarce a hope or fear in common with them. It is not character but incident that woos us out of our reserve. Something happens as we desire to have it happen to ourselves; some situation, that we have long dallied with in fancy, is realised in the story with enticing and appropriate details. Then we forget the characters; then we push the hero aside; then we plunge into the tale in our own person and bathe in fresh experience; and then, and then only, do we say we have been reading a romance. It is not only pleasurable things that we imagine in our day-dreams; there are lights in which we are willing to contemplate even the idea of our own death; ways

---

1-2. **The last . . . Feverel**, in Meredith's *The Ordeal of Richard Feverel*, 1859.   31-32. **The arrival . . . villa**, in George Sand's *Consuelo*, 1842.

1. **the Swiss Family Robinson**, in Johann Rudolph Wyss's book of that title, 1813. Its continued popularity proves that Stevenson's opinion of it is not accepted universally.   7. **Mysterious Island**, The, 1870, by Jules Verne.   36. **Eugène de Rastignac**, in Balzac's *Père Goriot*, 1834.

in which it seems as if it would amuse us to be cheated, wounded, or calumniated. It is thus possible to construct a story, even of tragic import, in which every incident, detail, and trick of circumstance shall be welcome to the reader's thoughts. Fiction is to the grown man what play is to the child; it is there that he changes the atmosphere and tenor of his life; and when the game so chimes with his fancy that he can join in it with all his heart, when it pleases him at every turn, when he loves to recall it and dwells upon its recollection with entire delight, fiction is called romance.

Walter Scott is out and away the king of the romantics. *The Lady of the Lake* has no indisputable claim to be a poem beyond the inherent fitness and desirability of the tale. It is just such a story as a man would make up for himself, walking, in the best health and temper, through just such scenes as it is laid in. Hence it is that a charm dwells undefinable among these slovenly verses, as the unseen cuckoo fills the mountains with his note; hence, even after we have flung the book aside, the scenery and adventures remain present to the mind, a new and green possession, not unworthy of that beautiful name, *The Lady of the Lake*, or that direct, romantic opening—one of the most spirited and poetical in literature—"The stag at eve had drunk his fill." The same strength and the same weaknesses adorn and disfigure the novels. In that ill-written, ragged book, *The Pirate*, the figure of Cleveland—cast up by the sea on the resounding foreland of Dunrossness—moving, with the blood on his hands and the Spanish words on his tongue, among the simple islanders—singing a serenade under the window of his Shetland mistress—is conceived in the very highest manner of romantic invention. The words of his song, "Through groves of palm," sung in such a scene and by such a lover, clench, as in a nutshell, the emphatic contrast upon which the tale is built. In *Guy Mannering*, again, every incident is delightful to the imagination; and the scene when Harry Bertram lands at Ellangowan is a model instance of romantic method.

"'I remember the tune well,' he says, 'though I cannot guess what should at present so strongly recall it to my memory.' He took his flageolet from his pocket and played a simple melody. Apparently the tune awoke the corresponding associations of a damsel. . . . She immediately took up the song—

   "'Are these the links of Forth,' she said;
    'Or are they the crooks of Dee,
   Or the bonny woods of Warroch Head
    That I so fain would see?'

"'By heaven!' said Bertram, 'it is the very ballad.'"

On this quotation two remarks fall to be made. First, as an instance of modern feeling for romance, this famous touch of the flageolet and the old song is selected by Miss Braddon for omission. Miss Braddon's idea of a story, like Mrs. Todgers's idea of a wooden leg, were something strange to have expounded. As a matter of personal experience, Meg's appearance to old Mr. Bertram on the road, the ruins of Derncleugh, the scene of the flageolet, and the Dominie's recognition of Harry, are the four strong notes that continue to ring in the mind after the book is laid aside. The second point is still more curious. The reader will observe a mark of excision in the passage as quoted by me. Well, here is how it runs in the original: "a damsel who, close behind a fine spring about half-way down the descent, and which had once supplied the castle with water, was engaged in bleaching linen." A man who gave in such copy would be discharged from the staff of a daily paper. Scott has forgotten to prepare the reader for the presence of the "damsel"; he has forgotten to mention the spring and its relation to the ruin; and now, face to face with his omission, instead of trying back and starting fair, crams all this matter, tail foremost, into a single shambling sentence. It is not merely bad English, or bad style; it is abominably bad narrative besides.

Certainly the contrast is remarkable; and it is one that throws a strong light upon the subject of this paper. For here we have a man of the finest creative instinct touching with perfect certainty and charm the romantic junctures of his story; and we find him utterly careless, almost, it would seem, incapable, in the technical matter of style, and not only frequently weak, but frequently wrong in points of drama. In character parts, indeed, and particularly in the Scotch, he was delicate, strong, and truthful; but the trite, obliterated features of too many of his heroes have already wearied two generations of readers. At times his characters will speak with something far beyond propriety—with a true heroic note; but on the next page they will be wading wearily forward with an ungrammatical and undramatic rigmarole of words. The man who could

7. **Miss Braddon,** Mary Elizabeth Braddon (1837–1915), author of *Lady Audley's Secret*, 1862, and many other bestsellers, was one of the most successful of the followers of Wilkie Collins. She had the bad judgment to try to "edit" Scott. 8. **Mrs. Todgers,** the keeper of a London boarding-house in Dickens's *Martin Chuzzlewit*, and a friend of Mr. Pecksniff, who, inebriated, suggests that he would "very much like to see Mrs. Todgers's notion of a wooden leg, if perfectly agreeable to herself."

conceive and write the character of Elspeth of the Craigburnfoot, as Scott has conceived and written it, had not only splendid romantic but splendid tragic gifts. How comes it, then, that he could so often fob us off with languid, inarticulate twaddle? It seems to me that the explanation is to be found in the very quality of his surprising merits. As his books are play to the reader, so were they play to him. He was a great day-dreamer, a seer of fit and beautiful and humorous visions, but hardly a great artist. He conjured up the romantic with delight, but he had hardly patience to describe it. Of the pleasures of his art he tasted fully; but of its cares and scruples never man knew less.

PULVIS ET UMBRA

Romanticism has a natural affinity with faith and hope. Stevenson's famous optimism was by no means entirely a matter of temperament; he suffered much unhappiness in his life, and there were times when he nearly succumbed to the forces of despair. He lived in a world in which a narrow interpretation of the truths of science was causing many men to abandon all belief in a spiritual interpretation of the universe. He found himself fundamentally out of sympathy with this attitude, and in "Pulvis et Umbra" he tried to meet the futilitarians on their own ground. Accepting all the basic contentions of science, he shows that values still exist, and achieves a magnificent expression of faith in man. The title—"Dust and Shadow"—is taken from Horace, *Odes*, Book IV, Ode 7, ll. 14–16.

WE look for some reward of our endeavours and are disappointed; not success, not happiness, not even peace of conscience, crowns our ineffectual efforts to do well. Our frailties are invincible, our virtues barren; the battle goes sore against us to the going down of the sun. The canting moralist tells us of right and wrong; and we look abroad, even on the face of our small earth, and find them change with every climate, and no country where some action is not honoured for a virtue and none where it is not branded for a vice; and we look in our experience, and find no vital congruity in the wisest rules, but at the best a municipal fitness. It is not strange if we are tempted to despair of good. We ask too much. Our religions and moralities have been trimmed to flatter us, till they are all emasculate and sentimentalised, and only please and weaken. Truth is of a rougher strain. In the harsh face of life, faith can read a bracing gospel. The human race is a thing more ancient than the ten commandments; and the bones and revolutions of

1–2. Elspeth of the Craigburnfoot, in *The Antiquary*.

the Kosmos, in whose joints we are but moss and fungus, more ancient still.

I

Of the Kosmos in the last resort, science reports many doubtful things and all of them appalling. There seems no substance to this solid globe on which we stamp:—nothing but symbols and ratios. Symbols and ratios carry us and bring us forth and beat us down; gravity that swings the incommensurable suns and worlds through space, is but a figment varying inversely as the squares of distances; and the suns and worlds themselves, imponderable figures of abstraction, NH_3 and H_2O. Consideration dares not dwell upon this view; that way madness lies; science carries us into zones of speculation, where there is no habitable city for the mind of man.

But take the Kosmos with a grosser faith, as our senses give it us. We behold space sown with rotatory islands, suns and worlds and the shards and wrecks of systems: some, like the sun, still blazing; some rotting, like the earth; others, like the moon, stable in desolation. All of these we take to be made of something we call matter: a thing which no analysis can help us to conceive; to whose incredible properties no familiarities can reconcile our minds. This stuff, when not purified by the lustration of fire, rots uncleanly into something we call life; seized through all its atoms with a pediculous malady; swelling in tumours that become independent, sometimes even (by an abhorrent prodigy) locomotory; one splitting into millions, millions cohering into one, as the malady proceeds through varying stages. This vital putrescence of the dust, used as we are to it, yet strikes us with occasional disgust, and the profusion of worms in a piece of ancient turf, or the air of a marsh darkened with insects, will sometimes check our breathing so that we aspire for cleaner places. But none is clean: the moving sand is infected with lice; the pure spring, where it bursts out of the mountain, is a mere issue of worms; even in the hard rock the crystal is forming.

In two main shapes this eruption covers the countenance of the earth: the animal and the vegetable: one in some degree the inversion of the other: the second rooted to the spot; the first coming detached out of its natal mud, and scurrying abroad with the myriad feet of insects or towering into the heavens on the wings of birds: a thing so inconceivable that, if it be well considered, the heart stops. To what passes with the anchored vermin, we

14. NH3 and H2O, the chemical formulas for ammonia and water.   **15–16. That way madness lies.** See *King Lear*, Act III, sc. 4, l. 21.

have little clue: doubtless they have their joys and sorrows, their delights and killing agonies,—it appears not how. But of the locomotory, to which we ourselves belong, we can tell more. These share with us a thousand miracles: the miracles of sight, of hearing, of the projection of sound, things that bridge space; the miracles of memory and reason, by which the present is conceived, and, when it is gone, its image kept living in the brains of man and brute; the miracle of reproduction, with its imperious desires and staggering consequences. And to put the last touch upon this mountain mass of the revolting and the inconceivable, all these prey upon each other, lives tearing other lives in pieces, cramming them inside themselves, and by that summary process, growing fat: the vegetarian, the whale, perhaps the tree, not less than the lion of the desert; for the vegetarian is only the eater of the dumb.

Meanwhile our rotatory island loaded with predatory life, and more drenched with blood, both animal and vegetable, than ever mutinied ship, scuds through space with unimaginable speed, and turns alternate cheeks to the reverberation of a blazing world, ninety million miles away.

2

What a monstrous spectre is this man, the disease of the agglutinated dust, lifting alternate feet or lying drugged with slumber; killing, feeding, growing, bringing forth small copies of himself; grown upon with hair like grass, fitted with eyes that move and glitter in his face; a thing to set children screaming;—and yet looked at nearlier, known as his fellows know him, how surprising are his attributes! Poor soul, here for so little, cast among so many hardships, filled with desires so incommensurate and so inconsistent, savagely surrounded, savagely descended, irremediably condemned to prey upon his fellow lives: who should have blamed him had he been of a piece with his destiny and a being merely barbarous? And we look and behold him instead filled with imperfect virtues: infinitely childish, often admirably valiant, often touchingly kind; sitting down, amidst his momentary life, to debate of right and wrong and the attributes of the deity; rising up to do battle for an egg or die for an idea; singling out his friends and his mate with cordial affection; bringing forth in pain, rearing with long-suffering solicitude, his young. To touch the heart of his mystery, we find in him one thought, strange to the point of lunacy: the thought of duty; the thought of something owing to himself, to his neighbour, to his God; an ideal of decency, to which he would rise if it were possible; a limit of shame, below

which, if it be possible, he will not stoop. The design in most men is one of conformity; here and there, in picked natures, it transcends itself and soars on the other side, arming martyrs with independence; but in all, in their degrees, it is a bosom thought:— Not in man alone, for we trace it in dogs and cats whom we know fairly well, and doubtless some similar point of honour sways the elephant, the oyster, and the louse, of whom we know so little:—But in man, at least, it sways with so complete an empire that merely selfish things come second, even with the selfish: that appetites are starved, fears are conquered, pains supported; that almost the dullest shrinks from the reproof of a glance, although it were a child's; and all but the most cowardly stand amid the risks of war; and the more noble, having strongly conceived an act as due to their ideal, affront and embrace death. Strange enough if, with their singular origin and perverted practice, they think they are to be rewarded in some future life: stranger still, if they are persuaded of the contrary, and think this blow, which they solicit, will strike them senseless for eternity. I shall be minded what a tragedy of misconception and misconduct man at large presents; of organised injustice, cowardly violence and treacherous crime; and of the damning imperfections of the best. They cannot be too darkly drawn. Man is indeed marked for failure in his efforts to do right. But where the best consistently miscarry, how tenfold more remarkable that all should continue to strive; and surely we should find it both touching and inspiriting, that in a field from which success is banished, our race should not cease to labour.

If the first view of this creature, stalking in his rotatory isle, be a thing to shake the courage of the stoutest, on this nearer sight he startles us with an admiring wonder. It matters not where we look, under what climate we observe him, in what state of society, in what depth of ignorance, burthened with what erroneous morality; by camp-fires in Assiniboia, the snow powdering his shoulders, the wind plucking his blanket, as he sits, passing the ceremonial calumet and uttering his grave opinions like a Roman senator; in ships at sea, a man inured to hardship and vile pleasures, his brightest hope a fiddle in a tavern and a bedizened trull who sells herself to rob him, and he for all that, simple, innocent, cheerful, kindly like a child, constant to toil, brave to drown, for others; in the slums of cities, moving among indifferent millions to mechanical employments, without hope of change in the future,

41–42. Assiniboia, now part of Saskatchewan.   **44. calumet,** the pipe of peace.

with scarce a pleasure in the present, and yet true to his virtues, honest up to his lights, kind to his neighbours, tempted perhaps in vain by the bright gin-palace, perhaps long-suffering with the drunken wife that ruins him; in India (a woman this time) kneeling with broken cries and streaming tears, as she drowns her child in the sacred river; in the brothel, the discard of society, living mainly on strong drink, fed with affronts, a fool, a thief, the comrade of thieves, and even here keeping the point of honour and the touch of pity, often repaying the world's scorn with service, often standing firm upon a scruple, and at a certain cost, rejecting riches:—everywhere some virtue cherished or affected, everywhere some decency of thought and carriage, everywhere the ensign of man's ineffectual goodness:—ah! if I could show you this! if I could show you these men and women, all the world over, in every stage of history, under every abuse of error, under every circumstance of failure, without hope, without help, without thanks, still obscurely fighting the lost fight of virtue, still clinging, in the brothel or on the scafford, to some rag of honour, the poor jewel of their souls! They may seek to escape, and yet they cannot; it is not alone their privilege and glory, but their doom; they are condemned to some nobility, all their lives long, the desire of good is at their heels, the implacable hunter.

Of all earth's meteors, here at least is the most strange and consoling: that this ennobled lemur, this hair-crowned bubble of the dust, this inheritor of a few years and sorrows, should yet deny himself his rare delights, and add to his frequent pains, and live for an ideal, however misconceived. Nor can we stop with man. A new doctrine, received with screams a little while ago by canting moralists, and still not properly worked into the body of our thoughts, lights us a step farther into the heart of this rough but noble universe. For nowadays the pride of man denies in vain his kinship with the original dust. He stands no longer like a thing apart. Close at his heels we see the dog, prince of another genus; and in him, too, we see dumbly testified the same cultus of an unattainable ideal, the same constancy in failure. Does it stop with the dog? We look at our feet where the ground is blackened with the swarming ant; a creature so small, so far from us in the hierarchy of brutes, that we can scarce trace and scarce comprehend his doings; and here also, in his ordered polities and rigorous justice, we see confessed the law of duty and the fact of individual sin. Does it stop, then, with the ant? Rather this desire of well-doing and this doom of frailty run through all the grades of life: rather is this earth, from the frosty top of Everest to the next margin of the internal fire, one stage of ineffectual virtues and one temple of pious tears and perseverance. The whole creation groaneth and travaileth together. It is the common and the godlike law of life. The browsers, the biters, the barkers, the hairy coats of field and forest, the squirrel in the oak, the thousand-footed creeper in the dust, as they share with us the gift of life, share with us the love of an ideal; strive like us—like us are tempted to grow weary of the struggle—to do well; like us receive at times unmerited refreshment, visitings of support, returns of courage; and are condemned like us to be crucified between that double law of the members and the will. Are they like us, I wonder, in the timid hope of some reward, some sugar with the drug? do they, too, stand aghast at unrewarded virtues, at the sufferings of those whom, in our partiality, we take to be just, and the prosperity of such as, in our blindness, we call wicked? It may be, and yet God knows what they should look for. Even while they look, even while they repent, the foot of man treads them by thousands in the dust, the yelping hounds burst upon their trail, the bullet speeds, the knives are heating in the den of the vivisectionist; or the dew falls, and the generation of a day is blotted out. For these are creatures compared with whom our weakness is strength, our ignorance wisdom, our brief span eternity.

And as we dwell, we living things, in our isle of terror and under the imminent hand of death, God forbid it should be man the erected, the reasoner, the wise in his own eyes—God forbid it should be man that wearies in welldoing, that despairs of unrewarded effort, or utters the language of complaint. Let it be enough for faith, that the whole creation groans in mortal frailty, strives with unconquerable constancy: Surely not all in vain.

---

7. **the sacred river,** the Ganges. 24. **jewel of their souls.** See *Othello,* Act III, sc. 3, ll. 155–56. 36. **A new doctrine,** the doctrine of evolution.

9. **Everest,** the world's highest known mountain, in the Himalayas. 12–13. **The whole creation . . . together.** See Romans 8: 22. 22–23. **that double law . . . the will.** See Romans 7: 23.

Oscar Wilde
1856–1900

Oscar Wilde was born in Dublin on October 15, 1856. His father was a distinguished physician (and a rake); his mother was a fantastic. At Oxford, where he won the Newdigate Prize for poetry, Oscar became the press agent of an estheticism whose outward signs included long hair, knee breeches, a velvet coat, a flowing tie, blue china, peacock feathers, the lily, the sunflower, and the green carnation. In 1881 he published his *Poems;* the next year he made a spectacular lecture tour in America (see Lloyd Lewis and Henry Justin Smith, *Oscar Wilde Discovers America*, Harcourt, Brace, 1936, and the introductory note to the selection from Gilbert's *Patience* on page 748 of this volume). Between 1888 and 1891 he published two volumes of fairy tales—*The Happy Prince* and *A House of Pomegranates* —a novel, *The Picture of Dorian Grey*, and a volume of essays, *Intentions*. His first plays—*Vera* and *The Duchess of Padua*—were not very successful, but between 1892 and 1895 he convinced the world that Britain had produced a dramatist who for brilliant epigram was unmatched since the days of Congreve. *The Importance of Being Earnest*, which is sheer glitter and banter, presented the Wildean comedy at its purest. *An Ideal Husband* was comparatively unimportant. *Lady Windermere's Fan* and *A Woman of No Importance* mingled epigram with "heart interest" and melodrama; from the point of view of the nineties, they were, in Bernard Shaw's sense of the term, "unpleasant" plays. *Salomé*, which was written in French for Sarah Bernhardt, though never produced by her, is a perverse, malodorous tragedy, based on the story of John the Baptist's martyrdom as told parenthetically in the sixth chapter of the Gospel according to St. Mark. The censorship forbade the use of Biblical subjects in the English theater; the play waited for its stage success until Richard Strauss made a music drama of it in 1905. But the book, illustrated by Aubrey Beardsley, the one figure as completely representative of the fin-de-siècle period as Wilde himself, remains one of the great monuments of the nineties.

In 1895 Wilde had the extremely bad judgment to bring a libel suit against the Marquis of Queensberry, who had resented his intimacy with the latter's son, Lord Alfred Douglas. His suit lost, Wilde himself was tried for statutory offenses and sentenced to two years at hard labor. His terrible sufferings found eloquent expression in "The Ballad of Reading Gaol" and the autobiographical *De Profundis,* which has been published only in part; but they were in no sense redemptive sufferings. Ruined in health, purse, and reputation, Wilde lived his last years in France as Sebastian Melmoth —Sebastian because St. Sebastian was martyred by being pierced with arrows, and the prison garb of English convicts is marked with arrows; Melmoth for the leading character in one of the most wonderful of British novels, *Melmoth the Wanderer*, by Wilde's great-uncle, Charles Robert Maturin—and slowly drank himself to death. The end came on November 30, 1900.

The Wilde "case" was more than a personal matter; it was a test of strength between estheticism and Philistinism. Decency was vindicated; it was unfortunate that smugness had to be glorified. Wilde himself was neither a monster nor a martyr; he was simply a man cursed with a terrible abnormality which neither his false training nor his false principles helped him to cure. His "art for art's sake" creed had obvious affinities with Pre-Raphaelitism and Paterism, but neither Rossetti nor Pater could have approved of the perverse lengths to which he carried it. Theoretically a strong case can be made for his central thesis—that esthetic values must be judged as esthetic values, not as moral or social values, but with his temperament he soon found himself, in practice, taking up the definitely antisocial position of an immoralist. He was less "free," he was less detached, consequently, than the Philistines he opposed.

Like Goldsmith, like Stevenson, Wilde was remarkable for his ability to do brilliant work in many different kinds of literature. Often he achieved beauty as well as brilliance, but much of his work is "sicklied o'er" with a fragile unreality, which is doubtless the reflection of his own curious self.

REQUIESCAT

This delicate poem is Wilde's dirge for his sister Isola, whose death in childhood moved him as profoundly as anything that ever happened to him. The Latin title means "May she rest [in peace]."

Tread lightly, she is near,
  Under the snow,
Speak gently, she can hear
  The daisies grow.

All her bright golden hair
  Tarnished with rust,
She that was young and fair
  Fallen to dust.

Lily-like, white as snow,
  She hardly knew   10

She was a woman, so
  Sweetly she grew.

Coffin-board, heavy stone,
  Lie on her breast,
I vex my heart alone,
  She is at rest.

Peace, Peace, she cannot hear
  Lyre or sonnet,
All my life's buried here,
  Heap earth upon it.   20

THE BALLAD OF READING GAOL

"The Ballad of Reading Gaol," which appeals to some readers because of its decadent horror and to others because of its strong social consciousness, is generally considered Wilde's most substantial achievement in poetry. It commemorates the execution, for the murder of his wife, of Charles T. Woolridge, of the Royal Horse Guards, during Wilde's term of imprisonment at Reading. The poem was written in Berneval, France, after the poet's release. It is interesting to compare with "The Rime of the Ancient Mariner" by Samuel Taylor Coleridge, page 77.

I

He did not wear his scarlet coat,
  For blood and wine are red,
And blood and wine were on his hands
  When they found him with the dead,
The poor dead woman whom he loved,
  And murdered in her bed.

He walked amongst the Trial Men
  In a suit of shabby gray;
A cricket cap was on his head,
  And his step seemed light and gay;   10
But I never saw a man who looked
  So wistfully at the day.

I never saw a man who looked
  With such a wistful eye
Upon that little tent of blue
  Which prisoners call the sky,
And at every drifting cloud that went
  With sails of silver by.

I walked, with other souls in pain,
  Within another ring,   20
And was wondering if the man had done
  A great or little thing,

The Ballad of Reading Gaol. **7. Trial Men,** criminals convicted under sentence subject to appeal.

When a voice behind me whispered low,
  "That fellow's got to swing."

Dear Christ! the very prison walls
  Suddenly seemed to reel,
And the sky above my head became
  Like a casque of scorching steel;
And, though I was a soul in pain,
  My pain I could not feel.   30

I only knew what hunted thought
  Quickened his step, and why
He looked upon the garish day
  With such a wistful eye;
The man had killed the thing he loved,
  And so he had to die.

Yet each man kills the thing he loves,
  By each let this be heard,
Some do it with a bitter look,
  Some with a flattering word,   40
The coward does it with a kiss,
  The brave man with a sword!

Some kill their love when they are young,
  And some when they are old;
Some strangle with the hands of Lust,
  Some with the hands of Gold:
The kindest use a knife, because
  The dead so soon grow cold.

Some love too little, some too long,
  Some sell, and others buy;   50
Some do the deed with many tears,
  And some without a sigh:
For each man kills the thing he loves,
  Yet each man does not die.

He does not die a death of shame
   On a day of dark disgrace,
Nor have a noose about his neck,
   Nor a cloth upon his face,
Nor drop feet foremost through the floor
   Into an empty space.   60

He does not sit with silent men
   Who watch him night and day;
Who watch him when he tries to weep,
   And when he tries to pray;
Who watch him lest himself should rob
   The prison of its prey.

He does not wake at dawn to see
   Dread figures throng his room,
The shivering Chaplain robed in white,
   The Sheriff stern with gloom,   70
And the Governor all in shiny black,
   With the yellow face of Doom.

He does not rise in piteous haste
   To put on convict-clothes,
While some coarse-mouthed Doctor gloats, and
     notes
   Each new and nerve-twitched pose,
Fingering a watch whose little ticks
   Are like horrible hammer-blows.

He does not know that sickening thirst
   That sands one's throat, before   80
The hangman with his gardener's gloves
   Slips through the padded door,
And binds one with three leathern thongs,
   That the throat may thirst no more.

He does not bend his head to hear
   The Burial Office read,
Nor, while the terror of his soul
   Tells him he is not dead,
Cross his own coffin, as he moves
   Into the hideous shed.   90

He does not stare upon the air
   Through a little roof of glass:
He does not pray with lips of clay
   For his agony to pass;
Nor feel upon his shuddering cheek
   The kiss of Caiaphas.

96. The kiss of Caiaphas. It was not the high priest
Caiaphas who kissed Jesus, but his own disciple, Judas
Iscariot, who betrayed him to Caiaphas. See Matthew 26.

2

Six weeks our guardsman walked the yard,
   In the suit of shabby gray:
His cricket cap was on his head,
   And his step seemed light and gay,   100
But I never saw a man who looked
   So wistfully at the day.

I never saw a man who looked
   With such a wistful eye
Upon that little tent of blue
   Which prisoners call the sky,
And at every wandering cloud that trailed
   Its ravelled fleeces by.

He did not wring his hands, as do
   Those witless men who dare   110
To try to rear the changeling Hope
   In the cave of black Despair:
He only looked upon the sun,
   And drank the morning air.

He did not wring his hands nor weep,
   Nor did he peek or pine,
But he drank the air as though it held
   Some healthful anodyne;
With open mouth he drank the sun
   As though it had been wine!   120

And I and all the souls in pain,
   Who tramped the other ring,
Forgot if we ourselves had done
   A great or little thing,
And watched with gaze of dull amaze
   The man who had to swing.

And strange it was to see him pass
   With a step so light and gay,
And strange it was to see him look
   So wistfully at the day,   130
And strange it was to think that he
   Had such a debt to pay.

For oak and elm have pleasant leaves
   That in the spring-time shoot:
But grim to see is the gallows-tree,
   With its adder-bitten root,
And, green or dry, a man must die
   Before it bears its fruit!

The loftiest place is that seat of grace
   For which all worldlings try: 140

116. peek, speak in a high, piping voice.

But who would stand in hempen band
  Upon a scaffold high,
And through a murderer's collar take
  His last look at the sky?

It is sweet to dance to violins
  When Love and Life are fair:
To dance to flutes, to dance to lutes
  Is delicate and rare:
But it is not sweet with nimble feet
  To dance upon the air!   150

So with curious eyes and sick surmise
  We watched him day by day,
And wondered if each one of us
  Would end the self-same way,
For none can tell to what red Hell
  His sightless soul may stray.

At last the dead man walked no more
  Amongst the Trial Men,
And I knew that he was standing up
  In the black dock's dreadful pen,   160
And that never would I see his face
  In God's sweet world again.

Like two doomed ships that pass in storm
  We had crossed each other's way:
But we made no sign, we said no word,
  We had no word to say;
For we did not meet in the holy night,
  But in the shameful day.

A prison wall was round us both,
  Two outcast men we were: 170
The world had thrust us from its heart,
  And God from out His care:
And the iron gin that waits for Sin
  Had caught us in its snare.

3

In Debtors' Yard the stones are hard,
  And the dripping wall is high,
So it was there he took the air
  Beneath the leaden sky,
And by each side a Warder walked,
  For fear the man might die.   180

Or else he sat with those who watched
  His anguish night and day;
Who watched him when he rose to weep,
  And when he crouched to pray;
Who watched him lest himself should rob
  Their scaffold of its prey.

The Governor was strong upon
  The Regulations Act:
The Doctor said that Death was but
  A scientific fact: 190
And twice a day the Chaplain called,
  And left a little tract.

And twice a day he smoked his pipe,
  And drank his quart of beer:
His soul was resolute, and held
  No hiding-place for fear;
He often said that he was glad
  The hangman's hands were near.

But why he said so strange a thing
  No warder dared to ask: 200
For he to whom a watcher's doom
  Is given as his task,
Must set a lock upon his lips,
  And make his face a mask.

Or else he might be moved, and try
  To comfort or console:
And what should Human Pity do
  Pent up in Murderers' Hole?
What word of grace in such a place
  Could help a brother's soul?   210

With slouch and swing around the ring
  We trod the Fools' Parade!
We did not care: we knew we were
  The Devil's Own Brigade:
And shaven head and feet of lead
  Make a merry masquerade.

We tore the tarry rope to shreds
  With blunt and bleeding nails;
We rubbed the doors, and scrubbed the floors,
  And cleaned the shining rails: 220
And, rank by rank, we soaped the plank,
  And clattered with the pails.

We sewed the sacks, we broke the stones,
  We turned the dusty drill:
We banged the tins, and bawled the hymns,
  And sweated on the mill:
But in the heart of every man
  Terror was lying still.

So still it lay that every day
  Crawled like a weed-clogged wave: 230

188. The Regulations Act, providing humane treatment
for prisoners.   **217. We . . . shreds,** to make oakum for
calking vessels.

And we forgot the bitter lot
   That waits for fool and knave,
Till once, as we trampled in from work,
   We passed an open grave.

With yawning mouth the yellow hole
   Gaped for a living thing;
The very mud cried out for blood
   To the thirsty asphalte ring:
And we knew that ere one dawn grew fair
   Some prisoner had to swing.   240

Right in we went, with soul intent
   On Death and Dread and Doom:
The hangman, with his little bag,
   Went shuffling through the gloom:
And each man trembled as he crept
   Into his numbered tomb.

That night the empty corridors
   Were full of forms of Fear,
And up and down the iron town
   Stole feet we could not hear,   250
And through the bars that hide the stars
   White faces seemed to peer.

He lay as one who lies and dreams
   In a pleasant meadow-land,
The watchers watched him as he slept,
   And could not understand
How one could sleep so sweet a sleep
   With a hangman close at hand.

But there is no sleep when men must weep
   Who never yet have wept: 260
So we—the fool, the fraud, the knave—
   That endless vigil kept,
And through each brain on hands of pain
   Another's terror crept.

Alas! it is a fearful thing
   To feel another's guilt!
For, right within, the sword of Sin
   Pierced to its poisoned hilt,
And as molten lead were the tears we shed
   For the blood we had not spilt.   270

The Warders with their shoes of felt
   Crept by each padlocked door,
And peeped and saw, with eyes of awe,
   Gray figures on the floor,
And wondered why men knelt to pray
   Who never prayed before.

All through the night we knelt and prayed,
   Mad mourners of a corse!
The troubled plumes of midnight were
   The plumes upon a hearse: 280
And bitter wine upon a sponge
   Was the savour of Remorse.

The gray cock crew, the red cock crew,
   But never came the day:
And crooked shapes of Terror crouched,
   In the corners where we lay:
And each evil sprite that walks by night
   Before us seemed to play.

They glided past, they glided fast,
   Like travellers through a mist: 290
They mocked the moon in a rigadoon
   Of delicate turn and twist,
And with formal pace and loathsome grace
   The phantoms kept their tryst.

With mop and mow, we saw them go,
   Slim shadows hand in hand:
About, about, in ghostly rout
   They trod a saraband:
And the damned grotesques made arabesques,
   Like the wind upon the sand!   300

With the pirouettes of marionettes,
   They tripped on pointed tread:
But with flutes of Fear they filled the ear,
   As their grisly masque they led,
And loud they sang, and long they sang,
   For they sang to wake the dead.

"*Oho!*" they cried, "*The world is wide,*
   But fettered limbs go lame!
And once, or twice, to throw the dice
   Is a gentlemanly game,   310
But he does not win who plays with Sin
   In the secret House of Shame."

No things of air these antics were,
   That frolicked with such glee:
To men whose lives were held in gyves,
   And whose feet might not go free,
Ah! wounds of Christ! they were living things,
   Most terrible to see.

Around, around, they waltzed and wound;
   Some wheeled in smirking pairs;   320

281. bitter wine . . . sponge. See Matthew 27:34.

With the mincing step of a demirep
  Some sidled up the stairs:
And with subtle sneer, and fawning leer,
  Each helped us at our prayers.

The morning wind began to moan,
  But still the night went on:
Through its giant loom the web of gloom
  Crept till each thread was spun:
And, as we prayed, we grew afraid
  Of the Justice of the Sun.   330

The moaning wind went wandering round
  The weeping prison-wall:
Till like a wheel of turning steel
  We felt the minutes crawl:
O moaning wind! what had we done
  To have such a seneschal?

At last I saw the shadowed bars,
  Like a lattice wrought in lead,
Move right across the whitewashed wall
  That faced my three-plank bed,   340
And I knew that somewhere in the world
  God's dreadful dawn was red.

At six o'clock we cleaned our cells,
  At seven all was still,
But the sough and swing of a mighty wing
  The prison seemed to fill,
For the Lord of Death with icy breath
  Had entered in to kill.

He did not pass in purple pomp,
  Nor ride a moon-white steed.   350
Three yards of cord and a sliding board
  Are all the gallows' need:
So with rope of shame the Herald came
  To do the secret deed.

We were as men who through a fen
  Of filthy darkness grope:
We did not dare to breathe a prayer,
  Or to give our anguish scope:
Something was dead in each of us,
  And what was dead was Hope.   360

For Man's grim Justice goes its way,
  And will not swerve aside:
It slays the weak, it slays the strong,
  It has a deadly stride:

With iron heel it slays the strong,
  The monstrous parricide!

We waited for the stroke of eight:
  Each tongue was thick with thirst:
For the stroke of eight is the stroke of Fate
  That makes a man accursed,   370
And Fate will use a running noose
  For the best man and the worst.

We had no other thing to do,
  Save to wait for the sign to come:
So, like things of stone in a valley lone,
  Quiet we sat and dumb:
But each man's heart beat thick and quick,
  Like a madman on a drum!

With sudden shock the prison-clock
  Smote on the shivering air,   380
And from all the gaol rose up a wail
  Of impotent despair,
Like the sound that frightened marshes hear
  From some leper in his lair.

And as one sees most fearful things
  In the crystal of a dream,
We saw the greasy hempen rope
  Hooked to the blackened beam,
And heard the prayer the hangman's snare
  Strangled into a scream.   390

And all the woe that moved him so
  That he gave that bitter cry,
And the wild regrets, and the bloody sweats,
  None knew so well as I:
For he who lives more lives than one
  More deaths than one must die.

4
There is no chapel on the day
  On which they hang a man:
The Chaplain's heart is far too sick,
  Or his face is far too wan,   400
Or there is that written in his eyes
  Which none should look upon.

So they kept us close till nigh on noon,
  And then they rang the bell,
And the Warders with their jingling keys
  Opened each listening cell,

395. **he,** the poet, the man of imagination. See Tennyson's
In Memoriam, Sec. 6, ll. 1–8, and note, page 500.

And down the iron stair we tramped,
    Each from his separate Hell.

Out into God's sweet air we went,
    But not in wonted way,   410
For this man's face was white with fear,
    And that man's face was gray,
And I never saw sad men who looked
    So wistfully at the day.

I never saw sad men who looked
    With such a wistful eye
Upon that little tent of blue
    We prisoners called the sky,
And at every careless cloud that passed
    In happy freedom by.   420

But there were those amongst us all
    Who walked with downcast head,
And knew that, had each got his due,
    They should have died instead:
He had but killed a thing that lived,
    Whilst they had killed the dead.

For he who sins a second time
    Wakes a dead soul to pain,
And draws it from its spotted shroud,
    And makes it bleed again,   430
And makes it bleed great gouts of blood,
    And makes it bleed in vain!

Like ape or clown, in monstrous garb
    With crooked arrows starred,
Silently we went round and round,
    The slippery asphalte yard;
Silently we went round and round,
    And no man spoke a word.

Silently we went round and round,
    And through each hollow mind   440
The Memory of dreadful things
    Rushed like a dreadful wind,
And Horror stalked before each man,
    And Terror crept behind.

The Warders strutted up and down,
    And kept their herd of brutes,
Their uniforms were spick and span,
    And they wore their Sunday suits,
But we knew the work they had been at,
    By the quicklime on their boots.   450

434. crooked arrows, marked on English prison garb.

For where a grave had opened wide,
    There was no grave at all:
Only a stretch of mud and sand
    By the hideous prison-wall,
And a little heap of burning lime,
    That the man should have his pall.

For he has a pall, this wretched man,
    Such as few men can claim:
Deep down below a prison-yard,
    Naked for greater shame,   460
He lies, with fetters on each foot,
    Wrapt in a sheet of flame!

And all the while the burning lime
    Eats flesh and bone away,
It eats the brittle bone by night,
    And the soft flesh by day,
It eats the flesh and bone by turns,
    But it eats the heart alway.

For three long years they will not sow
    Or root or seedling there: 470
For three long years the unblessed spot
    Will sterile be and bare,
And look upon the wondering sky
    With unreproachful stare.

They think a murderer's heart would taint
    Each simple seed they sow.
It is not true! God's kindly earth
    Is kindlier than men know,
And the red rose would but blow more red,
    The white rose whiter blow.   480

Out of his mouth a red, red rose!
    Out of his heart a white!
For who can say by what strange way,
    Christ brings His will to light,
Since the barren staff the pilgrim bore
    Bloomed in the great Pope's sight?

But neither milk-white rose nor red
    May bloom in prison air;
The shard, the pebble, and the flint,
    Are what they give us there: 490
For flowers have been known to heal
    A common man's despair.

485–86. Since . . . sight? Pope Urban IV declared that Tannhäuser's sin could not be forgiven until the pilgrim's staff burst into bloom; the ensuing miracle showed the superiority of God's mercy to that of humankind. See Wagner's opera.

So never will wine-red rose or white,
   Petal by petal, fall
On that stretch of mud and sand that lies
   By the hideous prison-wall,
To tell the men who tramp the yard
   That God's Son died for all.

Yet though the hideous prison-wall
   Still hems him round and round,   500
And a spirit may not walk by night
   That is with fetters bound,
And a spirit may but weep that lies
   In such unholy ground,

He is at peace—this wretched man—
   At peace, or will be soon:
There is no thing to make him mad,
   Nor does Terror walk at noon,
For the lampless Earth in which he lies
   Has neither Sun nor Moon.   510

They hanged him as a beast is hanged:
   They did not even toll
A requiem that might have brought
   Rest to his startled soul,
But hurriedly they took him out,
   And hid him in a hole.

They stripped him of his canvas clothes,
   And gave him to the flies:
They mocked the swollen purple throat,
   And the stark and staring eyes: 520
And with laughter loud they heaped the shroud
   In which their convict lies.

The Chaplain would not kneel to pray
   By his dishonoured grave:
Nor mark it with that blessed Cross
   That Christ for sinners gave,
Because the man was one of those
   Whom Christ came down to save.

Yet all is well; he has but passed
   To life's appointed bourne: 530
And alien tears will fill for him
   Pity's long-broken urn,
For his mourners will be outcast men,
   And outcasts always mourn.

5

I know not whether Laws be right,
   Or whether Laws be wrong;

All that we know who lie in gaol
   Is that the wall is strong;
And that each day is like a year,
   A year whose days are long.   540

But this I know; that every Law
   That men have made for Man,
Since first Man took his brother's life,
   And the sad world began,
But straws the wheat and saves the chaff
   With a most evil fan.

This too I know—and wise it were
   If each could know the same—
That every prison that men build
   Is built with bricks of shame,   550
And bound with bars lest Christ should see
   How men their brothers maim.

With bars they blur the gracious moon,
   And blind the goodly sun:
And they do well to hide their Hell,
   For in it things are done
That Son of God nor son of Man
   Ever should look upon!

The vilest deeds like poison weeds,
   Bloom well in prison-air;   560
It is only what is good in Man
   That wastes and withers there:
Pale Anguish keeps the heavy gate,
   And the Warder is Despair.

For they starve the little frightened child
   Till it weeps both night and day:
And they scourge the weak, and flog the fool,
   And gibe the old and gray,
And some grow mad, and all grow bad,
   And none a word may say.   570

Each narrow cell in which we dwell
   Is a foul and dark latrine,
And the fetid breath of living Death
   Chokes up each grated screen,
And all, but Lust, is turned to dust
   In Humanity's machine.

The brackish water that we drink
   Creeps with a loathsome slime,
And the bitter bread they weigh in scales
   Is full of chalk and lime,   580

545. **straws**, scatters. See Matthew 3:12.

And Sleep will not lie down, but walks
  Wild-eyed, and cries to Time.

But though lean Hunger and green Thirst
  Like asp with adder fight,
We have little care of prison fare,
  For what chills and kills outright
Is that every stone one lifts by day
  Becomes one's heart by night.

With midnight always in one's heart,
  And twilight in one's cell,   590
We turn the crank, or tear the rope,
  Each in his separate Hell,
And the silence is more awful far
  Than the sound of a brazen bell.

And never a human voice comes near
  To speak a gentle word:
And the eye that watches through the door
  Is pitiless and hard:
And by all forgot, we rot and rot,
  With soul and body marred.   600

And thus we rust Life's iron chain
  Degraded and alone:
And some men curse, and some men weep,
  And some men make no moan:
But God's eternal Laws are kind
  And break the heart of stone.

And every human heart that breaks,
  In prison-cell or yard,
Is as that broken box that gave
  Its treasure to the Lord,   610
And filled the unclean leper's house
  With the scent of costliest nard.

Ah! happy they whose hearts can break
  And peace of pardon win!
How else may man make straight his plan
  And cleanse his soul from Sin?
How else but through a broken heart
  May Lord Christ enter in?

And he of the swollen purple throat,
  And the stark and staring eyes,   620
Waits for the holy hands that took
  The Thief to Paradise;

609-12. that broken box . . . nard. The story is told in
Mark 14:3-9. 621-22. the holy hands . . . Paradise. See
Luke 23:39-43.

And a broken and a contrite heart
  The Lord will not despise.

The man in red who reads the Law
  Gave him three weeks of life,
Three little weeks in which to heal
  His soul of his soul's strife,
And cleanse from every blot of blood
  The hand that held the knife.   630

And with tears of blood he cleansed the hand,
  The hand that held the steel:
For only blood can wipe out blood,
  And only tears can heal:
And the crimson stain that was of Cain
  Became Christ's snow-white seal.

6

In Reading gaol by Reading town
  There is a pit of shame,
And in it lies a wretched man
  Eaten by teeth of flame,   640
In a burning winding-sheet he lies,
  And his grave has got no name.

And there, till Christ call forth the dead,
  In silence let him lie:
No need to waste the foolish tear,
  Or heave the windy sigh:
The man had killed the thing he loved,
  And so he had to die.

And all men kill the thing they love,
  By all let this be heard,   650
Some do it with a bitter look,
  Some with a flattering word,
The coward does it with a kiss,
  The brave man with a sword!

from THE DECAY OF LYING

THE DECAY OF LYING: A PROTEST

In Wilde's dialogue "The Decay of Lying" (*Intentions*,
1891), Vivian reads the following essay to his friend
Cyril. Wilde's impish perversity must not blind the student to the fact that he has presented a reasoned defense
of the romantic position. It is interesting to compare
Stevenson's "A Gossip on Romance," page 889.

623-24. broken . . . despise. See Psalm 51:17.
625. The man in red, the judge who passes sentence of
death. 633-36. For only blood . . . seal, a reference to
the Christian doctrine of the Atonement, according to which
the sacrifice of Christ redeemed humanity. For Cain, the
first murderer, see Genesis 4:1-15.

ONE of the chief causes that can be assigned for the curiously commonplace character of most of the literature of our age is undoubtedly the the decay of Lying as an art, a science, and a social pleasure. The ancient historians gave us delightful fiction in the form of fact; the modern novelist presents us with dull facts under the guise of fiction. The Blue-Book is rapidly becoming his ideal both for method and manner. He has his tedious *document humain*, his miserable little *coin de la création*, into which he peers with his microscope. He is to be found at the Librairie Nationale, or at the British Museum, shamelessly reading up his subject. He has not even the courage of other people's ideas, but insists on going directly to life for everything, and ultimately, between encyclopaedias and personal experience, he comes to the ground, having drawn his types from the family circle or from the weekly washerwoman, and having acquired an amount of useful information from which never, even in his most meditative moments, can he thoroughly free himself.

The loss that results to literature in general from this false ideal of our time can hardly be over-estimated. People have a careless way of talking about a "born liar," just as they talk about a "born poet." But in both cases they are wrong. Lying and poetry are arts—arts, as Plato saw, not unconnected with each other—and they require the most careful study, the most disinterested devotion. Indeed, they have their technique, just as the more material arts of painting and sculpture have, their subtle secrets of form and colour, their craft-mysteries, their deliberate artistic methods. As one knows the poet by his fine music, so one can recognise the liar by his rich rhythmic utterance, and in neither case will the casual inspiration of the moment suffice. Here, as elsewhere, practice must precede perfection. But in modern days while the fashion of writing poetry has become far too common, and should, if possible, be discouraged, the fashion of lying has almost fallen into disrepute. Many a young man starts in life with a natural gift for exaggeration which, if nurtured in congenial and sympathetic surroundings, or by the imitation of the best models, might grow into something really great and wonderful. But, as a rule, he comes to nothing. He either falls into careless habits of accuracy . . . or takes to frequenting the society of the aged and well-informed. Both things are equally fatal to his imagination, as indeed they would be fatal to the imagination of anybody, and in a short time he develops a morbid and unhealthy faculty of truth-telling, begins to verify all statements made in his presence, has no hesitation in contradicting people who are much younger than himself, and often ends by writing novels which are so lifelike that no one can possibly believe in their probability. This is no isolated instance that we are giving. It is simply one example out of many; and if something cannot be done to check, or at least to modify, our monstrous worship of facts, Art will become sterile, and beauty will pass away from the land.

Even Mr. Robert Louis Stevenson, that delightful master of delicate and fanciful prose, is tainted with this modern vice, for we know positively no other name for it. There is such a thing as robbing a story of its reality by trying to make it too true, and *The Black Arrow* is so inartistic as not to contain a single anachronism to boast of, while the transformation of Dr. Jekyll reads dangerously like an experiment out of the *Lancet*. As for Mr. Rider Haggard, who really has, or had once, the makings of a perfectly magnificent liar, he is now so afraid of being suspected of genius that when he does tell us anything marvellous, he feels bound to invent a personal reminiscence, and to put it into a footnote as a kind of cowardly corroboration. Nor are our other novelists much better. Mr. Henry James writes fiction as if it were a painful duty, and wastes upon mean motives and imperceptible "points of view" his neat literary style, his felicitous phrases, his swift and caustic satire. Mr. Hall Caine, it is true, aims at the grandiose, but then he writes at the top of his voice. He is so loud that one cannot hear what he says. Mr. James Payn is an adept in the art of concealing what is not worth finding. He hunts down the obvious with the enthusiasm of a short-sighted detective. As one turns over the pages, the suspense of the author becomes almost unbearable. The horses of Mr. William Black's phaeton

---

9–10. **document humain,** human document. **coin de la création,** corner of creation. Both are favorite phrases of the French naturalists.   28. **as Plato saw,** Wilde's reference is to the passage in Book III of the *Republic,* where Plato takes up the various kinds of fable that are to be drawn upon in teaching young children.

16. **Mr. Robert Louis Stevenson.** See page 897. 24. **Lancet,** British medical journal.   24–25. **Mr. Rider Haggard,** later Sir Henry Rider Haggard (1856–1925), British novelist, author of *She, King Solomon's Mines,* and many other tales of adventure. 31. **Mr. Henry James,** American-British novelist (1843–1916), one of the main influences upon the psychological trend of modern fiction. 35. **Mr. Hall Caine,** later Sir Hall Caine, sensational Isle of Man novelist (1853–1931), author of *The Deemster, The Christian, The Woman Thou Gavest Me,* and many other best-selling novels. 38. **Mr. James Payn,** novelist (1830–1898), editor of *Chambers's Journal* and the *Cornhill Magazine.* 43. **Mr. William Black,** author of *A Daughter of Heth* and more than thirty other novels, mostly of northern Scotland (1841–1898).

do not soar towards the sun. They merely frighten the sky at evening into violent chromolithographic effects. On seeing them approach, the peasants take refuge in dialect. Mrs. Oliphant prattles pleasantly about curates, lawn-tennis parties, domesticity, and other wearisome things. Mr. Marion Crawford has immolated himself upon the altar of local colour. He is like the lady in the French comedy who talks about "le beau ciel d'Italie." Besides, he has fallen into a bad habit of uttering moral platitudes. He is 10 always telling us that to be good is to be good, and that to be bad is to be wicked. At times he is almost edifying. *Robert Elsmere* is of course a masterpiece— a masterpiece of the "genre ennuyeux," the one form of literature that the English people seem thoroughly to enjoy. A thoughtful young friend of ours once told us that it reminded him of the sort of conversation that goes on at a meat tea in the house of a serious Nonconformist family, and we can quite believe it. Indeed it is only in England that 20 such a book could be produced. England is the home of lost ideas. As for that great and daily increasing school of novelists for whom the sun always rises in the East-End, the only thing that can be said about them is that they find life crude, and leave it raw.

In France, though nothing so deliberately tedious as *Robert Elsmere* has been produced, things are not much better. M. Guy de Maupassant, with his keen mordant irony and his hard vivid style, strips 30 life of the few poor rags that still cover her, and shows us foul sore and festering wound. He writes lurid little tragedies in which everybody is ridiculous; bitter comedies at which one cannot laugh for very tears. M. Zola, true to the lofty principle that he lays down in one of his pronunciamientos on literature, "L'homme de génie n'a jamais d'esprit," is determined to show that, if he has not got genius, he can at least be dull. And how well he succeeds! He is not without power. Indeed at 40 times, as in *Germinal*, there is something almost epic in his work. But his work is entirely wrong from

beginning to end, and wrong not on the ground of morals, but on the ground of art. From any ethical standpoint it is just what it should be. The author is perfectly truthful, and describes things exactly as they happen. What more can any moralist desire? We have no sympathy at all with the moral indignation of our time against M. Zola. It is simply the indignation of Tartuffe on being exposed. But from the standpoint of art, what can be said in favour of the author of *L'Assommoir*, *Nana*, and *Pot-Bouille?* Nothing. Mr. Ruskin once described the characters in George Eliot's novels as being like the sweepings of a Pentonville omnibus, but M. Zola's characters are much worse. They have their dreary vices, and their drearier virtues. The record of their lives is absolutely without interest. Who cares what happens to them? In literature we require distinction, charm, beauty, and imaginative power. We don't want to be harrowed and disgusted with an account of the doings of the lower orders. M. Daudet is better. He has wit, a light touch and an amusing style. But he has lately committed literary suicide. Nobody can possibly care for Delobelle with his "Il faut lutter pour l'art," or for Valmajour with his eternal refrain about the nightingale, or for the poet in *Jack* with his "mots cruels," now that we have learned from *Vingt Ans de ma Vie littéraire* that these characters were taken directly from life. To us they seem to have suddenly lost all their vitality, all the few qualities they ever possessed. The only real people are the people who never existed, and if a novelist is base enough to go to life for his personages he should at least pretend that they are creations, and not boast of them as copies. The justification of a character in a novel is not that other persons are what they are, but that the author is what he is. Otherwise the novel is not a work of art. As for M. Paul Bourget, the master of the *roman psychologique*, he commits the error of imagining that the men and women of modern life are capable of being infinitely analysed for an innumerable series of chapters. In point of fact, what is interesting about people in good society— and M. Bourget rarely moves out of the Faubourg St. Germain, except to come to London,—is the

4. **Mrs. Oliphant,** a phenomenally prolific writer of fiction and nonfiction alike (1828–1897). **6. Mr. Marion Crawford,** F. Marion Crawford (1854–1909), an international novelist, of American birth, very popular in the eighties and nineties. 9. "**le beau ciel d'Italie,**" the beautiful sky of Italy. 13. **Robert Elsmere.** Mrs. Humphry Ward's famous novel of faith and doubt in Victorian England (1888) was, of course, a much better book than Wilde gives it credit for being. 14. "**genre ennuyeux,**" tiresome genus. The phrase is used in Voltaire's preface to *L'enfant prodigue.* **29. M. Guy de Maupassant,** the great French master of the short story (1850–1893). **35. M. Zola,** Emile Zola, French novelist, the father of modern naturalism (1840–1902). **37–38.** "**L'homme . . . d'esprit.**" "The man of genius is never a wit."

8. **Tartuffe,** the hypocrite in Molière's famous play, 1664. 13. **Pentonville,** an ecclesiastical district in London. 21. **M. Daudet,** Alphonse Daudet (1840–1897), author of *Sapho* and many other works. 24. **Delobelle,** a character in *Fromont jeune et Risler aîné.* 24. "**Il faut lutter pour l'art.**" "One must fight for art." 25. **Valmajour,** a character in *Numa Roumestan.* **26–27.** "**mots cruels,**" desperate words. **27–28. Vingt Ans de ma Vie littéraire,** *Twenty Years of My Literary Life.* 38. **M. Paul Bourget,** 1852–1935. 39. **roman psychologique,** psychological novel. **44–45. Faubourg St. Germain,** Paris, the old residential center of the French gentry.

mask that each one of them wears, not the reality that lies behind the mask. It is a humiliating confession, but we are all of us made out of the same stuff. In Falstaff there is something of Hamlet, in Hamlet there is not a little of Falstaff. The fat knight has his moods of melancholy, and the young prince his moments of coarse humour. Where we differ from each other is purely in accidentals: in dress, manner, tone of voice, religious opinions, personal appearance, tricks of habit, and the like. The more one analyses people, the more all reasons for analysis disappear. Sooner or later one comes to that dreadful universal thing called human nature. Indeed, as any one who has ever worked among the poor knows only too well, the brotherhood of man is no mere poet's dream, it is a most depressing and humiliating reality; and if a writer insists upon analysing the upper classes, he might just as well write of match-girls and costermongers at once. . . .

The popular cry of our time is "Let us return to Life and Nature; they will recreate Art for us, and send the red blood coursing through her veins; they will shoe her feet with swiftness and make her hand strong." But, alas! we are mistaken in our amiable and well-meaning efforts. Nature is always behind the age. And as for Life, she is the solvent that breaks up Art, the enemy that lays waste her house. . . . Art begins with abstract decoration, with purely imaginative and pleasurable work dealing with what is unreal and non-existent. This is the first stage. Then Life becomes fascinated with this new wonder, and asks to be admitted into the charmed circle. Art takes life as part of her rough material, recreates it, and refashions it in fresh forms, is absolutely indifferent to fact, invents, imagines, dreams, and keeps between herself and reality the impenetrable barrier of beautiful style, of decorative or ideal treatment. The third stage is when Life gets the upper hand, and drives Art out into the wilderness. This is the true decadence, and it is from this that we are now suffering.

Take the case of the English drama. At first in the hands of the monks Dramatic Art was abstract, decorative and mythological. Then she enlisted Life in her service, and using some of life's external forms, she created an entirely new race of beings, whose sorrows were more terrible than any sorrow man has ever felt, whose joys were keener than lover's joys, who had the rage of the Titans and the calm of the gods, who had monstrous and marvellous sins, monstrous and marvellous virtues. To them she gave a language different from that of actual use, a language full of resonant music and sweet rhythm, made stately by solemn cadence, or made delicate by fanciful rhyme, jewelled with wonderful words, and enriched with lofty diction. She clothed her children in strange raiment and gave them masks, and at her bidding the antique world rose from its marble tomb. A new Caesar stalked through the streets of risen Rome, and with purple sail and flute-led oars another Cleopatra passed up the river to Antioch. Old myth and legend and dream took shape and substance. History was entirely re-written, and there was hardly one of the dramatists who did not recognise that the object of Art is not simple truth but complex beauty. In this they were perfectly right. Art itself is really a form of exaggeration; and selection, which is the very spirit of art, is nothing more than an intensified mode of over-emphasis.

But Life soon shattered the perfection of the form. Even in Shakespeare we can see the beginning of the end. It shows itself by the gradual breaking up of the blank-verse in the later plays, by the predominance given to prose, and by the over-importance assigned to characterisation. The passages in Shakespeare—and they are many— where the language is uncouth, vulgar, exaggerated, fantastic, obscene even, are entirely due to Life calling for an echo of her own voice, and rejecting the intervention of beautiful style, through which alone should life be suffered to find expression. Shakespeare is not by any means a flawless artist. He is too fond of going directly to life, and borrowing life's natural utterance. He forgets that when Art surrenders her imaginative medium she surrenders everything. Goethe says, somewhere—

"In der Beschränkung zeigt sich erst der Meister,"

"It is in working within limits that the master reveals himself," and the limitation, the very condition of any art is style. However, we need not linger any longer over Shakespeare's realism. *The Tempest* is the most perfect of palinodes. All that we desired to point out was, that the magnificent work of the Elizabethan and Jacobean artists contained within itself the seeds of its own dissolution, and that, if it drew some of its strength from using life as rough material, it drew all its weakness from using life as an artistic method. As the inevitable result of this substitution of an imitative for a creative medium, this surrender of an imaginative form, we have the modern English melodrama. The characters in these plays talk on the stage exactly as they would talk off it; they have neither aspirations nor aspirates; they are taken directly from life and repro-

6–8. with purple sail . . . to Antioch, as described by Shakespeare in *Antony and Cleopatra*, Act II, sc. 2, ll. 195 ff.

duce its vulgarity down to the smallest detail; they present the gait, manner, costume and accent of real people; they would pass unnoticed in a third-class railway carriage. And yet how wearisome the plays are! They do not succeed in producing even that impression of reality at which they aim, and which is their only reason for existing. As a method, realism is a complete failure.

What is true about the drama and the novel is no less true about those arts that we call the decorative arts. The whole history of these arts in Europe is the record of the struggle between Orientalism, with its frank rejection of imitation, its love of artistic convention, its dislike to the actual representation of any object in Nature, and our own imitative spirit. Wherever the former has been paramount, as in Byzantium, Sicily and Spain, by actual contact, or in the rest of Europe by the influence of the Crusades, we have had beautiful and imaginative work in which the visible things of life are transmuted into artistic conventions, and the things that Life has not are invented and fashioned for her delight. But wherever we have returned to Life and Nature, our work has always become vulgar, common and uninteresting. Modern tapestry, with its aërial effects, its elaborate perspective, its broad expanses of waste sky, its faithful and laborious realism, has no beauty whatsoever. The pictorial glass of Germany is absolutely detestable. We are beginning to weave possible carpets in England, but only because we have returned to the method and spirit of the East. Our rugs and carpets of twenty years ago, with their solemn depressing truths, their inane worship of Nature, their sordid reproductions of visible objects, have become, even to the Philistine, a source of laughter. A cultured Mahomedan once remarked to us, "You Christians are so occupied in misinterpreting the fourth commandment that you have never thought of making an artistic application of the second." He was perfectly right, and the whole truth of the matter is this: The proper school to learn art in is not Life but Art. . . .

It was not always thus. We need not say anything about the poets, for they, with the unfortunate exception of Mr. Wordsworth, have been really faithful to their high mission, and are universally recognised as being absolutely unreliable. But in the works of Herodotus, who, in spite of the shallow and ungenerous attempts of modern sciolists to verify his history, may justly be called the "Father of Lies"; in the published speeches of Cicero and the biographies of Suetonius; in Tacitus at his best; in Pliny's *Natural History;* in Hanno's *Periplus;* in all the early chronicles; in the Lives of the Saints; in Froissart and Sir Thomas Malory; in the travels of Marco Polo; in Olaus Magnus, and Aldrovandus, and Conrad Lycosthenes, with his magnificent *Prodigiorum et Ostentorum Chronicon;* in the autobiography of Benvenuto Cellini; in the memoirs of Casanova; in Defoe's *History of the Plague;* in Boswell's *Life of Johnson;* in Napoleon's despatches, and in the works of our own Carlyle, whose *French Revolution* is one of the most fascinating historical novels ever written, facts are either kept in their proper subordinate position, or else entirely excluded on the general ground of dulness. Now, everything is changed. Facts are not merely finding a footing-place in history, but they are usurping the domain of Fancy, and have invaded the kingdom of Romance. Their chilling touch is over everything. They are vulgarising mankind. The crude commercialism of America, its materialising spirit, its indifference to the poetical side of things, and its lack of imagination and of high unattainable ideals, are entirely due to that country having adopted for its national hero a man who, according to his own confession, was incapable of telling a lie, and it is not too much to say that the story of George Washington and the cherry-tree has done more harm, and in a shorter space of time, than any other moral tale in the whole of literature. . . .

39. the fourth commandment, "Remember the sabbath day, to keep it holy" (Exodus 20:8).   41. the second, "Thou shalt not make unto thee any graven image . . ." (Exodus 20:4).   46. Mr. Wordsworth, as his views are expressed, for example, in the preface to *Lyrical Ballads* (see page 29).   49. Herodotus, Greek historian (484?–425 B.C.).

4–5. Suetonius, author of *The Lives of the Caesars,* d. about 160 A.D. Tacitus, Roman historian (first century A.D.). Pliny, Roman naturalist (23–79 A.D.). Hanno, Carthaginian admiral, about 500 B.C., who explored the west coast of Africa, and whose account of his experiences is still extant in the Greek translation.   7. Froissart, French chronicler (1337?–1410?) of the Hundred Years' War. Sir Thomas Malory. See selections in Vol. I.   8. Marco Polo, Venetian traveler in China (1254–1323). Olaus Magnus, Swedish historian and cartographer (1490–1558). 9. Aldrovandus, Ulisse Aldrovandi (1522–1605), Italian naturalist.   9–10. Conrad Lycosthenes . . . Chronicon, German philologist and theologian (1518–1561). The text of the famous curious work cited by Wilde is "full of marvels with solemn annotations at the foot."   11. Benvenuto Cellini, Italian artist in metal (1500–1571), author of one of the world's most famous autobiographies.   12. Casanova, Giovanni Casanova de Seingalt (1725–1798), Italian poet and adventurer, celebrated for the extraordinary frankness of his *Memoirs.*   12–13. Defoe's History of the Plague, *Journal of the Plague Year,* 1722, a work of fiction, purportedly the account of an eyewitness of the great London plague of 1665. 13. Boswell's Life of Johnson. See selections in Vol. I. 31–32. the story of George Washington and the cherry-tree. "Father, I cannot tell a lie; I did it with my little hatchet." Mason Locke Weems told the story in his *Life of Washington,* 1800.

That some change will take place before this century has drawn to its close we have no doubt whatsoever. Bored by the tedious and improving conversation of those who have neither the wit to exaggerate nor the genius to romance, tired of the intelligent person whose reminiscences are always based upon memory, whose statements are invariably limited by probability, and who is at any time liable to be corroborated by the merest Philistine who happens to be present, Society [10] sooner or later must return to its lost leader, the cultured and fascinating liar. Who he was who first, without ever having gone out to the rude chase, told the wondering cavemen at sunset how he had dragged the Megatherium from the purple darkness of its jasper cave, or slain the Mammoth in single combat and brought back its gilded tusks, we cannot tell, and not one of our modern anthropologists, for all their much-boasted science, has had the ordinary courage to tell us. Whatever was [20] his name or race, he certainly was the true founder of social intercourse. For the aim of the liar is simply to charm, to delight, to give pleasure. He is the very basis of civilised society, and without him a dinner-party, even at the mansions of the great, is as dull as a lecture at the Royal Society, or a debate at the Incorporated Authors, or one of Mr. Burnand's farcical comedies.

Nor will he be welcomed by society alone. Art, breaking from the prison-house of realism, will [30] run to greet him, and will kiss his false, beautiful lips, knowing that he alone is in possession of the great secret of all her manifestations, the secret that Truth is entirely and absolutely a matter of style; while Life—poor, probable, uninteresting human life—tired of repeating herself for the benefit of Mr. Herbert Spencer, scientific historians, and the compilers of statistics in general, will follow meekly after him, and try to reproduce, in her own simple and untutored way, some of [40] the marvels of which he talks.

No doubt there will always be critics who, like a certain writer in the *Saturday Review*, will gravely censure the teller of fairy tales for his defective knowledge of natural history, who will measure imaginative work by their own lack of any imaginative faculty, and will hold up their ink-stained hands in horror if some honest gentleman, who has never been farther than the yew-trees of his own garden, pens a fascinating book of travels like Sir John Mandeville, or, like great Raleigh, writes a whole history of the world, without knowing anything whatsoever about the past. To excuse themselves they will try and shelter under the shield of him who made Prospero the magician, and gave him Caliban and Ariel as his servants, who heard the Tritons blowing their horns round the coral reefs of the Enchanted Isle, and the fairies singing to each other in a wood near Athens, who led the phantom kings in dim procession across the misty Scottish heath, and hid Hecate in a cave with the weird sisters. They will call upon Shakespeare—they always do—and will quote that hackneyed passage about Art holding the mirror up to Nature, forgetting that this unfortunate aphorism is deliberately said by Hamlet in order to convince the bystanders of his absolute insanity in all art-matters. . . .

Art finds her own perfection within, and not outside of, herself. She is not to be judged by any external standard of resemblance. She is a veil, rather than a mirror. She has flowers that no forests know of, birds that no woodland possesses. She makes and unmakes many worlds, and can draw the moon from heaven with a scarlet thread. Hers are the "forms more real than living man," and hers the great archetypes of which things that have existence are but unfinished copies. Nature has, in her eyes, no laws, no uniformity. She can work miracles at her will, and when she calls monsters from the deep they come. She can bid the almond-tree blossom in winter, and send the snow upon the ripe cornfield. At her word the frost lays its silver finger on the burning month of June, and the winged lions creep out from the hollows of the Lydian hills. The dryads peer from the thicket as she passes by, and the brown fauns smile strangely at her when she comes near them. She has hawk-faced gods that worship her, and the centaurs gallop at her side. . . .

What we have to do, what at any rate it is our

2. Sir John Mandeville. *The Travels of Sir John Mandeville*, a compilation of fact and fancy, is one of the most famous travel books in literature. Raleigh, Sir Walter Raleigh (c. 1552–1618). 6–7. Prospero . . . Caliban and Ariel are all characters in *The Tempest*, Shakespeare's play of the Enchanted Isle, but the reference to Tritons blowing their horns echoes Wordsworth's sonnet, "The World Is Too Much with Us" (page 67). 10. fairies . . . Athens, in *A Midsummer Night's Dream*. 11–13. led . . . sisters, *Macbeth*, Act IV, sc. 1. 15–19. that hackneyed passage . . . art-matters. *Hamlet*, Act III, sc. 2. Wilde here intentionally misinterprets Shakespeare's meaning. 27. "forms more real than living man," from Shelley's *Prometheus Unbound*, Act I. 31–32. when she calls monsters from the deep they come. See *I Henry IV*, Act III, sc. 1, ll. 53–55.

duty to do, is to revive this old art of Lying. Much of course may be done, in the way of educating the public, by amateurs in the domestic circle, at literary lunches, and at afternoon teas. But this is merely the light and graceful side of lying, such as was probably heard at Cretan dinner-parties. There are many other forms. Lying for the sake of gaining some immediate personal advantage, for instance—lying with a moral purpose, as it is usually called—though of late it has been rather 10 looked down upon, was extremely popular with the antique world. Athena laughs when Odysseus tells her "his words of sly devising," as Mr. William Morris phrases it, and the glory of mendacity illumines the pale brow of the stainless hero of Euripidean tragedy, and sets among the noble women of the past the young bride of one of Horace's most exquisite odes. Later on, what at first had been merely a natural instinct was elevated into a self-conscious science. Elaborate rules were 20 laid down for the guidance of mankind, and an important school of literature grew up round the subject. Indeed, when one remembers the excellent philosophical treatise of Sanchez on the whole question, one cannot help regretting that no one has ever thought of publishing a cheap and condensed edition of the works of that great casuist. A short primer, "When to Lie and How," if brought out in an attractive and not too expensive a form, would no doubt command a large sale, and would 30 prove of real practical service to many earnest and deep-thinking people. Lying for the sake of the improvement of the young, which is the basis of home education, still lingers amongst us, and its advantages are so admirably set forth in the early books of Plato's *Republic* that it is unnecessary to dwell upon them here. It is a mode of lying for which all good mothers have peculiar capabilities, but it is capable of still further development, and has been sadly overlooked by the School Board. 40

Lying for the sake of a monthly salary is of course well known in Fleet Street, and the profession of a political leader-writer is not without its advantages. But it is said to be a somewhat dull occupation, and it certainly does not lead to much beyond a kind of ostentatious obscurity. The only form of lying that is absolutely beyond reproach is lying for its own sake, and the highest development of this is, as we have already pointed out, Lying in Art. Just as those who do not love Plato more than Truth cannot pass beyond the threshold of the Academe, so those who do not love Beauty more than Truth never know the inmost shrine of Art. The solid stolid British intellect lies in the desert sands like the Sphinx in Flaubert's marvellous tale, and fantasy, *La Chimère*, dances round it, and calls to it with her false, flute-toned voice. It may not hear her now, but surely some day, when we are all bored to death with the commonplace character 20 of modern fiction, it will hearken to her and try to borrow her wings.

And when that day dawns, or sunset reddens, how joyous we shall all be! Facts will be regarded as discreditable, Truth will be found mourning over her fetters, and Romance, with her temper of wonder, will return to the land. The very aspect of the world will change to our startled eyes. Out of the sea will rise Behemoth and Leviathan, and sail round the high-pooped galleys, as they do on 30 the delightful maps of those ages when books on geography were actually readable. Dragons will wander about the waste places, and the phoenix will soar from her nest of fire into the air. We shall lay our hands upon the basilisk, and see the jewel in the toad's head. Champing his gilded oats, the Hippogriff will stand in our stalls, and over our heads will float the Blue Bird singing of beautiful and impossible things, of things that are lovely and that never happen, of things that are not and that should be. But before this comes to pass we 40 must cultivate the lost art of Lying.

13–14. **as Mr. William Morris phrases it,** in his translation of the *Odyssey*, 1867. 15–6. **the stainless hero . . . tragedy,** Orestes. 17–18. **the young bride . . . odes,** *Odes*, Book III, 11. The bride was Hypermnestra, her young husband Lynceus. 24. **Sanchez,** Thomas Sanchez of Cordova (1551–1610).

2. **Fleet Street,** the journalistic center of London. 15. **Flaubert,** Gustave Flaubert (1821–1880), author of *Madame Bovary* and *Salâmmbo*. 28. **Behemoth and Leviathan,** a huge beast and the crocodile, respectively, in Job 40–41.

Francis Thompson
1859–1907

Francis Thompson, whose aim was not "to be the poet of the return to Nature" but rather "the poet of the return to God," came to his destiny by a winding and difficult road. He was born in Lancashire, December 18, 1859, and was first intended for the Roman Catholic priesthood. He failed to qualify, turned next to his father's profession of medicine, and failed quite as ignominiously. From 1885 to 1888 he lived the life of an outcast on the streets of London, suffering both physical agony and mental torture, the latter greatly aggravated by the fact that he had contracted the opium habit during an illness. Wilfrid Meynell, the editor of *Merry England*, and his wife Alice, the distinguished poet, literally snatched him from the jaws of death, and gave him the means of working out his salvation as a man, as an artist, and as a human soul. He spent some time at the Premonstratensian Priory in Sussex, and later at a Capuchin monastery in Wales, where he became an intimate friend of Coventry Patmore. He died of tuberculosis in London, November 13, 1907.

Thompson published three volumes of poetry: *Poems*, 1893; *Sister Songs* (written for the Meynell children, whom he loved), 1895; *New Poems*, 1897. During the last ten years of his life he wrote only prose, including a fine essay on Shelley and a life of St. Ignatius Loyola. His work shows the influence of Shelley, but more strongly that of the metaphysical poets of the seventeenth century, especially Crashaw. In his own time, when the metaphysicals were less read than they are today, he was much reproached for the difficulty of his verse.

THE POPPY

To Monica

Summer set lip to earth's bosom bare,
And left the flushed print in a poppy there:
Like a yawn of fire from the grass it came,
And the fanning wind puffed it to flapping flame.

With burnt mouth, red like a lion's, it drank
The blood of the sun as he slaughtered sank,
And dipped its cup in the purpurate shine
When the eastern conduits ran with wine.

Monica, the daughter of Wilfred and Alice Meynell.
7. **purpurate**, purple.

Till it grew lethargied with fierce bliss,
And hot as a swinkèd gipsy is,   10
And drowsed in sleepy savageries,
With mouth wide a-pout for a sultry kiss.

A child and man paced side by side,
Treading the skirts of eventide;
But between the clasp of his hand and hers
Lay, felt not, twenty withered years.

She turned, with the rout of her dusk South hair,
And saw the sleeping gipsy there;
And snatched and snapped it in swift child's whim,
With—"Keep it, long as you live!"—to him.   20

And his smile, as nymphs from their laving meres,
Trembled up from a bath of tears;
And joy, like a mew sea-rocked apart,
Tossed on the waves of his troubled heart.

For *he* saw what she did not see,
That—as kindled by its own fervency—
The verge shrivelled inward smoulderingly:
And suddenly 'twixt his hand and hers
He knew the twenty withered years—
No flower, but twenty shrivelled years.   30

"Was never such thing until this hour,"
Low to his heart he said; "the flower
Of sleep brings wakening to me,
And of oblivion, memory."

"Was never this thing to me," he said,
"Though with bruisèd poppies my feet are red!"
And again to his own heart very low:
"Oh child! I love, for I love and know;

"But you, who love nor know at all
The diverse chambers in Love's guest-hall,   40
Where some rise early, few sit long:
In how differing accents hear the throng
His great Pentecostal tongue;

"Who know not love from amity,
Nor my reported self from me;
A fair fit gift is this, meseems,
You give—this withering flower of dreams.

10. **swinkèd**, exhausted from labor.   43. **Pentecostal**. See Acts 2.

"O frankly fickle, and fickly true,
Do you know what the days will do to you?
To your Love and you what the days will do,   50
O frankly fickle, and fickly true?

"You have loved me, Fair, three lives—or days;
'Twill pass with the passing of my face.
But where *I* go, your face goes too,
To watch lest I play false to you.

"I am but, my sweet, your foster-lover,
Knowing well when certain years are over
You vanish from me to another;
Yet I know, and love, like the foster-mother.

"So, frankly fickle, and fickly true!   60
For my brief life-while I take from you
This token, fair and fit, meseems,
For me—this withering flower of dreams."

The sleep-flower sways in the wheat its head,
Heavy with dreams, as that with bread:
The goodly grain and the sun-flushed sleeper
The reaper reaps, and Time the reaper.

I hang 'mid men my needless head,
And my fault is dreams, as theirs is bread!
The goodly men and the sun-hazed sleeper   70
Time shall reap; but after the reaper
The world shall glean of me, me the sleeper!

Love, love! your flower of withered dream
In leavèd rhyme lies safe, I deem,
Sheltered and shut in a nook of rhyme,
From the reaper man, and his reaper Time.

Love! I fall into the claws of Time;
But lasts within a leavèd rhyme
All that the world of me esteems—
My withered dreams, my withered dreams.   80

LITTLE JESUS

*Ex ore infantium Deus et lactentium
perfecisti laudem*

Little Jesus, wast Thou shy
Once, and just so small as I?
And what did it feel like to be
Out of heaven, and just like me?
Didst Thou sometimes think of *there*,
And ask where all the angels were?
I should think that I would cry
For my house all made of sky;
I would look about the air,

Ex . . . *laudem*. "Out of the mouths of babes and suck-
lings hast thou ordained strength." (Psalm 8:2; **Vulgate**)

And wonder where my angels were;   10
And at waking 'twould distress me—
Not an angel there to dress me!
Hadst Thou ever any toys
Like us little girls and boys?
And didst Thou play in Heaven with all
The angels, that were not too tall,
With stars for marbles? Did the things
Play *Can you see me?* through their wings?
And did Thy Mother let Thee spoil
Thy robes, with playing on *our* soil?
How nice to have them always new
In Heaven, because 'twas quite clean blue!

Didst Thou kneel at night to pray,
And didst Thou join Thy hands, this way?   20
And did they tire sometimes, being young,
And make the prayer seem very long?
And dost Thou like it best, that we
Should join our hands to pray to Thee?
I used to think, before I knew,
The prayer not said unless we do.
And did Thy Mother at the night
Kiss Thee, and fold the clothes in right?
And didst Thou feel quite good in bed,
Kissed, and sweet, and Thy prayers said?   30

Thou canst not have forgotten all
That it feels like to be small;
And Thou know'st I cannot pray
To Thee in my father's way—
When Thou wast so little, say,
Couldst Thou talk Thy Father's way?

So, a little Child, come down
And hear a child's tongue like Thy own;
Take me by the hand and walk,
And listen to my baby-talk.
To Thy Father show my prayer   40
(He will look, Thou art so fair),
And say: "O Father, I, Thy Son,
Bring the prayer of a little one."

And He will smile, that children's tongue
Has not changed since Thou wast young!

THE HOUND OF HEAVEN

The theme of this, one of the great English poems of religious experience, is well stated in the words of Father
J. F. X. O'Connor: "As the hound follows the hare, never
ceasing in its running, ever drawing nearer in the
chase . . . so does God follow the fleeing soul by his
Divine grace" (*A Study of Francis Thompson's "Hound of
Heaven,"* John Lane, 1912). It has been plausibly sug-

gested that the title may have come from Thompson's beloved Shelley, who speaks in *Promethus Unbound*, l. 34, of
"Heaven's wingèd hound."

I fled Him, down the nights and down the days;
　I fled Him, down the arches of the years;
　I fled Him, down the labyrinthine ways
Of my own mind; and in the mist of tears
I hid from Him, and under running laughter.
　　　Up vistaed hopes I sped;
　　　And shot, precipitated,
Adown Titanic glooms of chasmèd fears,
　From those strong Feet that followed, followed
　　　after.
　　　But with unhurrying chase,   10
　　　And unperturbèd pace,
　Deliberate speed, majestic instancy,
　　　They beat—and a Voice beat
　　　More instant than the Feet—
　"All things betray thee, who betrayest Me."

　　　I pleaded, outlaw-wise,
By many a hearted casement, curtained red,
　Trellised with intertwining charities;
(For, though I knew His love Who followèd,
　　　Yet was I sore adread   20
Lest, having Him, I must have naught beside)
But, if one little casement parted wide,
　The gust of His approach would clash it to.
　Fear wist not to evade, as Love wist to pursue.
Across the margent of the world I fled,
　And troubled the gold gateways of the stars,
　Smiting for shelter on their clangèd bars;
　　　Fretted to dulcet jars
And silvern chatter the pale ports o' the moon.
I said to Dawn: Be sudden—to Eve: Be soon;   30
　With thy young skiey blossoms heap me over
　　　From this tremendous Lover—
Float thy vague veil about me, lest He see!
　I tempted all His servitors, but to find
My own betrayal in their constancy,
In faith to Him their fickleness to me,
　Their traitorous trueness, and their loyal deceit.
To all swift things for swiftness did I sue;
　Clung to the whistling mane of every wind.
　　　But whether they swept, smoothly fleet,   40

1. I fled him. See Psalm 138:7-12. **14. instant,** pressing,
urgent. **16–18. I pleaded . . . charities.** "The casement,
being here the human heart, is trellised not merely with the
vine of the love of God but also with the love of creatures."—Francis P. LeBuffe, *The Hound of Heaven, An Interpretation,* Macmillan, 1921, page 34. **24. wist,** knew.
25. margent, margin, boundary. **30. I said . . . Be
soon.** See Deuteronomy 28:67. **34–37. I tempted . . .
deceit.** Since the poet sought in creatures what can only
be found in the Creator, they served God by refusing to
satisfy their ill-advised adorer.

The long savannahs of the blue;
　Or whether, Thunder-driven,
　They clanged his chariot 'thwart a heaven,
Plashy with flying lightnings round the spurn o'
　　　their feet:—
　Fear wist not to evade as Love wist to pursue.
　　　Still with unhurrying chase,
　　　And unperturbèd pace,
　Deliberate speed, majestic instancy,
　　　Came on the following Feet,
　　　And a Voice above their beat—   50
　"Naught shelters thee, who wilt not shelter
　　　Me."
I sought no more that after which I strayed,
　　　In face of man or maid;
But still within the little children's eyes
　　　Seems something, something that replies.
They at least are for me, surely for me!
I turned me to them very wistfully;
But just as their young eyes grew sudden fair
　　　With dawning answers there,
Their angel plucked them from me by the hair.   60
"Come then, ye other children, Nature's—share
With me" (said I) "your delicate fellowship;
　　　Let me greet you lip to lip,
　　　Let me twine with you caresses,
　　　　Wantoning
　With our Lady-Mother's vagrant tresses,
　　　Banqueting
　With her in her wind-walled palace,
　　　Underneath her azured daïs,
　Quaffing, as your taintless way is,   70
　　　From a chalice
Lucent-weeping out of the dayspring."
　　　So it was done;
I in their delicate fellowship was one—
Drew the bolt of Nature's secrecies.
　I knew all the swift importings
　On the wilful face of skies;
　I knew how the clouds arise
　Spumèd of the wild sea-snortings;
　　　All that's born or dies   80
　Rose and drooped with; made them shapers
Of mine own moods, or wailful or divine—
　With them joyed and was bereaven.
　　　I was heavy with the even,
　When she lit her glimmering tapers

41. savannahs of the blue, plains of the heavens.
60. Their angel, their guardian angel, who did not wish
the children to be the innocent means of deflecting the poet
from God. In this passage, and in that which immediately
follows, Thompson's Catholic dissent from the primitivistic
Nature-cult prominent in so many nineteenth-century poets
appears clearly.　**66. Lady-Mother's.** Nature's. **vagrant,**
wandering.　**72. Lucent-weeping,** dripping light.

Round the day's dead sanctities.
    I laughed in the morning's eyes.
I triumphed and I saddened with all weather,
    Heaven and I wept together,
And its sweet tears were salt with mortal mine;   90
Against the red throb of its sunset-heart
    I laid my own to beat,
    And share commingling heat;
But not by that, by that, was eased my human smart.
In vain my tears were wet on Heaven's grey cheek.
For ah! we know not what each other says,
    These things and I; in sound *I* speak—
Their sound is but their stir, they speak by silences.
Nature, poor stepdame, cannot slake my drouth;
    Let her, if she would owe me,   100
Drop yon blue bosom-veil of sky, and show me
    The breasts o' her tenderness:
Never did any milk of hers once bless
    My thirsting mouth.
    Nigh and nigh draws the chase.
    With unperturbèd pace,
Deliberate speed majestic instancy
    And past those noisèd Feet
    A voice comes yet more fleet—
"Lo! naught contents thee, who content'st
    not Me."   110

Naked I wait Thy love's uplifted stroke!
My harness piece by piece Thou hast hewn from me,
    And smitten me to my knee;
    I am defenceless utterly.
    I slept, methinks, and woke,
And, slowly gazing, find me stripped in sleep.
In the rash lustihead of my young powers,
    I shook the pillaring hours
And pulled my life upon me; grimed with smears,
I stand amid the dust o' the mounded years—   120
My mangled youth lies dead beneath the heap.
My days have crackled and gone up in smoke,
Have puffed and burst as sun-starts on a stream.
    Yea, faileth now even dream
The dreamer, and the lute the lutanist;
Even the linked fantasies, in whose blossomy twist
I swung the earth a trinket at my wrist,
Are yielding; cords of all too weak account
For earth with heavy griefs so overplussed.
    Ah! is Thy love indeed   130
A weed, albeit an amaranthine weed,

Suffering no flowers except its own to mount?
    Ah! must—
    Designer infinite!—
Ah! must Thou char the wood ere Thou canst limn
    with it?
My freshness spent its wavering shower i' the dust;
And now my heart is as a broken fount,
Wherein tear-drippings stagnate, spilt down ever
    From the dank thoughts that shiver
Upon the sighful branches of my mind.   140
    Such is; what is to be?
The pulp so bitter, how shall taste the rind?
I dimly guess what Time in mists confounds;
Yet ever and anon a trumpet sounds
From the hid battlements of Eternity,
Those shaken mists a space unsettle, then
Round the half-glimpsèd turrets slowly wash again.
    But not ere him who summoneth
    I first have seen, enwound
With glooming robes purpureal, cypress-crowned;
His name I know, and what his trumpet saith.   151
Whether man's heart or life it be which yields
    Thee harvest, must Thy harvest fields
    Be dunged with rotten death?

    Now of that long pursuit
    Comes on at hand the bruit;
That Voice is round me like a bursting sea:
    "And is thy earth so marred,
    Shattered in shard on shard?
Lo, all things fly thee, for thou fliest Me!   160
Strange, piteous, futile thing!
Wherefore should any set thee love apart?
Seeing none but I makes much of naught" (He
    said),
"And human love needs human meriting:
    How hast thou merited—
Of all man's clotted clay the dingiest clot?
    Alack, thou knowest not
How little worthy of any love thou art!
Whom wilt thou find to love ignoble thee,
    Save Me, save only Me?   170
All which I took from thee I did but take,
    Not for thy harms,
But just that thou might'st seek it in My arms.
    All which thy child's mistake
Fancies as lost, I have stored for thee at home:
    Rise, clasp My hand, and come!"

---

100. owe, own.   **108. noisèd**, making noise.   **115–21. I slept . . . heap.** Like Samson, in Judges 16. **122. My days . . . smoke.** See Psalm 101:4–7.   **123. sun-starts**, bubbles.   **126–27. linked fantasies . . . wrist**, his poetic dreams.   **131. A weed**, because it roots out all over loves. **amaranthine**, like the immortal amaranth. See *Paradise Lost*, Book III, ll. 353–57.

135. limn, draw.   **148. him**, "a symbol of death to self in the spirit of Christ."—Terence L. Connolly, in his annotated edition of Thompson's *Poems*, Appleton-Century, 1932. **150. purpureal**, purple. **cypress**, the symbol of death. **152–54. Whether . . . death.** So it was in the sacrifice of Christ, and so it is in the Christian's death to self. **156. bruit**, noise.

Halts by me that footfall:
Is my gloom, after all,
Shade of His hand, outstretched caressingly?
"Ah, fondest, blindest, weakest,　　　　　180
I am He Whom thou seekest!
Thou dravest love from thee, who dravest Me."

(since-old)

A FALLEN YEW

It seemed corrival of the world's great prime,
　　Made to un-edge the scythe of Time,
　　　　And last with stateliest rhyme.

No tender Dryad ever did indue
　　That rigid chiton of rough yew,
　　　　To fret her white flesh through:

But some god like to those grim Asgard lords,
　　Who walk the fables of the hordes
　　　　From Scandinavian fjords,

Upheaved its stubborn girth, and raised unriven, 10
　　Against the whirl-blast and the levin,
　　　　Defiant arms to Heaven.

When doom puffed out the stars, we might have
　　said,
　　It would decline its heavy head,
　　　　And see the world to bed.

For this firm yew did from the vassal leas,
　　And rain and air, its tributaries,
　　　　Its revenues increase,

And levy impost on the golden sun,
　　Take the blind years as they might run,　　　20
　　　　And no fate seek or shun.

But now our yew is strook, is fallen—yea,
　　Hacked like dull wood of every day
　　　　To this and that, men say.

Never!—To Hades' shadowy shipyards gone,
　　Dim barge of Dis, down Acheron
　　　　It drops, or Lethe wan.

179. **Shade of His hand.** See Isaiah 49 : 2. **1. corrival,**
companion. **4. Dryad,** in Greek mythology, a wood nymph
inhabiting a tree. **5. chiton,** shift or tunic. **7. Asgard,** the
home of the gods in Norse mythology. **11. levin,** lightning.
25. Hades, the Greek land of the dead. **26. Dis,** Pluto,
the ruler of Hades. **Acheron,** the river of sorrow in Hades.
27. Lethe, the river of forgetfulness.

Stirred by its fall—poor destined bark of Dis!—
　　Along my soul a bruit there is
　　　　Of echoing images,　　　　　　　30

Reverberations of mortality:
　　Spelt backward from its death, to me
　　　　Its life reads saddenedly.

Its breast was hollowed as the tooth of eld;
　　And boys, there creeping unbeheld,
　　　　A laughing moment dwelled.

Yet they, within its very heart so crept,
　　Reached not the heart that courage kept
　　　　With winds and years beswept.

And in its boughs did close and kindly nest　　40
　　The birds, as they within its breast,
　　　　By all its leaves caressed.

But bird nor child might touch by any art
　　Each other's or the tree's hid heart,
　　　　A whole God's breadth apart;

The breadth of God, the breadth of death and life!
　　Even so, even so, in undreamed strife
　　　　With pulseless Law, the wife,—

The sweetest wife on sweetest marriage-day,—
　　Their souls at grapple in mid-way,　　　　50
　　　　Sweet to her sweet may say:

"I take you to my inmost heart, my true!"
　　Ah, fool! but there is one heart you
　　　　Shall never take him to!

The hold that falls not when the town it got,
　　The heart's heart, whose immurèd plot
　　　　Hath keys yourself keep not!

Its ports you cannot burst—you are withstood—
　　For him that to your listening blood
　　　　Sends precepts as he would.　　　　60

Its gates are deaf to Love, high summoner;
　　Yea, Love's great warrant runs not there:
　　　　You are your prisoner.

Yourself are with yourself the sole consortress
　　In that unleaguerable fortress;
　　　　It knows you not for portress.

Its keys are at the cincture hung of God;
　　Its gates are trepidant to His nod;
　　　By Him its floors are trod.

And if His feet shall rock those floors in wrath, 70
　　Or blest aspersion sleek His path,
　　　Is only choice it hath.

Yea, in that ultimate heart's occult abode
　　To lie as in an oubliette of God,
　　　Or in a bower untrod,

Built by a secret Lover for His Spouse;—
　　Sole choice is this your life allows,
　　　Sad tree, whose perishing boughs
　　　　So few birds house!

FIELD–FLOWER

A Phantasy

God took a fit of Paradise-wind,
　　A slip of coerule weather, *blue*
A thought as simple as Himself,
　　And ravelled them together.
Unto His eyes He held it there,
To teach it gazing debonair
　　With memory of what, perdie,
A God's young innocences were.
His fingers pushed it through the sod—
It came up redolent of God,   10
Garrulous of the eyes of God
　　To all the breezes near it;
Musical of the mouth of God
　　To all had ears to hear it;
Mystical with the mirth of God,
　　That glow-like did ensphere it.
　　　　And—"Babble! babble! babble!" said;
　　　　"I'll tell the whole world one day!"
　　　　There was no blossom half so glad,
　　　　　Since sun of Christ's first Sunday.   20

A poet took a flaw of pain,
　　A hap of skiey pleasure,
A thought had in his cradle lain,
　　And mingled them in measure.
That chrism he laid upon his eyes,
And lips, and heart, for euphrasies,
　　That he might see, feel, sing, perdie,

---

68. **trepidant,** in a state of vibration.　71. **aspersion,**
sprinkling. **sleek,** make smooth.　76. **Lover,** God. **His**
Spouse, man's spiritual being.　1. **fit,** strain (a musical
term).　2. **coerule,** heavenly blue.　21. **flaw,** flake, fragment.　22. **hap,** a chance bit.　25. **chrism,** sacramental
anointment.　26. **euphrasies.** The herb euphrasy (eye-
bright) was supposed to have the power of restoring sight.

The simple things that are the wise.
Beside the flower he held his ways,
And leaned him to it gaze for gaze—   30
He took its meaning, gaze for gaze,
　　As baby looks on baby;
Its meaning passed into his gaze,
　　Native as meaning may be;
He rose with all his shining gaze
　　As children's eyes at play be.
　　　　And—"Babble! babble! babble!" said;
　　　　"I'll tell the whole world one day!"
　　　　There was no poet half so glad,
　　　　　Since man grew God that Sunday.   40

TO A SNOWFLAKE

What heart could have thought you?—
Past our devisal
(O filigree petal!)
Fashioned so purely,
Fragilely, surely,
From what Paradisal
Imagineless metal,
Too costly for cost?
Who hammered you, wrought you
From argentine vapour?—   10
　　God was my shaper.
Passing surmisal,
He hammered, He wrought me,
From curled silver vapour,
To lust of His mind;—
Thou could'st not have thought me!
So purely, so palely,
Tinily, surely,
Mightily, frailly,
Insculped and embossed,   20
With His hammer of wind,
And His graver of frost.

THE KINGDOM OF GOD

"In no Strange Land"

O world invisible, we view thee,
O world intangible, we touch thee,
O world unknowable, we know thee,
Inapprehensible, we clutch thee!

Does the fish soar to find the ocean,
The eagle plunge to find the air—
That we ask of the stars in motion
If they have rumour of thee there?

---

10. **argentine,** silvery.　"*In no Strange Land.*" See Exodus
2:22; Psalm 137:4.

Not where the wheeling systems darken,
And our benumbed conceiving soars!—   10
The drift of pinions, would we hearken,
Beats at our own clay-shuttered doors.

The angels keep their ancient places;—
Turn but a stone and start a wing!
'Tis ye, 'tis your estrangèd faces,
That miss the many-splendoured thing.

But (when so sad thou canst not sadder)
Cry;—and upon thy so sore loss
Shall shine the traffic of Jacob's ladder
Pitched betwixt Heaven and Charing Cross.   20

Yea, in the night, my Soul, my daughter,
Cry,—clinging Heaven by the hems;
And lo, Christ walking on the water
Not of Gennesareth, but Thames!

ENVOY

Go, songs, for ended is our brief, sweet play;
    Go, children of swift joy and tardy sorrow:
And some are sung, and that was yesterday,
    And some unsung, and that may be to-morrow.

Go forth; and if it be o'er stony way,
    Old joy can lend what newer grief must borrow:
And it was sweet, and that was yesterday,
    And sweet is sweet, though purchasèd with sorrow.

Go, songs, and come not back from your far
        way:
    And if men ask you why ye smile and sorrow,   10
Tell them ye grieve, for your hearts know To-day,
    Tell them ye smile, for your eyes know To-morrow.

Thomas Hardy
1840–1928

Hardy and Meredith, alone among English writers, achieved front rank both as novelist and as poet. Hardy began as a poet, writing only poetry until 1870, at which time his engagement to Emma Gifford made it seem advisable that he turn his attention to a more remunerative kind of writing. After the rough handling the critics gave the naturalistic *Jude the Obscure* in 1895, he abandoned the novel at the height of his powers; from then until the end of his long life in 1928, he again devoted himself exclusively to what was closest to his heart, poetry. In 1903–08 he published his vast epic-drama of the Napoleonic Wars, *The Dynasts*, which some critics consider the greatest literary achievement thus far in the twentieth century.

Hardy's prose and verse alike are mainly concerned with what he calls Wessex—"a province bounded on the north by the Thames, on the south by the English Channel, on the east by a line running from Hayling Island to Windsor Forest, and on the west by the Cornish coast." This region he has made definitely his own.

Though Hardy was often regarded as an iconoclast, no writer was ever more penetrated with a sense of the past. During his childhood in Dorsetshire, his neighbors were still discussing the threatened invasion of England by Napoleon at the beginning of the century in a dialect which clearly betrayed the Germanic origins of the English language, and Roman ruins, still standing, carried his mind back eighteen hundred years before Napoleon. Grown up, he became an ecclesiastical architect, and this profession helped to keep the older aspects of English civilization in his mind.

One cannot think of the past without thinking of the dead; it is not unnatural, therefore, that the dead should play a large part in Hardy's poems. For Hardy whatever has been, lives forever; nothing is ever lost or destroyed. The body has its resurrection in trees and flowers; less materially, the hands of the dead hover over the knobs of "Old Furniture," and the lineaments of the family face project themselves through the generations that perish. To purely human concerns (their own and their descendants') the dead are quite indifferent, yet they retain consciousness in their graves, and, as in Maeterlinck's *Blue Bird*, they die a second death when their memory fades. Those who die abroad—English soldiers in the Boer War, for

19. Jacob's ladder. See Genesis 28:12.   **20. Charing Cross**, in the heart of London.   **24. Gennesareth,** the Sea of Galilee; see Matthew 14:25–33. **Thames,** the river on which London is situated.

example—must leave their bodies in an alien clime, but their souls come home on the wings of the wind to an England quite indifferent to their military glory but happy to remember their quiet household ways in days gone by.

Men are so much like Nature in Hardy's world that an old woman's life can be likened to the leaves she rakes up in King's-Hintock Park. Yet Nature is perfectly indifferent to us, and we must enjoy the myriad beauties she presents without any thought that they were designed for our delectation. And God is as indifferent as Nature. God has actually forgotten that He ever made the world; it was one of his failures; He lost interest in it almost from the beginning. For that matter, God knows nothing of values. Values are a human invention; the very thing that Browning ("Saul") said could not happen has happened in Hardy's world. Some day, it may be, the Blind Will that neither good nor evil knows may come to wake and understand. But that time is not yet.

The social order men live in is the kind one would expect to find under such a dispensation. No "private" joy is possible; even as one sits down by the Christmas fire, a starving bird comes to the window, to suggest all the underprivileged ones who are being shut out in the cold. The country girl begins to get her share of the good things of life only when she is "ruined," and the rich woman cannot deck her body in furs without becoming responsible for the murder of the helpless creatures that were robbed of them and the equally helpless wage-slaves of her own kind who wrought them into a garment. Over everything else hovers the threat of war, once honorable, now utterly ruthless, senseless, stripped of every value war may once have possessed. Yet life goes on somehow, and love goes on; "In Time of 'The Breaking of Nations'" simply resets "Love among the Ruins" in a minor key.

Somber as Hardy's conception of life and the world is—and it should be remembered that he presents it suggestively, as a poet, not dogmatically, as a philosopher—it serves him well. It is challenging; it is original; it furnishes a complete standard of reference. And his technique as an artist is adequate to his conceptions. Both as poet and as novelist, he is guilty of numerous awkward infelicities; the sensuous harmonies of a Spenser or a Tennyson he no more desired in verse than he desired the sophisticated completeness of a Henry James in prose fiction. But what he loses in grace he more than makes up in rugged power.

Hardy's best novels are *Under the Greenwood Tree*, 1872; *Far From the Madding Crowd*, 1874; *The Return of the Native*, 1878; *The Mayor of Casterbridge*, 1886; *Tess of the D'Urbervilles*, 1891. In general, his short stories are far below the level of his best work; "The Three Strangers" (from *Wessex Tales*) is, however, an exception. His *Collected Poems*, 4th ed., Macmillan, 1932, includes *Wessex Poems*, 1898; *Poems of the Past and the Present*, 1902; *Time's Laughingstocks*, 1909; *Satires of Circumstance*, 1911–14; *Moments of Vision*, 1917; *Late Lyrics*, 1922; *Human Shows*, 1925; *Winter Words*, 1928.

THE SOULS OF THE SLAIN[1]

1

The thick lids of Night closed upon me
   Alone at the Bill
   Of the Isle by the Race—
Many-caverned, bald, wrinkled of face—
And with darkness and silence the spirit was on me
   To brood and be still.

2

No wind fanned the flats of the ocean,
   Or promontory sides,
   Or the ooze by the strand,
Or the bent-bearded slope of the land,   10
Whose base took its rest amid everlong motion
   Of criss-crossing tides.

3

Soon from out of the Southward seemed nearing
   A whirr, as of wings
   Waved by mighty-vanned flies,
Or by night-moths of measureless size,
And in softness and smoothness well-nigh beyond
   hearing
   Or corporal things.

4

And they bore to the bluff, and alighted—
   A dim-discerned train   20
   Of sprites without mould,
Frameless souls none might touch or might
   hold—
On the ledge by the turreted lantern, far-sighted
   By men of the main.

---

[1] This and the following poems by Thomas Hardy are from *Collected Poems*, 4th ed., 1932, The Macmillan Company. They are reprinted here by permission.
2–3. Bill . . . Race. "The 'Race' is the turbulent sea-area off the Bill of Portland, where contrary tides meet." (Hardy)
10. bent-bearded, covered with bent, a stiff, coarse grass.
15. vanned, winged.   **23. lantern,** lighthouse.

5

And I heard them say "Home!" and I knew them
  For souls of the felled
  On the earth's nether bord
Under Capricorn, whither they'd warred,
And I neared in my awe, and gave heedfulness to
    them
  With breathings inheld.   30

6

Then, it seemed, there approached from the
    northward
  A senior soul-flame
  Of the like filmy hue:
And he met them and spake: "Is it you,
O my men?" Said they, "Aye! We bear homeward
    and hearthward
  To feast on our fame!"

7

"I've flown there before you," he said then:
  "Your households are well;
  But—your kin linger less
On your glory and war-mightiness   40
Than on dearer things."—"Dearer?" cried these
    from the dead then,
  "Of what do they tell?"

8

"Some mothers muse sadly, and murmur
  Your doings as boys—
  Recall the quaint ways
Of your babyhood's innocent days.
Some pray that, ere dying, your faith had grown
    firmer,
  And higher your joys.

9

"A father broods: 'Would I had set him
  To some humble trade,
  And so slacked his high fire,   50
And his passionate martial desire;
Had told him no stories to woo him and whet him
  To this dire crusade!'"

10

"And, General, how hold out our sweethearts,
  Sworn loyal as doves?"
  —"Many mourn; many think
It is not unattractive to prink
Them in sables for heroes. Some fickle and fleet
    hearts
  Have found them new loves."   60

11

"And our wives?" quoth another resignedly,
  "Dwell they on our deeds?"
  —"Deeds of home; that live yet
Fresh as new—deeds of fondness or fret;
Ancient words that were kindly expressed or un-
    kindly,
  These, these have their heeds."

12

—"Alas! then it seems that our glory
  Weighs less in their thought
  Than our old homely acts,
And the long-ago commonplace facts   70
Of our lives—held by us as scarce part of our story,
  And rated as nought!"

13

Then bitterly some: "Was it wise now
  To raise the tomb-door
  For such knowledge? Away!"
But the rest: "Fame we prized till to-day;
Yet that hearts keep us green for old kindness we
    prize now
  A thousand times more!"

14

Thus speaking, the trooped apparitions
  Began to disband   80
  And resolve them in two:
Those whose record was lovely and true
Bore to northward for home: those of bitter tradi-
    tions
  Again left the land,

15

And, towering to seaward in legions,
  They paused at a spot
  Overbending the Race—
That engulphing, ghast, sinister place—
Whither headlong they plunged, to the fathomless
    regions
  Of myriads forgot.   90

16

And the spirits of those who were homing
  Passed on, rushingly,
  Like the Pentecost Wind;
And the whirr of their wayfaring thinned
And surceased on the sky, and but left in the gloam-
    ing
  Sea-mutterings and me.

93. Pentecost Wind. See Acts 2:2.

SHELLEY'S SKYLARK

(The Neighbourhood of Leghorn:
March 1887)

Somewhere afield here something lies
In Earth's oblivious eyeless trust
That moved a poet to prophecies—
A pinch of unseen, unguarded dust:

The dust of the lark that Shelley heard,
And made immortal through times to be;—
Though it only lived like another bird,
And knew not its immortality:

Lived its meek life; then, one day, fell—
A little ball of feather and bone;   10
And how it perished, when piped farewell,
And where it wastes, are alike unknown.

Maybe it rests in the loam I view,
Maybe it throbs in a myrtle's green,
Maybe it sleeps in the coming hue
Of a grape on the slopes of yon inland scene.

Go find it, faeries, go and find
That tiny pinch of priceless dust,
And bring a casket silver-lined,
And framed of gold that gems encrust;   20

And we will lay it safe therein,
And consecrate it to endless time;
For it inspired a bard to win
Ecstatic heights in thought and rhyme.

THE TO-BE-FORGOTTEN

I

I heard a small sad sound,
And stood awhile among the tombs around:
"Wherefore, old friends," said I, "are you distrest,
Now, screened from life's unrest?"

2

—"O not at being here;
But that our future second death is near;
When, with the living, memory of us numbs,
And blank oblivion comes!

3

"These, our sped ancestry,
Lie here embraced by deeper death than we;   10

Leghorn, Shelley's "To a Skylark" (see page 283) was
written at Leghorn.

Nor shape nor thought of theirs can **you descry**
With keenest backward eye.

4

"They count as quite forgot;
They are as men who have existed not;
Theirs is a loss past loss of fitful breath;
    It is the second death.

5

"We here, as yet, each day
Are blest with dear recall; as yet, can say
We hold in some soul loved continuance
    Of shape and voice and glance.   20

6

"But what has been will be—
First memory, then oblivion's swallowing sea;
Like men foregone, shall we merge into those
    Whose story no one knows.

7

"For which of us could hope
To show in life that world-awakening scope
Granted the few whose memory none lets die,
    But all men magnify?

8

"We were but Fortune's sport;
Things true, things lovely, things of good report   30
We neither shunned nor sought. . . . We see our
    bourne,
    And seeing it we mourn."

THE CURATE'S KINDNESS

A WORKHOUSE IRONY

I

I thought they'd be strangers aroun' me,
    But she's to be there!
Let me jump out o' waggon and go back and drown
    me
    At Pummery or Ten-Hatches Weir.

2

I thought: "Well, I've come to the Union—
    The workhouse at last—
After honest hard work all the week, and Commun-
    ion
    O' Zundays, these fifty years past.

30–31. **Things . . . sought.** See Philippians 4:8.
4. **Pummery,** Poundberry, near Dorchester. **Ten-Hatches
Weir,** a dammed pond near Dorchester.   5–6. **Union . . .
workhouse,** poorhouse.

3

"'Tis hard; but," I thought, "never mind it:
  There's gain in the end: 10
And when I get used to the place I shall find it
  A home, and may find there a friend.

4

"Life there will be better than t'other,
  For peace is assured.
The men in one wing and their wives in another
Is strictly the rule of the Board."

5

Just then one young Pa'son arriving
  Steps up out of breath
To the side o' the waggon wherein we were driving
  To Union; and calls out and saith: 20

6

"Old folks, that harsh order is altered,
  Be not sick of heart!
The Guardians they poohed and they pished and
    they paltered
  When urged not to keep you apart.

7

"'It is wrong,' I maintained, 'to divide them,
  Near forty years wed.'
'Very well, sir. We promise, then, they shall abide
    them
  In one wing together,' they said."

8

Then I sank—knew 'twas quite a foredone thing
  That misery should be   30
To the end! . . . To get freed of her there was the
    one thing
  Had made the change welcome to me.

9

To go there was ending but badly;
  'Twas shame and 'twas pain;
"But anyhow," thought I, "thereby I shall gladly
  Get free of this forty years' chain."

10

I thought they'd be strangers aroun' me,
  But she's to be there!
Let me jump out o' waggon and go back and drown
    me
  At Pummery or Ten-Hatches Weir.   40

AT CASTERBRIDGE FAIR

1

THE BALLAD-SINGER

Sing, Ballad-singer, raise a hearty tune;
Make me forget that there was ever a one
I walked with in the meek light of the moon
  When the day's work was done.

Rhyme, Ballad-rhymer, start a country song;
Make me forget that she whom I loved well
Swore she would love me dearly, love me long,
  Then—what I cannot tell!

Sing, Ballad-singer, from your little book;   9
Make me forget those heart-breaks, achings, fears;
Make me forget her name, her sweet sweet look—
  Make me forget her tears.

2

FORMER BEAUTIES

These market-dames, mid-aged, with lips thin-
    drawn,
  And tissues sere,
Are they the ones we loved in years agone,
  And courted here?

Are these the muslined pink young things to whom
  We vowed and swore
In nooks on summer Sundays by the Froom,
  Or Budmouth shore?

Do they remember those gay tunes we trod
  Clasped on the green;   10
Aye; trod till moonlight set on the beaten sod
  A satin sheen?

They must forget, forget! They cannot know
  What once they were,
Or memory would transfigure them, and show
  Them always fair.

3

AFTER THE CLUB-DANCE

Black'on frowns east on Maidon,
  And westward to the sea,

Casterbridge, Hardy's name for Dorchester, Dorsetshire, as
in his novel *The Mayor of Casterbridge.*   *Former Beauties.*
7. Froom, the river Frome.   **8. Budmouth,** Weymouth.
After the Club-Dance. **1. Black'on,** Blackdown Hill. **Maidon,**
Maiden Castle.

But on neither is his frown laden
  With scorn, as his frown on me!

At dawn my heart grew heavy,
  I could not sip the wine,
I left the jocund bevy
  And that young man o' mine.

The roadside elms pass by me,—
  Why do I sink with shame   10
When the birds a-perch there eye me?
  They, too, have done the same!

4

THE MARKET-GIRL

Nobody took any notice of her as she stood on the
  causey kerb,
All eager to sell her honey and apples and bunches
  of garden herb;
And if she had offered to give her wares and herself
  with them too that day,
I doubt if a soul would have cared to take a bargain
  so choice away.

But chancing to trace her sunburnt grace that morning as I passed nigh,
I went and I said "Poor maidy dear!—and will
  none of the people buy?"
And so it began; and soon we knew what the end of
  it all must be,
And I found that though no others had bid, a prize
  had been won by me.

5

THE INQUIRY

And are ye one of Hermitage—
Of Hermitage, by Ivel Road,
And do ye know, in Hermitage
A thatch-roofed house where sengreens grow?
And does John Waywood live there still—
He of the name that there abode
When father hurdled on the hill
    Some fifteen years ago?

Does he now speak o' Patty Beech,
The Patty Beech he used to—see,   10
Or ask at all if Patty Beech
Is known or heard of out this way?

—Ask if ever she's living yet,
And where her present home may be,
And how she bears life's fag and fret
    After so long a day?

In years agone at Hermitage
This faded face was counted fair,
None fairer; and at Hermitage
We swore to wed when he should thrive.   20
But never a chance had he or I,
And waiting made his wish outwear,
And Time, that dooms man's love to die,
    Preserves a maid's alive.

6

A WIFE WAITS

Will's at the dance in the Club-room below,
  Where the tall liquor-cups foam;
I on the pavement up here by the Bow,
  Wait, wait, to steady him home.

Will and his partner are treading a tune,
  Loving companions they be;
Willy, before we were married in June,
  Said he loved no one but me;

Said he would let his old pleasures all go
  Ever to live with his Dear.   10
Will's at the dance in the Club-room below,
  Shivering I wait for him here.

7

AFTER THE FAIR

The singers are gone from the Cornmarket-place
  With their broadsheets of rhymes,
The street rings no longer in treble and bass
  With their skits on the times,
And the Cross, lately thronged, is a dim naked space
  That but echoes the stammering chimes.

From Clock-corner steps, as each quarter ding-
    dongs,
  Away the folk roam
By the "Hart" and Grey's Bridge into byways and
    "drongs,"
  Or across the ridged loam;   10

The Inquiry.   **1. Hermitage,** a village near Dorchester.
2. Ivel Road, the road to Yeovil.   **4. sengreens,** plants
growing in the walls of houses.   **7. hurdled,** made hurdles
for enclosing farm or pasture land.

A Wife Waits.   **3. the Bow.** "The old name for a curved
corner by the cross-streets in the middle of Casterbridge."
(Hardy) *After the Fair.*   **1. Cornmarket-place,** the central
market in Dorchester.   **5. Cross,** the intersection of two
streets at Cornmarket-place.   **7. Clock-corner,** in Dorchester, near St. Peter's Church.   **9. "Hart,"** the White Hart,
an inn. **Grey's Bridge,** across a branch of the Frome.
"drongs," narrow lanes between walls.

The younger ones shrilling the lately heard songs,
    The old saying, "Would we were home."

The shy-seeming maiden so mute in the fair
    Now rattles and talks,
And that one who looked the most swaggering there
    Grows sad as she walks,
And she who seemed eaten by cankering care
    In statuesque sturdiness stalks.

And midnight clears High Street of all but the
    ghosts
    Of its buried burghees,   20
From the latest far back to those old Roman hosts
    Whose remains one yet sees,
Who loved, laughed, and fought, hailed their
    friends, drank their toasts
    At their meeting-times here, just as these!

NEW YEAR'S EVE

"I have finished another year," said God,
    "In grey, green, white, and brown;
I have strewn the leaf upon the sod,
Sealed up the worm within the clod,
    And let the last sun down."

"And what's the good of it?" I said.
    "What reasons made you call
From formless void this earth we tread,
When nine-and-ninety can be read
    Why nought should be at all?   10

"Yea, Sire; why shaped you us, 'who in
    This tabernacle groan'—
If ever a joy be found herein,
Such joy no man had wished to win
    If he had never known!"

Then he: "My labours—logicless—
    You may explain; not I:
Sense-sealed I have wrought, without a guess
That I evolved a Consciousness
    To ask for reasons why.   20

"Strange that ephemeral creatures who
    By my own ordering are,
Should see the shortness of my view,
Use ethic tests I never knew,
    Or made provision for!"

After the Fair. **19. High Street,** a main street in Dorchester.
New Year's Eve. **11–12. 'who in This tabernacle groan.'** See 2
Corinthians 5:4.

He sank to raptness as of yore,
    And opening New Year's Day
Wove it by rote as theretofore,
And went on working evermore
    In his unweeting way.   30

THE MAN HE KILLED

"Had he and I but met
    By some old ancient inn,
We should have sat us down to wet
    Right many a nipperkin!

"But ranged as infantry,
    And staring face to face,
I shot at him as he at me,
    And killed him in his place.

"I shot him dead because—
    Because he was my foe,   10
Just so: my foe of course he was;
    That's clear enough; although

"He thought he'd 'list, perhaps,
    Off-hand like—just as I—
Was out of work—had sold his traps—
    No other reason why.

"Yes; quaint and curious war is!
    You shoot a fellow down
You'd treat if met where any bar is,
    Or help to half-a-crown."   20

TO THE MOON

"What have you looked at, Moon,
    In your time,
Now long past your prime?"
"O, I have looked at, often looked at
    Sweet, sublime,
Sore things, shudderful, night and noon
    In my time."

"What have you mused on, Moon,
    In your day,
So aloof, so far away?"   10
"O, I have mused on, often mused on
    Growth, decay,
Nations alive, dead, mad, aswoon,
    In my day!"

"Have you much wondered, Moon,
　　On your rounds,
　　Self-wrapt, beyond Earth's bounds?"
"Yea, I have wondered, often wondered
　　At the sounds
Reaching me of the human tune　　　20
　　On my rounds."

"What do you think of it, Moon,
　　As you go?
　　Is Life much, or no?"
"O, I think of it, often think of it
　　As a show
God ought surely to shut up soon,
　　As I go."

OLD FURNITURE

I know not how it may be with others
　　Who sit amid relics of householdry
That date from the days of their mothers' mothers,
　　But well I know how it is with me
　　　Continually.

I see the hands of the generations
　　That owned each shiny familiar thing
In play on its knobs and indentations,
　　And with its ancient fashioning
　　　Still dallying:　　　10

Hands behind hands, growing paler and paler,
　　As in a mirror a candle-flame
Shows images of itself, each frailer
　　As it recedes, though the eye may frame
　　　Its shape the same.

On the clock's dull dial a foggy finger,
　　Moving to set the minutes right
With tentative touches that lift and linger
　　In the wont of a moth on a summer night,
　　　Creeps to my sight.　　　20

On this old viol, too, fingers are dancing—
　　As whilom—just over the strings by the nut,
The tip of a bow receding, advancing
　　In airy quivers, as if it would cut
　　　The plaintive gut.

And I see a face by that box for tinder,
　　Glowing forth in fits from the dark,
And fading again, as the linten cinder
　　Kindles to red at the flinty spark,
　　　Or goes out stark.　　　30

Well, well. It is best to be up and doing,
　　The world has no use for one to-day
Who eyes things thus—no aim pursuing!
　　He should not continue in this stay,
　　　But sink away.

THEN AND NOW

When battles were fought
With a chivalrous sense of Should and Ought,
　　In spirit men said,
　　"End we quick or dead,
　　Honour is some reward!
Let us fight fair—for our own best or worst;
　　So, Gentlemen of the Guard,
　　　Fire first!"

In the open they stood,
Man to man in his knightlihood:　　　10
　　They would not deign
　　To profit by a stain
　　On the honourable rules,
Knowing that practise perfidy no man durst
　　Who in the heroic schools
　　　Was nurst.

But now, behold, what
Is warfare wherein honour is not!
　　Rama laments
　　Its dead innocents:　　　20
　　Herod breathes: "Sly slaughter
Shall rule! Let us, by modes once called accurst,
　　Overhead, under water,
　　　Stab first."

THE THREE STRANGERS

AMONG the few features of agricultural England which retain an appearance but little
modified by the lapse of centuries, may be reckoned the long, grassy and furzy downs, coombs,
or ewe-leases, as they are called according to their
kind, that fill a large area of certain counties in the
south and south-west. If any mark of human occupation is met with hereon, it usually takes the
form of the solitary cottage of some shepherd.

Fifty years ago such a lovely cottage stood on
such a down, and may possibly be standing there
now. In spite of its loneliness, however, the spot,
by actual measurement, was not three miles from

19–21. Rama . . . Herod. See Matthew 2:13–18, which
refers back to Jeremiah 31:15.

a county-town. Yet that affected it little. Three miles of irregular upland, during the long inimical seasons, with their sleets, snows, rains, and mists, afford withdrawing space enough to isolate a Timon or a Nebuchadnezzar; much less, in fair weather, to please that less repellent tribe, the poets, philosophers, artists, and others who "conceive and meditate of pleasant things."

Some old earthen camp or barrow, some clump of trees, at least some starved fragment of ancient hedge is usually taken advantage of in the erection of these forlorn dwellings. But, in the present case, such a kind of shelter had been disregarded. Higher Crowstairs, as the house was called, stood quite detached and undefended. The only reason for its precise situation seemed to be the crossing of two footpaths at right angles hard by, which may have crossed there and thus for a good five hundred years. Hence the house was exposed to the elements on all sides. But, though the wind up here blew unmistakably when it did blow, and the rain hit hard whenever it fell, the various weathers of the winter season were not quite so formidable on the down as they were imagined to be by dwellers on low ground. The raw rimes were not so pernicious as in the hollows, and the frosts were scarcely so severe. When the shepherd and his family who tenanted the house were pitied for their sufferings from the exposure, they said that upon the whole they were less inconvenienced by "wuzzes and flames" (hoarses and phlegms) than when they had lived by the stream of a snug neighbouring valley.

The night of March 28, 182–, was precisely one of the nights that were wont to call forth these expressions of commiseration. The level rainstorm smote walls, slopes, and hedges like the clothyard shafts of Senlac and Crécy. Such sheep and outdoor animals as had no shelter stood with their buttocks to the winds; while the tails of little birds trying to roost on some scraggy thorn were blown inside-out like umbrellas. The gable-end of the cottage was stained with wet, and the eavesdroppings flapped against the wall. Yet never was commiseration for the shepherd more misplaced. For that cheerful rustic was entertaining a large party in glorification of the christening of his second girl.

The guests had arrived before the rain began to fall, and they were all now assembled in the chief or living room of the dwelling. A glance into the apartment at eight o'clock on this eventful evening would have resulted in the opinion that it was as cosy and comfortable a nook as could be wished for in boisterous weather. The calling of its inhabitant was proclaimed by a number of highly-polished sheep-crooks without stems that were hung ornamentally over the fireplace, the curl of each shining crook varying from the antiquated type engraved in the patriarchal pictures of old family Bibles to the most approved fashion of the last local sheep-fair. The room was lighted by half-a-dozen candles, having wicks only a trifle smaller than the grease which enveloped them, in candle-sticks that were never used but at high-days, holy-days, and family feasts. The lights were scattered about the room, two of them standing on the chimney-piece. This position of candles was in itself significant. Candles on the chimney-piece always meant a party.

On the hearth, in front of a back-brand to give substance, blazed a fire of thorns, that crackled "like the laughter of the fool."

Nineteen persons were gathered here. Of these, five women, wearing gowns of various bright hues, sat in chairs along the wall; girls shy and not shy filled the window-bench; four men, including Charley Jake the hedge-carpenter, Elijah New the parish-clerk, and John Pitcher, a neighbouring dairyman, the shepherd's father-in-law, lolled in the settle; a young man and maid, who were blushing over tentative *pourparlers* on a life-companionship, sat beneath the corner-cupboard; and an elderly engaged man of fifty or upward moved restlessly about from spots where his betrothed was not to the spot where she was. Enjoyment was pretty general, and so much the more prevailed in being unhampered by conventional restrictions. Absolute confidence in each other's good opinion begat perfect ease, while the finishing stroke of manner, amounting to a truly princely serenity, was lent to the majority by the absence of any expression or trait denoting that they wished to get on in the world, enlarge their minds, or do any eclipsing thing whatever—which nowadays so

5. **Timon,** the misanthrope in Shakespeare's play of that name, who takes up his residence in a cave in the woods, near the seashore. **Nebuchadnezzar.** So the Old Testament incorrectly names Nebuchadrezzar II, who reigned 604–561 B.C., and who carried the people of Judah captive into Babylonia. In the fourth chapter of the Book of Daniel, which was written in the second century B.C., Nebuchadnezzar appears, unhistorically, as having lost his mind and been "driven from men." This is the source of Hardy's reference to him. **38. Senlac,** Hastings, where William of Normandy defeated the Anglo-Saxons, 1066. **Crécy,** scene of the first great English victory of the Hundred Years' War, 1346.

28. **"like the laughter of a fool."** "For as the crackling of thorns under a pot, so is the laughter of the fool."—Ecclesiastes 7:6. **33. hedge-carpenter,** a mender of hedges **37. pourparlers,** conferences.

generally nips the bloom and *bonhomie* of all except the two extremes of the social scale.

Shepherd Fennel had married well, his wife being a dairyman's daughter from a vale at a distance, who brought fifty guineas in her pocket— and kept them there, till they should be required for ministering to the needs of a coming family. This frugal woman had been somewhat exercised as to the character that should be given to the gathering. A sit-still party had its advantages; but an undisturbed position of ease in chairs and settles was apt to lead on the men to such an unconscionable deal of toping that they would sometimes fairly drink the house dry. A dancing-party was the alternative; but this, while avoiding the foregoing objection on the score of good drink, had a counterbalancing disadvantage in the matter of good victuals, the ravenous appetites engendered by the exercise causing immense havoc in the buttery. Sheperdess Fennel fell back upon the intermediate plan of mingling short dances with short periods of talk and singing, so as to hinder any ungovernable rage in either. But this scheme was entirely confined to her own gentle mind: the shepherd himself was in the mood to exhibit the most reckless phases of hospitality.

The fiddler was a boy of those parts, about twelve years of age, who had a wonderful dexterity in jigs and reels, though his fingers were so small and short as to necessitate a constant shifting for the high notes, from which he scrambled back to the first position with sounds not of unmixed purity of tone. At seven the shrill tweedle-dee of this youngster had begun, accompanied by a booming ground-bass from Elijah New, the parish-clerk, who had thoughtfully brought with him his favourite musical instrument, the serpent. Dancing was instantaneous, Mrs. Fennel privately enjoining the players on no account to let the dance exceed the length of a quarter of an hour.

But Elijah and the boy in the excitement of their position quite forgot the injunction. Moreover, Oliver Giles, a man of seventeen, one of the dancers, who was enamoured of his partner, a fair girl of thirty-three rolling years, had recklessly handed a new crown-piece to the musicians, as a bribe to keep going as long as they had muscle and wind. Mrs. Fennel, seeing the steam begin to generate on the countenances of her guests, crossed over and touched the fiddler's elbow and put her hand on the serpent's mouth. But they took no notice, and fearing she might lose her character of genial hostess if she were to interfere too markedly, she retired and sat down helpless. And so the dance whizzed on with cumulative fury, the performers moving in their planet-like courses, direct and retrograde, from apogee to perigee, till the hand of the well-kicked clock at the bottom of the room had travelled over the circumference of an hour.

While these cheerful events were in course of enactment within Fennel's pastoral dwelling an incident having considerable bearing on the party had occurred in the gloomy night without. Mrs. Fennel's concern about the growing fierceness of the dance corresponded in point of time with the ascent of a human figure to the solitary hill of Higher Crowstairs from the direction of the distant town. This personage strode on through the rain without a pause, following the little-worn path which, further on in its course, skirted the shepherd's cottage.

It was nearly the time of full moon, and on this account, though the sky was lined with a uniform sheet of dripping cloud, ordinary objects out of doors were readily visible. The sad wan light revealed the lonely pedestrian to be a man of supple frame; his gait suggested that he had somewhat passed the period of perfect and instinctive agility, though not so far as to be otherwise than rapid of motion when occasion required. At a rough guess, he might have been about forty years of age. He appeared tall, but a recruiting sergeant, or other person accustomed to the judging of men's heights by the eye, would have discerned that this was chiefly owing to his gauntness, and that he was not more than five-feet-eight or nine.

Notwithstanding the regularity of his tread there was caution in it, as in that of one who mentally feels his way; and despite the fact that it was not a black coat nor a dark garment of any sort that he wore, there was something about him which suggested that he naturally belonged to the black-coated tribes of men. His clothes were of fustian, and his boots hobnailed, yet in his progress he showed not the mud-accustomed bearing of hobnailed and fustianed peasantry.

By the time that he had arrived abreast of the shepherd's premises the rain came down, or rather came along, with yet more determined violence. The outskirts of the little settlement partially

---

37. serpent, a now obsolete bass wind instrument, frequently mentioned by Hardy, who in his youth played in the orchestra of the village church. See his novel *Under the Greenwood Tree.*

15–18. the ascent . . . distant town. The mood and the image in this passage are both very Hardyesque. One of the characters in *The Return of the Native* descends from a summit of the heath "with the glide of a water-drop down a bud."

broke the force of wind and rain, and this induced him to stand still. The most salient of the shepherd's domestic erections was an empty sty at the forward corner of his hedgeless garden, for in these latitudes the principle of masking the homelier features of your establishment by a conventional frontage was unknown. The traveller's eye was attracted to this small building by the pallid shine of the wet slates that covered it. He turned aside, and, finding it empty, stood under the pent-roof for shelter.

While he stood the boom of the serpent within the adjacent house, and the lesser strains of the fiddler, reached the spot as an accompaniment to the surging hiss of the flying rain on the sod, its louder beating on the cabbage-leaves of the garden, on the straw hackles of eight or ten beehives just discernible by the path, and its dripping from the eaves into a row of buckets and pans that had been placed under the walls of the cottage. For at Higher Crowstairs, as at all such elevated domiciles, the grand difficulty of housekeeping was an insufficiency of water; and a casual rainfall was utilized by turning out, as catchers, every utensil that the house contained. Some queer stories might be told of the contrivances for economy in suds and dishwaters that are absolutely necessitated in upland habitations during the droughts of summer. But at this season there were no such exigencies; a mere acceptance of what the skies bestowed was sufficient for an abundant store.

At last the notes of the serpent ceased and the house was silent. This cessation of activity aroused the solitary pedestrian from the reverie into which he had lapsed, and, emerging from the shed, with an apparently new intention, he walked up the path to the house-door. Arrived here, his first act was to kneel down on a large stone beside the row of vessels, and to drink a copious draught from one of them. Having quenched his thirst he rose and lifted his hand to knock, but paused with his eye upon the panel. Since the dark surface of the wood revealed absolutely nothing, it was evident that he must be mentally looking through the door, as if he wished to measure thereby all the possibilities that a house of this sort might include, and how they might bear upon the question of his entry.

In his indecision he turned and surveyed the scene around. Not a soul was anywhere visible. The garden-path stretched downward from his feet, gleaming like the track of a snail; the roof of the little well (mostly dry), the well-cover, the top rail of the garden-gate, were varnished with the same dull liquid glaze; while, far away in the vale, a faint whiteness of more than usual extent showed that the rivers were high in the meads. Beyond all this winked a few bleared lamplights through the beating drops—lights that denoted the situation of the county-town from which he had appeared to come. The absence of all notes of life in that direction seemed to clinch his intentions, and he knocked at the door.

Within, a desultory chat had taken the place of movement and musical sound. The hedge-carpenter was suggesting a song to the company, which nobody just then was inclined to undertake, so that the knock afforded a not unwelcome diversion.

"Walk in!" said the shepherd promptly.

The latch clicked upward, and out of the night our pedestrian appeared upon the door-mat. The shepherd arose, snuffed two of the nearest candles, and turned to look at him.

Their light disclosed that the stranger was dark in complexion and not unprepossessing as to feature. His hat, which for a moment he did not remove, hung low over his eyes, without concealing that they were large, open, and determined, moving with a flash rather than a glance round the room. He seemed pleased with his survey, and baring his shaggy head, said, in a rich deep voice, "The rain is so heavy, friends, that I ask leave to come in and rest awhile."

"To be sure, stranger," said the shepherd. "And faith, you've been lucky in choosing your time, for we are having a bit of a fling for a glad cause—though, to be sure, a man could hardly wish that glad cause to happen more than once a year."

"Nor less," spoke up a woman. "For 'tis best to get your family over and done with, as soon as you can, so as to be all the earlier out of the fag o't."

"And what may be this glad cause?" asked the stranger.

"A birth and christening," said the shepherd.

The stranger hoped his host might not be made unhappy either by too many or too few of such episodes, and being invited by a gesture to a pull at the mug, he readily acquiesced. His manner, which, before entering, had been so dubious, was now altogether that of a careless and candid man.

"Late to be traipsing athwart this coomb—hey?" said the engaged man of fifty.

"Late it is, master, as you say.—I'll take a seat in the chimney-corner, if you have nothing to urge against it, ma'am; for I am a little moist on the side that was next the rain."

Mrs. Shepherd Fennel assented, and made room for the self-invited comer, who, having got com-

46. **traipsing,** tramping about idly or aimlessly.

pletely inside the chimney-corner, stretched out his legs and his arms with the expansiveness of a person quite at home.

"Yes, I am rather cracked in the vamp," he said freely, seeing that the eyes of the shepherd's wife fell upon his boots, "and I am not well fitted either. I have had some rough times lately, and have been forced to pick up what I can get in the way of wearing, but I must find a suit better fit for working-days when I reach home."

"One of hereabouts?" she inquired.

"Not quite that—further up the country."

"I thought so. And so be I; and by your tongue you come from my neighbourhood."

"But you would hardly have heard of me," he said quickly. "My time would be long before yours, ma'am, you see."

This testimony to the youthfulness of his hostess had the effect of stopping her cross-examination.

"There is only one thing more wanted to make 20 me happy," continued the new-comer. "And that is a little baccy, which I am sorry to say I am out of."

"I'll fill your pipe," said the shepherd.

"I must ask you to lend me a pipe likewise."

"A smoker, and no pipe about 'ee?"

"I have dropped it somewhere on the road."

The shepherd filled and handed him a new clay pipe, saying, as he did so, "Hand me your baccy-box—I'll fill that too, now I am about it."

The man went through the movement of search- 30 ing his pockets.

"Lost that too?" said his entertainer, with some surprise.

"I am afraid so," said the man with some confusion. "Give it to me in a screw of paper." Lighting his pipe at the candle with a suction that drew the whole flame into the bowl, he resettled himself in the corner and bent his looks upon the faint steam from his damp legs, as if he wished to say no more.

Meanwhile the general body of guests had been 40 taking little notice of this visitor by reason of an absorbing discussion in which they were engaged with the band about a tune for the next dance. The matter being settled, they were about to stand up when an interruption came in the shape of another knock at the door.

At sound of the same the man in the chimney-corner took up the poker and began stirring the brands as if doing it thoroughly were the one aim of his existence; and a second time the shepherd said, 50 "Walk in!" In a moment another man stood upon the straw-woven door-mat. He too was a stranger.

This individual was one of a type radically different from the first. There was more of the com-

monplace in his manner, and a certain jovial cosmopolitanism sat upon his features. He was several years older than the first arrival, his hair being slightly frosted, his eyebrows bristly, and his whiskers cut back from his cheeks. His face was rather full and flabby, and yet it was not altogether a face without power. A few grog-blossoms marked the neighbourhood of his nose. He flung back his long drab greatcoat, revealing that beneath it he 10 wore a suit of cinder-gray shade throughout, large heavy seals, of some metal or other that would take a polish, dangling from his fob as his only personal ornament. Shaking the water-drops from his low-crowned glazed hat, he said, "I must ask for a few minutes' shelter, comrades, or I shall be wetted to my skin before I get to Casterbridge."

"Make yourself at home, master," said the shepherd, perhaps a trifle less heartily than on the first occasion. Not that Fennel had the least tinge of 20 niggardliness in his composition; but the room was far from large, spare chairs were not numerous, and damp companions were not altogether desirable at close quarters for the women and girls in their bright-coloured gowns.

However, the second comer, after taking off his greatcoat, and hanging his hat on a nail in one of the ceiling-beams as if he been specially invited to put it there, advanced and sat down at the table. This had been pushed so closely into the chimney- 30 corner, to give all available room to the dancers, that its inner edge grazed the elbow of the man who had ensconced himself by the fire; and thus the two strangers were brought into close companionship. They nodded to each other by way of breaking the ice of unacquaintance, and the first stranger handed his neighbour the family mug—a huge vessel of brown ware, having its upper edge worn away like a threshold by the rub of whole generations of thirsty lips that had gone the way of all flesh, and 40 bearing the following inscription burnt upon its rotund side in yellow letters:—

THERE IS NO FUN

UNTiLL i CUM.

The other man, nothing loth, raised the mug to his lips, and drank on, and on, and on—till a curious blueness overspread the countenance of the shepherd's wife, who had regarded with no little surprise the first stranger's free offer to the second 50 of what did not belong to him to dispense.

"I knew it!" said the toper to the shepherd with

36–39. **a huge vessel . . . of all flesh.** See "Old Furniture," page 926.

much satisfaction. "When I walked up your garden before coming in, and saw the hives all of a row, I said to myself, 'Where there's bees there's honey, and where there's honey there's mead.' But mead of such a truly comfortable sort as this I really didn't expect to meet in my older days." He took yet another pull at the mug, till it assumed an ominous elevation.

"Glad you enjoy it!" said the shepherd warmly.

"It is goodish mead," assented Mrs. Fennel, with an absence of enthusiasm which seemed to say that it was possible to buy praise for one's cellar at too heavy a price. "It is trouble enough to make—and really I hardly think we shall make any more. For honey sells well, and we ourselves can make shift with a drop o' small mead and metheglin for common use from the comb-washings."

"O, but you'll never have the heart!" reproachfully cried the stranger in cinder-gray, after taking up the mug a third time and setting it down empty. "I love mead, when 'tis old like this, as I love to go to church o' Sundays, or to relieve the needy any day of the week."

"Ha, ha, ha!" said the man in the chimney-corner, who, in spite of the taciturnity induced by the pipe of tobacco, could not or would not refrain from this slight testimony to his comrade's humour.

Now the old mead of those days, brewed of the purest first-year or maiden honey, four pounds to the gallon—with its due complement of white of eggs, cinnamon, ginger, cloves, mace, rosemary, yeast, and processes of working, bottling, and cellaring—tasted remarkably strong; but it did not taste so strong as it actually was. Hence, presently, the stranger in cinder-gray at the table, moved by its creeping influence, unbuttoned his waistcoat, threw himself back in his chair, spread his legs, and made his presence felt in various ways.

"Well, well, as I say," he resumed, "I am going to Casterbridge, and to Casterbridge I must go. I should have been almost there by this time; but the rain drove me into your dwelling, and I'm not sorry for it."

"You don't live in Casterbridge?" said the shepherd.

"Not as yet; though I shortly mean to move there."

"Going to set up in trade, perhaps?"

"No, no," said the shepherd's wife. "It is easy to see that the gentleman is rich, and don't want to work at anything."

The cinder-gray stranger paused, as if to consider whether he would accept that definition of himself. He presently rejected it by answering, "Rich is not quite the word for me, dame. I do work, and I must work. And even if I only get to Casterbridge by midnight I must begin work there at eight to-morrow morning. Yes, het or wet, blow or snow, famine or sword, my day's work to-morrow must be done."

"Poor man! Then, in spite o' seeming, you be worse off than we?" replied the shepherd's wife.

" 'Tis the nature of my trade, men and maidens. 'Tis the nature of my trade more than my poverty. . . . But really and truly I must up and off, or I shan't get a lodging in the town." However, the speaker did not move, and directly added, "There's time for one more draught of friendship before I go; and I'd perform it at once if the mug were not dry."

"Here's a mug o' small," said Mrs. Fennel. "Small, we call it, though to me sure 'tis only the first wash o' the combs."

"No," said the stranger disdainfully. "I won't spoil your first kindness by partaking o' your second."

"Certainly not," broke in Fennel. "We don't increase and multiply every day, and I'll fill the mug again." He went away to the dark place under the stairs where the barrel stood. The shepherdess followed him.

"Why should you do this?" she said reproachfully, as soon as they were alone. "He's emptied it once, though it held enough for ten people; and now he's not contented wi' the small, but must needs call for more o' the strong! And a stranger unbeknown to any of us. For my part, I don't like the look o' the man at all."

"But he's in the house, my honey; and 'tis a wet night, and a christening. Daze it, what's a cup of mead more or less? There'll be plenty more next bee-burning."

"Very well—this time, then," she answered, looking wistfully at the barrel. "But what is the man's calling, and where is he one of, that he should come in and join us like this?"

"I don't know. I'll ask him again."

The catastrophe of having the mug drained dry at one pull by the stranger in cinder-gray was effectually guarded against this time by Mrs. Fennel. She poured out his allowance in a small cup, keeping the large one at a discreet distance from him. When he had tossed off his portion the shepherd renewed his inquiry about the stranger's occupation. The latter did not immediately reply, and the man in the chimney-corner, with sudden demonstrativeness, said, "Anybody may know my trade—I'm a wheelwright."

"A very good trade for these parts," said the shepherd.

"And anybody may know mine—if they've the sense to find it out," said the stranger in cinder-gray.

"You may generally tell what a man is by his claws," observed the hedge-carpenter, looking at his own hands, "My fingers be as full of thorns as an old pin-cushion is of pins."

The hands of the man in the chimney-corner instinctively sought the shade, and he gazed into the fire as he resumed his pipe. The man at the table took up the hedge-carpenter's remark, and added smartly, "True; but the oddity of my trade is that, instead of setting a mark upon me, it sets a mark upon my customers."

No observation being offered by anybody in elucidation of this enigma the shepherd's wife once more called for a song. The same obstacle presented themselves as at the former time—one had no voice, another had forgotten the first verse. The stranger at the table, whose soul had now risen to a good working temperature, relieved the difficulty by exclaiming that, to start the company, he would sing himself. Thrusting one thumb into the armhole of his waistcoat, he waved the other hand in the air, and, with an extemporizing gaze at the shining sheep-crooks above the mantelpiece, began:—

"O my trade it is the rarest one,
              Simple shepherds all—
   My trade is a sight to see;
For my customers I tie, and take them up on high,
   And waft 'em to a far countree!"

The room was silent when he had finished the verse—with one exception, that of the man in the chimney-corner, who, at the singer's word, "Chorus!" joined him in a deep bass voice of musical relish—

   "And waft 'em to a far countree!"

Oliver Giles, John Pitcher the dairyman, the parish-clerk, the engaged man of fifty, the row of young women against the wall, seemed lost in thought not of the gayest kind. The shepherd looked meditatively on the ground, the shepherdess gazed keenly at the singer, and with some suspicion; she was doubting whether this stranger were merely singing an old song from recollection, or was composing one there and then for the occasion. All were as perplexed at the obscure revelation as the guests at Belshazzar's Feast,[51] except the man in the chimney-corner, who quietly said, "Second verse, stranger," and smoked on.

51. **Belshazzar's Feast.** See Daniel 5.

The singer thoroughly moistened himself from his lips inwards, and went on with the next stanza as requested:—

"My tools are but common ones,
              Simple shepherds all—
   My tools are no sight to see:
A little hempen string, and a post whereon to swing,
   Are implements enough for me!"

Shepherd Fennel glanced round. There was no longer any doubt that the stranger was answering his question rhythmically. The guests one and all started back with suppressed exclamations. The young woman engaged to the man of fifty fainted half-way, and would have proceeded, but finding him wanting in alacrity for catching her she sat down trembling.

"O, he's the ——!" whispered the people in the background, mentioning the name of an ominous public officer. "He's come to do it! 'Tis to be at Casterbridge jail to-morrow—the man for sheep-stealing—the poor clock-maker we heard of, who used to live away at Shottsford and had no work to do—Timothy Summers, whose family were a-starving, and so he went out of Shottsford by the high-road, and took a sheep in open daylight, defying the farmer and the farmer's wife and the farmer's lad, and every man jack among 'em. He" (and they nodded towards the stranger of the deadly trade) "is come from up the country to do it because there's not enough to do in his own county-town, and he's got the place here now our own county man's dead; he's going to live in the same cottage under the prison wall."

The stranger in cinder-gray took no notice of this whispered string of observations, but again wetted his lips. Seeing that his friend in the chimney-corner was the only one who reciprocated his joviality in any way, he held out his cup towards that appreciative comrade, who also held out his own. They clinked together, the eyes of the rest of the room hanging upon the singer's actions. He parted his lips for the third verse; but at that moment another knock was audible upon the door. This time the knock was faint and hesitating.

The company seemed scared; the shepherd looked with consternation towards the entrance, and it was with some effort that he resisted his alarmed wife's deprecatory glance, and uttered for the third time the welcoming words, "Walk in!"

The door was gently opened, and another man stood upon the mat. He, like those who had preceded him, was a stranger. This time it was a short small personage, of fair complexion, and dressed in a decent suit of dark clothes.

"Can you tell me the way to —— ?" he began: when, gazing round the room to observe the nature of the company amongst whom he had fallen, his eyes lighted on the stranger in cinder-gray. It was just at the instant when the latter, who had thrown his mind into his song with such a will that he scarcely heeded the interruption, silenced all whispers and inquiries by bursting into his third verse:— 10

"To-morrow is my working day,
           Simple shepherds all—
To-morrow is a working day for me:
For the farmer's sheep is slain, and the lad who did
    it ta'en,
And on his soul may God ha' merc-y!"

The stranger in the chimney-corner, waving cups with the singer so heartily that his mead splashed over on the hearth, repeated in his bass voice as 20 before:—

"And on his soul may God ha' merc-y!"

All this time the third stranger had been standing in the doorway. Finding now that he did not come forward or go on speaking, the guests particularly regarded him. They noticed to their surprise that he stood before them the picture of abject terror— his knees trembling, his hand shaking so violently that the door-latch by which he supported himself 30 rattled audibly: his white lips were parted, and his eyes fixed on the merry officer of justice in the middle of the room. A moment more and he had turned, closed the door, and fled.

"What man can it be?" said the shepherd.

The rest, between the awfulness of their late discovery and the odd conduct of this third visitor, looked as if they knew not what to think, and said nothing. Instinctively they withdrew further and further from the grim gentleman in their midst, 40 whom some of them seemed to take for the Prince of Darkness himself, till they formed a remote circle, an empty space of floor being left between them and him—

". . . circulus, cujus centrum diabolus."

The room was so silent—though there were more than twenty people in it—that nothing could be heard but the patter of the rain against the window-shutters, accompanied by the occasional hiss of a 50 stray drop that fell down the chimney into the fire, and the steady puffing of the man in the

45. "circulus . . . diabolus," a circle whose center is the Devil.

corner, who had now resumed his pipe of long clay.

The stillness was unexpectedly broken. The distant sound of a gun reverberated through the air— apparently from the direction of the county-town.

"Be jiggered!" cried the stranger who had sung the song, jumping up.

"What does that mean?" asked several.

"A prisoner escaped from the jail—that's what it means."

All listened. The sound was repeated, and none of them spoke but the man in the chimney-corner, who said quietly, "I've often been told that in this county they fire a gun at such times; but I never heard it till now."

"I wonder if it is *my* man?" murmured the personage in cinder-gray.

"Surely it is!" said the shepherd involuntarily. "And surely we've zeed him! That little man who looked in at the door by now, and quivered like a leaf when he zeed ye and heard your song!"

"His teeth chattered, and the breath went out of his body," said the dairyman.

"And his heart seemed to sink within him like a stone," said Oliver Giles.

"And he bolted as if he'd been shot at," said the hedge-carpenter.

"True—his teeth chattered, and his heart seemed to sink; and he bolted as if he'd been shot at," slowly summed up the man in the chimney-corner.

"I didn't notice it," remarked the hangman.

"We were all a-wondering what made him run off in such a fright," faltered one of the women against the wall, "and now 'tis explained!"

The firing of the alarm-gun went on at intervals, low and sullenly, and their suspicions became a certainty. The sinister gentleman in cinder-gray roused himself. "Is there a constable here?" he asked, in thick tones. "If so, let him step forward."

The engaged man of fifty stepped quavering out from the wall, his betrothed beginning to sob on the back of the chair.

"You are a sworn constable?"

"I be, sir."

"Then pursue the criminal at once, with assistance, and bring him back here. He can't have gone far."

"I will, sir, I will—when I've got my staff. I'll go home and get it, and come sharp here, and start in a body."

"Staff!—never mind your staff; the man'll be gone!"

"But I can't do nothing without my staff—can I, William, and John, and Charles Jake? No; for there's the king's royal crown a painted on en in yaller and gold, and the lion and the unicorn, so as when I raise en up and hit my prisoner, 'tis made a lawful blow thereby. I wouldn't 'tempt to take up a man without my staff—no, not I. If I hadn't the law to gie me courage, why, instead o' my taking up him he might take up me!"

"Now, I'm a king's man myself, and can give you authority enough for this," said the formidable officer in gray. "Now then, all of ye, be ready. Have ye any lanterns?"

"Yes—have ye any lanterns?—I demand it!" said the constable.

"And the rest of you able-bodied——"

"Able-bodied men—yes—the rest of ye!" said the constable.

"Have you some good stout staves and pitchforks ——"

"Staves and pitchforks—in the name o' the law! And take 'em in yer hands and go in quest, and do as we in authority tell ye!"

Thus aroused, the men prepared to give chase. The evidence was, indeed, though circumstantial, so convincing, that but little argument was needed to show the shepherd's guests that after what they had seen it would look very much like connivance if they did not instantly pursue the unhappy third stranger, who could not as yet have gone more than a few hundred yards over such uneven country.

A shepherd is always well provided with lanterns; and, lighting these hastily, and with hurdle-staves in their hands, they poured out of the door, taking a direction along the crest of the hill, away from the town, the rain having fortunately a little abated.

Disturbed by the noise, or possibly by unpleasant dreams of her baptism, the child who had been christened began to cry heart-brokenly in the room overhead. These notes of grief came down through the chinks of the floor to the ears of the women below, who jumped up one by one, and seemed glad of the excuse to ascend and comfort the baby, for the incidents of the last half-hour greatly oppressed them. Thus in the space of two or three minutes the room on the ground-floor was deserted quite.

But it was not for long. Hardly had the sound of footsteps died away when a man returned round the corner of the house from the direction the pursuers had taken. Peeping in at the door, and seeing nobody there, he entered leisurely. It was the stranger of the chimney-corner, who had gone out with the rest. The motive of his return was shown

by his helping himself to a cut piece of skimmer-cake that lay on a ledge beside where he had sat, and which he had apparently forgotten to take with him. He also poured out half a cup more mead from the quantity that remained, ravenously eating and drinking these as he stood. He had not finished when another figure came in just as quietly—his friend in cinder-gray.

"O—you here?" said the latter, smiling. "I thought you had gone to help in the capture." And this speaker also revealed the object of his return by looking solicitously round for the fascinating mug of old mead.

"And I thought you had gone," said the other, continuing his skimmer-cake with some effort.

"Well, on second thoughts, I felt there were enough without me," said the first confidentially, "and such a night as it is, too. Besides, 'tis the business o' the Government to take care of its criminals—not mine."

"True; so it is. And I felt as you did, that there were enough without me."

"I don't want to break my limbs running over the humps and hollows of this wild country."

"Nor I neither, between you and me."

"These shepherd-people are used to it—simple-minded souls, you know, stirred up to anything in a moment. They'll have him ready for me before the morning, and no trouble to me at all."

"They'll have him, and we shall have saved ourselves all labour in the matter."

"True, true. Well, my way is to Casterbridge; and 'tis as much as my legs will do to take me that far. Going the same way?"

"No, I am sorry to say! I have to get home over there" (he nodded indefinitely to the right), "and I feel as you do, that it is quite enough for my legs to do before bedtime."

The other had by this time finished the mead in the mug, after which, shaking hands heartily at the door, and wishing each other well, they went their several ways.

In the meantime the company of pursuers had reached the end of the hog's-back elevation which dominated this part of the town. They had decided on no particular plan of action; and, finding that the man of the baleful trade was no longer in their company, they seemed quite unable to form any such plan now. They descended in all directions down the hill, and straightway several of the party fell into the snare set by Nature for all misguided midnight ramblers over this part of the cretaceous formation. The "lanchets," or flint slopes, which belted the escarpment at intervals of a dozen yards, took the less cautious ones unawares, and losing their footing on the rubbly steep they slid sharply downwards, the lanterns rolling from their hands to the bottom, and there lying on their sides till the horn was scorched through.

When they had again gathered themselves to-10gether the shepherd, as the man who knew the country best, took the lead, and guided them round these treacherous inclines. The lanterns, which seemed rather to dazzle their eyes and warn the fugitive than to assist them in the exploration, were extinguished, due silence was observed; and in this more rational order they plunged into the vale. It was a grassy, briery, moist defile, affording some shelter to any person who had sought it; but the party perambulated it in vain, and ascended on the 20other side. Here they wandered apart, and after an interval closed together again to report progress. At the second time of closing in they found themselves near a lonely ash, the single tree on this part of the coomb, probably sown there by a passing bird some fifty years before. And here, standing a little to one side of the trunk, as motionless as the trunk itself, appeared the man they were in quest of, his outline being well defined against the sky beyond. The band noiselessly drew up and faced 30him.

"Your money or your life!" said the constable sternly to the still figure.

"No, no," whispered John Pitcher. " 'Tisn't our side ought to say that. That's the doctrine of vaga-bonds like him, and we be on the side of the law."

"Well, well," replied the constable impatiently; "I must say something, mustn't I? and if you had all the weight o' this undertaking upon your mind, perhaps you'd say the wrong thing too!—Prisoner 40at the bar, surrender, in the name of the Father—the Crown, I mane!"

The man under the tree seemed now to notice them for the first time, and, giving them no oppor-tunity whatever for exhibiting their courage, he strolled slowly towards them. He was, indeed, the little man, the third stranger; but his trepidation had in a great measure gone.

"Well, travellers," he said, "did I hear ye speak to me?"

"You did: you've got to come and be our 50prisoner at once!" said the constable. "We arrest 'ee on the charge of not biding in Casterbridge jail in a decent proper manner to be hung to-morrow

morning. Neighbours, do your duty, and seize the culpet!"

On hearing the charge the man seemed enlight-ened, and, saying not another word, resigned him-self with preternatural civility to the search-party, who, with their staves in their hands, surrounded him on all sides, and marched him back towards the shepherd's cottage.

It was eleven o'clock by the time they arrived. The light shining from the open door, a sound of men's voices within, proclaimed to them as they approached the house that some new events had arisen in their absence. On entering they discovered the shepherd's living room to be invaded by two officers from Casterbridge jail, and a well-known magistrate who lived at the nearest county-seat, in-telligence of the escape having become generally circulated.

"Gentlemen," said the constable, "I have brought back your man—not without risk and danger; but every one must do his duty! He is in-side this circle of able-bodied persons, who have lent me useful aid, considering their ignorance of Crown work. Men, bring forward your prisoner!" And the third stranger was led to the light.

"Who is this?" said one of the officials.

"The man," said the constable.

"Certainly not," said the turnkey; and the first corroborated his statement.

"But how can it be otherwise?" asked the consta-ble. "Or why was he so terrified at sight o' the singing instrument of the law who sat there?" Here he related the strange behaviour of the third stran-ger on entering the house during the hangman's song.

"Can't understand it," said the officer coolly. "All I know is that it is not the condemned man. He's quite a different character from this one; a gauntish fellow, with dark hair and eyes, rather good-looking, and with a musical bass voice that if you heard it once you'd never mistake as long as you lived."

"Why, souls—'twas the man in the chimney-corner!"

"Hey—what?" said the magistrate, coming for-ward after inquiring particulars from the shepherd in the background. "Haven't you got the man after all?"

"Well, sir," said the constable, "he's the man we were in search of, that's true; and yet he's not the man we were in search of. For the man we were in search of was not the man we wanted, sir, if you understand my every-day way; for 'twas the man in the chimney-corner!"

"A pretty kettle of fish altogether!" said the magistrate. "You had better start for the other man at once."

The prisoner now spoke for the first time. The mention of the man in the chimney-corner seemed to have moved him as nothing else could do. "Sir," he said, stepping forward to the magistrate, "take no more trouble about me. The time is come when I may as well speak. I have done nothing; my crime is that the condemned man is my brother. Early this afternoon I left home at Shottsford to tramp it all the way to Casterbridge jail to bid him farewell. I was benighted, and called here to rest and ask the way. When I opened the door I saw before me the very man, my brother, that I thought to see in the condemned cell at Casterbridge. He was in this chimney-corner; and jammed close to him, so that he could not have got out if he had tried, was the executioner who'd come to take his life, singing a song about it and not knowing that it was his victim who was close by, joining in to save appearances. My brother threw a glance of agony at me, and I knew he meant, 'Don't reveal what you see; my life depends on it.' I was so terror-struck that I could hardly stand, and, not knowing what I did, I turned and hurried away."

The narrator's manner and tone had the stamp of truth, and his story made a great impression on all around. "And do you know where your brother is at the present time?" asked the magistrate.

"I do not. I have never seen him since I closed this door."

"I can testify to that, for we've been between ye ever since," said the constable.

"Where does he think to fly to?—what is his occupation?"

"He's a watch-and-clock-maker, sir."

"'A said 'a was a wheelwright—a wicked rogue," said the constable.

"The wheels of clocks and watches he meant, no doubt," said Shepherd Fennel. "I thought his hands were palish for's trade."

"Well, it appears to me that nothing can be gained by retaining this poor man in custody," said the magistrate; "your business lies with the other, unquestionably."

And so the little man was released off-hand; but he looked nothing the less sad on that account, it being beyond the power of magistrate or constable to raze out the written troubles in his brain, for they concerned another whom he regarded with more solicitude than himself. When this was done, and the man had gone his way, the night was found to be so far advanced that it was deemed useless to renew the search before the next morning.

Next day, accordingly, the quest for the clever sheep-stealer became general and keen, to all appearance at least. But the intended punishment was cruelly disproportioned to the transgression, and the sympathy of a great many country-folk in that district was strongly on the side of the fugitive. Moreover, his marvellous coolness and daring in hob-and-nobbing with the hangman, under the unprecedented circumstances of the shepherd's party, won their admiration. So that it may be questioned if all those who ostensibly made themselves so busy in exploring woods and fields and lanes were quite so thorough when it came to the private examination of their own lofts and outhouses. Stories were afloat of a mysterious figure being occasionally seen in some old overgrown trackway or other, remote from turnpike roads; but when a search was instituted in any of these suspected quarters nobody was found. Thus the day and weeks passed without tidings.

In brief, the bass-voiced man of the chimney-corner was never recaptured. Some said that he went across the sea, others that he did not, but buried himself in the depths of a populous city. At any rate, the gentleman in cinder-gray never did his morning's work at Casterbridge, nor met anywhere at all, for business purposes, the genial comrade with whom he had passed an hour of relaxation in the lonely house on the slope of the coomb.

The grass has long been green on the graves of Shepherd Fennel and his frugal wife; the guests who made up the christening party have mainly followed their entertainers to the tomb; the baby in whose honour they all had met is a matron in the sere and yellow leaf. But the arrival of the three strangers at the shepherd's that night, and the details connected therewith, is a story as well known as ever in the country about Higher Crowstairs.

2. **to raze . . . brain.** See *Macbeth*, Act V, sc. 3, l. 42.
43. **sere and yellow leaf.** See *Macbeth*, Act V, sc. 3, l. 25.

SUGGESTIONS FOR FURTHER READING

ABOUT THE PERIOD

See the final paragraph of the Introduction to The Victorian Period, page 385.

NOVELS

All Victorian novels are interesting reading. All that has been attempted here has been to mention a number of the most distinguished novelists, together with a good book to begin on in getting acquainted with each. The date given after each title is that of original publication.

Most of the great Victorian novels are available in Everyman's Library, Dutton. The editions mentioned specifically below are among those the editor particularly likes.

Brontë, Charlotte, *Jane Eyre*, 1847. Represents the triumph of Romanticism in Victorian fiction.

Brontë, Emily, *Wuthering Heights*, 1847; Heritage Press, 1940, illustrated by Barnett Freedman. The only English novel of cosmic scope before Hardy.

Bulwer-Lytton, Sir Edward, *The Last Days of Pompeii*, 1834; Scribner, 1926, illustrated by F. C. Yohn. Elaborate historical reconstruction and rich melodrama.

Collins, Wilkie, *The Moonstone*, 1868, and *The Woman in White*, 1860; "Modern Library Giant." The first English "mysteries" and still the best.

Dickens, Charles, *David Copperfield*, 1849–50; Heritage Press, 1935, illustrated by John Austen. The most beloved novel in the language.

Gaskell, Mrs., *Cranford*, 1853. Genteel people in English village life. A perfect idyll.

"George Eliot," *Adam Bede*, 1859; *The Mill on the Floss*, 1860; *Silas Marner*, 1861; *Romola*, 1862–63; "Modern Library Giant," an omnibus volume of the author's best books.

Hardy, Thomas, *The Return of the Native*, 1878; Harper, 1929, illustrated by Clare Leighton. One of the greatest "landscape novels" and the best expression of Hardy's feeling of the determinative effect of environment on character.

Kingsley, Charles, *Westward Ho!* 1855; Scribner, 1920, illustrated by N. C. Wyeth. Elizabethan sea rovers on the Spanish Main.

Meredith, George, *The Ordeal of Richard Feverel*, 1859. One of the most touching love stories in modern literature.

Reade, Charles, *The Cloister and the Hearth*, 1861. Holland and Renaissance Italy in one of the most exciting historical novels ever written.

Stevenson, Robert Louis, *The Master of Ballantrae*, 1889. Eighteenth-century Scotland. Probably Stevenson's closest approach to the novel.

Thackeray, William Makepeace, *Vanity Fair*, 1847–48; Heritage Press, 1940, with Thackeray's own illustrations. A picture and a criticism of English society at the time of Waterloo, with Becky Sharp, one of the grandest adventuresses in fiction.

PLAYS

Moses, Montrose J., ed., *Representative British Dramas, Victorian and Modern*, Little, Brown, 1931. An anthology.

OTHER PROSE OF THE PERIOD

Arnold, Matthew, *Essays and Poems*, ed. by F. W. Roe, Harcourt, Brace, 1934

Carlyle, Thomas, *Selections*, ed. by A. R. Benham, Harper, 1928

Huxley, T. H., *Readings*, ed. by C. Rinaker, Harcourt, Brace, 1934

Macaulay, T. B., *The Reader's Macaulay*, ed. by W. H. French and G. D. Sanders, American Book Co., 1936

Newman, John Henry, *Prose and Poetry*, ed. by G. N. Shuster, Allyn & Bacon, 1925

Pater, Walter, *Selections*, ed. by A. L. F. Snell, Houghton Mifflin, 1924

Ruskin, John, *Selections and Essays*, ed. by F. W. Roe, Scribner, 1918

Stevenson, Robert Louis, *Essays*, ed. by William Lyon Phelps, Scribner, 1918

Wilde, Oscar, *Writings*, Wise, 1931

POETRY

Browning, Robert, *Poetical Works*, ed. by A. Birrell and F. G. Kenyon, Macmillan, 1915. The fullest single-volume edition.

Brontë, Emily, *Complete Poems*, ed. by C. K. Shorter, Doran, 1924

Hardy, Thomas, *Collected Poems*, 4th ed., Macmillan, 1932. *The Dynasts*, new 1-vol. ed., Macmillan, 1931

Hopkins, Gerard Manley, *Poems*, ed. by R. Bridges and C. Williams, Oxford Press, 1937

Meredith, George, *Poetical Works*, ed. by G. M. Trevelyan, Scribner, 1912

Morris, William, *Selected Prose and Poetry*, Random House, 1935

Rossetti, Christina, *Poetical Works*, ed. by W. M. Rossetti, Macmillan, 1906. With memoir and annotations.

Rossetti, Dante Gabriel, *Complete Poetical Works*, ed. by W. M. Rossetti, Little, Brown, 1903; *The House of Life*, ed. by P. F. Baum, Harvard University Press, 1928

Swinburne, A. C., *Selections*, ed. by W. O. Raymond, Harcourt, Brace, 1925

Tennyson, Lord Alfred, *Works*, with notes by the author, ed. with a memoir by H. Tennyson, Macmillan, 1913. Complete except for two recent additions to the Tennyson canon—*The Devil and the Lady* and *Unpublished Early Poems*, both ed. by C. Tennyson, Macmillan, 1930, 1932.

BIOGRAPHY AND CRITICISM

Arnold, Matthew. Trilling, Leonard, *Matthew Arnold*, Norton, 1939. Penetrating critical study. Tinker, C. B., and Lowry, H. F., *The Poetry of Matthew Arnold: A Com-*

mentary, Oxford University Press, 1940. The standard handbook.

Brontë, Charlotte, Emily, and *Anne*. Sinclair, May, *The Three Brontës*, Hutchinson, 1912. A brilliant novelist's evaluation; despite some errors, still a fine general study of the Brontës. Ratchford, Fannie E., *The Brontë's Web of Dreams*, Columbia University Press, 1940. The latest word by a brilliant Brontë scholar.

Browning, Robert. DeVane, W. C., *A Browning Handbook*, Crofts, 1935. Indispensable repository of information. DeVane, W. C., *Browning's Parleyings: The Autobiography of a Mind*, Yale University Press, 1927. Distinguished critical study. Woolf, Virginia, *Flush, a Biography*, Harcourt, Brace, 1935. The most delightful of all Browning books, a picture of the famous courtship seen through the eyes of Miss Barrett's dog!

Carlyle, Thomas. Wilson, D. A., *The Life of Thomas Carlyle*, 6 vols. Dutton, 1923–34. A monumental biography. Perry, Bliss, *Thomas Carlyle*, Bobbs-Merrill, 1915. A good simple introduction.

Carroll, Lewis. De La Mare, Walter, *Lewis Carroll*, Faber and Faber, 1932. A beautiful tribute by a great writer.

Dickens, Charles. Chesterton, G. K., *Charles Dickens*, Dodd, Mead, 1906. A famous critical study. Wagenknecht, Edward, *The Man Charles Dickens*, Houghton Mifflin,

1929. The most elaborate study of Dickens's personality.

Hardy, Thomas. Weber, Carl J., *Hardy of Wessex*, Columbia University Press, 1940. A fine biographical and critical study.

Huxley, T. H. Peterson, Houston, *Huxley: Prophet of Science*, Longmans, 1932. Biography and evaluation.

Morris, William. Eshelman, Lloyd W., *Victorian Rebel: The Life of William Morris*, Scribner, 1940

Newman, John Henry. May, J. Lewis, *Cardinal Newman*, Longmans, 1937. A good modern biography.

Rossetti, Dante Gabriel. Winwar, Frances, *Poor Splendid Wings*, Little, Brown, 1933. A fascinating, almost novelized, account not only of the Rossettis but of Morris, Swinburne, and (less satisfactorily) of Ruskin.

Ruskin, John. Williams-Ellis, Amabel, *The Exquisite Tragedy: An Intimate Life of John Ruskin*, Doubleday, Doran, 1929. A vivid portrait.

Swinburne, A. C. Drinkwater, John, *Swinburne, An Estimate*, Dutton, 1924. An enthusiastic defense.

Tennyson, Lord Alfred. Nicolson, Harold, *Tennyson: Aspects of His Life, Character, and Poetry*, Houghton Mifflin, 1925. The best modern evaluation.

Wilde, Oscar. Winwar, Frances, *Oscar Wilde and the Yellow Nineties*, Harper, 1940. A thorough, sensible study of the great scandal.

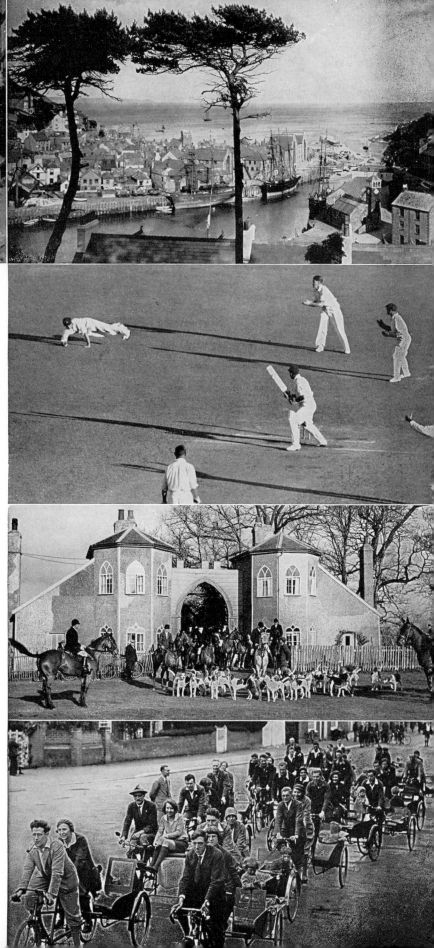

The Contemporary Period

Above. Clovelly, on the coast of Devon. *Above right.* Looe, on the coast of Cornwall. These two picturesque but typical English villages (one largely a resort, the other, a fishing town) suggest the importance of England's coastline. (Ewing Galloway)

A cricket game. Of all outdoor pastimes, cricket is most popular. Wherever Englishmen are, cricket is played. (Acme)

Meet of Essex and Suffolk Hunt. Large country estates, manorial houses, riding to hounds have persisted to the present day. For much of English aristocracy, life in the country means the long Edwardian week-end. (Acme)

Family cycling. Cycles provided with sidecars hold in England the place that the Ford holds in America. (Acme)

Fashionable Regent Street, looking toward Piccadilly, in the late 1930's. (Acme)

Billingsgate, the famous old London fish market. To speak "like a Billingsgate fishwife" still signifies strong language. (Ewing Galloway)

Piccadilly Circus, the hub of modern London. (Ewing Galloway)

The Strand, world-famous short and busy thoroughfare. (Burton Holmes, from Ewing Galloway)

Old Falstaff Inn at Gadshill. This famous old inn opposite the Charles Dickens home typifies enduring England, "the stables and the stout." (Ewing Galloway)

Airview of Southampton Harbor, in the 1930's. England has endured because of her tremendous merchant marine and naval power. (Ewing Galloway)

Pomp and pageantry still color the background of England. In the middle picture above, the Knights of the Garter, led by heralds, are passing through Windsor Castle to St. George's Chapel, 1937. This order of Chivalry was established by Edward III in 1348. (Acme)

Politics have played an important role in modern British life and thought. *Above left,* a mass meeting and protest demonstration in Trafalgar Square. *Above right,* 10 Downing Street (the home of the Prime Minister) caught while the household pet, a black cat, English symbol of good luck, keeps vigil outside. *Center right,* Lady Astor's Cliveden, the country house and grounds around which centered the famous "Cliveden Set." (Harris & Ewing and Acme)

Wightman Cup Doubles, 1938. Tennis is the Englishman's byword. The matches at Wimbledon rank as an international event. (Acme)

Factory for anti-aircraft guns. Britain's expanding industrial program was belatedly turned into an armament program. (Acme)

WOOLF

YEATS

GALSWORTHY

KIPLING

THE CONTEMPORARY PERIOD

Reaction and Reappraisal

THE age immediately preceding our own marked the consolidation of the power of the middle classes; our own era shows the middle classes on the defensive. The aggressive snobbery and confident assumptions of the moneyed middle classes, accepted by the Victorians, began to come under fire. By 1900 social, political, and industrial struggles were beginning. The lust for more wealth, intensified by the Empire's greed for more colonies, was paralleled by the rise in unemployment and the struggle of the labor unions. Discontent was occasional, not articulate; strikes were growing frequent. It was becoming clear that the unchecked domination of industrial capitalism presaged the decay of a whole economic system.

But the standards generally known as "Victorian" ruled in the minds of most people almost until the end of the nineteenth century. The changes were gradual. "You must remember that you always have to give England time," wrote Galsworthy. "She realizes things slowly." The Victorian contradictions were hushed by "good taste" and by a common consent so widespread as to seem a conspiracy. "High seriousness" excused the heavy pontifications; it concealed the disparity between the contending moral earnestness and industrial recklessness. A determined resignation, a spacious and pervading aura of "sweetness and light," somehow reconciled a gathering humanitarian impulse with a faster-growing commercialism. The conflicts between noble ideals and practical necessities, between religion and science, were resolved in a triumphant imperialism. The wealthy nation found comfort in its ledger and assurance in its literature; the Empire expanded in an ease that glittered and a security that was gold.

But voices of protest made themselves heard even before the end of the era. What began as easily adjusted disputes developed into irreconcilable discords; the lightly covered schisms became wide-open cleavages. The revolt against Victorianism was anticipated by the skepticism of Darwin and the agnosticism of John Stuart Mill in the 1860's; the last decade of the nineteenth century was marked by noticeable resistance to almost everything which Victoria had established, symbolized, and sanctified. The new forces questioned not only the conventions but the very framework of Victorian life. The younger men and women, especially the writers, differed in temperament, but they were all rebels, united in opposing the ideals of the age: the rigorous restraints, the decorous affectations, the "grand style," the sanctimonious platitudes, the immodest modesty, the prescribed patterns, and the general smugness. In fact, everything that was called "Victorian" they scorned.

The Esthetic Revolt

By 1890 several things besides the century were coming to an end. The "genteel tradition" was being everywhere opposed, not only by artists and writers, but by the ordinary individual. Audacity was in the air. The young women outraged their elders by daring to dispute them, brazenly discussing the possibility of woman suffrage, smoking cigarettes, and proposing to join men in what had been considered purely masculine games and occupations. Girls suddenly appeared on the golf course and the tennis court; they even appeared on bicycles—while England gasped. The young men of the nineties reacted against the immediate past with equal determination. They refused to attend evening prayers and went in for cards, slang, and Bohemianism. When the *Savoy* and the *Yellow Book* were hailed as the official organs of the young "intransigents," Max Beerbohm (1872–   ) wrote, "The Victorian era comes to its close, and the day of *sancta simplicitas* is ended." The phrase "fin de siècle," "end of a century," was not so much a characterizing term as a battle cry.

The term "fin de siècle" was allusive as well as exact; even its language was significant. The French Parnassians were discreetly collected and recklessly imitated by the English; the French journals dedicated to jolting the complacent (*épatant le bourgeois*) taught London how to shock itself. Parochial virtue was unfavorably compared with continental vice, and Paris became the literary center of England. By a neat trick of chronology, the death of Queen Victoria in 1901 brought Victorianism and the century to a simultaneous close. Anticipating the approaching end, the 1890's turned equally against a loose scientific materialism and a rigid respectability. The younger writers, with their eyes on French manners and their ears attuned to French sensibilities, cultivated queer attitudes and strained oversensitivity. They repudiated the principles of a morality which "fluctuated with the spiritual ebb and flow of the ages" and dedicated themselves to the cultural principles which do not shift with fashion, and to art itself, "which is eternal." Arthur Symons pronounced their credo while he defended the "immorality" of his own poems. "Show me," wrote Symons, "any commandment of the traditional code of morals which you are at present obeying, and I will show you its opposite among the commandments of some other code of morals which your forefathers once obeyed. . . . Is it for such a shifting guide that I am to forsake the sure and constant leading of art, which tells me that whatever I

find in humanity (passion, desire, the spirit or the senses, the hell or heaven of man's heart) is part of the eternal substance which nature weaves in the rough for art to combine cunningly into beautiful patterns!"

The contributors to the *Yellow Book* and the Rhymers' Club had no basic philosophical theory, but they had a common esthetic aim. It was to exalt art, to make "art for art's sake," to weave the strange colors and thin strands of fantasy "cunningly into beautiful patterns." Although the *Yellow Book* printed prose by Henry James (1843–1916), Kenneth Grahame (1859–1932), and Arnold Bennett (1867–1931), the characteristic figures of the 1890's were the poets. Some of these—Ernest Dowson (1867–1900), Lionel Johnson (1867–1902), Richard Le Gallienne (1867–   ), Victor Plarr (1863–1929), Arthur Symons (1865–   ), and William Butler Yeats (1865–1939)—belonged to the Rhymers' Club. Others, such as the artist Aubrey Beardsley (1872–1898), the poets Oscar Wilde (1856–1900), Lord Alfred Douglas (1870–   ), and George William Russell ("AE"; 1867–1935), were independent of the organization. Their program was unformulated, and vaguely defiant; it was not only limited, but diminished as time went on. They repudiated the worst of Tennyson (and often his best) while they luxuriated in a feeble wantonness more objectionable than any false purity. They devoted themselves self-consciously to a gaudy set of extravagances. The street lamps of London became "the iron lilies of the Strand," and the streetwalkers whom they apostrophized were "soiled doves" and "fallen Magdalens." They ridiculed the bad taste of their immediate predecessors by capitalizing a bad taste of their own; instead of being sentimental about virgins they were sentimental about prostitutes.

The sad young men were betrayed by their own affectations; attempting to live in a world of self-induced emotion and automatic sensation, they fell readily into decadence. Unable to see the strangeness of actual existence, they manufactured a prettiness which they mistook for beauty and an exoticism which they confused with vision.

Self-appraisal did not set in until the dawn of the twentieth century, but a few spirits were ready to question the narrow esthetic standards. In the midst of the subtle nineties Max Beerbohm mocked at the pretensions of Oscar Wilde, who had been acknowledged as the leader of the esthetic movement and whose Holy Grail (said Beerbohm) was the mot juste. Reviewing the period, Beerbohm wrote satirically: "Beauty had existed long before 1880. It was Mr. Oscar Wilde who managed her début. To study the period is to admit that to him was due no small part of the social vogue that Beauty began to enjoy. Fired by his fervid words, men and women hurled their mahogany into the streets and ransacked the curio-shops for the furniture of Annish days. . . . Into whatsoever ballroom you went, you would surely find half a score of comely ragamuffins in velvet, murmuring sonnets, posturing, waving their hands."

Soon the posturing ceased. Art could not live by sentimentality and rhetoric. (Yeats defined the difference when he said, "Sentimentality is deceiving one's self; rhetoric is deceiving other people.") The tinsel wore off; the essential shoddiness was revealed. Neither elegance nor perversity was sufficiently powerful to persist by itself, and when the reputation of Oscar Wilde collapsed beneath a social scandal, the movement collapsed with it. It was no longer fashionable to be notorious; wickedness as a way of art and life became not only unpopular but somewhat ridiculous.

Triumph of the Commonplace

The mannerisms of the esthetes were finally burlesqued to death by W. S. Gilbert (1836–1911) in *Patience* and by Robert Hichens (1864–   ) in *The Green Carnation*, 1894. Their literary leadership passed to a group of virile romanticists, of whom the most important were W. E. Henley (1849–1903) and Rudyard Kipling (1865–1936). This new group was equally opposed to the unctuous prudery of the Victorians and the languid corruption of the esthetes. It is significant, and perhaps inevitable, that the robust Henley-Kipling resurgence was almost concurrent with the final excesses of the esthetic movement.

Henley and Kipling influenced their contemporaries with prose as well as verse. Their work, opposed to the reticence of the Victorians, was forthright. In contradistinction to the anemic preciosity of the esthetes, it glorified the commonplace and exulted in a healthy vulgarity. It became the record of actual adventure, athletic, rousing, romantic, and violently patriotic.

The personality and influence of Henley exceeded his creative accomplishment. As critic and editor he sponsored a new breed of romanticists: Rudyard Kipling, Robert Louis Stevenson, H. G. Wells, William Butler Yeats, J. M. Barrie. Some of these men were older than Henley, some were much younger, but none could listen to him without being affected by his energy and enthusiasm. Henley was one of the first to call attention to the impressionism of Whistler and to defend the "crudity" of Rodin's sculptures. His "In Hospital" series dealt with unprepossessing material, but it turned into beauty what many considered too prosaic for poetry. A generation before vers libre became a fashion, he experimented boldly in unrhymed free verse. Revolting from poetic diction, he sounded the effectiveness of colloquial speech. He explored the city from the Tower to the slums with the sharp eye of a journalist.

"Life—give me life until the end!" Henley shouted. He prayed to be flung into the everlasting lull at the very top of his being, "the battle spirit shouting in my blood." It was no wonder that his voice sometimes grew boisterous and his overeagerness for red-blooded health sounded suspiciously neurotic. Besides being an enemy of defeatism, Henley was a cripple. His defiance of pain and cowardice was the honest expression of one who, "in the fell clutch of circumstance," had not winced nor cried aloud. His was a true heroism, not a set of heroic postures.

What Henley, because of a life too crowded with editorial duties, left unfinished, Kipling completed. Kipling emphasized the healthy, the robust and masculine, note, to the pitch of rowdiness. He did not theorize; he did not analyze; he accepted life in its paradoxical entirety and found it good. Kipling pierced the grimy exteriors and revealed the miracles of machinery, bridge-building, and the traffic of every day. Nothing, he insisted, was too harsh or too ugly for art. His contemporaries complained that his triumph was the triumph of the Philistine, that Kipling celebrated the strong at the expense of the subtle, and that he tried to strip the world of glamour. Kipling pointed to the new express trains and replied in justifiable sarcasm:

"Confound Romance! . . . And all unseen
Romance brought up the nine-fifteen."

Henley's valor was a general concept; Kipling particularized it. To Kipling the life of poetry was the life of action. He extended valor to the workers as well as to the dreamers. He struck up marches for the inglorious heroes of science; he composed swinging ballads for soldiers, sailors, mechanics, explorers, border thieves, ditch-diggers, tramps, even for housewives. Kipling's vision was not limited by his resources, but by his patriotism. His was an urgency not so much for the world as for the Empire; his Muse attempted to smile on all humanity, but she wore the sternly militant features of Britannia

Nevertheless, a burning faith shines through Kipling's drum-banging, and an invincible curiosity carries him beyond provincialism. Contemporary taste and shifting fashion may deprecate his uncritical enthusiasm and willful aggressiveness, but at his best—in a dozen stories and a score of poems—he is unsurpassed by any writer of his period.

A note of stoic heroism was sounded by A. E. Housman (1859–1936) in three small volumes of verse, one of which was posthumously published. Housman's was a quiet but forceful pessimism; it was achieved partly by the actuality of his Shropshire background, partly because of his terse, almost epigrammatic, idiom. A cloistered Latin scholar, Housman wrote with detachment about murder and suicide, personal betrayal and cosmic evil. His stanzas are miracles of incongruity; the most horrendous happenings shape themselves into measures which are a cross between a jig and hymn tune. His heroism is a far cry from the good world of the Victorians. Evil is a constant, but it must be borne. Cruelty is natural to the physical world, but it can be endured.

"Be still, be still, my soul; it is but for a season:
Let us endure an hour and see injustice done."

This was a new expression of the old stoic bitterness: a sense of suffering that is real but manfully restrained; a pervasive ill which, if gradually absorbed, creates an immunity against pain. Meanwhile the grim hedonist does not despair; there is love and laughter and enough liquor to go around. These, says Housman, echoing the Persian pleasure-seeker who wrote the *Rubáiyát*, are better than thinking—

"And malt does more than Milton can
To justify God's ways to man."

The Irish Movement: Revival and Rebellion

The robust romantic realism of Henley, Kipling, and Housman was toughened by a naturalistic fiction, which, like the esthetic movement, had its beginning in France. Zola was its acknowledged leader; George Moore (1853–1933) and George Gissing (1857–1903) were its disciples. The tendency extended into Ireland, where realism and estheticism joined to create a distinct and original movement. William Butler Yeats, George W. Russell ("AE"), Douglas Hyde (1860–   ), and George Moore were separated by taste and tradi-

tion, but they had a common aim: They proposed to create a national literature, which, though written in English, would express the unique spirit of Ireland and, founded upon strictly Irish lore and legendry, would create an independent tradition of its own. The plan was articulated by Yeats in *Ideas of Good and Evil*, 1903: "I would have Ireland recreate the ancient arts, the arts as they were understood in Judea, in India, in Scandinavia, in Greece and Rome, in every ancient land, as they were understood when they moved a whole people, and not a few people who have grown up in a leisure class and made this understanding their business."

Two movements for social and economic reform in Ireland sprang to life. The first, the Gaelic League (founded in 1893 by Douglas Hyde), had as its object the study of ancient Irish literature and the preservation of Irish as the racial language. The second, organized about six years later as the Irish Agricultural Organization Society by Horace Plunkett and abetted by George Russell, was a co-operative movement with a simple slogan: "Better farming; better business; better living." In its first year the co-operative society did a business of about $20,000; twelve years later statistics showed a business of more than $16,000,000. The social economy implicit in both movements strengthened the national culture. George Russell successfully combined agrarianism and mysticism; Douglas Hyde was able to unite folklore and warfare against the survival of the feudal system; William Butler Yeats dealt simultaneously in magic and politics. "Better living" turned from a poetic phrase into an accomplished fact. A nationalism began to be achieved; a new vision of life as well as a new literature maintained itself upon common effort and communal sense. The movements joined and became steadily more radical. Insurrections, suddenly rising and severely put down, grew increasingly violent; rebellion flamed everywhere; the hopes of a few dreamers became the battle cry of an embittered nation. The Irish renaissance ended in revolution; Eire was born of the blood of its poets. A poet, Douglas Hyde, became its President in 1938.

Much of the activity centered about the independent Irish Literary Theatre, later to be known as the Abbey Players because of the stirring performances in the Abbey Theatre in Dublin. It was for this theater that Yeats wrote his plays, plays that were atmospheric but compelling, symbolic but deeply emotional. The best of them communicated a sense of trance, a depth beyond ordinary reality. *Cathleen ni Houlihan*, a prose play first performed in 1902, lifted allegory to a plane of high patriotism. Even the most literal-minded members of the audience could not fail to see in the poor harried woman who had lost her fields and for whom men gladly died—a woman who never aged and who had "the walk of a queen"—the figure of Ireland. Among the other plays of Yeats which became famous for their summoning of the past in terms of the present are *The Land of Heart's Desire*, 1899; *Where There Is Nothing*, 1903; *The Hour Glass*, 1903; and *The King's Threshold*, 1904.

George Moore's contribution to the theater was by way of difficult, and finally abortive, collaboration. Douglas Hyde's work was chiefly in Gaelic. Lady Gregory (1859–1932) was the most prolific of the playwrights. Besides various translations she wrote twenty-four plays; though most of them are slender in theme, they are interesting in structure and characteristic in idiom.

The most powerful as well as the most original dramatist of the group was J. M. Synge (1871–1909). Synge's plays were few in number. But the longer pieces, such as *The Playboy of the Western World*, 1907, are rich in texture, and the one-act plays (especially *The Shadow of the Glen*, 1903, and *Riders to the Sea*, 1904) are masterpieces, classic in form and noble in conception. It may be said that Synge never imagined a commonplace character or wrote a mediocre line. Synge's language alone would have made a reputation for any writer. It was the language of simple people, peasants mostly, lifted into natural picturesqueness and spiced with fresh imagery, "to show that what is exalted or tender is not made by feeble blood." Language was Synge's preoccupation and his prime force. "I have thought," Synge wrote in an introduction to his bare and peat-flavored poems, "that at the side of the poetic diction, which everyone condemns, modern verse contains a great deal of poetic material, using poetic in the same special sense. The poetry of exaltation will be always the highest; but when men lose their poetic feeling for ordinary life, and cannot write of ordinary things, their exalted poetry is likely to lose its strength of exaltation, in the way men cease to build beautiful churches when they have lost happiness in building shops." It was not, as some maintain, a study of the Greek tragedies which disciplined Synge's mind and fortified his art; it was his own delicate sensibility playing against the rough life and elementary spirit of the Irish scene. No one recorded that life more graphically yet more colorfully; he not only crystallized it, he transfigured it. Synge echoed George Gissing's definition of art as "the expression, satisfying and

abiding, of the zest of life." Zest gave a vivid raciness to everything Synge wrote. A key to his strange combination, his fusion of reality and fantasy, of shyness and wildness, may be found in the introduction which he wrote to *The Playboy of the Western World*, quoted on page 1023.

Although the Irish renaissance began as a literary movement, it became a social synthesis which called forth every expression of creative and political thought. Poetry and drama were the forms which first attracted the writers of the group, but it was not long before wider experiences were embodied in a prose which varied from polemics to portraiture, from bitter wisdom to shrewd fancy. The outstanding writers of fiction and essays were George Moore, St. John Ervine (1883–   ), James Stephens (1882–   ), and Liam O'Flaherty (1897–   ), whose *The Informer*, 1926, won an English prize as a piece of fiction and the Motion Picture Academy award as a film.

George Moore spent his boyhood at the family estate in Mayo, which he inherited from his father, but Ireland did not attract him during his youth. It was not until the publication of *Parnell and His Island*, 1887, that he became interested in his early backgrounds, and the beginning of the Boer War (coincident with the appearance of *Evelyn Innes*, 1898, Moore's first sensational work) sent him back to the land of his fathers, where he remained twelve years. Although Moore subsequently insisted that he became part of the Celtic revival only out of curiosity, and although his avowedly subjective attitude owes much to Zola, the Irish scene as well as the Celtic spirit glimmers through *The Lake*, 1905, *The Untilled Field*, 1903, and the autobiographical *Hail and Farewell*, 1911–14. His interests, he claimed, were above personalities. But Moore was self-deceived. Portraits of his associates are everywhere in his work—Yeats is drawn (one might saw drawn and quartered) in Moore's memoirs as well as in *Evelyn Innes* in the character of Ulick Dean—and Moore himself, as a cultural David opposing a world of conventionally moral Goliaths, was his own favorite character.

St. John Ervine's work was far less varied than Moore's, but it struck deeper into the roots of the national consciousness. Known primarily for his realistic plays, Ervine brought to his novels and sketches an impersonality which, in its very detachment, was dramatic. Ervine wrote simply about simple people (*Mixed Marriage*, 1910; *Jane Clegg*, 1911; *John Ferguson*, 1914), but every characterization was fully illuminated. In the work of George Moore the style is far more memorable than the characters, whereas in Ervine the reader forgets the writing and remembers only the people.

James Stephens, in common with Yeats and "AE," brought a poet's equipment to his prose; he perfected a narrative tone utterly unlike that of Moore and Ervine. Its roots were in folklore, but it grew and flourished into a kind of legendry in which fact and fairy tale were inextricably mixed. Even before middle age Stephens was almost as legendary as his stories. It was said that he had been adopted by an apple woman in Belfast, that he had nearly died of cold and starvation, that he had been rescued by a streetwalker, and that he had roamed on foot through every corner of Ireland, ragged and unknown, until he was discovered by "AE." An extraordinary sympathy for the weak and bewildered manifests itself in all of Stephens's books. Sometimes the tone is wise and gentle, as in *The Crock of Gold*, 1912; sometimes it is fierce and blinding, as in *Here Are Ladies*, 1913, and *Etched in Moonlight*, 1928. One moment Stephens is capering with friendly goats, the next he is the intimate of austere gods, a lovable gamin and a beloved seer. No one has so fully articulated the double nature of the Irishman, the spirit that can turn from headlong gaiety to righteous anger, from childlike tenderness to uncontrollable rebellion.

The Scottish Renaissance

Unlike the Irish revival, the Scottish renaissance was scarcely an articulated movement. Its members belonged to no society, uttered no program, adhered to no particular center. Yet a group, scattered in locale and separated by temperament, emerged before the beginning of the twentieth century. Devoted to the village rather than to the town, the interpreters of rural life in Scotland grew so numerous and so devoted to the soil that Henley humorously referred to them as founders of the Kailyard (Cabbage Patch) School. Their objective, like that of the Irish, was to project a national feeling; but, unlike the contributors to the Celtic revival, they had no leadership, and their work lacked political significance. They pleased without disturbing; they aimed to entertain, to rouse a quick laugh or a light sigh, but not to provoke the deeper emotions.

John Watson (1850–1907), writing under the pseudonym of "Ian Maclaren," won a reputation for untroubled sentimentality, particularly with *Beside the Bonnie Briar Bush*, 1894. S. R. Crockett (1860–1914) rivaled "Maclaren" in popularity and

sententiousness. But their compatriot J. M. Barrie outlasted them both. The fame of James Matthew Barrie (1860–1937) grew steadily; it passed beyond national boundaries. Before he turned to the creation of the elfin whimsical *Peter Pan*, 1904, and the whimsically feminine *What Every Woman Knows*, 1908, Barrie employed a large part of Scotland and much of its vernacular for his effective plays and novels. Among Barrie's successes were the quaint and wholly Scottish *Auld Licht Idylls*, 1888; *A Window in Thrums*, 1889; *An Edinburgh Eleven*, 1888; *The Little Minister*, 1891; *Sentimental Tommy*, 1895; *Tommy and Grizel*, 1900, and the touching picture of his mother, *Margaret Ogilvy*, 1894.

The only discordant note was struck by George Douglas (1879–1902), whose first and only novel was published when the author was little more than twenty, and who died tragically shortly after its publication. *The House with the Green Shutters*, 1927, obviously autobiographical, was the very opposite of the light and charming sentiment fashioned by Douglas's compatriots; it was the "other side" of Scottish life; grim without alleviation, dark with conflict, and unflinchingly honest. It caused a sensation when it appeared, and more than one critic compared it to *Wuthering Heights* because of its communication of terror and painful intimacy.

Repudiated in its own country, Douglas's one volume spread its influence abroad; it stimulated a small but powerful movement in Wales. Rhys Davies (1903–   ) and Caradoc Evans (1890–   ) exploited the regional Welsh life with a primitive intensity. The exploitation of native strains was growing extreme; reality was emphasized to the point of cruelty, and, for a while, naturalism became synonymous with ruthless nationalism. A late manifestation of the Welsh spirit flowered—or, rather, erupted—in the fiercely summoned, word-intoxicated prose and verse of Dylan Thomas, whose work appeared in the late 1930's.

The Shifting Background

The twentieth century began on a high note of confident imperialism and all-encompassing certainty. Ten years later Englishmen understood why Kipling, at the height of the Diamond Jubilee, had warned them:

> "For heathen heart that puts her trust
> In reeking tube and iron shard,
> All valiant dust that builds on dust . . .
> For frantic boast and foolish word—"

By 1910 the frantic boasts had given way to uneasy apprehensions. British pride had been badly injured by the inglorious Boer War. There was little reason for complacency at home, where Liberals and Conservatives were waging a prolonged and aimless battle. Anglo-German relations were growing worse. Four years before the Kaiser's troops struck through Belgium, an Anglo-German war was taken for granted. The Kaiser, according to Philip Guedalla:

"made occasional attempts to reassure Great Britain; but, as their admirable purpose was obscured by his customary infelicity, they produced effects precisely contrary to those which he intended. . . . The world, perhaps excusably, was less interested in these blameless exercises than in the production of a new 13.5 naval gun and the performances of the new Zeppelin and the appearance of machine-gun sections at the last German manoeuvres." [1]

The World War of 1914-18 rapidly increased the sense of complexity. The future of science and the shape of things to come were too bewildering for cheerful prophecy. Eighteen years before the Armistice, Dr. Newell Dwight Hillis, clergyman and author, had hailed the brave new century: "For the first time government, invention, art, industry, and religion have served all the people." Now all the people were "served" by propaganda and poison gas, by a scorn of traditional faiths and a reckless pursuit of novelty, by suppressed depravity and unconcealed violence. Truth was a broken convention. As David Daiches summarized it:

"One by one the preconceptions of our fathers have been shattered, and instead of being replaced naturally with new beliefs as they die, they have been replaced by nothing. In terms of ethics and theory of value generally, if not with complete literalness, what ought to have been a brave new world has turned out a wasteland." [2]

Moral earnestness declined in favor of amoral curiosity. Such imponderables as the soul, the belief in immortality, the omniscient interest of a personal God, concerned the artist far less than a materialistic philosophy, the threat (or promise) of a new political order, and a general preoccupation with the daily life of all-too-mortal man. The virtues of the middle class were generally challenged; the domesticated ideals and exaggerated sentimentalities were exposed; the sexual standards were mocked and often repudiated. Private conscience blundered into social consciousness.

The rise of materialism, speeded on by the dominance of the machine, shifted attention from the spiritual universe to the world of science and physical sensation. Failing to find security in creeds and questionable faiths, men turned to research. They looked to psychoanalysis and socialism, in the hope of finding a way of life which could be integrated and controlled through the exercise of the intelligence.

New Tendencies in the Novel

The change in values brought about a new kind of novel. Subtleties of style and extraordinary techniques of communication were offered in compensation for the lost "community of belief." By the time the late Victorians gave way to the Edwardians, the tight form of the novel showed signs of breaking up. When the Edwardians were replaced by the Georgians, style, structure, and subject matter were altered almost beyond recognition. The rigid and complicated plot became increasingly flexible. With the chief Edwardian novelists (such as H. G. Wells, Arnold Bennett, and John Galsworthy) the plot was thinned out by extraneous commentaries, discursive polemics, and countless digressions. With the Georgians (such as D. H. Lawrence, James Joyce, Virginia Woolf, Dorothy Richardson, and Aldous Huxley) there was so much analysis, impressionism, experimentation, and intimate "atmosphere" that the plot almost disappeared.

The most interesting forerunner of the twentieth-century "naturalistic" novel was Samuel Butler (1835-1902). Son of a famous clergyman, grandson of a scholarly bishop, Butler was not only a pioneer but a rebel in the Victorian camp. His life was spent in conflict and controversy. Educated for the Church, he suddenly abandoned the family career, sailed to New Zealand, and became a sheep-rancher in the wild Rangitata district which, after his return to England, furnished a background for *Erewhon* (an anagram for "Nowhere"), 1872. *Erewhon* masqueraded as a romance, but it was an almost undisguised satire on the mores of contemporary England. *The Way of All Flesh*, 1903, which was part autobiography, part fiction, and part essay, was an even more devastating attack on the theological absurdities and domestic hypocrisies of Butler's generation. A permanent contribution to

[1] *The Hundred Years*. By Philip Guedalla. Doubleday, Doran and Company, Inc. 1937. [2] *The Novel and The Modern World*. By David Daiches. The University of Chicago Press. 1939.

literature, *The Way of All Flesh* was published—with an irony Butler would have cherished—a year after his death, but the technical importance of this one volume cannot be overestimated. It was a carry-all for the author's ideas; its freedom of form and range of interest prepared the way for the flexible plays and novels of the following quarter of a century. When George Bernard Shaw's critics accused him of being influenced by Ibsen, Shaw advised them to read "an almost unread Englishman by the name of Samuel Butler."

The work of H. G. Wells (1866–   ) mingled naturalism and romanticism; it combined carefully assembled data and imagination with inexhaustible enthusiasm. The most voluminous writer of the time, he was also the most versatile. Before he was seventy, Wells was the author of more than ninety volumes and thirty pamphlets; his fertility ranged from such full-length novels as *Kipps*, 1905, and *Tono-Bungay*, 1909 (which, like Butler's *The Way of All Flesh*, was a mixture of autobiography and invention) to a comprehensive review of humanity, *The Outline of History*, 1920; from the fantastic short stories of *Tales of Space and Time*, 1899, to prophecies of social reconstruction (*Men like Gods*, 1928; *The World Set Free*, 1914; and others)—from the library to the laboratory and back again. It has been said that Wells's natural creative power was increasingly weakened by his penchant for prophecy and social criticism; it has been charged against him that "he sold his birthright for a pot of message." But there can be no doubt that many of Wells's prophecies have been fulfilled, that his short stories are often as dynamic as they are surprising, and that the best of his novels are adroit in lifting the casual to the pitch of the extraordinary.

Another glorification of the commonplace was achieved by Arnold Bennett (1867–1931). If Bennett was not as prolific as Wells, he was even more versatile. Besides his many novels, short stories, essays, and memoirs, Bennett was a playwright, a musician, and a water-colorist. Bennett's novels differed from those of Wells not only in being more objective, more painstaking, and less passionate, but also in being far more slowly and solidly built. Bennett loved the minute, even the sordid, details of everyday existence. At the worst he was, as one of his critics complained, a "literary bricklayer," adding one small block of facts upon another. At his best—in *The Old Wives' Tale*, 1908, and the *Clayhanger* trilogy, 1910–16—Bennett was a painter in the Dutch manner; in a cleanly built prose he revealed an unsurpassed picture of the hard-working, unimaginative, and dominating middle class of England.

What *The Old Wives' Tale* did for the lower middle classes, Galsworthy's *The Forsyte Saga*, 1922, accomplished for the upper class. John Galsworthy (1867–1933) devoted himself to the genteel propertied society which was midway between the lower middle class and the aristocracy. Sensitive, sane, liberal without being radical, Galsworthy might have stepped out of one of his own novels. As a dramatist he was successful and, for the most part, convincing. More critical of society in his plays than in his novels, he dealt with the struggles of the weak and the unfortunate caught in the modern industrial machine. Such plays as *Strife*, 1909; *Justice*, 1910; and *Loyalties*, 1922, balance themselves on ethical and social problems; and, though Galsworthy impartially presented the just claims of the opposing points of view, there is no doubt that his sympathy was with the losers.

Joseph Conrad (1857–1924) differed from Galsworthy and Wells in being forceful without ethical purpose. Although Conrad repudiated "art for art's sake" almost as vigorously as he denied that he was a purely romantic novelist, he said: "The aim of creation cannot be ethical. I fondly believe that its object is purely spectacular—a spectacle for awe, love, adoration or hate if you like, but in this view—never for despair. These visions, delicious or poignant, are a moral end in themselves." Conrad (born Teodor Jozef Konrad Korzeniowski in the Ukraine) learned English through translations of Dickens and Shakespeare, and the help of Ford Madox Ford, with whom he collaborated. The nautical stories of Cooper and Marryat sent him to sea at the age of nineteen; his most characteristic tales are flung out against a panorama of dangerous waters, heavy skies, and mysterious reaches of space. Conrad employed a strange manner of narration which, in its very complication, allowed him to introduce "asides" and interpretations impossible in straightforward storytelling; but the very interruptions and digressions gave his fiction the air of scrupulous reality. Reality and artistry were Conrad's chief concern. He was eager, first of all "to make you *feel*, to make you *see*," and his force as well as his manner of telling a story or drawing a character (particularly in *The Heart of Darkness* and *Typhoon*, both 1902) succeeded in bringing "the light of magic suggestiveness to play for an evanescent instant over the commonplace surface of words worn thin by ages of careless usage."

E. M. Forster (1879–   ) dealt with the powers of a machine-driven civilization, but he did not worship them. On the contrary, he showed man beaten by brute conquest but triumphing over ruthlessness.

He pitted the individual against limitless size, and made size seem small. To Forster the physical events of life were less important than the personal relationships, the intricate human affections, the clash between basic passions and man's private integrities. ("Centuries of embracement, yet man is no nearer to understanding man.") His best novel, *A Passage to India*, 1925, is superficially a social-political tract; but it is first of all a subtle analysis of humanity, of the people of one race by a person of another. It renders no judgment, points no moral, but when it is finished the reader finds life larger and richer than before.

D. H. Lawrence (1885–1930) represented an extreme if not final revolt against Victorianism. More than that, he continually fought the standards of present society, challenged the ideal of democracy, and questioned civilization itself. An impassioned and maladjusted spirit, he was both realist and mystic, puritan and prophet. Forster wrote that Lawrence was "the only prophetic novelist writing to-day—all the rest are fantasists or preachers: the only living novelist in whom the song predominates, who has the rapt bardic quality. . . . What is valuable about him cannot be put into words; it is colour, gesture, and outline in people and things." Lawrence was fascinated by the nonreasonable (and even irrational) elements of human nature. He had an ideal of pure "mindlessness"; he never ceased to be fascinated by the role of the unconscious. It was an unusual unconsciousness which compelled him in *Sons and Lovers*, 1913, and *The Rainbow*, 1915: an unconscious with a conscience. Lashed by his self-contradictions, Lawrence tore himself to death. He worried flesh and spirit; he never ceased to agonize over dark and mystical demands which turned out to be twisted ethical problems.

James Joyce (1882–1941) carried the unconscious much further than Lawrence; he let its energy loose in the nightmare power and confusion of *Ulysses*. Joyce seemed to glory in the dissolution of ordinary human values without attempting to create new ones. He was not so much an experimenter as an exploder. *Ulysses*, 1922, preceded by the orderly *Dubliners*, 1914, and the organized *Portrait of the Artist as a Young Man*, 1916, is an explosive work disruptive in style, detonating with quasi-mythological allusions, immense knowledge, and private meanings. *Finnegan's Wake*, 1939, a conglomerate discharge of myths, puns, dreams, and violences of language, carries distortion to such a pitch that it is, for the most part, unintelligible to the average intelligent reader.

In the works of Virginia Woolf (1882–1941) the unconscious, with its outlet in the "stream of consciousness," was acknowledged, but it was strictly controlled. As a critic, her *The Common Reader*, 1925, and *A Room of One's Own*, 1929, were cleanly penetrating, witty without being malicious, and orthodox in manner. Her novels—notably *Mrs. Dalloway*, 1925; *To the Lighthouse*, 1927; *Orlando*, 1928; and *The Waves*, 1931—were far more experimental. They were a growing series of bold and successful techniques. Mrs. Woolf triumphed in impressionism; in the stylization of *Orlando*, a fantasy which is partly a history of the national spirit and partly a parody of literary styles; in the "interior monologue" of *The Waves*, a stylized soliloquy gradually revealing events and characters; in an almost complete abandonment of plot, and in a kind of writing which fluctuated between prose and poetry. Mrs. Woolf's quality was not so much a steady progress of experiences as a burst of unexpected flashes, a brilliant shower of impressions and reactions. The complexities and contradictions of her human beings were shown, as the London *Times* wrote, "by a gesture, an image, a perception. . . . Each character is much more conscious than we habitually are and utters not merely his sense of the moment, but, again and again, his secret individuality." Mrs. Woolf's combination of imaginative extravagance and artistic control caused admirers to stress her fluency—not the fluidity of a rushing river, nor the turbulence of a waterfall, but the upwelling of a deep spring which, subject to great pressure, "makes a high fountain in the air."

The novels of Aldous Huxley (1894–   ) show the gifted young Georgian as a hard-driven and disillusioned grandson of the illustrious scientist Thomas Henry Huxley. Like his grandfather, Aldous Huxley is skeptical about the moral sense, questions Christianity as a civilizing agency, and never ceases to wage war upon orthodox beliefs. He has turned, with equal loathing, from the ethics of the past and the standards of the present. His characters luxuriate in the pleasure of the intellect and plunge into sexuality only to be cheated by the mind and betrayed by the body. There are times when Huxley has written not only against his age but against his own creations. Even in the later novels, where Huxley attempts to repudiate the prolonged sterility of the early work, his characters live in a world of discontent and self-disgust. Rebecca West once analyzed him: "Notoriously the most fair-minded and honourably disposed person to his fellow men, he nevertheless continually makes statements about his own invented characters which have the poisonous quality of an anonymous letter. His individual creativeness forces him to invent these people and a good three-dimensional world for them to inhabit, and all would be beautiful and enduring art if it were not that the disillusionment which has been implanted in him makes him loathe himself for adding quantitatively to life, for increasing the horrid sum of experience." Finding no help in sensation, no faith in religion, and little hope in science, Huxley resigns himself to helplessness and, more recently, to passive mysticism—a commentary upon his decade as well as himself.

It is impossible to list all the novelists of the period; a consideration of the more important writers of fiction would require an encyclopedic work. But mention at least should be made of the heightened awareness and imaginative observation of W. H. Hudson (1841–1922); the cool detachment and expert craftsmanship of W. Somerset Maugham (1874–   ), especially in his *Of Human Bondage*, 1915, and *The Moon and Sixpence*, 1919; the delicate symbolism of Walter De La Mare (1873–   ), who, although known chiefly as a poet, composed, in *Memoirs of a Midget*, 1921, one of the memorable novels of the period; the prolific energy of Ford Madox Ford (1873–1939), who acted as mentor to Joseph Conrad when Conrad was learning to write in English, and whose "Tietjens" series, beginning with *Some Do Not*, 1924, vividly pictures the war years; the spirited regionalism of Sheila Kaye-Smith; the slow terror and almost overwhelming horror of Liam O'Flaherty; the dispassionate strength and uncompromising severity of Henry (born Henrietta) Handel Richardson, whose three-volume *The Fortunes of Richard Mahony*, 1917, is a masterpiece; the rare finesse and sensitivity of Rebecca West (1892–   ); the patient and detailed naturalism of Dorothy M. Richardson, who, like Joyce and Virginia Woolf, employed the "stream of consciousness" in *Pilgrimage*, 1938, which ran to twelve volumes; and the exquisite blend of satire and tenderness, whimsicality and wisdom, in the books of Sylvia Townsend Warner (1893–   ).

Rise of the Short Story

The period has been particularly rich in the development and diversity of its short stories. The reason for this is not far to seek. The increasingly rapid pace, the abruptly shifting tempo, the feverish alteration of standards, the continual exchange of quickly accepted and quickly discarded ideas, demanded a condensed form of fiction. The times called for a story which could be read between other

tasks at a single sitting. The short story served both as a stimulant and as an anodyne; it had always been a favorite medium of entertainment, both as a transcription of life and as a dramatization of it. But now the tellers of tales began to record many and significant changes. It may be said that in the twentieth century the short story came of age.

A comparison of the short stories of the present with those written during the last century will show an evolution not only of feeling but of form. The short story of the past moved quickly; it was firm in construction; it had a definite beginning and a climactic (and usually unexpected) end; it permitted no irrelevant details; it emphasized adroitness and surprise even at the expense of plausibility. The twentieth-century narrators have not been satisfied with the old formulas; they have insisted on new techniques to achieve new and more realistic effects. The elegant tone and crisp manner have given way to a colloquial leisure; the tale begins in the very midst of things and often comes to no particular conclusion; significant details are introduced not only for "atmosphere" but for characterizing elements; carefully "arranged" incidents are sacrificed for a pervading sense of actuality. Often, indeed, there is no "story" element. Instead there is presented a situation which seems trivial but which is charged with tension and untold possibilities.

The tradition of Poe and Maupassant, with its manipulated drama and skillfully patterned effects, clashed with the more recent tradition of Chekhov, in which no precise pattern was discernible. In the stories of James Joyce and Katherine Mansfield the manner is deceptively casual; instead of a tight and orderly progress there is maintained a flexibility of mood and a looseness which suggest the haphazard mystery of existence. Situation is the first requisite; sensibility is the touchstone. There is less of a prearranged dramatic tale and more of an actual transcript, "a slice of life."

W. Somerset Maugham, a critical compiler as well as an expert writer of short stories, summed up the differences. In an analytical introduction to his anthology, *Tellers of Tales*, Maugham wrote:

"People grow tired even of good things. They want change. To take an example from another art: domestic architecture during the (first) Georgian Era reached a rare perfection; the houses that were built then were good to look at and comfortable to live in. The rooms were spacious, airy, and well proportioned. You would have thought people would be content with such houses for ever. But no. The romantic era approached; they wanted the quaint, the fanciful, and the picturesque; and the architects, not unwilling, built them what they wanted. It is hard to invent such a story as Poe wrote and, as we know, even he, in his small output, more than once repeated himself. There is a good deal of trickiness in a narrative of this kind, and when, with the appearance and immediate popularity of the monthly magazine, the demand for such narratives became great, authors were not slow to learn the tricks. Craftsmen rather than artists, in order to make their stories effective they forced upon them a conventional design and presently deviated so far from plausibility in their delineation of life that their readers rebelled. They grew weary of stories written to a pattern they know only too well. They demanded greater realism." [3]

Thus the characteristics of the short story have adapted themselves not only to the fashion of the moment but also to the basic spirit of the age. Prompted by Poe, Maugham originally defined a short story as "a piece of fiction dealing with a single incident; it must sparkle, excite or impress; it must have unity of effect; it should move in an even line from its exposition to its close." Later tendencies, however, have amended and contracted the definition to a formula which is not derived from Poe and which permits the compiler to include stories which depend less on narration and more on implication. Maugham finally concluded that his definition could be simpler and more comprehensive: "I should define a short story as a piece of fiction that has unity of impression and that can be read at a single sitting. I should be inclined to say that the only test of its excellence is that it interests."

Most of the novelists already mentioned excelled in the writing of short stories. Besides these, several lesser authors developed an extraordinary subtlety. Among those who followed the Poe-Maupassant tradition, the most notable were Leonard Merrick (1864–   ), H. H. Munro ("Saki"; 1870–1916), A. E. Coppard (1878–   ), R. B. Cunninghame Graham (1874–   ), H. M. Tomlison (1873–   ), Hugh Walpole (1884–   ), and J. B. Priestley (1894–   ). Chekhov influenced the younger and more experimental writers, notably James Joyce and Katherine Mansfield (1888–1923), who implied far more than she told, who was precise but

[3] *Tellers of Tales: 100 Short Stories from England, the United States, France, Russia, and Germany*. Selected with an Introduction by W. Somerset Maugham. Doubleday, Doran & Company. 1939.

never finical, delicate without being precious, and who employed digression as a fine art.

The Analytical Biography

Perhaps the greatest change in tone and attitude was manifest in the writing of biography. The new biographers dedicated themselves to a lively skepticism. They were concerned with more than the facts of history; they probed behind the carefully assembled data to the living, disconcerting, and often disillusioning spirit. They felt that the account of a man and his age should be at least as interesting as fiction, and they knew that without creative imagination there could be no sense of reality.

The most remarkable biographer of the period was Lytton Strachey (1880–1932). Strachey may be said to have suddenly founded a whole school. It was a school of reappraisal which did not hesitate to apply relentless analysis, even psychoanalysis, to legendary heroes, saintly heroines, and pious rulers who had been considered sacrosant. Strachey cut through the pietism, the swaddled sentiment, the prudish reticences. His method was vivacious, his technique was innovating. His quest was a search for unsuspected truths, not for a restatement of recorded facts; his aim was esthetic, not ethical. For this he was equipped with an inquisitive subtlety, a devastating wit, and a bewildering brilliant style— "half butterfly and half gadfly." Although his field was literary history, he was not a detached historian. George Dangerfield, in the *Saturday Review of Literature*, July 23, 1938, pointed out that Strachey's attitude to the past was

"anti-clerical, aristocratic. If the word had not been deprived by the passage of years of almost all significance, you might say that it was a *Whig* attitude; and it is well to remember that there was Whig blood in his veins, a persistent fluid. But permeating and enriching this attitude of his was another quality, a quality not Whig at all: a strange and powerful romanticism. His characters move against a background of hints, of half-statements, of swift exposures, of vistas suddenly illumined and as suddenly veiled. It is a background which piques the reader's curiosity and inspires him with a longing to know more."

Philip Guedalla (1889–   ) has outlived Strachey in years, though not in popularity. Guedalla, frequently considered Strachey's rival, was consistently sharp and a little too determinedly epigram-matic. His scrutiny was closer than Strachey's, but the author of *Queen Victoria*, 1921, and *Elizabeth and Essex*, 1928, was the finer stylist. Guedalla special-ized in the figures and backgrounds of the nine-teenth century, and he dealt with them in a manner that was alternately suave and savage. On the whole Guedalla was a better historian than Strachey, but, as Dangerfield concluded, "he does not fill us with a longing to know more. The brilliant little needles of his perpetual epigrams prick the envelope of our curiosity until at last it subsides into utter defla-tion." Nevertheless, Guedalla's full-length *Wel-lington*, 1931, and *The Hundred Years*, 1936, are a necessary complement to the grace and malice of Strachey's *Eminent Victorians*, 1918, and his *Por-traits in Miniature*, 1931.

It should be added that the biographers of this period were often more dogmatic than their more guarded predecessors. They forgot Chesterton's reminder that our own time is only a time, and not the Day of Judgment. In an effort to avoid dullness at any cost, they sometimes sacrificed accuracy for brilliance and facts for prejudices. The cleverness of Guedalla produced shoddy imitations, and the wit of Strachey did not prevent this portraitist from be-ing frequently unfair to his sitter.

The biographer of the period frequently played the part of the essayist; often he became essayist and autobiographer in one. Among those who made the transition most skillfully were the older conserva-tives Hilaire Belloc (1870–   ), G. K. Chesterton (1874–1936), and Maurice Baring (1874–   ); the younger appraisers Lord David Cecil (1902–   ) and Harold Nicolson (1886–   ); and the poets Edmund Blunden (*Undertones of War*, 1928), Robert Graves (1895–   ; *Good-bye to All That*, 1929), and Siegfried Sassoon (1886–   ; *Memoirs of a Fox-Hunting Man*, 1928, and *Memoirs of an Infantry Officer*, 1930), all of whom turned to prose for their autobiographical records of the World War of 1914–18 and its crushing effects on sensibility and idealism.

The Changing Drama

Toward the end of the nineteenth century the drama began a rapid transition. The play of unreal situations and tricky romanticism gave way to the serious social drama, which, in turn, was sup-planted by the drama of social criticism and protest. The continental "tailor-made" plays of Sardou and Dumas dominated the English theater as late as

the 1880's, and when the realistic Ibsen was first performed in London he was howled down as "im-moral," "bestial," and "a chronicler of the abnor-mal." Yet it was not long before Ibsen became an influence. The social problems he posed were adapted and anglicized by Henry Arthur Jones (1851–1929) and Arthur Wing Pinero (1855–1934), both of whom, nevertheless, retained the technique of Sardou with its emphasis on calculated tension and "the big scene." Jones and Pinero kept them-selves well within the proprieties. They presumed to question Mrs. Grundy, but not actually to dispute her dictates; they were willing to be unconven-tional, but not to be unpopular.

Oscar Wilde (1856–1900) amused and shocked society without seriously challenging it. His were comedies of manners whose precursors were Con-greve, Sheridan, and the sophisticated Restoration dramatists. Wilde excelled in patently artificial situ-ations and trivial problems, but his flashing dialogue often concealed the unimportance of his themes. His influence may be traced not only in the light comedies of W. Somerset Maugham and the theat-rical flippancies of Noël Coward, but in the far more searching "plays for puritans" by George Bernard Shaw.

George Bernard Shaw (1856–   ) was a dynamo in the theater, an electric storm in the academies, and one of the most energizing forces in contem-porary culture. His early plays, notably *Widower's Houses*, 1892, and *Mrs. Warren's Profession*, 1898, bear the mark of Ibsen—Shaw's first critical study was entitled *The Quintessence of Ibsenism*, 1891—but his later work resembles in no way that of the grim Norwegian dramatist. Shaw succeeded in adding the dazzling repartee of Wilde to the fierce icono-clasm of Samuel Butler and in superimposing a bristling personality of his own. Shaw's manner was impertinent and paradoxical, but his purpose was serious. It was, moreover, intrepidly combative. Instead of complaining about Mrs. Grundy he hurled his challenge full at her. Unlike Wilde, he did not aim merely to surprise and shock, but to change men's thinking. His intention was that of Aristophanes, and the words spoken by the chorus in *The Acharnians* might have been addressed to his audiences by Shaw: "As for you, never lose him who will always fight for the cause of justice in his com-edies; he promises you that his precepts will lead you to happiness, though he uses neither flattery, nor intrigue, nor bribery, nor deceit; instead of loading you with praise, he will point you to the better way."

So great was the vitality of Shaw's ideas that at

eighty-four he spoke of writing a new "cycle" after *Geneva*, 1938, his fiftieth play. It was said, more or less facetiously, that he wrote plays as an excuse to write prefaces, and the prefaces were not only more thought-provoking than the plays but more dramatic. The Shaw formula, according to the American critic H. L. Mencken, was to put "the obvious in terms of the scandalous." But Shaw's continual attacks on enshrined convention and pious sham— from the romantic *Caesar and Cleopatra*, 1899, to the untheatrical *Misalliance*, 1910, and *Heartbreak House*, 1917, which are dramatized discussions— helped not only to change the form of the drama but to mold the social sense of the times. Shaw often complained that the last thing to be found in the theater was strictly contemporaneous thought, the prevalent idea. But even Shaw, as Lee Simonson wrote in *The Stage Is Set*,

"could not inject into a play ideas that had not permeated society long enough to create recognizable mouthpieces. . . . Shaw's emancipated mothers, daughters, and philanderers were not wholly invented but at least partially observed in Soho, Chelsea, and Mayfair. Shaw of course got the jump on his fellow playwrights by putting these and similar doctrinaires on the stage before their ideas had become truisms. But as a result many of their discoveries are now so commonplace that Shaw's plays, when revived, are often dismissed as being dated. They will not have a secure place in repertory until the passage of time takes from them the air of novelty with which Shaw himself ushered them on to the stage."[4]

Exceptions must be made to these plausible strictures, the outstanding exceptions being the extraordinary *Candida*, 1913, and the impassioned *Saint Joan of Arc*, 1923, in which the impudent Shaw becomes historian, timely critic, and timeless visionary.

The contributions to drama of the Irish renaissance, as well as the dramas of J. M. Barrie and John Galsworthy, have already been considered on preceding pages. The revival of the poetic drama was effected chiefly by Lascelles Abercrombie (1881–   ) and the American-born poet T. S. Eliot (1888–   ), whose *Murder in the Cathedral*, 1935, was as eloquent as it was theatrically effective. Meanwhile it is evident that the theater had again become not only an entertaining means of evasion, but

a center of criticism and a forum of provocative ideas.

Poetry of the Georgians

The Georgian poets were preceded by such traditionalists as Robert Bridges (1844–1930), Edmund Gosse (1849–1928), and T. Sturge Moore (1870–   ), the impassioned experimentalist Gerard Manley Hopkins (1844–1898), and the self-isolated Thomas Hardy (1844–1928). The Georgian poets consolidated the gains of their immediate predecessors, formed a loosely affiliated school, and issued a series of biennial collections, *Georgian Poetry*, from 1911 to 1922. They lacked a coherent philosophy, an intellectual core, but their technique was fresh and interesting. The tone was generally patterned on everyday speech; old-fashioned inversions were shunned; apostrophes were taboo; "poetic diction" was discarded in favor of an intensified but easily communicated language.

At first the spirit of the Georgian poets was as resolute as their speech. They seized on the commonplace with ardor. John Masefield (1874–   ) wrote about sailors, laborers, hunters, and murderers in such vigorous narratives as *The Widow in the Bye Street*, 1912; *Dauber*, 1913; *The Daffodil Fields*, 1913; and *Reynard the Fox*, 1919. Wilfrid Wilson Gibson (1878–   ) dramatized stonecutters, farmers, and ferrymen in *Daily Bread*, 1910, and *Livelihood*, 1917. D. H. Lawrence (1885–1930) put the almost inarticulate colliers and the overworked townspeople of his native Nottinghamshire into his early *Love Poems and Others*, 1913. But the gathering complexities bewildered the Georgians; war defeated and scattered them. As though betrayed by the upheaval, Masefield retreated into vague generalities about life and platitudes about beauty; Gibson fled to the security of remote associations and familiar stereotypes; Lawrence gave himself up to an increasingly baffled contemplation of the psyche. Perplexity grew; the movement became a movement of escape. The Georgians withdrew to the consoling English countryside, to a tender and prettified Nature, to the false solace of dreams. In their decline the Georgians staged a whole series of retreats; they attempted to return to romantic primitivism, to the belief that Nature was full of lovingkindness, that man was instinctively good, and that the nearer man got to Nature, the better he became. Since Nature is beautiful, "the beautiful is good." Man is a child of Nature; therefore, argued the Georgians, goodness and beauty will attend him as long as he shuns the evil city. They

[4] *The Stage Is Set*. By Lee Simonson. Harcourt, Brace and Company. 1932.

forgot that as early as 1845 Matthew Arnold had cautioned nature-worshipers:

"Man must begin, know this, where Nature ends;
Nature and man can never be fast friends."

The genuinely naïve and artless W. H. Davies (1871–1940) was followed by a coterie who capitalized the bucolic attitude. Theirs was an almost studied simplicity and a determined thoughtlessness. Ralph Hodgson (1871–   ) tuned the pastoral note to a music old in form but fresh in utterance; truly simple, Hodgson avoided mediocrity by the vitality of his emotion and the vigor of his imagination. Harold Monro (1879–1932) protected his hurt sensitivity by fantasies about ordinary objects and half-whimsical, half-metaphysical speculations about man's place in a mechanical world. Walter De La Mare (1873–   ) was obsessed by the unconscious mind, a mind half awake and faintly stirring beneath the conscious will. De La Mare did not altogether forget the active world, but he saw it—as in a reverie—a dream within a dream, part of a disembodied immeasurable universe.

The war inhibited and practically stopped Hodgson and others of his age. It killed such younger brilliant poets as Edward Thomas (1878–1918), Rupert Brooke (1887–1915), James Elroy Flecker (1884–1915), Wilfred Owen (1893–1918), Isaac Rosenberg (1890–1918), Francis Ledwidge (1891–1917), and the amazing boy Charles Hamilton Sorley (1895–1915), dead at twenty. The impetus of the Georgians was spent; the physical and intellectual lifeblood had been drained. Ironically enough, it took the threat of a new war to bring on a new vitalizing impulse.

Frustration and the Literature of Nerves

After the Treaty of Versailles England enjoyed a brief period of quiet, even of prosperity. But by 1920 the old troubles came back in more threatening forms. Unemployment increased alarmingly. Women continued to "agitate" for the vote that was not granted to women under thirty until 1928. Riots and pitched battles heralded the appearance of the Irish Free State as a fractious Dominion of the Crown. America, in what seemed the role of Brutus, added the last stab of the dagger by demanding payment of the war debt. Europe was bankrupt. The orthodox economics had failed; the old patterns of class and culture did not fit. The Labour Party was impotent.

The conflict between individualism and industrialism grew more violent, but produced no finality. The time spirit was sterile. Yet even frustration must express itself. Readers were no longer soothed by personal romanticism and pastoral assurances. Writers ceased to be charmed by erudite escapes and elaborate visions. They tried to create out of exasperation, to substitute contempt for faith, to give formlessness a form. A literature of nerves became apparent.

This exacerbated literature was, at times, expressive and eloquent, but its main expression was confusion. Here the artist was a true, if puzzled, recorder of his period. He attempted to depict a world assaulted by the midnight radio and the morning headlines, by the revelations of Freud and the wish fulfillments of the cinema, by all the isms from Socialism to Imagism, from Militarism to Cubism, Vorticism, Dadaism, and, later, Surrealism. The consequence was dislocation and disruption. Logic gave way to a free association of ideas; purposeful dissonances jarred the expected harmonies. The once orderly metaphor was forced to run wild, and the customary plausible progression was broken by startling chain images and interruptions abrupt as chain lightning.

The Sitwells were among the first to revolt against the wistful, falsely romantic, and vague "magic" of the Georgians. There were three of them: Edith Sitwell (1887–   ), Osbert Sitwell (1892–   ), and Sacheverell Sitwell (1897–   ). Mocking what they considered the false ingenuousness of their contemporaries, they created an even more artificial art. They specialized in grotesque unrealities, in a purposely overcolored rhetoric, in an approximation of the formalism of the ballet and the slapstick of the music hall. They advertised themselves impudently; they even capitalized their own absurdities. They distorted sense-effects and built a series of ivory towers inhabited (seemingly) by children and neurotics.

Although the average man could detect no sense in the wanderings of the new literature, it soon became evident that it was mad only north-northwest and that it had something significant if not pleasurable to say. The literature of nerves indicated another readjustment of values; it placarded new slogans and relied on eccentric efforts to show man's relation to a changing environment. Every distortion was used to evoke a disturbed mood or represent a shaken condition of the mind. No tenet seemed too extreme. Herbert Read (1893–   ), professor of fine art as well as a poet and a critic (*The Sense of Glory*, 1929; *The Meaning of Art*, 1932—published in the United States as *The Anatomy of Art*—and others) wrote: "Prose is constructive expression; poetry is creative expression. We now see that poetry may inhere in a single word, in a single syllable, and may therefore in an extreme case be without rhythm."

The critics thundered; prophets of doom were heard on every side. There was renewed talk of the disintegration of literature. But the conservatives and the radicals remained in their camps. They were united only when they sallied forth to attack the emerging postwar group.

Postwar Omens and Auguries

England muddled through postwar reconstruction, through the dole and the nightmare of European inflation, through the fall of the German Republic and the consequent rising specter of dictatorships. Until threatened with immediate disaster in 1939, Great Britain did nothing. As Harold Nicolson, author, diplomat, and member of Parliament, wrote:

"The British people, in common with other branches of the Anglo-Saxon race, are a mixture of realism and idealism. Being somewhat indolent by nature, it is only by dire necessity that they can be stirred to do unpleasant things. Yet when this necessity arises they like to make a virtue of it. This leads them at times to render unto God the things which are Caesar's and has earned them the reputation of hypocrisy. This is rather unfair. No Englishman feels really happy unless both his practical and his moral instincts are engaged." [5]

Before the Briton had a sense of acute danger he had a sense of prolonged confusion. Unable to return to orthodoxy, dissatisfied with blundering conservatism, he had depended on liberalism. But the liberal had changed his character. Hitherto the liberal had conveyed a sense of reserved power and certainty of purpose; now the liberal was sure of nothing but general distress and personal failure.

The modern temper was one of universal suspicion. It had been cheated by "causes," betrayed by slogans. Its symbols changed overnight. The airplane, which upon its trial flights only a few years ago seemed the symbol of liberation from earth, an image of free adventuring in the heavens, became a symbol of fear, of death that dropped casually from the skies.

[5] *Why Britain Is at War.* By Harold Nicolson. Penguin Books, Ltd. 1939.

Space shrank with the airplane; radio annihilated man's geographical boundaries. Yet governments grew more nationalistic and men less neighborly than ever. A reckless overproduction of goods and an aggressive selfishness impelled countries toward an economic breakdown which led to deliberately provoked wars. A decade that was financially irresponsible and morally insolvent was, in every sense, so shabby that it may well be known as the Threadbare Thirties.

There were those who hoped to see a new society rise from the ashes of the old. Conceived in the midst of tragedy, reared on tension, a new group arose in the early 1930's. They had more than youth and poetry in common; they shared the conviction that they were born in one war and seemed fated to die in another. Their predilections, their tastes, their social and political convictions, were equally opposed to those of the Georgians and the Sitwellians. They owed much of their technique to two experimental predecessors: Gerald Manley Hopkins, that fervent, richly associative, and most original poet who was neglected during his lifetime; and T. S. Eliot, who was influenced by the American poet Ezra Pound (1885–   ) and himself strongly influenced English poetry after 1925. Eliot prepared the way for the younger men; he celebrated and satirized the end of a cycle, the cultural decay of a period, and the approaching dissolution of a system. But Eliot retreated into Anglo-Catholicism and increasingly esoteric symbolism. Here the younger school broke with him; they refused to follow his desperate evasions and apparent defeatism.

The postwar group faced their world with suspicion rather than with confidence, with fearful intuition instead of calm experience. They came forward with hopeful gestures in place of certainties; they voiced prophecies rather than deliberate dogmas. The most notable of the group were W. H. Auden (1907–   ), Stephen Spender (1909–   ), Louis MacNeice (1907–   ), C. Day Lewis (1904–   ), and Christopher Isherwood (1904–   ).

Auden was the most intellectually daring of the group, the most experimental and brilliant in execution. His popularity was limited because of his very excess of energy, his willfullness and private satire, his rough improvisations and elaborate angers, his mixture of clear beauty and inexplicable allegory. Spender was less versatile but more intense; a genuine romantic as well as a rebel. Spender's emotion was fixed and forthright. He did not mask his passions or preoccupations; he translated the machine into poetry, announcing "the first powerful plain manifesto, the black statement of pistons." Christopher Isherwood, who collaborated with Auden in plays and travel books, emphasized in prose what his colleagues uttered in verse. Repudiation of the quiet countryside and the rejection of the devotional attitude were significant. As Alastair Miller summarized it in the *Saturday Review of Literature*, June 23, 1934:

"Nature is no longer considered anthropomorphically, nor love religiously. The poet no longer looks out of his window in the country and, blinding himself to the railway track, sees a beneficent Providence creating the pleasures and necessities of men: he sees electric pylons conveying imprisoned power, telegraph wires defying distance, motorploughs forcing fertility into the soil. There is no disrespect, as is sometimes maintained, for primroses and budding trees; but they are not accepted as a solution of, or consolation for, human misery."

To accomplish their ends, the postwar writers developed distinctive "attacks" and technical innovations. They substituted rapid allusions for definite relations. They proceeded from one image to another by inference and association rather than by natural sequence. Logic ceased to rule; often it was carelessly disdained, sometimes it was consciously discarded. The traditional "hero" continued to fascinate, but he was suspect; an idealized common man became "the coming man." The chief hope was in "the palpable and obvious love" of humanity. Spender, in particular, celebrated

"The names of those who in their lives fought for life,
Who wore at their hearts the fire's center.
Born of the sun they travelled a short while towards the sun,
And left the vivid air signed with their honour."

But before the postwar group had attained its top flight "the palpable and obvious love" of man was faced by a cataclysm. It was opposed, and almost destroyed, by the total war which began in September, 1939. Contemporary culture was riddled by the impact of unleashed frightfulness. Unsuspected political alignments cut across all loyalties; the errors of wishful thinking were pitifully exposed. A new force and the new weapon of mechanized warfare upset tactics, theories, and governments.

It is too early for a final appraisal of contemporary movements. Everyone sees the evidences of violent change, but no one can interpret them correctly. The world is thick with signs, but they appear too confusing, even too contradictory, to follow. For the moment chaos rules. Yet chaos is not a constant. And what seems the defeat of culture and the negation of all good may be the temporary "element of blank," the painful transition between the disappearance of one system of belief and the emergence of another. Creative power is not exhausted. It remains to be seen what form of expression it may inspire, and what kind of culture the future may reflect.

Joseph Conrad
1857–1924

Incongruous as it may seem, one of the greatest of modern British writers was by birth a Pole. Joseph Conrad was born Teodor Jozef Konrad Korzeniowski in 1857, in the Ukraine, then part of Russia. His parents were well-to-do Polish exiles with a broad cultural background; his father not only wrote poetry, but translated Shakespeare. After the death of his parents he was brought up by an uncle, who made it possible for him to enter the University of Cracow. Although a comfortable and gentlemanly career was planned for him, the boy decided to become a sailor and shipped as a seaman at sixteen. It was a strange choice for the son of Polish aristocrats whose homeland did not even touch the sea, but the

lad had already determined to be an Englishman, and, what is more, an English sailor. Before he was twenty-seven he had become a Master in the British Marine and a naturalized British subject, and had changed his name to Joseph Conrad.

He remained at sea for twenty years, not because he was sentimental about the element romanticized by landsmen, but because he was fascinated by the conflict between a sophisticated civilization and incalculable forces which can never be civilized. It seemed to him that men were most themselves when freed from the effects of organized society and pitted against a hostile universe. Sometimes this universe was actively threatening, sometimes it was cruelly apathetic; but it usually called forth man's integrity and, not infrequently, brought a submerged heroism to the surface.

The essentially tragic struggle between nobility and despair, high hope and defeat, is sounded in Conrad's first novel *Almayer's Folly*, 1895. Conrad was then almost forty. Within the next twenty years he had perfected a prose style and had become one of the great masters of modern English fiction. The books which elicited the most praise were the novels *The Nigger of the "Narcissus,"* 1898; *Lord Jim*, 1900; *Victory*, 1915; and the shorter tales *Typhoon*, 1902, *Youth*, 1902, *Heart of Darkness*, 1902, and *Within the Tides*, 1915. (A book of the complete short stories of Conrad was posthumously issued in 1933.) His first volume was published a few months after he left the sea (in 1894), married an Englishwoman, and settled in England. Although he learned the nuances of his adopted language from the simplest idioms to the most ornate figures of speech, he spoke with a foreign accent until the day of his death, August 3, 1924.

Conrad's attitude to life and art has been the subject of much controversy. It is an intellectual rather than a philosophical attitude. The spectacle of life fills him with pessimism—"if you take it to heart it becomes an unendurable tragedy"—but it is as a spectacle that he regards life. "I would fondly believe that its purpose is purely spectacular," he wrote, and such a conclusion explains Conrad's passion for observation and aloofness. Existence, to him, is full of terror and hidden evil, but Conrad devotes himself to a magic suggestiveness and "the few particles of truth floating in an ocean of insignificance." His indirect method of narration is famous and characteristic. Conrad is so anxious to appear objective, to avoid any possibility of being identified with his characters, that he goes to some length to remain outside of his work. Often he tells a story within the frame of another story or employs a narrator as disinterested agent and recording eye. Two of his most notable tales, *Youth* and *Heart of Darkness*, are "novellas," compromises between a short story and a novel, unfortunately too long to include here; and each is related through Marlow, a character used for no other purpose than to restrict the author's personal "point of view."

This method, employed even in the relatively short "The Inn of the Two Witches," results in a roundabout approach, a somewhat rambling beginning, and a tendency to slow up the narrative. But it makes for an almost complete detachment, and a sense of actuality of the thing recorded and retold rather than invented. Thus the tension in "The Inn of the Two Witches" does not seem to be manufactured; the horror grows naturally, and both the suspense and the terrible climax seem inevitable.

A small literature has grown up about Conrad and his work. Perhaps the most important are his own critical studies, *Notes on Life and Letters*, 1921, and *Notes on My Books*, 1921. A biography was published by Conrad's widow in 1935.

THE INN OF THE TWO WITCHES [1]

A FIND

THIS tale, episode, experience—call it how you will—was related in the fifties of the last century by a man who, by his own confession, was sixty years old at the time. Sixty is not a bad age—unless in perspective, when no doubt it is contemplated by the majority of us with mixed feelings. It is a calm age; the game is practically over by then; and standing aside one begins to remember with a certain vividness what a fine fellow one used to be. I have observed that, by an amiable attention of Providence, most people at sixty begin to take a romantic view of themselves. Their very failures exhale a charm of peculiar potency. And indeed the hopes of the future are a fine company to live with, exquisite forms, fascinating if you like, but—so to speak—naked, stripped for a run. The robes of glamour are luckily the property of the immovable past which, without them, would sit, a shivery sort of thing, under the gathering shadows.

I suppose it was the romanticism of growing age which set our man to relate his experience for his own satisfaction or for the wonder of his posterity. It could not have been for his glory, because the experience was simply that of an abominable fright —terror he calls it. You would have guessed that the relation alluded to in the very first lines was in writing.

This writing constitutes the Find declared in the sub-title. The title itself is my own contrivance (can't call it invention), and has the merit of veracity. We will be concerned with an inn here. As to the witches that's merely a conventional expression, and we must take our man's word for it that it fits the case.

The Find was made in a box of books bought in London, in a street which no longer exists, from a second-hand bookseller in the last stage of decay. As to the books themselves they were at least twentieth-hand, and on inspection turned out not worth the very small sum of money I disbursed. It might have been some premonition of the fact which made me say: "But I must have the box too." The decayed bookseller assented by the careless, tragic gesture of a man already doomed to extinction.

A litter of loose pages at the bottom of the box excited my curiosity but faintly. The close, neat, regular handwriting was not attractive at first sight. But in one place the statement that in A.D. 1813 the writer was twenty-two years old caught my eye. Two and twenty is an interesting age in which one is easily reckless and easily frightened; the faculty of reflection being weak and the power of imagination strong.

In another place the phrase: "At night we stood in again," arrested my languid attention, because it was a sea phrase. "Let's see what it is all about," I thought, without excitement.

Oh! but it was a dull-faced MS., each line resembling every other line in their close-set and regular order. It was like the drone of a monotonous voice. A treatise on sugar-refining (the dreariest subject I can think of) could have been given a more lively appearance. "In A.D. 1813 I was twenty-two years old," he begins earnestly, and goes on with every appearance of calm, horrible industry. Don't imagine, however, that there is anything archaic in my find. Diabolic ingenuity in invention though as old as the world is by no means a lost art. Lost art. Look at the telephones for shattering the little peace of mind given to us in this world, or at the machine guns for letting with dispatch life out of our bodies. Nowadays any blear-eyed old witch if only strong enough to turn an insignificant little handle could lay low a hundred young men of twenty in the twinkling of an eye.

If this isn't progress! . . . Why immense! We have moved on, and so you must expect to meet here a certain naïveness of contrivance and simplicity of aim appertaining to the remote epoch. And of course no motoring tourist can hope to find such an inn anywhere, now. This one, the one of the title, was situated in Spain. That much I discovered only from internal evidence, because a good many pages of that relation were missing—perhaps not a great misfortune after all. The writer seemed to have entered into a most elaborate detail of the why and wherefore of his presence on that coast—presumably the north coast of Spain. His experience has nothing to do with the sea, though. As far as I can make it out, he was an officer on board a sloop-of-war. There's nothing strange in that. At all stages of the long Peninsular campaign many of our men-

of-war of the smaller kind were cruising off the north coast of Spain—as risky and disagreeable a station as can be well imagined.

It looks as though that ship of his had had some special service to perform. A careful explanation of all the circumstances was to be expected from our man, only, as I've said, some of his pages (good tough paper too) were missing: gone in covers for jampots or in wadding for the fowling-pieces of his irreverent posterity. But it is to be seen clearly that communication with the shore and even the sending of messages inland was part of her service, either to obtain intelligence from or to transmit orders or advice to patriotic Spaniards, guerilleros, or secret juntas of the province. Something of the sort. All this can be only inferred from the preserved scraps of his conscientious writing.

Next we come upon the panegyric of a very fine sailor, a member of the ship's company, having the rating of the captain's coxswain. He was known on board as Cuba Tom; not because he was Cuban, however; he was indeed the best type of a genuine British tar of that time, and a man-of-war's man for years. He came by the name on account of some wonderful adventures he had in that island in his young days, adventures which were the favourite subject of the yarns he was in the habit of spinning to his shipmates of an evening on the forecastle head. He was intelligent, very strong, and of proved courage. Incidentally, we are told, so exact is our narrator, that Tom had the finest pigtail for thickness and length of any man in the Navy. This appendage, much cared for and sheathed tightly in a porpoise skin, hung half way down his broad back to the great admiration of all beholders and to the great envy of some.

Our young officer dwells on the manly qualities of Cuba Tom with something like affection. This sort of relation between officer and man was not then very rare. A youngster on joining the service was put under the charge of a trustworthy seaman, who slung his first hammock for him and often later on became a sort of humble friend to the junior officer. The narrator on joining the sloop had found this man on board after some years of separation. There is something touching in the warm pleasure he remembers and records at this meeting with the professional mentor of his boyhood.

We discover then that, no Spaniard being forthcoming for the service, this worthy seaman with the unique pigtail and a very high character for courage and steadiness had been selected as messenger for one of these missions inland which have been

14. **guerilleros,** guerillas, outlaws.   15. **juntas,** legislative groups.

mentioned. His preparations were not elaborate. One gloomy autumn morning the sloop ran close to a shallow cove where a landing could be made on that iron-bound shore. A boat was lowered, and pulled in with Tom Corbin (Cuba Tom) perched in the bow, and our young man (Mr. Edgar Byrne was his name on this earth which knows him no more) sitting in the stern-sheets.

A few inhabitants of a hamlet, whose grey stone houses could be seen a hundred yards or so up a deep ravine, had come down to the shore and watched the approach of the boat. The two Englishmen leaped ashore. Either from dullness or astonishment the peasants gave no greeting, and only fell back in silence.

Mr. Byrne had made up his mind to see Tom Corbin started fairly on his way. He looked round at the heavy surprised faces.

"There isn't much to get out of them," he said. "Let us walk up to the village. There will be a wine-shop for sure where we may find somebody more promising to talk to and get some information from."

"Aye, aye, sir," said Tom, falling into step behind his officer. "A bit of palaver as to courses and distances can do no harm; I crossed the broadest part of Cuba by the help of my tongue tho' knowing far less Spanish than I do now. As they say it themselves it was 'four words and no more' with me, that time when I got left behind on shore by the *Blanche*, frigate."

He made light of what was before him, which was but a day's journey into the mountains. It is true that there was a full day's journey before striking the mountain path, but that was nothing for a man who had crossed the island of Cuba on his two legs, and with no more than four words of the language to begin with.

The officer and the man were walking now on a thick sodden bed of dead leaves, which the peasants thereabouts accumulate in the streets of their villages to rot during the winter for field manure. Turning his head Mr. Byrne perceived that the whole male population of the hamlet was following them on the noiseless springy carpet. Women stared from the doors of the houses and the children had apparently gone into hiding. The village knew the ship by sight, afar off, but no stranger had landed on that spot perhaps for a hundred years or more. The cocked hat of Mr. Byrne, the bushy whiskers and the enormous pigtail of the sailor, filled them with mute wonder. They pressed behind the two Englishmen staring like those islanders discovered by Captain Cook in the South Seas.

It was then that Byrne had his first glimpse of the little cloaked man in a yellow hat. Faded and dingy as it was, this covering for his head made him noticeable.

The entrance to the wine-shop was like a rough hole in a wall of flints. The owner was the only person who was not in the street, for he came out from the darkness at the back where the inflated forms of wine skins hung on nails could be vaguely distinguished. He was a tall, one-eyed Asturian with scrubby, hollow cheeks; a grave expression of countenance contrasted enigmatically with the roaming restlessness of his solitary eye. On learning that the matter in hand was the sending on his way of that English mariner towards a certain Gonzales in the mountains, he closed his good eye for a moment as if in meditation. Then opened it, very lively again.

"Possibly, possibly. It could be done."

A friendly murmur arose in the group in the doorway at the name of Gonzales, the local leader against the French. Inquiring as to the safety of the road Byrne was glad to learn that no troops of that nation had been seen in the neighbourhood for months. Not the smallest little detachment of these impious *polizones*. While giving these answers the owner of the wine-shop busied himself in drawing into an earthenware jug some wine which he set before the heretic English, pocketing with grave abstraction the small piece of money the officer threw upon the table in recognition of the unwritten law that none may enter a wine-shop without buying drink. His eye was in constant motion as if it were trying to do the work of the two; but when Byrne made inquiries as to the possibility of hiring a mule, it became immovably fixed in the direction of the door which was closely besieged by the curious. In front of them, just within the threshold, the little man in the large cloak and yellow hat had taken his stand. He was a diminutive person, a mere homunculus, Byrne describes him, in a ridiculously mysterious yet assertive attitude, a corner of his cloak thrown cavalierly over his left shoulder, muffling his chin and mouth; while the broad-brimmed yellow hat hung on a corner of his square little head. He stood there taking snuff, repeatedly.

"A mule," repeated the wine-seller, his eyes fixed on that quaint and snuffy figure. . . . "No, señor officer! Decidedly no mule is to be got in this poor place."

The coxswain, who stood by with the true sailor's air of unconcern in strange surroundings, struck in quietly:

"If your honour will believe me Shank's pony's

25. **polizones**, vagrants, parasites.

the best for this job. I would have to leave the beast somewhere, anyhow, since the captain has told me that half my way will be along paths fit only for goats."

The diminutive man made a step forward, and speaking through the folds of the cloak which seemed to muffle a sarcastic intention——

"Sí, señor. They are too honest in this village to have a single mule amongst them for your worship's service. To that I can bear testimony. In these times 10 it's only rogues or very clever men who can manage to have mules or any other four-footed beasts and the wherewithal to keep them. But what this valiant mariner wants is a guide; and here, señor, behold my brother-in-law, Bernardino, wine-seller, and al-calde of this most Christian and hospitable village, who will find you one."

This, Mr. Byrne says in his relation, was the only thing to do. A youth in a ragged coat and goat-skin breeches was produced after some more talk. The 20 English officer stood treat to the whole village, and while the peasants drank he and Cuba Tom took their departure accompanied by the guide. The diminutive man in the cloak had disappeared.

Byrne went along with the coxswain out of the village. He wanted to see him fairly on his way; and he would have gone a greater distance if the seaman had not suggested respectfully the advisability of re-turn so as not to keep the ship a moment longer than necessary so close in with the shore on such an un- 30 promising looking morning. A wild gloomy sky hung over their heads when they took leave of each other, and their surroundings of rank bushes and stony fields were dreary.

"In four days' time," were Byrne's last words, "the ship will stand in and send a boat on shore if the weather permits. If not you'll have to make it out on shore the best you can till we come along to take you off."

"Right you are, sir," answered Tom, and strode 40 on. Byrne watched him step out on a narrow path. In a thick pea-jacket with a pair of pistols in his belt, a cutlass by his side, and a stout cudgel in his hand, he looked a sturdy figure and well able to take care of himself. He turned round for a mo-ment to wave his hand, giving to Byrne one more view of his honest bronzed face with bushy whiskers. The lad in goat-skin breeches looking, Byrne says, like a faun or a young satyr leaping ahead, stopped to wait for him, and then went off at a bound. Both 50 disappeared.

Byrne turned back. The hamlet was hidden in a fold of the ground, and the spot seemed the most

15–16. **alcalde,** mayor.

lonely corner of the earth and as if accursed in its uninhabited desolate barrenness. Before he had walked many yards, there appeared very suddenly from behind a bush the muffled up diminutive Spaniard. Naturally Bryne stopped short.

The other made a mysterious gesture with a tiny hand peeping from under his cloak. His hat hung very much at the side of his head. "Señor," he said without any preliminaries. "Caution! It is a positive fact that one-eyed Bernardino, my brother-in-law, has at this moment a mule in his stable. And why has he who is not clever a mule there? Because he is a rogue; a man without conscience. Because I had to give up the *macho* to him to secure for myself a roof to sleep under and a mouthful of *olla* to keep my soul in this insignificant body of mine. Yet, señor, it contains a heart many times bigger than the mean thing which beats in the breast of that brute connection of mine of which I am ashamed, though I opposed that marriage with all my power. Well, the misguided woman suffered enough. She had her purgatory on this earth—God rest her soul."

Byrne says he was so astonished by the sudden ap-pearance of that sprite-like being, and by the sar-donic bitterness of the speech, that he was unable to disentangle the significant fact from what seemed but a piece of family history fired out at him without rhyme or reason. Not at first. He was confounded and at the same time he was impressed by the rapid forcible delivery, quite different from the frothy ex-cited loquacity of an Italian. So he stared while the homunculus, letting his cloak fall about him, aspired an immense quantity of snuff out of the hollow of his palm.

"A mule," exclaimed Byrne, seizing at last the real aspect of the discourse. "You say he has got a mule? That's queer! Why did he refuse to let me have it?"

The diminutive Spaniard muffled himself up again with great dignity.

"*Quien sabe?*" he said coldly, with a shrug of his draped shoulders. "He is a great *politico* in every-thing he does. But one thing your worship may be certain of—that his intentions are always rascally. This husband of my *defunta* sister ought to have been married a long time ago to the widow with the wooden legs."

"I see. But remember that, whatever your mo-tives, your worship countenanced him in this lie."

14. **macho,** male animal, in this case the mule. 15. **olla,** food. 42. **"Quien sabe?"** "Who knows?" 46. **defunta,** deceased (woman). 47–48. **widow . . . legs,** the gallows, supposed to be "widowed" of the last executed criminal and waiting for another.

The bright unhappy eyes on each side of a predatory nose confronted Byrne without wincing, while with that testiness which lurks so often at the bottom of Spanish dignity——

"No doubt the señor officer would not lose an ounce of blood if I were stuck under the fifth rib," he retorted. "But what of this poor sinner here?" Then changing his tone: "Señor, by the necessities of the times I live here in exile, a Castilian and an old Christian, existing miserably in the midst of these brute Asturians, and dependent on the worst of them all, who has less conscience and scruples than a wolf. And being a man of intelligence I govern myself accordingly. Yet I can hardly contain my scorn. You have heard the way I spoke. A caballero of parts like your worship might have guessed that there was a cat in there."

"What cat?" said Byrne uneasily. "Oh, I see. Something suspicious. No, señor. I guessed nothing. My nation are not good guessers at that sort of thing; and, therefore, I ask you plainly whether that wine-seller has spoken the truth in other particulars?"

"There are certainly no Frenchmen anywhere about," said the little man with a return to his indifferent manner.

"Or robbers—*ladrones?*"

"*Ladrones en grande*—no! Assuredly not," was the answer in a cold philosophical tone. "What is there left for them to do after the French? And nobody travels in these times. But who can say! Opportunity makes the robber. Still that mariner of yours has a fierce aspect, and with the son of a cat rats will have no play. But there is a saying, too, that where honey is there will soon be flies."

This oracular discourse exasperated Byrne. "In the name of God," he cried, "tell me plainly if you think my man is reasonably safe on his journey."

The homunculus, undergoing one of his rapid changes, seized the officer's arm. The grip of his little hand was astonishing.

"Señor! Bernardino had taken notice of him. What more do you want? And listen—men have disappeared on this road—on a certain portion of this road, when Bernardino kept a *meson*, an inn, and I, his brother-in-law, had coaches and mules for hire. Now there are no travellers, no coaches. The French have ruined me. Bernardino has retired here for reasons of his own after my sister died. They were three to torment the life out of her, he and Erminia and Lucilla, two aunts of his—all affiliated to the devil. And now he has robbed me of my last mule. You are an armed man. Demand the *macho* from him, with a pistol to his head, señor—it

is not his, I tell you—and ride after your man who is so precious to you. And then you shall both be safe, for no two travellers have been ever known to disappear together in these days. As to the beast, I, its owner, I confide it to your honour."

They were staring hard at each other, and Byrne nearly burst into a laugh at the ingenuity and transparency of the little man's plot to regain possession of his mule. But he had no difficulty to keep a straight face because he felt deep within himself a strange inclination to do that very extraordinary thing. He did not laugh but his lip quivered; at which the diminutive Spaniard, detaching his black glittering eyes from Byrne's face, turned his back on him brusquely with a gesture and a fling of the cloak which somehow expressed contempt, bitterness, and discouragement all at once. He turned away and stood still, his hat aslant, muffled up to the ears. But he was not offended to the point of refusing the silver *duro* which Byrne offered him with a non-committal speech as if nothing extraordinary had passed between them.

"I must make haste on board now," said Byrne, then.

"*Vaya usted con Dios,*" muttered the gnome. And this interview ended with a sarcastic low sweep of the hat which was replaced at the same perilous angle as before.

Directly the boat had been hoisted the ship's sails were filled on the off-shore tack, and Byrne imparted the whole story to his captain, who was but a very few years older than himself. There was some amused indignation at it—but while they laughed they looked gravely at each other. A Spanish dwarf trying to beguile an officer of his majesty's navy into stealing a mule for him—that was too funny, too ridiculous, too incredible. Those were the exclamations of the captain. He couldn't get over the grotesqueness of it.

"Incredible. That's just it," murmured Byrne at last in a significant tone.

They exchanged a long stare. "It's as clear as daylight," affirmed the captain impatiently, because in his heart he was not certain. And Tom, the best seaman in the ship for one, the good humouredly deferential friend of his boyhood for the other, was becoming endowed with a compelling fascination, like a symbolic figure of loyalty appealing to their feelings and their conscience, so that they could not detach their thoughts from his safety. Several times they went up on deck, only to look at the coast, as if it could tell them something

25. "**Vaya usted con Dios**," "Go with God, God be with you."

of his fate. It stretched away, lengthening in the distance, mute, naked, and savage, veiled now and then by the slanting cold shafts of rain. The westerly swell rolled its interminable angry lines of foam, and big dark clouds flew over the ship in a sinister procession.

"I wish to goodness you had done what your little friend in the yellow hat wanted you to do," said the commander of the sloop late in the afternoon with visible exasperation.

"Do you, sir?" answered Byrne, bitter with positive anguish. "I wonder what you would have said afterwards? Why! I might have been kicked out of the service for looting a mule from a nation in alliance with His Majesty. Or I might have been battered to a pulp with flails and pitch-forks—a pretty tale to get abroad about one of your officers—while trying to steal a mule. Or chased ignominiously to the boat—for you would not have expected me to shoot down unoffending people for the sake of a mangy mule. . . . And yet," he added in a low voice, "I almost wished myself I had done it."

Before dark those two young men had worked themselves up into a highly complex psychological state of scornful scepticism and alarmed credulity. It tormented them exceedingly; and the thought that it would have to last for six days at least, and possibly be prolonged further for an indefinite time, was not to be borne. The ship was therefore put on the inshore tack at dark. All through the gusty dark night she went towards the land to look for her man, at times lying over in the heavy puffs, at others rolling idle in the swell, nearly stationary, as if she too had a mind of her own to swing perplexed between cool reason and warm impulse.

Then just at daybreak a boat put off from her and went on tossed by the seas towards the shallow cove where, with considerably difficulty, an officer in a thick coat and a round hat managed to land on a strip of shingle.

"It was my wish," writes Mr. Byrne, "a wish of which my captain approved, to land secretly if possible. I did not want to be seen either by my aggrieved friend in the yellow hat, whose motives were not clear, or by the one-eyed wine-seller, who may or may not have been affiliated to the devil, or indeed by any other dweller in that primitive village. But unfortunately the cove was the only possible landing place for miles; and from the steepness of the ravine I couldn't make a circuit to avoid the houses."

"Fortunately," he goes on, "all the people were yet in their beds. It was barely daylight when I found myself walking on the thick layer of sodden leaves filling the only street. No soul was stirring abroad, no dog barked. The silence was profound, and I had concluded with some wonder that apparently no dogs were kept in the hamlet, when I heard a low snarl, and from a noisome alley between two hovels emerged a vile cur with its tail between its legs. He slunk off silently showing me his teeth as he ran before me, and he disappeared so suddenly that he might have been the unclean incarnation of the Evil One. There was, too, something so weird in the manner of its coming and vanishing, that my spirits, already by no means very high, became further depressed by the revolting sight of this creature as if by an unlucky presage."

He got away from the coast unobserved, as far as he knew, then struggled manfully to the west against wind and rain, on a barren dark upland, under a sky of ashes. Far away the harsh and desolate mountains raising their scarped and denuded ridges seemed to wait for him menacingly. The evening found him fairly near to them, but, in sailor language, uncertain of his position, hungry, wet, and tired out by a day of steady tramping over broken ground during which he had seen very few people, and had been unable to obtain the slightest intelligence of Tom Corbin's passage. "On! on! I must push on," he had been saying to himself through the hours of solitary effort, spurred more by incertitude than by any definite fear or definite hope.

The lowering daylight died out quickly, leaving him faced by a broken bridge. He descended into the ravine, forded a narrow stream by the last gleam of rapid water, and clambering out on the other side was met by the night which fell like a bandage over his eyes. The wind sweeping in the darkness the broadside of the sierra worried his ears by a continuous roaring noise as of a maddened sea. He suspected that he had lost the road. Even in daylight, with its ruts and mudholes and ledges of outcropping stone, it was difficult to distinguish from the dreary waste of the moor interspersed with boulders and clumps of naked bushes. But, as he says, "he steered his course by the feel of the wind," his hat rammed low on his brow, his head down, stopping now and again from mere weariness of mind rather than of body—as if not his strength but his resolution were being overtaxed by the strain of endeavour half suspected to be vain, and by the unrest of his feelings.

In one of these pauses borne in the wind faintly as if from very far away he heard a sound of knocking, just knocking on wood. He noticed that the wind had lulled suddenly.

His heart started beating tumultuously because in

himself he carried the impression of the desert soli-tudes he had been traversing for the last six hours—the oppressive sense of an uninhabited world. When he raised his head a gleam of light, illusory as it often happens in dense darkness, swam before his eyes. While he peered, the sound of feeble knocking was repeated—and suddenly he felt rather than saw the existence of a massive obstacle in his path. What was it? The spur of a hill? Or was it a house! Yes. It was a house right close, as though it had risen from the ground or had come gliding to meet him, dumb and pallid, from some dark recess of the night. It towered loftily. He had come up under its lee; an-other three steps and he could have touched the wall with his hand. It was no doubt a *posada* and some other traveller was trying for admittance. He heard again the sound of cautious knocking.

Next moment a broad band of light fell into the night through the opened door. Byrne stepped ea-gerly into it, whereupon the person outside leaped with a stifled cry away into the night. An exclama-tion of surprise was heard too, from within. Byrne, flinging himself against the half-closed door, forced his way in against some considerable resistance.

A miserable candle, a mere rushlight, burned at the end of a long deal table. And in its light Byrne saw, staggering yet, the girl he had driven from the door. She had a short black skirt, an orange shawl, a dark complexion—and the escaped single hairs from the mass, sombre and thick like a forest and held up by a comb, made a black mist about her low forehead. A shrill lamentable howl of: "Miseri-cordia!" came in two voices from the further end of the long room, where the fire-light of an open hearth played between heavy shadows. The girl re-covering herself drew a hissing breath through her set teeth.

It is unnecessary to report the long process of questions and answers by which he soothed the fears of two old women who sat on each side of the fire, on which stood a large earthenware pot. Byrne thought at once of two witches watching the brewing of some deadly potion. But all the same, when one of them raising forward painfully her broken form lifted the cover of the pot, the escaping steam had an appetis-ing smell. The other did not budge, but sat hunched up, her head trembling all the time.

They were horrible. There was something gro-tesque in their decrepitude. Their toothless mouths, their hooked noses, the meagreness of the active one, and the hanging yellow cheeks of the other (the still one, whose head trembled) would have been laughable if the sight of their dreadful physi-

15. **posada,** inn, tavern.

cal degradation had not been appalling to one's eyes, had not gripped one's heart with poignant amazement at the unspeakable misery of age, at the awful persistency of life becoming at last an object of disgust and dread.

To get over it Byrne began to talk, saying that he was an Englishman, and that he was in search of a countryman who ought to have passed this way. Directly he had spoken the recollection of his part-ing with Tom came up in his mind with amazing vividness: the silent villagers, the angry gnome, the one-eyed wine-seller, Bernardino. Why? These two unspeakable frights must be that man's aunts—af-filiated to the devil.

Whatever they had been once it was impossible to imagine what use such feeble creatures could be to the devil, now, in the world of the living. Which was Lucilla and which was Erminia? They were now things without a name. A moment of sus-pended animation followed Byrne's words. The sorceress with the spoon ceased stirring the mess in the iron pot, the very trembling of the other's head stopped for the space of breath. In this infinitesimal fraction of a second Byrne had the sense of being really on his quest, of having reached the turn of the path, almost within hail of Tom.

"They have seen him," he thought with convic-tion. Here was at last somebody who had seen him. He made sure they would deny all knowledge of the Inglés; but on the contrary they were eager to tell him that he had eaten and slept the night in the house. They both started talking together, describ-ing his appearance and behaviour. An excitement quite fierce in its feebleness possessed them. The doubled-up sorceress flourished aloft her wooden spoon, the puffy monster got off her stool and screeched, stepping from one foot to the other, while the trembling of her head was accelerated to positive vibration. Byrne was quite disconcerted by their excited behaviour. . . . Yes! The big, fierce Inglés went away in the morning, after eating a piece of bread and drinking some wine. And if the caballero wished to follow the same path nothing could be easier—in the morning.

"You will give me somebody to show me the way?" said Byrne.

"Sí, señor. A proper youth. The man the cabal-lero saw going out."

"But he was knocking at the door," protested Byrne. "He only bolted when he saw me. He was coming in."

"No! No!" the two horrid witches screamed out together. "Going out. Going out!"

After all it may have been true. The sound of

knocking had been faint, elusive, reflected Byrne. Perhaps only the effect of his fancy. He asked:

"Who is that man?"

"Her *novio*." They screamed pointing to the girl. "He is gone home to a village far away from here. But he will return in the morning. Her *novio!* And she is an orphan—the child of poor Christian people. She lives with us for the love of God, for the love of God."

The orphan crouching on the corner of the 10 hearth had been looking at Byrne. He thought that she was more like a child of Satan kept there by these two weird harridans for the love of the Devil. Her eyes were a little oblique, her mouth rather thick, but admirably formed; her dark face had a wild beauty, voluptuous and untamed. As to the character of her steadfast gaze attached upon him with a sensuously savage attention, "to know what it was like," says Mr. Byrne, "you have only to observe a hungry cat watching a bird in a cage or a 20 mouse inside a trap."

It was she who served him the food, of which he was glad; though with those big slanting black eyes examining him at close range, as if he had something curious written on his face, she gave him an uncomfortable sensation. But anything was better than being approached by these blear-eyed nightmarish witches. His apprehensions somehow had been soothed; perhaps by the sensation of warmth after severe exposure and the ease of resting after the 30 exertion of fighting the gale inch by inch all the way. He had no doubt of Tom's safety. He was now sleeping in the mountain camp having been met by Gonzales' men.

Byrne rose, filled a tin goblet with wine out of a skin hanging on the wall, and sat down again. The witch with the mummy face began to talk to him, rambling of old times; she boasted of the inn's fame in those better days. Great people in their own coaches stopped there. An archbishop slept once in 40 the *casa*, a long, long time ago.

The witch with the puffy face seemed to be listening from her stool, motionless, except for the trembling of her head. The girl (Byrne was certain she was a casual gipsy admitted there for some reason or other) sat on the hearth stone in the glow of the embers. She hummed a tune to herself, rattling a pair of castanets slightly now and then. At the mention of the archbishop she chuckled impiously and turned her head to look at Byrne, so that the red 50 glow of the fire flashed in her black eyes and on her white teeth under the dark cowl of the enormous overmantel. And he smiled at her.

4. novio, betrothed, fiancé.   41. casa, house.

He rested now in the ease of security. His advent not having been expected there could be no plot against him in existence. Drowsiness stole upon his senses. He enjoyed it, but keeping a hold, so he thought at least, on his wits; but he must have been gone further than he thought because he was startled beyond measure by a fiendish uproar. He had never heard anything so pitilessly strident in his life. The witches had started a fierce quarrel about something or other. Whatever its origin they were now only abusing each other violently, without arguments; their senile screams expressed nothing but wicked anger and ferocious dismay. The gipsy girl's black eyes flew from one to the other. Never before had Byrne felt himself so removed from fellowship with human beings. Before he had really time to understand the subject of the quarrel, the girl jumped up rattling her castanets loudly. A silence fell. She came up to the table and bending over, her eyes in his——

"Señor," she said with decision, "you shall sleep in the archbishop's room."

Neither of the witches objected. The dried up one bent double was propped on a stick. The puffy-faced one had now a crutch.

Byrne got up, walked to the door, and turning the key in the enormous lock put it coolly in his pocket. This was clearly the only entrance, and he did not mean to be taken unawares by whatever danger there might have been lurking outside. When he turned from the door he saw the two witches "affiliated to the Devil" and the Satanic girl looking at him in silence. He wondered if Tom Corbin took the same precaution last night. And thinking of him he had again that queer impression of his nearness. The world was perfectly dumb. And in this stillness he heard the blood beating in his ears with a confused rushing noise, in which there seemed to be a voice uttering the words: "Mr. Byrne, look out, sir." Tom's voice. He shuddered; for the delusions of the sense of hearing are the most vivid of all, and from their nature have a compelling character.

It seemed impossible that Tom should not be there. Again a slight chill as of stealthy draught penetrated through his very clothes and passed over all his body. He shook off the impression with an effort.

It was the girl who preceded him upstairs carrying an iron lamp from the naked flame of which ascended a thin thread of smoke. Her soiled white stockings were full of holes.

With the same quiet resolution with which he had locked the door below, Byrne threw open one after another the doors in the corridor. All the rooms were empty except for some nondescript lumber in one or two. And the girl seeing what he would be at stopped every time, raising the smoky light in each doorway patiently. Meantime she observed him with sustained attention. The last door of all she threw open herself.

"You sleep here, señor," she murmured in a voice light like a child's breath, offering him the lamp.

"*Buenas noches, señorita*," he said politely, taking it from her.

She didn't return the wish audibly, though her lips did move a little, while her gaze black like a starless night never for a moment wavered before him. He stepped in, and as he turned to close the door she was still there motionless and disturbing, with her voluptuous mouth and slanting eyes, with the expression of expectant sensual ferocity of a baffled cat. He hesitated for a moment, and in the dumb house he heard again the blood pulsating ponderously in his ears, while once more the illusion of Tom's voice speaking earnestly somewhere near by was specially terrifying, because this time he could not make out the words.

He slammed the door in the girl's face at last, leaving her in the dark; and he opened it again almost on the instant. Nobody. She had vanished without the slightest sound. He closed the door quickly and bolted it with two heavy bolts.

A profound mistrust possessed him suddenly. Why did the witches quarrel about letting him sleep here? And what meant that stare of the girl as if she wanted to impress his features for ever in her mind? His own nervousness alarmed him. He seemed to himself to be removed very far from mankind.

He examined his room. It was not very high, just high enough to take the bed which stood under an enormous baldaquin-like canopy from which fell heavy curtains at foot and head; a bed certainly worthy of an archbishop. There was a heavy table carved all round the edges, some armchairs of enormous weight like the spoils of a grandee's palace; a tall shallow wardrobe placed against the wall and with double doors. He tried them. Locked. A suspicion came into his mind, and he snatched the lamp to make a closer examination. No, it was not a disguised entrance. That heavy, tall piece of furniture stood clear of the wall by quite an inch. He glanced at the bolts of his room door. No! No one could get at him treacherously while he slept. But would he be able to sleep? he asked himself anxiously. If only he had Tom there—the trusty seaman who had fought at his right hand in a cutting out affair or

9. **"Buenas noches,"** "Good night."

two, and had always preached to him the necessity to take care of himself. "For it's no great trick," he used to say, "to get yourself killed in a hot fight. Any fool can do that. The proper pastime is to fight the Frenchies and then live to fight another day."

Byrne found it a hard matter not to fall into listening to the silence. Somehow he had the conviction that nothing would break it unless he heard again the haunting sound of Tom's voice. He had heard it twice before. Odd! And yet no wonder, he argued with himself reasonably, since he had been thinking of the man for over thirty hours continuously and, what's more, inconclusively. For his anxiety for Tom had never taken a definite shape. "Disappear" was the only word connected with the idea of Tom's danger. It was very vague and awful. "Disappear!" What did that mean?

Byrne shuddered, and then said to himself that he must be a little feverish. But Tom had not disappeared. Byrne had just heard of him. And again the young man felt the blood beating in his ears. He sat still expecting every moment to hear through the pulsating strokes the sound of Tom's voice. He waited straining his ears, but nothing came. Suddenly the thought occurred to him: "He has not disappeared, but he cannot make himself heard."

He jumped up from the armchair. How absurd! Laying his pistol and his hanger on the table he took off his boots and, feeling suddenly too tired to stand, flung himself on the bed which he found soft and comfortable beyond his hopes.

He had felt very wakeful, but he must have dozed off after all, because the next thing he knew he was sitting up in bed and trying to recollect what it was that Tom's voice had said. Oh! He remembered it now. It had said: "Mr. Byrne! Look out, sir!" A warning this. But against what?

He landed with one leap in the middle of the floor, gasped once, then looked all round the room. The window was shuttered and barred with an iron bar. Again he ran his eyes slowly all round the bare walls, and even looked up at the ceiling, which was rather high. Afterwards he went to the door to examine the fastenings. They consisted of two enormous iron bolts sliding into holes made in the wall; and as the corridor outside was too narrow to admit of any battering arrangement or even to permit an axe to be swung, nothing could burst the door open—unless gunpowder. But while he was still making sure that the lower bolt was pushed well home, he received the impression of somebody's presence in the room. It was so strong that he spun round quicker than lightning. There was no one. Who could there be? And yet . . .

It was then that he lost the decorum and restraint a man keeps up for his own sake. He got down on his hands and knees, with the lamp on the floor, to look under the bed, like a silly girl. He saw a lot of dust and nothing else. He got up, his cheeks burning, and walked about discontented with his own behaviour and unreasonably angry with Tom for not leaving him alone. The words: "Mr. Byrne! Look out, sir," kept on repeating themselves in his head in a tone of warning.

"Hadn't I better just throw myself on the bed and try to go to sleep?" he asked himself. But his eyes fell on the tall wardrobe, and he went toward it feeling irritated with himself and yet unable to desist. How he could explain to-morrow the burglarious misdeed to the two odious witches he had no idea. Nevertheless he inserted the point of his hanger between the two halves of the door and tried to prize them open. They resisted. He swore, sticking now hotly to his purpose. His mutter: "I hope you will be satisfied, confound you," was addressed to the absent Tom. Just then the doors gave way and flew open.

He was there.

He—the trusty, sagacious, and courageous Tom was there, drawn up shadowy and stiff, in prudent silence, which his wide-open eyes by their fixed gleam seemed to command Byrne to respect. But Byrne was too startled to make a sound. Amazed, he stepped back a little—and on the instant the seaman flung himself forward headlong as if to clasp his officer round the neck. Instinctively, Byrne put out his faltering arms; he felt the horrible rigidity of the body and then the coldness of death as their heads knocked together and their faces came into contact. They reeled, Byrne hugging Tom close to his breast in order not to let him fall with a crash. He had just strength enough to lower the awful burden gently to the floor—then his head swam, his legs gave way, and he sank on his knees, leaning over the body with his hands resting on the breast of that man once full of generous life, and now as insensible as a stone.

"Dead! my poor Tom, dead," he repeated mentally. The light of the lamp standing near the edge of the table fell from above straight on the stony empty stare of these eyes which naturally had a mobile and merry expression. Byrne turned his own away from them. Tom's black silk neckerchief was not knotted on his breast. It was gone. The murderers had also taken off his shoes and stockings. And noticing this spoliation, the exposed throat, the bare upturned feet, Byrne felt his eyes run full of tears. In other respects the seaman was fully dressed; nei-

ther was his clothing disarranged as it must have been in a violent struggle. Only his checked shirt had been pulled a little out the waistband in one place, just enough to ascertain whether he had a money belt fastened round his body. Byrne began to sob into his handkerchief.

It was a nervous outburst which passed off quickly. Remaining on his knees he contemplated sadly the athletic body of as fine a seaman as ever had drawn a cutlass, laid a gun, or passed the weather earring in a gale, lying stiff and cold, his cheery, fearless spirit departed—perhaps turning to him, his boy chum, to his ship out there rolling on the grey seas off an iron-bound coast, at the very moment of its flight. He perceived that the six brass buttons of Tom's jacket had been cut off. He shuddered at the notion of the two miserable and repulsive witches busying themselves ghoulishly about the defenceless body of his friend. Cut off. Perhaps with the same knife which . . . The head of one trembled; the other was bent double, and their eyes were red and bleared, their infamous claws unsteady. . . . It must have been in this very room too, for Tom could not have been killed in the open and brought in here afterward. Of that Byrne was certain. Yet those devilish crones could not have killed him themselves even by taking him unawares —and Tom would be always on his guard of course. Tom was a very wide-awake wary man when engaged on any service. . . . And in fact how did they murder him? Who did? In what way?

Byrne jumped up, snatched the lamp off the table, and stooped swiftly over the body. The light revealed on the clothing no stain, no trace, no spot of blood anywhere. Byrne's hands began to shake so that he had to set the lamp on the floor and turn away his head in order to recover from this agitation.

Then he began to explore that cold, still, and rigid body for a stab, a gunshot wound, for the trace of some killing blow. He felt all over the skull anxiously. It was whole. He slipped his hand under the neck. It was unbroken. With terrified eyes he peered close under the chin and saw no marks of strangulation on the throat.

There were no signs anywhere. He was just dead.

Impulsively Byrne got away from the body as if the mystery of an incomprehensible death had changed his pity into suspicion and dread. The lamp on the floor near the set, still face of the seaman showed it staring at the ceiling as if despairingly. In the circle of light Byrne saw by the undisturbed patches of thick dust on the floor that there

11. **earring,** one of a ship's lines (correctly, earing).

had been no struggle in that room. "He has died outside," he thought. Yes, outside in that narrow corridor, where there was hardly room to turn, the mysterious death had come to his poor dear Tom. The impulse of snatching up his pistols and rushing out of the room abandoned Byrne suddenly. For Tom, too, had been armed—with just such powerless weapons as he himself possessed—pistols, a cutlass! And Tom had died a nameless death, by incomprehensible means.

A new thought came to Byrne. That stranger knocking at the door and fleeing so swiftly at his appearance had come there to remove the body. Aha! That was the guide the withered witch had promised would show the English officer the shortest way of rejoining his man. A promise, he saw it now, of dreadful import. He who had knocked would have two bodies to deal with. Man and officer would go forth from the house together. For Byrne was certain now that he would have to die before the morning—and in the same mysterious manner, leaving behind him an unmarked body.

The sight of a smashed head, of a cut throat, of a gaping gunshot wound, would have been an inexpressible relief. It would have soothed all his fears. His soul cried within him to that dead man whom he had never found wanting in danger. "Why don't you tell me what I am to look for, Tom? Why don't you?" But in rigid immobility, extended on his back, he seemed to preserve an austere silence, as if disdaining in the finality of his awful knowledge to hold converse with the living.

Suddenly Byrne flung himself on his knees by the side of the body, and dry-eyed, fierce, opened the shirt wide on the breast, as if to tear the secret forcibly from that cold heart which had been so loyal to him in life! Nothing! Nothing! He raised the lamp, and all the sign vouchsafed to him by that face which used to be so kindly in expression was a small bruise on the forehead—the least thing, a mere mark. The skin even was not broken. He stared at it a long time as if lost in a dreadful dream. Then he observed that Tom's hands were clenched as though he had fallen facing somebody in a fight with fists. His knuckles, on closer view, appeared somewhat abraded. Both hands.

The discovery of these slight signs was more appalling to Byrne than the absolute absence of every mark would have been. So Tom had died striking against something which could be hit, and yet could kill one without leaving a wound—by a breath.

Terror, hot terror, began to play about Byrne's heart like a tongue of flame that touches and withdraws before it turns a thing to ashes. He backed away from the body as far as he could, then came forward stealthily, casting fearful glances to steal another look at the bruised forehead. There would perhaps be such a faint bruise on his own forehead—before the morning.

"I can't bear it," he whispered to himself. Tom was for him now an object of horror, a sight at once tempting and revolting to his fear. He couldn't bear to look at him.

At last, desperation getting the better of his increasing horror, he stepped forward from the wall against which he had been leaning, seized the corpse under the armpits, and began to lug it over to the bed. The bare heels of the seaman trailed on the floor noiselessly. He was heavy with the dead weight of inanimate objects. With a last effort Byrne landed him face downward on the edge of the bed, rolled him over, snatched from under this stiff passive thing a sheet with which he covered it over. Then he spread the curtains at head and foot so that joining together as he shook their folds they hid the bed altogether from his sight.

He stumbled towards a chair, and fell on it. The perspiration poured from his face for a moment, and then his veins seemed to carry for a while a thin stream of half-frozen blood. Complete terror had possession of him now, a nameless terror which had turned his heart to ashes.

He sat upright in the straight-backed chair, the lamp burning at his feet, his pistols and his hanger at his left elbow on the end of the table, his eyes turning incessantly in their sockets round the walls, over the ceiling, over the floor, in the expectation of a mysterious and appalling vision. The thing which could deal death in a breath was outside that bolted door. But Byrne believed neither in walls nor bolts now. Unreasoning terror turning everything to account, his old-time boyish admiration of the athletic Tom, the undaunted Tom (he had seemed to him invincible), helped to paralyse his faculties, added to his despair.

He was no longer Edgar Byrne. He was a tortured soul suffering more anguish than any sinner's body had ever suffered from rack or boot. The depth of his torment may be measured when I say that this young man, as brave at least as the average of his kind, contemplated seizing a pistol and firing into his own head. But a deadly, chilly languor was spreading over his limbs. It was as if his flesh had been wet plaster stiffening slowly about his ribs. Presently, he thought, the two witches will be coming in, with crutch and stick—horrible, grotesque, monstrous—affiliated to the devil—to put a mark on his forehead, the tiny little bruise of death. And he wouldn't be able to do anything. Tom had struck out at something, but he was not like Tom. His limbs were dead already. He sat still, dying the death over and over again; and the only part of him which moved were his eyes, turning round and round in their sockets, running over the walls, the floor, the ceiling, again and again, till suddenly they became motionless and stony—starting out of his head fixed in the direction of the bed.

He had seen the heavy curtains stir and shake as 10 if the dead body they concealed had turned over and sat up. Byrne, who thought the world could hold no more terrors in store, felt his hair stir at the roots. He gripped the arms of the chair, his jaw fell, and the sweat broke out on his brow while his dry tongue clove suddenly to the roof of his mouth. Again the curtains stirred, but did not open. "Don't, Tom!" Byrne made effort to shout, but all he heard was a slight moan such as an uneasy sleeper may make. He felt that his brain was going, 20 for, now, it seemed to him that the ceiling over the bed had moved, had slanted, and came level again —and once more the closed curtains swayed gently as if about to part.

Byrne closed his eyes not to see the awful apparition of the seaman's corpse coming out animated by an evil spirit. In the profound silence of the room he endured a moment of frightful agony, then opened his eyes again. And he saw at once that the curtains remained closed still, but that the ceiling 30 over the bed had risen quite a foot. With the last gleam of reason left to him he understood that it was the enormous baldaquin over the bed which was coming down, while the curtains attached to it swayed softly, sinking gradually to the floor. His drooping jaw snapped to—and half rising in his chair he watched mutely the noiseless descent of the monstrous canopy. It came down in short smooth rushes till lowered half way or more, when it took a run and settled swiftly its turtle-back shape with 40 the deep border piece fitting exactly the edge of the bedstead. A slight crack or two of wood were heard, and the overpowering stillness of the room resumed its sway.

Byrne stood up, gasped for breath, and let out a cry of rage and dismay, the first sound which he is perfectly certain did make its way past his lips on this night of terrors. This then was the death he had escaped! This was the devilish artifice of murder poor Tom's soul had perhaps tried from beyond the 50 border to warn him of. For this was how he had died. Byrne was certain he had heard the voice of the seaman, faintly distinct in his familiar phrase, "Mr. Byrne! Look out, sir!" and again uttering

words he could not make out. But then the distance separating the living from the dead is so great! Poor Tom had tried. Byrne ran to the bed and attempted to lift up, to push off the horrible lid, smothering the body. It resisted his efforts, heavy as lead, immovable like a tombstone. The rage of vengeance made him desist; his head buzzed with chaotic thoughts of extermination, he turned round the room as if he could find neither his weapons nor the way out; and all the time he stammered awful menaces. . . .

A violent battering at the door of the inn recalled him to his soberer senses. He flew to the window, pulled the shutters open, and looked out. In the faint dawn he saw below him a mob of men. Ha! He would go and face at once this murderous lot collected no doubt for his undoing. After his struggle with nameless terrors he yearned for an open fray with armed enemies. But he must have remained yet bereft of his reason, because forgetting his weapons he rushed downstairs with a wild cry, unbarred the door while blows were raining on it outside, and flinging it open flew with his bare hands at the throat of the first man he saw before him. They rolled over together. Byrne's hazy intention was to break through, to fly up the mountain path, and come back presently with Gonzales' men to exact an exemplary vengeance. He fought furiously till a tree, a house, a mountain, seemed to crash down upon his head—and he knew no more.

Here Mr. Byrne describes in detail the skilful manner in which he found his broken head bandaged, informs us that he had lost a great deal of blood, and ascribes the preservation of his sanity to that circumstance. He sets down Gonzales' profuse apologies in full too. For it was Gonzales who, tired of waiting for news from the English, had come down to the inn with half his band, on his way to the sea. "His Excellency," he explained, "rushed out with fierce impetuosity, and, moreover, was not known to us for a friend, and so we . . ." etc., etc. When asked what had become of the witches, he only pointed his finger silently to the ground, then voiced calmly a moral reflection: "The passion for gold is pitiless in the very old, señor," he said. "No doubt in former days they have put many a solitary traveller to sleep in the archbishop's bed."

"There was also a gipsy girl there," said Byrne feebly from the improvised litter on which he was being carried to the coast by a squad of guerilleros.

"It was she who winched up that infernal machine, and it was she too who lowered it that night," was the answer.

"But why? Why?" exclaimed Byrne. "Why should she wish for my death?"

"No doubt for the sake of Your Excellency's coat buttons," said politely the saturnine Gonzales. "We found those of the dead mariner concealed on her person. But Your Excellency may rest assured that everything that is fitting has been done on this occasion."

Byrne asked no more questions. There was still another death which was considered by Gonzales as "fitting to the occasion." The one-eyed Bernardino stuck against the wall of his wine-shop received the charge of six escopettas into his breast. As the shots rang out the rough bier with Tom's body on it went past carried by a bandit-like gang of Spanish patriots down the ravine to the shore, where two boats from the ship were waiting for what was left on earth of her best seaman.

Mr. Byrne, very pale and weak, stepped into the boat which carried the body of his humble friend. For it was decided that Tom Corbin should rest far out in the bay of Biscay. The officer took the tiller and, turning his head for the last look at the shore, saw on the grey hillside something moving, which he made out to be a little man in a yellow hat mounted on a mule—that mule without which the fate of Tom Corbin would have remained mysterious for ever.

A. E. Housman
1859–1936

No English writer has ever been more closely identified with Shropshire than A(lfred) E(dward) Housman. Born there at the village of Bromsgrove, on March 26, 1859, Housman made Shropshire the scene of practically all his verse. He was educated at Oxford and became a Higher Division Clerk in the British Patent Office for ten years. In 1892 he left the Office, where he said he "did as little as possible," to become a teacher. As a professor of Latin (first at University College, London, later at Cambridge) he became one of the great scholars of his day. Shy in his personal life, his scholarly papers bristle with sarcasm and cold invective. The introductions to his editions of Manilius, 1903, revised in 1932, Juvenal, 1905, and Lucan, 1926, reveal Housman's admiration for chiseled form and his contempt for carelessness. But these were the preoccupations of the Latinist; as a person Housman discouraged controversies and avoided intimacies. A fellow poet, Wilfred Scawen Blunt, wrote of him, "He does not smoke, drinks little, and would, I think, be quite silent if he were allowed to be." Housman said that the description seemed accurate, except that Blunt offered him little to drink. A member of one of his classes remarked, "He was the only person I have known who so habitually and ominously looked down his nose." [1]

His edition of Manilius, published in 1932, represents an analysis of that author which occupied Housman for a full quarter of a century. A year after completion of this work, a weakness of the heart was manifest; Housman recognized the symptoms and foresaw the end. Nevertheless he continued to attend classes. Arguing that lecturing was a pleasure as well as a duty, he gave two lectures on Horace during the Lent term in 1936. He never completed the course. He died on April 30, 1936.

It is not, however, Housman's work as scholar and editor which spread his reputation beyond classical circles. Housman became internationally famous as the poet of A Shropshire Lad, 1896. His entire nonclassical output during his life consisted of two small volumes of poetry and one or two essays, of which The Name and Nature of Poetry, 1933, is the most trenchant and controversial. More than twenty-five years elapsed between the publication of A Shropshire Lad and an equally small volume significantly entitled Last Poems, 1922. A posthumous More Poems, edited by his brother Laurence, was published in 1936.

With the exception of Fitzgerald's translation of The Rubáiyát of Omar Khayyám no book of poetry of the period was more popular than A Shropshire Lad; none was so widely quoted. Although the former is Oriental and the latter Occidental, both books voice the same basic philosophy. It is a negative philosophy, a pessimistic extension of the theme "Eat, drink, and be merry, for tomorrow we die." Housman's fatalism is the darker of the two. Omar rejects a difficult and unjust world and comforts himself with a life of sheer sensation; Housman's lads escape only by suicide. That these volumes

[1] Quoted from A. E. Housman: A Sketch. By A. S. F. Gow. The Macmillan Company. 1936.

should have elicited so enthusiastic a response—especially from young people—is a strange phenomenon. But it is doubtful that readers paid much attention to the central philosophy. They were captivated by the quick turn of phrase, the charming sophistications and deceptive simplicities, the brisk rhythms, the appeal of easy recklessness.

It is a queer paradox which is presented by Housman's infectious verse. In the blithest measures he assures us that the world is evil, that men and girls are untrue, that we are roused to struggles that have no reason, and that Nature is only a little more inhuman than human nature. Train for ill and not for good, Housman warns us with fierce stoicism and bright jog-trot tunes. There is joy and beauty to be snatched, but there is endless injustice to be endured. The quiet countryside teaches us fortitude in its haphazard cruelty. Unkindness is native to man, but it is not peculiar to him; heaven and earth "ail from the prime foundation." "Luck's a chance, but trouble's sure," Housman repeats like a cheerful prophet of doom; but men are noblest when, realizing the futility of their efforts, they still struggle against frustration. Housman, remembering his favorite classics, ironically reminds us that we must be patient even in our disbelief; our tragedy is an ancient one.

"We for a certainty are not the first
    Have sat in taverns while the tempest hurled
Their hopeful plans to emptiness, and cursed
    Whatever brute and blackguard made the
        world."

There is no limit to the griefs of mortal flesh: "The troubles of our proud and angry dust are from eternity, and shall not fail." And, in another key:

        "Wanderers eastward, wanderers west,
        Know you why you cannot rest?
        'Tis that every mother's son
        Travails with a skeleton."

Grim this undoubtedly is; but the music is gay. With unsurpassed artistry Housman composed stanza after stanza which echo in the ear and cannot be shaken from the mind. His is a stripped verse, almost bare of decoration. But the spareness gives it precision, and the elimination of ornament gives it strength. Not since the Elizabethans have there been lyrics so delicate and yet so firm, so seemingly casual yet so inevitable. "Loveliest of Trees," "When I Was One-and-Twenty," "Reveille," "Is My Team Ploughing?" "To an Athlete Dying Young," "From Far, from Eve and Morn-

ing," "I Hoed and Trenched and Weeded"—to name only a few of the favorites—have the authority that comes with age and tradition. Although written in our own period, they seem part of the permanent literature of the English language. They are fastidious in the highest degree. They are small; they are limited in range and sometimes inflexible because of their overdisciplined line. But many of them are as nearly perfect as lyrics can hope to be.

LOVELIEST OF TREES [1]

Loveliest of trees, the cherry now
Is hung with bloom along the bough,
And stands about the woodland ride
Wearing white for Eastertide.

Now, of my threescore years and ten,
Twenty will not come again,
And take from seventy springs a score,
It only leaves me fifty more.

And since to look at things in bloom
Fifty springs are little room,   10
About the woodlands I will go
To see the cherry hung with snow.

WHEN SMOKE STOOD UP
FROM LUDLOW

When smoke stood up from Ludlow,
    And mist blew off from Teme,
And blithe afield to ploughing
    Against the morning beam
    I strode beside my team,

The blackbird in the coppice
    Looked out to see me stride,
And hearkened as I whistled
    The trampling team beside,
    And fluted and replied: 10

"Lie down, lie down, young yeoman;
    What use to rise and rise?
Rise man a thousand mornings
    Yet down at last he lies,
    And then the man is wise."

[1] The first fourteen poems are from *A Shropshire Lad*, Henry Holt and Company, Inc., authorized publishers.
Loveliest of Trees. **3. woodland ride,** a narrow forest road.
When Smoke Stood Up. **6. coppice,** a thicket, copse, underbrush.

I heard the tune he sang me,
  And spied his yellow bill;
I picked a stone and aimed it
  And threw it with a will:
    Then the bird was still.   20

Then my soul within me
  Took up the blackbird's strain,
And still beside the horses
  Along the dewy lane
    It sang the song again:

"Lie down, lie down, young yeoman;
  The sun moves always west;
The road one treads to labour
  Will lead one home to rest,
    And that will be the best."   30

FAREWELL TO BARN AND STACK AND TREE

"Farewell to barn and stack and tree,
  Farewell to Severn shore.
Terence, look your last at me,
  For I come home no more.

"The sun burns on the half-mown hill,
  By now the blood is dried;
And Maurice amongst the hay lies still
  And my knife is in his side.

"My mother thinks us long away;
  'Tis time the field were mown.   10
She had two sons at rising day,
  To-night she'll be alone.

"And here's a bloody hand to shake,
  And oh, man, here's good-bye;
We'll sweat no more on scythe and rake,
  My bloody hands and I.

"I wish you strength to bring you pride,
  And a love to keep you clean,
And I wish you luck, come Lammastide,
  At racing on the green.   20

"Long for me the rick will wait,
  And long will wait the fold,
And long will stand the empty plate,
  And dinner will be cold."

Farewell to Barn and Stack and Tree. **19. Lammastide**
August 1, formerly celebrated in England as a harvest festival.

REVEILLE

Wake: the silver dusk returning
  Up the beach of darkness brims,
And the ship of sunrise burning
  Strands upon the eastern rims.

Wake: the vaulted shadow shatters,
  Trampled to the floor it spanned,
And the tent of night in tatters
  Straws the sky-pavilioned land.

Up, lad, up, 'tis late for lying:
  Hear the drums of morning play;   10
Hark, the empty highways crying
  "Who'll beyond the hills away?"

Towns and countries woo together,
  Forelands beacon, belfries call;
Never lad that trod on leather
  Lived to feast his heart with all.

Up, lad: thews that lie and cumber
  Sunlit pallets never thrive;
Morns abed and daylight slumber
  Were not meant for man alive.   20

Clay lies still, but blood's a rover;
  Breath's a ware that will not keep.
Up, lad: when the journey's over
  There'll be time enough to sleep.

WHEN I WAS ONE-AND-TWENTY

When I was one-and-twenty
  I heard a wise man say,
"Give crowns and pounds and guineas,
  But not your heart away;
Give pearls away and rubies
  But keep your fancy free."
But I was one-and-twenty,
  No use to talk to me.

When I was one-and-twenty
  I heard him say again,   10
"The heart out of the bosom
  Was never given in vain;
'Tis paid with sighs a plenty
  And sold for endless rue."
And I am two-and-twenty,
  And oh, 'tis true, 'tis true.

TO AN ATHLETE DYING YOUNG

The time you won your town the race
We chaired you through the market-place;
Man and boy stood cheering by,
And home we brought you shoulder-high.

To-day, the road all runners come,
Shoulder-high we bring you home,
And set you at your threshold down,
Townsman of a stiller town.

Smart lad, to slip betimes away
From fields where glory does not stay   10
And early though the laurel grows
It withers quicker than the rose.

Eyes the shady night has shut
Cannot see the record cut,
And silence sounds no worse than cheers
After earth has stopped the ears:

Now you will not swell the rout
Of lads that wore their honours out,
Runners whom renown outran
And the name died before the man.   20

So set, before its echoes fade,
The fleet foot on the sill of shade,
And hold to the low lintel up
The still-defended challenge-cup.

And round that early-laurelled head
Will flock to gaze the strengthless dead,
And find unwithered on its curls
The garland briefer than a girl's.

IS MY TEAM PLOUGHING?

"Is my team ploughing,
That I was used to drive
And hear the harness jingle
When I was man alive?"

Ay, the horses trample,
The harness jingles now;
No change though you lie under
The land you used to plough.

"Is football playing
Along the river shore,   10
With lads to chase the leather,
Now I stand up no more?"

Ay, the ball is flying,
The lads play heart and soul;
The goal stands up, the keeper
Stands up to keep the goal.

"Is my girl happy,
That I thought hard to leave,
And has she tired of weeping
As she lies down at eve?"   20

Ay, she lies down lightly,
She lies not down to weep:
Your girl is well contented.
Be still, my lad, and sleep.

"Is my friend hearty,
Now I am thin and pine,
And has he found to sleep in
A better bed than mine?"

Yes, lad, I lie easy,
I lie as lads would choose;   30
I cheer a dead man's sweetheart,
Never ask me whose.

FROM FAR, FROM EVE AND MORNING

From far, from eve and morning
And yon twelve-winded sky,
The stuff of life to knit me
Blew hither: here am I.

Now—for a breath I tarry
Nor yet disperse apart—
Take my hand quick and tell me,
What have you in your heart.

Speak now, and I will answer;
How shall I help you, say;   10
Ere to the wind's twelve quarters
I take my endless way.

THE IMMORTAL PART

When I meet the morning beam
Or lay me down at night to dream,
I hear my bones within me say,
"Another night, another day.

"When shall this slough of sense be cast,
This dust of thoughts be laid at last,

The man of flesh and soul be slain
And the man of bone remain?

"This tongue that talks, these lungs that shout,
These thews that hustle us about,   10
This brain that fills the skull with schemes,
And its humming hive of dreams,—

"These to-day are proud in power
And lord it in their little hour:
The immortal bones obey control
Of dying flesh and dying soul.

"'Tis long till eve and morn are gone:
Slow the endless night comes on,
And late to fulness grows the birth
That shall last as long as earth.   20

"Wanderers eastward, wanderers west,
Know you why you cannot rest?
'Tis that every mother's son
Travails with a skeleton.

"Lie down in the bed of dust;
Bear the fruit that bear you must;
Bring the eternal seed to light,
And morn is all the same as night.

"Rest you so from trouble sore,
Fear the heat o' the sun no more,   30
Nor the snowing winter wild,
Now you labour not with child.

"Empty vessel, garment cast,
We that wore you long shall last.
—Another night, another day."
So my bones within me say.

Therefore they shall do my will
To-day while I am master still,
And flesh and soul, now both are strong,
Shall hale the sullen slaves along,   40

Before this fire of sense decay,
This smoke of thought blow clean away,
And leave with ancient night alone
The stedfast and enduring bone.

THE CARPENTER'S SON

"Here the hangman stops his cart:
Now the best of friends must part.
Fare you well, for ill fare I:
Live, lads, and I will die.

"Oh, at home had I but stayed
'Prenticed to my father's trade,
Had I stuck to plane and adze,
I had not been lost, my lads.

"Then I might have built perhaps
Gallows-trees for other chaps,   10
Never dangled on my own,
Had I but left ill alone.

"Now, you see, they hang me high,
And the people passing by
Stop to shake their fists and curse;
So 'tis come from ill to worse.

"Here hang I, and right and left
Two poor fellows hang for theft:
All the same's the luck we prove,
Though the midmost hangs for love.   20

"Comrades all, that stand and gaze,
Walk henceforth in other ways;
See my neck and save your own:
Comrades all, leave ill alone.

"Make some day a decent end,
Shrewder fellows than your friend.
Fare you well, for ill fare I:
Live, lads, and I will die."

BE STILL, MY SOUL, BE STILL

Be still, my soul, be still; the arms you bear are
    brittle,
    Earth and high heaven are fixt of old and founded
    strong.
Think rather,—call to thought, if now you grieve a
    little,
    The days when we had rest, O soul, for they were
    long.

Men loved unkindness then, but lightless in the
    quarry
    I slept and saw not; tears fell down, I did not
    mourn;
Sweat ran and blood sprang out and I was never
    sorry:
    Then it was well with me, in days ere I was born.

Now, and I muse for why and never find the reason,
    I pace the earth, and drink the air, and feel the
    sun.   10
Be still, be still, my soul; it is but for a season:
    Let us endure an hour and see injustice done.

Ay, look: high heaven and earth ail from the prime
   foundation;
   All thoughts to rive the heart are here, and all
   are vain:
Horror and scorn and hate and fear and indignation—
   Oh why did I awake? when shall I sleep again?

THE ISLE OF PORTLAND

The star-filled seas are smooth to-night
   From France to England strown;
Black towers above the Portland light
   The felon-quarried stone.

On yonder island, not to rise,
   Never to stir forth free,
Far from his folk a dead lad lies
   That once was friends with me.

Lie you easy, dream you light,
   And sleep you fast for aye;   10
And luckier may you find the night
   Than ever you found the day.

TERENCE, THIS IS STUPID STUFF

   "Terence, this is stupid stuff:
   You eat your victuals fast enough;
   There can't be much amiss, 'tis clear,
   To see the rate you drink your beer.
   But oh, good Lord, the verse you make,
   It gives a chap the belly-ache.
   The cow, the old cow, she is dead;
   It sleeps well, the hornèd head:
   We poor lads, 'tis our turn now
   To hear such tunes as killed the cow.   10
   Pretty friendship 'tis to rhyme
   Your friends to death before their time
   Moping melancholy mad:
   Come, pipe a tune to dance to, lad."

   Why, if 'tis dancing you would be,
   There's brisker pipes than poetry.
   Say, for what were hop-yards meant,
   Or why was Burton built on Trent?
   Oh many a peer of England brews
   Livelier liquor than the Muse,   20
   And malt does more than Milton can
   To justify God's way to man.

   18. Burton, Burton-on-Trent, site of England's most famous breweries.

Ale, man, ale's the stuff to drink
For fellows whom it hurts to think:
Look into the pewter pot
To see the world as the world's not.
And faith, 'tis pleasant till 'tis past:
The mischief is that 'twill not last.
Oh I have been to Ludlow fair
And left my necktie God knows where,   30
And carried half-way home, or near
Pints and quarts of Ludlow beer:
Then the world seemed none so bad,
And I myself a sterling lad;
And down in lovely muck I've lain,
Happy till I woke again.
Then I saw the morning sky:
Heigho, the tale was all a lie;
The world, it was the old world yet,
I was I, my things were wet,   40
And nothing now remained to do
But begin the game anew.

   Therefore, since the world has still
Much good, but much less good than ill,
And while the sun and moon endure
Luck's a chance, but trouble's sure,
I'd face it as a wise man would,
And train for ill and not for good.
'Tis true, the stuff I bring for sale
Is not so brisk a brew as ale: 50
Out of a stem that scored the hand
I wrung it in a weary land.
But take it: if the smack is sour,
The better for the embittered hour;
It should do good to heart and head
When your soul is in my soul's stead;
And I will friend you, if I may,
In the dark and cloudy day.

   There was a king reigned in the East:
There, when kings will sit to feast,   60
They got their fill before they think
With poisoned meat and poisoned drink.
He gathered all that springs to birth
From the many-venomed earth;
First a little, thence to more,
He sampled all her killing store;
And easy, smiling, seasoned sound,
Sate the king when healths went round.
They put arsenic in his meat
And stared aghast to watch him eat;   70
They poured strychnine in his cup
And shook to see him drink it up:
They shook, they stared as white's their shirt:
Them it was their poison hurt.

—I tell the tale that I heard told.
Mithridates, he died old.

I HOED AND TRENCHED
AND WEEDED

I hoed and trenched and weeded,
  And took the flowers to fair:
I brought them home unheeded;
  The hue was not the wear.

So up and down I sow them
  For lads like me to find,
When I shall lie below them,
  A dead man out of mind.

Some seed the birds devour,
  And some the season mars,   10
But here and there will flower
  The solitary stars,

And fields will yearly bear them
  As light-leaved spring comes on,
And luckless lads will wear them
  When I am dead and gone.

THE CHESTNUT CASTS HIS
FLAMBEAUX [1]

The chestnut casts his flambeaux, and the flowers
  Stream from the hawthorn on the wind away,
The doors clap to, the pane is blind with showers.
  Pass me the can, lad; there's an end of May.

There's one spoilt spring to scant our mortal lot,
  One season ruined of our little store.
May will be fine next year as like as not:
  Oh ay, but then we shall be twenty-four.

We for a certainty are not the first
  Have sat in taverns while the tempest hurled   10
Their hopeful plans to emptiness, and cursed
  Whatever brute and blackguard made the world.

It is in truth iniquity on high
  To cheat our sentenced souls of aught they crave,

And mar the merriment as you and I
  Fare on our long fool's errand to the grave.

Iniquity it is; but pass the can.
  My lad, no pair of kings our mothers bore;
Our only portion is the estate of man:
  We want the moon, but we shall get no more.   20

If here to-day the cloud of thunder lours
  To-morrow it will hie on far behests;
The flesh will grieve on other bones than ours
  Soon, and the soul will mourn in other breasts.

The troubles of our proud and angry dust
  Are from eternity, and shall not fail.
Bear them we can, and if we can we must.
  Shoulder the sky, my lad, and drink your ale.

EIGHT O'CLOCK

He stood, and heard the steeple
  Sprinkle the quarters on the morning town.
One, two, three, four, to market-place and people
  It tossed them down.

Strapped, noosed, nighing his hour,
  He stood and counted them and cursed his luck;
And then the clock collected in the tower
  Its strength, and struck.

THE LAWS OF GOD, THE LAWS
OF MAN

The laws of God, the laws of man,
He may keep that will and can;
Not I: let God and man decree
Laws for themselves and not for me;
And if my ways are not as theirs
Let them mind their own affairs.
Their deeds I judge and much condemn,
Yet when did I make laws for them?
Please yourselves, say I, and they
Need only look the other way.   10
But no, they will not; they must still
Wrest their neighbour to their will,
And make me dance as they desire
With jail and gallows and hell-fire.
And how am I to face the odds
Of man's bedevilment and God's?
I, a stranger and afraid
In a world I never made.
They will be master, right or wrong;

76. **Mithridates,** greatest of the kings of Pontus (c. 122–64 B.C.), who was presumed to have magical powers.
[1] This and the following three poems are from *Last Poems* by A. E. Housman, copyright, 1922, by Henry Holt and Company, Inc.   1. **flambeaux,** torches, sometimes decorated candlesticks; in this instance the torchlike flowering clusters of the chestnut tree.

21. **lours,** lowers, threatens.

Though both are foolish, both are strong.   20
And since, my soul, we cannot fly
To Saturn nor to Mercury,
Keep we must, if keep we can,
These foreign laws of God and man.

WHEN FIRST MY WAY TO FAIR I TOOK

When first my way to fair I took
Few pence in purse had I,

And long I used to stand and look
    At things I could not buy.

Now times are altered: if I care
    To buy a thing, I can;
The pence are here and here's the fair,
    But where's the lost young man?

—To think that two and two are four
    And neither five nor three   10
The heart of man has long been sore
    And long 'tis like to be.

Rudyard Kipling
1865–1936

India, the land where he began to write, saw the birth of (Joseph) Rudyard Kipling, at Bombay, on December 30, 1865. His parents were English; his father, John Lockwood Kipling, was professor of architectural sculpture, curator of the Lahore Museum, a painter, and an illustrator of some note. At six young Kipling was taken to England and educated at Westward Ho, in North Devon, and his experiences at the English school furnished the basis for the amusing *Stalky and Co.*, 1899. Returning to India, he engaged in journalism; at seventeen he became subeditor of the *Lahore Civil and Military Gazette*. At twenty-one he published his first volume, *Departmental Ditties*, 1886, a small book of light and occasional verse. A year later he challenged attention as a storyteller with *Plain Tales from the Hills*, 1887. Before he was twenty-four he had brought out six small collections of stories which showed his mastery in the form; among these early narratives are some of his best: *Under the Deodars*, *Soldiers Three*, *The Phantom Rickshaw*, and *Wee Willie Winkie*. They —and the stories which followed in rapid succession—were astonishing in their racy vigor, brilliant color, accurate observation, and, above all, their swift inventiveness. A new method as well as a new province was added to fiction: a realistic *Arabian Nights* transplanted to India and told by an Englishman.

With maturity, Kipling's gift grew in power and range. His soldier stories embodied characters which rank with those of Dickens. His stories for children —*The Jungle Books*, 1894–95; *Captains Courageous*, 1897; and *Just So Stories*, 1902—became contemporary classics. He appealed equally to youth and age

with *Kim*, 1901; *Puck of Pook's Hill*, 1906, *Rewards and Fairies*, 1910. His poems, from the early *Barrack-Room Ballads*, 1892, to the full-throated *The Five Nations*, 1903, impressed the craftsman with their skill and captivated the common reader with their gusto.

Between his twenty-third and twenty-sixth year Kipling traveled to China, Japan, India, and America. In England he found himself famous at twenty-seven. On a return visit to the United States in 1892 Kipling married an American, Caroline Starr Balestier, sister of Wolcott Balestier, with whom he wrote *The Naulahka*, 1891, and lived for a few years in Brattleboro, Vermont. Here he wrote several of his most popular works, including the animal stories in *Jungle Books*, and it seems likely that he would have remained in America if a quarrel with another brother-in-law, Beatty Balestier, and threats of legal action, had not driven him from Vermont back to England. Sensitive to criticism and increasingly wary of social contacts, Kipling withdrew from public life. He buried himself in a little Sussex village. He had lost a daughter; the death of a son during the World War embittered and almost silenced him. Although he had received the Nobel Prize for literature in 1907, changes in taste caused a reaction, a reaction directly chiefly against Kipling's militant "imperialism," which had once influenced British sentiment and, to some extent, its policies. Nevertheless, Kipling's work continued to grow in subtlety, if not in quantity, and he was at work on a collection of autobiographical notes when he died a few weeks after his seventieth birthday, January 17, 1936.

It has become the fashion in some quarters to

belittle Kipling's uncritical affirmations, his "inverted nostalgia" for Mandalay and the exotic regions "somewhere east of Suez," his patriotic fervor, and his "crude force." But if his energy is boisterous, it is irresistible. He not only discovered new scenes and fresh subject matter, he explored strange territories and established the "true romance" of bridge-builders, wireless operators, engineers, people familiar and unfamiliar up and down the world. As Somerset Maugham wrote: "He not only created characters, he created men. . . . Rudyard Kipling was the first to blaze the trail through new-found country, and no one has invested it with more glamour, no one has made it more exciting, and no one has presented it so vividly and with such a wealth of colour. . . . He had, like every writer, his shortcomings, but he remains notwithstanding the best short-story writer that England can boast of."

Rudyard Kipling was one of those rare writers who are equally at home in prose and in verse. Yet it seems likely that the dynamic poet will live even longer than the greatly gifted teller of tales. Kipling's prime quality as poet is his gusto, his rich and seemingly inexhaustible enthusiasm. Sometimes this exuberance defeats itself; the drum is often beaten so loudly that the music itself is drowned.

But Kipling is important for more than his brisk rhymes and marching rhythms. Coming at a time when poetry was surfeited with delicate languors and pastel imitations of antiquity, Kipling proclaimed the beauty as well as the liveliness of the actual world. Opposed to the affectations of romance, he offered realities which were far more romantic than the exaggerations. He invigorated the lifeblood of poetry with the simple expressions of men; he revived the ballad. He restored sincerity of tone, which the pre-Raphaelites had gone to some pains to lose; he added to vitality more grace than his critics are willing to concede.

Never has poetry possessed more verve, more forthright action. The lines vibrate with health; they communicate the tingle of salt spray, the snap of a banner, the tramp of boots, the lurch of the heart. But beneath the surge and rumble there is a delicacy, even a wistfulness, which is not immediately recognized. If Kipling is underpraised today because of the very qualities for which he was once overpraised, it is nothing more than the pendulum play of taste. He will be discovered again and again. He will be hailed not only for such perennial favorites as "Danny Deever" and "Mandalay," but for "The Sons of Martha," which celebrates inglorious domesticity, "The Land," which shows a large understanding of the soil and those who live close to it,

and "For to Admire" and "The Return," which carry nostalgic wanderlust to the pitch of high seriousness. It is more than possible that Kipling will outlive most of his generation and go down to posterity as a people's poet, a balladist whose songs were the popular measures of one age and the folk classics of another.

There is, as yet, no full-length biographical and critical study of Kipling. A year after his death there appeared *Something of Myself*, 1936, a collection of autobiographical notes containing memoirs, a sidelight on an era, and that "something" about the author which Kipling was willing to divulge.

MANDALAY [1]

By the old Moulmein Pagoda, lookin' eastward to
   the sea,
There's a Burma girl a-settin', an' I know she
   thinks o' me;
For the wind is in the palm-trees, and the temple-
   bells they say:
"Come you back, you British soldier; come you
   back to Mandalay!"
   Come you back to Mandalay,
   Where the old Flotilla lay:
   Can't you 'ear their paddles chunkin' from Ran-
   goon to Mandalay?
   On the road to Mandalay,
   Where the flyin'-fishes play,
   An' the dawn comes up like thunder outer China
   'crost the Bay!   10

'Er petticoat was yaller an' 'er little cap was green,
An' 'er name was Supi-yaw-lat—jes' the same as
   Theebaw's Queen,
An' I seed her first a-smokin' of a whackin' white
   cheroot,
An' a-wastin' Christian kisses on an 'eathen idol's
   foot:
   Bloomin' idol made o' mud—
   Wot they called the Great Gawd Budd—
   Plucky lot she cared for idols when I kissed 'er
   where she stud!
   On the road to Mandalay—

When the mist was on the rice-fields an' the sun was
   droppin' slow,
She'd git 'er little banjo an' she'd sing "*Kulla-lo-lo!*"

[1] This and the poems that follow are from *Departmental Ditties, Barrack-room Ballads and Other Verses* by Rudyard Kipling.

With 'er arm upon my shoulder an' her cheek agin
 my cheek   21
We useter watch the steamers an' the *hathis* pilin'
 teak.
 Elephints a-pilin' teak
 In the sludgy, squdgy creek,
 Where the silence 'ung that 'eavy you was 'arf
  afraid to speak!
 On the road to Mandalay—

But that's all shove be'ind me—long ago an' fur
 away,
An' there ain't no 'busses runnin' from the Bank to
 Mandalay;
An' I'm learnin' 'ere in London what the ten-year
 soldier tells:
"If you've 'eard the East a-callin', you won't never
 'eed naught else."   30
 No! you won't 'eed nothin' else
 But them spicy garlic smells,
 An' the sunshine an' the palm-trees an' the tinkly
  temple-bells;
 On the road to Mandalay—

I am sick o' wastin' leather on these gritty pavin'-
 stones,
An' the blasted Henglish drizzle wakes the fever in
 my bones;
Though I walks with fifty 'ousemaids outer Chelsea
 to the Strand,
An' they talks a lot o' lovin', but wot do they under-
 stand?
 Beefy face an' grubby 'and—
 Law! wot do they understand?   40
 I've a neater, sweeter maiden in a cleaner,
  greener land!
 On the road to Mandalay—

Ship me somewheres east of Suez, where the best is
 like the worst,
Where there aren't no Ten Commandments an' a
 man can raise a thirst;
For the temple-bells are callin', an' it's there that I
 would be—
By the old Moulmein Pagoda, lookin' lazy at the
 sea;
 On the road to Mandalay,
 Where the old Flotilla lay,
 With our sick beneath the awnings when we went
  to Mandalay!
 On the road to Mandalay,   50
 Where the flyin'-fishes play,
 An' the dawn comes up like thunder outer China
  'crost the Bay!

"FUZZY-WUZZY"

(Soudan Expeditionary Force)

We've fought with many men acrost the seas,
 An' some of 'em was brave an' some was not:
The Paythan an' the Zulu an' Burmese;
 But the Fuzzy was the finest o' the lot.
We never got a ha'porth's change of 'im:
 'E squatted in the scrub an' 'ocked our 'orses,
'E cut our sentries up at Suakim,
 An' 'e played the cat an' banjo with our forces.
  So 'ere's *to* you, Fuzzy-Wuzzy, at your 'ome in
   the Soudan;
  You're a pore benighted 'eathen but a first-
   class fightin' man;   10
  We gives you your certificate, an' if you want it
   signed
  We'll come an' 'ave a romp with you whenever
   you're inclined.

We took our chanst among the Kyber 'ills,
 The Boers knocked us silly at a mile,
The Burman give us Irriwaddy chills,
 An' a Zulu *impi* dished us up in style:
But all we ever got from such as they
 Was pop to what the Fuzzy made us swaller;
We 'eld our bloomin' own, the papers say,
 But man for man the Fuzzy knocked us 'oller. 20
  Then 'ere's *to* you, Fuzzy-Wuzzy, an' the missis
   and the kid;
  Our orders was to break you, an' of course we
   went an' did.
  We sloshed you with Martinis, an' it wasn't
   'ardly fair;
  But for all the odds agin' you, Fuzzy-Wuz, you
   broke the square.

'E 'asn't got no papers of 'is own,
 'E 'asn't got no medals nor rewards,
So we must certify the skill 'e's shown
 In usin' of 'is long two-'anded swords;
When 'e's 'oppin' in an' out among the bush
 With 'is coffin-'eaded shield an' shovel-spear, 30
A 'appy day with Fuzzy on the rush
 Will last an 'ealthy Tommy for a year.
  So 'ere's *to* you, Fuzzy-Wuzzy, an' your friends
   which are no more,
  If we 'adn't lost some messmates we would
   'elp you to deplore;
  But give an' take's the gospel, an' we'll call the
   bargain fair,
  For if you 'ave lost more than us, you crumpled
   up the square!

'E rushes at the smoke when we let drive,
    An', before we know, 'e's 'ackin' at our 'ead;
'E's all 'ot sand an' ginger when alive,
    An' 'e's generally shammin' when 'e's dead.   40
'E's a daisy, 'e's a ducky, 'e's a lamb!
    'E's a injia-rubber idiot on the spree,
'E's the on'y thing that doesn't care a damn
    For the Regiment o' British Infantree!
        So 'ere's *to* you, Fuzzy-Wuzzy, at your 'ome in
           the Soudan;
        You're a pore benighted 'eathen but a first-
           class fightin' man;
        An' 'ere's *to* you, Fuzzy-Wuzzy, with your
           'ayrick 'ead of 'air—
        You big black boundin' beggar—for you broke
           a British square!

DANNY DEEVER

"What are the bugles blowin' for?" said Files-on-
    Parade.
"To turn you out, to turn you out," the Color-
    Sergeant said.
"What makes you look so white, so white?" said
    Files-on-Parade.
"I'm dreadin' what I've got to watch," the Color-
    Sergeant said.
    For they're hangin' Danny Deever, you can hear
        the Dead March play,
    The regiment's in 'ollow square—they're hangin'
        him to-day;
    They've taken of his buttons off an' cut his stripes
        away,
    An' they're hangin' Danny Deever in the
        mornin'.

"What makes the rear-rank breathe so 'ard?" said
    Files-on-Parade.
"It's bitter cold, it's bitter cold," the Color-Ser-
    geant said.   10
"What makes that front-rank man fall down?" says
    Files-on-Parade.
"A touch o' sun, a touch o' sun," the Color-Ser-
    geant said.
    They are hangin' Danny Deever, they are
        marchin' of 'im round.
    They 'ave 'alted Danny Deever by 'is coffin on
        the ground;
    An' 'e'll swing in 'arf a minute for a sneakin'
        shootin' hound—
    O they're hangin' Danny Deever in the mornin'!

"'Is cot was right-'and cot to mine," said Files-on-
    Parade.
"'E's sleepin' out an' far to-night," the Color-Ser-
    geant said.
"I've drunk 'is beer a score o' times," said Files-on-
    Parade.
"'E's drinkin' bitter beer alone," the Color-Ser-
    geant said.   20
    They are hangin' Danny Deever, you must mark
        'im to 'is place,
    For 'e shot a comrade sleepin'—you must look
        'im in the face;
    Nine 'undred of 'is county an' the regiment's dis-
        grace,
    While they're hangin' Danny Deever in the
        mornin'.

"What's that so black agin the sun?" said Files-on-
    Parade.
"It's Danny fightin' 'ard for life," the Color-Ser-
    geant said.
"What's that that whimpers over'ead?" said Files-
    on-Parade.
"It's Danny's soul that's passin' now," the Color-
    Sergeant said.
    For they're done with Danny Deever, you can
        'ear the quickstep play,
    The regiment's in column, an' they're marchin'
        us away;   30
    Ho! the young recruits are shakin', an' they'll
        want their beer to-day,
    After hangin' Danny Deever in the mornin'!

RECESSIONAL

God of our fathers, known of old—
    Lord of our far-flung battle-line—
Beneath whose awful hand we hold
    Dominion over palm and pine—
Lord God of Hosts, be with us yet,
Lest we forget—lest we forget!

The tumult and the shouting dies—
    The Captains and the Kings depart—
Still stands Thine ancient sacrifice,
    An humble and a contrite heart.   10
Lord God of Hosts, be with us yet,
Lest we forget—lest we forget!

Far-called our navies melt away—
    On dune and headland sinks the fire—
Lo, all our pomp of yesterday
    Is one with Nineveh and Tyre!

Judge of the Nations, spare us yet,
Lest we forget—lest we forget!

If, drunk with sight of power, we loose
    Wild tongues that have not Thee in awe— 20
Such boastings as the Gentiles use,
    Or lesser breeds without the Law—
Lord God of Hosts, be with us yet,
Lest we forget—lest we forget!

For heathen heart that puts her trust
    In reeking tube and iron shard—
All valiant dust that builds on dust,
    And guarding calls not Thee to guard,
For frantic boast and foolish word,
Thy mercy on Thy People, Lord!   30

THE BALLAD OF EAST AND WEST

Oh, East is East, and West is West, and never the twain
    shall meet,
Till Earth and Sky stand presently at God's great Judg-
    ment Seat;
But there is neither East nor West, Border, nor Breed, nor
    Birth,
When two strong men stand face to face, though they come
    from the ends of the earth!

Kamal is out with twenty men to raise the Border
    side,
And he has lifted the Colonel's mare that is the
    Colonel's pride:
He has lifted her out of the stable-door between the
    dawn and the day,
And turned the calkins upon her feet, and ridden
    her far away.
Then up and spoke the Colonel's son that led a
    troop of the Guides:
"Is there never a man of all my men can say where
    Kamal hides?"   10
Then up and spoke Mahommed Khan, the son of
    the Ressaldar,
"If ye know the track of the morning-mist, ye know
    where his pickets are.
At dusk he harries the Abazai—at dawn he is into
    Bonair,
But he must go by Fort Bukloh to his own place to
    fare.
So if ye gallop to Fort Bukloh as fast as a bird can
    fly,
By the favor of God ye may cut him off ere he win
    to the Tongue of Jagai,

But if he be past the Tongue of Jagai, right swiftly
    turn ye then,
For the length and the breadth of that grisly plain is
    sown with Kamal's men.
There is rock to the left, and rock to the right, and
    low lean thorn between,
And ye may hear a breech-bolt snick where never a
    man is seen."   20
The Colonel's son has taken a horse, and a raw
    rough dun was he,
With the mouth of a bell and the heart of Hell, and
    the head of a gallows-tree.
The Colonel's son to the Fort has won, they bid him
    stay to eat—
Who rides at the tail of a Border thief, he sits not
    long at his meat.
He's up and away from Fort Bukloh as fast as he can
    fly,
Till he was aware of his father's mare in the gut of
    the Tongue of Jagai,
Till he was aware of his father's mare with Kamal
    upon her back,
And when he could spy the white of her eye, he
    made the pistol crack.
He has fired once, he has fired twice, but the whis-
    tling ball went wide.
"Ye shoot like a soldier," Kamal said. "Show now
    if ye can ride."   30
It's up and over the Tongue of Jagai, as blown dust-
    devils go,
The dun he fled like a stag of ten, but the mare like
    a barren doe.
The dun he leaned against the bit and slugged his
    head above,
But the red mare played with the snaffle-bars, as a
    maiden plays with a glove.
There was rock to the left and rock to the right, and
    low lean thorn between,
And thrice he heard a breech-bolt snick though
    never a man was seen.
They have ridden the low moon out of the sky, their
    hoofs drum up the dawn,
The dun he went like a wounded bull, but the mare
    like a new-roused fawn.
The dun he fell at a water-course—in a woful heap
    fell he,
And Kamal has turned the red mare back, and
    pulled the rider free.   40
He has knocked the pistol out of his hand—small
    room was there to strive,
"'Twas only by favor of mine," quoth he, "ye rode
    so long alive:
There was not a rock for twenty mile, there was not
    a clump of tree,

But covered a man of my own men with his rifle
    cocked on his knee.
If I had raised my bridle-hand, as I have held it
    low,
The little jackals that flee so fast, were feasting all in
    a row.
If I had bowed my head on my breast, as I have
    held it high,
The kite that whistles above us now were gorged till
    she could not fly."
Lightly answered the Colonel's son: "Do good to
    bird and beast,
But count who come for the broken meats before
    thou makest a feast.   50
If there should follow a thousand swords to carry
    my bones away,
Belike the price of a jackal's meal were more than a
    thief could pay.
They will feed their horse on the standing crop,
    their men on the garnered grain,
The thatch of the byres will serve their fires when
    all the cattle are slain.
But if thou thinkest the price be fair,—thy brethren
    wait to sup,
The hound is kin to the jackal-spawn,—howl, dog,
    and call them up!
And if thou thinkest the price be high, in steer and
    gear and stack,
Give me my father's mare again, and I'll fight my
    own way back!"
Kamal has gripped him by the hand and set him
    upon his feet.
"No talk shall be of dogs," said he, "when wolf and
    grey wolf meet.   60
May I eat dirt if thou hast hurt of me in deed or
    breath;
What dam of lances brought thee forth to jest at the
    dawn with Death?"
Lightly answered the Colonel's son: "I hold by the
    blood of my clan:
Take up the mare for my father's gift—by God, she
    has carried a man!"
The red mare ran to the Colonel's son, and nuzzled
    against his breast,
"We be two strong men," said Kamal then, "but
    she loveth the younger best.
So she shall go with a lifter's dower, my turquoise-
    studded rein,
My broidered saddle and saddle-cloth, and silver
    stirrups twain."
The Colonel's son a pistol drew and held it muzzle-
    end,
"Ye have taken the one from a foe," said he, "will
    ye take the mate from a friend?"   70

"A gift for a gift," said Kamal straight; "a limb for
    the risk of a limb.
Thy father has sent his son to me, I'll send my son to
    him!"
With that he whistled his only son, that dropped
    from a mountain-crest—
He trod the ling like a buck in spring, and he looked
    like a lance in rest.
"Now here is thy master," Kamal said, "who leads
    a troop of the Guides,
And thou must ride at his left side as shield on
    shoulder rides.
Till Death or I cut loose the tie, at camp and board
    and bed,
Thy life is his—thy fate it is to guard him with thy
    head.
So thou must eat the White Queen's meat, and all
    her foes are thine,
And thou must harry thy father's hold for the peace
    of the Border-line,   80
And thou must make a trooper tough and hack thy
    way to power—
Belike they will raise thee to Ressaldar when I am
    hanged in Peshawur!"

They have looked each other between the eyes, and
    there they have found no fault,
They have taken the Oath of the Brother-in-Blood
    on leavened bread and salt:
They have taken the Oath of the Brother-in-Blood
    on fire and fresh-cut sod,
On the hilt and the haft of the Khyber knife, and
    the Wondrous Names of God.
The Colonel's son he rides the mare and Kamal's
    boy the dun,
And two have come back to Fort Bukloh where
    there went forth but one.
And when they drew to the Quarter-Guard, full
    twenty swords flew clear—
There was not a man but carried his feud with the
    blood of the mountaineer.   90
"Ha' done! ha' done!" said the Colonel's son,
    "Put up the steel at your sides!
Last night ye had struck at a Border thief—to-night
    'tis a man of the Guides!"

*Oh, East is East and West is West, and never the twain
    shall meet,
Till Earth and Sky stand presently at God's great Judg-
    ment Seat;
But there is neither East nor West, Border, nor Breed, nor
    Birth,*

74. ling, heather.

When two strong men stand face to face, though they come
from the ends of the earth.

THE OVERLAND MAIL

(Foot-service to the Hills)

In the name of the Empress of India, make way,
  O Lords of the Jungle, wherever you roam,
The woods are astir at the close of the day—
  We exiles are waiting for letters from Home.
Let the robber retreat—let the tiger turn tail—
In the Name of the Empress, the Overland Mail!

With a jingle of bells as the dusk gathers in,
  He turns to the foot-path that heads up the hill—
The bags on his back and a cloth round his chin,
  And, tucked in his waistbelt, the Post Office
    bill:—   10
"Despatched on this date, as received by the rail,
  Per runner, two bags of the Overland Mail."

Is the torrent in spate? He must ford it or swim.
  Has the rain wrecked the road? He must climb by
    the cliff.
Does the tempest cry "Halt?" What are tempests to
    him?
  The Service admits not a "but" or an "if."
While the breath's in his mouth, he must bear with-
    out fail,
In the Name of the Empress, the Overland Mail.

From aloe to rose-oak, from rose-oak to fir,
  From level to upland, from upland to crest,   20
From rice-field to rock-ridge, from rock-ridge to
    spur,
  Fly the soft-sandalled feet, strains the brawny
    brown chest,
From rail to ravine—to the peak from the vale—
Up, up through the night goes the Overland Mail.

There's a speck on the hillside, a dot on the road—
  A jingle of bells on the footpath below—
There's a scuffle above in the monkey's abode—
  The world is awake, and the clouds are aglow.
For the great Sun himself must attend to the hail:—
  "In the name of the Empress, the Overland
    Mail!"   30

THE CONUNDRUM OF THE
WORKSHOPS

When the flush of a new-born sun fell first on Eden's
  green and gold,
Our father Adam sat under the Tree and scratched
  with a stick in the mould;

And the first rude sketch that the world had seen
  was joy to his mighty heart,
Till the Devil whispered behind the leaves: "It's
  pretty, but is it art?"

Wherefore he called to his wife, and fled to fashion
  his work anew—
The first of his race who cared a fig for the first,
  most dread review;
And he left his lore to the use of his sons—and that
  was a glorious gain
When the Devil chuckled "Is it art?" in the ear of
  the branded Cain.

They builded a tower to shiver the sky and wrench
  the stars apart,
Till the Devil grunted behind the bricks: "It's
  striking, but is it art?"   10
The stone was dropped at the quarry-side and the
  idle derrick swung,
While each man talked of the aims of art, and each
  in an alien tongue.

They fought and they talked in the north and the
  south, they talked and they fought in the west,
Till the waters rose on the jabbering land, and the
  poor Red Clay had rest—
Had rest till that dank blank-canvas dawn when
  the dove was preened to start,
And the Devil bubbled below the keel: "It's human,
  but is it art?"

The tale is as old as the Eden Tree—and new as the
  new-cut tooth—
For each man knows ere his lip-thatch grows he is
  master of art and truth;
And each man hears as the twilight nears, to the
  beat of his dying heart,
The Devil drum on the darkened pane: "You did it,
  but was it art?"   20

We have learned to whittle the Eden Tree to the
  shape of a surplice-peg,
We have learned to bottle our parents twain in the
  yolk of an addled egg,
We know that the tail must wag the dog, as the
  horse is drawn by the cart;
But the Devil whoops, as he whooped of old: "It's
  clever, but is it art?"

When the flicker of London sun falls faint on the
  club-room's green and gold,
The sons of Adam sit them down and scratch with
  their pens in the mould—

Mail set me down at Marwar Junction, where a funny little, happy-go-lucky, native-managed railway runs to Jodhpore. The Bombay Mail from Delhi makes a short halt at Marwar. She arrived as I got in, and I had just time to hurry to her platform and go down the carriages. There was only one Second-class on the train. I slipped the window and looked down upon a flaming red beard, half covered by a railway rug. That was my man, fast asleep, and I dug him gently in the ribs. He woke with a grunt, and I saw his face in the light of the lamps. It was a great and shining face.

"Tickets again?" said he.

"No," said I. "I am to tell you that he is gone South for the week. He is gone South for the week!"

The train had begun to move out. The red man rubbed his eyes. "He has gone South for the week," he repeated. "Now that's just like his impidence. Did he say that I was to give you anything? 'Cause I won't."

"He didn't," I said, and dropped away, and watched the red lights die out in the dark. It was horribly cold because the wind was blowing off the sands. I climbed into my own train—not an Intermediate Carriage this time—and went to sleep.

If the man with the beard had given me a rupee I should have kept it as a memento of a rather curious affair. But the consciousness of having done my duty was my only reward.

Later on I reflected that two gentlemen like my friends could not do any good if they foregathered and personated correspondents of newspapers, and might, if they black-mailed one of the little rat-trap states of Central India or Southern Rajputana, get themselves into serious difficulties. I therefore took some trouble to describe them as accurately as I could remember to people who would be interested in deporting them: and succeeded, so I was later informed, in having them headed back from the Degumber borders.

Then I became respectable, and returned to an Office where there were no Kings and no incidents outside the daily manufacture of a newspaper. A newspaper office seems to attract every conceivable sort of person, to the prejudice of discipline. Zenana-mission ladies arrive, and beg that the Editor will instantly abandon all his duties to describe a Christian prize-giving in a back slum of a perfectly inaccessible village; Colonels who have been overpassed for command sit down and sketch the outline of a series of ten, twelve, or twenty-four leading articles on Seniority *versus* Selection; missionaries wish to know why they have not been permitted to escape from their regular vehicles of abuse and swear at a brother-missionary under special patronage of the editorial We; stranded theatrical companies troop up to explain that they cannot pay for their advertisements, but on their return from New Zealand or Tahiti will do so with interest; inventors of patent punkah-pulling machines, carriage couplings and unbreakable swords and axle-trees call with specifications in their pockets and hours at their disposal; tea-companies enter and elaborate their prospectuses with the office pens; secretaries of ball-committees clamour to have the glories of their last dance more fully described; strange ladies rustle in and say: "I want a hundred lady's cards printed *at once*, please," which is manifestly part of an Editor's duty; and every dissolute ruffian that ever tramped the Grand Trunk Road makes it his business to ask for employment as a proof-reader. And, all the time, the telephone-bell is ringing madly, and Kings are being killed on the Continent, and Empires are saying—"You're another," and Mr. Gladstone is calling down brimstone upon the British Dominions, and the little black copy-boys are whining, "*kaa-pi chay-ha-yeh*" (copy wanted) like tired bees, and most of the paper is as blank as Modred's shield.

But that is the amusing part of the year. There are six other months when none ever come to call, and the thermometer walks inch by inch up to the top of the glass, and the office is darkened to just above reading-light, and the press-machines are red-hot of touch, and nobody writes anything but accounts of amusements in the Hill-stations or obituary notices. Then the telephone becomes a tinkling terror, because it tells you of the sudden deaths of men and women that you knew intimately, and the prickly-heat covers you as with a garment, and you sit down and write: "A slight increase of sickness is reported from the Khuda Janta Khan District. The outbreak is purely sporadic in its nature, and, thanks to the energetic efforts of the District authorities, is now almost at an end. It is, however, with deep regret we record the death," etc.

Then the sickness really breaks out, and the less recording and reporting the better for the peace of the subscribers. But the Empires and the Kings continue to divert themselves as selfishly as before, and the Foreman thinks that a daily paper really ought to come out once in twenty-four hours, and all the people at the Hill-stations in the middle of their amusements say: "Good gracious! Why can't the paper be sparkling? I'm sure there's plenty going on up here."

That is the dark half of the moon, and, as the advertisements say, "must be experienced to be appreciated."

It was in that season, and a remarkably evil season, that the paper began running the last issue of the week on Saturday night, which is to say Sunday morning, after the custom of a London paper. This was a great convenience, for immediately after the paper was put to bed, the dawn would lower the thermometer from 96° to almost 84° for half an hour, and in that chill—you have no idea how cold is 84° on the grass until you begin to pray for it—a very tired man could set off to sleep ere the heat 10 roused him.

One Saturday night it was my pleasant duty to put the paper to bed alone. A King or courtier or a courtesan or a Community was going to die or get a new Constitution, or do something that was important on the other side of the world, and the paper was to be held open till the latest possible minute in order to catch the telegram.

It was a pitchy black night, as stifling as a June night can be, and the *loo*, the red-hot wind from the 20 westward, was booming among the tinder-dry trees and pretending that the rain was on its heels. Now and again a spot of almost boiling water would fall on the dust with the flop of a frog, but all our weary world knew that was only pretence. It was a shade cooler in the press-room than the office, so I sat there, while the type ticked and clicked, and the night-jars hooted at the windows, and the all but naked compositors wiped the sweat from their foreheads, and called for water. The thing that was 30 keeping us back, whatever it was, would not come off, though the *loo* dropped and the last type was set, and the whole round earth stood still in the choking heat, with its finger on its lip, to wait the event. I drowsed, and wondered whether the telegraph was a blessing, and whether this dying man, or struggling people, was aware of the inconvenience the delay was causing. There was no special reason beyond the heat and worry to make tension, but, as the clock-hands crept up to three o'clock and 40 the machines spun their fly-wheels two and three times to see that all was in order, before I said the word that would set them off, I could have shrieked aloud.

Then the roar and rattle of the wheels shivered the quiet into little bits. I rose to go away, but two men in white clothes stood in front of me. The first one said: "It's him!" The second said: "So it is!" And they both laughed almost as loudly as the machinery roared, and mopped their foreheads. "We 50 seed there was a light burning across the road, and we were sleeping in that ditch there for coolness,

28. **night-jars,** nocturnal birds, sometimes called "goat-suckers," related to the American whippoorwill.

and I said to my friend here, The office is open. Let's come along and speak to him as turned us back from the Degumber State," said the smaller of the two. He was the man I had met in the Mhow train, and his fellow was the red-bearded man of Marwar Junction. There was no mistaking the eyebrows of the one or the beard of the other.

I was not pleased, because I wished to go to sleep, not to squabble with loafers. "What do you want?" I asked.

"Half an hour's talk with you, cool and comfortable, in the office," said the red-bearded man. "We'd *like* some drink—the Contrack doesn't begin yet, Peachey, so you needn't look—but what we really want is advice. We don't want money. We ask you as a favour, because you did us a bad turn about Degumber."

I led from the press-room to the stifling office with the maps on the walls, and the red-haired man rubbed his hands. "That's something like," said he, "This was the proper shop to come to. Now, Sir, let me introduce to you Brother Peachey Carnehan, that's him, and Brother Daniel Dravot, that is *me*, and the less said about our professions the better, for we have been most things in our time. Soldier, sailor, compositor, photographer, proof-reader, street-preacher, and correspondents of the *Backwoodsman* when we thought the paper wanted one. Carnehan is sober, and so am I. Look at us first, and see that's sure. It will save you cutting into my talk. We'll take one of your cigars apiece, and you shall see us light up."

I watched the test. The men were absolutely sober, so I gave them each a tepid whiskey and soda.

"Well *and* good," said Carnehan of the eyebrows, wiping the froth from his moustache. "Let me talk now, Dan. We have been all over India, mostly on foot. We have been boiler-fitters, engine-drivers, petty contractors, and all that, and we have decided that India isn't big enough for such as us."

They certainly were too big for the office. Dravot's beard seemed to fill half the room and Carnehan's shoulders the other half, as they sat on the big table. Carnehan continued: "The country isn't half worked out because they that governs it won't let you touch it. They spend all their blessed time in governing it, and you can't lift a spade, nor chip a rock, nor look for oil, nor anything like that without all the Government saying—'Leave it alone, and let us govern.' Therefore, such *as* it is, we will let it alone, and go away to some other place where a man isn't crowded and can come to his own. We are not little men, and there is nothing that we are afraid of except Drink, and we have signed a Contrack on that. *Therefore*, we are going away to be Kings."

"Kings in our own right," muttered Dravot.

"Yes, of course," I said. "You've been tramping in the sun, and it's a very warm night, and hadn't you better sleep over the notion? Come to-morrow."

"Neither drunk nor sunstruck," said Dravot. "We have slept over the notion half a year, and require to see Books and Atlases, and we have decided that there is only one place now in the world that two strong men can Sar-a-*whack*. They call it Kafiristan. By my reckoning it's the top right-hand corner of Afghanistan, not more than three hundred miles from Peshawur. They have two and thirty heathen idols there, and we'll be the thirty-third and fourth. It's a mountaineous country, and the women of those parts are very beautiful."

"But that is provided against in the Contrack," said Carnehan. "Neither Women nor Liqu-or, Daniel."

"And that's all we know, except that no one has gone there, and they fight, and in any place where they fight a man who knows how to drill men can always be a King. We shall go to those parts and say to any King we find—'D'you want to vanquish your foes?' and we will show him how to drill men; for that we know better than anything else. Then we will subvert that King and seize his Throne and establish a Dy-nasty."

"You'll be cut to pieces before you're fifty miles across the Border," I said. "You have to travel through Afghanistan to get to that country. It's one mass of mountains and peaks and glaciers, and no Englishman has been through it. The people are utter brutes, and even if you reached them you couldn't do anything."

"That's more like," said Carnehan. "If you could think us a little more mad we would be more pleased. We have come to you to know about this country, to read a book about it, and to be shown maps. We want you to tell us that we are fools and to show us your books." He turned to the bookcases.

"Are you at all in earnest?" I said.

"A little," said Dravot, sweetly. "As big a map as you have got, even if it's all blank where Kafiristan is, and any books you've got. We can read, though we aren't very educated."

I uncased the big thirty-two-miles-to-the-inch-map of India, and two smaller Frontier maps, hauled down volume INF-KAN of the "Encyclopaedia Britannica," and the men consulted them.

"See here!" said Dravot, his thumb on the map. "Up to Jagdallak, Peachey and me know the road.

We was there with Roberts' Army. We'll have to turn off to the right at Jagdallak through Laghmann territory. Then we get among the hills—fourteen thousand feet—fifteen thousand—it will be cold work there, but it don't look very far on the map."

I handed him Wood on the *Sources of the Oxus*. Carnehan was deep in the *Encyclopaedia*.

"They're a mixed lot," said Dravot, reflectively; "and it won't help us to know the names of their tribes. The more tribes the more they'll fight, and the better for us. From Jagdallak to Ashang. H'mm!"

"But all the information about the country is as sketchy and inaccurate as can be," I protested. "No one knows anything about it really. Here's the file of the *United Services' Institute*. Read what Bellew says."

"Blow Bellew!" said Carnehan. "Dan, they're a stinkin' lot of heathens, but this books here says they think they're related to us English."

I smoked while the men pored over *Raverty*, *Wood*, the maps, and the *Encyclopaedia*.

"There is no use your waiting," said Dravot politely. "It's about four o'clock now. We'll go before six o'clock if you want to sleep, and we won't steal any of the papers. Don't you sit up. We're two harmless lunatics, and if you come to-morrow evening down to the Serai we'll say good-bye to you."

"You *are* two fools," I answered. "You'll be turned back at the Frontier or cut up the minute you set foot in Afghanistan. Do you want any money or a recommendation down-country? I can help you to the chance of work next week."

"Next week we shall be hard at work ourselves, thank you," said Dravot. "It isn't so easy being a King as it looks. When we've got our Kingdom in going order we'll let you know, and you can come up and help us to govern it."

"Would two lunatics make a Contrack like that?" said Carnehan, with subdued pride, showing me a greasy half-sheet of note-paper on which was written the following. I copied it, then and there, as a curiosity—

This Contract between me and you persuing witnesseth in the name of God—Amen and so forth.

(*One*)   *That me and you will settle this matter together: i.e., to be Kings of Kafiristan.*

(*Two*)   *That you and me will not, while this matter is being settled, look at any Liquor, nor any Woman black, white or brown, so as to get mixed up with one or the other harmful.*

(Three) That we conduct ourselves with Dignity and
Discretion, and if one of us gets into trouble
the other will stay by him.
Signed by you and me this day.

Peachey Taliaferro Carnehan.
Daniel Dravot.
Both Gentlemen at Large.

"There was no need for the last article," said
Carnehan, blushing modestly; "but it looks regular.
Now you know the sort of men that loafers are—we
are loafers, Dan, until we get out of India—and *do*
you think that we would sign a Contrack like that
unless we was in earnest? We have kept away from
the two things that make life worth having."

"You won't enjoy your lives much longer if you
are going to try this idiotic adventure. Don't set the
office on fire," I said, "and go away before nine
o'clock."

I left them still poring over the maps and making
notes on the back of the "Contrack." "Be sure to
come down to the Serai to-morrow," were their
parting words.

The Kumharsen Serai is the great four-square
sink of humanity where the strings of camels and
horses from the North load and unload. All the na-
tionalities of Central Asia may be found there, and
most of the folk of India proper. Balkh and Bokhara there meet Bengal and Bombay, and try to
draw eye-teeth. You can buy ponies, turquoises,
Persian pussy-cats, saddle-bags, fat-tailed sheep and
musk in the Kumharsen Serai, and get many
strange things for nothing. In the afternoon I went
down there to see whether my friends intended to
keep their word or were lying there drunk.

A priest attired in fragments of ribbons and rags
stalked up to me, gravely twisting a child's paper
whirligig. Behind him was his servant bending under the load of a crate of mud toys. The two were
loading up two camels, and the inhabitants of the
Serai watched them with shrieks of laughter.

"The priest is mad," said a horse-dealer to me.
"He is going up to Kabul to sell toys to the Amir.
He will either be raised to honour or have his head
cut off. He came in here this morning and has been
behaving madly ever since."

"The witless are under the protection of God,"
stammered a flat-cheeked Usbeg in broken Hindi.
"They foretell future events."

"Would they could have foretold that my caravan would have been cut up by the Shinwaris almost within shadow of the Pass!" grunted the
Eusufzai agent of a Rajputana trading-house whose
goods had been diverted into the hands of other

robbers just across the Border, and whose misfortunes were the laughing-stock of the bazar. "Ohé,
priest, whence come you and whither do you go?"

"From Roum have I come," shouted the priest,
waving his whirligig; "from Roum, blown by the
breath of a hundred devils across the sea! O thieves,
robbers, liars, the blessing of Pir Khan on pigs,
dogs, and perjurers! Who will take the Protected of
God to the North to sell charms that are never still
to the Amir? The camels shall not gall, the sons
shall not fall sick, and the wives shall remain faithful while they are away, of the men who give me
place in their caravan. Who will assist me to slipper
the King of the Roos with a golden slipper with a
silver heel? The protection of Pir Khan be upon his
labours!" He spread out the skirts of his gaberdine
and pirouetted between the lines of tethered horses.

"There starts a caravan from Peshawur to Kabul
in twenty days, *Huzrut*," said the Eusufzai trader.
"My camels go therewith. Do thou also go and
bring us good-luck."

"I will go even now!" shouted the priest. "I will
depart upon my winged camels, and be at Peshawur in a day! Ho! Hazar Mir Khan," he yelled to
his servant, "drive out the camels, but let me first
mount my own."

He leaped on the back of his beast as it knelt,
and, turning round to me, cried: "Come thou
also, Sahib, a little along the road, and I will sell
thee a charm—an amulet that shall make thee
King of Kafiristan."

Then the light broke upon me, and I followed
the two camels out of the Serai till we reached open
road and the priest halted.

"What d'you think o' that?" said he in English.
"Carnehan can't talk their patter, so I've made him
my servant. He makes a handsome servant. 'Tisn't
for nothing that I've been knocking about the country for fourteen years. Didn't I do that talk neat?
We'll hitch on to a caravan at Peshawur till we get
to Jagdallak, and then we'll see if we can get don-
keys for our camels, and strike into Kafiristan.
Whirligigs for the Amir, O Lor! Put your hand under the camel-bags and tell me what you feel."

I felt the butt of a Martini, and another and another.

"Twenty of 'em," said Dravot placidly. "Twenty
of 'em and ammunition to correspond, under the
whirligigs and the mud dolls."

"Heaven help you if you are caught with those
things!" I said. "A Martini is worth her weight in
silver among the Pathans."

"Fifteen hundred rupees of capital—every rupee
we could beg, borrow, or steal—are invested on

these two camels," said Dravot. "We won't get caught. We're going through the Khaiber with a regular caravan. Who'd touch a poor mad priest?"

"Have you got everything you want?" I asked, overcome with astonishment.

"Not yet, but we shall soon. Give us a memento of your kindness, *Brother*. You did me a service yesterday, and that time in Marwar. Half my Kingdom shall you have, as the saying is." I slipped a small charm compass from my watch-chain and handed it up to the priest.

"Good-bye," said Dravot, giving me his hand cautiously. "It's the last time we'll shake hands with an Englishman these many days. Shake hands with him, Carnehan," he cried, as the second camel passed me.

Carnehan leaned down and shook hands. Then the camels passed away along the dusty road, and I was left alone to wonder. My eye could detect no failure in the disguises. The scene in Serai proved that they were complete to the native mind. There was just the chance, therefore, that Carnehan and Dravot would be able to wander through Afghanistan without detection. But, beyond, they would find death—certain and awful death.

Ten days later a native friend of mine, giving me the news of the day from Peshawur, wound up his letter with: "There has been much laughter here on account of a certain mad priest who is going in his estimation to sell petty gauds and insignificant trinkets which he ascribes as great charms to H. H. the Amir of Bokhara. He passed through Peshawur and associated himself to the Second Summer caravan that goes to Kabul. The merchants are pleased because through superstition they imagine that such mad fellows bring good-fortune."

The two, then, were beyond the Border. I would have prayed for them, but, that night, a real King died in Europe, and demanded an obituary notice.

The wheel of the world swings through the same phases again and again. Summer passed and winter thereafter, and came and passed again. The daily paper continued, and I with it, and upon the third summer there fell a hot night, a night-issue, and a strained waiting for something to be telegraphed from the other side of the world, exactly as had happened before. A few great men had died in the past two years, the machines worked with more clatter, and some of the trees in the Office garden were a few feet taller. But that was all the difference.

I passed over to the press-room, and went through just such a scene as I have already described. The nervous tension was stronger than it had been two years before, and I felt the heat more acutely. At three o'clock I cried, "Print off," and turned to go, when there crept to my chair what was left of a man. He was bent into a circle, his head was sunk between his shoulders, and he moved his feet one over the other like a bear. I could hardly see whether he walked or crawled—this rag-wrapped, whining cripple who addressed me by name, crying that he was come back, "Can you give me a drink?" he whimpered. "For the Lord's sake, give me a drink!"

I went back to the office, the man following with groans of pain, and I turned up the lamp.

"Don't you know me?" he gasped, dropping into a chair, and he turned his drawn face, surmounted by a shock of gray hair, to the light.

I looked at him intently. Once before had I seen eyebrows that met over the nose in an inch-broad black band, but for the life of me I could not tell where.

"I don't know you," I said, handing him the whiskey. "What can I do for you?"

He took a gulp of the spirit raw, and shivered in spite of the suffocating heat.

"I've come back," he repeated; "and I was the King of Kafiristan—me and Dravot—crowned Kings we was! In this office we settled it—you setting there and giving us the books. I am Peachey—Peachey Taliaferro Carnehan, and you've been setting here ever since—O Lord!"

I was more than a little astonished, and expressed my feelings accordingly.

"It's true," said Carnehan, with a dry cackle, nursing his feet, which were wrapped in rags. "True as gospel. Kings we were, with crowns upon our heads—me and Dravot—poor Dan—oh, poor, poor Dan, that would never take advice, not though I begged of him!"

"Take the whiskey," I said, "and take your own time. Tell me all you can recollect of everything from beginning to end. You got across the border on your camels. Dravot dressed as a mad priest and you his servant. Do you remember that?"

"I ain't mad—yet, but I shall be that way soon. Of course I remember. Keep looking at me, or maybe my words will go all to pieces. Keep looking at me in my eyes, and don't say anything."

I leaned forward and looked into his face as steadily as I could. He dropped one hand upon the table and I grasped it by the wrist. It was twisted like a bird's claw, and upon the back was a ragged, red, diamond-shaped scar.

"No, don't look there. Look at *me*," said Carnehan.

"That comes afterward, but for the Lord's sake don't distrack me! We left with that caravan, me and Dravot playing all sorts of antics to amuse the people we were with. Dravot used to make us laugh in the evenings when all the people was cooking their dinners—cooking their dinners, and . . . what did they do then? They lit little fires with sparks that went into Dravot's beard, and we all laughed—fit to die. Little red fires they was, going into Dravot's big red beard—so funny." His eyes left mine and he smiled foolishly.

"You went as far as Jagdallak with that caravan," I said, at a venture, "after you had lit those fires. To Jagdallak, where you turned off to try to get into Kafiristan."

"No, we didn't neither. What are you talking about? We turned off before Jagdallak, because we heard the roads was good. But they wasn't good enough for our two camels—mine and Dravot's. When we left the caravan, Dravot took off all his clothes and mine too, and said we would be heathen, because the Kafirs didn't allow Mohammedans to talk to them. So we dressed betwixt and between, and such a sight as Daniel Dravot I never saw yet nor expect to see again. He burned half his beard, and slung a sheep-skin over his shoulder, and shaved his head into patterns. He shaved mine, too, and made me wear outrageous things to look like a heathen. That was in a most mountaineous country, and our camels couldn't go along any more because of the mountains. They were tall and black, and coming home I saw them fight like wild goats—there are lots of goats in Kafiristan. And these mountains, they never keep still, no more than the goats. Always fighting they are, and don't let you sleep at night."

"Take some more whiskey," I said, very slowly. "What did you and Daniel Dravot do when the camels could go no further because of the rough roads that led into Kafiristan?"

"What did which do? There was a party called Peachey Taliaferro Carnehan that was with Dravot. Shall I tell you about him? He died out there in the cold. Slap from the bridge fell old Peachey, turning and twisting in the air like a penny whirligig that you can sell to the Amir. No; they was two for three ha'pence, those whirligigs, or I am much mistaken and woeful sore. And then these camels were no use, and Peachey said to Dravot—'For the Lord's sake, let's get out of this before our heads are chopped off,' and with that they killed the camels all among the mountains, not having anything in particular to eat, but first they took off the boxes with the guns and the ammunition, till two men came along driving four mules. Dravot up and dances in front of them, singing—'Sell me four mules.' Says the first man—'If you are rich enough to buy, you are rich enough to rob;' but before ever he could put his hand to his knife, Dravot breaks his neck over his knee, and the other party runs away. So Carnehan loaded the mules with the rifles that was taken off the camels, and together we starts forward into those bitter cold mountaineous parts, and never a road broader than the back of your hand."

He paused for a moment, while I asked him if he could remember the nature of the country through which he had journeyed.

"I am telling you as straight as I can, but my head isn't as good as it might be. They drove nails through it to make me hear better how Dravot died. The country was mountaineous and the mules were most contrary, and the inhabitants was dispersed and solitary. They went up and up, and down and down, and that other party, Carnehan, was imploring of Dravot not to sing and whistle so loud, for fear of bringing down the tremenjus avalanches. But Dravot says that if a King couldn't sing it wasn't worth being King, and whacked the mules over the rump, and never took no heed for ten cold days. We came to a big level valley all among the mountains, and the mules were near dead, so we killed them, not having anything in special for them or us to eat. We sat upon the boxes, and played odd and even with the cartridges that was jolted out.

"Then ten men with bows and arrows ran down that valley, chasing twenty men with bows and arrows, and the row was tremenjus. They was fair men—fairer than you or me—with yellow hair and remarkable well built. Says Dravot, unpacking the guns—'This is the beginning of the business. We'll fight for the ten men,' and with that he fires two rifles at the twenty men, and drops one of them at two hundred yards from the rock where we was sitting. The other men began to run, but Carnehan and Dravot sits on the boxes picking them off at all ranges, up and down the valley. Then we goes up to the ten men that had run across the snow too, and they fires a footy little arrow at us. Dravot he shoots above their heads and they all falls down flat. Then he walks over them and kicks them, and then he lifts them up and shakes hands all round to make them friendly like. He calls them and gives them the boxes to carry, and waves his hand for all the world as though he was King already. They takes the boxes and him across the valley and up the hill into a pine wood on the top, where there was half a dozen big stone idols. Dravot he goes to the biggest —a fellow they call Imbra—and lays a rifle and a cartridge at his feet, rubbing his nose respectful with his own nose, patting him on the head, and saluting in front of it. He turns round to the men and nods his head, and says,—'That's all right. I'm in the know, too, and all these old jim-jams are my friends.' Then he opens his mouth and points down it, and when the first man brings him food, he says —'No'; and when the second man brings him food, he says—'No'; but when one of the old priests and the boss of the village brings him food, he says— 'Yes'; very haughty, and eats it slow. That was how we came to our first village, without any trouble, just as though we had tumbled from the skies. But we tumbled from one of those damned ropebridges, you see, and—you couldn't expect a man to laugh much after that."

"Take some more whiskey and go on," I said. "That was the first village you came into. How did you get to be King?"

"I wasn't King," said Carnehan. "Dravot he was the King, and a handsome man he looked with the gold crown on his head, and all. Him and the other party stayed in that village, and every morning Dravot sat by the side of old Imbra, and the people came and worshipped. That was Dravot's order. Then a lot of men came into the valley, and Carnehand and Dravot picks them off with the rifles before they knew where they was, and runs down into the valley and up again the other side and finds another village, same as the first one, and the people all falls down flat on their faces, and Dravot says,— 'Now what is the trouble between you two villages?' and the people points to a woman, as fair as you or me, that was carried off, and Dravot takes her back to the first village and counts up the dead—eight there was. For each dead man Dravot pours a little milk on the ground and waves his arms like a whirligig, and 'That's all right,' says he. Then he and Carnehan takes the big boss of each village by the arm and walks them down into the valley, and shows them how to scratch a line with a spear right down the valley, and gives each a sod of turf from both sides of the line. Then all the people comes down and shouts like the devil and all, and Dravot says—'Go and dig the land, and be fruitful and multiply,' which they did, though they didn't understand. Then we asks the names of things in their lingo—bread and water and fire and idols and such, and Dravot leads the priest of each village up to the idol, and says he must sit there and judge the people, and if anything goes wrong he is to be shot.

"Next week they was all turning up the land in the valley as quiet as bees and much prettier, and the priests heard all the complaints and told Dravot in dumb show what it was about. 'That's just the beginning,' said Dravot. 'They think we're Gods.' He and Carnehan picks out twenty good men and shows them how to click off a rifle, and form fours, and advance in line, and they was very pleased to do so, and clever to see the hang of it. Then he takes out his pipe and his baccy-pouch and leaves one at one village and one at the other, and off we two goes to see what was to be done in the next valley. That was all rock, and there was a little village there, and Carnehan says—'Send 'em to the old valley to plant,' and takes 'em there and gives 'em some land that wasn't took before. They were a poor lot, and we blooded 'em with a kid before letting 'em into the new Kingdom. That was to impress the people, and then they settled down quiet, and Carnehan went back to Dravot, who had got into another valley, all snow and ice and most mountaineous. There was no people there and the Army got afraid, so Dravot shoots one of them, and goes on till he finds some people in a village, and the Army explains that unless the people wants to be killed they had better not shoot their little matchlocks; for they had matchlocks. We makes friends with the priest and I stays there alone with two of the Army, teaching the men how to drill; and a thundering big Chief comes across the snow with kettle-drums and horns twanging, because he heard there was a new God kicking about. Carnehan sights for the brown of the men half a mile across the snow and wings one of them. Then he sends a message to the Chief that, unless he wished to be killed, he must come and shake hands with me and leave his arms behind. The Chief comes alone first, and Carnehan shakes hands with him and whirls his arms about, same as Dravot used, and very much surprised that Chief was, and strokes my eyebrows. Then Carnehan goes alone to the Chief, and asks him in dumb show if he had an enemy he hated. 'I have,' says the Chief. So Carnehan weeds out the pick of his men, and sets the two of the Army to show them drill and at the end of two weeks the man can manoeuvre about as well as Volunteers. So he marches with the Chief to a great big plain on the top of a mountain, and the Chief's men rushes into a village and takes it; we three Martinis firing into the brown of the enemy. So we took that village too, and I gives the Chief a rag from my coat and says, 'Occupy till I come': which was scriptural. By way of a reminder, when me and the Army was eighteen hundred yards away, I drops a bullet near him standing on the snow, and all the people falls flat on their faces. Then I sends a letter to Dravot, wherever he be by land or by sea."

At the risk of throwing the creature out of train I interrupted,—"How could you write a letter up yonder?"

"The letter?—Oh!—The letter! Keep looking at me between the eyes, please. It was a string-talk letter, that we'd learned the way of it from a blind beggar in the Punjab."

I remember that there had once come to the office a blind man with a knotted twig and a piece of string which he wound round the twig according to some cipher of his own. He could, after the lapse of days or hours, repeat the sentence which he had reeled up. He had reduced the alphabet to eleven primitive sounds; and he tried to teach me his method, but I could not understand.

"I sent that letter to Dravot," said Carnehan; "and told him to come back because this Kingdom was growing too big for me to handle, and then I struck for the first valley, to see how the priests were working. They called the village we took along with the Chief, Bashkai, and the first village we took, Er-Heb. The priests at Er-Heb was doing all right, but they had a lot of pending cases about land to show me, and some men from another village had been firing arrows at night. I went out and looked for that village, and fired four rounds at it from a thousand yards. That used all the cartridges I cared to spend, and I waited for Dravot, who had been away two or three months, and I kept my people quiet.

"One morning I heard the devil's own noise of drums and horns, and Dan Dravot marches down the hill with his Army and a tail of hundreds of men, and, which was the most amazing, a great gold crown on his head. 'My Gord, Carnehan,' says Daniel, 'this is a tremenjus business, and we've got the whole country as far as it's worth having. I am the son of Alexander by Queen Semiramis, and you're my younger brother and a God too! It's the biggest thing we've ever seen. I've been marching and fighting for six weeks with the Army, and every footy little village for fifty miles has come in rejoiceful; and more than that, I've got the key of the whole show, as you'll see, and I've got a crown for you! I told 'em to make two of 'em at a place called Shu, where the gold lies in the rock like suet in mutton. Gold I've seen, and turquoise I've kicked out of the cliffs, and there's garnets in the sands of the river, and here's a chunk of amber that a man brought me. Call up all the priests and, here, take your crown.'

"One of the men opens a black hair bag, and I slips the crown on. It was too small and too heavy,

33. **tail,** a procession or long train.

but I wore it for the glory. Hammered gold it was—five pound weight, like a hoop of a barrel.

" 'Peachey,' says Dravot, 'we don't want to fight no more. The Craft's the trick, so help me!' and he brings forward that same Chief that I left at Bashkai—Billy Fish we called him afterwards, because he was so like Billy Fish that drove the big tank-engine at Mach on the Bolan in the old days. 'Shake hands with him,' says Dravot, and I shook hands and nearly dropped, for Billy Fish gave me the Grip. I said nothing, but tried him with the Fellow Craft Grip. He answers, all right, and I tried the Master's Grip, but that was a slip. 'A Fellow Craft he is!' I says to Dan. 'Does he know the word?'—'He does,' says Dan, 'and all the priests know. It's a miracle! The Chiefs and the priests can work a Fellow Craft Lodge in a way that's very like ours, and they've cut the marks on the rocks, but they don't know the Third Degree, and they've come to find out. It's Gord's Truth. I've known these long years that the Afghans knew up to the Fellow Craft Degree, but this is a miracle. A God and a Grand-Master of the Craft am I, and a Lodge in the Third Degree I will open, and we'll raise the head priests and the Chiefs of the villages.'

" 'It's against all the law,' I says, 'holding a Lodge without warrant from any one; and we never held office in any Lodge.'

" 'It's a master-stroke of policy,' says Dravot. 'It means running the country as easy as a four-wheeled bogie on a down grade. We can't stop to enquire now, or they'll turn against us. I've forty Chiefs at my heel, and passed and raised according to their merit they shall be. Billet these men on the villages, and see that we run up a Lodge of some kind. The temple of Imbra will do for the Lodge-room. The women must make aprons as you show them. I'll hold a levee of Chiefs to-night and Lodge to-morrow."

"I was fair run off my legs, but I wasn't such a fool as not to see what a pull this Craft business gave us. I showed the priests' families how to make aprons of the degrees, but for Dravot's apron the blue border and marks was made of turquoise lumps on white hide, not cloth.. We took a great square stone in the temple for the Master's chair, and little stones for the officers' chairs, and painted the black pavement with white squares, and did what we could to make things regular.

"At the levee which was held that night on the hillside with big bonfires, Dravot gives out that him and me were Gods and sons of Alexander, and Past Grand-Masters in the Craft, and was come to make Kafiristan a country where every man should eat in peace and drink in quiet, and specially obey us. Then the Chiefs come round to shake hands, and they was so hairy and white and fair it was just shaking hands with old friends. We gave them names according as they was like men we had known in India—Billy Fish, Holly Dilworth, Pikky Kergan, that was Bazar-master when I was at Mhow, and so on, and so on.

"*The* most amazing miracle was at Lodge next night. One of the old priests was watching us continuous, and I felt uneasy, for I knew we'd have to fudge the Ritual, and I didn't know what the men knew. The old priest was a stranger come in from beyond the village of Bashkai. The minute Dravot puts on the Master's apron that the girls had made for him, the priest fetches a whoop and a howl, and tries to overturn the stone that Dravot was sitting on. 'It's all up now,' I says. 'That comes of meddling with the Craft without warrant!' Dravot never winked an eye, not when ten priests took and tilted over the Grand-Master's chair—which was to say the stone of Imbra. The priest begins rubbing the bottom end of it to clear away the black dirt, and presently he shows all the other priests the Master's Mark, same as was on Dravot's apron, cut into the stone. Not even the priests of the temple of Imbra knew it was there. The old chap falls flat on his face at Dravot's feet and kisses 'em. 'Luck again,' says Dravot, across the Lodge to me, 'they say it's the missing Mark that no one could understand the why of. We're more than safe now.' Then he bangs the butt of his gun for a gavel and says: 'By virtue of the authority vested in me by my own right hand and the help of Peachey, I declare myself Grand-Master of all Freemasonry in Kafiristan in this the Mother Lodge o' the country, and King of Kafiristan equally with Peachey!' At that he puts on his crown and I puts on mine—I was doing Senior Warden—and we opens the Lodge in most ample form. It was an amazing miracle! The priests moved in Lodge through the first two degrees almost without telling, as if the memory was coming back to them. After that, Peachey and Dravot raised such as was worthy—high priests and Chiefs of far-off villages. Billy Fish was the first, and I can tell you we scared the soul out of him. It was not in any way according to Ritual, but it served our turn. We didn't raise more than ten of the biggest men, because we didn't want to make the Degree common. And they was clamouring to be raised.

" 'In another six months,' says Dravot, 'we'll hold another Communication, and see how you are working.' Then he asks them about their villages,

and learns that they was fighting one against the other, and were sick and tired of it. And when they wasn't doing that they was fighting with the Mohammedans. 'You can fight those when they come into our country,' says Dravot. 'Tell off every tenth man of your tribes for a Frontier guard, and send two hundred at a time to this valley to be drilled. Nobody is going to be shot or speared any more so long as he does well, and I know that you won't cheat me, because you're white people—sons of Alexander—and not like common, black Mohammedans. You are *my* people, and by God,' says he, running off into English at the end—"I'll make a damned fine Nation of you, or I'll die in the making!'

"I can't tell all we did for the next six months, because Dravot did a lot I couldn't see the hang of, and he learned their lingo in a way I never could. My work was to help the people plough, and now and again go out with some of the Army and see what the other villages were doing, and make 'em throw rope-bridges across the ravines which cut up the country horrid. Dravot was very kind to me, but when he walked up and down in the pine wood pulling that bloody red beard of his with both fists I knew he was thinking plans I could not advise him about, and I just waited for orders.

"But Dravot never showed me disrespect before the people. They were afraid of me and the Army, but they loved Dan. He was the best of friends with the priests and the Chiefs; but any one could come across the hills with a complaint and Dravot would hear him out fair, and call four priests together and say what was to be done. He used to call in Billy Fish from Bashkai, and Pikky Kergan from Shu, and an old Chief we called Kafuzelum—it was like enough to his real name—and hold councils with 'em when there was any fighting to be done in small villages. That was his Council of War, and the four priests of Bashkai, Shu, Khawak, and Madora was his Privy Council. Between the lot of 'em they sent me, with forty men and twenty rifles, and sixty men carrying turquoises, into the Ghorband country to buy those hand-made Martini rifles, that come out of the Amir's workshops at Kabul, from one of the Amir's Herati regiments that would have sold the very teeth out of their mouths for turquoises.

"I stayed in Ghorband a month, and gave the Governor there the pick of my baskets for hush-money, and bribed the Colonel of the regiment some more, and, between the two and the tribespeople, we got more than a hundred hand-made Martinis, a hundred good Kohat Jezails that'll throw to six hundred yards, and forty man-loads of

12. **fudge:** counterfeit or fake.

very bad ammunition for the rifles. I came back with what I had, and distributed 'em among the men that the Chiefs sent to me to drill. Dravot was too busy to attend to those things, but the old Army that we first made helped me, and we turned out five hundred men that could drill, and two hundred that knew how to hold arms pretty straight. Even those cork-screwed, hand-made guns was a miracle to them. Dravot talked big about powder-shops and factories, walking up and down in the pine wood when the winter was coming on.

" 'I won't make a Nation,' says he. 'I'll make an Empire! These men aren't niggers; they're English! Look at their eyes—look at their mouths. Look at the way they stand up. They sit on chairs in their own houses. They're the Lost Tribes, or something like it, and they've grown to be English. I'll take a census in the spring if the priests don't get frightened. There must be a fair two million of 'em in these hills. The villages are full o' little children. Two million people—two hundred and fifty thousand fighting men—and all English! They only want the rifles and a little drilling. Two hundred and fifty thousand men ready to cut in on Russia's right flank when she tries for India! Peachey, man,' he says, chewing his beard in great hunks, 'we shall be Emperors—Emperors of the Earth! Rajah Brooke will be a suckling to us. I'll treat with the Viceroy on equal terms. I'll ask him to send me twelve picked English—twelve that I know of—to help us govern a bit. There's Mackray, Sergeant-pensioner at Segowli—many's the good dinner he's given me, and his wife a pair of trousers. There's Donkin, the Warder of Tounghoo Jail; there's hundreds that I could lay my hand on if I was in India. The Viceroy shall do it for me, I'll send a man through in the spring for those men, and I'll write for a dispensation from the Grand Lodge for what I've done as Grand-Master. That—and all the Sniders that'll be thrown out when the native troops in India take up the Martini. They'll be worn smooth, but they'll do for fighting in these hills. Twelve English, a hundred thousand Sniders run through the Amir's country in driblets—I'd be content with twenty thousand in one year—and we'd be an Empire. When everything was shipshape, I'd hand over the crown—this crown I'm wearing now—to Queen Victoria on my knees, and she'd say: "Rise up, Sir Daniel Dravot." Oh, it's big! It's big, I tell you! But there's so much to be done in every place—Bashkai, Khawak, Shu, and everywhere else.'

" 'What is it?' I says. 'There are no more men coming in to be drilled this autumn. Look at those fat, black clouds. They're bringing the snow.'

" 'It isn't that,' says Daniel, putting his hand very hard on my shoulder; 'and I don't wish to say anything that's against you, for no other living man would have followed me and made me what I am as you have done. You're a first-class Commander-in-Chief, and the people know you; but—it's a big country, and somehow you can't help me, Peachey, in the way I want to be helped.'

" 'Go to your blasted priests, then!' I said, and I was sorry when I made that remark, but it did hurt me sore to find Daniel talking so superior when I'd drilled all the men, and done all he told me.

" 'Don't let's quarrel, Peachey,' says Daniel, without cursing. 'You're a King too, and the half of this Kingdom is yours; but can't you see, Peachey, we want cleverer men than us now—three or four of 'em, that we can scatter about for our Deputies. It's a hugeous great State, and I can't always tell the right thing to do, and I haven't time for all I want to do, and here's the winter coming on and all.' He put half his beard into his mouth, all red like the gold of his crown.

" 'I'm sorry, Daniel,' says I. 'I've done all I could. I've drilled the men and shown the people how to stack their oats better; and I've brought in those tinware rifles from Ghorband—but I know what you're driving at. I take it Kings always feel oppressed that way.'

" 'There's another thing too,' says Dravot, walking up and down. 'The winter's coming and these people won't be giving much trouble, and if they do we can't move about. I want a wife.'

" 'For Gord's sake leave the women alone!' I says. 'We've both got all the work we can, though I am a fool. Remember the Contrack, and keep clear o' women.'

" 'The Contrack only lasted till such time as we was Kings; and Kings we have been these months past,' says Dravot, weighing his crown in his hand. 'You go get a wife too, Peachey—a nice, strappin', plump girl that'll keep you warm in the winter. They're prettier than English girls, and we can take the pick of 'em. Boil 'em once or twice in hot water, and they'll come out like chicken and ham.'

" 'Don't tempt me!' I says. 'I will not have any dealings with a woman not till we are a dam' side more settled than we are now. I've been doing the work o' two men, and you've been doing the work o' three. Let's lie off a bit, and see if we can get some better tobacco from Afghan country and run in some good liquor; but no women.'

" 'Who's talking o' women?' says Dravot. 'I said wife—a Queen to breed a King's son for the King. A Queen out of the strongest tribe, that'll make them your blood-brothers, and that'll lie by your side and tell you all the people thinks about you and their own affairs. That's what I want.'

" 'Do you remember that Bengali woman I kept at Mogul Serai when I was a plate-layer?' says I. 'A fat lot o' good she was to me. She taught me the lingo and one or two other things; but what happened? She ran away with the Station Master's servant and half my month's pay. Then she turned up at Dadur Junction in tow of a half-caste, and had the impidence to say I was her husband—all among the drivers in the running-shed too!'

" 'We've done with that,' says Dravot, 'these women are whiter than you or me, and a Queen I will have for the winter months.'

" 'For the last time o' asking, Dan, do *not*,' I says. 'It'll only bring us harm. The Bible says that Kings ain't to waste their strength on women, 'specially when they've got a new raw Kingdom to work over.'

" 'For the last time of answering I will,' said Dravot, and he went away through the pine-trees looking like a big red devil, the sun being on his crown and beard and all.

"But getting a wife was not as easy as Dan thought. He put it before the Council, and there was no answer till Billy Fish said that he'd better ask the girls. Dravot damned them all round. 'What's wrong with me?' he shouts, standing by the idol Imbra. 'Am I a dog or am I not enough of a man for your wenches? Haven't I put the shadow of my hand over this country? Who stopped the last Afghan raid?' It was me really, but Dravot was too angry to remember. 'Who bought your guns? Who repaired the bridges? Who's the Grand-Master of the sign cut in the stone?' says he, and he thumped his hand on the block that he used to sit on in Lodge, and at Council, which opened like Lodge always. Billy Fish said nothing and no more did the others. 'Keep your hair on, Dan,' said I; 'and ask the girls. That's how it's done at Home, and these people are quite English.'

" 'The marriage of the King is a matter of State,' says Dan, in a white-hot rage, for he could feel, I hope, that he was going against his better mind. He walked out of the Council-room, and the others sat still, looking at the ground.

" 'Billy Fish,' says I to the Chief of Bashkai, 'what's the difficulty here? A straight answer to a true friend.'

" 'You know,' says Billy Fish. 'How should a man tell you who knows everything? How can daughters of men marry Gods or Devils? It's not proper.'

"I remember something like that in the Bible; but if, after seeing us as long as they had, they still believed we were Gods, it wasn't for me to undeceive them.

" 'A God can do anything,' says I. 'If the King is fond of a girl he'll not let her die.'

" 'She'll have to,' said Billy Fish. 'There are all sorts of Gods and Devils in these mountains, and now and again a girl marries one of them and isn't seen any more. Besides, you two know the Mark cut in the stone. Only the Gods know that. We thought you were men till you showed the sign of the Master.'

"I wished then that we had explained about the loss of the genuine secrets of a Master-Mason at the first go-off; but I said nothing. All that night there was a blowing of horns in a little dark temple halfway down the hill, and I heard a girl crying fit to die. One of the priests told us that she was being prepared to marry the King.

" 'I'll have no nonsense of that kind,' says Dan. 'I don't want to interfere with your customs, but I'll take my own wife.' 'The girl's a little bit afraid,' says the priest. 'She thinks she's going to die, and they are a-heartening of her up down in the temple.'

" 'Hearten her very tender, then,' says Dravot, 'or I'll hearten you with the butt of a gun so that you'll never want to be heartened again.' He licked his lips, did Dan, and stayed up walking about more than half the night, thinking of the wife that he was going to get in the morning. I wasn't by any means comfortable, for I knew that dealings with a woman in foreign parts, though you was a crowned King twenty times over, could not but be risky. I got up very early in the morning while Dravot was asleep, and I saw the priests talking together in whispers, and the Chiefs talking together too, and they looked at me out of the corners of their eyes.

" 'What is up, Fish?' I says to the Bashkai man, who was wrapped up in his furs and looking splendid to behold.

" 'I can't rightly say,' says he; 'but if you can induce the King to drop all this nonsense about marriage, you'll be doing him and me and yourself a great service.'

" 'That I do believe,' says I. 'But sure, you know, Billy, as well as me, having fought against and for us, that the King and me are nothing more than two of the finest men that God Almighty ever made. Nothing more, I do assure you.'

" 'That may be,' says Billy Fish, 'and yet I should be sorry if it was.' He sinks his head upon his great fur cloak for a minute and thinks. 'King,' says he, 'be you man or God or Devil, I'll stick by you today. I have twenty of my men with me, and they will follow me. We'll go to Bashkai until the storm blows over.'

"A little snow had fallen in the night, and every-thing was white except the greasy fat clouds that blew down and down from the north. Dravot came out with his crown on his head, swinging his arms and stamping his feet, and looking more pleased than Punch.

" 'For the last time, drop it, Dan,' says I, in a whisper. 'Billy Fish here says that there will be a row.'

" 'A row among my people!' says Dravot. 'Not much. Peachey, you're a fool not to get a wife too. Where's the girl?' says he, with a voice as loud as the braying of a jackass. 'Call up all the Chiefs and priests, and let the Emperor see if his wife suits him.'

"There was no need to call any one. They were all there leaning on their guns and spears round the clearing in the center of the pine wood. A deputa-tion of priests went down to the little temple to bring up the girl, and the horns blew up fit to wake the dead. Billy Fish saunters round and gets as close to Daniel as he could, and behind him stood his twenty men with matchlocks. Not a man of them under six feet. I was next to Dravot, and behind me was twenty men of the regular Army. Up comes the girl, and a strapping wench she was, covered with silver and turquoises but white as death, and looking back every minute at the priests.

" 'She'll do,' said Dan, looking her over. 'What's to be afraid of, lass? Come and kiss me.' He puts his arm round her. She shuts her eyes, gives a bit of a squeak, and down goes her face in the side of Dan's flaming red beard.

" 'The slut's bitten me!' says he, clapping his hand to his neck, and, sure enough, his hand was red with blood. Billy Fish and two of his matchlock-men catches hold of Dan by the shoulders and drags him into the Bashkai lot, while the priests howls in their lingo,—'Neither God nor Devil, but a man!' I was all taken aback, for a priest cut at me in front, and the Army behind began firing into the Bashkai men.

" 'God A'mighty!' says Dan. 'What is the mean-ing o' this?'

" 'Come back! Come away!' says Billy Fish. 'Ruin and Mutiny is the matter. We'll break for Bashkai if we can.'

"I tried to give some sort of orders to my men—the men o' the regular Army—but it was no use, so I fired into the brown of 'em with an English Mar-tini and drilled three beggars in a line. The valley was full of shouting, howling creatures, and every soul was shrieking, 'Not a God nor a Devil, but only a man!' The Bashkai troops stuck to Billy Fish all they were worth, but their matchlocks wasn't half as good as the Kabul breech-loaders, and four of them dropped. Dan was bellowing like a bull, for he was very wrathy; and Billy Fish had a hard job to pre-vent him running out at the crowd.

" 'We can't stand,' says Billy Fish. 'Make a run for it down the valley! The whole place is against us.' The matchlock-men ran, and we went down the valley in spite of Dravot. He was swearing horrible and crying out that he was a King. The priests rolled great stones on us, and the regular Army fired hard, and there wasn't more than six men, not counting Dan, Billy Fish, and Me, that came down to the bottom of the valley alive.

"Then they stopped firing, and the horns in the temple blew again. 'Come away—for Gord's sake come away!' says Billy Fish. 'They'll send runners out to all the villages before ever we get to Bashkai. I can protect you there, but I can't do anything now.'

"My own notion is that Dan began to go mad in his head from that hour. He stared up and down like a stuck pig. Then he was all for walking back alone and killing the priests with his bare hands; which he could have done. 'An Emperor am I,' says Daniel, 'and next year I shall be a Knight of the Queen.'

" 'All right, Dan,' says I; 'but come along now while there's time.'

" 'It's your fault,' says he, 'for not looking after your Army better. There was mutiny in the midst, and you didn't know—you damned engine-driving, plate-laying, missionary's-pass-hunting hound!' He sat upon a rock and called me every foul name he could lay tongue to. I was too heart-sick to care, though it was all his foolishness that brought the smash.

" 'I'm sorry, Dan,' says I, 'but there's no ac-counting for natives. This business is our Fifty-Seven. Maybe we'll make something out of it yet, when we've got to Bashkai.'

" 'Let's get to Bashkai, then,' says Dan, 'and, by God, when I come back here again I'll sweep the valley so there isn't a bug in a blanket left!'

"We walked all that day, and all that night Dan was stumping up and down on the snow, chewing his beard and muttering to himself.

" 'There's no hope o' getting clear,' said Billy Fish. 'The priests will have sent runners to the vil-lages to say that you are only men. Why didn't you stick on as Gods till things was more settled? I'm a dead man,' says Billy Fish, and he throws himself down on the snow and begins to pray to his Gods.

"Next morning we was in a cruel bad country—all up and down, no level ground at all, and no food either. The six Bashkai men looked at Billy Fish hungry-way as if they wanted to ask something, but they said never a word. At noon we came to the top of a flat mountain all covered with snow, and when we climbed up into it, behold, there was an Army in position waiting in the middle!

" 'The runners have been very quick,' says Billy Fish, with a little bit of a laugh. 'They are waiting for us.'

"Three or four men began to fire from the enemy's side, and a chance shot took Daniel in the calf of the leg. That brought him to his senses. He looks across the snow at the Army, and sees the rifles that we had brought into the country.

" 'We're done for,' says he. 'They are Englishmen, these people,—and it's my blasted nonsense that has brought you to this. Get back, Billy Fish, and take your men away; you've done what you could, and now cut for it. Carnehan,' says he, 'shake hands with me and go along with Billy. Maybe they won't kill you. I'll go and meet 'em alone. It's me that did it. Me, the King!'

" 'Go!' says I. 'Go to Hell, Dan. I'm with you here. Billy Fish, you clear out, and we two will meet those folk.'

" 'I'm a Chief,' says Billy Fish, quite quiet. 'I stay with you. My men can go.'

"The Bashkai fellows didn't wait for a second word but ran off; and Dan and Me and Billy Fish walked across to where the drums were drumming and the horns were horning. It was cold—awful cold. I've got that cold in the back of my head now. There's a lump of it there."

The punkah-coolies had gone to sleep. Two kerosene lamps were blazing in the office, and the perspiration poured down my face and splashed on the blotter as I leaned forward. Carnehan was shivering, and I feared that his mind might go. I wiped my face, took a fresh grip of the piteously mangled hands, and said: "What happened after that?"

The momentary shift of my eyes had broken the clear current.

"What was you pleased to say?" whined Carnehan. "They took them without any sound. Not a little whisper all along the snow, not though the King knocked down the first man that set hand on him—not though old Peachey fired his last cartridge into the brown of 'em. Not a single solitary sound did those swines make. They just closed up tight, and I tell you their furs stunk. There was a man called Billy Fish, a good friend of us all, and they cut his throat, Sir, then and there, like a pig; and the King kicks up the bloody snow and says: 'We've had a dashed fine run for our money. What's coming next?' But Peachey, Peachey Taliaferro, I tell you, Sir, in confidence as betwixt two friends, he lost his head, Sir. No, he didn't neither. The King lost his head, so he did, all along o' one of those cunning rope-bridges. Kindly let me have the papercutter, Sir. It tilted this way. They marched him a mile across that snow to a rope-bridge over a ravine with a river at the bottom. You may have seen such. They prodded him behind like an ox. 'Damn your eyes!' says the King. 'D'you suppose I can't die like a gentleman?' He turns to Peachey—Peachey that was crying like a child. 'I've brought you to this, Peachey,' says he. 'Brought you out of your happy life to be killed in Kafiristan, where you was late Commander-in-Chief of the Emperor's forces. Say you forgive me, Peachey.' 'I do,' says Peachey. 'Fully and freely do I forgive you, Dan.' 'Shake hands, Peachey,' says he. 'I'm going now.' Out he goes, looking neither right nor left, and when he was plumb in the middle of those dizzy dancing ropes. 'Cut, you beggars,' he shouts; and they cut, and old Dan fell, turning round and round and round, twenty thousand miles, for he took half an hour to fall till he struck the water, and I could see his body caught on a rock with the gold crown close beside.

"But do you know what they did to Peachey between two pine trees? They crucified him, Sir, as Peachey's hand will show. They used wooden pegs for his hands and his feet; and he didn't die. He hung there and screamed, and they took him down next day, and said it was a miracle that he wasn't dead. They took him down—poor old Peachey that hadn't done them any harm—that hadn't done them any. . . ."

He rocked to and fro and wept bitterly, wiping his eyes with the back of his scarred hands and moaning like a child for some ten minutes.

"They was cruel enough to feed him up in the temple, because they said he was more of a God than old Daniel that was a man. Then they turned him out on the snow, and told him to go home, and Peachey came home in about a year, begging along the roads quite safe; for Daniel Dravot he walked before and said: 'Come along, Peachey. It's a big thing we're doing.' The mountains they danced at night, and the mountains they tried to fall on Peachey's head, but Dan he held up his hand, and Peachey came along bent double. He never let go of Dan's hand, and he never let go of Dan's head. They gave it to him as a present in the temple, to remind him not to come again, and though the crown was pure gold, and Peachey was starving, never would Peachey sell the same. You knew Dravot. Sir!

You knew Right Worshipful Brother Dravot! Look at him now!"

He fumbled in the mass of rags round his bent waist; brought out a black horsehair bag embroidered with silver thread; and shook therefrom on to my table—the dried, withered head of Daniel Dravot! The morning sun that had long been paling the lamps struck the red beard and blind sunken eyes; struck, too, a heavy circlet of gold studded with raw turquoises, that Carnehan placed tenderly on the battered temples.

"You be'old now," said Carnehan, "the Emperor in his 'abit as he lived—the King of Kafiristan with his crown upon his head. Poor old Daniel that was a monarch once!"

I shuddered, for, in spite of defacements manifold, I recognized the head of the man of Marwar Junction. Carnehan rose to go. I attempted to stop him. He was not fit to walk abroad. "Let me take away the whiskey, and give me a little money," he gasped. "I was a King once. I'll go to the Deputy Commissioner and ask to set in the Poorhouse till I get my health. No, thank you, I can't wait till you get a carriage for me. I've urgent private affairs—in the south—at Marwar."

He shambled out of the office and departed in the direction of the Deputy Commissioner's house. That day at noon I had occasion to go down the blinding hot Mall, and I saw a crooked man crawling along the white dust of the roadside, his hat in his hand, quavering dolorously after the fashion of street-singers at Home. There was not a soul in sight, and he was out of all possible earshot of the houses. And he sang through his nose, turning his head from right to left:

> The Son of Man goes forth to war,
> 　A golden crown to gain;
> His blood-red banner streams afar—
> 　Who follows in his train?"

I waited to hear no more, but put the poor wretch into my carriage and drove him off to the nearest missionary for eventual transfer to the Asylum. He repeated the hymn twice while he was with me whom he did not in the least recognize, and I left him singing it to the missionary.

Two days later I enquired after his welfare of the Superintendent of the Asylum.

"He was admitted suffering from sun-stroke. He died early yesterday morning," said the Superintendent. "Is it true that he was half an hour bareheaded in the sun at midday?"

"Yes," said I, "but do you happen to know if he had anything upon him by any chance when he died?"

"Not to my knowledge," said the Superintendent. And there the matter rests.

William Butler Yeats
1865–1939

The family of William Butler Yeats was a distinguished one: his father was a well-known artist; his brother became a landscape-painter; one of his sisters established the Cuala Press, which presented many of the new writers of the Irish revival. Yeats was born June 13, 1865, at Sandymount, near Dublin, Ireland. When he was still a boy, his parents moved to London, and the child was sent to Godolphin School, but much of his youth was spent in the wilds of County Sligo. At fifteen, he returned to Ireland to attend the Erasmus Smith School in Dublin, and his vacations found him in the countryside sitting by turf fires and listening to folk tales.

At twenty-one Yeats published his first book, *Mosada: A Poem*, 1886. Immediately after its publication he went to London, became a contributor to the *Yellow Book*, formed the group known as the Rhymers' Club, and identified himself with those who made the 1890's a movement of elegantly mannered affectation. But Yeats's native integrity prevented him from integrating himself with the cult of the bizarre. Although he traveled abroad, he was rooted in Ireland. He helped found the Irish literary theater, dreamed of a national poetry that would be English in words but Irish in spirit, persuaded J. M. Synge to leave Paris and write for the Abbey Theatre in Dublin, and continued to direct as well as to inspire the multiple activities of the Irish Renaissance. The experimental poet grew into the national patriot. He was made Senator and served the Free State from 1922 to 1928. His influence grew in every field: as folklorist, playwright, champion of new tendencies (he was one of the first to hail such "strange" American phenomena as Vachel Lindsay and Ezra Pound), as essayist, and, perhaps most of all, as seer. The Nobel Prize for literature was awarded to him in 1924. The last years of his life were spent on the French and Italian Riviera. He died, after a brief illness, at Roquebrune, near Nice, January 28, 1939, and his body was taken to his native Ireland.

Although his essays and autobiography show him as an unusually intuitive spirit and a critic of the first order, it is as a poet that Yeats commands the reader's chief attention. His was a passion not only for poetry but for perfection. He was never fully satisfied with his work; it is said that he rewrote even more than he wrote. In continual attempts to refine and clarify his communication, he published many different editions of his *Collected Poems*, each edition completely superseding the previous volume.

The poetry of Yeats is of two sorts: the early verse, which charms because of its music, and the later poetry, which arrests because of its masterful imagery and metaphysical strength. *The Wanderings of Oisin*, 1889, *The Wind among the Reeds*, 1899, and *In the Seven Woods*, 1903, are extraordinary in their mixture of folk tone and personal fancy, of a music which is vague and a mythology which is both abstract and allusive. Sacrificing strength of thought to delicacy of phrase, Yeats first dealt with a small set of symbols, symbols that were colorful but which tended to become rhetorical and facile.

Responsibilities, 1914, *The Wild Swans at Coole*, 1917, and *Later Poems*, 1922, disclose a sudden change. The tone is sharper; the phrasing is direct rather than decorative. Even more significant is the poet's attitude to his subject matter. Yeats acknowledges this change implicitly in the poem wherein he declares that originally he had made his songs wear a romantic disguise, a coat

> "Covered with embroideries
> Out of old mythologies."

He says it explicitly in a dedication to his *Essays*, 1924: "My friends and I loved symbols, popular beliefs, and old scraps of verse that made Ireland romantic to herself; but the new Ireland, overwhelmed by responsibility, begins to long for psychological truth."

It is "psychological truth" which Yeats probed for, discovered, and revealed in his later writings. The artfully constructed fairylands and the elaborately allegorical gods of his youth are discarded for real people, immediate events, and the stripped facts of actual life. Pretty fancy is exchanged for mature imagination; the leaping fire is taught to burn slowly, but no less fiercely. "It is only when the in-

tellect has wrought the whole of life to drama, to crisis, that we may live for contemplation, yet keep our intensity," he says. In one of his most penetrating essays, "Poetry and Tradition," he amplifies the theme: "The raging fire and the destructive sword are portions of eternity too great for the eye of man, wrote Blake: and it is only before such things, before a love like that of Tristan and Iseult, before noble or ennobled death, that the free mind permits itself aught but brief sorrow. . . . Because there is submission in pure sorrow, we should sorrow alone over what is greater than ourselves."

"I am content to follow to its source every event in action or in thought," Yeats wrote in "A Dialogue of Self and Soul," and he concluded the poem with a Blake-like divination:

> "When such as I cast out remorse
> So great a sweetness flows into the breast
> We must laugh and we must sing,
> We are blest by everything,
> Everything we look upon is blest."

As Yeats grew old his intellectual power increased. *The Winding Stair*, 1932, *The King of the Great Clock Tower*, 1935, published in Yeats's seventieth year, and the posthumous *Last Poems and Plays*, 1940, contain magnificent expressions of "pure mind" or a clarification which is the completion of the partial mind. They also contain the utterances of a man not afraid to taste unpalatable truths and even less afraid to say that they are bitter. The later poems are weighted with a sense of isolation, with the disillusionments of the age—and of old age—with defeated dreams, with the decay of beauty (as reflected in Yeats's constant evocation of Maud Gonne, the beautiful Irish actress and revolutionary), with the death of friends and the degeneration of the contemporary world. Yet, though Yeats voiced his horror and even disgust in the later poems and plays, he did not despair. The ladder of happy fantasy was gone, but, even at the end, he was willing to begin the long ascent again.

> "I must lie down where all the ladders start,
> In the foul rag-and-bone shop of the heart."

Yeats separated his rational and intuitive self just as, in life, he separated the spiritual (and impersonal) poet from the violent (and personal) radicalism of Maud Gonne. The mysticism is not, however, an "escape"; it seems to be an extension of Yeats's theory that "nature, races, and individual men are unified by an image," that when men desert one myth they will substitute another. This is cumulatively proved by the verse. If Yeats's symbolism is complicated and questionable, the directness of his best poetry, the burning vision, "simple as flame," is undeniable.

THE LAKE ISLE OF INNISFREE [1]

I will arise and go now, and go to Innisfree,
And a small cabin build there, of clay and wattles
  made:
Nine bean-rows will I have there, a hive for the
  honey-bee,
And live alone in the bee-loud glade.

And I shall have some peace there, for peace comes
  dropping slow,
Dropping from the veils of the morning to where the
  cricket sings;
There midnight's all a glimmer, and noon a purple
  glow,
And evening full of the linnet's wings.

I will arise and go now, for always night and day
I hear lake water lapping with low sounds by the
  shore;   10
While I stand on the roadway, or on the pavements
  grey,
I hear it in the deep heart's core.

THE SONG OF WANDERING
AENGUS [1]

I went out to the hazel wood,
Because a fire was in my head,
And cut and peeled a hazel wand,
And hooked a berry to a thread;
And when white moths were on the wing,
And moth-like stars were flickering out,
I dropped the berry in a stream
And caught a little silver trout.

When I had laid it on the floor
I went to blow the fire aflame,   10
But something rustled on the floor,
And some one called me by my name:
It had become a glimmering girl
With apple blossoms in her hair
Who called me by my name and ran
And faded through the brightening air.

Though I am old with wandering
Through hollow lands and hilly lands,
I will find out where she has gone,
And kiss her lips and take her hands;   20
And walk among long dappled grass,
And pluck till time and times are done,
The silver apples of the moon,
The golden apples of the sun.

THE LOVER TELLS OF THE ROSE
IN HIS HEART [1]

All things uncomely and broken, all things worn out
  and old,
The cry of a child by the roadway, the creak of a
  lumbering cart,
The heavy steps of the ploughman, splashing the
  wintry mould,
Are wronging your image that blossoms a rose in
  the deeps of my heart.

The wrong of unshapely things is a wrong too great
  to be told;
I hunger to build them anew and sit on a green
  knoll apart,
With the earth and the sky and the water, re-made,
  like a casket of gold
For my dreams of your image that blossoms a rose
  in the deeps of my heart.

WHEN YOU ARE OLD [1]

When you are old and grey and full of sleep,
And nodding by the fire, take down this book,
And slowly read, and dream of the soft look
Your eyes had once, and of their shadows deep;

How many loved your moments of glad grace,
And loved your beauty with love false or true;
But one man loved the pilgrim soul in you,
And loved the sorrows of your changing face.

And bending down beside the glowing bars,
Murmur, a little sadly, how Love fled   10
And paced upon the mountains overhead
And hid his face amid a crowd of stars.

THE ROSE OF THE WORLD[1]

Who dreamed that beauty passes like a dream?
For these red lips, with all their mournful pride,
Mournful that no new wonder may betide,
Troy passed away in one high funeral gleam,
And Usna's children died.

We and the labouring world are passing by:
Amid men's souls, that waver and give place
Like the pale waters in their wintry race,
Under the passing stars, frame of the sky,
Lives on this lonely face.   10

Bow down, archangels, in your dim abode:
Before you were, or any hearts to beat,
Weary and kind one lingered by His seat;
He made the world to be a grassy road
Before her wandering feet.

DOWN BY THE SALLEY GARDENS[1]

Down by the salley gardens my love and I did meet;
She passed the salley gardens with little snow-white
    feet.
She bid me take love easy, as the leaves grow on the
    tree;
But I, being young and foolish, with her would not
    agree.

In a field by the river my love and I did stand,
And on my leaning shoulder she laid her snow-white
    hand.
She bid me take life easy, as the grass grows on the
    weirs;
But I was young and foolish, and now am full of
    tears.

Down by the Salley Gardens. **Salley,** willow. "This," Yeats
wrote in a footnote in one of the early editions (titled "An
Old Song Resung") "is an extension of three lines sung to me
by an old woman of Ballisodare."

LEDA AND THE SWAN[1]

In Greek mythology Leda while bathing was seduced
by Zeus, the god having disguised himself as a swan.

A sudden blow: the great wings beating still
Above the staggering girl, her thighs caressed
By the dark webs, her nape caught in his bill,
He holds her helpless breast upon his breast.

How can those terrified vague fingers push
The feathered glory from her loosening thighs?
And how can body, laid in that white rush,
But feel the strange heart beating where it lies?

A shudder in the loins engenders there
The broken wall, the burning roof and tower   10
And Agamemnon dead.
                        Being so caught up,
So mastered by the brute blood of the air,
Did she put on his knowledge with his power
Before the indifferent beak could let her drop?

AN IRISH AIRMAN FORESEES
HIS DEATH [1]

I know that I shall meet my fate
Somewhere among the clouds above;
Those that I fight I do not hate,
Those that I guard I do not love;
My country is Kiltartan Cross,
My countrymen Kiltartan's poor,
No likely end could bring them loss
Or leave them happier than before.
Nor law, nor duty bade me fight,
Nor public men, nor cheering crowds,   10
A lonely impulse of delight
Drove to this tumult in the clouds;
I balanced all, brought all to mind,
The years to come seemed waste of breath,
A waste of breath the years behind
In balance with this life, this death.

H. G. Wells
1866–

The most prolific of the English authors of our time, H(erbert) G(eorge) Wells, was born at Bromley, Kent, on September 21, 1866. His father was an unsuccessful shopkeeper, "a better cricketer than tradesman"; his mother was a worried housekeeper who had once been a lady's maid and whose chief ambition was to give her sons a "respectable" education. (Wells's early environment is reflected in the semiautobiographical *Kipps, Tono-Bungay,* and *The New Machiavelli.*) As a boy he read voraciously but haphazardly; he devoured Dickens and Washington Irving, but not Shakespeare; the novels of Scott bored him, but he learned *Marmion* and *The Lady of the Lake* by heart. At thirteen he became a draper's assistant, and remained in that capacity, working thirteen hours a day, for almost four years. At sixteen he became pupil and assistant master at a school in Midhurst; at seventeen, "a Cockney Adam out of a Sussex Eden," he entered the Royal College of Science, from which he graduated with honors at twenty-one.

At twenty-two he was teaching science, attempting journalism, and longing to be a writer. An account dated 1888 shows that he had burnt two novels, destroyed reams of poetry ("much of it comic"), sent away some humorous prose which never was returned, and sold exactly one short story. "Net profit One Pound. Some day I shall succeed, I really believe," he wrote, "but it is a weary game." At thirty, however, he published two novels and a collection of short stories: *The Time Machine, The Wonderful Visit,* and *The Stolen Bacillus and Other Incidents,* 1895. These publications were "scientific romances," fantasies with a scientific basis in the vein which many critics consider his best. The realistic and semiautobiographical novels, forerunners of a tendency in fiction which drew largely upon experience and actual life, followed later. Of these *Kipps: The Story of a Simple Soul,* 1905; *Tono-Bungay,* 1909; *The New Machiavelli,* 1911; *Mr. Britling Sees It Through,* 1916; and *The World of William Clissold,* 1926, were the most applauded.

Wells's sociological novels are less distinguished; it is difficult to draw the line between his pedagogical fiction and the political, philosophical, and ideological studies which have consumed most of his "later period." His admirers have regretted Wells's growing passion for prophecy. They mourn the loss of the author of remarkable short tales, and they deprecate his preoccupation with the World State, his speculations on the work and wealth of mankind, his countless discoveries of the future, and the prognostication of *The Shape of Things to Come.* As Wells grew older, he seemed less interested in the play of characters and the clash of circumstance than in propounding questions for which he alone had the answers. Yet, although the reviewers often treated Wells as an aging and repetitive oracle, *The Fate of Man,* 1939, published when Wells was seventy-three, proved to be one of the most comprehensive and forceful examinations of the democratic crisis, and this was followed by *The New World Order,* 1940, which was a sustained and probing examination, and which brought the number of his works to well over one hundred and thirty. It was not merely a facetious figure of speech that prompted references to him as "the inexhaustible Wells."

Perhaps the most illuminating summary of H. G. Wells has been written by the man himself. An article in the *Listener,* the weekly organ of the British Broadcasting Corporation, was reprinted in the *Living Age,* October, 1936, under the title "The Late H. G. Wells." Wells was very much alive at the time, but this is what he whimsically hoped would be said of him when the time came for his obituary. The opening paragraphs ran:

"The name of Mr. H. G. Wells, who died yesterday afternoon of heart failure in the Paddington Infirmary at the age of 97, will have few associations for the younger generation. But those listeners whose adult memories stretch back to the opening decades of the present century and who shared the miscellaneous reading of the period, may recall a number of titles of books he wrote and may even find in some odd attic an actual volume or so of his works. He was, indeed, one of the most prolific of the 'literary hacks' of that time. He not only wrote books himself but critical studies and even short volumes were written about him, and the number of entries under his name in the catalogue of that mighty mausoleum, the Reading Room (long since deserted by any readers) of the British Museum in London, amount to nearly six hundred.

"An interesting study of Wells was broadcast five years ago from the London Centre by Miss Phelps Lemon, and little has arisen since to modify her verdict. She describes him as something between a portent and a pioneer. He wrote a very frank and explicit autobiography which was published in 1934 and he added a supplement which, though it has never been printed, is accessible to the curious in the manuscript collection in the British Museum. From these documents we learn that his origins were common, and socially if not chronologically he reached back to the eighteenth century and the ascendancy of the British 'landed gentry.'

"His father was a gardener who became a small shopkeeper and professional cricketer, and his mother was the daughter of an old world innkeeper, and before her marriage, a 'lady's maid.' The most interesting thing about Wells was his refusal to accept the social inferiority to which he seemed to have been born, and the tenacity with which he insisted upon his rôle as the free citizen of a new world that was arising out of the debacle of the warring national states of the nineteenth and early twentieth centuries. He had a flair for what is coming. He was a liberal democrat in that he claimed an unlimited right to think, criticize, discuss and suggest, and he was a socialist in his antagonism to personal, racial or national monopolization."

Various collections and "omnibus" volumes of Wells's short stories and novels have appeared. One sees his ideas at work most vividly in *The Outline of History*, 1920; *The Short Stories of H. G. Wells*, 1927; and *The Scientific Romances of H. G. Wells*, published in America as *Seven Famous Novels*, 1934. The best full-length study is Geoffrey West's *H. G. Wells*, 1930, modestly subtitled *A Sketch for a Portrait*.

THE COUNTRY OF THE BLIND [1]

There are two versions of this story. The first dates from 1904; the second, which is the revised version printed here, was written a third of a century later. In an introduction to the second version Wells wrote that he "gave a new twist" to the central theme. "The essential idea," he concluded, "that a man with eyes falls into a valley of blind people and proves the falsity of the ancient saying that in the Country of the Blind the One-eyed Man is King, remains the same throughout, but the value attached to vision changes profoundly. It has been changed because there has been a change in the atmosphere of life about us. In 1904 the stress is upon the spiritual isolation

[1] From the revised edition, published by the Golden Cockerel Press. Reprinted by permission of Mr. H. G. Wells.

of those who see more keenly than their fellows and the tragedy of their incommunicable appreciation of life. The visionary dies, a worthless outcast, finding no other escape from his gift but death, and the blind world goes on, invincibly self-satisfied and secure. But in the later story vision becomes something altogether more tragic; it is no longer a story of disregarded loveliness and release; the visionary sees destruction sweeping down upon the whole blind world he has come to endure and even to love; he sees it plain, and he can do nothing to save it from its fate."

THREE hundred miles and more from Chimborazo, one hundred from the snows of Cotopaxi, in the wildest wastes of Ecuador's Andes, where the frost-and-sun-rotted rocks rise in vast pinnacles and cliffs above the snows, there was once a mysterious mountain valley, called the Country of the Blind. It was a legendary land, and until quite recently people doubted if it was anything more than a legend. Long years ago, ran the story, that valley lay so far open to the world that men, daring the incessant avalanches, might clamber at last through frightful gorges and over an icy pass into its equable meadows; and thither indeed men went and settled, a family or so of Peruvian half-breeds fleeing from the lust and tyranny of an evil Spanish ruler. Then came the stupendous outbreak of Mindobamba, when it was night in Quito for seventeen days, and the water was boiling at Yaguachi and all the fish floating dying even as far as Guayaquil; everywhere along the Pacific slopes there were landslips and swift thawings and sudden floods, and one whole side of the old Arauca crest slipped and came down in thunder, and cut off this Country of the Blind, as it seemed, for ever from the exploring feet of men.

But, said the story, one of these early settlers had chanced to be on the hither side of the gorge when the world had so terribly shaken itself, and perforce he had to forget his wife and his child and all the friends and possessions he declared he had left up there, and begin life again in the lower world.

He had a special reason to account for his return from that fastness, into which he had first been carried lashed to a llama, beside a vast bale of gear, when he was a child. The valley, he said, had in it all that the heart of man could desire—sweet water, pasture, an even climate, slopes of rich brown soil with tangles of a shrub that bore an excellent fruit, and on one side great hanging pine forests that held the avalanches high. Far overhead, a semi-circle of ice-capped precipices of grey-green rock brooded over that glowing garden; but the glacier stream flowed away by the farther slopes and only very rarely did an ice-fall reach the lower levels. In this valley it neither rained nor snowed, but the abundant springs gave a rich green pasture, that patient irrigation was spreading over all the valley space. The surplus water gathered at last in a little lake beneath the cirque and vanished with a roar into an unfathomable cavern. The settlers, he said, were doing very well indeed there. Their beasts did well and multiplied, and only one thing marred their happiness. Yet it was enough to mar it greatly; some sinister quality hidden in that sweet and bracing air. A strange disease had come upon them, and had made all the children born to them there—and indeed several older children also—blind. So that the whole valley seemed likely to become a valley of blind men.

It was, he said, to seek some charm or antidote against this plague of blindness that with infinite fatigue, danger and difficulty he had returned down the gorge. In those days, in such cases, men did not think of germs and infections but of sins; and it seemed to him that the reason of this affliction must lie in the negligence of these priestless immigrants to set up a shrine so soon as they entered the valley. He wanted a shrine—a handsome, cheap, effectual shrine—to be set up in the valley; he wanted relics and suchlike potent things of faith, blessed objects and mysterious medals and prayers. In his wallet he had a bar of native silver for which he would not account; he insisted there was none in the valley, with something of the insistence of an inexpert liar. The settlers had all clubbed their money and ornaments together, having little need for such treasure up there, he said, to buy them holy help against their ill. I figure this young mountaineer, sunburnt, gaunt and anxious, hat-brim clutched feverishly, a man all unused to the ways of the lower world, telling this story to some keen-eyed, attentive priest before the great convulsion; I can picture him presently seeking to return with pious and infallible remedies against that trouble, and the infinite dismay with which he must have faced the tumbled and still monstrously crumbling vastness where the gorge had once come out. But the rest of his tale of mischances is lost to me, save that I know he died of punishment in the mines. His offence I do not know.

But the idea of a valley of blind folk had just that appeal to the imagination that a legend requires if it is to live. It stimulates fantasy. It invents its own detail.

And recently this story has been most remarkably confirmed. We know now the whole history of this Country of the Blind from that beginning to its recent and tragic end.

We know now that amidst the little population of that now isolated and forgotten valley the contagion ran its course. Even the older children became groping and purblind, and the young saw but dimly, and the children that were born to them never saw at all. But life was very easy in that snow-rimmed basin, lost to all the world, with neither thorns nor briers, with food upon the bushes in its season, with no evil insects nor any beasts save the gentle breed of llamas they had lugged and thrust and followed up the beds of the shrunken rivers in the gorges by which they had come. The first generation had become purblind so gradually that they scarcely noted their loss. They guided the sightless youngsters who followed them hither and thither until they knew the whole valley marvellously, and when at last sight died out altogether among them the race lived on. They had even time to adapt themselves to the blind control of fire, which they made carefully in stoves of stone. They were a simple strain of people at the first, unlettered, only slightly touched with Spanish civilisation, but with something of a tradition of the arts of old Peru and its lost philosophy. Generation followed generation. They forgot many things; they devised many things. Their tradition of the greater world they came from became mythical in colour and uncertain. In all things save sight they were strong and able; and presently the chances of birth and heredity produced one who had an original mind and who could talk and persuade among them, and then afterwards another. These two passed, leaving their effects, and the little community grew in numbers and understanding, and met and settled all the social and economic problems that arose, sensibly and peaceably. There came a time when a child was born who was fifteen generations from that ancestor who went out of the valley with a bar of silver to seek God's aid, and who never returned. Then it chanced that a man came into this community from the outer world and troubled their minds very greatly. He lived with them for many months, and escaped very narrowly from their final disaster.

He was a mountaineer from the country near Quito, a man who had been down to the sea and had seen the world, and he was taken on by a party of Englishmen under Sir Charles Pointer, who had come out of Ecuador to climb mountains, to replace one of their three Swiss guides who had fallen ill. He climbed here and he climbed there, and then came the attempt on Parascotopetl, the "rotten" mountain, the Matterhorn of the Andes, in which he was lost to the outer world so that he was given up for dead.

Everyone who knew anything of the mountain-craft had warned the little expedition against the treachery of the rocks in this range, but apparently it was not a rock-fall that caught this man Nunez but an exceptional snow-cornice. The party had worked its difficult and almost vertical way up to the very foot of the last and greatest precipice, and had already built itself a night shelter upon a little shelf of rock amidst the snow, when the accident occurred. Suddenly they found that Nunez had disappeared, without a sound. They shouted, and there was no reply; they shouted and whistled, they made a cramped search for him, but their range of movement was very limited. There was no moon, and their electric torches had only a limited range.

As the morning broke they saw the traces of his fall. It seems impossible he could have uttered a cry. The depths had snatched him down. He had slipped eastward towards the unknown side of the mountain; far below he had struck a steep slope of snow, and ploughed his way down it in the midst of a snow avalanche. His track went straight to the edge of a frightful precipice, and beyond that everything was hidden. Far, far below, and hazy with distance, they could see trees rising out of a narrow, shut-in valley—the lost Country of the Blind. But they did not know it was the lost Country of the Blind, nor distinguish it in any way from any other narrow streak of sheltered upland valley. Unnerved by this disaster, they abandoned their attempt in the afternoon, and Pointer, who was financing the attempt, was called away to urgent private business before he could make another attack. To this day Parascotopetl lists an unconquered crest, and Pointer's shelter crumbles unvisited somewhere amidst the snows.

And this man who fell survived.

At the end of the slope he fell a thousand feet, and came down in the midst of a cloud of snow upon a snow slope even steeper than the one above. Down this he was whirled, stunned and insensible, but miraculously without a bone broken in his body; and then the gradients diminished, and at last he rolled out and lay still, buried amidst a softening heap of the white masses that had accompanied him and saved him. He came to himself with a dim fancy that he was ill in bed; then realised his position, worked himself loose and, after a rest or so, out until he saw the stars. He rested flat upon his chest for a space, wondering where he was and what had happened to him. He explored his limbs, they ached exceedingly but they were unbroken. He discovered that several of his buttons were gone and his coat turned over his head. His knife had gone from his pocket and his cap was lost, though it had been tied under his chin. His face was grazed; he was scratched and contused all over. He recalled that he had been looking for loose stones to raise a piece of the shelter wall. His ice-axe had disappeared.

He looked up to see, exaggerated by the ghastly light of the rising moon, the tremendous flight he had taken. For a while he lay, gazing blankly at that vast pale cliff towering above, rising moment by moment out of a subsiding tide of darkness. Since the light struck it first above it seemed to be streaming upward out of nothing. Its phantasmal mysterious beauty held him for space, and then he was seized with a paroxysm of sobbing laughter. . . .

After a great interval of time he became aware that he was near the lower edge of the snow. Below, down what was now a moonlit and practicable slope, he saw the dark and broken appearance of rock-strewn turf. He struggled to his feet, aching in every limb, got down painfully from the heaped loose snow about him, went downward until he was on the turf, and there dropped rather than lay beside a boulder, drank deep from the flask in his inner pocket, and instantly fell asleep. . . .

He was awakened by the singing of birds in trees far below.

He sat up stiffly and perceived he was on a little alp at the foot of a great precipice, grooved by the gulley down which he and his snow had come. Over against him another wall of jagged rock reared itself against the sky. The gorge between these precipices ran east and west and was full of the morning sunlight, which lit to the westward the mass of fallen mountain that had blocked the way to the world. Below him it seemed there was a precipice equally steep, but beyond the snow in the gulley he found a chimney dripping with snow-water down which a desperate man might venture. He found it easier than it looked, and came at last to another desolate alp, and then after a rock climb of no particular difficulty to a steep slope of trees. He took his bearings and turned his face eastward, for he saw it opened out above upon green meadows, among which he now glimpsed quite distinctly a cluster of stone huts of unfamiliar fashion. At times his progress was like clambering along the face of a wall, and after a time the rays of the rising sun were intercepted by a vast bastion, the voices of the singing birds died away, and the air grew cold and dark about him. But the distant valley with its houses seemed all the brighter for that. He presently came to talus, and among the rocks he noted—for he was an observant man—an unfamiliar fern that seemed to clutch out of the crevices with intense green hands. He picked a frond or so and gnawed its stalk and found it helpful. There were bushes but the fruit had not formed upon them.

About midday he emerged from the shadow of the great bluff into the sunlight again. And now he was only a few hundred yards from the valley meadows. He was weary and very stiff; he sat down in the shadow of a rock, filled up his nearly empty flask with water from a spring, drank it down, and rested for a time before he went on towards the houses.

They were very strange to his eyes, and indeed 10 the whole aspect of that valley became, as he regarded it, queerer and more unfamiliar. The greater part of its surface was lush green meadow, starred with many beautiful flowers, irrigated with extraordinary care, and bearing evidence of systematic cropping piece by piece. High up and ringing the valley about was a wall, and what appeared to be a circumferential water-channel, which received the runlets from the snows above and from which little trickles of water had been led to feed the meadows. 20 On the higher slopes above this wall, flocks of llamas cropped the scanty herbage amidst the tangled shrubs. Sheds, apparently shelters or feeding-places for the llamas, stood against the boundary wall here and there. The irrigation streams ran together into a main channel down the centre of the valley, that debouched into a little lake below a semi-circle of precipices, and this central canal was enclosed on either side by a wall breast-high. This wall gave a singularly urban quality to this secluded place, a 30 quality that was greatly enhanced by the fact that a number of paths paved with green, grey, black and white stones, and each with a curious little kerb at the side, ran hither and thither in an orderly manner. The houses of the central village were quite unlike the casual and higgledy-piggledy agglomeration of the mountain villages he knew; they stood in a continuous row on either side of a central street of astonishing cleanness; here and there their parti-coloured façade was pierced by a door, and not a 40 solitary window broke their even frontage. They were parti-coloured with extraordinary irregularity; smeared with a sort of plaster that was sometimes grey, sometimes drab, sometimes slate-coloured or dark-brown; and it was the sight of this wild plastering first brought the word "blind" into the thoughts of the explorer. "The good man who did that," he thought, "must have been as blind as a bat."

He descended a steep place and so came to the 50 wall and channel that ran about the valley, near where the latter spouted out its surplus contents into the lake. He could see now a number of men and women resting on piled heaps of grass, as if

taking a siesta; in the remoter part of the meadow, and nearer the village a number of recumbent children; and then nearer at hand three men carrying pails on yokes along a little path that ran from the encircling wall towards the houses. These latter were clad in garments of llama cloth and boots and belts of leather, and they wore caps of cloth with back and ear flaps. They followed one another in single file, walking slowly and yawning as they walked, like men who have been up all night. There was something so reassuringly prosperous and respectable in their bearing that after a moment's hesitation Nunez stood forward as conspicuously as possible upon his rock, and gave vent to a mighty shout that evoked a thousand echoes round and about the valley.

The three men stopped and moved their heads as if they were looking about them. They turned their faces this way and that, and Nunez gesticulated with freedom. But they did not appear to see him for all his gestures, and after a time, directing themselves towards the mountain far away to the right, they shouted as if in answer. Nunez bawled again and then once more, and as he gestured ineffectually the word "blind" came once more to the front of his thought. "The fools must be blind," he said.

When at last, after much shouting and irritation, Nunez crossed the stream by a little bridge, came through a gate in the wall, and approached them, he realised that they were indeed blind. He knew already that this was the Country of the Blind of which the legends told. Conviction had sprung upon him, and a sense of great and rather enviable adventure. The three stood side by side, not looking at him, but with their ears directed towards him, judging him by his unfamiliar steps. They stood close together like men a little afraid, and he could see their eyelids closed and shrunken, as if the very balls beneath them had shrunk away. There was an expression near awe on their faces.

"A man," one said, in hardly recognisable Spanish—"a man it is—a man or a beast that walks like a man—coming down from the rocks."

But Nunez advanced with the confident steps of a youth who enters upon life. All the old stories of the lost valley and the Country of the Blind had come back to his mind, and through his thoughts ran this old proverb, as if it were a refrain—

"In the Country of the Blind the One-Eyed Man is King."

"In the Country of the Blind the One-Eyed Man is King."

And very civilly he gave them greeting. He talked to them and used his eyes.

"Where does he come from, brother Pedro?" asked one.

"Down out of the rocks."

"Over the mountains I come," said Nunez, "out of the country beyond there—where men can see. From near Bogota, where there are a hundred thousands of people, and where the city passes out of sight."

"Sight?" muttered Pedro. "Sight?"

"He comes," said the second blind man, "out of the rocks."

The cloth of their coats Nunez saw was curiously fashioned, each with a different sort of stitching.

They startled him by a simultaneous movement towards him, each with a hand outstretched. He stepped back from the advance of these spread fingers.

"Come hither," said the third blind man, following his motion and clutching him neatly.

And they held Nunez and felt him over, saying no word further until they had done so.

"Carefully," he cried, when a finger was poked in his eye, and he realised that they thought that organ, with its fluttering lids, a queer thing in him. They felt over it again.

"A strange creature, Correa," said the one called Pedro. "Feel the coarseness of his hair. Like a llama's hair."

"Rough he is as the rocks that begot him," said Correa, investigating Nunez's unshaven chin with a soft and slightly moist hand. "Perhaps he will grow finer." Nunez struggled a little under their examination, but they gripped him firm.

"Carefully," he said again.

"He speaks," said the third man. "Certainly he is a man."

"Ugh!" said Pedro, at the roughness of his coat.

"And you have come into the world?" asked Pedro.

"*Out* of the world. Over mountains and glaciers; right over above there, half-way to the sun. Out of the great big world that goes down from here, twelve days' journey to the sea."

They scarcely seemed to heed him. "The fathers have told us men may be made by the forces of Nature," said Correa. "It is the warmth of things and moisture, and rottenness—rottenness."

"Let us lead him to the elders," said Pedro.

"Shout first," said Correa, "lest the children be afraid. This is a marvellous occasion."

So they shouted, and Pedro went first and took Nunez by the hand to lead him to the houses.

He drew his hand away. "I can see," he said.

"See?" said Correa.

"Yes, see," said Nunez, turning towards him, and stumbled against Pedro's pail.

"His senses are still imperfect," said the third blind man. "He stumbles, and talks unmeaning words. Lead him by the hand."

"As you will," said Nunez, and was led along smiling.

It seemed they knew nothing of sight.

Well, all in good time, he would teach them.

He heard people shouting, and saw a number of figures gathered together in the middle roadway of the village.

He found it taxed his nerve and patience more than he had anticipated, that first encounter with the population of the Country of the Blind. The place seemed larger as he drew near to it, and the smeared plasterings queerer, and a crowd of children and men and women (the women and girls, he was pleased to note, had some of them quite sweet faces, for all that their eyes were shut and sunken) came about him, and mobbed him, holding on to him, touching him with soft, sensitive hands, smelling at him, and listening for every word he spoke. Some of the maidens and children, however, kept aloof as if afraid, and indeed his voice seemed coarse and rude beside their softer notes. His three guides kept close to him with an effect of proprietorship, and said again and again, "A wild man out of the rocks."

"Bogota," he said. "Bogota. Over the mountain crests."

"A wild man—using wild words," said Pedro. "Did you hear that—*Bogota?* His mind is hardly formed yet. He has only the beginnings of speech."

A little boy nipped his head. "Bogota!" he said mockingly.

"Ay! A city to your village. I come from the great world—where men have eyes and see."

"His name's Bogota," they said.

"He stumbled," said Correa, "stumbled twice as we came hither."

"Bring him to the elders."

And they thrust him suddenly through a doorway into a room as black as pitch, save at the end there faintly glowed a fire. The crowd closed in behind him and shut out all but the faintest glimmer of day, and before he could arrest himself he had fallen headlong over the feet of a seated man. His arm, outflung, struck the face of someone else as he went down; he felt the soft impact of features and heard a cry of anger, and for a moment he struggled against a number of hands that clutched him. It was a one-sided fight. An inkling of the situation came to him, and he lay quiet.

"I fell down," he said, "I couldn't see in this pitchy darkness. Who could?"

There was a pause as if the unseen persons about him tried to understand his words. Then the voice of Correa said: "He is but newly formed. He stumbles as he walks and mingles words that mean nothing with his speech."

Others also said things about him that he heard or understood imperfectly.

"May I sit up?" he asked, in a pause. "I will not struggle against you again."

They consulted and let him rise.

The voice of an older man began to question him, and Nunez found himself trying to explain the great world out of which he had fallen, and the sky and mountains and sight and suchlike marvels, to these elders who sat in darkness in the Country of the Blind. And they would believe and understand nothing whatever he told them, a thing quite outside his expectation. They would not even understand many of his words. For fourteen generations these people had been blind and cut off from all the seeing world; the names for all the things of sight had faded and changed; the story of the outer world was faded and changed to a child's story; and they had ceased to concern themselves with anything beyond the rocky slopes above their circling wall. Blind men of genius had arisen among them and questioned the shreds of belief and tradition they had brought with them from their seeing days, and had dismissed all these things as idle fancies, and replaced them with new and saner explanations. Much of their imagination had shrivelled with their eyes, and they had made for themselves new imaginations with their ever more sensitive ears and finger-tips. Slowly Nunez realised this; that his expectation of wonder and reverence at his origin and his gifts was not to be borne out; and after his poor attempt to explain sight to them had been set aside as the confused version of a new-made being describing the marvels of his incoherent sensations, he subsided, a little dashed, into listening to their instruction.

The eldest of the blind men explained to him life and philosophy and religion, how that the world (meaning their valley) had been first an empty hollow in the rocks and then had come, first, inanimate things without the gift of touch, from these grass and bushes and after that llamas and a few other creatures that had little sense, and then men, and at last angels, whom one could hear singing and making fluttering sounds, but whom none could touch at all, which puzzled Nunez greatly until he thought of the birds.

The elder went on to tell Nunez how "by the Wisdom above us" time had been divided into the warm and the cold, which are the blind equivalents of day and night, and how it was good to sleep in the warm, and work during the cold, so that now, but for his advent, the whole town of the blind would have been asleep. He said Nunez must have been specially created to learn and serve the wisdom they had acquired, and for all his mental incoherency and stumbling behaviour he must have courage, and do his best to learn; and at that all the people in the doorway murmured encouragingly. He said the night—for the blind call their day night —was now far gone, and it behoved everyone to go back to sleep. He asked Nunez if he knew how to sleep, and Nunez said he did, but that before sleep he wanted food.

They brought him food, llama's milk in a bowl, and rough salted bread, and led him into a lonely place to eat out of their hearing, and afterwards to slumber, until the chill of the mountain evening roused them to begin their day again. But Nunez slumbered not at all.

Instead, he sat up in the place where they had left him, resting his limbs and turning the unanticipated circumstances of his arrival over and over in his mind.

Every now and then he laughed, sometimes with amusement and sometimes with indignation.

"Unformed mind!" he said. "Got no senses yet! They little know they've been insulting their heaven-sent king and master. I see I must bring them to reason. Let me think—let me think."

He was still thinking when the sun set.

Nunez had an eye for all beautiful things, and it seemed to him that the glow upon the snowfields and glaciers that rose about the valley on every side was the most beautiful thing he had ever seen. His eyes went from that inaccessible glory to the village and irrigated fields, fast sinking into the twilight, and suddenly a wave of emotion took him, and he thanked God from the bottom of his heart that the power of sight had been given him.

He heard a voice calling to him from out of the house of the elders.

"Ya ho there, Bogota! Come hither!"

At that he stood up smiling. He would show these people once and for all what sight would do for a man. They would seek him but not find him.

"You move not, Bogota," said the voice.

He laughed noiselessly, and made two stealthy steps aside from the path.

"Trample not on the grass, Bogota; that is not allowed."

Nunez had scarcely heard the sound he made himself. He stopped amazed.

The owner of the voice came running up the piebald path towards him.

"Why did you not come when I called you?" said the blind man. "Must you be led like a child? Cannot you hear the path as you walk?"

Nunez laughed. "I can see it," he said.

"There is no such word as *see*," said the blind man after a pause. "Cease this folly and follow the sound of my feet."

Nunez followed, a little annoyed.

"My time will come," he said.

"You'll learn," the blind man answered. "There is much to learn in the world."

"Has no one told you, 'In the Country of the Blind the One-eyed Man is King?'"

"What is blind?" asked the man carelessly over his shoulder.

Four days passed, and the fifth found the King of the Blind still incognito, as a clumsy and useless stranger among his subjects.

It was, he found, much more difficult to proclaim himself than he had supposed, and in the meantime, while he meditated his *coup d'état*, he did what he was told and learned the manners and customs of the Country of the Blind. He found working and going about at night a particularly irksome thing, and he decided that that should be the first thing he would change in his little kingdom.

They led a simple, laborious life, these people, with all the elements of virtue and happiness, as these things can be understood by men. They toiled, but not oppressively; they had food and clothing sufficient for their needs; they had days and seasons of rest; they made much of music and singing, and there was love among them, and little children.

It was marvellous with what confidence and precision they went about their ordered world. Everything, you see, had been made to fit their needs; each of the radiating paths of the valley area had a constant angle to the others, and was distinguished by a special notch upon its kerbing; all obstacles and irregularities of path and meadow had long since been cleared away; all their methods and procedure arose naturally from their special needs. Their senses had become marvellously acute; they could hear and judge the slightest gesture of a man a dozen paces away—could hear the very beating of his heart. Intonation had long replaced expression with them, and touches gesture, and their work with hoe and spade and fork was as free and confident as garden work can be. Their sense of smell was extraordinarily fine; they could distinguish individual differences as readily as a dog can, and they went about the tending of the llamas, who lived among the rocks above and came to the wall for food and shelter, with ease and confidence. It was only when at last Nunez sought to assert himself that he found how easy and confident their movements could be.

He rebelled only after he had tried persuasion.

At first on several occasions he sought to tell them of sight. "Look you here, you people," he said. "There are things you do not understand in me."

Once or twice one or two of them attended to him; they sat with faces downcast and ears turned intelligently towards him though with a faintly ironical smile on their lips, while he did his best to tell them what it was to see. Among his hearers was a girl, with eyes less red and sunken than the others, so that one could almost fancy she was hiding eyes, and she especially he hoped to persuade.

He spoke of the beauties of sight, of watching the mountains, of the sky and the sunrise, and they heard him with amused incredulity that presently became condemnatory. They told him that there were indeed no mountains at all, but that the end of the rocks where the llamas grazed was indeed the end of the world; the rocks became steeper and steeper, became pillars and thence sprang a cavernous roof of the universe, from which the dew and avalanches fell; and when he maintained stoutly the world had neither end nor roof such as they supposed, they were shocked and they said his thoughts were wicked. So far as he could describe sky and clouds and stars to them, his world seemed to them a hideous void, a terrible blankness in the place of the smooth roof to things in which they believed—it was an article of faith with them that above the rocks the cavern roof was exquisitely smooth to the touch. They called it the Wisdom Above.

He saw that in some manner he shocked them by his talk of clouds and stars, and so he gave up that aspect of the matter altogether, and tried to show them the practical value of sight. One morning he saw Pedro in the path called Seventeen and coming towards the central houses, but still too far off for hearing or scent, and he told them as much. "In a little while," he prophesied, "Pedro will be here." An old man remarked that Pedro had no business on Path Seventeen, and then, as if in confirmation, that individual as he drew near turned and went transversely into Path Ten, and so back with nimble paces to the outer wall. They mocked Nunez when Pedro did not arrive, and afterwards, when he asked

Pedro questions to clear his character, Pedro denied and outfaced him, and was afterwards hostile to him.

Then he induced them to let him go a long way up the sloping meadows towards the wall with one complacent individual, and to him he promised to describe all that happened among the houses. He noted certain comings and goings, but the things that really seemed to signify to these people happened inside of or behind the windowless houses— the only thing they took note of to test him by—and of these he could see or tell nothing; and it was after the failure of that attempt, and the ridicule they could not repress, that he resorted to force. He thought of seizing a spade and suddenly smiting one or two of them to earth, and so in fair combat showing the advantage of eyes. He went so far with that resolution as to seize his spade, and then he discovered a new thing about himself, and that was that it was impossible for him to hit a blind man in cold blood.

He hesitated and found them all aware that he had snatched up the spade. They stood alert, with their heads on one side, and bent ears towards him for what he would do next.

"Put that spade down," said one, and he felt a sort of helpless horror. He came near obedience.

Then he thrust one backwards against a house wall, and fled past him and out of the village.

He went athwart one of their meadows, leaving a track of trampled grass behind his feet, and presently sat down by the side of one of their ways. He felt something of the buoyancy that comes to all men in the beginning of a fight, but more perplexity. He began to realise that you cannot even fight happily with creatures that stand upon a different mental basis to yourself. Far away he saw a number of men carrying spades and sticks come out of the street of houses, and advance in a spreading line along the several paths towards him. They advanced slowly, speaking frequently to one another, and ever and again the whole cordon would halt and snuff the air and listen.

The first time they did this Nunez laughed. But afterwards he did not laugh.

One struck his trail in the meadow grass, and came stooping and feeling his way along it.

For five minutes he watched the slow extension of the cordon, and then his vague disposition to do something forthwith became frantic. He stood up, went a pace or so towards the circumferential wall, turned, and went back a little way. There they all stood in a crescent, still and listening.

He also stood still, gripping his spade very tightly in both hands. Should he charge them?

The pulse in his ears rang into the rhythm of "In the Country of the Blind the One-eyed Man is King!"

Should he charge them?

He looked back at the high and unclimbable wall behind—unclimbable because of its smooth plastering, but withal pierced by many little doors, and at the approaching line of seekers. Behind these, others were now coming out of the street of houses.

Should he charge them?

"Bogota!" called one. "Bogota! where are you!"

He gripped his spade still tighter and advanced down the meadows towards the place of habitations, and directly he moved they converged upon him. "I'll hit them if they touch me," he swore; "by Heaven I will. I'll hit." He called aloud, "Look here, I'm going to do what I like in this valley. Do you hear? I'm going to do what I like and go where I like!"

They were moving in upon him quickly, groping, yet moving rapidly. It was like playing blind man's buff, with everyone blindfolded except one. "Get hold of him!" cried one. He found himself in the arc of a loose curve of pursuers. He felt suddenly he must be active and resolute.

"You don't understand," he cried in a voice that was meant to be great and resolute, and which broke. "You are blind, and I can see. Leave me alone!"

"Bogota! Put down that spade, and come off the grass!"

The last order, grotesque in its urban familiarity, produced a gust of anger.

"I'll hurt you," he said, sobbing with emotion. "By Heaven, I'll hurt you. Leave me alone!"

He began to run, not knowing clearly where to run. He ran from the nearest blind man, because it was a horror to hit him. He stopped, and made a dash to escape from their closing ranks. He made for where a gap was wide, and the men on either side, with a quick perception of the approach of his paces, rushed in on one another. He sprang forward, and then saw he must be caught, and swish! the spade had struck. He felt the soft thud of hand and arm, and the man was down with a yell of pain, and he was through.

Through! And then he was close to the street of houses again, and blind men, whirling spades and stakes, were running with a sort of reasoned swiftness hither and thither.

He heard steps behind him just in time, and found a tall man rushing forward and swiping at the sound of him. He lost his nerve, hurled his spade a yard wide at his antagonist, and whirled about and fled, fairly yelling as he dodged another.

He was panic-stricken. He ran furiously to and fro, dodging when there was no need to dodge, and in his anxiety to see on every side of him at once, stumbling. For a moment he was down and they heard his fall. Far away in the circumferential wall a little doorway looked like Heaven, and he set off in a wild rush for it. He did not even look round at his pursuers until it was gained, and he had stumbled across the bridge, clambered a little way among the rocks, to the surprise and dismay of a young llama, who went leaping out of sight, and lay down sobbing for breath.

And so his *coup d'état* came to an end.

He stayed outside the wall of the Valley of the Blind for two nights and days without food or shelter, and meditated upon the unexpected. There were bushes, but the food on them was not ripe and hard and bitter. It weakened him to eat it. It lowered his courage. During these prowlings he repeated very frequently and always with a profounder note of derision that exploded proverb: "In the Country of the Blind the One-eyed Man is King." He thought chiefly of ways of fighting and conquering these people, and it grew clear that for him no practicable way was possible. He had no weapons, and now it would be hard to get one.

The canker of civilisation had got to him even in Bogota, and he could not find it in himself to go down and assassinate a blind man. Of course, if he did that, he might then dictate terms on the threat of assassinating them all. If he could get near enough to them, that is. And—sooner or later he must sleep! . . .

He tried also to find food among the pine trees, to be comfortable under pine boughs while the frost fell at night and—with less confidence—to catch a llama by artifice in order to try to kill it—perhaps by hammering it with a stone—and so finally, perhaps, to eat some of it. But the llamas had their doubts of him and regarded him with distrustful brown eyes, and spat when he drew near. Fear came on him the second day, an intense fatigue, and fits of shivering. Finally he crawled down to the wall of the Country of the Blind and tried to make terms. He crawled along by the stream shouting, until two blind men came out to the gate and talked to him.

"I was mad," he said. "But I was only newly made."

They said that was better.

He told them he was wiser now, and that he repented of all he had done.

Then he wept without intention, for he was very weak and ill, and they took that as a favourable sign.

They asked him if he still thought he could "*see*."

"No," he said, "that was folly. The word means nothing—less than nothing!"

They asked him what was overhead.

"About ten times the height of a man there is a roof above the world—of rock and wisdom and very, very smooth." . . .

He burst again into hysterical tears. "Before you ask me any more, give me some food or I shall die."

He expected dire punishments, but these blind people showed themselves capable of great toleration. They regarded his rebellion as but one more proof of his general idiocy and inferiority; and after they had whipped him they appointed him to do the simplest and heaviest work they had for anyone to do, and he, seeing no other way of living, did submissively what he was told.

He was ill for some days and they nursed him kindly. That refined his submission. But they insisted on his lying in the dark and that was a great misery. And the chief elders came and talked to him of the wicked levity of his mind, and reproved him so impressively for his doubts about the lid of rock that covered their cosmic casserole that he almost doubted whether indeed he was not the victim of hallucination in not seeing it overhead.

So Nunez humbled himself and became a common citizen of the Country of the Blind, and these people ceased to be a generalised people and became individualities and familiar to him, while the world beyond the mountains became more and more remote and unreal. There was Yacob, his master, a kindly man when not annoyed; there was Pedro, Yacob's nephew; and there was Medina-saroté, who was the youngest daughter of Yacob. She was little esteemed in the world of the blind, because she had a clear-cut face, and lacked the satisfying, glossy smoothness that is the blind man's ideal of feminine beauty; but Nunez thought her beautiful at first, and presently the most beautiful thing in the whole creation. Her closed eyelids were not sunken and red after the common way of the valley, but lay as though they might open again at any moment; and she had eyelashes, which were considered a grave disfigurement. And her voice was strong, and did not satisfy the acute hearing of the valley swains. So that she had no lover.

There came a time when Nunez thought that, could he win her, he would be resigned to live in the valley for all the rest of his days.

He watched her; he sought opportunities of doing her little services, and presently he found that she observed him. Once at a rest-day gathering they sat side by side in the dim starlight, and the music was sweet. His hand came upon hers and he dared to clasp it. Then very tenderly she returned his pressure. And one day, as they were at their meal in the darkness, he felt her hand very softly seeking him, and as it chanced the fire leaped then and he saw the tenderness of her face.

He sought to speak to her.

He went to her one day when she was sitting in the summer moonlight spinning. The light made her a thing of silver and mystery. He sat down at her feet and told her he loved her, and told her how beautiful she seemed to him. He had a lover's voice, he spoke with a tender reverence that came near to awe, and she had never before been touched by adoration. She made him no definite answer, but it was clear his words pleased her.

After that he talked to her whenever he could take an opportunity. The valley became the world for him, and the world beyond the mountains where men worked and went about in sunlight seemed no more than a fairy tale he would some day pour into her ears. Very tentatively and timidly he spoke to her of sight.

At first this sight seemed to her the most poetical of fancies, and she listened to his description of the stars and the mountains and her own sweet white-lit beauty as though it was a guilty indulgence. She did not believe, she could only half understand, but she was mysteriously delighted, and it seemed to him that she completely understood.

His love lost its awe and took courage. Presently he was for demanding her of Yacob and the elders in marriage, but she became fearful and delayed. And it was one of her sisters who first told Yacob that Medina-saroté and Nunez were in love.

From the first there was very great opposition to the marriage of Nunez and Medina-saroté; not so much because they valued her as because they held him as a being apart, an idiot, incompetent thing, below the permissible level of a man. Her sisters opposed it bitterly as bringing discredit on them all; and old Yacob, though he had formed a sort of liking for his clumsy, obedient serf, shook his head and said the thing could not be. The young men were all angry at the thought of corrupting the race, and one went so far as to revile and strike Nunez. He struck back. Then for the first time he found an advantage in seeing, even by twilight, and after that fight no one was disposed to lift a hand against him. But they still found his marriage impossible.

Old Yacob had a tenderness for his last little daughter, and was grieved to have her weep upon his shoulder.

"You see, my dear, he's an idiot! He has delusions; he can't do anything right."

"I know," wept Medina-saroté. "But he's better than he was. He's getting better. And he's strong, dear father, and kind—stronger and kinder than any other man in the world. And he loves me—and, father, I love him."

Old Yacob was greatly distressed to find her inconsolable, and, besides—what made it more distressing—he liked Nunez for many things. So he went and sat in the windowless council-chamber with the other elders, observing the trend of their talk, and said, at the proper time, "He's better than he was. Very likely, some day, we shall find him as sane as ourselves."

Then afterwards one of the elders, who thought deeply, had an idea. He was the great doctor among these people, their medicine man, and he had a very philosophical and inventive mind, and the idea of curing Nunez of his peculiarities appealed to him. One day when Yacob was present he turned to the topic of Nunez.

"I have examined Bogota," he said, "and the case is clearer to me. I think very probably he might be cured."

"That is what I have always hoped," said old Yacob.

"His brain is affected," said the blind doctor.

The elders murmured assent.

"Now, *what* affects it?"

"Ah!" said old Yacob.

"This," said the doctor, answering his own question. "Those queer things that are called the eyes, and which exist to make an agreeable soft depression in the face, are diseased, in the case of Bogota, in such a way as to affect his brain. They are greatly distended, he has eyelashes, and his eyelids move, and consequently his brain is in a state of constant irritation and distraction."

"Yes?" said old Yacob. "Yes?"

"And I think I may say with reasonable certainty that, in order to cure him completely, all that we need to do is a simple and easy surgical operation—namely, to remove those irritating bodies."

"And then he will be sane?"

"Then he will be perfectly sane, and a quite admirable citizen."

"Thank Heaven for the Wisdom beneath it!" said old Yacob, and went forth at once to tell Nunez of his happy hopes.

But Nunez's manner of receiving the good news struck him as being cold and disappointing.

"One might think," he said, "from the tone you take, that you did not care for my daughter."

It was Medina-saroté who persuaded Nunez to face the blind surgeons.

"*You* do not want me," he said, "to lose my gift of sight?"

She shook her head.

"My world is sight."

Her head dropped lower.

"There are beautiful things, the beautiful little things—the flowers, the lichens among the rocks, the lightness and visible softness on a piece of fur, the far sky with its drifting down of clouds, the sunsets and the stars. And there is *you*. For you alone it is good to have sight, to see your sweet, serene face, your kindly lips, your dear, dear, beautiful hands folded together. . . . It is these eyes of mine you won, these eyes that hold me to you, that these idiots seek. Instead, I must touch you, hear you, and never see you again. I must come under that roof of rock and stone and darkness, that horrible roof under which your imagination stoops. . . . No, you would not have me do that?"

She shuddered to hear him speak of the Wisdom Above in such terms. Her hands went to her ears.

A disagreeable doubt had arisen in him. He stopped, and left the thing a question.

"I wish," she said, "sometimes—" She paused.

"Yes?" said he, a little apprehensively.

"I wish sometimes—you would not talk like that."

"Like what?"

"It's your imagination. I love much of it, but not when you speak of the Wisdom Above. When you talked of those flowers and stars it was different. But now—"

He felt cold. "*Now?*" he said faintly.

She sat quite still.

"You mean—you think—I should be better, better, perhaps—"

He was realising things very swiftly. He felt anger, indeed, anger at the dull course of fate, but also sympathy for her lack of understanding—a sympathy near akin to pity.

"*Dear*," he said, and he could see by her whiteness how intensely her spirit pressed against the things she could not say. He put his arms about her, and kissed her ear, and they sat for a time in silence.

"If I were to consent to this?" he whispered at last, in a voice that was very gentle.

She flung her arms about him weeping wildly. "Oh, if you would," she sobbed, "if only you would!"

"And you have no doubt?"

"Dear heart!" she answered, and pressed his hands with all her strength.

"They will hurt you but little," she said; "and you would be going through this pain—you are going through it, dear lover, for *me*. . . . Dear; if a woman's heart and life can do it, I will repay you. My dearest one, my dearest with that rough, gentle voice, I will repay."

"So be it," he said.

And in silence he turned away from her. For the time he could sit by her no longer.

She could hear his slow retreating footsteps, and something in the rhythm of them threw her into a passion of weeping. . . .

He meant to go to a lonely place where the meadows were beautiful with white narcissus, but as he went he lifted up his eyes and saw the morning, the morning like an angel in golden armour, marching down the steeps. . . .

It seemed to him that before this splendour he, and this blind world in the valley, and his love, and all, were no better than the darkness of an anthill.

He did not turn aside to the narcissus fields as he had meant to do. Instead he went on, and passed through the wall of the circumference and out upon the rocks, and his eyes were always upon the sunlit ice and snow above.

He saw their infinite beauty, and his imagination soared over them to the things he would see no more.

He thought of that great free visible world he was to renounce for ever; the world that was his own, and beyond these encircling mountains; and he had a vision of those further slopes, distance beyond distance, with Bogota, a place of multitudinous stirring beauty, a glory by day, a luminous mystery by night, a place of palaces and fountains and statues and white houses, lying beautifully in the middle distance. He thought how for a day or so one might come down through passes, drawing ever nearer and nearer to its busy streets and ways. He thought of the river journey to follow, from great Bogota to the still vaster world beyond, through towns and villages, forest and desert places, the rushing river day by day, until its banks receded and the big steamers came splashing by, and one had reached the sea—the limitless sea, with its thousand islands, its thousands of islands, and its ships seen dimly far away in their incessant journeyings round and about the greater world. And there, unpent by mountains, one saw the sky—the sky, not such a disc as one saw it here, but a great arch of immeasurable blue, the blue of deeps in which the circling stars were floating.

His eyes scrutinised the imprisoning mountains with a keener enquiry.

It occurred to him that for many days now he had not looked at the cliffs and snow-slopes and gulleys by which he had slid and fallen and clambered down into the valley. He looked now; he looked but he could not find. Something had happened. Something had occurred to change and obliterate the familiar landmarks of his descent. He could not believe it; he rubbed his eyes and looked again. Perhaps he was forgetting. Some fresh fall of snow might have altered the lines and shapes of the exposed surfaces.

In another place too there had been slopes that he had studied very intently. For at times the thought of escape had been very urgent with him. Had they too changed? Had his memory begun to play tricks with him? In one place high up, five hundred feet or so, he had marked a great vein of green crystal that made a sort of slanting way upwards—but alas! died out to nothing. One might clamber to it, but above that there seemed no hope. That was still as it had been. But elsewhere?

Suddenly he stood up with a faint cry of horror in his throat.

"*No!*" he whispered crouching slightly. "No. It was there before!"

But he knew it had not been there before.

It was a long narrow scar of newly exposed rock running obliquely across the face of the precipice at its vastest. Above it and below it was weathered rock. He still struggled against that conviction. But there it was plain and undeniable and *raw*. There could be little doubt of the significance of that fresh scar. An enormous mass of that stupendous mountain wall had slipped. It had shifted a few feet forward and it was being held up for a time, by some inequality of the sustaining rocks. Maybe that would hold it now, but of the shift there was no doubt whatever. Could it settle down again in its new position? He could not tell. He scanned the distant surfaces. Above he saw little white threads of water from the snowfields pouring into this newmade crack. Below, water was already spouting freshly at a dozen points from the lower edge of the loosened mass. And then he saw that other, lesser fissures had also appeared in the mountain wall.

The more he studied that vast rock face the more he realised the possible urgency of its menace. If this movement continued the valley was doomed. He forgot his personal distress in a huge solicitude for this little community of which he had become a citizen. What ought these people to do? What could they do? Abandon their threatened houses? Make new ones on the slopes behind him? And how could he induce them to do it?

Suppose that lap of rock upon which the mass now rested *gave!*

The mountain would fall—he traced the possible fall with his extended hands—so and so and so. It would fall into and beyond the lake. It would bury the lower houses. It might bury the whole village. It might spell destruction for every living thing in the valley. Something they ought to do. Prepare refuges? Organise a possible evacuation? Set him to watch the mountains day by day? But how to make them understand?

If he went down now, very simply, very meekly, without excitement, speaking in low tones and abasing himself before them. If he said: "I am a foolish creature. I am a disgusting creature. I am unfit to touch the hem of the garment of the very least of your wise men. But for once, I pray you, believe in my vision! Believe in my vision! Sometimes such an idiot as I can *see*. Let me have some more tests about this seeing. Because indeed, indeed, I know of a great danger and I can help you to sustain it." . . .

But how could he convince them? What proofs could he give them? After his earlier failures. Suppose he went down now, with his warning fresh in his mind. Suppose he *insisted*.

"Vision. Sight." The mere words would be an outrage to them. They might not let him speak at all. And even then if he was permitted to speak, already it might be too late. At the best it would only set them discussing his case afresh. Almost certainly he would anger them, for how could he tell his tale and not question the Wisdom Above. They might take him and end the recurrent nuisance of him by putting out his eyes forthwith, and the only result of his intervention would be that he would be nursing his bloody eye sockets when the disaster fell. The mountain might hold for weeks and months yet, but again it might not wait at all. Even now it might be creeping. Even now the heat of the day must be expanding those sullen vast masses, thawing the night ice that held them together. Even now the trickling snow-water was lubricating the widening fissures.

Suddenly he saw, he saw plainly, a new crack leap across a shining green mass, and then across the valley came the sound of it like the shot of a gun that starts a race. The mass was moving *now!* There was no more time to waste. No more time for pleas and plans. "Stop!" he cried. "Stop!" and put out his hands as if to thrust back that slow deliberate catastrophe. It is preposterous but he believes he said, "Wait one minute!"

He ran headlong to the little bridge and the gate and rushed down towards the houses, waving his arms and shouting. "The mountain is falling," he screamed. "The whole mountain is falling upon you all. Medina-saroté! Medina-saroté!"

He clattered to the house of old Yacob and burst

in upon the sleepers. He shook them and shouted at them, going from one to the other.

"He's gone mad again," they cried aghast at him and even Medina-saroté cowered away from his excitement.

"Come," he said. "Come. Even now it is falling. The mountain is falling." And he seized her wrist in a grip of steel. "Come!" he cried so masterfully that in terror she obeyed him.

But outside the house there was a crowd that his shouts and noise had awakened, and a score of men had run out already and assembled outside the house and stood in his way.

"Let me pass," he cried. "Let me pass. And come with me—up the further slopes there before it is too late."

"This is too much. This is the last blasphemy," shrieked one of the elders. "Seize him. Hold him!"

"I tell you the mountain is falling. It is coming down upon you even now as you hold me here."

"The Wisdom Above us that loves and protects us *cannot* fall."

"Listen. That rumbling?"

"There has been rumbling like that before. The Wisdom is warning us. It is because of your blasphemies."

"And the ground rocking?"

"Brothers, cast him out! Cast him out of the valley. We have been foolish to harbour him so long. His sin is more than our Providence can endure."

"But I tell you the rocks are falling. The whole mountain is coming down. Listen and you can hear the crashing and the rending of them."

He was aware of a loud hoarse voice intoning through the uproar and drowning his own. "The Wisdom Above loves us. It protects us from all harm. No evil can touch us while the Wisdom is over us. Cast him forth! Cast him forth. Let him take our sins upon him and go!" "Out you go, Bogota," cried a chorus of voices. "Out you go."

"Medina-saroté! Come with me. Come out of this place!"

Pedro threw protective arms about his cousin.

"Medina-saroté!" cried Nunez. "Medina-saroté!"

They pushed him, struggling fiercely, up the path towards the boundaries. They showed all the cruelty now of frightened men. For the gathering noise of the advancing rocks dismayed them all. They wanted to out-do each other in repudiating him. They beat at his face with their fists and kicked his shins and ankles and feet. One or two jabbed at him with knives. He could not see Medina-saroté any longer and he could not see the shifting cliffs be-

cause of the blows and because of the blood that poured from a cut in his forehead, but the voices about him seemed to fade as the rumbling clatter of falling fragments wove together and rose into a thunderous roar. He shouted weeping for Medina-saroté to escape as they drove him before them.

They thrust him through a little door and flung him out on to a stony slope with a deliberate violence that sent a flock of llamas helter-skelter. He lay like a cast clout. "And there you stay—and starve," said one. "You and your—*seeing*."

He lifted his head for a last reply.

"I tell you. You will be dead before I am."

"You *fool!*" said the one he had fought, and came back to kick him again and again. "Will you never learn reason?" But he turned hastily to join his fellows when Nunez struggled clumsily to his feet.

He stood swaying like a drunken man.

He had no strength in his limbs. He did his best to wipe the blood from his eyes. He looked at the impending mountain-fall, he looked for a high rocky ledge he had noted that morning and then he turned a despairful face to the encircling doom of the valley. But he did not attempt to climb any further away.

"What's the good of going alone?" he said. "Even if I could. I shall only starve up there."

And then suddenly he saw Medina-saroté seeking him. She emerged from the little door and she was calling his name. In some manner she had contrived to slip away and come to search for him. "Bogota my darling!" she cried. "What have they done to you? Oh *what* have they *done* to you?"

He staggered to meet her, calling her name over and over again.

In another moment her hands were upon his face and she was wiping away the blood and searching softly and skilfully for his cuts and bruises.

"You must stay here now," she panted. "You must stay here for a time. Until you repent. Until you learn to repent. Why did you behave so madly? Why did you say those horrible blasphemies? You don't know you say them, but how are they to tell that? If you come back now they will certainly kill you. I will bring you food. Stay here."

"Neither of us can stay here. *Look!*"

She drew the air in sharply between her teeth at that horrible word "look" which showed that his madness was still upon him.

"There! That thunder!"

"What is it?"

"A stream of rocks are pouring down by the meadows and it is only the beginning of them. *Look* at them. Listen anyhow to the drumming and beating of them! What do you think those sounds mean? *That* and that! Stones! They are bouncing and dancing across the lower meadows by the lake and the waters of the lake are brimming over and rising up to the further houses. Come my darling. Come! Do not question, but come!"

She stood hesitating for a moment. There was a frightful menace now in the storm of sounds that filled the air. Then she crept into his arms. "I am afraid," she said.

He drew her to him and with a renewal of strength began to climb, guiding her feet. His blood smeared her face but there was no time to remedy that. At first she dragged upon him and then, perceiving the strain she caused, she helped and supported him. She was sobbing but also she obeyed.

He concentrated himself now upon reaching that distant shelf, but presently he had to halt for breath, and then only was he free to look back across the valley.

He saw that the foot of the cliff was sliding now down into the lake, scooping its waters before it towards the remoter houses, and that the cascade of rocks was now swifter and greater. They drove over the ground in leaps and bounds with a frightful suggestion in their movements as though they were hunting victims. They were smashing down trees and bushes and demolishing walls and buildings, and still the main bulk of the creeping mountain, deprived now of its supports, had to gather momen-30 tum and fall. It was breaking up as it came down. And now little figures appeared from the houses and ran hither and thither. . . .

For the first time Nunez was glad that Medina-saroté was blind.

"Climb! my darling," he said. "Climb!"

"I do not understand."

"Climb!"

A rush of terrified llamas came crowding up past them.

"It is so steep, so steep here. Why are these creatures coming with us?"

"Because they understand. Because they know we are with them. Push through them. Climb."

With an effect of extreme deliberation that mountain-side hung over the doomed valley. For some tense instants Nunez did not hear a sound. His whole being was concentrated in his eyes. Then came the fall and then a stunning concussion that struck his chest a giant's blow. Medina-saroté was 50 flung against the rocks and clung to them with clawing hands. Nunez had an instant's impression of a sea of rocks and earth and fragments of paths and walls and houses, pouring in a swift flood towards

him. A spray of wind-driven water bedewed him; they were pelted with mud and broken rock fragments, the wave of debris surged and receded a little and abruptly became still, and then colossal pillars of mist and dust rose up solemnly and deliberately and mounted towering overhead and unfolded and rolled together about them until they were in an impenetrable stinging fog. Silence fell again upon the world and the Valley of the Blind was 10 hidden from him for evermore.

Pallid to the centres of their souls, these two survivors climbed slowly to the crystalline ridge and crouched upon it.

And when some hour or so later that swirling veil of mist and dust had grown thinner and they could venture to move and plan what they would do, Nunez saw through a rent in it far away across a wilderness of tumbled broken rock and in a V-shaped cleft of the broken mountains, the green 20 rolling masses of the foothills, and far beyond them one shining glimpse of the ocean.

Two days later he and Medina-saroté were found by two hunters who had come to explore the scene of this disaster. They were trying to clamber down to the outer world and they were on the verge of exhaustion. They had lived upon water, fern roots and a few berries. They collapsed completely when the hunters hailed them.

They lived to tell their tale, and to settle in Quito among Nunez's people. There he is still living. He is a prosperous tradesman and plainly a very honest man. She is a sweet and gentle lady, her basketwork and her embroidery are marvellous, though of course she makes no use of colour, and she speaks Spanish with an old-fashioned accent very pleasant to the ear.

Greatly daring, I think, they have had four children and they are as stout and sturdy as their father 40 and they can see.

He will talk about his experience when the mood is on him but she says very little. One day however when she was sitting with my wife while Nunez and I were away, she talked a little of her childhood in the valley and of the simple faith and happiness of her upbringing. She spoke of it with manifest regret. It had been a life of gentle routines, free from all complications.

It was plain she loved her children and it was 50 plain she found them and much of the comings and goings about her difficult to understand. She had never been able to love and protect them as she had once loved and protected Nunez.

My wife ventured on a question she had long

wanted to ask. "You have never consulted oculists," she began.

"Never," said Medina-saroté. "I have never wanted to *see*."

"But colour—and form and distance!"

"I have no use for your colours and your stars," said Medina-saroté. "I do not want to lose my faith in the Wisdom Above."

"But after all that has happened! Don't you want to see Nunez; see what he is like?"   10

"But I know what he is like and seeing him might put us apart. He would not be so near to me. The loveliness of *your* world is a complicated and fearful loveliness and mine is simple and near. I had rather Nunez saw for me—because he knows nothing of fear."

"But the *beauty*!" cried my wife.

"It may be beautiful," said Medina-saroté, "but it must be very terrible to *see*."

John Galsworthy
1867–1933

It is not strange that John Galsworthy's life and work disclose an understanding of industrial acquisitiveness and a preference for analyzing the upper middle class, for he was the son of a successful lawyer, descended from an old Devonshire family. Significantly, his first successful novel was entitled *The Man of Property*, 1906.

Galsworthy was born at Coombe, Surrey (now a suburb of London) in 1867, and followed the best tradition of the gentry. He attended the smart preparatory school of Harrow, where he won acclaim as an athlete; finished his education at New College, Oxford; received an honor degree in law in 1889, was called to the bar a year later, but seldom practiced; traveled extensively and read novels continuously. Parochial in his life, he was international in his literary tastes. He enjoyed with equal enthusiasm the works of Dickens and Turgenev, Tolstoy and Anatole France. "Art," he declared, "is the one form of human energy which really works for union and destroys the barriers between man and man."

Little concerned with style, opposed to "art for art's sake," Galsworthy was a realist who believed that "the proper study of mankind is man." His concern with vagaries of humanity—and particularly with comfortable middle-class humanity—can be traced in all his work. It runs through the pleasant but mediocre verse in *Collected Poems*, 1934; the agreeable if not remarkable essays in *The Inn of Tranquillity*, 1912, and *Candelabra*, 1932; the many tales assembled in *Caravan*, 1925, and *On Forsyte 'Change*, 1930; the score of pamphlets, almost thirty plays, and more than twenty novels which made him famous and for which he was awarded the Nobel Prize for literature in 1932. Less than a year

after the coveted prize had been presented he died, January, 1933.

His first three novels and several uncollected short stories were printed over the pseudonym of "John Sinjohn." But it was not until Galsworthy printed *The Man of Property* that his characteristic note was sounded. With this volume he began the interrelated stories which, sixteen years later, were published as *The Forsyte Saga*, 1922. He returned to the theme again and again; no less than seven short stories extend the affairs of the family, and *One More River*, 1933, Galsworthy's last novel, is about lesser characters who had appeared in the Forsyte novels.

Well launched as a novelist, Galsworthy determined to be a dramatist. As a playwright he was esteemed by the critics and amply rewarded by the public. *The Silver Box*, 1906, employing the formula of Maupassant's "A Piece of String"; *Strife*, 1909; and *Justice*, 1910, were early successes. Even more popular on both sides of the Atlantic were *Loyalties*, 1922, and *Old English*, 1924, the latter founded on Galsworthy's short story "A Stoic." Most of the plays centered about intricate, and often tragic, human relationships. Seemingly detached, they were impartial but not impassive; they were, in the best sense, dramatized propaganda. *Strife* balanced the conflicting claims of capital and labor; *Justice* dealt with the cold ethics and inequalities of the law; *Loyalties* showed the disastrous folly of race prejudice. Although Galsworthy pretended to be a dispassionate commentator, his plays usually center about a person caught in a pitiless machine and a spirit destroyed by bewildering circumstance. The attitude throughout is that of the puzzled humanitarian: sympathetic with the weak, unafraid of the strong, but uncertain whether to blame society, the system, the mass—or whether to attempt to fix the blame at all.

The liberal attitude, dignified and cautious, is at its highest in Galsworthy's novels. In his full-length portrayal of the rise and decline of a great family, Galsworthy is both commentator and social critic. He purports to be a realistic observer, neither sentimental nor indignant; but it is not his objectivity which distinguishes *The Forsyte Saga*. It is the scope, the rich detail, and the compassion which set off the characters against their background. His concern for the characters is sometimes a defect. As a fellow craftsman, Joseph Conrad once advised him to be more indifferent to his "creatures." In one of his letters to Galsworthy, Conrad wrote: "Your attitude to them should be purely intellectual, more independent, freer, less rigorous than it is. You seem, for their sake, to hug your conceptions of right and wrong too closely."

Nevertheless, Galsworthy's intimacy with his subjects is a key to his power. His range and comprehensiveness—and unobtrusive symbolism—are seen even in the short stories, at least in the best of them. It is immediately apparent in "The Apple Tree," which is both realistic and symbolic. It is apparent even in as brief a story as "A Long-ago Affair," which is an almost perfect example of Galsworthy's technique in miniature.

When Galsworthy wrote of the postwar period, he failed because he was vague about what was happening, disturbed by new "standards," and worried about shifting values. But when he interpreted the stability of his own post-Victorian period, he approached—and sometimes attained—greatness.

A LONG–AGO AFFAIR [1]

HUBERT MARSLAND, the landscape painter, returning from a day's sketching on the river in the summer of 1921, had occasion to stay the progress of his two-seater about ten miles from London for a minor repair, and while his car was being seen to, strolled away from the garage to have a look at a house where he had often spent his holidays as a boy. Walking through a gateway and passing a large gravel-pit on his left, he was soon opposite the house, which stood back a little in its grounds. Very much changed! More pretentious, not so homely as when his Uncle and Aunt lived

there, and he used to play cricket on this warren opposite, where the cricket ground, it seemed, had been turned into a golf course. It was late—the dinner-hour, nobody playing, and passing on to the links he stood digesting the geography. Here must have been where the old pavilion was. And there—still turfed—where he had made that particularly nice stroke to leg, when he went in last and carried his bat for thirteen. Thirty-nine years ago—his sixteenth birthday. How vividly he remembered his new pads! A. P. Lucas had played against them and only made thirty-two—one founded one's style on A. P. Lucas in those days—feet in front of the bat, and pointed a little forward, elegant; you never saw it now, and a good thing too—one could sacrifice too much to style! Still, the tendency was all the other way; style was too much "off," perhaps!

He stepped back into the sun and sat down on the grass. Peaceful—very still! The haze of the distant downs was visible between his Uncle's old house and the next; and there was the clump of elms on the far side behind which the sun would be going down just as it used to then. He pressed the palms of his hands to the turf. A glorious summer—something like that summer of long ago. And warmth from the turf, or perhaps from the past, crept into his heart and made it ache a little. Just here he must have sat, after his innings, at Mrs. Monteith's feet peeping out of a flounced dress. Lord! The fools boys were! How headlong and uncalculating their devotions! A softness in voice and eyes, a smile, a touch or two —and they were slaves! Young fools, but good young fools. And, standing behind her chair—he could see him now—that other idol Captain Mac-Kay, with his face of browned ivory—just the colour of that elephant's tusk his Uncle had, which had gone so yellow—and his perfect black moustache, his white tie, check suit, carnation, spats, Malacca cane—all so fascinating! Mrs. Monteith, "the grass widow" they had called her! He remembered the look in people's eyes, the tone in their voices. Such a pretty woman! He had "fallen for her" at first sight, as the Yanks put it—her special scent, her daintiness, her voice! And that day on the river, when she made much of him, and Captain MacKay attended Evelyn Curtiss so assiduously that he was expected to propose. Quaint period! They used the word courting then, wore full skirts, high stays; and himself a blue elastic belt round his white-flannelled waist. And in the evening afterwards, his Aunt had said with an arch smile: "Good-night, *silly* boy!" Silly boy indeed, with a flower the grass widow had dropped pressed by his cheek into his pillow! What

[1] From *Caravan*, by permission of Charles Scribner's Sons.
1. warren, a field, usually enclosed, for keeping rabbits and other small game.

8–9. leg . . . thirteen, points and plays in cricket.

folly! And that next Sunday—looking forward to Church—passionately brushing his top hat; all through the service spying at her creamy profile, two pews in front on the left, between goat-bearded old Hallgrave her Uncle, and her pink, broad, white-haired Aunt; scheming to get near her when she came out, lingering, lurking, getting just a smile and the rustle of her flounces. Ah, ha! A little went a long way then! And the last day of his holidays and its nights with the first introduction to reality. Who said the Victorian Age was innocent?

Marsland put his palm up to his cheek. No! the dew was not yet falling! And his mind lightly turned and tossed his memories of women, as a man turns and tosses hay to air it; but nothing remembered gave him quite the feeling of that first experience.

His Aunt's dance! His first white waistcoat, bought *ad hoc*, from the local tailor, his tie laboriously imitating the hero—Captain MacKay's. All came back with such freshness in the quiet of the warren—the expectancy, the humble shy excitement, the breathless asking for a dance, the writing "Mrs. Monteith" twice on his little gilt-edged programme with its tiny tasselled white pencil; her slow-moving fan, her smile. And the first dance when it came; what infinite care not to tread on her white satin toes; what a thrill when her arm pressed his in the crush—such holy rapture, about all the first part of the evening, with yet another dance to come! If only he could have twirled her and "reversed" like his pattern, Captain MacKay! Then delirium growing as the second dance came near, making him cut his partner—the cool grass-scented air out on the dark terrace, with the chafers booming by, and in the starshine the poplars wondrously tall; the careful adjustment of his tie and waistcoat, the careful polishing of his hot face! A long breath then, and into the house to find her! Ballroom, supper-room, stairs, library, billiard-room, all drawn blank—"Estudiantina" going on and on, and he a wandering, white-waistcoated young ghost. Ah! The conservatory—and the hurrying there! And then the moment which had always been, was even now, such a blurred confused impression. Smothered voices from between a clump of flowers: "I saw her." "Who was the man?" A glimpse, gone past in a flash, of an ivory face, a black moustache! And then her voice: "Hubert"; and her hot hand clasping his, drawing him to her; her scent, her face smil-

ing, very set! A rustling behind the flowers, those people spying; and suddenly her lips on his cheek, the kiss sounding in his ears, her voice saying very softly: "Hubert, dear boy!" The rustle receded, ceased. What a long silent minute, then, among the ferns and blossoms in the dusk with her face close to his, pale, perturbed, before she led him out into the light, while he was slowly realising that she had made use of him to shelter her. A boy—not old enough to be her lover, but old enough to save her name and that of Captain MacKay! Her kiss—the last of many—but not upon *his* lips, *his* cheeks! Hard work realising that! A boy—of no account —a boy, who in a day would be at school again, kissed that *he* and *she* might renew their intrigue unsuspected!

How had he behaved the rest of that evening of romance bedrabbled? He hardly knew. Betrayed with a kiss! Two idols in the dust! And did they care what he was feeling? Not they! All they cared for was to cover up their tracks with him! But somehow —somehow—he had never shown her that he knew. Only, when their dance was over, and some one came and took her for the next, he escaped up to his little room, tore off his gloves, his waistcoat; lay on the bed, thought bitter thoughts. A boy! There he had stayed, with the thrum of the music in his ears, till at last it died away for good and the carriages were gone, and the night was quiet.

Squatting on the warren grass, still warm and dewless, Marsland rubbed his knees. Nothing like boys for generosity! And, with a little smile, he thought of his Aunt next morning, half-arch and half-concerned: "It isn't nice, dear, to sit out in dark corners, and—well, perhaps it wasn't your fault, but still, it isn't nice—not—quite——" and of how suddenly she had stopped, looking in his face, where his lips were curling in his first ironic laugh. She had never forgiven him that laugh—thinking him a cynical young Lothario? And Marsland thought: "Live and learn! Wonder what became of those two? Victorian Age! Hatches were battened down in those days! But, innocent—my hat!"

Ah! The sun was off, dew falling. He got up, rubbing his knees to take the stiffness out of them. Pigeons in the wood beyond were calling. A window in his Uncle's old home blazed like a jewel in the sun's last rays between the poplar trees. Heh! dear —a little long-ago affair!

From the *New Statesman*. See (H. H. Munro), copyright, 1920, by permission of the Viking Press, Inc., New York.

"Saki" (H. H. Munro)
1870–1916

Of Irish descent, H(ector) H(ugh) Munro was born in Burma, in 1870. His father and grandfather were army officers. Young Munro was sent to England at an early age; he was educated at Exmouth and Bedford and, later, in Europe by his father, who had retired. However, at twenty-three Munro returned to Burma, where he "imbibed" the spirit of the place and studied the contrasts of culture and colonization.

Three years later Munro came back to England and began to write sketches for the *Westminster Gazette* under the pseudonym of "Saki," the symbolic cupbearer in *The Rubáiyát* of Omar Khayyám. Journalism held him; he became foreign correspondent for the *Morning Post;* from 1902 to 1906 he was stationed in the Balkans, in Poland, in Russia, in Paris. The World War found him settled in London. He enlisted soon after the outbreak of hostilities, and was killed November 14, 1916.

"Saki" wrote one serious study, *The Rise of the Russian Empire*, 1900, two novels, and seven volumes of sketches and short stories. Most of the latter were assembled in *The Short Stories of "Saki,"* 1930. In an introduction to this volume Christopher Morley tacitly admitted the charge that "Saki" was an artificer, a teller of tales who carefully contrived his effects and usually "manipulated" his endings. But Morley, conceding a similarity to the American O. Henry, claimed that while both writers were 10 "masters of the park-bench setting," the Englishman was the sharper critic and often purged "the decorous amenities of an English week-end party with blasts of cyclone farce." Moreover, Morley maintained that "Saki" was less insistent than O. Henry "on twisting the story's tail, but an equal master of surprise," and that he was one of those writers "who ought to be enjoyed, not critichandled."

There can be no doubt about the enjoyment. 20 Most of "Saki's" stories are modernized and macabre fairy tales. The author delights to play in the territory between satire and burlesque. His extravaganzas remind the reader of G. K. Chesterton at one extreme, of P. G. Wodehouse at the other. He has an ingratiatingly light manner and a turn for the unforgettable phrase—the supposedly recent "no more privacy than a gold-

fish" originated in "Saki" shortly after the turn of the century.

Admirers have implied that "Saki" analyzed and "anatomized" the society of his day. However, the revived interest in this writer is not due to the reader's interest in social criticism, but rather to the sheer pleasure of such urbane and absurd and captivating stories as "Tobermory," "The She-Wolf," "The Mouse," "Mrs. Packletide's Tiger," "The Bag," "Laura," "The Background," and "The Seven Cream Jugs." Since, in spite of their brevity, it is obviously impossible to reprint all of these, the editor has selected the first as possibly the most improbable, and the most likely to tease the speculative imagination.

TOBERMORY[1]

IT was a chill, rain-washed afternoon of a late August day, that indefinite season when partridges are still in security or cold storage, and there is nothing to hunt—unless one is bounded on the north by the Bristol Channel, in which case one may lawfully gallop after fat red stags. Lady Blemley's house-party was not bounded on the north by the Bristol Channel, hence there was a full gathering of her guests round the tea-table on this particular afternoon. And, in spite of the blankness of the season and the triteness of the occasion, there was no trace in the company of that fatigued restlessness which means a dread of the pianola and a subdued hankering for auction bridge. The undisguised open-mouthed attention of the entire party was fixed on the homely negative personality of Mr. Cornelius Appin. Of all her guests, he was the one who had come to Lady Blemley with the vaguest reputation. Some one had said he was "clever," and he had got his invitation in the moderate expectation, on the part of his hostess, that some portion at least of his cleverness would be contributed to the general entertainment. Until tea-time that day she had been unable to discover in what direction, if any, his cleverness lay. He was neither a wit nor a

13. **pianola**, a mechanical self-playing piano.

croquet champion, a hypnotic force nor a begetter of amateur theatricals. Neither did his exterior suggest the sort of man in whom women are willing to pardon a generous measure of mental deficiency. He had subsided into mere Mr. Appin, and the Cornelius seemed a piece of transparent baptismal bluff. And now he was claiming to have launched on the world a discovery beside which the invention of gunpowder, of the printing-press, and of steam locomotion were inconsiderable trifles. Science had made bewildering strides in many directions during recent decades, but this thing seemed to belong to the domain of miracle rather than to scientific achievement.

"And do you really ask us to believe," Sir Wilfrid was saying, "that you have discovered a means for instructing animals in the art of human speech, and that dear old Tobermory has proved your first successful pupil?"

"It is a problem at which I have worked for the last seventeen years," said Mr. Appin, "but only during the last eight or nine months have I been rewarded with glimmerings of success. Of course I have experimented with thousands of animals, but latterly only with cats, those wonderful creatures which have assimilated themselves so marvellously with our civilization while retaining all their highly developed feral instincts. Here and there among cats one comes across an outstanding superior intellect, just as one does among the ruck of human beings, and when I made the acquaintance of Tobermory a week ago I saw at once that I was in contact with a 'Beyond-cat' of extraordinary intelligence. I had gone far along the road to success in recent experiments; with Tobermory, as you call him, I have reached the goal."

Mr. Appin concluded his remarkable statement in a voice which he strove to divest of a triumphant inflection. No one said "Rats," though Clovis's lips moved in a monosyllabic contortion which probably invoked those rodents of disbelief.

"And do you mean to say," asked Miss Resker, after a slight pause, "that you have taught Tobermory to say and understand easy sentences of one syllable?"

"My dear Miss Resker," said the wonder-worker patiently, "one teaches little children and savages and backward adults in that piecemeal fashion; when one has once solved the problem of making a beginning with an animal of highly developed intelligence one has no need for those halting methods. Tobermory can speak our language with perfect correctness."

This time Clovis very distinctly said, "Beyond-rats!" Sir Wilfrid was more polite, but equally sceptical.

"Hadn't we better have the cat in and judge for ourselves?" suggested Lady Blemley.

Sir Wilfrid went in search of the animal, and the company settled themselves down to the languid expectation of witnessing some more or less adroit drawing-room ventriloquism.

In a minute Sir Wilfrid was back in the room, his face white beneath its tan and his eyes dilated with excitement.

"By Gad, it's true!"

His agitation was unmistakably genuine, and his hearers started forward in a thrill of awakened interest.

Collapsing into an armchair he continued breathlessly: "I found him dozing in the smoking-room, and called out to him to come for his tea. He blinked at me in his usual way, and I said, 'Come on, Toby; don't keep us waiting'; and, by Gad! he drawled out in a most horribly natural voice that he'd come when he dashed well pleased! I nearly jumped out of my skin!"

Appin had preached to absolutely incredulous hearers; Sir Wilfrid's statement carried instant conviction. A Babel-like chorus of startled exclamation arose, amid which the scientist sat mutely enjoying the first fruit of his stupendous discovery.

In the midst of the clamour Tobermory entered the room and made his way with velvet tread and studied unconcern across to the group seated round the tea-table.

A sudden hush of awkwardness and constraint fell on the company. Somehow there seemed an element of embarrassment in addressing on equal terms a domestic cat of acknowledged mental ability.

"Will you have some milk, Tobermory?" asked Lady Blemley in a rather strained voice.

"I don't mind if I do," was the response, couched in a tone of even indifference. A shiver of suppressed excitement went through the listeners, and Lady Blemley might be excused for pouring out the saucerful of milk rather unsteadily.

"I'm afraid I've spilt a good deal of it," she said apologetically.

"After all, it's not my Axminster," was Tobermory's rejoinder.

Another silence fell on the group, and then Miss Resker, in her best district-visitor manner, asked if the human language had been difficult to learn. Tobermory looked squarely at her for a moment and then fixed his gaze serenely on the middle distance. It was obvious that boring questions lay outside his scheme of life.

"What do you think of human intelligence?" asked Mavis Pellington lamely.

"Of whose intelligence in particular?" asked Tobermory coldly.

"Oh, well, mine for instance," said Mavis, with a feeble laugh.

"You put me in an embarrassing position," said Tobermory, whose tone and attitude certainly did not suggest a shred of embarrassment. "When your inclusion in this house-party was suggested Sir Wilfrid protested that you were the most brainless woman of his acquaintance, and that there was a wide distinction between hospitality and the care of the feeble-minded. Lady Blemley replied that your lack of brain-power was the precise quality which had earned you your invitation, as you were the only person she could think of who might be idiotic enough to buy their old car. You know, the one they call 'The Envy of Sisyphus,' because it goes quite nicely up-hill if you push it."

Lady Blemley's protestations would have had greater effect if she had not casually suggested to Mavis only that morning that the car in question would be just the thing for her down at her Devonshire home.

Major Barfield plunged in heavily to effect a diversion.

"How about your carryings-on with the tortoise-shell puss up at the stables, eh?"

The moment he had said it every one realized the blunder.

"One does not usually discuss these matters in public," said Tobermory frigidly. "From a slight observation of your ways since you've been in this house I should imagine you'd find it inconvenient if I were to shift the conversation on to your own little affairs."

The panic which ensued was not confined to the Major.

"Would you like to go and see if cook has got your dinner ready?" suggested Lady Blemley hurriedly, affecting to ignore the fact that it wanted at least two hours to Tobermory's dinner-time.

"Thanks," said Tobermory, "not quite so soon after my tea. I don't want to die of indigestion."

"Cats have nine lives, you know," said Sir Wilfrid heartily.

"Possibly," answered Tobermory; "but only one liver."

"Adelaide!" said Mrs. Cornett, "do you mean to encourage that cat to go out and gossip about us in the servants' hall?"

The panic had indeed become general. A narrow ornamental balustrade ran in front of most of the bedroom windows at the Towers, and it was recalled with dismay that this had formed a favourite promenade for Tobermory at all hours, whence he could watch the pigeons—and heaven knew what else besides. If he intended to become reminiscent in his present outspoken strain the effect would be something more than disconcerting. Mrs. Cornett, who spent much time at her toilet table, and whose complexion was reputed to be of a nomadic though punctual disposition, looked as ill at ease as the Major. Miss Scrawen, who wrote fiercely sensuous poetry and led a blameless life, merely displayed irritation; if you are methodical and virtuous in private you don't necessarily want every one to know it. Bertie van Tahn, who was so depraved at seventeen that he had long ago given up trying to be any worse, turned a dull shade of gardenia white, but he did not commit the error of dashing out of the room like Odo Finsberry, a young gentleman who was understood to be reading for the Church and who was possibly disturbed at the thought of scandals he might hear concerning other people. Clovis had the presence of mind to maintain a composed exterior; privately he was calculating how long it would take to procure a box of fancy mice through the agency of the *Exchange and Mart* as a species of hush-money.

Even in a delicate situation like the present, Agnes Resker could not endure to remain too long in the background.

"Why did I ever come down here?" she asked dramatically.

Tobermory immediately accepted the opening.

"Judging by what you said to Mrs. Cornett on the croquet-lawn yesterday, you were out for food. You described the Blemleys as the dullest people to stay with that you knew, but said they were clever enough to employ a first-rate cook; otherwise they'd find it difficult to get any one to come down a second time."

"There's not a word of truth in it! I appeal to Mrs. Cornett——" exclaimed the discomfited Agnes.

"Mrs. Cornett repeated your remark afterwards to Bertie van Tahn," continued Tobermory, "and said, 'That woman is a regular Hunger Marcher; she'd go anywhere for four square meals a day,' and Bertie van Tahn said——"

At this point the chronicle mercifully ceased. Tobermory had caught a glimpse of the big yellow Tom from the Rectory working his way through the shrubbery towards the stable wing. In a flash he had vanished through the open French window.

With the disappearance of his too brilliant pupil Cornelius Appin found himself beset by a hurricane of bitter upbraiding, anxious inquiry, and frightened entreaty. The responsibility for the situation lay with him, and he must prevent matters from becoming worse. Could Tobermory impart his dangerous gift to other cats? was the first question he had to answer. It was possible, he replied, that he might have initiated his intimate friend the stable puss into his new accomplishment, but it was unlikely that his teaching could have taken a wider range as yet.

"Then," said Mrs. Cornett, "Tobermory may be a valuable cat and a great pet; but I'm sure you'll agree, Adelaide, that both he and the stable cat must be done away with without delay."

"You don't suppose I've enjoyed the last quarter of an hour, do you?" said Lady Blemley bitterly. "My husband and I are very fond of Tobermory—at least, we were before this horrible accomplishment was infused into him; but now, of course, the only thing is to have him destroyed as soon as possible."

"We can put some strychnine in the scraps he always gets at dinner-time," said Sir Wilfrid, "and I will go and drown the stable cat myself. The coachman will be very sore at losing his pet, but I'll say a very catching form of mange has broken out in both cats and we're afraid of it spreading to the kennels."

"But my great discovery!" expostulated Mr. Appin; "after all my years of research and experiment——"

"You can go and experiment on the short-horns at the farm, who are under proper control," said Mrs. Cornett, "or the elephants at the Zoological Gardens. They're said to be highly intelligent, and they have this recommendation, that they don't come creeping about our bedrooms and under chairs, and so forth."

An archangel ecstatically proclaiming the Millennium, and then finding that it clashed unpardonably with Henley and would have to be indefinitely postponed, could hardly have felt more crestfallen than Cornelius Appin at the reception of his wonderful achievement. Public opinion, however, was against him—in fact, had the general voice been consulted on the subject it is probable that a strong minority vote would have been in favour of including him in the strychnine diet.

Defective train arrangements and a nervous desire to see matters brought to a finish prevented an immediate dispersal of the party, but dinner that evening was not a social success. Sir Wilfrid had had rather a trying time with the stable cat and subsequently with the coachman. Agnes Resker ostentatiously limited her repast to a morsel of dry toast, which she bit as though it were a personal enemy; while Mavis Pellington maintained a vindictive silence throughout the meal. Lady Blemley kept up a flow of what she hoped was conversation, but her attention was fixed on the doorway. A plateful of carefully dosed fish scraps was in readiness on the sideboard, but sweets and savoury and dessert went their way, and no Tobermory appeared either in the dining-room or kitchen.

The sepulchral dinner was cheerful compared with the subsequent vigil in the smoking-room. Eating and drinking had at least supplied a distraction and cloak to the prevailing embarrassment. Bridge was out of the question in the general tension of nerves and tempers, and after Odo Finsberry had given a lugubrious rendering of "Mélisande in the Wood" to a frigid audience, music was tacitly avoided. At eleven the servants went to bed, announcing that the small window in the pantry had been left open as usual for Tobermory's private use. The guests read steadily through the current batch of magazines, and fell back gradually on the "Badminton Library" and bound volumes of *Punch*. Lady Blemley made periodic visits to the pantry, returning each time with an expression of listless depression which forestalled questioning.

At two o'clock Clovis broke the dominating silence.

"He won't turn up to-night. He's probably in the local newspaper office at the present moment, dictating the first instalment of his reminiscences. Lady What's-her-name's book won't be in it. It will be the event of the day."

Having made this contribution to the general cheerfulness, Clovis went to bed. At long intervals the various members of the house-party followed his example.

The servants taking round the early tea made a uniform announcement in reply to a uniform question. Tobermory had not returned.

Breakfast was, if anything, a more unpleasant function than dinner had been, but before its conclusion the situation was relieved. Tobermory's corpse was brought in from the shrubbery, where a gardener had just discovered it. From the bites on his throat and the yellow fur which coated his claws it was evident that he had fallen in unequal combat with the big Tom from the Rectory.

By midday most of the guests had quitted the

---

43. **Henley,** not the author, but the scene of the great annual regatta and races.

Towers, and after lunch Lady Blemley had sufficiently recovered her spirits to write an extremely nasty letter to the Rectory about the loss of her valuable pet.

Tobermory had been Appin's one successful pupil, and he was destined to have no successor. A few weeks later an elephant in the Dresden Zoological Garden, which had shown no previous signs of irritability, broke loose and killed an Englishman who had apparently been teasing it. The victim's name was variously reported in the papers as Oppin and Eppelin, but his front name was faithfully rendered Cornelius.

"If he was trying German irregular verbs on the poor beast," said Clovis, "he deserved all he got."

J. M. Synge
1871–1909

The Irish playwright J(ohn) M(illington) Synge was born at Rathfarnham, near Dublin, in 1871. His maternal grandfather was the Reverend Robert Traill, famous for his translation of Josephus. Words fascinated Synge from the beginning; as a child in Wicklow he listened to the quaint idioms of the countryfolk and fell into a half-rhythmical speech which was exact in its emphasis and yet blurred with a musical indefiniteness. Synge was graduated from Trinity College, Dublin, and went to Germany, undecided whether to be a musician or a scholar. He studied the theory of music, learned Hebrew and Gaelic, familiarized himself with Heine, and talked of translating the old German ballads into Irish. Then he went to Paris. In appearance he was arresting without being distinguished. Although of medium size, he was impressive in movement; a fierce mustache and a tuft on his nether lip gave him a somewhat French look. Spells of moody silence were followed by bursts of talk, when his speech "was like playing catch with an apple of banter, which one afterwards ate and forgot." Yeats describes him as "a drifting silent man full of hidden passion, one who loved wild islands, because there, set out in the light of day, he saw what lay hidden in himself."

It was in Paris that Yeats discovered Synge. He found him staying at a students' hotel in the Latin Quarter. Synge showed Yeats several of his tentative poems and essays; they were, according to Yeats, obsessed with methods of expression "and ways of looking upon life which come, not out of life, but out of literature, images reflected from mirror to mirror." Yeats, Synge's senior by only a few years, advised him to give up reading Racine, leave Paris, and return to Ireland. Synge obeyed Yeats to the letter. He went to the Aran Islands, lived primitively (chiefly upon salt fish and eggs), talked Irish, and became part of the life of the people. Most of all he listened to "the beautiful English which has grown up in Irish-speaking districts, and takes its vocabulary from the time of Malory and of the translators of the Bible but its idiom and its vivid metaphor from the Irish."

It was this homespun blend which Synge adapted to his purpose. Richly allusive, crammed with metaphor, and strengthened by intensity of feeling, it became his characterizing tongue. Synge's delight in language and passion for life was evident in his first work, *The Shadow of the Glen*, 1903. The reception of this play was typical of the hostility aroused by Synge's candor and penetration. The Irish audiences were willing to listen to satires of circumstances, particularly if they were concerned with city life, but they revolted against rustic satire; they would not permit the Irish peasant to be pictured in any but sentimental terms. Synge was assailed on every side, by the politicians, by the journalists, and by the professional patriots who accused him of "fouling his own nest." The hostility culminated after the performance of *The Playboy of the Western World*, 1907. This play, according to one journal, was "calumny gone raving mad"; at the second performance members of the Nationalist party shouted, blew trumpets, and caused such a disturbance that the actors could not be heard and police had to be called in. Similar demonstrations occurred when the play was produced in London and in New York. But Synge's coworkers, recognizing the complete individuality of his works, refused to be intimidated. Synge continued to compose plays for the Irish Theatre, and was at work on *Deirdre of the Sorrows*, in which he combined a favorite Irish myth with his own special dialect, when he died of an old illness in Dublin, in his thirty-ninth year, March 24, 1909.

Synge's work, matching his idiom, is condensed. In all he wrote only six plays—two of them extremely brief—a travel book, and one small volume of sharply tinctured poems and translations. Yet, even in his lifetime, admirers compared him to the masters of drama; it was claimed that he was "the greatest imaginative dramatist who has written English since Shakespeare." The enthusiasm was caused not only by Synge's adaptation of folk material, but by his sense of overbrimming life—"On the stage one must have reality, and one must have joy." In a preface to *The Tinker's Wedding*, 1907, Synge amplified this contention: "The drama is made serious—in the French sense of the word— not by the degree in which it is taken up with problems that are serious in themselves, but by the degree in which it gives the nourishment, not very easy to define, on which our imaginations live. . . . Of the things which nourish the imagination, humour is one of the most needful, and it is dangerous to limit or destroy it."

Humor alternately chuckles and riots through *The Playboy of the Western World*, which Yeats (in *Synge and the Ireland of His Time*, Ireland, 1911) considered "the strangest, the most beautiful expression in drama of that Irish fantasy which has come out of

Ireland" and which he claimed would be loved not only for its lyric utterance and violent laughter but "for holding so much of the mind of Ireland." In *The Playboy of the Western World*, where every speech is "as fully flavored as a nut or apple," tragedy turns into wild comedy. Christy Mahon, actually a bragging coward, becomes a hero fought over by the women and envied by the men; coarse realism is transformed into exotic romance and, when the glamorous word compels the grim deed, the climax is rough disillusion, comic but complete.

Just as Synge's imagination creates a drama which, though simple in plot, is greater than experience, so his characters speak a language which, though founded on the language of ordinary people, is richer than ordinary speech. The origin, as well as the vigor, of this speech is explained by Synge in the preface to *The Playboy of the Western World* which follows. "All art," Synge insists, "is a collaboration," and particular emphasis should be placed on the passage in which Synge describes how much aid he got from a chink in the floor of an old house which let him hear what was being said by the servants in the kitchen. In Synge's work, more than in most, the imagination of the artist is consciously linked with the imaginings of the people.

THE PLAYBOY OF THE WESTERN WORLD[1]

PREFACE

IN writing THE PLAYBOY OF THE WESTERN WORLD, as in my other plays, I have used one or two words only that I have not heard among the country people of Ireland, or spoken in my own nursery before I could read the newspapers. A certain number of the phrases I employ I have heard also from herds and fishermen along the coast from Kerry to Mayo, or from beggar-women and ballad-10 singers nearer Dublin; and I am glad to acknowledge how much I owe to the folk-imagination of these fine people. Anyone who has lived in real intimacy with the Irish peasantry will know that the wildest sayings and ideas in this play are tame indeed, compared with the fancies one may hear in any little hillside cabin in Geesala, or Carraroe, or Dingle Bay. All art is a collaboration; and there is little doubt that in the happy ages of literature, striking and beautiful phrases were as ready to the 20 story-teller's or the play-wright's hand, as the rich cloaks and dresses of his time. It is probable that when the Elizabethan dramatist took his ink-horn and sat down to his work he used many phrases that he had just heard, as he sat at dinner, from his

mother or his children. In Ireland, those of us who know the people have the same privilege. When I was writing *The Shadow of the Glen*, some years ago, I got more aid than any learning could have given me from a chink in the floor of the old Wicklow house where I was staying, that let me hear what was being said by the servant girls in the kitchen. This matter, I think, is of importance, for in countries where the imagination of the people, and the language they use, is rich and living, it is possible for a writer to be rich and copious in his words, and at the same time to give the reality, which is the root of all poetry, in a comprehensive and natural form. In the modern literature of towns, however, richness is found only in sonnets, or prose poems, or in one or two elaborate books that are far away from the profound and common interests of life. One has, on one side, Mallarmé and Huysmans producing this literature; and on the other, Ibsen and Zola dealing with the reality of life in joyless and pallid words. On the stage one must have reality, and one must have joy; and that is why the intellectual mod-

[1] Copyright, 1907, by J. M. Synge; copyright, 1935, by the Modern Library, Inc. Reprinted by permission of Random House, Inc.

ern drama has failed, and people have grown sick of the false joy of the musical comedy, that has been given them in place of the rich joy found only in what is superb and wild in reality. In a good play every speech should be as fully flavoured as a nut or apple, and such speeches cannot be written by anyone who works among people who have shut their lips on poetry. In Ireland, for a few years more, we have a popular imagination that is fiery, and magnificent, and tender; so that those of us who wish to 10 write start with a chance that is not given to writers in places where the springtime of the local life has been forgotten, and the harvest is a memory only, and the straw has been turned into bricks.

J. M. S.

January 21, 1907

PERSONS IN THE PLAY

CHRISTOPHER MAHON

OLD MAHON, his father, a squatter

MICHAEL JAMES FLAHERTY (called MICHAEL JAMES), a publican

MARGARET FLAHERTY (called PEGEEN MIKE), his daughter

WIDOW QUIN, a woman of about thirty

SHAWN KEOGH, her cousin, a young farmer

PHILLY CULLEN and JIMMY FARRELL, small farmers

SARA TANSEY, SUSAN BRADY, and HONOR BLAKE, village girls

A BELLMAN

SOME PEASANTS

The action takes place near a village, on a wild coast of Mayo. The first Act passes on an evening of autumn, the other two Acts on the following day.

ACT I

SCENE. *Country public-house or shebeen, very rough and untidy. There is a sort of counter on the right with shelves, holding many bottles and jugs, just seen above it. Empty barrels stand near the counter. At back, a little to left of counter, there is a door into the open air, then, more to the left, there is a settle with shelves above it, with more jugs, and a table beneath a window. At the left there is a large open fire-place, with turf fire, and a small door into inner room. PEGEEN, a wild-looking but fine girl, of about twenty, is writing at table. She is dressed in the usual peasant dress.*

Pegeen (slowly as she writes). Six yards of stuff for to make a yellow gown. A pair of lace boots with 50 lengthy heels on them and brassy eyes. A hat is suited for a wedding-day. A fine tooth comb. To be sent with three barrels of porter in Jimmy Farrell's creel cart on the evening of the coming Fair to Mis-

ter Michael James Flaherty. With the best compliments of this season. Margaret Flaherty.

Shawn Keogh (a fat and fair young man comes in as she signs, looks round awkwardly, when he sees she is alone). Where's himself?

Pegeen (without looking at him). He's coming. (*She directs the letter.*) To Mister Sheamus Mulroy, Wine and Spirit Dealer, Castlebar.

Shawn (uneasily). I didn't see him on the road.

Pegeen. How would you see him (*Licks stamp and puts it on letter.*) and it dark night this half hour gone by?

Shawn (turning towards door again). I stood a while outside wondering would I have a right to pass on or to walk in and see you, Pegeen Mike (*Comes to fire.*), and I could hear the cows breathing, and sighing in the stillness of the air, and not a step moving any place from this gate to the bridge.

Pegeen (putting letter in envelope). It's above at the 20 cross-roads he is, meeting Philly Cullen; and a couple more are going along with him to Kate Cassidy's wake.

Shawn (looking at her blankly). And he's going that length in the dark night.

Pegeen (impatiently). He is surely, and leaving me lonesome on the scruff of the hill. (*She gets up and puts envelope on dresser, then winds clock.*) Isn't it long the nights are now, Shawn Keogh, to be leaving a poor girl with her own self counting the hours to the 30 dawn of day?

Shawn (with awkward humour). If it is, when we're wedded in a short while you'll have no call to complain, for I've little will to be walking off to wakes or weddings in the darkness of the night.

Pegeen (with rather scornful good-humour). You're making mighty certain, Shaneen, that I'll wed you now.

Shawn. Aren't we after making a good bargain, the way we're only waiting these days on 40 Father Reilly's dispensation from the bishops, or the Court of Rome.

Pegeen (looking at him teasingly, washing up at dresser). It's a wonder, Shaneen, the Holy Father'd be taking notice of the likes of you; for if I was him I wouldn't bother with this place where you'll meet none but Red Linahan, has a squint in his eye, and Patcheen is lame in his heel, or the mad Mulrannies were driven from California and they lost in their wits. We're a queer lot these times to go troubling the Holy Father on his sacred seat.

Shawn (scandalized). If we are, we're as good this place as another, maybe, and as good these times as we were for ever.

Pegeen (with scorn). As good, is it? Where now will

you meet the like of Daneen Sullivan knocked the eye from a peeler; or Marcus Quin, God rest him, got six months for maiming ewes, and he a great warrant to tell stories of holy Ireland till he'd have the old women shedding down tears about their feet. Where will you find the like of them, I'm saying?

Shawn (*timidly*). If you don't, it's a good job, maybe; for (*with peculiar emphasis on the words*) Father Reilly has small conceit to have that kind walking around and talking to the girls.

Pegeen (*impatiently, throwing water from basin out of the door*). Stop tormenting me with Father Reilly (*Imitating his voice.*) when I'm asking only what way I'll pass these twelve hours of dark, and not take my death with the fear. (*Looking out of door.*)

Shawn (*timidly*). Would I fetch you the Widow Quin, maybe?

Pegeen. Is it the like of that murderer? You'll not, surely.

Shawn (*going to her, soothingly*). Then I'm thinking himself will stop along with you when he sees you taking on, for it'll be a long night-time with great darkness, and I'm after feeling a kind of fellow above in the furzy ditch, groaning wicked like a maddening dog, the way it's good cause you have, maybe, to be fearing now.

Pegeen (*turning on him sharply*). What's that? Is it a man you seen?

Shawn (*retreating*). I couldn't see him at all; but I heard him groaning out, and breaking his heart. It should have been a young man from his words speaking.

Pegeen (*going after him*). And you never went near to see was he hurted or what ailed him at all?

Shawn. I did not, Pegeen Mike. It was a dark, lonesome place to be hearing the like of him.

Pegeen. Well, you're a daring fellow, and if they find his corpse stretched above in the dews of dawn, what'll you say then to the peelers, or the Justice of the Peace?

Shawn (*thunderstruck*). I wasn't thinking of that. For the love of God, Pegeen Mike, don't let on I was speaking of him. Don't tell your father and the men is coming above; for if they heard that story, they'd have great blabbing this night at the wake.

Pegeen. I'll maybe tell them, and I'll maybe not.

Shawn. They are coming at the door. Will you whisht, I'm saying?

Pegeen. Whisht yourself.

[*She goes behind counter.* MICHAEL JAMES, *fat jovial publi-*

1. **peeler,** a policeman—so called from Sir Robert Peel, who organized the Irish constabulary. **49. whisht,** keep silent.

can, comes in followed by PHILLY CULLEN, *who is thin and mistrusting, and* JIMMY FARRELL, *who is fat and amorous, about forty-five.*]

Men (*together*). God bless you! The blessing of God on this place!

Pegeen. God bless you kindly.

Michael (*to men, who go to the counter*). Sit down now, and take your rest. (*Crosses to* SHAWN *at the fire.*) And how is it you are, Shawn Keogh? Are you coming over the sands to Kate Cassidy's wake?

Shawn. I am not, Michael James. I'm going home the short cut to my bed.

Pegeen (*speaking across the counter*). He's right too, and have you no shame, Michael James, to be quitting off for the whole night, and leaving myself lonesome in the shop?

Michael (*good-humouredly*). Isn't it the same whether I go for the whole night or a part only? and I'm thinking it's a queer daughter you are if you'd have me crossing backward through the Stooks of the Dead Women, with a drop taken.

Pegeen. If I am a queer daughter, it's a queer father'd be leaving me lonesome these twelve hours of dark, and I piling the turf with the dogs barking, and the calves mooing, and my own teeth rattling with the fear.

Jimmy (*flatteringly*). What is there to hurt you, and you a fine, hardy girl would knock the head of any two men in the place?

Pegeen (*working herself up*). Isn't there the harvest boys with their tongues red for drink, and the ten tinkers is camped in the east glen, and the thousand militia—bad cess to them!—walking idle through the land. There's lots surely to hurt me, and I won't stop alone in it, let himself do what he will.

Michael. If you're that afeard, let Shawn Keogh stop along with you. It's the will of God, I'm thinking, himself should be seeing to you now.

[*They all turn on* SHAWN.]

Shawn (*in horrified confusion*). I would and welcome, Michael James, but I'm afeard of Father Reilly; and what at all would the Holy Father and the Cardinals of Rome be saying if they heard I did the like of that?

Michael (*with contempt*). God help you! Can't you sit in by the hearth with the light lit and herself beyond in the room? You'll do that surely, for I've heard tell there's a queer fellow above, going mad or getting his death, maybe, in the gripe of the ditch, so she'd be safer this night with a person here.

Shawn (*with plaintive despair*). I'm afeard of Father Reilly, I'm saying. Let you not be tempting me, and we near married itself.

Philly (*with cold contempt*). Lock him in the west

room. He'll stay then and have no sin to be telling to the priest.

Michael (*to* SHAWN, *getting between him and the door*). Go up now.

Shawn (*at the top of his voice*). Don't stop me, Michael James. Let me out of the door, I'm saying, for the love of the Almighty God. Let me out (*Trying to dodge past him.*). Let me out of it, and may God grant you His indulgence in the hour of need.

Michael (*loudly*). Stop your noising, and sit down 10 by the hearth. (*Gives him a push and goes to counter laughing.*)

Shawn (*turning back, wringing his hands*). Oh, Father Reilly and the saints of God, where will I hide myself to-day? Oh, St. Joseph and St. Patrick and St. Brigid, and St. James, have mercy on me now!

[SHAWN *turns round, sees door clear, and makes a rush for it.*]

Michael (*catching him by the coat-tail*). You'd be going, is it?

Shawn (*screaming*). Leave me go, Michael James, leave me go, you old Pagan, leave me go, or I'll get the curse of the priests on you, and of the scarlet-coated bishops of the Courts of Rome.

[*With a sudden movement he pulls himself out of his coat, and disappears out of the door, leaving his coat in* MICHAEL's *hands.*]

Michael (*turning round, and holding up coat*). Well, there's the coat of a Christian man. Oh, there's sainted glory this day in the lonesome west; and by 30 the will of God I've got you a decent man, Pegeen, you'll have no call to be spying after if you've a score of young girls, maybe, weeding in your fields.

Pegeen (*taking up the defence of her property*). What right have you to be making game of a poor fellow for minding the priest, when it's your own fault is, not paying a penny pot-boy to stand along with me and give me courage in the doing of my work?

[*She snaps the coat away from him, and goes behind counter with it.*]

Michael (*taken aback*). Where would I get a pot-boy? Would you have me send the bell-man screaming in the streets of Castlebar?

Shawn (*opening the door a chink and putting in his head, in a small voice*). Michael James!

Michael (*imitating him*). What ails you?

Shawn. The queer dying fellow's beyond looking over the ditch. He's come up, I'm thinking, stealing your hens. (*Looks over his shoulder.*) God help me, he's following me now (*He runs into room.*), and if he's 50

37. **pot-boy**, a low-class servant.   42. **bell-man**, town crier. Pegeen's father, with humorous exaggeration, implies that if he keeps a servant the town crier will announce his bankruptcy.

heard what I said, he'll be having my life, and I going home lonesome in the darkness of the night.

[*For a perceptible moment they watch the door with curiosity. Some one coughs outside. Then* CHRISTY MAHON, *a slight young man, comes in very tired and frightened and dirty.*]

Christy (*in a small voice*). God save all here!

Men. God save you kindly!

Christy (*going to the counter*). I'd trouble you for a glass of porter, woman of the house. (*He puts down coin.*)

Pegeen (*serving him*). You're one of the tinkers, young fellow, is beyond camped in the glen?

Christy. I am not; but I'm destroyed walking.

Michael (*patronizingly*). Let you come up then to the fire. You're looking famished with the cold.

Christy. God reward you. (*He takes up his glass and goes a little way across to the left, then stops and looks about him.*) Is it often the polis do be coming into this 20 place, master of the house?

Michael. If you'd come in better hours, you'd have seen "Licensed for the Sale of Beer and Spirits, to be Consumed on the Premises," written in white letters above the door, and what would the polis want spying on me, and not a decent house within four miles, the way every living Christian is a bona fide, saving one widow alone?

Christy (*with relief*). It's a safe house, so.

[*He goes over to the fire, sighing and moaning. Then he sits down, putting his glass beside him and begins gnawing a turnip, too miserable to feel the others staring at him with curiosity.*]

Michael (*going after him*). Is it yourself is fearing the polis? You're wanting, maybe?

Christy. There's many wanting.

Michael. Many surely, with the broken harvest and the ended wars. (*He picks up some stockings, etc., that are near the fire, and carries them away furtively.*) It should be larceny, I'm thinking?

Christy (*dolefully*). I had it in my mind it was a dif- 40 ferent word and a bigger.

Pegeen. There's a queer lad. Were you never slapped in school, young fellow, that you don't know the name of your deed?

Christy (*bashfully*). I'm slow at learning, a middling scholar only.

Michael. If you're a dunce itself, you'd have a right to know that larceny's robbing and stealing. Is it for the like of that you're wanting?

Christy (*with a flash of family pride*). And I the son of 50 a strong farmer (*with a sudden qualm*), God rest his soul, could have bought up the whole of your old house a while since, from the butt of his tail-pocket, and not have missed the weight of it gone.

Michael (*impressed*). If it's not stealing, it's maybe something big.

Christy (*flattered*). Aye; it's maybe something big.

Jimmy. He's a wicked-looking young fellow. Maybe he followed after a young woman on a lonesome night.

Christy (*shocked*). Oh, the saints forbid, mister; I was all times a decent lad.

Philly (*turning on* JIMMY). You're a silly man, Jimmy Farrell. He said his father was a farmer a 10 while since, and there's himself now in a poor state. Maybe the land was grabbed from him, and he did what any decent man would do.

Michael (*to* CHRISTY, *mysteriously*). Was it bailiffs?

Christy. The divil a one.

Michael. Agents?

Christy. The divil a one.

Michael. Landlords?

Christy (*peevishly*). Ah, not at all, I'm saying. You'd see the like of them stories on any little paper 20 of a Munster town. But I'm not calling to mind any person, gentle, simple, judge or jury, did the like of me.

[*They all draw nearer with delighted curiosity.*]

Philly. Well, that lad's a puzzle-the-world.

Jimmy. He'd beat Dan Davies' circus, or the holy missioners making sermons on the villainy of man. Try him again, Philly.

Philly. Did you strike golden guineas out of solder, young fellow, or shilling coins itself? 30

Christy. I did not, mister, not sixpence nor a farthing coin.

Jimmy. Did you marry three wives maybe? I'm told there's a sprinkling have done that among the holy Luthers of the preaching north.

Christy (*shyly*). I never married with one, let alone with a couple or three.

Philly. Maybe he went fighting for the Boers, the like of the man beyond, was judged to be hanged, quartered, and drawn. Were you off east, young fel- 40 low, fighting bloody wars for Kruger and the freedom of the Boers?

Christy. I never left my own parish till Tuesday was a week.

Pegeen (*coming from counter*). He's done nothing, so. (*To* CHRISTY.) If you didn't commit murder or a bad, nasty thing, or false coining, or robbery, or butchery, or the like of them, there isn't anything that would be worth your troubling for to run from now. You did nothing at all. 50

Christy (*his feelings hurt*). That's an unkindly thing to be saying to a poor orphaned traveller, has a prison behind him, and hanging before, and hell's gap gaping below.

Pegeen (*with a sign to the men to be quiet*). You're only saying it. You did nothing at all. A soft lad the like of you wouldn't slit the windpipe of a screeching sow.

Christy (*offended*). You're not speaking the truth.

Pegeen (*in mock rage*). Not speaking the truth, is it? Would you have me knock the head of you with the butt of the broom?

Christy (*twisting round on her with a sharp cry of hor-* 10 *ror*). Don't strike me. I killed my poor father, Tuesday was a week, for doing the like of that.

Pegeen (*with blank amazement*). Is it killed your father?

Christy (*subsiding*). With the help of God I did surely, and that the Holy Immaculate Mother may intercede for his soul.

Philly (*retreating with* JIMMY). There's a daring fellow.

Jimmy. Oh, glory be to God!

Michael (*with great respect*). That was a hanging crime, mister honey. You should have had good reason for doing the like of that.

Christy (*in a very reasonable tone*). He was a dirty man, God forgive him, and he getting old and crusty, the way I couldn't put up with him at all.

Pegeen. And you shot him dead?

Christy (*shaking his head*). I never used weapons. I've no licence, and I'm a law-fearing man.

Michael. It was with a hilted knife maybe? I'm 30 told, in the big world it's bloody knives they use.

Christy (*loudly, scandalized*). Do you take me for a slaughter-boy?

Pegeen. You never hanged him, the way Jimmy Farrell hanged his dog from the licence, and had it screeching and wriggling three hours at the butt of a string, and himself swearing it was a dead dog, and the peelers swearing it had life?

Christy. I did not then. I just riz the loy and let fall the edge of it on the ridge of his skull, and he 40 went down at my feet like an empty sack, and never let a grunt or groan from him at all.

Michael (*making a sign to* PEGEEN *to fill* CHRISTY's *glass*). And what way weren't you hanged, mister? Did you bury him then?

Christy (*considering*). Aye. I buried him then. Wasn't I digging spuds in the field?

Michael. And the peelers never followed after you the eleven days that you're out?

Christy (*shaking his head*). Never a one of them, 50 and I walking forward facing hog, dog, or divil on the highway of the road.

Philly (*nodding wisely*). It's only with a common week-day kind of a murderer them lads would be

38. **loy,** a long, narrow spade.

trusting their carcase, and that man should be a great terror when his temper's roused.

Michael. He should then. (*To* CHRISTY.) And where was it, mister honey, that you did the deed?

Christy (*looking at him with suspicion*). Oh, a distant place, master of the house, a windy corner of high, distant hills.

Philly (*nodding with approval*). He's a close man, and he's right, surely.

Pegeen. That'd be a lad with the sense of Solomon to have for a pot-boy, Michael James, if it's the truth you're seeking one at all.

Philly. The peelers is fearing him, and if you'd that lad in the house there isn't one of them would come smelling around if the dogs itself were lapping poteen from the dung-pit of the yard.

Jimmy. Bravery's a treasure in a lonesome place, and a lad would kill his father, I'm thinking, would face a foxy divil with a pitchpike on the flags of hell.

Pegeen. It's the truth they're saying, and if I'd that lad in the house, I wouldn't be fearing the loosèd kharki cut-throats, or the walking dead.

Christy (*swelling with surprise and triumph*). Well, glory be to God!

Michael (*with deference*). Would you think well to stop here and be pot-boy, mister honey, if we gave you good wages, and didn't destroy you with the weight of work.

Shawn (*coming forward uneasily*). That'd be a queer kind to bring into a decent, quiet household with the like of Pegeen Mike.

Pegeen (*very sharply*). Will you whisht? Who's speaking to you?

Shawn (*retreating*). A bloody-handed murderer the like of . . .

Pegeen (*snapping at him*). Whisht, I am saying; we'll take no fooling from your like at all. (*To* CHRISTY *with a honeyed voice.*) And you, young fellow, you'd have a right to stop, I'm thinking, for we'd do our all and utmost to content your needs.

Christy (*overcome with wonder*). And I'd be safe in this place from the searching law?

Michael. You would, surely. If they're not fearing you, itself, the peelers in this place is decent, drouthy poor fellows, wouldn't touch a cur dog and not give warning in the dead of night.

Pegeen (*very kindly and persuasively*). Let you stop a short while anyhow. Aren't you destroyed walking with your feet in bleeding blisters, and your whole skin needing washing like a Wicklow sheep.

Christy (*looking round with satisfaction*). It's a nice

16. **poteen,** whisky made in private stills.

room, and if it's not humbugging me you are, I'm thinking that I'll surely stay.

Jimmy (*jumps up.*) Now, by the grace of God, herself will be safe this night, with a man killed his father holding danger from the door, and let you come on, Michael James, or they'll have the best stuff drunk at the wake.

Michael (*going to the door with men*). And begging your pardon, mister, what name will we call you, for we'd like to know?

Christy. Christopher Mahon.

Michael. Well, God bless you, Christy, and a good rest till we meet again when the sun'll be rising to the noon of day.

Christy. God bless you all.

Men. God bless you.

[*They go out except* SHAWN, *who lingers at door.*]

Shawn (*to* PEGEEN). Are you wanting me to stop along with you and keep you from harm?

Pegeen (*gruffly*). Didn't you say you were fearing Father Reilly?

Shawn. There'd be no harm staying now, I'm thinking, and himself in it too.

Pegeen. You wouldn't stay when there was need for you, and let you step off nimble this time when there's none.

Shawn. Didn't I say it was Father Reilly . . .

Pegeen. Go on, then, to Father Reilly (*In a jeering tone.*), and let him put you in the holy brotherhoods, and leave that lad to me.

Shawn. If I meet the Widow Quin . . .

Pegeen. Go on, I'm saying, and don't be waking this place with your noise. (*She hustles him out and bolts door.*) That lad would wear the spirits from the saints of peace. (*Bustles about, then takes off her apron and pins it up in the window as a blind,* CHRISTY *watching her timidly. Then she comes to him and speaks with bland good-humour.*) Let you stretch out now by the fire, young fellow. You should be destroyed travelling.

Christy (*shyly again, drawing off his boots*). I'm tired, surely, walking wild eleven days, and waking fearful in the night. (*He holds up one of his feet, feeling his blisters, and looking at them with compassion.*)

Pegeen (*standing beside him, watching him with delight*). You should have had great people in your family, I'm thinking, with the little, small feet you have, and you with a kind of a quality name, the like of what you'd find on the great powers and potentates of France and Spain.

Christy (*with pride*). We were great, surely, with wide and windy acres of rich Munster land.

Pegeen. Wasn't I telling you, and you a fine, handsome young fellow with a noble brow?

Christy (*with a flash of delighted surprise*). Is it me?

Pegeen. Aye. Did you never hear that from the young girls where you come from in the west or south?

Christy (*with venom*). I did not then. Oh, they're bloody liars in the naked parish where I grew a man.

Pegeen. If they are itself, you've heard it these days, I'm thinking, and you walking the world telling out your story to young girls or old.

Christy. I've told my story no place till this night, Pegeen Mike, and it's foolish I was here, maybe, to be talking free; but you're decent people, I'm thinking, and yourself a kindly woman, the way I wasn't fearing you at all.

Pegeen (*filling a sack with straw*). You've said the like of that, maybe, in every cot and cabin where you've met a young girl on your way.

Christy (*going over to her, gradually raising his voice*). I've said it nowhere till this night, I'm telling you; for I've seen none the like of you the eleven long days I am walking the world, looking over a low ditch or a high ditch on my north or my south, into stony, scattered fields, or scribes of bog, where you'd see young, limber girls, and fine, prancing women making laughter with the men.

Pegeen. If you weren't destroyed travelling, you'd have as much talk and streeleen, I'm thinking, as Owen Roe O'Sullivan or the poets of the Dingle Bay; and I've heard all times it's the poets are your like, fine, fiery fellows with great rages when their temper's roused.

Christy (*drawing a little nearer to her*). You've a power of rings, God bless you, and would there be any offence if I was asking are you single now?

Pegeen. What would I want wedding so young?

Christy (*with relief*). We're alike, so.

Pegeen (*she puts sack on settle and beats it up*). I never killed my father. I'd be afeard to do that, except I was the like of yourself with blind rages tearing me within, for I'm thinking you should have had great tussling when the end was come.

Christy (*expanding with delight at the first confidential talk he has ever had with a woman*). We had not then. It was a hard woman was come over the hill; and if he was always a crusty kind when he'd a hard woman setting him on, not the divil himself or his four fathers could put up with him at all.

Pegeen (*with curiosity*). And isn't it a great wonder that one wasn't fearing you?

Christy (*very confidentially*). Up to the day I killed my father, there wasn't a person in Ireland knew the kind I was, and I there drinking, waking, eating, sleeping, a quiet, simple poor fellow with no man giving me heed.

Pegeen (*getting a quilt out of the cupboard and putting it on the sack*). It was the girls were giving you heed maybe, and I'm thinking it's most conceit you'd have to be gaming with their like.

Christy (*shaking his head, with simplicity*). Not the girls itself, and I won't tell you a lie. There wasn't anyone heeding me in that place saving only the dumb beasts of the field. (*He sits down at fire.*)

Pegeen (*with disappointment*). And I thinking you should have been living the like of a king of Norway or the eastern world. (*She comes and sits beside him after placing bread and mug of milk on the table.*)

Christy (*laughing piteously*). The like of a king, is it? And I after toiling, moiling, digging, dodging from the dawn till dusk; with never a sight of joy or sport saving only when I'd be abroad in the dark night poaching rabbits on hills, for I was a devil to poach, God forgive me, (*Very naively.*) and I near got six months for going with a dung fork and stabbing a fish.

Pegeen. And it's that you'd call sport, is it, to be abroad in the darkness with yourself alone.

Christy. I did, God help me, and there I'd be as happy as the sunshine of St. Martin's Day, watching the light passing the north or the patches of fog, till I'd hear a rabbit starting to screech and I'd go running in the furze. Then, when I'd my full share, I'd come walking down where you'd see the ducks and geese stretched sleeping on the highway of the road, and before I'd pass the dunghill, I'd hear himself snoring out—a loud lonesome snore he'd be making all times, the while he was sleeping, and he a man'd be raging all times, the while he was waking, like a gaudy officer you'd hear cursing and damning and swearing oaths.

Pegeen. Providence and Mercy, spare us all!

Christy. It's that you'd say surely if you seen him and he after drinking for weeks, rising up in the red dawn, or before it maybe, and going out into the yard as naked as an ash tree in the moon of May, and shying clods against the visage of the stars till he'd put the fear of death into the banbhs and the screeching sows.

Pegeen. I'd be well-nigh afeard of that lad myself, I'm thinking. And there was no one in it but the two of you alone?

Christy. The divil a one, though he'd sons and daughters walking all great states and territories of the world, and not a one of them, to this day, but would say their seven curses on him, and they rous-

---

28. **streeleen,** wandering, adventuring.

45. **banbhs,** pigs.

ing up to let a cough or sneeze, maybe, in the deadness of the night.

Pegeen (*nodding her head*). Well, you should have been a queer lot. I never cursed my father the like of that, though I'm twenty and more years of age.

Christy. Then you'd have cursed mine, I'm telling you, and he a man never gave peace to any, saving when he'd get two months or three, or be locked in the asylums for battering peelers or assaulting men (*With depression.*), the way it was a bitter life he led me till I did up a Tuesday and halve his skull.

Pegeen (*putting her hand on his shoulder*). Well, you'll have peace in this place, Christy Mahon, and none to trouble you, and it's near time a fine lad like you should have your good share of the earth.

Christy. It's time surely, and I a seemly fellow with great strength in me and bravery of . . .

[*Some one knocks.*]

Christy (*clinging to* PEGEEN). Oh, glory! it's late for knocking, and this last while I'm in terror of the peelers, and the walking dead.

[*Knocking again.*]

Pegeen. Who's there?

Voice (*outside*). Me.

Pegeen. Who's me?

Voice. The Widow Quin.

Pegeen (*jumping up and giving him the bread and milk*). Go on now with your supper, and let on to be sleepy, for if she found you were such a warrant to talk, she'd be stringing gabble till the dawn of day.

[*He takes bread and sits shyly with his back to the door.*]

Pegeen (*opening door, with temper*). What ails you, or what is it you're wanting at this hour of the night?

Widow Quin (*coming in a step and peering at* CHRISTY). I'm after meeting Shawn Keogh and Father Reilly below, who told me of your curiosity man, and they fearing by this time he was maybe roaring, romping on your hands with drink.

Pegeen (*pointing to* CHRISTY). Look now is he roaring, and he stretched away drowsy with his supper and his mug of milk. Walk down and tell that to Father Reilly and to Shaneen Keogh.

Widow Quin (*coming forward*). I'll not see them again, for I've their word to lead that lad forward for to lodge with me.

Pegeen (*in blank amazement*). This night is it?

Widow Quin (*going over*). This night. "It isn't fitting," says the priesteen, "to have his likeness lodging with an orphaned girl." (*To* CHRISTY.) God save you, mister!

Christy (*shyly*). God save you kindly!

Widow Quin (*looking at him with half-amazed curiosity*). Well, aren't you a little smiling fellow? It

should have been great and bitter torments did rouse your spirits to a deed of blood.

Christy (*doubtfully*). It should, maybe.

Widow Quin. It's more than "maybe" I'm saying, and it'd soften my heart to see you sitting so simple with your cup and cake, and you fitter to be saying your catechism than slaying your da.

Pegeen (*at counter, washing glasses*). There's talking when any'd see he's fit to be holding his head high with the wonders of the world. Walk on from this, for I'll not have him tormented and he destroyed travelling since Tuesday was a week.

Widow Quin (*peaceably*). We'll be walking surely when his supper's done, and you'll find we're great company, young fellow, when it's of the like of you and me you'd hear the penny poets singing in an August Fair.

Christy (*innocently*). Did you kill your father?

Pegeen (*contemptuously*). She did not. She hit himself with a worn pick, and the rusted poison did corrode his blood the way he never overed it, and died after. That was a sneaky kind of murder did win small glory with the boys itself. (*She crosses to* CHRISTY'S *left.*)

Widow Quin (*with good-humour*). If it didn't, maybe all knows a widow woman has buried her children and destroyed her man is a wiser comrade for a young lad than a girl, the like of you, who'd go helter-skeltering after any man would let you a wink upon the road.

Pegeen (*breaking out into wild rage*). And you'll say that, Widow Quin, and you gasping with the rage you had racing the hill beyond to look on his face.

Widow Quin (*laughing derisively*). Me, is it? Well, Father Reilly has cuteness to divide you now. (*She pulls* CHRISTY *up.*) There's great temptation in a man did slay his da, and we'd best be going, young fellow; so rise up and come with me.

Pegeen (*seizing his arm*). He'll not stir. He's potboy in this place, and I'll not have him stolen off and kidnabbed while himself's abroad.

Widow Quin. It'd be a crazy pot-boy'd lodge him in the shebeen where he works by day, so you'd have a right to come on, young fellow, till you see my little houseen, a perch off on the rising hill.

Pegeen. Wait till morning, Christy Mahon. Wait till you lay eyes on her leaky thatch is growing more pasture for her buck goat than her square of fields, and she without a tramp itself to keep in order her place at all.

Widow Quin. When you see me contriving in my little gardens, Christy Mahon, you'll swear the Lord God formed me to be living lone, and that there

43. **shebeen**, a place where liquor is sold without a license.

isn't my match in Mayo for thatching, or mowing, or shearing a sheep.

Pegeen (with noisy scorn). It's true the Lord God formed you to contrive indeed. Doesn't the world know you reared a black ram at your own breast, so that the Lord Bishop of Connaught felt the elements of a Christian, and he eating it after in a kidney stew? Doesn't the world know you've been seen shaving the foxy skipper from France for a three-penny bit and a sop of grass tobacco would wring the liver from a mountain goat you'd meet leaping the hills?

Widow Quin (with amusement). Do you hear her now, young fellow? Do you hear the way she'll be rating at your own self when a week is by?

Pegeen (to CHRISTY). Don't heed her. Tell her to go into her pigsty and not plague us here.

Widow Quin. I'm going; but he'll come with me.

Pegeen (shaking him). Are you dumb, young fellow?

Christy (timidly, to WIDOW QUIN). God increase you; but I'm pot-boy in this place, and it's here I'd liefer stay.

Pegeen (triumphantly). Now you have heard him, and go on from this.

Widow Quin (looking round the room). It's lonesome this hour crossing the hill, and if he won't come along with me, I'd have a right maybe to stop this night with yourselves. Let me stretch out on the settle, Pegeen Mike; and himself can lie by the hearth.

Pegeen (short and fiercely). Faith, I won't. Quit off or I will send you now.

Widow Quin (gathering her shawl up). Well, it's a terror to be aged a score. (*To* CHRISTY, *going.*) God bless you now, young fellow, and let you be wary, or there's right torment will await you here if you go romancing with her like, and she waiting only, as they bade me say, on a sheepskin parchment to be wed with Shawn Keogh of Killakeen.

Christy (going to PEGEEN *as she bolts the door).* What's that she's after saying?

Pegeen. Lies and blather, you've no call to mind. Well, isn't Shawn Keogh an impudent fellow to send up spying on me? Wait till I lay hands on him. Let him wait, I'm saying.

Christy. And you're not wedding him at all?

Pegeen. I wouldn't wed him if a bishop came walking for to join us here.

Christy. That God in glory may be thanked for that.

Pegeen. There's your bed now. I've put a quilt upon you I'm after quilting a while since with my own two hands, and you'd best stretch out now for your sleep, and may God give you a good rest till I call you in the morning when the cocks will crow.

Christy (as she goes to inner room). May God and Mary and St. Patrick bless you and reward you, for your kindly talk. (*She shuts the door behind her. He settles his bed slowly, feeling the quilt with immense satisfaction.*) Well, it's a clean bed and soft with it, and it's great luck and company I've won me in the end of time—two fine women fighting for the likes of me—till I'm thinking this night wasn't I a foolish fellow not to kill my father in the years gone by.

[CURTAIN]

ACT II

SCENE, *as before. Brilliant morning light.* CHRISTY, *looking bright and cheerful, is cleaning a girl's boots.*

Christy (to himself, counting jugs on dresser). Half a hundred beyond. Ten there. A score that's above. Eighty jugs. Six cups and a broken one. Two plates. A power of glasses. Bottles, a school-master'd be hard set to count, and enough in them, I'm thinking, to drunken all the wealth and wisdom of the County Clare. (*He puts down the boot carefully.*) There's her boots now, nice and decent for her evening use, and isn't it grand brushes she has? (*He puts them down and goes by degrees to the looking-glass.*) Well, this'd be a fine place to be my whole life talking out with swearing Christians, in place of my old dogs and cat; and I stalking around, smoking my pipe and drinking my fill, and never a day's work but drawing a cork an odd time, or wiping a glass, or rinsing out a shiny tumbler for a decent man. (*He takes the looking-glass from the wall and puts it on the back of a chair; then sits down in front of it and begins washing his face.*) Didn't I know rightly I was handsome, though it was the divil's own mirror we had beyond, would twist a squint across an angel's brow; and I'll be growing fine from this day, the way I'll have a soft lovely skin on me and won't be the like of the clumsy young fellows do be ploughing all times in the earth and dung. (*He starts.*) Is she coming again? (*He looks out.*) Stranger girls. God help me, where'll I hide myself away and my long neck naked to the world? (*He looks out.*) I'd best go to the room maybe till I'm dressed again.

[*He gathers up his coat and the looking-glass, and runs into the inner room. The door is pushed open, and* SUSAN BRADY *looks in, and knocks on door.*]

Susan. There's nobody in it. (*Knocks again.*)

Nelly (pushing her in and following her, with HONOR BLAKE *and* SARA TANSEY). It'd be early for them both to be out walking the hill.

Susan. I'm thinking Shawn Keogh was making game of us, and there's no such man in it at all.

Honor (pointing to straw and quilt). Look at that. He's been sleeping there in the night. Well, it'll be a hard case if he's gone off now, the way we'll never set our eyes on a man killed his father, and we after rising early and destroying ourselves running fast on the hill.

Nelly. Are you thinking them's his boots?

Sara (taking them up). If they are, there should be his father's track on them. Did you never read in the papers the way murdered men do bleed and drip?

Susan. Is that blood there, Sara Tansey?

Sara (smelling it). That's bog water, I'm thinking, but it's his own they are, surely, for I never seen the like of them for whitey mud, and red mud, and turf on them, and the fine sands of the sea. That man's been walking, I'm telling you. *(She goes down right, putting on one of his boots.)*

Susan (going to window). Maybe he's stolen off to Belmullet with the boots of Michael James, and you'd have a right so to follow after him, Sara Tansey, and you the one yoked the ass cart and drove ten miles to set your eyes on the man bit the yellow lady's nostril on the northern shore. *(She looks out.)*

Sara (running to window, with one boot on). Don't be talking, and we fooled to-day. *(Putting on the other boot.)* There's a pair do fit me well, and I'll be keeping them for walking to the priest, when you'd be ashamed this place, going up winter and summer with nothing worth while to confess at all.

Honor (who has been listening at door). Whisht! there's some one inside the room. *(She pushes door a chink open.)* It's a man.

[SARA *kicks off boots and puts them where they were. They all stand in a line looking through chink.*]

Sara. I'll call him. Mister! Mister! *(He puts in his head.)* Is Pegeen within?

Christy (coming in as meek as a mouse, with the looking-glass held behind his back). She's above on the cnuceen, seeking the nanny goats, the way she'd have a sup of goat's milk for to colour my tea.

Sara. And asking your pardon, is it you's the man killed his father?

Christy (sidling toward the nail where the glass was hanging). I am, God help me!

Sara (taking eggs she has brought). Then my thousand welcomes to you, and I've run up with a brace of duck's eggs for your food to-day. Pegeen's ducks is no use, but these are the real rich sort. Hold out your hand and you'll see it's no lie I'm telling you.

42. cnuceen, little hill.

Christy (coming forward shyly, and holding out his left hand). They're a great and weighty size.

Susan. And I run up with a pat of butter, for it'd be a poor thing to have you eating your spuds dry, and you after running a great way since you did destroy your da.

Christy. Thank you kindly.

Honor. And I brought you a little cut of cake, for you should have a thin stomach on you, and you that length walking the world.

Nelly. And I brought you a little laying pullet— boiled and all she is—was crushed at the fall of night by the curate's car. Feel the fat of that breast, mister.

Christy. It's bursting, surely. *(He feels it with the back of his hand, in which he holds the presents.)*

Sara. Will you pinch it? Is your right hand too sacred for to use at all? *(She slips round behind him.)* It's a glass he has. Well, I never seen to this day a man with a looking-glass held to his back. Them that kills their fathers is a vain lot surely.

[*Girls giggle.*]

Christy (smiling innocently and piling presents on glass). I'm very thankful to you all to-day. . . .

Widow Quin (coming in quickly, at door). Sara Tansey, Susan Brady, Honor Blake! What in glory has you here at this hour of day?

Girls (giggling). That's the man killed his father.

Widow Quin (coming to them). I know well it's the man; and I'm after putting him down in the sports below for racing, leaping, pitching, and the Lord knows what.

Sara (exuberantly). That's right, Widow Quin. I'll bet my dowry that he'll lick the world.

Widow Quin. If you will, you'd have a right to have him fresh and nourished in place of nursing a feast. *(Taking presents.)* Are you fasting or fed, young fellow?

Christy. Fasting, if you please.

Widow Quin (loudly). Well, you're the lot. Stir up now and give him his breakfast. *(To* CHRISTY.*)* Come here to me *(She puts him on bench beside her while the girls make tea and get his breakfast.),* and let you tell us your story before Pegeen will come, in place of grinning your ears off like the moon of May.

Christy (beginning to be pleased). It's a long story; you'd be destroyed listening.

Widow Quin. Don't be letting on to be shy, a fine, gamey, treacherous lad the like of you. Was it in your house beyond you cracked his skull?

Christy (shy but flattered). It was not. We were digging spuds in his cold, sloping, stony, **divil's patch** of a field.

Widow Quin. And you went asking money of him, or making talk of getting a wife would drive him from his farm?

Christy. I did not, then; but there I was, digging and digging, and "You squinting idiot," says he, "let you walk down now and tell the priest you'll wed the Widow Casey in a score of days."

Widow Quin. And what kind was she?

Christy (with horror). A walking terror from beyond the hills, and she two score and five years, and two hundredweights and five pounds in the weighing scales, with a limping leg on her, and a blinded eye, and she a woman of noted misbehaviour with the old and young.

Girls (clustering round him, serving him). Glory be.

Widow Quin. And what did he want driving you to wed with her? *(She takes a bit of the chicken.)*

Christy (eating with growing satisfaction). He was letting on I was wanting a protector from the harshness of the world, and he without a thought the whole while but how he'd have her hut to live in and her gold to drink.

Widow Quin. There's maybe worse than a dry hearth and a widow woman and your glass at night. So you hit him then?

Christy (getting almost excited). I did not. "I won't wed her," says I, "when all know she did suckle me for six weeks when I came into the world, and she a hag this day with a tongue on her has the crows and seabirds scattered, the way they wouldn't cast a shadow on her garden with the dread of her curse."

Widow Quin (teasingly). That one should be right company.

Sara (eagerly). Don't mind her. Did you kill him then?

Christy. "She's too good for the like of you," says he, "and go on now or I'll flatten you out like a crawling beast has passed under a dray." "You will not if I can help it," says I. "Go on," says he, "or I'll have the divil making garters of your limbs to-night." "You will not if I can help it," says I. *(He sits up, brandishing his mug.)*

Sara. You were right surely.

Christy (impressively). With that the sun came out between the cloud and the hill, and it shining green in my face. "God have mercy on your soul," says he, lifting a scythe. "Or on your own," says I, raising the loy.

Susan. That's a grand story.

Honor. He tells it lovely.

Christy (flattered and confident, waving bone). He gave a drive with scythe, and I gave a lep to the east. Then I turned around with my back to the north,

and I hit a blow on the ridge of his skull, laid him stretched out, and he split to the knob of his gullet. *(He raises the chicken bone to his Adam's apple.)*

Girls (together). Well, you're a marvel! Oh, God bless you! You're the lad, surely!

Susan. I'm thinking the Lord God sent him this road to make a second husband to the Widow Quin, and she with a great yearning to be wedded, though all dread her here. Lift him on her knee, Sara Tansey.

Widow Quin. Don't tease him.

Sara (going over to dresser and counter very quickly, and getting two glasses and porter). You're heroes surely, and let you drink a supeen with your arms linked like the outlandish lovers in the sailor's song. *(She links their arms and gives them the glasses.)* There now. Drink a health to the wonders of the western world, the pirates, preachers, poteen-makers, with the jobbing jockies; parching peelers, and the juries fill their stomachs selling judgments of the English law *(Brandishing the bottle.).*

Widow Quin. That's a right toast, Sara Tansey. Now, Christy.

[*They drink with their arms linked, he drinking with his left hand, she with her right. As they are drinking,* PEGEEN MIKE *comes in with a milk-can and stands aghast. They all spring away from* CHRISTY. *He goes down left.* WIDOW QUIN *remains seated.*]

Pegeen (angrily, to SARA).What is it you're wanting?

Sara (twisting her apron). An ounce of tobacco.

Pegeen. Have you tuppence?

Sara. I've forgotten my purse.

Pegeen. Then you'd best be getting it and not fooling us here. *(To the* WIDOW QUIN, *with more elaborate scorn.)* And what is it you're wanting, Widow Quin?

Widow Quin (insolently). A penn'orth of starch.

Pegeen (breaking out). And you without a white shift or a shirt in your whole family since the drying of the flood. I've no starch for the like of you, and let you walk on now to Killamuck.

Widow Quin (turning to CHRISTY, *as she goes out with the girls).* Well, you're mighty huffy this day, Pegeen Mike, and, you young fellow, let you not forget the sports and racing when the noon is by.

[*They go out.*]

Pegeen (imperiously). Fling out that rubbish and put them cups away. *(*CHRISTY *tidies away in great haste.)* Shove in the bench by the wall. *(He does so.)* And hang that glass on the nail. What disturbed it at all?

Christy (very meekly). I was making myself decent only, and this a fine country for young lovely girls.

14. supeen, a sip.

Pegeen (*sharply*). Whisht your talking of girls. (*Goes to counter on right.*)

Christy. Wouldn't any wish to be decent in a place . . .

Pegeen. Whisht I'm saying.

Christy (*looks at her face for a moment with great misgivings, then as a last effort takes up a loy, and goes towards her, with feigned assurance*). It was with a loy the like of that I killed my father.

Pegeen (*still sharply*). You've told me that story 10 six times since the dawn of day.

Christy (*reproachfully*). It's a queer thing you wouldn't care to be hearing it and them girls after walking four miles to be listening to me now.

Pegeen (*turning round astonished*). Four miles?

Christy (*apologetically*). Didn't himself say there were only bona fides living in the place?

Pegeen. It's bona fides by the road they are, but that lot came over the river lepping the stones. It's not three perches when you go like that, and I was 20 down this morning looking on the papers the post-boy does have in his bag. (*With meaning and emphasis.*) For there was great news this day, Christopher Mahon. (*She goes into room on left.*)

Christy (*suspiciously*). Is it news of my murder?

Pegeen (*inside*). Murder, indeed.

Christy (*loudly*). A murdered da?

Pegeen (*coming in again and crossing right*). There was not, but a story filled half a page of the hanging of a man. Ah, that should be a fearful end, young 30 fellow, and it worst of all for a man who destroyed his da; for the like of him would get small mercies, and when it's dead he is they'd put him in a narrow grave, with cheap sacking wrapping him round, and pour down quicklime on his head, the way you'd see a woman pouring any frish-frash from a cup.

Christy (*very miserably*). Oh, God help me. Are you thinking I'm safe? You were saying at the fall of night I was shut of jeopardy and I here with 40 yourselves.

Pegeen (*severely*). You'll be shut of jeopardy no place if you go talking with a pack of wild girls the like of them do be walking abroad with the peelers, talking whispers at the fall of night.

Christy (*with terror*). And you're thinking they'd tell?

Pegeen (*with mock sympathy*). Who knows, God help you?

Christy (*loudly*). What joy would they have to 50 bring hanging to the likes of me?

Pegeen. It's queer joys they have, and who knows the thing they'd do, if it'd make the green stones cry itself to think of you swaying and swiggling at

the butt of a rope, and you with a fine, stout neck, God bless you! the way you'd be a half an hour, in great anguish, getting your death.

Christy (*getting his boots and putting them on*). If there's that terror of them, it'd be best, maybe, I went on wandering like Esau or Cain and Abel on the sides of Neifin or the Erris plain.

Pegeen (*beginning to play with him*). It would, maybe, for I've heard the Circuit Judges this place is a heartless crew.

Christy (*bitterly*). It's more than Judges this place is a heartless crew. (*Looking up at her.*) And isn't it a poor thing to be starting again and I a lonesome fellow will be looking out on women and girls the way the needy fallen spirits do be looking on the Lord?

Pegeen. What call have you to be that lonesome when there's poor girls walking Mayo in their thousands now?

Christy (*grimly*). It's well you know what call I have. It's well you know it's a lonesome thing to be passing small towns with the lights shining sideways when the night is down, or going in strange places with a dog noising before you and a dog noising behind, or drawn to the cities where you'd hear a voice kissing and talking deep love in every shadow of the ditch, and you passing on with an empty, hungry stomach failing from your heart.

Pegeen. I'm thinking you're an odd man, Christy Mahon. The oddest walking fellow I ever set my eyes on to this hour to-day.

Christy. What would any be but odd men and they living lonesome in the world?

Pegeen. I'm not odd, and I'm my whole life with my father only.

Christy (*with infinite admiration*). How would a lovely, handsome woman the like of you be lonesome when all men should be thronging around to hear the sweetness of your voice, and the little infant children should be pestering your steps I'm thinking, and you walking the roads.

Pegeen. I'm hard set to know what way a coaxing fellow the like of yourself should be lonesome either.

Christy. Coaxing.

Pegeen. Would you have me think a man never talked with the girls would have the words you've spoken to-day? It's only letting on you are to be lonesome, the way you'd get around me now.

Christy. I wish to God I was letting on; but I was lonesome all times, and born lonesome, I'm thinking, as the moon of dawn. (*Going to door.*)

Pegeen (*puzzled by his talk*). Well, it's a story I'm not understanding at all why you'd be worse than another, Christy Mahon, and you a fine lad with the great savagery to destroy your da.

Christy. It's little I'm understanding myself, saving only that my heart's scalded this day, and I going off stretching out the earth between us, the way I'll not be waking near you another dawn of the year till the two of us do arise to hope or judgment with the saints of God, and now I'd best be going with my wattle in my hand, for hanging is a poor thing (*Turning to go.*), and it's little welcome only is left me in this house to-day.

Pegeen (*sharply*). Christy! (*He turns round.*) Come here to me. (*He goes towards her.*) Lay down that switch and throw some sods on the fire. You're potboy in this place, and I'll not have you mitch off from us now.

Christy. You were saying I'd be hanged if I stay.

Pegeen (*quite kindly at last*). I'm after going down and reading the fearful crimes of Ireland for two weeks or three, and there wasn't a word of your murder. (*Getting up and going over to the counter.*) They've likely not found the body. You're safe so with ourselves.

Christy (*astonished, slowly*). It's making game of me you were (*Following her with fearful joy.*), and I can stay so, working at your side, and I not lonesome from this mortal day.

Pegeen. What's to hinder you from staying, except the widow woman or the young girls would inveigle you off?

Christy (*with rapture*). And I'll have your words from this day filling my ears, and that look is come upon you meeting my two eyes, and I watching you loafing around in the warm sun, or rinsing your ankles when the night is come.

Pegeen (*kindly, but a little embarrassed*). I'm thinking you'll be a loyal young lad to have working around, and if you vexed me a while since with your leaguing with the girls, I wouldn't give a thraneen for a lad hadn't a mighty spirit in him and a gamey heart.

[SHAWN KEOGH *runs in carrying a cleeve on his back, followed by the* WIDOW QUIN.]

Shawn (*to* PEGEEN). I was passing below, and I seen your mountainy sheep eating cabbages in Jimmy's field. Run up or they'll be bursting, surely.

Pegeen. Oh, God mend them!

[*She puts a shawl over her head and runs out.*

Christy (*looking from one to the other. Still in high spirits*). I'd best go to her aid maybe. I'm handy with ewes.

Widow Quin (*closing the door*). She can do that

much, and there is Shaneen has long speeches for to tell you now. (*She sits down with an amused smile.*)

Shawn (*taking something from his pocket and offering it to* CHRISTY). Do you see that, mister?

Christy (*looking at it*). The half of a ticket to the Western States!

Shawn (*trembling with anxiety*). I'll give it to you and my new hat (*Pulling it out of hamper.*); and my breeches with the double seat (*Pulling it off.*); and my new coat is woven from the blackest shearings for three miles around (*Giving him the coat.*); I'll give you the whole of them, and my blessing, and the blessing of Father Reilly itself, maybe, if you'll quit from this and leave us in the peace we had till last night at the fall of dark.

Christy (*with a new arrogance*). And for what is it you're wanting to get shut of me?

Shawn (*looking to the* WIDOW *for help*). I'm a poor scholar with middling faculties to coin a lie, so I'll tell you the truth, Christy Mahon. I'm wedding with Pegeen beyond, and I don't think well of having a clever, fearless man the like of you dwelling in her house.

Christy (*almost pugnaciously*). And you'd be using bribery for to banish me?

Shawn (*in an imploring voice*). Let you not take it badly, mister honey; isn't beyond the best place for you, where you'll have golden chains and shiny coats and you riding upon hunters with the ladies of the land. (*He makes an eager sign to the* WIDOW QUIN *to come to help him.*)

Widow Quin (*coming over*). It's true for him, and you'd best quit off and not have that poor girl setting her mind on you, for there's Shaneen thinks she wouldn't suit you, though all is saying that she'll wed you now.

[CHRISTY *beams with delight.*]

Shawn (*in terrified earnest*). She wouldn't suit you, and she with the divil's own temper the way you'd be strangling one another in a score of days. (*He makes the movement of strangling with his hands.*) It's the like of me only that she's fit for; a quiet simple fellow wouldn't raise a hand upon her if she scratched itself.

Widow Quin (*putting* SHAWN'S *hat on* CHRISTY). Fit them clothes on you anyhow, young fellow, and he'd maybe loan them to you for the sports. (*Pushing him towards inner door.*) Fit them on and you can give your answer when you have them tried.

Christy (*beaming, delighted with the clothes*). I will then. I'd like herself to see me in them tweeds and hat. (*He goes into room and shuts the door.*)

Shawn (*in great anxiety*). He'd like herself to see them. He'll not leave us, Widow Quin. He's a

---

9. wattle, flexible rod.   **15. mitch,** stray   **40. thraneen,** a blade of grass—any trifle.   **42. cleeve,** basket.

score of divils in him the way it's well nigh certain
he will wed Pegeen.

Widow Quin (*jeeringly*). It's true all girls are fond
of courage and do hate the like of you.

Shawn (*walking about in desperation*). Oh, Widow
Quin, what'll I be doing now? I'd inform again
him, but he'd burst from Kilmainham and he'd be
sure and certain to destroy me. If I wasn't so God-
fearing, I'd near have courage to come behind him
and run a pike into his side. Oh, it's a hard case to 10
be an orphan and not to have your father that
you're used to, and you'd easy kill and make yourself a hero in the sight of all. (*Coming up to her.*) Oh,
Widow Quin, will you find me some contrivance
when I've promised you a ewe?

Widow Quin. A ewe's a small thing, but what
would you give me if I did wed him and did save
you so?

Shawn (*with astonishment*). You?

Widow Quin. Aye. Would you give me the red 20
cow you have and the mountainy ram, and the
right of way across your rye path, and a load of
dung at Michaelmas, and turbary upon the western
hill?

Shawn (*radiant with hope*). I would surely, and I'd
give you the wedding-ring I have, and the loan of
a new suit, the way you'd have him decent on the
wedding-day. I'd give you two kids for your dinner,
and a gallon of poteen, and I'd call the piper on the
long car to your wedding from Crossmolina or from 30
Ballina. I'd give you . . .

Widow Quin. That'll do, so, and let you whisht,
for he's coming now again.

[CHRISTY *comes in very natty in the new clothes.* WIDOW
QUIN *goes to him admiringly.*]

Widow Quin. If you seen yourself now, I'm thinking you'd be too proud to speak to us at all, and
it'd be a pity surely to have your like sailing from
Mayo to the western world.

Christy (*as proud as a peacock*). I'm not going. If 40
this is a poor place itself, I'll make myself contented
to be lodging here.

[WIDOW QUIN *makes a sign to* SHAWN *to leave them.*]

Shawn. Well, I'm going measuring the racecourse
while the tide is low, so I'll leave you the garments
and my blessing for the sports to-day. God bless you!
                                        [*He wriggles out.*

Widow Quin (*admiring* CHRISTY). Well, you're
mighty spruce, young fellow. Sit down now while
you're quiet till you talk with me.

Christy (*swaggering*). I'm going abroad on the
hillside for to seek Pegeen.

23. **turbary,** the right to dig turf, or peat, upon another's
land.

Widow Quin. You'll have time and plenty for to
seek Pegeen, and you heard me saying at the fall
of night the two of us should be great company.

Christy. From this out I'll have no want of company when all sorts is bringing me their food and
clothing (*He swaggers to the door, tightening his belt.*),
the way they'd set their eyes upon a gallant orphan
cleft his father with one blow to the breeches belt.
(*He opens door, then staggers back.*) Saints of glory!
Holy angels from the throne of light!

Widow Quin (*going over*). What ails you?

Christy. It's the walking spirit of my murdered
da?

Widow Quin (*looking out*). Is it that tramper?

Christy (*wildly*). Where'll I hide my poor body
from that ghost of hell?

[*The door is pushed open, and old* MAHON *appears on
            threshold.* CHRISTY *darts in behind door.*]

Widow Quin (*in great amusement*). God save you,
my poor man.

Mahon (*gruffly*). Did you see a young lad passing
this way in the early morning or the fall of night?

Widow Quin. You're a queer kind to walk in not
saluting at all.

Mahon. Did you see the young lad?

Widow Quin (*stiffly*). What kind was he?

Mahon. An ugly young streeler with a murderous
gob on him, and a little switch in his hand. I met
a tramper seen him coming this way at the fall of
night.

Widow Quin. There's harvest hundreds do be
passing these days for the Sligo boat. For what is
it you're wanting him, my poor man?

Mahon. I want to destroy him for breaking the
head on me with the clout of a loy. (*He takes off a
big hat, and shows his head in a mass of bandages and
plaster, with some pride.*) It was he did that, and
amn't I a great wonder to think I've traced him
ten days with that rent in my crown?

Widow Quin (*taking his head in both hands and examining it with extreme delight*). That was a great blow.
And who hit you? A robber maybe?

Mahon. It was my own son hit me, and he the
divil a robber, or anything else, but a dirty, stuttering lout.

Widow Quin (*letting go his skull and wiping her hands
in her apron*). You'd best be wary of a mortified
scalp, I think they call it, lepping around with that
wound in the splendour of the sun. It was a bad
blow, surely, and you should have vexed him fearful
to make him strike that gash in his da.

Mahon. Is it me?

Widow Quin (*amusing herself*). Aye. And isn't it a

27. **streeler,** loafer.   28. **gob,** mouth.

great shame when the old and hardened do torment the young?

Mahon (*raging*). Torment him is it? And I after holding out with the patience of a martyred saint till there's nothing but destruction on, and I'm driven out in my old age with none to aid me.

Widow Quin (*greatly amused*). It's a sacred wonder the way that wickedness will spoil a man.

Mahon. My wickedness, is it? Amn't I after saying it is himself has me destroyed, and he a liar on walls, a talker of folly, a man you'd see stretched the half of the day in the brown ferns with his belly to the sun.

Widow Quin. Not working at all?

Mahon. The divil a work, or if he did itself, you'd see him raising up a haystack like the stalk of a rush, or driving our last cow till he broke her leg at the hip, and when he wasn't at that he'd be fooling over little birds he had—finches and felts— or making mugs at his own self in the bit of a glass we had hung on the wall.

Widow Quin (*looking at* CHRISTY). What way was he so foolish? It was running wild after the girls maybe?

Mahon (*with a shout of derision*). Running wild, is it? If he seen a red petticoat coming swinging over the hill, he'd be off to hide in the sticks, and you'd see him shooting out his sheep's eyes between the little twigs and the leaves, and his two ears rising like a hare looking out through a gap. Girls, indeed!

Widow Quin. It was drink, maybe?

Mahon. And he a poor fellow would get drunk on the smell of a pint. He'd a queer rotten stomach, I'm telling you, and when I gave him three pulls from my pipe a while since, he was taken with contortions till I had to send him in the ass-cart to the females' nurse.

Widow Quin (*clasping her hands*). Well, I never, till this day, heard tell of a man the like of that!

Mahon. I'd take a mighty oath you didn't, surely, and wasn't he the laughing joke of every female woman where four baronies meet, the way the girls would stop their weeding if they seen him coming the road to let a roar at him, and call him the looney of Mahon's.

Widow Quin. I'd give the world and all to see the like of him. What kind was he?

Mahon. A small, low fellow.

Widow Quin. And dark?

Mahon. Dark and dirty.

Widow Quin (*considering*). I'm thinking I seen him.

Mahon (*eagerly*). An ugly young blackguard.

19. felts, fieldfares.

Widow Quin. A hideous, fearful villain, and the spit of you.

Mahon. What way is he fled?

Widow Quin. Gone over the hills to catch a coasting steamer to the north or south.

Mahon. Could I pull up on him now?

Widow Quinn. If you'll cross the sands below where the tide is out, you'll be in it as soon as himself, for he had to go round ten miles by the top of the bay. (*She points to the door.*) Strike down by the head beyond and then follow on the roadway to the north and east.

[MAHON *goes abruptly.*

Widow Quin (*shouting after him*). Let you give him a good vengeance when you come up with him, but don't put yourself in the power of the law, for it'd be a poor thing to see a judge in his black cap reading out his sentence on a civil warrior the like of you. (*She swings the door to and looks at* CHRISTY, *who is cowering in terror, for a moment, then she bursts into a laugh.*) Well, you're the walking Playboy of the Western World, and that's the poor man you had divided to his breeches belt.

Christy (*looking out: then, to her*). What'll Pegeen say when she hears that story? What'll she be saying to me now?

Widow Quin. She'll knock the head of you, I'm thinking, and drive you from the door. God help her to be taking you for a wonder, and you a little schemer making up a story you destroyed you da.

Christy (*turning to the door, nearly speechless with rage, half to himself*). To be letting on he was dead, and coming back to his life, and following after me like an old weazel tracing a rat, and coming in here laying desolation between my own self and the fine women of Ireland, and he a kind of carcase that you'd fling upon the sea. . . .

Widow Quin (*more soberly*). There's talking for a man's one only son.

Christy (*breaking out*). His one son, is it? May I meet him with one tooth and it aching, and one eye to be seeing seven and seventy divils in the twists of the road, and one old timber leg on him to limp into the scalding grave. (*Looking out.*) There he is now crossing the strands, and that the Lord God would send a high wave to wash him from the world.

Widow Quin (*scandalized*). Have you no shame? (*Putting her hand on his shoulder and turning him round.*) What ails you? Near crying, is it?

Christy (*in despair and grief*). Amn't I after seeing the love-light of the star of knowledge shining from her brow, and hearing words would put you thinking on the holy Brigid speaking to the infant saints, and now she'll be turning again, and speaking hard words to me, like an old woman with a spavindy ass she'd have, urging on a hill.

Widow Quin. There's poetry talk for a girl you'd see itching and scratching, and she with a stale stink of poteen on her from selling in the shop.

Christy (*impatiently*). It's her like is fitted to be handling merchandise in the heavens above, and what'll I be doing now, I ask you, and I a kind of wonder was jilted by the heavens when a day was by.

[*There is a distant noise of girls' voices.* WIDOW QUIN *looks from window and comes to him, hurriedly.*]

Widow Quin. You'll be doing like myself, I'm thinking, when I did destroy my man, for I'm above many's the day, odd times in great spirits, abroad in the sunshine, darning a stocking or stitching a shift; and odd times again looking out on the schooners, hookers, trawlers is sailing the sea, and I thinking on the gallant hairy fellows are drifting beyond, and myself long years living alone.

Christy (*interested*). You're like me, so.

Widow Quin. I am your like, and it's for that I'm taking a fancy to you, and I wish my little houseen above where there'd be myself to tend you, and none to ask were you a murderer or what at all.

Christy. And what would I be doing if I left Pegeen?

Widow Quin. I've nice jobs you could be doing— gathering shells to make a white-wash for our hut within, building up a little goose-house, or stretching a new skin on an old curagh I have, and if my hut is far from all sides, it's there you'll meet the wisest old men, I tell you, at the corner of my wheel, and it's there yourself and me will have great times whispering and hugging. . . .

Voices (*outside, calling far away*). Christy! Christy Mahon! Christy!

Christy. Is it Pegeen Mike?

Widow Quin. It's the young girls, I'm thinking, coming to bring you to the sports below, and what is it you'll have me to tell them now?

Christy. Aid me for to win Pegeen. It's herself only that I'm seeking now. (WIDOW QUIN *gets up and goes to window.*) Aid me for to win her, and I'll be asking God to stretch a hand to you in the hour of death, and lead you short cuts through the Meadows of Ease, and up the floor of Heaven to the Footstool of the Virgin's Son.

Widow Quin. There's praying.

Voices (*nearer*). Christy! Christy Mahon!

2. **spavindy,** lamed and halting.   33. **curagh,** coracle, small boat with a wicker frame covered with hide.

Christy (*with agitation*). They're coming. Will you swear to aid and save me, for the love of Christ?

Widow Quin (*looks at him for a moment*). If I aid you, will you swear to give me a right of way I want, and a mountainy ram, and a load of dung at Michaelmas, the time that you'll be master here?

Christy. I will, by the elements and stars of night.

Widow Quin. Then we'll not say a word of the old fellow, the way Pegeen won't know your story till the end of time.

Christy. And if he chances to return again?

Widow Quin. We'll swear he's a maniac and not your da. I could take an oath I seen him raving on the sands to-day.

[*Girls run in.*]

Susan. Come on to the sports below. Pegeen says you're to come.

Sara Tansey. The lepping's beginning, and we've a jockey's suit to fit upon you for the mule race on the sands below.

Honor. Come on, will you?

Christy. I will then if Pegeen's beyond.

Sara Tansey. She's in the boreen making game of Shaneen Keogh.

Christy. Then I'll be going to her now.

[*He runs out followed by the girls.*]

Widow Quin. Well, if the worst comes in the end of all, it'll be great game to see there's none to pity him but a widow woman, the like of me, has buried her children and destroyed her man.

[*She goes out.*

[CURTAIN]

ACT III

SCENE.—*As before. Later in the day.* JIMMY *comes in, slightly drunk.*

Jimmy (*calls*). Pegeen! (*Crosses to inner door.*) Pegeen Mike! (*Comes back again into the room.*) Pegeen! (PHILLY *comes in in the same state.—To* PHILLY.) Did you see herself?

Philly. I did not; but I sent Shawn Keogh with the ass-cart for to bear him home. (*Trying cupboards which are locked.*) Well, isn't he a nasty man to get into such staggers at a morning wake; and isn't herself the divil's daughter for locking, and she so fussy after that young gaffer, you might take your death with drouth and none to heed you?

Jimmy. It's little wonder she'd be fussy, and he after bringing bankrupt ruin on the roulette man, and the trick-o'-the-loop man, and breaking the nose of the cockshot-man, and winning all in the

23. **boreen,** lane.

sports below, racing, lepping, dancing, and the Lord knows what! He's right luck, I'm telling you.

Philly. If he has, he'll be rightly hobbled yet, and he not able to say ten words without making a brag of the way he killed his father, and the great blow he hit with the loy.

Jimmy. A man can't hang by his own informing, and his father should be rotten by now.

[*Old* MAHON *passes window slowly.*]

Philly. Supposing a man's digging spuds in that field with a long spade, and supposing he flings up the two halves of that skull, what'll be said then in the papers and the courts of law?

Jimmy. They'd say it was an old Dane, maybe, was drowned in the flood. (*Old* MAHON *comes in and sits down near door listening.*) Did you never hear tell of the skulls they have in the city of Dublin, ranged out like blue jugs in a cabin of Connaught?

Philly. And you believe that?

Jimmy (*pugnaciously*). Didn't a lad see them and he after coming from harvesting in the Liverpool boat? "They have them there," says he, "making a show of the great people there was one time walking the world. White skulls and black skulls and yellow skulls, and some with full teeth, and some haven't only but one."

Philly. It was no lie, maybe, for when I was a young lad there was a graveyard beyond the house with the remnants of a man who had thighs as long as your arm. He was a horrid man, I'm telling you, and there was many a fine Sunday I'd put him together for fun, and he with shiny bones, you wouldn't meet the like of these days in the cities of the world.

Mahon (*getting up*). You wouldn't, is it? Lay your eyes on that skull, and tell me where and when there was another the like of it, is splintered only from the blow of a loy.

Philly. Glory be to God! And who hit you at all?

Mahon (*triumphantly*). It was my own son hit me. Would you believe that?

Jimmy. Well, there's wonders hidden in the heart of man!

Philly (*suspiciously*). And what way was it done?

Mahon (*wandering about the room*). I'm after walking hundreds and long scores of miles, winning clean beds and the fill of my belly four times in the day, and I doing nothing but telling stories of that naked truth. (*He comes to them a little aggressively.*) Give me a supeen and I'll tell you now.

[WIDOW QUIN *comes in and stands aghast behind him. He is facing* JIMMY *and* PHILLY, *who are on the left.*]

Jimmy. Ask herself beyond. She's the stuff hidden in her shawl.

Widow Quin (*coming to* MAHON *quickly*). You here, is it? You didn't go far at all?

Mahon. I seen the coasting steamer passing, and I got a drouth upon me and a cramping leg, so I said, "The divil go along with him," and turned again. (*Looking under her shawl.*) And let you give me a supeen, for I'm destroyed travelling since Tuesday was a week.

Widow Quin (*getting a glass, in a cajoling tone*). Sit down then by the fire and take your ease for a space. You've a right to be destroyed indeed, with your walking, and fighting, and facing the sun (*Giving him poteen from a stone jar she has brought in.*). There now is a drink for you, and may it be to your happiness and length of life.

Mahon (*taking glass greedily and sitting down by fire*). God increase you!

Widow Quin (*taking men to the right stealthily*). Do you know what? That man's raving from his wound to-day, for I met him a while since telling a rambling tale of a tinker had him destroyed. Then he heard of Christy's deed, and he up and says it was his son had cracked his skull. Oh, isn't madness a fright, for he'll go killing some one yet, and he thinking it's the man has struck him so?

Jimmy (*entirely convinced*). It's a fright, surely. I knew a party was kicked in the head by a red mare, and he went killing horses a great while, till he eat the insides of a clock and died after.

Philly (*with suspicion*). Did he see Christy?

Widow Quin. He didn't. (*With a warning gesture.*) Let you not be putting him in mind of him, or you'll be likely summoned if there's murder done. (*Looking round at* MAHON.) Whisht! He's listening. Wait now till you hear me taking him easy and unravelling all. (*She goes to* MAHON.) And what way are you feeling, mister? Are you in contentment now?

Mahon (*slightly emotional from his drink*). I'm poorly only, for it's a hard story the way I'm left to-day, when it was I did tend him from his hour of birth, and he a dunce never reached his second book, the way he'd come from school, many's the day, with his legs lamed under him, and he blackened with his beatings like a tinker's ass. It's a hard story, I'm saying, the way some do have their next and nighest raising up a hand of murder on them, and some is lonesome getting their death with lamentation in the dead of night.

Widow Quin (*not knowing what to say*). To hear you talking so quiet, who'd know you were the same fellow we seen pass to-day?

Mahon. I'm the same surely. The wrack and ruin of three-score years; and it's a terror to live that length, I tell you, and to have your sons going to the dogs against you, and you wore out scolding them, and skelping them, and God knows what.

Philly (*to* JIMMY). He's not raving. (*To* WIDOW QUIN.) Will you ask him what kind was his son?

Widow Quin (*to* MAHON, *with a peculiar look*). Was your son that hit you a lad of one year and a score maybe, a great hand at racing and lepping and licking the world?

Mahon (*turning on her with a roar of rage*). Didn't 10 you hear me say he was the fool of men, the way from this out he'll know the orphan's lot, with old and young making game of him, and they swearing, raging, kicking at him like a mangy cur.

[*A great burst of cheering outside, some way off.*]

Mahon (*putting his hands to his ears*). What in the name of God do they want roaring below?

Widow Quin (*with the shade of a smile*). They're cheering a young lad, the champion Playboy of the Western World.

[*More cheering.*] 20

Mahon (*going to window*). It'd split my heart to hear them, and I with pulses in my brain-pan for a week gone by. Is it racing they are?

Jimmy (*looking from door*). It is, then. They are mounting him for the mule race will be run upon the sands. That's the playboy on the winkered mule.

Mahon (*puzzled*). That lad, is it? If you said it was a fool he was, I'd have laid a mighty oath he 30 was the likeness of my wandering son. (*Uneasily, putting his hand to his head*.). Faith, I'm thinking I'll go walking for to view the race.

Widow Quin (*stopping him, sharply*). You will not. You'd best take the road to Belmullet, and not be dilly-dallying in this place where there isn't a spot you could sleep.

Philly (*coming forward*). Don't mind her. Mount there on the bench and you'll have a view of the whole. They're hurrying before the tide will rise, 40 and it'd be near over if you went down the pathway through the crags below.

Mahon (*mounts on bench*, WIDOW QUIN *beside him*). That's a right view again the edge of the sea. They're coming now from the point. He's leading. Who is he at all?

Widow Quin. He's the champion of the world, I tell you, and there isn't a hap'orth isn't falling lucky to his hands to-day.

Philly (*looking out, interested in the race*). Look at 50 that. They're pressing him now.

Jimmy. He'll win it yet.

Philly. Take your time, Jimmy Farrell. It's too soon to say.

Widow Quin (*shouting*). Watch him taking the gate. There's riding.

Jimmy (*cheering*). More power to the young lad!

Mahon. He's passing the third.

Jimmy. He'll lick them yet.

Widow Quin. He'd lick them if he was running races with a score itself.

Mahon. Look at the mule he has, kicking the stars.

Widow Quin. There was a lep! (*Catching hold of* MAHON *in her excitement*.) He's fallen! He's mounted again! Faith, he's passing them all!

Jimmy. Look at him skelping her!

Philly. And the mountain girls hooshing him on!

Jimmy. It's the last turn! The post's cleared for them now!

Mahon. Look at the narrow place. He'll be into the bogs! (*With a yell*.) Good rider! He's through it again!

Jimmy. He neck and neck!

Mahon. Good boy to him! Flames, but he's in!

[*Great cheering, in which all join.*]

Mahon (*with hesitation*). What's that? They're raising him up. They're coming this way. (*With a roar of rage and astonishment*.) It's Christy, by the stars of God! I'd know his way of spitting and he astride the moon. (*He jumps down and makes for the door, but* WIDOW QUIN *catches him and pulls him back*.)

Widow Quin. Stay quiet, will you? That's not your son. (*To* JIMMY.) Stop him, or you'll get a month for the abetting of manslaughter and be fined as well.

Jimmy. I'll hold him.

Mahon (*struggling*). Let me out! Let me out, the lot of you! till I have my vengeance on his head to-day.

Widow Quin (*shaking him, vehemently*). That's not your son. That's a man is going to make a marriage with the daughter of this house, a place with fine trade, with a licence, and with poteen too.

Mahon (*amazed*). That man marrying a decent and a moneyed girl! Is it mad yous are? Is it in a crazy-house for females that I'm landed now?

Widow Quin. It's mad yourself is with the blow upon your head. That lad is the wonder of the western world.

Mahon. I seen it's my son.

Widow Quin. You seen that you're mad. (*Cheering outside*.) Do you hear them cheering him in the zig-zags of the road? Aren't you after saying that your son's a fool, and how would they be cheering a true idiot born?

Mahon (*getting distressed*). It's maybe out of reason that that man's himself. (*Cheering again*.) There's none surely will go cheering him. Oh, I'm raving with a madness that would fright the world! (*He sits down with his hand to his head.*) There was one time I seen ten scarlet divils letting on they'd cork my spirit in a gallon can; and one time I seen rats as big as badgers sucking the life-blood from the butt of my lug; but I never till this day confused that dribbling idiot with a likely man. I'm destroyed surely.

Widow Quin. And who'd wonder when it's your brain-pan that is gaping now?

Mahon. Then the blight of the sacred drouth upon myself and him, for I never went mad to this day, and I not three weeks with the Limerick girls drinking myself silly and parlatic from the dusk to dawn. (*To* WIDOW QUIN, *suddenly.*) Is my visage astray?

Widow Quin. It is, then. You're a sniggering maniac, a child could see.

Mahon (*getting up more cheerfully*). Then I'd best be going to the union beyond, and there'll be a welcome before me, I tell you (*With great pride.*), and I a terrible and fearful case, the way that there I was one time, screeching in a straightened waistcoat, with seven doctors writing out my sayings in a printed book. Would you believe that?

Widow Quin. If you're a wonder itself, you'd best be hasty, for them lads caught a maniac one time and pelted the poor creature till he ran out, raving and foaming, and was drowned in the sea.

Mahon (*with philosophy*). It's true mankind is the divil when your head's astray. Let me out now and I'll slip down the boreen, and not see them so.

Widow Quin (*showing him out*). That's it. Run to the right, and not a one will see.

[*He runs off.*

Philly (*wisely*). You're at some gaming, Widow Quin; but I'll walk after him and give him his dinner and a time to rest, and I'll see then if he's raving or as sane as you.

Widow Quin (*annoyed*). If you go near that lad, let you be wary of your head, I'm saying. Didn't you hear him telling he was crazed at times?

Philly. I heard him telling a power; and I'm thinking we'll have right sport, before night will fall.

[*He goes out.*

Jimmy. Well, Philly's a conceited and foolish man. How could that madman have his senses and his brain-pan slit? I'll go after them and see him turn on Philly now.

[*He goes;* WIDOW QUIN *hides poteen behind counter. Then hubbub outside.*]

Voices. There you are! Good jumper! Grand

14. **parlatic,** paralytic.

lepper! Darlint boy! He's the racer! Bear him on, will you!

[CHRISTY *comes in, in jockey's dress, with* PEGEEN MIKE, SARA, *and other girls, and men.*]

Pegeen (*to crowd*). Go on now and don't destroy him and he drenching with sweat. Go along, I'm saying, and have your tug-of-warring till he's dried his skin.

Crowd. Here's his prizes! A bagpipes! A fiddle was played by a poet in the years gone by! A flat and three-thorned blackthorn would lick the scholars out of Dublin town!

Christy (*taking prizes from the men*). Thank you kindly, the lot of you. But you'd say it was little only I did this day if you'd seen me a while since striking my one single blow.

Town Crier (*outside, ringing a bell*). Take notice, last event of this day! Tug-of-warring on the green below! Come on, the lot of you! Great achievements for all Mayo men!

Pegeen. Go on, and leave him for to rest and dry. Go on, I tell you, for he'll do no more. (*She hustles crowd out;* WIDOW QUIN *following them.*)

Men (*going*). Come on then. Good luck for the while!

Pegeen (*radiantly, wiping his face with her shawl*). Well, you're the lad, and you'll have great times from this out when you could win that wealth of prizes, and you sweating in the heat of noon!

Christy (*looking at her with delight*). I'll have great times if I win the crowning prize I'm seeking now, and that's your promise that you'll wed me in a fortnight, when our banns is called.

Pegeen (*backing away from him*). You've right daring to go ask me that, when all knows you'll be starting to some girl in your own townland, when your father's rotten in four months, or five.

Christy (*indignantly*). Starting from you, is it? (*He follows her.*) I will not, then, and when the airs is warming in four months, or five, it's then yourself and me should be pacing Neifin in the dews of night, the times sweet smells do be rising, and you'd see a little shiny new moon, maybe, sinking on the hills.

Pegeen (*looking at him playfully*). And it's that kind of a poacher's love you'd make, Christy Mahon, on the sides of Neifin, when the night is down?

Christy. It's little you'll think if my love's a poacher's, or an earl's itself, when you'll feel my two hands stretched around you, and I squeezing kisses on your puckered lips, till I'd feel a kind of pity for the Lord God is all ages sitting lonesome in His golden chair.

Pegeen. That'll be right fun, Christy Mahon, and

any girl would walk her heart out before she'd meet a young man was your like for eloquence, or talk at all.

Christy (encouraged). Let you wait, to hear me talking, till we're astray in Erris, when Good Friday's by, drinking a sup from a well, and making mighty kisses with our wetted mouths, or gaming in a gap of sunshine, with yourself stretched back unto your necklace, in the flowers of the earth.

Pegeen (in a lower voice, moved by his tone). I'd be 10 nice so, is it?

Christy (with rapture). If the mitred bishops seen you that time, they'd be the like of the holy prophets, I'm thinking, do be straining the bars of Paradise to lay eyes on the Lady Helen of Troy, and she abroad, pacing back and forward, with a nosegay in her golden shawl.

Pegeen (with real tenderness). And what is it I have, Christy Mahon, to make me fitting entertainment for the like of you, that has such poet's talking, and 20 such bravery of heart.

Christy (in a low voice). Isn't there the light of seven heavens in your heart alone, the way you'll be an angel's lamp to me from this out, and I abroad in the darkness, spearing salmons in the Owen, or the Carrowmore?

Pegeen. If I was your wife I'd be along with you those nights, Christy Mahon, the way you'd see I was a great hand at coaxing bailiffs, or coining funny nicknames for the stars of night.

Christy. You, is it? Taking your death in the hailstones, or in the fogs of dawn.

Pegeen. Yourself and me would shelter easy in a narrow bush, (*With a qualm of dread.*); but we're only talking, maybe, for this would be a poor, thatched place to hold a fine lad is the like of you.

Christy (putting his arm round her). If I wasn't a good Christian, it's on my naked knees I'd be saying my prayers and paters to every jackstraw you have roofing your head, and every stony pebble is 40 paving the laneway to your door.

Pegeen (radiantly). If that's the truth I'll be burning candles from this out to the miracles of God that have brought you from the south to-day, and I with my gowns bought ready, the way that I can wed you, and not wait at all.

Christy. It's miracles, and that's the truth. Me there toiling a long while, and walking a long while, not knowing at all I was drawing all times nearer to this holy day.

Pegeen. And myself, a girl, was tempted often to 50 go sailing the seas till I'd marry a Jew-man, with ten kegs of gold, and I not knowing at all there was the like of you drawing nearer, like the stars of God.

Christy. And to think I'm long years hearing women talking that talk, to all bloody fools, and this the first time I've heard the like of your voice talking sweetly for my own delight.

Pegeen. And to think it's me is talking sweetly, Christy Mahon, and I the fright of seven townlands for my biting tongue. Well, the heart's a wonder; and, I'm thinking, there won't be our like in Mayo, for gallant lovers, from this hour to-day. (*Drunken singing is heard outside.*) There's my father coming from the wake, and when he's had his sleep we'll tell him, for he's peaceful then.

[*They separate.*]

Michael (singing outside).

The jailor and the turnkey
They quickly ran us down,
And brought us back as prisoners
Once more to Cavan town.

(*He comes in supported by* SHAWN.)

There we lay bewailing
All in a prison bound. . . .

[*He sees* CHRISTY. *Goes and shakes him drunkenly by the hand, while* PEGEEN *and* SHAWN *talk on the left.*]

Michael (to CHRISTY). The blessing of God and the holy angels on your head, young fellow. I hear tell you're after winning all in the sports below; and wasn't it a shame I didn't bear you along with me to Kate Cassidy's wake, a fine, stout lad, the like of you, for you'd never see the match of it for flows of drink, the way when we sunk her bones at noonday in her narrow grave, there were five men, aye, and six men, stretched out retching speechless on the holy stones.

Christy (uneasily, watching PEGEEN). Is that the truth?

Michael. It is, then; and aren't you a louty schemer to go burying your poor father unbeknownst when you'd a right to throw him on the crupper of a Kerry mule and drive him westwards, like holy Joseph in the days gone by, the way we could have given him a decent burial, and not have him rotting beyond, and not a Christian drinking a smart drop to the glory of his soul?

Christy (gruffly). It's well enough he's lying, for the likes of him.

Michael (slapping him on the back). Well, aren't you a hardened slayer? It'll be a poor thing for the household man where you go sniffing for a female wife; and (*Pointing to* SHAWN.) look beyond at that shy and decent Christian I have chosen for my

39. louty, loutish.

daughter's hand, and I after getting the gilded dispensation this day for to wed them now.

Christy. And you'll be wedding them this day, is it?

Michael (drawing himself up). Aye. Are you thinking, if I'm drunk itself, I'd leave my daughter living single with a little frisky rascal is the like of you?

Pegeen (breaking away from SHAWN*).* Is it the truth the dispensation's come?

Michael (triumphantly). Father Reilly's after reading it in gallous Latin, and "It's come in the nick of time," says he; "so I'll wed them in a hurry, dreading that young gaffer who'd capsize the stars."

Pegeen (fiercely). He's missed his nick of time, for it's that lad, Christy Mahon, that I'm wedding now.

Michael (loudly with horror). You'd be making him a son to me, and he wet and crusted with his father's blood?

Pegeen. Aye. Wouldn't it be a bitter thing for a girl to go marrying the like of Shaneen, and he a middling kind of a scarecrow, with no savagery or fine words in him at all?

Michael (gasping and sinking on a chair). Oh, aren't you a heathen daughter to go shaking the fat of my heart, and I swamped and drownded with the weight of drink? Would you have them turning on me the way that I'd be roaring to the dawn of day with the wind upon my heart? Have you not a word to aid me, Shaneen? Are you not jealous at all?

Shaneen (in great misery). I'd be afeard to be jealous of a man did slay his da.

Pegeen. Well, it'd be a poor thing to go marrying your like. I'm seeing there's a world of peril for an orphan girl, and isn't it a great blessing I didn't wed you before himself came walking from the west or south?

Shawn. It's a queer story you'd go picking a dirty tramp up from the highways of the world.

Pegeen (playfully). And you think you're a likely beau to go straying along with, the shiny Sundays of the opening year, when it's sooner on a bullock's liver you'd put a poor girl thinking than on the lily or the rose?

Shawn. And have you no mind of my weight of passion, and the holy dispensation, and the drift of heifers I am giving, and the golden ring?

Pegeen. I'm thinking you're too fine for the like of me, Shawn Keogh of Killakeen, and let you go off till you'd find a radiant lady with droves of bullocks on the plains of Meath, and herself bedizened in the diamond jewelleries of Pharaoh's ma. That'd be your match, Shaneen. So God save you now! (*She retreats behind* CHRISTY.)

Shawn. Won't you hear me telling you . . . ?

Christy (with ferocity). Take yourself from this, young fellow, or I'll maybe add a murder to my deeds to-day.

Michael (springing up with a shriek). Murder is it? Is it mad yous are? Would you go making murder in this place, and it piled with poteen for our drink to-night? Go on to the foreshore if it's fighting you want, where the rising tide will wash all traces from the memory of man. (*Pushing* SHAWN *towards* CHRISTY.)

Shawn (shaking himself free, and getting behind MICHAEL*).* I'll not fight him, Michael James. I'd liefer live a bachelor, simmering in passions to the end of time, than face a lepping savage the like of him has descended from the Lord knows where. Strike him yourself, Michael James, or you'll lose my drift of heifers and my blue bull from Sneem.

Michael. Is it me fight him, when it's father-slaying he's bred to now? (*Pushing* SHAWN.) Go on, you fool, and fight him now.

Shawn (coming forward a little). Will I strike him with my hand?

Michael. Take the loy is on your western side.

Shawn. I'd be afeard of the gallows if I struck with that.

Christy (taking up the loy). Then I'll make you face the gallows or quit off from this.

[SHAWN *flies out of the door.*

Christy. Well, fine weather be after him, (*Going to* MICHAEL, *coaxingly.*) and I'm thinking you wouldn't wish to have that quaking blackguard in your house at all. Let you give us your blessing and hear her swear her faith to me, for I'm mounted on the spring-tide of the stars of luck, the way it'll be good for any to have me in the house.

Pegeen (at the other side of MICHAEL*).* Bless us now, for I swear to God I'll wed him, and I'll not renege.

Michael (standing up in the centre, holding on to both of them). It's the will of God, I'm thinking, that all should win an easy or a cruel end, and it's the will of God that all should rear up lengthy families for the nurture of the earth. What's a single man, I ask you, eating a bit in one house and drinking a sup in another, and he with no place of his own, like an old braying jackass strayed upon the rocks? (*To* CHRISTY.) It's many would be in dread to bring your like into their house for to end them, maybe, with a sudden end; but I'm a decent man of Ireland, and I liefer face the grave untimely and I seeing a score of grandsons growing up little gallant swearers by the name of God, than go peopling my bedside with puny weeds the like of what you'd breed, I'm thinking, out of Shaneen Keogh. (*He joins their hands.*) A daring fellow is the jewel of the world, and a man did split his father's middle with a single clout should have the bravery of ten, so may God and Mary and St. Patrick bless you, and increase you from this mortal day.

Christy and Pegeen. Amen, O Lord!

[*Hubbub outside. Old* MAHON *rushes in, followed by all the crowd, and* WIDOW QUIN. *He makes a rush at* CHRISTY, *knocks him down, and begins to beat him.*]

Pegeen (*dragging back his arm*). Stop that, will you? 10 Who are you at all?

Mahon. His father, God forgive me!

Pegeen (*drawing back*). Is it rose from the dead?

Mahon. Do you think I look so easy quenched with the tap of a loy? (*Beats* CHRISTY *again.*)

Pegeen (*glaring at Christy*). And it's lies you told, letting on you had him slitted, and you nothing at all.

Christy (*catching* MAHON's *stick*). He's not my father. He's a raving maniac would scare the world. 20 (*Pointing to* WIDOW QUIN.) Herself knows it is true.

Crowd. You're fooling Pegeen! The Widow Quin seen him this day, and you likely knew! You're a liar!

Christy (*dumbfounded*). It's himself was a liar, lying stretched out with an open head on him, letting on he was dead.

Mahon. Weren't you off racing the hills before I got my breath with the start I had seeing you turn on me at all?   30

Pegeen. And to think of the coaxing glory we had given him, and he after doing nothing but hitting a soft blow and chasing northward in a sweat of fear. Quit off from this.

Christy (*piteously*). You've seen my doing this day, and let you save me from the old man; for why would you be in such a scorch of haste to spur me to destruction now?

Pegeen. It's there your treachery is spurring me, till I'm hard set to think you're the one I'm after 40 lacing in my heart-strings half-an-hour gone by. (*To* MAHON.) Take him on from this, for I think bad the world should see me raging for a Munster liar, and the fool of men.

Mahon. Rise up now to retribution, and come on with me.

Crowd (*jeeringly*). There's the playboy! There's the lad thought he'd rule the roost in Mayo. Slate him now, mister.

Christy (*getting up in shy terror*). What is it drives 50 you to torment me here, when I'd asked the thunders of the might of God to blast me if I ever did hurt to any saving only that one single blow.

Mahon (*loudly*). If you didn't, you're a poor good-

for-nothing, and isn't it by the like of you the sins of the whole world are committed?

Christy (*raising his hands*). In the name of the Almighty God . . .

Mahon. Leave troubling the Lord God. Would you have him sending down droughts, and fevers, and the old hen and the cholera morbus?

Christy (*to* WIDOW QUIN). Will you come between us and protect me now?

Widow Quin. I've tried a lot, God help me, and my share is done.

Christy (*looking round in desperation*). And I must go back into my torment is it, or run off like a vagabond straying through the unions with the dusts of August making mudstains in the gullet of my throat, or the winds of March blowing on me till I'd take an oath I felt them making whistles of my ribs within?

Sara. Ask Pegeen to aid you. Her like does often change.

Christy. I will not, then, for there's torment in the splendour of her like, and she a girl any moon of midnight would take pride to meet, facing southwards on the heaths of Keel. But what did I want crawling forward to scorch my understanding at her flaming brow?

Pegeen (*to* MAHON, *vehemently, fearing she will break into tears*). Take him on from this or I'll set the young lads to destroy him here.

Mahon (*going to him, shaking his stick*). Come on now if you wouldn't have the company to see you skelped.

Pegeen (*half laughing, through her tears*). That's it, now the world will see him pandied, and he an ugly liar was playing off the hero, and the fright of men.

Christy (*to* MAHON, *very sharply*). Leave me go!

Crowd. That's it. Now, Christy. If them two set fighting, it will lick the world.

Mahon (*making a grab at* CHRISTY). Come here to me.

Christy (*more threateningly*). Leave me go, I'm saying.

Mahon. I will, maybe, when your legs is limping, and your back is blue.

Crowd. Keep it up, the two of you. I'll back the old one. Now the playboy.

Christy (*in low and intense voice*). Shut your yelling, for if you're after making a mighty man of me this day by the power of a lie, you're setting me now to think if it's a poor thing to be lonesome it's worse, maybe, to go mixing with the fools of earth.

[MAHON *makes a movement towards him.*]

34. pandied, struck, whipped.

Christy (*almost shouting*). Keep off . . . lest I do show a blow unto the lot of you would set the guardian angels winking in the clouds above. (*He swings round with a sudden rapid movement and picks up a loy.*)

Crowd (*half-frightened, half-amused*). He's going mad! Mind yourselves! Run from the idiot!

Christy. If I am an idiot, I'm after hearing my voice this day saying words would raise the top-knot on a poet in a merchant's town. I've won your racing, and your lepping, and . . .

Mahon. Shut your gullet and come on with me.

Christy. I'm going, but I'll stretch you first.

[*He runs at old* MAHON *with the loy, chases him out of the door, followed by crowd and* WIDOW QUIN. *There is a great noise outside, then a yell, and dead silence for a moment.* CHRISTY *comes in, half-dazed, and goes to fire.*]

Widow Quin (*coming in, hurriedly, and going to him*). They're turning again you. Come on, or you'll be hanged, indeed.

Christy. I'm thinking, from this out, Pegeen'll be giving me praises the same as in the hours gone by.

Widow Quin (*impatiently*). Come by the back-door. I'd think bad to have you stifled on the gallows tree.

Christy (*indignantly*). I will not, then. What good'd be my lifetime if I left Pegeen?

Widow Quin. Come on, and you'll be no worse than you were last night; and you with a double murder this time to be telling to the girls.

Christy. I'll not leave Pegeen Mike.

Widow Quin (*impatiently*). Isn't there the match of her in every parish public, from Binghamstown unto the plain of Meath? Come on, I tell you, and I'll find you finer sweethearts at each waning moon.

Christy. It's Pegeen I'm seeking only, and what'd I care if you brought me a drift of chosen females, standing in their shifts itself, maybe, from this place to the eastern world?

Sara (*runs in, pulling off one of her petticoats*). They're going to hang him. (*Holding out petticoat and shawl.*) Fit these upon him, and let him run off to the east.

Widow Quin. He's raving now; but we'll fit them on him, and I'll take him in the ferry to the Achill boat.

Christy (*struggling feebly*). Leave me go, will you? when I'm thinking of my luck to-day, for she will wed me surely, and I a proven hero in the end of all.

[*They try to fasten petticoat round him.*]

Widow Quin. Take his left hand, and we'll pull him now. Come on, young fellow.

Christy (*suddenly starting up*). You'll be taking me from her? You're jealous, is it, of her wedding me?

Go on from this. (*He snatches up a stool, and threatens them with it.*)

Widow Quin (*going*). It's in the madhouse they should put him, not in jail, at all. We'll go by the back-door, to call the doctor, and we'll save him so.

[*She goes out, with* SARA, *through inner room. Men crowd in the doorway.* CHRISTY *sits down again by the fire.*]

Michael (*in a terrified whisper*). Is the old lad killed surely?

Philly. I'm after feeling the last gasps quitting his heart.

[*They peer in at* CHRISTY.]

Michael (*with a rope*). Look at the way he is. Twist a hangman's knot on it, and slip it over his head, while he's not minding at all.

Philly. Let you take it, Shaneen. You're the soberest of all that's here.

Shawn. Is it me to go near him, and he the wickedest and worst with me? Let you take it, Pegeen Mike.

Pegeen. Come on, so.

[*She goes forward with the others, and they drop the double hitch over his head.*]

Christy. What ails you?

Shawn (*triumphantly, as they pull the rope tight on his arms*). Come on to the peelers, till they stretch you now.

Christy. Me!

Michael. If we took pity on you the Lord God would, maybe, bring us ruin from the law to-day, so you'd best come easy, for hanging is an easy and a speedy end.

Christy. I'll not stir. (*To* PEGEEN.) And what is it you'll say to me, and I after doing it this time in the face of all?

Pegeen. I'll say, a strange man is a marvel, with his mighty talk; but what's a squabble in your backyard, and the blow of a loy, have taught me that there's a great gap between a gallous story and a dirty deed. (*To men.*) Take him on from this, or the lot of us will be likely put on trial for his deed to-day.

Christy (*with horror in his voice*). And it's yourself will send me off, to have a horny-fingered hangman hitching his bloody slipknots at the butt of my ear.

Men (*pulling rope*). Come on, will you?

[*He is pulled down on the floor.*]

Christy (*twisting his legs round the table*). Cut the rope, Pegeen, and I'll quit the lot of you, and live from this out, like the madmen of Keel, eating muck and green weeds on the faces of the cliffs.

Pegeen. And leave us to hang, is it, for a saucy liar, the like of you? (*To men.*) Take him on, out from this.

Shawn. Pull a twist on his neck, and squeeze him so.

Philly. Twist yourself. Sure he cannot hurt you, if you keep your distance from his teeth alone.

Shawn. I'm afeard of him. (*To* PEGEEN.) Lift a lighted sod, will you, and scorch his leg.

Pegeen (*blowing the fire with a bellows*). Leave go now, young fellow, or I'll scorch your shins.

Christy. You're blowing for to torture me. (*His voice rising and growing stronger.*) That's your kind, is it? Then let the lot of you be wary, for, if I've to face the gallows, I'll have a gay march down, I tell you, and shed the blood of some of you before I die.

Shawn (*in terror*). Keep a good hold, Philly. Be wary, for the love of God. For I'm thinking he would liefest wreak his pains on me.

Christy (*almost gaily*). If I do lay my hands on you, it's the way you'll be at the fall of night, hanging as a scarecrow for the fowls of hell. Ah, you'll have a gallous jaunt I'm saying, coaching out through Limbo with my father's ghost.

Shawn (*to* PEGEEN). Make haste, will you? Oh, isn't he a holy terror, and isn't it true for Father Reilly, that all drink's a curse that has the lot of you so shaky and uncertain now?

Christy. If I can wring a neck among you, I'll have a royal judgment looking on the trembling jury in the courts of law. And won't there be crying out in Mayo the day I'm stretched upon the rope, with ladies in their silks and satins snivelling in their lacy kerchiefs, and they rhyming songs and ballads on the terror of my fate? (*He squirms round on the floor and bites* SHAWN's *leg.*)

Shawn (*shrieking*). My leg's bit on me. He's the like of a mad dog, I'm thinking, the way that I will surely die.

Christy (*delighted with himself*). You will then, the way you can shake out hell's flags of welcome for my coming in two weeks or three, for I'm thinking Satan hasn't many have killed their da in Kerry, and in Mayo too.

[*Old* MAHON *comes in behind on all fours and looks on unnoticed.*]

Men (*to* PEGEEN). Bring the sod, will you?

Pegeen (*coming over*). God help him so. (*Burns his leg.*)

Christy (*kicking and screaming*). Oh, glory be to God! (*He kicks loose from the table, and they all drag him towards the door.*)

Jimmy (*seeing old* MAHON). Will you look what's come in?

[*They all drop* CHRISTY *and run left.*]

Christy (*scrambling on his knees face to face with old* MAHON). Are you coming to be killed a third time, or what ails you now?

Mahon. For what is it they have you tied?

Christy. They're taking me to the peelers to have me hanged for slaying you.

Michael (*apologetically*). It is the will of God that all should guard their little cabins from the treachery of law, and what would my daughter be doing if I was ruined or was hanged itself?

Mahon (*grimly, loosening* CHRISTY). It's little I care if you put a bag on her back, and went picking cockles till the hour of death; but my son and myself will be going our own way, and we'll have great times from this out telling stories of the villainy of Mayo, and the fools is here. (*To* CHRISTY, *who is freed.*) Come on now.

Christy. Go with you, is it? I will then, like a gallant captain with his heathen slave. Go on now and I'll see you from this day stewing my oatmeal and washing my spuds, for I'm master of all fights from now. (*Pushing* MAHON.) Go on, I'm saying.

Mahon. Is it me?

Christy. Not a word out of you. Go on from this.

Mahon (*walking out and looking back at* CHRISTY *over his shoulder*). Glory be to God! (*With a broad smile.*) I am crazy again!   [*Goes.*

Christy. Ten thousand blessings upon all that's here, for you've turned me a likely gaffer in the end of all, the way I'll go romancing through a romping lifetime from this hour to the dawning of the judgment day.   [*He goes out.*

Michael. By the will of God, we'll have peace now for our drinks. Will you draw the porter, Pegeen?

Shawn (*going up to her*). It's a miracle Father Reilly can wed us in the end of all, and we'll have none to trouble us when his vicious bite is healed.

Pegeen (*hitting him a box on the ear*). Quit my sight. (*Putting her shawl over her head and breaking out into wild lamentations.*) Oh, my grief, I've lost him surely. I've lost the only Playboy of the Western World.

[CURTAIN]

Max Beerbohm
1872–

Max Beerbohm was born in 1872 in London. Half-brother of the actor-manager Sir Herbert Beerbohm-Tree, he was educated at Charterhouse and Merton College. He was a prodigy as an undergraduate; his caricatures were praised for their critical acumen; his acid comments were quoted even in Cambridge. At twenty-three he said he had "written himself out"; at twenty-four he published a slender volume which, with a grand gesture of finality, he entitled *The Works of Max Beerbohm*, 1896. These witty essays were succeeded by *More*, 1899, *Yet Again*, 1909, *And Even Now*, 1920, books which showed mastery of an adroit style and gave finickiness a kind of splendor. Beerbohm wrote the 1890's to death; he used the technique of the decadents, and ridiculed them out of existence. If he made a cult of dandyism he also ended it; he never betrayed himself with false elegance. *The Happy Hypocrite: A Fairy Tale for Tired Men*, 1897, and *Zuleika Dobson: An Oxford Love Story*, 1911, somehow combine the trivial and the touching, the ultra-fastidious, the absurd, and the unexpectedly sentimental.

But Beerbohm cannot be disposed of by such generalities as "suave" and "exquisite," although both terms may well characterize him. Account must be taken of the biting appraisal of the elderly Swinburne and his "keeper," Watts Dunton, in "Number 2, the Pines" and the amazing tales in *Seven Men*, 1919. "A. V. Laider" is one of the best short stories of the period, a macabre short story in which idea and treatment, characterization and atmosphere, are fused in the crucible of style.

Beerbohm, the person, the caricaturist, and the writer, are one man—and here, if ever, the style is the man. In an article in the *New Republic* Philip Littell quoted Lytton Strachey from the latter's *Landmarks in French Literature*: "There is a kind of art, as everyone knows, that conceals itself; but there is another—and this is less often recognized—that displays itself, that *just* shows, charmingly but unmistakably, how beautifully contrived it is." This is particularly true of the art of Beerbohm, an art which is a style, and a style which does not disdain to reveal its smooth and malicious dexterity. Whether the author is shaping severely disciplined essays or spinning incredible tales, there is a continual delight in design for its own sake. Even the extravagances which color Beerbohm's prose are carefully controlled extravagances. As Philip Littell concluded:

"You cannot taste his sincerity apart from his artfulness, his common sense apart from his extravagance, his order and measure apart from his caprice. . . . Throughout the most preposterous events, fantastic or supernatural, their contriver keeps his air of recording them imperturbably, just as they happened, with smiling indifference to your ability or inability to perceive that he is weaving them into the most formal of designs, into remote and intimate pictures of man's wishes."[1]

"Smiling indifference . . . remote and intimate." . . . Perhaps there is no better way of summarizing Beerbohm's perfections and his seeming perversities, his sincerity and his irresponsibility, his apparent ease and his artfulness, which is an art in itself.

A. V. LAIDER [2]

I UNPACKED my things and went down to await luncheon.

It was good to be here again in this little old sleepy hostel by the sea. Hostel I say, though it spelt itself without an s and even placed a circumflex above the o. It made no other pretension. It was very cosy indeed.

I had been here just a year before, in mid-February, after an attack of influenza. Nothing was 10 changed. It had been raining when I left, and the waiter—there was but a single, a very old waiter—had told me it was only a shower. That waiter was still here, not a day older. And the shower had not ceased.

Steadfastly it fell on to the sands, steadfastly into the iron-grey sea. I stood looking out at it from the windows of the hall, admiring it very much. There seemed to be little else to do. What little there was I did. I mastered the contents of a blue hand-bill 20 which, pinned to the wall just beneath the framed engraving of Queen Victoria's Coronation, gave

---

[1] "Books and Things," *New Republic*, Feb. 25, 1920.
[2] From *Seven Men*, published by Alfred A. Knopf, Inc., copyright, 1920, by Max Beerbohm.

token of a concert that was to be held—or rather, was to have been held some weeks ago—in the Town Hall, for the benefit of the Life-Boat Fund. I looked at the barometer, tapped it, was not the wiser. I glanced at a pamphlet about Our Dying Industries (a theme on which Mr. Joseph Chamberlain was at that time trying to alarm us). I wandered to the letter-board.

These letter-boards always fascinate me. Usually some two or three of the envelopes stuck into the cross-garterings have a certain newness and freshness. They seem sure they will yet be claimed. Why not? Why *shouldn't* John Doe, Esq., or Mrs. Richard Roe, turn up at any moment? I do not know. I can only say that nothing in the world seems to me more unlikely. Thus it is that these young bright envelopes touch my heart even more than do their dusty and sallow seniors. Sour resignation is less touching than impatience for what will not be, than the eagerness that has to wane and wither. Soured beyond measure these old envelopes are. They are not nearly so nice as they should be to the young ones. They lose no chance of sneering and discouraging. Such dialogues as this are only too frequent:

A VERY YOUNG ENVELOPE. Something in me whispers that he will come to-day!

A VERY OLD ENVELOPE. He? Well, that's good! Ha, ha, ha! Why didn't he come last week, when *you* came? What reason have you for supposing he'll ever come *now?* It isn't as if he were a frequenter of the place. He's never been here. His name is utterly unknown here. You don't suppose he's coming on the chance of finding *you?*

A.V.Y.E. It may seem silly, but—something in me whispers—

A.V.O.E. Something in *you?* One has only to look at you to see there's nothing in you but a note scribbled to him by a cousin. Look at *me!* There are three sheets, closely written, in *me.* The lady to whom I am addressed—

A.V.Y.E. Yes, sir, yes; you told me all about her yesterday.

A.V.O.E. And I shall do so to-day and to-morrow and every day and all day long. That young lady was a widow. She stayed here many times. She was delicate, and the air suited her. She was poor, and the tariff was just within her means. She was lonely, and had need of love. I have in me for her a passionate avowal and strictly honourable proposal, written to her, after many rough copies, by a gentleman who had made her acquaintance under this very roof. He was rich, he was charming, he was in the prime of life. He had asked if he might write

to her. She had flutteringly granted his request. He posted me to her the day after his return to London. I looked forward to being torn open by her. I was very sure she would wear me and my contents next to her bosom. She was gone. She had left no address. She never returned. . . . This I tell you, and shall continue to tell you, not because I want any of your callow sympathy—no, *thank* you!—but that you may judge how much less than slight are the chances that you yourself——

But my reader has overheard these dialogues as often as I. He wants to know what was odd about this particular letter-board before which I was standing. At first glance I saw nothing odd about it. But presently I distinguished a handwriting that was vaguely familiar. It was mine. I stared, I wondered. There is always a slight shock in seeing an envelope of one's own after it has gone through the post. It looks as if it had gone through so much. But this was the first time I had ever seen an envelope of mine eating its heart out in bondage on a letter-board. This was outrageous. This was hardly to be believed. Sheer kindness had impelled me to write to "A. V. Laider, Esq.," and this was the result! I hadn't minded receiving no answer. Only now, indeed, did I remember that I hadn't received one. In multitudinous London the memory of A. V. Laider and his trouble had soon passed from my mind. But—well, what a lesson not to go out of one's way to write to casual acquaintances!

My envelope seemed not to recognise me as its writer. Its gaze was the more piteous for being blank. Even so had I once been gazed at by a dog that I had lost and, after many days, found in the Battersea Home. "I don't know who you are, but whoever you are, claim me, take me out of this!" That was my dog's appeal. This was the appeal of my envelope.

I raised my hand to the letter-board, meaning to effect a swift and lawless rescue, but paused at sound of a footstep behind me. The old waiter had come to tell me that my luncheon was ready. I followed him out of the hall, not, however, without a bright glance across my shoulder to reassure the little captive that I should come back.

I had the sharp appetite of the convalescent, and this sea-air had whetted already to a finer edge. In touch with a dozen oysters, and with stout, I soon shed away the unreasoning anger I had felt against A. V. Laider. I became merely sorry for him that he had not received a letter which might perhaps have comforted him. In touch with cutlets, I felt how sorely he had needed comfort. And anon, by the big bright fireside of that small dark smoking-room where, a year ago, on the last evening of my stay here, he and I had at length spoken to each other, I reviewed in detail the tragic experience he had told me; and I fairly revelled in reminiscent sympathy with him. . . .

A. V. Laider—I had looked him up in the visitors' book on the night of his arrival. I myself had arrived the day before, and had been rather sorry there was no one else staying here. A con- valescent by the sea likes to have some one to ob- serve, to wonder about, at meal-time. I was glad when, on my second evening, I found seated at the table opposite to mine another guest. I was the gladder because he was just the right kind of guest. He was enigmatic. By this I mean that he did not look soldierly nor financial nor artistic nor anything definite at all. He offered a clean slate for specula- tion. And thank heaven! he evidently wasn't going to spoil the fun by engaging me in conversation later on. A decently unsociable man, anxious to be left alone.

The heartiness of his appetite, in contrast with his extreme fragility of aspect and limpness of de- meanour, assured me that he, too, had just had in- fluenza. I liked him for that. Now and again our eyes met and were instantly parted. We managed, as a rule, to observe each other indirectly. I was sure it was not merely because he had been ill that he looked interesting. Nor did it seem to me that a spiritual melancholy, though I imagined him sad at the best of times, was his sole asset. I conjectured that he was clever. I thought he might also be im- aginative. At first glance I had mistrusted him. A shock of white hair, combined with a young face and dark eyebrows, does somehow make a man look like a charlatan. But it is foolish to be guided by an accident of colour. I had soon rejected my first impression of my fellow-diner. I found him very sympathetic.

Anywhere but in England it would be impossible for two solitary men, howsoever much reduced by influenza, to spend five or six days in the same hos- tel and not exchange a single word. That is one of the charms of England. Had Laider and I been born and bred in any other land we should have become acquainted before the end of our first eve- ning in the small smoking-room, and have found ourselves irrevocably committed to go on talking to each other throughout the rest of our visit. We might, it is true, have happened to like each other more than any one we had ever met. This off- chance may have occurred to us both. But it counted for nothing as against the certain surrender

of quietude and liberty. We slightly bowed to each other as we entered or left the dining-room or smoking-room, and as we met on the widespread sands or in the shop that had a small and faded cir- culating library. That was all. Our mutual aloofness was a positive bond between us.

Had he been much older than I, the responsi- bility for our silence would of course have been his alone. But he was not, I judged, more than five or six years ahead of me, and thus I might without impropriety have taken it on myself to perform that hard and perilous feat which English people call, with a shiver, "breaking the ice." He had reason, therefore, to be as grateful to me as I to him. Each of us, not the less frankly because si- lently, recognised his obligation to the other. And when, on the last evening of my stay, the ice actually was broken no ill-will rose between us: neither of us was to blame.

It was a Sunday evening. I had been out for a long last walk and had come in very late to dinner. Laider left his table almost immediately after I sat down to mine. When I entered the smoking-room I found him reading a weekly review which I had bought the day before. It was a crisis. He could not silently offer, nor could I have silently accepted, sixpence. It was a crisis. We faced it like men. He made, by word of mouth, a graceful apology. Ver- bally, not by signs, I besought him to go on read- ing. But this, of course, was a vain counsel of per- fection. The social code forced us to talk now. We obeyed it like men. To reassure him that our posi- tion was not so desperate as it might seem, I took the earliest opportunity to mention that I was going away early next morning. In the tone of his "Oh, are you?" he tried bravely to imply that he was sorry, even now, to hear that. In a way, per- haps, he really was sorry. We had got on so well together, he and I. Nothing could efface the mem- ory of that. Nay, we seemed to be hitting it off even now. Influenza was not our sole theme. We passed from that to the aforesaid weekly review, and to a correspondence that was raging therein on Faith and Reason.

This correspondence had now reached its fourth and penultimate stage—its Australian stage. It is hard to see why these correspondences spring up; one only knows that they do spring up, suddenly, like street crowds. There comes, it would seem, a moment when the whole English-speaking race is unconsciously bursting to have its say about some one thing—the split infinitive, or the habits of mi- gratory birds, or faith and reason, or what-not. Whatever weekly review happens at such a moment to contain a reference, however remote, to the theme in question reaps the storm. Gusts of letters blow in from all corners of the British Isles. These are presently reinforced by Canada in full blast. A few weeks later the Anglo-Indians weigh in. In due course we have the help of our Australian cousins. By that time, however, we of the Mother Country have got our second wind, and so determined are we to make the most of it that at last even the Editor suddenly loses patience and 10 says "This correspondence must now cease.—Ed." and wonders why on earth he ever allowed anything so tedious and idiotic to begin.

I pointed out to Laider one of the Australian letters that had especially pleased me in the current issue. It was from "A Melbourne Man," and was of the abrupt kind which declares that "all your correspondents have been groping in the dark" and then settles the whole matter in one short sharp flash. The flash in this instance was "Reason is 20 faith, faith reason—that is all we know on earth and all we need to know." The writer then inclosed his card and was, etc., "A Melbourne Man." I said to Laider how very restful it was, after influenza, to read anything that meant nothing whatsoever. Laider was inclined to take the letter more seriously than I, and to be mildly metaphysical. I said that for me faith and reason were two separate things, and (as I am no good at metaphysics, however mild) I offered a definite example, to coax the talk 30 on to ground where I should be safer. "Palmistry, for example," I said. "Deep down in my heart I believe in palmistry."

Laider turned in his chair. "You believe in palmistry?"

I hesitated. "Yes, somehow I do. Why? I haven't the slightest notion. I can give myself all sorts of reasons for laughing it to scorn. My common sense utterly rejects it. Of course the shape of the hand means something—is more or less an index of char- 40 acter. But the idea that my past and future are neatly mapped out on my palms—" I shrugged my shoulders.

"You don't like that idea?" asked Laider in his gentle, rather academic voice.

"I only say it's a grotesque idea."

"Yet you do believe in it?"

"I've a grotesque belief in it, yes."

"Are you sure your reason for calling this idea 'grotesque' isn't merely that you dislike it?" 50

"Well," I said, with the thrilling hope that he was a companion in absurdity, "doesn't it seem grotesque to *you?*"

"It seems strange."

"You believe in it?"

"Oh, absolutely."

"Hurrah!"

He smiled at my pleasure, and I, at the risk of re-entanglement in metaphysics, claimed him as standing shoulder to shoulder with me against "A Melbourne Man." This claim he gently disputed. "You may think me very prosaic," he said, "but I can't believe without evidence."

"Well, I'm equally prosaic and equally at a disadvantage: I can't take my own belief as evidence, and I've no other evidence to go on."

He asked me if I had ever made a study of palmistry. I said I had read one of Desbarolles' books years ago, and one of Heron-Allen's. But, he asked, had I tried to test them by the lines on my own hands or on the hands of my friends? I confessed that my actual practice in palmistry had been of a merely passive kind—the prompt extension of my palm to any one who would be so good as to "read" it and truckle for a few minutes to my egoism. (I hoped Laider might do this.)

"Then I almost wonder," he said, with his sad smile, "that you haven't lost your belief, after all the nonsense you must have heard. There are so many young girls who go in for palmistry. I am sure all the five foolish virgins were 'awfully keen on it' and used to say 'You can be led, but not driven,' and 'You are likely to have a serious illness between the ages of forty and forty-five,' and 'You are by nature rather lazy, but can be very energetic by fits and starts.' And most of the professionals, I'm told, are as silly as the young girls."

For the honour of the profession, I named three practitioners whom I had found really good at reading character. He asked whether any of them had been right about past events. I confessed that, as a matter of fact, all three of them had been right in the main. This seemed to amuse him. He asked whether any of them had predicted anything which 40 had since come true. I confessed that . . . all three had predicted that I should do several things which I had since done rather unexpectedly. He asked if I didn't accept this as at any rate a scrap of evidence. I said I could only regard it as a fluke— a rather remarkable fluke.

The superiority of his sad smile was beginning to get on my nerves. I wanted him to see that he was as absurd as I. "Suppose," I said, "suppose for sake 50 of argument that you and I are nothing but helpless automata created to do just this and that, and to have just that and this done to us. Suppose, in fact, we *haven't* any free will whatsoever. Is it likely or **conceivable** that the Power that fashioned us would take the trouble to jot down in cipher on our hands just what was in store for us?"

Laider did not answer this question, he did but annoyingly ask me another. "You believe in free will?"

"Yes, of course. I'll be hanged if I'm an automaton."

"And you believe in free will just as in palmistry—without any reason?"

"Oh, no. Everything points to our having free will."

"Everything? What, for instance?"

This rather cornered me. I dodged out, as lightly as I could, by saying "I suppose *you* would say it was written in my hand that I should be a believer in free will."

"Ah, I've no doubt it is."

I held out my palms. But, to my great disappointment, he looked quickly away from them. He had ceased to smile. There was agitation in his voice as he explained that he never looked at people's hands now. "Never now—never again." He shook his head as though to beat off some memory.

I was much embarrassed by my indiscretion. I hastened to tide over the awkward moment by saying that if *I* could read hands I wouldn't, for fear of the awful things I might see there.

"Awful things, yes," he whispered, nodding at the fire.

"Not," I said in self-defence, "that there's anything very awful, so far as I know, to read in *my* hands."

He turned his gaze from the fire to me. "You aren't a murderer, for example?"

"Oh, no," I replied, with a nervous laugh.

"*I* am."

This was a more than awkward, it was a painful, moment for me; and I am afraid I must have started or winced, for he instantly begged my pardon. "I don't know," he exclaimed, "why I said it. I'm usually a very reticent man. But sometimes—" He pressed his brow. "What you must think of me!"

I begged him to dismiss the matter from his mind.

"It's very good of you to say that; but—I've placed myself as well as you in a false position. I ask you to believe that I'm not the sort of man who is 'wanted' or ever was 'wanted' by the police. I should be bowed out of any police-station at which I gave myself up. I'm not a murderer in any bald sense of the word. No."

My face must have perceptibly brightened, for "Ah," he said, "don't imagine I'm not a murderer at all. Morally, I am." He looked at the clock. I

pointed out that the night was young. He assured me that his story was not a long one. I assured him that I hoped it was. He said I was very kind. I denied this. He warned me that what he had to tell might rather tend to stiffen my unwilling faith in palmistry, and to shake my opposite and cherished faith in free will. I said "Never mind." He stretched his hands pensively toward the fire. I settled myself back in my chair.

"My hands," he said staring at the backs of them, "are the hands of a very weak man. I dare say you know enough of palmistry to see that for yourself. You notice the slightness of the thumbs and of the two 'little' fingers. They are the hands of a weak and over-sensitive man—a man without confidence, a man who would certainly waver in an emergency. Rather Hamletish hands," he mused. "And I'm like Hamlet in other respects, too: I'm no fool, and I've rather a noble disposition, and I'm unlucky. But Hamlet was luckier than I in one thing: he was a murderer by accident, whereas the murders that I committed one day fourteen years ago—for I must tell you it wasn't one murder, but many murders that I committed—were all of them due to the wretched inherent weakness of my own wretched self.

"I was twenty-six—no, twenty-seven years old, and rather a nondescript person, as I am now. I was supposed to have been called to the Bar. In fact, I believe I *had* been called to the Bar. I hadn't listened to the call. I never intended to practise, and I never did practise. I only wanted an excuse in the eyes of the world for existing. I suppose the nearest I have ever come to practising is now at this moment: I am defending a murderer. My father had left me well enough provided with money. I was able to go my own desultory way, riding my hobbies where I would. I had a whole stableful of hobbies. Palmistry was one of them. I was rather ashamed of this one. It seemed to me absurd, as it seems to you. Like you, though, I believed in it. Unlike you, I had done more than merely read a book or so about it. I had read innumerable books about it. I had taken casts of all my friends' hands. I had tested and tested again the points at which Desbarolles dissented from the gypsies, and—well, enough that I had gone into it all rather thoroughly, and was as sound a palmist as a man may be without giving his whole life to palmistry.

"One of the first things I had seen in my own hand, as soon as I had learned to read it, was that at about the age of twenty-six I should have a narrow escape from death—from a violent death.

There was a clean break in the life-line, and a square joining it—the protective square, you know. The markings were precisely the same in both hands. It was to be the narrowest escape possible. And I wasn't going to escape without injury, either. That is what bothered me. There was a faint line connecting the break in the life-line with a star on the line of health. Against that star was another square. I was to recover from the injury, whatever it might be. Still, I didn't exactly look forward to it. Soon after I had reached the age of twenty-five, I began to feel uncomfortable. The thing might be going to happen at any moment. In palmistry, you know, it is impossible to pin an event down hard and fast to one year. This particular event was to be when I was *about* twenty-six; it mightn't be till I was twenty-seven; it might be while I was only twenty-five.

"And I used to tell myself that it mightn't be at all. My reason rebelled against the whole notion of palmistry, just as yours does. I despised my faith in the thing, just as you despise yours. I used to try not to be so ridiculously careful as I was whenever I crossed a street. I lived in London at that time. Motor-cars had not yet come in, but—what hours, all told, I must have spent standing on curbs, very circumspect, very lamentable! It was a pity, I suppose, that I had no definite occupation—something to take me out of myself. I was one of the victims of private means. There came a time when I drove in four-wheelers rather than in hansoms, and was doubtful of four-wheelers. Oh, I assure you, I was very lamentable indeed.

"If a railway-journey could be avoided, I avoided it. My uncle had a place in Hampshire. I was very fond of him and of his wife. Theirs was the only house I ever went to stay in now. I was there for a week in November, not long after my twenty-seventh birthday. There were other people staying there, and at the end of the week we all travelled back to London together. There were six of us in the carriage: Colonel Elbourn and his wife and their daughter, a girl of seventeen; and another married couple, the Blakes. I had been at Winchester with Blake, but had hardly seen him since that time. He was in the Indian Civil, and was home on leave. He was sailing for India next week. His wife was to remain in England for some months, and then join him out there. They had been married five years. She was now just twenty-four years old. He told me that this was her age.

"The Elbourns I had never met before. They

31. **four-wheelers,** carriages with four wheels seemed, somehow, safer than hansoms, which had two.

were charming people. We had all been very happy together. The only trouble had been that on the last night, at dinner, my uncle asked me if I still went in for 'the gypsy business,' as he always called it; and of course the three ladies were immensely excited, and implored me to 'do' their hands. I told them it was all nonsense, I said I had forgotten all I once knew, I made various excuses; and the matter dropped. It was quite true that I had given up reading hands. I avoided anything that might remind me of what was in my own hands. And so, next morning, it was a great bore to me when, soon after the train started, Mrs. Elbourn said it would be 'too cruel' of me if I refused to do their hands now. Her daughter and Mrs. Blake also said it would be 'brutal'; and they were all taking off their gloves, and—well, of course I had to give in.

"I went to work methodically on Mrs. Elbourn's hands, in the usual way, you know, first sketching the character from the backs of them; and there was the usual hush, broken by the usual little noises—grunts of assent from the husband, cooings of recognition from the daughter. Presently I asked to see the palms, and from them I filled in the details of Mrs. Elbourn's character before going on to the events in her life. But while I talked I was calculating how old Mrs. Elbourn might be. In my first glance at her palms I had seen that she could not have been less than twenty-five when she married. The daughter was seventeen. Suppose the daughter had been born a year later—how old would the mother be? Forty-three, yes. Not less than that, poor woman!"

Laider looked at me. "Why 'poor woman,' you wonder? Well, in that first glance I had seen other things than her marriage-line. I had seen a very complete break in the lines of life and of fate. I had seen violent death there. At what age? Not later, not possibly *later*, than forty-three. While I talked to her about the things that had happened in her girlhood, the back of my brain was hard at work on those marks of catastrophe. I was horribly wondering that she was still alive. It was impossible that between her and that catastrophe there could be more than a few short months. And all the time I was talking; and I suppose I acquitted myself well, for I remember that when I ceased I had a sort of ovation from the Elbourns.

"It was a relief to turn to another pair of hands. Mrs. Blake was an amusing young creature, and her hands were very characteristic, and prettily odd in form. I allowed myself to be rather whimsical about her nature, and, having begun in that vein, I went on in it—somehow—even after she had turned her palms. In those palms were reduplicated the signs I had seen in Mrs. Elbourn's. It was as though they had been copied neatly out. The only difference was in the placing of them; and it was this difference that was the most horrible point. The fatal age in Mrs. Blake's hands was—not past, no, for here *she* was. But she might have died when she was twenty-one. Twenty-three seemed to be the utmost span. She was twenty-four, you know.

"I have said that I am a weak man. And you will have a good proof of that directly. Yet I showed a certain amount of strength that day— yes, even on that day which has humiliated and saddened the rest of my life. Neither my face nor my voice betrayed me when in the palms of Dorothy Elbourn I was again confronted with those same signs. She was all for knowing the future, poor child! I believe I told her all manner of things that were to be. And she had no future—none, none in *this* world—except—

"And then, while I talked, there came to me suddenly a suspicion. I wondered it hadn't come before. You guess what it was? It made me feel very cold and strange. I went on talking. But, also, I went on—quite separately—thinking. The suspicion wasn't a certainty. This mother and daughter were always together. What was to befall the one might anywhere—anywhere—befall the other. But a like fate, in an equally near future, was in store for that other lady. The coincidence was curious, very. Here we all were together—here, they and I—I who was narrowly to escape, so soon now, what they, so soon now, were to suffer. Oh, here was an inference to be drawn. Not a *sure* inference, I told myself. And always I was talking, talking, and the train was swinging and swaying noisily along—to what? It was a fast train. Our carriage was near the engine. I was talking loudly. Full well I had known what I should see in the Colonel's hands. I told myself I had not known. I told myself that even now the thing I dreaded was not sure to be. Don't think I was dreading it for myself. I wasn't so 'lamentable' as all that—now. It was only of them that I thought—only for them. I hurried over the Colonel's character and career; I was perfunctory. It was Blake's hands that I wanted. *They* were the hands that mattered. If *they* had the marks—Remember, Blake was to start for India in the coming week, his wife was to remain in England. They would be apart. Therefore—

"And the marks were there. And I did nothing— nothing but hold forth on the subtleties of Blake's character. There was a thing for me to do. I wanted to do it. I wanted to spring to the window and pull the communication-cord. Quite a simple thing to do. Nothing easier than to stop a train. You just give a sharp pull, and the train slows down, comes to a standstill. And the Guard appears at your window. You explain to the Guard.

"Nothing easier than to tell him there is going to be a collision. Nothing easier than to insist that you and your friends and every other passenger in the train must get out at once. . . . There *are* easier things than this? Things that need less courage than this? Some of *them* I could have done, I daresay. This thing I was going to do. Oh, I was determined that I would do it—directly.

"I had said all I had to say about Blake's hands. I had brought my entertainment to an end. I had been thanked and complimented all round. I was quite at liberty. I was going to do what I had to do. I was determined, yes.

"We were near the outskirts of London. The air was grey, thickening; and Dorothy Elbourn had said, 'Oh, this horrible old London! I suppose there's the same old fog!' And presently I heard her father saying something about 'prevention' and 'a short act of Parliament' and 'anthracite.' And I sat and listened and agreed and—"

Laider closed his eyes. He passed his hand slowly through the air.

"I had a racking headache. And when I said so, I was told not to talk. I was in bed, and the nurses were always telling me not to talk. I was in a hospital. I knew that. But I didn't know why I was there. One day I thought I should like to know why, and so I asked. I was feeling much better now. They told me, by degrees, that I had had concussion of the brain. I had been brought there unconscious, and had remained unconscious for forty-eight hours. I had been in an accident—a railway accident. This seemed to me odd. I had arrived quite safely at my uncle's place, and I had no memory of any journey since that. In cases of concussion, you know, it's not uncommon for the patient to forget all that happened just before the accident; there may be a blank of several hours. So it was in my case. One day my uncle was allowed to come and see me. And somehow, suddenly, at sight of him, the blank was filled in. I remembered, in a flash, everything. I was quite calm, though. Or I made myself seem so, for I wanted to know how the collision had happened. My uncle told me that the engine-driver had failed to see a signal because of the fog, and our train had crashed into a goods-train. I didn't ask him about the people who were with me. You see, there was no need to ask. Very gently my uncle began to tell me, but—I had begun to talk strangely,

I suppose. I remember the frightened look of my uncle's face, and the nurse scolding him in whispers.

"After that, all a blur. It seems that I became very ill indeed, wasn't expected to live. However, I live."

There was a long silence. Laider did not look at me, nor I at him. The fire was burning low, and he watched it.

At length he spoke. "You despise me. Naturally. I despise myself."

"No, I don't despise you; but—"

"You blame me." I did not meet his gaze. "You blame me," he repeated.

"Yes."

"And there, if I may say so, you are a little unjust. It isn't my fault that I was born weak."

"But a man may conquer weakness."

"Yes, if he is endowed with the strength for that."

His fatalism drew from me a gesture of disgust. "Do you really mean," I asked, "that because you didn't pull that cord, you *couldn't* have pulled it?"

"Yes."

"And it's written in your hands that you couldn't?"

He looked at the palms of his hands. "They are the hands of a very weak man," he said.

"A man so weak that he cannot believe in the possibility of free will for himself or for any one?"

"They are the hands of an intelligent man, who can weigh evidence and see things as they are."

"But answer me: Was it fore-ordained that you should not pull that cord?"

"It was fore-ordained."

"And was it actually marked in your hands that you were not going to pull it?"

"Ah, well, you see, it is rather the things one *is* going to do that are actually marked. The things one *isn't* going to do,—the innumerable negative things,—how could one expect *them* to be marked?"

"But the consequences of what one leaves undone may be positive?"

"Horribly positive," he winced. "My hand is the hand of a man who suffered a great deal in later life."

"And was it the hand of a man *destined* to suffer?"

"Oh, yes. I thought I told you that."

There was a pause.

"Well," I said, with awkward sympathy, "I suppose all hands are the hands of people destined to suffer."

"Not of people destined to suffer so much as *I* have suffered—as I still suffer."

The insistence of his self-pity chilled me, and I harked back to a question he had not straightly answered. "Tell me: Was it marked in your hands that you were not going to pull that cord?"

Again he looked at his hands, and then, having pressed them for a moment to his face, "It was marked very clearly," he answered, "in *their* hands."

Two or three days after this colloquy there had occurred to me in London an idea—an ingenious and comfortable doubt. How was Laider to be sure that his brain, recovering from concussion, had *remembered* what happened in the course of that railway-journey? How was he to know that his brain hadn't simply, in its abeyance, *invented* all this for him? It might be that he had never seen those signs in those hands. Assuredly, here was a bright loop-hole. I had forthwith written to Laider, pointing it out.

This was the letter which now, at my second visit, I had found miserably pent on the letter-board. I remembered my promise to rescue it. I arose from the retaining fireside, stretched my arms, yawned, and went forth to fulfil my Christian purpose. There was no one in the hall. The "shower" had at length ceased. The sun had positively come out, and the front door had been thrown open in its honour. Everything along the sea-front was beautifully gleaming, drying, shimmering. But I was not to be diverted from my errand. I went to the letter-board. And—my letter was not there! Resourceful and plucky little thing—it had escaped! I did hope it would not be captured and brought back. Perhaps the alarm had already been raised by the tolling of that great bell which warns the inhabitants for miles around that a letter has broken loose from the letter-board. I had a vision of my envelope skimming wildly along the coast-line, pursued by the old but active waiter and a breathless pack of local worthies. I saw it out-distancing them all, dodging past coast-guards, doubling on its tracks, leaping breakwaters, unluckily injuring itself, losing speed, and at last, in a splendour of desperation, taking to the open sea. But suddenly I had another idea. Perhaps Laider had returned?

He had. I espied afar on the sands a form that was recognisably, by the listless droop of it, his. I was glad and sorry—rather glad, because he completed the scene of last year; and very sorry, because this time we should be at each other's mercy: no restful silence and liberty, for either of us, this time. Perhaps he had been told I was here, and had gone out to avoid me while he yet could. Oh weak, weak! Why palter? I put on my hat and coat, and marched out to meet him.

"Influenza, of course?" we asked simultaneously.

There is a limit to the time which one may spend in talking to another about his own influenza; and presently, as we paced the sands, I felt that Laider had passed this limit. I wondered that he didn't break off and thank me now for my letter. He must have read it. He ought to have thanked me for it at once. It was a very good letter, a remarkable letter. But surely he wasn't waiting to answer it by post? His silence about it gave me the absurd sense of having taken a liberty, confound him! He was evidently ill at ease while he talked. But it wasn't for me to help him out of his difficulty, whatever that might be. It was for him to remove the strain imposed on myself.

Abruptly, after a long pause, he did now manage to say, "It was—very good of you to—to write me that letter." He told me he had only just got it, and he drifted away into otiose explanations of this fact. I thought he might at least say it was a remarkable letter; and you can imagine my annoyance when he said, after another interval, "I was very much touched indeed." I had wished to be convincing, not touching. I can't bear to be called touching.

"Don't you," I asked, "think it *is* quite possible that your brain invented all those memories of what—what happened before that accident?"

He drew a sharp sigh. "You make me feel very guilty."

"That's exactly what I tried to make you *not* feel!"

"I know, yes. That's why I feel so guilty."

We had paused in our walk. He stood nervously prodding the hard wet sand with his walking-stick. "In a way," he said, "your theory was quite right. But—it didn't go far enough. It's not only possible, it's a fact, that I didn't see those signs in those hands. I never examined those hands. They weren't there. *I* wasn't there. I haven't an uncle in Hampshire, even. I never had."

I, too, prodded the sand. "Well," I said at length, "I do feel rather a fool."

"I've no right even to beg your pardon, but—"

"Oh, I'm not vexed. Only—I rather wish you hadn't told me this."

"I wish I hadn't had to. It was your kindness, you see, that forced me. By trying to take an imaginary load off my conscience, you laid a very real one on it."

"I'm sorry. But you, of your own free will, you know, exposed your conscience to me last year. I don't yet quite understand why you did that."

19. otiose, irrelevant and purposeless.

"No, of course not. I don't deserve that you should. But I think you will. May I explain? I'm afraid I've talked a great deal already about my influenza, and I shan't be able to keep it out of my explanation. Well, my weakest point—I told you this last year, but it happens to be perfectly true that my weakest point—is my will. Influenza, as you know, fastens unerringly on one's weakest point. It doesn't attempt to undermine my imagination. That would be a forlorn hope. I have, alas! a very strong imagination. At ordinary times my imagination allows itself to be governed by my will. My will keeps it in check by constant nagging. But when my will isn't strong enough even to nag, then my imagination stampedes. I become even as a little child. I tell myself the most preposterous fables, and—the trouble is—I can't help telling them to my friends. Until I've thoroughly shaken off influenza, I'm not fit company for any one. I perfectly realize this, and I have the good sense to go right away till I'm quite well again. I come here usually. It seems absurd, but I must confess I was sorry last year when we fell into conversation. I knew I should very soon be letting myself go, or rather, very soon be swept away. Perhaps I ought to have warned you; but—I'm a rather shy man. And then you mentioned the subject of palmistry. You said you believed in it. I wondered at that. I had once read Desbarolles' book about it, but I am bound to say I thought the whole thing very great nonsense indeed."

"Then," I gasped, "it isn't even true that you believe in palmistry?"

"Oh, no. But I wasn't able to tell you that. You had begun by saying that you believed in palmistry, and then you proceeded to scoff at it. While you scoffed I saw myself as a man with a terribly good reason for *not* scoffing; and in a flash I saw the terribly good reason; I had the whole story— at least I had the broad outlines of it—clear before me."

"You hadn't even thought of it before?" He shook his head. My eyes beamed. "The whole thing was a sheer improvisation?"

"Yes," said Laider, humbly, "I am as bad as all that. I don't say that all the details of the story I told you that evening were filled in at the very instant of its conception. I was filling them in while we talked about palmistry in general, and while I was waiting for the moment when the story would come in most effectively. And I've no doubt I added some extra touches in the course of the actual telling. Don't imagine that I took the slightest pleasure in deceiving you. It's only my will, not my conscience, that is weakened after influenza. I simply can't help telling what I've made up, and telling it to the best of my ability. But I'm thoroughly ashamed all the time."

"Not of your ability, surely?"

"Yes, of that, too," he said with his sad smile. "I always feel that I'm not doing justice to my idea."

"You are too stern a critic, believe me."

"It is very kind of you to say that. You are very kind altogether. Had I known that you were so essentially a man of the world—in the best sense of that term—I shouldn't have so much dreaded seeing you just now and having to confess to you. But I'm not going to take advantage of your urbanity and your easy-going ways. I hope that some day we may meet somewhere when I haven't had influenza and am a not wholly undesirable acquaintance. As it is, I refuse to let you associate with me. I am an older man that you, and so I may without impertinence warn you against having anything to do with me."

I deprecated this advice, of course; but, for a man of weakened will, he showed great firmness. "You," he said, "in your heart of hearts don't want to have to walk and talk continually with a person who might at any moment try to bamboozle you with some ridiculous tale. And I, for my part, don't want to degrade myself by trying to bamboozle any one—especially one whom I have taught to see through me. Let the two talks we have had be as though they have not been. Let us bow to each other, as last year, but let that be all. Let us follow in all things the precedent of last year."

With a smile that was almost gay he turned on his heel, and moved away with a step that was almost brisk. I was a little disconcerted. But I was

also more than a little glad. The restfulness of silence, the charm of liberty—these things were not, after all, forfeit. My heart thanked Laider for that; and throughout the week I loyally seconded him in the system he had laid down for us. All was as it had been last year. We did not smile to each other, we merely bowed, when we entered or left the dining-room or smoking-room, and when we met on the widespread sands or in that shop which had a small and faded, but circulating, library.

Once or twice in the course of the week it did occur to me that perhaps Laider had told the simple truth at our first interview and an ingenious lie at our second. I frowned at this possibility. The idea of any one wishing to be quit of *me* was most distasteful. However, I was to find reassurance. On the last evening of my stay, I suggested, in the small smoking-room, that he and I should, as sticklers for precedent, converse. We did so, very pleasantly. And after a while I happened to say that I had seen this afternoon a great number of sea-gulls flying close to the shore.

"Sea-gulls?" said Laider, turning in his chair.

"Yes. And I don't think I had ever realised how extraordinarily beautiful they are when their wings catch the light."

"Beautiful?" Laider threw a quick glance at me and away from me. "You think them beautiful?"

"Surely."

"Well, perhaps they are, yes; I suppose they are. But—I don't like seeing them. They always remind me of something—rather an awful thing—that once happened to me." . . .

It was a very awful thing indeed.

Walter De La Mare
1873–

Descended from a Huguenot family and distantly related to Browning, Walter (John) De La Mare was born April 25, 1873, at Charlton in Kent. He was educated at St. Paul's School in London. In his eighteenth year he entered business, and for almost twenty years he remained in the English branch of the Standard Oil Company.

A shy, almost withdrawn, person, De La Mare issued his first volume in 1902 under a pseudonym, "Walter Ramal." The title, *Songs of Childhood*, was significant, for, although De La Mare wrote and edited fifty books before he was sixty-five, he was most at home in the world of childhood. He lived in the realm of the half-juvenile, half-supernatural; his characters are innocents, fairies, witches, incredibly wide-eyed boys and girls, storybook goblins, love-torn ghosts, unhappy midgets, doomed princes, travelers in remote and scarcely imaginable regions. Even *Behold, This Dreamer*, 1939—an anthology in prose and verse of reverie, night, sleep, love dreams, nightmare, death, the unconscious, the imagination, divination, and kindred subjects—although published in De La Mare's sixty-seventh year, reflects the musings of an old and wondering child.

It is a strangely remembering quality which one finds in De La Mare. He is fascinated by the magic of dreams, "so various in their shocking disregard of our tastes and ideals," by the borderlands between hallucination and true vision, by the conflict between the outer event and the inward eye, by mystery *as* mystery. It is as if the experienced adult so feared or hated ordinary reality that his whole work was a defense against it, a retreat into a limbo where everything was veiled in an unearthly loveliness and the impossible was more likely to happen than not.

De La Mare would be the last to deny this. He has continually championed the extra-rational, the area of sensitivity beyond the realism which is a record of life. "Nature itself," he wrote, "resembles a veil over some further reality of which the imagination in its visionary moments seems to achieve a more direct evidence." It is toward illumination, rather than elucidation, that De La Mare strives. Yet (such is the pitch of his utterance) ecstasy and gloom, peace and horror, attain an incongruous similarity, a curious evenness of tone.

It is in this hushed and recessive mood that De La Mare triumphs. It is evidenced in his explorations into the other worlds. It is followed haphazardly in the books for children, from *Peacock Pie*, 1913, to *Down-adown-Derry*, 1922; gravely from the serious poems in *The Listeners*, 1912, where all is said by implication, to *Poems 1919–1934*, 1936; analytically in *Desert Islands and Robinson Crusoe*, 1930; poignantly in *Memoirs of a Midget*, 1921, one of the neglected masterpieces of contemporary prose.

Whether he is examining the spirit of fairy lore, or charting territories of immense solitude, or spinning sheer fantasies, De La Mare harks back to irresponsible childhood and irresistible romance, which is the never-aging child of the imagination. His "motto" might well be a verse from "Tom o' Bedlam's Song," an old anonymous poem which is one of De La Mare's favorites:

> "With a host of furious fancies,
>   Whereof I am commander;
>   With a burning spear,
>   And a horse of air,
> To the wilderness I wander."

It is as a "knight of ghosts" that De La Mare journeys forth. He is one of the few poets who have ventured "ten leagues beyond the wild world's end" and have returned to describe that unknown universe.

THE LISTENERS [1]

"Is there anybody there?" said the Traveller,
    Knocking on the moonlit door;
And his horse in the silence champed the grasses
    Of the forest's ferny floor.
And a bird flew up out of the turret,
    Above the Traveller's head:
And he smote upon the door again a second time;
    "Is there anybody there?" he said.
But no one descended to the Traveller;
    No head from the leaf-fringed sill   10

[1] From *The Listeners* by Walter De La Mare, Henry Holt and Company, Inc. Reprinted by permission.

Leaned over and looked into his grey eyes,
  Where he stood perplexed and still.
But only a host of phantom listeners
  That dwelt in the lone house then
Stood listening in the quiet of the moonlight
  To that voice from the world of men:
Stood thronging the faint moonbeams on the dark
    stair
  That goes down to the empty hall,
Hearkening in an air stirred and shaken
  By the lonely Traveller's call.   20
And he felt in his heart their strangeness,
  Their stillness answering his cry,
While his horse moved, cropping the dark turf,
  'Neath the starred and leafy sky;
For he suddenly smote on the door, even
  Louder, and lifted his head:—
"Tell them I came, and no one answered,
  That I kept my word," he said.
Never the least stir made the listeners,
  Though every word he spake   30
Fell echoing through the shadowiness of the still
    house
  From the one man left awake:
Ay, they heard his foot upon the stirrup,
  And the sound of iron on stone,
And how the silence surged softly backward,
  When the plunging hoofs were gone.

AN EPITAPH [1]

  Here lies a most beautiful lady,
    Light of step and heart was she;
  I think she was the most beautiful lady
    That ever was in the West Country.
  But beauty vanishes; beauty passes;
    However rare—rare it be;
  And when I crumble, who will remember
    This lady of the West Country?

THE GHOST

"Who knocks?" "I, who was beautiful,
  Beyond all dreams to restore,
I, from the roots of the dark thorn am hither,
  And knock on the door."

"Who speaks?" "I—once was my speech
  Sweet as the bird's on the air.
When echo lurks by the waters to heed;
  'Tis I speak thee fair."

[1] This and the next four poems are from the *Collected
Poems* of Walter De La Mare, 1901–1918, Henry Holt and
Company, Inc. Reprinted by permission.

"Dark is the hour!" "Ay, and cold."
  "Lone is my house." "Ah, but mine?"   10
"Sight, touch, lips, eyes yearned in vain."
  "Long dead these to thine. . . . "

Silence. Still faint on the porch
  Brake the flames of the stars.
In gloom groped a hope-wearied hand
  Over keys, bolts, and bars.

A face peered. All the grey night
  In chaos of vacancy shone;
Nought but vast sorrow was there—
  The sweet cheat gone.   20

NOD

Softly along the road of evening,
  In a twilight dim with rose,
Wrinkled with age, and drenched with dew,
  Old Nod, the shepherd, goes.

His drowsy flock streams on before him,
  Their fleeces charged with gold,
To where the sun's last beam leans low
  On Nod the shepherd's fold.

The hedge is quick and green with brier,
  From their sand the conies creep;   10
And all the birds that fly in heaven
  Flock singing home to sleep.

His lambs outnumber a noon's roses,
  Yet, when night's shadows fall,
His blind old sheep-dog, Slumber-soon,
  Misses not one of all.

His are the quiet steeps of dreamland,
  The waters of no-more-pain;
His ram's bell rings 'neath an arch of stars,
  "Rest, rest, and rest again."   20

THE SONG OF SHADOWS

Sweep thy faint strings, Musician,
  With thy long lean hand;
Downward the starry tapers burn,
  Sinks soft the waning sand;
The old hound whimpers couched in sleep,
  The embers smoulder low;
Across the walls the shadows
  Come, and go.

Sweep softly thy strings, Musician,
   The minutes mount to hours;   10
Frost on the windless casement weaves
   A labyrinth of flowers;
Ghosts linger in the darkening air,
   Hearken at the open door;
Music hath called them, dreaming,
   Home once more.

THE SONG OF FINIS

At the edge of All the Ages
   A Knight sate on his steed,
His armour red and thin with rust,

His soul from sorrow freed;
   And he lifted up his visor
From a face of skin and bone,
   And his horse turned head and whinnied
As the twain stood there alone.

No bird above that steep of time
   Sang of a livelong quest;   10
No wind breathed,
   Rest:
"Lone for an end!" cried Knight to steed,
   Loosed an eager rein—
Charged with his challenge into Space:
   And quiet did quiet remain.

G. K. Chesterton
1874–1936

The man often called the master of paradox, G(ilbert) K(eith) Chesterton, was born at Campden Hill, Kensington, now part of London, on May 29, 1874. After graduating from St. Paul's School and the Slade School of Art, he wavered between a career in art and a future in literature. He began by uniting both desires: he reviewed books of art. He never wholly discontinued his fondness for drawing; he illustrated several of his works, and about ten of the novels of his friend Hilaire Belloc. He delighted in debates, and the World War intensified his passion for controversy. Aware that something was wrong with the economic system, he revolted against both capitalism and socialism, and proclaimed a new order which was curiously like an old disorder: a confused and romanticized medievalism. Here Chesterton revealed his irrational rationalism. He wrote like an adult who lived in a world of childish fantasy, a serious thinker who thought only in terms of paradox, a philosopher who defended the obvious with the zeal of a fanatic crucified for his heresies.

His versatility matched his vigor. He traveled and lectured extensively; he became chief columnist on the *Daily News and Leader*, editor of *G. K.'s Weekly*, Fellow of the Royal Society of Literature, president of the Distributists League. When he died on June 14, 1936, he was the author of more than one hundred volumes of fiction, poetry, plays, biographies, criticisms, essays, and studies.

As a writer of fiction Chesterton delighted in high-flying surprise. His most characteristic novel, *The Man Who Was Thursday*, 1908, was subtitled "A Nightmare," and his Father Brown narratives—beginning with *The Innocence of Father Brown*, 1911, and ending with *The Scandal of Father Brown*, 1935—were a set of detective stories incongruously full of Christian symbols and faintly disguised sermons. A clue to Chesterton's tricky humor is contained in some of the other titles: *The Club of Queer Trades*, 1905; *The Unthinkable Theory of Professor Green*, 1925; *The Moderate Murderer*, 1929; *The Poet and the Lunatics*, 1929; *A Defence of Nonsense*, 1911.

In all these works there is a tremendous zest, a zest for the common people and the uncommon poet. Chesterton accomplishes new and dexterous combinations; he turns out journalistic articles which become poetic allegories, essays (like "A Piece of Chalk") which are parables. His is a robust eagerness that has its charm and which scarcely attempts to conceal its defects. The Chestertonian gusto plays with rhetoric, with winning but artificial simplicity, with a brilliant but calculated extravagance—all in a witty topsy-turvy land. His criticism of Mrs. Browning's style might well be applied to him:

"Whenever her verse is bad, it is bad from some violence of comparison, some kind of debauch of cleverness. Her nonsense never arises from weakness, but from a confusion of powers. . . . She cannot leave anything alone, she cannot write a line, without a conceit. She gives the reader the impression that she never declined a fancy."

Chesterton's liveliness and energy are at their best in his poetry—*New and Collected Poems*, 1929—in the tramping measures of "The rolling English drunkard who made the rolling English road," in the trumpeting rhymes and pounding rhythms of "Lepanto" and the "strong gongs groaning as the guns boom far." But he is likely to be remembered chiefly as a determined wielder of paradox, an author whose most characteristic volume was significantly entitled *Tremendous Trifles*, 1909, and who never ceased making verbal mountains out of intellectual molehills.

A biography, *G. K. Chesterton*, was written by Maurice Evans and published in 1939.

A PIECE OF CHALK [1]

I REMEMBER one splendid morning, all blue and silver, in the summer holidays, when I reluctantly tore myself away from the task of doing nothing in particular, and put on a hat of some sort and picked up a walking-stick, and put six very bright-coloured chalks in my pocket. I then went into the kitchen (which, along with the rest of the house, belonged to a very square and sensible old woman in a Sussex village), and asked the owner and occupant of the kitchen if she had any brown paper. She had a great deal; in fact, she had too much; and she mistook the purpose and the rationale of the existence of brown paper. She seemed to have an idea that if a person wanted brown paper he must be wanting to tie up parcels; which was the last thing I wanted to do; indeed, it is a thing which I have found to be beyond my mental capacity. Hence she dwelt very much on the varying qualities of toughness and endurance in the material. I explained to her that I only wanted to draw pictures on it, and that I did not want them to endure in the least; and that from my point of view, therefore, it was a question not of tough consistency, but of responsive surface, a thing comparatively irrelevant in a parcel. When she understood that I wanted to draw she offered to overwhelm me with note-paper, apparently supposing that I did my notes and correspondence on old brown paper wrappers from motives of economy.

I then tried to explain the rather delicate logical

shade, that I not only liked brown paper, but liked the quality of brownness in paper, just as I liked the quality of brownness in October woods, or in beer, or in the peat-streams of the North. Brown paper represents the primal twilight of the first toil of creation, and with a bright-coloured chalk or two you can pick out points of fire in it, sparks of gold, and blood-red, and sea-green, like the first fierce stars that sprang out of divine darkness. All this I said (in an off-hand way) to the old woman; and I put the brown paper in my pocket along with the chalks, and possibly other things. I suppose every one must have reflected how primeval and how poetical are the things that one carries in one's pocket; the pocket-knife, for instance, the type of all human tools, the infant of the sword. Once I planned to write a book of poems entirely about the things in my pocket. But I found it would be too long; and the age of the great epics is past.

With my stick and my knife, my chalks and my brown paper, I went out on to the great downs. I crawled across those colossal contours that express the best quality of England, because they are at the same time soft and strong. The smoothness of them has the same meaning as the smoothness of great cart-horses, or the smoothness of the beech-tree; it declares in the teeth of our timid and cruel theories that the mighty are merciful. As my eye swept the landscape, the landscape was as kindly as any of its cottages, but for power it was like an earthquake. The villages in the immense valley were safe, one could see, for centuries; yet the lifting of the whole land was like the lifting of one enormous wave to wash them all away.

I crossed one swell of living turf after another, looking for a place to sit down and draw. Do not, for heaven's sake, imagine I was going to sketch from Nature. I was going to draw devils and seraphim, and blind old gods that men worshipped before the dawn of right, and saints in robes of angry crimson, and seas of strange green, and all the sacred or monstrous symbols that look so well in bright colours on brown paper. They are much better worth drawing than Nature; also they are much easier to draw. When a cow came slouching by in the field next to me, a mere artist might have drawn it; but I always get wrong in the hind legs of quadrupeds. So I drew the soul of the cow; which I saw there plainly walking before me in the sunlight; and the soul was all purple and silver, and had seven horns and the mystery that belongs to all the beasts. But though I could not with a crayon get the best out of the landscape, it does not follow that the landscape was not getting the best out of me. And this, I think, is the mistake that people make about the old poets who lived before Wordsworth, and were supposed not to care very much about Nature because they did not describe it much.

They preferred writing about great men to writing about great hills; but they sat on the great hills to write it. They gave out much less about Nature, but they drank in, perhaps, much more. They painted the white robes of their holy virgins with the blinding snow, at which they stared all day. They blazoned the shields of their paladins with the purple and gold of many heraldic sunsets. The greenness of a thousand green leaves clustered into the live green figure of Robin Hood. The blueness of a score of forgotten skies became the blue robes of the Virgin. The inspiration went in like sunbeams and came out like Apollo.

But as I sat scrawling these silly figures on the brown paper, it began to dawn on me, to my great disgust, that I had left one chalk, and that a most exquisite and essential chalk, behind. I searched all my pockets, but I could not find any white chalk. Now, those who are acquainted with all the philosophy (nay, religion) which is typified in the art of drawing on brown paper, know that white is positive and essential. I cannot avoid remarking here upon a moral significance. One of the wise and awful truths which this brown-paper art reveals, is this, that white is a colour. It is not a mere absence of colour; it is a shining and affirmative thing, as fierce as red, as definite as black. When (so to speak) your pencil grows red-hot, it draws roses; when it grows white-hot, it draws stars. And one of the two or three defiant verities of the best religious morality, of real Christianity for example, is exactly this same thing; the chief assertion of religious morality is that white is a colour. Virtue is not the absence of vices or the avoidance of moral dangers; virtue is a vivid and separate thing, like pain or a particular smell. Mercy does not mean not being

cruel or sparing people revenge or punishment; it means a plain and positive thing like the sun, which one has either seen or not seen. Chastity does not mean abstention from sexual wrong; it means something flaming, like Joan of Arc. In a word, God paints in many colours; but He never paints so gorgeously, I had almost said gaudily, as when He paints in white. In a sense our age has realized this fact, and expressed it in our sullen costume. For if it were really true that white was a blank and colourless thing, negative and non-commital, then white would be used instead of black and grey for the funeral dress of this pessimistic period. We should see city gentlemen in frock coats of spotless silver linen, with top hats as white as wonderful arum lilies. Which is not the case.

Meanwhile, I could not find my chalk.

I sat on the hill in a sort of despair. There was no town nearer than Chichester at which it was even remotely probable that there would be such a thing as an artist's colourman. And yet, without white, my absurd little pictures would be as pointless as the world would be if there were no good people in it. I stared stupidly round, racking my brain for expedients. Then I suddenly stood up and roared with laughter, again and again, so that the cows stared at me and called a committee. Imagine a man in the Sahara regretting that he had no sand for his hour-glass. Imagine a gentleman in mid-ocean wishing that he had brought some salt water with him for his chemical experiments. I was sitting on an immense warehouse of white chalk. The landscape was made entirely out of white chalk. White chalk was piled mere miles until it met the sky. I stooped and broke a piece off the rock I sat on: it did not mark so well as the shop chalks do; but it gave the effect. And I stood there in a trance of pleasure, realizing that this Southern England is not only a grand peninsula, and a tradition and a civilization; it is something even more admirable. It is a piece of chalk.

W. Somerset Maugham
1874–

It was in Paris, where his father was connected with the British Embassy, that W(illiam) Somerset Maugham was born, January 25, 1874. He was, it seems, born to be a cosmopolitan, an inveterate traveler, and an insatiable reader. He had read all of Scott by the time he was ten; he taught himself to write by copying whole sections of the English classics. He was educated at King's School, Canterbury, Heidelberg University, and St. Thomas' Hospital. But although his father wanted him to be a doctor and although he dutifully took his degree, he never practiced. Nevertheless, his first volume, *Liza of Lambeth*, 1897, was written before he was twenty-three, while he was a medical student; the book grew out of his hospital experiences. Its frank revelation of slum conditions was considered sordid, even revolting, but it marked the advent of a new and extremely gifted apostle of candor.

Maugham wrote eighteen works between *Liza of Lambeth* and his next success. There were seven novels, a collection of short stories, a melodrama, several comedies and farces; but none of them made any particular impression. It was *Of Human Bondage*, 1915, which forced the critics to take Maugham seriously. *Of Human Bondage*, perhaps Maugham's most important contribution to the period, is semi-autobiographical; it returns to his days at the hospital and presents without mawkishness or false indignation a panorama of everyday, working-class existence. Superficially disinterested and detached, the author goes deep into ordinary life to achieve extraordinary scenes. Passages of extreme brutality are followed by moments of great pity and tenderness. *The Moon and Sixpence*, 1919, was a sudden and enormously popular change. Adapting the life story of the French artist Paul Gauguin in Tahiti, Maugham discovered the South Seas. For many years he luxuriated in the Orient, in actuality as well as in fiction. The mood of the public was "escapist," and Maugham, an unusually skilled craftsman, exploited that mood to the full. Some books of short stories of this period are *The Trembling of a Leaf*, 1921, which contained "Miss Thompson," a story that was successfully adapted for the stage and screen in *Rain; The Casuarina Tree*, 1929, in which appeared "The Letter," one of Maugham's greatest stage and screen successes; and *Ah King*, 1933.

The East also yielded such a tense novel as *The Painted Veil*, 1925, and such an original play as *East of Suez*, 1922.

By the time Maugham was sixty-five he had written and published more than fifty volumes, most of which enlarged his audience, enhanced his reputation, and swelled his increasing fortune. His plays were brilliant and financially dependable; among the dramatic "hits" of the London stage were *The Circle*, 1921; *Our Betters*, 1923; *The Letter*, 1925; and *The Constant Wife*, 1926. After his fifties, Maugham occupied himself largely with reminiscences and reappraisal. *Cakes and Ale, or, The Skeleton in the Cupboard*, 1930, is part fact, part fiction, and part caricature of a Grand Old Man of English letters (obviously Thomas Hardy), a facile literary opportunist (supposedly the novelist Hugh Walpole), and a gallery of shamelessly public "private lives." *The Summing Up*, 1938, is a frank and revealing "mental autobiography." *Altogether*, 1934, reassembles Maugham's collected short stories, many of which are delicate but penetrating social criticisms. *The Book Bag*, 1932, displays his acumen as a critic. As an anthologist, the selection in *Tellers of Tales*, 1939, proves his taste; the volume also contains a long and stimulating introductory essay on the art of writing. Maugham is possibly the only contemporary author who served his country as a spy—see *Ashenden, or The British Agent*, 1928—and whose garret was a magnificent villa on the Riviera.

Maugham's financial successes have made the critics overemphasize his adroitness and ability to please. The customary complaint has been that Maugham wrote just for the cynical and the sophisticated. But, as Richard Aldington pointed out: "Maugham's work gives the impression of coming from an accomplished man of the world and not from a man in a library. . . . His manner is entirely free of any trace of condescension, pretentiousness, and superciliousness. . . . It is not merely a question of good manners, but of an attitude to life which is superior to the limited interests and prejudices of cliques." [1]

"Successful," "cosmopolitan," "accomplished," "amazing" are the words usually employed to

[1] From "Somerset Maugham: An Appreciation," *Saturday Review of Literature*, Aug. 19, 1939.

characterize Maugham. If they are not altogether critical, they are fairly accurate descriptions of one who is, first and last, a teller of tales. Maugham is, in fact, so expert a weaver of plot and character that his style has attracted little notice. Yet he has a gift for repartee which is second only to that of his immediate predecessor, Oscar Wilde, and that of his contemporary, Bernard Shaw. The bitter phrase-making is at its best in his plays, but even his short stories disclose such epigrams as these: 10 "Modesty is a masculine virtue." "Women are always sensitive to the beauty of the self-sacrifice of others." "The romantics in this world only get by with their nonsense because they have at bottom a shrewd sense of reality. . . . The English are romantic; that is why other nations think them hypocritical. They are not: they set out in all sincerity for the Kingdom of God, but the journey is arduous and they have reason to pick up any gilt-edged investment that offers itself by the way." 20

"Red," the story given here, is reminiscent of *The Moon and Sixpence* in its haunting romantic mood and its poetic tone intermixed with blunt cynicism.

RED [1]

THE skipper thrust his hand into one of his trouser pockets and with difficulty, for they were not at the sides but in front and he was a portly 30 man, pulled out a large silver watch. He looked at it and then looked again at the declining sun. The Kanaka at the wheel gave him a glance, but did not speak. The skipper's eyes rested on the island they were approaching. A white line of foam marked the reef. He knew there was an opening large enough to get his ship through, and when they came a little nearer he counted on seeing it. They had nearly an hour of daylight still before them. In the lagoon the water was deep and they could anchor comfortably. 40 The chief of the village which he could already see among the coconut trees was a friend of the mate's, and it would be pleasant to go ashore for the night. The mate came forward at that minute and the skipper turned to him.

"We'll take a bottle of booze along with us and get some girls in to dance," he said.

"I don't see the opening," said the mate.

He was a Kanaka, a handsome swarthy fellow, with somewhat the look of a later Roman emperor, 50 inclined to stoutness; but his face was fine and clean-cut.

[1] From *The Trembling of a Leaf* by W. Somerset Maugham, copyright, 1921, by Doubleday, Doran and Company, Inc.

"I'm dead sure there's one right here," said the captain, looking through his glasses. "I can't understand why I can't pick it up. Send one of the boys up the mast to have a look."

The mate called one of the crew and gave him the order. The captain watched the Kanaka climb and waited for him to speak. But the Kanaka shouted down that he could see nothing but the unbroken line of foam. The captain spoke Samoan like a native, and he cursed him freely.

"Shall he stay up there?" asked the mate.

"What the hell good does that do?" answered the captain. "The blame fool can't see worth a cent. You bet your sweet life I'd find the opening if I was up there."

He looked at the slender mast with anger. It was all very well for a native who had been used to climbing up coconut trees all his life. He was fat and heavy.

"Come down," he shouted. "You're no more use than a dead dog. We'll just have to go along the reef till we find the opening."

It was a seventy-ton schooner with paraffin auxiliary, and it ran, when there was no head wind, between four and five knots an hour. It was a bedraggled object; it had been painted white a very long time ago, but it was now dirty, dingy, and mottled. It smelt strongly of paraffin and of the copra which was its usual cargo. They were within a hundred feet of the reef now and the captain told the steersman to run along it till they came to the opening. But when they had gone a couple of miles he realised that they had missed it. He went about and slowly worked back again. The white foam of the reef continued without interruption and now the sun was setting. With a curse at the stupidity of the crew the skipper resigned himself to waiting till next morning.

"Put her about," he said. "I can't anchor here."

They went out to sea a little and presently it was quite dark. They anchored. When the sail was furled the ship began to roll a good deal. They said in Apia that one day she would roll right over; and the owner, a German-American who managed one of the largest stores, said that no money was big enough to induce him to go out in her. The cook, a Chinese in white trousers, very dirty and ragged, and a thin white tunic, came to say that supper was ready, and when the skipper went into the cabin he found the engineer already seated at table. The engineer was a long lean man with a scraggy neck. He was dressed in blue overalls and a sleeveless jersey which showed his thin arms tattooed from elbow to wrist.

"Hell, having to spend the night outside," said the skipper.

The engineer did not answer, and they ate their supper in silence. The cabin was lit by a dim oil lamp. When they had eaten the canned apricots with which the meal finished, the Chink brought them a cup of tea. The skipper lit a cigar and went on the upper deck. The island now was only a darker mass against the night. The stars were very bright. The only sound was the ceaseless breaking of the surf. The skipper sank into a deck-chair and smoked idly. Presently three or four members of the crew came up and sat down. One of them had a banjo and another a concertina. They began to play, and one of them sang. The native song sounded strange on these instruments. Then to the singing a couple began to dance. It was a barbaric dance, savage and primeval, rapid, with quick movements of the hands and feet and contortions of the body; it was sensual, sexual even, but sexual without passion. It was very animal, direct, weird without mystery, natural in short, and one might almost say childlike. At last they grew tired. They stretched themselves on the deck and slept, and all was silent. The skipper lifted himself heavily out of his chair and clambered down the companion. He went into his cabin and got out of his clothes. He climbed into his bunk and lay there. He panted a little in the heat of the night.

But next morning, when the dawn crept over the tranquil sea, the opening in the reef which had eluded them the night before was seen a little to the east of where they lay. The schooner entered the lagoon. There was not a ripple on the surface of the water. Deep down among the coral rocks you saw little coloured fish swim. When he had anchored his ship the skipper ate his breakfast and went on deck. The sun shone from an unclouded sky, but in the early morning the air was grateful and cool. It was Sunday, and there was a feeling of quietness, a silence as though nature were at rest, which gave him a peculiar sense of comfort. He sat, looking at the wooded coast, and felt lazy and well at ease. Presently a slow smile moved his lips and he threw the stump of his cigar into the water.

"I guess I'll go ashore," he said. "Get the boat out."

He climbed stiffly down the ladder and was rowed to a little cove. The coconut trees came down to the water's edge, not in rows, but spaced out with an ordered formality. They were like a ballet of spinsters, elderly but flippant, standing in affected attitudes with the simpering graces of a bygone age. He sauntered idly through them, along a path that could be just seen winding its tortuous way, and it led him presently to a broad creek. There was a bridge across it, but a bridge constructed of single trunks of coconut trees, a dozen of them, placed end to end and supported where they met by a forked branch driven into the bed of the creek. You walked on a smooth, round surface, narrow and slippery, and there was no support for the hand. To cross such a bridge required sure feet and a stout heart. The skipper hesitated. But he saw on the other side, nestling among the trees, a white man's house; he made up his mind and, rather gingerly, began to walk. He watched his feet carefully, and where one trunk joined on to the next and there was a difference of level, he tottered a little. It was with a gasp of relief that he reached the last tree and finally set his feet on the firm ground of the other side. He had been so intent on the difficult crossing that he never noticed any one was watching him, and it was with surprise that he heard himself spoken to.

"It takes a bit of nerve to cross these bridges when you're not used to them."

He looked up and saw a man standing in front of him. He had evidently come out of the house which he had seen.

"I saw you hesitate," the man continued, with a smile on his lips, "and I was watching to see you fall in."

"Not on your life," said the captain, who had now recovered his confidence.

"I've fallen in myself before now. I remember, one evening I came back from shooting, and I fell in, gun and all. Now I get a boy to carry my gun for me."

He was a man no longer young, with a small beard, now somewhat grey, and a thin face. He was dressed in a singlet, without arms, and a pair of duck trousers. He wore neither shoes nor socks. He spoke English with a slight accent.

"Are you Neilson?" asked the skipper.

"I am."

"I've heard about you. I thought you lived somewheres round here."

The skipper followed his host into the little bungalow and sat down heavily in the chair which the other motioned him to take. While Neilson went out to fetch whisky and glasses he took a look round the room. It filled him with amazement. He had never seen so many books. The shelves reached from floor to ceiling on all four walls, and they were closely packed. There was a grand piano littered with music, and a large table on which books and magazines lay in disorder. The room made him feel embarrassed. He remembered that Neilson was a queer fellow. No one knew very much about him, although he had been in the islands for so many years, but those who knew him agreed that he was queer. He was a Swede.

"You've got one big heap of books here," he said, when Neilson returned.

"They do no harm," answered Neilson with a smile.

"Have you read them all?" asked the skipper.

"Most of them."

"I'm a bit of a reader myself. I have the *Saturday Evening Post* sent me regler."

Neilson poured his visitor a good stiff glass of whisky and gave him a cigar. The skipper volunteered a little information.

"I got in last night, but I couldn't find the opening, so I had to anchor outside. I never been this run before, but my people had some stuff they wanted to bring over here. Gray, d'you know him?"

"Yes, he's got a store a little way along."

"Well, there was a lot of canned stuff that he wanted over, an' he's got some copra. They thought I might just as well come over as lie idle at Apia. I run between Apia and Pago-Pago mostly, but they've got smallpox there just now, and there's nothing stirring."

He took a drink of his whisky and lit a cigar. He was a taciturn man, but there was something in Neilson that made him nervous, and his nervousness made him talk. The Swede was looking at him with large dark eyes in which there was an expression of faint amusement.

"This is a tidy little place you've got here."

"I've done my best with it."

"You must do pretty well with your trees. They look fine. With copra at the price it is now. I had a bit of a plantation myself once, in Upolu it was, but I had to sell it."

He looked round the room again, where all those books gave him a feeling of something incomprehensible and hostile.

"I guess you must find it a bit lonesome here though," he said.

"I've got used to it. I've been here for twenty-five years."

Now the captain could think of nothing more to say, and he smoked in silence. Neilson had apparently no wish to break it. He looked at his guest with a meditative eye. He was a tall man, more than six feet high, and very stout. His face was red and blotchy, with a network of little purple veins on the cheeks, and his features were sunk into its fatness. His eyes were bloodshot. His neck was buried in rolls of fat. But for a fringe of long curly hair, nearly white, at the back of his head, he was quite bald; and that immense, shiny surface of forehead, which might have given him a false look of intelligence, on the contrary gave him one of peculiar imbecility. He wore a blue flannel shirt, open at the neck and showing his fat chest covered with a mat of reddish hair, and a very old pair of blue serge trousers. He sat in his chair in a heavy ungainly attitude, his great belly thrust forward and his fat legs uncrossed. All elasticity had gone from his limbs. Neilson wondered idly what sort of man he had been in his youth. It was almost impossible to imagine that this creature of vast bulk had ever been a boy who ran about. The skipper finished his whisky, and Neilson pushed the bottle towards him.

"Help yourself."

The skipper leaned forward and with his great hand seized it.

"And how come you in these parts anyways?" he said.

"Oh, I came out to the islands for my health. My lungs were bad and they said I hadn't a year to live. You see they were wrong."

"I meant, how come you to settle down right here?"

"I am a sentimentalist."

"Oh!"

Neilson knew that the skipper had not an idea what he meant, and he looked at him with an ironical twinkle in his dark eyes. Perhaps just because the skipper was so gross and dull a man the whim seized him to talk further.

"You were too busy keeping your balance to notice, when you crossed the bridge, but this spot is generally considered rather pretty."

"It's a cute little house you've got here."

"Ah, that wasn't here when I first came. There was a native hut, with its beehive roof and its pillars, overshadowed by a great tree with red flowers; and the croton bushes, their leaves yellow and red and golden, made a pied fence around it. And then all about were the coconut trees, as fanciful as women, and as vain. They stood at the water's edge and spent all day looking at their reflections. I was a young man then—Good Heavens, it's a quarter of a century ago—and I wanted to enjoy all the loveliness of the world in the short time allotted to me before I passed into the darkness. I thought it was the most beautiful spot I had ever seen. The first time I saw it I had a catch at my heart, and I was afraid I was going to cry. I wasn't more than twenty-five, and though I put the best face I could on it, I didn't want to die. And somehow it seemed to me that the very beauty of this place made it easier for me to accept my fate. I felt when I came here that all my past life had fallen away, Stockholm and its University, and then Bonn: it all seemed the life of somebody else, as though now at last I had achieved the reality which our doctors of philosophy—I am one myself, you know—had discussed so much. 'A year,' I cried to myself. 'I have a year. I will spend it here and then I am content to die.'

"We are foolish and sentimental and melodramatic at twenty-five, but if we weren't perhaps we should be less wise at fifty.

"Now drink, my friend. Don't let the nonsense I talk interfere with you."

He waved his thin hand towards the bottle, and the skipper finished what remained in his glass.

"You ain't drinking nothin'," he said, reaching for the whisky.

"I am of a sober habit," smiled the Swede. "I intoxicate myself in ways which I fancy are more subtle. But perhaps that is only vanity. Anyhow, the effects are more lasting and the results less deleterious."

"They say there's a deal of cocaine taken in the States now," said the captain.

Neilson chuckled.

"But I do not see a white man often," he continued, "and for once I don't think a drop of whisky can do me any harm."

He poured himself out a little, added some soda, and took a sip.

"And presently I found out why the spot had such an unearthly loveliness. Here love had tarried for a moment like a migrant bird that happens on a ship in mid-ocean and for a little while folds its tired wings. The fragrance of a beautiful passion hovered over it like the fragrance of hawthorn in May in the meadows of my home. It seems to me that the places where men have loved or suffered keep about them always some faint aroma of something that has not wholly died. It is as though they had acquired a spiritual significance which mysteriously affects those who pass. I wish I could make myself clear." He smiled a little. "Though I cannot imagine that if I did you would understand."

He paused.

"I think this place was beautiful because here I had been loved beautifully." And now he shrugged his shoulders. "But perhaps it is only that my aesthetic sense is gratified by the happy conjunction of young love and a suitable setting."

Even a man less thick-witted than the skipper might have been forgiven if he were bewildered by

Neilson's words. For he seemed faintly to laugh at what he said. It was as though he spoke from emotion which his intellect found ridiculous. He had said himself that he was a sentimentalist, and when sentimentality is joined with scepticism there is often the devil to pay.

He was silent for an instant and looked at the captain with eyes in which there was a sudden perplexity.

"You know, I can't help thinking that I've seen you before somewhere or other," he said.

"I couldn't say as I remember you," returned the skipper.

"I have a curious feeling as though your face were familiar to me. It's been puzzling me for some time. But I can't situate my recollection in any place or at any time."

The skipper massively shrugged his heavy shoulders.

"It's thirty years since I first came to the islands. A man can't figure on remembering all the folk he meets in a while like that."

The Swede shook his head.

"You know how one sometimes has the feeling that a place one has never been to before is strangely familiar. That's how I seem to see you." He gave a whimsical smile. "Perhaps I knew you in some past existence. Perhaps, perhaps you were the master of a galley in ancient Rome and I was a slave at the oar. Thirty years have you been here?"

"Every bit of thirty years."

"I wonder if you knew a man called Red?"

"Red?"

"That is the only name I've ever known him by. I never knew him personally. I never even set eyes on him. And yet I seem to see him more clearly than many men, my brothers, for instance, with whom I passed my daily life for many years. He lives in my imagination with the distinctness of a Paolo Malatesta or a Romeo. But I daresay you have never read Dante or Shakespeare?"

"I can't say as I have," said the captain.

Neilson, smoking a cigar, leaned back in his chair and looked vacantly at the ring of smoke which floated in the still air. A smile played on his lips, but his eyes were grave. Then he looked at the captain. There was in his gross obesity something extraordinarily repellent. He had the plethoric self-satisfaction of the very fat. It was an outrage. It set Neilson's nerves on edge. But the contrast between the man before him and the man he had in mind was pleasant.

"It appears that Red was the most comely thing you ever saw. I've talked to quite a number of people who knew him in those days, white men, and they all agree that the first time you saw him his beauty just took your breath away. They called him Red on account of his flaming hair. It had a natural wave and he wore it long. It must have been of that wonderful colour that the pre-Raphaelites raved over. I don't think he was vain of it, he was much too ingenuous for that, but no one could have blamed him if he had been. He was tall, six feet and an inch or two—in the native house that used to 10 stand here was the mark of his height cut with a knife on the central trunk that supported the roof— and he was made like a Greek god, broad in the shoulders and thin in the flanks; he was like Apollo, with just that soft roundness which Praxiteles gave him, and that suave, feminine grace which has in it something troubling and mysterious. His skin was dazzling white, milky, like satin; his skin was like a woman's."

"I had kind of a white skin myself when I was 20 a kiddie," said the skipper, with a twinkle in his bloodshot eyes.

But Neilson paid no attention to him. He was telling his story now and interruption made him impatient.

"And his face was just as beautiful as his body. He had large blue eyes, very dark, so that some say they were black, and unlike most red-haired people he had dark eyebrows and long dark lashes. His features were perfectly regular and his mouth was 30 like a scarlet wound. He was twenty."

On these words the Swede stopped with a certain sense of the dramatic. He took a sip of whisky.

"He was unique. There never was any one more beautiful. There was no more reason for him than for a wonderful blossom to flower on a wild plant. He was a happy accident of nature.

"One day he landed at that cove into which you must have put this morning. He was an American sailor, and he had deserted from a man-of-war in 40 Apia. He had induced some good-humoured native to give him a passage on a cutter that happened to be sailing from Apia to Safoto, and he had been put ashore here in a dug-out. I do not know why he deserted. Perhaps life on a man-of-war with its restrictions irked him, perhaps he was in trouble, and perhaps it was the South Seas and these romantic islands that got into his bones. Every now and then they take a man strangely, and he finds himself like a fly in a spider's web. It may be that 50 there was a softness of fibre in him, and these green hills with their soft airs, this blue sea, took the northern strength from him as Delilah took the Nazarite's. Anyhow, he wanted to hide himself, and

he thought he would be safe in this secluded nook till his ship had sailed from Samoa.

"There was a native hut at the cove and as he stood there, wondering where exactly he should turn his steps, a young girl came out and invited him to enter. He knew scarcely two words of the native tongue and she as little English. But he understood well enough what her smiles meant, and her pretty gestures, and he followed her. He sat down on a 10 mat and she gave him slices of pineapple to eat. I can speak of Red only from hearsay, but I saw the girl three years after he first met her, and she was scarcely nineteen then. You cannot imagine how exquisite she was. She had the passionate grace of the hibiscus and the rich colour. She was rather tall, slim, with the delicate features of her race, and large eyes like pools of still water under the palm trees; her hair, black and curling, fell down her back, and she wore a wreath of scented flowers. Her 20 hands were lovely. They were so small, so exquisitely formed, they gave your heart-strings a wrench. And in those days she laughed easily. Her smile was so delightful that it made your knees shake. Her skin was like a field of ripe corn on a summer day. Good Heavens, how can I describe her? She was too beautiful to be real.

"And these two young things, she was sixteen and he was twenty, fell in love with one another at first sight. That is the real love, not the love that comes 30 from sympathy, common interests, or intellectual community, but love pure and simple. That is the love that Adam felt for Eve when he awoke and found her in the garden gazing at him with dewy eyes. That is the love that draws the beasts to one another, and the Gods. That is the love that makes the world a miracle. That is the love which gives life its pregnant meaning. You have never heard of the wise, cynical French duke who said that with two lovers there is always one who loves and one 40 who lets himself be loved; it is a bitter truth to which most of us have to resign ourselves; but now and then there are two who love and two who let themselves be loved. Then one might fancy that the sun stands still as it stood when Joshua prayed to the God of Israel.

"And even now after all these years, when I think of these two, so young, so fair, so simple, and of their love, I feel a pang. It tears my heart just as my heart is torn when on certain nights I watch 50 the full moon shining on the lagoon from an unclouded sky. There is always pain in the contemplation of perfect beauty.

"They were children. She was good and sweet and kind. I know nothing of him, and I like to think that then at all events he was ingenuous and frank. I like to think that his soul was as comely as his body. But I daresay he had no more soul than the creatures of the woods and forests who made pipes from reeds and bathed in the mountain streams when the world was young, and you might catch sight of little fauns galloping through the glade on the back of a bearded centaur. A soul is a troublesome possession and when man developed it he lost the Garden of Eden.

"Well, when Red came to the island it had recently been visited by one of those epidemics which the white man has brought to the South Seas, and one-third of the inhabitants had died. It seems that the girl had lost all her near kin and she lived now in the house of distant cousins. The household consisted of two ancient crones, bowed and wrinkled, two younger women, and a man and a boy. For a few days he stayed there. But perhaps he felt himself too near the shore, with the possibility that he might fall in with white men who would reveal his hiding-place; perhaps the lovers could not bear that the company of others should rob them for an instant of the delight of being together. One morning they set out, the pair of them, with the few things that belonged to the girl, and walked along a grassy path under the coconuts, till they came to the creek you see. They had to cross the bridge you crossed, and the girl laughed gleefully because he was afraid. She held his hand till they came to the end of the first tree, and then his courage failed him and he had to go back. He was obliged to take off all his clothes before he could risk it, and she carried them over for him on her head. They settled down in the empty hut that stood here. Whether she had any rights over it (land tenure is a complicated business in the islands), or whether the owner had died during the epidemic, I do not know, but anyhow no one questioned them, and they took possession. Their furniture consisted of a couple of grass mats on which they slept, a fragment of looking-glass, and a bowl or two. In this pleasant land that is enough to start housekeeping on.

"They say that happy people have no history, and certainly a happy love has none. They did nothing all day long and yet the days seemed all too short. The girl had a native name, but Red called her Sally. He picked up the easy language very quickly, and he used to lie on the mat for hours while she chattered gaily to him. He was a silent fellow, and perhaps his mind was lethargic. He smoked incessantly the cigarettes which she made him out of the native tobacco and pandanus leaf, and he watched her while with deft fingers she made grass mats. Often natives would come in and tell long stories of the old days when the island was disturbed by tribal wars. Sometimes he would go fishing on the reef, and bring home a basket full of coloured fish. Sometimes at night he would go out with a lantern to catch lobster. There were plantains round the hut and Sally would roast them for their frugal meal. She knew how to make delicious messes from coconuts, and the breadfruit tree by the side of the creek gave them its fruit. On feast-days they killed a little pig and cooked it on hot stones. They bathed together in the creek; and in the evening they went down to the lagoon and paddled about in a dug-out, with its great outrigger. The sea was deep blue, wine-coloured at sundown, like the sea of Homeric Greece; but in the lagoon the colour had an infinite variety, aquamarine and amethyst and emerald; and the setting sun turned it for a short moment to liquid gold. Then there was the colour of the coral, brown, white, pink, red, purple; and the shapes it took were marvellous. It was like a magic garden, and the hurrying fish were like butterflies. It strangely lacked reality. Among the coral were pools with a floor of white sand and here, where the water was dazzling clear, it was very good to bathe. Then, cool and happy, they wandered back in the gloaming over the soft grass road to the creek, walking hand in hand, and now the mynah birds filled the coconut trees with their clamour. And then the night, with that great sky shining with gold, that seemed to stretch more widely than the skies of Europe, and the soft airs that blew gently through the open hut, the long night again was all too short. She was sixteen and he was barely twenty. The dawn crept in among the wooden pillars of the hut and looked at those lovely children sleeping in one another's arms. The sun hid behind the great tattered leaves of the plantains so that it might not disturb them, and then, with playful malice, shot a golden ray, like the outstretched paw of a Persian cat, on their faces. They opened their sleepy eyes and they smiled to welcome another day. The weeks lengthened into months, and a year passed. They seemed to love one another as—I hesitate to say passionately, for passion has in it always a shade of sadness, a touch of bitterness or anguish, but as whole-heartedly, as simply and naturally as on that first day on which, meeting, they had recognized that a god was in them.

"If you had asked them I have no doubt that they would have thought it impossible to suppose their love could ever cease. Do we not know that the essential element of love is a belief in its own eternity? And yet perhaps in Red there was already a very little seed, unknown to himself and unsuspected by the girl, which would in time have grown to weariness. For one day one of the natives from the cove told them that some way down the coast at the anchorage was a British whaling-ship.

" 'Gee,' he said, 'I wonder if I could make a trade of some nuts and plantains for a pound or two of tobacco.'

"The pandanus cigarettes that Sally made him with untiring hands were strong and pleasant 10 enough to smoke, but they left him unsatisfied; and he yearned on a sudden for real tobacco, hard, rank, and pungent. He had not smoked a pipe for many months. His mouth watered at the thought of it. One would have thought some premonition of harm would have made Sally seek to dissuade him, but love possessed her so completely that it never occurred to her any power on earth could take him from her. They went up into the hills together and gathered a great basket of wild oranges, green, but 20 sweet and juicy; and they picked plantains from around the hut, and coconuts from their trees, and breadfruit and mangoes; and they carried them down to the cove. They loaded the unstable canoe with them, and Red and the native boy who had brought them the news of the ship paddled along outside the reef.

"It was the last time she ever saw him.

"Next day the boy came back alone. He was all in tears. This is the story he told. When after their 30 long paddle they reached the ship and Red hailed it, a white man looked over the side and told them to come on board. They took the fruit they had brought with them and Red piled it up on the deck. The white man and he began to talk, and they seemed to come to some agreement. One of them went below and brought up tobacco. Red took some at once and lit a pipe. The boy imitated the zest with which he blew a great cloud of smoke from his mouth. Then they said something to him and he 40 went into the cabin. Through the open door the boy, watching curiously, saw a bottle brought out and glasses. Red drank and smoked. They seemed to ask him something, for he shook his head and laughed. The man, the first man who had spoken to them, laughed too, and he filled Red's glass once more. They went on talking and drinking, and presently, growing tired of watching a sight that meant nothing to him, the boy curled himself up on the deck and slept. He was awakened by a kick; 50 and, jumping to his feet, he saw that the ship was slowly sailing out of the lagoon. He caught sight of Red seated at the table, with his head resting heavily on his arms, fast asleep. He made a move-ment towards him, intending to wake him, but a rough hand seized his arm, and a man, with a scowl and words which he did not understand, pointed to the side. He shouted to Red, but in a moment he was seized and flung overboard. Helpless, he swam round to his canoe which was drifting a little way off, and pushed it on to the reef. He climbed in and, sobbing all the way, paddled back to shore.

"What had happened was obvious enough. The whaler, by desertion or sickness, was short of hands, and the captain when Red came aboard had asked him to sign on; on his refusal he had made him drunk and kidnapped him.

"Sally was beside herself with grief. For three days she screamed and cried. The natives did what they could to comfort her, but she would not be comforted. She would not eat. And then, exhausted, she sank into a sullen apathy. She spent long days at the cove, watching the lagoon, in the vain hope that Red somehow or other would manage to escape. She sat on the white sand, hour after hour, with the tears running down her cheeks, and at night dragged herself wearily back across the creek to the little hut where she had been happy. The people with whom she had lived before Red came to the island wished her to return to them, but she would not; she was convinced that Red would come back, and she wanted him to find her where he had left her. Four months later she was delivered of a still-born child, and the old woman who had come to help her through her confinement remained with her in the hut. All joy was taken from her life. If her anguish with time became less intolerable it was replaced by a settled melancholy. You would not have thought that among these people, whose emotions, though so violent, are very transient, a woman could be found capable of so enduring a passion. She never lost the profound conviction that sooner or later Red would come back. She watched for him, and every time some one crossed this slender little bridge of coconut trees she looked. It might at last be he."

Neilson stopped talking and gave a faint sigh.

"And what happened to her in the end?" asked the skipper.

Neilson smiled bitterly.

"Oh, three years afterwards she took up with another white man."

The skipper gave a fat, cynical chuckle.

"That's generally what happens to them," he said.

The Swede shot him a look of hatred. He did not know why that gross, obese man excited in him so violent a repulsion. But his thoughts wandered and he found his mind filled with memories of the past. He went back five-and-twenty years. It was when he first came to the island, weary of Apia, with its heavy drinking, its gambling and coarse sensuality, a sick man, trying to resign himself to the loss of the career which had fired his imagination with ambitious thoughts. He set behind him resolutely all his hopes of making a great name for himself and strove to content himself with the few poor months of careful life which was all that he could count on. He was boarding with a half-caste trader who had a store a couple of miles along the coast at the edge of a native village; and one day, wandering aimlessly along the grassy paths of the coconut groves, he had come upon the hut in which Sally lived. The beauty of the spot had filled him with a rapture so great that it was almost painful, and then he had seen Sally. She was the loveliest creature he had ever seen, and the sadness in those dark, magnificent eyes of hers affected him strangely. The Kanakas were a handsome race, and beauty was not rare among them, but it was the beauty of shapely animals. It was empty. But those tragic eyes were dark with mystery, and you felt in them the bitter complexity of the groping, human soul. The trader told him the story and it moved him.

"Do you think he'll ever come back?" asked Neilson.

"No fear. Why, it'll be a couple of years before the ship is paid off, and by then he'll have forgotten all about her. I bet he was pretty mad when he woke up and found he'd been shanghaied, and I shouldn't wonder but he wanted to fight somebody. But he'd got to grin and bear it, and I guess in a month he was thinking it the best thing that had ever happened to him that he got away from the island."

But Neilson could not get the story out of his head. Perhaps because he was sick and weakly, the radiant health of Red appealed to his imagination. Himself an ugly man, insignificant of appearance, he prized very highly comeliness in others. He had never been passionately in love, and certainly he had never been passionately loved. The mutual attraction of those two young things gave him a singular delight. It had the ineffable beauty of the Absolute. He went again to the little hut by the creek. He had a gift for languages and an energetic mind, accustomed to work, and he had already given much time to the study of the local tongue. Old habit was strong in him and he was gathering together material for a paper on the Samoan speech. The old crone who shared the hut with Sally invited him to come in and sit down. She gave him *kava* to drink and cigarettes to smoke. She was glad to have some one to chat with and while she talked he looked at Sally. She reminded him of the Psyche in the museum at Naples. Her features had the same clear purity of line, and though she had borne a child she had still a virginal aspect.

It was not till he had seen her two or three times that he induced her to speak. Then it was only to ask him if he had seen in Apia a man called Red. Two years had passed since his disappearance, but it was plain that she still thought of him incessantly.

It did not take Neilson long to discover that he was in love with her. It was only by an effort of will now that he prevented himself from going every day to the creek, and when he was not with Sally his thoughts were. At first, looking upon himself as a dying man, he asked only to look at her, and occasionally hear her speak, and his love gave him a wonderful happiness. He exulted in its purity. He wanted nothing from her but the opportunity to weave around her graceful person a web of beautiful fancies. But the open air, the equable temperature, the rest, the simple fare, began to have an unexpected effect on his health. His temperature did not soar at night to such alarming heights, he coughed less and began to put on weight; six months passed without his having a haemorrhage; and on a sudden he saw the possibility that he might live. He had studied his disease carefully, and the hope dawned upon him that with great care he might arrest its course. It exhilarated him to look forward once more to the future. He made plans. It was evident that any active life was out of the question, but he could live on the islands, and the small income he had, insufficient elsewhere, would be ample to keep him. He could grow coconuts; that would give him an occupation; and he would send for his books and a piano; but his quick mind saw that in all this he was merely trying to conceal from himself the desire which obsessed him.

He wanted Sally. He loved not only her beauty, but that dim soul which he divined behind her suffering eyes. He would intoxicate her with his passion. In the end he would make her forget. And in an ecstasy of surrender he fancied himself giving her too the happiness which he had thought never to know again, but had now so miraculously achieved.

He asked her to live with him. She refused. He had expected that and did not let it depress him, for he was sure that sooner or later she would yield. His love was irresistible. He told the old woman of his wishes, and found somewhat to his surprise that she and the neighbours, long aware of them, were strongly urging Sally to accept his offer. After all, every native was glad to keep house for a white man.

and Neilson according to the standards of the island was a rich one. The trader with whom he boarded went to her and told her not to be a fool; such an opportunity would not come again, and after so long she could not still believe that Red would ever return. The girl's resistance only increased Neilson's desire, and what had been a very pure love now became an agonizing passion. He was determined that nothing should stand in his way. He gave Sally no peace. At last, worn out by his persistence and the persuasions, by turns pleading and angry, of every one around her, she consented. But the day after when, exultant, he went to see her he found that in the night she had burnt down the hut in which she and Red had lived together. The old crone ran towards him full of angry abuse of Sally, but he waved her aside; it did not matter; they would build a bungalow on the place where the hut had stood. A European house would really be more convenient if he wanted to bring out a piano and a vast number of books.

And so the little wooden house was built in which he had now lived for many years, and Sally became his wife. But after the first few weeks of rapture, during which he was satisfied with what she gave him, he had known little happiness. She had yielded to him, through weariness, but she had only yielded what she set no store on. The soul which he had dimly glimpsed escaped him. He knew that she cared nothing for him. She still loved Red, and all the time she was waiting for his return. At a sign from him, Neilson knew that, notwithstanding his love, his tenderness, his sympathy, his generosity, she would leave him without a moment's hesitation. She would never give a thought to his distress. Anguish seized him and he battered at that impenetrable self of hers which sullenly resisted him. His love became bitter. He tried to melt her heart with kindness, but it remained as hard as before; he feigned indifference, but she did not notice it. Sometimes he lost his temper and abused her, and then she wept silently. Sometimes he thought she was nothing but a fraud, and that soul simply an invention of his own, and that he could not get into the sanctuary of her heart because there was no sanctuary there. His love became a prison from which he longed to escape, but he had not the strength merely to open the door—that was all it needed—and walk out into the open air. It was torture and at last he became numb and hopeless. In the end the fire burnt itself out and, when he saw her eyes rest for an instant on the slender bridge, it was no longer rage that filled his heart but impatience. For many years now they had lived together bound by the ties

of habit and convenience, and it was with a smile that he looked back on his old passion. She was an old woman, for the women on the islands age quickly, and if he had no love for her any more he had tolerance. She left him alone. He was contented with his piano and his books.

His thoughts led him to a desire for words.

"When I look back now and reflect on that brief passionate love of Red and Sally, I think that perhaps they should thank the ruthless fate that separated them when their love seemed still to be at its height. They suffered, but they suffered in beauty. They were spared the real tragedy of love."

"I don't know exactly as I get you," said the skipper.

"The tragedy of love is not death or separation. How long do you think it would have been before one or other of them ceased to care? Oh, it is dreadfully bitter to look at a woman whom you have loved with all your heart and soul, so that you felt you could not bear to let her out of your sight, and realize that you would not mind if you never saw her again. The tragedy of love is indifference."

But while he was speaking a very extraordinary thing happened. Though he had been addressing the skipper he had not been talking to him, he had been putting his thoughts into words for himself, and with his eyes fixed on the man in front of him he had not seen him. But now an image presented itself to them, an image not of the man he saw, but of another man. It was as though he were looking into one of those distorting mirrors that make you extraordinarily squat or outrageously elongate, but here exactly the opposite took place, and in the obese, ugly old man he caught the shadowy glimpse of a stripling. He gave him now a quick, searching scrutiny. Why had a haphazard stroll brought him just to this place? A sudden tremor of his heart made him slightly breathless. An absurd suspicion seized him. What had occurred to him was impossible, and yet it might be a fact.

"What is your name?" he asked abruptly.

The skipper's face puckered and he gave a cunning chuckle. He looked then malicious and horribly vulgar.

"It's such a damned long time since I heard it that I almost forget it myself. But for thirty years now in the islands they've always called me Red."

His huge form shook as he gave a low, almost silent laugh. It was obscene. Neilson shuddered. Red was hugely amused, and from his bloodshot eyes tears ran down his cheeks.

Neilson gave a gasp, for at that moment a woman came in. She was a native, a woman of somewhat commanding presence, stout without being corpulent, dark, for the natives grow darker with age, with very grey hair. She wore a black Mother Hubbard, and its thinness showed her heavy breasts. The moment had come.

She made an observation to Neilson about some household matter and he answered. He wondered if his voice sounded as unnatural to her as it did to himself. She gave the man who was sitting in the chair by the window an indifferent glance, and went out of the room. The moment had come and gone.

Neilson for a moment could not speak. He was strangely shaken. Then he said:

"I'd be very glad if you'd stay and have a bit of dinner with me. Pot luck."

"I don't think I will," said Red. "I must go after this fellow Gray. I'll give him his stuff and then I'll get away. I want to be back in Apia to-morrow."

"I'll send a boy along with you to show you the way."

"That'll be fine."

Red heaved himself out of his chair, while the Swede called one of the boys who worked on the plantation. He told him where the skipper wanted to go, and the boy stepped along the bridge. Red prepared to follow him.

"Don't fall in," said Neilson.

"Not on your life."

Neilson watched him make his way across and when he had disappeared among the coconuts he looked still. Then he sank heavily in his chair. Was that the man who had prevented him from being happy? Was that the man whom Sally had loved all these years and for whom she had waited so desperately? It was grotesque. A sudden fury seized him so that he had an instinct to spring up and smash everything around him. He had been cheated. They had seen each other at last and had not known it. He began to laugh, mirthlessly, and his laughter grew till it became hysterical. The Gods had played him a cruel trick. And he was old now.

At last Sally came in to tell him dinner was ready. He sat down in front of her and tried to eat. He wondered what she would say if he told her now that the fat old man sitting in the chair was the lover whom she remembered still with the passionate abandonment of her youth. Years ago, when he hated her because she made him so unhappy, he would have been glad to tell her. He wanted to hurt her then as she hurt him, because his hatred was only love. But now he did not care. He shrugged his shoulders listlessly.

"What did that man want?" she asked presently.

He did not answer at once. She was old too, a fat old native woman. He wondered why he had ever loved her so madly. He had laid at her feet all the treasures of his soul, and she had cared nothing for them. Waste, what waste! And now, when he looked at her, he felt only contempt. His patience was at last exhausted. He answered her question.

"He's the captain of a schooner. He's come from Apia."

"Yes."

"He brought me news from home. My eldest brother is very ill and I must go back."

"Will you be gone long?"

He shrugged his shoulders.

John Masefield
1878–

John Masefield was born June 1, 1878, at Ledbury, Herefordshire. His father, a lawyer, died while Masefield was still a boy, and the lad was indentured to a merchant ship at fourteen. The first twenty years of his life were hard, dogged by poverty, venturesome but not adventurous. Masefield's wanderings took him to America, where he worked for a while in a carpet factory in Yonkers and in a Greenwich Village saloon in New York City.

Just before he returned to England in 1897 Masefield read Chaucer's *The Parlement of Foules*, and determined to be a poet. Five years later he published *Salt-Water Ballads*, 1902, a collection of swinging lyrics of sailors and the sea. It did not attract much attention, but the volume contained many of Masefield's most quoted verses. *The Everlasting Mercy*, 1911, was the first volume to achieve popular success; it was praised by the critics for its "Chaucerian vigor," relished by the lay reader for its plain speech and rhythmical heartiness. *The Widow in the Bye Street*, 1912, and *Dauber*, 1913, enlarged the author's reputation and increased his audience. Masefield's sympathy with ordinary workers and "common characters" often brought him to the verge of sentimentality—his dramatis personae usually "got religion" and reformed—but Masefield was one of the first to make the Georgian movement seem a movement of innovation, even of protest. Moreover he succeeded (if only temporarily) in bringing narrative verse back to favor. The popularity of his rude and sometimes shocking story-poems was great; they were liked for their gusto; they achieved a blend of personal strength and abstract vigor. But the World War, which outdid Masefield in intensity, did not stimulate a literature of violence. On the contrary, force lost its power and gave way to a literature of exhaustion. Immediately after the war, the poets with few exceptions turned from bugle calls to pastorals, and exchanged the field of battle for fields of buttercups and daisies. Masefield joined the movement of escape. Logically enough, he wrote "classic" sonnets, religious verse, and new versions of old myths such as *King Cole*, 1921, and *A Tale of Troy*, 1932. But in sacrificing his early vigor of epithet and plot he also sacrificed his individuality. Critical opinion changed. It began to be suspected that the rebellious Georgian was little more than a roughened Victorian.

Besides his poetry, the best of which can be found in *Collected Poems*, 1932, Masefield wrote more than a dozen plays (including translations from Racine); about twelve volumes of essays and studies which range from *Sea Life in Nelson's Time*, 1905, through *The Battle of the Somme*, 1919, to *Chaucer*, 1931; several books for boys; and "adventure" novels which capture his early robustiousness.

In 1930 Masefield succeeded Robert Bridges as poet laureate. It was said that *Reynard the Fox*, 1919, which vigorously expresses the spirit of rural England, did more than any other work to win him the honor.

A WANDERER'S SONG [1]

A wind's in the heart of me, a fire's in my heels,
I am tired of brick and stone and rumbling wagon-
      wheels;
I hunger for the sea's edge, the limits of the land,
Where the wild old Atlantic is shouting on the sand.

Oh I'll be going, leaving the noises of the street,
To where a lifting foresail-foot is yanking at the
      sheet;

[1] This and the following two poems are from *The Collected Poems of John Masefield*, copyright, 1923, by The Macmillan Company.

To a windy, tossing anchorage where yawls and
      ketches ride,
Oh I'll be going, going, until I meet the tide.

And first I'll hear the sea-wind, the mewing of the
      gulls,
The clucking, sucking of the sea about the rusty
      hulls,   10
The songs at the capstan in the hooker warping out,
And then the heart of me'll know I'm there or
      thereabout.

Oh I am sick of brick and stone, the heart of me is
      sick,
For windy green, unquiet sea, the realm of Moby
      Dick;
And I'll be going, going, from the roaring of the
      wheels,
For a wind's in the heart of me, a fire's in my heels.

SONNET

Flesh, I have knocked at many a dusty door,
Gone down full many a windy midnight lane,
Probed in old walls and felt along the floor,
Pressed in blind hope the lighted window-pane,
But useless all, though sometimes when the moon
Was full in heaven and the sea was full,
Along my body's alleys came a tune
Played in the tavern by the Beautiful.
Then for an instant I have felt at point
To find and seize her, whosoe'er she be,   10
Whether some saint whose glory doth anoint
Those whom she loves, or but a part of me,
Or something that the things not understood
Make for their uses out of flesh and blood.

LOLLINGTON DOWNS

[THE CHOICE]

The Kings go by with jewelled crowns;
Their horses gleam, their banners shake, their spears
      are many.
The sack of many-peopled towns
Is all their dream:
The way they take
Leaves but a ruin in the brake,
And, in the furrow that the ploughmen make,
A stampless penny: a tale, a dream.

The merchants reckon up their gold;
Their letters come, their ships arrive, their freights
      are glories;   10

The profits of their treasures sold
They tell and sum;
Their foremen drive
Their servants, starved to half-alive,
Whose labours do but make the earth a hive
Of stinking stories: a tale, a dream.

The priests are singing in their stalls;
Their singing lifts, their incense burns, their praying
   clamours;
Yet God is as the sparrow falls;
The ivy drifts,   20
The votive urns

Are all left void when Fortune turns;
The god is but a marble for the kerns
To break with hammers: a tale, a dream.

O Beauty, let me know again
The green earth cold, the April rain, the quiet
   waters figuring sky,
The one star risen.
So shall I pass into the feast
Not touched by King, merchant, or priest;
Know the red spirit of the beast,   30
Be the green grain;
Escape from prison.

Lytton Strachey
1880–1932

(Giles) Lytton Strachey was born in London in 1880. He was the son of General Sir Richard and Lady Jane Strachey; his cousin was St. Loe Strachey, editor of the *Spectator*. He was educated at Trinity College, Cambridge, where he won the Chancellor's Medal with a poem entitled *Ely*, a celebration of Cambridge and its poets. This was in Strachey's twenty-second year, and the judges who awarded the prize for the eminently traditional verses with their overtones of Tennyson and Arnold would never have predicted that Strachey would be one of the period's most famous tradition-smashers.

Strachey was an intellectual undergraduate but not a prodigy. His first book, *Landmarks in French Literature*, 1912, was published when he was thirty-two, and caused little comment and practically no surprise. It was not until Strachey was nearly forty that his *Eminent Victorians*, 1918, occasioned something of a furore. This was a strange sort of biography, brilliant, caustic, and dramatic; it bewildered the worshipers of tradition and delighted the rebels. Here was a historian who was making an art of biography—"that ill-digested mass of material, slipshod style, tedious panegyric"—and applying the psychoanalytical method to popular figures which had resisted analysis of any kind. With uninhibited candor and irrepressible curiosity, Strachey tore veil after veil from the shrines. It was not a rude iconoclasm but a cool elegance which accomplished such ironic reappraisals in *Queen Victoria*, 1921, *Books and Characters*, 1922, *Elizabeth and Essex*, 1928, and *Portraits in Miniature*, 1931.

Before he died, on January 21, 1932, Strachey had brought not only an unexpected verve but a critical selectiveness to biography. He wrote history like a novelist; his imaginative speculations, his acid skepticism, and his flair for epigrams started a vogue. The new type of biography found so many disciples that Strachey was often betrayed by his imitators. It has been charged against him that his forte was malicious attack, that he dipped his pen in vitriol to write poisonous letters about the defenseless dead. But Strachey's best work is neither vicious nor destructive; he knew gold wherever he might find it, and he makes the true metal of his effigies shine through their gilded reputations.

It is not merely the analytical criticism we remember in such a literary essay as the one on "Pope," but the dexterity with which the analysis is turned. Only a wit of high order could have spiced a technical discussion with such epigrams as: "Matthew Arnold was a poet, but his conception of poetry reminds us that he was also an inspector of schools." "Everything [in a poem by Pope] is obvious. The diction is a mass of clichés; the epithets are the most commonplace possible; the herds low, the brooks murmur, the flocks pant, the retreats are green, the flowers blush; the rhythm is that of a rocking horse; the sentiment is mere sugar. But what a relief! What a relief to have escaped for once from subtle elaboration of diction and metre, from complicated states of mind, and all the profound obscurities of Shakespeare and Mr. T. S. Eliot. How delightful to have no troubles at

23 kerns, barbarian soldiers, vandals.

all—to understand so very easily every single thing that is said!" And this, from the same essay, which might be pasted in the notebooks of every creator: "The essence of all art is the accomplishment of the impossible."

Strachey's successes and failures are bound up in his desire to humanize famous and little-known "names." The essay on "Lady Hester Stanhope" is as typical as it is quotable. The defects and the mannerisms are obvious; Strachey tended to cultivate a style for style's sake. Moreover, his sense of drama tempted him to impose undue significance upon small facts; and, though he prided himself upon his restraint, his irony compelled him to distort details. It is only necessary to compare Strachey's *Queen Victoria* with Sir Sidney Lee's book on the same subject to see what Strachey accomplished. Lee's book is dull; Strachey's is dazzling. Yet, as George Dangerfield concludes, Strachey's immediate influence was not good. "His style and his method were alike so personal that, though much could be learned from them, mere emulation could only result in caricature. His followers had a brief and dreary inning; they produced a series of so-called 'debunking' biographies, and their names were writ in water. But, before they disappeared, they had covered his reputation with clods of dull dirt." [1]

Whether or not that reputation will survive is a question that cannot yet be answered. It cannot be doubted, however, that, though his direct influence may have been harmful, Strachey indirectly changed the historian's entire approach. He brought to the writing of biography a dramatic incisiveness, a challenging imagination, and a fine prose rhythm. An antitraditionalist, he wrote in the tradition of those biographers who achieved a freedom of spirit, sharp revaluation, sudden brilliance, and, at times, a magnificence which can be accomplished only by the artist who has all his powers—factual and fictive—under strict control.

LADY HESTER STANHOPE [2]

THE Pitt nose has a curious history. One can watch its transmigrations through three lives. The tremendous hook of old Lord Chatham, under whose curve Empires came to birth, was succeeded by the bleak upward-pointing nose of William Pitt the younger—the rigid symbol of an indomitable *hauteur*. With Lady Hester Stanhope came the final stage. The nose, still with an upward tilt in it, had lost its masculinity; the hard bones of the uncle and the grandfather had disappeared. Lady Hester's was a nose of wild ambitions, of pride grown fantastical, a nose that scorned the earth, shooting off, one fancies, towards some eternally eccentric heaven. It was a nose, in fact, altogether in the air.

Noses, of course, are aristocratic things; and Lady Hester was the child of a great aristocracy. But, in her case, the aristocratic impulse, which had carried her predecessors to glory, had less fortunate results. There has always been a strong strain of extravagance in the governing families of England; from time to time they throw off some peculiarly ill-balanced member, who performs a strange meteoric course. A century earlier, Lady Mary Wortley Montagu was an illustrious example of this tendency: that splendid comet, after filling half the heavens, vanished suddenly into desolation and darkness. Lady Hester Stanhope's spirit was still more uncommon; and she met with a most uncommon fate.

She was born in 1776, the eldest daughter of that extraordinary Earl Stanhope, Jacobin and inventor, who made the first steamboat and the first calculating machine, who defended the French Revolution in the House of Lords and erased the armorial bearings—"damned aristocratical nonsense"—from his carriages and his plate. Her mother, Chatham's daughter and the favourite sister of Pitt, died when she was four years old. The second Lady Stanhope, a frigid woman of fashion, left her stepdaughters to the care of futile governesses, while "Citizen Stanhope" ruled the household from his laboratory with the violence of a tyrant. It was not until Lady Hester was twenty-four that she escaped from the slavery of her father's house, by going to live with her grandmother, Lady Chatham. On Lady Chatham's death, three years later, Pitt offered her his protection, and she remained with him until his death in 1806.

Her three years with Pitt, passed in the very centre of splendid power, were brilliant and exciting. She flung herself impetuously into the movement and the passion of that vigorous society; she ruled her uncle's household with high vivacity; she was liked and courted; if not beautiful, she was fascinating—very tall, with a very fair and clear complexion, and dark-blue eyes, and a countenance of wonderful expressiveness. Her talk, full of the trenchant nonchalance of those days, was both

[1] From George Dangerfield, "Lytton Strachey," a review, *Saturday Review of Literature*, July 23, 1938.   [2] From *Books and Characters* by Lytton Strachey, copyright, 1922, by Harcourt, Brace and Company, Inc.

amusing and alarming: "My dear Hester, what are you saying?" Pitt would call out to her from across the room. She was devoted to her uncle, who warmly returned her affection. She was devoted, too—but in a more dangerous fashion—to the intoxicating Antinous, Lord Granville Leveson Gower. The reckless manner in which she carried on this love-affair was the first indication of something overstrained, something wild and unaccountable, in her temperament. Lord Granville, after flirting with her outrageously, declared that he could never marry her, and went off on an embassy to St. Petersburg. Her distraction was extreme: she hinted that she would follow him to Russia; she threatened, and perhaps attempted, suicide; she went about telling everybody that he had jilted her. She was taken ill, and then there were rumours of an accouchement, which, it was said, she took care to *afficher*, by appearing without rouge and fainting on the slightest provocation. In the midst of these excursions and alarums there was a terrible and unexpected catastrophe. Pitt died. And Lady Hester suddenly found herself a dethroned princess, living in a small house in Montagu Square on a pension of £1,200 a year.

She did not abandon society, however, and the tongue of gossip continued to wag. Her immediate marriage with a former lover, Mr. Hill, was announced: "il est bien bon," said Lady Bessborough. Then it was whispered that Canning was "le régnant"—that he was with her "not only all day, but almost all night." She quarrelled with Canning and became attached to Sir John Moore. Whether she was actually engaged to marry him—as she seems to have asserted many years later—is doubtful; his letters to her, full as they are of respectful tenderness, hardly warrant the conclusion; but it is certain that he died with her name on his lips. Her favourite brother, Charles, was killed beside him; and it was natural that under this double blow she should have retired from London. She buried herself in Wales; but not for long. In 1810 she set sail for Gibraltar with her brother James, who was rejoining his regiment in the Peninsula. She never returned to England.

There can be no doubt that at the time of her departure the thought of a lifelong exile was far from her mind. It was only gradually, as she moved further and further eastward, that the prospect of life in England—at last even in Europe—grew distaste-

ful to her; as late as 1816 she was talking of a visit to Provence. Accompanied by two or three English fellow travellers, her English maid, Mrs. Fry, her private physician, Dr. Meryon, and a host of servants, she progressed, slowly and in a great state, through Malta and Athens, to Constantinople. She was conveyed in battleships, and lodged with governors and ambassadors. After spending many months in Constantinople, Lady Hester discovered that she was "dying to see Napoleon with her own eyes," and attempted accordingly to obtain passports to France. The project was stopped by Stratford Canning, the English Minister, upon which she decided to visit Egypt, and, chartering a Greek vessel, sailed for Alexandria in the winter of 1811. Off the island of Rhodes a violent storm sprang up; the whole party were forced to abandon the ship, and to take refuge upon a bare rock, where they remained without food or shelter for thirty hours. Eventually, after many severe privations, Alexandria was reached in safety; but this disastrous voyage was a turning-point in Lady Hester's career. At Rhodes she was forced to exchange her torn and dripping raiment for the attire of a Turkish gentleman—a dress which she never afterwards abandoned. It was the first step in her orientalization.

She passed the next two years in a triumphal progress. Her appearance in Cairo caused the greatest sensation, and she was received in state by the Pasha, Mehemet Ali. Her costume on this occasion was gorgeous: she wore a turban of cashmere, a brocaded waistcoat, a priceless pelisse, and a vast pair of purple velvet pantaloons embroidered all over in gold. She was ushered by chamberlains with silver wands through the inner courts of the palace to a pavilion in the harem, where the Pasha, rising to receive her, conversed with her for an hour. From Cairo she turned northwards, visiting Jaffa, Jerusalem, Acre, and Damascus. Her travelling dress was of scarlet cloth trimmed with gold, and, when on horseback, she wore over the whole a white-hooded and tasselled burnous. Her maid, too, was forced, protesting, into trousers, though she absolutely refused to ride astride. Poor Mrs. Fry had gone through various and dreadful sufferings—shipwreck and starvation, rats and blackbeetles unspeakable—but she retained her equanimity. Whatever her Ladyship might think fit to be, *she* was an Englishwoman to the last, and Philippaki was Philip Parker and Mustapha Mr. Farr.

Outside Damascus, Lady Hester was warned that the town was the most fanatical in Turkey,

30. **Canning,** George Canning (1770–1827), British statesman, orator, and wit; he favored the liberal movements and a foreign policy of nonintervention. 33. **Sir John Moore,** British general (1761–1809), especially famous for his Spanish campaign against Napoleon.

and that the scandal of a woman entering it in man's clothes, unveiled, would be so great as to be dangerous. She was begged to veil herself, and to make her entry under cover of darkness. "I must take the bull by the horns," she replied, and rode into the city unveiled at midday. The population were thunderstruck; but at last their amazement gave way to enthusiasm, and the incredible lady was hailed everywhere as Queen, crowds followed her, coffee was poured out before her, and the whole bazaar rose as she passed. Yet she was not satisfied with her triumphs; she would do something still more glorious and astonishing; she would plunge into the desert and visit the ruins of Palmyra, which only half-a-dozen of the boldest travellers had ever seen. The Pasha of Damascus offered her a military escort, but she preferred to throw herself upon the hospitality of the Bedouin Arabs, who, overcome by her horsemanship, her powers of sight, and her courage, enrolled her a member of their tribe. After a week's journey in their company, she reached Palmyra, where the inhabitants met her with wild enthusiasm, and under the Corinthian columns of Zenobia's temple crowned her head with flowers. This happened in March, 1813; it was the apogee of Lady Hester's life. Henceforward her fortunes gradually but steadily declined.

The rumour of her exploits had spread through Syria, and from the year 1813 onwards, her reputation was enormous. She was received everywhere as a royal, almost as a supernatural, personage: she progressed from town to town amid official prostrations and popular rejoicings. But she herself was in a state of hesitation and discontent. Her future was uncertain; she had grown scornful of the West—must she return to it? The East alone was sympathetic, the East alone was tolerable— but could she cut herself off for ever from the past? At Laodicea she was suddenly struck down by the plague, and, after months of illness, it was borne in upon her that all was vanity. She rented an empty monastery on the slopes of Mount Lebanon, not far from Sayda (the ancient Sidon), and took up her abode there. Then her mind took a new surprising turn; she dashed to Ascalon, and, with the permission of the Sultan, began excavations in a ruined temple with the object of discovering a hidden treasure of three million pieces of gold. Having unearthed nothing but an antique statue, which, in order to prove her disinterestedness, she ordered her appalled doctor to break into little bits, she returned to her monastery. Finally, in 1816, she moved to another house, further up Mount Lebanon, and near the village of Djoun; and at Djoun

she remained until her death, more than twenty years later.

Thus, almost accidentally as it seems, she came to the end of her wanderings, and the last, long, strange, mythical period of her existence began. Certainly the situation that she had chosen was sublime. Her house, on the top of a high bare hill among great mountains, was a one-storied group of buildings, with many ramifying courts and outhouses, and a garden of several acres surrounded by a rampart wall. The garden, which she herself had planted and tended with the utmost care, commanded a glorious prospect. On every side but one the vast mountains towered, but to the west there was an opening, through which, in the far distance, the deep blue Mediterranean was revealed. From this romantic hermitage, her singular renown spread over the world. European travellers who had been admitted to her presence brought back stories full of Eastern mystery; they told of a peculiar grandeur, a marvellous prestige, an imperial power. The precise nature of Lady Hester's empire was, indeed, dubious; she was in fact merely the tenant of her Djoun establishment, for which she paid a rent of £20 a year. But her dominion was not subject to such limitations. She ruled imaginatively, transcendentally; the solid glory of Chatham had been transmuted into the phantasy of an Arabian Night. No doubt she herself believed that she was something more than a chimerical Empress. When a French traveller was murdered in the desert, she issued orders for the punishment of the offenders; punished they were, and Lady Hester actually received the solemn thanks of the French Chamber. It seems probable, however, that it was the Sultan's orders rather than Lady Hester's which produced the desired effect. In her feud with her terrible neighbour, the Emir Beshyr, she maintained an undaunted front. She kept the tyrant at bay; but perhaps the Emir, who, so far as physical force was concerned, held her in the hollow of his hand, might have proceeded to extremities if he had not received a severe admonishment from Stratford Canning at Constantinople. What is certain is that the ignorant and superstitious populations around her feared and loved her, and that she, reacting to her own mysterious prestige, became at last even as they. She plunged into astrology and divination; she awaited the moment when, in accordance with prophecy, she should enter Jerusalem side by side with Mahdi, the Messiah; she kept two sacred horses, destined, by sure signs, to carry her and him to their last tri-

25. **£20,** about $100.

umph. The Orient had mastered her utterly. She was no longer an Englishwoman, she declared; she loathed England; she would never go there again; if she went anywhere it would be to Arabia, to "her own people."

Her expenses were immense—not only for herself but for others, for she poured out her hospitality with a noble hand. She ran into debt, and was swindled by the moneylenders; her steward cheated her, her servants pilfered her; her distress was at 10 last acute. She fell into fits of terrible depression, bursting into dreadful tears and savage cries. Her habits grew more and more eccentric. She lay in bed all day, and sat up all night, talking unceasingly for hour upon hour to Dr. Meryon, who, alone of her English attendants, remained with her, Mrs. Fry having withdrawn to more congenial scenes long since. The doctor was a poor-spirited and muddle-headed man, but he was a good listener; and there he sat while that extraordinary talk 20 flowed on—talk that scaled the heavens and ransacked the earth, talk in which memories of an abolished past—stories of Mr. Pitt and of George III., vituperations against Mr. Canning, mimicries of the Duchess of Devonshire—mingled phantasmagorically with doctrines of Fate and planetary influence, and speculations on the Arabian origin of the Scottish clans, and lamentations over the wickedness of servants; till the unaccountable figure, with its robes and its long pipe, loomed through the 30 tobacco-smoke like some vision of a Sibyl in a dream. She might be robbed and ruined, her house might crumble over her head; but she talked on. She grew ill and desperate; yet still she talked. Did she feel that the time was coming when she should talk no more?

Her melancholy deepened into a settled gloom when the news came of her brother James's death. She had quarrelled with all her English friends, except Lord Hardwicke—with her eldest brother, 40 with her sister, whose kind letters she left un-answered; she was at daggers drawn with the English consul at Alexandria, who worried her about her debts. Ill and harassed, she hardly moved from her bedroom, while her servants rifled her belongings and reduced the house to a condition of indescribable disorder and filth. Three dozen hungry cats ranged through the rooms, filling the courts with frightful noises. Dr. Meryon, in the midst of it all, knew not whether to cry or laugh. At moments the great lady regained her ancient fire; her bells pealed tumultuously for hours together; or she leapt up, and arraigned the whole trembling household before her, with her Arab war-mace in her hand. Her finances grew more and more involved—grew at length irremediable. It was in vain that the faithful Lord Hardwicke pressed her to return to England to settle her affairs. Return to England, indeed! To England, that ungrateful, miserable country, where, so far as she could see, they had forgotten the very name of Mr. Pitt! The final blow fell when a letter came from the English authorities threatening to cut off her pension for the payment of her debts. Upon that, after dispatching a series of furious missives to Lord Palmerston, to Queen Victoria, to the Duke of Wellington, she renounced the world. She commanded Dr. Meryon to return to Europe, and he—how could he have done it?—obeyed her. Her health was broken, she was over sixty, and, save for her vile servants, absolutely alone. She lived for nearly a year after he left her—we know no more. She had vowed never again to pass through the gate of her house; but did she sometimes totter to her garden—that beautiful garden which she had created, with its roses and its fountains, its alleys and its bowers—and look westward at the sea? The end came in June, 1839. Her servants immediately possessed themselves of every movable object in the house. But Lady Hester cared no longer: she was lying back in her bed—inexplicable, grand, preposterous, with her nose in the air.

P. G. Wodehouse
1881–

His full name—Pelham Grenville Wodehouse—sounds like that of one of Wodehouse's own characters. He was born at Guilford, October 15, 1881. Educated at Dulwich College, he began the literary life by writing for a boys' paper. His first volume, *The Pothunters*, 1902, appeared when Wodehouse was not quite twenty-one; since that time he has published an average of a book a year, to say nothing of plays, sketches, and scenarios. His activities for the theater include part authorship of nineteen musical comedies, most of which were produced in America; several of them—such as *Anything Goes*, 1934—were international successes. When the German army swept through France in May, 1939, Wodehouse was arrested in his villa in Le Touquet. From occupied France he was taken to Germany, where he was placed in a Silesian internment camp with more than a thousand other British subjects, his companions in confinement being truck-drivers, consuls, and coalheavers. A book about American crooks outwitted by their English victims was written in a room graciously furnished by his captors—a padded cell in an insane asylum.

A list of Wodehouse's volumes gives only a remote indication of the author's quality, although such titles as *Leave It to Psmith*, 1923; *The Inimitable Jeeves*, 1924; *The Code of the Woosters*, 1938; and *Uncle Fred in the Springtime*, 1939, suggest his gift for straight-faced absurdity. Wodehouse is indefatigable rather than versatile; he surprises not by any novelty in plot but by the continuing high spirits and perfection of his performance. His farces—and he has written practically nothing else—concern the same set of characters: idle young nincompoops floundering between bankruptcy and matrimony, snared by designing actresses or serious (but always beautiful) daughters of the aristocracy, attended by statesmanlike valets, and surrounded by armies of formidable aunts and incredibly eccentric uncles. Literary historians may well devote some time to a study of Wodehouse's distortions of a mad milieu and an insane period. In Wodehouse's crowded gallery of eccentrics there are no flat portraits. Here the admirable Jeeves stands like a combination Crichton and Machiavelli; here balmy or "potty" Lords and Earls lavish their affections on prize pigs, impersonate total strangers, and demolish drawing-room furniture with pokers and aplomb; here love and lunacy somehow find a way through the tortuous Psmith Psaga.

In a foreword to the omnibus *Nothing but Wodehouse*, 1932, Ogden Nash wrote:

"To inhabit the same world as Mr. Wodehouse is a high privilege; to inhabit the same volume, even as doorkeeper, is perilous. Not because people may make comparisons, for who is there to compare with him? Every schoolboy knows that no one can hold a candle to P. G. Wodehouse, and not for lack of effort either. The woods are full of ambitious candleholders, but none of them has yet come within scorching distance of the Old Master."

Critics may dispute Wodehouse's eminence. Analysts may be baffled by his unflagging popularity and the freshness with which he turns the same old tale. Readers may be divided in allegiance to Jeeves, Mulliner, Ukridge, Psmith, and Frederick Altamount Cornwallis Twistleton, fifth Earl of Ickenham. But to the true army of admirers (in which every reader seems to enlist himself) Wodehouse is neither a social satirist nor an irresponsible farceur. He is, as Nash declares, simply the Old Master.

UNCLE FRED FLITS BY [1]

IN order that they might enjoy their after-luncheon coffee in peace, the Crumpet had taken the guest whom he was entertaining at the Drones Club to the smaller and less frequented of the two smoking-rooms. In the other, he explained, though the conversation always touched an exceptionally high level of brilliance, there was apt to be a good deal of sugar thrown about.

The guest said he understood.

"Young blood, eh?"

"That's right. Young blood."

"And animal spirits."

[1] From *Young Men in Spats*, copyright by Pelham Grenville Wodehouse, 1936. Reprinted by permission of Mr. Wodehouse and the publishers, Doubleday, Doran and Company, Inc.

"And animal, as you say, spirits," agreed the Crumpet. "We get a fairish amount of those here."

"The complaint, however, is not, I observe, universal."

"Eh?"

The other drew his host's attention to the doorway, where a young man in form-fitting tweeds had just appeared. The aspect of this young man was haggard. His eyes glared wildly and he sucked at an empty cigarette-holder. If he had a mind, there was something on it. When the Crumpet called to him to come and join the party, he merely shook his head in a distraught sort of way and disappeared, looking like a character out of a Greek tragedy pursued by the Fates.

The Crumpet sighed.

"Poor old Pongo!"

"Pongo?"

"That was Pongo Twistleton. He's all broken up about his Uncle Fred."

"Dead?"

"No such luck. Coming up to London again tomorrow. Pongo had a wire this morning."

"And that upsets him?"

"Naturally. After what happened last time."

"What was that?"

"Ah!" said the Crumpet.

"What happened last time?"

"You may well ask."

"I do ask."

"Ah!" said the Crumpet.

Poor old Pongo (said the Crumpet) has often discussed his Uncle Fred with me, and if there weren't tears in his eyes when he did so, I don't know a tear in the eye when I see one. In round numbers the Earl of Ickenham, of Ickenham Hall, Ickenham, Hants, he lives in the country most of the year, but from time to time has a nasty way of slipping his collar and getting loose and descending upon Pongo at his flat in the Albany. And every time he does so, the unhappy young blighter is subjected to some soul-testing experience. Because the trouble with this uncle is that, though sixty if a day, he becomes on arriving in the metropolis as young as he feels—which is, apparently, a youngish twenty-two. I don't know if you happen to know what the word "excesses" means, but those are what Pongo's Uncle Fred from the country, when in London, invariably commits.

It wouldn't so much matter, mind you, if he would confine his activities to the club premises. We're pretty broad-minded here, and if you stop short of smashing the piano, there isn't much that

you can do at the Drones that will cause the raised eyebrow and the sharp intake of breath. The snag is that he will insist on lugging Pongo out in the open and there, right in the public eye, proceeding to step high, wide and plentiful.

So when, on the occasion to which I allude, he stood pink and genial on Pongo's hearth-rug, bulging with Pongo's lunch and wreathed in the smoke of one of Pongo's cigars, and said: "And now, my boy, for a pleasant and instructive afternoon," you will readily understand why the unfortunate young clam gazed at him as he would have gazed at twopenn'orth of dynamite, had he discovered it lighting up in his presence.

"A what?" he said, giving at the knees and paling beneath the tan a bit.

"A pleasant and instructive afternoon," repeated Lord Ickenham, rolling the words round his tongue. "I propose that you place yourself in my hands and leave the program entirely to me."

Now, owing to Pongo's circumstances being such as to necessitate his getting into the aged relative's ribs at intervals and shaking him down for an occasional much-needed tenner or what not, he isn't in a position to use the iron hand with the old buster. But at these words he displayed a manly firmness.

"You aren't going to get me to the dog races again."

"No, no."

"You remember what happened last June?"

"Quite," said Lord Ickenham, "quite. Though I still think that a wiser magistrate would have been content with a mere reprimand."

"And I won't—"

"Certainly not. Nothing of that kind at all. What I propose to do this afternoon is to take you to visit the home of your ancestors."

Pongo did not get this.

"I thought Ickenham was the home of my ancestors."

"It is one of the homes of your ancestors. They also resided rather nearer the heart of things, at a place called Mitching Hill."

"Down in the suburbs, do you mean?"

"The neighbourhood is now suburban, true. It is many years since the meadows where I sported as a child were sold and cut up into building lots. But when I was a boy Mitching Hill was open country. It was a vast, rolling estate belonging to your great-uncle, Marmaduke, a man with whiskers of a nature which you with your pure mind would scarcely credit, and I have long felt a sentimental urge to see what the hell the old place looks like now. Perfectly foul, I expect. Still, I think we should make the pious pilgrimage."

Pongo absolutely-ed heartily. He was all for the scheme. A great weight seemed to have rolled off his mind. The way he looked at it was that even an uncle within a short jump of the loony bin couldn't very well get into much trouble in a suburb. I mean, you know what suburbs are. They don't, as it were, offer the scope. One follows his reasoning, of course. "Fine!" he said. "Splendid! Topping!"

"Then put on your hat and rompers, my boy," said Lord Ickenham, "and let us be off. I fancy one gets there by omnibuses and things."

Well, Pongo hadn't expected much in the way of mental uplift from the sight of Mitching Hill, and he didn't get it. Alighting from the bus, he tells me, you found yourself in the middle of rows and rows of semi-detached villas, all looking exactly alike, and you went on and you came to more semi-detached villas, and those all looked exactly alike, too. Nevertheless, he did not repine. It was one of those early spring days which suddenly change to mid-winter and he had come out without his overcoat, and it looked like rain and he hadn't an umbrella, but despite this his mood was one of sober ecstasy. The hours were passing and his uncle had not yet made a goat of himself. At the Dog Races the other had been in the hands of the constabulary in the first ten minutes.

It began to seem to Pongo that with any luck he might be able to keep the old blister pottering harmlessly about here till nightfall, when he could shoot a bit of dinner into him and put him to bed. And as Lord Ickenham had specifically stated that his wife, Pongo's Aunt Jane, had expressed her intention of scalping him with a blunt knife if he wasn't back at the Hall by lunch time on the morrow, it really looked as if he might get through this visit without perpetrating a single major outrage on the public weal. It is rather interesting to note that as he thought this Pongo smiled, because it was the last time he smiled that day.

All this while, I should mention, Lord Ickenham had been stopping at intervals like a pointing dog and saying that it must have been just about here that he plugged the gardener in the trousers seat with his bow and arrow and that over there he had been sick after his first cigar, and he now paused in front of a villa which for some unknown reason called itself The Cedars. His face was tender and wistful.

"On this very spot, if I am not mistaken," he

6. **loony bin,** insane asylum.

said, heaving a bit of a sigh, "on this very spot, fifty years ago come Lammas Eve, I . . . Oh, blast it!"

The concluding remark had been caused by the fact that the rain, which had held off until now, suddenly began to buzz down like a shower-bath. With no further words, they leaped into the porch of the villa and there took shelter, exchanging glances with a gray parrot which hung in a cage in the window.

Not that you could really call it shelter. They were protected from above all right, but the moisture was now falling with a sort of swivel action, whipping in through the sides of the porch and tickling them up properly. And it was just after Pongo had turned up his collar and was huddling against the door that the door gave way. From the fact that a female of general-servant aspect was standing there he gathered that his uncle must have rung the bell.

This female wore a long mackintosh, and Lord Ickenham beamed upon her with a fairish spot of suavity.

"Good afternoon," he said.

The female said good afternoon.

"The Cedars?"

The female said yes, it was The Cedars.

"Are the old folks at home?"

The female said there was nobody at home.

"Ah? Well, never mind. I have come," said Lord Ickenham, edging in, "to clip the parrot's claws. My assistant, Mr. Walkinshaw, who applies the anaesthetic," he added, indicating Pongo with a gesture.

"Are you from the bird shop?"

"A very happy guess."

"Nobody told me you were coming."

"They keep things from you, do they?" said Lord Ickenham, sympathetically. "Too bad."

Continuing to edge, he had got into the parlor by now, Pongo following in a sort of dream and the female following Pongo.

"Well, I suppose it's all right," she said. "I was just going out. It's my afternoon."

"Go out," said Lord Ickenham cordially. "By all means go out. We will leave everything in order."

And presently the female, though still a bit on the dubious side, pushed off, and Lord Ickenham lit the gas-fire and drew a chair up.

"So here we are, my boy," he said. "A little tact, a little address, and here we are, snug and cozy and not catching our deaths of cold. You'll never go far wrong if you leave things to me."

"But, dash it, we can't stop here," said Pongo. Lord Ickenham raised his eyebrows.

"Not stop here? Are you suggesting that we go out into that rain? My dear lad, you are not aware of the grave issues involved. This morning, as I was leaving home, I had a rather painful disagreement with your aunt. She said the weather was treacherous and wished me to take my woolly muffler. I replied that the weather was not treacherous and that I would be dashed if I took my woolly muffler. 10 Eventually, by the exercise of an iron will, I had my way, and I ask you, my dear boy, to envisage what will happen if I return with a cold in the head. I shall sink to the level of a fifth-class power. Next time I came to London, it would be with a liver pad and a respirator. No! I shall remain here, toasting my toes at this really excellent fire. I had no idea that a gas-fire radiated such warmth. I feel all in a glow."

So did Pongo. His brow was wet with honest 20 sweat. He is reading for the Bar, and while he would be the first to admit that he hasn't yet got a complete toe-hold on the Law of Great Britain he had a sort of notion that oiling into a perfect stranger's semi-detached villa on the pretext of pruning the parrot was a tort or misdemeanor, if not actually barratry or soccage in fief or something like that. And apart from the legal aspect of the matter there was the embarrassment of the thing. Nobody is more of a whale on correctness and not 30 doing what's not done than Pongo, and the situation in which he now found himself caused him to chew the lower lip and, as I say, perspire a goodish deal.

"But suppose the blighter who owns this ghastly house comes back?" he asked. "Talking of envisaging things, try that one over on your pianola."

And, sure enough, as he spoke, the front door bell rang.

"There!" said Pongo.

"Don't say 'There!' my boy," said Lord Ickenham reprovingly. "It's the sort of thing your aunt says. I see no reason for alarm. Obviously this is some casual caller. A ratepayer would have used his latchkey. Glance cautiously out of the window and see if you can see anybody."

"It's a pink chap," said Pongo, having done so.

"How pink?"

"Pretty pink."

"Well, there you are, then. I told you so. It can't 50 be the big chief. The sort of fellows who own houses

like this are pale and sallow, owing to working in offices all day. Go and see what he wants."

"You go and see what he wants."

"We'll both go and see what he wants," said Lord Ickenham.

So they went and opened the front door, and there, as Pongo had said, was a pink chap. A small young pink chap, a bit moist about the shoulderblades.

"Pardon me," said this pink chap, "is Mr. Roddis in?"

"No," said Pongo.

"Yes," said Lord Ickenham. "Don't be silly, Douglas—of course I'm in. I am Mr. Roddis," he said to the pink chap. "This, such as he is, is my son Douglas. And you?"

"Name of Robinson."

"What about it?"

"My name's Robinson."

"Oh, *your* name's Robinson? Now we've got it straight. Delighted to see you, Mr. Robinson. Come right in and take your boots off."

They all trickled back to the parlour, Lord Ickenham pointing out objects of interest by the wayside to the chap, Pongo gulping for air a bit and trying to get himself abreast of this new twist in the scenario. His heart was becoming more and more bowed down with weight of woe. He hadn't liked being Mr. Walkinshaw, the anaesthetist, and 30 he didn't like it any better being Roddis Junior. In brief, he feared the worst. It was only too plain to him by now that his uncle had got it thoroughly up his nose and had settled down to one of his big afternoons, and he was asking himself, as he had so often asked himself before, what would the harvest be?

Arrived in the parlor, the pink chap proceeded to stand on one leg and look coy.

"Is Julia here?" he asked, simpering a bit, Pongo 40 says.

"Is she?" said Lord Ickenham to Pongo.

"No," said Pongo.

"No," said Lord Ickenham.

"She wired me she was coming here to-day."

"Ah, then we shall have a bridge four."

The pink chap stood on the other leg.

"I don't suppose you've ever met Julia. Bit of trouble in the family, she gave me to understand."

"It is often the way."

"The Julia I mean is your niece Julia Parker. Or, 50 rather, your wife's niece Julia Parker."

"Any niece of my wife is a niece of mine," said Lord Ickenham heartily. "We share and share alike."

"Julia and I want to get married."

"Well, go ahead."

"But they won't let us."

"Who won't?"

"Her mother and father. And Uncle Charlie Parker and Uncle Henry Parker and the rest of them. They don't think I'm good enough."

"The morality of the modern young man is notoriously lax."

"Class enough, I mean. They're a haughty lot."

"What makes them haughty? Are they earls?"

"No, they aren't earls."

"Then why the devil," said Lord Ickenham warmly, "are they haughty? Only earls have a right to be haughty. Earls are hot stuff. When you get an earl, you've got something."

"Besides, we've had words. Me and her father. One thing led to another, and in the end I called him a perishing old——Coo!" said the pink chap, breaking off suddenly.

He had been standing by the window, and he now leaped lissomely into the middle of the room, causing Pongo, whose nervous system was by this time definitely down among the wines and spirits and who hadn't been expecting this *adagio* stuff, to bite his tongue with some severity.

"They're on the doorstep! Julia and her mother and father. I didn't know they were all coming."

"You do not wish to meet them?"

"No, I don't!"

"Then duck behind the settee, Mr. Robinson," said Lord Ickenham, and the pink chap, weighing the advice and finding it good, did so. And as he disappeared the door bell rang.

Once more, Lord Ickenham led Pongo out into the hall.

"I say!" said Pongo, and a close observer might have noted that he was quivering like an aspen.

"Say on, my dear boy."

"I mean to say, what?"

"What?"

"You aren't going to let these bounders in, are you?"

"Certainly," said Lord Ickenham. "We Roddises keep open house. And as they are presumably aware that Mr. Roddis has no son, I think we had better return to the old layout. You are the local vet, my boy, come to minister to my parrot. When I return, I should like to find you by the cage, staring at the bird in a scientific manner. Tap your teeth from time to time with a pencil and try to smell of iodoform. It will help to add conviction."

So Pongo shifted back to the parrot's cage and stared so earnestly that it was only when a voice said "Well!" that he became aware that there was anybody in the room. Turning, he perceived that Hampshire's leading curse had come back, bringing the gang.

It consisted of a stern, thin, middle-aged woman, a middle-aged man and a girl.

You can generally accept Pongo's estimate of girls, and when he says that this one was a pippin one knows that he uses the term in its most exact sense. She was about nineteen, he thinks, and she wore a black béret, a dark-green leather coat, a shortish tweed skirt, silk stockings and high-heeled shoes. Her eyes were large and lustrous and her face like a dewy rosebud at daybreak on a June morning. So Pongo tells me. Not that I suppose he has ever seen a rosebud at daybreak on a June morning, because it's generally as much as you can do to lug him out of bed in time for nine-thirty breakfast. Still, one gets the idea.

"Well," said the woman, "you don't know who I am, I'll be bound. I'm Laura's sister Connie. This is Claude, my husband. And this is my daughter Julia. Is Laura in?"

"I regret to say, no," said Lord Ickenham.

The woman was looking at him as if he didn't come up to her specifications.

'I thought you were younger," she said.

"Younger than what?" said Lord Ickenham.

"Younger than you are."

"You can't be younger than you are, worse luck," said Lord Ickenham. "Still, one does one's best, and I am bound to say that of recent years I have made a pretty good go of it."

The woman caught sight of Pongo, and he didn't seem to please her, either.

"Who's that?"

"The local vet, clustering round my parrot."

"I can't talk in front of him."

"It is quite all right," Lord Ickenham assured her. "The poor fellow is stone deaf."

And with an imperious gesture at Pongo, as much as to bid him stare less at girls and more at parrots, he got the company seated.

"Now, then," he said.

There was silence for a moment, then a sort of muffled sob, which Pongo thinks proceeded from the girl. He couldn't see, of course, because his back was turned and he was looking at the parrot, which looked back at him—most offensively, he says, as parrots will, using one eye only for the purpose. It also asked him to have a nut.

The woman came into action again.

"Although," she said, "Laura never did me the honour to invite me to her wedding, for which reason I have not communicated with her for five years, necessity compels me to cross her threshold today. There comes a time when differences must be forgotten and relatives must stand shoulder to shoulder."

"I see what you mean," said Lord Ickenham. "Like the boys of the old brigade."

"What I say is, let bygones be begones. I would not have intruded on you, but needs must. I disregard the past and appeal to your sense of pity." 10

The thing began to look to Pongo like a touch, and he is convinced that the parrot thought so, too, for it winked and cleared its throat. But they were both wrong. The woman went on.

"I want you and Laura to take Julia into your home for a week or so, until I can make other arrangements for her. Julia is studying the piano, and she sits for her examination in two weeks' time, so until then she must remain in London. The trouble is, she has fallen in love. Or thinks she has."

"I know I have," said Julia.

Her voice was so attractive that Pongo was compelled to slew round and take another look at her. Her eyes, he says, were shining like twin stars and there was a sort of Soul's Awakening expression on her face, and what the dickens there was in a pink chap like the pink chap, who even as pink chaps go wasn't much of a pink chap, to make her look like that, was frankly, Pongo says, more than he could understand. The thing baffled him. He sought in 30 vain for a solution.

"Yesterday, Claude and I arrived in London from our Bexhill home to give Julia a pleasant surprise. We stayed, naturally, in the boarding-house where she has been living for the past six weeks. And what do you think we discovered?"

"Insects."

"Not insects. A letter. From a young man. I found to my horror that a young man of whom I knew nothing was arranging to marry my daugh- 40 ter. I sent for him immediately, and found him to be quite impossible. He jellies eels!"

"Does what?"

"He is an assistant at a jellied eel shop."

"But surely," said Lord Ickenham, "that speaks well for him. The capacity to jelly an eel seems to me to argue intelligence of a high order. It isn't everybody who can do it, by any means. I know if some one came to me and said 'Jelly this eel!' I should be nonplused. And so, or I am very much 50 mistaken, would Ramsay MacDonald and Winston Churchill."

51–52. **Ramsay MacDonald and Winston Churchill,** leading statesmen of the period.

The woman did not seem to see eye to eye.

"Tchah!" she said. "What do you suppose my husband's brother Charlie Parker would say if I allowed his niece to marry a man who jellies eels?"

"Ah!" said Claude, who, before we go any further, was a tall, drooping bird with a red soup-strainer moustache.

"Or my husband's brother, Henry Parker."

"Ah!" said Claude. "Or Cousin Alf Robbins, for that matter."

"Exactly. Cousin Alfred would die of shame."

The girl Julia hiccoughed passionately, so much so that Pongo says it was all he could do to stop himself nipping across and taking her hand in his and patting it.

"I've told you a hundred times, mother, that Wilberforce is only jellying eels till he finds something better."

"What is better than an eel?" asked Lord Ickenham, who had been following this discussion with the close attention it deserved. "For jellying purposes, I mean."

"He is ambitious. It won't be long," said the girl, "before Wilberforce suddenly rises in the world."

She never spoke a truer word. At this very moment, up he came from behind the settee like a leaping salmon.

"Julia!" he cried.

"Wilby!" yipped the girl.

And Pongo says he never saw anything more sickening in his life than the way she flung herself into the blighter's arms and clung there like the ivy on the old garden wall. It wasn't that he had anything specific against the pink chap, but this girl had made a deep impression on him and he resented her glueing herself to another in this manner.

Julia's mother, after just that brief moment which a woman needs in which to recover from her natural surprise at seeing eel-jelliers pop up from behind sofas, got moving and plucked her away like a referee breaking a couple of welter-weights.

"Julia Parker," she said, "I'm ashamed of you!"

"So am I," said Claude.

"I blush for you."

"Me, too," said Claude. "Hugging and kissing a man who called your father a perishing old bottle-nosed Gawd-help-us."

"I think," said Lord Ickenham, shoving his oar in, "that before proceeding any further we ought to go into that point. If he called you a perishing old bottle-nosed Gawd-help-us, it seems to me that the first thing to do is to decide whether he was right, and frankly, in my opinion . . ."

"Wilberforce will apologize."

"Certainly I'll apologize. It isn't fair to hold a remark passed in the heat of the moment against a chap . . ."

"Mr. Robinson," said the woman, "you know perfectly well that whatever remarks you may have seen fit to pass don't matter one way or the other. If you were listening to what I was saying you will understand . . ."

"Oh, I know, I know. Uncle Charlie Parker and Uncle Henry Parker and Cousin Alf Robbins and all that. Pack of snobs!"

"What!"

"Haughty, stuck-up snobs. Them and their class distinctions. Think themselves everybody just because they've got money. I'd like to know how they got it."

"What do you mean by that?"

"Never mind what I mean."

"If you are insinuating—"

"Well, of course, you know, Connie," said Lord Ickenham mildly, "he's quite right. You can't get away from that."

I don't know if you have ever seen a bull-terrier embarking on a scrap with an Airedale and just as it was getting down nicely to its work suddenly having an unexpected Kerry Blue sneak up behind it and bite it in the rear quarters. When this happens, it lets go of the Airedale and swivels round and fixes the butting-in animal with a pretty nasty eye. It was exactly the same with the woman Connie when Lord Ickenham spoke these words.

"What!"

"I was only wondering if you had forgotten how Charlie Parker made his pile."

"What are you talking about?"

"I know it is painful," said Lord Ickenham, "and one doesn't mention it as a rule, but, as we are on the subject, you must admit that lending money at two hundred and fifty per cent interest is not done in the best circles. The judge, if you remember, said so at the trial."

"I never knew that!" cried the girl Julia.

"Ah," said Lord Ickenham. "You kept it from the child? Quite right, quite right."

"It's a lie!"

"And when Henry Parker had all that fuss with the bank it was touch and go they didn't send him to prison. Between ourselves, Connie, has a bank official, even a brother of your husband, any right to sneak fifty pounds from the till in order to put it on a hundred to one shot for the Grand National? Not quite playing the game, Connie. Not the straight bat. Henry, I grant you, won five thousand

of the best and never looked back afterwards, but, though we applaud his judgment of form, we must surely look askance at his financial methods. As for Cousin Alf Robbins . . ."

The woman was making rummy stuttering sounds. Pongo tells me he once had a Pommery Seven which used to express itself in much the same way if you tried to get it to take a hill on high. A sort of mixture of gurgles and explosions.

"There is not a word of truth in this," she gasped at length, having managed to get the vocal cords disentangled. "Not a single word. I think you must have gone mad."

Lord Ickenham shrugged his shoulders.

"Have it your own way, Connie. I was only going to say that, while the jury were probably compelled on the evidence submitted to them to give Cousin Alf Robbins the benefit of the doubt when charged with smuggling dope, everybody knew that he had been doing it for years. I am not blaming him, mind you. If a man can smuggle cocaine and get away with it, good luck to him, say I. The only point I am trying to make is that we are hardly a family that can afford to put on dog and sneer at honest suitors for our daughters' hands. Speaking for myself, I consider that we are very lucky to have the chance of marrying even into eel-jellying circles."

"So do I," said Julia firmly.

"You don't believe what this man is saying?"

"I believe every word."

"So do I," said the pink chap.

The woman snorted. She seemed overwrought.

"Well," she said, "goodness knows I have never liked Laura, but I would never have wished her a husband like you!"

"Husband?" said Lord Ickenham, puzzled. "What gives you the impression that Laura and I are married?"

There was a weighty silence, during which the parrot threw out a general invitation to the company to join it in a nut. Then the girl Julia spoke.

"You'll have to let me marry Wilberforce now," she said. "He knows too much about us."

"I was rather thinking that myself," said Lord Ickenham. "Seal his lips, I say."

"You wouldn't mind marrying into a low family, would you, darling?" asked the girl, with a touch of anxiety.

"No family could be too low for me, dearest, if it was yours," said the pink chap.

"After all, we needn't see them."

"That's right."

"It isn't one's relations that matter: it's one-selves."

"That's right, too."

"Wilby!"

"Julia!"

They repeated the old ivy on the garden wall act. Pongo says he didn't like it any better than the first time, but his distaste wasn't in it with the woman Connie's.

"And what, may I ask," she said, "do you propose to marry on?"

This seemed to cast a damper. They came apart. They looked at each other. The girl looked at the pink chap, and the pink chap looked at the girl. You could see that a jarring note had been struck.

"Wilberforce is going to be a very rich man some day."

"Some day!"

"If I had a hundred pounds," said the pink chap, "I could buy a half-share in one of the best milk walks in South London to-morrow."

"If!" said the woman.

"Ah!" said Claude.

"Where are you going to get it?"

"Ah!" said Claude.

"Where," repeated the woman, plainly pleased with the snappy crack and loath to let it ride without an encore, "are you going to get it?"

"That," said Claude, "is the point. Where are you going to get a hundred pounds?"

"Why, bless my soul," said Lord Ickenham jovially, "from me, of course. Where else?"

And before Pongo's bulging eyes he fished out from the recesses of his costume a crackling bundle of notes and handed it over. And the agony of realizing that the old bounder had had all that stuff on him all this time and that he hadn't touched him for so much as a tithe of it was so keen, Pongo says, that before he knew what he was doing he had let out a sharp, whinnying cry which rang through the room like the yowl of a stepped-on puppy.

"Ah," said Lord Ickenham. "The vet wishes to speak to me. Yes, vet?"

This seemed to puzzle the cerise bloke a bit.

"I thought you said this chap was your son."

"If I had a son," said Lord Ickenham, a little hurt, "he would be a good deal better-looking than that. No, this is the local veterinary surgeon. I may have said I *looked* on him as a son. Perhaps that was what confused you."

He shifted across to Pongo and twiddled his hands enquiringly. Pongo gaped at him, and it was not until one of the hands caught him smartly in the lower ribs that he remembered he was deaf and started to twiddle back. Considering that he wasn t supposed to be dumb, I can't see why he should have twiddled, but no doubt there are moments when twiddling is about all a fellow feels himself equal to. For what seemed to him at least ten hours Pongo had been undergoing great mental stress, and one can't blame him for not being chatty. Anyway, be that as it may, he twiddled.

"I cannot quite understand what he says," announced Lord Ickenham at length, "because he sprained a finger this morning and that makes him stammer. But I gather that he wishes to have a word with me in private. Possibly my parrot has got something the matter with it which he is reluctant to mention even in sign language in front of a young unmarried girl. You know what parrots are. We will step outside."

"*We* will step outside," said Wilberforce.

"Yes," said the girl Julia. "I feel like a walk."

"And you?" said Lord Ickenham to the woman Connie, who was looking like a female Napoleon at Moscow. "Do you join the hikers?"

"I shall remain and make myself a cup of tea. You will not grudge us a cup of tea, I hope?"

"Far from it," said Lord Ickenham cordially. "This is Liberty Hall. Stick around and mop it up till your eyes bubble."

Outside, the girl, looking more like a dewy rosebud than ever, fawned on the old buster pretty considerably.

"I don't know how to thank you!" she said. And the pink chap said he didn't, either.

"Not at all, my dear, not at all," said Lord Ickenham.

"I think you're simply wonderful."

"No, no."

"You are. Perfectly marvellous."

"Tut, tut," said Lord Ickenham. "Don't give the matter another thought."

He kissed her on both cheeks, the chin, the forehead, the right eyebrow, and the tip of the nose, Pongo looking on the while in a baffled and discontented manner. Everybody seemed to be kissing this girl except him.

Eventually the degrading spectacle ceased and the girl and the pink chap shoved off, and Pongo was enabled to take up the matter of that hundred quid.

"Where," he asked, "did you get all that money?"

"Now, where did I?" mused Lord Ickenham. "I know your aunt gave it to me for some purpose. But what? To pay some bill or other, I rather fancy."

This cheered Pongo up slightly.

"She'll give you the devil when you get back," he said, with not a little relish. "I wouldn't be in your shoes for something. When you tell Aunt Jane," he said, with confidence, for he knew his Aunt Jane's emotional nature, "that you slipped her entire roll to a girl, and explain, as you will have to explain, that she was an extraordinarily pretty girl—a girl, in fine, who looked like something out of a beauty chorus of the better sort, I should think she would pluck down one of the ancestral battle-axes from the wall and jolly well strike you on the mazzard."

"Have no anxiety, my dear boy," said Lord Ickenham. "It is like your kind heart to be so concerned, but have no anxiety. I shall tell her that I was compelled to give the money to you to enable you to buy back some compromising letters from a Spanish *demimondaine*. She will scarcely be able to blame me for rescuing a fondly-loved nephew from the clutches of an adventuress. It may be that she will feel a little vexed with you for a while, and that you may have to allow a certain time to elapse before you visit Ickenham again, but then I shan't be wanting you at Ickenham till the ratting season starts, so all is well."

At this moment, there came toddling up to the gate of The Cedars a large red-faced man. He was just going in when Lord Ickenham hailed him.

"Mr. Roddis?"

"Hey?"

"Am I addressing Mr. Roddis?"

"That's me."

"I am Mr. J. G. Bulstrode from down the road," said Lord Ickenham. "This is my sister's husband's brother, Percy Frensham, in the lard and imported-butter business."

The red-faced bird said he was pleased to meet them. He asked Pongo if things were brisk in the lard and imported-butter business, and Pongo said they were all right, and the red-faced bird said he was glad to hear it.

"We have never met, Mr. Roddis," said Lord Ickenham, "but I think it would be only neighbourly to inform you that a short while ago I observed two suspicious-looking persons in your house."

"In my house? How on earth did they get there?"

"No doubt through a window at the back. They looked to me like cat burglars. If you creep up, you may be able to see them."

The red-faced bird crept, and came back not exactly foaming at the mouth but with the air of a man who for two pins would so foam.

12. **mazzard,** head.

"You're perfectly right. They're sitting in my parlor as cool as dammit, swigging my tea and buttered toast."

"I thought as much."

"And they've opened a pot of my raspberry jam."

"Ah, then you will be able to catch them red-handed. I should fetch a policeman."

"I will. Thank you, Mr. Bulstrode."

"Only too glad to have been able to render you this little service, Mr. Roddis," said Lord Ickenham. "Well, I must be moving along. I have an appointment. Pleasant after the rain, is it not? Come, Percy."

He lugged Pongo off.

"So that," he said, with satisfaction, "is that. On these visits of mine to the metropolis, my boy, I always make it my aim, if possible, to spread sweetness and light. I look about me, even in a foul hole like Mitching Hill, and I ask myself—How can I leave this foul hole a better and happier foul hole than I found it? And if I see a chance, I grab it. Here is our omnibus. Spring aboard, my boy, and on our way home we will be sketching out rough plans for the evening. If the old Leicester Grill is still in existence, we might look in there. It must be fully thirty-five years since I was last thrown out of the Leicester Grill. I wonder who is the bouncer there now."

Such (concluded the Crumpet) is Pongo Twistleton's Uncle Fred from the country, and you will have gathered by now a rough notion of why it is that when a telegram comes announcing his impending arrival in the great city Pongo blenches to the core and calls for a couple of quick ones.

The whole situation, Pongo says, is very complex. Looking at it from one angle, it is fine that the man lives in the country most of the year. If he didn't, he would have him in his midst all the time. On the other hand, by living in the country he generates, as it were, a store of loopiness which expends itself with frightful violence on his rare visits to the centre of things.

What it boils down to is this—Is it better to have a loopy uncle whose loopiness is perpetually on tap but spread out thin, so to speak, or one who lies low in distant Hants for three hundred and sixty days in the year and does himself proud in London for the other five? Dashed moot, of course, and Pongo has never been able to make up his mind on the point.

Naturally, the ideal thing would be if some one would chain the old hound up permanently and keep him from Jan. One to Dec. Thirty-one where he wouldn't do any harm—viz. among the spuds and tenantry. But this, Pongo admits, is a Utopian

dream. Nobody could work harder to that end than his Aunt Jane, and she has never been able to manage it.

Virginia Woolf
1882–1941

The third of four children of the eminent biographer and critic Sir Leslie Stephen by his second marriage, Virginia (Stephen) Woolf was born in London in 1882. Stephen's first wife was a daughter of Thackeray, and the Stephens were related to the Darwins, the Macaulays, the Trevelyans, the Stracheys, and other distinguished families. Her father's home, where Virginia Stephen received a thorough if informal education, was a focal point of culture. After her elder sister, Vanessa, married the art critic Clive Bell, Virginia married the author and publisher Leonard Woolf, in 1912, and became a part of the "Bloomsbury Group." This group, so called from the district of London in which most of them lived, included (besides the Woolfs and the Bells) the biographer Lytton Strachey, the economist John Maynard Keynes, the novelist E. M. Forster, and the painter Roger Fry. The members of the group, devoting themselves to "a pursuit of truth and a contemplation of beauty," opposed the genteel tradition; "in a gentlemanly society, they were ruthless . . . passionate in their devotion to what they thought good, brutal in their rejection of what they thought second-rate, resolute in their refusal to compromise."

Leonard and Virginia Woolf began printing limited editions from a small hand press; soon their publications were in demand, the editions grew larger, and the Hogarth Press was founded. Meanwhile, Virginia Woolf had been experimenting in the novel, the short story, and the essay. As a result, her books were fresh attempts to extend the gamut and enlarge the form. From the first, *The Voyage Out*, 1915, it was evident that a refined and highly sensitive intelligence was at work. *Night and Day*, 1919, struggled against the restrictions of the conventional novel; *Monday or Tuesday*, 1921, a set of short stories, alternated between prose statement and poetic implication; *Mrs. Dalloway*, 1925, imposed the past upon the present, and illumined a whole series of lives in eighteen hours of one woman's life.

Mrs. Dalloway marked the turning-point of

Virginia Woolf's creative power. Here her gifts were fused; she combined James Joyce's "stream of consciousness" technique, the current scientific inquiries regarding space and time as "fourth dimensions," and her own record of "tremendous trifles." Character, environment, and action were revealed in "the atoms as they fall upon the mind . . . by tracing the pattern, however disconnected and incoherent it appears, which each sight or incident scores upon the unconscious." This fusion was emphasized in *To the Lighthouse*, 1927, in which the atmosphere is even finer and more transparent than in the preceding work; in *Orlando*, 1928, which is an absorbing tour de force, a fantasy in which time is treated arbitrarily, the heroine nonchalantly changes her sex, and the author romps through English literature with stylistic bravura; in *The Waves*, 1931, and *The Years*, 1937, in which characters develop in terms of images, and in which Mrs. Woolf's gifts of observation and sensibility attain what seems to be an abstract virtuosity.

But Mrs. Woolf was not always experimental and involved. There is *Flush*, 1933, the "biography" of Elizabeth Barrett Browning's cocker spaniel, which is as sympathetic as it is shrewd; there is the straightforward and pointed *A Room of One's Own*, 1929; there are the apt and uncomplicated essays in *The Common Reader*, 1925, and *The Second Common Reader*, 1932. It may be that Mrs. Woolf will be remembered longest as one of the novelists who wrote during a suspension of faith and an unhappy search for new beliefs. The more serious novelists faced the situation with courage, if without solutions. "Joyce met the problem by retreating into a realm without values; Katherine Mansfield met it by endeavoring to cultivate an impossible purity of vision; Aldous Huxley met it by denunciation followed by romantic compensation; Virginia Woolf met it by trying to refine all life into a problem for the meditative intellect."[1]

On March 28, 1941, Mrs. Woolf took her stick

[1] David Daiches, *The Novel and the Modern World*, University of Chicago Press, 1939.

and went for her usual walk. When her disturbed household looked for her later, they found she had drowned herself. Her last book, *Between the Acts*, appeared a few months afterward. "Beau Brummell," for all its brevity, displays her in a combination of roles. It is no less winning, no less penetrating, for not being formidable.

BEAU BRUMMELL [1]

WHEN Cowper, in the seclusion of Olney, was roused to anger by the thought of the Duchess of Devonshire and predicted a time when "instead of a girdle there will be a rent, and instead of beauty, baldness," he was acknowledging the power of the lady whom he thought so despicable. Why, otherwise, should she haunt the damp solitudes of Olney? Why should the rustle of her silken skirts disturb those gloomy meditations? Undoubtedly the Duchess was a good haunter. Long after those words were written, when she was dead and buried beneath a tinsel coronet, her ghost mounted the stairs of a very different dwelling-place. An old man was sitting in his arm-chair at Caen. The door opened, and the servant announced, "The Duchess of Devonshire." Beau Brummell at once rose, went to the door and made a bow that would have graced the Court of St. James's. Only, unfortunately, there was nobody there. The cold air blew up the staircase of an Inn. The Duchess was long dead, and Beau Brummell, in his old age and imbecility, was dreaming that he was back in London again giving a party. Cowper's curse had come true for both of them. The Duchess lay in her shroud, and Brummell, whose clothes had been the envy of kings, had now only one pair of much-mended trousers, which he hid as best he could under a tattered cloak. As for his hair, that had been shaved by order of the doctor.

But though Cowper's sour predictions had thus come to pass, both the Duchess and the dandy might claim that they had had their day. They had been great figures in their time. Of the two, perhaps Brummell might boast the more miraculous career. He had no advantage of birth, and but little of fortune. His grandfather had let rooms in St. James's Street. He had only a moderate capital of thirty thousand pounds to begin with, and his

beauty, of figure rather than of face, was marred by a broken nose. Yet without a single noble, important, or valuable action to his credit he cuts a figure; he stands for a symbol; his ghost walks among us still. The reason for this eminence is now a little difficult to determine. Skill of hand and nicety of judgment were his, of course, otherwise he would not have brought the art of tying neck-cloths to perfection. The story is, perhaps, too well known—how he drew his head far back and sunk his chin slowly down so that the cloth wrinkled in perfect symmetry, or if one wrinkle were too deep or too shallow, the cloth was thrown into a basket and the attempt renewed, while the Prince of Wales sat, hour after hour, watching. Yet skill of hand and nicety of judgment were not enough. Brummell owed his ascendency to some curious combination of wit, of taste, of insolence, of independence—for he was never a toady—which it were too heavy handed to call a philosophy of life, but served the purpose. At any rate, ever since he was the most popular boy at Eton coolly jesting when they were for throwing a bargee into the river, "My good fellows, don't send him into the river; the man is evidently in a high state of perspiration, and it almost amounts to a certainty that he will catch cold," he floated buoyantly and gaily and without apparent effort to the top of whatever society he found himself among. Even when he was a captain in the Tenth Hussars and so scandalously inattentive to duty that he only knew his troop by "the very large blue nose" of one of the men, he was liked and tolerated. When he resigned his commission, for the regiment was to be sent to Manchester—and "I really could not go—think, your Royal Highness, Manchester!"—he had only to set up house in Chesterfield Street to become the head of the most jealous and exclusive society of his time. For example, he was at Almack's one night talking to Lord ——. The Duchess of —— was there, escorting her young daughter, Lady Louisa. The Duchess caught sight of Mr. Brummell, and at once warned her daughter that if that gentleman near the door came and spoke to them she was to be careful to impress him favourably, "for," and she sank her voice to a whisper, "he is the celebrated Mr. Brummell." Lady Louisa might well have wondered why a Mr. Brummell was celebrated, and why a Duke's daughter need take care to impress a Mr. Brummell. And then directly he began to move towards them the reason of her mother's warning became apparent. The grace of

[1] From *The Second Common Reader*, by Virginia Woolf, copyright, 1932, by Harcourt, Brace and Company, Inc.

11. Cowper, William Cowper (1731–1800), an English poet who, between periods of derangement, brought a fresh spirit of sympathy with the common man into English verse, anticipating the "enthusiasm of humanity" of Burns, Wordsworth, and Shelley.

23. bargee, a bargeman, who sometimes carried passengers down the Thames.

his carriage was so astonishing; his bows were so exquisite. Everybody looked over-dressed or badly dressed—some, indeed, looked positively dirty beside him. His clothes seemed to melt into each other with the perfection of their cut and the quiet harmony of their colour. Without a single point of emphasis everything was distinguished—from his bow to the way he opened his snuff-box, with his left hand invariably. He was the personification of freshness and cleanliness and order. One could well believe that he had his chair brought into his dressing-room and was deposited at Almack's without letting a puff of wind disturb his curls or a spot of mud stain his shoes. When he actually spoke to her, Lady Louisa would be at first enchanted—no one was more agreeable, more amusing, had a manner that was more flattering and enticing—and then she would be puzzled. It was quite possible that before the evening was out he would ask her to marry him, and yet his manner of doing it was such that the most ingenuous débutante could not believe that he meant it seriously. His odd grey eyes seemed to contradict his lips; they had a look in them which made the sincerity of his compliments very doubtful. And then he said very cutting things about other people. They were not exactly witty; they were certainly not profound; but they were so skilful, so adroit—they had a twist in them which made them slip into the mind and stay there when more important phrases were forgotten. He had downed the Regent himself with his dexterous "Who's your fat friend?" and his method was the same with humbler people who snubbed him or bored him. "Why, what could I do, my good fellow, but cut the connection? I discovered that Lady Mary actually ate cabbage!"—so he explained to a friend his failure to marry a lady. And, again, when some dull citizen pestered him about his tour to the North, "Which of the lakes do I admire?" he asked his valet. "Windermere, sir." "Ah, yes—Windermere, so it is—Windermere." That was his style, flickering, sneering, hovering on the verge of insolence, skimming the edge of nonsense, but always keeping within some curious mean, so that one knew the false Brummell story from the true by its exaggeration. Brummell could never have said, "Wales, ring the bell," any more than he could have worn a brightly coloured waistcoat or a glaring necktie. That "certain exquisite propriety" which Lord Byron remarked in his dress, stamped his whole being, and made him appear cool, refined, and debonair among the gentlemen who talked only of sport, which Brummell detested, and smelt of the stable, which Brummell never visited. Lady

Louisa might well be on tenter-hooks to impress Mr. Brummell favourably. Mr. Brummell's good opinion was of the utmost importance in the world of Lady Louisa.

And unless that world fell into ruins his rule seemed assured. Handsome, heartless, and cynical, the Beau seemed invulnerable. His taste was impeccable, his health admirable; and his figure as fine as ever. His rule had lasted many years and survived many vicissitudes. The French Revolution had passed over his head without disordering a single hair. Empires had risen and fallen while he experimented with the crease of a neck-cloth and criticised the cut of a coat. Now the battle of Waterloo had been fought and peace had come. The battle left him untouched; it was the peace that undid him. For some time past he had been winning and losing at the gaming-tables. Harriette Wilson had heard that he was ruined, and then, not without disappointment, that he was safe again. Now, with the armies disbanded, there was let loose upon London a horde of rough, ill-mannered men who had been fighting all those years and were determined to enjoy themselves. They flooded the gaming-houses. They played very high. Brummell was forced into competition. He lost and won and vowed never to play again, and then he did play again. At last his remaining ten thousand pounds was gone. He borrowed until he could borrow no more. And finally, to crown the loss of so many thousands, he lost the six-penny-bit with a hole in it which had always brought him good luck. He gave it by mistake to a hackney coachman: that rascal Rothschild got hold of it, he said, and that was the end of his luck. Such was his own account of the affair—other people put a less innocent interpretation on the matter. At any rate there came a day, 16th May 1816, to be precise—it was a day upon which everything was precise—when he dined alone off a cold fowl and a bottle of claret at Watier's, attended the opera, and then took coach for Dover. He drove rapidly all through the night and reached Calais the day after. He never set foot in England again.

And now a curious process of disintegration set in. The peculiar and highly artificial society of London had acted as a preservative; it had kept him in being; it had concentrated him into one single gem. Now that the pressure was removed, the odds and ends, so trifling separately, so brilliant in combination, which had made up the being

34. Rothschild, head of an enormously rich Jewish family whose exploits were legendary and whose financial powers were international.

of the Beau, fell asunder and revealed what lay beneath. At first his lustre seemed undiminished. His old friends crossed the water to see him and made a point of standing him a dinner and leaving a little present behind them at his bankers. He held his usual levee at his lodgings; he spent the usual hours washing and dressing; he rubbed his teeth with a red root, tweezed out hairs with a silver tweezer, tied his cravat to admiration, and issued at four precisely as perfectly equipped as if the Rue Royale had 10 been St. James's Street and the Prince himself had hung upon his arm. But the Rue Royale was not St. James's Street; the old French Countess who spat on the floor was not the Duchess of Devonshire; the good bourgeois who pressed him to dine off goose at four was not Lord Alvanley; and though he soon won for himself the title of Roi de Calais, and was known to workmen as "George, ring the bell," the praise was gross, the society coarse, and the amusements of Calais very slender. The Beau 20 had to fall back upon the resources of his own mind. These might have been considerable. According to Lady Hester Stanhope, he might have been, had he chosen, a very clever man; and when she told him so, the Beau admitted that he had wasted his talents because a dandy's way of life was the only one "which could place him in a prominent light, and enable him to separate himself from the ordinary herd of men, whom he held in considerable contempt." That way of life allowed of verse- 30 making—his verses, called "The Butterfly's Funeral," were much admired—and of singing, and of some dexterity with the pencil. But now, when the summer days were so long and so empty, he found that such accomplishments hardly served to while away the time. He tried to occupy himself with writing his memoirs; he bought a screen and spent hours pasting it with pictures of great men and beautiful ladies whose virtues and frailties were symbolised by hyenas, by wasps, by profusions 40 of cupids, fitted together with extraordinary skill; he collected Buhl furniture; he wrote letters in a curiously elegant and elaborate style to ladies. But these occupations palled. The resources of his mind had been whittled away in the course of years; now they failed him. And then the crumbling process went a little farther, and another organ was laid bare—the heart. He who had played at love all these years and kept so adroitly beyond the range of passion, now made violent advances to girls who 50 were young enough to be his daughters. He wrote such passionate letters to Mademoiselle Ellen of

23. **Lady Hester Stanhope.** See Lytton Strachey's essay on page 1075.

Caen that she did not know whether to laugh or to be angry. She was angry, and the Beau, who had tyrannised over the daughters of Dukes, prostrated himself before her in despair. But it was too late— the heart after all these years was not a very engaging object even to a simple country girl, and he seems at last to have lavished his affections upon animals. He mourned his terrier Vick for three weeks; he had a friendship with a mouse; he became the champion of all the neglected cats and starving dogs in Caen. Indeed, he said to a lady that if a man and a dog were drowning in the same pond he would prefer to save the dog—if, that is, there were nobody looking. But he was still per-suaded that everybody was looking; and his immense regard for appearances gave him a certain stoical endurance. Thus, when paralysis struck him at dinner he left the table without a sign; sunk deep in debt as he was, he still picked his way over the cobbles on the points of his toes to preserve his shoes, and when the terrible day came and he was thrown into prison he won the admiration of murderers and thieves by appearing among them as cool and courteous as if about to pay a morning call. But if he were to continue to act his part, it was essential that he should be supported—he must have a sufficiency of boot polish, gallons of eau-de-Cologne, and three changes of linen every day. His expenditure upon these items was enormous. Generous as his old friends were, and persistently as he supplicated them, there came a time when they could be squeezed no longer. It was decreed that he was to content himself with one change of linen daily, and his allowance was to admit of necessaries only. But how could a Brummell exist upon necessaries only? The demand was absurd. Soon afterwards he showed his sense of the gravity of the situation by mounting a black silk neck-cloth. Black silk neck-cloths had always been his aversion. It was a signal of despair, a sign that the end was in sight. After that everything that had supported him and kept him in being dissolved. His self-respect vanished. He would dine with any one who would pay the bill. His memory weakened and he told the same story over and over again till even the burghers of Caen were bored. Then his manners degenerated. His extreme cleanliness lapsed into carelessness, and then into positive filth. People objected to his presence in the dining-room of the hotel. Then his mind went—he thought that the Duchess of Devonshire was coming up the stairs when it was only the wind. At last but one passion remained intact among the crumbled debris of so many—an immense greed. To buy Rheims biscuits he sacrificed the greatest treasure that remained to him—he sold his snuff-box. And then nothing was left but a heap of disagreeables, a mass of corruption, a senile and disgusting old man fit only for the charity of nuns and the protection of an asylum. There the clergymen begged him to pray. " 'I do try,' he said, but he added something which made me doubt whether he understood me." Certainly, he would try; for the clergyman wished it and he had always been polite. He had 10 been polite to thieves and to duchesses and to God

Himself. But it was no use trying any longer. He could believe in nothing now except a hot fire, sweet biscuits, and another cup of coffee if he asked for it. And so there was nothing for it but that the Beau who had been compact of grace and sweetness should be shuffled into the grave like any other ill-dressed, ill-bred, unneeded old man. Still, one must remember that Byron, in his moments of dandyism, "always pronounced the name of Brummell with a mingled emotion of respect and jealousy."

James Joyce
1882–1941

James (Augustine Aloysius) Joyce was born in Dublin on February 2, 1882, and educated for the priesthood. For thirteen years he attended the best Jesuit schools in Ireland; his mind was thoroughly disciplined, but not his spirit. At twenty he wrote a blasphemous broadside, left his country, and repudiated his countrymen, "the most belated race in Europe."

From that time his life (according to Herbert Gorman, Joyce's official biographer) became "a constant struggle against terrific odds, prejudices, mob smugness, poverty, and physical disability." His work was censored, officially banned, and even burned; his books, forbidden by several governments, were illicitly published all over the world, and Joyce received no royalties from the pirated publications. He studied medicine in Paris; almost became a professional singer; taught languages in Trieste and Switzerland; wandered about the Continent until he finally settled in Paris. Illness and overwork necessitated ten eye operations in twenty years; Joyce was nearly blind after 1920. Writing was a painful effort for him; a few lines at a time scrawled on a large sheet of paper was all he could manage.

Joyce's literary debut was quiet and undistinguished: *Chamber Music*, 1907, a small volume of pseudo-Elizabethan verse in the traditional lyric manner. His next book marked the beginning of the artist's twofold struggle for recognition and for the right to pursue his own methods—methods which, depending upon the point of view, were lauded as pioneering or attacked as mere arrogance. (When introduced to William Butler Yeats, Joyce is said to have remarked, "We have met too late; you are

too old to be influenced by me.") A contract had been signed for a volume of short stories, *Dubliners*, in Joyce's twenty-fourth year. Six years later the book was still unpublished. Joyce was in Austria. The Irish firm of Maunsel made one objection after another to the book; they wanted names altered, phrases omitted, references canceled. Joyce reluctantly agreed to most of the demands, but the firm was still unsatisfied. They proposed that Joyce delete certain passages and one whole story. After long negotiation, Joyce consented, but the publishers, angered at Joyce's assaults on Dublin respectability, distributed the type and destroyed the books which had been printed. It was not until 1914 (eight years after the manuscript had been accepted) that *Dubliners* was published—in England, not in Ireland.

Such an incident suggests at least one reason for Joyce's self-imposed exile in France and his refusal to join the Celtic movement which was exploiting the "liberation" of Irish culture. *Dubliners*, like Synge's *The Playboy of the Western World*, was too frankly naturalistic for romantic folklorists and myth-lovers. It is significant that though Joyce was an ardent linguist and spoke Italian, German, French, and ten other languages, he never studied Gaelic. Contemplating the subject matter which Joyce transfuses into "the twilight sleep of his novels," Alfred Kazin wrote, "we have the extraordinary spectacle of an Irishman who hates Ireland, and can write of nothing else; a renegade Catholic whose novels owe their exaltation of blasphemy, their convoluted speech and scholastic imagery, to Irish catholicism; a member of the great nationalistic generation who has always despised Ireland's literary nationalism and the cult of the Gaelic, but whose novels, along with the poetry of Yeats, may yet be considered modern Ireland's finest literary testament." [1]

In his early thirties Joyce achieved full independence. *A Portrait of the Artist as a Young Man,* 1916, definitely breaks with tradition. It is a welter of moods and theories, a kaleidoscope of scenes which are both weird and commonplace. Obviously autobiographical, it displays the artist in a losing battle with his environment.

The central character of the *Artist as a Young Man,* Stephen Dedalus, becomes one of the chief figures in Joyce's *Ulysses,* 1922, banned for many years in the United States. *Ulysses,* another autobiographical extension of reality, is one of the strangest novels ever written and one of the most extraordinary works of the age. It is amazingly complex, yet compact. The protean "action," which involves many lives and runs to more than seven hundred crowded pages, takes place in a single day. In style and structure it is unlike anything which preceded it. Although the time background is eighteen hours in Dublin, the associations are epic—the epic from which the book derives its name. *Ulysses* is a macabre transformation of Homer's *Odyssey:* Leopold Bloom is Ulysses, Bloom's father is Tiresias, Paddy Dignam is Elpenor, Mr. Deasy is Nestor, Father Coffey is Cerberus, Mrs. Bloom is Penelope, Gerty MacDowell is Nausicaä, the newspaper office is the Cave of the Winds, the brothel is the court of Circe, the gluttons in the Burton are the Lestrygonians, and so on to the smallest detail of metamorphosis. The book itself is a mammoth exhibition of scholarliness and pornographic caricature, tragedy and horseplay, perverse obscurity and accomplished burlesque—one practically unintelligible chapter is composed of parodies of every style of English writing, from Anglo-Saxon to current journalese. Above all, *Ulysses* shows an unprecedented power of scrutiny joined to an insatiable thirst for analysis. As Herbert Gorman discovered in his first biography (*James Joyce,* 1924), "He left no stone unturned in Dublin, no scandal unexploited, no important personage ignored. Nothing has been left unsaid. It is all there to take or to leave as the reader will. Rabelais is pale beside it. . . . The *Satyricon* is the work of a child (an obscene child) beside it. Not a thought, not even the shadow of a thought, has been left unrevealed." Gorman failed to add that, while Rabelais constructed a world common to all humanity,

Joyce created a world where the crowd was unwelcome and the individual was lost.

Technically *Ulysses* is still a battleground of controversy. It violates all the so-called laws of unity, dispenses with quotation marks, jams together description and conversation, interrupts narratives with abrupt "interior monologues." The last forty-two pages are one long, unpunctuated sentence, an unbroken "stream of consciousness." Concerning this uninhibited record of a common woman's musings, Arnold Bennett wrote, "I have never read anything to surpass it, and I doubt if I have ever read anything to equal it."

With all its difficulties, *Ulysses* is crystal-clear compared to the book which followed. Rumors of the new work startled all but the most devout initiates; it became a legend during the fifteen years of its composition. From 1926 on parts of it appeared under puzzling titles: *Anna Livia Plurabelle,* 1928, *Tales Told of Shem and Shaun,* 1929, *Haveth Childers Everywhere,* 1930, *The Mime of Mick, Nick, and the Maggies,* 1934. Even before these installments were printed various admirers prepared a book of "explanations" succinctly entitled *Our Exagmination Round His Factification for Incamination of Work in Progress.*

When these parts were finally collected and supplemented they were entitled *Finnegan's Wake,* 1939, a work in which nothing was clear except its confusion. Apparently *Finnegan's Wake* was a head-on collision with the language of speech and literature, a colossal series of telescoped expressions that communicate little or nothing to the average reader, a crazy pattern of unknown words that Joyce had made up out of other words. A patient dissection revealed a set of characters who divide into multiple personalities; figures which dissolve into allusions; a nightmare distortion of history and legend, time and space; and a constant irruption of elaborate puns. Opinion was sharply divided: *Finnegan's Wake* was appraised as "literature of the fourth dimension," "the conception of a picture of life which is executed in words which say all things at once," "a triumph of free association," "a stupendous and erudite hoax," "the complete revolution of the word." Summarizing but declining to render a verdict, Clifton Fadiman wrote, "You pays your money and you takes your Joyce."

Dubliners is a naturalistic and impersonal collection in the best tradition of short-story writing. These stories, written by a man in his early twenties, are a proof of the inarticulate made articulate. Most of the people in *Dubliners,* wrote Padraic Colum, "live in little terraces and face the world with a

[1] Alfred Kazin, a review of Herbert S. Gorman's "James Joyce," *New York Herald Tribune: Books,* Feb. 18, 1940.

certain gentility. And those whose stories are the most memorable have been stirred by a look they have taken into the darkness." [1] "Counterparts" and "Ivy Day in the Committee Room" are "bridges" to Joyce's later work. The scenes in Davy Byrne's and Mulligan's pub (in "Counterparts") anticipate similar but more violent episodes in *Ulysses*.

A small library of reference has already grown up about Joyce and his books. The two most illu- [10] minating volumes are Stuart Gilbert's *James Joyce's Ulysses: A Study*, Knopf, 1930, and Herbert Gorman's amplification of his early biography, *James Joyce*, a full and intimate accounting (including extracts from Joyce's notebooks and letter files) published in 1940 by Farrar and Rinehart. Joyce died in Zurich, January 13, 1941.

COUNTERPARTS [2]

THE bell rang furiously and, when Miss Parker went to the tube, a furious voice called out in a piercing North of Ireland accent:

"Send Farrington here!"

Miss Parker returned to her machine, saying to a man who was writing at a desk:

"Mr. Alleyne wants you upstairs."

The man muttered "*Blast* him!" under his breath and pushed back his chair to stand up. When he [30] stood up he was tall and of great bulk. He had a hanging face, dark wine-coloured, with fair eyebrows and moustache: his eyes bulged forward slightly and the whites of them were dirty. He lifted up the counter and, passing by the clients, went out of the office with a heavy step.

He went heavily upstairs until he came to the second landing, where a door bore a brass plate with the inscription *Mr. Alleyne*. Here he halted, puffing with labour and vexation, and knocked. [40] The shrill voice cried:

"Come in!"

The man entered Mr. Alleyne's room. Simultaneously Mr. Alleyne, a little man wearing goldrimmed glasses on a clean-shaven face, shot his head up over a pile of documents. The head itself was so pink and hairless it seemed like a large egg reposing on the papers. Mr. Alleyne did not lose a moment:

"Farrington? What is the meaning of this? Why have I always to complain of you? May I ask you [50] why you haven't made a copy of that contract be-

[1] *Introduction to Dubliners*, Modern Library Edition, 1926.
[2] From *Dubliners* by James Joyce by permission of The Viking Press, Inc.

tween Bodley and Kirwan? I told you it must be ready by four o'clock."

"But Mr. Shelley said, sir—"

"*Mr. Shelley said, sir.* . . . Kindly attend to what I say and not to what *Mr. Shelley says, sir*. You have always some excuse or another for shirking work. Let me tell you that if the contract is not copied before this evening I'll lay the matter before Mr. Crosbie. . . . Do you hear me now?"

"Yes, sir."

"Do you hear me now? . . . Ay and another little matter! I might as well be talking to the wall as talking to you. Understand once for all that you get a half an hour for your lunch and not an hour and a half. How many courses do you want, I'd like to know. . . . Do you mind me now?"

"Yes, sir."

Mr. Alleyne bent his head again upon his pile of papers. The man stared fixedly at the polished [20] skull which directed the affairs of Crosbie & Alleyne, gauging its fragility. A spasm of rage gripped his throat for a few moments and then passed, leaving after it a sharp sensation of thirst. The man recognized the sensation and felt that he must have a good night's drinking. The middle of the month was passed and, if he could get the copy done in time, Mr. Alleyne might give him an order on the cashier. He stood still, gazing fixedly at the head upon the pile of papers. Suddenly Mr. [30] Alleyne began to upset all the papers, searching for something. Then, as if he had been unaware of the man's presence till that moment, he shot up his head again, saying:

"Eh? Are you going to stand there all day? Upon my word, Farrington, you take things easy!"

"I was waiting to see . . ."

"Very good, you needn't wait to see. Go downstairs and do your work."

The man walked heavily towards the door and, [40] as he went out of the room, he heard Mr. Alleyne cry after him that if the contract was not copied by evening Mr. Crosbie would hear of the matter.

He returned to his desk in the lower office and counted the sheets which remained to be copied. He took up his pen and dipped it in the ink, but he continued to stare stupidly at the last words he had written: *In no case shall the said Bernard Bodley be* . . . The evening was falling and in a few minutes they would be lighting the gas: then he could [50] write. He felt that he must slake the thirst in his throat. He stood up from his desk and, lifting the counter as before, passed out of the office. As he was passing out the chief clerk looked at him inquiringly.

"It's all right, Mr. Shelley," said the man, pointing with his finger to indicate the objective of his journey.

The chief clerk glanced at the hat-rack, but, seeing the row complete, offered no remark. As soon as he was on the landing the man pulled a shepherd's plaid cap out of his pocket, put it on his head and ran quickly down the rickety stairs. From the street door he walked on furtively on the inner side of the path towards the corner and all at once dived into a doorway. He was now safe in the dark snug of O'Neill's shop, and, filling up the little window that looked into the bar with his inflamed face, the colour of dark wine or dark meat, he called out:

"Here, Pat, give us a g.p., like a good fellow."

The curate brought him a glass of plain porter. The man drank it at a gulp and asked for a caraway seed. He put his penny on the counter and, leaving the curate to grope for it in the gloom, retreated out of the snug as furtively as he had entered it.

Darkness, accompanied by a thick fog, was gaining upon the dusk of February and the lamps in Eustace Street had been lit. The man went up by the houses until he reached the door of the office, wondering whether he could finish his copy in time. On the stairs a moist pungent odour of perfumes saluted his nose: evidently Miss Delacour had come while he was out in O'Neill's. He crammed his cap back again into his pocket and re-entered the office, assuming an air of absent-mindedness.

"Mr. Alleyne has been calling for you," said the chief clerk severely. "Where were you?"

The man glanced at the two clients who were standing at the counter as if to intimate that their presence prevented him from answering. As the clients were both male the chief clerk allowed himself a laugh.

"I know that game," he said. "Five times in one day is a little bit. . . . Well, you better look sharp and get a copy of our correspondence in the Delacour case for Mr. Alleyne."

This address in the presence of the public, his run upstairs and the porter he had gulped down so hastily confused the man and, as he sat down at his desk to get what was required, he realized how hopeless was the task of finishing his copy of the contract before half-past five. The dark damp night was coming and he longed to spend it in the bars, drinking with his friends amid the glare of gas and the clatter of glasses. He got out the Delacour correspondence and passed out of the office. He hoped

Mr. Alleyne would not discover that the last two letters were missing.

The moist pungent perfume lay all the way up to Mr. Alleyne's room. Miss Delacour was a middle-aged woman of Jewish appearance. Mr. Alleyne was said to be sweet on her or on her money. She came to the office often and stayed a long time when she came. She was sitting beside his desk now in an aroma of perfumes, smoothing the handle of her umbrella and nodding the great black feather in her hat. Mr. Alleyne had swivelled his chair round to face her and thrown his right foot jauntily upon his left knee. The man put the correspondence on the desk and bowed respectfully but neither Mr. Alleyne nor Miss Delacour took any notice of his bow. Mr. Alleyne tapped a finger on the correspondence and then flicked it towards him as if to say: "*That's all right: you can go.*"

The man returned to the lower office and sat down again at his desk. He stared intently at the incomplete phrase: *In no case shall the said Bernard Bodley be* . . . and thought how strange it was that the last three words began with the same letter. The chief clerk began to hurry Miss Parker, saying she would never have the letters typed in time for post. The man listened to the clicking of the machine for a few minutes and then set to work to finish his copy. But his head was not clear and his mind wandered away to the glare and rattle of the public-house. It was a night for hot punches. He struggled on with his copy, but when the clock struck five he had still fourteen pages to write. Blast it! He couldn't finish it in time. He longed to execrate aloud, to bring his fist down on something violently. He was so enraged that he wrote *Bernard Bernard* instead of *Bernard Bodley* and had to begin again on a clean sheet.

He felt strong enough to clear out the whole office single-handed. His body ached to do something, to rush out and revel in violence. All the indignities of his life enraged him. . . . Could he ask the cashier privately for an advance? No, the cashier was no good, no damn good: he wouldn't give an advance. . . . He knew where he would meet the boys: Leonard and O'Halloran and Nosey Flynn. The barometer of his emotional nature was set for a spell of riot.

His imagination had so abstracted him that his name was called twice before he answered. Mr. Alleyne and Miss Delacour were standing outside the counter and all the clerks had turned round in anticipation of something. The man got up from his desk. Mr. Alleyne began a tirade of abuse, saying that two letters were missing. The man an-

---

16. **curate,** ironic slang for bartender.   17–18. **caraway seed,** used, like cloves, to disguise the breath.

swered that he knew nothing about them, that he
had made a faithful copy. The tirade continued:
it was so bitter and violent that the man could
hardly restrain his fist from descending upon the
head of the manikin before him.

"I know nothing about any other two letters,"
he said stupidly.

"*You—know—nothing.* Of course you know nothing," said Mr. Alleyne. "Tell me," he added,
glancing first for approval to the lady beside him,
"do you take me for a fool? Do you think me an
utter fool?"

The man glanced from the lady's face to the little
egg-shaped head and back again; and, almost before
he was aware of it, his tongue had found a felicitous
moment:

"I don't think, sir," he said, "that that's a fair
question to put to me."

There was a pause in the very breathing of the
clerks. Every one was astounded (the author of the
witticism no less than his neighbours) and Miss
Delacour, who was a stout amiable person, began
to smile broadly. Mr. Alleyne flushed to the hue of
a wild rose and his mouth twitched with a dwarf's
passion. He shook his fist in the man's face till it
seemed to vibrate like the knob of some electric
machine:

"You impertinent ruffian! You impertinent
ruffian! I'll make short work of you! Wait till you
see! You'll apologize to me for your impertinence
or you'll quit the office instanter! You'll quit this,
I'm telling you, or you'll apologize to me!"

He stood in a doorway opposite the office,
watching to see if the cashier would come out alone.
All the clerks passed out and finally the cashier
came out with the chief clerk. It was no use trying
to say a word to him when he was with the chief
clerk. The man felt that his position was bad
enough. He had been obliged to offer an abject
apology to Mr. Alleyne for his impertinence, but he
knew what a hornet's nest the office would be for
him. He could remember the way in which Mr.
Alleyne had hounded little Peake out of the office
in order to make room for his own nephew. He felt
savage and thirsty and revengeful, annoyed with
himself and with every one else. Mr. Alleyne would
never give him an hour's rest; his life would be a
hell to him. He had made a proper fool of himself
this time. Could he not keep his tongue in his
cheek? But they had never pulled together from the
first, he and Mr. Alleyne, ever since the day Mr.
Alleyne had overheard him mimicking his North of
Ireland accent to amuse Higgins and Miss Parker:

that had been the beginning of it. He might have
tried Higgins for the money, but sure Higgins never
had anything for himself. A man with two establishments to keep up, of course he couldn't. . . .

He felt his great body again aching for the comfort of the public-house. The fog had begun to chill
him and he wondered could he touch Pat in
O'Neill's. He could not touch him for more than a
bob—and a bob was no use. Yet he must get money
somewhere or other: he had spent his last penny for
the g.p. and soon it would be too late for getting
money anywhere. Suddenly, as he was fingering his
watch chain, he thought of Terry Kelly's pawn-
office in Fleet Street. That was the dart! Why
didn't he think of it sooner?

He went through the narrow alley of Temple Bar
quickly, muttering to himself that they could all go
to hell, because he was going to have a good night
of it. The clerk in Terry Kelly's said *A crown!* but
the consignor held out for six shillings; and in the
end the six shillings was allowed him literally. He
came out of the pawn-office joyfully, making a little
cylinder of the coins between his thumb and fingers. In Westmoreland Street the footpaths were
crowded with young men and women returning
from business, and ragged urchins ran here and
there yelling out the names of the evening editions.
The man passed through the crowd, looking on the
spectacle generally with proud satisfaction and
staring masterfully at the office-girls. His head was
full of the noises of tram-gongs and swishing trolleys
and his nose already sniffed the curling fumes of
punch. As he walked on he preconsidered the terms
in which he would narrate the incident to the boys:

"So, I just looked at him—coolly, you know, and
looked at her. Then I looked back at him again—
taking my time you know. 'I don't think that that's
a fair question to put to me,' says I."

Nosey Flynn was sitting up in his usual corner of
Davy Byrne's and, when he heard the story, he
stood Farrington a half-one, saying it was as smart
a thing as ever he heard. Farrington stood a drink
in his turn. After a while O'Halloran and Paddy
Leonard came in and the story was repeated to
them. O'Halloran stood tailors of malt, hot, all
round and told the story of the retort he had made
to the chief clerk when he was in Callan's of
Fownes's Street; but, as the retort was after the
manner of the liberal shepherds in the eclogues, he
had to admit that it was not as clever as Farrington's retort. At this Farrington told the boys to
polish off that and have another.

Just as they were naming their poisons who
should come in but Higgins! Of course he had to

join in with the others. The men asked him to give his version of it, and he did so with great vivacity, for the sight of five small hot whiskies was very exhilarating. Every one roared laughing when he showed the way in which Mr. Alleyne shook his fist in Farrington's face. Then he imitated Farrington, saying, "*And here was my nabs, as cool as you please,*" while Farrington looked at the company out of his heavy dirty eyes, smiling and at times drawing forth stray drops of liquor from his moustache with the aid of his lower lip.

When that round was over there was a pause. O'Halloran had money, but neither of the other two seemed to have any; so the whole party left the shop somewhat regretfully. At the corner of Duke Street Higgins and Nosey Flynn bevelled off to the left while the other three turned back towards the city. Rain was drizzling down on the cold streets and, when they reached the Ballast Office, Farrington suggested the Scotch House. The bar was full of men and loud with the noise of tongues and glasses. The three men pushed past the whining match-sellers at the door and formed a little party at the corner of the counter. They began to exchange stories. Leonard introduced them to a young fellow named Weathers who was performing at the Tivoli as an acrobat and knockabout *artiste*. Farrington stood a drink all around. Weathers said he would take a small Irish and Apollinaris. Farrington, who had definite notions of what was what, asked the boys would they have an Apollinaris too; but the boys told Tim to make theirs hot. The talk became theatrical. O'Halloran stood a round and then Farrington stood another round, Weathers protesting that the hospitality was too Irish. He promised to get them in behind the scenes and introduce them to some nice girls. O'Halloran said that he and Leonard would go, but that Farrington wouldn't go because he was a married man; and Farrington's heavy dirty eyes leered at the company in token that he understood he was being chaffed. Weathers made them all have just one little tincture at his expense and promised to meet them later on at Mulligan's in Poolbeg Street.

When the Scotch House closed they went round to Mulligan's. They went into the parlour at the back and O'Halloran ordered small hot specials all round. They were all beginning to feel mellow. Farrington was just standing another round when Weathers came back. Much to Farrington's relief he drank a glass of bitter this time. Funds were getting low, but they had enough to keep them going. Presently two young women with big hats and a young man in a check suit came in and sat at a table close by. Weathers saluted them and told the company that they were out of the Tivoli. Farrington's eyes wandered at every moment in the direction of one of the young women. There was something striking in her appearance. An immense scarf of peacock-blue muslin was wound round her hat and knotted in a great bow under her chin; and she wore bright yellow gloves, reaching to the elbow. Farrington gazed admiringly at the plump arm which she moved very often and with much grace; and, when, after a little time, she answered his gaze he admired still more her large dark brown eyes. The oblique staring expression in them fascinated him. She glanced at him once or twice and, when the party was leaving the room, she brushed against his chair and said "*O, pardon!*" in a London accent. He watched her leave the room in the hope that she would look back at him, but he was disappointed. He cursed his want of money and cursed all the rounds he had stood, particularly all the whiskies and Apollinaris which he had stood to Weathers. If there was one thing that he hated it was a sponge. He was so angry that he lost count of the conversation of his friends.

When Paddy Leonard called him he found that they were talking about feats of strength. Weathers was showing his biceps muscle to the company and boasting so much that the other two had called on Farrington to uphold the national honour. Farrington pulled up his sleeve accordingly and showed his biceps muscle to the company. The two arms were examined and compared and finally it was agreed to have a trial of strength. The table was cleared and the two men rested their elbows on it, clasping hands. When Paddy Leonard said "Go!" each was to try to bring down the other's hand on to the table. Farrington looked very serious and determined.

The trial began. After about thirty seconds Weathers brought his opponent's hand slowly down on to the table. Farrington's dark wine-coloured face flushed darker still with anger and humiliation at having been defeated by such a stripling.

"You're not to put the weight of your body behind it. Play fair," he said.

"Who's not playing fair?" said the other.

"Come on again. The two best out of three."

The trial began again. The veins stood out on Farrington's forehead, and the pallor of Weathers' complexion changed to peony. Their hands and arms trembled under the stress. After a long struggle Weathers again brought his opponent's hand slowly on to the table. There was a murmur of applause from the spectators. The curate, who was standing beside the table, nodded his red head towards the victor and said with stupid familiarity:

"Ah! that's the knock!"

"What the hell do you know about it?" said Farrington fiercely, turning on the man. "What do you put in your gab for?"

"Sh, sh!" said O'Halloran, observing the violent expression of Farrington's face. "Pony up, boys. We'll have just one little smahan more and then we'll be off."

A very sullen-faced man stood at the corner of O'Connell Bridge waiting for the little Sandymount tram to take him home. He was full of smouldering anger and revengefulness. He felt humiliated and discontented; he did not even feel drunk; and he had only twopence in his pocket. He cursed everything. He had done for himself in the office, pawned his watch, spent all his money; and he had not even got drunk. He began to feel thirsty again and he longed to be back again in the hot, reeking public-house. He had lost his reputation as a strong man, having been defeated twice by a mere boy. His heart swelled with fury and, when he thought of the woman in the big hat who had brushed against him and said *Pardon!* his fury nearly choked him.

His tram let him down at Shelbourne Road and he steered his great body along in the shadow of the wall of the barracks. He loathed returning to his home. When he went in by the side-door he found the kitchen empty and the kitchen fire nearly out. He bawled upstairs:

"Ada! Ada!"

His wife was a little sharp-faced woman who bullied her husband when he was sober and was bullied by him when he was drunk. They had five children. A little boy came running down the stairs.

"Who is that?" said the man, peering through the darkness.

9. **smahan,** nip.

"Me, pa."

"Who are you? Charlie?"

"No, pa. Tom."

"Where's your mother?"

"She's out at the chapel."

"That's right. . . . Did she **think** of leaving **any** dinner for me?"

"Yes, pa. I——"

"Light the lamp. What do you mean by having the place in darkness? Are the other children in bed?"

The man sat down heavily on one of the chairs while the little boy lit the lamp. He began to mimic his son's flat accent, saying half to himself: "*At the chapel. At the chapel, if you please!*" When the lamp was lit he banged his fist on the table and shouted:

"What's for my dinner?"

"I'm going . . . to cook it, pa," said the little boy.

The man jumped up furiously and pointed to the fire.

"On that fire! You let the fire out! By God, I'll teach you to do that again!"

He took a step to the door and seized the walking-stick which was standing behind it.

"I'll teach you to let the fire out!" he said, rolling up his sleeve in order to give his arm free play.

The little boy cried "*O, pa!*" and ran whimpering round the table, but the man followed him and caught him by the coat. The little boy looked about him wildly but, seeing no way of escape, fell upon his knees.

"Now, you'll let the fire out the next time!" said the man, striking at him vigorously with the stick. "Take that, you little whelp!"

The boy uttered a squeal of pain as the stick cut his thigh. He clasped his hands together in the air and his voice shook with fright.

"O, pa," he cried. "Don't beat me, pa! And I'll . . . I'll say a *Hail Mary* for you. . . . I'll say a *Hail Mary* for you, pa, if you don't beat me. . . . I'll say a *Hail Mary*. . . ."

D. H. Lawrence
1885–1930

D(avid) H(erbert) Lawrence was born on September 11, 1885, at Eastwood, Nottinghamshire. Eastwood is a small colliery town, and Lawrence's father was a coal-miner, who when he was drunk (which was not infrequently) beat his wife and bullied his son. It is little wonder that the child developed an inordinate attachment to his mother, an attachment which is reflected in the autobiographical *Sons and Lovers*, 1913, one of Lawrence's early novels. Escaping the harshness of his environment, he took refuge in books and won a scholarship in the Nottingham high school. At sixteen he became a clerk; at eighteen, while he was still studying, he became a teacher in an elementary school; at nineteen he won another scholarship, but his poverty was such that he could not take advantage of it. At twenty-four a friend, who figures as "Miriam" in *Sons and Lovers*, copied out some of his poems and submitted them for publication. Five of the poems were accepted by Ford Madox Ford, who printed them in the *English Review*. Two years later, sponsored by Ford, Lawrence published his first novel, *The White Peacock*, 1911.

Lawrence had met and fallen in love with a married woman, Mrs. Ernest Weekley, born Baroness Frieda von Richthofen. The two eloped, lived abroad, were married, and came back to England to suffer through the World War. Lawrence was rejected for war service because of his tubercular condition; Frieda was suspected of being a German spy; the couple were harried and hounded throughout the duration of the war.

After the war Lawrence left England and, except for occasional visits, never returned to his homeland. He tried to establish himself in many parts of the world, but nowhere in the universe was he at home. All his life Lawrence was "departing in some rash fashion to some foolish place." He was alternately—and inconsistently—seeking a new world and the poet's lost security, the demolished ivory tower. He yearned for them in Florence, Sicily, Ceylon, Australia, Tahiti, Taos, Mexico, the Riviera—around the world and back again. Wherever he was, Lawrence wanted to be somewhere else.

Meanwhile, during his futile quest for "ultima Thule," Lawrence wrote thirteen novels, including *The Rainbow*, 1915, the most intensely poetic; and *Lady Chatterley's Lover*, 1928, the most openly scandalous; a dozen volumes of short stories; thirteen collections of poems, including a two-volume *Collected Poems*, 1928; four plays; twelve books of essays, three of travel, and a half-dozen translations. Three of the novels were suppressed; an exhibition of his paintings was raided by the police in London (1929); several of his canvases were not only banned but confiscated. Worn out by controversy, weary of travel, undermined in health, he died at Vence, near Nice, on March 2, 1930.

Lawrence's life, his letters, and his creative work are inextricably interknit. In everything he wrote and said his unhappy obsessions persist. He was possessed by and preoccupied with sex; he celebrated an almost fanatic primitivism and worshiped "the hot blood's blindfold art." A prophet of the "dark" subconscious, he glorified mindlessness with all his intellectuality. Suffering is rarely absent from his pages; the books reveal sexual torment and social defeat. The intensity is almost more than the reader can bear. Yet Lawrence's revolt against the intelligence is raised to a pitch of eloquence not attained by any writer of his generation. His great power is the articulation of blind instinct and his exploration of levels touched only by the probing psychoanalyst. As Edwin Muir wrote:

"His spirit is exalted only when it takes fire from his senses; his mind follows the fluctuations of his desires, intellectualizing them, not operating in its own right. . . . And that is because he is on the side of the instincts, and against all the forms, emasculated or deformed, in which they can be manifested in a civilized society." [1]

It is generally conceded that, as a novelist, Lawrence never surpassed *Sons and Lovers* and *The Rainbow*. But his status as a poet has not yet been established. It is as a poet, not as a prophet, that Lawrence is most compelling. His confusions and violences are sublimated in the sheer warmth of his poetry, a poetry which is full of kaleidoscopic images and complete honesty. The sex-fearful, sex-fascinated collier's son condenses a whole novel into the sequence of lyrics entitled "Whether or Not,"

[1] From an essay on D. H. Lawrence in *Transition*. By Edwin Muir. The Viking Press. 1026.

which has the background and idiom, even the dialect, of Lawrence's youth.

Lawrence became a legend in his day. He appeared, faintly disguised, in Osbert Sitwell's *Miracle on Sinai*, 1933; he and Frieda (called "Elsa") are pictured in the pathos of Kay Boyle's "Rest Cure"; he is "Mark Rampion" in Aldous Huxley's *Point Counter Point*, 1928. After his death a whole library of controversial books was written about him; Lawrence seems to have attracted a small army of warring biographers. *Contemporary British Literature*, 1935, lists more than one hundred references, and many more have appeared since the publication of that survey. The critical estimates range all the way from Horace Gregory's poetic interpretation, *Pilgrim of the Apocalypse*, 1933, to William York Tindall's mocking "exposure," *D. H. Lawrence and Susan His Cow*, 1939. No less than ten biographies and reminiscences have been printed. The most illuminating of these are Frieda Lawrence's *Not I, But the Wind*, 1934; Mabel Dodge Luhan's *Lorenzo in Taos*, 1932; and Hugh Kingsmill's *The Life of D. H. Lawrence*, 1938.

LIGHTNING [1]

I felt the lurch and halt of her heart
  Next my breast, where my own heart was beating;
And I laughed to feel it plunge and bound,
And strange in my blood-swept ears was the sound
  Of the words I kept repeating,
Repeating with tightened arms, and the hot blood's
  blindfold art.

Her breath flew warm against my neck,
  Warm as a flame in the close night air;
And the sense of her clinging flesh was sweet
Where her arms and my neck's blood-surge could
  meet.   10
  Holding her thus, did I care
That the black night hid her from me, blotted out
  every speck?

I leaned me forward to find her lips,
  And claim her utterly in a kiss,
When the lightning flew across her face,
And I saw her for the flaring space
  Of a second, like snow that slips
From a roof, inert with death, weeping "Not this!
  Not this!"

[1] This and the following poems are from *The Collected Poems* of D. H. Lawrence, copyright, 1929. Reprinted by permission of The Viking Press, Inc.

A moment there, like snow in the dark
  Her face lay pale against my breast,   20
Pale love lost in a thaw of fear,
And melted in an icy tear,
  And open lips, distressed;
A moment, then darkness shut the lid of the sacred
  ark.

I heard the thunder, and felt the rain,
  And my arms fell loose, and I was dumb.
Almost I hated her, sacrificed;
Hated myself, and the place, and the iced
  Rain that burnt on my rage; saying: "Come
Home, away home, the lightning has made it too
  plain."   30

A YOUTH MOWING

There are four men mowing down by the Isar;
I can hear the swish of the scythe-strokes, four
Sharp breaths taken; yea, and I
Am sorry for what's in store.

The first man out of the four that's mowing
Is mine, I claim him once and for all;
Though it's sorry I am, on his young feet, knowing
None of the trouble he's led to stall.

As he sees me bringing the dinner, he lifts
His head as proud as a deer that looks   10
Shoulder-deep out of the corn; and wipes
His scythe-blade bright, unhooks

The scythe-stone and over the stubble to me.
Lad, thou hast gotten a child in me,
Laddie, a man thou'lt ha'e to be,
Yea, though I'm sorry for thee.

WHETHER OR NOT

I

Dunna thee tell me it's his'n, mother,
  Dunna thee, dunna thee!
—Oh ay, he'll come an' tell thee his-sèn,
  Wench, wunna he?

Tha doesna mean ter say ter me, mother,
  He's gone wi' that—
—My gel, owt'll do for a man i' th' dark;
  Tha's got it flat!

Whether or Not. 3. his-sèn, himself.

But 'er's old, mother, 'er's twenty year
   Older nor him—   10
—Ay, an' yaller as a crowflower; an' yet i' th' dark
   Er'd do for Tim.

Tha niver believes it, does ter, mother?
   It's somebody's lies.
—Ax 'im thy-sèn, wench; a widder's lodger!
   It's no surprise.

2

A widow o' forty-five
Wi' a bitter, dirty skin,
To ha' 'ticed a lad o' twenty-five,
An' 'im to 'ave been took in!   20

A widow of forty-five
As 'as sludged like a horse all 'er life
Till 'er's tough as whit-leather, to slive
Atween a lad an' 'is wife!

A widow of forty-five!
A glum old otchel, wi' long
Witch teeth, an' 'er hawk-eyes, as I've
Mistrusted all along!

An' me as 'as kept my-sèn
Shut like a daisy bud,   30
Clean an' new an' nice, so's when
He wed he'd ha'e summat good!

An' 'im as nice an' fresh
As any man i' th' force,
To ha' gone an' given his clean young flesh
To a woman that coarse!

3

You're stout to brave this snow, Miss Stainwright,
   Are you makin' Brinsley way?
—I'm off up th' line to Underwood
   Wi' a dress as is wanted to-day.   40

Oh, are you goin' to Underwood?
   'Appen then you've 'eered!
—What's that as 'appen I've 'eered on, Missis?
   Speak up, you nedn't be feared.

Why, your young man an' Widow Naylor,
   'Er as 'e lodges wi'!
They say he's got 'er wi' childt; but there—
   It's nothing to do wi' me!

23. to slive, to slip, to interfere.

Though if it's true, they'll turn 'im out
   O' th' p'lice force, without fail;   50
An' if it's *not* true, you may back your life
   They'll listen to *her* tale.

—Well, I'm believin' no tale, Missis,
   I'm seein' for my-sèn.
An' when I know for sure, Missis,
   I'll talk *then*.

4

Nay, robin red-breast, tha needna
   Sit noddin' thy head at me!
My breast's as red as thine, I reckon,
   Flayed red, if tha could but see.   60

Nay, yo' blessed pee-whips,
   Yo' needna scraight at me!
I'm scraightin' my-sèn, but arena goin'
   Ter let iv'rybody see.

Tha *art* smock-ravelled, bunny,
   Larropin' neck an' crop
I' th' snow! but I's warrant thee
   I'm further ower th' top.

5

Now sithee theer at th' reelroad crossin'
Warmin' 'is-sèn at the stool o' fire   70
Under the tank as fills th' ingines,
If there isn't my dearly-beloved liar!

My constable, wi' 'is buttoned breast
As stout as the truth, my Sirs! an' 'is face
As bold as a robin! It's much he cares
For this nice old shame an' disgrace.

Oh, but 'e drops 'is flag when 'e sees me!
Yi, an' 'is face goes white! Oh yes,
Tha can stare at me wi' thy fierce blue eyes;
Tha won't stare me out, I guess.   80

6

Whativer brings thee out so far
   In a' this depth o' snow?
—I'm takin' 'ome a weddin'-dress,
   If yer mun know.

Why, is there a weddin' at Underwood
   As tha ne'd trudge up 'ere?
—It's Widder Naylor's weddin'-dress,
   'Er'll be wantin' it, I 'ear.

62. scraight, cry.   **65. smock-ravelled,** entangled, trapped.

'*Er* doesna want no weddin'-dress—
   Why—? but what dost mean?   90
—Doesn't ter know what I mean, Timmy?
   Yi, tha must ha' bin 'ard ter wean!

Tha'rt a good-un at suckin'-in yet, Timmy!
   But tell me, isn't it true
As 'er'll be wantin' my weddin'-dress
   In a wik or two?

—Tha's no 'casions ter ha'e me on,
   Lizzie; what's done is done.
—*Done*, I should think so! An' might I ask
   When tha begun?   100

It's thee as 'as done it, as much as me,
   So there, an' I tell thee flat.
—Me gotten a childt ter thy landlady?
   —Tha's gotten thy answer pat.

As tha allus 'ast; but let me tell thee
   Hasna ter sent me whoam, when I
Was a'most burstin' mad o' my-sèn,
   An' walkin' in agony?

After I'd kissed thee at night, Lizzie,
   An' tha's laid against me, an' melted   110
Into me, melted right into me, Lizzie,
   Till I was verily swelted.

An' if my landlady seed me like it,
   An' if 'er clawkin' eyes
Went through me as the light went out,
   Is it any cause for surprise?

—No cause for surprise at all, my lad;
   After kissin' an' cuddlin' wi' me, tha could
Turn thy mouth on a woman like that!
   I hope it did thee good.   120

—Ay, it did; but afterwards
   I could ha' killed 'er.
—Afterwards! how many times afterwards
   Could ter ha' killed 'er?

Say no more, Liz, dunna thee;
   'Er's as good as thee.
—Then I'll say good-bye to thee, Timothy;
   Take 'er i'stead o' me.

I'll ta'e thy word good-bye, Liz,
   Though I shonna marry 'er.   130
Nor 'er nor nub'dy.—It is
   Very brave of you, Sir!

106. **whoam**, home.   114. **clawkin'**, snatching.

—T' childt maun ta'e its luck, it mun,
   An' 'er maun ta'e '*er* luck.
F'r I tell yer I h'arena marryin' none
   On yer; yo'n got what yer took!

—That's spoken like a man, Timmy,
   That's spoken like a man!
"'E up an' fired 'is pistol,
   An' then away 'e ran!"   140

—I damn well shanna marry 'er,
   Nor yo', so chew it no more!
I'll chuck the flamin' lot o' you—
   —Yer nedn't 'ave swore!

7

There's 'is collar round th' candlestick,
An' there's the dark-blue tie I bought 'im!
An' these is the woman's kids 'es's so fond on,
An' 'ere comes the cat as caught 'im!

I dunno wheer 'is eyes was—a gret
Round-shouldered hag! My Sirs, to think   150
Of 'im stoopin' to 'er! You'd wonder 'e could
Throw 'imself down *that* sink!

I expect yer know who I am, Mrs. Naylor?
   —Who y'are? yis, you're Lizzie Stainwright.
An' 'appen you'd guess then what I've come for?
   —'Appen I mightn't, 'appen I might.

Yer knowed as I was courtin' Tim Merfin?
   —Yis, I knowed 'e wor courtin' thee.
An' yet yer've bin carryin' on wi' 'im!
   —Ay, an' 'im wi' me.   160

Well, now yer've got ter pay for it.
   —If I han, what's that ter thee?
'E isn't goin' ter marry yer.
   —Tha wants 'im thy-sèn, I see.

It 'asn't nothin' to do with me.
   —Then what art colleyfoglin' for?
I'm not 'avin' your orts an' slarts.
   —Which on us said you wor?

But I want you to know 'e's not *marryin'* you.
   —Tha wants 'im thy-sèn too bad.   170
Though I'll see as 'e pays you, an' does what's right.
   —Tha'rt for doin' a lot wi't' lad!

166. **colleyfoglin'**, carrying on.   167. **orts an' slarts**, leftovers, scraps.

8

To think I should 'ave ter 'affle an' caffle
    Wi' a woman, an' name 'er a price
For lettin' me marry the lad as I thought
    Ter marry wi' cabs an' rice!

But we'll go unbeknown ter th' registrar,
    An' give 'er the money there is;
For I won't be beholden to such as 'er,
    I won't, or my name's not Liz.   180

9

Ta'e off thy duty stripes, Tim,
    An' come in 'ere wi' me;
Ta'e off thy p'liceman's helmet
    An' look at me.

I wish tha hadna done it, Tim,
    I do, an' that I do!
For whenever I look thee i' th' face, I s'll see
    Her face too.

I wish I could wesh 'er off'n thee;
    'Appen I can, if I try.   190
But tha'll ha'e ter promise ter be true ter me
    Till I die. . . .

10

Twenty pounds o' thy own tha hast, an' fifty pound
    ha'e I;
Thine shall go ter pay the woman, an' wi' my bit
    we'll buy
All as we s'll want for furniture when tha leaves this
    place;
An' we'll be married at th' registrar—now lift thy
    face.

Lift thy face an' look at me, man! canna ter look at
    me?
Sorry I am for this business, an' sorry if ever I've
    driven thee
To do such a thing; though it's a poor tale, it is,
    that I'm bound to say,
Afore I can ta'e thee I've got a widder o' forty-five
    ter pay!   200

Dunnat thee think but what I've loved thee; I've
    loved thee too well.
An' 'deed an' I wish as this tale o' thine wor niver
    my tale to tell!
Deed an' I wish I c'd 'a' stood at th' altar wi' thee
    an' bin proud o' thee!
That I could 'a' bin first woman ter thee, as tha'rt
    first man ter me!

173. **'affle an' caffle,** bargain.

But we maun ma'e the best on't. So now rouse up
    an' look at me.
Look up an' say tha'rt sorry tha did it; say tha'rt
    sorry for me.
They'll turn thee out o' th' force, I doubt me; if
    they do, we can see
If my father can get thee a job on t'bank. Say tha'rt
    sorry, Timmy!

11

Ay, I'm sorry, I'm sorry,
    But what o' that!   210
Ay, I'm sorry! Tha needna worry
    Nor fret thy fat.

I'm sorry for thee, I'm sorry f'r 'er,
    I'm sorry f'r us a'.
But what then? Tha wants me, does ter
    After a'?

Ah'n put my-sèn i' th' wrong, Liz,
    An' 'er as well.
An' tha'rt that right, tha knows; 'tis
    Other folks in hell.   220

Tha *art* so sure tha'rt right, Liz!
    That damned sure!
But 'ark thee 'ere, that widder woman
    's less graspin', if 'er's poor.

What 'er gen, 'er gen me
    Beout a thought.
'Er gen me summat; I shanna
    Say it wor nought.

I'm sorry for th' trouble, ay
    As comes on us a'.   230
But sorry for what I had? why
    I'm not, that's a'.

As for marryin', I shanna marry
    Neither on yer.
Ah've 'ad a' as I can carry
    From you an' from 'er.

So I s'll go an' leave yer,
    Both on yer.
I don't like yer, Liz, I want ter
    Get away from yer.   240

212. fret thy fat, disturb yourself. **225. gen, gave.
226. Beout,** without.

An' I really like 'er neither,
　　Even though I've 'ad
More from 'er than from you; but either
　　Of yer's too much for this lad.

Let me go! what's good o' talkin'?
　　Let's a' ha' done.

Talk about love o' women!
　　Ter me it's no fun. . . .

I s'll say good-bye, Liz, to yer,
　　Yer too much i' th' right for me.　　250
An' wi' 'er somehow it isn't right.
　　So good-bye, an' let's let be!

Harold Nicolson
1886–

Harold (George) Nicolson was born in 1886 at Teheran, Persia, where his father, Sir Arthur Nicolson (later Baron Carnock), was chargé d'affaires. His early childhood was spent wherever the diplomatic service took his father: Persia, Turkey, Hungary, Bulgaria, Morocco. His formal education began at Wellington College, extended to Balliol, Oxford, where Nicolson took his M.A., and so to the Foreign Office. For twenty years (from 1909 to 1929) he was a popular diplomat in various capitals, where he acted largely as expert in Balkan affairs.

In 1929 Nicolson resigned from the diplomatic service, and a few months later joined the editorial staff of the London *Evening Standard*. He had already written four literary studies—*Paul Verlaine*, 1921; *Tennyson*, 1923; *Byron: The Last Journey*, 1924; and *Swinburne*, 1926—but now he devoted himself to a series of "indirect biographies." Differing from the formal or "pure" biography on the one hand and the half-poetic, half-psychoanalytical study on the other, Nicolson began writing contemporary history thinly veiled as fiction. Objective yet not altogether detached, he gave a gradually detailed picture of his times—and, more than incidentally, of himself—in such studies in diplomacy as the portrait of his father, *Sir Arthur Nicolson: First Lord Carnock*, 1930; *Peacemaking*, 1933; *Curzon: The Last Phase*, 1934; *Helen's Tower*, 1937, an account of his childhood through memories of his uncle, Lord Dufferin; in the incisive, pseudo-fictional *Some People*, 1926; and even in the collection of light essays *Small Talk*, 1937.

It is from the last volume that "The Edwardian Week-end" is reprinted. This delightful bit of reminiscence, nostalgic and malicious, is amplified in *The Edwardians*, written by his wife, V. Sackville-West, poet and novelist, "hero-heroine" of Virginia Woolf's *Orlando*.

THE EDWARDIAN WEEK-END [1]

THE Edwardian age will, we may presume, live in history as an age of comfort. *It was not.* It was an age of fevered luxury; at the same time it was an age of peculiar human ineptitude. People possessed false values, and they endeavoured, fortunately without success, to impose these values upon their children. The whole glittering decade passed in an atmosphere of plethoric friction. It is time that the jade and lobster of the Edwardian epoch were exposed.

In the first place, they ate excessively and competitively. No age, since that of Nero, can show such unlimited addiction to food. People were called by their valets at eight-thirty. These silent but hostile men would arrive bearing in their left hand a neat brass can of shaving water, and in their right hand a neat brass tray of tea, toast, and Marie biscuits. The Edwardian, blinking plethoric eyes above his pink silk eiderdown, would munch the biscuits and would sip the tea. He would then adjust his teeth, adjust his hair, adjust his Afghan dressing-robe, and slouch plethoric along the passage to the bathroom. If he were staying in a rich house (and all houses in the Edwardian epoch were rich), he would find in the bathroom the scented smell of his predecessor's indulgence, the half-empty bottles ("flacons" was the word they used) which contained Hammam Bouquet of Mr. Penthalicon. The guest would pour this unguent into the bath, from which his valet would already have removed the stains, the soapsuds and the other *disjecta membra* of the former occupant. The water would be tepid. Edwardian water was always tepid. The soap would also be tepid. His predecessor had left his signet ring in the soap-dish. Through the smell of Hammam Bouquet

[1] From *Small Talk* by Harold Nicolson, copyright, 1937, by Harcourt, Brace and Company, Inc.　**8. plethoric,** inflated.　**30. disjecta membra,** literally "scattered limbs."

would gradually pierce the smell of lavender bags and Sanitas. Disgusted and dyspeptic, the Edwardian would proceed with his bath. He shaved in it. All Edwardians, being at heart dirty folk, shaved in their baths.

When he returned to his bedroom, along the red pile carpet which marked the unending symmetry of the corridor, he would find that the windows had been slightly opened, and that his clothes had been laid ready for him upon the chintz settee. Taking a Régie cigarette from his Fabergé case he would contemplate these clothes with satisfaction. If he were a good Edwardian his shirt and collar would be all in one. A white shirt, somewhat frilled and tucked on the breast, ending in a stiff little upturned collar. Hard, expectant, circular—that collar would shortly encase his neck. Alternatively a Piccadilly collar of equal rigidity would be waiting for him on the dressing-table. Black clothes; a grey silk tie; a neat turquoise pin representing a pheasant walking slowly from left to right; a white cambric handkerchief; a dab of eau-de-Cologne; his purse; his card case; the smell of Euchrisma as he brushed his hair. Then he descended, down red pile staircases, to breakfast.

Only the really improper Edwardians had breakfast in their rooms. The others met, on that Sunday morning, in the dining-room. The smell of last night's port had given place to the smell of this morning's spirits of wine. Rows of little spirit-lamps warmed rows of large silver dishes. On a table to the right between the windows were grouped Hams, Tongues, Galantines, Cold Grouse, ditto Pheasant, ditto Partridge, ditto Ptarmigan. No Edwardian meal was complete without Ptarmigan. Hot or Cold. Just Ptarmigan. There would also be a little delicate rectangle of pressed beef from the shop of M. Benoist. On a further table, to the left between the doors, stood fruits of different calibre, and jugs of cold water, and jugs of lemonade. A fourth table contained porridge utensils. A fifth coffee, and pots of Indian and China tea. The latter were differentiated from each other by little ribbons of yellow (indicating China) and of red (indicating, without *arrière pensée*, our Indian Empire). The centre table, which was prepared for twenty-three people, would be bright with Malmaisons and toast-racks. No newspapers were, at that stage, allowed.

The atmosphere of the Edwardian dining-room at nine-thirty was essentially daring. A pleasant sense of confederacy and sin hung above the smell of the spirit-lamps. For had they not all been brought up to attend family prayers? And had they not all eluded that obligation? It was true, of course, that the host and hostess, with their niece, had at nine proceeded to the family chapel and heard the butler reading a short collect for the day. But the guests had for their part evaded these Victorian obligations. This corporate evasion gave to the proceedings an atmosphere of dash. There was no insincerity in the bright gaiety with which they greeted each other, with which they discussed how he or she had slept. "A little kedjiree, Lady Maude?" "Oh, thank you, Mr. Stapleton." Evidently it was all going very well.

Edwardian breakfasts were in no sense a hurried proceeding. The porridge was disposed of negligently, people walking about and watching the rain descend upon the Italian garden. Then would come whiting and omelette and devilled kidneys and little fishy messes in shells. And then tongue and ham and a slice of Ptarmigan. And then scones and honey and marmalade. And then a little melon, and a nectarine or two, and just one or two of those delicious raspberries. The men at that stage would drift (I employ the accepted term) to the smoking-room. The women would idle in the saloon watching the rain descend upon the Italian garden. It was then 10:30.

If the house possessed no private chapel (not all Edwardian houses possessed private chapels) the guests would then "assemble in the hall." There would be footmen fussing about in cockaded top-hats and long buff overcoats with gold buttons. A degree of jollity would be extracted from the process of deciding who would drive in the wagonette, who in the landau, who in the Victoria, who in the brougham. And who should walk. The latter category seized umbrellas and capes. People jingled off, clasping their prayer-books and the half-crown for the offertory. From the side door the children, wide-eyed and washed, would appear with their governesses. They crossed the park to the church beyond lodge.

With fervour would these Edwardians sing the psalms and the hymns, with reverence would they listen to the stories from the Old Testament. The smell of leather and wet mackintosh would permeate the damp little church. Every now and then an umbrella would tumble from a pew. The final benediction descended upon rows of bowed heads. The ladies' hats were rich with artificial flowers; the heads of the men were rich with the smell of Eu-

23. **Euchrisma,** a perfumed hair lotion.   45. **arrière pensée,** undisclosed reference, mental reservation.   47. **Malmaisons,** carnations.

12. **kedjiree,** an Indian dish composed of rice, butter, eggs, and spices; in England, a mixture of the above plus fish.

chrisma. They walked back to luncheon under dripping trees.

The half-hour before luncheon hung a little heavy on their hands. The women would repair to their rooms and deal with their hair and faces. The men would gather in the library, where they would shortly be joined by the curate, or, as the case might be, the house chaplain. A shy little man this, not knowing all these London people, not very certain how to modulate his voice. The younger men would come in later, having changed into tweeds. Great bowls of orchids and chrysanthemums were massed on the tables. There were silver vases of white roses, and cut glass vases in which the roses were red. The hostess, passing from group to group, would flick irritable emerald-laden fingers at these flowers, tugging them into different shapes. They would pass in to luncheon. The curate, hanging behind, would hang behind.

Edwardian luncheons were strained and bright. There was a theory that the good hostess should "draw her guests into conversation." This entailed a process of flinging conversational flies across the vast table and not waiting to see if the fish rose. "Colonel Westmacott, you simply must tell us about the Zambesi," and "Oh, Clara! Is it really true that dearest Evy has got to go to Nauheim?" There was a buzz of general talk. It would only be a buzz.

After luncheon they walked round the park. They did not visit the stables. Since the introduction of motors, the stables had become Victorian. The elder members of the party would drive over to Stonehenge in an open Daimler. They appeared, aged and flustered, in motoring veils of watered silk. Colonel Westmacott, in a tweed cape and spats, stumped off with Lady Moira to visit the quarries. Captain Fairfax took Miss Sinclair a drive in his De Dion. Professor Steinholtz slept.

Tea was served in the blue gallery. There were little ginger biscuits which one could only get from Biarritz and of which one kept a store in case the King came. All Edwardian houses kept stores of things like ginger biscuits and aubergines and French patissiers and bath salts in case the King came. And he did come. He came over and over again. And on Monday morning other people would read all about it in *The Morning Post*. It was only, however, when the King actually did come that one went so far as to have lobster salad for tea. Otherwise one just had scones, and egg sandwiches, and paté sandwiches and cucumber sandwiches, and chocolate cake, and walnut cake, and coffee cake, and cake. Also there were little plates,

with china-handled knives to match, from which people ate Tiptree jam with toast or brioches. The butler, the groom of the chambers, the under-butler and the footmen would move about offering food. But in the best houses (and most Edwardian houses were the best) the servants did not remain for tea.

After tea there would be bridge tables in the red drawing-room, and the men would not infrequently play billiards. Dinner was at half-past eight. The women would retire an hour before to change their tea-gowns for the other things which they donned to dine. The men also would change into clothes even more galling and restrictive than those they had worn all day. The guests would reassemble in the yellow saloon. The host by this time was already bored by his party, and would indicate a little irritably who was to take in whom. He held a fussy little piece of paper in his hand and would fuss from one man to another. The women, one by one, entered the room slowly, showing off their clothes. Then there would be dinner. Ptarmigan and champagne. Champagne and Ptarmigan. The hostess did not endeavour to stimulate general conversation at dinner. One only did that at luncheon. At dinner people talked, inclining their neat bodies sideways, to their neighbours. At nine forty-five the women swept, with backward glances, from the room. The host would take his glass of port, holding it with gingerly fingers from above, and move to the seat vacated by his wife. At ten-fifteen they joined the ladies in the music-gallery.

Bridge again. And at midnight, in the Holbein room, there would be devilled chicken, and more sandwiches, and every form of spirit and mineral water which man or woman could desire. In the corridors upstairs the ladies-maids would hang listlessly yawning. Fires would sparkle in the grates, reflected in brass bedstead and in mirror. The pink-silk reading-lamps were lit beside the beds. Upon the night-table stood bottles of Malvern Water and of Vichy, covered dishes of sandwiches. A ribboned coverlet of swans-down would be draped across the sofa. The kettle, by the fireplace, purred.

Next morning their valets would pack their Enos and their shooting-sticks. They would return by train to London. Their carriages would meet them, horses champing bits, at the arrival platform of Paddington. In the train coming up the members of the house-party would read in *The Morning Post* a list of the members of the house-party. They returned to Curzon Street feeling very pleased indeed. And next Saturday it would all begin again. . . .

2. brioches, light yeast-dough rolls popular in France.

43. **aubergines,** eggplant.   44. **patissiers,** pastry cooks.   44. **Enos,** laxative fruit salts.

Katherine Mansfield
1888–1923

Katherine Mansfield was born Kathleen Beauchamp near Wellington, New Zealand, on October 14, 1888. Third daughter of an eminent banker, Sir Harold Beauchamp, she was brought up in more than ordinary comfort. (Several charming episodes of her New Zealand childhood are recorded in *The Scrapbook of Katherine Mansfield*, 1940, which her husband published sixteen years after her death.) Even before she reached her teens, it was apparent that she would be a writer; her first story appeared in the magazine of Wellington Girls' College when she was nine. A little later she "published" a school magazine which she wrote out in longhand. Between her fourteenth and eighteenth years she was in England, where she attended Queen's College and edited the college paper. She returned to New Zealand in 1906 and, adopting the pseudonym by which she became known, contributed a series of articles to *The Native Companion*. But she was not happy. The hypersensitivity and restlessness which grew with the years was already taking possession of her. An inadequate allowance from her father increased her sense of lack; she craved isolation and dreaded it; she wanted opposites with stubborn intensity.

In her twentieth year she was allowed to return to England. But she would not stay in London. An excellent amateur musician, she joined a traveling opera company. But the hardships of "the road" were too much for her. The first of her breakdowns occurred, and, from that time on, she struggled between physical and mental distress, between actual illness and brooding neuroticism. She went to Germany for her health, and there she wrote "In a German Pension," which was printed by A. R. Orage in *The New Age*, 1911. Through Orage she met J. Middleton Murry, with whom she became associated on a literary review entitled *Rhythm*. Two years later (in 1913) she and Murry were married. With him and D. H. Lawrence she founded *Signature*, to which she made many contributions under a new pseudonym: "Matilda Berry."

By this time she was working under great stress. The World War intensified her nervous fears; she continually diagnosed herself for heart disease; the death of her brother at the front almost killed her, and she lived, she said, to write and justify him. Her *Journal* declared:

"I want to write about my own country till I simply exhaust my store. Not only because it is a 'sacred debt' that I pay to my country because my brother and I were born there, but also because in my thoughts I range with him over all the remembered places."

She wandered unhappily about Europe, coughing and changing one unpleasant lodging for another. She identified herself with two literary fellow sufferers, Chekhov and Keats, both of them tubercular, and, "reading between the lines" of their letters, she found affinities of thought and a conviction of doom. She fluctuated between England and France, finding peace nowhere. She was lonely, disillusioned in love, full of dread. She became overobservant and, in consequence, overwrought. She felt lost without Murry, and she was miserable with him.

"A day passed in the usual violent agitation such as J. only can fling me into. . . . At such times I feel I could never get well with him. It's like having a cannon-ball tied to one's feet when one is trying not to drown."

She retreated to Bandol, the Riviera, Italy, Switzerland, all to no avail. From Orage she learned of a place where her illness might be cured by "spiritual discipline." She attempted a kind of regeneration at the "brotherhood" in France, a final effort to purge herself of "the last trace of earthly degradation." She wanted to win back health in every sense—"to be rooted in life; to learn, to desire, to know, to feel, to think, to act." Here, at this combination of school and nursing home, following a way of life prescribed by Gurdjeff, she became calmer, but her physical condition grew worse. Her already wasted energy suddenly deserted her. She died of a violent hemorrhage January 9, 1923, at Fontainebleau.

The posthumous *Journal of Katherine Mansfield*, 1927, and *Letters of Katherine Mansfield*, 1928, both of which were edited by J. Middleton Murry, betray the sick woman whose illness exaggerated her intuitive state and intensified overwrought sensibilities. But they also reveal the tenderness and poignance which made her so sensitive. Hers was an understanding spirit, delicate, keen, seemingly detached and deeply emotional. She knew "the moment of direct feeling when we are most ourselves and least personal."

The person and the author were inseparable. She had a passion for perfection and destroyed much of her work, including the records of several years in "huge complaining diaries." Like her spirit, her work was frail but exquisite. She understood her limitations, but she was not inhibited by them. Following Chekhov, her greatest influence, she aimed at a literature which would be "an initiation into truth."

Almost all of Katherine Mansfield's work shows this dedication to truth in the smallest details of phrase and gesture. One remembers the evocations of mood and "atmosphere," the sharp stroke of characterization, rather than the narratives, in *Bliss*, 1920; *The Garden Party*, 1922; *The Doves' Nest*, 1923. Nowhere is her subtlety more skillfully employed than in "The Daughters of the Late Colonel." Here neurotic reality is achieved by fine nuances of implications, by the very blurring of the actual event and the train of memories it sets in motion. By suggestion and flashes into the past—flashes that are unprepared but perfectly convincing—a series of lives are revealed: the fluttering sisters living on frustrated dreams and genteel poverty; Kate, the domestic dragon, whom they dare not discharge; Nurse Andrews, whose affectations "point" the scene and whose concern with the butter emphasizes the situation; Cyril, the grandson, whose embarrassed casualness contrasts with the painful ceremoniousness of his worried aunts; and the old Colonel who, even in death, irascibly dominates them all. A tragicomic novel has been condensed into significant episodes and expressed in states of poignant sensibility.

Katherine Mansfield died prematurely at thirty-four; but she was not defeated. The woman struggled and lost; the artist survived. Her intensity triumphed in a few books which startle the reader with their swift illuminations. Her work as a writer, summarized Louis Kronenberger, "was an endless stalking of feelings, perceptions, language; it revealed—whatever its limitations, either in impulse or achievement—that amoral integrity which is the peculiar mark of the artist." [1]

[1] "Katherine Mansfield, a Review," *Nation*, Feb. 10, 1940.

THE DAUGHTERS OF THE LATE COLONEL [1]

I

THE week after was one of the busiest weeks of their lives. Even when they went to bed it was only their bodies that lay down and rested; their minds went on, thinking things out, talking things over, wondering, deciding, trying to remember where . . .

Constantia lay like a statue, her hands by her sides, her feet just overlapping each other, the sheet up to her chin. She stared at the ceiling.

"Do you think father would mind if we gave his top-hat to the porter?"

"The porter?" snapped Josephine. "Why ever the porter? What a very extraordinary idea!"

"Because," said Constantia slowly, "he must often have to go to funerals. And I noticed at—at the cemetery that he only had a bowler." She paused. "I thought then how very much he'd appreciate a top-hat. We ought to give him a present, too. He was always very nice to father."

"But," cried Josephine, flouncing on her pillow and staring across the dark at Constantia, "father's head!" And suddenly, for one awful moment, she nearly giggled. Not, of course, that she felt in the least like giggling. It must have been habit. Years ago, when they had stayed awake at night talking, their beds had simply heaved. And now the porter's head, disappearing, popped out, like a candle, under father's hat. . . . The giggle mounted, mounted; she clenched her hands; she fought it down; she frowned fiercely at the dark and said "Remember" terribly sternly.

"We can decide to-morrow," she sighed.

Constantia had noticed nothing; she sighed.

"Do you think we ought to have our dressing-gowns dyed as well?"

"Black?" almost shrieked Josephine.

"Well, what else?" said Constantia. "I was thinking—it doesn't seem quite sincere, in a way, to wear black out of doors and when we're fully dressed, and then when we're at home——"

"But nobody sees us," said Josephine. She gave the bedclothes such a twitch that both her feet became uncovered, and she had to creep up the pillows to get them well under again.

"Kate does," said Constantia. "And the postman very well might."

Josephine thought of her dark-red slippers, which

[1] From *The Garden Party* by Katherine Mansfield, copyright, 1922, by Alfred A. Knopf, Inc.

matched her dressing-gown, and of Constantia's favourite indefinite green ones which went with hers. Black! Two black dressing-gowns and two pairs of black woolly slippers, creeping off to the bathroom like black cats.

"I don't think it's absolutely necessary," said she.

Silence. Then Constantia said, "We shall have to post the papers with the notice in them to-morrow to catch the Ceylon mail. . . . How many letters have we had up till now?"

"Twenty-three."

Josephine had replied to them all, and twenty-three times when she came to "We miss our dear father so much" she had broken down and had to use her handkerchief, and on some of them even to soak up a very light-blue tear with an edge of blotting-paper. Strange! She couldn't have put it on—but twenty-three times. Even now, though, when she said over to herself sadly, "We miss our dear father *so* much" she could have cried if she'd wanted to.

"Have you got enough stamps?" came from Constantia.

"Oh, how can I tell?" said Josephine crossly. "What's the good of asking me that now?"

"I was just wondering," said Constantia mildly.

Silence again. There came a little rustle, a scurry, a hop.

"A mouse," said Constantia.

"It can't be a mouse because there aren't any crumbs," said Josephine.

"But it doesn't know there aren't," said Constantia.

A spasm of pity squeezed her heart. Poor little thing! She wished she'd left a tiny piece of biscuit on the dressing-table. It was awful to think of it not finding anything. What would it do?

"I can't think how they manage to live at all," she said slowly.

"Who?" demanded Josephine.

And Constantia said more loudly than she meant to, "Mice."

Josephine was furious. "Oh, what nonsense, Con!" she said. "What have mice got to do with it? You're asleep."

"I don't think I am," said Constantia. She shut her eyes to make sure. She was.

Josephine arched her spine, pulled up her knees, folded her arms so that her fists came under her ears, and pressed her cheek hard against the pillow.

2

Another thing which complicated matters was they had Nurse Andrews staying on with them that week. It was their own fault; they had asked her. It was Josephine's idea. On the morning—well, on the last morning, when the doctor had gone, Josephine had said to Constantia, "Don't you think it would be rather nice if we asked Nurse Andrews to stay on for a week as our guest?"

"Very nice," said Constantia.

"I thought," went on Josephine quickly, "I should just say this afternoon, after I've paid her, 'My sister and I would be very pleased, after all you've done for us, Nurse Andrews, if you would stay on for a week as our guest.' I'd have to put that in about being our guest in case——"

"Oh, but she could hardly expect to be paid!" cried Constantia.

"One never knows," said Josephine sagely.

Nurse Andrews had, of course, jumped at the idea. But it was a bother. It meant they had to have regular sit-down meals at the proper times, whereas if they'd been alone they could just have asked Kate if she wouldn't have minded bringing them a tray wherever they were. And meal-times now that the strain was over were rather a trial.

Nurse Andrews was simply fearful about butter. Really they couldn't help feeling that about butter, at least, she took advantage of their kindness. And she had that maddening habit of asking for just an inch more bread to finish what she had on her plate, and then, at the last mouthful, absent-mindedly—of course it wasn't absent-mindedly—taking another helping. Josephine got very red when this happened, and she fastened her small, bead-like eyes on the tablecloth as if she saw a minute strange insect creeping through the web of it. But Constantia's long, pale face lengthened and set, and she gazed away—away—far over the desert, to where that line of camels unwound like a thread of wool. . . .

"When I was with Lady Tukes," said Nurse Andrews, "she had such a dainty little contrayvance for the buttah. It was a silvah Cupid balanced on the—on the bordah of a glass dish, holding a tayny fork. And when you wanted some buttah you simply pressed his foot and he bent down and speared you a piece. It was quite a gayme."

Josephine could hardly bear that. But "I think those things are very extravagant" was all she said.

"But whey?" asked Nurse Andrews, beaming through her eyeglasses. "No one, surely, would take more buttah than one wanted—would one?"

"Ring, Con," cried Josephine. She couldn't trust herself to reply.

And proud young Kate, the enchanted princess, came in to see what the old tabbies wanted now. She snatched away their plates of mock something or other and slapped down a white, terrified blanc-mange.

"Jam, please, Kate," said Josephine kindly.

Kate knelt and burst open the sideboard, lifted the lid of the jam-pot, saw it was empty, put it on the table, and stalked off.

"I'm afraid," said Nurse Andrews a moment later, "there isn't any."

"Oh, what a bother!" said Josephine. She bit her lip. "What had we better do?"

Constantia looked dubious. "We can't disturb Kate again," she said softly.

Nurse Andrews waited, smiling at them both. Her eyes wandered, spying at everything behind her eye-glasses. Constantia in despair went back to her camels. Josephine frowned heavily—concentrated. If it hadn't been for this idiotic woman she and Con would, of course, have eaten their blanc-mange without. Suddenly the idea came.

"I know," she said. "Marmalade. There's some 20 marmalade in the sideboard. Get it, Con."

"I hope," laughed Nurse Andrews, and her laugh was like a spoon tinkling against a medicine-glass—"I hope it's not very bittah marmalayde."

3

But, after all, it was not long now, and then she'd be gone for good. And there was no getting over the fact that she had been very kind to father. She had nursed him day and night at the end. Indeed, both 30 Constantia and Josephine felt privately she had rather overdone the not leaving him at the very last. For when they had gone in to say good-bye Nurse Andrews had sat beside his bed the whole time, holding his wrist and pretending to look at her watch. It couldn't have been necessary. It was so tactless, too. Supposing father had wanted to say something—something private to them. Not that he had. Oh, far from it! He lay there, purple, a dark, angry purple in the face, and never even looked at 40 them when they came in. Then, as they were standing there, wondering what to do, he had suddenly opened one eye. Oh, what a difference it would have made, what a difference to their memory of him, how much easier to tell people about it, if he had only opened both! But no—one eye only. It glared at them a moment and then . . . went out.

4

It had made it very awkward for them when Mr. Farolles, of St. John's, called the same after-noon.

"The end was quite peaceful, I trust?" were the first words he said as he glided towards them through the dark drawing-room.

"Quite," said Josephine faintly. They both hung their heads. Both of them felt certain that eye wasn't at all a peaceful eye.

"Won't you sit down?" said Josephine.

"Thank you, Miss Pinner," said Mr. Farolles gratefully. He folded his coat-tails and began to lower himself into father's arm-chair, but just as he 10 touched it he almost sprang up and slid into the next chair instead.

He coughed. Josephine clasped her hands; Constantia looked vague.

"I want you to feel, Miss Pinner," said Mr. Farolles, "and you, Miss Constantia, that I'm try-ing to be helpful. I want to be helpful to you both, if you will let me. These are the times," said Mr. Farolles, very simply and earnestly, "when God means us to be helpful to one another."

"Thank you very much, Mr. Farolles," said Jo- 20 sephine and Constantia.

"Not at all," said Mr. Farolles gently. He drew his kid gloves through his fingers and leaned for-ward. "And if either of you would like a little Com-munion, either or both of you, here *and* now, you have only to tell me. A little Communion is often very help—a great comfort," he added tenderly.

But the idea of a little Communion terrified them. What! In the drawing-room by themselves—with no—no altar or anything! The piano would be much 30 too high, thought Constantia, and Mr. Farolles could not possibly lean over it with the chalice. And Kate would be sure to come bursting in and inter-rupt them, thought Josephine. And supposing the bell rang in the middle? It might be somebody im-portant—about their mourning. Would they get up reverently and go out, or would they have to wait . . . in torture?

"Perhaps you will send round a note by your good Kate if you would care for it later," said Mr. 40 Farolles.

"Oh yes, thank you very much!" they both said.

Mr. Farolles got up and took his black straw hat from the round table.

"And about the funeral," he said softly. "I may arrange that—as your dear father's old friend and yours, Miss Pinner—and Miss Constantia?"

Josephine and Constantia got up too.

"I should like it to be quite simple," said Jose- 50 phine firmly, "and not too expensive. At the same time, I should like——"

"A good one that will last," thought dreamy Constantia, as if Josephine were buying a night-gown. But of course Josephine didn't say that. "One suitable to our father's position." She was very nervous.

"I'll run round to our good friend Mr. Knight," said Mr. Farolles soothingly. "I will ask him to come and see you. I am sure you will find him very helpful indeed."

5

Well, at any rate, all that part of it was over, though neither of them could possibly believe that father was never coming back. Josephine had had a moment of absolute terror at the cemetery, while the coffin was lowered, to think that she and Constantia had done this thing without asking his permission. What would father say when he found out? For he was bound to find out sooner or later. He always did. "Buried. You two girls had me *buried!*" She heard his stick thumping. Oh, what would they say? What possible excuse could they make? It sounded such an appallingly heartless thing to do. Such a wicked advantage to take of a person because he happened to be helpless at the moment. The other people seemed to treat it all as a matter of course. They were strangers; they couldn't be expected to understand that father was the very last person for such a thing to happen to. No, the entire blame for it all would fall on her and Constantia. And the expense, she thought, stepping into the tight-buttoned cab. When she had to show him the bills. What would he say then?

She heard him absolutely roaring, "And do you expect me to pay for this gimcrack excursion of yours?"

"Oh," groaned poor Josephine aloud, "we shouldn't have done it, Con!"

And Constantia, pale as a lemon in all that blackness, said in a frightened whisper, "Done what, Jug?"

"Let them bu-bury father like that," said Josephine, breaking down and crying into her new, queer-smelling mourning handkerchief.

"But what else could we have done?" asked Constantia wonderingly. "We couldn't have kept him, Jug—we couldn't have kept him unburied. At any rate, not in a flat that size."

Josephine blew her nose; the cab was dreadfully stuffy.

"I don't know," she said forlornly. "It is all so dreadful. I feel we ought to have tried to, just for a time at least. To make perfectly sure. One thing's certain"—and her tears sprang out again—"father will never forgive us for this—never!"

6

Father would never forgive them. That was what they felt more than ever when, two mornings later, they went into his room to go through his things. They had discussed it quite calmly. It was even down on Josephine's list of things to be done. *Go through father's things and settle about them.* But that was a very different matter from saying after breakfast:

"Well, are you ready, Con?"

"Yes, Jug—when you are."

"Then I think we'd better get it over."

It was dark in the hall. It had been a rule for years never to disturb father in the morning, whatever happened. And now they were going to open the door without knocking even. . . . Constantia's eyes were enormous at the idea; Josephine felt weak in the knees.

"You—you go first," she gasped, pushing Constantia.

But Constantia said, as she always had said on those occasions, "No, Jug, that's not fair. You're eldest."

Josephine was just going to say—what at other times she wouldn't have owned to for the world— what she kept for her very last weapon, "But you're tallest," when they noticed that the kitchen door was open, and there stood Kate. . . .

"Very stiff," said Josephine, grasping the door-handle and doing her best to turn it. As if anything ever deceived Kate!

It couldn't be helped. That girl was . . . Then the door was shut behind them, but—but they weren't in father's room at all. They might have suddenly walked through the wall by mistake into a different flat altogether. Was the door just behind them? They were too frightened to look. Josephine knew that if it was it was holding itself tight shut; Constantia felt that, like the doors in dreams, it hadn't any handle at all. It was the coldness which made it so awful. Or the whiteness—which? Everything was covered. The blinds were down, a cloth hung over the mirror, a sheet hid the bed; a huge fan of white paper filled the fireplace. Constantia timidly put out her hand; she almost expected a snowflake to fall. Josephine felt a queer tingling in her nose, as if her nose was freezing. Then a cab klop-klopped over the cobbles below, and the quiet seemed to shake into little pieces.

"I had better pull up a blind," said Josephine bravely.

"Yes, it might be a good idea," whispered Constantia.

They only gave the blind a touch, but it flew up

and the cord flew after, rolling round the blind-stick, and the little tassel tapped as if trying to get free. That was too much for Constantia.

"Don't you think—don't you think we might put it off for another day?" she whispered.

"Why?" snapped Josephine, feeling, as usual, much better now that she knew for certain that Constantia was terrified. "It's got to be done. But I do wish you wouldn't whisper, Con."

"I didn't know I was whispering," whispered Constantia.

"And why do you keep on staring at the bed?" said Josephine, raising her voice almost defiantly.

"Oh, Jug, don't say so!" said poor Connie. "At any rate, not so loudly."

Josephine felt herself that she had gone too far. She took a wide swerve over to the chest of drawers, put out her hand, but quickly drew it back again.

"Connie!" she gasped, and she wheeled round and leaned with her back against the chest of drawers.

"Oh, Jug—what?"

Josephine could only glare. She had the most extraordinary feeling that she had just escaped something simply awful. But how could she explain to Constantia that father was in the chest of drawers? He was in the top drawer with his handkerchiefs and neckties, or in the next with his shirts and pyjamas, or in the lowest of all with his suits. He was watching there, hidden away—just behind the door-handle—ready to spring.

She pulled a funny old-fashioned face at Constantia, just as she used to in the old days when she was going to cry.

"I can't open," she nearly wailed.

"No, don't, Jug," whispered Constantia earnestly. "It's much better not to. Don't let's open anything. At any rate, not for a long time."

"But—but it seems so weak," said Josephine, breaking down.

"But why not be weak for once, Jug?" argued Constantia, whispering quite fiercely. "If it is weak." And her pale stare flew from the locked writing-table—so safe—to the huge glittering wardrobe, and she began to breathe in a queer, panting way. "Why shouldn't we be weak for once in our lives, Jug? It's quite excusable. Let's be weak—be weak, Jug. It's much nicer to be weak than to be strong."

And then she did one of those amazingly bold things that she'd done about twice before in their lives; she marched over to the wardrobe, turned the key, and took it out of the lock. Took it out of the lock and held it up to Josephine, showing Jose-phine by her extraordinary smile that she knew what she'd done, she'd risked deliberately father being in there among his overcoats.

If the huge wardrobe had lurched forward, had crashed down on Constantia, Josephine wouldn't have been surprised. On the contrary, she would have thought it the only suitable thing to happen. But nothing happened. Only the room seemed quieter than ever, and bigger flakes of cold air fell on Josephine's shoulders and knees. She began to shiver.

"Come, Jug," said Constantia, still with that awful callous smile, and Josephine followed just as she had that last time, when Constantia had pushed Benny into the round pond.

7

But the strain told on them when they were back in the dining-room. They sat down, very shaky, and looked at each other.

"I don't feel I can settle to anything," said Josephine, "until I've had something. Do you think we could ask Kate for two cups of hot water?"

"I really don't see why we shouldn't," said Constantia carefully. She was quite normal again. "I won't ring. I'll go to the kitchen door and ask her."

"Yes, do," said Josephine, sinking down into a chair. "Tell her, just two cups, Con, nothing else—on a tray."

"She needn't even put the jug on, need she?" said Constantia, as though Kate might very well complain if the jug had been there.

"Oh no, certainly not! The jug's not at all necessary. She can pour it direct out of the kettle," cried Josephine, feeling that would be a labour-saving indeed.

Their cold lips quivered at the greenish brims. Josephine curved her small red hands round the cup; Constantia sat up and blew on the wavy stream, making it flutter from one side to the other.

"Speaking of Benny," said Josephine.

And though Benny hadn't been mentioned Constantia immediately looked as though he had.

"He'll expect us to send him something of father's, of course. But it's so difficult to know what to send to Ceylon."

"You mean things get unstuck so on the voyage," murmured Constantia.

"No, lost," said Josephine sharply. "You know there's no post. Only runners."

Both paused to watch a black man in white linen drawers running through the pale fields for dear life, with a large brown-paper parcel in his hands. Josephine's black man was tiny; he scurried along glistening like an ant. But there was something blind and tireless about Constantia's tall, thin fellow, which made him, she decided, a very unpleasant person indeed. . . . On the veranda, dressed all in white and wearing a cork helmet, stood Benny. His right hand shook up and down, as father's did when he was impatient. And behind him, not in the least interested, sat Hilda, the unknown sister-in-law. She swung in a cane rocker and flicked over the leaves of the *Tatler*.

"I think his watch would be the most suitable present," said Josephine.

Constantia looked up; she seemed surprised.

"Oh, would you trust a gold watch to a native?"

"But of course I'd disguise it," said Josephine. "No one would know it was a watch." She liked the idea of having to make a parcel such a curious shape that no one could possibly guess what it was. She even thought for a moment of hiding the watch in a narrow cardboard corset-box that she'd kept by her for a long time, waiting for it to come in for something. It was such beautiful firm cardboard. But, no, it wouldn't be appropriate for this occasion. It had lettering on it: *Medium Women's 28. Extra Firm Busks*. It would be almost too much of a surprise for Benny to open that and find father's watch inside.

"And of course it isn't as though it would be going—ticking, I mean," said Constantia, who was still thinking of the native love of jewellery. "At least," she added, "it would be very strange if after all that time it was."

8

Josephine made no reply. She had flown off on one of her tangents. She had suddenly thought of Cyril. Wasn't it more usual for the only grandson to have the watch? And then dear Cyril was so appreciative, and a gold watch meant so much to a young man. Benny, in all probability, had quite got out of the habit of watches; men so seldom wore waistcoats in those hot climates. Whereas Cyril in London wore them from year's end to year's end. And it would be so nice for her and Constantia, when he came to tea, to know it was there. "I see you've got on grandfather's watch, Cyril." It would be somehow so satisfactory.

Dear boy! What a blow his sweet, sympathetic little note had been! Of course they quite understood; but it was most unfortunate.

"It would have been such a point, having him," said Josephine.

"And he would have enjoyed it so," said Constantia, not thinking what she was saying.

However, as soon as he got back he was coming to tea with his aunties. Cyril to tea was one of their rare treats.

"Now, Cyril, you mustn't be frightened of our cakes. Your Auntie Con and I bought them at Buszard's this morning. We know what a man's appetite is. So don't be ashamed of making a good tea."

Josephine cut recklessly into the rich dark cake that stood for her winter gloves or the soling and heeling of Constantia's only respectable shoes. But Cyril was most unmanlike in appetite.

"I say, Aunt Josephine, I simply can't. I've only just had lunch, you know."

"Oh, Cyril, that can't be true! It's after four," cried Josephine. Constantia sat with her knife poised over the chocolate-roll.

"It is, all the same," said Cyril. "I had to meet a man at Victoria, and he kept me hanging about till . . . there was only time to get lunch and to come on here. And he gave me—phew"—Cyril put his hand to his forehead—"a terrific blow-out," he said.

It was disappointing—to-day of all days. But still he couldn't be expected to know.

"But you'll have a meringue, won't you, Cyril?" said Aunt Josephine. "These meringues were bought specially for you. Your dear father was so fond of them. We were sure you are, too."

"I *am*, Aunt Josephine," cried Cyril ardently. "Do you mind if I take half to begin with?"

"Not at all, dear boy; but we mustn't let you off with that."

"Is your dear father still so fond of meringues?" asked Auntie Con gently. She winced faintly as she broke through the shell of hers.

"Well, I don't quite know, Auntie Con," said Cyril breezily.

At that they both looked up.

"Don't know?" almost snapped Josephine. "Don't know a thing like that about your own father, Cyril?"

"Surely," said Aunty Con softly.

Cyril tried to laugh it off. "Oh, well," he said, "it's such a long time since——" He faltered. He stopped. Their faces were too much for him.

"Even *so*," said Josephine.

And Auntie Con looked.

Cyril put down his teacup. "Wait a bit," he cried. "Wait a bit, Aunt Josephine. What am I thinking of?"

He looked up. They were beginning to brighten. Cyril slapped his knee.

"Of course," he said, "it was meringues. How

18. **Victoria,** one of the chief railroad stations of London.

could I have forgotten? Yes, Aunt Josephine, you're perfectly right. Father's most frightfully keen on meringues."

They didn't only beam. Aunt Josephine went scarlet with pleasure; Auntie Con gave a deep, deep sigh.

"And now, Cyril, you must come and see father," said Josephine. "He knows you were coming to-day."

"Right," said Cyril, very firmly and heartily. He got up from his chair; suddenly he glanced at the clock.

"I say, Auntie Con, isn't your clock a bit slow? I've got to meet a man at—at Paddington just after five. I'm afraid I shan't be able to stay very long with grandfather."

"Oh, he won't expect you to stay *very* long!" said Aunt Josephine.

Constantia was still gazing at the clock. She couldn't make up her mind if it was fast or slow. It was one or the other, she felt almost certain of that. At any rate, it had been.

Cyril still lingered. "Aren't you coming along, Auntie Con?"

"Of course," said Josephine, "we shall all go. Come on, Con."

9

They knocked at the door, and Cyril followed his aunts into grandfather's hot, sweetish room.

"Come on," said Grandfather Pinner. "Don't hang about. What is it? What've you been up to?"

He was sitting in front of a roaring fire, clasping his stick. He had a thick rug over his knees. On his lap there lay a beautiful pale yellow silk handker-chief.

"It's Cyril, father," said Josephine shyly. And she took Cyril's hand and led him forward.

"Good afternoon, grandfather," said Cyril, trying to take his hand out of Aunt Josephine's. Grand-father Pinner shot his eyes at Cyril in the way he was famous for. Where was Auntie Con? She stood on the other side of Aunt Josephine; her long arms hung down in front of her; her hands were clasped. She never took her eyes off grandfather.

"Well," said Grandfather Pinner, beginning to thump, "what have you got to tell me?"

What had he, what had he got to tell him? Cyril felt himself smiling like a perfect imbecile. The room was stifling, too.

But Aunt Josephine came to his rescue. She cried brightly, "Cyril says his father is still very fond of meringues, father dear."

"Eh?" said Grandfather Pinner, curving his hand like a purple meringue-shell over one ear.

Josephine repeated, "Cyril says his father is still very fond of meringues."

"Can't hear," said old Colonel Pinner. And he waved Josephine away with his stick, then pointed with his stick to Cyril. "Tell me what she's trying to say," he said.

(My God!) "Must I?" said Cyril, blushing and staring at Aunt Josephine.

"Do, dear," she smiled. "It will please him so much."

"Come on, out with it!" cried Colonel Pinner testily, beginning to thump again.

And Cyril leaned forward and yelled, "Father's still very fond of meringues."

At that Grandfather Pinner jumped as though he had been shot.

"Don't shout!" he cried. "What's the matter with the boy? *Meringues!* What about 'em?"

"Oh, Aunt Josephine, must we go on?" groaned Cyril desperately.

"It's quite all right, dear boy," said Aunt Jose-phine, as though he and she were at the dentist's together. "He'll understand in a minute." And she whispered to Cyril, "He's getting a bit deaf, you know." Then she leaned forward and really bawled at Grandfather Pinner, "Cyril only wanted to tell you, father dear, that *his* father is still very fond of meringues."

Colonel Pinner heard that time, heard and brooded, looking Cyril up and down.

"What an esstrordinary thing!" said old Grand-father Pinner. "What an esstrordinary thing to come all this way here to tell me!"

And Cyril felt it *was*.

"Yes, I shall send Cyril the watch," said Jose-phine.

"That would be very nice," said Constantia. "I seem to remember last time he came there was some little trouble about the time."

10

They were interrupted by Kate bursting through the door in her usual fashion, as though she had discovered some secret panel in the wall.

"Fried or boiled?" asked the bold voice.

Fried or boiled? Josephine and Constantia were quite bewildered for the moment. They could hardly take it in.

"Fried or boiled what, Kate?" asked Josephine, trying to begin to concentrate.

Kate gave a loud sniff. "Fish."

"Well, why didn't you say so immediately?" Josephine reproached her gently. "How could you expect us to understand, Kate? There are a great many things in this world, you know, which are fried or boiled." And after such a display of courage she said quite brightly to Constantia, "Which do you prefer, Con?"

"I think it might be nice to have it fried," said Constantia. "On the other hand, of course boiled fish is very nice. I think I prefer both equally well 10 . . . Unless you . . . In that case——"

"I shall fry it," said Kate, and she bounced back, leaving their door open and slamming the door of her kitchen.

Josephine gazed at Constantia; she raised her pale eyebrows until they rippled away into her pale hair. She got up. She said in a very lofty, imposing way, "Do you mind following me into the drawing-room, Constantia? I've something of great importance to discuss with you." 20

For it was always to the drawing-room they retired when they wanted to talk over Kate.

Josephine closed the door meaningly. "Sit down, Constantia," she said, still very grand. She might have been receiving Constantia for the first time. And Con looked round vaguely for a chair, as though she felt indeed quite a stranger.

"Now the question is," said Josephine, bending forward, "whether we shall keep her or not." 30

"That is the question," agreed Constantia.

"And this time," said Josephine firmly, "we must come to a definite decision."

Constantia looked for a moment as though she might begin going over all the other times, but she pulled herself together and said, "Yes, Jug."

"You see, Con," explained Josephine, "everything is so changed now." Constantia looked up quickly. "I mean," went on Josephine, "we're not 40 dependent on Kate as we were." And she blushed faintly. "There's not father to cook for."

"That is perfectly true," agreed Constantia. "Father certainly doesn't want any cooking now, whatever else——"

Josephine broke in sharply, "You're not sleepy, are you, Con?"

"Sleepy, Jug?" Constantia was wide-eyed.

"Well, concentrate more," said Josephine sharply, and she returned to the subject. "What it 50 comes to is, if we did"—and this she barely breathed, glancing at the door—"give Kate notice"—she raised her voice again—"we could manage our own food."

"Why not?" cried Constantia. She couldn't help smiling. The idea was so exciting. She clasped her hands. "What should we live on, Jug?"

"Oh, eggs in various forms!" said Jug, lofty again. "And, besides, there are all the cooked foods."

"But I've always heard," said Constantia, "they are considered so very expensive."

"Not if one buys them in moderation," said Josephine. But she tore herself away from this fascinating bypath and dragged Constantia after her.

"What we've got to decide now, however, is whether we really do trust Kate or not."

Constantia leaned back. Her flat little laugh flew from her lips.

"Isn't it curious, Jug," said she, "that just on this one subject I've never been able to quite make up my mind?"

II

She never had. The whole difficulty was to prove anything. How did one prove things, how could one? Suppose Kate had stood in front of her and deliberately made a face. Mightn't she very well have been in pain? Wasn't it impossible, at any rate, to ask Kate if she was making a face at her? If Kate answered "No"—and of course she would say "No"—what a position! How undignified! Then again Constantia suspected, she was almost certain that Kate went to her chest of drawers when she and Josephine were out, not to take things but to spy. Many times she had come back to find her amethyst cross in the most unlikely places, under her lace ties or on top of her evening Bertha. More than once she had laid a trap for Kate. She had arranged things in a special order and then called Josephine to witness.

"You see, Jug?"

"Quite, Con."

"Now we shall be able to tell."

But, oh dear, when she did go to look, she was as far off from a proof as ever! If anything was displaced, it might so very well have happened as she closed the drawer; a jolt might have done it so easily.

"You come, Jug, and decide. I really can't. It's too difficult."

But after a pause and a long glare Josephine would sigh, "Now you've put the doubt into my mind, Con, I'm sure I can't tell myself."

"Well, we can't postpone it again," said Josephine. "If we postpone it this time——"

12

But at that moment in the street below a barrel-organ struck up. Josephine and Constantia sprang to their feet together.

"Run, Con," said Josephine. "Run quickly. There's sixpence on the——"

Then they remembered. It didn't matter. They would never have to stop the organ-grinder again. Never again would she and Constantia be told to make that monkey take his noise somewhere else. Never would sound that loud, strange bellow when father thought they were not hurrying enough. The organ-grinder might play there all day and the stick would not thump.

It never will thump again,
It never will thump again,

played the barrel-organ.

What was Constantia thinking? She had such a strange smile; she looked different. She couldn't be going to cry.

"Jug, Jug," said Constantia softly, pressing her hands together. "Do you know what day it is? It's Saturday. It's a week to-day, a whole week."

A week since father died,
A week since father died,

cried the barrel-organ. And Josephine, too, forgot to be practical and sensible; she smiled faintly, strangely. On the Indian carpet there fell a square of sunlight, pale red; it came and went and came—and stayed, deepened—until it shone almost golden.

"The sun's out," said Josephine, as though it really mattered.

A perfect fountain of bubbling notes shook from the barrel-organ, round, bright notes, carelessly scattered.

Constantia lifted her big, cold hands as if to catch them, and then her hands fell again. She walked over to the mantelpiece to her favourite Buddha. And the stone and gilt image, whose smile always gave her such a queer feeling, almost a pain and yet a pleasant pain, seemed to-day to be more than smiling. He knew something; he had a secret. "I know something that you don't know," said her Buddha. Oh, what was it, what could it be? And yet she had always felt there was . . . something.

The sunlight pressed through the windows, thieved its way in, flashed its light over the furniture and the photographs. Josephine watched it. When it came to mother's photograph, the enlargement over the piano, it lingered as though puzzled to find so little remained of mother, except the earrings shaped like tiny pagodas and a black feather boa. Why did the photographs of dead people always fade so? wondered Josephine. As soon as a person was dead their photograph died too. But, of course, this one of mother was very old. It was thirty-five years old. Josephine remembered standing on a chair and pointing out that feather boa to Constantia and telling her that it was a snake that had killed their mother in Ceylon. . . . Would everything have been different if mother hadn't died? She didn't see why. Aunt Florence had lived with them until they had left school, and they had moved three times and had their yearly holiday and . . . and there'd been changes of servants, of course.

Some little sparrows, young sparrows they sounded, chirped on the window-ledge. *Yeep—eyeep—yeep.* But Josephine felt they were not sparrows, not on the window-ledge. It was inside her, that queer little crying noise. *Yeep—eyeep—yeep.* Ah, what was it crying, so weak and forlorn?

If mother had lived, might they have married? But there had been nobody for them to marry. There had been father's Anglo-Indian friends before he quarrelled with them. But after that she and Constantia never met a single man except clergymen. How did one meet men? Or even if they'd met them, how could they have got to know men well enough to be more than strangers? One read of people having adventures, being followed, and so on. But nobody had ever followed Constantia and her. Oh yes, there had been one year at East-bourne a mysterious man at their boarding-house who had put a note on the jug of hot water outside their bedroom door! But by the time Connie had found it the steam had made the writing too faint to read; they couldn't even make out to which of them it was addressed. And he had left next day. And that was all. The rest had been looking after father, and at the same time keeping out of father's way. But now? But now? The thieving sun touched Josephine gently. She lifted her face. She was drawn over to the window by gentle beams. . . .

Until the barrel-organ stopped playing Constantia stayed before the Buddha, wondering, but not as usual, not vaguely. This time her wonder was like longing. She remembered the times she had come in here, crept out of bed in her nightgown when the moon was full, and lain on the floor with her arms outstretched, as though she was crucified. Why? The big, pale moon had made her do it. The horrible dancing figures on the carved screen had leered at her and she hadn't minded. She remembered too how, whenever they were at the seaside, she had gone off by herself and got as close to the sea as she could, and sung something, something she had made up, while she gazed all over that restless water. There had been this other life, running out, bringing things home in bags, getting things on approval, discussing them with Jug, and taking them back to get more things on approval, and arranging father's trays and trying not to annoy father. But it all seemed to have happened in a kind of tunnel. It wasn't real. It was only when she came out of the tunnel into the moonlight or by the sea or into a thunderstorm that she really felt herself. What did it mean? What was it she was always wanting? What did it all lead to? Now? Now?

She turned away from the Buddha with one of her vague gestures. She went over to where Josephine was standing. She wanted to say something to Josephine, something frightfully important, about— about the future and what . . .

"Don't you think perhaps——" she began.

But Josephine interrupted her. "I was wondering if now——" she murmured. They stopped; they waited for each other.

"Go on, Con," said Josephine.

"No, no, Jug; after you," said Constantia.

"No, say what you were going to say. You began," said Josephine.

"I . . . I'd rather hear what you were going to say first," said Constantia.

"Don't be absurd, Con."

"Really, Jug."

"Connie!"

"Oh, *Jug!*"

A pause. Then Constantia said faintly, "I can't say what I was going to say, Jug, because I've forgotten what it was . . . that I was going to say."

Josephine was silent for a moment. She stared at a big cloud where the sun had been. Then she replied shortly, "I've forgotten too."

J. B. S. Haldane
1892–

J(ohn) B(urden) S(anderson) Haldane, son of the scientist J. S. Haldane, was born November 5, 1892. He was educated at Eton and at New College, Oxford. He became an authority on chemistry and was professor of biometry at University College, London, for many years. In 1938 his radical views brought him into conflict with the political arbiters and he was told to quit the university. Nevertheless, he carried on his experiments under conditions which, he wrote, were those of a siege.

He himself had been used "as an experimental animal" since the age of four. At eight he went down deep mines with his father, taking samples of air for later analysis. In the first World War he was an infantry officer, one of the first on whom gas masks were tested; he commanded a hand-grenade school, and was twice wounded. From 1919 to 1927 he did a number of experiments on himself. ("I think I hold the record for the amounts of ammonium, calcium, and strontium chloride which I have taken.") He went to Spain in 1936 to advise the Republican Government on gas protection. As a result he was drawn into politics and became a severe critic of the equivocal English Government.

On his return to London he was attacked by a gang of English Fascists.

Haldane has written many volumes of a highly technical nature, but he believes that a scientist is all the more use in the world "if, like Benjamin Franklin, he takes an active part in politics." Among the best of his books are *Animal Biology*, 1927, written in collaboration with Julian Huxley, brother of Aldous Huxley; *Daedalus: or Science and the Future*, 1924; *Callinicus: A Defence of Chemical Warfare*, 1925; *Possible Worlds and Other Essays*, 1927; *The Causes of Evolution*, 1932, a searching re-examination of Darwinism; and *Adventures of a Biologist*, 1940, a set of twenty-seven arresting essays published in England under the title of *Keeping Cool*.

Haldane stresses the social function of science. He shows that scientific explorations have increased man's wealth and his power to resist disease, but they have also brought about man's vicious exploitation of man and have multiplied the horrors of war. Science, capable of extending security and enriching life, has been used by mechanical excesses to speed up death. It has helped men, but it has almost destroyed mankind.

Haldane points out that until science is organized *for humanity* it will be not only aimless but vicious. He calls for new ways of thinking to match the new conditions. The twentieth century has presented problems which demand synthesis: combined social and scientific solution. Haldane implies that unless ideas are used as skillfully and sensitively as instruments, mankind may doom itself to a brilliant mechanical destruction.

Haldane's essay "Man's Destiny" should be read in connection with H. G. Wells's *The Fate of Man.* The diagnosis is similar to that of Alexander Carrel's *Man, the Unknown.* "For the first time in the history of humanity," wrote Dr. Carrel, "a crumbling civilization is capable of discerning the causes of its decay. For the first time it has at its disposal the gigantic strength of science. Will we utilize this knowledge and this power? It is our only hope of escaping the fate common to the civilizations of the past."

MAN'S DESTINY [1]

IF, as I am inclined to suspect, the human will is to some small extent free, there is no such thing as a destiny of the human race. There is a choice of destinies. Even if our actions are irrevocably predetermined we do not know our destiny. In either case, however, we can point to a limited number of probable fates for our species.

First let us consider the stage for our drama. The earth has existed for over a thousand million years. During most of this period its surface temperature has not been very different from that now prevailing. The sun has not cooled down appreciably during that time, and it will probably be only a little cooler a million million years hence, though somewhere about that time it is quite likely that the earth's surface will be destroyed owing to the disruption of the moon by tidal forces. Six hundred million years ago our ancestors were worms, ten thousand years ago they were savages. Both these periods are negligible compared with our possible future. Provided, therefore, that man has a future lasting for more than a few million years we can at once say that our descendants may, for anything we can see to the contrary, excel us a great deal more than we excel worms or jellyfish.

There are, however, several alternatives to this prospect. A catastrophe of an astronomical order, such as a collision with a stray heavenly body, is unlikely. The earth has lasted a long time without

any such disasters. The sun may possibly swell up temporarily, as similar stars occasionally do. In this case the human race will be very rapidly roasted. A disease may arise which will wipe out all, or almost all, mankind. But there is nothing in science to make such up-to-date versions of the apocalypse very probable.

Even if man does not perish in this dramatic manner, there is no reason why civilisation should not do so. All civilisation goes back to a common source less than 10,000 years ago, very probably in Egypt. It is a highly complicated invention which has probably been made only once. If it perished it might never be made again. When in the past its light was extinguished in one area—for example, when the Angles and Saxons wrecked Roman Britain—it could be lit again from elsewhere, as our savage ancestors were civilised from Italy and Ireland. A modern war followed by revolutions might destroy it all over the planet. If weapons are as much improved in the next century as in the last, this will probably happen.

But unless atomic energy can be tapped, which is wildly unlikely, we know that it will never be possible to box up very much more rapidly available energy in a given place, than we can already box up in a high explosive shell, nor has any vapour much more poisonous than "mustard gas" been discovered in the forty-one years that have elapsed since that substance was first produced. I think therefore that the odds are slightly against such a catastrophic end of civilisation.

But civilisation as we know it is a poor thing. And if it is to be improved there is no hope save in science. A hundred and forty years ago men, women and children were being hanged in England for stealing any property valued at over a shilling, miners were hereditary slaves in Scotland, criminals were publicly and legally tortured to death in France. Europe was definitely rather worse off, whether in health, wealth or morals, than the Roman Empire under Antoninus Pius in A.D. 150. Since then we have improved very greatly in all these respects. We are far from perfect; but we live about twice as long, and we do not hang starving children for stealing food, raid the coast of Africa for slaves, or imprison debtors for life. These advances are the direct and indirect consequences of science. Physics and chemistry have made us rich, biology healthy, and the application of scientific thought to ethics by such men as Bentham has done

---

[1] From *Possible Worlds and Other Papers* by J. B. S. Haldane, copyright, 1928, by Harper and Brothers.

51. Bentham, Jeremy Bentham (1748–1832), English philosopher and jurist, whose great work, *Principles of Morals and Legislation,* influenced political and moral thought.

more than any dozen saints to make us good. The process can only continue if science continues.

And pure science is a delicate plant. It has never flowered in Spain, and to-day it is almost dead in Italy. Everywhere there are strong forces working against it. Even where research is rewarded, the usual reward is a professorship with a full-time programme of teaching and administration. The bacteriologist can most easily earn a title and a fortune if he deserts research for medical practice. The potential physicist or chemist can often quadruple his income by taking up engineering or manufacture. In biology and psychology many lines of research are forbidden by law or public opinion. If science is to improve man as it has improved his environment, the experimental method must be applied to him. It is quite likely that the attempt to do so will rouse such fierce opposition that science will again be persecuted as it has been in the past. Such a persecution may quite well be successful, especially if it is supported by religion. A world-wide religious revival, whether Christian or not, would probably succeed in suppressing experimental inquiry into the human mind, which offers the only serious hope of improving it. Again, if scientific psychology and eugenics are used as weapons by one side in a political struggle, their opponents, if successful, will stamp them out. I think that it is quite as likely as not that scientific research may ultimately be strangled in some such way as this before mankind has learnt to control its own evolution.

If so, evolution will take its course. And that course has generally been downwards. The majority of species have degenerated and become extinct, or, what is perhaps worse, gradually lost many of their functions. The ancestors of oysters and barnacles had heads. Snakes have lost their limbs, and ostriches and penguins their power to flight. Man may just as easily lose his intelligence.

It is only a very few species that have developed into something higher. It is unlikely that man will do so unless he desires to and is prepared to pay the cost. If, as appears to be the case at present in most parts of Europe and North America, the less intelligent of our species continue to breed more rapidly than the able, we shall probably go the way of the dodo and the kiwi. We do not as yet know enough to avert this fate. If research continues for another two centuries, it is probable that we shall. But if, as is likely enough, the welfare of our descendants in the remote future can only be realized at a very considerable sacrifice of present happiness and liberty, it does not follow that such a sacrifice will be made.

4. **to-day.** This was written in 1926.

It is quite likely that, after a golden age of happiness and peace, during which all the immediately available benefits of science will be realized, mankind will very gradually deteriorate. Genius will become ever rarer, our bodies a little weaker in each generation; culture will slowly decline, and in a few thousand or a few hundred thousand years—it does not much matter which—mankind will return to barbarism, and finally become extinct. If this happens I venture to hope that we shall not have destroyed the rat, an animal of considerable enterprise which stands as good a chance as any other of evolving towards intelligence.

In the rather improbable event of man taking his own evolution in hand—in other words, of improving human nature, as opposed to environment—I can see no bounds at all to his progress. Less than a million years hence the average man or woman will realize all the possibilities that human life has so far shown. He or she will never know a minute's illness. He will be able to think like Newton, to write like Racine, to paint like Fra Angelico, to compose like Bach. He will be as incapable of hatred as St. Francis, and when death comes at the end of a life probably measured in thousands of years he will meet it with as little fear as . . . Arnold Von Winkelried. And every minute of his life will be lived with all the passion of a lover or a discoverer. We can form no idea whatever of the exceptional men of such a future.

Man will certainly attempt to leave the earth. The first voyagers into interstellar space will die. . . . There is no reason why their successors should not succeed in colonising some, at least, of the other planets of our system, and ultimately the planets, if such exist, revolving round other stars than our sun. There is no theoretical limit to man's material progress but the subjection to complete conscious control of every atom and every quantum of radiation in the universe. There is, perhaps, no limit at all to his intellectual and spiritual progress.

But, whether any of these possibilities will be realized depends, as far as we can see, very largely on the events of the next few centuries. If scientific research is regarded as a useful adjunct to the army, the factory, or the hospital, and not as the thing of all things most supremely worth doing, both for its own sake and that of its results, it is probable that the decisive steps will never be taken. And unless he

26. **Arnold Von Winkelried,** the Swiss patriot who "broke" the Austrian attack. He advanced toward the foe, and suddenly gathered a number of spears against his breast. Falling, he dragged them with him and opened a way through the enemy lines. 39. **quantum,** elemental unit of energy.

can control his own evolution as he is learning to control that of his domestic plants and animals, man

and all his works will go down into oblivion and darkness.

Wilfred Owen
1893–1918

Wilfred Owen was born March 18, 1893, in Oswestry, a town in Shropshire. His biography is tragically brief. He read Keats as a child, and entered London University at seventeen. At twenty he became a private tutor; at twenty-two he enlisted for the first World War in the Artists' Rifles; at twenty-four he was awarded the Military Cross for gallantry on the battlefield; at twenty-five he was killed. He died in action attempting to get his men across the Sambre Canal on November 4, 1918—exactly one week before the Armistice.

Owen published little during his short lifetime. He objected to the idea that his studies of war should be appraised as poetry. Yet of all the English war poets—including Robert Graves, Edmund Blunden, Siegfried Sassoon—Owen is the most powerful, as he is the most deeply passionate. His name was unknown until his friend Siegfried Sassoon assembled and arranged the contents of his posthumous *Poems*, 1920, later enlarged as *The Poems of Wilfred Owen*, 1931, edited by Edmund Blunden. These collections show Owen's attempts to extend the gamut of verse: experiments in assonance, rhyming consonants instead of vowels, shifts of accent and form. But his interest in technique was subservient to his subject, which was "War and the pity of War." He wrote of the brute horror of life in the trenches and the omnipresence of death. Without hysteria he uttered his bitter protests in "the abode of madness." "He never," said Sassoon, "wrote his poems (as so many more poets did) to make the effect of a personal gesture." He wrote as an individual who had discovered the tragedy of peoples, rather than of a person, in war. Such was the quality of his pity and his extraordinary restraint that his poetry has detached itself from the event and has become a thing of lasting beauty.

ANTHEM FOR DOOMED YOUTH [1]

What passing-bells for these who die as cattle?
 Only the monstrous anger of the guns.
 Only the stuttering rifles' rapid rattle

[1] This and the following poems are reprinted from *The*

Can patter out their hasty orisons.
No mockeries for them; no prayers or bells,
 Nor any voice of mourning save the choirs,—
The shrill, demented choirs of wailing shells;
 And bugles calling for them from sad shires.

What candles may be held to speed them all?
 Not in the hands of boys, but in their eyes   10
Shall shine the holy glimmers of good-byes.
 The pallor of girls' brows shall be their pall;
Their flowers the tenderness of silent minds,
And each slow dusk a drawing-down of blinds.

APOLOGIA PRO POEMATE MEO

I, too, saw God through mud,—
 The mud that cracked on cheeks when wretches smiled.
 War brought more glory to their eyes than blood,
 And gave their laughs more glee than shakes a child.

Merry it was to laugh there—
 Where death becomes absurd and life absurder.
 For power was on us as we slashed bones bare
 Not to feel sickness or remorse of murder.

I, too, have dropped off fear—
 Behind the barrage, dead as my platoon,   10
 And sailed my spirit surging, light and clear,
 Past the entanglement where hopes lay strewn;

And witnessed exultation—
 Faces that used to curse me, scowl for scowl,
 Shine and lift up with passion of oblation,
 Seraphic for an hour; though they were foul.

I have made fellowships—
 Untold of happy lovers in old song.
 For love is not the binding of fair lips
 With the soft silk of eyes that look and long,   20

Poems of Wilfred Owen by permission of The Viking Press, Inc.

By Joy, whose ribbon slips,—
    But wound with war's hard wire whose stakes are
        strong;
    Bound with the bandage of the arm that drips;
    Knit in the welding of the rifle-thong.

I have perceived much beauty
    In the hoarse oaths that kept our courage straight;
    Heard music in the silentness of duty;
    Found peace where shell-storms spouted reddest
        spate.

Nevertheless, except you share
    With them in hell the sorrowful dark of hell,   30
    Whose world is but the trembling of a flare,
    And heaven but as the highway for a shell,

You shall not hear their mirth:
    You shall not come to think them well content
    By any jest of mine. These men are worth
    Your tears. You are not worth their merriment.

GREATER LOVE

Red lips are not so red
    As the stained stones kissed by the English dead.
Kindness of wooed and wooer
Seems shame to their love pure.
O Love, your eyes lose lure
    When I behold eyes blinded in my stead!

Your slender attitude
    Trembles not exquisite like limbs knife-skewed,
Rolling and rolling there
Where God seems not to care;   10
Till the fierce Love they bear
    Cramps them in death's extreme decrepitude.

Your voice sings not so soft,—
    Though even as wind murmuring through raft-
        ered loft,—
Your dear voice is not clear,
Gentle, and evening clear,
As theirs whom none now hear,
    Now earth has stopped their piteous mouths that
        coughed.

Heart, you were never hot,
    Nor large, nor full like hearts made great with
        shot;   20
And though your hand be pale,
Paler are all which trail

Your cross through flame and hail:
    Weep, you may weep, for you may touch them
        not.

STRANGE MEETING

It seemed that out of battle I escaped
Down some profound dull tunnel, long since scooped
Through granites which titanic wars had groined.
Yet also there encumbered sleepers groaned,
Too fast in thought or death to be bestirred.
Then, as I probed them, one sprang up, and stared
With piteous recognition in fixed eyes,
Lifting distressful hands as if to bless.
And by his smile, I knew that sullen hall,
By his dead smile I knew we stood in Hell.   10
With a thousand fears that vision's face was grained;
Yet no blood reached there from the upper ground,
And no guns thumped, or down the flues made
    moan.
"Strange, friend," I said, "here is no cause to
    mourn."
"None," said the other, "save the undone years,
The hopelessness. Whatever hope is yours,
Was my life also; I went hunting wild
After the wildest beauty in the world,
Which lies not calm in eyes, or braided hair,
But mocks the steady running of the hour,   20
And if it grieves, grieves richlier than here.
For by my glee might many men have laughed,
And of my weeping something has been left,
Which must die now. I mean the truth untold,
The pity of war, the pity war distilled.
Now men will go content with what we spoiled,
Or, discontent, boil bloody, and be spilled.
They will be swift with swiftness of the tigress,
None will break ranks, though nations trek from
    progress.
Courage was mine, and I had mystery,   30
Wisdom was mine, and I had mastery;
To miss the march of this retreating world
Into vain citadels that are not walled.
Then, when much blood had clogged their chariot-
    wheels
I would go up and wash them from sweet wells,
Even with truths that lie too deep for taint.
I would have poured my spirit without stint
But not through wounds; not on the cess of war.
Foreheads of men have bled where no wounds were.
I am the enemy you killed, my friend.   40
I knew you in this dark; for so you frowned
Yesterday through me as you jabbed and killed.
I parried; but my hands were loath and cold.
Let us sleep now. . . . ."

Aldous Huxley
1894–

Aldous (Leonard) Huxley was born at Godalming on July 26, 1894. His father was the well-known writer, editor, and Greek scholar Leonard Huxley; his grandfather was the famous scientist Thomas Huxley; his great-uncle was Matthew Arnold. With so rich an inheritance Aldous Huxley represents the poverty-stricken end of a cycle: the failure of the classicist's standard of values and the defeat of the scientist's faith in science. Educated at Eton and at Balliol College, Oxford, Huxley intended to become a doctor, but serious trouble with his eyes prohibited the study of medicine, and, perfecting himself in touch-typing, he turned to literature.

Huxley's first publication was a book of verse, *The Burning Wheel,* 1916, and he has never quite relinquished his interest in poetic form; there have been five subsequent volumes of facile but undistinguished poetry. It was not until he was twenty-seven that Huxley devoted himself almost entirely to prose. A book of short stories, *Limbo,* 1920, and a novel, *Crome Yellow,* 1921, showed a new attitude, brilliant, erudite, and unhappy. In the twenty years between 1920 and 1940 Huxley published more than twenty-five volumes. Among the novels those which made the greatest impression are *Antic Hay,* 1923; *Point Counter Point,* 1928; *Brave New World,* 1932; and *After Many a Summer Dies the Swan,* 1940. The best of his short stories are in *Mortal Coils,* 1922; *Two or Three Graces,* 1926, and *Brief Candles,* 1930. His nonfictional prose, which some critics consider his most characteristic, includes the essays in *Proper Studies,* 1927; *Vulgarity in Literature,* 1930; *Music At Night,* 1931; *Ends and Means,* 1937; and the travel pieces in *Jesting Pilate,* 1926, and *Beyond the Mexique Bay,* 1934. Huxley, who was an intimate of D. H. Lawrence, Katherine Mansfield, and J. Middleton Murry—he joined Murry on the editorial staff of the *Athenaeum*—also edited *The Letters of D. H. Lawrence,* 1932.

In all the odd works of fiction as well as the other volumes, there is revealed a curious kind of writing: writing which disguises itself as entertainment in order to interest, but which neither respects the entertainment nor believes in the instruction. The aim, it seems, is satire, yet this is satire which frustrates itself. It begins to criticize life, then falters, then, disgusted with the human animal, turns away both from criticism and from life. Contemptuous of those who live on a "time-bound" plane, Huxley contemplates an "algebra of spiritual existence," yet he indicates no salvation for humanity in a Nirvana of abstract mathematics. His is a distortion of the mystic's way of thinking: he redeems the world in order to reject it.

The mystical vein—romantic, pacifist, nonresistant—increases in the later work; the early novels and stories are sufficiently realistic and cynical. Like Swift, to whom he is frequently compared, Huxley takes a sadistic delight in exposing human weakness and stripping the last rag of illusion from his own shabby and bewildered creatures. This savage disgust is, in itself, a confession of a personal hurt translated into a cosmic despair. As David Daiches analyzed it:

"Instead of justifying the optimistic belief in science and progress that, for example, his grandfather, the great T. H. Huxley, had held, the behavior of the upper middle classes at the time which Aldous began to sit up and take notice was such as to indicate the essential hollowness in the modern view, or lack of view, resulting from the disintegration of traditional values. You had killed, or your grandfather had killed, the bad bogieman—namely, Victorian superstition and convention; and what was the brave new world that modern science and freedom was then able to build? Dust and ashes. Not only was the splendor gone from moonlight and roses, but it was also gone from that other great stand-by of Victorian enlightenment—science and progress. The greater your desire to believe in what was gone, the greater your resentment at finding that it was not there. Hence you write satiric pictures of modern life, not out of a feeling of superiority or amused contempt or cynical indifference—not like Wells in some of his novels or like Shaw in his plays or yet like Norman Douglas in *South Wind*—but out of a feeling of horror, out of frustration, nostalgia, intense disappointment."[1]

Huxley himself defends his disinclination to accept the suffering world on its own terms. In *After*

[1] *The Novel and the Modern World.* By David Daiches. The University of Chicago Press. 1939.

Many a Summer Dies the Swan Huxley creates Mr. Propter, a mystical philosopher who echoes Huxley's deepest fears and his most devastating finalities. For example, Mr. Propter concludes that one of the enormous defects of so-called good literature was its acceptance of the conventional scale of values.

". . . it treated as though they were reasonable the mainly lunatic preoccupations of statesmen, lovers, business men, social climbers, parents. In a word, it took seriously the causes of suffering as well as the suffering. . . . So that even when a tragedy ended badly, the reader was hypnotized by the eloquence of the piece into imagining that it was all somehow noble and worth while. . . . No, a good satire was much more deeply truthful and, of course, much more profitable than good tragedy."

Huxley-Propter is no less disheartening when he turns from literature to life. He assures us that most of the things we have been taught do not deserve anything but cynicism.

"Yes, you've got to be cynical. Especially cynical about all the actions and feelings you've been taught to suppose were good. Most of them are not good. They're merely evils which happen to be regarded as creditable."

Where, then, is good to be found? Huxley gives us little comfort. Not on the human level, it seems, but "on the level below the human and on the level above." Here is a desperate choice: the level of the animal where good exists as "the proper functioning 10 of the organism in accordance with the laws of its own being," or the level of eternity, where good exists "in the form of knowledge of a world without desire or aversion." On the human level, which is never fully animal and rarely angelic, there is nothing, says Huxley, for which we can hope.

"The Gioconda Smile," one of Huxley's most skillful stories, illustrates the author's intellectuality and cynicism. Here his characters, typical of the social circle which is a microcosm of the pernicious 20 world, are buffeted about, "cheated by the mind and betrayed by the body." Huxley's genius for inventing unpleasant persons intensifies the narrative. The "hero" is a conceited puppet twitched by his unstable emotions, a comic flirt who becomes a tragic fool. His wife, although genuinely ill, is a born hypochondriac. Doris is a pretty moron. Miss Spence is a malevolent but simpering harpy. Even the doctor (Libbard) is, until the very denouement, a self-satisfied "soulful" prig. Yet they are not

"types." They are people, absurdly and terribly alive. They are drawn into the story with fateful casualness, or rather, they draw the story about them. They turn a satirical comedy into a shocking but plausible melodrama.

It is interesting to compare "The Gioconda Smile" with "Nuns at Luncheon," another of Huxley's remarkably effective short stories, reprinted in Somerset Maugham's omnibus *Tellers of Tales*. Here, too, is the picture of an evil world. But where the horror of "Nuns at Luncheon" ends by revolting the reader, "The Gioconda Smile" continues to trouble him with its persistent fascination of a degenerating society.

And this, says Huxley, this with all its self-deception and false values, its sexual excesses and its vast futility, is your lunatic sphere, the modern world. With only slight shifts in emphasis, he says it in all his highly readable work, over and over again.

THE GIOCONDA SMILE[1]

I

"MISS Spence will be down directly, sir."

"Thank you," said Mr. Hutton, without turning around. Janet Spence's parlourmaid was so ugly—ugly on purpose, it always seemed to him, malignantly, criminally ugly—that he could not bear to look at her more than was necessary. The door closed. Left to himself, Mr. Hutton got up and began to wander round the room, looking with meditative eyes at the familiar objects it contained.

Photographs of Greek statuary, photographs of the Roman Forum, coloured prints of Italian masterpieces, all very safe and well known. Poor, dear Janet, what a prig—what an intellectual snob! Her real taste was illustrated in that water-colour by the pavement artist, the one she had paid half a crown for (and thirty-five shillings for the frame). How often he had heard her tell the story, how often expatiate on the beauties of that skilful imitation of an oleograph! "A real Artist in the streets," and you could hear the capital A in Artist as she spoke the words. She made you feel that part of his glory had entered into Janet Spence when she tendered him that half-crown for the copy of the oleograph. She was implying a compliment to her own taste and penetration. A genuine Old Master for half a crown. Poor, dear Janet!

Mr. Hutton came to a pause in front of a small

[1] From *Mortal Coils* by Aldous Huxley, copyright, 1922, by Harper & Brothers.   **19. oleograph,** a lithograph copy of a painting, usually in gaudy colors.

oblong mirror. Stooping a little to get a full view of his face, he passed a white, well-manicured finger over his moustache. It was as curly, as freshly auburn as it had been twenty years ago. His hair still retained its colour, and there was no sign of baldness yet—only a certain elevation of the brow. "Shakespearean," thought Mr. Hutton, with a smile, as he surveyed the smooth and polished expanse of his forehead.

Others abide our question, thou art free. . . . Footsteps in the sea . . . Majesty . . . Shakespeare, thou shouldst be living at this hour. No, that was Milton, wasn't it? Milton, the Lady of Christ's. There was no lady about him. He was what women would call a manly man. That was why they liked him—for the curly auburn moustache and the discreet redolence of tobacco. Mr. Hutton smiled again; he enjoyed making fun of himself. Lady of Christ's? No, no. He was the Christ of Ladies. Very pretty, very pretty. The Christ of Ladies. Mr. Hutton wished there were somebody he could tell the joke to. Poor, dear Janet wouldn't appreciate it, alas!

He straightened himself up, patted his hair, and resumed his peregrination. Damn the Roman Forum; he hated those dreary photographs.

Suddenly he became aware that Janet Spence was in the room, standing near the door. Mr. Hutton started, as though he had been taken in some felonious act. To make these silent and spectral appearances was one of Janet Spence's peculiar talents. Perhaps she had been there all the time, had seen him looking at himself in the mirror. Impossible! But, still, it was disquieting.

"Oh, you gave me such a surprise," said Mr. Hutton, recovering his smile and advancing with outstretched hand to meet her.

Miss Spence was smiling too: her Gioconda smile, he had once called it in a moment of half-ironical flattery. Miss Spence had taken the compliment seriously, and always tried to live up to the Leonardo standard. She smiled on in silence while Mr. Hutton shook hands; that was part of the Gioconda business.

"I hope you're well," said Mr. Hutton. "You look it."

What a queer face she had! That small mouth pursed forward by the Gioconda expression into a little snout with a round hole in the middle as though for whistling—it was like a penholder seen from the front. Above the mouth a well-shaped nose,

finely aquiline. Eyes large, lustrous, and dark, with the largeness, lustre, and darkness that seems to invite sties and an occasional bloodshot suffusion. They were fine eyes, but unchangingly grave. The penholder might do its Gioconda trick, but the eyes never altered in their earnestness. Above them, a pair of boldly arched, heavily pencilled black eyebrows lent a surprising air of power, as of a Roman matron, to the upper portion of the face. Her hair was dark and equally Roman; Agrippina from the brows upward.

"I thought I'd just look in on my way home," Mr. Hutton went on. "Ah, it's good to be back here"—he indicated with a wave of his hand the flowers in the vases, the sunshine and greenery beyond the windows—"it's good to be back in the country after a stuffy day of business in town."

Miss Spence, who had sat down, pointed to a chair at her side.

"No, really, I can't sit down," Mr. Hutton protested. "I must get back to see how poor Emily is. She was rather seedy this morning." He sat down, nevertheless. "It's these wretched liver chills. She's always getting them. Women——" He broke off and coughed, so as to hide the fact that he had uttered. He was about to say that women with weak digestions ought not to marry; but the remark was too cruel, and he didn't really believe it. Janet Spence, moreover, was a believer in eternal flames and spiritual attachments. "She hopes to be well enough," he added, "to see you at luncheon tomorrow. Can you come? Do!" He smiled persuasively. "It's my invitation too, you know."

She dropped her eyes, and Mr. Hutton almost thought that he detected a certain reddening of the cheek. It was a tribute; he stroked his moustache.

"I should like to come if you think Emily's really well enough to have a visitor."

"Of course. You'll do her good. You'll do us both good. In married life three is often better company than two."

"Oh, you're cynical."

Mr. Hutton always had a desire to say "Bow-wow-wow" whenever that last word was spoken. It irritated him more than any other word in the language. But instead of barking he made haste to protest.

"No, no. I'm only speaking a melancholy truth. Reality doesn't always come up to the ideal, you know. But that doesn't make me believe any the less in the ideal. Indeed, I believe in it passionately—the ideal of a matrimony between two people in perfect accord. I think it's realisable. I'm sure it is."

38. **Gioconda smile,** the enigmatic expression on the face of Leonardo da Vinci's painting of "Mona Lisa," the wife of Francesco del Giocondo. See Pater on the subject, page 865.

He paused significantly and looked at her with an arch expression. A virgin of thirty-six, but still unwithered; she had her charms. And there was something really rather enigmatic about her. Miss Spence made no reply but continued to smile. There were times when Mr. Hutton got rather bored with the Gioconda. He stood up.

"I must really be going now. Farewell, mysterious Gioconda." The smile grew intenser, focused itself, as it were, in a narrower snout. Mr. Hutton made a Cinquecento gesture, and kissed her extended hand. It was the first time he had done such a thing; the action seemed not to be resented. "I look forward to to-morrow."

"Do you?"

For answer Mr. Hutton once more kissed her hand, then turned to go. Miss Spence accompanied him to the porch.

"Where's your car?" she asked.

"I left it at the gate of the drive."

"I'll come and see you off."

"No, no." Mr. Hutton was playful, but determined. "You must do no such a thing. I simply forbid you."

"But I should like to come," Miss Spence protested, throwing a rapid Gioconda at him.

Mr. Hutton held up his hand. "No," he repeated, and then, with a gesture that was almost the blowing of a kiss, he started to run down the drive, lightly on his toes, with long, bounding strides like a boy's. He was proud of that run; it was quite marvellously youthful. Still, he was glad the drive was no longer. At the last bend, before passing out of sight of the house, he halted and turned round. Miss Spence was still standing on the steps, smiling her smile. He waved his hand, and this time quite definitely and overtly wafted a kiss in her direction. Then, breaking once more into his magnificent canter, he rounded the last dark promontory of trees. Once out of sight of the house he let his high paces decline to a trot, and finally to a walk. He took out his handkerchief and began wiping his neck inside his collar. What fools, what fools! Had there ever been such an ass as poor, dear Janet Spence? Never, unless it was himself. Decidedly he was the more malignant fool, since he, at least, was aware of his folly and still persisted in it. Why did he persist? Ah, the problem that was himself, the problem that was other people.

He had reached the gate. A large, prosperous-looking motor was standing at the side of the road.

"Home, M'Nab." The chauffeur touched his cap.

"And stop at the cross-roads on the way, as usual," Mr. Hutton added, as he opened the door of the car. "Well?" he said, speaking into the obscurity that lurked within.

"Oh, Teddy Bear, what an age you've been!" It was a fresh and childish voice that spoke the words. There was the faintest hint of Cockney impurity about the vowel sounds.

Mr. Hutton bent his large form and darted into the car with the agility of an animal regaining its burrow.

"Have I?" he said, as he shut the door. The machine began to move. "You must have missed me a lot if you found the time so long." He sat back in the low seat; a cherishing warmth enveloped him.

"Teddy Bear . . ." and with a sigh of contentment a charming little head declined on to Mr. Hutton's shoulder. Ravished, he looked down sideways at the round, babyish face.

"Do you know, Doris, you look like the pictures of Louise de Kerouaille." He passed his fingers through a mass of curly hair.

"Who's Louise de Kera-whatever-it-is?" Doris spoke from remote distances.

"She was, alas! *Fuit*. We shall all be 'was' one of these days. Meanwhile . . ."

Mr. Hutton covered the babyish face with kisses. The car rushed smoothly along. M'Nab's back, through the front window, was stonily impassive, the back of a statue.

"Your hands," Doris whispered. "Oh, you mustn't touch me. They give me electric shocks."

Mr. Hutton adored her for the virgin imbecility of the words. How late in one's existence one makes the discovery of one's body!

"The electricity isn't in me, it's in you." He kissed her again, whispering her name several times: Doris, Doris, Doris. The scientific appellation of the sea-mouse, he was thinking as he kissed the throat she offered him, white and extended like the throat of a victim awaiting the sacrificial knife. The sea-mouse was a sausage with iridescent fur: very peculiar. Or was Doris the sea cucumber, which turns itself inside out in moments of alarm? He would really have to go to Naples again, just to see the aquarium. These sea creatures were fabulous, unbelievably fantastic.

"Oh, Teddy Bear!" (More zoology; but he was only a land animal. His poor little jokes!) "Teddy Bear, I'm so happy."

"So am I," said Mr. Hutton. Was it true?

"But I wish I knew if it were right. Tell me, Teddy Bear, is it right or wrong?"

11. **Cinquecento**, sixteenth century, the period of Leonardo da Vinci and the Gioconda.

25. **Fuit**, finished;—"she was."

"Ah, my dear, that's just what I've been wondering for the last thirty years."

"Be serious, Teddy Bear. I want to know if this is right; if it's right that I should be here with you and that we should love one another, and that it should give me electric shocks when you touch me."

"Right? Well, it's certainly good that you should have electric shocks rather than sexual repressions. Read Freud; repressions are the devil."

"Oh, you don't help me. Why aren't you ever serious? If only you knew how miserable I am sometimes, thinking it's not right. Perhaps, you know, there is a hell, and all that. I don't know what to do. Sometimes I think I ought to stop loving you."

"But could you?" asked Mr. Hutton, confident in the powers of his seduction and his moustache.

"No, Teddy Bear, you know I couldn't. But I could run away, I could hide from you, I could lock myself up and force myself not to come to you."

"Silly little thing!" He tightened his embrace.

"Oh, dear, I hope it isn't wrong. And there are times when I don't care if it is."

Mr. Hutton was touched. He had a certain protective affection for this little creature. He laid his cheek against her hair and so, interlaced, they sat in silence, while the car, swaying and pitching a little as it hastened along, seemed to draw in the white road and the dusty hedges towards it devouringly.

"Good-bye, good-bye."

The car moved on, gathered speed, vanished round a curve, and Doris was left standing by the sign-post at the cross-roads, still dizzy and weak with the languor born of those kisses and the electrical touch of those gentle hands. She had to take a deep breath, to draw herself up deliberately, before she was strong enough to start her homeward walk. She had half a mile in which to invent the necessary lies.

Alone, Mr. Hutton suddenly found himself the prey of an appalling boredom.

2

Mrs. Hutton was lying on the sofa in her boudoir, playing Patience. In spite of the warmth of the July evening a wood fire was burning on the hearth. A black Pomeranian, extenuated by the heat and the fatigues of digestion, slept before the blaze.

"Phew! Isn't it rather hot in here?" Mr. Hutton asked as he entered the room.

47. **Patience,** a game of cards played by one person; solitaire.

"You know I have to keep warm, dear." The voice seemed breaking on the verge of tears. "I get so shivery."

"I hope you're better this evening."

"Not much, I'm afraid."

The conversation stagnated. Mr. Hutton stood leaning his back against the mantelpiece. He looked down at the Pomeranian lying at his feet, and with the toe of his right boot he rolled the little dog over and rubbed its white-flecked chest and belly. The creature lay in an inert ecstasy. Mrs. Hutton continued to play Patience. Arrived at an *impasse*, she altered the position of one card, took back another, and went on playing. Her Patiences always came out.

"Dr. Libbard thinks I ought to go to Llandrindod Wells this summer."

"Well, go, my dear—go, most certainly."

Mr. Hutton was thinking of the events of the afternoon: how they had driven, Doris and he, up to the hanging wood, had left the car to wait for them under the shade of the trees, and walked together out into the windless sunshine of the chalk down.

"I'm to drink the waters for my liver, and he thinks I ought to have massage and electric treatment, too."

Hat in hand, Doris had stalked four blue butterflies that were dancing together round a scabious flower with a motion that was like the flickering of blue fire. The blue fire burst and scattered into whirling sparks; she had given chase, laughing and shouting like a child.

"I'm sure it will do you good, my dear."

"I was wondering if you'd come with me, dear."

"But you know I'm going to Scotland at the end of the month."

Mrs. Hutton looked up at him entreatingly. "It's the journey," she said. "The thought of it is such a nightmare. I don't know if I can manage it. And you know I can't sleep in hotels. And then there's the luggage and all the worries. I can't go alone."

"But you won't be alone. You'll have your maid with you." He spoke impatiently. The sick woman was usurping the place of the healthy one. He was being dragged back from the memory of the sunlit down and the quick, laughing girl, back to this unhealthy, overheated room and its complaining occupant.

"I don't think I shall be able to go."

"But you must, my dear, if the doctor tells you to. And, besides, a change will do you good."

"I don't think so."

"But Libbard thinks so, and he knows what he's talking about."

"No, I can't face it. I'm so weak. I can't go alone." Mrs. Hutton pulled a handkerchief out of her black silk bag, and put it to her eyes.

"Nonsense, my dear, you must make the effort."

"I had rather be left in peace to die here." She was crying in earnest now.

"O Lord! Now do be reasonable. Listen now, please." Mrs. Hutton only sobbed more violently. "Oh, what is one to do?" He shrugged his shoulders and walked out of the room.

Mr. Hutton was aware that he had not behaved with proper patience; but he could not help it. Very early in his manhood he had discovered that not only did he not feel sympathy for the poor, the weak, the diseased, and deformed; he actually hated them. Once, as an undergraduate, he spent three days at a mission in the East End. He had returned, filled with a profound and ineradicable disgust. Instead of pitying, he loathed the unfortunate. It was not, he knew, a very comely emotion; and he had been ashamed of it at first. In the end he had decided that it was temperamental, inevitable, and had felt no further qualms. Emily had been healthy and beautiful when he married her. He had loved her then. But now—was it his fault that she was like this?

Mr. Hutton dined alone. Food and drink left him more benevolent than he had been before dinner. To make amends for his show of exasperation he went up to his wife's room and offered to read to her. She was touched, gratefully accepted the offer, and Mr. Hutton, who was particularly proud of his accent, suggested a little light reading in French.

"French? I am so fond of French." Mrs. Hutton spoke of the language of Racine as though it were a dish of green peas.

Mr. Hutton ran down to the library and returned with a yellow volume. He began reading. The effort of pronouncing perfectly absorbed his whole attention. But how good his accent was! The fact of its goodness seemed to improve the quality of the novel he was reading.

At the end of fifteen pages an unmistakable sound aroused him. He looked up; Mrs. Hutton had gone to sleep. He sat still for a little while, looking with a dispassionate curiosity at the sleeping face. Once it had been beautiful; once, long ago, the sight of it, the recollection of it, had moved him with an emotion profounder, perhaps, than any he had felt before or since. Now it was lined and cadaverous. The skin was stretched tightly over the cheekbones, across the bridge of the sharp, bird-like nose. The closed eyes were set in profound bone-rimmed sockets. The lamplight striking on the face from the side emphasized with light and shade its cavities and projections. It was the face of a dead Christ by Morales.

"Le squelette était invisible
Au temps heureux de l'art païen."

He shivered a little, and tiptoed out of the room.

On the following day Mrs. Hutton came down to luncheon. She had had some unpleasant palpitation during the night, but she was feeling better now. Besides, she wanted to do honour to her guest. Miss Spence listened to her complaints about Llandrindod Wells, and was loud in sympathy, lavish with advice. Whatever she said was always said with intensity. She leaned forward, aimed, so to speak, like a gun, and fired her words. Bang! the charge in her soul was ignited, the words whizzed forth at the narrow barrel of her mouth. She was a machine-gun riddling her hostess with sympathy. Mr. Hutton had undergone similar bombardments, mostly of a literary or philosophic character—bombardments of Maeterlinck, of Mrs. Besant, of Bergson, of William James. To-day the missiles were medical. She talked about insomnia, she expatiated on the virtues of harmless drugs and beneficent specialists. Under the bombardment Mrs. Hutton opened out, like a flower in the sun.

Mr. Hutton looked on in silence. The spectacle of Janet Spence evoked in him an unfailing curiosity. He was not romantic enough to imagine that every face masked an interior physiognomy of beauty or strangeness, that every woman's small talk was like a vapour hanging over mysterious gulfs. His wife, for example, and Doris; they were nothing more than what they seemed to be. But with Janet Spence it was somehow different. Here one could be sure that there was some kind of a queer face behind the Gioconda smile and the Roman eyebrows. The only question was: What exactly was there? Mr. Hutton could never quite make out.

"But perhaps you won't have to go to Llandrindod after all," Miss Spence was saying. "If you get well quickly Dr. Libbard will let you off."

"I only hope so. Indeed, I do really feel rather better to-day."

Mr. Hutton felt ashamed. How much was it his own lack of sympathy that prevented her from feeling well every day? But he comforted himself by reflecting that it was only a case of feeling, not of being

7–8. "Le squelette . . . païen." "The skeleton was invisible in the happy days of pagan art."

better. Sympathy does not mend a diseased liver or a weak heart.

"My dear, I wouldn't eat those red currants if I were you," he said, suddenly solicitous. "You know that Libbard has banned everything with skins and pips."

"But I am so fond of them," Mrs. Hutton protested, "and I feel so well to-day."

"Don't be a tyrant," said Miss Spence, looking first at him and then at his wife. "Let the poor invalid have what she fancies; it will do her good." She laid her hand on Mrs. Hutton's arm and patted it affectionately two or three times.

"Thank you, my dear." Mrs. Hutton helped herself to the stewed currants.

"Well, don't blame me if they make you ill again."

"Do I ever blame you, dear?"

"You have nothing to blame me for," Mr. Hutton answered playfully. "I am the perfect husband."

They sat in the garden after luncheon. From the island of shade under the old cypress tree they looked out across a flat expanse of lawn, in which the parterres of flowers shone with a metallic brilliance.

Mr. Hutton took a deep breath of the warm and fragrant air. "It's good to be alive," he said.

"Just to be alive," his wife echoed, stretching one pale, knot-jointed hand into the sunlight.

A maid brought the coffee; the silver pots and the little blue cups were set on a folding table near the group of chairs.

"Oh, my medicine!" exclaimed Mrs. Hutton, "Run in and fetch it, Clara, will you? The white bottle on the sideboard."

"I'll go," said Mr. Hutton. "I've got to go and fetch a cigar in any case."

He ran in towards the house. On the threshold he turned round for an instant. The maid was walking back across the lawn. His wife was sitting up in her deck-chair, engaged in opening her white parasol. Miss Spence was bending over the table, pouring out the coffee. He passed into the cool obscurity of the house.

"Do you like sugar in your coffee?" Miss Spence inquired.

"Yes, please. Give me rather a lot. I'll drink it after my medicine to take the taste away."

Mrs. Hutton leaned back in her chair, lowering the sunshade over her eyes, so as to shut out from her vision the burning sky.

Behind her, Miss Spence was making a delicate clinking among the coffee-cups.

"I've given you three large spoonfuls. That ought to take the taste away. And here comes the medicine."

Mr. Hutton had reappeared, carrying a wineglass, half full of a pale liquid.

"It smells delicious," he said, as he handed it to his wife.

"That's only the flavouring." She drank it off at a gulp, shuddered, and made a grimace. "Ugh, it's so nasty. Give me my coffee."

Miss Spence gave her the cup; she sipped at it. "You've made it like syrup. But it's very nice, after that atrocious medicine."

At half-past three Mrs. Hutton complained that she did not feel as well as she had done, and went indoors to lie down. Her husband would have said something about the red currants, but checked himself; the triumph of an "I told you so" was too cheaply won. Instead, he was sympathetic, and gave her his arm to the house.

"A rest will do you good," he said. "By the way, I shan't be back till after dinner."

"But why? Where are you going?"

"I promised to go to Johnson's this evening. We have to discuss the war memorial, you know."

"Oh, I wish you weren't going." Mrs. Hutton was almost in tears. "Can't you stay? I don't like being alone in the house."

"But, my dear, I promised—weeks ago." It was a bother having to lie like this. "And now I must get back and look after Miss Spence."

He kissed her on the forehead and went out again into the garden. Miss Spence received him aimed and intense.

"Your wife is dreadfully ill," she fired off at him.

"I thought she cheered up so much when you came."

"That was purely nervous, purely nervous. I was watching her closely. With a heart in that condition and her digestion wrecked—yes, wrecked—anything might happen."

"Libbard doesn't take so gloomy a view of poor Emily's health." Mr. Hutton held open the gate that led from the garden into the drive; Miss Spence's car was standing by the front door.

"Libbard is only a country doctor. You ought to see a specialist."

He could not refrain from laughing. "You have a macabre passion for specialists."

Miss Spence held up her hand in protest. "I am serious. I think poor Emily is in a very bad state. Anything might happen—at any moment."

He handed her into the car and shut the door. The chauffeur started the engine and climbed into his place, ready to drive off.

"Shall I tell him to start?" He had no desire to continue the conversation.

Miss Spence leaned forward and shot a Gioconda in his direction. "Remember, I expect you to come and see me again soon."

Mechanically he grinned, made a polite noise, and, as the car moved forward, waved his hand. He was happy to be alone.

A few minutes afterwards Mr. Hutton himself drove away. Doris was waiting at the cross-roads. They dined together twenty miles from home, at a roadside hotel. It was one of those bad, expensive meals which are cooked only in country hotels frequented by motorists. It revolted Mr. Hutton, but Doris enjoyed it. She always enjoyed things. Mr. Hutton ordered a not very good brand of champagne. He was wishing he had spent the evening in his library.

When they started homewards Doris was a little tipsy and extremely affectionate. It was very dark inside the car, but looking forward, past the motionless form of M'Nab, they could see a bright and narrow universe of forms and colours scooped out of the night by the electric head-lamps.

It was after eleven when Mr. Hutton reached home. Dr. Libbard met him in the hall. He was a small man with delicate hands and well-formed features that were almost feminine. His brown eyes were large and melancholy. He used to waste a great deal of time sitting at the bedside of his patients, looking sadness through those eyes and talking in a sad, low voice about nothing in particular. His person exhaled a pleasing odour, decidedly antiseptic but at the same time suave and discreetly delicious.

"Libbard?" said Mr. Hutton in surprise. "You here? Is my wife ill?"

"We tried to fetch you earlier," the soft, melancholy voice replied. "It was thought you were at Mr. Johnson's, but they had no news of you there."

"No, I was detained. I had a breakdown," Mr. Hutton answered irritably. It was tiresome to be caught out in a lie.

"Your wife wanted to see you urgently."

"Well, I can go now." Mr. Hutton moved towards the stairs.

Dr. Libbard laid a hand on his arm. "I am afraid it's too late."

"Too late?" He began fumbling with his watch; it wouldn't come out of the pocket.

"Mrs. Hutton passed away half an hour ago."

The voice remained even in its softness, the melancholy of the eyes did not deepen. Dr. Libbard spoke of death as he would speak of a local cricket match. All things were equally vain and equally deplorable.

Mr. Hutton found himself thinking of Janet Spence's words. At any moment—at any moment. She had been extraordinarily right.

"What happened?" he asked. "What was the cause?"

Dr. Libbard explained. It was heart failure brought on by a violent attack of nausea, caused in its turn by the eating of something of an irritant nature. Red currants? Mr. Hutton suggested. Very likely. It had been too much for the heart. There was chronic valvular disease: something had collapsed under the strain. It was all over; she could not have suffered much.

3

"It's a pity they should have chosen the day of the Eton and Harrow match for the funeral," old General Grego was saying as he stood, his top hat in his hand, under the shadow of the lych gate, wiping his face with his handkerchief.

Mr. Hutton overheard the remark and with difficulty restrained a desire to inflict grievous bodily pain on the General. He would have liked to hit the old brute in the middle of his big red face. Monstrous great mulberry, spotted with meal! Was there no respect for the dead? Did nobody care? In theory he didn't much care; let the dead bury their dead. But here, at the graveside, he had found himself actually sobbing. Poor Emily, they had been pretty happy once. Now she was lying at the bottom of a seven-foot hole. And here was Grego complaining that he couldn't go to the Eton and Harrow match.

Mr. Hutton looked round at the groups of black figures that were drifting slowly out of the churchyard towards the fleet of cabs and motors assembled in the road outside. Against the brilliant background of the July grass and flowers and foliage, they had a horribly alien and unnatural appearance. It pleased him to think that all these people would soon be dead, too.

That evening Mr. Hutton sat up late in his library reading the life of Milton. There was no particular reason why he should have chosen Milton; it was the book that first came to hand, that was all. It was after midnight when he had finished. He got up from his armchair, unbolted the French windows, and stepped out on to the little paved terrace. The night was quiet and clear. Mr. Hutton looked at the stars and at the holes between them, dropped his eyes to the dim lawns and hueless flowers of the garden, and let them wander over the farther landscape, black and grey under the moon.

He began to think with a kind of confused violence. There were the stars, there was Milton. A man can be somehow the peer of stars and night. Greatness, nobility. But is there seriously a difference between the noble and the ignoble? Milton, the stars, death, and himself—himself. The soul, the body; the higher and the lower nature. Perhaps there was something in it, after all. Milton had a god on his side and righteousness. What had he? Nothing, nothing whatever. There was only Doris's little breasts. What was the point of it all? Milton, the stars, death, and Emily in her grave, Doris and himself—always himself . . .

Oh, he was a futile and disgusting being. Everything convinced him of it. It was a solemn moment. He spoke aloud: "I will, I will." The sound of his own voice in the darkness was appalling; it seemed to him that he had sworn that infernal oath which binds even the gods: "I will, I will." There had been New Year's days and solemn anniversaries in the past, when he had felt the same contritions and recorded similar resolutions. They had all thinned away, these resolutions, like smoke, into nothingness. But this was a greater moment and he had pronounced a more fearful oath. In the future it was to be different. Yes, he would live by reason, he would be industrious, he would curb his appetites, he would devote his life to some good purpose. It was resolved and it would be so.

In practice he saw himself spending his mornings in agricultural pursuits, riding round with the bailiff, seeing that his land was farmed in the best modern way—silos and artificial manures and continuous cropping, and all that. The remainder of the day should be devoted to serious study. There was that book he had been intending to write for so long—*The Effect of Diseases on Civilization*.

Mr. Hutton went to bed humble and contrite, but with a sense that grace had entered into him. He slept for seven and a half hours, and woke to find the sun brilliantly shining. The emotions of the evening before had been transformed by a good night's rest into his customary cheerfulness. It was not until a good many seconds after his return to conscious life that he remembered his resolution, his Stygian oath. Milton and death seemed somehow different in the sunlight. As for the stars, they were not there. But the resolutions were good; even in the daytime he could see that. He had his horse saddled after breakfast, and rode round the farm with the bailiff. After luncheon he read Thucydides on the plague at Athens. In the evening he made a few notes on malaria in Southern Italy. While he

31-32. **bailiff,** agent, farm-manager.

was undressing he remembered that there was a good anecdote in Skelton's jest-book about the Sweating Sickness. He would have made a note of it if only he could have found a pencil.

On the sixth morning of his new life Mr. Hutton found among his correspondence an envelope addressed in that peculiarly vulgar handwriting which he knew to be Doris's. He opened it, and began to read. She didn't know what to say; words were so inadequate. His wife dying like that, and so suddenly—it was too terrible. Mr. Hutton sighed, but his interest revived somewhat as he read on:

"Death is so frightening, I never think of it when I can help it. But when something like this happens, or when I am feeling ill or depressed, then I can't help remembering it is there so close, and I think about all the wicked things I have done and about you and me, and I wonder what will happen, and I am so frightened. I am so lonely, Teddy Bear, and so unhappy, and I don't know what to do. I can't get rid of the idea of dying, I am so wretched and helpless without you. I didn't mean to write to you; I meant to wait till you were out of mourning and could come and see me again, but I was so lonely and miserable, Teddy Bear, I had to write. I couldn't help it. Forgive me, I want you so much; I have nobody in the world but you. You are so good and gentle and understanding; there is nobody like you. I shall never forget how good and kind you have been to me, and you are so clever and know so much, I can't understand how you ever came to pay any attention to me, I am so dull and stupid, much less like me and love me, because you do love me a little don't you, Teddy Bear?"

Mr. Hutton was touched with shame and remorse. To be thanked like this, worshipped for having seduced the girl—it was too much. It had just been a piece of imbecile wantonness. Imbecile, idiotic: there was no other way to describe it. For, when all was said, he had derived very little pleasure from it. Taking all things together, he had probably been more bored than amused. Once upon a time he had believed himself to be a hedonist. But to be a hedonist implies a certain process of reasoning, a deliberate choice of known pleasures, a rejection of known pains. This had been done without reason, against it. For he knew beforehand—so well, so well—that there was no interest or pleasure to be derived from these wretched affairs. And yet each time the vague itch came upon him he suc-

45. **hedonist,** one who lives wholely for pleasure and sensation.

cumbed, involving himself once more in the old stupidity. There had been Maggie, his wife's maid, and Edith, the girl on the farm, and Mrs. Pringle, the waitress in London, and others—there seemed to be dozens of them. It had all been so stale and boring. He knew it would be; he always knew. And yet, and yet . . . Experience doesn't teach.

Poor little Doris! He would write to her kindly, comfortingly, but he wouldn't see her again. A servant came to tell him that his horse was saddled and waiting. He mounted and rode off. That morning the old bailiff was more irritating than usual.

Five days later Doris and Mr. Hutton were sitting together on the pier at Southend; Doris, in white muslin with pink garnishings, radiated happiness; Mr. Hutton, legs outstretched and chair tilted, had pushed the panama back from his forehead, and was trying to feel like a tripper. That night, when Doris was asleep, breathing and warm by his side, he recaptured, in this moment of darkness and physical fatigue, the rather cosmic emotion which had possessed him that evening, not a fortnight ago, when he had made his great resolution. And so his solemn oath had already gone the way of so many other resolutions. Unreason had triumphed; at the first itch of desire he had given away. He was hopeless, hopeless.

For a long time he lay with closed eyes, ruminating his humiliation. The girl stirred in her sleep. Mr. Hutton turned over and looked in her direction. Enough faint light crept in between the half-drawn curtains to show her bare arm and shoulder, her neck, and the dark tangle of hair on the pillow. She was beautiful, desirable. Why did he lie there moaning over his sins? What did it matter? If he were hopeless, then so be it; he would make the best of his hopelessness. A glorious sense of irresponsibility suddenly filled him. He was free, magnificently free. In a kind of exaltation he drew the girl towards him. She woke, bewildered, almost frightened under his rough kisses.

The storm of his desire subsided into a kind of serene merriment. The whole atmosphere seemed to be quivering with enormous silent laughter.

"Could anyone love you as much as I do, Teddy Bear?" The question came faintly from distant worlds of love.

"I think I know somebody who does," Mr. Hutton replied. The submarine laughter was swelling, rising, ready to break the surface of silence and resound.

"Who? Tell me. What do you mean?" The voice had come very close; charged with suspicion, an-

guish, indignation, it belonged to this immediate world.

"A-ah!"

"Who?"

"You'll never guess." Mr. Hutton kept up the joke until it began to grow tedious, and then pronounced the name "Janet Spence."

Doris was incredulous. "Miss Spence of the Manor? That old woman?" It was too ridiculous. Mr. Hutton laughed too.

"But it's quite true," he said. "She adores me." Oh, the vast joke! He would go and see her as soon as he returned—see and conquer. "I believe she wants to marry me," he added.

"But you wouldn't . . . you don't intend . . ."

The air was fairly crepitating with humour. Mr. Hutton laughed aloud. "I intend to marry you," he said. It seemed to him the best joke he had ever made in his life.

When Mr. Hutton left Southend he was once more a married man. It was agreed that, for the time being, the fact should be kept secret. In the autumn they would go abroad together, and the world should be informed. Meanwhile he was to go back to his own house and Doris to hers.

The day after his return he walked over in the afternoon to see Miss Spence. She received him with the old Gioconda.

"I was expecting you to come."

"I couldn't keep away," Mr. Hutton gallantly replied.

They sat in the summer-house. It was a pleasant place—a little old stucco temple bowered among dense bushes of evergreen. Miss Spence had left her mark on it by hanging up over the seat a blue-and-white Della Robbia plaque.

"I am thinking of going to Italy this autumn," said Mr. Hutton. He felt like a ginger-beer bottle, ready to pop with bubbling humorous excitement.

"Italy. . . ." Miss Spence closed her eyes ecstatically. "I feel drawn there, too."

"Why not let yourself be drawn?"

"I don't know. One somehow hasn't the energy and initiative to set out alone."

"Alone. . . ." Ah, sound of guitars and throaty singing! "Yes, travelling alone isn't much fun."

Miss Spence lay back in her chair without speaking. Her eyes were still closed. Mr. Hutton stroked his moustache. The silence prolonged itself for what seemed a very long time.

Pressed to stay to dinner, Mr. Hutton did not refuse. The fun had hardly started. The table was

36. **Della Robbia:** a famous fifteenth-century family of Italian artists who specialized in modeled majolica ware.

laid in the loggia. Through its arches they looked out on to the sloping garden, to the valley below and the farther hills. Light ebbed away; the heat and silence were oppressive. A huge cloud was mounting up the sky, and there were distant breathings of thunder. The thunder drew nearer, a wind began to blow, and the first drops of rain fell. The table was cleared. Miss Spence and Mr. Hutton sat on in the growing darkness.

Miss Spence broke a long silence by saying meditatively:

"I think everyone has a right to a certain amount of happiness, don't you?"

"Most certainly." But what was she leading up to? Nobody makes generalisations about life unless they mean to talk about themselves. Happiness: he looked back on his own life, and saw a cheerful, placid existence disturbed by no great griefs or discomforts or alarms. He had always had money and freedom; he had been able to do very much as he wanted. Yes, he supposed he had been happy—happier than most men. And now he was not merely happy; he had discovered in irresponsibility the secret of gaiety. He was about to say something about his happiness when Miss Spence went on speaking.

"People like you and me have a right to be happy some time in our lives."

"Me?" said Mr. Hutton, surprised.

"Poor Henry! Fate hasn't treated either of us very well."

"Oh, well, it might have treated me worse."

"You're being cheerful. That's brave of you. But don't think I can't see behind the mask."

Miss Spence spoke louder and louder as the rain came down more and more heavily. Periodically the thunder cut across her utterances. She talked on, shouting against the noise.

"I have understood you so well and for so long."

A flash revealed her, aimed and intent, leaning towards him. Her eyes were two profound and menacing gun-barrels. The darkness re-engulfed her.

"You were a lonely soul seeking a companion soul. I could sympathise with you in your solitude. Your marriage . . ."

The thunder cut short the sentence. Miss Spence's voice became audible once more with the words:

". . . could offer no companionship to a man of your stamp. You needed a soul mate."

A soul mate—he! a soul mate. It was incredibly fantastic. "Georgette Leblanc, the ex-soul mate of Maurice Maeterlinck." He had seen that in the

paper a few days ago. So it was thus that Janet Spence had painted him in her imagination—as a soul-mater. And for Doris he was a picture of goodness and the cleverest man in the world. And actually, really, he was what?—Who knows?

"My heart went out to you. I could understand; I was lonely, too." Miss Spence laid her hand on his knee. "You were so patient." Another flash. She was still aimed, dangerously. "You never complained. But I could guess—I could guess."

"How wonderful of you!" So he was an *âme incomprise*. "Only a woman's intuition . . ."

The thunder crashed and rumbled, died away, and only the sound of the rain was left. The thunder was his laughter, magnified, externalised. Flash and crash, there it was again, right on top of them.

"Don't you feel that you have within you something that is akin to this storm?" He could imagine her leaning forward as she uttered the words. "Passion makes one the equal of the elements."

What was his gambit now? Why, obviously, he should have said "Yes," and ventured on some unequivocal gesture. But Mr. Hutton suddenly took fright. The ginger beer in him had gone flat. The woman was serious—terribly serious. He was appalled.

Passion? "No," he desperately answered. "I am without passion."

But his remark was either unheard or unheeded, for Miss Spence went on with a growing exaltation, speaking so rapidly, however, and in such a burning intimate whisper that Mr. Hutton found it very difficult to distinguish what she was saying. She was telling him, as far as he could make out, the story of her life. The lightning was less frequent now, and there were long intervals of darkness. But at each flash he saw her still aiming towards him, still yearning forward with a terrifying intensity. Darkness, the rain, and then flash! her face was there, close at hand. A pale mask, greenish white; the large eyes, the narrow barrel of the mouth, the heavy eyebrows. Agrippina, or wasn't it rather—yes, wasn't it rather George Robey?"

He began devising absurd plans for escaping. He might suddenly jump up, pretending he had seen a burglar—Stop thief! stop thief!—and dash off into the night in pursuit. Or should he say that he felt faint, a heart attack? or that he had seen a ghost—Emily's ghost—in the garden? Absorbed in his childish plotting, he had ceased to pay any attention to

53. **Maurice Maeterlinck,** the Belgian essayist and dram-atist (1862–), author of *Pelleas and Mélisande, The Blue Bird,* and so on.   11–12. **âme incomprise,** a misunderstood soul.   44. **George Robey:** a famous comedian.

Miss Spence's words. The spasmodic clutching of her hand recalled his thoughts.

"I honoured you for that, Henry," she was saying.

Honoured him for what?

"Marriage is a sacred tie, and your respect for it, even when the marriage was, as it was in your case, an unhappy one, made me respect you and admire you, and—shall I dare say the word?—"

Oh, the burglar, the ghost in the garden! But it was too late.

". . . yes, love you, Henry, all the more. But we're free now, Henry."

Free? There was a movement in the dark, and she was kneeling on the floor by his chair.

"Oh, Henry, Henry, I have been unhappy, too."

Her arms embraced him, and by the shaking of her body he could feel that she was sobbing. She might have been a supplicant crying for mercy.

"You mustn't, Janet," he protested, Those tears were terrible, terrible. "Not now, not now! You must be calm; you must go to bed." He patted her shoulder, then got up, disengaging himself from her embrace. He left her still crouching on the floor beside the chair on which he had been sitting.

Groping his way into the hall, and without waiting to look for his hat, he went out of the house, taking infinite pains to close the front door noiselessly behind him. The clouds had blown over, and the moon was shining from a clear sky. There were puddles all along the road, and a noise of running water rose from the gutters and ditches. Mr. Hutton splashed along, not caring if he got wet.

How heartrendingly she had sobbed! With the emotions of pity and remorse that the recollection evoked in him there was a certain resentment: why couldn't she have played the game that he was playing—the heartless, amusing game? Yes, but he had known all the time that she wouldn't, she couldn't, play that game; he had known and persisted.

What had she said about passion and the elements? Something absurdly stale, but true, true. There she was, a cloud black-bosomed and charged with thunder, and he, like some absurd little Benjamin Franklin, had sent up a kite into the heart of the menace. Now he was complaining that his toy had drawn the lightning.

She was probably still kneeling by that chair in the loggia, crying.

But why hadn't he been able to keep up the game? Why had his irresponsibility deserted him, leaving him suddenly sober in a cold world? There was no answer to any of his questions. One idea burned steady and luminous in his mind—the idea of flight. He must get away at once.

4

"What are you thinking about, Teddy Bear?"

"Nothing."

There was a silence. Mr. Hutton remained motionless, his elbows on the parapet of the terrace, his chin in his hands, looking down over Florence. He had taken a villa on one of the hilltops to the south of the city. From a little raised terrace at the end of the garden one looked down a long fertile valley on to the town and beyond it to the bleak mass of Monte Morello and, eastward of it, to the peopled hill of Fiesole, dotted with white houses. Everything was clear and luminous in the September sunshine.

"Are you worried about anything?"

"No, thank you."

"Tell me, Teddy Bear."

"But, my dear, there's nothing to tell." Mr. Hutton turned around, smiled, and patted the girl's hand. "I think you'd better go in and have your siesta. It's too hot for you here."

"Very well, Teddy Bear. Are you coming too?"

"When I've finished my cigar."

"All right. But do hurry up and finish it, Teddy Bear." Slowly, reluctantly, she descended the steps of the terrace and walked towards the house.

Mr. Hutton continued his contemplation of Florence. He had need to be alone. It was good sometimes to escape from Doris and the restless solicitude of her passion. He had never known the pains of loving hopelessly, but he was experiencing now the pains of being loved. These last weeks had been a period of growing discomfort. Doris was always with him, like an obsession, like a guilty conscience. Yes, it was good to be alone.

He pulled an envelope out of his pocket and opened it; not without reluctance. He hated letters; they always contained something unpleasant—nowadays, since his second marriage. This was from his sister. He began skimming through the insulting home-truths of which it was composed. The words "indecent haste," "social suicide," "scarcely cold in her grave," "person of the lower classes," all occurred. They were inevitable now in any communication from a well-meaning and right-thinking relative. Impatient, he was about to tear the stupid letter to pieces when his eye fell on a sentence at the bottom of the third page. His heart beat with uncomfortable violence as he read it. It was too monstrous! Janet Spence was going about telling everyone that he had poisoned his wife in order to marry

Doris. What damnable malice! Ordinarily a man of the suavest temper, Mr. Hutton found himself trembling with rage. He took the childish satisfaction of calling names—he cursed the woman.

Then suddenly he saw the ridiculous side of the situation. The notion that he should have murdered anyone in order to marry Doris! If they only knew how miserably bored he was. Poor, dear Janet! She had tried to be malicious; she had only succeeded in being stupid.

A sound of footsteps aroused him; he looked around. In the garden below the little terrace the servant girl of the house was picking fruit. A Neapolitan, strayed somehow as far north as Florence, she was a specimen of the classical type—a little debased. Her profile might have been taken from a Sicilian coin of a bad period. Her features, carved floridly in the grand tradition, expressed an almost perfect stupidity. Her mouth was the most beautiful thing about her; the calligraphic hand of nature had richly curved it into an expression of mulish bad temper. . . . Under her hideous black clothes, Mr. Hutton divined a powerful body, firm and massive. He had looked at her before with a vague interest and curiosity. To-day the curiosity defined and focused itself into a desire. An idyll of Theocritus. Here was the woman; he, alas, was not precisely like a goatherd on the volcanic hills. He called to her.

"Armida!"

The smile with which she answered him was so provocative, attested so easy a virtue, that Mr. Hutton took fright. He was on the brink once more—on the brink. He must draw back, oh! quickly, quickly, before it was too late. The girl continued to look up at him.

"*Ha chiamato?*" she asked at last.

Stupidity or reason? Oh, there was no choice now. It was imbecility every time.

"*Scendo*," he called back to her. Twelve steps led from the garden to the terrace. Mr. Hutton counted them. Down, down, down, down. . . . He saw a vision of himself descending from one circle of the inferno to the next—from a darkness full of wind and hail to an abyss of stinking mud.

5

For a good many days the Hutton case had a place on the front page of every newspaper. There had been no more popular murder trial since George Smith had temporarily eclipsed the European War

26. **Theocritus**, Greek pastoral poet, c. third century B.C. 36. **"Ha chiamato?"** "Did you call?" 39. **"Scendo,"** "I am coming down."

by drowning in a warm bath his seventh bride. The public imagination was stirred by this tale of a murder brought to light months after the date of the crime. Here, it was felt, was one of those incidents in human life, so notable because they are so rare, which do definitely justify the ways of God to man. A wicked man had been moved by an illicit passion to kill his wife. For months he had lived in sin and fancied security—only to be dashed at last more horribly into the pit he had prepared for himself. Murder will out, and here was a case of it. The readers of the newspapers were in a position to follow every movement of the hand of God. There had been vague, but persistent, rumours in the neighbourhood; the police had taken action at last. Then came the exhumation order, the post-mortem examination, the inquest, the evidence of the experts, the verdict of the coroner's jury, the trial, the condemnation. For once Providence had done its duty, obviously, grossly, didactically, as in a melodrama. The newspapers were right in making of the case the staple intellectual food of a whole season.

Mr. Hutton's first emotion when he was summoned from Italy to give evidence at the inquest was one of indignation. It was a monstrous, a scandalous thing that the police should take such idle, malicious gossip seriously. When the inquest was over he would bring an action for malicious prosecution against the Chief Constable; he would sue the Spence woman for slander.

The inquest was opened; the astonishing evidence unrolled itself. The experts had examined the body, and had found traces of arsenic; they were of opinion that the late Mrs. Hutton had died of arsenic poisoning.

Arsenic poisoning. . . . Emily had died of arsenic poisoning? After that, Mr. Hutton learned with surprise that there was enough arsenicated insecticide in his greenhouses to poison an army.

It was now, quite suddenly, that he saw it: there was a case against him. Fascinated, he watched it growing, growing, like some monstrous tropical plant. It was enveloping him, surrounding him; he was lost in a tangled forest.

When was the poison administered? The experts agreed that it must have been swallowed eight or nine hours before death. About lunch-time? Yes, about lunch-time. Clara, the parlour-maid was called. Mrs. Hutton, she remembered, had asked her to go and fetch her medicine. Mr. Hutton had volunteered to go instead; he had gone alone. Miss Spence—ah, the memory of the storm, the white aimed face! the horror of it all!—Miss Spence confirmed Clara's statement, and added that Mr. Hutton had come back with the medicine already poured out in a wineglass, not in the bottle.

Mr. Hutton's indignation evaporated. He was dismayed, frightened. It was all too fantastic to be taken seriously, and yet the nightmare was a fact—it was actually happening.

M'Nab had seen them kissing, often. He had taken them for a drive on the day of Mrs. Hutton's death. He could see them reflected in the windscreen, sometimes out of the tail of his eye.

The inquest was adjourned. That evening Doris went to bed with a headache. When he went to her room after dinner, Mr. Hutton found her crying.

"What's the matter?" He sat down on the edge of her bed and began to stroke her hair. For a long time she did not answer, and he went on stroking her hair mechanically, almost unconsciously; sometimes, even, he bent down and kissed her bare shoulder. He had his own affairs, however, to think about. What had happened? How was it that the stupid gossip had actually come true? Emily had died of arsenic poisoning. It was absurd, impossible. The order of things had been broken, and he was at the mercy of an irresponsibility. What had happened, what was going to happen? He was interrupted in the midst of his thoughts.

"It's my fault—it's my fault!" Doris suddenly sobbed out. "I shouldn't have loved you; I oughtn't to have let you love me. Why was I ever born?"

Mr. Hutton didn't say anything, but looked down in silence at the abject figure of misery lying on the bed.

"If they do anything to you I shall kill myself."

She sat up, held him for a moment at arm's length, and looked at him with a kind of violence, as though she were never to see him again.

"I love you, I love you, I love you." She drew him, inert and passive, towards her, clasped him, pressed herself against him. "I didn't know you loved me as much as that, Teddy Bear. But why did you do it—why did you do it?"

Mr. Hutton undid her clasping arms and got up. His face became very red. "You seem to take it for granted that I murdered my wife," he said. "It's really too grotesque. What do you all take me for? A cinema hero?" He had begun to lose his temper. All the exasperation, all the fear and bewilderment of the day, was transformed into a violent anger against her. "It's all such damned stupidity. Haven't you any conception of a civilised man's mentality? Do I look the sort of man who'd go about slaughtering people? I suppose you imagine I was so insanely in love with you that I could commit any folly. When will you women understand that one isn't in-

sanely in love? All one asks for is a quiet life, which you won't allow one to have. I don't know what the devil ever induced me to marry you. It was all a damned stupid, practical joke. And now you go about saying I'm a murderer. I won't stand for it."

Mr. Hutton stamped towards the door. He had said horrible things, he knew—odious things that he ought speedily to unsay. But he wouldn't. He closed the door behind him.

"Teddy Bear!" He turned the handle; the latch clicked into place. "Teddy Bear!" The voice that came to him through the closed door was agonised. Should he go back? He ought to go back. He touched the handle, then withdrew his fingers and quickly walked away. When he was half-way down the stairs he halted. She might try to do something silly—throw herself out of the window or God knows what! He listened attentively; there was no sound. But he pictured her very clearly, tiptoeing across the room, lifting the sash as high as it would go, leaning out into the cold night air. It was raining a little. Under the window lay the paved terrace. How far below? Twenty-five or thirty feet? Once, when he was walking along Piccadilly, a dog had jumped out of a third-storey window of the Ritz. He had seen it fall; he had heard it strike the pavement. Should he go back? He was damned if he would; he hated her.

He sat for a long time in the library. What had happened? What was happening? He turned the question over and over in his mind and could find no answer. Suppose the nightmare dreamed itself out to its horrible conclusion. Death was waiting for him. His eyes filled with tears; he wanted so passionately to live. "Just to be alive." Poor Emily had wished it too, he remembered: "Just to be alive." There were still so many places in this astonishing world unvisited, so many queer delightful people still unknown, so many lovely women never so much as seen. The huge white oxen would still be dragging their wains along the Tuscan roads, the cypresses would still go up, straight as pillars, to the blue heaven; but he would not be there to see them. And the sweet southern wines—Tear of Christ and Blood of Judas—others would drink them, not he. Others would walk down the obscure and narrow lanes between the bookshelves in the London Library, sniffing the dusty perfume of good literature, peering at strange titles, discovering unknown names, exploring the fringes of vast domains of knowledge. He would be lying in a hole in the ground. But why, why? Confusedly he felt that some extraordinary kind of justice was being done. In the past he had been wanton and imbecile and irre-

40. **wains,** large wagons.

sponsible. Now Fate was playing as wantonly, as irresponsibly, with him. It was tit for tat, and God existed after all.

He felt that he would like to pray. Forty years ago he used to kneel by his bed every evening. The nightly formula of his childhood came to him almost unsought from some long unopened chamber of the memory. "God bless Father and Mother, Tom and Cissie and the Baby, Mademoiselle and Nurse, and everyone that I love, and make me a good boy. Amen." They were all dead now—all except Cissie.

His mind seemed to soften and dissolve; a great calm descended upon his spirit. He went upstairs to ask Doris's forgiveness. He found her lying on the couch at the foot of the bed. On the floor beside her stood a blue bottle of liniment, marked "Not to be taken"; she seemed to have drunk about half of it.

—"You didn't love me," was all she said when she opened her eyes to find him bending over her.

Dr. Libbard arrived in time to prevent any very serious consequences. "You mustn't do this again," he said while Mr. Hutton was out of the room.

"What's to prevent me?" she asked defiantly.

Dr. Libbard looked at her with his large, sad eyes. "There's nothing to prevent you," he said. "Only yourself and your baby. Isn't it rather bad luck on your baby, not allowing it to come into the world because you want to go out of it?"

Doris was silent for a time. "All right," she whispered. "I won't."

Mr. Hutton sat by her bedside for the rest of the night. He felt himself now to be indeed a murderer. For a time he persuaded himself that he loved this pitiable child. Dozing in his chair, he woke up, stiff and cold, to find himself drained dry, as it were, of every emotion. He had become nothing but a tired

and suffering carcass. At six o'clock he undressed and went to bed for a couple of hours' sleep. In the course of the same afternoon the coroner's jury brought in a verdict of "Wilful Murder," and Mr. Hutton was committed for trial.

6

Miss Spence was not at all well. She had found her public appearances in the witness-box very trying, and when it was all over she had something that was very nearly a breakdown. She slept badly, and suffered from nervous indigestion. Dr. Libbard used to call every other day. She talked to him a great deal—mostly about the Hutton case. . . . Her moral indignation was always on the boil. Wasn't it appalling to think that one had had a murderer in one's house. Wasn't it extraordinary that one could have been for so long mistaken about the man's character? (But she had had an inkling from the first.) And then the girl he had gone off with—so low class, so little better than a prostitute. The news that the second Mrs. Hutton was expecting a baby—the posthumous child of a condemned and executed criminal revolted her; the thing was shocking—an obscenity. Dr. Libbard answered her gently and vaguely, and prescribed bromide.

One morning he interrupted her in the midst of her customary tirade. "By the way," he said in his soft, melancholy voice, "I suppose it was really you who poisoned Mrs. Hutton."

Miss Spence stared at him for two or three seconds with enormous eyes, and then quietly said, "Yes." After that she started to cry.

"In the coffee, I suppose."

She seemed to nod assent. Dr. Libbard took out his fountain-pen, and in his neat, meticulous calligraphy wrote out a prescription for a sleeping-draught.

Stephen Spender
1909–

Stephen Spender was born near London, February 28, 1909. His mother was Violet Schuster; his father was Harold Spender, a well-known journalist. As a child Spender showed remarkable precocity; he interested himself in painting as well as poetry. At seventeen he revolted from formal education and tried to support himself; he bought a hand press and hoped to earn a living by printing chemists' labels. On this press Spender set up and printed in 1928 a paper-bound pamphlet of verse, *Nine Experiments*, which he had written in his seventeenth and eighteenth years. At nineteen he attended University College, Oxford, but did not wait to complete his course. *Twenty Poems*, 1930, was printed while he was an undergraduate, but Spender's name was unknown to America until the publication of *Poems*, 1933, which made something of a sensation in both England and America.

One of the reasons for its favorable reception was not only the quality of Spender's poetry but the evidence that new and vigorous poetry was again being written in England. The Georgians had lapsed into tired repetitions and stock gestures. The young poets—Stephen Spender, W. H. Auden, C. Day Lewis, Louis MacNeice—who emerged in the 1930's aroused readers by the force of their social convictions and the strength of their vocabulary. They accepted the modern scene with all its implications; they did not shrink from the necessity of the machine, nor did they sentimentalize it. They saw "electric pylons conveying imprisoned power, telegraph wires defying distance, motor ploughs forcing fertility into the soil." The change in subject matter was matched by a change in technique. As with D. H. Lawrence, their lyricism was livened by colloquialisms; like Gerard Manley Hopkins, they speeded up their verse with rapidly leaping images, enriched the line by unexpected internal rhyme, and achieved tension by strange syntactical ellipses. W. H. Auden was the most accomplished technician of the group; he mingled eloquence with banality, high rhetoric with the quick appeal of popular songs. Stephen Spender, less adroit, was far more intense. An almost Shelleyan fervor is apparent in such poems as "Not Palaces," "The Express," "The Funeral," and the exalted lines beginning "I think continually of those who were truly great." This last poem is one of the age's finest tributes to those

"Who wore at their hearts the fire's centre.
Born of the sun they travelled a short while towards the sun,
And left the vivid air signed with their honour."

"Not Palaces" is typical of Spender's idiom and the quick transit of his imagination. Here, in an abrupt set of images and half-evoked associations, is a call to youth, a call to co-operate with the changes taking place in a shifting world. The palaces are down; it is too late, the poet says, to sentimentalize over the past, too late for family pride and outworn prettiness, "beauty's filtered dusts." He insists that we must draw energy "As from the electric charge of a battery" if we are to be active spirits of our time. All our faculties must co-operate to appreciate this change—the eye, that quickly darting, delicately wandering gazelle; the ear, which "suspends on a chord The spirit drinking timelessness"; touch that intensifies all senses. These must equip us to realize a greater humanity, a humanity which will no longer be in love with war and death ("the programme of the antique Satan"), but which will proclaim death to the killers, "bringing light to life."

Trial of a Judge, 1938, is a dramatic allegory based on actual outrages committed by the Nazis in Germany. *The Still Centre*, 1939, is a collection of Spender's more meditative but no less impassioned poems. Besides his poetry Spender has written several volumes of prose, among the most distinguished of which are *The Burning Cactus*, 1936, a collection of five introspective short stories, and *The Destructive Element*, 1935, a study of modern writers and beliefs written from a political-moral standpoint.

THE EXPRESS [1]

After the first powerful plain manifesto
The black statement of pistons, without more fuss
But gliding like a queen, she leaves the station.
Without bowing and with restrained unconcern
She passes the houses which humbly crowd outside,
The gasworks and at last the heavy page

[1] This and the following poems are reprinted from *The Poems of Stephen Spender*, copyright, 1933, by permission of Random House, Inc.

Of death, printed by gravestones in the cemetery.
Beyond the town there lies the open country
Where, gathering speed, she acquires mystery,
The luminous self-possession of ships on ocean.   10
It is now she begins to sing—at first quite low
Then loud, and at last with a jazzy madness—
The song of her whistle screaming at curves,
Of deafening tunnels, brakes, innumerable bolts.
And always light, aerial, underneath
Goes the elate metre of her wheels.
Steaming through metal landscape on her lines
She plunges new eras of wild happiness
Where speed throws up strange shapes, broad curves
And parallels clean like the steel of guns.   20
At last, further than Edinburgh or Rome,
Beyond the crest of the world, she reaches night
Where only a low streamline brightness
Of phosphorus on the tossing hills is white.
Ah, like a comet through flame she moves entranced
Wrapt in her music no bird song, no, nor bough
Breaking with honey buds, shall ever equal.

THE LANDSCAPE NEAR AN AERODROME

More beautiful and soft than any moth
With burring, furred antennae feeling its huge path
Through dusk, the air-liner with shut-off engines
Glides over suburbs and the sleeves set trailing tall
To point the wind. Gently, broadly, she falls,
Scarcely disturbing charted currents of air.

Lulled by descent, the travellers across sea
And across feminine land indulging its easy limbs
In miles of softness, now let their eyes trained by
     watching
Penetrate through dusk the outskirts of this town   10
Here where industry shows a fraying edge.
Here they may see what is being done.

Beyond the winking masthead light
And the landing-ground, they observe the outposts
Of work: chimneys like lank black fingers
Or figures frightening and mad: and squat buildings
With their strange air behind trees, like women's
     faces
Shattered by grief. Here where few houses
Moan with faint light behind their blinds
They remark the unhomely sense of complaint, like
     a dog   20
Shut out and shivering at the foreign moon.

In the last sweep of love, they pass over fields
Behind the aerodrome, where boys play all day

Hacking dead grass: whose cries, like wild birds,
Settle upon the nearest roofs
But soon are hid under the loud city.

Then, as they land, they hear the tolling bell
Reaching across the landscape of hysteria
To where, larger than all the charcoaled batteries
And imaged towers against that dying sky,   30
Religion stands, the church blocking the sun.

THE FUNERAL

Death is another milestone on their way.
With laughter on their lips and with winds blowing
     round them
They record simply
How this one excelled all others in making driving-
     belts.

This is festivity, it is the time of statistics
When they record what one unit contributed:
They are glad as they lay him back in the earth
And thank him for what he gave them.

They walk home remembering the straining red
     flags,
And with pennons of song still fluttering through
     their blood   10
They speak of the world state
With its towns like brain-centres and its pulsing
     arteries.

They think how one life hums, revolves and toils,
One cog in a golden and singing hive:
Like spark from fire, its task happily achieved,
It falls away quietly.

No more are they haunted by the individual grief
Nor the crocodile tears of European genius,
The decline of a culture
Mourned by scholars who dream of the ghosts of
     Greek boys.   20

NOT PALACES

Not palaces, an era's crown
Where the mind dreams, intrigues, rests;
The architectural gold-leaved flower
From people ordered like a single mind,
I build. This only what I tell:
It is too late for rare accumulation
For family pride, for beauty's filtered dusts;
I say, stamping the words with emphasis,
Drink from here energy and only energy,
As from the electric charge of a battery,   10

To will this Time's change.
Eye, gazelle, delicate wanderer,
Drinker of horizon's fluid line;
Ear that suspends on a chord
The spirit drinking timelessness;
Touch, love, all senses;
Leave your gardens, your singing feasts,
Your dreams of suns circling before our sun,
Of heaven after our world.
Instead, watch images of flashing brass   20
That strike the outward sense, the polished will
Flag of our purpose which the wind engraves.
No spirit seek here rest. But this: No man
Shall hunger: Man shall spend equally.
Our goal which we compel: Man shall be man.

—That the programme of the antique Satan
Bristling with guns on the indented page
With battleship towering from hilly waves:
For what? Drive of a ruining purpose
Destroying all but its age-long exploiters.   30
Our programme like this, yet opposite,
Death to the killers, bringing light to life.

I THINK CONTINUALLY
OF THOSE

I think continually of those who were truly great.
Who, from the womb, remembered the soul's history

Through corridors of light where the hours are suns
Endless and singing. Whose lovely ambition
Was that their lips, still touched with fire,
Should tell of the Spirit clothed from head to foot in
   song.
And who hoarded from the Spring branches
The desires falling across their bodies like blossoms.

What is precious is never to forget
The delight of the blood drawn from ageless
   springs   10
Breaking through rocks in worlds before our earth.
Never to deny its pleasure in the simple morning
   light
Nor its grave evening demand for love.
Never to allow gradually the traffic to smother
With noise and fog the flowering of the spirit.

Near the snow, near the sun, in the highest fields
See how these names are fêted by the waving grass
And by the streamers of white cloud,
And whispers of wind in the listening sky.
The names of those who in their lives fought for
   life   20
Who wore at their hearts the fire's centre.
Born of the sun they travelled a short while towards
   the sun,
And left the vivid air signed with their honour.

SUGGESTIONS FOR FURTHER READING

The date given is that of original publication. The American publication date is sometimes later. The name of the publisher after the date tells where the book is now available.

NOVELS

Bennett, Arnold, *The Old Wives' Tale*, 1908; Modern Library
Chesterton, G. K., *The Flying Inn*, 1914; John Lane
Conrad, Joseph, *Lord Jim*, 1900; Modern Library
Douglas, Norman, *South Wind*, 1917; Modern Library
Forster, E. M., *A Passage to India*, 1924; Pocket Books
Galsworthy, John, *The Forsyte Saga*, 1922; Scribner
Garnett, David, *Lady into Fox*, 1922; Garden City Publishing Co.
Herbert, A. P., *The Water Gipsies*, 1930; Grosset & Dunlap
Hudson, W. H., *Green Mansions, A Romance of the Tropical Forest*, 1904; Modern Library
Huxley, Aldous, *Point Counter Point*, 1928; Modern Library
Joyce, James, *Ulysses*, 1922; Random House
Lawrence, D. H., *Sons and Lovers*, 1913; Modern Library
Maugham, W. Somerset, *Of Human Bondage*, 1915; Grosset (Doubleday)

Priestley, J. B., *The Good Companions*, 1929; Harper
Wells, H. G., *Tono-Bungay*, 1909
Woolf, Virginia, *To the Lighthouse*, 1927; Modern Library

SHORT STORY COLLECTIONS

Conrad, Joseph, *Sea Tales: Youth, Typhoon, The Shadow Line*, 1902; Garden City Publishing Co.
Coppard, A. E., *The Field of Mustard*, 1926; Knopf
Kipling, Rudyard, *Selected Prose and Poetry of Rudyard Kipling*, Garden City Publishing Co.—a one-volume edition including *Barrack-Room Ballads; The Light That Failed* (novel); *Plain Tales from the Hills* (short stories); *Soldiers Three* (tales); *The Phantom Rickshaw and other Ghost Stories; Wee Willie Winkie* (stories about children; *The Story of the Gadsbys*, etc.; Garden City Publishing Co., 1937
Mansfield, Katherine, *Short Stories*, 3 vols. in 1; Knopf, 1937
Maugham, W. Somerset, *The Favorite Short Stories of W. Somerset Maugham*, a 1-vol. edition including

"Rain," "Red," "The Letter," "The Vessel of Wrath,"
and ten other much-quoted tales. Doubleday, 1934
Munro ("Saki"), H. H., *The Short Stories of Saki*, 1930,
—complete; Viking Press

PLAYS

Barrie, Sir James M., *What Every Woman Knows*, 1918;
Scribner
Coward, Noel, *The Vortex: A Play in Three Acts*, 1924;
Doubleday, Doran
Dunsany, Lord Edward, *Plays of Gods and Men*, 1917;
Putnam
Galsworthy, John, *Plays: The Silver Box, Joy, Strife*,
1909; Scribner
O'Casey, Sean, *Two Plays: Juno and the Paycock, The
Shadow of a Gunman*, 1925; Macmillan
Shaw, George Bernard, *Nine Plays*, 1894-1924; Dodd,
Mead
Synge, J. M., *Complete Works*, 1935; Random House

POETRY

Auden, W. H., *Poems*, 1930; Faber & Faber
Brooke, Rupert, *Collected Poems*, 1932; Dodd, Mead
Eliot, T. S., *Collected Poems*, 1936; Harcourt, Brace
Housman, A. E., *The Collected Poems*, 4 vols. in 1, 1940;
Holt
Kipling, Rudyard, *Verses*, 1940; Doubleday, Doran
Masefield, John, *Reynard the Fox, or, The Ghost Heath Run*,
1919; Macmillan
Sassoon, Siegfried, *Counter-Attack*, 1918; Dutton
Untermeyer, Louis, *Modern British Poetry: A Critical An-
thology*, 1936; Harcourt, Brace
Yeats, W. B., *The Collected Poems of W. B. Yeats*, 1933;
Macmillan

BIOGRAPHY AND AUTOBIOGRAPHY

Graves, Robert, *Good-bye to All That: An Autobiography*,
1929; Blue Ribbon
Gregory, Lady Angda, *Our Irish Theatre: A Chapter of
Autobiography*, 1913; Putnam
Guedalla, Philip, *Palmerston*, 1926; Putnam
Hudson, W. H., *Far Away and Long Ago*, 1918; Dutton
Lawrence, T. E., *Revolt in the Desert*, 1927; Garden City
Publishing Co.
Moore, George, *Confessions of a Young Man*, 1888; Mod-
ern Library
Nicolson, Harold, *Some People*, 1927; World's Classics,
Oxford Press
Strachey, Lytton, *Queen Victoria*, 1921; Harbrace Edition,
Harcourt, Brace

ESSAYS AND SKETCHES

Belloc, Hilaire, *The Old Road*, 1904; Lippincott
Chesterton, G. K., *Tremendous Trifles*, 1918; Dodd, Mead
Cunninghame-Graham, R. B., *Rodeo*, 1936; Doubleday,
Doran—a collection of forty-seven sketches, essays, and
tales
Lucas, E. V., *A Fronded Isle and Other Essays*, 1927; Dou-
bleday, Doran
Tomlinson, H. M., *London River*, 1921; Knopf

GUIDES AND CRITICISM

Daiches, David, *The Novel and the Modern World*, Chicago
Press, 1939
Dobree, Bonamy, and Batho, Edith, *The Victorians and
After: 1830-1914*, McBride, 1938
Millett, Fred, Manly, John M., and Rickert, Edith,
Contemporary British Literature, 3d rev. and enl. ed.,
Harcourt, Brace, 1935

Though much I want which most would have,   c
Yet still my mind forbids to crave.   c

The sestet may also be composed of interlacing couplets, as in Shakespeare's "O Mistress Mine" from *Twelfth-Night*:

O mistress mine! where are you roaming?   a
O! stay and hear; your true love's coming,   a
   That can sing both high and low.   b
Trip no further, pretty sweeting;   a
Journeys end in lovers meeting,   a
   Every wise man's son doth know.   b

The sestet may be a mingling of rhymed and unrhymed lines, as in D. G. Rossetti's "The Blessed Damozel" (page 769 in Volume II), or the quaint arrangement which Robert Burns made his own in "To a Mouse" and "The Hermit":

In this lone cave, in garments lowly,   a
Alike a foe to noisy folly,   a
And brow-bent gloomy melancholy,   a
   I wear away   b
My life, and, in my office holy,   a
   Consume the day.   b

The term "sestet" is also used to designate the last six lines of the sonnet.

The *septet*, a rather uncommon but flexible seven-line form, is chiefly esteemed in the variation known as *rime royal*, so called because it was supposedly first employed by King James I of Scotland. Chaucer was fond of using it (see his "Tale of the Man of Law" and "Troilus and Criseyde" and "Parlement of Foules"); Masefield erected his "The Widow in the Bye Street," "Dauber," and others on this design.

On every bough the briddès herde I singe,   a
With voys of aungel in hir armonye;   b
Some besyd hem hir briddès forth to bringe;   a
The litel conyes to hir play gunne hye;   b
And further al aboute I gan espye   b
The dredful roe, the buck, the hart and hinde,   c
Squerels, and beastès smale of gentil kinde.   c

—Geoffrey Chaucer

The *octave*, a stanza of eight lines, presents infinite possibilities for the poet. It may be composed of the linking of two quatrains (*a-b-a-b-c-d-c-d*) or two triplets with an intervening pair of rhyming lines (*a-a-a-b-c-c-c-b*), as in the first example quoted below, or a quatrain, a triplet and an extra, final rhyme (*a-b-a-b-c-c-c-b*), as in the second example. Robert Bridges' "A Passer-by" presents still another arrangement (*a-b-a-b-b-c-b-c*).

Upon Saint Crispin's Day   a
Fought was this noble fray,   a
Which fame did not delay   a
   To England to carry.   b
O when shall English men   c
With such acts fill a pen?   c
Or England breed again   c
   Such a King Harry?   b

Agincourt— —Michael Drayton

From too much love of living,   a
   From hope and fear set free,   b
We thank with brief thanksgiving   a
   Whatever gods may be   b
That no life lives forever;   c
That dead men rise up never;   c
That even the weariest river   c
   Winds somewhere safe to sea.   b

The Garden of Proserpine— —A. C. Swinburne

Whither, O splendid ship, thy white sails crowding,   a
Leaning across the bosom of the urgent West,   b
That fearest nor sea rising nor sky clouding,   a
Whither away, fair rover, and what thy quest?   b
Ah! soon, when Winter has all our vales opprest,   b
When skies are cold and misty, and hail is hurling,   c
Wilt thou glide on the blue Pacific, or rest   b
In a summer haven asleep, thy white sails furling.   c

A Passer-by— —Robert Bridges

A particular form of the eight-line stanza is known as *ottava rima*, since it was adapted from the Italian. The arrangement is *a-b-a-b-a-b-c-c*, and examples of it are found in Byron's "Don Juan" and "The Vision of Judgment." An octave from the latter:

Saint Peter sat by the celestial gate,   a
   And nodded o'er his keys; when lo! there came   b
A wondrous noise he had not heard of late—   a
   A rushing sound of wind and stream and flame;   b
In short, a roar of things extremely great,   a
   Which would have made aught save a saint exclaim.   b
But he, with first a start and then a wink,   c
Said, "There's another star gone out, I think!"   c

The term "octave" is also used to designate the first eight lines of the sonnet.

The *Spenserian stanza* is a solemn, nine-line stanza, invented by Spenser. Its rhyme scheme is intricate (*a-b-a-b-b-c-b-c-c*) and the ninth line (called the *Alexandrine*) is one foot longer than the others, rounding out the stanza with an impressive sonority. Among the poems built on Spenserian stanza are Byron's "Childe Harold," Keats' "The Eve of St. Agnes," Shelley's "Adonais," and Spenser' *The Faerie Queene*, one stanza of which follows:

For take thy balance, if thou be so wise,	a
And weigh the wind that under heaven doth blow;	b
Or weigh the light that in the east doth rise;	a
Or weigh the thought that from man's mind doth flow:	b
But if the weight of these thou canst not show,	b
Weigh but one word which from thy lips doth fall:	c
For how canst thou these greater secrets know	c
That dost not know the least thing of them all?	c
Ill can he rule the great that cannot reach the small.	c

The ten-, eleven-, and twelve-line stanzas are combinations of smaller units and are rather uncommon. The fourteen-line stanza (the sonnet) has developed into one of the richest patterns in English poetry and must be considered separately.

THE BALLAD

Webster defines the *ballad* as follows: "A popular short narrative poem, especially a romantic poem characterized by simplicity of structure . . . usually founded on folk legend or tradition." There are, moreover, five features which characterize the ballad, no matter whether it is long or short.

1. The action is swift. There is no introduction and practically no explanation. No time is wasted in exposition; the characters leap at once into life.

2. The tale is simple and direct. The tone is straightforward and without elaboration; the language is the language of the people.

3. The story is moving. Whether it concerns an event of the day or something supernatural, the verses stir the emotion and the imagination.

4. The attitude is impersonal. The ballad-maker is a born storyteller, especially in the sense that he is outside of the story. He rarely comments or philosophizes upon the event; he scarcely ever renders judgment upon the characters.

5. With few exceptions, the story is concentrated upon one incident; it does not attempt to give all the events leading up to it, nor does it enlarge upon the consequences.

THE SONNET

The sonnets in these volumes are easily recognized. Although they show a variety of rhyme schemes, their basic structure is identical. All sonnets are built on fourteen lines, the lines themselves (with few exceptions) being composed of ten syllables—iambic pentameter. These fourteen lines are usually divided into the first eight (the octave) and the second six (the sestet). The three main types are the Petrarchan (or Italian), the Shakespearean, and the Miltonic sonnet.

The *Petrarchan sonnet* is the strictest; it permits only two rhymes in the octave and not more than three (often two) in the sestet. The octave is rhymed *a-b-b-a-a-b-b-a*. The sestet allows a variation in the line arrangement, the favorite pattern being either *c-d-e-c-d-e* or *c-d-c-d-c-d*. An example of the Petrarchan sonnet follows:

O Earth, lie heavily upon her eyes;	a
Seal her sweet eyes weary of watching, Earth;	b
Lie close around her; leave no room for mirth	b
With its harsh laughter, nor for sound of sighs.	a
She hath no questions, she hath no replies,	a
Hush'd in and curtain'd with a blessed dearth	b
Of all that irk'd her from the hour of birth;	b
With stillness that is almost Paradise.	a
Darkness more clear than noonday holdeth her,	c
Silence more musical than any song;	d
Even her very heart has ceased to stir:	c
Until the morning of Eternity	e
Her rest shall not begin nor end, but be;	e
And when she wakes she will not think it long.	d

Rest—   *—Christina Rossetti*

The *Shakespearean sonnet*, perfected but not invented by Shakespeare, completely departs from the finely interwoven Italian model. It is actually nothing more than a set of three quatrains concluded and cemented by a couplet. An example:

No longer mourn for me when I am dead	a
Than you shall hear the surly sullen bell	b
Give warning to the world that I am fled	a
From this vile world with vilest worms to dwell;	b
Nay, if you read this line, remember not	c
The hand that writ it, for I love you so	d
That I in your sweet thoughts would be forgot	c
If thinking on me then should make you woe.	d
O if, I say, you look upon this verse	e
When I perhaps compounded am with clay,	f
Do not so much as my poor name rehearse,	e
But let your love even with my life decay,	f
Lest the wise world should look into your moan	g
And mock you with me after I am gone.	g

from Sonnets—   *—William Shakespeare*

The *Miltonic sonnet* is an adaptation of the Petrarchan with a striking difference. The Italian model separated the octave and sestet by a break in thought; the octave usually presented a general idea while the sestet pointed it and made it particular. Instead of dividing his sonnets in two parts, Milton unrolled his thought and his rich music without interruption through the fourteen lines.

An example:

Avenge, O Lord, thy slaughtered Saints, whose bones	a
Lie scattered on the Alpine mountains cold;	b
Even them who kept thy truth so pure of old,	b
When all our fathers worshiped stocks and stones,	a
Forget not: in thy book record their groans	a
Who were thy sheep, and in their ancient fold	b
Slain by the bloody Piedmontese, that rolled	b
Mother with infant down the rocks. Their moans	a
The vale redoubled to the hills, and they	c
To heaven. Their martyred blood and ashes sow	d
O'er all the Italian fields, where still doth sway	c
The triple Tyrant; that from these may grow	d
A hundredfold, who, having learnt thy way,	c
Early may fly the Babylonian woe.	d

On the Late Massacre in Piedmont—   *—John Milton*

THE BALLADE

The ballade (not to be confused with the ballad) is the most popular as well as the most important of the strict forms brought over from France. Villon immortalized the form and Chaucer used it in England as early as the fourteenth century—see his "Ballade of Good Counsel." It is composed of three stanzas of eight lines and a half-stanza (the *envoy*) of four lines. The rhymes of the first stanza are arranged in the order *a-b-a-b-b-c-b-c*, and this arrangement is repeated in all the other stanzas—the envoy (or "message") being *b-c-b-c*. No rhyme word or rhyming sound may be repeated throughout the entire ballade.

The outstanding feature of the ballade is its *refrain*. The refrain is the line which ends all the stanzas and the envoy; it is repeated in its entirety and gives a unity to the poem.

I hid my heart in a nest of roses,	a
Out of the sun's way, hidden apart;	b
In a softer bed than the soft white snow's is,	a
Under the roses I hid my heart.	b
Why would it sleep not? Why should it start,	b
When never a leaf of the rose-tree stirred?	c
What made sleep flutter his wings and part?	b
Only the song of a secret bird.	c

Lie still, I said, for the wind's wing closes,	a
And mild leaves muffle the keen sun's dart;	b
Lie still, for the wind on the warm seas dozes,	a
And the wind is unquieter yet than thou art.	b
Does a thought in thee still as a thorn's wound smart?	b
Does the fang still fret thee of hope deferred?	c
What bids the lips of thy sleep dispart?	b
Only the song of a secret bird.	c

The green land's name that a charm encloses,	a
It never was writ in the traveller's chart,	b
And sweet on its trees as the fruit that grows is;	a
It never was sold in the merchant's mart.	b
The swallows of dreams through its dim fields dart,	b
And sleep's are the tunes in its tree-tops heard;	c
No hound's note wakens the wildwood hart,	b
Only the song of a secret bird.	c

ENVOI

In the world of dreams I have chosen my part,	b
To sleep for a season and hear no word	c
Of true love's truth or of light love's art,	b
Only the song of a secret bird.	c

A Ballade of Dreamland—   *—A. C. Swinburne*

THE RONDEAU

The *rondeau* is a nimbler form usually employed for sprightly themes, although it can be used gravely, as in the poem by Henley quoted below. It is composed of thirteen lines built on only two rhymes, the refrain being a repetition of the first part of the first line. Using *R* to represent the refrain, the rhyme-scheme would be *Ra-a-b-b-a, a-a-b-R, a-a-b-b-a-R*. An example:

What is to come we know not. But we know	Ra
That what has been was good—was good to show,	a
Better to hide, and best of all to bear.	b
We are the masters of the days that were:	b
We have lived, we have loved, we have suffered—even	
so.	a

Shall we not take the ebb who had the flow?	a
Life was our friend. Now, if it be our foe—	a
Dear, though it break and spoil us!—need we care	b
What is to come?	R

Let the great winds their worst and wildest blow,	a
Or the gold weather round us mellow slow:	a
We have fulfilled ourselves, and we can dare	b
And we can conquer, though we may not share	b
In the rich quiet of the afterglow.	a
What is to come?	R

What Is to Come—   *—W. E. Henley*

THE TRIOLET

In common with the ballade, the rondeau, and other forms imported from France, the *triolet* is founded on a strict rhyme scheme and constructed by skillful repetition. The smallest and shortest of the French forms, it consists of only eight lines— and three of the eight are repeated. The first line

(Ra) is repeated to make the fourth and seventh lines; the second line (Rb) is repeated to make the eighth line. An example of the triolet's nimbleness:

Under the sun	Ra
There's nothing new;	Rb
Poem or pun,	a
Under the sun,	Ra
Said Solomon,	a
And he said true.	b
"Under the sun	Ra
There's nothing new."	Rb

—*H. C. Beeching*

THE VILLANELLE

Originally used for pastoral subjects, the *villanelle* has become so stylized that its simplicity is quite artificial. It is composed of five three-line stanzas and a concluding stanza of four lines, each stanza ending with an alternating line of the first verse. In the last stanza both of these lines appear together as a concluding couplet. Only two rhymes are permitted throughout the verses. Henley has described the very essence of this form as follows:

A dainty thing's the Villanelle.	a 1
Sly, musical, a jewel in rhyme,	b
It serves its purpose passing well.	a 2
A double-clappered silver bell	a
That must be made to clink in chime,	b
A dainty thing's the Villanelle;	a 1
And if you wish to flute a spell,	a
Or ask a meeting 'neath the lime,	b
It serves its purpose passing well.	a 2
You must not ask of it the swell	a
Of organs grandiose and sublime—	b
A dainty thing's the Villanelle;	a 1
And, filled with sweetness, as a shell	a
Is filled with sound, and launched in time,	b
It serves its purpose passing well.	a 2
Still fair to see and good to smell	a
As in the quaintness of its prime,	b
A dainty thing's the Villanelle;	a 1
It serves its purpose passing well.	a 2

THE ODE

Derived from a Greek word meaning "song," the *ode*, according to the lexicographers, became "a form of stately and elaborate verse." Originally chanted, the ode was built on a set of themes and responses and sung by divided choirs, half the singers intoning the strophe, the other half replying with the antistrophe, and both uniting with the epode. Most of the odes in English verse depart from the Greek model, although Swinburne's "Athens" and some of his political odes preserve the antique mode, while Dryden's "Alexander's Feast" blends the responsive voices in the classical manner. Cowley invented a variation on the form which he called the *Pindaric ode*—an irregular, passionate declamation in which the form is swept aside on a wave of emotion—Cowley failing to comprehend that Pindar varied the verse arrangement of his odes but that each was consistently and strictly patterned.

Since Cowley, the shape of the ode has grown more and more uncertain. The odes of Coleridge, Wordsworth, and Tennyson, though eloquent, are irregular. The magnificent odes of Keats and Shelley are, in reality, extended and sustained lyrics. The term itself has been broadened; strophe and antistrophe have disappeared; the length and the stanza pattern are unpredictable. Today the ode may be recognized not by its form at all, but rather by its tone: an intense, richly elaborated, and often profound apostrophe.

BLANK VERSE

Blank verse may be defined as (1) any unrhymed regular measure or (2) unrhymed verse in iambic pentameter. Most scholars favor the second interpretation, although the unrhymed dactylic hexameter of Longfellow's *Evangeline* and the unrhymed trochaic tetrameter of his *Song of Hiawatha* are obviously a variety of blank verse. But the term "blank verse" seems attached to the iambic five-accented line first employed in English by Henry Howard, Earl of Surrey, and glorified by Shakespeare's dramas, Milton's epics, and Wordsworth's meditations. Along with its sonority, its great strength lies in its flexibility. It can deviate from strict metrical regularity without injuring the rolling line—in fact the departures, the endless variety of effects, reveal its never-exhausted power. Every master of blank verse has given the measure new modulations and stamped it with his characteristic idiom.

From the countless examples of eloquent blank verse five illustrative segments, ranging from the sixteenth to the twentieth century, have been chosen.

The stars move still, time runs, the clock will strike,
The devil will come, and Faustus must be damned.
O, I'll leap up to heaven!—Who pulls me down?—
See, where Christ's blood streams in the firmament!
One drop of blood will save me: O my Christ!—
Rend not my heart for naming of my Christ;
Yet will I call on him: O, spare me, Lucifer!—
Where is it now? 'tis gone:
And, see, a threatening arm, an angry brow!
Mountains and hills, come, come, and fall on me,
And hide me from the heavy wrath of heaven!

   Dr. Faustus—   *—Christopher Marlowe*

   There is a tide in the affairs of men,
   Which, taken at the flood, leads on to fortune;
   Omitted, all the voyage of their life
   Is bound in shallows and in miseries.
   On such a full sea are we now afloat;
   And we must take the current when it serves,
   Or lose our ventures. . .

    Julius Caesar—   *—William Shakespeare*

These are thy glorious works, Parent of good,
Almighty, Thine this universal frame,
Thus wondrous fair: Thyself how wondrous then!
Unspeakable, who sitt'st above these heavens
To us invisible, or dimly seen
In these thy lowest works; yet these declare
Thy goodness beyond thought, and power divine.
Speak, ye who best can tell, ye sons of light,
Angels, for ye behold Him, and with songs
And choral symphonies, day without night,
Circle His throne rejoicing, ye, in heaven,
On earth join all ye creatures to extol
Him first, Him last, Him midst, and without end.

   Paradise Lost—   *—John Milton*

   . . . That time is past,
   And all its aching joys are now no more,
   And all its dizzy raptures. Not for this
   Faint I, nor mourn nor murmur; other gifts
   Have followed; for such loss, I would believe,
   Abundant recompence. For I have learned
   To look on nature, not as in the hour
   Of thoughtless youth; but hearing oftentimes
   The still, sad music of humanity.

    Lines—   *—William Wordsworth*

See how these names are fêted by the waving grass . . .
The names of those who in their lives fought for life,
Who wore at their hearts the fire's centre.
Born of the sun they travelled a short while towards the
   sun,
And left the vivid air signed with their honour.

   I Think Continually of Those—   *—Stephen Spender*

VARIOUS DEVICES

Besides the patterns already defined, the poet has recourse to various devices. Some of the most easily recognizable are *alliteration, rhyme, assonance, onomatopoeia, metonymy, synecdoche, epithet, simile,* and *metaphor.*

Devices of Sound

Alliteration is the repetition of the same consonant sound in words or syllables succeeding each other at close intervals. Usually it refers to the repetition of a sound or letter at the beginning of words, as in

   Fields ever fresh and groves ever green.

But, besides the repetition of *f* and *g* in this line, there is alliteration of the *v* sounds, half buried in the midst of the words. It is the most recognizable of devices, often overused—Swinburne carried it to the point of parody—but it is extremely effective as an enrichment of rhyme, even a substitute for it, as in Anglo-Saxon poetry. A famous example is Tennyson's

   The moan of doves in immemorial elms,
   And murmuring of innumerable bees.

Rhyme, sometimes spelled *rime*, has been variously defined. However, the principle laid down by Thomas Hood still holds: "A rhyme must commence on an accented syllable. From the accented vowel of that syllable to the end, the words intended to rhyme must be *identical* in sound, but the letter or letters preceding the accented vowel must be *unlike* in sound." "Night" and "fight," for example, are true rhymes, but "night" and "knight" do not rhyme, there being nothing unlike in the sound preceding the vowel. Neither can "night" and "ride" be said to rhyme, for though the sound preceding the vowel is different, the sound *following* the vowel is not identical, as it should be to constitute a true rhyme. "Night" and "ride" is an instance of assonance.

Assonance is the matching of the vowel sound alone, irrespective of the consonant (or sound) which follows it. Thus "base" and "face" would be true rhyme, whereas "base" and "fade" would be assonance. The old ballads and folk poetry are full of assonance, sometimes purposeful, sometimes accidental, as in "Sir Patrick Spens":

The anchor broke, the topmast *split*,
    'Twas such a deadly *storm*.
The waves came over the broken *ship*
    Till all her sides were *torn*.

Onomatopoeia is the formation of words by the imitation of sounds; the words thus formed vividly suggest the object or action producing the sound. Such words are found in the cradle of the individual as well as in the infancy of the race: *bow-wow, ding-dong, hum, buzz*, and so on. Though not confined to verse, words like *whiz, crash, crunch, crackle, jangle, squeal, honk, hiss* have become properties of the poet.

When Keats wrote

The murmurous haunt of flies on summer eves

he not only suggested the presence of flies, he *imitated* the drone and buzzing of insects on a sultry evening.

Devices of Sense

Metonymy and *synecdoche* are related to metaphor and simile, being forms of comparison. Metonymy (literally "name change") is the substitution of one thing to represent another. Thus when Byron, describing the ball on the night before Waterloo says:

And Belgium's capital had gathered then
    Her beauty and her chivalry—

the word "beauty" represents "fair women" and the word "chivalry" symbolizes "brave men."

Synecdoche (literally, "receiving together") is a figure of speech in which a part represents the whole: in the cry

"A sail! A sail!"

the word "sail" symbolizes the entire ship. Both metonymy and synecdoche are "figures of association," and there is little real difference in the way they are used today.

An *epithet* is a word (usually an adjective) which describes its object with unusual exactness. It is the arresting term which not only points a description but reveals how imagination intensifies observation. This exactness and fancy may be seen in such epithets as: "*smooth-sliding* Mincius," "*brittle* beauty," "lazy, *leaden-stepping* hours," "the river *sweats* oil and tar," "the *strong* crust of *friendly* bread," "the *green hells* of the sea," "*full-throated* ease," "*embalmed* darkness."

Simile and *metaphor* are poetry's most constant properties. The power of each lies in establishing a kinship between two (usually unrelated) objects, and fixing the attention on one object by comparing it to another. When the comparison is direct and introduced by *like* or *as*, it is a simile; when the comparison is indirect or implied, without the use of *like* or *as*, it is a metaphor.

Among the many familiar similes, these three may be listed as often-quoted favorites:

O my luve is like a red, red rose (*Robert Burns*)

I wandered lonely as a cloud (*William Wordsworth*)

I have seen old ships sail like swans asleep (*James Elroy Flecker*)

The following are vivid examples of metaphor:

There is a garden in her face (*Thomas Campion*)

Life's but a walking shadow, a poor player (*William Shakespeare*)

O blackbird, what a boy you are! (*T. E. Brown*)

Without simile and metaphor the image would lose its swiftness and strength; poetry is founded on the vigor and range of the metaphorical mind. Its element is surprise. To relate the hitherto unrelated, to make the strange seem familiar and the familiar seem strange, is the aim of metaphor. Through this heightened awareness, poetry, though variously defined, is invariably pronounced and unmistakably perceived.

                                                          L. U.

GENERAL INDEX

The names of the authors whose selections are represented are shown in CAPITALS and SMALL CAPITALS.

The titles of selections quoted are shown in **bold face**.

The **bold-face** numbers refer to the pages on which authors are discussed in detail, and to the pages on which the quoted selections appear.

INDEX OF FIRST LINES

A LITERARY MAP OF England

60
50
40
30
20
10

Wells next the Sea

Great Grimsby

Flamborough Head

Scarborough

Sutton-on-the-Forest

Hull

THE WOLDS

Somersby

Boston

Swineshead Abbey

Lincoln

LINCOLN

R. Witham

Whitby

Coxwold

Stillington

Elvington

NOTTINGHAM

Newark

Nottingham

NORTH YORK MOORS

Leeds

York

Ouse R.

R. Trent

SHERWOOD FOREST

Newstead Abbey

Derby

Hartlepool

Hipswell

Pomfret Castle

Wakefield

Sheffield

DERBY

Derwent

Wearmouth

Jarrow

Tynemouth

Blyth

DURHAM

Tees

Swale R.

MARSTON MOOR

Haworth

Bradford

Halifax

THE PEAK

STAFFORD

Newcastle

West R.

Ure R.

Y O R K

LANCASTER

Manchester

Crewe

CHESTER

Chester

Hawarden

FLINT

Warkworth Castle

NORTHUMBERLAND

Appleby

WESTMORLAND

Grasmore

Lancaster

Liverpool

Birkenhead

Formby Pt.

FLINT

Wrexham

DENBIGH

Berwick-upon-Tweed

LINDESFARNE

FARNE IS.

Otterburn

CHEVIOT HILLS

Rydal Mt.

Ullswater

Keswick

Morecambe Bay

St. Asaph

Denbigh

Bangor

Holyhead

ANGLESEY

HOLY I.

Caernarvon

SNOWDON

CAERNARVON

FLODDEN FIELD

Dryburgh Abbey

Jedburgh

Melrose Abbey

Selkirk

Gretna Green

Carlisle

CUMBRIAN MTS.

MT. SKIDDAW

Cockermouth

Derwent Water

MT. HELVELLYN

Hawkshead

Brantwood

St. Bees Head

ISLE OF MAN

Douglas

Castletown

Abbotsford

Yarrow R.

Ettrick

Ecclefechan

Annan

Dumfries

Kirkcudbright

Solway Firth

LAMMERMOOR HILLS

Prestonpans

Edinburgh

Hawthornden

Firth of Forth

Greenock

Glasgow

Clyde

Kilmarnock

Auchinleck

Ayr

Alloway

Craigenputtock

R. Nith

R. Afton

Doon R.

Mull of Galloway

Loch Lomond

BUTE

ISLAND OF ARRAN

Firth of Clyde

KINTYRE

JURA

ISLAY

North Channel

Belfast

Dublin

I R I S H   S E A